Note to Reader

Developments since this B
for Press

On May 5, 2006 the Government announced the creation of a new Department for Communities and Local Government (DCLG). This will be the successor department to the Office of the Deputy Prime Minister (ODPM), to which there are a number of references throughout this book. The new Department will combine certain of the functions previously held by the Home Office with those that were undertaken by the ODPM, including planning and local government (see **1.4.1**).

The provisions relating to design and access statements foreshadowed at **13.3.5** are being brought into force in England on August 10, 2006 by virtue of SIs 2006 Nos 1062 (planning applications) and 1063 (applications for listed building consent).

The head office and London Region of English Heritage is to move, with effect from May 2006, to 1 Waterhouse Square, 138-142 Holborn, London EC1N 2ST (see **Appendix C**). Telephone numbers and other details remain as before.

LISTED BUILDINGS, CONSERVATION AREAS AND MONUMENTS

AUSTRALIA
Law Book Co.
Sydney

CANADA and USA
Carswell
Toronto, Canada

HONG KONG
Sweet & Maxwell
Asia

NEW ZEALAND
Brookers
Wellington

SINGAPORE and MALAYSIA
Sweet & Maxwell Asia
Singapore and Kuala Lumpur

LISTED BUILDINGS, CONSERVATION AREAS AND MONUMENTS

CHARLES MYNORS
FRTPI, MRICS, IHBC,
of the Middle Temple and the Inn of Court of Northern Ireland, Barrister;
Chancellor of the Diocese of Worcester;
Visiting Professor, Faculty of the Built Environment,
Oxford Brookes University

FOURTH EDITION

LONDON
SWEET & MAXWELL
2006

First edition published by Longman (1989)
Second edition published by FT Law & Tax (1995)
Third edition published by Sweet & Maxwell (1999)
Reprinted (2001)

Published in 2006 by
Sweet & Maxwell Limited
100 Avenue Road, London NW3 3PF
www.sweetandmaxwell.co.uk

Typeset by YHT Ltd, London

Printed and bound in Great Britain
by William Clowes Ltd, Beccles, Suffolk

No natural forests were destroyed to make this product,
only farmed timber was used and replaced.

The Thomson trademark and Star design are
trademarks of Thomson Financial S.A. used herein under licence.

ISBN 978 0421 75830 8

A CIP catalogue record for this book is available from The British Library.

Cover photograph © Getty Images
The cover picture shows the waterfront in Liverpool, maritime mercantile city, the
most recently declared of the United Kingdom's 21 world heritage sites.

For David

Foreword

I am very pleased to be asked to write the foreword for the fourth edition of what has become a classic work in this important field of the law.

My own involvement with the law of listed buildings goes back to my early days in planning chambers in the early 1970s. I well remember the interest created by the listing of key buildings in Covent Garden (by the then Secretary of State, Geoffrey Rippon Q.C., a member of my chambers), and the enforced abandonment of plans to bulldoze the whole area to make way for a major new highway. A visit to Covent Garden today is an object-lesson in the misguided thinking of the planners of the day, and how far, happily, we have come since then. Indeed, it is of interest that one of the two quotations given by the present author, by way of introduction to Part IV of this book, dates back to 1966, in an era which as he says saw the loss of some buildings of great importance, including the Euston Arch.

He cites the debate over the fate of Number 1 Poultry, in the City of London as the "most significant debate in recent years". Having acted for SAVE Britain's Heritage in that case, I am less happy with his comment that the buildings involved were not "of great consequence". Whatever one's views of the merits of the James Stirling building which has now replaced them, the decision to allow demolition of some eight listed buildings in the heart of an important conservation area was certainly seen at the time as controversial and of considerable general importance. However, as SAVE celebrates this year its 30th anniversary, with an exhibition at the Victoria and Albert Museum, it is perhaps more significant that this case was one of its few failures. It is almost unthinkable now that consent would be given for the destruction of a listed building of quality, other than for exceptional reasons in the public interest.

I found the historical introduction particularly interesting, as it shows the piecemeal way in which this area of the law has developed. The result, as in other areas of the law, is some unnecessary complexity. However, taken together, the controls represent a comprehensive, and on the whole effective, means of protecting the historic built environment, while allowing sufficient flexibility to enable such buildings to remain alive in the modern world. The interests of conservation are best served by an enlightened partnership between private owners and public authorities. The challenge for the latter is to provide practical guidance and regulation, without becoming over-fussy.

I commend this work as a friendly and dependable guide through the complexities of the legislation, for all involved—whether as owners, developers, regulators, or campaigners.

Lord Justice Carnwath CVO
Royal Courts of Justice
February 2006

Preface

"There are many, many types of books in the world, which makes good sense, because there are many, many types of people, and everybody wants to read something different. . . . But one type of book that practically no one likes to read is a book about the law. Books about the law are notorious for being very long, very dull, and very difficult to read."

Lemony Snicket, *A Series of Unfortunate Events: Book the First: The Bad Beginning* (Egmont Books, London, 2001)

This book has now more than doubled in length since the first edition, published around 16 years ago. The increase arises partly as a result of the greater complexity of this area of law and practice, including the consequences of much litigation; and partly due to easier access to materials. It now provides, hopefully, a comprehensive manual of the law and practice relating to historic buildings, areas and monuments ("the cultural heritage") throughout the United Kingdom.

This new edition is, hopefully, up-to-date as at January 1, 2006. It thus includes all the new legislation, so far as relevant, that has appeared in the last seven years—in particular the TCP (Trees) Regulations 1999; the various sets of Appeals Rules and Regulations of 2000; the Faculty Jurisdiction Rules 2000; ODPM-DCMS Circular 01/2001; the Enforcement Rules and Regulations of 2002; the various statutory instruments introducing separate procedures for Wales; the Planning (Amendment) (NI) Order 2003; and, most recently, the Planning and Compulsory Purchase Act 2004 and all the secondary legislation associated with it, some of which is still only in draft.

The 2004 Act—a measure rightly described recently as for the most part unnecessary, and complicating rather than simplifying the system[1]—contained little directly relating to the built heritage, but introduced a number of procedural changes that will be relevant. However, in the light of all the proposals put forward over many years for changes to the system, it represented the loss of a rare opportunity for parliamentary time to enact those changes that needed primary legislation. It was also the loss of a chance to reconnect the built heritage back into the mainstream planning system, where it belongs—reversing the process unwittingly started by the Law Commission 15 years ago when, by

---

[1] *Fragments from a Legal Landscape: Planning Law Update*, paper by Charles George Q.C. at the Joint Planning Law Conference 2005.

consolidating planning legislation into three Acts instead of one, it marginalised listed buildings and conservation areas, and accelerated by the Government when it set up the Department for the National Heritage (now the DCMS) in 1992.

Another lost opportunity is represented by the Heritage Protection Review, being undertaken in England by the DCMS, but not expected to come fully into effect until 2009 or 2010—if at all. For further information, see Appendix G.

Possibly of greater significance is the large number of recent court decisions included in this edition. This arises in part because there is simply a much greater number of cases reaching the courts. But it is also because almost all significant decisions of the Administrative Court (the successor to the Crown Office), as well as some rather less significant ones, are now available via web-based services such as Lawtel, Justis and Casetrack. And Government and other websites contain much additional relevant material (including more obscure legislation and consultation papers). How this will work out in the future—and whether, in particular, websites will be continually and adequately updated—remains to be seen; but for the moment there is a real problem in simply absorbing the material that is available out there.

However, users must be cautious in relying unthinkingly on all this case law. It is only really the decisions of the Court of Appeal and the House of Lords that should be relied on for broad principles. The numerous decisions at first instance may thus provide examples of how those principles are worked out in practice; and they may constitute interim guidance on some matters until they are considered by the higher courts, but they are not authoritative to the same extent.

Partly in the light of this new material, much of the book has been almost completely rewritten.

There is thus a new chapter on the international framework, reflecting the increased significance of world heritage sites. The chapter on listing has been split into two, with a new chapter covering more fully the extent of listing—including for the first time diagrams of the principal "curtilage" cases. And the chapter on repairs and maintenance has been expanded into three, dealing with the duties of owners, the powers of authorities to intervene short of acquiring the building or monument in question, and their powers of acquisition.

More radical changes have been made to Parts IV and V (works to historic buildings and monuments), where Chapter 12 deals with the need for the various types of permission and consent; Chapter 13 outlines the absurdly complicated rules governing the procedure for obtaining authorisation; Chapter 14 looks at the matters that need to be taken into account when considering whether works should be authorised; and Chapter 15 deals more fully with appeals and inquiries. The chapter on unauthorised works has been expanded into two—one on enforcement and one on prosecution (Chapters 18 and 19).

All of these chapters now give greater prominence to the provisions relating to planning permission, alongside those relating to listed building and scheduled monument consent—since almost all works to historic buildings require planning permission as well as (in some cases) the other consents; and most litigation relates to planning applications rather than applications for consent. Appendix G highlights possible changes to the law, including a proposal to eliminate listed building and scheduled monument consent altogether; a glance at the footnotes to this book, and especially those in Chapters 12 to 15 and 18, will underline the desirability of pursuing that.

Surprisingly, the area that has generated the most litigation since the third edition of this book has been the availability zero-rating for VAT of works to listed buildings. This is reflected in a completely new Chapter 17.

The other obvious change has been the incorporation throughout this book of references to legislation and policy applying in Scotland and Northern Ireland, alongside that for England and Wales. I have tried to incorporate the references principally in footnotes, so as not to disrupt the flow of the text; I apologise to readers from England and Wales who may nevertheless be irritated. However, shortage of space has meant that some of the more peripheral references are limited to the legislation applying in England and Wales; readers from Scotland and Northern Ireland will need to exercise caution accordingly.

As always, the production of a book (or a new edition) of this length relies to a large extent on assistance from others—always generously given.

I am thus especially grateful to Robert Carnwath for supplying (such a generous) Foreword; to Nigel Hewitson at English Heritage, who has kindly read the whole typescript in draft, and made a number of helpful suggestions; and to Bob Kindred, for the material in Appendix F. Many thanks also to the numerous local authority officers who supplied the material that forms the basis of the diagrams in Chapter 4, or patiently answered obscure queries; to Philip Morphy, for producing the diagrams so efficiently; to Peter Hoey, at Liverpool; and to Nick Butler at the National Trust. My prolonged absence from Chambers has placed an unreasonable burden on clients and, even more, on my clerks; I much appreciate the way in which they have borne the resulting inconvenience so cheerfully; also the moral support and encouragement from others in Chambers, including in particular Philip Petchey, Andrew Newcombe, and Alex Booth. I am grateful to Lyndsay Walker at Sweet & Maxwell, who has been a model of patience as the weeks to complete the typescript stretched into months, and Mat Beal for masterminding the final stages of turning it into a book.

It should also be mentioned that some of the new material in this edition appeared first in an article in the *Journal of Planning and Environment Law* or in pieces in *Context*, the magazine of the Institute of Historic Building Conservation (IHBC).

Finally, I continue to be hugely in debt to my long-suffering family; there have been moments when none of us thought this new edition would ever be finished; but Janet, in particular, has been a tower of strength throughout the whole process—without her support I very much doubt I would have had the patience to complete it. And David too has had to put up with me being at home more often, but available less; it is therefore to him (and not just because he supplied, entirely unprompted, the quotation at the start of this Preface) that this book is dedicated, with much love.

Charles Mynors
2 Harcourt Buildings, Temple, London EC4

Acknowledgments

Grateful acknowledgment is made to the owners of copyright in each of the following publications for their permission to quote from their works:

Jonathan Lynn and Anthony Jay, *Yes Minister: The Diaries of a Cabinet Minister* (1983), BBC Worldwide.

Lemony Snicket, *A Series of Unfortunate Events* (2001), Egmont Books.

David Eversley, *The Planner in Society: The Changing Role of the Profession* (1973), English Heritage.

Rt Hon. Richard Crossman, *The Diaries of a Cabinet Minister* (1976), Hamish Hamilton (now published by Penguin).

Sir John Betjeman, "Executive", from *A Nip in the Air* (1974), Hodder Headline.

Robert Hewitson, *The Heritage Industry* (1987), Methuen Publishing.

John Delafons, *Politics and Preservation* (1997), Taylor & Francis.

Sir Osbert Lancaster, "What should we preserve?" from Jane Fawcett (ed.), *The Future of the Past* (1976), Thames & Hudson.

English Heritage publications: *Power of Place: The Future of the Historic Environment* (2000); *Stopping the Rot: A Step-by-Step Guide to Serving Urgent Works and Repair Notices* (1998); Guidance Notes for Applicants on Acquisition Grants to Local Authorities to Underwrite Repairs Notices; Policy Statement on Enabling Development and the Conservation of Heritage Assets.

Extract from the Heritage Lottery Fund's 2004 accounts.

List of Abbreviations

The principal statutes governing this area of law, unfortunately, all have particularly lengthy and cumbersome names. In the main text, therefore, they have been shortened as follows:

"Ancient Monuments Act"	Ancient Monuments and Archaeological Areas Act 1979.
"Listed Buildings Act"	Planning (Listed Buildings and Conservation Areas) Act 1990
"Northern Ireland Order"	Planning (Northern Ireland) Order 1991
"Planning Act"	Town and Country Planning Act 1990
"Scottish Listed Buildings Act"	Planning (Listed Buildings and Conservation Areas) (Scotland) Act 1997
"Scottish Planning Act"	Town and Country Planning (Scotland) Act 1997

References to "the Department" are to the Office of the Deputy Prime Minister in respect of England (see **1.4.1**) and to the Welsh Assembly Government and the Scottish Executive (see **1.5**). The Historic Buildings and Monuments Commission for England is referred to under its popular name "English Heritage" (see **1.4.2**), and the agency of the Welsh Assembly Government dealing with historic buildings by its more commonly used title "Cadw" (see **1.5.2**). For Northern Ireland, see **1.5.5**.

The following abbreviations have been used in the footnotes, largely in order to shorten as far as possible the references to statutes, statutory instruments and Government guidance:

AMAAA	Ancient Monuments and Archaeological Areas Act
Circ.	Circular
DETR	Department of the Environment, Transport and the Regions
DCMS	Department for Culture, Media and Sport
DoE	Department of the Environment
DNH	Department of National Heritage
ECHR	European Convention on Human Rights and Fundamental Freedoms

Envt	Environment
HBAMA	Historic Buildings and Ancient Monuments Act
NI	Northern Ireland
ODPM	Office of the Deputy Prime Minister
P(A)(NI)O	Planning (Amendment) (Northern Ireland) Order
PCA	Planning and Compensation Act
PCPA	Planning and Compulsory Purchase Act
P(GD)O(NI)	Planning (General Development) Order (Northern Ireland)
P(LBCA)A	Planning (Listed Buildings and Conservation Areas) Act
P(LBCA) Regs	Planning (Listed Buildings and Conservation Areas) Regulations
P(LBCA)(S)A	Planning (Listed Buildings and Conservation Areas) (Scotland) Act
P(NI)O	Planning (Northern Ireland) Order
PPG	Planning Policy Guidance note
PPS	Planning Policy Statement
SI	Statutory Instrument
SRO	Statutory Rules and Orders
SSI	Scottish Statutory Instrument
TCP	Town and Country Planning
TCPA	Town and Country Planning Act
TCP(S)A	Town and Country Planning (Scotland) Act
TCP(GDP)O	TCP (General Development Procedure) Order
TCP(GDP)(S)O	TCP (General Development Procedure) (Scotland) Order
TCP(GPD)O	TCP (General Permitted Development) Order
TCP(GPD)(S)O	TCP (General Permitted Development) (Scotland) Order
TCP(LBCA)(S) Regs	TCP (Listed Buildings and Buildings in Conservation Areas) (Scotland) Regulations
WO	Welsh Office.

"HS Memorandum" refers to the *Memorandum of Guidance on Listed Buildings and Conservation Areas* published by Historic Scotland in 1998 (see **1.5.4**).

List of Figures

List of Tables

Contents

PART V. UNAUTHORISED WORKS

APPENDICES

INDEX

Full table of contents

Table of Cases

Table of Statutes and Measures

Table of Statutory Instruments

Table of Treaties, Conventions, Directives and Charters

Table of Government Policy Guidance

Part I

Introduction

"There is perhaps no one thing, which the most Polite part of Mankind have more universally agreed in: than the Value they have ever set upon the Remains of distant Times. Nor amongst the Severall kinds of those Antiquitys, are there any so much regarded, as those of Buildings: Some for their Magnificence, or curious workmanship; and others, as they move more lively and pleasing Reflections (than History without their Aid can do) on the Persons who have Inhabited them; On the Remarkable things which have been transacted in them, Or the extraordinary Occasions of Erecting them."

Sir John Vanbrugh, letter to the Duchess of Marlborough, 1709.

"Had we more faith in ourselves, and were more sure of our values, we would have less need to rely on the images and monuments of the past. We would also find that, far from being useless except as a diversion from the present, the past is indeed a cultural resource, that the ideas and values of the past—as in the Renaissance—can be the inspiration for fresh creation. But because we have abandoned our critical faculty for understanding the past, and have turned history into heritage, we no longer know what to do with it, except obsessively preserve it. The more dead the past becomes, the more we wish to enshrine its relics."

Robert Hewitson, *The Heritage Industry* (Methuen Publishing, London, 1987).

Introduction

Chapter 1

Introduction

1.1 The cultural heritage

1.1.1 Introduction

'What is the historic environment? Why does it matter?" So began *Power of Place*, the English Heritage review of policies relating to the historic environment of England, published in December 2000.

The answer to the first question was as follows:

"The historic environment is what generations of people have made of the places in which they lived. It is all about us. We are the trustees of that inheritance. It is, in every sense, a common wealth. Most of our towns and cities, and all of our countryside, are made up of layer upon layer of human activity. Each generation has made its mark. And each makes its decisions about the future in the context of what it has inherited. That context is irreplaceable. Once gone, it is gone forever."[1]

It is to be noted that this does not say that the historic environment is the best bits of what we have inherited; it is all of it.

As for the second question, the answer was more diffuse. It could be best summarised in the following passage:

"The future is not secure. In the past 50 years, much development simply ignored or trampled through its context, in city, town or countryside. Agricultural policy has taken little account of its impact on the rural landscape. The development of new transport links is destroying the tranquillity of the countryside, while both traffic and measures to control it seriously damage the appearance of historic towns and villages and thus the quality of life of the people who live in them. Poorly designed housing and commercial development have degraded the places where many people live. Good new architecture, especially in the context of historic areas, is often watered down through fear or ignorance on the part of decision-makers."[2]

---

[1] English Heritage, *Power of Place: the Future of the Historic Environment*, December 2000, para.02.

[2] *ibid.*, para.08. So much for a successful planning system.

But the problem is that everyone in principle values their surroundings as they are—in the well-known phrase of the old Government Circular, "the familiar and cherished local scene".[3] And change is generally welcomed by no-one, except possibly those in the development industry. On the other hand, development is still required, to provide new housing, new jobs and new facilities of various kinds—even though the beneficiaries of such initiatives will usually be those currently outside the area. A balance has to be found. It is easy to be cynical, and to caricature government statements in this area as being meaningless platitudes; but the problems are real, and there are no easy answers.

It is a truism that the historic cities and villages now so much admired would not exist if there had been planning policies in place at the relevant time to protect the countryside that presumably previously existed. And the principal buildings within them, now listed, would in many cases not be allowed under current policy, as they would not fit in with the surrounding townscape. And that applies not least to the buildings now listed at Grade I.[4] Whilst that is not a remotely original thought, it still needs to be repeated, as there is a climate abroad that is now strongly resistant to *any* change.

Against that background, the law seeks to achieve a balance—to avoid the needless or premature loss of that which should be protected, and to provide a procedural mechanism to enable the proper assessment of proposals for change. But the result is somewhat unsatisfactory:

"Since 1882, when the first legislation was passed, a complicated regulatory system has developed in England. . . . Owners of complex, sensitive sites may find themselves subject to a confusing plethora of different regulatory regimes operated by different authorities."[5]

It is significant this was the one area of established planning law that was considered sufficiently substantial to justify being hived off into a separate statute[6] in the 1990 consolidation. And even in the last six or seven years there have been well over 100 reported decisions of the courts, noted in this book, impinging directly on the heritage.

This chapter looks at the way the law has developed over the last 120 years into the complex code that exists at present, and which is the subject of the remainder of the book. It describes where the law is to be found; and it outlines the various bodies—central government, English Heritage, local authorities and others—

---

[3] Circ. 8/87, para.5. This phrase started its life in the speech of Lord Sandford in the House of Lords in 1973 : "The new approach . . . should take account of the growth of public opinion in favour of conserving the familiar and cherished local scene". By 1987, this had become "public opinion is now overwhelmingly in favour of enhancing the familiar and cherished local scene"—but it may be suspected that opinion is now in favour of preserving, or at least conserving (as in 1973), rather than enhancing it.

[4] Notwithstanding what has become known as "the Gummer exception", originally in PPG 7, para.3.21—which nearly disappeared in 2004, but which survived (albeit in a modified form) as para.11 of PPS 7, possibly due to representations by the RIBA and others.

[5] *Power of Place*, para.79.

[6] The Planning (Listed Buildings and Conservation Areas) Act 1990—hereafter "the Listed Buildings Act".

exercising key roles in its administration. And **Chapter 2** sets out the international framework for this area of law.

But, first, why is the law needed at all in this area?

1.1.2 What is to be conserved?

The first fundamental issue is that there has to be some enforceable consensus as to which buildings, monuments and areas are to be conserved. Thus, if the "historic environment" is simply defined as "what generations of people have made of the places in which they lived", that does not get us much further forward, since it includes everything; and it is neither possible nor desirable to save everything for ever. But if we are not to save everything, then what is to be selected? Most people would probably agree that at least some structures and places should be given protection—perhaps Westminster Abbey, Stonehenge, and Georgian Bath. But some enthusiasts would go further and wish to save almost all buildings built before, say, 1900—and many later ones too. There is thus not likely to be universal agreement as to what needs protection.

It would in theory be possible for a decision to be made as to the merits of a building each time there is some proposal which affects it; and indeed to some extent that is what happens, in that each new proposal is assessed on its merits, in the light of the value of the building and the surrounding area as it is perceived at the time. However, even if commendable in theory, such an approach would raise a number of obvious problems in practice if it were the only one employed—in particular, it would not enable a finer degree of control to be exercised automatically in certain situations (for example, to ensure that minor alterations only needed consent in the case of more important buildings). It would also mean that the evaluation process would need to be repeated on many occasions, and would lead to considerable uncertainty on the part of property owners, decision-makers and the general public.

In practice, therefore, the system adopted in the United Kingdom has always been that those considered to be appropriately qualified from time to time select particular monuments, buildings, and areas which are to receive special protection. This has been done in the case of archaeological monuments (now *scheduled monuments*) since 1882 and individual buildings (now *listed buildings*) since 1932—in theory by the Secretary of State, but in practice by his officials and (in England) since 1984 by English Heritage. Historic areas have since 1967 been selected, and designated as *conservation areas*, by local authorities.

The way in which that selection takes place, the criteria governing it, and the extent of the protection afforded, is the subject of **Part II** of this book. Chapters 4 to 7 thus describe in detail the systems most frequently encountered in practice: listed buildings (**Chapters 3 and 4**), conservation areas (**Chapter 5**), and scheduled monuments and areas of archaeological importance (**Chapter 6**). **Chapter 7** then catalogues a variety of other forms of protection—local lists, blue plaques, registered parks and gardens, trees, hedgerows, battlefields, and the historic landscape generally). It also looks at the special law relating to two of the largest owners of historic properties, the National Trusts.

It is these selected items—buildings, monuments, areas, gardens, battlefields and others—that together make up what has come to be known as "the cultural heritage". And it is they that make up the subject matter of this book.

1.1.3 Care of historic buildings and monuments

The next issue is the extent to which, once "special" buildings and areas have been selected, there is a duty or a power—on the part of either their owners or anyone else—to keep them in good repair or to allow access to them. It is, after all, obvious that old buildings often cost more to keep up than modern ones; and this may or may not be offset by increased property values: a beautiful Georgian rectory is likely to be worth more than the neighbouring 1950s house of the same size, even though the latter costs less to maintain, but a fine medieval parish church simply costs a lot to keep in good condition, and comparison with a modern equivalent is irrelevant.

Parliament could have imposed a duty to keep historic buildings in good repair, but it has chosen not to do so—no doubt for understandable political reasons. But the duties laid on all building owners, including in relation to ensuring access by disabled people, apply just as much to old buildings as to any others (see **Chapter 8**). It may occasionally be possible for owners to obtain financial assistance from English Heritage, local authorities and others; and there are tax concessions available in a few cases. However, the utility of such provisions (described in **Chapter 9**) is severely restricted by the limited moneys available—other than from the Lottery Fund.

Grant aid may not be enough; direct action may sometimes be more appropriate. To this end, there are a variety of statutory provisions (outlined in **Chapter 10**) enabling various authorities to carry out limited repairs in certain circumstances—again, subject to the availability of finance (although it is noteworthy that the most effective powers are often those designed primarily for purposes other than conservation).

Ultimately, however, it is in some cases the ownership of a historic building that is the problem. Thus, where the present owner is unable or unwilling to keep it in good repair, it may be necessary for a public authority to purchase it, either by agreement or under compulsory powers, in order to pass it on to someone else who will. The provisions enabling this to take place are explored in **Chapter 11**.

1.1.4 Works to historic buildings and monuments

Perhaps the most important role of the law in this area is to provide measures to control works affecting historic buildings and areas. Thus the loss of buildings of special value must be carefully controlled; but, at least as important, unsympathetic alterations must be restricted—or only allowed where there are good reasons. On the other hand, works that will not cause harm must be allowed, and even encouraged, since old buildings must wherever possible remain in active use. And the control process should also allow professional assistance to be given, so that wherever possible the needs and wishes of historic building owners can be accommodated in ways which do not harm the buildings. The way in which all this is achieved is thus the subject of the most significant section of this book (**Part IV**).

There are five types of consent that may need to be sought and obtained for works affecting historic buildings and areas. These are, in order of importance:

- *planning permission*, for most building operations and changes of use;

- *listed building consent*, for the alteration or demolition of listed buildings;

- *conservation area consent*, for the demolition of unlisted buildings in conservation areas;

- *scheduled monument consent*, for works to scheduled monuments; and

- *advertisements consent*, for the erection of signs and advertisements.

All but the most minor works need planning permission; although it will sometimes be granted automatically in the case of works categorised as "permitted development". Sometimes one of the other four will be required as well. The complex provisions governing the need for consent are considered at **Chapter 12**.

Once it has been decided that consent of some kind is required, one or more applications will need to be submitted to, processed and determined by the local planning authority. The procedural mechanics of this are outlined in **Chapter 13**. The policy considerations influencing whether consent will be forthcoming, not least with reference to the relevant guidance from central government, are outlined in **Chapter 14**; they have been the subject of much attention by the courts in recent years. And if consent cannot be obtained from the planning authority, there are various remedies open to disappointed owners and developers, notably appealing to the Secretary of State (see **Chapter 15**).

One of the more significant categories of historic buildings is places of worship. These have always been subject to different procedures and legislation, described here at **Chapter 16**.

By way of a consolation prize for the effort of obtaining consent for works to listed buildings and scheduled monuments, there is a significant concession available in that the cost of alterations to buildings occupied either as dwelling-houses or by charities are zero-rated for VAT. This too has been the subject of an apparently disproportionate amount of litigation, described in **Chapter 17**.

Finally, under this heading, the existence of controls achieves nothing if they are not adequately enforced. Where unauthorised works are carried out, resulting in harm to historic buildings and areas, authorities may take enforcement action if the harm is remediable (see **Chapter 18**); if it is not, it may be necessary to resort to prosecution (see **Chapter 19**).

1.1.5 Regional variations

The law described in this book applies generally throughout the United Kingdom.

The focus is on England, simply because there is a much greater number of historic buildings and areas there, and the majority of litigation has accordingly been in that context. This is subject to variations in particular cases, such as in London, and in national parks, which are noted where appropriate (and see in particular **1.4.4 and 1.4.5**).

The position in Wales is in principle just as in England—but in recent years the differences between the two are becoming more significant, although these almost entirely relate to policy and administration, rather than to the substance of the law. The law in Scotland and Northern Ireland is also broadly the same in substance, although the statutory basis is different; and there are a number of relatively minor variations in procedural details. Some of the key points are highlighted at **1.5**; and the relevant provisions are noted throughout the remainder of the book.

1.2 Historical background

1.2.1 The Ancient Monuments Acts 1882 to 1910

The need for the protection of buildings and monuments of special interest has now been recognised by Parliament for well over a century. Many of the features of the current legislation emerged relatively recently, in the Town and Country Planning Act 1947 and its successor statutes; but to appreciate fully the way in which the system developed, it is necessary to go back to the 19th-century Ancient Monuments Acts.

The first two of these Acts were passed as a result of the Parliamentary campaign in the 1870s led by Sir John Lubbock, who was Member of Parliament for Maidstone, a Trustee of the British Museum, and a keen antiquarian. This period also saw the foundation by William Morris, in 1877, of the first national amenity group, the Society for the Protection of Ancient Buildings. However, whilst the Society was created to protect medieval churches from Victorian "improvements", the ambit of the first legislation was much more restricted.

The Ancient Monuments Protection Act 1882 thus related solely to "ancient monuments", which were defined[7] to be the monuments listed in the Schedule to the Act, and "other monuments of a like character of which the Commissioners may consent to become the guardian", together with adjacent land required for the preservation of and access to the monuments. The Schedule to the Act listed some 26 monuments in England, 22 in Scotland, 18 in Ireland, and three in Wales. All of them were unoccupied prehistoric structures, such as dolmens, stone circles, barrows and pillars. The Act provided for the Commissioners of Works to become guardians or owners of "ancient monuments",[8] for inspectors appointed by the Commissioners to report to them on the condition of such monuments,[9] and for penalties to be imposed for damage to monuments.[10]

The Ancient Monuments Protection Act 1900 then empowered the Commissioners and, for the first time, county councils, to become guardians of any "monument" other than a dwelling,[11] and for the public to have access to any

---

[7] in s.11.
[8] ss 2 to 4.
[9] s.5.
[10] s.6.
[11] s.1.

monument in the ownership or guardianship of the Commissioners or a council. "Monument" was now defined, more widely than "ancient monument" under the 1882 Act, as "any structure, erection, or monument, of architectural or historic interest".[12] The Act also provided for a council to undertake or contribute towards the cost of preserving, maintaining and managing any monument, whether or not it was the owner or guardian of it; and the Commissioners were empowered to receive gifts and to assist the owners of monuments with the cost of repairs.

A Royal Commission reported in 1908, leading to a further short measure, the Ancient Monuments Protection Act 1910. That Act applied the provisions of s.4 of the 1882 Act (gifts of ancient monuments to the Commissioners) to any "monument" as defined by the 1900 Act; and it applied the penal provisions of the earlier Act to such monuments.

1.2.2 The Ancient Monuments Acts of 1913 and 1931

The next statute was the Ancient Monuments Consolidation and Amendment Act 1913, which repealed the three earlier Acts, and was very much what would be expected from its title. It provided for the Commissioners to set up an advisory board to be known as the Ancient Monuments Board. As previously, the Commissioners and local authorities could become owners or guardians of "ancient monuments"[13]; and an authority could assist with the cost of the preservation of any monument, whether or not under its control. In addition, the public was for the first time given a right of access to any monument in public ownership or guardianship.[14]

The 1913 Act introduced for the first time, in Pt III, the concept of a "preservation order", which could be placed on any ancient monument that was in danger. Such an order (which needed to be confirmed by Parliament) required all works to the monument to be approved by the Commissioners. It also introduced a duty on the Commissioners to prepare a list of "monuments" whose preservation seemed to the Ancient Monuments Board to be of national importance,[15] and such other monuments as the Commissioners saw fit to include. The owner of an ancient monument on the list had to notify the Commissioners of any proposed works, which presumably gave them an opportunity to impose a preservation order where appropriate.

Under the 1913 Act, "monument" was defined as any structure or erection other than one in ecclesiastical use,[16] and "ancient monument" as any monument that was in the Schedule to the 1882 Act (which remained in force), or any monument of a like character, or any monument the preservation of which was in the public interest by virtue of its special historic, architectural, traditional, artistic or archaeological interest, or the site of any such monument or its remains.

---

[12] s.6.
[13] Pts I and II of the Act.
[14] s.13.
[15] s.12.
[16] For the evolution of this exemption, see **Chapter 16** (places of worship).

Again, an ancient monument was defined so as to include adjoining land required for its preservation or for access to it.[17]

By 1931, some 3,000 ancient monuments had been included in the list, and around 200 were in the ownership or guardianship of the Commissioners. The 1913 Act was proving inadequate, however, and was accordingly strengthened by the Ancient Monuments Act 1931. The latter provided for the preparation of preservation schemes, which effectively restricted the carrying out of what would later be called "development" within the vicinity of an ancient monument, to ensure its preservation. It also enabled the Commissioners to defray the cost of a town planning scheme having the same effect under the Town and Country Planning Acts 1925 (and, in due course, the Act of 1932). The definitions were also amended (by s.15 of the 1931 Act), so that a "monument" was now "any building, structure, or other work, above or below the surface, and any cave or excavation", and an "ancient monument" was extended to include any monument on a list prepared under s.12 of the 1913 Act.

1.2.3 Buildings of special interest: the first Planning Acts

So far, protection had only been given to archaeological monuments. The protection of "areas" and "buildings" had to wait until the introduction of planning legislation.

In general, town planning schemes under the first planning Acts (of 1909 and 1919) could only apply to areas in the course of development or which seemed likely to be used for building—they thus excluded existing buildings. However, the Housing, etc., Act 1923 enabled the Minister to authorise the making of a scheme in an area that was already developed where "on account of the special architectural, historic or artistic interest attaching to a locality, it is expedient that [a scheme should be made] to protect [its] existing features".[18]

The Town and Country Planning Act 1932 then empowered a local authority that had resolved to prepare a scheme under the Act to make an order with respect to any building in its area, directing that the building could not be demolished without its consent.[19] The refusal of such consent was subject to a right of appeal to the Minister, but did not attract compensation; and demolition without obtaining consent was not a criminal offence. This produced the memorable outburst from the Marquis of Hartington (a member of the Royal Commission on Ancient and Historic and Historical Monuments) in the House of Lords:

"[Clause 17 of the 1932 Act] is an abominably bad clause. These buildings have been preserved to us not by Acts of Parliament but by the loving care of generations of free

---

[17] s.22.
[18] For the origins of this provision, see the article by Raymond Cocks at [1998] J.P.L. 203.
[19] s.17.

Englishmen who did not know what a Minister of Health was and who also did not know, in many cases, what a District Council was."[20]

These provisions were extended by the Town and Country Planning Act 1944, which introduced in embryonic form much of the scheme that operates today in relation to what are now known as "listed buildings". It thus enabled a preservation order to prohibit alteration or extension of a building in any way which was specified in the order, as well as its demolition.[21] The Act also for the first time made unauthorised works a criminal offence, punishable by a fine of up to £50; and a court could also order the payment of a sum for the purposes of restoring the building.[22] And authorities were empowered to acquire buildings in need of repair or management.[23]

These powers were, however, more theoretical than real; and anecdotal evidence suggests that, by the end of the Second World War, there were only a small handful of buildings subject to preservation orders—of which, apparently, almost half were in the town of Winchelsea in Kent.

The provisions of the 1932 and 1944 Acts were in any event swept away after the war by the Town and Country Planning Act 1947. Under s.29 of that Act, a "local planning authority" (a new concept introduced for the first time by the Act) could make a "building preservation order" in relation to a building—similar in concept to a "tree preservation order" under s.28. The new controls were kept separate from the scheduling of ancient monuments; a preservation order could thus not be served on a monument that had been scheduled under the 1913 or 1931 Acts (nor on an ecclesiastical building).

The order, once it had been confirmed by the Minister, required the consent of the authority to be obtained before any works were carried out to the building, and applied to the obtaining of such consent the provisions of the 1947 Act relating to applications for planning permission.[24] Because it was at that time (and for many years afterwards[25]) thought that planning permission was not needed for demolition, the works requiring consent under a building preservation order included demolition; consent was also required for works that would "seriously affect the character of the building",[26] a phrase that had first appeared in the 1944 Act.

In addition, under s.30 of the Act, the Minister was to produce a list of buildings of special architectural or historic interest, for the guidance of planning

---

[20] Elsewhere in the same debate, it was said of the noble Marquis by his kinsman the Viscount Cranborne that "the truth about him is that he is living in a period about 50 years ago." See Chapter 4 of John Delafons, *Politics and Preservation: a Policy History of the Built Heritage 1882–1996* (E. & F.N. Spon, London, 1997)—which is a fascinating read on this topic generally.
[21] By s.43(1).
[22] s.44(7).
[23] s.43(9),(10).
[24] TCP (Building Preservation Order) Regulations 1948 (SI 1948/1766).
[25] Until the decision of the Court of Appeal in *Cambridge City Council v Secretary of State* (1992) 64 P. & C.R. 257.
[26] s.29(3).

authorities. There was no requirement for consent to be obtained for works to a building included in such a list (over and above the normal requirement for planning permission), but proposed works were to be notified to the authority—presumably so that it could if it wished serve a preservation order. Failure to notify works to a building included in the Minister's list, or to obtain consent for works to a building subject to a preservation order, was a criminal offence, but still subject to a derisory penalty (£100).

The 1947 Act also retained the power for a local authority or the Minister to compulsorily acquire a building subject to a building preservation order,[27] and for an authority to acquire by agreement a building that was or could be subject to a preservation order,[28] so as in either case to secure its preservation.

The provisions of the 1947 Act, which applied only to England and Wales, were carried forward into the Town and Country Planning Act 1962, which was a consolidating measure, but otherwise remained broadly unaltered until 1968. The Town and Country Planning (Scotland) Act 1947 was similar, and also remained unaltered until 1969 (the Scots missed out on the 1962 consolidation).

1.2.4 *The Historic Buildings and Ancient Monuments Act 1953*

The two codes—relating to ancient monuments and historic buildings—came together briefly in the 1953 Act—which applied both to England and Wales and to Scotland. Parts II and III of this Act dealt with "ancient monuments", in particular, Pt II provided for a revised system of interim preservation notices and preservation orders, replacing the provisions of Pt III of the 1913 Act.[29] Part III of the 1953 Act made other, relatively minor amendments to the 1913 and 1931 Acts. No change was made to the definition of "monument" or "ancient monument".

Part I of the 1953 Act, on the other hand, dealt with "historic buildings"—a phrase that is nowhere defined. It set up three new Historic Buildings Councils (for England, Scotland and Wales), advising the Minister of Works,[30] as distinct from the three Ancient Monuments Boards, advising the Commissioners of Works, set up under the 1913 Act. It further provided for the making of grants by the Minister, on the advice of the appropriate council, for the repair and maintenance of "buildings of outstanding historic or architectural interest" and associated land or objects,[31] the acquisition by him of such buildings and land,[32] and the making of grants by him to the National Trusts for the acquisition of such buildings.[33]

No direct reference was made in the 1953 Act to buildings included in a list prepared by the Minister under the 1947 Act, or to those subject to building preservation orders made by local authorities under that Act—the forerunners to

---

[27] Under s.41(1),(2).
[28] Under s.41(6).
[29] As amended by s.4 of the 1931 Act. A Historic Buildings Council for Northern Ireland was to be set up in due course.
[30] ss 1 to 3.
[31] s.4.
[32] s.5.
[33] s.6(2)

today's "listed buildings"—although the Minister was authorised to make grants to local authorities to defray the cost of acquiring under s.41 of the 1947 Act buildings in poor repair[34]—which would have to be subject to preservation orders or capable of being so. And although the definition of "monument" has always included "building", the scheme of all the legislation up to and including the 1953 Act makes it clear that the two codes were always intended to remain distinct, as indeed they do until this day.

Further provision for the repair and maintenance of buildings of historic or architectural interest in England and Wales was made by the Local Authorities (Historic Buildings) Act 1962, which enabled local authorities to give grants and loans for that purpose.

1.2.5 The Civic Amenities Act 1967

The Civic Amenities Act 1967 started life as a private member's Bill promoted by Duncan Sandys, who had 10 years earlier founded the Civic Trust, and was until his death its president.[35] Its principal significance was that it introduced for the first time the concept of "conservation areas"—defined as "areas of special architectural or historic interest, the character or appearance of which it is desirable to preserve or enhance".[36] This resulted from the growing awareness at that time that whole areas could be of interest and value in their own right, as well as merely individual buildings and trees.

The legislation relating to conservation areas initially had very few teeth, however, in that the only specific measure of protection was the requirement for extra publicity to be given to applications for planning permission. More generally, though, there was a general requirement that special attention should be paid to the desirability of preserving or enhancing the character or appearance of the area.[37] That duty has in itself been considered important by the courts[38]; but no more specific provisions were included, and in particular there was no control over demolition, or works to trees.

The 1967 Act also introduced the power to carry out urgent works to unoccupied historic buildings (either subject to a building preservation order or included in the Minister's list); it increased the penalties for offences relating to such buildings; and it made a number of other minor procedural amendments relating to "listed buildings" (a phrase which appeared for the first time in the side notes to the Act).

The provisions of the 1967 Act, which applied both north and south of the border, were in due course incorporated into the consolidating Town and Country Planning Act 1971 and Town and Country Planning (Scotland) Act 1972.

---

[34] Under s.6(1) of the 1953 Act.
[35] He also chaired the Organising Committee of European Architectural Heritage Year, which led in due course to the Granada Convention (see **2.2.3**).
[36] s.1.
[37] s.1(5).
[38] see **5.3.2**.

1.2.6 The present system: the Town and Country Planning Act 1968

The first listing programme, which had started in 1947, was more or less complete for the whole of England by 1968. And it was the Town and Country Planning Act of that year which introduced in England and Wales the system of listed building control in more or less the form in which it exists today. It explicitly brought into use the concept of a "listed building", widened the scope of the matters to be taken into account by the Minister when considering whether to list a building,[38a] and for the first time defined a listed building so as to include objects attached to it or within its curtilage.[39]

More significantly, the 1968 Act widened the scope of control over works to historic buildings by providing that consent was automatically required for works to be carried out to any building included in the list produced by the Minister, without the need for the authority first to serve a building preservation order. However, whereas building preservation orders under the 1947 Act had simply applied to protected buildings the provisions of that Act relating to planning permission, the 1968 Act introduced for the first time the notion of a separate "listed building consent".[40] Where both types of consent were required, a grant of planning permission would automatically serve as listed building consent[41]—a link that was abolished by the Local Government, Planning and Land Act 1980.[42]

The 1968 Act also introduced for the first time the policy test to be applied in considering proposals for works to listed buildings:

"In considering whether to grant planning permission for development which consists of or includes works for the alteration or extension of a listed building, and in considering whether to grant listed building consent for any works, the local planning authority or the Minister, as the case may be, shall have regard to the desirability of preserving the building or any features of special architectural or historic interest which it possesses."[43]

That duty applied both to applications for planning permission and those for listed building consent. It was extended by the 1980 Act[44] so as to refer also to the setting of a listed building; but it still applies, in identical words, to both categories of application—even though, since the 1990 consolidation, it is now contained in two different sections.[45]

A further consequence of introducing "listed building consent" was that provision had to be made for applications procedures, along the lines of those relating to planning applications; they were tucked away in Pts I and II of Sch.5 to the 1968 Act, and when that Act was replaced by the consolidating TCPA 1971 they remained similarly hidden.[46] And parallel provisions were also introduced for

---

[38a] s.53.
[39] s.40(3).
[40] s.40.
[41] s.41(2).
[42] Sch.15, para.7. It is not entirely clear why.
[43] in s.41(3).
[44] Sch.15, para.7.
[45] P(LBCA)A 1990, ss 16(2) and 66(1).
[46] In Sch.11.

"listed building purchase notices"[47] and "listed building enforcement notices"[48]—the latter operating alongside the established criminal procedures. All of these are still basically in operation. Finally, the 1968 Act also allowed for the payment of compensation where listed building consent was refused for minor works of alteration or extension not requiring planning permission[49]—a right that was abolished in 1991.[50]

The Act also empowered planning authorities to serve "building preservation notices",[51] and required them to serve "repairs notices" prior to the compulsory purchase of listed buildings in poor repair[52]—these too remain in force today, more or less unaltered. Further, minor amendments were made to the procedures relating to planning applications in conservation areas; these were short-lived.

All of the changes introduced by the 1968 Act, which were explained in Circular 61/68 from the Ministry of Housing and Local Government, were carried forward into the 1971 Act. Similar changes were made in the Town and Country Planning (Scotland) Act 1969, and carried forward into the 1972 Act.

1.2.7 Conservation areas: the 1972 and 1974 Acts

The Town and Country Planning Act 1971, applying to England and Wales, incorporated all of the provisions of the 1962 Act, together with the amendments made in 1967 and the rather more numerous ones made in 1968. The new Act was almost immediately amended by the Local Government Act 1972, which set up the two-tier system of local planning authorities—with district councils responsible for heritage matters.

The Town and Country Planning (Scotland) Act 1972 similarly incorporated all of the remaining provisions of the 1947 Scottish Act, as amended in 1967 and 1969, and was itself similarly amended by the Local Government (Scotland) Act 1973. And the Planning (Northern Ireland) Order 1972 was much the same, save for the different administrative structure applying in the six counties.

Conservation areas were still, however, relegated right to the back of each of the new Acts: in England, they were to be found in Pt XV of the 1971 Act ("Miscellaneous and Supplementary Provisions"). It was soon recognised, however, that buildings in conservation areas also needed greater protection. As with listed buildings, there was initially a reluctance to introduce blanket control, so the TCP (Amendment) Act 1972 only enabled an authority to make a direction—similar in effect to a building preservation notice—applying to one or more buildings in a conservation area the provisions relating to listed building consent.[53] Such a direction required to be confirmed by the Secretary of State, or could come into force immediately.

---

[47] s.42 and Pt III of Sch.5.
[48] ss 44 to 47 and Pt IV of Sch.5.
[49] In s.43.
[50] See **15.4.3**.
[51] ss 48, 49; see **3.9**.
[52] ss 50–53; see **11.3.3**.
[53] s.8; Sch.2. See *R. v Endersby Properties* (1975) 32 P. & C.R. 399.

Hardly surprisingly, this was not a satisfactory mechanism. Two years later, therefore, the Town and Country Amenities Act 1974 introduced it on a blanket basis, requiring consent to be obtained for any almost demolition in a conservation area. Initially, this was referred to (confusingly) as "listed building consent"; surprisingly, it was the Town and Country Planning Act 1984, a little-noticed statute dealing with Crown land, which was the first to refer to it as "conservation area consent", a term which was wisely adopted by the Law Commission when the legislation was consolidated in 1990.[54]

The 1972 Act also introduced grants for works in conservation areas; and the 1974 Act also brought in for the first time some control over works to trees in conservation areas, requiring them to be notified to planning authorities. Both of these provisions—the latter somewhat unsatisfactory—are still in force.

Both Acts applied to Scotland as well as to England and Wales. Changes corresponding to those made in Great Britain in the 1968, 1972 and 1974 Acts were introduced in the Planning (Northern Ireland) Order 1982.

In England and Wales, meanwhile, the 1972 and 1974 Acts were followed by Circulars 86/72 and 102/74 from the Department of the Environment. These were in due course replaced by Circular 23/77, the first major piece of policy guidance in this area from central government.

1.2.8 Archaeology: the 1979 Act

The final major statute, the Ancient Monuments and Archaeological Areas Act 1979 (generally referred to in this book simply as "the Ancient Monuments Act") dealt with archaeology; it was the last bill to be introduced by the outgoing Labour administration in 1979.[55] This was to some extent a consolidating measure, in that it replaced the 1913 and 1931 Acts, and Pts II and III of the 1953 Act. But it did, significantly, introduce the concept of a schedule of monuments, to be prepared by the Secretary of State. Any works to a "scheduled monument" then required "scheduled monument consent" to be obtained from the Secretary of State, not from the local planning authority.

The other potentially major innovation was the concept of "areas of archaeological importance", which were the subject of Pt II of the Act. These have not in fact been greatly used; and it has been proposed for some while that Pt II should be repealed.[56]

The provisions of the 1979 Act, which apply equally to England, Wales and Scotland, remain almost entirely still in force.[57] The Historic Monuments and Archaeological Objects (Northern Ireland) Order 1995 is in very similar terms.[58]

---

[54] following the TCP (P(LBCA)A 1990) Regulations 1987—see TCPA 1971, s.55(3A), as substituted by the 1987 regulations, reg.12 and Sch.3.
[55] Which possibly explains why it is not the most expertly drafted statute in force.
[56] See **6.4**.
[57] See **Chapter 6, 12.8, 13.9, 14.8**.
[58] Save that it contains no provision for the designation of archaeological areas.

1.2.9 Amending legislation in the 1980s

In England at least, the second listing programme was finally completed by 1990, and the great majority of conservation areas had been designated by then. The 1980s saw no major new legislation, but rather a sequence of relatively minor amending statutes, dealing largely with procedural details.

The Local Government, Planning and Land Act 1980 thus introduced various minor changes, including—as well as the changes noted above[59]—certificates of immunity from listing, retrospective listing building consents, and certain specific conditions on listed building consents.[60] The following year, the Local Government and Planning (Amendment) Act 1981 tightened up various details of the enforcement mechanisms. These Acts were followed by new Government Circulars—12/81 in England, and 61/81 in Wales. Similar changes were made in the Local Government and Planning (Scotland) Act 1982

A more significant administrative change was made by the National Heritage Act 1983, which set up the Historic Buildings and Monument Commission for England (English Heritage), with consequential amendments to procedures. No similar changes were proposed or made for Wales or Scotland. And two years later, the Local Government Act 1985 abolished metropolitan county councils, including the Greater London Council (GLC), and English Heritage was given a correspondingly larger role in London.

The Housing and Planning Act 1986 then introduced (in England, Wales and Scotland) changes to the details relating to curtilage buildings, urgent works, subsequent approval of details, modification of conditions, works to ecclesiastical buildings, dangerous structures and applications for consent.[61] The coming into force of this Act was accompanied by an important new Circular, 8/87, from the Department of the Environment, parts of which remained in force until 1997.

Changes corresponding to those in the 1980 and 1986 Acts were introduced in the Planning and Building Regulations (Amendment) Northern Ireland) Order 1990.

1.2.10 The 1990 consolidation and the 1991 and 2004 Acts

As a result of the changes made in the 1970s and 1980s, even though most were in substance relatively minor, the provisions in the 1971 Act relevant to listed buildings and conservation areas increased from 24 sections to 36; and almost every one of those was further amended, in some cases several times.

The consolidation of planning legislation in 1990 in England and Wales swept all this away, and replaced the 1971 Act with four new statutes:

(1) the Town and Country Planning Act 1990 (referred to in this book as "the Planning Act"), which deals with mainstream planning control including, in particular, the need for planning permission for development, and control over works to trees and the display of advertisements;

---

[59] See **1.2.6**.
[60] In paras 5–12 of Sch.15.
[61] Sch.9.

(2) the Planning (Listed Buildings and Conservation Areas) Act 1990 ("the Listed Buildings Act"), particularly relevant to the topics dealt with in this book;

(3) the Planning (Hazardous Substances) Act 1990; and

(4) the Planning (Consequential Provisions) Act 1990.

It is indeed significant that listed buildings and conservation areas are now for the first time the subject of a separate Act. The opportunity was taken to incorporate into the new Act the provisions of the Local Authorities (Historic Buildings) Act 1962, which provided for historic buildings grants by local authorities, and some of the Redundant Churches and Other Religious Buildings Act 1969, both of which had escaped the 1971 consolidation.

The Planning and Listed Buildings Acts were themselves significantly amended by the Planning and Compensation Act 1991. The amendments introduced by that Act, in so far as they related to listed buildings and conservation areas, largely concerned enforcement procedures. A number of minor amendments were however made to other planning procedures.

Consolidation took place in Scotland in 1997, introducing four Acts similar to the English Acts of 1990—save that, happily, they were able to take on board the changes made in the Planning and Compensation Act 1991 and the Local Government etc. (Scotland) Act 1994. Northern Ireland was not so fortunate; consolidation took place into a single new instrument, the Planning (Northern Ireland) Order 1995; the changes made in Great Britain in 1991 had to wait until the Planning (Amendment) (Northern Ireland) Order 2003.

More recently, the 1990 Acts were again amended, by the Planning and Compulsory Purchase Act 2004—although few amendments of substance related directly to historic buildings and areas.[62] This time, unusually, the new Act made different provisions for England and for Wales. Corresponding legislation for Scotland is in the Planning (etc.) (Scotland) Bill, introduced in the Scottish Parliament at the end of 2005. Legislation for Northern Ireland is likely, as always, to take a little longer.

Finally, and almost as significant in practice as the actual legislation itself, new guidance was issued during the 1990s by central government, in the form of two important Planning Policy Guidance notes (PPGs).[63] PPG 16, appearing in 1990, covered archaeology, and is still in force more or less unaltered. PPG 15 first appeared in 1994, replacing Circ 8/87 (except for the directions, which remained in place until 1997). Both apply only to England; guidance now in force in Wales, Scotland and Northern Ireland is considered below.[64]

---

[62] The most significant amendment related to the development plan system (see **5.4**).
[63] See **1.3.5**.
[64] See **1.5**.

1.3 The sources of the law

1.3.1 Primary legislation

The principal source of the law that forms the subject of this book is primary legislation—that is, Acts passed by Parliament. The previous section of this chapter has outlined the evolutionary process by which the current statutes acquired their present form; of these, the most significant are the Planning (Listed Buildings and Conservation Areas) Act 1990 and its Scottish equivalent of 1997—referred to in this book simply as "the Listed Buildings Act" and "the Scottish Listed Buildings Act". Each of these is arranged as follows:

Part I. Listed Buildings.

Chapter I. Listing of special buildings.

Chapter II. Authorisation of works affecting listed buildings.
   Control of works in respect of listed buildings.
   Applications for listed building consent.
   Grant of consent subject to conditions.
   Appeals.
   Revocation and modification of consent.

Chapter III. Rights of owners, etc.
   Compensation.
   Listed building purchase notices.

Chapter IV. Enforcement.

Chapter V. Prevention of deterioration and damage.
   Compulsory acquisition of listed buildings in need of repair.
   Acquisition by agreement.
   Management of acquired buildings.

   Urgent preservation.
   Grants for repair and maintenance.
   Damage to listed buildings.

Chapter VI. Miscellaneous and supplemental.
   Exceptions for church buildings and ancient monuments.
   Validity of instruments, decisions and proceedings.
   Special considerations affecting planning functions.

Part II. Conservation areas.

Designation.
General duties of planning authorities.
Control of demolition.
Grants.
Town schemes.

Part III. General.

Authorities exercising functions under the Act.
Special cases.
Miscellaneous provisions.

Part IV. Supplemental.

Each Act is entirely a consolidation statute; although, as noted above, on the recommendation of the Law Commission, the opportunity was taken in 1990 to introduce the term "conservation area consent".

The other principal Acts which are relevant in Great Britain are:

(1)   the Historic Buildings and Ancient Monuments Act 1953, Pt I (dealing with grants etc);

(2)   the Ancient Monuments and Archaeological Areas Act 1979 ("the Ancient Monuments Act"); and

(3)   the Town and Country Planning Act 1990 ("the Planning Act") and the Town and Country Planning (Scotland) Act 1997 ("the Scottish Planning Act").

The first two have been amended in England by the National Heritage Act 1983, reflecting the creation of English Heritage.

Both the English Acts of 1990 were amended by the Planning and Compensation Act 1991 and the Planning and Compulsory Purchase Act 2004; the changes introduced by the 2004 Act are being brought into force gradually throughout 2005 and 2006, and are incorporated in this book as far as possible.

The relevant primary legislation in Northern Ireland is:

(1) the Planning (Northern Ireland) Order 1991, amended by the Planning (Amendment) (Northern Ireland) Order 2003 ("the Northern Ireland Order"); and

(2) the Historic Monuments and Archaeological Objects (Northern Ireland) Order 1995.[65]

1.3.2 Secondary legislation and directions

In addition to primary legislation, regulations may be made under powers in a number of sections of the Planning Act, the Listed Buildings Act and the equivalent legislation in Scotland and Northern Ireland.

The principal regulations currently in force in relation to the cultural heritage are the Planning (Listed Buildings and Conservation Areas) Regulations (referred to in this book as the P(LBCA) Regs) 1990).[66] These came into force on August 24, 1990, replacing the very similar TCP (Listed Buildings and Conservation Areas) Regulations 1987[67]—the differences being largely those necessary to reflect the 1990 consolidation of primary legislation. The 1990 Regulations provide for the detailed implementation of the Listed Buildings Act. The other statutory instruments that are particularly relevant to listed buildings and conservation areas are the TCP (General Permitted Development) and (General Development Procedure) Orders 1995.[68] These two orders together replaced the General Development Order 1988; the first sets out the categories of development for which planning permission is granted automatically.[69]

As for Scotland, the TCP (Listed Buildings and Buildings in Conservation Areas) (Scotland) Regulations 1987[70] and TCP (General Permitted Development) and (General Development Procedure) (Scotland) Orders 1992[71] are very similar to the equivalent instruments applying in England and Wales. Indeed, there are statutory instruments applying in Scotland that are equivalent in function and (usually) virtually identical in wording to almost all of those applying south of the border, except that (as in Wales) references to English Heritage are replaced by corresponding references to the Secretary of State.

---

[65] See **1.5.5**.
[66] SI 1990/1519.
[67] SI 1987/349.
[68] SI 1995/418 and 419.
[69] See **12.2.2**.
[70] SI 1987/1529 (S 112).
[71] SI 1992/223 and SI 1992/224.

Detailed procedural rules for Northern Ireland are contained in the Planning (Listed Buildings) Regulations (Northern Ireland) 1992,[72] the Planning (Conservation Areas) (Demolition) Regulations (Northern Ireland) 1988[73] and the Planning (General Development) Order 1993.[74]

In addition to those and other statutory instruments, the Secretary of State also has power to make directions to local planning authorities and others. Those currently in force in England are contained in Environment Circular 01/01[75]; they came into force on February 19, 2001. Those applying in Wales are in WO Circ. 1/98, which replaced from March 2, 1998 those in WO Circ. 61/96. It should however be noted that, unlike the remainder of the Circulars (and the PPG), these directions have the full force of law. They largely concern the circumstances in which applications for planning permission and listed building consent must be notified to particular bodies,[76] and the limits to the requirement for conservation area consent to be obtained for demolition of unlisted buildings.[77]

1.3.3 International law

As well as domestic law, international law is also relevant—at least in theory—as the background to the domestic law that is the subject of most of this book. Its impact has in practice so far been limited; but it is likely to grow. It is accordingly the subject of the following chapter.

1.3.4 Case law

The final source of law is the growing and evolving body of judicial decisions made in the higher courts, which are in general binding upon those deciding subsequent disputes, and which in particular guide inferior decision-makers such as inspectors and local planning authorities in their interpretation of the law. It should not be forgotten, however, that the function of this case law is largely just that—to interpret the legislative code produced by Parliament—and it is the legislation itself that is of the greatest importance.

The pattern of judicial decisions is in any event unavoidably dependent upon the chances of litigation; and the areas of statutory law which have received clarification in this way are thus somewhat random. But there can be no doubt that there have been in recent years many more cases in the courts—including a number in the Court of Appeal—involving the law relating to listed buildings and conservation areas. It is of course principally the decisions of that Court and the House of Lords that are significant in guiding the courts in reaching decisions on

---

[72] SR & O (NI) No.263.
[73] SR & O (NI) No.5.
[74] SR (NI) No.278
[75] Culture, Media and Sport Circ. 01/2001; this replaced DOE Circ. 14/97 (DCMS Circ. 1/97).
[76] See **13.5**.
[77] See **12.6**.

subsequent cases; but many other decisions noted here, from courts of first instance, are illustrative even if not strictly determinative.

Wherever possible, judicial decisions have been cited in the text by reference to Planning Law Reports (PLR), the Journal of Planning and Environment Law (JPL) or Property, Planning and Compensation Reports (P & CR), as these are probably the reports which are most readily available to practitioners, particularly those other than lawyers; for other citations, see the Table of Cases. Citation of cases that have not been reported in the traditional law reports are by reference to their neutral citation—generally "EWHC" or "EWCA". Transcripts of these sessions can generally be found in a web-based series such as Casetrack and Lawtel.

1.3.5 Central government policy guidance

Finally, it has already been mentioned that, in this as in many other areas of law and procedure, guidance from central government is almost as important as the actual legislation itself.

As with all government advice, these are not definitive (and indeed the courts gave from time to time overruled advice in a Circular or a PPG), but they provide a useful aid to the interpretation and implementation of the law. More generally, they provide an indication of current government policy, which is critical in determining whether or not particular proposals will be sympathetically received.

The two principal statements of relevant government policy in England are the Planning Policy Guidance notes:

- PPG 15, *Planning and the Historic Environment*, issued jointly by the DOE and the DNH in September 1994; and

- PPG 16, *Archaeology and Planning*, issued by the DOE in September 1990.

These are now showing their age, but each is still very valuable as a source information and guidance, and should be required reading for anyone working in the field. PPG15 was significantly amended by DOE Circ 14/97, largely following on the decision of the House of Lords in *Shimizu (UK) Ltd v Westminster CC*[78]; and then again by DETR Circ 01/01. The two PPGs are referred to at appropriate points throughout this book, and reproduced in an updated form at **Appendix A** and **Appendix B**. Each contained an appendix listing key bodies and organisations; a combined and updated list appears at **Appendix C**.

Policy guidance in other parts of the United Kingdom is considered towards the end of this Chapter.[79]

---

[78] [1996] 3 P.L.R. 89.
[79] See **1.5**.

1.4 The administration of control: England

1.4.1 Central government

Functions of central government are usually entrusted by Parliament to "the Secretary of State" generally, rather than to any specific Secretary of State. They can thus in practice be transferred from one department to another without the need for a specific Order under the Ministers of the Crown Act 1975. In this case, there are currently (and have been since 1992) two departments of central government with responsibility for the administration of control over listed buildings, conservation areas and monuments in England:

- the Office of the Deputy Prime Minister (ODPM); and

- the Department of Culture, Media and Sport (DCMS).

It may be helpful to set out briefly who does what, and how the present position arose.

Following the general election in 1992, some of the functions previously performed by the Department of the Environment (DoE) were transferred to the new Department for National Heritage.[80] So far as they are relevant to the topics covered in this book, they were as follows:

(1) listing of buildings[81];

(2) reserve powers in respect of the designation of conservation areas[82];

(3) scheduling monuments[83];

(4) grants to heritage bodies[84];

(5) dealing with urgent works notices, repairs notices and associated land acquisition[85];

(6) determining applications for scheduled monument consent[86]; and

(7) responsibilities in respect of the ecclesiastical exemption.[87]

---

[80] See DOE Circ. 20/92 (DNH Circ. 1/92), para.4. A few responsibilities had in the past been allocated specifically to the Secretary of State for the Environment; these were therefore explicitly transferred to the Department for National Heritage, by the Transfer of Functions (National Heritage) Order 1992 (SI 1992/1311), art.6. They include the role of the Secretary of State in relation to the management of certain monuments and buildings (which is in practice carried out on his or her behalf by English Heritage, under s.34 of the National Heritage Act 1983), the consideration of planning applications affecting Royal parks and palaces, and the membership of the Architectural Heritage Fund (see **9.7.2**), the Cathedrals Fabric Commission (see **16.8.1**), and the Chatham Historic Dockyard Trust.

[81] See **3.3**, **3.4**.

[82] See **5.5.2**.

[83] See **6.2**.

[84] See **Chapter 9**.

[85] See **10.3**, **10.4** and **Chapter 11**.

[86] See **13.9**.

[87] See **16.3** and **16.4**.

Following the election of a new Government in May 1997, the Department of National Heritage was renamed the Department for Culture, Media and Sport (DCMS).[88]

The Secretary of State for the Environment, on the other hand, retained all his powers in relation to general planning control. Since these to a considerable extent overlapped with his powers under the specific statutory regimes relating to listed buildings and conservation areas, the Department of the Environment also retained responsibility for the following casework:

(1) decisions on Art.4 directions[89] and

(2) the determination of called-in applications planning permission, listed building and conservation area consent, and applications by local planning authorities;

(3) determinations under the non-statutory procedure for dealing with proposals by government departments[90];

(4) procedures relating to the revocation or modification of permission and consent[91];

(5) the determination of appeals against refusal of permission and consent[92];

(6) procedures relating to listed building and conservation area purchase notices[93];

(7) consideration of proposals put forward by the Church Commissioners for the demolition of a redundant church that is listed or in a conservation area[94];

(8) procedures relating to listed building and conservation area enforcement notices[95]; and

(9) procedures relating to compensation in respect of the above.

The Department of the Environment was subsumed in 1998 into the Department of the Environment Transport and the Region (DETR), which metamorphosed in 2001 into the Department of Transport, Local Government and the Regions (DTLR) and then in May 2002 into the Office of the Deputy Prime Minister (ODPM).[96]

The two departments in practice work closely together, as shown by the joint production of PPG 15. Their roles are summarised at paras A2 and A3 of Annex A to the PPG.

---

[88] 1997 SI/1744, which came into force on August 22, 1997.
[89] See **7.4**.
[90] See **13.7, 13.10**.
[91] See **13.11**.
[92] See **15.3**.
[93] See **15.4**.
[94] See **16.3.8**.
[95] See **18.4, 18.5**
[96] SI 1997/2971; SI 2002/2626.

1.4.2 English Heritage

The Historic Buildings and Monuments Commission for England (referred to in this book, and almost everywhere else, as "English Heritage") was established in 1984, under the National Heritage Act 1983. That Act was amended by the National Heritage Act 2002 with effect from July 1, 2002.[97]

The powers and functions of English Heritage are formally defined in ss 33 to 35 of the 1983 Act; but its role is in practice fourfold:

(1) to manage monuments and historic buildings in public ownership;

(2) to advise the Secretaries of State on the exercise of their powers relating to listed buildings and conservation areas;

(3) to advise the Secretary of State for Culture, Media and Sport on the exercise of his or her powers relating to scheduled monuments;

(4) to act as a statutory consultee on the more significant applications for planning permission and listed building consent.

The first of these, which English Heritage carries out in succession to a long line of government departments stretching back to the Ministry of Works and beyond,[98] is the role which is more well-known to the public, and involves it in such matters as the controversy of the future care of Stonehenge. To this end, it may form companies, exploit intellectual property rights, acquire and other property, and sell souvenirs.[99] It is, however, largely beyond the scope of this book.

As to the second, English Heritage when it was first set up simply took over many of the tasks formerly performed by the Department of the Environment. Since then, however, it has taken a more independent line—not always to general public acclaim—and indeed has, on occasion, challenged the Government all the way to the High Court.[1] It now occupies (in England) a fundamentally important place in the system of control relating to listed buildings and conservation areas. Its functions in this field are summarised at paras A6–A9 of Annex A to PPG 15, and are referred to at appropriate places throughout this book. As to the third role, here too English Heritage is following its predecessors the Commissioners of Works.[2] Its functions in this area are summarised at para.2 of Annex 1 to PPG 16.

It is predominantly the fourth of the above functions that is the subject of much of this book.[3]

Until relatively recently, the recording (as opposed to identification) of the historic environment used to be principally the responsibility of the Royal Commission on Historical Monuments of England, a worthy body set up in the early years of the 20th century, and in more recent times often confused with English Heritage (not surprisingly, as the latter is consistently referred to in leg-

---

[97] Visit *www.english-heritage.org.uk*.
[98] See **1.2.1, 1.2.2**.
[99] National Heritage Act 1983, ss 33–35, as amended by National Heritage Act 2002.
[1] *Historic Buildings and Monuments Commission v Secretary of State* [1997] 3 P.L.R. 8, J.P.L. 424 (see **14.7.5, 14.9.5**).
[2] See **1.2**.
[3] See in particular **Chapters 13 and 14**.

islation as "the Commission"). It was finally subsumed into the newer body in 2002.[4]

The primary remit of English Heritage extends, obviously, only to England: there are no directly equivalent bodies in the other parts of the United Kingdom. However, it may now sell items relating to foreign buildings and monuments, and provide consultancy services in respect of such monuments.[5]

It should perhaps be emphasised that English Heritage is not part of government, however much it may sometimes behave as if it were. In that respect, it is fundamentally different from Cadw, Historic Scotland and the Environment and Heritage Service in Northern Ireland. And its role has gradually evolved over the 20 or so years since it was set up, in that it now perceives its role to be the promoter of the whole of England's historic environment, as defined at the start of this chapter, rather than just the agency that safeguards the best buildings and monuments from all change.

Finally, it is worth noting that English Heritage produces a wide range of useful, free publications covering the matters that are dealt with in this book; most are available in PDF format on its website.

1.4.3 Local planning authorities

Under the supervision of the Secretaries of State and the watchful eye of English Heritage, it is the local planning authority that has the leading role in securing the conservation of the historic environment in its area. It determines applications for planning permission, listed building consent and conservation area consent; it can takes enforcement action; it can make art.4 directions and tree preservation orders, and designate areas of special control over advertisements; it can serve notices to achieve the repair of historic buildings, and give grants and loans; and, not the least important, it has overall responsibility for planning policy in its area, which provides the framework within which all its other powers do or do not work.

In those areas where there is still a two-tier structure of local councils, the local planning authority is in general the district or borough council, subject to the variations noted below and at appropriate points throughout the remainder of the book. In some areas, however, the required range of knowledge and experience is beyond the resources of a single authority (particularly in the case of a smaller council whose area contains few listed buildings). In such cases, it is the county council which deals with all or most conservation matters, since it is able to provide a team of staff with the appropriate specialist skills.[6] In addition, authorities (of either tier) are able to call upon the advice of English Heritage in

---

[4]   The de facto merger took place in 1999; but the forma/merger could not be completed
      until after the passing of the NHA 2002, which for the first time gave English Heritage
      powers in relation to maritime archaeology previously possessed by the RCHM (see
      6.5). See also Authorisation of Works (Listed Buildings) (England) Order 2001 (SI 2001/
      24) (the effect of which is noted at **13.7.10**).
[5]   National Heritage Act 1983, ss 33A, 33B, inserted by National Heritage Act 2002, s.4.
[6]   Any local authority may delegate its functions to any other local authority: Local
      Government Act 1972, s.101.

appropriate cases. Some authorities obtain specialist advice from private consultants.

There have been unitary authorities in Greater London and the other metropolitan areas since 1986; that pattern was subsequently extended to a number of areas.[7] Such authorities are, obviously, responsible for all planning functions in their area—although they too may co-operate with neighbouring authorities if they consider it appropriate.

In practice, there are in some authorities a number of conservation officers with specialised training and experience; in other areas, by contrast, there are apparently no specialists, either in the county council or in any of the district councils.[8] The Institute of Historic Building Conservation (IHBC) exists to promote the wide availability of good advice and sound practice; and its journal *Context* is a useful source of advice and information.

The Secretary of State has stated that:

"The availability of advice from English Heritage, and from the national amenity societies on certain categories of listed building consent application, does not relieve authorities of the need to ensure that they have their own expert advice suitably deployed to enable them to deal both with day-to-day casework and with longer-term policy formulation. Whether this expertise should take the form of full-time conservation staff, or the use of consultancy expertise, is a matter for individual authorities to consider."[9]

He does have power to require district planning authorities to submit for his approval details of the arrangements they have made for the carrying out of their functions with relation to listed buildings and conservation areas, and to make appropriate directions if he is not satisfied that they are adequate.[10] In fact, of course, as with all local authority services, the quality of the expertise provided depends on the budget available.

More recently, the Government has recognised that there is a serious shortage of staff in local planning authority conservation sections.[11] It accordingly suggests that neighbouring authorities may want to enter partnerships with each other and with English Heritage in sub-regional groups. It also draws attention to the new HELM (Historic Environment Local Management) initiative.[12]

---

[7] All of the former (1974) counties of Avon, Berkshire, Cleveland, Herefordshire, Humberside, the Isle of Wight and Rutland; and the former districts of Blackburn, Blackpool, Bournemouth, Brighton and Hove, Darlington, Derby, Gillingham (Kent), Halton (Runcorn), Leicester, Luton, Milton Keynes, Nottingham, Peterborough, Plymouth, Poole, Portsmouth, Rochester, Southampton, Southend-on-Sea, Stoke-on-Trent, Thamesdown (Swindon), The Wrekin (Telford), Thurrock, Torbay, Warrington and York. See Local Government Act 1992, Local Government Changes for England Regulations 1994 (SI 1994/867) and the (Structural Change) Order made for each area under powers in the 1992 Act.

[8] For further details, see *Local Authority Conservation Provision in England*, a research project by Philip Grover of the School of the Built Environment at Oxford Brookes University, commissioned by English Heritage and the IHBC; the report, published in February 2003, is available on the English Heritage website.

[9] PPG 15, Annex A, para.A5.

[10] P(LBCA)A 1990, Sch.4, para.7.

[11] *Review of Heritage Protection: The Way Forward*, DCMS, June 2004.

[12] See website *www.helm.org.uk*

As for listed buildings owned by local authorities, they are subject to special rules relating to the obtaining of planning permission and listed building consent.[13] Authorities are also under a duty to have regard to the desirability of preserving features of special architectural or historic interest (and particularly listed buildings) when appropriating for other purposes land that they have acquired for general planning purposes—and when developing or disposing of such land.[14]

Finally, the law described in this book applies in the Isles of Scilly just as it does elsewhere in England, on the basis that the Council of the Isles is treated as if it were a unitary authority.[15]

1.4.4 Greater London

The law as described in this book generally applies throughout England. London has, however, always been slightly different from the rest of England with regard to planning law in general, and historic buildings law in particular. This was emphasised in 1986 when the Greater London Council was abolished. In the course of the emotional debate over abolition, much special pleading was made for the GLC's Historic Buildings Division, which had an international reputation for its high standards. As a result, the Division emerged from the ashes as the London Division of English Heritage.

The detailed procedures for handling applications are therefore somewhat different in Greater London. As with other areas with unitary authorities, the borough councils (including the Common Council of the City of London) are the local planning authorities in their areas, but English Heritage has a larger role than elsewhere. The Secretary of State therefore has a correspondingly reduced one.[16]

A further (slight) difference in London is the existence of the UK's only attempt at regional government—the Greater London Authority and the Mayor, set up under the Greater London Authority Act 1999. The Mayor has produced a spatial development strategy (entitled "the London Plan"), under powers in Pt VIII of that Act, which does contain a few policies relating to the historic environment.[17-18] Generally, however, his responsibilities for planning in the capital are focussed on strategic issues, and responsibility for the cultural heritage, including the determination of applications for listed building consent, remains with the borough councils, in consultation with English Heritage. The white paper, A Mayor and Assembly for London, suggested that the Mayor will have a role in appointments to English Heritage's London Advisory Committee.[19]

---

[13] See **13.10.5**.
[14] P(LBCA) A 1990, s.66 (2).
[15] P(LBCA)A 1990, s.92; SI 2005/2085.
[16] See **13.5**.
[17-18] Notably Policies 4B.10–14. The first states that "the Mayor will work with strategic partners to protect and enhance London's historic environment".
[19] Cm. 3897, para.5.76.

There used to be slightly different rules applying within the area of the London Docklands Development Corporation; but the Corporation was wound up in 1998.[20]

1.4.5 National parks, the Broads, the Cotswolds and the Chilterns

The administrative arrangements are also somewhat different in national parks and the Norfolk and Suffolk Broads. In these areas, the district councils have a much reduced role, and the responsibility is instead given to special ad hoc authorities.

In the seven English national parks (Dartmoor, Exmoor, the Lake District, Northumberland, the North York Moors, the Peak District and the Yorkshire Dales), special national park authorities were set up in 1997.[21] In the case of the Peak District and the Lake District, they replaced the special planning boards. Each new authority is the local planning authority for almost all purposes—including all matters relating to listed buildings and conservation areas.[22]

Since 1997, the purpose of designation of a national park has included the conservation and enhancement of the cultural heritage of the designated area.[23]

In the Broads, the local planning authority for most purposes will be the Broads Authority, set up under the Norfolk and Suffolk Broads Act 1988.

Planning control in areas of outstanding natural beauty (AONBs) is generally exercised as elsewhere—that is, the planning authority is the district council or unitary authority. However, the Countryside and Rights of Way Act introduced a power for the Secretary of State to establish a statutory board for any designated AONB, that would have certain functions concurrently with the other local authorities in the area.[24] Conservation Boards have now been established for the Cotswolds and Chilterns AONBs, with effect from October 22, 2004, and in each case the following functions, amongst others, have been conferred on them[25]:

(1)   the giving of grants for repair and maintenance of historic buildings[26];

(2)   the carrying out of urgent works to unoccupied historic buildings[27];

(3)   the acquisition and guardianship of ancient monuments[28]; and

(4)   the supervision of public access to monuments under public control.[29]

---

[20] SI 1997/2946. As to what might be considered its successors, the Thurrock and Thames Gateway Development Corporations, see **1.4.6**.

[21] Environment Act 1995, s.65; National Park Authorities (England) Order 1996 (SI 1996/1243).

[22] 1995 Act, Sch.9, para.13.

[23] 1995 Act, s.61(4).

[24] 2000 Act, s.86.

[25] The Cotswolds and Chilterns Areas of Outstanding Natural Beauty (Establishment of Conservation Board) Orders 2004 (SIs 2004/1777; 2004/1778), art.25.

[26] P(LBC)A 1990, ss 57, 58; see **9.6**.

[27] P(LBC)A 1990, ss 54, 55; see **10.3**.

[28] AMAAA 1979, ss 11, 12–17, 21; see **11.6**.

[29] AMAAA 1979, ss 19–20; see **11.6.5**.

It remains to see how the new boards will use their powers, which they can exercise concurrently with the existing local authorities in their areas.

1.4.6 Other special cases

There is power for the Secretary of State to designate an enterprise zone authority as the local planning authority for the purposes of the P(LBCA)A 1990.[30] He has, however, not chosen to do so for any of the zones so far declared. At present, therefore, the law and procedures described in this book apply in enterprise zones just as elsewhere.

A housing action trust, set up under powers in the Housing Act 1988, may also be designated the local planning authority for its area.[31] The Secretary of State is under a duty to ensure that trusts, when disposing of or developing their land, preserve any features of special architectural or historic interest, and particularly listed buildings.[32] Only six such trusts have so far been set up; and three of those have recently been dissolved.

Similarly, the Urban Regeneration Agency ("English Partnerships"), set up under Pt III of the Leasehold Reform, Housing and Urban Development Act 1993 to bring about the regeneration of vacant or derelict land, may be designated as the local planning authority for any area in which it operates, by an order under s.170 of the 1993 Act.[33]

In relation to any of these areas, references to "the local planning authority" should be interpreted accordingly.

The law and procedures relating to listed buildings and (subject to one exception[34]) those relating to conservation areas also applies in simplified planning zones just as elsewhere.

A number of urban development corporations were set up in the 1980s and early 1990s under powers in the Local Government Planning and Land Act 1980. Almost all were local planning authorities their area, for all purposes including those relating to listed buildings and conservation areas. All of those corporations have now been wound up, and their functions returned to district or borough councils. However, the idea seems to be enjoying a new lease of life, with three corporations being set up in 2003 and 2004[35]; two (Thurrock and Thames Gateway) have been designated as local planning authorities, but only for certain purposes.[36]

---

[30] s.81; TCPA 1990, s.6(2).
[31] TCPA 1990, s.8(1); 1988 Act, s.67. It appears that none of the trusts was in fact designated as a local planning authority.
[32] 1988 Act, s.66(3).
[33] TCPA 1990, s.8A, inserted by 1993 Act, Sch.21.
[34] See **5.3.1**.
[35] The Area and Constitution Orders are SI 2003/2896 (Thurrock); SI 2004/1641 (Thames Gateway); SI 2004/3370 (West Northamptonshire).
[36] The London Thames Gateway and Thurrock Development Corporation (Planning Functions) Orders 2005 (SIs 2005/2572 and 2005/2721); see **13.2.1**.

1.5 Law and practice in other parts of the United Kingdom

1.5.1 Introduction

The account earlier in this chapter of the historical process by which the present legislative code came to be as it is has mentioned in passing the legislation in parts of the United Kingdom outside England. From that brief account, it will be clear that the law in Wales is virtually identical to that in England, and the law in Scotland and Northern Ireland scarcely less so. But it is not quite the same—and the administrative arrangements, in particular, are significantly different.

Previous editions of this book have focussed principally on law and practice in England and Wales, and included a brief note at the end on differences in Scotland and Northern Ireland. In this edition, an attempt has been made for the first time to incorporate the law in Scotland and Northern Ireland into the main text—or at least into the footnotes, so that readers there may know where to look for more detail. This is, ironically, not least because practice and policy in Wales is increasingly differing from that in England; and if that is included, there seems no obvious reason to exclude practice and policy elsewhere in the United Kingdom.

References to the principal pieces of planning legislation—in particular, the Planning and Listed Building Acts of 1990, the Ancient Monuments Act, the 1987 Regulations and the General Development Order of 1992—are thus accompanied by references to their non-English equivalents. However, limitations of time and space have meant that it has not been possible to do the same for every peripheral reference; so readers outside England may have to exercise care accordingly.

This last section of the introductory chapter, therefore, merely seeks to highlight in outline the distinctive features of the systems within the United Kingdom outside England.

1.5.2 Wales: law

The law in Wales regarding listed buildings and conservation areas, and planning in general, is in principle identical to that applying in England; the details however are occasionally different—and a casual glance at the *Planning Law Encyclopedia* will make it clear that the extent of that difference is steadily increasing.

First, primary legislation in Wales is in principle identical to that in England.[37] However, as a result of the Government of Wales Act 1998, virtually all of the functions of the Secretary of State relating to planning, listed buildings and conservation areas were transferred to the National Assembly for Wales on July 6, 1999.[38] References in primary and secondary legislation (and in this book) to the Secretary of State should be construed accordingly. Further, this means in practice that the functions that are in England performed by departments of central government, including both the ODPM and the DCMS, are performed in Wales by "Welsh Assembly Government".

---

[37] See **1.3.1**.
[38] Government of Wales Act 1998, s.43; National Assembly for Wales (Transfer of Functions) Order 1999 (SI 672).

The powers of the Welsh Assembly Government are likely to be significantly extended following the enactment of the Government of Wales Bill, which was introduced into the House of Commons on December 8, 2005.

Since the remit of English Heritage does not extend to Wales, the changes introduced by the National Heritage Act 1983 largely apply to England only.[39] Thus in law the National Assembly has all the powers and duties ascribed in England either to the First Secretary of State or to the Secretary of State for Culture, Media and Sport—and most of those of English Heritage as well. In the exercise of its powers in relation to historic buildings, the Assembly is advised by the Historic Buildings Council for Wales[40]—an independent body whose members it appoints. It used to be advised in relation to archaeological matters by the Ancient Monuments Board for Wales, established in 1913, but that body is to be abolished on April 1, 2006.[41]

The agency within Welsh Assembly Government dealing on a day-to-day basis with historic buildings is known formally as "Cadw: Welsh Historic Monuments", based since January 2005 at Nantgarw. It is referred to in this book, as it is in practice, simply as "Cadw" (*cadw* is not an abbreviation, but a Welsh verb meaning to 'keep, preserve or save'). Cadw is in many ways similar to English Heritage—as is clear from comparing the draft versions of PPG 15 issued on either side of the border, which described the functions of the two bodies in identical terms.[42] Constitutionally, however, Cadw is part of central government, and therefore may not take an independent line (at, for example, highway inquiries). The implications of this were considered, in relation to Historic Scotland, in the *County Properties* case.[43]

Cadw is advised, particularly on grants but also more generally, by the Historic Buildings Council for Wales,[44] and provides the secretariat for the Council.

Secondly, the Local Government (Wales) Act 1994 introduced in 1996 unitary authorities throughout the principality—either county or county borough councils. These generally have responsibility for listed building control; and it was the policy of the Welsh Office to ensure that each new council has adequate conservation advice available to it. However, the comments above as to planning authorities apply generally to Wales as to England.[45]

Secondary legislation is also very similar to that applying in England—although it is important to note that, increasingly, regulations and orders are being issued separately (see the Table of Statutory Instruments). In addition, there

---

[39] See **1.4.2**.

[40] Established under HBAMA 1953, s.3.

[41] SI 2006/64.

[42] A draft version of PPG 15 (Wales) was issued at the end of 1993, which was virtually identical to the first draft of PPG 15 for England. However, no further progress was made on that; and no PPG 15 ever emerged in Wales (see **1.5.3**). Indeed, no planning policy guidance (on any subject) was issued for a long time.

[43] *County Properties v Scottish Ministers* [2001] 4 P.L.R. 122, overturning [2000] 4 P.L.R. 83, [2001] J.P.L. 170; see **1.5.4**.

[44] HBAMA 1953, ss 2, 3.

[45] See **1.4.3**, **1.4.5** and **1.4.6**. One minor difference is that the national park authorities in Wales—for the Brecon Beacons, the Pembrokeshire Coast, and Snowdonia—were set up in 1996, a year earlier than those in England (under SI 1995/2803).

are a few, relatively minor procedural differences—the directions in WO Circ. 1/ 98, for example, are slightly different to those in Environment Circ. 01/01 in relation to which classes of applications must be notified to the Assembly.[46] These largely arise as a result of the much smaller number of listed buildings in Wales,[47] and the correspondingly diminished role of local planning authorities—which rely heavily in practice on the advice of Cadw.

The Welsh language may be used alongside or instead of English in all proceedings; and Welsh forms have been prescribed.[48] These were drafted in relation to the TCPA 1971, as extended by s.2(2) of the Welsh Language Act 1967, but the forms prescribed in them can be used in connection with the Listed Buildings Act[49]—save that, obviously, references to "Deddf Cynllunio Gwlad a Thref 1971" should be replaced by references to "Deddf Cynllunio (Adeiladau Rhestredig ac Ardaloedd Cadwraeth) 1990".

Subject to the above, and to specific references elsewhere in this book, its contents may be relied on in Wales as in England.

Much useful information can be found in the report of the Welsh Affairs Committee of the House of Commons, published in May 1993, on *The Preservation of Historic Buildings and Ancient Monuments*,[50] the Government's response,[51] and the follow-up report, published, in March 1997.[52]

1.5.3 Wales: Government policy

The Welsh Assembly published in March 2002 a document entitled *Planning Policy Wales*, which provided general policy guidance on all topics—including those that are the subject of this book. On all other topics, that has been supplemented by more detailed Technical Advice Notes (TANs); historic buildings and conservation areas, however, are still the subject of WO Circ. 61/96, which replaced WO Circ. 61/81 with effect from December 5, 1996. That Circular was in turn amended slightly by WO Circ. 1/98, issued on February 2, 1998.

The guidance in the Welsh Circulars is broadly similar to that in the English PPG 15 (as amended), although it is in many cases slightly briefer. To save space, only the principal references to the Welsh guidance are given in the body of the text.

Guidance on archaeology in Wales is provided in WO Circ. 60/96, which replaced PPG 16 (Wales) on December 5, 1996.

1.5.4 Scotland

As from July 1, 1999, the Scotland Act 1998 brought into being a significantly different system of government in Scotland. Many central government responsi-

---

[46] See **13.7.3**.
[47] See **3.5.2**.
[48] Town and Country Planning (Listed Buildings in Wales and Buildings in Conservation Areas in Wales) (Welsh Forms) Regulations 1990 (SI 1990/1147).
[49] Planning (Consequential Provisions) Act 1990, s.2(4).
[50] HC 403, 2 vols including evidence.
[51] Cm 2416.
[52] HC 250.

bilities—including those under the Ancient Monuments Act and the Scottish Planning and Listed Buildings Acts of 1997—were transferred to the Scottish Executive; and the Scottish Ministers took over the responsibilities of the Secretary of State.[53]

Subject to that, the legislation relating to the cultural heritage in Scotland is in principle similar to that applying in Wales. The Ancient Monuments Act thus applies almost precisely is as it does to Wales; and the 1997 Scottish legislation, relating to listed buildings and conservation areas, is very similar to the 1990 legislation applying south of the border. The Planning and Compulsory Purchase Act 2004 does not apply to Scotland, but the Planning etc. (Scotland) Bill, introduced into the Scottish Parliament on December 19, 2005, contains broadly similar (but not identical) provisions. Practitioners in Scotland will need to be alert to see how it works in practice.[54]

The Scottish Ministers are now advised in relation both to archaeology and to historic buildings and areas by the Historic Environment Advisory Council for Scotland, a new body set up with effect from 2003, under the Public Appointments and Public Bodies etc. (Scotland) Act 2003—replacing both the Ancient Monuments Board for Scotland and the Historic Buildings Council for Scotland.[55] However, the Council does not have the executive powers of English Heritage—to which, indeed, there is no constitutionally equivalent Scottish body.

In practice, the responsibilities of the Scottish Ministers in relation to the historic environment—that is, ancient monuments and archaeological sites and landscapes, historic buildings, parks and gardens; conservation areas; and designed landscapes—are discharged by a body known as "Historic Scotland". This was set up in 1991, and is now an Agency of the Scottish Executive Education Department.[56] Its constitution is the *Framework Document* published in 2001. The position of Historic Scotland is thus constitutionally similar to Cadw[57] rather than English Heritage, although its resources and influence are greater than those of its Welsh counterpart.

The status and role of Historic Scotland has been considered by the courts in *County Properties Ltd v the Scottish Ministers*. Historic Scotland had objected to a proposal to demolish the Grade A listed house of "Greek" Thompson in Glasgow, to be replaced by a modern block—a proposal that had the broad support of the council. It had accordingly arranged for the Scottish Ministers to call it in for their decision, following a public inquiry. The developers objected to this, claiming that the Scottish Ministers could not make an unbiased decision on the application for listed building consent when their own executive agency, Historic Scotland, was known to be hostile. At first instance, the Outer House of the Court of Session agreed that the status of Historic Scotland as part of the Executive meant that the decision of the Ministers to call in the application, and to appoint a

---

[53] Scotland Act 1998, s.53

[54] Except that the changes made by the Planning and Compensation Act 1991 were incorporated into the 1997 Acts.

[55] Visit *www.heacs.org.uk*

[56] It succeeded "Historic Buildings and Monuments: Scotland", which was part of the Scottish Office Environment Department.

[57] See **1.5.2.**

reporter to hold an inquiry, would be a breach of the developers' human rights, under art.6 of the ECHR.[58]

However, on appeal, the Extra Division followed the decision of the House of Lords in the *Alconbury* litigation,[59] and held that, although the reporter would not be an "independent and impartial tribunal" for the purposes of art.6, that would not be fatal, since the rules of natural justice would be observed at the inquiry, and the decision reached would be subject to a right of statutory appeal to the courts on a point of law.[60] The reasoning behind the decision is somewhat opaque, and leads to more than a suspicion of pragmatic expediency; but the conclusion is clear enough: the status of Historic Scotland is not, as might have been thought, a constitutional problem. However, it does emphasise that in a case involving a central government agency, it is important for all concerned to pay scrupulous attention to the rules of natural justice.

The principal source of policy guidance from the Scottish Ministers is contained in the splendid *Memorandum of Guidance on Listed Buildings and Conservation Areas* produced by Historic Scotland, the most recent edition of which is still that which was produced in 1998.[61] Also relevant are national planning policy guidelines NPPG 5, *Archaeology and Planning*, produced in 1994; and NPPG 18, *Planning and the Historic Environment*, produced in April 1999.[62]

Local government in most areas of Scotland used to be divided between district and regional councils. Under this arrangement, as in England, the district councils were given almost all responsibility for listed building control. This was replaced with effect from April 1, 1996 by a new system of unitary authorities, under the provisions of the Local Government etc (Scotland) Act 1994.[63] There is provision for grouping of district authorities for structure planning purposes, but otherwise the new authorities will have full responsibility for planning, including listed buildings and conservation areas.[64] The existing unitary authorities will be retained in the Orkney, Shetland and Western Isles areas.

Two national parks were created in March 2003.[65] In the Trossachs and Loch Lomond National Park, created in July 2002, the national park authority is the sole planning authority, in place of the local authorities.[66] In the Cairngorms

---

[58] *County Properties v Scottish Ministers* [2000] 4 P.L.R. 83, [2001] J.P.L. 170 (Outer House, Court of Session).

[59] *R. (Holding and Barnes PLC) v Secretary of State; R. (Alconbury Developments Ltd) v Secretary of State* [2003] 2 A.C. 295, [2001] 2 P.L.R. 76, HL (in which it had been—unsuccessfully—claimed that the status of the Secretary of State as both landowner and tribunal meant that the determination of a planning application would inevitably lead to a breach of rights under art.6).

[60] *County Properties v Scottish Ministers* [2001] 4 P.L.R. 122 (Extra Division), overturning [2000] 4 P.L.R 83, [2001] J.P.L. 170.

[61] Available, price £20.00, including post and packing, from Historic Scotland.

[62] Available on the web at *www.scotland.gov.uk*

[63] Now incorporated into s.1 of the TCP (Scotland) Act 1997 and (by reference) into s.81(2) of the P(LBCA)(Scotland) Act 1997.

[64] TCP (Scotland) Act, s.5.

[65] Under the National Parks (Scotland) Act 2000.

[66] Loch Lomond and the Trossachs National Park Designation Order 2002 (SSI 201), art.7; structure planning remains with the local authorities.

National Park, on the other hand, the new authority (as from March 2003) has the power to make local plans, and to call in significant applications for planning permission and listed building consent, but otherwise the local authorities retain their normal planning role.[67] References to "planning authorities" in the remainder of the bok should be construed accordingly in relation to land and buildings within the area of the two park authorities.

1.5.5 Northern Ireland

The principal difference between planning control in Northern Ireland and elsewhere in the United Kingdom is centralised nature of planning control—that is, the Department of the Environment (NI) (referred to throughout the relevant legislation, and in this book, simply as "the Department") is both the relevant department of central government and the sole planning authority.[68] This leads to a considerable simplification of the legislation, since there is not the requirement for the elaborate schemes of notification and delegation that there is elsewhere.

In practice, there are two bodies responsible for the matters described in this book. The Environment and Heritage Service is responsible for the listing of buildings and the scheduling of monuments—much as the DCMS in England—advised by the Historic Buildings Council[69] and the Historic Monuments Council.[70] The function of the Councils is however similar to that of their Welsh counterparts[71] and is not as extensive as that of English Heritage. The Planning Service, on the other hand, is responsible for the production of development plans and the determination of applications for planning permission, listed building consent and conservation area consent.

The Planning Reform (Northern Ireland) Order 2006 was laid before Parliament on March 1, 2006, too late for its provisions to be included in this book. Its provisions broadly correspond to those in the Planning and Compulsory Purchase Act 2004.

Policy is contained principally in planning policy statements produced by the Planning Service, as well as development plans. The most relevant is PPS 6, *Planning, Archaeology and the Built Heritage*, produced in March 1999, which effectively the equivalent of both PPG 15 and PPG 16 in England. An addendum to this, *Areas of Townscape Character* was published in August 2005.[72] Also relevant are PPS 1, *General Principles* (March 1998)[73]; and PPS 6, *Quality Residential Environments* (June 2001).

---

[67] Cairngorms National Park Designation [etc.] Order 2003 (SSI 2003/1), art.7.
[68] All planning decisions up until October 14, 2002 were taken under the authority of the Minister for the Department of the Environment. Following the suspension of the Northern Ireland Assembly, the Parliamentary Under Secretary of State at the Northern Ireland Assembly has exercised that authority.
[69] 1991 Order, art.5 and Sch.3.
[70] art.22 of the Historic Monuments and Archaeological Objects (NI) Order 1995.
[71] See **1.5.2**.
[72] See **Chapter 12**.
[73] See in particular paras 14–22 and Annex 3.

Chapter 2

The International Framework

2.1 Introduction

All law within the United Kingdom and Ireland now has to be seen within a European and international context. That is true not least of environmental law generally, and planning law in particular. So far, international law has made relatively little impact on the law relating to the protection of the cultural heritage, which has generally developed in Great Britain independently, with Northern Ireland and, more recently, the Republic of Ireland[1] following on behind. But that may now be gradually changing.

This chapter therefore looks at three principal aspects of the international context within which to view the law regarding the identification and protection of the cultural heritage in the United Kingdom.

Firstly, the Government of the United Kingdom is a signatory to a number of other international conventions relating to the cultural heritage, including the Paris Convention of 1954, the Granada Convention of 1985, and the Valletta Convention of 1992 (see **2.2**). These have almost no direct effect in the UK, and are little known outside the conservation world, but very much form the background to the domestic legislation described in the rest of the book.

The second, and most striking, is the World Heritage Convention, signed in Paris in 1972 (see **2.3** and **2.4**). This does have some, limited, direct effect in UK practice and procedure; but the protection to be afforded to a world heritage site is largely achieved by the various other statutory mechanisms described in this part of this book—principally the listing or scheduling of the principle structures within it, and the designation of all or part of it as a conservation area.

And, thirdly, there a number of charters adopted by the International Council on Monuments and Sites (ICOMOS)—notably the Venice Charter of 1966, and the Burra Charter of 1999 (see **2.5**). These too are significant largely by way of background to the policy and practice described in the remainder of the book.

---

[1] There are of course a number of significant differences between law and practice in the Republic and those in the UK; see the Planning and Development Act 2001, especially Part 3 (Control of Development) and Part 4 (architectural heritage) and the Planning and Development Regulations 2001.

As for European law, its most significant impact specifically relating to this area is the requirement for prospective developers to carry out comprehensive environmental assessment of any proposed major development or other project; and one of the matters to be covered by such assessments is the impact of the proposal on the cultural heritage. However, since this has now been more or less fully incorporated into domestic legislation by the Planning and Compensation Act 1991[2], it is explored in detail later in this book, in the context of the procedures for obtaining the necessary permissions for carrying out works in historic areas.[3]

2.2 European treaties

2.2.1 Introduction

The United Kingdom is signatory to a number of international treaties relevant to the cultural heritage.

Potentially the most significant, at least in theory, is the Treaty of Rome. Article 128 of this, as inserted by the Treaty on European Union (Maastricht), provides that action may be taken by the Community to support or supplement the action of Member States in respect of the conservation and safeguarding of cultural heritage of European significance, as it contributes to the "flowering of the cultures of Member States".

This was until 2005 due to be replaced by the new Constitution for Europe, unanimously approved by the 25 members and three candidate states of the European Union on June 18, 2004 but, under the treaty of October 2004, only coming into force once adopted by each of the signatory countries in accordance with its own constitutional procedures—a state of affairs that now seems improbable. However, notwithstanding the uncertain future of the Constitution itself, it is perhaps significant that it stated right at the outset eight objectives of the Union, one of which was as follows:

"[The Union] shall respect its rich cultural and linguistic diversity, and shall ensure that Europe's cultural heritage is safeguarded and enhanced."[4]

Of the other European treaties to which the United Kingdom is a signatory, the most significant are:

- the European Cultural Convention (the Paris Convention of 1954);

- the Convention for the Protection of the Architectural Heritage of Europe (the Granada Convention of 1985); and

- the European Convention on the Protection of the Archaeological Heritage (the Valletta Convention of 1992).

---

[2] See now TCPA 1990, s.71A, inserted by Planning and Compensation Act 1991, s.15 [Scotland: TCP(S)A 1997, s.40; NI: P(NI)O 1991, art 25B, inserted by P(A)(NI)O 2003.]
[3] See **2.4.3** and **13.3.7**.
[4] Constitution for Europe, Pt I, Art.I–3(3). See *http://europa.eu.int/constitution/index_en.htm*

The text of each of these conventions may be found on the Council of Europe website[5], along with an explanatory report, and a note as to its coming into force in Member States.[6]

These conventions do not directly form part of the domestic law of the United Kingdom. As it has been put by the House of Lords, "treaties ... are not self-executing. Quite simply, a treaty is not part of English law unless and until it has been incorporated into the law by legislation."[7] This echoes the earlier dictum of the Court of Appeal, that "if the terms of the legislation are clear and unambiguous, they must be given effect to, whether or not they carry out Her Majesty's treaty obligations ..."[8]

On the other hand, the House of Lords has indicated that there is a value in considering treaties. First, they help to indicate the policy considerations that should guide the UK courts in interpreting the law:

"I do not doubt that conceptions of public policy should move with the times and that widely accepted treaties and statutes may point the direction in which such conceptions, as applied by the courts, ought to move."[9]

And, secondly, they may help to resolve ambiguities in legislation:

"it is a principle of construction of United Kingdom statutes ... that the words of a statute passed after the Treaty has been signed and dealing with the subject matter of the international obligation of the United Kingdom, are to be construed, if they are reasonably capable of bearing such a meaning, as intended to carry out the obligation, and not to be inconsistent with it."[10]

The relevant decisions of the higher courts, all of which were in the context of the European Convention on Human Rights (ECHR) prior to the enactment of the Human Rights Act 1998, are most usefully summarised in the decision of the House of Lords in *R. v Secretary of State, ex parte Brind*.[11]

As for the ECHR itself, that has of course now been incorporated into domestic law, in the 1998 Act, and thus now forms a new but essential element of the legal

---

[5]   *http://conventions.coe.int/*
[6]   The Council of Europe contains 46 Member States, which between them now extend to the whole of Europe including Russia and the former Soviet republics in the Caucasus, but excluding Belarus and the Holy See (the Vatican). The UK was one of the original members at the foundation of the Council in 1949. A convention is drawn up within the Council of Europe by a committee of experts, and adopted by a committee of relevant ministers from the Member States. It is then open for signature by states, and comes into force in each state once it has been signed and ratified (possibly subject to reservations)—subject to having been ratified by at least a minimum number of states (usually three).
[7]   *J H Rayner (Mincing Lane) Ltd. v Department of Trade and Industry* [1990] 2 A.C. 418, HL, *per* Lord Oliver of Aylmerton at p.500.
[8]   *Salomon v Commissioners of Customs and Excise* [1967] 2 Q.B. 116, per Diplock L.J. at p.143.
[9]   *Blathwayt v Baron Cawley* [1976] A.C. 397, HL, *per* Lord Wilberforce at p.426.
[10] *Garland v British Rail Engineering Ltd.* [1983] 2 A.C. 751, HL, per Lord Diplock at p.771. See also *R v Chief Immigration Officer, Heathrow Airport, ex p. Salamat Bibi* [1976] 1 W.L.R. 979, CA, *per* Lord Denning M.R. at p.984, and Geoffrey Lane L.J. at p.988, *Fernandes v Secretary of State for the Home Department* [1981] Imm AR 1, and *Chundawadra v Immigration Appeal Tribunal* [1988] Imm. A.R. 161.
[11] [1991] 1 A.C. 696, HL, per Lord Bridge at pp.747–8, and Lord Ackner at pp.760–2.

landscape in the United Kingdom. It is therefore referred to elsewhere in this book as appropriate.[12]

2.2.2 The Paris Convention of 1954

The European Cultural Convention[13] was opened for signature in Paris in 1954, and has since been ratified by all 46 Member States of the Council of Europe.[14] The United Kingdom became a contracting party on May 5, 1955, on which date the Convention came into force.[15]

The obligations of each contracting party, so far as relevant, are:

- to safeguard and to encourage the development of its national contribution to the common cultural heritage of Europe[16];

- to safeguard the objects of European cultural value placed under its control, as integral parts of the common cultural heritage of Europe, and

- to ensure reasonable access to such objects.[17]

In so far as these obligations relate to historic buildings and areas, their principal effect has been to bring into being the Granada Convention on the architectural heritage, and the London Convention, and later the Valletta Convention, on the archaeological heritage.

2.2.3 The Granada Convention of 1975

The European Charter of the Architectural Heritage was adopted in 1975 at the Congress of Amsterdam, the crowning event of European Architectural Heritage Year (EAHY).[18] That led 10 years later to the appearance of the Convention for the Protection of the Architectural Heritage of Europe,[19] which was opened for signature at the second European Conference of Ministers responsible for the Heritage, in Granada, Spain, on October 3, 1985. The United Kingdom was the fourth country to ratify it, in November 1987; it came into force there on March 1, 1988.[20] It has now been ratified by 36 of the Member States of the Council of Europe.[21]

The Convention first defines the architectural heritage as follows:

---

[12] See in particular **3.7** and **14.7.8**.
[13] European Treaty Series no.18.
[14] Belarus and the Holy See have also ratified the Paris Convention.
[15] The UK's ratification was extended to the Isle of Man in 1994, and to Jersey in 1999, but not yet to the other Channel Islands.
[16] Art.1.
[17] Art.5.
[18] It is perhaps significant that the chairman of the International Organising Committee of EAHY was Lord Duncan Sandys, the Minister of Housing and Local Government in the 1950s who had set up the Civic Trust. And the largest national delegation at the Amsterdam Congress was from the UK.
[19] European Treaty Series no.121.
[20] It also came into force on the same date in the Channel Islands and the Isle of Man.
[21] The principal non-joiners are Austria, Luxembourg, Poland and Ukraine.

"(1) monuments: all buildings and structures of conspicuous historical, archaeological, artistic, scientific, social or technical interest, including their fixtures and fittings;

(2) groups of buildings: homogeneous groups of urban or rural buildings conspicuous for their historical, archaeological, artistic, scientific, social or technical interest which are sufficiently coherent to form topographically definable units;

(3) sites: the combined works of man and nature, being areas which are partially built upon and sufficiently distinctive and homogeneous to be topographically definable and are of conspicuous historical, archaeological, artistic, scientific, social or technical interest."[22]

It will be observed that this is similar to the definition adopted by the World Heritage Convention,[23] but requires the monuments, etc. to be simply "of conspicuous ... interest" rather than of outstanding universal value. It is also noteworthy that the definition of "monuments" includes "fixtures and fittings".

Each state party undertakes to maintain an inventory of the heritage, and to take statutory measures for its protection.[24] That is to include the introduction of legislation:

- that requires consent to be obtained for the carrying out of works to protected buildings, or works that affect groups of buildings or the surroundings of individual buildings, with sanctions for non-compliance,

- that enables authorities to require owners to repair protected buildings and to carry out works in default if necessary;

- that enables protected properties to be compulsorily purchased.[25]

These are, of course, the basics of the statutory system that has now operated in the United Kingdom for many decades.[26] In addition, each party undertakes to provide adequate funding for conservation—but only within the limitations of the budget available—to promote measures for the general enhancement of the surroundings of buildings and groups, and to prevent their deterioration through pollution.[27]

Secondly, each party undertakes to adopt integrated conservation policies which:

"(1) include the protection of the architectural include the protection of the architectural heritage as an essential town and country planning objective, and ensure that this requirement is taken into account at all stages both in the drawing up of development plans and in the procedures for authorising work;

(2) promote programmes for the restoration and maintenance of the architectural heritage;

(3) make the conservation, promotion and enhancement of the architectural heritage a major feature of cultural, environmental and planning policies;

(4) facilitate whenever possible in the town and country planning process the conservation and use of certain buildings whose intrinsic importance would not war-

---

[22] Art.1.
[23] See **2.3.2**.
[24] Arts 2, 3.
[25] Arts 4, 5, 9. The second requirement (as to repairs) (Art.4(c)) does not apply in Northern Ireland.
[26] See **1.2**.
[27] Arts 6, 7, 8.

rant protection within the meaning of Article 3, paragraph 1, of this Convention but which are of interest from the point of view of their setting in the urban or rural environment and of the quality of life;

(5) foster, as being essential to the future of the architectural heritage, the application and development of traditional skills and materials."[28]

The following provisions of the Convention spell out in more detail how these aims are to be achieved. In particular, each party undertakes to foster the use of protected properties in the light of the needs of contemporary life, and their adaptation, when appropriate, for new uses.[29]

This is the basis for the local and national policies that guide the implementation of the legislation described in the remainder of this book.[30]

2.2.4 The London and Valletta Conventions

The Convention for the Protection of the Archaeological Heritage of Europe[31] arose out of a concern as to the effects of clandestine archaeological excavation. It was initially signed in London in 1969, and has since been ratified by 28 of the Member States of the Council of Europe. It was ratified by the United Kingdom in 1972, and came into force in 1973. Its concepts gradually became accepted practice throughout much of Europe.

By the 1980s, however, it was realised that the threat to the archaeological heritage was as much, if not more, due to large-scale construction projects. The Cultural Heritage Committee of the Council accordingly approved a revised Convention,[32] which was opened for signature in Valletta, Malta, on January 16, 1992, and has so far been ratified by 32 of the Member States. It was ratified in the United Kingdom[33] on September 19, 2000, and came into force on March 20, 2001.

The aim of the revised Convention is stated to be "to protect the archaeological heritage as a source of the European collective memory and as an instrument for historical and scientific study." It starts with a wide-ranging definition of the archaeological heritage:

"all remains and objects and any other traces of mankind from past epochs:

(i) the preservation and study of which help to retrace the history of mankind and its relation with the natural environment;

(ii) for which excavations or discoveries and other methods of research into mankind and the related environment are the main sources of information; and

(iii) which are located in any area within the jurisdiction of the Parties."[34]

State parties then undertake to institute a legal system that will make provision for the maintenance of an inventory of that heritage, the designation of protected monuments and areas, the preservation of the heritage for future study, and the

---

[28] Art.10.
[29] Art.11.
[30] See in particular **Chapter 14**.
[31] European Treaty Series no.66.
[32] European Treaty Series no.143.
[33] The ratification also extended (as from the same date) to Jersey and the Isle of Man.
[34] Art.1.

reporting to the authorities of chance finds. In particular, excavations and other archaeological activities, including the use of metal detectors, must be carefully controlled.[35]

The Convention also requires parties to allow for the input of trained archaeologists into the process of preparing planning policies, and into the various stages of implementing development schemes—not least by requiring environmental assessment (to include assessment of archaeological impact) to be carried out, allowing adequate time for an appropriate study to be made of sites, modifying plans in appropriate cases, conserving finds, and ensuring that arrangements for public access do not spoil the special interest of sites.[36] This is largely achieved within the United Kingdom by the various procedures described in the remainder of the book.[37]

State parties also undertake to fund archaeology, and in particular rescue archaeology, either from the public purse or private sector resources, as appropriate.

Finally, states are to prevent the illicit circulation of items found in archaeological sites; although this is recognised to be very difficult in practice.[38]

2.2.5 The Delphi Convention of 1985

The European Convention on Offences relating to Cultural Property[39] was opened for signature at Delphi, in Greece, in 1985. "Cultural property" includes elements of artistic or historical monuments or archaeological sites which have been dismembered. Some 20 years later, the Convention has yet to be ratified by any Member State. It is not immediately obvious what it adds to the Paris Convention of 1970.[40]

In the United Kingdom, the problem of the theft of objects removed from historic buildings and monuments has recently been addressed by the passing of the Dealing in Cultural Objects (Offences) Act 2003.[41]

2.2.6 ICOMOS charters

The international treaties discussed above were based at least in part on the charters and codes of practice produced by various specialist bodies. Pre-eminent among these were the charters published by ICOMOS and its national constituent bodies.

The first systematic attempt to set down an international code of practice was by the Athens Conference of 1931, organised by the International Museums Office. The resulting Athens Charter was superseded by the Venice Charter, approved in 1964 by the second Congress of Architects and Technicians of Historic Buildings and adopted by ICOMOS in 1965—under the title *International*

---

[35] Arts 2, 3.
[36] Art.5.
[37] See particularly **Chapter 6, 12.8, 13.9,** and **14.8.**
[38] Art.11.
[39] European Treaty Series no.119.
[40] See **2.5.2.**
[41] See **19.7.3.**

Charter for the Conservation and Restoration of Monuments and Sites. The Charter, which is not a lengthy document, sets out the basic principles of conservation and restoration, and provide a theoretical underpinning to much of the subsequent legislation and policy in this country and elsewhere. It repays study.

Other charters include those on historic gardens (Florence, 1981); historic towns and urban areas (Washington, 1987); the archaeological heritage (Lausanne, 1990); the underwater cultural heritage (Sofia, 1996); cultural tourism; the built vernacular heritage; and historic timber structures (all Mexico, 1999). The most recent is the ICOMOS Charter, *Principles for the Analysis, Conservation and Structural Restoration of Architectural Heritage*, ratified at Victoria Falls, Zimbabwe in 2003.

Some of the national committees of ICOMOS have also adopted charters. Much the most significant of these is the Burra Charter, from Australia, originally adopted in 1979 but updated in 1999. This sets out principles to guide those in the business of conserving places of cultural significance, and has been often referred to in the relevant technical literature.[42]

The text of all of the international and national charters referred to above can be obtained on the ICOMOS website.[43]

2.3 World heritage sites

2.3.1 The World Heritage Convention

Perhaps the most well-known of the international treaties relevant to this area of law is the Convention concerning the Protection of the World Cultural and Natural Heritage (usually referred to simply as the World Heritage Convention). This was adopted by the General Conference of the United Nations Educational, Scientific and Cultural Organisation (UNESCO) at its 17th session in Paris in 1972.[44] The preamble to the Convention recites that:

"... the cultural heritage and the natural heritage are increasingly threatened with destruction not only by the traditional causes of decay, but also by changing social and economic conditions which aggravate the situation with even more formidable phenomena of damage or destruction;

deterioration or disappearance of any item of the cultural or natural heritage constitutes a harmful impoverishment of the heritage of all the nations of the world."

That applies of course—in theory—to all items of the cultural heritage, however localised their significance. But the Convention is concerned principally with the items of more than local or even national significance. The preamble therefore goes on to note that:

"parts of the cultural or natural heritage are of outstanding interest and therefore need to be preserved as part of the world heritage of mankind as a whole".

---

[42] See also *The Illustrated Burra Charter*, published in 2004 and available from ICOMOS Australia.
[43] *www.icomos.org*
[44] For the text of the convention, visit *www.unesco.org/whc/world_he.htm*

It is against that background that the Convention seeks to put in place what it refers to as:

"an effective system of collective protection of the cultural and natural heritage of outstanding universal value, organised on a permanent basis and in accordance with modern scientific methods."

Part I defines what is to be considered to be the cultural and natural heritage for the purposes of the Convention,[45] and imposes on individual state parties a duty to identify and delineate particular properties within its territory that fall within those definitions.[46] Part II commits states to do all they can to ensure the identification, protection, conservation, presentation and transmission to future generations of the selected properties—each state party recognising that the duty to do that belongs primarily to that state.[47] In particular, each state party to the Convention undertakes that it will endeavour, so far as possible:

"to adopt a general policy which aims to give the cultural and natural heritage a function in the life of the community and to integrate the protection of that heritage into comprehensive planning programmes; [and]

to take the appropriate legal, scientific, technical, administrative and financial measures necessary for the identification, protection, presentation and rehabilitation of this heritage".[48]

Parts III and IV the Convention provides for a "World Heritage Committee"[49] and a "World Heritage Fund",[50] both of which have been in operation since 1976. In practice, the implementation of the Convention is overseen in Paris by the UNESCO World Heritage Centre,[51] and its two advisory bodies—ICCROM (the International Centre for the Study for the Preservation and Restoration of Cultural Property),[52] based in Rome, and ICOMOS (the International Council on Monuments and Sites),[53] also based in Paris. The websites of each of these organisations should be visited for current information.

Lastly, all state parties agree to co-operate with each other.[54]

2.3.2 Identification of the cultural heritage

The following are considered as "cultural heritage":

"(1) monuments: architectural works, works of monumental sculpture and painting, elements or structures of an archaeological nature, inscriptions, cave dwellings and combinations of features, which are of outstanding universal value from the point of view of history, art or science;

---

[45] Arts 1 and 2.
[46] Art.3.
[47] Art.4.
[48] Art.5(a), (d).
[49] Arts 8–14.
[50] Arts 15–28.
[51] whc.unesco.org
[52] www.iccrom.org
[53] www.icomos.org
[54] Articles 6, 7.

(2) groups of buildings: groups of separate or connected buildings which, because of their architecture, their homogeneity or their place in the landscape, are of out-standing universal value from the point of view of history, art or science; and

(3) sites: works of man or the combined works of nature and of man, and areas including archaeological sites which are of outstanding universal value from the historical, aesthetic, ethnological or anthropological points of view."[55]

The duties of the World Heritage Committee include the definition of criteria by reference to which properties may be assessed for inclusion in the list.[56] The current criteria are contained in the *Operational Guidelines for the Implementation of the World Heritage Convention*, updated most recently in February 2005.[57] Those relating to the cultural heritage are as follows:

"The Committee considers a property as having outstanding universal ... if the property meets one or more of the following criteria. Nominated properties shall therefore:

(i) represent a masterpiece of human creative genius;

(ii) exhibit an important interchange of human values, over a span of time or within a cultural area of the world, on developments in architecture or technology, monu-mental arts, town-planning or landscape design;

(iii) bear a unique or at least exceptional testimony to a cultural tradition or to a civilisation which is living or which has disappeared;

(iv) be an outstanding example of a type of building, architectural or technological ensemble or landscape which illustrates (a) significant stage(s) in human history;

(v) be an outstanding example of a traditional human settlement, land-use or sea-use which is representative of a culture (or cultures), or human interaction with the environment especially when it has become vulnerable under the impact of irre-versible change;

(vi) be directly or tangible associated with events or living traditions, with ideas, or with beliefs, with artistic works of outstanding universal significance. (The Committee considers that this criterion should preferably be used in conjunction with other criteria)...

To be deemed of outstanding universal value, a property must also meet the conditions of integrity and/or authenticity and must have an adequate protection and management system to ensure its safeguarding."

Following the annual meeting of the Committee in July 2005, 628 cultural sites, 160 natural sites and 24 mixed sites had been identified in 137 nations.[58] There is now strong emphasis on the establishment of a representative, balanced and

---

[55] World Heritage Convention, Art.1. Art.2 provides that the following are considered as "natural heritage": natural features consisting of physical and biological formations or groups of such formations, which are of outstanding universal value from an aesthetic or scientific point of view; geological and physiographical formations and precisely delineated areas which constitute the habitat of threatened species of animals and plants of outstanding universal value from the point of view of science or conservation; and natural sites or precisely delineated natural areas of outstanding universal value from the point of view of science or conservation.

[56] Art.11.

[57] Available at *http://whc.unesco.org/en/guidelines*. It is perhaps significant that, whereas in previous versions of the guidelines, the criteria for cultural and natural sites were sharply divided, they are now in a single list. The criteria for cultural sites, which used to be C(i) to C(vi), are now thus simply criteria (i) to (vi) of a list of 10 (the other four being those for natural sites).

[58] For the current list, updated following the meeting of the Committee in July each year, visit *http://whc.unesco.org/pg*

credible list—in other words, the west European states whose sites are currently well represented will in future find it more difficult to have further sites inscribed.[59]

2.3.3 Procedure

Article 11 of the Convention requires each state party is to select properties in its territory that conform to the above criteria, and submit an inventory of them to the World Heritage Committee. The Committee will then produce and periodically update a list of all such properties which it considers as having outstanding universal value.

The practical outworking of this is provided for in the *Operational Guidelines*. Where a state (in practice, the relevant department of the national government) considers that a property is suitable for inscription on the World Heritage List, it must first include it on the tentative list for the country concerned—after consultation with all relevant stakeholders, including site managers, local and regional authorities, local communities, non-governmental organisations, and any other interested parties. That list is then periodically (usually around every 10 years) updated, and submitted to the Secretariat of the World Heritage Centre, which enables all concerned to consider whether it would be appropriate for the properties concerned to be nominated and inscribed, in the light of the criteria considered above. A property can only be nominated once it has been on the tentative list for at least a year.[60]

A state may then nominate a site to the Secretariat. The advisory bodies will then be consulted for their views, seeking further information from the nominating government where necessary. The World Heritage Committee then meets once a year, in July, and decides whether or not to inscribe the property on the list. A property that is rejected may not be nominated again, other than in exceptional circumstances, such as where new information comes forward.

As for the extent of a world heritage site, the *Operational Guidelines* state that the delineation of boundaries is an essential requirement in the establishment of effective protection of nominated properties. Thus, for cultural sites,

"boundaries should be drawn to include all those areas and attributes which are a direct tangible expression of the outstanding universal value of the property, as well as those areas which in the light of future research possibilities offer potential to contribute to and enhance such understanding."[61]

The boundaries of the nominated property may coincide with one or more existing or proposed protected areas (such as, in the United Kingdom, conservation areas); but that will not always be appropriate. Wherever necessary for the proper conservation of the property, an adequate buffer zone should be provided.[62]

---

[59] There are, for example, 40 sites in Italy, compared with 65 in the whole of Africa.
[60] *Operational Guidelines*, 2005, paras 62–76.
[61] *ibid.*, paras 99–100, 132(1).
[62] *ibid.*, paras 103–107, 132(1).

Clearly the implications of this in practice will vary considerably, according to the type of site. It seems that the sites inscribed on the list in the first few years of its existence did not have precise boundaries; that is no doubt being gradually rectified.[63]

Since 1995, it has not been possible for a site to be inscribed without a management plan having previously been prepared; plans are still gradually being drawn up for sites inscribed prior to that date.[64]

Finally, the World Heritage Committee is to maintain a "List of World Heritage in Danger".[65] This flags up cases where urgent action needs to be taken to avoid the deterioration of the condition of the property to the point where it might have to be removed from the world heritage list; there are currently 35 properties in this position.[66]

2.3.4 World heritage sites in the United Kingdom

The United Kingdom became a party to the Convention in May 1984 (the 79th of the 180 countries who have done so to date).

As at July 2004, a total of 26 sites within the United Kingdom[67] had been inscribed on the World Heritage list, as follows:

England
Durham Castle and Cathedral (1986)—*(ii)*, *(iv)*, *(vi)*
Ironbridge Gorge (1986)—*(i)*, *(ii)*, *(iv)*, *(vi)*
Studley Royal Park, including the ruins of Fountains Abbey (1986)—*(i)*, *(iv)*
Stonehenge, Avebury and associated sites (1986)—*(i)*, *(ii)*, *(iii)*
Blenheim Palace (1987)—*(ii)*, *(iv)*
Palace of Westminster, Westminster Abbey and St Margaret's Church (1987)—*(i)*, *(ii)*, *(iv)*
City of Bath (1987)—*(i)*, *(ii)*, *(iv)*
Hadrian's Wall (1987)—*(ii)*, *(iii)*, *(iv)*
The Tower of London (1988)—*(ii)*, *(iv)*
Canterbury Cathedral, St Augustine's Abbey, and St Martin's Church (1988)—*(i)*, *(ii)*, *(vi)*
Maritime Greenwich (1997)—*(i)*, *(ii)*, *(iv)*, *(vi)*
Saltaire (2001)—*(ii)*, *(iv)*

Dorset and East Devon coast (2001)
Derwent Valley mills (2001)—*(ii)*, *(iv)*
Royal Botanic Gardens, Kew (2003)—*(ii)*, *(iii)*, *(iv)*
Liverpool—Maritime Mercantile City (2004)—*(ii)*, *(iii)*, *(iv)*

Wales
Castles and town walls of King Edward in Gwynedd (1986)—*(i)*, *(ii)*, *(iv)*
Blaenavon industrial landscape (2000)—*(iii)*, *(iv)*

Scotland
Saint Kilda (1986, 2004)—*(iii)*, *(v)*
Old and New Towns of Edinburgh (1995)—*(ii)*, *(iv)*
Heart of Neolithic Orkney (1999)—*(i)*, *(ii)*, *(iii)*, *(iv)*
New Lanark (2001)—*(ii)*, *(iv)*, *(vi)*

---

[63] The City of Bath world heritage site, for example, although inscribed almost 20 years ago, still has no formal boundary; Hadrian's Wall (inscribed the same year) only settled on one recently.

[64] *ibid.*, paragraphs 108–118; and see PPG 15, para.6.37

[65] World Heritage Convention, art.11(4).

[66] Only one is in Europe: Cologne Cathedral, Germany (Butrint, Albania was on the endangered list until July 2005). There was some concern in early 2005 that Hadrian's Wall might be placed on the list; but that was apparently unfounded.

[67] Including two in the Atlantic Ocean and one in the South Pacific—the remnants of empire ...

Northern Ireland
Giant's Causeway and Causeway Coast
(1986)

Elsewhere
Henderson Island (1988)
Gough Island and inaccessible islands
(1995, 2004)
Historic Town of St George and related
fortifications, Bermuda (2000)—*(iv)*

In the above list, against each site is noted the date on which it was first inscribed in the world heritage list, along with the applicable criteria justifying nomination in the case of each of the 21 cultural sites and the one mixed site (St Kilda[68]). The other four properties are natural sites.

In 2005, Hadrian's Wall became part of the *Frontiers of the Roman Empire* transnational World Heritage Site, along with the German-Raetian Limes—it is apparently hoped that other parts of the frontier, including some in Africa and Asia, will be added in due course.

2.3.5 Sites in the United Kingdom on the tentative list

As noted above, each state party is required to maintain a tentative list of sites which it intends to consider for nomination during the following years, and to resubmit it at least every 10 years. The current UK tentative list was drawn up in 1999, and includes the following properties:

England
Chatham Naval Dockyard—*(ii), (iii), (iv)*
Cornish Mining Industry—*(ii), (iii), (iv),*
(v)
Darwin's home and workplace: Down
House and environs—*(iii), (vi)*
The Lake District—*(ii), (iii), (v), (vi)*
Manchester and Salford (Ancoats,
Castlefield and Worsley)—*(ii), (iii), (iv)*
Monkwearmouth and Jarrow monastic
sites—*(iii), (iv), (vi)*
The New Forest—*(ii), (iii), (v)*
The Great Western Railway: Paddington-
Bristol (selected parts)—*(i), (ii), (iv), (vi)*
Shakespeare's Stratford—*(iii), (vi)*
The Wash and North Norfolk Coast

Wales
Pont-Cysyllte Aqueduct—*(i), (ii), (iv)*

Scotland
The Cairngorm Mountains
The Flow Country
The Forth Rail Bridge—*(i), (ii), (vi)*

Northern Ireland
Mount Stewart Gardens—*(ii), (vi)*

Elsewhere
Fountain Cavern, Anguilla—*(i), (ii), (iii)*
The Fortress of Gibraltar—*(i), (ii), (iii),*
(iv)

Again, the criteria claimed to justify nomination are noted against each of the 12 cultural sites and the two sites (the Lake District and the New Forest) that are both cultural and natural sites. The other three properties are natural sites.

It is likely that at least a few of these properties will be inscribed in the world heritage list during the currency of this book. And the tentative list will no doubt be updated. The current position should be checked on the ICOMOS website.[69]

---

[68] St Kilda was a natural site until July 2005.
[69] *www.icomos-uk.org/whs*

2.4 The consequences of inscription on the World Heritage List

2.4.1 Relationship with other designations

At the time of the previous edition of this book, some 15 sites within the United Kingdom itself[70] had been inscribed on the World Heritage List. That has now increased to 23, of which 20 are cultural sites, with a further 15 (including 12 cultural or joint sites) on the tentative list. And some of the sites are extensive urban areas. It remains to be seen whether the process will be subject to the same inflationary tendencies as have affected listing and scheduling; but there can be little doubt that world heritage sites will become of increasing significance in years to come.

Cultural sites on the World Heritage List—and indeed those on the tentative list—will by their nature in many cases be protected under the domestic legislation described in the remainder of this book. The specific buildings involved are generally listed buildings (many of Grade I or II*) or scheduled monuments[71]; and most of the sites will be in conservation areas. It is these designations, and the associated policies, that will protect world heritage sites in practice. It is thus an offence to demolish a Georgian building in Bath because it is listed, not because it is in a world heritage site—although that might of course be relevant in assessing the gravity of the offence.

Inclusion of a site on a world heritage list is thus not of itself a further instrument of control. On the other hand, it should not be forgotten that not all world heritage sites are protected by existing designations—the Blaenavon Industrial Landscape site in South Wales and the Cornish Mining Industry tentative site in England, for example, are not fully protected; and although the Lake District is a national park, that does not provide full protection to the buildings within it.

2.4.2 Development affecting a world heritage site

It has been noted in the course of a debate in the House of Lords that inscription of a site within the world heritage list highlights "the outstanding national and international importance of the site", as a material consideration to be taken into account by a local planning authority or the Secretary of State in determining an application for planning permission, listed building consent or scheduled monument consent.[72]

In particular, the Court of Appeal in the *Bath Society* case[73] held that where permission or consent is sought for development within a conservation area that is within a world heritage site:

---

[70] The author was, sadly, unable to research the relevant law and practice applying in Bermuda, Anguilla and the other locations outside the UK itself. The remainder of the chapter accordingly deals only with the position in Great Britain and Northern Ireland.

[71] See **Chapter 3** and **Chapter 6** respectively.

[72] *Hansard* (HL) Deb, February 13, 1989, col 57.

[73] See **14.7.3**.

"... the special attention which the inspector is bound to give to the provisions of [P(LBCA)A 1990, s.72 (the duty to pay special attention to the desirability of preserving or enhancing a conservation area)] is of particular importance where the site concerned is of 'such universal value that protecting it is the concern of all mankind'. This fact ... requires at least that it must be manifest from the terms of the inspector's report that very close consideration has been given to the provisions of this section, and it is insufficient that it is possible to spell out from the terms of the report that the inspector has, in some way, the terms of the section in mind."[74]

But it will be noted again that this is stating that the fact that a property is within a world heritage site emphasises the importance of the conservation area duty; it does not introduce a free-standing duty of itself.

A more recent decision of the courts considering in greater detail the importance of world heritage sites was *Coal Contractors Ltd v Secretary of State*,[75] relating to Hadrian's Wall—scheduled as an ancient monument in 1982 and designated as a world heritage site in 1987. Permission was refused for opencast coal extraction within the setting of the Wall. The applicant appealed; and the inspector considered that amongst the main issues raised by the proposal was its impact on an area of great landscape value and on the setting of Hadrian's Wall. He considered, however, that the applicant had complied with the need to avoid an adverse impact. However, the Secretary of State disagreed with that recommendation, saying that a further issue must be the impact of the proposal on a world heritage site; that impact would be unacceptable, and the proposal should accordingly be rejected.

The mineral operator challenged the Secretary of State's decision in the High Court, on the grounds that he had been perverse to distinguish the impact on the world heritage site as a separate issue. The deputy judge dismissed the challenge, drawing attention to the ministerial statement in the House of Lords noted above, and confirming that world heritage site designation was a material factor in planning decisions. The Secretary of State had accepted that there was no demonstrable harm; but that did not mean that he had to accept every conclusion as to visual impact. He had elevated the world heritage site issue to be a main consideration, but that did not render his reasoning obscure or perverse.

Further advice is given in central government policy[76] on the formulation of planning policies relating to world heritage sites, and the scrutiny to be given to development proposals affecting them; but that is brief, and in the blandest terms.

It is thus up to the relevant local planning authorities, and the Secretary of State on appeal, to ensure the preservation and enhancement of world heritage sites through the normal development control process. It will in particular be essential for authorities to include within their local development frameworks suitable policies to ensure the protection of sites—particularly in cases where no formal protection is provided by means of other designations.[77] The issues arising

---

[74] *Bath Society v Secretary of State* [1991] 2 P.L.R. 51 *per* Stocker L.J. at p.66.

[75] (1993) 68 P. & C.R. 285, [1995] J.P.L. 421.

[76] PPG 15, paras 2.22 and 2.23; WO Circ. 61/96, paras 14 and 15; HS Memorandum, para.2.24. Ironically, the corresponding guidance in Northern Ireland (in PPS 6, s.4) is the fullest.

[77] See **2.4.1**.

from this are the same as with the preparation of policies for the protection of conservation areas, and are accordingly considered later.[78]

2.4.3 Environmental assessment

One specific way in which extra protection is given to world heritage sites is that those undertaking projects of any kind within them are subject to a more stringent requirement as to the submission of an assessment of their likely environmental impact than would apply elsewhere. This reflects the principle that a minor proposal in a highly sensitive location can be as significant, and thus as deserving of careful assessment, as a much more major one in a much less sensitive site.

Thus the 1985 European directive on environmental impact assessment (EIA) requires that, in principle, all projects in the categories listed in Annex I (that is, really major ones such as motorways and large chemical plants) must be the subject of an impact assessment; whereas those in Annex II need only be the subject of an assessment if they fall within certain criteria, set out at Annex III.[79] These include the environmental sensitivity of the areas likely to be affected by the project in question, having regard, in particular, to landscapes of historical, cultural or archaeological significance.[80] This requirement has been transposed into UK domestic legislation in the form of a suite of regulations, relating to various categories of projects.[81]

The regulations most often come across are those relating to projects that require planning permission. These provide that an environmental statement must be submitted along with the application in all cases involving Sch.1 development (major projects) and, within a world heritage site or other sensitive area, for all Sch.2 development likely to have a significant effect on the environment by virtue of factors such as its nature, size or location.[82] Outside such sensitive areas, statements only have to be submitted for Sch.2 development where it is on a significant scale (determined by reference to criteria appropriate to the category of development involved).

Most of the other regulations make similar provisions for projects in world heritage sites.[83]

---

[78] See **5.4**.
[79] Dir. 85/337 (OJ L175/40), Art.4, substituted by Dir. 97/11.
[80] Dir. 85/337 (OJ L175/40), Annex III, para.2, inserted by Dir. 97/11.
[81] England, Wales and Scotland: fish farming in marine waters (SI 1999/367); gas pipelines (SI 1999/1672); nuclear reactors (SI 1999/2892); harbour works (SI 1999/3445). England and Wales: projects requiring planning permission (SI 1999/293, amended by SI 2000/2867); highways (SI 1999/369); land drainage (SI 1999/1783); forestry (SI 1999/2228); electricity works (SI 2000/1927); pipe-lines (SI 2000/1928); Transport and Works Act proposals (SI 2000/2190), cultivation for intensive agriculture of previously uncultivated or semi-natural land (SI 2001/3966 (Eng), SI 2002/2127 (W)). Scotland: development (SSI 1999/1, amended by SSI 2002/324), forestry (SSI 1999/43); electricity (SSI 2000/320); cultivation (SSI 2002/6); water management (SSI 2003/341).
[82] TCP (Environmental Impact Assessment) (England and Wales) Regulations 1999, reg.2(1).
[83] Of those listed at fn 81 above, the only exceptions are those relating to land drainage, nuclear reactors, and the cultivation of previously uncultivated land; presumably all projects in these categories need special assessment.

More recently, a further European directive has been issued on the assessment of plans and programmes, which has been transposed into domestic legislation as the Environmental Assessment of Plans and Programmes Regulations 2004.[84] These require that an environmental assessment is to be carried out as part of the preparation of more or less any land-use-related plan or programme where it is likely to have significant environmental effects on, amongst other things, areas or landscapes that have a recognised national, European or international protection status.[85] That would obviously include inscribed and tentative world heritage sites.

The net result of all these provisions is that development plans and proposals (in the broadest sense of that term) within a world heritage site is likely to be much more carefully scrutinised than it might be elsewhere.

Environmental impact assessment is considered further in a later chapter, in the context of the procedures for obtaining permission for development proposals affecting historic areas.[86-87]

2.5 Other UNESCO Conventions

2.5.1 The Hague Convention of 1954

The Convention for the Protection of Cultural Property in the Event of Armed Conflict was signed at the Hague on May 14, 1954.[88] The Convention provides for a system of general and special protection of cultural property in situations of international and domestic armed conflict. "Cultural property" for this purpose is defined as:

> "(a) movable or immovable property of great importance to the cultural heritage of every people, such as monuments of architecture, art or history, whether religious or secular; archaeological sites; groups of buildings which, as a whole, are of historical or artistic interest; . . .;
> (b) buildings whose main and effective purpose is to preserve or exhibit the movable cultural property defined in sub-paragraph (a) . . . .;
> (c) centres containing a large amount of cultural property as defined in subparagraphs (a) and (b), to be known as 'centres containing monuments'.[89]"

In time of armed conflict, parties to the Convention are required to respect cultural property situated within their own territory as well as within the territory of other parties, by refraining from using such property for military purposes and by refraining from committing any hostile act against it. However, this "general protection" can be waived on the ground of imperative military necessity.

The Second Protocol to the Convention was adopted in 1999. It clarified the protection to be given to cultural property in peacetime, and specified the circumstances that would amount to "imperative military necessity". The Protocol

---

[84] Dir. 2001/42. The relevant regulations are SI 2004/1633 (England), SI 2004/1656 (Wales) and SSI 2004/258 (Scotland).
[85] SI 2004, 1633, regs 5, 9, Sch.1, para.2(g).
[86-87] See **13.3.7**.
[88] For the text of the Convention and the two Protocols, see *www.unesco.org/culture*
[89] 1954 Convention, art.1.

also created a new, further category of protection, called "enhanced protection", for certain cultural heritage which is of the greatest importance for humanity and which must not be used for military purposes or to shield military sites.

The Government of the United Kingdom decided not to ratify the Hague Convention when it was first drafted because, along with a number of other countries, it considered that it did not provide an effective regime for the protection of cultural property. It has, however, welcomed the production of the Second Protocol, and now intends to ratify the Convention and both Protocols.[90]

The proposal is that, in relation to the immovable cultural heritage, the general protection afforded by the Convention should be given to:

- UK world heritage sites (excluding those that are only inscribed as natural sites);

- Grade I buildings in England and Wales, and Grade A in Scotland and Northern Ireland (together amounting to around 11,000 list entries); and

- Grade I registered parks and gardens in England (around 126 list entries).

It is suggested that "enhanced protection" is given just to world heritage sites.[91]

2.5.2 The Paris Convention of 1970

The Convention on the Means of Prohibiting and Preventing the Illicit Import, Export and Transfer of Ownership of Cultural Property was signed in Paris on November 14, 1970. For this purpose, "cultural property" includes "products of archaeological excavations (including regular and clandestine) or of archaeological discoveries; [and] elements of artistic or historical monuments or archaeological sites which have been dismembered". It thus includes items removed from or formerly part of historic buildings and monuments. Article 3 declares that the import, export or transfer of ownership of cultural property effected contrary to the provisions of the Convention to be illicit.

The United Kingdom signed up to the Paris Convention in 2002, one of the most recent of the 102 states to do so. In practice, some protection is now given by the Dealing in Cultural Objects (Offences) Act 2003.[92]

---

[90] DCMS Consultation Paper, September 2005—in which the Minister for Culture states, without apparent irony, that he believes that "the UK's declared intention to ratify the 1954 Hague Convention [more than 60 years after it was first drafted] is an important signal of the priority we attach to the protection of cultural property in the event of armed conflict, both nationally and internationally."

[91] See **12.3**.

[92] See **19.7.3**.

Part II

Identifying and recording the cultural heritage

"A great deal of what is now supposed to be our priceless heritage was regarded as extravagant Victorian rubbish forty years ago, and may well be so regarded a generation hence ... The planner's task is not to set up his own aesthetic yardsticks half-way between the preciousness of the knightly dictators and the total lack of all taste by the great majority of the population, but to point out the costs of conservation and the benefits of destruction—as they affect the whole community."

David Eversley, *The Planner in Society: The Changing Role of the Profession* (Faber, London, 1973).

"No yardstick of aesthetic judgment is of universal validity; time and distance both produce the strangest reversals. No educated person would today contemplate the destruction of Chartres with equanimity, but in the eighteenth century many would have regarded it as welcome deliverance too long delayed. And can we be certain that the obvious necessity for preserving Paestum would be self-evident to one brought up in the shadow of Angkor Wat? However, the consciousness that all judgments on such matters are relative does not absolve us from making them."

Sir Osbert Lancaster, "What should we preserve?" in Jane Fawcett (ed.), *The Future of the Past: Attitudes to Conservation, 1174–1974* (Thames & Hudson, London, 1976).

Chapter 3

Listed Buildings

3.1 Introduction

If special protection is to be given to certain buildings of particular merit or interest, it follows that the first requirement is that they should be identified.[1]

In an ideal world, it should be possible for the architectural and historic interest of a building to be taken into account automatically by all those considering the desirability of any proposal affecting it. In reality, however, opinions are bound to differ widely as to the merits of a particular building; and this is particularly so when it is under threat. It is remarkable that a building that has stood totally unnoticed for years can suddenly be extolled by amenity groups as having been a gem of its particular type—the day after it has been demolished. Of more concern, perhaps, is the fate of a building which is widely admired and enjoyed, but condemned by a developer as being a mediocre example of an uninteresting style.

The Planning (Listed Buildings and Conservation Areas) Act 1990 in England and Wales, and the 1997 Act in Scotland, following all the planning Acts since 1932,[2] therefore recognise that certain buildings have to be identified as being not just of some interest, but of "special architectural or historic interest". The Secretary of State is thus under a duty to compile a list of such buildings.[3] Works to these buildings are then subject to the need for *listed building consent*, in addition to the normal requirement for planning permission[4]; and those responsible for unauthorised works can be penalised.[5]

The present system of listed building consent replaces the old system of *building preservation orders* in force prior to January 1969.[6]

---

[1]   And see art.2 of the Granada Convention (noted at **2.2.3**).
[2]   See **1.2**.
[3]   P(LBCA)A 1990, s.1(5). [Scotland: P(LBCA)(S)A 1997, s.1(1).] In Northern Ireland, the duty lies on the Department (P(NI)O 1991, art.42).
[4]   See **12.3**, **12.4** and **12.5**.
[5]   See **Chapters 18 and 19**.
[6]   See **1.2.3**.

The basic definition of a "listed building" is a building that is for the time being included in a list compiled under the relevant Act.[7] This chapter considers what kinds of "buildings" can be and have in fact been selected for listing (see **3.2**), what is the procedure by which they come to be listed, what can be done to overturn a listing, and what remedies are available if they are not listed (**3.3**). Listing may be unwelcome in some cases; it is possible to seek a certificate from immunity from listing (see **3.4**). These three sections focus on law and procedure in England; the following section (**3.5**) looks at the differences in Wales, Scotland and Northern Ireland.

The consequences of listing are summarised at **3.6** (and of course explored in greater detail in the remainder of the book). It is sometimes argued that listing is a breach of human rights; this thorny question is considered at **3.7**. The procedure for removing a building from the list, briefly explained at **3.8**.

Finally, it sometimes occurs that a building is perceived to need urgently the protection afforded by listing, but there is no time to seek the involvement of central government or English Heritage. In that situation, a local authority may without further ado impose a building preservation notice (see **3.9**)—which gives protection on a temporary basis—but only on the understanding that, if the building is not eventually listed, compensation will be payable.

The trickier question of the extent of the listing, once a building has been selected, is considered fully in the following chapter.

3.2 The selection of buildings to be listed

3.2.1 What may be listed

To state the obvious, it is only possible to list a "building". A "building" is defined to include a structure or erection, and any part of a building as so defined, but does not include plant or machinery comprised in a building.[8] Neither "structure" nor (in this context) "erection" is defined.

One of the earliest attempts to define a "building" suggested that it was "something that is artificial, the construction of man, put together of bricks and mortar, and used for a particular purpose".[9] The Exchequer Division thus considered that arches similar to the vaults of a conventional London town house were a "building". This definition was subsequently widened in relation to the planning Acts since, as has been observed a long time ago in the courts, a "building", by virtue of the relevant definition sections, includes a "structure", and therefore things which would not ordinarily be called buildings are included in that term where it is used in the Acts.[10] Some years later, Lord Parker C.J. concluded (albeit probably obiter) in *Cheshire CC v Woodward* that the Act is referring to "any structure or erection which can be said to form part of the realty,

---

[7] P(LBCA)A 1990, s.1(5). [Scotland: P(LBCA)(S)A 1997, s.1(4); NI: P(NI)O 1991, art.42(7).]

[8] TCPA 1990, s.336, as applied by P(LBCA)A 1990, s.91(2). [Scotland: TCPA(S)A 1997, s.277(1), as applied by P(LBCA)(S)A 1990, s.81(2); NI: P(NI)O 1991, art.2(2).]

[9] *Thompson v Sunderland Gas Co.* (1877) 2 Ex. D. 429, at 435.

[10] *Mills & Rockleys v Leicester CC* [1946] 1 All E.R. 424, per Lord Goddard C.J. at p.427.

and to change the physical character of the land".[11] This would certainly be just as relevant today in the context of listed "buildings".

As to what is a "structure", this has been considered principally in the context of other statutes. It has thus been defined, in its most general terms, as a "construction of related parts",[12] and in more detail as:

"something artificially erected, constructed, put together, of a certain degree of size or permanence, which is still maintained as an artificial erection, or which though not so maintained, has not become indistinguishable in bounds from the natural earth surrounding."[13]

A building, eligible for listing, can thus be as large as a palace or as small as a bollard—provided it is at least a "structure". It would also be perfectly possible to list apparently temporary structures such as holiday chalets,[14] and horizontal surfaces such as areas of stone setts, pavements and flights of steps[15]—provided of course that they were of sufficient interest. And indeed a surprising variety of structures have been listed over the years—including, for example, statues, grave stones, lamp posts, train sheds, water troughs, mews arches and tunnels.[16]

The exclusion of "plant and machinery comprised in a building" means that artefacts such as industrial equipment, engines and so forth may not be listed in their own right—however great their interest as items of industrial archaeology. The proper course to protect such items is for the Secretary of State to list the building containing them, as they will then be included in the listing.[17] It must also be doubtful whether it is right to list an "object", such as a bronze sculpture made of a single piece of metal or concrete.[17a]

Finally, it should be noted that it is, theoretically, possible to list part of a building—perhaps where the remainder is of no special interest—as noted by Lord Ackner, in the dissenting speech in *Debenhams PLC v Westminster CC*[18] and, more recently, by Lord Hope in *Shimizu UK Ltd v Westminster CC*.[19] In practice, however, this is very rarely done[20]; although it would enable the listing of a single house within a terrace, perhaps because of its historic interest.[21] It can also occur where only a small part of an earlier structure remains, now forming part of a more recent structure—as with the entrance to the old Bishopsgate Goods Station in east London.[22] And sometimes, where a structure (such as a

---

[11] [1962] 2 QB 126.

[12] *Black v Shaw* (1913) 33 N.Z.L.R. 194 at 196.

[13] *Inland Revenue Commissioners v Smyth* [1914] 3 K.B. 406, at pp.421–422.

[14] *R. v Swansea CC, ex p. Elitestone)* [1992] J.P.L. 1143, upheld at [1993] 2 P.L.R. 65.

[15] *IRC v Smyth*, above.

[16] The Ancient Monuments Society regularly records in its Newsletter further examples of unusual structures included in the list.

[17] See **4.3.5**.

[17a] But see *R. (Judge) v Secretary of State and Middlesbrough BC* [2005] EWCA Civ. (statue; see **4.2.3**).

[18] [1987] A.C. 396 at p.411.

[19] [1996] 3 P.L.R. 89 at 102D.

[20] See article at [1997] J.P.L. 503, 603.

[21] *Shimizu* at 101G.

[22] *R. (Hammerton) v London Underground Limited* [2002] E.W.H.C. 2307; [2003] J.P.L. 984, para.33–43. And see **4.2.1**.

bridge) spans the boundary between the areas of two neighbouring local authorities, one half may be listed some years before the other.[23]

3.2.2 Criteria for selection

Buildings in England are chosen for inclusion in the statutory list on the basis of
definite criteria, originally drawn up by the Historic Buildings Council (the
forerunner of English Heritage).[24] The criteria in their current form are set out at
paras 6.10–6.16 of PPG 15.[25]

The principal factors taken into account are categorised as follows:

"(1) *architectural interest*: the lists are meant to include all buildings which are of
    importance to the nation for the interest of their architectural design, decoration
    and craftsmanship; also important examples of particular building types and
    techniques (*e.g.* buildings displaying technological innovation or virtuosity) and
    significant plan forms;
  (2) *historic interest*: this includes buildings which illustrate important aspects of the
    nation's social, economic, cultural or military history;
  (3) *close historical associations* with nationally important people or events;
  (4) *group value*, especially where buildings comprise an important architectural or
    historical unity or a fine example of planning (*e.g.* squares, terraces or model
    villages)."

The requirement in the Act that listed buildings should be of "special" interest is
interpreted by the Secretary of State as requiring that they should usually be of
national rather than local interest.[26] It is questionable whether that is right; a
building might be only of local interest, but still "special".

The first of these criteria ("architectural interest") is usually fairly straightforward. It will usually be reflected in the external appearance of a building—both
its intrinsic architectural merit and any group value—which is indeed the basis on
which most people judge a building's interest. The PPG makes it clear that the
existence of other buildings of similar quality elsewhere is not likely to be a major
consideration.[27] It also, correctly, points out that the special architectural interest
of a building will not always be reflected in visual quality: "buildings which are
important for reasons of technological innovation, or as illustrating by particular
aspects of social or economic history, may well have little external visual
interest".[28]

This has been explored at length in a recent decision of the Administrative
Court, relating to a decision by the Secretary of State not to list Pimlico School in
London, a famous building designed in the early 1960s by a group within the
GLC Architects' Department under the leadership of John Bancroft. English

---

[23] This happened in the case of some of the bridges over the Thames in London, which
   were listed in two halves as part of the routine re-survey of buildings in each of the
   boroughs concerned.
[24] For an interesting account tracing the gradual evolution over the years of the listing
   criteria, see Delafons, *Politics and Preservation: a Policy History of the Built Heritage
   1882–1996* (E. & F.N. Spon, London, 1997).
[25] For Wales, Scotland and Northern Ireland, see **3.5**.
[26] PPG 16, para.6.16.
[27] para.6.13.
[28] para.6.14.

Heritage initially (in 1993) recommended that it should not be listed, taking the view that buildings less than 30 years old should only be listed if they were of sufficient quality to justify Grade I or II*; but its later changed its mind, recommending it for listing at Grade II. The Secretary of State disagreed, considering that its design was fundamentally flawed, and refused to list it—and granted a certificate of immunity from listing.[29] Bancroft challenged her decision; and Gibbs J. held as follows:

"It seems to me that the profession of architecture is generally regarded as not only an art but a science; a profession devoted not solely to providing aesthetic pleasure, but rather a profession which seeks to provide aesthetically original or pleasing solutions to the practical and functional challenges presented by its briefs. It follows in my judgment that the Secretary of State was entitled to take into account any design flaws in the building and the seriousness or otherwise of their consequences in determining whether to list the building."[30]

The "historic interest" of a building is a more difficult concept. The listing of buildings primarily for historical reasons is to a greater extent a comparative exercise; the aim will be to list the best examples of each type that is of special historical interest[31]—for example, the most interesting Victorian mill and factory buildings). As to a building with historical associations, the Secretary of State is of the view that, where these are well-documented and of national importance, they will increase the case for its listing, and may justify a higher grading[32]; but he considers that "either the building should be of some architectural merit in itself, or it should be well preserved in a form which directly illustrates and confirms its historical associations (*e.g.* because of the survival of internal features)".[33] This may be of particular importance where alterations to the buildings are subsequently proposed.

As to the last of the four criteria, the Secretary of State has since 1968 been obliged to consider the contribution (presumably by virtue of its architectural or historic interest) that a building makes to any group of which it forms part.[34] This requirement was possibly introduced in the light of the decision by the Court of Appeal in *Earl of Iveagh v Minister of Housing and Local Government*, relating to two Adam houses in St James's Square ("[they] are situated in the least spoilt corner of one of the most famous of the historic squares in central London and form part of a continuous frontage presenting the general appearance of the square as it existed in the late eighteenth and early nineteenth centuries"), in which the Court concluded that a building might be of special interest by reason of its setting as one of a group.[35]

---

[29] See **3.4**.
[30] *R. (Bancroft) v Secretary of State for Culture, Media and Sport* [2005] J.P.L. 477, per Gibb J. at paras 54–55.
[31] para.6.13.
[32] See **3.2.4**.
[33] PPG 15, para.6.15.
[34] P(LBCA)A 1990, s.1(3)(a). [Scotland: P(LBCA)(S)A 1997, s.1(2)(a); NI: P(NI)O 1991, art.42(2)(a).]
[35] [1964] 1 Q.B. 395, upholding [1962] 2 QB 147.

Finally, when considering whether or not to list a particular building, of any period, the Secretary of State is to take into account the merits of not only the building itself, but also those of any object or structure fixed to the building or within its curtilage.[36] These may indeed be the principal or even only reason for the building being listed—as with, for example, a nondescript pumping station listed for the sake of the magnificent beam engine inside; the beam engine itself could not be listed as such, since "building" excludes "plant and machinery".[37] Certainly, as explained in the following chapter, once the building itself has been listed, those ancillary items will be protected just as much, so it makes sense for the Secretary of State to have to consider what those items will be at the time he is considering protecting them.

3.2.3 Application of criteria

PPG 15 makes it clear that the intention is that, as a result of the exercise over many years of the above criteria, the following buildings in England should now be listed:

(1) *before 1700*: all buildings, which survive in anything like their original condition;

(2) *1700 to 1840*: most buildings, although some selection is necessary;

(3) *1840 to 1914*: only buildings of definite quality and character, including the best examples of particular building types;

(4) *after 1914*: only selected buildings:

- *between 30 and 10 years old*: only buildings which are of outstanding quality and under threat; and
- *less than 10 years old:* none.[38]

The first listing programme in England ran from 1947 to 1968. The lists produced were somewhat patchy—especially the earlier ones. A second nationwide resurvey was therefore carried out from 1969. It was accelerated in 1982, and the fieldwork for it was completed by the spring of 1989. New lists, sometimes known as "green backs", have been prepared for each local authority area, incorporating and replacing earlier lists.

The emphasis was then on listing arising out of more precisely targeted research-based studies of particular building types, known to be under-represented in the lists. Further studies were carried out to identify key buildings of the twentieth century, including those of the post-war period. Proposals for listing followed as each phase of the research was completed.[39]

The present position as to the number and nature of listed buildings in England, along with much other relevant information, is to be found in the useful pub-

---

[36] P(LBCA)A 1990, s.1(3)(b). [Scotland: P(LBCA)(S)A 1997, s.1(2)(b); NI: P(NI)O 1991, art.42(2)(b).] And see **Chapter 4**.

[37] See **3.2.1**.

[38] PPG 15, para.6.11.

[39] PPG 15, para.6.12.

lication by English Heritage entitled *Heritage Counts*.[40] This states that the total number of listed buildings in England at April 2005 (when English Heritage took a more active part in the listing process) was 372,038.[41]

This figure should be treated with considerable caution, since it relates to entries in the list rather than, necessarily, to individual properties. A "building" may thus be a single house, a terrace of 20 houses, or a gate pier. Further, the figure for the number of list entries at the start of 1998 was 451,287[42]; it has been suggested that the apparent reduction between the two figures is the result of "action taken to refine and improve the archive of information on listed buildings."[43]

However, if listed buildings are counted so that, for example, a terrace is treated as a number of separate buildings, it is likely that the total number of listed buildings in England has been more or less stable for the last 10 years, in the region of 500,000.[44] This represents about 2 per cent of all buildings.

Finally, it may be noted that standards can change quite quickly. The buildings in St James' Square whose listing in 1960 (with the support of Westminster City Council) was upheld by the Court of Appeal had been the subject of a grant of planning permission only five years earlier for redevelopment.[45] It is inconceivable that anyone would now consider demolishing them; indeed, one has since been upgraded to Grade II*. And more recently the passage of six years caused English Heritage to change its view over the suitability for listing of one of the iconic buildings from the 1960s.[46]

3.2.4 Grades

Not all listed buildings are of equal worth. Listed buildings in England are generally classified into three grades: Grade I, Grade II* and Grade II. It has always been slightly puzzling that the grading system is wholly non-statutory, given that a number of procedural requirements (in secondary legislation) depend on the grade assigned to a building. However, the most recent guidance from the DCMS (albeit only in draft form) has clarified that Grade I buildings are those of exceptional

---

[40] Published in November 2005; the latest in a series of annual reports available free from English Heritage, or online at *www.historicenvironment.org.uk*. The first, published in November 2002, was entitled *State of the Historic Environment Report 2002*. The second and third, *Heritage Counts 2003 and 2004*, were published in November 2003 and December 2004. These reports superseded *English Heritage Monitor*, published for many years by the English Tourist Board. As the years go by, these reports are increasingly interesting as background information on the built heritage generally,with each year a focus on a specific aspect of it; but decreasingly useful as a source of detailed statistical information.

[41] A very slight increase from 371,591 in August 2003 and 371,971 in August 2004.

[42] See the previous edition of this book for more details.

[43] Whatever that means. See *Heritage Counts 2004*, p.44.

[44] That is the figure given in PPG 15 (published in 1994), para.6.6, and again in *Heritage Counts 2004* (published 10 years later), p.44.

[45] *Earl of Iveagh v Minister of Housing and Local Government* [1964] 1 Q.B. 395, upholding [1962] 2 Q.B. 147 (see **3.2.2**).

[46] *R. (Bancroft) v Secretary of State for Culture, Media and Sport* [2005] J.P.L. 477; although that was (probably) not enough to save the building, as the Secretary of State had not changed her mind (see **3.2.2**).

interest; Grade II* buildings are particularly important buildings of more than special interest; and Grade II buildings are of special interest, warranting every effort to preserve them.[47]

Of the 371,214 graded list entries at mid-March 2005, 9,140 (just under 2½ per cent) were Grade I, and 20,904 (5.6 per cent) Grade II*.[48] The remainder (91.9 per cent) were Grade II.

Note that there is no truth in the widespread misconception that buildings are classified as Grade II* because of their interior. Nor is it true that the interiors of buildings of Grade II (unstarred) are not listed, and can thus be altered with impunity. Grade II* is simply an intermediate grade. Every part of a listed building, of whatever grade, is as a matter of law all equally listed—albeit, of course, that some parts may well be more important than others as a matter of merit.

Older lists used to contain some buildings classified as Grade III. These were buildings of local interest, but not statutorily "listed" buildings. They did not therefore obtain the protection afforded to buildings of other grades. However, when these earlier lists were revised, such buildings were frequently upgraded to Grade II—particularly where they were of group value; for a summary of the types of building thus upgraded, see para.2 of the Appendix to DoE Circ. 102/74.[49] In addition, many of them will also be in conservation areas, and their demolition will for that reason require consent.[50] Some authorities also compile "local lists"; these are considered later.[51]

The full significance of the grading of listed buildings will become apparent when considering the availability of financial assistance for repairs[52] and the details of procedure for processing planning and listed building consent applications.[53] Grading is also regarded by the Secretary of State as important in determining applications and appeals.[54]

Buildings are very rarely downgraded; but it is not that uncommon to come across a building that has been upgraded in the light of changing standards or new information or research becoming available. Over the years, therefore, the percentage of listed buildings in the higher grades (I and II*) has slightly risen—for example, from what was said to be a total of 6 per cent in 1994[55] to almost exactly 8 per cent in 2005. But the general picture remains the same—the great majority of listed buildings are Grade II.

---

[47] *Revisions to Principles of Selection for Listing Buildings: PPG 15*, consultation document, DCMS, July 2005.

[48] Figures from English Heritage National Monuments Record. Oddly, there were also at that date 199 listed buildings that had no grade.

[49] For an account of the (rather curious) evolution of the grading system generally, see Delafons, pp.66–68, 107.

[50] See **12.6**.

[51] See **7.2**.

[52] See **Chapter 9**.

[53] See **Chapter 13**.

[54] See PPG 15, paras 3.6 and 3.17; WO Circ. 61/96, paras 71 and 91.

[55] PPG 15, para.3.6—although that figure may have been slightly too small even then.

Church of England churches (and one or two other buildings) were in the earlier lists classified as Grades A, B or C, but in more recent lists have been assigned to Grades I, II* and II.[56] The special criteria governing the selection and grading of churches are described later in the book.[57]

3.2.5 Revision of criteria

The DCMS announced in July 2005 that it was proposing to revise the criteria for the selection of buildings suitable to be listed. It accordingly issued a draft circular, the final version of which is expected to be issued during 2006, containing new criteria and associated guidance to replace the guidance currently to be found in paragraphs 6.1 to 6.16 of PPG 15, and considered above.[58]

The new criteria proposed are essentially identical to those currently applying,[59] save that they rightly accept that buildings which are less than 10 years old may be listed under the most exceptional circumstances. They also clarify that the state of repair of a building is not a relevant consideration when deciding whether a building meets the test of special architectural or historic interest—save where the state of a building's disrepair has detracted from its interest to the point where it can no longer be considered "special".

The most significant innovation in the proposed new guidance is that it contains criteria for each of 20 building types,[60] against which the Secretary of State will assess the special interest of a building proposed for listing. An example of this is the proposed criteria for selecting places of worship for listing, reproduced later in this book.[61] It is hoped that this will make it simpler for everyone to understand what features are considered to be significant when assessing buildings from very different periods, different regions, or completely different styles. And English Heritage will publish on its website more detailed selection guides for each building type, to be periodically updated as required.

The new guidance will not affect listing in Wales, Scotland or Northern Ireland.

3.3 Listing procedure (England)

3.3.1 Production of the list

The Secretary of State is to compile a list of buildings of special architectural or historic interest, following consultation with experts in the field of historic

---

[56] There were in 2005 still 38 buildings of Grade A, 413 of Grade B, and 289 of Grade C— mainly but (apparently) not exclusively churches.

[57] See **16.1.2**.

[58] *Revisions to Principles of Selection for Listing Buildings: Planning Policy Guidance Note 15*, consultation document, DCMS, July 2005.

[59] See **3.2.2, 3.2.3**.

[60] Agricultural; commemorative; commercial; communications; culture and recreation; domestic (country house, suburban house, town house, 20th-century house, vernacular buildings); educational; buildings in gardens, parks and open spaces; health and welfare; industrial; law and government; military; places of worship; street furniture; transport; utilities.

[61] See **16.1.2**.

buildings (including, specifically, English Heritage).[62] He or she may approve lists produced by others—such as local authorities, consultants, or amenity groups— and may, in particular, approve lists prepared by English Heritage.[63]

There is in principle a list for the area of each local authority (district or borough council). In practice, the first lists came into force in the 1940s; and they are constantly being amended. Amendment usually takes the form of:

(1)   the inclusion of one or more new buildings in the list;

(2)   the alteration of the grade ascribed to a building already on the list;

(3)   the removal of a building from the list (because it has been altered, demolished, or burned, or its merit proves to have been misjudged, or it was listed in error); or

(4)   the issue of a complete new list for an authority's area.

The last of these will generally be done only as part of a programmed resurvey of the whole country (see above); and the list produced will normally include all buildings listed previously, although possibly with updated descriptions or grades. More common is the ad hoc addition to the list of a particular building, terrace or group—possibly as a result of the identification of key modern buildings or other research-based studies[64] or as a "spot-listing".[65] The past few years have thus seen a succession of announcements by the Secretary of State that he or she has listed a group of tube stations, or theatres, or sculptures, or whatever.

In practice, the survey work is carried out by a team of specialist inspectors employed by or acting as consultants to English Heritage. They will assess the buildings concerned on the basis of the criteria outlined above, possibly carrying out appropriate research.

There is no requirement for the Secretary of State or English Heritage to consult the owners of buildings to be listed, or local authorities, or anyone else. However, the Code of Conduct for resurvey teams now emphasises the need for publicity before a survey is carried out, and co-operation while it is in progress. Except where an inspector has been warned or has reasonable grounds to suspect that there is a threat of pre-emptive demolition, he or she will now contact the owner or occupier of the property being inspected—or leave a visiting card—and also the relevant local planning authority.

There is a statutory power (under s.88) for anyone duly authorised by the Secretary of State to enter any land at any reasonable time to survey any building (either on that land or on any other land) in connection with a proposal to include it in, or exclude it from, the statutory list.[66] There must, therefore, presumably be at least some grounds for thinking that the building is worthy of being listed (or de-listed, as the case may be). That would extend to entering a building, since

[62]   s.1(4).
[63]   P(LBCA)A 1990, s.1(1).
[64]   See **3.2.3**.
[65]   See **3.3.2**.
[66]   P(LBCA)A 1990, s.88(1). Note, incidentally, that s.88 was amended, and ss 88A and 88B were inserted, by the Planning and Compensation Act 1991.

"land" includes "building".[67] A person carrying out such a survey must, if required, give at least 24 hours' notice,[68] unless a warrant has been issued under s.88A. If the property is damaged, compensation is payable.[69] Moreover, anyone obstructing a person exercising a right of entry under ss 88 or 88A is liable to a fine not exceeding level 3 on the standard scale.[70]

Once a building or group of buildings have been surveyed, and any comments made by the owner and local authority have been considered, the inspector concerned will reach a conclusion on their suitability for listing. If they are reckoned to be suitable, a draft amendment to the list (or, as appropriate, a new list) will be sent with a supporting report to the Secretary of State, who will then either list the buildings or decline to do so.[71] If approved, the new list is typed, signed and dated by a principal on behalf of the Secretary of State. It is that date that determines conclusively when the building becomes listed.

This process was examined in some detail in the *John Walker* case.[72] The details, in that case, proved to be of crucial importance: on September 25, 1973, the parties signed a contract in which the defendants agreed to sell a Victorian warehouse to the plaintiffs, with a view to its demolition prior to the redevelopment of the site, for £1,710,000. Two days later, on September 27, the list (containing 1,500 other buildings throughout the London Borough of Tower Hamlets as well as the warehouse) was signed, and the warehouse became effectively "listed". The evidence was that, once listed, it was worth only £210,000.

3.3.2 Spot listing

Anyone (including a local authority) may request the Secretary of State to include a building on the statutory list—and indeed in 2004 there were a number of such requests in England. Where such a request is successful, the result is known as "spot-listing". In England, now that the national resurvey has largely been completed, the significance of spot-listing has increased as a way of achieving protection for a building under threat.

It is of course only the Secretary of State who has power to list buildings, but in practice it is best to address a request for listing to the Heritage Protection Operations Department at English Heritage, sending a copy to the DCMS. And although a local authority cannot list a building, it is sensible to seek its support— not least since it may be able to point out that, for example, the building in question was recently proposed for listing, but rejected.

A request should be accompanied by the following:

---

[67] Interpretation Act 1978, s.5 and Sch.1.

[68] s.88(1).

[69] s.88B(7); *Six Carpenters' Case* (1610) 8 Co. Rep. 146a.

[70] s.88B(3); *R. v Chief Constable of Devon and Cornwall, ex p. CEGB* [1981] 3 All E.R. 826.

[71] Prior to April 1, 2005, English Heritage officers used to report to officials in the DCMS, who then prepared a further report to the Secretary of State, which was obviously somewhat wasteful of professional time.

[72] *Amalgamated Investment and Property Co. Ltd v John Walker and Sons Ltd* [1976] 3 All E.R. 509; Buckley L.J. (at p.512) found the evidence with regard to the listing procedures to be "rather startling". But it should be noted that that case refers to the procedures as they were some 30 years ago.

(1) a location plan (such as an Ordnance Survey map extract) showing, wherever possible, the position of any other listed buildings nearby;

(2) the name and contact details of the owner.

(3) clear up-to-date photographic prints of the main elevations of the building;

(4) any information about the building, for example:
— the date(s) of its construction;
— any specialised function it may have performed;
— any historical associations;
— the name of its architect (if known);
— its group value in the street scene;
— details of any interior features of interest; and

(5) a justification for adding the building to the list.[73]

The last of these is particularly important. Where an area has been recently resurveyed, it is unlikely that a building will be added to the list without cogent evidence as to why it might have been overlooked. See **Form D1** in Appendix D for an example of a request.

Once such a request is received, an investigator will be dispatched to inspect the building, except in a case of urgency where the information supplied is adequate for the building to be assessed without a visit. It will then, if appropriate, be listed in the normal way.

The spot-listing of a building may be awkward for its owner and any prospective purchasers, especially where there are well advanced proposals for its demolition and the redevelopment of its site. The Department thus advises that it is preferable from all points of view for a building to be assessed for possible listing as early as possible, and in particular before permission is granted for any redevelopment.[74] A local authority keen to save a building can of course serve a building pre-servation notice, which secures immediate, if temporary, preservation.[75]

3.3.3 Notification of local authority, owners and occupiers

Once a list or an amendment has been signed, a copy is immediately sent to all the local authorities covering the area concerned (county council and district or borough council).[76] Usually a certified copy is sent to the town clerk or chief executive, with extra copies for general use as required. In addition, copies of lists are to be sent as follows:

(1) *in Greater London*: to English Heritage[77];

---

[73] PPG 15, para.6.22.
[74] PPG 15, para.6.21. The corresponding advice for Scotland (at para.1.17 of the HS Memorandum) has twice recently formed the basis of a successful challenge in the courts to listing (see **3.3.5**).
[75] See **3.9**.
[76] P(LBCA)A 1990, s.2(1), amended by Local Government (Wales) Act 1994, Sch.6.
[77] s.2(1)(a).

(2) *in national parks*: to the national park authority[78]; and

(3) *in the Broads*: to the Broads Authority.[79]

Letters are also sent by the Department to "the owner/occupier" of every building newly listed, together with a copy of an explanatory leaflet. However, these will not reach everyone with an interest in the building, particularly where it is leasehold, or in multiple occupation, or currently vacant. The local authority (district or borough council) is therefore under a duty to inform every owner and occupier of the building "as soon as possible" after being notified by the Secretary of State.[80] This means that the authority first has to find out who are all the owners (including absent freeholders, tenants of blocks of flats, etc.) and occupiers. This can be done by personal inspection, or using the authority's statutory powers to obtain information[81]—possibly using a standard questionnaire.

The notification can take place almost immediately in the case of a single building being added to the list; but where a new list is produced for the whole of an authority's area, the paperwork involved can be very time-consuming, and has to be fitted in amongst other routine work. It is not surprising, therefore, that notification can be delayed for several months. The actual notification is to be "in the prescribed form".[82]

However, since the listing (and hence the need for listed building consent[83]) takes effect from the date the list is signed (see above), and since in certain circumstances the owner may not be informed of it until some while later, there is a real risk that the owner can carry out works to the building which require consent, without being aware of the need for it. It is thus possible for an owner (or his or her contractor or other agent) to commit, quite unintentionally, an offence punishable by imprisonment—which is particularly unfortunate since the offence is one of strict liability.[84] Authorities have therefore rightly been reminded of the need to notify owners "as soon as possible".[85]

Thus in one case in North Wales, two derelict cottages were listed in November 1998, just after they had been bought by a new owner. He restored them in late 1999, in a way that needed listed building consent, but this only came to the light when the local authority's building control officer visited the site. The owner was not served the official notification that the cottages had been listed until August 2000, by which time he was facing enforcement action, requiring the cottage to be restored properly. The Local Government Ombudsman considered that he should

---

[78] s.2(1)(b)(ii); TCPA 1990, s.4A(2), inserted by Environment Act 1995, s.67.

[79] s.2(1)(b)(iii) and Sch.4, para.5(a).

[80] s.2(3), amended by 1994 Act, Sch.6.

[81] TCPA 1990, s.330 applied by P(LBCA)A 1990, s.89(1); Local Government (Miscellaneous Provisions) Act 1976, s.16.

[82] s.2(3)(b). The current form is at Sch.4 to the P(LBCA) Regs 1990, as substituted by SI/2005, 1085—the new notice (finally, after 13 years!) takes account of the fact that listing is carried out by DCMS rather than the DOE.

[83] See **12.2, 12.5**.

[84] since *R. v Wells Street Metropolitan Stipendiary Magistrate, ex p. Westminster CC* [1986] 1 W.L.R. 1046: see 10.2.2.

[85] PPG 15, para.6.17; WO Circ. 61/96, para.50.

be reimbursed for the cost of the corrective works, architect's fees and some legal fees as well.[86]

The dangers of incorrect notification have recently been highlighted in a case relating to a tree preservation order, where the wrong owner who notified and the order declared invalid as a result.[87] It must be doubted whether this would apply to listing, given that many more people are involved; but certainly, the risk of such problems should be minimised.

The fact that a building is listed, upgraded, or deleted from the list is to be a local land charge.[88] This has the effect of ensuring that any future prospective purchaser of the building, as well as the present owners and occupiers, is made aware of its listing, and can therefore find out from the planning authority what effect this may have on any proposed development. Such a charge is to be entered in Pt 10 of the Local Land Charges Register ("listed buildings charges").[89]

Failure to register the charge does not affect its enforceability—although it may lead to an entitlement to compensation.[90] The extent of this entitlement has been recently considered in *Pound v Ashford BC*,[91] which concerned a farmhouse that had been listed in 1977 without the listing having been registered. The claimant acquired the building in 1984, and both he and the planning authority were unaware that it was listed. In 1990 and 1995, planning permission was granted for development on neighbouring land, which reduced the value of the listed farmhouse possibly by up to £100,000, and which arguably might not have occurred had its listed status been known. The court held that compensation for the failure to register the listing was payable, if at all, only to the initial purchaser. And secondly, compensation would only be payable if the listing was enforced against the purchaser—if, for example, he had to undo alterations for which he had not obtained listed building consent.

Thus, in *Aquis Estates v Minton*,[92] a property company had agreed to purchase the remaining few years of a long leasehold of an old factory in Southwark, subject to there being no adverse entry on the purchaser's local land charge search. The building was subsequently listed, largely for its industrial historical interest. The purchaser then sought to rescind the contract. It was held that the listing did constitute an "adverse entry", since it would clearly hamper a developer in plans to convert the building for office use. However, although this amounted to a breach of a term of the contract which would have allowed the purchaser to rescind, he had chosen to continue to negotiate, and had invited the vendor to make a non-statutory appeal against the listing.[93] That, not surpris-

---

[86] Gwynedd Council; ombudsman reference 2001/0569/CN/251.
[87] *Knowles v Chorley BC* [1998] J.P.L. 593.
[88] s.2(2).
[89] Local Land Charge Rules 1977, r.3.
[90] Local Land Charges Act 1975, s.10(1).
[91] [2003] 2 PLR 83. But note that the claimant, although unsuccessful in his claim for compensation, did not have to pay the authority's costs, by virtue of s.10(9) of the 1975 Act: *Pound v Ashford (No. 2)* Lawtel AC9200527.
[92] [1975] 1 W.L.R. 1452.
[93] See **3.3.4**.

ingly, was unsuccessful. But the purchaser, having thus elected to affirm the contract by negotiating, could not repudiate it now.

Finally, the listing of a building—or the deposit of a copy of the relevant list with the local authority—between the date on which its purchase is complete and that on which the purchase is registered does not affect the force of the listing. This was the (unsurprising) conclusion of the House of Lords, albeit probably *obiter*, in *Abbey National Building Society v Cann*,[94] following an examination of relevant property law principles.

3.3.4 Appeals against listing

There is no statutory right to appeal against the inclusion of a building in the list. But anyone who is unhappy with a decision by the Secretary of State to list a building may write to the DCMS within 28 days requesting that it be reconsidered. Indeed, anyone can at any time write to the Secretary of State claiming that a building should not be listed (after an initial survey has been carried out), or that it should be removed from the list.

The Department issued during 1994 a revised version of its leaflet *How to Appeal Against Listing*, available from the Listing Branch. There are no forms to fill in, no set procedures to go through, and no time limits.

"You should be aware, however, that buildings are listed for their special architectural or historic interest. ... We cannot take a building off the list just because an owner feels aggrieved. We have to be convinced that a mistake has been made in adding the building in the first place; or that a building has become so altered or mutilated over the years that it is no longer worthy of listing."

The information required is as for spot-listing (see above)—location plan, photographs and other details as appropriate.[95]

Such approaches may lead to a decision being overturned. In the *Aquis Estates* case,[96] none of the parties held out any hope that it would be successful, and the listing was referred to as being "in practice impossible to rescind". In fact, however, it may be noted that in 1992, for example, about half of the 141 appeals received were successful (this should be compared to some 1,840 buildings being listed that year).

There was much discussion in the House of Lords in 1991, during the debate on the Housing and Planning Bill, as to the possibility of a statutory right of appeal against listing. However, after a somewhat confused debate in Committee, their lordships voted at report stage not to provide for such a right. But it is likely that the issue will reappear in connection with the proposed revisions to the listing process.[97]

There is of course at present a statutory right to appeal against the listing of a building if listed building consent is refused for works to it,[98] or if a listed building

---

[94] [1990] 1 All E.R. 1085 (per Lord Oliver at 1095j and Lord Jauncey at 1110b).
[95] See PPG 15, para.6.26; WO Circ. 61/96, para.58.
[96] See **3.3.3**.
[97] See **Appendix G**.
[98] P(LBCA)A 1990, s.21(3).

enforcement notice is issued.[99] This is the first time when the listing of a building directly affects its owner adversely. For that reason, the Secretary of State is not generally prepared to entertain an application for de-listing if the building in question is the subject of an application for listed building consent, or an appeal following an application.[1] As to the uncertainty resulting from listing (in other words, from the need to obtain listed building consent), this is no worse than that which arises from the need to obtain planning permission for development.

3.3.5 Judicial review of listing

An alternative to the non-statutory review by the Secretary of State of his or her decision to list is to seek to overturn the decision in the courts. Thus, while the decision whether or not to list a building (or to de-list one already listed) is inevitably a matter of discretion, that discretion must be exercised reasonably, and is subject to judicial review. A decision not to list a building was recently challenged, unsuccessfully, in *R. (Bancroft) v Secretary of State*.[2] The courts are likely to be unenthusiastic about an application to challenge a listing, on the grounds that whether or not a particular building has special interest is very much a matter for the discretion of the Secretary of State and for English Heritage, her adviser.

However, the Court of Session in Scotland has recently had before it two separate applications for judicial review of decisions by the Scottish Ministers to list buildings in circumstances similar to the present. Both challenges focused on the *Memorandum of Guidance* produced in 1998 by Historic Scotland, and in particular on para.1.17, which stated:

"A building will not normally be listed once a planning application in respect of it has been lodged, or whilst works which have received planning permission are under way, and will certainly not be listed in the course of an appeal period or current appeal against refusal of planning permission."

In *R. v Scottish Ministers (ex p. Sovereign Land (Mearns) Ltd*,[3] planning permission had been sought unsuccessfully for the carrying out of new development (the construction of a car park, to serve an adjacent shopping centre) on the site of the Newton Mearns Primary School. The developers accordingly intended to exercise their right to appeal to the Scottish Ministers against the decision of the planning authority. However, before they had submitted their appeal, the Ministers included the school in the statutory list. The developers therefore sought judicial review on the ground (amongst others) that, in deciding to list the school in the course of the appeal period, the Ministers had failed to take account of a relevant consideration, had frustrated the petitioner's legitimate expectation that the above policy would be followed, had exercised their powers in an unreasonable, arbitrary or perverse manner, and had acted unfairly by listing a building in the course of the determination of an application for planning

---

[99] s.39(1)(a).

[1] PPG 15, para.6.27; WO Circ. 61/96, para.59.

[2] [2005] JPL 477; see **3.2.2**. Technically, this was a decision to issue a certificate of immunity (see **3.4**)—but the issues involved are those that would arise in a challenge to a decision to list (or not to list) a building.

[3] Decision to list the building dated September 24, 2003.

permission and during the appeal period without giving the developers an opportunity to make representations on the listing of the building and on the intention of the respondents to depart from policy.

In the second case, *R. v Scottish Ministers (ex p. Tesco Stores Ltd)*,[4] planning permission had been sought for the erection of a new store, on land in Galashiels. Part of that land was occupied by the Scottish Woollen Technical College. Before the application had been determined by the planning authority, the Ministers listed the college. Again, their decision was challenged—on virtually identical grounds to those relied on in the *Newton Mearns* case.

In both cases, the Scottish Ministers allowed the petition to be granted unopposed, and the decision of Historic Scotland "reduced" (the equivalent in Scotland of being quashed). Unfortunately there is as a result no formal decision of the Court, but it is perhaps significant that Historic Scotland gave way not once but twice.[5]

The corresponding guidance in England, at para.6.21 of PPG 15, not quite as strongly worded as para.1.17 of the Scottish *Memorandum*, but it is clearly to the same effect—planning authorities should notify the Department as soon as possible of buildings threatened by development, and buildings should not be listed once planning permission has been granted for redevelopment.[6]

Arguably, therefore, the Secretary of State should not list a building while the planning process for its replacement is underway, since to do so would be to fly in the face of the guidance in PPG 15, which—just as with the corresponding guidance in Scotland—creates a legitimate interest that buildings will not be listed once planning permission has been granted. It would therefore arguably be unlawful and capable of being quashed by way of an application for judicial review. That argument has been accepted twice by the Scottish Ministers, and there is no logical reason why it should apply any less in relation to listing by the Secretary of State for Culture, Media and Sport in England.

3.3.6 Compensation for listing

The financial consequences of a building being listed can in some cases be disastrous for an owner or prospective purchaser. This may be due to the inability of a developer to demolish it and do something more profitable with the site (as in the *John Walker* case[7]). Or it may be that an owner of a listed building is faced with huge repair bills, lowering its market value—as in *Cavendish Funding Ltd v Henry Spencer & Sons Ltd*,[8] in which a listed manor house was initially valued in 1991 at around £1.5 million, but, due to its poor state of repair and the obligation

---

[4]   Decision to list dated February 23, 2004.
[5]   For completeness, it may be noted that there was in each case a second argument alleging that the whole listing exercise was a breach of human rights. The Scottish Ministers, in conceding defeat, explicitly declined to accept that argument, and conceded only on the first argument, noted above.
[6]   See **3.3.2**.
[7]   *Amalgamated Investment and Property Co. Ltd v John Walker and Sons Ltd* [1976] 3 All E.R. 509; see **3.3.1**.
[8]   [1998] 1 E.G.L.R. 104, CA.

which was perceived to fall upon the owners due to the listing, was agreed to be actually worth in the order of about £250,000.

In other cases listing may be advantageous, as is shown by the number of estate agents' particulars which make a feature of it; indeed the RICS and English Heritage produce an annual survey *The Investment Performance of Listed Buildings*, which suggests that—at least in the long term—listed office buildings outperform unlisted buildings in investment terms.

Either way, however, it has always been accepted by the courts that the possibility of a building being listed is something that has to be accepted. Thus Buckley L.J. in *John Walker* commented:

"It seems to me that the risk of property being listed as property of architectural or historical interest is a risk which inheres in all ownership of buildings. In many cases it may be an extremely remote risk. In many cases it may be a marginal risk. In some cases it may be a substantial risk. But it is a risk, I think, which attaches to all buildings and it is a risk that every owner and every purchaser of property must recognise that he is subject to."[9]

The same point had been implicitly accepted in *Aquis Estates v Minton*.[10]

There is, in particular, no right to any compensation—either for any future increase in the cost of maintenance or repairs due to the requirement to use traditional materials, or for any restriction on the right to alter and, eventually, demolish the building. There was, until 1990, a very limited right to compensation where listed building consent was refused, but that has now been abolished.[11]

3.3.7 Appeals against refusal to list

Local residents, amenity groups and even, occasionally, local authorities may sometimes request the Secretary of State to list a building, but without success. It is questionable whether there is in such a situation any means of redress.

This is similar, but not identical, to the situation which occurred in *R. v Secretary of State, ex p. Rose Theatre Trust*,[12] which concerned an application for judicial review of the Secretary of State's decision not to include in the schedule of ancient monuments the remains of the Rose Theatre in London. The Secretary of State's position under the Ancient Monuments Act[13] is that he may include in the schedule any monument which appears to him to be of national importance. In that case he agreed that the remains of the theatre were important, but decided for various reasons not to schedule them. Schiemann J. noted that there was no dispute that the Secretary of State had agreed that the theatre was of national importance, but decided that he had a broad discretion as to whether to include it in the schedule. He also decided, in a judgment that was later to give rise to some concern, that neither a concerned member of the public, such as an eminent

---

[9] At 517a.
[10] [1975] 1 W.L.R. 1452 (see **3.3.3**).
[11] See **15.4.2**.
[12] [1990] 1 P.L.R. 39.
[13] AMAAA 1979, s.1(3).

archaeologist, nor a group of such people, had a sufficient interest[14] to justify an application for judicial review.[15]

A decision by the Secretary of State not to list a building is somewhat different, in that he or she has a duty, not a power, to compile a list of buildings of special interest.[16] Arguably, therefore, once the Secretary of State has formed the view that a building is of special interest—as to which there must be a considerable element of discretion, since perceptions of such matters differ widely—he or she then has no option but to list it. The only likely ground of challenge would thus be if the Secretary of State had been *Wednesbury* unreasonable in reaching a decision as to whether or not the building was of interest.[17]

The *Rose Theatre* case still causes problems, though, on the "sufficient interest" point; it would seem that a private individual or a local amenity group might not have a sufficient interest to challenge a refusal to list. Arguably, however, the owner of the building, its occupier, the developer, and—possibly—the local authority and English Heritage would all have a sufficient interest; but the point has not yet been tested in the courts.

The court has recently considered the failure by the Secretary of State to list Pimlico School, in London, in spite of a recommendation to do so by English Heritage.[18] The challenge was nominally to the decision to issue a certificate of immunity, but the issues raised would be those that would have to be raised in a challenge to a failure to list a building. The fact that the court allowed such a challenge to be brought by a claimant whose only interest was that he had designed the building in question some 40 years earlier indicates that the court has relaxed its restrictive attitude to "sufficient interest" since the *Rose Theatre* case; but the reasons he failed are such that it seems that the courts would require huge persuasion to overturn a decision not to list a building.

3.3.8 *Where to inspect the list*

Lists must be kept available for inspection by the public at reasonable hours, free of charge, by all local authorities, English Heritage (lists for Greater London only), national park authorities, the Broads Authority and the Secretary of State.[19]

Lists for the whole of England are available at English Heritage's National Monuments Record. Alternatively, queries about the contents of the lists can be sent to the Listing Branch of the Department of Culture, Media and Sport, which has recently completed the major exercise of computerising and indexing all the statutory lists. Perhaps the most useful source of information is the Images of England website[20], which contains list descriptions for (almost) every listed

---

[14] In the terms of the Supreme Court Act 1981, s.31(3).
[15] See **15.7**.
[16] Under P(LBCA)A 1990, s.1.
[17] *Associated Provincial Picture Houses v Wednesbury Corporation* [1948] 1 K.B. 223.
[18] *R. (Bancroft) v Secretary of State for Culture, Media and Sport* [2005] J.P.L. 477 (see **3.2.2, 3.3.5**).
[19] P(LBCA)A 1990, s.2(4), (6).
[20] *www.imagesofengland.org.uk*

building in England, searchable by reference to a wide variety of indicators; it also features photographs in some cases.

It is often prudent for enquirers to apply to the appropriate local authority for information, however, for they will then also be able to find out whether or not the building is in a conservation area. If it is, it will be subject to some control (notably over demolition) even if it is not listed.

3.3.9 Changes to the listing system prior to new legislation

The consultation paper issued by the Government in June 2004 proposed a number of changes to the listing system. Most required new primary legislation; they are outlined briefly in **Appendix G**. However, it also included one or two administrative changes to be introduced in relation to the existing system.[21]

First, there is to be more openness and transparency in the listing process—including, unsurprisingly, greater consultation with the owners of buildings being considered for listing. This has been proposed periodically, and is therefore nothing new. Second, the DCMS is introducing a procedure to allow for a more formal review of listing—with effect from the taking over by English Heritage of responsibility for listing, so that angry, unhappy or simply puzzled owners can seek further information and, if necessary, the decision to list can be reversed. This replaces the previous informal appeal system.

In the absence of statutory backing, neither of these proposals would seem to amount to a great deal; and any move towards greater consultation with owners would obviously have to be subject to safeguards to prevent abuse.

Linked to both of these proposals, there will also be information packs for the owners of newly listed buildings, explaining why they have been listed, and encouraging them to be proud of the asset they own and to want to look after it. This is a development of the leaflet that currently accompanies notifications of listing.

Third, there may be increased clarity as to the extent of listing; this is considered at the end of the next chapter.[22]

3.4 Certificates of immunity from listing

Partly as a result of the *John Walker* case,[23] it was recognised that the listing of a building at a late stage in redevelopment proposals can cause great inconvenience or hardship. It is therefore possible to apply for a *certificate of immunity from listing*. This is a legal guarantee that a building will not be listed during the five years starting with the date on which the certificate is signed.[24] It also prevents the local authority from serving a building preservation notice on the building during that period.[25]

---

[21] *Review of Heritage Protection: The Way Forward*, DCMS, June 2004.
[22] See **4.6.4**.
[23] See **3.3.1**.
[24] P(LBCA)A 1990, s.6(2).
[25] See **3.9**.

An application for a certificate can be made by anyone, whether or not they own the building, provided that planning permission has been granted for works involving its alteration or demolition or that a planning application has been submitted for such works.[26] This means that it is not possible for a vendor (or prospective purchaser) to apply for a certificate before placing a property on the market, in order to assist in determining its value. In such a case, however, it would presumably be possible to make an application after first submitting a token application for a minor alteration.

The application is made—in England—to the Listing Branch of the DCMS; the Department of National Heritage (the predecessor to the DCMS) published during 1994 a revised guide to certificates of immunity. There is no prescribed form; nor is there any charge—although there will of course be a fee payable for the planning application which must have preceded the application for a certificate. A copy of the application for a certificate, and of all the accompanying material, must be sent to the local planning authority[27]—that is, to the district or borough council and, outside London and the metropolitan areas, to the county council or national park authority.[28] In addition, where the building is in London, a copy should be sent to English Heritage[29] and, where it is in the Broads, to the Broads Authority.[30]

The application should include:

(1) the full address of the building;

(2) a copy of the relevant planning application or permission;

(3) the same information that would be required for a spot-listing application[31]; and

(4) confirmation that the application has been copied to the appropriate authority (as above).

For a sample application, see **Form D2** in Appendix D.

On receipt of the application, a thorough inspection of the building will be arranged and the relevant governmental department will ask the local authority if it wishes to make any comments. It is also noteworthy that PPG 15 reminds applicants that "it should not be assumed that even a recent decision by the Secretary of State not to list a building necessarily means that he will grant a certificate of immunity".[32] This bears out the observation from experience that the perceived merit of a building can change in a short time.[33]

---

[26] s.6(1).

[27] s.6(3).

[28] TCPA 1990, ss 1(1), (1B), (2) and 2, amended by Local Government (Wales) Act 1994, s.18.

[29] P(LBCA)A 1990, s.6(4).

[30] P(LBCA)A 1990, Sch.4, para.5(b).

[31] See **3.3.2**.

[32] PPG 15, para.6.29.

[33] *Earl of Iveagh v Minister of Housing and Local Government* [1964] 1 Q.B. 395, upholding [1962] 2 Q.B. 147; *R. (Bancroft) v Secretary of State for Culture, Media and Sport* [2005] J.P.L. 477 (see **3.2.3**).

The working of this procedure has been considered by the Administrative Courts recently in *R. (Bancroft) v Secretary of State*, from which it is clear that the courts are—not surprisingly—going to be very unwilling to interfere with a decision of the Secretary of State, provided that there is at least some basis on which she or he could properly have made it.[34]

A certificate takes the form of a letter to the applicant, signed on behalf of the Secretary of State. If one is issued, the Department will notify the district or borough council and the county council (and, in London, English Heritage). The existence of a certificate is not a local land charge; but it has been suggested that it should be disclosed in response to enquiries by prospective purchasers.[35]

Note that a certificate does not preclude the local authority from including the property within a conservation area, which would mean that consent could still be required for its demolition. The official line is that "it is not practicable to extend the certificate procedure to provide immunity from the effects of conservation area designation".[36] It is not quite clear why this should be so, and it arguably renders the whole procedure slightly pointless.

If a certificate is not issued, the building will of course be listed; but at least this removes some uncertainty.

3.5 Listing in Wales, Scotland and Northern Ireland

3.5.1 Introduction

The principles explained above in relation to practice in England apply equally to Wales, Scotland and Northern Ireland. Thus the primary legislation (ss 1 and 2 of the Listed Buildings Act) applying in Wales is identical to that in England; that in Scotland and Northern Ireland (ss 1 and 2 of the Scottish Listed Buildings Act and art.42 of the Northern Ireland Order) is very similar. This section accordingly concentrates only on the principal differences.

3.5.2 Wales

The principles underlying the listing process, outlined above in relation to England, apply equally to Wales. And the primary and secondary legislation are identical, with Welsh language forms prescribed[37]; and the policy and guidance in the relevant Welsh Office circulars is similar to that applying in England.[38] Their practical outworking is, however, somewhat different.

The criteria for the selection of listed buildings in Wales are generally as set out in WO Circ. 61/96,[39] which are almost identical to those in PPG 15.[40] However,

---

[34] See **3.2.2**.
[35] para.6.33.
[36] para.6.30.
[37] SI 1990/1147. But note that these forms pre-date the coming into being of the Welsh Assembly Government, and may need to be updated accordingly (and see **1.5.2**).
[38] For convenience, references to Welsh guidance are given in **3.3**.
[39] WO Circ. 61/96, para.48 and Annex C.
[40] See **3.2.2**.

the Welsh Affairs Committee of the House of Commons in its 1997 report indicate that it was disappointed that not enough protection was being given to distinctively Welsh building types.[41] As a result, the policy guidance on listing for historical association[42] was replaced with new wording at Appendix F to WO Circ. 1/98. The grades used are identical to those in England.

The Welsh Office took over responsibility for listing from the Department of the Environment in 1981, when there were relatively few listed buildings in the principality. By 1997, the Welsh Affairs Committee report noted with approval the progress being made on the resurvey (by then being carried out by Cadw): in some areas it was almost complete, although in others it was still to begin.[43] And by 1998, a gradual resurvey had led to a total of over 20,000 list entries.[44] By May 2005, the figure had risen to 28,285—again, the precise figure for the number of actual buildings involved depending, as in England, on how they are counted.

The resurvey being carried out by Cadw, now a department within the Welsh Assembly Government, is expected to be complete by the end of 2005. It is still estimated that the eventual number of listed building entries in Wales will be in the region of 30,000.

Lists for Wales are available at Cadw and at the RCAHMW in Aberystwyth, as well as at the offices of the relevant council.

The procedure for immunity certificates operates in Wales entirely as in England; policy guidance is in WO Circ. 61/96.[45]

3.5.3 Scotland

Criteria for the selection of listed buildings in Scotland are as follows:

(a) *before 1840*: all buildings that are of any quality, even if plain, and survive in anything like their original form;

(b) *1840 to 1914*: buildings that are of definite quality and character, either individually or as a group;

(c) *1914 to 1945*: buildings that are good examples of the work of an important architect, or of a particular style (whether traditional, progressive or international modern);

(d) *after 1945*: buildings of outstanding quality and some vintage (a very high degree of selection is exercised).[46]

It will be noted that these are significantly different to the criteria operating in England in one or two details.

---

[41] HC 250; see **1.5.2.**
[42] WO Circ. 61/96, Annex C, para.5.
[43] HC 250.
[44] Of these, 371 were of Grade I, 1,241 of Grade II*, 18,566 of Grade II, and 483 "others". The latter category reflects that the older lists classified churches differently—into Grades A, B, C, and — [*sic*].
[45] WO Circ. 61/96, paras 60–64.
[46] HS Memorandum, para.1.8.

The "categories" (corresponding to "grades" in England) used in the statutory list are:

"A   Buildings of national or international importance, either architectural or historic, or fine little-altered examples of some particular period, style or building type.

B   Buildings of regional or more than local importance, or major examples of some period, style or building type which may have been altered.

C(S) Buildings of local importance, lesser examples of any period, style or building type, as originally constructed or altered; and simple traditional buildings which group well with categories A and B or are part of a planned group such as an estate or an industrial complex."[47]

There is a further C (non-statutory) category, equivalent to the English Grade III, but this and the B for Group category are being phased out in the current resurvey, of which two-thirds had been completed by mid-1998.

At May 2005 there were 46,867 listed buildings in Scotland—including 3,649 of Category A, 26,168 of Category B (including B for Group) and 17,050 of Category C(s).[48] From these figures, it will be appreciated that the significance of the categories in Scotland is somewhat different to that of the grades in England and Wales.

One unique feature of the Scottish system relates to groups of buildings:

"Buildings which relate together in townscape terms, or as planned layouts in urban, rural or landed estate contexts, often have their value stressed by inclusion within A or B Groups (C groups are being phased out). The group category does not alter the individual category, but emphasises that the value of individual buildings is enhanced by association with others in the group. In considering an application for listed building consent, planning authorities should bear in mind the effect of a proposal, not only on the individual building, but on the group as a whole. The A or B category indicates the overall value of the group."[49]

There were in 2005 a total of 1,081 listed buildings included in Grade A groups and 1,383 in Grade B groups. That suggests that the process of allocating buildings to graded groups is still far from complete.

Copies of lists in Scotland are available for inspection at offices of planning authorities and at the headquarters of Historic Scotland in Edinburgh.[50] Listing is not (as it is in England and Wales) a local land charge, as there is no such system of registration in Scotland. This makes it all the more important for the Secretary of State and local authorities to notify owners of listing as promptly as possible.[51]

There is for some reason no procedure in Scotland to obtain a certificate of immunity from listing.

3.5.4 Northern Ireland

Buildings in Northern Ireland are listed by the Environment and Heritage Service of the Department of the Environment, following consultation with the Historic

---

[47] HS Memorandum, para.1.6. Note that A, B and C do not just refer to ecclesiastical buildings, as in old English lists.

[48] There are also still 432 buildings in Grade C (non-statutory).

[49] HS Memorandum, para.1.7.

[50] See **Appendix C**.

[51] HS Memorandum, para.1.14.

Buildings Council and the relevant district council.[52] The first survey began in 1974, and a second survey started in 1995; by May 2005 there were some 8,235 list entries.

The criteria for selecting listed buildings are in Annex C to (NI) PPS 6. Buildings are assessed in relation to their architectural interest, their historic interest and their group value. In general, buildings dating from the 19th century, if they survive in anything like their original form, will qualify for listing; after that, the choice is progressively more selective due to the greater number of surviving buildings. The number of post-1914 buildings is relatively small; normally nothing is listed if it is less than 30 years old. Unlike the criteria in Great Britain, these broad principles are sensibly elaborated in greater detail.[53]

There were, in 2005, 188 buildings listed at Grade A (as with Grade I in England, around 2½ per cent of the total)—those of the greatest importance to Northern Ireland—and 464 (5 per cent) at Grade B +. The buildings allocated to Grade B + are those that would have merited Grade A but for additions or alterations, and those that would have been in Grade B but for some exceptional features or interiors.

The remaining 7,583 listed buildings, in Grade B, are gradually being banded into two groups: those with a wide selection of attributes in Grade B1, those with fewer in Grade B2. Also in Grade B2 are those that are within a conservation area but whose quality is appreciably above the average. Around three quarters of the Grade B buildings have so far been banded—60 per cent to Grade B1 and 40 per cent to Grade B2.

Lists are available for inspection at the offices of the Environment and Heritage Service at Hill Street, Belfast, and at Divisional Planning Offices.[54]

A certificate of immunity may be sought from the Department[55] which, again, will consult with the Historic Buildings Council and the district council.

3.6 The consequences of listing

3.6.1 Planning legislation

The effect of a building being listed is that it is declared openly to be "of special architectural or historic interest".[56] This does not imply that there is any presumption in favour of the building being preserved—compare the definition of a conservation area, which is defined as an area "the character or appearance of which it is desirable to preserve or enhance". But it is stated in the Act that the inclusion of a building in the list is "with a view to the guidance of local planning authorities in the performance of their functions under this Act in relation to historic buildings".[57]

[52] P(NI)O 1991, art.42.
[53] NI PPS 6, Annex C, paras C3 to C8.
[54] As required by art.42(6) of the Order.
[55] art.43.
[56] P(LBCA)A 1990, s.1(1).
[57] s.1(1).

The most important of these functions is probably the determining of applications for planning permission and listed building consent. Accordingly, the Act provides that:

"In considering whether to grant planning permission for development which affects a listed building or its setting, the local planning authority or as the case may be, the Secretary of State, shall have special regard to the desirability of preserving the building or its setting or any features of special architectural or historic interest which it possesses."[58]

An identical duty is laid upon those considering whether to grant listed building consent for any works.[59]

There is, in neither case, a statutory presumption in law in favour of the building being preserved—but the planning authority is at least to consider the desirability of that being achieved; this is considered in more detail later.[60] "Listing" a building therefore in theory means precisely that—merely including it in a list, as an aide memoire to all concerned to ensure that it is not demolished or damaged by unsuitable alterations without careful thought being given to its preservation.

In practice, however, the Secretaries of State have made it clear that as a matter of policy buildings of special interest in England should be preserved.[61] Policy in Wales is less emphatic, but broadly similar.[62] The House of Lords, too, shares this view:

"... the public interest in the preservation of buildings of special architectural or historic interest needs no emphasis. Once a building has been listed, that public interest has been declared".[63]

To assist in achieving this, planning legislation has over the years been developed so that there are now a number of special provisions regarding listed buildings. These are explored in more detail in the remainder of this book, but can be summarised as follows:

(1) the procedure for making art.4 directions (requiring planning permission to be obtained for works that would otherwise be permitted development) is slightly different[64];

(2) a local authority or the Secretary of State is able to take some steps to ensure that a listed building is maintained in good repair[65];

(3) the "permitted development" limits are significantly more restricted[66];

---

[58] P(LBCA)A 1990, s.66(1).
[59] s.16(2).
[60] See **14.4**.
[61] PPG 15, para.3.3; quoted at **14.4.2**.
[62] At *Planning Guidance (Wales): Planning Policy*, para.19, and WO Circ. 61/96, para.68.
[63] *Robbins v Secretary of State* [1989] 1 W.L.R. 204 per Lord Bridge at 211 H.
[64] See **7.4.3**.
[65] See **Chapter 10**.
[66] See **12.4.3, 12.5.2**.

(4) "listed building consent" is required for the demolition of a listed building, and for any other works which affect its special character (usually as well as planning permission)[67];

(5) extra publicity is given by local planning authorities to planning applications affecting the setting of a listed building[68];

(6) authorities are to consider the desirability of preserving the building and its setting when considering such applications[69];

(7) the local authority or the Secretary of State may take enforcement action or institute a criminal prosecution if unauthorised works are carried out.[70]

Note too that if a building is listed, that may prevent the implementation of a planning permission already given, unless listed building consent can be obtained. Alternatively, it may be possible to seek approval for a revised scheme—or for revised details following an outline permission.[71]

These points should all be borne in mind by those proposing to purchase a listed building, particularly if they are considering carrying out building works. In addition, the Court of Appeal has recently confirmed that owners and occupiers of listed buildings are at risk of receiving a listed building enforcement notice in respect of any unauthorised works carried out, by whomsoever, since the date of the listing:

"purchasers of such buildings should be most careful to ensure that they are not liable to be enforced against for unauthorised works by their predecessors going back perhaps over many years. It may be that pre-contract enquiries should be more specifically directed to this risk than has hitherto been the case."[72]

Conveyancers should take note.

3.6.2 Other legislation

The listing of a building may have other consequences in addition to the more general valuation implications considered briefly above.[73] The following are some of the miscellaneous provisions that may be relevant in particular cases; most are discussed in more detail later in the book.

First, there are a number of other statutes which impose general "environmental duties" on various bodies, which are relevant to listed buildings.[74]

Second, limited financial assistance may occasionally be available from various sources for the repair and restoration of listed buildings and there are certain tax

---

[67] See **12.2.3**.
[68] See **13.5.8, 13.5.9**.
[69] See **14.6**.
[70] See **Chapters 18 and 19**.
[71] As in *Heron Corporation v Manchester CC* [1977] 1 E.G.L.R. 131.
[72] *Braun v Secretary of State* [2003] 1 P.L.R. 90, CA, *per* Simon Brown L.J. at para.18. In fact, the liability probably extends only back to the date of listing or January 1, 1969 in the case of buildings listed before that date (see **18.3.5**)
[73] See **3.3.1, 3.3.5**.
[74] See **8.6**.

concessions applicable in the case of properties of outstanding interest.[75] And where listed buildings in non-domestic use are unoccupied, rates are not payable.[76] Other than in exceptional cases, however, these do little to mitigate any extra costs that may arise due to the higher standard of works required of owners of listed buildings.

Third, the Secretary of State is under a duty to ensure that the Building Regulations are drafted with an eye to the preservation of the character of listed buildings.[77]

Fourth, where works are carried out to listed buildings that are in residential use or occupied by a charity, provided that they have been the subject of a grant of listed building consent, VAT is not payable.[78]

Fifth, where a building is let subject to a term in the lease requiring the tenant to demolish and redevelop, the landlord is not entitled to forfeit and re-enter if the building is subsequently listed, so that demolition is no longer realistically possible.[79] It must remain an open question as to what the position would be if the building were already listed at the time the lease is entered into.

Finally, where a church is listed, special rules apply to modify the procedures for the approval of works to it.[80]

However, the duty that is often supposed to exist, but does not, is a general duty on owners and occupiers of listed buildings to keep them in good repair.[81]

3.7 Listing as a possible breach of human rights

3.7.1 Article 1 to the First Protocol (right to peaceful enjoyment)

It is sometimes suggested that the listing of a building might constitute a breach of human rights, as defined by the European Convention for the Protection of Human Rights and Fundamental Freedoms.[82] The incorporation of the Convention directly into UK domestic law via the Human Rights Act 1998 makes the question more immediate.

It could thus be argued that the imposition of the restrictions necessarily involved in listing amounts to a form of compulsory purchase and that the absence of any effective right of appeal and any compensation[83] renders it in breach of Art.1 of the First Protocol to the Europe Convention on Human Rights. That provides as follows:

"Every natural or legal person is entitled to the peaceful enjoyment of his possessions. No-one shall be deprived of his possessions except in the public interest and subject to the

---

[75] See **Chapter 9**.
[76] See **9.8**.
[77] Sustainable and Secure Buildings Act 2004, s.2.
[78] See **Chapter 17**. The concession is also available for works to listed places of worship.
[79] *John Lewis Properties PLC v Viscount Chelsea* (1993) 67 P. & C.R. 120.
[80] See **Chapter 16**.
[81] See **8.2**.
[82] See, for example, Crow, "Fair Trial? The Human Rights Act and the listing of buildings" [2003] J.P.L. 793.
[83] See **3.3.4, 3.3.5**.

conditions provided for by law and by the general principles of international law. The preceding provisions shall not, however, in any way impair the right of a State to enforce such laws as it deems necessary to control the use of property in accordance with the general interest or to secure the payment of taxes or other contributions or penalties."

However, it may be noted that—as with most of the rights under the Convention—this right is not unqualified. Deprivation of property is thus justifiable where it is in the public interest, and the control of its use where it is in the general interest. The European Court of Human Rights has ruled that the state will only be responsible for interferences which affect the economic value of property, or can be expressed in economic terms.[84] In any case, the Article makes no mention of compensation, although the Court has made it clear that interferences less than deprivation do not have a right to compensation attached.[85] This may be the case even where there may be a reduction in the value of the property.[86]

Following from that, the Court has found that expectations do not have the necessary degree of certainty to amount to possessions.[87] Therefore, the loss of development value (as in *Amalgamated Investment v John Walker*[88]) would not of itself engage Art.1. Further, the listing of a building, however onerous, would not be considered more than a control of the use of property, since such a control would not be capable of amounting to expropriation unless it involved the actual or effective extinction of all rights or the deprivation of any meaningful use.[89]

The test to be applied is one of "fair balance", not dissimilar to the notion of proportionality within general European jurisprudence:

"For the purposes of the ... provision, the Court must determine whether a fair balance was struck between the demands of the general interest of the community and the requirements of the protection of the individual's fundamental rights. The search for this balance is inherent in the whole of the Convention and is also reflected in the structure of Article 1."[90]

The listing of a building, therefore, must be justified in the general interest. And it may be noted that states have been consistently allowed a wide margin of appreciation in achieving the balance between individual rights and the general interest, provided that any interference with property has a legitimate aim.[91]

---

[84] *S v France* (1990) 65 D.R. 250, 261, EComm HR.

[85] *Pinnacle Meat Processors v UK*, Application 33298/96, October 21, 1998, EComm HR (Admissibility decision).

[86] *James v United Kingdom* (1986) 8 E.H.R.R. 123.

[87] See, for example, *Batelaan and Huiges v Netherlands* (1984) 41 D.R. 170 at 173.

[88] *Amalgamated Investment and Property Co. Ltd v John Walker and Sons Ltd* [1976] 3 All E.R. 509; see **3.3.1, 3.3.6**.

[89] *Lithgow v United Kingdom* (1986) 8 E.H.R.R. 329. See also *Papamichalopoulos v Greece* (1993) 16 E.H.R.R. 440.

[90] *Sporrong and Lonnroth v Sweden* (1983) 5 E.H.R.R. 35 (at paragraph 69). See also *Fredin v Sweden (No. 1)* (1991) 13 E.H.R.R. 784 at para.51; *Mellacher v Austria* (1989) 12 E.H.R.R. 391.

[91] Clayton and Tomlinson, *The Law of Human Rights*, (Oxford: Oxford University Press, 2000), p1314.

3.7.2 Article 8 (right to respect for private life)

Secondly, it could be argued that listing is in breach of Art.8 of the Convention, which provides:

> "1. Everyone has the right to respect for his private and family life, his home, and his correspondence.
>
> 2. There shall be no interference by a public authority with the exercise of this right except such as is in accordance with the law and is necessary in a democratic society in the interests of national security, public safety or the economic well-being of the country, for the prevention of disorder or crime, for the protection of health or morals, or for the protection of the rights and freedoms of others."

However, like Art.1 of the First Protocol, this right too is qualified and may afford the state a wide margin of appreciation—not least in the area of planning control. The state may in particular justify proportionate interference with the right contained in para.1 by reference to the exceptions contained at para.2; as with Art.1, a fair balance must be arrived at. The Court noted in *Buckley v United Kingdom* that it is necessary, in the particular context, to construe Art.8 consistently with Art.1 of the First Protocol.[92]

Furthermore, although development control issues have been found to engage Art.8, they are something of a footnote in the case law which it has generated—other than in a number of cases relating to gypsies and travellers.[93] It is therefore difficult to draw any direct analogy with listed buildings, since those cases go to whether it is permissible to prevent, by refusal of planning permission, an individual or household actually living on a particular piece of land, taking all material considerations into account. In the gypsy cases, the decision to do so was held to be proportionate, notwithstanding that in each instance the applicant actually owned the land. It is difficult to imagine the situation where the listed buildings procedures would actually prevent an owner from occupying, or meaningfully occupying, his or her home.

3.7.3 Article 6 (right to a fair hearing)

It has been noted that it is possible to request an informal review of a decision by the Secretary of State to list a building, but that this is in practice carried out by an officer of English Heritage, the body that initially recommended the building to be listed.[94] The decision of the Secretary of State is also susceptible to judicial review, although it is hard to see under what circumstances it might be quashed since the decision to list is one of judgement[95].

Given that that there is thus no formal right of appeal or statutory review available in respect of listing, it could be considered that the whole procedure is in breach of Art.6(1), which provides as follows:

[92] (1997) 23 E.H.R.R. 101, at para.67.
[93] See for example *Buckley*, and *Chapman v United Kingdom* (2001) 33 E.H.R.R. 18.
[94] See **3.3.4**.
[95] But see *R. (Bancroft) v Secretary of State for Culture, Media and Sport* [2005] J.P.L. 477 (noted at **3.2.2**).

"In the determination of his civil rights and obligations or of any criminal charge against him, everyone is entitled to a fair and public hearing within a reasonable time by an independent and impartial tribunal established by law...."

As to whether the listing of a building amounts to the determination of the "civil rights and obligations" of its owner or occupier, the jurisprudence of the Court of Human Rights has historically interpreted the phrase as rooted in private rights, and there has been much discussion as to the extent to which administrative law decisions attract procedural rights. Nevertheless, it is clear that real and personal property rights arising in the context of planning are regarded by the Court as civil rights.[96] There is little doubt, therefore, that for the purposes of the procedure as a whole, the rights of owners of listed buildings come within the ambit of Art.6.

Whether the listing procedure itself can be said to be determinative of those rights is less certain. Proceedings are said to be determinative when the outcome is directly decisive of them.[97] The starting point is the comments made by Lord Clyde in the *Alconbury* case:

"It is clear that Article 6(1) is engaged where the decision which is to be given is of an administrative character, that is to say one given in the exercise of a discretionary power, as well as a dispute in a court of law regarding the private rights of the citizen, provided that it directly affects civil rights and obligations and is of a genuine and serious nature."[98]

This was considered recently in *R. (Aggregate Industries UK Ltd) v English Nature*.[99] The applicant's land had been designated as an SSSI, which severely restricted the use to which it could put it, and it argued that the confirmation of the designation by English Nature engaged Art.6(1). Forbes J. considered that, "for Article 6(1) to be engaged, the relevant decision-making process which resolves the dispute between the parties must be 'directly decisive' of the civil rights and obligations in question". In that case, however, the article was engaged by the process of notification and confirmation of the SSSI, and, once the applicant had objected to the notification, a serious dispute had arisen as to whether the designation should be confirmed. That was determinative of the applicant's civil rights to use and enjoy its property. *Aggregates Industries* went further than any previous decision in accepting that the Article was engaged by a purely administrative decision.

The Court in *Aggregates Industries* accepted that, Art.6(1) having been engaged, English Nature did not have the requisite appearance of independence and impartiality in confirming the designation, given that its decision was based on a report by its own officers which recommended confirmation after those officers had considered and rejected the applicant's objections. Nevertheless, the decision-making procedure had to be considered as a whole in order to assess whether it complied with the article; and it was held that there were sufficient procedural safeguards which could be relied upon to produce fair and reasonable

---

[96] *Bryan v United Kingdom* [1996] 1 P.L.R. 47.

[97] *Ringeisin v Austria (No. 1)* (1971) 1 E.H.R.R. 455.

[98] *R. (Alconbury Developments Limited and others) v Secretary of State for the Environment, Transport and the Regions etc* [2003] 2 A.C. 295, at para.150.

[99] [2003] Env.L.R. 3.

decisions and that the decision to confirm the designation was essentially one of policy and expediency. This, when added to the court's powers of judicial review, meant that the procedure as a whole was compliant with Art.6(1).

The same approach would seem to apply to listing—considering the process as a whole, there are sufficient procedural safeguards which could be relied upon to produce fair and reasonable decisions. And there is a real opportunity for representations to be made by the owner of the property is at the consent stage, where it can be argued that the building is not worthy of its listing. Finally, it may be noted that the components of a fair trial required by Art.6 do not specifically include an appeal.

3.7.4 Application to listing

Since the coming into force of the Human Rights Act 1998, the issue of whether the listing of a buildings is a breach of the Convention has not as such come before the courts in the United Kingdom. However, it was considered in passing in *R. (Chant) v Secretary of State*,[1] in the context of a challenge to a discontinuance order which had been confirmed by the Secretary of State following an inquiry. The order required that the use of property at the edge of a village (including a farmhouse and a barn, each listed Grade II) for agricultural, storage and industrial uses should cease—partly in order to safeguard the future of the buildings. The Claimant had claimed at the inquiry that the order was an interference which violated his rights under Art.1 of the First Protocol and Art.8.

Sullivan J. rejected these arguments and stated that the preservation of listed buildings was a proper planning consideration. In particular he noted:

"Although set in the context of a consideration of the objectors' rights under Article 1 of the First Protocol, the Secretary of State is, in substance, carrying out the same balancing exercise as is required under section 102 in deciding whether or not it is 'expedient' to make the order in the public interest. ... Thus both the Inspector and the Secretary of State applied the correct statutory test and there was ample material on which they were entitled to conclude that it was expedient in the interests of the proper planning of Somerton to confirm the order. It could not possibly be said, in the light of the Inspector's conclusions on the planning merits, that the Secretary of State's decision was either unreasonable or in any way disproportionate."[2]

In a recent Scottish case, *Cannell v The Scottish Ministers*,[3] the claimant argued that the burden of the system of control of listed buildings on him should be regarded as excessive, considering particularly the number and length of the various procedures involved in the enforcement of the control, the cost to him, the sanctions engaged or threatened in connection with those procedures, the lack of fault on his part, the power to recover expenses from him and the practical consequences of listing. He relied in particular on the system's alleged deficiency in respect of expenses. As a result, he submitted, Arts 1 and 8 had been violated because the burden was disproportionate to its legitimate aims. The conclusion of

---

[1] [2002] E.W.H.C. 1440; see **10.9.1**.
[2] [2002] E.W.H.C. 1440, at paras 46–7.
[3] 2003 S.C. 404.

the Court was that the system was proportionate and that it was "going too far" to say otherwise.[4]

In *R. (Brennon) v Bromsgrove DC*,[5] which concerned the making of a tree protection order, a challenge was made to the order on the ground that it interfered with the claimant's right to enjoyment of his property in a way that was excessive and disproportionate. Richards J. rejected that submission, stating:

"So far as concerns Art.1 of Protocol 1, the short answer, in my view, is that the statutory regime concerning tree preservation orders represents a fair balance between the general interest of the community and the requirements of the protection of the individual's rights, to use the language of the court in *James v United Kingdom*[6] at para.[50]. An order may be made only where it is needed in the interests of amenity to do so. There are elaborate procedural safeguards, including the right to make representations before an order is made and the right to seek consent under the order and to appeal to an inspector against any refusal to give such consent. One sees in all of this a striking of the balance by the legislature, and one does not need to accord a wide margin of discretion to the legislature in order to reach the conclusion that the balance has been struck appropriately. Exactly the same considerations apply to justification of interference under Art.8."[7]

The tree protection system is comparable by analogy with that of listing buildings, so that this is a clear rejection of the engagement of convention rights.

It is thus highly unlikely that it would be found that the listing of a building is a violation of Art.1, or any of the other provisions of the Convention mentioned above. The pattern of jurisprudence, both domestically and in Europe, suggests that the aim of listing is legitimate and the system itself, taken as a whole, would be found to be proportionate.

3.8 Removal of a building from the list

A building should obviously be removed from the list if it is totally or substantially demolished. In that case, the relevant department should be informed in writing, and sent photographs as appropriate.

A building could also be removed if it were to be no longer considered of special architectural or historic interest, or because it has been substantially altered, or because it was entered on the list by mistake, or because someone has successfully appealed against the listing.[8]

Once the Secretary of State has decided or agreed to remove a building from the list, or to alter its grade, the procedure is exactly as for listing.[9] Again, the relevant form to be sent to the owner is prescribed in regulations.[10]

---

[4] See para.35.
[5] [2003] 2 P. & C.R. 33.
[6] (1986) 8 E.H.R.R. 123.
[7] [2003] 2 P. & C.R. 33 at para.33.
[8] See **3.3.4**.
[9] See **3.3.1, 3.3.3**.
[10] P(LBCA) Regs 1990, Sch.4, as substituted by SI 2005/1085.

3.9 Temporary listing: building preservation notices

3.9.1 The need for building preservation notices

It will be clear from the above description that the listing process is, inevitably, slow; and it is also incomplete. A building of merit may therefore be at risk until it is listed at the next routine resurvey of the area. Or it may have been overlooked in the last one—particularly if its distinctive features are not readily apparent from an external survey.

In such a case the local authority, an amenity group or any individual can always write to the appropriate department requesting that the building be "spot-listed".[11] In the majority of cases, however, even this process takes considerable time. It is therefore not suitable where a building of special interest is under immediate threat of demolition or drastic alteration.

To help solve this problem, a provision was introduced in the Town and Country Planning Act 1968—now in ss 3 and 4 of the Listed Buildings Act and the Scottish Listed Buildings Act—whereby a local planning authority in Great Britain could effectively list a building on a temporary basis by serving a *building preservation notice* on its owner and occupier. The procedure may be used only in respect of an unlisted building that is:

(1) of special architectural or historic interest; and

(2) in danger of being altered or demolished.[12]

A building preservation notice may not be served on an ecclesiastical building[13] or a scheduled monument.[14] Nor may it be served on a building in England or Wales that has been the subject of a certificate of immunity from listing within the previous five years.[15]

Note that a building preservation notice should not be confused with a "building preservation order", the provisions relating to which were repealed by the 1968 Act.[16]

3.9.2 Procedure

A building preservation notice must:

(1) state that the building appears to the authority to be of special architectural or historic interest;

(2) state that the Secretary of State has been asked to list it; and

(3) explain the effect of the notice (see below).[17]

---

[11] See **3.3.2**.
[12] P(LBCA)A 1990, s.3(1). [Scotland: P(LBCA)(S) 1997, 3(1).]
[13] P(LBCA)A 1990, s.60. [P(LBCA)(S) 1997, s.54.] See **Chapter 16**.
[14] P(LBCA)A 1990, s.61. [P(LBCA)(S) 1997, s.55.] See **Chapter 6**.
[15] P(LBCA)A 1990, s.6(2)(b). See **3.4**.
[16] See **1.2.3**.
[17] P(LBCA)A 1990, s.3(2). [P(LBCA)(S)A 1997, s.3(2).]

The need to serve a building preservation notice will often be urgent, not allowing for decisions to be taken by committees. The power to take the initial decision to serve one may therefore usefully be delegated to appropriate officers of the authority, so as to save time.[18] Once the decision has been taken to serve a notice, it should be prepared as soon as possible, and a copy served on all those involved. The most important person is usually the occupier of the building; it will be prudent wherever possible to ensure that he or she is given a copy personally. Where there are several occupiers (as, for example, with a residential building in multiple occupation, or an urban building with different retail tenants on the ground floor), postal service by recorded delivery may be more practical. A copy must also be served on the owner (if different, such as in the case of leasehold property). As to the importance of correct service, see *Knowles v Chorley BC*.[19]

Given that, in most cases, a building preservation notice is only used where there is a development proposal pending, it is obviously sensible for the authority to serve a copy on all those involved in the development (who will usually be known)—these might include architects, project managers, contractors and (not the least important, if matters have progressed to an advanced stage) demolition contractors. In each case, again, delivery is best by hand or by recorded mail.

It is not permissible to serve a building preservation notice solely by email.[20] However, where the email address of any of the relevant people or firms is known, it would do no harm to use electronic as well as traditional means—not least since it enables large numbers of people to be informed immediately.

Where any of the above cannot be found, it may be sensible, especially in cases of urgency, to fix a copy of the notice to the building or to a prominent object on the site (such as the main gate or doorway). This may of course also be done in addition to serving copies on owners and occupiers. It is indeed possible to fix the notice on the building without serving any copies on owners and occupiers; but if this is the only way in which the notice is published, the notice so fixed must itself state that.[21] This procedure was introduced to overturn the effect of the decision in *Maltglade Ltd v St Albans RDC*.[22]

Where a notice is handed or sent to any of those noted above, it will usually be helpful to attach an accompanying letter in clear English saying what it means; the "explanation" demanded by the Act is often itself not as clear as it might be. For a sample notice, see Form D3 in Appendix D.

At the same time as serving the notice, the authority must also immediately request the Secretary of State formally to list the building. Such a request should include a copy of the notice, a location plan, and photographs of the building.[23]

There is no statutory right of appeal by the owner or occupier against the serving of a building preservation notice. But, as with listing, it is always possible

---

[18] Local Government Act 1972, s.101.
[19] [1998] J.P.L. 593.
[20] P(LBCA)A 1990, s.89(1A)(a), inserted by SI 2003/956 (England) and SI 2004/3157 (Wales). [P(LBCA)(S)A 1997, s.79(1A), inserted by SI 2004/332.]
[21] P(LBCA)A 1990, s.4. [P(LBCA)(S)A 1997, s.4.]
[22] [1972] 1 WLR 1230
[23] PPG 15, para.6.24; WO Circ. 61/96, para.56. HS Memorandum, paras 1.16, 1.18.

, make an informal appeal to the Secretary of State.[24] If listed building consent is subsequently applied for, and refused or granted subject to adverse conditions, it is possible to appeal on the ground (amongst any others) that the building should not be listed.[25]

A building preservation notice may be served in England by a local planning authority, other than a county planning authority.[26] In general, this will be the district or borough council.[27] The Thurrock and Thames Gateway urban development corporations have the sole responsibility for serving notices in their areas.[28] In addition, English Heritage may serve a notice in respect of a building in Greater London.[29] In Wales, a notice is to be served by the county or county borough council.[30] In national parks, the relevant authority will be the national park authority[31], and in the Broads it will be the Broads Authority.[32] In Scotland, the notice is to be served by the planning authority.[33]

3.9.3 The consequences of a building preservation notice

A building preservation notice comes into force as soon as it has been served on both the owner and the occupier of the building.[34] Its effect is that, for as long as it remains effective, the building is effectively a listed building.[35] In particular, works for its alteration or demolition require listed building consent[36]; and if such works are carried out without consent being obtained, the local authority can take enforcement action or can institute criminal proceedings.[37]

However, such protection lasts only for six months. If within that period the Secretary of State decides that the building should be listed, then the owner and occupier and the local authority will be notified in the usual way,[38] and the building will thereafter have precisely the same status as that of any other listed building.

Alternatively, the Secretary of State may decide not to list the building. In that case, he or she will notify the planning authority, which will in turn notify the

---

[24] See **3.3.4**.
[25] P(LBCA)A 1990, s.21(4). [P(LBCA)(S)A 1997, s.19(4).]
[26] P(LBCA)A 1990, ss 3(1), 4(1).
[27] TCPA 1990, s.1(1), (2).
[28] Thurrock Development Corporation (Planning Functions) Order 2005 (SI 2005/2572), art.4, Sch.; London Thames Gateway Development Corporation (Planning Functions) Order 2005 (SI 2005/2721), art.5, Sch.
[29] P(LBCA)A 1990, ss 3(8), 4(4).
[30] Local Government (Wales) Act 1994, s.18, Sch.6.
[31] TCPA 1990, s.4A(2), inserted by Environment Act 1995, s.67.
[32] P(LBCA)A, 1990, Sch.4, para.5.
[33] P(LBCA)(S)A 1997, ss 3(1), 4(1).
[34] P(LBCA)A 1990, s.3(3)(a). [P(LBCA)(S)A 1997, s.3(3)(a).]
[35] P(LBCA)A 1990, s.3(5). [P(LBCA)(S)A 1997, s.3(5).] The only provision that applies to a building that is actually listed but not, for some reason, to one that is merely subject to a building preservation notice, is the specific offence of criminal damage to a listed building (see **19.2.3**).
[36] See **12.2.3**.
[37] See **Chapters 18 and 19**.
[38] See **3.3.3**.

owner and occupier.[39] The effect of the notice will lapse; and any application for listed building consent that is outstanding will lapse, as will any outstanding enforcement proceedings. However, if unauthorised work was carried out while the notice was in force, anyone responsible is still liable to criminal prosecution, and any expenses incurred by the authority in taking enforcement action will still be recoverable.[40]

If the service of the notice caused any financial damage, including any payment of damages resulting from a breach of contract for building or demolition works, the authority is then liable to pay compensation; although only to anyone who had an interest in the building at the time when the notice was served.[41] This means that anyone else who may be out of pocket (contractors, etc.) can only recover damages if they are able successfully to sue the building owner, who could then recover from the authority.

A claim for compensation under this provision must be submitted within six months.[42]

Finally, if the Secretary of State decides not to list the building, the local authority may not serve another building preservation notice on it within 12 months of his decision,[43] which contains the interesting implication, borne out by experience, that the perceived architectural or historic interest of a building may change significantly in only a year!

If, however, the Secretary of State takes no action within the six-month period, the notice will also lapse.[44] The consequences will be the same as if there had been a formal decision not to list the building[45]; except that, in this case, there is nothing to stop the authority immediately serving another notice, and thus in effect prolonging the original notice for a further six months.

3.9.4 Northern Ireland

There was until recently no similar procedure in Northern Ireland—no doubt partly due to the unitary system of planning control in place there. However, art.25 of the Planning (Amendment) (Northern Ireland) Order 2003 introduced, with effect from April 2003, a system that is in all material respects identical to that operating in Great Britain, save that, not surprisingly, it is the Department (rather than the local authority) that serves a building preservation notice on the owner and occupier of the building under threat, and the Department that eventually lists it.[46]

---

[39] P(LBCA)A 1990, s.3(4)(b), (6). [P(LBCA)(S)A 1997, s.3(4)(b), (6)(a).]
[40] P(LBCA)A 1990, Sch.2. [P(LBCA)(S)A 1997, Sch.2.]
[41] P(LBCA)A 1990, s.29. [P(LBCA)(S)A 1997, s.26.]
[42] P(LBCA) Regs 1990, reg.9. [P(LBCA)(S) Regs 1987, reg.9.]
[43] P(LBCA)A 1990, s.3(7). [P(LBCA)(S)A 1997, s.3(6)(b).]
[44] P(LBCA)A 1990, s.3(3)(b). [P(LBCA)(S)A 1997, s.3(3)(b).]
[45] P(LBCA)A 1990, Sch.2, para.1(a). [P(LBCA)(S)A 1997, Sch.2, para.1(a).]
[46] P(NI)O 1991, ss 42A and 42B (equivalent to P(LBCA)A 1990, ss 3 and 4) and 42C (equivalent to Sch.2), inserted by Planning (Amendment) (NI) Order 2003, art.25(1).

Here, too, compensation is available in the event that a building preservation notice is withdrawn without the building being formally listed.[47]

---

[47] P(NI)O 1991, s.67A (equivalent to P(LBCA)A 1990, s.29), inserted by 2003 Order, art.25(3).

Chapter 4

The Extent of Listing

4.1 Introduction

4.1.1 The problem

It is obvious that, in many cases, there will be a number of objects of interest and subsidiary buildings associated with a building of special interest. Thus, for example, a fine mansion house from the eighteenth century will invariably have been listed by the Secretary of State as a building of special architectural or historic interest. But do the protection, and the restrictions, imposed by the listing extend to the stables block next to it, or the gate piers at the bottom of the drive? And what about the gardener's cottage some way from the main house, or the modern potting shed just beyond the stables? Inside the mansion, whilst the removal of the main staircase would no doubt be subject to some form of control, what about replacing a chandelier? Or a bath tap?

It is therefore important to know just what is comprised within the listing of a building, principally because this will help to determine whether or not listed building consent is needed for any works proposed. If a farmhouse was listed in 1965, and a new roof is to be put on a barn nearby that has recently been converted to separate residential use,[1] does the listing of the house extend to the barn? If it does not, work can proceed without any consent at all; but if it does, listed building consent is needed, and failure to obtain it may lead to enforcement or even criminal prosecution.

It will also have various other consequences, such as in relation to the procedures to be adopted in processing planning applications. It has also been held in the leading case on this point that, once the extent of the listing has been determined under the planning Acts, this will also apply in considering any other statutory code, such as those governing the payment of VAT and non-domestic rates, which refer to listed buildings[2]—although caution is needed, particularly in relation to VAT.[3]

---

[1] As occurred in *Morris v Wrexham CBC and the National Assembly* [2002] 2 P. & C.R. 7.
[2] *Debenhams PLC v Westminster CC* [1987] A.C. 396, *per* Lord Keith at 404E, and Lord Ackner (who dissented on the main point at issue) at p.412E.
[3] *Zielinski Baker and Partners v Customs and Excise Commissioners* [2004] 1 W.L.R. 707, HL; see **17.2.2**.

These difficulties also occur in other areas of law, such as landlord and tenant (at the end of a tenancy, which items can be removed by the tenant and which go with the building)[4]; conveyancing (what passes with the property, and what can be removed by the vendor)[5]; inheritance (which items are part of the property, which are chattels)[6]; mortgages[7]; and insurance. This is therefore not a new problem; and the statutory controls governing listed buildings need to be seen in this light, building on to provisions of the common law that have been evolving for centuries.

It might at first sight seem to be desirable that those selecting buildings for special protection should specifically list all the associated items that are also to be protected. But a moment's thought will make it clear that that is impractical—it would be relatively straightforward to show the curtilage of a listed building on a map, but it would not be feasible to catalogue all the subsidiary structures within that curtilage that are to come within the listing, and even less so all the items worthy of protection inside the building. The solution, however tiresome it may be in practice, therefore has to be a statutory formula prescribing in general what is to be included and what, by inference, is outside the scope of protection.

4.1.2 The relevant statutory provisions

The key provision in relation to England and Wales is s.1(5) of the Listed Buildings Act, which states as follows:

"In this Act, 'listed building' means a building which is for the time being included in a list compiled or approved by the Secretary of State under this section; and for the purposes of this Act—

(a) any object or structure fixed to the building; and
(b) any object or structure within the curtilage of the building which, although not fixed to the building, forms part of the land and has done so since before July 1, 1948

shall be treated as part of the building."

This was introduced by the Town and Country Planning Act 1968.[8] Prior to that, the 1947 and 1962 Acts merely indicated that protection could be given to "a building", without elaborating further.

Section 1(4) of the Scottish Listed Buildings Act is in identical terms. Article 42(7) of the Northern Ireland Order is similar, save that the date in paragraph (b) is October 1, 1973.

Bearing in mind that the curtilage of a building may be small or may be quite extensive, it is clear that a "listed building", as defined by the Act, is not simply an actual physical building that happens to be of special interest and has been

---

[4] *Leigh v Taylor* [1902] A.C. 157, HL (tenant for life and remainderman); *Spyer v Phillipson* [1931] 2 Ch.183.

[5] *Hamp v Bygrave* [1983] 1 E.G.L.R. 174; *Berkeley v Poulett* [1977] 1 E.G.L.R. 86, CA (see **4.4.2**).

[6] *re Whaley* [1908] 1 Ch.615.

[7] *Botham v TSB* (1997) 73 P. & C.R. D.1, CA.

[8] TCPA 1968, s.40(3)—although the exclusion of post-1948 curtilage structures was introduced by the Housing and Planning Act 1968, Sch.9, para.1(1).

recognised as such. It is, rather, a legal concept, and may extend so as to encompass a whole range of objects and structures, of which some may themselves be buildings.

The extent of listing is also significant in the light of the decision of the House of Lords in *Shimizu*[9] that the phrase "listed building" effectively means the whole of the building—including, presumably, all the objects and structures referred to in s.1(5).

The current position of the Secretary of State is set out in the relevant policy guidance.[10]

This chapter now looks in more detail at each element of that definition in turn, to see what is at issue: what is encompassed in respect of the actual building in the list (**4.2**); what is meant by "objects and structures" in principle (**4.3**), and in more detail those fixed to a building in the list (**4.4**) and those in its curtilage (**4.5**). The position is summarised at **4.6**, along with a consideration of how to proceed in cases of doubt.

To aid the comprehension of the reports of the principal cases, plans have been provided highlighting the principal features referred to. In each case, the building included in the list is shown with an asterisk.[11]

4.2. The building in the list

4.2.1 The whole of the building

The first element in the definition is the building that is itself included in the list. The Secretary of State can list a "building"[12]—and a "building" is defined to include any structure or erection, and any part of any building as so defined.[13] That means that it is possible to list a whole building or structure or (in theory at least[14]) part of one; but once the favoured item has been selected, every part of it is in law equally "listed".

This means in particular that the interior is thus just as much listed as the exterior—whether or not it is in itself of any interest—and regardless of the grade of the listing.[15] And all the features on the exterior of the building are equally listed. Listed, too, would be any unattractive later additions to an old building; and modern replacement windows and doors. Statements that, for example, the exterior of a building, or a particularly fine Victorian shopfront, are listed mean

---

9 *Shimizu (U.K.) Ltd v Westminster CC* [1996] 3 P.L.R. 89, [1997] 1 W.L.R. 168 HL at p.182.

10 PPG 15, paras 3.30–3.36.; WO Circ. 61/96, paras 84–90; HS Memorandum, paras 1.2–1.4; NI PPS 6, Annex C, paras C14–C18.

11 The author is grateful to the officers of the relevant planning authorities who kindly supplied the material on which these plans (and one or two that were not used due to shortage of space) were based.

12 P(LBCA)A 1990, s.1(1) [Scotland: P(LBCA)(S)A 1997, NI: P(NI)O 1991, art.42(1).]

13 TCPA 1990, s.336, applied by P(LBCA)A 1990, s.91(2) [Scotland: TCP(S)A 1997, s.277(1), applied by P(LBCA)(S)A 1997, s.81(2); NI: P(NI)O 1991, art.2].

14 It is rare in practice; see **3.2.1**.

15 See **3.2.4**. An example of this in practice was an appeal decision reported at [1983] J.P.L. 751, regarding works to the interior of a late-Victorian pub.

nothing—the exterior, or the shopfront, may well be the reason why the building has been included in the list; but either the whole building is listed, including the interior, or none of it.

Clearly, the building or structure that is being included in the list is the one that exists at the date of listing, even though that will normally include work from a number of different dates. So, for example, the nasty 1930s extension at the back of the Georgian mansion is just as much listed as the remainder (although of course it may well be much easier to obtain consent to remove it).

Further, it would seem that where a building is altered or extended—with or without consent—after it has been listed, the new work is generally included in the listing just as much as the old. This has recently been confirmed in *Richardson Developments Ltd v Birmingham City Council*.[16] Any other conclusion would be unworkable.

But that will not always be the case. One exception is where an extension to a listed building is on such a scale that it dwarfs the original building—as happened in *Richardson*. The case concerned a complex known as St Chad's Court in Edgbaston, which, at the time of the listing, in 1982, comprised a central core, built in the eighteenth century, and two wings built in the 1930s (which were expressly excluded from the listing). In 1994, the two wings had been demolished and replaced with modern office blocks. The council now sought payment of non-domestic rates for the office blocks, on the basis that, since the office accommodation was more substantial in size than the listed structure, and capable of occupation independent of the latter, it could not be said to attract the listing of the principal building.[17]

Whilst Dyson J. rejected the proposition that only such extensions as were constructed at the date of listing fell within the confines of s.1(5)(a), he equally resisted the argument that any extension to a listed building of whatever size automatically attracts the listing of the original building.[18] Extensions, too, as with any other "object or structure" attached to a building in the list, must be subsidiary to it if they are to share in the protection afforded by listing.

It has been noted that, occasionally, only part of a building is listed.[19] Where that happens, the remainder of the building may be included in the listing—where, for example, one half of a structure straddling a local authority boundary is included in the list on a routine resurvey, it is likely that the unlisted half would be considered a structure fixed to it or in its curtilage. But where a deliberate decision is made to list only part of a much larger structure, it is likely that the remainder will not be included—were it otherwise, the listed tail would be wagging the affixed dog.[20]

The question of what kinds of buildings and structures are chosen for listing has been considered already.[21]

---

[16] [1999] J.P.L. 1001 at p.1006.
[17] On non-domestic rating of unoccupied listed buildings, see **9.9**.
[18] p.1006.
[19] See **3.2.1**.
[20] That was the approach (and terminology) adopted by Ouseley J. in an obiter comment in *R. (Hammerton) v London Underground Limited* [2003] J.P.L. 984, at para.43.
[21] At **3.2**.

4.2.2 The list description

In virtually all statutory lists, there is a description provided for each item included. This is purely to aid identification, and does not mean that any feature not noted is of no importance—it would be possible to write a substantial book on each of the larger listed buildings (a cathedral, for instance), without mentioning every one of its notable features.[22] But the description does (or at least should) make clear which building is being highlighted. This can be useful, especially where an older building or structure is itself within the grounds of a newer one (such as a medieval wall enclosing the garden of a nondescript Victorian house). And, at least in more modern English listings, the descriptions will include mention of those features which led English Heritage to recommend listing.[23]

The list description may also be helpful where it is a group of structures that is sought to be preserved, as with the memorial to Sir Samuel Sadler in Middlesbrough that was the subject of *R. (Judge) v Secretary of State*.[23a] The description there makes it clear that the "building" in the list included the statue itself, the supporting pedestal, and the steps, walls and piers.

The significance of the list description was considered by the House of Lords in *City of Edinburgh Council v Secretary of State for Scotland*.[24] Lord Hope, who delivered the leading judgment in relation to the listed buildings aspect of the case, noted that the prescribed notice of listing sent to owners of buildings newly listed allowed only for the specification of the building, without any description.[25] He also considered that the imprecise language used in some of the description in this particular case (which related to a large group of buildings) meant that it was clearly not designed to be a definitive description of the entire premises within the curtilage. It was, however, legitimate to refer to the description to resolve any ambiguity in the "name of building listed" (such as existed in that case).

Thus, for example, if a listing refers to "Church Farm, and stables block to south-east", where there are in fact two stables blocks to the south east, it would be permissible to refer to the list description to see which was meant. It would, on the other hand, not be correct to assume that the absence of a reference to the sundial on the wall of the farm meant that it was not included in the listing, or that its removal did or did not require listed building consent. Having said that, it is true that it will often be helpful for both developers and decision makers, to know what the features were which persuaded the Secretary of State that a building should be listed.[26]

The description also assists in determining the weight to be ascribed to the listing. Thus, for example, if two structures out of a group of three in a single

---

[22] The list description of Hereford Cathedral, for example, is startlingly brief—but no-one is in any doubt as to which building the Secretary of State was intending to list.

[23] See PPG 15, para.6.19; WO Circ. 61/96, para.52.

[23a] *R. (Judge) v Secretary of State and Middlesbrough BC* [2005] EWCA, unreported, July 22, 2005, CA; affirming [2005] EWHC 887 (Admin), unreported, April 28, 2005. See also **4.2.3**.

[24] [1997] 3 P.L.R. 71.

[25] See 4.2.3.

[26] As Lord Hope remarked in *Edinburgh*, at 77A.

curtilage are specifically mentioned in the list, that does not alter the need for consent to be obtained to demolish the third[27]—but it does suggest that such consent might more readily be forthcoming.

It may be noted that list descriptions are generally compiled by enthusiasts, who sometimes include items that are definitely not covered by the listing.[28]

4.2.3 The status of a listed building after being dismantled or removed

Finally, it may also be noted that a "building" that has been included in the list may remain "a listed building" even after it has been dismantled or moved. A notorious example was the case of Stagbatch Barn in Herefordshire, which was dismantled into numbered sections, for export to America. The planning authority sought an injunction to secure its return from Southampton Dock to its original location, and its re-erection. Hoffman J. granted one, observing that the word "building" is perfectly capable of meaning something which had been a listed building but which had since been demolished.[28a]

The authority then took enforcement action against the company that was now the owner of the pieces of the barn, whose appeal to the Secretary of State was unsuccessful.[28b] The company challenged the validity of the action in the High Court. Mann J. followed the approach of Hoffman J., and accepted that, even though the pieces had now arguably changed from realty to personalty, with the prospect reincarnation as a corporeal hereditament, that was irrelevant; they still constituted a "building" for the purposes of the Listed Buildings Act, and the question of ownership should be decided accordingly.[28]

That decision was recently followed by Sullivan J. (whose decision was in turn subsequently affirmed by the Court of Appeal) in *R. (Judge) v Secretary of State*,[28d] in which it was accepted that it was possible to grant listed building consent for the removal of a listed building (in this case, a memorial statute) from its original location, subject to a condition that it be re-erected at a prescribed spot elsewhere.

4.3 Objects and structures associated with the building in the list

4.3.1 General principles

It has been noted above that a listed building is defined to include any object or structure fixed to the building or in its curtilage.[29] The phrase "object or structure" is a fairly general one, and would seem to include almost anything—for

---

[27] See 4.5.4.
[28] Such as the skeleton referred to in the description of the Leeds Medical School (listed Grade II*).
[28a] *Leominster DC v British Historic Buildings and SPS Shipping* [1987] J.P.L. 350; see **18.7.3.**
[28b] The decision of the Secretary of State is noted at [1987] J.P.L. 798; see **18.4.8.**
[28c] *R. v Leominster DC, ex p. Antique Country Buildings Ltd* [1988] J.P.L. 554.
[28d] *R. (Judge) v Secretary of State and Middlesbrough BC* [2005] EWCA, unreported, July 22, 2005, CA; affirming [2005] EWHC 887 (Admin), unreported, April 28, 2005.
[29] P(LBCA)A 1990, s.1(5).

example, a door handle, a sundial, a conservatory, or an immediately adjoining building (which would clearly be a "structure"). It may even include an earthwork; see the comments below on *Watson-Smyth v Secretary of State*.[30] A climbing plant would not be included, as it would be attached to the ground, and thus part of it.

It should be remembered that the object or structure associated with the building that is itself included in the list is by virtue of s.1(5) to be regarded as part of *that* building. That is, the associated object or structure is not to be considered as if it was listed in its own right—section 1(5) does not import any special interest to something that in fact has none.

4.3.2 Ancillary buildings: Calderdale and Debenhams

A particular problem that often arises in practice is where the "structure" attached to or in the curtilage of a listed building is itself a building, such as a garage, associated with a (listed) house; or one house (not listed in its own right) attached to or in the curtilage of another (listed). Is the "associated" structure in each case to be considered as much subject to listed building control as the principal building, clearly included in the list, with which it is associated?

The two leading decisions on this, both cited in all the subsequent cases, are those of the Court of Appeal in *A.-G. v Calderdale BC*[31] and of the Court of Appeal and the House of Lords in *Debenhams PLC v Westminster CC*.[32]

In *Calderdale*, the building that was actually included in the list was a disused mill, listed in 1971. Attached to this was a stone bridge, and attached to the other end of the bridge was a terrace of 15 millworkers' cottages, also disused (see **Figure 4.1**). The ownership of the terrace and the mill was split in 1973. The dispute centred on the contention that, since a structure B fixed to a listed building A is deemed to be part of the building, structure C fixed to structure B is also part of building A.

In the opinion of Stephenson L.J., the purpose of the statute[33] was to bring within control works to objects and structures which might not be intrinsically of interest, but which were so closely related to a listed building that their removal might adversely affect it.[34] On this basis, he favoured a broad approach to the construction of the subsection and thus concluded that:

"although at first sight it seemed unlikely that [the far end] of this terrace could be regarded as fixed to the mill, he thought the judge [at first instance] was right in concluding that this terrace was a structure fixed to the mill in the ordinary sense of those words."

This decision was reviewed, not entirely favourably, by the House of Lords in *Debenhams*. That was a rating case, concerning a group of several buildings in the West End of London which were within the same hereditament for rating purposes, but only some of which (including the former Hamley's toy shop in 200/202 Regent Street and its rear portion, 51–52 Kingly Street) were listed in their own

---

[30] [1992] J.P.L. 451; see 4.5.8.
[31] (1983) 46 P. & C.R. 399, [1983] J.P.L 310.
[32] [1987] A.C. 396, overturning [1986] J.P.L 671.
[33] At that time TCPA 1971, s.54(9). the predecessor to P(LBCA)A 1990, s.1(5).
[34] See, for example, P(LBCA)A 1990, s.16(2) and Circ. 8/87, para.25.

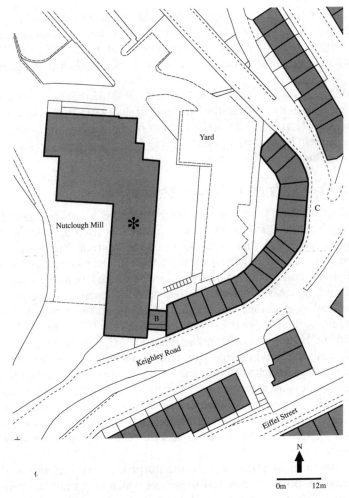

Figure 4.1 Nutclough Mill, Hebden Bridge, West Yorkshire (*A.-G. v Calderdale BC*)

right. 27–28 Kingly Street was not listed in its own right, but had been linked to the others by a footbridge at second floor level and a subway (see **Figure 4.2**). The two buildings were in fact entirely different in character, and were only ever linked for a short period by an accident of history. But it was held in the Court of Appeal (following *Calderdale*) that Number 27–28 was a structure fixed to the admittedly listed building, and was therefore part of it.

However, this was overturned by the majority on appeal to the House of Lords. After considering *Calderdale*, and reviewing the wording of what is now s.1(5), Keith L.J. concluded as follows:

"In my opinion to construe the word 'structure' here as embracing a complete building not subordinate to the building of which it is to be treated as forming part would ... produce an unreasonable result ... All these considerations and the general tenor of the second sentence of [subs (5)] satisfy me that the word ... is intended to convey a limitation to such structures as are ancillary to the listed building itself, for example the stable block of a

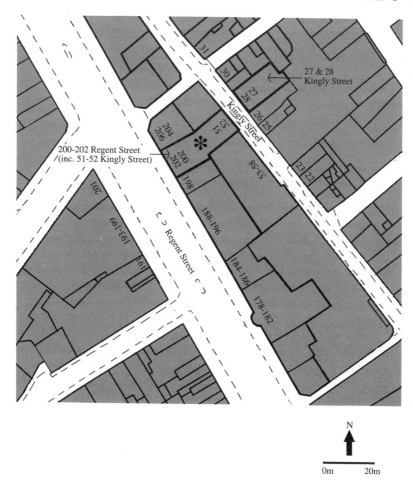

Figure 4.2 Kingly Street, Westminster, London W1 (*Debenhams PLC v Westminster CC*)

mansion house, or the steading of a farmhouse, either fixed to the main building or within its curtilage. In my opinion, the concept envisaged is that of principal and accessory."[35]

The definition of "steading", so far as is relevant, is "a farmhouse and out-buildings; the outbuildings in contrast to the farmhouse".[36] This makes it clear that, in the common situation of a farmhouse being listed the other building (cowsheds, stables, etc.) in the same group are also included within the listing—although the very use of the word "outbuilding" indicates a building that has a subsidiary function.

As to what is "ancillary", Lord Keith considered that:

"[the Kingly Street building] was not of its nature ancillary to [the Regent Street building], in the sort of sense that a steading is ancillary to a farmhouse. It was historically an independent building."

---

[35] [1987] A.C. 396 at p.403D.
[36] "Steading" is a Scots word (Lord Keith is a Scot).

It appears that, at the date of the listing, the former was being occupied for a use ancillary to that of the latter, and was in the same ownership; but that was not enough. "On a broad perspective", it was not ancillary.

It also appears that Lord Keith (with whom Lords Templeman and Griffiths agreed) may have accepted the decision in *Calderdale* on the basis that, presumably at the date of the listing, the terrace of cottages was ancillary to the mill, whereas Lord Mackay (with whom Lord Griffiths also agreed) considered it possible that, by reason of the ownership position at that date, the mill and the terrace were part of a single unit.[37]

4.3.3 Ancillary buildings: case law since Debenhams

The principles in *Calderdale* and *Debenhams* were subsequently developed by the courts in a number of cases, notably *Watts v Secretary of State*[38], *R v Camden LBC, ex p. Bellamy*,[39] and *Morris v Wrexham CBC and the National Assembly*.[40]

Watts concerned the demolition of part of a wall (running from A to D in **Figure 4.3**) that ran alongside a road, between Bix Manor, in Oxfordshire, and a nearby barn. The barn had been in the curtilage of the Manor House until 1981, when the owner of both properties sold the Manor House but retained the barn in its own curtilage. The Manor House was listed in 1985, together with other ancillary buildings to the south; but the listing did not include either the barn to the north or the wall. A section of wall (from B to C) was removed; and the planning authority took enforcement action to secure its reinstatement.

The deputy judge, after considering at length the judgments in *Calderdale* and *Debenhams*, held as follows:

"At the date of the listing, the section of wall formed part of the curtilage of a property separate from the listed building in terms of ownership and physical occupation. That property was being put to a wholly independent use unassociated with Bix Manor ... At the time of listing there was no functional connection and that section of wall did not in any sense serve the listed building. It was clearly ancillary to another separate building and, in my judgment, was not a structure ancillary to Bix Manor".[41]

The wall was thus not subject to listed building control.

If, therefore, an object or structure is to be treated as part of a listed building, it must at the date of listing be associated with the building that is itself included in the list, and not merely associated with a building that is only treated as being part of that building by virtue of s.1(5).

R. v Camden LBC, ex p. Bellamy concerned two buildings in Hampstead, north London. 22 Perrin's Walk, which was not itself included in the list, had originally formed the stable or coach house for 22 Church Row, which had been included in the list in 1950 (see **Figure 4.4**). It was agreed that the two properties had been in the same ownership until 1970; and the garden between them was used at all

---

[37] That was at any rate the conclusion of Graham Eyre Q.C., sitting as deputy judge, in *Watts v Secretary of State* [1991] 1 P.L.R. 61 at 72D.

[38] [1991] 1 P.L.R. 61.

[39] [1991] J.P.L. 255.

[40] [2002] 2 P. & C.R. 7.

[41] [1991] 1 P.L.R. 61 at p.72F.

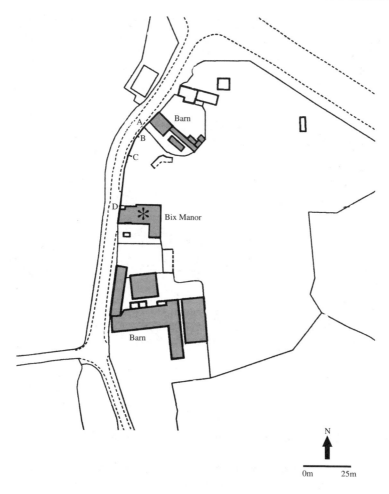

Figure 4.3 Bix Manor, Oxfordshire (*Watts v Secretary of State*)

material times by the owners and occupiers of 22 Church Row. There was however a dispute as to the use of 22 Perrin's Walk at the date of listing—it may have been used as a garage for 22 Church Row, or it may have been used separately for car repairs on a commercial basis. Nolan L.J. concluded:

"The legal position was by no means simple, but if, at the time of listing in 1950, 22 Perrin's Walk was in use as the garage or coach house of 22 Church Row, then on the basis of the test laid down in the *Calderdale* and *Debenhams* cases it had to be taken to have been included in the listing."[42]

In other words, the requirement is that the object or structure—or, as in this case, building—must have been ancillary to the building in the list at the date of the listing.

The most recent of these three case, *Morris*, concerned a property known as The Lodge, near Wrexham in north Wales. The landholding comprised not only

---

[42] [1992] J.P.L. 255.

Figure 4.4 Church Row, Hampstead, London NW3 (*R. v Camden LBC, Ex p. Bellamy*)

the principal building, which was specifically included in the list, but also numerous outbuildings, which had historically been used for agricultural purposes by successive residents of The Lodge (see **Figure 4.5**). However, although at the date of listing, in 1966, the entirety of the holding had been in one freehold ownership, The Lodge and the outbuildings had been occupied by different parties. The freeholders, a farming family named Evans, made use of outbuildings for agricultural purposes, whilst they leased The Lodge to a retired Colonel for use as a house.

In determining that the outbuildings were not ancillary to The Lodge, Jackson J. emphasised the lack of any functional link between the principal building and the ancillary structures at the date of listing. He stated that:

"While matters of past history are relevant, the primary focus of enquiry should be upon the state of affairs existing in January 1966, when The Lodge was listed.... It is true that the Evans family owned The Lodge, subject to Colonel Bromilow's lease, and also owned and used the north-east outbuildings. However, this circumstance cannot have the effect of bringing the north-east outbuildings within the curtilage of The Lodge".[43]

---

[43] At p.94.

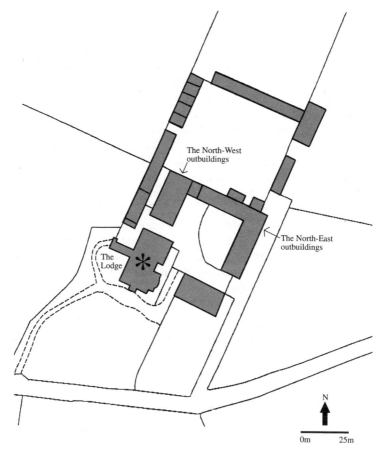

Figure 4.5 The Lodge, Halton, Clwyd (*Morris v Wrexham CBC and the National Assembly*)

4.3.4 Pre-1969 listings

The conclusion from the foregoing analysis is that, to see whether a structure that is not included in the list in its own right is nevertheless subject to listed building control, the correct approach is to consider the position as it was at the date of listing, and to see whether the unlisted structure was then ancillary to the listed building. That at any rate is the test that clearly emerges from the cases. However, there may be a problem in relation to buildings listed prior to 1969.

As already noted, the provision that is now s.1(5) of the Listed Buildings Act was only enacted in the 1968 Planning Act,[43a] coming into effect on January 1, 1969. Prior to that date, the relevant provisions of the 1947 and 1962 Acts simply referred to the power of the Minister to list a building, which imposed a requirement for two months' notice to be given to the planning authority before any works were carried out to "the building"—with a fine for non-compliance.[44]

[43a] s.40(3), 54.
[44] TCPA 1947, s.30(6),(9).

There was thus no reference to objects or structures attached to the building or in its curtilage.

Clearly, from the start of 1969, the Minister must be taken to have had regard to the existence of the new provision, so that the protection afforded to any building listed thereafter would, from the date of its listing, have extended to included any relevant ancillary objects and structures. However, in relation to buildings listed prior to 1969, that new provision would presumably not have operated retrospectively—so as to mean that, for example, someone was now liable to prosecution in respect of works that had been carried out without notice in 1965 to a barn associated with a farmhouse that had been listed in 1950.

But that leaves uncertain the question of a building listed at some date prior to 1969 where the situation on the ground had changed between the date of listing and the coming into force of the new provision. Where, for example, a farmhouse was listed in 1950, and a barn was then used for agricultural purposes ancillary to the occupation of the farmhouse, but in 1960 the barn started to be entirely separately occupied for purposes wholly unrelated to the use of the farmhouse, it would be surprising if the effect of the 1968 provision was to include the barn within the listing, even though the Secretary of State would not have had any regard to the barn back in 1950 and it was by 1969 no longer associated with the farmhouse.

A different problem might arise if the barn—historically associated with the farmhouse—had come to be in separate ownership and unrelated occupation by the date the farmhouse was listed in 1950, but was reunited with it prior to 1969. Fifty years later, is the barn to be protected by the listing of the farmhouse?

As it happens, Nutclough Mill and Hamley's (the listed buildings in *Calderdale* and *Debenhams*) were both included in the list after 1968, as was Bix Manor (in *Watts*). And although the listed buildings in *ex p. Bellamy* and *Morris* were listed pre-1969, it appears that this point was not raised at all. It would seem that the most logical approach is to regard the key date as January 1, 1969 for those buildings already listed by then, as Parliament may be taken to have considered the position as it was at that date when it enacted the new provision. The rule would thus become that, in relation to a building listed prior to January 1, 1969, the position should be considered as at that date, not the date of listing, to see which objects and structures were ancillary to it and either attached to it or in its curtilage.

It remains to be seen whether this approach—for which, it is admitted, there is no judicial authority whatsoever—would find favour with the courts were the point to arise. Alternatively, and preferably, Parliament could make explicit on the face of the statute the date at which the position is to be considered.

4.3.5 Plant and machinery

The question of plant and machinery associated with a listed building can sometimes cause problems.

A "building", which can be listed, is specifically defined to exclude "plant or machinery comprised in a building".[45] However, s.1(5) refers to, amongst other

---

[45] TCPA 1990, s.336, applied by P(LBCA)A 1990, s.91(1).

things, an *object* attached to a building or in its curtilage, which would suggest something additional to a building, as defined in s.336. There seems no reason, therefore, why an item of plant or machinery, which will clearly be an object, should be excluded from the effect of listing—provided of course that it passes the test, considered below, of being a "fixture" or "part of the land".

This argument was put forward on behalf of the Secretary of State, and accepted by the court, in *R. v Secretary of State for Wales ex p. Kennedy*.[46]

4.4 Objects and structures fixed to a listed building

4.4.1 The general rule

It is clear that a listed building is not just a bare brick box. Its appeal usually if not always lies as much in the numerous elements that go to make up its finished appearance. Thus, a country house contains numerous building elements—window surrounds, skirting boards, staircases, chimney pieces and so on—each of which is clearly an integral part of it. It also contains even more elements—such as curtains, free-standing furniture, table lamps, and pictures simply hanging on the wall—that are equally clearly not part of the house itself, however much they may contribute to its character.

But between these two groups there are, inevitably, items whose status is less straightforward. Chandeliers, weighing many hundreds of kilograms; panelling and tapestries, made or adapted specifically for the house; sculptures, in purpose-designed settings; clocks and bells, built into turrets; all have been the subject of protracted arguments. Such items add immensely to the character of the buildings in which they are found, and those seeking to preserve that character are keen that they remain there. However, as long as they do, their value is, at best, negligible[47]—whereas, once severed from the building, they may be worth thousands or even millions of pounds.

As already noted, this type of problem has often arisen over the centuries in other contexts, and has given rise to a substantial body of case law.[48] The approach adopted by the courts in relation to listed buildings has therefore been to assume that the formula in the listed building legislation (referring to "any object or structure fixed to the building"[49]) simply incorporates the principles arising from those cases. Thus, in the leading case, *Debenhams PLC v Westminster*

---

[46] [1996] 1 P.L.R. 97 at 102B, D.

[47] Arguably, the value of such an item is only the difference it makes to the value of the property of which it forms part—which may be nil. But it may rise eventually, if circumstances (such as the declining viability of maintaining the property) suggest that it may be worthwhile for a speculative purchaser to acquire it, subject to the need for it to remain a least for the present on the property, in the hope that one day consent for its removal may be forthcoming.

[48] See **4.1.1**.

[49] P(LBCA)A 1990, s.1(5)(a); [Scotland: P(LBCA)(S)A 1997, s.1(4)(a); NI: P(NI)O 1991, art.42)7)(a).]

CC,[50] Lord Mackay considered the predecessor to s.1(5) of the Listed Buildings Act,[51] concluding as follows:

"It appears to me that the word 'fixed' is intended in section 54(9) to have the same connotation as in the law of fixtures, and that what is achieved by the latter part of section 54(9) is that the ordinary rule of the common law is applied so that any object or structure fixed to a building should be treated as part of it."[52]

It follows that, in cases of doubt, the critical test to determine whether or not an object is included in the listing would be whether it is a "fixture" (such as carved wood panelling) or a "fitting" (such as furniture or paintings).

It should be noted, incidentally, that to be protected by listed building control, an object has to be fixed to "the building"—that is, a building included in a list— not fixed to a building that is itself fixed to or in the curtilage of a building in the list. And a post-1948 addition to a listed building is still "listed"; it was only post-1948 structures in the curtilage of the building, not fixed to it, that were in 1987 excluded from the listing.[53]

In the present context, it is also important to remember that whether an object is or is not a "fixture", and thus part of a listed building by virtue of s.1(5), is independent of any merit that it may or may not possess. But whether or not its alteration or removal will need listed building consent depends on whether the works will affect the character of the building as a building of special architectural or historic interest.[54] Clearly the removal of fine fifteenth-century carvings[55] will affect the building's special character, and will therefore require consent; the removal of a bath tap (just as much a fixture) will not.

Indeed, in theory the question of whether an object is part of the listed building is wholly distinct from the question of whether its removal requires listed building consent or, if it does, whether such consent would be forthcoming. In practice, however, a dispute on this issue only arises where there is a strong desire on the part of the planning authority to retain an item of interest in a listed building; if, therefore, the correct analysis is that consent is required for its removal, it is unlikely to be forthcoming. The determination of the proper status in law of the item in question is thus often the key to whether it is possible to remove it.[56]

4.4.2 The common law rules

This "ordinary rule of the common law", imported by Lord Mackay in *Debenhams* into the statutory code relating to listed buildings, is far from straightforward. Indeed, many of the decisions—which go back to the earliest years of the nineteenth century—note the impossibility of arriving at any entirely satisfactory synthesis.

[50] [1987] A.C. 396.
[51] TCPA 1971, s.54(9).
[52] At 408.
[53] Housing and Planning Act 1986, Sch.9, paras 1 and 13.
[54] P(LBCA)A 1990, s.7; see 9.1.3.
[55] *Corthorn Land and Timber Co v MOHLG* (1966) 17 P. & C.R. 210, and *Re Chesterfield* [1911] 1 Ch.237.
[56] But not always; see the Noseley Hall case, noted at **4.4.3**.

The two principal tests to be applied in considering whether any particular object is a fixture, and thus part of the building, were most clearly propounded by the Court of Appeal in *Berkeley v Poulett*, in which Scarman L.J., as he then was, held as follows:

"As so often, the difficulty is not the formulation but the application of the law. I think there is now no need to enter into research into the case law prior to *Leigh v Taylor*.[57] The answer today to the question whether objects which were originally chattels have become fixtures, that is to say part of the freehold, depends on the application of two tests:

(1) the method and degree of annexation;
(2) the object and purpose of the annexation.

Since *Leigh v Taylor*, the question is really one of fact. .... a degree of annexation which in earlier times the law would have treated as conclusive may now prove nothing. If the purpose of annexation be for the better enjoyment of the object itself, it remains a chattel, notwithstanding a high degree of physical annexation. Clearly, however, it remains significant to discover the extent of physical disturbance of the building of the land involved in the removal of the object. If an object cannot be removed without serious damage to, or destruction of, some part of the realty, the case for its having become a fixture is a strong one. .... Conversely, an object affixed to realty but capable of being removed without much difficulty may yet be a fixture if, for example, the purpose of its affixing be that 'of creating a beautiful room as a whole' (Neville J. in *Re Whaley*[58]). .... Today so great are the technical skills of affixing and removing objects to land or buildings that the second test is more likely than the first to be decisive. Perhaps the enduring significance of the first test is a reminder that there must be some degree of physical annexation before a chattel can be treated as part of the realty."[59]

So, for example, tapestries, fixed to the wall, were considered fixtures in *Re Whaley*, but not in *Leigh v Taylor*. In the first of these, it was considered that "the ornaments were inserted primarily for the purpose of creating a beautiful room as a whole, and not intended for the mere display and enjoyment of the chattels themselves", whereas in the second "the tapestry was never intended in any way to become part of the house".

In the light of the plethora of early authority, it is encouraging to note the words of Scarman L.J. as to there being no need to go back before *Leigh v Taylor*. That case was decided in 1901; so the many nineteenth-century cases should, in theory, only be looked into in any detail so far as they relate to the specific facts of a current dispute; and the focus should be on more recent decisions.[60] In practice,

---

[57] [1902] A.C. 157, HL.

[58] [1908] 1 Ch.615 at p.619.

[59] *Berkeley v Poulett* [1977] 1 E.G.L.R. 86, CA, at pp.88G–89B.

[60] See, for example, *Lyon v London City and Midland Bank* [1903] 2 K.B. 135 and *Vaudeville Electric Cinema v Muriset* [1923] 2 Ch.74 (fixed furniture); *Reynolds v Ashby* [1904] A.C. 466, HL and *Jordan v May* [1947] 1 K.B. 427, CA (machinery); *Re Whaley* [1908] 1 Ch.615 (tapestries); *Re Lord Chesterfield's Settled Estates* [1911] 1 Ch.237 (carvings); *Boswell v Crucible Steel Co* [1925] 1 K.B. 119, CA (windows); *Spyer v Phillipson* [1931] 2 Ch.183, CA (panelling); *Hamp v Bygrave* [1983] 1 E.G.L.R. 174 (garden ornaments); *Botham v TSB*, (1997) 73 P. & C.R. D1, CA.

of course, judges in more recent cases have continued to go back to those older authorities, which thus continue to be useful.[61]

The first test is thus to consider how solidly and permanently the item in question is physically fixed to the building—which will include considerations such as how much work was done to it and to the building to bring them together (was the picture simply hung on a hook on the wall, or was it painted onto a panel that was cut specially to fit a specific alcove?), and how much damage would be caused by its removal. But even a free-standing object, attached to the building solely by its own weight, may exceptionally be a fixture if there is enough evidence to indicate the intention behind its placing in that position.[62]

The second test is to consider why the object was placed in that location—was it to show off the object as an object, or was it to create a beautiful room? But that test is more clearly stated than applied. A picture, for example, or a chandelier cannot readily be seen or enjoyed unless they are hung on a wall or from a ceiling; and there would be no point in displaying ether if they did not fit in with overall decorative scheme of the room. In practice, therefore, each case has to be decided on its facts.

4.4.3 Fixtures and fittings: examples

A notable example of the outworking of these principles was provided by the controversy over the removal from the tempietto at Woburn Abbey of Canova's statue known as *The Three Graces*. The Secretary of State initially considered that the statue was a fixture, but stated that he did not propose to take listed building enforcement action. SAVE Britain's Heritage then applied to the High Court for judicial review of that decision. As a result, the Secretary of State took further advice, and reached the view that the statue was not part of the building within the meaning of s.1(5), and that the question of taking enforcement action thus did not arise.

In his letter to the owners of the statue setting out his modified position,[63] the Secretary of State accepted Lord Mackay's view (in *Debenhams*) that the correct test to be applied was the same as is applied at common law to decide whether an article is a fixture, namely the degree and purpose of annexation. He also by implication confirmed that the relevant date was that on which the tempietto was listed. After considering carefully the history of the sculpture and the gallery, he concluded as follows:

"The tests, although easily stated, are not so easily applied. The degree of annexation was not great. The plinth [upon which the statue stood] was fastened to the floor, but apparently not in such a way as to make the removal particularly difficult. The statue itself was freestanding. As to the purpose of annexation, the Secretary of State now takes the view, on further consideration, even accepting that the tempietto was specifically built or mod-

---

[61] Including, in particular, *Hellawell v Eastwood* (1851) 6 Exch. 295, *D'Eyncourt v Gregory* (1866) 3 L.R. Eq. 382 and *Holland v Hodgson* (1872) L.R. 7 C.P. 328, Ex. Ch. (noted at **4.5.5** below). But there are over 30 other reported 19th-century authorities, cited in the various standard works on real property law.

[62] *Monti v Barnes* [1900] 1 Q.B. 205 (dog grates).

[63] Reproduced at [1991] J.P.L. 401.

ified to house the statue, that this does not of itself mean that the statue became part of the building...

[He] considers that, even if the degree of annexation, looked at in isolation, could have been sufficient to satisfy the relevant test (which he doubts), here the purpose of annexation was not such as to make the statue part of the building. If the position is judged objectively, and without regard to the way in which the owners have regarded and treated the statue, it seems to him that the object or purpose of installing the statue in the tempietto was not to dedicate it to the land or to incorporate it into the land, but to show off the statue."

Consent for removal was accordingly judged not to be necessary.

Two subsequent appeal decisions explored these matters in some detail. The first, related to the removal from Leighton Hall in mid-Wales of three substantial chandeliers and an elaborate turret-clock.[64] The dealer to whom they had been sold argued that they were not fixtures, and thus not subject to listed building control, but that, even if they were, their removal would improve the building as they were stylistically wholly at odds with the interior of the Hall. On the first point, the inspector (whose view was supported by the Secretary of State) concluded as follows:

"From the extensive case law submitted by the parties, it is clear that the tests to be applied in this appeal are, firstly, the degree to which the objects are fixed to the building, including the ease with which they can be removed and any damage caused to the structure or object by their removal, and secondly, the objective or purpose of their annexation to the building, whether for the improvement of the property or for ornamentation and the enjoyment of the objects themselves. As both parties have emphasised, the second test also touches upon the architectural merit of the pieces and their place in the design of the listed building as a whole."

The Secretary of State's decision was subsequently challenged in the High Court, but the inspector's report (which he had adopted) was described as "not only a model of thoroughness, but its group of legal principles and their relationship and application to the facts as found cannot legitimately be faulted"; the challenge accordingly failed.[65]

The second case related to the removal from the Time & Life building in New Bond Street, London of four valuable works of modern art. In that case, too, the inspector agreed with the parties that the critical tests were the degree of annexation and the purpose of annexation; but he chose to apply those tests to the situation as it was at the date of listing (1988), rather than (as would seem to be more logical) as it was at the date when the artworks first arrived in the building (the early 1950s).[66] His decision too was therefore challenged in the High Court, and was quashed by consent. A further inquiry was held, leading to a decision by the Secretary of State to uphold the enforcement notices and require all four works to be returned—even though, in the absence of listed building control, the Time Life Company (which had installed them when the building was first built)

[64] Reported at [1995] J.P.L. 256.

[65] See *Kennedy v Secretary of State for Wales* [1996] 1 P.L.R. 97. For a further development in the saga of the clock at Leighton Hall, see **18.6.4**.

[66] The first decision is reported at [1995] J.P.L. 241.

might, as a matter of property law, have enjoyed a right to remove them at the end of its tenancy.

A more recent case concerned two sets of paintings at Noseley Hall in Leicestershire.[67] The Secretary of State agreed with his inspector that two huge horse paintings in the main hall of the house were found not to be fixtures, so that listed building consent was not required for their removal; although, interestingly, the inspector had concluded that, if they had been fixtures, he would have recommended that consent should be given. But a series of paintings in the study, each secured to the wall simply by mirror plates, were considered to be fixtures, on the grounds of their contribution to the decoration of the room as a whole; listed building consent for their removal was accordingly refused.

4.4.4 Is the conventional view of the law correct?

It may be worth bearing in mind that Lord Mackay's observations in *Debenhams*[68] were not necessarily correct. For one thing, they were arguably only obiter, that case being primarily about the relationship between principal and ancillary buildings, rather than fixtures and fittings. Secondly, the "ordinary rule of the common law" to which he referred depends, amongst other things, on whether a building is held freehold or leasehold, whether or not it is subject to a mortgage, whether it is occupied for domestic, trade or other purposes, and whether the item in question is utilitarian or ornamental—matters which are mostly irrelevant in the context of historic buildings.

An alternative view would thus be that the phrase "the building that is included in the list" itself includes any thing that is part of the building by the operation of the ordinary rule, and thus any item which is a "fixture". An "object affixed to the building" therefore means something over and above that, and would thus include any item screwed or otherwise attached to the building as thus defined—including some items that might be rightly classified as fittings under the ordinary rule.

Such an approach would provide a more logical interpretation of s.1(5)(a), which is otherwise at least arguably otiose except as regards plant and machinery. It would also enable protection to be given to items whose removal would unquestionably affect the character of a historic building—such as, for example, mirrors, wall lights, electroliers, pelmet boards and tapestries, which are generally considered to be outside the scope of the Act. That would doubtless be considered by some to be a major advantage, and by others (notably property owners) as wholly impractical.

However, attractive or not, such a view flies in the face of the plain words of the decision of the House of Lords in *Debenhams*, followed by the High Court subsequently[69] and by the Secretary of State in appeal decisions.[70] At least for the moment, therefore, the law should be taken to be as explained above.

---

[67] Noted at [1999] J.P.L. 1145.
[68] See **4.4.1**.
[69] for example, in *Kennedy v Secretary of State for Wales* [1996] 1 P.L.R. 97.
[70] See **4.4.3**.

4.5 Objects and structures in the curtilage of a listed building

4.5.1 The general rule

It is not surprising that a listed building is defined to include objects and structures fixed to the building. They are, after all, very obviously part of the building. It is perhaps less immediately apparent that the listing extends to any object (such as a statue or birdbath) or structure (such as a garden pavilion or wall) in the vicinity of the building.

This protection obviously makes sense in the case of, for example, a large country house whose grounds contain numerous temples, statues, grottoes and so on; they may indeed in some cases be one of the reasons, or indeed the principal reason, why the building was listed.[71] On the other hand, they are still affected by the restrictions involved in the listing process even if they are of no interest whatever (such as a decaying garden shed). As with fixtures, it should be borne in mind that listed building consent would only be needed for their alteration or removal if the proposed works would affect the character of the listed building as a whole.

However, a line has to be drawn somewhere. Particularly in the countryside, listed buildings may be associated with large landholdings, sometimes extending to many hundreds of hectares; and it would be ridiculous if all objects and structures within them were to be theoretically protected. The planning Acts accordingly have (since 1968) granted protection to "any object or structure within the curtilage of the building which, although not fixed to the building, forms part of the land and has done so since before July 1, 1948".[72]

The listing thus extends to pre-1948 objects and structures within the *curtilage* of the building actually included in the list. In principle, the dictionary definition of "curtilage" is "an area of land attached to a house and forming one enclosure with it".[73] It derives from the Old French word *courtil*, meaning "small court". It is a conveyancing term often used in property transactions; and it turns up in various modern statutes.

Although the use of the word is thus relatively widespread (at least in legal contexts), it may in practice sometimes be far from straightforward to determine what is the curtilage of a particular building—or, of greater significance, whether one structure is in the curtilage of another. Although much is sometimes made of this, when considering whether ancillary object or structure is to be taken as being protected by the listing of a nearby building, it is often more important to consider whether the associated structure is "ancillary" to the listed building (already considered earlier in this chapter[74]). This is certainly what emerges from the

---

[71] s.1(3)(b); see **3.2.2**.

[72] P(LBCA)A 1990, s.1(5)(b); [Scotland: P(LBCA)(S)A 1997, s.1(4)(b). NI: P(NI)O 1991, art.42)7)(b), although the cut-off date there is October 1, 1973.]

[73] *New Oxford Dictionary of English* (Clarendon, Oxford, 1988).

[74] See **4.3**.

decision of the House of Lords in *Debenhams plc v Westminster CC*[75] and those of the High Court in *Watts, ex p. Bellamy* and *Morris*.[76]

Nevertheless, it is in some instances necessary to consider the definition of curtilage. There are numerous decided cases dealing with this, some in contexts other than specifically relating to listed buildings, and those referred to here are only a selection. This discussion below accordingly considers, first, the cases specifically relating to the curtilage of listed buildings, then the decisions relating to the extent of a curtilage, decided in the context of permitted development rights[77] and under other statutes. Finally, there is a brief look at some of the decisions from other areas of law, referred to in the statutory cases.

4.5.2 The extent of curtilage: listed buildings cases

The principal case dealing explicitly with the definition of curtilage in the context of listed buildings is *Attorney-General v Calderdale BC*, relating to Nutclough Mill at Hebden Bridge in West Yorkshire.[78]

Counsel for the applicants had conceded that buildings in different ownerships might be within the same curtilage; but he had contended (rightly, in the view of Stephenson L.J.) that they fell less easily within the same curtilage if they were in different ownerships. Counsel for the planning authority had also submitted that less attention, should be paid to title and division of ownership, otherwise listed building control could easily be evaded by colourable transfers of title; and more weight should be given to historical association and proximity.

In its judgment, the Court of Appeal referred to a number of decisions (including *Methuen-Campbell v Walters*,[79] *Pilbrow v Vestry of the Parish of St Leonard, Shoreditch*[80] and *Vestry of St Martin's in the Fields v Bird*[81]), showing that different facts might lead to different conclusions, and indeed that the same facts might lead to different judicial opinions. However, there was at the end of the argument before the court agreement that:

"three factors had to be taken into account in deciding whether a structure (or object) was within the meaning of [s.1(5)], whatever might be the strict conveyancing interpretation of the ancient and somewhat obscure word 'curtilage'. They are:

(1) the physical 'layout' of the listed building and the structure;
(2) their ownership, past and present; and
(3) their use or function, past and present."

Stephenson L.J. thus held that the terrace had definitely been within the curtilage of the mill when they were both built in 1870, and therefore came ultimately to the conclusion, not without doubt, that:

---

[75] [1987] A.C. 396.
[76] *Watts v Secretary of State* [1991] P.L.R. 61, *R. v Camden LBC, ex p. Bellamy* [1991] J.P.L. 255, and *Morris v Wrexham CBC and the National Assembly*; see **4.3.3**.
[77] See **12.2.2**.
[78] [1983] J.P.L. 310 (see **4.3.2** and **Figure 4.1** for the facts).
[79] (1979) Q.B. 525; see **4.5.4**.
[80] [1985] 1 Q.B. 433.
[81] [1985] 1 Q.B. 428.

"the terrace has not been taken out of the curtilage by the changes which had taken place, and remained so closely related physically or geographically to the mill as to constitute with it a single unit and to be comprised within its curtilage in the sense that those words were used in this subsection."

The threefold test set out in *Calderdale* remains the key to analysing this issue, and has been applied by the court in a number of subsequent cases that have explored particular aspects of this problem.

The extent of curtilage in the case of structures such as ice houses, garden temples and ha-has in the grounds of a country house was considered by Sir Frank Layfield, sitting as deputy judge in *Watson-Smyth v Secretary of State*.[82] He concluded, first, that where one structure that is clearly ancillary to a listed principal building is listed in its own right, that does not of itself mean that the ancillary structure is outside the curtilage of the principal building. Many such structures are listed because of their own merit, but are clearly within the curtilage of listed buildings. Second, it cannot be assumed that each structure in such a group has its own, distinct curtilage, for that might lead to the splitting up of a single, clearly defined curtilage into indefinable parcels.

As to the situation that sometimes occurs where there are within a single area of land a number of buildings, some but not all of which are listed, and none of which is more significant than the others, this was considered in *Re West Norwood Cemetery*, in the context of a large municipal cemetery. It was held that "the effect of listing 67 buildings and monuments within a clearly defined area means that ... the whole of the cemetery is effectively within the listing".[83] That may have been correct on the particular facts of that case, but the approach should not be pushed too far.

On the other hand, it has been confirmed that not every building has or is capable of having a curtilage.[84] At the Bishopsgate Goods Yard, in east London, the Secretary of State had listed some while earlier the entrance to an older structure, of which most of the remainder had perished; and more recently a historic viaduct running through the middle. In relation to the former, Ouseley J. held that "it seems odd to suppose the gates and walls themselves had a curtilage and that those other parts lay within the curtilage".[85] The same would no doubt apply to features such as gate lodges, boundary walls, bollards, and monuments that have been listed in their own right—frequently they will be within the curtilage of other buildings that have also been listed, but, where they are not, the listing of a bollard does not give rise to protection for the unremarkable building in the forecourt of which it is standing.

Visual matters may occasionally be significant. This has not yet been tested in the courts, but was the subject of an appeal decision, relating to a group of buildings surrounding a farmyard in Chipping Campden in Gloucestershire.[86] The farmhouse on one side was included in the list in 1960. The other buildings surrounding the yard were by that date probably no longer in agricultural use,

---

[82] [1992] J.P.L. 451.

[83] [1994] Fam. 210 at 225F (Southwark Consistory Court).

[84] *R. (Hammerton) v London Underground Limited* [2003] J.P.L. 984, at para.170.

[85] *Hammerton* at para.43.

[86] ref. App/G/92/ F1610/1.

and were by the date of the appeal in separate ownership; one had been turned into a separate dwelling. The Secretary of State considered that, although a substantial portion of the other buildings surrounding the farmyard were now ancillary to the new dwelling in the practical sense, the visual function of those buildings, and of the new dwelling itself, continued to relate to the former farmhouse; he thus decided that all the buildings surrounding the yard were within the curtilage of the farmhouse (even though described in the list as being of no special interest).

This should be contrasted with *Morris v Wrexham CBC and the National Assembly*, discussed earlier in this chapter, which suggests that the sole question was what was the position at the date of the listing—subsequent events are irrelevant.[87]

The Court of Appeal has considered the issue of "curtilage" relatively recently, in the case of *Skerritts of Nottingham Ltd v Secretary of State*,[88] which concerned the Grade II listed Grimsdyke Hotel, in Harrow (the former residence of WS Gilbert). Skerritts, the owners of the hotel, had installed double glazing in a stable block, situated some 200 metres from the hotel (see **Figure 4.6**). No listed building consent had been sought for the operation. The local authority began enforcement proceedings, on the basis that the stable block lay within the curtilage of the hotel, so that consent should have first been obtained. Skerritts maintained that, on the basis of the decision in *Dyer*,[89] no listed building consent was required, since the curtilage of a building must be small. This latter view was accepted by Mr George Bartlett Q.C., sitting as a deputy judge, when the matter came before him.[90]

The Secretary of State appealed successfully to the Court of Appeal. In giving judgement, Robert Walker L.J. maintained that:

"whilst the decision in *Dyer* was plainly correct ... this court went further than it was necessary to go in expressing the view that the curtilage of a building must always be small, or that the notion of smallness is inherent in the expression".[91]

The Court did not see fit to give any further detailed guidance upon the matter, other than to reiterate the proposition established in *Dyer* that curtilage will always be a question of fact and degree. Accordingly, it appears that whilst in any given instance it will be necessary to have regard to all the circumstances, the starting position for consideration can no longer be an assumption that a curtilage is necessarily limited in extent.

The decision in *Dyer* was also applied in an appeal decision relating to the demolition of a lodge building in Warwick.[92] The lodge was some 200m from the main (listed) house, which had subsequently been used as a school, and the two buildings had been in the same ownership and related use until the date of the listing. There was then a hedge partially enclosing the lodge, but it was still open

---

[87] [2002] 2 P. & C.R. 7; see **4.3.3** and **Figure 4.5**.
[88] [2000] 2 P.L.R. 84, [2001] Q.B. 59.
[89] *Dyer v Dorset CC* [1989] Q.B. 346, CA; see **4.5.4**.
[90] [1999] 2 P.L.R. 109.
[91] At p.91E.
[92] [2003] J.P.L. 769.

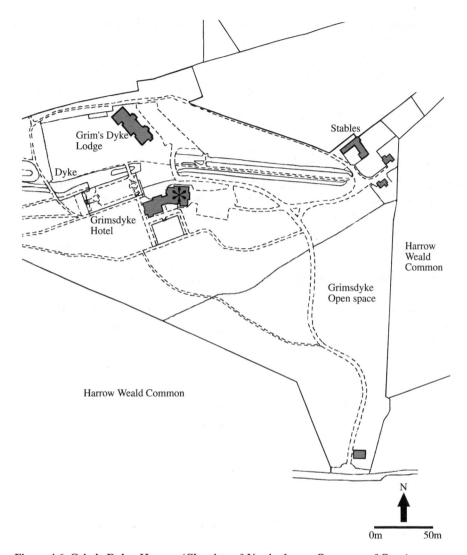

Figure 4.6 Grim's Dyke, Harrow (*Skerritts of Nottingham v Secretary of State*)

to the drive, and visible form the front of the main house. The grounds had been used for modern residential development, but that was not sufficient to negate the original relationship; and the inspector accordingly found the lodge to be ancillary to and in the curtilage of the house, so that consent was required for its demolition.

The position is thus that, for the purposes of establishing what is the extent of a listed building, the position must be examined as it was at the date of listing (or, possibly, as it was at January 1, 1969 in relation to buildings listed before then[93]), in the light of the criteria in *Calderdale*. And once a decision has been reached, the

[93] See **4.3.4**.

courts will be slow to interfere—as Sullivan J. expressed it in *R. v North Devon DC, ex p. Tarn*:

"Whether a particular structure is within the curtilage of a particular listed building is a question of fact for the local planning authority or the Secretary of State to decide. On such a question of fact, I would interfere with the district council's decision that, in this case, the hedgebank was not within the curtilage of Prospect Lodge only if I thought it had erred in principle in some way, or if there was no evidence to support its decision or, to put it another way, if its conclusion in this respect was perverse."[94]

4.5.3 Definition of "curtilage": other planning cases

The courts have on a number of occasions considered the extent of the curtilage of a dwellinghouse, to determine whether the construction of garden buildings and enclosures would be permitted by the TCP (General Permitted Development) Order 1995 or its predecessors.[95]

Collins v Secretary of State[96] related to a cottage set in 4.5 acres of gardens, of which the part nearest to the cottage was well-cut lawn and the remainder was rough grass, largely neglected. The appellant constructed a summerhouse in the rough part of the gardens, which was the subject of an enforcement notice. On the subsequent appeal to the high court against the inspector's upholding of the notice, Sir Graham Eyre Q.C., sitting as deputy judge, considered that in determining the nature and extent of the curtilage of a dwellinghouse, it is important that it should serve the purposes of the dwelling in some necessary or useful manner (echoing the test in *Sinclair-Lockhart's Trustees*[97]). On the facts in this case, the rough part of the garden could not be described as part of the curtilage of the cottage, since it did not serve the cottage.

The facts in *James v Secretary of State*[98] were not dissimilar; a tennis court was constructed towards the further end of a 0.5-hectare parcel of land surrounding a detached house set in wooded countryside. Sir Graham Eyre Q.C. (again) held that the extent of the curtilage is "quintessentially a matter of fact". The inspector considered that the field on which the court had been constructed was within the same ownership as the house; and found that there was a functional association between them. However, on the facts, the inspector found that the field was quite separate and distinct from the cultivated garden attached to the house, and the house and the tennis court did not have the appearance of close association or of being within the same enclosure. His decision, that the field was not in the curtilage of the house was thus entirely satisfactory.

A third decision, *McAlpine v Secretary of State*,[99] again related to the construction of a swimming pool and tennis court in a paddock beyond the bottom of a generous garden. Nigel Macleod Q.C., sitting as deputy judge, confirmed that the decision as to whether the pool was in the curtilage of the house was essentially a matter of fact and degree for the inspector. He also suggested that it is

[94] February 20, 1998, unreported.
[95] See **12.2.2**.
[96] [1989] E.G.C.S. 15.
[97] See **4.5.4**.
[98] [1991] 1 P.L.R. 58.
[99] [1995] 1 P.L.R. 16.

allowable for inspectors, in appropriate cases, to consider historical evidence where it assists the determination of a present curtilage boundary.

The most recent of these GPDO cases is *Lowe v The First Secretary of State*,[1] in which the court emphasised that the curtilage of a building was not necessarily to be equated to the land in the same ownership as it.

It should be noted that, when determining what is the extent of a listed building, the key question is what was the extent of the curtilage of the building in the list at the date on which it was listed[2]; however, when determining what permitted development rights apply, the key question is what is the extent of the curtilage of the building in question at the date of the development.[3] The principles are the same in either case, but the date on which they fall to be applied is different.

National and local planning policies sometimes refer to various types of development being acceptable within the curtilage of existing buildings. PPG 3 thus encourages housing development to take place on previously development land, which is defined to include the curtilage of previously existing buildings or infrastructure[4]; this was considered by Sullivan J. in *Withers v Secretary of State*.[5] A similar policy in a local plan was considered by Harrison J. in *Wheeler v The First Secretary of State*.[6]

Finally, where a building or structure is on a sea coast, a tidal river or an estuary, the tidal water and the land beneath it are excluded from its curtilage.[7]

4.5.4 Definition of "curtilage": cases decided under other statutory regimes

One definition of "curtilage" often cited is "the ground which is used for the comfortable enjoyment of the house or building ... serving the purpose of the house or building in some necessary or reasonably useful way" This formulation, from *Sinclair-Lockhart's Trustees v Central Land Board*,[8] is not very precise; and it might also include, for example, a neighbour's garden which could serve a house in a very useful way by providing an attractive view. But the test in *Sinclair* was used by the inspector whose decision was the subject of judicial criticism in *Wheeler*, on the basis that he had applied the test incorrectly, when determining that an ancillary structure "*must* serve the house or building in some necessary [or] reasonable way".[9]

In *Stephens v Cuckfield RDC*,[10] a case in which the court generally shied away from defining "curtilage",[11] it was pointed out that one can have a garden which is

---

[1] [2003] 1 P.L.R. 81; see **12.5.2.**
[2] See **4.5.2.**
[3] See **12.5.2.**
[4] PPG 3, *Housing*, para.23 and Annex C.
[5] *Wheeler v Secretary of State* [2002] 4 P.L.R. 102.
[6] [2003] E.W.H.C. 1194 Admin.
[7] *Assessor for Lothian Region v BP Oil Grangemouth Refinery* [1985] S.L.T. 228.
[8] (1951) 1 P. & C.R. 195 at 204.
[9] [2003] E.W.H.C. 1194 Admin, at para.10.
[10] [1959] 1 Q.B. 516.
[11] Particularly at p.526.

not within the curtilage of anything.[12] Further, in *Caledonian Railway Co. v Turcan*,[13] it was held by the House of Lords that an accessway leading to a yard could in appropriate circumstances be part of the curtilage of the building adjoining the yard.

It is thus not surprising that, in *Re St George's Church, Oakdale*,[14] it was held that the territorial extent of the curtilage "will depend on the facts of the individual case and the circumstances of the particular site." And in *Methuen-Campbell v Walters*,[15] Buckley J. held that it was not enough that the land and its curtilage were conveyed or demised together. Nor is the test whether the enjoyment of one is advantageous or convenient or necessary for the full enjoyment of the other:

"For one corporeal hereditament to fall within the curtilage of another, the former must be so intimately associated with the latter as to lead to the conclusion that the former in truth forms part and parcel of the latter. There can be very few houses indeed that do not have associated with them at least some few square yards of land, constituting a yard or basement area or passageway or something of the kind ... which on a reasonable view could only be regarded as part of the messuage, and such small pieces of land would be held to fall within the curtilage of the messuage. This may extend to ancillary buildings, structures or areas such as outhouses, a garage, a driveway, a garden, and so forth. How far it is appropriate to regard this identity as part of one messuage or parcel of land as extending must depend on the character and circumstances under consideration. To the extent that it is reasonable to regard them as constituting one messuage or parcel of land, they will be properly regarded as all falling within one curtilage; they constitute an integral whole".[16]

The leading case on this point, *Dyer v Dorset CC*,[17] concerned a provision in the Housing Act 1980 giving an owner of a dwellinghouse the right to buy it where it "either forms part of, or is within the curtilage of, the building".[18] This particular case concerned a college of agriculture, which comprised an estate of about 100 acres containing the main house, Kingston Maurward, which was its headquarters, extensive gardens, a park and a mass of outbuildings (see **Figure 4.7**)—a situation similar to a number of larger listed buildings in extensive grounds used for institutional purposes.[19] The lecturers' houses, including the one whose status was in dispute, were on the edge of the estate, facing a road which provided the only vehicular access. They were fenced off at the back, although there was pedestrian access to the rest of the college grounds.

The Court of Appeal held that the issue of whether a particular dwellinghouse was within the curtilage of another building, being a question of fact and degree, was primarily for the trial judge. Lord Donaldson M.R. examined the numerous authorities, including most of those referred to above, and concluded that the word "curtilage" seemed always to have to be read in context. Accordingly, if in

---

[12] At 520.
[13] [1898] A.C. 256.
[14] [1975] 2 All E.R. 870.
[15] (1979) Q.B. 525.
[16] At pp 543–4.
[17] [1989] Q.B. 346, CA. Leave to appeal to the House of Lords was refused: [1988] 1 W.L.R. 1284.
[18] Housing Act 1980, Sch.1, amended by the Housing Act 1984.
[19] Kingston Maurward House itself is indeed listed, Grade I.

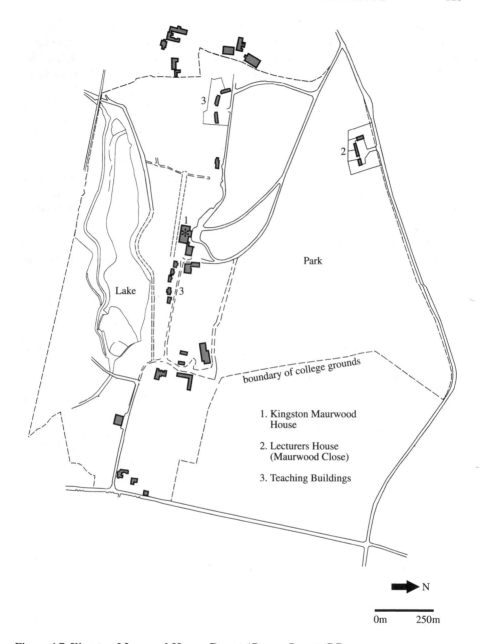

Figure 4.7 Kingston Maurward House, Dorset (*Dyer v Dorset CC*)

this case the relevant words were the "curtilage of the college", he would have had little doubt that, despite the fact that the house was on the edge of the campus and divided from it by a fence, it would have rightly been held to have been within that curtilage. But those were not the relevant words, and he was quite unable to find that the house lay within the curtilage of any other college building or collection of buildings.

This suggests that a subsidiary building that might have been within the curtilage of a principal building in large grounds will probably be considered to be not within that curtilage once it has been enclosed within its own curtilage. See also the decision of the Scottish Lands Tribunal in *Shipman v Lothian Regional Council*,[20] dealing with the curtilage of schools in the context of similar legislation. and *Barwick v Kent County Council*,[21] concerned with a house allegedly within the curtilage of a fire station".

4.5.5 Structures forming part of the land

As with objects and structures attached to the building,[22] the first critical test is not any intrinsic worth that the object or structure may or may not possess, but whether it "forms part of the land." The normal rules for distinguishing between fixtures and fittings will therefore apply. Thus greenhouses, not secured to the ground but standing by their own weight on concrete dollies, were held not to be part of the land[23]; whereas in *Holland v Hodgson*[24] a dry stone wall was held to be clearly a fixture. In the latter case, the position was summarised as follows:

"Perhaps the true rule is, that articles not otherwise attached to the land than by their own weight are not to be considered as part of the land, unless the circumstances are such as to show that they are intended to be part of the land; the onus of showing that they were so intended is on those who assert that they have ceased to be chattels; and that, on the contrary, an article which is affixed to the land even slightly is to be considered as part of the land, unless the circumstances are such as to show that it was intended all along to continue a chattel, the onus lying on those who contend it is a chattel".[25]

In a notable borderline case carved figures on the stairs, sculptured marble vases in the hall, a pair of marble lions at the head of a flight of garden steps and 16 stone garden seats, all of which merely rested on their own weight, were all held to be fixtures; the test was whether the items were "part of the architectural design ... and put in there as such, as distinguished from mere ornaments to be afterwards added".[26] Gardens of special interest are considered generally in a later chapter.[27]

The listing does extend to structures forming part of the layout of the grounds of a building. This was considered in *Watson-Smyth v Secretary of State and Cherwell DC*,[28] in the context of a ha-ha (a ditch and wall constructed so as to form a boundary to the garden of a country house while not interrupting the view of the countryside beyond). The owner of North Aston Hall (listed Grade II) had constructed a new dry stone wall using stones from the wall from the ha-ha, and had then filled in the ditch. The owner appealed against the resulting listed building enforcement notice, first (unsuccessfully) to the Secretary of State and

---

[20] (1989) S.L.T. (Lands Tr) 82.
[21] (1992) 24 H.L.R. 341, [1992] E.G.C.S. 12.
[22] See **4.4**.
[23] *HE Dibble v Moore* [1970] 2 Q.B. 181, CA.
[24] (1872) L.R. 7 C.P. 328, Ex. Ch.
[25] p.335.
[26] *D'Eyncourt v Gregory* (1866) 3 LR Eq 382 *per* Lord Romilly M.R. at p.396.
[27] See **7.5**.
[28] [1992] J.P.L. 451.

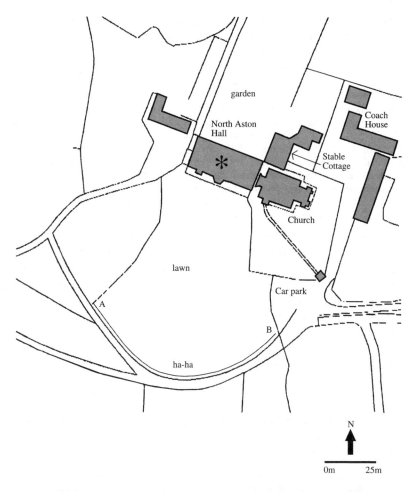

Figure 4.8 North Aston Hall, Oxfordshire (*Watson-Smyth v Secretary of State*)

then to the court. Sir Frank Layfield Q.C., sitting as deputy judge, appeared to accept without question the finding of the inspector that the two main elements of the ha-ha, the ditch and the wall, were integral parts of the structure, and thus that they could form part of the listed building provided that the ha-ha was within its curtilage.

The decision in *Watson-Smyth* is clearly correct as far as it relates to the wall, and confirms that structures such as terraces, balustrades, flights of steps and so forth are structures capable of being treated as part of a listed building by virtue of s.1(5). It is less clear, however, that a ditch can be an object or structure, albeit that its construction (if it is of significant size) may involve an engineering operation. The decision should be read alongside that in *Cotswold DC v Secretary of State*,[29] where it was held that the listing of a building did not extend to the actual ground surrounding it.

---

[29] [1985] J.P.L. 407; see **12.5.3**.

Pre-1948 walls and other means of enclosure are also included in the listing, provided (as will normally be the case) that they are ancillary to a principal building and not to a building that is itself ancillary.[30]

On the other hand, a hedgebank adjoining a road in Devon was held not to be part of a listed house standing nearby:

"The hedgebank is to be distinguished from the ha-ha in *Watson-Smyth*. Very often the function of a ha-ha is to define the curtilage around a hall or mansion, separating it physically, but not visually from the surrounding parkland. There is nothing to suggest that this hedgebank is contemporaneous with Prospect Lodge [the listed building]. The evidence suggests that it may be of some antiquity/ it seems likely that it is an old field boundary, since it extends along the whole length of the frontage ... When Prospect Lodge was built in 1820, it no doubt served to enclose the parkland that then enclosed the house, but there is nothing to suggest that the whole of that parkland should be treated as being within the curtilage of Prospect Lodge."[31]

Since April 1, 1987, structures in the curtilage of a listed building were not subject to listed building control if they have been erected since before 1948. This removes from the need for consent many trivial operations in the grounds of listed buildings. It incidentally also removes the anomaly whereby listed building consent could in some circumstances be required for the demolition of a garden shed erected (quite possibly under permitted development rights) in the 1960s.

4.6 Conclusion

4.6.1 Summary

In the light of the above analysis, which confirms the view of Nolan L.J. in *ex p. Bellamy*[32] that the legal position is "by no means simple", the correct approach would seem to be as follows.

(1) The building that is itself included in the list ("the principal building") must first be identified from the list—the description should only be referred to where the identification of the building is ambiguous.[33]

(2) The whole of the principal building, including its interior, will be covered by the listing.

(3) Any object (such as a sundial or panelling) fixed to the principal building at the date of listing will be included, provided that it is a "fixture" according to the normal rules of land law.[34]

(4) Any structure fixed to the principal building at the date of listing will be included, provided that, if it is itself a building, it was "ancillary" to the

[30] See *Watts v Secretary of State* [1991] 1 P.L.R. 61 at 72H.
[31] *R. v North Devon DC, ex p. Tarn* February 20, 1998, unreported.
[32] *R. v Camden LBC, ex p. Bellamy* [1991] JPL 255, at p.262.
[33] *City of Edinburgh* (per Lord Hope).
[34] *Debenhams* (per Lord Mackay).

principal building at the date of listing[35] (or possibly at January 1, 1969 in the case of buildings listed prior to that date[36]).

(5) The curtilage of the principal building must then be identified, which will be "quintessentially a matter of fact".[37] Relevant matters will be the physical layout of the principal building and any other buildings that might or might not be within its curtilage; their ownership, past and present; and their function, past and present. Not all the land in the same ownership as the principal building will necessarily be included[38]; some land in separate ownership may be included.[39] Not every structure has a curtilage.[40]

(6) Any pre-1948 structure that was in the curtilage of the principal building at the date of listing (or possibly January 1, 1969) will be included in the listing, provided that it is a fixture, and is ancillary to the principal building.

The practical effect of the inclusion in the listing of ancillary structures is limited by the requirement that listed building consent is only needed for works to the "listed building" (to include the building in the list and all the ancillary items) where they affect the special character of the listed building as a whole.[41] And, of course, if an ancillary structure has been erected since 1948, it would now only be included within the listing if it was actually (directly or indirectly) "fixed" to the principal building.

4.6.2 Cases of doubt

In view of the preceding comments, it will be clear that it will not always be easy to determine whether or not a particular building, object or structure is within the scope of the listing.

If in doubt, therefore, the safest course is to ask the local planning authority. It is, after all, the authority that would, in the first instance, decide whether or not to take enforcement action or to institute a prosecution if works are carried out for which listed building consent should (in its view) have been obtained; and one critical element which the authority will take into account is whether the building, object or structure concerned is deemed by the Act to be part of a listed building. Any opinion which the local authority may express will not bind it[42]; and its view may well change if faced subsequently with a specific proposal—and resulting public pressure.

[35] *Debenhams* (per Lord Keith); *Morris*.
[36] See **4.3.4**.
[37] *James*.
[38] *Collins; James*; and *Lowe*.
[39] *Calderdale*.
[40] *Hammerton*.
[41] P(LBCA)A 1990, s.7.
[42] *Western Fish Products v Penwith D.C.* [1981] 2 All E.R. 204.

This problem is considered later in the book,[43] in the context of specific works being actually proposed.

Where no works are currently in prospect, one somewhat artificial device that may be effective is to seek a certificate of lawfulness of proposed use or development,[44] for the carrying out of works which are automatically permitted by the TCP (General Permitted Development) Order 1995 except where they are in the curtilage of a listed building. So, for example, the construction or alteration of a low wall is permitted by the Order, except where it would involve development within the curtilage of a listed building, or development to a wall surrounding a listed building.[45] If the authority refuses to grant such a certificate in respect of a hypothetical proposed low wall around a building, that can only be because it considers that the building is indeed included in the listing.

The advantage of such an approach is not only that it forces the authority to make a decision that binds it, but also that it provides a right of appeal to the Secretary of State[46] if the authority appears to have taken the wrong decision—or if it declines to make any decision at all. It was just such a device that led to the decision of the Secretary of State in relation to the barn at Chipping Campden.[47]

The problem in practice with approaching the local authority for clarification is that it may express the view that consent is required for works, in truth because it wishes that it were; and once such a view has been expressed, it could be tricky to go ahead with the works, and face potential criminal prosecution.

Partly with that in mind, it would, in theory, be possible to seek a declaration in the courts to put the matter beyond doubt. However, in the light of the time and expense involved, such a course of action would probably only be appropriate (if at all) when a specific project is in contemplation.[48] And the courts may in any event be reluctant to become involved in what will be, at least to some extent, a matter of opinion (particularly in the case of fixtures).[49]

4.6.3 Reform

It would be difficult not to share the views expressed in the peroration of the judgment in *ex p. Bellamy*:

"...In conclusion, I would express sympathy for the parties—especially for Camden and for other local planning authorities for whom this is a potentially recurring problem—at being faced many years after the event with the question whether or not a particular structure had to be taken to have been included in the original listing. I would hope that as a general rule it might be possible for the description in the list, whether original or amended, to specify the main ancillary structures which were included together with the principal building."[50]

---

[43] See **12.10**.
[44] Under TCPA 1990, s.192 (inserted by PCA 1991, s.10).
[45] TCP (GPD) Order, Sch.2, Pt 2, Class A: see **12.5.2**.
[46] TCPA 1990, s.195, amended by Planning and Compensation Act 1991, Sch.7.
[47] See **4.5.2**.
[48] See **12.10.4**, and **Form D12** in Appendix D.
[49] See the reservations expressed by Ouseley J in *R. (Hammerton) v London Underground Limited* [2003] J.P.L. 984, at para.154ff.
[50] *R. v Camden LBC, Ex p. Bellamy* [1991] J.P.L. 255 at p.263.

Lord Montagu (the then chairman of English Heritage), in response to similar concerns expressed in the course of the House of Lords debate on the Housing and Planning Bill, commented that:

"...the practice of the Department now and of my officers who advise the Department is to consider individually all the structures and buildings on a site which can be construed as separate buildings and to list those, and only those, which qualify. The new lists therefore will leave little room for doubt whether a building is listed or not".[51]

This is echoed in the comment in Government guidance that:

"...following recent case law, the Secretary of State for National Heritage has attempted to consider individually all the structures and buildings on a site which can be construed as separate buildings, and to list those which qualify for listing."[52]

This applies principally to listings subsequent to Lord Montagu's statement in the Lords.

The passage of time suggests that this optimism is only partially justified. The increasing precision of modern listing descriptions is to be welcomed, since it is important to be able to identify the principal building in each case, so as to be able to determine whether any other structure is ancillary to it.[53] However, even if such a practice were to be universally followed, under the law as it stands the "listed" status would still not extend to ancillary structures outside the curtilage of the principal building, and at least some uncertainty would thus remain.

4.6.4 Proposed further reform

The consultation paper issued by the Government in June 2004 indicated that, in order to make the listing decision more transparent and to remove uncertainty, English Heritage will now issue with every listing (from April 2005) a "summary of importance", to show the owner of the building in question what is included and why it has been listed.[54] There is the perhaps inevitable caveat that it must be understood that such a summary must not be taken as a definitive list of all the features of interest in a building—as impressions of a building's merit change over the years. It is therefore difficult to see how this new "summary" differs significantly from a traditional list description (at least one of the more recent ones).[55]

Perhaps more helpfully, it is suggested that such summaries of importance should be accompanied by a map indicating the extent of designation. This will presumably lessen the scope for the somewhat arid arguments that not infrequently arise as to what is or is not the "curtilage" of a listed building—as evidenced by the extensive case law outlined earlier in this chapter.[56] The old curtilage rule will presumably still apply to all pre-2004 listings, so the effectiveness of this change will only be gradual. However, it is undoubtedly a step in the right direction. In the light of the decision of the Court of Appeal (in *R. v Bovis*

---

[51] *Hansard* (HL) Deb, October 13, 1986, col 623.
[52] At para.3.33 of PPG 15. Para.87 of WO Circ. 61/96 is in similar terms.
[53] As noted above, and emphasised by Lord Hope in *Edinburgh*.
[54] *Review of Heritage Protection: The Way Forward*, DCMS, June 2004. See also **3.3.9**.
[55] See **4.2.2**, **4.6.3**.
[56] See **4.5**.

Construction Ltd[57]) that the extent of a scheduled monument is as shown on the map accompanying the entry in the schedule, the courts may take the same line in relation to the new maps; although it would be greatly preferable for the matter to be placed beyond doubt by legislation.

[57] [1994] Crim L.R. 938, CA; see **6.2.5**.

Chapter 5

Conservation Areas

5.1 Introduction

Some 20 years after the production of the first lists of buildings of special interest, it was recognised that whole areas could also need special protection. They might or might not contain any buildings of particular architectural merit or historical importance; but "public opinion is now overwhelmingly in favour of enhancing the familiar and cherished local scene".[1]

The Civic Amenities Act 1967 therefore introduced the concept of *conservation areas*; the legislation was significantly strengthened in 1972 and 1974.[2] Four areas were designated in England in 1967; around 6,000 in the following 20 years, and 3,000 since 1987; the estimated total at the middle of 2005 was 9,374 conservation areas.[3] The number of buildings in each area varies from a handful to several thousand; there must by now be well over a million buildings within a conservation area—several times as many as are listed in their own right. Every district in England now has at least one conservation area.

There were at the middle of 2005 about 502 conservation areas in Wales,[4] around 650 in Scotland and 59 in Northern Ireland.

Some conservation areas were, prior to 1980, declared as being "of outstanding interest". This accolade was solely for the purpose of determining eligibility for grants under the 1972 Act,[5] and was scrapped by the Local Government, Planning and Land Act 1980[6]; it is therefore now of no further significance.

---

[1] Circ. 8/87, para.5.
[2] See **1.2.5** and **1.2.7**.
[3] An increase of 234 since the previous year's figure of 9,140; *Heritage Counts 2004*, EH, section 3.2.1 and Indicator A2.1 (the latter being a graph showing the rise in the number of areas designated since 1977). The corresponding figures for 2002 and 2003 were 9,027 and 9,080.
[4] A good source of information on conservation areas in Wales is *Conservation Areas in Wales: Management and Urban Design*, produced in 1999 jointly by Civic Trust Wales and Cardiff University, and available at *www.civictrustwales.org/report_site*
[5] Now P(LBCA)A 1990, s.77 (see **9.4.2**).
[6] 1980 Act, Sch.15, para.27.

This chapter considers, first, the process by which conservation areas come to be designated (**5.2**). It then summarises (at **5.3**) the consequences of designation, most of which are explored in more detail throughout the remainder of the book, and considers the specific issue of policies and proposals relating to conservation areas (**5.4**).

This book largely relates to buildings, monuments and the built heritage generally; and the consequences of conservation area designation are thus generally explored in that context. However, one other important consequence relates to the protection afforded to trees in conservation areas. This is explored in full detail elsewhere, along with the law relating to trees generally[7]; but it is summarised in the last section of this chapter (**5.5**). The related topic of tree preservation orders is considered briefly in **Chapter 7**, along with other forms of protection given to the heritage.[8]

5.2 Designation of conservation areas

5.2.1 Eligibility for designation

The statutory definition of a conservation area is "an area of special architectural or historic interest, the character or appearance of which it is desirable to preserve or enhance".[9]

The criteria adopted by different planning authorities, and by a single authority as time goes on, are bound to vary widely. The Act does not specify to whom the preservation or enhancement of the area must be desirable; and opinion is scarcely likely to be unanimous. It is however clear that, in general, it is the local planning authority which is obliged to determine which parts of its area are of special interest. In fulfilling that duty, the weight to be given to any particular factor is for the authority.[10]

Government guidance in England is as follows:

"It is the quality and interest of areas, rather than individual buildings, which should be the prime consideration in identifying conservation areas. There has been increasing recognition in recent years that our experience of a historic area depends on much more than the quality of individual buildings—on the historic layout of property boundaries and thoroughfares; on a particular 'mix' of uses; on characteristic materials; on appropriate scaling and detailing of contemporary buildings; on the quality of advertisements, shop fronts, street furniture and hard and soft surfaces; on vistas along streets and between buildings; and on the extent to which traffic intrudes and limits pedestrian use of spaces between buildings. Conservation area designation should be seen as the means of recognising the importance of all these factors and of ensuring that conservation policy addresses the

---

[7] See Mynors, *The Law of Trees, Forests and Hedgerows* (London, Sweet & Maxwell, 2002).

[8] See **7.6**.

[9] P(LBCA)A 1990, s.69(1). [Scotland: P(LBCA)(S) 1997, s.61(1); NI: P(NI)O 1991, art.50(1).]

[10] *R. v Surrey CC ex p. Oakimber Ltd* (1995) 70 P. & C.R. 649.

quality of townscape in its broadest sense as well as the protection of individual buildings".[11]

The areas that have been designated have in fact varied widely in character. The first ones were mainly town centres (such as Stamford) and architectural set pieces (such as Bath). Others have included villages, model housing layouts (as at Saltaire), open spaces (Princes Park, Liverpool, with its formal approach) and areas of attractive if unremarkable suburbia. Some include groups of quite recent buildings (such as Silver End Estate in Essex). There are also conservation areas that are almost entirely rural and are very large indeed. Some areas have unfortunately been declared for reasons that were perhaps only tenuously connected with their architectural or historical character (such as parts of Kensington High Street, and Hammersmith Broadway). And some of the areas designated most recently seem, unsurprisingly, to be rather less "special" than those designated in the 1970s and 80s.

The courts have also confirmed (in *R. v Canterbury CC, ex p. Halford*[12]) that it is in order to designate an area to include the setting of buildings that form its focus (in that case, fields surrounding the village of Barham, in Kent). And it is permissible to include docks and harbours, provided that they are within the jurisdiction of the relevant planning authority.[13] The few cases in which the designation of conservation areas have been reviewed by the courts are considered below.[14]

There is unfortunately no "immunity certificate" procedure available to guarantee against a property being included within a conservation area.[15]

5.2.2 Authorities empowered to designate conservation areas

A conservation area may be designated in Great Britain by "any local planning authority"[16]—that is, by any of the following:

(1) *in Greater London and the metropolitan counties*: the borough council[17];

(2) *in a national park outside a metropolitan area*: the national park authority[18];

(3) *in the Broads*: the Broads Authority[19];

---

[11] PPG 15, para.4.2. WO Circ. 61/96, para.20 is similar, but by no means identical. Guidance for Scotland (more extensive) is in HS Memorandum, paras 4.1–4.4. There is no equivalent guidance for Northern Ireland (see PPS 6, para.2.18).

[12] [1992] 2 P.L.R. 137.

[13] *R. v Easington DC, ex p. Seaham Harbour Dock Company* [1999] 3 P.L.C.R. 225.

[14] At **5.2.5**.

[15] See **3.4**.

[16] P(LBCA)A 1990, s.69(1). [Scotland: P(LBCA)(S)A 1997, s.61(1) ("any planning authority").]

[17] TCPA 1990, s.1(2).

[18] P(LBCA)A 1990, Sch.4, para.4(1) (b); TCPA 1990, s.4A(2), inserted by the Environment Act 1995, s.67.

[19] P(LBCA)A 1990, Sch.4, paras 4(1)(c), 5.

(4) *elsewhere in England*: either the district council or the county council[20];

(5) *elsewhere in Wales*: the county or county borough council[21];

(6) *in Scotland*: any local authority.[22]

A county council or national park authority may not designate an area without first consulting the relevant district council.[23] A district council is not under a duty to consult the county before making a designation; but:

"... it is clearly desirable that there should be continuing consultation between county and district with a view to formulating joint policies and arrangements for making the best use of staff".[24]

English Heritage may designate conservation areas in Greater London, after consulting the relevant borough council and obtaining the consent of the Secretary of State.[25] Again, such consent is likely to be given only in very exceptional cases.[26] English Heritage did in fact in 1995 exercise its powers to designate a conservation area in Wandsworth, in the face of a threat by the Borough Council to carry out unsuitable works to its own housing.

In practice, therefore, most if not all designations are made by local authorities—albeit often at the instigation of local residents or amenity groups.

The Secretary of State is also empowered to designate conservation areas, and to cancel designations, after consulting the relevant local planning authority (see above).[27] He has stated that his policy is to use his powers only "in exceptional cases"[28]; and they have apparently never in fact been used. The local planning authority (see above) and, in England, English Heritage must be notified of any designation or cancellation made by the Secretary of State.[29]

In Northern Ireland, conservation areas are designated by the Department, after consultation with the Historic Buildings Council, the relevant district council and such other bodies as may be prescribed.[30]

5.2.3 Designation procedure

The first stage in designating a conservation area should normally be the carrying out of a survey, to determine whether the area is of sufficient quality, and to define carefully what is its special architectural or historic character. The latter may prove to be important subsequently, when the authority comes to determine

---

[20] P(LBCA)A 1990, Sch.4, para.1; TCPA 1990, s.1(1).
[21] TCPA 1990, s.1(1B), inserted by the Local Government (Wales) Act 1994, s.18.
[22] P(LBCA)(S)A 1997, s.61(1); TCP(S)A 1997, s.1.
[23] P(LBCA)A 1990, Sch.4, para.4(2), amended by the Environment Act 1995, Sch.20.
[24] Circ. 8/87, para.56.
[25] P(LBCA)A 1990, s.70(1), (2), (4).
[26] PPG 15, para.4.8.
[27] P(LBCA)A 1990, ss 69(3), 70(3). [Scotland: P(LBCA)(S)A 1997, s.61(2).]
[28] in PPG 15, para.4.8. [Scotland: HS Memorandum, para.4.5.]
[29] P(LBCA)A 1990, s.70(6). [Scotland: P(LBCA)(S) 1997, s.62(2).]
[30] P(NI)O 1991, art.50(1), to be amended by Planning Reform (NI) Order 2006.

planning applications, in order to enable it to establish whether (and if so how) proposed development would affect that character.[31] Brief policy advice on this is contained in Government guidance[32]; but there is much other, more useful guidance available.[33]

Once an area has been identified by officers of the authority as being suitable for designation, or an existing area for extension, a report will be submitted to the appropriate committee, and a resolution will be passed to designate the area. The area involved should be specified accurately, since the designation will significantly affect the rights of property owners living within it. In most cases, this is best done by preparing a schedule of all the properties to be included, which should be appended to the resolution.

It is also sensible to include in the committee report a note as to all the relevant consequences of designation (for example, as to the protection of trees[34] or the availability of grants[35]); "it would be a folly and indeed misleading not to indicate what are the possible results."[36] However, it is only the architectural and historic interest of the area that should be taken into account, so those making the decision may have to be careful to exclude from their mind irrelevant considerations.[37]

In particular, where—as not infrequently occurs in the case of more recent designations—there is development pressure in the vicinity of land to be included in (or excluded from) a conservation area, it would be prudent for the authority to have a clear record of the reasons for the proposed inclusion or exclusion, to avoid later accusations of impropriety. Thus, in *Blanefield Property Co. v Salisbury DC*,[38] an early military airfield at Old Sarum was designated as a conservation area, following an English Heritage recommendation to that effect; the designation was then cancelled. The local plan review process was proceeding at the same time; and it was subsequently alleged that the cancellation had not been sufficiently taken into account in the decision to remove the site from a special landscape area (and thus increase the chances of it being developed). In the event, the court was satisfied that there was no connection between the local plan review process and the conservation area designation and cancellation; but such litigation is best avoided.

It will be helpful at an early stage to prepare a map of the proposed area—both for the purposes of public consultation and to inform the members of the authority. In the event of any conflict between the schedule and the map, it is the former which will prevail; and in a densely built-up area, a map of sufficient scale

---

[31] See, for example, *R. (Waveney DC) v Secretary of State* [2003] J.P.L. 1058, and many of the other cases cited in **14.7**.

[32] PPG 15, para.4.4 and 4.5; WO Circ. 61/96, para.21.

[33] In particular, the guides published by English Heritage: *Informed Conservation* (Clark, 2001), and *Understanding Place: Guidance on Conservation Area Appraisals* (2005); also *Conservation Area Management—A Practical Guide*, English Historic Towns Forum (EHTF), 1998.

[34] *R. v Canterbury CC, ex p. Halford* [1992] 2 P.L.R. 137.

[35] *R. v Easington DC, ex p. Seaham Harbour Dock Company* [1999] 3 P.L.C.R. 225.

[36] *ex p. Seaham Harbour Dock Company* [1999] 3 P.L.C.R. 225, *per* Owen J. at p.231E.

[37] *R. v Secretary of State, ex p. Royal Society for the Protection of Birds* [1996] J.P.L. 844.

[38] February 25, 2004, unreported (available on Lawtel) (see **5.2.4**).

to indicate beyond all doubt the boundaries of a large conservation area will have to be of considerable size. A schedule removes any uncertainty as to whether or not a particular property is included—as will be necessary when registering the designation as a local land charge (see below)—and can be transmitted by telephone and more easily photocopied and faxed. But both the map and the schedule need to be prepared with care.

The papers relating to the designation of a conservation area must be available for three clear days before the meeting of the relevant committee or subcommittee.[39] However, if the decision of a subcommittee is defective because insufficient notice was given, or for any other reason, the subsequent ratification of the purported decision by a committee will be sufficient to validate the designation.[40]

It is the date of the appropriate formal resolution by the local authority that is the date of the designation, not the date of any subsequent advertisement.

5.2.4 Publicity

As noted above, the designation of a conservation area should be preceded by some kind of survey; and this may well be accompanied by a public consultation exercise. It may be noted that the one successful challenge to a conservation area designation led to it being quashed by consent, due to "deeply flawed" procedures in relation to consultation—although it is not clear what the flaws were.[41]

However there is no statutory requirement for consultation; and authorities can, and occasionally do, designate or extend areas without any prior notice. They have therefore been reminded that it is important that proposals to designate new areas or to extend existing ones should be made known in the locality.[42] This is not least so that developers and those living in the area may be aware of the existence of the designation, and thus aware of the need to apply for consent for the demolition of unlisted buildings, and to notify the authority of works to trees.

Once an area has been designated or extended, however, the authority must place an advertisement in at least one local newspaper and in the *London Gazette*. This must contain sufficient details to enable the area to be identified (presumably a schedule of properties included; see above), and a note as to the effects of the designation.[43] For a sample notice, see **Form D4** in Appendix D. The authority must also notify the Secretary of State and (in England) English Heritage of the designation.[44]

In contrast to the compulsory notification of owners and occupiers of a building that is listed,[45] no notice has to be given to those living or working in the

---

[39] Local Government Act 1972, s.100B(2), inserted by Local Government (Access to Information) Act 1985.

[40] *R. v Swansea CC ex p. Elitestone Ltd* [1993] 2 P.L.R. 65.

[41] Noted in passing in *Blanefield Property Co Ltd v Salisbury DC*, unreported, February 25, 2004 (available on Lawtel) at para.9.

[42] PPG 15, para.4.7; WO Circ. 61/96, para.25; HS Memorandum, para.4.11.

[43] P(LBCA)A 1990, s.70(7), (8). [Scotland: P(LBCA)(S) 1997, s.62(4); NI: P(NI)O 1991, art.50(4).]

[44] P(LBCA)A 1990, s.70(5); PPG 15, para.4.7. [Scotland: P(LBCA)(S) 1997, s.62(1).]

[45] See **3.3.3**.

area. Parliament must have either assumed that they will spot the announcement in the local press, which is somewhat naive since it is usually in small print in the "statutory notices" section, or else considered that to notify them individually would be desirable but impossibly expensive. This means that there is an even greater likelihood of an owner or developer carrying out works without being aware that consent is required.[46] However, in England and Wales the designation is to be registered as a local land charge, which means that future purchasers of property in the area will be warned of its existence.[47]

Unlike listing, which is a separate category of local land charge, the inclusion of a building in a conservation area is a "planning charge." It is thus to be included in Part 3 of the Register.[48]

5.2.5 Challenging a conservation area designation

As with the listing of buildings, there is no statutory right of appeal against a building being included in a conservation area. There is nothing to stop an individual owner writing to the local authority and asking it to cancel the designation; but the chances of success are likely to be remote.

Alternatively it is, at least in theory, possible to seek judicial review of an authority's decision to designate a conservation area.[49] Again, the chances of success are slim—there are only five reported challenges to conservation area designations, of which three were unsuccessful, and one simply led to the authority re-making the decision.[50] The principles underlying such a challenge have been considered in *R. v Canterbury CC, ex p. Halford*[51] and *R. v Swansea CC ex p. Elitestone Ltd.*[52]

The *Canterbury* case concerned the extension of a conservation area. The owner of some land in the proposed area, which was at the time the subject of an inquiry into the refusal of planning permission, sought judicial review of the designation.

The application was granted, and the designation quashed, but only on the limited ground that the report recommending that the area be extended stressed that this would protect some trees in the proposed area,[53] but failed to point out to the committee that a preservation order already protected them. The first test in considering any designation is thus to consider whether or not the authority

---

[46] See **19.5.2**.

[47] s.69(4).

[48] Local Land Charges Rules 1977, rr 2(2), 3.

[49] For judicial review procedures, see **15.7**.

[50] The unsuccessful challenges were *R. v Swansea CC ex p. Elitestone Ltd* [1992] J.P.L. 1143, upheld at [1993] 2 PLR 65; *R. v Surrey CC ex p. Oakimber Ltd* (1995) 70 P. & C.R. 649; *R. v Easington DC, ex p. Seaham Harbour Dock Company* [1999] 3 PLCR 225. The successful challenge leading to re-making the decision was *R. v Canterbury CC, ex p. Halford* [1992] 2 PLR 137. The fifth challenge (noted in passing in *Blanefield Property Co Ltd v Salisbury DC*, unreported, February 25, 2004 (available on Lawtel) at para.9) led to the designation being quashed by consent; see **5.2.4**. The author would be grateful to anyone who has information about any other challenge to a designation—successful or otherwise.

[51] [1992] 2 P.L.R. 137.

[52] [1992] J.P.L. 1143, upheld at [1993] 2 P.L.R. 65.

[53] See **5.5**.

demonstrably took into account all relevant factors, including the likely effect of designation. Subject to that, the test is merely one of reasonableness; thus, in this case, there had been reports from time to time suggesting that the conservation area should be extended; so there was nothing perverse in the council's decision.

The Court held that it was perfectly proper to seek to conserve the setting of a village, including greens and paddocks, trees and fields; although this was not to say that it was correct to seek to impose a buffer zone. It would be impossible to draw the line firmly between those two concepts; again, the only test was whether in a particular case an authority had been *Wednesbury* unreasonable. More generally, there was no need to look separately at every piece of land in a proposed conservation area to see whether it was of architectural or historic interest; the intention of Parliament must have been that a planning authority would consider the whole of an area as an entity which might give rise to the special interest.

The *Elitestone* case concerned a group of 26 or so chalets, in a secluded woodland setting, originally built as holiday homes but now permanently occupied. The chalets would have been of minimal interest in the eyes of many, but the council was perfectly entitled to take the view that the area as it was and with its own individual buildings and system of tenure was of historic interest, as an example of "plot land development"—"a unique part of the nation's built legacy". The Court was not a court of appeal from such a decision.

This approach was also taken by the court in dismissing the more recent challenge to the designation of virtually the whole of Brooklands race track and airfield as a conservation area.[54]

This echoes, too, the approach adopted by the Queen's Bench Division in *Sweet v Secretary of State*,[55] in considering the validity of an order designating a site of special scientific interest. The judge considered that the inspector recommending the designation was entitled to conclude that, while only part of the land was of national importance, the whole of the land constituted a single environment; the Secretary of State, in accepting that recommendation, was thus entitled to treat the site as a whole and find that it was of national importance.

It follows from this that it is perfectly legitimate to argue (for example, at a planning inquiry) that, while a conservation area as a whole is of special interest, not all parts of it are of equal value.

5.2.6 Review of conservation areas

Every local planning authority is under a continuing duty to consider whether it should designate new conservation areas, or extend existing ones—as is English Heritage in Greater London.[56] In *R. v Canterbury CC ex p. Halford*,[57] for example, the council was quite properly carrying out a thorough survey of its

---

[54] *R. v Surrey CC ex p. Oakimber Ltd* (1995) 70 P. & C.R. 649.

[55] [1989] 2 P.L.R. 14.

[56] P(LBCA)A 1990, s.69(2), 70(1). There is no corresponding requirement in Scotland or Northern Ireland; but the Secretary of State has urged authorities to keep boundaries under review anyway (HS Memorandum, para.4.14).

[57] [1992] 2 P.L.R. 137 (see **5.2.5**).

area—albeit over a prolonged period. It is possible, although rare, for a past designation to be cancelled[58]—18 were cancelled in 1990, and 19 in 1991 (the only two years for which figures are available).

Authorities in England were urged to indicate their strategy for designating areas at the time they prepare local plans and unitary development plans, as this helps to give publicity to any proposals that may emerge.[59] A Government proposal (in 1989) that this should be the *only* means of designation was not pursued. However, there is much to be said in favour of designating conservation areas at the same time as preparing local development documents (the successors to local plans and UDPs, under the new regime introduced by the Planning and Compulsory Purchase Act 2004[60]), as it enables conservation policies to be seen in the context of the more general land use planning process; it also enables interested parties other than the planning authority to put forward suggestions.

More generally, PPG 15 draws attention to the duty to review areas and designate further ones, and rightly advises as follows:

"Authorities should bear in mind that it is important that conservation areas are seen to justify their status and that the concept is not devalued by the designation of areas lacking any special interest."[61]

A total of over 2,000 conservation areas have now been amended, largely but not exclusively by way of extension.

Where appropriate, conservation area may be varied or cancelled as a result of such reviews, using the same procedures as those that applied to their initial designation.[62]

5.2.7 Where to find information

Information as to whether a particular property is within a conservation area, or is likely to be included within one, can be found out from the planning department of the appropriate district or borough council, county council, or national park authority.[63] There will usually be a "conservation officer" who will be able to advise on the specific implications of any particular existing or proposed designation.

It should be borne in mind that the precise boundaries of areas are altered from time to time, and new areas designated, so that it is important to ensure that any information is right up to date.

---

[58] s.70(5), (6), (8).
[59] In PPG 15, para.2.9.
[60] See **5.4, 14.3**.
[61] At para.4.3.
[62] P(LBCA)A 1990, s.70(5). [Scotland: P(LBCA)(S) 1997, s.62; NI: P(NI)O 1991, art.50(2),(3).]
[63] P(LBCA)(S)A 1997, s.62(5). There is apparently no statutory requirement in England or Wales, presumably because of the requirement to register designation as a local land charge; but it is good practice.

5.3 The consequences of conservation area designation

5.3.1 General consequences

In the 40 years or so since the first conservation areas were designated, there has been a slow but steady increase in the number of specific statutory provisions aimed at assisting in their preservation and enhancement. The principal effects of the designation of a conservation area are explored in more detail in the remainder of the book, but may be summarised as follows:

(1) the local planning authority is under a general duty to ensure the preservation and enhancement of conservation areas (see below), and a particular duty to prepare proposals to that end[64];

(2) notice must be given to the local authority before works are carried out to any tree in the area[65];

(3) conservation area consent is required for the demolition of any unlisted building in the area[66]; and the local authority or the Secretary of State may take enforcement action or institute a criminal prosecution if consent is not obtained[67];

(4) the details as to the limits of what works may be carried out without planning permission are somewhat different[68]; and

(5) extra publicity is given to planning applications affecting conservation areas[69]; and the planning authority is to take into account the desirability of preserving and enhancing the character of the area when determining such applications.[70]

Other consequences, less significant in practice, are as follows:

(6) the making of art.4 directions, limiting permitted development rights, is more straightforward[71];

(7) limited financial assistance may be available for the upkeep of a building in the area[72];

(8) the local authority or the Secretary of State may be able to take steps to ensure that a building in a conservation area is kept in good repair[73];

---

[64] See **5.4**.
[65] See **5.5**.
[66] See **12.6**
[67] See **Chapters 18 and 19**.
[68] See **12.7**.
[69] See **13.6**.
[70] See **5.3.2** and **Chapter 14**.
[71] See **7.4**.
[72] See **Chapter 9**.
[73] See **Chapter 10**.

(9) the display of advertisements may be somewhat more restricted than elsewhere[74].

Further relevant duties are contained in other legislation, touched upon later in the book,[75] including the Housing Act 1985, the Electricity Act 1989, the Water Industry Act 1991, the Land Drainage Acts 1991 and 1994, and the Environment Act 1995. These are expressed in general terms, and do not specifically refer to conservation areas, but the bodies to which the Acts relate will do well to be aware of conservation area designations.

In addition, it may be noted that land within a conservation area may not be included within a simplified planning zone.[76] Where land that has been included in a simplified planning zone is subsequently included in a conservation area, however, that does not take it out of the zone.[77]

5.3.2 *The statutory duty*

The fundamentally important statutory provision is now contained in s.72(1) of the Listed Buildings Act, which states that the basic conservation area duty is as follows:

"In the exercise, with respect to any buildings or other land in a conservation area, of any functions under or by virtue of any of the provisions mentioned in subsection (2), special attention shall be paid to the desirability of preserving or enhancing the character or appearance of that area."[78]

Section 64(1) of the Scottish Listed Buildings Act is in identical terms.

The provisions referred to are:

(1) the planning Acts (or the Scottish planning Acts);

(2) Part I of the Historic Buildings and Ancient Monuments Act 1953; and

(3) in England and Wales, ss 70 and 73 of the Leasehold Reform, Housing and Urban Development Act 1993 (estate management schemes).

The main thrust of the statutory conservation area duty relates to the exercise of functions under the planning Acts—whether by planning authorities, the Secretary of State, inspectors or anyone else. Of the four Acts, the most significant are the Town and Country Planning Act 1990 and the Planning (Listed Buildings and Conservation Areas) Act 1990.[79]

In relation to England and Wales, the most relevant of the many and various powers under or by virtue of Planning Act include the following:

(1) the preparation of development plans under Pt II of the Act;

---

[74] See **12.10**.
[75] See **8.6**.
[76] TCPA 1990, s.87(1).
[77] s.87(2).
[78] P(LBCA)A 1990, s.72(1), as amended by the Leasehold Reform, Housing and Urban Development Act 1993, Sch.21, para.30.
[79] For details of the four Acts, see 1.2.10. In Scotland, there are corresponding Acts of 1997; in Northern Ireland, they are all subsumed into the P(NI)O 1991.

(2) the control of development under Pt III;

(3) the enforcement of that control under Pt VII;

(4) the controls under Pt VIII relating to trees,[80] advertisements[81] and property in need of maintenance; and

(5) the exercise of highways powers under Pt X.

The most relevant of the powers and duties under the Listed Buildings Act include the following:

(1) the control of works to listed buildings (under ss 7–26);

(2) the enforcement of that control (under ss 38–46);

(3) the giving of grants for the repair and maintenance of buildings (under ss 57, 58);

(4) the preparation of proposals under s.71;

(5) the control of demolition (under ss 74, 75); and

(6) the carrying out of urgent works to preserve unoccupied buildings (s.76).

There are equivalent provisions to all of these in the Scottish Planning Act and Listed Buildings Act.

The most notable example of the use of those powers is in the determination of planning applications. The precise extent and scope of the duty under s.72 has thus in recent years been the subject of much litigation in that context; see in particular the series of cases from *Steinberg v Secretary of State*[82] to *South Lakeland DC v Secretary of State*.[83] That litigation is considered in detail in a later chapter[84]; but the conclusion is clear—the duty is an important one, to which authorities must devote careful attention.

The other powers referred to above are considered elsewhere in this book.[85]

The 1953 Act authorises the giving of grants or loans,[86] and will only be of limited relevance to conservation areas. The duty as it relates to the 1993 Act is considered below.[87]

Article 50(1) of the Northern Ireland Order is in substance the same as the English section 72(1), save that all of the other statutory provisions referred to are in the Order itself (including historic buildings grants, under Pt X).

Helpful general advice for local authorities (and all involved with the management of and development in conservation areas) is to be found in policy

[80] *Sherwood and Sherwood v Secretary of State* [1996] J.P.L. 925; see **5.5, 7.6**.
[81] *R. (Clear Channel UK Ltd) v Secretary of State* [2005] J.P.L. 704; see **12.9**.
[82] [1989] 2 P.L.R.9.
[83] [1992] 2 W.L.R. 204.
[84] See **14.7**.
[85] See **5.3.1** above.
[86] See **9.4**.
[87] See **5.3.5** and **5.3.6**.

guidance from central government[88]; also in two English Heritage publications, produced in August 2005: *Guidance on the Management of Conservation Areas*, and *Guidance on Conservation Area Appraisals*; both are available on the English Heritage website.

5.3.3 Conservation area advisory committees

Planning authorities have also been asked to consider setting up conservation area advisory committees, consisting primarily of people who are not members of the authority. The composition of such committees will vary, depending on the locality; advice is given in PPG 15.[89] It may be appropriate to set up a committee for each conservation area, possibly meeting locally; or else one covering the whole or part of an authority's area.

Such committees frequently have a strong membership, comprising experienced and respected local practitioners, when first set up. In some areas, it has proved possible to retain this high level of commitment. In others, however, the initial enthusiasm has waned somewhat. This in part reflects the general acceptance of the desirability of conservation, leading to lack of interest or complacency. The committed membership of amenity groups, who often provide the membership for advisory committees, has similarly declined in such areas in recent years. And conservation area designation may be perceived by local authorities to be politically undesirable, since it is held to be partially responsible for house prices rising faster (or falling more slowly). Such councils also feel that conservation deflects resources from other tasks regarded as more important, such as providing homes and jobs. Here advisory committees, where they exist, exercise only marginal influence; and any representations by amenity groups are often counterproductive.

The role of such a committee is usually to advise on applications for planning permission, listed building consent and conservation area consent which affect the conservation area(s) in question, to comment on other issues that may affect the area (such as traffic management schemes), and to help formulate positive proposals for its enhancement. But the High Court has recently emphasised (in *Costas Georgiou v Enfield LBC*[90]) that caution needs to be exercised by advisory committees when considering applications for planning permission and other consents—and, by extension, preliminary proposals for schemes that subsequently go forward as formal applications.

Richards J. pointed out that the membership of the conservation area group (CAG) in that case overlapped with that of the planning committee; that, although the remit of the CAG was to consider only the conservation implications of the proposals in question, its conclusion was expressed simply as unqualified support; and that, when the matter came to the planning committee charged with determining the applications, nothing was said about the limited function of the CAG or about the need for those with dual membership to put on one side the

---

[88] PPG 15, Section 4; WO Circ. 61/96, Part 2; HS Memorandum, Ch.4; and NI PPS 6, Ch.7.

[89] PPG 15, para.4.13 (WO Circ. 61/96, para.28).

[90] [2005] J.P.L. 62.

support expressed in the CAG and to examine all the relevant planning issues before reaching a decision. He accordingly concluded:

"In those circumstances, I take the view, though not without a degree of hesitation, that a fair-minded and informed observer would conclude that there was a real possibility of bias, in the sense of the decisions being approached with closed minds, and without impartial consideration of all the planning issues, as a result of the support expressed by the CAG being carried over into support for the applications in the context of the planning committee's decisions."[91]

This is a salutary warning not just to conservation area committees but to all those who make representations, to remember that their remit is a limited one. They are not there to "decide" on applications, but simply to advise on their conservation or design implications; and those who are on both the conservation area committee and the main committee must re-consider each application afresh when it comes up for formal determination by the latter, taking into account but not slavishly following the recommendation of the conservation area committee.

However, the above reflections should not lead to an abandonment of conservation area committees, which can perform a valuable role in giving proposal a level of scrutiny which is not possible to a planning committee with limited time.

5.3.4 Local authority development in conservation areas

One situation in which a planning authority needs to be particularly careful is when it is itself carrying out development in a conservation area. The precise scope of the duty that is laid upon it in such a case came under scrutiny in the High Court, in *R. v Lambeth LBC, ex p. Sharp*.[92] The Borough Council wished to construct a stadium in part of Brockwell Park in south-east London, which was in a conservation area. It used the procedure under the Town and Country Planning General Regulations 1976, whereby it could grant itself deemed permission, and as part of that procedure erected one site notice. It also held a well-attended public meeting, at which the effect on the conservation area of the proposed development was fully discussed, but it transpired that when the initial decision had been made by the relevant council officer to seek deemed permission, he had not taken into account the fact that Brockwell Park had by then been designated as a conservation area. He had therefore failed to take into account the effect of the proposal on the conservation area, as the council was required to do by the 1971 Act.

The way the council took the decision, including the meeting and the representations received subsequently, indicated, when viewed as a whole, that they were fully aware of the conservation issues. But it was held that the initial failure to consider the council's duty under what is now s.72 meant that the notice to seek deemed permission was bad, and that everything that followed was bad, and the deemed planning permission was therefore quashed. This decision was upheld in the Court of Appeal,[93] although the issue of the council's general duty was not raised there.

---

[91] [2005] J.P.L. 62. at para.33.
[92] [1986] J.P.L. 201.
[93] Reported at [1987] J.P.L. 440.

Those officers and members of a local authority who are directly and regularly involved in the planning process should be aware of the significance of conservation area designation, and should not cause the authority to be caught out in this way. The precise problem that arose in that case would not arise now, since the successor to the 1976 Regulations do not contain provisions corresponding to those that led to the problem[94]; the importance of this decision in the present context therefore lies in its implications for those elsewhere within the authority, in departments such as engineers, housing, recreation, and so on. Thus, in this case,

"it was said that the inference to be drawn from the sequence of events was that all [the officer] did was to carry out the policy that the amenity services committee was set on ... It was not, however, possible to separate the functions of the borough council [in this way]."[95]

The existence of conservation areas, and the implication of designation, therefore needs to be brought to the attention of any officers and members of a local authority who are responsible for carrying out activities that require deemed planning permission.

5.3.5 Leasehold enfranchisement in conservation areas

Many of the great residential estates of the eighteenth and nineteenth centuries were constructed by landlords who kept control of their subsequent maintenance and development through the imposition of covenants—both negative and positive—in the leases. The matters over which control could thus be exercised by the landlord (so as, for example, to ensure regular, uniform painting of terraces) far exceeded those which could be controlled by a mere planning authority. This ensured that large areas of central London (such as Belgravia) and other cities (such as the Canning area of Liverpool) retained their original, broadly homogenous appearance.

However, there has been over the years a gradual extension of leasehold enfranchisement—that is, the right of tenants to require the sale to them of the freehold of their property—under a series of statutes from the Leasehold Reform Act 1967 to the Leasehold Reform, Housing and Urban Development Act 1993. The scope for the exercise of control by landlords has thus diminished, with a correspondingly increased risk of damage to the appearance of previously uniform estates. This risk has to some extent been diminished by the introduction of estate management schemes; see now s.69 of the 1993 Act. These enable landlords:

(1)   to retain control over the appearance of the properties of which they once owned the freehold;

(2)   to inspect them, and to carry out necessary repairs and renewals; and

(3)   to require the occupiers of the properties to maintain them.

An application for such a scheme must be made to a leasehold valuation tribunal by the landlord, normally made within two years of the coming into force of

---

[94]   See **13.10.5**.
[95]   [1986] J.P.L. 201 at 204 *per* Croom-Johnson L.J.

s.70 of the 1993 Act—that is, on or before October 30, 1995. It is, however, possible for an application to be made later, but only with the consent of the Secretary of State.[96] In all cases, the tribunal must consider the past development and present character of the area and any relevant architectural and historical considerations[97]—and the Secretary of State must consider those matters when considering whether to approve the making of a late application.[98] Additionally, where a proposed scheme is for an area within a conservation area, an opportunity must be given for comment to be made by the local planning authority and (in England) English Heritage.[99]

Where the landlord does not make an application under s.70 or s.72 to set up a scheme, the planning authority and English Heritage may do so, but only during the period of six months starting with the end of the relevant period during which the landlord could have done so. This too applies only in the case of a conservation area.

Finally, to avoid any loss of estate management control in particularly sensitive cases, rights of leasehold enfranchisement do not apply in three specific situations, as follows:

(1)   property which has been accepted by the Inland Revenue as being of outstanding interest in connection with inheritance tax relief[1];

(2)   property owned by the National Trust[2]; and

(3)   property within the precinct of a Church of England cathedral, within the meaning of the Care of Cathedrals Measure 1990.[3]

5.4 Policies and proposals

5.4.1 The local development framework

It has already been noted that planning authorities in England should consider the possibility of designating or extending conservation areas at the time when they prepare local development documents (LDDs) under Pt 2 of the Planning and Compulsory Purchase Act 2004.[4]

More importantly, authorities should include appropriate policies within LDDs, to clarify their general approach with regard to existing as well as future conservation areas:

---

[96]   1993 Act, s.72.
[97]   s.70(3).
[98]   s.72(3).
[99]   s.70(5); and see PPG 15, para.4.30.
[1]   Leasehold Reform Act 1967, s.32A, inserted by 1993 Act, s.68 (see **9.9.2**).
[2]   1993 Act, s.95; see **7.10**.
[3]   1993 Act, s.96; see **16.8.1**.
[4]   See **5.2.6** above. For Wales, Scotland and Northern Ireland, see **5.4.4**.

"the local development documents must (taken as a whole) set out the authority's policies (however expressed) relating to the development and use of land in their area".[5]

Issues covered could thus include:

(1) the promotion of suitable development (including pedestrian schemes or the creation of open space) to be carried out by the authority itself or by other agencies;

(2) the encouragement of high standards of design in new development and the alteration of existing buildings;

(3) the encouragement of suitable new uses for neglected historic buildings;

(4) the seeking of planning obligations to bring about improvements;

(5) the control of potentially unsuitable development (either in a particular area, or in all areas);

(6) the enhancement of the appearance of the area through measures to divert parking and through traffic elsewhere; and

(7) appropriate policies in respect of trees and advertisements.

The key principle is thus s.38(6) of the 2004 Act, which provides that:

"If regard is to be had to the development plan for the purpose of any determination to be made under the planning Acts, the determination must be made in accordance with the plan unless material considerations indicate otherwise."[6]

That principle applies in particular to the determination by local planning authorities (and the Secretary of State) of applications for planning permission, and to planning applications affecting conservation areas and listed buildings just as much as to any others.

In addition, although s.38 does not apply directly to the determination of applications for conservation area consent, since there is no explicit duty to take into account the development plan, such applications are very often associated with applications for planning permission. If, therefore, an authority wishes to resist inappropriate new development in a conservation area, and to counter the oft-repeated argument that there is a presumption in favour of permission being granted, it is vital to have available a well-written set of conservation policies in an adopted local plan, not just an attractive but informal series of guidelines.[7] And see below on the need to justify carefully a requirement that a particular conservation area must be enhanced, and not simply preserved.[8]

On the other hand, not all development is unsuitable in every conservation area; and not every existing building must be kept forever. The duty of an authority is after all to enhance, as well as to preserve, the character of its con-

---

[5] Planning and Compulsory Purchase Act 2004, s.17; local planning authorities for this purpose are district and borough councils, unitary authorities, national park authorities and the Broads Authority (see s.37).

[6] This is of course the successor to s.54A of the 1990 Act.

[7] See PPG 15, para.2.4; WO Circ. 61/96, para.4.

[8] See **14.7.5**.

servation areas.[9] It follows that positive policies, encouraging neighbourliness and good design, may be in some cases just as important as negative policies restricting almost all new development.

It is likely that the Secretary of State will reject policies in a local development document which are too detailed—so that policies in the draft Unitary Development Plan for a London borough requiring that the paving, kerbstones and even coal-hole covers in a particular conservation area must be kept intact were rejected as being "prescriptive, onerous and restrictive".[10] On the other hand, detailed policies for a conservation area may be appropriate when it is subject to particular development pressure. Authorities should therefore contact the regional office of the Department when considering the level of detail of conservation policies to be included in LDDs.

It is also important to bear in mind that other policies in the development plan, which were not designed to be directly relevant to conservation, may prove to be critical. Thus in *Bath Society v Secretary of State*,[11] the inspector considering the draft local plan recommended that it should be amended so as to include a policy not to permit any building on a particular site in a conservation area. The inspector, at the subsequent appeal relating to a proposal to build on the site, failed to take into account that recommendation; and this was sufficient to result in his decision being overturned[12]—quite apart from his failure to carry out his duty under s.72 of the Listed Buildings Act.[13]

5.4.2 The local development scheme and the development plan documents

The proposed LDDs for each planning authority's area must be specified in the local development scheme, along with such other documents as the authority thinks appropriate.[14] A scheme will specify which LDDs are to be development plan documents (DPDs)—that is, those which are to go, or have been, through the full scrutiny process, comprising community involvement, consultation and independent examination by an inspector. It is only DPDs that are accorded the full status of being part of the development plan for the purposes of s.38 of the 2004.[15]

The details of the new system are provided by the Town and Country Planning (Local Development) (England) Regulations 2004; guidance is available in PPS 12, *Local Development Frameworks*.[16] PPS 12 explains that the local development framework should include the following development plan documents:

---

[9] P(LBCA)A 1990, s.72.
[10] *R. v Secretary of State, ex p. Islington LBC* [1995] J.P.L. 121.
[11] [1991] 1 W.L.R. 1303.
[12] See p.1313D.
[13] See **14.7.3** for further discussion of this case.
[14] Schemes should have been prepared for all areas within six months of the coming into force of Pt 2 of the Act—that is, by March 28, 2005.
[15] See **5.4.1**.
[16] Available at *www.odpm.gov.uk*, along with *Creating Local Development Frameworks: A companion guide to PPS12*, published by the ODPM in 2004.

- the core strategy;

- site-specific allocations of land; and

- area action plans (where needed).[17]

The core strategy will normally be the first DPD to be produced, and will set out the authority's spatial vision and strategic objectives for its area. In other words, it will contain the broad policies and the key land-use allocations, but not the more or less comprehensive suite of platitudinous development policies found in so many old-style local plans (not least in relation to conservation and design):

"Local planning authorities should avoid producing a compendium of use-related development control policies which can be repetitive and quickly become out of date. The focus, instead, should be on topic-related policies such as protecting residential amenity; protecting landscape and natural resources; nature conservation; addressing accessibility; highway and transport issues; protecting vitality and viability; and addressing visual impact etc."[18]

It will be note that there is no mention here of the historic environment.

Area action plans should be used to provide the planning framework for areas where significant change or conservation is needed—with the focus clearly on implementation: criteria may be set in the core strategy for identifying locations and priorities for preparing area action plans. They should, amongst other things, protect areas particularly sensitive to change, and resolve conflicting objectives in areas subject to development pressures. But the focus is on short-term action, normally over three years, rather than on inactive preservation. Whilst, therefore, some conservation areas will no doubt be the subject of, or included in, area action plans, the emphasis will be on regeneration; any conservation benefit will be an added bonus.

An adopted proposals map will also be needed, to illustrate the spatial extent of policies, with inset maps as necessary. That map will also identify areas of protection, including conservation areas. The inset maps may be used to show policies for particular parts of an authority's area—such as those covered by area action plans.

In all of this, it may be observed that the emphasis is definitely, and probably rightly, on planning for those areas (and topics) which require intervention, rather than attempting to provide policies for those large tracts of land, including many conservation areas, where no particular action is required.

The structure and local plans now in existence for most if not all areas of England will cease to have any status three years after the start of the new system (that is, by September 2007), unless—as seems likely to occur—the Secretary of State prolongs their life in particular cases. This emphasises the need for authorities to ensure that new-style local development documents are put in place rapidly; and for those who feel so inclined to ensure that they include suitable policies relating to the historic environment and, in particular, an over-arching policy in the core strategy to form the basis for related supplementary planning documents and area action plans.

---

[17] PPS 12, s.2.
[18] PPS 12, para.2.29.

5.4.3 Supplementary planning documents

The problem of overly detailed policies being included in LDDs has already been noted. One possible solution is to include them instead in non-statutory, supplementary guidance.

Thus the new policy-making framework introduced by the 2004 Act envisaged the preparation of other planning documents—supplementary planning documents (SPDs)—that are within the same policy framework, but not necessarily the subject of an independent examination. Such documents are part of the planning framework for the area, although they do not form part of the statutory development plan, and thus not attracting the priority given by s.38 to development plan policies in the determination of planning applications.

SPDs may be particularly relevant to conservation areas. Guidance in PPS 12 is as follows:

"Supplementary planning documents may cover a range of issues, both thematic and site-specific, which may expand policy or provide further detail to policies in a development plan document. They must not, however, be used to allocate land. Supplementary planning documents may take the form of design guides, area development briefs, master plan or issue-based documents which supplement policies in a development plan document."[19]

This emphasises that they must be tied back to a relevant policy in a development plan document. They must also be produced with community involvement and supported by a sustainability appraisal report.

Such an SPD could be used to set out an authority's generic policies for its conservation areas; but it is very different in concept to character appraisals and management proposals prepared under s.71 of the Listed Buildings Act.[20] One approach might be for an authority to propose a single SPD covering all of the conservation areas in its area, which could point to proposals for individual conservation areas prepared under s.71.

5.4.4 Wales, Scotland and Northern Ireland

The arrangements for Wales are somewhat different. There is not a local development framework for each local authority area but, instead, there will be local development plans (LDPs). A Welsh Assembly Guidance Note issued in revised form in November 2004 provided initial advice; more detailed guidance will no doubt be issued when Pt 6 of the Act is brought into force later in 2005. The principles are, not surprisingly, similar to those applying to the LDDs in England. In particular, the Assembly Government encourages authorities to produce shorter plans, not overly burdened by detailed development control policies.

But there can be more detailed area policies:

"Where there are proposals for significant change in the use or development of land or conservation of one or more areas, LDPs should contain more detailed policies. These should provide the context for that area as a whole. Detailed design guidance and masterplanning should not be included in the development plan but should be covered in

---

[19] PPS 12, para.2.43; see also paras 4.39–4.44.
[20] See **5.4.5**.

supplementary planning guidance (SPG), such as development briefs, which can be a material consideration in deciding planning applications."[21]

The new arrangements described above do not apply in Scotland; separate legislation, not along precisely the same lines, was introduced into the Scottish Parliament at the end of 2005.[22] In the meanwhile, the old development plan system remains north of the border. Northern Ireland also has different arrangements, due to its single-tier planning system.

However, in both Scotland and Northern Ireland, the development plan has primacy, just as in England and Wales.[23]

5.4.5 Conservation area proposals

In addition to the development plan, authorities in Great Britain are under a specific duty (under s.71 of the Listed Buildings Act[24]) from time to time to "formulate and publish proposals for the preservation and enhancement of any parts of their area which are conservation areas". No timing is laid down; nor is there in the Act any detailed requirement as to the form or content of such proposals.

Proposals under s.71 must be submitted to a public meeting locally, theoretically within the actual conservation area itself.[25] Usually of more value will be the involvement of local residents, professionals and amenity groups. It may be useful for the authority to form a joint working party with such groups—to meet both before the proposals are formally prepared, to discuss ideas, and afterwards, to ensure that they are implemented. Wider publicity for the authority's policies for a conservation area is also, sensibly, advocated in PPG 15.[26]

Such proposals are outside the local development framework, as they would not be tied back to a policy in a development plan document; although it may be possible to link them back to a supplementary planning document.[27] However, it may be noted that the ODPM has recently included a new three-part Best Value Performance Indicator, under the Local Government Act 1999, relating to conservation areas:

- the total number of conservation areas in an authority's area;

- the percentage of conservation areas in its area with an up-to-date character appraisal; and

---

[21] Draft Guidance, 2004, para.28
[22] See Planning etc. (Scotland) Bill.
[23] Scotland: TCP(S)A 1997, s.25. NI: P(NI)O 1991, art.4(2A), inserted by Planning (Amendment) (NI) Order 2003, art.30—although the new provision has yet to be brought into force.
[24] Scotland: P(LBCA)(S)A 1997, s.63.
[25] s.71(2).
[26] PPG 15, para.4.12 (WO Circ. 61/96, para.27).
[27] See **5.4.3**.

- the percentage with published management proposals.[28]

The "management proposals" there referred to are those prepared under s.71, not the formal development plan documents or supplementary planning documents.

Conservation area character appraisals and management proposals, prepared under s.71, might cover in more detail the same topics as were mentioned in connection with development plans, as well as other more specific items. Thus "proposals for preservation" would presumably include policies for the avoidance of harmful change, which may need to be supplemented by proposals for Art.4 directions[29] where the powers available would otherwise be inadequate. They might also include proposals for restoration work assisted by grants or loans, to avoid demolition taking place that would otherwise become necessary.

"Proposals for enhancement" of the conservation area would include proposals for:

(1) the removal of all that presently harms its character (such as unsightly street furniture to be removed or upgraded, and vacant sites to be land-scaped or sensitively developed); and

(2) the promotion of positive improvements (such as design policies for specific sites or new buildings generally, paving schemes, and grant-aiding the replacement of missing architectural details).

County councils, where they still exist, may be able to assist district councils in the preparation of such appraisals and proposals; they may have a larger budget, and relevant facilities such as graphics support; and their officers will often have wider experience of the technical and policy issues involved. In addition, English Heritage has recently issued practical guidance, under the general heading *Understanding Place*.

Local authorities have in practice interpreted the requirement to prepare conservation area proposals in widely differing ways. Some have proposed, and carried out, very imaginative schemes for specific physical enhancements (such as pedestrianising and paving a market square). Others have produced short leaflets setting out detailed policies and proposals for a particular terrace. A few have produced what are virtually (non-statutory) local plans. Most authorities have done little or nothing. The problem is that it is much easier (and cheaper) to "formulate and publish" proposals than to implement them.

In Northern Ireland, although there is a general duty to pay special attention to the desirability of preserving or enhancing the character or appearance of a conservation area once it has been declared,[30] there is no specific duty to prepare proposals to that end. However, the Department has in fact prepared designation documents and design guides for most of the conservation areas in the six counties.

---

[28] BV219. It is perhaps significant that these are included in the list of BVPI indicators under the heading "culture", rather than "planning", presumably because the BVPI was promoted by the DCMS.
[29] See **7.4**.
[30] 1991 Order, art.50(5); see **5.3.1**.

5.4.6 Highways and historic areas

Finally, Chapter 5 of PPG 15, on transport and traffic management, helpfully draws attention to the importance of ensuring that new traffic routes, traffic management schemes, and the treatment of "floorscape" and street furniture, actually enhance rather than detract from the character and appearance of historic areas.[31]

Reference is also made to a number of other useful publications which are relevant to this increasingly significant aspect of conservation area management (updated to 2005 in the version of PPG 15 that appears at **Appendix A** to this book).

5.5 Trees in conservation areas

5.5.1 Notice to be given to the planning authority before carrying out works

It is the character and appearance of conservation areas as a whole that planning authorities are required to preserve and enhance, not just that of the buildings within them. A major element in the character and appearance of many areas is the trees and open spaces within them. The latter, inevitably and rightly, are not suitable for any but very limited "control", although at least some of the most important parks and gardens are now recorded.[32] However, ill-considered works to trees may not only lead to the loss of the trees themselves, but also ruin the appearance of the area surrounding them and spoil the setting of any buildings nearby. Since this is particularly unfortunate in conservation areas, whose appearance is (by definition) both special and worth preserving, local authorities have been given at least some powers to control works to trees there.

Accordingly, under s.211 of the Planning Act, anyone proposing to carry out any works to a tree that is in a conservation area in England or Wales must almost always give written notice of at least six weeks to the local planning authority.[33] The works to be notified under this provision are the "cutting down, topping, lopping, uprooting, wilful damage, or wilful destruction" of any tree.[34] As to the meaning of "destruction", see below[35]; as to the vexed question of what is a tree, the High Court has held that:

"Bushes and scrub nobody, I suppose, would call 'trees', nor indeed shrubs, but it seems to me that anything that ordinarily one would call a tree is a 'tree' within this group of sections [in the Planning Act]."[36]

This requirement, which seems to be relatively unknown by owners of property in conservation areas (or at any rate is not widely observed), was introduced by the Town and Country Amenities Act 1974, the same Act that provided for

---

[31] Advice for Northern Ireland is at Annex A of PPS 6. There is no corresponding advice for Wales or Scotland.

[32] See **7.5**.

[33] TCPA 1990, s.211(1)(3).

[34] ss 211(1), 198(3)(a).

[35] See **5.5.5**.

[36] *Bullock v Secretary of State* (1980) 40 P. & C.R. 246, *per* Phillips J. at p.251.

effective control over demolition in conservation areas.[37] However, it is subject to
a number of exceptions, considered below.

Current Government guidance is given in Chapter 9 of the DETR publication
Tree Preservation Orders: A Guide to the Law and Good Practice.[38]

An identical requirement applies in Scotland and Northern Ireland, under s.172
of the Scottish Planning Act and art.66A of the Northern Ireland Order—the
latter only since November 12, 2003.[39]

5.5.2 Exceptions to the need to notify the local authority

There are, inevitably, a number of exceptions to the general requirement to notify
works to trees in conservation areas, set out in regulations made under s.212 of
the Planning Act[40]; see currently the TCP (Trees) Regulations 1999. By virtue of
reg.10, it is not necessary to notify the authority in any of the following
circumstances:

(1) the cutting down, uprooting, topping or lopping of a tree in any of the
    circumstances specified in s.198(6) of the Act[41];

(2) the cutting down, uprooting, topping or lopping of a tree:

   — where carried out by any one of a variety of statutory undertakers,
     river authorities, airport authorities, etc. (either on their own opera-
     tional land, or to ensure safety of electricity cables and plant, or to
     prevent interference with watercourses and land drains)[42];
   — which is a fruit tree in a commercial orchard cultivated for fruit
     production[43]; or
   — in order to carry out development for which detailed planning per-
     mission has been granted (but not merely in order to carry out per-
     mitted development[44]);

(3) the pruning of any fruit tree[45];

(4) the cutting down of a tree in accordance with a felling licence under the
    Forestry Act 1967, or in accordance with a plan of operations approved by
    the Forestry Commission[46];

---

[37] See **1.2.7**.
[38] The Guide, published in 2000, effectively replaces DoE Circ. 36/78; although that
     Circular, at least in theory, remains in force in Wales (as WO Circ. 64/78). There is also
     very limited guidance in PPG 15, paras 4.38–4.40 (and WO Circ. 61/96, paras 42–44).
     For a comprehensive treatment of this subject, see Mynors, *The Law of Trees, Forests
     and Hedgerows* (Sweet & Maxwell, London, 2002), especially Chapters 19–21.
[39] Planning (Amendment) (NI) Order 2003, art.26(4).
[40] Scotland: TCP(S)A 1997, s.172; NI: P(NI)O 1991, art.66B.
[41] 1999 Regulations, Schedule, art.10(1)(a); see **5.5.3**.
[42] TCP (Trees) Regulations 1999, Schedule (model TPO), art.5(1)(a),(e)–(g), (2), applied
     by reg.10(1)(a).
[43] 1999 Regulations, Schedule, art.5(1)(b), applied by reg.10(1)(a).
[44] 1999 Regulations, Schedule, art.5(1)(d), applied by reg.10(1)(a); for "permitted devel-
     opment", see **12.2.2**.
[45] 1999 Regulations, Schedule, art.5(1)(c), applied (somewhat inelegantly) by reg.10(1)(a).
[46] 1999 Regulations, Schedule, reg.10(1)(b),(c).

(5) the cutting down, uprooting, topping or lopping of a tree by or on behalf of a local authority[47];

(6) the cutting down, uprooting, topping or lopping of a tree with a diameter of not more than 75mm at 1.5m above ground level; or the cutting down or uprooting of a tree with a diameter of not more than 100mm at that height solely to improve the growth of other trees.[48]

Most of these categories are straightforward; they were tightened up in 1999, following a review of the law relating to tree preservation orders generally. There are corresponding exemptions in Scotland and Northern Ireland; the former[49] are slightly different, but are likely soon to be brought into line with those applying in England and Wales; the latter are almost identical.[50]

5.5.3 Exceptions specified in section 198(6) of the Planning Act

The Planning Act specifies in s.198(6) certain circumstances in which consent is not required to carry out works to a tree in England or Wales that is protected by a tree preservation order.[51] An identical provision is in art.65(3) of the Northern Ireland Order; a similar but not identical provision is in s.160(6) of the Scottish Planning Act. This is then carried over into the conservation areas regime, so that there is no need either to notify the planning authority of such works to trees in conservation areas, either.[52]

The works specified are the cutting down, uprooting, topping or lopping of any tree:

(1) in England, Wales and Northern Ireland, because the tree is dead, dying or has become dangerous; in Scotland, because the works are urgently necessary in the interests of safety;

(2) in order to comply with any obligations imposed by any Act of Parliament or subsidiary legislation; or

(3) so far as may be necessary to prevent or abate any nuisance.

---

[47] 1999 Regulations, Schedule, reg.10(1)(d).

[48] 1999 Regulations, Schedule, reg.10(1)(e),(f), (2)(b). In the case of multi-stemmed trees, the size limits will be taken to be exceeded where any of the stems exceeds the relevant limit (see reg.10(2)(a)).

[49] TCP (TPO and Trees in Conservation Areas) (Scotland) Regulations 1975 (SI 1975/1204), amended by SI 1985/1385 and SI 1984, 329.

[50] Planning (Trees) Regulations (NI) 2003 (SR 444), reg.9. There is no exemption for forestry and works by local authorities, and the statutory undertakers exemption is, unsurprisingly, slightly different.

[51] See 20.2.

[52] TCPA 1990, s.212(4); 1999 Regulations, Schedule, art.10(1)(a). [Scotland, 1975 Regulations; NI, 12003 Regulations, reg.9(1)(a).] See **5.5.2**.

As to the first of these, whether a tree is dead or dying or has become dangerous is likely to be a matter of fact and degree.[53] The exemption for "dying" trees would seem to apply where the death of a tree is both certain and imminent.[54]

The meaning of the word "dangerous" was considered by the court in *Smith v Oliver*,[55] which concerned a number of trees in a conservation area growing next to a fence adjoining a footway. Farquharson J. held that, in deciding whether a tree has become dangerous, the justices should look at the state of the tree, its size, its position, and such effect as any of those factors have so far had. It is permissible to look at what might happen in the future: if a tree has already shown signs of disturbing a fence or pavement, or indeed a house itself;

"...it is not necessary to wait for the fence to fall down on some passing pedestrian or the condition of the pavement to be such that somebody falls and is injured, or that the house begins to subside."

But, he said, the danger must be reasonably immediate—not far off, or remote.

That judgment, with respect, needs to be read with caution on this point. A tree cannot be classified as "dangerous" *merely* by virtue of its size and position, but only where its characteristics—perhaps disease, defective form, vehicle impact or whatever—mean that it is likely to fall or shed branches, and where its location is such that a failure would be likely to cause harm. Another way of looking at it is to say that where the condition and location of a tree, taken together, are such that the occupier of the land on which it is growing is under a duty, either at common law or under the Occupiers' Liability Acts, to take action if he is to avoid being sued, then the tree is "dangerous".

The exemption is thus to avoid the occupier being prevented by the planning authority from doing what he is obliged to do under the common law.

As to the third category noted above, many trees will be perceived to be a nuisance in the everyday sense of that word, but what is envisaged here is a nuisance at law—that is, where something that happens on one property prevents the enjoyment of the neighbouring property. It follows that where a tree is a "nuisance" only in the colloquial sense, because it is impeding the enjoyment of the property on which it stands, that cannot be of itself enough to justify not getting consent.[56]

The actual encroachment of a tree on to neighbouring land is regarded as a nuisance rather than a trespass[57]—whether it takes the form of the penetration of roots from one property to another[58] or by the overhanging of branches.[59] But whilst at common law the property owner suffering the nuisance is entitled to the self-help remedy of abatement—by cutting back the branches or roots to the boundary line—it may be that no action would lie in the courts in the absence of

---

[53]   *Smith v Oliver* [1989] 2 P.L.R. 1.

[54]   The Government stated in its 1994 review that this element of the exemption was to be repealed in England and Wales; it does not apply in Scotland anyway.

[55]   [1989] 2 P.L.R. 1.

[56]   *Edgeborough Building Co Ltd v Woking UDC* (1966) 198 E.G. 581.

[57]   *Lemmon v Webb* [1895] A.C. 1, HL.

[58]   *Davey* and *Bunclark v Hertfordshire CC* [1977] 2 E.G.L.R. 114.

[59]   *Lemmon v Webb* [1895] A.C. 1, HL, *Smith v Giddy* [1904] 2 K.B. 448 and *British Road Services Ltd v Slater* [1964] 1 W.L.R. 498.

any damage.[60] The exemption from control under the Planning Act may, therefore, similarly apply only where there is actual damage as opposed to merely an encroachment over a neighbour's air space.

That is, not surprisingly, the interpretation favoured by the Department and by most local authorities, and has been followed in at least one (unreported) Crown Court decision.[61] However, it does fly in the face of the clear wording of the Act; and the better view would seem to be that the exemption relates to any works to prevent or abate any encroachment of a tree onto neighbouring land, regardless of whether any damage is being caused.

As for nuisance caused by trees growing in the highway, see *Paterson v Humberside CC*.[62]

The Court of Appeal (in *R. v Alath Construction Ltd*[63]) has emphasised that it is the duty of the person cutting down a tree without consent to prove that he or she comes within one of the exceptions. In that case, which concerned a beech tree that was felled after the 1987 gales, the owner claimed that it had been dangerous. The court agreed that the person cutting down the tree is in a unique position to know the true condition of it at the time of the act. It is thus important, if subsequent prosecution is to be avoided, that evidence of the tree's condition (photographs, or specialists' reports) is obtained at the time it is felled, and that that evidence is retained.

Where a tree in a conservation area is removed in any of the circumstances specified in s.198(6), it must be replaced by another.[64]

5.5.4 Notification procedure

Notice must be given in writing to the relevant planning authority, specifying the trees concerned and the works proposed.[65] It is also advisable to state the reasons for the works, and whether any replacement planting is proposed. Some authorities issue a standard form for this purpose; others are content for notice to be given by letter. Once notice has been given, the works must not be carried out until either the authority has granted consent or no response has been received after six weeks have elapsed.[66]

In England and Wales, the planning authority for this purpose is in general the district planning authority—that is, in England, the district or borough council[67] or, in Wales, the county or county borough council.[68] In a national park outside a metropolitan county, the national park authority has concurrent powers[69]; but the

---

[60] *per* Kennedy J., obiter, in *Smith v Giddy* at 451.

[61] *Sun Timber Company v Leeds City Council* (1980) Leeds Crown Court (unreported). That decision relies on a misreading of *King v Taylor* [1976] 1 E.G.L.R. 132.

[62] (1996) 12 Const. L.J. 64, QBD.

[63] [1990] 1 W.L.R. 1255.

[64] s.213(1)(b). [Scotland: TCP(S)A 1997, s.174(1)(b); NI: P(NI)O 1991, art.82C(1)(b).] See **5.5.6**.

[65] TCPA 1990, s.211(3)(a). [TCP(S)A 1997, s.172(3)(a); P(NI)O 1991, art.66A(3)(a).]

[66] s.211(3)(b). [TCP(S)A 1997, s.172(3)(b); P(NI)O 1991, art.66A(3)(b).]

[67] TCPA 1990, Sch.1, para.14, s.1(1)(b), (2).

[68] TCPA 1990, s.1B, inserted by the Local Government (Wales) Act 1994, s.18.

[69] ss 4(2), 2(1); s.4A(4), inserted by the Environment Act 1995, s.67.

Broads Authority has sole powers in its area.[70] In Northern Ireland, the notice is to be given to the Department.[71]

The authority is to maintain a register of all notices given to it under this provision.[72]

In considering whether to grant or withhold consent, an authority must pay special attention to the desirability of preserving or enhancing the character of appearance of the conservation area.[73] For the meaning of this formula, see the sequence of cases discussed in connection with building works in conservation areas.[74]

Where consent is granted, there is in theory no provision for any conditions to be attached. In practice, however, there would seem to be no reason why an authority could not achieve the same result by indicating that it was willing to grant unconditional consent if the works were carried out in a particular way, but that otherwise it would impose a tree preservation order on the tree, and refuse consent. Thus, where an authority wishes to refuse consent for the works, or wishes to impose any conditions on a grant of consent, the only (cumbersome) way in which this can be done is for it first to make a tree preservation order, and then refuse consent under that order. There is then a right of appeal against such refusal.[75]

Where no response is received, the works can proceed without further ado. If however, there is then a charge for an offence under s.211, the burden of proof will be on the person who did the act in question, to show that notice was indeed given to the authority. The fact that the six-week period has elapsed does not prevent the authority from making a tree preservation order—although such an order would obviously not be effective to prohibit works carried out between the end of the six-week period and the making of the order.[76] A further notification will be required if the works are to be carried out more than two years after the original notice.[77]

Finally, where a tree in a conservation area is already subject to a tree preservation order, it is necessary to obtain consent under the order for any works proposed, rather than to give notice under s.211.[78] This means that it is not sufficient merely to wait six weeks after notifying the authority of the proposed works; a formal consent will be required before the works can be carried out with impunity.

---

[70] s.5(2), (3).
[71] P(NI)O 1991, art.66A(3)(a).
[72] s.214; Circ. 36/78, Memorandum, para.64.
[73] P(LBCA)A 1990, s.72; *Sherwood v Secretary of State* [1996] J.P.L. 925. [Scotland: P(LBCA)(S)A 1997, s.64; NI: P(NI)O 1991, art.50(5).]
[74] See **14.7**.
[75] See **7.6**.
[76] *R. v North Hertfordshire D.C., ex p. Hyde* [1989] 3 P.L.R. 89.
[77] TCPA 1990, s.211(3)(b) (ii). [Scotland: TCP(S)A 1997, s.172(3)(b)(ii); P(NI)O 1991, art.66A(3)(b)(ii).]
[78] See **7.6.3**.

5.5.5 Unauthorised works

It is an offence under s.211(1) of the Planning Act:

(1) to carry out any works to a tree in a conservation area without giving notice to the authority, unless the works are in one of the exempted categories[79]; or

(2) to carry out any such works where consent has been refused.

Note that none of the exempted categories includes the wilful damage or destruction of any tree. This therefore always remains an offence. The "destruction" of a tree has been held to include the carrying out of any act, such as severing its root system, as a result of which it ceases to have any further use as an amenity; that is, it is no longer worth preserving.[80]

This offence is probably one of strict liability—that is, it would not be a necessary ingredient that the accused was aware that the tree was within a conservation area.[81] In the event of a conviction, however, it would be open to the defence to argue for a reduced sentence—at least where the property has not changed hands since the conservation area was designated—since there is no requirement to notify the owner of a building in a conservation area of its designation (unlike the owner of a building that is listed, or a tree that is subjected to a tree preservation order, each of whom must immediately be informed). This would not be open to a subsequent owner, of course, since the existence of a conservation area is a local land charge.[82]

If the unauthorised works consist of:

(1) the cutting down, uprooting or wilful destruction of a tree; or

(2) the wilful damage, lopping or topping of a tree in such a manner as is likely to destroy it,

the offence is triable either way, and is subject to a fine of up to £20,000 on summary conviction, or an unlimited fine on indictment.[83] Where an offender is convicted, either by the magistrates or in the Crown Court, the court must bear in mind in determining the appropriate fine any financial benefit that has accrued or is likely to accrue as a result of the offence (as with unauthorised works to listed buildings).[84] Thus if the removal of a tree unlocks a development site, the fine should in theory be substantial. In practice, however, possibly even more than with other offences described in this book, any fines imposed are likely to be very small, especially in the magistrates' courts. See **Chapter 19** on sentencing, and on criminal procedure generally.

Where several trees are cut down without the requisite notice having been given, each tree should be the subject of a separate count on the indictment. If

---

[79] Listed in **5.5.2**.
[80] *Barnet LBC v Eastern Electricity Board* [1973] 1 W.L.R. 430.
[81] See **19.3.2**.
[82] See **5.2.4**.
[83] TCPA 1990, ss 210, 211(4), amended by PCA 1991, s.23.
[84] ss 210(3), 211(4), as amended by PCA 1991, s.23.

found guilty in such a case, each count will lead to a separate fine; so the total may in the end be quite substantial (especially when the authority's costs are taken into account).

If the unauthorised works consist of any other topping or lopping of a tree, the offence is triable only summarily, and the maximum penalty on conviction is a fine of up to level 4 on the standard scale.[85] In a case of urgency, a local planning authority may apply to the court for an injunction to restrain an actual or apprehended offence under s.211.[86]

The authority may enter any land to determine whether an offence under s.211 has been committed.[87] If the land is occupied, 24 hours' notice must be given, except in a case of urgency, where a warrant must first be obtained from a justice of the peace.

Precisely the same applies in Scotland[88] and Northern Ireland save that, in the latter, the maximum fine on summary conviction is £30,000.[89]

5.5.6 The requirement to plant a replacement

Where a tree in a conservation area is removed because it is dead, dying or dangerous, or to comply with an Act of Parliament, or to prevent or abate a nuisance,[90] a replacement tree must be planted. The same applies where a tree in a conservation area is removed without notice having first been given to the authority.[91] In such circumstances, a tree "of an appropriate size and species" must normally be planted "at the same place" as the tree that has been removed, as soon as is reasonable.[92] However, this requirement can be dispensed with or varied if the authority is notified and states in writing that it is agreeable.[93]

The appropriateness of the size and species would presumably be determined in the light of all the circumstances after the removal of the previous tree: where, for example, an old oak tree was removed from a small, recently created suburban garden, its replacement should obviously not be another large oak. Similarly, the replacement would in many cases have to be "near" the same place as the old tree, since its remaining roots will often render planting "at" exactly the same place either impossible (without enormous expense) or undesirable, and it would be absurd for the authority to be notified in every such case.

If a new tree is not planted when it is required, the planning authority may serve on the owner of the land concerned at any time within the following four years a notice under s.207, requiring the planting of a tree or trees of a size and species to be specified.[94] Note that the duty to plant passes with the ownership of the land,

---

[85] ss 210(4), 211(4). See **Appendix F**.
[86] s.214A, inserted by PCA 1991, s.23. On injunctions generally, see **18.7**.
[87] s.214B, inserted by PCA 1991.
[88] TCP(S)A 1997, ss 171, 172(4).
[89] P(NI)O 1991, arts 66, 66A(4), as amended and inserted by Planning (Amendment) (NI) Order 2003, art.26.
[90] See **5.5.3**.
[91] See **5.5.5**.
[92] TCPA 1990, s.213(1).
[93] ss 206(2), 213(2).
[94] TCPA 1990, ss 207(1), 213(3).

and can be enforced by the authority accordingly.[95] The authority may enter any land to determine whether a notice should be served.[96]

The notice will take effect on a date specified in it, which must be at least 28 days after it is served on the owner of the land concerned.[97] At any time before it comes into effect, the owner may appeal to the Secretary of State against the notice, on the following grounds:

(a) that the requirement to replant does not apply;

(aa) that the requirement should be dispensed with;

(b) that the size or species specified, or the time within which the planting is to be carried out, is unreasonable;

(c) that the planting is not required in the interests of amenity, or would be contrary to good forestry practice; or

(d) that the location for the planting is unsuitable.[98]

The appeal is to be in writing, including the grounds on which it is based; and either the owner or the planning authority can insist on an inquiry. The notice is of no effect until the appeal is finally determined.[99] The Secretary of State or the inspector can uphold or quash the notice, or can vary it if that can be done without causing injustice to either party.[1]

If the notice is upheld, with or without variations, and the trees are still not planted, the authority can enter the land, do the work itself, and reclaim the cost from the current owner of the land, together with a reasonable sum in respect of its establishment charges.[2] This is recoverable as a simple contract debt. The current owner may in turn recover it from whoever was responsible for the replanting requirement arising in the first place.[3] It seems that it would be possible for the authority to plant only some of the required trees under this provision.[4]

Again, precisely the same applies in Scotland[5] and Northern Ireland[6]; note that the procedures in Northern Ireland were amended in 2003.

---

[95] ss 206(5), 213(3).
[96] ss 214B(1)(c), 214C, inserted by PCA 1991, s.23.
[97] s.208(1), amended by PCA 1991, s.23.
[98] s.207(4), substituted by PCA 1991, s.23.
[99] As to which, see **18.6.1**.
[1] s.208(7), (8), substituted by PCA 1991, s.23.
[2] s.209(1), LGA 1974, s.36.
[3] TCPA 1990, s.209(2).
[4] *Arcam Demolition and Construction Co. Ltd v Worcestershire C.C.* [1964] 1 W.L.R. 661.
[5] TCP(S)A 1997, ss 174, 168–170.
[6] P(NI)O 1991, arts 82–82C.

Chapter 6

Ancient Monuments

6.1 Introduction

The evolution of the legislation protecting the cultural heritage has been outlined earlier in the book.[1] From that account, it will be readily apparent that the initial initiatives in Parliament all related to what would now be thought of as "ancient monuments", as opposed to "historic buildings". Indeed, by 1882 (when the first Ancient Monuments Act was passed), a significant proportion of the buildings now listed were only a few years old—or were yet to be built.

In that first Act, somewhat limited protection was afforded to 69 prehistoric monuments—including some in what is now the Republic of Ireland. Almost exactly a hundred years later, the legislation relating to the protection of ancient monuments was consolidated and amended by the Ancient Monuments and Archaeological Areas Act 1979 (generally referred to in this book simply as "the Ancient Monuments Act"), which replaced the previous "preservation orders" with a new system of "scheduled monuments".[2]

The 1979 Act applies to England, Wales and Scotland. Since it was significantly amended by the National Heritage Act 1983, English Heritage has had most of the functions originally performed by the Secretary of State for the Environment in relation to monuments in England.[3] In Wales and Scotland, responsibility for archaeological matters rests with the Welsh Assembly and the Scottish Ministers, and all their duties are in practice carried out by Cadw and Historic Scotland. Government guidance on archaeology in England and Wales is given in PPG 16, *Archaeology and Planning*, reproduced as **Appendix B,** and WO Circ. 60/96. Policy for Scotland is in Planning Advice Note PAN 42, *Archaeology* and National Planning Policy Guidance note NPPG 5, *Archaeology and Planning*, both published in January 1994 and available on the web.[4]

---

[1] See **1.2.**
[2] See below.
[3] National Heritage Act 1983, Sch.4, paras 25–69
[4] *www.scotland.gov.uk/publications/search*

Similar protection for monuments in Northern Ireland is provided by the Environment and Heritage Service,[5] under the Historic Monuments and Archaeological Objects (Northern Ireland) Order 1995, with policy guidance in PPS 6.

This chapter considers the mechanisms afforded by the 1979 Act and the 1995 Order for the protection of archaeological sites and monuments, in particular the scheduling of ancient monuments of national importance—the scheduling process is described in **6.2;** and the consequences of scheduling in **6.3**.

However, there are many more sites that are of archaeological interest than simply those that have been classified as scheduled monuments. In particular, the assessment of development proposals regularly involves the consideration of archaeological issues. The 1979 Act accordingly provided for the designation of "areas of archaeological importance" (see **6.4**), where special protection is available.

Finally, there is a special regime relating to maritime archaeology, noted briefly at **6.5**, which may come to be of increasing significance in the future.

6.2 Ancient monuments

6.2.1 Definitions

The Ancient Monuments Act and (in Northern Ireland) the 1995 Order define several categories of monuments. First, "monument" itself is defined as follows:

"(a) any building, structure or work, whether above or below the surface of the land, and any cave or excavation,
  (b) any site comprising the remains of any such building, structure, or work or of any cave or excavation, and
  (c) any site comprising, or comprising the remains of, any vehicle, vessel or aircraft or other movable structure or part thereof which neither constitutes nor forms part of any work which is a monument within paragraph (a) above."[6]

This is a very wide definition, although para.(a) specifically excludes an ecclesiastical building in ecclesiastical use[7] and para.(c) excludes a wreck protected by the Protection of Wrecks Act 1973.[8] Nor will a site come within s.61(7)(c) unless the situation of the vehicle, vessel, etc. at that particular location is a matter of public interest. "Remains" in this context includes "any trace or sign of the previous existence of the thing in question".[9]

A "monument" includes any machinery attached to it if it could not be detached without being dismantled[10]—this provides protection for industrial machinery, beam engines, and so forth. References to a monument should also be taken to include its site[11]; and the site of a monument is defined to include, as well

---

[5] Part of the Department of the Environment; see *www.ehsni.gov.uk*
[6] AMAAA 1979, s.61(7). [NI: HMAO(NI)O 1995, art.2(6).]
[7] See **Chapter 16**.
[8] s.61(8). [NI: art.2(7).] As to maritime archaeology generally, see **6.5**.
[9] s.61(13). [NI: art.2(11).] And see the Protection of Military Remains Act 1986.
[10] s.61(7). [NI: art.2(6).]
[11] s.61(10)(a). [NI: art.2(9)(a).]

as the land on which it stands, any adjacent land which (in the opinion of the Secretary of State or English Heritage or a local authority) is essential for its support or preservation.[12]

Secondly, a "scheduled monument" is defined as a monument included by the Secretary of State in the schedule of monuments which he or she is required to compile, under s.1 of the 1979 Act.[13] The schedule was initially to include every monument that had been included, or proposed for inclusion, in the list prepared by him under s.12 of the Ancient Monuments Consolidation Act 1913.[14] He or she may then include any monument which appears to be "of national importance"—a phrase that is nowhere defined, but which is considered below.[15]

A "monument" is explicitly defined to include part of a monument,[16] but a "scheduled monument" is not defined to include part of a scheduled monument. It would seem, therefore, that the problems raised in the context of listed buildings by the decision in *Shimizu (UK) Ltd v Westminster CC*[17] would apply equally to scheduled monuments. That is, the Secretary of State may schedule all or part of a monument, but, once that has been done, it is the whole of the scheduled monument that is to be considered, not any particular part of it.

Thirdly, an "ancient monument" is defined as:

(a) any scheduled monument; and

(b) any other monument which in the opinion of the Secretary of State is of public interest by reason of the historic, architectural, traditional, artistic or archaeological interest attaching to it.[18]

Note that this is not quite the same as the definition of "ancient monument" in the Ancient Monuments Acts 1913 to 1953, which referred to (as well as any monument that was on the list under the 1931 Act or subject to a preservation order) any monument "the preservation of which was of public interest" by reason of its special historic, etc., interest. This means that the classification of a monument as an ancient monument now says nothing about the desirability or otherwise of its preservation. The principal significance of this definition is that the powers of acquisition and guardianship apply to "ancient monuments", and not just to "scheduled monuments".[19]

In Northern Ireland, the phrase "historic monument" has exactly the same meaning and significance as the phrase "ancient monument" in Great Britain.[20]

Finally, the 1979 Act and the 1995 Order further define a "protected monument" as any scheduled monument and any monument under the ownership or

---

[12] s.61(9). [NI: art.2(8).] But see **6.2.5** on the extent of a scheduled monument.
[13] AMAAA 1979, s.1(10); curiously, section 61(1) suggests that a "scheduled monument" is defined in s.1(11)—but there is no s.1(11). [NI: HMAO(NI)O 1995, arts 2(2), 3(2)— the schedule is prepared by the Department.]
[14] See **1.2.2**. [In Northern Ireland, the Historic Monuments Act (Northern Ireland) 1971.]
[15] See **6.2.2**.
[16] s.61(10)(b). [NI: art.2(9)(b).]
[17] [1997] 1 W.L.R. 168, HL, [1996] 3 P.L.R. 89, HL; see **12.6.2**, **12.6.3**.
[18] s.61(12).
[19] AMAAA 1979, ss 10–12. See **11.6**.
[20] HMAO(NI)O 1995, art.2(1).

guardianship of the Secretary of State or English Heritage or a local authority,[21] and a "protected place" as the site of a protected monument or any place within an area of archaeological importance.[22] Both of these terms are used only in connection with the definition of offences relating to archaeological sites.[23]

6.2.2 Scheduled monuments

The Secretary of State is only empowered, not required, by the Act to include in the schedule monuments that appear to be of national importance (compare the *duty* to list buildings of special architectural or historic interest). This gives him or her a broad discretion as to what to include. This is just as well, not least because—given the wide definition of "monument", including any building, structure or work—he would otherwise have to "schedule" most if not all of the buildings that he has "listed". And indeed there has always been some degree of overlap between the two systems, which is probably inevitable.

Some buildings and structures are thus both scheduled under the Ancient Monuments Act and listed under the Listed Buildings Act. These are mainly unoccupied buildings, such as medieval barns and dove-cotes, old bridges, and some urban buildings, such as guildhalls and medieval city walls. In England at least, the Government's intention is that, as the Monuments Protection Programme continues, buildings and monuments will in future be accorded whichever type of protection seems most suitable.[24] The problem of overlapping controls should thus gradually diminish.

The great majority of "monuments", however, have in fact always tended to be archaeological sites and structures. So, for example, of the 594 monuments scheduled during 1997, 29 per cent were barrows, cairns or burial mounds, 22 per cent were stone crosses, 7 per cent were rock or stone carvings, 6 per cent were moated sites, 6 per cent were lead mines, and 5 per cent were Roman remains. Other significant categories of monuments scheduled in the past include camps and settlements, castles and fortifications, deserted villages, disused ecclesiastical buildings, bridges, linear earthworks, and industrial monuments. The Secretary of State is not entitled to schedule any structure occupied as a dwelling (other than by a caretaker).[25]

The non-statutory criteria used by the Secretary of State (and in England by English Heritage, acting on his or her behalf) for assessing the importance of a monument and considering whether scheduling is appropriate were first formulated in 1983. They are currently set out at Annex 4 to PPG 16, and (in identical terms) in Annex 3 to WO Circ. 60/96. They relate to:

(1)   whether it characterises a particular category or period;

(2)   whether the category of monument is regionally or nationally rare;

---

[21]   AMAAA 1979, s.28(3). [NI: HMAO(NI)O 1995, art.30(3).]
[22]   AMAAA 1979, s.42(2). [NI: HMAO(NI)O 1995, art.29(2).]
[23]   See **19.7**.
[24]   See PPG 15, para.6.34, and PPG 16, Annex 3, para.4.
[25]   AMAAA 1979, s.1(4). [NI: HMAO(NI)O 1995, art.3(5).]

(3) the existence of related documentation;

(4) the association of this monument with others;

(5) the extent of its survival and its current condition;

(6) whether it is particularly fragile or vulnerable;

(7) whether it possesses a number of features of interest;

(8) whether there is potential for future discoveries.

Similar, but by no means identical, criteria for Scotland are at para.47 of Planning Advice Note PAN 42.

6.2.3 The discretion not to schedule a monument

Even once the Secretary of State has decided that a monument is "of national importance", he or she does not have to include it in the schedule. Thus, where English Heritage recommended that a semi-submerged Bronze Age timber circle on the Norfolk foreshore was of national importance, but was likely to be destroyed by wave action, the Secretary of State agreed not to schedule it, but to authorise its removal elsewhere for conservation.[26]

The extent of this discretion was also considered by the High Court following a challenge to the decision not to schedule the site of the Rose Theatre in London.[27]

Schiemann J. held that the Secretary of State was entitled to regard as a relevant factor the possibility that compensation might be payable.[28] Moreover, it was open to him to balance the desirability of preserving archaeological remains against the need for redevelopment in central London, and to consider the implications for future co-operation by other landowners; he was thus not obliged to schedule the monument, and then to carry out the balancing exercise when application was made to him for scheduled monument consent. He was also entitled to take the view that in this particular case the monument was as well protected by not being scheduled as by being scheduled. The court accordingly declined to quash the Secretary of State's decision.[29]

6.2.4 The scheduling process

It is the Secretary of State, not a local authority, who has power to include a monument in the schedule—or remove one from it.[30] In England, that power is exercised by the Secretary of State for Culture, Media and Sport, but only after consulting English Heritage; and in practice English Heritage, using either its own staff or consultants acting on its behalf, carries out all the survey work leading to the decision to schedule. In Wales and Scotland, the survey work is carried out by

---

[26] *HBMC v Nolan and others*, Ch D, 6th July 1999, unreported (available on Lawtel).

[27] *R. v Secretary of State, ex p. Rose Theatre Trust* [1990] 1 P.L.R. 39.

[28] See **15.4.3**.

[29] The court also held that, although the Rose Theatre Trust had been formed specifically to fight the decision, it nevertheless had insufficient *locus* (standing) to seek judicial review (see **15.7.2**).

[30] AMAAA 1979, s.1(1)–(3),(5)

Cadw and Historic Scotland, both constitutionally part of central government—or, again, by consultants on their behalf.

Any person duly authorised by the Secretary of State may enter any land to carry out a survey in order to record matters of archaeological or historic interest[31]—this power would obviously be relevant to the scheduling process. The owner of a site or monument is usually consulted before it is added to the schedule, although this is not required by the Act, and may obviously be inappropriate in some cases.[32]

Once a monument has been included in or excluded from the schedule, the Secretary of State (in England) is to inform English Heritage, and to send it a copy of the new or amended entry in the schedule.[33] English Heritage is then to notify the owner and occupier of the monument, and any local authority in whose area it is.[34] In Wales and Scotland, the Secretary of State himself (that is, Cadw or Historic Scotland) informs owners, occupiers and authorities.[35] A local authority for this purpose means any county, county borough, borough or district council,[36] the Broads Authority,[37] and any national park authority.[38] Note that it is a defence to a charge under s.2 (relating to unauthorised works to a scheduled monument) that the accused did not know and had no reason to believe that the monument was scheduled.[39] It is accordingly important that owners and occupiers are informed of the scheduling as soon as possible.

The inclusion of a monument in the schedule in England and Wales is a local land charge.[40]

Current records of scheduled monuments in England are maintained by English Heritage, and by Cadw and Historic Scotland in respect of Wales and Scotland.[41] They produce from time to time a list for each county, and should be contacted to ascertain whether a particular monument is scheduled. Enquiries concerning the county lists in England should be directed to the DCMS.[42] An alternative source of information is the relevant County Sites and Monuments Record in England—where one still exists following local government reorganisation[43]; County Records in Wales are held by the Regional Archaeological Trusts.[44] These records contain information not only on scheduled sites in their area but also on virtually all non-scheduled sites of archaeological interest.

[31] s.26.
[32] See PPG 16, Annex 3, para.2. [Scotland: PAN 42, para.42.]
[33] s.1(6A).
[34] s.1A.
[35] s.1(6).
[36] s.61(1).
[37] s.52A.
[38] Environment Act 1995, Sch.9, para.10.
[39] s.2(8).
[40] s.1(9).
[41] As required respectively by ss 1A and 1(7).
[42] PPG 16, para.2.
[43] Addresses were at Annex 2 to PPG 16; but they are probably somewhat out-of-date (and for that reason not reproduced at **Appendix B** to this book).
[44] Again, for addresses, see Annex 2 to WO Circ. 60/96.

In Northern Ireland, the 1995 Order provides for the preparation by the Department of a schedule of monuments.[45] Further information may be obtained from the Environment and Heritage Service.

6.2.5 The extent of a scheduled monument

The question of how far the listing of a building extends is one that not infrequently arises in practice, and to which there is sometimes not an easy answer. The position is, however, somewhat more straightforward in relation to monuments.

It has already been noted that a "monument" includes its site[46]; and the site of a monument is defined to include, as well as the land on which it stands, any adjacent land which (in the opinion of the Secretary of State or English Heritage or a local authority) is essential for its support or preservation.[47] But it has until relatively recently been far from clear how far this should extend. That may cause a substantial problem where a monument of one period is underneath a building of a later period—or even several.

The Court of Appeal considered this problem in the context of two appeals against convictions for unauthorised works, *R. v Bovis Construction Ltd* (relating to the palace of the governor of Roman Londinium, the remains of which survive beneath Cannon Street Railway Station) and *R. v Jackson* (relating to Mettingham Castle in Suffolk).[48] In *Bovis*, drainage works had been carried out that affected the soil surrounding the remains of the palace, but not the palace itself; and in *Jackson*, a householder had demolished part of a 20th century boundary wall between his garden and the castle, which adjoined it.

The court held in *Bovis* that the extent of the scheduling is as shown on the map accompanying the entry in the schedule; and that it extends to include not just any known buildings, artefacts and other items, but also the soil within which they are lying. This makes sense, since many archaeological sites will, or at least may, contain objects whose existence or precise whereabouts are unknown. It was also held that, where land is included under s.61(9)—that is, as being necessary for the support or preservation of the monument—it is simply necessary to refer to the map. Thus, if the question arises as to whether scheduled monument consent is needed for works to within such land, or in the event of a prosecution where such works have been carried out without consent, it is not for the jury to re-determine the matter of which ancillary land should properly have been included within the initial scheduling.

In *Jackson*, on the other hand, the map accompanying the entry in the schedule was unclear—in particular, as to whether or not the scheduling extended to include the castle's boundary wall. It was held that certainty is of vital impor-

---

[45] art.3.

[46] AMAAA 1979, s.61(10)(a). [NI: HMAO(NI)O 1995, art.2(9)(a).] See **6.2.1**.

[47] s.61(9). [NI: art.2(8).]

[48] Both decided on May 6, 1994, and both unreported. A brief note of *Bovis* is at [1994] Crim. L.R. 938, CA; a fuller account appears in an article in *Context* 63 (September 1999). A transcript of *Jackson* is available on Lawtel.

tance, and that any ambiguity must be resolved in favour of the defendant who had carried out works that might constitute a criminal offence.

The rule therefore appears to be that the map accompanying the schedule entry is definitive as to the land that is protected save that, where there is doubt as to whether or not any particular item or piece of land is included, it should be assumed to be excluded.

6.2.6 The progress of scheduling

By the start of 1986, some 10,000 monuments had been scheduled in England; and plans were then announced for a major exercise, to be known as the Monuments Protection Programme, to be carried out by English Heritage with the aim of bringing the total up to about 60,000. In the previous edition of this book, it was noted that by 1997 that figure had been reduced somewhat, so that it was then envisaged that there would eventually be some 45,000 scheduled monuments— about 7.5 per cent of the total estimated number of unprotected archaeological sites in England.[49] It was also noted that some 17,351 ancient monuments had been scheduled at that time, a figure that was expected to rise to 36,000 by 2003.

In the event, the number of scheduled monuments in England as at May 2005 was 19,750.[50] That figure which should be compared to the 500,000 or so buildings which had by that date been listed, and the many more that are in a conservation area. The Secretary of State has indicated that, broadly speaking, scheduled monuments rank in importance with listed buildings of Grade I and II*.[51]

As at the start of May 2005, there were around 3,200 scheduled monuments in Wales, and around 8,000 in Scotland. In Northern Ireland, there were some 1,716 scheduled monuments, of which 181 were in state care.

6.3 The consequences of scheduling

6.3.1 Repairs, grants and tax concessions

Once a monument has been being scheduled, grants may be available to assist with its acquisition or preservation[52]; and, if that is not enough to secure it for posterity, it may be the subject of public acquisition and guardianship.[53]

These provisions also apply to an "ancient monument" that is not scheduled— that is, any monument that in the opinion of the Secretary of State is of public interest[54]—but it is likely that priority will be given to the support of those monuments that have been scheduled, not least as the requirement for scheduled

---

[49] The total number was estimated to be in the region of 600,000 by the Department of National Heritage, in its 1997 Annual Report (Cm.3611).

[50] For figures a year earlier, see *Heritage Counts 2004*, para.3.1.2. That total had risen by 148 in the 12 months to the end of March 2004; and 123 in the following 12 months.

[51] PPG 16, Annex 3, para.4; WO Circ. 60/96, Annex 1, para.4. There are in England about 30,000 listed buildings of Grade I and II* (see **3.2.4**).

[52] See **9.4.3**.

[53] See **11.6**.

[54] See **6.2.1**.

monument consent means that the investment made by way of financial support can be protected through the ability to control works in the future.

Other related provisions grant exemption from the payment of non-domestic rates where a scheduled monument is unoccupied[55]; and enable urgent works to be carried out for its preservation.[56]

6.3.2 Works to scheduled monuments

It is obvious that ancient monuments and archaeological sites are inherently vulnerable to being damaged by the carrying out of unsuitable works—or indeed, in some cases, almost any works. Accordingly, special considerations apply to the processing and determination of planning and listed building consent applications for proposals with archaeological implications.[57]

In addition, however, extra protection is given to those monuments that have been scheduled, in that, just as works to listed buildings require listed building consent as well as planning permission, so virtually all works affecting scheduled monuments require *scheduled monument consent*.[58] This requirement was introduced in its present form in the Ancient Monuments Act, and replaced the previous system whereby the consent of the Minister was required for the carrying out of any works to a monument that was subject to an interim preservation notice or preservation order under the 1953 Act.[59]

The precise extent of the need for scheduled monument consent is considered later in the book,[60] as are the procedure for obtaining it and the remedies available if it is not forthcoming.[61] If works are carried out that have been the subject of a grant of scheduled monument consent, they will be zero-rated for VAT.[62]

6.3.3 Criminal offences

As with listed buildings, the carrying out of works to a scheduled monument without scheduled monument consent is a criminal offence.[63] So also is the destroying or damaging of any protected monument, whether or not scheduled[64]—although, here too, it is more likely that this provision would be used in connection with a monument that is in fact scheduled.

Further, it is an offence to use without authorisation a metal detector (or, in Northern Ireland, any "detecting device") at the site of a scheduled monument or a monument in public ownership or guardianship.[65]

---

[55] See **9.8.2**.
[56] See **10.4**.
[57] See **13.6.3**; **13.6.4** (procedures) and **14.8** (matters to be taken into account).
[58] See **12.2.5**.
[59] See **1.2.4**
[60] See **12.8.3**; **12.8.4**.
[61] See **13.9**, **15.4.3**.
[62] See **17.2.6**.
[63] See **19.6.1**.
[64] See **19.6.7**.
[65] See **19.7.1**. In addition, Pt III of the 1995 order contains a restriction on searching for archaeological objects anywhere in Northern Ireland (see **19.7.2**); there is no corresponding provision in Great Britain.

And if any object is removed from the site of a monument without consent, it is an offence to subsequently dispose of it.[65a]

6.4 Areas of archaeological importance

6.4.1 Introduction

The problems of development affecting the site or setting of a known ancient monument are considered later in this book.[66] Rather different considerations arise, however, where redevelopment is proposed on a site which is already built on or otherwise in use, but which is known or suspected to be of archaeological significance. Such a situation occurs often in connection with redevelopment in the centre of older cities.

In practice, developers in such situations will often be willing to provide time (and sometimes money) to enable archaeological exploration to take place before development starts. This may be as a result of an entirely voluntary arrangement, or it may be required by a planning authority as a condition of granting planning permission.[67]

It used to be considered, however, that in a few cases such voluntary or semi-voluntary arrangements would not be sufficient, so that a formal mechanism was required whereby an appropriate body could be given a chance to investigate and record any items of significance. The Ancient Monuments Act accordingly introduced for the first time the concept of "areas of archaeological importance". They are the subject of Pt II of that Act, which was brought into force on April 14, 1982.[68]

Five areas were designated in 1984, comprising the historic centres of Canterbury, Chester, Exeter, Hereford and York. In a *Memorandum* to the House of Commons Environment Committee in 1986, the Department of the Environment observed that the designations were something of an experiment:

"Broadly speaking, the statutory powers associated with designation are intended to help prevent important archaeological sites being damaged or destroyed without there first being at least an opportunity for proper archaeological investigation and record. Thus, designation is essentially about gaining time for rescue archaeology, where appropriate, as opposed to the conservation of artefacts below ground. There is therefore a crucial difference between these powers and the controls under Part I of the 1979 Act affecting scheduled ancient monuments."[69]

The special procedures relating to the handling of planning applications in the archaeological areas that have been designated are outlined later.[70]

No further designations were in fact ever made; and it now seems that the arrangements outlined in PPG 16 provide a measure of protection for archae-

[65a] Dealing in Cultural Objects (Offences Act 2003 (see **19.7.3**).
[66] See **12.8**, **13.6.3**, **13.9**, **14.8**.
[67] See **14.8.2**.
[68] By SI 1982/362.
[69] Reproduced in the First Report of the Committee, session 1986–1987 (ref 146) Vol. 2, p.19.
[70] See **13.6.4**, **13.6.5**.

ological deposits of this kind that is at least as effective as the somewhat cumbersome system provided for by the Act. It is accordingly envisaged that the whole system of archaeological areas will be abandoned at the first appropriate legislative opportunity.[71] However, the legislation remains in force for the moment, and there follows, if only for completeness, a brief account of the designation procedure.

There is no provision in Northern Ireland for the designation of archaeological areas.

6.4.2 Designating an area of archaeological importance

An area of archaeological importance can be designated by the Secretary of State (after consulting with English Heritage in England), a local authority, the Broads Authority, or (in London only) English Heritage itself.[72] The designation order must contain a map, but is otherwise in whatever form the Secretary of State considers appropriate.[73]

If it is the Secretary of State who is proposing the designation, he or she should first consult with the local authorities in the area and (in England) with English Heritage, and then advertise the proposal in the *London Gazette* and in a local newspaper. The draft order must then be kept available for inspection, by the relevant local authorities, English Heritage and by the Secretary of State. Once at least six weeks have elapsed after the publication of the advertisements, the Secretary of State may make the final designation order—either as the draft, or designating a reduced area—and must then publicise that (as before) and send copies to the local authorities and English Heritage.[74]

If it is English Heritage or a local authority that wishes to designate an area, the procedure is basically the same, save that it must submit the draft designation order to the Secretary of State for confirmation.[75] Further details of the procedure may be prescribed by the Secretary of State in regulations,[76] but no regulations have been made.

A designation order comes into effect six months after it is made (if by the Secretary of State) or otherwise six months after it is confirmed. As with the designation of a conservation area, those living and working in the area do not have to be informed of the designation of an archaeological area, but a copy of the designation order (if made by the Secretary of State) has to be deposited with each local authority concerned[77]; and its existence is a local land charge.[78]

---

[71] See the Government's Green Paper *Protecting the Heritage*, published in May 1996, para.4.8.
[72] AMAAA 1979, s.33.
[73] Sch.2, paras 1,8.
[74] Sch.2, paras 1–7.
[75] Sch.2, paras 8–15A.
[76] paras 8, 10(2), 15.
[77] Sch.2, para.7(b).
[78] s.33(5).

The Secretary of State may (after consulting English Heritage in relation to an area in England) reduce the extent of an area or revoke the designation order altogether.[79]

6.4.3 Investigating authorities

For each archaeological area, the Secretary of State is to appoint an investigating authority, which is to have the powers prescribed by ss 35–39 of the 1979 Act relating to the carrying out of archaeological investigations at sites that are the subject of proposed development.[80]

The investigating authority is to be a person considered by the Secretary of State to be "competent to undertake archaeological investigations".[81] In practice, it is a local archaeological unit. English Heritage is to be consulted in relation to making or cancelling any appointment in England; and the appointment (or its cancellation) is to be notified to each local authority covering the area concerned. Where no appointment has been made for the time being, English Heritage or Cadw is to fulfil the role by default.[82]

The investigating authority may delegate the exercise of its powers to any person duly authorised in writing.[83]

6.4.4 The effect of designation

The principal effect of the designation of an archaeological area is that proposed development needs to be specially notified, to enable the investigating authority to consider whether it wishes to carry out archaeological investigations; and, if it does wish to do so, it must be given access to the site once it has been cleared.[84] Non-compliance with this requirement is a criminal offence.[85]

In addition, the unauthorised use of a metal detector in an archaeological area is an offence.[86]

6.5 Maritime archaeology

6.5.1 Scheduled monuments in territorial waters

There are in practice a number of archaeological sites along the coast line—including fish traps, defensive structures, harbours, and numerous submerged vessels. The National Monuments Record (NMR) contains over 40,000 records of wreck sites and seabed archaeological features, documentary references to marine casualities and fishermen's net fastenings.

---

[79] s.33(4); and see Sch.2, paras 17,18.
[80] s.34.
[81] s.34(1).
[82] s.34(2)–(4).
[83] s.34(5).
[84] See **13.6.4**.
[85] See **13.6.5**.
[86] See **19.7.1**.

The Ancient Monuments Act (and the 1995 Order in Northern Ireland) explicitly state that a monument within the seaward limits of the territorial waters of the United Kingdom—that is, generally, within 22.22km (12 nautical miles) of the low water line[87]—may be scheduled.[88] The entry in the schedule relating to any such monument is to state that it is lying off the coast of England, Wales, Scotland or Northern Ireland; and the monument is thereafter deemed to be within that country.

So far, very little use has been made of this provision—save for the designation by Historic Scotland as a scheduled monument of the seven remaining warships from the German High Seas Fleet scuttled in Scapa Flow after the First World War.[89] However, this is likely to be of increasing significance—not least if, as currently predicted, the shore lines of the United Kingdom recede as a result of climate change. Thus, for example, the Secretary of State considered scheduling a Bronze Age timber circle on the Norfolk foreshore, although in the event he decided instead that it should be removed elsewhere and conserved.[90]

6.5.2 Other legislation

Other relevant legislation relates principally to submerged wrecks of ships and aircraft.[91]

The basic rights of salvage, intended to encourage people at sea to help vessels in distress and to save property that would otherwise be lost, are controlled by the Merchant Shipping Act 1995, which incorporates the International Convention on Salvage 1989.[92] These apply as much to historic wrecks and their contents as they do to any other shipwrecks, and require finders of wrecks to report finds to the Receiver of Wreck, who may then—in the absence of a claim from its owner—dispose of the find as she sees fit, with a reward (possibly part of the find itself) going to the finder.

Against that background, the Protection of Wrecks Act 1973 was introduced (as a private member's Bill) as a stop-gap measure to provide some measure of protection for designated wrecks of historic, archaeological or artistic importance. Some 58 sites have so far been designated.[93] It is an offence to tamper with any vessel at a site designated under the Act, or to carry out any exploration there, or

---

[87] Territorial Sea Act 1987.

[88] AMAAA 1979, s.53(1). [NI: HMAO(NI)O 1995, art.38.]

[89] Cadw has also scheduled the remains of the *Louisa*, now within the enclosed area of Cardiff Bay.

[90] *HBMC v Nolan and others*, Ch D, July 6, 1999, unreported (available on Lawtel).

[91] For a useful summary, see the DMS consultation paper of March 2004, *Protecting our Marine Historic Environment: Making the System Work Better*; for a comprehensive account, see the paper produced in 2003 for EH by the University of Wolverhampton entitled *Marine Archaeology Legislation Project*.

[92] Reproduced at Sch.11 to the 1995 Act. The 1995 Act otherwise largely replicates the Merchant Shipping Act 1894.

[93] Including six off the coast of Wales, eight off Scotland, and one off Northern Ireland. Perhaps the most famous of the designated sites is the *Mary Rose*, off Portsmouth—the second to be designated. Two sites have subsequently been revoked.

to enter the site of a vessel considered to be dangerous, other than with a licence obtained from the Secretary of State.[94]

The operation of the 1973 Act is the responsibility of the DCMS Advisory Committee on Historic Wreck Sites, which is now administered (on a UK-wide basis) by English Heritage. And since 2002 English Heritage has been able to provide financial assistance towards the exploration of protected wrecks.[95]

Finally, it is an offence to tamper with or enter the site of any military aircraft or vessel that has been designated by the Secretary of State as a protected place or a controlled site under the Protection of Military Remains Act 1986.[96] Again, a licence can be obtained (from the Ministry of Defence).

---

[94] 1973 Act, ss 1(3), 2(3).
[95] National Heritage Act 1983, s.33C, inserted by National Heritage Act 2002, s.6.
[96] The Secretary of State for Defence announced in 2001 a set of criteria for designation of sites under the Act, including their historic significance—and stated that 16 vessels, in UK waters, would be designated as controlled sites, and five, in international waters, as protected places.

Chapter 7

Other Forms of Protection

7.1 Introduction

The previous chapters in this part of the book have described the principal ways in which the buildings, monuments and areas that make up the cultural heritage have been identified, so as to facilitate their protection and enhancement—as world heritage sites, listed buildings, conservation areas and scheduled monuments. But there are a variety of other forms of protection recognised by law and custom; this chapter considers a few of the most notable.

First, there are various means of identifying and protecting buildings, other than by listing.

There are thus a number of buildings that are of interest, but not of sufficient merit to justify being listed. These may be included by the local authority on a local or supplementary list (**7.2**). And a few buildings are particularly noted for their historical associations with particular people or events. These may be highlighted by special plaques, of which the most famous are the blue plaques in London and elsewhere (see **7.3**).

Some buildings, notably some in conservation areas, are in need of extra protection from the various types of minor alteration and disfigurement that can normally be carried out under "permitted development" rights.[1] This can be achieved by the imposition of Art.4 directions (**7.4**), which require planning permission to be obtained for such minor works—although there may be an entitlement to compensation if permission is refused.

Secondly, there is the cultural heritage apart from buildings and monuments. The protection of parks and gardens of special value, albeit largely by persuasion rather than coercion, was thus put on a semi-statutory footing—at least in England—over 20 years ago (see **7.5**).

Trees of particular value—often essential elements in the setting of historic buildings, in the character of conservation areas, and the appearance of the rural landscape—have been given special protection since the 1940s (see **7.6**); other elements of the landscape, such as hedgerows (**7.7**) and battlefields (**7.8**), are now also increasingly being safeguarded, or at least identified. But there is in addition a

---

[1]   See **12.2.2**.

growing appreciation of the wider landscape as part of the cultural heritage (see **7.9**). And within that broader picture, the National Trust has always had a special role, and legal status, in relation to both buildings and, more especially, landscape (see **7.10**).

7.2 Buildings of local interest

7.2.1 The production of a local list

It is self-evident that not all buildings are of equal merit or interest. It is equally obvious that there will inevitably be a number of buildings that are not listed nor even of listable quality, at least not yet, but which are nevertheless of more interest than their neighbours.

A number of local planning authorities have recognised this, and have prepared lists of such buildings. These lists are given a variety of names—including "local list", "supplementary list", "list of buildings of local interest". Buildings on such lists may or may not be within a conservation area. They will frequently include local landmarks (such as ornate corner buildings), curiosities, and buildings which are too modern or in some other respect fail to meet the criteria for listing.[2]

The preparation of such a list can be a useful policy tool, in that clearly not all non-listed buildings are of no merit whatsoever. One proper approach to preparing one would be to produce the list, on the basis of a survey or in conjunction with local amenity groups, and have it available for public comment, prior to the preparation of the local plan. When that plan is produced, the list can be included as an appendix, and policies included in the body of the plan for the protection of the buildings on it. Those policies, and the selection of buildings to which they are to apply, can then be the subject of the normal local plan objection procedure.

Appropriate policies for a building on a local list might thus be that alterations and extensions to it, and any development affecting its setting, should be designed with particular care. Once such policies have been included in an adopted local plan, they will have considerable weight.[3]

What is not appropriate is for policies in a local plan to refer to the protection of buildings on a local list that is yet to be produced, since that would be to negate the possibility of objections being made. It is of course possible for an informal local list to be prepared subsequent to the preparation of the plan, but it would have relatively little weight (for example, at an appeal) prior to its incorporation into the plan when it is next amended or replaced. In the same way, to add a further building on an informal basis to a list that is properly included in a local plan will achieve little.

It is not uncommon for owners of buildings included in local lists to complain that there is no statutory basis for the practice. However, it is noteworthy that the High Court has considered at least two challenges relating to locally listed

---

[2] See **3.2.2**.
[3] Planning and Compulsory Purchase Act 2004, s.38(6). [Scotland: TCP(S)A 1997, s.25; NI: P(NI)O 1991, art.4(2A), to be inserted by Planning (Amendment) (NI) Order 2003, art.30 (not yet in force).] (See **14.3.1**).

buildings[4]; and more recently the Court of Appeal compiled a local plan policy relating to "buildings of townscape merit" (in *R. (Springhall) v Richmond-upon-Thames LBC*[4a])—and in none of these cases was any adverse comment made, either on the existence of a local list or on the policies in the development plan relating to locally listed buildings.

7.2.2 Effect of the inclusion of a building in a local list

The inclusion of a building in a local list, and the production of relevant policies in the local plan as indicated above, will not have any immediate effect in law.

In particular, the inclusion of a building in a local list will not lead to any changes to the permitted development rights relating to its extension or alteration, which will thus apply just as they do to any other unlisted building—although there will of course be restrictions if the building happens to be in a conservation area.[5] For that reason, it may well be appropriate to impose an art.4 direction, requiring specific planning permission to be obtained for such works, thus enabling control to be obtained over design and detailing.

Unless a locally listed building is in a conservation area, no consent will be required for its demolition. Nor, in general, will planning permission be needed.[6] However, in the case of a dwellinghouse, notice will need to be given to the planning authority before it can be demolished[7]; and this will enable an authority, if it feels sufficiently strongly, to protect a locally listed building by imposing an art.4 direction so that demolition is no longer permitted automatically.[8]

This was considered recently in *R. (Magauran) v Secretary of State*, in which a council sought to protect a locally listed house by refusing planning permission for its replacement with a bock of flats. The owner appealed, and the inspector determining the appeal concluded firstly that permission simply for the demolition of the house would not be required; and secondly that, had the house been demolished prior to the appeal, there would have been no basis for refusing permission for the replacement. She accordingly allowed the appeal and granted permission, notwithstanding the local plan policy seeking to retain such buildings. The court found nothing wrong with that approach[9] (although it is not entirely clear what the inspector found to outweigh the policy).

Policies in a local plan should thus be phrased cautiously—for example, "the Council will, as far as possible, resist the loss of any building on the local list" or "the Council will only grant permission for a replacement building in the site of a locally listed building in exceptional circumstances". The latter might enable a planning authority to refuse permission for any replacement building until a

---

[4] *R. (Magauran) v Secretary of State*, unreported, July 12, 2005 (available on Lawtel); and *St Albans DC v Secretary of State* [1993] J.P.L. 374.
[4a] [2006] EWCA Civ 19, unreported, January 24, 2006; affirming [2005] EWHC 52 (Admin), unreported, January 18, 2005.
[5] See **12.7.2**.
[6] See **12.2.2**.
[7] TCP (General Permitted Development) Order 1995, Sch.2, Pt 31.
[8] See **7.4**.
[9] Unreported, July 12, 2005.

proposal emerges for one that is actually an improvement on what exists, or until it is possible to point to some exceptional circumstances justifying the erection of a new building. Such an approach will not guarantee the retention of the locally listed building—since, as pointed out in *Magauran*, no permission is needed for its demolition—but it may avoid it being removed on a speculative basis.

Finally, there will, for example, be no compulsion to publicise planning applications affecting the setting of a locally building (as there would be with a statutorily listed one)—although that may be sensible.

7.3 Buildings of historic interest: blue plaques

Some buildings—which may or may not be on the statutory or local list—are noted for their historical associations with particular people or events. These may be highlighted by special plaques, of which the most famous are the "blue plaques" in London and, more recently, elsewhere.

On the abolition of the Greater London Council (GLC) in 1985, special powers were given in London to English Heritage and to London borough councils to provide and erect plaques commemorating events or people connected with buildings or sites.[10] That gave statutory authority to the scheme that had been run for many years by the GLC and its predecessor, the London County Council, and is now maintained by English Heritage.

Other authorities and special interest groups, and English Heritage outside London, operate similar schemes on a non-statutory basis.

It would seem that the erection of such signs would require express consent under the TCP (Control of Advertisements) Regulations—the deemed consent under Class 2A applies only a sign displayed "for the purpose of identification, direction or warning with respect to the building on which it is displayed",[11] whereas the plaques erected under these schemes are for information.

7.4 Article 4 directions

7.4.1 Effect of an article 4 direction

Some areas, and some buildings, are particularly susceptible to harm caused by a succession of small changes—things that might in other circumstances be of no consequence. So, for example, a row of traditional cottages might be spoiled if the occupier of one of them replaced the traditional windows with modern ones with crude plastic frames. And what one does, others are likely to copy.

Where the buildings in question are listed, this problem is avoided through the requirement for listed building consent to be obtained for even the smallest

---

[10] Local Government Act 1985, Sch.2, para.4. It is not clear why there was a need for any specific statutory provision; this may have been a sop to those concerned about the abolition of the world-famous Historic Buildings Division of the GLC.

[11] TCP (Control of Advertisements) Regulations 1992, Sch.3, Class 2A. [Scotland: 1984 Regulations, Sch.4, Class IIA; NI: 1992 Regulations, Sch.3, Class 2A.]

changes.[12] In the case of unlisted buildings, the only protection is through the requirement for planning permission to be obtained. However, the normal rule is that small alterations, which are generally acceptable, are granted planning permission automatically by the TCP (General Permitted Development) Order 1995[13]—they are what is generally known as "permitted development".[13a] This can have most unfortunate consequences where the buildings and their surroundings are vulnerable to the type of development concerned.

A local planning authority may therefore sometimes wish to restrict the right of landowners to carry out certain categories of development which would otherwise be automatically permitted. This can be achieved by making an *article 4 direction*—it is art.3 of the 1995 Order which "permits" those classes of development specified in Sch.2, and art.4 that enables a planning authority to restrict that permission. A direction can be made covering one or more properties, and can restrict one or more classes of permitted development, or part of one class (for example, "alterations to any part of any elevation of the dwellinghouse fronting a highway"[14]).

The effect of an article 4 direction being made on a property in respect of a particular category of permitted development is thus not that development within that category can never be carried out, but simply that it is no longer automatically permitted—that is, it is no longer permitted by the Order, but must instead be the subject of a specific planning application. This does not necessarily mean that the planning authority will refuse permission, but it does enable it to retain some control over design and detailing—and possibly to grant permission subject to appropriate conditions.

Directions may thus be particularly useful where an authority wishes:

(1)   to control the precise details of minor works (such as the design of window surrounds on new side extensions, or the materials used in new front garden walls);

(2)   to control the location of development (for example, to allow extensions to dwellinghouses, but only at the rear rather than the side);

(3)   to prevent completely a particular type of development (such as the painting of previously unpainted brickwork, or alterations to the front elevations of dwellinghouses); or

(4)   exceptionally, to prevent all development however minor (such as on a site of known archaeological significance).

The procedure may thus be appropriate to enable a planning authority to control development in, for example, all or part of a conservation area—and may be employed as part of a general policy for the area. It may also be useful to protect

---

[12]   See **12.4.4**.

[13]   And the TCP (General Permitted Development) (Scotland) Order 1992 and the Planning (General Development) Order (NI) 1993.

[13a]   See **12.2.2**.

[14]   Currently within Pt 1, Class A of Sch.2.

locally listed buildings[15] or the setting of a group of listed ones, or in a world heritage site.[16]

However, it should not be forgotten that where an application for planning permission is made following the imposition of an article 4 direction, compensation may be payable if permission is refused.[17]

Directions will usually be made covering a group of properties, or a wider area, although it has been held that an article 4 direction can be made in respect of a single site.[18] The existence of a direction should be entered by the local authority as a local land charge in Pt 3 of the register as a "planning charge".[19]

Note that a direction cannot invalidate development that has been lawfully completed by the date it is made.[20]

In relation to England and Wales, there are essentially three types of direction:

(1)   directions under article 4(2) affecting conservation areas;

(2)   directions under article 4(1) affecting only listed buildings;

(3)   directions under article 4(1) affecting other land.

Each of these is dealt with in turn. The key distinction between them is that those in the third category require the approval of the Secretary of State (except in cases of urgency); the others do not.

A direction (under either article 4(1) or article 4(2)) may be made either by the district or county planning authority in relation to a conservation area, but in other case only by the authority that would determine an application for development of the type covered by the direction.[21] In areas where there are two tiers of local authority, a direction made by a district council must be notified to the county council, and vice versa.[22] The Secretary of State may also make a direction.[23]

A direction cannot be made under article 4 to restrict permitted development rights to mineral exploration, under Parts 22 and 23 of the 1995 Order.[24] Instead, the procedure under article 7 is used.[25]

7.4.2 Article 4(2) directions

It has already been noted that certain types of permitted development, particularly relating to dwellinghouses, if carried out in an insensitive manner, can have unfortunate effects upon the character and appearance of conservation areas. A

[15]   See **7.2**.
[16]   See **2.3**.
[17]   See **15.4.1**.
[18]   *Thanet DC v Ninedrive* [1978] 1 All E.R. 703.
[19]   Local Land Charges Rules 1977, rr 2(2), 3.
[20]   *Cole v Somerset CC* [1956] 3 All E.R. 531.
[21]   art.4(6).
[22]   arts 5(2), 6(6).
[23]   art.4(1).
[24]   art.4(1).
[25]   See **7.4.9**.

simplified procedure is accordingly available to enable art.4(2) directions to be made in such cases, without the need for approval by the Secretary of State.[26]

An article 4(2) direction may be made where it is to restrict the carrying out, in relation to a building or land that fronts "a relevant location" (that is, a highway, waterway or open space) in conservation area, of development in one or more of the following categories[27]:

(1)   the enlargement, improvement or other alteration of a dwellinghouse; any alteration to its roof; the construction of a porch; the provision within its curtilage of a building, enclosure, swimming pool, etc; the provision of a hard surface; or the installation etc of a satellite antenna[28];

(2)   the erection, construction, maintenance, improvement or alteration of a gate, fence, wall or other means of enclosure within the curtilage of a dwellinghouse[29];

(3)   the painting of the exterior of any part of a dwellinghouse or of a building or enclosure within the curtilage of a dwellinghouse[30]; and

(4)   the demolition of all or part of a gate, fence, wall or other means of enclosure within the curtilage of a dwellinghouse.[31]

A direction under article 4(2) may also be made to restrict the erection, alteration or removal of a chimney on a dwellinghouse or on a building in the curtilage of a dwellinghouse, whether or not it fronts a relevant location.

Note that all of the above categories relate to "dwellinghouses", which exclude houses converted into flats. Where it is desired to control a particular category of development (other than one normally permitted under Part 1 of Schedule 2) in relation to a group of buildings of which some are dwellinghouses and some have been converted into flats, it may be best to make a direction for the whole group under article 4(1), with the approval of the Secretary of State.[32]

One particular use of article 4 directions that may be appropriate is to restrict the creation of front garden parking spaces by the partial removal of front boundary walls—since such walls are an important feature in many conservation areas. Where the whole of a front wall more than one metre high is removed, this would probably constitute "demolition" and would thus require conservation area consent, which could simply be refused, but where only part is removed, this is not demolition, and therefore does not require that consent.[33] However, the

---

[26]   This procedure was introduced in 1995; but a survey carried out in 1997 by the English Historic Towns Forum suggested that very few authorities had in fact used the new powers available to them.

[27]   Listed in art.4(5).

[28]   Normally permitted under Classes A, C to F, or H of Pt 1 of Sch.2 to the 1995 Order.

[29]   Pt 2, Class A.

[30]   Pt 2, Class C.

[31]   Pt 31, Class B.

[32]   See **7.4.5**.

[33]   *Shimizu (UK) Ltd v Westminster CC* [1996] 3 P.L.R. 89.

latter clearly a building operation, however, and is thus development which is permitted under the 1995 Order[34]—unless an article 4 direction is made.

Another type of direction that sometimes causes problems is one covering painting[35] with the aim of bringing about or maintaining a uniform colour scheme for a formal group of buildings. It is in such a case essential to prepare beforehand a colour code, possibly in conjunction with any local amenity groups. Such a code should be drafted with reference to the numbered British Standard colours,[36] not to general descriptions (for example, "cream") or manufacturers' own brand names ("almond blossom"). It is more likely to be effective if a single colour scheme is stipulated, and well publicised. But in practice it may prove very difficult to enforce any scheme without extensive co-operation from property owners.

It is perhaps more realistic only to attempt to control painting in the case of buildings where *any* paint would be highly unfortunate, such as those faced with stone, or with elaborate decorations in terracotta. In such cases it may be best to frame the direction so as to restrict only "painting of hitherto unpainted parts of the elevation, being development within Part 2, Class C"; this has the effect of leaving outside control the repainting of woodwork and pipework.

7.4.3 Directions under article 4(1) affecting only listed buildings

It will not often be necessary to make article 4 directions concerning alterations and extensions to listed buildings themselves, as these will virtually always require listed building consent, and thus be within the control of the planning authority. It may however be appropriate in a few cases for an authority to make a direction restricting permitted development within the curtilage of a listed building, since this will not require listed building consent and would otherwise be outside control.

There are in fact very few types of development affecting a listed building which do not require a specific planning permission.[37] However, one example where a direction might be appropriate would be to restrict the provision of hard surfaces or satellite dishes in the curtilage of listed dwellinghouses.[38] Another would be to restrict unsuitable curtilage development associated with agricultural buildings.[39]

A direction does not normally require the approval or confirmation of the Secretary of State if it relates only to:

(a) a listed building;

(b) a building which is notified to the authority by the Secretary of State as a building of architectural or historic interest; or

(c) development within the curtilage of a listed building.[40]

---

[34] Pt 2, Class A of Sch.2.
[35] Normally permitted under Class C of Pt 2 of Sch.2 to the 1995 Order.
[36] Derived from BS 4800.
[37] See **12.4.3**.
[38] Still permitted development within Pt 1, Classes F and H respectively.
[39] PPG 15, para.2.20.
[40] TCP (General Permitted Development) Order 1995, art.5(3).

It is not clear to what the second category refers.

In such a case, the direction is therefore made by the planning authority, and notified to the owners and occupiers of the land concerned. It comes into force on the date of the notification.[41] Note however that it must still be approved by the Secretary of State if it is made to restrict the carrying out of routine works by statutory undertakers.[42]

7.4.4 Directions under article 4(1) in other cases

Where a direction is made under article 4(1) in relation to unlisted buildings, the approval of the Secretary of State is still required. This would still apply to:

(1) directions restricting permitted development on dwellinghouses in conservation areas not fronting on to highways, waterways or open spaces;

(2) directions relating to other types of property in conservation areas (for example, restricting the alteration or demolition of gates and walls outside buildings converted to flats); and

(3) directions relating to properties not in a conservation area.

The Government's general approach to the making of art.4 directions is that permitted development rights should be withdrawn only in exceptional circumstances, where there is a real and specific threat of development being carried out which would damage an interest of acknowledged importance.[43]

In relation to directions in conservation areas, the current policy of the Secretary of State is set out in PPG 15. In summary, in those cases in which a direction still requires approval, this is reasonably likely to be forthcoming where:

(1) the planning authority has undertaken an assessment of the special architectural and historic interest of the conservation area concerned;

(2) the proposed direction helps to protect features that are key elements in that area, and whose importance to the special interest of the area can be demonstrated;

(3) there is local support for the direction; and

(4) the direction involves the minimum withdrawal of permitted development rights (in terms of both area and types of development) necessary to achieve its objective.[44]

The Secretary of State has also advised authorities to consider the use of article 4 directions where they are aware of real and specific threats to known archae-

---

[41] art.5(10).

[42] arts 4(4)), 5(3).

[43] DoE Circ. 9/95 (WO Circ. 26/95), App. D, para.1. As to directions relating to development by Electronic Communications Code operators, see para.19 of PPG 8, *Telecommunications*.

[44] PPG 15, para.4.23. Policy for Wales used to be at Appendix II to WO Circ. 61/81. That has been cancelled, but no new guidance appears to have been issued.

ological sites as a result of the potential exercise of permitted development rights.[45]

7.4.5 Normal procedure

A direction, whether under article 4(2) or under article 4(1), must be drawn up accurately. The planning authority must therefore first consider carefully which properties are to be covered, and which Classes, or which parts of which Classes, of permitted development are to be restricted. These should generally both be kept to the minimum possible: if a direction covers too much, it is more difficult to draft accurately, more time-consuming to prepare, less likely to be effectively enforced, and therefore more likely to be ignored by owners. In addition, the Secretary of State has stated that, in cases where his approval is required, it is unlikely to be forthcoming where a direction is drawn too widely.

The best approach is probably to introduce smaller directions more often, rather than to attempt to cover everything in one large direction.

The properties involved must be specified with precision, particularly in the case of a direction covering a large area. This may best be done both on a map and on a list. The choice of categories of development to be controlled needs to be considered carefully, and defined precisely but clearly. This is particularly important where a direction relates to only some categories of development within Class A of Part 1, since this covers a wide variety of different types of work. The direction will be a formal document but, if it is to be effective, it must also be capable of being understood by property owners and occupiers.

Where an authority makes a direction under article 4(2), it must then publicise it by inserting a notice in a local newspaper.[46] This must:

(1)   set out the properties and classes of development involved;

(2)   explain the effect of the direction, and that it is made under article 4(2);

(3)   name a place where the direction (together with a map showing the area affected) may be inspected; and

(4)   specify a period (of at least 21 days) within which representations may be made to the local planning authority in relation to the direction.

The authority must also serve a similar notice on the owner and occupier of every dwellinghouse affected by the direction, unless it considers that it is impracticable to do so.[47] The direction comes into force in relation to any property on the date on which notice is served on the owner and occupier; where no such notice is served, it comes into force on the date of the newspaper advertisement.

The advertisement procedure should not be the sole method of publicising a direction except where really unavoidable, as the owners and occupiers are then unlikely to become aware of it. It is probably best in the case of a direction

---

[45] PPG 16, para.18; WO Circ. 60/96, para.10.
[46] art.6(1)(a).
[47] art.6(4), (5).

covering a large area to deliver a notice to each dwellinghouse concerned, addressed to "the owner/occupier", and then to place an advertisement in the paper to comply with the formal requirements. Nor does it matter particularly, in the case of a direction restricting development in Part 1, if a notice is served on a property which, unknown to the authority, has been converted into some use other than a dwellinghouse—since permitted development rights under that Part would not apply anyway.

The notice served on owners and occupiers will usually be a formal legal document. It should therefore wherever possible be accompanied by a leaflet explaining in simple language what an article 4 direction is, and why one has been served in this particular case. The draft text of such a leaflet might also be a convenient way for officers of an authority to explain to the relevant committee why the direction should be made in the first place.

The authority must then consider any representations made in response to the notices published. It may then confirm the direction, not less than 28 days after the last notice was published and not more than six months after it was made.[48] If the authority does confirm it, it must give notice of the confirmation in the same way that it notified the making of the order. If it does not confirm the order within six months of making it, it will lapse.

Where an authority makes a direction under article 4(1), it must send it in draft to the Secretary of State for approval (except where it relates only to a listed building[49]). The authority must then wherever possible promptly notify every owner and occupier of any land affected, since the direction takes effect in relation to any property only on the date on which it is notified to its owner and occupier.[50] As with article 4(2) directions, if the authority considers that individual notification is impracticable, it may as an alternative rely on a notice in the local press; the direction in this case takes effect on the date of the press notice[51]—but, here too, press notices should not generally be relied upon as the sole means of publicising an order except where unavoidable.

7.4.6 Article 4(1) directions: procedure in cases of urgency

Where an authority wishes to make a direction under article 4(1) to counter an immediate threat of unsuitable permitted development occurring, the above procedure will take too long. There is accordingly an alternative procedure available in some cases, which can be used where the authority considers that proposed development would be "prejudicial to the proper planning of their area or would constitute a threat to the amenities of their area".[52] It is however only possible to use this procedure to restrict permitted development in Parts 1 to 4.[53] This means, in particular, that it cannot be used to stop permitted development

---

[48] art.6(7)–(9).
[49] See **7.4.3**.
[50] art.5(10).
[51] art.5(15).
[52] TCP (General Permitted Development) Order 1995, art.5(4).
[53] See **12.2.2** for details.

carried out by statutory undertakers and Electronic Communications Code operators.[54]

Where a direction is made under article 4(1) in reliance on article 5(4), it does not require the approval of the Secretary of State. As soon as it has been made, notice should be given to the owners and occupiers concerned, or an advertisement be placed in the press, in the same way as when a direction has been approved in a non-urgent case[55]; the direction comes into force on the date of the notice or advertisement.[56] However, it only remains in force for six months unless it is confirmed by the Secretary of State, with or without modifications, within that period. A copy of the direction should therefore be sent to the Department as soon as it is made.[57]

When the direction has in due course been either confirmed or disallowed by the Secretary of State, further notice must be given in the same manner.[58]

It is probably best for an authority faced with an immediate threat of unsuitable development that would otherwise be permitted in one of Parts 1–4 to make at once a direction under article 5(4), covering only the property directly affected, and send it for confirmation to the Secretary of State. It should then consider whether similar development is likely to take place elsewhere in the immediate area; if so, it should make a second, more comprehensive direction under the normal procedure covering the wider area (including the first property). It can then cancel the earlier urgent direction once the subsequent one has been approved.

7.4.7 Appeal against making of an article 4 direction

There is no formal right of appeal against the making of an article 4 direction. But where an owner or occupier becomes aware, by whatever means, that the local planning authority is proposing to make a direction affecting his or her property, it is of course open to him or her to object.[59] Indeed, under the procedures for article 4(2) directions, authorities must take into account representations made by owners and occupiers. Similarly, it is possible to object after receiving notice that a direction has been made under the speedier procedure.[60] Such an objection should be in the form of a letter to the authority, stating why it is considered that the carrying out of the relevant category of permitted development would not be harmful. In the case of a direction requiring the confirmation of the Secretary of State, a second copy of the letter should be enclosed, together with a request that it should be sent to the officer at the Department who is dealing with the case.

An informal approach of this kind is not likely to succeed in persuading the authority to cancel the direction; but it may occasionally persuade the Secretary of State not to approve it.

---

[54] See **12.7.3** for Code operators.
[55] See **7.4.5**.
[56] art.5(10), (12)–(15).
[57] art.5(5), (7), (8).
[58] art.5(8), (11)–(15).
[59] As with appealing against a building being listed; see **3.3.4**.
[60] See **7.4.6**.

7.4.8 Scotland and Northern Ireland

Article 4 directions may be made by any planning authority in Scotland, under the provisions of the TCP (General Permitted Development) (Scotland) Order 1995.[61] However, they always require the approval of the Secretary of State except where they only affect listed buildings.[62] There is thus no equivalent to the procedure under article 4(2) available in relation to conservation areas in England and Wales. In addition, they must be notified to occupiers of the properties concerned—a press notice is never sufficient. A sample direction is at Schedule 3 to the Order.

In Northern Ireland, an article 4 direction may be made by the Department, under the Planning (General Development) Order (NI) 1993.[63] It may be notified either to the occupiers of the properties concerned, or where necessary by means of a press notice.[64]

7.4.9 Minerals: article 7 directions

The TCP (General Permitted Development) Order 1995 relates, amongst other things, to the carrying out of exploration for minerals for up to six months[65] and the removal of material from a mineral-working deposit.[66] An article 4 direction may not be made in respect of either of these categories of permitted development.[67] Instead, the prospective developer must in every case give at least 28 days written notice to the mineral planning authority.[68] The authority may then, at any time up to 21 days after receiving such notice, decide to make a direction under article 7 of the Order.

By virtue of article 7(2), an article 7 direction may be made where (amongst other criteria) the proposed operation:

(1) is in a "site of archaeological interest", that is:

— land included in the site of a scheduled monument or a site registered in the Sites and Monuments Record,[69] or
— land within an area of archaeological importance[70];

(2) would cause serious detriment to the area; or

(3) would adversely affect the setting of a Grade I listed building.[71]

---

[61] 1992 Order, arts 4 and 5.
[62] art.4(3),(5).
[63] 1993 Order, arts 4 and 5.
[64] art.5.
[65] Pt 22, Class B.
[66] Pt 23, Class B.
[67] art.4(1). Where there is not a unitary authority, the relevant authority will generally be the county council or national park authority
[68] TCPA 1990, s.1(4).
[69] See **6.2.4**.
[70] See **6.4**.
[71] See **13.5.8**.

As to the first of these (development at an archaeological site), a direction may not be made, where the operation is in one of the categories on the list of operations which do not need to be notified to planning authorities in archaeological areas.[72]

The effect of an article 7 direction is that the relevant permitted development right no longer applies, so that a specific application for planning permission has to be made. Once it has made a direction, the authority must immediately send a copy to the developer and to the Secretary of State; the latter then has 28 days (which cannot be extended) in which to disallow the direction. In effect, therefore, the permitted development rights under Part 22 or Part 23 can only be actually exercised once the possibility of making an article 7 direction has been explored both by the authority and the Secretary of State.

The procedure in Scotland is identical.[73] In Northern Ireland, a similar direction may be made, but only in relation to mineral exploration, where it is likely to affect (amongst other things) an archaeological site, a listed building of any grade, or a conservation area.[74]

7.5 Historic parks and gardens

7.5.1 Statutory protection

Gardens are a major feature of the setting of many listed buildings and of many conservation areas. They clearly cannot be "preserved"—in the sense of being kept unaltered for all time—but they can be kept safe from harm.

Although the ground within the curtilage of a listed building will not itself be listed,[75] any "structures" such as walls, statues, staircases, gazebos, temples, ha-has and (probably) terraces will be.[76] The need for listed building consent to alter or remove these features will also help to protect the garden itself.

Further, it has been recognised by the Court of Appeal that a pattern of private gardens in a conservation area might be a feature of the area which it would be desirable to preserve or enhance[77]; any development in such gardens would thus need to be considered accordingly, in the light of the test in *Bath Society v Secretary of State*.[78] The need for any works to trees in a conservation area to be notified to the planning authority also provides some degree of protection.[79]

Finally, whether or not a garden is in the curtilage of a listed building or in a conservation area, any important trees should be subject to tree preservation orders, and the need for works to such trees to be approved also protects the garden as a whole.[80]

---

[72] Specified in the Schedule to the Areas of Archaeological Importance (Notification of Operations) (Exemptions) Order 1984: see **13.6.4**.
[73] TCP (General Permitted Development) (Scotland) Order 1995, art.7.
[74] Planning (General Development) Order (NI) 1993, art.6.
[75] *Cotswold DC v Secretary of State and Pearson* [1985] J.P.L. 407.
[76] *Watson-Smyth v Secretary of State and Cherwell D.C.* [1992] J.P.L. 451 (see **4.5.5**).
[77] *Ward v Secretary of State* [1990] 1 P.L.R. 85.
[78] [1992] P.L.R. 51 (see **14.7.3**).
[79] See **5.5**.
[80] See **7.6**.

7.5.2 *Register of Historic Parks and Gardens in England*

It will be apparent from the above that the degree of formal protection given to parks and gardens—as opposed to structures and trees within them—is not great. It would therefore be a pity if there was not at least some record of the best ones. Further, it is often claimed that proposed development will harm an important park or garden—but some mechanism is necessary to enable all concerned to assess the relative significance of the land involved.

Accordingly, when English Heritage was set up in 1983, it was given a new power, to compile a register of gardens of special historic interest in England.[81] The criteria for selecting parks and gardens to be included in the register were as follows:

(1) parks and gardens formed before 1750 where the original layout is still in evidence;

(2) most parks and gardens laid out between 1750 and 1820 if they still reflect the intentions of the original layout; and

(3), (4) the best parks and gardens laid out between 1820 and 1939 which are in good or (if pre-1880) fair condition and of aesthetic merit.

When a more detailed assessment of a site is possible, particular attention could also be paid to:

(5) parks and gardens which were influential in the development of taste, whether through contemporary reputation or through reference in contemporary theoretical literature;

(6) parks and gardens which are early or representative examples of a genre of layout or a designer of national statute;

(7) parks and gardens having an association with significant historical events or persons; and

(8) parks and gardens with group value, especially as an integral part of the layout surrounding a major house or as part of a town planning scheme.

English Heritage published a Register of Historic Parks and Gardens for each county, containing between them some 1,085 sites throughout England. These volumes are being gradually updated, and by May 1998 included 1,295 parks and gardens, ranging from major man-made landscapes like Blenheim to quite small gardens such as the one hectare garden at Marsh Court in Hampshire.

The same grades are used as for listed buildings: Grade I (those of exceptional interest), Grade II* (of great interest), and Grade II (of special interest). However, the proportion in each grade is somewhat different—around 10 per cent are Grade I, 28 per cent Grade II*, and 62 per cent Grade II.

The rate of inclusion has diminished since the first county registers were

---

[81] HBAMA 1953, s.8C, inserted by NHA 1983.

completed, but new entries are still made. The criteria for selection and grading have remained constant. Where a park or garden is included in the register for the first time, a copy of the new entry is to be sent to the owner and occupier of the garden concerned, the district and county planning authority for the area, and the Secretary of State.

All general enquiries about the register should be made to the Inspector of Historic Parks and Gardens, English Heritage.[82]

7.5.3 Significance of inclusion in the Register

The significance of a site being included within the Register is explained in PPG 15 as follows:

"Local planning authorities should protect registered parks and gardens in preparing development plans and in determining planning applications. The effect of proposed development on a registered park or garden or its setting is a material consideration in determining a planning application. Planning and highways authorities should also try to safeguard registered parks or gardens when themselves planning new developments or road schemes."[83]

The same paragraph of PPG 15 states that no additional statutory controls follow from the inclusion of a site in the Register. This is now no longer quite true, however, since planning authorities are now required to notify English Heritage any planning applications affecting Grade I or II* registered parks or gardens.[84] It would also be sensible to notify English Heritage of proposals which would have an exceptional impact on Grade II parks and gardens. The Garden History Society must also be consulted by authorities before they grant planning permission for any development which will affect any registered park or garden, of any grade.[85]

Perhaps at least as significantly, an increasing number of development plans and local development documents contain policies relating to development affecting registered parks and gardens. Local authorities have in particular been advised to avoid registered parks and gardens when drawing up road proposals—although it is recognised that a balance has to be struck between conservation, other environmental concerns, economics, safety and engineering feasibility.[86] And there has been much concern about the effect of proposals for golf courses affecting historic parks and gardens.[87]

---

[82] See also para.4 of Appendix B to DoE Circ. 9/95.

[83] PPG 15, para.2.24.

[84] TCP (General Development Procedure) Order 1995, art.10(1)(o).

[85] TCP (Consultation with the Garden History Society) Direction 1995, reproduced as Appendix C to Circ. 9/95. Further information is at para.5 of Appendix B to that Circular.

[86] PPG 13, para.5.20; PPG 15, para.5.5. See *Robert Hitchin Ltd v Bovis Homes* (1996) 72 P&CR 579 at p.596 (a battlefields case; see **7.8**).

[87] *R. v Secretary of State, ex p. Maltzahn* [1998] E.G.C.S. 43 (see **14.3.1**). See also guidance produced by English Heritage in June 1991 (now out of print).

Finally, there are specific powers for English Heritage and (in Wales and Scotland) the Secretary of State to offer grants for the upkeep of gardens of outstanding interest,[88] and for English Heritage to acquire such gardens.[89]

7.5.4 Register of Historic Landscapes, Parks and Gardens (Wales)

There is no statutory power for the Secretary of State to maintain a register of historic landscapes, parks and gardens in Wales.

Cadw is nevertheless preparing such a register. The first part, covering Historic Parks and Gardens, is being prepared as a series of volumes by county, on the same lines as the Register maintained by English Heritage. The criteria for the selection of sites are set out at Annex B to WO Circular 61/96; they are similar but not identical to those applying in England.

It appears that the Register, albeit non-statutory, is to have similar weight, as a material consideration in determining planning applications, as its English equivalent.[90] There is no formal requirement for applications affecting registered gardens to be notified to the Garden History Society, but planning authorities have been "asked" to consult Cadw on planning applications in respect of Grade I and II* sites, and the Garden History Society on applications affecting gardens on the Register, of any grade.[91]

7.5.5 Scotland and Northern Ireland

There is no statutory register of gardens in Scotland; but there has for many years been in existence a non-statutory Inventory of Gardens and Designed Landscapes. Planning authorities are required to consult the Secretary of State in relation to any proposed development that would affect land in the Inventory[92]— which appeared three years before any similar requirement was introduced in England. And clearly the inclusion of land within the Inventory will be a material consideration in the assessment of proposals for development affecting it.

In Northern Ireland, the preparation of the Register of Historic Parks, Gardens and Demesnes is somewhat less advanced. However, that too will be a material consideration in the assessment of development.

For further details, see Chapter 5 of the Historic Scotland *Memorandum* and Chapter 5 of PPS 6, each of which (but particularly the former) provides guidance in considerably more detail than available in England or Wales.

---

[88] HBAMA 1953, s.3A (England) (see **9.4.1**), s.4 (Wales and Scotland) (see **9.5.1**), both as amended by National Heritage Act 1983.

[89] HBAMA 1953, as amended by National Heritage Act 1983; see **11.2.3**).

[90] WO Circ. 61/96, para.16.

[91] See WO Circ. 29/95, Appendix B, para.7, and WO Circ. 1/98, para.23.

[92] art.15(1)(j)(iv) of the TCP (General Development Procedure) (Scotland) Order 1992 (SI 1992/224 (s.18).

7.6 Tree preservation orders

7.6.1 When a tree preservation order may be made

As well as the limited general protection given to trees in conservation areas under section 211 of the Planning Act,[93] and sometimes as a result of it, it will sometimes be desirable for individual trees or groups of trees to be specially protected. This may also be appropriate in some cases in registered parks and gardens.

This is to some extent achieved through local authorities being given powers to make *tree preservation orders*, under section 198 of the Act. These are inaptly named, for no amount of legislation can "preserve" a tree beyond its natural life-span. However they at least provide some control over unsuitable works being carried out which would damage or destroy the health or appearance of selected trees.

A local authority may make tree preservation orders where it appears to be expedient to do so in the interests of "amenity".[94] It has been held in the Court of Appeal[95] that:

"the word 'amenity' still connotes in a statute what Scrutton L.J. thought it did[96] on its first appearance in the Housing and Town Planning etc Act of 1909: 'pleasant circumstances or features, advantages'."

In an Australian decision of 1955, it was held:

"...the word may be taken to express that element in the appearance and layout of town and country which makes for a comfortable and pleasant life rather than a mere existence."[97]

And it has been held that the amenity of land may be defined as "[its] visual appearance and the pleasure of its enjoyment".[98] A current dictionary definition is "the pleasantness or attractiveness of a place".[99]

Current government guidance in England and Wales (in the *Guide to the Law and Good Practice*, published by DETR in 2000[1]) on this issue provides a useful (but not exhaustive) checklist of factors which may be relevant:

"In the Secretary of State's view, tree preservation orders should be used to protect selected trees and woodlands if their removal would have a significant impact on the local environment and its enjoyment by the public. Local planning authorities should be able to show that a reasonable degree of public benefit would accrue before orders are made or confirmed. The trees, or at least part of them, should therefore normally be visible from a public place, such as a road or footpath, although, exceptionally, the inclusion of other trees may be justified.

•   The benefit may be present or future;

---

[93]   See **5.5.1**—which also refers to a definition of what is a "tree" for these purposes.
[94]   TCPA 1990, s.198(1).
[95]   *FFF Estates v Hackney LBC* [1981] Q.B. 503, CA.
[96]   In *Re Ellis and Ruislip-Northwood UDC* [1920] 1 K.B. 343 at p.370.
[97]   *Re Parramatta City Council, ex p. Tooth & Co* (1955) 55 SR (NSW) 282 at pp.306, 308.
[98]   *Cartwright v Post Office* [1968] 2 All E.R. 646 at p.648.
[99]   *The New Oxford Dictionary of English* (1st ed., Clarendon, Oxford, 1988).
[1]   See **5.5.1**.

- trees may be worthy of preservation for their intrinsic beauty or for their contribution to the landscape;
- [they may be worthy of preservation] because they serve to screen an eyesore or future development;
- the value of trees may be enhanced by their scarcity; and
- the value of a group of trees or woodland may be collective only.

Other factors, such as importance as a wildlife habitat, may be taken into account which alone would not be sufficient to warrant a TPO."[2]

This emphasises in particular that orders should in general only be made to protect trees which are publicly visible, and only rarely those in rear gardens—although a tree at the centre of a large block of urban gardens may in fact be seen by more people, and give more pleasure, than one beside a remote country lane.

Also relevant will be general statutory duties. Thus the general duty of planning authorities to preserve and enhance the appearance of conservation areas,[3] will mean that they should consider making orders covering the trees in them. Suitable occasions for this will be when notice is given to them of proposed works to trees, under the section 211 procedure; for an example of this, see *Sherwood and Sherwood v Secretary of State*.[4] In addition, authorities should consider protecting trees when they are surveying their areas in connection with preparing local development documents, and enhancement proposals under section 71 of the Listed Buildings Act.[5]

Authorities are also under a special duty to consider the desirability of making orders when granting planning permission for development on sites containing existing trees.[6] This would apply particularly where an authority is considering an application for listed building consent or planning permission for works to a listed building, since it is then under a duty to consider the desirability of preserving the setting of the building, which may well include trees.[7] Finally, it may be appropriate to make orders to protect new trees to be planted in connection with development (often as a result of a condition attached to the planning permission).[8] Where orders are made in any of these circumstances to protect trees from damage or loss as a result of impending building works, they will almost always need to be made under the section 201 procedure.[9]

In the light of the absence of any right of appeal to the Secretary of State against the making of an order,[10] it is particularly important for a local authority to give proper consideration to the making of the order in the first place, and not to take into account any immaterial considerations.[11] Since the only material

---

[2] *Tree Preservation Orders: a Guide to the Law and Good Practice*, DETR (cited below as "*DETR Guide*"), 2000, paragraph 3.2 [bullet points added for clarity]; Wales: see Technical Advice Note (TAN) 10, *Tree Preservation Orders* ("TAN 10"), 1997, para.15.
[3] P(LBCA)A 1990, s.72; see **5.3.2**.
[4] [1996] J.P.L. 925; and see **5.5**.
[5] See **5.4**; see also paras 4.38–4.40 of PPG 15, and paras 42–44 of WO Circ. 61/96.
[6] TCPA 1990, s.197.
[7] P(LBCA)A 1990, ss 16(2), 66(1).
[8] TCPA 1990, ss 197(b), 198(5).
[9] See 20.2.4.
[10] See 20.2.4.
[11] *Bellcross Co. Ltd v Mid Bedfordshire D.C.* [1988] 15 E.G. 106.

consideration is "amenity", it would be improper to take into account, for example, the desire to impede an unpopular development taking place on a site currently occupied by trees of no particular amenity value.

This is not the place for a more detailed discussion of the circumstances where the making of a tree preservation order would be appropriate, or the procedure for making one. These matters, along with the consequences of making an order, have now been exhaustively covered elsewhere.[12]

7.6.2 Making a tree preservation order

The form of a tree preservation order is provided for in regulations—those currently in force being the TCP (Trees) Regulations 1999. An order is to be in the form, or "substantially" in the form, of the model order set out as the Schedule to these.[13] The body of the order, together with the second and third schedules to it, is to set out the requirement for consent to be obtained, the procedure for obtaining it and various consequential provisions as to replacement planting, compensation and so forth.[14]

The first schedule to the order is to specify the trees to be protected by the order (which area is also to be shown on a map). They are to be categorised into trees specified individually, trees specified by reference to an area, groups of trees, and woodlands. These classifications can be significant when it comes to the requirement to plant replacement trees.[15]

The procedure for making an order is set out in the 1999 Regulations. The relevant local authority must, after making the draft order, have it available for public inspection.[16] It must also send copies to the owners and occupiers of any land affected by the order (which would in many cases include neighbouring properties), and anyone else entitled to fell any of the trees affected by the order (such as tree surgeons, builders and surveyors) together with a notice stating the reasons for the making of the order, and explaining their right to object to the authority.[17] It is important that the owners and occupiers of the land are correctly identified, as incorrect service may invalidate any subsequent prosecution.[18]

Objections can then be made to the authority, which can if it wishes hold an inquiry to consider them. It may then confirm the order with or without modifications, but if any modifications have been made, those who were initially notified must be told.[19] Any "modifications" to an order must be just that,

---

[12] See Part IV of Mynors, *Law of Trees, Forests and Hedgerows* (Sweet & Maxwell, London, 2002).
[13] reg.4.
[14] See **7.6.3–7.6.7**.
[15] s.206(1); *Bush v Secretary of State for the Environment* [1988] J.P.L. 108; *Evans v Waverley B.C.* [1995] E.G.C.S. 132, CA.
[16] This will generally be the district council in areas where there are two tiers of local authority; orders may also be made by national park authorities, the Broads Authority and, exceptionally, by county councils (TCPA 1990, s.1; s.4A(4), inserted by the Environment Act 1995, s.67; Sch.1, para.13).
[17] reg.5.
[18] *Knowles v Chorley B.C.* [1998] J.P.L. 593.
[19] regs 7–9.

however—that is, they cannot have the effect of producing a quite different order—such as by turning an "area" order into a "woodland" order.[20]

The order in theory takes effect only once it has been confirmed.[21] However, where it appears to the authority that the order should take effect at once, it can insert in the order a direction[22] to achieve this. It must then also explain to the owners and occupiers concerned that this means that the order comes into effect immediately, so that consent is needed for any works to the trees involved from the date of the order.[23] Since orders will often be made in circumstances where their purpose will be frustrated if they do not come into effect immediately, it is difficult to see any particular merit in the s.199 procedure. However, where the section 201 procedure is used, the order must be confirmed within six months, or else it lapses.

Once an order has been confirmed, its validity cannot be challenged except by application to the High Court.[24] Such an application must be made within six weeks of the date of the confirmation of the order[25]; although the order continues in force until the end of any legal proceedings.[26]

Once the order is in force, a copy of it must still be retained for public inspection by the local authority that made it.[27] If it is not, any subsequent prosecution for a breach of the order may fail.[28]

7.6.3 Need for consent under a tree preservation order

Where works are to be carried out for the cutting down, topping, lopping, uprooting, wilful damage, or wilful destruction of a tree that is protected by a preservation order, consent must normally be obtained from the local authority.[29] Consent may also be required by an order to cause or permit a tree to be cut down.[30]

Consent will not be required for the cutting down, uprooting, topping or lopping of a tree because it is dying, dead or dangerous, or in order to comply with an Act of Parliament, or to prevent or abate a nuisance.[31] However, where a tree is removed solely because it is dying, dead or dangerous, a replacement will normally have to be planted.[32]

Nor will consent be needed in any of the circumstances listed in the order itself as exemptions, generally relating to works by statutory undertakers, works to

---

[20] *Evans v Waverley B.C.* [1995] 3 P.L.R. 80, CA, overturning [1995] 2 P.L.R. 46, QB.
[21] s.199(1).
[22] Under s.201.
[23] reg.5(c)(v).
[24] TCPA 1990, ss 284(1)(e), (2)(c), 288(4).
[25] s.288(3); *R. v Secretary of State for the Environment, ex p. Ostler* [1977] Q.B. 122.
[26] s.288(5)(a).
[27] reg.5(a).
[28] *Vale of Glamorgan B.C. v Palmer* [1984] J.P.L. 334.
[29] TCPA 1990, s.198(3)(a).
[30] *R. v Bournemouth J.J., ex p. Bournemouth Corporation* (1970) 21 P. & C.R. 163.
[31] s.198(6); see **5.5.3**. The "dead or dying" exemption does not apply in Scotland.
[32] s.206(1)(b); the requirement is enforced just as for unauthorised works in conservation areas (see **5.5.6**).

fruit trees, or works necessary to carry out development.[33] It should be noted that the terms of the particular order in question need to be read with care—the primary or secondary legislation may have changed since it was issued (several times in the case of older orders); and it is the wording of the order, not that of the current legislation, that is authoritative.

Finally, where the volume of timber to be felled is such that a felling licence is required,[34] an application should be made not to the local authority but only to the Forestry Commission.[35]

7.6.4 Applications for consent

An application for consent to carry out works to a tree protected by a tree preservation order is to be made to the same authority that made the order. Usually the authority will have a standard form, but sometimes a letter will suffice. Either way, the application should contain the following details:

(1)   the location, size and species of the trees concerned;

(2)   the works to be carried out;

(3)   the reason for the works; and

(4)   any replanting proposed.

There is no fee payable.

Again, it is the terms of the order in question that will determine the details of the procedure.

Consent can be refused or granted subject to conditions; and conditions may in particular be imposed requiring one or more trees to be planted to replace the one that is to be removed. A condition requiring replacement planting can be enforced by a notice under section 207.[36]

The function of granting or refusing consent under a preservation order relating to a tree in a conservation area is one to which section 72 of the Listed Buildings Act applies.[37] Accordingly, an authority should have regard to the desirability of preserving or enhancing the area and, if it considers that the loss of the tree—even with replacement—will harm the area, it should refuse consent.[38]

There is a right of appeal against the planning authority's decision to the Secretary of State, who will (if required to do so by either party) hold an inquiry or, more normally, an informal hearing.[39]

If the decision to refuse consent or to grant it subject to onerous conditions leads to a loss in the value of the land, this is generally recoverable from the planning authority by way of compensation under the relevant article of the

---

[33]   See categories (2) and (3) in **5.5.2**.
[34]   Under Forestry Act 1967, s.9.
[35]   s.10.
[36]   s.207(1)(b); see **5.5.6**.
[37]   See **5.3.2**.
[38]   *Sherwood and Sherwood v Secretary of State* [1996] J.P.L. 925.
[39]   See the Order for details.

order.[40] The quantum of such compensation is not limited to the commercial value of the timber which cannot now be realised.[41] No compensation is however payable in the case of a refusal of consent under a pre-1999 order, if a certificate is issued by the authority (as it frequently will be), under article 5 of the order, to the effect that:

(1) the decision was in the interests of good forestry; or

(2) the trees concerned are of outstanding or special amenity value.

As a result of widespread concern following the decision of the Court of Appeal in the *Canterbury* case, such a certificate may now be issued in connection with woodlands as well as in other situations.[42] There is however in all cases a right of appeal against an article 5 certificate.[43]

Consent may also be modified or revoked, where continued operations are damaging the area.[44]

7.6.5 Unauthorised works

It is an offence under s.210 of the Planning Act:

(1) to carry out works to a tree that is subject to a tree preservation order without obtaining consent from the local authority, unless the works are in one of the exempted categories[45]; or

(2) to carry out any such works where consent has been refused.

The considerations which apply here are identical to those applying to offences under section 211.[46] In particular, the penalties are identical[47]; and an offender must plant trees to replace any that have been lost.[48]

The offence is one of strict liability, that is, ignorance of the order is no defence.[49] The only exceptions to this are where the planning authority has omitted to notify the owner of the making of the order,[50] and where it has failed to keep a copy of it available for inspection.[51] And an owner is not liable for unauthorised works carried out to trees on his or her land by independent contractors acting against express instructions.[52]

---

[40] TCPA 1990, s.203.

[41] *Bell v Canterbury C.C.* [1986] J.P.L. 844.

[42] art.5 of model order, in Schedule to TCP (Trees Preservation Order) Regulations 1969, as amended by TCP (Tree Preservation Order) (Amendment) Regulations 1988.

[43] TCPA 1962, s.62 [now TCPA 1990, s.78(1)], applied by Model order, Sch.3.

[44] *Mills v Secretary of State* [1998] 3 P.L.R. 12.

[45] See 12.2.5.

[46] See **5.5.5**.

[47] s.210(2)–(4), amended by PCA 1991, s.23.

[48] s.206(1)(a); here too, the requirement is enforced just as for unauthorised works in conservation areas (see **5.5.6**).

[49] *Maidstone B.C. v Mortimer* [1981] J.P.L. 112; and see 10.2.2.

[50] *Knowles v Chorley B.C.* [1998] J.P.L. 593.

[51] *Vale of Glamorgan B.C. v Palmer* [1984] J.P.L. 334.

[52] *Groveside Homes v Elmbridge B.C.* (1987) 284 E.G. 940.

A threatened breach of a tree preservation order can be restrained by the use of an injunction, even where no prosecution for breach of the order has been instituted.[53] Committal for a breach of such an injunction could lead to imprisonment in appropriate cases.[54]

7.6.6 Scotland and Northern Ireland

More or less identical provisions exist in relation to Scotland and Northern Ireland.

The primary legislation relating to Scotland is at ss 160–171 of the Scottish Planning Act. The relevant regulations are the TCP (TPO and Trees in Conservation Areas) (Scotland) 1975[55]; these are likely to be replaced in the relatively near future, and the law brought more closely into line with that applying in England and Wales under the TCP (Trees) 1999 Regulations.

That updating process has already taken place in Northern Ireland, resulting in the appearance of the Planning (Trees) Regulations 2003, which are in very similar terms to the 1999 Regulations. The primary legislation is in arts 65–66 of the Northern Ireland Order.[56] As always, the principal difference is that the Department has the key role in relation to tree preservation orders, rather than local authorities.

7.7 Hedgerows of historical or archaeological interest

7.7.1 The Hedgerows Regulations 1997

In addition to specific trees, one specific feature of the countryside that may be of considerable historic (and, occasionally, archaeological) significance is hedgerows. For this reason, as well as for their contribution to the overall appearance of the landscape and their value as homes of plants and wildlife, some measure of protection was given to important hedgerows in England and Wales by the Environment Act 1995.

The Hedgerows Regulations 1997,[57] made under s.95 of that Act, prescribe the complex mechanism that enables the removal of hedgerows to be controlled in certain circumstances. It should be noted that the drafting of the Regulations was widely criticised when they first appeared, possibly because they were the very last item emerging from Parliament under the Government that went out of office in April 1997; the incoming Government accordingly undertook almost immediately to carry out a thorough review, which was expected to lead in due course to

---

[53] s.214A, inserted by PCA 1991, s.23 (see 10.9).

[54] *Kent C.C. v Batchelor* (1976) 33 P. & C.R. 185. See also *Attorney General v Melville Construction Co. Ltd* (1968) 20 P & CR 131, *Kent C.C. v Batchelor (No. 2)* [1979] 1 W.L.R. 213, and *Newport B.C. v Khan* [1990] 1 W.L.R. 1185.

[55] Amended by SI 1985/1385 and SI 1984/329.

[56] art.65 amended, and arts 65A and 65B inserted, by Planning (Amendment) (NI) Order 2003, art.26.

[57] SI 1997/1160.

revisions, possibly substantial. However, no amending legislation had emerged by the end of 2005.

The provisions of the Regulations are only considered briefly here; for more details see the helpful booklet published by the Department of the Environment, *The Hedgerows Regulations 1997: A Guide to the Law and Good Practice*.[58] There are no corresponding provisions relating to Scotland and Northern Ireland.

The Regulations affect all hedgerows of more than 20 metres in length, or which join other hedgerows, provided that they adjoin land used for agriculture, forestry, or the keeping or breeding of horses or donkeys, or common land, a village green, a site of special scientific interest or a local nature reserve. However, they do not apply to hedgerows within or adjoining the curtilage of a dwellinghouse.[59]

Anyone intending to remove such a hedgerow (except in certain limited cases[60]) must notify the appropriate local authority (district or borough council, national park authority or the Broads Authority). The authority may then decide whether the hedgerow is "important" according to eight criteria, specified in Schedule 1 to the Regulations.

If the hedgerow is not "important", the authority is unable to prevent its removal; but if it is important, there is a presumption in favour of it being retained,[61] and the authority may then issue a "hedgerow retention notice"— which is to specify which of the criteria in Schedule 1 applies.[62] There is a right of appeal to the Secretary of State against a notice.[63] If no response is received from the authority within six weeks, the hedgerow may be removed in any event.[64] To remove a hedgerow without notifying the authority, or after it has issued a hedgerow retention notice, is an offence[65]; it may also lead to a requirement for the hedgerow to be replaced.[66]

The eight criteria, specified in Part II of Schedule 1 to the Regulations, against which the importance of a hedgerow is determined include five relating to archaeology and history, considered below. The other three criteria relate to wildlife and landscape, and are very much more complex.

7.7.2 Important hedgerows: criteria relating to history and archaeology

Criterion 1 is that a hedgerow marks the boundary of a parish or township existing before 1850[67]; the best evidence in relation to this will be the historical maps mentioned below. The year 1850 was selected so as to pre-date the rationalisation of parish boundaries which created current civil parishes. The

---

[58] Available, price £5.50, from the Publications Sales Centre, Unit 8, Goldthorpe Industrial Estate, Goldthorpe, Rotherham, S63 9BL. See also Mynors, *op. cit.*, Chapter 24.
[59] 1997 Regulations, reg.3. For the definition of "curtilage", see **4.5**.
[60] reg.6.
[61] reg.5(5).
[62] reg.5(7).
[63] reg.9.
[64] reg.5(6).
[65] reg.7.
[66] reg.8.
[67] 1997 Regulations, Sch.1, Pt II, para.1.

effectiveness of this criterion will be limited in heavily populated areas by the exclusion from protection of hedgerows bounding residential curtilages.

Criterion 2 is that a hedgerow incorporates an archaeological feature that is a scheduled monument at the date of the proposal[68] or that was recorded in a sites and monuments record (SMR) at the relevant date.[69] Criterion 3 is that a hedgerow is wholly or partly on land that is within a site that is a scheduled monument at the date of the proposal or that is recorded in an SMR at the relevant date, and is associated with any monument or feature on that site.[70] "Archaeological feature" and "incorporates" are not defined. SMRs are not always up to date, and the "relevant date" approach means that information subsequently recorded in an SMR cannot be taken into account, which is unfortunate. SMRs do not usually define accurately (or at all) the precise boundaries of sites within them.

Criterion 4 is that a hedgerow marks the boundary of a pre-1600 estate or manor recorded at the relevant date in an SMR or in a document held in a record office, or is visibly related to a building or other feature of such an estate or manor.[71] The record office means the Public Record Office, the British Library (Manuscript Collection) and the National Library of Wales (Department of Manuscripts and Records) and other national and local record offices and libraries. The most fruitful source of information is likely to be the Public Record Office at Kew and the relevant County Record Office.

Relevant documents are likely to be estate maps (from 1580 onwards), tithe maps and awards (usually from the 1840s, and usually where there had been no previous Inclosure Acts), inclosure maps and early Ordnance Survey maps (together with their field books, now in the British Museum). Earlier charters and manorial records will need to be translated into modern English, but this has been done in some cases; and they sometimes provide useful information by their description of estate boundaries in the form of "perambulations", which may mention hedges and other features.

The results of research carried out by ADAS for the Department of the Environment suggested that in practice criteria 2, 3 and perhaps 4 will have very little effect.[72]

Criterion 5 is that a hedgerow:

(1) is recorded in a document held in a record office as an integral part of a field system pre-dating the Inclosure Acts, or

(2) is part of, or visibly related to, any building or other feature associated with such a system which:

---

[68] See **6.2.2**.

[69] 1997 Regulations, Sch.1, Pt II, para.2. As to SMRs, see **6.2.3**.

[70] 1997 Regulations, Sch.1, Pt II, para.3. As to the extent of the site of a scheduled monument, see **6.2.5**.

[71] 1997 Regulations, Sch.1, Pt II, para.4.

[72] *The Hedgerows Evaluation System: A System for Identifying Important Hedgerows*, a contract report by ADAS for the Department of the Environment, 1996, paragraph 4.2.2.

(i) is substantially complete, or

(ii) which is identified by the local planning authority in a relevant development control document as a key landscape characteristic.[73]

It is not clear what is meant by "integral" or "substantially complete"; but it is noteworthy that the 1998 edition of the *Hedgerows Guide* (unlike the original, 1997, edition) comments[74] as follows:

"the phrase 'pre-dating the Inclosure Acts' should be taken to mean before 1845 (whether or not Inclosure Acts exist for the area in question), that being the earliest of the Acts known by the collective title given by the Short Titles Act 1896.

Any document used in support of paragraph 5(a) should identify the hedgerow in relation to the wider field pattern. Whether the hedgerow is an 'integral part of the field system is a matter of judgment, on the basis of what the field pattern now is (rather than that recorded in the document) and whether the pattern would no longer be discernible if the hedgerow was removed."

This suggests that this criterion may be of greater significance than might have been thought.

It is not clear what will be the scope of documentation prepared by the planning authority for the purposes of development control. Here too, it is unfortunate that research subsequent to the relevant date cannot be taken into account.

7.7.3 Inclosure Act hedgerows

Many hedgerows and other field boundaries in England are the result of the inclosure movement of the 18th and 19th centuries—that is, they were planted to demarcate the parcels of land allotted by the awards made under the various Inclosure Acts.[75] It had been generally supposed until the 1990s that those Acts were of no continuing significance. However, they were then resuscitated by environmental campaigners, as a means to prevent development perceived to be undesirable, by forcing the owners of Inclosure Acts hedges to maintain them intact.

The most notorious of the ensuing cases was an action brought in the Hull County Court, *Seymour v Flamborough Parish Council*,[76] to enforce the terms of an 18th-century inclosure award relating to a hedge in Yorkshire. It was held that the award was still enforceable. The judgment in that case was for a number of reasons somewhat unsatisfactory; but it was nevertheless widely reported (in the popular press, not the law reports), in terms which suggested that it had established that all Inclosure Acts were fully enforceable.

Unsurprisingly, other litigation followed; and some reached the courts.[77] However, in both the cases directly considering the enforceability of awards under inclosure Acts, *Marlton v Turner*[78] (relating to a hedge at Field Dalling, in Nor-

---

[73] 1997 Regulations, Sch.1, Pt II, para.5.

[74] *Hedgerows Guide*, 1998 edition, paras 7.22, 7.23.

[75] On the Inclosure Act hedgerows generally, see Mynors, *op. cit.*, Chapter 23, and the sources cited therein.

[76] 1996, unreported.

[77] There must, presumably, be other cases than the two highlighted here; the author would welcome details (or, better, a transcript) of any other relevant decision.

[78] Noted briefly at [1997] C.L.Y. 4233.

folk) and *Meddick v Shiplake PC*[79] (in Oxfordshire), the courts explicitly declined to follow the decision in *Flamborough*, and both claims failed. And in *R. v Solihull BC, ex p. Berkswell PC*,[80-81] the High Court carefully avoided the question.

It would seem therefore that, in spite of the outcome of the litigation in *Flamborough*, it is likely that the courts will only rarely uphold the enforceability of an old inclosure award.

7.7.4 Hedgebanks and drystone walls

In some parts of the United Kingdom, notably in Devon and Cornwall, old hedgebanks and drystone walls are a notable feature of the landscape. However, the protection given to them is limited.

In so far as they are classifiable as hedgerows, they are capable of being subject to the procedure under the Hedgerows Regulations 1997, outlined above. Indeed, old hedgebanks would probably classify as "important" hedgerows for the purposes of the Regulations. However, during the debate on what became the Environment Act 1995, the Government confirmed that a wall or bank on its own would not qualify for protection.

In so far as they are structures, and thus buildings within the meaning of the Planning Act, hedgebanks and walls would qualify for being listed by the Secretary of State; but it is thought that this has only rarely, if ever, happened. And if they are not listed, but in a conservation area, little protection is given, since to remove part of a structure is not usually demolition, and thus does not require conservation area consent.[82]

7.8 Battlefields

A further specific feature of the historic countryside is the site of a historic battle. A pilot study was accordingly launched by English Heritage in 1992, to identify notable sites for inclusion in a register of battlefields. This was prompted not least by the widespread public concern over the routeing of what became the A14 across the site of the Battle of Naseby.[83]

The first Register was duly published in March 1995, and now lists some 43 battlefields throughout England.[84]

It is stated in PPG 15 that the Register will be comparable in status with the Register of Parks and Gardens (considered above). That is clearly not quite accurate, in that the Parks Register is at least recognised in primary and secondary legislation, albeit that inclusion in it confers little protection, whereas the Battlefields Register is wholly non-statutory. Whether this will in due course become a statutory register remains to be seen; further public consultation has been promised.[85]

---

[79] December 1999, unreported.
[80-81] (1998) 77 P. & C.R. 312.
[82] See appeal noted at [2001] J.P.L. 390.
[83] See, for example, *R. v Secretary of State for Transport, Ex p. Blacket* [1992] J.P.L. 1401.
[84] For further details, visit *www.battlefieldstrust.com*.
[85] See also PPG 15, paras 2.25 and 6.39.

Some such sites are also identified in local plans, and their protection thus becomes a material consideration in the determination of planning applications, including those for highway proposals. Further, as with parks and gardens, local authorities have also been advised to avoid registered battlefields when drawing up road proposals—although here too a balance has to be struck.[86]

There is no corresponding initiative in Wales.

7.9 The wider landscape

7.9.1 The historic landscape generally

The most important historic parks, gardens, trees, hedgerows, and battlefields have for some time been given at least some protection.[87] Awareness has however grown in recent years as to the importance of the wider historic landscape. Some guidance on this is given in PPG 15, although it is sensibly pointed out that:

"Appraisals based on assessment of the historic character of the whole countryside will be more flexible, and more likely to be effectively integrated with the aims of the planning process, than an attempt to define selected areas for additional control. It is unlikely therefore to be feasible to prepare a definitive register at a national level of England's wider historic landscape. The whole of the landscape, to varying degrees and in different ways, is an archaeological and historic artefact, the product of complex historic processes and past land-use."[88]

At present, therefore, there is no particular statutory mechanism, nor any non-statutory register, for the protection of historic landscape as such, other than through the normal process of development control. Areas of particular significance and key landscape characteristics have accordingly been identified in some structure and local plans; details should be sought from local planning authorities.

Notwithstanding these problems, a non-statutory register of historic landscape in Wales has been prepared by Cadw, as the second part of its Register of Landscapes, Parks and Gardens, and issued for consultation.[89]

There is no direct equivalent in Scotland or Northern Ireland.

7.9.2 Environmentally sensitive areas

Much of the wider landscape is of course in agricultural use, and is thus outside the scope of normal planning control. There is therefore a provision whereby the Secretary of State (in practice, DEFRA—or its opposite numbers in Wales, Scotland and Northern Ireland) can designate "environmentally sensitive areas" under s.18 of the Agriculture Act 1986. The purpose of such a designation is (amongst other things) to conserve and enhance the natural beauty of an area, and to protect buildings or other objects of archaeological, architectural or his-

---

[86] PPG 13, para.5.20; PPG 15, para.5.5; *Robert Hitchin Ltd v Bovis Homes* (1996) 72 P&CR 579 at p.596. See **7.7.3**.
[87] See **7.5** to **7.8**.
[88] PPG 15, para.6.40; see also para.2.26.
[89] WO Circ. 61/96, para.16.

toric interest through the maintenance or adoption of particular agricultural methods. English Heritage is a consultee in the designation process.[90]

Designation may facilitate the protection of archaeological sites and monuments (whether or not scheduled), but it may also assist in the protection of the wider historic landscape. So, for example, payments may be made to farmers for the management of archaeological features, and the restoration of traditional and heritage features, such as traditional farm buildings, gates, pillars and posts, at rates specified in the relevant designation order and updated from time to time.

The next stage is usually the drawing up of management agreements,[91] which may be used in ways analogous to those discussed later in connection with agreements under s.17 of the Ancient Monuments Act.[92]

Some 44 areas were designated, and extended (in some cases several times), by a series of statutory instruments in the 1990s.[93] Those in England and Northern Ireland were then re-designated in 2000 and 2005 respectively.[94]

7.10 The National Trusts

7.10.1 The organisation and objectives of the National Trusts

The National Trust—or, to give it its full name, the National Trust for Places of Historic Interest or Natural Beauty—is a charitable body, founded in 1895 and incorporated by the National Trust Act 1907, operating in England, Wales and Northern Ireland. It now protects and opens to the public some 300 or so historic houses and gardens, and 49 industrial monuments and mills—most if not all of which will be listed, scheduled or on the gardens register. It also owns around 250,000 hectares of countryside, and 1100km (700 miles) of outstanding coast.[95]

But as well as its principal properties, the grand country houses, the Trust owns a total of over 20,000 buildings, on the estates associated with the houses, or associated with its landholdings of open countryside; and it holds protective covenants over many more.[96] Many of these too will be listed or in conservation areas. It is thus a major player in the cultural heritage world; and it has the unique feature that it is able to hold land inalienably.

The organisation and management of the Trust are laid down in the National Trust Act 1907, the National Trust Charity Scheme Confirmation Act 1919, the

---

[90] Agriculture Act 1986, s.19(2), (3).
[91] Under s.18(3).
[92] See **11.6.6**.
[93] 22 in England, seven in Wales, 10 in Scotland, and five in Northern Ireland.
[94] Environmentally Sensitive Areas (Stages I to IV) Designation Orders 2000, SIs 3049–3052. [NI: SR 2005/276.]
[95] The total coastline of England, Wales and Northern Ireland is 4,959km (3,082 miles).
[96] Visit *www.nationaltrust.org.uk/historicproperties*.

National Trust Acts of 1937, 1939, 1953 and 1971[97], and the Charities (National Trust) Order 2005.[98] The National Trust for Scotland is a separate but similar organisation, set up in 1931 and governed by the National Trust for Scotland Order Confirmation Acts 1935 to 1973.[99]

The purposes of the National Trust were originally defined, in the 1907 Act, as being to promote:

(1) the permanent preservation of land of beauty and historic interest

— for the benefit of the nation, and
— for the preservation (so far as practicable) of their natural aspect features and animal and plant life; and

(2) the permanent preservation of buildings of beauty and historic interest for the benefit of the nation.[1]

They were then extended to include the promotion of the following:

(3) the preservation of

— buildings of national interest or architectural, historic or artistic interest, and
— places of natural interest or beauty;

(4) the protection and augmentation of the amenities of such buildings and places and their surroundings;

(5) the preservation of furniture and pictures and chattels of any description having national or historic or artistic interest; and

(6) the access to and enjoyment of such buildings, places and chattels by the public.[2]

Whilst the language used is not quite the same as that of the Ancient Monuments and Listed Buildings Acts, the underlying purpose is similar. The key differences are, as would be expected, an emphasis on open land as well as buildings—the natural as well as the cultural heritage—but also an explicit recognition of the value of furniture, pictures and other chattels of interest, which are largely outside the scope of the general legislation considered in the remainder of this book.

---

[97] The six Acts together may be referred to as "the NT Acts of 1907 to 1971" (see 1971 Act, s.1(2)). Note that only the 1909 and 1919 Acts apply to Northern Ireland. The 1971 Act was extensively amended by the 2005 Order.

[98] SI 2005/712, made under s.17 of the Charities Act 1993, applying only to England and Wales, and coming into force on March 25, 2005. It is the Order that contains the basic mechanics of how the Trust operates as an organisation in the 21st century.

[99] Visit *www.nts.org.uk*.

[1] NT Act 1907, s.4(1); National Trust for Scotland Order Confirmation Act 1935.

[2] NT Act 1937, s.3; National Trust for Scotland Order Confirmation Act 1938. It is far from clear why these new purposes were thought necessary—or why they could not have simply replaced the old. Indeed, the Acts as a whole would benefit from consolidation and rationalisation. The extended purposes do not apply in Northern Ireland, as the 1937 Act does not extend to Northern Ireland.

The National Trust has published a series of three papers describing the out-working in practice of these statutory purposes in relation to the cultural heritage: *Opening Historic Houses* and *Historic Buildings: The Conservation of their Fix-tures, Fittings, Decorations and Contents* (1996); and *Curatorship in the National Trust* (2000). The operations of the National Trust for Scotland are governed by a series of policies and principles, including a set of *Conservation Principles* adopted in July 2003.

7.10.2 Special status of National Trust land

The National Trusts generally own land and buildings just as any other freehold owner, and is subject to exactly the same statutory constraints as anyone else. However, given their statutory purposes, there should usually be no conflict between their aims and the conservation policies of local planning authorities and the Secretary of State.[3]

The distinctive feature of property owned by either of the Trusts is that much (but not all) of it is held inalienably—that is, it is to be held by the Trust in perpetuity, for preservation for the benefit of the nation in accordance with the objects of the Trust.[4] It may also be, and frequently is, the subject of a lease, on such terms as the Trust thinks fit, but only subject to the approval of the Charity Commission having regard to the Trust's statutory purposes.[5] In the light of those purposes, the Trust is well aware of its duties and those of its tenants to care for the buildings and structures on its land; and the rents passing will reflect, amongst other things, the liability to repair and maintain them with appropriate materials and traditional techniques.

Where land is passed to the Trust, possibly in lieu of taxes, the donor will often draw up a memorandum of wishes, setting out the way in which he or she wishes the property to be occupied and managed in future—possibly with the donor and family continuing to live in part. The true status in law of such an agreement remains somewhat uncertain.

If the National Trust is approached by a public body, developer or road builder wishing to build on its land, it may not simply sell it; and indeed it would only rarely wish to do so. But there may be circumstances where the Trust is willing to co-operate—where, for example, only a thin sliver of land is being taken, and appropriate exchange land elsewhere is being offered in return. In such a situation, the land can be purchased, but only by an authority possessing compulsory powers. Trust land may thus in practice be alienated, but only subject to the possibility of a public local inquiry; and the Secretary of State would no doubt be

---

[3] For a rather less sympathetic account, see "Misguided Tours", by Patrick Wright, in *New Socialist*, 1986. He comments: "The National Trust lacks the capability to think positively of history as transformation, discontinuity or change. [It] arrives at its superior definition of the nation through a purifying cult of permanence, continuity and endurance. The nation is not seen as a heterogeneous society that makes its own history as it moves forward, however chaotically, in the future. Instead, it is portrayed as an *already achieved* and timeless historical identity which demands only appropriate reverence and protection in the present."

[4] NT Act 1907, s.21(1).

[5] NT Charity Scheme Confirmation Act 1919.

very reluctant to make or confirm such an order in the event of widespread opposition.

If, on the other hand, the Trust itself objects to the compulsory purchase of its land, the order has to be confirmed by special parliamentary procedure.[6]

---

[6] Acquisition of Land Act 1981, s.18; Statutory Orders (Special Procedure) Act 1945.

Part III

Repair, maintenance, finance, and public acquisition

"Whereas the surviving monuments or architecture are among the most important and interesting evidences of history, in that from them may be inferred the former customs, culture and civil condition of the nation, and therefore their preservation is greatly to be wished, we decree as follows:...

It is the duty of all public authorities to take the greatest possible care of the monuments made known in the foresaid inventory, to which end the same shall be printed and communicated to them"

Louis X, Grand Duke of Hesse, decree of 1818.

"I do some mild developing. The sort of place I need
Is a quiet country market town that's rather run to seed.
A luncheon and a drink or two, a little *savoir faire*—
I fix the Planning Officer, the Town Clerk and the Mayor.

And if some preservationist attempts to interfere
A 'dangerous structure notice' from the Borough Engineer
Will settle any buildings that are standing in our way—
The modern style, sir, with respect, has really come to stay."

Excerpt from John Betjeman, "Executive", in *A Nip in the Air* (J. Murray, London, 1974)

Chapter 8

Duties of Owners and Occupiers of Historic Buildings

8.1 Introduction

Part II of this book has considered the way in which different categories of historic buildings, areas and monuments are listed, designated and scheduled. But does such identification impose on the owners and occupiers of the structures involved any duties over and above those that apply to all buildings? The short answer is "no"—other than, obviously, the duty to obtain consent for works to them, considered in Part IV of this book, which describes the various measures designed to ensure that they are protected from unnecessary demolition and unsuitable alterations.

There are, however, certain duties that do indeed apply in connection with all buildings, but which may pose particular problems in relation to historic structures. There is thus a limited duty on the occupiers of premises to ensure that those on the land and on neighbouring land are reasonably safe; and this may lead in some cases to a duty to carry out appropriate repairs (see **8.2** and **8.3**). Insurance may also be an issue of particular concern (**8.4**).

There is in general no duty to admit the public to historic buildings—unless that is imposed as a condition of a grant or loan or under an agreement with the Revenue.[1] But if the public are admitted anyway—either generally, as with a ruined castle, or a railway station, or as part of the business of the occupier, as with a hotel—suitable provision must be made for those members of the public who are disabled. The new requirements relating to this (see **8.5**), that came into force relatively recently, may pose particular problems in relation to older buildings.

And finally, a number of public authorities are under specific duties to pay special regard to the cultural heritage when carrying out their various functions (see **8.6**).

---

[1] See **9.4.5** (English Heritage grants); **9.6.1** (local authority grants); and **9.9.2** (exemption from inheritance tax).

Public authorities have various powers (described in **Chapter 9**) to give financial assistance to the owners and occupiers of historic buildings, which may act as an incentive to carrying out necessary repairs. They may intervene in certain cases to carry out such repairs themselves (see **Chapter 10**). And if all else fails they may step in and acquire important buildings and monuments, partly where they are in dire need of repair, or to ensure public access (see **Chapter 11**). Generally, though, the responsibility for the upkeep of such buildings lies with their owners—if only because public authorities have very modest funds with which to exercise their powers.

But that responsibility remains largely a moral one, since the duties laid upon owners and occupiers by law—which form the subject matter of this chapter—are surprisingly limited. The statutory regime governing the cultural heritage thus places surprisingly little emphasis on positive management; as one recent study has perceptively commented:

"the listed building regime remains, by statute and Government policy, an overwhelmingly passive one, requiring only the granting of prior consent for certain works. The current regime does not embrace the concept of an active, building-specific management strategy designed to preserve, enhance or recover significance, 'built on a constructive relationship between land owners and managers and the officers of the conservation agencies', as is now proposed for SSSIs. . . .

Active management of listed buildings is clearly more demanding of both human and financial resources. Even if the resources were available, such an approach would not always be justified at a level below that of systematic monitoring of the building stock of an area as a whole, particularly for buildings in stable management and use."[2]

8.2 The duty to inspect and maintain

8.2.1 Importance of maintenance

The most immediate problem facing the owner of many a historic building is that of ensuring that it is kept in reasonable condition, and trying to pay for the maintenance and repair that this involves. Where a building has not been properly looked after, so that more or less drastic restoration is now necessary, the problems, and the bills, will be greater still.

Ultimately, neglect of a building may threaten its survival. English Heritage carried out a sample survey, the results of which were published in January 1992.[3] That suggested that 7 per cent of listed buildings in England—that is, nearly 37,000 buildings—were then in danger from neglect, and that twice that number were in danger of falling into that state. In recent years, English Heritage has produced an annual *Buildings at Risk* survey, covering listed buildings of Grade I and II* and structural scheduled monuments. The 2005 survey[4] suggests that 1,302 buildings and monuments are currently "at risk"—including around 1 in 30 of all Grade I and II* listed buildings (at 3.4 per cent, a slight drop from the figure

---

[2] *Streamlining listed building consent: lessons from the use of management agreements*, research report for English Heritage, June 2003, paras 5.2.2, 5.2.5.
[3] *Buildings at Risk*.
[4] Available on the English Heritage website.

of 3.8 per cent in the first survey, in 1999). As for buildings of Grade II, just over half of all local authorities in England maintain their own register of buildings at risk.

All of the registers indicate that there is a major regional disparity, with significantly more buildings in disrepair in the north than in the south; and the costs of repair are much greater there.

Local authorities will be concerned to ensure that the historic buildings in their area are in good repair. It is of little comfort to prevent one fine listed building from demolition if at the same time whole streets of old buildings are falling into disrepair through neglect of repair and maintenance. This is emphasised in Government policy:

"Regular maintenance and repair are the key to the preservation of historic buildings. Modest expenditure on repairs keeps a building weather-tight, and routine maintenance (especially roof repairs and the regular clearance of gutters and downpipes) can prevent much more expensive work becoming necessary at a later date."[5]

8.2.2 Duty to inspect

The first stage in keeping a historic building, or indeed any building, in good repair is to carry out regular maintenance. That in turn is made easier by the carrying out of a regular inspection.

There is in general no duty to carry out such an inspection; however, some corporate property owners do have a system of regular inspections, often at around five-year intervals. That in turn enables schedules of maintenance and repairs to be drawn up on a sensible basis, and the necessary works carried out— and funded—as part of a rolling programme.

The only statutory basis for such a scheme applies in the case of places of worship in use by the Church of England. In most cases, this is under the Inspection of Churches Measure 1955, which applies in essence to all parish churches and to all other Church of England buildings that have chosen to opt into the faculty system under the Care of Places of Worship Measure 1999.[6] In the case of cathedrals, it is under section 14 of the Care of Cathedrals Measure 1990.

Under the 1955 Measure, the synod of each diocese is required to establish a scheme to ensure that an inspection of the fabric of every parish church is carried out, at least (in theory) once every five years.[7] The inspection is to be made by an architect or building surveyor appointed in accordance with the scheme and approved by the diocesan advisory committee (DAC).[8] He or she is to make a report and send copies both to the archdeacon and to the parochial church council (PCC) of the church concerned.[9] The cost of the inspection is usually, but not always, paid from a special fund set up under the scheme. If a church council

---

[5]   PPG 15, para.7.1.
[6]   See **16.3.5**.
[7]   1955 Measure, s.1.
[8]   1955 Measure, s.1, amended by Care of Churches and Ecclesiastical Jurisdiction Measure 1991, Sch.3. For the DAC, see **16.6.3**.
[9]   In the case of a place of worship included in the scheme by virtue of the 1999 Measure, the report is to be sent to the archdeacon and the Council for the Care of Churches (1999 Measure, s.3(4)).

does not itself arrange for an inspection to be carried out, the archdeacon can require it to do so, and, if necessary, he can arrange it himself.[10]

Similar arrangements apply on a non-statutory basis in relation to places of worship in use by most if not all of the other Christian denominations[11]; also to properties owned by the National Trust, operational property assets of Network Rail, properties owned by some local authorities, and no doubt many other larger landowners.

A regular inspection of this kind, at whatever frequency, can be very valuable, since it alerts both the owner and occupier of the building concerned and those responsible for its maintenance to impending problems. It thus enables them, finances permitting, to arrange for appropriate maintenance or repairs to be carried out, obviating the need for more expensive works later on—and indeed to ensure in good time that finances are available. And, whilst such arrangements generally do not apply only to historic buildings, they can be particularly valuable in such cases, since the cost of maintenance and repairs can be proportionately greater.

8.3 The duty to repair

8.3.1 The general rule

There is no specific obligation on the owner of a building that is listed or in a conservation area to keep it in good repair—any more than there is such an obligation in the case of any other building. This may at first sight seem surprising; but it is not clear how such a duty could be enforced, or to what standard, or at whose expense.

Instead, the law allows for grants and loans to be given by public authorities to assist with the cost of repairs—but not usually to meet them entirely. And there are a few, very limited, tax concessions.[12] In addition, there are some powers available to local authorities (acting as either the planning authority or the housing authority) which they may use in certain circumstances to persuade or, in some cases, to force owners to carry out repair works. Some of these apply to all buildings, and some specifically to historic buildings.[13] And, finally, authorities may in extreme cases purchase buildings in poor repair, and either carry out the necessary repairs themselves or pass them on to others who will.[14] However, it will be noted that all these powers are simply permissive—that is, they provide a statutory mechanism to enable works to be carried out where an authority has the political will, backed up by the necessary financial muscle.

But the freedom of owners of historic buildings to let them fall into disrepair reflects the basic rule that the owner of any property has a right to enjoy it as he or she wishes. This freedom has of course been substantially eroded in the last 100

[10] 1955 Measure, s.2.
[11] See, for example, Constitution of the Church in Wales, Chapter IV, 17; Methodist Church Standing Order 952.
[12] See **9.9**.
[13] See **Chapter 10**.
[14] See **Chapter 11**.

years, not least by planning and other statutory controls; but it still remains true that there is no general obligation to keep a building—of any age—in good repair. Further, there is no obligation on the owners of old buildings to put them into a condition where they are capable of resisting "not only all ordinary but also all extraordinary forces that may be let loose to operate against them"—such as vibration caused by building operations on neighbouring land.[15]

To this general principle there are, however, certain limited exceptions, principally applying in cases where a building is not merely in poor condition or unsightly, but is positively dangerous.

8.3.2 Liability for safety of buildings

By virtue of the Occupiers' Liability Act 1957, occupiers of property are under a duty (the "common duty of care") to take "such care as is reasonable in all the circumstances" to see that their visitors will be reasonably safe for the purpose for which they are invited or permitted to be there.[16] And under the Occupiers' Liability Act 1984, occupiers of property in England and Wales are to protect anyone on their premises (including trespassers) from any danger of which they are aware or which they have grounds to suspect, where it is reasonable to offer such protection.[17]

In deciding which Act applies, it should be noted that an entrant may often be (explicitly or implicitly) permitted to be on some of the occupier's land, but not necessarily on all of it; as one judge put it graphically, "when you invite a person into your house to use the staircase, you do not invite him to slide down the banisters"[18]; so the election canvasser is (thankfully) not entitled to inspect your bedroom. Where a person who is a lawful visitor to part of premises strays onto a part to which he or she is not invited, he or she ceases to be a "visitor", protected by the 1957 Act, and becomes instead a trespasser, protected only by the 1984 Act.[19]

The duty under the 1957 and 1984 Acts to keep a building safe for visitors normally falls on whoever has control over it. Thus, in the case of leasehold property, the duty is normally placed on the tenant. However where a building is occupied under a licence, the absentee freeholder may be liable.[20] The freeholder will also be liable if he or she has undertaken to carry out repairs, or has reserved a power to do so.[21] If the building is vacant, the last "occupier" may still be liable.[22]

As for who is to be protected, the law sensibly recognises that children will need special consideration.[23] Those with special knowledge, on the other hand—such as

---

[15] *Hoare v McAlpine* [1923] 1 Ch.167.
[16] Occupiers' Liability Act 1957, s.2. [Scotland: Occupiers' Liability (Scotland) Act 1960, s.2.]
[17] Occupiers' Liability Act 1984, s.1.
[18] *The Carlgarth* [1927] P.93, *per* Scrutton L.J. at p.110.
[19] *Hillen v ICI (Alkali) Ltd* [1936] A.C. 65 at pp.69–70.
[20] *Wheat v Lacon* [1966] A.C. 552, HL.
[21] Defective Premises Act 1972, s.4.
[22] *Harris v Birkenhead Corporation* [1976] 1 W.L.R. 279.
[23] 1957 Act, s.2(3)(a).

builders, specialist subcontractors and possibly local authority conservation officers—can be left to look after (and insure) themselves, to avoid being hit by falling masonry.

The standard of protection to be offered in each case is only what is "reasonable". One of the factors that will be relevant in considering this will presumably be the nature and age of the property. Thus in one case, relating to Pendennis Castle in Cornwall, built in 1540, it was noted that: "Hadrian's Wall is not to be judged by the standards of Haringey Town Hall".[24] It will also be important to consider the likely use of the area where there are risks, and to prioritise any programme of repairs accordingly—so that the archway over the drive leading to a historic house should be repaired before the attic of a disused outbuilding.

Occasionally, it may be possible for occupiers of buildings to avoid the possibility of being sued under the Occupiers' Liability Acts by closing the part of the building that is considered dangerous, or by erecting suitable signs—but only where there is an opportunity for those reading them to take evasive action. Where, for example, a tower of an unoccupied castle is dangerous, it can simply be fenced off; but where a section of wall is liable to collapse onto those walking up from the car park to the ticket office, it is not enough to put up a sign pointing out the danger; it has to be dealt with properly.

And usually the way for occupiers to avoid liability is to carry out suitable repairs.

8.3.3 Exclusion of occupiers' liability

Where people are allowed onto land as part of the business of the occupier of that land, or as part of another business, the occupier may not exclude his liability for death or personal injury, and may not unreasonably exclude or restrict his liability for other damage (for example, to parked cars).[25] "Business" for this purpose includes the activities of "any government department or local or public authority"[26]. Where access to land is granted for recreational or educational purposes, that will only come within these provisions if the allowing of such access itself falls within the business activities of the occupier[27].

So, for example, the occupier of a private house may allow someone to look round the house on the strict understanding that she is not liable for any harm that may occur due to its poor condition, since occupying a house is not a business; it is then up to the visitor to decide whether to take up the offer—and, if harm does in fact occur, it would then be up to the owner to establish the existence of the agreement. But the proprietor of a hotel may not exclude liability for harm caused by the state of it, since running a hotel is a business.

---

[24] *Hogg v Historic Buildings and Monuments Commission* [1989] C.L.Y. 2573.
[25] Unfair Contract Terms Act 1977, s.2(1),(2).
[26] 1977 Act, s.14.
[27] 1977 Act, s.1(3), as amended by Occupiers' Liability Act 1984, s.2.

8.3.4 Liability to users of the highway

Where a building immediately adjoins a highway, if it becomes dangerous and in a state where it could collapse and injure a passer-by or a neighbour, the occupier will be liable under the law of nuisance[28] or negligence. This will be so particularly if the occupier is under a contractual liability to keep the building in repair, such as a covenant in a lease (see below). Furthermore, the occupier will be liable whether or not he or she knew or ought to have known of the problem, and even if a contractor had been employed to sort it out.[29] In some cases, such as where a small dwellinghouse is let on a short lease, the freehold owner may be responsible as well as the occupier—even if there was no covenant in the lease for the landlord to carry out repairs.[30]

This could be particularly relevant in the case of older buildings of a more ornate style in urban areas—stucco, for example, is liable to become loose after a bad winter, and portions of details such as ornamental cornices may fall onto the footway.

8.3.5 Repair of leasehold property

The tenant of a leasehold building is under an implied obligation to use the premises in a tenant-like manner—that is, " must take proper care of the place" and "must do the little jobs about the place which a reasonable tenant would do".[31] A tenant is also bound by any repairing covenants in the lease—typically, "to repair and keep the demised premises in good tenantable repair and condition"—which will be of greater consequence in most cases.

The significant point for present purpose is the appropriate standard of repair is construed with reference to the age, character and locality of the premises at the time the lease commenced.[32] Further:

"The age of the house must be taken into account, because nobody could reasonably expect that a house 200 years old should be in the same condition as a house lately built; the character of the house must be taken into account, because the same class of repair as would be necessary to a palace would be wholly unnecessary to a cottage; and the locality of the house must be taken into account, because the state of repair necessary for a house in Grosvenor Square would be wholly different from the state of repair necessary for a house in Spitalfields".[33]

The language of the judgment reflects the times in which it was given; but it remains to be seen what effect, if any, the listing of a building would have on the scope of a tenant's obligation under such a repairing covenant. Certainly there is no liability to repair inherent defects—which may be particularly relevant in the case of historic buildings.[34]

---

28 *Wringe v Cohen* [1940] 1 K.B. 229.
29 *Tarry v Ashton* (1876) 1 Q.B.D. 314.
30 *Mint v Good* [1951] 1 K.B. 517, CA.
31 *Warren v Keen* [1954] 1 Q.B. 15, CA at 20.
32 *Lurcott v Wakely and Wheeler* [1911] 1 K.B. 905, CA.
33 *Proudfoot v Hart* (1890) 25 Q.B.D. 42 *per* Lord Esher M.R. at 52.
34 *Lister v Lane and Nesham* [1893] 2 Q.B. 212, CA and *Collins v Flynn* [1963] 2 All E.R. 1068.

A landlord, on the other hand, has in general no obligation to repair leased premises, unless required to do so by a specific covenant in the lease. But in the case of a dwellinghouse (which in this context includes a flat) let after October 24, 1961 on a lease for a term of less than seven years, the landlord is under an implied obligation to keep in good repair the exterior and structure of the building.[35] In particular,

"In determining the standard of repair required by the lessor's repairing covenant, regard shall be had to the age, character and prospective life of the dwellinghouse."[36]

Any purported attempt to include in the lease a clause excluding this liability will be void.

The liability may be extensive in the case of historic buildings—in one case, for example, a landlord was held liable to insert a new damp-proof course in order to eradicate dampness in a late Victorian mansion block.[37] On the other hand, the Court of Appeal held more recently that it was sufficient to carry out running repairs to the roof of an old building, listed Grade I, even where the landlord knew that it would be highly beneficial for it to completely replaced, in the light of the age and character of the dwelling concerned.[38] And it has been specifically held that there is no greater liability on the landlord to repair listed buildings than applies in any other case.[39]

For further discussion of the extent of this liability, see *Encyclopedia of Housing Law and Practice*.

8.3.6 Need for consent for repairs

It should be noted that it may be necessary to obtain listed building consent or, occasionally, planning permission before repair works are carried out. For convenience, this is considered along with the obtaining of consent for more major works.[40–41]

8.4 The duty to insure

The owner of a listed building should insure it for enough to enable it to be properly rebuilt; if the building is lost, and the insurance is insufficient, the planning authority will either have to accept a substandard replacement or else provide very substantial grant aid. But there is no duty to insure as such.

The question of what constitutes "reinstatement" for insurance purposes was considered in *Beaumont v Humberts*.[42] That case concerned a Grade II listed farmhouse, thatched and built principally of brick and flint but with some original

---

[35] Landlord and Tenant Act 1985, ss 11–14.
[36] 1985 Act, s.11(3).
[37] *Elmcroft Developments v Tankersley-Sawyer* [1984] 270 E.G. 140, CA.
[38] *Trustees of Dame Margaret Hungerford Charity v Beazley*, The Times, May 17, 1993, CA.
[39] *Corporate Body of Norwich Cathedral v Gaskin* [2004] E.W.H.C. 1918 (Ch)
[40–41] See **12.4.6**.
[42] [1990] 2 E.G.L.R. 166, CA.

cob walls filled with a mixture of mud and cow dung. One wall had settled over the centuries and was some four inches out of true. A surveyor was asked to value the building "for insurance reinstatement purposes".

There were three possible interpretations of "reinstatement". The first was the provision of an exact copy, including cob in the walls and one wall four inches out of true. No one contended that that was what the surveyor should have estimated for, not least because it would have involved certain sections of the house having no foundation, but simply resting on the earth, which would be contrary to present building regulations. Alternatively, he could have estimated for a replacement which was as near as practicable an exact copy of the existing house (approximately £300,000).

What the surveyor actually did was to estimate for a sensible reconstruction in the same style and general shape, and with the same general accommodation, but redesigned in parts to make it more liveable-in and more convenient. The "higgledy-piggledy back additions", one of the staircases and certain other features would not be replaced, and the walls would not be three feet thick. This led to a figure of around £175,000. The Court of Appeal upheld (albeit only by a majority) the finding that that third approach was not negligent. If what had been wanted had been an estimate for what would be as nearly as practicable an exact copy, it should have been asked for in plain terms.

More generally, English Heritage and the Royal Institution of Chartered Surveyors jointly published in 1994 two pamphlets entitled *Insuring Your Historic Building*, one dealing with houses and commercial buildings[43] and one on churches and chapels.[44] Each of these is a very useful source of guidance on some of the technical difficulties likely to be encountered. The leaflet on houses and commercial buildings does however suggest that:

"If a building is entirely gutted, but a substantial masonry shell survives, repair of the external walls and reinstatement of the roof to their pre-fire appearance is likely to be required, even if there is scope for a contemporary approach within."

No source for the supposed "requirement" is given, and it is indeed not at all clear on what basis such repair and reinstatement could be insisted upon.[45]

8.5 The duty to adapt for disabled people

8.5.1 The Disability Discrimination Act 1995

Whilst there is no general duty to admit the public to historic buildings, some of the more important ones (country houses, castles and so on) are in fact open to the public as tourist attractions. And very many more historic buildings (and more recent buildings in historic areas) are open to the public by virtue of their use—for example, as offices, shops, churches, hotels, railway stations and so on. Unfortunately, however, many such buildings have flights of steps, heavy doors,

[43] Revised in March 1997.
[44] August 1996.
[45] See 10.7.3.

uneven floors, and other features that make them very unwelcoming for the less mobile, the partially sighted and other disabled people.

Under Part III of the Disability Discrimination Act 1995—which, unusually, applies throughout the United Kingdom[46]—it is unlawful for any *provider of services* to the public to *discriminate* against *disabled people*.[47] Each of these key terms is defined in the Act. The operation of Part III of the Act is the subject of a very useful *Code of Practice*,[48] produced in 2002 by the Disability Rights Commission (DRC).[49] The provisions of the *Code* are not in themselves binding, but must be taken into account in deciding what is reasonable[50]; it is accordingly essential reading for all service providers and those advising them. The 1995 Act has been significantly amended by the Disability Rights Commission Act 1999 and extended by the Disability Discrimination Act 2005.

A "provider of services" is effectively a person or organisation who provides almost any service to the public—whether for payment or otherwise.[51] The *Code of Practice* provides numerous examples; but it certainly includes, for example, shops, offices, banks, hotels, recreational facilities, churches, pubs, restaurants, and tourist attractions—many of which will be housed in historic buildings or operate within historic areas.

Secondly, the term "discrimination" is defined so as to encompass a situation in which there is an objectively discernible act of discrimination, but without a subjective belief (at the time) that the act is justified. Discrimination can take two forms—

(1) for a reason which relates to a disabled person's disability, treating him or her less favourably than others to whom that reason does not or would not apply[52]; and

(2) failing to comply with a section 21 duty (to make adjustments to the way in which the service is offered) in circumstances in which the effect of that failure is to make it impossible or unreasonably difficult for the disabled person to make use of the service.[53]

However, in either case, the act or omission is not discriminatory if it can be shown to be justified.[54] It is the second limb of this duty that is important in the present context, and is accordingly considered below in more detail.

---

[46] The Act applies to Northern Ireland subject to some modifications set out in Sch.8, but they are not relevant for present purposes.

[47] 1995 Act, s.19(1).

[48] *Disability Discrimination Act 1995: Code of Practice: Goods, Facilities, Service and Premises* (produced by Disability Rights Commission, under s.53A(1) of the 1995 Act; brought into force on May 27, 2002, by SI 2000/720—available from TSO, £13.95).

[49] The DRC was set up under the Disability Rights Commission Act 1999. Visit *www.drc.gov.uk*

[50] 1995 Act, s.53A.

[51] 1995 Act, s.19(2),(3).

[52] 1995 Act, s.20(1).

[53] 1995 Act, ss 19(1)(b), 20(2).

[54] 1995 Act, s.20(3)–(9).

The third key concept is that of a "disabled person". This is defined in Part I of and Schedule 1 to the 1995 Act, which make it clear that "disability" is broad and all-embracing, in that it is:

"any physical or mental impairment which has a substantial and long-term effect on the ability of the person concerned to carry out normal day-to-day activities, with reference to mobility, manual dexterity, physical co-ordination, continence, ability to lift, carry or otherwise move everyday objects, speech, hearing or eyesight, memory or ability to concentrate, learn or understand, or perception of the risk of physical danger".[55]

It therefore extends not just to people in wheelchairs, the totally blind and the deaf, but also to those with arthritis, partial sight, progressive Altzheimer's Disease, and many, many others.

The number of such people is not certain. The DRC estimates it at 8.5 million in the UK, or around 15 per cent of the population.[56] And it should not be forgotten that any changes specifically for the benefit of those who are given rights by the Act will also benefit the elderly, the heavily pregnant, those who are excessively large or small, infants and those in charge of them, the sick, and the temporarily injured—which sooner or later includes everyone.

It should be emphasised that Pt III of the 1995 Act is concerned with the provision of services generally, not specifically with buildings. Further, the whole Act and all the guidance focuses on the duties of service providers, and does not address some of the consequential problems that arise for others—such as planning authorities. Thus, the key question is not, for example, whether wheelchair users can get through a particular door into a shop or hotel, but rather whether everyone (including wheelchair users, the blind and those with reduced hearing) can have the benefit of all of the various services offered by the shopkeeper or hotelier.

8.5.2 The duties under the 1995 Act

When the 1995 Act first came into force, in December 1996, the duty not to discriminate was essentially non-specific, and in particular did not involve any duty to adapt premises. So, for example, the a hairdresser operating in an old building that had steps up to the only entrance or the management of a hotel whose restaurant was accessible only through a very narrow door would have been able to argue that they were not discriminating against disabled people, but were simply unable to provide them with the services of the hairdresser or the full services of the hotel due to the particular features of the building.

The Act then began to bite in December 1999, when it became necessary for service providers to make any reasonable adjustments to their practices, policies

---

[55] 1995 Act, Schedule 1, para.4. See also the Appendix to the *Code of Practice*.
[56] Over 5.2 million disabled people are of working age (18 per cent of the working population), yet only 42 per cent are in employment (compared to 81 per cent of non-disabled people of working age). One in four customers either has a disability or has a closed relative or friend who is disabled; the estimated annual purchasing power of people with disabilities is £40–50 billion.

or procedures so as to ensure that it was not impossible or unreasonably difficult for disabled people to make use of the services provided.[57] Secondly, where the features of the building in which the services were provided meant that it was impossible or unreasonably difficult for disabled people to make use of them, an alternative means of getting access to the services had to be provided—for example, by a hairdresser offering to give customers haircuts at their homes—although that was clearly not possible in all cases (a hotel cannot provide a restaurant off-site).[58] But there was still no duty to adapt premises.

However, in October 2004, Part III of the 1995 Act finally came fully into force, some nine years after the Act was first passed. As a result, service providers are now under a positive duty, under section 21, to make any necessary adjustments not only to the way in which they provide the service in question, but also to the premises in which they provide it, so as to ensure as far as is reasonable that everyone, able-bodied or otherwise, has equal access to the service.[59] The Court of Appeal has recently affirmed that the policy of the Act is "to provide access to a service as close as it is reasonably possible to get to the standard normally offered to the public at large."[60]

The duty of service providers under section 21(2) is thus now as follows:

"Where a physical feature (for example, one arising from the design or construction of a building or the approach or access to premises) makes it impossible or unreasonably difficult for disabled persons to make use of such a service, it is the duty of the provider of that service to take such steps as it is reasonable, in all the circumstances of the case, for him to have to take in order to—

    (a) remove that feature;
    (b) alter it so that it no longer has that effect;
    (c) provide a reasonable means of avoiding the feature; or
    (d) provide a reasonable alternative method of making the service in question available to disabled persons."[61]

It will be noted that there is no order of priorities as between the different limbs of the duty under section 21; which, if any, of the steps specified must be taken will depend simply on what is "reasonable, in all the circumstances of the case". As to what is a "physical feature", this is the subject of regulations that provide that more or less anything is capable of being a feature attracting the duty under the Act, including any feature arising from the design or construction or any fixtures or fittings in a building occupied by the service provider.[62]

---

[57] 1995 Act, s.21(1). For example, a restaurant operating a "no dogs" policy should relax it so as to allow guide dogs for the blind.

[58] S.21(2)(d).

[59] 1995 Act, s.21. See **8.5.4**.

[60] *Roads v Central Trains Ltd* [2004] E.W.C.A. Civ. 1541 and *Ross v Ryanair Ltd* [2005] 1 W.L.R. 2447 at para.32, both following *Re Holy Cross, Pershore* [2002] Fam. 1, para.105.

[61] 1995 Act, s.21(2)(a)–(c).

[62] Disability Discrimination (Service Providers and Public Authorities Carrying out Functions) Regulations 2005 (SI 2005/2901), reg.9 (replacing Disability Discrimination (Services and Premises) Regulations 1999 (SI 1999/1191), reg.3, from December 4, 2006).

There is no criminal liability for failure by service providers to comply with duties under the 1995 Act. And there is no entitlement for a local authority, or the DRC, or anyone else, simply to enforce those duties in the abstract. Instead, a disabled person who claims to have been the subject of discrimination has a right of action to sue the relevant service provider in the county court—and may seek damages (amongst other things, as compensation for injury to feelings).[63] It may also be possible to seek an injunction, which would have the effect of assisting other disabled people in future. Clearly, in response to such an action, a service provider would need to show that it had taken "such steps as it was reasonable, in all the circumstances of the case, for it to have taken".

8.5.3 What are reasonable steps to have to take

It has been noted that the duty of the service provider is in all cases only to take "such steps as it is reasonable, in all the circumstances, for him to have to take".[64] What, in practice, is likely to be "reasonable"? In the past, duties to take "reasonable" care have tended to be in the context of a requirement to do something that would be likely to be done in any event. Thus, for example, occupiers have for many years been under a duty to take reasonable care for the safety of their visitors[65]; and employers under a duty to take reasonable care of their employees. But, in both cases, they would probably have done that anyway. This is a rare example of a Parliament imposing a duty on a person to do something that is against his or her commercial interests.

It remains to be seen what approach the courts will take. One key factor, however, will be the guidance in the *Code of Practice*. This states as follows—

"What is a reasonable step for a particular service provider to have to take depends on all the circumstances of the case. It will vary according to:

— the type of service being provided;
— the nature of the service provider and its size and resources;
— the effect of the disability on the individual disabled person.

However, without intending to be exhaustive, the following are some of the factors which might be taken into account when considering what is reasonable:

— whether taking any particular steps would be effective in overcoming the difficulty that disabled people face in assessing the services in question;
— the extent to which it is practicable for the service provider to take the steps;
— the financial and other costs of making the adjustment;
— the extent of any disruption which taking the steps would cause;
— the extent of the service provider's financial and other resources;
— the amount of any resources already spent on making adjustments;
— the availability of financial and other assistance."[66]

The *Code* gives a number of useful examples of how this works out in particular cases.

---

[63] 1995 Act, s.25 and Sch.3, Pt II.
[64] 1995 Act, s.21.
[65] See **8.3.2**.
[66] *Code of Practice*, paras 4.21–22.

8.5.4 The duty to remove or alter physical features of a building

Two of the steps that may be appropriate for a service provider to take, under section 21 of the 1995 Act, are to remove any physical features that impede access by disabled people to the service provided and to alter them so that they no longer have that effect.

However, that does not mean that premises have to be altered in all cases; there are often measures that can be taken, costing little or nothing, to enable disabled people to have access to at least most of the services provided. So, for example, in the case of a hotel it may be necessary to ensure that there is a side door open, that is accessible without steps (or with fewer steps) as well as the main door up a flight of steps—that may be a perfectly acceptable alternative to providing a costly ramp up to the main door, especially where the hotel is listed. Or a museum may have to accommodate the special exhibition, or the evening lecture, in a room which has good access for the less mobile, rather than in a gallery up a few steps or an upstairs room.

It is thus foolish to spend money on physical alterations—particularly to historic buildings—where a little thought and imagination may be able to find an alternative solution that will involve less expense and effort, and less loss of historic fabric. Sometimes, however, merely altering procedures will not be enough; the only solution will be to alter the building itself.

The first physical feature to be considered is usually steps. These are obviously difficult for those in wheelchairs—but also for those with children in pushchairs, and those who are generally less agile. So a ramp can be provided. But a ramp must not be too steep, or it may cause as many problems as it solves; and some disabled people positively prefer steps to ramps—so it is best to have both. And the top step of a flight should have a tactile surface to alert the blind to a potential falling hazard. Nor should it be forgotten that, to avoid the problems caused by external steps, it may be easier to alter the ground level around the building—although care should be taken not to impair the operation of any damp-proof courses.

In practice, at least as tricky as steps are heavy doors, which can be very difficult for those in wheelchairs (and those with pushchairs), and also for the frail and arthritic. But providing automatically opening doors may create a danger if they allow smaller children to run out unsupervised onto a road or car park. It is thus important to ensure that making life easier for one group does not create major hazards for others. Occupiers of buildings do, after all, have a duty of care to all their visitors, not just those who are disabled. So, for example, the removal of a Victorian draught lobby at Dorchester Abbey in Oxfordshire was said to be necessary to allow entrance to the Abbey by wheelchairs; of the two alternatives considered, one would have impeded exit in case of fire; and the other would have caused difficulties for the partially sighted. None of the options proposed was ideal; but the best compromise had to be found.[67]

In particular, it is better wherever possible to arrange for all who use the building to be able to do so in the same way, rather than to provide an "alter-

---

[67] Oxford Consistory Court, October 7, 2002, unreported.

native" for the disabled. This is the approach known as "inclusive design". The *Code of Practice* rightly points out that:

"Although the Act does not place the different options for overcoming a physical feature in any form of hierarchy, it is recognised good practice for a service provider to consider first whether a physical feature which creates a barrier for disabled people can be removed or altered. This is because removing or altering the barriers is an 'inclusive' approach to adjustments. It makes the services available to everyone in the same way. In contrast, an alternative method of service offers disabled people a different form of service than is provided for non-disabled people."[68]

Note that it will not be necessary to do something that alters the very nature of the service being provided.[69] Thus, for example, a historic building open to the public may contain winding staircases up remote towers; they are part of its charm, and it would be unnecessary to provide a way to avoid them (although, of course, it is still desirable to provide alternative routes through buildings as far as possible to maximise access for all).

In the light of all these various considerations, working out in detail what is most appropriate is thus clearly a matter for specialist advice. In practice, the owners of many historic and other buildings will procure an access audit, to highlight the particular problems faced by disabled people and to suggest ways of avoiding or at least minimising them. It may in particular be suitable to consider these matters in connection with the conducting of other surveys, or when building works are carried out for other reasons.

A number of examples of complying with the duty under the Act are given in the *Code*. More detailed guidance as to what this means in practice in particular cases is contained in numerous publications now available.[70] And there are now a very large number of specialist organisations dealing with particular forms of disability.[71]

8.5.5 Overlap with historic buildings legislation

Nothing in the 1995 Act obviates the need for the appropriate consents to be obtained before carrying out works that seem to be desirable. Thus, listed building consent will be required for works (other than the most minor) to listed buildings, such as the installation of ramps or the widening of doors, and planning permission for works affecting the external appearance of buildings whether or not they are listed[72]; and a faculty for alterations to Church of England buildings.[73] Indeed, the relevant secondary legislation provides specifically that where

---

[68] *Code of Practice*, paras 5.38, 5.39.
[69] s.21(6).
[70] See, for example Tessa Palfryman, *Designing for Accessibility: an Introductory Guide* (CAE, London, 2000); Lisa Foster, *Access to the Historic Environment: Meeting the Needs of Disabled People* (Donhead Publishing, Shaftesbury, 1997); Sylvester Bone, *Buildings for All to Use: Good Practice Guidance for Improving Existing Public Buildings for People with Disabilities* (Construction Industry Research and Information Association (CIRIA), 1996); and *Easy Access to Historic Properties* (English Heritage, 1995).
[71] See the DRC website at *www.drc.org.uk*.
[72] See **12.4**, **12.7**.
[73] See **16.6.4**, **16.6.8**.

consent is required for the carrying out of works that may reasonably be required under the Act, there is no duty to carry out those works before that consent has been obtained.[74]

So, for example, in the Dorchester case, the chancellor observed:

"However, although [the requirements of section 21 of the 1995 Act] are binding statutory obligations, they do not oust the faculty jurisdiction. Nothing can be done without first obtaining the authority of a faculty. ...

It is here that there may arise a seeming conflict between the provisions of the 1995 Act and the faculty jurisdiction. This is because there may be cases where the value of a particular architectural item sought to be removed in pursuance of the 1995 Act is so great that it nonetheless ought to remain unaltered for posterity; in such a case, the removal or alteration would in itself be unreasonable when seen within the wider context of the national heritage. In those circumstances, it would be the duty of the consistory court to rule that the presumption for its retention outweighs the argument for change based on disability discrimination. Each case, of course, will depend on its individual facts, but the service provider will fulfil his or her obligation to take such steps [under section 21] as are reasonable by pursuing the petition to the court."

It is likely that the same approach will be adopted by planning authorities (and by the Secretary of State on appeal) in cases involving secular historic buildings.

As for the duty of planning authorities to have regard to the duties under the 1995 Act when considering applications for planning permission and listed building consent, this is considered later.[75]

The duties under 1995 Act should also be taken into account in considering any alterations to buildings, as well as those specifically aimed to make them more accessible. It would after all be foolish from every point of view to alter a building (for whatever reason) in a way that made it less accessible by disabled people, or which hindered the implementation of adjustments to make it more accessible at some time in the future.

8.6 Duties of public authorities

8.6.1 Introduction

A large number of historic buildings, and buildings and structures in historic areas, are owned by public authorities of various kinds. The operations of these bodies are governed by a wide variety of statutes, obviously dealing principally with topics apparently quite unrelated to the cultural heritage, but many of which impose general "environmental" duties that are very relevant to historic buildings and areas. The scope and enforceability of duties "to have regard to the desirability of" various matters is considered below.[76]

The duties under these non-planning statutes are of course additional to (and in some cases more extensive than) those arising under the statutes relating directly

---

[74] Disability Discrimination (Service Providers and Public Authorities Carrying out Functions) Regulations 2005 (SI 2005/2901), reg.10 (replacing Disability Discrimination (Providers of Services) (Adjustment of Premises) Regulations 2001 (SI 2001/3253), reg.3(2) from December 4, 2006).
[75] See **14.4.10**.
[76] See **14.4.1**.

to listed buildings, conservation areas and ancient monuments (notably the 1990 and 1979 Acts).

The importance of such statutory duties has been recently emphasised in *Heatherington UK Ltd v Secretary of State*,[77] where duties had been laid upon decision makers by two statutes. It was clear that the inspector had applied one, but far from clear that he had applied the other, and his decision was accordingly quashed. Further, in *Kent CC v Secretary of State*,[78] it was made clear that duties under other legislation (such as provisions in the highways Acts aimed at road safety) should not necessarily take precedence over duties in the planning Acts relating to listed buildings and conservation areas.

8.6.2 Local authorities

First, the Secretaries of State have asked local authorities to deal with their own buildings in ways which will provide examples of good practice to other owners—notably by finding for them suitable alternative uses or owners.[79]

For a slightly bizarre example of how not to do it, see the appeal relating to Pontypool Town Hall—described by the inspector as "an outstandingly handsome building". An application for retrospective consent for the replacement of traditional timber-framed windows by new ones with uPVC frames had been referred to the Secretary of State.[80] The Inspector at the resulting appeal commented:

"Why the windows were ever removed remains a mystery to me. However, even if any of them needed to be replaced, suitably treated replica windows made of selected timber could have been used. It is impossible to conclude whether replacing the windows in uPVC was cheaper than replacing them with timber would have been because the Council did not work out the cost of the latter. I am not sure, in any case, that such a consideration is relevant. I believe that it is widely understood by most owners of listed buildings, whether public bodies or private individuals, that they have a duty to preserve the special character of such buildings—even though repair and restoration works might be more expensive than would be the case if the building were not listed. It is particularly important that local planning authorities take this attitude and set an example to others."[81]

As has been noted above, there may be a moral duty on the owners of listed buildings to preserve their special character, but there is only a very limited one in law.

However, local authorities are under a special duty to preserve any listed buildings (and indeed any "features of interest" even if not listed) when they are in the process of appropriating, developing and disposing of land for general planning purposes.[82] This might apply where, for example, an authority is assembling land for a town centre redevelopment scheme.

---

[77] [1995] J.P.L. 228 (see **14.2.2**).
[78] [1995] J.P.L. 610.
[79] PPG 15, paras 3.37–3.38; WO Circ. 61/96, para.127.
[80] under P(LBCA)A Regs 1990, reg.13; see **13.10.5**.
[81] [1993] J.P.L. 604.
[82] P(LBCA)A 1990, s.66(2).

In addition, local housing authorities in preparing any proposals for the provision of housing accommodation, or in taking any action under the Act, are to have regard to:

(1) the beauty of the landscape or countryside;

(2) the other amenities of the locality; and

(3) the desirability of preserving existing works of architectural, historic or artistic interest.[83]

This is particularly relevant in the context of repairs and associated demolition works, and is considered in a later chapter along with other more specific provisions in housing legislation and policy guidance.[84] Note that this duty also applies to authorities when considering what action to take in relation to the giving of grants[85] and the declaration of renewal areas.[86]

8.6.3 Public utilities

Secondly, there is a general environmental duty laid upon the Secretary of State, the Environment Agency, internal drainage boards, water undertakers and sewerage undertakers, when formulating or considering any proposals relating to any functions of the Agency or any such board or undertaker.[87]

The duty is twofold. The first part is to have regard to the desirability of:

(1) protecting and conserving buildings, sites and objects of archaeological, architectural or historic interest; and

(2) maintaining the availability to the public of any facility for visiting or inspecting any such building, site or object.

The second is to take into account any effect which the proposals would have:

(1) on any such buildings, sites or objects; or

(2) on the availability of any such facility for visiting or inspecting them; or

(3) on the beauty or amenity of any rural or urban area.

Secondly, a similar but less extensive duty is imposed upon any body licensed to generate, transmit or supply electricity, or exempt from the need for such a licence.[88] Under the Electricity Act 1989, such bodies, when formulating any proposals for generating stations, transmission lines or other works, must:

---

[83] Housing Act 1985, s.607.
[84] See **10.2**.
[85] 1985 Act, s.605 (as substituted by Local Government and Housing Act 1989, Sch.9, para.85); and 1989 Act, Pt VIII (see **9.6.5**).
[86] 1989 Act, Pt VII (see **10.8.5**).
[87] Water Industry Act 1991, s.3, Environment Act 1995, s.7, and Land Drainage Act 1991, s.61A (inserted by Land Drainage Act 1994). The same applies to local authorities, when exercising functions under the Land Drainage Act 1991 (see s.61B).
[88] Electricity Act 1989, ss 5 and 6, amended by the Utilities Act 2000.

(1) have regard to the desirability of protecting sites, buildings, and objects of architectural, historic or archaeological interest; and

(2) do what it reasonably can to mitigate any effect which the proposals would have on any such sites, buildings or objects.[89]

When considering whether or not to give consent for such proposals, the Secretary of State is also to have regard to the extent to which they have mitigated any effect on any such sites, buildings or objects. Every licence holder must also prepare, within 12 months of the grant of the licence, a statement setting out the way in which it will perform its duty; and before preparing such a statement it must consult with English Heritage or the Historic Buildings Council for Wales.[90]

There are no similar duties imposed on gas suppliers.[91]

Electronic communications code operators (that is, BT and other operators of local broadband cable systems and 3G networks) operate under the terms of the Electronic Communications Code, monitored by OFCOM.[92] This Code requires special notifications to or consultation with the local planning authority in the case of listed buildings or in conservation areas, and in many cases requires new lines to be placed underground.[93]

8.6.4 The coal industry

Finally, now that the coal industry has unfortunately almost ceased to exist as such, the Coal Authority is formulating proposals for dealing with land no longer required for mining operations. In doing so, it is to have regard to the desirability of (amongst many other things) protecting sites, buildings, structures and objects of architectural, historic or archaeological interest; and it must take into account the effect of its proposals on such sites, buildings, structures or objects.[94]

Where new proposals are put forward for coal mining (including operations incidental to mining, and the restoration of land used in connection with mining), either by the Coal Authority or by anyone else, the same matters must be taken into account. In addition, proposals must be put forward to mitigate as far as reasonably practicable any adverse effects which the coal mining will have on sites, buildings, objects and structures of interest.[95] Further, these matters must all be taken into account by the planning authority determining the planning application for the mining proposals[96]—although it is difficult to imagine that it would not have regard to them in any event.

---

[89] 1989 Act, Sch.9, para.1.
[90] 1989 Act, Sch.9, para.2.
[91] Under the Gas Acts 1986 and 1995. However, the Secretary of State is now required to issue guidance to the Gas and Electricity Markets Authority as to its contributions towards the attainment of environmental policies (Gas Act 1986, s.4AB, inserted by Utilities Act 2000.
[92] Communications Act 2003, s.106ff. The Code is in Sch.2 to the Telecommunications Act 1984, as amended by Schedule 3 to the 2003 Act.
[93] For the need for planning permission to be obtained, see **12.7.3**.
[94] Coal Industry Act 1994, s.3(7).
[95] 1994 Act, s.53(3).
[96] s.53(2).

New coal mining operations also require a licence from the Coal Authority; and in granting or withholding a licence, the Authority is to have regard to the above considerations.[97]

By virtue of section 19 of the Coal Mining Subsidence Act 1991, special provisions apply where an ancient monument (whether or not scheduled[98]) or a listed building is affected by subsidence, so that its special character as a property of historic, architectural, archaeological or other special interest is affected. In such cases, the affected property must be restored to its condition before the subsidence occurred, and the provision[99] which enables payment to be made in lieu of carrying out restoration works is deemed not to apply.

Subsidence damage due to coal mining affects around a thousand properties each year; and in the past few years there have been at least 36 claims under the Act relating to listed buildings and ancient monuments. The operation of section 19 was accordingly considered in the recent decision of the Technology and Construction Court (TCC) in *Coal Authority v Nostell Trustees and others*, an appeal from the award of an arbitrator appointed to determine the amount of compensation payable for damage caused by subsidence to the Stable Block at Nostell Priory (listed Grade I):

"... this means that if, for instance, the building in question had a listed stone façade of special interest which cracked due to subsidence damage, then the repair or replacement of those parts of the façade which cracked must be such as to leave the building with a stone façade in the same general condition as it was before the cracking occurred, so as to maintain the special interest of that face which had led to it being listed in the first place. It does not mean that, simply because the façade was listed, special stone of particular durability, and/or stone of considerably higher quality than the stone already in place and only available at huge expense, should be paid for by the Authority."[1]

---

[97] 1994 Act, s.28(1).
[98] See **6.2**.
[99] 1991 Act, s.10.
[1] January 28, 2005, transcript available on Lawtel, at para.21.

Chapter 9

Grants, Loans and Tax Concessions

9.1 Introduction

The special control mechanisms applying to historic buildings, and indeed the few powers that are available to encourage repairs, inevitably involve an element of restriction on the freedom of the owners of such buildings to do what they like with them. The justification for such restriction is presumably that Parliament has decided that it is desirable that such buildings and areas should wherever possible be conserved in the national interest.

Furthermore, the inclusion of a building in the statutory list or within a conservation area will in many cases sooner or later involve its owner in extra expense. Decaying stone slates that might otherwise be replaced with concrete tiles must be restored with slates to match the original. Crumbling cornices cannot be simply removed; they must be carefully restored to the same pattern. And so on. Almost all works to an old building are expensive; and this should be taken into account by a prudent purchaser when acquiring or renting one. But this is especially so where the building is "preserved" by law.

Seen from this perspective, listing is a form of compulsory acquisition of owners' rights, but with the critical feature that there is no financial compensation.[1] It might therefore be reasonable to expect that this should be offset by a system of generous grants, loans and other financial incentives to assist repairs and restoration. It might even appear from the legislation that this is so. In fact, however, almost all that is to be found are permissive powers, even though there are a surprisingly large number of them.

This book is primarily concerned to explain the law, and this chapter therefore outlines the relevant statutory provisions relating to grants and loans for the built heritage. The principal source of funds is the Heritage Lottery Fund (see **9.3**); but there are specific powers for English Heritage (**9.4**) central Government in Wales, Scotland and Northern Ireland (**9.5**) and local authorities (**9.6**) to provide funding in relation to buildings and monuments. And there are a variety of further sources of funding, some earmarked specifically to achieve conservation purposes, and

---

[1] See **3.3.6**.

some designed principally with other purposes in mind, but which may be available in appropriate cases to restore historic buildings and areas (**9.7**).

Finally, liability to local and central taxation generally falls on owners and occupiers of historic buildings just as on any other tax payers. However, in partial recognition of the financial burdens imposed on such owners by the constant need for high-cost maintenance and repairs, some special reliefs are given in certain, very limited circumstances (see **9.8**). Thus where a non-domestic listed building is unoccupied, it will normally be exempt from payment of the uniform business rate. And there are in addition some general reliefs relating to capital taxation which may be of particular relevance to historic buildings; but further reliefs are available where a building is of "outstanding interest".

An additional concession is that supplies made in connection with alterations to listed buildings and scheduled monuments are normally zero-rated for VAT purposes. This is considered in Part IV of this book, as it only applies where listed building consent or scheduled monument consent has been obtained for the works.[2]

9.2 Grants and loans: general points

9.2.1 General points to be considered by applicants for grant aid

Anyone considering applying for financial assistance should remember that all grants and loans, from whatever source, are only discretionary (with the very limited exception of some housing grants[3]), and that the actual availability of assistance in any particular case is critically dependent upon the availability of finance, and the spending priorities of the various bodies involved.

The focus of each scheme, and the conditions on which money is given, have shifted over time, and will doubtless continue to do so. The current position in relation to England and Wales can be found on the very useful website *Funds for Historic Buildings*, maintained by the Architectural Heritage Fund.[4] This not only guides potential enquirers to suitable sources of finance, but also provides links to other relevant websites. The comprehensive booklet *Sources of Financial Help for Scotland's Historic Buildings*, produced jointly by the Scottish Civic Trust and Historic Scotland and updated and reprinted in 2002, is available on the Historic Scotland website. A second edition of the Directory of Funds for Historic Buildings Northern Ireland was published in 2004, and is available on the website of the Ulster Architectural Heritage Society.[5]

Finally, prospective applicants would also be wise to bear in mind the following points—quoted from a guidance note produced in April 2004 by English Heritage, but applying equally to grant aid from any public body:

"We aim to secure a sustainable future for the historic environment by ensuring that work carried out with our grants is:

[2] See **Chapter 17**.
[3] See **9.6.5**.
[4] *www.ffhb.org.uk*
[5] *www.uahs.co.uk*.

- sympathetic to the character and importance of the building, monument or landscape;
- supported by proper planning and adequate investigation of projects, reducing risk and improving cost control;
- completed to an appropriate standard; and

that subsequent regular maintenance is carried out."[6]

9.2.2 General points to be considered by funding authorities

Grants may be given by the Heritage Lottery Fund for a wide range of projects involving the heritage.[7] Grants and loans may be given towards the cost of restoring individual historic buildings of outstanding interest by English Heritage, Cadw, or Historic Scotland, depending on location.[8] Finance can be made available for other individual historic buildings (whether or not they are "outstanding") by local authorities, of either tier,[9] by English Heritage (in London)[10] and by the Department of the Environment in Northern Ireland.[11]

These individual grants may be useful in specific cases, particularly where the building to be restored is individually of exceptional interest; but the buildings thus benefiting will tend to be widely scattered geographically, and the overall effect therefore very limited. An alternative approach, which in some cases can be much more effective, is for a local authority to concentrate on restoring a specific group of properties, such as a terrace or a row of uniform villas.

Such a restoration scheme can have a number of facets. Grants and loans can be offered for specified improvements (such as painting, or the restoration of particular missing features—cornices, window surrounds, porches, roof slates, and so on). Article 4 directions[12] can be made in appropriate cases, to ensure that, for example, painting is carried out according to a coordinated colour scheme. Technical advice can be made available. Publicity can be given to the whole programme, through the distribution of suitable leaflets and visits to individual property owners. In these and other ways, the financial and manpower resources of the authority can be concentrated on a single area, to achieve the maximum effect. Further, a relatively limited financial input from a local authority can attract much greater investment by others—in Calderdale, for example, £11.5 million of new investment was stimulated in five years by just £800,000 in Council expenditure.

The financial element in such a package can be grants and loans under the 1985 or 1990 Acts (see above). Alternatively or (better) in addition, English Heritage may offer conservation area grants.[13] Or it may be possible to set up a town scheme or a conservation area partnership scheme, enabling finance to be

---

[6] *Grants for Historic Buildings, Monuments and Designed Landscapes* (see **9.4.1**).
[7] See **9.3**.
[8] Under HBAMA 1953 (see **9.4.1** (English Heritage) and **9.5.1–9.5.3** (Wales and Scotland)).
[9] Under P(LBCA)A 1990 and P(LBCA)(S)A 1997 (see **9.6.1–9.6.3**).
[10] Under the Local Government Act 1985 (see **9.4.4**).
[11] Under P(NI)O 1991 (see **9.5.4**).
[12] See **7.4**.
[13] See **9.4.2**.

obtained from both the local authority and English Heritage or Cadw or Historic Scotland[14]—or from the Heritage Lottery Fund under its Townscape Heritage Initiative.

In residential areas, it may be appropriate for a local authority to offer grants or declare a renewal area under the Housing Acts,[15] leading to the greater availability of grant aid, with subsidies from central government. It may also be sensible for an authority to carry out some works itself, either to buildings or to the surrounding area.

9.2.3 Exercise of discretion

Procedures for allocating grants and loans need to be considered carefully by funding authorities. The powers of local authorities in this area are in most cases entirely discretionary, but such discretion must actually be exercised by the local authority (that is, the full council or the relevant committee or subcommittee as authorised by its standing orders). In practice, it would in many cases be impracticable for a committee or subcommittee to consider every application for grant aid, and an officer will have to do so. This type of delegation is allowed for,[16] but it should be formally agreed; and such agreement should state clearly the terms and limits of the delegation. The officer exercising the delegated power may not in turn delegate it to a junior officer.

Similarly, it is probably sensible for an authority to adopt a policy as to the circumstances in which grant aid will normally be given or withheld, so as to maximise consistency and fairness, and minimise the time spent on considering each application. However, such a policy should not be followed blindly. Every case must be considered on its own merits and decided as the public interest requires at the time.[17] Where an applicant insists on being heard, the relevant committee should at least consider any written representations made, especially in view of the absence of any statutory right of appeal against the refusal of a grant.[18]

In particular, it has been held that it is unlawful to adhere unthinkingly to a policy of not giving grants for works which are already under way at the time of the application.[19] Such a policy may well be prudent—and is indeed widely followed—but individual applications must still be given proper attention.

---

[14] See **9.6.4**. See also PPG 15, para.4.10.
[15] See **9.6.5**.
[16] By Local Government Act 1972, s.101(1)(a).
[17] See, for example, *Att-Gen, ex rel Tilley v Wandsworth LBC* [1981] 1 W.L.R. 854; *R. v Port of London Authority, ex p. Kynoch Ltd* [1919] 1 K.B. 176 at 185; and *R. v London County Council, Ex p. Corrie* [1918] 1 K.B. 68.
[18] See *Corrie* at p.75.
[19] *R. v Secretary of State for Transport, ex p. Sheriff* (1986) *The Times*, December 18, 1986.

9.3 Grants from the National Heritage Memorial Fund and the Heritage Lottery Fund

9.3.1 The National Heritage Memorial Fund

The National Heritage Memorial Fund (NHMF) was established under the National Heritage Act 1980, as a memorial to those who died for the United Kingdom. It has become, in effect, the fund of last resort to enable exceptional but expensive objects, places and landscapes to be saved for the nation. In the 25 years since it was set up, it has given over 1,000 grants.[20]

The Fund has power to give financial assistance in the case of "things of any kind which are of scenic, historic, archaeological, aesthetic, architectural, engineering, artistic or scientific interest". To that end, it may give grants under sections 3 and 3A of the Act towards any project that appears to be of public benefit, for the purposes of securing the preservation or enhancement of such things, the study and understanding of them, and access to and enjoyment of them; it may also give financial support to exhibitions and archives.[21]

As well as giving grants, the Fund may also (under section 4) finance the acquisition, maintenance and preservation of:

"(a) any land, building or structure which in the opinion of the Trustees is of outstanding scenic, historic, archaeological, aesthetic, architectural, engineering or scientific interest;

(b) any object which in their opinion is of outstanding historic, artistic or scientific interest;

(c) any collection or group of objects, being a collection or group which taken as a whole is in their opinion of outstanding historic, artistic or scientific interest;

(d) any land or object not falling within paragraph (a), (b) or (c) above the acquisition, maintenance or preservation of which is in their opinion desirable by reason of its connection with land or a building or structure falling within paragraph (a) above; or

(e) any rights in or over land the acquisition of which is in their opinion desirable for the benefit of land or a building or structure falling within paragraph (a) or (d) above."[22]

In practice, the NHMF makes relatively few grants each year; but they are substantial; thus in 2003–04 it awarded eight grants totalling £7.8 million. Generally, in spite of the wide scope of its statutory remit, it focuses on aspects of the heritage other than buildings; but in the previous year it contributed £17.5 million (the largest grant in its history) towards the purchase by the National Trust of the Tyntesfield estate near Bristol.

However, in the present context the most important feature of the NMHF's operations is that it administers the Heritage Lottery Fund.

[20] National Heritage Memorial Fund, *Annual Report and Accounts, 2003–2004*.
[21] National Heritage Act 1980, ss 3, 3A, substituted by National Heritage Act 1997, s.1.
[22] National Heritage Act 1980, s.4(2), substituted by National Heritage Act 1997, Sch.

9.3.2 The National Lottery

In the last ten years, by far the most significant sources of funding for conservation projects has been from the proceeds of the National Lottery.

The Lottery was established under the National Lottery etc. Act 1993, and is under the direction of the National Lottery Commission, which licences a company to run it.[23] A condition of the licence is that a specified proportion of the proceeds are paid to the Secretary of State, who in turn pays them into the National Lottery Distribution Fund.[24] After payment of expenses, the proceeds are allocated to various "good causes"; $16^2/_3$ per cent is to go towards "expenditure on or connected with the national heritage".[25] The latter phrase is defined to include any expenditure for any purpose for which money may be spent by the NHMF under sections 3, 3A or 4 of the National Heritage Act 1980 (see above).[26]

The money allocated to the heritage is then passed by the Distribution Fund to the NHMF.[27] It in turn administers the money under the name the Heritage Lottery Fund (HLF), and distributes grants to appropriate projects, as detailed in the report that it submits each year to Parliament.[28] As a result of this somewhat complex mechanism, it is the Heritage Lottery Fund that pays out grants, and to whom enquiries should be made.[29]

Where a project falls within the scope of two or more of the good causes, the application for funding may be dealt with by only one of the distributing bodies.[30]

9.3.3 Heritage Lottery Fund grant schemes

The Heritage Lottery Fund operates on the basis of a series of policy imperatives, including the following:

> "(a) the need to continue to distribute money for projects which promote the public good (including the widening of public access) or charitable purposes, and which are not intended primarily for private gain;

---

[23] National Lottery etc. Act 1993, amended by National Lottery Act 1998, s.1.

[24] 1993 Act, ss 5(6), 21. The Secretary of State for this purpose is the Secretary of State for Culture, Media and Sport. Under a new s.5 of the 1993 Act, to be inserted by clause 4 of the National Lottery Bill, introduced into Parliament in June 2005, the licensee is to pay the relevant proportion of the proceeds direct to the Distribution Fund, cutting out the role of the Secretary of State as middle-woman.

[25] 1993 Act, s.22(3)(c), amended by 1998 Act, s.6(5). The other causes are the arts and sport ($16^2/_3$ per cent each) (s.22(3)(a), (b)). Under a new s.22(3)(d), to be inserted by clause 7 of the National Lottery Bill, the remaining 50 per cent will go to charitable expenditure, health, education and the environment, following the winding up of the Millennium Commission, the New Opportunities Fund and the National Lottery Charities Board.

[26] 1993 Act, s.44, amended by NHA 1997.

[27] 1993 Act, s.23(3).

[28] 1993 Act, s.34(3).

[29] See **Appendix C** for contact details.

[30] As in *R. v Arts Council of England, ex p. Women's Playhouse Trust* 1997, *The Times*, August 20, 1997, which concerned an application for Lottery funds to restore the Wapping Hydraulic Power Station (listed Grade II*) and convert it into a cultural centre.

(b) the need to ensure that the Fund considers applications which relate to the complete range of activities connected with the national heritage;

(c) the need to promote access, for people from all sections of society, to heritage objects and collections, to the built and natural heritage and to projects which relate to the history, natural history and landscape of the United Kingdom;

(d) the need to promote knowledge of and interest in the heritage by children and young people;

(e) the need to further the objectives of sustainable development;

(f) the need for funding to be applied to projects that are fir a specific, time-limited purpose;

(g) the need for applicants to demonstrate the financial viability of a project for the period of the grant;

(h) the need for projects to be supported by an element of partnership funding, and/or contributions in kind, from other sources."[31]

In the 11 years since it was set up (to March 31, 2005), the HLF has awarded grants totalling just over £3.3 billion to 16,700 projects across the UK. This represents around 1,500 projects each year, being awarded an average grant of £200,000 per project; this should be compared with the annual figure of around 2,500 applications for grants. In recent years there has been increasing emphasis on smaller awards, so that the number of awards of under £50,000 (under the scheme entitled *Your Heritage*) has increased from less than 100 in 1995/96 to over 2,000 in 2003/04. And the *Awards for All* scheme offers grants of between £500 and £5,000 to small groups, paid jointly by the HLF and the other lottery distributors. Larger projects (involving heritage assets of any kind) will still be eligible for *Heritage Grants* of over £50,000.

There are in addition a range of more specific schemes, as follows:

- *Townscape Heritage Initiative*: contributions of between £250,000 and £2 million towards the cost of repairs to historic buildings and bringing back into use empty buildings, in conservation areas;

- *Public Parks Initiative*: grants of over £50,000 for regeneration of parks;

- *Landscape Partnerships Initiative*: grants of over £250,000 towards the conservation of landscape areas of distinct local character;

- *Repair Grants for Places of Worship*: grants for urgent repairs to places of worship (other than cathedrals) in use, costing between £10,000 and £200,000[32]; and

- *Young Roots*: grants of between £5,000 and £25,000 towards projects involving young people (13–20 years old) in the heritage.

Separate guidelines and application packs have been produced for each scheme, available on-line.[33] A full account of the first ten years of the Fund's operation is contained in *Heritage Counts 2004*, from English Heritage.

---

[31] Heritage Lottery Fund, *Lottery Distribution Accounts for the year ended 31st March 2004*.

[32] Administered jointly with English Heritage in England and with Historic Scotland.

[33] *www.hlf.org.uk*

9.4 Grants and loans from English Heritage

9.4.1 Finance for buildings and gardens of outstanding interest

Grants have been available for over half a century for the repair and maintenance of buildings of outstanding interest. The provisions relevant to England are now to be found in section 3A of the Historic Buildings and Ancient Monuments Act 1953.[34] This enables English Heritage to make grants for the purpose of defraying in whole or in part any expenditure incurred or to be incurred:

> "[1] in the repair or maintenance of a building which is situated in England which appears to [it] to be of outstanding historic or architectural interest, or
> [2] in the upkeep of any land ... which comprises, or is contiguous or adjacent to, any such building, or
> [3] in the repair or maintenance of any objects ordinarily kept in any such building, or
> [4] in the upkeep of a garden or other land ... which appears to [it] to be of outstanding historic interest but which is not contiguous or adjacent to such a building."[35]

Grants made under section 3A can be recovered under section 4A of the 1953 Act[36] in the following circumstances:

(1) if any condition attached to the offer of the grant is not complied with[37]; or

(2) if at any time within ten years of the payment of the grant:

> — the recipient disposes of the building[38]; or
> — the recipient gives the building (other than on death) to another, and he or she disposes of it.[39]

A "disposal" for this purpose means a sale, exchange or lease for 21 years or more.[40] But it does not include the creation of a mortgage, and a sale by a mortgagee does not therefore result in the grant having to be repaid.[41] This power to demand the repayment of a grant is entirely discretionary.

English Heritage may also make loans for the same purposes.[42] Loans under section 3A may be subject to whatever terms as to repayment and interest as seem appropriate.[43]

Where a grant is given by English Heritage to the National Trust for the repair and maintenance of a building of outstanding interest, it may take the form of a capital endowment, the income from which can then be used to defray the relevant maintenance or repair costs over a longer period (so long as it is reasonably

---

[34] Inserted by National Heritage Act 1983.
[35] s.3A(1) (numbering added).
[36] Inserted by Ancient Monuments and Archaeological Areas Act 1979 and amended by National Heritage Act 1983.
[37] s.4A(2).
[38] s.4A(4).
[39] s.4A(6), (7).
[40] s.4A(5).
[41] *Canterbury C.C. v Quine* (1987) 55 P. & C.R. 1.
[42] s.3A(2).
[43] s.3A(5).

practicable to give effect to the purposes of the endowment").[44] Such an arrangement may be secured by a contract, trust or other arrangement as appropriate. It is also possible for the Trust to be given a grant by English Heritage to defray all or part of the cost of acquiring any building of outstanding historic or architectural interest, or land adjacent to such a building, or any other garden or land of outstanding historic interest.[45]

In considering whether to give a grant or loan under the 1953 Act, English Heritage is to have regard not only to the building itself, but also to the desirability of preserving and enhancing the character and appearance of any conservation area in which it is located.[46]

9.4.2 Finance for conservation areas

Grants may be made by English Heritage under section 77 of the Listed Buildings Act to defray the whole or part of "any relevant expenditure [which] has made or will make a significant contribution towards the preservation or enhancement of the character or appearance of any conservation area or any part of any conservation area situated in England".[47] Grants may be subject to any conditions thought suitable.[48] In particular, they may by virtue of section 78 be recovered in appropriate cases if the property changes hands within 10 years, exactly as for grants under the 1953 Act.[49]

A further option is for English Heritage and one or more local authorities to enter into a "town scheme agreement" under section 79, whereby they identify a group of buildings in a conservation area that would benefit from a programme of repairs and enhancement works.[50] English Heritage may then offer grants under section 80 towards the cost of such works.

Loans may also be made under these powers, and may be subject to any terms as to interest and repayment that seem to be appropriate.[51] It is thought that few if any loans have however actually been offered.

9.4.3 Finance for ancient monuments

Grants to assist the acquisition and preservation of ancient monuments have been available since the beginning of the century, no doubt on the basis that ancient monuments by their nature are often expensive to maintain and produce no income.[52] The relevant statutory provision is now section 24 of the Ancient Monuments and Archaeological Areas Act 1979.[53]

---

[44] ss 3A(3).
[45] ss 5B(2), 6(2)(4).
[46] P(LBCA)A 1990, s.72.
[47] P(LBCA)A 1990, s.77(1).
[48] s.77(4).
[49] See **9.4.1**.
[50] See **9.6.4.**
[51] s.77(4)–(6).
[52] See **1.2.1**.
[53] As amended by the National Heritage Act 1983.

First, subsections (1) and (3A) provide for English Heritage to defray or contribute towards the cost of the acquisition of an ancient monument by any person (which could include a local authority or other public body). Secondly, subsections (2) and (3A) enable it to defray or contribute towards the cost of the preservation, maintenance and management of an ancient monument, or indeed to undertake all or part of the work itself. English Heritage may also fund the removal of the monument in whole or part to a new site to ensure its preservation. It will be noted that the above powers relate to any "ancient monument", whether or not scheduled[54]—but in practice English Heritage normally restricts its grants to scheduled monuments.

Finally, English Heritage may contribute towards (but not pay the whole of) the cost of the provision of facilities by a local authority at an ancient monument.[55]

9.4.4 London grants

English Heritage has always had wider powers in Greater London than elsewhere in England, following the abolition of the Greater London Council in 1986.

In particular, it took over the GLC's historic buildings grant programme, being given special powers (in the Local Government Act 1985) to "undertake, or contribute towards, the cost of preserving, maintaining and managing any building or place of historical or architectural interest in Greater London".[56] This is somewhat wider than the corresponding provision in the Listed Buildings Act[57], since English Heritage can carry out the work and pay for the entire cost itself if it wishes. It can also "preserve" and "manage" a building, not just "repair" and "maintain it". It may assist any "place" of interest, rather than just any "building", which would seem to extend to financing enhancements to the street scene, and other such works.

There is no specific provision however for the recovery of any grant made under the 1985 Act, although in practice grants are often subject to a condition that they must be repaid if the property changes hands within 10 years.[58] Nor may a loan be offered under these powers.

9.4.5 English Heritage grant schemes in practice

In practice, English Heritage aims to give a wide range of grants using all of the powers mentioned above, particularly focussing on those cases which where significant elements of the historic environment are at risk, or where there is a lack of alternative sources of funding. It will also be necessary for applicants for grant aid to demonstrate financial need. Full details, including application forms, may be found on the grants section of the English Heritage website; prospective

---

[54] See **6.2**.
[55] 1979 Act, s.24(3), (3A).
[56] Local Government Act 1985, Sch.2, para.3(1)(b).
[57] See **9.6.1**.
[58] As for s.77 grants; see 9.4.1.

applicants are recommended to consult the relevant English Heritage regional office at an early stage.

The principal scheme is for *Historic Buildings, Monuments and Designed Landscapes*. To qualify for a grant under this scheme, a project would normally have to involve a building listed at Grade I or II*, a scheduled monument, or a designed landscape that is included in the Register of Historic Parks and Gardens at Grade I or II*.[59] Grants may also be offered to projects within conservation areas of in Greater London, involving buildings that are unlisted or building or gardens listed at Grade II, but only exceptionally.

Grants will usually be of not less than £10,000; applications for grants of more than £200,000 should be submitted by January 31 each year.

Grants under the scheme will be subject to a number of conditions, including that some public access may be given, at a level appropriate to the nature of the property. In fact many of the buildings given grant aid in 1986–87 already offer some form of public access, either through opening to the public generally or by appointment, or by the nature of their use (such as hotels or theatres). Problems may however arise where private houses in rural areas are to be opened to the public; and arrangements as to access, parking and so on should be considered carefully.[60] And for the possible effect of an access requirement on valuation for rating, see below.[61]

In some cases, a condition may require that the grant is repaid if the property changes hands within 10 or 15 years after it is given.

Secondly, English Heritage administers along with the Heritage Lottery Fund a scheme for the *Repair of Places of Worship*. Grants will normally be given to projects costing between £10,000 and £200,000 (including fees and VAT). Applications for buildings of Grade I or II* have to be made by June 30 each year; those for buildings of Grade II by September 30. Repairs to Church of England and Roman Catholic cathedrals (which are not eligible for HLF funding) are the subject of a separate scheme.

A condition that is sometimes imposed requires that any further alterations or additions to the building must be approved by English Heritage. The purpose of this is to protect the value of the investment made by ensuring that the effect of the grant-aided works is not diluted by further inappropriate works. This can be particularly significant in the case of grants for places of worship, since works to the interior of churches (and cathedrals) in use are otherwise outside the scope of listed building control[62]; the imposition of such conditions thus gives English Heritage a means of becoming involved.

There is also a special scheme for grants for the repair and conservation of war memorials in England—although it is not clear on what statutory basis.

---

[59] See **7.5**.
[60] See *Rosling v Pinnegar* (1987) 54 P. & C.R. 124 at p.126; revisited by the Court of Appeal in 1998 (unreported, but available on Lawtel).
[61] See **9.8.1**.
[62] See **16.3**.

Finally, grants are available to local authorities to offset their costs incurred in employing conservation officers,[63] carrying out urgent repairs to historic buildings,[64] and acquiring listed buildings in need of repair.[65] And small grants may be available to national voluntary organisations for projects that promote the conservation and understanding of the historic environment (under the *National Capacity Building* programme).

Some £24 million was offered by English Heritage in 2003/04 in grants towards the repair of historic buildings. And an average of around £35,000 per annum was offered to places of worship over the last 10 years under the English Heritage / Heritage Lottery Fund joint scheme. These figures compare with the £270,000 awarded by the HLF in 2003/04.

9.5 Grants and loans from central government in Wales, Scotland and Northern Ireland

9.5.1 Statutory powers in Wales and Scotland

The powers of the National Assembly for Wales (in practice, Cadw) and the Scottish Ministers (Historic Scotland) to make grants and loans under the 1953 Act in relation to buildings and land of outstanding interest in Wales and Scotland are more or less identical to those of English Heritage in relation to items in England.[66]

The terms under which grants are made (under section 4) in Wales are thus the same as those applying to section 3A grants in England, except that the Welsh Assembly, before making any grant under this provision, must consult the Historic Buildings Council for Wales (other than in cases of urgency).[67] The Scottish Ministers used to be under a similar duty to consult the Historic Buildings Council for Scotland before making grants under section 4, but they now have merely the option to consult the Historic Environment Advisory Council for Scotland.[68] A grant made under section 4 can be recovered under section 4A just as a section 3A grant in England.

Loans may also be given by the Assembly and the Scottish Ministers for any of the above purposes. Such loans may be on whatever terms they thinks fit, subject to the approval of the Treasury.[69]

Similarly, grants and loans may also be made by Cadw, again on the advice of the Historic Buildings Council for Wales, and by Historic Scotland, for expen-

[63] See now PPG 15, para.4.10. (and see **1.4.3**).
[64] See **10.3.6**.
[65] See **11.5.2**.
[66] HBAMA 1953, ss 4, 6, amended by Town and Country Amenities Act 1974 and National Heritage Act 1983; see **9.4.1**.
[67] s.4(4).
[68] Public Appointments and Public Bodies etc. (Scotland) Act 2003, s.16.
[69] 1953 Act, s.4(1), extended by Civic Amenities Act 1967, s.4(1).

diture to preserve and enhance the character of conservation areas, and grants to assist with the funding of works in town schemes.[70]

The powers of the Welsh Assembly and the Scottish Ministers to give assistance in relation to the preservation of ancient monuments in Wales and Scotland, under section 24 of the Ancient Monuments Act, are exactly the same as those of English Heritage in relation to England.[71]

9.5.2 Grants available from Cadw

Cadw makes grants to historic buildings of outstanding architectural or historic interest—that is, the best historic buildings in Wales. It places particular importance on the need to preserve such buildings where they are currently in danger of disrepair or dereliction. It also assists works in buildings that are judged to make a significant contribution to the preservation and enhancement of conservation areas; and encourages Townscape Heritage Initiative schemes and townscape schemes in conjunction with the Heritage Lottery Fund and other partners.

The practical outworking of this, with likely rates of grant support and application procedures, are explained in a booklet entitled *Historic Buildings Grants & Conservation Area Grants*, most recently updated in 2004 and available on the Cadw website.

Grants are also occasionally given by Cadw toward the upkeep of ancient monuments; again, a guidance booklet is available on the website. Financial support for parks and gardens is provided in conjunction with the Lottery Fund, the Countryside Commission for Wales and the Forestry Commission. And small grants are made to help voluntary organisations such as local civic societies (under the *Civic Initiative Grants* programme).

9.5.3 Grants available from Historic Scotland

Historic Scotland gives grants of around £10 million each year, to assist with repairs worth over £40 million. The principal scheme is the *Historic Building Repair Grants Scheme*, which offers help to private owners to meet the cost of high quality repairs using traditional materials and specialist craftsmen, to conserve original features in buildings of special interest. In return, owners undertake to insure and maintain the building, an allow some access to visitors. Applications are invited by the end of January, May and September each year, and need to demonstrate that the building concerned is of sufficient interest, that it is at serious risk from neglect or disrepair, and the grant is needed.

There is also a special *Places of Worship Repair Grants Scheme*, run jointly with the Lottery Fund, for which applications musty be made by the end of March and September.

Local authorities may also seek grants of up to £1.5 million from the Historic Scotland *Historic Environment Regeneration Fund* to help with the establishment

---

[70] Wales: P(LBCA)A 1990, ss 77,78,80. Scotland: P(LBCA)(S)A 1997, ss 69,70,72; see **9.4.2** and **9.6.4**.
[71] See **9.4.3**.

of a conservation area regeneration scheme or a Townscape Heritage Initiative scheme supported by the Lottery Fund.

9.5.4 Northern Ireland

Because of the way planning and listed building control is administered in Northern Ireland, there is not the plethora of grant giving powers that exist in Great Britain. Instead, the Northern Ireland Order simply provides that the Department may make grants or loans:

(1) towards all or part of the cost of repair and maintenance of listed buildings, land adjacent to them, or objects kept in them[72]; and

(2) to defray all or part of any expenditure in connection with the preservation or enhancement of conservation areas.[73]

Note that the buildings do not have to be of "outstanding" interest.

Assistance may also be offered in relation to the cost of preserving, maintaining and managing ancient monuments.[74]

Brief details of the availability of grants for historic buildings are available on the website of the Environment and Heritage Service. It should be noted that the grants scheme is currently under review, and details and terms may therefore change; further information should be therefore sought from their office in relation to particular schemes.

9.6 Grants and loans from local authorities and similar bodies

9.6.1 Grants for historic buildings and monuments

A local authority (in England or Wales) may offer a grant under section 57 of the Listed Buildings Act to contribute towards the cost of the repair or maintenance of:

(1) any listed building in or in the vicinity of its area[75]; or

(2) any other (unlisted) building of architectural or historic interest in its area.[76]

It is uncertain what would be sufficient "interest" to justify the giving of a grant to an unlisted building; but arguably any building which an authority is prepared to pay money to see repaired and maintained must be of at least some interest.

Grants can be given by county councils, district councils, county borough councils, joint planning boards, the Broads Authority, national park authorities

---

[72] P(NI)O 1991, art.106.
[73] art.52.
[74] Historic Monuments and Archaeological Objects (NI) Order 1995, art.23.
[75] P(LBCA)A 1990, s.57(1)(a).
[76] s.57(1)(b).

and the Cotswold and Chilterns Conservation Boards.[77] Advice was given by central government to local authorities in England and Wales on the use of their powers under the Local Authorities (Historic Buildings) Act 1962, the predecessor to s.57.[78] There is now no such current advice of any consequence.

Similar powers are available to local authorities in Scotland, under s.51 of the Scottish Listed Buildings Act. There is no similar power in Northern Ireland; instead, grants are available from the Environment and Heritage Service.[79]

In the case of an expensive programme of works, it may be appropriate for two authorities (county and district council) each to give a grant towards a building, to achieve the maximum benefit. Similarly, in the case of an important building on or near the boundary between two districts, it may be desirable for the two district (or county) authorities to share the cost, although in this case the building must be listed.[80] In either of these situations it will often be advantageous for the grant to be administered and the repair works to be checked by only one of the funding authorities, acting as agent for the other.[81]

Grants may only be by way of a contribution towards the cost of the works, although there is no limit as to the proportion of the cost that can be met by way of grant, provided it is less than 100 per cent. This would seem to mean that, if the works are carried out by the authority itself, the owner of the building must make a contribution (even if only a nominal one) towards the cost.

The availability, and size, of grants varies enormously as between different authorities—a few projects attracting grants of over £100,000, and some trivial amounts. Some authorities allocate funds on a "first-come-first-served" basis, others according to carefully thought-out criteria; for example, according to types of building or geographical areas; but see the comments earlier in this chapter on the application of such criteria.[82] Details as to the availability of grants under s.57 should be sought from each of the various authorities as relevant: in some areas schemes are administered by county councils, in others by district councils. The only common feature is that almost all councils are short of funds and, however willing they are to support restoration works in principle, will require consider-able persuasion actually to part with money.

As a condition of receiving a grant under the 1990 Act, the recipient may be required to enter into an agreement with the authority whereby the public can have access to the building.[83] Sensible advice was given in an earlier Government Circular (now cancelled):

"A requirement as to access will not be appropriate in all cases. Some buildings may not be sufficiently large or significant to justify this. Sometimes the value of a building attracting a

---

[77] s.57(7), amended by the Local Government (Wales) Act 1994, Sch.6 and extended by the Environment Act 1995, Sch.9, para.13(4)(b); Cotswolds and Chilterns Areas of Out-standing Natural Beauty (Establishment of Conservation Board) Orders 2004 (SIs 2004/ 1777; 2004/1778), art.25.

[78] In App. VI of Circ. 8/87 and App. VI of WO Circ. 61/81.

[79] See **9.5.4**.

[80] P(LBCA)A 1990, s.57(1)(a); P(LBCA)(S)A 1997, s.51(1)(a).

[81] As is provided for by Local Government Act 1972, s.101(1)(b).

[82] See **9.2.3**.

[83] P(LBCA)A 1990, s.57(6). [Scotland: P(LBCA)(S)A 1997, s.51(6).]

grant may lie in its external appearance seen from a street or other public place. On the other hand where the building is not reasonably visible from a public place or where its value lies partly or wholly in its interior, opportunities for public access at specified times or by appointment to the building or to the appropriate parts of it should be considered.

The extent and duration of public access must clearly be decided with regard to the circumstances of each case. A requirement that would be so onerous upon the owner or occupier of the building as to discourage the acceptance of a grant would, of course, tend to defeat the object of the Act".[84]

And see the cases, noted already in connection with similar requirements attached to English Heritage grants, as to problems that may arise in connection with requiring access.[85]

At the same time as assisting towards the cost of the repair and maintenance of a building under the Listed Buildings Acts, an authority may also make a grant towards the cost of the upkeep of any garden that is occupied with it.[86] "It will often be unsatisfactory for public funds to be spent on preserving a building if the surrounding garden, which might be part of the architectural concept or at least a pleasant setting for the building, could not be kept in reasonable order".[87] Grants cannot however be given towards gardens other than in connection with grants or loans for buildings associated with them (unlike grants under the 1953 Act[88]).

A local authorities may also defray or contribute towards the cost of the preservation, maintenance and management of any ancient monument—whether or not scheduled—or indeed may undertake all or part of the work itself.[89]

9.6.2 Repayment of local authority grants

A grant made under the 1990 Act can be recovered by the local authority that paid it if, at any time within the following three years, the recipient either:

(1) disposes of the building[90]; or

(2) gives it (other than on death) to another, and he or she disposes of it.[91]

A "disposal" for this purposes means a sale, exchange or lease for 21 years or more.[92] But it does not include the creation of a mortgage, and a sale by a mortgagee does not lead to the grant having to be repaid.[93]

It is also possible for an authority to seek to recover the grant if any condition attached to its offer (for example, as to letting the public have access to the

---

[84] Circ. 8/87, App VI, paras 7, 8.
[85] *Rosling v Pinnegar* (1987) 54 P. & C.R. 124 and 1998 (unreported), and *Hauptfuhrer v Thompson* [1978] 1 E.G.L.R. 183; see **9.4.5**—also **9.9.2** on access requirements in connection with tax concessions.
[86] P(LBCA)A 1990, s.57(2). [Scotland: P(LBCA)(S)A 1997, s.51(2).]
[87] Circ. 8/87, App VI, para.4.
[88] See **9.4.1**.
[89] AMAAA 1979, s.24(4).
[90] P(LBCA)A 1990, s.58(1). [Scotland: P(LBCA)(S)A 1997, s.52(1).]
[91] s.58(2), (3); s.52(2),(3).
[92] s.58(1); s.52(1).
[93] *Canterbury CC v Quine* (1987) 55 P. & C.R. 1.

building) is not complied with.[94] This provision was introduced following a recommendation by the Law Commission[95], to bring local authority grants into line with section 77 grants.[96] In order that it should not operate unfairly, however, it did not apply in the case of grants made prior to the coming into force of the 1990 Act.[97]

This power to demand the repayment of a grant is entirely discretionary:

"The object ... is to deter speculators and to prevent profit-making attributable to the grant from public funds. It will not always be right to recover the grant ... For example the works towards the cost of which grant was paid might have been done at the request of the local authority in order to retain the architectural advantage of the building, perhaps by having a new stone tile roof instead of concrete tiles or by replacing a decaying ornamental feature, and might have no functional advantage. Again, a preservation society may sometimes propose to buy a building for restoration and apply for a grant, making it clear at the outset that their intention would be to re-sell the building. In such circumstances it would appear right to recover the grant only to such extent as is possible after the preservation society have recouped their expenditure."[98]

9.6.3 Loans for historic buildings

As an alternative to making a grant, a local authority may offer a loan for the same purposes.[99] This may be upon such terms and conditions as it wishes.[1] In particular, an authority may make low-interest or interest-free loans; and it may renounce its right to repayment at any time, or subsequently vary the interest rate or other conditions with the agreement of the owner.[2] The generality of the power to impose terms and conditions would seem to admit the possibility of requiring public access, as for grants.[3]

The setting up of a programme of loans may be a cost-effective way for an authority to bring about the repair, maintenance and restoration of historic buildings, since the funds can be recycled as the loans are repaid. Experience would tend to suggest, however, that—particularly in a time of low interest rates generally—such a programme will only be attractive if the loans are interest-free (which implies a hidden element of grant aid), and if the bureaucracy is kept to the absolute minimum.

9.6.4 Town schemes

As noted above, it may in some cases be helpful for the relevant national funding body to work in partnership with one or more local authorities.

One way to achieve this is by means of a "town scheme agreement" under section 79 of the Listed Buildings Act, which authorises English Heritage or Cadw

---

[94] s.58(4); s.52(4).
[95] Cm. 958, para.44.
[96] See 9.4.1.
[97] Planning (Consequential Provisions) Act 1990, Sch.3, para.17.
[98] Circ. 8/87, App. VI, para.11.
[99] P(LBCA)A 1990, s.57(3). [Scotland: P(LBCA)(S)A 1997, s.51(3).]
[1] s.57(4); s.51(4).
[2] s.57(5); s.51(4).
[3] Although Circ. 8/87, App. VI, para.6 suggested otherwise.

and the relevant local authority or authorities each to agree to allocate an annual sum to be given in grants over a specified number of years for the repair of a specified group of properties. The properties involved (which must be in a conservation area) are included in a list or shown on a map.[4] This mechanism spreads the cost of the work and maximises the effectiveness of the money spent.

The repair of any of the buildings in the scheme can then be assisted by a grant, which comprises two elements:

(1) part from the local authority or authorities concerned[5]; and

(2) part from English Heritage or Cadw (under s.80).[6]

Where both the county council and the district council are involved, they may split the local authority portion of the grant between them as they see fit. The Broads Authority and national park authorities are also able to enter into town scheme agreements.[7] The organisation that is supervising a scheme—which could be either the national body or one of the local authorities involved—will be responsible for giving grants to applicants, including the share contributed by the other partner organisation.[8]

A grant may be reclaimed by the body that gave it, exactly as for any other local authority grant under the 1990 Act,[9] in the following circumstances:

(1) where a property changes hands within three years of a grant being paid[10]; or

(2) in the case of a grant paid after August 1990, where a condition on the grant has been breached.[11]

This arrangement used to be used reasonably frequently in England, more recently under the title *Conservation Area Partnership* scheme. However, the programme is currently under review. In Wales, town scheme agreements are in practice the main channel through which Cadw grants are given for repairs in conservation areas.[12]

Corresponding provisions for Scotland are in sections 71 and 72 of the Scottish Listed Buildings Act. There is obviously no need for such a scheme in Northern Ireland, in view of the unitary system of planning control.

9.6.5 Housing grants

Where historic buildings are in residential use, grants by local authorities under Housing Grants, Construction and Regeneration Act 1996 can in some cases be much more effective to bring about their restoration than grants aimed specifically

---

4   s.79(1).
5   Using powers under s.57, as to which see **9.6.1**.
6   Using its powers under s.80(1).
7   s.79(3), amended by Environment Act 1995, Sch.10.
8   s.80(5), (6).
9   See **9.6.2**.
10   s.80(7).
11   s.80(7); Planning (Consequential Provisions) Act, Sch.3, para.17.
12   WO Circ. 61/96, para.141.

at historic buildings.[13] From the point of view of the building owner, where such grants are available at all they are likely to be easier to obtain, since the authority's funds available for housing are likely to be very much greater than those available for conservation. In a few cases, grants are available as of right. The advantage for the authority is that they will attract financial support from central government.

In appropriate cases, it may be sensible for an applicant to seek, or an authority to offer, a housing grant under the 1996 Act in addition to any historic buildings grants that may be offered under the 1953 or 1990 Acts, since the former can be used for improvement and conversion works, whereas the latter will be limited to repair and maintenance. This can enable modern amenities to be provided, which in turn can make the restoration of an old house a viable proposition.

The new arrangements provide for a co-ordinated strategy of grant aids with the following types of grant available:

(1) *renovation grants*, for the improvement or repair of a dwelling or the provision of dwellings by the conversion of a house or other building;

(2) *common parts grants*, for the improvement or repair of the common parts of a building;

(3) *disabled facilities grants*;

(4) *HMO grants*, for the improvement or repair of a house in multiple occupations, or for the provision of one by conversion;

(5) grants for *group repair schemes*; and

(6) *home repair assistance*, replacing minor works assistance under the 1989 Act.

The strategy is described fully in relevant government guidance,[14] to which reference should be made for further details.

Unlike the scheme for grants under the 1985 Act there are no limits of eligible expenses—and thus no higher limits for listed buildings. Instead, the principal factor determining the entitlement to grant aid is the extent of the financial resources of the applicant.

Advice on grant-aid in relation to historic buildings is given in of PPG 15:

"Where a local planning authority proposes to grant-aid renovation work to a listed house or a house in a conservation area, care should be taken to ensure that standard grant conditions (*e.g.* for damp proofing or insulation) are not imposed in a way which would be damaging to the historic character of the building. In such cases housing and environmental health departments should consult with the authority's conservation officer or seek expert advice from other sources."[15]

---

[13] The 1996 Act replaced Pt VIII of the Local Government and Housing Act 1989 with effect from December 1996. Relaxations were made to the statutory scheme under the 1996 Act by the Regulatory Reform (Housing Assistance) Order 2002.

[14] Including DoE and DETR Circulars 17/96, 04/97, 17/97, 04/98, 06/99, 03/00, 05/01 and 03/02.

[15] PPG 15, para.3.29 (and see WO Circ. 61/96, para.126).

The advice also stresses the need for a sympathetic approach in applying the requirements of Building Regulations and Fire Regulations to the repair or conversion of older buildings.[16]

9.7 Financial assistance from other sources

9.7.1 Private trusts

In addition to those already described, there are a number of other possible sources of finance for the repair, maintenance and restoration of historic buildings. Not the least significant of these are the significant number of private charitable trusts concerned (either exclusively or as one of several objects) with preservation.[17] English Heritage has estimated that in the region of 750 projects each year have been assisted from such bodies, with a total of £6 million in grants.[18]

There are in particular over 60 private trusts listed on the AHF database (*Funds for Historic Buildings*[19]), of which almost exactly half are restricted to the support of projects in particular parts of the country, and 21 are concerned exclusively concerned with the repair and maintenance of places of worship—and there are undoubtedly many more that are not, yet, on the database.

Further possibilities may be found in the *Directory of Grant-Making Trusts*, published every year by the Directory of Social Change in association with Charities Aid Foundation, and *A Guide to Major Grant-making Trusts*, published annually by the DSC; both are generally available in reference libraries, as are a range of regional directories. It may also be worth inspecting the Register of Local Charities, available both at the offices of the local authority and at the Charity Commission in London. In many areas there are longstanding charities with suitable objects, whose trustees could be approached.

9.7.2 Building preservation trusts

A building preservation trust is a non-profiting organisation set up to bring about the restoration of historic buildings by purchasing them, carrying out the required works, and then reselling them on the open market. The theory is that the addition to the value of each building dealt with in this way will gradually increase the capital assets of the trust, and enable it to buy and restore an ever increasing number of buildings.

A trust can raise money from wherever it wishes, and may apply for grants and loans under any or all of the schemes described so far in this chapter. It can also

---

[16] PPG 15, paras 3.26 and 3.27, and WO Circ. 61/96, para.124.

[17] It may be relevant to note that the Charities Bill introduced in May 2005 clarified the meaning of "charitable purposes", to include (amongst many other things) "the advancement of arts, culture, the heritage or science"; "the advancement of environmental protection or improvement"; and analogous purposes. (Charities Bill, as brought to the Commons, November 2005, clause 2(2)(f),(i), (4)(b)).

[18] *Heritage Counts 2004*, s.4.3.2.

[19] *www.ffhb.org.uk*

borrow money on a short-term low-interest loan from the Architectural Heritage Fund, which had working capital of £13.3 million at July 2005; over the last 30 years, the Fund has thus made working capital loans of £82 million. The Fund in turn is able to be grant aided by the Secretary of State (in England, Wales and Scotland) and by English Heritage.[20] The Fund and the trusts themselves are registered charities.

By mid-2005, there were over 250 trusts in the United Kingdom—generally local to particular parts of the country. Further details are available from the Fund.[21]

9.7.3 Public bodies

There are various public sector bodies who make grants which are aimed primarily at other objectives, but which may be used to assist restoration works.

The repair, maintenance and presentation of historic buildings and gardens are closely related to the tourist industry. It is for this reason that the national Tourist Boards used to give grants[22] for any project which will provide or improve tourist amenities and facilities. But DEFRA, amongst others, operates a system of grants for tourism projects in rural areas. Local authorities, too, may be more willing to give grants, under any of their various powers, if they can be convinced that a restoration project will boost local tourism.

British Coal assists suitable preventive or restoration works to buildings in areas of mining subsidence.[23] The Council for Small Industries in Rural Areas (COSIRA) and the Countryside Commission both give grants for the conversion of redundant buildings in rural areas. The Welsh Development Agency may assist the creation of jobs through the reuse of redundant buildings. The Sports Council, the Crafts Council and other similar bodies may in appropriate cases be able to help.

Where historic buildings and areas are in inner cities, it may be possible to achieve conservation objectives through the use of financial incentives and other powers under the Government's urban regeneration programme. This includes the setting up of urban development corporations and housing action trusts and the designation of enterprise zones and simplified planning zones, as well as the more recent creation of English Partnerships[24] and regional development agencies.[25] The details of these are beyond the scope of this book, but the relevant authorities in each case may be willing to use its powers in a way that is helpful to conservation rather than otherwise—English Heritage has estimated that three

[20] Under their powers in the Ancient Monuments and Archaeological Areas Act 1979, s.49, amended by National Heritage Act 1983. Its annual funding from English Heritage increased to £185,000 for 2005–06—an increase of 18 per cent over the amount in previous years.

[21] *www.ahfund.org.uk*. And see PPG 15, Annex A, para.A.18 and WO Circ. 61/96, Annex A, para.16.

[22] Under the Development of Tourism Act 1969, s.4; grants under this power have not been available for some years now.

[23] Under the Coal Mining (Subsidence) Act 1991; although see **8.6.4**.

[24] Under the Leasehold Reform, Housing and Urban Development Act 1993.

[25] Under the Regional Development Agencies Act 1998.

regional development agencies alone were responsible for projects involving historic buildings worth some £9.8 million in 2003/04.[26]

There are also various tax-related schemes that may be used creatively to fund heritage-related projects. These include the Landfill Tax Credit Scheme, under which landfill operators may direct up to 20 per cent of their tax liability in any year to fund approved environmental projects, and the Aggregate Levy Sustainability Fund.

Any grants that are obtained from such sources will of course be even more effective if they are used together with funding from other sources, such as grants or loans from English Heritage, Cadw or Historic Scotland.

Once again, details of some of these, and other possibilities, are contained on the website *Funds for Historic Buildings*.[27]

9.8 Rating

9.8.1 Valuation

Listed buildings and other historic structures are generally valued for rating purposes as any other property. However, some concessions may occasionally be made.

Firstly, where a rating hereditament comprises or includes a group of listed buildings, with a substantial repairing liability and some element of limitation as to user, that must be taken into account in valuing it. But the resulting reduction may not be large—possibly only 5 per cent.[28] Similarly, where a grant is given subject to a requirement as to giving public access, a reduction may be given, to compensate for the drawbacks of visitors, but not a great deal—see *Hauptfuhrer v Thompson*,[29] relating to a Grade I Palladian villa at Richmond, Surrey.

Secondly, guidance was given by the Court of Appeal as to the techniques to be adopted in the valuation of a large stately home, in the case of *National Trust v Hoare*[30]—relating to Petworth House and Castle Drogo. In such cases, where there is realistically only one possible occupier, the result will be that it would pay only a nominal hypothetical rent; that in turn should lead to the conclusion that there should be a nil rental value, and thus nil rates payable.

9.8.2 Unoccupied historic buildings

Rates are in principle payable in respect of the occupation of all non-domestic property—and thus not in respect of unoccupied property. That applies to historic buildings just as to any others.

However, the Secretary of State has power (under the Local Government Finance Act 1988[31]) to determine that rates *are* to be payable in respect of all

[26] *Heritage Counts 2004*, s.4.3.2.
[27] www.ffhb.org.uk
[28] *McPhail v Saul* [1995] R.A. 39, LT.
[29] [1978] 1 E.G.L.R. 183.
[30] (1999) 77 P. & C.R. 366, [1999] 1 E.G.L.R. 155, CA.
[31] s.45(1).

unoccupied non-domestic property other than that within certain exempted categories, prescribed in regulations. Using that power, he has prescribed that non-domestic rating does apply to unoccupied buildings, but not to those that are listed, or subject to a building preservation notice,[32] or scheduled under the 1979 Act.[33]

The exemption does not apply to an unlisted building in a conservation area, or to an ancient monument that is not "scheduled".[34]

Problems have arisen with the scope of this exemption, since the extent of a "hereditament" for rating purposes may be quite different—larger or smaller—than that of a "listed building" (with, or even without, its curtilage) as defined by section 1(5) of the Listed Buildings Act.[35] The first is a concept arising from the characteristics of how a building is occupied; the second arises from its physical (architectural and topographical) features. Therefore in some cases it may not be very meaningful to discuss, as the 1989 Regulations do, whether or not a hereditament "is included" in the list.

The scope of this exemption was considered in *Providence Properties Ltd v. Liverpool CC*,[36] decided under the General Rate Act 1967.[37] The rating hereditament in that case comprised three warehouses, of which one was listed and two were not. The Divisional Court held that the exemption from rating would not apply. This approach was upheld by the House of Lords in *Debenhams plc v Westminster CC*.[38] After finding on the facts that one of the two buildings comprising the hereditament was listed and one was not, Lord Keith agreed that the whole hereditament was liable to the payment of rates. He also specifically considered the position where a building preservation notice is served on one building within a hereditament, so that it could be said without any undue straining of language that the hereditament as such is the subject of the notice, but considered that even here the whole hereditament would be liable to the payment of rates.[39]

As to whether or not a hereditament is "unoccupied", so as to give rise to the possibility of the exemption coming into play, this is a matter of general rating law beyond the scope of this book; but see in particular *R. v St Pancras Assessment Committee*[40] and *London County Council v Wilkins*.[41]

---

[32] See **7.3.9**.
[33] Non-Domestic Rating (Unoccupied Property) Regulations 1989 (SI 1989/2261), reg.2(2)(a), (e).
[34] See **6.2**.
[35] See **4.1.2**.
[36] [1980] R.A. 189.
[37] para.2(c) of Sch.1 to the 1967 Act contained a similar exemption to that in the 1989 Regulations.
[38] [1987] A.C. 396, HL. For the facts, see **4.3.2**.
[39] At pp.347–8.
[40] (1877) 2 Q.B.D. 581.
[41] [1957] A.C. 362, HL.

9.9 Capital taxation

9.9.1 Capital taxation: general reliefs

Finally, there are some provisions which operate so as to give a measure of relief to the owners of all buildings, which may be particularly relevant in the case of historic buildings.

First, a historic building will in many cases be the only or principal residence of an individual private taxpayer. Where this is so, capital gains tax is not payable on its disposal.[42] Where the taxpayer owns and occupies two or more houses, he or she may elect as to which is to be treated as the "principal" one.

Secondly, gifts of property may attract relief from capital gains tax or inheritance tax (IHT). There is a general roll-over relief applicable to a capital gain accruing on the gift of any asset, provided that both the donor and the recipient apply to the Revenue (formerly the Inland Revenue, now a branch of Revenue and Customs). The net effect of this is to transfer the payment of any capital gains tax due, until (at least) the next disposal of the asset.[43] Gifts of property to charities and to certain heritage bodies are subject to a similar roll-over relief,[44] and are also exempt from inheritance tax if the gift is on the death of the donor.[45] A gift of property will not attract inheritance tax anyway if it is made at least seven years before the death of the donor—and if the donor dies within the seven-year period, tax is payable but at a tapering rate.[46]

The heritage bodies referred to in the previous paragraph are those generally concerned with the preservation of "the heritage", and include English Heritage, the National Trust, the Historic Churches Preservation Trust, the Nature Conservancy Council, any local authority, any government department, and any university.[47]

9.9.2 Capital taxation and buildings of outstanding interest

A gift of an historic building on the death of the donor, or where the donor dies within the seven years following the gift, will not attract the inheritance tax that would otherwise be payable, provided that the new owner (or other appropriate person) gives an undertaking under section 31 of the IHT Act 1985, to the satisfaction of the Revenue, that:

(1) the building is of outstanding historic or architectural interest[48];

(2) the new owner undertakes that reasonable access will be provided for the public and that the building will be properly maintained.[49]

---

[42] Taxation of Chargeable Gains Act 1992, ss 222–226.
[43] 1992 Act, s.260.
[44] s.257.
[45] IHT Act 1984, ss 23, 25, 26, 32.
[46] Finance Act 1986, s.101 and Sch.19.
[47] IHT Act 1984, Sch.3.
[48] IHT Act 1984, s.31(1)(c).
[49] section 31(4)–(4F), as amended by Finance Act 1985, Sch.26.

The requirements as to access were tightened up with effect from July 1998, in that owners are now no longer able to opt for public access only by prior appointment.[50] Revenue and Customs can in appropriate cases seek a direction whereby heritage property that previously attracted conditional exemption on the basis of limited access should now be open to the public on open days without appointment. However, such a direction will not be given where the burden on the property owner of such increased access is disproportionate to the public benefit.[51]

Once a property has thus been accepted for conditional exemption, the undertaking given under section 31 will be monitored, and any breach will normally lead to the loss of the exemption[52]; but the Revenue will usually first give the person concerned due notice, and an opportunity to remedy the situation.

Special rules apply where a gift is made during the lifetime of the donor, and within the following seven years the property is given or sold to one of the heritage bodies referred to above, or is accepted by the Revenue in satisfaction of tax—see below.[53] In such cases, no further undertakings need to be given, and the "conditional" exemption then becomes absolute.

Conditional exemption is not lost on the disposal of heritage property on the subsequent death of the recipient, or on a subsequent lifetime transfer, or gift to spouse or heritage body. In each case, however, the undertakings as to access and maintenance must be renewed by the new owner.

Secondly, inheritance tax is not payable where such a building is accepted by the Revenue in satisfaction of inheritance tax liability generally (in which case there will be no liability to capital gains tax, stamp duty or value added tax either).[54]

Thirdly, where a fund is set up for the maintenance of a building of outstanding interest, further reliefs are available. Neither capital gains tax nor inheritance tax will be payable on property transferred to the fund when it is set up,[55] and inheritance tax will not be payable when capital is spent from the fund for a purpose connected with the property. The person setting up the fund (that is, the owner of the building) can elect that any income from it is to be assessable to income tax on the trustees at a favourable rate, rather than on him or herself, so long as it is spent on such purposes. The capital of the fund, however, must be used for the preservation or repair of the property, or for providing public access to it, or to meet the expenses of the trustees. The details of how such funds are to be operated are provided in Schedule 4 to the 1984 Act.

The test of whether a building is "outstanding" for these purposes is inevitably imprecise. The offer of a grant under the 1953 Act[56] is usually accepted by the Revenue as evidence of sufficient quality; but broadly any building that is listed

---

[50] Finance Act 1998, Sch.25.
[51] *In the matter of applications to vary the undertakings of "A" and "B" (SpC 439) (2004)* (2005) STC (SCD) 103. See also **9.4.5** and **9.6.1** on corresponding requirements in connection with the giving of grants.
[52] s.32(2).
[53] IHT Act 1984; s.26A, introduced by Finance Act 1986, Sch.19.
[54] IHT Act 1984, s.230.
[55] s.27.
[56] See **9.4.1**, **9.5.1**.

Grade I or II*, or any scheduled monument, might be accepted, and even one of Grade II in exceptional circumstances. Where a building is accepted as being of sufficient interest, any reliefs apply to land and objects associated with the building as they do to the building itself[57]; but special rules apply to such associated property, to ensure that it is not broken up.[58]

The above comments are inevitably only in very broad outline. Those seeking further information should seek specialist tax advice.[59]

Finally, it may be noted that one of the aims of providing special tax treatment in such cases is to prevent the break-up of an estate. The Housing and Urban Development Bill was accordingly amended during its passage through Parliament to ensure that rights of leasehold enfranchisement[60] do not apply in the case of property which has been accepted by the Revenue as being "outstanding" for these purposes.[61]

---

[57] 1984 Act, s.31(1)(d), (e).
[58] s.32A, inserted by Finance Act 1985, Sch.26.
[59] There used to be a helpful booklet published by the Inland Revenue, Capital Taxation and the National Heritage (IR67). However, that has long been out of print; and there appears to be no up-to-date equivalent.
[60] See 5.3.5.
[61] Leasehold Reform, Housing and Urban Development Act 1993, s.68.

Chapter 10

Repairs and Restoration: Powers of Public Authorities

10.1 Introduction

10.1.1 Powers available

Where a building falls into disrepair, the liability of its owner under common law and statute (outlined in **Chapter 8**) and the powers for the Lottery Fund and public authorities to give grants (outlined in **Chapter 9**) will between them rarely be sufficient to ensure that it is restored. Parliament has therefore decided that local authorities, central government and English Heritage should be given statutory powers to enable them to intervene in certain cases—to carry out themselves works on behalf of the owner, and in appropriate cases to charge the owner for the privilege. Those powers are the subject of this chapter.

The most serious situation is where a building is in such a poor state of repair as to be positively dangerous. The local authority then has powers (under the Building Act 1984 and corresponding legislation in inner London; see **10.2**) to require the owner to demolish it or make it safe—or for the authority to do so itself and recharge the owner. However, the insensitive or unthinking use of these powers can be a real impediment to conservation, especially since they are often administered by officers whose principal aims, quite rightly, lie elsewhere. Those Acts are therefore now subject to modification in the case of buildings that are listed or in a conservation area.

Secondly, where listed buildings (and, exceptionally, unlisted buildings in conservation areas) are in need of urgent repairs—particularly to render them watertight and weatherproof—planning authorities may require the owners to carry them out (under sections 54 and 76 of the Listed Buildings Act; see **10.3**). Here too, the authority may alternatively do the work itself and charge the owner of the building. Separate arrangements (under section 5 of the Ancient Monuments Act) apply to scheduled monuments in need of urgent repairs, since these pose somewhat different problems from those arising in connection with buildings that are (at least potentially) more actively in use (see **10.4**).

Thirdly, there are other wide-ranging powers enabling authorities to secure the improvement of unsightly land (including demolition sites), which enable local authorities to do works in certain cases to enhance listed buildings, monuments and their settings, and conservation areas. The choice of which statutory procedure to use depends on whether or not the authority wishes to recoup the cost of the works from the owner (see **10.5** to **10.7**).

Fourthly, local authorities have powers under the Housing Acts to deal with unfit houses and to declare clearance areas and renewal areas. These provisions are not primarily intended to achieve the preservation of historic buildings; but they can in appropriate cases be used by an imaginative local authority to that end. The expenditure involved will usually be met from environmental health and housing budgets, which will often be much larger than the small allocation specifically earmarked for "conservation". Again, however, the provisions are modified in their application to listed buildings and conservation areas (see **10.8**).

It may be the use of a building that is leading to its poor condition: the only solution then may be for the planning authority to take discontinuance action, and pay compensation as appropriate (see **10.9**).

Powers equivalent to those mentioned above are available to local authorities in Scotland as in England, and to the Department in Northern Ireland.

Of course, in many instances, the simplest, cheapest and often the most effective course of action is to offer specialist guidance. This may take the form of advice to building owners from suitably trained officers. Or where the same problems recur frequently, it may be sensible to produce appropriate technical leaflets, possibly in collaboration with other authorities whose areas contain similar buildings:

"Owners of listed buildings should be encouraged to seek expert advice on . . . the best way to carry out any works to their property. Many will need to obtain professional advice anyway, but the Secretaries of State hope that local authorities will give owners all the informal advice they can or guide them to other sources where they can get advice for themselves. English Heritage publishes much specialist advice on the care of historic buildings and can sometimes give advice on individual cases, especially where unusual problems are encountered. The national amenity societies are willing to offer advice to individual owners whenever possible. The Royal Commission on the Historical Monuments of England may have a record of a building and its reports and photographs may be available for guidance in understanding the structure and its evolution".[1]

Authorities have also been encouraged to identify buildings at risk, so as to be able to provide advice to owners as early as possible.[2]

Finally, however, in a few cases the problem may be so serious that the only way to solve it is for the building or monument to be acquired by a public authority. This is the subject of the following chapter.

10.1.2 Choice of procedure

The law directly relating to listed buildings in poor repair has always placed greater emphasis on the powers of the local planning authority than on the duties of either the authority or building owners. Financial restrictions perhaps make this inevitable.

---

[1]   PPG 15, para.3.25.
[2]   PPG 15, para.7.2.

But even the existence of a power imposes by implication a duty to consider whether it should be exercised. This emerged clearly in *R. v Stroud D.C., ex p. Goodenough*[3], where the local authority had served a notice requiring the owners of two buildings to make them safe or demolish them within eight weeks. Three members of a local action group thereupon applied for an order of *mandamus* to force the authority to take steps to secure the preservation of the buildings.

It was held in the Divisional Court that:

"...a planning authority ... should exercise great circumspection to see whether or not there was some other alternative open to them to prevent the demolition taking place when this was not desirable. If a planning authority did not take into account all its relevant powers when doing this then it was failing to perform its function properly under the legislation".[4]

This is no more than a standard principle of administrative law:

"...it has been so often decided as to have become an axiom, that, in public statutes, words only directory, permissory or enabling may have a compulsory force where the thing to be done is for the public benefit or in advancement of public justice".[5]

The difficulty for interested third parties such as amenity groups or neighbours will still be to prove that an authority has not merely decided not to use these powers, for whatever reasons, but has failed even to consider doing so:

"The very concept of administrative discretion involves a right to choose between more than one possible course of action upon which there is room for reasonable people to hold differing opinions as to which is to be preferred".[6]

10.1.3 An example of the use of local authority powers in practice

A notable example of the use of the various procedures, together with grant aid, featured Pell Wall Hall near Market Drayton in Shropshire—a country house by Soane, much altered in the Victorian and Edwardian periods.

The owner had allowed it to deteriorate since acquiring it in the mid-1960s, and in 1984 the local authority served a repairs notice under the predecessor to section 48 of the Listed Buildings Act[6a]. It then started compulsory purchase proceedings, including in the draft compulsory purchase order a direction for minimum compensation.[7] It intended to sell the building to a building preservation trust,[8] at a loss of £100,000. The owner appealed without success to the magistrates' court against the order, and thence (equally unsuccessfully) to the Crown Court, the High Court and the Court of Appeal—the latter in July 1987.[9] In 1986, fire had reduced the building to a shell, and during 1987 emergency works were carried out

---

[3] [1982] JPL 246.

[4] *per* Woolf J. at p.247.

[5] *R. v Tithe Commissioners* (1849) 14 Q.B. 459 *per* Coleridge J. at 474.

[6] *Secretary of State for Education and Science v Tameside M.B.C.* [1977] A.C. 1014 *per* Lord Diplock at 1064.

[6a] See **11.3**.

[7] See **11.4.3**.

[8] See **9.7.2**.

[9] Reported as *Rolf v North Shropshire D.C.* [1988] J.P.L. 103. See **11.3.5**.

by the authority, under the predecessor to section 54, with grant aid from English Heritage.[9a]

The compulsory purchase order was finally confirmed in January 1988, and the building passed to the authority. The authority in due course passed it on, for £1, to a new building preservation trust formed especially for the purpose. In 1994, a grant of £1 million was offered by English Heritage, and a loan was offered by the Architectural Heritage Fund. Planning permission and listed building consent were granted for the demolition of the less important parts of the building and for the restoration of the remainder, which was completed in 1998: the shell of the house, as designed by Soane, is now in good condition and looking splendid— more so, indeed, than for over a century. The trust then sought a Lottery grant[10] to fund the restoration of the interior, and passed on the Hall to a private owner, who is continuing to restore it gradually.

There is, therefore, now a reasonable chance that the building will one day be completely restored and brought back into full use. However, the saga—which has been continuing for twenty years—demonstrates that the whole exercise requires a great deal of patience and stamina, as well as money, on the part of all concerned.

10.2 Dangerous structures

10.2.1 General provisions

Where a building seems to an authority to be not merely in disrepair but dangerous, it may apply to the magistrates' court, and the court may make an order under section 77 of the Building Act 1984 requiring the owner:

(1) to make it safe; or

(2) to demolish all or part of it and remove any rubbish resulting from the demolition work.[11]

The owner need not specify that the works should be carried out in a particular way—by demolition, rebuilding or otherwise.[12]

If the owner fails to comply with the notice, the authority can carry out the necessary works itself. It may also recover any expenses incurred; and the owner is liable to a fine of up to level 1 on the standard scale.[13]

In emergency, the authority can proceed to carry out any necessary works immediately, without first applying to the court, relying on section 78 of the 1984 Act. Such works might, in particular, include fencing off the building to protect passers-by from possible danger, or merely arranging for it to be watched—but they might, in extreme cases, involve the demolition of all or part of the build-

---

[9a] See **10.3**.
[10] See **9.3**.
[11] Building Act 1984, s.77.
[12] *R. v Bolton Recorder, ex p. McVittie* [1940] 1 K.B. 290.
[13] See **Appendix F**.

ing.[14] However, it should if possible notify the owner and occupier of its intention before taking action. Here too, it is able to claim expenses afterwards. If it takes this course of action, however, the court in awarding expenses may take into account whether the situation was sufficiently urgent to justify the shorter procedure.[15]

Thirdly, where a building seems to the authority to be "ruinous or dilapidated" (but not necessarily dangerous), it may serve on the owner a notice under section 79, requiring him or her to carry out works of repair or restoration.[16] The owner is, however, normally able to demolish all or part of the building as an alternative to carrying out the required works.

The "works" envisaged in this context are "something in the nature of semi-permanent work to the building itself which would make it reasonably safe in respect of a person who might happen to go into it".[17]

The Building Act 1984 (like those portions of the Public Health Act 1936 which it replaced) does not apply to inner London[18]; but broadly similar provisions are contained in the London Building Acts (Amendment) Act 1939. However, the procedure is somewhat different, in that the district surveyor is to notify the borough council of any dangerous structure in its area.[19] Either the district surveyor or the council will then carry out any works necessary, and recover their expenses from the owner, or else the council may prop up the building and require the owner to carry them out.[20] A notice can also be served on the owner of a neglected structure.[21]

10.2.2 Modification in the case of listed buildings and conservation areas

A notice under any of the various powers in the 1984 Act is usually served by the environmental health department of the local authority, who will not be directly concerned with historic buildings matters. Section 56 of the Listed Buildings Act therefore requires that, before taking any steps with a view to making a dangerous structure order under section 77 in respect of a building that is listed or in a conservation area, an authority must consider:

(1) if repair works are urgently necessary, carrying them out under section 54 of the Listed Buildings Act,[22] and

(2) (in the case of a listed building), serving a repairs notice under section 48 of that Act[23], with a view to then compulsorily acquiring it; or

---

[14] 1984 Act, s.78(4).
[15] 1984 Act, s.78(1).
[16] 1984 Act, s.79.
[17] *Holme v Crosby Corporation* (1949) unreported; see *Encyclopedia of Environmental Health*, para.2–1484.
[18] 1984 Act, Sch.3, Pt II.
[19] 1939 Act, s.61; *London CC v Herring* [1894] 2 Q.B. 522.
[20] ss 62–66.
[21] s.69.
[22] See **10.5**.
[23] See **11.3.3**.

Secondly, where a notice is served under either section 77 or 79, the building owner who receives it may not be aware (or may choose to forget) that, if the building is listed or in a conservation area, the appropriate consent will still be needed before demolition can proceed. Both sections accordingly contain a provision making it explicitly clear that any requirement to carry out works in response to orders under those sections do not override the need for consent to be obtained under the Listed Buildings Act in the case of buildings that are listed or in conservation areas.[24] The same applies in the case of the 1939 Act in relation to London. The purpose of the provision is:

"... to make it clear that the orders or notices do not override listed building control. That should once and for all dispel any notion that listed building consent is not required if a building is the subject of a dangerous structure order or notice. Either listed building consent must be obtained or notice must be given in accordance with the new provision in [what is now P(LBCA)A 1990, s.9(3)], if the defence offered by that subsection is to be relied on".[25]

Thus any works to a listed building specified in a dangerous structure order require listed building consent—unless they are so minor that they do not affect the special character of the building.[26] Similarly, any demolition required by an order requires conservation area consent if the building concerned is in a conservation area. A defence is provided if consent is not obtained,[27] but it lays a substantial burden of proof on the owner if such a defence is to be successful[28]; it is not enough merely to state that the building was subject to a dangerous structure order. The Secretary of State sensibly suggests that an authority serving a dangerous structure order should remind the building owner of the need to obtain the appropriate consent or give notice under section 8(2)(d).[29]

Section 78 of the 1984 Act, on the other hand, provides that "[a local authority] may take steps as may be necessary [to remove the danger]." This provision of itself would seem to be "authorisation" within the meaning of section 7 of the Listed Buildings Act; it is after all difficult to conceive of a higher form of authorisation than an Act of Parliament. It is also noteworthy that sections 77 and 79 of the 1984 Act (under which an authority may serve a notice requiring an owner to carry out certain works to a building) each contain a final subsection explicitly stating that the power to serve a notice is subject to the provisions of the 1990 Act regarding listed buildings, whereas section 78 contains no such subsection.

---

[24] 1984 Act, ss 77, 79; 1939 Act, ss 62, 65, 69; new final subsections inserted by Housing and Planning Act 1986, and amended by Planning (Consequential Provisions) Act 1990, Sch.2.

[25] *Hansard* (HL), October 13, 1986, cols 587–8.

[26] See **12.4.4**.

[27] By P(LBCA)A 1990, s.8(2).

[28] See **12.4.7, 19.4.2**.

[29] PPG 15, Annex B, para.B.16; WO Circ. 61/96, para.123.

In other words, a private owner always needs authorisation (in the form of listed building consent and, where appropriate, planning permission) to carry out works, urgent or not, whereas a local authority is authorised by the Act to carry out works where they are urgent.[30]

The corresponding provisions for Scotland are in sections 10, 11, 13 and 17 of the Building (Scotland) Act 1959; guidance (much fuller than that for England) is in the *HS Memorandum*.[31] Where a local authority in Scotland serves a notice in respect of a listed building in its ownership requiring it to be demolished or substantial works to it to be carried out, it must immediately notify the Secretary of State (if necessary, orally) by virtue of section 56 of the Scottish Listed Buildings Act (one of the few provisions in that Act with no English equivalent).

10.3 Urgent repairs to historic buildings

10.3.1 Urgent repairs to listed buildings

It may sometimes occur that a historic building is in disrepair, possibly serious disrepair, but that relatively minor repairs works would arrest its decline, and obviate the need for even more substantial repairs in future.

Local authorities—that is, any district, country borough, borough or county council—are accordingly given power under section 54 of the Listed Buildings Act and section 49 of the Scottish Listed Buildings Act to carry out urgent works for the preservation of any listed building in their area, and (if they wish) to recover the cost of them from the building owner. Similar powers are given to national park authorities in England and Wales, the Broads Authority,[32] the Thurrock and Thames Gateway urban development corporations[33] and the Cotswold and Chilterns Conservation Boards.[34] In Northern Ireland, the Department has the same power.[35]

This power was originally designed for use in connection with unoccupied buildings. However, since 1987, it may also be used in respect of a building that is occupied, but only to secure the preservation of a part of it that is "not in use".[36] This is in spite of the side note to the section, which still reads "urgent works to preserve unoccupied listed buildings".

In addition, it should also be borne in mind that a "listed building" includes:

---

[30] The only other interpretation of the Act would be that an authority may carry out the works under s.78, but that it requires listed building consent—which would be from the Secretary of State. That would either impose a major delay, or mean that works would in practice almost always be authorised (retrospectively).

[31] HS Memorandum, paras 3.12–3.16.

[32] P(LBCA)A 1990, s.91(6); Environment Act 1995, Sch.9, para.13(4)(a).

[33] Thurrock Development Corporation (Planning Functions) Order 2005 (SI 2005/2572), art.4, Sch. London Thames Gateway Development Corporation (Planning Functions) Order 2005 (SI 2005/2721), art.5, Sch.

[34] The Cotswolds and Chilterns Areas of Outstanding Natural Beauty (Establishment of Conservation Board) Orders 2004 (SIs 2004/1777; 2004/1778), art.25.

[35] P(NI)O 1991, art.80.

[36] s.54(4).

(1) any object or structure fixed to the building; and

(2) any object or structure which has been within the curtilage of the building since before 1948.[37]

There is therefore no reason why an authority could not carry out works under section 54 to save a particular feature of a listed building or its curtilage (such as a fine plaster ceiling, or a garden temple). The only requirement is that the part of the building concerned is "not in use", which is likely to be the case if it requires urgent work for its preservation. The use of the phrase "not in use", rather than (as previously) the word "unoccupied" also means that, for example, a ceiling void may be eligible under this heading.

Note that works may not be carried out under section 54 to a building in ecclesiastical use[38] or to a scheduled monument.[39] Urgent works to an ancient monument may, however, be carried out under the Ancient Monuments Act.[40]

As well as local authorities, English Heritage may also take action under section 54, if authorised by the Secretary of State to act on his or her behalf in relation to a building in England.[41] PPG 15 suggests that this authority would be given in exceptional circumstances only[42]—as it was in the case of the Grade I Revesby Abbey, Lincolnshire, where £120,000 was spent in 1988 on urgent works (the recovery of which from the owner was subsequently authorised by the Secretary of State), although it might be appropriate where the building was owned by a local authority or other public body, or a foreign government. In London, English Heritage may carry out works on its own initiative.[43]

In Wales and Scotland, the National Assembly and the Scottish Ministers may also carry out works without further ado[44]—although, again, this will happen only exceptionally.[45]

10.3.2 Urgent repairs to unlisted buildings in conservation areas

The powers of authorities in England and Wales under section 54 of the Listed Buildings Act, and the corresponding powers in relation to Greater London, Scotland and Northern Ireland, may also be used in respect of an unlisted building in a conservation area.[46] In this case, however, the Secretary of State (or equivalent) must first give a direction that the procedure can be used, on the

---

[37] s.1(5); see **Chapter 4**.
[38] s.60(1), (2).
[39] s.61.
[40] AMAAA 1979, s.5; see **10.4**.
[41] P(LBCA)A 1990, s.54(2)(a). It is noteworthy that, if the Secretary of State considers that works are necessary, he is required to authorise English Heritage to take action— although that does not seem to require English Heritage to take that action once it is authorised to do so.
[42] At para.7.6.
[43] s.54(7).
[44] Wales: P(LBCA) 1990, s.54(2)(b); Scotland: P(LBCA)(S)A 1997, s.49(2).
[45] WO Circ. 61/96, para.131.
[46] P(LBCA)A 1990, s.76.

grounds that the preservation of the building is important for maintaining the character or appearance of the area.[47]

A local authority wishing to use its power under this section in connection with a particular unlisted building, and amenity groups or individual members of the public attempting to persuade an authority to do so, should seek a direction under section 76(1) by (in England) writing to the DCMS, enclosing photographs or other suitable evidence. The Secretary of State has stated that he will consider sympathetically the making of such a direction in respect of an unlisted building, provided that it makes a positive contribution to a conservation area.[48] Before doing so, he or she is to consult with English Heritage.[49] In Wales and Scotland, the authority or other interested party should seek a direction by writing to Cadw or Historic Scotland.[50]

Similarly, English Heritage may carry out urgent works to an unlisted building in a conservation area outside Greater London, if authorised by the Secretary of State; and Cadw and Historic Scotland may carry out urgent works to unlisted buildings in conservation areas.[51] And in Northern Ireland, the Department may carry out works to an unlisted building whose preservation it considers important to a conservation area.[52]

Subject to the need for a direction to be obtained, the procedure is identical to urgent works carried out to listed buildings.

10.3.3 Types of works envisaged

The works specified in the notice must be "urgently necessary for the preservation of the building".[53] As to what is envisaged, the view of the Secretary of State in England is that:

"[the use of these powers] should be restricted to emergency repairs, for example works to keep a building wind- and weather-proof and safe from collapse, or action to prevent vandalism or theft. The steps taken should be the minimum consistent with achieving this objective, and should not involve an owner in great expense".[54]

Guidance in Wales and Scotland is similar, save that, oddly, in the former case it omits the advice against involving the owner in great expense.[55]

This is self-explanatory. However, it still leaves open the question of what repairs would be appropriate in the case of an unoccupied building that is deteriorating, but only gradually. If repair works are not carried out, the building may stand for some time to come, and it might therefore be difficult to classify them as "urgent". Sooner or later, the building will collapse and, on the day before that, the works will indeed be "urgent", and the service of a notice will be too late. This

---

[47] s.76(1).
[48] PPG 15, para.7.5.
[49] s.76(2).
[50] WO Circ. 61/96, para.130; HS Memorandum, paras 4.42–4.43.
[51] s.54(2), applied by s.76.
[52] P(NI)O 1991, art.80(1)(b),(2).
[53] P(LBCA)A 1990, s.54(1).
[54] PPG 15, para.7.7.
[55] WO Circ. 61/96, para.132; HS Memorandum, paras 3.18 to 3.21.

may be a particular problem where only part of a building (such as a room, or a ceiling) is under threat from, for example, dry rot or beetle infestation. In any such case, therefore, it will be a matter for individual judgment by the local authority as to when a section 54 notice can be justified.

These provisions were considered by the High Court in *R. v Secretary of State for Wales, ex p. Swansea CC.*[56] The Council had served a notice under section 54, stating that it considered certain works to be urgently necessary for the preservation of the building in question, and then carried them out, and sought to recover the cost. The Secretary of State found that some of the works had indeed been urgently necessary but that the remainder, although necessary for the preservation of the building, had not been *urgently* necessary. The court determined that in those circumstances, the cost of all the works was recoverable—and, by implication, that the Council had been justified in serving the notice. All that is necessary is that the specified works are at least necessary:

"I should have found it surprising if Parliament had intended to allow an owner who had neglected to carry out work that was necessary to preserve a listed building to escape liability for the cost of carrying out that work simply because the authority had decided that the work was urgently necessary when, in fact, it was not. What is urgently necessary may be a difficult question to determine. How urgent is urgent? Opinions may reasonably differ. As [counsel for the Secretary of State] points out. Section 54 creates an emergency procedure. Authorities are expected to decide what may be difficult questions quickly. In those circumstances, a balance has to be struck between the interests of owners and the interests of society in the preservation of listed buildings. ... Subject to the other statutory defences given by section 55(4), the defaulting owner is liable to pay the cost of necessary work, provided that the authority reasonably thought that the work was urgently necessary."[57]

In addition, it is specifically provided that the works may consist of or include temporary support for the building—such as scaffolding, props or shelter.[58] This overturns the ruling by the Court of Appeal in *R. v Secretary of State, ex p. Hampshire CC.*[59]

10.3.4 Initial procedure

Any person duly authorised in writing by the appropriate local authority may enter any land (including, for example, a building next door to the one in need of preservation) to determine whether or not the authority should exercise its powers under section 54.[60] The general comments on entry to private property that were made in connection with the survey of buildings for listing would apply here too.[61] Twenty-four hours' notice must normally be given.[62] However, it is possible in

---

[56] [1999] 2 P.L.R. 14.
[57] [1999] 2 P.L.R. 14 *per* Dyson J. at p.17.
[58] s.54(3).
[59] [1981] J.P.L. 47 *per* Donaldson L.J. at 49.
[60] P(LBCA)A 1990, s.88(3)(b), amended by the Planning and Compensation Act 1991, Sch.3.
[61] See **3.3.1**.
[62] s.88B(1), inserted by the 1991 Act.

cases of urgency to obtain a warrant from a justice of the peace authorising immediate entry at any time.[63]

If it is decided that works are to be done, the authority must give at least seven days' written notice to the owner.[64] A sample notice is at **Form D5** in Appendix D. The purpose of this requirement is to enable the owner to discuss the matter with the authority, and perhaps to arrange for the works to be carried out without the need for any further persuasion.

The notice must "describe the works proposed to be carried out".[65] That is, it must "contain some detail of what works [are] contemplated", preferably with an estimate: it is no good requiring the owner "to support the building in a manner to the satisfaction of the Council to prevent its collapse",[66] or to carry out "all such steps as may be necessary to preserve the structure of the building".[67] The requirement to describe the works in detail is also important in that it enables the owner to decide whether to appeal against the notice (see below), in accordance with the rules of natural justice.[68]

If the authority wishes to reclaim the cost of the works, the owner has a right to appeal (see below). Thus the notice may come under careful scrutiny both from the owner and from the Secretary of State or the Assembly. It is therefore important for the works carried out by the authority to be carefully considered— both as to their extent and as to their cost. Any decisions need to be fully supported by factual evidence and accurately recorded for use in case of any appeal. See also the comments below on *Bolton MBC v Jolley*.[69]

The extent of the work that may be included was considered, in passing, by the House of Lords in *Robbins v Secretary of State*.[70] Lord Bridge there made it clear that they could only be those works which are urgently necessary to preserve the building as it subsists when the works are undertaken; that is, they cannot extend to works which may have been, or may soon become necessary.[71]

A frugal authority may insist on obtaining several tenders and accepting only the lowest. As a result, the works may be significantly delayed, and eventually carried out to a poor standard, leading to yet further deterioration of the building. On the other hand, an authority carrying out the works immediately, and accepting the first estimate available, may find that the Secretary of State disallows some of the costs on appeal. In practice, speed is often essential to prevent further disrepair.

The works described on the notice may be such that they would, in other circumstances, require planning permission or listed building consent. However,

---

[63] s.88A(1)(b)(ii), (4)(b), inserted by the 1991 Act.

[64] s.54(5).

[65] s.54(6).

[66] *R. v Secretary of State for the Environment, ex p. Hampshire CC* [1981] JPL 47.

[67] *R. v Camden LBC, ex p. Comyn Ching & Co. (London) Ltd and another* [1984] J.P.L. 661 at 661 and 666.

[68] See, for example, *Cooper v The Board of Works for Wandsworth* (1863) 14 C.B. (NS) 180.

[69] [1989] 1 P.L.R. 97; see **10.3.6**.

[70] [1989] 1 W.L.R. 201.

[71] See p.211D.

section 54 provides that "a local authority *may* execute works which appear to [it] to be urgently necessary for the preservation of a listed building". As with section 78 of the Buildings Act 1984[72], this of itself would seem to be "authorisation"; specific listed building consent is thus not required. It follows that, although an authority in reliance on section 54 may carry out works in such a way that they might be open to criticism (and enforcement action or even prosecution) if they were to be done by anyone else without listed building consent, the authority cannot be impugned in any formal action.[73] It also follows that an authority should be assiduous not to misuse its powers by carrying out unsuitable works in reliance on this procedure.

10.3.5 Carrying out the works

Once the notice has been served on the owner, there may of course be a satisfactory response—an undertaking by the owner that the works will be carried out, possibly accompanied by an application for listed building consent (and, where appropriate, planning permission[74]) to carry out more substantial works of restoration or conversion. The owner may also seek, or the authority may offer, a grant or loan.[75]

If, however, no satisfactory response is forthcoming, the authority serving the notice can then proceed to carry out the necessary works itself.[76] If the owner explains that the works will be carried out "in due course", that would not be satisfactory. In the absence of any firm proposals, and given that the works are by definition at least claimed to be urgent, the authority would probably be justified in proceeding.

Where the owner of an unoccupied building is unknown or cannot be traced, the authority may proceed at least seven days after putting up a notice addressed "to the owner/occupier" and setting out the details of what works are proposed. If no response is received to such a notice within the seven-day period (and a response is for obvious reasons unlikely), the authority may proceed with the works, although it will in practice have to meet the cost from its own resources.

There is, again, a right of entry to carry out the works.[77] This requires either the issue of a warrant[78] or 24 hours' notice.[79] It is not clear whether the latter requirement would be met by the service of the notice under section 54(5), or whether a second notice would be required—it may therefore be prudent to issue a second one to avoid possible challenge, or to obtain a warrant in case of urgency.

---

[72] See **10.2.2**.
[73] This became an issue in the notorious case of Sproughton Mill in Suffolk, where works were carried out in reliance on s.54 that were said by the owner to have been substandard.
[74] See **12.4**.
[75] See **Chapter 9**.
[76] s.54.
[77] Under s.88(3)(c) (amended by the Planning and Compensation Act 1991, Sch.3).
[78] Under s.88A.
[79] Under s.88B(1).

10.3.6 Recovery of the cost of the works

Once the works have been carried out by a local authority, it can then, if it wishes, recover their cost.[80] To achieve this, it must first serve on the "owner" of the building a further notice setting out the cost, and asking him or her to pay. An example is at **Form D6** in Appendix D. Such a notice should state clearly that it is a notice under section 55; and should also explain the mechanism for making representations to the Secretary of State under section 55(4). The Court of Appeal in *Bolton MBC v Jolley* commended as "models of their kind" the notices served by the Council in that case.[81] Corresponding provisions are at section 50 of the Scottish Listed Buildings Act and article 80(5)–(10) of the Northern Ireland Order.

The authority is not obliged to recover anything, and there is no reason in law why it should not seek to recover only part of the cost, or none—subject to considering any subsequent criticism from the District Auditor if it acts capriciously. This might be appropriate where, for example, the owner was an individual with limited means, or a charity—particularly in the case of a large building, where even limited repairs are likely to be expensive. In other cases, there might in practice be no way of recovering any of the cost, such as where the owner is overseas, bankrupt or unknown (see above). If an authority intends to try to recover any or all of the cost of the works, it should in any event take into account from the outset the financial circumstances of the owner[82]—again, there is no corresponding advice in Wales,[83] but it would still be necessary, since it is possible for the owner, even in Wales, to appeal on the grounds of hardship (see below).

The "owner" from whom the money can be recovered[84] is presumably, in the absence of any more specific provision, the same "owner" as the one on whom notice was first served of the authority's intention to carry out the works.[85] There is no provision for the authority to claim it from a new owner; nor can the cost of the works be registered as a local land charge. Therefore, in order to prevent possible problems arising in the event of the property changing hands, the authority should seek to recover the cost as soon as possible after the works have been carried out. If necessary, the cost of the works, together with a reasonable sum in respect of establishment charges, can be recovered as a simple contract debt.[86]

If English Heritage has carried out the works, as the agent of the Secretary of State, it is the Secretary of State who is entitled to recover the cost.[87]

Within 28 days of receiving a demand for payment, an owner may make representations to the Secretary of State on any of the following grounds:

---

[80] P(LBCA)A 1990, s.55.
[81] [1989] 1 P.L.R. 97.
[82] PPG 15, para.7.8.
[83] Compare WO Circ. 61/96, para.133.
[84] Under s.55(2).
[85] s.54(5).
[86] County Courts Act 1984, s.16, as amended by SI 1991/724; Local Government Act 1974, s.36.
[87] s.51(1).

(1) that some or all of the works were unnecessary for the preservation of the building;

(2) that the amount specified in the notice is unreasonable; or

(3) that the recovery of it would cause hardship.[88]

Where the works involved include temporary support or shelter for the building (see above), the continuing expenses involved are recoverable from the owner, and may be billed on an interim basis.[89] However, the owner may claim, as one of the grounds of appeal against the recovery of expenses, that the temporary works have continued for an unreasonable length of time.[90]

There is no requirement to send a copy of such representations to the local authority, but to do so would be sensible—not least so that it may be aware why it has not been reimbursed.

The Secretary of State will take all such representations into account before determining the amount to be recovered, and will be particularly concerned to establish whether the works carried out were the minimum required to secure the building's preservation and prevent further deterioration.[91]

The Divisional Court has declined to express a general view as to what would amount to "hardship", save to note that it shared with the elephant impossibility of definition combined with ease of recognition.[92]

The Secretary of State will notify his decision, and the reasons for it, to the owner, and to the local authority (or English Heritage if it carried out the works).[93] In some cases such appeals have been decided only after a long delay, and even then the alterations made to the sums claimed were relatively trivial.

Finally, it may be noted that English Heritage has power to give grants to local authorities to assist them in defraying the cost of carrying out urgent works.[94] An application form is included with the leaflet *Grants to local authorities to underwrite urgent repairs notices*, which states that it is willing to give grants of up to 80 per cent of the irrecoverable cost of undertaking urgent works in appropriate cases. It will generally assist only in the case of works to Grade I and II* buildings, or Grade II buildings in Greater London, or unlisted buildings in conservation areas where a direction has been made under section 76.[95] No grant will be paid for works carried out prior to an application for grant aid being determined, but it aims to determine 80 per cent of such applications within six weeks.

---

[88] s.55(4) (a), (c), (d).

[89] s.55(3).

[90] s.55(4)(b).

[91] See PPG 15, para.7.8; WO Circ. 61/96, para.133.

[92] *R. v Secretary of State for the Environment, ex p. Hampshire C.C.* [1981] J.P.L. 47, *per* Donaldson L.J. at p.49.

[93] s.55(5).

[94] Under Historic Buildings and Ancient Monuments Act 1953, s.3A, in the case of buildings of Grade I and II* (see **9.4.1**), or under P(LBCA)A 1990, s.77(1), in the case of buildings (listed or not) in conservation areas (see **9.4.2**).

[95] See **10.3.2**.

Again, corresponding powers (if not finance) are given to Cadw and Historic Scotland.[96]

In Northern Ireland, there is a right of appeal to the Planning Appeals Commission against any demand by the Department for repayment of the cost of the works carried out.[97]

10.4 Urgent repairs to scheduled monuments

The Secretary of State, the Welsh Assembly or the Scottish Ministers may themselves carry out works that are urgently necessary for the preservation of a scheduled monument, under section 5 of the Ancient Monuments Act. Before doing so, the owner of the monument and the occupier (if not the owner) must be given seven days' written notice. Equivalent powers are given to the Department in Northern Ireland, under article 7 of the 1995 Order, although it only needs to give 48 hours of proposed works.

As to the meaning of "preservation", there would seem to be no reason not to apply the approach of the House of Lords in *South Lakeland DC v Secretary of State*: "preserve" means "to keep safe from harm".[98]

This power may be used simply to carry out works required in the normal course of events—such as to repair storm damage—in which case it will not be possible to recover the cost of them from anyone (other than by negotiation). In some cases, however, such works may be needed to repair damage deliberately caused to the monument. Where the perpetrator is known and has been convicted of criminal damage, a compensation order will probably have been made by the sentencing court,[99] and such order will then be enforceable as if it had been originally been made in favour of the Secretary of State.[100]

Alternatively, English Heritage may be authorised by the Secretary of State to carry out such works to a monument in England.[1] The procedure is identical to that applying to the carrying out of works by the Secretary of State.

Local authorities do not have any powers under this provision.

In addition to these powers, which relate only to urgent works, there are also more general powers for public authorities to carry out, at their own expense, repairs to ancient monuments.[2]

---

[96] Under s.4 of the 1953 Act and s.77(2) of the 1990 Act.
[97] See **15.8.1**.
[98] [1992] 2 W.L.R. 204 (see 8.8.3).
[99] Under Powers of Criminal Courts Act 1973, s.35.
[100] AMAAA 1979, s.5(2).
[1] AMAAA 1979, s.5(3) to (5), inserted by National Heritage Act 1983, Sch.4.
[2] See **10.7.2**.

10.5 Requiring repairs to be carried out by or at the expense of the property owner

10.5.1 Background

A local planning authority may serve a notice under section 215 of the Town and Country Planning Act 1990 on the owner and occupier of any building or other land whose condition is adversely affecting the amenity of the neighbourhood, requiring the recipient to remedy its poor condition (subject to a right of appeal[3]). If the necessary works are not carried out, the authority can then carry out the necessary works itself and reclaim the cost from the owner.[4]

A section 215 notice can be served in connection with any "land"; and "land" is defined to include "a building".[5] There is no need for the building to be listed or for the land to be in a conservation area, but the section 215 procedure is particularly appropriate to a neglected historic building. It would be equally applicable to occupied, partly occupied or vacant buildings. It could also be used for churches and scheduled monuments (unlike notices under section 48 or section 54 of the Listed Buildings Act[6]). The local authority simply has to be satisfied, before serving the notice, that the condition of the property is "adversely affecting" the "amenity" of any part of its area or the area of any neighbouring authority.[7]

In considering what works can sensibly be required in a section 215 notice in a particular case, it is essential to consider carefully the statutory grounds of appeal (considered below), in order to see whether they could be relied upon successfully. Thus a notice could not be used to require internal works to be carried out, or to remedy disrepair resulting naturally from the lawful use of the building.

The Government has issued useful best practice guidance to local authorities in England in January 2005, encouraging them to consider using their powers under section 215 in relation to listed buildings and their settings, and in the enhancement of conservation areas.[8] It points out that one (unidentified) planning authority has taken action under section 215 resulting in improvements being carried out to 41 listed buildings and 104 unlisted buildings in conservation areas.

The law in Scotland, under sections 179–1181 of the Scottish Planning Act, is similar to that in England and Wales—the principal difference being that the appeal against a section 179 notice is to the Scottish Ministers rather than to the magistrates' court. There is no equivalent procedure in Northern Ireland.

---

[3] See **10.5.4**.
[4] See **10.5.8**.
[5] TCPA 1990, s.336; also Interpretation Act 1978, s.5 and Sch.1.
[6] See **11.3** and **10.3** respectively.
[7] TCPA 1990, s.215(1).
[8] *Town and Country Planning Act 1990: Section 215: Best Practice Guidance*, available on the ODPM website. See also the research report *Derelict Land and Section 215 Powers*, commissioned in 1999.

10.5.2 Initial procedure

A section 215 notice may in general be served by a district or borough council[9] or, in Wales, by a county or county borough council.[10] In a national park, it may be served only by a national park authority[11] and, in the Broads, only by the Broads Authority.[12] In Scotland, a section 179 notice may be served by a planning authority.[13]

The authority must "serve the notice on the owner and occupier" of the land.[14] It will often be prudent for the authority to find out first who are the owners and occupiers (see below).

The notice must specify:

(1)   what steps the authority requires to be taken to remedy the condition of the building, and the period within which those steps are to be taken[15]; and

(2)   the period at the end of which it is to come into effect.[16]

As to the steps to be taken, the notice must specify these with sufficient accuracy for the recipient to know exactly what he or she has to do, and by when it has to be done. This requirement has been considered at length by the courts in the context of the steps required to be taken by an enforcement notice.[17] If the notice does not specify the works at all, or is hopelessly vague, it will be a nullity, and the recipient will not be under any duty to comply with it.

The specification of the works required would usually best be done by way of a schedule of repairs attached to the notice (as is standard practice with repairs notices under the Housing Acts).

As to what works are suitable to be the subject of a section 215 notice, this will clearly depend on the facts of each case. But a planning authority, when drafting a notice, and a property owner, when considering whether to appeal against one, should bear in mind that amongst the four possible grounds of appeal against a notice are that the remedial works required to be carried out are excessive; and that the time within which those works are to be carried out is unreasonably short.[18]

10.5.3 Service and coming into effect of notice

The ODPM *Best Practice Guide* sensibly suggests that the process starts with negotiation between the authority and the owner of the building concerned. It also includes sample "first warning" letters. Simply the implied threat of formal

---

[9]   TCPA 1990, s.1(1) (2), Sch.1, para.14.

[10]   s.1B, inserted by the Local Government (Wales) Act 1994, s.18.

[11]   s.4A(4), inserted by the Environment Act 1995, s.67.

[12]   s.5(2).

[13]   P(LBCA)(S)A 1997, s.179(1).

[14]   TCPA 1990, s.215(1).

[15]   s.215(2).

[16]   s.215(3).

[17]   See, in particular, the comments of Upjohn L.J. in *Miller-Mead v Minister of Housing and Local Government* [1963] 2 Q.B. 196 at 232, often followed subsequently.

[18]   s.217(1) (c), (d); see **10.5.6**.

action under section 215 may be sufficient to bring about the improvement of the building.

A section 215 notice, once it has been served, comes into effect at the end of the period stated within it. This must be at least 28 days from the date of service.[19] Note that the wording of this requirement is different from that of the corresponding provision relating to the issue of enforcement notices.[20] Since it is the notice itself, and not a copy, which is served on each owner and occupier, the date on which it comes into force must be the same for each recipient. If, therefore, notices are served on different dates, the periods specified in each must be calculated so as to expire simultaneously. This requires very careful drafting to avoid errors. It is also prudent to choose a date for the notice to come into effect which allows for the possibility of notices not being delivered and having to be re-addressed. If the different recipients of the same notice are in effect told that it is to come into effect on different dates, the notice will probably be a nullity, and all recipients will then be able to ignore it.[21]

Because of potential procedural challenges, therefore, it is best to ensure that, as far as possible, the notice is served on *all* the relevant owners and occupiers on the same date. To achieve this, it will usually be necessary to serve a preliminary notice on any known owner or occupier seeking the full name and address of any others. A planning authority can require these details to be supplied within a period of 14 days, on penalty of a fine of up to level 5 on the standard scale.[22] There is also a power to obtain much more information from owners, to be supplied within a period of up to 21 days on pain of a fine of up to level 3.[23]

Some of these problems arise because the procedural requirements as to the service of section 215 notices were badly drafted. The section in its revised form still uses the language of the pre–1981 provisions concerning the service of enforcement notices.[24] Those were significantly amended by the Local Government and Planning (Amendment) Act 1981, because a number of practical procedural difficulties arose where there were many owners and occupiers involved. It may therefore be relevant to consult pre–1981 editions of standard texts for details of the possible pitfalls (for both the local authority and the building owner).

10.5.4 Appeal against a section 215 notice

Anyone receiving a section 215 notice may appeal against it—in England and Wales, to the magistrates' court for the area containing the land.[25] Such an appeal must be made before the notice comes into effect, which will be at least 28 days after its service to owners and occupiers (see above). There is then a further right of appeal, by either the appellant or the planning authority who served the notice,

---

[19] TCPA 1990, s.215(3).
[20] In TCPA 1990, s.172 (as substituted by the Planning and Compensation Act 1991, s.5.
[21] *Bambury v Hounslow LBC* [1966] 2 Q.B. 204; *Stevens v Bromley LBC* [1972] Ch.39; 400, CA.
[22] Local Government (Miscellaneous Provisions) Act 1976, s.16, as amended by the Criminal Justice Act 1982; see **Apendix F**.
[23] TCPA 1990, s.330.
[24] See, for example, TCPA 1971, s.87(7) as originally drafted.
[25] TCPA 1990, s.217(1), (2).

to the Crown Court.[26] In Scotland, an appeal against a section 179 notice is—much more appropriately—to be made to the Scottish Ministers.[27]

Where an appeal has been made, the notice is suspended until the matter is finally determined.[28] This means, in England, until the time for appealing to the Crown Court has expired or, if such an appeal has been made, until the appropriate time limits for appeals to higher courts have expired.[29]

Whoever the appeal is made to, it may only be on the prescribed statutory grounds—four in England and Wales, five in Scotland, considered in detail below. An appeal to the magistrates' court may also raise the issue of *vires*, even if proceedings for judicial review are in prospect. Since the *vires* challenge could clearly be raised by way of a defence to prosecution under section 216, it must be in order for it to be raised at the earlier appeal as well.[30]

When determining an appeal against a section 215 notice, the magistrates' court may quash it, or may uphold it with or without alteration. Such alteration may only be made if it does not cause any injustice to the appellant.[31] The court may also correct any informality, defect or error in the notice if it is satisfied that the mistake is not "material".[32] The wording of these provisions again follows that of the pre–1981 enforcement provisions; and the scope of the court's power is thus now considerably narrower than that of the Secretary of State's power to vary enforcement notices.[33]

The *Best Practice Guidance* suggests that "very few section 215 notices are appealed and of those that are only a small proportion are upheld." It is presumably the appeals that are generally not being upheld, rather than the notices.

10.5.5 *Grounds of appeal: the condition of the land*

The first two grounds of appeal against a section 215 notice are as follows:

"(a) that the condition of the land to which the notice relates does not adversely affect the amenity of any part of the area of the local planning authority which served the notice, or of any adjoining area;

(b) that the condition of the land to which the notice relates is attributable to, and such as results in the ordinary course of events from, the carrying on of operations or a use of land which is not in contravention of Part III [of the TCPA 1990]."[34]

These are grounds (a) and (d) in Scotland.

Note that, if a recipient of a notice wants to appeal against it on grounds (a) or (b), an appeal to the magistrates' court or the Scottish Ministers is the only way to proceed.[35]

---

[26] s.218.
[27] TCP(S)A 1997, s.180.
[28] s.217(3).
[29] *Garland v Westminster CC* (1970) 21 P. & C.R. 555.
[30] See *R. v Oxford Crown Court, ex p. Smith* (1989) *The Times*, December 27, 1989.
[31] TCPA 1990, s.217(5).
[32] s.217(4).
[33] See TCPA 1990, s.176, as amended by the Planning and Compensation Act 1991, Sch.7.
[34] Under TCPA 1990, s.217(1)(a), (b).
[35] TCPA 1990, s.285(1).

The first of these should be straightforward. Any dispute is likely to be a simple matter of fact or opinion. The meaning of "amenity" has been considered earlier.[36] The phrase "adversely affecting" was introduced by the Housing and Planning Act 1986; but its meaning has not yet been explored by the courts. The requirement in the Act as originally drafted was that the condition of the land should "seriously injure" its surroundings; the new phrase implies that something less than serious injury would suffice to justify a notice. A building that is "derelict" would thus almost certainly fall within the scope of the section 215 power; one that was merely "in disrepair" might or might not. The side-note to the section is "power to require proper maintenance of land." This would appear to justify an authority serving a notice on a building that was merely in need of maintenance, rather than only on buildings that were in danger of collapse.

The second ground of appeal is less straightforward. It means basically that the section 215 procedure can be used either:

(1) where the poor condition of the property arises from a building or other operation or a use of the property that *is* in contravention of planning control[37]; or

(2) where the poor condition of the property happens to arise in this case, but need not inevitably arise, from an operation or use of the property that is perfectly in order.

In the second of these situations, therefore, it is necessary to consider whether the poor condition of the property is "such as results in the ordinary course of events from" that operation or use. So, for example, if planning permission has been granted to use a site for car-breaking, it would not be possible to use a section 215 notice to control the unsightly appearance which would no doubt ensue. Yet if a building is used quite lawfully for residential purposes—or indeed is vacant after such use has stopped—there is no reason why, *in the ordinary course of events*, that use should lead to the building being in poor condition. If therefore such a building is in poor condition, so as to lead to the amenity of the surrounding area being affected, it would be perfectly in order to use the section 215 procedure to bring about its improvement.

10.5.6 Grounds of appeal: the remedial works required

The third and fourth grounds of appeal against a section 215 notice are as follows:

"(c) that the requirements of the notice exceed what is necessary for preventing the condition of the land from adversely affecting the amenity of any part of the area of the local planning authority who served the notice, or of any adjoining area;

(d) that the period specified in the notice as the period within which any steps required by the notice are to be taken falls short of what should reasonably be allowed."[38]

---

[36] See **7.6.1**.
[37] See TCPA 1990, s.171A, as substituted by PCA 1991, s.4.
[38] s.217(1)(c), (d).

These are grounds (b) and (c) in Scotland. There is also a ground (e) in Scotland, that the notice was served wrongly. If it is claimed that a notice was incorrectly served in England or Wales, an application for judicial review may be made.[39]

As to the first of these grounds, this will normally mean that a notice can only require the carrying out of external works, such as:

(1)   the repair or restoration of crumbling cornices, porticoes, pinnacles and other details;

(2)   the repainting of particular details or of a whole facade;

(3)   the repair, restoration or repainting of other features such as walls, railings, gates and fences; or

(4)   the tidying up of gardens and other open land (particularly where adjacent to a road).

In most cases, internal works to a building could not be included, however necessary they might be for its long-term health, since they make little difference to its effect on the amenity of the area. It might be argued that, where a building is in such poor condition as to be on the verge of partial or total collapse, it would be appropriate to prevent this by serving a section 215 notice requiring more substantial structural work. However, this would probably not withstand challenge. A notice can only be served where the amenity of the area is (currently) affected by the condition of the land or building,[40] not where it is merely likely to be affected in the future. Accordingly, the works required in the notice can only be those needed to alleviate a present problem, not those desirable (or even necessary) to prevent a future one.

In addition, the works required should only be the minimum needed to improve the external appearance of the property, since any other specification would be open to being challenged on appeal. In considering what is this minimum level of works, it would be relevant to take into account whether the building is listed or in a conservation area. Thus, for example, suppose that a uniform Grade I terrace of stucco town houses which is otherwise in perfect condition contains one house that has been neglected, with peeling stucco and missing features. Only its complete external restoration to the same state as the others would be adequate to alleviate the effect it currently has on the area. But if the building in poor condition is one of a group of mixed styles within a not particularly distinguished conservation area, then the scope of works which could reasonably be required by a section 215 notice would obviously be more limited.

As to the second ground, relating to time for compliance, the courts have held—when considering the corresponding ground of appeal against an enforcement notice[41]—that it is correct to take a realistic approach, looking at the

---

[39]   Under CPR Part 54; see **15.7**.

[40]   s.215(1).

[41]   Now TCPA 1990, s.174(2)(g)), as substituted by the Planning and Compensation Act 1991, s.6.

whole history of the site and taking previous delays and prevarications into account.[42]

In general, it will be a matter for the discretion of the magistrates as to whether or not the requirements of the notice are excessive on either or both of these grounds.

10.5.7 Non-compliance with a section 215 notice

Unless it is quashed on appeal, a section 215 notice will sooner or later come into effect—either at the end of the period stated within it, or when any appeals have been finally disposed of. The recipient must then carry out the remedial works specified in it, within the time specified or within such longer period as may be allowed by the authority. If the works are not carried out, the local authority can institute a prosecution in the magistrates' court. Anyone convicted will then be liable to a fine of level 3.[43]

If, after being convicted, the owner or occupier of the property still does not do everything possible to ensure that the original notice is complied with, he or she is guilty of a further offence, and can on conviction be liable to a daily fine of up to one-tenth of level 3.[44] To be convicted of the further offence, no further specific act is required; all that is necessary is to take no action to improve the condition of the property.

Where, the recipient of the notice is no longer the owner or occupier of the property, the present owner or occupier may be substituted as defendant in any prosecution.[45] Similarly, if the failure to comply with the notice is through no fault of the person served with the notice, the person who is responsible may be convicted instead.[46]

10.5.8 Carrying out of the required works by the local authority

In spite of the possibility of the owner and occupier being convicted under section 216(2) or 216(6), the required remedial works may still not be carried out. The local authority will then have to step in and carry them out itself. If it does so, it may recover the cost of the works from the current owner of the property.[47]

If the current owner was not responsible for the state of affairs which gave rise to the notice in the first place, he or she may in turn claim the cost of the works from whomever was responsible.[48] The service of a section 215 notice is a local land charge, to be registered in Part 3 of the Register as a "planning charge".[49] Any prospective purchaser should therefore be in a position to adjust the purchase price accordingly. The liability to pay the expenses recovered by the authority has, since January 8, 1998, been registrable as a charge on the land, so

---

[42] *Mercer v Uckfield RDC* (1962) 60 L.G.R. 226.
[43] TCPA 1990, s.216(2). See **Appendix F**.
[44] s.216(6), amended by the Planning and Compensation Act 1991, Sch.7.
[45] s.216(3), (4).
[46] s.216(5).
[47] TCPA 1990, s.219(1).
[48] s.219(2).
[49] Local Land Charges Rules 1977, rr 2(2), 3.

that it may be recovered on any future transfer of ownership.[50] Alternatively, the authority may recover the cost of the works, together with a reasonable sum in respect of its establishment charges, as a simple contract debt.[51]

These provisions mean that this is now a very effective way of getting repairs done. It should not be too difficult for the authority to serve the notice, resist any appeal, enter the land and carry out the necessary works. In practice, it may be appropriate for the authority to volunteer to do the works itself, and simply recharge the cost of them to the owner or, if the owner is unable or unwilling to pay, to register the cost as a charge on the property.[52] The *Best Practice Guidance* suggests that authorities have generally not experienced great difficulties recovering their costs.

If anyone with an interest in the land other than the owner (such as a tenant in occupation) prevents the authority from carrying out the works, the owner may complain to the magistrates' court. The court may then order that other person to desist.[53]

10.6 Land in poor condition following demolition works

One specific problem that can arise is where the collapse or demolition of a building leads to such a quantity or type of rubbish or other material lying on the site of the building, or on any adjoining land, that the land is in such a condition as to be "seriously detrimental to the amenities of the neighbourhood". In such a situation, as an alternative to serving a section 215 notice, the local authority may serve on the owner of the land a notice under section 79 of the Building Act 1984, requiring the owner to take such steps as may be necessary to clear up the site.[54]

This in effect gives an authority the power to deal with such a site on a once-only basis.

The corresponding power available to a borough council in inner London to deal with derelict, neglected or unsightly land is contained in London Government Act 1963.[55] Anyone receiving a notice served under that Act may appeal against it to a magistrates' court.

10.7 Carrying out of repairs by an authority at its own expense

10.7.1 General powers to carry out repairs

The use of section 215 notices may be useful where an authority wants repairs to be carried out by or at the expense of a property owner. But there may be

---

[50] s.219(5); TCP General Regulations 1992, reg.14(3), inserted by SI 1997/3006.
[51] Country Court Act 1984, s.16, as amended by SI 1991/724; Local Government Act 1974, s.36.
[52] Environment Circ. 02/98, para.7.
[53] Public Health Act 1936, s.289, as applied with modifications by TCPA 1990, s.219(3) and TCP General Regulations 1992, reg.14(1).
[54] Building Act 1984, s.79(2).
[55] 1963 Act, s.40(3), Sch.11, Pt II, para.9

circumstances where an authority perfectly properly decides to carry out works to historic buildings and in historic areas in circumstances where the owner is unwilling or unable to fund them—or where the owner is unknown.

Any local authority is thus able to carry out (at its own expense) works it considers expedient for the purpose of reclaiming or improving land which is "derelict, neglected or unsightly"—which may be useful to bring about the restoration and improvement of historic areas and the setting of historic buildings. And since "land" includes "building",[56] it would empower an authority to repair a derelict, neglected or unsightly building. The relevant power is in, of all places, section 89(2) of the National Parks and Access to the Countryside Act 1949[57]—but in spite of the title of the Act, its exercise is not restricted to rural areas. Nor is it restricted to any specific categories of land or buildings.

As to the meaning of the phrase "derelict, neglected or unsightly", the view of the Secretary of State—albeit in the context of open land, rather than buildings— is that:

"there are no statutory definitions of these words and so they are to be given their natural, common-sense meaning. It is preferable, wherever possible, to consider the words taken together, as there is a considerable overlap between all three. The word "unsightly" is clearly directed to the appearance of the land, but an untidy or uncared for appearance may also be relevant in considering whether the land is derelict or neglected. Land may be "neglected" without ever having been the subject of any operations by man (such as building, dumping or excavating), but it may be inappropriate to describe such land as "derelict".[58]

The power may be particularly useful in the case of buildings or groups of buildings that are simply neglected, as it enables an authority to carry out basic enhancement works, albeit at its own expense. The authority must obtain the consent of the owner of all of the buildings involved, but is then able simply to get on with and pay for the necessary works itself. Alternatively, it may do a deal with an owner, or a group of owners, to split the cost of works on any basis that seems sensible.

Further, the authority may compulsorily purchase such land if it needs to[59]: for example, if the owner is unknown or very uncooperative. Advice on the exercise of this power is contained in Appendix F to DoE Circular 02/2003.[60-61]

10.7.2 Repairs to ancient monuments

As with historic buildings, ancient monuments are mostly in private hands. Many, for example, are in or underneath fields that are part of working farms. Since it would in some cases be unreasonable for a private landowner to have to meet the full costs of maintaining, say, an iron-age hill fort or a deserted medieval village, there are powers for public authorities to carry out at their own expense, works for the preservation of ancient monuments.

---

[56] Interpretation Act 1978, s.5 and Sch.1.
[57] As inserted by s.3 of the Derelict Land Act 1982.
[58] ODPM Circ. 02/2003, Appendix F, para.5.
[59] 1949 Act, s.89(5).
[60-61] Appendix M.

Repair works generally may be carried out to any ancient monument—whether or not scheduled[62]—by English Heritage, the National Assembly for Wales (Cadw), the Scottish Ministers (Historic Scotland), or any local authority, relying on powers in section 24 of the Ancient Monuments Act.[63] "Local authority" for this purpose includes the Broads Authority[64], and any national park authority.[65] The works that may be carried out under this provision are the "preservation, maintenance and management" of the monument. Alternatively, the public authority may simply "assist in" such works—either financially or otherwise.

The meaning of "preservation" has already been considered.[66] "Maintenance" is defined to include:

"fencing, repairing, and covering in, of a monument and the doing of any other act or thing which may be required for the purpose of repairing the monument or protecting it from decay or injury."[67]

"Management" is not defined, but could clearly include works carried out over a longer period. The consent of the owner (but not necessarily that of the occupier) must be obtained. Subject to that, there would thus seem to be scope for all kinds of arrangements, with either the owner or the occupier or the public authority carrying out the works or the management, and either the owner or the occupier or one or more public authorities paying for them. It may be prudent to formalise such arrangements by an agreement under section 17 of the 1979 Act.[68]

English Heritage, Cadw and Historic Scotland may also remove a monument or any part of it to another place to ensure its preservation, or pay for all or some of the cost of that being done.[69] Perhaps slightly surprisingly, the consent of the owner is not required.

Finally, they may give advice as to the treatment of any ancient monument, and may supervise the carrying out of any works to it—if invited to do so by the owner, or if they consider it advisable (with or without such invitation!).[70] This service may be charged for, or may be carried out voluntarily.

Here too, if all else fails, the monument may need to be taken into public control—either guardianship or outright ownership. This is considered in **Chapter 11**.

---

[62] See **6.2**.
[63] AMAAA 1979.
[64] s.52A.
[65] Environment Act 1995, Sch.9, para.10.
[66] See **10.4**.
[67] AMAAA 1979, s.13(7).
[68] See **11.6.6**.
[69] s.24(2),(3A).
[70] s.25.

10.8 Unfit houses and clearance areas

10.8.1 General provisions

Under Part IX of the Housing Act 1985, where a local housing authority[71] was satisfied that a house was "unfit for human occupation",[72] it was required to decide whether to serve a repairs notice, a closure order, a demolition order, or a clearance order.[73] In reaching its decision, it had to take account of the criteria laid down in the Act, as well as relevant government guidance.[74] The Housing Act 2004 has introduced a new system of assessing housing conditions and enforcing housing standards, by reference to the existence on the premises of category 1 or category 2 hazards (as prescribed by regulations).[75]

Both the old and the new systems paid special regard to the problems that obviously arise where houses that are in poor condition are also of architectural or historic interest.[76] This is in addition to the general duty of a housing authority under s.607 of the 1985 Act (which remains in force), in taking any action under the 1985 Act, to have regard to:

(1) the beauty of the landscape or the countryside;

(2) the other amenities of the locality; and

(3) the desirability of preserving existing works of architectural, historic or artistic interest.

As to the meaning of the "amenity" of land, this has been considered earlier (albeit in a different context).[77]

10.8.2 Listed buildings

There are a number of specific duties laid on housing authorities in dealing with run-down buildings that are of special architectural or historic interest.

First, where an authority is satisfied that a house is in very poor condition (a concept that is obviously defined with some care[78]) may make an order requiring that the premises be vacated and demolished.[79] However, a demolition order may not be served on a building if:

---

[71] District council or borough council: Housing Act 1985, s.1.

[72] "Unfitness" was judged by reference to the standards prescribed by s.604 of the 1985 Act and elaborated in Departmental Circulars (see most recently Circular 17/96).

[73] Under Housing Act 1985, ss 189, 264, 265 or 289. Note that all of those provisions were substituted or substantially amended by the Local Government and Housing Act 1989.

[74] s.604A.

[75] Housing Act 2004, s.2; to be brought into force on a date to be announced. Note that some of the new provisions are in the form of new or amended provisions inserted into the 1985 Act; others are freestanding provisions in the new Act.

[76] Housing Act 1985, s.265(6), to be substituted by 2004 Act, s.46 for existing s.265(3).

[77] See **7.6.1** (tree preservation orders).

[78] 1985 Act, s.265, to be substituted by 2004 Act, s.46.

[79] 1985 Act, s.266(1), to remain in force.

(1) it is a listed building[80]; or

(2) the Secretary of State has served a notice stating that "its architectural or historic interest is sufficient to render it inexpedient that it should be demolished pending determination of the question whether it should be a listed building"[81]; note that there is no reference anywhere in the Listed Buildings Act to such a notice of "impending listing".

Where a building that is already subject to a demolition order is listed, the authority is to determine the order (so that it no longer has any effect).[82] Note that the demolition order will not determine automatically, so that the authority must still actually take action.

Secondly, where a listed building is included in a clearance area, the housing authority must within three months apply to the Secretary of State for listed building consent before it can be demolished.[83] In practice such an application might well be aired at the inquiry into the compulsory purchase order.[84] A notice to treat (following the confirmation of the order) may not be served until consent has been granted.[85] Where a listed building has been included in a clearance area but is not unfit, the authority must apply to the Secretary of State for listed building consent before it can be demolished; if consent is not obtained, the building ceases to be in the clearance area, and the compulsory purchase order ceases to have effect.[86]

Similarly, if a building is listed after being included in a clearance area and acquired (either by agreement or using compulsory purchase powers), listed building consent must be applied for within three months of the listing.[87] If consent is not obtained, the authority may not demolish it under section 291, but is instead deemed to have purchased it under Part II of the 1985 Act (that is, to provide housing accommodation) or, if it is not a house, under Part IX of the TCPA 1990 (that is, land purchased for general planning purposes); again, this will mean that the authority itself will then have to restore the building.

The Government formerly advised that a building that is listed or subject to a building preservation notice should only be included in a clearance area in exceptional circumstances[88]; and only where listed building consent has been given for its demolition. More specific guidance on the application of Pt IX of the 1985 Act (under the old system) to listed buildings and conservation areas was given in Appendix C to DETR Circ. 01/2001 and Appendix E to WO Circ. 1/98.

---

[80] 1985 Act, s.304(1), to be substituted by 2004 Act, Sch.15 for existing s.304(1).

[81] 1985 Act, s.304(4), to be substituted by 2004 Act, Sch.15 for existing s.304(3).

[82] 1985 Act, s.304(2), to be substituted by 2004 Act, Sch.15 for existing s.304(2). On the former arrangement, whereby the authority had to make a closure order instead of a demolition order in such circumstances, see the decision of the Court of Appeal in *Beaney v Branchett* [1987] 2 E.G.L.R. 115, CA.

[83] 1985 Act, s.305(1), to remain in force.

[84] Under 1985 Act, s.290.

[85] 1985 Act, s.305(2), to remain in force.

[86] 1985 Act, s.305(4), to remain in force.

[87] 1985 Act, s.306, to remain in force.

[88] Annex B to DoE Circ. 17/96 and WO Circ. 59/96.

10.8.3 Application to conservation areas

In deciding whether to serve a repair notice, the authority must take into account, amongst other things, "proposals for the area in which the premises are situated, and in particular whether they are within a conservation area or renewal area".[89] Similarly, in considering the service of a closing order, it must:

"...take into account the existence of a conservation area and proposals generally for the area in which the premises are situated. Short term closure may be an option if the long term objective is revitalisation of the area".[90]

An unlisted building in a conservation area may be subject to a demolition order under section 265 or to a compulsory purchase order under section 290 which is confirmed by the Secretary of State following the declaration of a clearance area. The housing authority does not then need conservation area consent before it can demolish it.[91] However this is subject to the general duty of the authority under section 607 to have regard to environmental considerations.[92]

10.8.4 Application to ancient monuments

Land which is the site of an ancient monument or other object of archaeological interest cannot be acquired for the purposes of clearance under Pt IX of the 1985 Act.[93] It is not clear what is envisaged by "object of archaeological interest"; but "ancient monument" presumably has the some meaning as in the Ancient Monuments Act.[94]

In addition, such land may only be acquired for housing purposes (presumably as part of a larger area) by compulsory purchase, and not by agreement.[95-97] That ensures that there is the possibility of an inquiry, and in any event the need for confirmation by the Secretary of State.

10.8.5 Area improvement

In addition to its powers with respect to individual buildings and pieces of land, a local authority may also take steps to bring about the improvement of a whole area, by declaring a renewal area under Part VII of the Local Government and Housing Act 1989. It may be appropriate in some cases to coordinate this action with other initiatives aimed more specifically at historic buildings.

On one hand, the declaration of a renewal area brings with it greater involvement and activity by the authority. If the area contains a number of listed or other historic buildings, any improvement works will need to be carefully monitored to ensure that they take account of the special features of each building.

---

[89] DoE Circ. 17/96, Annex F, para.18.
[90] para.19.
[91] DETR Circ. 01/2001, para.31(1)(i),(j); WO Circ. 1/98, para.20(1)(i); see **12.6.7**.
[92] See **10.8.1**
[93] Housing Act 1985, s.608(a), amended by Local Government and Housing Act 1989; see **10.8.1**.
[94] See **5.6.2**.
[95-97] s.608(b).

On the other hand, and more positively, this increased building activity—and financial commitment—can be an excellent opportunity to bring about the restoration of historic buildings and areas on a scale which would otherwise be impossible. This is not least because the improvement programme is financed from the local authority's housing budget, which is usually considerably larger than its planning budget that finances the enhancement of historic buildings. It can also be a good opportunity to carry out general environmental works to an area—landscaping, paving schemes, road closures and so on. These can make a significant improvement to the setting of a listed building or to the appearance of a conservation area. In addition, the declaration of a special area leads to much greater availability of subsidy by central government.

The provisions of Part VII of the 1989 Act relating to renewal areas are described in detail in the relevant government guidance, which also provide useful policy guidance on how they can be applied in practice. In particular, housing authorities have been advised that renewal area strategies should take full account of any statutory planning framework already established for the area—which would include the existence of any listed buildings or the designation of any conservation areas. It is thus clear that an authority's renewal area strategy should be fully harmonised with its conservation strategy.

For further details of renewal areas, texts on housing law and practice should be consulted.

10.9 Buildings in poor condition due to inappropriate use

10.9.1 Need for discontinuance action

It may sometimes arise that a historic building is being used, perfectly lawfully, for a purpose that is inevitably leading to its disrepair—and perhaps, slowly but surely, to its eventual collapse. For example, a group of listed farm buildings may be used for a variety of informal uses such as vehicle repairs, storage of building materials, and miscellaneous light industry, with complete disrespect for the condition of the buildings and their setting—as occurred in the recent case of *Chant v Secretary of State*.[98]

In such a situation, there is no point in serving an urgent repairs notice—the problem is real, but not immediate. Nor is it appropriate to serve a section 215 notice—since it would be possible to appeal against it on the ground that the condition of the building is due to the carrying on of operations or a use of land which is not in contravention of planning control.[99] And it may be that, in such circumstances, compulsory purchase of the building would not achieve anything either, since a new owner would not be willing to spend the money necessary to repair the buildings if they were still going to be used in an unsuitable way.

In other words, it is the use that is the problem; and until that is brought to an end, the condition of the buildings will not improve, and they may in the long run be lost altogether. But where that use is lawful (whether or not it has been the

[98] [2003] J.P.L. 1200, (2002) 28 E.G. 127 (CS).
[99] See **10.5.5**.

result of a formal grant of planning permission) enforcement action will not succeed in bringing it to an end. Thus the only option in such a case is for the planning authority to make a discontinuance order under the Planning Act—and to pay compensation.

The same would apply where buildings (including sheds and so forth) spoiling the setting of listed buildings or monuments—or alterations or extensions to unlisted buildings—have been allowed to remain for more than four years, so that it is no longer possible to take enforcement action to secure their removal.[1]

Thus, section 102 of the Act provides as follows:

"If, having regard to the development plan and to any other material considerations, it appears to a local planning authority that it is expedient that in the interests in the proper planning of the area (including the interests of amenity),

  (a) that any use of land should be discontinued, or that any conditions should be imposed on the continuance of a use of land; or

  (b) that any buildings or works should be altered or removed, they may be order—

    (i) require the discontinuance of that use, or

    (ii) impose such conditions as may be specified in the order on the continuance of it, or

    (iii) require such steps as may be so specified to be taken for the alteration or removal of the buildings or works,

as the case may be."[2]

As for the meaning of the word "amenity", that has already been considered in general terms.[3] The Administrative Court confirmed in *Chant* that "the proper planning of the area" and "the interests of amenity" could include the preservation of listed buildings—particularly where the development plan included (as most such plans do) policies encouraging the preservation of listed buildings. The same approach would doubtless apply where a discontinuance notice was to be served to improve the setting of a listed building, or land in a conservation area.

Equivalent provisions are in section 71 of the Scottish Planning Act and article 39 of the Northern Ireland Order.

10.9.2 Procedure

The relevant planning authority should consider carefully what it wishes to achieve. It may thus make a discontinuance notice to bring about the cessation of any lawful use or buildings, stating what use is to be stopped or modified, or what buildings are to be removed. It may couple this with an enforcement notice bringing to an end any unlawful activities on the site; or with a grant of planning permission for some alternative use or building.[4]

---

[1] Alterations to listed buildings themselves can of course be the subject of enforcement action indefinitely—see **18.3.5**.

[2] TCPA 1990, s.102(1)

[3] See **7.6**.

[4] TCPA 1990, s.102(2)

A discontinuance must be sent to the Secretary of State for confirmation. A copy is to be sent to the owner, who is entitled to object at an inquiry.[5] There is no particular burden of proof on the authority making the order, simply a requirement to justify that the proposed action is expedient. Nor is the making of an order a breach of human rights under article 1 of the Protocol to the ECHR.[6] Useful guidance on how this operates in practice is to be found in *Chant*.[7]

Compensation is to be paid, under s.115, to anyone who suffers loss as a result of the making of a discontinuance order.[8]

---

[5] TCPA 1990, s.103. In Northern Ireland, a notice is issued by the Department, but still has to be sent to the owner, who can object at an inquiry (P(NI)O 1991, art.39(4)).

[6] See **3.7.4**.

[7] *Chant v Secretary of State* [2003] J.P.L. 1200.

[8] Scotland: TCP(S) A 1990, s.83.

Chapter 11

Acquisition of Historic Buildings and Monuments by Public Authorities

11.1 Introduction

Where a listed building is in poor condition, this is in some cases the result of the owner or occupier being unwilling or unable to carry out the necessary works. This may be because the building is deliberately being allowed to fall into disrepair, so as to force the planning authority to grant listed building consent for its demolition. Or it may be because the owner would be very willing to repair it, but simply cannot afford to.

In such a situation, the local authority or English Heritage may occasionally be willing to offer grants or loans (see **Chapter 9**). But these will usually only cover part of the cost of the works, and the owner will still need to find the balance, and, again, may be unwilling or unable to do. If the works are urgent, the procedure under section 54 of the Listed Buildings Act) may be used.[1] But this is only effective in limited circumstances and cannot, in particular, bring about works other than those immediately necessary. Further, even if a way can be found to assist or persuade the owner to carry out the works needed to bring the building into good or at least reasonable repair, it still has to be maintained in the future, which may (especially in the case of a large building) be a very onerous responsibility.

The basic problem thus arises from the ownership of the building. The existing owner cannot or will not maintain it; those who could and would do not own it. The Listed Buildings Act accordingly provides special procedures whereby a listed building may be acquired by a public authority.[2]

This may be done by agreement (see **11.2**). Indeed, a public authority may acquire by agreement a building of special architectural or historic interest whether or not it is scheduled, listed or in a conservation area; and whether or not it is in poor repair. This also enables a building to be transferred from a private owner

---

[1] See **10.3**.
[2] P(LBCA)A 1990, ss 47–52. [Scotland: P(LBCA)(S)A 1997, ss 42–48; NI: P(NI)O 1991, arts 107–109.]

to a public authority so that the latter can make appropriate arrangements for the public to have access to it.

If the owner is unwilling to sell by agreement, the authority may have to resort to special compulsory purchase powers. There are special powers under the Listed Buildings Act available in relation to listed buildings in poor repair; the procedure is in general as for any other compulsory purchase, save that the first step in the procedure is the service of a repairs notice (see **11.3**). Indeed, the service of a repairs notice, with the explicit threat of compulsory purchase to follow, is in most cases sufficient either for the carrying out of the necessary repairs by the current owner or the sale of the building to someone else who will carry them out. Alternatively, it would be possible for a planning authority to acquire any historic building using compulsory powers where it could show that to be necessary for the proper planning of its area.

As with all compulsory purchase, the difficult issues arise in relation to compensation, and there are, perhaps unsurprisingly, special rules governing the assessment of compensation payable for any compulsory purchase of historic buildings (see **11.4**).

Once historic buildings have been acquired, they need to be managed or, more often, disposed of. The options are considered at **11.5**.

Finally, certain ancient monuments are of such a character that it may be more suitable for them to be in public ownership. The ancient monuments Acts have accordingly always contained provisions allowing for the acquisition and ownership or guardianship of monuments; the powers in the 1979 Act are set out in **11.6**.

11.2 Acquisition of historic buildings by agreement

11.2.1 Acquisition by a local authority of a historic building in poor repair

A local authority in England or Wales may acquire by agreement any building which it considers to be of special architectural or historic interest, under section 52 of the Listed Buildings Act.[3] A "local authority" is any county, district or borough council,[4] save that in relation to a national park it is the national park authority (only).[5]

A "building" may be any "structure or erection", but not plant or machinery.[6] There is no need for it to be scheduled or listed, or even in a conservation area. The Act states specifically that the statutory list is prepared for the guidance of local authorities in performing their functions under the Act[7]; and there will therefore be a presumption in favour of this power being used in connection with listed buildings. However, an authority may quite legitimately disagree with the Secretary of State as to the merit of a building.

---

[3] P(LBCA)A 1990, s.52(1)(a)), amended by the Local Government (Wales) Act 1994, Sch.6.
[4] s.52(1).
[5] Environment Act 1995, Sch.9, para.13(2).
[6] TCPA 1990, s.336, applied by P(LBCA)A 1990, s.91(2).
[7] P(LBCA)A 1990, s.1(1).

In Scotland, such a building may be acquired by agreement by any planning authority.[8]

One situation in which an authority might wish to acquire a historic building is where the building is in poor repair, and its owner is either unwilling or unable to do the necessary works. The authority, following the completion of the acquisition, may then either carry out the works itself or pass it on to others to do so.[9] In this situation, if there is a break-down in negotiations to acquire a building by agreement, the authority may wish to use its compulsory powers instead; although this will only be possible if the building is both listed and in poor repair.[10]

An authority may also acquire by agreement any land that is necessary for preserving a building acquired under section 52, or necessary for preserving its amenities[11] or for affording access to it or for its control and management. In this case, unlike the acquisition of the building itself, the authority must (in England and Wales) obtain the confirmation of the Secretary of State or the Welsh Assembly.[12]

Acquisition of property by agreement is more straightforward than compulsory purchase, and will be suitable where the owner and the local authority—possibly after consultation with English Heritage—are agreed that purchase by the authority is the best means of securing the future of the building. Since the terms and conditions of the purchase will be by mutual agreement, there is no reason why an authority should not in appropriate cases pay a reduced price for a dilapidated building in need of major restoration.

Alternatively, acquisition by agreement may be suitable where the owner of a building in poor repair realises that compulsory acquisition is practically inevitable sooner or later, and does not want to go through the inconvenience of the repairs notice and compulsory purchase procedure.

However, both the authority and the owner should always be aware that, if negotiations—whether amicable or through gritted teeth—break down, the authority can still use its compulsory powers. It follows that the compensation payable for acquisition by agreement will be the same as following compulsory purchase—if a larger price was paid, the authority would be in trouble with the District Auditor; and if a price was paid that seemed too small, the owner would insist on compulsory powers being used, with recourse to the Lands Tribunal to settle the compensation.

English Heritage (or the Welsh Assembly or the Scottish Ministers) may be willing to make a financial contribution towards the cost of an authority acquiring property under section 52.[13]

---

[8]   P(LBCA)(S)A 1997, s.52(1)(a).
[9]   See **11.5**.
[10] See **11.3**.
[11] See **6.13.5**.
[12] s.52(1)(b). [There is no such requirement in relation to Scotland: P(LBCA)(S)A 1997, s.47(1)(b).]
[13] HBAMA 1953, ss 5B(1), 6, inserted and amended by National Heritage Act 1983.

The ways in which a building may be dealt with following acquisition—such as resale to a new owner, refurbishment by a developer, or leaseback to the original owner—are dealt with later in this chapter.[14]

11.2.2 Acquisition of other historic buildings by a local authority

There is no requirement under section 52 for a historic building to be in poor repair before it can be passed by agreement to a local authority; and an authority may wish to acquire a building of particular interest from a private owner to enable the public to have access to it. Or an owner of a historic building may simply wish to be absolved from the responsibilities of caring for it, and transfer to a local authority—possibly for use for some public purpose—may be an appropriate course of action.

In these circumstances, where the building is not in need of repair, there is no explicit power to enable it to be compulsorily purchased—although that may be possible in some situations.[15] This may affect the price payable—but otherwise the position is as described above.

11.2.3 Acquisition by central government and by English Heritage

The Secretary of State (in England[16]), the Welsh Assembly and the Scottish Ministers have power to acquire by agreement, or to accept as a gift, any building which appears to them to be "of outstanding historic or architectural interest" and any land contiguous or adjacent to such a building.[17] Here too, there is no requirement that the building should be in need of repair.

As to the meaning of "outstanding interest", this has already been considered in relation to grants.[18]

They may also accept a capital endowment to provide income for the upkeep of a historic building.[19] This avoids problems that might otherwise occur, as such an endowment (unless it were charitable) would fail as a non-charitable purpose trust.

English Heritage may acquire (by purchase, lease or gift) any property in England that is:

(1)   a building of outstanding historic or architectural interest; or

(2)   a building that is in a conservation area, and of special historic or architectural interest; or

(3)   land associated with a building in either of those categories; or

---

[14] P(LBCA)A 1990, s.53(1). [Scotland: P(LBCA)(S)A 1997, s.48(1).] See **11.5**.
[15] Where it can be shown that the acquisition is necessary for the proper planning of the area (TCPA, s.226, amended by the Planning and Compulsory Purchase Act 2004).
[16] That is, the Secretary of State for Culture, Media and Sport (see **1.4.1**).
[17] HBAMA 1953, s.5(1).
[18] See **9.4.1**.
[19] 1953 Act, s.8

(4) any other garden or land that is of outstanding historic or architectural interest.[20]

Here too it is possible for an endowment for the upkeep of such a building or garden to be accepted.[21]

The Secretary of State, the Assembly and the Scottish Ministers may also purchase by agreement, or accept as a gift, any objects (such as paintings or furniture) associated with such a building, provided that the building is in their ownership or control or that of the relevant National Trust.[22] And English Heritage has similar powers in relation to objects associated with buildings in England.[23]

Following acquisition, the Secretary of State [etc.] or English Heritage may then make whatever arrangements seem to be appropriate for the disposal, custody and management of the property.[24]

Except in cases of urgency, any acquisition or disposal of property in England by the Secretary of State must in any event be the subject of consultation with English Heritage; and any acquisition or disposal of property in Wales by the Assembly with the Historic Buildings Council for Wales.[25] And any such action by English Heritage itself must have the consent of the Secretary of State.[26] In Scotland, there is no longer any requirement for the Secretary of State to consult anyone, but in practice it is likely that he or she will consult the Historic Environment Advisory Council for Scotland.

11.2.4 Northern Ireland

The Department may acquire by agreement any historic building, and any contiguous or adjacent land, under article 107 of the Northern Ireland Order.

11.3 Compulsory purchase of listed buildings in need of repair

11.3.1 Overview

Where a local authority wants to acquire a listed building in poor repair, it will usually be worth seeking to do so by agreement with the owner.[27] However, in some cases, this will be impossible—possibly because the owner is unwilling to sell at an appropriate price, or at all, or is unknown. In such case, the authority may have to resort to using compulsory purchase powers. And even where the owner is not altogether unwilling to sell by agreement, sometimes the availability of such

[20] 1953 Act, s.5A, inserted by National Heritage Act 1983 and amended by Planning (Consequential Provisions) Act 1990.
[21] 1953 Act, s.8A, 8B, inserted by National Heritage Act 1983.
[22] 1953 Act, ss 5(2). For the National Trust, see **7.10**.
[23] 1953 Act, ss 5A(2), inserted by National Heritage Act 1983.
[24] s.5(3), (3A).
[25] s.5(4), amended by the 1983 Act. See **11.3.2** for an example of an acquisition of a listed building (Apethorpe Hall) by the Secretary of State.
[26] s.5A(4), inserted by the 1983 Act.
[27] See **11.2**.

powers may help to concentrate the mind. The Listed Buildings Act accordingly contains (in section 47) special powers to enable this to occur.

The first step in the procedure is for the authority to serve a repairs notice on the owner of the building specifying the works that authority considers to be necessary for its preservation.[28] The notice of itself does not impose any liability on the owner, but simply enables the authority to start compulsory purchase procedures if those works are not carried out. It also enables an owner to be clear as to what precisely is required—otherwise an authority would be able constantly to increase its demands, and the owner could never entirely relax.

In practice, the service of a notice—and the associated negotiation—will often be sufficient to bring about at least some of the necessary works. On the other hand, the authority needs to be aware that it may have to go all the way to actually acquiring the building if it is to achieve anything—although note that it may be able to obtain financial assistance from English Heritage, Cadw or Historic Scotland.[29]

This is illustrated by the survey published by the Association of Conservation Officers[30] describing the use that was made of repairs notices over a period of six years. 31 per cent of English local authorities had authorised the service of one or more repairs notices, involving a total of 287 listed buildings. 162 notices were in the event served: 38 resulted in a public inquiry; and five compulsory purchase orders were finally confirmed. The survey (now slightly dated, but still the most authoritative source of information[31]) contains much valuable information on how the procedure works in practice, together with copious examples of clauses for inclusion in the schedule to a notice specifying the works to be carried out.

Some of the possible courses of action open to the authority once a listed building has been acquired under section 47 are considered later in this chapter.[32] A notable instance of the use of this procedure was the action taken by North Shropshire District Council to bring about the repair of Pell Wall Hall.[33]

This procedure may not be used in the case of an unlisted building, which may therefore normally only be acquired by agreement.[34] Nor may it be used to acquire a building in ecclesiastical use,[35] or a scheduled monument.[36] The latter may however be compulsorily acquired under the Ancient Monuments Act.[37]

Similar powers are available in section 42 of the Scottish Listed Buildings Act and article 109 of the Northern Ireland Order.

---

[28] See **11.3.3**.
[29] See **11.5.2**.
[30] The predecessor to the Institute of Historic Building Conservation.
[31] Available, price £4, from the author, Bob Kindred, 4 Henley Road, Ipswich IP1 3SF.
[32] See **11.5.1**.
[33] *Rolf v North Shropshire D.C.* [1988] J.P.L. 103; see **10.1.3**.
[34] See **11.2**.
[35] s.60(1),(2); see **Chapter 16**.
[36] s.61.
[37] See **11.6.2**. On repairs to ancient monuments generally, see **10.4**, **10.7.2**, **11.6**.

11.3.2 Acquiring authorities

Generally, the compulsory purchase of a listed building under section 47 will be carried out in England or Wales by a local authority (county, county borough, district or borough council), by English Heritage (in London only), or by the Broads Authority. These are referred to in the Act as "the appropriate authority".[38] National park authorities and the Thurrock and Thames Gateway urban development corporations are the sole appropriate authority in their area.[39] In Scotland, acquisition is generally by the planning authority.[40] A listed building in Northern Ireland can only be acquired by the Department.[41]

There is no reason why (in England) a county council and a district council should not operate together. The former will sometimes have greater specialist expertise in historic buildings matters, and may have experience of using this procedure elsewhere in the county. The latter will be responsible for the grant of planning permission and listed building consent for any subsequent rehabilitation of the building. English Heritage may also be involved, either in Greater London or elsewhere—both as a source of technical expertise and to provide financial assistance where appropriate.

In addition, the Secretary of State may compulsorily purchase a listed building in England (after consultation with English Heritage).[42] He has stated that he will only use this power himself in "exceptional circumstances".[43] This has in fact occurred only twice. The first was in December 1992, when a repairs notice was served in relation to the Crescent in Buxton, Derbyshire—which prompted the owners of the building to sell it to the local council. More recently, the current Secretary of State served a compulsory purchase order in respect of Apethorpe Hall in Northamptonshire, a remarkable 15th-century country house (listed Grade I) which had been in English Heritage's Buildings at Risk register since it was first prepared in 1998, and had fallen into serious disrepair. Here too, this prompted the owner to sell the house by agreement—with a substantial deposit being paid by the Secretary of State in return for being allowed into possession early, to start the necessary repair works.

The Welsh Assembly and the Scottish Ministers may similarly use these powers—although, again, they will in practice only do so in exceptional cases.[44]

11.3.3 Repairs notices

The first formal stage in the procedure is that a "repairs notice" must be served on the owner and occupier.[45] The notice must firstly "specify the works which [the

---

[38] See ss 47(1)(a), (7), amended by the Local Government (Wales) Act 1994, Sch.6.
[39] Environment Act 1995, Sch.9, para.13(1); Thurrock Development Corporation (Planning Functions) Order 2005 (SI 2005/2572), art.4, Sch.; London Thames Gateway Development Corporation (Planning Functions) Order 2005 (SI 2005/2721), art.5, Sch.
[40] P(LBCA)(S)A 1997, s.42(1)(a).
[41] P(NI)O 1991, art.109(1).
[42] ss 47(1)(b), (3)(a), 48(4).
[43] PPG 15, para.7.11.
[44] Wales: ss 47(1)(b), 48(4); Scotland: P(LBCA)(S)A 1997, s.42(1)(b).
[45] P(LBCA)A 1990, s.48(1).

authority considers] reasonably necessary for the proper preservation of the building". This provision—and the repairs notice procedure generally—was considered by the House of Lords in the leading case of *Robbins v Secretary of State*, which concerned the Willesborough Windmill in Kent. That case made it clear that the works to be specified in a repairs notice can be those necessary for the preservation of the building in the state in which it was at the date of listing, rather than at the date of the notice.[46]

This is probably best achieved by means of a detailed report by an appropriately qualified surveyor or architect, with detailed experience of the repair and maintenance of the type of building in question. It is not clear whether the word "specify", used in the Act, means that the notice must include a "specification" in sufficient detail to enable it to be used by a builder without more ado, or whether it merely implies a report adequate to form the basis of such a specification. It presumably means a description of the works sufficient to identify exactly what is needed, without specifying the number of bricks to be used. It is noticeable that the corresponding provision relating to urgent works[47] states that a notice under that section need only "describe" the works; that suggests that the use of the word "specify" does require a greater level of detail.

In practice, it will usually be appropriate to discuss the works specified with whoever is actually going to carry them out. This in turn means that the authority (in an appropriate case in conjunction with the county council or English Heritage[48]) should have clearly thought through what it intends to do once it has purchased the building—see below for some suggestions. Note that the authority does not have to take into account the owner's means when specifying the works[49]—this contrasts with the section 54 procedure, where the owner can appeal against a claim for recovery of the cost of urgent works carried out on the grounds that it would cause hardship.

Most of all, it is vital wherever possible for the authority to enter communication with the owner of the building. As the English Heritage guide *Stopping The Rot* observes:

"Often, a written warning of an impending repairs notice and possible compulsory purchase will be sufficient to encourage the owner to repair the property, or alternatively to sell it to a third party who will undertake the repairs".

That guide accordingly suggests an initial informal approach, followed by warning letters—of which useful precedents are provided—before a formal repairs notice is served.

The notice should not specify works over and above those that the authority considers to be "reasonably necessary for the proper preservation of the building".[50] Thus in *Robbins* the notice served under section 48 required works to be done to the windmill which went beyond mere repairs, and included measures aimed at "restoring it to its former glory". It was held that this did not invalidate

---

[46] *Robbins v Secretary of State* [1989] 1 W.L.R. 201 at 212B.
[47] In s.54(6) (see **10.5.3**).
[48] See **11.3.2**.
[49] *Rolf v North Shropshire D.C.* [1988] J.P.L. 103 at 105.
[50] s.48(1)(a).

the subsequent approval by the Secretary of State of the authority's compulsory purchase order; as the deputy judge hearing the case at first instance pointed out:

"...there was an obvious public interest, where listed buildings were concerned, in expecting owners to make reasonable efforts to comply with those parts of repairs notices which they know to require work which could lawfully be required."[51]

In that case, the owner had carried out no works at all. But authorities should not use this as an excuse to avoid considering carefully what works are currently necessary, as opposed to desirable. More extensive works, however worthwhile, should not be included in the notice, but obviously can be carried out later at the authority's discretion, once it owns the building. Perhaps surprisingly, the Secretary of State has stated, in relation to buildings in England,[52] that he considers it to be legitimate to include in a repairs notice repairs that are necessary to preserve what remains of the rest of the building—for example, a roof that was defective at the time of listing. The corresponding Welsh guidance[53] does not go as far.

The fact that the notice is to specify the works (presumably all the works) necessary for the preservation of the building would seem to mean that it is not possible to serve several notices in respect of the same building. Further, the building referred to is the listed building to be purchased, which must be the whole building—including all curtilage structures.[54] Of course, if several buildings in a group are separately listed, there would be nothing to prevent one notice being served in relation to each, followed by a single compulsory purchase order for the whole group. Generally, however, the procedure should be focussed on one listed building (that is, building in the list plus its curtilage structures[55]).

The procedure may, incidentally, be used (unlike urgent repairs notices under section 54[56]) to secure the repair of buildings which are wholly in use.

The repairs notice must also explain the effects of sections 47 to 50 of the Act (or the equivalent in Scotland or Northern Ireland)—that is, it must set out what is the compulsory purchase procedure, including the provisions as to compensation.[57] For a sample notice, see **Form D7** in Appendix D. The Act only requires the notice must be served on the owner of the building—that is, the freeholder or, where appropriate, the leaseholder or sub-lessee entitled to receive the market rent.[58] But it would also be sensible for a copy to be served on the occupier(s) of the building, and any other interested parties (such as any prospective purchasers and their professional advisers, English Heritage, and the district or county council).

---

[51] [1988] J.P.L. 349 at p.356.
[52] PPG 15, para.7.10.
[53] WO Circ. 61/96, para.138.
[54] See *Shimizu (U.K.) Ltd v Westminster C.C.* [1996] 3 PLR 89, in which Lord Hope explicitly stated (at 105C) that he had not found any provision in the Act where "listed building" needed to be interpreted as including "part of a listed building".
[55] See **Chapter 4**.
[56] See **10.3**.
[57] s.48(1)(b). [Scotland: P(LBCA)(S)A 1997, s.43(1)(b); NI: P(NI)O 1991, art.109(4)(b).]
[58] s.48(1), 91(2); *London Corporation v Cusack-Smith* [1955] AC 337, upheld in *Pollway Nominees v Croydon LBC* [1986] 2 All E.R. 849.

Where a notice has been served under section 48, the owner is barred from serving either a purchase notice or a listed building purchase notice on the authority at any time within the succeeding three months—or, if compulsory purchase proceedings are started within that three-month period, at any time until they are concluded.[59]

Finally, where the owner of the building is not known or cannot be traced, a notice should be affixed to the building (see the comments as to the corresponding procedure for section 54 notices[60]). The compulsory purchase proceedings can then be started two months after the notice was put up, under the special procedure in the Compulsory Purchase Act 1965.[61]

If a repairs notice is withdrawn at any stage, notice of the withdrawal must be given to all concerned.[62]

11.3.4 Compulsory purchase: initial procedure

The detailed procedure is broadly as for any compulsory purchase, and is governed in England and Wales by the Acquisition of Land Act 1981[63] and associated subordinate legislation made in 2004.[64] However, there is a special right of appeal to the magistrates' court.[65] Some guidance is given in ODPM Circular 02/03; although it unfortunately predates the 2004 Regulations.

The acquiring authority first makes a draft compulsory purchase order, in the prescribed form set out as Form 1 in the Schedule to the relevant Regulations; for a sample order, see **Form D8** in Appendix D to this book. Where a direction for minimum compensation is made[66], an additional paragraph 3 must also be included in the draft order.[67] The land to be acquired is defined in the order by reference to a schedule and a map. Authorities have been warned to take care when preparing orders—a high proportion of orders submitted to the Secretary of State for confirmation contain errors or omissions.[68]

The order may include not only the listed building itself, but also any adjoining land whose purchase is appropriate.[69] This would, for example, apply to land required for preserving the building or its amenities (such as the garden of a town house), or for affording access to it, or for its proper control or management (such

---

[59] s.48(5), (6). [Scotland: P(LBCA)(S)A 1997, s.43(4),(5)]

[60] At **10.3.5**.

[61] 1965 Act, Sch.2.

[62] s.48(3). [Scotland: P(LBCA)(S)A 1997, s.43(3); NI: P(NI)O 1991, art.109(6).]

[63] P(LBCA)A 1990, s.47(2).

[64] England: Compulsory Purchase of Land (Written Representations Procedure) (Ministers) Regulations 2004, and Compulsory Purchase of Land (Prescribed Forms) (Ministers) Regulations 2004 (SIs 2004/2594 and 2004/2595); Wales: Compulsory Purchase of Land (Written Representations Procedure) (National Assembly for Wales) Regulations 2004, and Compulsory Purchase of Land (Prescribed Forms) (National Assembly for Wales) Regulations 2004 (SIs 2004/2730 and 2004/2732). These together replaced the 1994 Regulations (SI 1994/2145) with effect from October 31, 2004.

[65] s.47(4); see **11.3.5**.

[66] See **11.4.3**.

[67] SIs 2004/2595 and 2004/2732, reg.4(a).

[68] Circ. 6/85, para.3.

[69] s.47(1), (7).

as the outbuildings of a country house, or the lodge of an institutional building). The proper extent of land to be included was considered in an appeal decision relating to a listed farmhouse in Reigate, Surrey,[70] in which the Secretary of State considered that the order land should include the adjacent agricultural buildings, and a nearby lake, but not the more distant fields.

In relation to the acquisition of land said to be necessary to secure the continuing viability of the listed building, the English Heritage guide *Stopping the Rot* notes as follows:

"The amount of land could be crucial in determining the economic viability of the building. This will depend on the building's location, scope for re-use, and repair and refurbishment costs. A CPO was recently confirmed in respect of a modest Grade II listed house comprising a land area of approximately 600 m^2, in recognition of the need to provide additional development to subsidise the listed building repair costs (*Radford v East Hampshire DC*)."

The East Hampshire case there referred to concerned a site where a building was to be compulsorily acquired together with land that might be independently developed. The Inspector holding the inquiry into the compulsory purchase order concluded as follows:

"the whole site should continue to be treated as one planning unit; the future of the whole site should be considered on a comprehensive basis; new development of the adjoining land should be designed in conjunction with development proposals for the listed building; the amenities of the listed building might thereby be preserved; and profit from any new development can be directed to fund the necessary repairs, so that the land [adjacent to the listed building] would be required 'indirectly' for the preservation of the building."[71]

The authority then advertises the order for at least two weeks in the local press, and serves separate notices on each owner, lessee and occupier of the land.[72] The notice is to be in the form of Form 8 in the Schedule to the Regulations, with in every case the inclusion of additional paras 3 and 5 from the second part of that form; and where a direction for minimum compensation is to be included, an additional para.4 must also be included in the notice.[73] For an example, see **Form D9** in Appendix D to this book; for guidance, see Appendix K to Circular 02/03.

The compulsory purchase of the building cannot start until at least two months after the repairs notice has been served.[74] For this purpose, the "start" of the compulsory purchase means the service of the notices on the owners, etc. of the land.[75] The press advertisement and the notice to the owners, etc., must both state the date by which any objections may be made. This must be at least 21 days from the making of the draft order.

In the Reigate appeal decision, noted above, the land owner agreed not to object to the order provided that the council undertook not to implement it if it

---

[70] Noted at [1998] J.P.L. 612.

[71] Inspector's report relating to 26–30 Normandy Street, Alton, paras 79–80; the same approach has been adopted in at least one subsequent inquiry (relating to 116 High Street, Boston, Lincolnshire (ref: HSD/68/02/40)).

[72] Acquisition of Land Act 1981, ss 11, 12.

[73] SIs 2004/2595 and 2004/2732, reg.4(b).

[74] P(LBCA)A 1990, s.48(1).

[75] section 48(6); 1981 Act, s.12.

was confirmed, subject to the required works being carried out by an agreed date. That seems a sensible way forward—although it is not clear how such an agreement would be enforced.

11.3.5 Appeal to magistrates' court

In addition to the normal method of objecting to any compulsory purchase order, described below, there is an additional right to appeal to the local magistrates' court. This was described by Lord Bridge in *Robbins* as being tailor-made to solve the dilemma of determining whether the works required in a repairs notice are excessive.[76] An alternative view is that it is somewhat anomalous, and a hangover from the days when appeals against enforcement notices were to the magistrates.

Under this provision, anyone served with notice of the order may, within the following 28 days, apply to the court for an order staying further proceedings on the compulsory purchase order.[77] On receipt of the complaint by the building owner, the court will issue a summons on complaint[78]; an example is at **Form D10** in Appendix D. The local authority concerned will then attend to answer the complaint. But there appears to be no provision for the authority to set out a statement of its case; nor for the production of proofs by expert witnesses. In practice, however, evidence is likely to be by way of proofs.

In any event, an order staying the proceedings must be granted if, but only if, the court is satisfied that "reasonable steps have been taken for properly preserving the building". But the steps must have already been taken by the date of the hearing; a mere promise will not be enough. In practice, therefore, it is not worth applying to the magistrates' court unless there is reasonably clear evidence as to the works that have been done and the resulting condition of the building.

Anyone aggrieved by the decision of the magistrates' court can appeal to the Crown Court.[79] It was as a result of such an appeal that the Pell Wall Hall case eventually reached the Court of Appeal.[80]

11.3.6 Confirmation of compulsory purchase order

Objections to the draft compulsory purchase order are likely to fall into two categories:

(1) those against the principle of compulsory purchase; and

(2) those referring only to the amount of compensation to be paid.

If there are no objections, or if the authority considers that all the objections are in the second category, the Secretary of State is then entitled to confirm the order without further ado. If, however, there are any objections which are or might be in the first category, there must first be a public inquiry, unless the objectors agree

---

[76] [1989] 1 W.L.R. 201 at pp.213, 214.
[77] P(LBCA)A 1990, s.47(4).
[78] In Form 99; see *Stone's Justices' Manual*, 1998 ed., para.9–591; Magistrates' Court Act 1980, ss 51, 52; Magistrates' Court Rules 1981, rr 34, 98.
[79] s.47(6).
[80] [1988] J.P.L. 103 at 104; and see **10.1.3**.

that the matter should be dealt with by way of written representations (a new procedure available only since 2004).[81] Curiously, objectors other than owners, lessees and occupiers, such as neighbours or amenity societies, have a right to be heard, but the Secretary of State is entitled to disregard their objections.[82] Otherwise, the procedure is as for other similar inquiries.[83]

Before confirming the order, in the case of a building in England, the Secretary of State must consult English Heritage—except, obviously, in the case of a draft order made by English Heritage itself in London.[84]

Of more significance, a compulsory purchase order must not be confirmed unless the Secretary of State is satisfied as to three matters:

(1) that reasonable steps are not being taken to preserve the building properly[85]; and

(2) that it is expedient that provision should be made for its preservation[86]; and

(3) that it is expedient that the building should be compulsorily purchased to secure its preservation.[87]

Thus if the works specified in the repairs notice had been carried out in their entirety, the Secretary of State would normally refuse to confirm a compulsory purchase order, on the first ground above—although in theory the acquisition could be authorised in order to ensure that other works, considered to be necessary for the preservation of the building but which had not been specified in the notice were carried out.

Note that the requirement is in the present tense—it may be sufficient for an owner to claim that he or she intends to carry out repairs, but it would seem that what is required to defeat an order is probably at the very least a binding contract for the carrying out of the repairs. It may also be insufficient to show that only some of the works have been carried out; but where a notice contains more than is strictly required for the building's preservation, the owner would only need to show that those works that were actually necessary had been carried out.[88] Note too that the works must be such as to preserve the building "properly"—a mere temporary operation would not suffice.

The Secretary of State has stated that he will also need to be satisfied that the means and the resources necessary for securing the building's repair will be

---

[81] Acquisition of Land Act 1981, ss 13–13C, inserted by Planning and Compulsory Purchase Act 2004, s.100(6).

[82] *Middlesex CC v Minister of Local Government and Planning* [1953] 1 Q.B. 12, CA.

[83] Compulsory Purchase by Non-Ministerial Acquiring Authorities (Inquiries Procedure) Rules 1990 (these are likely to be soon replaced following the coming into force of Pt 8 of the Planning and Compulsory Purchase Act 2004; *Local Government Board v Arlidge* [1915] A.C. 120. For inquiries generally, see **15.3**.

[84] P(LBCA)A 1990, s.47(3)(a).

[85] s.47(1).

[86] s.47(3)(b).

[87] s.47(3)(b).

[88] *Robbins v Secretary of State and Ashford BC*; see **11.3.3**.

available.[89] The acquiring authority should therefore have in place a scheme to deal with the building—either to put it on the open market (where the building is such that it will clearly be bought by someone) or to pass it to a specialist body who can restore it and then dispose of it.[90]

If the order is confirmed, possibly in a modified form, notices must once again be publicised in the press and sent to the owners and occupiers of the land.[91]

11.3.7 Scotland and Northern Ireland

The procedure for compulsory purchase of listed buildings in poor repair in Scotland is in principle the same as in England and Wales, but under the Acquisition of Land (Authorisation Procedure) (Scotland) Act 1947[92]—with a right to apply to a sheriff and, on appeal, to the Court of Session.

In Northern Ireland, the procedure is by way of vesting order, governed by the Local Government Act (Northern Ireland) 1972, as modified by Schedule 2 to the Planning (Northern Ireland) Order 1991.[93]

11.4 Compensation for compulsory purchase of listed buildings

11.4.1 General principles

The compensation payable for the compulsory purchase of a historic building is, in principle, assessed on the same basis as in any other case. However, there are some particular problems which may occur, reflected in the rules for compensation in section 5 of the Land Compensation Act 1961; and there are some specific statutory assumptions—as a result of section 49 of the Listed Buildings Act—that must be made in the case of any compulsory purchase of a listed building. They thus apply where a listed building is to be compulsorily purchased to bring about its repair, but equally where a listed building happens to be included within a town centre redevelopment scheme.

The basic principle (rule 2 in the 1961 Act) is that the price to be paid for land being compulsorily acquired is its value "if sold on the open market by a willing seller". In determining what this open market value is, the normal rules will apply. Historic buildings will often be capable of being valued on this basis just like any other building.

However, in some cases it may be more appropriate to value them in accordance with rule 5, which applies "where land is, and but for the compulsory acquisition would continue to be, devoted to a purpose of such a nature that there is no general demand or market for land for that purpose". This would apply to, for example, churches and chapels, and ornamental structures serving no useful purpose. It has been estimated that these two groups comprise respectively 5 per

---

[89] PPG 15, para.7.12; WO Circ. 61/96, para.136.

[90] See **11.5**.

[91] 1981 Act, s.15, substituted by 2004 Act, s.100(7).

[92] P(LBCA)(S) 1997, s.42(3).

[93] P(NI)O 1991, art.87(2), applied by art.109(3). Note that there is no provision in Northern Ireland for a direction for minimum compensation (see **11.4.3**).

cent and 16 per cent of all listed buildings. Clearly, in such circumstances, to pay open market value (which might be nil) would be unjust, and the compensation payable is therefore the reasonable cost of equivalent reinstatement elsewhere, if that is bona fide intended by the landowner. However, what cost is "reasonable" may be difficult to determine. The replacement of monumental Victorian architecture by a modern functional building often makes it difficult to decide what is genuinely "equivalent" or comparable.

A further problem arises where such a structure is redundant. In this case, rule 5 no longer applies, since the land would no longer be used for its last purpose, even if it were not being compulsorily purchased, and there is no intention to reinstate. The appropriate value would therefore again be that obtainable on the open market; which would presumably be the value in some alternative use, if there is any, or otherwise might be zero or even negative.[94]

In addition, the planning position needs to be investigated carefully to ascertain what, if any, planning permission might be forthcoming which would increase the value of the property. The relevant statutory assumptions that are to be made include the following:

(1) planning permission would be granted for development specified in Schedule 3 to the Planning Act—principally rebuilding, subject to the volume of the original building not being increased by more than one tenth—subject to the condition set out in Schedule 10 to that Act[95];

(2) listed building consent would be granted for any demolition involved in carrying out such development[96], but not necessarily for any other demolition; and

(3) listed building consent would be granted for any alteration or extension of the building.[97]

The only other relevant assumption that can be made (by virtue of section 16 of the 1961 Act) is that planning permission would be granted for development for a purpose specified in the development plan[98]—but only if permission might reasonably expect to have been granted,[99] and in deciding that, it would of course have been taken into account that the building is listed.[1] Otherwise, it cannot be assumed that planning permission would be granted for alterations and extensions; and without planning permission, the grant of listed building consent (under assumption (3)) is of little value.

The net effect of these assumptions is therefore that the only (small) additional value that can be relied on is that arising from the possibility of carrying out:

---

[94] See, for example, *Essex Incorporated Congregational Union v Colchester BC* [1982] 2 E.G.L.R. 178.

[95] 1961 Act, s.15, substituted by PCA 1991, Sch.6.

[96] P(LBCA)A 1990, s.49(b).

[97] s.49(a). There was, prior to 1992, a limited exception to the third of these assumptions, but that was removed by PCA 1991, Sch.6, para.45.

[98] 1961 Act, s.16(2)(a), (3)(a).

[99] s.16(2)(b), (3)(b).

[1] See **12.3** to **12.5**.

(1) works for which planning permission can be assumed to be granted, by virtue of assumption (1) above;

(2) works for which permission can be assumed by virtue of section 16 (see above), but which involve only alteration and extension, and no demolition;

(3) works for which planning permission has already been granted by a development order (other than demolition); or

(4) works which are not development, and for which planning permission is not required.

This does not mean that planning permission and listed building consent would necessarily be refused for any other works to the building[2]—merely that they cannot be assumed. In practice, and particularly in the situation of compulsory purchase, the likelihood of obtaining either permission or consent might well be small—and that will be reflected in the value that can be obtained for the building.

Compensation in Scotland will be determined in accordance with Land Compensation (Scotland) Act 1963, with modifications relating to listed buildings (similar to those applying in England and Wales, described above) set out in section 44 of the Scottish Listed Buildings Act. There are apparently no corresponding provisions relating to Northern Ireland.

Any dispute over the amount of compensation is to be referred to the relevant Lands Tribunal.[3]

11.4.2 Compensation for acquisition under section 47

In general, the compulsory acquisition of a listed building in poor repair, under section 47 of the Listed Buildings Act, will lead to compensation being payable on the same basis as for any other compulsory purchase of a listed building, as outlined above.[4]

The planning position may need to be considered more carefully where the acquiring authority is willing to grant planning permission for refurbishment proposals involving a change of use or some new building works.

But there is no assumption that listed building consent would be granted for any other works amounting to total or partial demolition of the building.[5] It should be borne in mind here that some works of "alteration or extension" will include an element of (at least partial) demolition,[6] and that it therefore cannot be assumed that consent will automatically be granted for them. In the case of a building being purchased under section 47, which is likely to be considered to be of particular interest by the acquiring authority, such consent would indeed probably not be forthcoming. This would also put a severe restraint on any additional value to be reflected in the purchase price.

[2] And see 1961 Act, s.15(3).
[3] 1961 Act, s.1.
[4] See **11.4.1**.
[5] P(LBCA)A 1990, s.49.
[6] See **12.6.2**, **12.6.3**.

One useful example illustrating the arithmetic involved in a typical case is *Taylor v Cheltenham BC*,[7] which related to the compulsory purchase in the late 1970s of 22 Lansdown Parade, Cheltenham. All the other properties in the terrace were in first class repair and the council had successfully restored the whole parade. The owner of number 22, who was in an old people's home, had allowed his house to deteriorate to the extent that the cost of putting it into good condition (allowing for both improvement grants and historic building grants) was £12,100, whereas its value once restored was only £11,000. The Lands Tribunal accepted that mathematically the property had a minus value and would thus not be bought by a householder for occupation—but that a speculative purchaser might be prepared to accept it at a knockdown price. Compensation was accordingly awarded at a notional figure of £2,000.

A similar approach was taken by the Tribunal in the more recent (1995) case of *Bellamy v Great Yarmouth BC*, where it accepted that a residual valuation resulted in a dilapidated Victorian building being valued at £1. However, it preferred to adopt a "robust approach", recognising that a speculator or entrepreneur might well purchase the property for future use or development, and accordingly assessing its value at £17,5000, along with severance and injurious affection of £2,500.[8] A similar approach was adopted in *Hale v Blaenau Gwent CBC*, where a redundant chapel was valued by the Tribunal at a notional £5,000.[9]

11.4.3 Compensation for building deliberately left derelict

One further feature of compulsory purchase under section 47 of the 1990 Act is that there is a special method of assessing the compensation payable where the listed building to be acquired has been deliberately left derelict.[10]

This only applies, however, where the acquiring authority is satisfied that the building has been deliberately allowed to fall into disrepair for the purpose of justifying:

(1) its demolition, and

(2) the development or redevelopment of the site or any adjoining site.[11]

In other words, to justify the use of this procedure, it must be proved by the authority that the neglect of the building was not merely deliberate or reckless, but also that the underlying motive was to facilitate demolition and redevelopment. Such a claim would be difficult to justify in the face of a counterclaim by the owner that he or she had no such motive, but was simply unable to afford to maintain the building properly.

Where such a claim can be substantiated, the authority may include in the draft compulsory purchase order a "direction for minimum compensation"; and if it does so, it must state this in the notice served on the owners and occupiers

---

[7] (1978) 246 E.G., LT.
[8] [1996] R.V.R. 41, LT.
[9] Lands Tribunal, August 26, 1999, unreported (available on Lawtel).
[10] P(LBCA)A 1990, s.50.
[11] s.50(1) (b), (2).

informing them of the order.[12] See paragraph 3 of the sample order (**Form D8**) in the Appendix D to this book, and paragraph 4 of the sample notice (**Form D9**).

The effect of such a direction is that the compensation payable by the authority for the purchase of the building is not to be assessed on the basis of the usual assumptions as to planning permission contained in the Land Compensation Act 1961.[13] Instead, it is to be assumed that planning permission and listed building consent would only be granted for those works which are necessary for restoring the building and maintaining it in a proper state of repair.[14] This would stifle any hope that the owner might have entertained of obtaining an inflated "development" value for the site. The Secretary of State has commented that:

"It is hoped that authorities will not often have to resort to this power, but its existence should act as a deterrent against the sort of deliberate neglect which has caused the loss of listed buildings in the past."[15]

Anyone who is served with notice of a compulsory purchase order containing a direction for minimum compensation can apply within 28 days to the local magistrates' court for an order that the direction is deleted from the purchase order. If the court is satisfied that the reason for the state of the building is not to facilitate its demolition and redevelopment, then it must delete the direction from the purchase order.[16] The procedure for such an application is as for an application under section 47(4).[17] There is also a right of appeal to the Crown Court against the decision of the magistrates' court.[18]

For an example of the use of a minimum compensation direction, see *Rolf v North Shropshire DC*.[19]

There is a corresponding provision for a direction for minimum compensation in Scotland, under section 45 of the Scottish Listed Buildings Act, but not in Northern Ireland.

11.5 Options after the acquisition of a historic building

11.5.1 Possible options

Once a historic building is in public ownership, the acquiring authority then has a number of options. In principle, it can make such arrangements for its management, use or disposal as it considers appropriate to ensure its preservation.[20]

It could, for example, carry out the necessary repairs itself, and then either retain it for its own purposes, or sell or lease it to another owner. Alternatively, it could transfer it to another owner straight away, but subject to a requirement that

---

[12] s.50(3); SIs 2004/2595 and 2004/2732, reg.4. A model for such a direction is provided in Appendix K to ODPM Circular 02/03, but it is in the same form as in the Regulations.
[13] See **11.4.1**.
[14] s.50(4).
[15] Circ. 8/87, para.136.
[16] s.50(6).
[17] See **11.3.5**.
[18] s.50(8).
[19] [1988] J.P.L. 103 at 104 (see **10.1.2**).
[20] P(LBCA)A 1990, s.53; and see *Rolf v North Shropshire DC* [1988] J.P.L. 103 at 107.

the owner carry out the repairs. The latter is likely to be the simplest and best option where the property is of a kind that is readily saleable—albeit at a discount reflecting the condition. Thus, for example, a house in west London that has been neglected for years by an elderly absentee owner could simply be put on the open market, whereas a decaying medieval castle in mid-Wales may be less straightforward.

If a subsequent owner can be identified prior to the completion of the compulsory purchase, the authority could enter into a conditional contract of sale with him or her, to be completed at the moment the authority itself acquires the building. In this way, it would receive the proceeds of the subsequent sale at the same time as it had to pay for the initial purchase. The authority would thus not be out of pocket for more than a very short time—and in determining the level of capital receipts of an authority under section 9 of the Local Government Act 2003, allowance is made for back-to-back deals of this sort.[21] Authorities would thus need to be particularly careful to ensure that the building was passed on promptly to its new owners, and in any event within two years so as to avoid unnecessarily increasing their spending, and thereby attracting financial penalties.[22]

The procedure could therefore be used in several different ways. The simplest option is where the owner of a listed building (for example, a town house owned by an absentee landlord and let as flats) has allowed it to fall into very poor condition, but is not interested in doing any repairs (since the capital outlay would not be reflected in extra rental income). Here the local authority can purchase the building, repair it, and sell it to a new owner, who can either continue to use it for the same purpose or apply to change its use. Alternatively, the authority could sell the building subject to a requirement that it must be repaired, possibly offering a grant as an inducement to carry out detailed work to the correct specifications.

Secondly, where, for example, a listed building in poor condition is occupied by a charity or other organisation that has very limited capital to carry out repairs, a local authority can purchase the building, carry out the works at its own expense (or with assistance from English Heritage or other grant-giving bodies), and lease it back to the original occupiers on a lease containing a landlord's repairing covenant.

Thirdly, the procedure could be used where a substantial listed building (such as a country house or a church) is no longer required or suitable for its original function. In such a case, the authority could serve a repairs notice setting out precisely what repairs it considers are needed to the building (see above). It can then seek offers from suitable developers for a total rehabilitation scheme, which will include all the specified repairs, together with (probably) a change of use and (possibly) considerable alterations. A contract should then be entered into for the sale of the building by the authority to the developer, conditional on the suc-

---

[21] The current rules are in the Local Authorities (Capital Finance and Accounting) (England) Regulations 2003 (SI 2003/3146).

[22] And see PPG 15, para.7.13 and WO Circ. 61/96, para.14—although note that these were written in the light of the Local Government and Housing Act 1989; the new Regulations, made under the 2003 Act, are nothing like as extensive in their effect as the 1990 and 1997 Regulations, made under the 1989 Act.

cessful completion of its compulsory purchase from the existing owner. Where planning permission is needed for the proposed works, the contract could be linked to a planning obligation, to ensure that the necessary repairs are carried out. Such an obligation—either an agreement or a unilateral undertaking—can be made under section 106 of the Planning Act.[23] It needs to be very carefully drafted, if it is to bind all parties as intended—many section 106 agreements contain errors, or turn out to be unenforceable. A simple example of an undertaking is shown at **Form D15** in Appendix D.

Fourthly, the authority could sell the building to a building preservation trust,[24] for the trust to carry out the repairs and any appropriate refurbishment works. The financial details of such a transaction would need to be worked out carefully so as to minimise the burden on the trust; it might well be appropriate for the resale to include an element of grant aid, again from English Heritage or elsewhere.

These are only a few examples of how the procedure could be used creatively. What is certain is that, once an authority has acquired experience of the procedure in practice, it is much easier to do it again, and to find ways of maximising the benefit to all concerned.

The view of the Secretary of State is that:

"... privately owned historic buildings should, wherever possible, remain in the private sector. Local planning authorities are encouraged to identify a private individual or body, such as a building preservation trust, which has access to funds to carry out the necessary repairs and to which the building will be sold on as quickly as possible. Suitable covenants should be negotiated to ensure that repairs will be carried out by the purchaser."[25]

11.5.2 Contribution towards authorities' expenses

English Heritage has power to assist a local authority using its powers under sections 47–50 of the Listed Buildings Act to purchase a listed building—of any grade—in England.[26] It has accordingly set up a scheme of *Acquisition grants to local authorities to underwrite repairs notices*. In its guidance notes for applicants, it emphasises the importance of local authorities using these powers, and states that:

"this should not be seen as a last resort, but as a logical step to be taken as soon as it is evident that a building capable of beneficial use is deteriorating significantly as a result of neglect, and well before it decays to the extent that it will cost more to repair than it is worth. ...

We are therefore prepared to use the powers which allow English Heritage to assist in the acquisition of historic buildings, in appropriate cases to underwrite up to 80% of an authority's potential irrecoverable costs in pursuing acquisition of buildings at risk, including the cost of serving and following up Repairs Notices. ...

---

[23] As substituted by PCA 1991, s.12. This will be overtaken during the lifetime of this book by the coming into force of ss 46 to 48 of the Planning and Compulsory Purchase Act 2004 and regulations made under it. In Scotland, see s.75 of the Scottish Planning Act.

[24] See **9.7.2**.

[25] In PPG 15, para.7.13, and WO Circ. 61/96, para.137.

[26] HBAMA 1953, s.5B(1), inserted by NHA 1983 and amended by Planning (Consequential Provisions) Act 1990.

Before offering grant, we will obviously expect to see a convincing strategy for resolving the long-term future of the listed building—including, where it has negative value, how the 'conservation deficit' could be funded. A 'back-to-back' agreement, often (although not necessarily) with a building preservation trust, to take the building from the local planning authority if and when they acquire it, commonly forms part of a solution, although a building with a positive value might equally be sold on the open market, with suitable safeguards to ensure its repair."[27]

Cadw and Historic Scotland have similar powers.[28]

11.6 Public ownership and guardianship of ancient monuments

11.6.1 Introduction

As with historic buildings, ancient monuments are mostly in private hands. Many, for example, are in or underneath fields that are part of working farms. It has already been noted that there are powers for public authorities to give grants for works for the preservation of ancient monuments,[29] and for them to carry out such works at their own expense.[30]

However, as with listed buildings, where a private owner is unwilling or unable to co-operate in preserving or maintaining a monument, the only option may be to take it into public control. This may be suitable anyway for the most important monuments, as one means of ensuring that the public are able to gain access to them.

The Ancient Monuments Act accordingly provides for two methods of taking monuments into public control: acquisition of ownership, or guardianship. Both apply in principle to any "ancient monument" in Great Britain, as defined in the Act[31]—although, in practice, it is highly likely that any monument that is sufficiently important to be worth taking into public control will in fact be scheduled.

11.6.2 Acquisition of ancient monuments

The Secretary of State (in England, Wales or Scotland) may acquire any ancient monument by compulsory purchase, under section 10 of the Act,[32] and may also acquire any land adjoining or in the vicinity of the monument (or any easement, such as a right of way, over such land) needed for the maintenance of the monument or its amenities, or to provide or facilitate access to it, or for its management, or to provide access and facilities to the public.[33] The procedure is as set out in the Acquisition of Land Act 1981 or the Acquisition of Land (Authorisation Procedure) (Scotland) Act 1947. When the 1979 Act was going through Parliament, the Secretary of State undertook that the compulsory power

---

[27] *Guidance notes for applicants*, undated, available (along with application form) on the English Heritage website.
[28] 1953 Act, s.6, amended by the 1983 and 1990 Acts.
[29] See **9.4.3** (central government) and **9.6.1** (local authorities).
[30] See **10.4** (urgent works) and **10.7.2** (other repairs).
[31] AMAAA 1979, s.61(12) (see **6.2**).
[32] AMAAA 1979, s.10.
[33] ss 15, 16.

would never be used except where it was the only way of securing the preservation of a monument.[34]

Local authorities do not have powers under the Ancient Monuments Act to acquire monuments compulsorily; but they could do so under the Planning Act where such acquisition would be necessary for the proper planning of the area, and its "environmental well-being".[35]

An ancient monument may also be acquired by agreement or as a gift by the Secretary of State (after consulting English Heritage in relation to a monument in England),[36] and by English Heritage (after obtaining the consent of the Secretary of State).[37] Monuments may also be acquired by local authorities and similar bodies[38]—that is, county, county borough, borough and district councils,[39] the Broads Authority,[40] national park authorities[41] and the Cotswolds and Chilterns Conservation Boards.[42] This may be assisted by grants from by English Heritage, Cadw or Historic Scotland.[43] These provisions also extend to associated land and easements over it, as for compulsory purchase.[44]

Once a monument is in the ownership of one of the public bodies referred to above, it may then be passed to any of the others.[45] And once land has been acquired under the Act, it may only be disposed of on such terms as will secure the preservation of the monument, except where its preservation is no longer practical.[46] A local authority and English Heritage may only dispose of such land after consulting with the Secretary of State; and the Secretary of State must consult with English Heritage before doing so in relation to a monument in England.

11.6.3 Guardianship of ancient monuments

An alternative to the outright acquisition of an ancient monument by a public authority is a guardianship arrangement. Essentially, the owner of the monument does give up ownership, but passes it to the care of a public body which then has the duty to maintain it for as long as it is guardian.[47] The guardian may be the Secretary of State (after consultation with English Heritage in relation to a

---

[34] Hansard, H.C. Debs, vol. 965, col. 1361 (April 4, 1979).
[35] TCPA 1990, s.226(1),(1A), as inserted by Planning and Compulsory Purchase Act 2004, s.99. For valuation, see *Kemis v Salisbury DC*, May 3, 1994, unreported, LT (summary available on Lawtel).
[36] AMAAA 1979, s.11(1),(3).
[37] s.11(3A), (1A).
[38] s.11(2).
[39] s.61(1).
[40] s.52A.
[41] Environment Act 1995, Sch.9, para.10.
[42] The Cotswolds and Chilterns Areas of Outstanding Natural Beauty (Establishment of Conservation Board) Orders 2004 (SIs 2004/1777; 2004/1778), art.25.
[43] under s.24; see **9.4.3** (England), **9.5.1** (Wales, Scotland).
[44] ss 15,16.
[45] s.21.
[46] s.30.
[47] AMAAA 1979, s.13(1).

monument in England), English Heritage (after consultation with the Secretary of State), or a local authority [etc].[48]

A guardianship arrangement is to be created by deed, by the owner of the land. The "owner" for this purpose will normally be the freeholder, the holder of a lease of which at least 45 years is unexpired, or the owner of a life interest.[49] A guardianship arrangement can, however, also be created by an owner of a limited interest in the land—such as a tenant for life, trustees for sale, a corporate body, or charitable trustees.[50] The occupier of the monument, if there is one other than the owner, must be a party to the deed.[51] The deed, which is a local land charge,[52] binds almost any subsequent owner of the monument.[53] For as long as it lasts, the existence of the deed does not affect the estate or interest of any other person in the monument.[54]

Associated land nearby may also be taken into guardianship, just as with compulsory purchase (see above).[55] Rights over such land may also be acquired by the guardian of the monument, and may be enforced by it as if it were the owner of the monument for as long as the guardianship arrangement subsists, and the existence of such a right is for that period a local land charge.[56] The owner of a limited interest (see above) in such land may also grant an easement to the guardian of a nearby monument.[57]

In addition, either the Secretary of State or English Heritage may purchase or accept as a gift any object associated with a monument in their guardianship.[58] They may also accept a capital endowment to provide income for the upkeep of such a monument.[59]

The effect of a guardianship arrangement is set out in section 13 of the 1979 Act. In particular, in order to enable it to fulfil its (sometimes extremely onerous) duty to maintain the monument, the guardian has full control and management of it, and may do whatever is necessary to exercise that control and management; it may enter the site of the monument at any reasonable time; and it may open up or examine it.[60] All these powers are to be exercised to ensure the preservation of the monument; and all are subject to any explicit provisions of the relevant guardianship deed.[61]

---

[48] s.12(1)–(2).
[49] s.12(3).
[50] s.18(1).
[51] s.12(4).
[52] s.12(7).
[53] s.12(9).
[54] s.12(11).
[55] s.15.
[56] s.16(4)–(9).
[57] s.18(2)(a).
[58] HBAMA 1953, s.5(2)(b), (3A).
[59] HBAMA 1953, ss 8(1)(c), 8A(1)(c); and see **11.2.3**.
[60] s.13(1)–(5).
[61] s.13(6).

The operation of guardianship in practice has recently been considered by the Outer House of the Court of Session in *Duffield Morgan Ltd v Historic Scotland*.[62] The court there accepted in particular that the statutory scheme had the effect that guardianship extended to any road necessary to gain access to the monument from the highway, even if in fact the guardian had not exercised its power to admit the public to the monument in its care.

Under these provisions, English Heritage and the relevant arm of central government (in practice the DCMS, Cadw and Historic Scotland) each have a substantial number of properties in their care subject to guardianship arrangements. The DCMS entrusts English Heritage with the care of the properties of which it is guardian. And English Heritage spends considerable sums each years maintaining such properties.

Guardianship may be passed from English Heritage, the Secretary of State or a local authority to any of the others, or to another authority.[63] The existing guardian must obtain the consent of anyone immediately affected by the operation of the guardianship (such as the owner of the land, and anyone entitled to future interests in it) before passing it to another body.

11.6.4 Termination of guardianship

A guardianship arrangement may be terminated at any time by an occupier of the monument who has a sufficient interest to qualify him or her to enter into a guardianship but who is not bound by the original deed. That will only rarely, if ever, occur, however; and, until it does, the guardianship continues in effect until the guardian enters into an agreement ("a termination agreement") with all the parties currently affected, whereby the guardianship is either renounced or varied.[64] Such an agreement may be entered into by a local authority only with the consent of the Secretary of State, and by the Secretary of State in England only after consulting English Heritage.[65] Variation of the guardianship will usually be by the exclusion from it of part of the monument.

A termination agreement may not be entered into unless the guardian of the monument is satisfied that satisfactory arrangements have been made for its preservation following the termination or variation of the guardianship, or that it is no longer practicable to preserve the monument.[66] The guardian, in considering whether the proposed arrangements for the future care of the monument are satisfactory, is likely to require evidence as to their financial viability. Past expenditure by the guardian on the upkeep of the monument is not an issue when considering whether to enter into a termination agreement; it is only the future that is relevant.

---

[62] *Duffield Morgan Ltd v Lord Advocate as representing Historic Scotland*, 2004 S.L.T. 413, OH.
[63] s.21.
[64] AMAAA 1979, s.14(1).
[65] s.14(2).
[66] s.14(3).

A termination agreement may perfectly properly be associated with an agreement under section 17,[67] which would enable financial arrangements to be put in place. Note, however, that all of these provisions allow only for "agreements"; so neither the guardian nor the owner can force the other to act.

Following the termination of the guardianship, any rights acquired over neighbouring land under s.16 may be revoked[68].

11.6.5 Access to monuments in public control

The public must be allowed access to any monument that is either owned by English Heritage, the Secretary of State or a local authority or is in the guardianship of any of them[69]—that is, after all, one of the purposes of such public control, even though the main aim of it will usually be simply the preservation of the monument. The Cotswolds and Chilterns Conservation Boards may also supervise access to monuments in their areas.[70]

The provision of such access will be controlled by virtue of regulations made by the owner or guardian of the monument, which may make appropriate provisions for opening times, and other measures to ensure the preservation of the monument.[71] Access may in fact be limited to particular parts of the monument, or excluded altogether for a time, if that is necessary for its protection or for safety. Access may also be refused to particular persons, considered likely to damage the monument.[72] Regulations have been made under these powers relating to access to Stonehenge.[73]

The breach of such regulations is an offence, attracting a penalty on summary conviction of up to level 3 on the standard scale.[74]

The Secretary of State, English Heritage, or a local authority may provide facilities for the public at any monument in public ownership or guardianship.[75] Such facilities may be provided on the site itself or on any land associated with it, and appropriate charges may be made for their use. The provision of such facilities, if it amounts to development (for example, the erection of "visitor centres"), will usually either require planning permission or need to be notified to the local planning authority.[76]

11.6.6 Agreements relating to ancient monuments

As an alternative to ownership or guardianship, the Secretary of State, English Heritage or a local authority may enter into an agreement under section 17 of the

---

[67] See **11.6.6**.
[68] s.16(6).
[69] AMAAA 1979, s.19(1).
[70] The Cotswolds and Chilterns Areas of Outstanding Natural Beauty (Establishment of Conservation Board) Orders 2004 (SIs 2004/1777; 2004/1778), art.25.
[71] s.19(2)–(5).
[72] s.19(6).
[73] SI 1997/2038.
[74] s.19(7), amended by Criminal Justice Act 1982; Criminal Penalties etc (Increase) Order 1984.
[75] s.20.
[76] See **Chapter 12**.

1979 Act with the occupier of any ancient monument or of any land nearby. The owner of such land, if not the occupier, may—but need not—also be a party to such an agreement. Such an agreement may also bind successors in title to the original parties[77]; and may be entered into by the owner of a limited interest in the land concerned (see above).[78]

This provides a useful mechanism to achieve a number of purposes, including the maintenance of the monument, the carrying out of necessary works to it, the provision of public access, restricting the use of it, prohibiting particular activities, and the making of payments by the relevant public body.[79] It may provide effectively for guardianship; but it may be used more creatively. It might, for example, contain a deal whereby the owner and the public body share the cost of maintenance and improvement works, and thereafter split any proceeds arising from public access. It could restrict certain activities (such as filming) without the consent of the public body, but provide for that body to receive part of any receipts once consent is granted. Or it could ensure the repayment of all or part of any public investment in improvements on the termination of the agreement.

PPG 16 also suggests that a section 17 agreement could be used to provide for the beneficial management of an archaeological site by its owner—for example, the use by a farmer of appropriate agricultural practices on land containing prehistoric earthworks or the site of a deserted village.[80] Such an agreement could reward the farmer by the making of appropriate payments, either on a regular basis, or as a one-off capital sum to pay for measures such as protective fencing.

A monument subject to an agreement under section 17 is not subject to the automatic public right of access under section 19,[81] but such access may in practice be provided under the terms of the agreement.

11.6.7 Licence to carry out works

One other alternative to ownership is the acquisition of a licence to carry out exploratory or conservation work. Thus, for example, English Heritage was able to obtain a licence from the owner of the foreshore at Holme-Next-the-Sea in Norfolk, to enable it to examine a Bronze Age timber circle. It then decided that the circle was in imminent danger of being lost due to wave action, and accordingly took steps to remove it for conservation elsewhere. When its efforts were obstructed by local people and druids (who regarded the site as sacred), it then obtained an injunction against both known and unknown people to enable it to complete the exercise.[82]

---

[77] s.17(5).
[78] s.18(2)(b).
[79] s.18(4).
[80] PPG 16, Annex 3, para.16.
[81] See **11.6.5** above.
[82] *HBMC v Nolan and others*, Ch D, July 6, 1999, unreported (available on Lawtel).

Part IV

Carrying out works to historic buildings and monuments

"One of the area in which I took a particular interest was historic buildings. ... This kind of work was utterly despised by Dame Evelyn [Sharp]. She regarded it as pure sentimentalism and she called it 'preservationism', a word of abuse. She, who counted herself a modern iconoclast, took the extremely—yes, I will say it—illiterate view that there was a clear-cut conflict between 'modern' planning and 'reactionary' preservation. During my time as Minister, in speech after speech, I tried to break down this false dichotomy and to establish a new and sensible relationship between planning and preservation."

Rt Hon. Richard Crossman, *The Diaries of a Cabinet Minister* (London, Cape, 1976)

"Too many consents and permissions are required before a historic building can be altered or adapted. The listing system is important in obliging developers to recognise the value of historic buildings and to adopt a more creative approach. However, the listing system lacks transparency and appears haphazard, and so can delay regeneration schemes."

House of Commons ODPM Housing, Planning, Local Government and the Regions Committee, report on *The Role of Historic Buildings in Urban Regeneration*, July 2004.

Chapter 12

Works affecting Historic Buildings and Monuments: the Need for Consent

12.1 Introduction

12.1.1 Overview

The previous parts of this book have considered how the various components of the cultural heritage are identified by central and local authorities (**Part II**) and what, if any, powers and duties exist to ensure their upkeep (**Part III**). However, the most important matters from the point of view of the law are those arising where building works are proposed that affect historic buildings and areas.

In truth, very few significant historic buildings have actually been lost in recent years, and the major debates as to whether such a building should be demolished, which used to be a feature of the early years of the planning system, have largely disappeared.[1] But many have been altered, sometimes with unfortunate results; and many have been spoilt through the impoverishment of their setting. It is thus common for schemes—whether for minor alterations to dwellinghouses or for major city centre redevelopments—to be rejected due to their perceived impact, or to be delayed while improvements are negotiated. No doubt many more have not even surfaced, for the same reason. On the one hand, some of those with positions of power in local authorities, English Heritage and elsewhere feel that the heritage must be defended fearlessly from all change, or at least all adverse change; others feel equally strongly that the system of control and protection has got out of hand, and is unnecessarily impeding much-needed improvements.

This part of the book accordingly sets out the law that governs the making of changes to the historic environment. This chapter considers what consents are needed for various categories of works; and **Chapter 13** explains how they may be obtained; both focus largely on procedures, and the statutory rules governing

---

[1] The first quotation on the previous page thus comes from an era which saw the loss of the Coal Exchange and the Euston Arch in London (1962) and Eldon Square in Newcastle (1966). Perhaps the most significant debate in recent years was over the fate of No.1 Poultry, in the City of London (see *Save Britain's Heritage v the Secretary of State* [1991] 1 W.L.R. 153); but that was now some while ago, and the building involved was not in fact of great consequence.

them. **Chapter 14** looks at the wide range of issues that arise in considering whether or not consent should be granted, and attempts to summarise the many cases decided by the courts. **Chapter 15** explores what options are available to developers and others by way of appeals and other remedies if the resulting decision is unfavourable. Special rules have always applied to works to churches and other places or worship; these are considered in **Chapter 16**. And, finally, the cost of carrying out works to protected buildings (essentially listed buildings and scheduled monuments) is zero-rated for VAT; that has given rise to a surprising amount of litigation in recent years, considered in **Chapter 17**.

Where work that requires consent is carried out without that consent having been obtained, it may be possible for the relevant planning authority to take enforcement action to remedy the situation; or criminal prosecution may be more appropriate. This is considered in the final section of the book (**Part V**).

12.1.2 The need for consent

There are various types of consent that may be required for the carrying out of works to existing buildings and for the construction of new ones, including the following:

- planning permission, listed building consent, conservation area consent, scheduled monument consent, and consent under the Control of Advertisements Regulations;

- special consent for works to places of worship;

- authorisation under the Building Act, and under the Building Regulations.

This chapter considers the various consents in the first group. The scope of each is briefly outlined in **12.2**. The remainder of the chapter then considers the way in which the requirements of the law operate in practice, in relation to various categories of works, as follows:

- works affecting listed buildings—demolition and alteration of listed buildings (**12.3** and **12.4**), and the erection of new buildings and other works affecting them (**12.5**);

- works in conservation areas—the demolition of existing unlisted buildings (**12.6**); and the alteration of existing buildings and the erection of new ones (**12.7**);

- works affecting scheduled monuments (**12.8**); and

- signs and advertisements (**12.9**).

The last section of the chapter (**12.10**) considers briefly the possible courses of action in the event of uncertainty as to whether or not consent is required.

As noted above, works to places of worship are the subject of a separate chapter.[2] And this book does not deal with authorisation under the Building Act

---

[2] See **Chapter 16**.

and the Building Regulations,[3] which raise rather different issues; although it should not be forgotten that such authorisation will frequently be required in addition to the consents under the planning Acts that are the main focus of the discussion in this and the following chapters.[4]

Finally, it should not be forgotten that, where a proposal involves the loss of one or more trees, further consent may be required—although not if the tree is to be felled as a direct result of works fir which planning permission has been granted.[5]

12.1.3 Special cases

Buildings and ancient monuments on Crown land, as thus defined, may be—and frequently are—listed[6] and scheduled.[7] And many are in conservation areas. However, planning permission, listed building consent, conservation area consent and advertisements consent are not currently required as such for works carried out by the Crown on its own land. Instead, the developing department submits a Notice of Proposed Development to the local planning authority that it is intending to carry out works for which permission or other consent would generally be required.[8] The net result is that Crown developers (including government departments) are required to notify planning authorities in precisely the same circumstances as other developers need to submit ordinary applications.

This arrangement is due to be changed shortly, when Crown immunity is abolished as a result of the Planning and Compulsory Purchase Act 2004. Crown developers will then be in the same position as everyone else in terms of the need for consent.[8a]

English Heritage is not a government department, but is treated as one in some respects. It also has particular rights to carry out certain works without the need to submit an application for planning permission or scheduled monument consent.

Local authorities have no exemption from the need for planning permission or other consents; but the procedure for applications by authorities for their own development works is slightly different from that applying in other cases. Similarly, works to be authorised under the Transport and Works Act 1992 still

---

[3] In England and Wales, the Building Act 1984, and the Building Regulations 2000. The corresponding legislation in Scotland and Northern Ireland is somewhat different.

[4] The local authority and others, such as neighbours and various statutory authorities, will generally have to be notified of any proposed demolition works (other than in inner London) under the Building Act 1984, ss 80–83.

[5] See **5.5.2** (trees in a conservation area) and **7.6.3** (trees subject to a tree preservation order).

[6] P(LBCA)A 1990, s.83(1)(a). [Scotland: P(LBCA)(S)A 1997, s.74(1)(a); NI: P(NI)O 1991, art.113(1)(c).]

[7] AMAAA 1979, s.50(1)(a). [NI: Historic Monuments and Archaeological Objects (NI) Order 1995, art.37(1)(a).]

[8] The procedure is prescribed in Circ. 18/84 (WO Circ. 37/84). SDD Circ. 21/84 is in similar terms; see **13.10.1**.

[8a] See **13.10.2**.

require listed building consent, conservation area consent and scheduled monument consent just as in other case, but the procedure is slightly modified.

In all these cases, the need for works to be authorised is thus broadly as in other cases, as described in this chapter, but it is the procedure for obtaining that authorisation that is slightly modified. The details are accordingly explored in the following chapter (see **13.10**).

12.2 Consents that may be required

12.2.1 Planning permission

The law governing the need for planning permission has been developing for many years, and is now complex; reference should be made to standard works on planning law for a general exposition. The discussion in this chapter focuses on the need for planning permission for works affecting listed buildings, conservation areas and ancient monuments.

The fundamental principle of the planning system in the United Kingdom is thus that anyone wishing to carry out development, including most building or engineering works, must obtain planning permission from the local planning authority or the Secretary of State.[9] And this applies to works to or affecting historic buildings and areas—including places of worship and scheduled monuments—just as it does to those affecting any others.

"Development" is defined as follows:

"the carrying out of building, engineering, mining or other operations in, on, over or under land, or the making of any material change in the use of any buildings or other land.[10]

"Building operations" obviously includes the erection of any building or structure.[11] But it also includes:

"(a) demolition of buildings;
(b) rebuilding;
(c) structural alterations of or additions to buildings; and
(d) other operations normally undertaken by a person carrying on business as a builder."[12]

However, the definition of "development" specifically excludes:

"the carrying out for the maintenance, improvement or other alteration of any building of works which—

(i) affect only the interior of the building; or
(ii) do not materially affect the external appearance of the building;

---

[9] Or in Northern Ireland from the Department of the Environment ("the Department").
[10] s.55(1). [Scotland: TCP(S)A 1997, s.26(1); NI: P(NI)O 1991, art.11(1).]
[11] Even if as small as a model village (as at Bekonscot in Buckinghamshire: *Buckinghamshire CC v Callingham* [1952] 2 Q.B. 515).
[12] s.55(1A), inserted by the Planning and Compensation Act 1991, s.13. [Scotland: TCP(S)A 1997, s.26(4); NI: P(NI)O 1991, art.11(1A), inserted by Planning (Amendment) (NI) Order 2003.]

unless they are works for making good war damage, or for the alteration of a building by providing additional space below ground".[13]

The precise definition of maintenance, etc. will depend on the facts in each case. But the restoration to the same design of a building, of which only the original foundations, damp course and two walls remained, has been held—not surprisingly, perhaps—to be reconstruction, constituting development, and not maintenance or repair,[14] as has the replacement of a hedge by a corrugated iron fence.[15] Similarly, a proposal to rebuild substantially a derelict, listed, house was held on appeal to require planning permission as well as listed building consent, both of which were refused.[16]

"Engineering operations" include the formation of any means of access, whether public or private, for vehicles or pedestrians.[17] The laying of hardcore on a garden after the removal of the front and side walls has on appeal been held to be the formation of an access, and hence to constitute development requiring planning permission.[18] This could be significant in that such development can often have a very unfortunate effect on the character of a conservation area. But note that this will often be permitted development, not normally requiring specific permission.[19]

Also excluded from the scope of "development" is demolition in any category specified in a direction by the Secretary of State.[20] The current direction applying in England and Wales is the TCP (Demolition—Description of Buildings) Direction 1995, which excludes from the scope of "development" the demolition of any of the following categories of building or structure:

"(1) any building which is a listed building . . .;
(2) any building in a conservation area [other than the whole or any part of any gate, fence, wall or other means of enclosure];
(3) any building which is a scheduled monument . . .;
(4) . . . any building other than a dwellinghouse or a building adjoining a dwellinghouse;
(5) any building the cubic content of which, measured externally, does not exceed 50 cubic metres; and
(6) the whole of any gate, fence, wall or other means of enclosure [outside a conservation area]."

The TCP (Demolition Which is Not Development) (Scotland) Direction 2001[21] is in virtually identical terms.

---

[13] TCPA 1990, s.55(2)(a). [Scotland: TCP(S)A 1997, s.26(2)(a).; NI: P(NI)O 1991, art.11(2)(a).]
[14] *Street v Essex CC* (1965) 193 E.G. 537.
[15] *Scholes v Heysham BC* (1966) 197 E.G. 563.
[16] See [1985] J.P.L. 807.
[17] TCPA 1990, s.336. [Scotland: TCP(S)A 1997, s.277; NI: P(NI)O 1991, art 2.]
[18] [1972] JPL 109.
[19] See **12.2.2**.
[20] s.55(2)(g). [Scotland: TCP(S)A 1997, s.26(2)(g); NI: P(NI)O 1991, art.11(2)(f).]
[21] In SDD Circ. 1/2001.

The primary legislation in Northern Ireland relating to demolition only came into line with that in Great Britain at the end of 2004.[22] However, the Planning (Demolition—Description of Buildings) Direction 2005 is markedly distinct from the directions in Great Britain, in that the demolition of a building within an area of townscape character or an area of village character is not excluded from the definition of development, and thus generally requires planning permission; but the demolition of dwellinghouses and buildings adjoining them does not otherwise require planning permission.[23]

Planning permission is also needed to change the use of a listed building, and for building works and changes of use affecting its setting—none of which will necessarily require listed building consent. And it is generally needed for all building operations in conservation areas—whereas conservation area consent is only rarely needed (for the demolition of all or nearly all of a building[24]). Indeed, the requirement for planning applications to be made in such cases is often the only means available to a planning authority to control development which, on its own or cumulatively, may have a serious effect on the setting of a listed building or the character and appearance of a conservation area, which is why special rules apply.

To obtain planning permission, it is usually necessary to submit a planning application to the local planning authority.[25] The exception is where what is proposed is "permitted development", which is (in most cases) permitted automatically by a development order[26]—unless the authority has made an "Article 4 direction", so that an application is still required.[27]

In very many cases where listed building consent is required for works to a listed building, planning permission will also be required. Two applications will therefore have to be made (except where the works are permitted development); but they will generally be decided together. Further, although planning permission is not generally required for demolition, listed building consent or conservation area consent will be required; and such consent will frequently be sought in conjunction with planning permission for the redevelopment of the site; and in practice in such a situation the two applications will often stand or fall together.[28]

12.2.2 Permitted development

As noted above, the definition of "development", for which planning permission is generally needed, is very wide-ranging. It therefore includes a large number of

---

[22] 2004 SR&O 489 brought into force art.18 of the Planning (Amendment) (NI) Order 2003, which inserted new paras (1A) and (2)(e) into art.11 of the P(NI)O 1991, with effect from December 1, 2004.

[23] Planning (Demolition—Description of Buildings) Direction 2005, which came into effect on May 11, 2005, replacing a similar direction of 2004; and see **12.6.1**. For policy guidance, see Addendum to PPS 6, published in August 2005.

[24] See **12.6.2**.

[25] The planning authority in Scotland, the Department in Northern Ireland.

[26] See **12.2.2**.

[27] See **7.4**.

[28] See for example *Henry Davis & Co v Secretary of State* [1992] J.P.L. 1162. And see **G3** in Appendix G for possible reform.

relatively inconsequential building and other operations, which are in most cases entirely uncontroversial. And it would be a huge waste of resources on the part of all concerned if in every such case a planning application had to be submitted and determined. The Secretary of State accordingly has power to grant permission, by general or special development order, for particular categories of minor works— for which a planning application is then generally unnecessary. They are usually referred to as *permitted development*.

The general development order currently in force in England and Wales is the TCP (General Permitted Development) Order 1995. The 1995 Order includes 84 "Classes" of permitted development, grouped into the three "Parts" of Schedule 2. They include, for example, the construction of small extensions to dwelling-houses, the painting of buildings, and works by various public bodies. They are subject in almost all cases to numerous restrictions as to volume, dimensions, location and other details, a few of which are tighter where the relevant works affect a listed building or its curtilage or where the land concerned is in a conservation area.[29]

The Parts and Classes most relevant to listed buildings and conservation areas are set out in **Table 12.1.**

Demolition (which is anyway only "development" in relatively few cases, principally involving dwellinghouses[30]) will be permitted by Part 31; but notice must first be given to the planning authority, to enable it to decide whether it requires an opportunity to approve the method of the proposed demolition and any proposed restoration of the site. For further details of the procedure to be followed in such cases, see DoE Circular 10/95.[31]

The formation of any means of access, whether public or private, for vehicles or pedestrians will be permitted development, if it is within the curtilage of a dwellinghouse or in connection with other permitted development.[32]

The 1995 Order was amended in 1996, to take account of local government reorganisation in Wales[33]; and on a number of occasions more recently, princi-pally in relation to telecommunications development.[34] It is almost inevitable that it will be further amended during the currency of this book, so care must always be taken to check the current position. Slightly surprisingly, it has been held by the courts that, in determining whether a planning application is required to carry out development, the relevant law to consider is that which applied when the development was begun, not when it was completed.[35] If therefore building works are begun which are permitted development, but before they are complete the Order is altered so that they would no longer be permitted development, a planning application is still not required.

---

[29] See **12.4.3** and **12.7.2**.
[30] See **12.2.1**.
[31] WO Circ. 31/95. In Scotland, Class 70 in Sch.1 to the 1992 Order (inserted in 1995) is similar; but there is no corresponding provision in Northern Ireland.
[32] TCP (General Permitted Development) Order 1995, Sch.2, Pt 1, Class F; Pt 2, Class B.
[33] By SI 1996/528.
[34] By SIs 1998/462, 1999/1661, 2001/2718 (England), 2002/828 (England), 2002/1878 (Wales) and, most recently, 2005/2935 (England) and 2006/124 (Wales); see **12.7.3**.
[35] *Dawson v Secretary of State and Barnet LBC* [1983] J.P.L 544.

Table 12.1 Relevant categories of permitted development

Part 1 Development within the curtilage of a dwellinghouse[36]:
   Class A Alterations and small extensions
   Class B Alterations to the roof affecting its shape
   Class C Other alterations to the roof
   Class D Porches
   Class E Garden structures (sheds, swimming pools, etc.)[37]
   Class F Hardstandings for domestic vehicles
   Class G Storage tanks for heating oil
   Class H Small satellite antennas

Part 2 Minor operations:
   Class A Gates, fences and walls
   Class B Means of access
   Class C Painting[38]

Part 4, Class A Temporary buildings

Parts 6 and 7 Agricultural and forestry buildings and operations

Part 8 Industrial and warehouse development[39]

Parts 9 and 10 Repairs to streets, private ways and services

Part 11 Development authorised by local or private Acts of Parliament or orders

Parts 12 to 18 Minor development by various public bodies

Parts 22 and 23 Mineral exploration[40]

Parts 24 and 25 Telecommunications development[41]

Part 26 Works by or on behalf of English Heritage[42]

Part 31 Demolition works

Part 32 Minor development relating to schools, colleges, universities and hospitals[43]

Part 33 Closed circuit television cameras.[44]

Source: TCP (General Permitted Development) Order 1995, Sch.1

Note, however, that specific planning permission is needed to carry out works which would otherwise be permitted by the Order in several instances:

(1)   where the right to do so has been withdrawn by a condition on a previous grant of planning permission[45];

(2)   where the existing building or use of the land is unlawful[46];

(3)   where the works would involve making or widening an access to a trunk or classified road, or would create a danger to the users of any road[47]; or

---

[36]   See **12.4.3, 12.4.6, 12.7.2.**
[37]   See **12.5.2.**
[38]   See **12.4.5.**
[39]   See **12.7.2.**
[40]   See **7.4.9.**
[41]   See **12.7.3.**
[42]   See **13.10.3.**
[43]   See **12.7.2.**
[44]   See **12.7.2.**
[45]   1995 Order, art.3(4).
[46]   art.3(5).
[47]   art.3(6).

(4) where the relevant permitted development rights have been withdrawn by an article 4 direction.[48]

Finally, the Planning and Compulsory Purchase Act 2004 also introduced for the first time (in England and Wales) a procedure enabling a local planning authority to make a local development order, which has the effect of granting planning permission for development specified in the order—which may be either a specific project or a general category of development.[49] It remains to be seen what use will be made of this power or whether, like simplified planning zones, it proves to be more complicated than it is worth. However, the Government has proposed that it will not apply so as to grant planning permission for development affecting a listed building or within a conservation area.[50]

The corresponding provisions in Scotland and Northern Ireland are the TCP (General Permitted Development) (Scotland) Order 1992 and the Planning (General Development) Order (NI) 1993, both of which have also been amended a number of times since they were first made. These are broadly similar to the 1995 Order, but there are some slight differences generally noted here; the actual orders should accordingly be checked carefully.

12.2.3 Listed building consent

As noted above, planning permission is needed for most building works to a listed building or affecting the setting of one; and the following chapters describe the requirement for extra publicity to be given to applications for such works,[51] and the extra care that is to be taken by planning authorities in processing such applications.[52] However, planning permission is not generally needed for demolition; nor for interior works or very minor external works. In most cases, such works are likely to be of little consequence—but that may not be so in the case of listed buildings, the character of which can be sensitive to even the slightest alterations.

It would have been possible to adjust the definition of "development" in its application to listed buildings; however, the mechanism actually adopted was to introduce a separate control regime, operating alongside the need for planning permission.[53] Almost all works to a listed building therefore now need to be authorised by a grant of *listed building consent* by the appropriate local planning authority, whether or not they need or have been granted planning permission. Section 7 of the Listed Buildings Act thus provides that:

"no person shall execute or cause to be executed any works for the demolition of a listed building or for its alteration or extension in any manner which would affect its

---

[48] See **7.4**.
[49] TCPA 1990, ss 61A to 61C, to be inserted by Planning and Compulsory Purchase Act 2004, s.40. There are no equivalent provisions (yet) in Scotland or Northern Ireland.
[50] Draft TCP (General Development Procedure) (Amendment) (No 2) (England) Order 2005, art.2A(15), annexed to *Changes to the Development Control System: Second Consultation Paper*, ODPM 2005.
[51] See **13.5**.
[52] See **14.4–14.6**.
[53] See **1.2.3** and **1.2.6** for a historical account of how this emerged.

character as a building of special architectural or historic interest, unless the works are authorised ...".[54]

It is unfortunately not clear whether the limitation ("in any manner", etc.) refers just to the "alteration or extension" or also to the "demolition"—and there is no punctuation to help either. The provision was first introduced as section 43(5) of the Town and County Planning Act 1944.[55] It was there made quite clear that the limitation referred only to the alteration or extension of a building. The 1947 Act condensed the wording to its present form, thus introducing the ambiguity retained by all subsequent planning Acts up to and including the Listed Buildings Act in 1990. That history would tend to suggest that the meaning of the provision is that consent is required for:

(1) any works to a listed building that can properly be characterised as being for its "demolition"; and

(2) any other works to it, for its alteration or extension, if they affect its character.

This interpretation was favoured by the Court of Appeal in *Shimizu (UK) Ltd v Westminster CC*[56]—and not questioned in the House of Lords.[57]

The carrying out of unauthorised works (that is, works for which listed building consent is needed but has not been obtained) is a criminal offence.[58] This is in contrast to the carrying out of development for which planning permission is required but has not been obtained, which is only a breach of planning control— the criminal offence in that case only occurs if the planning authority chooses to serve an enforcement notice, and the developer fails to comply with it. See **Chapter 18** for a further discussion of unauthorised works.

It should be borne in mind when considering what works need listed building consent that, as explained in detail in **Chapter 4**, a "listed building" includes:

(1) the building itself;

(2) any object or structure fixed to it; and

(3) any other object or structure that has been in its curtilage since 1948.[59]

However, whilst a "building" also includes any part of a building as so defined,[60] the House of Lords has held that the phrase "listed building", at every place where it occurs in the Listed Buildings Act, means the whole building, and does not include "part of a listed building".[61]

---

[54] P(LBCA)A 1990, s.7. [Scotland: P(LBCA)(S)A 1997, s.6; NI: P(NI)O 1991, art.44(1).]
[55] See **1.2.3**.
[56] [1995] 23 E.G. 118 at 123.
[57] [1996] 3 P.L.R. 89.
[58] P(LBCA)A 1990, s.9. [Scotland: P(LBCA)(S)A 1997, s.8; NI: P(NI)O 1991, art.44(2).]
[59] P(LBCA)A 1990, s.1(5). [Scotland: P(LBCA)(S)A 1997, s.1(4); NI: P(NI)O 1991, art.42(7).]
[60] P(LBCA)A 1990, s.91(2); TCPA 1990, s.336. [Scotland: P(LBCA)(S)A 1997, s.81(2); TCP(S)A 1997, s.277; NI: P(NI)O 1991, art.2.]
[61] *Shimizu*, see above.

Finally, it is probable that the phrase "works *for* the demolition of a listed building or *for* its alteration [etc.]" implies an element of premeditated or planned action. Accidental damage, for example by vehicle impact or by fire, would thus not require subsequent consent. This interpretation has been favoured in decisions by the Secretary of State relating to "demolition" and "alteration" caused by vehicles.[62] Needless to say, it may in some cases be necessary to provide cogent evidence to prove that the damage really was accidental.

Like planning permission, listed building consent is obtained from the local planning authority or, on appeal, from the Secretary of State.[63]

There is no equivalent in listed buildings legislation to the mechanism whereby some minor works ("permitted development") are granted planning permission automatically.[64] It is noteworthy that there is a corresponding mechanism whereby certain, very limited works are automatically granted scheduled monument consent; but these are largely routine maintenance and urgent works necessary to secure safety.[65] Consideration has been given to introducing a system whereby works to a particular listed building could be authorised in advance on a blanket basis, possibly as part of a management plan. Such an approach would be valuable particularly in relation to large modern buildings or groups of buildings that have been listed; but it would lead to problems of definitions, and might create almost as many problems as it solves.[66]

It should also be borne in mind that, if listed building consent is sought and obtained for proposed works, their cost will not be subject to value added tax.[67] This may be a partial incentive to outweigh any delay involved in applying for consent.

12.2.4 Conservation area consent

In principle, section 74 of the Listed Buildings Act provides that conservation area consent is now needed for the demolition of almost any building within a conservation area.[68]

The scheme of the legislation is to apply almost all the provisions of the Listed Buildings Act regarding "listed building consent" to "conservation area consent", subject to any variation that may be prescribed in regulations. The sections of that Act which may thus be applied to unlisted buildings in conservation areas are listed in section 74(3) of the Act; and the modifications that have in fact been

---

[62] Noted at [1990] J.P.L. 445 and [1981] J.P.L. 443 respectively.

[63] See **Chapter 13** and **Chapter 15**. The Secretary of State may also grant consent where he calls in an application for his or her own determination—an event that, these days, occurs only rarely (see **13.7.6**).

[64] See **12.2.2**.

[65] See **12.8.4**.

[66] *Streamlining listed building consent: lessons from the use of management agreements*, research report for English Heritage, June 2003.

[67] See **Chapter 17**.

[68] For the slightly tortuous way in which this requirement (and the term "conservation area consent") first emerged, see **1.2.7**.

made in their application to unlisted buildings are set out as Schedule 3 to the
P(LBCA) Regulations 1990.[69]

As a result of this peculiarly unlovely statutory scheme, the only really significant
difference between listed building consent and conservation area consent is that the
latter is not required for the "alteration or extension" of an unlisted building, but
only for its "demolition". This distinction has caused considerable problems in
practice, not least following the decision of the House of Lords in *Shimizu (UK)
Ltd v Westminster CC*.[70] There are also a number of exemptions from the need for
conservation area consent. These points are considered further below.[71]

As with listed building consent, it is a criminal offence to carry out works that
require conservation area consent without that consent having first been
obtained.[72]

12.2.5 Scheduled monument consent

Scheduled monument consent is required for almost any works affecting a
scheduled monument.[73]

Scheduled monument consent is generally obtained in response to an application to the Secretary of State[74]; the local planning authority has little if any part to
play in the process.[75] However, as with planning permission (but not listed
building consent), because the definition of operations that require scheduled
monument consent is very wide-ranging, certain categories of relatively minor
works are granted consent automatically.[76]

As with works to listed buildings, the carrying out of works to a scheduled
monument without scheduled monument consent is a criminal offence.[77] So also is
the destroying or damaging of any protected monument, whether or not
scheduled.[78]

12.2.6 Consent under the Advertisements Regulations

One feature of the urban scene which causes particular concern in some conservation areas is inappropriate signage and advertising. This may be in the form
of traditional advertisement hoardings, or may be on shop fascias, canopies,

---

[69] Those sections, as thus modified, are set out as the Appendix to the text of the 1990 Act
as reproduced in Volume 3 of the *Encyclopedia of Planning Law and Practice*. The
corresponding provisions in Scotland are P(LBCA)(S)A 1997, s.66(3), and TCP
(P(LBCA)A 1990) (S) Regs 1987, Sch.4; in Northern Ireland, P(NI)O 1991, art.51(3)
and Planning (Conservation Areas) (Demolition) Regulations (NI).]

[70] [1996] 3 P.L.R. 89.

[71] See **12.6**.

[72] See **19.5**.

[73] The annual number of applications in the four years from 1993–94 to 1996–97 was 901,
1,088, 971, and 950 respectively.

[74] The DCMS in England; elsewhere, Cadw, Historic Scotland, and the Department in
Northern Ireland.

[75] See **13.9.3**.

[76] See **12.8.4**.

[77] See **19.6**.

[78] See **19.6.7**.

placards, displays at petrol stations, estate agents' boards, flags or even balloons. Fly-posting, too, can be a problem in some urban areas. In addition, signs and advertisements can often detract from the appearance of listed buildings and their settings.

The display of outdoor advertisements—in so far as it amounts to "development"[79]—has always been exempt from normal planning control.[80] It is instead controlled under special regulations made under powers in the planning Acts.[81] The regulations currently in force are the TCP (Control of Advertisements) Regulations 1992,[82] which provide that:

- advertisements in the classes in Schedule 2 to the 1992 Regulations, which are almost always either trivial (such as signs on petrol pumps) or else desirable in the public interest (such as national flags or election posters), are exempt from control altogether,

- those in the classes in Schedule 3, which are usually inoffensive (such name boards on buildings), are granted "deemed consent" automatically; and

- all other advertisements require "express consent" from the local planning authority or the Secretary of State.

Deemed consent can however be withdrawn in a specific case by means of a discontinuance notice (subject to a right of appeal by the advertiser).[83]

Unauthorised advertising is a criminal offence.[84]

Policy advice on the control of advertising in England is currently contained in DoE Circular 5/92 and 15/94 and PPG 19.[85] Advertising in conservation areas is also covered in passing in PPG 15 and WO Circular 61/96.[86]

Consent for signs and advertisements is considered further at **12.9**.

12.2.7 Works carried out in emergency

Finally, it has already been noted that section 78 of the Building Act 1984 provides that a local authority "may take steps as may be necessary" to remove a danger. And s.54 of the Listed Buildings Act provides that an authority "may

---

[79] See **12.2.1**.

[80] TCPA 1990, s.222; see **12.9.1**. [Scotland: TCP(S)A 1997, s.184; NI: P(NI)O 1991, art.67(5).]

[81] ss 220, 221, amended by the Planning and Compensation Act 1991, Schs 6 and 7. [Scotland: TCP(S)A 1997, ss 182, 183; NI: P(NI)O 1991, art.67(1)–(4).]

[82] The 1992 Regulations (SI No 666) have been slightly amended by SIs 1994/2351, 1996/396, and 1999/1810. The Planning (Control of Advertisements) (NI) Regulations 1992 (amended in 1998) are very similar. TCP (Control of Advertisements) (Scotland) Regulations 1984 are drafted somewhat differently, but with the same result.

[83] See **12.9.5**.

[84] See **19.8**.

[85] WO Circs. 14/92 and 70/94, *Planning Guidance (Wales): Planning Policy*, paras 194, 195, and WO TAN 7. For Northern Ireland, a draft PPS 17, *The Control of Outdoor Advertisements*, was produced in February 2004. The corresponding guidance for Scotland is still SDD Circular 10/84.

[86] PPG 15, paras 4.31–4.36; WO Circ. 61/96, paras 36–41.

execute works which appear to be necessary for the preservation of a listed building".[87] In either case, the steps taken or works executed may be such that they would otherwise require planning permission or listed building or conservation area consent.

Technically, the Planning Act merely requires that all building operations—including those carried out by planning authorities—require planning permission to be obtained; and there is specific provision for permission to be obtained after the completion of works.[88] In practice, however, it would be ridiculous for an authority to object to works it had carried out itself. But the exact position in law is not entirely clear.

The Listed Buildings Act, by contrast, provides that no works may be carried out to a listed building unless they are "authorised"—which would, arguably, include authorisation by Act of Parliament.[89] That would seem to remove the possibility of criminal sanctions in such a situation.

This might appear to be a technicality, but it may become a live issue where the works carried out by the authority (almost inevitably in a hurry, without the time for extended consultation and discussion) are controversial—and those done under section 78 of the 1984 Act may include demolition.

12.3 Demolition of a listed building[90]

12.3.1 The need for planning permission

In principle, the demolition of a listed building requires listed building consent, but not planning permission.

It has been noted that "development", for which planning permission will generally be required, includes demolition. However, the Secretary of State has directed that development does not include, amongst other things, the demolition of "any building which is a listed building as defined in s.1(5) of the [Listed Buildings Act]."[91] The total demolition of all or most of a listed building thus clearly does not require planning permission.

The direction was no doubt intended to avoid any need for planning permission to be obtained as well as listed building consent, so as to avoid the overlap of controls.[92] However, in the light of the decision of the House of Lords in *Shimizu (UK) Ltd v Westminster CC*,[93] that demolition in effect means the removal of enough of a building to lead to a site for redevelopment, and the fact that "a listed

---

[87] See **10.2.2** and **10.3.4**.
[88] TCPA 1990, ss 57, 73A. [Scotland: TCP(S)A 1997, ss 28, 33; NI: P(NI)O 1991, arts 12, 29.]
[89] P(LBCA)A 1990, s.7. [Scotland: P(LBCA)(S)A 1997, s.6; NI: P(NI)O 1991, art.44(1).]
[90] See **Table 12.2**.
[91] TCPA 1990, s.55(2)(g); TCP (Demolition—Description of Buildings) Direction 1995 (in DOE Circ. 10/95, Appendix A), para.(1)(a); see **12.2.1**. The directions in Scotland and Northern Ireland are identical.
[92] Although no such considerations seem to have avoided the need for both planning permission and listed building consent to be obtained for alterations to listed buildings.
[93] [1996] 3 P.L.R. 89.

building as defined in section 1(5)" may in fact comprise several buildings, it is not entirely clear how this would operate in the case of the demolition of a subsidiary building that is not itself listed—a stables block, for example—in the curtilage of a listed building. Thus the demolition of the curtilage building is not the "demolition of a listed building"; but it is still the demolition of a building, and therefore excluded from the definition of development by the 1995 Direction.

In practice, however, this is likely to be somewhat academic in most cases, since planning permission will of course be needed if there are any alterations or other building or rebuilding works associated with the "demolition".

Slightly oddly, therefore, the partial demolition (in the non-technical sense of the term) of a building listed in its own right will not need planning permission if it is on a fairly substantial scale, relative to the building, although it will need listed building consent. If it is more limited, it will amount to alteration, and will thus almost certainly need planning permission—as well as listed building consent.[94]

A further oddity is that, in the exceptional case where part only of a building is listed, planning permission is required (in addition to listed building consent) for the demolition of just that part, since the exemption in the 1995 Direction does not apply to "part of a building". However, the demolition of the whole of the building does not require planning permission (again, in addition to listed building consent in respect of the listed part).[95]

12.3.2 The need for listed building consent

Listed building consent will generally be required for any works to a listed building that are properly described as "demolition".[96] The only exceptions are:

- the demolition of a listed building that is also a scheduled monument, which requires scheduled monument consent instead of listed building consent[97];

- the demolition of a Church of England place of worship in pursuance of a pastoral or redundancy scheme.[98]

This is reasonably straightforward; but problems may occasionally occur where only part of a listed building is to be removed. That should generally be treated as "alteration", rather than as "demolition" as such—the House of Lords in *Shimizu* confirmed that "listed building" does not include "part of a listed building"; and that "demolition" implies works on such a scale as to result in a site for redevelopment.[99] However, since the alteration of a listed building also requires listed building consent if it affect the character of the building as one of special architectural or historic interest, the distinction is again likely to be only of academic interest.

---

[94] See **12.4**.
[95] *R. (Hammerton) v London Underground Ltd)*, [2003] J.P.L. 984, at para.149.
[96] P(LBCA)A 1990, ss 7, 8. [Scotland: P(LBCA)(S)A 1997, ss 6, 7; NI: P(NI)O 1991, art.44.]
[97] See **12.8**.
[98] P(LCA)A 1990, s.60(7); see **16.10**.
[99] [1997] 1 W.L.R. 168 at p.182. And see now Appendix D to Circ. 01/01.

Listed building consent would thus probably be required under this heading for works such as the removal of an internal wall or front garden railings—as being "alterations" that affect the character of the building as a building of special architectural or historic interest. The removal of a fireplace, or a wrought-iron balcony, on the other hand, might or might not need consent—depending on whether or not it affected the special character of the building as one of special architectural or historic interest. The removal of plaster mouldings, previously damaged by traffic, was held by the Secretary of State on appeal to be an alteration which did not affect the character of the building.[1]

Since "a listed building" includes some structures in its curtilage, it is possible to envisage works which would clearly be "demolition" in the non-technical sense (the removal of a pre-war potting shed within the curtilage of a country house but at some distance from it, for example) but which might equally clearly not affect the character of the "building" (that is, the listed building itself plus all the buildings and structures in its curtilage[2]), and would therefore be an alteration not requiring consent. That apart, there are probably in practice not many works of partial demolition which would not alter the character of a building, and those require consent for that reason.

For a further discussion as to the difference between these categories, see **12.6**.

In addition, where proposed works include any demolition, as opposed to alteration or extension, notice must be given before starting to English Heritage (the successor to the Royal Commission on Historical Monuments since February 19, 2001).[3] Indeed, this was one of the principal matters which led the Court of Appeal in *Shimizu* to decide that "demolition" was to be definitely distinguished from "alteration".[4] In Wales and Scotland, notice is to be given to the Royal Commission on Ancient and Historical Monuments; and in Northern Ireland, to the Department.[5]

The demolition a listed place of worship of any of the other exempt denominations other than the Church of England[6] is, in theory, exempt from the need for listed building consent, but only as long as the building remains "used for ecclesiastical purposes" following the works, which would seem to be impossible if it is being demolished so as to create a site for redevelopment.[7]

---

[1] [1981] J.P.L. 443.

[2] P(LBCA)A 1990, s.1(5); see **Chapter 4**. [Scotland: P(LBCA)(S)A 1997, s.1(4); NI: P(NI)O 1991, art.42(7).]

[3] P(LBCA)A 1990, s.8(2)(b), (c), amended by Authorisation of Works (Listed Buildings) (England) Order 2001. And see **13.7.10**.

[4] See **12.6.3**.

[5] Wales: P(LBCA)A 1990, s.8(2)(b), (c); Scotland: P(LBCA)(S)A 1997, s.7(2),(4)); NI: P(NI)O 1991, art.44(2).

[6] See **16.3.4**.

[7] P(LBCA)A 1990, s.60(1). [Scotland: P(LBCA)(S)A 1997, s.54(1); NI: P(NI)O 1991, art.44(8)(a).]

Table 12.2 Works to a listed building: permissions and consents needed

Type of work	Planning application	Application for listed building consent
1. Total demolition of building	Not needed	Always needed
2. Partial demolition	Not needed	Almost always needed
3. External alteration or extension of building (not "permitted development"[8])	Always needed	Always needed
4. External alteration or extension building (permitted development)	Needed only where required by an Article 4 direction[9] or a condition on a previous permission	Needed except where the works do not affect the character of the building as one of special interest
5. Minor external alteration to building (not "development")	Not needed	Needed except where the works do not affect the character of the building as one of special interest
6. Alteration to interior of building	Not needed	Needed except where the works do not affect the character of the building as one of special interest
7. Demolition of pre-1948 building in the curtilage of listed building[10]	Not needed	Needed where the works affect that special character of the "listed building" (that is, the building in the list plus the curtilage buildings)
8. Alteration or extension of pre-1948 curtilage building	As for 3 to 6 above	As for 7 above
9. Demolition of post-1948 curtilage building	Not needed	Not needed
10. Alteration or extension of post-1948 curtilage building	As for 3 to 6 above	Not needed
11. Works to a listed scheduled monument	As for 1 to 6 above	Not needed; but application for scheduled monument consent will almost always be needed
12. Erection of new building in curtilage of listed building	Almost always needed	Not needed
13. Works to exterior of a listed place of worship of exempt denomination	As for 3 to 6 above	Not needed; but consent under denomination's own procedures will be needed
14. Works to interior of a listed place of worship of exempt denomination	Not needed	Not needed; but consent under denomination's own procedures will be needed
15. Works to listed place of worship of non-exempt denomination	As for 1 to 6 above	As for 1 to 6 above

---

[8] See **12.2.2**.
[9] See **7.4**.
[10] See **4.5**.

12.4 Alterations and extensions of a listed building[11]

12.4.1 The general rule

Any alterations or extensions to the exterior of a building that forms part of a listed building need planning permission, so long as they materially affect the external appearance of that building.[12] Listed building consent, on the other hand, is required for any alterations (internal or external) or extensions to a such a building if they affect the character of the whole listed building as a building of special architectural or historic interest.[13]

The two tests are distinct, but in practice their meaning is likely to be similar if not identical in most cases involving external works. Certainly, almost any works of any consequence to the exterior of a principal listed building (that is, the one that is itself included in the list, rather than an ancillary structure included merely by virtue of section 1(5)) are likely to need both planning permission and listed building consent.

The chief distinction between the two types of consent is therefore that listed building consent is needed for at least some works to the interior of a listed building, whereas planning permission can never be. And where works are carried out to an ancillary building in the curtilage of a listed building, planning permission will be needed where the works materially affect the appearance of that building, whereas listed building consent will only be needed if they affect the special character of the listed building as a whole (including the principal building and all the ancillary buildings).

12.4.2 The need for planning permission

Where building operations are to be carried out for the maintenance, improvement or other alteration of any building—whether a building listed in its own right, or a building in the curtilage of such a building, or indeed any other building, they will need planning permission unless "they affect only the interior of the building, or do not materially affect [its] external appearance".[14]

The question of what "materially affects the external appearance of a building" was considered by the High Court in *Burroughs Day v Bristol CC*,[15] which concerned a listed Georgian building in a conservation area. The proposed works consisted of alterations to the roof, which would be invisible except from balloons or from the top floors of a nearby office block, and the restoration of the original glazing pattern on the front elevation. Richard Southwell, Q.C., sitting as deputy judge, summarised as follows the factors to be taken into account:

    (1) what must be affected is "the external appearance", and not simply the exterior of the building. The alteration must be one which affects the way

---

[11] See **Table 12.2**.
[12] See **12.4.2**.
[13] See **12.4.4**.
[14] TCPA 1990, s.55(1), (1A), (2)(a). See **12.2.1**. [Scotland: TCP(S)A 1997, s.26(1),(2)(a),(4); NI: P(NI)O 1991, art.11(1),(1A),(2)(a).]
[15] [1996] 1 P.L.R. 78.

in which the exterior of the building is or can be seen by an observer outside the building;

(2) roof alterations may affect the external appearance of the building if they can be seen from any normal vantage point on the ground, or on or in a neighbouring building;

(3) the external appearance must be "materially" affected, which depends in part on the degree of visibility;

(4) whether a proposal is material is likely to depend on both the nature of the building (as to which its status as being listed or in a conservation area may be relevant) and the nature of the alteration;

(5) materiality is to be judged in relation to the whole building, not simply the part directly affected.

He also indicated that factual evidence will be required, including plans and photographs, showing the nature of the building and the proposed alteration, and the extent to which the altered appearance of the building will be visible; but he pointed out that the role of those providing such evidence was not to interpret the law.

The checklist thus provided is helpful. But the deputy judge possibly erred in going on to suggest that a change in window details that removes the original pattern of fenestration could be regarded as material, because of the damage it might do to the appearance of the building, even though a change the other way, restoring the original design, would not be material because of not involving any such damage. That would seem to be confusing "material" with "harmful", which is not justified. However, the deputy judge did specifically state that his comments on that issue were *obiter*.

The decision in *Burroughs Day* confirms that, in the case of a building that is listed in its own right, the great majority of external alterations will need planning permission. Where, on the other hand, a building forms part of a listed building by virtue of being in the curtilage of a building included in the list, a situation that did not arise in that case, it is necessary to consider solely the curtilage building on its own. That may be less sensitive to minor alterations (for example, where a new window is to be inserted a 1930s structure in the far corner of the garden of a listed house); they may therefore not require planning permission. But, if in doubt, the planning authority should be consulted.

Floodlighting is in general not development.[16] This would not be the case however if the equipment used to provide the illumination is so substantial or permanently fixed to the building or the ground that its installation amounts to an engineering operation.

The construction of a new shopfront would be a building operation, and thus development requiring planning permission. However, the fixing of a sign to a listed building would require no planning permission but advertisements consent.[17]

---

[16] *Kensington and Chelsea RBC v CG Hotels* [1981] J.P.L. 190.
[17] See **12.9.3**.

12.4.3 Permitted development

Having established that almost all alterations to a listed building are development, and thus require planning permission, the next question is to see whether any are permitted automatically by the General Development Order. The most relevant categories of permitted development have already been noted.[18] They generally apply to listed buildings just as in any other case. But there are some significant differences.

Firstly, where the building in question is a dwellinghouse, almost any extension, of whatever volume, requires planning permission. This is because paragraph A.1(g) of Part 1 of Schedule 2 to the 1995 Order provides that "the erection of a building within the curtilage of a listed building" is not permitted development. The intention of the draftsman was probably to refer only to freestanding buildings. But any statutory instrument must be interpreted in the context of its parent Act.[19] And in this case the Planning Act specifically provides that "building" includes "part of a building".[20] That is of course "except in so far as the context otherwise requires", but here the context is that of the enlargement or alteration of a dwellinghouse. The "building" within the curtilage of the listed dwellinghouse, whose erection is stated not to be permitted development, would thus include an extension to the listed house itself, which, after all, must almost inevitably be within its own curtilage.[21]

This also ensures that the erection of a conservatory loosely attached to a listed building, which arguably does not require listed building consent, does require a planning application (even though listed building consent would not necessarily be required for its removal[22]). However, an application is not required if the extension takes the form of a porch or a dormer on a rear roof slope outside a conservation area, as these are still permitted developments under Classes B and D respectively in Part 1.

Secondly, the permitted development right to install closed-circuit television cameras does not apply to listed buildings—which would include buildings and structures included within the listing by virtue of section 1(5) of the Listed Buildings Act, such as boundary walls.[23] There is no corresponding restriction in Scotland—presumably because it is considered that the need for listed building consent is a sufficient control.

Thirdly, the installation of antennas (including dish aerials) by Electronic Communications Code operators is not permitted development on a listed building (other than a dwellinghouse).[24] In Scotland, the restriction applies only

---

[18] See **12.2.2**.

[19] Interpretation Act 1978, s.11.

[20] TCPA 1990, s.336. [Scotland: TCP(S)A 1997, s.277; NI: P(NI)O 1991, art.2.]

[21] For a possible alternative view, see the Scottish case of *Whyte v Bruce* (1900) 7 S.L.T. 423, which suggested that the extension of a building might not constitute the erection of a building. And see the correspondence in the J.P.L. at [1982] 667, [1984] 327 and [1987] 308.

[22] See appeal decision at [2000] J.P.L. 324.

[23] 1995 Order, Sch.2, Pt 33, para.A.1(a).

[24] Pt 24, para.A.1(g)(iv), (h)(iii); see also **12.7.3**. [NI: Planning (General Development) Order 1993, Pt 17, substituted in 2003.]

to a Grade A building, but it does apply also to its setting.[25] More generally, where a satellite dish is attached to a listed building, listed building consent will be needed since it will almost inevitably affect its character[26]; the permitted development rules are accordingly the same as for unlisted buildings.

It may also be noted that where an article 4 direction is made by a local planning authority withdrawing permitted development rights from one or more listed buildings, it does not require the approval of the Secretary of State.[27]

12.4.4 The need for listed building consent

Listed building consent is required for the carrying out of any works for the alteration or extension of a listed building in any manner which would affect its character as a building of special architectural or historic interest.[28] This covers a larger spectrum of works than those for which planning permission is required, and includes in particular works which are not "development" at all either because they affect only the interior of the building or because they do not "materially" affect its external appearance.[29]

It also includes alterations and extensions that are classified as being "development", but which are permitted automatically by the General Development Order and thus do not normally need to be the subject of a planning application.[30]

What types of works are sufficient to "affect the character" of a listed building as a building of special architectural or historic interest? The phrase is a fairly general one, and is open to wide interpretation. By way of example, it has been held by the Secretary of State in appeal decisions that listed building consent was required for the erection of shutters,[31] the installation of new double glazed windows,[32] the replacement of Victorian stained glass with clear glazing,[33] the removal of a partition and other internal alterations to a smoke room in a public house,[34] the painting of stonework,[35] and the application of self-adhesive lettering to windows.[36]

It is perhaps important to repeat here that the description (if any) of the building in the statutory list does not necessarily include all of its features of merit[37]—even though it is true, as noted in *City of Edinburgh Council v Secretary of State for Scotland*,[38] that the description will often be "helpful". Thus to alter a feature not noted in the description of a building, and in particular the interior,

---

[25] TCP (General Development) Order 1992, Sch.1, Pt 20, Class 67, substituted in 2001.
[26] See **12.4.4**.
[27] See **7.4.5**.
[28] P(LBCA)A 1990, s.7, 8; see **12.2.3**. [Scotland: P(LBCA)(S)A 1997, ss 6, 7; NI: P(NI)O 1991, art.44.]
[29] See **12.2.1**.
[30] See **12.2.2**.
[31] [1981] J.P.L. 607.
[32] [1988] J.P.L. 194.
[33] [1984] J.P.L. 899.
[34] [1983] J.P.L. 751.
[35] [1979] J.P.L. 782; and see **12.4.5**.
[36] [2001] J.P.L. 252.
[37] See **4.2.2**.
[38] [1997] 3 P.L.R. 71, at p.77A.

might still be to affect its character, and therefore require listed building consent. Note that, contrary to a popular misconception, this applies regardless of the grade of the building (it does not just apply to buildings of Grade I or II*).

In particular, the removal of fixtures from the interior of a listed building may be considered an alteration affecting its character, and therefore requiring consent. The removal of the chandeliers and clock from Leighton Hall and that of four works of modern art from the Time and Life Building are good examples of this.[39]

On the other hand, in considering the character of "the building" as one of special interest, what is at issue is the character of the whole building—that is, the whole of the building listed in its own right plus all the pre-1948 structures and objects in its curtilage, and not just that of either the main building by itself or the particular structure or building to be altered.[40] However, in the case of a listed building set in large grounds, presumably to alter a minor structure (such as an outhouse) at some distance from either the main building or any subsidiary buildings that are intrinsically of any interest would be unlikely to affect the character of the whole, and would therefore only rarely require consent.

Affixing a sign or advertisement to a listed building will almost always require listed building consent (whether or not it requires express consent under the advertisements regulations), as it will affect the appearance of the building.

As with demolition works (see above), the courts are the ultimate arbiter of whether proposed works would affect the character of a listed building sufficiently to require listed building consent. In practice, however, common sense will usually supply the answer—consent will only very exceptionally be needed, for example, for very minor works such as rewiring or redecorating. But it should not be forgotten that sincerely held views on such matters can differ strongly; and that failure to obtain listed building consent when it is required is a criminal offence, and can end up in a fine, or worse. If in any doubt, anyone contemplating virtually any works to a listed building (of any grade) should seek advice from the planning authority, or just submit an application to be safe.

Finally, it may be noted that some piers are listed, and extend well beyond the low-water mark. This may mean that in some cases there is, theoretically, only limited control over works to them. In others, planning control—and hence listed building control—is expressly extended to include such structures.[41]

12.4.5 Painting

The painting of a building often does not materially affect its external appearance—where, for example, it is already painted and the new coat is in the same colour or one that is not significantly different—and is thus not development. However, where the external appearance is affected (such as where unpainted brickwork is to be painted for the first time, or where a white house is to painted

---

[39] See **4.4.3**; and **4.4** generally on fixtures and fittings.
[40] s.1(5). [Scotland: P(LBCA)(S)A 1997, s.1(4); NI: P(NI)O 1991, art.42(7).]
[41] For example, the Isle of Wight, by virtue of the Isle of Wight Act 1980, s.45; and see *R. v Easington DC, Ex p. Seaham Harbour Dock Company* [1999] P.L.C.R. 225. For a discussion of the issues involved, see the *Encyclopedia of Planning Law*, para.P57.13.

purple), such work is generally, in the absence of an article 4 direction, permitted development—even in the case of a listed building.[42] This does not apply, however, in Scotland, where the painting of a listed building—if it is development at all—is not permitted development, and therefore requires a planning application.[43]

As for listed building consent, there can be little doubt that painting a hitherto unpainted listed building (or a hitherto unpainted part of one) affects its character, and thus requires listed building consent. Thus, as noted above, it has been held on appeal that consent should have been obtained for the painting of stonework.[44] In one case in Lincolnshire, the owner of a listed stone building who had painted it red was successfully prosecuted in the magistrates' court, and had to remove the paint.[45]

Repainting existing paintwork in a different colour can be more difficult. In a notorious appeal in 1972, the Secretary of State considered that listed building consent should have been obtained for the repainting of a front door of a listed building (22 Royal Crescent in Bath, listed Grade I).[46] On the planning merits, however, he went on to find that, since the repainting, the colour of the door had faded to such an innocuous shade of pale primrose yellow that it no longer affected the building's character. Since the effect of time and weathering had been such as to eliminate that particular breach of listed building control, the listed building enforcement notice was suitably varied.

In *Windsor and Maidenhead RBC v Secretary of State*,[47] on the other hand, the offending paintwork was rather more noticeable. A listed building enforcement notice had been served on the owners of 2 and 2A Clarence Crescent in Windsor alleging a breach of listed building control by:

"painting the exterior of the building in colours of deep pink with black detailing on, *inter alia*, pilasters, string course, window cills, window frames, the base area of the main wall on the front elevation and the front porch."

The inspector reported that "It is my view that the character of the appeal premises has been altered to a point which constitutes a contravention of section 55 of the Act [the predecessor to section 7]". However, the Secretary of State in his decision disagreed:

"There are occasions when the painting of the facade of a listed building is undoubtedly an alteration which affects its character because it obliterates features of interest, eg brickwork, timbering or lettering or other details which are architecturally or historically important. In such cases, consent is, in the opinion of the Secretary of State, needed. In the present case he notes that the facade of the building was already painted and the action of repainting cannot therefore be said to have constituted works of alteration".[48]

---

[42] 1995 Order, Sch.2, Pt 2, Class C. [NI: 1993 Order, Sch.1, Pt 2, Class C.]
[43] 1992 Order, Sch.1, Pt 2, Class 9(2)(b).
[44] [1979] J.P.L. 782.
[45] [1984] J.P.L. 578.
[46] Noted at [1972] J.P.L. 650.
[47] [1988] J.P.L. 410.
[48] p.411.

This echoed his advice as it then was.[49] The Council appealed against the Secretary of State's decision; and Mann J., as he then was, considered that the critical question is whether the repainting affects the character of the building as a building of special interest—as it did here.[50] He did not think that there was any sensible distinction to be drawn between painting and repainting, and accordingly remitted the matter to the Secretary of State with a direction to dismiss the appeal and uphold the enforcement notice. Circular 8/87 was subsequently amended[51] to reflect this judgment.[52]

That decision makes it clear that the need for consent turns on the extent to which the painting or repainting affects the character of the building. Thus in a terrace of white stucco town houses, to paint one house cream would probably not need listed building consent; but to paint one dark blue[53] would need consent—and would probably not get it!

Painting the interior of a building can never be development, and can therefore never require planning permission.[54] But to paint the interior of a listed building, or even some feature of the interior, may require listed building consent, if it affects the character of the building. Thus the painting of wooden panelling at Sutton Place, Surrey (listed Grade I) was held by the Secretary of State, disagreeing with his inspector, to be an alteration requiring consent, although he agreed with the inspector that consent should be granted, as the painting unified the appearance of the panelling, which was of mixed dates and styles, and some of which was of poor quality.[55]

12.4.6 Repairs

Repairs and restoration works to a listed building may constitute development if they materially affect its external appearance. For example, where a building has been allowed to decay seriously, or even become semi-derelict, then works of repair (however desirable) may well affect its appearance, and therefore be "development". However, in the case of a dwellinghouse, such works will be permitted by Class A of Part 2.[56]

In practice, an application for planning permission will only rarely be insisted upon, since repairs will anyway require listed building consent if they comprise alterations which would affect its special character.[57] The fact that the works may be required by a dangerous structures order or repair notice is irrelevant.[58] It is

---

[49] Circ. 8/87 para.93.
[50] At 414.
[51] By Circ. 18/88.
[52] See now PPG 15, para.3.2 and WO Circ. 61/96, para.67.
[53] See appeal decision at [2002] J.P.L. 774.
[54] TCPA 1990, s.55(2)(a)(i). [Scotland: TCP(S)A 1997, s.26(2)(a)(i); NI: P(NI)O 1991, art.11(2)(a)(i).]
[55] [1984] J.P.L. 899 at 902, 904.
[56] And repairs to other categories of building may also be permitted development: for example, non-residential agricultural buildings (Class A of Pt 6).
[57] See PPG 15, para.3.2 and WO Circ. 61/96, para.67.
[58] Building Act 1984, ss 77, 79; London Building Acts (Amendment) Act 1939, ss 62, 65, 69; final subsections inserted by Housing Planning Act 1986; see **10.2**.

also irrelevant that the proposed works may have been the subject of an offer of a grant, from whatever source.

Careful thought needs to be given to the precise way in which the repairs are carried out, and the materials used. If the details of the works are appropriate, then not only is listed building consent more likely to be granted, but it may not be needed at all—since a repair using materials virtually identical to those used in the original building and carried out to the same design can scarcely be said to affect its character.

On the other hand, the carrying out of repairs using new materials may constitute works affecting the character of the building, and may therefore require consent. In *Bath CC v Secretary of State and Grosvenor Hotel*,[59] for example, it was agreed by all the parties involved, including the owner of the (Grade I) building, that the replacement of a leaking roof comprising some Welsh slates and some asbestos "slates" with a new roof of just asbestos slates was an alteration requiring consent. It was also held in this case that the supposed urgency of the works in no way obviated the need for consent at least to be applied for before works were started. If it had been, the owners would have immediately become aware both that listed building consent would only be granted for re-roofing entirely in Welsh slates, and that financial assistance might be available to assist with the cost of the works.[60]

As to cleaning and restoration, the view of the Secretary of State in England is that:

"Cleaning a building usually requires listed building consent. This is not only because cleaning can have a marked effect on the character of buildings, but also because cleaning processes can affect the historic fabric."[61]

This is probably correct in relation to the whole or a significant part of a building, but may be overly restrictive in relation to smaller operations, such as cleaning a balustrade. It is noteworthy that the subsequent guidance for Wales omits this advice.[62]

12.4.7 Urgent works

Works may sometimes have to be carried out to a listed building as a matter of urgency, either by way of emergency repairs, or to forestall imminent collapse. This might involve the demolition of a whole building which is suddenly found to be unsafe; or it might mean something less drastic (for example, hacking off the remainder of a stucco cornice after part had fallen onto the street below). Such works will require planning permission or listed building consent or both, just as in any other case—that is, if they amount to demolition or if they affect the special character of the building. The fact that the works may be required by a dangerous structures order or similar notice is irrelevant (see above).

---

[59] [1983] J.P.L. 737.
[60] See **18.4.8** for further details of this case.
[61] PPG 15, Annex C, para.C.18.
[62] Appendix to Annex D to WO Circ. 61/96.

Wherever possible, planning permission or listed building consent, as appropriate, should be obtained, or at least applied for, in advance. If there should be any subsequent dispute, the application will be a useful indication, if not proof, that the applicant is not attempting to flout the law. The conservation officer of the local authority may be able to give some guidance on how the works could best be carried out.

In some cases, however, the urgency may be such that it is not practical to obtain authorisation in advance. It will then be necessary to obtain planning permission and listed building consent to retain the works which have already been carried out.[63] In all cases, unless it is absolutely certain that listed building consent is not required at all,[64] written notice (even if not a formal application for consent) must be given to the local planning authority "as soon as reasonably practicable", either before or after the works, to avoid any possible liability to criminal prosecution for carrying out works without consent. Such notice must justify in detail why the works are being or were carried out, and in particular must explain:

(1) that they were urgently necessary in the interests of safety or health or for the preservation of the building;

(2) that the same result could not be achieved by repair works or temporary support or shelter; and

(3) that the works were limited to the minimum measures immediately necessary.[65]

It has been noted above that listed building consent is probably not required for accidental damage.[66] Following such an accident—for example, where a building has been partly demolished by fire or vehicle impact, or has partially collapsed in the course of building works—it may be necessary to carry out further works to render safe what remains; even, in some cases, to the extent of completely demolishing the building. Such further works, if they are in truth urgently necessary, would be covered by the above provision,[67] but as well as notifying the authority it would be appropriate to record (with photographs) the condition of the building after the initial damage and before the further works, to avoid any subsequent suggestion of impropriety.

Where works are carried out as a matter of urgency that are thought at the time to be necessary but which, in fact, are subsequently shown not to have been, it may, exceptionally, be possible to avoid conviction by relying on the common-law defence of duress of circumstances.[68] To avoid this loophole being abused,

---

[63] TCPA 1990, s.73A (planning permission); P(LBCA)A 1990, s.8(3) (listed building consent). [Scotland: TCP(S)A 1997, s.33, P(LBCA)(S)A 1997, s.7(3); NI: P(NI)O 1991, arts 29, 44(3).]

[64] See **12.4.4**.

[65] P(LBCA)A 1990, s.9(3); and see **19.4.2**. [Scotland: P(LBCA)(S)A 1997, s.8(3); NI: P(NI)O 1991, art.44(7).]

[66] See **12.2.3**.

[67] See for example the appeal decision noted at [1990] J.P.L. 444.

[68] See **19.2**.

authorities should be astute to issue very promptly in appropriate cases a written statement explaining that in the opinion of the relevant officer, there is no need for the building in question to be demolished; for a sample notice, see **Form D11** in Appendix D.

12.4.8 Moving a listed building

Where a listed building or structure is to be moved in its entirety from one location to another, it seems that listed building consent is required for its dismantling. Such consent, if granted, is likely to be subject to a condition requiring it to be re-erected at the chosen new location. And the re-erection would presumably require planning permission—particularly if there are ancillary works necessary to accommodate the building in its new site. For a recent example of this, see *R. (Judge) v Secretary of State.*[68a]

12.4.9 Changes of use

Planning permission is almost always required for a material change in the use of a building, unless the existing and proposed uses are within the same use class.[69] The use classes are currently prescribed in the TCP (Use Classes) Order 1987.[70]

However, listed building consent will only be required for a change in the use of a building if its physical consequences involve some demolition works, or if they affect the character of a listed building.

It will therefore sometimes happen that applications for two types of consent will be needed, for example where a listed house is being converted into offices. In such a case, the two applications will be determined on the basis of different criteria, and it could well happen that one is refused and the other is granted.

12.4.10 Places of worship

Works to listed churches need planning permission as much as for those affecting any other category of building; nor is there is any relevant category of "permitted development".

They were in the past always to a large extent outside the need for listed building consent. However, the rules were significantly changed in 1994. The current position is described in detail in **Chapter 16**, but is broadly as follows:

(1) listed building consent is almost never required for works to a listed Church of England church or cathedral, whether it is in use or redundant[71];

[68a] *R (Judge) v Secretary of State and Middlesbrough BC* [2005] EWCA, unreported, July 22, 2005, CA; affirming [2005] EWHC 887 (Admin), unreported, April 28, 2005.

[69] TCPA 1990, s.55(1),(2)(f). [Scotland: TCP(S)A 1997, s.26(1), (2)(f); NI: P(NI)O 1991, art.11(1),(2)(f).]

[70] The 1987 Order has been amended a number of times, but most notably by SI 2005/84, with effect from April 21, 2005; see Circular 03/05. [Scotland: TCP (Use Classes) (Scotland) Order 1989; NI: Planning (Use Classes) (NI) Order 1989.]

[71] See **16.3.3** (churches in use); **16.3.5** (cathedrals); **16.3.8** (redundant buildings).

(2) consent is only required for works to a listed place of worship of the other principal Christian denominations if the religious use of the building has ceased[72]; and

(3) consent is required for works to any other "ecclesiastical building" as in any other case.[73]

12.5 Other works affecting a listed building

12.5.1 The need for planning permission

The discussion above has focussed on works being carried out to a building that is itself listed. However, a listed building may also be affected by works carried out to other buildings nearby, and by the erection of new buildings or structures, which are in its curtilage or affect its setting.

Thus, the carrying out of development in the vicinity of a listed building, but not actually affecting the building itself, will not require listed building consent,[74] but will require the submission of a planning application unless it is permitted by the General Development Order. Such works may significantly affect the setting of the listed building, which is why applications to carry them out require special publicity.[75] However, there are no special rules regarding the definition of development, and thus the need for planning permission, in relation to works that affect the curtilage or setting of a listed building.

12.5.2 Permitted development: works in the curtilage of a listed building

The rules as to what categories of development are permitted by the General Development Order are significantly different in relation to works carried out in the curtilage of a listed building.

First, almost any development in the curtilage of a listed dwellinghouse needs specific planning permission. Class E in Part 1 of Schedule 2 to the Order provides that "the provision within the curtilage of a dwellinghouse of any building or enclosure, swimming or other pool required for a purpose incidental to the enjoyment of the dwellinghouse, or the maintenance, improvement or other alteration of such a building or enclosure" is normally permitted development. But this only applies to operations within the curtilage of a dwellinghouse that is listed if the volume of the building to be built, altered or improved is less than $10m^3$.[76] To make doubly certain, since (in England, Wales and Northern Ireland) such an operation if it is in a conservation area is to be treated as though it were

---

[72] See **16.3.4**, **16.3.8**.
[73] See **16.3.6**
[74] See **12.5.3**.
[75] See **13.5**.
[76] 1995 Order, Sch.1, Pt 1, para.E.1(f). [NI: 1993 Order, Sch.1, para.D.1(e).] In Scotland, the floor area must be no more than 4 sq m (TCP (General Permitted Development) (Scotland) Order, Class 3(2)(f)).

the enlargement of the dwellinghouse itself,[77] the Order provides that this still does not mean that the erection of a building in the curtilage of a listed building is permitted development.[78]

Secondly, the "erection, construction, maintenance, improvement or alteration of a gate, fence, wall or other means of enclosure" (normally permitted development if not more than 1m high fronting a highway or 2m elsewhere) is not permitted by the Order if it is within or enclosing the curtilage of a listed building.[79]

These two changes were introduced because such works do not need listed building consent,[80] and were until 1988 almost entirely outside the control of the planning authority, even if they had a highly undesirable effect on the setting of a listed building.

As to the meaning of "curtilage", this has been defined as "an area of land attached to a house and forming one enclosure with it."[81] The precise extent of the curtilage of a building has been considered by the courts on many occasions. The conclusions to be drawn from this litigation were considered in an earlier chapter, as it may be crucial to know the extent of the curtilage of a listed building in order to determine whether an ancillary structure comes within the ambit of the listing, by virtue of section 1(5) of the Listed Buildings Act.[82] And it may be noted that four of the cases cited there, *Collins v Secretary of State*,[83] *James v Secretary of State*,[84] *McAlpine v Secretary of State*,[85] and *Lowe v The First Secretary of State*[86] were decided in the context of assessing whether development was permitted by the General Development Order.

In *Lowe*, the owner of a Grade II listed building erected a 1.8m-high chain-link fence along the length of the property's 650m driveway. Such a fence would ordinarily be permitted by the 1995 Order, but the local authority nevertheless took enforcement action. It considered that the fence had been erected within the curtilage of the listed building, with the result that permitted development rights were not applicable. On appeal to the Secretary of State, the Inspector concurred with the authority's view, concluding that the fence had been erected with a view to enclosing land within the appellant's ownership. The Inspector considered that, given the purpose of the fence, it necessarily defined the curtilage and also fell within it. However, on the matter being appealed to the High Court, Sir Richard Tucker determined that:

---

[77] 1995 Order, Sch.2, Pt 1, para.A3(a)(i); see **12.7.2**. [NI: 1993 Order, Sch.1, Pt 1, para.A.2(a)]

[78] 1995 Order, Sch.2, Pt 1, para.A.1(g). [NI: 1993 Order, Sch.1, Pt 1, para.A.1(i).]

[79] 1995 Order, Sch.2, Pt 2, para.A.1(d). [Scotland: Part 2, Class 7; NI: 1993 Order, Sch.1, Pt 2, para.A.1(d).]

[80] See **12.5.3**.

[81] *New Oxford Dictionary of English, op cit.*

[82] See **4.5**.

[83] [1989] E.G.C.S. 15.

[84] [1991] 1 P.L.R. 58.

[85] [1995] 1 P.L.R. 16.

[86] [2003] 1 P.L.R. 81.

"The Inspector fell into error in taking into consideration and relying upon the reason for the erection of the fence. That reason cannot affect the character of the land upon which it was erected, nor the question of whether or not that land fell within the curtilage of the hall".[87]

It should also be noted that, when determining what permitted development rights apply, the key question is what is the extent of the curtilage of the building in question at the date of the development.[88] This is to be contrasted with the approach to be adopted when determining what is the extent of a listed building, where the key question is what was the extent of the curtilage of the building in the list at the date on which it was listed.[89] The principles are the same in either case, but the date on which they fall to be applied is different.[90]

In other words, to determine whether, for example, a proposal to erect a small structure near a listed dwellinghouse would be permitted development, the correct test is first to identify what is the building referred to in the list, and what was the curtilage of that building at the date of listing (which may of course be some while ago). That will enable the extent of the "listed building" to be determined for the purposes of s.1(5). Then it is necessary to consider what is now the curtilage of that listed building (which may be smaller or larger than its curtilage at the date of listing), and whether it currently includes the location of the proposed structure. If it does, the permitted development rights would be modified as indicated above.

12.5.3 The need for listed building consent

The High Court has decided (in *Cotswold DC v Secretary of State*) that building consent cannot be required for the erection of a new building within the curtilage or affecting the setting of a listed building, unless it is physically attached to the existing building, since the definition of a listed building does not include the ground.[91] For similar reasons, it has been decided by the Secretary of State on appeal that the placing of two strips of York stone paving in the front garden of a listed house did not need consent.[92]

These decisions should be contrasted with the earlier case of *Watson-Smyth v Secretary of State*,[93] in which it was held that the removing stones from the wall of a ha-ha and filling in the adjoining ditch would require listed building consent.

---

[87] At p.87.
[88] See **4.5.2**.
[89] *Watts v Secretary of State* [1991] 1 P.L.R. 61, *R. v Camden LBC, EX p. Bellamy* [1991] J.P.L. 255, and *Morris v Wrexham CBC and the National Assembly* [2002] 2 P. & C.R. 7. See **4.3.3**.
[90] See **4.5.3**.
[91] [1985] J.P.L. 407; see also the appeal at [1984] J.P.L. 55, and *Bradfield v Commissioners of Customs & Excise*, 1990, unreported, a decision of the VAT Tribunal noted at **17.3.4**.
[92] [1975] J.P.L. 690.
[93] (1992) 64 P. & C.R. 156, [1992] J.P.L. 451; see **4.5.5**.

12.6 Demolition of an unlisted building in a conservation area[94]

12.6.1 The need for planning permission

The general rule is that where works to a building are on such a scale as to amount to its demolition, as opposed to its alteration, they need conservation area consent, but not (except in the case of gates, walls, etc.) planning permission. Where they are on a lesser scale, they are properly categorised as alteration, and will need planning permission.[95] And some relatively small-scale operations to remove parts of buildings (such as windows and parts of front garden walls) may constitute permitted development, which can therefore be carried out without any consent at all, in the absence of an article 4 direction.[96]

The basis for this is that the Secretary of State, who has power to direct that certain categories of demolition shall not be development,[97] has directed that development generally does not include, amongst other things, the demolition of a building in a conservation area.[98] The approach of the House of Lords in *Shimizu* presumably applies here too, so that the demolition of all or most of such a building does not require planning permission.

However, the exemption does not extend to the demolition of the whole or part of any gate, fence, wall or other means of enclosure. Such demolition will therefore be "development". However, it will normally be permitted development, by virtue of Class B of Part 31 of Schedule 2 to the GPDO, so that no planning application will have to be submitted.[99] Planning authorities could make article 4 directions[1] controlling such demolition in appropriate cases—which might be appropriate, for example, to restrict the loss of front garden walls in conservation areas.

The direction applying in Scotland is identical.[2]

In Northern Ireland, the 2005 Direction excludes the demolition of buildings in conservation areas (which therefore needs only conservation area consent, as in England), but it does not exclude the demolition of buildings in areas of townscape character and areas of village character, the demolition of which thus generally requires planning permission.[3] These areas are listed in two schedules to the Direction or designated in a development plan. There are a number of exceptions to this requirement—broadly similar to the exemptions from the

---

[94] See **Table 12.3**.
[95] See **12.7.1**.
[96] See **12.7.2**.
[97] See **12.2.1**.
[98] TCP (Demolition—Description of Buildings) Direction 1995 (in DOE Circ. 10/95, Appendix A), paras (1)(b), (2).
[99] See **12.2.2**.
[1] See **7.4**.
[2] TCP (Demolition Which is Not Development) (Scotland) Direction 2001 (see SDD Circ. 1/2001), para.1(1)(c).
[3] Planning (Demolition—Description of Buildings) Direction 2005, para.2(d). For policy guidance, see Addendum to PPS 6, published in August 2005.

requirement for conservation area consent (that is, works of demolition that are essentially trivial or that are authorised under other procedures[4]).

12.6.2 The need for conservation area consent

By virtue of s.74(1) of the Listed Buildings Act, conservation area consent is needed from the local planning authority for almost any works for the demolition of all or almost all of any building within a conservation area.[5]

By virtue of s.75(1), however, consent is *not* needed for the following:

(1)   the demolition of a listed building (for which listed building consent is needed instead[6]);

(2)   the demolition of a scheduled monument (for which scheduled monument consent is needed instead[7]); or

(3)   the demolition of a building in any of the exempted categories set out in a direction by the Secretary of State.[8]

The demolition of any unlisted place of worship in a conservation area, in theory, does not require building consent, but—as with listed churches—only as long as the building remains "for the time being used for ecclesiastical purposes", which is impossible if it is being demolished.[9]

Because conservation area consent is needed for "demolition", but not for "alteration" or "extension"[10], it is important to know into which category any particular works will fall. The difficulty arises because a "building" is defined to include a structure or erection, *and any part of a building or structure or erection.*[11] It might therefore be thought that to remove part of a building—such as the ridge tiles, or the windows—is "demolition" requiring consent; and indeed that used to be the general view prior to the decision of the House of Lords in *Shimizu (UK) Ltd v Westminster CC.*[12] Since then, however, it has been accepted that conservation area consent is required only for the demolition of all or at least most of a building.

12.6.3 The Shimizu decision

The whole issue was considered fully by the Court of Appeal and the House of Lords in *Shimizu (UK) Ltd v Westminster CC.* The case concerned the inter-

---

[4]   2005 Direction, para.3; see **12.6.5**.
[5]   P(LBCA)A 1990, s.74(1). [Scotland: P(LBCA)(S)A 1997, s.66(1); NI: P(NI)O 1991, art.51(2).]
[6]   See **12.3.2**.
[7]   See **12.8.3**.
[8]   See **12.6.5**.
[9]   P(LBCA)A 1990, s.75(1)(b); see **16.4**. [Scotland: P(LBCA)(S)A 1997, s.67(1)(b); NI: P(NI)O 1991, art.51(1)(b).]
[10]   See **12.2.4**.
[11]   See TCPA 1990, s.336; emphasis added. [Scotland: TCP(S)A 1997, s.277; NI: P(NI)O 1991, art.2.]
[12]   [1996] 3 P.L.R. 89. See the previous edition of this book for a discussion of the law prior to the decision in *Shimizu.*

Table 12.3 Works to an unlisted building in a conservation area: permissions and consents needed

Type of work	Planning application	Application for conservation area consent
1. Demolition of building whose total volume is less than 115 cu m	Not needed	Not needed
2. Demolition of wall etc. less than 1 m high fronting highway, waterway or open space, or 2 m elsewhere	Not needed	Not needed
3. Total demolition of agricultural building	Not needed	Only needed for pre-1914 building
4. Demolition works required or permitted under certain legislation	Not needed	Not needed
5. Total demolition of any other building	Not needed	Always needed
6. Demolition of entire building except façade, prior to redevelopment	Probably needed	Probably needed
7. Other partial demolition	Not needed	Needed if the works amount to a building operation
8. External alteration or extension of building (not "permitted development"[13])	Always needed	Not needed
9. External alteration or extension building (permitted development)	Needed only where required by an Article 4 direction[14] or a condition on a previous permission	Not needed
10. Minor external alteration to building (not "development")	Not needed	Not needed
11. Alteration to interior of building	Not needed	Not needed
12. Works to a scheduled monument in a conservation area	As for 5 to 11 above	Not needed; but application for scheduled monument consent will almost always be needed
13. Erection of new building	Almost always needed	Not needed
13. Works to exterior of a place of worship of exempt denomination	As for 5 to 11 above	Not needed; but consent under denomination's own procedures will be needed
14. Works to interior of a place of worship of exempt denomination	Not needed	Not needed; but consent under denomination's own procedures will be needed
15. Works to place of worship of non-exempt denomination	As for 5 to 11 above	As for 5 to 11 above

[13] See **12.2.2**.
[14] See **7.4**.

pretation of section 27 of the Listed Buildings Act, which provided that compensation was payable following the refusal of listed building consent for the alteration or extension of a listed building, but not following the refusal of consent for its demolition.[15] That provision had in fact been repealed prior to the start of the *Shimizu* litigation, but the statutory scheme underlying the control of works to listed buildings and in conservation areas is such that the principles applying to the interpretation of section 27 of the Act would apply equally to that of s.74, whereby conservation area consent is required for demolition but not for alteration or extension.

In *Shimizu*, listed building consent had been granted for the removal of virtually the whole of the building (formerly known as Qantas House) on the corner of Bond Street and Piccadilly in London, leaving only the façade, the chimney breasts and the chimney stacks, so as to enable the construction of a new interior. The building then changed hands, and the new owners wished to maximise the floorspace in the new building; they accordingly sought consent to remove the chimney breasts as well. They were unsuccessful, and sought compensation, claiming that the removal of the chimney breasts was "alteration", not "demolition", a view which was supported by the Lands Tribunal at first instance.[16] The compensating authority appealed to the Court of Appeal.[17]

Russell L.J., in a dissenting judgment, considered that the words "demolition" and "alteration" should be given their ordinary meaning; and that to ascertain which of them is apt is the task of the tribunal of fact. The member of the Lands Tribunal had in this case been perfectly entitled to regard the works proposed as being an alteration of part of the building, confined to the interior in both the horizontal and vertical planes. Millett L.J. and Sir Ralph Gibson disagreed, however. The former held that:

"... demolition, with or without replacement, on the one hand and alteration on the other are mutually exclusive concepts. The demolition and replacement of part of a building cannot constitute a mere alteration of that part. The old part has gone. Its replacement is a substitute for the old, not an alteration of it".[18]

Sir Ralph Gibson, in the most thorough of the three judgments, noted that for works of demolition to be authorised, it was necessary both for the authority to issue consent for them and for the Royal Commission to be notified—but that only the former was necessary in relation to works of alteration or extension. This emphasised the separation of the two categories, and showed that demolition of part of a building is not capable of being included in and treated as part of the works for alteration. The judge did however go on to accept (albeit probably *obiter*) that:

"The notion of demolition is not apt to include all and any work of removal of part. For example, the removal of part of a wall for insertion of windows or of doors would not, I think, properly be regarded as demolition of part of the building but as alteration of it".[19]

---

[15] See **15.4.2**.
[16] [1994] 1 E.G.L.R. 214.
[17] [1995] 1 P.L.R. 72.
[18] p.120.
[19] p.124.

Both judges also implied that the way in which an applicant described his or her proposal, and the way in which the planning authority categorised it, would not influence its true nature.

The *Shimizu* litigation then proceeded to the House of Lords.[20] The leading judgment was given by Lord Hope, who considered the meaning of "listed building" and found that, wherever it occurred in the Act, it appeared to mean the whole of the building, not part of it. It followed that the "demolition of a listed building" means the removal or destruction of the whole of that building; the removal or destruction of part is only the "alteration" of the whole.

He further held that the definition of what constitutes "demolition", as opposed to "alteration", is still ultimately a question of fact, for the tribunal of fact, and that no more precise definition of the expression was required—although he did specifically note that "demolition" could apply not only to the pulling down of every single part of a building but also to the clearing of a whole site for redevelopment whilst leaving the façade of the building standing. He thus came to the conclusion that there was in any event nothing in the instant case to justify overturning the original decision of the Lands Tribunal; compensation was thus to be awarded.

12.6.4 Application of the Shimizu doctrine to conservation areas

In the course of his speech in *Shimizu*, Lord Hope explicitly considered the question of the need for conservation area consent. He dealt with the point thus:

"It was suggested that the provisions of section 74 ... were inconsistent with this interpretation. Subsection (1) of section 74 provides that a building in a conservation area shall not be demolished without the consent of the appropriate authority, and subsection (3) provides that various sections in Part I of the Act have effect in relation to buildings in conservation areas as they have effect in relation to listed buildings. I do not think that there is any inconsistency as long as it is appreciated that a listed building can consist of part of a building. Buildings in a conservation area are put on the same footing as buildings of special architectural or historic interest, or any part of a building which has that character, which [are] for the time being included in the list. In the context of section 74(1), subject to any exceptions or modifications which may have been prescribed under subsection (3) of that section, *the reference to the demolition of a building in a conservation area must be taken to mean the removal of the whole building*, in the same way as section 17(3) appears to contemplate works to a listed building which will produce a site for redevelopment."[21]

It is arguable that these observations are obiter; but the better view would seem to be that they formed an integral part of his analysis of the statutory code, and thus of the decision.

The conclusion is thus simple: conservation area consent will only be needed for the carrying out of works in a conservation area provided that they are, as a matter of fact, carried out on such a scale as to amount to the "demolition" of a whole building. This would include, for example, the removal of an entire building; or the removal of all of it except the façade; or the removal of an entire front garden wall. But it would not include the removal of a single window, or a

[20] [1996] 3 P.L.R. 89.
[21] [1996] 3 P.L.R. 89 at 105E; emphasis added.

whole shop front; nor the removal of one wall of a building, prior to adding on an extension (even before consent had been granted for the new work); nor the removal of a porch, or the knocking of a hole into a wall; nor the removal of architectural details such as finials, gate-piers and so on. These would all be "alterations".

There is in practice a whole range of minor operations—particularly in the context of dwellinghouses—which do not require a specific planning application because they are "permitted development"[22]; notable examples would be the making of elevational alterations, and the removal of part of a front garden wall to create a parking space. It had always been thought that such works were nevertheless within the control of the planning authority, as they were partial demolition, requiring conservation area consent. Now, however, it is clear that they do not, and so are outside all planning control (unless the authority makes an article 4 direction,[23] with the consequential liability to pay compensation).

The decision in *Shimizu* largely settled the debate as to the distinction between "alteration" and "demolition". It overruled the earlier decision in *R. v North Hertfordshire*,[24] and meant that that paragraph 4.28 of PPG 15 (as originally issued) was also wrong. The latter was therefore cancelled, and replaced with new guidance, now in Appendix B to Circular 01/01; the text of PPG 15 at **Appendix A** to this book incorporates the revisions. Paragraph 3.19 of WO Circular 61/96 was similarly replaced by Appendix B to WO Circular 1/98.[25]

12.6.5 *Other exceptions to the need for conservation area consent*

The Secretary of State has power to make directions exempting certain categories of demolition from the need for conservation area consent to be obtained.[26]

The direction currently applying to England is contained in paragraph 31 of Circular 01/01, which is virtually identical to its predecessor,[27] which it replaced with effect from January 18, 2001. The direction applying to Wales, in paragraph 20 of WO Circular 1/98, came into effect on March 2, 1998.[28] They broadly apply to two categories of works:

- those that are (at least in most cases) relatively trivial, not justifying the extra control; and

- those that are authorised under some other procedure.

Each is considered in turn.

---

[22] See **12.2.2**.
[23] See **7.4**.
[24] [1981] J.P.L. 752.
[25] Scotland: NPPG 18, para.49.
[26] P(LBCA)A 1990, s.75(1)(d), (2), (4). [Scotland: P(LBCA)(S)A 1997, s.67(2); NI: P(NI)O 1991, art.51(3).]
[27] The direction in para.28 of Circ. 14/97, which replaced that in para.97 of DoE Circ. 8/87.
[28] It replaced the short-lived direction in para.31 of WO Circ. 61/96, which was identical to the old (1987) English direction. The 1996 direction (which came into force on December 5, 1996) had replaced its predecessor, in para.70 of WO Circ. 61/81.

The direction applying in Scotland, in Annex IV of SDD Circular 17/1987, is generally similar to the direction that used to apply in England since 1987. The direction currently applying in Northern Ireland was made on February 3, 1988, and is broadly in line with that applying in Wales. It is to be expected that both directions will be updated in due course.

12.6.6 Minor demolition works

The first group of categories of demolition works which are exempted from the need for conservation area consent comprises various minor works which are presumably reckoned to be generally harmless.[29] This represents a mechanism similar to "permitted development", whereby planning permission is granted automatically for certain types of generally harmless development.[30] But note that there is no equivalent of the "article 4 direction" procedure,[31] so it is not possible for a local authority to bring within control any demolition in the exempted categories, except by seeking to have the building concerned listed or serving on it a building preservation notice.[32]

Conservation area consent is thus not needed for the demolition of the following categories of unlisted building:

"(a) any building with a total cubic content not exceeding 115 cubic metres (as ascertained by external measurement) or any part of such a building, other than a pre-1925 tombstone;

(b) any gate, wall, fence or means of enclosure which is less than one metre high where abutting on a highway (including a public footpath or bridleway), waterway or open space, or less than two metres high in any other case;

(c) any building erected since January 1, 1914 and in use, or last used, for the purposes of agriculture or forestry."

Category (a) allows the demolition without consent of small structures (such as garden sheds). This used to be carefully distinguished from the "demolition" of small parts of larger structures and buildings, which was not exempt; however, since *Shimizu*, it is now clear that such partial demolition does not need conservation area consent anyway.[33]

The only exception to this provision is that the demolition of a pre-1925 tombstone, of whatever size, needs consent if it is in a conservation area—unless it is within the curtilage of a church belonging to one of the exempt denominations, when it would be solely under the control of the relevant denominational authorities.[34] This means that, for example, the removal of older monuments in municipal cemeteries and cemeteries attached to synagogues and closed churches would require conservation area consent.

The second category is reasonably straightforward. It should be noted that, in measuring the height of a wall, ground level is to be taken as the level of the

---

[29] Circ. 01/01, para.28(1)(*a*)–(*c*); WO Circ. 1/98, para.20(1) (a)–(c).
[30] See **12.2.2**.
[31] See **7.4**.
[32] See **3.9**.
[33] See **12.6.4**.
[34] Ecclesiastical Exemption (Listed Buildings and Conservation Areas) Order 1994 (SI 1994/1771), art.5(1)(d); see **16.4.1**. And see Circ. 01/01, para.34.

highest part of the surface of the ground adjacent to it.[35] The lower height limit now applies to walls etc abutting waterways as well as those abutting highways and open spaces. However, note that the removal of such a wall may require the submission of a planning application where the local authority has made an article 4 direction in respect of the land in question.[36]

The third category probably reflects the view that the design of most post-1914 agriculture and forestry buildings is such that their removal would probably be an advantage!

There used to be a further category under this heading, allowing for the demolition without consent of part of an industrial building.[37] Again, however, since the decision in *Shimizu*, it is clear that such partial "demolition" is more correctly categorised as "alteration", and thus does not require conservation area consent anyway.

12.6.7 Demolition authorised under other procedures

The second group of exceptions refers to various circumstances where demolition can be authorised or required under other procedures.[38]

Conservation area consent is thus not needed in England for demolition works required by any of the following:

(d) a discontinuance order;

(e) a planning obligation under s.106 of the Planning Act;

(f) an enforcement notice or a listed building enforcement notice;

(g) a condition attached to a planning permission;

(h) a notice under section 215 of the Planning Act;[39]

(i) a demolition order under the Housing Act 1985;[40]

(j) a compulsory purchase order under the 1985 Act (but only where the order has been approved by the Secretary of State)[41]; and

(k) a pastoral scheme or a redundancy scheme under the Pastoral Measure 1983 (providing for the demolition of a redundant Church of England church[42]).

The presumption here is that further consent is unnecessary, since in most of these cases the demolition works will have already been either permitted or indeed

---

[35] Circ. 01/01, para.7.
[36] See **12.6.1**.
[37] DOE Circ. 8/87, para.97(d); W.O. Circ. 61/96, para.31(d).
[38] Circ. 01/01, para.31(d)–(k).
[39] See **10.5**.
[40] See **10.8**.
[41] See **10.8.3**.
[42] See **16.10**.

required by the local authority, which will have presumably taken into account their effect on the appearance of the conservation area[43].

For the exemption in category (e) to operate, the agreement must actually "require" the demolition of the building, rather than merely facilitate the development of its site—see *Windsor and Maidenhead RBC v Brandrose Investments Ltd*[44], decided in relation to the old law on agreements (prior to the introduction of the present "planning obligations" provisions).[45]

A change was made in 1987 to the wording of what is now category (g), whereby a local planning authority could no longer give itself planning permission for a new building in a conservation area, and incorporate as a condition a requirement that the existing building on the site should be demolished. In such a case, conservation area consent therefore had to be obtained from the Secretary of State.[46] That change appears to have been lost in the 1997 redrafting.

Category (j) ensures that a local authority cannot demolish a house in a conservation area that has been acquired by agreement under Housing Act powers without first obtaining the approval of the Secretary of State.

All these categories also apply to Wales, except that category (i) relates to "any building included in an operative clearance order or compulsory purchase order under Part IX of the 1985 Act or subject to a demolition order under Part II of that Act", and category (j) to any building subject to Part IX of the Act that is purchased by a local authority by agreement.[47] The reason for the difference between England and Wales is not clear.

It was proposed that demolition should be exempt from the need for conservation area consent if it results from the implementation of a planning permission granted before the conservation area in question was designated.[48] No such change was made when the 1997/1998 directions were made, however, so that such demolition does still require consent.

12.6.8 Demolition in cases of urgency

Where works have to be carried out as a matter of urgency for the demolition of an unlisted building in a conservation area, the same considerations apply as in the case of urgent works to a listed building. Conservation area consent is still required, but if the urgency is such that the works have to be done before consent has been obtained, prosecution may be avoided provided that written notice is given to the planning authority as soon as reasonably practicable, explaining that:

- that the works were urgently necessary for safety or health,

- that the same result could not be achieved by repair works or temporary support or shelter; and

---

[43] As required by P(LBCA)A 1990, s.72.
[44] [1983] J.P.L. 374 at 375.
[45] By PCA 1991, s.12.
[46] P(LBCA)A 1990, s.74(2)(a).
[47] WO Circ. 1/98, para.20(1)(d)–(k).
[48] Draft PPG 15, Annex 8, para.22.

- that the works were limited to the minimum measures immediately necessary.[49]

12.7 Other operations in a conservation area[50]

12.7.1 The need for planning permission

Whereas listed building consent is needed for the demolition, alteration or extension of a listed building, conservation area consent is needed only for the demolition of an unlisted building in a conservation area, but not for its alteration or extension.

However, planning permission is needed for "building operations" of any consequence, including most alterations and extensions to existing buildings. This has recently acquired greater significance, following the decision of the House of Lords in *Shimizu* that conservation area consent is not needed for works of partial, as opposed to total, demolition, and that such works are, presumably, better categorised as "alterations".[51]

Where such alterations require the making of a planning application (as with, say, the removal of architectural features from a building in commercial use), the planning authority retains control. Where, however, planning permission is granted automatically by the TCP (General Permitted Development) Order,[52] as with the removal of features from a dwelling-house, or of part of a front garden wall, the authority is powerless to intervene except by imposing an article 4 direction.[53]

The definition of "development" specifically excludes "the carrying out for the maintenance, improvement or other alteration of any building of works which affect only the interior of the building, or do not materially affect the external appearance of the building..."[54]

This means that, generally, neither planning permission nor any other consent is needed for the carrying out of internal works to an unlisted building in a conservation area. However, where such works are on a sufficient scale as to amount to the gutting of the building in question, so as to leave a clear site for constructing what is in effect a new building but surrounded by all or some of the original external walls (the practice known as "façadism"), it may be that conservation area consent is needed[55]; and it may well be that such works would also require planning permission, as they would probably have some effect on the external appearance of the building.

---

[49] P(LBCA)A 1990, s.9(3), applied by s.74; and see **12.4.7**. [Scotland: P(LBCA)(S)A 1997, s.8(3), applied by s.66; NI: P(NI)O 1991, art.44(7), applied by art.51.]
[50] See **Table 12.3**.
[51] *Shimizu (U.K.) Ltd v Westminster CC* [1996] 3 P.L.R. 89.
[52] See **12.2.2**.
[53] See **7.4**.
[54] TCPA 1990, s.55 (2)(a); see **12.2.1**. [Scotland: TCP(S)A 1997, s.26(2)(a); NI: P(NI)O 1991, art.11(2)(a).]
[55] See **12.6.4**.

The question of what "materially affects the external appearance of a building" was considered by the High Court in *Burroughs Day v Bristol CC*, and has been discussed earlier.[56] But it may be noted that the court explicitly stated that, in considering the effect on the appearance of a building of a particular operation, the fact that it is in a conservation area may well be material. So, for example, an inspector cited the decision in *Burroughs Day* in agreeing with a planning authority that the installation of replacement uPVC windows in a building in a conservation area was development.[57]

Planning permission will also, obviously, be needed for the construction of a new building in a conservation area, just as elsewhere—there are no special rules regarding the definition of "development" in relation to such works. This enables the authority to have some influence over changes in the character of the area, which is why special publicity is needed for such applications.[58]

12.7.2 Permitted development rights in conservation areas

Since conservation area consent is not needed for the erection of new buildings or for the alteration of existing ones, the need for planning permission to be obtained is the only way in which a planning authority can control works which may significantly affect the character or appearance of a conservation area. However, if the works are permitted development, then no planning application is normally needed, and the authority has no control at all, except by making an article 4 direction covering the property and the type of development concerned.

For example, the character of a conservation area that mainly comprises terraces of small Victorian cottages opening off the back of the pavement can be totally transformed by the replacement of the original sliding sash windows with modern glazing. Such work is permitted development,[59] and no planning application is therefore required. Therefore unless the cottages are listed or subject to an article 4 direction, the planning authority is powerless to intervene.

The limits of what is permitted development within a conservation area can therefore be of considerable significance. There are accordingly certain differences between permitted development limits generally and those applying in conservation areas. The more restricted limits apply also in various other categories of sensitive areas, as well as in conservation areas—together referred to in the Order as "Article 1(5) land". And note that the modified limits apply regardless of when the area in question was designated. The principal differences are now as follows (the complex provisions regarding telecommunications development are considered in the following section[60]).

First, extensions to dwellinghouses in conservation areas are only permitted development if they do not add more than 10 per cent or 50 cu. m. (whichever is

---

[56] [1996] 1 P.L.R. 78 (see **12.4.2**).

[57] Appeal decision at [2004] J.P.L. 855.

[58] See, for example, *Steinberg v Secretary of State* [1989] 2 P.L.R. 9, and the cases which followed it (discussed here at **14.7**).

[59] 1995 Order, Sch.2, Pt 1, Class A. [Scotland: 1992 Order, Sch.1, Pt 1, Class 1; NI: 1993 Order, Sch.1, Pt 1, Class A.]

[60] See **12.7.3**.

greater) to the volume of the original building.[61] The limits elsewhere are 15 per cent or 70 cu. m. except in the case of terrace houses.[62] Nor are the following permitted development within a conservation area:

(1) the cladding of any part of the exterior of a dwellinghouse with stone, artificial stone, timber, plastic or tiles[63]; or

(2) any alterations to the roof of a dwellinghouse resulting in a material alteration to its shape, notably dormer windows.[64]

Cement and pebbledash rendering is, however, still permitted development.[65]

Secondly, Class E in Part 1 of the Schedule to the GPDO—which provides that the erection within the curtilage of a dwellinghouse of various buildings and enclosures is normally permitted development[66]—applies generally within a conservation area just as elsewhere; but if the volume of the building to be built, altered or improved (the "curtilage building") is greater than 10 cubic metres, and the dwellinghouse is in a conservation area, the operation is to be treated as though it were the enlargement of the dwellinghouse itself.[67] The relevant limits in Class A in Part 1 therefore apply, as to height, size, location and so on. Outside conservation areas, this applies only if the curtilage building will be within 5m of the dwellinghouse.[68]

Thirdly, the painting of a building will often not be development.[69] However, where the external appearance of the building is affected, such work is generally, in the absence of an article 4 direction, permitted development—even if it seriously spoils the appearance of a group of buildings in a conservation area.[70] This does not apply, however, in Scotland, where the painting of a building in a conservation area—if it is development at all—is not permitted development, and therefore requires a planning application.[71]

Fourthly, in England and Wales, extensions and alterations of industrial and warehouse buildings and electricity undertakers' buildings are only permitted development in conservation areas if they do not add more than 10 per cent to the volume of the original building, or 500 sq. m. to its aggregate floor space; elsewhere the limits are 25 per cent and 1,000 sq. m. respectively.[72] In Scotland, the limits for industrial and warehouse building are the same in conservation areas as elsewhere; those for electricity undertakers' buildings are as in England.[73] In

---

[61] Sch.2, Pt 1, para.A.1 (a)(i).

[62] para.A.1(a)(i), (ii).

[63] para.A.2.

[64] para.B.1(e).

[65] *Tower Hamlets LBC v Secretary of State and Nolan* [1995] J.P.L. 112.

[66] See **12.2.2**.

[67] paras E.1(f), A.3(a)(i). Note that this no longer applies only to garages and coachhouses, as was the case prior to 1988.

[68] para.A.3(a)(ii).

[69] See **12.4.5**.

[70] 1995 Order, Sch.2, Pt 2, Class C. [NI: 1993 Order, Sch.1, Pt 2, Class C.]

[71] 1992 Order, Sch.1, Pt 2, Class 9(2)(b).

[72] 1995 Order, Sch.2, Pt 8, para.A.1(a),(e); Pt 17, para.G.1(c).

[73] 1992 Order, Sch.1, Pt 8, Class 23; Pt 13, Class 40.

Northern Ireland, no such extensions or alterations are permitted development in conservation areas, regardless of size.[74]

Fifthly, where a building is erected or extended on the site of any school, college, university or hospital in England or Wales, in reliance upon permitted development rights in Part 32, any materials used are required to be of a similar appearance to those used for the original buildings if the site is within a conservation area.[75]

Finally, the permitted development right to install closed-circuit television cameras does not apply at all in conservation areas in Scotland.[76]

12.7.3 Satellite dishes and other telecommunications equipment

The rules as to what satellite dishes and other telecommunications equipment may be erected without the need for a planning application are notoriously complex, and have been changed a number of times in recent years. Most recently, the rules in England and Wales were changed to bring into line the requirements relating to all microwave antennae—whether satellite dishes or any other kind.[77]

Firstly, then, in England and Wales, in the case of either a dwellinghouse or a building under 15m high, the permitted development rights allow the erection of a single antenna, up to 60cm long where mounted on a chimney and 100cm in any other case; and a second antenna up to 60cm long. Where there is a chimney stack, antennas should not exceed the highest part of the roof by more than 60cm, or the highest part of the chimney, whichever is the lower; where there is no stack, they should not exceed the highest part of the roof.[78] In the case of a building (other than a dwellinghouse) more than 15m high, up to four antennas may be erected under permitted development rights—up to 60cm long where mounted on a chimney and up to 130cm long elsewhere.[78a] In all cases antennas must be located so that their effect on the external appearance of the building is minimised.[78b]

However, in all cases, the rules are significantly tighter in conservation areas, in that such installations are not permitted development if they are on a chimney, wall or roof slope which both faces onto and is visible from a highway—or a waterway in the Broads.[79]

In Scotland, such an installation of an antenna is only permitted development in a conservation area only where it is on any part of a dwellinghouse not fronting

---

[74] 1993 Order, Sch.1, Pt 8, Class A; Pt 13, Class C.
[75] 1995 Order, Sch.2, Pt 32, para.A.2.
[76] 1992 Order, Sch.1, Pt 25, Class 72 (inserted in 1996).
[77] By SIs 2005/2935 (England) and 2006/124 (Wales) (which are virtually identical). For Government guidance on the new rules, see ODPM Circ. 10/2005.
[78] 1995 Order, Sch 2, Pt 1, Class H (installation on a dwellinghouse or in its curtilage); Pt 25, Class A (on other buildings less than 15 m high).
[78a] 1995 Order, Sch 2, Pt 25, Class B.
[78b] 1995 Order, Sch 2, Pt 1, Class H, para.H.2(a); Pt 25, Class A, para.A.2(a); Pt 25, Class B, para.B.2(a).
[79] 1995 Order, Sch 2, Pt 1, Class H, para.H.1(d); Pt 25, Class A, para.A.1(i); Pt 25, Class B, para.B.1(g).

a road.[80] In Northern Ireland, no such installations are permitted development anywhere in a conservation area.[81]

In cases where the installation is not permitted development, a specific planning application will be required—and it may be guessed that that permission will probably not be granted.

Secondly, as a result of advances in the relevant technology, a number of operators have been designated by OFCOM under the Communications Act 2003 as providers of designated electronic communications networks or services.[82] These include BT and other operators of local broadband cable systems and 3G networks. The Electronic Communications Code, which may applied to operators at their request or as a result of a direction by OFCOM, allows them to install in the street and on private property apparatus such as wires, poles, masts, street cabinets, microwave dishes and other antennas.[83]

Under Part 24 of Schedule 2 to the 1995 Order, such installations, on the operator's own land or elsewhere, are permitted development provided that they conform to the terms of the Code.[84] In addition, the installation of antennas (including dish aerials) by operators is not permitted development within a conservation area, except for a small antenna on a dwellinghouse less than 15m in height, and even then it must not be on a chimney or a wall or roof slope fronting a highway.[85] And radio equipment housing is only permitted development in a conservation area if it is less than 2.5 cu. m. in volume.[86] The restrictions in Scotland and Northern Ireland are broadly similar.[87]

An operator must (except in emergency) give at least eight weeks' notice to the planning authority of any other works which it proposes to carry out within a conservation area on its own land, relying on the permission in Part 24.[88] This gives the authority a chance to require the operator to obtain its approval to the siting and appearance of the equipment or, in appropriate cases, to withdraw the permitted development right by means of an article 4 direction.[89] For further details, see the 2001 edition of PPG 8, *Telecommunications*, in particular Annex 1 to the Appendix, which attempts to explain the prior approval procedures.

---

[80] 1992 Order, Sch.1, Pt 1, Class 6, para.6(2)(d) (dwellinghouses), Pt 21, Class 68, para.68(2)(f) (other cases).

[81] 1993 Order, Sch.1, Pt 1, Class G, para.G.1(f) (dwellinghouses), Pt 18, Class A, para.A.1(g) (other cases).

[82] Under s.33 of the Communications Act 2003. This is the successor to the system of licensing of public telecommunications operators under s.7 of the Telecommunications Act 1984 (repealed by s.147 of the 2003 Act).

[83] Communications Act 2003, s.106 ff. The Code is in Sch.2 to the Telecommunications Act 1984, as amended by Sch.3 to the 2003 Act. See **8.6.3**.

[84] A new Pt 24 was substituted for England by TCP (General Permitted Development) (Amendment) (England) Order 2001; a slightly different Pt 24 was substituted for Wales by SI 2002/1879. These were both amended by the Communications Act 2003 (Consequential Amendments Order 2003 (SI 2003/2155).

[85] para.A.1(i), (n), (o).

[86] para.A.1(l)(iii).

[87] Scotland: 1992 Order, Sch.1, Part 20, Class 67, as substituted by SSI 2001/266 and amended by SI 2003/2155. NI: 1993 Order, Pt 17, substituted by SR 2003/98.

[88] para A.2(4).

[89] See **7.4**. See PPG 8, *Telecommunications*, 2001, para.19.

Where prior approval is obtained for an installation, and the land in question is then included in a conservation area before the works are carried out, that does not have the effect of withdrawing the permission already given; the only option open to an authority that wants, in effect, to revoke the approval already given is to make an article 4 direction.[90]

12.7.4 The need for other consents

Where work is to be carried out to a listed building or a scheduled monument that happens to be in a conservation area, listed building consent or scheduled monument consent will be required as in other case.

Where a sign or advertisement is attached to a building in a conservation area, advertisements consent (but not planning permission) will be required—although if it is erected as part of a larger project (even, for example, the creation of a new shopfront), planning permission will be required as well.

12.8 Works affecting ancient monuments

12.8.1 The need for planning permission

In principle, planning permission is needed for works affecting an ancient monument, whether or not scheduled, just as in any other case. The significance of this is that, where a monument is scheduled, an application for scheduled monument consent will almost always be required, but that will be to the Secretary of State. Where planning permission is required, on the other hand, the application will be to the local planning authority. Secondly, by no means all ancient monuments and archaeological remains are scheduled. And a change of use, if it involves no physical works at all, might (at least in theory) need planning permission but not scheduled monument consent.

The High Court in *Burroughs Day v Bristol CC*[91] confirmed that, in considering whether building operations materially affect the external appearance of a building, it is appropriate to take into account whether it is listed or in a conservation area; and the same approach would presumably apply where building or engineering operations are proposed to an above-ground ancient monument. It is thus likely that most if not all works to an above-ground monument would be categorised as "development", requiring planning permission.

Works to below-ground archaeological remains would be development, requiring planning permission, if they can be categorised as "engineering operations".[92]

There are no special rules about permitted development relating to ancient monuments, save that the installation by Electronic Communications Code operators of antennas (including dish aerials) on a scheduled monument is not

---

[90] *R. (Orange PCS Limited and others) v Islington LBC* [2005] E.W.H.C. 963 Admin, May 9, 2005, upheld in the Court of Appeal, January 19, 2006—a decision that is interesting in relation to the prior approval process generally.

[91] [1996] 1 P.L.R. 78; see **12.4.2**.

[92] See **12.2.1**.

permitted development.[93] And the permitted development right to install closed-circuit television cameras (in England and Wales) does not apply to scheduled monuments.[94]

For the considerations that arise where a monument is scheduled after the making of a planning application but before the grant of planning permission, see *R. v West Oxfordshire DC, Ex p. Pearce Homes Ltd.*[95] Where on the other hand the scheduling takes place after the formal grant of permission, and scheduled monument consent is subsequently refused, compensation may be payable.[96] The interaction between planning permission and archaeological sites, and the special considerations that apply to the processing and determination of planning applications for proposals with archaeological implications, are considered further in following chapters.[97]

12.8.2 The need for listed building consent and conservation area consent

It is possible for a building that is listed under the Listed Buildings Act also to be a scheduled monument under the Ancient Monuments Act.[98] Thus some agricultural buildings, such as medieval barns or dovecotes, are both scheduled and listed, as are some bridges, urban buildings (for example, market halls and guildhalls) and, increasingly, industrial monuments.

Almost any works to a scheduled monument require scheduled monument consent.[99] However, if the monument is listed, listed building consent would not be needed as well.[1]

This avoids duplication of controls. It is in some cases unfortunate that, since applications for scheduled monument consent are determined solely by the Secretary of State, the conservation officers of the local planning authority, who may have considerable local knowledge, are not necessarily involved. However, planning permission will often still be required; and this will give the authority an opportunity to become involved.[2]

Similarly, where a building in a conservation area that is or is on the site of a scheduled monument is to be demolished, scheduled monument consent will be required but not conservation area consent.[3]

Where an ancient monument is not scheduled, but is listed or in a conservation area, works to it will of course need listed building consent or conservation area consent just as with works to any other building or structure.[4]

---

[93] 1995 Order, Sch.2, Pt 24, para.A.1(g)(iv), (h)(iii); see also **12.7.3**.
[94] 1995 Order, Sch.2, Pt 33, para.A.1(a).
[95] [1986] J.P.L. 523.
[96] See **15.4.3**.
[97] See **13.6.3**, **14.8** and **15.4.3**.
[98] See **Chapter 3** and **Chapter 6**.
[99] See **12.8.3**.
[1] P(LBCA)A 1990, s.61. [Scotland: P(LBCA)(S)A 1997, s.55; NI: P(NI)O 1991, art.44(8)(b).]
[2] See **12.8.1**.
[3] P(LBCA)A 1990, s.75(1)(c). [Scotland: P(LBCA)(S)A 1997, s.67(1)(c); NI: P(NI)O 1991, arts 55(1)(b), 44(8)(b).]
[4] See **12.3** to **12.7**.

12.8.3 The need for scheduled monument consent

Over and above the extra scrutiny given to planning applications affecting ancient monuments, extra protection is given to the most significant ancient monuments, in that, just as works to listed buildings require listed building consent as well as planning permission, so virtually all works affecting scheduled monuments require *scheduled monument consent*. This requirement was first introduced in its present form in 1979 as section 2 of the Ancient Monuments Act, which applies to England, Wales and Scotland. It replaced the previous system whereby the consent of the Minister was required for the carrying out of any works to a monument that was subject to an interim preservation notice or preservation order under the 1953 Act.[5]

Scheduled monument consent is required for almost any works affecting a scheduled monument. By virtue of section 2(2) of the Ancient Monuments Act, consent is in particular required for:

"(a) any works resulting in

- the demolition or destruction of a scheduled monument;
- any damage to it;

(b) any works for the purpose of:

- removing or repairing a scheduled monument or any part of it;
- making any alterations or additions to it; and

(c) any flooding or tipping operations on land in, or under which there is a scheduled monument."[6]

It will be readily appreciated that this is a much broader class of operations than those for which planning permission or listed building consent is required, especially bearing in mind that a "monument", and thus a scheduled monument, is defined to include:

(1) any machinery attached to the monument, if it could not be detached without being dismantled[7];

(2) the land on which the monument stands;

(3) any adjacent land which (in the opinion of the Secretary of State or English Heritage or any local authority) is essential for the support or preservation of the monument[8]; and

(4) any part of a monument as thus defined.[9]

This means in particular that works which interfere with the ground (such as soil moving, many agricultural operations, and the laying of a pipe or cable, as well as the erection of a new building or structure) will require scheduled monument consent. This is unlike the position with listed building consent, which is only

---

[5] See **1.2.4**
[6] Bullets added for clarity.
[7] AMAAA 1979, s.61(7).
[8] s.61(9).
[9] s.61(10)(b).

required for the carrying out of works that actually affect the listed building itself, not the ground in its curtilage.[10] In addition, by virtue of section 2(2)(a), consent is required for works that actually result in the demolition or destruction of or damage to all or part of a monument, even if the person responsible has no intention to bring about such a result.

The range of works for which consent is in fact sought is very wide—from minor repair works to an above-ground monument (such as repointing of stonework) through to a major new development proposal on a site with a below-ground scheduled monument in one corner.[11]

The corresponding requirement in Northern Ireland is now in art.4 of the Historic Monuments and Archaeological Objects (NI) Order 1995.

12.8.4 *Schedule monument consent granted by order*

Just as planning permission is granted automatically for certain categories of relatively minor development,[12] there are a number of operations affecting scheduled monuments which are normally of little consequence, and for which as a result scheduled monument consent is granted automatically, by means of an order made by the Secretary of State or the Scottish Ministers under section 3 of the Ancient Monuments Act. In England, such an order has to be the subject of consultation with English Heritage.

The categories of works that are currently granted consent in this way in England and Wales are listed in the Schedule to the Ancient Monuments (Class Consents) Order 1994.[13] The corresponding order for Scotland is SI 1996/1507; that Order should be consulted for the detailed wording of the various classes and the exceptions to each class.[14] The equivalent provision in Northern Ireland is the Historic Monuments (Class Consents) Order (Northern Ireland) 2001.

Class 1 comprises agricultural, horticultural and forestry works—including the tilling of domestic gardens and allotments. This is on the basis that such works are carried out regularly, so that they will not cause any new damage. Unsurprisingly, therefore, the consent applies only where the works are carried out at the same spot as others of the same kind that have been carried out at some time in the previous six years (not five years as in the 1981 Order).[15] Further, there are a number of specific categories of works which are excluded from the general consent under this Class—largely those which cause greater disturbance to the ground, or involve the erection or removal of buildings or walls. The Government

---

[10] *Cotswold DC v Secretary of State* [1985] J.P.L. 407 (see **12.5.3**).

[11] The annual number of applications in the four years from 1993–94 to 1996–97 was 901, 1,088, 971, and 950 respectively.

[12] See **12.2.2**.

[13] SI 1994/1381. This replaced the previous Order, made in 1981 and amended in 1984; but note that it is that (1981) Order that is reproduced at Annex 4 of PPG 16, and the current Order in WO Circ. 60/96.

[14] Reproduced as Annex 3 to PAN 42, which stated that the 1996 Order was "shortly" to be replaced. Classes I to V in Scotland are broadly similar to Classes 1 to 5 in England and Wales.

[15] The corresponding period in Scotland is also six years (but 10 years in the case of ploughed land); in Northern Ireland, it is three years.

has undertaken to review this Class, in an attempt to provide better protection of important archaeological sites from ploughing.[16]

Class 2 consists of coal mining[17] at a depth of greater than 10m—deep enough, that is, to have no impact on any archaeological material near the surface. This allows more than the previous Order, which only granted consent for mining deeper than 100m below ground.

Class 3 is essential works by the British Waterways Board for the functioning of a canal; and Class 4 is works for the repair or maintenance of any machinery—provided, in either case, that they do not involve any "material alteration" to a scheduled monument.[18] These are necessary because a monument is defined to include machinery attached to it.[19]

Class 5 is works urgently necessary for safety or health. They are only granted consent in this way, however, if they are limited to the minimum measures immediately necessary and if they are notified in writing (together with a justification for them) to the Secretary of State as soon as is reasonably practicable.[20] This is similar to the provisions under which urgent works to listed buildings can be justified,[21] save that there is no explicit requirement to prove that the same result could not be achieved by repair works or temporary support or shelter. Note that the carrying out of urgent works of this kind is specifically provided as a defence to a charge under section 2 of the Ancient Monuments Act[22], although under that section there is no requirement to prove that the works were the minimum necessary—if they were not, if it is difficult to see how they could be said to be "urgently necessary".

Under Class 6, consent is granted for any works executed by English Heritage. Since it is the body relied on by the Secretary of State in deciding whether to grant or withhold consent in every other case in England[23], there is little point in requiring it to recommend all its own proposals. This Class is significant, however, when it is remembered that over 400 monuments—including many of the most important ones—are managed by English Heritage. Such works, where they amount to "development", will also be permitted automatically by Part 26 of Schedule 2 to the TCP (General Permitted Development) Order 1995.[24]

The remaining classes relate to work authorised or approved under the Act itself; all were included for the first time in 1994. Class 7 permits the carrying out of exploratory works (approved by the Secretary of State or English Heritage) in connection with an application for full scheduled monument consent. Class 8 permits works for the maintenance or preservation of a monument as a result of

---

[16] *Review of Heritage Protection: The Way Forward*, DCMS, June 2004.

[17] Either by the British Coal Corporation or any holder of a license under the Coal Industry Nationalisation Act 1946, s.36(2). There is no corresponding class in Northern Ireland since there is no coal there.

[18] These are classes 2 and 3 in Northern Ireland.

[19] AMAA 1979, s.61(7); see **6.2.5**.

[20] Class 4 in Northern Ireland; notice is, obviously, to be given to the Department.

[21] P(LBCA)A 1990, s.9(3) (see **12.4.7**).

[22] See **19.6.6**.

[23] See **13.9.3**.

[24] See **12.2.2**.

an agreement made between the occupier of the monument and the Secretary of State or English Heritage, under section 17 of the Act.[25] Class 9 is works that are the subject of grant aid under section 24.[26] In each case, the works must have already been approved by English Heritage or by the Secretary of State, so there is little point in requiring them to be approved again. Class 10 consists of the placing of markers (not deeper than 300mm into the ground) by the RCAHMW[27], for the purpose of surveying the visible remains of a monument.

There is a power for consent granted by an Order this way to be subject to conditions[28]; that power has not yet been exercised.

The powers of entry relating to a grant of scheduled monument consent[29] apply equally to a grant of consent by an order under section 3.[30] This ensures that any finds that come to light may be recorded, and that if necessary the class consent can be withdrawn where it seems that the works being carried out in reliance on it are having an unacceptable effect on the monument. The Secretary of State can thus exclude the provisions of the Order in a particular case by a specific direction[31], so that a specific application has to be made for consent—a procedure that is analogous to an article 4 direction.[32] That power, too, appears not to have ever been exercised.

If the consent granted by an order is effectively revoked—either as a result of the order being amended, or by means of a direction being made under s.3(3)—and consent is subsequently applied for and is either granted subject to onerous conditions or refused, compensation is payable—by English Heritage, or by the Secretary of State in Wales.[33] This is similar to an award of compensation following the refusal of planning permission as a result of the imposition of an article 4 direction.[34]

12.9 Signs and advertisements

12.9.1 The need for planning permission

The erection of large advertisement hoardings, or fascias forming part of shopfronts, may be on a sufficiently substantial scale to amount to a building operation. And the use of a plot of land for advertising may be a material change in use.

---

[25] See **11.6.6**. This is the only one of this group of classes that applies in Northern Ireland (as Class 5).
[26] See **9.4.3**.
[27] The Royal Commission on Ancient and Historic Monuments in Wales. Class 10 also authorises such operations by the Royal Commission in England; it appears that the Order has not yet been amended to recognise the operational merger of that body into English Heritage (see **1.4.2**).
[28] AMAAA 1979, s.3(2).
[29] See **13.9**.
[30] ss 6(6), 6A(5).
[31] Under s.3(3).
[32] See **7.4**.
[33] s.9(1),(2),(3).
[34] As to compensation generally, see **15.4.3**.

Advertising may thus sometimes be properly classified as "development" under the Planning Act.

However, provided the advertising is properly authorised under the Advertisements Regulations, planning permission is deemed to be granted, and an application for planning permission is never needed.[35]

12.9.2 The need for listed building consent and scheduled monument consent

The display of insensitively designed or sited advertisements can spoil the appearance of a listed building, or detract from its setting. The erection of a sign or advertisement of any size on or attached to a listed building would almost always require listed building consent, as it would be likely to constitute an alteration which affected its special character.[36] This is so even if the display is for one reason or another outside the scope of the Advertisements Regulations.[37] And it has already been noted that the painting of a listed building in such a way as to draw attention to it, which might be done with the intention of advertising the presence of a commercial occupier, would usually listed building consent.[38]

On the other hand, the replacement of one sign on a listed building with another of similar design would not require listed building consent so long as it does not affect the special character of the building. And if a sign or advertisement is not actually attached to a listed building, it would not require listed building consent,[39] however much it might ruin its setting.

12.9.3 The need for advertisements consent

The principal method of controlling signs and advertisements is by means of the need for consent under the Town and Country Planning (Control of Advertisements) Regulations 1992, and the equivalent regulations for Scotland and Northern Ireland.[40]

Lack of space precludes a detailed examination of the precise mechanics of the control. Briefly, however, "express consent" is required from the local authority for the display of any advertisement unless either:

(1) it falls outside the scope of the Regulations altogether; or

(2) it is granted "deemed consent" by the Regulations.

The definition of "advertisement", which is in section 336 of the Planning Act,[41] is extremely wide:

---

[35] TCPA 1990, s.222. [Scotland: TCP(S)A 1997, s.184; NI: P(NI)O 1991, art.67(5).]

[36] See **12.4.4**.

[37] See **12.9.3**.

[38] See **12.4.5**.

[39] *Cotswold DC v Secretary of State and Pearson* [1985] J.P.L. 407.

[40] TCP (Control of Adverts) (Scotland) Regulations 1984 (SI 1984/467), and Planning (Control of Adverts) Regulations (NI) 1992 (SR&O No 448).

[41] Amended by Planning and Compensation Act 1991, s.20. [Scotland: TCP(S)A 1997, s.277; NI: P(NI)O 1991, art.2, amended by Planning (Amendment) (NI) Order 2003.]

"'Advertisement' *means* any word, letter, model, sign, placard, board, notice, awning, blind, device or representation, whether illuminated or not, that is:

[i] in the nature [of advertisement, announcement or direction; and]

[ii] employed wholly or partly for the purposes of advertisement, announcement or direction; and

without prejudice to the previous provisions of this definition, 'advertisement' *includes*:

[a] any hoarding or similar structure used, or designed or adapted for use, for the display of advertisements; and

[b] anything else used, or designed, or principally adapted principally for use, for such display;

and reference to the display of advertisements shall be construed accordingly."[42]

The word "device" means an emblem or "logo".[43] The definition explicitly includes blinds and awnings, to remove the confusion caused by contradictory decisions of courts in Scotland and England.[44] Perhaps surprisingly, the use of a hologram to display images on clouds can constitute a display of advertisements.[45]

This obviously covers a wide range of signs which are wholly unexceptionable. The 1992 Regulations accordingly provide, in regulation 5, that the display of an advertisement in any of the ten classes in Schedule 2 is outside control altogether, regardless of how much or little effect it may have on the appearance of the surrounding area. The classes are as follows:

(A) an advertisements displayed on or consisting of a balloon[46];

(B) an advertisements on enclosed land;

(C) an advertisements on or in a vehicle[47];

(D) an advertisement incorporated in the fabric of a building[48];

(E) an advertisements referring to an article for sale;

(F) an advertisement relating to a pending election[49];

(G) an advertisement required to be displayed by Parliament or by a statute;

(H) a traffic sign[50];

---

[42] Material in square brackets and emphasis added for clarity.

[43] *McDonald v Howard Cook Advertising Ltd* [1972] 1 W.L.R. 90, following *Arthur Maiden Ltd v Lanark CC (No. 1)* [1958] J.P.L. 417.

[44] *Glasgow DC v Secretary of State for Scotland* [1989] 1 P.L.R. 84 and *Westminster CC v Secretary of State* [1990] 1 P.L.R. 30.

[45] *Great Yarmouth BC v Secretary of State; Newport BC v Secretary of State for Wales* (1996) 74 P. & C.R. 147.

[46] *Wadham Stringer (Fareham) Ltd v Fareham BC* [1987] J.P.L. 715, and the Civil Aviation (Aerial Advertising) (Captive Balloon) Regulations 1984 (SI 1984/474).

[47] *Torbay BC v Gorvin* (1987), unreported.

[48] *Kensington and Chelsea RBC v Harvey Nichols* [2001] 3 P.L.R. 71, CA (shroud advertising, surrounding a building site).

[49] Including an election for the European Parliament or the Welsh Assembly.

[50] As defined by the Road Traffic Registration Act 1984; see the Traffic Signs Regulations and General Directions 2002.

(I)   the national flag of any country; and

(J)   an advertisement inside a building.

Schedule 2 to the Regulations should be consulted for the precise scope of each class—which (with one minor exception relating to balloons[51]) does not depend on whether the site is in a conservation area or within the curtilage or setting of a listed building or scheduled monument.

The corresponding provisions in Scotland are in regulation 3 of the 1984 Scottish Regulations; they are the same, except that advertisements in [English] Classes F, G and H are granted deemed consent rather than being exempt from consent altogether. In Northern Ireland, regulation 4 of and Schedule 2 to the 1992 (NI) Regulations are identical to those in England.

12.9.4 Deemed consent under the Advertisements Regulations

Perhaps the most important provision of the scheme of control is that deemed consent is granted automatically by regulation 6 for advertising in any of the Classes in Schedule 3 to the 1992 Regulations. The Classes including the following:

(1)   various official signs and advertisements;

(2)   miscellaneous small signs; small notices advertising trades and professions (such as doctors' brass plates); signs relating to churches, hotels and so on;

(3)   estate agents' boards[52]; site boards at building sites; advertisements for fetes, sales, and other temporary events;

(4)   illuminated signs on business premises in retail parks, advertising the business itself or the goods or services available there (other than in sensitive areas);

(5)   other signs on business premises, advertising the business or the goods or services available[53];

(6)   signs on forecourts of business premises[54];

(7)   advertisements on flags (excluding the display by housebuilders of flags in sensitive areas);

---

[51] Express consent is required within conservation areas, national parks, areas of outstanding natural beauty and the Broads for the display of an advertisement on a tethered balloon for any length of time (which elsewhere requires consent only if the display is for more than ten days in any year).

[52] *Porter v Honey* [1988] 1 W.L.R. 1420, HL, overturning [1988] J.P.L. 632.

[53] *Arthur Maiden Ltd v Lanark CC (No 1)* [1958] J.P.L. 417, and *Havering LBC v Network Signs Ltd* (1998), *The Times*, January 2, 1998.

[54] *Cooper v Bailey* (1956) 6 P. & C.R. 261, *Blakemore v Heron Service Stations Ltd* (1971) 22 P. & C.R. 601, and *Heron Service Stations Ltd v Coope* [1973] 1 W.L.R. 502, HL.

(8) posters on hoardings surrounding building sites (other than in sensitive areas)[55];

(9) four-sheet poster panels displayed on purpose-designed highway structures[56];

(10) Neighbourhood Watch signs;

(11) temporary signs to housebuilders' sites; and

(12) advertisements inside a building.

All these classes are subject to various limitations as to size and location; and advertisements (other than those in Classes 4, 7 or 12) are not normally granted deemed consent if they are illuminated. And there are slightly more restrictive provisions applying within conservation areas and other sensitive areas.[57]

The classes of advertisements granted deemed consent are drafted somewhat differently in Scotland, but the result is that there are equivalents to all of the English classes except 4A, 7, 9, 10 and 11.[58] The Northern Ireland Regulations are identical to the English ones save for the absence of Class 9.[59]

Deemed consent is also granted, under Class 13, for advertisements displayed on a site used for advertising on April 1, 1974.[60] In order to obtain consent under this heading, there must have been "no substantial increase in the extent, or alteration in the manner", of the use of the site for advertising since 1974. This allowed the display with deemed consent of a modern billboard on a gable end wall which had some years earlier been painted to form an advertisement.[61] And it may (exceptionally) allow the addition of illumination to a previously un-illu-minated advertisement.[62] The corresponding date in Scotland is August 16, 1948[63]; there is no similar provision in Northern Ireland.

As to the meaning of "site", this appears to be the parcel of land on which an advertisement is displayed, rather than the specific position within that parcel of land at which the advertisement is located.[64]

Finally, Class 14 grants deemed consent for advertisements that were granted express consent, after that consent has expired. In Scotland, the same result is achieved by regulation 19 of the 1984 Regulations. In Northern Ireland, however,

---

[55] *Wandsworth LBC v Mills and Allen Ltd* (1998) 76 P. & C.R. 214; *Postermobile PLC v Kensington and Chelsea RBC*, (2000) P. & C.R. 524; *Cal Brown v Hounslow LBC* [2002] 2 P. & C.R. 22; *Brent LBC v Maiden Outdoor Advertising*, 2002.

[56] Highways Act 1980, Pt VIIA.

[57] National parks, areas of outstanding natural beauty and the Broads.

[58] TCP (Control of Adverts) (Scotland) Regulations 1984, Sch.4.

[59] Planning (Control of Adverts) Regulations (NI) 1992, Sch.3, as amended by SR 1998. 147.

[60] Sch.3, Class 13.

[61] *Mills and Allen Ltd v City of Glasgow (No 2)* [1980] J.P.L. 409) following *Arthur Maiden Ltd v Lanark CC* (No. 2) [1958] J.P.L. 422.

[62] *R. (Maiden Outdoor Advertising) v Lambeth LBC* [2004] J.P.L. 820.

[63] TCP (Control of Adverts) (Scotland) Regulations 1984, reg.13.

[64] *Barking and Dagenham LBC v Mills and Allen Ltd* [1997] 3 P.L.R. 1, following *Scotts Restaurant PLC v City of Westminster* [1993] J.P.L. B34.

there is no equivalent provision, so that all express consents are effectively of indefinite duration.

A local planning authority may seek a direction under regulation 7 restricting the display of advertising in one of the above classes.[65] The effect of such a direction is somewhat similar to that of an article 4 direction[66]—that is, it means that an advertisement in the particular category can be displayed, but only if it has been the subject of a grant of express consent.

12.9.5 Discontinuance notices

Where an advertisement is being displayed with the benefit of deemed consent, a planning authority (in England, Wales and Scotland) may serve a discontinuance notice on the owner and occupier of the land and on the advertiser, requiring it to be removed, where it considers the removal to be necessary "to remedy a substantial injury to the amenity of the locality or a danger to members of the public".[67] It might well be expedient for an authority to use this procedure where a particular advertisement is disfiguring a conservation area or the setting of a listed building.

It is possible for an advertiser to appeal to the Secretary of State against a discontinuance notice.[68] If the advertisement to be discontinued was being displayed in 1948, any expenses incurred in complying with the notice can be recovered from the planning authority, although this right does not extend to reclaiming the present value of any future loss of income.[69]

By way of example, Westminster City Council used this procedure to try to bring about the improvement of the appearance of the Pimlico Conservation Area through the removal of illuminated box signs on hotels, and their replacement with more suitable signs.[70] This was considered by the court to be a perfectly reasonable aim; and it was noted that what is now regulation 4(1)(a) provided that, in exercising its powers under the Regulations in the interests of amenity, an authority was entitled to assess the general characteristics of an area disregarding any advertisements already being displayed there.

The Secretary of State, in dealing with any appeal against a discontinuance notice in such a case, therefore, should not just consider the merits or otherwise of the particular advertisement concerned, but should also bear in mind the prospective removal of others in the area.

Similarly, in *Cheque Point UK Ltd v Secretary of State*,[71] the Council had taken action to bring about the removal of a shopfront sign in a conservation area. The

---

[65] TCP (Control of Adverts) (Scotland) Regulations 1984, reg.11; Planning (Control of Adverts) Regulations (NI) 1992, reg.6.

[66] See **7.4**.

[67] reg.8(1); TCP (Control of Adverts) (Scotland) Regulations 1984, reg.14. As to service of a discontinuance notices generally, see *Swishbrook Ltd v Secretary of State* [1990] J.P.L. 137, 824 and *Nahlis v Secretary of State* [1995] 3 P.L.R. 95. There is no such procedure in Northern Ireland.

[68] reg.15(3); (Scotland) Regulations 1984, reg.21.

[69] TCPA 1990, s.223. [Scotland: TCP(S)A 1997, s.185; NI: P(NI)O 1991.]

[70] *Westminster CC v Secretary of State* [1988] 3 P.L.R. 104.

[71] [1996] 72 P. & C.R. 415.

Secretary of State, determining the appeal against the discontinuance notice, considered that the sign was out of keeping with the remaining original features of the shopfront surround, and was exposed to view from the frontages of wholly residential properties in an attractive square directly opposite the premises. The sign was thus "substantially injurious to the interests of amenity and incompatible with the conservation states of the locality". The court held that the Secretary of State had used the correct test.

The most recent example of the use of this procedure is *R. (Clear Channel UK Ltd) v Secretary of State*,[72] which related to advertisement panels surrounding a cleared site in a conservation area adjacent to a listed building. Express consent was granted (on appeal) for their display as a short-term expedient, and they subsequently obtained deemed consent under Class 13. Ten years later the planning authority brought about their removal by means of a discontinuance notice, which was the subject of an unsuccessful appeal to the Secretary of State; the decision of the inspector, who considered the display of the panels to harm the setting of the listed building and the conservation area, was upheld by the High Court.

12.9.6 Advertising in conservation areas

The 1990 Act itself specifically states that regulations may make special provision with respect to the control of advertisements in conservation areas.[73] In fact, however, the 1992 Regulations apply to land in conservation areas almost exactly as elsewhere, with only four minor exceptions, already noted.[74]

In general, local planning authorities have been advised that:

"It is reasonable to expect that more exacting standards of advertisement control will prevail in conservation areas ... Many conservation areas are thriving commercial centres where the normal range of advertisements on commercial premises is to be expected, provided they do not detract from amenity. [They] should use advertisement controls flexibly in such areas, so as to conserve or enhance particular features of architectural or historic interest."[75]

The guidance in PPG 15 and WO Circ. 61/96 is in similar terms.[76]

Specific advice has also been given on deciding applications and appeals involving poster sites:

"Poster advertising may be appropriate in the predominantly shopping and business parts of conservation areas, though particular care to ensure that the method of presentation of any posters displayed in a conservation area is compatible with the area's architectural or historic features is essential. In some areas, the smaller sizes of poster panel will be more appropriate to the scale of the buildings."[77]

---

[72] [2005] J.P.L. 704.
[73] TCPA 1990, s.221(1)(a); TCP(S)A 1997, s.183(1)(a). There is no such provision in Northern Ireland.
[74] See **12.9.3** and **12.9.4**.
[75] PPG 19, para.22; WO Tan 7, para.17 is similar.
[76] PPG 15, paras 4.31 and 4.32; WO Circ. 61/96, paras 36 and 37.
[77] PPG 19, Annex, para.14; WO TAN 7, Annex, para.A14.

It has also been explicitly recognised in the courts that the control of advertisements is one of the functions of a planning authority which must be carried out with special attention being given to the desirability of preserving or enhancing the character or appearance of any conservation area involved, most recently in *R. (Clear Channel UK Ltd) v Secretary of State.*[78]

And it has already been noted that the use of discontinuance notices may be appropriate in conservation areas.[79]

The Secretaries of State have also advocated the benefits of authorities liaising with traders and other advertisers in conservation areas, so as to explain their policies and seek cooperation.[80] If all else fails, they will be prepared to make a regulation 7 direction,[81] imposing stricter control. That has so far been successfully tried in relation to estate agents' boards in conservation areas in London and Bath.[82]

12.9.7 *Areas of special control of advertisements*

The definition by a local authority of an *area of special control* of advertisements may also be appropriate within all or part of a conservation area. This is an area within which the control of advertisements appears to be much stricter than elsewhere.[83]

Except in rural areas, however, the approval of the Secretary of State is needed before an area of special control can be defined. Current advice is that designation as a conservation area, although it may not be decisive, will be a material factor:

"For example, the proposed area may be a small enclave, in an otherwise mainly commercial city-centre, where there are important architectural, archaeological, historical or visual characteristics. Such an area might comprise the precincts of a cathedral and neighbouring ecclesiastical buildings, or a historic market-place".[84]

As to the relationship between conservation areas and areas of special control, the courts have held as follows:

"[it was] said that the conservation area was covered by the reference ... to the area of special control of advertisements, but this cannot be correct. An area of special control may well ... cover many areas which are not designated as conservation areas. Conservation is a separate and additional control, as is recognised by s.277(8) of the Act [now s.72]."[85]

The Government published in 1996 a consultation paper proposing to abolish areas of special control, arguing (correctly) that the extra control actually pro-

---

[78] [2005] J.P.L. 704. See also *South Hams DC v Secretary of State* [1988] 3 P.L.R. 57 at 59; *Westminster CC v Secretary of State* [1988] 3 P.L.R. 104 at 105.

[79] See **12.9.5.**

[80] PPG 15, paras 4.35, 4.36; WO Circ. 61/96, paras 40,41.

[81] See **12.9.4.**

[82] Generally granted deemed consent under Sch.3, class 3A.

[83] regs 18, 19; TCP (Control of Adverts) (Scotland) Regulations 1984, regs 8, 9. There is no equivalent designation in Northern Ireland.

[84] PPG 19, para.27; WO TAN 7, para.21. On areas of special control generally, see DoE Circ. 5/92 (WO Circ. 14/92), Annex, paras 22–24; PPG 19, paras 25–27; and WO TAN 7, paras 19–21.

[85] *South Hams DC v Secretary of State* [1988] 3 PLR 57, *per* Mr David Widdicombe Q.C., sitting as a deputy High Court judge, at p.60.

vided was almost none. The proposal was not pursued, however, as the amenity societies felt uneasy at the loss of even the apparent protection. The proposal will surface again, no doubt, in due course.

12.10 Procedure in cases of uncertainty

12.10.1 The need for planning permission

In a borderline case, the planning authority should be consulted as to whether planning permission is needed for proposed works. The authority may be willing to give an informal view; but a formal procedure is available to obtain a determination that is binding on it in the event of future disagreement, known as a certificate of lawfulness of proposed use or development (CLOPUD).[86] In the event of an unfavourable decision, it is possible to appeal to the Secretary of State.

Alternatively, in the case of works proposed to a listed building, it will often be prudent to submit an application for planning permission. An application for listed building consent will almost always be required anyway, and the two applications can therefore be submitted and processed at the same time—the same drawings can after all be used for both. If the building is unlisted, but in a conservation area, both the planning authority and any local amenity groups may be particularly vigilant to spot apparently unauthorised alterations; and the submission of an application may therefore avoid much trouble later on.

12.10.2 The need for listed building consent

There are two principal reasons why there may be doubt regarding the need for listed building consent to be obtained for works which are proposed or which have just been carried out. Either or both may quite properly give rise to considerable uncertainty.

First, there may be doubt as to whether the relevant building, object or structure involved is by virtue of section 1(5) of the Listed Buildings Act to be treated as being part of a listed building—that is, effectively, whether or not it is listed at all. This has been considered in some detail in **Chapter 4**; but the legal position, which was admitted by Nolan L.J. in *R. v Camden LBC, Ex p. Bellamy*[87] to be "by no means simple", means that doubts may well remain.

Secondly, even if the building is listed, or the object or structure is to be treated as part of a listed building, do the works proposed affect the character of the building as one of special architectural or historic interest? The decision must inevitably be one of fact and degree, which will equally inevitably lead sometimes to considerable dispute.

Here too, if in doubt, and particularly where the works concerned are likely to be unobjectionable, the safest course is usually to ask the local planning authority.

---

[86] Under TCPA 1990, s.192. If the works have already taken place, what will be needed is a certificate of lawfulness of existing use or development (CLEUD), under s.191. [Scotland: TCP(S)A 1997, ss 151, 150; NI: P(NI)O 1991, arts 83B, 83A, inserted by Planning (Amendment) (NI) Order 2003.]

[87] [1992] J.P.L. 255; see **4.3.3**.

It is, after all, the authority that decides whether or not to take enforcement action or to institute a prosecution if works are carried out for which listed building consent should (in its view) have been obtained. It is always possible, when served with a copy of a listed building enforcement notice, to appeal against it on the ground that consent was not required for the works.[88] But it is more sensible to ask for the authority's view in the first place.

However, this is not always straightforward, since the answer obtained will depend on the ability of the relevant officer of the authority to decide accurately what is the extent of the listing and, often more tricky in practice, his or her view of what affects the character of the building. Thus in one VAT case, the Customs & Excise were told by "the senior planning officer" in writing that certain internal works to a Grade I listed building did not require listed building consent, whereas the owner of the building had dealt with a different officer who had been "a good deal more difficult to satisfy than the one who wrote the letter".[89] Persistence may pay dividends.

In addition, it has recently been held (in the context of the Advertisements Regulations) that it is an abuse of process for a local authority to bring, or continue, a prosecution where the defendant has acted on the basis of an assurance by the authority's officers that consent was not required.[90] The same would presumably apply where officers indicate that listed building consent is not required. For that reason, it is preferable if at all possible to seek the authority's view by reference to plans of the building and written specifications of the works, and to obtain confirmation of the authority's view in writing.

Note that unauthorised development is merely a breach of planning control. This means that it may sometimes be appropriate for practitioners in borderline cases to advise a client to seek planning permission for development, after it has taken place, only if requested to do so by the planning authority or on receipt of a planning contravention notice.[91] To carry out works to a listed building without listed building consent is, by contrast, a criminal offence; any listed building consent obtained subsequently does not alter any existing liability.[92] To advise a client to carry out such works and only seek consent later would thus never be correct.

There is, however, no formal administrative procedure to enable an owner to ascertain definitively whether or not listed building consent would be required for a particular operation he or she has in mind. Any opinion offered by a local authority officer must, therefore, be just that—it will not and cannot legally bind the authority.[93] It is unfortunate that the Government's view is that the intro-

---

[88] P(LBCA)A 1990, s.39(1)(c), substituted by PCA 1991, Sch.3. [Scotland: P(LBCA)(S)A 1997, s.35(1)(c); NI: P(NI)O 1991, art.78(1)(b), substituted by Planning (Amendment) (NI) Order 2003.]

[89] *Owen v Customs and Excise Commissioners*, London Tribunal Centre, April 23, 2004 (transcript available on HM Revenue and Customs website) (see **17.3.4**).

[90] *Postermobile Ltd v Brent LBC* (1997) *The Times*, December 8, 1997.

[91] TCPA 1990, s.171C, inserted by PCA 1991, s.1. [Scotland: TCP(S)A 1997, s.125; NI: P(NI)O 1991, art.81A, inserted by Planning (Amendment) (NI) Order 2003.]

[92] See **Chapter 19**.

[93] *Western Fish Products v Penwith DC* [1981] 2 All E.R. 204.

duction of a formal certificate procedure equivalent to certificates of lawfulness of proposed development[94] is "unnecessarily complex" and "confusing"[95]—the more so since just such a procedure exists in Northern Ireland.[96]

English Heritage has recently made plain its support for guidelines issued jointly by itself, the local planning authority and the owner of a listed building, to indicate those works which would not affect the character of the building, and which would thus not require consent. This might be helpful in some cases—for example, large 20th-century buildings—but cannot be definitive. See the research report produced in 2003 for English Heritage entitled *Streamlining Listed Building Consent*.[97]

12.10.3 The need for conservation area consent

The same considerations would apply to the need to obtain conservation area consent—particularly following the *Shimizu* decision.[98] As with listed building consent, there is no formal mechanism to obtain a determination that is binding on the planning authority.

12.10.4 Action for a declaration

One remaining possible course of action is to seek a declaration, in the Chancery Division of the High Court, to put the matter beyond challenge—either as to whether a particular building or structure forms part of a listed building, or whether particular works to a listed building affect its character.

The Court has a discretionary power to make a binding declaration, whether or not any other remedy is being claimed.[99] When considering whether the power should be exercised, the Court should take into account the justice to the claimant, the justice to the defendant, whether the declaration would serve any useful purpose, and whether there are any other special reasons why such an order should be made.[1]

It is likely that such an action would involve a dispute as to facts, so that a Pt 7 claim would be appropriate; see **Form D12** in Appendix D for a sample particulars of claim. However, litigation of this kind is time-consuming and expensive, with uncertain results, and should not be embarked upon lightly or without legal advice.

---

[94] See **12.10.1**.
[95] (*Hansard* (HL) Deb, January 29, 1991, col 668.
[96] P(NI)O 1991, art.48. There is a fee of £45 for such an application (Planning (Fees) Regulations (NI) 2005, reg.17). This formal procedure is apparently very rarely used; see *Streamlining Listed Building Consent*, English Heritage, 2003, para.5.4.10.
[97] Issued in June 1995.
[98] See **12.6.4**.
[99] Civil Procedure Rules, Part 40, r.20.
[1] *Financial Services Authority v Rouke*, *The Times*, November 12, 2001; see also *Wallersteiner v Moir* [1974] 1 W.L.R. 991, CA, *per* Scarman L.J. at p.1031

Chapter 13

Works affecting Historic Buildings and Monuments: Application Procedures

13.1 Introduction

13.1.1 Overview

Once it has been determined which of the various forms of permission and consent are required before a project can be lawfully carried out (as spelled out in detail in **Chapter 12**), the next step is to seek the necessary consents—unless planning permission is granted automatically by the General Permitted Development Order, scheduled monument consent by the Class Consents Order or deemed advertisement consent by the Advertisements Regulations.[1]

In the great majority of cases, where a proposal involves works being carried out to listed buildings, it will be necessary to seek both planning permission and listed building consent. Where it involves works that affect the setting of a listed building, but do not actually affect the listed building itself, or works in a conservation area, it will usually require planning permission only—but conservation area consent may exceptionally be needed where it includes the demolition of all or most of an unlisted building in a conservation area. And if a proposal involves signs or advertisements, express consent under the advertisements regulations may be needed as well.

In all of these cases, the relevant permission or consent will have to be sought from the relevant planning authority.[2] And where more than one type of consent is required, in practice they are sought together, and the applications are processed together, and determined alike—advice from central government is, rightly, that this is generally preferable for both the applicant and the authority.[3] First, though, it may in some cases be well worth considering pre-application discussions with the authority (see **13.2**). The appropriate applications must then be made, containing sufficient detail to enable the authority to be certain precisely

---

[1] See **12.2.2, 12.8.4, 12.9.4** respectively.
[2] In Northern Ireland, the Planning Service of the Department of the Environment ("the Department") (see **13.2.1**).
[3] PPG 15, para.2.12; WO Circ. 61/96, para.8.

what is proposed, and to evaluate the likely impact of the proposal in question (**13.3**).

The authority will then acknowledge receipt of the applications (**13.4**), publicise them, and notify those who are likely to have useful views (see **13.5** and **13.6**). The procedures relating to the submission and determination of applications for listed building consent are particularly complex and bureaucratic; they are accordingly summarised diagrammatically in **Figure 13.1**.

Occasionally, but only rarely, the Secretary of State (in England), the Welsh Assembly or the Scottish Ministers will call in applications for their own decision. Much more commonly, the authority itself will either grant permission or consent or it will refuse them (**13.7**). Where permission or consent is granted, either by the authority or the Secretary of State, it will be subject to conditions (**13.8**). As to the basis on which such applications are determined, this is in principle a matter of policy rather than law; but that has been the subject of considerable litigation in recent years—considered in **Chapter 14**.

A quite different procedure relates to the submission and determination of applications for scheduled monument consent. These are to be made not to the planning authority but to the Secretary of State or equivalent (**13.9**).

Special rules apply to the submission, processing and determination of applications for permission and consent made by central government departments and English Heritage on Crown land, and by local authorities; also for works that are the subject of an application for an order under the Transport and Works Act 1992 (see **13.10**).

Finally, once permission and consent have been granted, they can (in theory) be revoked or modified (**13.11**).

13.1.2 The sources of the procedural requirements

The rules governing the submission and processing of planning applications (that is, applications for outline and detailed planning permission, approval of reserved matters and approval of details) have been developed over many years. In relation to England and Wales, the relevant primary legislation is now to be found principally in sections 62 to 67 and 91 to 96 of the Planning Act. However, it should be noted that these sections were significantly amended by the Planning and Compulsory Purchase Act 2004. Some of the relevant provisions in that Act are already in force in England; the remainder are expected to come into force during 2006.

At least as important as the Act itself is the secondary legislation made under powers in it—including in particular the TCP (Applications) Regulations 1988 and the TCP (General Development Procedure) Order 1995. The 1995 Order has also been significantly amended, at least in England, as a result of the changes in the 2004 Act; further changes are expected to come into force in 2006, when the 1988 Regulations will be revoked.[4]

---

[4]   The relevant statutory instrument will now be made under s.62 of the TCPA 1990, as inserted by s.42 of the 2004 Act. A draft (the (TCP) General Development Procedure) (Amendment No.2) (England) Order 2005) was published in March 2005, along with *Changes to the Development Control System: Second Consultation Paper.*

As is becoming increasingly common with new legislation, the new arrangements are expected to come into force in Wales slightly after England; practitioners in Wales therefore need to check the current position as to what is in force, and as to the extent to which the secondary legislation, once introduced, is the same there as in England.

These rules are discussed comprehensively in standard texts on planning law. They are designed to apply in a wide variety of circumstances, some of which are irrelevant in the context of the subject matter of this book. This chapter accordingly focuses on those matters that are most relevant in that context—particularly bearing in mind that planning applications will often be submitted and determined in parallel with applications for listed building and other consents.

Planning applications in Scotland and Northern Ireland are governed by the TCP (General Development Procedure) (Scotland) Order 1992 and the Planning (General Development) Order (NI) 1993—each amended several times since first made.

The rules of procedure regarding applications for listed building consent are likewise to be found in several places. First, sections 10–26 of the Listed Buildings Act provide the basic rules. This was one of the happier results of the 1990 consolidation, since these sections replaced the rather obscure provisions of Schedule 11 to the TCPA 1971.[5] Secondly, section 10(3) of the Act gives the Secretary of State powers to make regulations setting out detailed procedures. The regulations currently in force are the Planning (Listed Buildings and Buildings in Conservation Areas) Regulations 1990.[6] These provisions of the Act and the Regulations will also be significantly amended by the 2004 Act, with effect from late 2005 or early 2006.[7]

Thirdly, the Secretary of State is also empowered to give directions exempting certain types of application from compliance with some of those procedures.[8] The directions currently in force in England are included within Circular 01/01, which on February 19, 2001 replaced those in DoE Circular 14/97.[9] The directions in force in Wales are in WO Circular 1/98, which came into force on March 2, 1998, replacing the directions in WO Circular 61/96[10]; there are (in a few cases) significant differences from those applying in England.

The procedures for handling applications for listed building consent in England were set out in tabular form in Part II of PPG 15, Annex B; but this must now be read alongside the Table in Appendix A to Circular 01/01, which helpfully

---

[5] See **1.2.6**.

[6] SI 1990/1519; referred to throughout this book as P(LBCA) Regs 1990; see **1.3.2**.

[7] A draft of the relevant statutory instrument (Planning (Listed Buildings and Conservation Areas) (Amendment) (England) Regulations 2005) was published in March 2005, along with *Changes to the Development Control System: Second Consultation Paper*. Again, similar regulations will no doubt be published in due course for Wales.

[8] P(LBCA)A 1990, s.15.

[9] The directions in Circ. 14/97 had themselves on October 1, 1997 replaced those in DoE Circ. 18/87 (which had remained in force despite the cancellation of the policy content of that Circular by PPG 15).

[10] Which had in turn replaced those in WO Circ. 61/81.

summarises the requirements for notification, consultation and referral. For Wales, the corresponding references are Annex E to WO Circular 61/96 and Appendix A to WO Circular 1/98.

The sources of the procedural rules regarding conservation area consent are as for listed building consent, although the 1990 Act is slightly modified in its application to conservation areas by Schedule 3 to the 1990 Regulations.[11] The comments in Annex B to PPG 15 regarding listed building consent applications are specifically extended to apply to conservation area consent except where otherwise stated.[12]

Procedures for listed building and conservation area consent applications in Scotland and Northern Ireland are governed by the TCP (Listed Buildings and Buildings in Conservation Areas) (Scotland) Regulations 1987[13] and the Planning (Listed Buildings) Regulations (NI) 1992.[14]

The procedure for applications for scheduled monument consent is prescribed in the Ancient Monuments (Applications for Scheduled Monument Consent) Regulations 1981.[15]

The procedure for the submission and determination of applications for express consent for signs and advertisements is provided for in the relevant Control of Advertisements Regulations.[16]

13.2 Preliminaries

13.2.1 The planning authority

An application for planning permission or listed building or conservation area consent in England or Wales should be made to and determined by "the local planning authority".[17] That will in general be the district or borough council in England.[18] In Wales, it will generally be the county or county borough council.[19] In a national park it will be the national park authority[20]; and in the Broads, the Broads Authority.[21]

In the area of the Thurrock Urban Development Corporations and part of the area of the Thames Gateway Corporation, with effect from October 2005, those

---

[11] P(LBCA)A 1990, s.74(3).
[12] PPG 15, para.4.25; Pt 3 of WO Circ. 61/96 is similarly extended by para.32.
[13] SI 1987/1529.
[14] SR&O (NI) 263.
[15] See **13.9**.
[16] See **13.5.10**.
[17] TCPA 1990, s.62(1); P(LBCA)A 1990, s.10(1).
[18] TCPA 1990, s.1(1)(b), (2); P(LBCA)A 1990, s.81, Sch.4, para.2.
[19] TCPA 1990, s.1(1B), inserted by the Local Government (Wales) Act 1994, s.18; P(LBCA)A 1990, s.81, Sch.4, para.1(2).
[20] TCPA 1990, s.4; s.4A(2), inserted by the Environment Act 1995, s.67; P(LBCA)A 1990, s.81, Sch.4, para.3.
[21] TCPA 1990, s.5; P(LBCA)A 1990, Sch.4, para.5.

corporations have been designated as local planning authorities, but only for major planning applications (defined in the relevant planning functions orders[22]). However, throughout their areas, the corporations have been designated as planning authorities for all functions relating to listed buildings (but not applications for conservation area consent).[23] This means that a proposal for works to a listed building may need to be the subject of an application for planning permission made to the appropriate district council and an application for listed building consent to the development corporation.

Once permission or consent has been granted (or purported to be granted), its validity cannot be questioned on the ground that it should have been granted by some other authority.[24]

Applications are thus in most cases to be determined formally by district or borough planning authorities. However, in certain areas some, or even almost all, applications are referred to the county council (where there is one), as it will have the necessary specialist expertise.[25]

In Scotland applications should be made to the "planning authority".[26]

As for Northern Ireland, it has a unitary system of planning control—so that all applications for planning permission, listed building and conservation area consent, and advertisements consent are made to the Planning Service of the Department in Belfast. References to "the planning authority" should be understood accordingly.

In addition, authorities may in some cases call upon the advice of English Heritage, Cadw or Historic Scotland, even where they are not obliged to consult them formally—although limitations on resources may mean that such advice will only be forthcoming in exceptional circumstances.

For simplicity, the remainder of this chapter generally refers to "the planning authority"—this should be understood to be "the local planning authority" in England and Wales, "the planning authority" in Scotland, and the Department in Northern Ireland. And references to "the Secretary of State" should be understood to be to the Welsh Assembly or the Scottish Ministers as appropriate.

13.2.2 Pre-application discussions

Before submitting a formal application for planning permission or listed building consent, a prospective applicant should always consider whether it might be fruitful to have a preliminary meeting with the appropriate planning authority (see above). Wherever possible, such a meeting should be with the officers of the authority who will actually deal with the application—including, where possible, the conservation officer. It may also usefully involve officers of the county

---

[22] Thurrock Development Corporation (Planning Functions) Order 2005 (SI 2572), art.3; London Thames Gateway Development Corporation (Planning Functions) Order 2005 (SI 2721), art.4.

[23] Thurrock Development Corporation (Planning Functions) Order 2005 (SI 2572), art.4, Sch.; London Thames Gateway Development Corporation (Planning Functions) Order 2005 (SI 2721), art.5, Sch.

[24] TCPA 1990, s.286(1); P(LBCA)A 1990, Sch.4, para.6.

[25] See **1.4.3**.

[26] TCP(S)A 1997, s.1; P(LBCA)(S)A 1997, s.9.

authority, English Heritage, Cadw or Historic Scotland (see above). Advice from central government encourages such early consultation in relation to development proposals affecting historic buildings and areas, as well as liaison with English Heritage in appropriate cases.[27]

Preliminary meetings could be either on site—which is preferable, at least for the first meeting—or at the authority's offices. In the latter case, detailed photographs of the buildings should be available. The timing of a pre-application meeting needs thought. It should be after sufficient details of the proposed works have been considered for the scheme to be clear, but before it has become unchangeable. Note that, where an officer expresses a view as to the outcome of an application, that does not commit the authority. And such involvement does not disentitle the officer concerned from taking part in the processing of a subsequent, identical application.[28]

The House of Lords (in *McCarthy & Stone (Developments) v Richmond-upon-Thames LBC*[29]) made it clear that it was not lawful for authorities to make a charge for such meetings. However, that decision has now been overturned by section 53 of the Planning and Compulsory Purchase Act 2004, which enables planning authorities to charge for performing any of their functions, and for doing anything incidental to those functions.[30] It remains to be seen how authorities will exercise their new powers.

Applicants in Wales should note that it is particularly important to obtain any advice from Cadw prior to the submission of a formal application, as its professional officers will not take part in informal discussions once an application has been submitted unless the planning authority is also represented. Further, if the Secretary of State is considering whether to call-in an application, officers of Cadw will not engage in discussions with either applicants or the authority. This apparently unco-operative stance is simply the inevitable result of Cadw's position as an executive agency within the Welsh Assembly Government.[31] The same problem may occur in relation to Historic Scotland.

It will also often be sensible for those contemplating works to buildings to discuss them with any neighbours likely to be affected and (in appropriate cases) with national and local amenity societies and residents groups—they are likely to be consulted anyway by the planning authority,[32] and it is prudent for applicants to seek their support at an early stage, to avoid problems later. Such consultation may also lead to constructive suggestions for modifications at an early stage.

---

[27] See PPG 15, para, 2.11; WO Circ. 61/96, para.6.
[28] *R. v Canterbury CC, Ex p. Cox* [1993] E.G.C.S. 159.
[29] [1992] 1 P.L.R. 131.
[30] TCPA 1990, s.303, as amended by Planning and Compulsory Purchase Act 2004, s.53 (with effect from March 7, 2005).
[31] WO Circ. 61/96, paras 100–102.
[32] See **13.4, 13.5**.

13.2.3 Applications for works to scheduled monuments

It is highly likely that development affecting a scheduled monument will need scheduled monument consent (from the Secretary of State) as well as planning permission.[33] It would therefore be prudent for the two applications to be submitted and considered concurrently; any alterations needed to obtain one consent will need to be considered in connection with the obtaining of the other.

13.3 Submission of applications to the planning authority

13.3.1 Overview

Any application to a planning authority for permission or consent will require:

- a completed application form;

- a completed ownership certificate;

- material identifying precisely the land and buildings involved, and describing what is proposed;

- (from early 2006) a design and access statement;

- in the case of an application for planning permission or advertisements consent,[34] a fee;

- in the case of a planning application for a major proposal, an environmental assessment; and

- other relevant supporting material as appropriate.

Each of these is considered in turn.

Where applications are submitted at the same time for more than one type of consent, the same drawings and supporting material can obviously be used for each; but the number of copies will need to take into account all the relevant procedural requirements. In particular, planning applications require a total of four copies of the application form and each drawing, and applications for listed building consent require three copies; if both applications are submitted together, that will therefore require four copies of one form, three of the other, seven copies of the drawings, and two copies of the design and access statement and other supporting material.

The significance in law of the various requirements described here is currently governed by the ruling of the Court of Appeal in *Main v Swansea*[35]—which held that the validity of a planning permission should not hinge on the distinction between serious and minor irregularities, but should be judged in the light of all the circumstances, the nature and effect of the irregularity, the identity of the complainant and the time that has elapsed before the complaint.

---

[33] See **12.8**.
[34] Or listed building or conservation area consent in Northern Ireland.
[35] (1985) 49 P. & C.R. 26, CA.

However, this may change—at least in England and Wales—once the new arrangements introduced by the Planning and Compulsory Purchase Act 2004 are in place (probably in late 2005 or early 2006). That Act inserts a new section 327A into the Planning Act, which provides that a planning authority "must not" entertain an application for planning permission or advertisements consent if it does not comply with relevant requirements as to the matters to be submitted.[36] This will also apply to applications for listed building and conservation area consent.[37] It is likely that the courts in future will be much less lenient towards failures to comply with procedural requirements.[38]

The existence of s.327A makes all the more disturbing a slightly odd decision of the Court of Appeal, in *Fenland DC v Reuben Rose (Properties) Ltd*,[39] in which it was held that the court—either the County Court or the High Court—did have jurisdiction to entertain an application by a planning authority for an injunction to prevent works being carried out to a listed building, even though they had apparently been the subject a grant of planning permission and listed building consent by the authority some four years earlier, because the issue of the consent had been flawed by a procedural irregularity (albeit one relating to the processing of the application rather than its initial submission). Judge L.J. thus in effect held that the validity of a listed building consent (and thus, presumably also a planning permission) could in principle be questioned long after its issue by this route—which could of course be extremely inconvenient for a developer who was in possession of what it understandably took to be a perfectly valid consent. However, he explicitly recognised that the granting of an injunction was discretionary; and left open the question of whether that discretion should be exercised in favour of the council or the developer.[40]

On that basis, and bearing in mind the presumed intention of Parliament in enacting section 327A, it may be that in the future the courts will be more inclined to quash permissions and consents where they are based on applications that are subsequently found to have been improperly made or processed.

13.3.2 Application forms

Each application must be submitted on the relevant form which should be obtained from the appropriate planning authority.[41] There is currently no standard form; each authority (or in some cases each group of authorities) issues its own—not least so that the information supplied on it can then be recorded onto computer. And some authorities already allow information to be submitted

---

[36] TCPA 1990, s.327A, to be inserted by Planning and Compulsory Purchase Act 2004, s.42(5)

[37] P(LBCA)A 1990, s.89(1), to be inserted by 2004 Act, s.42(9).

[38] See, for example, the attitude of the court in *R. (Wall) v Brighton* [2005] 1 P. & C.R. 33 in relation to the new requirement to give reasons for permissions (see **13.7.8**).

[39] [2000] P.L.C.R. 376, CA.

[40] It is understood that the Council took the hint, and proceeded no further with the matter.

[41] TCP (Applications) Regulations 1988, reg.3(1)(a)(i); P(LBCA) Regs 1990, reg.3(1). [Scotland: TCP (General Development Procedure) (Scotland) Order 1992, art.3(a); P(LBCA) (S) Regs 1987, reg.3(1).]

on an electronic form. Note that there may be a few authorities still issuing "listed building consent" forms for use with applications for conservation area consent.

Part of the new arrangements to be introduced by the 2004 Act in England and Wales, probably during 2006, will be standardised application forms. It is expected that there will in future be, in principle, one form for each type of application, which can be downloaded from the web and completed electronically. This will require an applicant to supply only the information that is relevant to the type of proposal concerned—so that, for example, someone seeking permission to build a new hospital will have to answer many more questions than someone seeking a small residential extension. There will also be new application forms for listed building and conservation area consents, and advertisements consent, constructed on a similar basis.

A range of forms in hard copy will still be available for those who require them. And existing forms issued by authorities will still be acceptable for a transitional period (probably lasting a year) following the introduction of the new ones.

Applications for planning permission in England and Wales require a total of four copies of the relevant form.[42] In Scotland, they require as many as specified by the planning authority, up to a maximum of four[43]; and in Northern Ireland, a total of seven copies, unless the Department indicates otherwise.[44] Applications for listed building and conservation area consent require three.[45] And if two applications are being submitted at the same time (for example, for planning permission and listed building consent), the two forms to be completed will be similar in concept, but different in detail.

13.3.3 Ownership certificates

If the applicant is not the owner of the building that is to be altered or demolished, or the land on which development is to be carried out, the planning authority will wish to know the views of the person who does own it. By virtue of section 65 of the Planning Act and section 11 of the Listed Buildings Act, therefore, every application for planning permission, listed building or conservation area consent must be accompanied by one copy of a certificate indicating the ownership of the building. This will be evidence of one of the following:

(1) that the applicant is the only owner of the building (Certificate A);

(2) that the applicant has informed all the other owners of the building of the application (Certificate B);

(3) that the applicant has informed all the other known owners of the building of the application, and has taken reasonable steps (in practice, usually by inserting a notice in the local press) to notify the unknown owners of it (Certificate C); or

---

[42] TCP (Applications) Regulations 1988, reg.3(1)(c). This is not expected to change with the new requirements to be introduced in 2006 (see footnotes 4 and 7 above).
[43] TCP (General Development Procedure) (Scotland) Order 1992, art.3(c)(ii).
[44] Planning (General Development) Order (NI) 1993, art.7.
[45] P(LBCA) Regs 1990, reg.3(1). This too is not expected to change with the new requirements to be introduced in 2006. [Scotland: P(LBCA) (S) Regs 1987, reg.3(1).]

(4) that the applicant does not know of any of the owners of the building, but has taken reasonable steps to notify them of the application (Certificate D).

The "owner" in this context means anyone who, 20 days before the date of the application, had a freehold interest in the building, or a leasehold interest with at least seven years unexpired. The certificates and notices to be used are set out as Schedule 2 to the General Development Procedure Order (planning applications) and Schedule 2 to the 1990 Regulations (applications for listed building and conservation area consent).[46]

To submit a false certificate deliberately or recklessly is a criminal offence, punishable by a fine of up to level 3.[47] Hitherto, the submission of an incorrect certificate has only rarely invalidated any permission or consent eventually granted, following the decision of the Court of Appeal in *Main v Swansea CC*.[48] However, a permission will be quashed where it arises from an application accompanied by a certificate known to be false. Thus, in *R. (Pridmore) v Salisbury DC and Docking*,[49] the Court held that it is one thing to fail to give notice of an application to an unidentified owner of part of the land, as in *Main*, but quite another to certify that notice had been given on a stated date (Certificate B), knowing that notice had not been given either on that date or at all. It is likely that the attitude of the courts will in any event be less lenient once the new arrangements introduced by the 2004 Act are in place (probably in 2006).[50]

In order that, having thus been notified, the owners (as defined above) have a chance to make representations, the authority must not determine the application until 21 days have elapsed since the last owner was informed of the application or since it was advertised in the press (whichever was the later). And when it does determine the application, it must also take into account any such representations made within the 21-day period.[51]

If two applications are being submitted at the same time (for example, for planning permission and listed building consent), two ownership certificates will need to be completed.

An application for advertisements consent does not need to be accompanied by an ownership certificate.

The equivalent provisions for Scotland and Northern Ireland are in section 35 of the Scottish Planning Act and section 10 of the Scottish Listed Buildings Act; and article 22 and paragraph 3 of Schedule 1 to the Northern Ireland Order.[52]

---

[46] Welsh language equivalents are at Sch.2 to SI 1995/3336 (planning applications) and Sch.2 to SI 1990/1147 (applications for listed building and conservation area consent).

[47] s.11(6).

[48] (1985) 49 P. & C.R. 26. See **13.3.1**.

[49] [2005] J.P.L. 655, 1 P. & C.R. 32.

[50] TCPA 1990, s.327A, to be introduced in England and Wales by s.42(5) of the 2004 Act; see **13.3.1**.

[51] TCP (General Development Procedure) Order 1995, art.19; P(LBCA)A Regs 1990, reg.6(3).

[52] The certificates are in TCP (General Development Procedure) (Scotland) Order 1992, Sch.3 (planning applications) and P(LBCA) (S) Regs 1987, Sch.2 (LBC and CAC applications); and Sch.2 to the Planning (General Development) Order (NI) 1993.

13.3.4 *Material identifying the land and buildings involved, and describing what is proposed*

Any application must identify the land or buildings to which it relates, and must describe what is proposed—whether by plans, drawings, photo-montages, models or other material—at a suitable level of detail.[53] This is so that it is possible for the planning authority and others to assess properly the impact of what is proposed, and for all (including subsequent purchasers of the land involved) to see precisely what is the subject of any permission or consent that may eventually emerge.

Where works are proposed to alter or extend listed buildings, the drawings and supporting material required for the listed building consent application will need to be in considerable detail, including specifications of materials and proprietary products to be used in any new works or repairs, and will therefore almost certainly be adequate for the planning application as well. The most recent guidance suggests:

"The Secretary of State considers that, to avoid any doubt about what is required by way of information from an applicant, authorities should set out at the beginning of discussions exactly what information they will require to enable them to consider an application for listed building consent. For all but the simplest work this should normally include a plan to identify the building in question; measured drawings of all floor plans; and external or internal elevations affected by the proposed works. Drawings should also show the building as existing and as proposed. The inclusion of photographs is particularly helpful—in relation to all elevations in demolition cases, or of the part of the building affected (interior or exterior) in alteration or extension cases. Other plans and drawings as are necessary to describe the works proposed would be helpful."[54]

This new guidance is said to be by way of "clarification" of previous advice[55] but in fact it adds little—although it echoes the comments of the inspector, supported by the High Court, in *Stocks Hotel v Secretary of State*.[56]

It is sensibly proposed that all drawings will in future have to be to an identified scale, and show the direction of north.[57]

The photographs referred to need not be taken professionally, but should clearly show the architectural details of the building.

Planning applications for works affecting conservation areas and listed buildings, whether or not they are accompanied by applications for other types of consent, will be subject to the same rules as to the submission of forms and supporting material.[58] But in practice the requirements of planning authorities as to the amount of information that should be submitted about the materials and details of proposed development will often be more demanding in such cases than elsewhere.

---

[53] TCP (Applications) Regulations 1988, reg.3(2) (planning applications); P(LBCA) Regs 1990, reg.3(1) (LBC and CAC applications).

[54] App. C to Circ. 14/97, repeated in App B to Circ. 01/01; App. C to WO Circ. 1/98.

[55] At para.B.3 of Annex B to PPG 15, and para.104 of WO Circ. 61/96.

[56] [1996] E.G.C.S. 165 (see **13.4.1**).

[57] Draft TCP (General Development Procedure) (Amendment) (No. 2) (England) Order 2005, art.5, and draft Planning (LBCA) (Amendment) (England) Regulations 2005, reg.3, annexed to *Changes to the Development Control System: Second Consultation Paper*, ODPM 2005.

[58] TCP (Applications) Regulations 1988, reg.3.

Some authorities are tempted to seek from applicants an excessive amount of supporting information—further or more detailed drawings and so forth—before they will render an application as valid. The legitimacy of this practice was considered by the Court of Appeal in *R. v Secretary of State, Ex p. Bath and NE Somerset DC*.[59] The Court held that applicants for planning permission and listed building consent should provide appropriate detail with their applications, and co-operate with planning authorities; however, it held, if an applicant is aggrieved by a request for what is perceived to be an excessive information, he may appeal to the Secretary of State, who may determine the question of the validity of the application as well as that of the desirability of the proposal.

In the case of an application for outline planning permission, details need not be supplied of the reserved matters.[60]

13.3.5 Design and access statements

The changes to be introduced by the 2004 Act will for the first time require in most if not all cases applicants to submit with applications for planning permission in England and Wales:

"(a) a statement about the design principles and concepts that have been applied to the development; [and]
(b) a statement about how issues relating to access to the development have been dealt with".[61]

However, the requirement will probably not apply to applications for engineering or mining operations, changes of use, or (more significantly) development within the curtilage of a dwellinghouse other than within a designated area such as a world heritage site or conservation area.[62]

It is envisaged that all applications for listed building and conservation area consent will be subject to a requirement in virtually identical terms.[63]

Similar requirements are to be introduced into Northern Ireland by the Planning Reform (NI) Order 2006.

The new statutory provision is drafted by reference to two statements. However, the Government's intention is that this requirement will take the form of applicants for permission or consent having to submit a single "design and access statement". The level of detail required in such a statement will depend on the scale and complexity of the application; where it relates only to householder development, for example, it could be very short. As to its content, the intention is as follows:

---

[59] [1999] 2 PLR 120, CA, upholding *The Times*, January 28, 1999, [1999] J.P.L. B160.
[60] TCP (Applications) Regulations 1988, reg.3(2); see **13.3.9**.
[61] TCPA 1990, s.62(5), inserted by 2004 Act, s.42(1).
[62] Draft TCP (General Development Procedure) (Amendment) (No. 2) (England) Order 2005, art.6, annexed to *Changes to the Development Control System: Second Consultation Paper*, ODPM 2005.
[63] P(LBCA)A 1990, s.10(4), inserted by 2004 Act, s.42(8); draft Planning (LBCA) (Amendment) (England) Regulations 2005, reg.4, annexed to *Changes to the Development Control System: Second Consultation Paper*.

"the design component of a statement would cover seven elements:

- response to context. This means how the physical, social, economic and policy context of the development has informed its design in relation to each of the six other design elements below;
- quantum or amount of development proposed for each use...
- use or mix of uses proposed;
- layout, the buildings, routes and open spaces proposed within the development, and their relationship to buildings and spaces outside the development;
- scale, height and width of each proposed building;
- appearance, aspects of a building or place which determine the visual impression it makes, including the external built form of a development; and
- landscaping, enhancement or protection of the amenities of the site and the area in which it is situated, including screening and planting.

Where an application for listed building consent was involved, the design component of a statement would cover use, layout, scale and appearance. In addition, it should include a brief explanation of how design policies and approaches have taken account of paragraph 3.5 of PPG 15 *Planning and the Historic Environment*, and in particular:

- the historic and architectural importance of the building;
- the particular physical features of the building that justify its designation as a listed building;
- the building's setting.

The access component of a statement would cover the following points:

(a) the policy or approach adopted to access, and how policies relating to access in local development documents have been taken into account;
(b) what, if any, consultation has been undertaken as to the access and what account has been taken of the outcome of any such consultation;
(c) how any specific issues which might affect access to the development have been addressed;
(d) how prospective users will be able to access the development from the existing transport network, and why the main points of access to the site and the layout of access routes within the site have been chosen; and
(e) how features which ensure access to the development will be maintained.

This information should be integral to the statement, and should be dealt with within any of the seven elements listed above, and not just the access section.

Where an application for listed building consent was involved, the statement would include components (a) (explanation of policy and approach to access), (b) (details of consultation), and (e) (maintenance policies), along with the following:

- a brief explanation of how the approach to access takes account of the building being listed, with reference to paragraph 3.5 of PPG 15; and
- a brief explanation of the range of access solutions considered, including an explanation of any specific issues affecting access to the listed building."[64]

It is likely that this the introduction of this requirement (probably during 2006) will be accompanied by policy advice from central government, which will need to be checked to see how it interprets the requirement. It remains to be seen whether it gives rise to the growth of a body of litigation similar to that which followed the introduction of the requirement for environmental impact assessment.

---

[64] *Changes to the Development Control System: Second Consultation Paper*, paras 2.27–2.31.

The new requirement does not (yet) operate in Scotland or Northern Ireland on a statutory basis; but it is likely that authorities there will appreciate the submission of such a statement on a voluntary basis, by way of justification for what is proposed.

Where it is proposed to replace a building that is listed or in a conservation area with a new building, the quality of the replacement will be a material consideration.[65] Details of that replacement should accordingly be submitted with the application for listed building or conservation area consent.

13.3.6 Fees

A fee is required with an application for planning permission or advertisements consent, calculated in accordance with the current scale.[66] The only exception is where the proposed development requires specific permission because of either a condition on an earlier permission or an article 4 direction.[67]

There is no fee payable for an application for listed building or conservation area consent, except in Northern Ireland.[68] But if an application for planning permission or advertisements consent is submitted at the same time, the correct fee (if any) should be submitted with it, otherwise both applications may be delayed.

13.3.7 Environmental statements

Prospective developers are required to carry out comprehensive environmental assessment of any proposed development or other project of any consequence. In order to determine what proposals are of consequence for these purposes, it is necessary to consider not just the nature and scale of the proposal, but also the importance and sensitivity of the area in which it is to take place. Thus, a minor proposal in a highly sensitive location can be as significant, and thus as deserving of careful assessment, as a much more major one in a much less sensitive site.

This principle is reflected in the European directive on environmental impact assessment[69], which has been transposed into UK domestic legislation in the form

---

[65] See **14.4.7, 14.7.6**.
[66] The current regulations are the TCP (Fees for Applications and Deemed Applications) Regulations 1989, as amended by the TCP (Fees [etc.]) (Amendment) (England) Regulations 2005 (SI 2005/843) with effect from April 1, 2005. At the previous round, separate Amendment Regulations were issued for Wales; no doubt they will be this time too. [Scotland: TCP (Fees [etc.]) (Scotland) Regulations 2004 (SI 2004/219); NI: Planning (Fees) Regulations (NI) 2005 (SR 2005/222).]
[67] TCP (Fees [etc]) Regulations 1989, regs 5, 6. Scottish Regulations, regs 5, 6.
[68] Planning (Fees) Regulations (NI) 2005, reg.15 (the fee is £50).
[69] Directive 85/337 (OJ L175/40), art.4, substituted by Directive 97/11.

of a suite of regulations, relating to various categories of projects.[70] Under the principal regulations, relating to the carrying out of development that requires planning permission, a planning application must be accompanied (or followed) by an environmental statement where the development to which it relates is within one of the categories in Schedule 1 to the Regulations (that is, really major ones). An environmental statement will also be required in relation to an application for a project that.

- is within one of the categories in Schedule 2 (of which the most significant in the present context is probably "infrastructure projects"[71]), and

- is either within a sensitive area (including a world heritage site[72] or a scheduled monument), or is such that its scale exceeds certain prescribed thresholds set out in the Schedule, and

- is likely to have significant effects on the environment by virtue of its nature, size and location—by reference to the matters set out in Schedule 3, which include the characteristics of the proposed development, and the environmental sensitive of the geographical areas likely to be affected by it, having regard to (amongst other things) landscapes of historic, cultural or archaeological significance.

As to the third of these, the key issue is whether the effects of the proposed development are likely to be "significant"—whether beneficial or adverse: "in this context benefit, like beauty, is in the eye of the beholder".[73]

Where there is any doubt as to whether a project is one that requires the submission of an environmental statement, a screening opinion may be obtained from the planning authority.

Where a statement is required, it must contain as far as is reasonable the material prescribed in Schedule 4, including:

"1. A description of the development, including in particular (a) a description of the physical characteristics of the whole development and the land-use requirements during the construction and operational phases...
2. An outline of the main alternatives studied...

---

[70] The relevant regulations applying in England are as follows: SI 1999/293, amended by SI 2000/2867 (projects requiring planning permission); SI 1999/367 (fish farming in marine waters); SI 1999/369 (highways); SI 1999/1672 gas pipelines); SI 1999/1783 (land drainage); SI 1999/2228 (forestry); SI 1999/2892 (nuclear reactors); SI 1999/3445 (harbour works); SI 2000/1927 (electricity works); SI 2000/2190 (Transport and Works Act proposals), and SI 2001/3966, SI 2002/2127 (projects on uncultivated and semi-natural land). Most of these either apply in Wales, Scotland and Northern Ireland, are have equivalents that do.

[71] Including industrial estates, shopping centres, car parks, sports stadiums, leisure centres, multiplex cinemas, other urban development projects, railways, airfields, roads, harbours and ports, inland waterways, dams, tramways, light railways, pipelines, aqueducts, coastal defence works, groundwater abstraction, and motorway service areas (see TCP (Environmental Impact Assessment) (England and Wales) Regulations 1999, Sch.2, Class 10.)

[72] See **2.3**.

[73] *British Telecommunications PLC v Gloucester City Council* [2002] J.P.L. 993, at para.69.

3. A description of the aspects of the environment likely to be significantly affected by the development, including, in particular, population, fauna, flora, soil, water, air, climatic factors, *material assets, including the architectural and archaeological heritage*, landscape and the relationship between the above factors.
4. A description of the likely significant effects of the development on the environment, which should cover the direct effects and any indirect, secondary, cumulative, short, medium and long term, permanent and temporary, positive and negative effects of the development...
5. A description of the measures envisaged to prevent, reduce and where possible offset any significant adverse effects on the environment.
6 A non-technical summary of the information provided under paragraphs 1 to 5..."[74]

For further details, see DoE Circular 02/99 and WO Circular 11/99. The other regulations, relating to projects that do not require the submission of planning applications, are broadly similar.[75]

These requirements have given rise to a good deal of litigation in recent years, much of which is beyond the scope of this book.[76] However, the impact of proposed development on listed buildings, conservation areas, ancient monuments, and the cultural heritage generally, will clearly be a significant element both in the assessment of whether an environmental assessment is required at all and, if it is, in the statement that will need to be produced.

13.3.8 Other supporting material

In many cases, a design and access statement will be required; and in the case of major developments, an environmental statement will also need to be produced.[77] But it is still necessary for applicants to consider whether they need to submit additional material, to explain what is proposed, and why it is either necessary or desirable. This may not always be needed—where, for example, a proposal is routine, and obviously sensible; or where it has been the subject of discussion with the planning authority, indicating that there will be no problem. In other cases, however, more elaborate supporting material may be necessary. And it is not sensible to wait for the planning authority to ask for extra material, which may lead to delay.

In particular, policy as to works to listed buildings is contained in PPG 15:

"Applicants for listed building consent must be able to justify their proposals. They will need to show why works which would affect the character of a listed building are desirable or necessary. They should provide the local planning authority with full information, to enable [it] to assess the likely impact of their proposals on the special architectural or historic interest of the building and on its setting."[78]

---

[74] 1999 Regulations, Sch.4—emphasis added.
[75] See footnote 70 above.
[76] See, in particular, *Berkeley v Secretary of State (No. 1)* [2002] 1 A.C. 603, [2001] Env. L.R. 16, (2001) 81 P. & C.R. 492, [2000] 3 All E.R. 897, HL, overturning [1998] 3 P.L.R. 39, P.L.C.R. 97, CA; *R. (Prokopp) v London Underground Limited and others* [2004] 1 P. & C.R. 31, CA, reversing [2003] E.G.C.S. 119; and the other decisions helpfully summarised in the *Encyclopedia of Planning Law* paras 3B–949.362.1 et seq.
[77] See **13.3.6** and **13.3.7**.
[78] para.3.4; WO Circ. 61/96, para.69.

The same would in principle apply to applications for planning permission and conservation area consent.

As to what should be covered by such supporting material, it should be sufficient to ensure that the planning authority has all the information it needs (as opposed to wants[79]) on all the topics that are relevant to the particular proposal. This might be, for example, very detailed drawings of a particular doorway; or a photomontage showing how a new building will fit in with a conservation area; or samples of the materials to be used; or examples of other similar projects successfully completed. The following Chapter highlights some of the issues that have arisen in particular cases that have reached the courts; but what are the key issues in relation to any particular proposal will obviously need to be considered on a case-by-case basis.

In particular, in certain cases—where, for example, it is being argued that it is not economically viable to restore a building, or to keep it in its existing use—it may be sensible for an applicant to submit a financial appraisal of the proposed works; for an example, see **Form D12** in Appendix D.[80]

Where proposed development affects a site of archaeological significance, whether or not scheduled, it is important that sufficient detail accompanies the planning application to enable the planning authority, and anyone it consults, to make an informed decision. The matters to be considered will be:

(1) an assessment of what archaeological material is actually present;

(2) the possibility of preserving that material *in situ*;

(3) the likely impact of the proposal on the archaeological value of the site;

(4) the possibility of mitigating that impact;

(5) the recording of the material prior to and during the course of the development.

The production of such supporting material will be in the form of an assessment, involving desk-based research, and an evaluation, using the results of fieldwork where necessary. The Institute of Field Archaeologists have produced relevant standards and guidance as to what is required at each of the two stages.[81]

13.3.9 Outline applications

Finally, where an applicant wishes to know the views of the planning authority on the principle of a particular category of development on a site, without having to go to the trouble and expense of submitting all the details at the outset, it is possible to make an outline planning application. By this mechanism, the applicant can specify that the siting, design, external appearance, means of access and

---

[79] *R. v Secretary of State, Ex p. Bath and NE Somerset DC* [1999] 2 P.L.R. 120, CA, upholding *The Times*, January 28, 1999, [1999] J.P.L. B160 (see **13.3.4**).

[80] And see **14.4.6**.

[81] And see PPG 16, paras 20–22, and WO Circ. 60/96, paras 12–14.

landscaping—or any combination of them—are to be reserved for subsequent approval.[82]

It is likely that this will not often be suitable in relation to proposals involving historic buildings and areas, as a decision on the acceptability or otherwise of the details is in most cases an integral element in the determination of the application.[83] Some authorities indeed will not accept outline applications in some or all of their conservation areas. An authority is entitled to do this wherever it is of the opinion that in a particular case an outline application for planning permission would be unsuitable, because the general principle involved "ought not to be considered separately from all or any of the reserved matters".[84]

Where an authority has required more details under this procedure, an applicant can either provide them, or else immediately appeal to the Secretary of State—as if the application had been non-determined. The six-month period for making such an appeal starts with the date on which the demand was made.[85] The Secretary of State can also ask for more details in any event.

It is noticeable that the planning applications that were considered in *Ward v Secretary of State*[86] and *Unex Dumpton v Secretary of State*[87] were both outline applications—highlighting the potential for difficulty and confusion that can arise.[88]

On the other hand, it may sometimes be appropriate for a planning authority (or the Secretary of State) to grant outline permission in such cases. Thus, in *Gloucester City Council v Secretary of State*,[89] a developer submitted one outline planning application and one detailed application in respect of land at Gloucester Docks; and the Secretary of State granted the former but refused the latter. The council appealed against the grant of permission, on the ground that the proposal affected two conservation areas, and the setting of several listed buildings, and could not possibly be determined in the absence of a detailed scheme. The court rejected that proposition. Provided the decision maker is satisfied that an appropriate design could in principle be achieved, it is perfectly proper to leave the preparation and approval of that design to the stage of the approval of reserved matters.

The provisions as to outline applications are in any event to be tightened up as part of the reforms introduced by the Planning and Compulsory Purchase Act 2004.[90]

---

[82] TCPA 1990, s.92 [Scotland, TCP(S)A 1997, s.59; NI: P(NI) O 1991, art.35].

[83] PPG 15, para.4.18.

[84] TCP (General Development Procedure) Order 1995, art.3(2); see PPG 15, para.4.18. [Scotland: TCP(GDP)(S)O 1992, art.4(3); NI: Planning (General Development) Order (NI) 1993, art.8(2).]

[85] art.23(2)(c).

[86] [1990] 1 P.L.R. 85.

[87] [1990] 2 P.L.R. 1.

[88] See **14.7.2**.

[89] [2001] J.P.L. B380. For the subsequent approval of reserved matters, see *British Telecommunications PLC v Gloucester City Council* [2002] J.P.L. 993.

[90] See *Changes to the Development Control System: Second Consultation Paper*, ODPM 2005.

The distinction between a grant of outline permission and a grant of full permission subject to a condition requiring some details to be approved subsequently by the planning authority[91] is that the latter will arise from a full planning application, with all details supplied (including in relation to those matters as to which the authority wishes to see more information)—whereas an outline application does not need to contain any details of the reserved matters. Once permission has been granted, however, the distinction between the two types of permission is often far from clear in practice.

It is not possible to submit an outline listed building or conservation area consent application—although, again, it is possible for a planning authority to grant consent subject to a condition requiring details to be approved subsequently.

13.4 Processing of applications by the planning authority

13.4.1 Initial action by planning authority

Once an application has been received, the authority must check that it has been validly made—that is, that it contains the required forms, drawings, photographs and other details as appropriate, ownership certificate, fee, design and access statement (where relevant), and other relevant supporting material.[92]

Once the planning authority is satisfied that an application has been validly made, it must acknowledge receipt of it as soon as reasonably practicable.[93] A form of acknowledgement is set out as one of the Schedules to each of the relevant regulations.[94]

In practice, many applications are accompanied by drawings which are either missing one or two details, or simply generally insufficient to explain and justify what is proposed; the authority may therefore ask the applicant for any further details it requires.[95] The matter is well summarised in WO Circular 61/96:

"Drawings are the principal record of changes to historic buildings, and the foundation of proper control. They will also make the consultation on procedure more effective. Local planning authorities should not accept applications with inadequate drawings."[96]

On the other hand, this approach should not be pushed too far—a realistic approach must be adopted as to how much information is really necessary, as opposed to merely desirable.[97]

---

[91] See **13.8.4**.
[92] See **13.3**.
[93] TCP (General Development Procedure) Order 1992, art.5; P(LBCA) Regs 1990, reg.3(2). [Scotland: TCP (GDP) (S) O 1992, art.12.]
[94] TCP (GDP)O 1995, Sch.1, Pt I (planning applications); P(LBCA) Regs 1990, Sch.1, Pt I (LBC and CAC applications); Welsh language equivalents are at Pt I of Sch.1 to SIs 1995/3336 and 1990/1147 respectively. [Scotland: TCP (GDP) (S) O 1992, Sch.6.]
[95] P(LBCA)A 1990, s.10(2); P(LBCA) Regs 1990, reg.3(3).
[96] para.103: there is no corresponding guidance in England.
[97] *R. v Secretary of State, ex p. Bath and NE Somerset DC* [1999] 2 P.L.R. 120, upholding *The Times*, January 28, 1999, [1999] J.P.L. B160; see **13.3.4**.

Where drawings are submitted which an authority considers are inadequate, it should say so promptly. Thus in *Stocks Hotel v Secretary of State*,[98] the council had refused planning permission and listed building consent for a new wing to be added onto as 18th-century listed building in the Chilterns, and the inspector agreed that the submitted drawings were barely adequate. However, although he went on to dismiss the appeal on its merits, he awarded costs against the council for its failure to use its powers under s.10 of the Listed Buildings Act to give advance notice of the degree of detail required in the plans and drawings accompanying the application.

Guidance was issued by the ODPM in March 2005 on the validation of planning applications, in relation to the existing legislation. The requirements are to be slightly tightened up as part of the package of reforms introduced by the Planning and Compulsory Purchase Act 2004.[99]

13.4.2 Checking that permission or consent is necessary

As a matter of good practice, a planning authority should check that the relevant permission or consent is actually required for the works proposed.[1] In particular, it has already been demonstrated that there can be considerable uncertainty both as to whether a particular structure is or is deemed to be listed[2] and as to whether the works will affect its character. It is therefore not surprising that applications are sometimes submitted unnecessarily, arising from either an excess of caution or a mistaken interpretation of the law.

Clearly, if the authority forms the view that permission or consent is not required, the applications should be promptly returned, together with any supporting material submitted (although it may be prudent to retain one set of drawings for reference in the event of any subsequent complaints)—and any fee paid.

13.4.3 Repeat applications

A planning authority may decline to determine an application for planning permission or listed building or conservation area consent where it is similar to (that is, the same or substantially the same as) one previously made without success. This power is designed to prevent the submission of repeated applications with the intention of, over time, wearing down opposition to undesirable proposals.

It is thus now possible for a planning authority in England to decline to determine an application for permission or consent where during the previous two years:

(1) the Secretary of State has called-in a previous, similar application, and refused it; or

---

[98] [1996] E.G.C.S. 165.
[99] Draft TCP (General Development Procedure) (Amendment) (No. 2) (England) Order 2005, art.7, annexed to *Changes to the Development Control System: Second Consultation Paper*, ODPM 2005.
[1] See **Chapter 12**.
[2] See **Chapter 4**.

(2) the Secretary of State has dismissed an appeal in respect of a similar application; or

(3) the authority has refused more than one similar application, without an appeal having been made.[3]

This power, as it relates to declining to determine planning applications the first two of these situations, was introduced by the Planning and Compensation Act 1991, and still applies in that form in Scotland and Northern Ireland.[4] It was more recently significantly extended by section 43 of the Planning and Compulsory Purchase Act 2004—in particular, so as to add the third to the list of cases in which the power may be exercised, and to extend the procedure to applications for listed building and conservation area consent. Section 43 was brought into force in England on August 24, 2005, and will no doubt be brought into force in Wales shortly. Policy advice is in ODPM Circular 08/2005.

A similar change is to be introduced in Northern Ireland by the Planning Reform (NI) Order 2006.

13.4.4 Consultation and publicity

Once an authority has accepted an application as valid, before it even starts to consider whether to grant or refuse listed building consent, it must give publicity to the application, and give notice of it to national and local bodies with access to specialist knowledge and wider experience, as well as those likely to be immediately affected (in particular those living and working in nearby properties).

It will thus be helpful for authorities to consult those known to have a special interest or expertise in the area, the particular type of building or materials involved, or the actual building itself. Local amenity groups, architects, local historians, and many others all may have valuable contributions to make. So too may county council officers, even where they are not directly involved. Often the national amenity societies or the Civic Trust may be able to provide names of relevant experts. And it may well be appropriate for applications for proposals affecting a conservation area to be referred for comment to the conservation area advisory committee.[5]

In some areas, although not required to do so by law, district planning authorities also notify county authorities of proposals affecting historic buildings and areas. This enables the specialist conservation officers in the county authority to provide helpful advice, both to the district authority and to the applicant. The proportion of applications notified in this way varies from nil in some districts to almost all in others.

In addition to such professionals and experts, local residents' groups and individuals living or working nearby may have comments to make. These will vary considerably in value—from uninformed "not in my back yard" reaction to

---

[3] TCPA 1990, s.70A, as substituted by Planning and Compulsory Purchase Act 2004, s.43, and P(LBCA)A 1990, s.81A, as inserted by 2004 Act, s.43.

[4] Scotland: TCP(S)A 1997, s.39; NI: P(NI)O 1991, art.25A, inserted by Planning (Amendment) (NI) Order 2003, art.20.

[5] See **5.3.3**.

sensible contributions; but much goodwill may needlessly be lost if it is perceived that local people are not being kept informed. The Secretaries of State have stated that they "attach particular importance to the activities of the voluntary sector in heritage matters, and hope that local authorities will work in close co-operation with national and local amenity bodies and draw on their expertise to the full".[6]

Further, in the event of any subsequent appeal, the support of both informed professional opinion and those with local knowledge may be of great assistance to the authority.

In order to ensure that at least a reasonable amount of informed professional input is available in at least the most significant cases, there are a number of special requirements as to publicity and notification, highlighted in the following sections—**13.5** relates to proposals affecting listed buildings, and **13.6** to other proposals. The procedure for listed building consent applications in England and Wales is shown diagrammatically in **Figure 13.1**. But these should be in practice merely the minimum; and authorities should consider carefully how far to publicise each application on a case-by-case basis.

The process of notification and publicity was recently considered by the Court of Appeal, in *R. (Wainwright) v Richmond-upon-Thames LBC*. As to the placing of advertisements in the local press (generally in small print in the "Statutory Notices" section of newspapers circulating in the relevant area), which is a feature of a number of the statutory requirements catalogued below—the court commented:

"While it is unlikely that, for the most part, individuals read such notices, the notices are of value to local interest groups who tend to look out for such notices in the local press and, in my judgment, would have found the notices sufficient to prompt further enquiries and, if appropriate, make representations to the council."[7]

As to mailing local people, it emphasised that this must be done carefully—so that, for example, more than one letter is put through the letterbox in houses in flats.

The court also confirmed in the same case that the duty to publicise something must encompass a duty to consider representations received in response to such a notice, since there would otherwise be no point in representations being made if they were not going to be considered.

Finally, it must not be forgotten by those responding to such consultation and publicity that their role is only to make an input into the decision-taking process. So, for example, they may perfectly properly say "the erection of an extension on the east side of the house will spoil that elevation and diminish the overall interest of the building as the last unaltered villa of its kind in this area ..." That may be a helpful and accurate viewpoint. However, in many cases, in practice such representations conclude "... and the application should therefore be refused." It may be that the conservation issues are the only issues at stake, in which case such a proposal should indeed be refused. But it may be that there are other considerations involved, pointing the other way. A proper conclusion might thus be

---

[6] PPG 15, Annex A, para.A. 17.
[7] *R. (Wainwright) v Richmond-upon-Thames LBC, The Times*, January 16, 2002, CA, at para.26.

Figure 13.1 Listed building consent applications in England and Wales: summary of procedures

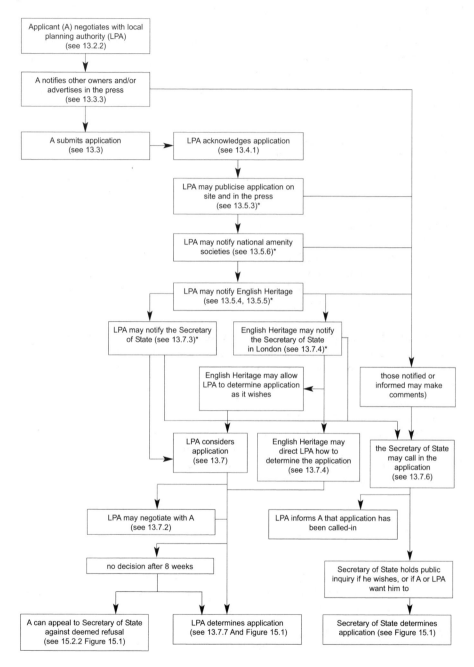

Note: The stages indicated with an asterix only occur in certain cases; see the relevant text for details

that a proposal is slightly undesirable on conservation grounds, but hugely desirable for some other reason, so that on balance it should be permitted. That balancing exercise is thus for the planning authority or the Secretary of State, not for the interest group.

Indeed, arguably, a specialist lobby group—whether in the interests of building conservation or the preservation of newts—is the last person to make a disinterested assessment of the overall merits of a proposal. It can fight its corner, but it must not seek to imply that its specialist interest is of necessity the *only* material consideration; it may be, but it may well not be.[8]

13.4.5 *Notification of major proposals to the Commission for Architecture and the Built Environment (CABE)*

The Commission for Architecture and the Built Environment (CABE) is the successor to the Royal Fine Arts Commission, which was wound up in 2001. It was initially a limited company, but became a statutory body, operating in England and elsewhere as it thinks appropriate, upon the passing of Part 8 of the Clean Neighbourhoods and Environment Act 2005.

The functions of CABE include the promotion of high standards in architecture and the design, management and maintenance of the built environment, and to that end providing advice and developing and reviewing projects (whether or not it is requested to do so). The built environment includes any structure or area built or designed for human use (such as squares, parks and recreation areas), and any area available for public use in the vicinity of such a structure or area.[9] One way in which it discharges its functions is to review the design of projects which have been submitted for planning permission; it is also devoting a high proportion of its efforts to becoming involved in projects at an early stage, helping clients, designers and planning authorities to achieve the best possible quality.

The Government agreed, in a letter of May 15, 2001 from DETR to planning authorities, that CABE should be a non-statutory consultee for the purposes of planning applications. However, because it has limited resources, CABE wishes to be consulted only in connection with projects which are significant in some way. These may include the following:

(1) proposals which are significant because of their size or the uses they contain (including large buildings or groups of buildings, infrastructure projects, and major changes in the public realm such as pedestrianisation schemes);

(2) proposals which are significant because of their site (including those which affect important views—into a world heritage site, for example—or are site so as to give rise to exceptional effects on their locality);

(3) proposals with an importance than their size, use or site would suggest (including those which are likely to establish a pattern for future devel-

---

[8]   *Georgiou v Enfield LBC* [2005] J.P.L. 62 (see **5.3.3** and **14.9.1**).
[9]   Clean Neighbourhoods and Environment Act 2005, s.88.

opment, and those which are out of the ordinary because of their scale, form or materials).

In the present context, it may be appropriate for authorities to consult CABE about significant proposals affecting world heritage sites, conservation areas and the setting of important listed buildings and scheduled monuments—as early as possible, and indeed quite possibly prior to the submission of a formal application.

Any consultation with CABE is wholly separate from any consultation or notification that may be carried out as a result of the various statutory requirements described in the following two sections.

13.5 Publicity for proposals affecting listed buildings

13.5.1 Publicity for planning applications and notification of neighbours

There is no specific requirement for planning applications for works affecting listed buildings to be publicised any more than any other planning applications. However, all planning applications must be publicised by the planning authority at least to some degree—the extent of such publicity depending on the scale of what is proposed.[10]

A planning application for development that is such that either it requires an environmental statement[11] or it is not in accordance with the development plan or it affects a public right of way must be publicised both by placing an advertisement in the local press and by displaying a notice on or near the site.

An application for other major development (including residential development of 10 or more houses, or on a site of more than ½ hectare; other development creating more than 1,000 sq. m. of floorspace, or on a site of more than 1 hectare) must be publicised both by advertising in the local press and by either displaying a site notice or a serving a notice on the owners and occupiers of any land adjacent to the site of the proposed development. As to which of the latter is more appropriate, it will depend on how much interest is likely to be generated by the proposal[12]; it could be argued that more extensive publicity would be appropriate for a proposal affecting one or more listed buildings.

All other planning applications must be publicised by either a site notice or a notice served on adjoining owners and occupiers.

In each case, any site notice must be displayed for at least 21 days; and the planning authority must take reasonable care to protect it from defacement. And the notice placed in the local press or sent to neighbouring owners and occupiers must provide a period of at least 21 days in which responses can be sent to the planning authority.[13] When determining the application, the authority must also

---

[10] TCP (General Development Procedure) Order 1995, art.8.
[11] See **13.3.7**.
[12] See Circ. 15/92, *Publicity for Planning Applications.*
[13] TCP (General Development Procedure) Order 1995, Sch.3.

take into account any representations made in responses to the publicity and notification made within the 21-day period.[14]

This requirement is taken seriously by the courts. Thus, in *R. v Bolsover DC, ex p. Paterson*,[15] the owner of Brookhill Hall in Derbyshire (listed Grade II) was proposing to replace an existing wooden garage with a new, large brick one. The conservation officer, in the course of preliminary discussions, had agreed that the proposed structure would not significantly affect either the setting of the Hall or that of the separately listed Coach House. However, when the application was submitted, the officer carrying out the notification had failed to spot that the Coach House and the Groom's Cottage (both former outbuildings of the Hall) were separately occupied, and had failed to notify them.

The owner of the Coach House successfully sought judicial review to have the resulting grant of planning permission quashed, the Court accepting that he and the owner of Groom's Cottage were entitled to have a proper opportunity to put their case properly to the Council—even though such arguments might not prevail.

In Scotland, it is the applicant for planning permission (not the planning authority) who must notify the owners and occupiers of adjoining or nearby land of proposed development.[16]

In Northern Ireland, the Department is to publish in the local press a notice of every planning application it receives in a conservation area, and elsewhere every application other than one for the improvement or alteration of a dwellinghouse or the provision or alteration of a building or enclosure within its curtilage.[17]

13.5.2 Notification of planning applications

Any works to a listed building (as opposed to works affecting its setting) that require planning permission will almost always require listed building consent as well. Accordingly, the principal requirements as to notification relate to applications for listed building consent—since that will ensure that proposals for such works come to the attention of those who need or wish to know about them.

However, Circ. 01/01 notes that it would be helpful if authorities outside London would notify English Heritage of planning applications involving demolition or alteration of Grade I or II* buildings.[18] There is as yet no statutory power to require this—an amendment to the TCP (General Development Procedure) Order 1995 may be made in due course.

And where a planning application is submitted for works involving the demolition or material alteration of a listed building (of any grade) in London, the planning authority must consult English Heritage.[19] As to the meaning and extent

---

[14] TCP (General Development Procedure) Order 1995, art.19.
[15] [2000] E.G.C.S. 83, [2001] J.P.L. 211 (see also **14.6.1**).
[16] TCP (GDP) (S) O 1992, art.9 and Sch.4. See art.2 as to the definition of "neighbouring land".
[17] P(NI)O 1991, art.21; Planning Applications (Exemption from Publication) Order (NI) 1999 (SR 338). For the definition of "curtilage", see **4.5**.
[18] Circ. 01/01, para.11.
[19] TCP (General Development) Procedure Order 1995, art.10(1)(m).

of "consultation", see *R. v Secretary of State for Social Services ex parte Association of Metropolitan Authorities*,[20] and DoE Circular 9/95.[21] In this case there is initially a 14-day limit for responses, although responses received late must still be taken into account.[22]

Planning authorities in Scotland are to consult with the Scottish Ministers (Historic Scotland) in respect of all planning applications affecting a Category A listed building.[23]

Proposals for works that affect the setting of a listed building (whether or not they also actually affect the building itself) are subject to a completely separate set of requirements;[24] but these are in addition to those described above.

13.5.3 Publicity for listed building consent applications

A planning authority in England must publicise any application for listed building consent affecting a building of Grade I or II*, and any application which affects the exterior of a Grade II building, by inserting a notice in the local press (or, in the London Borough of Camden, on the Council's website) and one on or near the building.[25] Each notice must state where the application (including any plans and photographs submitted) can be inspected—which can be a website where the authority maintains one.[26] In the case of a listed building in large grounds, it would obviously be prudent for the authority to erect a notice at the boundary of a site as well as on the building itself.

In Scotland, the planning authority must publicise every application for listed building consent, regardless of the grade of building involved, by placing a notice in the Edinburgh Gazette, in a local newspaper and on or near the building.[27] And in Northern Ireland the Department is to publicise every such application in the local press.[28]

The authority must not determine the application until at least 21 days have elapsed since the latest of the two notices was published or erected.[29] When it does determine it, it must take into account any representations made as a result of the notices within the 21-day period.

Note that different rules that apply where an application is for the works that are the subject of a concurrent application under the Transport and Works Act 1992.[30]

---

[20] [1986] 1 W.L.R. 1.
[21] App B, para.3 (WO Circ. 29/95).
[22] art.10(4),(5).
[23] TCP (General Development Procedure) (Scotland) Order 1992, art.15(j)(v).
[24] See **13.5.8, 13.5.9**.
[25] P(LBCA) Regs 1990, reg.5(1), (1A), (3), as amended (in respect of England) by SI 2004/2210.
[26] P(LBCA) Regs 1990, reg.8A, as inserted by SI 2003/956 (England) and SI 2004/3156 (Wales).
[27] P(LBCA)(S) Regs 1987, reg.5.
[28] P(NI)O 1991, Sch.1, para.2.
[29] In Northern Ireland, the time limit is 14 days.
[30] See **13.10.6**.

13.5.4 Notification to English Heritage of listed building consent applications (England outside London)

Planning authorities in England outside Greater London, under section 13 of the Listed Buildings Act, must notify English Heritage of all applications for listed building consent, except those in categories prescribed by the Secretary of State under section 15 of the Act.

The current direction by the Secretary of State, which is to be found in paragraph 15 of ODPM / DCMS Circ. 01/01, requires that English Heritage must be notified of all applications for listed building consent relating to:

(1) any works to a Grade I or II* building;

(2) the total demolition of a principal Grade II building;

(3) the demolition of a principal external wall of such a building; or

(4) the demolition of all or a substantial part of the interior of such a building.[31]

The reference to a "principal" Grade II building means a building listed in its own right, as opposed to a building that forms part of a listed building by being in its curtilage.[32] Any proposal to retain less than 50 per cent of an elevation, including the vertical plane of any roof, is to be treated as being the demolition of a principal external wall; and the demolition of a substantial part of an interior includes the removal of any principal internal element of the structure, such as a staircase, load-bearing wall, floor structure or roof structure.[33] This may cause problems of interpretation in a few cases; but it is probable that the courts would interpret this direction as "directory" rather than "mandatory", so that only a blatant failure to comply with it would be sufficient to lead to a subsequent decision being invalidated.[34]

The aim of this notification is to enable English Heritage to become involved at the earliest possible stage, and to offer helpful comments before an authority has made up its mind, if it feels that a particular proposal is of sufficient importance. In extreme cases it can request the Secretary of State to call-in the application for his or her own decision. However it has no power to give a binding direction to an authority as to how an application is to be determined.

Notification of an application should be sent to the appropriate regional office of English Heritage as soon as it is received, and regardless of whether or not the authority intends to grant consent. Supporting information (plans, photographs, and other relevant documents) should be included wherever possible. The Circular suggests that two copies should be sent, so that English Heritage may operate both in its advisory role and as recording agency in succession to the RCHM.[35] This seems to be somewhat profligate in cases not involving demoli-

---

[31] In Circ. 01/01, para.15(2)(a)—replacing the previous one in DoE Circ. 14/97, para.15(2)(a).

[32] Circ. 01/01, para.7.

[33] Circ. 01/01, para.15(3). Further guidance is given in para.24 of Circ. 01/01.

[34] *Howard v Bodington* (1877) 2 P.D. 203 *per* Lord Penzance at p.211.

[35] Circ. 01/01; see **13.5.7**.

tion—except that it does enable English Heritage to decide whether or not it wants a chance to record any features of a building if consent is granted. If it does, it should request the authority to impose an appropriate condition on the consent.

An authority should allow 28 days for English Heritage to comment before it determines an application[36]—although English Heritage in practice now aims to turn round applications in 21 days.

13.5.5 Notification to English Heritage of listed building consent applications in London

Authorities in Greater London are required to notify the London Region of English Heritage of every application for listed building consent, under section 14, except where the authority has decided to refuse it, or the Secretary of State has directed otherwise (under section 15). English Heritage will then in turn notify the Secretary of State, except where it directs the authority to refuse the application.[37]

The position used to be that authorities had to notify English Heritage of all applications, whether for the demolition, alteration or extension of all or any part of any listed building, of any grade.[38] Instead, since 2001, they are required to notify it of applications in the four categories noted in **13.5.4**—that is, broadly, any works to a building of Grade I or II* and the demolition of a all or most of a building of Grade II (exactly as outside London)—and also all proposals for other works to Grade II buildings in the following categories:

(1) railway stations (including Underground stations), theatres, cinemas, bridges across the Thames;

(2) buildings in the curtilage of railway stations (including Underground stations); and

(3) buildings owned by local planning authorities where the application is by someone other than the authority.[39]

The significance of the first two additional categories is explained as follows in the Circular:

"Railway stations are included ... to enable English Heritage to assist the boroughs in adopting a consistent approach to this London-wide network of buildings. ... It would be helpful for English Heritage to be involved at the earliest stage on applications relating to listed theatres and cinemas, as these can be particularly problematic. Bridges across the Thames straddle borough boundaries and ... an English Heritage overview would therefore be useful. The revised notification arrangements will also apply to curtilage buildings to railway stations. This is because, in these cases, it is not uncommon for there to be a complex of buildings which are of interest."

As for the third extra category, applications by local planning authorities for works to their own listed buildings are determined by the Secretary of State; but in

---

[36] PPG 15, Annex B, Pt II, para.(3). Note that the change to a 21-day period for responding to consultations introduced by PCPA 2004, s.54 does not apply in this case (see ODPM Cicular 08/2005).

[37] See **13.7.4**.

[38] P(LBCA)A 1990, s.15(5); Circ. 14/97, para.15(2)(b).

[39] In Circ. 01/01, para.15(2)(b).

the absence of this direction, anyone else (such as a tenant or a prospective purchaser) could apply to the authority for consent, in spite of the obvious potential conflict of interest. That loophole has now been blocked, at least in London, by the need for all such applications to be referred to English Heritage.

The Secretary of State has stated that he will require from English Heritage a fully detailed submission in the case of an application for the demolition of a principal listed building (of any grade) or the demolition of a principal external wall or substantially all of the interior of a Grade I or II* building.[40] It follows that authorities must in these cases send English Heritage enough material for it to be able to pass on a set to the Secretary of State.

Slightly different rules used to apply in the area of the London Docklands Development Corporation[41]; but that direction is no longer of any effect following its dissolution. No special directions have yet been made for any of the new urban development corporations.[42]

13.5.6 Notification to national amenity societies of listed building consent applications

Planning authorities in England and Wales must notify the major national amenity societies of any application to demolish all or part of a listed building (of whatever grade), as soon as it is received.[43] By virtue of the current directions, the societies which must be consulted in this way are the following:

(1)   the Ancient Monuments Society

(2)   the Council for British Archaeology

(3)   the Georgian Group

(4)   the Society for the Protection of Ancient Buildings;

(5)   the Victorian Society; and

(6)   the Twentieth Century Society.[44]

The previous directions, now superseded, required notification of "all applications to demolish a listed building".[45] This was assumed to include applications for the removal of a part of a listed building. However, in the light of the decision of the House of Lords in *Shimizu (U.K.) Ltd v Westminster CC*,[46] that assumption is now seen to have been wrong, so the new directions refer to applications "for works for the demolition of a listed building, or for works for the alteration of a

---

[40] Circ. 01/01, paras 29, 30; see **13.7.4**. For the meaning of "principal building", see **13.5.4**.
[41] Set out most recently at para.16 of Circ. 14/97.
[42] See **1.4.6**.
[43] P(LBCA)A 1990, s.15(5)(a).
[44] In ODPM Circ. 09/2005, Annex A—which replaced the direction in Circ. 01/01, para.15(1) with effect from October 6, 2005. WO Circ. 1/98, para.1B is in the same terms, save that it omits the Twentieth Century Society—no doubt it will be replaced soon by a new direction identical to that applying in England.
[45] in DoE Circ. 8/87 (para.81) and WO Circ. 61/81 (para.52).
[46] [1996] 3 P.L.R. 89 (see 11.2.3).

listed building which comprise or include the demolition of any part of that building". The position is thus now restored to what it was always thought to have been.

As to the distinction between "demolition" of part of a building and "alteration" of it, this is a new concept, and so there is as yet no case law. The discussion in the previous Chapter of what constitutes "demolition" of a whole building will clearly be relevant however.[47] And it may be noted that the case of *R. v North Hertfordshire DC*,[48] mentioned there, arose because of the contention of a neighbour that the planning authority should have notified the national amenity societies of an application for the "extension" of a listed building. It was held in the High Court that, in the circumstances of that case, the extension did involve sufficient demolition of the existing structure to amount to demolition of part of it, and that the societies should therefore have been notified.

The specific concerns of each society are explained in paragraphs A.15 and A.16 of Annex A to PPG 15; and their current addresses are given at **Appendix C** of this book. The notification should include a copy of the relevant entry in the statutory list describing the building concerned, and should include appropriate supporting information.[49] In the case of partial demolition, the authority should also state whether it will in due course be notifying the Secretary of State of the application. Clearly, where the application is, for example, for consent to demolish a Georgian building, it would be appropriate to send full details to the Georgian Group, but only a brief note to the Victorian Society.

There is of course no bar on sending to the appropriate national amenity societies notice of other applications—such as those for significant extensions to listed buildings or for new buildings in conservation areas. This can in some cases be a valuable means of bringing informed and articulate professional opinion and comment to bear on a particular proposal.

As for Scotland, the fact that all listed building consent applications are advertised in the press and the *Edinburgh Gazette* means that the national societies can discover them from that source; there is as a result no specific requirement to notify them—although this well may be appropriate in particular cases.[50] Nor is there a formal requirement to notify the societies in Northern Ireland.

13.5.7 Notification to Royal Commission on Historical Monuments of listed building consent applications

Planning authorities in England used to give notice of any application for listed building consent for the total or partial demolition of any listed building to the Royal Commission on Historical Monuments of England.[51] The purpose here was that the Commission should be alerted to the possible need to record the building for posterity should consent be given.

---

[47] See **12.6.4**.
[48] [1981] J.P.L. 752.
[49] Circ. 01/01, para.18; WO Circ. 1/98, para.12.
[50] See *HS Memorandum*, para.2.37.
[51] Circ. 14/97, para.15(1).

The Royal Commission (sometimes referred to as RCHM(E)), which was set up in 1908 with the aim of recording historic buildings in England, was distinct from the Historic Buildings and Monuments Commission for England (referred to in this book as "English Heritage"), set up in 1983. The two bodies merged in January 2001, since when English Heritage has taken on the role of recording buildings that are to be demolished.[52] There is thus now no direction to send copies of applications for demolition to English Heritage, since all such applications have to be sent to it anyway—but it would be sensible for authorities to comply with the request to send an extra copy.[53]

In Wales, applications for demolition must still be sent to the Royal Commission on Ancient and Historical Monuments in Wales—in precisely the same cases as they are to be sent to the national amenity societies.[54] The relevant direction in this case is in paragraph 10 of WO Circular 1/98.[55] It is not necessary for an authority to send to the Commission an extract from the statutory list; but it should send all other appropriate supporting information, together with an indication of whether it will in due course be notifying the Secretary of State of the application.

The Royal Commission on the Ancient and Historical Monuments of Scotland must similarly be notified of applications for demolition of listed buildings in Scotland.[56]

In Northern Ireland, the recording of buildings to be demolished is carried out by the Department, so no specific requirement as to the notification of applications arises.

13.5.8 Works affecting the setting of a listed building: publicity for planning applications

The statutory requirements described so far all relate to proposals for works to a listed building itself. However, a listed building may also be harmed, possibly seriously, by works carried out that affect its setting. And it has already been noted that such works may well require neither listed building consent nor conservation area consent.[57] The need for planning permission to be obtained is therefore the only means open to a planning authority to exercise any control in these cases. It is therefore not surprising that the authority is under a duty (under section 67 of the Listed Buildings Act) to publicise such applications, in order to obtain a wider cross-section of public opinion.

This duty thus applies where the application is for *any* development which, in the opinion of the planning authority, would affect the setting of a listed building.[58] As to how far this extends, helpful advice is given in paragraph 2.17 of PPG

---

[52] Authorisation of Works (Listed Buildings) (England) Order 2001 (SI 2001/24).
[53] See **13.5.4**.
[54] See **13.5.6**.
[55] See also para.12 of that circular, and para.105 of WO Circ. 61/96.
[56] See *HS Memorandum*, para.2.37.
[57] See **12.5.3**.
[58] P(LBCA)A 1990, s.67(1).

15.[59] In summary, "this provision should not be interpreted too narrowly ... if there is doubt about the precise extent of a building's setting, it is better to publish a notice".

The scope of the corresponding guidance in Circular 8/87[60] was considered in *R. v South Herefordshire DC, Ex p. Felton*[61], in the context of a planning application for the erection of a potato store near Bollitree Castle, near Ross-on-Wye. The castle is a notable example of a mid 18th-century gothic sham castle developed around an imposing house of circa 1700. The nearest part of the stores was to be some 77 metres from the castle. On the question of whether the new building would affect the setting of the listed building, McCowan J. commented that:

"... it does seem to me ... that [the officer of the planning authority] appears to think that what he has got to have to regard to is whether you can see the potato store from the house. He certainly there does not appear to be appreciating that that is not the whole answer when one considers whether the setting of the listed buildings will be affected. There is, of course, to be taken into consideration the view of the listed buildings in relation to the new building seen from other positions, ..."

[counsel for the applicant] says "affect" must mean materially affect. That may well be so, but in my judgment what is striking is that the words are not "substantially affect the setting of a listed building" ... I am bound to say that I am amazed that anybody could have thought that a building of the nature of the potato store, of the sheer bulk of the potato store, would not affect the setting of the listed buildings."[62]

More recently, it has been held that in considering the setting of a listed building or ancient monument, it is proper to have regard to the view from the building or monument towards the proposed development, or from the proposed development towards the building or monument, or from any relevant view from the side (that is, presumably, any point from which it is possible to see both the building or monument and the proposed development).[63] Note in particular that the setting of a building, as thus defined, is likely to be considerably more extensive than its curtilage.[64]

It should be noted that the requirement arises where the proposed works will affect the setting of the listed building—whether beneficially or adversely: in this context, as with determining the need for environmental assessment, "benefit, like beauty, is in the eye of the beholder".[65]

Where an authority considers that proposed development would affect the setting of a listed building, as thus defined, it is to publicise the application by:

(1) a notice in a local newspaper; and

(2) a notice on or near the land concerned, which must be displayed for at least seven days.[66]

---

[59] And, more briefly, in WO Circ. 61/96, para.7.
[60] para.27.
[61] [1989] 3 P.L.R. 81.
[62] pp 86, 87.
[63] *Revival Properties v Secretary of State* [1996] B86.
[64] See **4.5**.
[65] *British Telecommunications PLC v Gloucester City Council* [2002] J.P.L. 993, at para.69; see **13.3.7**.
[66] P(LBCA) Regs 1990, reg.5A, inserted by SI 2004/2210.

Each notice must indicate the nature of the development in question, and must name a place or website where further details (that is, the drawings and supporting material) can be inspected. Those details must then be obtainable there for at least 21 days from the date of the press notice. Note that it is the planning authority that is under a duty to give such publicity, not the applicant.

Whether such publicity is of value must remain open to question. Authorities are in any event obliged to give at least some publicity to every application,[67] and many authorities choose to publicise applications (including those outside conservation areas) much more widely than they are required to by law. They will thus often inform neighbours and local amenity groups. See DoE Circular 15/92 for advice on good practice.[68]

Where it falls to the district council to carry out such publicity in connection with an application which will be dealt with by the county council (for example, for minerals or waste disposal), it must notify the county council of the publicity it has carried out as soon as possible.[69]

The planning authority must not determine the application until 21 days after the appearance of the press notice or the putting up of the site notice, whichever was the later; and it must take into account any representations received during that period as a result of the publicity.[70]

Finally, it should be noted that the requirements as to publicity and notifying English Heritage (see below) apply only to an application "for planning permission".[71] This clearly includes a simple "planning application" (either detailed or outline). It also includes an application for permission to develop land without compliance with conditions attached to a previous grant of permission,[72] but not a retrospective application under section 73A.[73] Nor does it include:

(1) an application for approval of reserved matters following an outline grant of planning permission;

(2) an application for any other approval by the planning authority needed as a result of a condition attached to a previous grant of detailed permission;

(3) an application for any approval required by a condition attached to the permission granted by the TCP (General Permitted Development) Order 1995 (including, for example, certain agricultural development in sensitive areas[74] or development permitted by private Acts[75]; or

(4) an application for consent under the Advertisements Regulations.[76]

---

[67] See **13.5.1**.
[68] WO Circ. 32/92.
[69] P(LBCA)A 1990, Sch.4, para.4(3).
[70] s.67(7).
[71] s.67(1).
[72] under TCPA 1990, s.73.
[73] P(LBCA)A, s.67(8), as substituted by PCA 1991, Sch.7.
[74] Pt 6, conditions A2(2) (i), (ii).
[75] Pt 11, condition A1.
[76] See **13.5.10**.

The corresponding requirement in Scotland is in section 60 of the Scottish Listed Buildings Act.

13.5.9 Works affecting the setting of a listed building: notification of planning applications

As well as publicising all planning applications for development affecting the setting of a listed building, planning authorities in England must notify English Heritage of those affecting the setting of a Grade II* or Grade I building.[77]

In addition, authorities in London must notify English Heritage of applications for development affecting the setting of a Grade II building if:

(1)   it is in the curtilage of the building; or

(2)   it involves the provision of more than 1,000 sq m of gross floor space; or

(3)   it involves the construction of a building more than 20m in height.[78]

Where a group of listed buildings contains buildings of different grades, a planning authority should usually assume that a development proposal affecting the setting of any one of the group affects the setting of all, and notify English Heritage accordingly. This was considered in *R. v South Herefordshire DC, ex p. Felton*.[79] The listed building in question, Bollitree Castle, was, for listing purposes, divided into five parts—one Grade I, one Grade II*, and three Grade II. The judge was unimpressed with the argument that only the Grade II buildings in the group were affected.

"True, three of the buildings were only Grade II, but of the remaining two, one was Grade I and the other Grade II*. I have no doubt that the proposed building affected the setting of the last two, as well as of the others. The words are: 'affect the setting of a listed building', and it is impossible, in my judgment, to cut this grouping of listed buildings at the castle into sections. Some parts are no doubt of greater architectural merit and importance than others. None the less, this is a setting".[80]

He held accordingly that English Heritage should have been notified; and the planning permission that had been issued was therefore quashed. His "careful and thorough" judgment was subsequently upheld in the Court of Appeal.[81]

It has already been noted that a building or structure is also deemed to be part of a listed building if it is attached to it or if it has been within its curtilage of a listed building since before June 1948.[82] However, such buildings are not normally mentioned in the list, and are therefore not allocated a grade. This can cause problems where an authority has to decide what procedure to follow with regard to an application for works to a building, not listed in its own right, that is within the curtilage of two buildings of different grades. In practice, where there is any doubt it would seem to be sensible to regard such a building as being of the higher

[77]   P(LBCA)A 1990, s.67(3), (4); Circ. 01/01, para.8(1), (2)(a), (3)(a).
[78]   P(LBCA)A 1990, s.67(3), (4); Circ. 01/01, para.8(1), (2)(b),(c).
[79]   [1989] 3 P.L.R. 81 (see **13.5.8** for the facts).
[80]   p.87.
[81]   [1991] J.P.L. 633.
[82]   See **4.5**.

of the two grades, since works to it could be said to affect the setting of the more important of the admittedly listed buildings. Where the curtilage building is obviously of no interest at all, so that this would be absurd, and the procedure appropriate to the lower grade is therefore followed, the reason for this should be clearly recorded, to protect against any subsequent legal challenge.

Authorities should send a copy of the press notice[83] as soon as possible, enclosing a copy of the application (including all accompanying documentation and drawings[84]). The aim of those provisions is to enable English Heritage to comment helpfully on applications at the earliest possible stage and before authorities have reached their own conclusions. All that is strictly necessary is to send the briefest details. In practice, however, so many applications are notified each year that it is almost impossible for English Heritage to discriminate between them or to make any very useful response. Authorities have therefore been encouraged to send some more details, at least in the more significant cases.

There is no specification in the Circular as to the period which must elapse before it can be assumed that English Heritage has no comment to make—it merely refers to "the relevant period of notice".[85] An earlier Circular suggested that if nothing was heard within 28 days, it could be assumed that it has no comment.[86] There is a time limit specified in the Act, however, in that representations (including, presumably, those by English Heritage) only have to be taken into account if they are made within 21 days of the display of the site notice or the publication of the press notice, whichever is the later.[87] English Heritage does not in any event have a right to require the authority to determine an application in a particular way; it merely has a right to make representations, which the authority must "take into account".[88] Here too, in practice, English Heritage aims to respond within 21 days.

There are no corresponding requirement that all planning applications affecting the setting of listed buildings in Wales should be notified to the Welsh Assembly (Cadw).

Planning authorities in Scotland are to consult with the Scottish Ministers (Historic Scotland) in respect of all planning applications affecting the setting of a Category A listed building.[89]

13.5.10 Advertisements consent applications

The erection of signs and advertisements actually attached to listed buildings will almost always need listed building consent as well as consent under the Advertisements Regulations. The requirements described above as to the publicity for and notification of applications for listed building consent should accordingly be

---

[83] See **13.5.8**.
[84] Circ. 01/01, para.13.
[85] para.13.
[86] Circ. 8/87, para.30.
[87] s.67(7).
[88] TCPA 1990, s.71(1), substituted by the Planning and Compensation Act 1991; 1995 Order, art.10(5).
[89] TCP (General Development Procedure) (Scotland) Order 1992, art.15(j)(v), amended by SI 1994/3293.

sufficient to ensure that such proposals are adequately publicised and scrutinised. There is accordingly no requirement for applications for express advertisements consent to be specially publicised.

Signs and advertisements affecting the setting of a listed building will in most cases only cause serious harm where they are both large and permanent—and so will require express consent rather than deemed consent. Clearly the effect of such a proposal on the setting of the building will be a material consideration in the decision by the planning authority as to whether consent should be granted; but there is nevertheless no specific requirement as to publicity or notification.

13.6 Publicity for proposals other than those affecting listed buildings

13.6.1 Development affecting conservation areas (planning applications)

The carrying out of development in a conservation area will only require conservation area consent if it includes demolition; the ability to scrutinise planning applications for such development is therefore the most important power available to an authority in carrying out its duty to preserve and enhance the area's character and appearance.

It has already been noted that at least some publicity must be given to all planning applications[90]—and this applies to applications for development in conservation areas just as much as elsewhere. In addition, however, planning authorities are required (under section 73 of the Listed Buildings Act and section 65 of the Scottish Listed Buildings Act) to publicise all applications for development that would affect the character or appearance of a conservation area.[91] Note that this would include development of land outside the area but still affecting it. Such publicity is exactly as for development affecting the setting of listed buildings (that is, a notice in the press and on or near the site).[92]

It has already been noted that in Northern Ireland, the Department is to publish in the local press a notice of every planning application it receives in a conservation area.[93]

In addition, authorities in England must notify English Heritage of any development affecting the character or appearance of a conservation area, if it involves:

(1) the erection of a new building or the extension of an existing building where the site area is more than 1,000 sq m;

(2) the change of use of a building on such a site; or

(3) the construction of any building of more than 20m in height.[94]

---

[90] See **13.5.1**.
[91] P(LBCA)A 1990, s.73.
[92] See **13.5.8**.
[93] P(NI)O 1991, art.21; Planning Applications (Exemption from Publication) Order (NI) 1999 (SR 338); see **13.5.1**.
[94] Circ. 01/01, para.8(2)(d) for London, para.8(3)(b) elsewhere.

In general, the comments above on notification apply in this case too.[95]

There are no corresponding requirement that all planning applications affecting and conservation areas in Wales and Scotland should be notified to the Welsh Assembly (Cadw) and Historic Scotland.

13.6.2 Demolition in conservation areas (applications for conservation area consent)

On receipt of an application for conservation area consent, the planning authority must publicise it by placing a notice on site and in the local press, and take into account any representations made as a result.[96]

Authorities are not required to notify the national amenity societies of conservation area applications, nor (in Wales or Scotland) the Royal Commission on Historical Monuments; neither section 13 of the Listed Buildings Act, nor the directions in paragraph 15 of Circular 01/01 and paragraph 10 of WO Circular 61/96 applies to unlisted buildings. But there is no reason why it should not notify one or more of them of any particular application if it wishes—for example, where proposed demolition in a conservation area affects the setting of a listed building of a particular period. And there is no requirement for the Secretary of State to be notified either.

Similarly, an authority outside London is not required to send any application for conservation area consent to English Heritage, although of course it may if it wishes.

However, within Greater London, the London Region of English Heritage must be notified of every application for conservation area consent. Further, the planning authority must not determine the application until 28 days have elapsed after English Heritage was notified, and must take into account any representations made by it.[97] Note that English Heritage is not empowered to direct the authority how to determine the application; it may merely comment. Moreover, it is not required to consult the Secretary of State before making any such comment.

In Scotland, the planning authority must publicise every application for conservation area consent by placing a notice in the *Edinburgh Gazette*, in a local newspaper and on or near the building.[98]

13.6.3 Works affecting archaeological sites

It is obvious that the carrying out of development—even if relatively minor—may affect archaeological sites. It is therefore important that, where a site is known (or even suspected) to be of archaeological significance, a chance is given to those

---

[95] in **13.5.2**.
[96] P(LBCA) Regs 1990, reg.5(1), (2).
[97] P(LBCA)A 1990, s.14, as substituted in respect of unlisted buildings in conservation areas by P(LBCA) Regs 1990, Sch.3. The draft PPG 15 (Annex 8, para.20) suggested that in due course this requirement will apply only to applications in London which relate to the total demolition of a building, the substantial demolition of a building, so that only its street or principal façade is retained, or the demolition of the street or principal façade of a building. No such change has yet been made.
[98] P(LBCA)(S) Regs 1987, reg.5.

with appropriate specialist knowledge to assess its true importance and what is likely to be the impact of the proposed development.

In fact, however, the only statutory requirement is that planning authorities should consult English Heritage (or Cadw in Wales) when they receive planning applications for development likely to affect the site of a scheduled monument.[99] There is a 14-day limit for responses to such consultation, but responses received later must be still taken into account.[1] In Scotland, planning authorities are required to consult the Scottish Ministers (Historic Scotland) in relation to planning applications affecting the site or setting of a scheduled monument.[2]

However, given the relatively small number of scheduled monuments in comparison to the estimated number of unprotected archaeological sites,[3] it is clear that the above requirements will of themselves only be of limited use; and planning authorities in England have been advised to consult English Heritage more generally on non-scheduled sites.[4] Developers and planning authorities are accordingly recommended to consult the County Archaeological Officer or equivalent who holds the Sites and Monuments Record, or English Heritage in London.[5] In Wales, consultation should be with the appropriate local authority or national park authority archaeological officer or Regional Archaeological Trust.[6]

It may also be appropriate to give notice to the above bodies of applications for listed building consent for works that affect ancient monuments and archaeological sites—although there is no statutory requirement to do so.

13.6.4 Works affecting areas of archaeological importance

Special arrangements apply to the processing of planning applications in an area of archaeological importance, designated under Part II of the Ancient Monuments Act.[7] Any developer wishing to carry out on any site within the area any operations which disturb the ground, or any flooding or tipping operations, must serve on the local borough or district council an operations notice.[8] If the operations involve the clearance of the site, the developer must serve a further notice on the investigating authority[9] (under section 35(7)) once the site is clear.[10]

The "developer" for these purposes is anyone with a relevant interest in the site, or a statutory undertaker, or a body with compulsory purchase powers.[11] If the council is itself the developer, it must serve the relevant notices on the Secretary of

[99] TCP (General Development Procedure) Order 1995, art.10(1)(n).
[1] art.10(4),(5).
[2] TCP (General Development Procedure) (Scotland) Order 1992, art.15(j)(vi), amended by SI 1994/3293. As to the extent of the "site" of a monument, see **6.2.5**; and as to the meaning and extent of "consultation", see **13.5.2**.
[3] See **6.2.6**.
[4] PPG 16, para.23.
[5] PPG 16, paras 19, 23.
[6] WO Circ. 60/96, paras 11,15.
[7] See **6.4**.
[8] 1979 Act, s.35(1)–(5).
[9] See **6.3.3**.
[10] See **13.6.5** for the consequences of failure to serve a notice.
[11] s.36.

State.[12] The form of an operations notice, and indeed of all notices to be served under this procedure, is prescribed in regulations.[13]

The requirement to notify the investigating authority does not however apply where the authority itself has already given its consent to the proposed works.[14] Nor does it apply where the works have been exempted by order of the Secretary of State. The current Order lists 11 categories of operations:

(1) agriculture, horticulture and forestry to a depth of 600mm;

(2) landscaping and gardening to a depth of 600mm;

(3) tunnelling or other works at a depth of more than 10m;

(4) mining operations in accordance with the Code of Practice for Minerals Operators dated August 1982;

(5)–(9) routine operations by various statutory undertakers and similar bodies;

(10) operations on a site for which another operations notice has been served less than five years ago; and

(11) operations that have been granted scheduled monument consent.[15]

It will be seen that this list still leaves most types of development needing to be notified; in particular, minor works such as small extensions to buildings, which might not even need a planning application,[16] will need to be the subject of an operations notice.

Once it has received an operations notice, the investigating authority can enter the site to determine whether archaeological excavation would be worthwhile, and generally to watch operations.[17] At any time within four weeks of the notice, it can in turn serve a notice on the developer, the authority, the Secretary of State and English Heritage, stating that it intends to excavate.[18] It then has a right to investigate the site for a period of four months and two weeks, starting:

(1) on a date six weeks after the service of the operations notice; or

(2) the date the site has been cleared, as notified under section 35(7) (see above); or

(3) any earlier date agreed between the developer and the investigating authority.[19]

---

[12] s.35(5)(c).

[13] Areas of Archaeological Importance (Forms of Notices etc) Regulations 1984 (SI 1984/1285).

[14] s.37(1).

[15] Areas of Archaeological Importance (Notification of Operations) (Exemption) Regulations 1984 (SI 1984/1286).

[16] See 12.2.2.

[17] s.38(1).

[18] s.38(3).

[19] s.38(4).

If nothing has been heard from the investigating authority six weeks after the service of the operations notice, the developer may proceed with impunity. The investigating authority still has a right to excavate, but only in such a way as not to impede the development.[20]

The effect of this procedure is that a developer can be sure that, although there is a chance that it will not be possible to touch the site for up to six months after serving an operations notice, the time allowed for excavations cannot be extended beyond that six-month period without its voluntary agreement.

13.6.5 Failure to notify works in an area of archaeological importance

It is an offence under section 35(1) for a developer to carry out any operations in an area of archaeological importance, other than those exempted by order of the Secretary of State (see above), without having served an operations notice, or within six weeks of having served one. It is also an offence to carry out operations after a site has been cleared without having first notified the investigating authority of the clearance under section 35(7).

In proceedings for such an offence, it is a defence for the accused to prove:

(1) that he or she took all reasonable precautions and exercised all due diligence to avoid or prevent disturbance of the ground;

(2) that he or she did not know and had no reason to believe that the site of the operations was in an area of archaeological importance; or

(3) that the operations were urgently necessary in the interests of safety or health, and that written notice of the need for them was given to the Secretary of State as soon as reasonably practicable.[21]

The offences are triable either way.[22] The developer would be liable on summary conviction to a fine of up to the statutory maximum (currently £5,000) or, on conviction on indictment to an unlimited fine.

13.6.6 Works affecting historic parks and gardens

Planning authorities receiving applications for development in England affecting any garden or park of special historic interest, registered on the statutory register and classified as Grade I or Grade II*, must consult English Heritage.[23] As to the meaning of "consult", see above.

This requirement does not apply in Wales, as the register maintained by Cadw is non-statutory, although Welsh authorities are nevertheless asked to consult Cadw on all planning applications affecting Grade I and II* sites.[24]

There is a further requirement, also applying in England only, for authorities to notify to the Garden History Society of all planning applications affecting any

---

[20] s.38(5).
[21] s.37(5),(6).
[22] s.35(9); see **Chapter 19** on criminal offences generally; and **Appendix F** on penalties.
[23] See **7.5**. As to the meaning of "consult", see **13.5.2**.
[24] WO Circ. 1/98, para.23.

garden included in the register, regardless of its grade, unless they are proposing to refuse them.[25]

There is no reason why authorities in Wales and Scotland should not also notify the Society, on a voluntary basis, in appropriate cases, and they have been asked to do so in connection with every application affecting a registered garden, of whatever grade.[26]

13.7 Determination of applications

13.7.1 Timetable

It may at this point be helpful to summarise the various time limits contained in the above discussion of procedures.

First, the planning authority must not determine an application for planning permission or listed building consent until at least 21 days after the latest of the following:

(1) the notification by the applicant of other owners of the building (if any); or the publication of a notice in the local paper by the applicant, where he or she does not know of some or any of the other owners of the building[27];

(2) the placing of a notice by the authority on or near the building, in the press or the sending of a copy to neighbouring owners and occupiers.[28]

Secondly, where an authority has notified an application for planning permission to English Heritage, it may not determine it for at least 14 days.[29] And where an application for listed building or conservation area consent has been referred to English Heritage for comment, it can be assumed that there is no comment if no response is received within 28 days.[30] The same applies where (any) authority has notified the national amenity societies of an application for listed building consent: 28 days should be allowed for comment.[31] And no decision must be made on an application for planning permission in an archaeological area until 28 days has elapsed following its notification to the investigating authority.[32]

Finally, unless the Secretary of State calls in the application for his or her own decision, the authority is under a duty to determine it within eight weeks. The eight-week period starts on the date on which the application was first received, or the date on which it was first agreed to be valid, if that was later (where, for example, the initial submission was accompanied by the wrong ownership

---

[25] TCP (Consultation with Garden History Society) Direction 1995, reproduced as Appendix C to DoE Circ. 9/95.
[26] WO Circ. 1/98, para.23.
[27] See **13.3.3**.
[28] See **13.5.1, 13.5.3**.
[29] See **13.5.2**.
[30] PPG 15, Annex B, Pt II, para.(3). See **13.5.4, 13.5.5, 13.6.2**
[31] PPG 15, Annex B, Pt II, para.(4). See **13.5.6**.
[32] See **13.6.4**.

certificate, or inadequate drawings).[33] This period may be extended by written agreement between the applicant and the authority.

13.7.2 Communication with the applicant

Authorities have been urged to give decisions on applications as quickly as possible after the various statutory periods for representations have expired.[34] They should in the meanwhile keep applicants informed about the progress of applications; and any potential difficulties about their proposals should be discussed with them to try to resolve the problems in a mutually satisfactory way. In practice, many applications take longer than eight weeks to determine; and authorities do not always notify applicants of likely delay, particularly if it will not be substantial.

Where the application is called in by the Secretary of State (see below), the authority must inform the applicant of this within the eight-week period (or, again, a longer period if agreed).[35]

If an applicant has not received by the end of the eight-week period (or whatever extended period has been agreed) either a decision on the application or a notice that it has been called in, he or she is entitled to appeal to the Secretary of State. Such an appeal is on the basis that the application is deemed to have been refused.[36] Since many decisions take longer than eight weeks to be reached, it is only worth an applicant appealing under this provision where:

(1) it appears certain that the application is going to be refused, and he or she merely wishes to get the appeal started as soon as possible; or

(2) the consultation process has got out of hand, and the application is clearly going to take much longer than eight weeks to be dealt with by the planning authority; or

(3) it appears that the authority is unwilling to reach any decision at all.

It is in any event always worthwhile for the applicant and the relevant officer of the planning authority to keep in touch while the application is being processed. By doing this, it should be possible to minimise, and hopefully to avoid altogether, any disagreements and misunderstandings that might otherwise arise. If, however, it appears that an application is likely (or certain) to be refused, it may be prudent for the applicant to put in writing a summary of his or her case, to be considered by the relevant local authority officer or committee before reaching a decision.[37]

---

[33] P(LBCA) Regs 1990, reg.3(4).
[34] PPG 15, Annex B, Pt II, para.(6).
[35] TCP (General Development Procedure) Order 1995, art.18; P(LBCA) Regs 1990, reg.3(4), (5).
[36] TCPA 1990, s.78(2), P(LBCA)A 1990, s.20(2); and see **15.2.2**.
[37] See **Form D14** in Appendix D for an example.

13.7.3 Listed building and conservation area consent applications in England (outside London) and Wales

An authority is free to refuse any application for listed building consent without notifying the Secretary of State.[38] If, however, it wishes to grant consent for works of any consequence, it must first notify him or her, so that there is an opportunity for the application to be called-in.

The application procedures are thus designed to ensure that the Department is made aware of the more important cases by requiring that, in principle, it is sent a copy of any application which a planning authority intends to grant. To avoid a flood of trivial applications being referred, however, section 15 of the Listed Buildings Act provides that the Secretary of State may direct which categories of application are *not* to be notified (any direction with respect to buildings in England must be made in consultation with English Heritage).

The direction currently in force in England is at paragraph 26 of Circular 01/01.[39] As a result, a planning authority outside Greater London must notify the Secretary of State of every application for listed building consent, unless it is going to refuse it, if it relates to:

(1) any works to a Grade I or II* building;

(2) the total demolition of a principal Grade II building;

(3) the demolition of a principal external wall of such a building; or

(4) the demolition of all or a substantial part of the interior of such a building.

These categories are identical to those which have to be notified to English Heritage.[40] This means that, by the time the Secretary of State becomes involved with an application, and consults English Heritage, it will already have been aware of it for a while, and should be able to give advice promptly as to whether or not it should be called-in.

The Government has recently proposed that, in future, applications (in England) will only need to be notified to the Secretary of State where a written objection has been made by English Heritage.[40a] It remains to be seen whether this proposal will be adopted.

In addition, the Secretary of State is able to require a planning authority to refer to the Department any application, or any class of applications, for listed building consent, even if it falls within a category of applications which it would not normally see.[41] Thus an amenity group, for example, could ask him or her to inspect a particularly contentious application for the alteration or extension of a Grade II building, with a view to possibly calling it in.

The notification is to be on the form provided at the end of Annex B to PPG 15. That form lists the items to be sent along with the notification. It should be sent to

---

[38] P(LBCA)A 1990, s.13(1).
[39] Replacing the previous one in Circ. 14/97, para.22.
[40] See **13.5.4**.
[40a] *Listed Buildings Casework*, ODPM consultation paper, February 2006.
[41] P(LBCA)A 1990, s.15(4).

the appropriate Government regional office. The Secretary of State, on receiving the notification, will consult English Heritage and, if he or she wishes to call-in an application for his/her decision, must do so within 28 days of being notified of it, or must during that period ask for more time.[42] If nothing is heard from the Department by the end of the 28-day period, the authority may determine the application without more ado. If, however, within that period more time has been sought, the authority may not determine the application until it has received the Department's final ruling—however long that takes.

In Wales, a planning authority must notify the Welsh Assembly (in practice, Cadw) of almost any application for listed building consent which it proposes to grant.[43] The only exception is where it refers only to works to the interior of a building of Grade II; and even that does not apply where a grant by Cadw has been given or is being contemplated (although that will only rarely occur with a Grade II building). The current direction to that effect is in WO Circ. 1/98, para.15.[44]

If a planning authority fails to notify the Secretary of State or the Assembly under these provisions, and then purports to grant listed building consent, the courts may declare that the consent is not valid. Thus, in *Fenland DC v Reuben Rose (Properties) Ltd*,[45] the Council purported to grant listed building consent for the demolition of a listed building without having first notified the application to the Secretary of State; some four years later, it sought an injunction in the county court to prevent a developer carrying out the demolition in reliance on the consent. The Court of Appeal accepted that there was no valid consent, and that the demolition was unauthorised—although it left open the question of whether an injunction should be granted.[46]

No application for conservation area consent in England or Wales has to be referred to the Secretary of State or the Assembly.

13.7.4 Listed building and conservation area consent applications in London

Within Greater London, a planning authority (in practice, the borough council) does not need to refer any listed building consent applications direct to the Secretary of State. Instead, it notifies English Heritage, in the circumstances set out above—broadly, any works to a building of Grade I or II*, the demolition of a all or most of a building of Grade II, and other works to Grade II buildings in certain specific categories.[47]

---

[42] P(LBCA)A 1990, s.13(2).

[43] s.13(1).

[44] Identical to the direction previously in force since 1981. The Welsh Office issued in 1994 a consultation paper suggesting that authorities should be allowed to decide most applications affecting Grade II buildings without reference to Cadw, provided they could satisfy the Welsh Office that they had in place the necessary expertise. However, in the light of responses received to that paper, it was decided to retain in place the existing arrangements at least for the moment.

[45] [2000] P.L.C.R. 376, E.G.C.S. 46, CA.

[46] See **13.3.1**.

[47] See **13.5.5**.

English Heritage may then without further ado direct the council to refuse the application. Alternatively, it may direct it to grant the application, or authorise it to determine the application as it wishes. However, before English Heritage either directs or allows a council to grant consent, it must first notify the Secretary of State of the application.[48] Once he or she has been consulted, the Secretary of State then has 28 days in which to call it in for his or her own decision, or to seek more time in which to consider the matter.[49]

The Secretary of State has stated that he has not exercised his power to intervene in recent years, and will consider amending section 15(1) when the opportunity arises, so that he will then be able to disapply only part of section 14 (and thus require to be notified of only some of the applications of which English Heritage is notified). Until then, he is content to receive in most cases only a brief description of the proposed works and the building involved. However, a fully detailed submission will be required in the case of an application for:

(1) the demolition of a principal listed building (of any grade) or

(2) the demolition of a principal external wall or substantially all of the interior of a Grade I or II* building.[50]

If a borough council is directed by English Heritage to refuse an application, and it is unwilling to accept the direction, it may, within 28 days of receiving it, refer the whole matter to the Secretary of State, who may then call it in.[51] If the authority does not do so, or if it does not hear from the Secretary of State within 28 days of referring the application (or such longer period as the Secretary of State has requested), it must comply with the original direction from English Heritage.[52]

Every conservation area consent application in Greater London must be notified to English Heritage by the planning authority; but English Heritage does not have to notify it to the Secretary of State.[53]

13.7.5 Notification of applications to the Scottish Ministers

Planning authorities in Scotland are required to notify the Scottish Ministers of: planning applications for planning permission that have been the subject of consultation with the Secretary of State under article 15 of the General Development Procedure) (Scotland) Order (that is, those affecting a Category A listed building or its setting, or a scheduled monument or its site or setting[54])—but only where they have been advised to refuse permission or grant it subject to conditions, and they are minded not to follow that advice.[55]

---

[48] Circ. 01/01, para.26(2).
[49] P(LBCA)A 1990, s.14(5),(6).
[50] Circ. 01/01, paras 29, 30. For the meaning of "principal building", see **13.5.4**.
[51] See **13.7.6**.
[52] P(LBCA)A 1990, s.14(4), (7); PPG 15, Annex B, Pt II, para.(9).
[53] See **13.6.2**.
[54] See **13.5.2, 13.5.9, 13.6.3**.
[55] Scottish Development Department Circular 4/1997, Annex A.

The Scottish Ministers must also be notified of applications for listed building consent for the demolition of any listed building or for the alteration or extension of any building of Grade A or B (not B for Group), and all applications for conservation area consent.[56]

13.7.6 Call-in by central government

The Secretary of State, the Welsh Assembly, or the Scottish Ministers may occasionally decide that an application for planning permission, listed building or conservation area consent should be "called in" for their own decision, rather than being left to be decided by the planning authority. This may happen as a result of an application being notified to them under the statutory procedures outlined above, or because of pressure from English Heritage, national or local amenity societies, or even interested individuals.[57]

If this happens, the relevant Government Office will direct the planning authority to refer to it the application (or, where more than one application is involved, all of them)—that is, the forms, together with all supporting drawings, photographs and other details, along with any representations that have been made by owners, amenity societies, neighbours, and others.[58] The authority may also wish to send a statement of its own views on the application.

The authority must notify the applicant in writing that the Secretary of State has called in the application.[59]

Where an application is called in, the Department treats it as if it were the subject of an appeal.[60] That is, it first offers the applicant and the planning authority a chance to be heard at a public local inquiry if either wishes.[61] It is also likely that English Heritage will become involved in such a case in England.[62] It may happen that one or other local authority (district or county council) is perfectly satisfied with the proposed works, and is therefore on the same "side" as the applicant—with the other authority, English Heritage, local or national groups, or individuals, or some combination of them, in opposition.

In London, where a borough council does not wish to accept a direction by English Heritage that it should refuse an application for listed building consent,[63] and it notifies the Secretary of State as a result,[63a] the Secretary of State may call it in. In that case, too, there will be an offer of a public inquiry if the applicant, the authority or English Heritage wishes.[64]

---

[56] Scottish Development Department Circular 17/1987, Annex III.

[57] TCPA 1990, s.77; P(LBCA)A 1990, s.12. [Scotland: TCP(S)A 1997, s.46; P(P(LBCA)(S)A 1997, s.11.]

[58] s.77(3); s.12(3); see **13.3**.

[59] TCP (General Development Procedure) Order 1995, art.18; P(LBCA) Regs 1990, reg.3(4), (5).

[60] See **Chapter 15**.

[61] s.77(5); s.12(4).

[62] National Heritage Act 1983, s.33.

[63] See **13.7.4**.

[63a] Under PLCBA 1990, s.14(4).

[64] P(LBCA)A 1990, s.14(8).

The Secretary of State has stated that his policy is to be very selective about calling-in planning applications:

"[The Secretary of State] will, in general, only take this step if planning issues of more than local importance are involved. Such case may include, for example, those which in his opinion:

- may conflict with national policies on important matters;
- could have significant effects beyond their immediate locality;
- give rise to substantial regional or national controversy;
- raise significant architectural or urban design issues; or
- may involve the interests of national security or of foreign governments."[65]

The fourth of these criteria may sometimes arise in cases involving significant listed buildings, or major schemes in conservation areas.

Similarly, applications for listed building consent are only likely to be called-in where the Secretary of State considers that a proposal raises issues of "exceptional significance or controversy", or where it is associated with another matter (a planning appeal, called-in planning application or compulsory purchase order) that is also before him or her.[66]

In Wales, once an application has been called in, Cadw cannot be a party at any resulting inquiry, since it is part of the Welsh Office. It will, however, give advice to the Secretary of State, in the form of a brief statement.[67]

There is obviously no right of appeal against a called-in decision, other than to the courts on a point of law.[68]

An application for works that are the subject of a concurrent application for an order under the Transport and Works Act 1992 will be referred to the Secretary of State for decision, without the need for any specific direction.[69]

It has been argued that the call-in of applications by the Scottish Ministers at the request of Historic Scotland is a breach of human rights, since Historic Scotland is an executive agency of the Ministers. The appointment of a reporter (inspector) by the Minister to hold an inquiry would therefore mean that the Ministers would not be acting as an independent and impartial tribunal within the meaning of article 6 of the European Convention on Human Rights. The argument was dismissed, however, on the basis that the reporter, although possibly not such a tribunal, would nevertheless be required to conduct his inquiry in accordance with the rules of natural justice, subject to the control of the courts.[70] The same would apply to a decision by the Welsh Assembly to call-in an application at the request of Cadw.

Finally, the Secretary of State has recently held in, a decision on a called-in case, that his previous decision not to call in the application (for the demolition of

---

[65] *Hansard*, June 16, 1999, col 138. See also *R. v Secretary of State, ex p. Adlard* [2002] 1 W.L.R. 2525, H.R.L.R. 37.

[66] PPG 15, paras 3.20–3.21 and WO Circ. 61/96, paras 76–77.

[67] WO Circ. 61/96, para.78.

[68] s.12(5); see **15.6**.

[69] s.12(3), inserted by 1992 Act, s.17; see **13.10.6**.

[70] *County Properties Ltd v Scottish Ministers* [2001] 4 P.L.R. 122, overturning [2000] H.R.L.R. 677, [2001] J.P.L. 170.

a significant 20th-century house) did not give rise to a legitimate expectation that he would not review that decision and decide the application himself anyway.[71]

13.7.7 Decision by planning authority

The matters that should be taken into account in reaching that final decision are considered in detail in the following chapter.

The law governing the actual making of the decision, whether by a committee or subcommittee of the planning authority or by an officer under delegated powers, is the same as in any other case.[72] In particular, a decision made by elected councillors will be on the basis of a report produced by officers; and part of the officers' function is to assess how much information needs to be presented. As pointed out in *British Telecommunications PLC v Gloucester CC*:

"The fact is that members can be intimidated and discouraged by too much detail, just as they may be ill-equipped if there is too little. It is important that the principal issues and key information are put to them, but it is not necessary, or indeed desirable, that the report should be exhaustive."[73]

It may well be appropriate for decisions relating to historic buildings and areas to be the subject of a preliminary assessment by a conservation advisory group within the planning authority; care must then be taken that the views of that group are treated as an input into the final decision-taking process, which takes into account on an equal footing all relevant issues.[74]

A planning authority (or, come to that, the Secretary of State or equivalent) may either:

- refuse an application for planning permission, listed building consent or conservation area consent, or

- grant it subject to conditions (even if only as to the duration of the consent[75]).

As to the power to impose conditions, see below.[76]

Where a proposal is for a package of works, it is possible for consent to be granted for some and refused for others. This can only happen where each group is clearly defined and could have formed the basis of a separate freestanding application of itself. See for example an appeal regarding where consent was granted for the construction of a mansard roof on a house (to replace the existing decayed one), but refused for unsympathetic alterations to windows on the front façade; and more recently where consent was granted for the relocation of

---

[71] Runnymede BC, inspectorate reference APP/Q3630/V/04/1145659,1156052 (Greenside). See also **14.4.4**.

[72] See, for example, the considerations outlined at paras P70.53–64 of the *Encyclopedia of Planning Law and Practice*.

[73] [2002] J.P.L. 993 at para.117; see paras 102–120 generally; also *R. v Selby DC, ex p. Oxton Farms* [1997] E.G.C.S. 60, CA, and *Mendip DC, ex p. Fabre* [2000] J.P.L. 810.

[74] *Georgiou v Enfield LBC* [2005] J.P.L. 62 (see **5.3.2** and **14.7.1**).

[75] See **13.8.3**.

[76] See **13.8**.

external pipes so as to run internally and the installation of new French doors, but refused for the installation of new windows generally.[77]

13.7.8 Notification of decision

Whatever the decision, written notice of it must be given as soon as possible to the applicant.

In England, the notification of the decision must include the reasons for the refusal or grant and for any conditions imposed on a grant.[78] Elsewhere, the notification must include the reasons for a refusal or the imposition of any decisions, but not for the grant of permission or consent.[79] In the case of a planning application in England or Wales, whatever the decision, the notification must also include a list of the relevant development plan policies and proposals.[80] Note that the requirement for giving reasons for a grant of permission, introduced in 2003, appears to be mandatory—so that a decision without reasons would almost always be quashed by the court.[81] Further, it is not enough simply to refer to the committee report and minutes; the reasons must comprise a free-standing statement, not requiring reference to another documents.[82]

A form of notification, which includes a statement of the applicant's rights to appeal against a refusal of permission or consent or any of the conditions is set out in a Schedule to each of the relevant orders and regulations.[83]

In any case where English Heritage, Cadw or the national amenity societies were initially notified of an application for listed building consent, they must also be informed of any decision on it.[84] And English Heritage must be notified of the outcome of every application for conservation area consent in London.[85] There is no corresponding requirement to inform those who were notified of planning applications.

---

[77] [1984] J.P.L. 525 (Bristol); [2003] J.P.L. 914 (East Bergholt).

[78] TCP (General Development Procedure) Order 1995, art.22(1), substituted by SI 2003/2047, art.5 (England) and amended by SI 2004/1434, art.3 (Wales); P(LBCA) Regs 1990, art.3(5), substituted by SI 2003/2048.

[79] Wales: TCP (General Development Procedure) Order 1995, art.22(1), amended by SI 2004/1434, art.3; P(LBCA) Regs 1990, reg.3(5). Scotland: TCP (General Development Procedure) (Scotland) Order 1992, art.22(1); TCP(LBCA) (S) Regs, art.3(4).

[80] TCP (General Development Procedure) Order 1995, art.22(1), substituted / amended as above.

[81] R. (Wall) v Brighton and Hove City Council [2005] 1 P. & C.R. 33.

[82] R. (Chisnell) v Richmond-upon-Thames LBC, April 26, 2005, unreported.

[83] TCP (General Development Procedure) Order 1995, Sch.1, Pt 2 (planning applications); P(LBCA) Regs 1990, Sch.1, Pt 2 (LBC and CAC applications). Welsh equivalents are at SI 1995/3336, Sch.1, Pt 2 (planning applications) and SI 1990/1147, Sch., Pt 2. [Scotland: TCP (General Development Procedure) (Scotland) Order 1992, Sch.9; TCP(LBCA) (S) Regs, Sch.1, Pt 2).

[84] P(LBCA)A 1990, s.15(5)(b); Circ. 01/01, para.15, WO Circ. 1/98, para.10; see **13.5**.

[85] P(LBCA)A 1990, s.14, modified by 1990 Regs, Sch.3.

13.7.9 Temporary or personal consents

Where permission or consent is granted, it will always be subject to a condition requiring that the permitted works are started within a specified period.[86] However, subject to that, it will generally last indefinitely,[87] except where:

(1) it specifically states otherwise; or

(2) it is revoked or modified, when compensation may be payable.[88]

The first of these, which refers to what is in effect a temporary grant of permission or consent, will not often be suitable. Where it is granted, it should normally be subject to conditions:

(1) that the works are carried out in such a way that they can be removed at the end of the temporary period without any adverse effect on the building or land concerned; and

(2) that they are thus removed at the end of the period.[89]

Where a temporary listed building consent is granted in this way, if the works are not removed as required, the owner would have committed a criminal offence, and could therefore be prosecuted and (presumably) made to remove them.[90]

A grant of permission or consent can be acted on by anyone interested in the building for the time being—again, unless it states otherwise.[91] A "personal" grant of listed building consent would not often be suitable, since the considerations to be taken into account by an authority determining an application for listed building consent (as opposed to one for planning permission) primarily concern the building, not its owners or occupiers.[92] See *Gwinnell v Secretary of State*[93] for an example.

13.7.10 The grant of listed building consent for demolition

In addition to needing listed building consent, works for the demolition of a listed building are not fully authorised until they have been notified to the relevant recording body. In England, this is English Heritage (as the successor to the Royal Commission on Historical Monuments of England[93a]); elsewhere it is the relevant

---

[86] See **13.8.3**.
[87] TCPA 1990, s.75(1); P(LBCA)A 1990, s.16(3). [Scotland: TCP(S)A 1997, s.44(1); P(LBCA)(S)A 1997, s.14(3); NI: P(NI)O 1991, art.30(1); Sch.1, para.6.]
[88] See **13.12**.
[89] See appeal decision at [2001] J.P.L. 1124.
[90] P(LBCA)A 1990, ss 7, 8(1)(b), (2)(d), 9(1).
[91] TCPA 1990, s.75(1); P(LBCA)A 1990, s.16(3). [Scotland: TCP(S)A 1997, s.44(1); P(LBCA)(S)A 1997, s.14(3); NI: P(NI)O 1991, art.30(1); Sch.1, para.6.]
[92] P(LBCA)A 1990, s.16(2). [Scotland: P(LBCA)(S)A 1997, s.14(2); NI: P(NI)O 1991, art.45(1).]
[93] [1994] E.G.C.S. 81 (discussed at **14.9.2**).
[93a] P(LBCA)A 1990, s.8(2), amended by Authorisation of Works (Listd Buildings) Order 2001 (SI 2001/24).

Royal Commission in Wales and Scotland, or the Department in Northern Ireland.[94] Reasonable access must be then given to the officers of the recording body for a period of at least a month (three in Scotland) so that they can record the building, unless they state in writing that they do not wish to or have already done so. Authorities have been asked to draw this requirement to the attention of all applicants for consent for demolition—preferably by a suitable note on the relevant application form.[95]

Where listed building consent is granted for the total demolition of a building, the authority should remind the applicant of his or her obligation to allow access to officers of the relevant recording body to record the building.[96] In the case of consent being granted for partial demolition or major alterations, there is no automatic right for a recording body to be given access, but such a consent could be subject to a condition requiring that access be given for a month, as for total demolition.[97] This might apply in any case where a major feature is likely to be lost or radically changed.[98]

In either case, an authority in England should also send the applicant a copy of the form Stat E, on which to give notice of the intention to demolish.[99]

A copy of the decision should be sent to the relevant recording body, English Heritage or the Royal Commission, as an advance warning.

Authorities have also been reminded that, where consent has been granted for the demolition of a building, it should be kept at least weather-proof and vandal-proof until work actually starts (the same applies in the case of major alterations); and that, once the building has actually been demolished, the Department of Culture, Media and Sport should be notified so that it can be removed from the list.[1]

There is no need for either the authority or the applicant to notify English Heritage or the Royal Commission of any decision to grant conservation area consent for demolition.

13.7.11 Applications for advertisements consent

An application for express consent for the display of advertisements is processed in much the same way as an application for planning permission or listed building consent, and consent is either granted subject to conditions or refused; the procedure is provided for in the relevant Control of Advertisements Regulations.[2]

---

[94] P(LBCA)A 1990, s.8(2) Wales. [Scotland: P(LBCA)(S)A 1997, s.7(2); NI: P(NI)O 1991, art.44(2)(b).]

[95] PPG 15, Annex B, para.B.4.

[96] PPG 15, Annex B, para.B.4; and see 9.4.6.

[97] See **Appendix E**.

[98] PPG 15, para.3.22, and Circ. 01/01, para.18.

[99] The form is available from English Heritage.

[1] PPG 15, Annex B, paras B.6, B.7; WO Circ. 61/96, paras 107, 108.

[2] TCP (Control of Advertisements) Regulations 1992, regs 9–17. [Scotland: TCP (Control of Advertisements) Regulations 1984, regs 15–23; NI: TCP (Control of Advertisements) (NI) Regulations, regs 7–14.] See also **12.2.6**.

Express consent is normally limited to five years. However, after the expiry of that period, deemed consent is granted automatically.[3] In Northern Ireland, consents are of indefinite duration.

13.8 Conditions and obligations

13.8.1 Statutory powers to impose conditions

In considering whether or not to grant planning permission, listed building consent or conservation area consent, the ability to impose conditions often plays a most important part in the decision. Frequently, permission or consent would not be given at all unless conditions were imposed safeguarding the treatment of the building concerned or requiring works to be carried out in a certain way.

Planning authorities, and the Secretary of State, have a general power to impose any conditions on a grant of permission or consent.[4] Some types of conditions are specifically provided for by statute; but that is specifically stated to be without prejudice to the general power to impose conditions. A breach of any condition attached to a grant of listed building or conservation area consent is an offence liable to attract the same maximum penalties as carrying out work without consent at all.[5]

However, the general power to impose conditions cannot be exercised without any limits. Thus "the planning authority are not at liberty to use their powers for an ulterior object, however desirable that object may seem to them to be in the public interest".[6] Rather, the power to impose conditions on a grant of planning permission must be exercised in pursuance of the aims of planning control—that is, in accordance with the development plan and all other material considerations and, where there is conflict, the development plan must take precedence.[7]

In relation to listed buildings, the decision as to whether to grant planning permission for development that affects a listed building or its setting must be exercised in the light of the general duty "to have regard to the desirability of preserving the building or its setting or any features of special architectural or historic interest which it possesses."[8] That same duty would seem to apply to the imposition of conditions on planning permissions. It would also seem to apply, on precisely the same basis, to the imposition of conditions on listed building consents.[9] The imposition of conditions on planning permission for development in a conservation area, or on conservation area consent, is subject to the general duty

3   1992 Regulations, Schedule 3, Pt I, Class 14. [Scotland: reg.19.]
4   TCPA 1990, ss 70(1), 72(1); P(LBCA)A 1990, ss 16(1), 17. [Scotland: TCP(S)A 1997, ss 37(1), 40; P(LBCA)(S)A 1997, ss 14(1), 15; NI: P(NI)O 1991, arts 25(1), 27, 45.]
5   P(LBCA)A 1990, s.9(2),(4); see **19.2.2**.
6   *per* Lord Denning in *Pyx Granite Co. Ltd v Minister of Housing and Local Government* [1958] 1 Q.B. 554 at 572.
7   TCPA 1990, s.70(2); Planning and Compulsory Purchase Act 2004, s.38(6). [Scotland: TCP(S)A 1997, ss 25, 37(2); NI: P(NI)O 1991, arts 4(2A), 25(1).]
8   P(LBCA)A 1990, s.66(1). [Scotland: P(LBCA)(S)A 1997, s.59(1); NI: P(NI)O 1991, art.45(1).]
9   P(LBCA)A 1990, s.16(2). [Scotland: P(LBCA)(S)A 1997, s.14(2); NI: P(NI)O 1991, art.45(1).]

to pay special attention to the desirability of preserving or enhancing the character or appearance of the area.[10] The outworking of these duties is considered in more detail in the following chapter.

The courts will only intervene to overturn a condition if they consider that it is one which "no reasonable authority, acting within the four corners of their jurisdiction, could have decided to impose". To prove this "would require something overwhelming".[11] On the other hand, authorities should be wary of imposing more conditions than are strictly necessary.

13.8.2 Policy advice

Comprehensive ministerial advice on the imposition of conditions on planning permissions is given in DoE Circular 11/95. This lays down a number of tests, which it summarises in the well-known formula that:

"conditions should be:

  (i)   necessary,
  (ii) relevant to planning,
  (iii) relevant to the development to be permitted,
  (iv) enforceable,
  (v)   precise, and
  (vi) reasonable in all other respects."[12]

That Circular should be consulted for further comments on the practical application of those tests.

This is repeated in PPG 15, in relation to listed building and conservation area consents, save that the second and third considerations are rolled up in the single requirement that conditions must be "relevant"[13]; which presumably means relevant both to listed building control generally and to the particular works permitted. There is otherwise no general ministerial guidance relating to conditions on listed building and conservation area consents equivalent to that in Circular 11/95. However, the considerations in that Circular, suitably adapted, are equally relevant to conditions on such consents.

The power to impose conditions was considered by the Outer House of the Court of Session in *Edinburgh City Council v Scottish Ministers*,[14], in which a reporter granted listed building consent for the retention of an internal partition wall, subject to a condition that it be removed within one month of either the permanent cessation of the use of the relevant room as a bedroom, or the removal of net curtains, or that of the privet hedge outside. The court emphasised the need to ensure that conditions are drafted with care and precision, and held that the present condition failed that test, and should be quashed.

---

[10] P(LBCA)A 1990, s.72. [Scotland: P(LBCA)(S)A 1997, s.64; NI: P(NI)O 1991, art.50(5).]
[11] *Associated Provincial Picture Houses v Wednesbury Corporation* [1948] 1 K.B. 223, *per* Lord Greene M.R. at 233 and 230; cited with approval in the House of Lords in *Fawcett Properties Ltd v Buckinghamshire CC* [1961] A.C. 636 at 6612, 6789 and 685.
[12] DoE Circ. 11/95 (WO Circ. 35/95), para.14. [Scotland: NPPG 8, para.44.]
[13] Annex B, para.B.8; WO Circ. 61/96, para.109.
[14] [2002] 4 P.L.R. 54, [2003] J.P.L. 903; see also **18.2.4**.

The Court of Appeal also rejected a well-intentioned attempt by a planning authority to secure the removal of an unsightly barn, which harmed the setting of a listed building, by way of a condition attached to a grant of planning permission for the change of use of the building. The Court agreed that a condition seeking demolition of an ancillary structure could not be said to relate to a change of use that did not affect the external appearance of the listed building.[15]

No sample conditions for listed building consents are provided in PPG 15 or Circular 01/01. However, Annex F to WO Circular 61/96 contains examples of conditions which may be appropriate to listed building consents. These are the basis of many of those included in as **Appendix E** to this book.

13.8.3 Duration of permission and consent

Every planning permission and listed building or conservation area consent granted since 1980 has been subject to an implied condition that the works permitted by it must be begun within five years of the date of the grant, unless there is an explicit condition stating a different time-limit, which could be either longer or shorter.[16] This period was reduced to three years by section 51 of the Planning and Compulsory Purchase Act 2004 in respect of England and Wales[17] (the five-year limit remains elsewhere); although a limit of four or five years might be more appropriate where a planning authority grants permission or consent subject to a large number of matters to be sorted out before any of the permitted works can be started.

The reason for such a condition is commonly given as "as required by the [1990 Act]". That is incorrect, as the 1990 Act does not require any particular time limit. The correct reason is more accurately stated as "to ensure that the planning authority retains the right to review unimplemented consents."

There have been a number of cases over the years clarifying the extent of precisely what constitutes "beginning" work in the context of planning permission—from which it appears that very little needs to be done in order to implement a permission.[18] There is no corresponding provision in relation to listed building consent; however, by analogy with the provisions applying to planning permissions, it would seem that, for works to be "begun", it will be sufficient for an owner to have carried out almost any part of them.

Once works have thus been begun, their completion can be delayed indefinitely.[19] A planning authority cannot force an unwilling owner to complete works for which planning permission has been granted, but it can serve a "completion notice", the effect of which is that the permission will expire on a specified date, at

---

[15] *Delta Design and Engineering Ltd v Secretary of State* (2000) 80 P. & C.R. 76, CA, overturning [1999] J.P.L. 612.

[16] TCPA 1990, s.91; P(LBCA)A 1990, s.18. [Scotland: TCP(S)A 1997, s.58; P(LBCA)(S)A 1997, s.16; NI: P(NI)O 1991 arts 34, 46.]

[17] The new time limit applies automatically only in the case of permissions and consents granted on or after August 24, 2005 in England; the commencement date for Wales will no doubt follow in due course.

[18] See, for example, *Malvern Hills DC v Secretary of State* [1982] J.P.L. 439; *Thayer v Secretary of State* [1992] J.P.L. 264.

[19] *Spackman v Wiltshire CC* (1976) 33 P. & C.R. 430.

least a year away.[20] There is no corresponding provision in relation to listed building consent. Thus if, for example, listed building consent is granted for removing the existing windows from a building and replacing them with suitable alternatives, and the owner merely removes the existing ones without replacement, the only remedies open to the authority to achieve the completion of the works would be to prosecute him or her for not carrying them out in accordance with the consent,[21] to carry out the works itself as a matter of urgency,[22] or to serve a repairs notice.[23]

One way to avoid this problem, where a building is unoccupied during conversion works, might be to impose a *Grampian* condition on the listed building consent, to the effect that the building should not be reoccupied until all the works have been completed to the satisfaction of the planning authority.[24] This was the option preferred by the Secretary of State in connection with the conversion of County Hall to a hotel.[25] The Inspector had favoured the setting up of a contingency fund to safeguard the future of the building in the event of the permitted development not being completed—Battersea Power Station having been cited as a notable example of another large listed building where grand proposals had (and still have) failed to come to fruition. Unfortunately, however, there was no statutory power to enable the creation of such a fund, and he therefore recommended that consent should still be granted, even without it—but subject to the *Grampian* condition.

Where planning permission or listed building consent is obtained for the carrying out of works, but is not implemented within the specified period, it will lapse; and a further application must be made to review it. DoE Circular 11/95[26] advises that a planning application made in those circumstances should generally be granted unless there has been some change in planning circumstances since the previous permission was granted, or continued failure to begin the works will lead to uncertainty.[27] There seems to be no reason why the same approach should not apply to applications for the renewal of listed building consent (see for example *Stocks Hotel v Secretary of State*[28]).

13.8.4 Subsequent approval of details

It has already been noted that a planning authority may grant "outline planning permission", reserving certain matters for subsequent approval.[29] Alternatively, the authority may respond to a full planning application—that is, one containing details of all aspects of the proposed development—by granting full planning

---

[20] TCPA 1990, s.94. [Scotland: TCP(S)A 1997, s.61; NI: P(NI)O 1991, art.37 (in Northern Ireland, the term is "completion order").]
[21] Under P(LBCA)A 1990, s.9(1); see **19.2.2**.
[22] under PLBCA 1990, s.54; see **10.3**.
[23] under s.48; see **11.3**.
[24] *Grampian Regional Council v City of Aberdeen DC* (1983) 47 P. & C.R. 633.
[25] *Lambeth LBC v Secretary of State* [1992] J.P.L. 759, upholding [1992] E.G.C.S. 17.
[26] WO Circ. 35/95.
[27] See para.60.
[28] [1996] E.G.C.S. 165.
[29] See **13.3.9**.

permission but subject to conditions reserving particular details for later approval.

Similarly, an authority may grant listed building consent subject to a condition reserving details for later approval.[30] This is not intended to be "outline listed building consent" under another name, as is emphasised by the placing within the Act itself of the requirement that *every* application for consent must be accompanied by sufficient details to describe the works.[31] Thus, even if an applicant desires to obtain consent subject to such a condition, and the authority is willing to grant it, the initial application must still be accompanied by full details.

The grant of permission or consent subject to such conditions means that, where enough information about proposed works has been supplied for their general effect to be assessed, they can now be authorised in principle, even though more negotiation may be needed as to the fine tuning—such as the materials to be used, or the detailing of a particular element of an alteration or a new building. However, authorities should avoid the temptation to impose numerous conditions of this kind requiring further approval to be given for matters as to which they in fact already have perfectly adequate information.

Such conditions should state whether the subsequent approval is to be by the planning authority or by the Secretary of State or the Scottish Ministers.[32]

Where subsequent approval of details by the planning authority is required, an application should be made as if for straightforward planning permission or listed building consent. If approval is not forthcoming, there is a right of appeal against refusal or non-determination, as for a straightforward application.[33]

13.8.5 Other statutory conditions

There are several other conditions which are specifically stated in the Act to be capable of being attached to a grant of listed building or conservation area consent. These include:

(1) that particular features of the building are to be preserved, either as part of it or after severance from it[34];

(2) that any damage caused by the works permitted is made good after they are complete; and

(3) that the building, or a specified part of it, is reconstructed following the execution of the works, with:

---

[30] P(LBCA)A 1990, s.17(2). [Scotland: P(LBCA)(S)A 1997, s.15(2); NI: P(NI)O 1991, art.45(4).]

[31] P(LBCA)A 1990, s.10(2) (b); PPG 15, Annex B, para.B. 10; WO Circ. 61/96, para.111. [Scotland: P(LBCA)(S)A 1997, s.9(2)(b); NI: P(NI)O 1991, Sch.1, para.1(1).]

[32] P(LBCA)A 1990, s.17(2). [Scotland: P(LBCA)(S)A 1997, s.15(2).]

[33] TCPA 1990, s.78(1)(b), (2); P(LBCA)A 1990, s.20(1) (c), (2); see **15.2.2**.

[34] For examples of appeal decisions where listed building consent was granted subject to such conditions, see [1987] J.P.L. 299 (balusters to be retained after the demolition of a house), and [1985] J.P.L. 652 (a Union Set—a double row of barrels—to be retained after the demolition of a brewery).

- the use of original materials so far as practicable; and
- such alterations of the interior of the building as may be specified.[35]

These are reasonably straightforward. The precise wording of conditions to be used in a particular case will obviously need to be considered very carefully, since many historic buildings are unique; and it will in many cases be best if the conditions are drafted, or at least finalised, in conjunction with the person who will actually carry out the works, to avoid the possibility of any misunderstanding or dispute later on.

One variant of this is where part of a building is to be demolished or substantially altered, in such a way as to render the remaining part liable to collapse. It may then be appropriate not just to require that the vulnerable part should remain, but in addition to insist on the submission for prior approval of a detailed scheme to ensure that this actually occurs.

Where a listed building is to be moved in its entirety from one location to another, that may be the subject of a grant of listed building consent subject to a condition requiring it to be re-erected at the chosen new location, and no doubt also requiring the prior approval of the details of the moving and re-erection process.[35a]

Consent may also be granted subject to a condition that the building shall not be demolished until:

- a contract for the carrying out of works of redevelopment of the site has been made; and
- planning permission has been granted for that redevelopment.[36]

Such a condition would be used where an authority wishes to ensure that premature demolition does not take place and leave an empty gap long before planning permission is sought and rebuilding starts. The Secretary of State has urged authorities to impose it wherever listed building consent (and, by inference, conservation area consent) is granted for demolition.[37] The use of such a condition will also be appropriate in cases where only the main façade of a building is to be retained in front of a completely rebuilt interior or, as is now preferred, the front range of a property is to be retained. Here it should be linked to a series of other conditions to ensure that the retention is in fact possible.

Examples of such conditions are at **Appendix E**.

---

[35] P(LBCA)A 1990, s.17(1). [Scotland: P(LBCA)(S)A 1997, s.15(1); NI: P(NI)O 1991, art.45(3).]

[35a] For a notorious recent example, see *R (Judge) v Secretary of State and Middlesbrough BC* [2005] EWCA, unreported, July 22, 2005, CA; affirming [2005] EWHC 887 (Admin), unreported, April 28, 2005.

[36] P(LBCA)A 1990, s.17(3). [Scotland: P(LBCA)(S)A 1997, s.15(3); NI: P(NI)O 1991, art.45(5).]

[37] PPG 15, Annex B, para.B.5; WO Circ. 61/96, para.106. For an example, see the appeal decision at [1987] J.P.L. 299.

As for the effect of such a condition being imposed on the assessment of whether a landlord intends to demolish and rebuild, see the decision of the Court of Appeal in *Parlisade Investments Ltd v Collin Estates Ltd*.[38]

There are no corresponding statutory conditions in relation to a grant of planning permission—although those noted above could perfectly properly be used in that context.

13.8.6 Other conditions

It is important to ensure by condition that features are kept safe during the course of building works. Authorities have been advised to impose conditions relating to the recording of architectural features likely to be lost or altered in proposed works, and those which may be discovered during the course of them.[39] The same principle applies to the protection and recording of archaeological features.[40]

In addition, it would be appropriate, in any case involving either total demolition or the removal or radical alteration of any major feature of the building, to impose a condition requiring that access be given to English Heritage, the relevant Royal Commission or some other appropriate recording body to enable it to record the building or feature.[41] This is particularly important in the case of what used to be referred to as "partial demolition", but is now more accurately categorised as alteration consisting of the removal of part of the building[42]—since in such cases the recording body does not have an automatic right of access.[43]

As well as the conditions referred to above, which are those specifically envisaged either in statute or in government guidance, there will be a number of others that will be appropriate in particular cases. Indeed, it is important to draft conditions carefully, rather than simply use without thought those on a list of standard conditions. It is also worth considering how the conditions are grouped and ordered, to avoid the apparently random scattering commonly found in practice. It may thus be most convenient, both for the applicant and the planning authority, if conditions are grouped as follows (so far as relevant):

(1) the duration of the consent;

(2) details to be resolved before the start of any works (so that the scope of the permission and consent is known);

(3) no works of demolition to start until construction of replacement building has been properly secured;

(4) practical matters to be dealt with before the start of any other works (such as recording of items to be removed or destroyed; protection of items of

---

[38] [1992] 2 E.G.L.R. 94.
[39] PPG 15, paras 3.23–3.24.
[40] See **14.8.2, 14.8.3**.
[41] See **13.7.10**.
[42] Since the decision of the House of Lords in *Shimizu (UK) Ltd v Westminster CC* [1996] 3 P.L.R. 89; see **12.6.3**.
[43] Advice is given at PPG 15, paras 3.22–3.24 and WO Circ. 61/96, paras 81–83.

value to remain on site; access from the highway and parking within the site);

(5) the way in which works are to be carried out;

(6) the completed building not to be occupied until the works have been fully completed;

(7) damage to be made good;

(8) the way in which the completed development is to be used;

(9) the restoration of any temporary works.

Conditions in categories (2), (4) and (6) (and possibly others) could alternatively be framed on a phase-by-phase basis in the case of larger schemes.

Thus, for example, all the conditions requiring approval of particular matters before the start of any works should be grouped together. In this way, it should be possible for the applicant to know what he or she has to do at any given stage, and in particular what further approvals are necessary. And the authority can check, in appropriate cases, that there is no need for enforcement action to be taken.

13.8.7 Applications to modify conditions

It has already been noted that conditions are often very important. Nevertheless it may sometimes be desirable to seek to have a condition altered or removed.

From the point of view of the applicant, he or she may seek to have conditions varied or discharged where they have become too onerous—either because circumstances have changed; or because the current owner is not the original applicant; or because the works already carried out have revealed that the remaining approved works are now likely to be unexpectedly expensive to complete. Examples of this might be where dry rot is more extensive than thought; or where other structural problems arise.[44] As always, if (as often occurs) both planning permission and listed building consent have been subject to similar conditions, it is necessary to modify both sets of conditions.

From the point of view of the planning authority, on the other hand, there may be occasions where the approved scheme was less than ideal, and where revised conditions may be appropriate once better solutions for the treatment of the building have been devised. It may also be sensible to reconsider conditions attached to the original consent if older and more interesting features are revealed once works have begun. An authority in such a case can only invite the applicant to submit an application to modify the relevant conditions. If the applicant is unwilling, the authority would have to modify the consent, which is possible, but which carries with it a possible liability to pay compensation.[45]

The provision relating to planning permissions allows for a planning authority or the Secretary of State to grant permission for development but without compliance with conditions previously attached; but if they consider it appropriate,

---

[44] PPG 15, Annex B, para.B.11; WO Circ. 61/96, para.112.
[45] See **13.11**.

they may grant permission subject to "conditions differing from those subject to which the previous permission was granted".[46] The wording of the corresponding provision relating to listed building and conservation area consent allows for the planning authority or the Secretary of State to "vary or discharge the conditions attached to the consent, and [to] add new conditions consequential upon the variation or discharge".[47] The phrase "variation of condition" would clearly include the alteration of minor details (such as materials) specified in approved drawings.

In the case of conditions on a grant of planning permission (and in relation to listed building and conservation area consent in Northern Ireland), such an application may be made by anyone; but in relation to listed building and conservation area consent in England, Wales and Scotland, it may be made only by a person "interested in" a listed building.[48] That is, presumably, the applicant need not "have an interest in" it; so a prospective purchaser, or even conceivably an amenity group, could apply. This can be contrasted with, for example, the enforcement provisions[49] which use the latter phrase, which clearly has a more precise legal meaning. The more general phrase may lead to disputes as to *locus standi*. Thus in *Bearmans Ltd v Metropolitan Police District Receiver*, Devlin L.J. said: "The word 'interested' is not a word which has any well defined meaning ... it is essential ... to look at the scope and purpose of the Act."[50] See also *R. v Dudley Crown Court, Ex p. Pask*:

"... there is no reason here to import into the word 'interest' a requirement that the interest be a legal or equitable one in the special property sense."[51]

That case concerned the grant of a licence to a person "interested" in any premises. In a planning case concerning compensation payable under what it now section 107 of the Planning Act to any person "interested" in land, Eveleigh and Kerr L.JJ. held that someone with a mere contractual right to occupy land, probably not substantial enough to amount to a licence, was "interested" in it; Stephenson L.J. on the other hand preferred limiting the word to meaning "holding a proprietary interest in" (that is, either a legal or an equitable interest, including possibly an interest arising as a result of estoppel).[52] That narrower view was also supported in the earlier case of *Jones v Secretary of State for Wales*.[53]

The intention behind the provision in the Listed Building Act is clear, however. The initial guidance thus stated:

"... it has been decided to restrict the making of the application to a person interested in the building to avoid applications by third parties who may try to have the consent altered without having the responsibility for carrying out the work".[54]

---

[46] TCPA 1990, s.73. [Scotland: TCP(S)A 1997, s.42; NI: P(NI)O 1991, art.28.]
[47] P(LBCA)A 1990, 19. [Scotland: P(LBCA)(S)A 1997, s.17; NI: P(NI)O 1991, Sch.1, para.5.]
[48] P(LBCA)A 1990, s.19(1). [Scotland: P(LBCA)(S)A 1997, s.17(1).]
[49] P(LBCA)A 1990, ss 38(4) (b)), 39(1).
[50] [1961] 1 WLR 634 at p.655.
[51] (1983) *The Times*, June 18, 1983.
[52] *Pennine Raceway Ltd v Kirklees MDC* [1982] 3 All E.R. 628.
[53] (1974) 28 P. & C.R. 280.
[54] Circ. 8/87, para.78.

The current guidance merely state that an application can be made by persons with a legal interest in the building.[55]

An application for the variation or discharge of a condition is (obviously) to specify the condition at issue; otherwise the procedural provisions follow almost exactly those applying to an ordinary application for consent.[56] The form to be sent to the applicant notifying him or her of the decision is at Part III of Schedule 1 to the 1990 Regulations.[57] And there is a right of appeal to the Secretary of State if such an application is refused, or is granted subject to the imposition of further conditions, or is not determined.[58]

13.8.8 Planning obligations

Consideration of some of the issues raised in the following chapter may lead a developer to the conclusion that certain benefits may usefully be offered, such as the restoration of a historic building, or restrictions imposed, such as the removal of unsuitable alterations that were carried out by a previous owner. In England and Wales, this may in some instances best be achieved by the entering into of a planning obligation under section 106 of the Planning Act, or its successor sections 46 to 48 of the Planning and Compulsory Purchase Act 2004 (once in force)[59]—either an agreement between the developer and the planning authority, or a unilateral undertaking. A very simple example of the latter is included at **Form D15** in Appendix D.

The provisions applying in Scotland are the same as section 106 of the 1990 Act as initially enacted (and its predecessor, section 52 of the 1971 Act), and do not allow for unilateral undertakings.[60] In Northern Ireland, they are (since August 2005) now the same as section 106 following the changes made in 1991.[61]

For a planning authority or the Secretary of State to take into account a planning obligation, the developer must be able to demonstrate that he or she can in fact deliver what has been promised. Thus in *South Oxfordshire DC v Secretary of State*,[62] a unilateral undertaking was submitted by the Trustees of a large estate, containing many historic buildings, intended to ensure that the income from the proposed development would indeed be used to finance the restoration works. The council was concerned that the undertaking did not define what repair works were to be carried out, and was thus unenforceable; it accordingly could not constitute a planning obligation under the Act. However, Sir Graham Eyre Q.C., sitting as deputy judge, considered that section 106 of the Act, as amended, now gave wide powers to developers to conclude undertakings provided that they met planning objectives; and there was no need (as there had been previously) to seek agreement with the planning authority. In this case, the Trustees had wide

[55] PPG 15, Annex B, para.B.11; WO Circ. 16/96, para.112.
[56] P(LBCA)A 1990, s.19(2), (3); P(LBCA) Regs 1990, reg.4.
[57] The Welsh language equivalent is at Pt III of Sch.1 to SI 1990/1147.
[58] s.20(1)(b), (2); see **15.2.2**.
[59] sections described by the learned editor of the *Planning Encyclopedia* as "easily the most puzzling to have found their way into the new Act".
[60] TCP(S)A 1997, s.75.
[61] P(NI)O 1991, arts 40–40B. inserted by Planning (Amendment) (NI) Order 2003.
[62] [1995] J.P.L. 213 (see **14.9.4**).

powers to ensure that the buildings on the Estate were repaired, and they had undertaken to use their best endeavours to ensure that this in fact occurred. The undertaking was thus a valid planning obligation.

No doubt the inspector in the *South Oxfordshire* case, in being influenced by the undertaking so as to grant planning permission, was reassured by the thought that the Trustees had already carried out many repairs of the kind now proposed; others may find more difficulty in convincing authorities and inspectors that their intentions are genuine.

In *Hart DC v Secretary of State*,[63] the Council challenged an inspector's decision, on the ground (amongst others) that he had failed to take into account deficiencies in the section 106 obligation, including the absence of a requirement to restore and maintain the park land or to continue the equestrian use of the stables and the absence of any provision to ensure that sufficient funds would be available for the restoration or maintenance of the listed buildings and the park land. The challenge failed, as the court found that the inspector had considered these matters with care; and he was not required to address every detail of the proposed agreement.

For further details on planning obligations, reference should be made to a general planning law textbook applying in the relevant jurisdiction.[64]

13.9 Applications for scheduled monument consent

13.9.1 Submission of application

All applications for scheduled monument consent in England are to be made to the Secretary of State—that is, the DCMS—and not to the planning authority or to English Heritage. However, anyone even contemplating carrying out any works to a scheduled monument would do well to consult English Heritage at the earliest possible opportunity, since the DCMS will "as soon as practicable" send a copy of any application it receives to English Heritage,[65] and it will be English Heritage's officers who will in practice be dealing with it. Preliminary discussions will ensure that there are minimum problems later on.

In Wales and Scotland, applications for consent are to be made to the Welsh Assembly and the Scottish Ministers—in practice, Cadw and Historic Scotland, who should be consulted by prospective applicants. References here to "the determining body" should be construed accordingly.

The procedure is set out in Part I of Schedule 1 to the Ancient Monuments Act, and in the two sets of Ancient Monuments (Applications for Scheduled Monument) Consent Regulations issued in 1981—one for England and Wales, and one for Scotland.[66]

---

[63] [1997] J.P.L. B125 (see **14.6.2**).
[64] And see ODPM Circ. 05/2005, *Planning Obligations*.
[65] 1979 Act, Sch.1, para.2A.
[66] SI 1981/1301.

An application is to be made on the form prescribed in Schedule 1 to the 1981 Regulations.[67] The form used in practice, Form AM112 is available, together with supporting guidance notes, from DCMS (Buildings, Monuments and Sites Division, Branch 2), or Cadw (Ancient Monuments Administration).[68] The corresponding form for Scotland is available from Historic Scotland. The Form must be accompanied by plans and drawings sufficient to identify the monument and describe the works proposed.[69] By the nature of ancient monuments, the works may need to be described in considerable detail, to enable their effect on the monument to be ascertained adequately. The determining body can always ask for further information if it wishes.[70]

In Northern Ireland applications are to be made to the Environment and Heritage Service of the Department, under the terms of the Historic Monuments and Archaeological Objects (Northern Ireland) Order 1995.

13.9.2 Notification of other owners

An application for scheduled monument consent should be accompanied by a certificate as to the ownership of the monument, similar to that needed with applications for planning permission and listed building consent.[71] However, unlike the position with regard to those applications, the determining body does have jurisdiction to entertain an application for scheduled monument consent if it is not accompanied by a certificate.[72] The form in which that notice is to be given to other owners of the land is prescribed by Part II of Schedule 2 to the Regulations; it states that:

"... an opportunity to make representations with respect to the application will be afforded by the Secretary of State before the application is determined."

That wording might suggest to an owner that the determining body would, at some date following the receipt of the application, write to all the owners other than the applicant, to seek their views. In fact, however, at least until recently, the practice of the Secretary of State was to regard the receipt of the notice in the prescribed form as itself being the opportunity to make representations. This led to a successful challenge to a grant of consent for the erection of a telecommunications aerial on Morpeth Castle in Northumberland. The owner of the Castle (which happened to be the local council) was notified of the application by the telecommunications operator, in the prescribed form, and awaited its promised opportunity to make representations; but the next thing it heard was that consent had been granted. The Council applied to the High Court under section

---

[67] reg.2(1).
[68] For current addresses etc, see **Appendix C**. Note that those in PPG 16 are out of date. Welsh language forms are available, in 2001/1438.
[69] reg.2(2).
[70] reg.2(3).
[71] 1979 Act, Sch.1, para.2; 1981 Regulations, reg.3, Sch.2, Pt I. [NI: HMAO(NI)O 1995, Sch.1, para.2.]
[72] Compare, for example, AMAAA 1979, Sch.1, para.2(1) with P(LBCA) Regs 1990, reg.6(1).

55 of the Act for the decision of the Secretary of State to be quashed,[73] and the matter was referred back to her for a further decision, following her submission to judgment.

Following that incident, owners and planning authorities are now given a proper opportunity to comment; but those (owners and others) notified of an application should make representations promptly, and not wait to be asked.

13.9.3 Determination of application

English Heritage or (outside England) the determining body will consider the application. In practice, they will often be aware of the proposals already, as a result of preliminary discussions (see above). There is a specific power for anyone duly authorised to enter any land for the purpose of inspecting any scheduled monument in connection with an application for consent for works to it.[74]

In relation to a monument in England, English Heritage will make a recommendation to the Secretary of State. There is no timetable laid down in the Act or the Regulations, but it aims to do so within three months of being initially notified of the application. The Secretary of State (that is, the DCMS) in turn aims to decide every case within one month following receipt of a recommendation from English Heritage.

The determining body must take into account any representations made as a result of the notice given by the applicant to other owners of the land.[75] As for the other matters to be taken into account, these are considered in the following chapter.[76]

It may also give publicity to an application if it seems appropriate, and if so must consider any representations made as a result. He or she must in any event also take into account any representations made by anybody, regardless of how they arose.[77] There is no other formal requirement for an application for consent to be publicised—either to neighbours, or on site or in the press. This is a curious lacuna, which should be rectified at some suitable opportunity. In practice, however, English Heritage and Cadw normally do consult local authorities, regional archaeological trusts in Wales, and other bodies as appropriate.[78]

The determining body, before coming to a final decision on an application, is obliged either to hold a public inquiry or at least to give an opportunity to the applicant and anyone else considered appropriate to be heard before an inspector; and he or she must then take into account the report of the person holding that inquiry or hearing.[79] This is an important procedural safeguard, since there is no right of appeal against the decision of the determining body—other than to the High Court. Presumably English Heritage would always be able to be a party to any such inquiry or hearing, even though it has no actual statutory right to do so.

---

[73] See **15.6.1**.
[74] AMAAA 1979, ss 6(2)(a), 6A(3). [NI: HMAO(NI)O 1995, arts 8(2),(3).]
[75] See **13.9.2**.
[76] See **14.8**, particularly **14.8.4**.
[77] AMAAA 1979, Sch.1, para.3(3)(a). [NI: HMAO(NI)O 1995, Sch.1, para.3(3)(a).]
[78] PPG 16, Annex 3, para.8; WO Circ. 60/96, Annex 1, para.8.
[79] Sch.1, para.3(3)(b). [NI: HMAO(NI)O 1995, Sch.1, para.3(3)(b).]

There is a power to make an award as to the payment of the costs of the parties to such an inquiry.[80]

In practice, very few inquiries indeed are held under this provision. Where a proposal involves applications for both planning permission and scheduled monument consent, the determining body will generally make every attempt to ensure that both are the subject of a single inquiry.[81] To assist applicants to decide whether to insist on a hearing, the current practice is to send them a provisional decision based on the material submitted with the application together with the representations made by those consulted.[82]

Once the determining body has reached a decision, notice of it must be given to the applicant and to everyone else who has made representations with respect to the application.[83] Curiously, there is no requirement in the 1979 Act to give reasons for any conditions or for the refusal of consent; but they are in any event required as a result of section 10(1)(6) of the Tribunals and Inquiries Act 1992; and full reasons should always be given as a matter of good practice.

13.9.4 Grant of consent

Consent may be given for all the works that were the subject of the application, or only for some of them.[84] Out of the 1,000 or so applications decided each year, only a mere handful (often less than 10) are refused; but many of the remainder are the subject of negotiations, sometimes protracted; and all consents are subject to conditions, in some cases stringent, designed to protect the monument in question.

Conditions may be imposed in relation to the manner in which or the persons by whom the works are to be carried out.[85] They may also require a person authorised by English Heritage or (outside England) the relevant determining body to be given an opportunity to examine the monument and its site before any works are carried out, and carry out such excavation as appears to be desirable for the purposes of archaeological investigation.[86] In practice, it is likely that a condition will require reasonable access to be given before or during the carrying out of works, as appropriate, either to English Heritage or to a nominated archaeological unit. There is also a general power to impose conditions; but this will be subject to the requirements as to conditions generally.[87]

If conditions are imposed which are onerous, there is an entitlement to claim compensation in exactly the same circumstances as where consent is refused.[88]

Every scheduled monument consent is subject to a condition that the works to which it relates must be started within five years, unless stated otherwise.[89] See

[80] Sch.1, para.4. There is no equivalent power in Northern Ireland.
[81] PPG 16, Annex 3, para.9; WO Circ. 60/96, Annex 1, para.9.
[82] PPG 16, Annex 3, para.9; WO Circ. 60/96, Annex 1, para.10.
[83] AMAAA 1979, Sch.1, para.3(4). [NI: HMAO(NI)O 1995, Sch.1, para.3(4).]
[84] AMAAA 1979, Sch.1, para.3(1). [NI: HMAO(NI)O 1995, Sch.1, para.3(1).]
[85] AMAAA 1979, s.2(4). [NI: HMAO(NI)O 1995, art.4(4).]
[86] AMAAA 1979, s.2(5). [NI: HMAO(NI)O 1995, art.4(5).]
[87] AMAAA 1979, s.2(4); see 13.8. [NI: HMAO(NI)O 1995, art.4(4).]
[88] AMAAA 1979, s.7(1); see 15.4.3. [NI: HBAO (NI)O 1995, art.9.]
[89] AMAAA 1979, s.4; see 13.8.3. [NI: HBAO (NI)O 1995, art.6.]

above as to the similar provision relating to planning permission and listed building consent—and note that the five year rule in this case was not changed by the 2004 Act.

There is a power for anyone authorised by the determining body or English Heritage to enter any land at any reasonable time to ensure that works authorised by a scheduled monument consent are being carried out in accordance with its terms.[90] There is a further power for anyone authorised by the determining body (presumably including English Heritage, although there is no specific provision to that effect) to enter land while the works are being carried out, to inspect the land and to watch the works, so as to record any matters of archaeological or historical interest.[91]

13.9.5 Refusal of consent

Where scheduled monument consent is refused, or granted subject to onerous conditions, there is no right of appeal (other than by way of a challenge in the High Court on a point of law[92]). There is however a very limited right to compensation, under s.7 of the Ancient Monuments Act.[93]

13.10 Special cases

13.10.1 Works by central government: the existing law

Crown land is at present, and in general, immune from planning control, and from listed building control in particular.[94] "Crown land" for this purpose includes land owned by the monarch in right of the Crown or of the Duchy of Lancaster, land owned by the Duchy of Cornwall and (most significantly) land owned by or held in trust for a Government department.[95]

Cadw and Historic Scotland are agencies of Welsh Assembly Government and the Scottish Executive; works carried out by them are therefore in the same position as works carried out by any other government department. The Secretary of State is the police authority for the metropolitan police district, and works on land owned by the Metropolitan Police thus benefit from Crown immunity.[96] Health authorities, and other health service bodies, on the other hand, have ceased to enjoy any such immunity since 1991.[97]

Planning permission, listed building consent, conservation area consent and advertisements consent are thus not currently required for works carried out by the Crown on its own land. However, instead, the developing department (that is, the government department or whatever) submits a Notice of Proposed Devel-

---

[90] AMAAA 1979, ss 6(3), 6A(2). [NI: HBAO (NI)O 1995, art.8(3).]
[91] AMAAA 1979, s.6(4). [NI: HBAO (NI)O 1995, art.8(4).]
[92] See **15.6.1**.
[93] See **15.4.3**.
[94] *Lord Advocate v Dumbarton DC* [1990] 2 A.C. 580, 1 All E.R. 1, HL.
[95] TCPA 1990, s.293. [Scotland: TCP(S)A 1997, s.242; NI: P(NI)O 1991, art.118.]
[96] Police Act 1964, Sch.8.
[97] National Health Service and Community Care Act 1990, s.60.

opment to the planning authority that it is intending to carry out works for which permission or consent would otherwise be required, under the arrangement described in Part IV of DoE Circular 18/84.[98]

The authority then deals with the Notice of Proposed Development as if it were a normal application for permission or consent, and advertises it in the press, notifies the national amenity societies and so on, in the usual way (see the earlier sections of this chapter for details). In particular, where a proposal affects the character of a conservation area or the setting of a listed building, authorities have been asked to advertise it and notify English Heritage in cases where they would do so if the same development were to be carried out by any other developer.[99] Any objections received are passed to the developing department, which will then consider whether to proceed. Any unresolved dispute between that department and the planning authority is referred to the ODPM, which will either deal with the matter on the basis of written representations, or hold a non-statutory public inquiry.

Works by government departments to scheduled monuments in their ownership do not need scheduled monument consent (it would, after all, be odd for one arm of central government to be required to obtain consent from another). Instead, the procedure will be as for works to listed buildings in Crown ownership, except that it is the Secretary of State, the Welsh Assembly or the Scottish Ministers (that is, the DCMS, Cadw or Historic Scotland) who are to be notified, rather than the planning authority.

Similarly, in Northern Ireland, proposals for Crown development are submitted to the Department.

However, where the owner of any other interest in Crown land (such as a lessee or licensee) wishes to carry out development—or to demolish, alter or extend a listed building, demolish an unlisted building in a conservation area, carry out works to a scheduled monument, or display an advertisement—permission or consent will be required in the normal way.[1] In such a case, the relevant Crown department would need to be consulted by the owner under the normal arrangements for notifying other owners.[2] Note that a scheduled monument in the guardianship of the Secretary of State is not "owned" by the Crown, and accordingly works to it require scheduled monument consent in the normal way.

Where a government department wishes to dispose of its interest in land, and wishes to carry out development or other works, possibly because it considers that the land would be more valuable, it may seek planning permission or other consents as appropriate from the planning authority.[3] Such applications are dealt with in the same way as if it were made by any other owner.

---

[98] WO Circ. 37/84. SDD Circ. 21/84 is in similar terms.
[99] Circ. 18/84, para.18.
[1] P(LBCA)A 1990, s.83(1)(b). [Scotland: P(LBCA)(S)A 1997, s.74(1)(b); NI: P(NI)O 1991, art.113(1)(b).]
[2] See 13.3.3.
[3] TCPA 1990, s.299(1); P(LBCA)A 1990, s.84.

13.10.2 Abolition of Crown immunity

The above arrangements are to be swept away by reforms introduced by Part 7 of the Planning and Compulsory Purchase Act 2004 and Part IV of the Planning Reform (NI) Order 2006. These will generally subject Crown land in England, Wales and Scotland to precisely the same regime as any other land. Applications will thus be required in the same circumstances as other case—save in the case of works that are both urgent and in the national interest. However, criminal sanctions will not be available where works have been carried out without listed building consent, conservation area consent or scheduled monument consent, or where a planning enforcement notice is not complied with.

When the new arrangements come into force, probably during 2006 in relation to Great Britain, any notice issued by a planning authority in response to a Notice of Proposed Development will be treated as if it was a grant or refusal of planning permission, with a right of appeal accordingly.[4] Circular 18/84 will no doubt then be replaced by a new Circular, explaining the new procedure in detail; but until then, the existing procedure, outlined above, will continue to operate.

13.10.3 Works by English Heritage

English Heritage is not part of central government. However, when it was first set up, it was given the same status as a government department in respect of works carried out on behalf of the Secretary of State—that is, works to any monuments, buildings or land that had previously been owned by the Department of National Heritage (the predecessor to the DCMS) for which it then became responsible.[5-6] In general, therefore, such works do not currently require planning permission or listed building consent as such, but will be notified to planning authorities under Circular 18/84, in the same way as works by government departments.[7] This will obviously change when Crown immunity is abolished.[8]

Otherwise, the carrying out of development by English Heritage generally require planning permission to the same extent as works by any other developer. However, certain works for the preservation or repair of buildings or monuments in its ownership or control are permitted development.[9] These include:

(1) the maintenance, repair or restoration of a building or monument (but not its extension);

(2) the erection of protective screens or fencing, for a period of six months (or longer if agreed by the planning authority); and

(3) works to stabilise any cliff, watercourse or coastline.

This does not include development associated with the promotion of buildings and monuments as visitor attractions. The construction of car parks, ticket

---

[4] Planning and Compulsory Purchase Act 2004, Sch.4.
[5-6] National Heritage Act 1983, s.34(2), Sch.3, para.2(3); Circ. 18/84, Pt IV, para.2.
[7] See **13.10.1**.
[8] See **13.10.2**.
[9] TCP (General Permitted Development) Order 1995, Sch.2, Pt 26.

booths, refreshment shops, heritage interpretation centres and the like will thus still need to be notified to the planning authority, or to form the subject of a planning application, depending on whether or not the works are to be carried out in respect of a property which English Heritage manages by virtue of a direction of the Secretary of State.

Similarly, listed building consent and conservation area consent is generally required for works by English Heritage where they are not carried out on behalf of the Department—where, for example, it is seeking approval for works to be carried out to buildings which it is proposing to purchase. Planning authorities have been directed to refer direct to the Secretary of State for his or her decision all applications for such consent made by English Heritage in respect of the carrying out of works to any building which is in its ownership, guardianship or otherwise under its control or of which it is the prospective purchaser.[10] Authorities should advertise such applications in the usual way and forward any comments received, together with their own comments, to the government regional office.

Where works by English Heritage require scheduled monument consent, that is granted automatically.[11]

13.10.4 Works by foreign governments

Where a foreign government wishes to carry out building works, it requires planning permission, listed building consent and so on in the same way as any other building owner. In practice, planning authorities do grant consent for, for example, works to embassy buildings (many of which are listed). However, where an authority wishes to refuse consent, it will refer the application to the ODPM, which will deal with it (where appropriate, in conjunction with the Foreign and Commonwealth Office) as if it were a called-in application.

13.10.5 Works by local authorities

A local authority, at the moment unlike a central government department, needs planning permission, listed building consent or conservation area consent just like anyone else.[12]

Local authorities wishing to carry out their own development may in effect grant themselves planning permission, by the relevant committees merely passing the appropriate resolutions—although note that an application for such development must not be determined by a committee, subcommittee or officer responsible for the management of the land or building involved.[13] This applies even if the proposal affects the setting of a listed building or the character of a conservation area. A local authority must also notify English Heritage of its own development proposals in cases where any other developer would have to do so— since the requirement for it to be notified applies to any application for devel-

---

[10] Direction in Circ. 01/01, para.35, identical to that in DoE Circ. 14/97, para.32.
[11] Class 6 of the Ancient Monuments (Class Consents) Order 1994 (see 12.8.5).
[12] TCPA 1990, s.316; P(LBCA)A 1990, s.82(2), (3).
[13] TCP General Regulations 1992, reg.10.

opment in the relevant categories, regardless of by whom such application is made.[14]

However, applications by local authorities themselves for listed building consent to demolish their listed buildings, or to alter or extend them, must be made to the Secretary of State.[15]

This incidentally means that where an authority wishes to dispose of a listed building on the open market, it may grant itself planning permission for a change of use; but if the change involves any alterations to the building, listed building consent must still be obtained from the Secretary of State. It is possible that in such circumstances the Secretary of State might call-in any concurrent planning application for his or her own decision, so that the two applications can be determined together.

The application for listed building consent is made in the form of an application to the authority, and is deemed to have been referred to the Secretary of State under the call-in provisions.[16] The authority must therefore advertise the application on site and in the press, except in the case of works which affect only the interior of a Grade II building.[17] It should also advertise the application elsewhere as it deems fit, and must notify the national amenity societies where appropriate.[18] An authority in England should also, "as a matter of good practice", notify English Heritage at the earliest possible stage.[19] It must then send the application to the Secretary of State, along with any representations received.[20] An application by a district council is made direct to the Secretary of State, and one by a county council is made to the district council, which passes it on to him.[21] The Secretary of State will then reach a decision, after holding a public inquiry if the authority wishes.[22]

There is an unfortunate loophole, however, in that anyone other than a local authority may apply to the authority (not to the Secretary of State) for listed building consent to carry out works to a building owned by the authority. A lessee or licensee of a Grade II listed building owned by a local authority (or indeed someone with no interest in the building at all) may therefore apply for consent to alter it, and the authority itself may grant consent, without any reference to English Heritage or the Secretary of State.[23]

The same applies in principle to applications by local authorities to demolish their own unlisted buildings in conservation areas, which must be made to the Secretary of State.[24] Thus, for example, the Greater London Council was able in

[14] In Circ. 01/01; see **13.5.2**.
[15] s.82(4)(a)); P(LBCA) Regs 1990, reg.13(2).
[16] reg.13(3) (see **13.7.6**).
[17] regs 13(4), (5).
[18] See **13.5.3–13.5.9**.
[19] Circ. 01/01, para.20.
[20] reg.13(3), (6).
[21] reg.13(7).
[22] reg.13(3); P(LBCA)A 1990, s.12(1).
[23] For concern expressed by the Court in relation to a similar loophole that used to apply under the old (pre-1992) arrangements regarding planning applications for works to listed buildings, see *R. v Merton LBC, Ex p. Burnett* [1990] 1 P.L.R. 72.
[24] P(LBCA)A 1990, s.74(2)(a); P (LBCA) Regs 1990, reg.13.

1982 to prevent (at least for a while) the demolition of Kensington Town Hall by the local council, by including it within a conservation area. At the time the designation order came into effect, half of the building had been perfectly lawfully demolished. As a result of the designation, before the demolition works could be completed, the Borough Council then had to seek consent from the Secretary of State, which in the event he readily gave—he had also declined to list the building a few years earlier.

Works to a scheduled monument owned by a local authority, and works carried out by an authority to any other monument, require scheduled monument consent from the Secretary of State just as much as do any other works.

13.10.6 Works to be authorised under the Transport and Works Act

Proposals (such as those for harbours, docks and light railways) which would have previously been authorised by private bills now have to be authorised by orders made under the Transport and Works Act 1992 (which applies to England, Wales and Scotland). The Secretary of State, if he decides to make an order under section 1 or section 3 of the Act, will normally at the same time direct that planning permission be deemed to be granted for the proposal, to the extent to which it involves the carrying out of any development.[25]

However, where such a proposal involves works to a listed building, listed building consent is required and has to be applied for separately.[26] The same applies in respect of conservation area consent or scheduled monument consent where a proposal involves the demolition of an unlisted building in a conservation area or any works to a scheduled monument.

An application for listed building or conservation area consent that relates to works that are the subject of a concurrent application for an order under the 1992 Act is made to the planning authority, but the administrative requirements are subject to slight modifications, prescribed in the regulations made under section 15 of the 1992 Act.[27] They apply where the application for consent is made either concurrently with the application under that Act or not more than 10 weeks after it, or in any other case where the Secretary of State considers them appropriate. The Department of Transport, which is the Department responsible for processing applications under the 1992 Act, has indicated that the modified procedure under the 1992 Regulations will apply wherever it is practicable.[28]

Where the 1992 Regulations apply, an applicant may submit either full details of the works proposed, as with any other application, or appropriate extracts from the details supplied with the application under the 1992 Act. In some cases, however, it may not be practicable to supply full details of the works proposed, as they may not be known at the time the application is made; in this case, the application should include a clear written description of the works proposed,

---

[25] TCPA 1990, s.90(2A), inserted by 1992 Act, s.16(1).

[26] 1992 Act, s.17.

[27] Transport and Works Applications (Listed Buildings, Conservation Areas and Ancient Monuments Procedure) Regulations 1992 (SI 1992/3138).

[28] At para.7.9 of the *Guide to Procedures*.

supported by such other materials as the applicant is reasonably able to provide.[29]

The Department of Transport has indicated that it will only exceptionally be appropriate to reserve full details of the works for later approval[30]—for example, where the promoters of an underground railway scheme are unable to predict the exact requirements for underpinning of a listed building until soil surveys have been carried out, which may not be feasible until after the order under the 1992 Act has been made. Applicants are thus warned that, in general, the ODPM, which will still be responsible for processing the application for listed building or conservation area consent, will want to see proposals in full.

It is the responsibility of the applicant, not that of the planning authority, to advertise the application for consent.[31] The advertisement must be made before the application itself is submitted to the authority (within the period of 14 days ending with the date of the application), but may be combined with the advertisement of the application under the 1992 Act. The drawings and so on submitted with the application must be kept available for a period of 42 (not, as normally, 21) days after the application is submitted.

Instead of submitting one of the normal ownership certificates,[32] the applicant must include a certificate (Certificate AA) stating that all the relevant owners of the building have been served with notices under the 1992 Act, and that each notice stated that an application was also being made for listed building consent.[33] Note that "owner" in this case includes also the owner of a leasehold interest with at least *three* years' unexpired.[34] The form of the certificate is at para.2(7).

It is still the authority's responsibility to post the notices on site.[35]

The authority will then automatically refer the application to the Secretary of State for his or her decision. In such a case, if inquiries are held into both of the two applications, they have to be held concurrently.[36] The procedure at such a joint inquiry will be that governing an inquiry into an application under the 1992 Act.[37]

Similar requirements apply to the making of an application for scheduled monument consent concurrently with an application for an order under the 1992 Act.[38]

The relevant considerations are set out in full (together with the procedure for applications under the 1992 Act generally) in a useful booklet produced by the

---

[29] P(LBCA)A 1990, s.10(2)(b), as substituted by 1992 Regulations, Sch.1, para.1.
[30] at para.7.11 of the *Guide*.
[31] P(LBCA) Regs 1990, reg.5(1)(a), as substituted by 1992 Regulations, Sch.1, para.2(3).
[32] See **13.3.3**.
[33] P(LBCA) Regs 1990, reg.6(1)(aa), as inserted by 1992 Regulations, Sch.1, para.2(5).
[34] reg.6(4), as substituted by 1992 Regulations, Sch.1, para.2(6).
[35] P(LBCA) Regs 1990, reg.5(1)(b), as substituted by 1992 Regulations, Sch.1, para.2(3); see **13.5.3**.
[36] Transport and Works Applications (Listed Buildings, Conservation Areas and Ancient Monuments Procedure) Regulations 1992, reg.5.
[37] Transport and Works (Inquiries Procedure) Rules 1992 (SI 1992/2817).
[38] 1992 Regulations, Sch.2.

Department of Transport.[39] It may be noted that a consultation paper was issued in mid-2005 on proposals to improve the procedure for making orders.[40]

13.11 Revocation or modification of permission or consent

13.11.1 Overview

It may occasionally happen that a planning authority wishes to revoke or modify a planning permission or listed building or conservation area consent that has been granted, either by itself or by the Secretary of State. The procedure to be followed in such cases is set out in sections 97–100 of the Planning Act and sections 23–26 of the Listed Buildings Act.

In considering whether to revoke or modify either planning permission or listed building or conservation area consent, the planning authority or the Secretary of State must generally have regard to the development plan and to any other material considerations.[41] They must also have regard to the desirability of preserving and enhancing any conservation area involved.[42] Examples of occasions where modification of conditions might be desirable were noted above.[43]

Equivalent provisions are in sections 64–68 and 76 of the Scottish Planning Act and sections 21–24 and 25 of the Scottish Listed Buildings Act. As so often, the procedure in Northern Ireland is much simpler due to the single-tier system of planning control.[44] And similar provisions are available under the Ancient Monuments Act to enable scheduled monument consent to be revoked and modified where appropriate.

However, not surprisingly, the general entitlement to compensation in each case ensures that these power to revoke and modify permissions and consents are used only rarely.

13.11.2 Procedure

The planning authority should first make a revocation (or modification) order. It must then notify the owners and any occupiers of the building, and anyone else likely to be involved, such as architects, surveyors, builders, and (sometimes the most important!) demolition contractors. It should then normally submit the

---

[39] *Transport and Works Act 1992: a Guide to Procedures*, ISBN 0115511598, HMSO, £7.55.

[40] Available on the Department of Transport website.

[41] TCPA 1990, s.97(2), P(LBCA)A 1990, ss 23(2), 26(2); Planning and Compulsory Purchase Act 2004, s.38(6). This is a slightly curious provision insofar as it relates to listed building or conservation area consent, as there is no requirement to consider the development plan when granting such consent in the first place (see **Chapter 14**). Odder still, the Secretary of State appears to be under a duty to consider the development plan when considering whether to revoke listed building consent, but not when considering revoking a planning permission (TCPA 1990, s.100(1)).

[42] P(LBCA)A 1990, s.72. [Scotland: P(LBCA)(S)A 1997, s.64; NI: P(NI)O 1991, art.50(5).]

[43] See **13.8.7**.

[44] P(NI)O 1991, arts 38 and 47. The availability of compensation is still under the P(NI)O 1972, which was not wholly repealed by the 1991 Order.

order to the Secretary of State for confirmation, unless all those notified have stated in writing that they have no objection to it, in which case the expedited procedure can be used. There is then a period of (at least) 28 days during which any of those notified can insist that the Secretary of State holds a public inquiry before confirming the order. At such an inquiry, only the person requiring it to be held and the local authority have a right to appear, but presumably other interested parties would in practice be heard.[45] Whether or not there is an inquiry, the order only takes effect once the Secretary of State has confirmed it (with or without alterations).

The effect of an order is to revoke or modify permission or consent for any works other than those already carried out.[46] This means that the revocation procedure is scarcely if ever likely to be effective as an emergency measure to stop a building being demolished in reliance upon a listed building consent which the authority now regrets having given.

The Secretary of State may also revoke or modify a permission or consent, after consultation with the planning authority—not least in circumstances where there is some doubt as to the probity of the process that led to the initial grant. He or she should make the draft order, serve copies as above and, if required to do so, hold an inquiry before actually finalising it.[47]

Of crucial importance is that compensation is payable by the planning authority where permission or consent is revoked or modified, to anyone who can show that they have suffered loss or damage as a result. The measure of the compensation payable will be:

(1) the cost of works carried out subsequent to the grant of listed building consent and before the confirmation of the order, insofar as they are rendered abortive by the revocation or modification; plus

(2) the cost of the preparation of drawings etc necessary to carry out the work; plus

(3) any other loss or damage directly attributable (such as any loss in the value of the land).[48]

Compensation is not payable in respect of any expenditure incurred prior to the grant of permission or consent—as that must have always been speculative in any event.

A claim for compensation must be submitted to the appropriate local authority within six months of the revocation or modification taking effect.[49]

13.11.3 Expedited procedure where no objections are made

An expedited procedure (under section 98 of the Planning Act and section 25 of the Listed Buildings Act) applies where all of those notified of the draft order

---

[45] TCPA 1990, s.98; P(LBCA)A 1990, s.24.
[46] TCPA 1990, s.97(4); P(LBCA)A 1990, s.23(3).
[47] TCPA 1990, s.100; P(LBCA)A 1990, s.26.
[48] TCPA 1990, s.107; P(LBCA)A 1990, s.28.
[49] TCP General Regulations 1992, reg.12; P(LBCA) Regs 1990, reg.9.

revoking or modifying planning permission or listed building consent have stated in writing that they do not object to it. Where this applies, the planning authority must advertise that fact in a local newspaper.[50] The advertisement must also specify:

(1) a period (of at least 28 days) within which anyone else can object to the draft order and require the Secretary of State to hold an inquiry; and

(2) a further period (of at least 14 days after the expiration of the 28-day period) at the end of which the order will take effect automatically if no such objections have been made.

A copy of the advertisement must be sent to the Secretary of State within three days of its publication. Copies must also be sent to all those originally notified, presumably to give them a second chance to object. If no objections are made as a result of the advertisement and the notifications, and the Secretary of State does not request the authority to send the order for his or her confirmation, it takes effect automatically at the end of the 14-day period.[51]

This expedited procedure is not available to revoke or modify planning permissions or listed building consents granted originally by the Secretary of State.[52] Where it is used, compensation is payable for the revocation or modification of planning permission, but not for that of listed building or conservation area consent.[53]

13.11.4 Revocation or modification of scheduled monument consent

Once consent has been granted in relation to a monument in England under the Ancient Monuments Act, it is theoretically possible for the Secretary of State to modify or revoke it (after consulting English Heritage), in particular by altering the period within which the works must be started.[54] Similarly, the Welsh Assembly and the Scottish Ministers may revoke or modify a consent granted under that Act, and the Department may modify a consent under the Historic Monuments and Archaeological Objects (NI) Order 1991.[55] To assist in the consideration of whether to take such action, there is a power for anyone authorised by the Secretary of State [etc.] to enter any land for that purpose.[56]

The procedure for modifying or revoking consent is set out in Part II of Schedule 1 to the Ancient Monuments Act, which should be checked for detailed provisions.[57] In outline, however, the relevant government body must serve on the owner and occupier of the monument a notice of the proposal, together with the reasons for it. Where the proposal is to revoke the consent altogether, or to

---

[50] TCPA 1990, s.99; TCP General Regulations 1992, reg.17; P(LBCA)A 1990, s.25; P(LBCA) Regs 1990, reg.10.
[51] TCPA 1990, s.99(2)–(7); P(LBCA)A 1990, s.(25)(2),(3).
[52] TCPA 1990, s.99(8); P(LBCA)A 1990, s.25(1)(a).
[53] P(LBCA)A 1990, s.28(1).
[54] AMAAA 1979, s.4(3)–(5).
[55] HMAO(NI)O 1995, art.6(3)–(5).
[56] AMAAA 1979, s.6(2)(b). [NI: HMAO(NI)O 1995, art.8(2)(b).]
[57] in Northern Ireland, Pt II of Sch.1 to HMAO(NI)O 1995.

modify it so as to exclude some works, the notice will have the effect of halting immediately those works which are now unauthorised. The owner and occupier then have 28 days in which to object. If there are no objections, the consent may simply be modified or revoked without further ado. If there are objections, there must first be an inquiry or hearing if any objector wishes one. Notice of the outcome must be given to the owner and occupier and anyone who appeared at the inquiry.

Compensation can be claimed either on the issue of a notice of a proposal to modify or revoke consent, or where consent actually is modified or revoked.[58] The heads of entitlement are as for the revocation or modification of planning permission or listed building consent.[59]

Compensation is payable under the Ancient Monuments Act by English Heritage or by Cadw or Historic Scotland.[60] The amount payable is assessed in accordance with the rules in section 5 of the Land Compensation Act 1961; and special rules apply where the land is subject to a mortgage.[61] Disputes as to compensation are to be determined by the Lands Tribunal, under sections 2 and 4 of the 1961 Act, as though references to the acquiring authority were references to English Heritage or Cadw or Historic Scotland as appropriate.[62] In Northern Ireland, compensation is payable by the Department.[63]

---

[58] AMAAA 1979, s.9. [NI:]
[59] See **13.11.2**.
[60] AMAAA 1979, s.9(1).
[61] AMAAA 1979, s.27.
[62] s.47; *Currie's Executors v Secretary of State for Scotland* [1993] 2 E.G.L.R. 221 (see **15.4.3**).
[63] HMAO(NI)O 1995, art.11.

Chapter 14

Works affecting Historic Buildings and Monuments: Matters to be Considered

14.1 Introduction

It has been explained in **Chapter 12** that one or more types of consent may be required before building and other works can be carried out lawfully—including in particular planning permission, listed building consent, conservation area consent, scheduled monument consent, advertisements consent.[1] **Chapter 13** then outlined the various procedural requirements as to how those consents may be sought, and how applications should be determined. This chapter now considers on what basis those consents are to be granted or withheld. This is vitally important not only for planning authorities, which have to determine applications, but also for landowners and developers—who need to be able to maximise their chances of obtaining consent as expeditiously as possible—and for those who wish to frustrate unwelcome proposals.

The basic principles are those underlying all administrative law—notably, that the discretion of a public authority must be exercised reasonably: to use the classic formulation of Lord Greene in *Wednesbury*:

"a person entrusted with a discretion must, so to speak, direct himself properly in law. He must call his own attention to the matters he is bound to consider. He must exclude from his consideration matters which are irrelevant to what he has to consider. If he does not obey those rules, he may truly be said, and often is said, to be acting 'unreasonably'."[2]

And in the planning field, there are a number of statutory powers and duties that must be firmly borne in mind:

"Parliament must have conferred the discretion with the intention that it should be used to promote the policy and objects of the Act; the policy and objects of the Act must be determined by construing the Act as a whole, and construction is always a matter for the court."[3]

---

[1] See **Chapter 12**.
[2] *Associated Provincial Picture Houses v Wednesbury Corpn* [1948] 1 K.B. 223, *per* Lord Greene M.R. at p.30.
[3] *Padfield v Minister of Agriculture, Fisheries and Food* [1968] A.C. 997, HL, *per* Lord Reid at p.1030.

There has been an incessant stream of litigation in the courts over what should or should not be taken into account in planning decisions. This chapter focusses particularly on the considerations that are of key importance in the context of decisions relating to works affecting historic buildings and areas. It accordingly considers first (in **14.2**) the nature of the basic statutory duties relevant to each of the various types of consent. It looks (briefly) at the development plan (**14.3**), and then in rather more detail at the particular duties relating to listed buildings (**14.4–14.6**), conservation areas (**14.7**) and ancient monuments (**14.8**). It then summarises some of the other factors that must be borne in mind (**14.9**).

As well as the various items of government guidance, referred to below as appropriate, useful guidance is also to be found in a number of (free) publications produced by English Heritage—including *Development in the Historic Environment* (June 1995), *Conservation Area Practice* (July 1995) and *Informed Conservation* (2001).

14.2 The basic requirements

14.2.1 Applications for planning permission

The basic duty laid upon those determining planning applications—either planning authorities or the Secretary of State—is that that they must do so "having regard to the development plan, so far as material to the application, and to any other material considerations". This principle has been in all planning Acts since 1947, and is currently in section 70(2) of the Planning Act (and section 37(2) of the Scottish Planning Act and article 25(1) of the Northern Ireland Order).

Further, section 38(6) of the Planning and Compulsory Purchase 2004 (the successor to section 54A of the 1990 Act) provides that the determination must be made "in accordance with the development plan" unless material considerations indicate otherwise—that is, the development plan always comes first. Section 25 of the Scottish Planning Act and article 4(2A) of the Northern Ireland Order[4] are to the same effect. This is considered further below.[5]

Secondly, any planning application should be considered in the light of the effect of the proposed development on any building directly involved and on the surrounding area—regardless of whether or not it forms part of the setting of a listed building or is designated as a conservation area. Thus it has been held in the House of Lords that:

"though the relevant statute does not refer expressly to a particular consideration, nevertheless, there will be some matters so obviously material to a decision on a particular project that anything short of direct consideration of them by the ministers ... would not be in accordance with the intention of the Act."[6]

---

[4] To be inserted by the Planning (Amendment) (NI) Order 2003, art.30, and again (bizarrely) by Planning Reform (NI) Order 2006, art.4, with effect from a date to be announced.

[5] See **14.3**.

[6] *Re Findlay* [1985] A.C. 318, HL, per Lord Scarman at pp.333–334, quoting *Creed NZ Inc v Governor-General* [1981] 1 N.Z.L.R. 172 at p.183; cited in *Bath Society v Secretary of State* [1991] 2 P.L.R. 51, CA.

See, for example, *Cotswold DC v Secretary of State*,[7] where an inspector thought that the site of a proposed development was within a conservation area, where in fact it was not. And, by extension, a proposal to alter or extend any existing building must always be considered in the light of its effect on the character and appearance of that building itself.

However, where a proposal directly or indirectly affects a listed building or a conservation area, formal duties are laid upon the planning authority and the Secretary of State, by the Listed Buildings Acts.

Thus, in relation to development affecting listed buildings, section 66(1) of the Listed Buildings Act provides as follows:

"In considering whether to grant planning permission for development which affects a listed building or its setting, the local planning authority or, as the case may be, the Secretary of State, shall have special regard to the desirability of preserving the building or its setting or any features of special architectural or historic interest which it possesses."

The implications of this are considered in detail at **14.4**.

In relation to conservation areas, section 72(1) of that Act states that:

"In the exercise, with respect to any buildings or other land in a conservation area, of any functions under or by virtue of any of the provisions mentioned in subsection (2), special attention shall be paid to the desirability of preserving or enhancing the character or appearance of that area."[8]

This duty, which has generated a surprising amount of litigation, is considered at **14.7**.

Corresponding provisions, in identical terms, are to be found in sections 59(1) and 64(1) of the Scottish Listed Buildings Act, and articles 45(1) and 50(5) of the Northern Ireland Order.

There is no explicit statutory duty relating to planning applications affecting ancient monuments (scheduled or otherwise), archaeological areas, world heritage sites or locally listed buildings.

Planning authorities are also under a duty to take into account the responses to the consultation and publicity exercise they have carried out.[9] And they must also have regard to any relevant Government policy.[10] More generally, they must consider any other relevant matters—what these will be in any particular case will of course be a matter for careful consideration. These considerations, which apply equally to other types of applications, are considered towards the end of the chapter.[11]

14.2.2 Overlapping statutory duties

As to the relative importance of the requirements outlined above, Glidewell L.J. noted in *Bolton MBC v Secretary of State* that "there is clearly a distinction between matters which a decision maker is obliged by statute to take into account

---

[7] [1998] J.P.L. B116.
[8] P(LBCA)A 1990, s.72(1).
[9] See **Chapter 13**.
[10] *Gransden (EC) Ltd v Secretary of State* (1987) 54 P. & C.R. 361, CA, affirming (1987) 54 P. & C.R. 86.
[11] See **14.9**.

and those where the obligation to take into account is to be implied from the nature of the decision and of the matter in question."[12] A year later, the same judge, in *Bath Society v Secretary of State*, considered the matter in relation to the conservation area duty (under what is now section 72 of the Listed Buildings Act). He held as follows:

"In my opinion, in a conservation area the requirement under [s.72] to pay 'special attention' should be the first consideration for the decision-maker. It is true that the desirability of preserving or enhancing the character or appearance of the conservation area is, in formal terms, a 'material consideration' within [s.70(2)]. Since, however, it is a consideration to which special attention is to be paid as a matter of statutory duty, it must be regarded as having considerable importance and weight."[13]

The same would presumably have applied to the listed buildings duty under section 66. Since that judgment, the enactment of section 54A of the Planning Act (now section 38(6) of the 2004 Act), has made it clear that the development plan is, in general, to take precedence over any other material considerations. It follows that the duties under the Listed Buildings Act are subordinate to the duty to have regard to the plan, but that they are still more important than the duty to have regard to any other material consideration.

In *St Albans DC v Secretary of State*,[14] the first High Court decision to confront directly the meaning of section 54A, the deputy judge noted that an inspector determining an appeal had rightly been concerned with the requirements of section 72, but "that did not mean that the development plan could be ignored". However, he held, although the inspector in his decision had not explicitly mentioned the development plan policies relating to the conservation area (or those relating to locally listed buildings[15]), he had clearly been aware of them and had in effect found that there was no breach, and there was thus no inconsistency with the approach required by section 54A.

Subsequent decisions suggest that the courts are more likely to follow the approach taken in *Heatherington UK Ltd v Secretary of State*,[16] which emphasised the importance of considering explicitly all the statutory duties laid upon decision makers. That case concerned a property in Mayfair, originally residential, whose freehold owners sought unsuccessfully a further temporary permission to use the first floor as offices; at appeal, the inspector concluded that there were no special circumstances justifying an exception to the normal policy in the development plan resisting such proposals, and refused permission. On appeal by the applicant, the deputy judge noted the statutory provisions outlined above, and concluded that, in this case, it was clear that the inspector had applied section 54A, but far from clear that he had applied section 66 of the Listed Buildings Act. On the balance of probabilities, therefore, he had been in breach of his statutory duty under the latter Act, and his decision should therefore be remitted for reconsideration.

---

[12] (1990) 61 P. & C.R. 343, CA, following *Creed (NZ) Incorporated v Governor-General* [1981] 1 N.Z.L.R. 172.
[13] [1991] 2 P.L.R. 51, CA, at p.64H (see **14.7.3** for the facts).
[14] [1993] J.P.L. 374.
[15] See **7.2**.
[16] [1995] J.P.L. 228 (considered in more detail at 7.6.1).

The same principle would apply where development affects a building that is both listed and in a conservation area—so that the duty under section 66 (listed buildings) would fall to be considered alongside that under section 72 of that Act (conservation areas). Both must be taken fully into account, so that the effect of the proposal must be considered both in relation to the immediate surroundings (the listed building and its setting) and in the light of its effect on the conservation area. This was emphasised in *R. v Camden LBC, Ex p. Bellamy*.[17] Thus alterations to a listed building in a conservation area may be judged acceptable in relation to the character of the conservation area, but unacceptable in relation to that of the building itself, and therefore refused.[18]

These decisions highlight the problems arising where there are several statutory tests applicable; it is important for decision makers not merely to select the one they prefer. As for the order of preference, it must be:

(1) the development plan, so far as material;

(2) the effect of the proposed development on any listed buildings or their setting or on any conservation area;

(3) the responses to publicity and consultation; and then

(4) any other material considerations.

14.2.3 Applications for listed building consent

There is no explicit requirement for decision makers to take any notice of the development plan when determining applications for listed building consent (for the demolition, alteration or extension of listed buildings[19]), although policies in it will clearly be relevant.[20]

There is on the other hand an explicit duty, under section 16(2) the Listed Buildings Act (s.14(2) of the Scottish Listed Buildings Act and article 45(1) of the Northern Ireland Order), as follows:

"In considering whether to grant listed building consent for any works, the local planning authority or the Secretary of State shall have special regard to the desirability of preserving the building or its setting or any features of special architectural or historic interest which it possesses."

It will be noted that this duty is virtually identical to that applying to the determination of planning applications[21]—indeed, until 1980, the duties were in the same subsection (as they still are in Northern Ireland). It is considered in more detail below.[22]

Where the listed building in question in question is in a conservation area, s.72(1) of the Listed Buildings Act will mean that it will also be necessary for the authority or the Secretary of State to pay special attention to the desirability of

---

[17] [1991] J.P.L. 255.
[18] See, for example, the appeal at [2003] J.P.L. 914 (East Bergholt).
[19] See **12.2.3**.
[20] See **14.3**.
[21] See **14.2.1**.
[22] See **14.4**.

preserving or enhancing the character or appearance of that area.[23] This will mean that both duties are engaged, and both must be taken fully into account.

In addition, any responses to consultation and publicity[24] must be taken into account, along with Government policy and anything else that is relevant.[25]

14.2.4 Applications for conservation area consent

There is no explicit statutory duty specifically relating to the determination of applications for conservation area consent (for the demolition of unlisted buildings in conservation areas[26]). However, the duty under section 72(1) of the Listed Buildings Act, requiring special attention to be paid to the desirability of preserving or enhancing the character or appearance of the conservation area in question, will clearly be relevant.[27] So too will the need to consider the development plan, since demolition of a building in a conservation area is usually associated with the construction of something to replace it—which will require planning permission and thus be subject to the plan.

Here too, any responses to consultation and publicity[28] must be taken into account, along with Government policy and anything else that is relevant.[29]

14.2.5 Applications for scheduled monument consent

There is no explicit statutory duty specifically relating to the determination of applications for scheduled monument consent (for the carrying out of any works to scheduled monuments[30]). Nor do any of the duties under Planning Act (relating to the development plan) or the Listed Buildings Act (relating to listed buildings and conservation areas) apply.

However, it will still be necessary for the Secretary of State (or equivalent in other jurisdictions) to take into account any responses to consultation and publicity,[31] along with Government policy and anything else that is relevant—which may of course in appropriate cases include the effect of the proposed works on the setting of a nearby listed building, or on a conservation area.[32]

14.2.6 Applications for advertisements consent

When considering whether or not to grant consent for the display of advertisements, a planning authority may only take into account two considerations—

---

[23] P(LBCA)A 1990, s.72(1). [Scotland: P(LBCA)(S)A 1997 s.64(1); NI: P(NI)O 1991, art.50(5).] See **5.3.2** and **14.7**.
[24] See **Chapter 13**.
[25] See **14.1.1** and **14.9**.
[26] See **12.2.4**.
[27] P(LBCA)A 1990, s.72(1). [Scotland: P(LBCA)(S)A 1997 s.64(1); NI: P(NI)O 1991, art.50(5).] See **14.7**.
[28] See **Chapter 13**.
[29] See **14.1.1** and **14.9**.
[30] See **12.2.5**.
[31] See **13.9**.
[32] See **14.1.1** and **14.9**.

"amenity" and public safety.[33] Matters such as the commercial need for a particular advertisement, or the desirability or otherwise of its contents, are therefore totally irrelevant.

The need to consider amenity means that the authority is required to consider the effect of a proposed advertisement "in the light of the general characteristics of the locality, including the presence therein of any feature of historic, architectural, cultural or similar interest".[34] One such feature would be any listed building that was affected by a proposed advertisement. And the authority is required to have special regard to the desirability of preserving the character and appearance of conservation areas when exercising any of its powers under the Planning 1990, of which the control of advertisements is one.[35] Indeed, the duty under what is now section 72 of the Listed Buildings Act was considered first in a case relating to the control of advertisements.[36]

A decision by the Secretary of State to grant consent for a carefully designed non-illuminated advance warning sign was thus overturned by the courts because, although he had considered the effect of the proposed sign on the setting of a nearby listed building, he had not considered its effect on the conservation area. In particular, he had ignored the comment of his Inspector that "too great a multiplicity of individual signs is likely to prove both unsatisfactory and detrimental to the exceptionally attractive landscapes of the South Hams".[37]

14.3 The development plan

14.3.1 Relevance of the development plan

Section 38(6) of the Planning and Compulsory Purchase Act 2004 provides that, where any decision is to be made under the planning Acts having regard to the development plan, it must be made in accordance with the development plan unless material considerations indicate otherwise.[38] This clearly relates to the determination of planning applications, and to the taking of a wide variety of other decisions relating to planning—such as whether to take enforcement action, or to revoke a planning permission—which are explicitly stated in the Act as requiring to be undertaken with regard to the development plan.

The development plan may contain many policies, at various levels of generality, relating to any particular application—thus, for example, a proposal to replace a listed house with a new office block will probably be the subject of policies relating to the loss of housing stock, the location of new office development, and the level of parking provision, as well as (almost inevitably) a policy in

---

[33] reg.4. As to the meaning of the word "amenity" generally, see **7.6**.

[34] reg.4(1)(a).

[35] P(LBCA)A 1990, s.72(1) (see **14.7**). [Scotland: P(LBCA)(S)A 1997 s.64(1); NI: P(NI)O 1991, art.50(5).] *R. (Clear Channel UK Ltd) v Secretary of State* [2005] J.P.L. 704.

[36] *Westminster CC v Secretary of State* [1983] 3 P.L.R. 104; see **14.7.2**.

[37] *South Hams DC v Secretary of State* [1988] 3 P.L.R. 57.

[38] Scotland: Scotland: TCP(S)A 1997, s.25; NI: P(NI)O 1991, art.4(2A) (to be inserted by the Planning (Amendment) (NI) Order 2003, art.30, and by Planning Reform (NI) Order 2006, art.4, with effect from a date to be announced).

both the structure plan and (if there is one) the local plan severely restricting the demolition of listed buildings. And there may be a new local plan or other development plan document emerging. All of those will need to be considered, and balanced against each other, to see what is "in accordance with the development plan".

Thus, for example, in *R. v Secretary of State, ex p. Maltzahn*, a developer had appealed unsuccessfully against a planning authority's refusal of permission for a proposed golf course on the basis of a policy in the local plan that contained a presumption against development harming historic parkland; the officer's report to the committee had failed to mention a policy in the emerging plan introducing a presumption in favour of golf course proposals. The court, upholding the inspector's decision, noted that the policy in the emerging plan applied only where proposals did not adversely affect the setting of a listed building, archaeological site or historic parkland, and that it was clear that the council had focussed on the effect of the present proposal on the historic parkland, so the Council's failure to refer to the policy had not been not unreasonable.

However, to avoid challenges of this kind, it is important for authorities to consider carefully, and to note explicitly, all relevant policies. And the new requirement in England and Wales to include a list of all such policies with the notice of the decision means that it may be difficult for authorities to introduce new policies in the event of a subsequent appeal.[39]

This is not the case, however, with regard to the determination of applications for listed building consent—the only statutory duty is that under section 16 of the Listed Buildings Act,[40] and no reference at all is made to the development plan. It follows that there is no explicit requirement even to consider the plan, let alone to determine applications in accordance with it. Section 38(6) is thus of no relevance. This has been accepted by the High Court in *St Albans DC v Secretary of State*[41]—although the point was not argued—and by the Secretary of State at paragraph 2.4 of PPG 15 and paragraph 5 of WO Circular 61/96.

The development plan may contain policies which are relevant to the exercise of listed building control—even if only because a proposal requires planning permission as well as listed building consent, and the application for the former will need to be made in accordance with the plan. But PPG 15 suggests that policies relating to proposals which require *only* listed building consent (such as demolition or internal works) should be contained in supplementary planning guidance, referred to in the development plan, rather than in the plan itself.[42]

This may all be somewhat academic, however, since the policies relating to listed buildings and conservation areas in most local and unitary development plans tend to be drafted in similar terms to the relevant duties prescribed in legislation and Government policy, which clearly do apply the determination of applications for listed building and conservation area consent. In any event, the

---

[39] TCP (General Development Procedure) Order 1995, art.22(1), substituted by SI 2003/2047, art.5 (England) and amended by SI 2004/1434, art.3 (Wales); see **13.7.8**.
[40] See **14.4**.
[41] [1993] J.P.L. 374.
[42] PPG 15, para.2.5.

policy framework—whether in statute, development plan, Government policy or supplementary planning guidance—is usually straightforward (all proposals affecting listed buildings or their settings or conservation areas must preserve and/ or enhance them, as relevant); the more interesting question is how they apply in particular situations.

14.3.2 Identifying the development plan

The definition of "the development plan" in England and Wales has been changed by the Planning and Compulsory Purchase Act 2004, with effect from September 28, 2004. In the short term—that is, until September 28, 2007 at the latest—the development plan will still comprise:

- the regional spatial strategy (RSS) or, in Greater London, the spatial development strategy; and

- in areas in England with unitary authorities and in Wales, the adopted unitary development plan; and

- in other areas in England, the adopted structure plan and local plan.[43]

Once new-style development plan documents (or, in Wales, a local development plan) have been adopted, they will supersede the UDP, structure plan and local plan[44]—which will in any event cease to have effect on September 28, 2007, unless the Secretary of State directs otherwise. "Development plan documents" are local development documents (LDDs) that form part of the development plan[45]; the somewhat convoluted scheme that results from the new provisions has been outlined earlier.[46]

In Scotland, the development plan consists of the adopted structure plan and any adopted local plan.[47] In Northern Ireland, the development plan is an adopted plan produced by the Department.[48]

Clearly, emerging plans are relevant to the determination of applications—the more so as they near completion, and particularly where the plans being replaced are of some antiquity. Also relevant, although of less weight, will be supplementary planning documents of various kinds.[49]

14.4 Demolition, alteration and extension of listed buildings

14.4.1 General principles

There are four principal categories of works affecting listed buildings:

---

[43] TCPA 1990, ss 27, 54; Planning and Compulsory Purchase Act 2004, Sch.8, para.1.
[44] Planning and Compulsory Purchase Act 2004, s.38(1)–(4).
[45] 2004 Act, s.37(3).
[46] See **5.4.2** (England) and **5.4.4** (Wales).
[47] TCP(S)A 1997, s.24(1).
[48] P(NI)O 1991, art.4.
[49] See **5.4.3**.

(1) the demolition of a listed building (requiring only listed building consent[50]);

(2) the carrying out of works for the alteration or extension of a listed building (virtually always requiring listed building consent, and very often planning permission as well[51]);

(3) the change of use of a listed building (requiring only planning permission[52]); and

(4) the carrying out of operations which affect the setting of a listed building, or which make financially viable its restoration (generally requiring only planning permission—although works to one listed building, requiring listed building consent as well as planning permission, may also affect another[53]).

The first two of these are considered in this section; the third and fourth in the following ones.

When determining applications for listed building consent and planning permission in any of these situations, the crucial duty is that contained in the Listed Buildings Act, which provides that, in considering whether to grant planning permission for development which affects a listed building or its setting, or listed building consent for any works, the local planning authority or the Secretary of State shall have special regard to the desirability of preserving:

- the building itself, or

- its setting, or

- any features of special architectural or historic interest which it possesses.[53a]

Corresponding provisions are to be found in the Scottish Listed Buildings Act and the Northern Ireland Order.[53b]

By "the building" is meant, presumably, the listed building itself, which of course includes all the objects and structures fixed to it and all the post-1948 objects and structures within its curtilage.[54] In some case, the relevant entry in the statutory list refers to a group of buildings (notably in the case of a terrace of houses); it is then not clear which building is to be considered. However, it is likely that such a group will be uniform in character, so that the effect of any proposals will be on the group as a whole as much (or as little) as on the individual building

---

[50] See **12.3**.
[51] See **12.4**.
[52] See **12.4.9**.
[53] See **12.5**.
[53a] P(LBCA)A 1990, s.66(1) (planning permission) (see **14.2.1**); s.16(1) (listed building consent) (**14.2.3**).
[53b] P(LBCA)(S)A 1997, s.59(1) (planning permission); s.14(2) (listed building consent); P(NI)O 1991, art.45(1).
[54] s.1(5); see **Chapter 4**

within it. As to the "setting" of a listed building, this is considered later in the chapter.[55]

The use of the word "features" suggests more than simply structures and fixtures; so that it may be appropriate for the decision-maker to consider the desirability of preserving such items as pictures, artworks, contents generally, and gardens, so long as those items are features of the building. Arguably, some items that are to a greater or lesser extent intangible, such as evidence of the history of a building, the uniformity of its fenestration, or the layout of its grounds, may also fall to be considered under this heading.

The Court of Appeal has held, in the context of conservation areas, that "preserving" means "keeping safe from harm"[56]; there seems to be no reason why this interpretation should not apply to section 16 (listed buildings) just as much as it does to section 72 (conservation areas).

The nature of this duty has been considered in *Bristol Meeting Room Trust v Secretary of State and Bristol CC*,[57] where the deputy judge considered that it made it "clear that the legislation required that the preservation of a listed building had to operate as a paramount consideration." This echoes the comment of Glidewell L.J. in *Bath Society v Secretary of State*[58] that the corresponding duty under s.72 should be "the first consideration for the decision maker".[59] It is questionable, however, whether the learned deputy judge was strictly correct, since the legislation does not (as is commonly thought) require that the building must be preserved, but merely that the decision-maker must consider whether or not it is desirable that it should be. This is emphasised by the use of the word "or" between "the building", "its setting" and "any features [etc.]", which itself necessarily implies that it might not be desirable to preserve one or more of those items.

Form D16 in Appendix D is an outline of a typical proof of evidence relating to conservation matters, in connection with an appeal against the refusal of planning permission for works to a listed building in a conservation area. It provides a checklist of the issues that may be relevant in such cases, and as such could equally form the basis of a local authority officer's committee report, or an applicant's letter in support of an application (see also **Form D14**).

Finally, it is sometimes alleged that the application of the listed buildings test under section 16 or 66 of the Listed Buildings Act—so as to refuse an application for planning permission for works affecting a listed building or an application for listed building consent—is a breach of human rights. This argument is not known ever to have succeeded; certainly it failed in relation to the conservation area duty under section 72.[60] It also received short shrift in the recent decision of the

---

[55] See **14.6.1**.
[56] *per* Mann L.J. in *South Lakeland DC* [1991] 2 P.L.R. 97; see **14.7.3**.
[57] [1991] J.P.L. 152; see **14.4.2**.
[58] [1991] 2 P.L.R. 51.
[59] See 8.8.7.
[60] *Sabi v Secretary of State* June 18, 2002 (Forbes J.) (leave to appeal refused, October 8, 2002, CA) (see **14.7.8**).

Secretary of State to refuse listed building consent for the demolition of Greenside in Surrey.[61]

The remainder of this section considers the outworking of this test in practice, in particular in relation to demolition, changes of use alterations and extensions of listed buildings,[62] works affecting their setting,[63] and works said to be necessary in order to fund their restoration.[64] First, however, it may be appropriate to highlight briefly Government policy relating to this area.

14.4.2 Government policy

One vital factor to be considered in assessing any proposal for the demolition or alteration of a listed building is the declared policy of the Secretary of State (or the Assembly, the Scottish Ministers or the Department, as appropriate). This will clearly be relevant where an application is refused, and the applicant appeals against the refusal, or where it is called-in, since it will then be the relevant central government agency that will determine the application. In reaching such a decision, it is in general obliged to take into account its own declared policy, or else to state explicitly why this is not appropriate on any particular occasion.[65] Thus, for example, the Mappin and Webb case, considered above was a case where the Secretary of State explicitly declined to follow his normal policy, and was required to give reasons for doing so.[66]

But the considerations which will influence the Secretary of State in such cases are equally relevant to decisions by planning authorities, since—although authorities may determine applications for listed building consent as they see fit (subject to any directions by English Heritage)—they will not wish to make decisions that are likely to be overturned on appeal.

Government policy relating to works to listed buildings in England is principally in PPG 15, produced originally in 1994 and reproduced (in an updated form) as **Appendix 5** to this book—see in particular paragraphs 2.11 to 2.19 (planning applications) and paragraphs 3.1 to 3.19 (applications for listed building consent).

Relevant advice for other parts of the United Kingdom is in paragraphs 66 to 71 and 93 to 98 of Welsh Office Circular 61/96, paragraphs 2.15 to 2.22 of the *Memorandum of Guidance* produced by Historic Scotland, and paragraphs 6.1 to 6.18 and 6.28 to 6.32 of PPS 6, produced by the Planning Service in Northern Ireland.[67] The guidance in these publications is very similar, but not always identical either in detail or emphasis, to the English equivalent; they should be checked for actual wording.[68] Further, while it is not unknown for English gui-

---

[61] See **14.4.4**
[62] See **14.4**; **14.5**.
[63] See **14.6.1**.
[64] See **14.6.2** to **14.6.5**.
[65] *Sears Blok v Secretary of State and Southwark LBC* [1982] J.P.L. 248, *JA Pye (Oxford) Estates Ltd v West Oxfordshire DC and Secretary of State* <u>REF</u>
[66] *Save Britain's Heritage v No 1 Poultry Ltd and Secretary of State* [1991] 1 W.L.R. 153; see **14.4.7**.
[67] See **1.5**.
[68] All recent Government guidance is freely available on the relevant website.

dance to be cited by applicants and appellants elsewhere, it is always preferable to cite the local guidance whenever possible.

Underlying all the detailed advice, these documents (and their predecessors over many years) have always made it abundantly clear that as a matter of policy, as opposed to law, listed buildings *should* be preserved—whatever the strict interpretation of the statutory provisions. The final version of PPG 15 (unlike the draft) thus retains the general presumption in favour of preserving listed buildings, found in all previous guidance.[69] The basic policy approach is summed up as follows:

"The importance which the Government attaches to the protection of the historic environment was explained in paragraphs 1.1–1.7 above. Once lost, listed buildings cannot be replaced; and they can be robbed of their special interest as surely by unsuitable alteration as by outright demolition. They represent a finite resource and an irreplaceable asset. There should be a general presumption in favour of the preservation of listed buildings, except where a convincing case can be made out, against the criteria set out in this section, for alteration or demolition. While the listing of a building should not be seen as a bar to all future change, the starting point for the exercise of listed building control is the statutory requirement on local planning authorities to 'have special regard to the desirability of preserving the building [etc.]' (section 16). This reflects the great importance to society of protecting listed buildings from unnecessary demolition and from unsuitable and insensitive alteration, and should be the prime consideration for authorities in determining an application for consent."[70]

As to the extent to which a report to a planning authority committee needs to refer explicitly to Government policy—and to PPG 15 in particular—this was considered by the High Court in *British Telecommunications PLC v Gloucester CC.* Elias J. said that he would have been surprised if the members of the authority's committee had been unaware of the relevant principles (not least because they had just a few months earlier dealt with another application in the same conservation area); but he accepted that it would not be right automatically to assume that relevant guidance is always known and has been considered either by officers or members, even though no express mention is made of it in the relevant report.[71]

This emphasises the need to ensure that those who make decisions are kept fully informed as to current Government policy.

14.4.3 The Secretary of State's criteria for determining applications

The problem in practice, of course, is to determine which demolition is "unnecessary", and which alterations are "unsuitable" or "insensitive". The Secretary of State has accordingly provided at paragraph 3.5 of PPG 15 guidance on the criteria to be taken into account by a local authority when considering any application for listed building consent to demolish or alter a listed building, and by inspectors when deciding appeals:

---

[69] See for example Circ. 8/87, para.38.
[70] PPG 15, para.3.3. Para.116 of *Planning Guidance (Wales): Planning Policy* is similar but much more succinct.
[71] [2002] J.P.L. 993 at para.111; see also *Boulevard Land v Secretary of State* [1998] J.P.L. 983 at p.991.

"(i) the importance of the building—its intrinsic architectural and historic interest and rarity, in both national and local terms ("historic interest" is further explained in paragraph 6.11);

(ii) the particular physical features of the building (which may include its design, plan, materials or location) which justify its inclusion in the list: list descriptions may draw attention to features of particular interest or value, but they are not exhaustive and other features of importance (eg interiors) may come to light after the building's inclusion in the list;

(iii) the building's setting and its contribution to the local scene, which may be very important, *e.g.* where it forms an element in a group, park, garden or other townscape or landscape, or where it shares particular architectural forms or details with other buildings nearby;

(iv) the extent to which the proposed works would bring substantial benefits for the community, in particular by contributing to the economic regeneration of the area or the enhancement of its environment (including other listed buildings)."

The corresponding guidance for Wales is at WO Circular 61/96, paragraph 70; "historic interest" is further explained in Appendix F to WO Circular 1/98.[72] Guidance for Northern Ireland, at paragraph 6.5 of PPS 6, is identical to that in England.

These considerations will also be relevant to applications for planning permission to alter or extend listed buildings.

The first three of the criteria mentioned above relate to the importance of the building, both in its own right and in relation to its setting. See, for example, the appeals noted in the *Journal of Planning and Environment Law* relating to an important early cinema in the centre of Swansea, an area almost devoid of listed buildings and other buildings of distinction (to be retained),[73] and a redundant public house in Hampshire of no apparent interest or beauty (consent granted to demolish).[74] And it seems that the perceived mediocrity of the Mappin and Webb building in the City of London was one of the factors which led to the grant of listed building consent for its demolition.[75]

The grading of a building is clearly relevant,[76] but only to a limited extent— there are, after all, almost 500,000 buildings of Grade II, which cannot all be of equal merit!

However, whilst the quality of a building is, in theory, obviously of considerable relevance, it is a difficult topic on which to produce convincing evidence—as opposed to mere opinion:

"When one is dealing with questions of aesthetic value, I very much doubt whether experts are necessarily of any use at all ... It would not, ... really help, it seems to me, if one is dealing with pure aesthetic values, to call witnesses to say that a painting was beautiful. It would be of considerable assistance, of course, if it were relevant, to call experts to say that it was worth £50,000, but not that it was beautiful or that a piece of architecture was of high quality, and the reason for that seems to me to be this: that experts do tend to differ, and for every expert that one could find who said, looking at pure aesthetics, that some-

---

[72] See **3.5.2**.
[73] [1986] J.P.L. 141.
[74] [1987] J.P.L. 297.
[75] See **14.4.7**.
[76] PPG 15, paras 3.6, 3.14; WO Circ. 61/96, paras 71, 96.

thing was exceptionally fine one might quite easily find another expert who took exactly the opposite view."[77]

For a case where it was of relevance, see *General Accident v Secretary of State*,[78] where the key issue was whether a listed building, in the gothic revival style, fitted into the Cheltenham Conservation Area—all parties agreed it was of some interest. Such an assessment was accepted to be a matter for the inspector and the Secretary of State.

As to the list description mentioned in the second of the above criteria, this was also considered (albeit *obiter*) by Lord Hope in *City of Edinburgh Council v Secretary of State for Scotland*:

"both the decision maker and the developer will, no doubt, find it helpful to know what the features were which persuaded the Secretary of State that the building should be listed as being of special architectural or historic interest."[79]

But note that this does not mean that consent should necessarily be given for the removal or alteration of a feature not included in the list, or withheld for a feature that is included.

The fourth of the above criteria relates to the provision of benefits. This was largely new when it first appeared in the PPG, and appears to have been relatively little used in practice. But it would seem, in principle, to justify—for example—the alteration of a listed building so far as necessary to create some new community facility, or the demolition of such a building if that was essential to enable the construction of a bypass. However, there would of course need to be a balancing exercise carried out, involving the merits (and possible costs) of preserving the building in its present condition as against the merits of the benefits to be provided following its alteration or loss.

14.4.4 Demolition

Applications for listed building consent for the demolition of listed buildings are invariably considered extremely carefully, and are very unlikely to be granted. And not only is it hard to gain consent, but is getting harder. In the years from 1990 to 1994, an average of just over 300 applications were made each year for the demolition of a listed building. These led to only 83 consents being granted each year—a fifth of the figure ten years earlier, in spite of the massive increase in the number of listed buildings. And in the three years following 1994, the number of consents dropped again—to an average of only 55.

In addition to the general principles set out at paragraph 3.5 of PPG 15 (see above), the basic approach of the Government towards applications for demolition in England is set out at paragraph 3.16:

"The destruction of historic buildings is in fact very seldom necessary for reasons of good planning: more often it is the result of neglect, or of failure to make imaginative efforts to find new uses for them or to incorporate them into new development."

---

[77] *Winchester CC v Secretary of State* (1978) 36 P. & C.R. 455, *per* Forbes J. at 472.
[78] [1977] 1 E.G.L.R. 130.
[79] [1997] 3 P.L.R. 71 at pp.76–77.

Paragraph 3.17 then makes it clear that the demolition of any Grade I or Grade II* building should be wholly exceptional and should require the strongest justification.

Secondly, consent should not be given for the total or substantial demolition of any listed building without clear and convincing evidence being provided to show:

(1) that all reasonable efforts have been made to sustain existing uses or find viable new uses, and that those efforts have failed; and

(2) that preservation in some form of charitable or community use[80] is not possible or suitable; or

(3) that redevelopment would produce substantial benefits for the community which would decisively outweigh the loss resulting from demolition.

Proposals should therefore be judged by local planning authorities against the following criteria, set out in full at paragraph 3.19:

(1) the condition of the building, and the cost of repairing and maintaining it in relation to its importance and to the value derived from its continued use;

(2) the adequacy of efforts made to retain the building in use; and

(3) the merits of alternative proposals for the site.

The first two of these essentially relate to the relative viability of restoring the building for its existing use, refurbishing it (possibly with substantial alterations) for a new use, or demolishing it to make way for a replacement.[81] The third criterion is considered below.[82]

For a well-publicised example of the application of these criteria in practice, see the recent decision of the Secretary of State on a retrospective application for consent to demolish Greenside, described as "a very significant building of the International Modern Movement in Britain" and listed Grade II.[83] He noted that the building required substantial repairs, but not so as to render it incapable of being occupied. And he accepted that it had been marketed for two years, but not at a price reflecting its condition. He accordingly refused consent—and also, significantly, refused planning permission for the construction of a replacement dwelling, due to the location of the site in the green belt.

Similar guidance for Wales, Scotland and Northern Ireland is at paragraphs 90 to 92 of WO Circular 61/96, paragraphs 2.10 to 2.14 of the Historic Scotland *Memorandum of Guidance*, and Policy BH10 and paragraphs 6.22 to 6.27 of PPS 6.

The policy guidance in PPG 15 is considered further below, in the context of works to listed buildings other than demolition.

---

[80] See PPG 15, para.3.11
[81] See **14.4.2**
[82] See **14.4.3**.
[83] Runnymede BC, inspectorate reference APP/Q3630/V/04/1145659,1156052.

14.4.5 Financial viability of restoration

One of the most important factors determining whether or not an historic building can be preserved or restored is whether a use can be found for it that is both suitable for the building and financially viable. The duty laid upon the decision-maker has thus been summarised as follows by Collins J. in *Thompson v Secretary of State*:

"There are two aspects to listed building consent. First, the decision has to be made whether what is proposed will harm the listed building. If it will not, or the decision is that any such harm is such as can be regarded as sufficiently slight to justify the development, then the further issue, as to justification despite harm, will not have to be considered. But if it is considered that the harm is such as would normally justify refusal, the decision-maker has to go on to consider whether, notwithstanding that, in the circumstances it is necessary to grant the permission because otherwise the listed building would be lost, and it would be lost if it was economically viable to maintain its existence unless some form of development such as was requested is permitted to go ahead."[84a]

This slightly confuses the position by using the word "development", which is, strictly, no appropriate in the context of listed building consent; but the principle is sound—first, consider the harm; then go on to consider whether, in spite of any harm, there may nevertheless be reasons suggesting that consent should be granted.

The Secretary of State's policy on this, in the context of applications to demolish listed buildings,[84] was considered in *Bristol Meeting Room Trust v Secretary of State and Bristol CC*.[85] The owners of a listed building in poor repair sought listed building consent for its demolition.[86] The City Council claimed at the ensuing appeal that, once restored, the house would have a value in excess of the costs of restoration; and the appellants should have put the building on the open market. The inspector agreed; and noted that only one estimate had been obtained for each element of the repairs. The Secretary of State also agreed that, in accordance with the criteria mentioned in paragraph 90 of Circular 8/87,[87] there were no grounds overriding the presumption in favour of preserving the listed building. He accordingly upheld the inspector's recommendation, and dismissed the appeal.

The owners appealed against the decision of the Secretary of State refusing listed building consent on the grounds that the policy in Circular 8/87—and in particular the advice in paragraph 89 relating to the placing of buildings on the market[88]—was unlawful because it was rigid and did not admit of special circumstances. Sir Graham Eyre Q.C., sitting as deputy judge, considered the advice, and considered that special circumstances of an applicant would only exceptionally be relevant. In this case, for example, the matters put forward by the appellants were hardly germane to the fundamental question of the desirability of

[84a] *Thompson v Secretary of State and Barnsley MBC* [2004] EWHC, unreported, June 16, 2004, QBD; transcript available via Casetrack, *per* Collins J. at para.16.
[84] See 9.7.5.
[85] [1991] J.P.L. 152.
[86] See 8.7.8 for the facts.
[87] See now PPG 15, paras 3.5 and 3.19, WO Circ. 61/96, paras 70 and 92.
[88] Now PPG 15, para.3.19(ii); WO Circ. 61/96, para.92(iii).

preserving the building. He concluded that the future use of the building had not been sufficiently investigated.

However, the advice, relating to the condition of a building and the cost of repair,[89] was also relevant. The Secretary of State, in his decision, had accepted the inspector's opinion that, although the building was in a poor state of repair, it was nevertheless capable of economic restoration. In fact, however, the inspector in this case had not found that the building was capable of restoration. There had been no material of a conclusive nature before him; and he had therefore been unable to go any further than indicate that he was not satisfied that the building was incapable of economic restoration. The Secretary of State had accordingly wholly misunderstood the inspector's reasoning; and his decision was therefore vitiated. For an earlier case where there was a substantial difference between experts as to the cost of restoration, see *Thanet DC v Secretary of State*.[90]

In *Henry Davis & Co. v Secretary of State*,[91] the Inspector was again not satisfied that he had enough evidence on the matter of repairs; in particular, he had received no evidence at all as to costs and values, merely comment. The case had been dealt with by written representations, and the appellants subsequently argued that they had not presented such evidence because the point was "blindingly obvious": but it was plainly not obvious to the inspector.

In the light of this, it will be sensible for an applicant to include with his application a financial appraisal, highlighting the matters noted above. **Form D13** in Appendix D is an example of a development appraisal indicating that the repair and refurbishment of a listed building is not viable, whereas a more substantial scheme of reordering (requiring listed building consent) would be profitable. If even that is not viable, a further appraisal would be needed, to prove that demolition and redevelopment is the only realistic option.

Applicants should be aware, however, that the assumptions underlying such appraisals may be examined thoroughly in the event of a subsequent appeal—not least because (as can be seen by comparing the two valuations in the Appendix) relatively slight alterations to key variables can have a surprisingly great effect on the outcome. And those intent on saving a threatened building will often tend to underestimate the extent of the repairs necessary before it can sensibly be re-used, just as developers exaggerate the problems.[92] A report by a building surveyor may therefore be required to support any estimates of the cost of restoration or redevelopment, along with an analysis of genuinely comparable values.

The economics of restoration will sometimes not determine the issue. Thus in *Cullimore v Secretary of State*[93] the court noted that the inspector had considered the question of costs and the economics of rebuilding, but that this was only one factor at issue; it found that, even if he had not considered that matter, he would have still reached the same decision. Most importantly, no sufficient reason had been found to override the presumption in favour of retaining the building.

[89] para.3.19(i)/para.92(i).
[90] [1978] 1 E.G.L.R. 142.
[91] [1992] J.P.L. 1162.
[92] *P G Murdoch v Secretary of State* [2001] J.P.L. 841; this point only emerges from the transcript (available on Lawtel).
[93] [1992] E.G.C.S. 69.

Even where rehabilitation of a listed building is not economically viable for its owner, consent may still be refused where there is a reasonable prospect of it being purchased and restored by a new owner, such as an amenity group or a building preservation trust.[94] Conversely, there may be no need to require the owner of a building to put it on the market where the economics of restoration are acknowledged by all to be marginal.[95]

14.4.6 Financial evaluation of proposed redevelopment

Where, as will often be the case, it is proposed to redevelop the site of a listed building with another building, it appears that the following considerations are relevant:

(1) the cost of putting the listed building into good repair;

(2) the value of the building for any purpose if put into good repair;

(3) accordingly, the extent to which such restoration is an economic proposition;

(4) whether any, and if so what, replacement building is feasible; and

(5) the cost and value of any such replacement.[96]

A similar approach was adopted in *Thanet DC v Secretary of State*, where it was considered that the likely cost of restoration was such as to render the whole proposal impracticable.[97]

Several reported appeal decisions regarding redundant buildings also illustrate this principle. In 1985, listed building consent was granted for the demolition of the Bass No. 2 Brewery at Burton-on-Trent in Staffordshire, since no scheme that was financially viable could be found for its re-use.[98] The following year, consent was refused for the demolition of the Maltings at Sleaford, to allow more time to seek alternative uses for the buildings, and for investigating the best form of redevelopment.[99] By contrast, where listed building consent was sought for the demolition of a redundant brick-kiln in Reading, it was granted on the grounds that no other use could be found for the building other than to restore it as a "controlled" ruin having only local, and extremely limited, interest, and that this could not justify the high cost of both the restoration works themselves and the subsequent maintenance that would be required.[1]

The general view of the Government is clear:

"The Secretaries of State would not expect consent for demolition to be given simply because redevelopment is economically more attractive to the developer than repair and re-use of a historic building, or because the developer acquired the building at a price that

---

[94] See, for example, the appeal at [1984] J.P.L. 679.
[95] *R. (Sullivan) v Warwick DC* [2003] J.P.L. 1545, 2 P.L.R. 56 at para.4.3.
[96] *Kent Messenger Ltd v Secretary of State* [1976] J.P.L. 372.
[97] [1978] J.P.L. 251.
[98] [1985] J.P.L. 652.
[99] [1986] J.P.L. 55.
[1] [1984] J.P.L. 121.

reflected the potential for development rather than the condition and constraints of the existing historic building."[2]

Further, it has been held that, where a listed building forms only part of a redevelopment site, or part of a group of buildings, it is legitimate to consider the economic viability of restoration as against redevelopment in the context of the site or the group of buildings as a whole, rather than just a particular building on its own—not least because a comprehensive development of a whole area may have beneficial effects on the value of each building in it.[3]

14.4.7 Design of proposed redevelopment

As to the design quality (as opposed to the financial viability) of any proposed redevelopment, the Secretary of State in *Kent Messenger* had taken the view that it was not a material consideration, but the High Court specifically left the question open. In *Godden*, Stuart Smith J. considered that:

"Where an area ... was an obvious candidate for redevelopment in a potentially attractive area, then such potential development was a material consideration but it was probably not one to which great weight would be attached unless the nature of the development was reasonably well known ... But weight was a matter for the Inspector and the Secretary of State."[4]

One notable case where the quality of a new building was considered to be a relevant matter in deciding whether to grant consent for the demolition of the listed building which it was to replace was the demolition of the Mappin and Webb building and seven other listed buildings in the City of London. The owners of the important site wished to demolish these and replace them with a modern building designed by James Stirling. The inspector at the inquiry considered that the existing buildings on the site were of less value than others in the area, that the proposed replacement "might just be a masterpiece", and that this was sufficient to override the undoubted presumption in favour of retaining listed buildings. The Secretary of State accordingly granted planning permission, listed building consent and conservation area consent.

Save Britain's Heritage, a national amenity group, applied to have the decision quashed. Simon Brown J. upheld it at first instance, but his judgment was overturned by the Court of Appeal,[5] Woolf L.J. considered that the reasoning of the Secretary of State was defective, and accordingly quashed the decision. The owners appealed to the House of Lords,[6] which reversed the decision of the Court of Appeal. The Secretary of State's general policy in favour of retaining listed buildings[7] was not absolute, and could in very special circumstances be overridden. This case was one of those special circumstances, the Secretary of State

---

[2] PPG 15, para.3.17; WO Circ. 61/96, para.91.
[3] *Godden v Secretary of State* [1988] J.P.L. 99; *P G Murdoch v Secretary of State* [2001] J.P.L. 841.
[4] [1988] J.P.L. 99 at 1001.
[5] [1990] 3 P.L.R. 50; (1990) 60 P. & C.R. 539.
[6] *Save Britain's Heritage v No 1 Poultry Ltd and Secretary of State* [1991] 1 W.L.R. 153.
[7] In Circ. 8/87, para.89; see now PPG 15, para.3.3, quoted at **14.4.2**.

had specifically considered his general policy, and he had explicitly stated his reasons for departing from it.

This case, albeit widely reported, might well not have reached the House of Lords had it not concerned such a prominent site, or a design by such a notorious architect; and the Secretary of State's decision letter made it clear that the outcome was not to be regarded as a general precedent leading to the loss of listed buildings. And since then, the Secretaries of State have made it plain that "subjective claims for the architectural merits of proposed replacement buildings should not in themselves be held to justify the demolition of any listed building".[8]

A more typical case is *Henry Davis & Co v Secretary of State*,[9] which concerned a proposal to replace a recently listed building in a conservation area with a new office block. Malcolm Spence Q.C., sitting as deputy judge, started with the guidance in paragraph 95 of Circular 8/87, which strictly relates to conservation area consent: "consent to demolish should normally be given only where there are acceptable and detailed plans for redevelopment."[10] He held that this applied even more to the demolition of listed buildings. He accordingly found it "quite impossible to imagine that listed building consent would have been granted by this inspector for the demolition of this listed building without there being in place a suitable redevelopment scheme".

Similarly in *Kent CC v Secretary of State*,[11] the court upheld a refusal by the Secretary of State to grant conservation area consent for demolition, in the absence of a satisfactory replacement structure.[12]

As to the assessment of design quality, see the comments of Forbes J. in *Winchester CC v Secretary of State*, quoted earlier.[13] It is difficult enough assessing the quality of an existing building; evaluating a proposed replacement will be even harder. See also the comments below on the design of the alterations.[14]

14.4.8 *Proposals for major alterations and extensions*

The success rate of applicants in obtaining consent for alterations and extensions to listed buildings is significantly lower than for other buildings. Appeals relating to alterations, generally at the front of the building, succeed in only around 20 per cent of cases; those relating to extensions, generally at the rear, in 35 per cent.

One particular issue that sometimes proves particularly contentious is the exercise of control by planning authorities over design—either of extensions to existing listed buildings or of new buildings affecting their setting. Where a proposal is for an extension, as opposed to an alteration, to a listed building, this will be judged on its merits; but the most common reason for refusal, however it is

---

[8]   PPG 15, para.3.19(iii); WO Circ. 61/96, para.92(iii).
[9]   [1992] J.P.L. 1162.
[10] See now PPG 15, para.4.27; WO Circ. 61/96, para.33.
[11] [1995] J.P.L. 610.
[12] See **14.7.6**.
[13] (1987) 36 P. & C. R. 455; see **14.4.3**.
[14] See **14.4.8**.

phrased, is likely to be that used by the inspector in *Stocks Hotel v Secretary of State*[15]—the "mundane" character of the proposed new work.[16]

Where an existing building is altered or extended, the general design, detailing and choice of materials of the new work should obviously respect those of the original building. In some cases, this may mean that the new work must match the old exactly. Elsewhere, it may be possible to incorporate new designs, but thought should still be given to such details as matching up storey heights, and echoing the rhythm of solid and void in the original elevation. The choice of materials will also need particularly careful consideration.

It should also be borne in mind when considering the desirability of proposed alterations to an existing building that they will have an effect not just on the appearance of the building itself but also on that of the area in which it is set. Thus, for example, where planning permission was sought for the addition of an extra floor in the form of a mansard roof on a listed house within the Kingsdown Conservation Area in Bristol, the recommendation of the inspector (that it should be allowed) was influenced both by the effect of the extra storey on the appearance of the house itself and by its impact on the skyline of the conservation area as a whole.[17]

As for the design of a proposed alteration, while it is legitimate to argue about its merit, it should be borne in mind that most inspectors find such argument of limited value.[18]

The subjective nature of such issues is also reflected in the recognition by the courts that one inspector may disagree with another on matters such as aesthetics, even though no reason is given (*Standard Securities v Secretary of State*[19]; *Speyroc Construction Ltd v Secretary of State*[20]). And the Court of Appeal has recently emphasised that such issues are for the initial decision-maker (planning authority or inspector), not for the court—even where the court is a deputy judge with a "huge experience in the field of planning inquiries".[21]

PPG 15 also points out that much of its advice on demolition proposals would also be relevant to the consideration of more substantial alterations, in particular where they involve the demolition of a significant part of the listed building.[22] As to whether a particular part of a listed building is "significant" for these purposes, this will be a question of fact in each case, requiring an assessment of both the proportion of the building represented by the part to be lost and the qualitative significance of that part.[23] Thus, in general, the greater the part of a listed building

---

[15] [1996] E.G.C.S. 165.

[16] General policy advice is at PPG 15, Annex C, para.C.7, and WO Circ. 61/96, Annex D, para.9.

[17] [1984] J.P.L. 525.

[18] *Winchester CC v Secretary of State* (1978) 36 P. & C.R. 455; see **14.4.3, 14.4.7**.

[19] [1992] E.G.C.S. 129.

[20] [1993] E.G.C.S. 55.

[21] See *R. v Leominster DC, ex p. Pothecary* [1998] J.P.L. 335, overturning [1997] E.G.C.S. 02.

[22] paras 3.7 and 3.15A (the latter inserted by Envt Circ. 14/97, App. E, and retained by Circ. 01/01).

[23] *R. (Sullivan) v Warwick DC* [2003] JPL 1545, 2 P.L.R. 56. *The Times*, June 12, 2003, at para.43.

that is to be removed, the more likely it is that the tests in PPG 15 relating to demolition should be applied; but that might also be the case with the removal of a small but crucial part of the building's original character.

Finally, in the unusual situation of a building having been substantially damaged by a fire, the effect of a proposal should be assessed in relation to the building as it now exists, rather than as it was previously.[24]

14.4.9 Proposals for repairs and minor alterations

Planning authorities are likely to scrutinise very carefully all proposals to carry out alterations to listed buildings. The importance of good design has already been emphasised in relation to proposal for more major alterations and extensions[25]; but the same principles apply equally to proposals for repairs and minor alterations.

Careful and intelligent advice on the principles to be adopted in altering listed buildings is given in PPG 15.[26] More detailed advice on particular types of alteration is at Annex C to the PPG, prepared by English Heritage, covering external elevation, roofs, external doors, windows, shopfronts, interiors, floors, minor additions and new services, and the even more comprehensive Appendix 1 to the Historic Scotland *Memorandum*.

In addition, much specialist advice is available from English Heritage, the national amenity societies[27] and elsewhere—both in the form of published material and by way of comment on particular cases.[28] The PPG also refers to *The Repair of Historic Buildings: Advice on Principles and Methods* by Christopher Brereton, which is a scholarly if at times somewhat purist manual of detailed advice, published by English Heritage.[29]

The corresponding advice for Wales is in WO Circ. 61/96.[30] Specialist advice is obviously available from Cadw although only on a limited basis.[31]

Amongst appeals which have been reported have been the following (listed building consent was refused in every case):

— new replacement windows[32];

— plastic blinds on a Victorian shop front[33]; a PVC canopy outside a night club in a conservation area[34]; and

— a glazed door to enclose a brick storm porch.[35]

---

[24] *Re Tonbridge School Chapel* [1993] 1 W.L.R. 1138, at p.1144.
[25] See **14.4.8**; see also **14.6.1** on the design of new buildings affecting the setting of listed buildings.
[26] PPG 15, paras 3.12 to 3.15.
[27] See **13.5.6, Appendix C**.
[28] See PPG 15, para.3.25.
[29] PPG 15, Annex C, para.C.1
[30] WO Circ. 61/96, paras 93–98A and Annex D.
[31] WO Circ. 61/96. paras 100–102 (see 9.3.2).
[32] [1987] J.P.L. 806 and [1988] J.P.L. 194 and [1993] J.P.L. 604 (see **8.6.2**).
[33] [1986] J.P.L. 928.
[34] [1985] J.P.L. 669.
[35] [1985] J.P.L. 416.

Also of interest is the decision of the Secretary of State on a called-in listed building consent application and several associated appeals regarding a number of proposed alterations to Sutton Place in Surrey (listed Grade I).[36] Amongst the issues considered relevant were the following:

(1) the contribution made by the building to the appearance and character of the general locality (in this case, limited);

(2) the purpose of the proposed works (some of the proposed alterations, for example, were to provide fire exits);

(3) the fact that some of the alterations had the effect of restoring the appearance of the building at an earlier date[37];

(4) the condition, age and quality of features to be removed or obscured by the alterations (here, wood panelling of various dates, to be covered with paint);

(5) the historical importance of the features (in this case, stained glass illustrating an aspect of the history of the ownership of the house); and

(6) the possibility of retaining some of the features in alternative locations.

PPG 15 sensibly suggests that authorities should consider drawing up policies for alterations to listed buildings, outside the development plan:

"Such guidance will carry greater weight to the extent that it has been the subject of public consultation, has been formally adopted by the authority, and is published in a format which gives clear advice and is readily available to the public."[38]

Neighbouring authorities with areas containing similar types of buildings could also produce such guidance jointly, which would be able to draw on a wider ranger of experience, as well as saving cost and producing policies that would have greater credibility and weight.

One particular type of alteration to historic buildings which seems to give rise to numerous problems in practice is the conversion of barns and other agricultural buildings. This is encouraged in principle by government guidance,[39] but can lead to the loss of character: see the English Heritage leaflet on this subject, *The Conversion of Historic Farm Buildings*.[40]

14.4.10 *Adjustments to buildings to facilitate access by disabled people*

One particular category of alteration that is likely to be more frequent in coming years is the carrying out of alterations to a listed building to make it more

---

[36] [1984] J.P.L. 899.
[37] See **183.6**.
[38] PPG 15, para.2.5.
[39] PPG 2, para.16 (green belts), PPS 7, paras 17, 18 (countryside) and *Planning Guidance (Wales): Planning Policy*, paras 156 and 190.
[40] Published in a revised edition in May 1993.

accessible by the less mobile—in the light of the duties on service providers under the Disability Discrimination Act 1995, considered earlier in the book.[41]

There is at present no statutory or other duty on planning authorities to have special regard to disability issues. However, as from December 4, 2006, all public authorities in carrying out their functions are to have due regard to "the need to eliminate discrimination that is unlawful under the 1995 Act" (note, not the desirability of eliminating such discrimination).[42] This new duty will have to balanced against the existing duties to have special regard to the preservation of historic buildings and areas.[43] In any event, it is perhaps wise for authorities (and for applicants) to reflect on the guidance of the Secretary of State in PPG 15:

"It is important in principle that disabled people should have dignified easy access to and within historic buildings. If it is treated as part of an integrated review of access arrangements for all visitors or users, and a flexible and pragmatic approach is taken, it should normally be possible to plan suitable access for disabled people without compromising a building's special interest. Alternative routes or re-organising the use of spaces may achieve the desired result, without the need for damaging alterations."[44]

This is all elaborated in the comprehensive *Good Practice Guide* issued relatively recently by the ODPM, which also provides a list of useful contacts.[45]

14.4.11 Listed buildings and archaeology

Some listed buildings are scheduled ancient monuments, and many others are either of intrinsic archaeological interest or stand on ground which contains archaeological remains.[46] In such cases, appropriate arrangements should be made to ensure that the archaeological implications of development proposals are adequately assessed before planning permission or listed building consent is granted for works affecting them, and that archaeological discoveries made during the works are properly recorded.[47]

14.5 The use of listed buildings

14.5.1 The existing use

The discussion so far has focussed on building works to listed buildings (including demolition). But often the key to the preservation of a listed building will be to find a suitable use. Thus some uses are more or less appropriate in terms of their physical effect on the building, and may inevitably involve alterations (which may be either beneficial, leading to restoration of a ruin, or harmful) now or in the

---

[41] See **8.5**.
[42] Disability Discrimination Act 1995, s.49A, inserted by Disability Discrimination Act 2005, s.3 (and see SI 2005/2774).
[43] See **14.4.1** and **14.7.1**.
[44] PPG 15, *Planning and the Historic Environment*, para.3.28.
[45] *Planning and Access for Disabled People: a Good Practice Guide*. See particularly Chapter 10.
[46] PPG 16, para.2.15; WO Circ. 61/96, para.10.
[47] See also **14.8**.

future. And clearly different uses yield different economic returns, with consequences for viability.

The Secretary of State has rightly noted that:

"the best use [for a historic building] will very often be the use for which [it] was originally designed, and the continuation or reinstatement of that use should certainly be the first option when the future of a building is considered."[48]

The PPG sounds a note of caution, however: not all original uses will now be viable or even necessarily appropriate. And there must be a realistic prospect of such a use continuing, if permission is to be refused for a change of use. Thus, in considering an application for a change of use of County Hall in London to a hotel, the inspector stated that the most appropriate use for the main building was to maintain it for local government use. There was however (at least at that time) no probability that it would be put to such a use if permission was refused. Whilst therefore the Secretary of State had to pay special regard to the desirability of preserving the building and its setting, he had no duty to enquire further than this; the building thus had to be put to an alternative use which would respect its special features.[49]

A more typical example of how this principle works out in practice is given by an appeal against the refusal of planning permission for the conversion into offices of a residential building in Winchester (then listed Grade II, and about to be upgraded to II*). The Inspector, in his report dismissing the appeal, stated as follows:

"In my opinion the main issues in this appeal are whether the change of use of the Mill House to offices is necessary in order to preserve this listed building; and whether such a use would maintain the integrity of the structure and the attractiveness of its setting.

I agree with the parties that the Mill House is a fine listed building and all steps should be taken to ensure its preservation. In my opinion, national and local policies would justify granting planning permission for the change of use to offices provided it could be established that, because there was no demand for a residential use, the house would not again be used for that purpose and would fall into decay if permission were not granted . . .

From the evidence submitted I am not satisfied that the Mill House is incapable of continued residential use . . . Bearing in mind the quality of the house and its setting, the likely cost of such works is not so great as to mean that the house would not command a reasonable price for residential use in today's market.

The other main issue which I identified only falls to be considered in detail if it is established that the Mill House is incapable of residential use. While an office use could on your evidence provide a sufficient return to enable the property to be restored and maintained in good order, such a use would in my view make it difficult to retain the integrity of structure, as works beyond those necessary for domestic use would be needed if the house were to be used for offices."[50]

---

[48] PPG 15, para.3.10.
[49] *Lambeth LBC v Secretary of State* [1992] E.G.C.S. 17 (upheld in the Court of Appeal [1992] J.P.L. 759; see also **13.8.3**.
[50] [1988] J.P.L. 285 at pp.286–8.

Where a building is in a specialised use, it may be necessary to obtain appropriate specialist advice—either as to the generality of the trade or business concerned, or as to the suitability of the particular building.[51]

14.5.2 New uses for listed buildings

Planning authorities have been urged to relax controls over land use allocation, density, plot ratio and daylighting, and to apply Building Regulations and fire safety legislation sensitively and sensibly, where this would enable historic buildings to be given a new lease of life.[52] The same would no doubt apply to the Disability Discrimination Act 1995.

This theme is central to the reasoning behind many decisions (by local planning authorities and by inspectors at appeals) on applications for changes of use of listed buildings. The PPG sums it up as follows:

"In principle the aim should be to identify the optimum viable use that is compatible with the fabric, interior and setting of the historic building. This may not necessarily be the most profitable use if that would entail more destructive alterations than other viable uses."[53]

It points out that grant aid may assist in enabling restoration for a use that is not viable; and where a building is particularly sensitive, it may be possible to secure its future by community or charitable ownership, preserving it for its own sake. These solutions will, however, be appropriate only in exceptional cases; and the general message is clear—viability is of the essence.[54]

This will sometimes lead to permission being sought for the change of use of a listed building to a use that would otherwise be against policy (possibly because of, for example, the extent of traffic likely to be generated), but which is said to be necessary in order to generate sufficient income to restore the building. In such case, the considerations set out in the English Heritage policy statement on enabling development, considered below, will be relevant.[55]

Accordingly, where permission is sought for a proposal that includes the change of use of a listed building (possibly in connection with alterations to it or development affecting its setting), it may be desirable for the applicant to produce detailed financial calculations to show that the continuation of the present use is not sufficiently profitable to enable the building to be restored. See **Form D13** in Appendix D for an example of a development appraisal; it may be appropriate to carry out a similar exercise both for the existing use and for the suggested alternative (and see below on such appraisals generally). Similarly, it may be

---

[51] See, for example, the note produced by the Campaign for Real Ale on the viability of public houses (available on *www.pubsweek.org*).

[52] PPG 15, paras 2.18, 3.26–3.27; WO Circ. 61/96, paras 12, 124. And see *Building Regulations and Historic Buildings*, an interim guidance note on the application of Part L (energy conservation) produced by English Heritage in 2002.

[53] PPG 15, para.3.9

[54] paras 3.8–3.11; *Planning Guidance (Wales): Planning Policy*, para.118 is similar.

[55] *Enabling Development and the Conservation of Heritage Assets: Policy Statement*, English Heritage, 2001 (see **14.6.4**). For an example, see *R. (Davey) v Aylesbury Vale DC and Mentmore Towers Ltd*, March 11, 2005, unreported (transcript available on Lawtel).

appropriate for the planning authority to take its own specialist advice to assess the information supplied in connection with a particular proposal.

As with appraisals of the viability of restoring old buildings, the amount of detail that will be required from applicants, and the amount that should be supplied to the committee determining the applications, will vary from case to case.[56]

Whilst it may thus be in order for a planning authority to relax its land-use policies to achieve conservation aims, the Government has made clear its opposition to tightening policy to that end.[57]

An unusual example of these principles being applied was in *Tower Hamlets LBC v Secretary of State and Lane*,[58] where permission was granted for the conversion of a listed residential building into offices, which would otherwise have been against policy, in order to secure its restoration. In that case, the restoration works were carried out, but the new use was not implemented. When permission was sought to renew the permission, it was held that it was legitimate for the inspector to take into account the benefit of the restoration works which had already taken place.

14.6 Other development affecting listed buildings

14.6.1 Works affecting the setting of a listed building

Listed buildings will obviously be affected by proposals for their demolition, alteration and extension, and changes to their use. But they can also be affected, and sometimes just as radically, by development nearby—such as the construction of an insensitive office block towering over a small listed cottage next door, or the removal of insensitively located pipework and extensions from a building next to a fine manor house. Indeed, the alteration of one listed building may have an effect (beneficial or otherwise) on the setting of another.

Accordingly, in considering whether to grant planning permission for development which affects the setting of a listed building, the planning authority or the Secretary of State is to have special regard to, amongst other things, the desirability of preserving that setting.[59]

In particular, where a new building is prosposed that affects the setting of a listed building, it will be important to ensure that it is sensitively designed. Advice is given in PPG 15, as follows:

"The design of new buildings intended to stand alongside historic buildings needs very careful consideration. In general it is better that old buildings are not set apart but are woven into the fabric of the living and working community. This can be done, provided that the new buildings are carefully designed to respect their setting, follow fundamental architectural principles of scale, height, massing and alignment, and use appropriate materials. This does not mean that new buildings have to copy their older neighbours in

---

[56] *Davey*, above.
[57] See PPG 15, para.2.18, and WO Circ. 61/96, para.12.
[58] [1983] J.P.L. 315.
[59] P(LBCA)A 1990, ss 16(2) and 66(1) (see **14.4.1**). [Scotland: P(LBCA)(S)A 1997, ss 14(2), 59(1); NI: P(NI)O 1991, art.45(1).]

detail: some of the most interesting streets in our towns and villages include a variety of building styles, materials, and forms of construction, of many different periods, but together forming a harmonious group."[59a]

As for Wales, see Technical Advice Note TAN 5, *Design*.

There will be more scope for new designs here than would be the case with alterations to an existing building (pastiche neo-Georgian is not always, or even often, the right answer) but local authorities (and amenity groups) will understandably be more concerned with architectural and aesthetic aspects of new proposals in such locations than they would be elsewhere.

In general, planning authorities have been criticised, both by architects and developers and by the Government, for becoming too involved in the design of proposed new development; but it has been recognised that historic buildings and areas are a special case. And see the comments in the previous chapter in relation to design statements to be submitted with applications in England and Wales.[59b] See also the comment above on the design of alterations to listed buildings,[59c] which apply with even greater force to new buildings affecting their setting of exsiting ones.

The extent of the "setting" of a listed building has already been considered; but it may mean something wider than just its curtilage, or just the land that can be seen from it.[60] In practice, the question is not—as it is with "curtilage"—what is the boundary of the setting, but rather does a particular proposed development affect the setting of a listed building in the vicinity. The answer to this is likely to depend on the nature of the proposal as much as on that of the listed building. Thus the erection of a tall radio mast may affect the setting of a number of listed buildings, some a considerable distance from it; whereas the erection of a small shed in the garden of a listed house is likely to affect its setting only if it is reasonably close.

This is reasonably straightforward; but it is important to take into account not just the setting of the listed building nearest to the proposed development, but also the settings of those further away, if they are also likely to be affected. Thus, in *R. v Bolsover DC, Ex p. Paterson*, it was argued that the council had taken account of the effect of a proposed development on the setting of one nearby listed building, but not on that of another. The court accepted the evidence of the planning officer that he had considered both, and would not have quashed the resulting permission had there not also been a fatal procedural defect.[61] But such challenges should be avoided, by ensuring that the record makes it clear (usually within the report to the relevant committee, and in the reasons for refusal) that the effect of the proposal has been considered in relation to each of the nearby listed buildings.

In *Ryan v Secretary of State*, on the other hand, the Court quashed a grant of planning permission for the extension of 17 Upper Mall, Hammersmith (listed Grade II) on the basis that the inspector had considered the effect of the extension on No. 17 itself and its setting, and on the conservation area within which it lay,

[59a] PPG 15, para.2.14.
[59b] See **13.3.5**.
[59c] See **14.4.8**.
[60] *R. v South Herefordshire DC, ex p. Felton* [1989] 3 P.L.R. 81; see **13.5.8, 13.5.9**.
[61] [2000] E.G.C.S. 83, [2001] J.P.L. 211 (see **13.5.1** for the facts).

but not had not fully considered its effect on the setting of Sussex House (on the opposite side of the street to No. 17, and listed Grade II*). The deputy judge accepted that the character and appearance of the conservation area, which had been considered, undoubtedly included the view of Sussex House from the river or the towpath, and to that extent its setting had been considered. However, he held that its setting also included the view out from the House across the river—which had not been fully taken into account—and therefore, after some hesitation, remitted the decision for re-determination.

Ryan is a slightly strange decision, in that it appears to establish that, although there is generally considered to be no right in law to a view from a building, there is if it is listed. However, it is a helpful reminder that all listed buildings near to the site of a proposed development must be considered, not just the one that is directly involved.

But there are limits. Where a proposal on a site close to a large number of listed buildings, as with a major redevelopment scheme in a historic town centre, it may be unrealistic to expect an officer's report to draw attention specifically to the effect on the setting of each one—particularly where visual material, such as drawings and models, is also available.[62]

Policy advice on works affecting the setting of a listed building is in paragraphs 2.16 and 2.17 of PPG 15 and paragraph 11 of WO Circular 61/96.

14.6.2 *Restoration of historic buildings as planning gain ("enabling development")*

It has already been noted that the preservation of a historic building may be a factor justifying the grant of planning permission for an otherwise unacceptable change in its use. This principle has in some cases been carried further, where the preservation of one building is only possible if funds are made available through the realisation of profits from another, otherwise unacceptable, development. Here too, the development "affects" the listed building, not directly as with an alteration or extension, nor by its geographical proximity to it, but by virtue of its economic effect. It follows that in this situation, too, the determination of the planning application is subject to the duty under the Listed Buildings Act to have special regard to the desirability of preserving a listed building or its setting or special features.[63]

Thus in *Brighton BC v Secretary of State*, a school sought permission to develop an unused area of one of their playing fields as a housing estate.[64] On appeal, the decision to grant permission (against the policies of the development plan) was influenced by the desire of the school to realise sufficient profit from the sale of the site to allow them to refurbish the main school buildings, which were listed Grade II and in a conservation area.

The *Brighton* decision was cited with approval in *R. v Westminster CC, ex p. Monahan*, in relation to the partial redevelopment of Covent Garden Opera

---

[62] *British Telecommunications PLC v Gloucester CC* [2002] J.P.L. 993 at para.118.

[63] P(LBCA)A 1990, ss 66(1) and 16(2) (see **14.4.1**). [Scotland: P(LBCA)(S)A 1997, ss 59(1), 14(2); NI: P(NI)O 1991, art.45(1).]

[64] *Brighton BC v Secretary of State for the Environment* (1978) 39 P. & C.R. 46.

House in London. Here the planning authority was satisfied that the restoration of the principal parts of the (Grade I) Opera House (only half of the cost of which could be raised by donations) justified the raising of finance by demolishing other listed buildings of less importance in order to carry out an otherwise unacceptable office development. The local residents objected, and challenged by way of judicial review the resolution of the authority to grant planning permission.[65] Webster J. in the High Court held that the fact that the finances made available from the commercial development would enable the improvements to be carried out was capable of being a material consideration, and could thus be taken into account by the authority. This decision was subsequently upheld by the Court of Appeal.[66] See also *Northumberland CC v Secretary of State*.[67]

A further example was the quashing by the High Court of a decision of the Secretary of State to refuse planning permission for development in the grounds of Formby Hall in Lancashire. He stated that everything possible should be done to preserve and restore the building, and noted that the proposals appeared to offer a last opportunity to preserve and restore it, but did not consider that sufficient to overrule the presumption against substantial new buildings in the green belt. His decision was considered to be perverse, and could not stand.[68] This indicates that the possibility of such restoration might be sufficient to overturn other policy objections to a proposal.

However, the court refused to quash the decision of an inspector granting permission for the construction of 22 houses at Hawley Grove and works to the Grade II listed Hawley Park House and its stable block, on the basis that the new development would finance the restoration of the house.[69] Robin Purchas Q.C., sitting as deputy judge, considered that the inspector had clearly considered with care all of the matters raised by the council, including possible difficulties in enforcing the restoration conditions if the owner for the time being was without funds; and that there was no need for the inspector to have considered whether there might be alternative, less harmful, means of achieving the desired objective of restoration.

Other relevant appeal decisions from this period, noted in previous editions of this book, are those relating to Broadlands House in Hampshire and Croome Court, Worcestershire (both important Grade I listed buildings).[70]

Finally, if a planning authority wishes to save a listed building by granting planning permission for development associated with it, suitable wording must be used in the grant of permission to ensure that the hoped-for linkage does in fact occur—otherwise a developer may become insolvent after the associated development has taken place but before the listed building has been restored. Alternatively, the listed building may collapse either naturally (as in *Burhill Estates v Woking BC*[71]) or otherwise, and the validity of the permission may be called into

[65] [1988] J.P.L. 557.
[66] [1989] 1 P.L.R. 36.
[67] [1989] J.P.L. 700.
[68] *Care Link v Secretary of State* [1989] 2 P.L.R. 47.
[69] *Hart DC v Secretary of State* [1997] J.P.L. B125.
[70] [1990] J.P.L. 453; [1990] J.P.L. 622.
[71] [1995] J.P.L. 147.

question. One way to avoid such problems is to impose suitable conditions on the planning permission—such as one to prohibit the occupation of the new building until the listed building has been restored. An alternative is to seek a planning obligation.[72]

14.6.3 Enabling development in the Court of Appeal: the restoration of Downe Hall

Downe Hall in Dorset is a fine late 18th-century listed building, Grade II*, set in a registered park and within a conservation area. By 1994 it was in very poor condition, and neither the owner nor the local authority was able to fund the necessary repairs. The only way forward was to transfer the property to someone who was able and willing to carry them out. The position was later summarised as follows by Schiemann L.J. when the matter came before the Court of Appeal:

"No private person acceptable to the owner had come forward. Any developer would only be prepared to do the work if he considered that the totality of what he was allowed to do on the site would show him a sufficient profit to make it financially worthwhile. In the context of the present case, he would almost invariably ask to be permitted to do work which would, on the one hand, harm the setting of the Hall but which would, on the other hand, finance the preservation of the building. So there was a tension between these two desiderata. A developer will in general try and persuade the Council that he must be permitted to do that which gives him the maximum amount of profit. This might, depending on his view of the market and the costs of restoration of the Hall, lead him to ask for permission for more, or it may be bigger, houses than are, in truth, required to make it worthwhile in his opinion to proceed. A further complicating factor can be that the setting of the building may be less harmed than by a larger beautifully designed development than by a smaller off-the-shelf development.

This sort of situation leaves a council with complex judgments to be made. How adverse is the effect of the proposed development in the grounds on the setting of the Hall? Is the developer bluffing when he sets out what he claims are his minimum terms? Can he be trusted to fulfil his engagements? Is it sensible to reject the so-called minimum terms and hope that the owner will want to find, and in due course will find, some other solution which is more acceptable in planning terms? Will the owner just let matters continue to slide as she had in times past, while the building decays? Is the building in danger of further serious harm while the ideal solution is being sought? Will the search for the best inhibit the achievement of the good?"[73]

These are the issues that commonly arise in this type of case.

A developer was duly found, who prepared a scheme (turning the Hall into five dwelling units, with eight new units in the grounds) that was acceptable to the council and to English Heritage. The developer produced a financial appraisal indicating that the scheme would yield a residual value for the Hall, after the carrying out of the repairs, of £250,000; in the absence of the scheme, the property had a substantial negative value. It was contrary to the development plan, in that it harmed the setting of the Hall, the registered park and the conservation area, as well as raising concerns as to landscape, nature conservation, residential amenity and traffic generation. On the other hand, it would save the Hall.

---

[72] See **13.8.8**.
[73] *R. v West Dorset DC, Ex p. Searle* [1999] J.P.L. 331.

The council considered that this type of development was not ideal, but was acceptable; the benefits of the scheme outweighed the harm, and approved the package in principle. The developer would not reduce the number of houses, and the council had recently lost a similar scheme elsewhere because of delay due to its insistence on too much information; it accordingly did not carry out an independent assessment of the developer's appraisal. It accordingly granted the necessary planning permission and listed building consent, subject to a s.106 agreement to ensure that the promised restoration did actually take place.[74]

The local objectors challenged the decision, in the High Court (unsuccessfully) and in the Court of Appeal, which considered that the council had made the right decision. There was no obligation on a developer to produce an appraisal, and no requirement for the council to appraise any appraisal that might be produced. In effect, by failing to consider the proposal in more depth, the council was saying either that no other suitable developer would be found, or that no other suitable scheme would be produced, or simply that—in view of the state of the Hall—it was not willing to take a chance. It had, after all, been well aware of the views of those opposed to the development.

14.6.4 The English Heritage Practical Guide

In the light of such considerations, English Heritage produced in 1999 a policy statement entitled *Enabling Development and the Conservation of Heritage Assets*. The term "heritage asset" is used as shorthand for any component of the historic environment, including scheduled monuments and other archaeological remains, historic buildings (listed or of local significance), conservation areas, and historic landscapes (including registered parks, gardens and battlefields).

The principles in that policy statement were then amplified further in the useful *Practical Guide to Assessment*, produced in June 2001, which effectively superseded it.[75] That *Guide* also included helpful precedents for relevant documents, including a section 106 agreement to secure the objective of enabling development, incorporating a form of bond. The *Guide* is now an essential starting point for discussions on any schemes involving enabling development—and is regularly relied on at relevant inquiries.

The basic principles are as follows:

"English Heritage believes that there should be a general presumption against 'enabling development' which does not meet all of the following criteria:

(1) the enabling development will not materially detract from the archaeological, architectural, historic, landscape or biodiversity interest of the asset, or materially harm its setting;

(2) the proposal avoids detrimental fragmentation of management of the heritage asset;

(3) the enabling development will secure the long-term future of the heritage asset and, where applicable, its continued use for a sympathetic purpose;

---

[74] The houses were indeed built, and the Hall saved—and the challenger apparently lost a great deal of money in legal fees (exacerbated because the judge, exceptionally, ordered her to pay two sets of costs).

[75] Available from English Heritage.

(4) the problem arises from the inherent needs of the heritage asset, rather than the circumstances of the present owner or the purchase price paid;

(5) sufficient financial assistance is not available from any other source;

(6) it is demonstrated that the amount of enabling development is the minimum necessary to secure the future of the heritage asset, and that its form minimises disbenefits; and

(7) the value or benefit of the survival or enhancement of the heritage asset outweighs the long-term cost to the community (i.e. the disbenefits) of providing the enabling development.

If it is decided that a scheme of enabling development meets all these criteria, English Heritage believes that planning permission should only be granted if:

(1) the impact of the development is precisely defined at the outset, normally through the granting of full rather than outline permission;

(2) the achievement of the heritage objective is securely and enforceably linked to it, bearing in mind the guidance in Circular 01/97, *Planning Obligations*;

(3) the heritage asset is repaired to an agreed standard, or the funds to do so made available, as early as possible in the course of enabling development, ideally at the outset and certainly before completion or occupation; and

(4) the planning authority closely monitors implementation, if necessary acting promptly to ensure a satisfactory outcome."

Crucially, the *Guide* added the clear statement that the policy applies only in the case of proposed development contrary to established planning policy (the development plan). It thus does not apply to proposals that are in accordance with the statutory development plan and national policy. This was explored by the Court of Appeal in *R. (Young) v Oxford City Council*, which concerned the erection of a new mews development in the grounds of a decaying listed building in Headington, to unlock funds for its restoration. The Court accepted that the decision-making process in such a case now potentially involves two stages:

"The committee should first have considered whether the mew development was acceptable, in planning terms, on its merits. If so, permission should have been granted. If not, the committee should have gone on to consider whether permission should have been granted to [sic] the project as enabling development within the meaning of the [English Heritage] policy statement. That would involve a consideration of the policy statement and its application to the facts of the case."[76]

14.6.5 Application of the English Heritage Guide

The English Heritage Guide has now been accepted as a material consideration in several cases in the courts since *Young*. In *Jewson Holdings v Secretary of State*,[77] the court upheld the conclusion of an inspector pointing out that the Statement stresses that developers should explore a range of development strategies. The inspector was not persuaded that the developer in that case had fully and objectively explored the council's suggestion that the listed buildings could be repaired and put to a beneficial low-key use, such as storage, without the need for enabling development. Further, he considered that the figures put forward by the developer for the cost of the essential repairs to the buildings did not necessarily represent a fair assessment. Such conclusions are common in disputes of this kind.

---

[76] [2002] 3 P.L.R. 86, CA, overturning the decision of Ouseley J., *per* Pill L.J. at para.21.

[77] March 21, 2003, unreported (transcript available on Casetrack).

The Guide was also accepted as a key consideration in *Valente v Secretary of State*,[78] in which the principal issue was the extent of the restoration works to a listed barn that should be taken into account in assessing whether to grant permission for a hotel that had an acceptable impact on neighbouring listed buildings but was otherwise unacceptable development in the green belt.

Most recently, in *R. (Davey) v Aylesbury Vale DC and Mentmore Towers Ltd*,[79] the court has stressed that the guidance contained in the English Heritage document is not mandatory; it is not part of the development plan, and stands instead as a material consideration. That case related to the change of use of Mentmore Towers in Buckinghamshire into a luxury hotel, along with the construction of a new wing in the grounds. The officer's report had referred to the Policy Statement, but the Council had received specialist advice that the scale of the proposed development was about right and that, in all the circumstances, no benefit was to be gained by "going through all the further hoops" (to use counsel's expression) theoretically required by the Statement.

In short, the Practical Guide is to be regarded as an essential guide, but—as with all policy—it is to be interpreted in the light of all the circumstances.

14.7 Works affecting conservation areas

14.7.1 General principles

There are four principal categories of works affecting conservation areas:

(1) the demolition of listed buildings in a conservation area (requiring only listed building consent);

(2) the alteration and extension of listed buildings (requiring planning permission and listed building consent);

(3) the demolition of unlisted buildings in a conservation area (requiring conservation area consent);

(4) the alteration and extension of existing unlisted buildings, the change of use of existing buildings (listed or otherwise), and the construction of new buildings (requiring only planning permission).

Some of the considerations applying in the case of works in the first two categories—by virtue of the fact that the building in question is listed—have already been considered[80]; but these will need to be taken into account alongside the factors applying to any proposals in conservation areas. And see the comments earlier in the chapter as to the position where a decision-maker is subject to overlapping statutory duties.[81]

When determining applications for planning permission, listed building consent and conservation area consent in any of these situations, the decision maker will

---

[78] May 14, 2003, unreported (transcript available on Lawtel).
[79] March 11, 2005, unreported (transcript available on Lawtel), at para.30.
[80] See **14.4**.
[81] See **14.2.2**.

be subject to the duty in section 72(1) of the Listed Buildings Act, which states that

"in the exercise, with respect to any buildings or other land in a conservation area, of any functions under or by virtue of [the Planning or Listed Buildings Acts], special attention shall be paid to the desirability of preserving or enhancing the character or appearance of that area."

Corresponding provisions are to be found in section 64(1) of the Scottish Listed Buildings Act, and article 50(5) of the Northern Ireland Order.

The scope of the duty under section 72, which first appeared in the Civic Amenities Act 1967, has been the subject of much litigation, of which the first notable decision was that of Lionel Read Q.C. in *Steinberg v Secretary of State*.[82] The next section accordingly considers that decision and those that preceded and followed it; **14.7.3** considers the decision of the Court of Appeal in *Bath Society* and that of the House of Lords in *South Lakeland DC v Secretary of State*.[83] **14.7.4** and **14.7.5** consider the meaning of "character or appearance" and "preservation or enhance"; **14.7.6** reviews the position with regard to demolition, and **14.4.7** considers changes of use and other related development; **14.7.8** attempts to set out some conclusions.

It is noteworthy that the High Court has held that planning authorities, inspectors and other decision-takers are under a statutory duty under s.72 to consider the effect of proposed development on any conservation area affected, even if no-one else raises the point.[84]

It should not be forgotten that, in relation to applications for planning permission, the duty under section 72 is subordinate to that under section 38(6) of the Planning and Compensation Act 1986, to make decisions in accordance with the development plan.[85] However, as already noted, policies in development plans are generally in terms very similar to those of section 72; there is therefore, in reality, little if any conflict between the two duties.

Secondly, both applicants and authorities should be aware of the policy of the Secretaries of State. This is summarised as follows:

"Many conservation areas include the commercial centres of the towns and villages of which they form part. While conservation (whether by preservation or enhancement) of their character or appearance must be a major consideration, this cannot realistically take the form of preventing all new development: the emphasis will generally need to be on controlled and positive management of change. Policies will need to be designed to allow the area to remain alive and prosperous, and to avoid unnecessarily detailed controls over businesses and householders, but at the same time to ensure that any new development accords with the area's special architectural and historic interest.

Many conservation areas include gap sites, or buildings that make no positive contribution to, or indeed detract from, the character or appearance of the area; their replacement should be a stimulus to imaginative, high quality design, and seen as an opportunity to enhance the area's character and appearance. What is important is not that new

---

[82] [1989] 2 P.L.R. 9.
[83] [1991] 2 P.L.R. 97.
[84] *Kids Co v Secretary of State*, July 26, 2002, unreported (transcript available from Lawtel), para.33.
[85] Scotland: TCP(S)A 1997, s.25; NI: P(NI)O 1991, art.4(2A) (inserted by the Planning (Amendment) (NI) Order 2003, s.30, with effect from a date to be announced).

buildings should directly imitate earlier styles, but that they should be designed with respect for their context, as part of a larger whole which has a well-established character and appearance of its own."[86]

Paragraph 30 of WO Circular 61/96 is similar.

Thirdly, many of the considerations arising in the context of proposed development affecting listed buildings and their settings (in the previous sections of this chapter) will apply almost equally to proposals in conservation areas. It will thus often be relevant to consider in particular such matters as the possible reuse of buildings that, whilst not of sufficient merit to justify being listed, may still be worthy of retention by virtue of their importance in the area as a whole.[87] And the discussion relating to the design of new buildings, and alterations and extensions to existing ones, will also be just as relevant to buildings in conservation areas.[88]

Similarly, the law and guidance relating to enabling development, considered above in relation to listed buildings, applies equally—in principle—to development said to be necessary to finance the restoration of an unlisted building in a conservation area. The English Heritage Policy Statement, in particular, explicitly drafted to refer to "heritage assets", including conservation areas.[89] However, since an unlisted building is, by definition, of less value than a listed one, it will probably not often occur that the restoration of such a building will be found to be a factor justifying development that would otherwise be unacceptable.

Finally, the Court will not be sympathetic to planning appeals being used "as a kind of oblique addition to judicial review proceedings" with the real aim of challenging the propriety of a conservation area designation.[90]

14.7.2 The conservation area duty: cases before Bath Society

The duty under what is now section 72 was considered first in a case relating to the control of advertisements in a conservation area. Malcolm Spence Q.C., sitting as deputy judge, held that, because the Secretary of State did not consider whether the discontinuation of the advertisements would enhance the character of the area, his decision was not within the powers of the Act.[91]

Lionel Read Q.C. then held in the more widely known case of *Steinberg v Secretary of State* that:

"... there is a world of difference between the issue which the Inspector defined for himself—whether the proposed development would 'harm' the character of the conservation area—and the need to pay special attention to the desirability of preserving or enhancing the character or appearance of the conservation area. In short, harm is one thing; preservation or enhancement is another."[92]

---

[86] PPG 15, paras 4.16–4.17.
[87] See also **Form D14** and **Form D16** in Appendix D, and the comments on them at **14.4.1**; and **14.4.8, 14.4.9**.
[88] See **14.4–14.4.10**.
[89] See **14.6.4**.
[90] See *Elitestone Ltd v Secretary of State for Wales* [1992] J.P.L. 1143 at 1148.
[91] *Westminster CC v Secretary of State* [1988] 3 P.L.R. 104.
[92] [1989] 2 P.L.R. 9.

That approach was followed by McCowan J. in *Bromley LBC v SSE*.[93] He considered that an approach which said, as in that case, that the proposed development "is not good, but is not quite as bad as we thought" or that "it does not detract quite as much from the area as it seemed to a couple of years ago" was a long way from holding that it preserved or enhanced the character or appearance of the conservation area.

However, in *Unex Dumpton Ltd v Secretary of State*[94], Roy Vandermeer Q.C., sitting as deputy judge, stressed that it is relevant at least to consider the question of harm. He also pointed out that it is the conservation area as a whole whose character and appearance has to be considered, not simply each individual component of it, and that it was possible that a proposal to replace one building with another might have no material effect upon the conservation area; certainly it would not automatically follow that such a proposal would have an adverse effect.

The matter was then considered by the Court of Appeal in *Ward v Secretary of State*.[95] This concerned a proposal to build houses on land that currently formed private gardens. Woolf L.J., as he then was, considered that the wording of the inspector's decision letter was unfortunate, in that it concentrated on whether the development would cause an unacceptable degree of harm; but no real significance should be attached to that. What was of more concern to the court was that the inspector had appeared to consider that private gardens could not form part of the character of the area which it was required to preserve or enhance,[96] and had failed to consider whether the proposed development was more or less beneficial to the area than what existed on the site at present.

Then, in *Harrow LBC v Secretary of State*,[97] Graham Eyre Q.C., sitting as deputy judge, said that he did not read the *Steinberg* case as saying that an inspector has to put out of his mind an approach which involves the investigation of harm: "The question of harm may still be important, and in particular in the context of the obligation in respect of preservation".[98] He emphasised that it must be apparent from the decision letter read as a whole that the inspector has discharged the duty imposed by section 72; an awareness of that duty does not need to be slavishly rehearsed at every juncture in a report or decision letter.

In a further decision by Graham Eyre Q.C. (*South West Regional Health Authority v Secretary of State*[99]), on the following day, he again emphasised the relevance of considering harm—where a proposal in one respect preserves or enhances the character of an area but in another would have a harmful effect, the decision maker should balance the preservation and enhancement against the harm.

[93] [1990] J.P.L. 53.
[94] [1990] 2 P.L.R. 1.
[95] [1990] 1 P.L.R. 85.
[96] See 7.5.1.
[97] [1990] 2 P.L.R. 62, [1991] J.P.L. 137.
[98] p.67E.
[99] [1991] J.P.L. 141.

14.7.3 The Bath Society and South Lakeland decisions

The two most significant decisions in this sequence of litigation were those of the Court of Appeal in *Bath Society v Secretary of State*[1] and of the House of Lords in *South Lakeland DC v Secretary of State*.[2]

The *Bath Society* case related to land within a conservation area, which had been allocated as open space in the local plan, following a recommendation to that effect by the local plan Inspector. Developers now wished to construct a block of flats on the land. They failed to obtain planning permission from the City Council, and appealed to the Secretary of State, who granted planning permission, following the recommendation of the Inspector who had held an inquiry. The Bath Society appealed against his decision.

The Court of Appeal, overturning the decision at first instance, held that the Secretary of State's decision should be overturned, on two grounds. First, the recommendation by the local plan inspector was so obviously material that anything short of direct consideration of it by the Secretary of State could not be in accordance with the intention of the Act. Secondly, the Inspector had not given proper consideration to the desirability of preserving or enhancing the conservation area, as required by the predecessor to section 72.[3] The decision in fact rested largely on the first point, relating to the local plan. Glidewell L.J. nevertheless provided some helpful guidelines as to how decisions in conservation areas should be approached.[4]

Just over a month after the decision in the *Bath Society* case, a differently constituted Court of Appeal considered conservation areas again, in *South Lakeland DC v Secretary of State*.[5] This related to an application for permission to build a new vicarage within the Cartmel Conservation Area, which was refused by the district council. An appeal followed, and permission was granted by an inspector, following an inquiry. He found that the proposed new building would neither harm nor enhance the area (largely because it was to be constructed in a location where it would be only visible from very limited viewpoints).

The inspector's decision was quashed by Lionel Read Q.C., sitting as deputy judge.[6] The deputy judge, not surprisingly, followed his own approach in *Steinberg*[7]—the inspector had considered whether the proposed development would cause harm to the conservation area, rather than whether it would preserve or enhance it; his decision was thus flawed and should be quashed. The Court of Appeal quashed the deputy judge's decision—and, in doing so, effectively overturned his decision in *Steinberg*. "Preserve" had its normal meaning—"to keep safe from harm"; the preservation of the character or appearance of a conservation area, stated in the Act to be desirable, could be achieved either by a

---

[1] [1991] 2 P.L.R. 51.
[2] [1991] 2 P.L.R. 97.
[3] TCPA 1971, s.277.
[4] See **14.2.2**.
[5] [1991] 2 P.L.R. 97.
[6] [1991] J.P.L. 144.
[7] See **14.7.2**.

positive contribution to preservation, or by development which (as in this case) left it unharmed.

The ruling of the Court of Appeal was upheld in the House of Lords.[8]

14.7.4 Character or appearance

The Act makes it clear that the character and the appearance of a conservation area must each be considered separately—although they may in some cases effectively mean the same thing. This has been in recent years the subject of a number of High Court challenges to decisions of planning authorities and inspectors. Most of these have failed, on the basis that the assessment of the character and appearance of a conservation area is entirely a matter for the decision-maker, as is the effect of a particular proposal on that character and appearance.

See, for example, *Trafford MBC v Secretary of State*[9] (development in rear garden); *Kids Co v Secretary of State*[10] (after-school club in South London); *Swindon BC v Secretary of State*[11] (road-rail interchange minerals adjoining conservation area in Swindon); *Ludlum v Secretary of State*[12] (alterations to stable block in rural village); and *R. (University College London) v Secretary of State*[13] (new student accommodation block in Bloomsbury)—which incidentally illustrate well the huge range of circumstances in which conservation area issues can arise. Each of these decisions was specific to its own facts, and in each the court refused to intervene.

As to the character of an area, this is often difficult to determine with any precision. It is thus all the more important for planning authorities to decide what exactly they think is the character of their conservation areas, preferably as soon as possible following designation, as this will (or at least should) provide useful objective analysis of survey material, and thus a starting point for any debate. The recent policy statements from English Heritage on conservation areas should be of assistance here.[14]

Sullivan J. in *R. (Waveney DC) v Secretary of State*[15] also pointed out that it is possible that development that may harm the character of a particular (unlisted) building within a conservation area may nevertheless have a neutral effect on the character of the area as a whole, where that character has already been eroded through numerous examples of similar development. This is particularly relevant in the case of relatively minor works, such as the replacement of traditional windows with modern ones, where they have been carried out already (with or without permission) elsewhere.[16] But it would also seem to apply where the

---

[8] [1992] 2 A.C. 141, 1 P.L.R. 143, HL.
[9] [2001] J.P.L. 115.
[10] July 26, 2002, unreported (transcript available from Lawtel), para.33.
[11] April 2, 2003, unreported (transcript available on Lawtel).
[12] January 23, 2004, unreported (transcript available on Lawtel).
[13] [2005] J.P.L. 975.
[14] See **5.2.3** and **5.3.2**.
[15] [2003] J.P.L. 1058.
[16] See also *Historic Buildings and Monuments Commission v Secretary of State* [1997] J.P.L. 424.

character of an area is very mixed—what may spoil one property may not harm the character of the area as a whole.

Conversely, it has been suggested by the courts that it is permissible to consider the impact of proposed development on the part of the conservation area in which it is to be carried out, even if that part is a creation of relatively recent development, and its character not one of the special qualities that led to the designation of the area as a whole.[16a]

An unusual argument arose in *Kensington and Chelsea RBC v Secretary of State and Earl Properties*,[17] where an inspector had granted permission on appeal for an underground car park, on the basis that anyone looking at the finished result would not know it was there. The council was unsuccessful in arguing that the character of the conservation area was harmed because the integrity of the garden square was destroyed by the mere existence of the car park. The court supported the Inspector's view that the integrity of the car park would be restored, and the character of the area thus unharmed.

As to appearance, this was considered by the High Court in *Chorley and James v Secretary of State*.[18] This related to a decision by an inspector refusing planning permission for the demolition of a shed and the erection of a house in a rural conservation area, who had stated that the main issue was the effect of the proposal on the character of the area, and refused permission. The deputy judge, quashing the inspector's decision, noted that she had considered the main issue in the context of the development plan, and its policies relating to the rural area, not those relating to the conservation area; nor had she considered the overall picture of the conservation area. Insofar as she had considered the effect of the proposal on the conservation area, it was only as to the effect on its character, as a rural area; she had not (as she should have done) considered also the effect on its appearance. The inspector had thus failed to take into account a material consideration, and her reasoning was defective.

Finally, note that it is the existing character and appearance of the conservation area, as it is, that must be considered, not its character and appearance as the decision-maker might like it to be.[19]

14.7.5 Preservation or enhancement

Decision-makers are to consider the desirability of preserving *or* enhancing the conservation area.[20] So far, most of the litigation has considered the question of whether development which does not harm the area can be said to "preserve" it. However, it may be that enhancement is desirable, not simply preservation. Thus, in an attractive part of a conservation area, it will usually be sufficient to ensure that development preserves—that is, does not harm—its character. But where a site in its present condition is an eyesore in the middle of an otherwise attractive

---

[16a] *University College London v First Secretary of State* [2005] J.P.L. 975.

[17] [1998] J.P.L. B15.

[18] [1993] J.P.L. 927.

[19] *Historic Buildings and Monuments Commission v Secretary of State* [1997] J.P.L. 424: see **14.7.5**.

[20] P(LBCA)A 1990, s.72; emphasis added.

area, it would be eminently sensible for a planning authority to try to achieve development that positively "enhances" the area, by replacing what is there with something better.

This was doubted by Malcolm Spence Q.C., sitting as deputy judge, in *Revival Properties v Secretary of State*, whose judgment was summarised as follows:

"It was perfectly lawful for the inspector and then the Secretary of State first to consider the question of preservation and then to dismiss the point about enhancement peremptorily, as that approach satisfies section 72(1) of the [Act]. Once the inspector had decided that the proposal would preserve the character and appearance of the conservation area, the requirement of the section was fulfilled. The proposal did not in addition have to enhance the character and appearance of the conservation area. That position cannot possibly be altered simply because a party submits at the inquiry that the proposal needs to enhance the character and appearance of the conservation area."[21]

From the very brief report of the decision, it is impossible to be certain whether that approach was justified on the particular circumstances of the case; but it seems doubtful that it could always be correct. The duty under section 72 applies not just to the determination of planning applications, but also to the exercise of any functions under the planning Acts and Part I of the 1953 Act.[22] That includes (amongst other things) the giving of grants for buildings in need of repair[23] and the repair of buildings and the enhancement of land in poor condition,[24] both of which indicate an assessment that an area needs enhancement and not just preservation—at least in respect of the particular building or land concerned.

It presumably could not be right to accept that a derelict 1950s infill building in the middle of a fine historic area should be replaced by a poorly designed modern building, simply because it was no worse and thus on balance did not harm the character of the area. It would not be correct, however, in every case—or even often—to say that a particular development should not be allowed because it "only" preserved the area and did not enhance it; that might, and indeed usually would, be sufficient. For such an argument to be advanced with any chance of success, it would be necessary for cogent evidence to be produced as to why the site in its present condition detracted from the area and why, as a result, it was desirable to enhance the character of the area by improving it, rather than merely preserving it.

Thus in the "Wirksworth door" case, the court rejected the argument put forward by English Heritage that the many existing unattractive doors in the area should be ignored, and held that the duty of the decision-maker was to consider the conservation area as he or she found it, faults and all, and to ensure that it was not harmed.[25] That might have been right in that case, as the desirability of enhancement had not been explicitly argued in front of the inspector—even if he had considered the point, he would not have had any evidence on which to base a

---

[21] [1996] J.P.L. B86.
[22] See **5.3.2**.
[23] See **Chapter 9**.
[24] See **Chapter 10**.
[25] *Historic Buildings and Monuments Commission v Secretary of State* [1997] 3 P.L.R. 8; J.P.L. 424; see also **14.9.5**.

conclusion. But generally it would seem to be necessary to consider, amongst other things, whether it is desirable to enhance an area, and not just to preserve it.

It is sometimes argued that, even though one proposal might preserve or enhance a conservation area, its implementation would prevent that of another scheme that would be even better. The Court of Appeal (in *R. (Mount Cook Land Ltd) v Westminster CC*[26]) held that, where one proposal satisfied the test under section 72, that was all that was needed to justify a grant of planning permission; and that the merits of an alternative scheme would rarely be relevant.

Finally, it should not be forgotten that an authority is perfectly entitled to insert into its local plan a policy that a particular part of a conservation area, or a particular site in it, is in need of enhancement—indeed it is under a duty to consider doing so, as the preparation of development plans is one of its functions to which the duty under section 72 applies.[27] Once such a policy has been included in a local plan that has been adopted, it then becomes a very material consideration in the determination of any subsequent planning application affecting the area concerned. Such an approach is in practice more likely to sway an inspector at an inquiry than a last-minute attempt to criticise a proposal because it does not enhance the area.

14.7.6 Demolition of unlisted buildings in conservation areas

The determination of an application for conservation area consent, for the demolition of an unlisted building in a conservation area, is subject to the duty under section 72 of the Listed Buildings Act just as much as the determination of planning applications. In assessing whether or not consent should be granted, the planning authority must thus have regard to the desirability of preserving or enhancing the character or appearance of the conservation area in which the building is situated.[28]

In brief, if, for example, a proposal is to demolish an eyesore which at present spoils the area, consent should be granted; if on the other hand it is to demolish a building that is in itself unremarkable but fits in perfectly as part of a pleasant, homogeneous area, it should—in the absence of any other, overriding reasons— be refused. The key factor to be considered is thus undoubtedly the appearance and character of the area, not that of the building itself. PPG 15 sums it up as follows:

"... account should clearly be taken of the part played in the architectural and historic interest of the area by the building for which demolition is proposed, and in particular of the wider effects of demolition on the building's surroundings and on the conservation area as a whole."[29]

In addition, there is for the first time stated in government guidance a "general presumption in favour of retaining buildings which make a positive contribution

---

[26] [2004] 2 P. & C.R. 22, 1 P.L.R. 29, CA.
[27] See **5.4.1**.
[28] P(LBCA)A 1990, s.72. [Scotland: P(LBCA)(S)A 1997 s.64(1); NI: P(NI)O 1991, art.50(5).]
[29] PPG 15, para.4.26

to the character or appearance of a conservation area"[30]—"a positive contribution" meaning simply "something more than 'little or no contribution'."[31] Proposals to demolish such buildings are thus to be judged in the light of the relevant guidance relating to the demolition of listed buildings.[32] It is arguable that this policy approach is fundamentally misconceived, as it imports to unlisted buildings a status almost equal to that of listed buildings. However, inspectors are obliged to follow Government policy, misconceived or otherwise.

In one, slightly unusual, case, conservation area consent was refused for the demolition of a wendy house, which was found by an inspector to be "a delightful garden building with furniture and furnishings inside". The High Court upheld his decision, on the basis of his overall conclusion that the building made a positive contribution to the garden and to the conservation area.[33]

Where (as is often the case) the demolition of a building is to be followed by the redevelopment of the site, consent for demolition should not normally be given unless there are acceptable and detailed plans for any redevelopment.[34] Government guidance draws attention to *Richmond-upon-Thames LBC v Secretary of State*,[35] in which Sir Douglas Frank, sitting as deputy judge of the High Court, held that the function of giving consent to demolish an unlisted building in a conservation area could not be performed without seeing what was to be substituted and how it would fit into the area. Arguably, however, if the demolition of an existing building in a conservation area contributes nothing to the preservation or enhancement of the character of the area, consent should be refused; and the consideration of any replacement building then becomes irrelevant. That principle was been taken somewhat further, in the context of the demolition of a listed building (albeit, as it happened, in a conservation area) in *Henry Davis & Co. v Secretary of State*.[36]

The *Richmond* case was also followed in *Kent CC v Secretary of State*,[37] where the court upheld the Secretary of State's refusal to grant conservation area consent to a highway authority for the demolition of two bridges in a conservation area. It was agreed that the bridges were not of themselves of any particular merit; and that they did not meet current road safety standards. However, the proposed replacement scheme was not in keeping with the character of the conservation area; and until that was improved, consent for demolition should be withheld.

Also relevant here will be the considerations raised in *Kent Messenger Ltd v Secretary of State*[38] and *Thanet DC v Secretary of State*[39] on the economics of the replacement building—the first of these was considered by the judge in the

[30] PPG 15, para.4.27; WO Circ. 61/96, para.33.
[31] *Fulford v Secretary of State* March 26, 1997, unreported (transcript available on Lawtel).
[32] PPG 15, paras 3.16–3.19; WO Circ. 61/96, paras 91, 92 (see **14.4.4, 14.4.6**).
[33] *Cadogan Holding Company v Secretary of State* [1997] J.P.L. B154.
[34] PPG 15, para.4.27; WO Circ. 61/96, para.3.3.
[35] (1978) 37 P. & C.R. 151.
[36] [1992] J.P.L. 1162; see **14.4.7**.
[37] [1995] J.P.L. 610.
[38] [1976] J.P.L. 372.
[39] [1978] J.P.L. 251.

Richmond case (above)—and *Godden v Secretary of State*[40] on the redevelopment of larger areas.[41] And it may be wise for the developer to submit, or the planning authority to require—a financial appraisal of restoration as against demolition and replacement; but the failure to do so will not necessarily be fatal, if there is enough relevant evidence to support the case for demolition.[42]

14.7.7 Changes of use and similar proposals

As well as proposals for building works, which will (or at least may) clearly affect the architectural character of a conservation area, there will be other proposals for development, in particular for changes of use, which may not change the appearance of the area but may nevertheless affect its character.

Thus Roy Vandermeer Q.C. sitting as deputy judge in *Archer and Thompson v Secretary of State*, held that it seemed quite plain that matters such as the nature of a use and its effect could be of consequence.[43] A change of use might, for example, affect the historic interest of an area; or its character might be affected by noise. He wholly rejected the proposition that the test was limited so that the only considerations that could be brought within the compass of section 72 were matters affecting physical structures. That case concerned the change of use of premises in a conservation area at Causewayhead, Penzance, into a "family entertainment centre"; the inspector deciding the appeal had rejected it largely on conservation grounds. And in *Penwith DC v Secretary of State*[44] it was held that it had been reasonable for an inspector to decide that, in general, an amusement arcade was not appropriate in a conservation area, unless particular circumstances suggested otherwise.

Similarly, in *Fugler v Secretary of State*[45], the duty under section 72 was one reason for an inspector refusing permission for the change of use of a basement in a central London conservation area to a wine bar, on the grounds that it would cause noise and disturbance to local residents. In *R. v Secretary of State, ex p. Romer*,[46] permission was refused for the conversion of a basement in north London into a self-contained flat due to the effect of the resulting higher density on the character of the conservation area. And in *Kids Co v Secretary of State*,[47] permission was refused for an after-school club in south London partly because of the effect of the noise and disturbance together with activity spilling out onto surrounding streets, leading to material harm to the character and appearance of the conservation area. In all three cases, the decisions were upheld by the courts.

However, the similar decision by an inspector to uphold an enforcement notice relating to the use of premises in the Chinatown area of Soho as a hostess bar was

---

[40] [1988] J.P.L. 99.
[41] And see **14.4.6**.
[42] *R. v Bristol City Cl, ex p. Anderson* [1998] E.G.C.S. 44.
[43] [1991] J.P.L. 1027.
[44] [1986] 1 E.G.L.R. 193.
[45] [1993] E.G.C.S. 48.
[46] May 2, 2002, unreported (transcript available from Lawtel).
[47] July 26, 2002, unreported (transcript available from Lawtel), para.33.

quashed—albeit largely on the basis that the claimant had not had a chance to deal with the point at the inquiry.[48]

This principle does not mean, however, that any application for a change of use in a conservation area can be opposed on such grounds. Thus in *Bristol CC v Secretary of State*,[49] the city council had refused to allow the demolition and replacement of a shopfront and the change of use of the ground floor to a restaurant, partly on the grounds of the effect of the resulting traffic on the conservation area. The resulting appeal was allowed, and the council's appeal against the inspector's decision was unsuccessful. He had not said that the new use would have no effect, but only that its effect would not be significant. In *Westminster CC v Secretary of State*,[50] the planning authority was equally unsuccessful in seeking to overturn the decision of an inspector allowing the use of a flat roof as a roof terrace, on the basis that it did not look out of place in the conservation area. And in *Gloucester CC v Secretary of State*,[51] the authority did not even attempt to overturn the finding of an inspector that an amusement centre in the city centre would maintain the vitality of the conservation area, and preserve its character and appearance.

It was implicitly accepted by the Court in *Swindon BC v Secretary of State*[52] that the nature of the use of a proposed use of land adjacent to a conservation area (in that case, a road-rail minerals transfer depot across the line from the Railway Conservation Area in Swindon) was a material consideration in the determination of a planning application.

Finally, it may happen that a proposal has an indirect effect upon a conservation area some way away, but that may be sufficient to be a material consideration in determining the application. Thus in *Wansdyke DC v Secretary of State*, the court upheld the decision of an inspector permitting a proposal for a sports facility within Bathampton Conservation Area even though it harmed that conservation area—for example, because it would be floodlit.[53] This was because there was a real possibility that it would enable the provision of other development on the site of the existing sports ground over a mile away, which would ease the appalling traffic congestion in the centre of Bath itself, and thus enhance that internationally important conservation area. This decision is also noteworthy in that it demonstrates that it may be necessary to balance the effect (direct or indirect) of a proposal on two conservation areas.

14.7.8 Conclusions

As a result of this stream of litigation, the approach to be adopted would seem to be as follows.

---

[48] *Entertainu Ltd v Secretary of State*, May 6, 2003 (transcript available from Lawtel).
[49] [1992] E.G.C.S. 22. Since the ruling in *Shimizu*, the removal of the shopfront would have required planning permission rather than conservation area consent.
[50] July 21, 2003, unreported (transcript available on Lawtel).
[51] March 10, 2003, unreported (transcript avialbale on Casetrack).
[52] April 2, 2003, unreported (transcript available on Lawtel).
[53] [1992] J.P.L. 1168.

First, the duty under section 72 must be the first consideration for the decision-maker—first, that is, after the development plan.[54] Secondly, both the character and the appearance of the area must be considered[55]—but as it is, not as it might be.[56] Thirdly, where development in a conservation area neither enhances the character or appearance of the area nor harms it—where its effect is, in other words, neutral—it may be said to preserve that character or appearance.[57] Fourthly, development that would not affect physical structures may nevertheless affect the character of an area.[58]

In thus considering the effect of a proposal on the character or appearance of a conservation area, the decision-maker must reach one of three possible conclusions:

(1) the development will either enhance or preserve (that is, in the light of *South Lakeland*, if it will not harm) the character or appearance of the area;

(2) the development will simultaneously enhance the character or appearance of the area and cause some detriment[59] or it may enhance one conservation area and harm another[60]; or

(3) the development will neither enhance nor even preserve the character or appearance of the area.

The first conclusion must be a major point in favour of allowing the development. In the second situation, the detriment identified is a material consideration, and the decision-maker should weigh up the enhancement against the detriment.

If the decision-maker reached the third conclusion, then it is almost inevitable that the development will have some detrimental, or harmful, effect on that character or appearance. Such a conclusion will be a consideration of considerable importance and weight; and in such a situation any presumption in favour of development is rebutted. That does not necessarily mean that the application should be refused; but it should be permitted only if there is some advantage or benefit out-weighing the failure to satisfy the test in section 72 and such detriment as may inevitably follow from that.

The House of Lords in *South Lakeland* summarised it thus:

"There is no dispute that the intention of [s.72] is that planning decisions in respect of development proposed to be carried out in a conservation area must give a high priority to the objective of preserving or enhancing the character or appearance of the area. If any proposed development would conflict with that objective, there will be a strong presumption against the grant of planning permission, though in exceptional cases the pre-

---

[54] *Bath Society v Secretary of State* [1991] 2 P.L.R. 51 at p.64; see **14.2.2**.
[55] *Chorley and James v Secretary of State* [1993] J.P.L. 927.
[56] *Historic Buildings and Monuments Commission v Secretary of State* [1997] J.P.L. 424.
[57] *per* Mann L.J. in *South Lakeland* [1991] 2 P.L.R. 97 at 101E.
[58] *Archer and Thompson v Secretary of State* [1991] J.P.L. 1027, *Wansdyke DC v Secretary of State* [1992] J.P.L. 1168; see **14.6.5**.
[59] As in *Harrow LBC v Secretary of State* [1990] 2 P.L.R. 62.
[60] As in *Wansdyke*.

sumption may be overridden in favour of development which is desirable on the ground of some other public interest."[61]

The PPG adopts that formulation[62]; and the draft PPG 15 suggested that examples of such public interest might be "a local or national need for the development in question, or the prospect of wider environmental benefits outweighing the direct loss to the conservation area in question".[63]

Finally, it has been argued that the application of conservation area policies, and the duty under section 72 of the Act, is a breach of the Human Rights Act 1998 insofar as it restricts private householders from doing what they wish with their own property, such as erecting gates and fences for security purposes. This argument was rejected in *Sabi v Secretary of State*, where a householder living in Hampstead Garden Suburb, north London, had erected gates and fences after a spate of burglaries and other incidents; the court held that the protection of the environment—including the preservation of the character of the conservation area—was appropriate and legitimate aim to be pursued in the public interest, and thus not in breach of the 1998 Act.[64]

And it has already been noted that the duty under section 72 also applies to the determination of applications for express consent for advertisements and appeals against discontinuance notices.[65]

14.8 Works affecting archaeological remains

14.8.1 Proposed development affecting archaeological deposits

There is no statutory duty, equivalent to those under the Listed Buildings Act considered above, relating to the determination of planning applications for proposals affecting ancient monuments or other archaeological deposits. Maybe there should be, but there is not. The only relevant duties are therefore those applying to all planning determinations—namely, to determine such applications in accordance with the development plan, and all other material considerations.

The effect of a proposal on the archaeological value of a site or on the special interest of an ancient monument is a material consideration in the determination of a planning application, even though—unlike listed buildings and conservation areas—it is not explicitly recognised as such by statute. And this has been clearly recognised by central government:

"The desirability of preserving an ancient monument and its setting is a material consideration in determining planning applications whether that monument is scheduled or unscheduled."[66]

---

[61] [1992] 2 A.C. 141 *per* Lord Bridge at 146F.
[62] PPG 15, para.4.19; *Planning Guidance (Wales); Planning Policy*, para.126.
[63] At para.4.21.
[64] June 18, 2002 (Forbes J) (leave to appeal refused, October 8, 2002, CA).
[65] *R. (Clear Channel UK Ltd) v Secretary of State* [2005] J.P.L. 704. See **14.2.6**.
[66] PPG 16, para.18; WO Circ. 60/96, para.10. [Scotland, NPPG 5. para.25; NI, PPS 6, para.3.3.]

Thus, even before the introduction of the system of scheduled monuments, in *Hoveringham Gravels Ltd v Secretary of State*, a case relating to sand and gravel extraction on a site protected by a preservation order under the 1913 Act,[67] Lord Denning M.R. commented:

"But now I turn back to the extraction of sand and gravel for commercial purposes ... Even if there had been no preservation orders, they would never have got permission for that purpose ... They actually applied for planning permission—long before any preservation orders were made—and were refused. The cause of this refusal ... lies in the very nature of Berry Mound Camp itself. It was known to the planning authorities to be an iron age fort of great archaeological interest, so much so that it was of national importance that it should be preserved and not destroyed. That was a perfectly legitimate reason for refusing planning permission. It was just as legitimate to refuse for archaeological reasons as for amenity reasons."[68]

It may also occur that archaeological explorations, carried out before a planning permission is formally issued, reveal important remains; in that situation, the remains may or may not be scheduled, depending on their importance, but it is perfectly in order to rescind the decision to grant permission, on the grounds of the need to protect them. This is what occurred in *R. v West Oxfordshire DC, ex p. Pearce Homes Ltd,*[69] where the council resolved to grant permission for development on the site of the 12th-century palace subject to the finalisation of a section 52 (now section 106) agreement; but, before that permission was issued, archaeological work revealed the true importance of the remains. The council accordingly reconsidered the matter, and refused permission, so as to protect the palace—particularly in view of its location in the conservation area and in close proximity to the parish church. The court held that, since no permission had actually been issued, it was proper for the council to change its mind. There was thus no permission to "revoke", and therefore no compensation payable to the unlucky developer. The moral to this tale is that whilst preliminary archaeological work is in principle highly desirable, and encouraged by the Government,[70] developers have to be aware of the risks entailed.

And the Government has clearly underlined the value of archaeological deposits, and the importance of protecting them, in its general policy guidance in PPG 16. That document should be read thoroughly by anyone involved in carrying out or assessing development affecting archaeological remains in England. The overall approach is as follows:

"Archaeological remains should be seen as a finite, and non-renewable resource, in many cases highly fragile and vulnerable to damage and destruction. Appropriate management is therefore essential to ensure that they survive in good condition. In particular, care must be taken to ensure that archaeological remains are not needlessly or thoughtlessly destroyed.
Where nationally important archaeological remains, whether scheduled or not, and their settings, are affected by proposed development, there should be a presumption in favour of their physical preservation."[71]

---

[67] See 1.2.2.
[68] [1975] Q.B. 754 at 763.
[69] [1986] J.P.L. 523.
[70] See PPG 16, paras 20–22; WO Circ. 60/96, paras 12–14; see also **13.3.8.**
[71] PPG 16, paras 6 and 18. Corresponding guidance for Wales is at para.3 of WO Circ. 60/96 and para.134 of *Planning Guidance (Wales): Planning Policy.*

Corresponding guidance for Wales is principally in Welsh Office Circular 60/96. Guidance in Scotland is to be found in NPPG 5, *Archaeology and Planning*, and PAN 42, *Archaeology*, both published in January 1994. The most recent (1999) policy guidance is in Northern Ireland, where PPS 6 extends to archaeology as well as other aspects of building conservation.[72]

14.8.2 *Preservation in situ*

The above extract from PPG 16 emphasises that the priority should be, wherever possible, to preserve archaeological remains in situ, rather than to dig them up for examination and recording—once they have gone, they cannot be returned. The more recent guidance for Wales states the principle clearly:

"From the archaeological point of view, excavation should be regarded as a second-best option. The science of archaeology is developing rapidly. Excavation means the total destruction of evidence (apart from removable artefacts) from which future techniques could almost certainly extract more information than is currently possible. Excavation can be expensive and time-consuming, and discoveries may have to be evaluated in a hurry against an inadequate research framework. The preservation in situ of important archaeological remains is therefore to be preferred."[73]

Where archaeological material is to be preserved on a development site, it is important to ensure that it is protected. This is usually achieved by a condition: the Secretary of State has suggested the following:

"No development shall take place until fencing has been erected, in a manner to be agreed with the local planning authority, about [name of monument]; and no works shall take place within the area inside that fencing without the written consent of the authority."[74]

Within a building, it may be necessary to secure appropriate designs, particularly with regard to foundations, to preserve as much as possible of the archaeological deposits; and this too may need to be the result of negotiation and amendment of the proposal. In the final analysis, however, government guidance recognises that authorities may have to consider refusing permission where developers do not seek to accommodate important remains (as happened in the *Hoveringham Gravels* case, above).[75]

14.8.3 *Preservation by record*

Physical preservation in situ may not always be practically possible; or in some cases its desirability may be overridden by other considerations—where, for example, a monument of only minor importance lies underneath the site on which it is proposed to carry out an otherwise desirable development. The Government has recognised this problem, and allows for planning authorities to satisfy themselves that the developer has made appropriate provision for the excavation

---

[72] See Chapter 3, and Policies BH1–BH4.
[73] WO Circ. 60/96, at para.19.
[74] Appendix A to DoE Circ. 11/95, WO Circ. 35/95, Appendix A, model condition 53.
[75] PPG 16, at para.28; WO Circ. 60/96, para.18.

and recording of the remains—either prior to the start of the development or whilst it is being carried out (by means of a watching brief).[76]

Again, this will need to be regulated; and this can be done in simple cases by means of appropriate conditions on any planning permission granted. Appropriate conditions, based on those suggested by the Secretary of State, might be as follows:

"No development shall take place within the area indicated [this would be the area of archaeological interest] until the applicant, or its agent or successor in title, has secured the implementation of a programme of archaeological work in accordance with a written scheme of investigation which has been submitted by the applicant and approved in writing by the local planning authority.

The developer shall afford access at all reasonable times to any archaeologist nominated or approved in writing by the local planning authority, and shall allow him to observe the excavations and record items of interest and finds."[77]

The scope of the programme of work envisaged by the first of these conditions would depend on the results of the assessment and evaluation carried out prior to the application.[78] Somewhat analogous to a landscaping scheme, it matters not who carries out the work or how much it costs, but simply whether it will be sufficient in all of the circumstances of the case.

As to the second condition, it is of course possible that—in spite of the best intentions of all concerned—such monitoring and observation will reveal the presence of a hitherto unsuspected archaeological deposit, leading to a desire for more extensive exploration. In that situation, government guidance advises that in the majority of cases it should prove possible for the parties to resolve their differences through voluntary discussion and for a satisfactory compromise to be reached.[79] No doubt, but in some cases a discovery of significant remains could be a major problem. The authority could revoke the planning permission, but only with the payment of compensation.[80] Or the Secretary of State could schedule the remains under the Ancient Monuments Act, and refuse the resulting application for scheduled monument consent; but that too would lead to a demand for compensation.[81] The guidance sensibly suggests that developers may in any event wish to take out appropriate insurance.

As an alternative to a condition, the developer and the planning authority may enter into a planning obligation under section 106 of the Planning Act. Reference should be made to the Code of Practice produced by the British Archaeologists' and Developers' Liaison Group and the model agreements produced by the British Property Federation.

14.8.4 Applications for scheduled monument consent

There is no specific statutory provision as to the matters to be considered in determining an application for scheduled monument consent, but the most recent

---

[76] PPG 16, paras 24–26; cf. WO Circ. 60/96, paras 18–21.
[77] See model conditions 55 and 54 in Appendix A to DoE Circ. 11/95, WO Circ. 35/95.
[78] See **13.3.8**.
[79] PPG 16, para.31; WO Circ. 60/96, para.24.
[80] TCPA 1990, ss 97–100, 107–113; see **13.11**.
[81] See **15.4.3**.

expression of Government policy is in WO Circular 60/96, which is likely to reflect policy in other parts of the United Kingdom as well:

"The Secretary of State regards the main purpose of scheduling as ensuring the preservation of ancient monuments. Thus there should be a presumption in favour of their physical preservation when considering applications for consent to undertake works to them, *i.e.* a presumption against proposals which would involve significant alteration or cause damage, or which would have a significant impact on the setting of visible remains. In considering applications for scheduled monument consent, therefore, the Secretary of State will expect applicants (particularly where underground pipelines, cables or sewers are to be laid) to demonstrate that no practicable alternative route or location, avoiding the monument, exists; and that the need to undertake the works outweighs the presumption in favour of the protection of a monument of national importance."[82]

Where a scheduled monument is also listed, the Secretary of State has stated that he will also have regard to his published policies relating to listed buildings, particularly with regard to the need to explore alternative uses and to retain important features.[83]

14.9 Other matters to be taken into account

14.9.1 Specific duties

As well as the specific duties laid upon decision makers to have regard to the development plan, listed buildings and conservation areas, there are a handful of other duties,[84] most of which are generally not relevant to proposals of the kind being considered here.

However, the one specific duty laid on the decision-taking authority in almost every case is to take into account any representations made:

(1) by owners of the building who were notified by the applicant or were alerted by the advertisement placed in the press[85]; or

(2) as a result of the notices placed on site and in the press by the authority.[86]

The authority is only obliged to take into account such representations if they are made within the relevant 21-day period (after the notification or advertisement). In practice it would be unwise to ignore any comments received, whether as a result of the publicity or otherwise, before the actual date of the decision.

Any representations received in response to the notification of English Heritage, Cadw and the national amenity societies[87] should also be a major factor in considering an application.[88]

---

[82] Annex 1, para.11.

[83] In WO Circ. 60/96, Annex 1, para.12.

[84] Such as those relating to the protection of the countryside and natural habitats, and the management of waste disposal and landfill.

[85] TCP (General Development Procedure) Order 1995, art.19; P(LBCA) Regs 1990, reg.6(3); see **13.3.3**.

[86] reg.5; see **13.5.1** to **13.5.3**, **13.5.8**.

[87] See **13.5.4** to **13.5.7**.

[88] *R. v Tandridge DC, ex p. Al Fayed, The Times*, January 28, 1999, [1999] E.G.C.S. 6; upheld by CA, (2000) 79 P. & C.R. 227.

Responses from local amenity societies,[89] although theoretically of less weight than those from the national bodies, will tend to vary between erudite comment, based on wide local knowledge, and unthinking objection to all change. They should in any event be given careful consideration. Responses from private individuals, neighbours, local architects and so forth will similarly vary in quality, but should all be conscientiously taken into account. However, it should be remembered—both by planning authorities and by objectors—that it is the cogency of an objection that is critical, rather than the number of people by whom it is raised.[90]

Further, those who make representations—English Heritage, national and local amenity groups, special conservation committees, and of course individual residents—often perfectly properly put forward views based solely on the heritage issues involved arising in connection with a particular proposal. But it may be that there are other considerations involved, such as highways, or economic impact, and these may be more or less significant than conservation. This was highlighted recently in *Georgiou v Enfield LBC*.[91] As it happens, in that case, the conservation issues militated in favour of permission being granted, whereas highways and other issues indicated a refusal. Often it is the other way round. But whichever way the various considerations point, they must be given appropriate weight, and then considered as a whole, when an application is being finally determined by the planning authority or the Secretary of State.

The other relevant specific duty is to take into account any environmental statement accompanying a planning application.[92]

14.9.2 Special circumstances

In some cases, the personal circumstances of the owners or occupiers of a building may be relevant. Thus, in the context of planning applications, it has been held by the House of Lords that:

"Personal circumstances of an occupier, personal hardship, the difficulties of businesses which are of value to the character of a community are not to be ignored in the administration of planning control. It would be inhuman pedantry to exclude from the control of our environment the human factor. The human factor is always present, of course, indirectly as the background to the consideration of the character of land use. It can, however, and sometimes should, be given direct effect as an exceptional or special circumstance. But such circumstances, when they arise, fall to be considered not as a general rule but as exceptions to a general rule to be met in special cases. If a planning authority is to give effect to them, a specific case has to be made and the planning authority must give reasons for accepting it. It follows that, though the existence of such cases may be mentioned in a plan, this will only be necessary where it is prudent to emphasise that, notwithstanding the general policy, exceptions cannot be wholly excluded from consideration in the administration of planning control."[93]

---

[89] See **13.4.4**.
[90] See PPG 15, Annex A, para.A.17.
[91] [2005] J.P.L. 62. See also **13.4.4**.
[92] TCP (Assessment of Environmental Effect) Regulations 1999, reg.2(1). See also **13.3.7**.
[93] *Great Portland Estates plc v Westminster CC* [1985] A.C. 661, HL, *per* Lord Scarman at pp.669–670.

The same is true of applications for listed building consent.

A case illustrating the significance of personal circumstances was *Gwinnell v Secretary of State*.[94] This concerned a pair of listed semi-detached houses in Islington, north London, both of which were owned by a couple in ill-health. Listed building consent had been granted in 1989 for the making of an opening in the party wall between the back rooms of the two houses, to enable the two neighbouring ground floors to be used together as a single unit. A further consent was granted in 1990 for an opening between the front rooms—but, this time, subject to a condition that it should be blocked up at the end of five years or after the applicants vacated the house, whichever was the longer. The applicants appealed against the condition, but the inspector dismissed their appeal, feeling that the condition was reasonable as a balance between a desire to secure the long-term preservation of the building and a compassionate concern for particular physical needs. The applicants appealed.

Nigel Macleod Q.C., sitting as deputy judge, allowed the appeal. He considered that, by refusing to lift the condition, the inspector had been defending a principle—the integrity of the listed building—that could be breached by the implementation of the earlier permission (which had had no condition). He was clearly aware of the earlier permission, which had indeed formed a major part of the appellants' case on appeal, but chose to determine the appeal solely on the merits of the current application. The right approach was to consider the likelihood of the fall-back position coming into play[95]; this the inspector had failed to do, and his decision should thus be quashed.

These kinds of issues also typically crop up in retrospective applications, to retain works that have already been carried out, as in *South Lakeland DC v SSE and Rowbotham*.[96]

Such decisions should be treated with caution, however, since in both cases there were other factors that made them unusual. In *Gwinnell*, the court did not criticise the inspector for upholding the condition, so as to secure the preservation of the building, but merely for failing to take into account sufficiently the previous consent. Similarly, in *South Lakeland*, it is clear that the inspector's decision to allow the retention of windows that had been fitted without consent was strongly influenced by the fact that they had already been installed and that, even on this type of compassionate grounds, a straightforward appeal against refusal of listed building consent would probably not have succeeded; indeed, two subsequent appeals for the retention of similar windows in the same terrace were refused.[97]

The conclusion therefore would seem to be that personal circumstances of particular owners and occupiers are relevant, but that they will usually lead merely to an attempt to achieve a sensitive compromise (permit some new windows, but only sympathetic ones; or allow a connecting door, but only for a limited period), rather than to a complete reversal of normal conservation principles. And they will sometimes not lead to any relaxation of normal conservation

---

[94] [1994] E.G.C.S. 81.
[95] *Snowden v Secretary of State* [1980] J.P.L. 749.
[96] [1991] J.P.L. 440.
[97] See **18.2.4**.

policies—as, for example, where the owner of a statue (itself listed Grade II*) wanted to remove it to a more secure location elsewhere in the grounds (listed building consent refused on appeal),[98] or where a householder living in a conservation area had erected gates and fences after a spate of burglaries and other incidents (enforcement notice upheld by inspector and High Court).[99]

This is illustrated by the case of *Bristol Meeting Room Trust v Secretary of State and Bristol CC*.[1] The appellants owned a meeting room attracting many cars and coaches. Parking arrangements were inadequate; and they therefore acquired the house next door, with the intention of demolishing it so as to gain extra parking space. The building was listed in the following year. It was not occupied, and was now in a poor state of repair. An application for listed building consent for demolition was refused by the City Council, and the Secretary of State dismissed the subsequent appeal. The Trust appealed, partly on the grounds that the Secretary of State had not had regard to the special circumstances that did in fact apply in this particular case.

Sir Graham Eyre Q.C., sitting as deputy judge, started from the requirement that the decision maker must "have special regard to the desirability of preserving the building or its setting or any feature of special ... interest."[2] It was therefore clear, he said, that the legislation required that the preservation of a listed building had to operate "as a paramount consideration". Special circumstances of an applicant would not often be relevant—but they might be exceptionally. In this case, the Secretary of State had considered a number of matters put forward by the appellants, but they were hardly germane to the fundamental question of the desirability of preserving the building. He concluded that the future use of the building had not been sufficiently investigated, and he was entitled to take that view.

Consent may also occasionally have to be granted for the demolition of a building not with a view to the redevelopment of its site, but simply because its owner (even with the benefit of any grants available) cannot afford to keep it in a safe condition, let alone in good repair, and where as a result there is no alternative to demolition. The Secretary of State thus ended his decision letter granting consent for the demolition of a Victorian Methodist church in Barnsley with this slightly pathetic plea:

"In all the circumstances of this unfortunate case has concluded with regret that he would not be justified in adhering to his normal policy of withholding consent for demolition where it is not clear that all avenues for further use have been explored. He points out that a listed building consent is permissive and not mandatory, and trusts that in the event that, even at this late stage, some aid is offered which would enable the Church Council at least to retain the temporary scaffolding support, they would not exercise the consent.[3]

---

[98] Appeal decision at [200] J.P.L. 1125 (Painswick).
[99] *Sabi v Secretary of State*, June 18, 2002 (Forbes J.) (leave to appeal refused, 8th October 2002, CA) (see **14.7.8**).
[1] [1991] J.P.L. 152.
[2] LBCA, s.70.
[3] [1984] J.P.L. 363 at 366.

14.9.3 Other material considerations

It will be recalled that an authority, in determining applications, must have "special regard" to the desirability of preserving the building, its setting and its features, and pay "special attention" to the desirability of preserving and enhancing conservation areas.[4] However, the use of the word "special" in each case indicates that while the principal concern of the authority is to consider the desirability of preservation, that is not the only issue that it can take into account. This opens the way for it to bear in mind any other "material considerations"—a phrase that is used explicitly only in connection with planning applications,[5] but which has been considered at length in the courts, most recently in *R. v Westminster CC, ex p. Monahan*.[6]

As to what may be taken into account, this will obviously vary from case to case. The classic explanation is that given by Cooke J. in *Stringer v Minister of Housing and Local Government*:

"In principle, it seems to me that any consideration which relates to the use and development of land is capable of being a planning consideration. Whether a particular consideration falling within that broad class is material in any given case will depend on the circumstances."[7]

A number of relevant considerations have been touched upon in passing earlier in this chapter. As for others, a full analysis is beyond the scope of this book; but a summary of the current position, as it emerges from copious litigation, is to be found in the *Planning Encyclopedia*.[8]

14.9.4 Balancing opposing factors

It is important not to consider one issue to the exclusion of all others. This is of course the essence of making any planning decision; but it is easy for those who are particularly enthusiastic about a specific issue (not least in the field of conservation) to feel that it should be supported and encouraged to the exclusion of all others. This has been emphasised in two decisions of the High Court.

The first, *Worsted Investments v Secretary of State*,[9] related to Thremhall Priory, a semi-derelict Grade II listed building in Essex. A scheme was approved in 1991 to rebuild it with additions and an office extension, but that was not financially viable on its own. An application was therefore now submitted for outline permission for new buildings in its grounds. The planning authority refused it, as did the inspector on appeal. He considered that, although the proposal would assist in restoring the Priory, it would significantly harm its setting, and that the harm would not be outweighed by the benefit of restoration—particularly in view of how little of the original Priory remained. The appellants appealed, arguing that the inspector had found that every effort should be made

---

[4]   P(LBCA)A 1990, ss 16(2), 66(1), 72(1). [Scotland: P(LBCA)(S)A 1997, ss 14(2), 59(1), 64(1); NI: P(NI)O 1991, arts 45(1), 50(5).]
[5]   TCPA 1990, s.70(2). [Scotland: TCP(S)A 1997, s.37(2); NI: P(NI)O 1991, art.25(1).]
[6]   [1988] J.P.L. 557 (see **14.6.2**).
[7]   [1971] 1 All E.R. 65, at p.77.
[8]   *Encyclopedia of Planning Law and Practice*, paras 70.15 to 70.52.
[9]   [1994] E.G.C.S. 66.

to restore the building, and could not therefore now conclude that the benefit of restoration would be outweighed by the harm caused.

David Keene Q.C., (then) sitting as deputy judge, considered the advice in Appendix I to Circular 8/87 that "every effort should be made" to preserve a Grade II building; but he held that it did not mean that restoration would justify any degree of harm. The inspector had properly carried out a crucial balancing exercise, reaching the conclusion that the harm outweighed the benefit. He accordingly dismissed the appeal. The quoted phrase does not appear in the PPG; but the principle still holds good.

The second decision, *South Oxfordshire DC v Secretary of State*,[10] also concerned new building works which were stated to be necessary partly in order to finance restoration works—this time within the Mapledurham Estate in Berkshire, which is a conservation area and in an area of outstanding natural beauty. Almost all the houses in the village are listed, and a number have over the years been restored by the Trustees of the Estate—in particular the main house and the watermill, now open to the public. They now sought permission for a golf course and clubhouse, to fund further repairs. The planning authority refused permission, so the Trustees appealed to the Secretary of State. In his decision, the inspector accepted that the proposal would harm the character of the area, but considered that there were compensating advantages. In particular, the Trustees had undertaken to carry out restoration works.[11] He accordingly granted permission. The planning authority in turn appealed to the courts.

Here too, however, the court upheld the inspector's decision, considering that he had properly undertaken a balancing exercise—although in this instance he had come to the conclusion that the benefit of the proposal outweighed the harm, and allowed the appeal.

Both these decisions emphasise that, merely because central government and local policy recognises the preservation of listed buildings as being desirable, that does not mean that it outweighs any harm caused to every other objective.

A rather different situation arose in *Isaac v Secretary of State*,[12] in which the National Rivers Authority (then responsible for tidal defence) had sought permission for a scheme that would protect Bideford in Devon against flooding. The inspector accepted that the scheme would harm the setting of a listed medieval long bridge over the river, and detract from the character and appearance of the conservation area, but concluded that those objections were offset by the need for the flood defences; the alternative scheme proposed would have less impact, but would also be less effective.

Conversely, even where a proposed development may be desirable on other grounds, it may still be refused on conservation considerations. Thus, in *R. (University College London) v Secretary of State*, an application for a new student accommodation block was turned down both by the planning authority and the Secretary of State on appeal, on the basis of its effect on the Bloomsbury Con-

[10] [1995] J.P.L. 213.
[11] See **13.8.8**.
[12] [2003] Env. L.R. 23.

servation Area, even though it was generally accepted that—other things being equal—new accommodation would be desirable.[13]

14.9.5 Planning applications following imposition of an article 4 direction

Finally, it has already been noted that a planning authority may make an art.4 direction, the effect of which is that anyone wishing to carry out the relevant type of development has to apply for a specific grant of planning permission.[14]

If such permission is refused, or granted subject to onerous conditions, it will then of course be possible to appeal against the decision to the Secretary of State. At such an appeal, the argument that the development which the authority wishes to restrict is normally permitted automatically will certainly be a very material consideration, in favour of the applicant. On the other hand, so too will be the argument that the very existence of the direction indicates the importance of the area, and the harm that will be caused to it by what would otherwise be a minor change.

Generally, however, once a direction has been made, the resulting planning application should be determined on the same basis as any other: there is not automatically any duty on the decision-maker to apply any more stringent test. So, for example, in a conservation area there is no requirement for development to enhance, rather than merely to preserve, the area—unless the authority or someone else puts forward that argument and can justify it on the particular facts of the case, if necessary at inquiry.[15]

The above conclusions emerged out of an unsuccessful High Court challenge by English Heritage to an inspector's decision allowing a uPVC door on appeal at Wirksworth in Derbyshire.[16] The inspector decided that the door did not harm the area—there were others nearby that were worse. English Heritage argued that he should have considered the issue of precedent: one plastic door might be relatively harmless, but a multitude of them would ruin the area. But the court was unimpressed—since the inspector had found no harm, any number of doors would still cause no harm. If therefore an authority wishes to run that argument, it should seek to persuade the inspector that 50 doors of this character would cause harm, therefore each of them does—including the first.

And it has already been noted that what may cause harm to one property in a conservation area may nevertheless leave unharmed the character of the area as a whole.[17]

It should also be noted that there is potentially a right to compensation where planning permission is refused for development that only requires a planning application as a result of an art.4 direction.[18] This may also be a material consideration.

---

[13] [2005] J.P.L. 975.

[14] See **7.4**.

[15] See **14.7.5**.

[16] *Historic Buildings and Monuments Commission v Secretary of State* [1997] 3 P.L.R. 8, J.P.L. 424.

[17] *R. (Waveney DC) v Secretary of State* [2003] J.P.L. 1058 (see **14.7.4**).

[18] See **15.4.1**.

Chapter 15

Appeals and Other Remedies

15.1 Introduction

It will, inevitably, sometimes happen that the outcome of the application process described in the previous chapters upsets someone. If permission or consent is refused, or granted subject to onerous decisions, the applicant will be dissatisfied. If on the other hand permission is granted, objectors (whether neighbours, amenity groups or rival developers) may be disappointed—or outraged.

In the first situation, the best course of action for the aggrieved applicant may well be to negotiate with the planning authority, to secure permission and consent for an acceptable alternative proposal. However, failing that, there is a statutory right to appeal to the Secretary of State (or equivalent) against the authority's decision (see **15.2**). It is also possible to make such an appeal where the authority makes no decision at all. Appeals may be dealt with by written representations, an informal hearing or a public inquiry (**15.3**).

There is in principle only a very limited right to compensation for adverse decisions (see **15.4**). However, where the refusal of permission or consent leads to the land being utterly worthless, it may be possible for a purchase notice to be served on the authority, requiring it to take the land—at an appropriate value (**15.5**).

The outcome of all these procedures may still be unsatisfactory—either to the property owner or to the authority or to one of the other parties involved—and there is therefore a further right of appeal against the decision of the Secretary of State, but only on a point of law, to the courts (see **15.6**). There is also a right of appeal to the courts (again, only on a point of law) against the decision of the Secretary of State on a called-in application for planning permission or listed building consent or on an application for scheduled monument consent but, again, only on a point of law.

Figure 15.1 illustrates diagrammatically the various possible courses of action open to an applicant for listed building consent who receives an adverse decision—either a refusal, or a grant subject to onerous conditions—or no decision at all. The position is similar in relation to decisions on planning applications.

In the second situation, where permission or consent is granted, there is no right of appeal to the Secretary of State; instead, an aggrieved objector may seek

Figure 15.1 Possible responses to an adverse decision

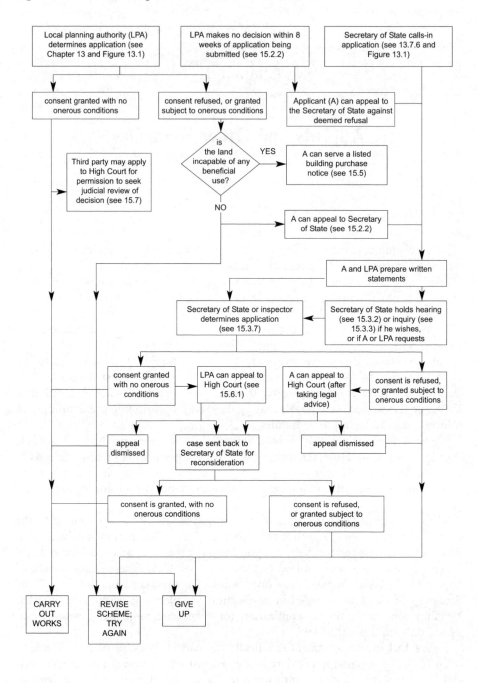

judicial review of the offending decision, but only on a point of law, and only with the permission of the court (see **15.7**).

For simplicity, this chapter has been drafted by reference to appeals to "the Secretary of State"—readers in Wales and Scotland should assume the law applies equally to appeals to the Welsh Assembly or the Scottish Ministers, except as noted. Further, the right to appeal in relation to decisions on applications for conservation area consent is exactly as for listed building consent decisions; all the comments in the remainder of this chapter about listed building consent appeals apply, in general, equally to conservation area consent appeals.[1]

In Northern Ireland, the appeal system is in a number of respects slightly different; it is briefly considered here at **15.8**.

15.2 Appeal to the Secretary of State

15.2.1 Negotiation on a compromise

Where planning permission or listed building consent has been refused, or granted subject to onerous conditions, it is always sensible for the aggrieved applicant to consider first entering into (or continuing) negotiations with the planning authority, either instead of or as well as immediately submitting an appeal to the Secretary of State. If there are relatively few disputed matters, even a successful appeal may not be worth the delay and expense involved.

Alternatively, since no fee is payable either for a further planning application within 12 months of one that was refused[2] or for a listed building consent application, it may be worth submitting an application or applications for a compromise proposal at the same time as submitting an appeal on the refused proposal. If the former is successful, possibly following negotiations with the authority and further amendment, that may obviate the need for proceeding further with the latter.

A further tactic that is sometimes used, especially where a refusal is anticipated in relation to a larger scheme, is what is known as "twin-tracking". This is where two identical applications are submitted, so that one can be appealed for non-determination after eight weeks have elapsed, while negotiations with the planning authority can continue on the other (in cases involving listed buildings, this would need to be done with both the planning application and the listed building consent application). If those negotiations lead to the grant of permission and consent, possibly following amendments, then the appeal on the first application can be withdrawn; if they do not, the appeal is already in the queue for the allocation of an inquiry date—and indeed the drawings etc. of the scheme in its revised form, following the negotiations on the second application, may be substituted for those accompanying the first application, so as to maximise the chances of success.

---

[1] P(LBCA) Regs 1990, reg.12 and Sch.3. [Scotland: TCP(LBCA)(S) Regs 1987, reg.13 and Sch.4.]

[2] TCP (Fees [etc]) Regulations 1989, reg.8.

The Government has always been, for some reason, unenthusiastic about twin-tracking, and has introduced, in England and Wales, a power for planning authorities to decline to accept duplicate applications[3]—although it seems that this will be discretionary. Further, there is to be a new power for an authority to continue to determine an application, even after an appeal has been submitted for non-determination; if it then grants permission or consent, the applicant can continue to appeal, but only against the conditions; but if it refuses, there will be clear reasons for refusal.[4]

15.2.2 *The right of appeal*

The broad statutory framework for appeals to the Secretary of State in respect of decisions relating to planning applications is provided in sections 78 and 79 of the Planning Act (in relation to England and Wales), and sections 47 and 48 of the Scottish Planning Act. The corresponding provisions in relation to appeals relating to decisions on listed building and conservation area consent applications are in sections 21 and 22 of the Listed Buildings Act and sections 18 and 19 of the Scottish Listed Buildings Act.

The principal right of appeal applies where an applicant who is refused planning permission or listed building consent by a planning authority, or considers that a condition attached to a grant of permission or consent is unreasonable or onerous. In such circumstances, an appeal may be made to the Secretary of State within six months of the authority's decision.[5] Note that the time-limit was briefly reduced (in England) to three months; however, following widespread unhappiness, the six-month limit was rapidly restored—albeit with minimum publicity.[6]

Secondly, there is an identical right of appeal against the decision of a local planning authority not to vary or remove onerous conditions on a previous grant of permission or consent—or to vary or remove those conditions but only subject to the imposition of further conditions.[7] The same time-limit applies.

Thirdly, it is possible to appeal against a deemed refusal if the authority fails to make any decision within eight weeks of receiving any of the above types of application (or such longer period as has been agreed); again, the applicant must lodge the appeal within six months of the expiry of the relevant period.[8]

An extension of these six-month periods is possible, but only with the consent of the Secretary of State, which is unlikely to be forthcoming except in very

---

[3] TCPA 1990, s.70B, and P(LBCA)A 1990, s.81B, both to be introduced by PCPA 2004, s.43.

[4] TCPA 1990, s.78A, and P(LBCA)A 1990, s.20A, both to be introduced by PCPA 2004, s.50.

[5] TCPA 1990, s.78(1)(b), TCP(GDP)O 1995, art.23(1) (planning appeals); P(LBCA)A 1990, s.20(1)(a); P(LBCA) Regs 1990, reg.8(1) (listed building and conservation area consent appeals).

[6] The six-month time limit now applies to all decisions by planning authorities made on or after October 14, 2004. For the background to the changes ("mea culpa"), see the explanatory memorandum to SI 2004/3340.

[7] See **13.8.7**.

[8] TCPA 19890, s.78(2),(4), TCP(GDP)O 1995, arts 20, 23(2); P(LBCA)A 1990, s.20(2), (3)(a); regs 3(4), 8(1): see **13.7.2**.

abnormal circumstances. Once the time limit has elapsed, it is therefore necessary to submit a new application, using the same drawings. On the assumption that it will be determined in the same way as the previous one, an appeal against non-determination can then be lodged as soon as eight weeks have elapsed.

There is, finally, a right of appeal against the refusal of an authority to approve details as required by a condition on an earlier grant of permission or consent, and against the approval of such details subject only to further conditions.[9] It is also possible to appeal against the non-determination by an authority within eight weeks of an application for such approval.[10]

15.2.3 Procedure

Appeal procedures are covered fully in general texts on planning law and procedure; they will therefore only be described in outline here, with particular emphasis on those features peculiar to listed buildings appeals.

Appeals are to be made, on the appropriate form, to the Planning Inspectorate at Bristol or Cardiff or the [Scottish Executive] Inquiry Reporters Unit at Falkirk, as appropriate. Note that where particular works required both planning permission and listed building consent, and both were refused or granted subject to adverse conditions (or both applications were not decided), *two* appeals will be necessary, each on the appropriate form. All the relevant forms are available on the website of the Inspectorate[11]—with different forms for England and Wales—or that of the Inquiry Reporters Unit.[12] They are updated from time to time; and the current version should be downloaded when required. It is expected that it will soon once again be possible for the forms to be completed electronically.

Along with the relevant form, a copy of each of the following must also be submitted:

(1) the application, and all relevant drawings and other supporting material (including the ownership certificate and ownership details) submitted with the application[13];

(2) any revised or additional drawings or other material;

(3) the planning authority's decision (if any);

(4) a plan showing the site outlined in red (preferably on a 1:10,000 OS plan); and

---

[9] TCPA 1990, s.78(1)(b), (2); P(LBCA)A 1990, s.20(1)(c),(2); see **13.8.4**.

[10] In the case of appeals arising out of listed building consents, there is no possibility of extending the eight-week limit (P(LBCA)A 1990, s.20(3)(b)).

[11] *www.planning-inspectorate.gov.uk*. Forms are also available on request in large print, on audiotape, in Braille or in another language.

[12] *http://www.scottishexecutive.gov.uk/Topics/Planning-Appeals* (or simply go to the Scottish Executive website and proceed on instinct; there does not appear to be a straightforward website address).

[13] See **13.3**.

(5)   all relevant correspondence with the planning authority (both before and after the submission of the application).[14]

Where the appeal is against the refusal of matters reserved in an outline permission, or details required to be approved under a condition, that first permission should accompany the appeal. And where an environmental statement was produced in association with the original application, a copy should accompany the appeal.

Where the inspectorate considers that the information supplied is inadequate to describe the proposal, it will reject the appeal—even if the authority (possibly reluctantly) considered it to be just adequate. Equally, where the inspectorate considers the information to be sufficient, it is entitled to accept and determine the appeal, even the authority may vociferously maintain that more information should be supplied.[15]

Each appeal form incorporates a further ownership certificate (as prescribed in regulations[16]). This will probably require the same information as was submitted with the original application(s), but it may not, since it refers to the position as it is 20 days before the date of the appeal, which may be many months after the date of the application. The appellant will also have to notify the owners once again and insert further press notices as appropriate.

Where an appeal is made following an adverse planning decision, the appeal form and the accompanying material should be sent to the Inspectorate; and a further copy should be sent to the planning authority (other than so much of the accompanying material as the authority already possesses). The Inspectorate asks those making listed building and conservation area consent appeals also to send a copy of the relevant appeal form and other material to the planning authority, although there is no statutory authority for this since there is no provision in the Listed Buildings Regulations corresponding to article 23(1)(b) of the General Development Procedure Order 1995.[17] But it is a sensible procedure, and saves time, and thus should normally be followed.

In many cases, two appeals will be required, one against refusal of planning permission, and one against refusal of listed building consent. The six-month time limit will apply to both, and the two appeals will generally be dealt with, and decided, together. This applies, for example, where applications have been refused both for listed building consent for the demolition of a listed building (or an unlisted building in a conservation area) and for planning permission for the subsequent redevelopment of its site, or where both listed building consent and planning permission are required for the alteration or extension of a listed building.

---

[14] TCP(GDP)O 1995, art.23(3) (planning appeals); P(LBCA) Regs 1990, reg.8(2) (listed building and conservation area consent appeals). [Scotland: TCP(GDP)(S)O 1992, art.23, P(LBCA)(S) Regs 1987, reg.8(2).]

[15] *R. v Secretary of State, ex p. Bath and North East Somerset DC* [1999] 2 P.L.R. 120, CA (see **13.3.4**).

[16] TCP(GDP)O 1995, arts 7, 9; P(LBCA) Regs 1990, reg.6(5), Sch.2. [Scotland: TCP(GDP)(S)O 1992, art.24, Sch.10, P(LBCA)(S) Regs 1987, reg.8(2), Sch.2.]

[17] Nor in Scotland.

The Planning Inspectorate has issued various helpful advice on appeals, including *Making your Planning Appeal*, describing the procedure from the point of view of the appellant; and *Guide to Taking Part in Planning Appeals*, designed for those who wish to comment on someone else's appeal. Both are written primarily to cover appeals against refusal of planning permission, but they do apply broadly to listed building and conservation area consent appeals as well. The Inquiry Reporters Unit has issued *Planning Appeals in Scotland*. Each of these is periodically updated and available in PDF format on the relevant website.[18]

15.2.4 Grounds of appeal

An appellant may use any ground of appeal that seems appropriate. Needless to say, the considerations influencing decisions by planning authorities on applications for planning permission or listed building consent, outlined in the previous chapter, will be equally relevant to decisions on appeals—indeed, decisions by authorities are strongly influenced by an awareness of the basis on which appeals will be determined. The appellant's grounds of appeal, and supporting argument, and the planning authority's response, should be drafted accordingly.

A checklist of some of the issues that will often be relevant is provided at **Form D16** in Appendix D. It relates to an appeal against the refusal of listed building consent and planning permission for works to a listed building in a conservation area, and could form the basis either for a statement accompanying an appeal to be decided on written representations or for a proof of evidence to be used at an inquiry.

In particular, in the case of an application for consent for the total demolition of a building that is listed or in a conservation area, the appellant will need to be able to show that every avenue which could lead to its retention has been explored. And where (as is more usual) works are proposed for the alteration or extension of such a building, it is necessary to demonstrate either that they are inherently desirable or, if they are not, that they are necessary (so that it is not viable to retain the building in its existing form).

Where an appeal relates to a listed building, it is possible—and sometimes (although not often) appropriate—for an appellant to claim that the building in question is not of special architectural or historic interest, and should not therefore be listed as such.[19] This ground is likely to become used more often as the number of listed buildings increases. It is also particularly relevant where the building is not listed but is subject to a building preservation notice.[20] Where this argument is advanced, the DCMS or Cadw will be consulted.[21]

If such a ground of appeal is used, it should not be the only one relied on. If the Secretary of State decides that the building is of merit, disagreeing with the appellant, it will still be necessary to show why it should not be kept unaltered.

---

[18] The most recent editions are currently those of May 2005, in relation to England, and April 2003, for Wales; but check the website for more recent versions.

[19] P(LBCA)A 1990, s.21(3). [Scotland: P(LBCA)(S)A 1997, s.19(3).]

[20] s.21(4); see **3.9**. [Scotland: P(LBCA)(S)A 1997, s.19(4).]

[21] PPG 15, Annex B, para.B.12; WO Circ. 61/96, para.113.

The appeal should thus be framed in the alternative: the building is of no special value but, even if it is of value, it is not economic to retain it (etc.).

There is no corresponding provision applying to conservation area appeals; indeed, no specific grounds of appeal are mentioned. But there is no reason why, for example—in relation to any appeal relating to proposed works in a conservation area—an appellant should not include in the ground of appeal either or both of the following:

(1) "that the area in which the building lies is not an area of special architectural or historic interest, and ought not to be designated as a conservation area", and/or

(2) "that the character and appearance of the area in which the building lies are not desirable to preserve and enhance, and that it ought not to be designated as a conservation area".

More generally, the notification of the refusal of planning permission (or the imposition of conditions on a grant) will provide full reasons and, for decisions on applications in England and Wales, a list of development plan policies relied on.[22] Those should form the basis of the grounds of appeal—together with any other policies suggesting that permission should be granted. Listed building and conservation area consent appeals should be based on the policies in the relevant government guidance.

15.2.5 Choice of procedure

Around 80 per cent of appeals in England are decided on the basis of an exchange of written representations followed by a site visit, 16 per cent following an informal hearing, and only 4 per cent following a public inquiry. The Inspectorate, acutely conscious of the time involved for all concerned, and under pressure from central government to speed up the process as far as possible, strongly urges all appellants to use the written procedure.

However, the Secretary of State is obliged to hold a hearing or inquiry if either the appellant or the local planning authority wishes it.[23] In practice, where one or both of the principal parties opt to be heard, the Inspectorate will decide which of the two procedures is more suitable, bearing in mind the expressed wishes of the parties—the indicative criteria used in respect of appeals in England are available on the Inspectorate website.

The details of the various procedures are set out below; but it must be remembered at all times that the relevant time limits are to be strictly adhered to. The English circular issued in 2000 stated that "failure to comply with deadlines in the Rules will, except in extraordinary circumstances, result in a party's representations (which may be a statement of case or proofs of evidence) not

---

[22] See **13.7.8**.
[23] TCPA 1990, s.79(2); P(LBCA)A 1990, s.22(2). [Scotland: TCP(S)A 1997, s.48(2); P(LBCA)(S)A 1997, s.20(2).]

being taken into account."[24] Experience since then has made it abundantly clear that this was not mere bluff.

The written representations procedure precludes the possibility of testing the opposing party's evidence by cross-examination, and is not suitable where the issues are complex or the factual position is uncertain. It is also not possible for parties to claim costs from the opposing party if the written procedure is used—although applications for costs at hearings and inquiries are not often successful, and the written procedure is in any event a good deal cheaper.

An inquiry, as opposed to a hearing, will be suitable if the case will take longer than a day to hear, or if there is a need for formal cross-examination, or there is substantial third-party interest.

The Inspectorate estimated at the start of 2006 that, in England, the average time for a decision on appeal dealt with by written representations would be around 18 weeks from the start date. Most inquiries and hearings would both take almost a year to arrange; decisions would then be made within four weeks (hearings) or six weeks (inquiries); but cases involving proposals for 10 or more dwellings would be dealt with significantly quicker. In Wales, decisions would be made within 16, 22 or 30 weeks, depending on which method was used; in Scotland, the target in 2004 was to determine 80 per cent of appeals within 20 weeks (written representations) or 38 weeks (inquiries). These times should be treated with caution, as sometimes hearings and inquiries may be arranged much sooner than they would indicate; and, obviously, long inquiries into complex appeals may take much longer.

Guidance on each of the procedures is provided in the relevant government circulars (noted below), which should be mandatory reading for all involved in the appeal process.

15.2.6 Appeal against refusal of advertisements consent

If advertisements consent is refused by the local authority, it is possible to appeal to the Secretary of State.[25] It is also possible to appeal where a discontinuance notice is served, restricting the right to display advertisements that normally obtain deemed consent.

In practice, all such appeals are determined on the basis of written representations or informal hearings. In determining any appeal, the inspector or reporter will be guided by the same considerations as guide planning authorities—namely, amenity and safety.[26]

---

[24] DETR Circ. 05/2000, *Planning Appeals: Procedures (including Inquiries into Called-in Applications)*, para.9.
[25] TCP (Control of Advertisements) Regulations 1992, reg.15(1). [Scotland: TCP (CA) (Scotland) Regulations 1992, reg.22.]
[26] See **14.2.6**.

15.3 The determination of appeals

15.3.1 The written representations procedure

As already noted, around four out of five appeals are decided following the exchange of written representations, without either a hearing or an inquiry. The relevant procedures have for some years now been set out in Regulations:

- TCP (Appeals) (Written Representations Procedure) (England) Regulations 2000[27];

- TCP (Referrals and Appeals) (Written Representations Procedure) (Wales) Regulations 2003[28]; and

- TCP (Appeals) (Written Submissions Procedure) (Scotland) Regulations 1990.[29]

Guidance is provided in Annex 1 to DETR Circular 05/2000 and Annex 1 to WAG (Welsh Assembly Government) Circular 07/2003, which are in almost identical terms, and (for Scotland) in SEDD Circular 1/2000.

Oddly, the rules for Wales and Scotland apply both to planning and listed building and conservation area consent appeals; but those for England apply only to planning appeals.[30] The procedure for listed building consent (and conservation area consent) appeals in England decided on the basis of written representations therefore remains non-statutory. However, it is sensible to deal with such appeals as if the 2000 Regulations applied to them as well, not least since the Inspectorate certainly does so.

On receipt of an appeal, the Inspectorate will determine "the starting date", and give notice of that to the appellant and the planning authority.[31] The appeal form and any accompanying documents will comprise the appellant's case—so it is not worth submitting an appeal until completely ready; although further representations can be made within six weeks of the starting date. The authority must send a completed appeal questionnaire (which contains answers to a series of questions designed to elicit all the relevant basic information in respect of the site, its history, the application, and the relevant policy framework) and supporting documents within two weeks of the starting date, and any further representations it may wish to make within six weeks.[32] The preferred format for such statements (from either side) is indicated in the relevant circular.

The authority must advertise the appeal on the site, and give notice of it to relevant third parties (including amenity societies, neighbours, etc.)—particularly those who made representations on the original application. Any submissions by

---

[27] SI 2000/1628.
[28] SI 2003/390.
[29] SI 1990/507.
[30] English and Welsh Regulations, reg.2. [Scottish Regulations, reg.3, Sch., para.8.]
[31] English and Welsh Regulations, reg.4.
[32] English and Welsh Regulations, reg.6,7.

third parties must be submitted to the Inspectorate within the same six-week period (in Scotland, within four weeks of the receipt of the appeal).[33]

There is then a chance for each side to comment on the representations of all the other parties, provided that such comments are received by the Inspectorate within nine weeks of the starting date. There will then be a site inspection by an inspector (in England and Wales) or reporter (in Scotland), at which he or she will be accompanied by representatives of both parties or neither.

The inspector or reporter will then issue his or her decision, in the form of a letter to the appellant, copied to the other parties. A decision letter following an appeal decided by written representations may quite properly be shorter than would be appropriate in a case subject to an inquiry, but it must still identify the main issues, the inspector's conclusions and the reasons for them.[34]

15.3.2 Informal hearings

The informal hearing is a relatively recent introduction, but is now used four times as often as a formal inquiry. Its purpose is to enable the case for each party to be tested, but without the formality of a public inquiry. The relevant procedures were relatively recently set out for the first time in formal Rules for England and Wales[35], and explained in Annex 2 to DETR Circular 05/2000 and Annex 2 to WAG Circular 07/2003. Procedures in Scotland remain non-statutory, and are set out as Annex F to SDD Circular 17/1998. All apply equally to planning appeals and to listed building and conservation area consent appeals.

Here too there is a clear timetable. The authority must submit the questionnaire to the Inspectorate within two weeks of the starting date, and notify all those who made representations on the original application[36]—note that a failure to notify such persons may invalidate the eventual decision, if a person who had a legitimate expectation of being consulted can show that his or her representations might have made a difference to the decision.[37] The principal parties must then submit hearing statements (together with supporting documents) within six weeks; and any written comments on the statements of other parties within nine weeks.[38] Guidance on the format of a hearing statement is in the relevant circular, and along with details the procedure at the hearing itself.

The date of the hearing will then be fixed—theoretically within 12 weeks of the starting date, or as soon after that as practicable, although it has already been noted that much longer delays may be anticipated in practice.[38a]

As for the hearing itself, it is to take the form of a discussion led by the inspector; cross-examination is not to be permitted, unless the inspector considers

---

[33] English and Welsh Regulations, reg.5. [Scottish Regulations, reg.4.]
[34] *Henry Davis & Co v Secretary of State* [1992] J.P.L. 1162.
[35] TCP (Hearings Procedure) (England) Rules 2000 (SI 2000/1626) and (Wales) Rules 2003 (SI 2003/1271).
[36] English and Welsh Hearings Rules, r.4.
[37] *Rubin v Secretary of State* (2004) February 9, 2004 (unreported; summary available on Lawtel).
[38] English and Welsh Hearings Rules, r.6.
[38a] See **15.2.5**.

that to be necessary to ensure a thorough examination of the main issues.[39] That rule may have been drafted in the light of the decision of the Court of Appeal in *Dyason v Secretary of State*:

"Planning permission having been refused, conflicting propositions and evidence would often be placed before an inspector on appeal. Whatever procedure was followed, the strength of a case could only be determined upon an understanding of that case, and by testing it with reference to propositions in the opposing case. At a public local inquiry, the inspector, in performing that task, usually had the benefit of cross-examination. If cross-examination disappeared, the need to examine propositions in that way did not disappear with it. ... A fair and thorough investigation can in my judgment be expected by a party who has the right to be heard whichever procedure is followed."[40]

The inspector is able to close a hearing at any stage, and arrange for an inquiry to be held instead (and the parties can urge him or her to do so).[41] And the hearing may be adjourned to continue at the site—a course of action that may often be appropriate in cases involving listed buildings.

An award of costs may be sought by either party to an appeal, if it is determined by an informal hearing. The rules are as for a planning inquiry and are summarised in DoE Circular 8/93.[42]

There will then be a site inspection, and the inspector will in due course issue his or her decision.

15.3.3 Public inquiries: preliminary points

Inquiries are used for only 4 per cent of appeals, that is, 1 in 25; but, inevitably, they will in general be the most complex or high-profile ones. In the great majority of cases, the actual decision will be taken by the inspector or reporter holding the inquiry but, in a few instances, it will be taken by "the Secretary of State" (or equivalent)—that is, in practice, a civil servant in the Government regional office or the Assembly Government or the Scottish Executive, as the case may be.

In England and Wales, inspectors are thus now empowered to determine all appeals relating to applications for planning permission, and appeals against the refusal or conditional grant of listed building consent for any works to almost any Grade II listed building, and all appeals against the refusal of conservation area consent.[43] However, the Secretary of State or the Welsh Assembly will still always determine any listed building consent appeal referring to a building of Grade I or II* or to a building (of any grade) if it has been the subject of a repairs grant under the 1953 Act—although such grants are in practice only given to buildings of Grade II* or Grade I anyway.[44] It has recently been proposed by the Government that all appeals will be determined by inspectors, including those relating

---

[39] English and Welsh Hearings Rules, r.11.
[40] [1998] J.P.L. 778, 2 P.L.R. 54.
[41] English and Welsh Hearings Rules, r.8.
[42] WO Circ. 29/93; see **15.3.6**.
[43] TCP (Determination of Appeals by Appointed Persons) (Prescribed Classes) Regulations 1997, reg.3.
[44] See **9.4.1** (England), **9.5.1** (Wales)

to Grade II and II* buildings, except where grants have been given under the 1953 Act.[44a] In Scotland, all appeals may be determined by reporters.[45]

Notwithstanding those general rules, the Secretary of State (or equivalent) will still determine an appeal where it is associated with some other form of appeal that cannot be determined by an inspector—such as one against a compulsory purchase order, a road scheme, an order under the Transport and Works Act 1992, or a decision on an application for consent under a pre-1999 tree preservation order. And of course an appeal against the refusal of planning permission for works to a Grade I or II* listed building will presumably be decided by the Secretary of State, along with the associated listed building consent appeal. And the Secretary of State may also chose to recover an appeal for his or her own determination even if it is in a category normally decided by an inspector, particularly where there is a great deal of public interest, or the case is complex or the proposal is of regional or national significance. The Scottish Ministers have stated that they may themselves chose to determine cases relating to Grade A buildings.[46]

The procedures are prescribed in Rules, with in each case one set for those decided by inspectors and one for those decided by the Secretary of State. The rules much more commonly encountered in practice will be those governing inquiries for appeals determined by inspectors and reporters, as follows:

- TCP Appeals (Determination by Inspectors) (Inquiries Procedure) (England) Rules 2000[47];

- TCP Appeals (Determination by Inspectors) (Inquiries Procedure) (Wales) Rules 2003[48]; and

- Town and Country Planning Appeals (Determination by Appointed Person) (Inquiries Procedure) (Scotland) Rules 1997.[49]

They all apply both to planning and listed building and conservation area consent appeals. The brief discussion below is framed by reference to these rules, but the corresponding rules for appeals being determined by the Secretary of State (or equivalent)[50] are very similar. Guidance is provided in Annex 3 to DETR Circ. 05/2000, Annex 3 to WAG Circ. 07/2003, and Annexes B and C to SEDD Circ. 17/1998.

It may, incidentally, be noted that the procedure described here applies in principle also to the processing of applications called-in by the Secretary of State where one or other party wants an inquiry. And a further set of rules deals with

---

[44a] *Listed Buildings Casework*, ODPM consultation paper, February 2006.
[45] TCP (Determination of Appeals by Appointed Persons) (Prescribed Classes) (Scotland) Regulations 1987 (SI 1987/1531), amended by SI 1989/577.
[46] HS Memorandum, para.7.10.
[47] SI 2000/1625 ("English Inquiries Rules").
[48] SI 2003/1267 ("Welsh Inquiries Rules").
[49] SI 1997/750, amended by SI 1998/2312 ("Scottish Inquiries Rules").
[50] SI 2000/1624; SI 2003/1266; and SI 1997/796, amended by SI 1998/2311.

inquiries relating to major infrastructure projects[51]—but they are generally beyond the scope of this book.

15.3.4 Procedure prior to an inquiry

As with the other procedures, the first step is the announcement by the Inspectorate to all concerned of "the starting date". The planning authority must then, within two weeks, send the completed questionnaire to the Inspectorate (or the Scottish Executive Inquiry Reporters Unit), and notify all concerned that an appeal has been made.[52]

Within six weeks, each principal party must submit a statement of case (sometimes referred to as a "rule 6 statement"), which must set out the full basis of its case and a list of all documents on which it proposes to rely at the inquiry.[53] This is designed to assist each party to know the basis of the case it will have to answer; but it is in practice at least as valuable as a means of encouraging each party to think through in depth (possibly for the first time, particularly in the case of planning authorities) what its own case actually is. Any comments on the statements of case must be served on the Inspectorate within nine weeks of the starting date. The Secretary of State or the Inspectorate may also require a statement to be submitted by any other party who has indicated an intention to be present.[54]

Where an inquiry in England or Wales is expected to last for more than two weeks, a pre-inquiry meeting will normally be held (theoretically within 12 weeks of the starting date), and the inspector must draw up a timetable for the inquiry.[55] A pre-inquiry meeting may also occur in other cases—such as where the two sides are wholly unable to agree on anything. In Scotland, the holding of a pre-inquiry meeting is entirely at the discretion of the reporter.[56]

The inquiry will then be fixed, if possible at a date within 20 weeks of the starting date, or as soon after that as can be arranged (currently there is in many cases a delay of many months, even for inquiries of a day or two).[57] Note that the parties will usually be given one chance to refuse the date offered by the Inspectorate, which will then simply impose a date. It is important to let the Inspectorate know as soon as possible if the length of time allocated seems inadequate, so that the hall (and the inspector) can be booked accordingly.

All the procedural rules and guidance for inquiries are drafted on the assumption that there are just two main parties—the appellant and the planning authority. However, representations may well have been made in relation to the original application by English Heritage, or by national or local amenity societies, or other public authorities; and these bodies may well wish to be involved at the

---

[51] TCP (Major Infrastructure Project Inquiries Procedure) (England) Rules 2005 (SI 2005/2115); and see ODPM Circ. 08/2005.
[52] English and Welsh Inquiries Rules, r.4(4). Scottish Inquiries Rules, r.4.
[53] English and Welsh Inquiries Rules, r.6. Scottish Inquiries Rules, rr 7, 8.
[54] English and Welsh Inquiries Rules, r.6(6). Scottish Inquiries Rules, r.9.
[55] English and Welsh Inquiries Rules, rr 7, 8.
[56] Scottish Inquiries Rules, r.6.
[57] English and Welsh Inquiries Rules, r.10. Scottish Inquiries Rules, r.14.

appeal stage. The inspector is entitled to permit any person or body to appear at an inquiry[58]; and in practice the involvement of amenity groups and other third parties is welcomed.

In particular, where English Heritage has been consulted in relation to a planning application in London, or given a direction to a London borough council as to how an application for listed building consent should be determined,[59] and this results in an appeal, the council may require it to provide a statement setting out its reasons for the direction.[60] And, whether or not a formal direction was given, English Heritage has a formal right to be heard at any inquiry relating to a listed building consent appeal in Greater London.[61]

Cadw and Historic Scotland, by contrast, will not appear at inquiries, since they are constitutionally parts of the Welsh Assembly Government and the Scottish Executive, by whom the appeal is to be determined.

15.3.5 Evidence at inquiries

Written evidence must be sent—whether by post, by courier or otherwise—to the Inspectorate so as to arrive no later than four weeks before the start of the inquiry. This date is crucially important, as documents sent late will simply be returned unread.

The first element in the written evidence is the statement of common ground.[62] This is to be prepared by the two main parties—although if, as noted above, there is to be significant involvement by a third party at the inquiry, it should be involved also in the preparation of the statement of common ground. The statement is likely to be a relatively short document, accompanied by copies of other plans, reports, policies or other documents as appropriate. In a typical case, it might well include some or all of the following:

A. the dates when each of the various existing buildings involved was built and extended;

B. the date on which each building or monument was listed or scheduled (with statutory list or schedule description), and a plan showing the extent of its curtilage;

C. the date on which each conservation area was designated and extended, and a map of the boundaries at each stage;

D. the relevant planning history of the appeal site prior to the present proposal/s (with details of previous applications and decisions);

E. photographs of the area, and plan showing points from which they were taken (and, if appropriate, details of the lenses, etc. used to take them);

---

[58] English and Welsh Inquiries Rules, r.11(2). Scottish Inquiries Rules, r.15(2).
[59] See **13.5.5**.
[60] English Inquiries Rules, rr 4(2), (3).
[61] English Inquiries Rules, r.11(1)(g).
[62] English and Welsh Inquiries Rules, r.15.

F. the precise details of the current proposal or proposals (with copies of all relevant drawings reduced to A3 size);

G. the history of the present proposal/s (with all relevant correspondence, committee reports, minutes of meetings etc, all in date order);

H. map showing points from which all or specific parts of the site or the appeal proposal will be visible;

I. relevant extracts from all policies in the development plan and any emerging development plan documents that are considered relevant by either or both parties;

J. relevant extracts from all other relevant policy documents (including central government guidance, English Heritage policy statements, local design guides, village policies, etc.);

K. agreed evidence relating to each of the specialist topics.

There is no reason why any of the above matters (and there may well be others) needs to be in the slightest degree controversial; but it would save everyone time and effort if such a bundle could be agreed and prepared right at the outset. Once one copy of such a bundle has been prepared, preferably in a looseleaf binder, and paginated (so that the pages in section F are numbered F1, F2 and so on), it can be copied to all concerned, and further pages added from time to time if appropriate. In particular, it would minimise the extent to which witnesses on either side had to reproduce material in their proofs.

There is no formal requirement for a statement of common ground in Scotland, but the joint preparation of such a document would still have the same benefits.

The second element in the written evidence is a proof from each witness.[63] Thought needs to be given as to who should be the witnesses—in a simple case, a single architect/planner on each side may be all that is needed; in more complex cases, relevant consultants—building surveyors, archaeologists, millwrights, glass experts and many others—will also be useful, both to the planning authority and to the building owner. Conservation officers from the county council, where available, may on occasion be useful at inquiries to support the evidence of a district council, both because of their specialist technical knowledge and as a result of their wider experience.

It should not need to be said that each witness is to give his or her unvarnished professional opinion, regardless of whether or not it is helpful to his or her client (or employer, in the case of a local authority officer acting as witness). Obviously it is unwise for a party to chose a witness who is hostile to the point of view being promoted, but equally a witness must be able genuinely to support the views that he or she is advancing. Further, a specialist witness is there not to express a view as to the way in which the appeal should be determined, but solely as to his or her assessment of the likely effect of the proposal in respect of the particular matters on which he or she is an expert.[64] The High Court in *Burroughs Day v Bristol CC*

---

[63] English and Welsh Inquiries Rules, r.14.
[64] See the comments on the decision in *Georgious v Enfield LBC* [2005] J.P.L. 62.

has considered the role of expert witnesses in relation to inquiries, and criticised in particular the practice of experts in non-legal proceedings acting effectively as advocates for their client and getting drawn into legal argument.[65] It drew attention to the summary of the duties and responsibilities of an expert witness in the decision of the Court of Appeal in *The Ikarian Reefer*,[66] and indicated that the same principles should apply to expert witnesses at planning and listed building inquiries.

On the other hand, the job of the planning witness is not just to recite all the relevant policies, but to carry out a balancing exercise between all the various factors involved (or which conservation will often only be one), so as to reach a conclusion as to how the appeal should be determined.

As for the proofs of evidence for inquiries in England and Wales, the Circulars contain useful advice on their preparation, both as to principles and as to practical details; see also the statement produced by the Planning Inspectorate entitled *Better Presentation of Evidence-in-Chief*.[67] For an example of the structure of a typical proof of evidence, see **Form D16** in Appendix D. A summary of the proof will be required, also four weeks in advance of the inquiry, where the proof exceeds 1,500 words.

In Scotland, each witnesses is to prepare a precognition, and send a copy to the Inquiry Reporters Unit 2 weeks before the inquiry, together with a summary where the precognition is more than 2,000 words long.[68]

15.3.6 Procedure at an inquiry

At the inquiry, the inspector will open by explaining the procedure, and outlining what seem to be the principal issues. The advocates for the appellant and the planning authority will then make brief opening statements.

The planning authority will then present its case, by its advocate calling witnesses who will each be invited to read their written summary (unless, as often occurs, both parties and the inspector are content to take that as read) and make any additional comments—for example, in the light of material produced by other parties. They will then be questioned by the advocate for the appellant. The appellant will then present its case. The third parties will generally go last, although the inspector generally allows them to interpose their evidence at any appropriate point, in the light of the time constraints of all involved. In Scotland, the appellant goes first, rather than the authority.

The advocates for the authority and the appellant will then make closing submissions, summarising their case and their assessments of the evidence presented, and making any legal points. They are required to make available to the inspector a written copy of their submissions in cases where an inquiry is expected to last for eight or more days, and encouraged to do so in other cases. The

---

[65] [1996] 1 P.L.R. 78; see **12.4.2**.
[66] [1993] 2 E.G.L.R. 183, upheld in the Court of Appeal at [1995] Lloyd's Rep.455.
[67] Available on the Planning Inspectorate website, but only (for some reason) on the Welsh section.
[68] Scottish Inquiries Rules, r.11.

inspector will generally give an indication at the close of the inquiry as to the expected date of his or her report.

Whilst the foregoing is the normal pattern, the detailed programming of an inquiry is at the discretion of the inspector.[69] The inspector will also make an accompanied site inspection at some point—usually after the end of the inquiry, sometimes at a convenient point during it, or even (occasionally) before it opens.[70] If more evidence emerges at the site inspection, this should be reported to the parties, so that they have a chance to comment on it.[71]

Finally, an award of costs may be sought by either party to an appeal (or indeed by both). In general, each party is to bear its own costs; but it may be required to bear some or all of the other side's if:

- it has behaved unreasonably in relation to the substance of the appeal (that is, an authority has unreasonably refused consent, or an application has unreasonably appealed against a refusal); or

- it has behaved unreasonably in relation to procedure (for example, by producing new evidence so as to require an adjournment), and

- in either case, its behaviour has put the other side to extra expense.

The rules are elaborated in DoE Circular 8/93.[72] Exceptionally, costs may be awarded against the successful party.[73]

15.3.7 The decision

In the vast majority of cases, the final decision on an appeal will be taken by the inspector who held the inquiry.[74] He or she will issue a letter setting out the cases presented by the parties, and a reasoned decision.[75] If there has been an application for costs, that will be the subject of a separate decision.

The inspector, where he or she is not making the decision, will submit a report analysing the facts of the case to the Secretary of State, the Assembly or the Scottish Ministers. In *Godden v Secretary of State* (a case regarding the demolition of a listed building of considerable historic interest in Folkestone), Stuart Smith J. considered that:

"He felt that he should not approach consideration of the Inspector's report and reasons as if it were a statute or contract where each word or phrase may have to be carefully weighed, but liberally and according to its intent and purpose. Moreover, it was addressed to informed readers, those who had knowledge of the issues and the evidence given at the inquiry. It was also the decision of a technically qualified Inspector who had inspected the

---

[69] English and Welsh Inquiries Rules, r.16. Scottish Inquiries Rules, r.19.
[70] English and Welsh Inquiries Rules, r.17. Scottish Inquiries Rules, r.20.
[71] *Kids Co v Secretary of State* (2002), July 26 (unreported, transcript available from Lawtel).
[72] WO Circ. 29/93. [Scotland: SDD Circ. 6/1990.]
[73] As in *Stocks Hotel v Secretary of State* [1996] E.G.C.S. 165; see 9.4.1
[74] See **15.3.3**.
[75] English and Welsh Inquiries Rules, r.19. Scottish Inquiries Rules, r.22.

building and the site, and who not only might but was expected to use his own knowledge and expertise in reaching a decision where that knowledge and expertise was relevant."[76]

Further, the decision must be accompanied by proper and adequate reasons for it, which must be "clear and intelligible and deal with the substantial points which had been raised".[77]

The inspector is not entitled to form his own view on a matter which was not canvassed by either party to an inquiry. Thus, where an inspector refused listed building consent for the removal of an air-raid shelter that was attached to a Tudor wall, he did so on the basis of his finding as to what would be involved, not founded on any evidence given at the inquiry; and his decision was accordingly quashed.[78]

The same would presumably apply to an appeal decided on the basis of written representations or following an informal hearing.

The inspector and the Secretary of State will decide the appeal from first principles; they are not there merely to see whether the decision of the planning authority was justified on the basis of its stated reasons. In particular, they may vary the authority's decision in whole or in part, even if the part varied was not subject to appeal.[79] This can be important where an appeal is against conditions attached to permission or consent—there is always a danger that the appeal might result in the permission or consent being refused altogether. The standard practice however is that appellants are informed if an inspector is minded to add stricter conditions or take away the permission or consent altogether—so that they have a chance to withdraw their appeal and at least retain what they have.[80]

As well as allowing or dismissing the appeal, either the Secretary of State or an inspector may vary the list by removing from it the building involved.[81] If, however, the building is not listed but is merely subject to a building preservation notice,[82] the Secretary of State (but not an inspector) may direct that it is not to be included in the list, and notify the planning authority accordingly.[83]

15.3.8 The outcome

The importance given by the Government to this area of planning control is demonstrated by the relatively low success rate for appeals relating to listed buildings. Proposals for outright demolition are only very rarely granted consent. Appeals relating to alterations succeed in around 20 per cent of cases; extensions (generally at the rear) in around 35 per cent. These figures are well below the success rates for appeals generally.

The detailed consideration of appeal decisions is beyond the scope of this book—not least because they so often depend on the specific circumstances of the

---

[76] [1988] J.P.L. 99 at p.102.
[77] ibid.
[78] *Cadogan Holding Company v Secretary of State* [1997] J.P.L. B154.
[79] s.22(1).
[80] See *Making Your Planning Appeal*, para.2.12, on the Inspectorate website.
[81] s.22(1)(b); Sch.3, para.2(1)(a).
[82] See **3.9**.
[83] s.3(4)(a).

case, and are of little general applicability. They are however noted occasionally in the *Journal of Planning and Environment Law* and regularly in *Context*, the journal of the Institute of Historic Buildings Conservation; and a significant number are summarised in *Development Control Practice*, a very useful looseleaf work, and in the weekly newspaper *Planning* from the same publishers.[84]

15.4 Compensation

15.4.1 Compensation for refusal of planning permission

Generally, compensation is not payable following the refusal or conditional grant of planning permission. However, if permission is refused following an application that was only required as a result of an article 4 direction, it may be possible to claim compensation from the authority under section 108 of the Planning Act. The assessment of the quantum of compensation payable is provided for by section 107.[85]

As a result, if the development that the authority wishes to restrict consists of an alteration to a building that would increase its value (such as an extension), it may have to pay compensation, quantified as the difference between the value of the land if the development were to have been carried out (less the cost of the works) and its value in its existing state. In arriving at the latter figure it is to be assumed that some development of the kind listed in Schedule 3 to the Planning Act (notably rebuilding) would be allowable.[86] A further sum will also be payable by the authority in respect of any work that is rendered abortive by the making of the direction.[87] The calculation of the total sum is a complex matter, requiring specialist legal and valuation advice.

Generally, therefore, compensation probably would not be payable in the first two of the four cases identified in **7.4.1**—since, for example, the control of the colour in which a building is painted will have little if any adverse effect on its value—but it might well be in the third and fourth cases.

It would seem that the rights to compensation under section 108 apply where permitted development rights are withdrawn by an article 7 direction, just as much as where they are withdrawn by an article 4 direction.[87a]

15.4.2 Compensation for refusal of listed building and conservation area consent

There used to be in certain limited circumstances a right to claim compensation where listed building consent was refused or granted subject to adverse conditions. For this to apply, the works for which consent was refused had to fulfil two criteria:

---

[84] Ambit Publications of Gloucester.
[85] TCPA 1990, s.108(1), as amended by PCA 1991, Sch.6. [Scotland: TCP(S)A 1997, s.77(1).]
[86] s.107(4), applied by s.108(1).
[87] s.107(1),(2), applied by s.108(1).
[87a] See **7.4.9**.

(1) they had to constitute "alteration or extension" of a listed building, not "demolition"; and

(2) either they were not "development" at all or else they were "permitted development".[88]

In other words, they had to be in the category of works for which listed building consent was required, but not planning permission.

This right was, however, abolished in 1990.[89]

There has never been any right to compensation for refusal of conservation area consent.

15.4.3 Compensation for refusal of scheduled monument consent

Where scheduled monument consent is refused, or granted subject to onerous conditions, there is no right of appeal (other than by way of a challenge in the High Court on a point of law[90]). There is however a very limited right to compensation, under s.7 of the 1979 Act.

First, compensation is payable where planning permission has been granted, and scheduled monument consent is refused for the carrying out of the development thus authorised—provided that the permission was granted prior to the scheduling of the monument, and is still extant at the date of the refusal.[91] This should not occur often, as preliminary investigation in connection with the consideration of the planning application should reveal the existence of the monument, so that planning permission can then be refused on archaeological grounds (whether or not the monument is scheduled)—and there is of course generally no compensation where planning permission is refused for any reason. This is what occurred in *R. v West Oxfordshire DC, ex p. Pearce Homes Ltd.*[92] It was the threat of compensation having to be paid under this provision that contributed to the decision of the Secretary of State not to schedule the remains of the Rose Theatre in London, after planning permission had been granted.[93]

Secondly, compensation is payable where scheduled monument consent is refused for works which are "permitted development" or which are not "development" at all.[94] It is not payable, however, where any of the works would or might result in the total or partial demolition of the monument, unless the works are involved in or incidental to the use of the site for agricultural or forestry.[95]

---

[88] P(LBCA)A 1990, s.27(1)(b) (see **12.2.1** and **12.2.2**).

[89] by PCA 1991, s.31(3). Although note that it was claims that had been made under s.27 before it was repealed that gave rise several years later to the decision of the Queen's Bench Division in *Burroughs Day v Bristol CC* [1996] 1 P.L.R. 78 (see **14.4.2**) and that of the House of Lords in *Shimizu (U.K). Ltd v Westminster C.C.* [1996] 3 P.L.R. 89 (see in particular **12.3.2** and **12.6.3**), both of which have proved to have considerable impact in relation to other areas of law considered in this book.

[90] See **15.6** below.

[91] s.7(2)(a).

[92] [1986] J.P.L. 523 (see **14.8.1**).

[93] *R. v Secretary of State, Ex p. Rose Theatre Trust* [1990] 1 P.L.R. 39 (see 4.1.3).

[94] s.7(2)(b); see **12.2.2** and **12.2.1**.

[95] s.7(4).

Thus, for example, compensation would be payable if consent were refused for the laying of a sewer across the site of a scheduled monument,[96] provided the laying of the sewer, if allowed, would not lead to the complete loss of the monument. It would also be payable where the site of a monument was to be ploughed up by a farmer (which is not development), even if that would lead to the monument being destroyed altogether.

Thirdly, where a monument is included in the Schedule, scheduled monument consent may now be required to continue the current use of the site (for example, for waste tipping or mineral extraction). If that consent is refused, or granted subject to onerous conditions, resulting in the continuation of that use being effectively impossible, compensation may be payable.[97]

The net effect of these provisions is to preserve any value attaching to the land by virtue of either:

(1) any express planning permission (not in the TCP (General Permitted Development) Order) granted before the monument was scheduled; or

(2) any right to carry out works that do not require planning permission.

Otherwise, compensation is limited to the amount lost by being unable to continue the use of the site that subsisted at the date of scheduling. Thus in *Hoveringham Gravels v Secretary of State*,[98] consent was (in effect) refused both for gravel working and for agriculture, but compensation was only payable for the second refusal, since the agricultural works would not have been development.

Compensation is assessed in accordance with the provisions of the Land Compensation Act 1961.[99] The date at which it falls to be assessed is the date of the refusal of consent. Thus, in *Currie's Executors v Secretary of State for Scotland*,[1] 100 hectares of the Isle of Arran had been scheduled in 1987, as containing an important complex of hut circles, field systems and clearance cairns, dating from the Bronze Age. Scheduled monument consent was in 1989 refused for the afforestation of the land, and compensation was sought from the Secretary of State. The Lands Tribunal for Scotland found that the value of forestry land had fallen considerably between 1987 and 1989, due to the removal of tax concessions. Further, even if consent had been granted in 1989, the Forestry Commission would not have given a grant under the Woodland Grant Scheme due to the presence of the archaeological material, so the afforestation would probably not have proceeded in any event; there was accordingly no loss in the value of the land, and no compensation payable.

Finally, if compensation has been paid for the refusal of consent, but consent is subsequently granted for some or all of the same works, then the compensation in respect of those works can be recovered in whole or part—which is not unreasonable.[2] The way this is achieved is by the granting of consent subject to a

---

[96] Which would be permitted development under Pt 16 of Sch.2 to the TCP(GPD)O 1995.
[97] s.7(2) (c), (5).
[98] [1975] Q.B. 754 (see 8.9.1).
[99] AMAAA 1979, ss 27, 47; see **13.11.2**.
[1] [1993] 2 E.G.L.R. 221.
[2] AMAAA 1979, s.8.

condition that the works thus authorised may not be carried out until the compensation has been repaid. Compensation is similarly repayable where consent is granted subject to onerous conditions which are subsequently modified or removed.

15.5 Purchase notices

15.5.1 Overview

The planning and listed building control procedures inevitably involve restricting to some degree the freedom of owners of land and buildings to do what they like with them. In most cases, it is still possible to use, or to sell, the property, albeit perhaps not in the way (or at the price) the owner might have liked, or with the same financial reward. In a very few instances, however, an owner of land or buildings may be unable to use them for anything, and thus be left with a valueless asset. In such a situation, he or she can seek to force the local authority to purchase them, together with any land adjacent or contiguous to it in the same ownership, by serving on it a *purchase notice* or a *listed building purchase notice*— or, of course, both. The service of such a notice is thus, in effect, a form of compulsory purchase in reverse.

A purchase notice may be served where an application for planning permission is refused, or is granted but subject to onerous conditions, or where permission is granted but then subsequently revoked or modified.[3] Similarly, a listed building or conservation area purchase notice may be served where an application for listed building or conservation area consent is refused, or is granted but subject to onerous conditions, or where consent is revoked or modified.[4]

15.5.2 Service of a purchase notice

In each case, to justify the service of a purchase notice, the owner must be able to show that the land in question is "incapable of beneficial use" as a result of the refusal, revocation or conditions.[5] That is, it must be demonstrated:

(1) that the land is useless in its existing state; and

(2) where permission or consent has been granted, but subject to conditions, or modified by the imposition of conditions, that the land cannot be rendered usable by the carrying out of the works for which the consent was granted, because of those conditions; and

(3) that there is no other purpose which would render it capable of being used beneficially for which planning permission and listed building consent has been or can be obtained.

---

[3] TCPA 1990, s.137. [Scotland: TCP(S)A 1997, s.88.]
[4] P(LBCA)A 1990, s.32 (applied to conservation area consent) by P(LBCA) Regs 1990, reg.12 and Sch.3. [Scotland: P(LBCA)(S)A 1997, s.28; TCP(LBCA)(S) Regs 1990, reg.13 and Sch.4.]
[5] TCPA 1990, s.137(2); P(LBCA)A 1990, s.32(2).

It may sometimes happen that an old building has been allowed to decay, deliberately or otherwise, so that the only way in which its site can be used beneficially is by the building first being demolished. In such a case, if the planning authority refuses listed building consent, the site will be useless. Arguably, it is the decay, which is the owner's responsibility—or at any rate not the authority's—which has caused the impasse, not the refusal of consent. However, a listed building purchase notice which was served in just those circumstances was upheld in *Leominster BC v Minister of Housing and Local Government*[6]; the local authority's argument that the Minister should have considered the history of the building's gradual decay was rejected.

As to the meaning of "beneficial use" in general, the standard planning law texts should be consulted. See DoE Circular 13/83[7] with regard to this and on purchase notices generally.

In the case of a purchase notice, the land to be considered is the whole of the land that was subject to the planning decision in question.[8] In the case of a listed building purchase notice, the "land" to be considered is the listed building itself, together with any adjacent land in the same ownership whose use is claimed by its owner to be inseparable from that of the building.[9] The listed building means the whole of the building included in the list, together with all of the pre-1948 objects and structures (and buildings) in its curtilage—so that it is not possible to serve a listed building purchase notice requiring an authority to purchase, for example, a set of outbuildings that are redundant but cannot be demolished, without the principal buildings.[10]

Where the above conditions are satisfied, the owner must serve on the relevant authority a notice within 12 months of the decision, or later if the period is extended by the Secretary of State.[11] The relevant authority for this purpose is the district or London borough council in England, or county or county borough council in Wales.[12] In a national park a notice may be served on the national park authority.[13] In Scotland, a notice must be served on the planning authority.[14]

For a model form of listed building purchase notice, see **Form D17** in Appendix D.

[6] (1971) 218 E.G. 1419.
[7] WO Circ. 22/83.
[8] *Cook and Woodham v Winchester CC* (1994) 69 P. & C.R. 99.
[9] s.32(3).
[10] *Shimizu Ltd v Westminster CC* [1997] 1 W.L.R. 168, HL at pp.182–183. See appeal decision at [2000] J.P.L. 857.
[11] TCP General Regulations 1992, reg.12; P(LBCA) Regs 1990, reg.9(2).
[12] TCPA 1990, s.137(2), P(LBCA)A 1990, s.32(1)—both as amended by Local Government (Wales) Act 1994, Sch.6.
[13] TCPA 1990, s.147A, P(LBCA)A 1990, s.32(4A)—both inserted by the Environment Act 1995. It appears that the intention was that the authority should not share this function with any other council, although the drafting of the new provisions is not entirely clear
[14] TCP(S)A 1997, s.88(2).

15.5.3 Procedure after service of notice

The procedure following the service of a purchase notice or listed building purchase notice is set out at sections 139–143 of the Planning Act and sections 33–37 of the Listed Buildings Act, which are in very similar terms.[15]

On receipt of a notice, the council may agree to purchase the land in question, or it may pass on the notice to another authority (including the Broads Authority) or statutory undertaker who is willing to purchase it. If no authority can be found to purchase the land willingly, then the council on which the notice was first served must within three months of the date of that service send it on to the Secretary of State, who must notify all concerned of his or her intention, and hold a public inquiry if required to do so.

As an alternative to confirming a purchase notice, the Secretary of State can do one of the following:

(1) where the purchase notice was served as a result of permission or consent being refused, grant it;

(2) where it was served as a result of permission or consent being granted subject to onerous conditions, remove them;

(3) where it was served as a result of permission or consent being revoked or modified, cancel or vary the revocation or modification order;

(4) where he or she considers that the site could be beneficially used for some other purpose, direct that any necessary planning permission or listed building consent should be granted if an application were to be made.

Or of course the notice may be confirmed—thus forcing the council to acquire the land. If no action is taken within nine months, the notice is deemed to be confirmed anyway. Alternatively, the notice may be confirmed only in respect of part of the land, or with the substitution of another public authority for the council on whom it was originally served. Before reaching any conclusion on a notice, the Secretary of State.

A listed building purchase notice should not be confirmed unless the Secretary of State is satisfied that all of the land concerned is contiguous or adjacent to the listed building in question, and is necessary for the preservation of the building or its amenities (which presumably include its immediate setting), or for access to it or for its proper control or management.[16]

Once a notice has been confirmed, the authority purchasing the land is deemed to be authorised to acquire it compulsorily, and to have served a notice to treat on the owner. The acquisition procedure thereafter follows the normal pattern of compulsory purchase. The valuation assumptions as to the compensation payable are complex; specialist advice should be obtained. In particular, if a listed building purchase notice is served as a result of listed building consent being revoked or modified, and the planning authority is therefore forced to pay compensation under section 28 as well as to purchase the land under section 32, then the price

[15] Scotland: TCP(S)A 1997, ss 90–94; P(LBCA)(S)A 1990, ss 29–33.
[16] P(LBCA)A 1990, s.35(3). [Scotland: P(LBCA)(S)A 1997, s.31(3).]

payable for the land is to be reduced by the amount of that compensation, to avoid double counting.[17]

The general assumptions applying wherever a listed building is compulsorily purchased apply here too[18]; and see *Essex Incorporated Congregational Union v Colchester BC*[19] on valuation following the service of a listed building purchase notice.

Where a local authority is required to purchase land wholly or partly in the interests of a service provided by a government department, the minister responsible for that service may make a contribution towards the purchase cost.[20]

15.6 Challenging decisions of the Secretary of State

15.6.1 Right to challenge

The decision of the Secretary of State, the Welsh Assembly or the Scottish Ministers (or that of an inspector or reporter on their behalf) on a called-in application or an appeal—whether in relation to planning permission or listed building or conservation area consent—is final with regard to issues of fact and policy.[21] But it is possible for anyone aggrieved by such a decision to apply to the High Court (or the Court of Session in Scotland) for it to be quashed, on a point of law.

The same applies to a decision by the Secretary of State to revoke or modify a planning permission or listed building or conservation area consent, to confirm a purchase notice or listed building or conservation area purchase notice, or to serve a discontinuance notice (amongst other things).

In each case, the relevant statutory provision (section 288 of the Planning Act, section 63 of the Listed Buildings Act, section 239 of the Scottish Planning Act, and section 58 of the Scottish Listed Buildings Act) provides a route for challenging the offending decision—sometimes known as a "statutory challenge", to distinguish it from a claim for judicial review—but it makes clear that the validity of the decision may not otherwise be challenged in any legal proceedings whatsoever.[22]

The phrase "a person aggrieved" has been considered at length in the courts. It undoubtedly includes the applicant/appellant in all cases; and English Heritage in cases where it has been involved.[23] It probably also includes anyone who made representations in writing or at the hearing or inquiry, such as a local amenity

---

[17] P(LBCA)A 1990, s.37. See **15.4**. [Scotland: P(LBCA)(S)A 1997, s.33.]

[18] P(LBCA)A 1990, s.49; see **11.4**. [Scotland: P(LBCA)(S)A 1997, s.44.]

[19] [1982] 2 E.G.L.R. 178.

[20] TCPA 1990, s.305(1), P(LBCA)A 1990, s.90(1); and see Cm. 958, para.50. [Scotland: TCP(S)A 1997, s.254(1), P(LBCA)(S)A 1997, s.80(1).]

[21] TCPA 1990, ss 77(7), 79(5); P(LBCA)A 1990, ss 12(5), 22(3). [Scotland: TCP(S)A 1997, ss 46(7), 48(6); P(LBCA)(S)A 1997, ss 11(5), 20(3).]

[22] TCPA 1990, s.284(1); P(LBCA)A 1990, s.62(1). [Scotland: TCP(S)A 1997, s.237(1); P(LBCA)(S)A 1990, s.57(1).]

[23] *Historic Buildings and Monuments Commission v Secretary of State* [1997] 3 P.L.R. 8.

society[24] and people living nearby,[25] particularly in the light of the more relaxed approach being taken—in most instances—with claims for judicial review.[26] The local planning authority directly concerned has a separate but similar right of challenge.[27]

There is also a right to appeal to the courts (under section 55 of the Ancient Monuments Act) against a decision of the Secretary of State to grant or withhold scheduled monument consent, or to revoke consent.[28] The relevant provisions of that Act are identical to the corresponding provisions of the Planning and Listed Buildings Acts.

It may be noted that, although a statutory challenge is often colloquially, and wrongly, referred to as "judicial review", it is significantly different. Firstly, where the statutory conditions are satisfied, the right to apply to the court is automatic, with no need for permission to be obtained. Secondly, the challenge must be brought within six weeks, rather than simply "promptly", and there is no possibility of that time limit being extended.

15.6.2 Grounds of challenge

The only grounds on which an application may be made under any of the above statutory provisions are:

(1) that the decision was not within the powers under the relevant Act; or

(2) that any of the relevant requirements have not been complied with in relation to it, and that the interests of the aggrieved person have been prejudiced as a result.[29]

This includes almost any failure of the Secretary of State (etc.) to comply either with the numerous specific procedural requirements of the relevant Act or the subsidiary legislation made under it, or with any of the general principles of administrative law. Challenges may thus be made based on, for example, a failure by the decision-maker to take into account representations from interested parties (especially those with a statutory right to be consulted), a failure to consider material facts, or a failure to give a clear and reasoned decision.[30]

A detailed analysis of this lies beyond the scope of the present work, but the classic formulation of the possible grounds of challenge was given by Lord

---

[24] *Turner v Secretary of State* (1973) 28 P. & C.R. 123.

[25] *Bernard Hollis v Secretary of State* [1983] J.P.L. 164.

[26] See **15.7.2**.

[27] TCPA 1990, s.288(2),(10); P(LBCA)A 1990, s.63(2), (7). [Scotland: TCP(S)A 1997, s.239(2),(10); P(LBCA)(S)A 1990, s.58(2),(7).]

[28] AMAAA 1979, s.55 (see **13.9.2** for the only challenge known to have been made under s.55). The same procedure could be used to challenge the designation of an archaeological area under Pt II of the 1979 Act, if there were ever to be another area designated (see **6.4**).

[29] TCPA 1990, ss 284(1)(f),(3)(a),(b), 288(1)(b),(5)(b); P(LBCA)A 1990, ss 62(1)(b), (2)(a), 63(1),(4)(b). [Scotland: TCP(S)A 1997, ss 237(1)(f),(3)(a),(b), 239(1)(b),(5)(b); P(LBCA) (S)A 1990, ss 57(1)(c),(2)(a), 58(1),(4)(b).] AMAAA 1979, s.55(5).

[30] *Godden v Secretary of State* [1988] J.P.L. 99.

Denning M.R. in *Ashbridge Investments Ltd v Minister of Housing and Local Government*:

"... it seems to me that the court can interfere with the Minister's decision if he has acted on no evidence; or if he has come to a conclusion to which on the evidence he could not reasonably have come; or if he has given a wrong interpretation of the words of the statute; or if he has taken into consideration matters which he ought not to have taken into account, or *vice versa*."[31]

This has been criticised as being an extension of the statutory provisions; but it has been repeatedly followed by the courts ever since; "so it is the accepted interpretation".[32] Another oft-cited summary is that of Forbes J. in *Seddon Properties v Secretary of State*.[33]

A large number of challenges to decisions of the Secretary of State or of an inspector are based on an alleged failure to take into account particular matters raised at the inquiry, or on the taking into account of matters not raised. The courts are reluctant to quash decisions on this basis; as noted in the House of Lords:

"if there is one principle of planning law more firmly settled than any other, it is that matters of planning judgment are within the exclusive province of the local planning authority or the Secretary of State."[34]

The permissible grounds of challenge thus do not include a mere disagreement with the substance of the decision, or the policy underlying it, however strongly or sincerely felt. Out of many cases, *General Accident v Secretary of State*[35] is typical—the key issue was whether the listed building in question was worth preserving; and that had been explored by all parties and by the inspector. Other issues were subordinate to that, and would not have altered the decision.

Sadly, a not uncommon feature of cases in which applicants appear in person is a conclusion such as this:

"Having considered, I hope, sufficiently ... all the points raised, I have to say that, whilst in every way sympathising with his disappointment at a decision which refuses him planning permission ... he is not entitled to apply to this court for the relief he seeks. His true complaint is dissatisfaction with the merits of the decision, as opposed to the process by which it has been arrived at and the power to arrive at it—which are the sole matters which this court can take into account in exercising its jurisdiction. Accordingly, I will dismiss this appeal."[36]

On the other hand, where an inspector has misunderstood a point being raised by a party, or has failed altogether to take it into account, and where it is genuinely not clear what the decision would have been if that point had been properly taken

---

[31] [1965] 1 W.L.R. 1320 at 1326.
[32] *R. v Secretary of State, ex p. Ostler* [1977] Q.B. 122, *per* Lord Denning at p.134.
[33] [1978] J.P.L. 835. See also, for example, the rather more recent decision of Sullivan J. in *Newsmith Stainless Ltd v Secretary of State* [2001] E.W.H.C. Admin 74.
[34] *Tesco Stores v Secretary of State* [1995] 1 W.L.R. 759, HL, *per* Lord Hoffmann at p.780.
[35] [1977] 1 E.G.L.R. 130.
[36] *Robinson v Secretary of State*, September 11, 2002 (unreported, transcript available on Lawtel).

into account, the court may be persuaded to quash the decision and send it for re-determination.[36a]

A challenge to the adequacy of the reasons for a decision is sometimes made as a make-weight, to support a more substantial challenge on other grounds, and is treated by the Court accordingly. However, it may sometimes be appropriate; indeed, in *Thanet DC v Secretary of State*,[37] the deputy judge expressly stated that the challenge (to a decision relating to the cost of restoring a listed building) should have been brought on the grounds that the reasons were unintelligible, and therefore were not reasons at all. The principles governing the consideration by the courts of a challenge to the adequacy of reasons given by the Secretary of State or an inspector were considered carefully by the House of Lords in *Save Britain's Heritage v No 1 Poultry Ltd* (the Mansion House case)[38] and more recently in *South Buckinghamshire DC v Porter (No.2)*.[39]

Other decisions of the courts—arising out of either a statutory challenge or a claim for judicial review—are cited elsewhere throughout this book.

15.6.3 Procedure

An application under any of the above statutory provisions must be made within six weeks from the date on which the decision letter being challenged is put in the post.[40] There is no means of extending the six-week period—even if the applicant did not know, and could not reasonably have been expected to have known, of the decision being challenged.[41]

An application in England or Wales is made by way of a Pt 8 claim form, lodged in the Administrative Court in London, notice of which must be served on the Treasury Solicitor (on behalf of the Secretary of State or the Assembly) and on the authority, or, if the application is by the authority, on any party or parties who would be entitled to apply in their own right.[42] No permission is required from the court.

Evidence will almost always be by witness statement, exhibiting the decision in question and any relevant documents necessary to make sense of the claimant's argument. Witness statements in support of a claim must be filed in the court within 14 days of the service of the claim, and served on the other parties. And evidence by a respondent or third party in opposition to the application must then be filed within 21 days of receipt of the evidence in support. Skeleton arguments must be filed 21 days prior to the hearing by counsel for those parties intending to

---

[36a] *Thompson v Secretary of State and Barnsley MBC* [2004] EWHC, unreported, June 16, 2004, QBD; transcript available via Casetrack.

[37] [1978] 1 E.G.L.R. 142.

[38] [1997] 1 W.L.R. 153, HL; see **14.4.7**.

[39] [2004] 1 W.L.R. 1953, HL.

[40] TCPA 1990, s.288(3); P(LBCA)A 1990, s.63(3); AMAAA 1979, s.55(1); *Griffiths v Secretary of State* [1983] 2 A.C. 51. [Scotland: TCP(S)A 1997, s.239(3); P(LBCA)(S)A 1990, s.58(3).]

[41] *R. v Secretary of State, Ex p. Ostler* [1977] Q.B. 122; *R. v Secretary of State, Ex p. Kent* [1990] 1 P.L.R. 128, CA.

[42] CPR, Sch.1, RSC Ord. 94, rr 1, 2.

be represented. The case will then be heard by a single judge of the Queen's Bench Division.

Even where the court finds that there has been an error, it has a discretion not to quash the offending decision if satisfied that there has been no prejudice.[43] And where it does overturn the decision, the court will not simply quash it, but rather order that the matter be remitted to the decision-maker for reconsideration. So, although countless applications and appeals are no doubt procedurally imperfect at some point (the complexity of the rules makes this almost inevitable), it is only worth considering an application to the courts if it is possible that the alleged error contributed substantially to the wrong decision being made. And whilst a successful court challenge only rarely leads to the Secretary of State coming to a different decision the second time round, such reverses do occasionally occur.[44]

It should also be borne firmly in mind by anyone contemplating a legal challenge that the costs penalty in the event of failure may be severe.

An application in Scotland is made by a petition presented in the Inner House of the Court of Session, lodged in the Petitions Department in Edinburgh.[45]

15.6.4 Appeal to the higher courts

It is possible to appeal to the Court of Appeal, but (since 1999) only with the permission of the High Court or the Court of Appeal itself.[46] Such permission will only be given if there is considered to be a real chance of success, or there is some other compelling reason why an appeal should be heard.

Further appeal to the House of Lords is only possible with leave from either the Court of Appeal or the House of Lords itself.[47]

15.7 Challenging other decisions: claims for judicial review

15.7.1 Right to a challenge

The statutory procedure described above applies only to challenge the decisions in the categories listed in the relevant sections of the various Acts. In particular, it applies to most (but not quite all) decisions of the Secretary of State, the Welsh Assembly and the Scottish Ministers. However, there are certain types of decisions not listed there—notably decisions by the Secretary of State to list buildings, or to schedule monuments (or not to do so), and all decisions made by planning authorities. These may, in principle, be the subject of challenge by way of a claim for judicial review.

Where the decision of an authority is that permission or consent should be withheld, or granted subject to onerous conditions, the disappointed applicant/owner/developer has of course a right of appeal to the Secretary of State, con-

---

[43] *Miller v Weymouth and Melcombe Regis Corpn* (1974) 27 P. & C.R. 468.
[44] See the saga of the artwork in the Time and Life Building, noted at **4.4.3**.
[45] TCP(S)A 1997, s.239; P(LBCA)(S)A 1990, s.58. Rules of the Court of Session 1994, Chapter 14.
[46] CPR, Order 52.
[47] Administration of Justice (Appeals) Act 1934.

sidered earlier in this chapter; and if an appeal is made that still results in an unsatisfactory outcome, there is the right of statutory challenge. But if planning permission or listed building or conservation area consent is granted, those who objected to the development—such as neighbours, amenity groups and rival developers—do not have a right of appeal. Instead, they may make a claim for judicial review of the decision, but only on a point of law. Thus, for example, in *R. v North Hertfordshire DC, ex p. Sullivan*,[48] a neighbour challenged the propriety of a planning authority's decision to grant listed building consent for what was alleged to be demolition without first consulting the national amenity societies.[49]

For a judicial review claim to succeed, it will be necessary to show that the particular act or decision complained of was illegal, unreasonable, or procedurally improper.[50] Generally, many of the same considerations noted above in connection with statutory challenges[51] will apply equally to claims for judicial review.

Decisions of the Secretary of State [etc.] and inspectors on costs applications at hearings and inquiries are also in principle capable of being challenged by way of a claim for judicial review, but the costs of such a claim are likely to be equal to or greater than the costs at stake, so disgruntled applicants should think long and hard before embarking on such a challenge.[52]

An alternative, but often unsatisfactory, remedy is to refer the decision of a planning authority to the local government ombudsman. However, the decision of the ombudsman is likely to take some time to emerge; so a claim for judicial review should not await the outcome of such a reference.

15.7.2 *Who may bring a claim for judicial review*

The practice of the courts as to who can bring a claim for judicial review has become more liberal over the last twenty years or so. Schiemann J. in 1990 considered a challenge by the Rose Theatre Trust—a group of local residents, archaeologists, theatre enthusiasts and others, formed specifically to fight the decision of the Secretary of State not to schedule the Theatre as an ancient monument—and concluded that it had no standing to challenge a decision.[53] That decision attracted widespread criticism[54]; and more recent challenges to the *locus standi* of groups have tended to fail.

The current position is thus that various categories of national and local groups—including a national lobby group,[55] an unincorporated association of

---

[48] [1981] J.P.L. 752.
[49] See **13.5.6**.
[50] *Council of Civil Service Unions v Minister for the Civil Service* [1984] 3 All E.R. 935 *per* Lord Diplock at 950.
[51] See **15.6.2**.
[52] *R. v Secretary of State, ex p. Ealing LBC*, April 22, 1999, Sullivan J.
[53] *R. v Secretary of State, ex p. Rose Theatre Trust* [1990] 1 P.L.R. 39; see also *Locus Standi*, an article by Schiemann at [1990] P.L. 342.
[54] Notably by Sedley J. in *R. v Somerset CC ex p. Dixon* [1997] J.P.L. 1030.
[55] *R. v HMIP, ex p. Greenpeace Ltd* [1994] All E.R. 321.

local residents,[56] a company established by a local residents' group,[57] and a parish council[58]—have been allowed to bring claims.

Individuals bringing claims have, similarly, been treated increasingly sympathetically by the courts in recent years (as in *Ex p. Sullivan*, above, or *R. v Stroud DC, ex p. Goodenough*[59]). And the Administrative Court recently took a much more relaxed approach in relation to a challenge by the architect of a notable modern building to a decision of the Secretary of State not to list it[60]—thus coming full circle from the decision 15 years earlier in the Rose Theatre case.

The practice of the Scottish courts as to who may bring an action for judicial review has generally been more restrictive than in England.[61]

15.7.3 Procedure

The procedure for making a claim for judicial review is in Part 54 of the Civil Procedure Rules, and the accompanying practice direction.[62]

It is necessary to seek permission to begin an action for judicial review. An application for permission must be made by lodging the appropriate claim form

"(a) promptly; and
(b) in any event not later than 3 months after the grounds to make the claim first arose."[63]

It has been stressed that this does not mean that there is a three-month time-limit.[64] With the increase in the number of planning cases, including listed buildings challenges, a practice started to emerge whereby the courts were in effect requiring that in such cases the six-week time-limit applying to statutory appeals[65] should be observed in making claims for judicial review.[66] However, that was rightly rejected by the House of Lords in *R. v Hammersmith and Fulham LBC, ex p. Burkett*, which emphasised that "promptly" meant just that; the application to the court must thus be made "with the utmost celerity"[67] and "with the utmost

---

[56] *R. v Sheffield CC, ex p. Power* [1994] E.G.C.S. 101.
[57] *R. v Secretary of State, ex p. Kirkstall Valley Campaign Ltd* [1996] 3 All E.R. 304; *R. v Leicestershire CC, Ex p. Blckfordby & Boothcare Action Group Ltd* [2001] Env. L.R. 2.
[58] *R. v Cotswold DC, Ex p. Barrington PC* [1997] E.G.C.S. 66; *R. v Oxfordshire CC, ex p. Sunningwell PC* [2000] A.C. 335.
[59] (1980) 43 P. & C.R. 59 (see **10.1.2**). See also, for example, *R. (Kides) v South Cambridgeshire DC* [2003] 1 P. & C.R. 4, overturning [2001] EWHC Admin 839; *R (Hammerton) v London Underground Ltd* [2003] J.P.L. 984.
[60] *R. (Bancroft) v Secretary of State for Culture* [2005] J.P.L. 477; see **3.3.7**.
[61] *Scottish Old People's Welfare Council, Petrs*, 1987 S.L.T. 179.
[62] There is also a pre-action protocol for judicial review claims, but his will not be appropriate where the decision being challenged cannot be altered by the decision-maker (as will be the case with a grant of planning permission or listed building consent).
[63] CPR, Pt 54, r.54.5. The appropriate claim form for England and Wales is Form N461.
[64] *R. v Cotswold DC, Ex p. Barrington PC* (1997) 75 P. & C.R. 515 at p.523.
[65] See **15.6.3**.
[66] See, for example, *R. v Ceredigion CC Ex p. Mckeown* [1998] 2 P.L.R. 1.
[67] *R. v Exeter DC, Ex p. Thomas* [1989] 3 P.L.R. 61 *per* Simon Brown J.

seek an extension of the three-month limit; but
granted.

the defendant, and the name of any interested

s seeking permission, and details of the remedies

the grounds for the claim, and a statement of the

for extension of time, if appropriate, and any application for directions (for example, for expedition in a case of urgency); and

(5) a time estimate for the hearing of the substantive hearing, if permission is granted.

The form must also be accompanied by any evidence, usually in the form of a formal witness statement, exhibiting all of the necessary documents. It will be appreciated that the proper preparation of a claim takes more than a few minutes, and so the decision to proceed should not be left until the last moment.

Where it is a decision of a planning authority that is being challenged, it is dangerous to seek evidence as to the basis on which members reached their decision; reliance should generally be placed on the recorded decision of the committee, together with the officers' report leading up to it.[69]

The claim form must be filed in the Administrative Court Office in London or Cardiff, and served on the other parties within seven days. The court will then proceed to determine, on the basis of the papers, whether permission should be granted. If it is withheld, the claimant may seek to persuade a judge at an oral hearing. In practice, this permission hearing often amounts to a dress rehearsal for the hearing of the substantive claim; but if the respondent authority chooses to be represented at the hearing, it will not normally be able to claim its costs of doing so from the claimant.[70] In some cases, particularly where there is an element of urgency, the two hearings may be conflated into one.

If the court finds that the impugned decision was indeed defective, it still has a discretion whether or not to quash it; and it may well decline to do so if there is little or no prejudice to the claimant, or if good administration demands otherwise.

In Scotland, an action for judicial review is made by lodging a petition at the Petitions Office.[71] The procedure is governed by Part 58 of the Rules of the Court of Session; note that the recommendations in the Bowman Report, reflected in Part 54 of the Civil Procedure Rules in England, do not apply in Scotland. There

---

[68] *R. v Independent Television Commission, Ex p. TVNI Ltd* (1991) *The Times*, December 30.
[69] *R. (Young) v Oxford City Council* [2002] 3 P.L.R. 86, CA, *per* Pill L.J. at para.20.
[70] *R. (Mount Cook Land Ltd) v Westminster CC* [2004] 1 P.L.R. 29, CA.
[71] The appropriate form is Form 58.6.

is no time limit for lodging a petition; and no requirement to obtain a petition. There is no paper hearing; instead, a first hearing will be fixed, at which a second hearing may be arranged.

15.7.4 Appeal to the higher courts

The right of appeal against a decision of the High Court (to the Court of Appeal and on to the House of Lords) is the same in relation to a claim for judicial review as it is in relation to a statutory challenge.[72]

15.8 Northern Ireland

15.8.1 Appeals to the Planning Appeals Commission

In Northern Ireland, appeals relating to planning applications are covered by articles 32 and 33 of the Northern Ireland Order, and those relating to listed building and conservation area consent appeals by paragraphs 7 and 8 of Schedule 1 to the Order. Appeals are made to the Planning Appeals Commission (PAC), which is an independent body. The procedure is described in a useful booklet entitled *Procedures for Planning Appeals*, the current edition of which is available on the PAC website.[73]

An appeal is made on the appropriate form, which is available in hard copy or on the web. A fee must be submitted with the appeal (other than one relating solely to the display of an advertisement), and a certificate of land ownership. There are four types of procedure for appeals: written representations with or without an accompanied site visit, informal hearing, and formal hearing. Even formal hearings are generally less formal than inquiries elsewhere; there are, for example, no closing submissions. As in Great Britain, there are strict time-limits for the submission of statements of case.

Whichever procedure is used, the case is considered by the appointed Commissioner, who reports to the PAC at its next meeting; the PAC then issues its collective decision—at the earliest, between 17 and 26 weeks after the initial making of a valid appeal, depending on the procedure used. Where an inquiry has been held, the decision of the PAC is to be sent to the Department, which must then consider it.[74]

15.8.2 Compensation and purchase notices

There used to be a right to compensation where listed building consent was refused or granted conditionally for the alteration or extension of a building, in circumstances where the works would normally be permitted development, under article 64(2) of the Planning (NI) Order 1972. However, that right was abolished

---

[72] See **15.6.4**.
[73] *www.pacni.gov.uk*. The most recent edition is dated September 2005.
[74] P(NI)O 1991, art.111(6).

by the Planning (Compensation etc) Act (NI) 2001.[75] The law in the six counties is thus now the same as it has been in Great Britain since the enactment of the Planning and Compensation Act 1991.

As in Great Britain, compensation is payable where scheduled monument consent is refused for works that have already been granted planning permission, or which are permitted development or not development at all, or for the continuing of the existing use of the land.[76]

Where planning permission or listed building consent is refused, granted subject to adverse conditions, revoked or modified, a purchase notice may be served under article 94 of the Planning (Northern Ireland) Order 1991 where the land has become incapable of beneficial use—as in Great Britain.[77]

15.8.3 Application to the High Court

There is no equivalent of the statutory challenge under the Planning and Listed Buildings Acts in Great Britain. Instead, all administrative decisions, whether by the Department or the PAC, can be challenged by an application for judicial review.[78]

Procedure is governed by Order 53 of the Rules of the Supreme Court (NI) 1980, and is similar to that applying in England (under RSC Order 53) prior to the introduction of the Civil Procedure Rules. Thus the application must be made promptly, and in any event within three months of the decision being impugned; and leave is required.

A right of appeal lies to the Court of Appeal (in Belfast) and thence to the House of Lords in London.

---

[75] 2001 Act, s.3. By virtue of s.4, the change took effect in relation to any application for listed building consent made on or after October 23, 2000.
[76] Historic Monuments and Archaeological Objects (NI) Order 1995, art.9. See **15.4.3**.
[77] See **15.5**.
[78] *Re Meekatharra Ltd* [1995] 6 B.N.I.L. 105.

Chapter 16

Places of Worship

16.1 Introduction

16.1.1 Background

Among the most notable of all Britain's historic buildings must be its churches and cathedrals. Over half (approximately 8,500) of the places of worship of the Church of England date from before the Reformation; almost all of these are listed. A further 4,500 post-Reformation buildings are listed, including the Wren churches, and many fine examples of Victorian architecture. These figures include the cathedrals, as well as many buildings formerly but no longer used for Anglican worship. In addition, a significant proportion of Church of England buildings are in conservation areas—in many cases, indeed, a conservation area will have a church or cathedral as its focal point.

There are also over 3,000 other listed Christian places of worship in England. The Methodists alone have an estimated 700 listed chapels (including a dozen of Grade I or II*), and a further 900 in conservation areas, largely from the Victorian period. The United Reformed Church has around 400, and the Baptists around 350. The Roman Catholics, too, have in the region of 800 listed buildings, particularly in the larger cities, including a number of Grade I or II*. The Quakers and the Unitarians have fewer buildings, but in each case a higher proportion of them are of architectural interest, particularly those built in the 18th century.

In addition it may be noted that, as part of the move to list more recent buildings,[1] many 20th-century places of worship have been listed in England, including several from the period since the 1939–45 War. Coventry Cathedral, for example, was listed Grade I in March 1988, and a significant selection were listed in September 1998.

Listed places of worship of the Church of England and the Church in Wales used to be graded A, B and C, rather than I, II* and II; but in lists issued (or updated) since 1977 the "secular" grading system[2] has sensibly been used for religious buildings of all faiths and all denominations, whether in use or

---

[1] See **3.2.3**
[2] See **3.2.4**.

redundant. There are inevitably a very much higher proportion of listed places of worship classified as Grade I or II* than is the case with listed buildings generally: at the beginning of 2006, in England, 4,700 had been listed Grade I (over half of all Grade I buildings)—including a handful of non-conformist and Roman Catholic buildings—and a further 4,900 were Grade II*.[2a]

Jews in the British Isles, unlike those in continental Europe, have enjoyed 300 years of continuous settlement. As a result, there is a significant number of synagogues of architectural or historic interest, of which at least 35 are listed in England alone. The Bevis Marks synagogue, on the fringe of the City of London, in use since 1701, is thus listed Grade I. The only two surviving Georgian synagogues (in Plymouth and Exeter), and a handful of Victorian ones, have been upgraded to Grade II*, and there are a number listed at Grade II. It is not known how many synagogues are in conservation areas, although there are probably (relatively) fewer than churches.

As for buildings of other faiths, not many have yet been listed, although there are at least seven listed mosques—including the first mosque in England (in Woking), purpose-built in 1889, and recently upgraded to Grade II*. The others are converted Christian churches—including the grade II*-listed mosque in Fournier Street, Spitalfields (in east London), which was originally a Huguenot chapel, and was then used successively as a Methodist chapel and a synagogue, reflecting the changing ethnic make-up of the local area. There are also several listed former church buildings, now used as places of worship by other faiths, including four temples (two Sikh, one Hindu and one Buddhist).

And since there are now a large number of mosques, Hindu and Sikh temples and gurdwaras in the United Kingdom, it is inevitable that some must be in conservation areas.

16.1.2 Principles of selection for listing

Places of worship have always been a major feature of the statutory lists; and the principles on which they have been selected for listing have been drawn up to reflect their distinctive architectural and historical character. The most recent re-formulation of those principles was in the DCMS consultation document of July 2005, on the proposed revision to the principles of selection for listed buildings generally. This included criteria for the identification of buildings suitable for listing by reference to a number of use categories; the section on places of worship was as follows:

"The range of places of worship is huge and diverse, extending from great cathedrals to humble chapels and from the synagogue to the mosque. Places of worship fulfil two main functions: to provide a dignified setting for worship, and to act as a shelter for the congregation. Different traditions place different emphasis on these. Many churches pay special attention to embellishing the sacred space around the altar; others, like non-conformist chapels, emphasise preaching, their plans favouring audibility and clear sight lines; while synagogues focus on the holy texts placed centrally for all to see. Some faith communities attach little significance to the fabric, considering the church to be the people

[2a] Estimates based on the Images of England database (*www.imagesofengland.org.uk*)

who can meet anywhere; others see the building as representing continuity, and invest heavily in decoration and monuments.

Clearly the physical expression of one tradition cannot be measured against that of another, and the modest 1830s mud and thatch meeting house needs to be assessed in its own terms and not that of the iconic fourteenth-century parish church. Historic interest in a place of worship derives from one or, more likely, a combination of factors concerning the building and its fittings:

- architectural and artistic quality;
- setting;
- historic associations that are special to the community;
- the extent to which the building reflects patterns of patronage or changes in liturgy and devotional practice;
- age and rarity;
- intactness.

While some places of worship are elaborate examples of high art, others are modest and functional but still provide important evidence of past cultures and the aspirations of local communities and traditional craftsmen. All these issues need to be taken into account when assessing significance and determining grade. Thresholds for designation become higher as buildings become more recent in date. For modern buildings, clear levels of special architectural or historic interest will be required."[3]

16.1.3 Works to historic places of worship

It has already been noted that most of the main Christian denominations require that places of worship are regularly inspected, so that repairs and maintenance can be carried out on a regular basis.[4]

Where works (either repairs and maintenance or more major alterations) are to be carried out to places of worship, the need for planning permission will be just as with any other building type—that is, it will generally required for almost any external works to existing buildings, and for any building operations in their curtilages (see **16.2**).

However, where a listed place of worship belongs to one of the six principal Christian denominations, and is in use as such, listed building consent is never required for internal works, and is required for external works only where they affect structures (other than the place of worship itself) that are listed in their own right, such as memorials or lychgates (see **16.3**). This is the result of an arrangement known as the "ecclesiastical exemption". Conservation area consent is for the same reason only very rarely needed for any works to such a building (**16.4**). Works to places of worship of other denominations and faiths will require listed building and conservation area consent as in any other case.

Places of worship in use are rarely if ever scheduled as monuments; but works to scheduled structures in their curtilage will require scheduled monument consent as in other cases; there is no "ecclesiastical exemption" from such control (see **16.5**).

The ecclesiastical exemption arises from the fact that each of the main Christian denominations has its own system of controlling works to places of worship in

---

[3] *Revisions to Principles of Selection for Listed Buildings*, consultation document, DCMS, July 2005, paragraphs 6.64–6.65 of proposed text to be substituted in PPG 15; see **3.2.5**.

[4] See **8.2.2**.

use, which has been accepted by the Government as affording a level of protection at least equivalent to that afforded by the secular system of listed building and conservation area consent. The most widespread of these systems, the faculty jurisdiction of the Church of England, is described at **16.6** and **16.7**; works to other Church of England buildings (outside the faculty system) are considered at **16.8**, and works to buildings of the other five exempt denominations at **16.9**.

Works to redundant places of worship are considered at **16.10**.

Unauthorised works to places of worship are considered in **Chapter 18**.[4a]

16.2 Planning Permission

16.2.1 The need for planning permission

Building works to churches and other buildings used for religious activities require planning permission as much as works affecting any other building type.[5] This is regardless of the religion or denomination of the building in question, or whether it is in use or redundant. It is also regardless of whether or not it is listed, scheduled, or in a conservation area. Further, there is no category of "permitted development"[6] applying specifically to places of worship.

Planning permission will therefore very often be required for works to the exterior of such buildings that would also require listed building consent were it not for the ecclesiastical exemption (see below)—notably for alterations affecting the exterior of a building, and extensions, of whatever size. It will also be needed for relatively minor matters such as new window guards and, in some cases, repairs, where they affect the appearance of the building.

Planning permission will also in many cases be required for the carrying out of works in the curtilage of a place of worship or affecting its setting—such as alterations to paths, walls, gates and other structures. Works to gates, fences and walls will generally be permitted by the General Permitted Development Order,[7] but not within the curtilage of a listed building.

The effect of these provisions is to give the planning authority, in theory, almost as much control as it would have had if there had been no ecclesiastical exemption—although it seems that authorities are curiously unwilling to exercise that control in practice.[8] The crucial difference lies only in that, where the exemption still applies, there is no "secular" control over works to church interiors, which can often be both architecturally and artistically of great importance.

16.2.2 The determination of planning applications

The explicit approval of the local planning authority is thus needed for almost any external alterations to a place of worship, unless they do not materially affect

---

[4a] See **18.9**.
[5] TCPA 1990, s.55(2) (a); see **12.2.1**. [Scotland: TCP(S)A 1997, s.26(2)(a); NI: P(NI)O 1991, art.11(2)(a).]
[6] See **12.2.2**.
[7] TCP(GPD)O 1995, Sch.2, Pt 2, Class A.
[8] And see **16.3.8**, highlighting the slightly strange set-up in Scotland.

its appearance, and for many other works affecting its setting. Further, in determining any planning application for works affecting a listed building or its setting, an authority must have special regard to the desirability of preserving it, or any features of special interest that it possesses.[9] And in determining an application for works in a conservation area, it must consider the desirability of preserving the character and appearance of that area.[10]

Where planning permission is required for works to a place of worship that is listed or in a conservation area, the application should be determined in accordance with any relevant policies in the development plan—including in particular those relating to works to listed buildings and in conservation areas.[11] It would also seem to be appropriate to take into account the relevant Government policies relating to listed building control,[12] as well as those relating to development control.[13]

In addition, it will often be helpful to refer to the very helpful English Heritage policy statement *New Work in Historic Churches*, a new edition of which was issued in 2003.[14] This considers in particular the vexed question of how best to provide for the changing needs—and expectations—of contemporary congregations, not least for additional space and modern facilities, without compromising the integrity of important historic buildings.

Planning authorities should also bear in mind that, once planning permission has been granted for a proposal—such as an extension—Church courts will usually be reluctant to revisit the matters that were considered by the planning authority.[15]

16.3 Listed building consent

16.3.1 Consent for works to ecclesiastical buildings in use

In spite of their architectural and historic importance, places of worship that are in use have always been largely outside the scope of normal listed building control. This is by virtue of what is known as the *ecclesiastical exemption*, which provides that the need for listed building consent to be obtained does not generally apply to works to "an ecclesiastical building which is for the time being in ecclesiastical use". This provision is currently to be found in section 60(1) the Listed Buildings Act, s.54(1) of the Scottish Listed Buildings Act, and article 44(8) of the Northern Ireland Order.

---

[9] P(LBCA)A 1990, s.66(1); see **14.4.1**. [Scotland: P(LBCA)(S)A 1997, s.59(1); NI: P(NI)O 1991, art.45(1).]

[10] P(LBCA)A 1990, s.72(1); see **14.7.1**. [Scotland: P(LBCA)(S)A 1997, s.64(1); NI: P(NI)O 1991, art.50(5).]

[11] See **14.3**.

[12] In PPG 15, s.3 and Annex C; WO Circ. 61/96, Pt 3 and Annex D; HS Memorandum Pt 2 and Appendix 1; (NI) PPS 6, Chapter 6, Annex E.

[13] In PPG 15, s.2; WO Circ. 61/96, Pt I.

[14] Available in the "free publications" section of the English Heritage website.

[15] *Re St Laurence Alvechurch* (2003) *The Times*, September 4, [2004] J.P.L. 1162 (Worcester Consistory Court); see also **16.7.4**.

The term "ecclesiastical building" is not defined, other than by noting that it does not include "a building used or available for use by a minister of religion wholly or mainly as a residence from which to perform the duties of his office".[16] That exception was introduced to reverse the ruling in *Phillips v Minister of Housing and Local Government*.[17] More generally, the phrase has been considered by the House of Lords in *Attorney General, ex rel Bedfordshire CC v Howard United Reformed Church Trustees, Bedford*,[18] the leading case on this subject. Lord Cross in that case first stated clearly that "ecclesiastical" does not mean "Anglican", that is, it certainly includes the free churches and the Roman Catholic Church.[19] He further agreed with the Court of Appeal that a building that is now vacant but which was used as a church and has never been used for any other purpose is still an "ecclesiastical building".[20] Unfortunately he declined to consider questions such as whether the ownership of the building was relevant, or whether it makes a difference if the building had not originally been built as a church.

Similarly, the term "ecclesiastical purposes" is not defined. The Court of Appeal in *Howard* considered that the term meant "church purposes as distinct from social purposes", and thought that the use of the building for church meetings, elders' meetings, and a carol service, but for no other worship, was sufficient to constitute "use for ecclesiastical purposes".[21] Lord Cross considered that it was:

"... a vague phrase which might mean only purposes connected with the use of the building for corporate worship or might extend to any purposes which the church authorities might think likely to foster Christian fellowship among the members of the congregation".[22]

The legislation further provides that a building shall be taken to be used for ecclesiastical purposes if it would be so used but for works that are currently taking place.[23] The implications of that provision were also considered at length in *Howard*.

The practical effect of this exemption is that, where it applies, listed building consent is not required for the alteration or extension of a listed ecclesiastical building of any denomination provided that it is used for ecclesiastical purposes (however defined) both before and after the works. Further, it would seem that consent is not required where an ecclesiastical building is to be partly demolished, provided that ecclesiastical use is to continue in the part of the building that remains. This would have allowed the Catholic Archdiocese of Liverpool to demolish St Francis Xavier's Church, even though it was listed, because one small chapel was to be retained for worship. This did not in fact take place, owing to

---

[16] P(LBCA)A 1990, s.60(3). [Scotland: P(LBCA)(S)A 1997, s.54(3); NI: P(NI)O 1991, art.44(8).]

[17] [1965] 1 Q.B. 156.

[18] [1976] A.C. 363.

[19] At p.376.

[20] At p.377.

[21] [1974] 3 All E.R. 273 at 277.

[22] [1976] A.C. 363 at 377.

[23] P(LBCA)A 1990, s.60(4). [Scotland: P(LBCA)(S)A 1997, s.54(4); NI: P(NI)O 1991, art.44(8).]

vociferous public protest. But those who tried to save the Jesmond Methodist Church in Newcastle were not so fortunate: it was demolished, without listed building consent, two years after it was listed, because the attached Sunday School building was retained.

16.3.2 The extent of the exemption: England and Wales

The ecclesiastical exemption was introduced in the Ancient Monuments [etc.] Act 1913, on the basis that all churches that were then considered to be of any historical interest belonged to the Church of England, and the Church of England had its own effective system of control.[24] The other side of the bargain was that the Church agreed not to seek financial assistance for the cost of repair and maintenance of its buildings.

Since then, the exemption has been incorporated into the provisions relating to listed building control, and (effectively) extended to other denominations, even though until relatively recently they had no systems of control comparable to the Church of England's faculty system. Not surprisingly, therefore, the exemption was strongly resented by many within the conservation movement—and defended vigorously by the churches.[25] As a result of the widespread concern, the Secretary of State was in 1987 given powers[26] to make a direction excluding from the exemption particular buildings or particular categories of building.

The scope of the exemption in England and Wales now applies only to works to buildings owned by religious bodies which have in place satisfactory internal systems of control, approved by the Secretary of State for Culture, Media and Sport. Such approval will only be given if the denomination's decision-making process embodies a number of principles, set out in PPG 15 and WO Circular 61/96.[27] The effect of those is principally that:

(1) the assessment of works to churches that are listed or in a conservation area should be undertaken by a body that is independent of the local congregation concerned, and that has available to it expert advice;

(2) such proposals should be publicised, and notified to English Heritage or Cadw, amenity societies, and the local planning authority;

(3) the decision-making body should take into account the architectural and historic interest of the building concerned along with other factors;

(4) there should be an appeal mechanism where a proposal is refused;

(5) there should be records of how the procedure operates in each case;

(6) there should be an effective mechanism to prevent breaches of control, and to effect reinstatement where appropriate;

(7) churches should be regularly inspected and maintained.

---

[24] See **1.2.2**.

[25] The arguments were summarised in an article at [1985] J.P.L. 599.

[26] Now in P(LBCA)A 1990, s.60(5).

[27] PPG 15, para.8.4; WO Circ. 61/96, para.142.

These principles are also set out in more detail at para.6.0 of a helpful (free) booklet produced in September 1994 by the Department of National Heritage and Cadw: *The Ecclesiastical Exemption—What It Is and How It Works.*[28]

The position now is thus that all works to any listed building should be under at least some system of effective, independent control—whether administered by a special body within the religious organisation concerned or as part of the normal "secular" system of listed building control.

The only direction made so far under section 60(5) is the Ecclesiastical Exemption (Listed Buildings and Conservation Areas) Order 1994[29], which came into effect on October 1, 1994. The denominations which were in article 4 of that Order identified as having a system of control justifying them remaining within the exemption are:

(1)   the Church of England,

(2)   the Church in Wales,

(3)   the Roman Catholic Church,

(4)   the Methodist Church,

(5)   the Baptist Union, and

(6)   the United Reformed Church.

In each case, the basic extent of the exemption is set out in the somewhat tortuous provisions of article 5 of the 1994 Order[30]; and its applicability to some special cases is identified in article 6.[31]

16.3.3   Listed building control: Church of England buildings

The buildings of the Church of England can for the present purpose be divided into three categories: those subject to the faculty jurisdiction; the cathedrals; and the remainder.

In the case of a Church of England building that is subject to the faculty jurisdiction—that is, broadly, almost any place of worship other than a cathedral—the exemption from listed building control only applies to:

(1)   a church building itself, and any object or structure within it[32]; and

(2)   any object or structure fixed to a church building or within its curtilage, unless that object or structure is itself a separately listed building.[33]

So, for example, to remove the pews from inside a listed church, or to paint the ceiling, requires neither planning permission (since the works are internal) nor listed building consent (because of the exemption). The enlargement of a window,

---

[28]   Available from the DCMS at 2–4 Cockspur Street, London SW1Y 5DH.
[29]   SI 1994/1771.
[30]   See **16.3.3** (Church of England); **16.3.4** (other exempt denominations).
[31]   See **16.3.5**.
[32]   1994 Order, art.5(1)(a),(b).
[33]   art.5(1)(c),(d) and (3).

on the other hand, requires planning permission (because it affects the external appearance of the building), but not listed building consent (because of the exemption).

Works to an object or structure, such as a funerary monument, that is deemed to be part of a listed church building solely by virtue of being within its curtilage,[34] are still exempt from control[35]—although they may require planning permission if on a sufficient scale to amount to a "building operation". However, where such a monument is listed in its own right, listed building consent would be required as well.

As for Church of England cathedrals, a plan has been approved by the Secretary of State and deposited with the local planning authority in relation to each one. The exemption then applies to:

(1) any building, object or structure that is within the precincts of the cathedral for the purposes of the Care of Cathedrals Measure 1990[36] and within the red line on the relevant plan;

(2) any place of worship that is within the precinct but outside the red line— but not any object or structure fixed to it or within its curtilage; and

(3) any funerary monument in a graveyard, that is within the precinct but outside the red line—but not if it is listed in its own right.[37]

As for other Church of England buildings, some are exempt on a temporary basis (under art.6 of the 1994 Order), notably those within a Church of England peculiar.[38]

16.3.4 Buildings of other denominations subject to the exemption

In relation to buildings in ecclesiastical use other than within the Church of England, the exemption is retained (by virtue of article 4 of the 1994 Order) in the following cases:

(1) buildings of the Church in Wales vested in the Representative Body of the Church in Wales or any other representative body[39];

(2) buildings held in trust by the diocesan trustees of a diocese of the Roman Catholic Church;

(3) buildings owned by or held in trust or for the purposes of the Methodist Church or any connexional or local organisation of the Methodist Church;

(4) buildings held in trust for a church in membership with the Baptist Union of Great Britain or the Baptist Union of Wales by one of the trust corporations set out in Schedule 1 to the Order; and

---

[34] Under P(LBCA)A 1990, s.1(5), see **4.5**.
[35] 1994 Order, art.5(4).
[36] See **16.8.1**.
[37] 1994 Order, art.5(2).
[38] See **16.3.5** and **16.8.2**.
[39] Under Welsh Church Act 1914, s.13(2).

    (5)   buildings in any of the provinces of the United Reformed Church held on the trusts set out in the United Reformed Church Acts of 1972 and 1981.[40]

As with Church of England buildings subject to faculty control, in each of the above cases the exemption only extends to works to a church building itself and any object or structure within it, and any object or structure fixed to a church building or within its curtilage—unless that object or structure is itself a separately listed building.[41] It also applies only where the works are carried out by the relevant official church body, so that control can be maintained by the relevant denomination's own internal procedure.[42]

However, broadly speaking, almost any works to a church, chapel or (where applicable) cathedral of any of these five denominations are exempt from secular listed building control provided that they are controlled instead by the denomination itself.

Here too, there are also a few other buildings of these denominations which are exempt from secular control on a temporary basis.[43]

16.3.5 Special cases

By virtue of article 6 of the 1994 Order, the ecclesiastical exemption also applies, but only on a temporary basis, to works to a building that is:

    (1)   within a Church of England peculiar[44] or religious community (monastery, etc.);

    (2)   used for worship by any of the six exempt denominations within any university, college, school, hospital, Inn of Court, or other public or charitable institution;

    (3)   subject to a sharing agreement under the Sharing of Church Buildings Act 1969 made by any of the exempt denominations or by any church in membership of the Baptist Unions; or

    (4)   owned by or for a Roman Catholic Religious Institute or Society of Apostolic Life.

It might appear that the exemption applies in these cases to any building. However, it should be remembered that this is subject to the requirement that, for works to a listed building to be exempt from listed building control under this provision, the building in question must still be "in use for ecclesiastical purposes"—so that the exemption would not extend to the many buildings in such situations that are in other uses—such as the residential buildings of an Oxbridge college, or the laundry at a convent.

---

[40] United Reformed Church Act 1972, Sch.2, Pt I, and United Reformed Church Act 1981, Sch.2, Pt I.
[41] art.5(1),(3).
[42] art.5(5).
[43] See **16.3.5**.
[44] See **16.8.2**.

The Care of Places of Worship Measure 1999 introduced a new mechanism whereby Church of England places of worship that are outside both the faculty jurisdiction and the Cathedrals Measure could be entered on a special list maintained by the Council for the Care of Churches (the CCC). A building is thus eligible for inclusion in the CCC list if it is in any of the first three of the four categories above, or a chapel forming part of an Episcopal residence.[45] The effect of inclusion is that the building then becomes subject to the faculty jurisdiction, and thus exempt from secular listed building control—but by virtue of article 4 (buildings subject to faculty jurisdiction) rather than article 6 (temporary exemptions).

It is envisaged that the temporary exemption under article 6 will be withdrawn, as part of the proposals in the heritage protection review.[46] From same date in the future, therefore, works to all listed places of worship will be under control either by means of the internal system of the relevant denomination (such as the faculty system of the Church of England), or by the normal secular system of listed building consent administered by local planning authorities.

Finally, the exemption applies to any building in England and Wales used for worship by the three principal Scottish denominations.[47] This will be reviewed in due course when the Government has decided upon the scope of the corresponding exemption applying in Scotland.

16.3.6 Buildings in use by other denominations and religions

Buildings in use for ecclesiastical purposes which belong to Christian denominations other than those identified in a direction under section 60(5) no longer benefit from the exemption. This means that currently, as a result of the 1994 Order[48], full listed building control applies to all listed buildings in England and Wales belonging to any Christian denomination other than the Church of England, the Church in Wales, the Roman Catholic Church, the Methodist Church, the Baptist Union and the United Reformed Church.

As to places of worship of other (non-Christian) faiths,[49] these were touched upon briefly by Lord Cross in *Attorney General, ex rel Bedfordshire CC v Howard URC Trustees, Bedford*,[50] but he specifically declined to consider whether the expression "ecclesiastical building" extended to synagogues and mosques. The Act now implies that it does, in that the power to exclude buildings from the exemption is specifically stated to apply to buildings "of different religious faiths".[51] In the event, however, none of the non-Christian religions have so far

---

[45] Care of Places of Worship Measure 1999, s.1(2). The procedure for applying for inclusion in the list is provided in the Care of Places of Worship Rules (SI 1999/2111). Further details, and notes for applicants, may be obtained from the CCC (see **Appendix C**).

[46] See **16.3.9**.

[47] 1994 Order, art.6(2)(f); the denominations are the Church of Scotland, the Free Church of Scotland, and the Free Presbyterian Church.

[48] See **16.3.2**.

[49] See **16.1.1**.

[50] [1976] A.C. 363 (see **16.3.2**).

[51] In s.60(6)(b).

been accepted as satisfying the criteria to justify the exemption continuing; full listed building control will therefore apply to all of them.

The principles governing the exercise of listed building control over works to places of worship in all cases where the exemption does not apply are set out at paragraph 8.12 of PPG 15.[52] That states that liturgical matters should be given due weight as a material consideration, and that among the matters which should be taken into account are whether the changes proposed:

(1) are necessitated by a change in the worship needs of the congregation;

(2) are necessitated by an increase or reduction in congregation size;

(3) are directed at accommodating other activities within the building to help ensure its continued viability;

(4) would involve substantial structural changes, eg subdivision of important existing spaces;

(5) would involve removal or destruction of important fixtures and fittings, or are more in the nature of a reversible re-ordering of internal features; and

(6) would involve disturbance of archaeologically important remains below ground.

The PPG also contains a number of more detailed guidelines[53]; and emphasises that, where consent is required, the general policies in it apply equally to works to ecclesiastical buildings.

16.3.7 The extent of the exemption: Scotland and Northern Ireland

The Scottish Ministers have the same powers as the Secretary of State in England to make an order restricting the scope of the ecclesiastical exemption.[54] However, no formal order has yet been made.

Instead of a formal order, a non-statutory pilot scheme was introduced in 2002, to control works to the exterior of a place of worship that would have required listed building consent in the absence of the exemption. Under the scheme, those proposing to undertake such works applied for listed building consent to the planning authority, and the authority notified Historic Scotland of the application. If agreement was reached between all three parties, the works could then proceed without further ado. However, if either the authority or (in the case of buildings listed Grade A or B) Historic Scotland objected, the matter was referred to the denomination's own decision making body, which was to make a decision in accordance with the guidance set out in the HS Memorandum.[55]

---

[52] para.143 of WO Circ. 61/96.

[53] PPG 15, para.8.11.

[54] Scotland: P(LBCA)(S)A 1997, s.54(5); NI: P(NI)O 1991, art.44(9).

[55] See *Pilot Scheme to Apply Listed Building Control to Exterior of Churches in Ecclesiastical Use 2002 to 2004: Guidance Notes*, available on the Historic Scotland website.

The pilot scheme did not apply to internal works, which thus remained entirely outside secular control. And even in relation to external works, it only applied to the buildings of the principal Christian denominations.[56]

The scheme operated for a three-year period, until the end of December 2004. It is not entirely clear what it was intended to achieve, since—as already noted[57]— external works required planning permission anyway; and the application for informal consent under the scheme would not seem to have added anything. However, it was considered a success, in that a number of proposals were referred to authorities and to Historic Scotland that would not otherwise have been.

It may well be that a permanent scheme, along the same or similar lines as the pilot scheme, will be introduced on a more formal basis during 2006—possibly extended to all ecclesiastical buildings (including those of other faiths).

In Northern Ireland, the Department has the power to make an order restricting the scope of the exemption.[58] However, here too, no formal order has been made; and the exemption therefore applies to all ecclesiastical buildings in ecclesiastical use, regardless of faith or denomination.[59]

16.3.8 Listed building consent for works to redundant buildings

Buildings no longer in use for public worship clearly cannot be within the terms of the ecclesiastical exemption, as they are not "for the time being used for ecclesiastical purposes". Works to them are therefore subject to full listed building control.

The only exception to this is the demolition of redundant buildings of the Church of England, which are dealt with according to a special procedure governed by the Pastoral Measure 1983.[60] Such works, if carried out within the terms of a pastoral or redundancy scheme under the Measure, are exempt from listed building control not by virtue of section 60(1) of the Listed Buildings Act, but as a result of section 60(7). The latter provision, which originated in the Redundant Churches and Other Religious Buildings Act 1969, is entirely separate from the general ecclesiastical exemption described above, and is thus not affected at all by the 1994 Order.[61]

The justification for the exemption under s.60(7) is not immediately apparent, since there can be no interference with religious freedom in the case of a building that is redundant—especially where it is to be demolished. As a result of concern

---

[56] That is, those within the Scottish Churches Committee: the Associated Presbyterian Churches, the Baptist Union of Scotland, the Free Church of Scotland, the Free Presbyterian Church, the Methodist Church in Scotland, the Roman Catholic Church in Scotland, the Scottish Episcopal Church, the United Free Church of Scotland, and the United Reformed Church Scotland Synod.

[57] See **16.2.1**.

[58] P(NI)O 1991, art.44(9).

[59] The Environment and Heritage Service website suggests that "[the exemption] does not remove the owner's obligation to ensure that the building's character is maintained." It is not entirely clear what is the "obligation" there referred to.

[60] See **16.10**.

[61] See **16.3.2**.

that it could be thought to lead to abuse, agreement was reached between the Government and the Church of England as follows:

"... the Church Commissioners have agreed to ask the Secretary of State for the Environment whether he wishes to hold a non-statutory local public inquiry into any such proposals for demolition (which would otherwise fall within the scope of those controls) where English Heritage, the Advisory Board for Redundant Churches, the local planning authority or a national amenity society have lodged objections. The Church Commissioners have also undertaken to accept a recommendation from the Secretary of State following such an inquiry that the church is of sufficient importance to be vested in the Churches Conservation Trust (formerly the Redundant Churches Fund) or, in cases where the recommendation was not that the building should go to the Trust, to make further efforts to find an alternative use and to engage in further consultation with the Secretary of State before using the Pastoral Measure powers to demolish. In considering what recommendation he will make, following a non-statutory inquiry, the Secretary of State will take into account the financial implications of retaining a church building as well as the architectural and historic interest of the church and other planning and social factors, and will consult the Secretary of State for National Heritage."[62]

The demolition of a listed church would normally only be carried out under a pastoral or redundancy scheme. If, however, (exceptionally) it were to be carried out under the faculty procedure,[63] it would not be within the exemption in section 60(7); nor would it be within the exemption in section 60(1), as the building would not be "used for ecclesiastical purposes". Listed building consent would therefore be required.

Also, perhaps surprisingly, it is only the *demolition* of a redundant church under the Pastoral Measure that is exempt from the need for listed building consent to be obtained. The alteration or extension of a redundant building, even as part of a scheme under the Measure, thus requires listed building consent. The distinction between "demolition" and "alteration" has been considered earlier[64]; and note that, since the decision of the House of Lords in *Shimizu (UK) Ltd v Westminster CC*,[65] works of "partial demolition" are properly categorised as "alteration", so that works to a listed building carried out under the Pastoral Measure are not exempt from the need for listed building consent unless they are for its total demolition.

16.3.9 The future of the ecclesiastical exemption

The ecclesiastical exemption was for many years derided by those who saw it as the churches effectively granting themselves permission to alter their own buildings, many of which were of considerable historic and architectural interest. The churches, by contrast saw the freedom from secular control as necessary to enable them to use their places of worship in the way that was most appropriate for worship and mission.[66]

As a result, the faculty system of the Church of England and the Church in Wales was amended significantly in the late 1980s to take account of conservation

---

[62] PPG 15, para.8.15.
[63] See **16.6.9**.
[64] See **12.6.3**.
[65] [1996] 3 P.L.R. 89, HL.
[66] The arguments were summarised in an article at [1985] J.P.L. 599.

concerns; and the exemption was in 1994 restricted to those denominations that had internal systems of control perceived to be adequate.[67] Dr John Newman was then appointed by the Government to review the whole issue; his report, published in 1997, recommended that the exemption should continue, but that the denominations concerned should be encouraged to improve their systems.[68]

The systems of all the exempt denominations have continued to be tightened up, and to give greater weight to heritage concerns, so that each is to a large extent now a relatively sophisticated control mechanism, providing an adequate alternative system of controlling works to places of worship of special interest.[69] Further, each of the various committees involved has available to it a wealth of specialist knowledge and experience that could not be matched by a planning authority. Mr Peter Howell carried out in 2004 for the Welsh Assembly Government a further review of the system as it operates in Wales[70]; many of his conclusions would apply equally to England.

In England, the DCMS published in February 2004 a consultation paper on *The Future of the Ecclesiastical Exemption*; and in July 2005 an analysis of the responses to that paper, *The Ecclesiastical Exemption: the Way Forward*. That set out the Government's view that:

- those denominations that currently operate their own systems of control over works to historic places of worship should continue to do so, with exemption from secular listed building control;

- the exemption will not be extended beyond those denominations; and

- the operation of the exemption will continue to be monitored periodically.

It also proposed the extension to ecclesiastical buildings, and in particular cathedrals and their precincts, of the heritage partnership agreement (HPA) approach being put forward for secular buildings[71]. It is far from clear how that would work in practice, but pilot projects are being implemented to enable best practice to be developed.

16.4 Conservation area consent

16.4.1 Ecclesiastical buildings in use

Conservation area consent is not needed, in principle, for the demolition of an unlisted ecclesiastical building if it is for the time being in use for ecclesiastical purposes[72]—the meaning of those terms has already been considered, in connection with the exemption from listed building consent.[73]

---

[67] See **16.3.2**.
[68] See the previous edition of this book, at 13.8.
[69] See **16.6** to **16.9**.
[70] Available on the Cadw website.
[71] See **Appendix G**.
[72] P(LBCA)A 1990, s.75(1)(b). [Scotland: P(LBCA)(S)A 1997, s.67(1)(b); NI: P(NI)O 1991, arts 44(8), 51(5).]
[73] See **16.3.1**.

As with listed buildings, however, the Secretary of State (or equivalent) has power[74] to make orders restricting the operation of the exemption from control to certain buildings or categories of building. Using that power, the Secretary of State has made the Ecclesiastical Exemption (Listed Buildings and Conservation Areas) Order 1994, to exempt ecclesiastical buildings in use in England and Wales from conservation area control in precisely the same circumstances as from listed building control.[75] No corresponding orders have yet been made in Scotland or Northern Ireland.

This exemption is actually now usually irrelevant in that, since the decision of the House of Lords in *Shimizu*, above, it is clear that conservation area consent is only required for the total (or near-total) demolition of the whole of a building—in which case, ecclesiastical use could not continue in any event. The partial demolition of an unlisted ecclesiastical building (of any denomination) in a conservation area thus does not need conservation area consent, not because of the ecclesiastical exemption, but because partial "demolition" (of any building) does not need consent anyway. The exemption might still apply, however, where a major part of the building is to be demolished, with ecclesiastical use continuing in what remains.

The removal of an unlisted building or structure (such as a funerary monument) in the curtilage of a place of worship in use by one of the exempt denominations is exempt from secular control by virtue of the 1994 Order.[76] And the removal of a post-1925 monument does not need conservation area consent, by virtue of the direction in Circular 01/01.[77] Consent will still be required for the removal of a pre-1925 monument if it is in the curtilage of a non-exempt place of worship, or in a cemetery not attached to a place of worship in use.

16.4.2 Redundant buildings

The total or partial demolition of buildings in conservation areas that are no longer in use for public worship does not come within the scope of the exemption, and the works will thus generally require consent.

As with listed buildings, however, consent is not required for the demolition of redundant buildings of the Church of England under the terms of the Pastoral Measure[78]—in this case, by virtue of the directions in Circular 01/01 and WO Circular 1/98.[79]

16.5 Archaeology

Before the birth of listing in its modern form, churches in use were at least to some extent exempt from the protection afforded to ancient monuments and archae-

---

[74] P(LBCA)A 1990, s.75(7),(8). [Scotland: P(LBCA)(S)A 1997, s.67(7),(8); NI: P(NI)O 1991, arts 44(9), 51(5).]
[75] SI 1994/177; see **16.3.2**.
[76] 1994 Order, art.5(1)9(d).
[77] Circ. 01/01, para.28(1)(a); WO Circ. 1/98, para.20(1)(a) (see **12.6.6**).
[78] See **16.10**.
[79] Envt Circ. 01/01, para.28(1)(k); WO Circ. 1/98, para.20(1)(k).

ological sites, in that the "ecclesiastical exemption" first surfaced in the context of the Ancient Monuments Act of 1913.[80] Even today the definition of monument specifically excludes "an ecclesiastical building in use for ecclesiastical purposes".[81]

There are however a number of examples of churches and churchyards, of all denominations but particularly within the Church of England, which contain objects and structures of considerable archaeological value—not least because churchyards will in many cases have been used for the same purpose for many centuries. Known sites within churchyards may be, and in some cases are, scheduled under the 1979 Act, and where work is proposed which would affect them, scheduled monument consent is needed just as in any other case[82]: there is no ecclesiastical exemption from that requirement.

In many other cases, archaeological sites are not scheduled, or are within or beneath a place of worship in use, and thus cannot be scheduled. In such cases, where planning permission is required for any works (such as for an extension to a church), the same principles apply as in other cases where development proposals have archaeological implications.[83] Where planning permission is not required (for example, for internal works) or is granted by the TCP (General Permitted Development) Order 1995 (such as for the digging of trenches for pipes and cables across churchyards), it is up to the relevant church authorities[84] to exercise control responsibly, after taking appropriate advice.

16.6 The faculty jurisdiction of the Church of England: procedures

16.6.1 Introduction

The most well-known of the internal systems of control operated by the various exempt denominations is the faculty system applying to most buildings of the Church of England.

The faculty jurisdiction has been in existence for many centuries. However, as a result of concern by the Church of England that it might lose the ecclesiastical exemption,[85] the procedures were significantly tightened up in 1993, so as to increase the weight given to aesthetic concerns, particularly in the case of places of worship which are listed or in conservation areas. Following the 1997 report by Dr John Newman on the ecclesiastical exemption generally, further changes were made to the arrangements relating to works to such buildings. It is therefore probably now true to say that the long-standing faculty jurisdiction is "more sophisticated" than the secular system of listed building control.[86]

---

[80] See **1.2.2**.
[81] AMAAAA 1979, s.61(7). For the meaning of the quoted phrase, see **16.3.1**.
[82] See **12.8.3**.
[83] See **14.8**.
[84] See **16.6** to **16.9**.
[85] See **16.3.9**.
[86] See the comments of Sir John Owen, Dean of the Arches, in *Re All Saints Melbourn* [1990] 1 W.L.R. 833 at 841A.

The basis of the faculty jurisdiction is now to be found largely in the Care of Churches and Ecclesiastical Jurisdiction Measure 1991, which almost entirely superseded the Faculty Jurisdiction Measure 1964. The detailed rules governing procedure are in the Faculty Jurisdiction Rules 2000, which came into force on January 1, 2001 (replacing the 1992 Rules of the same name).[87] In broad principle, all works to Church of England places of worship must be authorised either by the relevant archdeacon or by the chancellor of the diocese concerned, in either case on the advice of the diocesan advisory committee (the DAC).

The DAC is the body which provides advice to parishes, as well as to the bishop and the chancellor, on all matters relating to church buildings and churchyards. There are to be at least twelve members appointed in addition to the chairman and all the archdeacons in the diocese; of these, three are to be appointed after consultation with English Heritage, the national amenity societies[88] and the local authority associations. The members of the committee must between them have knowledge of, amongst other matters, the history, development and use of church buildings, architecture, archaeology, art and history, and experience of the care of historic buildings and their contents.[89]

In addition to parish churches, the faculty jurisdiction now also extends to buildings that have been included in the list maintained by the Council for the Care of Churches under the Care of Places of Worship Measure 1999.[90] The procedure governing applications for faculties in such cases will be governed by the Faculty Jurisdiction (Care of Places of Worship) Rules 2000,[91] which are in very similar terms to the general Faculty Rules.

The principles underlying the faculty system have been explained elsewhere.[92] The remainder of this section of this book merely highlights the features of the faculty procedure that are of particular relevance in the case of works to churches that are of special architectural, historic or archaeological interest. The matters to be taken into account in determining petitions for such works are considered in the following section.

Separate rules govern the procedure to be followed in the case of unauthorised works.[93]

---

[87] SI 2000/2047. It is these Rules that are referred to below as "the 2000 Rules". Measures and Rules approved by the General Synod of the Church of England have the same force as Acts of Parliament and SIs, and are published by and obtainable from the Stationery Office (and available on *www.opsi.gov.uk*).

[88] The Council for British Archaeology, the Georgian Group, the Society for the Protection of Ancient Buildings, the Victorian Society, and any other body designated by the Dean of the Arches (see 1991 Measure, s.31(1)). The corresponding definition in the 2000 Rules adds the Twentieth Century Society—which has been accepted as a statutory consultee for listed building consent applications since October 6, 2005 (see also **16.6.4**).

[89] 1991 Measure, Sch.1, para.4.

[90] See **16.3.5**.

[91] SI 2000/2048.

[92] See Mark Hill, *Ecclesiastical Law* (2nd ed., Oxford University Press, Oxford, 2001). There used to be a splendidly clear and practical *Code of Practice*, issued by Church House Publishing, containing much useful advice on best practice; sadly, it is now out of print, as is G. H. Newsom, *Faculty Jurisdiction of the Church of England*, (2nd ed., Sweet & Maxwell, London, 1993).

[93] The Faculty Jurisdiction (Injunctions and Restoration Orders) Rules 1992 (see **18.9**).

16.6.2 *Need for a faculty*

The requirement for a faculty to be obtained is basically a means of ensuring that the desirability of proposals for works to be carried out to churches is considered carefully, with due regard being paid both to the needs of the worshipping community and to the wider concerns of the public. A faculty is thus needed for all works of any consequence to:

(1) a Church of England parish church or its churchyard[94];

(2) any other consecrated building[95], including unconsecrated land within its curtilage[96];

(3) any building licensed for public worship before March 1, 1993 if it was brought within the faculty jurisdiction by the bishop[97];

(4) any building licensed for public worship after March 1, 1993 unless it has specifically been taken outside the faculty jurisdiction by the bishop[98]; and

(5) any building that has been the subject of a successful application to be included in the list maintained by the CCC under the Care of Places of Worship Measure 1999.[99]

The meaning of "curtilage" has been considered extensively earlier in this book; indeed, it is noteworthy that some of the cases cited there arose from applications for faculties.[1]

A faculty will also be required for the introduction or removal of fittings (which would not require listed building consent in the case of secular buildings). However, it will not be needed for minor works—a list of such works, sometimes referred to as the *de minimis* list, is prepared by the chancellor of each diocese.[2] In some cases, the archdeacon must first be notified. For details, the secretary of the relevant DAC should be consulted.

A faculty is not required for works to cathedrals, which are subject to the procedure under the Care of Cathedrals Measure 1990.[3] Also outside the faculty jurisdiction are works to other non-parochial buildings used for Church of England worship—such as those in ecclesiastical peculiars or religious communities, those within any university, college, school, hospital, almshouse, Inn of Court, or other public or charitable institution, and those subject to a sharing

---

[94]   1991 Measure, s.11(1).
[95]   *Re St John, Chelsea* [1962] 1 W.L.R. 706 (London Consistory Court) at 708.
[96]   1964 Measure, s.7.
[97]   1964 Measure, s.6(1), amended by 1991 Measure, Sch.7.
[98]   1991 Measure, s.11(2),(3).
[99]   See **16.3.5**.
[1]   *Pilbrow v Vestry of the Parish of St Leonard, Shoreditch* [1985] 1 Q.B. 433; *Vestry of St Martin's in the Fields v Bird* [1985] 1 Q.B. 428; *Re West Norwood Cemetery* [1994] Fam. 210 (Southwark Consistory Court) at 225F (see **4.5**).
[2]   1991 Measure, s.11(8). In practice, there is an increasing degree of standardisation as between the *de minmis* lists in different dioceses.
[3]   See **16.8.1**.

agreement under the Sharing of Church Buildings Act 1969—unless they have been included in the CCC list maintained under the 1999 Measure.

This means that virtually all Church of England buildings are within the faculty jurisdiction, including many that have in the past been treated as though they were exempt both from the faculty system (by custom) and from the secular system of listed building control (by virtue of the ecclesiastical exemption[4]). The normal faculty system thus controls works to all school and hospital chapels[5], all university and college chapels subject to the above exceptions, cemetery chapels (regardless of ownership[6]), and private chapels owned by unincorporated bodies.[7]

The requirement for a faculty applies to a place of worship that is listed or within a conservation area at least as much as in any other case—indeed, some of the items on the *de minimis* list do not apply in the case of works to such buildings.

16.6.3 Preliminary discussions with the diocesan advisory committee (DAC)

In order to ensure that proposed works are properly designed, particularly where they affect buildings of special interest, parishes should obtain proper design advice: "if a PCC has sufficient enthusiasm for a project to wish to obtain a faculty, then the reasonable cost of professional advice and assistance must be allowed for in the overall cost of the scheme."[8] They should also, where appropriate, consider documents such as English Heritage's policy statement *New Works in Historic Places of Worship*.[9] That statement also sensibly recommends that the starting point is to understand fully the architectural and historical significance of the building, and to identify carefully what are the needs of the worshipping community.

Parishes would also be well advised to consult the diocesan advisory committee (DAC) as early as possible—possibly while drawing up the brief to the architect. They are in any event required to seek the advice of the DAC before lodging a "petition" (application) for a faculty for any works.[10] They should provide the DAC with plans, photographs and other material necessary to explain what is intended; and where the proposal involves significant changes to a listed church, they should also submit:

- a statement of significance—a document that summarises the historical development of the building and identifies the important features that make major contributions to its character; and

---

4 See **16.3.2**.
5 See for example *Re Tonbridge School Chapel* [1993] 1 W.L.R. 1138 (Rochester Consistory Court) at 1142.
6 See *Re Dixon* [1892] P.386, *Re Coleford Cemetery* [1984] 1 W.L.R. 1369 and *Re West Norwood Cemetery* [1994] 3 W.L.R. 820 (Southwark Consistory Court).
7 *Sutton v Bowden* [1913] Ch.518.
8 *Re St George the Martyr, Holborn* (1997) 5 Ecc. L.J. 67 (London Consistory Court), *per* Cameron Ch.
9 See **16.2.2**.
10 2000 Rules, r.3(1).

- a statement of needs—a document that sets out the reasons why the needs of the parish cannot be met without making changes to the building and why those changes are necessary to the worship and mission of the church.

The preparation of these documents—the need for which was introduced for the first time in the 2000 Rules—will assist the parish as well as the DAC (and, in due course, the chancellor) to focus on the key issues. Guidance on the preparation of statements has been issued by many DACs.

The fact that the DAC contains a number of specialist members[11] ensures that the architectural and historic importance of a church is fully taken into account both in the drawing up of any scheme for its alteration and in any decision concerning its future. Frequently a proposal of any significance (particularly to a church that is listed or in a conservation area) will be the subject of extensive discussion, in order to iron out problems; the members of the DAC will between them have a great deal of experience of works to churches. Such consultations may take time; but the chancellor must not make a decision on a faculty petition without the advice of the DAC, except in emergency.[12]

In due course, the DAC will issue a certificate recommending the works to the chancellor or the archdeacon, or not recommending them, or (if it wishes to sit on the fence) simply not objecting to them.[13]

16.6.4 Discussions with heritage bodies and the planning authority

Parishes contemplating carrying out works are under a duty to consult English Heritage, the local planning authority and any relevant national amenity society in certain cases, set out at Appendix B to the 2000 Rules, at the same time as seeking the advice of the DAC[14]—although it must be questionable how far this requirement is observed in practice. Again, however, it is sensible to consult such bodies as early as possible, since they have a great deal of experience of works of this kind.

Thus, where proposed works involve the alteration of or extension to a listed church to such an extent as is likely to affect its character as a building of special architectural or historic interest, parishes should consult English Heritage. In relation to Grade I or II* buildings, even small alterations should be the subject of consultation; but in relation to Grade II buildings consultation is only required in the case of works involving the demolition or removal of all or a substantial part of the structure of the interior (such as a staircase, gallery, load-bearing wall, floor structure, roof structure, or major internal fixtures such as fixed pews, rood screen or organ).[15]

The local planning authority and any relevant national amenity society (depending on the age of the building) should also be consulted in relation to alterations and extension to listed churches (of whatever grade) likely to affect

[11] See **16.6.1**.
[12] 2000 Rules, r.14.
[13] As Form 1 in Appendix C to the 2000 Rules.
[14] 2000 Rules, Appendix B, para.1.
[15] 2000 Rules, Appendix B, para.1(a), 2(i),(ii).

their special character, where they involve the demolition or removal of all or a substantial part of the structure of the interior or the addition of a significant new element (such as the creation of a new space through sub-division).[16]

Where works are likely to affect the archaeological importance of a church or archaeological remains existing within the church or its curtilage, consultation should take place with English Heritage, the local planning authority and any relevant national amenity society (in practice, the Council for British Archaeology).[17]

Finally, where works involve "demolition affecting the exterior of an unlisted building in a conservation area", parishes should consult the local planning authority and any relevant national amenity society (depending on the age of the building), but not English Heritage.

Whether or not parishes do carry out such consultation, they will be advised by the DAC to do so in appropriate cases. Thus the certificate issued by the DAC will state whether or not it considers that some or all of the works or proposals.

> "(i) involve alteration of or extension to a listed church to such an extent as is likely to affect its character as a building of special architectural or historic interest, or
> (ii) are likely to affect the archaeological importance of the church or archaeological remains existing within the church or its curtilage;
> (iii) will involve demolition affecting the exterior of an unlisted building in a conservation area".[18]

It would seem to be no coincidence that the first of these uses the same words as are used as in section 7 of the Listed Buildings Act, which determines whether listed building consent is needed for works to a building other than one in ecclesiastical use.[18a] A DAC in its consideration of works to a listed place of worship should thus, in effect, consider whether they are such that, were the exemption not in place, they would require listed building consent. The third may have been intended to be the same as the test for whether conservation area consent is required, although it fails to take into account the consequences of *Shimizu UK Ltd v Westminster CC*.[19]

If the DAC considers that proposed works will have one or more of these effects, it will also recommend that the parish consult English Heritage, the local planning authority, the appropriate national amenity society, the CCC, or some other body or person. This is a very useful provision, as it will alert the parish to the need for such consultation at the earliest possible stage, so as to avoid intervention (and consequential delay) later on in the process, when everyone has become committed to a scheme. It also, incidentally, means that the national societies may be consulted on proposals for alterations and extensions, whereas in the case of secular buildings they are only required to be notified of proposals for demolition.[20]

---

[16] 2000 Rules, Appendix B, para.1(a), 3, 4, 5. As to the societies to be consulted, see **16.6.1**.
[17] 2000 Rules, Appendix B, para.1(b), 2(iii), 3, 4.
[18] 2000 Rules, Appendix C, Form 1; see **16.6.3**.
[18a] See **12.2.3**.
[19] [1996] 3 P.L.R. 89, HL; see **12.6**.
[20] See **13.5.6**.

Those bodies and persons being consulted in relation to a faculty petition (or prior to submission of one) should remember the general principle set out in s.1 of the Care of Churches and Ecclesiastical Jurisdiction Measure 1991:

"Any person or body carrying out functions of care and conservation under this Measure or under any other enactment or rule of law relating to churches shall have due regard to the role of a church as a local centre of worship and mission."

This certainly applies to diocesan advisory committees, and to the CCC. It arguably applies to the other consultees mentioned above. Note, however, that this is not stated to be a principle overriding all other considerations, merely a consideration which must be given "due" regard.[21]

As for the outcome of such consultations, this will often lead to a proposal being modified—the emergence of a scheme that gives the parish what it wants, whilst at the same time being sensitive to the character of the building concerned, is likely to be well worth the time and effort involved in negotiation. On the other hand, as emphasised by one chancellor,

"consultation must not be confused with subjugation. A parish should not feel obliged to take on board each and every comment from an amenity society or consultee. It should give them adequate weight, but should not incorporate every aspect of sometimes mutually contradictory advice, as a valid project may thereafter be compromised."[22]

16.6.5 Petition for a faculty

Once the views of the DAC have been obtained, a formal petition may be lodged with the diocesan registry. This must be accompanied by the appropriate form,[23] along with all necessary drawings, etc. to describe what is proposed. Where the building concerned is listed or in a conservation area, petitioners should bear in mind the observations of the chancellor in *Re St Mary's Banbury*:

"I am not prepared to grant the faculty on the basis of the plans and other material adduced at the hearing. This is a Grade A [now Grade I] listed building; and any proposal to alter the structure of such a building must be approached with the same care and be subject to the same detailed consideration as would be necessary if the churches were to lose their ecclesiastical immunity and if, therefore, this were an application for listed building consent under the Town and Country Planning Act 1971."[24]

Similarly, in considering a petition for a substantial re-ordering of a Grade II* listed church in London[25], the chancellor expressed sympathy with English Heritage, the Victorian Society and the Council for the Care of Churches, who had been hampered in their consideration of parts of the scheme by the lack of detailed plans. She stated:

"Whilst I fully understand the need for prudence in relation to spending the limited resources usually available to a PCC, I regard the approach which was adopted here as a

---

[21]   *Re St Luke the Evangelist, Maidstone* [1995] Fam. 1, Court of Arches, at 7E.
[22]   *Re St Mary Magdalene and St Denys, Midhurst* (2002) 6 Ecc. L.J. 99. And see **16.7.4**.
[23]   2000 Rules, Appendix C, Form 2.
[24]   [1985] 2 All E.R. 611 (Oxford Consistory Court), *per* Boydell Ch at 618. He went on to direct that a further and more detailed petition be submitted.
[25]   *Re St George the Martyr, Holborn* (1997) 5 Ecc. L.J. 67 (London Consistory Court), *per* Cameron Ch.

false economy. A scheme such as that originally proposed in this case, involving alteration to the fabric and furnishings of a listed church, requires to be properly prepared by an architect or surveyor, so that all bodies which have a legitimate concern about the proposal can see exactly what is involved. Far from arousing opposition, such plans are likely to alleviate concern. In addition, they form the basis for a dialogue between an experienced church architect or surveyor and the bodies concerned with conservation, which frequently, in my experience, can result in some variation being agreed, which will meet the conservation objection whilst at the same time still preserving the substance of the petitioner's works.

For the benefit of other parishes in the future, I make it quite clear that plans in support of a major scheme of alteration of a listed church will have to be prepared in sufficient detail to enable me, and the bodies concerned with conservation, to understand easily what the details of the proposed works are."

As for what needs to be included, other than drawings and other material sufficient to describe what is proposed, the courts have consistently maintained that the onus of proving the need for any proposal and its appropriateness lies on the petitioner; see, for example, the authoritative decision in *Peek v Trower*,[26], which long predates the listing system. This means that, where there is a dispute either as to the need for proposed works or as to their effect, more information will be required—and the more important the church, or the more major the alterations to it, the greater will be the need for supporting evidence.[27] Otherwise, the same material will be required as for the initial discussions with the DAC— obviously modified as seems appropriate in the light of those discussions.

At the same time as lodging the petition, the petitioners must for 28 days display a public notice describing the proposed works and explaining that representations may be made to the registrar.[28]

16.6.6 Determination of petitions: procedure

Petitions for faculties are determined either by the chancellor or, where they are for relatively minor matters, the archdeacon.[29] The archdeacon may, in particular, not determine a faculty for works falling within rule 13(3)—that is, works that involve alteration to or extension of a listed church to such an extent as is likely to affect its character as a building of special architectural or historic interest, or are likely to affect the archaeological importance of the church or archaeological remains existing within the church or its curtilage, or involve demolition affecting the exterior of an unlisted church in a conservation area.[30] It is partly for this reason that the DAC is required to certify whether works come within those categories.[31]

In addition to the general public notice, the chancellor may in addition direct that particular people or organisations should be specially cited, or other publicity given. This could apply where, for example, he or she is aware that a local amenity group has been actively involved in the formulation of the proposals, or is known

---

[26] (1881) 7 P.D. 21 at 27.
[27] *Re St Paul the Apostle* (2000) 6 Ecc. L.J. 162 (Wakefield Consistory Court).
[28] 2000 Rules, Appendix C, Form 3.
[29] 2000 Rules, Appendix A.
[30] 2000 Rules, rr 7(1), 9(1)(a), 10(1)(c).
[31] See **16.6.3**.

to have strong views (either for or against). Where proposals fall within rule 13(3), the chancellor must direct that English Heritage, the local planning authority and any appropriate national amenity society[32] should be specially notified, unless they are known to have been notified of the proposal already (as they should have been[33]), and have no further comment.[34] However, this should not often be necessary, as intending petitioners should have consulted the relevant bodies before submitting the faculty and, even if they have not, they should have been reminded to do so by the DAC.[35]

Further, where the works are likely to affect the character of Grade I or II* building, or to involve demolition of the exterior of an unlisted building in a conservation area, the petition must be advertised in the local press.[36]

16.6.7 Responses to notification and publicity

Following the consultation and notification, all who wish may then make representations for or against the proposal. Those who have been specifically notified have 28 days to respond. In practice, all those who respond before the actual decision is made will probably have their representations taken into account. Since 2000, it has been possible for those making written representations to have them taken into account by the chancellor, without the need for giving oral evidence in the event of a hearing.[37]

The following are entitled to object to any proposal:

(1) a person living in the parish or on the church electoral roll;

(2) the archdeacon;

(3) the parochial church council;

(4) the local planning authority;

(5) any national amenity society, whether or not it has been specially notified of the proposal; and

(6) anyone else known to the chancellor to have an interest in the proposals (for example, a local amenity society).[38]

The local planning authority for these purposes is the authority which is responsible for the exercise of listed building control under the 1990 Act.[39] This will generally be the district or borough council[40]; but where there is more another

---

[32] See **16.6.1**. For this purpose, the national amenity societies include the Twentieth Century Society (see 2000 Rules, r.1).

[33] See **16.6.3**.

[34] r.13(3).

[35] See **16.6.3**.

[36] r.13(4).

[37] r.16(3)–(5).

[38] r.16(1),(2).

[39] 1991 Measure, s.31(1).

[40] See **13.2.1**.

public authority interested (such as a county council or national park authority), it would presumably be able to appear on the same basis as a local society.

This gives a good opportunity for those—such as the local planning authority—concerned as to the architectural or historic interest of a place of worship or its surroundings to ensure that their views are properly aired, either in writing or, if they feel strongly enough, at an oral hearing. Indeed, with the enhanced role now given to amenity societies, English Heritage and, more especially, local planning authorities, it is surprising that their involvement in the faculty process has not been greater. But it is important for those (such as planning authorities and amenity groups) wishing to be involved actively in the decision-making process to have in place a system to enable them to respond promptly to petitions, and to present considered representations (in support or opposition) as appropriate. And where such bodies support a proposal, that may outweigh widespread local opposition in the form of a petition.[41]

Faculty proceedings are almost always determined upon the basis of written representations,[42] but this procedure is unlikely to be appropriate in a case involving major alterations to a listed building, or where there are objections on aesthetic grounds.[43] Indeed, one advantage of the faculty procedure, as compared with applications for planning permission or listed building consent, is that objectors are entitled to insist upon an oral hearing. On the other hand, there is a slight risk that objectors considered to have behaved unreasonably may be penalised by having to pay the petitioners' costs.[44]

In any case where it has been specially cited under rule 13(3), and in any other case where it applies to the registrar, English Heritage has a right to give evidence at the hearing, as a judge's witness, without being formally made a party to the proceedings.[45] This has the advantage that it is not at risk as to costs. The same principle applies to the CCC, which is required to be notified by the registrar of any proposal involving any building or article of historic or artistic interest.[46]

A faculty may be refused or granted, possibly subject to conditions—including as to the subsequent approval of details, which may be particularly appropriate in the case of more sensitive buildings or larger schemes. Where a large programme of works is envisaged, it may be appropriate to grant a faculty for the whole, subject to each phase being the subject of a further and more detailed petition.[47]

16.6.8 Overlap with other controls

Where works affect the exterior of a building, planning permission will be required and, exceptionally, where the exemption does not apply (for example, in

---

[41] *Re St Augustine, Scissett* (2004) 7 Ecc. L.J. 495 (Liverpool Consistory Court).

[42] r.26.

[43] *Re St James, New Malden* [1994] Fam. 44 (Southwark Consistory Court) at pp.47–48.

[44] See, for example, *Re All Saints, Small Heath* (1998) 5 Ecc. L.J. 211 (Birmingham Consistory Court). Costs are more generally dealt with in *Re St Mary, Sherborne* [1996] Fam. 63 (Court of Arches).

[45] r.24.

[46] rr 15, 23.

[47] *Re Holy Cross, Pershore* [2002] Fam. 1, 6 Ecc. L.J. 86 (Worcester Consistory Court); *Re St Paul, Birkenshaw* (2001) 6 Ecc. L.J. 170 (Wakefield Consistory Court).

the case of some structures in the churchyards), listed building consent or conservation area consent may be needed as well. Where a church grant has been given in the past by English Heritage, its consent may be required too—even for works that would otherwise be within the exemption.[48] Applicants have been advised that, in such cases, these other approvals should be obtained before a faculty is applied for[49]—so that, if alterations have to be made, there will be no need to apply for a further faculty for the works as thus amended.

The same logic would of course apply the other way—so that, if the diocesan advisory committee or the chancellor seeks amendments before a faculty will be granted, further consent may be required from the secular authorities. However, in practice, it is normal for the chancellor to decline to grant a faculty until the secular authorities are satisfied with a proposal.

16.6.9 Faculties for demolition

The demolition of a church will normally be authorised under a pastoral or redundancy scheme, under the Pastoral Measure 1983, rather than by a faculty.[50] The procedure under the 1983 Measure may also be suitable for a proposal to demolish a church that is listed or in a conservation area, in order to test whether demolition could be avoided by finding an alternative use for the building or (exceptionally) vesting it in the Churches Conservation Trust.[51]

A faculty may, however, be granted for the total or partial demolition of a church where a new church will take the place of the demolished building or part[52]; and for partial demolition where the part left standing will still be used for Church of England worship.[53] As to the distinction between "demolition" and "alteration" in this context, see *Re St James, Callow End*[54]; and note that the principles in *Shimizu (UK) Ltd v Westminster CC*[55] should here be applied with caution, since section 17 of the Measure, unlike the Listed Buildings Act, specifically refers to "demolition or partial demolition".

Where a church that is listed or in a conservation area is to be demolished in reliance on the procedure under section 17(2) or section 17(3)(a), the diocesan registrar must give notice to the Secretary of State, the local planning authority, English Heritage and the national amenity societies[56]; and the chancellor must then consider any advice tendered by those consulted.[57] If a faculty is granted, the Measure provides that the Royal Commission on Historical Monuments must be given at least a month's notice of the works, to enable it to record the building or part before it is demolished.[58] Following the abolition of the Royal Commission,

---

[48] See **9.4.5**.
[49] *Code of Practice* (see **16.6.1**), para.133.
[50] See **16.10**.
[51] *Code of Practice* (see 16.6.1), para.190.
[52] 1991 Measure, s.17(2).
[53] s.17(3)(a).
[54] [2001] 1 W.L.R. 835 (Worcester Consistory Court).
[55] [1996] 3 P.L.R. 89 (see **12.6.3**).
[56] See **16.6.1**.
[57] s.17(5)(a), (b); 1992 Rules, r.12(7).
[58] s.17(5)(c).

notice should presumably now be given to English Heritage instead—as with the grant of listed building consent for demolition.[59]

In addition, a faculty may be granted for partial demolition where it is necessary for the repair or alteration of the church or the reconstruction of the part demolished.[60] If a church that is listed or in a conservation area is to be demolished for this reason, the requirements described in the previous paragraph must be complied with unless the chancellor is satisfied, after consulting the diocesan advisory committee, that the demolition will not materially affect the external or internal appearance of the church or its architectural, archaeological, artistic or historic character.[61] These requirements are of course additional to those that apply in the case of any petition for a faculty.[62]

The points which should be addressed in any report prepared in connection with a petition under section 17 were considered in *Re St Barnabas Dulwich*,[63] and summarised as follows:

"(1) the needs of the parish (in terms of its pastoral role);
(2) the architectural or historic importance of the building to be demolished, particularly where the building is listed or in a conservation area;
(3) its contribution, if any, to the area in which it stands;
(4) the cost of restoration, and the sources from which that could be raised; and
(5) the extent to which it would be possible to restore the church to its previous appearance."[64]

The total or partial demolition of a church may in any event only be authorised by a faculty where the bishop has given his written approval; and any such proposal must be publicised in the *London Gazette* and in the local press, and the diocesan advisory committee and the Council for the Care of Churches must be informed.[65]

Note that, where the total demolition of a church that is listed or in a conservation area is carried out relying on a faculty rather than a scheme under the 1983 Measure,[66] listed building consent or conservation area consent will be required.[67]

Where all or part of a church has to be demolished in the interests of safety or health or in the interests of the preservation of the building, and where there is no time to obtain a faculty, the chancellor may authorise the necessary works in writing, without going through the faculty procedure.[68] Where the church is listed or in a conservation area, the chancellor must be satisfied that:

---

[59] See **13.7.10**
[60] s.17(3)(b).
[61] s.17(6).
[62] See **16.6.5**.
[63] [1994] Fam. 124 (Southwark Consistory Court).
[64] At p.133A. See also *Re All Saints, Elland* (1999) Ecc. L.J. 390 (Wakefield Consistory Court).
[65] s.17(4).
[66] See **16.10**.
[67] See **16.3.8** and **16.4.2**.
[68] 1991 Measure, s.18(1); see *Re Christchurch Sparkbrook*, October 10, 2005 (unreported, transcript available on Lawtel) (Birmingham Consistory Court) (demolition of unlisted church authorised following damage by tornado).

(1) it is not possible to achieve the same object by means of carrying out repairs or providing temporary support or shelter; and

(2) the works to be carried out are limited to the minimum measures immediately necessary.[69]

The chancellor's approval may require the carrying out of restoration works. It will in any event require the local planning authority to be informed in writing of the works carried out; and the approval must itself be sent to the authority, and to the CCC.[70] These requirements echo those under section 9(3) of the Listed Buildings Act.[71] However, this procedure is highly exceptional; and the planning authority should, if at all possible, be consulted before any works are carried out.[72]

16.6.10 Appeals

Following the decision of the consistory court, either the petitioners or any of the objectors may appeal:

(1) in a case involving a question of doctrine, ritual or ceremonial, to the Court of Ecclesiastical Causes Reserved; or

(2) in any other case, to the Arches Court of Canterbury or the Chancery Court of York, as appropriate.

The relevant procedures are in the Faculty Jurisdiction (Appeals) Rules 1998.[73] There is provision for English Heritage, any of the national amenity societies or the local planning authority to be notified of an appeal, regardless of whether it was a party at the consistory court.[74] Further, any of those bodies may in exceptional circumstances be heard at an appeal—but only with the leave of the relevant appeal court.[75]

16.7 The faculty system: matters to be considered

16.7.1 Significance of a church being listed

The general principles of administrative law underlying to the making of any decision have been considered briefly in the context of applications for planning permission and listed building consent.[76] They apply equally to the granting or withholding of faculties. A chancellor (or archdeacon) must thus take into account anything that is relevant, and disregard whatever is irrelevant. In particular, he or she should pay due regard to the role of a church as a local centre of

---

[69] s.18(1)(b).
[70] s.18(2), (3).
[71] See **12.4.7, 12.6.8** and **19.4.2**.
[72] *Code of Practice* (see **6.6.1**), para.214.
[73] SI 1998/1713.
[74] Appeals Rules, r.7(4).
[75] Appeals Rules, r.14.
[76] *Associated Provincial Picture Houses v Wednesbury Corpn* [[1948] 1 K.B. 223 (see **14.1.1**).

worship and mission—the duty under section 1 of the 1991 Measure, perhaps surprisingly, does not directly apply to chancellors; but the Court of Arches has observed that, even if it had applied, it would have added nothing to their existing duty and practice.[77]

There are no other statutory duties laid upon those determining faculty petitions; but there has been a great deal of case law. In particular, where a place of worship is listed, the fact of the listing will be extremely relevant. This has been considered in a number of cases in the Church's Appeal Courts.[78]

In the first, *Re St Mary's Banbury*,[79] the Court of Arches (the appellate court from consistory courts in almost all cases) considered the relevant principles and stated that a faculty for works which would affect the character of a listed church as such should only be granted in wholly exceptional circumstances, which show clearly the necessity for such a change. The reference to "proved necessity" in *Banbury* was criticised in the second case, *Re St Stephen's Wallbrook*,[80] by the Court of Ecclesiastical Causes Reserved, since no such concept appeared in the secular legislation relating to listed building consent. The latter court, however, hears only appeals in cases involving doctrine or ceremonial, and its decisions are thus strictly binding only in the very rare cases of that kind. The Court of Arches noted that criticism when it next considered the matter, in *Re All Saints, Melbourn*,[81] but modified its stance only slightly, to the effect that a faculty should be granted only in wholly exceptional circumstances for works which *adversely* affected the character of a listed church.

In the light of those authorities, the matter was then considered by the London Consistory Court in *Re St Helen's, Bishopsgate*.[82] She identified three questions to be addressed by the court in a case involving a listed building:

"(1) Have the petitioners proved a necessity for some or all of the proposed works, either because they are necessary for the pastoral well-being of St Helen's or for some other compelling reason?
(2) Will some or all of the works adversely affect the character of the church as a building of special architectural interest?
(3) If the answer to (2) is yes, then is the necessity proved by the petitioners such that, in the exercise of the court's discretion, a faculty should be granted for some or all of the works?"

16.7.2 The decisions in St Luke's, Maidstone and Sherborne Abbey

The Court of Arches has issued two leading judgments on the matter of works to listed churches, in *Re St Luke's, Maidstone*[83] and *Re St Mary, Sherborne*.[84]

---

[77] *Re St Luke the Evangelist, Maidstone* [1995] Fam. 1 (Court of Arches) at 7A,D. See **16.7.2**.
[78] See **16.6.10**.
[79] [1987] (Court of Arches) Fam. 136.
[80] [1987] (CECR) Fam. 146.
[81] [1990] 1 W.L.R. 833 (Court of Arches).
[82] 1993, unreported (London Consistory Court).
[83] [1995] Fam. 1 (Court of Arches).
[84] [1996] Fam. 63 (Court of Arches).

The appeal in *Maidstone* related to a proposal for a major re-ordering of the interior of a Grade II listed church which had been turned down by the commissary-general (the equivalent of the chancellor in the Diocese of Canterbury). The dispute was concerned, in the words of the judgment, with:

"...two potentially conflicting and, from the viewpoint of the proponents, perfectly valid arguments. The first is that a church is the House of God, and that any alteration which is seen by the incumbent and congregation to be desirable in order to encourage and assist true worship should be permitted without outside restraint. The second is that most of the churches in this land are national treasures of which the present incumbent and the present congregation are merely temporary occupiers and custodians with no right to make unnecessary or, as some would seem to argue, any alterations."[85]

In the most important passage of the judgment, the court then held as follows:

"As the newly constituted Arches Court, we hope it may be helpful if we set out certain guidelines, emphasising that they are not rules of law but guidance designed to assist chancellors in arriving at decisions in cases where there are valid but clearly conflicting interests and arguments ... We consider that, in deciding upon alterations to a church, a chancellor should have in mind that:

(i) the persons most concerned with worship in a church are those who worship there regularly, although other members of the church who are not regular worshippers may also be concerned.

(ii) where a church is listed, there is a strong presumption against change which would adversely affect its character as a building of special architectural or historic interest. In order to rebut that presumption, there must be evidence of sufficient weight to show a necessity for such a change for some compelling reason, which could include the pastoral well-being of the church.

(iii) whether a church is listed or not, a chancellor should always have in mind not only the religious interest but also the aesthetic, architectural and communal interests relevant to the church in question.

(iv) although the present and future needs of worshippers must be given proper weight, a change which is permanent and cannot be reversed is to be avoided wherever possible."[86]

The court also commended the approach of the chancellor in *Re St Helen's, Bishopsgate*,[87] set out above. As a result, what have gradually become known as "the *Bishopsgate* questions" have been since then applied by all chancellors, albeit with differing degrees of emphasis.[88]

In that case, on its facts, the refusal at first instance was overturned, and a faculty granted subject to a condition that the pews should be retained until a new home for them could be found; in the event, that proved to be impossible, and a further faculty was therefore granted for their disposal.[89]

The *Bishopsgate* formulation was re-visited two years later by the Court of Arches, in relation to a proposal to replace the Victorian west window of Sherborne Abbey (listed Grade I) with a more modern one. The Court first considered the question of "necessity":

---

[85] [1995] Fam. 1 at p4E.

[86] p.8B.

[87] 1993, unreported (see **16.7.1**).

[88] See **16.7.3**.

[89] *Re St Luke, Maidstone (No. 2)* (1998) 5 Ecc. L.J. 131 (Canterbury Commissary Court).

"The word 'necessity' has caused some trouble mainly because it has an objective and compulsive element. It is possible to argue that, if a change is necessary, it is a change which must be allowed, no matter what objections there may be. However, we believe that in using this word in the context of there being three relevant questions, we are not indicating an absolute; we are indicating the approach which a responsible Church must have to listed buildings. The presumption is that there shall be no change."[90]

The Court re-emphasised that presumption, in considering the order of the questions posed in *St Helen, Bishopsgate*:

"It might be said that logic demands that [the effect of the works on the character of the church] should be the first question, with the present first question only being asked if this second question is answered in the affirmative. However, we do not accept this comment, as by the questions and their order we wish to stress the fact that, with listed buildings, the presumption is so strongly in favour of no alteration that the first question which must be asked is: are the alterations necessary? The present order of questions emphasises that for listed buildings the presumption is heavily against change. To change the order of questions would, we believe, cause confusion and might seem to some to indicate a relaxation of the requirements before change will be authorised. No such relaxation is intended or desired by this court."[91]

This is if anything an even more stringent test than that applying to proposals for works to secular listed buildings: PPG 15 states that applicants must show why works which would affect the character of a listed building are desirable or necessary,[92] which effectively reverses the order of the first two questions.

16.7.3 The application of the Bishopsgate test in the consistory courts

The approach outlined in *St Helen, Bishopsgate*, and approved by the Court of Arches in *Maidstone* and *Sherborne*, has now been applied by diocesan chancellors in numerous subsequent decisions. Each of those is strictly binding only in relation to the diocese where it was made but—in so far as it deals with a point of principle rather than simply turning on its own facts—will generally be followed in others.[93] Such decisions should thus be treated with caution, but may be useful to refer to, particularly where works are proposed affecting specific items.

The meaning of "necessity" in the *Bishopsgate* formula, highlighted in *Sherborne*, was considered again in *Re St John the Evangelist*, where the chancellor concluded that it meant:

"something less than essential, but more than merely desirable or convenient; in other words, something that is requisite or reasonably necessary."[94]

---

[90] [1996] Fam. 63 (Court of Arches) at p.77C.
[91] [1996] Fam. 63 at p.77H.
[92] PPG 15, para.3.4.
[93] Decisions of the consistory courts are now regularly summarised in the Ecclesiastical Law Journal (Ecc. L.J.), available from the Editor at 1 The Sanctuary, London SW1P 3JT (tel 020 7222 5381); index available at *www.ecclawsoc.org.uk*. Transcripts of decisions of the consistory courts are available in the Middle Temple Library.
[94] (1998) 5 Ecc. L.J. 217 (Southwark Consistory Court), following *Sharkey v Secretary of State* [1992] 2 P.L.R. 11, CA at p.19.

This has been followed in some cases[95], but was criticised in *Re Dorchester Abbey* for failing to stress that there must be a "compelling" reason for change in order for it to be sanctioned.[96]

One factor in assessing the necessity for proposed works will be the pastoral well-being of the parish; but this should not necessarily be paramount.[97] Another issue that may often be relevant will be the duty of the parish, as a service provider under the terms of the Disability Discrimination Act 1995, to adapt a place of worship to accommodate the needs of disabled people.[98]

The effect of proposed works on the character of a place of worship as a building of special architectural or historic interest will be assessed just as it would in the case of an application for listed building consent affecting any other building type. As it was put in one recent case:

"There is thus no requirement in law either that a church should be maintained for all time in the state in which it happens to be at present, or that it should automatically be changed in accordance with the latest liturgical fashion. That applies irrespective of whether the church is listed, or is objectively of any particular special architectural or historic interest, since many otherwise unremarkable churches are nevertheless of great concern to those who worship in or visit them. It does however apply just as much to those churches that are of special interest; and it is unfortunate that many seem to believe sincerely that it is reasonable to fight to retain every shred of evidence of numerous past alterations, whilst resisting equally strongly any future changes. Just as history did not stop in the reign of Edward VII, no more did it stop yesterday, and it is important that those responsible for churches do not neglect their responsibilities to future generations to create something that they will be able to value as their heritage."[99]

The problem with the *Bishopsgate* questions, and more especially the order in which they are posed, is that they seem to rule out alterations to places of worship that are considered to be desirable, possibly highly desirable, but which could not on any basis be said to be "necessary". This was considered—in relation to millennium windows—in *Re St Gregory Offchurch*, in which the chancellor effectively reversed the order of the first two questions, by asking first whether the proposed new window adversely affected the character of the building.[100] Some chancellors have since then followed that approach in relation to works to listed buildings generally, whilst emphasising that they are not in any way seeking to undermine the presumption against change to listed churches.[1]

---

[95] *Re Holy Cross, Pershore* [2002] Fam. 1, 6 Ecc. L.J. 86 (Worcester Consistory Court) at para.78; *Re St Paul, Birkenshaw* (2001) 6 Ecc. L.J. 170 (Wakefield Consistory Court).

[96] (2002) 7 Ecc. L.J. 105 (Oxford Consistory Court). See also *Re St Mary the Virgin, Essendon* (2001) 6 Ecc. L.J. 415 (St Albans Consistory Court).

[97] *Re Holy Cross, Pershore* at para.86 (doubted in *Re Wadsley Parish Church* (2001) 6 Ecc. L.J. 172 (Sheffield Consistory Court) and *Re St Mary, Longstock* (2005, unreported, Chichester Consistory Court)).

[98] *Re Holy Cross, Pershore* at paras 98–106; *Re Dorchester Abbey*. See also **14.4.10**.

[99] *Re Holy Cross, Pershore* at para.75.

[100] [2001] 1 W.L.R. 2471, 4 All E.R. 378 (Coventry Consistory Court).

[1] *Re St Thomas, Stourbridge* (2001, unreported) (Worcester Consistory Court), followed in *Re St Peter, Walworth* (2002) 7 Ec LJ 103 (Southwark Consistory Court); *Re All Saints, Crondall* (2002) 6 Ecc. L.J. 420 (Guildford Consistory Court); *Re Dorchester Abbey*; and *Re St Mary, Longstock* (2005, unreported, Chichester Consistory Court).

Some petitions have thus failed due to the inability on the part of the parish to prove sufficiently the necessity for proposed works that were found to have had an adverse effect on the character of the building concerned. A classic example is the recent decision to refuse a faculty for a timber platform at the chancel arch of a Grade I church in Somerset to accommodate a nave altar—the parish was far from unanimously in support of the proposal, and the heritage bodies were all in opposition.[2] Other cases have involved the removal of part of a magnificent rood screen, the main feature of the original design of a church in Newquay now listed Grade II*,[3] and an oak screen from the entrance to a chancel, because it was an integral part of the beauty of a church in Kirkby-in-Ashfield, listed Grade II.[4] The same test was held to apply to the disposal of surplus items, removed earlier; merely because they are gathering dust in a corner does not justify their removal.[5]

On the other hand, in *Re St Peter and St Paul, River*,[6] a faculty was granted for a substantial extension to a Grade II listed church and the re-ordering of the interior, following a grant of planning permission in spite of local objection, since the parish had proved the necessity for the works, and that they would not adversely affect the church as a building of special interest. Necessity was also found to have been proved in relation to a proposal to remove a screen from a church in Sussex, although the chancellor also noted that the screen was not in its original position, nor all of one date.[7]

The above considerations have generally been applied hitherto to cases relating to works to the interior of places of worship, which require a faculty but not listed building consent. They have also been accepted as being correct also for cases affecting the exterior, such as extensions.[8] That in turn suggests that they would presumably also apply, although no doubt with less weight, to cases relating to unlisted churches in conservation areas—although probably not where the proposed works affected only the interior of a church.

Finally, where a building having been substantially damaged by a fire, the effect of a proposal should be assessed in relation to the building as it now exists, rather than as it was previously.[9]

16.7.4 Other factors

In a number of cases, where planning permission has been granted (for external works) in spite of local opposition, chancellors have been unmoved by objectors

---

[2] *Re St Andrew, Banwell*, unreported 2006 (Bath and Wells Consitory Court).
[3] *Re St Michael the Archangel, Newquay* (1995) 4 Ecc. L.J. 526 (Truro Consistory Court).
[4] *Re St Wilfrid, Kirkby-in-Ashfield* (1995) 4 Ecc. L.J. 604 (Southwell Consistory Court).
[5] *Re St Peter, Great Berkhamsted* (2000) 6 Ecc. L.J. 165 (St Albans Consistory Court).
[6] (1997) 5 Ecc. L.J. 130 (Canterbury Commissary Court).
[7] *Re St Peter, Ardingly* (1999) 5 Ecc. L.J. 386 (Chichester Consistory Court). See also *Re St Nicholas, Kenilworth* (2003) 7 Ecc. L.J. 492 (Coventry Consistory Court).
[8] *Re St Mary, St Giles and All Saints, Canwell* (1997) 5 Ecc. L.J. 71 (Lichfield Consistory Court).
[9] *re Tonbridge School Chapel* [1993] 1 W.L.R. 1138, at p.1144 (Rochester Consistory Court).

maintaining their opposition in the consistory court, and have granted a faculty.[10] That approach was followed in *Re St Laurence, Alvechurch*, a case involving the construction of an extension to a church that was both listed and in a conservation area, and thus required planning permission.[11] The scheme had been supported by all the statutory consultees, and planning permission had been granted, in spite of local opposition. The chancellor held that it should be assumed in such cases that the local planning authority in granting permission had had regard to the desirability of preserving the building and the character of the area, and that its decision on such matters should therefore generally be followed—unless there was convincing evidence to the contrary, or the building had been listed since the decision of the planning authority, or there were issues relating to the junction of the new and old work.

The views of the various bodies that have to be consulted will always be taken into account. Thus, for example, where the Georgian Group strongly opposed the introduction of an unsuitable lighting scheme into a Grade I church, and the chancellor agreed.[12] In another scheme, by contrast, an objector considered that the furnishings in a church were important, but English Heritage, specially notified, considered that the building (by a prominent Arts and Crafts architect) was special, but not outstanding, and that the proposal to alter the furnishings was on balance unobjectionable; a faculty was accordingly granted, on condition that the furnishings were kept so that the alterations could one day be reversed.[13] And in some cases the consultees may not agree on the desired outcome, in which case the chancellor cannot please everyone.[14]

Sometimes, however, the most appropriate solution will be a compromise. Thus, where a Victorian church (listed Grade II) needed re-roofing, the planning authority wanted to see the existing tiles reused. In the event, the chancellor considered that the salvaged tiles were unsuitable; but that clay tiles would be better than the modern concrete tiles preferred by the parish, and not too much more expensive in view of the significant improvement in the end result.[15] It may therefore be helpful for objectors to a scheme to promote an alternative, so that the court can consider all of the possible options, rather than simply refuse one.[16] On the other hand, such compromise may be unsatisfactory—as where the planning authority insisted on the retention of a tower following a disastrous fire that destroyed the remainder of a church; the resulting scheme seemed to satisfy no-one.[17]

---

[10] *Re Holy Trinity, Louth* (1996) 4 Ecc. L.J. 763 (Lincoln Consistory Court); *Re St Mary, St Giles and All Saints, Canwell* (1997) 5 Ecc. L.J. 71 (Lichfield Consistory Court); *Re St Peter and St Paul, River* (1997) 5 Ecc. L.J. 130 (Canterbury Commissary Court); *Re St Mary, King's Worthy* (1998) 5 Ecc. L.J. 133 (Winchester Consistory Court); *Re St James, Stalmine* (2000) 6 Ecc. L.J. 81 (Blackburn Consistory Court).

[11] (2003) *The Times*, September 4 (Worcester Consistory Court); see also *Re All Saints Hordle* (2002) 6 Ecc. L.J. 238 (Winchester Consistory Court).

[12] *St Peter, Horbury* (1995) 4 Ecc. L.J. 684 (Wakefield Consistory Court).

[13] *Re St Agnes, Moseley* (1996) 4 Ecc. L.J. 685 (Birmingham Consistory Court).

[14] *Re Holy Trinity, Louth* (1996) 4 Ecc. L.J. 763 (Lincoln Consistory Court).

[15] *Re St Matthias, Hanford* (1995) 4 Ecc. L.J. 607 (Lichfield Consistory Court).

[16] As in *Re Holy Cross, Pershore* [2002] Fam. 1 (Worcester Consistory Court).

[17] *Re Holy Trinity, Louth* (1996) 4 Ecc. L.J. 763 (Lincoln Consistory Court).

Particular problems may arise in relation to the removal of valuable works of art from places of worship, generally alleged to be necessary for reasons of security. This as considered in *Re St Peter, Racton*, where a faculty was not granted for the removal of a marble bust by Rysbrack, on the grounds that it could be more securely fixed to the monument of which it formed part, and that a resin replica would discolour over time.[18] The introduction of works of art, on the other hand, should generally be allowed, provided that it does not adversely affect the structure of the church.[19]

Floodlighting is an example of a category of proposal that generally does require a faculty, even though the secular courts have accepted that it does not require planning permission. In a number of instances it leads to opposition from those living nearby, but it has usually been allowed, as an enhancement to the building.[20]

16.8 Buildings of the Church of England outside the faculty jurisdiction

16.8.1 Cathedrals

The cathedrals of the Church of England are among the finest historic buildings in the world but, as ecclesiastical buildings in ecclesiastical use, they were (and are) exempt from listed building control[21]; and they are not subject to faculty control either. Works to them were accordingly not subject to any form of supervision by any outside body. This was altered in 1991, with the coming into effect of the Care of Cathedrals Measure 1990, which provided for the establishment of a Cathedrals Fabric Commission, a national body, and a fabric advisory committee for each cathedral.[22] Each body is to include representatives of particular experience and learning.

That Measure has since been amended by the Care of Cathedrals (Supplementary Provisions) Measure 1994 and the Care of Cathedrals (Amendment) Measure 2005—the latter to be brought into force during 2006.

The approval of the Commission under section 6(1) is required for any proposal for:

(1) works which would permanently alter the fabric of the cathedral itself or of any ecclesiastical building within its precinct;

(2) the demolition of any part of a cathedral or such building;

---

[18] (2001) 6 Ecc. L.J. 291 (Chichester Consistory Court).
[19] *Re St Matthew, Westminster* (2002) 6 Ecc. L.J. 2002 (London Consistory Court).
[20] *Re SS Peter and Paul, Wantage* (1999) 5 Ecc. L.J. 306 (Oxford Consistory Court); *Re St Mary, Leigh* (2000) 6 Ecc. L.J. 167 (Rochester Consistory Court); *Re All Saints, Hough on the Hill* (2001) 6 Ecc. L.J. (Lincoln Consistory Court).
[21] See **16.3.3**.
[22] Exceptionally, the Cathedral of Christ Church in Oxford is not subject to the 1990 Measure, but is instead classified as a peculiar (s.20(1)).

(3) the disturbance of any archaeological remains within the precinct; or

(4) the sale, loan or other disposal of any object of outstanding interest.

The last category enables control over proposals such as the ill-fated attempt by the Dean of Hereford Cathedral to sell the Mappa Mundi in the 1980s.

The Commission, before deciding any application, must first advertise it, and send notice of it to the relevant fabric advisory committee, English Heritage, the national amenity societies, and (except in case (4) above) the local planning authority; and it must take into account any representations received as a result.[23]

The approval of the relevant fabric advisory committee is required for any other works which would materially affect:

(1) the architectural, archaeological, artistic or historic character of the cathedral or any ecclesiastical building within its precinct;

(2) the immediate setting of the cathedral; or

(3) any archaeological remains within the precinct.[24]

Any application to the committee for a proposal in any of the above categories must be notified by it to English Heritage, the national societies and the local planning authority.[25] The approval of the committee is also required for the disposal of any object in the cathedral of interest (other than one of outstanding interest) and for the addition to the cathedral of any object which would affect its character. If the committee refuses to approve a proposal, the chapter may appeal to the Commission.[26]

In the event of doubt as to which is the appropriate authority in respect of any particular works, the Commission has power to determine the matter.[27] Where a proposal requires planning permission, listed building consent or scheduled monument consent, and the Commission is satisfied that the planning authority has taken into account all considerations relevant to the preservation of the immediate setting of the cathedral church, it may issue a written declaration that no approval is required under the Measure.[28]

There has hitherto been a provision whereby a parish church cathedral (that is, one where there is no dean and chapter, such as Sheffield) could opt to be either under the jurisdiction of the Cathedrals Fabric Commission or under the faculty jurisdiction that is to be repealed by the 2005 Measure.[28a]

The Commission is also to be notified of any application for listed building consent that is proposed to be made by the administrative body of any cathedral—before that application is made.[29] This would apply to any works to a building in the ownership of the chapter other than one in ecclesiastical use, since

---

[23] s.8.
[24] ss 2, 6.
[25] s.7, to be amended by Care of Cathedrals (Amendment) Measure 2005.
[26] s.9.
[27] s.6(2)–(2B), as amended by the 2005 Measure, s.5.
[28] s.6(2C),(2D), to be inserted by the 2005 Measure, s.5.
[28a] s.18, to be repealed by the 2005 Measure, s.16.
[29] s.10.

works to the latter would not of course require listed building consent in any event.[30]

Where it appears that works have been or are about to be carried out in contravention of the 1990 Measure, the Bishop is to make a special visitation to the cathedral concerned, and give such directions as appear to be necessary.[31] If those directions are insufficient, he may then seek from the Vicar General's Court of the province an injunction or restoration order, as appropriate.

16.8.2 Peculiars

The peculiars are those institutions of the Church of England which are outside the jurisdiction of the diocesan bishop. They are thus institutions, rather than (as popularly supposed) buildings.

Almost all peculiar jurisdictions were abolished by Order-in-Council made between 1836 and 1852, under the Ecclesiastical Commissioners Acts 1836 and 1850. The cathedrals were left alone by those Orders-in-Council; but they are now with one exception subject to the provisions of the Care of Cathedrals Measure 1990.[32] The other peculiars that were expressly left alone are still in existence, and works to the ecclesiastical buildings within them are thus subject neither to the provisions of the 1990 Measure nor to those of the Care of Churches and Ecclesiastical Jurisdiction Measure 1991.[33] They are very few in number, as follows:

(1) Westminster Abbey;

(2) St George's Chapel, Windsor;

(3) some or possibly all of the chapels in royal residences;

(4) the chapels in some or possibly all of the pre-Reformation colleges at Oxford and Cambridge; and

(5) the Cathedral of Christ Church, Oxford.[34]

It is probable that the Temple and the Tower of London also remain as peculiars in spite of the Orders-in-Council, since they were at the relevant date between two dioceses; and it is conceivable that there may have been one or two others that survived for that or some other reason.[35]

The General Synod has reformed this situation somewhat, in that those responsible for each peculiar are now able to bring it within the faculty jurisdiction, by inviting the Council for the Care of Churches to include it in the list maintained under the Care of Places Worship Measure 1999. The effect of inclusion in that list is that there is then a duty to carry out a quinquennial

---

[30] See **16.3.1**.
[31] Care of Cathedrals (Supplementary Provisions) Measure 1994.
[32] See **16.8.1**.
[33] See **16.6**.
[34] Care of Cathedrals Measure 1990, s.20(1)
[35] For further information on peculiars, see the article by Paul Barber at [1994] 3 Ecc. L.J. 299.

inspection (under the Inspection of Churches Measure 1955)[36]; and works to places of worship within the peculiar are then subject to the faculty jurisdiction.[37] The intention of the Government is that, for those peculiars which opt not to be included in the CCC list, the exemption from secular control will be withdrawn.

16.9 Internal procedures of exempt denominations other than the Church of England

16.9.1 Introduction

Each of the other denominations whose places of worship are exempt from secular listed building control has an internal system of control broadly similar in effect to the faculty system of the Church of England. Each also conforms to a greater or lesser extent with the principles summarised in PPG 15 and WO Circular 61/96.[38]

Only brief details of each denomination's system are given below; further information may be obtained from the websites and other sources indicated.[39]

Basic contact details for each of the denominations concerned are given in **Appendix C**; the relevant web-site should be explored for details of local bodies (such as Church in Wales and Roman Catholic dioceses, Baptist trust corporations and URC synods).

The "national amenity societies" referred to below are those which must be notified of proposals to demolish secular listed buildings[40]—the Ancient Monuments Society, the Council for British Archaeology, the Society for the Protection of Ancient Buildings, the Georgian Group, the Victorian Society, and the Twentieth Century Society.

16.9.2 The Church in Wales

The Church in Wales was disestablished in 1920, although it remains part of the Anglican Communion. As with the Church of England, a large proportion of its places of worship (1,100 out of a total of 1,500) are listed.

The Church in Wales has long had a faculty system broadly similar to that operating in the Church of England.[41] The key difference between the two is that church buildings and churchyards are vested not in the parishes but in the Representative Body of the Church; this facilitates the development of country-wide policies in relation to the care and control of churches. In addition, the faculty system applies to cathedrals as well as parish churches. The relevant procedures are set out in the Faculty Rules of the Diocesan Courts of the Church in Wales, which were amended in 1995; they are available on the Church in Wales website. Also on that website is a very useful guide to Parochial Administration.

---

[36] See **8.2.2.**
[37] See **16.3.5** and **16.6.**
[38] PPG 15, para.8.4; WO Circ. 61/96, para.142; see **16.3.2.**
[39] See also the DNH booklet, Ecclesiastical Exemption, referred to at **16.3.2.**
[40] See **13.5.6.**
[41] See **16.6, 16.7.**

As with the Church of England, any proposal to carry out works to a church or cathedral, listed or otherwise, requires a faculty to be obtained from the consistory court. The chancellor receives advice from the diocesan advisory committee (DAC), which has members with appropriate specialist expertise: Cadw and the national amenity societies are consulted about membership.[42] Further, petitions affecting a place of worship that is listed or in a conservation area must be advertised by the petitioner in the press, and notified by the secretary of the DAC to Cadw, the local planning authority and (if the works affect the character of such a building or its archaeological interest) the national societies.[43]

The Faculty Rules are enforceable by the Representative Body in the civil courts. There is provision for the service of injunctions at the behest of any interested person or body to prevent unauthorised works to churches or cathedrals, and restoration orders where such works have already taken place.

16.9.3 The Roman Catholic Church

The relevant procedures of the Roman Catholic Church are set out in the *Directory on the Ecclesiastical Exemption from Listed Building Control*, issued by the Bishop's Conference of England and Wales (Department for Christian Life and Worship) in March 2001.[44] This is available on the Historic Churches section of the website of the Patrimony Committee and Subcommittee of the Liturgy Office, along with some useful *Notes and Guidance* issued in 2004.[45]

Decisions on works to historic churches are taken by 12 Historic Churches Committees—one for the five dioceses along the south of England, one for the four in the north-west, one for the three in Wales and Herefordshire, and one for each of the other dioceses. Each Committee has members with expertise in historic buildings issues, including (on a non-voting basis) a representative of English Heritage or Cadw, an officer from one of the local planning authorities in its area, and a representative of the national amenity societies.[46] The Catholic Church is unique amongst the six exempt denominations in that it is the same body which both provides the specialist advice on proposals and also adjudicates on them.

A decree has thus been issued by each Catholic diocese, providing that a faculty is required from the relevant Committee for the carrying out of any internal or external works (short of outright demolition) to any listed church, oratory or chapel owned by the diocese, the parish or any other ecclesiastical organisation subject to the Bishop and used for worship, or any other listed ecclesiastical building (except a presbytery) belonging to a religious institution and used for ecclesiastical purposes.

An application for a faculty is made to the Committee (possibly preceded by informal consultation in less straightforward cases). The Secretary of the Committee will notify the relevant conservation bodies, including the local planning

---

[42] Third Schedule to the Rules.
[43] Rules 8, 9.
[44] This replaces the *Provisions for Implementing the new Code of Practice*, approved by the Bishops' Conference in April 1994.
[45] *www.catholic-ew.org.uk/liturgy*
[46] *Directory*, paras 12–15.

authority, and (except in the case of works to the interior of a Grade II building) advertise the proposal on the exterior of the building and in the local press. In practice, an application will be followed by a site visit by the Committee, possibly attended also by representatives of the conservation bodies and the local authority; and the meeting of the Committee where the decision is made can be addressed by the applicant. The decision will be notified to all the conservation bodies.[47]

There is a right of appeal by either the applicant or an objector; but it is to the Diocesan Bishop, who will establish an appeals commission to resolve the matter, in accordance with canonical norms. Guidelines for Appeals have been issued by the Church Patrimony Sub-committee.[48]

Where works are carried out without the approval of the Historic Churches Committee, the Chairman is to issue a Cessation of Unauthorised Works Order, requiring the unauthorised works to stop immediately. A copy of the Order is sent to the Bishop. A retrospective application must then be submitted, and if that is not approved, the parish may be required to reinstate what has been removed, damaged or demolished.

For further details, consult the Liturgy Department of the Bishops' Conference, or the relevant Historic Churches Committee.

16.9.4 The Methodist Church

The Methodist Church, unlike any of the other exempt denominations, maintains a highly centralised system of control of works to buildings which are listed or in a conservation area. It is also alone in employing a full-time conservation officer. The procedures are determined by the relevant provisions in the Model Trusts and Standing Orders, which were amended by Conference following the amendments to the ecclesiastical exemption in 1994.[49]

All proposals for such works have to be approved in due course by the Property Committee of the Property Division, even for works which might not require such approval in the case of a non-listed building.[50] Proposals should initially be notified to the Property Committee, along with a Statement of Significance and a Statement of Needs. The Committee will in appropriate cases consult English Heritage or Cadw and the national amenity societies. Once the managing trustees have finalised their proposal, taking into account any views expressed as a result of the initial negotiations, it should be forwarded through the Circuit meeting and District Committees to the Property Committee.[51] That Committee then sends

---

[47] *Directory*, paras 16–29.

[48] Also available on the website. Appeals were made, under the old *Provisions*, in the cases of *Re St Mary and All Angels, Canton, Cardiff* (1999) 6 Ecc. L.J. 78; *Re St Werburgh, Grosvenor Park Road, Chester* (2000) unreported; and *Re St Michael, Newport* (2001) 6 Ecc. L.J. 412.

[49] See **16.3.9**. Some further information is available on the Methodist Church website (*www.methodist.org.uk*).

[50] Standing Order (SO) 930(2)(viii).

[51] SO 930(1),(5).

details to the planning authority and the conservation bodies, and the managing trustees must advertise the proposal on site and in the local press.[52]

The Listed Buildings Advisory Committee will then consider any representations received, and make a recommendation for approval or refusal to the Property Committee, which will then proceed to a decision. The LBAC has members who between them possess an appropriate range of expertise but, surprisingly (and unlike the other exempt denominations) it does not have members nominated by the national amenity societies.[53] Notwithstanding that, the administration of the system is generally regarded as efficient.

In reaching its decision, the Committee is to take into account, in addition to any other relevant factors, the desirability of preserving historic church buildings, the importance of protecting features of architectural merit and historic interest and the archaeological implications of the scheme.[54] The decision will be notified to the planning authority and the conservation bodies—and, where demolition is involved, English Heritage (as successor to the Royal Commission on Historical Monuments).

In practice, decisions of the Property Committee are delegated to the Connexional Property Secretary, who generally adopts the view of the conservation officer, which in turn will embody the views of the LBAC and the conservation bodies. Appeals are made to the board of the Property Division through a District Representative.

Where works are carried out without authorisation, the Property Committee will request the managing trustees to rectify the damage, after the LBAC has recommended (in conjunction with the conservation bodies) a schedule of works to be carried out. Where such works are carried out, a charge may be brought against the managing trustees, which may lead to their suspension, and the cost of the work may be charged to them.[55]

16.9.5 The Baptist Union

The exemption from secular control applies only to buildings that are held in trust with one of the Baptist trust corporations. There are in addition many Baptist churches, particularly those of the Strict and Particular Baptists, which are not in membership with one of these unions, and are as a result outside the exemption.

A proposal for relevant works is to be sent to the relevant trust corporation, which will then send them on to a single national Listed Buildings Advisory Committee, whose members have between them appropriate expertise (and three of whom are appointed following consultation with English Heritage, Cadw, the national amenity societies, and the local government associations). The Committee will notify the heritage bodies, and take into account any representations made when reaching its decision—which will, if endorsed by the trust corporation, be issued to the applicant and notified to the heritage bodies.

---

[52] SO 982.
[53] SO 332.
[54] SO 983.
[55] SO 985.

If consent is refused, the church may appeal to the Legal Committee of the Baptist Union, which will appoint an independent adjudicator to determine the matter.

Where works have been or are about to be carried out without the consent of the trust corporation, it will take such steps as are open to it to rectify the damage caused or to prevent the works starting, as the case may be. It is far from clear how, if at all, effective this system is.

Further information is available in a series of leaflets that can be downloaded from the Baptist Union Corporation Downloads section of the Baptist Church website:

LB.1: Introducing the Listed Buildings Advisory Committee

LB.2: Making Application to the Listed Buildings Advisory Committee

LB.3: Advising Churches on Applications to the Listed Buildings Advisory Committee.[56]

It is also important for churches contemplating doing works to discuss their proposals with their holding trust corporation.

16.9.6 The United Reformed Church

The United Reformed Church (URC) was created in 1972 by the union of the Congregational Church in England and Wales and the Presbyterian Church of England. Details of the procedure for obtaining approval for works to URC places of worship are contained in the Property Handbook, to be found the URC website.[57]

Each Synod of the United Reformed Church has its own listed buildings advisory committee (LBAC), with which proposals should be discussed at the earliest possible stage.[58] Having obtained approval from the Church Meeting and the District (or Synod) Council, churches should then apply to the Provincial (or Synod) Property Committee and the LBAC. The Property Committee will then consult English Heritage, the planning authority and the national amenity societies, whose views it will take into account along with those of the LBAC when it decides to grant or withhold consent.

There is an appeal procedure in the event that consent is not forthcoming.

16.10 Closure of places of worship

16.10.1 Church of England buildings: proposals under the Pastoral Measure

As well as the routine procedures for ensuring that Church of England buildings are regularly surveyed, and that any alterations that may be proposed in the

---

[56] www.baptist.org.uk/resources/guidelines.htm
[57] www.urc.org.uk/plato. The Handbook is produced by PLATO (the Provincial Legal Administrative and Trust Officers' Association).
[58] URC Procedure, para.2.13.

course of their regular use are approved,[59] there is provision for the continuous review of the arrangements for pastoral care within each diocese as a whole and in each parish, and for the making of any proposals for changes that may be considered appropriate as a result of such a review. The significance of this in the present context is that such changes may (and often do) involve alterations to parish churches, changes in their use, construction of new ones or demolition of existing ones. However, since these will often concern not just the church communities involved but also the wider community (including, amongst others, local authorities and amenity societies), there are elaborate arrangements to ensure that at each stage all such views are heard (even if they are not always listened to).

The relevant procedure is set out in the Pastoral Measure 1983, as amended in 1993.[60] Further amendments to the 1983 Measure are proposed in the Dioceses, Pastoral and Mission Measure, currently (2006) before the General Synod. That Measure, if implemented, will amongst other things provide for the Council for the Care of Churches (CCC) to take over the role of the Advisory Board for Redundant Churches. The intention is that there will in due course be a new, consolidating Measure to replace the 1983 and 1993 Measures and the new Measure.

Each diocese has a pastoral committee, which prepares as necessary *pastoral schemes* for the rearrangement of parishes, clergy, churches and vicarages, and for other related matters. In future, where such a scheme contain a provision which, if implemented, would result in a church being declared closed for public worship, it will be known as a pastoral church scheme.[61] The committee sends such schemes in draft to the bishop, after consulting all "interested parties".[62] These are principally the vicars, patrons and church councils of the parishes involved, the archdeacons and, usually, the local planning authority (in this context, the district or borough council[63]).

In any case involving the closure of a church for public worship, the committee is required not merely to consult the local planning authority, but actually to ascertain its views.[64] In such a case, the committee must also consult the CCC, which must then prepare a report on:

(a)   the historic interest and architectural quality of the churches involved and of others in the area;

(b)   the historic interest and aesthetic quality of their contents; and

(c)   the special features of any churchyards involved.[65]

In future, the report will also have to contain any relevant information on architectural and structural changes that might be necessary as a result of any of

---

[59]   See **8.2.2**, **16.6** and **16.7**.
[60]   Pastoral (Amendment) Measure 1993, s.13. Other technical amendments were made to the 1983 Measure by the Church of England (Miscellaneous Provisions) Measure 2005.
[61]   Draft Dioceses, Pastoral and Mission Measure, cl. 23.
[62]   1983 Measure, s.3.
[63]   s.87.
[64]   By s.3(7).
[65]   s.3(8).

the buildings involved being either closed for worship or converted to mixed use.[66]

The bishop may amend the proposed scheme, with the agreement of the pastoral committee, and will then send it on to the Church Commissioners.[67] Where a proposal provides for the closure of a church for worship, and its alteration or demolition, or its transfer to the Churches Conservation Trust, the Commissioners must consult with the Advisory Board (or, in future, the CCC).[68] The Commissioners will then prepare a draft scheme and send copies to all interested parties. They will consider any comments made, finalise the scheme, and send it for formal approval by Her Majesty in Council.[69]

16.10.2 Provision made by a pastoral scheme

Where a building is to be closed for public worship as a result of a pastoral scheme under the 1983 Measure, the scheme itself will not normally provide for its future use or for its demolition.[70] However a pastoral scheme may make such provision where the building is to be replaced by a new place of worship (which will not necessarily, or often, be a new building) and where one of the following conditions are satisfied:

(1)   the Advisory Board states that the church is of no merit; or

(2)   it is satisfied with a proposal to move its principal features to another church; or

(3)   the Commissioners are satisfied (in spite of any advice to the contrary given by the Advisory Board) "for reasons regarded by them as sufficient" that the church should be demolished; or

(4)   they are satisfied as to the future use proposed for the church.[71]

In the future, the pastoral committee will be under a duty in respect of any building that is to be closed for regular worship, if it is listed or in a conservation area, to make every endeavour to provide a suitable alternative use or uses for it; and where the CCC is satisfied with the use or uses thus suggested, the scheme may provide for that to be come into effect.[72]

In addition (even where a replacement place of worship is not, yet, available), a pastoral scheme may provide for an alternative use for the building to be closed if there is one already known which is acceptable to the Commissioners. Finally, a scheme may provide for a church to be transferred to the Churches Conservation Trust where no alternative use is likely to be found, and where the building is "of such historic and archaeological interest or architectural quality that it ought to

---

[66]   Draft Dioceses [etc.] Measure, cl. 35.
[67]   s.4.
[68]   s.5(2), to be amended by Dioceses [etc.] Measure, cl. 36.
[69]   ss 6–10.
[70]   s.28.
[71]   s.46.
[72]   1983 Measure, s.42(1), to be inserted by Dioceses [etc.] Measure, cl. 40; s.46(1), to be substituted by Dioceses [etc.] Measure, cl.41.

be preserved in the interests of the nation and the Church of England".[73] Since 1993, a church may only be transferred to the Trust (either under section 47 or under section 51[74]) if the Commissioners are satisfied that it will have sufficient resources to repair and maintain it.[75] The Trust is jointly financed by the Church Commissioners and English Heritage.

Except in the specific cases mentioned above, a pastoral scheme will only provide that a church is to become redundant. The ultimate fate of the building in most cases has to be the subject of a *redundancy scheme* (in future to be known as a "pastoral (church disposal) scheme").[76]

16.10.3 Redundancy schemes

A redundancy scheme will provide for the future of a building that has been declared in a pastoral scheme to be closed for public worship, in one of the following ways:

(1) an alternative use for the building;

(2) the transfer of the building, if it is of great interest (see above), to the Churches Conservation Trust;

(3) the diocesan board of finance to retain control of it; or

(4) the demolition of the building.[77]

The scheme will also, in practice, make other related provisions as to the future of any land attached, and the disposal of the proceeds of any sale.

A scheme must not normally be made for at least six months after the formal declaration of redundancy (that is, the approval of the pastoral scheme), but it must be made within three years from then, unless that would be impracticable.[78] During the waiting period, the church council has no further responsibility for the redundant building, except to assist the diocesan board of finance (which takes full charge of it) with its preservation. The quinquennial inspection is no longer required.[79] The Church Commissioners may however, before the six-month period is up, prepare a draft redundancy scheme providing for either:

(1) the demolition of the building (if the Advisory Board for Redundant Churches) is satisfied that it is of no interest at all); or

(2) an approved alternative use.[80]

In future, it will not be possible for a pastoral (church disposal) scheme to provide for the demolition of a church that is either a listed building or in a conservation

---

[73] s.47.
[74] See **16.10.3**.
[75] Pastoral (Amendment) Measure 1993, ss 3, 4.
[76] s.48, to be amended by Dioceses [etc.] Measure, Sch.5.
[77] s.51.
[78] s.50(1). The period will in future be two years (Dioceses [etc.] Measure, cl. 44.)
[79] See **8.2.2**.
[80] s.49.

area, unless the Commissioners (after consultation with the CCC) are satisfied that there is no objection to the demolition.[81]

The Commissioners, before preparing a draft redundancy scheme that involves any demolition of the building (in whole or in part) or any architectural or structural changes to it, must consult the Advisory Board. They must, in any event, consult the bishop, and serve a copy of the draft scheme on the following (among others):

(1) the diocesan board of finance;

(2) the Advisory Board;

(3) the Churches Conservation Trust (if it is proposed to transfer the building to it); and

(4) the local planning authority.[82]

They must also advertise the draft scheme in a local paper, stating where it can be inspected in detail.[83] They must bear in mind all the comments made, and they may then decide to proceed with the scheme or to amend it—in the latter case, they must then start the whole process all over again.

Once a redundancy scheme is confirmed by Her Majesty in Council, the faculty procedure[84] will no longer apply and, except in the case of buildings transferred to the Trust, the legal effects of consecration will cease.[85]

At any stage of the process, the board of finance or the Churches Conservation Trust may transfer a redundant building to the Secretary of State or, with his or her agreement, to English Heritage.[86]

Since 1969, when the present system came into operation, around 1,679 churches have been declared redundant. Of these, 22 per cent have been demolished, 57 per cent converted to other uses, and 21 per cent preserved (almost always by means of transfer to the Redundant Churches Fund or the Churches Conservation Trust).[87]

16.10.4 Buildings of other denominations closed for worship

Each of the exempted denominations other than the Church of England has its own system for dealing with buildings no longer required for worship. These are summarised very briefly in the booklet on the ecclesiastical exemption published by the Department for National Heritage[88]; and further details are available from the addresses in **Appendix C**.

The key feature in each case should be that the relevant denominational body will notify the local planning authority when a building becomes redundant, as

[81] s.49(1), to be substituted by Dioceses [etc.] Measure, cl. 43.
[82] See **16.10.1**.
[83] s.50.
[84] See **16.6**.
[85] s.61, amended by 1993 Measure, s.7.
[86] s.66, amended by National Heritage Act 1983.
[87] Church Commissioners Annual Report, 2004.
[88] See **16.3.2**.

the denomination's own procedure will cease to apply to it, and it will be instead subject to normal full listed building control. In the case of the United Reformed and Baptist Churches, however, this does not take place; and the Newman Report recommended that this should be rectified.

In Wales, the exemption from listed building and conservation area consent applies (in the case of buildings closed for public worship) only to the few Church of England churches there[89]; it does not apply to redundant buildings of the Church in Wales, which are thus subject to normal secular control.

---

[89] WO Circ. 1/98, para.20(1)(k).

Chapter 17

Value Added Tax

17.1 Introduction

17.1.1 Background

Prior to 1984, all alterations to buildings were zero-rated for VAT. The Government then introduced VAT at standard rate on alterations, but retained the relief for listed buildings and scheduled monuments, in response to pressure from the heritage lobby.[1] However, as with many tax "concessions", the benefit is more apparent than real. In particular, following the decision of the European Court of Justice in *Commission of the European Communities v UK*,[2] the relief was significantly curtailed by the Finance Act 1989, so that it now only applies where the building is used after the works in question for residential or charitable purposes.[3]

The relevant legislation is now contained in the VAT Act 1994, which contains a number of "Groups" of items that are zero-rated.[4] Those that are principally relevant in the present context are:

- Group 5 (construction of buildings etc); and

- Group 6 (protected buildings).

Shortly after the coming into force of the 1994 Act, a new version of each of these two Groups was substituted by statutory order, with effect from March 1, 1995.[5] The commentary here relates to the Act as thus amended. Note that, as with almost all tax legislation, the VAT Acts apply throughout the United Kingdom.

---

[1] VAT Act 1983, Group 8A, added by Finance Act 1984, s.10, and Sch.6, art.8; amended by VAT (Protected Buildings) Order 1985 (SI 1985/18). See further, on the historical background, *Customs and Excise Commissioners ("Commissioners") v Zielinski Baker & Partners* [2004] 1 WLR, HL 707 at paras 27–30, 42.

[2] [1988] S.T.C. 456, [1990] 2 Q.B. 130.

[3] Finance Act 1989, Sch.3, para.2.

[4] VAT Act 1994, s.30, Sch.8.

[5] Group 5 substituted by Value Added Tax (Construction of Buildings) Order 1995 (SI 1995/280), and subsequently amended by other SIs, but not in relation to the matters discussed here; Group 6 substituted by Value Added Tax (Protected Buildings) Order 1995 (SI 1995/283), and subsequently amended by the Historic Monuments and Archaeological Objects (Northern Ireland) Order 1995 and the P(LBCA)(S)A 1997.

Further details can be obtained in a useful free leaflet *Buildings and Construction* (Notice 708), issued in July 2002 by HM Customs and Excise—the predecessor in respect of VAT matters to HM Revenue and Customs (HMRC)), obtainable from local VAT offices and on the HMRC website.[6]

In addition to the statutory scheme, a further concession is operated by DCMS to enable the reclaim of the VAT payable on repairs to places of worship.

17.1.2 Overview

As a result of the provisions described above, the current position is now as follows:

(1) the cost of "approved alterations" to "protected buildings" is zero-rated;

(2) other alterations to protected buildings are liable to tax at the standard rate (currently) 17.5 per cent;

(3) tax paid on the cost of the repair and maintenance of listed places of worship can be recovered in full;

(4) the repair and maintenance of other buildings ("protected" or otherwise) is liable to tax at standard rate; and

(5) the disposal of a protected building after it has been substantially reconstructed is zero-rated.

The effect of this is that, where works to a listed building are carried out in such a way that they do not affect its special character, no listed building consent is required, and their cost does not attract VAT relief. Where on the other hand the works do affect the character of the building, so that consent is required, VAT relief will be available. The relief in its present form thus arguably encourages works to be carried out in a less sensitive manner, and as a result has been the subject of much criticism; it was described by a previous Secretary of State for the National Heritage as "a wholly indefensible anomaly". The Treasury has nevertheless stoutly resisted all moves for reform.

However, the Court of Appeal has held that it is appropriate to consider the purpose of the exemption—that is, that Parliament must have had in mind the onerous responsibilities imposed upon the owners of listed buildings. While the onus is on a taxpayer to show on the balance of probabilities that he or she comes within the zero-rating provisions, therefore, it is reasonable in borderline cases or where they are unclear to construe those provisions in favour of the taxpayer.[7]

This chapter first considers in more detail the question of what is a "protected building" (see **17.2**). It then explains what are "approved alterations", and in particular how they differ from repair and maintenance (**17.3**); and what supplies of services and goods are the subject of zero-rating (**17.4**). The special position of

---

[6] *http://customs.hmrc.gov.uk* in the "Public Notices" section.
[7] *Commissioners v Arbib* [1995] E.G.C.S. 56; (1995) S.T.C. 490. On the other hand, the Tribunal in the same dispute observed that "common sense and the law applicable to VAT are not well acquainted" (November 25, 1995 (11486)).

places of worship is considered in **17.5**. The last section deals with zero-rating on disposals of protected buildings (see **17.6**).

Finally, it should be noted at the outset that the statutory provisions have been the subject of a very substantial amount of litigation in recent years, sometimes in the courts and more often in the VAT Tribunals. The decisions are occasionally reported in the law reports,[8] but more often in various web-based services (including the HMRC website).[9] As to the decisions of tribunals, it has been observed by the Court of Appeal that:

> "a series of reasoned judgments such as the tribunal gives is bound to disclose the general principles upon which it proceeds. I think that that is not only inevitable but also desirable. It makes for uniformity of treatment and it is helpful to the industry and to its advisers to know in a general way how particular classes of applications are likely to be treated."[10]

Decisions of particular Tribunals are therefore noted here, as they are often cited in subsequent High Court litigation, and are helpful to indicate the way in which particular provisions are interpreted in practice; but it should be borne in mind that they are not binding on other tribunals. The Commissioners of Customs and Excise are referred to in case citations in this Chapter simply as "Commissioners".

17.2 Protected buildings

17.2.1 The statutory formula

In the context of historic buildings, zero-rating applies by virtue of Group 6 in Schedule 8 to the VAT Act 1994 to the following:

- the supply of goods and services in connection with the carrying out of approved alterations to a protected building; and

- the disposal of a protected building following its substantial reconstruction.[11]

It will be observed that the common feature of these is the concept of a "protected building". It is therefore essential to understand at the outset what is meant by that term.

Group 6 contains a number of Notes which interpret the terms used in the Items. Note (1) defines a "protected building" as follows:

> ". . . a building which is designed to remain as or become a dwelling or number of dwellings (as defined in Note (2) below) or is intended for use solely for a relevant residential purpose or a relevant charitable purpose after the reconstruction or alteration and which, in either case, is
>
> (a) a listed building, within the meaning of [the Listed Buildings Act] or [the Scottish Listed Buildings Act] or [the Northern Ireland Order]; or

---

[8] The court decisions in particular are generally reported in *Simon's Tax Cases* (STC).
[9] Particularly Lawtel. Decisions noted here by reference to the *Value Added Tax Encyclopaedia* pre-date the web.
[10] *Merchandise Transport Ltd v British Transport Commission* [1962] 2 Q.B. 173, CA (transport tribunals) *per* Devlin L.J. at p.193.
[11] VAT Act 1994, Sch.8, Group 6; for the actual wording used, see **17.4.1** and **17.6**.

(b) a scheduled monument within the meaning of [the Ancient Monuments Act] or the Historic Monuments and Archaeological Objects (Northern Ireland) Order 1995"[12]

This formulation has recently been considered at length by the House of Lords in the leading case of *Commissioners v Zielinski Baker and Partners*. Lord Walker held that it can be divided into three "integers": a protected building is thus:

(1) a building,

(2) which is designed to remain as or become a dwelling [or be used for a residential or charitable purpose], and

(3) which is a listed building [or scheduled monument] within the meaning of the relevant legislation.[13]

17.2.2 Dwellings

The type of building most commonly encountered in cases relating to zero-rating is "a building designed to remain as or become a dwelling or a number of dwellings."[14] A building falls into this category if each dwelling within it satisfies the following conditions:

(a) the "dwelling" consists of self-contained living accommodation;

(b) there is no provision for direct internal access to any other dwelling or part of a dwelling; and

(c) there is no restrictive covenant or planning restriction preventing such use.[15]

It thus includes both a conventional house and a flat.

However, works to a building that constitutes ancillary accommodation to a dwelling will not be not zero-rated, since such a building cannot itself be a dwelling, and thus cannot be a protected building—even where it is in the curtilage of a listed building.

This provision was the subject of the decision of the House of Lords, in *Zielinski Baker*.[16] Works were carried out to an outbuilding at the Mere, Little Houghton, in Northamptonshire, a listed building of around 1830. The outbuilding, built at around the same time as the main house and connected to it by an ornamental wall, was initially a stable and carriage shed and latterly a garage and laundry. The outbuilding was not listed in its own right, but was undoubtedly in the curtilage of the listed house, and thus part of a listed building within the meaning of section 1(5) of the Listed Buildings Act.[16a] Listed building consent had

---

[12] VAT Act 1994, Sch.8, Group 6, Note (1), amended by the Historic Monuments and Archaeological Objects (Northern Ireland) Order 1995, Sch.3 and Planning (Consequential Provisions) (Scotland) Act 1997, Sch.2.

[13] [2004] 1 W.L.R. 707, HL, at para.40. The term "integer" he adopted from patent law.

[14] VAT Act 1994, Sched. 8, Group 6, Note (1). There are around 190,000 listed dwellings in England (38 per cent of all listed buildings).

[15] Group 6, Note (2).

[16] [2004] 1 W.L.R. 707, HL, at para.40.

[16a] See **4.5** and **17.2.5**.

been given for the conversion of the outbuilding into changing and games facilities; the question was whether the cost of those works could be zero-rated for VAT.

The VAT and Duties Tribunal initially held that it was[17]; that was overturned by Etherton J. in the Chancery Division[18]; his decision was in turn reversed (but only by a majority) by the Court of Appeal.[19] That was then overturned in the House of Lords, who held—albeit, again, only by a majority—that the works were not zero-rated.[20] That, if nothing else, indicates that the law is not altogether straightforward. The outbuilding in the instant case was accepted by all to be a separate building, and it was—to use Lord Hoffman's precise formulation—"a listed building, or more accurately part of a notional listed building".[21] But it was not itself to remain or become a dwelling; and it therefore failed to comply with the second of Lord Walker's integers. It was thus not a protected building within the meaning of the VAT Act; and works for its alteration would therefore not qualify for zero-rating.

It is therefore not enough that a building should be within the curtilage of a building listed in its own right, so that listed building consent is required for its alteration. The decision in *Zielinski Baker* confirms the earlier decisions of the London VAT Tribunal, that a garage and shed complex, built in 1917, just under 15m from a listed Elizabethan house, was not a protected building,[22] so that alterations to it should not be zero-rated; that a barn (listed in its own right) within the curtilage of a listed house was not part of the house, even though it was to be converted to form an adjunct to the dwelling[23]; and that an out-building 6m from a listed house and 3m from a later conservatory built onto it was not a "dwelling".[24]

Those earlier cases would probably still be decided the same way now, but they should nevertheless be considered with caution, since they pre-date the introduction in 1995 of the proviso to the definition of a dwelling, whereby a building is not a dwelling if it its use as a separate dwelling is prohibited by a covenant, planning condition or other restriction.[25] Thus in three more recent cases, each relating to the conversion of a barn or outbuilding to form guest accommodation to be occupied in association with a nearby house, the tribunal noted that there was in existence just such a restriction, and declined to accept zero-rating.[26] The

[17] Birmingham VAT Tribunal (July 4, 2000; summary available on Lawtel).
[18] [2001] S.T.C. 585.
[19] [2002] S.T.C. 829, CA.
[20] The only consolation for the tax payer being that his costs in the Lords were paid by the Customs and Excise.
[21] [2004] 1 W.L.R. 707, HL, at para.10.
[22] *Orme v Commissioners*, February 1993 (9975) (noted in *Value Added Tax Encyclopaedia*, vol.2).
[23] *MKM Builders v Commissioners*, May 1993 (10511) (noted in *Encyclopaedia*).
[24] *Lee v Commissioners*, June 1993 (10662) (noted in *Encyclopaedia*).
[25] Group 6, Note (2)(c), introduced by Value Added Tax (Protected Buildings) Order 1995 (SI 1995/283).
[26] *Ford v Commissioners*, September 10, 1999 (16271), *Clamp v Commissioners*, December 14, 1999 (16422) (transcripts of both available on Lawtel); *Smith v Commissioners*, May 5, 2005 (LON/03/0681) (transcript available on HMRC web-site).

same conclusion has also been reached in another case where there was no condition restricting separate disposal.[27]

The one exception to this principle is that the Act specifically provides that a
dwelling does include a garage occupied with the dwelling, provided that it was
built at the same time as the dwelling—or, where the dwelling was substantially
reconstructed, at the same time as that reconstruction. This has recently been
interpreted by a tribunal as meaning that, to justify zero-rating, the building to
which the approved alterations are carried out must at the time of the alterations
be used for the storage of vehicles, regardless of the purpose for which it was
built.[28] As a result of that decision, HMRC now accepts that the key test is that
the building in question should have been in use as a garage before the works and
continue to be used as one afterwards.[29]

17.2.3 Other buildings in residential use

A building may also be a protected building if it is intended for use for a "relevant
residential purpose". That includes use as communal living accommodation, such
as a children's home, nursing home, students' hostel, barracks, home for the
elderly, hospice or monastery—but not a hospital, a prison or a hotel.[30] Note (3).
The key consideration is whether the residential element is primary (as in a home
providing residential accommodation, with care for those who need it), in which
case zero-rating is allowable, or secondary (as in a hospital, principally providing
medical care).[31]

This was considered by a tribunal in relation to a group of three former agricultural buildings in Herefordshire converted to form respectively a nursing home
(in the former farmhouse, listed in its own right), sheltered housing (in a barn
attached to the farmhouse by a link block), and associated administration (in
another building attached to the barn by screen walls).[32] The tribunal accepted
that the three buildings had originally formed one complex; and that it was
perfectly reasonable for the administration function to be in a separate building.
Accordingly it allowed zero-rating on all of the conversion works. This decision is
not altogether easy to reconcile with the barn cases noted above; but it would
seem to indicate that a more relaxed approach might be allowed where a group of
buildings are all used for a "relevant residential purpose" than would be appropriate in the case of a building ancillary to a "dwelling".

---

[27] *Hopewell-Smith v Commissioners*, June 30, 2000 (16725) (transcript available on
   Lawtel).
[28] *Grange Builders (Quainton) Ltd v Commissioners*, January 17, 2005 (LON/02/982)
   (transcript available on HMRC website). That decision noted that the rationale for the
   requirement as to simultaneous construction was "hard to discover".
[29] *HMRC Business Brief 11/05*, May 18, 2005.
[30] Group 5, Note (4), applied by Group 6, Note (3).
[31] *Revenue & Customs Commissioners v Fenwood Developments Ltd*, 2005, *The Times*,
   December 26, (transcript available via Lawtel).
[32] *Hill Ash Developments v Commissioners*, July 18, 2000 (16747) (transcript available on
   Lawtel).

17.2.4 Buildings in charitable use

The other broad category of listed buildings and monuments (alongside residential buildings) that attract zero-rating is "buildings in use for a relevant charitable purpose." A "relevant charitable purpose" means use by a charity:

> "(a) otherwise than in the course or furtherance of a business;
> (b) as a village hall or similarly in providing social or recreational facilities for a local community."[33]

The first limb of this definition thus includes any building used by a charity for its principal charitable operations, but excludes buildings operated by charitable businesses such as private schools[34] and Oxfam shops.

The meaning of the second phrase in the definition was considered by the Court of Appeal in *Commissioners v Jubilee Hall Recreation Centre.*[35] It noted that a village hall is not run on a commercial basis, although it may occasionally be let out at a commercial rent to raise money to pay for its maintenance, and held that the use of the word "similarly" means that charities providing facilities to a local community must be predominantly—although not necessarily exclusively—operated on a charitable basis for social, including recreational, purposes. Jubilee Hall was used for the provision of leisure facilities to those living in the locality—centred on Covent Garden in central London—but its clientele and staff were drawn from a wide area, and included tourists and those working in the area; that was fatal to the claim for zero-rating.

17.2.5 Listed buildings

It has been noted that a building, to be a protected building, may be "a listed building within the meaning of the Listed Buildings Act, the Scottish Listed Buildings Act or the Northern Ireland Order".[36] This therefore brings in the definition of "listed building" in those statutes, which is as follows:

> "In this Act, 'listed building' means a building which is for the time being included in a list compiled or approved by the Secretary of State under this section; and for the purposes of this Act—
>
> (a) any object or structure fixed to the building; and
> (b) any object or structure within the curtilage of the building which, although not fixed to the building, forms part of the land and has done so since before July 1, 1948
>
> shall be treated as part of the building."[37]

---

[33] Group 5, Note (6), applied by Group 6, Note (3).

[34] *Commissioners v St Dunstan's Educational Foundation* [1999] S.T.C. 381; although this did not seem to be an issue in *Christ's Hospital v Revenue & Customs*, June 16, 2005 (LON/04/1041) (transcript available via Lawtel).

[35] [1998] E.G.C.S. 184, *The Times*, December 31, 1998; [1999] S.T.C. 381.

[36] VAT Act 1994, Sch.8, Group 6, Note (1)(a), amended by Planning (Consequential Provisions) (Scotland) Act 1997, Sch.2.

[37] P(LBCA)A 1990, s.1(5); P(LBCA)(S)A 1997, s.1(4); P(NI)O 1991, art.42(7) is similar, save that the date in para.(b) is October 1, 1973.

It thus includes the building in the list itself, and the objects or structures associated with it.[38] This is in line with the decision of the House of Lords in *Debenhams plc v Westminster CC*[39] which was concerned with rating, rather than VAT.[39a] However, the phrase used in the VAT Act is "a building which is . . . a listed building". Whilst therefore a non-listed structure and a listed building to which it is attached might together form a single "building" capable of being a dwelling (or a building used for a relevant residential or charitable purpose), a listed house and an outbuilding in its curtilage cannot together form a "building", whether or not they together form a dwelling.

This means that it will not be possible to claim zero-rating on the cost of works to a curtilage structure, such as a barn or stables block, unless it is itself to remain or become a dwelling. This has recently been confirmed by the decision of the House of Lords in *Zielinski Baker*, noted above along with a number of decisions of VAT Tribunals to the same effect.[40] That decision seems to be correct; but it highlights the problem with the definition of "listed building" in section 1(5) of the Listed Buildings Act, in that that effectively refers not (just) to a single building but (at least in some cases) to a group of buildings or structures, so that the concept (in the VAT Act) of "a building that is a listed building" does not really make sense. It is to be hoped that the forthcoming review of the legislation addresses this problem.

17.2.6 Scheduled monuments

A building, to be a protected building, may alternatively be "a scheduled monument within the meaning of [the Ancient Monuments Act] or the Historic Monuments and Archaeological Objects (Northern Ireland) Order 1995."[41] This therefore brings in the definition of "scheduled monument" in those statutes— that is, a monument included by the Secretary of State in the schedule of monuments which he or she is required to compile.[42] The 1979 Act and the 1995 Order also provide that a "monument" includes any machinery attached to it; as well as its site, that is, the land on which it stands together with any adjacent land which (in the opinion of the Secretary of State or English Heritage or a local authority) is essential for its support or preservation.[43]

In general, the comments in this chapter relating to VAT on works to listed buildings apply equally to works to scheduled monuments. Indeed, it was the inclusion of scheduled monuments in the definition of "protected building" that was one of the factors leading the House of Lords to its conclusions in *Zielinski*

---

[38] See **Chapter 4** for an extensive discussion of this.

[39] [1987] A.C. 396 at pp.404E, 412E.

[39a] See **9.8.2**.

[40] [2004] 1 W.L.R. 707, HL; see **17.2.2**.

[41] VAT Act 1994, Sch.8, Group 6, Note (1), amended by the 1995 Order, Sch.3.

[42] AMAAA 1979, s.1(10). [NI: HMAO(NI)O 1995, arts 2(2), 3(2)—the schedule is prepared by the Department.] See **6.2.1**.

[43] s.61(7),(9),(10)(a). [NI: art.2(6),(8),(9)(a).] See **6.2.5** on the extent of a scheduled monument generally.

Baker.[44] However, it may be noted that houses cannot, generally, be scheduled (as opposed to listed); and so this aspect of the exemption is of little utility in practice.

17.2.7 Other historic buildings

A building which is subject to a building preservation notice,[45] but which has not yet been listed, is not a "protected building" for the purposes of VAT legislation; nor is an unlisted building in a conservation area,[46] nor one in a local list.[47]

17.3 Approved alterations

17.3.1 The statutory formula

Zero-rating is available on the supply of goods and services in the course of an "approved alteration to a protected building. Note (6) of Group 6 provides as follows:

" 'Approved alteration' means—

(a) in the case of a protected building which is an ecclesiastical building to which section 60 of the Planning (Listed Buildings and Conservation Areas) Act 1990 applies, any works of alteration;

(c) in any other case, works of alteration which may not, or but for the existence of a Crown interest or Duchy interest could not, be carried out unless authorised under, or under any provision of—

    (i) Part I of the of [the Listed Buildings Act],

    (ii) Part I of the of [the Scottish Listed Buildings Act],

    (iii) Part V of [the Northern Ireland Order],

    (iv) Part I of [the Ancient Monuments Act], or

    (v) Part II of the Historic Monuments and Archaeological Objects (Northern Ireland) Order 1995

and for which, except in the case of a Crown interest or Duchy interest, consent has been obtained under any provision of that Part,

but does not include any works of repair or maintenance, or any incidental alteration to the fabric of a building which results from the carrying out of repairs, or maintenance work."[48]

This requires three conditions to be satisfied:

(1) there should be an alteration to a protected building (as distinct from new works);

(2) that alteration should be neither works of repairs or maintenance nor incidental alterations resulting from such works; and

---

[44] [2004] 1 W.L.R. 707, HL at paras 19, 20, 36; see **17.2.2**.
[45] See **3.9**.
[46] See **Chapter 5**.
[47] See **7.2**.
[48] VAT Act 1994, Sch.8, Group 6, Note (6), amended by the Historic Monuments and Archaeological Objects (Northern Ireland) Order 1995, Sch.3 and Planning (Consequential Provisions) (Scotland) Act 1997, Sch.2. Note that para.(b) was repealed by the 1995 Order.

(3) the alteration should be approved—that is, the subject of a grant of listed
     building consent or scheduled monument consent as appropriate (except in
     the case of works to churches or buildings owned by the Crown).[49]

17.3.2 Alterations distinguished from new works

The construction of a new building separate from, but in the curtilage of, a
protected building is in any event specifically excluded from the definition of
"approved alteration".[50] On the other hand, where a protected building is
extended, it is possible to claim zero-rating on the ground that the extension is an
alteration. The difficulty may be to distinguish between the two where a new, free-
standing structure is constructed so as to abut the existing building.

An extreme example of this problem occurred in *Customs & Excise Commissioners v Arbib*,[51] in which the court considered the status of works to demolish a
barn and replace it with a new building housing a swimming pool. The new
building was attached to the main house, listed Grade II, by a brick garden wall
and covered way. The Commissioners would have accepted the new building as an
extension to the existing building if the walkway had been enclosed on two sides—
showing how fine was the distinction to be resolved. The VAT tribunal noted that
the planning authority had required listed building consent to be obtained, on the
ground that the work constituted an extension to the listed house, and had
accordingly granted zero-rating; its decision was upheld in the High Court.

But this approach should not be carried too far. The High Court in *Revenue &
Customs Commissioners v Tinsley*,[52] following *Zielinski Baker*, recently held that
works to create a number of terraces in the garden of Narborough Hall (a listed
building and a dwelling), with the top terrace immediately abutting the Hall, were
not zero-rated. The court also doubted the correctness of the earlier decision of a
tribunal that had allowed zero-rating for the construction of a new boundary wall
abutting onto, but not tied into, a listed cottage.[53]

17.3.3 Alterations distinguished from repairs and maintenance

It may in some cases be difficult to draw a clear distinction between "repairs and
maintenance" and "alterations". However, works that are properly categorised as
repair and maintenance can never be "an approved alteration", even if they are
included within the terms of the relevant listed building or scheduled monument
consent. Such works can therefore never be zero-rated.[54]

The distinction between "alteration" and "repair and maintenance" has been
the subject of much litigation in tribunals and the courts. In particular, the House

---

[49] *Commissioners v Moorish* [1998] E.G.C.S. 111.
[50] Group 6, Note (10). This explicitly applies the ruling in *Cotswold* (see **17.3.4**). Note that
the construction of a new building may be zero-rated, but under Group 5 rather than
Group 6, where it is to be occupied for residential or charitable purposes.
[51] [1995] E.G.C.S., S.T.C. 490.
[52] June 10, 2005 (unreported, transcript available on Lawtel).
[53] *Mason v Commissioners*, September 2, 1999 (unreported; transcript available via
Lawtel).
[54] VAT Act 1994, Sch.8, Group 6, Note (6).

of Lords has considered the point in the context of pre–1984 legislation, which applied zero-rating to any alterations (including to non-listed buildings), in two leading cases—*ACT Construction v Commissioners*[55] and *Commissioners v Viva Gas Appliances*.[56] In the first of these, which concerned substantial works of underpinning, the House of Lords declined to define "repair and maintenance", which should be given their ordinary meaning; but it approved the statement by Brandon L.J. in the Court of Appeal:

"In the present case, the work done was not done to any existing part of a building; it was entirely new work. It involved a radical and fundamental alteration to the construction of the building as it had been before. It involved an extension of the existing building in a downward direction. Such work in my view is not capable of coming within the expression 'maintenance' in the ordinary and natural meaning of that word."[57]

In *Viva Gas Appliances*, the House of Lords held that "alteration" must affect the fabric of the building, short of demolition, and be more than "de minimis". That decision has been applied in numerous subsequent tribunal decisions, allowing zero-rating for the replacement of a derelict lighting system in a church with a completely new installation,[58] and the insertion of new damp insulation and drainage system,[59] but not for the construction of a trench outside the base of an external wall (also of a church), to avoid damp penetration (classified as "maintenance" and thus not zero-rated[60]).

Sometimes works that would otherwise be classified as repair and maintenance may be classified as alteration if carried out at the same time as other works:

"A house could be divided into flats. ... As part of the division of the property, rooms which had previously existed would have to be redecorated. As long as this was an integral part of the alterations, the redecoration would be treated in the same way as the alteration, even though, if the rooms had been redecorated otherwise than in the course of the alterations, the work would have been standard-rated."[61]

In the specific context of works to a protected building, one tribunal has considered that there is a distinction between works which, after completion, enabled part of a building to perform the same function in the same way as it did before the works were carried out, even using different materials, and works which enabled that part to perform the same function in a different way to that in which it was before. Thus the replacement of an old gutter with a new one of a different design leading to different outlet points—with the incidental effect of making repair of the old gutter unnecessary—was considered to be an alteration.[62]

---

[55] [1981] 1 W.L.R. 1542.

[56] [1983] 1 W.L.R. 1445.

[57] [1981] 1 W.L.R. 49, 1 All E.R. 324.

[58] *All Saints with St Nicholas Icklesham v Commissioners*, October 21, 1999 (19321) (transcript available via Lawtel).

[59] *Carr v Commissioners*, September 30, 2005 (19267) (transcript available via Lawtel).

[60] *St Petroc Minor (Vicar and PCC) v Commissioners*, January 12, 2000 (16450) (transcript available via Lawtel).

[61] *St Luke's Church (PCC) v Commissioners* (1982) S.T.C. 856, *per* Woolf J at p.861.

[62] *All Saints Church v Commissioners*, May 1993 (10490) (noted in *Value Added Tax Encyclopaedia*, vol.2).

That decision was applied by the High Court in *Commissioners v Windflower Housing Association*, concerning the replacement of an entire roof on a listed building. The new roof was constructed using modern materials, which necessitated the raising of the roof plane, which on its own would suggest that the works were not repair and maintenance. However, apart from the raising of the roof, the work done was "maintenance", defined as "a task designed by the owner or occupier to minimise, for as long as possible, the need for, and future scale and cost of further attention to the fabric of the building."[63] Taking the works as a whole, therefore, they were repair and maintenance, and any changes in the roof were either de minimis or dictated exclusively by the nature and use of modern building materials.

The substitution of new windows (double-glazed, with fake astragals) for old ones does not constitute an alteration—even if it is granted listed building consent.[64] But zero-rating was given for the removal of a gutter and a drainpipe, and adding an extra layer of slates onto the roof of a bay, so that rainwater from the roof would in future simply fall onto the pavement.[65] Clearly such cases will need to be decided on their facts; decisions of tribunals should therefore be treated as illustrative and not determinative.

Where a building is not merely altered but reconstructed, for example following a severe fire, that will amount to new building work, and may be zero-rated under Group 5 rather than Group 6—although, obviously, only if it is to be used for a relevant residential or charitable purpose.[66]

17.3.4 The need for approval

Part of the test as to whether alterations are approved is whether:

- they are such that they may not be carried out unless authorised; and

- such authorisation has actually been granted.

Usually this means that work for which listed building or scheduled monument consent has been granted will be accepted (other things being equal) for zero-rating. But the need for consent cannot simply be assumed.

The Revenue and Customs are sometimes willing to accept that, if listed building consent has been obtained for particular works, it must have been needed, and that those works are therefore approved alterations—as in *Arbib*, noted above.[67] However, this does not always apply. Thus the Tribunal did not accept that listed building consent was required for the construction of a new, detached garage in the grounds of a listed building—even though the planning authority had granted it.[68]

---

[63] (1995) S.T.C. 860.
[64] *Moore v Commissioners*, June 8, 2004 (EDN/03/85) (transcript available on HMRC website).
[65] *Starr v Commissioners*, July 21, 2005 (MAN/05/0043) (transcript available via Lawtel).
[66] *Commissioners v Moorish* [1998] E.G.C.S. 111.
[67] See **17.3.2**.
[68] *Bradfield v Commissioners*, 1990 (5339) (noted in *Value Added Tax Encyclopaedia*, vol.2), following *Cotswold DC v Secretary of State* (1984) 51 P. & C.R. 139 (see **12.5.3**).

Conversely, where a substantial set of stud walls, with cupboards and doorways, were installed within a large bedroom in a Grade I listed castle, as part of a larger programme of internal works, the tribunal was prepared to accept that they required listed building consent.[69] Presumably that was on the basis that it considered that the grant of listed building consent related to the package of works as a whole, including the new wall, even though an officer of the planning authority had indicated to the Customs and Excise that consent would not be required for the wall on its own.

It will be noted that alterations carried out to listed buildings and scheduled monuments are only zero-rated if the relevant consent has actually been obtained beforehand. Where works are carried out without consent, it may be possible subsequently to obtain consent for their retention—either by making an application for consent or by appealing against an enforcement notice. However, such consent is not retrospective, so it will not be possible to claim zero-rating.

In the unusual situation where a house is partially destroyed by fire, and then shortly afterwards the remaining part is demolished—before consent has been obtained—it will not be possible to justify zero-rating the demolition under Group 6, since the works have not been formally authorised. However, if a new house is then built on the site, it will be possible to zero-rate the demolition under Group 5, as a preliminary part of the construction of a new dwelling.[70]

17.3.5 Special cases

It has been noted earlier that, until now, works to Crown buildings have generally not required listed building or scheduled monument consent.[71] Zero-rating in such cases is thus applied to alterations that would require such consent if they were carried out to any other building.[72]

Once the exemption of Crown land from planning control has finally been abolished, as a result of the Planning and Compulsory Purchase Act 2004, the provisions of Note (6) to Group 6 will no doubt be amended so as to bring alterations to Crown buildings into line with other cases.

Works to listed places of worship also do not generally require listed building consent; they also are therefore subject to special rules, considered below.[73]

17.4 The supply of services and goods

17.4.1 The statutory formula

By virtue of Items 2 and 3 in Group 6, zero-rating applies to:

---

[69] *Owen v Commissioners*, June 21, 2004 (LON/03/462) (transcript available on HMRC website).

[70] *Dart Major Works Ltd v Commissioners*, October 1, 2004 (LON/03/1133) (transcript available via Lawtel).

[71] See **13.10**.

[72] VAT Act 1994, Sch.8, Group 6, Notes (6)(c), (8).

[73] See **17.5**.

"2.   the supply, in the course of an approved alteration of a protected building, of any services other than the services of an architect, surveyor or any other person acting as consultant or in a supervisory capacity; and

3.   the supply of building materials to a person to whom the supplier is supplying services within Item 2 of this Group which include the incorporation of the materials into the building (or its site) in question."[74]

The meaning of "protected building" and "approved alteration" has been considered already.[75]

The result of this is that contractors and subcontractors carrying out approved alterations to protected buildings may zero-rate both the labour cost of the works (under Item 2), and the cost of materials (under Item 3). Since both are zero-rated, there is no need to distinguish between them in invoices, provided that there is no element of works on items properly classified as "repairs and maintenance".

Note that the supply of materials is only zero-rated if they are supplied as part of a building project carried out by contractors, and if the materials are supplied by those contractors. There is thus no scope for private owners of protected buildings being able to reclaim VAT paid on goods bought for use by themselves in carrying out DIY alterations to protected buildings. Nor can contractors claim zero-rating on goods delivered to site by suppliers not carrying out any installation.[76]

The relief does apply to the supply and installation of items normally built into the structure of a building such as space and water heating devices, alarm systems, fitted kitchen furniture, and lifts; but not to other domestic electrical or gas appliances (such as washing machines and telephones) or other fitted furniture (such as bookcases) or materials supplied to make it; nor to carpets.[77] However, where a major installation of internal walls, doors and cupboards is inserted into a listed house, the Customs may be prepared to accept that it is not simply fitted cupboards, and thus may be eligible for zero-rating.[78] And in a major refurbishment project, some fitted items may be allowable for zero-rating, while others may attract tax at standard rate.[79]

Professional fees are not zero-rated.

17.4.2 Cases of uncertainty

HM Customs and Excise suggests that, to justify zero-rating any supplies, a contractor will need in addition to the usual records:

(1)   for listed buildings, including churches, evidence that it was a listed building when the works were done (either a copy of the entry in the relevant statutory list or in the local land charges register, or a copy of the

---

[74]   VAT Act 1994, Sch.8, Group 6, Items 2 and 3.
[75]   See **17.2** and **17.3** above.
[76]   *Commissioners v Jeffs*, 1995, *The Independent*, July 3, (transcript available via Lawtel).
[77]   Group 5, Notes (22), (23), applied by Group 6, Note (3).
[78]   *Owen v Commissioners*, June 21, 2004 (LON/03/462) (transcript available on HMRC website).
[79]   *Christ's Hospital v Revenue & Customs*, June 16, 2005 (LON/04/1041) (transcript available via Lawtel).

statutory notice sent out by the local authority at the time the building was listed)[80];

(2) for listed buildings other than churches, evidence that the alteration works received listed building consent (a copy of the consent together with any associated schedules, correspondence and drawings showing what works obtained listed building consent); and

(3) for buildings other than dwellings (that is, other buildings in relevant residential use and charitable buildings), a certificate in the form indicated in Appendix A to VAT leaflet 708.[81]

Where works consist only in part of approved alterations, an apportionment is to be made between those and the remainder.[82]

In cases of uncertainty, an approach should be made for a ruling to the local VAT office dealing with the contractor. This should be done by supplying full details of the proposed works, as for the listed building consent application (and using the same numbered drawings).[83]

Once a ruling has been obtained stating that the works are zero-rated, this will normally be honoured by the Customs and Excise in the event of any subsequent dispute.[84]

17.5 Works to places of worship

17.5.1 Eligible alterations

Works to listed places of worship in use by any of the six exempt denominations in England and Wales (the Church of England, the Church in Wales, the Roman Catholic Church, the Methodist Church, the Baptist Union and the United Reformed Church) are exempt from the need for listed building consent, by virtue of the "ecclesiastical exemption" from listed building control.[85] The rules about "approved alterations" are accordingly different in such cases.

Where the ecclesiastical exemption applies, all alterations other than repair and maintenance are approved alterations for the purposes of zero-rating for VAT, by virtue of Note (6)(a) to Group 6. This used to be significant—it is noticeable that a number of the tribunal decisions cited earlier in this chapter relate to works carried out to places of worship[86]—although it may prove to be less so in the future, at least for as long as the Listed Places of Worship Scheme (see below) continues in existence.

---

[80] See **3.3**.
[81] Group 5, Note (12)(b), applied by Group 6, Note (3).
[82] Group 6, Note (9); see also *All Saints Church*.
[83] See **13.3.4**.
[84] *Hansard*, (HL) Deb July 21, 1978, cols 426–7.
[85] See **16.3**.
[86] *St Luke's Church* (1982) S.T.C. 856; *All Saints Church*, 1993; *All Saints with St Nicholas Icklesham*, 1999; *St Petroc Minor*, 2000 (see **17.3.3**).

Unsurprisingly, the exemption does not apply to a minister's house; although it would when the house is listed in its own right. Nor does it apply to curtilage structures such as walls, gates and tombstones, since they are not ecclesiastical buildings.[87] Works to listed places of worship of non-exempt denominations and religions (such as Quaker meeting houses and synagogues) are still be eligible for zero-rating, but under Note (6)(c), since they would require listed building consent—provided of course that such consent has been obtained.

Oddly, places of worship in Scotland and Northern Ireland (of all denominations and religions) appear to miss out on zero-rating. This is because works to them are not alterations to "ecclesiastical buildings to which section 60 of the (English) Listed Buildings Act applies", but nor (probably) are they works requiring to be authorised by the Scottish Listed Buildings Act or the Northern Ireland Order. They are thus zero-rated neither by Note (6)(a) nor by Note (6)(c). Until this anomaly is rectified, it is to be hoped that HMRC will give zero-rating as a non-statutory concession.

17.5.2 Repairs and maintenance

Works of repair and maintenance to listed places of worship are not eligible for zero-rating, any more than such works to other listed buildings.

However, the Government has made proposals to the European Commission for a reduced rate of 5 per cent on such works. This is being considered in the Commission's review, currently under way, of the permitted reduced rates in the sixth VAT directive.

In the meanwhile, the Chancellor announced in the 2001 Budget that he would introduce an interim grant scheme, the effect of which would be to return in grant aid the difference between 5 per cent and the actual amount spent on VAT on the cost of eligible repairs to listed places of worship. That was extended in the 2004 Budget to cover the full amount of VAT for eligible works carried out on April 1, 2004. The scheme, known as the Listed Places of Worship Grant Scheme, is to continue until March 31, 2008, unless a reduced rate is achieved earlier; experience suggests that it may well be extended, but those potentially eligible should check the position at the time.

The Scheme is administered by the DCMS, but applies to listed buildings throughout the United Kingdom that are used solely or mainly as places of worship for any religion, including redundant buildings owned by certain specified organisations.[88] It is non-discretionary.

Further details and an application form are available on a special website.[89]

---

[87] Note (7).
[88] Including the Churches Conservation Trust, Historic Chapels Trust, the Friends of Friendless Churches, the Welsh Religious Buildings Trust and the Scottish Redundant Churches Trust.
[89] www.lpwscheme.org.uk

17.6 The disposal of reconstructed buildings

As well as the supply of goods and services in connection with an approved alteration to a protected building, there is a further relief available whereby zero-rating applies also to:

"1. The first grant by a person substantially reconstructing a protected building of a major interest in, or in any part of, the building or its site."[90]

For a building to be "substantially reconstructed" it must be gutted, so that only the outside walls and significant external features remain (such as roofs, domes, colonnnades, porches); and at least 60 per cent of the total cost of the works are wholly attributable to "approved alterations".[91] Where the building is partly in use for a qualifying (residential or charitable) purposes and partly in use for some other purpose, the amount payable is zero-rated only in relation to that portion of it that relates to the portion of the building in use for the qualifying purpose.[92]

The disposal must be by way of grant, assignment or surrender of a freehold or long (more than 21 years) leasehold interest.[93] Where the disposal is by way of a lease, with a premium, the premium is zero-rated, but not the rent subsequently payable; where there is no premium, only the first payment of rent is zero-rated.[94]

Helpful guidance on the interpretation of these provisions is given by a decision of a tribunal relating to the reconstruction of a ruined house in Wiltshire,[95] in which it was accepted that the words "substantially reconstructing" are to be taken together and given their ordinary everyday meaning. Each case will be a matter of impression. In that case, the builder had preserved what he could, and reused what materials he could, and had painstakingly recreated the original building but using much new material. As for the 60 per cent test, that requires not a detailed analysis of each item, to see if it is alteration or repair, but rather a broader perspective.

That decision was distinguished in a more recent case concerning a major refurbishment of a listed house that was in poor repair, but not ruinous; the tribunal considered that what had been done was better categorised as "minor enlargement of a building and a modernisation of its interior" as opposed to "substantial reconstruction".[96]

---

[90] VAT Act 1994, Sch.8, Group 6, Item 1.
[91] Group 6, Note (4); as to approved alterations, see **17.3** above.
[92] Group 6, Note (5).
[93] VAT Act 1994, s.96(1); and Sch.8, Group 5, Note (1), applied by Group 6, Note (3).
[94] VAT Act 1994, Sch.8, Group 5, Note (14), applied by Group 6, Note (3).
[95] *Lordsregal Ltd v Commissioners*, March 17, 2004 (LON/01/1243) (transcript available via Lawtel).
[96] *Southlong East Midlands v Commissioners*, February 18, 2005 ((LON/03/789) (transcript available via Lawtel), adopting *Barraclough v Commissioners*, 1986 (2529).

Part V

Unauthorised works

"The British system of conservation has evolved mainly in response to growing public concern for the heritage. Sustainable conservation requires the support of public opinion. There is some evidence that attitudes may be changing or, at least, that doubts are being expressed about the extent and intensity of conservation policies."

John Delafons, *Politics and Preservation* (E. & F. N. Spon, London, 1997)

"Find out what the children are doing, and tell them to stop it."

The Duchess, in Lewis Carroll, *Alice's Adventures in Wonderland* (1865)

Chapter 18

Unauthorised Works: Enforcement

18.1 Introduction

18.1.1 Background

Part IV of this book outlined in some detail the occasions on which various forms of permission or consent are required for works to historic buildings and monuments, and development in historic areas, and how such permission can be obtained (or at least sought).

What happens, however, if such works take place without permission or consent? This would include not only major works (such as the total demolition of an important listed building), but also alterations that may be minor but which are still significant (such as changing the pattern of glazing bars on a house in a uniform terrace). Or consent might be granted for the demolition of part of an unsafe building but only subject to a condition that it must be reconstructed in the original materials—what if no further works take place after demolition? In the face of such problems, the whole system of control would be very weak if there were no effective means of enforcing it.

The carrying out of works to a listed building without listed building consent is a criminal offence—as is the demolition of a building in a conservation area without conservation area consent, and the carrying out of works to a scheduled monument without scheduled monument consent. It is therefore possible for those responsible to be prosecuted. This is considered in detail in the following chapter, but is far from straightforward; and it is by no means always appropriate.

In practice, therefore, it is always sensible for a planning authority to consider at the outset options other than prosecution. And of these the first option to be considered is whether to invite an application or applications for retrospective authorisation of the works that have been carried out (see **18.2**). A further possibility in appropriate cases is to serve a breach of condition notice, against which there is no right of appeal.

In some cases, however, the best option will be to take enforcement action—that is, to issue a planning enforcement notice or a listed building enforcement notice or both (see **18.3**). This has the advantage of forcing owners of property (or those who carried out the works) to take practical steps to alleviate the effect of their misdeeds—and usually an authority is, or should be, more concerned to alleviate the effects of unauthorised works rather than to punish those responsible. And of course there is no reason why an authority should not at the same time take enforcement action and mount a criminal prosecution, thus securing at least the possibility of both restitution and punishment.

Note that there is no power to take enforcement action to bring about the restoration of an ancient monument, or the removal of an unauthorised advertisement[1]—in each case, therefore, prosecution is the only option.

If an enforcement notice is issued, there is a right to appeal against it to the Secretary of State (see **18.4**). However, if no appeal is made, or if any appeal is unsuccessful, it will have to be complied with (**18.5, 18.6**).

In cases of urgency, it may be necessary for the authority to issue of a stop notice or seek an injunction from the courts; these are considered in **18.7**.

Finally, special regimes apply in the case of unauthorised signs and advertisements and unauthorised works to places of worship. These are briefly considered in **18.8** and **18.9**.

18.1.2 Legislation and policy

The Planning and Listed Buildings Acts of 1990, applying in England and Wales, were significantly amended in relation to enforcement procedures by the Planning and Compensation Act 1991 to incorporate the recommendations of the report of Robert Carnwath Q.C. on *Enforcing Planning Control*. All references in this chapter to sections 171A to 196C of the Planning Act and sections 38 to 46 of the Listed Buildings Act are thus to those sections as amended or inserted by Schedule 3 to the 1991 Act.

Virtually identical changes were made in 1991 to the relevant Scottish legislation, but they have subsequently been incorporated in the Scottish Planning and Listed Buildings Acts of 1997. And similar changes have now been made in Northern Ireland, in the Planning (Amendment) (Northern Ireland) Order 2003, as from November 12, 2003[2]; references to the Northern Ireland Order should accordingly be understood to be to the Order as amended in 2003 (and references to "a planning authority" should be interpreted as a reference to the Department).

It should be emphasised that the enforcement of planning control is a very complex subject, that has generated over the years a great deal of highly technical litigation and legislation. This chapter accordingly does not attempt to cover all aspects of the topic, but merely to draw attention to the relevant legislation and to highlight some of the issues that may arise in the context of works affecting historic buildings and areas.

Guidance on enforcement generally, including in relation to listed buildings and conservation areas, is contained (for England and Wales) in *Enforcing Planning Control: Good Practice Guide for Local Planning Authorities*, issued by the DETR

---

[1]   Except, for some reason, for advertisements in Scotland: see **18.8**.
[2]   2003 S.R. 443 (C34).

in 1997, and in ODPM Circular 02/2002 and NAW Circular 08/2003, both entitled *Enforcement Appeals Procedures*.[3] Guidance for Scotland is in SDD Circular 4/1999, *Planning Enforcement: Town and Country Planning (Scotland) Act 1997*, and Planning Advice Note PAN 54, *Planning Enforcement*; although it relates only to enforcement against breaches of planning control, with no reference to listed buildings and conservation areas.[4] Guidance on all aspects of enforcement in Northern Ireland is in Planning Policy Statement PPS 9, *The Enforcement of Planning Control*.[5]

18.2 Possible courses of action

18.2.1 Enforcement or prosecution?

The first decision to be made by an authority when confronted by apparently unauthorised works to listed buildings or scheduled monuments, or affecting their setting, or unauthorised works in a conservation area, is whether:

- to take no action;

- to authorise (reluctantly or otherwise) what has been done;

- to take some form of enforcement action to undo what has been done, or at least mitigate its effect,

- to apply for an injunction[6] to prevent further works, or

- to prosecute those responsible.

The carrying out of works to a listed building for which listed building consent ought to have been, but was not obtained, is a criminal offence. The same is true of carrying out works without conservation area consent or scheduled monument consent. This is in contrast to the position regarding development for which specific planning permission is required but has not been obtained, which is only a breach of planning control. In the latter case, a criminal offence occurs only if an enforcement notice is issued and not complied with. It is therefore possible for a local authority (or English Heritage or an amenity group or, come to that, anyone interested) to mount a criminal prosecution. The following chapter examines the details of pursuing such a prosecution, since they are not covered in any depth in standard planning law texts.

But it should not be assumed that that approach will be appropriate in every case, or even often, particularly in view of the large amount of time that is involved, and the relatively low penalties that are likely to be obtained. In summary, prosecution will usually be suitable only when the works that have been carried out are irreversible (such as in the case of total or partial demolition, or

---

[3] The former not to be confused with DTLR Circ. 02/02 (on major infrastructure projects).

[4] Available on the Scottish Executive website (*www.scotland.gov.uk/Topics/Planning-Building/Planning*).

[5] Available on the Planning Service website (*www.planningni.gov.uk*)

[6] Interdict in Scotland.

the removal of a significant feature that cannot be recovered or satisfactorily replaced) or where there is a need to discourage repetition (such as where a builder is replacing traditional timber windows with unsuitable plastic ones in a number of properties in a conservation area) or limitation.

Further, in a criminal prosecution, an authority must prove "beyond reasonable doubt" that an offence has occurred, and that the accused was responsible. In enforcement proceedings, by contrast, it is only necessary to prove on the balance of probabilities that unauthorised works have taken place; and it does not matter who was responsible.

It is therefore usually sensible for an authority to take enforcement action wherever possible, as opposed to prosecution. However, it is necessary at least to consider prosecution at the outset since, if it is only contemplated once enforcement proceedings have been finally exhausted, that could be some time in the future, long after the memories of all concerned have faded, so that it may be difficult to obtain sufficient evidence to secure a conviction. It may therefore be sensible—if prosecution is to be an option—at least to undertake any initial investigations reasonably promptly, while any enforcement action is under way.

And before even doing that, the first stage is to consider whether it is really necessary to take any action at all, and whether it may be best simply to authorise what has been done—possibly subject to suitable conditions designed to minimise its effect.

18.2.2 Initial procedure

The first initial step in enforcement action—before deciding what, if any, action to take—will usually be for the planning authority to obtain enough information.

Where it appears to an authority that there may have been a breach of planning, as opposed to listed building control, it may serve a "planning contravention notice" (under section 171C of the Planning Act[7]) on the owner or occupier of the land in question, or on any person carrying out operations on it. The notice will require the recipient to provide information on (amongst other things) who owns the land, what is taking place or has taken place on it, and why that has or does not need planning permission. A failure to comply with a planning contravention notice without a reasonable excuse is an offence.[8]

Where the breach seems to be a failure to have obtained listed building or conservation area consent, as opposed to planning permission, it is not possible for a planning authority to serve a planning contravention notice, but it (or English Heritage in London) may obtain information as to the ownership of land by serving a notice under section 330 of the Planning Act.[9]

Quite apart from these statutory powers, it is always worth an authority exploring carefully what actually has been or is going on, rather than relying on highly coloured accounts supplied by informants. But care needs to be exercised by all concerned where works may have constituted a breach of any requirement

---

[7] Scotland: TCP(S)A 1997, s.125; NI: P(NI)O 1991, art.67C.
[8] TCPA 1990, s.171D. [Scotland: TCP(S)A 1997, s.126; NI: P(NI)O 1991, art.67D.]
[9] Applied by P(LBCA)A 1990, s.89(1). [Scotland: TCP(S)A 1997, s.272, applied by P(LBCA)(S)A 1997, s.79(1); NI: P(NI)O 1991, art.125.]

for listed building or conservation area consent, since that would constitute a criminal offence. It may therefore be appropriate for the authority to issue a caution under the Police and Criminal Evidence Act 1984 to avoid the possibility of problems arising should the authority in due course institute criminal proceedings.

18.2.3 Works that are unauthorised but not unacceptable

Firstly, works may have been carried out that were right on the borderline of what does or does not materially affect the external appearance of a building, or affect the character of a listed building as a building of special architectural or historic interest, such that the need for permission or consent is highly arguable. Or the works may be such that they do indeed technically require planning permission or listed building consent—albeit only just—but are in fact very minor and quite unexceptionable. Or planning permission or listed building consent may have been granted for some works, similar but not identical to works currently being carried out.

In such instances, unless the property owner wishes to obtain permission or consent in order to regularise the position, it may be prudent for all concerned to take no further action at all. Alternatively, the planning authority may wish to send the owner a brief letter stating for the record that it does not intend to take further action; that may be useful if further works are carried out at a later date.

A slight complication is that, if the works were such that they required listed building consent—either in addition to planning permission or otherwise—then carrying them out without consent, or not strictly in accordance with any consent that has been granted, would have been a criminal offence. Further, there is no time-limit on either taking enforcement action or issuing criminal proceedings—and a planning authority cannot fetter its discretion by undertaking never to take any such action. In those circumstances, it may be wise for the owner (or prospective owner) to obtain written authorisation from the authority to avoid later difficulties.

Secondly, works may have been carried out that were sufficiently major that they undoubtedly required planning permission or listed building or consent, but which are such that permission or consent would equally certainly have been readily forthcoming if only it had been sought. This could include the re-roofing of a listed building in stone slates that are different from, but better than, the asbestos slates that were there before; the construction of a perfectly satisfactory extension to a house that exceeds by a few centimetres the size of one that would be granted permission by the General Permitted Development Order; or the removal of a hideous porch that was erected some while ago.

In such a situation, it would be unreasonable for an authority to take punitive or enforcement action; but equally it would be imprudent for the owner to take no action at all—not least because problems may arise when the property subsequently changes hands. Here the right way forward is for the authority to invite the owner to submit the necessary application or applications to retain the works carried out, or for the owner to submit them voluntarily. Such applications are submitted and processed just like any others,[10] although the fact that the works have already been carried out means that their effect on the building should be much easier to ascertain, and that as a result it will only be necessary to submit relatively few (if indeed any) details of what has been done.

In any of the above cases, planning authorities should be astute to avoid being drawn into what are alleged to be major breaches of planning control and violations of the heritage, but are actually simply the result of neighbour disputes. Such cases soak up time (and public money) to an extent that is wholly disproportionate to any conceivable public benefit.

18.2.4 Unauthorised works that are not wholly acceptable

Works may have been carried out to a listed building, without consent, which are not altogether satisfactory and which would therefore have been opposed had consent been sought. Alternatively, works may be carried out that are significantly different from those that have been permitted, such that the difference is objectionable. In some such cases, it may not be right for an authority to take a firm line, and institute enforcement action or criminal proceedings—either because it is now unrealistic in all the circumstances to expect the building to be restored to its former state; or because to do so would be undesirable (where, for example, its former state was even worse than its present one); or because of personal or other special reasons.[11]

Here too the least undesirable course may be for an application to be submitted for planning permission or listed building or conservation area consent, as appropriate, to retain the unauthorised works. The Court of Appeal has recognised that, in some cases, even where an authority would not have give permission for a proposal if asked in advance, it may be not so objectionable as to require it to be undone; and that to do so would be a disproportionate sanction for the breach of the law concerned.[12] A graphic example is the case of the unauthorised windows that ended up, some 17 years after they were installed, in front of Scott Baker J.:

"It seems to me that the state of affairs that has arisen in this case is an extremely unfortunate one. Mr and Mrs Wigham have replaced old windows in their house, beginning in 1985 and doing the work bit by bit. Nobody complained until their house was put on the market in January 2001. It was at that point that an astute planning officer noticed that the work appeared to be in breach of the listed building regulations. How it happened that there was no complaint whatsoever over the previous 16 years is difficult to understand. No one, either local authority or member of the public, appears to have been bothered by the new windows. One of the problems in the case is that there was apparently correspondence between the Wighams and the Council but it is no longer in existence. The Wighams thought the Council was content with what they were doing.

. . . It does seem to me surprising that a local authority stands by for many, many years and then suddenly swoops on something that has been done with a listed building, without

[10] P(LBCA)A 1990, s.8(3).
[11] See **14.9.2**.
[12] *R. v Leominster DC, ex p Pothecary* [1998] J.P.L. 335.

considering exercising a discretion whether to take action, a considerable period of time having gone by without apparent complaint from anybody.

Be that as it may, it seems to me that the underlying problem ought to be looked at. The fact is that it would be very expensive now for the Wighams to replace these PVC windows back in their original state. I do rhetorically ask the question whether and to what extent this is really necessary. It seems to me desirable that the local authority and the Wighams, if necessary with some independent person, sit down and try and plot the way ahead, to the mutual satisfaction of all parties."[13]

Sometimes the best approach in such a situation is for the authority to decide formally to take no action in view of the particular circumstances, but making it clear that this is not to constitute a precedent for other properties.

Another example of this in the listed building field came before the court in *South Lakeland DC v SSE and Rowbotham*.[14] The occupier of No.3 The Square, Burton, a Grade II listed terrace in a conservation area in Cumbria, replaced (without listed building consent) the original timber sash windows with modern casement windows. An application was submitted to retain the new windows; it was refused, on the grounds that "the window frames as installed materially detract from the character and appearance of this building". The occupier appealed, putting forward a strong case on compassionate grounds. She was 84 years old, frail, and unable to open and close sash windows; and double glazing was essential to shut out noise, and to conserve heat. The observations of the planning authority as to the effect of the alterations on the character of the building were disputed, and it was argued that the original sash windows, or indeed any sash windows, would be unsuitable for efficient double glazing.

The council responded in detail, emphasising the importance of the house at the historic core of the village and explaining its view that the windows had a serious adverse effect on the character of the building and of the conservation area. The inspector, an architect, found in the council's favour on that issue. He was also satisfied that, if the original windows were not capable of adaptation and improvement, a more sympathetic solution could have been arrived at which would still have achieved the requirements of sound and heat insulation and draught-proofing. However, after considering the special circumstances, including the costs and disruption to the occupier in having the windows replaced again and the benefits that had already accrued to her, he granted listed building consent for the retention of the windows; and his decision was upheld in the High Court.

A more recent instance of this approach was the decision of the Court of Appeal in *Braun v Secretary of State*, in which, after remitting the matter to the Secretary of State for reconsideration, the court commented that it was surely questionable whether the enforcement notice should be taken further, and that the building owner and the council should resolve the matter by some form of compromise.[15] Unfortunately that proved impossible in respect of all the works involved, and the matter duly ended up in front of another inspector; but he took

---

[13] *R. (Wigham) v Secretary of State*, September 12, 2002, unreported (transcript available via Lawtel). A planning authority in such a situation might reflect with advantage on what is commonly supposed to be the better part of valour...

[14] [1991] J.P.L. 440.

[15] [2001] 1 P.L.R. 90, CA, at para.30.

the hint, and sought pragmatic solutions, whilst "endeavouring to safeguard this engaging listed building." He accordingly allowed the appeal and quashed the notice in respect of the remaining items.[16]

Thus, it may in some circumstances be appropriate for an authority to take a more lenient approach on a retrospective application than would be appropriate were consent to be applied for in advance. However, in many cases, authorities will rightly take a rather more robust attitude. Thus, following the court decision in *South Lakeland*, the occupiers of two other properties in the same terrace in Burton also installed similar new windows without consent, and the planning authority took enforcement action. The inspector upheld both enforcement notices, observing in relation to one of them:

"I have taken into account the similar windows at No.3. However, in my view, the fact that inappropriate windows have been granted consent makes it more, and not less, important to ensure that appropriate windows are installed elsewhere in the front façade. Consequently I find no merit in the suggestion that, for uniformity, inappropriate windows should be installed in all the windows on the front elevation of Nos 1–4. I have taken into account cost and disturbance in relation to your personal, financial and marital circumstances ... while I have sympathy for your situation, I conclude, on balance, that the objections [to the windows] are not outweighed by other material considerations."[17]

And authorities have been advised not to grant consent in such circumstances merely to recognise a fait accompli.[18] A planning authority, faced with works that have already been carried out, should thus first consider whether it would have granted permission of consent had it been sought in advance—in the light of the considerations outlined earlier in this book[19]—and then take into account any subsequent matters which may be relevant. If it would not have done so, it should then go on to consider whether there are nevertheless compelling personal or other circumstances that suggest that consent should be granted for the works to be retained.

If permission or consent is granted in such a situation, it is open to the authority, or the Secretary of State if the application is called-in, to impose whatever conditions seem suitable to ensure that the effect of the works is minimised, and that any consequential damage is made good.[20] If the owner resents any of the conditions imposed, it is possible either to apply to the planning authority to have them varied[21] or to appeal against them to the Secretary of State.[22]

18.2.5 Submission notices

In Northern Ireland, where it appears to the Department that development has been carried out in the previous four years without planning permission granted

---

[16] PINS ref APP/H5390/F/01/1056763.
[17] Appeal refs: T/APP/F/91/M0933/608899 (quoted) and T/APP/F/91/M0933/609379–80.
[18] PPG 15, para.3.42; WO Circ. 61/96, para.121. See also *Edinburgh CC v Scottish Ministers* [2002] 4 P.L.R. 54, [2003] J.P.L. 903 (quoted at **18.4.6**); and **13.8.2**.
[19] See **Chapter 14**.
[20] See **13.8.5**.
[21] See **13.8.7**.
[22] See **15.2.2**.

either by a development order or in response to an application, it may issue a notice under article 23 of the Northern Ireland Order, requiring an application for permission to be made within 28 days. Anyone failing to comply is guilty of an offence, and liable on summary conviction to a fine of Level 3 on the standard scale.

There is a right to appeal against a submission notice to the Planning Appeals Commission.[23]

There is no equivalent procedure to enable the Department to require the submission of an application for listed building or conservation area consent. And there is no similar procedure in England, Wales or Scotland.

18.2.6 The effect of permission and consent to retain works already carried out

If planning permission or listed building or conservation area consent is granted after enforcement action is under way, the permission or consent will automatically negate any enforcement notice that may have been issued insofar as it relates to the works now authorised.[24]

However, if listed building or conservation area consent is granted to retain works which have already been carried out, it is not "retrospective"—even though it is often for convenience referred to as such. That is, it does not absolve the owner from liability to criminal prosecution for the fact that consent was not obtained in the first place—although, in the event of conviction in such circumstances, the fact that consent had subsequently been granted would no doubt be taken into account in sentencing.[25]

18.2.7 Breach of conditions

A further possibility is that works are granted planning permission (and, if necessary, listed building consent) but are then carried out in breach of one or more of the conditions attached. Here, too, the first matter to be considered is whether the result is acceptable or unacceptable.

Thus, for example, a condition may require that no works are to start until details of all materials to be used have been approved by the planning authority. If works start without such approval having been obtained, but the materials actually used are perfectly appropriate, there may be no point in taking any action—other than, possibly, inviting a retrospective application to put the record straight. And permission is often granted for works subject to a condition that they be carried out in accordance with the drawings, but it may become apparent once works start that the details may need to be revised: if the discrepancy is very minor, the answer may then be to do nothing; bearing in mind, again, that non-compliance with a condition on a listed building consent is a criminal offence.

---

[23] P(NI)O 1991, art.24. See the guidance available on the PAC website (*www.pacni.gov.uk*).
[24] TCPA 1990, s.180; P(LBCA)A 1990, s.44(1) [Scotland: TCP(S)A 1997, s.137; P(LBCA)(S)A 1997, s.40(1); NI: P(NI)O 1991, arts 75, 79(1),(2).]
[25] P(LBCA)A 1990, s.44(2) [Scotland: P(LBCA)(S)A 1997, s.40(2); NI: P(NI)O 1991, arts 79(3).]

Alternatively, the authority may invite, or the developer may submit, an application to modify or remove the conditions in question. This has been considered earlier.[26]

It may be, however, that a failure to comply with a condition is far from acceptable—where, for example, planning permission and listed building consent are granted for the construction of an extension to a historic building, but the materials and detailing employed are seriously sub-standard.

Where the works were the subject of a grant of planning permission (whether or not accompanied by listed building consent), the planning authority may serve a breach of condition notice, under section 187A of the Planning Act.[27] A breach of condition notice can be served on the person carrying out the development in question, and is to require him or her to comply with the condition or conditions specified in the notice. It is in particular to specify the steps the authority considers should be taken to secure compliance with the condition (such as, in the present context, the removal of the unauthorised roof tiles and their replacement by approved ones), and the time by when they are to be taken (at least 28 days).

There is no right of appeal to the Secretary of State against a breach of condition notice—on the basis that a person who was granted planning permission had a right to appeal against the conditions attached to it; if therefore he or she implements that permission, the conditions should be complied with. If the person receiving the notice has not within the specified time complied with its requirements, he or she will have committed an offence, unless it can be shown that all reasonable measures have been taken to secure compliance.

There is no corresponding provision to bring about compliance with conditions attached to a grant of listed building consent. However, a consent is usually granted at the same time as a planning permission for the same works, and subject to the same conditions; so the successful service of a notice to secure compliance with a condition on a permission will incidentally also secure compliance with the corresponding condition on the consent. Failing which, it would be possible to institute a prosecution.[28]

18.2.8 Unauthorised works to scheduled monuments

If unauthorised works are carried out to a scheduled monument, there is no provision in the 1979 Act for "enforcement action" to be taken, as there is with unauthorised works to a listed building; an ancient monument by its nature usually cannot be "restored". This means, at least in theory, that the only measure that could possibly be effective, either as a punishment or as a deterrent to others, is criminal prosecution.[29]

[26] See **13.8.7**.
[27] Scotland: TCP(S)A 1997, s.145; NI: P(NI)O 1991, art.76A.
[28] See **19.2.2**.
[29] See **19.6.1**.

It follows from the fact that there is no enforcement procedure that there is no provision for scheduled monument consent to be sought to retain the monument as it now stands, following the execution of unauthorised works.[30]

However, where the works carried are in fact not controversial, there would seem to be no reason why an approach should not be made to English Heritage (or Cadw, Historic Scotland, or the Department in Northern Ireland) to obtain its confirmation that, had consent been sought, it would have been granted—possibly subject to conditions. If such a letter of confirmation is obtained, it is not "consent", and has no formal status; but it would in practice mean that, subject to any suggested conditions being complied with, the likelihood of prosecution is effectively removed. The risk of such a course of action, of course, is that, if the works are in fact not considered acceptable, the authorities are alerted to the possibility of prosecution.

18.3 The issue of enforcement notices

18.3.1 Unauthorised works to listed buildings

The most usual route to obtain the undoing of undesirable works that have been carried out is the issue of enforcement notices.

As with many of the other procedures described in this book, it must be remembered that most works to listed buildings require both planning permission and listed building consent. Accordingly, when it appears that unauthorised works to a listed building have taken place, it will be necessary for the planning authority to consider serving both:

- an enforcement notice under section 172 of the Planning Act (referred to in this Chapter as a "planning enforcement notice"), insofar as development has been carried out without planning permission granted either by the General Permitted Development Order or in response to an application; and

- a "listed building enforcement notice" (under section 38 of the Listed Buildings Act), in so far as works to listed buildings have been carried out without listed building consent.

The carrying out of development without planning permission is not a criminal offence, but merely a breach of planning control under the Planning Act. If such a breach should come to the attention of the planning authority, it has complete discretion as to whether or not to issue a planning enforcement notice. If the authority does issue a notice, anyone served with a copy is entitled to appeal against it to the Secretary of State. However, unless such an appeal is allowed, it is then a criminal offence not to comply with the notice.

The same principles are applied by the Listed Buildings Act to works to a listed building carried out without listed building consent. The authority thus has

---

[30] Compare the provision relating to listed building consent under P(LBCA)A 1990, s.8(3); see **18.2.3**

complete discretion whether to issue a listed building enforcement notice. Again, subject to a right of appeal, non-compliance with the notice is then an offence. However, as well as the points made earlier in this chapter, there are several aspects of the procedures which should be borne in mind at the outset:

(1) the issue of a listed building enforcement notice is an alternative (or may be in addition) to the criminal prosecution of those responsible for allegedly unauthorised works[31];

(2) there is no time limit for the issue of a listed building enforcement notice equivalent to the "four-year rule" and "ten-year rule" applying in relation to planning enforcement notices[32]; and

(3) there is no equivalent to the "stop notice" procedure in relation to works being carried out without listed building consent, nor any equivalent to the "temporary stop notice" introduced by the Planning and Compulsory Purchase Act 2004—instead, an injunction must be served in cases of urgency.[33]

The implications of the second of these points is considered further below.[34]

18.3.2 Unauthorised works in a conservation area

If a planning authority is concerned about unauthorised development that has taken place in a conservation area—either the alteration of an existing, unlisted building or the erection of a new building—its only option will usually be to issue a planning enforcement notice.

In theory, it is possible to issue a "conservation area enforcement notice" where an unlisted building in a conservation area has been demolished without conservation area consent. However, the House of Lords in *Shimizu* has made it clear that conservation area consent is only required where demolition is carried out so as to result in a site for new development[35]; and it is likely that it will not be practicable to reverse demolition on that scale—and indeed, even if it is possible, it will only rarely be desirable, since, by definition, the building involved will not be listed. It is therefore difficult to envisage many circumstances where it might be sensible to issue a conservation area enforcement notice.[36]

The discussion in the remainder of this chapter thus concentrates almost entirely on planning enforcement notices and listed building enforcement notices; but the rules as to the issue of a conservation area enforcement notice are exactly as for the issue of a listed building enforcement notice—save for there being (unsurprisingly) slightly different grounds of appeal, as noted below.[37]

---

[31] See **Chapter 19**

[32] In this respect, a listed building enforcement notice resembles a planning enforcement notice concerning an unauthorised change of use issued prior to the changes introduced by the Planning and Compensation Act 1991.

[33] See **18.7**.

[34] See **18.3.5, 18.4.5**.

[35] *Shimizu PLC v Westminster CC* [1996] 3 P.L.R. 89, HL; see **12.6.3**.

[36] For an exception, see the interesting appeal decision noted at [2004] J.P.L. 97.

[37] See **18.4.7**.

18.3.3 *Authorities empowered to take enforcement action*

Enforcement action may be taken by the local planning authority[38]—that is, in general, the district or borough council in England,[39] the county or county borough council in Wales[40]—the planning authority in Scotland,[41] and the Department in Northern Ireland.[42] National park authorities in England and Wales[43] and the Broads Authority[44] each have jurisdiction in their respective areas.

In Greater London, English Heritage has the same powers as a borough council in relation to the issue of listed building and conservation area enforcement notices (but not planning enforcement notices)[45]; and it does not have to consult the borough council before issuing a notice. Slightly more oddly, the new urban development corporations in Thurrock and the Thames Gateway have also been given powers in relation to the issue of listed building and conservation area enforcement notices (in place of the relevant borough or district council), but not in relation to planning enforcement notices.[46]

In addition, the Secretary of State or the Scottish Ministers, after consultation with the planning authority, as defined above, may issue a notice. English Heritage must be consulted in relation to a listed building and conservation area enforcement notice issued in England. A notice issued by the Secretary of State has the same effect as one issued by a local authority.[47] The use of this power is rare; but it could be appropriate where it is a local authority itself (or English Heritage!) that has carried out the unauthorised works.

18.3.4 *The decision to issue an enforcement notice*

The relevant authority (or the Secretary of State) may issue an enforcement notice if:

(1) it appears that works have been carried out without planning permission or listed building or conservation area consent or in breach of a condition attached to a grant of permission or consent; and

---

[38] TCPA 1990, s.172; P(LBCA)A 1990, s.38(1).

[39] TCPA 1990, s.1(1), (2); P(LBCA)A 1990, Sch.4, para.2.

[40] TCPA 1990, s.1(1B), inserted by the Local Government (Wales) Act 1994, s.18.

[41] TCP(S)A 1997, s.1, P(LBCA)(S)A 1997, s.81(2).

[42] P(NI)O 1991, arts 68(1), 77(1).

[43] TCPA 1990, s.4A(2), inserted by the Environment Act 1995, s.67.

[44] TCPA 1990, s.5; P(LBCA)A 1990, Sch.4, para.5.

[45] P(LBCA)A 1990, s.45.

[46] SI 2005/2572, art.4, Sch. (Thurrock); SI 2005/2721, art.5, Sch. (Thames Gateway). The official Explanatory Memorandum to each SI states that "the Order does not give the Corporation enforcement powers under the Planning Act, because of the administrative and resource burden involved. The Order does, however, give the Corporation enforcement powers under the Listed Buildings Act because they do not pose the same burden." That may be an explanation; it is not a good reason.

[47] TCPA 1990, s.182; P(LBCA)A 1990, s.46. [Scotland: TCP(S)A 1997, s.139; P(LBCA)(S)A 1997, s.41.] There is, obviously, no corresponding provision in Northern Ireland.

(2)   the authority considers it "expedient" to do so having regard to:

- in the case of a planning enforcement notice, the provisions of the development plan and any other material considerations[48];
- in the case of a listed building enforcement notice, the effect of the works on the special character of the listed building in question[49]; and
- in the case of any works affecting a conservation area, their effect on its character and appearance.[50]

As to the first of these, it does not matter who carried out the works (provided that they were not too long ago: see below[51]). Where, for example, a previous owner has built an extension, or a vandal has removed a fireplace or some panelling, it is perfectly in order to issue a listed building enforcement notice requiring the present owner to carry out the necessary restoration works—to remove the unauthorised works, replace the missing items, or make good the damage.[52] This may at first sight seem unfair, but if the damage was done by a previous owner, the purchase price should have been adjusted to reflect the liability on the new owner to repair it; and if it was done by a vandal, a conscientious property owner should carry appropriate insurance.

As to the second criterion, expediency, this is important. Thus, the most usual reason for enforcement action being taken is that complaints are made to the authority by amenity groups and members of the public; but authorities must actually consider what action is expedient—and not issue enforcement notices merely because permission or consent has not been obtained. Thus, for example, it is significant that an authority is required, when considering whether to issue a listed building enforcement notice, to take into account not merely whether the effect of the works carried out on the character of the building is such that they required consent, but whether their effect was sufficient to justify enforcement action.

An authority should also consider carefully what, if any, grounds of appeal are likely to be relied on if it issues a planning or listed building enforcement notice, and on what basis it would counter those grounds. So, for example, a very basic point to consider is whether the works actually needed permission or consent; and, if they did, whether it would have been granted.

In particular, listed building consent should be sought for works which significantly improve the appearance of a building just as much as for those which detract from it; but if, in the former case, consent had not been sought before works were carried out, it would quite possibly not be "expedient" for the authority to take enforcement action. It would of course be imprudent for an

---

[48] TCPA 1990, s.172(1). [Scotland: TCP(S)A 1997, s.127(1); NI: P(NI)O 1991, art.68(1).]
[49] P(LBCA)A 1990, s.38(1). [Scotland: P(LBCA)(S)A 1997, s.34(1); NI: P(NI)O 1991, art.77(1).]
[50] P(LBCA)A 1990, s.72; and s.38(1), applied by s.74(3) and modified by P(LBCA) Regs 1990, reg.12 and Sch.3. [Scotland: P(LBCA)(S)A 1997, s.64; and s.34(1), applied by s.66(3); NI: P(NI)O 1991, art.50(3); and art.77(1), applied by art.51(5).]
[51] See **18.3.5**.
[52] *Braun v Secretary of State* [2003] 2 P.L.R. 90, CA, at paras 14, 15.

owner in such a situation to rely on an authority taking no action; and an application to retain the works should therefore be submitted.[53]

What, if any, action an authority takes is of course entirely at its discretion. The advice of the Secretaries of State is as follows:

"Enforcement may be intrinsically desirable for the benefit of the building in question, while the work entailed by enforcement may also represent a sufficient response to the offence. However, unauthorised work may often destroy historic fabric the special interest of which cannot be restored by enforcement. Moreover, well-publicised successful prosecutions can provide a valuable deterrent to wilful damage to, or destruction of, listed buildings, and it is the Secretary of State's policy to encourage proceedings where it is considered that a good case can be sustained".[54]

An authority cannot be forced to take action of any kind if it chooses not to do so, unless it can be shown that its refusal is unreasonable or arbitrary.[55] Thus, where a council declined to take enforcement action in relation to works carried out to a listed boundary wall, the court found that the council had dealt with the greatest care with the numerous representations of the complainant neighbour; it had a power to act and not a duty, and had exercised its discretion correctly. It accordingly not only declined to quash the council's action, but awarded costs against the neighbour on an indemnity basis.[56] Otherwise, the only remedies available to a dissatisfied complainant would be a private prosecution in the case of a person carrying out works to a listed building (which will not often be a realistic option) or a complaint to the ombudsman (which is not likely to achieve a great deal either).

Where works have been carried out leading to a conviction for failure to obtain listed building or conservation area consent, this would be a powerful element in the case for the planning authority in the event of a subsequent inquiry into any appeal against an enforcement notice relating to the same works. However, where such a prosecution leads to an acquittal, this does not necessarily preclude the authority from persisting with enforcement action, since (as already noted) the issues at stake are somewhat different, and a jury is not required to give reasons for acquitting.[57]

18.3.5 Time-limits

Where building or other works are carried out—either to construct a new building or to alter an existing one—a planning enforcement notice may not be issued more than four years after the works are substantially complete.[58]

---

[53] See **18.2.3**.
[54] PPG 15, para.3.47 (WO Circ. 61/96, para.121 is similar). And see HS Memorandum, paras 3.1, 3.2.
[55] *Perry v Stanborough (Developments) Ltd* (1977) 244 E.G. 551.
[56] *R. v Cotswold DC, ex p. Kissel* [1997] J.P.L. 1395.
[57] *Braun v Secretary of State*, December 19, 2002, Ouseley J. at paras 26, 27 (upheld on different grounds at [2003] 1 P.L.R. 90, CA). For an example of this in practice, see also the appeal decision noted at [2004] J.P.L. 97.
[58] TCPA 1990, s.171B(2). [Scotland: TCP(S)A 1997, s.124(1); NI: P(NI)O 1991, art.67B(1).]

However, there is no corresponding time-limit for the issue of a listed building or conservation area enforcement notice. This was confirmed by the Court of Appeal in *Braun v Secretary of State*, in which Simon Brown L.J. held as follows:

"Of course, an owner cannot be prosecuted under sections 7 and 9 [of the Listed Buildings Act] for unauthorised contravening work carried out by his predecessors in title. But section 38 is concerned not with prosecution, but rather with enforcement, and enforcement is available against works provided only that they did in fact involve a contravention, whenever and by whomsoever they were carried out. I say whenever: until, of course, the building is listed, there can be no contravention by anyone."[59]

A listed building or conservation area notice may thus not be issued where the offending works were carried out before the building in question was listed or included in a conservation area—since, obviously, such works would not have required consent.

However, it must be respectfully questioned whether the Court of Appeal in *Braun* was entirely correct. The requirement for listed building consent to be obtained for works to listed buildings was only introduced (in the Town and Country Planning Act 1968) on January 1, 1969, so works carried out prior to that date cannot generally be the subject of the issue of a listed building enforcement notice. The only exception might be where a building was prior to that date subject to a building preservation order,[60] since it would have then been necessary to obtain the consent of the planning authority for works to demolish it or seriously affect its character. It might therefore, in theory, still be possible for enforcement action to be taken where such works were carried out without consent; although it is difficult to imagine that being "expedient" more than 35 years later.

Indeed, the issue of a listed building enforcement notice after an unreasonably long time has elapsed since the alleged breach of control might be considered to be a breach of human rights under Article 6.

In Northern Ireland, a listed building enforcement notice cannot be issued in respect of works carried out before December 9, 1978.[61]

Note that where works were carried out to a listed building more than four years ago, without either planning permission or listed building consent, it would be possible for the planning authority to issue a listed building enforcement notice to require them to be reinstated, even though it could not issue a planning enforcement notice in respect of the same works.

18.3.6 Contents of an enforcement notice

An enforcement notice is to specify clearly:

(1) the alleged contravention;

(2) what the authority wishes to see done about it;

---

[59] [2003] 1 PLR 90, CA, *per* Simon Brown L.J. at para.14.
[60] See **1.2.3**.
[61] P(NI)O 1991, art.78(1)(a). That is the date on which the relevant provisions of the Planning Amendment (NI) Order 1978 came into force.

(3) the time in which that must be done; and

(4) the date on which the notice is to come into effect.[62]

The general test which must be satisfied by any enforcement notice is "does it tell [the recipient] fairly what he has done wrong and what he must do to remedy it?".[63] For a sample listed building enforcement notice, see **Form D18** in Appendix D.

As for the contravention, this must be set out clearly, so that the recipient can decide whether to claim that the specified works have been not carried out or, if they have, that they have been the subject of a grant of permission or consent. This is particularly important in relation to a listed building enforcement notice, since the absence of a time limit means that a notice may in principle relate to works carried out over many years.[64]

As for the steps which the authority can require to be carried out, a planning enforcement notice can specify those that are necessary to remedy injury to amenity that has been caused by the unauthorised works—including:

- the alteration or removal of any buildings or works, or

- the carrying out of any building or other operations.

Similarly, a listed building enforcement notice can specify:

- steps for restoring the building to its former state; or if that would not be reasonably practicable or would be undesirable,

- steps necessary to alleviate the effect of the unauthorised works.

And either type of notice may require works to be carried out to bring about what would have occurred if the terms and conditions of any permission or consent which has been granted for the works had been complied with.[65]

The reference to the "former state" of a building refers to its state immediately before the allegedly unauthorised works were carried out. Thus in his report on the appeal against listed building enforcement notices served in respect of Sutton Place, Surrey, the inspector noted drily that:

"...it seems to me that the 'former state' of the building referred to in the notice means its state immediately prior to the removal of the stained glass and not, as suggested in the grounds of appeal, its state in the 16th century".[66]

---

[62] TCPA 1990, s.173, P(LBCA)A 1990, s.38(2),(3). [Scotland: TCP(S)A 1997, s.128, P(LBCA)(S)A 1997, s.34(2),(5); NI: P(NI)O 1991, arts 68A, 77.]

[63] *Miller-Mead v Minister of Housing and Local Government* [1963] 2 Q.B. 196 at 232 *per* Upjohn L.J.

[64] *Braun v Secretary of State* [2003] 1 P.L.R. 90, CA, at paras 19–29.

[65] TCPA 1990, s.173(4),(5), P(LBCA)A 1990, s.38(2). [Scotland: TCP(S)A 1997, s.128(4),(5), P(LBCA)(S)A 1997, s.34(2); NI: P(NI)O 1991, arts 68A(4),(5), 77(1).]

[66] [1984]) J.P.L. 899; and see **14.4.9**.

Where a building has been dismantled into pieces that are capable of being re-assembled,[66a] or removed as a single piece to a new location, a notice may also require that to be done.

It will often happen that the restoration of the building will either be impracticable, because of the irreversible nature of the works carried out, or undesirable, because the former state was even worse than it is now. The second category of remedial works in relation to each type of notice was therefore added to enable a planning authority to require the owner to carry out whatever further works might be desirable in all the circumstances. Where a notice specifies works in this category, they are deemed to be granted planning permission or listed building consent if they are carried out in accordance with that specification.[67] Conversely, a notice should not require works to be carried out that are in breach of some other statutory code.[68]

Where a building has been subject both to specific unlawful alterations and to general decay, it is perfectly lawful to issue a notice seeking the rectification of the alterations even if that has the effect of making the owner carry out some general repairs as well.[69]

The drafting of any enforcement notice needs care, if it is not to be open to a successful appeal. This is particularly so with regard to the specification of the remedial works required by the authority.[70] Where a period feature has been removed, the authority should thus consider carefully whether it should require:

(1) the return of the original item (if its whereabouts are known);

(2) the insertion of an exact facsimile (if appropriate details are available);

(3) the insertion of a similar item of the same period;

(4) the insertion of a modern item performing the same function: or

(5) the making good of the damage to the building caused by the removal of the item (either on its own or in combination with one of the above options).

An authority must also ensure that the remedial works are specified with sufficient precision to avoid the need for any subsequent approval to be obtained. If a notice contains a requirement for the authority's approval to be obtained for the

---

[66a] As happened in the case of Stagbatch Barn (see **4.2.3**). The decision of the Secretary of State is noted at [1987] J.P.L. 798; see **18.4.8**; it was upheld in *R. v Leominster DC, ex p. Antique Country Buildings Ltd* [1988] J.P.L. 554. See also *R. (Judge) v Secretary of State and Middlesbrough BC* [2005] EWCA, unreported, July 22, 2005, CA; affirming [2005] EWHC 887 (Admin), unreported, April 28, 2005.

[67] TCPA 1990, s.173(11),(12), P(LBCA)A 1990, s.38(7). [Scotland: TCP(S)A 1997, s.128(13),(14), P(LBCA)(S)A 1997, s.34(4); NI: P(NI)O 1991, arts 68A(11),(12), 77(5).]

[68] *Mackay v Secretary of State* [1994] J.P.L. 806, doubted in *South Hams DC v Halsey* [1996] J.P.L. 761

[69] *R. v Elmbridge BC, ex p. Active Office Ltd* [1998] J.P.L. B43 above.

[70] See **18.4.8**.

details of the required works, that will render the notice a nullity, incapable of correction by either the authority or an inspector on appeal.[70a]

A planning enforcement notice must specify the reasons why it was issued and the relevant development plan policies.[71] There is, curiously, no corresponding requirement in relation to a listed building enforcement notice, although to include a statement of reasons would seem to be good practice.

18.3.7 Service of copies of the notice

Once the notice has been "issued" by the local authority (that is, a resolution to that effect has been passed by the appropriate committee, sub-committee or officer acting under delegated powers) or by English Heritage or the Secretary of State, copies of it must be served within 28 days on the owners and occupiers of the property and on anyone else who "has an interest in it".[72]

In the unusual case of a building having been dismantled partially or wholly, a copy of the notice should also be served on whoever now owns most of the pieces.[73] Similarly, where part of a building is removed from the remainder, copies should be served both on the owner of the main building and on the apparent owner of the part removed. If works are actually in progress, it would also be prudent for the authority to serve copies on any builders, demolition contractors, architects, surveyors and others involved, and possibly to fix a copy to the building itself.

Where a notice relates to two properties, or to a boundary wall between them, care must be taken to draft it correctly and to serve copies on all involved—in one such case, the notice was served on one owner only, and sought to reclaim the costs of the restoration works off the other. Not only did the authority concerned fail to reclaim those costs, but it had to pay the second owner's costs of litigation on an indemnity basis.[74]

An authority which has issued an enforcement notice should send to each person involved two copies of it, so that the recipient can retain one and send one with any appeal.[75] The authority should also send with each copy of a planning enforcement notice details of the right to appeal against it, and a note of the fee payable for an appeal. Many authorities fulfil this requirement by including with the notice a copy of the booklet *Making Your Enforcement Notice Appeal*, toge-

---

[70a] *Kaur v Secretary of State* (1989) 61 P. & C.R. 249; *Payne v National Assembly for Wales and Caerphilly CBC* [2006] EWHC 596 (Admin) unreported, January 5, 2006.

[71] TCPA 1990, s.173(10), TCP (Enforcement Notices and Appeals) (England) Regulations 2002 (SI 2002/2682) (England), reg.4, TCP (Enforcement Notices and Appeals) (Wales) Regulations 2003 (SI 2003/394), reg.3. [Scotland: TCP(S)A 1997, s.128(11); NI: P(NI)O 1991, art.68A(10).]

[72] TCPA 1990, s.172(2), P(LBCA)A 1990, s.38(4). [Scotland: TCP(S)A 1997, s.127(2), P(LBCA)(S)A 1997, s.34(6); NI: P(NI)O 1991, art.68(2), 77(6).] As to the meaning of the latter phrase, see **13.8.7**.

[73] *R. v Leominster DC Ex p. Antique Country Buildings Ltd* [1988] J.P.L. 554; see **4.2.3** and **18.3.6**.

[74] *Browning v Tameside MBC* [1997] E.G.C.S. 38.

[75] TCP (Enforcement Notices and Appeals) (England) Regulations 2002 (SI 2002/2682) (England), reg.5; (Wales) Regulations 2003 (SI 2003/394), reg.4. See ODPM Circ. 02/2002, Annex 1; and NAW Circ. 08/2003. [Scotland: ; NI: .]

ther with the official appeal form.[76] Again, there are no corresponding requirements in relation to listed building enforcement notices, although to include the
same material would seem to be good practice.[77]

18.3.8 Register of enforcement notices

A register is to be kept of planning enforcement notices, thus ensuring that
prospective purchasers of property and subsequent owners are aware of potential
problems.[78]

A register of listed building and conservation area enforcement notices only has
to be kept in Scotland and Northern Ireland.[79] In England and Wales, in the
absence of such a register, a subsequent owner, who will be responsible for
compliance with such a notice (and liable to being prosecuted for non-compliance), may quite legitimately be unaware of its existence. This is an unfortunate
loophole, which should be promptly rectified. In the meanwhile, it would be good
practice for authorities in England and Wales too to record such notices on a non-
statutory basis.

18.3.9 Special cases

No enforcement notice may be issued in respect of works carried out by the
Crown (that is, in practice, by government departments[80]) on its own land.[81] In
respect of other works carried out to a building owned by the Crown, for example
by a tenant, a notice can only be issued with the consent of "the appropriate
authority"—that is, usually, the relevant department or the Crown Estates
Commissioners. This will shortly change when Crown immunity is lifted (at least
in Great Britain).[82]

Where the owner of a listed building is a foreign government (many of the
embassies in London, for example, are listed), enforcement action is not in
practice possible, since the buildings and land used for the purposes of a diplomatic mission are declared to be inviolable by the 1961 Vienna Convention on
Diplomatic Relations.[83] In practice, therefore, an authority in such a case should
invite the ODPM to request the Foreign and Commonwealth Office to intervene
on its behalf.

---

[76] See **18.4.1**.
[77] Except that there is no fee payable for listed building and conservation area enforcement
notice appeals.
[78] TCPA 1990, s.188. [Scotland: TCP(S)A 1997, s.147; NI: P(NI)O 1991, art.124(1)(d).]
[79] P(LBCA)(S)A 1997, s.34(9); NI: P(NI)O 1991, art.124(1)(d).
[80] See **13.10.1**.
[81] TCPA 1990, s.296(2)(a), P(LBCA)A 1990, s.83(3). [Scotland: TCP(S)A 1997,
s.245(2)(a), P(LBCA)(S)A 1997, s.74(3); NI: P(NI)O 1991, art.113(3), (4).]
[82] PCPA 2004, s.84 (England and Wales), s.94 (Scotland) (see also **13.10.2**). For Northern
Ireland, see Planning Reform (NI) Order 2006.
[83] art.22(1), applied in the UK by the Diplomatic Privileges Act 1964.

18.4 Appealing against enforcement notices

18.4.1 Submission of appeal

An appeal against an enforcement notice may be made at any time before the notice is due to come into effect; note that no extensions of that time limit are allowed in any circumstances.[84] It may be made:

- in England, Wales and Northern Ireland, by anyone either having an interest in the building, or occupying it by virtue of a licence both at the time the notice is served and at the date of the appeal[85];

- in Scotland, by anyone having an interest in the land or on whom the notice was served.[86]

The appeal may be made on the appropriate form, similar to the one used for appealing against the refusal of permission or consent, issued by the Planning Inspectorate (in England and Wales), the Scottish Executive Inquiry Reporters Unit or the Planning Appeals Commission in Northern Ireland. The form is in each case available on the relevant website[87]; and a copy should have been sent with the notice itself. The use of the form is not mandatory—it is possible to appeal simply by letter—but the grounds relied upon should be set out clearly.

Whether or not the official form is used, the appeal must be in writing. The only grounds that can be relied on are those set out in the relevant statutory provisions; they are also listed on the appeal form. The appellant need not specify which grounds are being relied on when the appeal is first made; it is in theory adequate to state no more than the address of the building and the name of the local authority involved. But it is helpful to all parties if at least some statement accompanies the appeal. A statement must in any event be provided within 14 days of it being requested by the Secretary of State, specifying the grounds relied on and stating briefly the facts on which it is proposed to rely in support of each of those grounds.[88]

The statutory grounds of appeal against each type of notice are set out in the table at **Figure 18.1**, and considered in more detail below.[89] Those relating to a planning enforcement notice are set out in section 174 of the Planning Act (those in section 130 of the Scottish Planning Act and article 69 of the Northern Ireland Order are identical). Those relating to a listed building enforcement notice, which are similar (albeit in a different order), are in section 39 of the Listed Buildings

---

[84] *Howard v Secretary of State for the Environment* [1975] Q.B. 235; *Lenlyn Ltd v Secretary of State* [1985] J.P.L. 482; *R. v Secretary of State, Ex p. Jackson* [1987] J.P.L. 790.

[85] TCPA 1990, s.174(1),(6); P(LBCA)A 1990, s.39(1), (7). [NI: P(NI)O 1991, arts 69(1),(2), 78(1),(2).]

[86] TCP(S)A 1997, s.130(1); P(LBCA)(S)A 1997, s.35(1).

[87] See **15.2.3** (England, Wales and Scotland) and **15.8.1** (Northern Ireland).

[88] TCPA 1990, s.174(4), P(LBCA)A 1990, s.39(4); TCP (Enforcement Notices and Appeals) (England) Regulations 2002, reg.6; (Wales) Regulations 2003, reg.5. [Scotland: TCP (Enforcement of Control) (No. 2) (Scotland) Regulations 1992 (SI 1992/2086), reg.5.

[89] See **18.4.2** to **18.4.8**.

Act and section 35 of the Scottish Listed Buildings Act; those applying in Northern Ireland (in aricle 78 of the Order) are almost the same, except as noted in the table. The grounds of appeal against a conservation area enforcement notice are identical to those against a listed building enforcement notice, except as noted.

The choice of grounds need to be considered with care, as it is not possible to add others later. And if an appellant relies on more than one ground of appeal, but only provides supporting information in respect of some of them, the appeal may be decided without any consideration being given to the other grounds.[90] And if works have been carried out to a listed building, which are alleged to require both planning permission and listed building consent, two notices will have to be served, and hence two appeals made; and the grounds will need to be harmonised appropriately.

The appeal should also be accompanied by a copy of the notice being appealed against, and any other relevant documents. If the appeal involves a planning enforcement notice, a fee should also be included (which will generally be twice the fee that would be payable for a planning application for the same type of development). It must be sent so as to reach the relevant agency by the date on which the notice would otherwise come into effect, by first-class post and recorded delivery. The envelope should be clearly marked "Enforcement Notice Appeal", to ensure that there is no delay.

Useful guidance on submitting an appeal in England and Wales is contained in the publication *Making Your Enforcement Appeal*, a copy of which should be sent by the planning authority to everyone receiving a copy of an enforcement notice. It is also available on the Inspectorate website. Similarly useful guidance is on the websites of the Planning Appeals Commission in Northern Ireland. Limited guidance is available from the Scottish Executive Inquiry Reporters' Unit.

Table 18.1 Grounds of appeal against enforcement notices

Planning enforcement notices	*Listed building enforcement notices and conservation area enforcement notices*
(e) That copies of the enforcement notice were not served as required by section 172 [of the Planning Act].	(f) That copies of the notice were not served as required by section 38(4) [of the Listed Buildings Act].
(b) That the matters stated in the notice [as constituting a breach of planning control] have not occurred.	(b) That the matters alleged to constitute a contravention of section 9(1) or (2) [of the Listed Buildings Act] have not occurred.
(c) That those matters (if they occurred) do not constitute a breach of planning control.	(c) That those matters (if they occurred) do not constitute such a contravention.[91]
	(d) That works to the building were urgently necessary in the interests of safety or health or for the preservation of the building [etc].[92]

---

[90] TCPA 1990, s.174(5), P(LBCA)A 1990, s.39(5).
[91] Ground (a) in Northern Ireland.
[92] See **18.4.4**.

(d) That, at the date the notice was issued, no enforcement action could be taken in respect of any breach of planning control which may be constituted by those matters.

(a) That, in respect of any breach of planning control which may be constituted by the matters stated in the notice, planning permission ought to be granted, or

[that] the condition or limitation concerned ought to be discharged

(f) That the steps required by the notice to be taken ... exceed what is necessary to remedy any breach of planning control which may be constituted by those matters or, as the case may be, to remedy any injury to amenity which has been caused by any such breach.

(g) That any period specified in the notice [at the end of which any steps are required to have been taken] falls short of what should reasonably be allowed

(c) That the contravention alleged in the notice occurred before 9th December 1978. [Northern Ireland only]

(e) That listed building consent ought to be granted for the works, or

that any relevant condition of such consent as has been granted ought to be discharged, or different conditions substituted.

(a) That the building is not of special architectural or historic interest.[93] *[LBEN only]*

(a) That retention of the building is not necessary in the interests of preserving the character or appearance of the conservation area in which it is situated.[94] *[CAEN only]*

(g) That the requirements of the notice [for restoring the building to its former state] exceed what is necessary for restoring the building to its condition before the works were carried out.[95]

(i) That the steps required by the notice for the purpose of restoring the character of the building to its former state would not serve that purpose *[LBEN only]*.

(j) That the steps required to be taken [to alleviate the effects of the works which were carried out] exceed what is necessary [for that purpose].

(k) That the steps required to be taken [to bring the building to the state in which it would have been if the consent which has been granted had been complied with] exceed what is necessary [for that purpose].

(h) That the period specified in the notice as the period within which any step is to be taken falls short of what should reasonably be allowed.[96]

18.4.2 Ground of appeal: service of the notice defective

Logically, the first ground of appeal (actually ground (e) against a planning enforcement notice and ground (f) against a listed building enforcement notice) is that copies of the relevant notice were not served as required by the relevant

---

[93] Does not apply in Northern Ireland.
[94] Does not apply in Northern Ireland.
[95] Ground (h) in Northern Ireland.
[96] Ground (g) in Northern Ireland.

statutory provision.[97] If it can be substantiated, the notice is defective, and the authority would simply have to issue another one.

However, it should be borne in mind that, even if it can be proved that a copy of the notice was not served on a person who should have had one, the Secretary of State may disregard that if he or she considers that neither that person nor the appellant was substantially prejudiced by the error.[98] So, for example, it may not be enough to show that a mortgagee was not served with a copy of the notice, as was the case with the enforcement notice in the Stagbatch Barn case.[99] Where someone appeals to the Secretary of State against a notice, it is not then possible for anyone else subsequently to appeal to the courts on the grounds that it was not properly served on that person.[1]

18.4.3 Grounds of appeal: no contravention of the Act

The second ground to be considered (happily it is ground (b) in all cases) is that the matters alleged to constitute a breach of planning control or a contravention of section 9(1) or (2) of the Listed Buildings Act have not occurred. As to the two offences referred to, see the following chapter.[2] This is in principle a matter of fact—either the works described in the notice have occurred or they have not; either the listed building has been altered or demolished, or it has not. However, the precise wording of the notice should be checked; it may be that works have taken place, or the building has been altered, but not in the way or to the extent specified there.

The third ground (ground (c) in almost all cases[3]) is that the matters alleged to constitute a breach of planning control or a contravention of section 9(1) or (2) do not constitute such a breach or contravention. This, unlike ground (b), is largely a matter of law and depends on the matters set out earlier in this book. Professional advice will be needed if this ground is relied on. To prove that a breach of planning control or a contravention of section 9 has occurred, the authority must be able to point to some development that has occurred without planning permission having being granted, or some "works" for the alteration or demolition of the building without listed building consent. Conversely, the appellant must seek to show either that permission or consent was not needed, or that it was granted—either by the General Permitted Development Order or in response to an application.

Those works need not have been carried out by the present owner[4]; but the Secretary of State has taken the view that damage caused by something outside

---

[97] See **18.3.7**.
[98] TCPA 1990, s.176(5), P(LBCA)A 1990, s.41(5). [Scotland: TCP(S)A 1997, s.132(4), Scotland: P(LBCA)(S)A 1997, s.37(2)(b); NI: P(NI)O 1991, arts 70(3), 78(3).]
[99] See the appeal decision reported at [1987] J.P.L. 798; also **4.2.3**, **18.4.8**, **18.7.3**.
[1] TCPA 1990, s.175(5), P(LBCA)A 1990, s.39(6). There appear to be no corresponding provisions in Scotland or Northern Ireland.
[2] See **19.2.1** and **19.2.2**.
[3] Ground (a) in an appeal against a listed building or conservation area enforcement notice in Northern Ireland.
[4] *R. v Elmbridge BC, ex p. Active Office Ltd* [1998] J.P.L. B43, (1998) 10 Admin L.R. 561.

the owner's control, such as impact by a passing car, does not amount to "works".[5] Reinstatement in such cases is thus beyond the scope of the enforcement procedure.[6]

In some cases permission or consent will have been granted, but it is not clear whether the permitted works include those that have actually been carried out. In such a case, it is necessary to check all the relevant paperwork in order to work out what precisely has been permitted (the drawings and other material that was submitted with the original applications may have subsequently been altered several times)—not least where planning permission and listed building consent have both been granted, sometimes at different times or for different works.[7] And it seems that it just might be possible for a planning authority to argue that a consent was defective (even if given some while ago), for example because it was issued without a statutory consultee having been consulted—although that is a very unattractive tactic.[8]

If either of these grounds is successfully relied on, the only option open to the Secretary of State would be to allow the appeal and quash the notice.[9]

18.4.4 Ground of appeal: works urgently necessary

Sometimes it will be claimed that works that required planning permission or (more often) listed building consent were carried out as a matter of urgency, before authorisation could be obtained. Permission and consent will still be needed in such cases; but clearly cannot always be obtained in advance. On the other hand, it is easy to claim after the event, falsely, that works were urgently necessary. This has been considered earlier, and it was pointed out that—if prosecution is to be avoided—any works carried out to a listed building must be limited to the minimum necessary and notified to the planning authority as soon as reasonably practicable, by virtue of the defence in section 9(3) of the Listed Buildings Act.[10]

Where the authority is not convinced that the works were genuinely necessary, it may issue an enforcement notice. Where it is alleged that the works required planning permission, so that a planning enforcement notice is issued, it will be necessary for the appellant to rely on ground (c) (that the works did not need permission) and ground (a) (that permission should be granted). Where the works were to a listed building, the corresponding grounds of appeal against a listed building enforcement notice are (c) and (e). There is, however, an additional ground of appeal (ground (d)) against a listed building enforcement notice, as follows:

---

[5] In two appeal decisions noted at [1981] J.P.L. 443 and [1990] J.P.L. 444.
[6] See **8.4** as to insurance.
[7] See for example *Regent Inns PLC v Secretary of State* [2002] E.W.H.C. 2270 Admin, unreported (transcript available via Casetrack).
[8] It was accepted in *Fenland DC v Reuben Rose (Properties) Ltd* [2000] P.L.C.R. 376 (an injunction case; see **18.7.2**).
[9] s.41(2).
[10] See **12.4.7**.

"[i] that works to the building were urgently necessary in the interests of safety or health or for the preservation of the building, and

[ii] that it was not practicable to secure safety or health or, as the case may be, the preservation of the building by works of repair or works for affording temporary support or shelter, and

[iii] that the works carried out were limited to the minimum measures necessary."[11]

This reflects the wording of section 9(3). Factual evidence will be needed as to the condition of the building prior to the works, and professional evidence (from, say, a building surveyor or structural engineer) as to the cost and feasibility of both the works that were carried out and any alternatives that may be suggested.

Note that, even if this ground is successfully relied on, consent should still have been obtained for the works, so that ground (e) should always be relied on as well (as well as ground (c) if the works were relatively minor).

18.4.5 Ground of appeal: enforcement action time barred

The question of time limits has already been considered in the context of the decision to take enforcement action.[12]

Where a planning enforcement notice is issued in relation to building or other works that were substantially completed more than four years ago, an appeal should be made against a planning enforcement notice on ground (d). There is no corresponding time limit for enforcement action in relation to allegedly unauthorised works to listed buildings or demolition in conservation areas, and therefore no corresponding ground of appeal against a listed building or conservation area enforcement notice.

Where a listed building or conservation area notice is issued in respect of works that were carried out before the building in question was listed or included in a conservation area, or before January 1, 1969 (if the building was listed prior to that date), an appeal should be made relying on ground (c) (that the works did not need consent).[13]

18.4.6 Grounds of appeal: permission or consent should be granted

The grounds considered so far are effectively that the notice is invalid, that the works did not take place, that they did not need permission or consent, that they were justified because they were urgently necessary, and that enforcement was time-barred. In other words, one way or another, the authority should not have taken enforcement action.

However, unless an appellant is absolutely 100 per cent certain of success on one or more of those grounds—and whatever other grounds (if any) may be relied on—any appeal should always include a claim that planning permission or listed building or conservation area consent (or, as appropriate, both) should be granted for the works that have been carried out. Similarly, where a condition of a per-

---

[11] P(LBCA)A 1990, s.39(1)(d) (material in square brackets added for clarity). [Scotland: P(LBCA)(S)A 1997, s.35(1)(d); NI: P(NI)O 1991, art.78(1)(d).]

[12] See **18.3.5**.

[13] The corresponding date in Northern Ireland is December 9, 1978 (P(NI)O 1991, art.78(1)(a)).

mission or consent has allegedly not been complied with, it should be claimed that the condition should be varied or discharged. That is, the grounds of almost every appeal should include ground (a) in relation to a planning enforcement notice and ground (e) in relation to a listed building or conservation area enforcement notice.

Further, whether or not those grounds are explicitly relied on, the Secretary of State or the Inspector, in deciding the appeal, may grant planning permission or listed building consent, in response to an application deemed to have been made.[14] It is therefore always prudent to consider what could be put forward to justify what has been done, on its merits. In doing this, the issues at stake will primarily be those that are relevant to an ordinary application for permission or consent or the variation of conditions.[15]

The one factor that is different, however, is that the works will by definition have been already carried out—at least in part. If therefore the notice is upheld they will have to be undone, and the original state of the building restored. That may be impossible, impracticable or unreasonable. The first case—where, for example, features have been destroyed—is unlikely to arise, since prosecution would be more appropriate than enforcement action. The second case—where it is said that reinstatement would be difficult or expensive, but not impossible— demands an exercise of judgment by the inspector. The third might occur where, for example, the personal circumstances of an appellant mean that it would be unreasonable to insist on reinstatement.

As for the considerations that would apply in such cases, these are very much the same as those that apply in the case of retrospective applications generally, considered earlier in this chapter.[16] In particular, inspectors should be astute to consider the desirability of what has been done, rather than just the possibility of mitigating its effects. The Court of Session thus criticised a reporter [inspector] who had allowed an enforcement notice appeal, subject to conditions:

"I appreciate that the reporter adopted what he recognised to be a 'pragmatic' approach, and it is possible to sympathise with him to some extent in that approach. I also appreciate that, in some cases, the distinction between

- asking oneself the question whether it is reasonable that an offending structure be removed, and
- asking oneself the question whether a proposal *ab ante* to construct such a structure should receive consent,

may be a fine one. But, in my view, the two questions are truly different questions, and to apply the former test may risk deploying, in favour of the property owner who has carried out the development or alteration without the consent required by the law, a practical advantage not enjoyed by those owners more careful or scrupulous in their attention to the requirements of the legislation. It also invites the imposition of inappropriate conditions directed, not to the grant of consent, but to the cessation and removal of an unauthorised

---

[14] TCPA 1990, s.177, P(LBCA)A 1990, ss 41(6)(a),(b), (7). [Scotland: TCP(S)A 1997, s.133, P(LBCA)(S)A 1997, s.37(4)(a),(b),(5); NI: P(NI)O 1991, arts 71(1), 78(4).]
[15] See **Chapter 14**.
[16] See **18.2.2**; also **Chapter 14**.

alteration to a listed building for which consent might never have been granted *ab ante*. To apply the former test is, in my view, an error in law."[17]

However, the personal circumstances of an owner should not be ignored.[18]

18.4.7 Grounds of appeal: the building not of special interest

One specific reason for an appeal on the basis that permission or consent should be granted is that the building or area in question is not of special architectural or historic interest. This is not a specific ground in relation to a planning enforcement notice, but it is ground (a) in relation to a listed building enforcement notice.

As to whether reliance on this ground is justified, this is a straightforward matter of fact and opinion, as to which professional witnesses should be called—but bear in mind the limited value of such evidence in some cases.[19] If the Secretary of State agrees, he will be able to remove the building from the list, so that listed building consent is no longer required for the works.[20] Note that the time at which the merit of the building should be assessed is before the carrying out of allegedly unauthorised works. Thus where a K6 telephone kiosk had been accidentally destroyed by a car, it was its interest prior to the collision that fell to be considered, not that in its crumpled state afterwards.[21]

It is thought that this ground rarely succeeds, but it should be relied on in some cases to back up the general claim that consent should be granted. If it is accepted, the Secretary of State has power to remove the building from the list.[22]

In relation to an appeal against a conservation area enforcement notice, ground (a) becomes: "that retention of the building is not necessary in the interests of preserving or enhancing the character of the conservation area in which it is situated". It thus cannot be claimed as a specific ground that the area in question is not suitable to be designated as a conservation area, however much that might seem to be justified, since the list of statutory grounds is exhaustive. However, there is no reason why such a claim cannot be made in support of an appeal against either a planning enforcement notice or a conservation area enforcement notice (or even a listed building enforcement notice, come to that) on the ground that permission and consent should be granted.

18.4.8 Grounds of appeal: requirements of the notice excessive

Even if it is accepted that permission or consent should not be granted for the works that have been carried out, it may still be reasonably argued that the steps to rectify their effect are impractical or excessive.

---

[17] *Edinburgh CC v Scottish Ministers* [2002] 4 P.L.R. 54, [2003] J.P.L. 903 (bullet points added). See also **13.8.2**.
[18] *Hounslow LBC v Secretary of State* [1997] J.P.L. 141 (considered at **18.4.9** below).
[19] And see the comment of Forbes J. in *Winchester CC v Secretary of State* (1978) 36 P. & C.R. 455, quoted at **14.4.3**.
[20] s.41(6)(c).
[21] See [1990] J.P.L. 445.
[22] P(LBCA)A 1990, ss 41(6)(c). [Scotland: P(LBCA)(S)A 1997, s.37(4)(c). There is no corresponding provision in Northern Ireland.]

In relation to a planning enforcement notice, there is a single ground—(ground f)—that the steps required by the notice to be taken exceed what is necessary to remedy any breach of planning control which may be constituted by the offending works or any injury to amenity which has been caused by any such breach.

This was considered in an appeal against an enforcement notice requiring the removal of uPVC-framed windows that had been installed in place of metal casement windows in an unlisted building in a conservation area (subject to an article 4 direction) in Hart, and their replacement with new windows of "traditional materials". The inspector considered this requirement to be ambiguous, and in any event seeking an improvement over what was in existence prior to the unauthorised works; the notice was varied accordingly.[23]

In relation to listed building enforcement notices, the grounds are more specific:

"(g) That the requirements of the notice [for restoring the building to its former state] exceed what is necessary for restoring the building to its condition before the works were carried out.[24]

(i) That the steps required by the notice for the purpose of restoring the character of the building to its former state would not serve that purpose.

(j) That the steps required to be taken [to alleviate the effects of the works which were carried out] exceed what is necessary [for that purpose].

(k) That the steps required to be taken [to bring the building to the state in which it would have been if the consent which has been granted had been complied with] exceed what is necessary [for that purpose]."

The first, ground (g), is a simple claim that what is required is excessive; the second, ground (i), is a claim that it would not even achieve the stated purpose anyway. Reliance on either ground, even if successful, is likely to lead to the notice being varied rather than quashed. Note that ground (i) does not apply in relation to an appeal against a conservation area enforcement notice.

A notorious example of the successful use of ground (g) in practice was the case of the Grosvenor Hotel in Bath. The building, which was listed Grade I, had originally been roofed with stone tiles. At some later date, these had been replaced with natural Welsh slates. These in turn had gradually deteriorated, and the owners had therefore patched up its roof over the years in a piecemeal fashion so that approximately two-thirds of it was now covered in Welsh slates, and one-third in asbestos slates, but some parts in various other materials including corrugated sheeting. They then decided to completely re-roof the building, using asbestos slates. The builders were starting to do this when the local authority issued a listed building enforcement notice, requiring them to stop work, and re-roof the whole building in natural slates.

The owners appealed to the Secretary of State against the notice on a number of grounds including (g). He allowed the appeal on that ground, but only because he felt:

(1) that the steps specified in the notice were more than was required to restore the building "to its former state", which was by implication neither with its

---

[23] Appeal ref.APP/N1730/c/01/1062678, noted at [2002] J.P.L. 130.
[24] Ground (h) in Northern Ireland.

original roof of stone tiles, nor with its later roof entirely of Welsh slates, but with its patchwork roof as it had been prior to the recent re-roofing; and

(2) that it would not be possible for the notice to be amended so as to require the roof to be reinstated to that previous patchwork condition.

The City Council then appealed to the High Court.[25] On the first point, Woolf J., as he then was, agreed with the Secretary of State:

"...the power which was given could not be properly used to achieve what the planning authority, for the best of reasons, would like to achieve here, namely a result which would be an improvement so far as this roof was concerned from a situation which existed prior to the unauthorised works being carried out. At that time there were asbestos slates and although the company, no doubt, were very wrong in carrying out the work which they did without consent, the object of the new provision was not to provide a punishment for them in the form of a requirement to carry out work which was over and above the work which was required to remedy the works which were done without consent."[26]

On the second point, however, he disagreed with the Secretary of State, since he felt that the notice could be amended, but whether that would be desirable in this case would be a matter for him (the Secretary of State) and the City Council. The notice was accordingly remitted to him for further consideration, and he decided that ground (g) succeeded, and that the notice should therefore be quashed.[27]

That decision was considered and applied in the more recent decision of Rafferty J. in *Foxlow v Secretary of State*, upholding the dismissal of an appeal against a listed building enforcement notice requiring the reinstatement of a chimney stack in a Grade II* building in Harrogate.[28]

On the other hand, in the appeal against the listed building enforcement notice served by Leominster District Council requiring the reconstruction of Stagbatch Barn,[29] the Secretary of State noted that Woolf J. had said in the *Bath* case:

"If works were carried out without the necessary building consent then it may be that an indirect consequence was that the person carrying out those works which were necessary to comply with a proper enforcement notice will have to carry out more work than was strictly required by the ... notice. That would not be a ground for challenging [its] validity because the person carrying out the works should be in the best position to know what steps were needed to rectify the breach of the listed building provisions which he had committed..."[30]

He therefore considered that in this case it was not unduly onerous to require the owners to rebuild the barn, particularly since it had been carefully packed and stored ready for re-erection elsewhere.

Ground (j) is that the steps required by the notice to be taken exceed what is necessary to alleviate the effect of the unauthorised works executed to the building. Ground (k) is that the required steps exceed what is necessary to bring the building to the state in which it would have been if the consent which had been

---

[25] *Bath CC v Secretary of State for the Environment and Grosvenor Hotel* [1983] J.P.L. 737.
[26] pp 740–1.
[27] See [1984] J.P.L. 285.
[28] [2001] J.P.L. B1215 (transcript available via Lawtel).
[29] [1987] J.P.L. 798; for the facts, see **4.2.3** and **18.7.3**.
[30] *Bath, per* Woolf J. at p.741.

granted had been complied with. These two grounds raise similar considerations to ground (g).

18.4.9 Grounds of appeal: insufficient time for compliance

Finally, whatever other grounds are relied on, it can always be argued that the time for compliance with the notice is insufficient—ground (g) in relation to planning enforcement notices, and ground (h) in relation to listed building and conservation area enforcement notices.

However, this ground should never be used on its own except as a last resort, for, although it is frequently accepted by the Secretary of State, it almost invariably leads to the notice being varied so as to allow for a longer period in which to carry out the specified works. It thus merely postpones the inevitable.[31] Exceptionally, it may be appropriate for a substantially extended period to be allowed. This can occur where a building is in a very poor state, and needs to be put in good repair before it is worth restoring or returning decorative items.

Alternatively, the personal circumstances of an owner may suggest a longer period. In *Hounslow LBC v Secretary of State*,[32] for example, a disabled owner of an upper-floor flat in a listed building installed a lift without consent. The council issued a listed building enforcement notice, which an inspector upheld on appeal, but with the period for compliance extended so as to expire on the owner's 60th birthday—by which time he could make alternative arrangements. The court, on appeal, raised an eyebrow at such a prolonged period, but considered it was not irrational—merely generous.

18.5 The determination of enforcement appeals

18.5.1 Appeal procedures

As with appeals against the refusal of planning permission and listed building consent, there are three different procedures for dealing with appeals against enforcement notices; an exchange of written representations, an informal hearing, or an inquiry. These have largely been explained already, in **Chapter 15**, and more or less the same procedures and time limits apply in connection with enforcement appeals.

The Secretary of State (or equivalent) has power to dismiss an appeal or quash an enforcement notice, without any inquiry, where one side or the other fails to produce a statement when asked to do so.[33] In any other case, and in any event in Northern Ireland, either a hearing or a public local inquiry must be held if either the appellant or the local authority wishes to be heard.[34]

---

[31] See also **18.6.1** on compliance periods.
[32] [1997] J.P.L. 141.
[33] TCPA 1990, s.176(3),(4); P(LBCA)A 1990, s.41(3), (4). [Scotland: TCP(S)A 1997, s.132(3).] This does not apply in Northern Ireland.
[34] TCPA 1990, s.175(3); P(LBCA)A 1990, s.40(2). [Scotland: TCP(S)A 1997, s.131(2), NI: P(NI)O 1991, art.69(6).]

The detailed procedures for appeals in England—against either planning enforcement notices or listed building enforcement notices—are contained within five statutory instruments:

- TCP (Enforcement Notices and Appeals) (England) Regulations 2002[35];

- TCP (Enforcement) (Written Representations Procedure) (England) Regulations 2002[36];

- TCP (Enforcement) (Hearings Procedure) (England) Rules 2002[37];

- TCP (Enforcement) (Determination by Inspectors) (Inquiries Procedure) (England) Rules 2002[38]; and

- TCP (Enforcement) (Inquiries Procedure) (England) Rules 2002.[39]

The last of these is used in the rare cases where an enforcement appeal is determined by the Secretary of State rather than an inspector. Corresponding rules, very similar to the English ones, were made a year later in Wales.[40] Guidance on the operation of each procedure is in the relevant Annex to ODPM Circular 02/2002 or NAW Circular 08/2003.

In Scotland, much more sensibly, precisely the same regulations and rules apply to enforcement appeals as to other types of appeal.[41] Those regulations and rules apply to listed building and conservation area enforcement notices as well as to planning enforcement notices; but the relevant guidance, at Annex E to SDD Circular 4/1999, applies only to the latter. The procedures in Northern Ireland are described in the publication produced by the Planning Appeals Commission entitled *Procedures for Enforcement Notice, Listed Building and Submission Notice Appeals* available on its website.[42]

The proportion of cases dealt with by inquiry is much higher than with appeals against refusals, as enforcement disputes often involve disputes of fact and complex legal submissions, and are therefore not suitable either for written representations or informal hearings. An inquiry will in particular be more

---

[35] SI 2002/2682.
[36] SI 2002/2683.
[37] SI 2002/2684.
[38] SI 2002/2685.
[39] SI 2002/2686
[40] TCP (Enforcement Notices and Appeals) (Wales) Regulations 2003 (SI 2003/394); TCP (Enforcement) (Written Representations Procedure) (Wales) Regulations 2003 (SI 2003/395); TCP (Enforcement) (Hearings Procedure) (Wales) Rules 2003 (SI 2003/1268); TCP (Enforcement) (Determination by Inspectors) (Inquiries Procedure) (Wales) Rules 2003 (SI 2003/1270); and TCP (Enforcement) (Inquiries Procedure) (Wales) Rules 2003 (SI 2003/1269).
[41] TCP (Enforcement of Control) (No. 2) (Scotland) Regulations 1992 (SI 1992/2086); TCP Appeals) (Written Submissions Procedure) (Scotland) Regulations 1990 (SI 1990/507); TCP Appeals (Determination by Appointed Person) (Inquiries Procedure) (Scotland) Rules 1997 (SI 1997/750) (amended by SI 1998/2312); and TCP Appeals (Inquiries Procedure) (Scotland) Rules 1997 (SI 1997/796) (amended by SI 1998/2311) (see **15.3**).
[42] *www.pacni.gov.uk*. The most recent edition is dated September 2005.

appropriate than a hearing in cases where evidence as to fact is to be taken into account.

18.5.2 The decision on an enforcement appeal

The power to decide enforcement notice appeals in England and Wales has been delegated to inspectors in almost all cases.[43] The only exception is listed building enforcement notices relating to Grade I and II* buildings, and Grade II buildings where a grant has been given under the Historic Buildings and Ancient Monuments Act 1953—which will be rare.[44] In Scotland, all appeals may be determined by reporters.[45] As with other appeals, the Secretary of State, the Welsh Assembly and the Scottish Ministers are entitled to recover an enforcement appeal for his or her own decision if it seems appropriate.[46]

All enforcement notice appeals in Northern Ireland are made by the Planning Appeals Commission.

In determining an appeal, the decision-maker may quash the notice.[47] He or she may grant planning permission or listed building or conservation area consent for all or part of the works carried out, or discharge any condition attached to a permission or consent that has already been granted, or substitute another.[48] And in the case of a listed building enforcement notice appeal (other than in Northern Ireland), the building may be removed from the statutory list.[49]

Alternatively, the decision-maker may uphold the notice, but may also correct any minor defect in its drafting, or vary its terms, provided that this can be done without causing injustice.[50] Thus, for example, in a decision letter by the Secretary of State regarding the unauthorised installation of replacement windows, window frames and doors, he stated:

"[He] has regard to the term 'sliding casement' in the schedule to the enforcement notice, which it is agreed could be misunderstood. The Council would appear to be seeking replacement of the three uPVC windows with traditional timber windows of the horizontal sliding sash type. The Secretary of State is thus of the view that the enforcement notice as served by the Council is imprecise, but that it can be varied. Accordingly the appeal against the listed building enforcement notice has been considered on that basis".[51]

---

[43] TCP (Determination of Appeals by Appointed Persons) (Prescribed Classes) Regulations 1997. It has recently been proposed that all appeals should in future be determined by inspectors, other than where a grant has been made under the 1953 Act (see *Listed Buildings Casework: a consultation paper*, ODPM, February 2006).

[44] See **9.4.1** (England) and **9.5.1** (Wales).

[45] TCP (Determination of Appeals by Appointed Persons) (Prescribed Classes) (Scotland) Regulations 1987 (SI 1987/1531), amended by SI 1989/577.

[46] See **15.3.3**.

[47] TCPA 1990, s.176(2), P(LBCA)A 1990, s.41(2). [Scotland: TCP(S)A 1997, s.132(1); P(LBCA)(S)A 1997, s.37(1); NI: P(NI)O 1991, arts 70(1), 78(3).]

[48] TCPA 1990, s.177(1)(a),(b), P(LBCA)A 1990, s.41(6)(a),(b). [Scotland: TCP(S)A 1997, s.133(1)(a),(b); (LBCA)(S)A 1997, s.37(4)(a),(b); NI: P(NI)O 1991, arts 71(1)(a),(b), 78(4)(a),(b).]

[49] P(LBCA)A 1990, s.41(6)(c). [Scotland: (LBCA)(S)A 1997, s.37(4)(c).]

[50] TCPA 1990, s.176(1), P(LBCA)A 1990, s.41(1). [Scotland: TCP(S)A 1997, s.132(2); P(LBCA)(S)A 1997, s.37(2); NI: P(NI)O 1991, arts 70(2), 78(3).]

[51] [1987] J.P.L. 804.

18.5.3 Challenge to a grant of permission or consent following an enforcement appeal

A decision by the Secretary of State or an inspector to grant planning permission or listed building consent following an appeal against an enforcement notice in England or Wales may be challenged by way of an application to the High Court, exactly as though it was a decision following an appeal against the refusal of permission or consent.[52] Such a challenge may be made by any aggrieved party, without any need for permission from the court, but must be brought within six weeks of the decision, without any right of extension.[53]

The same applies to *any* decision on an enforcement notice appeal in Scotland (whether to quash the notice or to uphold it); an appeal may be made to the Court of Session within six weeks.[54] However, no challenge can be brought on any ground that could have been relied on in an appeal to the Scottish Ministers.[55] This includes, obviously, the argument that the building in question was not protected by the listing.[56]

18.5.4 Other challenges to a decision on an enforcement appeal

The decision of an inspector or the Secretary of State on an appeal against a listed building enforcement notice in England or Wales (other than a decision to grant permission or consent[57]) may be challenged on a point of law in the High Court.[58] Here too, no challenge can be brought on any ground that could have been relied on in an appeal to the Secretary of State.[59] This includes, obviously, the argument that the building in question was not protected by the listing.[60]

A challenge under this provision may not be made without the permission of the court having first been obtained.[61] The relevant procedure is prescribed in RSC Order 94.[62] An application for permission must be made within 28 days of the decision being challenged. There is a discretionary power for the court to extend the time,[63] but this will only be exercised sparingly; an application for an extension of time should be made along with the application for leave.

The application for permission must be in writing, setting out the facts relied on, and must be served, along with a draft appellant's notice, and a witness statement or affidavit verifying any facts relied on must be served on the Secretary of State (in practice the Treasury Solicitor), the planning authority or the

---

[52] TCPA 1990, ss 284(3)(e), 288(4); P(LBCA)A 1990, ss 62(2)(c) and 63.
[53] TCPA 1990, s.288(3); P(LBCA)A 1990, s.63(3) For further details, see **15.6**.
[54] TCP(S)A 1997, s.237(3)(d); P(LBCA)(S)A 1997, s.57(2)(c).
[55] Scotland: TCP(S)A 1997, s.134; P(LBCA)(S)A 1997, s.37(6).
[56] See *R. v Dacorum BC, Ex p. Cannon* [1996] 2 P.L.R. 45.
[57] As to which, see **18.5.2**.
[58] TCPA 1990, s.289, P(LBCA)A 1990, s.65.
[59] TCPA 1990, s.285(1), LBCA, s.64.
[60] See *R. v Dacorum BC, Ex p. Cannon* [1996] 2 P.L.R. 45.
[61] TCPA 1990, s.289(6), P(LBCA)A 1990, s.65(5).
[62] RSC Ord 94, rr 12 and 13, substituted by SI 1992/638; included (in amended form) in Sch.1 to the Civil Procedure Rules 1998; and subsequently amended by Civil Procedure(Amendment) Rules 2000.
[63] Under CPR, Part 3, r.3.1(2)(a). See also Pt 2, r.2.11.

appellant, and any other person having an interest in the land.[64] All of these, together with a copy of the decision being challenged and an affidavit as to service, must then be filed in the Administrative Court (formerly the Crown Office).[65] At any stage, during either the application for permission or the substantive hearing, the court may order that the enforcement notice shall continue to have effect (either wholly or partially), pending the final disposal of the matter[66]—although that provision does not seem to be particularly relevant to listed buildings. There is no right of appeal against a decision of the court on an application for permission.[67]

The substantive appeal is brought by way of a Part 8 claim form, served on those notified of the application for permission. It will be heard by a single judge, unless the court directs that it should go to a divisional court. If the appeal is successful, there is no power for the court to quash or set aside the notice[68]; it will instead normally remit it to the Secretary of State for rehearing.

Further appeal is to the Court of Appeal, again only with leave,[69] and finally to the House of Lords.[70]

18.5.5 Application for judicial review

The right of appeal to the High Court under the above provisions is confined to the appellant, the planning authority, and anyone with an interest in the land to which the notice related.[71] There seems however to be no reason why a decision to quash a notice on the basis of the merits of the works carried out—which does not go to the "validity" of the notice—could not be challenged by way of an application for judicial review, possibly by an amenity group which had appeared at the public inquiry.

And any challenge to a decision of the Planning Appeals Commission in Northern Ireland must be by way of an application for judicial review.[72]

18.6 Carrying out works required by enforcement notices

18.6.1 Coming into effect of the notice

An enforcement notice comes into effect on a date stated in it, which must be at least 28 days after copies of it were issued to those who had to receive them.[73] At

---

[64] Ord 94, rr 12(2) (d), 13(5).

[65] Ord 94, r.12(2) (c), (e).

[66] TCPA s.289(5A); P(LBCA)A 1990, s.65(3A).

[67] *Huggett v Secretary of State* (1995), *The Times* March 1, CA.

[68] Ord.94, r.13(8).

[69] TCPA 1990, s.289(6), P(LBCA)A 1990, s.65(5).

[70] See **15.6.4**.

[71] s.65(1). By virtue of s.45, English Heritage could appeal against a decision relating to a notice it had issued (in Greater London)

[72] See **15.8.3**.

[73] TCPA 1990, ss 172(3), 173(8); P(LBCA)A 1990, s.38(3),(4). [Scotland: TCP(S)A 1997, ss 127(3), 128(8), P(LBCA)(S)A 1997, s.34(5); NI: P(NI)O 1991, arts 68(3), 68A(8), 77(4),(6).]

any time before that date, the local authority may withdraw it (although it can always issue another) or the owner may appeal against it to the Secretary of State.[74] If an appeal is made, the notice then only comes into effect once the appeal has been withdrawn or "finally determined".[75] The effect of these provisions is that, in the absence of any appeal to the High Court, the notice comes into effect:

(1)　on the date stated in it, or

(2)　if there is an appeal against the notice, which is subsequently withdrawn, on the date of the withdrawal, or

(3)　if the appeal is not withdrawn, when the Secretary of State determines it, and the time for appealing against that determination has elapsed.

As to the coming into effect of a notice where an appeal is made to the High Court, see above.[76]

If planning permission or listed building consent is subsequently granted to retain all or some of the works which are the subject of the enforcement notice, the notice will then cease to have effect as far as it relates to those works.[77] That will however not affect the liability to prosecution for past non-compliance with the notice[78]; nor, in the case of unauthorised works to listed buildings or demolition in a conservation area, the liability to prosecution for the original contravention.

18.6.2 Compliance with the notice

Once an enforcement notice has finally come into force, and all possibility of appeal has been exhausted,[79] the remedial works specified in it must be carried out within the stated period, subject to any extension that may have been won on appeal, or that may have been allowed by the planning authority (it is possible for a notice to specify different periods for different works).[80]

The carrying out of the works is now the responsibility of whoever owns it when the time for compliance expires, and of any subsequent owner for as long as the works remain incomplete. If the works are not carried out, he or she is liable

---

[74]　TCPA 1990, s.173A, P(LBCA)A 1990, ss 38(5),(6), 39(1). [Scotland: TCP(S)A 1997, s.129, P(LBCA)(S)A 1997, s.34(7),(8); NI: P(NI)O 1991, arts 68B, 77(6).]

[75]　TCPA 1990, s.175(4), P(LBCA)A 1990, s.39(3). [Scotland: TCP(S)A 1997, ss 131(3); P(LBCA)(S)A 1997, s.35(3); NI: P(NI)O 1991, arts 69(8).]

[76]　See **18.5.4.**

[77]　TCPA 1990, s.180(1), P(LBCA)A 1990, s.44(1). [Scotland: TCP(S)A 1997, ss 137(1); P(LBCA)(S)A 1997, s.40(1); NI: P(NI)O 1991, arts 75(1), 79(1).]

[78]　TCPA 1990, s.180(2), P(LBCA)A 1990, s.44(2). [Scotland: TCP(S)A 1997, ss 137(3); P(LBCA)(S)A 1997, s.40(2); NI: P(NI)O 1991, arts 75(3), 79(3).]

[79]　See **18.5.**

[80]　TCPA 1990, ss 173(9), 173A(1)(b), P(LBCA)A 1990, s.38(3)(b),(5)(b). [Scotland: TCP(S)A 1997, ss 128(9), 129(1)(b), P(LBCA)(S)A 1997, s.34(5)(b),(7)(b); NI: P(NI)O 1991, arts 68A(8), 77(4)(b).]

to be prosecuted for non-compliance.[81] This is an offence triable either way.[82] The maximum penalty is a fine of up to £20,000 on summary conviction (£30,000 in Northern Ireland), or an unlimited fine on indictment; and in determining the amount of any fine, the court is in particular to take into account any benefit accruing as a result of non-compliance with the notice[83] and the means of the offender.[84] See the following chapter and **Appendix F** on sentencing generally.

There are two statutory defences to such a charge. The first is that the owner has done everything that he or she could be expected to do to comply with the notice.[85] This may be a suitable defence where the building is let to or occupied by another, and particularly relevant in the case of works to the interior of a building. It may also succeed where an owner has instructed works to be carried out to comply with a notice, and the contractors have (through no fault of the owner) not yet done them.[86]

Secondly, it is possible to prosecute someone for failure to comply with a listed building enforcement notice even where the works to which the notice relates were carried out by someone else.[87] However, to avoid this operating unfairly, a person being prosecuted may claim as a defence that:

(1) that he or she was not served with a copy of the notice, and

(2) in the case of a planning enforcement notice,[88] or a listed building or conservation area enforcement notice in Scotland or Northern Ireland,[89] that it was not in the appropriate register; or in the case of a listed building or conservation area enforcement notice in England or Wales, that he or she was unaware of its existence.[90]

The difference in the defences arises as a result of the absence of a statutory register of listed building and conservation area enforcement notices in England and Wales, and the fact that a subsequent owner may be genuinely unaware of the existence of such a notice.[91] Before prosecuting in such a case (and indeed probably in every case) an authority should therefore draw the attention of the

---

[81] TCPA 1990, s.179(1),(2), P(LBCA)A 1990, s.43(1),(2). [Scotland: TCP(S)A 1997, s.136(1),(2); P(LBCA)(S)A 1997, s.39(1),(2); NI: P(NI)O 1991, arts 72(1),(2), 77(6).]

[82] See **Appendix F**.

[83] TCPA 1990, s.179(8),(9), P(LBCA)A 1990, s.43(5),(6). [Scotland: TCP(S)A 1997, s.136(8),(9); P(LBCA)(S)A 1997, s.39(5),(6); NI: P(NI)O 1991, arts 72(8), 77(6).]

[84] Powers of Criminal Courts (Sentencing) Act 2000, s.128; *R. v Browning* [1996] 1 P.L.R. 61.

[85] TCPA 1990, s.179(3), P(LBCA)A 1990, s.43(4)(a). [Scotland: TCP(S)A 1997, s.136(3); P(LBCA)(S)A 1997, s.39(4)(a); NI: P(NI)O 1991, arts 72(3), 77(6).]

[86] That was the position in *Mid-Devon v Avery* (1992) 65 P. & C.R. 47, where builders were instructed to install traditional wooden windows to replace unauthorised modern ones whose removal was required by an enforcement notice. That case however was decided under the old law, where this defence was not available, and is thus no longer applicable.

[87] *R. v Elmbridge BC, ex p. Active Office Ltd* [1998] J.P.L. B43 (1998) 10 Admin L.R. 561.

[88] TCPA 1990, s.179(7). [Scotland: TCP(S)A 1997, s.136(7); NI: P(NI)O 1991, art.72(7).]

[89] P(LBCA)(S)A 1997, s.39(4)(b); P(NI)O 1991, arts 72(7), 77(6).

[90] P(LBCA)A 1990, s.43(4)(b).

[91] See **18.3.8**.

current owner to the existence of the notice, and only institute proceedings after a reasonable time for compliance.

Following a conviction for non-compliance, if the required works are still not carried out, the person convicted, or any subsequent owner, may be prosecuted again. This is not a separate offence; it is, rather, the same offence but to be charged by reference to a subsequent period.[92] The penalties are accordingly the same.

18.6.3 Execution of the required works by the planning authority

Finally, if all else fails, the planning authority may enter the land, carry out the required works itself, and reclaim the cost of doing so from whoever is currently the owner of the land.[93] This is recoverable as a simple contract debt.[94] A local authority, but not English Heritage, may also recover a reasonable sum in respect of its establishment charges.[95]

Any sum recovered from the owner may in turn be recovered from whoever was responsible for the unauthorised works in the first place.[96]

Detailed provisions as to for the procedures applicable to the carrying out of the works in England and Wales are contained in the relevant provisions of the Public Health Act 1936.[97]

18.6.4 Seeking an injunction to achieve compliance

Where an item is removed from a listed building or a monument without consent, and an enforcement notice comes into effect to require its return, it may not be possible for an authority to prosecute the possessor of the item, as he or she may not be the owner of the building. Nor would it be possible to secure compliance by entering the land, since the item is not there. The only course open in such a situation seems to be to seek a mandatory injunction from the High Court requiring the item to be returned forthwith. Such an application would be the subject of a full trial, if resisted by the possessor of the item in question; and the application for a permanent mandatory injunction should accordingly be accompanied by an application for an interlocutory injunction restraining the possessor of the item from disposing of it prior to trial.

Thus in *Powys CC v Kennedy* 1998 the dealer to whom a clock had been sold following its removal from Leighton Hall in mid-Wales[98] declined to return it even though required to do so by an enforcement notice which had come into effect

---

[92] TCPA 1990, s.179(6), P(LBCA)A 1990, s.43(3). [Scotland: TCP(S)A 1997, s.136(6); P(LBCA)(S)A 1997, s.39(3); NI: P(NI)O 1991, arts 72(6), 77(6).]

[93] TCPA 1990, s.178(1), P(LBCA)A 1990, s.42(1). [Scotland: TCP(S)A 1997, s.135(1); P(LBCA)(S)A 1997, s.38(1); NI: P(NI)O 1991, arts 74(1), 77(6).]

[94] County Court Act 1984, s.16.

[95] Local Government Act 1974, s.36.

[96] TCPA 1990, s.178(2), P(LBCA)A 1990, s.42(2). [Scotland: TCP(S)A 1997, s.135(4); P(LBCA)(S)A 1997, s.38(2); NI: P(NI)O 1991, arts 74(2), 77(6).]

[97] PHA 1936, ss 276, 289 and 294; applied by TCPA 1990, s.178(3), TCP General Regulations 1992, reg.14, and P(LBCA)A 1990, s.42(3) and P(LBCA) Regulations 1990, reg.11.

[98] Unreported; and see **4.4.3**.

following an unsuccessful appeal. The planning authority accordingly obtained an interlocutory injunction, not least because the court considered that it had a strong case in support of its application for a permanent injunction—although the deputy judge was also critical of the authority's delay in coming to court. In the event, the clock was returned without the need for a mandatory injunction.

It is now also possible in some such cases to pursue those in possession of objects removed from listed buildings or monuments under the Dealing in Cultural Objects (Offences) Act 2003.[99]

18.7 Cases of urgency: stop notices and injunctions

18.7.1 Introduction

The previous parts of this chapter have dealt with the courses of action open to achieve the restoration of a building after a planning authority after unauthorised works have taken place. However, prevention is always better than cure; and, where it is known that such works are about to take place, it may be necessary for the authority to take pre-emptive action. Thus there will inevitably be a few cases where urgent action is required to stop a listed building being demolished or substantially altered in the very near future—possibly within 24 hours; or to halt unauthorised works which are actually in progress.

In such situations, it will be of limited use to institute criminal proceedings: even if the offenders are successfully prosecuted, it will usually be much too late to stop the works being completed. It will also be useless to issue a listed building enforcement notice on its own. If the works have not started, there has been no breach to be enforced; and if they are under way, it may not be possible to resurrect the building. In the latter case, however, if there is any possibility of the effect of the works being remedied, a notice should still be issued, even if it eventually proves ineffective.

Where a planning enforcement notice is issued to stop undesirable development being carried out without planning permission, it is possible to issue a "stop notice" which has the effect of bringing the enforcement notice into effect within three days—or even less in appropriate circumstances.[100]

However, there is no equivalent procedure with breaches of the listed building control system. Instead, it is possible for a planning authority in England or Wales or English Heritage to apply to the High Court or the county court for an injunction under s.44A of the Listed Buildings Act restraining the owner of the building (or anyone else who may be thought suitable) from carrying out, or continuing, any unauthorised works to it. Indeed, an injunction may be sought, as an alternative to a stop notice, to restrain a breach of planning control.[1]

In Scotland, a planning authority may make an application to the Court of Session or the court of sheriff for interdict to restrain a breach of planning control, but there is non-explicit power to make an application for interdict merely to

---

[99] See **19.7.3**.
[100] TCPA 1990, s.183. [Scotland: TCP(S)A 1997, s.140; NI: P(NI)O 1991, art.73.]
[1] TCPA 1990, s.187B.

prevent a contravention of listed building control.[2] This distinction possibly reflects a marked reluctance on the part of the Scottish courts in the past to allow actions for interdict in planning matters. However, where works are to be carried out to a listed building that would require both planning permission and listed building consent, it would be possible for an authority to mount an application for interdict.

In Northern Ireland, the Department may apply to the High Court or the county court for an injunction to restrain either a breach of planning control or a contravention of listed building or conservation area control.[3]

It is also sometimes necessary to restrain an apprehended breach of scheduled monument control, or to stop unauthorised works from proceeding any further. It is therefore possible for injunctions to be sought by the Secretary of State, through the agency of the Attorney-General, or by English Heritage, under a specific power in the National Heritage Act 1983.[4]

If such an injunction (known as *quia timet*) or interdict is granted, and its terms are then flouted, a further action can be brought for contempt of court. The courts consider actions for contempt very seriously, and it is thus likely that any penalties imposed at that stage would be severe, including, in appropriate cases, imprisonment.[5]

18.7.2 Principles governing the exercise of the court's discretion

Although there is no doubt as to the powers of authorities to seek injunctions, the remedy remains a discretionary one. An injunction will, understandably, only be granted where it is really necessary. The correct approach has been expressed by the Court of Appeal:

"...the court should bear in mind that the duty of a local planning authority under the planning legislation was not merely to enforce penalties for past offences but was also to do all within [its] power to ensure, through properly observed planning control, the natural amenities of [its] area; and that the local planning authority could take the view, in an appropriate case, that it was necessary to resort to relief at civil law in order to prevent irreparable damage, which might well not be prevented by the process of a magistrates' court."[6]

This overrides the test, previously much quoted, of whether the act complained of is a "deliberate and flagrant breach of the criminal law".[7] It has subsequently been held that an injunction should be granted only if it appeared that the unlawful

---

[2] TCP(S)A 1997, s.146.
[3] P(NI)O 1991, art.76B; brought into effect on April 22, 2003 (SR 2003/188).
[4] NHA 1983, s.33(2A)(b).
[5] As in *Maidstone BC v Batchelor* (1983) (unreported): contempt of court for flouting an injunction issued to uphold a tree preservation order.
[6] *Runnymede BC v Ball and Others* [1986] J.P.L. 288, as summarised by Millett J. in *Runnymede BC v Smith and Others* [1986] J.P.L. 592 at 597.
[7] First formulated in *Stafford BC v Elkenford Ltd* (1976) 121 S.J. 34.

operations would continue unless and until effectively restrained by the law, and that nothing short of an injunction would be effective.[8]

In any event, a *quia timet* injunction would in principle be an entirely appropriate remedy where a listed building is about to be or is being demolished, since the damage will usually be both irreparable and unable to be prevented in any other way. There are no formal grounds of appeal against an injunction, as there are against an enforcement notice or listed building enforcement notice; but the person wishing to proceed with the works will have to consider many of the same issues—in particular, is the building listed? Do the works require consent? And has consent been granted?

As with works that are the subject of enforcement notices, there will in some cases be in existence a permission or consent, but not (at least in the view of the authority) for precisely the works that are now about to be carried out. It is then necessary to check all the relevant paperwork in order to work out what precisely has been permitted. And it seems that it may occasionally be permissible for a planning authority to argue that an apparently valid consent is defective, for example because it was issued without a statutory consultee having been consulted—although the courts are unlikely to be sympathetic.[9]

It would also be possible to use injunctions to halt the unauthorised demolition of unlisted buildings in conservation areas in the same circumstances as apply in the case of works to listed buildings, since section 44A of the Listed Buildings Act is included in the list of provisions applied by section 74(3). It could be more difficult to persuade a court to issue an injunction in connection with an unlisted building; but it might be possible, particularly in the case of a fagrant breach[10–11] or a persistent offender.

It will be noted that much of the case law predates the introduction by the Planning and Compensation Act 1991 of the explicit power to seek an injunction, when local authorities were increasingly often using their general power to seek an injunction to enforce planning law.[12] It may be that the courts in Scotland will be willing to act similarly in relation to anticipated breaches of listed building control even in the absence of a specific statutory provision in the Scottish Listed Buildings Act—in which case the pre-1991 English case law would be particularly relevant.

18.7.3 Interlocutory injunctions

An interlocutory injunction may sometimes be appropriate to halt works to a listed building pending the resolution of other litigation—where, for example, there is a dispute over the precise extent of the works permitted by a listed building consent. In such a situation, a refusal to grant an injunction may result in

---

[8] *Wychavon DC v Midland Events (Special Events) Ltd* (1987) 86 L.G.R. 83 at 89, cited with approval in *City of London Corporation v Bovis Construction Ltd* (1988) *The Times*, April 21.

[9] The Court of Appeal reluctantly legitimised this tactic in *Fenland DC v Reuben Rose (Properties) Ltd* [2000] P.L.C.R. 376.

[10–11] For an example, see the saga that led to the appeal decision noted at [2004] J.P.L. 97.

[12] Local Government Act 1972, s.222.

the building being altered or demolished, and would thus effectively render further litigation pointless. It has thus been recognised by the House of Lords in *Kirklees MBC v Wickes Building Supplies Ltd* that "an injunction may be granted in an emergency to restrain an infringement of the law, for example the cutting down of a tree in breach of a tree preservation order".[13]

In general, whether an interlocutory injunction will be granted in any particular instance will be determined at the inter partes hearing according to the principles set out by the House of Lords in *American Cyanamid Co v Ethicon Ltd.*[14] Thus the party seeking the injunction (in this case, the authority) must show:

(1) that there is a serious question to be tried: this should not be too difficult if the works are about to start or are under way, although there will need to be proof; and where the works are already well advanced (particularly in the case of demolition), it must be shown that it will be possible for their effect to be reversed;

(2) that an award of damages will not compensate the authority for the loss of or damage to the building (which will plainly be the case, since it is seeking the injunction on behalf of the public, not in its own right); and

(3) that damages would compensate the defendants if it subsequently transpired that its case was defective (if, for example, it turned out that the building was not in fact listed, or that a building preservation notice had not been properly served).

If an award of damages will adequately compensate the defendants in the event of the authority eventually losing, the court should then grant the injunction. This had led in the past to the enforcing authority being required to give an undertaking in damages. That could be quite an onerous requirement—particularly where a large development scheme is held up pending the resolution of the dispute. The House of Lords in *Kirklees* (above) decided, however, that an undertaking was not needed where an authority was required to enforce the law.[15] In the case of listed buildings legislation, the planning authority is empowered, but not required to take enforcement action, but it is likely that the reasoning behind the decision in *Kirklees* would lead to the authority not being required to give an undertaking.

If, on the other hand, an award of damages will not compensate the defendants, the court must decide where the public interest lies; and usually it will favour the maintenance of the status quo, which in a listed building case will also result in it granting the injunction.

The operation of these principles is illustrated by the case of Stagbatch Barn in Herefordshire. It came to the attention of the local authority on August 5, 1986 that a listed medieval cruck barn had been dismantled, and that its timbers were about to be exported to the USA. An injunction was granted ex parte that same

---

[13] [1992] 3 W.L.R. 170 at 178H, following *Newport BC v Khan* [1990] 1 W.L.R. 1185.
[14] [1975] A.C. 396.
[15] As it was in that case, under s.71(1) of the Shops Act 1950; see [1992] 3 W.L.R. 170 at 182G.

day; and the local authority issued a listed building enforcement notice on August 8 requiring its re-erection.[16] The injunction was renewed on August 11 after an inter partes hearing by Hoffman J.[17] He considered the application of the *Cyanamid* guidelines, and decided that the balance of convenience plainly favoured the retention of the timbers within the country until the matter could be resolved.

Although the Stagbatch case is not directly to point, because it concerns the export of a building which had already been demolished (which will not often occur), the same principles would seem to apply where demolition or other unauthorised works are about to happen or are currently taking place.

18.7.4 Authorities empowered to seek injunctions

An injunction under section 44A may be sought either by the local planning authority[18] or, in England, by English Heritage.[19] The local planning authority will in general be in England either the county council (where one exists) or the district or borough council.[20] In Wales, it will generally be the county or county borough council.[21] The Broads Authority may also serve an injunction in respect of a building in the Broads.[22] In a national park, however, only the national park authority may act.[23]

Note that circumstances justifying seeking an injunction to restrain a breach of planning or listed building control are likely to arise unexpectedly, and without sufficient time to obtain committee authorisation for action. An authority should therefore have in place a scheme of delegation entitling an appropriate officer to make the decision that an injunction should be sought. Conversely, those on the receiving end of such an injunction should check that the authority had in place such an arrangement, as its absence would be fatal.[24]

18.7.5 Procedure

An application for an injunction in these circumstances is best brought in the High Court. The first step, if time permits, is for the authority to issue Pt 7 claim form informing the defendants (the owners of the building and all others concerned) that the court will be moved by counsel for an interlocutory injunction in the terms specified in the notice. This notice must be served at least two days before the motion is heard, and will need to be accompanied by an affidavit setting

---

[16] As to which, see **18.4.8**.
[17] Reported as *Leominster D.C. v British Historic Buildings and SPS Shipping* [1987] J.P.L. 350; see **4.2.3**.
[18] P(LBCA)A 1990, s.44A(1).
[19] P(LBCA)A 1990, s.44A (4).
[20] TCPA 1990, s.1(1), (2); P(LBCA)A 1990, s.81.
[21] TCPA 1990, s.1 (1B), inserted by Local Government (Wales) Act 1994, s.18.
[22] P(LBCA)A 1990, Sch.4, para.5.
[23] TCPA 1990, s.4(1); s.4A(2), inserted by Environment Act 1995, s.67.
[24] *Kirklees BC v Brook* [2005] 2 P. & C.R. 318.

out the relevant facts and a draft order.[25] The claim will then be heard in open court, and the injunction will, if granted, take effect immediately.

Where greater speed is required, the authority should apply at once to the court on a "without notice" (previously *ex parte*) basis—that is, without the defendants being present. In extreme cases, where the court is not sitting, application may be made at any time to a judge at his or her home; the authority's solicitors should telephone the Royal Courts of Justice, which will be able to put them in touch with a judge available for the hearing of urgent applications. The authority will have to produce a witness statement or affidavit as to the merits of its case, and an undertaking both to serve the notice of motion on the defendants as soon as possible (that is, in the following 24 hours) and to compensate them if it transpires that it was not entitled to the relief sought. If it is successful, the court will issue an interim injunction which will be effective only for a short period (usually five days or a week), until an application on notice (*inter partes*) can be heard, so that the defendants can state their case.

Alternatively an injunction may be sought in the county court.[26] The Court of Appeal in *Newport* warned that the jurisdiction should be sparingly used, however.

Finally, it is possible to seek an injunction against a person whose identity is unknown.[27] This is designed to help to assist in halting works by dubious "cowboy" builders. The relevant procedure is to be provided for in RSC Order 110[28]: it will still be necessary to describe in some way the person against whom the injunction is sought, and to verify by witness statement or affidavit that it was not possible in the time available to identity him or her more precisely.

Although, following *Kirklees*, an undertaking in damages will probably not be required,[29] an authority seeking an injunction will nevertheless be liable for the costs of the defendant if it is unable to make out its case—even though it no doubt considers that the proceedings were brought in the public interest.[30]

When an injunction has been made, copies should be served on all those likely to be affected. In the Newmarket case,[31] copies of the injunction were secured all over the site, including on ladders and a cement mixer.

18.7.6 Breach of an injunction

In the event of unauthorised works continuing even after the issue of an injunction, proceedings for contempt should be started in the High Court. For these to succeed it will be necessary to produce evidence to prove that all the relevant papers have been served; and witness statements or affidavits to that effect will be required from the officers concerned.

---

[25] Samples are at Forms D19 to D21 in **Appendix D**.
[26] P(LBCA)A 1990, s.44A(5), confirming *Newport BC v Khan* [1990] 1 W.L.R. 1185.
[27] P(LBCA)A 1990, s.44A(3).
[28] Now in Sch.1 to the Civil Procedure Rules 1998.
[29] See **18.7.3**.
[30] *Re Southbourne Ltd* [1993] 1 W.L.R. 244 at 250G.
[31] See **18.7.6**.

In April 1990, for example, the director of a property company was fined £25,000, believed to be a record fine at the time, after both he and the company were found to be in contempt of court for breaking an injunction taken out by the district council. He had started covering the red back elevation of Palace House Mansion, a distinguished Georgian House in Newmarket (listed Grade II) in a cement rendering; when he was asked by council officers to desist, he refused, claiming the works were "repairs". A High Court injunction was accordingly obtained, which was ignored. At the hearing in proceedings for contempt, the defendants undertook to pay for restorative and remedial works to the brickwork, and were ordered to pay the council's costs. Following the case, English Heritage commented: "Owners and developers must be made aware of the serious nature of offences of this kind. The legislation has teeth which can and will bite hard, as the courts have now shown".[32]

18.8 Unauthorised signs and advertisements

In general, the remedy for an authority concerned about an unauthorised display of advertising is to prosecute those responsible.[33]

The display of an advertisement, if it involves development[34] (as with, for example, a roadside hoarding), will not be deemed to be granted planning permission if it is in breach of the Advertisements Regulations.[35] It follows that it would in theory be possible for a planning authority In England or Wales, or the Department in Northern Ireland, to take enforcement action, requiring such a display to be removed. It is known that the ODPM is unhappy with this view, but it seems to be a perfectly appropriate mechanism to employ if the concern of an authority is to remove the advertisement rather than to punish the advertiser.[36] But it would not apply, even in theory, to those advertisement displays that do not involve development.

The Advertisements Regulations in Scotland are somewhat different, in that they explicitly apply to the advertisement control regime the provisions of the planning enforcement legislation considered earlier in this chapter, so as to enable a planning authority to serve in respect of an unauthorised display of advertisements an enforcement notice, against which there is a right of appeal to the Scottish Ministers.[37] If the notice comes into effect, the authority may then carry out the necessary works to remove the advertisement. There is no equivalent provision elsewhere in the United Kingdom.

Alternatively, a local authority (district or borough council) may remove or obliterate any placard or poster displayed in contravention of the Regulations.

---

[32] [1990] J.P.L. 398.

[33] See **19.8**.

[34] See **12.2.1**.

[35] Deemed planning permission is normally granted for the display of advertising by TCPA 1990, s.222 (see **12.2.6**). [Scotland: TCP(S)A 1997, s.184; NI: P(NI)O 1991, art.67(5).]

[36] Although see *Torridge DC v Jarrad* (1998) *The Times*, April 13, for a different view.

[37] TCP (Control of Advertisements) (Scotland) Regulations 1984, Part VII. And see Scottish Development Department (SDD) Circular 10/84, Annex A, paras 27–30.

Where it does not identify who is responsible, this can be done at once; where it does, that person only has to be given two days' notice.[38] This procedure, which enables an authority to control fly-posting, has been little used. It appears to be very straightforward, however, and would be appropriate where unauthorised posters are disfiguring a listed building, or spoiling the setting of one or the appearance of a conservation area.

In London, a local authority may charge the advertiser for the cost of removing a placard or poster under section 225.[39] In addition, authorities in London may take similar action against an unauthorised hoarding after giving 21 days' notice on the person responsible.[40] They may also deface signs or graffiti which are detrimental to the amenity of an area, even if not "advertisements" within the definition in the 1990 Act.[41] These provisions too seem useful, and will hopefully be extended nationwide in due course.

In Northern Ireland, the position is a for England and Wales, save that the provision in the 1991 Order whereby the Department may invite a planning application is also applied to advertisements.[42]

18.9 Unauthorised works to a place of worship

Where planning permission or (exceptionally) listed building consent is required for works to a place of worship, or in the curtilage of one, and is not obtained, enforcement action may be taken by a planning authority as in any other case.

However, as explained earlier, most works to places of worship (in particular, those to interiors) are controlled in practice by the internal systems of control of the exempt denominations.[43] An essential part of each of those systems is a procedure for the enforcement of control. As one Church of England chancellor remarked, following the carrying out of various works to a Grade I listed church without a faculty,

"because the Church of England and therefore its officers such as the minister and churchwardens are trustees of the heritage for the parish, the diocese and the nation, ignorance of the law and even well-intentioned breaches of the law cannot and will not be tolerated."[44]

---

[38] TCPA 1990 s.225.

[39] A modified s.225(3)–(9) was substituted in relation to Greater London except Tower Hamlets by the London Local Authorities Act 1995, s.10, and in relation to Tower Hamlets by the London Local Authorities Act 1996, s.27.

[40] 1995 Act, s.11. For an example of the use of this procedure, see *Cal Brown Ltd v Hounslow LBC* [2002] 2 P. & C.R. 22. And for an example of a spectacularly inept misuse of it, see *R. (Maiden Outdoor Advertising) v Lambeth LBC* [2004] J.P.L. 820— "Lambeth got virtually everything one could think of wrong ... a perfect example of how not to behave by a local authority".

[41] s.12.

[42] P(NI)O 1991, arts 23, 24, applied by Planning (Control of Advertisements) Regulations (NI) 1992, and modified by Sch.4.

[43] See **16.6–16.9**.

[44] *Re St Giles, Durham*, (1998) 5 Ecc. L.J. 301 (Durham Consistory Court). See also *Re St Edburga, Leigh*, 2004, unreported (Worcester Consistory Court).

Where works are carried out in such circumstances, the chancellor may issue an injunction to halt any unauthorised works which are proceeding or which appear likely to proceed, or make a restoration order to restore the position to that which existed before they were carried out.[45] The procedure in either case is governed by the Faculty Jurisdiction (Injunctions and Restoration Orders) Rules 1992.

An injunction may be issued or a restoration order may be made on the application of any person appearing to the chancellor to have a sufficient interest in the matter.[46] This includes, amongst others, English Heritage, the national amenity societies and the local planning authority; and it is perhaps significant that one of the first injunctions to be obtained under the new procedures was at the behest of a planning authority.[47] As with all injunctive relief, an injunction may in an emergency be obtained almost immediately; in the first instance, the diocesan registrar should be approached.

Details of the procedures of the other exempt denominations should be sought from their national offices (or on the relevant website[48]).

---

[45] s.13(4),(5).

[46] s.13(6).

[47] *Wycombe DC v St Margaret, Tylers Green*, 1994, unreported (Oxford Consistory Court).

[48] See **16.9**.

Chapter 19

Criminal Offences

19.1 Introduction

The carrying out of almost any works to a listed building or a scheduled monument without having obtained consent is a criminal offence, as is the unauthorised demolition of a building in a conservation area.

The fact that Parliament has made a breach of these statutory codes a criminal offence may reflect its view of the importance of our heritage, and the seriousness of unauthorised acts resulting in the loss of any of it. More pragmatically, however, it also arises from the nature of such an offence. To erect an unsatisfactory building without planning permission is no doubt an evil, but it is one which can readily be cured, by the simple expedient of issuing an enforcement notice requiring the offending structure to be demolished. But to knock down a fine old building, or indeed any building, whether or not it is a great evil, is not an act that can easily be reversed; it is in many cases simply not possible to resurrect old buildings (even a reconstruction in facsimile is still lacking the "age" which is often such a feature of historic fabric). It is essential, therefore, if the law is to have any force at all, for it to be backed up by the availability of criminal sanctions.

The unauthorised display of advertisements is also a criminal offence—presumably not because it is irreversible, but on the contrary because it is easy to erect signs and hoardings resulting in substantial financial rewards whilst enforcement action is under way.

The relevant legislation therefore provides for a number of criminal offences relating to historic buildings and monuments. The principal ones are those relating to the carrying out of unauthorised works, as follows:

- carrying out of unauthorised works to a listed building or to a building protected by a building preservation notice (see **19.2** to **19.4**);

- unauthorised demolition of an unlisted building in a conservation area (**19.5**); and

- carrying out of unauthorised works to a scheduled monument (**19.6**).

Even though it should now be somewhat simpler to obtain a conviction for these offences since the decision of the Court of Appeal in *R. v Sandhu*,[1] criminal procedure is not straightforward, particularly to those not encountering it often. It may be for this reason that in 2001, 82 per cent of local authorities in England brought no prosecutions at all.[2] The ODPM is expected to issue during 2006 guidance to local authorities on prosecution procedures.

Further, prosecuting those responsible may not always, or even often, be the most appropriate response when confronted by unauthorised works. In particular, where the consequences of the works can be reversed (for example, where a traditional window in a listed building has been replaced with an inappropriate modern one, or an unsightly extension erected), it may be more appropriate for a planning authority to take one of various forms of enforcement action, as described in the previous chapter.[3] However, there is no power to take enforcement action to bring about the restoration of an ancient monument.

A further group of offences relating to historic buildings are considered in **19.7**, as follows:

- damage to historic buildings;

- unauthorised use of a metal detector; and

- dealing in cultural objects.

The unauthorised display of advertisements is considered at **19.8**.
General points as to procedure (relevant to all of the above offences) are outlined in **19.9**, and matters relating to sentencing in **19.10**. Appeals are touched upon briefly at **19.11**. Further details on these aspects of procedure should be sought in standard works on criminal procedure.

Finally, it may be noted that much of the commentary in this chapter will be equally relevant to some of the other offences mentioned briefly earlier in this book:

- failing to notify works in an area of archaeological importance[4];

- carrying out works to a tree in a conservation area without notifying the planning authority[5]; and

- carrying out works to a tree subject to a tree preservation order without consent under the order.[6]

---

[1] [1997] JPL 853, CA (see **19.9.6**).
[2] *Local Authority Conservation Provision*, research carried out for English Heritage by P. Grover (available on the EH website).
[3] See **18.2.1**, **18.3.4**.
[4] See **13.6.5**.
[5] See **5.5.5**; for more details, see Mynors, *The Law of Trees, Forests and Hedgerows* (Sweet & Maxwell, London, 2002), Chapter 21.
[6] See **7.6.5**; for more details, see Mynors, *ibid.*, Chapter 19.

19.2 Unauthorised works to listed buildings: the offences

19.2.1 Unauthorised works to a listed building

There are two offences created by section 9 of the Listed Buildings Act. The first, in section 9(1), is simply "contravention of section 7". That section in turn provides as follows:

"Subject to the following provisions of this Act, no person shall execute or cause to be executed any works for the demolition of a listed building or for its alteration or extension in any manner which would affect its character as a building of special architectural or historic interest, unless the works are authorised."

Section 8(1) of the Scottish Listed Buildings Act similarly refers simply to contravention of section 6 of that Act; and the corresponding offence in Northern Ireland is in article 44(1) of the Order.

The elements of the offence created by sections 7 and 9(1) are as follows:

(1) the building in question is listed;

(2) works are carried out for its demolition, alteration or extension;

(3) if the works are for the alteration or extension of the building, they affect its character as a building of special architectural or historic interest;

(4) the works are executed, or caused to be executed, by the defendant; and

(5) the works are unauthorised.

This reflects the analysis of the offence in *R. v Sandhu*[7]; although that decision related only to alteration, not to demolition.

To obtain a conviction, the prosecution must prove (beyond reasonable doubt) all but the last of these. Conversely, to achieve an acquittal, the accused must prove (on the balance of probabilities) either that the works were authorised, or that he or she can rely on any available defence—notably the statutory defence that the works were urgently necessary for health or safety or the common law defence of duress of circumstances.[8]

In practice, there is likely to be little disagreement on most of the above items in any particular case. However, difficulties may arise in relation to some points, including the following:

- in the case of a structure attached to a listed building, or in its curtilage, was it included in the list?

- were the works *for* the demolition etc of the building, or were they the result of an accident?

- in the case of works short of total demolition, did they affect the special character of the listed building?

- who actually carried out the works, and on whose orders?

---

[7] [1997] J.P.L. 853, CA (see **19.9.6**).
[8] See **19.4**.

- if there was a listed building consent in existence, did it cover the works actually carried out?

- were the works urgently necessary?

- did the accused think that they were necessary to avoid a danger, and were they limited to what was reasonable?

These points are considered further below.

The offence created by sections 7 and 9(1) is triable either way. The penalty on summary conviction (in a magistrates' court) is a fine of up to £20,000 (£30,000 in Northern Ireland) or a jail sentence of up to six months; on conviction on indictment, an unlimited fine or imprisonment for up to two years.[9]

19.2.2 Non-compliance with conditions attached to listed building consent

The second offence created by section 9 of the Listed Buildings Act is contained in subsection (2), as follows:

"Without prejudice to subsection (1), if a person executing or causing to be executed any works in relation to a listed building under a listed building consent fails to comply with any condition attached to the consent, he shall be guilty of an offence."

Section 8(2) of the Scottish Listed Buildings Act and article 44(5) of the Northern Ireland Order are identical.

The elements of this offence are as follows:

(1) the building in question is listed;

(2) works are carried out

- for its demolition, or
- for its alteration or extension in a manner that affects its character as a building of special architectural or historic interest;

(3) the works are executed or caused to be executed, by the defendant;

(4) the works are authorised by a grant of consent;

(5) the conditions on that consent having not been complied with.

To secure a conviction, all of these must be proved by the prosecution. Most will usually be relatively straightforward; although many of the problems noted above in connection with section 9(1) may occur equally in connection with section 9(2). In addition, difficulties may arise is if the wording of the relevant condition is obscure.

It is a defence to a charge under section 9(2) that the works carried out in breach of a condition were urgently necessary for health and safety[10] (or thought

---

[9] P(LBCA)A 1990, s.9(4); see **19.10**. [Scotland: P(LBCA)(S)A 1997, s.8(4); NI: P(NI)O 1991, art.44(6), substituted by art.14 of the Planning (Amendment) (NI) Order 2003.]

[10] P(LBCA)A 1990, s.9(3). [Scotland: P(LBCA)(S)A 1997, s.8(3); NI: P(NI)O 1991, art.44(7).]

to be necessary); but the same requirements concerning proof apply as when this defence is used in response to a charge under section 9(1).[11]

Examples of situations in which a charge under section 9(2) rather than section 9(1) might be appropriate would include cases where demolition was not followed by reconstruction as required by a condition, or where items from the building were not retained after the completion of the works. In the case of alterations, section 9(2) might be invoked where works have been carried out using the wrong materials or to the wrong design.

The offence created by section 9(2) is triable either way, and carries the same penalties on conviction as an offence under section 9(1).[12]

19.2.3 Damage to a listed building

As an alternative to a charge under section 9 of the Listed Buildings Act, it may occasionally be appropriate for an authority to bring a charge under s.59(1), which provides as follows:

"If, with the intention of causing damage to a listed building, any relevant person does or permits the doing of any act which causes or is likely to result in damage in damage to the building, he shall be guilty of an offence..."

Section 53(1) of the Scottish Listed Buildings Act is identical; s.49(1) of the Northern Ireland Order is to the same effect.

The elements of this offence are as follows:

(1) the building in question is listed;

(2) an act is carried out which:

- causes damage to the building, or
- is likely to result in such damage;

(3) the act is done or permitted by the defendant;

(4) the defendant is a "relevant person"; and

(5) he or she has the intention of causing damage to the building.

Note that this offence can only be committed by a "relevant person"—that is, someone who, but for this section, would be entitled to do or permit the act in question.[13] That is, in general, it can only be committed by or on behalf of the owner or occupier of the land. Thus, in the case of a building occupied under a lease or licence, the terms of the occupancy agreement would need to be checked to see who would be entitled to do works to the building.

If works causing damage are carried out by anyone not entitled to do them at all, the correct course would be to charge under section 1 of the Criminal Damage Act 1971, rather than under section 59 of the Listed Buildings Act. The effect of

---

[11] See **19.4**.

[12] P(LBCA)A 1990, s.9(4); see **19.2.2**. [Scotland: P(LBCA)(S)A 1997, s.8(4); NI: P(NI)O 1991, art.44(6), substituted by art.14 of the Planning (Amendment) (NI) Order 2003.]

[13] P(LBCA)A 1990, s.59(2). [Scotland: P(LBCA)(S)A 1997, s.53(2); NI: P(NI)O 1991, art.49(1).]

section 59 is thus to extend the provisions of the 1971 Act, which do not apply to acts carried out by or on behalf of owners of property, so as to include acts carried out by their owners in the case of listed buildings.

The offence does not apply in the case of a listed building that is a place of worship belonging to one of the six exempt denominations and is in ecclesiastical use; although it will apply to a redundant church, even one of the Church of England.[14] Nor will it apply if the building is a scheduled monument as well as a listed building[15]; although it would then be possible in certain cases to bring a charge under section 28 of the Ancient Monuments Act.[16]

Nor does the offence apply in the case of acts authorised either:

- by a grant of planning permission or deemed planning permission (but not planning permission granted by a development order); or

- by a grant of listed building consent.

To secure a conviction, the prosecution must be able to prove all of the five elements noted above. Conversely, to achieve an acquittal, the accused must prove either that the building in question is an exempted ecclesiastical building or scheduled monument, or that the works have been authorised (as above).

The offence under section 59 can only be tried summarily (that is, before a magistrate); and the maximum penalty on conviction is a fine of level 3 on the standard scale.[17] As to procedure generally, and principles of sentencing, see below; although not all of the points discussed there will necessarily be relevant to an offence under section 59.

If a person after being convicted of an offence under s.59(1) fails to take such reasonable steps as may be necessary to prevent any damage or further damage resulting from the act which led to the conviction, he or she is guilty of a further offence under section 59(4). This is also only triable summarily and, if found guilty, the offender is liable for each day that the failure continues to a fine of one-tenth of level 3 (see above).[18]

19.2.4 Unauthorised works to a building subject to a building preservation notice

Section 9 of the Listed Buildings Act applies to a building in respect of which a building preservation notice has been served[19] as it does to a listed building.[20] It is therefore an offence either:

---

[14] P(LBCA)A 1990, s.60; see **16.3.2**. [Scotland: P(LBCA)(S)A 1997, s.54; NI: P(NI)O 1991, arts 44(8)(a), 49(1).]

[15] P(LBCA)A 1990, s.61. [Scotland: P(LBCA)(S)A 1997, s.55; NI: P(NI)O 1991, arts 44(8)(b), 49(1).]

[16] See **19.6.7**.

[17] P(LBCA)A 1990, s.59(1); see **Appendix F**. [Scotland: P(LBCA)(S)A 1997, s.53(1); NI: P(NI)O 1991, art.49(1).]

[18] P(LBCA)A s.59(4), amended by PCA 1991, Sch.7, para.58. [Scotland: P(LBCA)(S)A 1997, s.53(4); NI: P(NI)O 1991, art.49(3).]

[19] See **3.9**.

[20] P(LBCA)A 1990, s.3(5).

(1) to carry out works for the demolition of such a building, or for its alteration or extension in any way which affects its character as a building of special interest, without listed building consent having been granted,[21] or

(2) where consent has been granted for such works, to carry them out in breach of any condition attached to it.[22]

The same applies in respect of the corresponding provisions in Scotland and, since April 2003, Northern Ireland.[23]

The elements of the offences under these provisions, the statutory and common-law defences available in respect of a charge,[24] and the penalties in the event of a conviction, are exactly the same as for the corresponding offence in connection with works to a building that is actually listed.[25] The comments below relating to those offences[26] thus apply here too, save that (obviously) it will be necessary to prove that a building preservation notice has been properly served in respect of the building, rather than that it has been listed. In particular, the date on which the notice was actually served will need to be proved where it is critical (where, for example, the unauthorised works started at around the same time). Service through the post cannot be presumed.[27]

The offence under section 59 of "causing damage" does not apply to a building subject to a building preservation notice.

19.2.5 Alternative charges

Finally, it is worth considering what alternatives are available to charges under section 9(1) (unauthorised works to a listed building) or under section 9(2) (works carried out in breach of a condition)—and note that those two may occasionally be alternatives to each other.

First, in some cases it may be difficult to prove that the works were either sufficiently substantial to amount to demolition, especially since the decision of the House of Lords in *Shimizu (UK) Ltd v Westminster CC*[28] or, if they were for the alteration of the building, that they affected its character, but somewhat easier to prove that carrying them out damaged the building, and therefore constituted an offence under section 59 of the Listed Buildings Act. The required *mens rea* (intention) is different—there must be an intention to cause damage for a successful prosecution under section 59—and the maximum penalty is lower. If it is nevertheless felt to be appropriate to consider a charge under section 59 as an alternative to one under section 9(1), the indictment should be framed to contain

---

[21] P(LBCA)A 1990, ss 7, 9(1), applied by s.3(5).
[22] P(LBCA)A 1990, s.9(2), applied by s.3(5).
[23] Scotland: P(LBCA)(S)A 1997, ss 6, 8(1),(2), applied by s.3(5); NI: P(NI)O 1991, art.44(1),(5), applied by art.25(5), inserted by art.25 of the Planning (Amendment) (NI) Order 2003.
[24] See **19.4**.
[25] See **19.2.1**.
[26] See **19.3** and **19.4**.
[27] *Maltglade v St Albans RDC* [1972] 3 All E.R. 129.
[28] [1997] 3 P.L.R. 89 (see **12.6.3**).

both counts; the magistrates or (on indictment) the jury would then be able to convict on whichever count proves to be justified by the evidence.

However, discretion is needed. If, for example, the impecunious owner of a listed building replaces the natural slates on the roof with asbestos slates, it may be impossible to secure a conviction either under section 9(1) (because the court does not consider that the works harmed the character of the building) or under s.59 (because there is no evidence that the owner intended to cause damage—quite the reverse: the owner wanted to re-roof the building to prevent damage, but could not afford the correct slates). In such a case, it might be more appropriate for the authority to take enforcement action. It may be easier to convince an inspector at the appeal against the enforcement notice that the works affected the character of the building, and at least it might then be possible to get the slates restored, perhaps with a grant.

The same applies in relation to the corresponding offences in Scotland and Northern Ireland.[29-31]

Secondly, where a building thought to have been listed or subject to a building preservation notice has been demolished (as opposed to altered), if it transpires that it was after all not listed, or that the notice had not been properly served, it would be possible if the building is in a conservation area for the prosecution to seek to amend the indictment so as to allege that the offence is now under section 9 of the Listed Buildings Act as applied by section 74(3)[32], rather than under section 9 *simpliciter*.

Thirdly, where a property is intentionally or recklessly destroyed by fire, the matter should be referred to the police, who will consider prosecuting those responsible for arson.[33] The maximum penalty on conviction is six months' imprisonment or a fine of the statutory maximum; or, where life is endangered, life imprisonment.[34]

19.3 Unauthorised works to a listed building: the matters to be proved by the prosecution

19.3.1 Proving that the building was listed

The first element of the offences under sections 9(1), 9(2) and 59 of the Listed Buildings Act[35] requires the prosecuting authority to prove that the relevant building or structure had been included in the list in its own right at the date on which the offending works were carried out, or that it was at that date an object or structure attached to a building in the list, or a pre-1948 structure in the curtilage of such a building.

[29-31] Scotland: P(LBCA)(S)A 1997, ss 8(1),(2), 53(1); NI: P(NI)O 1991, arts 44(1),(5),49(1).
[32] As to which, see **19.5**. [Scotland: P(LBCA)(S)A 1997, s.8 applied by s.66(3); NI: P(NI)O 1991, art.44, applied by art.51(5).]
[33] Criminal Damage Act 1971, s.1(3).
[34] Criminal Damage Act 1971, s.4(1).
[35] Scotland: P(LBCA)(S)A 1997, ss 8(1),(2), 53(1); NI: P(NI)O 1991, arts 44(1),(5),49(1).

The starting point will be the production (usually by the authority) of all the relevant paperwork; and it must be completely in order. This will include a certified copy of the extract from the official list, signed by the officer of the relevant central government department. It must also be shown that the then owner of the building was notified in writing when it was first listed, and that a copy of the list has been kept available for public inspection by the authority and by the Secretary of State at all times subsequently.[36] Thus it has been held that liability under the tree preservation order legislation did not apply where a defendant was ignorant of the order either because the local planning authority had failed to notify the correct owner of the land of its existence[37] or because the authority had failed to make it available for public inspection.[38] The requirement to place on deposit a certified copy of the order and the accompanying map[39] was held to be mandatory, and not merely directory, and the absence of the order and the map were fatal to the chances of a successful prosecution. Since there is a similar requirement for a copy of the list to be deposited with the relevant local authority, the same principles would apply to a listed building prosecution.

Even having established that the building in question is listed, there may still be a dispute as to the extent of the listing—as with, for example, the removal of panelling alleged to be fixed to a listed building and thus to form part of it, or the alteration of a barn supposedly in the curtilage of a nearby listed farmhouse. This can cause significant problems in some instances, and has been considered at length in **Chapter 4**. In such cases, it will be necessary for both prosecution and defence to call appropriate professionals to give evidence.

19.3.2 Knowledge that the building was listed

The carrying out of unauthorised works to a listed building is an offence of strict liability. That is, it makes no difference if the person carrying out the works did not know that the building was listed.

In *R. v Wells Street Metropolitan Stipendiary Magistrate, ex p. Westminster CC*,[40] the city council was concerned to prosecute people caught in the act of removing valuable architectural features from a listed building in Wimpole Street. The stipendiary magistrate decided that committal proceedings could not be continued since there was no evidence that the accused knew that the building was listed. He accordingly refused to commit them for trial by jury. On the matter being referred to the High Court, however, Watkins L.J. held that the offence under what is now section 9 was one of strict liability, and that it was therefore enough to prove that the act had been carried out. The case was accordingly remitted back to the magistrate to continue the hearing.

Strict liability normally applies to more minor offences, usually those punishable only by fine. In the case of listed buildings offences, it is theoretically possible

---

[36] As required by P(LBCA)A 1990, s.2(4), (5). [Scotland: P(LBCA)(S)A 1997, s.2(3),(4); NI: P(NI)O 1991, art.6.]
[37] *Knowles v Chorley BC* [1998] J.P.L. 593.
[38] *Vale of Glamorgan BC v Palmer* [1984] J.P.L. 334.
[39] Currently under TCP (Tree Preservation Order) Regulations 1999, reg.6(c).
[40] [1986] 1 W.L.R. 1046.

to be imprisoned on conviction, but that would be at the discretion of the court, and is not of itself sufficient to require that proof of knowledge would always be needed to secure a conviction. In the course of his judgment, Watkins L.J. relied on the decision of the Privy Council in *Gammon (Hong Kong) Ltd v AG of Hong Kong*[41]—which, significantly, concerned breaches of the Building Regulations (albeit in Hong Kong). Lord Scarman, in what is now the classic statement of the law on offences of strict liability, had held in that case that there is a presumption in law that *mens rea* (intent) is required before a person can be held guilty of any criminal offence, including a statutory offence.[42] This presumption can be displaced only if this is clearly or by necessary implication the effect of the statute, and in addition only if it can be shown that the creation of strict liability will be effective to promote the objects of the statute by encouraging greater vigilance to prevent the commission of the prohibited act.

The outcome of *Ex p. Westminster* is in line with an earlier judgment that the carrying out of unauthorised works to a tree that is protected by a tree preservation order is an offence of strict liability.[43] The combined effect of these decisions is to indicate that a whole group of offences under the planning Acts are offences of strict liability, including in particular damage to a listed building,[44] unauthorised demolition of a building in a conservation area,[45] and the carrying out of works to a tree in a conservation area without giving notice to the planning authority.[46]

One of the implications of an offence being one of strict liability is that no evidence needs to be called as to knowledge or intent of the accused, as that is irrelevant to the question of guilt. Indeed, the Court of Appeal has held that because it is irrelevant, and is highly likely to be prejudicial to the accused, such evidence is inadmissible.[47]

Where, as will usually be the case, the unauthorised works are carried out by a builder or demolition company, rather than by the owner in person, liability only attaches to the owner if he or she was vicariously liable for the acts of the contractor at the time the works were carried out. Thus where a protected tree was uprooted by an independent tree contractor, contrary to the express instructions of the owner, the owner was held not liable.[48]

19.3.3 The works carried out: a charge under section 9

Where unauthorised works are alleged to have been carried out to a listed building, and as a result a prosecution is brought under section 9 of the Listed

---

[41] [1984] 2 All E.R. 503.
[42] At p.507.
[43] TCPA 1990, s.210(1); *Maidstone BC v Mortimer* [1981] J.P.L. 112.
[44] Under P(LBCA)A 1990, s.59(1); see **19.2.3**. [Scotland: P(LBCA)(S)A 1997, s.53(1); NI: P(NI)O 1991, art.49(1).]
[45] Under P(LBCA)A 1990, s.9(1), applied by s.74(3); see **19.5**. [Scotland: P(LBCA)(S)A 1997, s.8 applied by s.66(3); NI: P(NI)O 1991, art.44, applied by art.51(5).]
[46] Under TCPA 1990, s.211(1); see **5.5**. [Scotland: TCP(S)A 1997, s.172; NI: P(NI)O 1991, art.66A, inserted by art.26 of the Planning (Amendment) (NI) Order 2003.]
[47] *R. v Sandhu* [1997] J.P.L. 853, CA (see **19.9.6**).
[48] *Groveside Homes v Elmbridge BC* (1987) 284 E.G. 940; see also **19.3.5**.

Buildings Act,[49] there will usually be no doubt that some works were actually carried out.

However, where it is alleged that a building was damaged due to vehicle impact, fire, or other "accidental" cause, the authority must be able to prove that works were carried out by the defendant, as opposed to damage being caused by an act of God or the accidental intervention of a third party. And it must also be shown that the works were "for" its demolition, alteration or extension; there must, in other words, be an element of intent. Where, for example, a rotten window is removed allegedly so as to enable its replacement in facsimile, and in the process the whole gable collapses, the prosecution must show that this was not an accident.

A variation of this is where some damage occurs as a result of a "genuine" accident, and then the owner decides to finish off the job by demolishing what remained, but subsequently claims that it simply fell down (or that its conscious removal was necessary for safety reasons). No complaint is made as to the initial accident (or maybe it is not possible to prove conclusively that it was deliberate); but the authority feels that what was left could have been saved. In such a case, there may be substantial problems in assembling sufficient evidence to justify prosecution—once the building has gone, it may be difficult to determine how and why it went; and the owner is of course under no duty to assist in any investigation.

The distinction between "demolition" and "alteration" has now been clarified by the decision of the House of Lords in *Shimizu (UK) Ltd v Westminster CC*.[50] If the works in question are properly categorised as "demolition", it will not be necessary to prove that they affected the character of the building; see the decision of the Court of Appeal in *Shimizu*.[51] If, on the other hand, the works consist of alteration or extension, as is more usual, it will be necessary to prove that they affect the character of the building. This may lead to problems of proof in borderline cases,[52] and will have to be the subject of expert evidence by both sides. Ultimately, however, it is up to the prosecution to prove that the works did affect the character of the building, not up to the defence to prove that they did not.

One particular problem is where a comprehensive programme of repair or maintenance work is carried out, without listed building consent. In practice, works such as re-wiring, renewal of rotten timber skirting, and renewal of plumbing will involve the removal of much old material before the new is brought in to replace it. If therefore the authority inspects the building once the first part of the work has been done, it may understandably form the view that major work has taken place without consent; but once the new items have been inserted, the net result will probably be more or less imperceptible, with no overall effect on the special character of the building. Prosecution in such circumstances would probably only be justifiable where the insertion of the new pipes or cables or whatever led to the destruction of much original fabric (beams, laths or plaster).

---

[49] Scotland: P(LBCA)(S)A 1997, s.8; NI: P(NI)O 1991, art.44.
[50] [1996] 3 P.L.R. 89 (see **12.6.3**).
[51] [1995] 23 E.G. 118 at 123 (and see **12.2.3**).
[52] See **12.4.4**.

If the building has only recently been listed, it will be necessary to produce evidence of the date when the works were started.

It is also essential for the prosecution to be able to prove that the works were carried out, or caused by the defendant. This is considered further below, in the context of choosing who to prosecute.[53]

19.3.4 The works carried out: a charge under section 59

Where works are carried out to a listed building that are not sufficient to amount to "alteration" or "extension", it would be more appropriate to frame a charge by reference to section 59 of the Listed Buildings Act—that is, so as to refer to acts that cause—or are likely to result in—damage to the building.[54] A charge under this section might also be appropriate where the works in question are such that listed building consent was probably (but not definitely) required, but was not sought. That has the advantage that it is not necessary to prove that the works "affected the character of the building".[55]

As to works "likely to result in damage to" a listed building, one type of damage that could be envisaged here is work that is sufficiently substantial to harm the building (and possibly to lead to its decay and eventual demolition)—and therefore undesirable—but not substantial enough either to "cause" damage, or to require listed building consent.[56] Thus it could be difficult to show that the removal of a few slates from the roof of a redundant listed building, so as to let in the rain and eventually cause major structural problems, in itself actually "caused" any damage. And the removal of a tile could scarcely be said to affect the special character of the building, and thus require consent. But it might be possible to show "beyond reasonable doubt" that it would be likely to result in damage. On the other hand, the maximum sentence is not great.

If a prosecution under section 59 is to be successful, it will be necessary to prove that the person doing the prohibited act actually intended to cause the damage resulting (or likely to result). It will not be enough merely to prove that he or she was reckless as to whether damage would be caused.[57] As to the meaning of "intend", see standard texts on criminal law.[58] On the other hand, knowledge that the building was listed would probably not need to be proved, following *R. v Wells Street Metropolitan Stipendiary Magistrate*,[59] although no case under section 59 has yet been reported.

To commit an offence under section 59, it is necessary to do a prohibited act, or to permit another to do so. It is not enough to unwittingly cause another to do it; knowledge or recklessness would be required.[60]

---

[53] See **19.9.3**.
[54] Scotland: P(LBCA)(S)A 1997, s.53; NI: P(NI)O 1991, art.49.
[55] See **19.2.3**.
[56] See **12.4.4**.
[57] Contrast the wording of, for example, Criminal Damage Act 1971, s.1.
[58] And, in particular, Criminal Justice Act 1967, s.8, and *R. v Moloney* [1985] A.C. 905.
[59] [1986] 1 W.L.R. 1046 (see **19.3.2**).
[60] *Sweet v Parsley* [1970] A.C. 132 at 162 *per* Lord Diplock.

19.3.5 Liability for carrying out the works

The final matter to be proved by the prosecution is that the accused was actually responsible for the works which were carried out to the building. In the case of a charge under section 9, it must prove that the accused executed or caused to be executed the works in question. For a charge under section 59 (damage), it is necessary to prove that he or she did the act in question or permitted it to be done.

This may be straightforward—where, for example, the landowner or contractor was actually seen and photographed on-site whilst the works were taking place. But it may be less so where the planning authority only becomes aware of the works some while afterwards.

An offence is also committed, under the Accessories and Abbettors Act 1861 or the Magistrates Court Act 1980, if a person aids, abets, counsels or procures someone else to commit an offence. A landowner who instructs a contractor is thus vicariously liable for the actions of the contractor, and thus for any unauthorised works carried out by the contractor. However, that does not extend to the situation where, for example, a landowner hires a contractor to carry out works but specifically tells the contractor not to remove more than a certain amount of a wall, and the contractor nevertheless does so. In that situation, although the contractor is clearly liable for the breach of listed building control, it has gone beyond its authority in carrying out the unauthorised works, and the landowner is not also liable.[61]

Where, as will not infrequently occur, the actual act is carried out by an employee of a company, or indeed an individual trading as a company, the company will be liable as well as the individual—although, again, that would not apply if the company can show that the employee was acting outside the scope of his authority.

Conversely, where unauthorised works to a listed building are carried out by a company—for example, a firm of contractors, or a corporate property owner employing a contractor—it is possible to prosecute not only the company concerned, but also (except in Northern Ireland) any officer of the company who consented to or connived in the commission of the offence, or whose negligence contributed to it.[62] This may help to ensure non-recurrence, especially by developers who are habitually dealing with historic buildings and areas. So, for example, in *R. v Alath Construction Ltd; R. v Brightman*[63] (a tree case), a development company (A) was fined £500 for felling a protected tree, and the managing director of the company (B) a further £500—and each had to pay £1,000 towards the costs of the prosecution.

For a prosecution to succeed against the officer of a company, however, it will be necessary to show that the officer concerned was a decision-maker within the company with the power and responsibility to decide corporate policy and strategy.[64]

---

[61] *Groveside Homes v Elmbridge BC* [1987] 2 E.G.L.R. 199.
[62] TCPA 1990, s.331. [Scotland: TCP(S)A 1997, s.273;
[63] [1990] 1 W.L.R. 1255, CA; [1991] 1 P.L.R. 25; see **19.4.4.**
[64] *Woodhouse v Walsall MBC* [1994] Env L.R. 30.

Note that, for some reason, it is not possible to prosecute the officers of a company as well as the company itself for an offence of damage to a listed building.[65]

19.3.6 Burden and standard of proof

The burden of proof in a criminal trial lies in general on the prosecution, which must prove all the elements of the offence charged, to the normal criminal standard (sufficient for a jury to be "satisfied beyond reasonable doubt so that they feel sure"[66]). It is therefore up to the prosecution to prove that the works were carried out, that the defendant was responsible, and that the building was listed. It is also for the prosecution to prove (in appropriate cases) that the works affected the character of the building[67]—that is, the defendant does not have to prove that the works did *not* affect its character.

19.4 Unauthorised works to a listed building: matters to be proved by the defence

19.4.1 The existence of consent

A person carrying out works to a listed building will not be committing an offence under section 9 of the Listed Buildings Act (or the equivalent provisions in Scotland and Northern Ireland) if those works are authorised—that is, if:

(1) the local planning authority or the Secretary of State has granted listed building consent in writing for the execution of the works;

(2) the works are executed in accordance with the terms of:
- the consent, and
- any conditions attached; and

(3) in the case of works involving total demolition of the building, notice of the proposal has been given to the relevant recording body[68] and thereafter either:
- for at least one month following the grant of consent, and before the start of the works, reasonable access to the building has been made available to that body for the purpose of recording it; or
- it has stated that it has completed its recording of the building, or that it does not wish to record it.[69]

This is reasonably straightforward; see the relevant sections of **Chapter 13** for further details. That is, a person carrying out any of the specified operations will not be committing an offence if he or she has obtained the consent of the local

---

[65] P(LBCA)A 1990, s.89(2). [Scotland: P(LBCA)(S)A 1997, s.79(2).]

[66] *Ferguson v R.* [1979] 1 W.L.R. 94, PC.

[67] *Gatland v Commissioner of Police of the Metropolis* [1968] 2 Q.B. 279.

[68] English Heritage or the relevant Royal Commission (see **13.5.7**).

[69] ss 8(1), 8(2); and see **13.7.10**. [Scotland: P(LBCA)(S)A 1997, s.7(1),(2); NI: P(NI)O 1991; art.44(2).]

planning authority or the Secretary of State, and carries out the operations in accordance with the conditions attached to such consent.

The burden is on the accused to prove that consent has been obtained, and that any conditions have been complied with—not on the prosecution to prove the converse (which is in any event logically impossible):

"In *R v Edwards*,[70] the Court of Appeal expressed their conclusion in the form of an exception to what they said was the fundamental rule of our criminal law, that the prosecution must prove every element of the offence charged. They said that the exception 'is limited to offences arising under enactments which prohibit the doing of an act save in specified circumstances or by persons of specified classes or with specified qualifications or with the licence of specified authorities.' "[71]

It is important, if prosecution is to be avoided, that the consent in question does cover precisely the works that have been carried out. In some cases, it is clear that there is a consent, which must authorise something, but far from clear precisely what. *Richmond-upon-Thames v Secretary of State*[72] was a tree case illustrating the problems that can arise where an authority attempts to enforce against works carried out allegedly in excess of those permitted by an imprecisely worded consent (in that case "to remove the two longest branches overhanging [the neighbouring property]"). However, unless the consent is so vague as to be a nullity, a court would simply have to look at the consent and all the circumstances and try to work out what was intended by the authority. But note that the interpretation of a consent is a matter of law, for the judge, not one of fact for the decision of the jury.[73]

It has already been noted that a grant of (so-called) retrospective listed building consent for the retention of works already carried out is not sufficient to avoid criminal prosecution.[74] But it must be open to doubt whether the courts would consider very seriously such a prosecution were it to be mounted after consent had thus been granted.

In relation to a charge under section 59 (damage to a listed building), it is merely necessary for the accused to prove the existence of planning permission or listed building consent; it is not necessary to show that the relevant recording body has been notified.

Finally, sections 9 and 59 of the Listed Buildings Act do not apply to ecclesiastical buildings exempted from listed building control,[75] nor to scheduled monuments. In an appropriate case, it is up to the defence to prove that the building in question falls into one of these categories.

---

[70] [1975] Q.B. 27, at pp.39–40.

[71] *R. v Hunt* [1987] A.C. 352, HL, *per* Lord Griffiths at p.375; quoted in *R. v Alath Construction Ltd; R. v Brightman* [1990] 1 W.L.R. 1255, CA at p.1259C.

[72] [2001] E.W.H.C. Admin 205, March 5, 2001, unreported.

[73] *R. v Bovis Construction Ltd* [1994] Crim. L. R. 938, CA (Crim) (a scheduled monument case), following *R. v Spens* (1991) 93 CAR 194.

[74] Under P(LBCA)A 1990, s.8(3); see **18.2.4**. [Scotland: P(LBCA)(S)A 1997, s.7(3); NI: P(NI)O 1991, art.44(3).]

[75] See **16.3.2**.

19.4.2 Urgency of works as defence

It has always been recognised that it will sometimes be necessary to carry out works as a matter of urgency, for safety reasons. In practice, of course, this has always been an obvious loophole since, once a building has been totally demolished, it is easy for an owner to claim that its removal was "necessary", but difficult for an authority—and sometimes even more difficult for a vigilant amenity group—to prove otherwise.

It is therefore possible to avoid conviction under section 9 where works are carried out without consent only where the person responsible is able to prove all of the following:

"(a) that works to the building were urgently necessary in the interests of safety or health or for the preservation of the building,
 (b) that it was not practicable to secure safety or health or, as the case may be, the preservation of the building by works of repair or works for affording temporary support or shelter,
 (c) that the works carried out were limited to the minimum measures immediately necessary, and
 (d) that notice in writing justifying in detail the carrying out of the works was given to the local planning authority as soon as reasonably practicable."[76]

The above wording, which is reasonably self-explanatory, is the result of an amendment made by the Housing and Planning Act 1986, and should deter demolition companies that might otherwise be willing to deal with allegedly "unsafe" listed buildings on Friday nights. It minimises (but does not remove entirely) the problem of an unscrupulous property owner who demolishes all or part of a listed building, thus removing the evidence. But it is probably as far as the law can go; and it is difficult to see how that particular problem could ever be entirely satisfactorily solved.

It will be noted that the planning authority must still be informed "as soon as reasonably practicable". Since the authority has the power to grant listed building consent for the works already carried out,[77] such consent could then be subject to suitable conditions, and thus, in theory, the authority could require restoration of the building, or the making good of any damage.

There is no corresponding urgent works defence to a charge (under section 59) of damage to a listed building.

19.4.3 Buildings considered to be dangerous: duress of circumstances

Where works are carried out because a building is dangerous, there is no need for consent to be obtained, as a result of the statutory exemption discussed above. However, that does not apply where a building is not dangerous, but where the owner thinks it is, and takes action to avoid the perceived harm. This may happen where, for example, an owner considers a dangerous situation has arisen following a listed building being damaged by fire or vehicle impact, and demolishes it

---

[76] P(LBCA)A 1990, s.9(3). [Scotland: P(LBCA)(S)A 1997, s.8(3); NI: P(NI)O 1991, art.44(7).]

[77] P(LBCA)A 1990, s.8(3); see **18.1.2**. [Scotland: P(LBCA)(S)A 1997, s.7(3); NI: P(NI)O 1991, art.44(3).]

(or what is left of it). Once it has gone, it will usually be impossible for the authority to prove conclusively that it had not been dangerous at the time it was demolished—but equally difficult for the owner or contractor to prove the contrary.

There is, or at least may be, a further possibility open to the owner, if the authority persists in prosecuting in such circumstances: to rely on what is known as the defence of "duress of circumstances". The principles governing this defence were set out by the Court of Appeal in *R. v Martin*:

"... the defence is available only if, from an objective standpoint, the accused can be said to be acting reasonably and proportionately in order to avoid a threat of death or serious injury.
... assuming the defence to be open to the accused on his account of the facts, the issue should be left to the jury, who should be directed to determine these two questions:

- first, was the accused, or may he have been, impelled to act as he did because, as a result of what he reasonably believed to be the situation, he had good cause to fear that otherwise death or serious physical injury would result?
- second, if so, may a sober person of reasonable firmness, sharing the characteristics of the accused, have responded to that situation by acting as he acted?

If the answer to both those questions was yes, then the jury would acquit: the defence of necessity would have been established."[78]

In other words, if the owner of a building genuinely believes that it is likely to cause death or serious injury—perhaps, for example, by wholly or partly collapsing onto a path—he or she may remove the cause of the danger. The applicability of this defence to listed buildings cases was confirmed by the Crown Court in Winchester in *Basingstoke and Deane BC v Palmer*, as a preliminary point in a trial where a building had been partly destroyed by fire, and the remainder demolished the following day to prevent it collapsing onto a pavement.[79]

In order to avoid conviction on this basis, the accused must first be able to show that the defence is available on his or her account of the facts; that is, assuming that the factual evidence called by the defence is accurate, might the collapse of the building have caused death or serious physical injury? Secondly, it must be proved that the response by the accused to the perceived threat was both reasonable and proportionate. There may be several ways in which to deal with a possibly dangerous building, such as preventing access to the land onto which it is likely to collapse until a specialist opinion can be obtained as to its state. It is therefore important, if this defence is to be relied on in any subsequent prosecution, for the owner of the structure or the contractor carrying out the works to assemble as much evidence as possible before the works are done.

It would of course be possible for this defence to be relied upon inappropriately. To minimise the risk of this, an authority that is notified of a potentially dangerous structure should send a properly qualified officer to inspect it as soon as possible and take photographs and any other evidence. If the officer forms the

---

[78] (1989) 88 C.R. App. R. 343, *per* Simon Brown J. at p.346 (following the earlier decision in *Conway* (1988) 88 Cr. App. R. 159, [1988] 3 All E.R. 1025, CA; see also *R. v Pommell* [1995] 2 Cr. App. R. 607, and *Archbold*, 2005, para.17–128.
[79] Unreported, June 5, 2000.

view either that it is not dangerous or that there are other ways of dealing with it, written advice to that effect should be given to the owner (for an example, see Form D11 in **Appendix D**), who should sign a note acknowledging that the advice has been received. It would then be difficult for the owner to prove subsequently that it was reasonable to act in some way other than as recommended.

19.4.4 Burden and standard of proof

Where a statute creates an exception or a defence, it is for the defendant to show that it applies in the particular case.[80] It is thus up to him or her to prove that the works were properly authorised, that is, that listed building consent had been granted and (in cases involving demolition) that the relevant recording body had been notified. It is not necessary (and, indeed, arguably it would not be logically possible) for the authority to prove that the works were not authorised.

If the defence is based on the claim that the works were urgently necessary for safety or health,[81] it is for the defendant to prove all the elements of that defence. Thus in *R. v Alath Construction Ltd; R. v Brightman*,[82] the Court of Appeal confirmed that, where a tree had been felled in apparent contravention of a tree preservation order, it was up to the accused to show that the tree had indeed been dangerous, or that the works fell within one of the other statutory categories which were exempt from the need for consent.[83] The same principle would apply to works to listed buildings. Similarly, it is up to the accused to prove in appropriate cases that consent was not required.[84]

The House of Lords has recently accepted that a reverse burden of proof (whereby it is for the accused rather than the prosecution to prove the existence or absence of a particular matter) is not a breach of human rights.[85]

Where the burden of proof rests on the defendant rather than on the prosecution, the standard of proof required is merely the balance of probabilities.[86]

19.5 Unauthorised demolition in a conservation area

19.5.1 Unauthorised demolition

The demolition of an unlisted building in a conservation area without conservation area consent is a criminal offence, except in the circumstances where such consent is not required.[87] Subject to that, the same considerations would

---

[80] Magistrates' Courts Act 1980, s.101; *R. v Edwards* [1975] Q.B. 27, CA.
[81] See **19.4.2**, above.
[82] [1991] 1 P.L.R. 25.
[83] See **7.6.3**.
[84] See **19.4.1**.
[85] *R. v Johnstobe* [2003] 1 W.L.R. 1736, HL. See also *Att-Gen's Reference (No. 1 of 2004)* sub nom *R. v Edwards and others* [2004] 1 W.L.R. 2111, CA.
[86] *R. v Carr-Briant* [1943] K.B. 607, CCA.
[87] P(LBCA)A 1990, ss 7 and 9(1) as applied by s.74(3). For the exceptions, see **12.6.5**. [Scotland: P(LBCA)(S)A 1997, ss 6 and 8(1), applied by s.66(3); NI: P(NI)O 1991, art.44(1), applied by art.55(5).]

generally apply as to proceedings under section 9(1) in connection with listed buildings.[88] In particular, the elements of the offence are as follows:

(1) the building in question is in a conservation area;

(2) works are carried out for its demolition;

(3) the works are executed, or caused to be executed, by the defendant; and

(4) the works are unauthorised.

The burden would thus be on the planning authority (or whoever mounted the prosecution) to prove (beyond reasonable doubt) that the building was in a conservation area, that the demolition had taken place, and that it had been carried out by the defendant. It would be up to the accused, on the other hand, to prove (on the balance of probabilities) either:

(1) that conservation area consent was not required; or

(2) that conservation area consent had been obtained; or

(3) that one of the defences could be relied on.

It is also an offence to carry out demolition works for which conservation area consent has been given without complying with a condition attached to the consent.[89] The factors noted above in connection with non-compliance with conditions on a listed building consent would apply here too.[90]

The offences under section 9(1) and section 9(2), as applied to unlisted buildings in conservation areas, are triable either way, and carry the same maximum penalties as the corresponding listed building offence.[91]

It is not an offence under the Listed Buildings Act to "damage" an unlisted building in a conservation area, unless that damage amounts to demolition of part of the building, since section 59 applies to listed buildings only.

19.5.2 Matters to be proved by the prosecution

The burden will be on the prosecution to prove first that the demolition has taken place. This may cause problems following the judgment of the House of Lords in *Shimizu (UK) Ltd v Westminster CC*.[92] In relation to the demolition of part of a building, it will be necessary to show that the works were on a sufficient scale to amount to demolition, so as to leave a site for redevelopment, rather than alteration.

Secondly, it must be shown by the prosecution that the building was in a conservation area at the relevant time. In proving this, particular care would be needed to ensure that the relevant paperwork (including copies of the advertise-

---

[88] See **19.3** and **19.4**.
[89] P(LBCA)A 1990, s.9(2), applied by s.74(3). [Scotland: P(LBCA)(S)A 1997, s.8(2), applied by s.66(3); NI: P(NI)O 1991, art.44(5), applied by art.55(5).]
[90] See **19.2.2**.
[91] P(LBCA)A 1990, s.9(4), applied by s.74(3); see **19.2.1**. [Scotland: P(LBCA)(S)A 1997, s.8(4), applied by s.66(3); NI: P(NI)O 1991, art.44(6), applied by art.55(5).]
[92] [1997] 3 P.L.R. 89.

ment in the local newspaper and the *London Gazette*[93]) was in order; the procedures followed by some authorities in designating conservation areas might not stand up very well under cross-examination.[94]

It would seem that both offences are strict liability; that is, it is not necessary for the prosecution to prove that the accused knew that the building was in a conservation area.[95] On the other hand, whereas the owner and occupier of a building must be informed as soon as it is listed, there is no such requirement when property is included in a conservation area—there is merely a requirement to register the designation as a local land charge,[96] so that *subsequent* owners are made aware of it. It follows that, if an accused can show that he or she has owned the building since before the designation of the conservation area, and was genuinely unaware of it, it may be possible to secure a greatly reduced penalty. On sentencing generally, see below.[97]

19.5.3 Defences

As to possible defences, those applying to works to listed buildings apply equally to demolition of unlisted buildings in conservation areas.[98] In particular, the accused would be able to escape conviction if he or she were able to show:

- that consent had been granted for the works carried out; or

- that the works were urgently necessary in the interests of safety or health or for the preservation of the building, and that it was not practicable to secure safety or health or the preservation of the building by works of repair or works for affording temporary support or shelter, and that the works carried out were limited to the minimum measures immediately necessary, and that notice in writing justifying the works in detail was given to the local planning authority as soon as reasonably practicable[99]; or

- that he or she genuinely believed that the works were necessary to avoid death or serious physical injury, and that what was done was a reasonable response to that belief.[1]

In addition, it has earlier been explained that there are a number circumstances where conservation area consent is not needed for demolition, by virtue of section 75(1) of the Listed Buildings Act, in particular where the works are either relatively trivial, or else are authorised under some other procedure (as set out in the relevant direction by the Secretary of State).[2] Where this is considered to be

---

93   As required by s.70(8); see **5.2.4**.
94   *Vale of Glamorgan BC v Palmer* [1984] J.P.L. 334.
95   *R. v Wells Street Metropolitan Stipendiary Magistrate, Ex p. Westminster CC* [1986] 1 W.L.R. 1046; see **19.3.2**.
96   See **5.2.4**.
97   See **19.10**.
98   See **19.4**.
99   P(LBCA)A 1990, s.9(3), applied by s.74(3); see **19.4.2**. [Scotland: P(LBCA)(S)A 1997, s.8(3), applied by s.66(3); NI: P(NI)O 1991, art.44(7), applied by art.55(5).]
1   See **19.4.3**.
2   See **12.6.5**.

relevant, the burden is on the defence to prove that the demolition is in one of those excepted categories, rather than on the prosecution to prove that it is not.

This was confirmed by the Court of Appeal in *R. v Alath Construction*,[3] in relation to the corresponding provision in the Planning Act relating to the need for consent for works to protected trees, which is specifically stated not to apply in certain circumstances.[4] Russell L.J. considered that this was a true exception or exemption,[5] and does not provide an essential ingredient of the offence, so that it was for the defence to prove that it applies.

19.6 Unauthorised works to an ancient monument

19.6.1 Unauthorised works: prosecution under section 2(1)

It is offence under section 2(1) of the Ancient Monuments Act (which applies in England, Wales and Scotland) to execute or cause or permit to be executed to a scheduled monument any of the works specified in section 2(2) without having obtained scheduled monument consent.[6] There are three limbs to this offence, each with its own defences.

As to the general principles regarding the need for the prosecution to prove every element of an offence, and for the proof by the accused of one or more relevant defences, see the discussion above relating to unauthorised works to listed buildings.[7] For examples of a conviction under section 2, see *R. v Bovis Construction Ltd*[8] and *R. v Jackson*,[9] both of which emphasised the importance of establishing the extent of a scheduled monument, and construing carefully the scope of works authorised by a grant of scheduled monument consent.

An offence under section 2(1) is triable either way—that is, in the magistrates' court or in front of a jury.[10] A person found guilty is liable on summary conviction to a fine of up to the "statutory maximum".[11] On conviction on indictment, there is liability to an unlimited fine. See below on sentencing generally; and note that three of the reported decisions of the Court of Appeal on sentencing[12] relate to offences under the 1979 Act.

The corresponding offence in Northern Ireland is under article 3 of the Historic Monuments and Archaeological Objects (NI) Order 1995.

---

[3] [1990] 1 W.L.R. 1255.
[4] See now TCPA 1990, s.198(6) (see **7.6.3** and **19.4.4**).
[5] Unlike the position in *R. v Hunt* [1987] A.C. 352.
[6] AMAAA 1979, s.2(1).
[7] See **19.3** and **19.4**.
[8] [1994] Crim. L. R. 938, CA (Crim); see **6.2.5**.
[9] (1994) unreported; transcript available via Lawtel. See **6.2.5**.
[10] See **19.4.4**.
[11] Currently £5,000: Magistrates' Courts Act 1980, s.32; see **Appendix F**.
[12] *R. v Seymour* [1988] 1 PLR 19, *R. v JO Sims Ltd* (1993) 14 Cr. App. R (S) 213, and *R. v Simpson* (1993) 14 Cr. App. R. (S) 602; see **19.10.1**.

19.6.2 Demolition or destruction of a monument (section 2(2)(a))

The first category of proscribed works is the carrying out of any unauthorised works which result in the demolition or destruction of a monument, or any damage to it.[13] It should be remembered that the definition of a monument includes any part of it, and all or part of its site.[14]

It is a defence to a charge under this first heading to prove:

(1)   that the accused "took all reasonable precautions and exercised all due diligence to avoid or prevent damage to the monument"[15]; or

(2)   that (in the case of a monument in Great Britain) the accused did not know and had no reason to believe:

- that the monument was within the area affected by the works, or
- that it was scheduled.[16]

With regard to the first of these two statutory defences, it does not matter whether the accused knew or intended that the works would have a particular result; all that is necessary is for the prosecution to prove that the accused did actually carry out the works, and that they had the result specified. This avoids defences based on feigned surprise as to the effect of what was done. It also means that, as with listed buildings prosecutions, following the decision of the Court of Appeal in *R. v Sandhu*,[17] the prosecution should not call evidence as to the knowledge or intention of the accused; that would be relevant only to sentencing.

The second of the two statutory defences means that, except in Northern Ireland, the offence is only to a limited extent one of strict liability. However, to avoid a conviction, it is not enough for an accused to show that he or she was unaware that the monument was likely to be affected, or that it was scheduled; it must also be proved (on the balance of probability) that he or she had no reason to believe it was. That may be difficult, unless it can be shown that, for example, the owner of a monument deliberately supplied false information to the contractor who did the damage—in which case, the contractor could escape prosecution but the owner would be liable for prosecution for the works carried out by the contractor as his or her agent.

19.6.3 Other works to a scheduled monument (section 2(2)(b))

The second category of unauthorised works is the carrying out of any unauthorised works for the purpose of removing or repairing a scheduled monument or any part of it, or making any alterations or additions to it.[18]

There is no need (as there is with the corresponding listed buildings offence) for the prosecution to prove that the alteration affected the special character of the

---

[13]   AMAAA 1979, s.2(2)(a). [NI: Historic Monuments and Archaeological Objects (NI) Order, art.4(2)(a).]

[14]   AMAAA 1979, s.61(10). [NI: 1995 Order, art.2(9).]

[15]   AMAAA 1979, s.2(7). [NI: 1995 Order, art.4(7).]

[16]   s.2(8).

[17]   [1997] J.P.L. 141 (see **19.9.6**).

[18]   AMAAA 1979, s.2(2)(b). [NI: 1995 Order, art.4(2)(b).]

monument as one of archaeological or historic interest. And, again, since the "monument" includes its site (see above), the scope of "alterations or additions" must be considerable, although some very minor works will of course be permitted by the general class consent under section 3.[19] Note that there is in this case no specific defence based on lack of knowledge of the scheduled status of the monument; this suggests that this limb of the offence at any rate is one of strict liability.[20]

The essential distinction between sections 2(2)(a) and 2(2)(b) is that the former relates to acts resulting in the total loss of a monument; the latter refers to lesser works, for its alteration. It would often be appropriate to frame a charge in the alternative, by reference to both section 2(2)(a) and section 2(2)(b)).

19.6.4 Flooding and tipping (section 2(2)(c))

The third limb of the offence under section 2(1) or the 1979 Act is the carrying out of unauthorised flooding or tipping operations on land in, on or under which there is a scheduled monument.[21] In this case, there need be no interference with the monument itself, but merely with the land on or under which it is situated.

Here too it is a defence (except in Northern Ireland) to prove that the accused did not know and had no reason to believe that the monument was within the area affected by the works or that it was scheduled.[22]

19.6.5 Breach of a condition on scheduled monument consent

Where the works have been given scheduled monument consent, but are carried out in breach of any condition attached to it, that is a further offence, under section 2(6) of the Ancient Monuments Act. The penalties are as for a charge under section 2(1).[23]

It is a defence to a charge under section 2(6) for the accused to prove that he or she took "all reasonable precautions and exercised all due diligence to avoid contravening the condition".[24]

19.6.6 Defences to charges under section 2

It is of course a defence to a charge under section 2(1) of the Act to prove that the works in question were authorised—that is, that they had received scheduled monument consent from the Secretary of State (or the Department in Northern Ireland) and that they had been carried out in accordance with the terms and conditions of such consent.[25]

---

[19] See **12.8.4**.
[20] Again, for the implications of this, see below.
[21] AMAAA 1979, s.2(2)(c). [NI: 1995 Order, art.4(2)(c).]
[22] AMAAA 1979, s.2(8).
[23] See **19.6.1**.
[24] AMAAA 1979, s.2(6). [NI: 1995 Order, art.4(6).]
[25] AMAAA 1979, s.2(3). [NI: 1995 Order, art.4(3).]

It is also a defence (to a charge under either section 2(1) or section 2(6)) to prove both

- that the works were urgently necessary in the interests of safety and health, and

- that written notice of the need for them was given to the Secretary of State as soon as reasonably practicable.[26]

This is easy to claim after the event, and difficult for the prosecution to disprove, and thus represents an unfortunate loophole which could be exploited by an unscrupulous owner of a monument. It is in fact drafted identically to the corresponding provision in the listed buildings code as it was before being tightened up by the Housing and Planning Act 1986, and should be tightened up as was that provision.[27]

If the unauthorised works constitute serious "damage" to a scheduled monument, it may be preferable to frame a charge under section 28, as this carries a higher maximum sentence.[28] On the other hand, for a charge under section 28 to succeed, the required *mens rea* of intent or recklessness must be proved. Where works are carried out to an ancient monument that is not scheduled, it will not be possible to bring a charge under section 2 of the 1979 Act; instead, the charge will have to be under section 1 of the Criminal Damage Act 1971—which again requires recklessness or intent.

19.6.7 Damaging a protected monument (section 28)

Quite apart from the offence under section 2 of the Ancient Monuments Act, there is a further offence committed, under section 28, by anyone who;

(1) without lawful excuse destroys or damages a protected monument; and:

(2) knows that it is a protected monument; and

(3) either intends to destroy or damage the monument, or is reckless as to whether it would be destroyed or damaged.[29]

This applies to acts done by anyone, including the owner, other than those for which scheduled monument consent has been obtained (or granted by an order under section 3[30]).

A *protected monument* is defined for this purpose as any monument which is either:

(1) a scheduled monument[31]; or

(2) in the ownership or guardianship of the Secretary of State, the Department (in Northern Ireland), English Heritage, or a local authority.[32]

---

[26] AMAAA 1979, s.2(9). [NI: 1995 Order, art.4(8).]
[27] TCPA 1971, s.55(6) (see **19.4.2**).
[28] See **19.6.7**.
[29] AMAAA 1979, s.28(1). [NI: 1995 Order, art.30(1).]
[30] See **12.8.4**.
[31] See **6.2.2**.
[32] See **11.11.6**.

Unlike the offence of damaging a listed building,[33] this is not an offence of strict liability, in that it must be proved that the defendant knew that the monument was protected. On the other hand, it will in many cases be difficult for an accused to prove the absence of such knowledge, especially where there are signs and other evidence. On the other hand, it is not necessary to prove "intent" to carry out the act in question; mere "recklessness" is sufficient. The wording of the offence follows that used in section 1 of the Criminal Damage Act 1971, so that the necessary state of mind is as described by Lord Diplock in *R. v Caldwell*.[34]

A charge of damaging a monument is likely to be considered more seriously by the courts than one of damaging a listed building—and indeed carries higher penalties than one under section 2. It is triable either way (that is, by magistrates or in the Crown Court).[35] It attracts on summary conviction a fine of up to the statutory maximum, or a prison sentence of up to six months, or both. On conviction on indictment, the maximum penalty is an unlimited fine, or imprisonment for up to two years, or both. Where, as a result of such a conviction, a compensation order is made under section 35 of the Powers of Criminal Courts Act 1973, it may in appropriate cases be in favour of the guardian of the monument rather than the owner.[36]

In some cases, it might also be appropriate to consider a charge of attempted damage.[37] This would attract a fine of up to £2,000 or six months' imprisonment.[38]

19.7 Other offences relating to historic buildings and monuments

19.7.1 Using a metal detector in a protected place

Perhaps surprisingly, the most common offence under the Ancient Monuments Act is the unauthorised use of a metal detector in a protected place.[39] A metal detector is defined as "any device designed or adapted for detecting or locating any metal or mineral in the ground", which includes some equipment used by bona fide archaeologists as well as the machines used by amateur treasure hunters. A "protected place" means the site of a scheduled monument[40] or of a monument under the ownership or guardianship of the Secretary of State, English Heritage, or a local authority,[41] or anywhere within an area of archaeological importance designated under Part II of the Act.[42]

Anyone charged with this offence is liable on summary conviction to a fine of up to level 3 on the standard scale.[43] The owner of land may be charged just as

---

[33] See **19.2.3**.
[34] [1982] A.C. 341 at p.354.
[35] AMAAA 1979, s.28(4)
[36] AMAAA 1979, s.29. In Northern Ireland, an order is made under art.14 of the Criminal Justice (NI) Order 1994, in favour of the Department (see 1995 Order, art.31).
[37] Under Criminal Attempts Act 1981, s.1(1).
[38] 1981 Act, s.4(1)(c).
[39] AMAAA 1979, s.42(1).
[40] See **6.2.2**.
[41] See **11.6**.
[42] See **6.4**.
[43] AMAAA 1979, s.42(1). [£200 ???]

much as anyone else. The mere possession, as opposed to the use, of a metal detector at a protected site might be triable either as an offence of attempt[44] or as one of possessing an article for use to damage property.[45]

In Northern Ireland, it is an offence simply to possess, without authorisation, any "detecting device" (not just a metal detector) in a protected place, whether or not it is used.[46] The penalty is a fine of up to level 4 on the standard scale.

The real problem, however, is not the use of a metal detector but the subsequent removal from the site of any objects discovered as a result of its use. Accordingly it is a more serious offence to remove from a protected place, without consent, any object of archaeological or historic interest—note: not "special" interest— discovered with the use of a metal detector (or any detecting device in Northern Ireland).[47] This is triable either way, and attracts on summary conviction a fine of up to the statutory maximum[48] and, on conviction on indictment, an unlimited fine. Alternatively, dealing in such objects may be the subject of a conviction under the Dealing in Cultural Objects (Offences) Act 2003.[49]

Consent—either for the use of a detector or for the removal from the site of anything discovered—must be obtained from English Heritage, the Welsh Assembly (Cadw), the Scottish Ministers (Historic Scotland) or the Heritage Service in Northern Ireland. It normally takes the form of a licence, which will be subject to conditions; and a failure to comply with a condition is an offence attracting the same maximum penalty as the failure to obtain consent altogether.[50]

It is a defence to proceedings under section 42 to prove:

(1)   that the metal detector was being used for purposes other than to locate objects of archaeological or historic interest; or

(2)   that the accused had taken all reasonable steps to discover whether the site was a protected place, and as a result did not believe that it was.[51]

19.7.2 Searching for archaeological objects

In Northern Ireland, Part III of the Historic Monuments and Archaeological Objects Order 1995 makes it a summary offence to search for archaeological objects anywhere (not just at a site of archaeological interest), without a licence from the Department.[52] The maximum penalty is a fine of level 3 on the standard scale. If a licence is obtained from the Department for such searching, it does not authorise entry onto private land, so the consent of the owner is still required.[53]

---

[44]   Under Criminal Attempts Act 1981, s.1(1).
[45]   Criminal Damage Act 1971, s.3(a).
[46]   Historic Monuments and Archaeological Objects (NI) Order 1995, art.29(1).
[47]   AMAAA 1979, s.42(3). [NI : 1995 Order, art.29(3).]
[48]   See **Appendix F**.
[49]   See **19.7.3**.
[50]   AMAAA 1979, s.42(4),(5). [NI: 1995 Order, art.29(4),(5).]
[51]   AMAAA 1979, s.42(6),(7). [NI: 1995 Order, art.29(6).]
[52]   1995 Order, art.41(1).
[53]   1995 Order, art.41(3).

Anything that is found must be reported within 14 days to the Director of the Ulster Museum, the Department, or the local police.[54] It must then not be passed on to anyone else for a further period of three months without consent.

A conviction for any breach of these requirements attracts a fine of up to level 3 on the standard scale.

There is no corresponding provision elsewhere in the United Kingdom.

19.7.3 Dealing in cultural objects

Architectural theft—that is, the removal of and trade in objects of interest (fireplaces, panelling, stone carvings, etc) from historic buildings—is a growing problem. This led recently to the enactment of the Dealing in Cultural Objects (Offences) Act 2003. By virtue of section 1 of the Act, which extends only to England and Wales, it is an offence to deal in a tainted cultural object.

A "cultural object" is any object of historical, architectural or archaeological interest—whether or not the person dealing in it knows or believes it to be of any interest at all. The test is thus presumably an objective one, as to which it would be necessary to call appropriate evidence if the point were to be challenged. A cultural object is "tainted" if:

- it has been removed after December 30, 2003 from a building, structure or monument[55] of historical, architectural or archaeological interest, either in the United Kingdom or elsewhere, or has been excavated;

- if the removal was from a building or structure, as opposed to a monument, the object at one time formed part of it (not necessarily immediately prior to the removal); and

- the removal or excavation constituted at the time a criminal offence, under either UK or foreign law.[56]

To deal with an object is to buy, hire, borrow, accept, sell let on hire, lend, give, import or export it, or to agree with someone else or to make an arrangement for any of those things to be done (whether in the UK or elsewhere).[57] And where an offence is committed by a body corporate, but with the consent or connivance of a senior officer or member of the body, or due to the neglect of such a person, both the body and the person are liable to be prosecuted.[58]

In practice, therefore, an offence under the 2003 Act is committed not when the object in question is first removed from the building or monument, but when, following such removal, it is sold, given or lent to someone else—or exported —either the first such disposal, or any subsequent one. But for a conviction to succeed, it is not enough to show that the object was initially removed without

[54] 1995 Order, art.42(1).
[55] A monument for these purposes has the same definition as in AMAAA 1979, s.61(7) save that it does not exclude a building or structure—but that is purely because buildings and structures are included in any event.
[56] 2003 Act, s.2.
[57] 2003 Act, s.3.
[58] 2003 Act, s.5.

consent; it must be shown that the subsequent disposal was "dishonest": that is, for example, that the person disposing of the object concealed its true provenance, or represented that the necessary consent had been obtained.

The penalties for the offence under section 1 are on summary conviction a fine of up to the statutory maximum, or a term of imprisonment of up to six months; on conviction on indictment (in the Crown Court) an unlimited fine or imprisonment for up to seven years—a longer maximum term than for demolishing a building or monument outright.[59] Where the offence involves the export or import of such objects, the prosecution can be brought by the Revenue and Customs[60]; otherwise, it is likely to be brought by English Heritage or, possibly, local authorities.

The result of this Act is that it will now be possible to prosecute those dealing in, for example, fireplaces, panelling, sculpture and other objects that previously formed art of a listed building and which were removed without listed building consent; also objects found on archaeological sites with the use of an unlicensed metal detector. And if a register is prepared of objects known to have been illegally removed from historic buildings and monuments, and circulated to dealers, they will be fixed with notice that the objects are tainted, and thus will hopefully decline to deal with them—so increasing the difficulty of disposing of such items.

19.8 Unauthorised advertising

It has already been noted that the display of unsuitable signs and advertisements may have a significant impact on historic buildings, areas and monuments and their settings; planning authorities are accordingly able to maintain detailed control over such displays, under the Control of Advertisements Regulations.[61]

In practice, many advertisements are displayed without consent. Lack of space precludes a detailed analysis of all of the options available to planning authorities to bring about their removal; but, in short, it is an offence to display an advertisement in contravention of the Regulations, under section 224(3) of the Planning Act. This is a summary offence, attracting a maximum penalty of a fine of up to level 4 on the standard scale for displays in England and Wales (recently increased from level 3, which still applies to displays in Scotland and Northern Ireland).[62] This penalty is still low in comparison to the rewards that may be obtained from display of advertisements at a prime location; although note that the display of a series of advertisements at a single site constitutes a series of offences, not a single offence.[63]

---

[59] 2003 Act, s.1(3).
[60] 2003 Act, s.4.
[61] See **12.2.6, 12.9**.
[62] Maximum fine in England and Wales increased by Anti-Social Behaviour Act 2003, s.53; increase in Northern Ireland to be introduced by Planning Reform (Northern Ireland) Order 2006. See **Appendix F** for current levels.
[63] *Kingston-upon-Thames RBC v National Solus Sites* [1994] J.P.L. 251.

The decision to prosecute is not limited to cases where it is in the interests of amenity and public safety[64]—although it is difficult to imagine any other motive. It is an abuse of process to bring, or continue, a prosecution where the defendants have acted on the basis of an assurance by the authority's officers that no consent was required for the display of the advertisement in question.[65]

An advertisement is deemed to be displayed by the owner and occupier of the land on which it is, and by the person whose goods or services are being advertised—as well as, obviously, by the poster contractor.[66] All may therefore be prosecuted in an appropriate case. However, a person who is only deemed to be displaying an advertisement by virtue of this provision cannot be convicted of an offence under section 224(3) (in England or Wales) if he or she is able to show either:

- that the display was without his or her knowledge, or

- that he or she had taken all reasonable steps to prevent or remove the display.[67]

This follows the ruling of the Divisional Court in *Preston v BUAV*,[68] but overturns its later, reluctant conclusion (in *Wycombe DC v Michael Shanly Group Ltd*[69]) that it was sufficient for a defendant to prove simply that he or she had withheld consent for a display—although it would seem that the latter still applies in Scotland and Northern Ireland).

It is for the defence to prove the existence of consent—either deemed consent under the Regulations[70] or express consent—not for the prosecution to prove the absence of consent.[71] Nor is it possible to rely on the 10-year time limit relating to breaches of planning control, since a breach of the 1992 Advertisements Regulations is not of itself a "breach of planning control", the Regulations are designed to provide a complete, self-contained code of control.[72]

If, following a conviction, the offending advertisement is not removed, a further offence will have been committed, attracting for each day that the offence continues a fine of one-tenth of level 4 (in England, Wales or Northern Ireland)[73] or one-tenth of level 3 (in Scotland).[74] A prosecution for this offence can be brought even where an appeal against the initial conviction is pending—although if the

---

[64] *Kingsley v Hammersmith & Fulham LBC* (1991) 62 P. & C.R. 589; more recently, see *Butler v Derby City Council* (November 22, 2005, unreported; transcript available via Lawtel).

[65] *Postermobile PLC v Brent LBC* (1997), *The Times*, December 8.

[66] TCPA 1990, s.224(5). [Scotland: TCP(S)A 1997, s.186(4); NI: P(NI)O 1991, art.84(3).]

[67] TCPA 1990, s.224(6), inserted by Clean Neighbourhoods and Environment Act 2005, s.33 (England and Wales only).

[68] (1985), *The Times*, July 24.

[69] [1994] 1 E.G.L.R. 200, DC, following *Merton LBC v Edmonds* (1993), *The Times*, July 6.

[70] See **12.9.4**.

[71] *O'Brien v Hertsmere DC* (1997) 74 P. & C.R. 264, following *R. v Edwards* [1975] Q.B. 27. and see **19.4.1**.

[72] *Torridge DC v Jarrad* (1998), *The Times*, April 13.

[73] TCPA 1990, s.224(3), amended by Anti-Social Behaviour Act 2003, s.53. [NI: P(NI)O 1991, art.84(2), to be amended by Planning Reform (NI) Order 2006.]

[74] TCP(S)A 1997, s.186(3).

initial; conviction is subsequently overturned, the subsequent one would fall with it.[75] This does not apply, however, where the unauthorised advertisement is removed following a prosecution, and later replaced after a break.[76]

Where a prosecution fails, due to the defence being able to prove the existence of deemed consent, it is possible for the planning authority to serve a discontinuance notice bringing to an end the consent. Unless the notice is overturned (on appeal to the Secretary of State), it is then possible for the authority to institute new proceedings against the same advertiser.[77]

19.9 Procedure

19.9.1 Initial investigation

Anyone is entitled to bring a prosecution in respect of unauthorised works to a listed building. And some of the most effective prosecutions have been by amenity groups such as the Society for the Protection of Ancient Buildings.

However, in practice, of the relatively few prosecutions that have been brought, the great majority have been by planning authorities. An authority is likely to become aware of the carrying out of apparently unauthorised works as a result of a complaint by a neighbouring resident, passer-by, or amenity group; or it may be one of its own officers or councillors who makes the discovery. The cooperation of the local planning authority, and possibly of English Heritage, would in any event be invaluable to any other body (or individual) contemplating a prosecution.

Sometimes the informer (or council officer) will actually see the works taking place, and who is carrying them out. In that case, he or she should take photographs if at all possible, and prepare and sign a written statement promptly (within a few days), before the recollection of what was seen has faded. If there is eventually a prosecution, it will then be possible for the maker of such a statement to use it in court to refresh his or her memory. Any photographs taken should be retained by the authority, along with a note of who took them, and when, and who processed them. Clearly, the evidence of someone who was present and saw what occurred will be very helpful if the authority is to secure a conviction.

The usual practice is for a full record of events to be made contemporaneously in a notebook (referred to as a "memory refreshing document"). A signed statement[78] can then be prepared if and when a prosecution is instituted.

Where possible, anyone who seems to be responsible for the carrying out the works, or associated with them in any way—such as the owner and/or occupier of the land, and any contractors involved—should be briefly interviewed to establish what is going on. This will assist the authority to decide subsequently whether to mount a prosecution, but it will also enable the person responsible to point to any defence which seems to be relevant—such as, that the building was dangerous, or that the works had in fact been permitted. Thus it may well be that it quickly

---

[75] *O'Brien v Hertsmere DC* (1998) 76 P. & C.R. 441.
[76] *Kensington and Chelsea RBC v Elmton* [1978] 1 E.G.L.R. 147, DC.
[77] *O'Brien v Croydon LBC* (1998) 77 P. & C.R. 126.
[78] Under Criminal Justice Act 1967, s.9.

becomes clear that no offence has been committed, and the matter can be allowed to drop without further ado. Alternatively such an interview may enable the authority officer to take photographs and other evidence.

However, care must be used in talking to people who may have committed a criminal offence. Those likely to be in the position of conducting such interviews should read the code issued by the Home Secretary under the Police and Criminal Evidence Act (PACE) 1984, entitled *Code C: The Detention, Treatment and Questioning of Persons by Police Officers*[79]—before the problem arises, since there may be no time to read it then. In spite of its name, the Code applies to officers of a local authority investigating possible offences just as much as it does to police officers;[80] and a copy of the Code should be readily available at the authority's offices, for consultation by all concerned.[81] In particular, persons under suspicion must be cautioned that they do not have to say anything, but that anything that is said may later be used in court;[82] further, they must be given a chance to obtain legal advice if they wish.

In practice, if a prosecution does take place, a conversation at the site may provide useful evidence, but it should have been recorded in a notebook, signed both by the suspect and by the officer—and of course it must have been under caution. From the point of view of the suspect, such a conversation by-passes the safeguards provided by a taped interview, and is therefore discouraged by the Code. After a relatively brief interview at the site, any further conversations are likely to take place at the authority's premises.

In some cases, the incident will only come to light after the works have been completed. The same principles still apply—as much information as possible must be gathered as soon as possible, and recorded accurately. In some such cases, the person who carried out the works may be willing to admit having done so, possibly with qualifications ("I carried out the works because I was told the building was unsafe"). In the event of subsequent court proceedings, such a statement, referred to as a "confession" under the terms of PACE, may be the best evidence available to the prosecuting authority; it follows that it is vital that the caution must be administered right at the start of any interview, otherwise the confession will be inadmissible.

Others willing to give evidence (neighbours and so on) should also be interviewed as soon as possible, so as to enable the authority to make an informed decision as to whether to prosecute. Such people should also be kept informed of the progress of the prosecution.

Finally, it may be noted that the 1990 Act provides rights for officers of the local planning authority to enter land to ascertain whether an offence has been

---

[79] Available in the Home Office publication *Police and Criminal Evidence Act 1984 (section 66): Codes of Practice*, available from the Stationery Office. Note that revised Codes of Practice (available on the Home Office website) were issued for consultation in 2002.

[80] Police and Criminal Evidence Act 1984, s.67(9).

[81] Code C, para.1.2.

[82] See s.10 of the Code on cautions generally, and in particular para.10.4 as to the wording of the caution to be given.

committed; these are identical to the rights that exist where a building is initially being considered for listing.[83]

19.9.2 *The decision to prosecute*

In principle, the first question to be asked is whether, in relation to a particular act or series of acts carried out to a protected building or structure, it appears that all of the ingredients of one of the relevant offences under can be proved.[84] If they can, and if none of the relevant exemptions or defences seem to apply, it is in principle possible to mount a prosecution of those responsible. However, merely because works have taken place to a protected building without the necessary consent does not of course mean that those responsible must inevitably be prosecuted.

For example, it may well be inappropriate for a planning authority to prosecute where consent would have been readily forthcoming had it been sought, or where the works carried out differed only marginally from those for which consent had already been permitted. In such a case, it is true that consent should have been sought; but the failure to have done so would not be a major wrong, and would only rarely deserve a criminal penalty; it would usually be more appropriate for the authority either to invite the submission of a retrospective application (in the case of works to a listed building or in a conservation area) or to take no further action.

And it may not be appropriate to prosecute a householder who was genuinely ignorant of the existence of the need for consent, or someone who believed, perhaps wrongly, that one of the exemptions applied.[85] It has also been recently held—in the context of the Advertisements Regulations (see above)—that it is an abuse of process to bring, or continue, a prosecution where the defendants have acted on the basis of an assurance by the authority's offices that no consent was required for the works in question.[86]

Nor should it be forgotten that it is possible in some cases to take enforcement action, requiring the effect of the unauthorised works to be reversed.[87] This may be a sufficient response to the works—and may negate any gain achieved by those who carried them out. On the other hand, where an important building has been cynically demolished in order to facilitate a development scheme, there is no possibility of achieving a restitution, and little point in seeking a replacement in facsimile, prosecution may be more appropriate.

The Code for Crown Prosecutors, issued by the Director of Public Prosecutions under section 10 of the Prosecution of Offences Act 1985, sets out a two stage test in considering whether to mount a prosecution. The first question to be asked is

---

[83] P(LBCA)A 1990, ss 88 to 88B (especially s.88(2)(c)); see **3.3.1**. [Scotland: P(LBCA)(S)A 1997, ss 76 to 78 (especially s.76(2)(b); NI: P(NI)O 1991, art.121(1)(c)(i)).

[84] See **19.3** to **19.6**.

[85] See **12.6.5**, **12.8.4**, **12.9.4**.

[86] *Postermobile P.L.C v Brent LBC* (1997) *The Times*, December 8.

[87] See **Chapter 8**, particularly **18.2.1**.

whether there is sufficient evidence available to provide a "realistic prospect of conviction".[88] Since the decision of the Court of Appeal in *R. v Sandhu*,[88a] it is clear that relatively little evidence has to be brought to secure a conviction, so that mounting a successful prosecution should—at least in theory—be relatively straightforward.

However, even if there is sufficient evidence to secure a conviction, the prosecutor must then go on to ask whether a prosecution would be in the public interest. Among the factors listed militating against prosecution are the following:

"(a) the court is likely to impose a nominal penalty; . . .
(c) the offence was committed as a result of a genuine mistake or misunderstanding (these factors must be balanced against the seriousness of the offence);
(d) the loss or harm can be described as minor and was the result of a single incident, particularly if it was caused by a misjudgement;
(e) there has been a long delay between the offence taking place and the date of the trial, unless:

- the offence is serious;
- the delay has been caused in part by the defendant;
- the offence has only recently come to light; or
- the complexity of the offence has meant that there has been a long investigation; . . .

(h) the defendant has put right the loss or harm that was caused. . . ."[89]

The same principles would presumably apply to a prosecution by a local authority or other enforcement agency. And it should be borne in mind that, whereas a well-publicised successful prosecution may be useful to deter others from breaching orders, equally a well-publicised acquittal may be distinctly unhelpful.

19.9.3 Who should be prosecuted

Thought needs to be given as to who should be prosecuted. In a typical case of unauthorised works having been carried out to a listed building, bearing in mind the position already explained as to prosecuting those who aid and abet the commission of an offence,[90] it may in principle possible to prosecute the owner of the building, the contractors and sub-contractors involved, and any of the professionals (architect, surveyor, project manager etc).

However, it would probably be best practice to single out those actually responsible—and, possibly, those who are likely to re-offend. Thus, where an autocratic owner orders a timid contractor to demolish a building, the owner should be prosecuted and the contractor warned not to offend again. But where a bullish salesman persuades a gullible householder to install new windows without consent, the glazing company should be prosecuted, and the householder served with a copy of an enforcement notice—the cost and inconvenience of having a further set of windows installed will be punishment enough.

---

[88] Code for Crown Prosecutors, s.5. The current Code, the current (fifth) edition of which was issued in 2004, is available (in nine languages) on the CPS website (*www.cps.gov.uk*).
[88a] [1997] J.P.L. 141 (see **19.9.6**).
[89] Code for Crown Prosecutors, para.5.10.
[90] See **19.3.5**.

19.9.4 Procedure before the trial: offences triable either way

The more serious of the offences noted above are "triable either way"—that is, either by the magistrates or by a jury in the Crown Court. The procedure in these cases will generally be as for any other criminal trial brought by a local authority in relation to an either-way offence. This applies to the offences listed in Part 1 of **Figure 19.1**, including in particular:

- carrying out unauthorised works to a listed building, a building subject to a building preservation notice, or a scheduled monument;

- unauthorised demolition of a building in a conservation area;

- damaging a protected monument; and

- in England and Wales only, dealing with a tainted cultural object.

The first stage of the prosecution in such cases will be that an information will be laid before the relevant magistrates, setting out the bare bones of what the accused is alleged to have done. Sample informations are at **Form D22** in **Appendix D**. There is no time-limit for laying an information for an either-way offence, but it may be considered oppressive if a prosecution is brought too long after an alleged offence, in the absence of any reason justifying such a delay.

Difficulties may arise where a substantial programme of unauthorised works were carried out. It may or may not be appropriate to charge them all together as one offence, depending on the circumstances. The general rule was explained as follows in *DPP v Merriman*:

"When two or more acts of a similar nature committed by one defendant are connected with one another in the time or place of their commission, or by their common purpose, in such a way that they can be fairly be regarded as forming part of the same transaction or criminal enterprise, they can be charged as one offence in a single indictment."[91]

For example, in *Cullen v Jardine*,[92] it was held that an information charging the unlawful felling of 90 trees (in contravention of the Forestry Act 1967) was not bad for duplicity even though the felling had occurred over three days. It is likely that more than one count will be preferable where different considerations apply—for example, where some works were definitely unauthorised, but others were at least arguably the subject of consent; or where some alterations to a building undoubtedly affected its character, but others were more marginal.

There will then be a "plea before venue" hearing at the magistrates' court, at which the accused will be asked to indicate his or her likely plea. If the accused pleads guilty, the magistrates proceed as they would following a guilty plea at a summary trial; and in practice they will proceed to sentencing unless they feel that their powers of sentence are inadequate.

If the accused pleads not guilty, the prosecution and the defence will be invited to make representations as to the appropriate mode of trial—by magistrates or in the Crown Court—and the magistrates will then state their opinion. In reaching

---

[91] [1973] A.C. 584, HL, at p.607.
[92] [1985] Crim. L.R., 668, *The Times*, April 29. And see *R. v Wilson* (1979) 69 Cr. App. R. 83.

their decision, they will be guided by the general principles laid down in the *Mode of Trial Guidelines*, issued in 1995,[93] which include the following:

"...(d) where cases involve complex questions of fact or difficult questions of law, the court should consider [transfer] for trial; ...

(f) in general, except where otherwise stated, either-way offences should be tried summarily unless the court considers that the particular case has one or more of the features set out in the following pages and that its sentencing powers are insufficient;

(g) the court should also consider its powers to commit an offender for sentence,[94] if information emerges during the course of the hearing which leads them to conclude that the offence is so serious ... that their powers to sentence him are inadequate."

The first of these is likely to be relevant where, as will sometimes be the case, the magistrates are unfamiliar with offences of this kind.

As to the second and third, all four of the above offences carry a higher maximum sentence on conviction in the Crown Court than in the magistrates' courts. The general tenor of the advice is nevertheless that either-way offences should be tried by magistrates; and experience suggests that such an approach is correct in relation to offences of this kind. There is in any event a right of appeal from the decision of the magistrates to the Crown Court, against a guilty verdict or sentence.[95]

If all concerned agree to a summary trial, that will then take place in the normal way.

However, the accused is always entitled to a jury trial if he or she wishes it.[96] If that is the choice, or if the magistrates decide that it is the most appropriate, the authority will then prefer a bill of indictment (on similar lines to the information), and the matter will proceed to the Crown Court. There will then be a brief plea and directions hearing (PDH)[97]; and, where appropriate, any preliminary points of law can be dealt with at a separate pre-trial hearing.[98] Thereafter, the trial will proceed as any other jury trial.

19.9.5 Procedure: offences triable only in the magistrates' court

Less serious offences, known as "summary only offences", can be tried only by the magistrates. In the present context, this applies to the offences listed in Part 2 of **Figure 19.1**, including:

- damaging a listed building;

- unauthorised use of a metal detector in a protected place;

---

[93] Unreported, but quoted at Blackstone, *Criminal Practice*, D3.7, and *Archbold*, 2005, para.1–40; similar (although by no means identical) to those issued five years earlier, reported at [1990] 1 W.L.R. 216.

[94] Now under Powers of the Criminal Court (Sentencing) Act 2000, s.3.

[95] See **19.11**.

[96] At least for the moment.

[97] See the rules in *Practice Direction: Crown Court (Plea and Directions Hearings)* [1995] 1 W.L.R. 1318; and the judge's questionnaire annexed to them.

[98] Under the Criminal Procedure and Investigations Act 1996, s.40.

- in Northern Ireland, unlicensed searching for archaeological objects; and

- unauthorised display of advertisements.

The trial in such cases will be as for any other summary trial, with an automatic right of appeal to the Crown Court or, by way of case stated, to the Divisional Court.

Perhaps the most significant procedural point to be highlighted is that the information[99] must be laid within six months of the date on which the offence was committed.

19.9.6 Evidence

It is essential for a body mounting a prosecution under these provisions to ensure that the required evidence is available. Conversely, anyone wishing to avoid a conviction must know what case the prosecution has to establish, if he or she is to be able successfully to discredit it, and to call evidence accordingly. Reference should be made to the discussion above as to the elements of each of the various relevant offences, and what needs to be proved—and by whom. It is thus vital to remember that the prosecution must prove all of the elements of the offence in question, each beyond reasonable doubt, if it is to achieve a conviction.

In particular, it is improper for magistrates or members of the jury to use their own experience to fill in gaps in the evidence—so, for example, where there is no evidence as to whether works were carried out before or after a building was listed, it is not open to the magistrates to simply guess on the basis of their own knowledge of having seen the building in question at various dates.[1]

In a trial for an offence of this kind, it is worthwhile for the parties to agree as much as possible in advance, by way of "formal admissions"[2]—it makes life easier for them, and also pleases magistrates and judges by expediting the progress of the trial. This may apply to, for example, details such as the identity of the owner and occupier of the property in question; the details of the works carried out (date and time, and extent); and any other factual details not in dispute. This will enable the trial to concentrate on the issues that are not agreed—such as whether the works affected the character of the building; or whether they were included in the scope of those for which consent had been given.

Where matters are not agreed, evidence will have to be called by each side. Deciding what evidence to call will obviously be a matter of judgment in each case; but it is important that, in relation to matters other than pure fact, those giving evidence are appropriately qualified. Thus, for example, where the issue in question is whether particular works affected the character of the building, it will be necessary to call a witness with specialist knowledge of the type of building in question, and experience of other similar cases, rather than merely any architect or surveyor. But if the issue is the structural stability of a building following partial loss by fire, the witness should be a building surveyor or engineer (rather than a town planner). In either case, they must have seen the building and be able

---

[99] See **19.9.4**.
[1] *Carter v Eastbourne BC* [2000] 2 P.L.R. 60.
[2] See Criminal Evidence Act 1967, s.10.

to talk confidently and knowledgeably—it is no good a building control officer or engineer giving evidence, solely on the basis of some blurred photographs, about the condition of a building demolished some while ago.

Finally, the one category of evidence that should *not* be produced, at least until after conviction, is any evidence as to the motives or knowledge of the accused. Such material will be inadmissible, and may render any conviction liable to be quashed. Thus, in *R. v Sandhu*, the Court of Appeal overturned the conviction of the appellant, for carrying out unauthorised alterations to Hainhault Hall in Essex (Grade II listed), as the trial judge in the Crown Court had allowed the prosecution to lead evidence to the effect that the accused had been clearly warned both by the local authority and by his own surveyor as to what he could or could not do. The Court of Appeal held that such evidence was relevant as to sentencing, but not as to liability:

"evidence should not have been admitted to prove matters not relevant to establish the charges but which were simply likely to prejudice the jury's mind against the appellant."[3]

This means that particular caution must be exercised in leading evidence—thus, key questions are "were the works carried out in such a way as to affect the character of the building?" and "were they authorised?", not whether (in either case) the defendant knew or thought they were. Note, however, that such evidence may be very relevant when it comes to sentencing.[4]

19.10 Sentencing

19.10.1 General principles

The starting point is the statutory provision relating to each of the relevant offences, which lays down the maximum penalty in the event of conviction. This has already been noted above, but in summary the maxima are as shown in **Figure 19.1**.

The principles on which the correct fine should be assessed have been considered in a number of guideline cases in the Court of Appeal, Criminal Division—both those relating directly to listed buildings and scheduled monuments and those relating to the analogous legislation relating to protected trees. These are perhaps at least as significant in practice as the statutory maxima, and are of course in addition to those which will be potentially relevant in all criminal cases, such as the means of the defendant,[5] his or her previous record (so far as relevant), any guilty plea, and the extent of the defence's co-operation with the prosecution.

Thus, in *R. v Seymour*,[6] following a conviction for damage to a scheduled monument,[7] the Court of Appeal (Criminal Division) reduced the fine from £10,000 to £3,000, considering:

---

[3] *R. v Sandhu* [1997] J.P.L. 853.
[4] See **19.10.4**.
[5] Powers of the Criminal Court (Sentencing) Act 2000, s.128; *R. v Duckworth*, (1995) 16 Cr. App. R. (S) 529, at p.531; *R. v Browning* [1996] 1 P.L.R. 61, CA.
[6] [1988] 1 P.L.R. 19, (1988) 9 Cr. App. R. (S) 395.
[7] Under AMAAA 1979, s.2(1).

Table 19.1 Maximum penalties for criminal offences

Offence	Statutory provision (Great Britain[8])	Maximum penalty on summary conviction	Maximum penalty on indictment
1. Triable either way offences			
Unauthorised works to a listed building	Listed Buildings Act, s.9; Scottish Listed Buildings Act, s.8	Fine of £20,000 (£30,000 in Northern Ireland) or 6 months imprisonment	Unlimited fine or 2 years imprisonment
Unauthorised works to a building subject to a building preservation notice	Listed Buildings Act, s.9, as applied by s.3(5); Scottish Listed Buildings Act, applied by s.3(5)	Fine of £20,000 (£30,000 in Northern Ireland) or 6 months imprisonment	Unlimited fine or 2 years imprisonment
Unauthorised demolition of a building in a conservation area	Listed Buildings Act, s.9, as applied by s.74(3); Scottish Listed Buildings Act, s.9, applied by s.66(3)	Fine of £20,000 (£30,000 in Northern Ireland) or 6 months imprisonment	Unlimited fine or 2 years imprisonment
Damaging a protected monument	Ancient Monuments Act, s.28	Fine of statutory maximum, or 6 months imprisonment	Unlimited fine, or 2 years imprisonment
Unauthorised works to a scheduled monument	Ancient Monuments Act, s.2	Fine of statutory maximum (currently £2,000)	Unlimited fine
Unlicensed removal of object found with metal detector	Ancient Monuments Act, s.42(3)	Fine of statutory maximum	Unlimited fine
Dealing with a tainted cultural object *(England and Wales only)*	Dealing in Cultural Objects (Offences) Act 2003, s.1	Fine of statutory maximum, or 6 months imprisonment	Unlimited fine, or 7 years imprisonment
2. Summary only offences			
Damage to a listed building	Listed Buildings Act, s.59	Fine of Level 3 (currently £1,000).	...
Unauthorised use of a metal detector in a protected place	Ancient Monuments Act, s.42	Fine of Level 3 (currently £1,000).	...
Unlicensed searching for archaeological objects *(NI only)*	Historic Monuments and Archaeological Objects Order 1995, art 41	Fine of Level 3	...
Unauthorised display of advertisements	Planning Act 1990, s.224; Scottish Planning Act, s.186	Fine of Level 4 (currently £2,500) (Level 3 in Scotland and NI)	...

[8] For statutory provisions in Northern Ireland, see the relevant section earlier in this chapter.

"we have to do the best we can and relate the fine, so far as is practicable to do so, to the status and resources of the appellant, so that it is in fact a penalty and not something derisory, but at the same time reflects the fact that this was not a deliberate and conscious assault upon our national heritage but was due to a misunderstanding or, perhaps more accurately, a failure to take adequate advice in time".[9]

R. v JO Sims Ltd, a further decision under the Ancient Monuments Act, related to the destruction of Winchester Palace, an important monument on the south bank of the River Thames in London.[10] The defendant had carried out building works which had destroyed some of the remains of the Palace, in circumstances which showed clearly that it had been negligent. As against that, it had pleaded guilty; it had stopped work as soon as it realised the problem; and it had as a result made a substantial loss from being unable to let the new office accommodation it had hoped to complete. The fine of £75,000 imposed by the Crown Court was around 75 per cent of its annual profits. It was accordingly reduced on appeal to £15,000. A similar approach was adopted by the Court of Appeal in *R. v Simpson*, reducing fines for the negligent damage to a Roman fort from £33,000 to £15,000.[11]

These last two decisions, and the earlier decisions referred to in them, were considered by the Court of Appeal in the guideline case of *R. v Duckworth*.[12] This related to the demolition without consent of parts of Dowles Manor, near Bewdley. An additional charge, of demolishing the first floor, was dismissed by the jury, but they found the defendant guilty of demolishing the ground floor. The Court indicated that the factors that should guide courts in arriving at an appropriate sentence in a case of this kind are as follows:

(1)   the degree of damage to the historic structure;

(2)   the degree of financial gain that the defendant has attempted to achieve; and

(3)   most importantly, the degree of culpability.

Each of these is considered in turn.

19.10.2 *The degree of damage to the historic structure*

Both the Court of Appeal in *Duckworth*[13] and the Sentencing Advisory Panel, in its recent advice to the Court of Appeal on sentencing for environmental offences,[14] have accepted that the extent of the damage will be a relevant factor. This involves two matters—the importance of the structure being damaged (for example, is it a Grade I building, or a structure in the curtilage of a Grade II building?); and the significance of the damage (total demolition, or the removal of a door handle?).

[9]   p.24.
[10]   (1993) 14 Cr. App. R. (S) 213.
[11]   (1993) 14 Cr. App. R. (S) 602.
[12]   (1995) 16 Cr. App. R. (S) 529.
[13]   (1995) 16 Cr. App. R. (S) 529.
[14]   Under Crime and Disorder Act 1998, s.81(3). See *www.sentencing-advisory-panel.gov.uk*.

In the relatively rare case of a building being totally demolished, or a monument totally destroyed, only the first of these will be relevant. But where the unauthorised works are something less—alteration or extension—both need to be considered together. It may also be relevant to establish what enforcement action, if any, is contemplated (or has already taken place), so as to understand the true impact of the offending alterations.

Further, although a challenge to the validity of the listing, conservation area designation or scheduling cannot be raised as a defence to a prosecution, evidence as to the poor quality of what has been lost (or altered) may be raised as a mitigating factor to secure a lower sentence. On the other hand, a court might take the view that even if, for example, the building that had been altered was of little merit when first listed, or had been substantially altered since then, the right course of action by the landowner would have been to seek consent for works to it, if necessary from the Secretary of State on appeal, rather than simply to carry them out regardless; and that a reduction in sentence may therefore not be appropriate.

19.10.3 The benefit accruing from the offence

Section 9(5) of the Listed Buildings Act specifically provides that, in passing sentence, the court must in particular "have regard to any financial benefit which has accrued or appears likely to accrue to [a person convicted] in consequence of the offence".[15]

Logically, if the court is to have proper regard to the financial benefit accruing to the defendant, the sentence should in most cases be no less than that benefit—even if that means a fine that is in hundreds of thousands of pounds in extreme cases. Thus if, in the circumstances of the *John Walker* case,[16] the building had been illegally demolished, the benefit accruing would have been £1.5 million—at 1973 prices. A fine of a few thousand pounds would thus not have been a great deterrent. However, such large fines are not encountered in practice.

Nevertheless, it may be appropriate for cases involving a substantial financial benefit to be sent to the Crown Court for sentencing. This occurred, for example, in the case of the recent demolition of Greenside, even though the actual fine imposed by the Crown Court was less than £20,000.

The Sentencing Advisory Panel summarised the position as follows:

"As a general principle, individuals and companies should not profit from their offences. It is important that the sentence takes account of any economic gain achieved by the offender to take appropriate precautions; it should not be cheaper to offend than to prevent the commission of an offence."[17]

---

[15] P(LBCA)A 1990, s.9(5), amended by PCA 1991, Sch.3, para.1. Since 199, this has applied both to the magistrates and to the Crown Court. [Scotland: P(LBCA)(S)A 1997, s.8(5); NI: P(NI)O 1991, art.44(6), substituted by Planning (Amendment) (NI) Order 2003, art.13.]

[16] See **3.3.1**.

[17] *Environmental Offences: The Sentencing Advisory Panel's Advice to the Court of Appeal*, March 1, 2000, para.16.

The offences being considered by the panel, such as air or water pollution, are perhaps generally more serious than offences relating to historic buildings and structures; but the underlying approach would seem to be equally valid in relation to such offences.

In this context, too, it will be important to establish in any case whether the planning authority will be taking enforcement action, requiring the damage to be undone, and whether any such requirement will be challenged. So, for example, if a building has been demolished, and is not going to be replaced, with the result that access can now be obtained to a development site which is thus worth many hundreds of thousands of pounds, that should lead to a very substantial fine. If on the other hand a building has been altered by the insertion of new doors and windows, which will now have to be replaced, and perhaps have already been replaced, there may well be no benefit accruing at all.

The decision in *R. v Palmer*[18] related to the felling by the accused of a tree that had been subject to a tree preservation order, in order to avoid having to install a root barrier between it and his house. The judgment of the Court of Appeal is directly relevant to many cases where a listed building is deliberately altered without consent, to save the expense of carrying out some works that would otherwise be necessary. It took as its starting point the cost (just under £1,000) of the works that were no longer necessary following the unlawful felling, and deduced from that an appropriate penalty to reflect "the deliberate defiance by the appellant" of the order, arriving at a figure of £3,000.

In *R. v M and G Contractors Ltd*,[19] listed building consent had been given for the conversion of a 17th-century barn. In due course, virtually all of the original timber frame was removed, so that what was left was no longer worthy of being listed. The judge accepted that it had probably cost more to try to retain the old structure and then gradually replace it than it would have done simply to build a completely new house, so that the unauthorised demolition had not led to any profit. Nevertheless, he held:

"Whilst I do not take the view that this should involve a heavy penalty, having regard to the amounts involved here, it has got to be one that shows that people must at all times, especially in dealing with these historic buildings, behave strictly in accordance with the conditions which have been imposed upon them."

The Court of Appeal agreed, and dismissed the appeal against the sentence of £6,000.

19.10.4 The degree of culpability of the defendant

In *R. v Duckworth*,[20] the Court of Appeal considered the culpability of the accused to be "in many respects the most important" of the factors in sentencing, commenting as follows:

"These offences can be committed in a number of circumstances. They are sometimes described as offences of strict liability, whether or not that term is strictly accurate. But the

---

[18] (1989) 11 Cr. App. R. (S) 407.
[19] (1986) 8 Cr. App. R. (S) 474.
[20] (1995) 16 Cr. App. R. (S) 529: see **19.10.1**.

offence may be committed though a lack of care on the part of the defendant or indeed through ignorance of his proper responsibilities in the relevant matter. On the other hand, it may be a case where the defendant has acted wilfully, in disregard of the need to obtain consent, or he has even acted wilfully, with an intent to destroy an historic structure.

...This man is a chartered surveyor. He is experienced in the relevant matters, and to suggest that he acted in any way other than in a wilful disregard of a necessity to obtain consents is, in our judgment, fanciful."[21]

The Court accordingly held that the fine of £15,000 imposed in the Crown Court was, in the circumstances, not inappropriate or wrong in principle (although it did reduce it because of the appellant's financial circumstances)—although, given that the offence resulted in a gain of £150,000, that still leaves a worrying net gain of £135,000, which seems to go against the approach adopted in *Palmer* of increasing the amount of the gain to arrive at the fine.

Similarly, in *R. v Sandhu*,[22] another listed buildings case, Bingham L.J. held that it was relevant to sentence that the appellant, before carrying out the unauthorised works, had been warned and advised of the dangers, chose an incompetent builder, and was generally happy to ride roughshod over the regulations. At the end of Lord Bingham's judgment in that case, he stated:

"It was, in our judgment, bound to sway the jury against the defendant and distract attention from the principal issue if the jury were told, as they were, that the appellant, before causing the execution of the alterations objected to, was warned and advised of the dangers, chose to ignore that advice, chose an incompetent builder and was generally happy to ride roughshod over the regulations. *Those are all matters relevant to sentence ...*" (emphasis added).

This factor will also involve consideration of the status and occupation of the defendant. Indeed, a surprising number of defendants are (or should be) perfectly well aware of the relevant law. And the extent to which the defendant was aware of the importance of what was destroyed will also be relevant.

On the other hand, although there is no need for the authority to prove that the accused knew of the existence of the tree preservation order in order to secure a conviction, the presence or absence of such knowledge may be highly relevant to the penalty imposed. Thus, in *Maidstone BC v Mortimer*,[23] a tree case, the accused was a tree-feller by occupation, but had been told by the landowner (incorrectly, as it turned out) that she had obtained the necessary consent from the council. The Divisional Court held that his lack of knowledge was insufficient for him to escape conviction, but "that fact can be reflected in the penalty imposed on him".[24]

Finally, the advice given to the Court of Appeal by the Sentencing Advisory Panel[25] on sentencing for environmental offences also emphasised the culpability

---

[21] *per* Hobhouse L.J. at pp.531, 532.
[22] [1997] J.P.L. 853; see **19.9.6**.
[23] [1980] 3 All E.R. 552; [1981] J.P.L. 319.
[24] [1980] 3 All E.R. 552, *per* Park J. at p.555f.
[25] See **19.6.2**.

of a defendant as a factor in assessing an appropriate sentence—either aggravating or reducing the seriousness of an offence.[26]

19.10.5 Penalties in practice

The way these principles work out in practice can be seen by looking at the table of convictions at **Appendix F**. This is derived from research carried out by Bob Kindred on behalf of the Institute of Historic Building Conservation, largely on the basis of reports in the national, local and professional press and information supplied by local authorities, and relates to the period since 1991, when the maximum fines were increased.[27] The 97 decisions noted there must represent a reasonable cross-section of all convictions, although it should obviously be borne in mind that the table does not include acquittals.

Various factors emerge. First, unsurprisingly, custodial sentences are extremely rare, and only imposed in very extreme cases—although there are two instances of courts making clear that the defendant only just avoided imprisonment (*Carter Hall, Eckington*, and *Liberty PH, Great Yarmouth*).

Secondly, also predictably, fines are increasing—partly because of inflation, but also because magistrates are becoming more familiar with this type of offence. The other side of this coin is that certain authorities, too, are becoming more familiar with prosecution procedures, and are therefore instituting prosecutions more often, and with "better" results (from their point of view). Over the 14 years covered by the table, there were 19 instances of fines of £10,000 or more; and a further 19 between £5,000 and £9,999.

Finally, it is noticeable that the defendants include two Members of Parliament, two councillors, and several members of the relevant professions—all of whom ought to know better. In the case of architects and surveyors, it is possible that conviction may lead to disciplinary proceedings by the RIBA or the RICS.

It should not be forgotten, either, that penalties can be imposed in other ways. Thus, when Monkspath Hall, Solihull (18th century, listed Grade II) was demolished, allegedly by mistake, the bulldozer driver was fined £1,500, and the demolition company (of which he was a director) £2,000. The local council, which had employed them to demolish (unlisted) farm buildings across the road, then used them under their contract, as a result of which the company had to pay for the cost of rebuilding and preserving the remaining parts of the Hall, estimated in 1985 at £200,000.[28]

19.10.6 Sentencing procedure

The sentencing procedure, which obviously occurs after the accused has either pleaded guilty or been found guilty following trial, is in most cases relatively

---

[26] See *Environmental Offences: The Panel's Advice to the Court of Appeal*, March 1, 2000, paras 6, 12.

[27] For the preceding period, see the previous edition of this book.

[28] *Solihull BC v D Doyle Contractors (Birmingham) Ltd and Keenan*, reported as a news item in *The Times*, November 7, 1985.

straightforward. However, sentencing has the potential to be the most contentious element in a prosecution for offences relating to listed buildings and monuments.

In cases of works for the alteration or extension of a listed building, the extent of the damage may have been dealt with prior to conviction, since the importance of the building and the extent of the works carried out may need to have been explored in order to assess whether the works affected its character as a building of special interest. On the other hand, if there is no doubt that the works affected the character of the building, or if they were for its demolition anyway, such matters might be prejudicial at the earlier stage of the trial, and would therefore be inadmissible (following *R. v Sandhu*[29]). And matters such as the benefit arising from the offence, and the culpability of the accused, are wholly irrelevant to the issue of liability, and thus for the same reason inadmissible. However, such matters are all very relevant to sentencing, and they will therefore have to be explored following conviction and prior to sentencing.

Where such further evidence is required, the proper procedure to be followed, following the decision in *Sandhu*, is what is sometimes referred to as a *Newton* hearing.[30] Witnesses are called and cross-examined just as in a full trial, to establish the various matters relevant to sentencing—such as the state of the defendant's knowledge, the degree of financial gain realised or expected, the financial means of the defendant and, possibly, the degree of damage to the building.[31] The trial thus effectively splits into two parts.

Strictly speaking, a *Newton* hearing is only correct after a guilty plea, in which case no evidence at all will have been called prior to conviction. The Court of Appeal has however advocated a similar procedure where a conviction follows a non-guilty plea, and where there is still relevant evidence to be canvassed as to the mental state of the defendant, or some other similar issue.[32]

It should also not be forgotten that, whilst the duty of those appearing for the defendant is to achieve the lowest possible sentence, it does not follow that the duty of the prosecution is to achieve the maximum possible; rather, it is to assist the court to achieve a level of penalty that is fair in all the circumstances.[33]

Where the magistrates, after a summary trial, convict the defendant, they may decide in the light of all the evidence they have heard that the case should be committed to the Crown Court for sentencing, because it deserves a greater sentence than the maximum they can impose. Before doing so, however, they may seek further details of the defendant—for example, as to financial status and previous convictions.

19.10.7 Costs

Finally, in the event of a conviction in a case of this kind, the prosecution will usually seek to recover all or part of its costs from the defendant. Indeed, it will be obvious from the table at **Appendix F** that, in many cases, the amount of the costs

---

[29] [1997] J.P.L. 853; see **19.9.6**.
[30] *R. v Newton* (1982) 77 Cr. App. R. 13. See the note on *R. v Hill* [1997] Crim. L.R. 459.
[31] *R. v Duckworth* (1995) 16 Cr. App. R.(S) 529; see **19.10.1**.
[32] *R. v Robinson* (1968) 53 Cr. App. R. 314 and *R. v Finch* (1992) 14 Cr. App. R. (S) 226.
[33] *R. v Banks* [1916] 2 K.B. 621.

awarded can be a significant part of the overall penalty; and in some case the costs can exceed the fine.

In general, the computation of allowable costs is beyond the scope of this book; but, in broad terms, section 18 of the Prosecution of Offences Act 1985 provides that the court may order the defendant to pay to the prosecutor such costs "as it considers just and reasonable". A similar provision[34] was considered in *Neville v Gardner Merchant Ltd*,[35] where it was held that magistrates could order the defendant to pay the costs of investigating the offence, even though it was done by a salaried employee of the prosecuting authority. However, in *R. v Seymour*,[36] a case under the Ancient Monuments Act,[37] the appellant was prosecuted by the Crown Prosecution Service, following an investigation by English Heritage, and the costs of the investigation were held by the Court of Appeal not to be properly included in the order to pay prosecution costs.

The two decisions were considered by the Court of Appeal in *R. v Associated Octel Ltd*,[38] which decided that *Seymour* had been decided *per incuriam*, and that *Neville* was to be preferred. The costs of the prosecution, for the purposes of the 1985 Act, may thus include the costs of the prosecuting authority in carrying out investigations with a view to prosecution, where it results in a conviction. It was therefore just and reasonable for the defendant to be ordered to pay all such costs—even if the prosecution eventually modified its case. The Court in *Associated Octel* did however make the following, eminently sensible, observations as to procedure:

(i) The prosecution should serve on the defence, at the earliest time, full details of its costs, so as to give the defence a proper opportunity to consider them and make representations on them, if appropriate.

(ii) If the defendant, once served with a schedule of the prosecution's costs, wished to dispute the whole or any part of the schedule, he should give proper notice to the prosecution of the objections which it was proposed to make; at least it should be made clear to the court what the objections were. It might be that in some exceptional cases a full hearing would need to be held for the objections to be resolved, as there was no provision for the taxation of the prosecution's costs in a criminal case.

Note that this applies to all prosecution costs (including those of attending the hearing), not just to those of investigating the offence. These principles are clearly relevant to a local planning authority seeking to recover its costs—both those of the hearing and those of the investigation leading up to it.

In practice, having considered the means of the defendant and all the circumstances, the court will often order the defendant to pay a proportion of the prosecuting authority's costs, rather than the whole of them. The amount

---

[34] In the Costs in Criminal Cases Act 1973, s.2(2).
[35] (1983) 5 Cr. App. R. (S.) 349.
[36] [1988] 1 P.L.R. 19.
[37] See **19.10.1**.
[38] Discussed at [1997] Crim. L.R. 144.

recovered can (exceptionally) exceed the amount of the fine, although it should never be "grossly disproportionate" to it.[39]

If the prosecution proves in the event to be unable to make its case, it will have to pay the costs of the defendant—there is no special rule as to costs in proceedings brought in the public interest.[40]

19.11 Appeals

It is possible for the defendant to appeal against a decision of the magistrates—either a conviction (following a non-guilty plea) or sentence—to the Crown Court. Such an appeal must be made within 21 days, and is heard by a bench consisting of a Crown Court Judge sitting with two magistrates, without a jury. They will rehear the whole matter afresh, and the procedure is exactly the same as in the magistrates' court.

Alternatively, an appeal on a point of law can be made, either by the defence or the prosecution, to the Divisional Court by way of case stated. The Divisional Court (which will consist of one High Court Judge and one Appeal Court Judge), if it allows the appeal, will either direct the magistrates to acquit or convict, or leave it to them to reach a new decision on a proper legal basis. Such an appeal can also be made following an appeal to the Crown Court.

Where a case is heard in the first instance in the Crown Court, appeal lies to the Court of Appeal (Criminal Division)—again, either as to sentence or conviction—but only with leave, which is not often forthcoming. There is no right of appeal by the prosecution against acquittal.

---

[39] *R. v Northallerton Magistrates' Court, Ex p. Dove* (1999) 163 J.P. 657.
[40] *Re Southbourne Ltd* [1993] 1 W.L.R. 244 at 250G.

Appendices

"Bernard nodded. 'The Corn Exchange is a listed building. So it's one of [the Department of the Environment's] planning inspectors who will be conducting the inquiry. Sir Humphrey and the Department will be laying down some 'informal' guidelines for him. ... Guidelines are perfectly proper. Everyone has guidelines for their work.'

"It didn't sound perfectly proper to me. 'I thought planning inspectors were impartial', I said.

"Bernard chuckled. 'Oh *really* Minister! So they are! Railway trains are impartial too. But if you lay down the lines for them, that's the way they go.'"

Jonathan Lynn and Antony Jay, *Yes Minister: The Diaries of a Cabinet Minister by the Right Hon. James Hacker MP* (BBC, London, 1983)

Appendix A

Planning Policy Guidance Note PPG15:
Planning and the Historic Environment

Note: this Appendix reproduces the PPG, originally published in September 1994 jointly by the Department of the Environment and the Department of National Heritage, as it stands following amendment by Circular 01/01[1] (which itself incorporated and superseded amendments to the PPG that had previously been made by Circular 14/97[2]) and with references to legislation and guidance updated as appropriate. Material added, omitted or updated is indicated by the use of square brackets, as is editorial material in the footnotes.

Planning policy guidance notes set out Government policy on planning issues and provide guidance to local authorities and others on the operation of the planning system. They also explain the relationship between planning policies and other policies which have an important bearing on issues of development and land use. Local planning authorities must take their content into account in preparing their development plans. The guidance may also be material to decisions on individual planning applications and appeals.

INTRODUCTION

1. This PPG provides a full statement of Government policies for the identification and protection of historic buildings, conservation areas, and other elements of the historic environment. It explains the role played by the planning system in their protection. It complements the guidance on archaeology and planning given in PPG 16.[3]

2. In addition to normal development controls, the Planning (Listed Buildings and Conservation Areas) Act 1990[4] provides specific protection for buildings and areas of special architectural or historic interest. In many instances there is a close link between controls over listed buildings and conservation areas and development control decisions. In such cases development and conservation issues will generally need to be considered together.

---

[1] [Department of the Environment, Transport and the Regions (DETR) Circ. 01/01 (DCMS Circ. 01/01), *Arrangements for Handling Heritage Applications—Notification and Directions by the Secretary of State*, Appendix B.]

[2] [Department of the Environment (DOE) Circ. 14/97 (DCMS Circ. 01/97), *Planning and the Historic Environment—Notification and Directions by the Secretary of State*, Appendix E.]

[3] [Reproduced at **Appendix B** of this book.]

[4] Referred to [throughout the PPG] as "the Act"; the Town and Country Planning Act 1990 is referred to as "the principal Act".

3. This guidance is not only for local authorities, but also for other public authorities, property owners, developers, amenity bodies and all members of the public with an interest in the conservation of the historic environment. It updates the advice in Department of the Environment Circular 8/87, within the existing legislative framework. The policy content of Circular 8/87 is hereby cancelled, along with all of Circular 18/88. The directions in Circular 8/87 will continue in force until new directions have been made.[5] Such directions will be made at the same time as related changes to the Town and Country Planning General Development Order 1988 (the GDO)[6], and the Planning (Listed Buildings and Conservation Areas) Regulations 1990, and will be the subject of a separate Circular.[7]

4. The guidance given in this PPG should not involve any significant additional expenditure for local planning authorities. New duties placed on authorities by subordinate legislation—e.g. directions, the GDO, and the Ecclesiastical Exemption (Listed Buildings and Conservation Areas) Order 1994—are the subject of separate consultation with the local authority associations.

Structure of the PPG

5. Part 1 of the PPG deals with those aspects of conservation policy which interact most directly with the planning system, whose operation is the responsibility of [the First Secretary of State[8]] for the Environment. Decisions on called-in applications for, and appeals against refusals of, listed building or conservation area consent are the responsibility of [the First Secretary of State] because of their frequent close links with issues of development control.

6. Part 2 of the PPG deals with aspects of conservation policy which are less directly linked to the planning system, and which are for the most part the responsibility of [the Secretary of State for Culture, Media and Sport[9]].

7. There is however no sharp distinction between the two areas of responsibility. For instance, both Secretaries of State have an interest in policies for the designation and protection of conservation areas; and protection of the wider aspects of the historic environment (e.g. historic landscapes) is effected mainly through the operation of the planning system. 8. In Part 1 of the PPG and in Annex B[10], references to "the Secretary of State" are, unless otherwise stated, references to [the First Secretary of State]; in Part 2 and in Annex A[11], "the Secretary of State" refers to [the Secretary of State for Culture, Media and Sport].

---

[5] [New directions were made, in Environment Circ. 14/97, which were in turn replaced by further new directions in Environment Circ. 01/01. See **12.6.5** and **13.5**.]

[6] [See now the Town and Country Planning (General Permitted Development) Order 1995 (SI 1995/418) and the Town and Country Planning (General Development Procedure) Order 1995 (SI 1995/419).]

[7] [See now Environment Circ. 01/01.]

[8] [In practice, the Office of the Deputy Prime Minister (ODPM); see **1.4.1**.]

[9] [The successor to the Secretary of State for National Heritage since 1997; see **1.4.1**.]

[10] [Annex B to the PPG is a summary of listed building control procedures, not reproduced in this book.]

[11] [Annex A to the PPG is a list of the main heritage bodies in England. An updated list is at Appendix C to this book.]

PART 1

1. Planning and conservation

1.1 It is fundamental to the Government's policies for environmental stewardship that there should be effective protection for all aspects of the historic environment. The physical survivals of our past are to be valued and protected for their own sake, as a central part of our cultural heritage and our sense of national identity. They are an irreplaceable record which contributes, through formal education and in many other ways, to our understanding of both the present and the past. Their presence adds to the quality of our lives, by enhancing the familiar and cherished local scene and sustaining the sense of local distinctiveness which is so important an aspect of the character and appearance of our towns, villages and countryside. The historic environment is also of immense importance for leisure and recreation.

The role of the planning system

1.2 The function of the planning system is to regulate the development and use of land in the public interest. It has to take account of the Government's objective of promoting sustainable economic growth, and make provision for development to meet the economic and social needs of the community. As [PPS 1] makes clear, planning is also an important instrument for protecting and enhancing the environment in town and country, and preserving the built and natural heritage. The objective of planning processes should be to reconcile the need for economic growth with the need to protect the natural and historic environment.

1.3 The Government has committed itself to the concept of sustainable development—of not sacrificing what future generations will value for the sake of short-term and often illusory gains. This approach is set out in [*A Better Quality of Life—A Strategy for Sustainable Development for the UK*[12]]. It is also a key element of the development plan system, as set out in [PPS 12]. This commitment has particular relevance to the preservation of the historic environment, which by its nature is irreplaceable. Yet the historic environment of England is all-pervasive, and it cannot in practice be preserved unchanged. We must ensure that the means are available to identify what is special in the historic environment; to define through the development plan system its capacity for change; and, when proposals for new development come forward, to assess their impact on the historic environment and give full weight, alongside other considerations.

Conservation and economic prosperity

1.4 Though choices sometimes have to be made, conservation and sustainable economic growth are complementary objectives and should not generally be seen as in opposition to one another. Most historic buildings can still be put to good economic use in, for example, commercial or residential occupation. They are a valuable material resource and can contribute to the prosperity of the economy, provided that they are properly maintained: the avoidable loss of fabric through neglect is a waste of economic as well as environmental resources. In return, economic prosperity can secure the continued vitality of conservation areas, and the continued use and maintenance of historic buildings, provided that there is a sufficiently realistic and imaginative approach to their alteration and change of use, to reflect the needs of a rapidly changing world.

---

[12] [CM 4345, Stationery Office, 1999; the Strategy is currently under review. Note that references in the original PPG to other publications have here been updated wherever possible to refer to the most appropriate equivalent current publications.]

1.5 Conservation can itself play a key part in promoting economic prosperity by ensuring that an area offers attractive living and working conditions which will encourage inward investment—environmental quality is increasingly a key factor in many commercial decisions. The historic environment is of particular importance for tourism and leisure, and Government policy encourages the growth and development of tourism in response to the market so long as this is compatible with proper long-term conservation. Further advice on tourist aspects of conservation is given in PPG 21 and the English Tourist Board's publication *Maintaining the Balance*[13].

Stewardship: the role of local authorities and others

1.6 The Government urges local authorities to maintain and strengthen their commitment to stewardship of the historic environment, and to reflect it in their policies and their allocation of resources. It is important that, as planning authorities, they adopt suitable policies in their development plans, and give practical effect to them through their development control decisions. As highway authorities too, their policies and activities should reflect the need to protect the historic environment and to promote sustainable economic growth, for roads can have a particular impact at all levels—not only through strategic decisions on the siting of new roads, but also through the more detailed aspects of road building and road maintenance, such as the quality of street furniture and surfaces. Above all, local authorities should ensure that they can call on sufficient specialist conservation advice, whether individually or jointly, to inform their decision-making and to assist owners and other members of the public.

1.7 However, the responsibility of stewardship is shared by everyone—not only by central and local government, but also by business, voluntary bodies, churches, and by individual citizens as owners, users and visitors of historic buildings. The historic environment cannot be preserved unless there is broad public support and understanding, and it is a key element of Government policy for conservation that there should be adequate processes of consultation and education to facilitate this.

2. Development plans and development control

2.1 The principal Act (as amended) requires development plans to include policies for "the conservation of the natural beauty and amenity of the land" and for "the improvement of the physical environment". The Town and Country Planning (Development Plan) Regulations [1999] require authorities to have regard to environmental considerations in preparing their plan policies and proposals. The protection of the historic environment, whether individual listed buildings, conservation areas, parks and gardens, battlefields or the wider historic landscape, is a key aspect of these wider environmental responsibilities, and will need to be taken fully into account both in the formulation of authorities' planning policies and in development control.

Development plans

2.2 Structure, local, and unitary development plans [and, since 2004, local development frameworks] are the main vehicle for ensuring that conservation policies are co-ordinated and integrated with other planning policies affecting the historic environment. Imaginative planning policies can not only reduce threats to it, but increase its contribution to local amenity. By including suitable policies in their plans, local authorities can give encouragement to the satisfactory reuse of neglected historic buildings, particularly where major

---

[13] [English Tourist Board, 1991. See also *Making the Connections—a Practical Guide to Tourism Management in Historic Towns*, English Historic Towns Forum, 1999.]

groups of buildings need to be tackled comprehensively, and where other planning factors, such as traffic problems, may be discouraging reuse.

2.3 [Section 38 of the Planning and Compensation Act 2004][14] provides that where, in making any determination under the planning Acts, regard is to be had to the development plan, the determination must be made in accordance with the development plan unless material considerations indicate otherwise. It is therefore important that plans include all the criteria on the basis of which planning decisions will be made. Plans should set out clearly all conservation policies relevant to the exercise of an authority's development control functions, and also policies which are relevant to cases where development and conservation issues are linked and will need to be addressed together.

2.4 The Courts have accepted that section 54A [of the principal Act] does not apply to decisions on applications for listed building consent or conservation area consent, since in those cases there is no statutory requirement to have regard to the provisions of the development plan. [The same principle would presumably to section 38 of the 2004 Act.] However, authorities should ensure that aspects of conservation policy that are relevant, directly or indirectly, to development control decisions are included—for instance, policies for alterations or extensions to listed buildings that also constitute development (to which [section 38] will directly apply). In view of the statutory requirements that authorities should have special regard to the desirability of preserving any listed building or its setting, or any features of special architectural or historic interest which it possesses, and should pay special attention to the desirability of preserving or enhancing the character or appearance of any conservation area in exercising their development control functions, plans should also include policies for works of demolition or alteration which, while not in themselves constituting development, could affect an authority's decision on a related application for planning permission.

2.5 There may be some detailed conservation policies which have no bearing on issues of development control—for instance, policies for the treatment of some internal features of listed buildings where this would not affect consideration of planning applications but might require listed building consent. Other examples may relate to certain types of alteration, repairs, maintenance or decoration. These policies should be presented as supplementary guidance rather than included in the plan itself. Such guidance will carry greater weight to the extent that it has been the subject of public consultation, has been formally adopted by the authority, and is published in a format which gives clear advice and is readily available to the public. Development plans should contain a reference to such policies in the reasoned justification, together with a clear indication of where those policies may be seen in full.

2.6 Full guidance on the preparation of plans is given in PPG 12. Structure plans and the first part of unitary development plans provide a statement of the overall strategy for a county, borough or metropolitan district area, and should include conservation of the historic environment as one of their key topics, taking account of any broad strategic objectives or constraints set out in relevant regional planning guidance. The structure plan should provide a broad planning framework, guiding the approach to be adopted in local plans to such issues as the capacity of historic towns to sustain development, the relief of pressure on historic central areas by the identification of opportunities for growth elsewhere, and the provision of transport infrastructure which respects the historic environment.

2.7 Local plans and the second part of unitary development plans should set out more detailed development control policies for an authority's area: they should include both the policies which will apply over the area as a whole, and any policies and proposals which will apply to particular neighbourhoods. Both policies and proposals should be illustrated on the proposals map (see paragraph 7.14 of PPG 12).

---

[14] [This replaced s.54A of the principal Act with effect from September 28, 2004.]

2.8 Local plans should set out clearly the planning authority's policies for the preservation and enhancement of the historic environment in their area, and the factors which will be taken into account in assessing different types of planning application—for example, proposals for the change of use of particular types of historic building or for new development which would affect their setting. It is important that clear policies are formulated for cases where new development is proposed in order to provide income for the upkeep of historic buildings (see [DETR Circular 16/97]). Plans should also include a strategy for the economic regeneration of rundown areas, and in particular seek to identify the opportunities which the historic fabric of an area can offer as a focus for regeneration. Excessively detailed or inflexible policies concerning individual buildings or groups of buildings should be avoided.

2.9 Plans should set out authorities' broad criteria for the designation of new conservation areas and for the review of existing conservation area boundaries; and, where possible, which particular areas are in mind for both. The process of assessment, detailed definition or revision of boundaries, and formulation of proposals for individual conservation areas (as required by section 71 of the Act) should involve extensive local consultation and should be pursued separately from the local plan process itself. But the plan should provide a policy framework, making clear to the public how detailed assessment documents and statements of proposals for individual conservation areas relate to the plan, and what weight will be given to them in decisions on applications for planning permission and conservation area consent. (See also paragraphs 4.3–4.7, 4.10 and 4.15). Designation strategies should take account of the fact that authorities now have general powers to control the demolition of dwelling houses outside conservation areas (see Department of the Environment [Circular 10/95]).

2.10 English Heritage is a statutory consultee on draft plans, but is also able to offer specialist advice at preparation stage. In conjunction with [the Countryside Agency] and English Nature, it is also issuing guidance on conservation in strategic and local plans. There will often be advantage in consultation at an early stage in plan preparation with other statutory agencies and with the national amenity societies and local conservation bodies, as well as wider public consultation at the formal deposit stage.

[Guidance on the preparation and content of local development frameworks is contained in PPS 12].

Development control

2.11 The Secretary of State attaches particular importance to early consultation with the local planning authority on development proposals which would affect historic sites and structures, whether listed buildings, conservation areas, parks and gardens, battlefields or the wider historic landscape. There is likely to be much more scope for refinement and revision of proposals if consultation takes place before intentions become firm and timescales inflexible. Local planning authorities should indicate their readiness to discuss proposals with developers before formal planning applications are submitted. They should expect developers to assess the likely impact of their proposals on the special interest of the site or structure in question, and to provide such written information or drawings as may be required to understand the significance of a site or structure before an application is determined. The principle of early consultation should extend to English Heritage and the national amenity societies on cases where a formal planning or listed building consent application would be notifiable to them by direction or under the [General Development Procedure Order].

2.12 It is generally preferable for both the applicant and the planning authority if related applications for planning permission and for listed building or conservation area consent are considered concurrently. Authorities are required by section 66(1) of the Act, in considering whether to grant planning permission for development which affects a listed building or its setting, to have special regard to the desirability of preserving the building or its setting or any features of architectural or historic interest which it possesses. It is unlikely that they will be able to do so effectively unless the planning application is accompanied by a listed building consent application (where the development in question requires one) or at least contains an equivalent amount of information. If an authority is asked to consider a planning application in isolation, a decision on that application cannot be taken as predetermining the outcome of a subsequent application for listed building consent. Authorities are also required by section 72 of the Act, in the exercise in a conservation area of their powers under the Planning Acts (and Part I of the Historic Buildings and Ancient Monuments Act 1953), to pay special attention to the desirability of preserving or enhancing the character or appearance of that area. In the case of unlisted buildings in conservation areas, the Courts have held that consent for the demolition of a building may involve consideration of what is to take its place (see paragraph 4.27).

2.13 Local planning authorities are urged to ensure that they have appropriately qualified specialist advice on any development which, by its character or location, might be held to have an adverse effect on any sites or structures of the historic environment. The need for environmental assessment of major development proposals affecting historic areas should be considered in the light of the advice given in [DETR Circular 02/99]. Authorities should ensure that [the Commission for Architecture and the Built Environment (CABE)] is consulted on all planning applications raising conservation issues of more than local importance, and should take [CABE's] views fully into account in reaching their decisions.

2.14 The design of new buildings intended to stand alongside historic buildings needs very careful consideration. In general it is better that old buildings are not set apart, but are woven into the fabric of the living and working community. This can be done, provided that the new buildings are carefully designed to respect their setting, follow fundamental architectural principles of scale, height, massing and alignment, and use appropriate materials. This does not mean that new buildings have to copy their older neighbours in detail: some of the most interesting streets in our towns and villages include a variety of building styles, materials, and forms of construction, of many different periods, but together forming a harmonious group. Further general advice on design considerations which are relevant to the exercise of planning controls is given in [paragraphs 33 to 39 of PPS 1].

2.15 Some historic buildings are scheduled ancient monuments, and many which are not scheduled are either of intrinsic archaeological interest or stand on ground which contains archaeological remains. It is important in such cases that there should be appropriate assessment of the archaeological implications of development proposals before applications are determined; and that, where permission is to be granted, authorities should consider whether adequate arrangements have been made for recording remains that would be lost in the course of works for which permission is being sought. Further advice on archaeology and planning is given in PPG 16.

The setting of listed buildings

2.16 Sections 16 and 66 of the Act require authorities considering applications for planning permission or listed building consent for works which affect a listed building to have special regard to certain matters, including the desirability of preserving the setting of the building. The setting is often an essential part of the building's character, especially if a garden or grounds have been laid out to complement its design or function. Also, the economic viability as well as the character of historic buildings may suffer and they can be robbed of much of their interest, and of the contribution they make to townscape or the countryside, if they become isolated from their surroundings, e.g. by new traffic routes, car parks, or other development.

2.17 Local planning authorities are required under section 67 of the Act to publish a notice of all applications they receive for planning permission for any development which, in their opinion, affects the setting of a listed building. This provision should not be interpreted too narrowly: the setting of a building may be limited to obviously ancillary land, but may often include land some distance from it. Even where a building has no ancillary land—for example in a crowded urban street—the setting may encompass a number of other properties. The setting of individual listed buildings very often owes its character to the harmony produced by a particular grouping of buildings (not necessarily all of great individual merit) and to the quality of the spaces created between them. Such areas require careful appraisal when proposals for development are under consideration, even if the redevelopment would only replace a building which is neither itself listed nor immediately adjacent to a listed building. Where a listed building forms an important visual element in a street, it would probably be right to regard any development in the street as being within the setting of the building. A proposed high or bulky building might also affect the setting of a listed building some distance away, or alter views of a historic skyline. In some cases, setting can only be defined by a historical assessment of a building's surroundings. If there is doubt about the precise extent of a building's setting, it is better to publish a notice.

Changes of use

2.18 New uses may often be the key to a building's or area's preservation, and controls over land use, density, plot ratio, daylighting and other planning matters should be exercised sympathetically where this would enable a historic building or area to be given a new lease of life. The Secretary of State is not generally in favour of tightening development controls over changes of use as a specific instrument of conservation policy. He considers that, in general, the same provisions on change of use should apply to historic buildings as to all others. Patterns of economic activity inevitably change over time, and it would be unrealistic to seek to prevent such change by the use of planning controls.

2.19 Advice on the planning aspects of re-use and adaptation of rural buildings is given in [paragraphs 17 and 18 of PPS 7]. English Heritage has also issued guidance entitled *The Conversion of Historic Farm Buildings*[15]. Special considerations apply in Green Belts (see PPG 2).

Article 4 directions for listed buildings

2.20 Under article 5 of [the General Development Procedure Order (GDPO)], directions under article 4 bringing certain categories of permitted development within planning control can be made by local authorities without the need for approval by the Secretary of State if they relate solely to a listed building or to development within the curtilage of a listed building, provided they do not affect the carrying out of development by a statutory undertaker. Authorities are reminded that permitted development rights should not be restricted without good reason; but there will nevertheless be cases where it will be desirable to invoke this power to ensure that the immediate setting of a listed building is protected when minor development is proposed. For example, farm buildings converted to new uses may otherwise generate curtilage developments—such as garages, fuel tanks or fences—that may not be suitable in an agricultural setting.

Planning controls and other aspects of the historic environment

2.21 Listed buildings and conservation areas are treated in sections 3 and 4 below. Other aspects of the historic environment are considered briefly here.

---

[15] [1993. Now out of print.]

World Heritage Sites

2.22 Details of World Heritage Sites in England are given in paragraph 6.35. No additional statutory controls follow from the inclusion of a site in the World Heritage list. Inclusion does, however, highlight the outstanding international importance of the site as a key material consideration to be taken into account by local planning authorities in determining planning and listed building consent applications, and by the Secretary of State in determining cases on appeal or following call-in.

2.23 Each local authority concerned, taking account of World Heritage Site designation and other relevant statutory designations, should formulate specific planning policies for protecting these sites and include these policies in their development plans. Policies should reflect the fact that all these sites have been designated for their outstanding universal value, and they should place great weight on the need to protect them for the benefit of future generations as well as our own. Development proposals affecting these sites or their setting may be compatible with this objective, but should always be carefully scrutinised for their likely effect on the site or its setting in the longer term. Significant development proposals affecting World Heritage Sites will generally require formal environmental assessment, to ensure that their immediate impact and their implications for the longer term are fully evaluated (see paragraph 2.13 above).

Historic parks and gardens

2.24 Again no additional statutory controls follow from the inclusion of a site in English Heritage's Register of Parks and Gardens of Special Historic Interest (see paragraph 6.38), but local planning authorities should protect registered parks and gardens in preparing development plans and in determining planning applications. The effect of proposed development on a registered park or garden or its setting is a material consideration in the determination of a planning application. Planning and highway authorities should also safeguard registered parks or gardens when themselves planning new developments or road schemes.

Historic battlefields

2.25 A similar non-statutory Register of Historic Battlefields [has been] prepared by English Heritage (see paragraph 6.39). This [does] not entail additional statutory controls, but [. . .] will need to be taken into account by local planning authorities. The effects of any development on the limited number of registered sites will form a material consideration to be taken into account in determining planning applications.

The wider historic landscape

2.26 Conservation of the wider historic landscape greatly depends on active land management, but there is nevertheless a significant role for local planning authorities. In defining planning policies for the countryside, authorities should take account of the historical dimension of the landscape as a whole rather than concentrate on selected areas. Adequate understanding is an essential preliminary and authorities should assess the wider historic landscape at an early stage in development plan preparation. Plans should protect its most important components and encourage development that is consistent with maintaining its overall historic character. Indeed, policies to strengthen the rural economy through environmentally sensitive diversification may be among the most important for its conservation.

3. Listed building control

3.1 Section 1 of the Act imposes on the Secretary of State for National Heritage a duty to compile or approve lists of buildings of special architectural or historic interest. The Secretary of State's policy for the listing of such buildings is set out in paragraphs 6.10–6.16. Once a building is listed (or is the subject of a building preservation notice), section 7 of the Act provides that consent is normally required for its demolition [. . .][16], and for any works of alteration or extension which would affect its character as a building of special architectural or historic interest. It is a criminal offence to carry out such works without consent, which should be sought from the local planning authority. This section sets out the main elements of Government policy for listed building controls. Details of the procedures are summarised in Annex B[17].

3.2 Controls apply to all works, both external and internal, that would affect a building's special interest, whether or not the particular feature concerned is specifically mentioned in the list description. Consent is not normally required for repairs, but, where repairs involve alterations which would affect the character of the listed building, consent is required. Whether repairs actually constitute alterations which require consent is a matter of fact and degree which must be determined in each case. Where painting or repainting the exterior or interior of a listed building would affect the building's character, consent is required. Further detailed guidance on alterations to listed buildings, prepared by English Heritage, is given in Annex C[18]. The Secretaries of State commend this guidance and ask all local planning authorities to take it into account in their exercise of listed building and development controls. Whether proposed works constitute alterations or a demolition is again a matter of fact and degree. Fixtures and curtilage buildings—i.e. any object or structure which is fixed to the building, or is within the curtilage and forms part of the land and has done so since before July 1948—are also treated as part of the building for the purposes of listed building control (see paragraphs 3.30–3.36 below).

3.3 The importance which the Government attaches to the protection of the historic environment was explained in paragraphs 1.1–1.7 above. Once lost, listed buildings cannot be replaced; and they can be robbed of their special interest as surely by unsuitable alteration as by outright demolition. They represent a finite resource and an irreplaceable asset. There should be a general presumption in favour of the preservation of listed buildings, except where a convincing case can be made out, against the criteria set out in this section, for alteration or demolition. While the listing of a building should not be seen as a bar to all future change, the starting point for the exercise of listed building control is the statutory requirement on local planning authorities to "have special regard to the desirability of preserving the building or its setting or any features of special architectural or historic interest which it possesses" (section 16). This reflects the great importance to society of protecting listed buildings from unnecessary demolition and from unsuitable and insensitive alteration and should be the prime consideration for authorities in determining an application for consent.

3.4 Applicants for listed building consent must be able to justify their proposals. They will need to show why works which would affect the character of a listed building are desirable or necessary. They should provide the local planning authority with full information, to enable them to assess the likely impact of their proposals on the special architectural or historic interest of the building and on its setting.

[16] [The words ", in whole or in part" were deleted by Environment Circ. 14/97, Appendix E.]
[17] [Not reproduced in this book.]
[18] [Not reproduced in this book.]

General criteria

3.5 The issues that are generally relevant to the consideration of all listed building consent applications are:

(i) the importance of the building, its intrinsic architectural and historic interest and rarity, in both national and local terms ("historic interest" is further explained in paragraph 6.11);

(ii) the particular physical features of the building (which may include its design, plan, materials or location) which justify its inclusion in the list: list descriptions may draw attention to features of particular interest or value, but they are not exhaustive and other features of importance (e.g. interiors) may come to light after the building's inclusion in the list;

(iii) the building's setting and its contribution to the local scene, which may be very important, e.g. where it forms an element in a group, park, garden or other townscape or landscape, or where it shares particular architectural forms or details with other buildings nearby;

(iv) the extent to which the proposed works would bring substantial benefits for the community, in particular by contributing to the economic regeneration of the area or the enhancement of its environment (including other listed buildings).

3.6 The grading of a building in the statutory lists is clearly a material consideration for the exercise of listed building control. Grades I and II* identify the outstanding architectural or historic interest of a small proportion (about 6 per cent) of all listed buildings. These buildings are of particularly great importance to the nation's built heritage: their significance will generally be beyond dispute. But it should be emphasised that the statutory controls apply equally to all listed buildings, irrespective of grade; and since Grade II includes about 94 per cent of all listed buildings, representing a major element in the historic quality of our towns, villages and countryside, failure to give careful scrutiny to proposals for their alteration or demolition could lead to widespread damage to the historic environment.

3.7 The following paragraphs deal first with alterations and extensions and then with demolitions, though considerations relevant to the two types of case to some extent overlap. For instance, some of the considerations set out in paragraph 3.19, in relation to demolitions, may also be relevant to substantial works of alteration or extension which would significantly alter the character of a listed building. Since listed building consent applications will often raise the issue of the most appropriate use for a building, the question of use is also discussed here.

Use

3.8 Generally the best way of securing the upkeep of historic buildings and areas is to keep them in active use. For the great majority this must mean economically viable uses if they are to survive, and new, and even continuing, uses will often necessitate some degree of adaptation. The range and acceptability of possible uses must therefore usually be a major consideration when the future of listed buildings or buildings in conservation areas is in question.

3.9 Judging the best use is one of the most important and sensitive assessments that local planning authorities and other bodies involved in conservation have to make. It requires balancing the economic viability of possible uses against the effect of any changes they entail in the special architectural and historic interest of the building or area in question. In principle the aim should be to identify the optimum viable use that is compatible with the fabric, interior, and setting of the historic building. This may not necessarily be the most profitable use if that would entail more destructive alterations than other viable uses.

Where a particular compatible use is to be preferred but restoration for that use is unlikely to be economically viable, grant assistance from the authority, English Heritage or other sources may need to be considered.

3.10 The best use will very often be the use for which the building was originally designed, and the continuation or reinstatement of that use should certainly be the first option when the future of a building is considered. But not all original uses will now be viable or even necessarily appropriate: the nature of uses can change over time, so that in some cases the original use may now be less compatible with the building than an alternative. For example, some business or light industrial uses may now require less damaging alterations to historic farm buildings than some types of modern agricultural operation. Policies for development and listed building controls should recognise the need for flexibility where new uses have to be considered to secure a building's survival.

3.11 If a building is so sensitive that it cannot sustain any alterations to keep it in viable economic use, its future may nevertheless be secured by charitable or community ownership, preserved for its own sake for local people and for the visiting public, where possible with non-destructive opportunity uses such as meeting rooms. Many listed buildings subsist successfully in this way—from the great houses of the National Trust to buildings such as guildhalls, churches and windmills cared for by local authorities or trusts—and this possibility may need to be considered. The Secretaries of State attach particular importance to the activities of the voluntary sector in heritage matters: it is well placed to tap local support, resources and loyalty, and buildings preserved in its care can make a contribution to community life, to local education, and to the local economy.

Alterations and extensions

3.12 Many listed buildings are already in well-established uses, and any changes need be considered only in this context. But where new uses are proposed, it is important to balance the effect of any changes on the special interest of the listed building against the viability of any proposed use and of alternative, and possibly less damaging, uses. In judging the effect of any alteration or extension it is essential to have assessed the elements that make up the special interest of the building in question. They may comprise not only obvious visual features such as a decorative facade or, internally, staircases or decorated plaster ceilings, but the spaces and layout of the building and the archaeological or technological interest of the surviving structure and surfaces. These elements are often just as important in simple vernacular and functional buildings as in grander architecture.

3.13 Many listed buildings can sustain some degree of sensitive alteration or extension to accommodate continuing or new uses. Indeed, cumulative changes reflecting the history of use and ownership are themselves an aspect of the special interest of some buildings, and the merit of some new alterations or additions, especially where they are generated within a secure and committed long-term ownership, should not be discounted. Nevertheless, listed buildings do vary greatly in the extent to which they can accommodate change without loss of special interest. Some may be sensitive even to slight alterations; this is especially true of buildings with important interiors and fittings—not just great houses, but also, for example, chapels with historic fittings or industrial structures with surviving machinery. Some listed buildings are the subject of successive applications for alteration or extension: in such cases it needs to be borne in mind that minor works of indifferent quality, which may seem individually of little importance, can cumulatively be very destructive of a building's special interest.

3.14 As noted above, the listing grade is a material consideration but is not of itself a reliable guide to the sensitivity of a building to alteration or extension. For example, many Grade II buildings are of humble and once common building types and have been listed precisely because they are relatively unaltered examples of a particular building type; so they can as readily have their special interest ruined by unsuitable alteration or extension as can Grade I or II* structures.

3.15 Achieving a proper balance between the special interest of a listed building and proposals for alterations or extensions is demanding and should always be based on specialist expertise; but it is rarely impossible, if reasonable flexibility and imagination are shown by all parties involved. Thus, a better solution may be possible if a local planning authority is prepared to apply normal development control policies flexibly; or if an applicant is willing to exploit unorthodox spaces rather than set a standardized requirement; or if an architect can respect the structural limitations of a building and abandon conventional design solutions in favour of a more imaginative approach. For example, standard commercial office floor-loadings are rarely needed in all parts of a building, and any unusually heavy loads can often be accommodated in stronger areas such as basements. The preservation of facades alone, and the gutting and reconstruction of interiors, is not normally an acceptable approach to the re-use of listed buildings: it can destroy much of a building's special interest and create problems for the long-term stability of the structure.

[3.15A Where works of alteration involve the demolition of a significant part of the listed building, the considerations set out in paragraph 3.19 should be addressed.][19]

Demolitions

3.16 While it is an objective of Government policy to secure the preservation of historic buildings, there will very occasionally be cases where demolition is unavoidable. Listed building controls ensure that proposals for demolition are fully scrutinised before any decision is reached. These controls have been successful in recent years in keeping the number of total demolitions very low. The destruction of historic buildings is in fact very seldom necessary for reasons of good planning: more often it is the result of neglect, or of failure to make imaginative efforts to find new uses for them or to incorporate them into new development.

3.17 There are many outstanding buildings for which it is in practice almost inconceivable that consent for demolition would ever be granted. The demolition of any Grade I or Grade II* building should be wholly exceptional and should require the strongest justification. Indeed, the Secretaries of State would not expect consent to be given for the total or substantial demolition of any listed building without clear and convincing evidence that all reasonable efforts have been made to sustain existing uses or find viable new uses, and these efforts have failed; that preservation in some form of charitable or community ownership is not possible or suitable (see paragraph 3.11); or that redevelopment would produce substantial benefits for the community which would decisively outweigh the loss resulting from demolition. The Secretaries of State would not expect consent to demolition to be given simply because redevelopment is economically more attractive to the developer than repair and re-use of a historic building, or because the developer acquired the building at a price that reflected the potential for redevelopment rather than the condition and constraints of the existing historic building.

[3.18 ...][20]

3.19 Where proposed works would result in the total or substantial demolition of the listed building [...][21], the Secretaries of State would expect the authority, in addition to the general considerations set out in paragraph 3.5 above, to address the following considerations:

[19] [Inserted by Environment Circ. 14/97, Appendix E.]
[20] [Paragraph deleted by Environment Circ. 14/97, Appendix E.]
[21] [The words ", or any significant part of it" were deleted by Environment Circ. 14/97, Appendix E.]

(i) the condition of the building, the cost of repairing and maintaining it in relation to its importance and to the value derived from its continued use. Any such assessment should be based on consistent and long-term assumptions. Less favourable levels of rents and yields cannot automatically be assumed for historic buildings. Also, they may offer proven technical performance, physical attractive ness and functional spaces that, in an age of rapid change, may outlast the short-lived and inflexible technical specifications that have sometimes shaped new developments. Any assessment should also take account of the possibility of tax allowances and exemptions and of grants from public or charitable sources. In the rare cases where it is clear that a building has been deliberately neglected in the hope of obtaining consent for demolition, less weight should be given to the costs of repair;

(ii) the adequacy of efforts made to retain the building in use. The Secretaries of State would not expect listed building consent to be granted for demolition unless the authority (or where appropriate the Secretary of State himself) is satisfied that real efforts have been made without success to continue the present use or to find compatible alternative uses for the building. This should include the offer of the unrestricted freehold of the building on the open market at a realistic price reflecting the building's condition (the offer of a lease only, or the imposition of restrictive covenants, would normally reduce the chances of finding a new use for the building);

(iii) the merits of alternative proposals for the site. Whilst these are a material consideration, the Secretaries of State take the view that subjective claims for the architectural merits of proposed replacement buildings should not in themselves be held to justify the demolition of any listed building. There may very exceptionally be cases where the proposed works would bring substantial benefits for the community which have to be weighed against the arguments in favour of preservation. Even here, it will often be feasible to incorporate listed buildings within new development, and this option should be carefully considered: the challenge presented by retaining listed buildings can be a stimulus to imaginative new design to accommodate them.

Called-in applications

3.20 The Secretary of State may require applications for listed building consent to be referred to him for decision, but this call-in power has only been exercised in a small number of cases per year in recent years. The policy of the Secretary of State is to be very selective about calling in listed building consent cases.

3.21 Cases are likely to be called in where the Secretary of State considers that the proposals raise issues of exceptional significance or controversy. It may also happen that an application for listed building consent is received by a local planning authority when a related matter (e.g. a planning appeal, a called-in planning application or a compulsory purchase order) is being considered by the Secretary of State. Unless it is clear that the listed building consent application can reasonably be dealt with separately, such an application will normally be called in.

Recording buildings

3.22 [English Heritage][22] must be notified of all proposals to demolish listed buildings, and allowed access to buildings which it wishes to record before demolition takes place. There are other circumstances where notification may also be appropriate—for instance, where the exterior of a building is likely to be radically changed as a consequence of major repairs,

---

[22] [Substituted by DETR Circ. 01/01, Appendix B.]

alteration or extension, or where interior work of significance will be lost, affected by sub-division, or substantially rebuilt.

3.23 Local planning authorities should also consider, in all cases of alteration or demoli-tion, whether it would be appropriate to make it a condition of consent that applicants arrange suitable programmes of recording of features that would be destroyed in the course of the works for which consent is being sought. Authorities should not, however, require applicants to finance such programmes in return for the granting of consent. Nor should applicants expect to be granted consent merely because they have arranged suitable pro-grammes. (For recording of archaeological remains see paragraph 2.15).

3.24 Hidden features of interest are sometimes revealed during works of alteration, espe-cially in older or larger buildings: chimney pieces, fireplaces, early windows and doors, panelling, wattle-and-daub partitions and even wall-paintings may come to light. Appli-cants for listed building consent should be made aware of this possibility and should seek the advice of the local planning authority when such things are found. If there is any likelihood that hidden features will be revealed, the local planning authority should attach an appropriate condition to the listed building consent to ensure their retention or proper recording, or should require exploratory opening up, with listed building consent as necessary, before considering consent for the main works.

Advice to owners

3.25 Owners of listed buildings should be encouraged to seek expert advice on whether proposed works require listed building consent, and on the best way to carry out any such works to their property. Many will need to obtain professional advice anyway, but the Secretaries of State hope that local planning authorities will give owners informal advice where they can or guide them to other sources where they can get advice for themselves. English Heritage publishes much specialist advice on the care of historic buildings and can sometimes give advice on individual cases, especially where unusual problems are encountered. [In addition, English Heritage's National Monuments Record Centre may have a record of a building, and its reports and photographs may be available for guidance in understanding the structure and its evolution. The national amenity societies are willing to offer advice to individual owners whenever possible.][23]

Building and fire legislation; access for disabled people; house renovation grants

3.26 In exercising their responsibilities for the safety of buildings under the building and fire legislation, local planning authorities should deal sympathetically with proposals for the repair or conversion of historic buildings. The Building Regulations should be operated in a way which avoids removal of features which contribute to the character of a listed building and are part of the reason for its being listed. Sufficient flexibility exists within the Building Regulations and Fire Precautions Act systems for authorities to have regard to the possible impact of proposals on the historical or architectural value of a building, and authorities should consult their own conservation officers, or seek expert advice from other sources, when handling difficult situations. It is particularly important that there should be a flexible approach to structural matters, to ensure that any changes are in character with the rest of the building and that there is no unacceptable damage to the fabric. In order to ensure that requirements which are unacceptable in terms of a historic building can be considered as part of a listed building consent application, the precise Building and Fire Regulations requirements should be made explicit *before* an application has been deter-mined. A successful outcome is more likely to be negotiated if the authorities have been consulted from the outset.

[23] [Substituted by DETR Circ. 01/01, Appendix B.]

3.27 For the longer term, local planning authorities should be aware of the *Report of the Review of the Fire Safety Legislation and Enforcement*[24] which was published on 22 June 1994. The scrutiny was asked to review all legislation for which the Home Office, the Department of the Environment and the Health and Safety Executive have policy responsibility in relation to fire safety; to review the arrangements for enforcing the legislation; and to examine the practicability of bringing policy responsibility for fire safety together in a single department. The Report makes 61 recommendations, but Ministers are committed to full consultation before any proposals for changing the existing arrangements are made.

3.28 It is important in principle that disabled people should have dignified easy access to and within historic buildings. If it is treated as part of an integrated review of access requirements for all visitors or users, and a flexible and pragmatic approach is taken, it should normally be possible to plan suitable access for disabled people without compromising a building's special interest. Alternative routes or re-organizing the use of spaces may achieve the desired result without the need for damaging alterations.

3.29 Where a local planning authority proposes to grant-aid renovation work to a listed house or a house in a conservation area, care should be taken to ensure that standard grant conditions (e.g. for damp proofing or insulation) are not imposed in a way which would be damaging to the historic character of the building. In such cases housing and environmental health departments should consult with the authority's conservation officer or seek expert advice from other sources. Details of grants available are given in the Department of the Environment publication House Renovation Grants.

Fixtures and curtilage structures

3.30 It is important to know the extent of a listing, not just to determine whether listed building consent is needed for works, but also to determine the payment of VAT and business rates. List descriptions are for the purposes of identification and are not a comprehensive or exclusive record of all features—see paragraph 6.19. Section 1(5) of the Act sets out the meaning of a listed building for the purposes of the Act: a listed building is one included in a list compiled or approved by the Secretary of State and includes "any object or structure fixed to the building" and "any object or structure within the curtilage of the building which, although not fixed to the building, forms part of the land and has done so since before 1 July 1948". The Courts have considered in a number of cases in this context the meaning of "any object or structure fixed to the building" and "curtilage".

3.31 The listing of a building confers protection not only on the building, but also on any object or structure fixed to the building which is ancillary to the building. The word "fixed" has the same connotation as in the law of fixtures. These well-known rules provide that any object or structure fixed to a building should be treated as part of it. It is a test therefore of fact in each case as to whether a structure is free-standing or physically fixed to the building. Generally it would be reasonable to expect some degree of physical annexation, together with indications that the annexation was carried out with the intention of making the object an integral part of the land or building. In the light of this test, items such as chimney-pieces, wall panelling and painted or plastered ceilings will normally be found to be part of the building.

3.32 It may be difficult in some individual cases to decide whether a particular object or structure is a fixture or not. Free-standing objects, e.g. statues, may be fixtures if they were put in place as part of an overall architectural design; this could include objects specially designed or made to fit in a particular space or room. But works of art which were placed in a building primarily to be enjoyed as objects in their own right, rather than forming part of the land or the building, are not likely to be properly considered as fixtures. Each case must

[24] [Home Office, 1994.]

be treated in the light of its own facts, and owners who are contemplating works are advised to contact their local planning authority first.

3.33 The listing of a building confers protection also on any object or structure within its curtilage which forms part of the land and has done so since before 1 July 1948. Following recent case law, [the Secretary of State for Culture, Media and Sport] has attempted to consider individually all the structures and buildings on a site which can be construed as separate buildings and to list those which qualify for listing. There will still be circumstances, however, where a structure or building forms part of land which surrounds or is connected to or serves a listed building, and landowners and local planning authorities will need to consider on the facts of each case whether it forms part of the land and falls within the curtilage of the listed building.

3.34 The principal tests as to whether an object or structure is within the curtilage of a listed building relate to the physical layout of the land surrounding the listed building at the date of the statutory listing and the relationship of the structures on the surrounding land to each other. Changes in ownership, occupation or use after the listing date will not bring about the de-listing of a building which formed part of the principal building at the date of listing. The Courts have held that for a structure or building within the curtilage of a listed building to be part of a listed building it must be ancillary to the principal building, that is it must have served the purposes of the principal building at the date of listing, or at a recent time before the date of listing, in a necessary or reasonably useful way and must not be historically an independent building. Where a self-contained building was fenced or walled-off from the remainder of the site at the date of listing, regardless of the purpose for which it was erected and is occupied, it is likely to be regarded as having a separate curtilage. The structure or building must still form part of the land, and this probably means that there must be some degree of physical annexation to the land.

3.35 Considerations which may assist local planning authorities in forming their own views, or giving advice if requested, include:

- the historical independence of the building;

- the physical layout of the principal building and other buildings;

- the ownership of the buildings now and at the time of listing;

- whether the structure forms part of the land;

- the use and function of the buildings, and whether a building is ancillary or subordinate to the principal building.

3.36 It is always necessary to recognise, however, that the question of whether a building, structure or object is within the curtilage of, or is fixed to, the principal building, unless specifically included in the listing, is in any particular case a matter of fact and ultimately a matter for the Courts. Great caution must, therefore, be exercised in attempting to extrapolate any general principles from recent decisions and this guidance does not purport to be definitive.

Local authority applications

3.37 A county council (where not a local planning authority) is required to make its applications for listed building consent to the relevant district planning authority, which should consider them against the normal criteria. Local planning authorities are normally required to make their own applications to the Secretary of State, whether or not they themselves own the listed building in question. The Secretaries of State ask authorities to deal with their own buildings in ways which will provide examples of good practice to other owners. It is particularly important that every effort should be made to maintain historic buildings in good condition, and to find appropriate new uses for buildings in authority ownership which are no longer in active use. Prompt disposal is important: empty buildings should not be retained on a contingency basis, with all the risk of neglect and disrepair that this can create.

3.38 The Secretary of State will be particularly concerned to ensure that local planning authorities take full account of the policies set out in this PPG, and will not be disposed to grant consent for the demolition of listed buildings in authorities' ownership unless there is clear and convincing evidence that alternative possibilities for new ownership and new uses have been thoroughly explored.

Churches and Crown buildings

3.39 Special provisions apply to ecclesiastical buildings in use for ecclesiastical purposes, which are in some circumstances exempt from listed building and conservation area controls. Details of the arrangements which apply to such buildings are given in section 8.

3.40 The Crown is currently exempt from listed building and conservation area controls; but the Government has undertaken that Crown bodies will normally operate as if these controls did apply (see Department of the Environment Circular 18/84). English Heritage should be notified of Crown developments on the same basis as normal applications. [Part 7 of the 2004 Act contains provisions removing] Crown exemption in planning and conservation matters[25]; pending [the coming into effect of those provisions], the arrangements in Circular 18/84 continue to apply.

3.41 Works by English Heritage on monuments, buildings or land which are owned by or in the care of [the Secretary of State for Culture, Media and Sport] and which they are managing on his behalf are treated as Crown development and the procedures in Circular 18/84 will apply. If English Heritage wishes to carry out works to other listed buildings, or demolish an unlisted building in a conservation area, it must obtain listed building or conservation area consent. The Secretary of State has directed that all such applications should be referred to him. The authority should advertise such applications as they would any other private application and forward any representations received, together with their own comments, to the appropriate regional Government Office.

Listed building consent for works already executed

3.42 Section 8(3) of the Act allows listed building consent to be sought even though the works have already been completed. Applications for consent to retain such works should follow the same procedures as other listed building consent applications and should contain sufficient information (see Annex B paragraph B.3[26]). Local planning authorities should not grant consent merely to recognise a *fait accompli*; they should consider whether they would have granted consent for the works had it been sought before they were carried out, while having regard to any subsequent matters which may be relevant. If the work is not of a suitable type or standard, consent should not normally be given, and the risk of prosecution or enforcement action will remain. If consent is granted, it is not retrospective; the works are authorised only from the date of the consent. A prosecution may still be brought for the initial offence.

Enforcement

3.43 If work is carried out without consent, a local planning authority can issue a listed building enforcement notice (section 38). The notice may (a) require the building to be brought back to its former state; or (b), if that is not reasonably practicable or desirable, require other works specified in the notice to alleviate the effects of the unauthorised works; or (c) require the building to be brought into the state it would have been in if the terms of

[25] [See **13.10.2**.]
[26] [Not reproduced in this book.]

any listed building consent had been observed. It was held in the case of *Bath City Council v Secretary of State for the Environment* [1983] JPL 737 that this provision could not be used to secure an improvement to a listed building compared to its state before the unauthorised works were carried out. There is a right of appeal to the Secretary of State against a notice; the appeal procedures are generally similar to those for enforcement of development control following the Planning and Compensation Act 1991, although there are no provisions equivalent to a planning contravention notice, nor is there any limitation on the period within which a listed building enforcement notice must be issued. If works subject to a listed building enforcement notice are later authorised under section 8(3), the enforcement notice will cease to have effect in relation to those works, although the liability to prosecution for an offence committed before the date of consent remains. Breach of a listed building enforcement notice is itself an offence, with financial penalties parallel to those for a breach of listed building control.

Prosecutions

3.44 It is a criminal offence to execute, or cause to be executed, without first obtaining listed building consent any works for the demolition [. . .][27] of a listed building or any works of alteration or extension which would affect its special interest, or to fail to comply with the terms of any condition attached to a consent (section 9). This includes the theft of architectural fixtures. The current penalty for conviction in a magistrates' court is a fine of up to £20,000 or imprisonment for up to six months (or both), whilst on conviction in the Crown Court an unlimited fine or a prison sentence of up to two years (or both) may be imposed. In determining the amount of any fine, a magistrates' court or the Crown Court must have regard to any financial benefit which has accrued or may accrue from the offence.

3.45 In proceedings for an offence under section 9 it is a defence to prove all of the following matters:

(a) that works to the building were urgently necessary in the interests of safety or health or for the preservation of the building;

(b) that it was not practicable to secure safety or health or, as the case may be, to preserve the building by works of repair or works for affording temporary support or shelter;

(c) that the works carried out were limited to the minimum measures immediately necessary; and

(d) that notice in writing justifying in detail the carrying out of the works was given to the local planning authority as soon as reasonably practicable.

3.46 Anyone—individuals as well as English Heritage and local planning authorities—can start proceedings. English Heritage and planning authorities can also seek injunctions for breaches of listed building control. A prosecution may also be initiated under section 59 where deliberate damage is caused to a listed building by an owner or his agent, for which financial penalties are provided.

3.47 Local planning authorities will obviously need to consider, when faced with a breach of listed building control, whether to take enforcement action or to prosecute or both. Enforcement may be intrinsically desirable for the benefit of the building in question, while the work entailed by enforcement may also represent a sufficient response to the offence. However, unauthorised work may often destroy historic fabric the special interest of which cannot be restored by enforcement. Moreover, well-publicised successful prosecutions can provide a valuable deterrent to wilful damage to, or destruction of, listed buildings, and it is

---

[27] [The words ", in whole or in part," were deleted by Environment Circ. 14/97, Appendix E.]

the Secretary of State's policy to encourage proceedings where it is considered that a good case can be sustained.

3.48 Prosecution and enforcement relate to breaches of listed building control that have already occurred. Where such a breach is continuing or there is good reason to suppose it is about to occur, authorities should consider seeking an injunction to stop or prevent it. Since a breach of listed building control (unlike development control) is itself a criminal offence, there is no need or statutory provision for stop notices. Authorities may, of course, find written warnings useful deterrents. Injunctions can be obtained speedily from the Court even where the actual or expected offender is not present before the Court, or indeed where his or her identity is not known; the essential ingredient is to satisfy the Court that the application is soundly based. In the case of an interim injunction the Court would normally ask the applicant to compensate the restrained party for any costs the latter might incur as a result of the interim injunction if the Court refuse to grant a final injunction. Anyone who refuses to comply with an injunction is in contempt of Court and may be fined or imprisoned (or both).

4. Conservation areas

4.1 Section 69 of the Act imposes a duty on local planning authorities to designate as conservation areas any "areas of special architectural or historic interest the character or appearance of which it is desirable to preserve or enhance". There are now more than 8,000 conservation areas in England.[28] Whilst listing procedures are focused on the protection of individual buildings, conservation area designation is the main instrument available to authorities to give effect to conservation policies for a particular neighbourhood or area. Designation introduces a general control over the demolition of unlisted buildings and provides the basis for policies designed to preserve or enhance all the aspects of character or appearance that define an area's special interest.

Assessment and designation of conservation areas

4.2 It is the quality and interest of areas, rather than that of individual buildings, which should be the prime consideration in identifying conservation areas. There has been increasing recognition in recent years that our experience of a historic area depends on much more than the quality of individual buildings—on the historic layout of property boundaries and thoroughfares; on a particular "mix" of uses; on characteristic materials; on appropriate scaling and detailing of contemporary buildings; on the quality of advertisements, shop fronts, street furniture and hard and soft surfaces; on vistas along streets and between buildings; and on the extent to which traffic intrudes and limits pedestrian use of spaces between buildings. Conservation area designation should be seen as the means of recognising the importance of all these factors and of ensuring that conservation policy addresses the quality of townscape in its broadest sense as well as the protection of individual buildings.

4.3 Local planning authorities also have under section 69 a duty to review their areas from time to time to consider whether further designation of conservation areas is called for. In some districts, areas suitable for designation may have been fully identified already; and in considering further designations authorities should bear in mind that it is important that conservation areas are seen to justify their status and that the concept is not devalued by the designation of areas lacking any special interest. Authorities should seek to establish consistent local standards for their designations and should periodically review existing conservation areas and their boundaries against those standards: cancellation of designa-

---

[28] [There were an estimated 9,140 conservation areas in England in 2004 (see *Heritage Counts 2004*, s.3.2.1).]

tion should be considered where an area or part of an area is no longer considered to possess the special interest which led to its original designation.

4.4 The more clearly the special architectural or historic interest that justifies designation is defined and recorded, the sounder will be the basis for local plan policies and development control decisions, as well as for the formulation of proposals for the preservation and enhancement of the character or appearance of an area. The definition of an area's special interest should derive from an assessment of the elements that contribute to (and detract from) it. Conservation areas vary greatly, but certain aspects will almost always form the basis for a coherent assessment: the topography—for example, thoroughfares and property boundaries—and its historical development; the archaeological significance and potential; the prevalent building materials; the character and hierarchy of spaces; the quality and relationship of buildings in the area and also of trees and other green features. The assessment should always note those unlisted buildings which make a positive contribution to the special interest of the area. More detailed advice on assessment and on other aspects of the management of conservation areas is set out in English Heritage's guidance note *Conservation Area Practice*[29].

4.5 The principal concern of a local planning authority in considering the designation of a conservation area should be to form a judgement on whether the area is of special archi-tectural or historic interest the character or appearance of which it is desirable to preserve or enhance. In deciding whether it is desirable to designate, an authority may take into account the resources likely to be required, not only for the administration of conservation area controls, but also for consultation with local residents and formulation of policies for a new area: without follow-up, designation is unlikely to be effective in itself. An authority's justification for designation, as reflected in its assessment of an area's special interest and its character and appearance, is a factor which the Secretary of State will take into account in considering appeals against refusals of conservation area consent for demolition, and appeals against refusals of planning permission (see also paragraph 2.9).

4.6 Given the nature of conservation area controls—essentially controls over demolition; strengthened controls over minor development; and the protection of trees—designation is not likely to be appropriate as a means of protecting landscape features, except where they form an integral part of the historic built environment and that factor needs to be taken into account in considering any planning applications which would affect them. The Courts have held that it is legitimate in appropriate circumstances to include within a conservation area the setting of buildings that form the heart of that area (*R. v Canterbury City Council, ex p Halford* [1992] 2 PLR 137). Designation is clearly not a proper means of controlling activities (e.g. agricultural operations) which do not fall within the definition of develop-ment. Designation may well, however, be suitable for historic parks or gardens and other areas of historic landscape containing structures that contribute to their special interest and that fall within the categories subject to conservation area controls. Where there are no other reasons for designating a conservation area, trees may instead be protected by means of a tree preservation order.

4.7 There is no statutory requirement to consult prior to designation or cancellation of designation, but it will be highly desirable that there should be consultation with local residents, businesses and other local interests (e.g. amenity bodies) over both the identifi-cation of areas and the definition of their boundaries. The greater the public support that can be enlisted for designation before it takes place, the more likely it is that policies for the area will be implemented voluntarily and without the need for additional statutory con-trols. Local planning authorities should advise English Heritage and the appropriate regional Government Office when conservation areas are designated.

---

[29] [English Heritage, 1993; now out of print. See also *Conservation Area Appraisals*, English Heritage, 2005.]

4.8 English Heritage and [the Secretary of State for Culture, Media and Sport] also have powers to designate conservation areas, but look to local planning authorities in the first instance to consider the case for designation. English Heritage's powers relate to London only, where they are required to consult the London borough council concerned and to obtain the Secretary of State's consent to designation. The Secretary of State must also consult the authorities concerned before using his powers of designation. His policy is to use his own powers only in exceptional cases, for instance where an area is of more than local interest; or where there is evidence to suggest that an authority's ownership of important buildings may have influenced a decision not to use its own powers, and there is a clear threat to the character or appearance of the area. The Secretary of State may also apply such criteria when requested to approve the use of English Heritage's powers.

Policies for conservation areas

4.9 Section 71 of the Act places a duty on local planning authorities to formulate and publish proposals for the preservation and enhancement of conservation areas. It is important that designation is not seen as an end in itself: policies will almost always need to be developed which clearly identify what it is about the character or appearance of the area which should be preserved or enhanced, and set out the means by which that objective is to be pursued. Clear assessment and definition of an area's special interest and the action needed to protect it will help to generate awareness and encourage local property owners to take the right sort of action for themselves.

4.10 The Act requires proposals for the preservation and enhancement of a conservation area to be submitted for consideration to a "public meeting" in the area, but wider consultation will almost always be desirable, both on the assessment of special interest and on proposals for the area. Consultation should be undertaken not only with local residents and amenity societies but also with chambers of commerce, public utilities, and the highway authority. The character and appearance of many conservation areas is heavily dependent on the treatment of roads, pavements and other public spaces (see paragraphs 5.13–5.18). It is important that conservation policies are fully integrated with other policies for the area, e.g. for shopping and traffic management. Account should also be taken of wider policies (e.g. for house renovation grants) which may affect the area's character or appearance. The preparation of local plans provides the best opportunity for integrating conservation policies with wider policies for the area, though a local planning authority's detailed statement of proposals for the conservation area should not itself be part of the development plan (see paragraphs 2.9 above and 4.15 below). Carefully targeted grant schemes using the authority's powers under section 57 of the Act to help with repair and enhancement should also be considered as part of the policy for an area. In certain cases English Heritage Conservation Area Partnership funding may be available.

Vacant premises over shops

4.11 Bringing vacant upper floors back into use, particularly residential use, not only provides additional income and security for the shop owner, but also helps to ensure that what are often important townscape buildings are kept in good repair it meets a widespread need for small housing units and helps to sustain activity in town centres after working hours. Local planning authorities are urged to develop policies to secure better use of vacant upper premises, e.g. by giving careful consideration to planning applications for shop conversions which would eliminate separate accesses to upper floors; by working with housing associations to secure residential conversions; and through the house renovation grant system.

Local information and consultation

4.12 Once policies for a particular area have been formulated, they should be made available to local residents and businesses in leaflet form, setting out clearly why the area has been designated; what its specially valuable features are; how individual householders can help to protect its character and appearance; and what additional controls and opportunities for assistance designation brings with it. Without such information, the support of local residents is not likely to be realised to the full. (English Heritage's guidance note on conservation areas gives advice on such publicity.)

4.13 Local planning authorities are asked to consider setting up conservation area advisory committees, both to assist in formulating policies for the conservation area (or for several areas in a particular neighbourhood), and also as a continuing source of advice on planning and other applications which could affect an area. Committees should consist mainly of people who are not members of the authority; local residential and business interests should be fully represented. In addition to local historical, civic and amenity societies, and local chambers of commerce, the authority may wish to seek nominations (depending on the character of the area) from national bodies such as the national amenity societies and the Civic Trust. Authorities should consider whether there is scope for the involvement of local people on a voluntary basis in practical work for the enhancement of an area.

Use of planning powers in conservation areas

4.14 Section 72 of the Act requires that special attention shall be paid in the exercise of planning functions to the desirability of preserving or enhancing the character or appearance of a conservation area. This requirement extends to all powers under the Planning Acts, not only those which relate directly to historic buildings. The desirability of preserving or enhancing the area should also, in the Secretary of State's view, be a material consideration in the planning authority's handling of development proposals which are outside the conservation area but would affect its setting, or views into or out of the area. Local planning authorities are required by section 73 to publish a notice of planning applications for development which would in their opinion affect the character or appearance of a conservation area.

4.15 The status now accorded to the development plan by [section 38 of the 2004 Act] makes it particularly important that an authority's policies for its conservation areas, insofar as they bear on the exercise of development controls, should be set out in the local plan. There should also be a clear indication of the relationship between the plan itself and detailed assessment documents or statements of proposals for particular conservation areas, making clear that development proposals will be judged for their effect on the character and appearance of the area as identified in the assessment document.

4.16 Many conservation areas include the commercial centres of the towns and villages of which they form part. While conservation (whether by preservation or enhancement) of their character or appearance must be a major consideration, this cannot realistically take the form of preventing all new development: the emphasis will generally need to be on controlled and positive management of change. Policies will need to be designed to allow the area to remain alive and prosperous, and to avoid unnecessarily detailed controls over businesses and householders, but at the same time to ensure that any new development accords with the area's special architectural and historic interest.

4.17 Many conservation areas include gap sites, or buildings that make no positive contribution to, or indeed detract from, the character or appearance of the area; their replacement should be a stimulus to imaginative, high quality design, and seen as an opportunity to enhance the area. What is important is not that new buildings should directly imitate earlier styles, but that they should be designed with respect for their context, as part of a larger whole which has a well-established character and appearance of its own.

4.18 Local planning authorities will often need to ask for detailed plans and drawings of proposed new development, including elevations which show the new development in its setting, before considering a planning application. In addition to adopted local plan policies, it may be helpful to prepare design briefs for individually important "opportunity" sites. Special regard should be had for such matters as scale, height, form, massing, respect for the traditional pattern of frontages, vertical or horizontal emphasis, and detailed design (e.g. the scale and spacing of window openings, and the nature and quality of materials). General planning standards should be applied sensitively in the interests of harmonising the new development with its neighbours in the conservation area.

4.19 The Courts have recently confirmed that planning decisions in respect of development proposed to be carried out in a conservation area must give a high priority to the objective of preserving or enhancing the character or appearance of the area. If any proposed development would conflict with that objective, there will be a strong presumption against the grant of planning permission, though in exceptional cases the presumption may be overridden in favour of development which is desirable on the ground of some other public interest.

4.20 As to the precise interpretation of "preserve or enhance", the Courts have held (*South Lakeland District Council v Secretary of State for the Environment* [1992] 2 WLR 204) that there is no requirement in the legislation that conservation areas should be protected from all development which does not enhance or positively preserve. Whilst the character and appearance of conservation areas should always be given full weight in planning decisions, the objective of preservation can be achieved either by development which makes a positive contribution to an area's character or appearance, or by development which leaves character and appearance unharmed.

Permitted development in conservation areas

4.21 The [General Permitted Development Order (GPDO)] requires planning applications for certain types of development in conservation areas which are elsewhere classified as permitted development. These include various types of cladding; the insertion of dormer windows into roof slopes; the erection of satellite dishes on walls, roofs or chimneys fronting a highway; and the installation of radio masts, antennae or radio equipment housing with a volume in excess of two cubic metres (unless the development is carried out in an emergency). The size of house and industrial extensions that may be carried out without specific planning permission is also more restricted.

4.22 On 30 March 1994 the Government announced a new proposal to enable local planning authorities to make directions withdrawing permitted development rights for a prescribed range of development materially affecting some aspects of the external appearance of dwellinghouses, such as doors, windows, roofs and frontages. There would be no requirement to obtain the Secretary of State's approval for such directions, but authorities would have to publicise their proposals in advance and have regard to the views of local people. Further details of these new arrangements will be published by circular shortly.

4.23 The withdrawal of permitted development rights outside these categories will continue to require Article 4 directions for which the Secretary of State's approval is generally needed before they can become effective. The Secretary of State takes the view that permitted development rights should not be withdrawn without clear justification and that, wherever possible, residents in conservation areas should continue to enjoy the same freedom to undertake development as residents elsewhere. He does not consider that the designation of a conservation area in itself automatically justifies making an Article 4 direction. Such directions may, however, have a role to play if they would help to protect features that are key elements of particular conservation areas and do not come within the categories that will be subject to the arrangements set out in paragraph 4.22 above. The

Secretary of State will generally be in favour of approving directions in conservation areas where these are backed by a clear assessment of an area's special architectural and historic interest, where the importance to that special interest of the features in question is established, where the local planning authority can demonstrate local support for the direction, and where the direction involves the minimum withdrawal of permitted development rights (in terms of both area and types of development) necessary to achieve its objective.

4.24 Sections 107 and 108 of the principal Act make provision for the payment of compensation in certain circumstances where permitted development rights have been withdrawn by an Article 4 direction or an amendment to [the GPDO].

Conservation area control over demolition

4.25 Conservation area designation introduces control over the demolition of most buildings within conservation areas (section 74 of the Act); exceptions are specified in section 75 and in the relevant direction. Applications for consent to demolish must be made to the local planning authority or, on appeal or call-in, to the Secretary of State. Procedures are essentially the same as for listed building consent applications. Authorities' own applications must be made to the Secretary of State. Scheduled ancient monuments are exempt from conservation area control: scheduled monument consent for proposed works must be sought from [the Secretary of State for Culture, Media and Sport] (see PPG 16).

4.26 In exercising conservation area controls, local planning authorities are required to pay special attention to the desirability of preserving or enhancing the character or appearance of the area in question; and, as with listed building controls, this should be the prime consideration in determining a consent application. In the case of conservation area controls, however, account should clearly be taken of the part played in the architectural or historic interest of the area by the building for which demolition is proposed, and in particular of the wider effects of demolition on the building's surroundings and on the conservation area as a whole.

4.27 The general presumption should be in favour of retaining buildings which make a positive contribution to the character or appearance of a conservation area. The Secretary of State expects that proposals to demolish such buildings should be assessed against the same broad criteria as proposals to demolish listed buildings (paragraphs 3.16–3.19 above). In less clear-cut cases—for instance, where a building makes little or no such contribution—the local planning authority will need to have full information about what is proposed for the site after demolition. Consent for demolition should not be given unless there are acceptable and detailed plans for any redevelopment. It has been held that the decision-maker is entitled to consider the merits of any proposed development in determining whether consent should be given for the demolition of an unlisted building in a conservation area.

[4.28 The House of Lords judgment in the recent case of *Shimizu (United Kingdom) Ltd v Westminster City Council* [1997] 1 All ER. 481 affected the long-accepted practice of interpreting the term "listed building" throughout the Planning (Listed Buildings and Conservation Areas) Act 1990 as including "part of a listed building". This means that whether work amounts to demolition or alteration of a listed building must be considered in the context of the whole of the listed building and that "demolition" refers to pulling down a building so that it is destroyed completely or [at] least to a very significant extent. It follows that a scheme of works which involves the demolition of part only of a listed building, falling short of the destruction of the whole listed building, will be works for alteration of the listed building and will not constitute demolition for the purposes of the Planning (Listed Buildings and Conservation Areas) Act 1990 unless they amount to a clearing of the site of the listed building for redevelopment.

4.28A Whether works are for demolition or alteration is still a matter of fact and degree in each case, to be decided in the light of guidance given by the House of Lords. Major works which comprise or include acts of demolition falling short of the complete destruction of a listed building, *e.g.* façade retention schemes, may still constitute works for demolition, therefore, depending on their extent. However, many works which were previously regarded as demolition, because they involved the destruction of part of the fabric of the building, will now fall into the category of alterations and will require consent only if they affect the building's character as a building of special architectural or historic interest. The demolition of a curtilage building is likely to fall within this category.

4.28B The House of Lords also considered that works for the demolition of an unlisted building in a conservation area must also involve the total or substantial destruction of the building concerned. This means that many works which involve the destruction of the fabric of part only of a building will not be works of demolition and will not require conservation area consent.][30]

4.29 It will often be appropriate to impose on the grant of consent for demolition a condition under section 17(3)of the Act, as applied by section 74(3), to provide that demolition shall not take place until a contract for the carrying out of works of redevelopment has been made and planning permission for those works has been granted. In the past, ugly gaps have sometimes appeared in conservation areas as a result of demolition far in advance of redevelopment.

Leasehold reform

4.30 The extended arrangements for leasehold enfranchisement under the Leasehold Reform, Housing and Urban Development Act 1993 included wider provisions for estate management schemes aimed at maintaining the appearance and amenity of areas currently under a single landlord's control. Schemes can be applied for by landlords or representative bodies such as residents' associations up to 30 October 1995 (in some exceptional cases later with the Secretary of State's agreement) and, when approved, transferred to local planning authorities or specially constituted bodies. Within conservation areas, schemes can by default be promoted by authorities or English Heritage between that deadline and 30 April 1996. The costs of management under such schemes fall to be met by the freeholders. In considering whether to approve a scheme the leasehold valuation tribunal is required to have regard *inter alia* to the past development and present character of the area and to architectural or historical considerations. Moreover, in conservation areas, applicants for schemes are required to notify English Heritage and the local planning authority and invite them to make representations to the tribunal. These provisions should enable authorities in appropriate cases to help maintain the appearance of an architecturally unified estate through regulation of the development, use and appearance of property beyond what can be enforced under the planning system (e.g. by regulating external decoration and cleaning), and through being able to require proper maintenance and repair of the structure and external elements of the buildings. Further information is available from English Heritage.

Advertisement control

4.31 All outdoor advertisements affect the appearance of the building or the neighbourhood where they are displayed. The main purpose of the advertisement control system is to help everyone involved in the display of outdoor advertising to contribute positively to the appearance of an attractive and cared-for environment. So it is reasonable to expect that the local planning authority's duty to pay special attention to the desirability of preserving or enhancing the character or appearance of a conservation area will result in practice in

---

[30] [The advice in these three paragraphs was substituted for the original para.4.28 by Environment Circ. 14/97, Appendix E. The new advice is also at Appendix D to DETR Circ. 01/01.]

applying more exacting standards when the authority consider whether to grant consent for a proposed advertisement in such an area.

4.32 In conservation areas it is important for local planning authorities to be sensitive in the use of their powers under the Town and Country Planning (Control of Advertisements) Regulations 1992, because many areas include retail and commercial premises, ranging from small corner-shops to thriving commercial centres. Outdoor advertising is essential to commercial activity in a free and diverse economy, and the success of local businesses will usually help owners and tenants of commercial premises to maintain buildings in good repair and attractive appearance.

4.33 Local planning authorities may wish to adopt advertisement control policies as part of their duty to formulate and publish proposals for the preservation and enhancement of conservation areas. Such policies can inform prospective advertisers about the type of displays likely to prove acceptable in an area; and they should provide a rational and consistent basis for decision-making on all advertisement control matters, including the serving of discontinuance notices.

4.34 Because of the special interest of most conservation areas, certain categories of "deemed consent" advertisements which may have a significant visual impact are not permitted for display in a conservation area without the local planning authority's specific consent. But a general prohibition of the display of certain classes of advertisement, or the withdrawal or limitation of those which may be displayed with deemed consent, is not usually justified solely because of designation.

4.35 Attention is drawn to the value of education and co-operation to help prevent unsympathetic advertisements. Local planning authorities may wish to consider mounting programmes, in association with local businesses, to promote advertisement policies by providing advice about the design and siting of suitable displays which respect the character and appearance of an area (either by the publication of design guidelines, the mounting of exhibitions, the setting-up of an advisory service in a Planning Department, or a combination of these approaches).

4.36 Where a local planning authority has pursued this approach, but considers that it has not prevented unsuitable or harmful advertisement displays, the Secretary of State will be prepared to consider making a direction under regulation 7 of the 1992 Regulations referred to above, if the authority can justify it. In seeking such additional control, authorities will be expected to show that they have well-formulated policies for the display of advertisements in the area and that the vigorous use of normal powers of control has proved inadequate. Similarly, when considering whether an advertisement is causing "substantial injury to amenity", so that its display should be discontinued, the Secretary of State will particularly consider any evidence, on appeal, that the authority have acted in accordance with a well-formulated advertisement control policy.

4.37 Further advice on outdoor advertisement control, including in conservation areas, is given in PPG 19.

Trees in conservation areas

4.38 Trees are valued features of our towns and countryside and make an important contribution to the character of the local environment. Under Part VIII of the principal Act, local planning authorities have a power to protect trees and woodlands in the interests of amenity by making tree preservation orders. In addition to this general power, authorities are under a duty to make adequate provision for the preservation and planting of trees when granting planning permission for the development of land. They do this by a combination of planning conditions and tree preservation orders.

4.39 Many trees in conservation areas are the subject of tree preservation orders, which means that the local planning authority's consent must be obtained before they can be cut down, topped or lopped. In addition to these controls, and in view of the contribution that trees can make to the character and appearance of a conservation area, the principal Act makes special provision for trees in conservation areas which are not the subject of tree preservation orders. Under section 211, subject to a range of exceptions, (including small trees and ones that are dead, dying or dangerous), anyone proposing to cut down, top or lop a tree in a conservation area is required to give six weeks' notice to the local planning authority. The purpose of this requirement is to give the authority an opportunity to consider bringing the tree under their general control by making a tree preservation order in respect of it. Penalties for contravention, which may include a requirement to replant, are similar to those for tree preservation orders. For guidance on these matters see [*Tree Preservation Orders: A Guide to the Law and Good Practice*, DETR, 2000].

4.40 When considering whether to extend protection to trees in conservation areas, local planning authorities should always take into account the visual, historic and amenity contribution of trees. In some instances new plantings or re-plantings may be desirable where this would be consistent with the character and appearance of the area.

5. Transport and traffic management

5.1 The Government's commitment to sustainable development entails greater integration of transport with other aspects of land-use planning in order to reduce the need for travel, to moderate future traffic growth, and to minimise the environmental impacts of transport. This may lead to a greater concentration of development on existing centres, including historic towns. In developing policies and projects it is essential, therefore, that local highway and planning authorities take full account of the wider costs of transport choices, including impact on the historic environment.

5.2 Major new transport infrastructure developments can have an especially wide-ranging impact on the historic environment, not just visually and physically, but indirectly, for example, by altering patterns of movement or commerce and generating new development pressures or opportunities in historic areas. Local highway and planning authorities should therefore integrate their activities and should take great care to avoid or minimise impacts on the various elements of the historic environment and their settings.

5.3 The Secretaries of State also attach particular importance to early consultation on traffic management and highway maintenance schemes, and associated development proposals which would affect listed buildings or conservation areas or parks, gardens or battlefields and their settings. Local highway and planning authorities should take great care to assess the impact on existing roads of new projects, e.g. for the rerouting of traffic or for pedestrianisation. They are urged to seek the advice of English Heritage, where appropriate, before determining any such proposals.

New traffic routes

5.4 When contemplating a new route, authorities should consider whether the need for it, and any impact on the environment, might be obviated by an alternative package of transport management such as parking and charging policies, park-and-ride schemes, and public transport priority. New roads should not be built just to facilitate more commuting into already congested areas. This is especially true in historic towns where the character and layout cannot easily absorb radical changes such as new roads.

5.5 If a new route is unavoidable, authorities should initially identify any features of the historic environment—including parks, gardens, battlefields and archaeological sites as well as buildings and areas—and evaluate their importance. Wherever possible, new roads (and any other transport infrastructure) should be kept away from listed buildings, conservation areas and other historic sites. However, in each case a suitable balance has to be struck between conservation, other environmental concerns, economics, safety and engineering feasibility. Highway and planning authorities should set common objectives wherever possible and are advised to consult each other about transport proposals affecting historic areas. Such proposals are subject to the same constraints as other major development proposals in areas of protection, and authorities will have to obtain listed building consent or conservation area consent where appropriate. Further advice is given in PPG 13 on how authorities should seek to manage demand and improve the attractiveness of local centres through their transport and planning policies.

5.6 Where work to listed structures or those in conservation areas, such as historic bridges, is needed to meet new national or European requirements, this should be carried out with great care. Many bridges are of considerable age and represent important features of the cultural heritage. Their survival to this day owes a great deal to the care of past generations, and, where remedial or strengthening works are found to be necessary, proposals should seek to retain the character of these structures for the benefit of future generations. Traditional materials should only be replaced where it can be proved that this is essential in the interests of structural stability. Sympathetic remedial measures, which restore the carrying capacity and extend the life of these structures while retaining their character, are preferable to complete reconstruction, and will normally prove more cost-effective. Authorities are urged to consider sympathetic alterations where necessary to carry heavier traffic, or, where new construction is the only realistic course, to retain and restore the old structure for use by pedestrians and cyclists. Authorities are also urged to exercise flexibility over the design of parapets on historic bridges.

5.7 When the opportunity occurs, the possibility of reusing structures for new transport schemes should always be examined. Disused railway viaducts and bridges provide an environmentally advantageous solution for such schemes, in both rural and urban areas, especially in environmentally sensitive areas. The restoration and conversion of historic structures such as these can be a positive benefit from a transport scheme.

Schemes promoted under the Transport and Works Act 1992

5.8 Since 1 January 1993, when Part I of the Transport and Works Act 1992 came into force, proposals which would have previously been authorised under private Bill procedure have instead had to be authorised by Orders made under that Act. Such proposals include the construction or operation of railways, tramways, trolley vehicle systems, other guided transport systems, inland waterways, and structures interfering with rights of navigation. The Act brings the procedures for authorising such schemes more into line with those which have applied for years to highways projects. If the relevant Secretary of State decides to make an Order under the Act, he may at the same time direct that planning permission be deemed to be granted for the proposal, to the extent to which it involves carrying out any development.

5.9 Where the proposal involves works to a listed building, or demolition of an unlisted building in a conservation area, a separate application must be made to the local planning authority for listed building consent or conservation area consent respectively. The regulations which normally apply to such consent applications are subject to minor modifications so that they may more easily be progressed in parallel with the application for the related order. These changes are set out in the Transport and Works Applications (Listed Buildings, Conservation Areas and Ancient Monuments Procedures) Regulations 1992. An application for listed building or conservation area consent made concurrently with an application for an order under the 1992 Act will automatically be referred by the local planning authority to the Secretary of State for the Environment for his decision, without the need for any specific direction. Where there is need for a public local inquiry, the related applications will be considered at a concurrent inquiry. This means that one Inspector will be able to make mutually compatible recommendations about the different applications.

5.10 A fuller description of these concurrent procedures (together with the procedure for applications under the 1992 Act generally) is set out in the Department of Transport publication *Transport and Works Act 1992: A Guide to Procedures*[31].

Roads in centres or settlements

5.11 Local highway authorities should take measures to protect the historic environment from the worst effects of traffic. They have powers to create vehicle-restricted areas or pedestrian zones and to introduce traffic-calming measures where appropriate. However, there is increasing recognition that in some historic areas the total exclusion of traffic combined with extensive pedestrianisation can create sterile precincts, particularly at night. In some cases, it may be preferable to consider limited access at selected times for all traffic or particular classes of traffic (e.g. buses, trams, service vehicles), or shared streets and other spaces designed to encourage motorists to modify their driving behaviour when mixing with pedestrians. Park and Ride schemes may also have a part to play in areas where it is desirable to limit car access to historic centres and conservation areas. Advice is available in the English Historic Towns Forum publication *Bus-based Park and Ride: Good Practice Guide*[32]. All these measures, together with encouraging a variety of uses on the ground floors of developments, can help to increase the attractiveness of town centres, and will also help to meet the policy objectives of PPG 6 and PPG 13, and Department of the Environment Circular 5/94.

5.12 Vehicle restrictions and traffic-calming measures can often be effective in reducing the speeds at which people choose to drive. The Department of Transport issues advice on pedestrianisation and a range of traffic-calming features which may be introduced. The Highways (Traffic Calming) Regulations [1999] give authorities the flexibility to use a wide variety of traffic-calming features, in addition to road humps, which can constrain vehicle speeds. These include chicanes, build-outs, pinch points, gateways, rumble devices, islands and overrun areas. However, some designs can be difficult to integrate into an older streetscape and there can be no standard solution. Each feature or device should relate in its design and materials to the overall townscape to ensure that traffic-calming reinforces rather than diminishes local character. Traffic-calming measures using a combination of traditional materials and devices may help to secure the right balance. For instance, the use of traditional cobbles or stone setts may prove effective in keeping down traffic speeds, though they are likely to increase levels of road surface noise; they will also not always find favour with cyclists and disabled people. Authorities should also consult with the emergency services before laying such surfaces to ensure that their response times are not unduly increased. Advice is available to local authorities in the English Historic Towns Forum publication *Traffic Measures in Historic Towns*[33]. Authorities should consider the extent to which these different kinds of traffic-calming measures need to be signed, and ensure that signing is kept to the minimum necessary to ensure safety and comply with legal requirements.

Floorscape and street furniture

5.13 Floorscape and street furniture often make a vital contribution to the appearance of a conservation area. Traditional stone, or in some cases brick, surfaces and layouts should be retained wherever possible, or re-introduced where there is historical evidence for them. In particular, where there is a tradition of rectangular slab paving, small block paviours and arbitrary new patterns should be avoided. In many small towns and villages, rammed earth, hoggin or aggregate, in modern times finished with tarmac, was always the traditional

---

[31]   [A new edition of the *Guide* was issued to take account of changed inquiry procedures taking effect in August 2004.]

[32]   [Second edition, 2000.]

[33]   [EHTF, 1994. See also *Transport Demand Management—A Guide to Management*, EHTF, 1999.]

surface. Tarmac, preferably dressed with a suitable local aggregate, remains an appropriate and inexpensive finish for many conservation areas. Wherever practical, natural earth, hoggin, or aggregate footpaths or drives should be retained and protected for their semi-rural character. If a street is to be pedestrianised, it is important to retain the traditional relationship between footways and carriageway, including kerb lines. Wall-to-wall surfaces are often unsuitable and the scale, texture, colour and laying patterns of any new materials should be sympathetic to the area's appearance.

5.14 In certain circumstances grants may be available from English Heritage towards the cost of street improvement schemes which incorporate the use of traditional paving features. English Heritage's publication *Street Improvements in Historic Areas*[34] offers guidance on the treatment of streets and public open spaces in historic areas, to encourage wider recognition of the important contribution they make to townscape quality. The New Roads and Street Works Act 1991 makes statutory undertakers responsible for carrying out the permanent reinstatement of the highway where they disturb it. They are now required to reinstate the same materials as previously existed, or the closest possible match if the materials cannot be reused. Local authorities play an important role in ensuring that statutory undertakers and their contractors carry out reinstatement to an appropriate specification and timetable.

5.15 Even the smallest towns contain a wealth of street furniture of historic or architectural interest, such as pillar boxes, telephone kiosks, drinking fountains, railings, clocks and many others, often of local distinctiveness. The appearance of historic streets can be improved by preserving or reinstating such items where appropriate (see *Street Improvements in Historic Areas*). Authorities contemplating modern tramway systems should consider the effects that catenary supports and other associated street furniture and electrical equipment may have on historic streetscapes.

5.16 Road signs and markings can also have a significant impact on a street's appearance. These should be of an appropriate character and quality, without unnecessary duplication of signs and posts. Wherever possible signs should be fixed to existing posts or street furniture. Traffic signs are only needed to direct drivers to their desired destinations or to particular facilities, warn them of hazards and indicate mandatory requirements. Signs which do none of these things may not be necessary at all, and much can be done to eliminate sign clutter simply by removing redundant signs, or by combining separate signs onto a single backing board. Regular "street audits" are valuable and local amenity societies may be able to help with these. Further advice is available in *Traffic Measures in Historic Towns*. Where the Traffic Signs Regulations[35] and the Department of Transport's *Traffic Signs Manual*[36] provide for some degree of flexibility in size, siting and colour, authorities should take advantage of this in historic areas. Parking restriction signs in particular can be sited on buildings where appropriate, thus eliminating the need in many cases for a pole with a single sign. Authorities' attention is drawn to the flexibility permitted in respect of no-waiting lines: a narrower line of a different colour is permitted in environmentally sensitive areas. Consideration should be given to applying waiting restrictions to areas, where appropriate, and removing yellow lines.

5.17 Authorities should seek advice on the selection and positioning of street lighting equipment appropriate to the age and character of the surrounding area. The Department of Transport publication *Road Lighting and the Environment*[37], for example, provides helpful advice. High pressure sodium lamps (with controlled light spillage) may be preferable in environmentally sensitive areas as they provide a whiter light with a more natural rendition of colour. Off-the-peg "period" columns and lanterns are not universally

---

[34] [English Heritage, 1993. Now out of print.]
[35] [SI 2002/3113 (The Stationery Office, 2003).]
[36] [Department of Transport, 2003 (The Stationery Office).]
[37] [1993. Now out of print.]

appropriate in historic areas. Special designs reflecting established local styles or motifs, or simple modern designs, may be preferable.

5.18 The effects of road works and other transport projects on trees in conservation areas, or trees which form part of the setting of listed buildings, can be particularly damaging. Authorities should stress the need for statutory undertakers and others to take care when excavating, or diverting services, near existing trees in order to avoid damage to roots. Where root damage occurs, this may not show in a tree's health for several years.

PART 2

6. Identifying and recording the historic environment

[NOTE: the Government proposes to replace the existing paras 6.1 to 6.9, set out below, with revised guidance, slightly updated to reflect recent thinking about the management of the historic environment and in particular the importance of treating different components of the historic environment in a holistic way.[38]]

6.1 In its broadest sense, the historic environment embraces all those aspects of the country that reflect the shaping hand of human history. Scarcely any part of England is untouched by the interaction between people and nature which has taken place over thousands of years. Some of the most obvious features of this environment are historic buildings. England is exceptionally rich in these—great churches, houses, and civic buildings—but our understanding of the historic environment now encompasses a much wider range of features, and in particular stresses the relationship between individual buildings, and also the value of historic townscape and landscape as a whole.

6.2 There is growing appreciation not just of the architectural set pieces, but of many more structures, especially industrial, agricultural and other vernacular buildings that, although sometimes individually unassuming, collectively reflect some of the most distinctive and creative aspects of English history. More than this, our understanding and appreciation of the historic environment now stretches beyond buildings to the spaces and semi-natural features which people have also moulded, and which are often inseparable from the buildings themselves. For example, the pattern of roads and open spaces and the views they create within historic townscapes may be as valuable as the buildings. In the countryside, the detailed patterns of fields and farms, of hedgerows and walls, and of hamlets and villages, are among the most highly valued aspects of our environment. England is particularly rich in the designed landscapes of parks and gardens, and the built and natural features they contain: the greatest of these are as important to national, and indeed international, culture as are our greatest buildings.

6.3 Processes of classification are necessary for the practical purposes of identifying and protecting individual sites and areas. This is achieved through the statutory systems for scheduling ancient monuments, listing historic buildings and designating conservation areas. Scheduling and listing are undertaken by the Secretary of State; designation of conservation areas is the responsibility of local planning authorities. In addition, English Heritage compiles registers of parks and gardens of special historic interest, and of historic battlefields. Identified in these ways, the historic environment may be protected through the development control system and, in the case of listed buildings and conservation areas, through the complementary systems of listed building and conservation area control.

6.4 The first part of this PPG explained how these control systems work, and how they relate to the broader planning system for development control. This part of the PPG sets

---

[38] *[Revisions to Principles of Selection for Listing Buildings: PPG 15,* issued by DCMS for consultation, July 2005; see **3.2.5**.]

out Government policy for the listing of historic buildings, and for the identification of certain other aspects of the historic environment. It also gives guidance on the upkeep of historic buildings, and on the powers available to local authorities and to the Secretary of State to secure repairs to neglected historic buildings.

6.5 Archaeology plays an essential role in informing and widening our understanding of the historic environment. Many important sites and structures of archaeological interest are identified and protected through the statutory schedule of ancient monuments maintained by the [Department of Culture, Media and Sport]. The principles of selection are set out in PPG 16. Other known sites are included in the National Monuments Record of [English Heritage][39], and in county sites and monuments records.

Historic buildings

6.6 Historic buildings listed by the Secretary of State under section 1 of the Act are placed in one of three grades to give an indication of their relative importance. The current listing position in England is (to the nearest thousand):

List Entries (England, 1993)[40]

Grade I	9,000	(2%)
Grade II*	19,000	(4%)
Grade II	416,000	(94%)
	443,000	

About 500,000 individual buildings are estimated to be protected: some list entries cover several buildings. Some churches in older lists are still Grades A, B and C (which in the context of planning and listed building consent applications should all be treated in the same way as Grade I and II* buildings). Gradings can be changed following revaluation after damage or alteration, or as more evidence of a building's history comes to light.

Identification of buildings for listing

6.7 Buildings are added to the statutory lists in two main ways:

(i) as a result of systematic resurvey or review of particular areas or building types; or

(ii) following proposals from local authorities, amenity societies or other bodies or individuals that particular buildings should be added to the list ("spot listing").

6.8 Before including buildings in the statutory lists the Secretary of State is required to consult English Heritage and such other persons as he may consider appropriate as having special knowledge of, or interest in, buildings of architectural or historic interest. Expert advisers appointed by English Heritage normally visit and report on buildings before they are listed. In the case of systematic resurveys and reviews there will normally be close consultation between English Heritage and the local planning authority before recommendations for listing are submitted to the Secretary of State. Wherever possible the Secretary of State will consider the views of others, but it is not his practice to advertise proposals for new listings.

6.9 The number of listed buildings has increased fourfold since 1970 as a result of 24 years' work to resurvey England's built heritage. Some of the lists deriving from the earlier years of the resurvey are currently being reviewed, but the priority in future will be on more precisely targeted, research-based studies of particular building types which are known to be under-represented in the lists, rather than area surveys.

---

[39] [Substituted by DETR Circ. 01/01, Appendix B.]
[40] [For current figures, see **3.2**.]

Principles of selection

[NOTE: the Government proposes to replace the existing paras 6.10 to 6.16, set out below, with revised guidance. The general principles are to remain largely unchanged, although they are to be redrafted in places to try and make them clearer. Those principles are to be illustrated with detailed criteria for listing relating to 20 specific building types.[41]]

6.10 The following are the main criteria which the Secretary of State applies as appropriate in deciding which buildings to include in the statutory lists:

architectural interest: the lists are meant to include all buildings which are of importance to the nation for the interest of their architectural design, decoration and craftsmanship; also important examples of particular building types and techniques (e.g. buildings displaying technological innovation or virtuosity) and significant plan forms;

historic interest: this includes buildings which illustrate important aspects of the nation's social, economic, cultural or military history;

close historical association: with nationally important people or events;

group value, especially where buildings comprise an important architectural or historic unity or a fine example of planning (e.g. squares, terraces or model villages).

Not all these criteria will be relevant to every case, but a particular building may qualify for listing under more than one of them.

6.11 Age and rarity are relevant considerations, particularly where buildings are proposed for listing on the strength of their historic interest. The older a building is, and the fewer the surviving examples of its kind, the more likely it is to have historic importance. Thus, all buildings built before 1700 which survive in anything like their original condition are listed; and most buildings of about 1700 to 1840 are listed, though some selection is necessary. After about 1840, because of the greatly increased number of buildings erected and the much larger numbers that have survived, greater selection is necessary to identify the best examples of particular building types, and only buildings of definite quality and character are listed. For the same reasons, only selected buildings from the period after 1914 are normally listed. Buildings which are less than 30 years old are normally listed only if they are of outstanding quality and under threat. Buildings which are less than ten years old are not listed.

6.12 The approach adopted for twentieth century listing is to identify key exemplars for each of a range of building types industrial, educational, residential, etc.—and to treat these exemplars as broadly defining a standard against which to judge proposals for further additions to the list. This approach has already been successfully applied to the inter-war period, and English Heritage is now engaged on a three-year research programme to extend it to the post-war period (subject to the "30 year rule" mentioned above). Proposals for listings in each building type will be made as each stage of the research is completed.

Selectivity

6.13 Where a building qualifies for listing primarily on the strength of its intrinsic architectural quality or its group value, the fact that there are other buildings of similar quality elsewhere is not likely to be a major consideration. But, as noted above, the listing of buildings primarily for historical reasons is to a greater extent a comparative exercise, and needs to be selective where a substantial number of buildings of a similar type and quality survive. In such cases the Secretary of State's aim will be to list the best examples of the type which are of special historic interest.

---

[41] [*Revisions to Principles of Selection for Listing Buildings: PPG 15*, issued by DCMS for consultation, July 2005; see **3.2.5**.]

Aesthetic merits

6.14 The external appearance of a building—both its intrinsic architectural merit and any group value—is a key consideration in judging listing proposals, but the special interest of a building will not always be reflected in obvious visual quality. Buildings which are important for reasons of technological innovation, or as illustrating particular aspects of social or economic history, may well have little external visual quality.

Historical associations

6.15 Well-documented historical associations of national importance will increase the case for the inclusion of a building in the statutory list. They may justify a higher grading than would otherwise be appropriate, and may occasionally be the deciding factor. But in the Secretary of State's view there should normally be some quality or interest in the physical fabric of the building itself to justify the statutory protection afforded by listing. Either the building should be of some architectural merit in itself, or it should be well preserved in a form which directly illustrates and confirms its historical associations (e.g. because of the survival of internal features). Where otherwise unremarkable buildings have historical associations, the Secretary of State's view is that they are normally best commemorated by other means (e.g. by a plaque), and that listing will be appropriate only in exceptional cases.

National and local interest

6.16 The emphasis in these criteria is on national significance, though this cannot be defined precisely. For instance, the best examples of local vernacular building types will normally be listed. But many buildings which are valued for their contribution to the local scene, or for local historical associations, will not merit listing. Such buildings will often be protected by conservation area designation (see paragraphs 4.2 ff). It is also open to planning authorities to draw up lists of locally important buildings, and to formulate local plan policies for their protection, through normal development control procedures. But policies should make clear that such buildings do not enjoy the full protection of statutory listing.

[NOTE: the Government proposes to cancel the existing paras 6.17 to 6.40, as they relate to procedure rather than policy, and have in any event been overtaken by the procedural and administrative changes at the DCMS and English Heritage.[42]*]*

7. The upkeep and repair of historic buildings

7.1 Regular maintenance and repair are the key to the preservation of historic buildings. Modest expenditure on repairs keeps a building weathertight, and routine maintenance (especially roof repairs and the regular clearance of gutters and downpipes) can prevent much more expensive work becoming necessary at a later date. It is a common misunderstanding that historic buildings have a fixed lifespan, and that gradual decay of their fabric is inevitable. On the contrary, unless there are intrinsic defects of design or materials, the lifespan of a historic building may be indefinite provided that timely maintenance, and occasional major repairs such as the renewal of roof coverings and other features, are regularly undertaken. Major problems are very often the result of neglect and, if tackled earlier, can be prevented or reduced in scale. Regular inspection is invaluable.

---

[42] [*Revisions to Principles of Selection for Listing Buildings: PPG 15*, issued by DCMS for consultation, July 2005; see **3.2.5**.]

7.2 The effective use of local planning authorities' controls set out in Part 1 is essential, but it will not of itself prevent historic buildings falling into neglect or disuse. The timely use of urgent works and repairs notice powers, described below, should always be considered, but authorities' resources for conservation will be used to best effect if some are devoted to identifying buildings at risk—from neglect or inappropriate changes—as early as possible and providing advice, encouragement and (where appropriate) grants to owners. Monitoring listed buildings, and unlisted buildings which make a positive contribution to conservation areas, by means of simple, regularly updated condition surveys is a valuable element of this approach. Dated photographs will provide a record of changes (and useful evidence in the event of statutory action being needed). Positive involvement of this kind by authorities will help prevent unnecessary loss of historic fabric, not to mention the probable cost and discord of action at a later stage.

7.3 The theft of architectural features, statuary, monuments and specialist materials has increased in recent years, and local authorities and owners are recommended to take precautions to safeguard them, especially when historic buildings are vacant or being refurbished. This may involve careful removal for safe and secure storage on site. Theft is a criminal offence and adequate records and photographs of vulnerable items will help the police recover them if stolen.

Repair

7.4 There is no specific duty on owners to keep their buildings in a good state of repair (though it will normally be in their interests to do so), but local authorities have powers to take action where a historic building has deteriorated to the extent that its preservation may be at risk. These powers take two forms.

Urgent works

7.5 Section 54 of the Act enables a local authority (or English Heritage in London) to carry out urgent works for the preservation of listed buildings in their area after giving notice to the owner. These powers can be used only in respect of an unoccupied building, or the unused part of a partly occupied building. Section 76 of the Act enables the Secretary of State to direct (after consulting English Heritage) that the powers shall apply to an unlisted building in a conservation area if it appears to him that its preservation is important for maintaining the character or appearance of that area. The Secretary of State will consider sympathetically the making of such a direction in respect of an unlisted building which makes a positive contribution to a conservation area. Authorities or members of the public may ask the Secretary of State to make such a direction; such requests should be supported by evidence confirming the importance of the building.

7.6 The Secretary of State can also exercise these powers himself, but under the terms of the legislation he must authorise English Heritage to give notice and carry out the works on his behalf. His policy is to use his powers only in exceptional cases, for instance where a building is of exceptional interest or is in local authority ownership; or where a conservation area is of more than local interest and either the building in question is so important to the area that failure to carry out urgent works to it would seriously damage the character or appearance of the area, or the building, as well as meeting the basic section 76 criterion, in local authority ownership. In all such cases he would normally only consider the use of his own powers where the local authority concerned has decided not to take action itself.

7.7 Authorities will note that these powers are confined to *urgent* works: in the Secretary of State's view, their use should be restricted to emergency repairs, for example works to keep a building wind- and weather-proof and safe from collapse, or action to prevent vandalism or theft. The steps taken should be the minimum consistent with achieving this objective, and should not involve an owner in great expense. English Heritage has published [*Stop-*

ping the Rot: a Guide to Serving Urgent Works and Repairs Notices,[43] which includes advice on methods of temporary repair.

7.8 Local authorities (or English Heritage in London, or the Secretary of State) may recover from owners the cost of urgent works carried out under these provisions, subject to the owner's right to make representations to the Secretary of State. Representations may be made on the grounds that some or all of the works were unnecessary; that temporary arrangements have continued for an unreasonable length of time; or that amounts are unreasonable or their recovery would cause hardship. The Secretary of State will take all such representations into account before determining the amount to be recovered, and will be particularly concerned to establish whether the works carried out were the minimum required to secure the building's preservation and prevent further deterioration. If an authority intends to attempt to recover the cost of the works, the financial circumstances of the owner should be taken into account at the outset and any sums the authority wishes to recover from an owner should not be unreasonable in relation to his or her means.

Repairs notices

7.9 If a local planning authority (or English Heritage in London) considers that a listed building is not being properly preserved, it may serve a repairs notice on the owner (under section 48 of the Act). This notice must specify the works which the authority considers reasonably necessary for the proper preservation of the building, and must explain the relevant provisions of the legislation, which are described briefly below. These powers are not confined to urgent works or to unoccupied buildings, and authorities should consider their use in cases where protracted failure by an owner to keep a listed building in reasonable repair places the building at risk.

7.10 A House of Lords judgment (*Robbins v Secretary of State for the Environment* [1989] 1 All ER 878) has provided guidance on the nature of the works which may properly be specified in a repairs notice. The judgment held that, while the definition of works reasonably necessary for the proper preservation of the building will always relate to the circumstances of the individual case, and involve judgments about what is reasonable, the word "preservation" has to be given its ordinary meaning in contrast to "restoration", and this imposes an objective limitation which must be applied in considering the scope of works to be specified in a notice. The judgment also made clear that a notice can include works for the preservation of a building having regard to its condition at the date when it was listed: in other words, where a building has suffered damage or disrepair since being listed, the repairs notice procedure can be used to secure the building's preservation as at the date of listing, but should not be used to restore other features. If, however, repairs are necessary to preserve what remains of the rest of the building—for example, to a roof that was defective at the time of listing—it is legitimate, in the Secretary of State's view, to include them in a repairs notice.

7.11 Repairs notice powers may also be exercised by the Secretary of State, but, as with urgent works, his policy is to treat these powers essentially as reserve powers, and to use them only in exceptional circumstances. It is not open to the Secretary of State to authorise the use of repairs notices in respect of unlisted buildings in conservation areas.

Compulsory acquisition of listed buildings in need of repair

7.12 If at least two months have elapsed following the service of a repairs notice, and it appears to the body who served the notice that reasonable steps are not being taken for the proper preservation of the building, they may begin compulsory purchase proceedings. Compulsory purchase orders (CPOs) made by a local planning authority or by English Heritage require the Secretary of State's confirmation, and the Secretary of State must

---

[43] [Published in 1998, available at *www.english-heritage.org.uk*]

consult English Heritage before making an order himself or confirming an authority's order. In making or confirming an order, the Secretary of State must be satisfied that it is expedient to make provision for the preservation of the building and to authorise its compulsory acquisition for that purpose. The Secretary of State will also need to be satisfied that the means and the resources necessary for securing the building's repair will be available. A listed building CPO may also include land which an authority wishes to acquire for the purposes of access, amenity or management in connection with the building ("relevant land" in the Act).

7.13 The Secretary of State considers that privately owned historic buildings should, wherever possible, remain in the private sector. Local planning authorities are encouraged to identify a private individual or body, such as a building preservation trust, which has access to funds to carry out the necessary repairs and to which the building will be sold on as quickly as possible. Suitable covenants should be negotiated to ensure that repairs will be carried out by a purchaser. Authorities should be aware that where they wish to acquire a listed building pass it on, "back to back" deals are possible. These are [. . .] set out in [the Local Authorities (Capital Finance and Accounting) (England) Regulations 2003]. Authorities are reminded that where a historic building is disposed of (either by freehold sale or long lease) within two years of its acquisition (or, where disposal was contracted for, but not implemented, in that period, within three years of acquisition), and the price received on resale is no more than the price paid, use of the capital receipt is unrestricted. Acquisitions under arrangements for immediate onward sale should, therefore, have no adverse financial implications for the authority, though there will clearly be other resource costs involved in securing confirmation of a CPO.

7.14 Any person who has an interest in a listed building which a local planning authority wishes to acquire compulsorily, and who has been served with a notice under the Acquisition of Land Act 1981, may apply to a magistrates' court for an order staying further proceedings on the compulsory purchase order. If an applicant is aggrieved by the decision of the magistrates' court, he or she may appeal to the Crown Court. Authorities should also be aware that where a compulsory purchase order is objected to, and a local public inquiry held (and also where representations against the recovery of expenses for works carried out under section 54 are heard as part of a related planning matter), the Secretary of State may make an order as to the costs of the parties at the inquiry (see Department of the Environment Circular 8/93).

General considerations

7.15 The possible need to follow up with a CPO is clearly something which local planning authorities should take into account when contemplating repairs notice action. But the following are also relevant considerations:

a recent study (*Listed Building Repairs Notices*[44]) has shown that in over 60 per cent of cases authorisation or formal service of a notice was itself sufficient to prompt owners either to begin repairs or to sell the building in question on to a third party: in only 13 per cent of cases did the matter reach a CPO inquiry;

the purpose of compulsory purchase is to ensure that reasonable steps are taken for properly preserving a listed building: it is not a requirement that the local authority should itself carry out the repairs or pay for them. Indeed in the Secretary of State's view it is preferable, as stated in paragraph 7.13 above, for the authority to obtain a firm commitment from a private purchaser to repair the building and meet the costs (perhaps with the assistance of any relevant grant-aid available);

[44] [By Bob Kindred; published by the Association of Conservation Officers (the predecessor of the Institute of Historic Building Conservation) in 1992.]

the Act contains provisions for minimum compensation where an owner has deliberately allowed a building to fall into disrepair in order to justify its demolition and secure permission for redevelopment of the site (section 50 of the Act); minimum compensation should however be sought only where there is clear evidence of such an intention;

where the minimum compensation provisions do not apply, normal market value rules apply (as laid down in the Land Compensation Act 1961); but even here, high costs of repair, combined with limited possibilities for development, may indicate a very low or even nominal value.

Authorities also have powers under section 52 of the Act to acquire land and buildings by agreement.

8. Churches and the ecclesiastical exemption

8.1 Ecclesiastical buildings are fully subject to planning control, but ecclesiastical buildings which are for the time being used for ecclesiastical purposes are exempt from listed building and conservation area controls, except in so far as the Secretary of State provides otherwise by Order under section 60(5) and 75(7) of the Act. Ecclesiastical exemption does not apply to the residences of ministers of religion (section 60(3)).

8.2 The context of the exemption is provided by an undertaking by the Church of England that its historic buildings would be subject to a separate Church system of control which took account of the historical and architectural importance of churches. This system, known as faculty jurisdiction, has developed over time, in particular in a series of ecclesiastical measures passed by the General Synod and approved by Parliament, and in subordinate arrangements approved by the General Synod; a separate system covers Church of England cathedrals. The exemption has, however, extended to ecclesiastical buildings of all denominations, not just those of the Church of England.

8.3 Following public consultation in 1992 the Secretary of State, in conjunction with the Secretary of State for Wales, announced that an Order would be made to provide that the exemption would in future apply only to the Church of England and to other denominations and faiths which set up acceptable internal systems of control embodying the principles set out in the Government's code of practice. The Ecclesiastical Exemption (Listed Buildings and Conservation Areas) Order 1994 has now been made and [came] into force on 1 October 1994.

Code of practice for denominations' internal control systems

8.4 The Government's code comprises the following points:

1. proposals for relevant works should be submitted by the local congregation or minister for the approval of a body independent of them;

2. that body should include, or have arrangements for obtaining advice from, people with expert knowledge of historic church buildings;

3. the decision-making process should provide for:

    (a) consultation with the local planning authority, English Heritage and national amenity societies, allowing them (except in cases of emergency) 28 days to comment;
    (b) the display for the same 28-day period of a notice in a prominent position outside the building describing the proposed works and similarly inviting comments;
    (c) the publication of a similar notice in a local newspaper;

(d) in cases of demolition, notification [, for purposes of statutory recording, of English Heritage][45] (see also paragraph 3.22).

4. the decision-making body should be required, in considering proposals submitted to it, to take into account any representations made and, along with other factors, the desirability of preserving historic church buildings and the importance of protecting features of architectural merit and historic interest (including fixtures—see paragraphs 3.13 and 8.11);

5. there should be a clear and fair procedure for settling all disputes between the local congregation or minister and the decision-making body as to whether proposals should proceed;

6. there should be procedures for dealing with any breach of the control system, including provision for reinstatement where works to historic church buildings have been carried out without consent;

7. there should be arrangements for recording how the above procedures were implemented in each case and the nature of the decision taken; for making such records available for public inspection during reasonable hours; and for notifying the decision to the above consultees;

8. There should be arrangements to ensure the proper maintenance of historic church buildings including thorough inspections on a fixed cycle of not more than five years.

So far as a denomination's circumstances permit, these points should be incorporated in legally binding procedures.

8.5 In considering proposals for such works, any effects on the archaeological importance of the church or archaeological remains existing within it or its curtilage should be taken into account along with other relevant factors. Where works of repair or alteration are to be carried out which would affect the fabric of listed churches or churches in conservation areas, denominations should attach any necessary conditions for proper recording in accordance with the principles set out in paragraphs 3.22–3.24 and, in respect of archaeological remains, in paragraph 2.15.

Future scope of the exemption

8.6 For those denominations and faiths which retain the exemption, its scope is reduced by the Order to the following:

• any church building;

• any object or structure within a church building;

• any object or structure fixed to the exterior of a church building, unless the object or structure is itself a listed building;

• any object or structure within the curtilage of a church building which, although not fixed to that building, forms part of the land, unless the object or structure is itself a listed building.

("Church building" is defined as a building whose primary use is as a place of worship.)

8.7 The Order provides continued exemption on this reduced basis (to the extent specified in it) for the Church of England and also for the Church in Wales, the Roman Catholic Church, the Methodist Church, the Baptist Union of Great Britain, the Baptist Union of Wales and the United Reformed Church. Ecclesiastical buildings of these denominations

---

[45] [substituted by DETR Circ. 01/01, Appendix B.]

are covered by acceptable internal systems of control broadly conforming to the principles in the Government's code of practice. It is intended to monitor these arrangements and review them after two years. (Further Orders can be made if any other denominations or faiths are subsequently accepted as qualifying.)

8.8 Details of these denominations' arrangements will be published in a separate leaflet circulated to all local authorities. This will include the special arrangements made for Church of England cathedrals where all buildings, objects or structures within an area designated by [the Secretary of State for Culture, Media and Sport], after consulting the Cathedrals Fabric Commission for England, and places of worship and unlisted tomb-stones and other monuments elsewhere within the cathedral precinct, are exempt. A list of addresses for the denominations concerned, and related bodies, is included in Annex A[46].

8.9 The Order also provides continued exemption for ecclesiastical buildings of these denominations in various categories where insufficient information is currently available (e.g. buildings of ... Roman Catholic religious communities; and school and other insti-tutional chapels). The intention is that by the end of a limited period all buildings within these categories will either become subject to the normal local authority controls or be included within the scope of an exempted denomination's internal system of control. [The Care of Places of Worship Measure 1999 extended the scope of the Church of England faculty system so as to cover buildings of "peculiars", and those of Church of England religious communities. The other] bodies concerned have been notified of the Order and invited to consider what future arrangements would be appropriate for them.

Exercise of controls over non-exempt church buildings

8.10 For denominations, faiths and independent congregations not listed in the Order, their places of worship [have been] fully subject to listed building and conservation area control from 1 October 1994. For non-exempt denominations, works begun or contracted for before 1 October 1994 are exempt. Conservation area control [extends] to memorials, monuments and tombstones of whatever size erected prior to 1925, in order to bring authorities' controls into alignment with those which [are] operated by the denominations listed in the Order; this [has been] done by a direction made under section 75(2) by the Secretary of State.[47]

8.11 Much of the architectural character and historic interest of places of worship lies in the arrangement and furnishing of their interiors. The great majority of furnishings are likely to be fixed and so form part of the listed building (paragraphs 3.30–3.32), and their architectural coherence and quality will need to be taken into account when considering any proposals for re-ordering. It is probable that some changes have taken place in the past, and before considering further alterations the chronology and completeness of the existing arrangements should be carefully assessed. It is particularly important to identify, and where possible retain, the spatial arrangements and fixtures that belong to the principal period of building. When considering proposals for creating cleared areas for multi-pur-pose use, the possibility of making fixed seating capable of being dismantled or moved should be investigated. Proper recording in accordance with the principles set out in paragraphs 3.22–3.24 and, in respect of archaeological remains, paragraph 2.15, should always be considered. Where extensive re-ordering takes place, some examples of the replaced furnishings should be retained wherever possible and, where appropriate, mate-rials such as panelling should be re-used within the building or offered for re-use in a similar context, rather than destroyed.

8.12 In considering applications for consent relating to buildings used for worship authorities are advised that, in addition to the general considerations set out in section 3,

---

[46] [See **Appendix C.**]

[47] [At para.31(1)(a),(2) of Environment Circ. 01/01. See **12.6.6.**]

the following matters (mainly relating to interiors) should be given due weight as material considerations, *viz.* whether the changes proposed:

(i) are necessitated by a change in the worship needs of the congregation;

(ii) are necessitated by an increase or a reduction in congregation size;

(iii) are directed at accommodating other activities within the building to help ensure its continued viability primarily as a place of worship;

(iv) would involve substantial structural changes, e.g. subdivision of important existing spaces;

(v) would involve the removal or destruction of important fixtures and fittings, or are more in the nature of a reversible re-ordering of internal features;

(vi) would involve disturbance of archaeologically important remains below ground.

8.13 English Heritage has published guidance entitled [*New Works to Historic Places of Worship*[48]] which local planning authorities may find useful in respect of buildings of all denominations. The Church of England has published a *Code of Practice on the Care of Churches and Ecclesiastical Jurisdiction Measure*[49] which gives detailed guidance on many of the procedures to be followed and recommended practice under its own system of control (other than for cathedrals).

8.14 The Secretary of State will continue to have the power to bring within normal listed building or conservation area controls by a further Order any individual ecclesiastical building where it seems likely that potentially damaging works will be carried out without the necessary authorisation having been obtained under an exempt denomination's procedures, and without legal sanctions being available to the denomination internally.

Buildings no longer in ecclesiastical use

8.15 [In the case of the Church of England, works for the demolition of a redundant building or part of such building][50] in pursuance of a pastoral measure or redundancy scheme under the Pastoral Measure 1983 are exempt from listed building control by virtue of section 60(7) of the Act, and demolition of such a building is exempt from conservation area consent by a direction under s.75(2). The Church Commissioners have, however, agreed to ask [the First Secretary of State] whether he wishes to hold a non-statutory public local inquiry into any such proposal for works of demolition (which would otherwise fall within the scope of those controls)] where English Heritage, the Advisory Board for Redundant Churches, the local planning authority or a national amenity society have lodged reasoned objections. The Church Commissioners have also undertaken to accept a recommendation from the Secretary of State [. . .] following such an inquiry that the church is of sufficient importance to be vested in the Churches Conservation Trust (formerly the Redundant Churches Fund) or, in cases where the recommendation was not that the building should go to the Trust, to make further efforts to find an alternative use and to engage in further consultation with the Secretary of State for the Environment before using the Pastoral Measure powers to demolish. In considering what recommendation he will make, following a non-statutory inquiry, [the First Secretary of State] will take into account the financial implications of retaining a church building as well as the architectural and historic interest of the church and other planning and social factors, and will consult [the Secretary of State for Culture, Media and Sport].

---

[48] [Published in 2003, available at *www.english-heritage.org.uk*]
[49] [Now out of print.]
[50] [Substituted by DETR Circ. 01/01, Appendix B.]

8.16 Total demolition by faculty is not exempt but would require listed building and conservation area consent in the normal way, as would total demolition by exempt denominations other than the Church of England. This is because the exemption only applies to a building in ecclesiastical use, and the view of the Courts has been that a building cannot be considered to be in such use if it is being totally demolished. Denominations have been asked to notify the local authority concerned when a church building covered by the exemption ceases to be used primarily for worship. Where total demolition is proposed, denominations may find it useful, before applying to the local planning authority for consent, to see that the proposal has been scrutinised through their normal procedures where these apply.

8.17 Except as mentioned above, Church of England buildings which are no longer in regular ecclesiastical use are fully subject to the normal listed building and conservation area controls once a declaration of redundancy under the Pastoral Measure comes into operation. These controls also cover buildings vested in the Churches Conservation Trust, in most of which church services are still held on an occasional basis. During the waiting period between a declaration of redundancy under the Pastoral Measure and the coming into operation of a redundancy scheme authorities are advised to discuss the application of the controls with the diocesan or parish bodies concerned where the authority is considering taking action under the urgent works provisions of section 54 of the Act or where the diocesan board of finance considers it necessary to remove fixtures for safe keeping under section 49(2) of the Pastoral Measure.

8.18 Many churches, of all denominations, when no longer required for worship may nevertheless have a continuing and valuable contribution to make to the community in terms of architecture, art, social and local or national history. They often occupy central and convenient positions in villages and towns and can, therefore, offer suitable venues for a variety of social and community purposes, such as meetings, concerts, exhibitions, indoor sports and evening classes. Even where the building itself is not worthy of individual listing as of architectural or historic interest, it may nevertheless be a familiar and important feature of an urban or rural landscape—while a surrounding churchyard may possess considerable ecological interest. It is important that once a church becomes redundant no unnecessary delay should occur in finding an alternative use for it. Conversion to another use which preserves the most interesting elements, internal and external, is to be preferred to demolition.

ANNEX A. THE LEGISLATION AND THE MAIN HERITAGE BODIES

[An updated list of these bodies, or their successors, appears at Appendix C to this book.]

ANNEX B. LISTED BUILDING CONTROL PROCEDURES

ANNEX C. GUIDANCE ON ALTERATIONS TO LISTED BUILDINGS

ANNEX D. BIBLIOGRAPHY

[These Annexes are not reproduced in this book.]

Appendix B

Planning Policy Guidance Note PPG16: *Archaeology and Planning*

Note: this Appendix reproduces the PPG, originally published in September 1990 by the Department of the Environment, with references to legislation and guidance updated as appropriate. Material added, omitted or updated is indicated by the use of square brackets, as is editorial material in the footnotes.

INTRODUCTION

1. This guidance is for planning authorities in England, property owners, developers, archaeologists, amenity societies and the general public. It sets out the Secretary of State's policy on archaeological remains on land, and how they should be preserved or recorded both in an urban setting and in the countryside. It gives advice on the handling of archaeological remains and discoveries under the development plan and control systems, including the weight to be given to them in planning decisions and the use of planning conditions. (Separate controls exist for scheduled monuments—See Annex 3.) The guidance pulls together and expands existing advice, within the existing legislative framework. It places no new duties on local authorities, and should not place any significant additional burden on local authorities.

2. The guidance is arranged as follows:

A. The importance of archaeology: a general introduction (paragraphs 3–14).

B. Advice on the handling of archaeological matters in the planning process:

   — Development plans (paragraphs 15–16)
   — Sites and monuments Records—SMRs (paragraph 17)
   — Planning applications (paragraphs 18–26)
   — Planning decisions (paragraphs 27–28)
   — Planning conditions (paragraphs 29–30)
   — Discovery of archaeological remains during development (paragraph 31).

Annex 1. Key bodies and organisations.[1]

Annex 2. Contact Addresses for County Archaeological Officers and SMRs.[2]

---

[1] [Not reproduced in this book. An updated list appears at **Appendix C**.]
[2] [Not reproduced in this book.]

Annex 3. Legislative arrangements: scheduling of ancient monuments, control of scheduled monuments and their management; Offences; Metal Detectors; Areas of Archaeological Importance (AAIs); Environmental Assessment; Simplified Planning Zones (SPZs).[3]

Annex 4. Secretary of State's criteria for scheduling.

Annex 5. Ancient Monuments (Class Consent) Order 1981.[4]

A. THE IMPORTANCE OF ARCHAEOLOGY

3. Archaeological remains are irreplaceable. They are evidence—for prehistoric periods, the only evidence—of the past development of our civilization.

4. Today's archaeological landscape is the product of human activity over thousands of years. It ranges through settlements and remains of every period, from the camps of the early hunter gatherers 400,000 years ago to remains of early 20th century activities. It includes places of worship, defence installations, burial grounds, farms and fields, and sites of manufacture.

5. These remains vary enormously in their state of preservation and in the extent of their appeal to the public. "Upstanding" remains are familiar enough—the great stone circles, the castle and abbey ruins of the Middle Ages or abandoned coastal defence systems. But less obvious archaeological remains, such as ancient settlements and field systems, are also to be found across large parts of the country. Some prehistoric sites in wetland areas contain important wood and organic remains. Many buildings in older towns lie on top of Roman, Anglo-Saxon or medieval structures.

6. Archaeological remains should be seen as a finite and non-renewable resource, in many cases highly fragile and vulnerable to damage and destruction. Appropriate management is therefore essential to ensure that they survive in good condition. In particular, care must be taken to ensure that archaeological remains are not needlessly or thoughtlessly destroyed. They can contain irreplaceable information about our past and the potential for an increase in future knowledge. They are part of our sense of national identity and are valuable both for their own sake and for their role in education, leisure and tourism.

7. The present century has been a period of striking environmental change. Some changes, like the erosion of coastal areas, have occurred naturally. But much archaeological heritage has been destroyed by human activity—for example, by modern construction methods in urban development and expansion of the road network, by modern agricultural techniques (in particular deep ploughing or drainage of wetlands), and by mineral extraction.

8. With the many demands of modern society, it is not always feasible to save all archaeological remains. The key question is where and how to strike the right balance. Where nationally important archaeological remains, whether scheduled or not, and their settings, are affected by proposed development there should be a presumption in favour of their physical preservation. Cases involving archaeological remains of lesser importance will not always be so clear cut and planning authorities will need to weigh the relative importance of archaeology against other factors including the need for the proposed development (see also paragraph 27). Regardless of the circumstances, taking decisions is much easier if any archaeological aspects of a development site can be considered early on in the planning and development control process. This is discussed in Section B.

9. Archaeological records for England currently contain around 600,000 sites and monuments. Some 13,000 nationally important cases enjoy special protection as

---

[3]   [Not reproduced in this book.]
[4]   [See now the Ancient Monuments (Class Consents) Order (SI 1994/1381).]

"scheduled monuments", under the Ancient Monuments and Archaeological Areas Act 1979.[5] English Heritage have embarked on a survey programme which is expected to result in significant additional numbers being given this statutory protection (see Annex 3).

10. Scheduling archaeological remains ensures that the case for preservation is fully considered given any proposals for development or other work which might damage the monument. The planning system, as paragraph 18 emphasises, is equally in a position to consider the desirability of preserving archaeological remains, and the various options open to planning authorities for dealing with archaeological remains are considered in Section B. Much can be achieved within the wider planning process when developers are prepared to enter into discussions with archaeologists and consider fully the needs of archaeology. This voluntary approach to considering the needs of archaeology is a well-established and growing practice and has been formalized in Codes of Practice by the British Archaeologists' and Developers' Liaison Group (BADLG)[6] (see paragraph 26; also Annex 1, paragraph 9), and the Confederation of British Industry (CBI) Code for Mineral Operators.

11. Archaeological issues are often important in minerals planning, particularly in the extraction of sand and gravel. River valleys have provided an attractive place for man to settle but at the same time these areas often contain valuable sand and gravel resources. Minerals can clearly only be worked where they are found so they often differ from other forms of development in that there is not the same flexibility of choice of location. The CBI's revised Code of Practice for Mineral Operators on archaeological investigations provides advice on how minerals operators should consult archaeological interests in formulating planning applications, to ensure that archaeological factors are fully taken into account in the planning decision process.

12. The key to informed and reasonable planning decisions, as emphasised in paragraphs 19 and 20, is for consideration to be given early, before formal planning applications are made, to the question whether archaeological remains exist on a site where development is planned and the implications for the development proposal. When important remains are known to exist or when archaeologists have good reason to believe that important remains exist, developers will be able to help by preparing sympathetic designs using, for example, foundations which avoid disturbing the remains altogether or minimise damage by raising ground levels under a proposed new structure, or by the careful siting of landscaped or open areas. There are techniques available for sealing archaeological remains underneath buildings or landscaping, thus securing their preservation for the future even though they remain inaccessible for the time being.

13. If physical preservation *in situ* is not feasible, an archaeological excavation for the purposes of "preservation by record", may be an acceptable alternative (see also paragraphs 24 and 25). From the archaeological point of view this should be regarded as a second best option. The science of archaeology is developing rapidly. Excavation means the total destruction of evidence (apart from removable artefacts) from which future techniques could almost certainly extract more information than is currently possible. Excavation is also expensive and time-consuming, and discoveries may have to be evaluated in a hurry against an inadequate research framework. The preservation *in situ* of important archaeological remains is therefore nearly always to be preferred.

14. Positive planning and management can help to bring about sensible solutions to the treatment of sites with archaeological remains and reduce the areas of potential conflict between development and preservation. Both central government and English Heritage have important roles to play (see Annex 1). But the key to the future of the great majority of archaeological sites and historic landscapes lies with local authorities, acting within the framework set by central government, in their various capacities as planning, education

---

[5] [As at March 2005, there were 19,700 sites recorded in England.]
[6] [See **Appendix C** for address.]

and recreational authorities, as well as with the owners of sites themselves. Appropriate planning policies in development plans and their implementation through development control will be especially important.

B. ADVICE ON THE HANDLING OF ARCHAEOLOGICAL MATTERS IN THE PLANNING PROCESS

Development Plans

15. Development plans should reconcile the need for development with the interests of conservation including archaeology. Detailed development plans (ie local plans and unitary development plans [and local development frameworks]) should include policies for the protection, enhancement and preservation of sites of archaeological interest and of their settings. The proposals map should define the areas and sites to which the policies and proposals apply. These policies will provide an important part of the framework for the consideration of individual proposals for development which affect archaeological remains and they will help guide developers preparing planning applications.

16. Although the surviving numbers of archaeological remains are finite and irreplaceable, obviously not all of them are of equal importance. Planning authorities may therefore wish to base their detailed development plan policies and proposals on an evaluation of the archaeological remains in their area. Archaeological remains identified and scheduled as being of national importance should normally be earmarked in development plans for preservation. Authorities should bear in mind that not all nationally important remains meriting preservation will necessarily be scheduled; such remains and, in appropriate circumstances, other unscheduled archaeological remains of more local importance, may also be identified in development plans as particularly worthy of preservation.

Sites and Monuments Records—SMRs

17. All shire counties now maintain Sites and Monuments Records (SMRs) staffed by at least one professional officer, usually employed by the County Council. In London the SMR is maintained by English Heritage. In ex-Metropolitan county areas centralised SMRs are jointly maintained by Metropolitan Boroughs. An increasing number of non-metropolitan District Councils now employ archaeological staff within their planning departments. All planning authorities should make full use of the expertise of County Archaeological Officers or their equivalents (see Annex 1 paragraphs 4–6). English Heritage is ready to advise on the archaeological policies proposed for inclusion in draft plans. Consultation with English Heritage, as suggested by [Planning Policy Statement PPS 12, Annex E], may be of particular help in urban areas where important archaeological remains may not be adequately identified by scheduling.

Planning Applications

18. The desirability of preserving an ancient monument and its setting is a material consideration in determining planning applications whether that monument is scheduled or unscheduled. Developers and local authorities should take into account archaeological considerations and deal with them from the beginning of the development control process. Where local planning authorities are aware of a real and specific threat to a known archaeological site as a result of the potential exercise of *permitted development rights* (as set out in Schedule 2 to [the Town and Country Planning (General Permitted Development) Order 1995]) they may wish to consider the use of their powers under Article 4 of that

Order to withdraw those rights and to require specific planning permission to be obtained before development can proceed. Most such directions require the Secretary of State's approval, either before they come into effect or within six months of being made, unless they relate solely to a listed building. Further advice on the use of Article 4 Directions is given in Appendix D to [DOE Circular 9/95].

(a) The First Step: Early Consultations between Developers and Planning Authorities

19. The needs of archaeology and development can be reconciled, and potential conflict very much reduced, if developers discuss their preliminary plans for development with the planning authority at an early stage. Once detailed designs have been prepared and finance lined up, flexibility becomes much more difficult and expensive to achieve. In their own interests, therefore, prospective developers should in all cases include as part of their research into the development potential of a site, which they undertake before making a planning application, an initial assessment of whether the site is known or likely to contain archaeological remains. The first step will be to contact the County Archaeological Officer or equivalent who holds the SMR, or English Heritage in London. The SMR provides information about the locations where archaeological remains are known or thought likely to exist. Where important remains are known to exist or where the indications are that the remains are likely to prove important, English Heritage are also ready to join in early discussions and provide expert advice. Special notification requirements apply in designated Areas of Archaeological Importance—see Annex 3, paragraphs 19–20.

20. These consultations will help to provide prospective developers with advance warning of the archaeological sensitivity of a site. As a result they may wish to commission their own archaeological assessment by a professionally qualified archaeological organisation or consultant. This need not involve fieldwork. Assessment normally involves desk-based evaluation of existing information: it can make effective use of records of previous discoveries, including any historic maps held by the County archive and local museums and record offices, or of geophysical survey techniques.

(b) Field Evaluations

21. Where early discussions with local planning authorities or the developer's own research indicate that important archaeological remains may exist, it is reasonable for the planning authority to request the prospective developer to arrange for an archaeological field evaluation to be carried out before any decision on the planning application is taken. This sort of evaluation is quite distinct from full archaeological excavation. It is normally a rapid and inexpensive operation, involving ground survey and small-scale trial trenching, but it should be carried out by a professionally qualified archaeological organisation or archaeologist. The Institute of Field Archaeologists[7], publishes a Directory of members, which developers may wish to consult. Evaluations of this kind help to define the character and extent of the archaeological remains that exist in the area of a proposed development, and thus indicate the weight which ought to be attached to their preservation. They also provide information useful for identifying potential options for minimising or avoiding damage. On this basis, an informed and reasonable planning decision can be taken.

22. Local planning authorities can expect developers to provide the results of such assessments and evaluations as part of their application for sites where there is a good reason to believe there are remains of archaeological importance. If developers are not prepared to do so voluntarily, the planning authority may wish to consider whether it would be appropriate to direct the applicant to supply further information under the provisions of Regulation 4 of the Town and Country Planning (Applications) Regulations

---

[7]   [See **Appendix C** for address.]

1988 and if necessary authorities will need to consider refusing permission for proposals which are inadequately documented. In some circumstances a formal Environmental Assessment may be necessary. For further details see Annex 3, paragraphs 21 and 22.

(c) Consultations by Planning Authorities

23. When planning applications are made without prior discussion with the local planning authorities, the authorities should seek to identify those applications which have archaeological implications, and to assess their likely archaeological impact by consulting the County Archaeological Officer or equivalent and the County Sites and Monuments Record. When it is evident that a particular development proposal is likely to affect archaeological remains, applicants may need to be asked to provide more detailed information about their scheme—for example, the type of foundations to be used—or they may be asked to carry out an evaluation. Planning authorities should also ensure that they are fully informed about the nature and importance of the archaeological site and its setting. They should therefore seek archaeological advice, normally from the County Archaeological Officer or equivalent who in turn may wish to consult locally based museums and archaeological units and societies. In the case of a development proposal that is likely to affect the site of a scheduled ancient monument [Article 10(1)(n) of the Town and Country Planning (General Development Procedure) Order 1995], requires local planning authorities to consult English Heritage. Local planning authorities may find it helpful to consult more generally with English Heritage on applications for development that affect non-scheduled sites. Existing information about a site is often sufficient to allow authorities to make planning decisions which take into account all material considerations.

(d) Arrangements For Preservation By Record Including Funding

24. The Secretary of State recognises that the extent to which remains can or should be preserved will depend upon a number of factors, including the intrinsic importance of the remains. Where it is not feasible to preserve remains, an acceptable alternative may be to arrange prior excavation, during which the archaeological evidence is recorded.

25. Planning authorities should not include in their development plans policies requiring developers to finance archaeological works in return for the grant of planning permission. By the same token developers should not expect to obtain planning permission for archaeologically damaging development merely because they arrange for the recording of sites whose physical preservation *in situ* is both desirable (because of their level of importance) and feasible. Where planning authorities decide that the physical preservation *in situ* of archaeological remains is not justified in the circumstances of the case and that development resulting in the destruction of the archaeological remains should proceed, it would be entirely reasonable for the planning authority to satisfy itself before granting planning permission, that the developer has made appropriate and satisfactory provision for the excavation and recording of the remains. Such excavation and recording should be carried out before development commences, working to a project brief prepared by the planning authority and taking advice from archaeological consultants. This can be achieved through agreements reached between the developer, the archaeologist and the planning authority (see following paragraph). Such agreements should also provide for the subsequent publication of the results of the excavation. In the absence of such agreements planning authorities can secure excavation and recording by imposing conditions (see paragraphs 29 and 30). In particular cases where the developer is a non-profit making community body, such as a charitable trust or housing association, which is unable to raise the funds to provide for excavation and subsequent recording without undue hardship, or in the case of an individual who similarly does not have the means to fund such work, an application for financial assistance may be made to English Heritage.

26. Agreements covering excavation, recording and the publication of the results may take different forms. For example, developers or their archaeological consultants and local

planning authorities may wish to conclude a voluntary planning agreement under section 106 of the Town and Country Planning Act 1990 or other similar powers. The Secretary of State is pleased to note the increasing number of agreements being reached within the terms and spirit of the British Archaeologists' and Developers' Code of Practice. Model agreements between developers and the appropriate archaeological body regulating archaeological site investigations and excavations can be obtained from the British Property Federation. These agreements can provide for the excavation and recording of sites before development work starts. Voluntary agreements are likely to provide more flexibility and be of greater mutual benefit to all the parties than could be provided for by alternative statutory means. They have the advantage of setting out clearly the extent of the developer's commitment, thereby reducing both uncertainty over the financial implications of having to accommodate any archaeological constraints and the possibility of unforeseen delays to the construction programme.

Planning Decisions

27. Once the planning authority has sufficient information, there is a range of options for the determination of planning applications affecting archaeological remains and their settings. As stated in paragraph 8, where nationally important archaeological remains, whether scheduled or not, and their settings, are affected by proposed development there should be a presumption in favour of their physical preservation *in situ*, ie, a presumption against proposals which would involve significant alteration or cause damage, or which would have a significant impact on the setting of visible remains. The case for the preservation of archaeological remains must however be assessed on the individual merits of each case, taking into account the archaeological policies in detailed development plans, together with all other relevant policies and material considerations, including the intrinsic importance of the remains and weighing these against the need for the proposed development.

28. There will no doubt be occasions, particularly where remains of lesser importance are involved, when planning authorities may decide that the significance of the archaeological remains is not sufficient when weighed against all other material considerations, including the need for development, to justify their physical preservation *in situ*, and that the proposed development should proceed. As paragraph 25 explains, planning authorities will, in such cases, need to satisfy themselves that the developer has made appropriate and satisfactory arrangements for the excavation and recording of the archaeological remains and the publication of the results. If this has not already been secured through some form of voluntary agreement, planning authorities can consider granting planning permission subject to conditions which provide for the excavation and recording of the remains before development takes place (see following section). Local planning authorities may, as a matter of last resort, need to consider refusing planning permission where developers do not seek to accommodate important remains.

Planning Conditions

29. Planning authorities should seek to ensure that potential conflicts are resolved and agreements with developers concluded before planning permission is granted. Where the use of planning conditions is necessary, authorities should ensure that, in accordance with [DOE Circular 11/95], they are fair, reasonable and practicable. It is however open to the local planning authority to impose conditions designed to protect a monument and to ensure that reasonable access is given to a nominated archaeologist—either to hold a "watching brief" during the construction period or specifically to carry out archaeological investigation and recording in the course of the permitted operations on site. Conditions on these lines help to ensure that if remains of archaeological significance are disturbed in the course of the work, they can be recorded and, if necessary, emergency salvage undertaken.

30. In cases when planning authorities have decided that planning permission may be granted but wish to secure the provision of archaeological excavation and the subsequent

recording of the remains, it is open to them to do so by the use of a negative condition i.e. a condition prohibiting the carrying out of development until such time as works or other action, e.g. an excavation, have been carried out by a third party. In such cases the following model is suggested:

"No development shall take place within the area indicated (this would be the area of archaeological interest) until the applicant has secured the implementation of a programme of archaeological work in accordance with a written scheme of investigation which has been submitted by the applicant and approved by the Planning Authority."

(Developers will wish to ensure that in drawing up a scheme, the timetable for the investigation is included within the details of the agreed scheme).

The use of this model is also advocated in the CBI Code of Practice for Mineral Operators. The advice on the use of the above condition should be regarded as supplementary to that contained in [DOE Circular 11/95] relating to archaeology.[8]

---

[8] [Circ. 11/95, *Use of Conditions in planning permission*, provides as follows:

Sites of Archaeological Interest
80. Scheduled ancient monuments are protected by Part I of the Ancient Monuments and Archaeological Areas Act 1979, and investigation for archaeological purposes is provided for in designated areas by Part II of that Act. Where these provisions apply, their effect should not be duplicated by planning conditions (cf paragraphs 21–23 above), although authorities granting planning permission in such circumstances are advised to draw the attention of the applicant to the relevant provisions of the 1979 Act.
81. Where, however, planning permission is being granted for development which might affect a monument which has not been scheduled, or which might affect land in an area which is considered to be of archaeological interest but which has not been formally designated as such under section 33 of the 1979 Act, the local planning authority may wish to impose conditions designed to protect the monument or ensure that reasonable access is given to a nominated archaeologist—either to hold a "watching brief" during the construction period or specifically to carry out archaeological investigation and recording before or in the course of the permitted operations on the site. (For further advice on archaeology and planning conditions see paragraphs 29 and 30 of PPG 16: Archaeology and Planning or PPG 16 (Wales), and model conditions 53–55).

Appendix A. Suggested models of acceptable conditions: Sites of archaeological interest (not scheduled or designated under 1979 Act)
53. No development shall take place until fencing has been erected, in a manner to be agreed with the local planning authority, about [insert name of monument]; and no works shall take place within the area inside that fencing without the consent of the local planning authority *(paragraphs 80–81)*.
54. The developer shall afford access at all reasonable times to any archaeologist nominated by the local planning authority, and shall allow him to observe the excavations and record items of interest and finds *(paragraphs 80–81)*.
Conditions should not require work to be held up while archaeological investigation takes place, though some developers may be willing to give such facilities.
55. No development shall take place within the area indicated (this would be the area of archaeological interest) until the applicant, or their agents or successors in title, has secured the implementation of a programme of archaeological work in accordance with a written scheme of investigation which has been submitted by the applicant and approved in writing by the local planning authority.
Developers will wish to ensure that in drawing up a scheme, the timetable for the investigation is included within the details of the agreed scheme.]

Discovery of Archaeological Remains during Development

31. The preceding guidance (paragraphs 19 and 20 in particular) has been framed to minimise occasions when totally unexpected problems arise while development is in progress. Nevertheless, and in spite of the best pre-planning application research, there may be occasions when the presence of archaeological remains only becomes apparent once development has commenced. Developers may wish to consider insuring themselves against the risk of a substantial loss while safeguarding the interest of historic remains unexpectedly discovered on the site. Conflicts that may otherwise arise between developers and archaeologists may not be easy to solve although English Heritage, who have a great deal of experience in handling these situations, are ready to offer practical advice, as is the British Archaeologists' and Developers' Liaison Group[9]. Where fresh archaeological discoveries are deemed by the Secretary of State, on English Heritage's advice, to be of national importance, in accordance with his published criteria (see Annex 4), the Secretary of State for [Culture, Media and Sport] has power to schedule the remains. In that event developers would need to seek separate scheduled monument consent before they continue work. It is also open to a planning authority or the Secretary of State to revoke a planning permission if deemed necessary, in which case there is provision for compensation. In the majority of cases, however, it should prove possible for the parties to resolve their differences through voluntary discussion and for a satisfactory compromise to be reached.

ANNEX 1. KEY BODIES AND ORGANISATIONS.

[*An updated list of these bodies, or their successors, appears at Appendix C to this book.*]

ANNEX 2. CONTACT ADDRESSES FOR COUNTY ARCHAEOLOGICAL OFFICERS AND SMRS

ANNEX 3. LEGISLATIVE ARRANGEMENTS

[*These Annexes are not reproduced in this book.*]

ANNEX 4. SECRETARY OF STATE'S CRITERIA FOR SCHEDULING

The following criteria (which are not in any order of ranking), are used for assessing the national importance of an ancient monument and considering whether scheduling is appropriate. The criteria should not however be regarded as definitive; rather they are indicators which contribute to a wider judgement based on the individual circumstances of a case.

- (*i*) *Period*: all types of monuments that characterise a category or period should be considered for preservation.

- (*ii*) *Rarity*: there are some monument categories which in certain periods are so scarce that all surviving examples which still retain some archaeological potential should be preserved. In general, however, a selection must be made which portrays the typical and commonplace as well as the rare. This process should take account of all aspects of the distribution of a particular class of monument, both in a national and a regional context.

---

[9]   [See **Appendix C** for address.]

(iii) *Documentation*: the significance of a monument may be enhanced by the existence of records of previous investigation or, in the case of more recent monuments, by the supporting evidence of contemporary written records.

(iv) *Group Value*: the value of a single monument (such as a field system) may be greatly enhanced by its association with related contemporary monuments (such as a settlement and cemetery) or with monuments of different periods. In some cases, it is preferable to protect the complete group of monuments, including associated and adjacent land, rather than to protect isolated monuments within the group.

(v) *Survival/Condition*: the survival of a monument's archaeological potential both above and below ground is a particularly important consideration and should be assessed in relation to its present condition and surviving features.

(vi) *Fragility/Vulnerability*: highly important archaeological evidence from some field monuments can be destroyed by a single ploughing or unsympathetic treatment; vulnerable monuments of this nature would particulary benefit from the statutory protection which scheduling confers. There are also existing standing structures of particular form or complexity whose value can again be severely reduced by neglect or careless treatment and which are similarly well suited by scheduled monument protection, even if these structures are already listed historic buildings.

(vii) *Diversity*: some monuments may be selected for scheduling because they possess a combination of high quality features, others because of a single important attribute.

(viii) *Potential*: on occasion, the nature of the evidence cannot be specified precisely but it may still be possible to document reasons anticipating its existence and importance and so to demonstrate the justification for scheduling. This is usually confined to sites rather than upstanding monuments.

ANNEX 5. ANCIENT MONUMENTS (CLASS CONSENT) ORDER 1981

[*see now the Ancient Monuments (Class Consents) Order 1994 (SI 1994/1381).*]

Appendix C

Key bodies and organisations

Note: this Appendix includes most of the organisations referred to in Annex A of PPG 15 and Annex 1 of PPG 16, updated and supplemented as appropriate.

C1. CENTRAL GOVERNMENT

Office of the Deputy Prime Minister (ODPM)
Web: *www.odpm.gov.uk*
Eland House, Bressenden Place, London, SW1E 5DU
Tel: 020 7944 3985 (Planning Development Control Policy Division A)

Department for Culture Media and Sport (DCMS)
Web: *www.culture.gov.uk*
2–4 Cockspur Street, London, SW1Y 5DH
Tel: 020 7211 6000

National Assembly for Wales (Welsh Assembly Government: Llywdraeth Cynulliad Cymru)
Web: *www.wales.gov.uk*
Cardiff Bay, Cardiff, CF99 1NA
Tel: 029 2082 5111

Cadw: Welsh Historic Monuments
Web: *www.cadw.wales.gov.uk*
Plas Carew, Unit 5/7 Cefn Coed, Parc Nantgarw, Cardiff, CF15 7QQ
Tel: 01443 336000

Planning Inspectorate
Web: *www.planning-inspectorate.gov.uk*
Temple Quay House, 2 The Square, Bristol, BS1 6PN
Tel: 0117 372 6372
Crown Buildings, Cathays Park, Cardiff, CF10 3NQ
Tel: 029 2082 3866

Scottish Executive Development Department
Web: *www.scotland.gov.uk*
Victoria Quay, Edinburgh, EH6 6QQ
Tel: 0131 556 8400

Historic Scotland
Web: *www.historic-scotland.gov.uk*
Longmore House, Salisbury Place, Edinburgh, EH9 1SH
Tel: 0131 668 8600

Planning Service (NI)
Web: *www.planningni.gov.uk*
Millennium House, 19–25 Great Victoria Street, Belfast, BT2 7BN
Tel: 028 9041 6700

Environment and Heritage Service (NI)
Web: *www.ehsni.gov.uk*
Waterman House, 5–33 Hill Street, Belfast, BT1 2LA
Tel: 028 9054 3034/3145

C2. ENGLISH HERITAGE

(Historic Buildings and Monuments Commission for England)
Web: *www.english-heritage.org.uk*
London Region
Fortress House, 23 Savile Row London, W1S 2ET
Tel: 020 7973 3000

East Midlands Region
44 Derngate, Northampton, NN1 1UH
Tel: 01604 735400

East of England Region
Brooklands House, 24 Brooklands Avenue, Cambridge, CB2 2BU
Tel: 01223 582700

North East Region
Bessie Surtees House, 41–44 Sandhill, Newcastle-upon-Tyne, NE1 3JF
Tel: 0191 261 1585

North West Region
Canada House, 3 Chepstow Street, Manchester, M1 5FW
Tel: 0161 242 1400

South East Region
Eastgate Court, 195–205 High Street, Guildford, GU1 3EH
Tel: 01483 252000

South West Region
29 Queen Square, Bristol, BS1 4ND
Tel: 0117 975 0700

West Midlands Region
112 Colmore Row, Birmingham, B3 3AG
Tel: 0121 625 6820

Yorkshire Region
37 Tanner Row, York, YO1 6WP
Tel: 01904 601901

National Monument Record (NMR)
Alexander House, 19 Fleming Way, Swindon, SN1 2NG
Tel: 01793 414600

C3. LOCAL GOVERNMENT

Local Government Association
Web: *www.lga.gov.uk*
Local Government House, Smith Square, London, SW1P3HZ
Tel: 020 7644 3131

Association of London Government
Web: *www.alg.gov.uk*
59½ Southwark Street, London, SE1 0AL
Tel: 020 7934 9999

Welsh Local Government Association (Cymdeithas Llwdraeth Leol Cymru)
Web: *www.wlga.gov.uk*
Local Government House, Drake Walk, Cardiff, CF10 4LG
Tel: 029 2046 8600

C4. NATIONAL AMENITY SOCIETIES

Ancient Monuments Society
Web: *www.ancientmonumentssociety.org.uk*
St. Ann's Vestry, 2 Church Entry, London, EC4V 5HB
Tel: 020 7236 3934

Council for British Archaeology
Web: *www.britarch.ac.uk*
66 Bootham, York, YO30 7BZ
Tel: 01904 671417

Garden History Society
Web: *www.gardenhistory.org*
70 Cowcross Street, London, EC1M 6EJ
Tel: 020 7608 2409

Georgian Group
Web: *www.georgiangroup.org.uk*
6 Fitzroy Square, London, W1T 5DX
Tel: 0871 750 2936

Joint Committee of the National Amenity Societies
Web: *www.jcnas.org.uk*
1 Priory Gardens, Bedford Park, London, W4 1TT
Tel: 020 8994 1019

Society for the Protection of Ancient Buildings (SPAB)
Web: *www.spab.org.uk*
37 Spital Square, London, E1 6DY
Tel: 020 7377 1644

Twentieth Century Society
Web: *www.c20society.org.uk*
70 Cowcross Street, London, EC1M 6EJ
Tel: 020 7250 3857

Victorian Society
Web: *www.victorian-society.org.uk*
1 Priory Gardens, Bedford Park, London, W4 1TT
Tel: 020 8994 1019

C5. PROFESSIONAL ASSOCIATIONS

Association of Local Government Archaeological Officers (ALGAO)
Web: *www.algao.org.uk*
Tel: 019755 64071

Institute of Field Archaeologists (IFA)
Web: *www.archaeologists.net*
SHES, Whiteknights, University of Reading, PO Box 227, Reading, RG6 6AB
Tel: 0118 378 6446

Institute of Historic Building Conservation (IHBC)
Web: *www.ihbc.org.uk*
Jubilee House, High Street, Tisbury, Wiltshire, SP3 6HA
Tel: 01747 873133

Royal Institution of Chartered Surveyors (RICS)
Web: *www.rics.org*
12 Great George Street, Parliament Square, London, SW1P 3AD
Tel: 020 7222 7000

Royal Town Planning Institute (RTPI)
Web: *www.rtpi.org.uk*
41 Botolph Lane, London, EC3R 8DL
Tel: 020 7929 9494

C6. MISCELLANEOUS BODIES RELATED TO THE BUILT HERITAGE

Architectural Heritage Fund
Web: *www.ahfund.org.uk*
Alhambra House, 27–31 Charing Cross Road, London WC2H 0AU
Tel: 020 7925 0199

Association of Building Preservation Trusts
Web: *www.heritage.co.uk/apt/*
Clareville House, 26/27 Oxendon Street, London, SW1Y 4EL
Tel: 020 7930 1629

Churches Conservation Trust
Web: *www.visitchurches.org.uk*
1 West Smithfield, London EC1A 9EE
Tel: 020 7213 0660

Civic Trust
Web: *www.civictrust.org.uk*
Essex Hall, 1–6 Essex Street, London WC2R 3HU
Tel: 020 7359 7900

Commission for Architecture and the Built Environment (CABE)
Web: *www.cabe.org.uk*
1 Kemble Street, London, WC2B 4AN
Tel: 020 7960 2400

English Historic Towns Forum
Web: *www.ehtf.org.uk*
PO Box 22, Bristol, BS16 1RZ
Tel: 0117 975 0459

Heritage Lottery Fund
Web: *www.hlf.org.uk*
7 Holbein Place, London SW1W 8NR
Tel: 020 7591 6000

Historic Chapels Trust
Web: *www.hct.org.uk*
St George's Lutheran Church, 55 Alie Street, London, E1 8EB
Tel: 020 7481 0533

International Council on Monuments and Sites
Web: *www.icomos.org/uk*
70 Cowcross Street, London, EC1M 6EJ
Tel: 020 7566 0031

Museums, Libraries and Archives Council
Web: *www.mla.gov.uk*
Victoria House, Southampton Row, London, WC1B 4EA
Tel: 020 7273 1444

National Trust
Web: *www.nationaltrust.org.uk*
36 Queen Anne's Gate, London, SW1H 9AS
Tel: 01793 817400

National Trust for Scotland
Web: *www.nts.org.uk*
Wemyss House, 28 Charlotte Square, Edinburgh, EH2 4ET
Tel: 0131 243 9300

Theatres Trust
Web: *www.theatrestrust.org.uk*
22 Charing Cross Road, London, WC2H 0QL
Tel: 020 7836 8591

C7. RELIGIOUS DENOMINATIONS EXEMPT FROM LISTED BUILDING CONTROL

Baptist Union of Great Britain
Web: *www.baptist.org.uk*
Baptist Union Corporation Ltd, Baptist House, PO Box 44, 129 Broadway, Didcot, Oxfordshire, OX11 8RT
Tel: 01235 517700

Church in Wales (Yr Eglwys yng Nghymru)
Web: *www.churchinwales.org.uk*
39 Cathedral Road, Cardiff, CF11 9XF
Tel: 029 2034 8200

General Synod of the Church Of England
Web: *www.cofe.anglican.org/about/builtheritage*
Church House, Great Smith Street, London, SW1P 3NZ
Tel: 020 7898 1000

  Council For The Care Of Churches
  Web: *www.churchcare.co.uk*
  Tel: 020 7898 1866

  Cathedrals Fabric Commission for England
  Tel: 020 7898 1863

  Church Commissioners for England
  Web: *www.cofe.anglican.org/about/churchcommissioners*
  1 Millbank, London, SW1P 3JZ
  Tel: 020 7898 1619

  Advisory Board for Redundant Churches
  Cowley House, Little College Street, London, SW1P 3SH
  Tel: 020 7898 1871

Methodist Church
Web: *www.methodist.org.uk*
Methodist Property Office, Central Buildings, Oldham Street, Manchester, M1 1JQ
Tel: 0161 236 5194

Roman Catholic Church
Web: *www.catholic-ew.org.uk/liturgy/Department/Patrimony.html*
Catholic Bishops' Conference of England & Wales, Department for Christian Life and Worship, 39 Eccleston Square, London, SW1V 1PL
Tel: 020 7901 4850

United Reformed Church
Web: *www.urc.org.uk/plato*
c/o Towns, Needham, Solicitors, Kingsgate, 51/53 South King Street, Manchester, M2 6DE
Tel: 0161 832 3721

Appendix D

Forms and Precedents

Where a form is prescribed, and is readily accessible, it is not reproduced here, but its location is noted at the appropriate point in the main text. This Appendix contains sample forms and precedents for use in those situations where no official form is prescribed, or where the official form either is hard to find or requires adaptation.

As with all sample forms and precedents, caution should be exercised in using these, to ensure that they are appropriately adapted to fit particular circumstances. In general, square brackets have been used to indicate items that may need to be omitted or altered. The local planning authority has been referred to as "the Council", as it will in most cases be a council, and that is probably the way in which most non-professionals are likely to think of it; notices served by English Heritage or by or on other types of local planning authority (see **1.4.5, 1.4.6**) should obviously be adjusted as appropriate.

Detailed examples have largely been avoided, so as to make the precedents of more general applicability. In some instances, however, to omit all details would render the precedents useless; particular care should be taken in these cases to make all necessary adaptations.

For simplicity, the samples forms and precedents have been drafted for use in England; those in other parts of the United Kingdom will have to adapt them appropriately.

D1. Request for building to be spot-listed

[see **3.3.2**]

To: English Heritage

<u>Planning (Listed Building and Conservation Areas) Act 1990, Section 1:</u>
(*name and address of building*)

The above building appears to be a building of special architectural or historic interest, of sufficient quality to be included within the list of such buildings maintained by the Secretary of State.

The principal reasons why it is of special interest are as follows:
   (*specify*).

[I am aware that this area has been recently resurveyed, in (*date*); but I consider that this building is likely to have been overlooked because (*specify*)].

[This request is a matter of extreme urgency, as it is believed that an application is about to be made to *or* an application has been made to or planning permission has been granted by (*name of local planning authority*) for development involving the alteration *or* extension *or* demolition of the building.]

A plan is attached to this application showing the position of the building (outlined in red), and photographs are enclosed showing each principal elevation [together with the following notable features of it: (*specify*)]

[The building has group value in the street scene; this illustrated by photographs (*specify*)].

The approximate date of the building in (*date*); its architect is believed to be the (*name*) [*or* is unknown, but it is similar to (*specify*), designed by (*name*)].

[A schedule describing the particular features of architectural or historic interest is attached (*this should include details of any specialised function the building may have performed; its historical associations; and interior features of interest*)]

For the above reasons, I request English Heritage to recommend that the Secretary of State to list the building at the earliest appropriate opportunity [or as a matter of extreme urgency].

A copy of this request has been sent to (*name of local planning authority*) and to the Department of Culture, Media and Sport.

(*signature of or on behalf of applicant*)
(*date*)

D2. Application for certificate of immunity from listing

[see **3.4**]

To: the Secretary of State for Culture, Media and Sport

<u>Planning (Listed Buildings and Conservation Areas) Act 1990, Section 38:</u>
(*name and address of buildings*)

An application has been made to [or planning permission has been granted by] (*name of local planning authority*) for development involving the alteration [*or* extension *or* demolition] of the above building. A plan is attached to this application showing the position of the building (outlined in red), and photographs are enclosed showing each principal elevation [together with the following notable feature of the building: (*specify*)]

The approximate date of the building is (*date*); its architect is believed to be (*name*) [*or* is unknown, but the building is similar to (*specify*), designed by (*name*)]. [A schedule describing the particular features of architectural or historic interest is attached (*this should include details of: any specialised function the building may have performed; its historical associations; and interior features of interest*)]

Notice of this application has been given to (*name of local planning authority*), the local planning authority for the area in which the building is situated, by letter date (specify).

(*signature of or on behalf of applicant*)
(*date*)

D3. Building preservation notice

[see 3.9]

BUILDING PRESERVATION NOTICE

(*NAME OF LOCAL PLANNING AUTHORITY*)

PLANNING (LISTED BUILDINGS AND CONSERVATION AREAS) ACT
1990, SECTION 3

To: (*name and address of owner/occupier*)

[*or* (*in case of notice put up on site, under section 4 of the Act*) TO WHOM IT
MAY CONCERN]

1. (*Name of local planning authority*) ("the Council") is the local planning
authority for the purposes of section 3 of the Planning (Listed Buildings and
Conservation Areas) Act 1990 for the area containing (*address of building to be
preserved*) ("the Building"). The Building is shown on the map attached to this
Notice edged in red [and is more fully described, for identification purposes only,
in the Schedule to this Notice].

2. It appears to the Council that the Building, which has not been listed, is
nevertheless of special architectural or historic interest, and is in danger of being
demolished or altered in such a way as to effect its character as a building of
special architectural or historic interest.

3. The Council has therefore requested the Secretary of State for Culture, Media
and Sport to consider including the Building in the list of buildings of special
architectural or historic interest compiled or approved under section 1 of the 1990
Act.

4. As a result of section 3(3) and 3(4) of the Act, this Notice will come into force
as soon as it has been served on the owner/s and occupier/s of the Building.

5. It will remain in force for six months from the date on which it was served (that
is, the date at the foot of this Notice). However, it will cease to be in force if,
before the end of that six-month period, the Secretary of State either includes the
Building in the list under section 1, or notifies the Council that he does not intend
to do so. In the latter case, the Council will then immediately notify the owner/s
and occupier/s of the Building.

6. For as long as this Notice is in force, the provisions of the Act (other than
section 59) shall have effect in relation to the Building as if it were a listed
building. The principal effect of this is that you will need to apply to the Council
for "listed building consent" if you wish to demolish the Building, or if you wish
to alter or extend it in any way which will affect its character as a building of
special architectural or historic interest.

7. IF, WHILE THE NOTICE IS IN FORCE, YOU CARRY OUT SUCH
WORKS TO THE BUILDING WITHOUT CONSENT, YOU WILL BE

LIABLE TO CRIMINAL PROSECUTION, EXCEPT IN CERTAIN CIRCUMSTANCES WHERE THE WORKS ARE URGENTLY NECESSARY IN THE INTERESTS OF SAFETY OR HEALTH OR FOR THE PRESERVATION OF THE BUILDING (IN WHICH CASE YOU SHOULD NOTIFY THE COUNCIL AT THE EARLIEST POSSIBLE OPPORTUNITY).

8. If the Notice ceases to be in force because six months have elapsed since it was served, or because the Secretary of State during that period notifies the Council that he does not intend to include the Building in the list, the provisions of Schedule 2 to the Act will then apply. Under that Schedule:

(a) the fact that the Notice has ceased to be in force will not affect the criminal liability of any person for having committed offences in relation to the Building while it was in force;

(b) any proceedings relating to any application for listed building consent for works to the Building, made while the Notice was in force, will lapse, as will any consent granted while it was in force;

(c) any listed building enforcement notice served in relation to the Building while this Notice was in force shall cease to have effect, and any related appeal proceedings will lapse; and

(d) the fact that the Notice has ceased to be in force will not affect the ability of the Council or a subsequent owner of the Building to recover, from a person who carried out unauthorised works to the Building, the costs of any remedial works required by a listed building enforcement notice relating to the Building.

(*signature on behalf of local planning authority*)
(*date*)

[SCHEDULE

(*description of building: only required where a simple address is insufficient to identify it*)]

If you require further information regarding this Notice, you should contact: (*specify*)

D4. Notice of designation or enlargement of conservation area

[see **5.2.4**]

(*NAME OF LOCAL PLANNING AUTHORITY*)

PLANNING (LISTED BUILDINGS AND CONSERVATION AREAS) ACT
1990, SECTION 69

(*SPECIFY BY NAME*) CONSERVATION AREA

NOTICE IS GIVEN under the provisions of the 1990 Act that (*name of local planning authority*) [*or* the (*name*) County Council *or* the Historic Buildings and Monuments Commission for England (English Heritage), after consulting with (*name of local planning authority*),] has determined that the area described in the Schedule to this Notice is an area of special architectural or historic interest, and that it is desirable to preserve or enhance its character or appearance. It has accordingly designated the area as a "conservation area" [*or* it has accordingly extended the (*specify existing conservation area*) Conservation Area, so as to include this area].

The principal effects of this area being designated as a conservation area [*or* being included within a conservation area] are as follows:

1. The Council is under a duty to prepare proposals to ensure the preservation or enhancement of the area.

2. Consent must be obtained from the Council for the demolition of any building in the area.

3. Special publicity must be given to planning applications for development in the area.

4. In carrying out any functions under the planning Acts (and, in particular, in determining applications for planning permission and listed building consent), the Council and the Secretary of State are required to take into account the desirability of preserving or enhancing the character or appearance of the area.

5. Six weeks' notice must be given to the Council before works are carried out to any tree in the area.

SCHEDULE

(*list of properties to be included in conservation area, or other precise description*)

(*signature on behalf of local planning authority*)
(*date*)

Further information regarding conservation areas may be obtained from: (*specify*)

D5. Notice of intention to carry out urgent works

[see **10.3.4**]

NOTICE OF INTENTION TO CARRY OUT URGENT WORKS

(*NAME OF LOCAL PLANNING AUTHORITY*)

PLANNING (LISTED BUILDINGS AND CONSERVATION AREAS ACT) 1990, SECTION 54

To: (*name and address of owner*)

[or, *where owner is unknown*: TO WHOM IT MAY CONCERN]

1. The building known as (*specify*) ("the Building") is a listed building within the meaning given to that term by section 1(5) of the Planning (Listed Buildings and Conservation Areas) Act 1990 ("the Act"). The Building is shown on the map attached to this Notice edged in red [and is more fully described, for identification purposes only, in Schedule One to this Notice].

[or The building known as (*specify*) ("the Building") is within a conservation area designated under section 69 of the Planning (Listed Buildings and Conservation Areas) Act 1990 ("the Act"). The Secretary of State has by a letter dated (*date*) given a direction under section 76 of the Act that the preservation of the building is important for maintaining the character and [*or or*] appearance of that area. Section 54 of the Act therefore relates to the Building as if it were a listed building. The Building is shown on the map attached to this Notice edged in red [and is more fully described, for identification purposes only, in Schedule One to this Notice].]

2. (*Name of local planning authority*) ("the Council") is a local authority whose area includes the Building.

3. It appears to the Council that the works described in the Schedule [*or* Schedule Two] to this Notice ("the Works") are urgently required for the preservation of the Building. The Council has obtained estimates which suggest that the initial cost of the Works is likely to be in the region of £(*specify*).

4. Unless by (*date: at least seven days after the date of the notice*) the Council is satisfied that the Works are being carried out or that they will be started in the very near future, the Council may itself enter the Land on which the Building stands, and carry them out.

5. If the Council does decide to carry out the Works itself, you will be given as much warning as possible. You should be aware however that the Council is not obliged to give any warning after issuing this Notice. If therefore it considers that the need for the Works has become so urgent that they must be carried out without any delay, you will not be given any further warning.

[6. Items (*specify*) in the Schedule [*or* Schedule Two] are works for affording temporary support [*or* shelter] for the Building; the support [*or* shelter] thus provided may be retained in place for as long as is necessary. The continuing cost of this is likely to be in the region of £(*specify*) per month.]

[7. When the Council has carried out the Works, you will be sent a further notice indicating the expenses incurred by the Council in doing so, and requiring you to reimburse it.] [You will [also] be sent further notices from time to time asking you to reimburse the Council for the ongoing expenses incurred in continuing to provide temporary support [*or* shelter].]

8. If the Council seeks at any stage to recover from you the expenses incurred by it in carrying out the Works, you will be given an opportunity to make representations to the Secretary of State—

   (a) that some or all of the Works were unnecessary for the preservation of the Building; or

   [(b) in the case of the items referred to in paragraph 6 above, that the temporary arrangements have continued for an unreasonable length of time; or]

   (c) that the amount being sought is unreasonable; or

   (d) that the recovery of that amount would cause you hardship.

The Secretary of State will then determine to what extent your representations are justified.

9. If you wish to discuss the need for the Works, or any other matter relevant to them, you should as soon as possible, and in any event before the date specified in paragraph 4 above, contact: (*specify*).

(*signature on behalf of local authority*)
(*date*)

[SCHEDULE ONE

(*description of building: only required where a simple address is insufficient to identify it*)]

SCHEDULE [TWO]

(*description of works to be carried out*)

D6. Carrying out urgent works: notice requiring owner to pay expenses

[see **10.3.6**]

DEMAND FOR PAYMENT: THIS NOTICE REQUIRES YOUR
URGENT ATTENTION

(*NAME OF LOCAL PLANNING AUTHORITY*)

PLANNING (LISTED BUILDINGS AND CONSERVATION AREAS ACT)
1990, SECTION 55

To: (*name and address of owner*)

1. The building known as (*specify*) ("the Building") is a listed building within the meaning given to that term by section 1(5) of the Planning (Listed Buildings and Conservation Areas) Act 1990 ("the Act"). [*or* The building known as (*specify*) ("the Building") is within a conservation area designated under section 69 of the Planning (Listed Buildings and Conservation Areas) Act 1990 ("the Act"). The Secretary of State has by a letter dated (*date*) given a direction under section 76 of the Act that the preservation of the building is important for maintaining the character and [*or* or] appearance of that area. Section 54 of the Act therefore relates to the Building as if it were a listed building.] The Building is shown on the map attached to this Notice edged in red [and is more fully described, for identification purposes only, in Schedule One to this Notice.]

2. (*Name of local planning authority*) ("the Council") is a local authority whose area includes the Building.

3. It appeared to the Council that certain works were urgently for the preservation of the Building. The Council informed you by a notice dated (*specify*) that, unless by (*date*) it was satisfied that those works were being carried out or that they would be started in the very near future, it would itself enter the Land on which the Building stands, and carry them out.

4. No satisfactory response was received to that notice [, nor to the subsequent letters it sent to you on (*dates*)]. The Council has therefore carried out itself [*or* arranged to be carried out on its behalf by a contractor] the works itemised in the Schedule [*or* Schedule Two] to this Notice ("the Works"). The expenses that were incurred by it in carrying out those Works [*or* arranging for those Works to be carried out] were as indicated in that Schedule.

5. The Council has resolved to require you to pay [part of] the expense of carrying out the Works.

6. YOU MUST THEREFORE NOW PAY THE SUM OF £ (*SPECIFY*) TO THE COUNCIL BY (*DATE: AT LEAST 28 DAYS FROM DATE OF NOTICE*). THIS MAY BE DONE BY ANY OF THE METHODS SPECIFIED IN THE ANNEX TO THIS NOTICE.

7. You may if you wish, at any time before (*date 28 days from date of notice*), make representations to the Secretary of State—

(a) that some or all of the Works were unnecessary for the preservation of the Building; or

(b) that the amount being sought is unreasonable; or

(c) that the recovery of that amount would cause you hardship.

Such representations should be sent to: (*specify*). A copy should also be sent to the Council.

8. When the Secretary of State has received any representations made to him [her], he [she] will determine to what extent they are justified, and will notify you of his [her] decision, the reasons for it and the amount that he [she] considers is reasonably recoverable. You will then be liable to pay that amount to the Council.

[9. Items (*specify*) in the Schedule [*or* Schedule Two] were works for affording temporary support [*or* shelter] for the Building; the support [*or* shelter] thus provided will be retained in place for as long as is necessary. The continuing cost of this is likely to be in the region of £(*specify*) per month. Further requests for payment will be sent to you from time to time. The right to make representations to the Secretary of State will apply to these further demands for payment as they do to the present demand. You will in addition be entitled to make representations to him [her] that the temporary arrangements have continued for an unreasonable length of time.]

10. If you wish to discuss the need for the Works, or any other matter relevant to them, you should as soon as possible, and in any event before the date specified in paragraph 7 above, contact: (*specify*).

(*signature on behalf of local authority*)
(*date*)

[SCHEDULE ONE

(*description of building: only required where a simple address is insufficient to identify it*)]

SCHEDULE [TWO]

(*description of works that have been carried out, together with cost*)

ANNEX

(*methods of payment*)

D7. Listed building repairs notice

[see **11.3.3**]

LISTED BUILDING REPAIRS NOTICE

(*NAME OF LOCAL PLANNING AUTHORITY*)

PLANNING (LISTED BUILDINGS AND CONSERVATION AREAS) ACT
1990, SECTION 48

To: (*name and address of owner/occupier*)

1. (*Name of local planning authority*) ("the Council") is the appropriate authority for the purposes of section 48 of the 1990 Act ("the Act") for the area containing (*address of building to be repaired*) ("the Building"). The Building is shown on the map attached to this Notice edged in red [and is more fully described, for identification purposes only, in Schedule One to this Notice].

2. It appears to the Council that the works specified in Schedule Two to this notice are reasonably necessary for the proper preservation of the Building, which is listed.

3. Once two months have elapsed following the date on which you are served with this notice, if the notice has not been withdrawn, the Council may request the First Secretary of State to authorise it to acquire compulsorily:

   (a) the Building; and

   (b) any land contiguous or adjacent to it which appears to him to be necessary for preserving the building or its amenities, or for affording access to it, or for its proper control or upkeep.

4. The Secretary of State may make or confirm an order for the compulsory purchase of the Building if:

   (a) it appears to him that reasonable steps are not being taken for the proper preservation of the Building;

   (b) he is satisfied that it is expedient to make provision for its preservation; and

   (c) he is satisfied that it is expedient for that purpose for it to be acquired compulsorily.

5. If compulsory purchase procedures are initiated, you will have the right to apply to the magistrates' court within 28 days of the service on you of the notice to treat, for an order staying the proceedings on the ground that reasonable steps have been taken for properly preserving the Building.

6. If the Building is compulsorily purchased following the service of this Notice, it shall be assumed for the purpose of assessing the compensation that is payable that listed building consent would be granted for any works:

(a) for the alteration or extension of the Building; or

(b) for its demolition for the purpose of carrying out development of any class specified in Schedule 3 to the Town and Country Planning Act 1990.

7. If the Secretary of State is satisfied that the Building has been deliberately allowed to fall into disrepair, for the purpose of justifying its demolition and the development or redevelopment of its site or any adjoining site, he may include in the compulsory purchase order a "direction for minimum compensation".

8. The effect of a direction for minimum compensation is that, for the purpose of assessing the compensation that is payable, it shall be assumed that:

(a) planning permission would not be granted for any development or re-development of the site of the Building; and

(b) listed building consent would not be granted for any works other than those necessary for restoring the Building and maintaining it in a proper state of repair.

9. Where a direction for minimum compensation is included in a compulsory purchase order or draft order, you will have the right to apply to the magistrates' court within 28 days of the service on you of the notice stating the effect of the order or draft order, for an order that no such direction should be included.

(signature on behalf of local authority)
(date)

If you require further information regarding this notice, you should contact: *(specify)*

[SCHEDULE ONE

(description of building: only required where a simple address is insufficient to identify it)]

SCHEDULE TWO

(specification of works to be carried out)

D8. Compulsory purchase following service of repairs notice: draft order

[see **11.3.4**]

THE BARCHESTER CITY COUNCIL (NO 5 DEANERY CLOSE)
COMPULSORY PURCHASE ORDER 2006

PLANNING (LISTED BUILDINGS AND CONSERVATION AREAS) ACT
1990, SECTION 47; ACQUISITION OF LAND ACT 1981

Barchester City Council (in this order called "the acquiring authority") makes the following order—

1. Subject to the provisions of this order, the acquiring authority is, under section 47 of the Planning (Listed Buildings and Conservation Areas) Act 1990 ("the Listed Buildings Act"), hereby authorised to purchase compulsorily [the land] [and the rights over land] described in paragraph 2 for the purpose of preserving the listed building known as No. 5 Deanery Close ("the Building").

2. (1) The land authorised to be purchased compulsorily under this order is the land described in Table 1 in the Schedule and delineated and shown in red on a map prepared in duplicate, sealed with the common seal of the acquiring authority and marked "Map referred to in the Barchester City Council (No 5 Deanery Close) Compulsory Purchase Order 2006".

[(2) The new rights to be purchased compulsorily over land under this order are described in Table 2 in the Schedule and the land is shown in green on the said map.][1]

[3. Under section 50 of the Listed Buildings Act"), the acquiring authority makes the following direction, being satisfied that the Building has been deliberately allowed to fall into disrepair for the purpose of justifying its demolition and the development or redevelopment of the site or any adjoining site:

For the purpose of assessing compensation and notwithstanding anything to the contrary in the Land Compensation Act 1961, the Town and Country Planning Act 1990 or the Listed Buildings Act, it is hereby directed that it shall be assumed:

(a) that planning permission would not be granted for the development or redevelopment of the site of the Building; and

(b) that listed building consent would not be granted for any works for the demolition, alteration or extension of the Building, other than development or works necessary for restoring it to and maintaining it in a proper state of repair.][2]

---

[1] para.2(2) is only to be included where it is necessary to purchase an interest in a parcel of land other than the Building itself.

[2] para.3 is only to be included where the building has been deliberately allowed to fall into disrepair for the purpose of justifying its demolition and the development or redevelopment of the site or any adjoining site (see **11.4.3**).

SCHEDULE

Table 1

Number on map (1)	Extent, description and situation of the land (2)	Qualifying persons under section 12(2)(a) of the Acquisition of Land Act 1981—name and address (3)			
		Owners or reputed owners	Lessees or reputed lessees	Tenants or reputed tenants (other than lessees)	Occupiers
1.	5, Deanery Close, Barchester: house and garden	[name]	[name]	[name]	[name]

Table 2

Number on map (4)	Other qualifying persons under section 12(2A)(a) of the Acquisition of Land Act 1981 (5)		Other qualifying persons under section 12(2A)(b) of the Acquisition of Land Act 1981—not otherwise shown in Tables 1 & 2 (6)	
	Name and address	Description of interest to be acquired	Name and address	Description of the land for which the person in adjoining column is likely to make a claim
2.	[name], 7, Deanery Close, Barchester	Right of way along northern boundary	[name]	7 Deanery Close

(*Date*)

[Attestation Clause]

D9. Compulsory purchase following service of repairs notice: notice to owner

[see **11.3.4, 11.4.3**]

THE BARCHESTER CITY COUNCIL (NO 5 DEANERY CLOSE) COMPULSORY PURCHASE ORDER 2006
PLANNING (LISTED BUILDINGS AND CONSERVATION AREAS) ACT 1990, SECTION 47; ACQUISITION OF LAND ACT 1981

1. Barchester City Council ("the Council") made on the (*date*) the Barchester City Council (No 5 Deanery Close) Compulsory Purchase Order 2006, under section 47 of the section 47 of the Planning (Listed Buildings and Conservation Areas) Act 1990 ("the Listed Buildings Act"). It is about to submit this order to the First Secretary of State for confirmation, and if confirmed, the order will authorise the Council to purchase compulsorily the land and the rights described below for the purpose of preserving the listed building known as No. 5 Deanery Close ("the Building").

2. A copy of the order and of the map referred to in it have been deposited at (*specify*), and may be seen at all reasonable hours.

3. Under section 47 of the Listed Buildings Act, any person having an interest in a listed building which it is proposed to acquire compulsorily under that section may, within 28 days after the service of this notice, apply to the magistrates' court for an order staying further proceedings on the compulsory purchase order; and if the court is satisfied that reasonable steps have been taken for properly preserving the Building, the court must make an order accordingly.

[4. The Council has included in the order a direction for minimum compensation (the meaning of which is explained in Schedule Two to this notice). Under section 50 of the Listed Buildings Act, any person having an interest in the building may, within 28 days after the service of this notice, apply to the magistrates' court for an order that the direction be not included in the order as confirmed; and if the court is satisfied that the Building has not been deliberately allowed to fall into disrepair for the purpose of justifying its demolition and the development or redevelopment of the site or any adjoining site, the court must make the order applied for.][3]

5. Subject to any action taken under the Listed Buildings Act (which also provides for appeals against decisions of the court), the position with respect to this order is set out below.

6. If no relevant objection as defined in section 13(6) of or paragraph 4(6) of Schedule 1 to the Acquisition of Land Act 1981 is made, or if all such objections made are withdrawn, or if the Secretary of State is satisfied that every objection

---

[3]   para.4 of the Notice and Sch.2 are only to be included where a direction for minimum compensation is to be included; see **11.4.3**.

made relates exclusively to matters of compensation which can be dealt with by the Lands Tribunal, the Secretary of State may confirm the order with or without modifications.

7. In any other case where a relevant objection has been made which is not withdrawn or disregarded, the Secretary of State is required, before confirming the order either—

    (i) to cause a public local inquiry to be held; or

    (ii) to afford to the objector an opportunity of appearing before and being heard by a person appointed by the Secretary of State for the purpose; or

    (iii) with the consent of the objector to follow a written representations procedure.

8. The Secretary of State may then, after considering the objection and the report of the person who held the inquiry or hearing or considered the written representations, confirm the order with or without modifications. In the event that there is no objection, whether by a qualifying person or otherwise, the confirming authority may in certain circumstances permit the acquiring authority to determine confirmation of the order.

9. Any objection to the order must be made in writing to the Council before (*date: at least 21 days after the date of the service of the Notice*) and should state the title of the order, the grounds of objection and the objector's address and interests in the land.

(*Signature on behalf of planning authority*)
(*date*)

SCHEDULE [ONE]. DESCRIPTION OF LAND [AND RIGHTS] TO BE ACQUIRED

(*description of all land and rights to be purchased: as to Schedule One to the draft order—see* **Form D8**)

[SCHEDULE TWO

1. If the Secretary of State is satisfied that the Building has been deliberately allowed to fall into disrepair, for the purpose of justifying its demolition and the development or redevelopment of its site or any adjoining site, he may include in the compulsory purchase order as confirmed a "direction for minimum compensation".

2. The effect of a direction for minimum compensation is that, for the purpose of assessing the compensation that is payable, it shall be assumed that:

    (a) planning permission would not be granted for any development or redevelopment of the site of the Building; and

    (b) listed building consent would not be granted for any works other than those necessary for restoring the Building and maintaining it in a proper state of repair.]

D10. Compulsory purchase order following service of repairs notice: application to magistrates' court to stay proceedings: complaint and summons

[see **11.3.5**]

(NAME) MAGISTRATES' COURT

(<i>Date</i>)

To the Defendant (<i>name of authority which issued the notice</i>) of (<i>address</i>)

You are hereby summoned to appear on (<i>date</i>) at (<i>time</i>) before the Magistrates' Court at (<i>address</i>) to answer the following complaint:

MATTER OF COMPLAINT: The Complainant is a person having an interest in (<i>address of building</i>), which is a listed building ("the Building"). He [She] states that reasonable steps are being taken for properly preserving the Building, but that under powers in section 47 of the Planning (Listed Buildings and Conservation Areas) Act 1990 the (<i>name of local authority</i>) has been authorised by the Secretary of State to acquire compulsorily the building [together with (<i>specify</i>) hectares of land adjacent or contiguous to it];

AND the Complainant now applies for an order staying all further proceedings for the compulsory acquisition of the Building [and associated land].

The grounds of this application are:

(<i>specify steps taken for the preservation of the building</i>)

The complaint of: (<i>signature of or on behalf of complainant</i>) (<i>Address and telephone number</i>) who upon oath [or affirmation] states that the Defendant is responsible for the matter of complaint of which particulars are given above.

TAKEN [and sworn [or affirmed]] before me this (<i>date</i>)

(<i>signature</i>) Justice of the Peace [or Justices' Clerk]

D11. Notice to be issued after partial collapse of listed building

[see **12.4.7, 19.4.3**]

[NAME OF LISTED BUILDING]

PLANNING (LISTED BUILDINGS AND CONSERVATION AREAS) ACT 1990, SECTION 47

IMPORTANT AND URGENT NOTICE

To (*name of owner/occupier*)

[To whom it may concern][4]

1. (*name of building*) ("the Building") is a building listed by the Secretary of State as a building of special architectural or historic interest, under the Planning (Listed Buildings and Conservation Areas) Act 1990. (*name of authority*) ("the Council") is the local planning authority for the area including the Building.

2. It has come to the attention of the Council that on or about (*date; and approx time if appropriate*) the Building sustained damage by virtue of [fire] [vehicle impact] [partial collapse during the course of building operations] [*specify*].

3. The remaining part of the building consists of: (*specify*). This is still a listed building for the purposes of the Act until it has been removed from the list by the Secretary of State.

4. This remaining structure was inspected on (*date; and approx time if appropriate*) by (*names of Council officers or other professionals involved*) on behalf of the Council.

5. [The remaining structure appears to be safe for the time being, without the need for any further works to be undertaken.] [*or* The remaining structure may be unsafe; but any danger to the public can be eliminated by erecting fencing in the position as shown on the plan.] [*or* The remaining structure may be unsafe; but any danger to the public can be eliminated by (*specify remedial works urgently necessary*).]

6. Any works other than those specified in the previous paragraph will require listed building consent, which should be sought as a matter of urgency from the Council. Failure to obtain such consent may lead to prosecution under sections 7 and 9 of the 1990 Act.

7. If in spite of this notice you decide or are advised that further works are urgently necessary for health or safety reasons, you should inform the Council immediately to discuss the position. The officer dealing with this matter is (*specify*), on telephone number (*specify*). Out of office hours, you should contact (*specify*), who should be also contacted in the event of any queries.

---

[4] Where the name of the owner or occupier is unknown.

D12. Need for listed building consent: action for a declaration: particulars of claim to accompany Part 7 claim form

[see **4.6.2** and **12.10.4**]

(*Royal Arms*)

In the High Court of Justice   Claim No. CO/   /2006
Queen's Bench Division
Administrative Court list

Between:

A. B.

Claimant

—and—

The Barchester City Council

Defendant

PARTICULARS OF CLAIM

1. The building known as Barchester New Mill, Barchester ("the Listed Building") was included on May 12, 1989 within a list of buildings of special architectural or historic interest approved or compiled by the Secretary of State under section 1 of the Planning (Listed Buildings and Conservation Areas) Act 1990 ("the Act").

2. The Claimant has been since 1887 and is the freehold owner of land at (*address*) ("the Land"). The Land contains a group of buildings including the Listed Building and the building known as Barchester Old Mill ("the Old Mill"). The Claimant bought the land on (*date*) 1887 from [B], who had bought it on (*date*) 1852 from [A]. [A] had owned the Land prior to 1852.

3. The Listed Building was built in around 1890, and has been used from then until 1985 for the manufacture of cloth and for ancillary activities. Since 1985 it has been largely vacant.

4. The Old Mill is a building approximately 23 metres to the south of the Listed Building. It was built in or around 1855, and was used for the manufacture of cloth until 1887, when it was converted for use for the storage of cloth made in the Listed Building. A row of lean-to sheds spanning from the Old Mill to the Listed Building was constructed at unknown dates between 1907 and 1958. From 1982 until 1989 the Old Mill was vacant, and since a date in or around June 1989 it has been used by [C] for storage of electronic equipment. From February 1 1989 a part of the Land containing the Old Mill has been leased to [C].

5. The Claimant now intends to carry out works ("the Works") to alter and extend the Old Mill, to convert it for use for flats, as follows: (*specify*).

6. The Defendant is the local planning authority for the district of Barchester, which includes the Listed Building and the Old Mill.

7. No listed building consent has been sought or granted in relation to the Works.

8. The Defendant has indicated by a letter of (*date*) that it considers that to carry out the Works without listed building consent would constitute a contravention of section 9(1) of the Act. It has further indicated that, if an application for listed building consent were to be made to authorise the Works, it is unlikely that consent would be granted having regard to the desirability of preserving the Listed Building, its setting and the features of architectural or historic interest which it possesses.

AND the Claimant claims:

1. a declaration that the Old Mill is not to be treated as part of the Listed Building for the purposes of section 1(5) of the Act in that:

   (a) the Old Mill was not at the date on which the Listed Building was listed within its curtilage;

   (b) further or alternatively, the Old Mill is not an object or structure attached to the Listed Building;

2. further or alternatively, a declaration that listed building consent is not required for the carrying out of the Works in that they are not works for the demolition of the Listed Building or any part of it or for the alteration or extension of the Listed Building or any part of it in any manner which would affect its character as a building of special architectural interest;

3. further or other relief; and

4. costs.

Statement of truth

Served etc

D13. Application for listed building consent: financial evaluation of proposal

[see **13.3.8, 14.4.6**]

WORKS TO 142 LONDON ROAD, BARCHESTER DEVELOPMENT APPRAISAL SUMMARY

Scheme 1: repair and refurbishment for residential use (without need for listed building consent)

price that can be paid for land	£540,000

Scheme 2: refurbishment and alteration for office use (with listed building consent):

price that can be paid for land	£1,140,000

Existing (residential) use:

value in current condition	£600,000

Conclusion: Scheme 1 is not viable; scheme 2 is viable

SCHEME 1: REPAIR AND REFURBISHMENT FOR RESIDENTIAL USE (WITHOUT NEED FOR LISTED BUILDING CONSENT)

To yield building of floor area 1,500 sq m gross, 1,100 sq m net,

(a) Capital value on completion

Rent of £140 per sq m on net floor area of 1,100 sq m	154,000	
Capitalised at 7% (14.29 YP)	2,200,000	
Less purchaser's costs at 2.75%	60,500	
		2,140,000

(b) Deduct building costs

Construction costs of £500 per sq m on gross floor area of 1,500 sq m		750,000	
Professional fees at 12.5%		93,750	
		843,750	
Finance costs at 14% for 12 months		59,050	
Legal fees	8,000		
Agents: Letting	19,000		
Sale	46,000		
Promotion	15,000		
		80,000	
			991,000

(c) Gross margin [value (a) minus cost (b)]

available for land purchase and profit element   1,149,000

(d) Land acquisition costs

Price of land	x
Finance at 14% for 2 years on price of land (x)	0.3x
Acquisition costs	0.04x
	1.34x

(e) Developer's profit

at, say, 25% of costs [(b) plus (d)]   247,750 + 0.333x

Total of (d) and (e)   247,750 + 1.673x

Price that can be paid for land $= \dfrac{1,149,000 - 247,750}{1.67}$

= £539,670

say £540,000

SCHEME 2: REFURBISHMENT AND ALTERATION FOR OFFICE USE (WITH LISTED BUILDING CONSENT)

To yield building of floor area 1,500 sq m gross, 1,200 sq m net,

(a) *Capital value on completion*

Rent of £150 per sq m on net floor area of 1,200 sq m	180,000	
Capitalised at 6% (16.66 YP)	3,000,000	
Less purchaser's costs at 2.75%	82,500	
		2,917,500

(b) *Deduct building costs*

Construction costs of £450 per sq m on gross floor area of 1,500 sq m		675,000	
Professional fees at 12.5%		84,375	
		759,375	
Finance costs at 14% for 12 months		53,155	
Legal fees	8,000		
Agents: Letting	19,000		
Sale	46,000		
Promotion	15,000		
		80,000	
			900,500

(c) *Gross margin [value (a) minus cost (b)]*

available for land purchase and profit element	2,017,000

(d) *Land acquisition costs*

Price of land	x
Finance at 14% for 2 years on price of land (x)	0.3x
Acquisition costs	0.04x
	1.34x

(e) *Developer's profit*

at, say, 20% of costs [(b) plus (d)]	180,100 + 0.27x

Total of (d) and (e)	180,100 + 1.61x

Price that can be paid for land = $\dfrac{2{,}017{,}000 - 180{,}100}{1.61}$

$$= £1{,}140{,}931$$

say £1,140,000

D14. Application for listed building consent: supporting letter to local planning authority

[see **13.7.2**, **14.4.1**, **14.7.1**]

Cllr Slope,
Chair, Planning and Development Committee,
Barchester City Council,
Civic Centre,
Barchester BR1 4EA   September 7, 2005

Dear Cllr Slope,

142 London Road, Barchester: Applications nos TP/05/724,725/L

I understand that your Committee is to consider the above applications (for planning permission and listed building consent) at its meeting on 16 September. They concern a proposal to refurbish and upgrade the interior of a fine Grade II listed building, and to replace a later extension to the rear with a more suitable modern one. The purpose of these works is to create a regional office for Universal Computer Products PLC, which is a successful and expanding company providing a number of jobs in your area.

You will be aware that the villas along the north side of this part of London Road were built in around 1853, in a somewhat florid Italianate style, to house the newly wealthy merchants of that period. Number 142, in common with most of the others, was converted into flats after the war. More recently (in about 1964) it was subdivided further into small bed-sitters—largely used by student nurses from the nearby Hospital. The house became increasingly seedy, and has been partly vacant since 1994. By the time our client purchased a 99-year lease in 2003, the property was in a poor state of repair.

One or two of the villas in this group were demolished in the 1950s, but an application (by the former owner) to demolish No 142 was refused in 1997. Our client is now very keen to save the building and restore it to its former glory, to avoid its eventual demolition—which would not be in accordance with policy ENV 6.

The proposed works to the interior of the building are necessary partly by way of repair, in view of its current dilapidated state, and partly in order to bring it up to the standards of modern office accommodation elsewhere. We have however tried to retain all the principal internal features of any merit. The new accommodation will also be entirely level-access, so as to enable the Company to comply fully with the Disability Discrimination Act 1995.

The existing rear extension is of no particular value, in that it appears to have been tacked on in the 1930s, to provide extra space for kitchens etc. Our proposal is to replace this with a slightly larger but more sensitively designed extension. This will also provide additional floor-space that will in turn reduce the need to alter the main building.

The removal of the existing extension and the construction of sensitively designed replacement will also improve the setting of the neighbouring property, no 140, which is also a listed building—particularly when seen from the Park to the rear. It thus complies with Local Plan policy ENV 7.

As to the change from residential to office use, a financial appraisal was submitted with the application, showing that the only viable alternative was to demolish the whole building. To refurbish it for residential use would not yield a high enough residual value to do more than cover the cost of the works. There is space for an attractively landscaped car park area, to accommodate sufficient parking spaces for both cars and bicycles, to comply with policy MOV 5; London Road is also served by a number of bus routes, thus reducing the need for car use.

In the light of the above, I trust that you will agree that this proposal should be welcomed as a way of bringing this important building back into productive use— and thus also of enhancing the character and appearance of the surrounding London Road conservation area, in line with policy ENV 8.

If you have any queries, please do not hesitate to get in touch.

Yours sincerely,
S. Harding
Design Group

D15. Application for planning permission and listed building consent: unilateral undertaking

[see **11.5.1, 13.8.8**]

UNILATERAL UNDERTAKING

THIS UNILATERAL UNDERTAKING is given this   day of 20

BY (*NAME*) of (*address*) ("the Applicant")

TO (*name of local planning authority*) ("the Council")

WHEREAS:

(A) The Council is the local planning authority for the purposes of the Town and Country Planning Act 1990 ("the Planning Act") and the Planning (Listed Buildings and Conservation Areas) Act 1990 ("the Listed Buildings Act") for the area within which is the freehold land referred to in this Undertaking;

(B) The Applicant owns the freehold interest in land and buildings known as (*specify*) ("the Land"), shown edged red on the plan annexed to this Undertaking;

(C) The building known as *specify*) ("the Building") is included in the list of buildings of special architectural and historic interest maintained by the Secretary of State under the provisions of the Listed Buildings Act;

(D) The applicant has submitted on (*date*) to the Council two applications (together referred to as "the Applications"), as follows:

   (i)   an applicant for planning permission to change the use of the Building and to carry out certain building operations on the Land ("the First Application"), Council reference (*specify*); and

   (ii) an application for listed building consent to carry out those building operations ("the Second Application"), Council reference (*specify*); and

(E) The Council has refused those applications;

(F) The Applicant has appealed to the Secretary of State against those refusals;

(G) The Applicant has indicated that the applications should be granted, either subject to conditions or subject both to conditions and to the entering into of an undertaking;

NOW THIS UNDERTAKING WITNESSES as follows:

1. This Undertaking is made under section 106 of the Planning Act (and is a planning obligation for the purposes of that section).

2. The Council is the local planning authority by which the provisions of this Undertaking are intended to be enforceable.

3. Except as shall be specifically provided in the remainder of this Undertaking, no person shall be liable for any breach of the covenants restrictions or obligations contained in this Undertaking occurring after he has parted with his interest in the Land, or the part in respect of which such breach occurs.

4. This Undertaking shall come into effect only when the Secretary of State or an inspector on his behalf shall have granted the planning permission and listed building consent for the works that are the subject of the Applications:

5. If any permission or consent thus granted is quashed or is revoked or withdrawn or (without the consent of the Applicant) is modified by any statutory procedure, this Undertaking shall cease to have effect.

6. If the Applications are granted by or on behalf of the Secretary of State, the applicant undertakes to observe and perform the restrictions and obligations set out in the Schedule to this Undertaking.

7. The applicant further undertakes to pay on demand any legal costs reasonably incurred by the Council as a result of this undertaking.

8. The Applicant recognises that this Undertaking will be registered as a local land charge in the Register of Local Land Charges maintained by the Council.

9. Save where the context otherwise requires, references in this Undertaking to any party shall include the successor in title to that party.

IN WITNESS OF THE ABOVE the Applicant has duly executed this Undertaking as a deed and has caused its common seal to be affixed to it on the day and year first before written.

THE COMMON SEAL of (*name of applicant*)

was affixed to
this Undertaking
in the presence of:

SCHEDULE

RESTRICTIONS AND OBLIGATIONS TO BE OBSERVED AND PERFORMED

1. The Applicant will (*specify*)

D16. Appeal against refusal of planning permission and listed building consent: content of proof of evidence

[see **14.4.1, 14.7.1, 15.3.5**]

EVIDENCE OF (*NAME*) IN SUPPORT OF [THE APPEAL BY (*NAME*) AGAINST] THE REFUSAL BY BARCHESTER CITY COUNCIL OF PLANNING PERMISSION AND LISTED BUILDING CONSENT FOR A CHANGE OF USE TO OFFICES OF 142 LONDON ROAD, BARCHESTER AND NEW OFFICE EXTENSION IN THE REAR GARDEN

1.   Qualifications and experience of witness

    1.1 Qualifications
    1.2 Experience in previous employment
    1.3 Present role

2.   Barchester: historical background

    2.1 General (outline) history
    2.2 History of London Road area pre-1990
    2.3 Recent history of London Road area

3.   Conservation areas affected by proposal

    3.1 Initial designation of the London Road Conservation Area
    3.2 Later extensions
    3.3 Character of the London Road Conservation Area
    3.4 Appearance of Conservation Area
    3.5 Assessment of importance
    3.6 Other conservation areas potentially affected

4.   142 London Road

    4.1 History pre-1914
    4.2 History since 1914
    4.3 Features of building
    4.4 Setting of building
    4.5 Assessment of importance
    4.6 Shortcomings of present accommodation

5.   Other listed buildings affected by proposal

    5.1 Description of buildings
    5.2 Setting of buildings
    5.3 Assessment of importance

6.   Archaeological potential

    6.1 Archaeological significance of area
    6.2 Exploratory work carried out to date

7. Description of proposal

    7.1 Planning history of site

    7.2 Evolution of present proposal

    7.3 Description of appeal proposal

    7.4 Negotiations following the submission of the application

    7.5 Accommodation of needs of disabled people

    7.6 Distinction between alternative schemes before the inquiry

8. Impact of proposals

    8.1 Impact on 142 London Road itself and its features

    8.2 Impact on setting of 142 London Road

    8.3 Impact on setting of other listed buildings

    8.4 Impact on London Road Conservation Area

    8.5 Impact on other conservation areas

    8.6 Impact on archaeological potential of area

9. Assessment by reference to the local development framework

    9.1 Introduction

    9.2 Structure plan

    9.3 Draft replacement structure plan

    9.4 Local plan: site-specific policies

    9.5 Local plan: other policies

    9.6 Deposit draft modifications to local plan

10. Assessment by reference to central government policy

    10.1 PPG 15 (Historic Buildings and Conservation Areas)

    10.2 PPG 16 (Archaeology and Planning)

11. Assessment by reference to other published policy documents

    11.1 Site brief

    11.2 English Heritage policy statement on conservation areas

    11.3 Council non-statutory policy for conservation area

12. Miscellaneous points

    12.1 [etc]

13. Other comments on grounds of appeal

14. Suggested conditions

15. Conclusions

Appendices

A   Barchester: history

    A1 Map showing historical development of City

B   Conservation areas

    B1 Map showing present extent of London Road Conservation Area and neighbouring conservation areas

    B2 Initial designation of London Road Conservation Area: Committee report of February 14, 1972

    B3 First extension (report of July 17, 1985)

    B4 Second extension (report of December 13, 1991)

C   142 London Road

    C1 Plan showing ages of parts of main building and curtilage buildings

D   Listed buildings affected by proposal

    D1 Map showing location, grades and assumed curtilages of listed buildings

    D2 List descriptions of buildings

E   Archaeological potential

    E1 Map showing location of exploratory work carried out to date

F   Impact of proposals

    F1 Map showing area from which new building will be visible

    F2 Sections through site showing visibility of roof

    F3 Elevation from rear, showing actual line of existing roofs

    F4 Elevation of east side of London Road, showing impact of proposal

G   The local development framework: extracts

    G1 Structure plan

    G2 Draft replacement structure plan

    G3 Local plan

    G4 Deposit draft modifications to local plan

H   Government policy: extracts

    H1 PPG 15 (Historical Buildings and Conservation Areas)

    H2 PPG 16 (Archaeology and Planning)

I   Other published policy documents: extracts

    I1 English Heritage policy statement on conservation areas

    I2 Council non-statutory policy for conservation area

J   Suggested conditions

D17. Listed building purchase notice

[see **15.5.2**]

LISTED BUILDING PURCHASE NOTICE
(*NAME OF LOCAL PLANNING AUTHORITY*)
PLANNING (LISTED BUILDINGS AND CONSERVATION AREAS) ACT 1990, SECTION 32

To the Chief Executive (*or other title as appropriate*) of (*name of local planning authority*) ("the Council").

(*name and address of listed building*)

The above listed building ("the Building") was the subject of an application for listed building consent (planning authority reference (*specify*)) dated (*date*) [to (*insert name of local planning authority if not the same as Council on whom this notice is served*). That application was refused [*or* was granted subject to conditions] on (*date*).

The land at (*address*) which is shown on the map attached to this Notice edged in red [and which is more fully described for identification purposes only, in the Schedule to this Notice] ("the Land") is land contiguous [*or* adjacent] to the Building. The use of the Land is substantially inseparable from the use of the Building, and the Land and the Building ought therefore to be treated together as a single holding.

As a result of that refusal of consent, the Building and Land have become incapable of reasonably beneficial use in their existing state.

[*or* As a result of the conditions attached to that consent, the Building and Land cannot be rendered capable of reasonably beneficial use by the carrying out of the works for which consent was granted.]

Further, the Building and Land cannot be rendered capable of reasonably beneficial use by the carrying out of any works for which listed building consent has been granted, or in respect of which the local planning authority or the Secretary of State have undertaken to grant consent.

I [We] therefore require the Council to purchase my [our] interest in the Land, which is (*specify*).

All correspondence on this matter should be sent to me [us] [or my [our] agent, (*name*)] at (*address and telephone number*).

(*signature of or on behalf of owner*)

(*date*)

D18. Listed building enforcement notice

[see **18.3.6**]

(*NAME OF LOCAL PLANNING AUTHORITY*)

PLANNING (LISTED BUILDINGS AND CONSERVATION AREAS) ACT
1990, SECTION 38

TO: (*name of recipient*)

1. (*Name of local planning authority*) ("the Council") is the local planning authority for the purposes of section 38 of the 1990 Act ("the Act") for the area containing (*address of building*) ("the Building"). The Building is shown on the map attached to this Notice edged in red [and is more fully described, for identification purposes only, in the Schedule to this Notice].

2. The Building is included within a list of buildings of special architectural or historic interest approved or compiled by the Secretary of State under section 1 of the Act [*or* is the subject of a building preservation notice under section 3 of the Act].

3. It appears to the Council that the works specified in the Second Schedule to this Notice ("the Works") have been [*or* are being] executed to the Building.

4. It appears to the Council that the Works are such as to constitute a contravention of section 9(1) [*or* 9(2)] of the Act.

5. The Council considers it expedient to issue this notice having regard to the effect of the unauthorised works on the character of the Building as one of special architectural or historic interest, and for the reasons set out in the Annex to this Notice.

THE COUNCIL GIVES NOTICE that, under section 38 of the Act, it requires the steps specified in the Third Schedule to this Notice to be taken within (*a period of at least 28 days*) from the date on which this Notice takes effect, for the purpose of [restoring the Building to its former state] [*or* alleviating the effect of the Works, since it considers that the restoration of the Building to its former state would not be reasonably practicable or would be undesirable] [*or* bringing the Building to the state in which it would have been if the terms and conditions of the listed building consent specified in the Fourth Schedule to this Notice had been complied with].

This Notice shall take effect on (*date: at least 28 days after the date of the notice*), subject to the provisions of section 39 of the Act (relating to appeals to the Secretary of State).

(*signature on behalf of local planning authority*)
(*date*)

If you require further information regarding this Notice, you should contact:
(*specify*)

FIRST SCHEDULE

(*description of building: only required where a simple address is insufficient to identify it*)

SECOND SCHEDULE

[The demolition without listed building consent of part of the Building, namely (*specify part demolished*)]

[The alteration [or extension] of the Building without listed building consent by (*specify works of alteration or extension*)]

[The removal without listed building consent of objects [or structures] forming part of the Building, namely: (*specify objects or structures removed*)]

THIRD SCHEDULE

(*specify works to be carried out*)

FOURTH SCHEDULE

(*details of listed building consent, if any, granted*)

ANNEX

REASONS FOR ISSUING ENFORCEMENT NOTICE

(*example relates to removal of object or structure; to be adapted for other cases*)

1. The panelling in the Great Hall was prior to its removal fixed to the walls of the Great Hall of Barchester Castle ("the Building"), and was part of the original architectural scheme of the Hall; it was thus fixed to the Building. The staircase leading from the south terrace down to the lawn is a structure within the curtilage of the Building. By virtue of section 1(5) of the Planning (Listed Buildings and Conservation Areas) Act 1990, each was therefore to treated as part of the building for the purposes of the Act.

2. The said panelling was chosen and fixed to the walls of the Great Hall by the original owner of the Building, and were part of its original concept and design. Before its removal, it was a feature of special architectural and historic interest, and contributed significantly to the character and appearance of the Great Hall, and thus to that of the Building as a whole.

3. The staircase was built by a subsequent owner of the Hall as part of the laying out of the grounds in 1886. Before its removal, it contributed significantly to the setting of the Building.

4. The removal of the panelling and of the staircase represented partial demolition of the Building, or alternatively its alteration in such a manner as to affect its character as a building of architectural or historic interest, within the meaning of section 7 of the Act.

5. The Council considers that listed building consent should not be granted for the removal of the panelling or the staircase, having regard to the desirability of preserving the Building, its setting and all the features of special architectural or historic interest which it possesses.

D19. Injunction to prevent unauthorised works to listed building: particulars of claim to accompany Part 7 claim form

[see **18.7.5**]

(*Royal Arms*)

In the High Court of Justice
Queen's Bench Division
Administrative Court list
Between:

Claim No. CO/   /2006

Barchester City Council

Claimant

—and—

A. B.

Defendant

PARTICULARS OF CLAIM

1. The Claimant is the local planning authority for the district of [Barchester], which includes the building known as [Barchester Hall, Barchester] ("the Building").

2. The Building is included within a list of buildings of special architectural or historic interest approved or compiled by the Secretary of State under section 1 of the Act [*or* is the subject of a building preservation notice under section 3 of the Act].

3. [It appears to the Claimant that] works have been [*or* are being] carried out to the Building on or about (*date*), as follows:

(*specify*)

4. The Defendant has indicated [in a letter to the Claimant of (*date*)] his intention [*or* The Claimant has discovered that the Defendant intends] to carry out [further] works [*or* to continue carrying out works] to the Building ("the Intended Works"), as follows:

(*specify*)

5. The nature of the Intended Works is such that it would not subsequently be possible or reasonably practicable to restore the building to the state in which it was prior to their carrying out.

6. No listed building consent has been granted in relation to the Intended Works [*or* listed building consent was granted on (*date*) for (*specify*), but the Intended Works are not within the terms of that consent], and they therefore constitute a contravention of section 9(1) [*or* 9(2)] of the Act.

7. If an application for listed building consent were to be made to authorise the Intended Works, it is unlikely that consent would be granted having regard to the

desirability of preserving the Building, its setting and the features of architectural or historic interest which it possesses.

8. The Claimant fears that, unless the Defendant is restrained by this honourable court, he will carry out [or continue carrying out] the Intended Works and/or other works for the demolition of the Building [or for the alteration or extension of the Building in a manner which would affect its character as a building of special architectural interest].
AND the Claimant claims:

(1)   an injunction restraining the Defendant by himself his servants or agents from carrying out without listed building consent any works for the demolition of the Building or for its alteration or extension in any manner which would affect its character as a building of special architectural interest;

(2)   further or other relief; and

(3)   costs.

(*Signed*) etc

Served on (*date*) by (*name*) [,agents for (*name and address*)], solicitors for the Claimant

D20. Injunction to prevent unauthorised works to listed building: witness statement to accompany claim form

[see **18.7.5**]

Claimant; *J Smith; 1st; (date)*

In the High Court of Justice   Claim No. CO/   /2006
Queen's Bench Division

Administrative Court list

Between:

Barchester City Council

Claimant

—and—

A. B.

Defendant

I, [*John Smith*] of (*address*), [*town planner*], say as follows:

1. I am [an assistant planning officer] employed by the Claimant, and am duly authorised to make this affidavit on its behalf. The facts deposed to in it are, except as noted, true to the best of my knowledge and belief.

2. The Claimant is the local planning authority for the district of [Barchester], which includes the building known as (*specify*) ("the Building").

3. There is now produced and shown to me marked ["JS 1"] a bundle containing the following documents:

(a) the extract from the list compiled and maintained by the Secretary of State under section 1 of the Planning (Listed Buildings and Conservation Areas) Act 1990, including the entry for [*or* the building preservation notice served on (*date*) in relation to] the Building;

(b) photographs of the Building taken on (*date*) [, before the carrying out of the recent works];

(c) extracts from the Claimant's file relating to the Building, containing past correspondence, applications for planning permission and listed building consent, and relevant decisions of the Secretary of State on appeals;

(d) an exchange of correspondence between the Claimant and the Defendant relating to the carrying out of recent works to the Building;

(e) letters to the Claimant from [the secretary of the Barchester Society and from others], regarding threats made by the Defendant to carry out [further] works [*or* to continue to carry out works] to the Building.

4. The Building is a listed building of considerable interest, but is currently in a poor state of repair. It is, however, capable of restoration at reasonable expense.

5. The Defendant is the owner of the Building, and has on several occasions sought consent to alter or extend it; he has also recently applied for planning permission for new housing in its curtilage. He has also carried out various minor works to the Building without listed building consent on or about (*date*); the Claimant is currently considering whether to take enforcement action.]

6. [The letters received by the Claimant from the secretary of the Barchester Society and from others indicate that the Defendant intends to demolish the Building in the next few days.]

7. [By letters dated (*dates*), the Claimant reminded the Defendant that the Building was listed [*or* subject to a building preservation notice], and that listed building consent would be required for its demolition or for its alteration or extension or extension in any way which affected its character. No replies were received to any of those letters. I telephoned the Defendant on (*date*), and he told me not to waste my time writing letters as he would ignore them, that he did not need permission, and that he could do what he chose with his own building.]

8. It is my belief that, unless restrained by the Court, the Defendant intends to demolish all or at any rate a substantial part of [*or* carry out substantial alterations to] the Building. I consider that listed building consent would be required for those works.

9. No listed building consent has been granted in relation to the works which I believe are to be carried out [*or* listed building consent was granted on (*date*) for (*specify*), but the works which I believe are to be carried out are not within the terms of that consent], and they therefore constitute a contravention of section 9(1) [*or* 9(2)] of the Act.

10. My understanding is that the nature of the intended works is such that it would not subsequently be possible or reasonably practicable to restore the Building to its present state. It would therefore not be practical to take enforcement action once the works have been carried out.

11. I also consider that, if an application for listed building consent were to be made to authorise the intended works, it is unlikely that consent would be granted, having regard to the desirability of preserving the Building, its setting and the features of architectural or historic interest which it possesses.

12. I respectfully request this Honourable Court to grant the Order sought in the Claimant's summons.

Statement of truth [etc]

This Statement is filed on behalf of the Claimant.

D21. Injunction to prevent unauthorised works to listed building: draft order

[see **18.7.5**]

(*Royal Arms*)

In the High Court of Justice   Claim No. CO/   /2006
Queen's Bench Division
Administrative Court list

The Hon Mr Justice (*name*)
(*day and date*)

Between:

Barchester City Council

Claimant

—and—

A. B.

Defendant

Defendant

UPON MOTION for an injunction made today to this Court by Counsel for the Claimant

AND UPON READING the Claim Form issued on (*date*) and the witness statement of [John Smith] filed on the same day in support of the Claimant and the exhibits referred to in that statement,

AND UPON HEARING Counsel for the Claimant,

AND the Claimant undertaking by its Counsel

(1) to abide by any order that this Court may make as to damages in case this Court shall hereafter be of the opinion that the Defendant by reason of this Order shall have sustained any which the Claimant ought to pay, and

(2) to notify the Defendant forthwith of the making of this Order,

THIS COURT ORDERS that the Defendant be restrained whether by himself his servants or agents from carrying out without listed building consent any works for the demolition of (*specify the building*) or for its alteration or extension in any manner which would affect its character as a building of special architectural interest

Costs reserved.

NOTICE: IF YOU (*NAME*) DISOBEY THIS ORDER YOU WILL BE LIABLE TO PROCESS OF EXECUTION FOR THE PURPOSE OF COMPELLING YOU TO OBEY THE SAME.

D22. Informations to be laid before magistrates

[see **19.9.4**]

JOHN SMITH on or about 1st January 2006 carried out without authorisation works for the alteration of a listed building, namely 1 Cathedral Close, Barchester, in a manner that affected its character as a building of special architectural or historic interest, namely:

(*specify unauthorised works*)

contrary to sections 7 and 9(1) of the Planning (Listed Buildings and Conservation Areas) Act 1990.

JOHN SMITH on or about 1st January 2006 carried out works to a listed building, namely 2 Cathedral Close, Barchester, for its alteration in a manner that affected its character as a building of special architectural or historic interest, namely (*specify unauthorised works, as described in the listed building consent*), in breach of conditions [2 and 3] of the consent ref. (*specify*) granted on (*date*), in that

(*specify breaches of conditions*)

contrary to sections 7 and 9(2) of the Planning (Listed Buildings and Conservation Areas) Act 1990.

JOHN SMITH, being the freehold owner of a listed building, namely 21 Cathedral Close, Barchester, on or about 1st January 2006 or permitted to be carried out without authorisation acts which caused or were likely to result in damage to that building, namely:

(*specify unauthorised acts*)

contrary to section 59(1) of the Planning (Listed Buildings and Conservation Areas) Act 1990.

JOHN SMITH on or about 1st January 2006 carried out without authorisation works for the demolition of a building subject to a building preservation notice, namely 99 Cathedral Close, Barchester, contrary to sections 7 and 9(1) of the Planning (Listed Buildings and Conservation Areas) Act 1990, as applied by section 3(5) of that Act.

JOHN SMITH on or about 1st January 2006 carried out without authorisation works for the demolition of an unlisted building in a conservation area, namely 190 London Road, Barchester, contrary to sections 7 and 9(1) of the Planning (Listed Buildings and Conservation Areas) Act 1990, as applied by section 74(3) of that Act.

Appendix E

Conditions on listed building consents

These sample conditions are based on those in Annex F to Welsh Office Circ. 61/96. For a general discussion on conditions, see **13.8**. Note that, as with all precedents, these conditions will need to be adapted to suit particular circumstances.

The author would welcome any suggestions for additions, to be included in a future edition of this book.

E1. The duration of consent

1. The works to which this condition relates shall be begun not later than [three] years from the date of this consent.

E2. Matters to be resolved before the start of works

2. No works shall be carried out on the site until details of [the detailing of the new windows on the east elevation] [*or* the method of safeguarding of the Michelangelo sculpture in the main hall during the course of the works] [*or* the matters specified in Schedule One] [*etc*] have been supplied to and approved in writing by the local planning authority, and the work shall then be carried out in accordance with those details.

3. No works shall be carried out to the [plaster ceiling of the Chinese Library] until details of [its restoration] have been supplied to and approved in writing by the local planning authority, and the work shall then be carried out in accordance with those details.

4. The building [*or specified part*] shall not be demolished before:
   (a) a contract for the carrying out of the works of redevelopment of the site has been made, and
   (b) planning permission has been granted for the redevelopment for which that contract provides.

5. The building [*or specified part*] shall not be demolished [*or specified element of the building* shall not be removed from the building] until:

(a) notice has been given in writing to [English Heritage] [*or* the Royal Commission on the Ancient and Historical Monuments in Wales *or* Scotland *or* the Department];

(b) reasonable access to the building [*or* the part to be demolished or removed] has been made available for at least one month to the members and officers of [English Heritage] [*etc.*] for the purpose of recording it; and

(c) a duly authorised officer of [English Heritage] [*etc.*] has stated in writing either that it has completed its recording of the building or that it does not wish to record it.

6. For a period of [14 days] before work starts, [*name of person or body*] shall be given access to the building to enable to take photographs of the interior [or make measured drawings].[1]

7. In respect of [the removal of the panelling from the dining room], the local planning authority shall be given [14 days] notice of the intention to carry out the works, and [*name of person or body*] shall be allowed access to the building to enable to take photographs [*or* make measured drawings] of any fabric of historical or architectural interest before it is covered up [*or* removed] in continuance of the work for which consent has been given.[2]

E3. The carrying out of the works

8. The demolition of the [wall/roof/porch/etc.] shall be carried out by hand [*or* by tools held in the hand other than power-driven tools] and the materials stored for re-use.[3]

9. The staircase/panelling/chimney-piece] in [*location*] [*or* the items listed in Schedule Two] shall be removed and stored under cover [*or* in a location approved in writing by the local planning authority] for re-use in the building as part of the works permitted by this consent [*or* elsewhere] [*or* at a location approved in writing by the local planning authority].

10. The [plaster ceiling/wall painting] in the room identified as GF 2 on Plan no. 123A shall be removed under the supervision of a contractor specialising in this type of work, appointed by the developer/applicant and approved by the local planning authority. It shall thereafter be stored under cover [*or* at a location approved in writing by the authority] for re-use [*etc*].

[1] This condition must not specify who is to pay for the photographs or drawn records (although, if the applicant or owner has in fact offered to make a satisfactory record him herself, that can be required, in terms reflecting the offer made). The time allowed must be reasonably short, and must not unreasonably interfere with the execution of the authorised works. This condition does not affect the obligation to allow access to the relevant recording body (see Condition 5 above, and **13.7.10**).

[2] See note 1.

[3] Demolition by hand is expensive, and this condition should only be used where it is essential to avoid damage to the part of the building which is to remain standing.

11. The internal features [*specify wherever possible*] which are removed in accordance with this consent, together with as much as practicable of the original external materials, shall be incorporated in the new buildings.

12. Dado weatherboarding from [*or to match that in*] the existing rear wall of the cottage shall be used on the rear wall of the extension hereby permitted.

13. The front range of this building, as shown in red on Plan 124A, shall be retained and incorporated into any new development on this site.[4]

14. Before any work is undertaken to demolish any part of the building, the applicant shall take such steps and carry out such works as shall, during the progress of the works permitted by this consent, secure the safety and stability of that part of the building which is to be retained in accordance with condition [13] above. Such steps and works shall where necessary include, in relation to any part of the building to be retained, measures:

   (a) to strengthen any wall or vertical surface;
   (b) to support any floor, roof and horizontal surface; and
   (c) to provide protection for the building against the weather during the progress of the works.[5]

15. The carved entrance doorway, surround, balcony and panelling, extending across the whole width of the western end of the building, as shown in green on Plan 125A, shall be retained in situ and shall be protected during the whole period of alterations by a plywood box cover mounted on a timber frame, to the satisfaction of the local planning authority.

16. The windows in the extension to which this consent relates shall be side-hung casements in plain glass without any glazing bars.

17. The door in the extension to which this consent relates shall be timberboarded.

E4. The completion of the works

18. The building [*or a specified part*] shall not be re-occupied following the start of the works until all the works [*or a specified element of the works*] have been completed to the satisfaction of the local planning authority.

19. Any damage caused by or during the course of the carrying out of the works hereby permitted shall be made good after they are complete.

---

[4] This condition should be linked to the following one; and should be accompanied by one similar to no.4 above.
[5] This condition should be linked to the preceding one.

E5. Personal or temporary consents

20. When the building ceases to be used by [*named occupier*], the works hereby permitted shall be reversed, and the building shall as far as practicable be restored to the condition in which it is immediately prior to the carrying out of the permitted works, with such alterations as the local planning authority may approve in writing.

Appendix F

Penalties for Criminal Offences

F1. The standard scale

A number of statutes referred to at various points in this book provide for certain activities in certain circumstances to be criminal offences. Where such a statute only refers to the maximum penalty on summary conviction—that is, following trial in a magistrates' court—the offence is referred to as a "summary offence". Where a higher maximum penalty is provided in the event of conviction on indictment—that is, following trial in the Crown Court (by a jury)—the offence is referred to as a "triable either way" offence.

In either case, maximum penalties following summary conviction are fixed by reference to the standard scale prescribed by statute.[1] The current scale is as follows:

Level on the scale	Amount of fine
1	£200
2	£500
3	£1,000
4	£2,500
5	£5,000

Where a statutory provision refers to "the statutory maximum", that is equal to the "prescribed sum", which is currently £5,000.[2]

All of the above amounts may be increased by order, to reflect the changing value of money.[3] However, no such order has in fact ever been made—even

---

[1] Criminal Justice Act 1982, s.37(2), as substituted by Criminal Justice Act 1991, s.17(1). [Scotland: Criminal Procedure (Scotland) Act 1995, s.225; NI: Fines and Penalties (NI) Order 1984, art.5(2), as substituted by Criminal Justice (NI) Order 1994, art.3(2).

[2] Magistrates' Courts Act 1980, s.32(9), amended by Criminal Justice Act 1991, s.17(2). [Scotland: 1995 Act, s.225(8); NI: 1984 Order, art.4(8), as amended by 1994 Order, art.3(1).]

[3] Magistrates' Courts Act 1980, s.43, as amended by Criminal Justice Act 1982, s.48. [Scotland: 1995 Act, s.225(4), NI: 1984 Order, art.17(4), as substituted by 1994 Order, art.9.]

though the present scale and statutory maximum have been in place since 1992 (or, in Northern Ireland, 1995).

F2. Fines in practice

Some indication as to the level of fines imposed in practice is given by the following tables, based on data collected for the Institute of Historic Building Conservation (IHBC) by Bob Kindred, and reproduced here with his permission. Details of further recent convictions, and of future ones, should be sent to him at 4 Henley Road, Ipswich IP1 3SF. All the cases noted here are subsequent to the change in levels of penalties in 1991, when the maximum fine for an offence under section 7 of the Listed Buildings Act was increased to £20,000 in the magistrates' court (unlimited in the Crown Court).

For brief commentary, see **19.10.5**.

(a) The Crown Court

1991

Binchester, Co. Durham: Roman Fort (scheduled monument) damaged by negligence; owner pleaded guilty to three counts, fined on each £11,000, reduced on appeal to £5,000: costs £10,000, not reduced on appeal.[4]

1992

Dartmouth, Devon: demolition of Methodist chapel (Grade II), using explosives; developer jailed for four months, the explosives expert also four months, three months suspended for two years. [South Hams DC].

Market Bosworth, Leics: alterations to the Old Rectory (Grade II); listed status disputed; protracted and expensive case; owner fined £1,000 on two counts, plus (substantial) costs, and required to re-build (cost £25,000). [Hinckley BC].

Downley, Bucks: replaced all timber-framed sash windows of farmhouse (Grade II*) with uPVC; enforcement action failed to secure replacement; after two years, double-glazing firm fined £5,000 ("national company should have known better") and owner £250; plus costs of £200. [Wycombe DC].

Southwark, London: remains of Winchester Palace (scheduled monument) partially destroyed by building works; developer fined £75,000 (plus £1,000 costs), reduced on appeal to £15,000.[5]

1993

Bewdley, Worcs: rebuilding and partial demolition of Dowles Manor (Grade II, downgraded from Grade II* following fire), after obtaining consent for extensive

---

[4] *R. v Simpson* (1993) 14 Cr. App. R. (S) 602; see **19.10.1**.
[5] *R. v J.O. Sims Ltd* (1993) 14 Cr. App. R.(S) 213; see **19.10.1**.

repairs; owner fined £15,000 (plus £15,000 costs), halved by Court of Appeal.[6] [Wyre Forest DC].

1994

Hampton Lucy, Warwicks: demolition of central chimney-stack and other alterations to Grovefields Farmhouse (Grade II); case transferred by Magistrates to Crown Court; owner (also developer) fined £5,000 (plus £1,167 costs). [Stratford-upon-Avon DC].

Stoke Newington, London: works to roof, and rear extension; fine on roof works lowered on appeal, but fine for extension doubled (and costs increased); total fine £5,000 (plus £5,300 costs). [Islington LBC].

1996

Chigwell, Essex: alterations to windows of Hainault Hall (Grade II); six charges; owner fined £3,500 (plus £17,500 costs); conviction overturned by Court of Appeal.[7] [Epping Forest DC].

1997

Wakefield, W. Yorks: removal of 16th and 17th-century oak panelling and fireplaces; owner pleaded guilty to two of eight charges; fined £6,000 on each (plus £25,490 costs). [Wakefield MBC].

Eckington, Derbyshire: major alterations to roof and interior of Carter Hall (Grade II); owner fined £6,000 (plus £19,720 costs); only escaped imprisonment because of guilty plea and agreement to reinstate features. [NE Derbyshire DC].

1998

Newport, Gwent: partial demolition of Stelvio House (Grade II) one day after listing; owners pleaded guilty; categorised by judge as "cynical commercial act"; fined £200,000, based on likely profit from redevelopment of site (plus £13,000 costs). [Newport CBC].

2000

Rangemore, Staffordshire: three owners sold fireplaces from Grade II* Hall to antique dealer; claimed theft; listed building enforcement notices served; prosecuted under Fraud Act; two pleaded guilty, sentenced to nine months; one pleaded not guilty, convicted and sentenced to 12 months. [East Staffordshire DC].

2005

Virginia Water, Surrey: demolition of Greenside (iconic 20th-century house), following application for listed building consent but while Secretary of State was

---

[6] *R. v Duckworth* (1995) Cr. App. R. (S) 529; see **19.10.1**, **19.10.4**.

[7] *R. v Sandhu* [1997] J.P.L. 853; see **19.9.6**, **19.10.4**.

considering whether to call it in (retrospective consent subsequently refused); guilty plea; fined £15,000 (plus £10,000 costs). [Runnymede BC].

(b) Magistrates Courts

1991

Norwich: installation of solid roller shutter to shopfront (Grade II); defendant a TV personality targeted by animal rights activists; absolute discharge; enforcement notice upheld requiring removal. [Norwich CC].

Odstone, Leicestershire: demolition of barn in curtilage of farm (Grade II); owner claimed barn not listed and dangerous; two charges; fined total of £500 (plus £500 costs); gain from sale of bricks ignored; not required to rebuild. [Hinckley BC].

Northchurch, Herts: demolition of 17th-century dovecote (Grade II); claimed structure was dilapidated and action not deliberate; owner (MP) and wife (county councillor) fined £500 each, plus costs (unknown). [Dacorum DC].

1992

Trumpington, Cambs: demolition of curtilage building and alteration of two others (unlisted); fined £21,500 (plus £2,460 costs); on appeal, Crown Court waived fine (but not costs), but required building to be re-erected.

Marlborough, Wilts: satellite dish on Cricketers Arms PH (Grade II); owner fined £100 (plus £250 costs). [Kennet DC].

Orchardleigh, Gloucs: removal of overmantle and fender from country house (Grade II*); executor of estate fined £2,000, plus costs; conviction overturned on appeal. [Mendip DC].

Scotter, Lincs: demolition of garage and store, in curtilage of Manor House (Grade II); owner claimed ignorance; fined £250, and his company £400; plus costs of £250. [West Linsey BC].

Bridgnorth, Shropshire: external alterations to Grade II building; defendant (of no fixed abode) fined £350 (plus £150 costs)

Welshpool, Powys: removal of statue of Icarus (separately listed Grade II*) from pond at Leighton Hall; owner pleaded guilty, but claimed removal was to avoid theft; fined £500; statue (valued at £50,000) later returned. [Montgomery DC].

Legsby, Lincs: demolition of farmhouse (Grade II) in spite of condition on consent requiring repair; husband and wife owners each fined £1,250 on each of two charges (plus £4,000 costs). [West Linsey DC].

Orgreave, Staffs: failure to comply with LBEN requiring removal of unauthorised lift shaft from Grade II building; owner fined £3,000 (no costs). [Lichfield DC].

1993

Barnsley, S. Yorks: replacement of timber sash windows by uPVC; owners (who were chartered surveyors) refused consent for retention; fined £1,000 (plus £1,125 costs). [Barnsley MBC].

Broseley, Shropshire: works to Grade II building; fine of £200 (plus £200 costs); because of personal circumstances of defendant, payment allowed at £20 per week. [Bridgnorth DC].

Thurgarton, Notts: alterations including concrete window lintels and uPVC rainwater goods, to Rose Cottage (Grade II); fine of £250 (plus £70 costs). [Newark & Sherwood DC].

Clerkenwell, London WC1: demolition of all except front wall of Grade II building; two charges of failing to comply with conditions and causing demolition; architect fined £2,000; owner (housing assn) £1,000; costs (£5,500) split equally. [Camden LBC].

Hingham, Norfolk: signs on shop (Grade II), following enforcement action and two warnings of prosecution; guilty plea; fine of £200 (plus costs of £614). [South Norfolk DC].

1994

Long Stratton, Norfolk: signs painted onto 17th c. brickwork of Wig & Dickle PH (Grade II); works authorised by brewery; lessee fined £5,000 (plus £787 costs). [South Norfolk DC].

Kirklington, Notts: removal of roof timbers from barn in curtilage of Greet Farmhouse (Grade II); fine of £5,000, reduced on appeal to Crown Court to £1,000, plus costs of £120, reduced on appeal to nil. [Newark & Sherwood DC].

Burton-upon-Trent, Staffs: non-compliance with condition on consent requiring record to be made of redundant machinery before removal from mill (Grade II) and re-use elsewhere; owner fined £3,000 (plus £6,000 costs). [East Staffordshire BC].

Stoke Newington, London N16: alterations to Grade II building; three charges; owner fined £5,000 (plus £5,300 costs); appealed to Crown Court; fine for roof works reduced, but fine for rear extension doubled. [Hackney LBC].

Stillingfleet, N. Yorks: demolition of east wing of Stillingfleet House (Grade II) after consent granted for demolition of minor outbuildings and internal alterations; owner fined £500 (plus £1,000 costs). [Selby DC].

Iver, Bucks: demolition of Love Green Farmhouse (Grade II), following consent for alteration and extension; allegedly unsafe; owner instructed contractor; owner fined £10,000, reduced on appeal to Crown Court to £8,320; costs of £433. [South Bucks DC].

Ipswich, Suffolk: failure to reinstate three sliding sash windows on 98 St Helens Street (listed Grade II); because of financial circumstances of defendant, allowed conditional discharge, but still required to pay £100 costs and to reinstate windows.[8] [Ipswich BC].

Ramsbury, Wilts: demolition of chimneystack and internal walls and floors at the Institute (Grade II); developer claimed building in poor repair and relied on s.9(3) unsuccessfully; fined £10,000 (plus £1,750 costs). [Kennet DC].

1995

Bicester, Oxon: removal of rare Venetian window from Kings Arms Hotel (Grade II); owner (brewery) not prosecuted; design consultants fined £2,000 (plus £375 costs). [Cherwell DC].

Eardington, Shropshire: removal of fireplace from the Knowle (Grade II); absolute discharge, because defendant bankrupt. [Bridgnorth DC].

Much Wenlock, Shropshire: total demolition of Grade II building; prosecution under s.80 of Building Act 1984 (see **9.1.2**) as well as under P(LBCA)A 1990; owner fined £1,800, two contractors fined £1,200 and £600; plus costs of £4,850. [Bridgnorth DC].

Heytesbury, Wilts: refusal to restore redundant entrance gates to Grade II house (temporarily in storage after estate severed by bypass); fined £10,000; reduced on appeal to Crown Court to £500; plus costs (unknown). [West Wiltshire DC].

Kensington, London W8: removal of plasterwork from three floors of noted 1862 interior of 18 Holland Park (Grade II), as part of conversion from flats back to house; owner (chartered surveyor) fined £3,000 (plus £2,000 costs). [Kensington & Chelsea RBC].

Bilsthorpe, Notts: demolition of chimneys and cart lodge wings of Rectory Farm (unlisted in conservation area); fine of £500 (plus costs of £250); enforcement action secured rebuilding. [Newark & Sherwood DC].

Uppey, Dorset: demolition of leucomb at Uppey House (Grade II); no financial benefit from works; loss of English Heritage grant greater than maximum fine; owner required to reinstate; absolute discharge. [Weymouth BC].

Ascott-under-Wychwood, Oxon: extension and alterations to Langley Mill (Grade II); owner fined £3,500 (plus £300 costs). [West Oxfordshire DC].

Great Yarmouth, Norfolk: signs, lighting, etc. on 18th-century Liberty's wine bar "in wild defiance of local authority", owner fined £1,500 on each of seven charges plus £500 for unauthorised laser advertisement, plus £365 costs (Recorder: "most fortunate to escape imprisonment"); appeal to Crown Court unsuccessful, but £300 further costs. [Great Yarmouth BC].

---

[8] See second offence in 2001.

Hoveringham, Notts: non-compliance with request for information and breach of condition notice relating to Homeleigh (Grade II); Council pointed to neglect of building; defence pleaded poverty; fined £650 and £800 (plus £840 costs). [Newark & Sherwood DC].

Stoke Goldington, Bucks: demolition and rebuilding of barn at Chestnut Farm (unlisted in conservation area) following consent to convert; owner failed to notify Council; pleaded not guilty; fined £600, based on income, plus £1,400 costs. [Milton Keynes BC].

Newton Blossomville, Bucks: demolition of barn at Home Farm (unlisted in conservation area); owner (councillor) did not gain financially; pleaded guilty; fined £1,000, plus £235 costs. [Milton Keynes BC].

1996

Atlow, Derbyshire: numerous internal and external alterations to the Parsonage (Grade II), despite prior site meeting with Council; all alterations treated as one charge; new purchasers (husband and wife) each fined £1,000 (plus £250 costs); remedial works cost £25,000. [Derbyshire Dales DC].

Kirby, Merseyside: alterations including imitation windows and uPVC guttering to Grade II building; owner fined £2,000 (plus £225 costs); remedial works not done; further prosecution; owner pleaded guilty; fined further £500 (plus further £150 costs). [Knowsley MBC].

Soho, London W1: alterations to 27–28 St Anne's Court (Grade II), including removal of panelling (c. 1710), and opening up between buildings; leaseholder pleaded guilty; fined £650 on each of seven charges; enforcement notice complied with. [Westminster CC].

Brewood, Staffs: failure to comply with condition on LBC forbidding use of power tools for raking out pointing of Grade II house. Defendant contractor had been paid less than half cost of works; pleaded guilty; fined £2,000 (plus £200 costs). [South Staffs DC].

Northampton: rendered brick rear elevation, reduced chimney stack on 19th-century building (Grade II); retrospective application for consent (refused); fined £100 (plus £100 costs). [Northampton BC].

Orsett, Essex: various alterations to Old Hall Farmhouse (Grade II); owners (MP and husband) each fined £3,000 plus £4,000 costs; enforcement action largely successful in achieving reinstatement. [Thurrock BC].

King's Cross, London N1: gutting of 19th-century house (Grade II), removing all period features, to convert to bed-sits; described by Magistrate as "serious and flagrant offence"; charge against owner dropped; his company fined £10,000 (plus £3,000 costs). [Islington LBC].

1997

Enville, Staffs: demolition of of grade II cottage in poor condition, to replace with carport; plea changed to guilty prior to trial; fined £2,000 (plus £500 costs). [South Staffs DC].

Edingley, Notts: alteration of farm buildings in curtilage of Goldhill Farm (Grade II) including raising roof, inserting rooflights; listed status not accepted; owner fined £9,000 (plus £1,600 costs); appeal to Crown Court unsuccessful. [Newark & Sherwood DC].

Pickering, N Yorks: various alterations to Grade II building, four to five months after being advised by Council to stop works; owner fined £3,250 (plus £100 costs); reduced on appeal to Crown Court to £1,500). [Ryedale DC].

Ramsgate, Kent: alterations to roof of Grade II building; non-compliance with enforcement notice requiring reinstatement; owner fined £500 (plus £300 costs). [Thanet DC].

Debenham, Suffolk: numerous alterations to Grade II* building; owner given absolute discharge, builder conditional discharge plus costs (amount unknown). [Mid-Suffolk DC].

Ipswich, Suffolk: internal alterations and damage to medieval fabric of Old Bell Inn (Grade II), to install new beer chilling equipment; installer cautioned; owner prosecuted on three charges of damage; pleaded guilty; fined £3,000 (plus £350 costs). [Ipswich BC].

Ramsgate, Kent: painting brickwork on end-of-terrace flank wall of Grade II house; owners pleaded guilty; fined £200 (plus £75 costs). [Thanet DC].

Utling, Essex: various alterations to the Granery, Utling Hall (Grade II); conditional discharge (plus £50 costs). [Maldon DC].

1998

Esher, Surrey: non-compliance with listed building enforcement notice requiring restoration of Sandown House (Grade II) following removal of internal features by owners for safety and by vandals; unsuccessful challenge in High Court[9]; owners fined £5,000 (plus £5,000 costs). [Elmbridge BC].

Haydon Wick, Wilts: alterations to the Manor Farmhouse (Grade II) to insert extractor fans, and demolition of two curtilage walls; owners (brewery) pleaded guilty to four charges; fined £5,000 on each, plus £2,000 costs. [Swindon BC].

Salmesbury, Lancs: various alterations to the Campions pub (Grade II); guilty plea; fined £5,000 (plus £600 costs). [South Ribble DC].

Eynsham, Oxon: internal alterations (staircases, galleries) to two barns (listed Grade II); contractor fined £1,200 (plus £1,300 costs). [West Oxon DC].

[9] *R. v Elmbridge BC v Active Office Ltd* [1998] J.P.L. B43, (1998) 10 Admin L.R. 561; see **18.6.2**.

Farnham, Surrey: alterations to Grade II building; owner, surveyor, two builders pleaded guilty (surveyor only after hearing evidence); owner, surveyor given conditional discharges; builders fined £500 (plus £5,000 costs). [Waverley BC].

Wereham, Norfolk: timber-framed windows in PH (Grade II) replaced with uPVC; court accepted that proper windows had been replaced by trial; fined 1,500 (plus £800 costs). [Kings Lynn BC].

Totteridge, London: internal alterations to Grade II cottages; guilty plea to 14 specimen charges for removal of windows, doors etc; fined total £7,500 (plus £1,000 costs). [Barnet LBC].

1999

Lerwick, Shetlands: contractor removed of c.1900 shopfront from Grade C building, prior to consent being obtained, despite being told to keep it; fined £10,000 (plus costs). [Shetland Islands Council].[10]

Southwark, London: demolition of Grade II building; owner and company each fined £10,000 (plus £4,000 costs); appeal to Crown Court dismissed (judge would have increased fine if he could). [Southwark LBC].

2000

Totteridge, London: replacement of 1950s metal-framed windows with new sash windows at Grade II house; owner pleaded guilty; fined £2,000 per window (plus £850 costs).

Stadhampton, Oxon: internal works to pub (listed Grade II) allegedly done before purchase; listed building enforcement notice; appeal failed; non-compliance; guilty plea; fined £15,000 (plus £577 costs). [South Oxfordshire DC].

Ipswich, Suffolk: installed poor-quality BT shopfront in Grade II building; refused listed building consent; corrected before trial; guilty plea; fined £10,000 ("major retailer should have known better") (plus £600 costs). [Ipswich BC].

Ipswich, Suffolk: external and internal alterations; listed building and planning enforcement notices; seven charges of non-compliance; plea changed to guilty on day of trial; fined £6,500 (plus £1,500 costs). [Ipswich BC].

Kelvedon, Essex: remarkably unaltered medieval hall house (Grade II*); sand-blasting of timbers, removal of windows, staircase etc; non-guilty plea; some plea bargaining; contractor fined £1,000, owner fined £2,000 (plus £2,150 costs). [Braintree DC].

2001

Ipswich, Suffolk: features removed from Grade II building; enforcement notice on new owner; not complied with; fined £2,000 (plus £200 costs). [Ipswich BC].

---

[10] Sheriffs Court.

Stanmore, Middx: international style house (unlisted, CA); inappropriate render and new windows; non-compliance with enforcement notice; husband and wife (separated) each fined £2,100 (plus £700 costs each). [Harrow LBC].

Hammersmith, London: alterations to interior; four items charged as one offence; only one proved; absolute discharge.[11]

Ipswich, Suffolk: early 18th-century doorcase removed from 98 St Helens Street, with modern replacement; non-compliance with listed building enforcement notice even in extended timescale; second offence[12]; fined £500 (plus £350 costs). [Ipswich BC].

Buxton, Derbys: 18th-century mill by Arkwright, consent for conversion, unauthorised demolition of part; guilty plea; fined £12,500 (plus £6,000 costs). [Peak District NPA].

Islington, London: alteration and extension of Grade II house; guilty plea; individual owner and company prosecuted; fined total £12,500 (plus £9,200 costs). [Islington LBC].

Thorpe Underwood, N Yorks: removal of chimney stack, Grade II* house; fined £4,00 (stack) and £2,000 (consequential removal of chimneybreast) (plus £30,000 costs). [Harrogate BC].

2002

Bramshaw, Hants: demolition of granary in curtilage of Grade II house; poor condition not accepted as justification for failure to obtain consent; fined £5,000 (plus £1,750 costs). [New Forest DC].

Iden Green, Kent: alterations to Grade II listed farmhouse; 22 charges; five guilty pleas; charges dropped after meeting authority's costs (£45,000; in addition to defendant's costs estimated at £50,000). [Tunbridge Wells BC].

Belton, Lincs: demolition of c.1750 building (Grade II) in poor repair; plea changed to guilty in court; fined £3,000 (plus £3,000 costs). [North Lincolnshire DC].

Knightsbridge, London: additional storey on listed (Grade II) house; designer claimed authorised by planning permission and listed building consent; pleaded not guilty; fined £1,200 (plus £4,000 costs). [Kensington & Chelsea RBC].

Brewood, Staffs: removal of features, inappropriate re-pointing etc at Hall, Stables and Gazebo (Grade II* and II); six offences under s.9, two under s.59; guilty plea; fines between £500 and £10,000, total £40,550 (plus £32,415 costs). [S Staffordshire DC].

---

[11] See *Braun v First Secretary of State* [2003] 2 P.L.R. 90, CA for the subsequent enforcement action and High Court proceedings; and see **18.3.5**.
[12] For first offence, see 1994.

2003

Tallentine, Cumbria: demolition of curtilage barn; argument as to danger from fallen masonry not accepted; fined £15,000 (plus £5,000 costs); on appeal to Crown Court, fine upheld and costs increased to £6,200.

Doune, Stirlingshire: demolition of house (Grade B), on buildings at risk register since 1992; claimed dangerous; fine £1,000 (plus £50 costs). [Stirlingshire Council].[13]

2004

Ormskirk, Lancs: total demolition of unlisted cottages in CA; failure to obtain CA consent or to notify under Building Act; no commercial gain,, guilty plea; fined £13,000 (plus £727 costs). [West Lancashire DC].

Hethe, Oxon: alterations to floor and tie-beams carried out by owner himself; pleaded guilty; sought community service penalty due to financial hardship; fined £5,000 (plus £500 costs). [Cherwell DC].

Ipswich, Suffolk: internal alterations to Grade II building; claim that work done partly by squatters not accepted; failed to notify authority; guilty plea, fined £8,000 (plus £2,000 costs). [Ipswich LBC].

2005

Banbury, Oxon: total demolition of two unlisted houses in conservation area; developer and contractor each pleaded guilty; plea in mitigation (work undertaken in good faith for health and safety) accepted by court, would otherwise have referred to Crown Court for sentence; each fined £15,000 plus £13,000 (plus costs of £5150). [Cherwell DC].

Aspartia, Cumbria: demolition of offshoot building and internal wall; Grade II farmhouse; guilty plea; £3,000 fine for offshoot, £2,000 for wall (plus costs of £300). [Allerdale DC].

---

[13] Sheriffs Court.

Appendix G

Possible Changes to the Law

G1. Introduction

The Planning and Compensation Act 1991 and the Planning and Compulsory Purchase Act 2004 both contained very few provisions directly relevant to the cultural heritage. In the course of the debate in the House of Lords on the former, the spokesman for the Government observed that the heritage was so important that it deserved a separate bill to itself—when parliamentary time permitted, of course. Fifteen years later, that bill has yet to appear.

However, over the last 10 years, the Government has issued a number of consultation papers. Those in England include the following—

- *Protecting our Heritage*, issued by the Department for National Heritage in May 1996;

- *The Power of Place*, produced by English Heritage in December 2000;

- *A Force for Our Future*, produced by the DCMS December 2001, at the same time as the green papers that led eventually to the Planning and Compulsory Purchase Act 2004;

- *Protecting our Historic Environment: Making the System Work Better*, produced by the DCMS in July 2003; and

- *The Future of the Ecclesiastical Exemption: a Consultation Paper for England*, produced by the DCMS in February 2004.

Protecting Our Heritage was issued jointly with the Welsh Office; in the same year, a similar (but not, of course, altogether identical) paper was produced by the Scottish Office, entitled *Protecting the Built Heritage* (Cm. 3267). The Welsh Assembly has produced *Review of the Historic Environment in Wales: a Consultation Document* and *Protection of Historical Assets in Wales: a Consultation Document* in March and September 2003; the Assembly's response to the representations in response to the former was published in January 2004.

In addition, the ODPM has commissioned a number of reports from consultants, including a review of the General Permitted Development Order by Nathaniel Lichfield & Partners in September 2003.

The most recent proposals from the Government, for England, are contained in the *Review of Heritage Protection: the Way Forward*, produced by the DCMS in June 2004. This is by way of a follow-up to the responses to the July 2003 consultation document, and contains proposals for the way forward, to be implemented in two stages—the first being those changes that did not require primary legislation, which could be brought in relatively quickly. Some of the changes outlined in that document have thus already been put into effect (notably the marginally increased role for English Heritage in the listing process, the increased user-friendliness of the listing system, the review of listing criteria, an informal right of appeal against listing, and a summary of importance and map). Those have already been noted in the main text as appropriate.[1]

The other principal initiatives put forward in the June 2004 document cannot be implemented in the absence of primary legislation; they will be further outlined in a White Paper, expected to appear sometime in the first half of 2006. The necessary bill is not expected until the Parliamentary session 2007/08 at the earliest, after which there will then be a need for regulations, and then a new version of PPG 15 and PPG 16, probably to be merged into a single document. The new system is thus not expected to be fully in place until around 2010—assuming no slippage!

In a separate initiative, the ODPM commissioned the Halcrow Group to look at the possible unification of the various consent regimes; the resulting report was published in June 2004, at the same time as *The Way Forward*.

This appendix outlines the proposals put forward by the Government that are expected to be taken forward in any new legislation; and summarises the conclusions of the Halcrow report. It then itemises a number of other possible changes that could be considered.

G2. Changes proposed by the Government

A new single register

The principal change on the horizon is that the Government has decided that there will be a new, single document entitled the "Register of Historic Sites and Buildings of England". This will contain two parts. The first, the main section, will be compiled by English Heritage, and will incorporate:

- world heritage sites;

- the existing statutory regimes of listed buildings and scheduled monuments; and

- the non-statutory regimes of historic parks and gardens, and battlefields.

The second will be a local section, compiled by planning authorities, and will include:

---

[1]   See **3.2.5, 3.3.1, 3.3.8, 4.6.4** and **12.8.4**.

- conservation areas, and

- locally listed buildings.

English Heritage will set the standards and criteria for entries in the local section.

The paper claims that "this arrangement is intended to demonstrate clearly that significance in the historic environment is assessed and owned from both ends, national and local. There is also an international dimension in World Heritage Sites". An alternative view is that the new register is trying to be all things to all people; in attempting to include such a wide variety of categories of heritage assets in a single register, there will be considerable confusion. Further, the change will be wholly irrelevant for the great majority of the 500,000 buildings already listed, where there is no need for any new designation.

It is to be hoped that any legislation introducing the new system will make it clear precisely what is intended to be included along with each item in each category, to avoid the difficulties that presently arise with the curtilage of listed buildings—although it is difficult to see how any system of registration will remove such problems altogether. It would also be good to ensure that the details of items that are available included in the new register—with detailed maps of each site—are on the web from the outset (following the admirable example of the registers of access land maintained by DEFRA and the CCW).

The new system will presumably sweep up the decision made some years ago to do away with areas of archaeological importance.

The Government also proposes to put on the face of the statute "an overarching definition of historic assets". It is not clear what that is supposed to mean; possibly, like "sustainable development", it will be the subject of much debate. However, the criteria for listing / scheduling are to be reviewed (again), with specific standards being set for each of the various categories of asset—archaeological remains, buildings, underwater assets, landscapes, battlefields and historic areas. The decision to include an item in the register will not take into account considerations—such as, in particular, regeneration and redevelopment issues—other than merit.

One interesting offshoot of this integrated approach is that there will in some cases be in effect an area designation at national level. This would apply, for example, to sites where there are numerous distinct but linked elements of the historic environment, such as a country house with its associated buildings, park and gardens, or a university campus with buildings of different ages. It would also apply in cases where current regimes do not really work, such as areas (both rural and urban) with extensive archaeological remains.

There is now in place a series of 15 pilot studies, launched by English Heritage, to test out a more integrated or holistic approach to protection, in relation to a wide variety of different types of heritage assets. These projects will no doubt focus primarily on designation; but hopefully they will also consider carefully the way in which buildings and land in each of these different categories can be most effectively protected after they have been identified and catalogued. The results will be fed into the next exercise; and more especially into the process of drafting the second-stage legislation.

Listing: other changes

Linked to the previous proposal is a commitment to give English Heritage statutory responsibility for listing in England. English Heritage has of course for
many years been responsible in practice.[2] So there would seem to be little change
in reality. But further proposals are designed to bolster this; in particular, that
there will be a policy framework set by the Secretary of State; and a statutory
right of appeal to him/her, as well as a power of call-in.

There is also, yet again, the oft-repeated pledge to make the listing system more
open—so that owners would be consulted before their building was included in
the register. Such a procedure would, obviously, need to be linked to a system of
interim protection, so as to avoid the hasty alteration or demolition of a building
being considered for inclusion in the register. Whilst therefore there is some
commitment to greater openness in the first stage of the reforms,[3] it is only at the
second stage, when there is the possibility of legislative changes to bring in the
interim protection, that the new system can really become effective.

However, even though 96 per cent of those responding to the 2003 consultation
exercise agreed with this approach, it may nevertheless be questionable how much
benefit will actually accrue. The whole process of listing is after all simply one of
"experts" (either actual experts or so-called ones) registering that a building is of
interest to them—the views of laymen may therefore be of limited relevance at
that stage. Later on, once there is a particular proposal, it may well be sensible to
balance the views of professionals who wish to see a building retained[4] against
those of the owners who wish to alter or demolish it; but that is a different
scenario from the initial selection process.

Almost everyone responding to the consultation felt that the grading system
should be maintained. The Government has accepted this, and proposes that the
present system of grading be made clearer, by the merging of Grades I and II*
into a new, unified, super grade of listing—Grade 1. That is sensible, but scarcely
revolutionary. On the other hand, there was a proposal in the consultation paper
that some buildings currently classified as Grade II should be reassigned to local
lists, but this was unpopular, and is not to be pursued. That is scarcely surprising,
politically, but is nevertheless unfortunate. There are after all almost half a million
listed buildings in England alone, of which around 96 per cent are Grade II; and it
simply cannot be true that all are of equal value. Some form of assessment would
be helpful to decision makers—both in considering proposals for alterations, and
in allocating scarce money for repairs. But it not likely that half of the listed
building owners in the land would wish to be "downgraded" to a new Grade 3,
whether statutory or otherwise. Nor is it clear how a system of grading will fit in
with a unified register of assets.

The Government has recognised the importance of Historic Environment
Records (HERs), the successors to the old Sites and Monuments Records, as they
underpin the new system of integrated registers. It accordingly proposes that local
authorities should all either maintain or have access to HERs, and that such

---

[2]   See **3.3.1**.
[3]   See **3.3.9**.
[4]   See **6.2.4**.

records should be placed on a statutory footing. This is particularly important in rural areas.

Works to historic buildings

Of greater concern in practice is the system for protecting historic buildings and areas from unsuitable changes. The first proposal here is that listed building consent and scheduled monument consent should be integrated into a single system. This makes sense, and would echo the integration of the two types of assets into a single register.

Secondly, there will be a system of statutory management agreements—provisionally to be called "Heritage Partnership Agreements" (HPAs)—enabling works in defined categories to be carried out on a regular basis without the need for detailed applications to be made in each case. This would be particularly suitable for large scale buildings, sites and landscapes; for complex historic entities that comprise more than one type of asset; and for assets better managed alongside other statutory regimes. Indeed, arguably, it is only sites in these categories that would benefit from the proposed new single register. Such an approach might also be suitable for assets of a similar type in single ownership but in dispersed locations—such as historic bridges and underground stations.

Perhaps surprisingly, this approach has also been recommended in the separate paper issued by the DCMS in July 2005 on works to historic places of worship.[5] It suggests, somewhat incoherently, that HPAs could be issued at area level—even though such buildings vary hugely, and no standard specification would be appropriate. However, pilot schemes are being set up to see whether such an approach would work—particularly in relation to buildings in cathedral precincts.

Finally, there has been for some while a commitment to replace PPG 15 (historic buildings) and PPG 16 (archaeology) with a single new planning policy statement (PPS). However, in view of the impending new legislation that would be needed to implement the changes outlined above, and consequential rules and regulations, it now seems unlikely that any new guidance will be produced until after the dust has settled on the new system.

Conclusion

Overall, the changes outlined here, taken as a whole, represent a partly worthwhile package of reforms, albeit scarcely radical. However, given that the great bulk of the country's historic assets have already been identified under the one or other of the existing regimes, it is difficult to see what is the real value in changing the designation / listing system now—is it perhaps a case of closing the stable door after the horse has bolted?

---

[5] *The Ecclesiastical Exemption: the Way Forward* (see **16.3.9**).

G3. The Unification of Consent Regimes

In a separate initiative, the Halcrow report (*Unification of Consent Regimes*) also supported the unification of listed building and scheduled monument consents as a first stage. It also noted that conservation area consent is in fact only rarely required, and recommended that it be rolled up into planning permission, which is after all needed for all development, including demolition—the current exemption from the definition of "development" of the demolition of buildings that are listed or in a conservation area arises solely as a result of a ministerial direction, which could easily be reversed.

Looking further ahead, the authors of the report—after considering a number of possible models, as well as the system in other countries—considered that there was much to be said for the merging all four consents into one. This would seem to offer a huge degree of simplification, with no loss of control.[6] Surprisingly few amendments would need to be made to the planning application procedures to enable the incorporation within it of all the distinctive features of the present listed building consent procedures—in particular, as to consultation and publicity for particular categories of proposed works. Such a change would also automatically absorb many of the other suggested amendments noted at **G4** below.

The scope of the works for which planning permission is required would thus need to be slightly enlarged, so as to include all demolition, all alterations and extensions affecting the character of listed buildings, all works to scheduled monuments, and all advertising. That would then enable the repealing of the requirement for separate systems of listed building consent, conservation area consent, scheduled monument consent, and consent under the Advertisements Regulations—many works requiring these other forms of consent also require planning permission anyway. It is noteworthy that local planning authorities and even High Court judges frequently muddle up the terminology relating to the different types of permission and consent.

Such a system of unified consent would have obvious administrative advantages, with only one application, one committee report, one appeal, one enforcement notice, etc. for each proposal. At present, the two types of application are in almost all cases dealt with together. It would involve no loss of control, as all those works which presently require listed building consent would still require permission; and breach of that requirement would still be a criminal offence, marking the importance of listed buildings.

Such a change would make no difference in policy terms, as precisely the same policy test applies at present to both types of application—currently under section 16 of the Listed Buildings Act in relation to listed building consent and section 66 of that Act in relation to planning permission.[7] And the duty in relation to works in conservation areas applies equally to the determination of both types of

---

[6] This was an idea first canvassed in an article at [1998] J.P.L. 101, and in the previous edition of this book, and then explored in greater depth in a paper published by the Society of Advanced Legal Studies on *The Simplification of the Planning System*.

[7] See **14.2.1** and **14.2.3**.

application.[8] The abolition of a separate system of listed building consent would, more positively, bring the control of works to listed buildings into the mainstream of planning control, so that heritage issues can be considered on an equal footing alongside other issues such as employment, traffic, retail prosperity, and accessibility. It would also reconnect the built heritage back into the mainstream planning system, where it belongs—reversing the process unwittingly started by the Law Commission 16 years ago when, by consolidating planning legislation into three Acts instead of one, it marginalised listed buildings and conservation areas, and accelerated by the Government when it set up the Department for the National Heritage (now the DCMS) in 1992.

The House of Commons ODPM Housing, Planning, Local Government and the Regions Committee, welcomed this proposal, in its report on *The Role of Historic Buildings in Urban Regeneration*, issued in July 2004. But the Government has not yet promised any legislation, although it has undertaken to consider the way forward. However, in practice, it is likely that the unification proposal, if is to be implemented at all, would best be dealt with at the same time as the other matters referred to above (and below) that require primary legislation.

G4 Other possible changes

In the course of the preparation of the English Heritage consultation document *Power of Place* in 2000, a paper was prepared summarising a number of possible changes to this area of law—some left over from the 1996 document *Protecting Our Heritage*, some suggested in the previous edition of this book, and others coming from a variety of sources. The notes below highlight the most significant of those that have not either been adopted by the Government, in the course of the various initiatives noted earlier in this Appendix, or else overtaken by the passage of time. They are not necessarily commended by the present author (indeed a few seem impractical or positively unhelpful), but they are all are gathered together here for completeness.

The order of these suggestions generally follows that of the main book; reference should be made to the Chapters indicated for further details of the existing law and procedures. For simplicity, they have been drafted by reference to law and practice in England; but most would apply equally to Wales, Scotland and Northern Ireland.

Administrative and general (Chapter 1)

The responsibility for heritage matters in England could be given to a single Government department, instead of being split between the ODPM and the DCMS. Conversely, every Government department could be given a statutory responsibility towards the historic environment, with one Department taking the lead.

The name of the Historic Buildings and Monuments Commission could be formally changed to "English Heritage", and its statutory duties and functions, under the National Heritage Act 1983, conflated. Its accountability, and the

---

[8] See **14.7.1**.

openness of its decision-making procedures, could be improved. In addition, its powers in Greater London could be extended so as to apply to the rest of England. And it could be given a more formal role in the development and revision of any legislation and Government initiatives affecting the heritage (such as building regulations).

The content of legislation and policy could be harmonised as between the different parts of the United Kingdom, except where there is good reason for local differences. There could be broad duties relating to the cultural heritage imposed on all public bodies.

Listed buildings (Chapters 3 and 4)

The Secretary of State could be given discretion not to list a building in circumstances where its demolition or alteration is required in order to implement a valid planning permission, where it is clear that conservation issues have already been considered—or to direct that listed building consent would not be needed for works carried out in pursuance of a valid planning permission granted prior to listing. He/she could also be given discretion not to list a building if it was clear that its important features were already adequately protected by being within a conservation area.

The Secretary of State could be given power to list only the exterior of a building; or the listing could protect only those features noted in the list description. The significance of the listing description could in any event be made clear on the face of the statute. The Act could be clarified to identify which structures fixed to listed building are protected, and specifically to include plant and machinery attached to a listed building. The Act could be modified so as to refer to "principal listed buildings" and "ancillary objects and structures", thus enabling greater protection to be given to the former. The Act could make explicit the relevant date for considering the extent of curtilage and the extent of listing generally. Post-1948 curtilage structures could be included in the listing where the building itself is post-1948.

The system of grading listed buildings could be made statutory.

There could be a right to compensation for owners of buildings that are listed (or land that is scheduled).

The wording of the exemptions relating to listed buildings in the rating and VAT legislation could be reconsidered, to resolve the anomalies arising from the use of phrases such as "a hereditament that is a listed building" (rating) or "a building that is a listed building" (VAT).

It could be possible for anyone to apply for a certificate of immunity from listing, without first having to submit a planning application. Consultation could take place on applications for certificates of immunity (as for listing proposals, see above). The Secretary of State could be required to notify the planning authority of an application for a certificate. There could be a right of appeal against the refusal of a certificate. And the immunity certificate system could be extended to Scotland.

If there are still any unlisted buildings subject to building preservation orders, they could now be listed, and the provisions relating to building preservation orders in Schedule 1 to the Listed Buildings Act could then be repealed.

Conservation areas (Chapter 5)

It might be appropriate to require public consultation before conservation areas are designated. It might also be appropriate to require future designations to be part of the development plan process, or to be approved by the Secretary of State. The certificate of immunity system could be extended to provide protection from inclusion in a conservation area.

Greater emphasis could be placed on the duty of authorities to review existing conservation areas. Conservation areas could be graded, as with listed buildings and registered gardens.

The duty under section 71 could be strengthened so as to require local planning authorities to prepare statements as to the character and appearance of their conservation areas. And the status of the proposals prepared under the existing section 71 could be clarified in relation to the new system of development plan documents under the 2004 Act.

Alternatively, conservation area designation could be phased out, in favour of a duty to manage the whole historic environment with regard to preserving its character.

Other forms of protection (Chapters 2, 6 and 7)

The existence of world heritage sites in the United Kingdom could be put on a statutory footing.

The definition of ancient monument in the National Heritage Act 1983 (in the context of English Heritage's powers) could be brought into line with that in the Ancient Monuments Act 1979. In addition, now that more monuments are scheduled, there seems to be no need for a further class of "ancient monument".

The powers available to a guardian of an ancient monument could be clarified, to enable it to have in effect the full powers of an owner (other than to dispose of the land or any interest in it). The power to enter management agreements (under section 17 of the 1979 Act) could be extended to the Broads Authority and other appropriate bodies. English Heritage could also be able to enter contracts with appropriate bodies (local authorities or others) to exercise their powers and duties under such agreements.

As with listed buildings, the grading of parks and gardens could be put on a statutory footing. And the Welsh register of parks and gardens of special interest could be given a statutory basis.

English Heritage could be given a statutory power to compile other registers of land and other items of special interest, or to approve such registers compiled by others.

Duties of owners; grants, loans and tax concessions (Chapters 8, 9 and 17)

There could be a statutory duty of care on owners and occupiers of listed buildings to carry out appropriate repairs and maintenance, either when a building is first listed or on a continuing basis.

The giving of a grant by English Heritage or the Secretary of State (and possibly by a local authority), subject to a condition requiring repayment if the property changes hands, could be registerable as a local and charge, to facilitate recovery.

English Heritage could have powers to give grants directly to building preservation trusts, rather than (as at present) only through a local authority or the Architectural Heritage Fund. It could also be given explicit statutory powers to grant aid a local authority to enable it to employ conservation staff.

The diverse legislation providing for grants and loans, as well as for the acquisition and ownership of property, could be rationalised into a single statutory code. Or there could be a central fund for the repair of listed buildings and the enhancement of conservation areas.

The imposition of VAT on repairs could be abolished, or fixed at a lower rate. Or there could be a right to set the cost of repairs against tax.

Repairs and restoration: powers of public authorities (Chapters 10 and 11)

The definition of the works that may be the subject of an urgent repairs notice could be clarified. And there could be a power for the Secretary of State to direct (in cases of hardship) that the cost of urgent works is recoverable, but not without further consent (except where the property subsequently changes hands). In addition, the cost of urgent works carried out by English Heritage could be recoverable by it directly from the owner, rather than by the Secretary of State on its behalf; and there could be no right to object to such recovery on the grounds that the works are unnecessary.

The power to serve a repairs notice could be extended to listed buildings which are also scheduled monuments, to scheduled monuments that are not listed, and to unlisted buildings in a conservation area. The repairs notice provisions could be clarified to ensure that a repairs notice served on the owner of a building can be relied upon to justify compulsory purchase from a subsequent owner.

The various provisions relating to repairs could be extended so as to enable English Heritage (not just in London) and all types of planning authority to take any appropriate action, and so as to apply buildings owned by the Crown.

Appeals against repairs notices (and directions for minimum compensation) could be to the Secretary of State rather than to the magistrates' courts. The statutory basis for compulsory purchased be amended, so as to increase the significance of a building being listed. A planning authority could be given powers to carry out works required by a repairs notice; or to serve an injunction requiring action by the owner of the building.

The power relating to the repair of monuments could be strengthened.

Works affecting historic buildings and monuments: the need for consent (Chapters 12 and 16)

Following the abolition of archaeological areas (see above), there could be a restriction on permitted development rights at or near the site of any scheduled monument.

The need for listed building consent could only apply to works for the demolition of a listed building where they affect its special character. The need for listed building consent for works to curtilage structures could be dispensed with except for demolition, extension and alteration affecting the exterior.

The need for conservation area consent for partial demolition could be clarified, following the *Shimizu* decision. The need for conservation area consent could be harmonised as between the different parts of the UK.

A procedure could be introduced to enable anyone to find out whether particular works would require listed building or conservation area consent.

It could be made clear that scheduled monument consent is required for operations which disturb the ground at the site of a monument.

The need for scheduled monument consent for works to monuments that form part of churches and cathedrals of the Church of England could be removed. On the other hand, the exemption from the need for listed building consent could be withdrawn from redundant Church of England buildings.

Application and appeal procedures (Chapters 13 and 15)

There could be a standard form for listed building consent applications, to be used throughout the country. There could be a duty on planning authorities to reject applications not accompanied by sufficient information. There could be a requirement for an impact assessment to accompany certain listed building and conservation area consent applications. There could be a requirement to maintain a register of listed building and conservation area consents.

The requirements for certain applications to be notified to the Secretary of State could be replaced with a requirement to notify English Heritage instead. There could be a central clearing house for applications notified to national amenity societies.

Procedures for processing listed building consent applications in London could be brought into line with those in the rest of England. In particular, the power of English Heritage to direct authorities in London as to the way in which to determine listed building consent applications could be gradually phased out.

There could be a standard condition on listed building and scheduled monument consents that information discovered in the course of preparing and implementing proposals must be deposited in a publicly maintained archive. It could be made clear that a planning obligation could be entered into in connection with a grant of listed building consent.

The ability of a local authority to grant listed building consent for works to one of its own buildings could cease. Or applications by local authorities could be determined by English Heritage, with a right of appeal to the Secretary of State.

The determination of applications for scheduled monument consent could be devolved to local planning authorities.

The TCP (Appeals) (Written Representations) Procedure Regulations could be amended so as to refer explicitly to listed building consent appeals in England.

There could be a right of appeal by third parties against decisions of planning authorities (as in Ireland).

Works affecting historic buildings and monuments: matters to be considered (Chapter 14)

The balance between preservation and development could be adjusted, by replacing the duty to have special regard to the desirability of preservation with a positive duty to avoid harm. There could be broad duties relating to the cultural heritage imposed on all decision makers.

There could be a special statutory duty to have regard to preserving world heritage sites, ancient monuments, registered parks and gardens, and their setting in determining planning applications (equivalent to that applying to listed buildings and conservation areas).

There could be a special duty on public utilities carrying out routine works under the highway to respect the character of conservation areas and the setting of other heritage assets.

Unauthorised works (Chapters 18 and 19)

There could be a requirement to maintain a register of listed building and conservation area enforcement notices.[9]

A new power could be introduced to serve a listed building stop notice, to bring to a halt unauthorised works more easily than by an injunction.

There could be a system of enforcement action in relation to unauthorised works to scheduled monuments, parallel to that applying to listed buildings, either as an alternative or in addition to prosecution (as with listed buildings). There could also be an explicit power for local authorities (as well as English Heritage) to seek injunctions to halt unauthorised works.

The penalty for carrying out unauthorised works to a monument could be increased to be the same as that for unauthorised works to a listed building. There could also be a power to impose a custodial sentence. And it could be an offence to remove finds from a scheduled site without consent (not merely, as at present, where there is damage to the monument or where a metal detector is used).

English Heritage could have powers to enter onto land to protect and record monuments exposed by unauthorised works.

The "urgent works defence" to prosecution under the Ancient Monuments Act could be brought into line with the corresponding provision relating to listed buildings, and the defence of ignorance of a monument's status could be removed.

The provisions relating to conservation area enforcement notices and purchase notices are largely otiose, and could be repealed without any loss.

---

[9] See **18.6.2**.

Index

St Paul's Sc

APPOSITION 2024

FIDE ET LITERIS

O Wang

GLUCKSTEIN PRIZE - Computing

High Master

NUMERICAL METHODS FOR SCIENTIFIC COMPUTING

THE DEFINITIVE MANUAL FOR MATH GEEKS

Second Edition

KYLE NOVAK

EQUAL
SHARE
PRESS

Cover illustration: The Rayleigh quotient with its three basins of attraction for a symmetric three-dimensional matrix. The Rayleigh quotient method, an iterative technique for finding eigenvalue–eigenvector pairs, is developed on page 99. The solution to the Swift–Hohenberg equation with random initial conditions, which models Rayleigh–Bénard convection, is discussed on page 473.

Pardon the dust: This book is in continuous development, published using an agile mindset of making it available sooner so that it can be of use and providing steady improvements. Great efforts have been made to identify and correct mistakes. Nonetheless, to borrow a Piet Hein grook: "The road to wisdom? Well, it's plain and simple to express: err and err and err again but less and less and less." Your comments, suggestions, corrections, and criticisms are appreciated: kyle.novak@equalsharepress.com. The latest digital version of this book is available at https://www.equalsharepress.com/media/NMFSC.pdf.

Equal Share Press
1919 Clarendon Boulevard
Arlington, Virginia 22201

www.equalsharepress.com

Your feedback is important. Use this QR code to leave a comment, make a suggestion, or report errata.

Dedicated to Laura

$$(x^2 + y^2 - 1)^3 - x^2 y^3 = 0$$
$$(x^2 + y^2)^2 - 2(x^2 - y^2) = 0$$

Contents

Numerical Analysis

Numerical Differential Equations

Preface

This book was born out of a set of lecture notes I wrote for a sequence of three numerical methods courses taught at the Air Force Institute of Technology. The courses Numerical Linear Algebra, Numerical Analysis, and Numerical Methods for Partial Differential Equations were taken primarily by mathematics, physics, and engineering graduate students. My goals in these courses were to present the foundational principles and essential tools of scientific computing, provide practical applications of the principles, and generate interest in the topic. These notes were themselves inspired by lectures from a two-sequence numerical analysis course taught by my doctoral advisor Shi Jin at the University of Wisconsin.

The purpose of my notes was first to guide the lectures and discussion, and second, to provide students with a bridge to more rigorous and complete, but also more mathematically dense textbooks and references. To this end, the notes acted as a summary to help students learn the key mathematical ideas and explain the principles intuitively. I favored simple picture proofs and explanations over more rigorous but abstruse analytic derivations. Students who wanted the details could find them in any number of other numerical mathematics texts.

In moving from a set of supplementary lecture notes to a stand-alone book, I wondered whether to make them into a handbook, a guidebook, or a textbook. My goal in writing and subsequently revising this book was to provide a concise treatment of the core ideas, algorithms, proofs, and pitfalls of numerical methods for scientific computing. I aimed to present the topics in a way that might be consumed in bits and pieces—a handbook. I wanted them weaved together into a grand mathematical journey, with enough detail to elicit an occasional "aha" but not so much as to become overbearing—a guidebook. Finally, I wanted to present the ideas using a pedagogical framework to help anyone with a good understanding of multivariate calculus and linear algebra learn valuable mathematical skills—a textbook. Ultimately, I decided on a tongue-in-cheek "definitive manual for math geeks." To be clear, it's definitely not definitive. And, it need not be. If a person knows the right questions to ask, they can find a dozen answers through a Google search, a Github tutorial, a Wikipedia article, a Stack Exchange snippet, or a YouTube video.

When I published the first edition of this book several years ago, I did so with an agile development mindset. Get it out quickly with minimal bugs so that it can be of use to others. Then iterate and improve. Make it affordable. When textbooks often sell for over a hundred dollars, keep the print version under twenty and the electronic one free. Publish it independently to be able to make rapid improvements and to keep costs down. While I had moderate aspirations, the Just Barely Good Enough (JBGE) first edition was panned. A reviewer named Ben summarized it on Goodreads: "Typos, a terrible index. Pretty sure it was self published. It does a good job as a primer, but functionally speaking, it's a terrible textbook." Another reviewer who goes by Nineball stated on Amazon: "This text is riddled with typos and errors. You can tell the author had great objectives for making concise book for numerical methods, however the number of errors significantly detracts from the message and provides a substantial barrier to understanding." This JBGE++ edition fixes hundreds of typos, mistakes, and coding glitches. Still, there are undoubtedly errors I missed and ones I inadvertently introduced during revision. Truth be told, I'd rather spend my time watching *The Great British Bake Off* with my beautiful wife than hunting down every last typo. I also learned that designing a good index is a real challenge. The index in this book is still a work in progress. I apologize to anyone who struggled with the JBGE edition. And I apologize in advance for any mistakes that appear in this one. I understand that Donald Knuth would personally send a check for $2.56 to anyone who found errors in his books. I can't do that, but if you ever find yourself in my town, I'll happily buy you a beer to ease your frustration. That offers goes out to you, especially, Ben and Nineball.

Paul Halmos once said about writing mathematics to "pretend that you are explaining the subject to a friend on a long walk in the woods, with no paper available." I wonder what he would have said about writing about numerical methods. Would he have said "with no computer available?" I believe so. Understanding Newton's method, for instance, has more to do with the Banach fixed-point theorem than addition assignment operators. While a mathematics book should be agnostic about scientific programming languages, snippets of code can help explain the underlying theory and make it more practical. In the first edition of this book, I focused entirely on Matlab. With this edition, I've embraced Julia. To help understand the switch, one need only consider that Matlab was first released forty years ago, placing its development closer to the 1940s ENIAC than today's grammar of graphics, dataframes, reactive notebooks, and cloud computing. Python's NumPy and SciPy are twenty years old. Julia is barely ten. Still, Matlab and Python are both immensely important languages.

Michael Mol's Rosetta Code (http://www.rosettacode.org), a wiki he describes as a "program chrestomathy," inspired me to include both in the back matter.

In designing this book, I repurposed the first five aphorisms of Tim Peter's "The Zen of Python." *Beautiful is better than ugly.* I've chosen the printed page because it provides the most expressive mathematical typography and consistency in notation. I've rendered graphics in this book almost entirely within the LATEX environment to maintain visual unity. *Explicit is better than implicit.* I've provided solutions to most exercises because they are invaluable to self-study. And I've included working Julia, Python, and Matlab code to encourage tinkering and exploration. All of the code is available as Jupyter notebooks. *Simple is better than complex.* I've kept the code to minimum working examples to enable the underlying mathematics to more readily be seen—something that mathematician Nick Trefethen has dubbed "ten-digit algorithms." These are programs that are "ten digits, five seconds, and just one page." Such programs must run fast enough to permit students to explore, iterate, adjust, and experiment. They must be concise enough to communicate how the algorithm works. And, they must have scientific accuracy, i.e., at least ten digits. I've tried to keep unity in notation throughout the book wherever possible. I've favored intuitive explanations over rigorous ones that require unnecessary mathematical machinery. *Complex is better than complicated.* But, I've introduced heavy mathematical machinery when necessary. *Universal is better than specialized.* I've focused on the mathematics over the algorithm and the algorithm over the code.

Let me express a few words of gratitude. This book has been an ongoing struggle—at times, demoralizing and annoying, and at others, meditative and therapeutic. I am most grateful to the support and patience of my mind-blowingly awesome wife. Thank you, Laura. I am grateful to the open-source community for developing tools such as tools Octave, R, Python, Julia, LATEX, and Inkscape. I am grateful to the countless authors who volunteer answers on Wikipedia, StackExchange, Reddit, and GitHub. I am grateful to all who provided feedback to improve this book, particularly the significant contributions by Kristina Williams, Chris Rackauckas, and Mariano Mateos. Finally, I am grateful for the tinkers and the teachers. The world is a better place because of people like you. This book project is me paying it forward.

Kyle A. Novak
Washington, D.C.
February 2022

About the Author

Kyle Novak is an applied mathematician, data scientist, and policy advisor with twenty-five years of experience in finding solutions to real problems. Kyle examined the national security threats of autonomous air systems while at the Air Force Research Laboratory, served as a cryptologic mathematician at the National Security Agency, taught graduate students at the Air Force Institute of Technology, and provided decision analysis to senior military leaders at the Pentagon. As a science and technology policy fellow at the U.S. Agency for International Development, Kyle explored the use of digital technologies and data science toward ending extreme poverty and promoting resilient, democratic societies. He subsequently served as an advisor on science and technology, national security, defense, and foreign policy in the U.S. Senate. In his most recent position at the National Institute of Justice, Kyle guides research on the application of artificial intelligence and mathematical modeling in criminal justice and policing.

Kyle Novak has been featured in the American Mathematical Society's *101 Careers in Mathematics*. His book *Special Functions of Mathematical Physics: A Tourist's Guidebook* explores the quintessential special functions that arise from solving differential equations and develops the mathematical tools and intuition for working with them. Kyle holds a PhD in mathematics from the University of Wisconsin–Madison.

Introduction

Scientific computing is the study and use of computers to solve scientific problems. Numerical methods are techniques designed to solve those problems efficiently and accurately using numerical approximation. Numerical methods have been around for centuries. Indeed, some four thousand years ago, Babylonians used a technique for approximating square roots. And over two thousand years ago, Archimedes developed a method for approximating π by inscribing and circumscribing a circle with polygons. With the progress of mathematical thought, with the discovery of new scientific problems requiring novel and efficient approaches, and more recently, with the proliferation of cheap and powerful computers, numerical methods have worked their way into all aspects of our lives, although mostly hidden from view.

Eighteenth-century mathematicians Joseph Raphson and Thomas Simpson used Newton's then recently invented Calculus to develop numerical methods for finding the zeros of functions. Their approaches are at the heart of gradient descent, making today's deep learning algorithms possible. In solving problems of heat transfer, nineteenth-century mathematician Joseph Fourier discovered that any continuous function could be written as an infinite series of sines and cosines. At the same time, Carl Friedrich Gauss invented though never published a numerical method to compute the coefficients of Fourier's series recursively. It wasn't until the 1960s that mathematicians James Cooley and John Tukey reinvented Gauss' fast Fourier transform, this time spurred by a Cold War necessity of detecting nuclear detonations. Computers themselves have enabled mathematical discovery. Shortly after World War I, French mathematicians Pierre Fatou and Gaston Julia developed a new field of mathematics that examined the dynamical structure of iterated complex functions. Sixty years later, Benoit Mandelbrot, a researcher at IBM, used computers to discover the intricate fractal worlds hidden in these simple recursive formulas.

Today, numerical methods are accelerating the convergence of different scientific disciplines, in which artificial intelligence uses techniques of nonlinear optimization and dimensionality reduction to generate implicit solutions to complex systems. In the early nineteenth century, Ada Lovelace envisioned the first computer program to compute Bernoulli numbers for a hypothetical invention of Charles Babbage, an invention that wouldn't be built until almost a hundred years later. In the 1980s, physicist Richard Feynman postulated that solving some physics problems such as simulating quantum systems would require an entirely new kind of computer, a quantum computer. A decade later, mathematician Peter Shor developed an algorithm of prime factorization that could only be run on such a hypothetical computer. Today, quantum computing is being realized. One can wonder what numerical methods are yet to be developed to solve complex scientific problems on future biocomputers.

This book examines many of the essential numerical methods used today, the mathematics behind these methods, and the scientific problems they were developed to solve. The book is structured into three parts—numerical methods for linear algebra, numerical methods for analysis, and numerical methods for differential equations.

▷ Numerical methods for linear algebra

There are two fundamental problems in linear algebra: solving a system of linear equations and solving the eigenvalue problem. Succinctly, the first problem says

1. Given an operator $\mathbf{A}$ and a vector $\mathbf{b}$, find the vector $\mathbf{x}$ such that $\mathbf{A}\mathbf{x} = \mathbf{b}$.

Such a problem frequently arises in science and engineering applications. For example, find the polynomial $p(x) = \sum_{i=0}^{n} c_i x^i$ passing through the points $\{(x_0, y_0), (x_1, y_1), \ldots, (x_n, y_n)\}$. Another example, solve the Poisson equation, which models the steady-state heat distribution $u(x, y)$,

$$-\left(\frac{\partial^2}{\partial x^2} + \frac{\partial^2}{\partial y^2} \right) u(x, y) = f(x, y) \quad \text{for} \quad (x, y) \in \Omega$$

$$u(x, y) = g(x, y) \quad \text{for} \quad (x, y) \in \partial\Omega$$

where $f(x, y)$ is the source term and $g(x, y)$ is the boundary value. Numerically, we can solve this problem by first considering a discrete approximation and then solving the often large resultant system of linear equations. When solving the problem, getting the solution is primarily left up to a black box. Part One of this book breaks open that black box.

Numerically, one can solve the problem $\mathbf{A}\mathbf{x} = \mathbf{b}$ either directly or iteratively. The primary direct solver is Gaussian elimination. We can get more efficient methods such as banded solvers, block solvers, and Cholesky decomposition by taking advantage of a matrix's properties, such as low bandwidth and symmetry. Chapter 2 looks at direct methods. Large, sparse matrices often arise in the numerical methods for partial differential equations and machine learning. We can efficiently solve such systems by using iterative methods. Iterative methods rely on matrix multiplication to find an approximate solution. Chapter 5 looks at iterative methods such as the Jacobi, Gauss–Seidel, SOR, and Krylov methods like the conjugate gradient method. It also examines multigrid methods.

In some cases, a solution to $\mathbf{Ax} = \mathbf{b}$ may not exist. Or, if one does exist, it may not be unique. In the real world, such an answer is often unacceptable. Therefore, we can consider the modified problem

$1'$. Find the "best" $\mathbf{x}$ that satisfies $\mathbf{Ax} = \mathbf{b}$.

Of course, what "best" means needs to be rigorously defined. Chapter 3 does this by looking at the least squares problem. In most applications, the best solution results from an orthogonal projection. A few different algorithms get us the orthogonal decomposition of a matrix, namely the Gram–Schmidt process, Givens rotations, and Householder reflections. Singular value decomposition provides yet another way of finding the least squares solution.

We can state the second fundamental problem of linear algebra as

2. Given an operator $\mathbf{A}$, find the scalar λ and the vector $\mathbf{x}$ such that $\mathbf{Ax} = \lambda\mathbf{x}$.

Eigenvalue problems arise in the study of stability, steady-state behavior, and ordinary differential equations. It is impossible to solve the eigenvalue problem directly, so we must instead use iterative methods. In Chapter 4, we look at how to do this.

Finally, Chapter 6 looks at the fast Fourier transform, which has revolutionized computational mathematics, signal processing, imaging, and a host of other fields.

▷ Numerical methods for analysis

Numerical analysis develops tools and methods for problem-solving methods in such a manner that they can be implemented *efficiently* and *accurately* using a computer. Because of this, one can study numerical analysis from a rather theoretical framework, heavy in functional analysis. But one can also study it by looking at its application in solving problems—an approach often called scientific computing. As mathematics research becomes more and more interdisciplinary, numerical analysis is leaning more towards scientific computing.

The general strategy of scientific computing is to find a simple and efficient method to solve a difficult problem. Infinite dimensions are replaced with finite dimensions, nonlinear problems are localized as linear problems, and continuous models are exchanged for discrete models. In this way, numerical analysis is foremost a study of numerical approximation. Chapter 7 gives a quick discussion of the preliminaries: convergence, stability, and sources of errors of a numerical method. Chapter 8 introduces iterative methods to find the approximate solutions to nonlinear equations and the roots of polynomials and extends the results to nonlinear systems. Chapter 9 considers methods of interpolating data using polynomial expansion, splines, and so forth. Chapter 10 looks at methods of approximating whole functions using basis functions such as orthogonal polynomials, wavelets, and neural nets. It also discusses the nonlinear least squares problem. Finally, Chapter 11 provides an overview of numerical differentiation and integration.

▷ Numerical methods for differential equations

Part Three examines ordinary differential equations and three classifications of partial differential equations: parabolic, hyperbolic and elliptic. Parabolic equations include the heat or diffusion equation. Solutions are always smooth and grow smoother over time. An important related set of problems includes the reaction-diffusion equations, which model ice melting in a pool of water, the patterning of stripes on a zebra or spots on a leopard, and the aggregation of bacteria or tumor cells in response to chemical signals. Hyperbolic equations are often used to model low viscosity gas and particle dynamics. Nonlinear hyperbolic equations are synonymous with shock waves and are used to model anything from supersonic flight to bomb blasts to tsunamis to traffic flow. Without a smoothing term, discontinuities may appear but do not disappear. An alternative weak solution is needed to handle these equations mathematically. Adding viscosity to the equation regularizes the solution and brings us back to parabolic equations. In some regards, elliptic equations may be viewed as the steady-state solutions to parabolic equations. They include the Laplace equation and the Poisson equation. Unlike parabolic and hyperbolic equations, which are typically time-dependent, elliptic equations are often time-independent. They are used to model strain in materials, steady-state distribution of electric charge, and so forth. Often, a problem does not neatly fit into any given category. And sometimes, the problem behaves very differently over different length and time scales. For example, the Navier–Stokes equation describing fluid flow is predominantly diffusive on small length and time scales, but it is predominately advective on large scales. The melting of ice occurs only at the thin interface region separating the liquid and solid. Deflagration (and detonation) has two timescales—a slow diffusion and a fast chemical reaction timescale. These so-called stiff problems require careful consideration.

Part Three also examines three essential numerical tools for solving partial differential equations: finite difference methods, finite element methods, and Fourier spectral methods. Finite difference (and finite volume) methods are the oldest. They were employed in the 1950s and developed throughout the twentieth century (and before that). Their simple formulation allows them to be applied to a large class of problems. However, finite difference methods become cumbersome when the boundaries are complicated. Finite element methods were developed in the 1960s to solve problems for which finite difference methods were not well adapted, such as handling complicated boundaries. Hence, finite element methods provide attractive solutions to engineering problems. Finite element methods often require more numerical and mathematical machinery than finite difference methods. Fourier spectral methods were also developed in the 1960s following the (re)discovery of the fast Fourier transform. They are important in fluid modeling and analysis where boundary effects can be assumed to be periodic.

Finally, Part Three explores three mathematical requirements for a numerical method: consistency, stability, and convergence. Consistency says that the discrete numerical method is a correct approximation to the continuous problem. Stability says that the numerical solution does not blow up. Finally, convergence says you can always reduce error in the numerical solution by refining the mesh. In other words, convergence says you get the correct solution.

▷ Doing mathematics

Mathematician Paul Halmos once remarked, "the only way to learn mathematics is to do mathematics." Doing mathematics involves visualizing complex data structures, thinking logically and creatively, and gaining conceptual understanding and insight. Doing mathematics is about problem-solving and pattern recognition. It is recognizing that the same family of equations that models the response of tumor cells to chemical signals also models an ice cube melting in a glass of water and the patterning of spots on a leopard. It is appreciating that the equations of fluid dynamics can apply in one instance to tsunamis, in the next to traffic flow, and in a third to supersonic flight. Ultimately, mathematics is about understanding the world, and doing mathematics is learning to see that. Of course, one must learn the mechanics and structure of mathematics to have the familiarization, technique, and confidence to start doing mathematics. Each chapter concludes with a set of problems. Solutions to problems marked with a ✍ are provided in the Back Matter.

▷ Julia, Python, Matlab

Not surprisingly, programming plays a starring role in scientific computing. There are several scientific programming languages that one might use—Julia, Python with SciPy and NumPy, MATLAB or its open-source alternatives Octave and Scilab, R, Mathematica and Maple, SageMath, C, Fortran, and perhaps even JavaScript. This book emphasizes Julia because of the language's freshness, versatility, simplicity, growing popularity, and notation and syntax that accurately mirror mathematical expressions. That's not to say that the book ignores other scientific programming languages. Indeed, the Back Matter includes a chapter devoted to Python and Matlab. Every Julia commentary—identified with the ♣ glyph—has a matching commentary for Python and Matlab. Every snippet of

Julia code has a matching snippet of Python and Matlab code. The code may not be entirely Julian, Pythonic, or Matlabesque, as some effort was taken to bridge all of the languages with similar syntax to elucidate the underlying mathematical concepts. The code is likely not the fastest implementation—in some cases, it is downright slow. Furthermore, the code may overlook some coding best practices, such as exception handling in favor of brevity. And, let's be honest, long blocks of code are dull. All of the code is available as a Jupyter notebook:

https://nbviewer.jupyter.org/github/nmfsc/julia/blob/main/julia.ipynb

The code in this book was written and tested in Julia version 1.9.2. To cut down on redundancy, the LinearAlgebra.jl and Plots.jl packages are implicitly assumed always to be imported and available, while other packages will be explicitly imported in the code blocks. Additionally, we'll use the variable bucket to reference the GitHub directory of data files.

```
using LinearAlgebra, Plots
bucket = "https://raw.githubusercontent.com/nmfsc/data/master/";
```

▷ QR links

When I was a young boy, I would thumb through my father's copy of *The Restless Universe* by physicist Max Born. (Max Born is best known as a Nobel laureate for his contributions to fundamental research in quantum mechanics and lesser known as a grandfather to 80s pop icon Olivia–Newton John.) While I didn't understand much of the book, I marveled at the illustrations. The book, first published in 1936, featured in its margins a set of what Born called "films," what the publisher called "mutoscopic pictures," and what we today would call flipbooks. By flicking the pages with one's thumb, simple animations emerged from the pages that helped the reader visualize the physics a little bit better. In designing this book, I wanted to repurpose Max Born's idea. I decided to use QR codes at the footers of several pages as a hopefully unobtrusive version of a digital flipbook to animate an illustration or concept discussed on that page. As a starting example, the QR code on this page contains one of Max Born's original films animating gas molecules. Simply unlock the code using your smartphone—I promise no Rick Astley. But you can also ignore them altogether.

gas molecules film
from *The Restless Universe*

Numerical Methods for
Linear Algebra

Chapter 1

A Review of Linear Algebra

We'll start by reviewing some essential concepts and definitions of linear algebra. This chapter is brief, so please check out other linear algebra texts such as Peter Lax's book *Linear Algebra and Its Applications*, Gilbert Strang's identically titled book, or David Watkins' book *Fundamentals of Matrix Computations* for missing details.

1.1 Vector spaces

Simply stated, a *vector space* is a set V that is closed under linear combinations of its elements called *vectors*. If any two vectors of V are added together, the resultant vector is also in V; and if any vector is multiplied by a scalar, the resultant vector is also in V. The scalar is often an element of the real numbers $\mathbb{R}$ or the complex numbers $\mathbb{C}$, but it could also be an element of any other field $\mathbb{F}$. We often say that V is a vector space over the field $\mathbb{F}$ to remove the ambiguity. Once we have the vector space's basis—which we'll come to shortly—we can express and manipulate vectors as arrays of elements of the field with a computer.

What are some examples of vector spaces? The set of points in an n-dimensional space is a vector space. The set of polynomials $p_n(x) = \sum_{k=0}^{n} a_k x^k$ is another vector space. The set of piecewise linear functions over the interval $[0, 1]$ is yet another vector space—this one is important for the finite-element method. The set of all differentiable functions over the interval $[0, 1]$ that vanish at the endpoints is also a vector space. Another is the vector space over the Galois field $GF(p^n)$ with characteristic p and n terms. For example, $GF(2^8)$

gives byte xor arithmetic,

$$\{11011011\} \text{ xor } \{10001101\} = \{01010110\}.$$

If V is a vector space over $\mathbb{F}$, then a subset W of V is a *subspace* if W is a vector space over $\mathbb{F}$. Consider a system of n vectors $\{\mathbf{v}_1, \mathbf{v}_2, \ldots, \mathbf{v}_n\} \in V$. The set of all linear combinations of the system *generates* a subspace W of V. We call W the *span* of the system and denote it by $W = \text{span}\{\mathbf{v}_1, \mathbf{v}_2, \ldots, \mathbf{v}_n\}$. The system $\{\mathbf{v}_1, \mathbf{v}_2, \ldots, \mathbf{v}_n\}$ is called the *spanning set* or the *generators* of W.

The system of vectors $\{\mathbf{v}_1, \mathbf{v}_2, \ldots, \mathbf{v}_n\}$ of a vector space V is said to be *linearly independent* if all linear combinations are unique. That is,

$$a_1\mathbf{v}_1 + a_2\mathbf{v}_2 + \cdots + a_n\mathbf{v}_n = 0$$

if and only if the scalars $a_1, a_2, \ldots, a_n$ are all zero. Otherwise, we say that the system is *linearly dependent*.

A *basis* of V is a system of linearly independent generators of V. For example, the monomials $\{1, x, x^2, \ldots, x^k\}$ are a basis for the space of kth-order polynomials. The number of elements in a basis of a vector space V is the *dimension* of V. Not every vector space can be generated by a finite number of elements. Take, for instance, the space of smooth functions over the interval $(0, 1)$ that vanish at the endpoints. Functions in this space can be represented as a Fourier sine series, and the vector space is spanned by the vectors $\sin m\pi x$ with $m = 1, 2, 3, \ldots$. Such a vector space is said to be infinite-dimensional. If $\{\mathbf{u}_1, \mathbf{u}_2, \ldots, \mathbf{u}_n\}$ is a basis of V, then any vector in $\mathbf{v} \in V$ has a unique decomposition with respect to the basis:

$$\mathbf{v} = v_1\mathbf{u}_1 + v_2\mathbf{u}_2 + \cdots + v_n\mathbf{u}_n.$$

This decomposition can be expressed in matrix representation as the vector

$$\mathbf{v} = (v_1, v_2, \ldots, v_n)$$

where the basis is implicitly understood. Hence, any n-dimensional vector space over $\mathbb{R}$ is isomorphic to $\mathbb{R}^n$. The standard basis of $\mathbb{R}^n$ is $\{\boldsymbol{\xi}_1, \boldsymbol{\xi}_2, \ldots, \boldsymbol{\xi}_n\}$ where

$$\boldsymbol{\xi}_i = (\underbrace{0, \ldots, 0, 1, 0, \ldots, 0}_{i-1}).$$

It should be emphasized that the choice of a basis is not unique, although the representation of a vector in that basis is unique. For example, consider the space of quadratic polynomials $\mathbb{P}_2$. One basis for this space is the set of monomials $\{1, x, x^2\}$. Another basis is the first three Legendre polynomials $\{1, x, \frac{1}{2}(3x^2 - 1)\}$. Both of these sets span $\mathbb{P}_2$ and the elements of each set are linearly independent—we can't form x^2 by combining x and 1. Given a basis, any vector in $\mathbb{P}_2$ has a unique representation in $\mathbb{R}^3$. The vector $1 + x^2$ can be represented as $(1, 0, 1)$ in the basis $\{1, x, x^2\}$. The same vector $1 + x^2$ can be represented $\left(\frac{4}{3}, 0, \frac{2}{3}\right)$ in the Legendre basis $\left\{1, x, \frac{1}{2}(3x^2 - 1)\right\}$.

▷ Matrices

Let V and W be vector spaces over $\mathbb{C}$. A *linear map* from V into W is a function $f : V \to W$ such that $f(\alpha\mathbf{x} + \beta\mathbf{y}) = \alpha f(\mathbf{x}) + \beta f(\mathbf{y})$ for all $\alpha, \beta \in \mathbb{C}$ and $\mathbf{x}, \mathbf{y} \in V$. For any linear map f, there exists a unique matrix $\mathbf{A} \in \mathbb{C}^{m \times n}$ such that $f(\mathbf{x}) = \mathbf{A}\mathbf{x}$ for all $\mathbf{x} \in \mathbb{C}^n$. Every n-dimensional vector space over $\mathbb{C}$ is isomorphic to $\mathbb{C}^n$. And every linear map from an n-dimensional vector space into an m-dimensional vector space can be represented by an $m \times n$ matrix.

⁂ A column vector can be formed using the syntax [1,2,3,4], [1;2;3;4], [(1:4)...], or [i for i ∈1:4]. A row vector has the syntax [1 2 3 4].

Example.   Consider the derivative operator defined over the space of quadratic polynomials $\left(\frac{\mathrm{d}}{\mathrm{d}x} : \mathbb{P}_2 \mapsto \mathbb{P}_2\right)$. It's easy to confirm that the derivative operator is a linear operator. Let's determine its matrix representation. First, we need to assign a basis for $\mathbb{P}_2$. Let's take the monomial basis $\{1, x, x^2\}$. Note that $\frac{\mathrm{d}}{\mathrm{d}x}\left(a + bx + cx^2\right) = b + 2cx$. It follows from

$$
\begin{bmatrix} 0 & 1 & 0 \\ 0 & 0 & 2 \\ 0 & 0 & 0 \end{bmatrix} \begin{bmatrix} a \\ b \\ c \end{bmatrix} = \begin{bmatrix} b \\ 2c \\ 0 \end{bmatrix} \quad \text{that} \quad \frac{\mathrm{d}}{\mathrm{d}x} \equiv \begin{bmatrix} 0 & 1 & 0 \\ 0 & 0 & 2 \\ 0 & 0 & 0 \end{bmatrix}
$$

for quadratic polynomials using the monomial basis.   ◀

A matrix represents a mapping from one vector space to another one—or possibly the same one. And matrix multiplication represents the composition of mappings from one vector space to another one to a subsequent one. Two matrices can be multiplied together only if their dimensions are compatible, i.e., the number of columns of the first equals the number of rows of the second. Matrices can also be combined through element-wise operations like addition or the Hadamard product if they are compatible, i.e., their dimensions agree.

⁂ Julia uses the "dot" operation to broadcast arithmetic operators by expanding scalars and arrays to compatible sizes. If A = rand(4,4) and B = rand(4,4), then A*B is matrix multiplication, while A.*B is the component-wise Hadamard product. If x = rand(4,1), then A.*x is computed by first implicitly replicating the column vector x to first produce a 4 × 4 array. The dot syntax can also be applied to functions. For example, sin.(A) will take the sine of each element of A and return a 4 × 4 array. Furthermore, the @. macro applies dots to all operations in an expression.

The *transpose* $\mathbf{A}^\mathsf{T}$ of an $m \times n$ matrix $\mathbf{A}$ is the $n \times m$ matrix obtained by interchanging the rows of $\mathbf{A}$ with columns of $\mathbf{A}$. That is, $[\mathbf{A}^\mathsf{T}]_{ij} = [\mathbf{A}]_{ji}$. The transpose has a few well-known and easily proved properties: $(\mathbf{A}^\mathsf{T})^\mathsf{T} = \mathbf{A}$,

$(\mathbf{A} + \mathbf{B})^\mathsf{T} = \mathbf{A}^\mathsf{T} + \mathbf{B}^\mathsf{T}$, $(\mathbf{AB})^\mathsf{T} = \mathbf{B}^\mathsf{T}\mathbf{A}^\mathsf{T}$, and $(\mathbf{A}^{-1})^\mathsf{T} = (\mathbf{A}^\mathsf{T})^{-1}$. The *conjugate transpose* or *adjoint* $\mathbf{A}^\mathsf{H}$ of a matrix $\mathbf{A} \in \mathbb{C}^{m\times n}$ is the $n \times m$ matrix obtained by exchanging the row of $\mathbf{A}$ with complex conjugates of columns of $\mathbf{A}$.

⁂ The transpose of A is transpose(A), and the conjugate transpose is A'.

Consider a matrix $\mathbf{A} \in \mathbb{C}^{m\times n}$. The *column space* (or range) of $\mathbf{A}$ is the subspace of $\mathbb{C}^n$ generated by the columns of $\mathbf{A}$. The dimension of the column space $\mathbf{A}$ equals the dimension of the rows space of $\mathbf{A}$ and is called the *rank* of $\mathbf{A}$. The *null space* or *kernel* of $\mathbf{A}$ is the subspace of $\mathbb{C}^n$ generated by the vectors $\mathbf{x} \in \mathbb{C}^n$ such that $\mathbf{Ax} = \mathbf{0}$. The dimension of the null space is called the *nullity* of $\mathbf{A}$. The *row space* is a subspace of $\mathbb{C}^m$ generated by the rows of $\mathbf{A}$ (the columns of $\mathbf{A}^\mathsf{T}$). The *left null space* is a subspace of $\mathbb{C}^m$ generated by the vectors $\mathbf{x} \in \mathbb{C}^m$ with $\mathbf{xA} = \mathbf{0}$. In other words, the left null space of $\mathbf{A}$ is the null space of $\mathbf{A}^\mathsf{T}$. For a system $\mathbf{Ax} = \mathbf{b}$, we have[1]

$$\mathbf{A}(\mathbf{x}_{\text{row}} + \mathbf{x}_{\text{null}}) = \mathbf{b}_{\text{column}} + \mathbf{b}_{\text{left null}}.$$

A nonzero null space leads to an undetermined system with infinite solutions. A nonzero left null space leads to an inconsistent solution with zero solutions.

Example.   Consider the derivative operator over the space of quadratic polynomials using the monomial basis $\{1, x, x^2\}$. The derivative operator maps constants to zero, so the null space of the derivative operator is span$\{1\}$ or equivalently span$\{(1, 0, 0)\}$. The derivative of a quadratic polynomial spans $\{1, x\}$, so the column space is span$\{1, x\}$ or equivalently span$\{(1, 0, 0), (0, 1, 0)\}$. The left null space is the complement to the column space, so it follows that the left null space is span$\{x^2\}$ or span$\{(0, 0, 1)\}$.   ◄

Several important types of matrices are listed on page 8. Remember, all vector spaces over $\mathbb{R}^n$ are isomorphic to $\mathbb{R}^n$. So by considering maps in $\mathbb{R}^n$, we have a nice geometric interpretation of linear maps. Take $\mathbb{R}^2$. A circle (centered at the origin) is mapped to an ellipse (also centered at the origin), and a square is mapped to a parallelogram. In higher dimensions, a sphere is mapped to an ellipsoid, and a cube is mapped to a parallelepiped.

1.2   Eigenspaces

A number λ is called an *eigenvalue* of a square matrix $\mathbf{A}$ if there exists a nonzero vector $\mathbf{x}$, called the *eigenvector*, such that $\mathbf{Ax} = \lambda\mathbf{x}$. The set of eigenvectors

---

[1]These set of statements relating the four fundamental subspaces (the row space, null space, column space, and left null space) is often called the fundamental theorem of linear algebra, a term popularized by Gilbert Strang.

associated with an eigenvalue λ is called the *eigenspace*. A subspace S is said to be *invariant* with respect to a square matrix $\mathbf{A}$ if any vector in S stays in S under mapping by $\mathbf{A}$. In other words $\mathbf{A}S \subset S$. An eigenspace is invariant, and specifically, an eigenvector is directionally invariant. The set of eigenvalues $\{\lambda_1, \lambda_2, \ldots, \lambda_n\}$ of $\mathbf{A}$ is called its *spectrum* and denoted by $\lambda(\mathbf{A})$. The *spectral radius* of $\mathbf{A}$ is the largest absolute value of its eigenvalues: $\rho(\mathbf{A}) = \max\{|\lambda_1|, |\lambda_2|, \ldots, |\lambda_n|\}$.

Eigenvectors have a simple geometric interpretation. Let's take $\mathbb{R}^2$. Start with two unit eigenvectors for $\mathbf{A}$. They fit in a unit circle. The matrix $\mathbf{A}$ will stretch the eigenvectors by their respective eigenvalues, and our unit circle becomes an ellipse. The vectors that lie along the semi-major and semi-minor axes of our new ellipse are called *singular vectors*. The semi-major and semi-minor radii are called singular values. If the matrix $\mathbf{A}$ happens to be a normal matrix, i.e., $\mathbf{A}^\mathsf{T}\mathbf{A} = \mathbf{A}\mathbf{A}^\mathsf{T}$, then the eigenvectors are all mutually orthogonal. In this case, the eigenvectors are the singular vectors and the eigenvalues are the singular values.

▷ Similar matrices

Two square matrices $\mathbf{A}$ and $\tilde{\mathbf{A}}$ are *similar* if there exists a matrix $\mathbf{C}$ such that $\mathbf{A} = \mathbf{C}\tilde{\mathbf{A}}\mathbf{C}^{-1}$. Such a transformation is called a *similarity transform*. The mapping by $\tilde{\mathbf{A}}$ is the same transformation in the standard basis as the mapping by $\mathbf{A}$ in the basis given by the columns of $\mathbf{C}$. That is, $\mathbf{C}\tilde{\mathbf{A}}\mathbf{C}^{-1}$ means simply "change to the basis given by the columns of $\mathbf{C}$, apply $\tilde{\mathbf{A}}$ and then change back to the standard basis."

If $\mathbf{C}$ is a unitary matrix, we say that $\tilde{\mathbf{A}}$ and $\mathbf{A}$ are *unitarily similar*. Similarity transformations can simplify a problem by transforming a matrix into a diagonal or triangular matrix. By analogy, it is often faster to take two detours and hook up with a superhighway than take the direct route.

▷ Diagonalization

A matrix that has a complete set of eigenvectors is said to be *nondefective*. For nondefective matrices, we can rewrite the eigenvalue problem $\mathbf{A}\mathbf{x} = \lambda\mathbf{x}$ as $\mathbf{A}\mathbf{S} = \mathbf{S}\mathbf{\Lambda}$, where $\mathbf{S}$ is a matrix of the eigenvectors and $\mathbf{\Lambda}$ is a diagonal matrix of eigenvalues. This formulation leads to the *diagonalization* of $\mathbf{A}$ as $\mathbf{A} = \mathbf{S}\mathbf{\Lambda}\mathbf{S}^{-1}$, which says that $\mathbf{A}$ is similar to the diagonal matrix $\mathbf{\Lambda}$ in its eigenvector basis. The system is uncoupled in this eigenvector basis and much easier to manipulate.

Some important types of matrices

Symmetric: $\mathbf{A}^\mathsf{T} = \mathbf{A}$.

Hermitian or *self-adjoint*: $\mathbf{A}^\mathsf{H} = \mathbf{A}$.

Positive definite: a Hermitian matrix $\mathbf{A}$ such that $\mathbf{x}^\mathsf{H}\mathbf{A}\mathbf{x} > 0$ for any nonzero vector $\mathbf{x}$.

Orthogonal: $\mathbf{Q}^\mathsf{T}\mathbf{Q} = \mathbf{I}$.

Unitary: $\mathbf{U}^\mathsf{H}\mathbf{U} = \mathbf{I}$. Columns of orthogonal matrices and unitary matrices are mutually orthonormal. Orthogonal and unitary matrices are geometrically equivalent to rotations and reflections.

Permutation: A permutation matrix is an orthogonal matrix whose columns are permutations of the identity matrix. Geometrically, a permutation matrix is a type of reflection.

Normal: $\mathbf{A}^\mathsf{H}\mathbf{A} = \mathbf{A}\mathbf{A}^\mathsf{H}$. Examples of normal matrices include unitary, Hermitian, and skew-Hermitian ($\mathbf{A}^\mathsf{H} = -\mathbf{A}$) matrices.

Projection: $\mathbf{P}^2 = \mathbf{P}$.

Orthogonal projection: $\mathbf{P}^2 = \mathbf{P}$ and $\mathbf{P}^\mathsf{T} = \mathbf{P}$. The matrix $\mathbf{P} = \mathbf{A}(\mathbf{A}^\mathsf{T}\mathbf{A})^{-1}\mathbf{A}^\mathsf{T}$ maps vectors into the column space of $\mathbf{A}$ but does not change vectors already in that subspace. Any vector orthogonal to the column space of $\mathbf{A}$ is mapped to the zero vector, i.e., if $\mathbf{A}^\mathsf{T}\mathbf{B} = \mathbf{0}$, then $\mathbf{P}\mathbf{B} = \mathbf{0}$.

Diagonal: $a_{ij} = 0$ for $i \neq j$. We denote it as $\mathrm{diag}(a_{11}, a_{22}, \ldots, a_{nn})$.

Upper triangular: $a_{ij} = 0$ for $i > j$.

Tridiagonal: $a_{ij} = 0$ if $|i - j| > 1$.

Banded: $a_{ij} = 0$ if $i - j > m_l$ or $j - i < m_u$. The number $m_u + m_l + 1$ is called the *bandwidth*.

Upper Hessenberg: $a_{ij} = 0$ for $i > j + 1$.

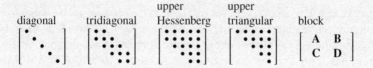

diagonal   tridiagonal   upper Hessenberg   upper triangular   block

| unit eigenvectors | stretched by eigenvalues | singular vectors |

Example. We can evaluate a function of a matrix $f(\mathbf{A})$ by using the Taylor series expansion of f and the diagonalization of the matrix:

$$f(\mathbf{A}) = \sum_{k=0}^{\infty} c_k \mathbf{A}^k = \sum_{k=0}^{\infty} c_k \left(\mathbf{SAS}^{-1}\right)^k = \sum_{k=0}^{\infty} c_k \mathbf{SA}^k \mathbf{S}^{-1} = \mathbf{S} \left(\sum_{k=0}^{\infty} c_k \mathbf{\Lambda}^k\right) \mathbf{S}^{-1}.$$

So $f(\mathbf{A})$ is $\mathbf{S} \operatorname{diag}(f(\lambda_1), f(\lambda_2), \ldots, f(\lambda_n))\mathbf{S}^{-1}$. For instance, the system of differential equations

$$\frac{\mathrm{d}}{\mathrm{d}t}\mathbf{u} = \mathbf{A}\mathbf{u} \quad \text{has the formal solution} \quad \mathbf{u}(t) = e^{t\mathbf{A}}\mathbf{u}(0).$$

The solution can be evaluated as $\mathbf{u}(t) = \mathbf{S} \operatorname{diag}\left(e^{\lambda_1 t}, e^{\lambda_2 t}, \ldots, e^{\lambda_n t}\right) \mathbf{S}^{-1}\mathbf{u}(0)$ or simply as $\mathbf{v}(t) = \operatorname{diag}\left(e^{\lambda_1 t}, e^{\lambda_2 t}, \ldots, e^{\lambda_n t}\right) \mathbf{v}(0)$ where $\mathbf{v}(t) = \mathbf{S}^{-1}\mathbf{u}(t)$, completely decoupling the system. If $\mathbf{A}$ happens to be a circulant matrix (the type of matrix that often arises when solving a partial differential equation with periodic boundary conditions), $\mathbf{S}$ is easy and fast to compute—it's a discrete Fourier transform. We'll come back to the discrete Fourier transform in Chapter 6. ◄

▷ Schur and spectral decompositions

Every square matrix is unitarily similar to an upper triangle matrix whose diagonal elements are the eigenvalues of the original matrix, a representation called the Shur decomposition. Furthermore, every normal matrix is unitarily similar to a diagonal matrix whose elements are the eigenvalues of the original matrix, a representation called spectral decomposition.

Theorem 1 (Schur decomposition). *Every square matrix is unitarily similar to an upper triangular matrix. In other words, given $\mathbf{A}$, there exists a unitary matrix $\mathbf{U}$ and an upper triangular matrix $\mathbf{T}$ such that $\mathbf{T} = \mathbf{U}^H\mathbf{A}\mathbf{U}$. Furthermore, the diagonal elements of $\mathbf{T}$ are the eigenvalues of $\mathbf{A}$.*

Proof. We can prove this by induction. Take $\mathbf{A} \in \mathbb{C}^{n \times n}$. When $n = 1$, the hypothesis is clearly true: $\mathbf{A} = \lambda$ is already an upper triangular 1×1 matrix with $\mathbf{U} = 1$. Now, assume that the hypothesis holds for $n - 1$ and show that it also holds for n. Let λ be an eigenvalue of $\mathbf{A}$ and $\mathbf{v}$ be the associated eigenvector with $\|\mathbf{v}\|_2 = 1$. Let $\mathbf{U}_1$ be a unitary matrix whose first column is $\mathbf{v}$:

$$\mathbf{U}_1 = \begin{bmatrix} \mathbf{v} & \mathbf{W} \end{bmatrix}$$

where $\mathbf{W}$ is the $n \times (n-1)$ matrix of remaining columns. Let $\mathbf{A}_1 = \mathbf{U}_1^H \mathbf{A} \mathbf{U}_1$. Then

$$\mathbf{A}_1 = \begin{bmatrix} \mathbf{v}^H \\ \mathbf{W}^H \end{bmatrix} \mathbf{A} \begin{bmatrix} \mathbf{v} & \mathbf{W} \end{bmatrix} = \begin{bmatrix} \mathbf{v}^H \mathbf{A} \mathbf{v} & \mathbf{v}^H \mathbf{A} \mathbf{W} \\ \mathbf{W}^H \mathbf{A} \mathbf{v} & \mathbf{W}^H \mathbf{A} \mathbf{W} \end{bmatrix} = \begin{bmatrix} \lambda & \mathbf{v}^H \mathbf{A} \mathbf{W} \\ \mathbf{0} & \mathbf{W}^H \mathbf{A} \mathbf{W} \end{bmatrix} = \left[\begin{array}{c|ccc} \lambda & * & \cdots & * \\ \hline 0 & & & \\ \vdots & & \hat{\mathbf{A}} & \\ 0 & & & \end{array} \right]$$

where $\hat{\mathbf{A}} = \mathbf{W}^H \mathbf{A} \mathbf{W} \in \mathbf{C}^{(n-1) \times (n-1)}$. By the induction hypothesis, there exists a unitary matrix $\hat{\mathbf{U}}_1$ and an upper triangular matrix $\hat{\mathbf{T}}$ such that $\hat{\mathbf{T}} = \hat{\mathbf{U}}_1^H \hat{\mathbf{A}} \hat{\mathbf{U}}_1$. Let

$$\mathbf{U}_2 = \left[\begin{array}{c|ccc} \lambda & * & \cdots & * \\ \hline 0 & & & \\ \vdots & & \hat{\mathbf{U}}_1 & \\ 0 & & & \end{array} \right].$$

Then $\mathbf{U}_2$ is unitary and

$$\mathbf{U}_2^H \mathbf{A}_1 \mathbf{U}_2 = \left[\begin{array}{c|ccc} \lambda & * & \cdots & * \\ \hline 0 & & & \\ \vdots & & \hat{\mathbf{U}}_1^H \hat{\mathbf{A}}_1 \hat{\mathbf{U}}_1 & \\ 0 & & & \end{array} \right] = \left[\begin{array}{c|ccc} \lambda & * & \cdots & * \\ \hline 0 & & & \\ \vdots & & \hat{\mathbf{T}} & \\ 0 & & & \end{array} \right]$$

is an upper triangular matrix. Call it $\mathbf{T}$. So

$$\mathbf{T} = \mathbf{U}_2^H \mathbf{A}_1 \mathbf{U}_2 = \mathbf{U}_2^H \mathbf{U}_1^H \mathbf{A} \mathbf{U}_1 \mathbf{U}_2 = \mathbf{U}^H \mathbf{A} \mathbf{U}. \qquad \square$$

Theorem 2 (Spectral theorem). *If $\mathbf{A}$ is a normal matrix $(\mathbf{A}^H \mathbf{A} = \mathbf{A} \mathbf{A}^H)$, then $\mathbf{A} = \mathbf{U} \mathbf{\Lambda} \mathbf{U}^H$ where $\mathbf{U}$ is a unitary matrix whose columns are eigenvalues of $\mathbf{A}$ and $\mathbf{\Lambda}$ is a diagonal matrix whose elements are the eigenvalues of $\mathbf{A}$. Furthermore, the eigenvalues of a Hermitian matrix are real.*

Proof. As a consequence of the Shur decomposition theorem, $\mathbf{A} = \mathbf{U} \mathbf{\Lambda} \mathbf{U}^H$ where $\mathbf{\Lambda}$ is an upper triangular matrix whose diagonal elements are eigenvalues of $\mathbf{A}$ and $\mathbf{U}$ is a unitary matrix. It follows that

$$\mathbf{A}^H \mathbf{A} = \mathbf{U} \mathbf{\Lambda}^H \mathbf{U}^H \mathbf{U} \mathbf{\Lambda} \mathbf{U}^H = \mathbf{U} \mathbf{\Lambda}^H \mathbf{\Lambda} \mathbf{U}^H \quad \text{and}$$
$$\mathbf{A} \mathbf{A}^H = \mathbf{U} \mathbf{\Lambda} \mathbf{U}^H \mathbf{U} \mathbf{\Lambda}^H \mathbf{U}^H = \mathbf{U} \mathbf{\Lambda} \mathbf{\Lambda}^H \mathbf{U}^H.$$

$\mathbf{\Lambda}^H \mathbf{\Lambda} = \mathbf{\Lambda} \mathbf{\Lambda}^H$ looks like

$$\begin{bmatrix} \times & & & \\ \times & \times & & \\ \times & \times & \times & \\ \times & \times & \times & \times \end{bmatrix} \begin{bmatrix} \times & \times & \times & \times \\ & \times & \times & \times \\ & & \times & \times \\ & & & \times \end{bmatrix} = \begin{bmatrix} \times & \times & \times & \times \\ & \times & \times & \times \\ & & \times & \times \\ & & & \times \end{bmatrix} \begin{bmatrix} \times & & & \\ \times & \times & & \\ \times & \times & \times & \\ \times & \times & \times & \times \end{bmatrix}.$$

Let's look just at the diagonal elements of the product $\boldsymbol{\Lambda}^H\boldsymbol{\Lambda} = \boldsymbol{\Lambda}\boldsymbol{\Lambda}^H$. Starting with the $(1, 1)$-element:

$$t_{11}^2 = \sum_{k=1}^{n} t_{1k}^2.$$

So $t_{1k} = 0$ for $k > 1$. Hence $\boldsymbol{\Lambda}^H\boldsymbol{\Lambda} = \boldsymbol{\Lambda}\boldsymbol{\Lambda}^H$ looks like

$$\begin{bmatrix} \times & & & \\ & \times & & \\ & \times & \times & \\ & \times & \times & \times \end{bmatrix}\begin{bmatrix} \times & \times & \times & \times \\ & \times & \times & \times \\ & & \times & \times \\ & & & \times \end{bmatrix} = \begin{bmatrix} \times & \times & \times & \times \\ & \times & \times & \times \\ & & \times & \times \\ & & & \times \end{bmatrix}\begin{bmatrix} \times & & & \\ & \times & & \\ & \times & \times & \\ & \times & \times & \times \end{bmatrix}.$$

Now, move to the $(2, 2)$-element:

$$t_{22}^2 = \sum_{k=2}^{n} t_{2k}^2.$$

So $t_{2k} = 0$ for $k > 2$. Hence $\boldsymbol{\Lambda}^H\boldsymbol{\Lambda} = \boldsymbol{\Lambda}\boldsymbol{\Lambda}^H$ looks like

$$\begin{bmatrix} \times & & & \\ & \times & & \\ & & \times & \\ & & \times & \times \end{bmatrix}\begin{bmatrix} \times & & & \\ & \times & \times & \\ & & \times & \times \\ & & & \times \end{bmatrix} = \begin{bmatrix} \times & & & \\ & \times & & \\ & & \times & \times \\ & & & \times \end{bmatrix}\begin{bmatrix} \times & & & \\ & \times & & \\ & & \times & \\ & & \times & \times \end{bmatrix}.$$

Continuing like this, it follows that $\boldsymbol{\Lambda}$ is a diagonal matrix. When $\mathbf{A}$ is also a Hermitian matrix, $\mathbf{A} = \mathbf{A}^H$, from which it follows that $\boldsymbol{\Lambda} = \boldsymbol{\Lambda}^H$. So the eigenvalues of a Hermitian matrix are real. $\square$

By the spectral theorem, a Hermitian matrix $\mathbf{A}$ is unitarily similar to a diagonal matrix $\mathbf{A} = \mathbf{Q}\boldsymbol{\Lambda}\mathbf{Q}^H$ where $\mathbf{Q}$ is a unitary matrix of the eigenvectors. Geometrically, this says that a real, symmetric matrix behaves like a diagonal operator in a rotated (and reflected) basis. Also,

$$\mathbf{A} = \lambda_1\mathbf{q}_1\mathbf{q}_1^H + \lambda_2\mathbf{q}_2\mathbf{q}_2^H + \cdots + \lambda_n\mathbf{q}_n\mathbf{q}_n^H$$

where $\mathbf{q}_k\mathbf{q}_k^H$ is an orthogonal projection matrix onto the unit eigenvector $\mathbf{q}_k$. This decomposition is known as the *spectral decomposition* of $\mathbf{A}$.

Example. A circulant matrix

$$\mathbf{C} = \begin{bmatrix} c_1 & c_2 & \cdots & c_{n-1} & c_n \\ c_n & c_1 & c_2 & & c_{n-1} \\ \vdots & c_n & c_1 & \ddots & \vdots \\ c_3 & & \ddots & \ddots & c_2 \\ c_2 & c_3 & \cdots & c_n & c_1 \end{bmatrix}$$

is a normal matrix. Circulant matrices often appear in practice as the discrete approximation to the Laplacian and as convolution operators on a periodic domain. They are unitarily similar to diagonal matrices $\mathbf{\Lambda} = \mathbf{FCF}^H$ where $\mathbf{F}$ is the discrete Fourier transform. By making a change of basis using $\mathbf{F}$, we trade a complicated operator $\mathbf{C}$ for a simple diagonal one $\mathbf{\Lambda}$. With the invention of the fast Fourier transform, the two changes of the bases $\mathbf{F}$ and $\mathbf{F}^H$ are relatively quick steps.   ◀

▷ Singular value decomposition

We can generalize spectral decomposition to non-symmetric and even non-square matrices. Such a decomposition is called the *singular value decomposition* or simply the SVD. Let $\mathbf{A} \in \mathbb{C}^{m \times n}$. There exist two unitary matrices $\mathbf{U} \in \mathbb{C}^{m \times m}$ and $\mathbf{V} \in \mathbb{C}^{n \times n}$ such that

$$\mathbf{U}^H \mathbf{AV} = \mathbf{\Sigma} = \mathrm{diag}(\sigma_1, \ldots, \sigma_n)$$

with $\sigma_1 \geq \cdots \geq \sigma_n \geq 0$. The numbers σ_i are called the *singular values* of $\mathbf{A}$ and are given by

$$\sigma_i(\mathbf{A}) = \sqrt{\lambda_i(\mathbf{A}^H \mathbf{A})}.$$

The unitary matrix $\mathbf{U}$ is the matrix of eigenvectors of $\mathbf{AA}^H$ and the unitary matrix $\mathbf{V}$ is the matrix of eigenvectors of $\mathbf{A}^H \mathbf{A}$.

Singular value decomposition has an intuitive geometric interpretation: $\mathbf{AV} = \mathbf{U\Sigma}$. Any matrix $\mathbf{A}$ maps a sphere with axes along the columns of $\mathbf{V}$ into an ellipsoid $\mathbf{U\Sigma}$ with some dimensions possibly zero. The singular values give the radii of the ellipsoid. The right singular vectors are mapped into the left singular vectors, which form the semiprincipal axes of the ellipsoid. The largest singular value gives the maximum magnification of the matrix. The smallest singular value gives the smallest magnification of the matrix.

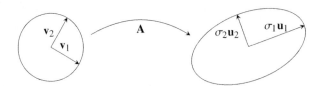

Example. A 2×2 matrix maps points on the unit circle to points on an ellipse. Such a mapping can have two, one, or zero real eigenvectors. See Figure 1.1. Here we consider equivalent matrices with singular values $\sigma_1 = 2$ and $\sigma_2 = 1$ formed by changing the right singular vectors of the singular value decomposition. Think of twisting the unit circle by different angles. Eigenvectors lie along the radial direction. When the right and left singular matrices are the same, the matrix is symmetric and has a pair of orthogonal eigenvectors that are identical

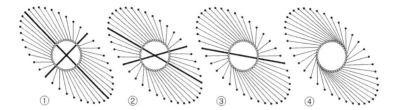

Figure 1.1: A matrix maps points on the unit circle to points on an ellipse. Such a mapping has two, one, or zero real eigenvectors (thick line segments) running along the radial directions.

to the left and right singular vectors ①. If we adjust the right singular vector slightly by twisting the unit circle, the eigenvectors move toward one another ② until they are colinear ③, and finally they become complex ④. A matrix that does not have a complete basis of eigenvectors is called defective.   ◀

1.3   Measuring vectors and matrices

▷ **Inner products**

An *inner product* on the vector space V is any map $(\cdot, \cdot)$ from $V \times V$ into $\mathbb{R}$ or $\mathbb{C}$ with the three properties—linearity, Hermiticity, and positive definiteness:

1. $(a\mathbf{u} + b\mathbf{v}, \mathbf{w}) = a\,(\mathbf{u}, \mathbf{w}) + b\,(\mathbf{v}, \mathbf{w})$ for all $\mathbf{u}, \mathbf{v}, \mathbf{w} \in V$ and $a, b \in \mathbb{C}$;

2. $(\mathbf{u}, \mathbf{v}) = \overline{(\mathbf{v}, \mathbf{u})}$; and

3. $(\mathbf{u}, \mathbf{u}) \geq 0$ and $(\mathbf{u}, \mathbf{u}) = 0$ if and only if $\mathbf{u} = 0$.

Two vectors $\mathbf{u}$ and $\mathbf{v}$ are *orthogonal* if $(\mathbf{u}, \mathbf{v}) = 0$. Important examples of inner products include the *Euclidean inner product* $(\mathbf{u}, \mathbf{v})_2 = \mathbf{u}^\mathsf{T}\mathbf{v}$ and the *A-energy inner product* $(\mathbf{u}, \mathbf{v})_\mathbf{A} = \mathbf{u}^\mathsf{T}\mathbf{A}\mathbf{v}$ where $\mathbf{A}$ is symmetric, positive definite. Vectors that are orthogonal under the A-energy inner product are said to be A-orthogonal or A-conjugate. We can visualize two vectors $\mathbf{u}$ and $\mathbf{v}$ that are orthogonal under the Euclidean inner product as being perpendicular in space. What can we make of A-orthogonal vectors? Because $\mathbf{A}$ is a symmetric, positive-definite matrix, it has the spectral decomposition $\mathbf{A} = \mathbf{Q}\mathbf{\Lambda}\mathbf{Q}^{-1}$, where $\mathbf{Q}$ is an orthogonal matrix of eigenvectors. Then $(\mathbf{u}, \mathbf{v})_\mathbf{A}$ is simply $(\mathbf{\Lambda}^{1/2}\mathbf{Q}^{-1}\mathbf{u})^\mathsf{T}(\mathbf{\Lambda}^{1/2}\mathbf{Q}^{-1}\mathbf{v})$. That is, the $\mathbf{u}$ and $\mathbf{v}$ are perpendicular in the scaled eigenbasis of $\mathbf{A}$.

▷ **Vector norms**

A *vector norm* on the vector space V is any map $\| \cdot \|$ from V into $\mathbb{R}$ with the three properties—positivity, homogeneity, and subadditivity:

1. $\|\mathbf{v}\| \geq 0$ for all $\mathbf{v} \in V$ and $\|\mathbf{v}\| = 0$ if and only if $\mathbf{v} = 0$;

2. $\|\alpha\mathbf{v}\| = |\alpha|\|\mathbf{v}\|$; and

3. $\|\mathbf{v} + \mathbf{w}\| \leq \|\mathbf{v}\| + \|\mathbf{w}\|$.

The *p-norm* is an important class of vector norms:[2]

$$\|\mathbf{u}\|_p = \left(\sum_{i=1}^{n} |u_i|^p \right)^{1/p} \qquad \text{for } 1 \leq p < \infty.$$

Specific cases of the p-norm include the 1-norm

$$\|\mathbf{u}\|_1 = \sum_{i=1}^{n} |u_i|,$$

the *Euclidean norm* or 2-norm

$$\|\mathbf{u}\|_2 = \left(\sum_{i=1}^{n} |u_i|^2 \right)^{1/2} = \sqrt{(\mathbf{u}, \mathbf{u})_2},$$

and the ∞-norm (taking $p \to \infty$)

$$\|\mathbf{u}\|_\infty = \max_{1 \leq i \leq n} |u_i|.$$

Another important class of vector norms is the *energy norm*

$$\|\mathbf{u}\|_\mathbf{A} = \sqrt{(\mathbf{u}, \mathbf{u})_\mathbf{A}} \qquad \text{where } \mathbf{A} \text{ is symmetric, positive definite.}$$

Let's make a couple of observations about vector norms. First, every inner product *induces* a vector norm: $\|\mathbf{u}\|^2 = (\mathbf{u}, \mathbf{u})$. All such induced vector norms satisfy the *Cauchy–Schwarz inequality* $(\mathbf{x}, \mathbf{y}) \leq \|\mathbf{x}\|\|\mathbf{y}\|$. To see this, note that for any value α we have

$$0 \leq \|\mathbf{x} - \alpha\mathbf{y}\|^2 = \|\mathbf{x}\|^2 - 2\alpha(\mathbf{x}, \mathbf{y}) + |\alpha|^2\|\mathbf{y}\|^2.$$

By taking $\alpha = (\mathbf{x}, \mathbf{y})/\|\mathbf{y}\|^2$, it follows that $0 \leq \|\mathbf{x}\|^2\|\mathbf{y}\|^2 - (\mathbf{x}, \mathbf{y})^2$. Second, the Euclidean norm is invariant under orthogonal transformations $\|\mathbf{Q}\mathbf{x}\|_2 = \|\mathbf{x}\|_2$. This result should be clear from the geometric interpretation of the Euclidean norm and orthogonal transformation, but you can crosscheck it with simple algebra: $\|\mathbf{Q}\mathbf{x}\|_2^2 = \|\mathbf{x}^\mathsf{T}\mathbf{Q}^\mathsf{T}\mathbf{Q}\mathbf{x}\|_2 = \|\mathbf{x}^\mathsf{T}\mathbf{x}\|_2 = \|\mathbf{x}\|_2^2$.

Two norms $\|\cdot\|_\alpha$ and $\|\cdot\|_\beta$ on a vector space V are *equivalent* if there are positive constants c and C such that $c\|\mathbf{u}\|_\alpha \leq \|\mathbf{u}\|_\beta \leq C\|\mathbf{u}\|_\alpha$ for all vectors $\mathbf{u} \in V$. All norms on finite-dimensional vector spaces are equivalent. This means that we can often choose a convenient norm with which to work and the results will hold with respect to the other norms.

---

[2] The p-norm is the discrete, finite-dimensional analog to an ℓ^p-norm for an infinite-dimensional vector space and an L^p-norm for a continuous vector space.

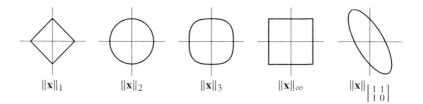

Figure 1.2: Unit circles in different norms on $\mathbb{R}^2$.

Example. Let's first show that the 1- and 2-norms are equivalent and then show that the 2- and ∞-norms are equivalent. We'll take $V = \mathbb{R}^n$.

 The hypercube $\|\mathbf{x}\|_1 = 1$ can be inscribed in the hypersphere $\|\mathbf{x}\|_2 = 1$, which can itself be inscribed in the hypercube $\|\mathbf{x}\|_1 = \sqrt{n}$. So $\frac{1}{\sqrt{n}}\|\mathbf{x}\|_1 \le \|\mathbf{x}\|_2 \le \|\mathbf{x}\|_1$.

 The hypercube $\|\mathbf{x}\|_\infty = 1/\sqrt{n}$ can be inscribed in the hypersphere $\|\mathbf{x}\|_2 = 1$, which can be inscribed in the hypercube $\|\mathbf{x}\|_\infty = 1$. So $\|\mathbf{x}\|_\infty \le \|\mathbf{x}\|_2 \le \sqrt{n}\|\mathbf{x}\|_\infty$.   ◀

▷ Matrix norms

A *matrix norm* is map $\|\cdot\|$ from $\mathbb{R}^{m\times n}$ into $\mathbb{R}$ with the three properties—positivity, homogeneity, and subadditivity:

1. $\|\mathbf{A}\| \ge 0$ and $\|\mathbf{A}\| = 0$ if and only if $\mathbf{A} = 0$;

2. $\|\alpha\mathbf{A}\| = |\alpha|\|\mathbf{A}\|$; and

3. $\|\mathbf{A} + \mathbf{B}\| \le \|\mathbf{A}\| + \|\mathbf{B}\|$.

A matrix norm is said to be *submultiplicative* if it has the additional property

4. $\|\mathbf{AB}\| \le \|\mathbf{A}\|\|\mathbf{B}\|$.

A matrix norm $\|\cdot\|$ is said to be *compatible* or *consistent* with a vector norm $\|\cdot\|$ if $\|\mathbf{Ax}\| \le \|\mathbf{A}\|\|\mathbf{x}\|$ for all $\mathbf{x} \in \mathbb{R}^n$. One might ask "what is the smallest matrix norm that is compatible with a vector norm?" We call such a norm the *induced matrix norm*:

$$\|\mathbf{A}\| = \sup_{\mathbf{x}\neq 0} \frac{\|\mathbf{Ax}\|}{\|\mathbf{x}\|} = \sup_{\|\mathbf{x}\|=1} \|\mathbf{Ax}\|.$$

The induced norm is the most that a matrix can stretch a vector in a vector norm.

Theorem 3. *An induced norm is compatible with its associated vector norm. An induced norm of the identity matrix is one. An induced norm is submultiplicative.*

Proof.

1. $\|\mathbf{Ax}\| = \dfrac{\|\mathbf{Ax}\|}{\|\mathbf{x}\|}\|\mathbf{x}\| \leq \left(\sup\limits_{\mathbf{x}\neq 0} \dfrac{\|\mathbf{Ax}\|}{\|\mathbf{x}\|}\right)\|\mathbf{x}\| = \|\mathbf{A}\|\,\|\mathbf{x}\|$

2. $\|\mathbf{I}\| = \sup\limits_{\|\mathbf{x}\|=1} \|\mathbf{x}\| = 1$

3. $\|\mathbf{AB}\| = \sup\limits_{\|\mathbf{x}\|=1} \|\mathbf{ABx}\| \leq \sup\limits_{\|\mathbf{x}\|=1} \|\mathbf{A}\|\,\|\mathbf{Bx}\| = \|\mathbf{A}\|\,\|\mathbf{B}\|$ □

Arguably, the most important induced matrix norms are the *p*-norms

$$\|\mathbf{A}\|_p = \sup\limits_{\|\mathbf{x}\|=1} \|\mathbf{Ax}\|_p$$

In particular, the 2-, 1-, and ∞-norms arise frequently in numerical methods. So, it's good to get a geometric intuition about each one. See the Figure 1.3 on the next page.

We'll start with the 2-norm or the *spectral norm*. A circle ($\mathbf{x}$) is mapped to an ellipse ($\mathbf{Ax}$) under a linear transformation ($\mathbf{A}$), and sup $\|\mathbf{Ax}\|_2$ corresponds to the largest radius of the ellipse. So $\|\mathbf{A}\|_2 = \sigma_{\max}(\mathbf{A})$.

Next, consider the unit circle of the 1-norm. The square ($\mathbf{x}$) is mapped to a parallelogram ($\mathbf{Ax}$). The supremum of $\|\mathbf{Ax}\|_1$ must come from one of the vertices of the parallelogram. The vertices of the parallelogram are mapped from the corners of the square, each of which corresponds to one of the standard basis elements $\pm\boldsymbol{\xi}_j$, e.g., in three-dimensions $(\pm 1, 0, 0)$, $(0, \pm 1, 0)$ or $(0, 0, \pm 1)$. Then $\mathbf{A}\boldsymbol{\xi}_j$ returns (plus or minus) the *j*th column of $\mathbf{A}$. Therefore,

$$\|\mathbf{A}\|_1 = \max\limits_{1\leq j\leq n} \sum\limits_{i=1}^{m} |a_{ij}|.$$

Finally, consider the unit circle for the ∞-norm. Again, a square ($\mathbf{x}$) is mapped to a parallelogram ($\mathbf{Ax}$). The supremum of $\|\mathbf{Ax}\|_1$ must originate from the corners of the square. This time the corners are at $(\pm 1, \pm 1, \ldots, \pm 1)$. Explicitly,

$$\begin{bmatrix} a_{11} & a_{12} & a_{13} \\ a_{21} & a_{22} & a_{23} \\ a_{31} & a_{32} & a_{33} \end{bmatrix} \begin{bmatrix} \pm 1 \\ \pm 1 \\ \pm 1 \end{bmatrix} = \begin{bmatrix} \pm a_{11} \pm a_{12} \pm a_{13} \\ \pm a_{21} \pm a_{22} \pm a_{23} \\ \pm a_{31} \pm a_{32} \pm a_{33} \end{bmatrix}.$$

By taking the largest possible element, we have

$$\|\mathbf{A}\|_\infty = \max\limits_{1\leq i\leq n} \sum\limits_{j=1}^{m} |a_{ij}|.$$

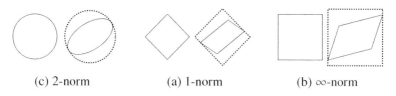

(c) 2-norm   (a) 1-norm   (b) ∞-norm

Figure 1.3: Mapping of unit circles by $\frac{1}{4}\begin{bmatrix} 1 & 1 \\ 1 & 3 \end{bmatrix}$.

Note that $\|\mathbf{A}\|_\infty = \|\mathbf{A}^T\|_1$. You can use the superscripts of the 1- and ∞-norms as a mnemonic to remember in which direction to take the sums. The "1" runs vertically, so take the maximum of the sums down the columns. The "∞" lies horizontally, so take the maximum of the sums along the rows. For example,

$$\mathbf{A} = \begin{bmatrix} 1 & 2 & 3 \\ 2 & 1 & 1 \\ 1 & 4 & 0 \end{bmatrix}, \qquad \|\mathbf{A}\|_1 = 7, \quad \|\mathbf{A}\|_\infty = 6.$$

⁂ The LinearAlgebra.jl function opnorm(A,p) computes the p-norm of a matrix $\mathbf{A}$, where the optional argument p can be either 1, 2 (default), or Inf. The LinearAlgebra function norm(A) returns the Frobenius norm.

Theorem 4. $\|\mathbf{A}\|_2$ *equals the largest singular value of* $\mathbf{A}$. *If* $\mathbf{A}$ *is Hermitian, then* $\|\mathbf{A}\|_2$ *equals the spectral radius of* $\mathbf{A}$. *If* $\mathbf{A}$ *is unitary, then* $\|\mathbf{A}\|_2 = 1$.

Proof. This theorem has the easy picture proof mentioned above and depicted in Figure 1.3 above. A circle is mapped to an ellipse, and the induced 2-norm corresponds to the largest radius of the ellipse. If the matrix is Hermitian, then the singular values are the same as the eigenvalues. If the matrix is unitary, the ellipse is simply another unit circle.

If you're not satisfied with this picture proof, here's an algebraic proof. Take $\mathbf{A} \in \mathbb{C}^{n \times n}$. $\mathbf{A}^H\mathbf{A}$ is Hermitian, so there exists a unitary matrix $\mathbf{U}$ such that

$$\mathbf{U}^H\mathbf{A}^H\mathbf{A}\mathbf{U} = \text{diag}(\lambda_1, \lambda_2, \ldots \lambda_n)$$

where λ_i are the nonnegative eigenvalues of $\mathbf{A}^H\mathbf{A}$. Let $\mathbf{y} = \mathbf{U}^H\mathbf{x}$. Then

$$\|\mathbf{A}\|_2 = \sup_{\|\mathbf{x}\|_2=1} \sqrt{\mathbf{x}^H\mathbf{A}^H\mathbf{A}\mathbf{x}} = \sup_{\|\mathbf{x}\|_2=1} \sqrt{\mathbf{y}^H\mathbf{U}^H\mathbf{A}^H\mathbf{A}\mathbf{U}\mathbf{y}}$$

$$= \sup_{\|\mathbf{y}\|_2=1} \sqrt{\sum_{i=1}^{n} \lambda_i|y_i|^2} = \sqrt{\max_{1 \le i \le n} \lambda_i}.$$

Furthermore, if $\mathbf{A}$ is Hermitian, then the singular values of $\mathbf{A}$ equal its eigenvalues. If $\mathbf{A}$ is unitary, $\mathbf{A}^H\mathbf{A} = \mathbf{I}$.   □

Theorem 5. $\rho(\mathbf{A}) \leq \|\mathbf{A}\|$ *where* $\|\cdot\|$ *is an induced norm. Furthermore, for symmetric matrices,* $\|\mathbf{A}\|_{\max} \leq \rho(\mathbf{A})$ *where the max norm* $\|\mathbf{A}\|_{\max} = \max_{i,j} |a_{ij}|$.

Proof. If λ is an eigenvalue of $\mathbf{A}$, then $\mathbf{A}\mathbf{x} = \lambda\mathbf{x}$ for some vector $\mathbf{x}$. So $\|\mathbf{A}\mathbf{x}\| = |\lambda|\|\mathbf{x}\|$. From this it follows that $|\lambda| = \|\mathbf{A}\mathbf{x}\|/\|\mathbf{x}\|$, and hence

$$\rho(\mathbf{A}) = \max_{\lambda \in \lambda(\mathbf{A})} |\lambda| \leq \sup_{\mathbf{x} \neq 0} \frac{\|\mathbf{A}\|}{\|\mathbf{x}\|} = \|\mathbf{A}\|.$$

A standard basis vector $\boldsymbol{\xi}_j$ is mapped to the jth column of $\mathbf{A}$. So $\|\mathbf{A}\|_{\max}$ must be equal to or smaller than the largest component $\mathbf{A}\boldsymbol{\xi}_j$ for some $\boldsymbol{\xi}_j$. The largest component of $\mathbf{A}\boldsymbol{\xi}_j$ must be equal to or smaller than the length of $\mathbf{A}\boldsymbol{\xi}_j$. So $\|\mathbf{A}\|_{\max} \leq \max_j \|\mathbf{A}\boldsymbol{\xi}_j\|_1 \leq \sigma_{\max}(\mathbf{A})$.   □

Example.   We can put a lower and upper bound on the spectral radius of a symmetric matrix using $\|\mathbf{A}\|_{\max} \leq \rho(\mathbf{A}) \leq \|\mathbf{A}\|_\infty$. For the following matrix

$$\begin{bmatrix} 5 & 1 & 2 & 1 \\ 1 & 2 & 2 & 3 \\ 2 & 2 & 4 & 2 \\ 1 & 3 & 2 & 6 \end{bmatrix}$$

we find that $6 \leq \rho(\mathbf{A}) \leq 12$. The computed value is $\rho(\mathbf{A}) \approx 10.03$.   ◀

▷ **Quadratic forms**

The quadratic form of a real, symmetric $n \times n$ matrix $\mathbf{A}$ is defined as $q(\mathbf{x}) = \mathbf{x}^\mathsf{T}\mathbf{A}\mathbf{x}$. In component form,

$$q(x_1, x_2, \ldots, x_n) = \sum_{i,j=1}^{n} a_{ij} x_i x_j.$$

In the case of a 2×2 matrix,

$$q(x, y) = \begin{bmatrix} x & y \end{bmatrix} \begin{bmatrix} a & b \\ b & c \end{bmatrix} \begin{bmatrix} x \\ y \end{bmatrix} = ax^2 + 2bxy + cy^2 :$$

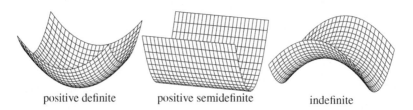

positive definite   positive semidefinite   indefinite

A matrix $\mathbf{A}$ is said to be *positive definite*, if $\mathbf{x}^\mathsf{T}\mathbf{A}\mathbf{x} > 0$ for all $\mathbf{x} \neq 0$. Likewise, a matrix $\mathbf{A}$ is said to be negative definite, if $\mathbf{x}^\mathsf{T}\mathbf{A}\mathbf{x} < 0$ for all $\mathbf{x} \neq 0$. A matrix $\mathbf{A}$ is positive semidefinite if $\mathbf{x}^\mathsf{T}\mathbf{A}\mathbf{x} \geq 0$ and negative semidefinite if $\mathbf{x}^\mathsf{T}\mathbf{A}\mathbf{x} \leq 0$. Otherwise, the matrix is indefinite.

Theorem 6. *A symmetric matrix is positive definite if and only if it has only positive eigenvalues.*

Proof. Suppose that $\mathbf{A}$ is positive definite. Then $\mathbf{x}^\mathsf{T}\mathbf{A}\mathbf{x} > 0$ for any nonzero vector $\mathbf{x}$. If $\mathbf{x}$ is an eigenvector, $\mathbf{x}^\mathsf{T}\mathbf{A}\mathbf{x} = \mathbf{x}^\mathsf{T}\lambda\mathbf{x} = \lambda\|\mathbf{x}\|^2$. It follows that $\lambda > 0$. On the other hand, suppose that $\mathbf{A}$ has only positive eigenvalues λ_i. Because $\mathbf{A}$ is symmetric, any vector $\mathbf{x}$ can be written as a linear combination of orthogonal unit eigenvectors $\mathbf{x} = c_1\mathbf{q}_1 + c_2\mathbf{q}_2 + \cdots + c_n\mathbf{q}_n$. Then the quadratic form

$$\mathbf{x}^\mathsf{T}\mathbf{A}\mathbf{x} = (c_1\mathbf{q}_1 + c_2\mathbf{q}_2 + \cdots + c_n\mathbf{q}_n)^\mathsf{T}(c_1\lambda_1\mathbf{q}_1 + c_2\lambda_2\mathbf{q}_2 + \cdots + c_n\lambda_n\mathbf{q}_n)$$

$$= c_1^2\lambda_1\|\mathbf{q}_1\|^2 + c_2^2\lambda_2\|\mathbf{q}_2\|^2 + \cdots + c_n^2\lambda_n\|\mathbf{q}_n\|^2 = \sum_{i=1}^{n}\lambda_i x_i^2$$

by orthogonality of the eigenvectors. Because the $\lambda_i > 0$ for all i, it follows that $\mathbf{x}^\mathsf{T}\mathbf{A}\mathbf{x} > 0$. □

A matrix $\mathbf{A}$ is said to be *congruent* to a matrix $\mathbf{B}$ if there is an invertible matrix $\mathbf{S}$ such that $\mathbf{B} = \mathbf{S}^\mathsf{T}\mathbf{A}\mathbf{S}$. Congruent matrices have the same quadratic forms in different bases:

$$q_B(\mathbf{x}) = \mathbf{x}^\mathsf{T}\mathbf{B}\mathbf{x} = \mathbf{x}^\mathsf{T}\mathbf{S}^\mathsf{T}\mathbf{A}\mathbf{S}\mathbf{x} = (\mathbf{S}\mathbf{x})^\mathsf{T}\mathbf{A}\mathbf{S}\mathbf{x} = \mathbf{y}^\mathsf{T}\mathbf{A}\mathbf{y} = q_A(\mathbf{y}) \text{ for } \mathbf{y} = \mathbf{S}\mathbf{x}.$$

Example. Linear algebra used in quantum physics has its own unique notation. When quantum theory was developed in the early twentieth century, linear algebra was not widely taught in physics (or mathematics) departments, so the quantum pioneer Paul Dirac invented his own notation. A solution $\psi(x)$ to Schrödinger's equation $\mathbf{H}\psi = E\psi$, with the Hamiltonian operator $\mathbf{H} = -(\hbar^2/2m)\Delta + V(x)$ and the real-valued energy E, is a vector of an infinite-dimensional vector space W. In Dirac or bra–ket notation, a vector ψ is denoted by a special symbol $\rangle$. We can then express the vector $\alpha\psi$ as $\alpha\rangle$. Because this notation is ambiguous when working with more than one vector, say ψ_1 and ψ_2, we use an additional label, say 1 and 2, to write the vectors as $|1\rangle$ and $|2\rangle$. Note that the label is simply enclosed in $|$ and $\rangle$. Such an object is called a "ket." We can then express $\alpha\psi_1$ as $\alpha|1\rangle$. Bear in mind that anything between $|$ and $\rangle$ is simply a label, so $|\alpha 1\rangle \neq \alpha|1\rangle$ and $|1 + 2\rangle \neq |1\rangle + |2\rangle$. The space of kets spans the vector space W, and we can choose a basis of kets.

A linear functional mapping $W \to \mathbb{C}$ is often called a *covector*. The space of linear functionals, which forms the dual space to the vector space, is itself a vector space. A vector in the dual space of Hermitian operators is denoted by $\langle$. Define a linear functional $\langle = (\phi, \cdot) = \int_{-\infty}^{\infty} \phi^* \cdot dx$, where $\phi^*(x)$ is the complex conjugate of a function $\phi(x)$. We can now write an inner product $(\phi, \psi) = \int_{-\infty}^{\infty} \phi^* \psi \, dx$ as $\langle \rangle$. Just as we used labels to make $\rangle$ unambiguous, we can do the same for $\langle$. To denote a specific operator $\langle$, we can similarly enclose a label a between $\langle$ and $|$ to get $\langle a|$. We call such a linear operators a "bra." Let's take an orthonormal basis for W: $\{|0\rangle, |1\rangle, |2\rangle, \dots\}$. For each ket there is a corresponding bra $\{\langle 0|, \langle 1|, \langle 2|, \dots\}$, and the inner product $\langle i|j\rangle = \delta_{ij}$. (By convention, it is not necessary to write $|$ twice when combining a bra with a ket.) Furthermore, the projection operator is simply the outer product $\mathbf{P}_i = |i\rangle \langle i|$. This allows us to decompose an arbitrary vector

$$\psi = \alpha_0 |0\rangle + \alpha_1 |1\rangle + \cdots + \alpha_i |i\rangle + \cdots$$

into its orthonormal basis vector components

$$\mathbf{P}_i \psi = |i\rangle \langle i| \psi = \alpha_0 |i\rangle \langle i|0\rangle + \alpha_1 |i\rangle \langle i|1\rangle + \cdots + \alpha_i |i\rangle \langle i|i\rangle + \cdots = \alpha_i |i\rangle.$$

States are the solutions to the Schrödinger equation $\mathbf{H}\psi = E\psi$. Recognize that the Schrödinger equation is simply an eigenvalue equation (an eigenequation). The eigenvalue solutions of it are called eigenstates. The complex-valued solutions ψ are called wave functions, and by convention are normalized over space $\int_{-\infty}^{\infty} \psi^* \psi dx = 1$. This gives a wavefunction ψ the interpretation of a probability distribution $\rho(x) = |\psi(x)|^2$, the probability density of a particle at position x. Because the Schrödinger equation is an eigenvalue problem, we can find the spectral decomposition of the Hamiltonian operator

$$\mathbf{H} = E_0 |0\rangle \langle 0| + E_1 |1\rangle \langle 1| + E_2 |2\rangle \langle 2| + \cdots.$$

The Schrödinger equation can be solved in terms of its eigenvector components. Recall that the eigenvalues of Hermitian operators are real and the eigenvectors are orthogonal. When a physicist says that ψ a superposition of states, they are saying that the vector ψ is a linear combination of the orthonormal basis vectors $|0\rangle, |1\rangle, |2\rangle, \dots$.

Hermitian operators and unitary operators both play key roles in quantum physics. The Hermitian operators that have starring roles include the position operator $\mathbf{x} = x$, the momentum operator $\mathbf{p} = -i\hbar\nabla$, and the Hamiltonian operator $\mathbf{H}$. For example, applying the position operator is the same as multiplying by x: $\mathbf{x}\rangle = x\rangle$. The composition $\langle \mathbf{x}\rangle$ represents the expected value of the probability distribution $\int_{-\infty}^{\infty} \psi^* x \psi dx = \int_{-\infty}^{\infty} x|\psi|^2 dx$. The composition $\langle \mathbf{p}\rangle$ represents the expected value of the momentum $-i\hbar \int_{-\infty}^{\infty} \psi^* (\partial/\partial x)\psi dx$. And $\langle \mathbf{H}\rangle$ represents the expected value of the energy. ◄

1.4   Stability

It's convenient to solve problems by using black-box methods—letting an algorithm in a computer, for example, take care of the tedious computation. This book is largely about prying open those black boxes to inspect and tinker with their algorithmic cogwheels. Still, regardless of the algorithm: garbage in, garbage out. How can we know whether a problem will have a meaningful solution? The problem may have no solution. The problem may have multiple solutions. Perhaps the problem is so sensitive to change that a method cannot replicate the output if the input changes by even the slightest amount. To address this concern, French mathematician Jacques Hadamard introduced the concept of mathematical well-posedness in 1923. A problem is said to be *well-posed* if

1. a solution for the problem *exists*;
2. the solution is *unique*; and
3. this solution is *stable* under small perturbations in the data.

If any of these conditions fail to hold, the problem is *ill-posed*. A solution $\mathbf{x}$ to the linear problem $\mathbf{Ax} = \mathbf{b}$ exists if $\mathbf{b}$ is in the column space of $\mathbf{A}$. The solution $\mathbf{x}$ is unique if the null space of $\mathbf{A}$ is only the zero vector. As long as the matrix $\mathbf{A}$ is invertible, a unique solution exists. We will examine the case when $\mathbf{A}$ is not invertible in Chapter 3. In this section, we look at stability.

Let $\mathbf{b} = \mathbf{Ax}$. Suppose that we perturb the input data $\mathbf{x}$, perhaps due to round-off error or errors in measurement. How does this perturbation affect our numerical computation of $\mathbf{b}$? Alternatively, how does perturbing $\mathbf{A}$ affect our computation? Or, if we are solving $\mathbf{Ax} = \mathbf{b}$, what is the effect of perturbing $\mathbf{b}$?

As we will see, the first and third questions are equivalent. Put more precisely, how does the relative change in the input vector $\|\delta\mathbf{x}\|/\|\mathbf{x}\|$ affect the relative change in the output vector $\|\delta\mathbf{b}\|/\|\mathbf{b}\|$? Take

$$\mathbf{b} + \delta\mathbf{b} = \mathbf{A}(\mathbf{x} + \delta\mathbf{x}).$$

By linearity, $\delta\mathbf{b} = \mathbf{A}\delta\mathbf{x}$, from which it follows that

$$\|\delta\mathbf{b}\| = \|\mathbf{A}\delta\mathbf{x}\| \leq \|\mathbf{A}\|\|\delta\mathbf{x}\|.$$

Furthermore, from $\mathbf{x} = \mathbf{A}^{-1}\mathbf{b}$ we have

$$\|\mathbf{x}\| = \|\mathbf{A}^{-1}\mathbf{b}\| \leq \|\mathbf{A}^{-1}\|\|\mathbf{b}\|.$$

Combining these two inequalities,

$$\frac{\|\delta\mathbf{b}\|}{\|\mathbf{b}\|} \leq \|\mathbf{A}^{-1}\|\|\mathbf{A}\|\frac{\|\delta\mathbf{x}\|}{\|\mathbf{x}\|}.$$

The factor $\|\mathbf{A}^{-1}\|\|\mathbf{A}\|$ is called the *condition number* of the matrix $\mathbf{A}$ and is denoted by $\kappa(\mathbf{A})$. The condition number of the p-norm of $\mathbf{A}$ is denoted by $\kappa_p(\mathbf{A})$.

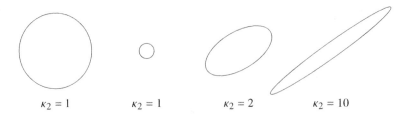

$\kappa_2 = 1$ $\kappa_2 = 1$ $\kappa_2 = 2$ $\kappa_2 = 10$

Figure 1.4: Images of unit circles under different linear transformations and their associated condition numbers.

When the condition number is small, a small perturbation $\delta \mathbf{x}$ on $\mathbf{x}$ results in a small change $\delta \mathbf{b}$ in $\mathbf{b}$. In this case, we say that $\mathbf{b}$ *depends continuously* on the data $\mathbf{x}$.

Let's look at the condition number another way. For any induced norm, the condition number $\kappa(\mathbf{A}) \geq 1$:

$$\kappa(\mathbf{A}) = \|\mathbf{A}\| \|\mathbf{A}^{-1}\| \geq \|\mathbf{A}\mathbf{A}^{-1}\| = \|\mathbf{I}\| = 1.$$

Furthermore, since

$$\|\mathbf{A}^{-1}\| = \sup_{\|\mathbf{x}\|=1} \|\mathbf{A}^{-1}\mathbf{x}\| = \sup_{\mathbf{x}\neq 0} \frac{\|\mathbf{A}^{-1}\mathbf{x}\|}{\|\mathbf{x}\|} = \sup_{\mathbf{y}\neq 0} \frac{\|\mathbf{A}^{-1}\mathbf{y}\|}{\|\mathbf{y}\|} \quad \text{where } \mathbf{y} = \mathbf{A}\mathbf{x}$$

$$= \sup_{\mathbf{x}\neq 0} \frac{\|\mathbf{A}^{-1}\mathbf{A}\mathbf{x}\|}{\|\mathbf{A}\mathbf{x}\|} = \sup_{\mathbf{x}\neq 0} \frac{\|\mathbf{x}\|}{\|\mathbf{A}\mathbf{x}\|} = \sup_{\|\mathbf{x}\|=1} \frac{1}{\|\mathbf{A}\mathbf{x}\|} = \frac{1}{\inf_{\|\mathbf{x}\|=1} \|\mathbf{A}\mathbf{x}\|},$$

it follows that

$$\kappa(\mathbf{A}) = \frac{\sup_{\|\mathbf{x}\|=1} \|\mathbf{A}\mathbf{x}\|}{\inf_{\|\mathbf{x}\|=1} \|\mathbf{A}\mathbf{x}\|}.$$

Therefore, a geometric interpretation of the condition number is

$$\kappa(\mathbf{A}) = \frac{\text{maximum magnification}}{\text{minimum magnification}}.$$

Specifically, the condition number in the Euclidean norm is $\kappa_2(\mathbf{A}) = \sigma_{\max}/\sigma_{\min}$, the ratio of radii of the semi-major to semi-minor axes of an ellipsoid image of a matrix. See the figure above.

Another way to think of the condition number is as a measure of linear dependency of the columns. A matrix $\mathbf{A}$ is *ill-conditioned* if $\kappa(\mathbf{A}) \gg 1$. If $\mathbf{A}$ is singular, $\kappa(\mathbf{A}) = \infty$. If $\mathbf{A}$ is a unitary or orthogonal matrix, then $\kappa_2(\mathbf{A}) = 1$. This makes orthogonal matrices numerically quite appealing because multiplying by them does not introduce numerical instability.

Now, the second question: how does the perturbation $\mathbf{A} + \delta\mathbf{A}$ affect our computation? Take the singular value decomposition of $\mathbf{\Sigma} = \mathbf{U}^H\mathbf{A}\mathbf{V}$. Perturbation of $\mathbf{A}$ says $\mathbf{U}^H(\mathbf{A} + \delta\mathbf{A})\mathbf{V} = \mathbf{\Sigma} + \delta\mathbf{\Sigma}$ and hence $\mathbf{U}^H\delta\mathbf{A}\mathbf{V} = \delta\mathbf{\Sigma}$. Because $\mathbf{U}$ and $\mathbf{V}$ are unitary, they are 2-norm preserving. So $\|\delta\mathbf{A}\|_2 = \|\delta\mathbf{\Sigma}\|_2$. Perturbations in a matrix cause perturbations of roughly the same size in its singular values. See Watkins' book *Fundamentals of Matrix Computations* for an analysis of simultaneous perturbations in both the matrix and the input vectors.

Example.   A Hilbert matrix is an example of an ill-conditioned matrix. The 4×4 Hilbert matrix is

$$\mathbf{H} = \begin{bmatrix} 1 & 1/2 & 1/3 & 1/4 \\ 1/2 & 1/3 & 1/4 & 1/5 \\ 1/3 & 1/4 & 1/5 & 1/6 \\ 1/4 & 1/5 & 1/6 & 1/7 \end{bmatrix}$$

and the elements of a general Hilbert matrix are $h_{ij} = (i + j - 1)^{-1}$. We can construct a Hilbert matrix using Julia with the function

```
hilbert(n) = [1/(i+j-1) for i=1:n, j=1:n]
```

and display the density plot of $\mathbf{H}^{-1}\mathbf{H}$ by explicitly converting it to type `Gray`:

```
using Images
[Gray.(1 .- abs.(hilbert(n)\hilbert(n))) for n ∈ (10,15,20,25,50)]
```

$n = 10$	$n = 15$	$n = 20$	$n = 25$	$n = 50$

Zero values are white, values with magnitude one or greater are black, and intermediate values are shades of gray. An identity matrix is represented by a diagonal of black in a field of white. While the numerical computation appears to be more-or-less correct for $n \leq 10$, it produces substantial round-off error for even moderately low dimensions such as $n = 15$.   ◄

🔩 The LinearAlgebra.jl function `cond(A,p)` returns the p-condition number of A for p either 2 (default), 1, or `Inf`.

🔩 The SpecialMatrices.jl function `hilbert(n)` returns a Hilbert matrix as rationals.

1.5   Geometric interpretation of linear algebra

This chapter reviewed several fundamental concepts of linear algebra. Many of these concepts have simple geometric analogs that help develop an intuition of abstract and sometimes abstruse notions.

Consider the space $\mathbb{R}^n$. A vector is a point in space, and a unit vector is a point on a unit circle (n-sphere). The unit vector is the direction of a vector. The zero vector is the origin. A matrix, as a linear transformation, maps a circle (n-sphere) centered at the origin to an ellipse (ellipsoid) centered at the origin. An affine transformation adds translation, but a linear transformation keeps the origin fixed. Similarly, a square is mapped to a parallelogram, and an n-cube is mapped to a parallelepiped. An $m \times n$ matrix maps vectors from $\mathbb{R}^n$ to $\mathbb{R}^m$. The rank is the number of dimensions of the resultant ellipsoid. The null space is the space of the vectors that are mapped by the matrix to the zero vector. The column space is the space spanned by the ellipsoid.

A diagonal matrix stretches along coordinate axes. A unit upper triangular matrix or unit lower triangular matrix shears an image like a deck of cards sliding on top of one another. A projection matrix squashes all of the vectors in some direction to a pancake. A vector in the column space is already in the pancake and doesn't move. Orthogonal projection squashes perpendicularly. An orthogonal matrix is a generalized rotation or reflection. A permutation reorders the coordinate axes by successively swapping rows of a matrix. If there is an even number of exchanges, the signature is even and the orientation is right-handed. Otherwise, it is left-handed. A determinant is the signed volume of the parallelepiped spanned by the column vectors of a square matrix. The absolute value of the determinant is the relative change in volume between the n-cube and the associated parallelepiped. The sign of the determinant is the orientation of the associated permutation. The Jacobian determinant (familiar from calculus) measures the relative, local change in volume caused by a change of variables.

An eigenvector of a matrix is any vector whose direction is not changed by the matrix. An eigenvalue is the amount by which an eigenvector is stretched. A matrix maps a unit circle into an ellipse, and the singular values are the lengths of the radii of the ellipsoid. A basis is the underlying set of vectors on which we create a coordinate system. The standard basis consists of an orthogonal unit vectors. Sometimes, it is more convenient to choose another basis, like the eigenbasis.

A vector norm is the length of a vector—that is, the distance to the origin. Often, we think of distance in terms of a Euclidean norm (the 2-norm). But other norms are useful, particularly the 1-norm and the ∞-norm. The 1-norm is the sum of the absolute values of the coordinates of a vector in the standard basis, and the ∞-norm is the magnitude of the largest coordinate of a vector in the standard basis. The 2-norm is invariant under an orthogonal change of basis, while the 1- and ∞-norms are not. We can extend the concept of a norm to a matrix. An induced norm is the most that any vector could be stretched by the matrix. Norms also help us measure the condition of a matrix. An ill-conditioned matrix maps a circle to a very eccentric ellipse. The 2-condition number is the ratio of the semi-major to semi-minor radii.

1.6 Exercises

1.1. Show that if $\mathbf{x}$ is an eigenvector of a nonsingular matrix $\mathbf{A}$ with eigenvalue λ, then $\mathbf{x}$ is also an eigenvector of $\mathbf{A}^{-1}$ with eigenvalue $1/\lambda$. Also, show that $\mathbf{x}$ is an eigenvector of $\mathbf{A} - c\mathbf{I}$ with eigenvalue $\lambda - c$.

1.2. Prove that similar matrices have the same spectrum of eigenvalues.

1.3. Krylov subspaces are important tools in the computation of eigenvalues of large matrices. An order-r Krylov subspace $\mathcal{K}_r(\mathbf{A}, \mathbf{x})$ generated by the $n \times n$ matrix $\mathbf{A}$ and a vector $\mathbf{x}$ is the subspace spanned by $\{\mathbf{x}, \mathbf{A}\mathbf{x}, \mathbf{A}^2\mathbf{x}, \ldots, \mathbf{A}^{r-1}\mathbf{x}\}$.

  (a) What is the dimension of the Krylov subspace if $\mathbf{x}$ is an eigenvector of $\mathbf{A}$?

  (b) What is the dimension of the Krylov subspace if $\mathbf{x}$ is the sum of two linearly independent eigenvectors of $\mathbf{A}$?

  (c) What is the maximum possible dimension that the Krylov subspace can have if $\mathbf{A}$ is a projection operator?

  (d) What is the maximum possible dimension that the Krylov subspace can have if the nullity of $\mathbf{A}$ is m?

1.4. A $(0,1)$-matrix is a matrix whose elements are either zero or one. Such matrices are important in graph theory and combinatorics. How many of them are invertible? This is an easy problem when the matrix is small. For example, there are two 1×1 $(0,1)$-matrices, namely, $[0]$ and $[1]$. So half are invertible. There are sixteen 2×2 matrices whose entries are ones and zeros:

Singular: $\begin{bmatrix} 0 & 0 \\ 0 & 0 \end{bmatrix} \begin{bmatrix} 0 & 1 \\ 0 & 0 \end{bmatrix} \begin{bmatrix} 1 & 0 \\ 0 & 0 \end{bmatrix} \begin{bmatrix} 1 & 1 \\ 0 & 0 \end{bmatrix} \begin{bmatrix} 0 & 0 \\ 0 & 1 \end{bmatrix} \begin{bmatrix} 0 & 0 \\ 1 & 0 \end{bmatrix} \begin{bmatrix} 0 & 0 \\ 1 & 1 \end{bmatrix} \begin{bmatrix} 0 & 1 \\ 0 & 1 \end{bmatrix} \begin{bmatrix} 1 & 0 \\ 1 & 0 \end{bmatrix} \begin{bmatrix} 1 & 1 \\ 1 & 1 \end{bmatrix}$

Invertible: $\begin{bmatrix} 1 & 0 \\ 0 & 1 \end{bmatrix} \begin{bmatrix} 0 & 1 \\ 1 & 0 \end{bmatrix} \begin{bmatrix} 1 & 1 \\ 1 & 0 \end{bmatrix} \begin{bmatrix} 1 & 1 \\ 0 & 1 \end{bmatrix} \begin{bmatrix} 1 & 0 \\ 1 & 1 \end{bmatrix} \begin{bmatrix} 0 & 1 \\ 1 & 1 \end{bmatrix}$

So three-eighths are invertible. Estimate how many $n \times n$ $(0,1)$-matrices are invertible. Plot the ratio of invertible matrices as a function of size n for $n = 1, 2, \ldots, 20$ and explain the results. *Note:* There are 2^{n^2} $n \times n$ $(0,1)$-matrices—for instance, roughly 10^{19} 8×8 matrices. To check each 8×8 matrix using a 100 petaflop supercomputer would take over 100 years. Instead, we can approximate the number of invertible matrices by using a random sample of

(0, 1)-matrices. Test a large number (perhaps 10,000) of such matrices for each $n = 1, 2, \ldots, 20$.

1.5. Consider the $n \times n$ matrix used to approximate a second-derivative

$$
\mathbf{D} = \begin{bmatrix}
-2 & 1 & & & & \\
1 & -2 & 1 & & & \\
& \ddots & \ddots & \ddots & & \\
& & 1 & -2 & 1 \\
& & & 1 & -2
\end{bmatrix}.
$$

(a) Find the eigenvalues of $\mathbf{D}$.

(b) Compute the spectral radius $\rho(\mathbf{D} + 2\mathbf{I})$.

(c) Determine the condition number $\kappa_2(\mathbf{D})$ and discuss its behavior as $n \to \infty$.

(d) Confirm your answers numerically.

1.6. Prove that the induced norm is a matrix norm.

1.7. Consider the matrix $\mathbf{A}$ that maps $\mathbb{R}^3$ into $\mathbb{R}^2$:

$$
\mathbf{A} = \begin{bmatrix}
4 & -3 \\
-2 & 6 \\
4 & 6
\end{bmatrix}.
$$

(a) Compute the SVD of $\mathbf{A}$ by hand and use it to find the null space of $\mathbf{A}$.

(b) What vector is magnified the most in the 2-norm? By how much and what is the resultant vector?

1.8. Let $\mathbf{P}$ be an orthogonal projection matrix. Prove that $\mathbf{I} - \mathbf{P}$ is also a projection matrix and that $\mathbf{I} - 2\mathbf{P}$ is a symmetric, orthogonal matrix. Describe geometrically what each operator does. Determine the eigenvalues.

1.9. The Frobenius norm is defined as $\|\mathbf{A}\|_F = \sqrt{\sum_{i,j} a_{ij}^2}$. This norm is particularly useful in image processing.

(a) Prove that the Frobenius norm is a matrix norm by showing that the three properties of matrix norms hold.

(b) Determine $\|\mathbf{Q}\|_F$ where $\mathbf{Q}$ is an $n \times n$ orthogonal matrix.

(c) Prove that the Frobenius norm is invariant under orthogonal transformations $\|\mathbf{QA}\|_F = \|\mathbf{A}\|_F$.

(d) Prove that $\|\mathbf{A}\|_F = \sqrt{\sum_i \sigma_i^2}$, where σ_i is the ith singular value of $\mathbf{A}$.

(e) Prove that $\|\mathbf{A}\|_F^2$ equals the trace of $\mathbf{A}^T\mathbf{A}$.

(f) Prove that the Frobenius norm is compatible with the Euclidean vector norm.

(g) Prove that the Frobenius norm is also submultiplicative.

Hint: Don't solve this problem sequentially. Spoiler: Start with (e).

1.10. Cleve Moler and Charles van Loan's article "Nineteen dubious ways to compute the exponential of a matrix" presents several methods of computing $e^{\mathbf{A}}$ for a matrix $\mathbf{A}$. Discuss or implement one of the methods. How is a matrix exponent computed in practice?

Chapter 2

Direct Methods for Linear Systems

Finding solutions to linear systems is a core problem of scientific computing. The problem is so fundamental that functions are widely available in optimized software libraries for numerical linear algebra, such as LAPACK (Linear Algebra Package) and the Intel Math Kernel Library. So it's unlikely that one would ever need to program any of these algorithms explicitly. However, it is worthwhile to understand the mathematics underpinning these packages to be aware of potential pitfalls. This chapter discusses direct methods for solving the problem $\mathbf{Ax} = \mathbf{b}$ when $\mathbf{A}$ is invertible. We will discuss methods for solving $\mathbf{Ax} = \mathbf{b}$ when $\mathbf{A}$ is not invertible in Chapter 3. And we will discuss iterative methods for solving $\mathbf{Ax} = \mathbf{b}$ in Chapter 5.

There are several ways to solve $\mathbf{Ax} = \mathbf{b}$ in Julia. For a 2000×2000 matrix, A\b takes about 0.15 seconds and inv(A)*b takes 0.42 seconds. The (\) function solves the system by first determining the structure of the square matrix A. It then applies specialized routines—dividing by diagonal elements of diagonal matrices, using backward or forward substitution on upper or lower triangular matrices, or applying general LU decomposition on square matrices. The LinearAlgebra.jl package provides further optimized methods to factorize special matrix types, such as Tridiagonal and Cholesky. Such routines are significantly faster than those for general arrays. For example, computing A\b using a 2000×2000 tridiagonal matrix explicitly cast as type Tridiagonal is about a thousand times faster than performing the same operation on one that was not.

♣ The macro @less shows the Julia code for a method. The command can help you know what's happening inside the black box.

29

⚐ The macros @time and @elapsed provide run times. Use the begin...end block for compound statements. Julia precompiles your code on the first run, so run it twice and take the time from the second run.

2.1 Gaussian elimination

Elementary row operations leave a matrix in row equivalent form, i.e., they do not fundamentally change the underlying system of equations but instead return an equivalent system of equations. The three elementary row operations are

1. multiply a row by a scalar,
2. add a scalar multiple of a row to another row, and
3. interchange two rows.

We can solve $\mathbf{Ax} = \mathbf{b}$ by using elementary row operations on the augmented matrix $\begin{bmatrix} \mathbf{A} | \mathbf{b} \end{bmatrix}$ to get a reduced row echelon matrix.

There is a clear benefit to interchanging two rows to simplify computation using a pencil and paper. On the other hand, every floating-point calculation takes just as much work as any other floating-point calculation using a computer. So let's start by writing an algorithm that does not interchange rows. Getting a matrix into reduced row echelon form is a two-stage procedure.

1. Forward elimination. Starting with the first column, successively march through the columns zeroing out the elements below the diagonal.

$$\begin{bmatrix} \times \times \times \times & | & \times \\ \times \times \times \times & | & \times \\ \times \times \times \times & | & \times \\ \times \times \times \times & | & \times \end{bmatrix} \rightarrow \begin{bmatrix} \times \times \times \times & | & \times \\ \times \times \times & | & \times \\ \times \times \times & | & \times \\ \times \times \times & | & \times \end{bmatrix} \rightarrow \begin{bmatrix} \times \times \times \times & | & \times \\ \times \times \times & | & \times \\ \times \times & | & \times \\ \times \times & | & \times \end{bmatrix} \rightarrow \begin{bmatrix} \times \times \times \times & | & \times \\ \times \times \times & | & \times \\ \times \times & | & \times \\ \times & | & \times \end{bmatrix}$$

2. Backward elimination. Starting with the last column, successively march through the columns zeroing out the elements above the diagonal.

$$\begin{bmatrix} \times \times \times \times & | & \times \\ \times \times \times & | & \times \\ \times \times & | & \times \\ \times & | & \times \end{bmatrix} \rightarrow \begin{bmatrix} \times \times \times & & | & \times \\ \times \times & & | & \times \\ \times & | & \times \\ \times & | & \times \end{bmatrix} \rightarrow \begin{bmatrix} \times \times & & | & \times \\ \times & & | & \times \\ \times & | & \times \\ \times & | & \times \end{bmatrix} \rightarrow \begin{bmatrix} \times & & & | & \times \\ \times & & | & \times \\ \times & | & \times \\ \times & | & \times \end{bmatrix}$$

⚐ The RowEchelon.jl function rref returns the reduced row echelon form.

The first stage (forward elimination) requires the most effort because we need to compute using entire rows. We need to operate on n^2 elements to zero out the elements below the first pivot, $(n - 1)^2$ elements to zero out the elements below the second pivot, and so forth. The second stage (backward elimination) is relatively fast because we only need to work on one column at each iteration. Zeroing out the elements above the last pivot requires changing n elements, zeroing out the elements above the second pivot requires $n - 1$ elements, and so forth. By saving the intermediate terms of forward elimination, we can express a matrix $\mathbf{A}$ as the product $\mathbf{A} = \mathbf{LU}$, where $\mathbf{L}$ is a unit lower triangular matrix (with ones along the diagonal) and $\mathbf{U}$ is an upper triangular matrix. If such a decomposition exists, it is unique. This decomposition allows us to solve the problem $\mathbf{Ax} = \mathbf{b}$ in three steps:

1. Compute $\mathbf{L}$ and $\mathbf{U}$.
2. Solve $\mathbf{Ly} = \mathbf{b}$ for $\mathbf{y}$.
3. Solve $\mathbf{Ux} = \mathbf{y}$ for $\mathbf{x}$.

This process is called *Gaussian elimination*. Contrary to its name, Gaussian elimination did not originate with Carl Friedrich Gauss. The technique is well over two thousand years old and was commonly known as just "elimination" until the 1950s, when the influential mathematician George Forsythe misattributed it to Gauss. John von Neumann and Herman Goldstine developed Gaussian elimination in its modern matrix form as "the combination of two tricks" in their foundational 1947 article "Numerical Inverting of Matrices of High Order." (Grcar [2011]) The first trick, specified in step 1 to decompose a matrix into a product of two triangular matrices, is called *LU decomposition*. The second trick, specified in steps 2 and 3, solves the triangular systems inductively. Let's look at each of these tricks, starting with the second.

▷ Solving triangular systems

Steps 2 and 3 are relatively straightforward. The lower triangular system

$$
\begin{bmatrix}
1 & & & \\
l_{21} & 1 & & \\
\vdots & & \ddots & \\
l_{n1} & l_{n2} & \cdots & 1
\end{bmatrix}
\begin{bmatrix}
y_1 \\ y_2 \\ \vdots \\ y_n
\end{bmatrix}
=
\begin{bmatrix}
b_1 \\ b_2 \\ \vdots \\ b_n
\end{bmatrix}
$$

can be solved using forward elimination, starting from the top and working down. From the ith row

$$
l_{i1}y_1 + \cdots + l_{i,i-1}y_{i-1} + y_i = b_i,
$$

we have

$$
y_i = b_i - \sum_{j=1}^{i-1} l_{ij}y_j,
$$

where each y_i is determined from the y_j coming before it. It is often convenient to overwrite the array $\mathbf{b}$ with the values $\mathbf{y}$ to save computer memory.

Now, let's implement step 3 to solve the upper triangular system

$$\begin{bmatrix} u_{11} & u_{12} & \cdots & u_{1n} \\ & u_{22} & \cdots & u_{2n} \\ & & \ddots & \vdots \\ & & & u_{nn} \end{bmatrix} \begin{bmatrix} x_1 \\ x_2 \\ \vdots \\ x_n \end{bmatrix} = \begin{bmatrix} y_1 \\ y_2 \\ \vdots \\ y_n \end{bmatrix}$$

using backward elimination (starting from the bottom and working up). From the ith row

$$u_{ii}x_i + u_{i,i+1}x_{i+1} + \cdots + u_{in}x_n = y_i,$$

we have

$$x_i = \frac{1}{u_{ii}} \left(y_i - \sum_{j=1+i}^{n} u_{ij}x_j \right).$$

As before, we can overwrite the array $\mathbf{b}$ with the values $\mathbf{x}$. Note that we never need to change the elements of $\mathbf{L}$ or $\mathbf{U}$ when solving the triangular systems. So, once we have the LU decomposition of a matrix, we can use it over and over again.

▷ LU decomposition

Now, let's implement the LU decomposition itself (step 1). On a practical note, computer memory is valuable when n is large. So it's important to make efficient use of it. Storing the full matrices $\mathbf{A}$, $\mathbf{L}$, and $\mathbf{U}$ in computer memory takes $3n^2$ floating-point numbers (at eight bytes each). The matrices $\mathbf{L}$ and $\mathbf{U}$ together have the same effective information $\mathbf{A}$, so keeping $\mathbf{A}$ is unnecessary. Also, $\mathbf{L}$ and $\mathbf{U}$ are almost half-filled with zeros—wasted memory. Now, the smart idea! Note that except along the diagonal, the nonzero elements of $\mathbf{L}$ and $\mathbf{U}$ are mutually exclusive. In fact, since the diagonal of $\mathbf{L}$ is defined to be all ones, we can store the information in these two matrices in the same array as

$$\begin{bmatrix} u_{11} & u_{12} & \cdots & u_{1n} \\ l_{21} & u_{22} & \cdots & u_{2n} \\ \vdots & & \ddots & \vdots \\ l_{n1} & l_{n2} & \cdots & u_{nn} \end{bmatrix}.$$

Now, the really smart idea! Overwrite $\mathbf{A}$ with the elements of $\mathbf{L}$ and $\mathbf{U}$. When performing LU decomposition, we work from the top-left to the bottom-right. We zero out the elements of the ith column below the ith row and fill up the corresponding elements in $\mathbf{L}$. There is no conflict if we store this information in the same matrix. Furthermore, since we are moving diagonally down the matrix $\mathbf{A}$, there is no conflict if we simply overwrite the elements of $\mathbf{A}$. For example,

$$\begin{bmatrix} 2 & 4 & 2 & 3 \\ -2 & -5 & -3 & -2 \\ 4 & 7 & 6 & 8 \\ 6 & 10 & 1 & 12 \end{bmatrix} \rightarrow \begin{bmatrix} 2 & 4 & 2 & 3 \\ -1 & -1 & -1 & 1 \\ 2 & -1 & 2 & 2 \\ 3 & -2 & -5 & 3 \end{bmatrix} \rightarrow \begin{bmatrix} 2 & 4 & 2 & 3 \\ -1 & -1 & -1 & 1 \\ 1 & 3 & 1 \\ 3 & 2 & -3 & 1 \end{bmatrix} \rightarrow \begin{bmatrix} 2 & 4 & 2 & 3 \\ -1 & -1 & -1 & 1 \\ 2 & 1 & 3 & 1 \\ 3 & 2 & -1 & 2 \end{bmatrix}.$$

Let's implement this algorithm. Starting with the first column, we move right. We zero out each element in the jth column below the jth row using elementary row operations. And here's the switch—we backfill those zeros with the values from **L**.

$$\left.\begin{array}{l} \text{for } j = 1, \ldots, n \\ \quad \left[\begin{array}{l} \text{for } i = j+1, \ldots, n \\ \quad \left[\begin{array}{l} a_{ij} \leftarrow a_{ij}/a_{jj} \\ \text{for } k = j+1, \ldots, n \\ \quad \left[a_{ik} \leftarrow a_{ik} - a_{ij}a_{jk} \right. \end{array}\right. \end{array}\right. \end{array}\right\} \text{LU decomposition}$$

$$\left.\begin{array}{l} \text{for } i = 2, \ldots, n \\ \quad \left[b_i \leftarrow b_i - \sum_{j=1}^{i-1} a_{ij}b_j \right. \end{array}\right\} \text{forward elimination}$$

$$\left.\begin{array}{l} \text{for } i = n, n-1, \cdots, 1 \\ \quad \left[b_i \leftarrow \left(b_i - \sum_{j=i+1}^{n} a_{ij}b_j \right)/a_{ii} \right. \end{array}\right\} \text{backward elimination}$$

The corresponding Julia code is

```julia
function gaussian_elimination(A,b)
  n = size(A,1)
  for j in 1:n
    A[j+1:n,j] /= A[j,j]
    A[j+1:n,j+1:n] -= A[j+1:n,j:j].*A[j:j,j+1:n]
  end
  for i in 2:n
    b[i:i] -= A[i:i,1:i-1]*b[1:i-1]
  end
  for i in n:-1:1
    b[i:i] = ( b[i] .- A[i:i,i+1:n]*b[i+1:n] )/A[i,i]
  end
  return b
end
```

Julia's built-in LAPACK functions for Gaussian elimination are substantially faster than the above script. The code above takes about 4 seconds to solve a 1000×1000 system, whereas Julia's built-in function takes about 0.02 seconds.

▷ **Operation count**

We can count the number of operations to gauge the complexity of Gaussian elimination. To produce the LU decomposition of an $n \times n$ matrix requires

$$\sum_{j=1}^{n} \sum_{i=j+1}^{n} \left(1 + \sum_{k=j+1}^{n} 2 \right) = \tfrac{2}{3}n^3 - \tfrac{1}{2}n^2 - \tfrac{1}{6}n$$

additions and multiplications. Forward and backward elimination each requires

$$\sum_{i=1}^{n} \left(2 + \sum_{j=1}^{i-1} 2 \right) = n^2 + n$$

operations. When n is large, Gaussian elimination requires about $\tfrac{2}{3}n^3$ operations to get the initial decomposition and $2n^2$ to solve the two triangular systems.

Breaking Gaussian elimination into an LU decomposition step and forward-backward elimination steps saves time when solving a system like $\mathbf{A}\mathbf{x}(t) = \mathbf{b}(t)$ where the term $\mathbf{b}(t)$ changes in time. For example, we might want to determine the changing heat distribution $\mathbf{x}(t)$ in a room with a heat source $\mathbf{b}(t)$. Computing the LU decomposition is the most expensive step requiring $\tfrac{2}{3}n^3$ operations. But we only need to do it once. After that, we only need to perform $2n^2$ operations at each time step to solve the two triangular systems.

▷ **Pivoting**

Gaussian elimination fails if the pivot a_{ii} is zero at any step because we are dividing by zero. In practice, even if a pivot is close to zero, Gaussian elimination may be unstable because round-off errors get amplified. Consider the following matrix and its LU decomposition without row exchanges

$$\mathbf{A} = \begin{bmatrix} 1 & 1 & 2 \\ 2 & 2+\varepsilon & 0 \\ 4 & 14 & 4 \end{bmatrix} = \begin{bmatrix} 1 & 0 & 0 \\ 2 & 1 & 0 \\ 4 & 10/\varepsilon & 1 \end{bmatrix} \begin{bmatrix} 1 & 1 & 2 \\ 0 & \varepsilon & -4 \\ 0 & 0 & 40/\varepsilon - 4 \end{bmatrix}.$$

Let $\varepsilon = 10^{-15}$, or about five times machine epsilon. The 2-norm condition number of this matrix is about 10.3, so it is numerically pretty well-conditioned. But because of round-off error, the computed LU decomposition is

$$\tilde{\mathbf{A}} = \begin{bmatrix} 1 & 0 & 0 \\ 2 & 1 & 0 \\ 4 & 10/\varepsilon & 1 \end{bmatrix} \begin{bmatrix} 1 & 1 & 2 \\ 0 & \varepsilon & -4 \\ 0 & 0 & 40/\varepsilon \end{bmatrix} = \begin{bmatrix} 1 & 1 & 2 \\ 2 & 2+\varepsilon & 0 \\ 4 & 14 & 8 \end{bmatrix}.$$

The original matrix $\mathbf{A}$ and the reconstructed matrix $\tilde{\mathbf{A}}$ differ in the bottom-right elements. Let's see how well our naïve function gaussian_elimination does in solving $\mathbf{A}\mathbf{x} = \mathbf{b}$ when $\mathbf{b} = (-5, 10, 0)$.

```
ε = 1e-15; A = [1 1 2;2 2+ε 0; 4 14 4]; b = [-5;10;0.0]
A\b, gaussian_elimination(A,b)
```

The function fails horribly, returning a solution of about $(1, 4, -5)$ instead of the correct answer $(5, 0, -5)$. The numerical instability results from dividing by a small pivot. We can avoid it by permuting the rows or columns at each iteration so that a large number is in the pivot position.

In *partial pivoting*, we permute the rows of the matrix to put the largest element in the pivot position a_{ii}. With each step of LU factorization, we find $r = \arg\max_{k \geq i} |a_{kj}|$ and interchange row i and row r. To permute the rows, we left-multiply by a permutation matrix $\mathbf{P}$ that keeps track of all the row interchangesc$\mathbf{PA} = \mathbf{LU}$. As a result of pivoting, the magnitudes of all of the values of matrix $\mathbf{L}$ are less than or equal to one.

In *complete pivoting*, we permute both the rows *and* the columns to put the maximum element in the pivot position a_{ii}. With each step of LU factorization, find $r, c = \arg\max_{k,l \geq i} |a_{kl}|$, and interchange row i and row r and interchange column i and column c. To interchange rows, we left-multiply by a permutation matrix $\mathbf{P}$, and to interchange columns, we right-multiply by a permutation matrix $\mathbf{Q}$—i.e., $\mathbf{PAQ} = \mathbf{LU}$. Applied to the problem $\mathbf{Ax} = \mathbf{b}$, complete pivoting yields $\mathbf{LU}(\mathbf{Q}^{-1}\mathbf{x}) = \mathbf{P}^{-1}\mathbf{b}$. Generally, complete pivoting is unnecessary, and partial pivoting is sufficient.

2.2 Cholesky decomposition

A symmetric, positive-definite matrix $\mathbf{A}$ has the factorization $\mathbf{R}^\mathsf{T}\mathbf{R}$, where $\mathbf{R}$ is an upper triangular matrix. This factorization is called the Cholesky decomposition. Let's prove this property and then examine how to implement it numerically.

Theorem 7. *A symmetric, positive-definite matrix $\mathbf{A}$ has the decomposition $\mathbf{R}^\mathsf{T}\mathbf{R}$ where $\mathbf{R} = \mathbf{LD}^{1/2}$.*

Proof. The proof has several steps. First, we show that the inverse of a unit lower triangular matrix is a unit lower triangular matrix. It is easy to confirm the block matrix identity

$$\begin{bmatrix} \mathbf{A} & \mathbf{0} \\ \mathbf{C} & \mathbf{D} \end{bmatrix}^{-1} = \begin{bmatrix} \mathbf{A}^{-1} & \mathbf{0} \\ -\mathbf{D}^{-1}\mathbf{CA}^{-1} & \mathbf{D}^{-1} \end{bmatrix}.$$

The hypothesis is certainly true for 1×1 matrix $\begin{bmatrix} 1 \end{bmatrix}$. Suppose that the hypothesis is true for an $n \times n$ unit lower triangular matrix. By letting $\mathbf{D}$ be such a matrix and $\mathbf{A} = \begin{bmatrix} 1 \end{bmatrix}$, then the claim follows for an $(n + 1) \times (n + 1)$ matrix.

Next, we show that if $\mathbf{A}$ is symmetric and invertible, then $\mathbf{A}$ has the decomposition $\mathbf{A} = \mathbf{LDL}^\mathsf{T}$, where $\mathbf{L}$ is a unit lower triangular matrix and $\mathbf{D}$ is a diagonal matrix. $\mathbf{A}$ has the decomposition $\mathbf{LDM}^\mathsf{T}$, where $\mathbf{M}$ is a unit lower triangular matrix. We only need to show that $\mathbf{M} = \mathbf{L}$. We left multiply $\mathbf{A} = \mathbf{L}\mathbf{D}\mathbf{M}^\mathsf{T}$ by $\mathbf{M}^{-1}$ and right multiply it by $\mathbf{M}^{-\mathsf{T}}$, giving us

$$\mathbf{M}^{-1}\mathbf{A}\mathbf{M}^{-\mathsf{T}} = \mathbf{M}^{-1}\mathbf{L}\mathbf{D}.$$

Note that $\mathbf{M}^{-1}\mathbf{A}\mathbf{M}^{-\mathsf{T}}$ is a symmetric matrix, and by theorem 7, the matrix $\mathbf{M}^{-1}\mathbf{L}\mathbf{D}$ is lower triangular with diagonal $\mathbf{D}$. Hence, $\mathbf{M}^{-1}\mathbf{A}\mathbf{M}^{-\mathsf{T}}$ must be the diagonal matrix $\mathbf{D}$. So,

$$\mathbf{A} = \mathbf{L}\mathbf{D}\mathbf{M}^\mathsf{T} = \mathbf{M}^{-1}\mathbf{A}\mathbf{M}^{-\mathsf{T}}\mathbf{M}^\mathsf{T} = \mathbf{L}\mathbf{M}^{-1}\mathbf{A}$$

from which it follows that $\mathbf{L}\mathbf{M}^{-1} = \mathbf{I}$, or equivalently $\mathbf{L} = \mathbf{M}$.

Now, we show that if $\mathbf{A}$ is an $n \times n$ symmetric, positive-definite matrix and $\mathbf{X}$ is an $n \times k$ matrix with $\mathrm{rank}(\mathbf{X}) = k$, then $\mathbf{B} = \mathbf{X}^\mathsf{T}\mathbf{A}\mathbf{X}$ is symmetric, positive definite. (We say that $\mathbf{B}$ is *congruent* to $\mathbf{A}$ if there exists an invertible $\mathbf{X}$ such that $\mathbf{B} = \mathbf{X}^\mathsf{T}\mathbf{A}\mathbf{X}$.) Take $\mathbf{x} \in \mathbb{R}^k$. Then

$$\mathbf{x}^\mathsf{T}\mathbf{B}\mathbf{x} = (\mathbf{X}\mathbf{x})^\mathsf{T}\mathbf{A}(\mathbf{X}\mathbf{x}) \geq 0$$

and it equals 0 if and only if $\mathbf{X}\mathbf{x} = \mathbf{0}$. Since the $\mathrm{rank}(\mathbf{X}) = k$, $\mathbf{x}$ must be $\mathbf{0}$. Therefore, $\mathbf{B}$ is positive definite.

Finally, we finish the proof. Because $\mathbf{A} = \mathbf{L}\mathbf{D}\mathbf{L}^\mathsf{T}$ where $\mathbf{L}$ is a unit lower triangular matrix and $\mathbf{D} = \mathbf{L}^{-1}\mathbf{A}\mathbf{L}^{-\mathsf{T}}$ is positive definite, it follows that the eigenvalues of $\mathbf{D}$ (the diagonal elements of $\mathbf{D}$) are positive. So we can define $\mathbf{R}^\mathsf{T} = \mathbf{L}\mathbf{D}^{1/2}$. $\qquad\square$

As one might expect, the algorithm for Cholesky decomposition is similar to the algorithm for LU decomposition without pivoting. We'll formulate the algorithm by looking at how $\mathbf{R}^\mathsf{T}$ multiplies with $\mathbf{R}$ to give us $\mathbf{A}$:

$$\begin{bmatrix} r_{11} & & & \\ r_{12} & r_{22} & & \\ \vdots & & \ddots & \\ r_{1n} & r_{2n} & \cdots & r_{nn} \end{bmatrix}\begin{bmatrix} r_{11} & r_{12} & \cdots & r_{1n} \\ & r_{22} & & r_{2n} \\ & & \ddots & \vdots \\ & & & r_{nn} \end{bmatrix} = \begin{bmatrix} a_{11} & a_{12} & \cdots & a_{1n} \\ a_{12} & a_{22} & \cdots & a_{2n} \\ \vdots & \vdots & \ddots & \vdots \\ a_{1n} & a_{2n} & \cdots & a_{nn} \end{bmatrix}$$

Starting with a_{11}:

$$r_{11}r_{11} = a_{11} \qquad \text{from which} \qquad r_{11} = \sqrt{a_{11}}$$

$$\begin{bmatrix} \bullet & & & \\ \circ & \circ & & \\ \circ & \circ & \circ & \\ \circ & \circ & \circ & \circ \end{bmatrix}\begin{bmatrix} \bullet & \circ & \circ & \circ \\ & \circ & \circ & \circ \\ & & \circ & \circ \\ & & & \circ \end{bmatrix} = \begin{bmatrix} \times & \times & \times & \times \\ \times & \times & \times & \times \\ \times & \times & \times & \times \\ \times & \times & \times & \times \end{bmatrix}$$

where $\bullet$ is the now known and can be used in subsequent steps and $\circ$ are still unknowns. Once we have r_{11} we can find all other elements of the first column:

$$r_{11}r_{1i} = a_{1i} \qquad \text{from which} \qquad r_{1i} = a_{1i}/r_{1i}$$

$$\begin{bmatrix} \bullet & & & \\ \bullet & \circ & & \\ \bullet & \circ & \circ & \\ \bullet & \circ & \circ & \circ \end{bmatrix} \begin{bmatrix} \bullet & \bullet & \bullet & \bullet \\ & \circ & \circ & \circ \\ & & \circ & \circ \\ & & & \circ \end{bmatrix} = \begin{bmatrix} \times & \times & \times & \times \\ \times & \times & \times & \times \\ \times & \times & \times & \times \\ \times & \times & \times & \times \end{bmatrix}$$

We continue for each remaining $n - 1$ columns of $\mathbf{R}$ by first finding the ith diagonal element:

$$\sum_{k=1}^{i} r_{kj} r_{ki} = a_{ii} \qquad \text{from which} \qquad r_{ii} = \left(a_{ii} - \sum_{k=1}^{i-1} r_{ki}^2 \right)^{\frac{1}{2}}$$

$$\begin{bmatrix} \bullet & & & \\ \bullet & \bullet & & \\ \bullet & \circ & \circ & \\ \bullet & \circ & \circ & \circ \end{bmatrix} \begin{bmatrix} \bullet & \bullet & \bullet & \bullet \\ & \bullet & \circ & \circ \\ & & \circ & \circ \\ & & & \circ \end{bmatrix} = \begin{bmatrix} \times & \times & \times & \times \\ \times & \times & \times & \times \\ \times & \times & \times & \times \\ \times & \times & \times & \times \end{bmatrix}$$

Once we have the diagonal, we fill in the remaining elements from that column:

$$\sum_{k=1}^{i} r_{kj} r_{ki} = a_{ji} \qquad \text{from which} \qquad r_{ji} = \frac{1}{r_{ii}} \left(a_{ji} - \sum_{k=1}^{i-1} r_{kj} r_{ki} \right)$$

$$\begin{bmatrix} \bullet & & & \\ \bullet & \bullet & & \\ \bullet & \bullet & \circ & \\ \bullet & \bullet & \circ & \circ \end{bmatrix} \begin{bmatrix} \bullet & \bullet & \bullet & \bullet \\ & \bullet & \bullet & \bullet \\ & & \circ & \circ \\ & & & \circ \end{bmatrix} = \begin{bmatrix} \times & \times & \times & \times \\ \times & \times & \times & \times \\ \times & \times & \times & \times \\ \times & \times & \times & \times \end{bmatrix}$$

We can write this algorithm as the following pseudocode:

$$\begin{aligned} &\text{for } i = 1, \ldots, n \\ &\quad \left[\begin{aligned} &r_{ii} \leftarrow \left(a_{ii} - \sum_{k=1}^{i-1} a_{ik}^2 \right)^{1/2} \\ &\text{for } j = 2, \ldots, i \\ &\quad \left[\; r_{ij} \leftarrow \frac{1}{r_{ii}} \left(a_{ji} - \sum_{k=1}^{i-1} r_{kj} r_{ki} \right) \right. \end{aligned} \right. \end{aligned}$$

We can successively overwrite the matrix $\mathbf{A}$, just as in LU decomposition. Cholesky decomposition requires $\frac{1}{3} n^3$ operations instead of $\frac{2}{3} n^3$ operations that general LU decomposition requires. Furthermore, pivoting is not needed in Cholesky decomposition because the matrix is symmetric, positive definite.

2.3   Linear programming and the simplex method

Linear programming was developed in the 1940s by mathematicians George Dantzig, John von Neumann, and Leonid Kantorovich to solve large-scale industrial and military production, management, and logistics problems. This development coincided with the development of digital computers that were needed to implement such solutions. A "program" is a schedule or plan of things to do.[1] By analyzing a system, determining the objective to be fulfilled, and

---

[1] The word "program" has found its way into many different contexts referring to schedules or plans: an economic program, a theater program, a television program, a computer program.

constructing a statement of actions to perform (a program), the system can be represented by a mathematical model. The use of such mathematical models is called mathematical programming. That a number of military, economic, and industrial problems can be approximated by mathematical systems of linear inequalities and equations gives rise to linear programming (LP).[2]

As a typical example of an LP problem, imagine that you are tasked with shipping canned tomatoes from several factories to different warehouses scattered around the United States. Each of the factories can fill a certain number of cases per day, and similarly each of the warehouses can sell a fixed number of cases per day. The cost of shipment from each factory to each warehouse varies by location. How do you schedule or program shipment to minimize the total transportation cost? An LP problem consists of decision variables (the quantities that the decision-maker controls), a linear objective function (the quantity to be maximized or minimized), and linear constraints (conditions that the solution must satisfy). The decision variables of the cannery problem are the number of cases to ship from each factory to each warehouse. The linear objective function is the cost of shipping all of the cases. And the constraints are the number of cases each factory can fill and each store can sell.

Example.   The Stigler diet problem is another typical LP problem. In 1944 economist George Stigler wondered what the least amount of money a typical person would need to spend on food to maintain good health was. To do this, he examined 77 different foods along with nine nutrients (calories, protein, calcium, etc.). In this problem, the decision variables are the quantities of foods, the objective function is the total dollars spent, and the constraints are the minimum nutritional requirements. (Stigler [1945]) The simplex method, which we'll discuss below, wouldn't be developed for a few more years. Instead, Stigler found a solution heuristically by eliminating all but fifteen foods and then searching for the answer: $39.93 per year (in 1939 prices or around $730 today).

In 1947 Jack Laderman, working at the National Bureau of Standards, revisited the Stigler diet problem using the recently developed simplex method and a team of nine clerks, each armed with a hand-operated desk calculator. The team took approximately 120 person-days to obtain the optimal solution: $39.69 per year, just a little better than Stigler.

George Dantzig revisited the problem in the 1950s, this time with the aid of a computer, to find himself a personal diet in an effort to lose weight. He adjusted the objective function to "maximize the feeling of feeling full," which

---

[2]The term *linear programming* says nothing about the problems' primary challenge, that of solving a system of inequalities. Just a few years after its introduction, physicist Phillip M. Morse lamented, "it seems to me that the term 'linear programming' is a most unfortunate phrase for this promising technique, particularly since many possible extensions appear to be in nonlinear directions. A more general yet more descriptive term, such as 'bounded optimization,' might have been a happier choice."

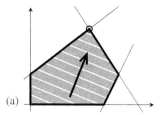 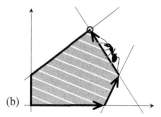

Figure 2.1: A two-dimensional simplex. (a) The objective function reaches its maximum and minimum at vertices of the simplex. (b) The simplex method steps along edges from vertex to vertex in a direction that increases the objective function, just as an ant might crawl, until it finally reaches a maximum.

he then interpreted as the weight of food minus the weight of water content. He collected data on over 500 different foods, punched onto cards and fed into an IBM 701 computer. Dantzig recalled that the optimal diet was "a bit weird but conceivable," except that it also included several hundred gallons of vinegar. Reexamining the data, he noted that vinegar was listed as a weak acid with zero water content. Fixing the data, he tried to solve the problem again. This time it called for hundreds of bouillon cubes per day. No one at the time had thought to put upper limits on sodium intake. So, he added an upper constraint for salt. But now, the program demanded two pounds of bran each day. And when he added an upper constraint on bran, it prescribed an equal amount of blackstrap molasses. At this point, he gave up. (Dantzig [1990]) ◄

The standard form of an LP problem is

Find the maximum of the objective function $z = \mathbf{c}^T\mathbf{x}$ subject to constraint $\mathbf{Ax} \leq \mathbf{b}$ and nonnegativity restriction $\mathbf{x} \geq 0$.

We'll take $\mathbf{A}$ to be an $m \times n$ matrix. If a problem is not already in standard form, there are several things we can do to put it there. Instead of finding the minimum of the objective function $\mathbf{c}^T\mathbf{x}$, we find the maximum of $-\mathbf{c}^T\mathbf{x}$. In place of a constraint $\mathbf{a}^T\mathbf{x} \geq b$, we write the constraint as $-\mathbf{a}^T\mathbf{x} \leq -b$. In place of an equation constraint $\mathbf{a}^T\mathbf{x} = b$, we use two inequality constraints $\mathbf{a}^T\mathbf{x} \leq b$ and $-\mathbf{a}^T\mathbf{x} \leq -b$. If a decision variable x is negative, we can take $-x$; and if the variable x is not restricted, we can redefine it $x = x^{(1)} - x^{(2)}$ where $x^{(1)}, x^{(2)} \geq 0$.

We can better understand the structure of an LP problem by sketching out the feasible region—the set of all possible points that satisfy the constraints. See the figure above. The nonnegativity condition restricts us to the positive orthant (the upper right quadrant for two dimensions). The system $\mathbf{Ax} = \mathbf{b}$ describes a set of hyperplanes (a set of lines in the two dimensions). So, assuming that the constraints are not inconsistent, the set $\mathbf{Ax} \leq \mathbf{b}$ carves out a convex n-polytype, also known as a simplex, in the positive orthant (a convex polygon in the upper right quadrant in two dimensions). The objective function $\mathbf{c}^\mathsf{T}\mathbf{x}$ is itself easy enough to describe. The objective function increases linearly in the direction of its gradient $\mathbf{c}$. Imagine water slowly filling a convex polyhedral vessel in the direction opposite of a gravitational force vector $\mathbf{c}$. The water's surface is a level set given by $z = \mathbf{c}^\mathsf{T}\mathbf{x}$. As the water finally fills the vessel, its surface will either come to a vertex of the polyhedron (a unique solution) or to a face or edge of the polyhedron (infinitely many solutions). This characterization is often called the fundamental theorem of linear programming.

Theorem 8. *The maxima of a linear functional over a convex polytope occur at its vertices. If the values are at k vertices, then they must be along the k-cell between them.*

Proof. Let $\mathbf{x}^*$ be a maximum of $\mathbf{c}^\mathsf{T}\mathbf{x}$ subject to $\mathbf{Ax} \leq \mathbf{b}$. Suppose that $\mathbf{x}^*$ is in the interior of the polytope. Then we can move a small distance ε from $\mathbf{x}^*$ in any direction and still be in the interior. Take the direction $\mathbf{c}/\|\mathbf{c}\|$. Then $\mathbf{c}^\mathsf{T}(\mathbf{x}^* + \varepsilon\mathbf{c}/\|\mathbf{c}\|) = \mathbf{c}^\mathsf{T}\mathbf{x}^* + \varepsilon\|\mathbf{c}\| > \mathbf{c}^\mathsf{T}\mathbf{x}^*$. But this says that $\mathbf{x}^*$ is not a maximum. It follows that $\mathbf{x}^*$ must be on the boundary of the polytope. If $\mathbf{x}^*$ is not a vertex, then it is the convex combination of vertices: $\mathbf{x}^* = \sum_{i=1}^{k} \lambda_i \mathbf{x}_i$ with $\sum_{i=1}^{k} \lambda_i = 1$ and $\lambda_i \geq 0$. Then

$$0 = \mathbf{c}^\mathsf{T}\left(\mathbf{x}^* - \sum_{i=1}^{k} \lambda_i \mathbf{x}_i\right) = \sum_{i=1}^{k} \lambda_i \left(\mathbf{c}^\mathsf{T}\mathbf{x}^* - \mathbf{c}^\mathsf{T}\mathbf{x}_i\right).$$

Because $\mathbf{x}^*$ is a maximum, $\mathbf{c}^\mathsf{T}\mathbf{x}^* \geq \mathbf{c}^\mathsf{T}\mathbf{x}_i$ for all i. And it follows that each term of the sum is nonnegative. The sum itself is zero, so all the terms must be zero. Hence, $\mathbf{c}^\mathsf{T}\mathbf{x}_i = \mathbf{c}^\mathsf{T}\mathbf{x}^*$ for each $\mathbf{x}_i$, i.e., every $\mathbf{x}_i$ is maximal. Therefore, all the points on the k-cell whose vertices are $\{\mathbf{x}_1, \mathbf{x}_2, \ldots, \mathbf{x}_p\}$ are maximal.   □

The diet problem that George Stigler solved had 15 decision variables along with 9 constraints. So, there are as many as $\binom{15}{9} = 5005$ possible vertices from which to choose a solution. That's not so many that the problem couldn't be solved using clever heuristics. But, the original problem with 77 decision variables has as many as $\binom{77}{9}$ or over 160 billion possibilities. How can we systematically pick the solution among all of these possibilities? George Dantzig's simplex solution was to pick any vertex and examine the edges leading away from that vertex, choosing any edge along which the cost variable was positive. If the edge is finite, then it connects to another vertex. Here you examine its edges and choose yet another one along which the cost variable is positive. Now continue like that, traversing from vertex to vertex along edges much as an ant might do as it climbs the simplex until arriving at a vertex for which no direction is strictly increasing. This vertex is the maximum. See Figure 2.1.

We can rewrite the system of constraints $\mathbf{Ax} \leq \mathbf{b}$ as a system of equations by introducing nonnegative slack variables $\mathbf{s}$ such that $\mathbf{Ax} + \mathbf{s} = \mathbf{b}$. For "greater than" inequalities, slack variables are called surplus variables and are subtracted. From this, we have the standard equational form of the LP problem:

Find the maximum of the objective function $z = \mathbf{c}^\mathsf{T}\mathbf{x}$ subject to constraint $\mathbf{Ax} \pm \mathbf{s} = \mathbf{b}$ and nonnegativity restriction $\mathbf{x}, \mathbf{s}, \mathbf{b} \geq 0$.

If any elements of $\mathbf{b}$ are negative, we can simply multiply the corresponding rows of $\mathbf{A}$ by minus one to make $\mathbf{b}$ nonnegative. The $\pm$ operator is applied componentwise—i.e., to enforce nonnegativity of both $\mathbf{b}$ and $\mathbf{s}$ we either add or subtract the slack or surplus variables accordingly. We can write the objective function $z = \mathbf{c}^\mathsf{T}\mathbf{x}$ as $\mathbf{c}^\mathsf{T}\mathbf{x} + \mathbf{0}^\mathsf{T}\mathbf{s} - z = 0$ where z is our still unknown cost and $\mathbf{0}$ is an m-dimensional vector of zeros called the reduced cost. The problem is now one of simplifying the system

$$\begin{bmatrix} \mathbf{A} & \mathbf{I} & \mathbf{0} \\ \mathbf{c}^\mathsf{T} & \mathbf{0}^\mathsf{T} & 1 \end{bmatrix} \begin{bmatrix} \mathbf{x} \\ \mathbf{s} \\ -z \end{bmatrix} = \begin{bmatrix} \mathbf{b} \\ 0 \end{bmatrix} \quad \text{where} \quad \mathbf{x}, \mathbf{s} \geq 0.$$

The matrix $\mathbf{I}$ is a diagonal matrix of $\{+1, -1\}$ depending on whether the initial constraint was a "less than" inequality (leading to a slack variable) or a "greater than" inequality (leading to a surplus variable). Equality constraints lead to an equation with a slack variable and an equation with a surplus variable. Consider the identical system

$$\begin{bmatrix} \bar{\mathbf{A}} & \mathbf{0} \\ \bar{\mathbf{c}} & 1 \end{bmatrix} \begin{bmatrix} \bar{\mathbf{x}} \\ -z \end{bmatrix} = \begin{bmatrix} \mathbf{b} \\ 0 \end{bmatrix} \quad \text{where } \bar{\mathbf{A}} = \begin{bmatrix} \mathbf{A} & \mathbf{I} \end{bmatrix}, \ \bar{\mathbf{x}} = \begin{bmatrix} \mathbf{x} \\ \mathbf{s} \end{bmatrix}, \ \bar{\mathbf{c}} = \begin{bmatrix} \mathbf{c} \\ \mathbf{0} \end{bmatrix}, \ \text{and } \bar{\mathbf{x}} \geq \mathbf{0}.$$

To help organize calculations, Dantzig introduced a tableau, which is updated at each iteration of the simplex method:

$$\begin{array}{c|c|c} \bar{\mathbf{A}} & \mathbf{0} & \mathbf{b} \\ \hline \bar{\mathbf{c}}^\mathsf{T} & 1 & 0 \end{array} \tag{2.1}$$

The matrix $\bar{\mathbf{A}}$ has m rows and $m + n$ columns, so its rank is at most m. We'll assume that the rank is n to simplify the discussion. Otherwise, we need to consider a few extra steps. We can choose m linearly independent columns as the basis for the column space of $\bar{\mathbf{A}}$. Let $\mathbf{A}_B$ be the submatrix formed by these columns. The variables $\mathbf{x}_B$ associated with these columns are called *basic variables*. The remaining n columns form a submatrix $\mathbf{A}_N$, and the variables $\mathbf{x}_N$ associated with it are called the *nonbasic variables*. Altogether, we have $\bar{\mathbf{A}}\bar{\mathbf{x}} = \mathbf{A}_B\mathbf{x}_B + \mathbf{A}_N\mathbf{x}_N = \mathbf{b}$. By setting all nonbasic variables to zero, the solution is simply given by the basic variables. Such a solution is called a *basic feasible solution* when the nonnegativity restriction $\bar{\mathbf{x}} \geq 0$ is enforced. How do we ensure that it is enforced?

Our strategy will be to start with the basic feasible solution equal to the slack variables and then systematically swap nonbasic and basic variables so that the cost function increases and the nonnegativity restrictions are not broken. At each step, we choose an entering variable from $\mathbf{x}_N$ and a leaving variable from $\mathbf{x}_B$, along with their respective columns in $\mathbf{A}_N$ and $\mathbf{A}_B$. We can use elementary row operations to convert the newly added column in $\mathbf{A}_B$ to a standard basis vector (a column of the identity matrix). In this way, by taking nonbasic vectors $\mathbf{x}_N = \mathbf{0}$, we will always keep $\mathbf{x}_B = \mathbf{b}$, up to a permutation. If $\mathbf{b}$ is nonnegative, then we know that $\mathbf{x}$ is nonnegative. So, we need to choose prospective pivots accordingly. The entering basic variable determines the pivot column, and the leaving basic variable determines the pivot row. At each iteration, we want to increase the objective function. So choose any column j for which c_j is positive. Next, we want to ensure that none of the elements of $\mathbf{b}$ ever become negative when we perform row reduction. So, we will choose the row i for which a_{ij} is positive and the ratio b_i/a_{ij} is the smallest. Because we will always set nonbasic variables to zero, using row operations to zero out the cost function on the entering basic variable will automatically update the objective value: $-z + \bar{\mathbf{c}}^\top \bar{\mathbf{x}} = 0$. We can summarize the simplex algorithm as

1. Build a simplex tableau (2.1) using $\mathbf{A}$, $\mathbf{b}$, and $\mathbf{c}$.
2. Take the basic variables to initially be the set of slack variables.
3. Repeat the following steps until no positive elements of $\bar{\mathbf{c}}$ remain:

   a) Choose a pivot column j with positive $\bar{c}_j$
   b) Choose the pivot row $i = \arg\min_i \{b_i/a_{ij} \text{ with } a_{ij} > 0\}$.
   c) Use elementary row operations to set the pivot to one and zero out all other elements in the column.

The following Julia code implements a naïve simplex method. We start by defining the function used for pivot selection and row reduction. We don't need to explicitly track entering and leaving variables because we can sort it out in the end. The $\begin{bmatrix} 0 & 1 \end{bmatrix}^\top$ column of the tableau (2.1) doesn't change, so we don't need to include it in the code. We can write the row reduction function as an in-place assignment operator.

```
function row_reduce!(tableau)
  (i,j) = get_pivot(tableau)
  G = tableau[i:i,:]/tableau[i,j]
  tableau[:,:] -= tableau[:,j:j]*G
  tableau[i,:] = G
end
```

```
function get_pivot(tableau)
  j = argmax(tableau[end,1:end-1])
  a, b = tableau[1:end-1,j], tableau[1:end-1,end]
  k = findall(a.>0)
  i = k[argmin(b[k]./a[k])]
  return(i,j)
end
```

Now we can write the simplex algorithm:

```
function simplex(c,A,b)
  (m,n) = size(A)
  tableau = [[A I b] ; [c' zeros(1,m) 0]]
  while (any(tableau[end,1:n].>0))
    row_reduce!(tableau)
  end
  p = findall(tableau[end,1:n].==0)
  x = zeros(n,1)
  [x[i]=tableau[:,i]·tableau[:,end] for i∈p]
  z = -tableau[end,end]
  y = -tableau[end,n.+(1:m)]
  return((z=z, x=x, y=y))
end
```

Example.   Consider the following LP problem: "Find the maximum of the objective function $2x + y + z$ subject to the constraints $2x + z \leq 3$, $4x + y + 2z \leq 2$, and $x + y \leq 1$." The program can be solved using

```
A = [2 0 1;4 1 2;1 1 0]; c = [2;1;1]; b = [3;2;1]
solution = simplex(c,A,b)
```

To better illustrate the simplex method, we can add the command

```
display(round.(tableau,digits=2))
```

to the `while` loop. The initial tableau consists of six blocks $\mathbf{A}$, $\mathbf{I}$, $\mathbf{b}$, $\mathbf{c}^T$, $\mathbf{0}$ and 0:

2.00	0.00	1.00	1.00	0.00	0.00	3.00
4.00	1.00	2.00	0.00	1.00	0.00	2.00
1.00	1.00	0.00	0.00	0.00	1.00	1.00
2.00	1.00	1.00	0.00	0.00	0.00	0.00

The simplex algorithm scans the bottom row for the largest value and chooses that column as pivot column. It next determines the pivot row by selecting the largest positive element in that column relative to the matching element in the last column.

$$
\begin{array}{ccccccc}
2.00 & 0.00 & 1.00 & 1.00 & 0.00 & 0.00 & 3.00 \\
4.00 & 1.00 & 2.00 & 0.00 & 1.00 & 0.00 & 2.00 \\
1.00 & 1.00 & 0.00 & 0.00 & 0.00 & 1.00 & 1.00 \\
2.00 & 1.00 & 1.00 & 0.00 & 0.00 & 0.00 & 0.00
\end{array}
$$

The algorithm then uses row reduction to zero out the elements in the pivot column and set the coefficient of the pivot row to one. It repeats the loop choosing the next pivot column and pivot row.

$$
\begin{array}{ccccccc}
0.00 & -0.50 & 0.00 & 1.00 & -0.50 & 0.00 & 2.00 \\
1.00 & 0.25 & 0.50 & 0.00 & 0.25 & 0.00 & 0.50 \\
0.00 & 0.75 & -0.50 & 0.00 & -0.25 & 1.00 & 0.50 \\
0.00 & 0.50 & 0.00 & 0.00 & -0.50 & 0.00 & -1.00
\end{array}
$$

The algorithm repeats row reduction and pivot column and row selection.

$$
\begin{array}{ccccccc}
0.00 & 0.00 & -0.33 & 1.00 & -0.67 & 0.67 & 2.33 \\
1.00 & 0.00 & 0.67 & 0.00 & 0.33 & -0.33 & 0.33 \\
0.00 & 1.00 & -0.67 & 0.00 & -0.33 & 1.33 & 0.67 \\
0.00 & 0.00 & 0.33 & 0.00 & -0.33 & -0.67 & -1.33
\end{array}
$$

After row reduction, there are more remaining positive values in the bottom row. The simplex algorithm has found a solution.

$$
\begin{array}{ccccccc}
0.50 & 0.00 & 0.00 & 1.00 & -0.50 & 0.50 & 2.50 \\
1.50 & 0.00 & 1.00 & 0.00 & 0.50 & -0.50 & 0.50 \\
1.00 & 1.00 & 0.00 & 0.00 & 0.00 & 1.00 & 1.00 \\
-0.50 & 0.00 & 0.00 & 0.00 & -0.50 & -0.50 & -1.50
\end{array}
$$

The negative value of the cost variable solution.z is in the lower-left corner. The second and third columns are reduced—they correspond to basic variables. The first column is not reduced—it corresponds to a nonbasic variable, which we set to zero. From the values in the right-most column, we have that the solution solution.x is $(x, y, z) = (0, 1.0, 0.5)$. ◄

The bottom row of the reduced tableau also gives us the solution to a related problem. An LP problem has two related formulations—the primal problem and the dual problem. Every variable of the primal LP is a constraint in the dual LP, every constraint of the primal LP is a variable in the dual LP, and a maximum objective function in the primal is a minimum in the dual (and vice versa). Until now, we've only considered the primal problem:

Find the maximum of the objective function $z = \mathbf{c}^T\mathbf{x}$ subject to constraint $\mathbf{Ax} \le \mathbf{b}$ and nonnegativity restriction $\mathbf{x}, \mathbf{b} \ge 0$.

The dual of this problem is

> Find the minimum of the objective function $z = \mathbf{b}^T\mathbf{y}$ subject to constraint $\mathbf{A}^T\mathbf{y} \geq \mathbf{c}$ and nonnegativity restriction $\mathbf{y}, \mathbf{c} \geq 0$.

The strong duality theorem states four possibilities: 1. both the primal and dual are infeasible (no feasible solutions); 2. the primal is infeasible and the dual is unbounded; 3. the dual is infeasible and the primal is unbounded; or 4. both the primal and dual have feasible solutions and their values are the same. This means that we can solve the dual problem instead of the primal problem.

Example. The LP problem "find the minimum of the objective function $3x + 2y + z$ subject to the constraints $2x + 4y + z \leq 2$, $y + z \leq 1$, and $x + 2y \leq 1$" is the dual to the primal LP problem in the previous example. Its solution is given by solution.y, or $(x, y, z) = (0, 0.5, 0.5)$ where cost function has a minimum value of 1.5. ◄

> ⚙ JuMP.jl ("Julia for Mathematical Programming") is a modeling language for for-mulating optimization problems in Julia. JuMP interfaces with several external solvers such as GLPK.jl, COSMO.jl, and Tulip.jl.

2.4 Sparse matrices

James H. Wilkinson defines a *sparse matrix* as "any matrix with enough zeros that it pays to take advantage of them" in terms of memory and computation time. If we are smart about implementing Gaussian elimination, each zero in a matrix means potentially many saved computations. So it is worthwhile to use algorithms that maintain sparsity by preventing fill-in. In Chapter 5, we'll look at iterative methods for sparse matrices.

Suppose that we have the 4×6 full matrix

$$\mathbf{A} = \begin{bmatrix} 11 & 0 & 0 & 14 & 0 & 16 \\ 0 & 22 & 0 & 0 & 25 & 26 \\ 0 & 0 & 33 & 34 & 0 & 36 \\ 41 & 0 & 43 & 44 & 0 & 46 \end{bmatrix}.$$

If the number of nonzero elements is small, we could store the matrix more efficiently by just recording the locations and values of the nonzero elements. For example,

column	1	1	2	3	3	4	4	4	5	6	6	6	6
row	1	4	2	3	4	1	3	4	2	1	2	3	4
value	11	41	22	33	43	14	34	44	25	16	26	36	46

To store this array in memory, we can go a step further and use *compressed sparse column* (CSC) format. Rather than saving explicit column numbers, compressed column format data structure only saves pointers to where the new columns begin

index	1		3	4		6			9	10				14
row		1	4	2	3	4	1	3	4	2	1	2	3	4
value		11	41	22	33	43	14	34	44	25	16	26	36	46

Similarly, the compressed sparse row (CSR) format indexes arrays by rows instead of columns. A CSC format is most efficient for languages like Julia, Matlab, R, and Fortran, which use a column-major order convention to store data. A CSR format is most efficient for languages like Python and C, which use a row-major convention.

♣ SparseArrays.jl includes several utilities for constructing sparse matrices.

♣ Julia's backslash and forward slash operators use UMFPACK (pronounced "Umph Pack") to solve nonsymmetric, sparse systems directly.

The *density* of a sparse matrix is the number of nonzero elements divided by the total number of elements. Conversely, the *sparsity* is the number of zero elements divided by the total number of elements. Julia's SparseArrays.jl function nnz returns the number of nonzero elements of sparse matrix. For example, A = sprand(60,80,0.2) will construct a 60-by-80 sparse, random matrix with a density of 0.2 and nonzero elements uniformly distributed over the unit interval. The command nnz(A) returns an integer in the neighborhood of 960. The Plots.jl function spy(A) draws the sparsity plot of matrix A, a row-column scatter plot of its nonzero values. The spy command is not always needed as simply outputting A to the console in Julia will provide a sparsity pattern printed using the Unicode braille pattern.

▷ Graphs

In 1735 mathematician Leonhard Euler solved a puzzle asking whether it was possible to walk about the city of Königsberg, crossing each of the seven bridges connecting the banks of the Pregel River and its two islands exactly once—no backtracking or double crossing.[3]

---

[3] Euler published his paper in 1741. A hundred years later, Königsberg native Gustav Kirchhoff published his eponymous electrical circuits laws. One can wonder if walking along the bridges inspired him. Königsberg is now Kalingrad, Russia. Only two of the original bridges remain today. One was completely rebuilt in 1935, two were destroyed during the bombing of Königsberg in World War II, and two others were later demolished to make way for a modern highway.

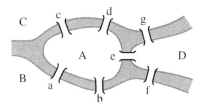 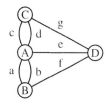

Euler found the solution by replacing the islands and mainland river banks with points called *vertices* or *nodes* and the bridges with line segments called *edges* that linked the vertices together. By counting the *degree* of each vertex—that is, the number of edges associated with each vertex—Euler was able to confidently answer "no." A *path* or *walk* is a sequence of edges that join a sequence of vertices. An Eulerian path is a path that visits every edge exactly once, the type of path that the Königsberg bridge puzzle sought to find. An Eulerian path can have at most two vertices with odd degree—one for the start of the walk and one for the end of it. The vertices of the Königsberg graph have degrees 5, 3, 3, and 3. This puzzle laid the foundation for the mathematical discipline called graph theory, which examines mathematical structures that model pairwise relationships between objects.

Nowadays, we use graph theory to describe any number of things. When describing the internet, vertices are websites, and edges are hyperlinks connecting those websites together. In social networks, vertices are people, and edges are the social bonds between pairs of individuals. In an electrical circuit, vertices are junctions, and edges are resistors, inductors, capacitors, and other components.

We can use sparse matrices to analyze graph structure. Similarly, we can use graphs to visualize the structure of sparse matrices. An *adjacency matrix* $\mathbf{A}$ is a symmetric $(0, 1)$-matrix indicating whether or not pairs of vertices are adjacent. The square of an adjacency matrix $\mathbf{A}^2$ tells us the number of paths of length two joining a particular vertex with another particular one. The kth power of an adjacency matrix $\mathbf{A}^k$ tells us the number of paths of length k joining a particular vertex with another particular one. A graph is said to be *connected* if a path exists between every two vertices. Otherwise, the graph consists of multiple components, the sets of all vertices connected by paths and connected to no other vertices of the graph.

One way to measure the connectivity of a graph is by examining the Laplacian matrix of a graph. The *Laplacian matrix* (sometimes called the graph Laplacian or Kirchhoff matrix) for a graph is $\mathbf{L} = \mathbf{D} - \mathbf{A}$, where the *degree matrix* $\mathbf{D}$ is a diagonal matrix that counts the degrees of each vertex and $\mathbf{A}$ is the adjacency matrix. The matrix $\mathbf{L}$ is symmetric and positive semidefinite. Because $\mathbf{L}$ is symmetric, its eigenvectors are all orthogonal. The row and column sums of $\mathbf{L}$ are zero. It follows that the vector of ones is in the nullspace, i.e., the vector of ones is an eigenvector. Finally, the number of connected components equals the dimension of the nullspace, i.e., the multiplicity of the zero eigenvalue.

As its name might suggest, the Laplacian matrix also has a physical interpretation. Imagine an initial heat distribution $\mathbf{u}$ across a graph where u_i is the temperature at vertex i. Suppose that heat moves from vertex i to vertex j proportional to $u_i - u_j$ if the two vertices share an edge. We can model the heat flow in the network as

$$\frac{d\mathbf{u}}{dt} = -(\mathbf{D} - \mathbf{A})\mathbf{u} = -\mathbf{L}\mathbf{u},$$

which is simply the heat equation if we replace $-\mathbf{L}$ with the Laplacian Δ. We can write the solution $\mathbf{u}(t)$ using the eigenvector basis $\mathbf{L}$. Namely,

$$\mathbf{u}(t) = \sum_{i=1}^{n} c_i(t)\mathbf{v}$$

for eigenvalues $\mathbf{v}$, where $c_i(0)$ is the spectral projection of the initial state $\mathbf{u}(0)$. The solution to the decoupled system is $c_i(t) = c_i(0)e^{-\lambda_i t}$, where the eigenvalues of $\mathbf{L}$ are $0 = \lambda_1 \le \lambda_2 \le \cdots \le \lambda_n$. What happens to the solution as $t \to \infty$? If the graph is simply connected, the equilibrium solution is given by the eigenvector associated with the zero eigenvalue, i.e., the null space of $\mathbf{L}$. In other words, the distribution across the vertices converges to the average value of the initial state across all vertices—what we should expect from the heat equation.[4]

In moving from a perturbed initial state to the equilibrium state, the large-eigenvalue components decay rapidly and the small-eigenvalue components linger. The zero eigenvector is the smoothest and corresponds to all constants. The next eigenvector is the next smoothest, and so on. The solution can be approximated using the smallest eigenvalues λ_2 and λ_3 near equilibrium. This approximation gives us a way to draw the graph in two dimensions in a meaningful way—compute the two smallest nonzero eigenvalues of the graph Laplacian and the unit eigenvectors associates with these eigenvalues. Place vertex i at the coordinates given by the ith component of $\mathbf{v}_2$ and the ith component of $\mathbf{v}_3$. This approach is called spectral layout drawing. To dig deeper, see Fan Chung and Ronald Graham's *Spectral Graph Theory*.

Another popular method for drawing graphs also uses an equilibrium solution to a physical problem. The force-directed graph drawing (developed by Thomas Fruchterman and Edward Reingold in 1991) models edges as springs that obey Hooke's law and vertices as electrical charges that obey Coulomb's law. The force at each node is given by $f_{ij} = a_{ij} + r_{ij}$, where

$$a_{ij} = k^{-1}\|\mathbf{x}_i - \mathbf{x}_j\|, \qquad \text{if } i \text{ connects to } j$$
$$r_{ij} = -\alpha k^2\|\mathbf{x}_i - \mathbf{x}_j\|^{-2}, \qquad \text{if } i \ne j$$

---

[4]Alternatively, we can imagine the graph as a set of nodes linked together by springs. In this case, the governing equation is the wave equation $\mathbf{u}_{tt} = -\mathbf{L}\mathbf{u}$. The solution that minimizes the Dirichlet energy is the one that minimizes oscillations making the solution as smooth as possible.

and the parameters k and α adjust the optimal distance between vertices. To keep the graph to a two-dimensional unit square, we might choose the parameter k to be one over the square root of the number of vertices. Because we are simply trying to get a visually pleasing graph with separated vertices, we don't need to solve the problem precisely. We start with random placement of the nodes. Then we iterate, updating the position of each vertex sequentially

$$\mathbf{x}_i \leftarrow \mathbf{x}_i + \Delta t \sum_{i=1}^{n} f_{ij} \frac{\mathbf{x}_i - \mathbf{x}_j}{\|\mathbf{x}_i - \mathbf{x}_j\|},$$

where the step size Δt is chosen sufficiently small to ensure stability. Because the force on each vertex is affected by the position of every other vertex and because it may potentially take hundreds of iterations to reach the equilibrium solution, force-directed graph drawing may require significant computation time.

♣ The Graphs.jl and GraphPlot.jl libraries provide utilities for constructing, analyzing, and visualizing graphs.

Example.   The bottlenose dolphins living in Doubtful Sound, a fjord in the far southwest of New Zealand, form a small population that has decreased significantly over the past thirty years. Researchers studying this community of 62 dolphins observed that they appeared to have greater cooperation and group stability to survive in the ecological constraints of the southern fjord. (Lusseau et al. [2003]) Their data set provides a glimpse into the social dynamics of the dolphins. The adjacency matrix is available from the SuiteSparse Matrix Collection (https://sparse.tamu.edu) maintained by Timothy Davis.[5] Let's draw the graph of the frequent associations of the dolphins.   First, we'll define a helper function to download and build a sparse adjacency matrix.

```
using DelimitedFiles, SparseArrays
function get_adjacency_matrix(filename)
  ij = readdlm(download(bucket*filename*".csv"),',',Int)
  sparse(ij[:,1],ij[:,2],one.(ij[:,1]))
end
```

Then, we'll plot the graph.

```
using Graphs, GraphPlot
g = get_adjacency_matrix("dolphins") |> Graph
gplot(g,layout=spectral_layout)
```

---

[5]The collection is a curated set of around 3000 sparse matrices that occur in applications such as computational fluid dynamics, financial modeling, and structural engineering. SuiteSparse also maintains the software library of sparse matrix routines such as UMFPACK, SSMULT, and SPQR used in Julia, Python, and Matlab.

spectral layout   force-directed layout   circular layout

Figure 2.2: Graph drawing layouts for the bottlenose dolphin network.

The graphs using `spectral_layout`, `spring_layout`, and `circular_layout` are shown in the figure above. We can see in the force-directed layout how the dolphin group appears to consist of two smaller two pods. The circular layout draws the vertices at equally spaced points along a circle's circumference. It is difficult to interpret the associations between the dolphins using this layout because there are so many crossings. In the next section, we'll develop a method of sorting the vertices to minimize the bandwidth. ◄

▷ **Preserving sparsity**

A matrix is a *banded matrix* with lower bandwidth p and upper bandwidth q if the ij-elements are zero except when $j - q \le i \le j + p$. For example, a diagonal matrix has lower and upper bandwidths of 0, and a tridiagonal matrix has lower and upper bandwidths of 1. Banded matrices often arise in finite difference approximations to one-dimensional partial differential equations.

A banded matrix with lower bandwidth p and an upper bandwidth q has an LU decomposition with a lower bandwidth of p and an upper bandwidth of q. The number of multiplications and additions is approximately $2npq$. Forward and backward substitution requires an additional $2np + 2nq$ operations.

Consider the simple example of the following sparse matrix:

with a tremendous fill-in. But, if we reorder the rows and columns first by moving

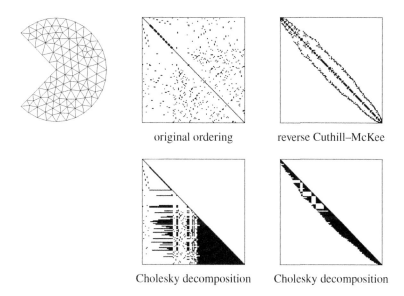

original ordering   reverse Cuthill–McKee

Cholesky decomposition   Cholesky decomposition

Figure 2.3: The original ordering and the reverse Cuthill–McKee ordering of the sparsity plot for the Laplacian operator in a finite element solution for a pacman domain. The Cholesky decompositions for each ordering are directly below.

the first row to the bottom and the first column to the end, then

has the LU decomposition

In the $n \times n$ case, the original matrix requires $O(n^3)$ operations to compute the LU decomposition plus another $O(n^2)$ operations to solve the problem. Furthermore, we need to store all n^2 terms of the LU decomposition. The reordered matrix, on the other hand, suffers from no fill-in. It only needs $4n$ operations (additions and multiplications) for the LU decomposition and $8n$ operations to solve the system.

We can lower the bandwidth of a sparse matrix and reduce the fill-in by reordering the rows and columns to get the nonzero elements as close to the diagonal as possible. The Cuthill–McKee algorithm does this for symmetric matrices by using a breadth-first search to traverse the associated graph.[6] The algorithm builds a permutation sequence starting with an empty set:

---

[6]Dijkstra's algorithm also uses breadth-first search—this time to determine the shortest path between nodes on a graph. Imagine that nodes represent intersections on a street map and the weighted edges are the travel times between intersections. Then, Dijkstra's algorithm can help route

1. Choose a vertex with the lowest degree and add it to the permutation set.
2. For each vertex added to the permutation set, progressively add its adjacent vertices from lowest degree to highest degree, skipping any already vertex.
3. If the graph is connected, repeating step 2 will eventually run through all vertices—at which point we're done. If the graph is disconnected, repeating step 2 will terminate without reaching all of the vertices. In this case, we'll need to go back to step 1 with the remaining vertices.

Consider the 12×12 matrix in the figure on the facing page. We start the Cuthill–McKee algorithm by selecting a column of the matrix with the fewest off-diagonal nonzero elements. Column 5 has one nonzero element in row 10, so we start with that one. We now find the uncounted nonzero elements in column 10–rows 3 and 12. We repeat the process, looking at column 3 and skipping any vertices we've already counted. We continue in this fashion until we've run through all the columns to build a tree. To get the permutation, start with the root node and subsequently collect vertices at each lower level to get $\{5, 10, 12, 3, 1, 7, 8, 9, 2, 4, 11, 6\}$. In practice, one typically uses the *reverse Cuthill–McKee* algorithm, which simply reverses the ordering of the relabeled vertices $\{6, 11, 4, 3, 9, 8, 7, 1, 3, 12, 10, 5\}$. The new graph is isomorphic to the original graph—the labels have changed but nothing else. Relabeling the vertices of the graph is identical to permuting the rows and columns of the symmetric matrix. Other sorting methods include minimum degree and nested dissection.

⣿ Finite element packages such as JuliaFEM.jl and FinEtools.jl include functions for the Cuthill–McKee algorithm.

▷ Revised simplex method

Linear programming problems often involve large, sparse systems. Unfortunately, the simplex tableau, which may start with very few nonzero entries, can fill in with each iteration. In practice, it's not necessary to store or compute with the entire tableau at each iteration. We only need to select the basic variables so that the objective function increases. The revised simplex method does exactly that. Remember the LP problem:

Find the maximum of the objective function $z = \bar{\mathbf{c}}^T \bar{\mathbf{x}}$ subject to constraint $\bar{\mathbf{A}}\bar{\mathbf{x}} = \mathbf{b}$ and nonnegativity restriction $\bar{\mathbf{x}}, \mathbf{b} \geq 0$,

which has the tableau

$$\begin{array}{c|c|c} \bar{\mathbf{A}} & \mathbf{0} & \mathbf{b} \\ \hline \bar{\mathbf{c}}^T & 1 & 0 \end{array}.$$

the fastest travel from one part of a city to another. In contrast, a depth-first search explores a path as far as possible before backtracking to take a different path—a strategy one might use to solve mazes.

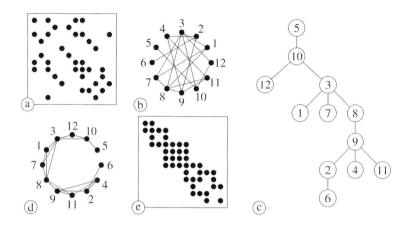

Figure 2.4: Cuthill–McKee sorting: (a) original sparsity pattern; (b) associated graph; (c) completed breadth-first search tree; (d) reordered graph; (e) sparsity pattern of column-and-row-permuted matrix.

At its simplest level, the simplex method involves sorting the basic variables from the nonbasic variables. We can decompose the augmented matrix into basis and nonbasis columns $\bar{\mathbf{A}} = \begin{bmatrix} \mathbf{A}_N & \mathbf{A}_B \end{bmatrix}$ such that $\mathbf{A}_N \mathbf{x}_N + \mathbf{A}_B \mathbf{x}_B = \mathbf{b}$. Although we represent them as grouped together, the columns of $\mathbf{A}_N$ and the columns of $\mathbf{A}_B$ may come from anywhere in $\bar{\mathbf{A}}$ as long as they are mutually exclusive. As with the regular simplex method, we'll again assume that $\bar{\mathbf{A}}$ has full rank. In this case, $\mathbf{A}_B$ is invertible and

$$\mathbf{A}_B^{-1}\mathbf{A}_N\mathbf{x}_N + \mathbf{x}_B = \mathbf{A}_B^{-1}\mathbf{b}. \qquad (2.2)$$

By setting the nonbasic variables $\mathbf{x}_N$ to zero, we have the solution $\mathbf{x}_B = \mathbf{A}_B^{-1}\mathbf{b}$. We choose the basic variables, and hence the columns of $\mathbf{A}_B$, to maximize the objective function

$$z = \mathbf{c}_N^{\mathsf{T}}\mathbf{x}_N + \mathbf{c}_B^{\mathsf{T}}\mathbf{x}_B = (\mathbf{c}_N^{\mathsf{T}} - \mathbf{c}_B^{\mathsf{T}}\mathbf{A}_B^{-1}\mathbf{A}_N)\mathbf{x}_N + \mathbf{c}_B^{\mathsf{T}}\mathbf{A}_B^{-1}\mathbf{b}. \qquad (2.3)$$

We can build a tableau from (2.2) and (2.3):

$$\begin{array}{cc|c|c} \mathbf{A}_B^{-1}\mathbf{A}_N & \mathbf{I} & \mathbf{0} & \mathbf{A}_B^{-1}\mathbf{b} \\ \hline \mathbf{c}_N^{\mathsf{T}} - \mathbf{c}_B^{\mathsf{T}}\mathbf{A}_B^{-1}\mathbf{A}_N & \mathbf{0} & 1 & -\mathbf{c}_B^{\mathsf{T}}\mathbf{A}_B^{-1}\mathbf{b} \end{array}.$$

At each iteration, we need to keep track of which variables are basic and which ones are nonbasic, but it will save us quite a bit of computing time if we also keep track of $\mathbf{A}_B^{-1}$.

We start with $\mathbf{A}_N = \mathbf{A}$ and $\mathbf{A}_B = \mathbf{I}$. At each iteration, we choose a new entering variable—associated with the pivot column—by looking for any (the first) positive element among the reduced cost variables $\mathbf{c}_N^T - \mathbf{c}_B^T \mathbf{A}_B^{-1} \mathbf{A}_N$. Let $\mathbf{q}$ be that jth column of $\mathbf{A}_N$ and $\hat{\mathbf{q}}$ be jth column of $\mathbf{A}_B^{-1} \mathbf{A}_N$, i.e. $\hat{\mathbf{q}} = \mathbf{A}_B^{-1} \mathbf{A}_N \boldsymbol{\xi}_j$, where $\boldsymbol{\xi}_j$ is the jth standard basis vector. With our pivot column in hand, we now look for a pivot row i that will correspond to our leaving variable. We take $i = \arg\min_i x_i/q_i$ with $q_i > 0$ to ensure that $\mathbf{x}_B = \mathbf{A}_B^{-1} \mathbf{b}$ remains nonnegative. Let $\mathbf{p}$ be the ith column of $\mathbf{A}_B$, the column associated with the leaving variable.

After swapping columns $\mathbf{p}$ and $\mathbf{q}$ between $\mathbf{A}_B$ and $\mathbf{A}_N$, we'll need to update $\mathbf{A}_B^{-1}$. Fortunately, we don't need to recompute the inverse entirely. Instead, we can use the Sherman–Morrison formula, which gives a rank-one perturbation of the inverse of a matrix:

$$(\mathbf{A} + \mathbf{u}\mathbf{v}^T)^{-1} = \mathbf{A}^{-1} - \frac{\mathbf{A}^{-1}\mathbf{u}\mathbf{v}^T\mathbf{A}^{-1}}{1 + \mathbf{v}^T\mathbf{A}^{-1}\mathbf{u}}.$$

By taking $\mathbf{u} = \mathbf{q} - \mathbf{p}$ and $\mathbf{v} = \boldsymbol{\xi}_i$, we have

$$(\mathbf{A}_B + (\mathbf{q} - \mathbf{p})\boldsymbol{\xi}_i^T)^{-1} = \mathbf{A}_B^{-1} - \hat{q}_i^{-1}(\hat{\mathbf{q}} - \boldsymbol{\xi}_i)\boldsymbol{\xi}_i^T\mathbf{A}_B^{-1}$$

where $\hat{\mathbf{q}} = \mathbf{A}_B^{-1}\mathbf{q}$, $\hat{q}_i = \boldsymbol{\xi}_i^T\mathbf{A}_B^{-1}\mathbf{q}$, and $\mathbf{A}_B^{-1}\mathbf{p} = \boldsymbol{\xi}_i$. Note that this is equivalent to row reduction.

Let's implement the revised simplex method in Julia. We'll take ABinv to be $\mathbf{A}_B^{-1}$ and B and N to be the list of columns of $\bar{\mathbf{A}}$ in $\mathbf{A}_B$ and $\mathbf{A}_N$, respectively. We define a method $\xi(i)$ to return a unit vector. In practice, we can save and update $\begin{bmatrix} \mathbf{A}_B^{-1} & \mathbf{A}_B^{-1}\mathbf{b} \end{bmatrix}$ instead of simply $\mathbf{B}^{-1}$ and stop as soon as we find the first j.

```julia
using SparseArrays
function revised_simplex(c,A,b)
  (m,n) = size(A)
  ξ = i -> (z=spzeros(m);z[i]=1;z)
  N = Vector(1:n); B = Vector(n .+ (1:m))
  A = [A sparse(I, m, m)]
  ABinv = sparse(I, m, m)
  c = [c;spzeros(m,1)]
  while(true)
    j = findfirst(x->x>0,(c[N]'.-(c[B]'*ABinv)*A[:,N])[:])
    if isnothing(j); break; end
    q = ABinv*A[:,N[j]]
    k = findall(q.>0)
    i = k[argmin(ABinv[k,:]*b./q[k])]
    B[i], N[j] = N[j], B[i]
    ABinv -= ((q - ξ(i))/q[i])*ABinv[i:i,:]
  end
  i = findall(B.≤n)
  x = zeros(n,1)
  x[B[i]] = ABinv[i,:]*b
  return((z=c[1:n]'*x, x=x, y=c[B]'*ABinv))
end
```

2.5   Exercises

2.1. Modify the function `gaussian_elimination` program on page 33 to include partial pivoting. Use both functions to solve the system $\mathbf{Ax} = \mathbf{b}$, where

$$\mathbf{A} = \begin{bmatrix} 1 & 1 & 2 \\ 2 & 2+\varepsilon & 0 \\ 4 & 14 & 4 \end{bmatrix} \quad \text{and} \quad \mathbf{b} = \begin{bmatrix} -5 \\ 10 \\ 0 \end{bmatrix}$$

with $\varepsilon = 10^{-15}$ (or about five times machine epsilon).

2.2. Write the LU decomposition of the block matrix: $\begin{bmatrix} \mathbf{A} & \mathbf{B} \\ \mathbf{C} & \mathbf{D} \end{bmatrix}$.

2.3. LU decomposition provides an efficient way to compute the determinant of a matrix. (Julia, Python, and Matlab all use this approach.) Write a program to find a determinant using LU decomposition. ✍

2.4. In the film *Good Will Hunting*, Professor Gerald Lambeau presents what he considers a challenging problem to his students, with the promise that the solver would "go on to fame and fortune." The problem is as follows:

G is the graph

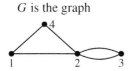

Find
1) the adjacency matrix $\mathbf{A}$
2) the matrix giving the number of 3-step walks
3) the generating function for walks from $i \to j$
4) the generating function for walks from $1 \to 3$.

A generating function of a given sequence is the function whose power series coefficients equal the terms of that sequence, in this case the number of walks between two given points. Solve Professor Lambeau's problem. Check your solution by writing a numerical function that computes the number of walks between two points. ✍

2.5. Write a program to implement the reverse Cuthill–McKee algorithm for symmetric matrices. ✍

2.6. Use the Cuthill–McKee algorithm to reorder the vertices in the circular graph layout of the bottlenose dolphin network in the example on page 49. ✍

2.7. The nematode *Caenorhabditis elegans* is the first and only organism whose complete connectome, consisting of 277 interconnected neurons, has been mapped. The adjacency matrix for the connectome is available as edges of a bipartite graph *celegans.csv* from https://github.com/nmfsc/data (from Choe et al. [2004]). Use the Cuthill–McKee algorithm to order the nodes to minimize the bandwidth. See Reid and Scott's article "Reducing the total bandwidth of a sparse unsymmetric matrix" for different approaches.

2.8. Use the simplex method to solve the Stigler diet problem to find the diet that meets minimum nutritional requirements at the lowest cost. The data from Stigler's 1945 paper is available as *diet.csv* from https://github.com/nmfsc/data (nutritional values of foods are normalized per dollar of expenditure).   △

2.9. In 1929 Hungarian author Frigyes Karinthy hypothesized that any person could be connected to any other person through a chain consisting of at most five intermediary acquaintances, a hypothesis now called six degrees of separation.[7] In a contemporary version of Karinthy's game called "six degrees of Kevin Bacon," players attempt to trace an arbitrary actor to Kevin Bacon by identifying a chain of movies coappearances.[8] The length of the shortest path is called the Bacon number. Kevin Bacon's Bacon number is zero. Anyone who has acted in a movie with him has a Bacon number of one. Anyone who has acted with someone who has acted with Kevin Bacon has a Bacon number of two. For example, John Belushi starred in the movie *Animal House* with Kevin Bacon, so his Bacon number is one. Danny DeVito never appeared in a movie with Kevin Bacon. But he did appear in the movie *Goin' South* with John Belushi, so his Bacon number is two. The path connecting Danny DeVito to Kevin Bacon isn't unique. Danny DeVito also acted in *The Jewel of the Nile* with Holland Taylor, who acted with Kevin Bacon in *She's Having a Baby*.

Write a graph search algorithm to find the path connecting two arbitrary actors. You can use the corpus of narrative American feature films from 1972 to 2012 to test your algorithm. The data, scraped from Wikipedia, is available at https://github.com/nmfsc/data/. The file *actors.txt* is a list of the actors, the file *movies.txt* is a list of the movies, and the CSV file *actor-movie.csv* identifies the edges of the bipartite graph. Because Wikipedia content is crowd-sourced across thousands of editors, there are inconsistencies across articles.   △

2.10. The CSC and CSR formats require some overhead to store a sparse matrix. What is the break-even point in terms of the density?   △

---

[7] In Karinthy's short story "Láncszemek" ("Chains"), the author explains how he is two steps removed from Nobel laureate Selma Lagerlöf and no more than four steps away from an anonymous riveter at the Ford Motor Company.

[8] Mathematicians sometimes play a nerdier game by tracking the chain of co-authors on research papers to the prolific Hungarian mathematician Paul Erdős.

Chapter 3

Inconsistent Systems

In the last chapter, we examined solutions to square, consistent systems. Now, we turn our attention to nonsquare matrices. We can solve a nonsquare system $\mathbf{Ax} = \mathbf{b}$ like the square system in Julia using the (\) function. Computing A\b for a 2000×1999 matrix takes 1.54 seconds, considerably longer than the 0.15 seconds to solve a 2000×2000 matrix. Alternatively, solving the same nonsquare system using the pseudoinverse pinv(A)*b takes 5.6 seconds—the inverse inv(A)*b takes 0.42 seconds for the square system. Both approaches—the backslash operator and the pseudoinverse—use orthogonal projection to reduce a problem to a lower-dimensional subspace in which it has a unique solution. This chapter examines how QR decomposition and singular value decomposition are used to generate such subspaces. We also look at several applications of low-rank approximation.

3.1 Overdetermined systems

Perhaps we want to solve a problem with noisy input data. The problem might be curve fitting, image recognition, or statistical modeling. We may have sufficient data, but they are inconsistent, so the problem is ill-posed. The solution is to filter out the noise leaving us with consistent data. It is not difficult for us to mentally filter out the noise in the figures on the next page and recognize the letter on the left or the slope of the line on the right.

In this chapter, we'll develop the mathematical tools to instruct a computer to do the same. Consider the overdetermined system $\mathbf{Ax} = \mathbf{b}$ where $\mathbf{A} \in \mathbb{R}^{m \times n}$, $\mathbf{x} \in \mathbb{R}^n$, and $\mathbf{b} \in \mathbb{R}^m$ with $m > n$. The linear system does not have a solution unless $\mathbf{b}$ is in the column space of $\mathbf{A}$, i.e., unless $\mathbf{b}$ is a linear combination of the columns of $\mathbf{A}$. While we may not be able to find "the" solution $\mathbf{x}$, we will often be able to find a "best" solution $\tilde{\mathbf{x}}$ so that $\mathbf{A}\tilde{\mathbf{x}}$ is closest to $\mathbf{b}$. In this case, we want to choose $\tilde{\mathbf{x}}$ that minimizes the norm of the *residual* $\tilde{\mathbf{r}} = \mathbf{b} - \mathbf{A}\tilde{\mathbf{x}}$.

So, which norm? The 1-, 2- and ∞-norms are all relevant norms, but the 2-norm is Goldilocks' baby bear of norms—not too hard and not too soft. The 1-norm minimizes the importance of outliers, the ∞-norm only looks at the outliers, and the 2-norm takes the middle of the road. Also, some problems are ill-posed in the 1- and ∞-norms. So, the 2-norm seems to be a natural choice. But wait, there's more! Perhaps the nicest property of the 2-norm is that the problem of finding a solution that minimizes the 2-norm of the residual is a linear problem. Recently, the 1-norm has gained some popularity in research and applications because it handles noisy data better than the 2-norm by minimizing the influence of outliers (Candè and Wakin [2008]). But because the minimization problem in the 1-norm is nonlinear, more complex solvers must be used.[1]

▷ **The normal equation**

Suppose that $\tilde{\mathbf{x}}$ minimizes $\|\mathbf{Ax} - \mathbf{b}\|_2^2$. Then for any arbitrary vector $\mathbf{y}$

$$\|\mathbf{A}(\tilde{\mathbf{x}} + \mathbf{y}) - \mathbf{b}\|_2^2 \geq \|\mathbf{A}\tilde{\mathbf{x}} - \mathbf{b}\|_2^2.$$

By rearranging the terms on the left-hand side, we have

$$\|(\mathbf{A}\tilde{\mathbf{x}} - \mathbf{b}) + \mathbf{Ay}\|_2^2 \geq \|\mathbf{A}\tilde{\mathbf{x}} - \mathbf{b}\|_2^2.$$

And expanding,

$$\|\mathbf{A}\tilde{\mathbf{x}} - \mathbf{b}\|_2^2 + \|\mathbf{Ay}\|_2^2 + 2\mathbf{y}\mathbf{A}^\mathsf{T}\mathbf{Ax} - 2\mathbf{y}^\mathsf{T}\mathbf{A}^\mathsf{T}\mathbf{b} \geq \|\mathbf{A}\tilde{\mathbf{x}} - \mathbf{b}\|_2^2,$$

which says

$$\|\mathbf{Ay}\|_2^2 + 2\mathbf{y}^\mathsf{T}\mathbf{A}^\mathsf{T}\mathbf{A}\tilde{\mathbf{x}} - 2\mathbf{y}^\mathsf{T}\mathbf{A}^\mathsf{T}\mathbf{b} \geq 0,$$

---

[1] In statistics and machine learning applications, the 2-norm arises from the maximum likelihood estimation using a Gaussian distribution $\exp(-x^2)$. The 1-norm comes from maximum likelihood estimation using the Laplace distribution $\exp(-|x|)$.

or equivalently
$$2\mathbf{y}^\mathsf{T}(\mathbf{A}^\mathsf{T}\mathbf{A}\tilde{\mathbf{x}} - \mathbf{A}^\mathsf{T}\mathbf{b}) \geq -\|\mathbf{A}\mathbf{y}\|_2^2.$$

Because this expression holds for any $\mathbf{y}$ and because $\mathbf{A}^\mathsf{T}\mathbf{A}\tilde{\mathbf{x}} - \mathbf{A}^\mathsf{T}\mathbf{b}$ is independent of $\mathbf{y}$, it must follow that
$$\mathbf{A}^\mathsf{T}\mathbf{A}\tilde{\mathbf{x}} - \mathbf{A}^\mathsf{T}\mathbf{b} = 0.$$

From this, we get the *normal equation*

$$\mathbf{A}^\mathsf{T}\mathbf{A}\tilde{\mathbf{x}} = \mathbf{A}^\mathsf{T}\mathbf{b}.$$

Here's another way to get this equation. The residual $\|\mathbf{r}(\tilde{\mathbf{x}})\|_2$ is minimized when the gradient of $\|\mathbf{r}(\tilde{\mathbf{x}})\|_2$ is zero—equivalently when the gradient of $\|\mathbf{r}(\tilde{\mathbf{x}})\|_2^2$ is zero. Taking the gradient of

$$\|\mathbf{r}(\tilde{\mathbf{x}})\|_2^2 = \|\mathbf{A}\tilde{\mathbf{x}} - \mathbf{b}\|_2^2 = \tilde{\mathbf{x}}^\mathsf{T}\mathbf{A}^\mathsf{T}\mathbf{A}\tilde{\mathbf{x}} - 2\tilde{\mathbf{x}}^\mathsf{T}\mathbf{A}^\mathsf{T}\mathbf{b} + \mathbf{b}^\mathsf{T}\mathbf{b}$$

gives us
$$0 = 2\mathbf{A}^\mathsf{T}\mathbf{A}\tilde{\mathbf{x}} - 2\mathbf{A}^\mathsf{T}\mathbf{b}.$$

Therefore, $\mathbf{A}^\mathsf{T}\mathbf{A}\tilde{\mathbf{x}} = \mathbf{A}^\mathsf{T}\mathbf{b}$.

Let's examine the normal equation by looking at the error $\mathbf{e} = \mathbf{x} - \tilde{\mathbf{x}}$ and the residual $\mathbf{r} = \mathbf{A}\mathbf{e} = \mathbf{b} - \delta\mathbf{b}$ where $\delta\mathbf{b} = \mathbf{A}\mathbf{e}$. The solution to the normal equation is

$$\tilde{\mathbf{x}} = (\mathbf{A}^\mathsf{T}\mathbf{A})^{-1}\mathbf{A}^\mathsf{T}\mathbf{b},$$

from which
$$\tilde{\mathbf{b}} = \mathbf{A}\tilde{\mathbf{x}} = \mathbf{A}(\mathbf{A}^\mathsf{T}\mathbf{A})^{-1}\mathbf{A}^\mathsf{T}\mathbf{b} = \mathbf{P}_\mathbf{A}\mathbf{b},$$

where $\mathbf{P}_\mathbf{A}$ is the orthogonal projection matrix into the column space of $\mathbf{A}$. The residual is simply

$$\mathbf{r} = \mathbf{b} - \tilde{\mathbf{b}} = (\mathbf{I} - \mathbf{P}_\mathbf{A})\mathbf{b} = \mathbf{P}_{N(\mathbf{A}^\mathsf{T})}\mathbf{b},$$

where $\mathbf{P}_{N(\mathbf{A}^\mathsf{T})}$ is the orthogonal projection matrix into the left null space of $\mathbf{A}$. Whatever of the origins of the term *normal equation*,[2] it serves as a useful pneumonic that the residual $\mathbf{b} - \mathbf{A}\tilde{\mathbf{x}}$ is *normal* to the column space of $\mathbf{A}$. Recall that we can write $\mathbf{A}\mathbf{x} = \mathbf{b}$ as

$$\mathbf{A}(\mathbf{x}_{\text{row}} + \mathbf{x}_{\text{null}}) = \mathbf{b}_{\text{column}} + \mathbf{b}_{\text{left null}}.$$

The system is inconsistent because $\mathbf{b}_{\text{left null}} \neq 0$. By simply zeroing out $\mathbf{b}_{\text{left null}}$, we get a solution. Put another way, we want to solve the problem $\mathbf{A}\mathbf{x} = \mathbf{b}$. But we can't because it has no solutions. So instead, we adjust the problem to be

---

[2] According to William Kruskal and Stephen Stigler, Gauss introduced term (*Normalgleichungen*) in an 1822 paper without motive. They offer possibilities about its origin but nothing dominates.

$Ax = b - \delta b$ where the δb puts the right-hand side into the column space of A. The residual δb is none other than the left null space component of b. Pretty remarkable! Furthermore, zeroing out x_{null} will get a unique solution. We'll come back to this idea later in the chapter.

Direct implementation of the normal equation can make a difficult problem even worse because the condition number $\kappa(A^TA)$ equals $\kappa(A)^2$, and the condition number $\kappa((A^TA)^{-1}A^T)$ may be even larger. A moderately ill-conditioned matrix can lead to a very ill-conditioned problem. Instead, let's look at an alternative means of solving an overdetermined system by applying an orthogonal matrix to the original problem. Such an approach is more robust (numerically stable) and is almost as efficient as solving the normal equation.

▷ QR decomposition

Every real $m \times n$ matrix A can be written as the product of an $m \times m$ orthogonal matrix Q and an $m \times n$ upper triangular matrix R. We'll constructively prove this later. This decomposition, known as *QR decomposition*, is the key idea of this chapter and will be used extensively in the next chapter as well. Let's see how we can use it.

We'll start with the normal equation $A^TAx = A^Tb$. Taking $A = QR$, then

$$(QR)^TQRx = (QR)^Tb,$$

which reduces to

$$R^TRx = R^TQ^Tb.$$

Note that we simply have the Cholesky decomposition R^TR of A^TA on the left-hand side. By rearranging the terms of this equality, we have

$$R^T(Rx - Q^Tb) = 0,$$

which says $Rx - Q^Tb$ is in the null space of R^T (the left null space of R):

$$
\begin{bmatrix} \bullet\,0\,0\,0\,0\,0 \\ \bullet\,\bullet\,0\,0\,0\,0 \\ \bullet\,\bullet\,\bullet\,0\,0\,0 \\ \bullet\,\bullet\,\bullet\,\bullet\,0\,0\,0 \end{bmatrix}
\begin{bmatrix} 0 \\ 0 \\ 0 \\ 0 \\ \bullet \\ \bullet \end{bmatrix}
=
\begin{bmatrix} 0 \\ 0 \\ 0 \\ 0 \\ 0 \\ 0 \end{bmatrix}.
$$

So Rx must equal Q^Tb in the first m rows. In the other $m - n$ rows, it can be anything. Let's come at this again. Suppose that we have the overdetermined system $Ax = b$:

$$
\begin{bmatrix} \bullet\,\bullet\,\bullet\,\bullet \\ \bullet\,\bullet\,\bullet\,\bullet \\ \bullet\,\bullet\,\bullet\,\bullet \\ \bullet\,\bullet\,\bullet\,\bullet \\ \bullet\,\bullet\,\bullet\,\bullet \\ \bullet\,\bullet\,\bullet\,\bullet \end{bmatrix}
x =
\begin{bmatrix} \bullet \\ \bullet \\ \bullet \\ \bullet \\ \bullet \\ \bullet \end{bmatrix}.
$$

The matrix $\mathbf{A} = \mathbf{QR}$ for some $\mathbf{Q}$. By applying $\mathbf{Q}^{\mathsf{T}} = \mathbf{Q}^{-1}$ to both sides of the equation, we get the triangular system $\mathbf{Rx} = \mathbf{Q}^{\mathsf{T}}\mathbf{b}$:

$$\begin{bmatrix} \bullet & \bullet & \bullet & \bullet \\ 0 & \bullet & \bullet & \bullet \\ 0 & 0 & \bullet & \bullet \\ 0 & 0 & 0 & \bullet \\ 0 & 0 & 0 & 0 \\ 0 & 0 & 0 & 0 \\ 0 & 0 & 0 & 0 \\ 0 & 0 & 0 & 0 \end{bmatrix} \mathbf{x} = \begin{bmatrix} \bullet \\ \bullet \\ \bullet \\ \bullet \\ \bullet \\ \bullet \\ \bullet \\ \bullet \end{bmatrix}.$$

We discard the inconsistent bottom equations and solve the system

$$\begin{bmatrix} \bullet & \bullet & \bullet & \bullet \\ 0 & \bullet & \bullet & \bullet \\ 0 & 0 & \bullet & \bullet \\ 0 & 0 & 0 & \bullet \end{bmatrix} \mathbf{x} = \begin{bmatrix} \bullet \\ \bullet \\ \bullet \\ \bullet \end{bmatrix}.$$

In the next chapter, we'll use orthogonal matrices to help us find eigenvalues. One reason orthogonal matrices are particularly lovely is that they don't change the lengths of vectors in the 2-norm. The 2-condition number of an orthogonal matrix is one. So the errors don't blow up when we iterate. How do we find the orthogonal matrix $\mathbf{Q}$? We typically use Gram–Schmidt orthogonalization, a series of Givens rotations, or a series of Householder reflections. Let's examine each of these methods of QR decomposition.

▷ Gram–Schmidt orthogonalization

The Gram–Schmidt process generates an orthonormal basis for a subspace by successively projecting out the nonorthogonal components. The orthogonal projection matrix for a general matrix $\mathbf{A}$ is $\mathbf{P_A} = \mathbf{A}(\mathbf{A}^{\mathsf{T}}\mathbf{A})^{-1}\mathbf{A}^{\mathsf{T}}$. For a vector $\mathbf{v}$, the projection matrix is $\mathbf{P_v} = (\mathbf{vv}^{\mathsf{T}})/(\mathbf{v}^{\mathsf{T}}\mathbf{v})$. And, for a unit length vector $\mathbf{q}$, the projection matrix is simply $\mathbf{P_q} = \mathbf{qq}^{\mathsf{T}}$.

Suppose that we have the vectors $\mathbf{v}_1, \mathbf{v}_2, \ldots, \mathbf{v}_n$. Let's find an orthonormal basis $\mathbf{q}_1, \mathbf{q}_2, \ldots, \mathbf{q}_n$ for the subspace spanned by $\mathbf{v}_1, \mathbf{v}_2, \ldots, \mathbf{v}_n$.

1. Take $\mathbf{w}_1 = \mathbf{v}_1$ and normalize it to get $\mathbf{q}_1 = \mathbf{w}_1/\|\mathbf{w}_1\|_2$.

2. We want to find $\mathbf{q}_2$ such that $(\mathbf{q}_2, \mathbf{q}_1)_2 = 0$. We can do this by subtracting the $\mathbf{q}_1$ component of $\mathbf{v}_2$ from $\mathbf{v}_2$. Taking $\mathbf{w}_2 = \mathbf{v}_2 - \mathbf{P}_{\mathbf{q}_1}\mathbf{v}_2$ and noting that $\mathbf{P}_{\mathbf{q}_j}\mathbf{v}_k = \mathbf{q}_j^{\mathsf{T}}\mathbf{q}_j\mathbf{v}_k = (\mathbf{q}_j, \mathbf{v}_k)_2\,\mathbf{q}_j$ we have

$$\mathbf{w}_2 = \mathbf{v}_2 - (\mathbf{q}_1, \mathbf{v}_2)_2\,\mathbf{q}_1.$$

This step finds the closest vector to $\mathbf{v}_2$ (in the 2-norm) that is orthogonal to $\mathbf{w}_1$. Now, normalize $\mathbf{w}_2$ to get $\mathbf{q}_2 = \mathbf{w}_2/\|\mathbf{w}_2\|_2$.

3. To get $\mathbf{q}_3$, subtract the $\mathrm{span}\{\mathbf{q}_1, \mathbf{q}_2\}$ components of $\mathbf{v}_3$ from $\mathbf{v}_3$ and normalize:

$$\mathbf{w}_3 = \mathbf{v}_3 - \mathbf{P}_{\mathbf{q}_1}\mathbf{v}_3 - \mathbf{P}_{\mathbf{q}_2}\mathbf{v}_3 = \mathbf{v}_3 - (\mathbf{q}_1, \mathbf{v}_3)_2\,\mathbf{q}_1 - (\mathbf{q}_2, \mathbf{v}_3)_2\,\mathbf{q}_2.$$

This step finds the closest vector to $\mathbf{v}_3$ which is orthogonal to both $\mathbf{w}_1$ and $\mathbf{w}_2$. Now, normalize $\mathbf{w}_3$ to get $\mathbf{q}_3 = \mathbf{w}_3/\|\mathbf{w}_3\|_2$.

4. In general, at the kth step we compute $\mathbf{q}_k = \mathbf{w}_k / \|\mathbf{w}_k\|_2$ with

$$\mathbf{w}_k = \mathbf{v}_k - \sum_{j=1}^{k-1} r_{jk} \mathbf{q}_j \quad \text{where} \quad r_{jk} = (\mathbf{q}_j, \mathbf{v}_k).$$

We continue to get the remaining $\mathbf{q}_4, \mathbf{q}_5, \dots, \mathbf{q}_n$.

The classical Gram–Schmidt method that subtracts the projection all at once can be numerically unstable because unless the vectors are already close to orthogonal, the orthogonal component is small. A better implementation is the modified Gram–Schmidt process that subtracts the projections successively:

for $k = 1, \dots, n$
$\quad \mathbf{q}_k \leftarrow \mathbf{v}_k$
$\quad$ for $j = 1, \dots, k-1$
$\quad\quad r_{jk} = (\mathbf{q}_j, \mathbf{v}_k)$
$\quad\quad \mathbf{q}_k \leftarrow \mathbf{q}_k - r_{jk} \mathbf{q}_j$
$\quad r_{kk} \leftarrow \|\mathbf{q}_k\|_2$
$\quad \mathbf{q}_k \leftarrow \mathbf{q}_k / r_{kk}$

▷ Givens rotations

A faster way to get the QR decomposition of $\mathbf{A}$ is to use a series of rotation matrices applied to $\mathbf{A}$. Let's see how we can get an upper triangular matrix this way. A rotation in the plane is given by

$$\mathbf{Q} = \begin{bmatrix} \cos\theta & -\sin\theta \\ \sin\theta & \cos\theta \end{bmatrix}.$$

By choosing θ appropriately, we can rotate a vector to zero out either the first or the second components. For example, for a vector $\mathbf{x} = (x_1, x_2)$, we can get

$$\hat{\mathbf{x}} = \mathbf{Q}\mathbf{x} = \begin{bmatrix} \sqrt{x_1^2 + x_2^2} \\ 0 \end{bmatrix}$$

by taking

$$\cos\theta = \frac{x_1}{\sqrt{x_1^2 + x_2^2}} \quad \text{and} \quad \sin\theta = -\frac{x_2}{\sqrt{x_1^2 + x_2^2}}.$$

By applying a right rotation $\mathbf{Q}$ to a 2×2 matrix $\mathbf{A}$, we can get

$$\begin{bmatrix} c & -s \\ s & c \end{bmatrix} \begin{bmatrix} a_{11} & a_{12} \\ a_{21} & a_{22} \end{bmatrix} = \begin{bmatrix} * & * \\ 0 & * \end{bmatrix}$$

where for ease of notation we take $c \equiv \cos\theta$ and $s \equiv \sin\theta$.

We can similarly rotate a vector in a plane in higher dimensions. Consider the rotation of the 5×5 matrix $\mathbf{A}$ in the 2–5 plane

$$\mathbf{Q}_{52} = \begin{bmatrix} 1 & & & & \\ & c & & & -s \\ & & 1 & & \\ & & & 1 & \\ & s & & & c \end{bmatrix},$$

which zeros out element 5-2. The product $\mathbf{Q}_{52}\mathbf{A}$ equals

$$\begin{bmatrix} 1 & & & & \\ & c & & & -s \\ & & 1 & & \\ & & & 1 & \\ & s & & & c \end{bmatrix}\begin{bmatrix} a_{11} & a_{12} & a_{13} & a_{14} & a_{15} \\ a_{21} & a_{22} & a_{23} & a_{24} & a_{25} \\ a_{31} & a_{32} & a_{33} & a_{34} & a_{35} \\ a_{41} & a_{42} & a_{43} & a_{44} & a_{45} \\ a_{51} & a_{52} & a_{53} & a_{54} & a_{55} \end{bmatrix} = \begin{bmatrix} a_{11} & a_{12} & a_{13} & a_{14} & a_{15} \\ * & * & * & * & * \\ a_{31} & a_{32} & a_{33} & a_{34} & a_{35} \\ a_{41} & a_{42} & a_{43} & a_{44} & a_{45} \\ * & 0 & * & * & * \end{bmatrix}$$

where rows two and five of the new matrix are simply linear combinations of rows two and five of the original matrix. We can create an upper triangular matrix by starting from the left and working to the right,

For example, consider a 4×4 matrix

$$\mathbf{A} = \begin{bmatrix} \times & \times & \times & \times \\ \times & \times & \times & \times \\ \times & \times & \times & \times \\ \times & \times & \times & \times \end{bmatrix}.$$

By applying three Givens rotations, we can zero out the elements below the first pivot:

$$\mathbf{Q}_{41}\mathbf{Q}_{31}\mathbf{Q}_{21}\mathbf{A} = \begin{bmatrix} \times & \times & \times & \times \\ 0 & \times & \times & \times \\ 0 & \times & \times & \times \\ 0 & \times & \times & \times \end{bmatrix}.$$

By applying another two Givens rotations, we can zero out the elements below the second pivot:

$$\mathbf{Q}_{42}\mathbf{Q}_{32}\mathbf{Q}_{41}\mathbf{Q}_{31}\mathbf{Q}_{21}\mathbf{A} = \begin{bmatrix} \times & \times & \times & \times \\ 0 & \times & \times & \times \\ 0 & 0 & \times & \times \\ 0 & 0 & \times & \times \end{bmatrix}.$$

And by applying one more Givens rotations, we can zero out the element below the third pivot:

$$\mathbf{Q}_{43}\mathbf{Q}_{42}\mathbf{Q}_{32}\mathbf{Q}_{41}\mathbf{Q}_{31}\mathbf{Q}_{21}\mathbf{A} = \begin{bmatrix} \times & \times & \times & \times \\ 0 & \times & \times & \times \\ 0 & 0 & \times & \times \\ 0 & 0 & 0 & \times \end{bmatrix} = \mathbf{R}.$$

So, formally

$$\mathbf{A} = \mathbf{Q}\mathbf{A} = (\mathbf{Q}_{43}\mathbf{Q}_{42}\mathbf{Q}_{32}\mathbf{Q}_{41}\mathbf{Q}_{31}\mathbf{Q}_{21})^{-1}\mathbf{R}.$$

To solve the problem $\mathbf{A}\mathbf{x} = \mathbf{b}$, we instead solve

$$\mathbf{R}\mathbf{x} = \mathbf{Q}_{43}\mathbf{Q}_{42}\mathbf{Q}_{32}\mathbf{Q}_{41}\mathbf{Q}_{31}\mathbf{Q}_{21}\mathbf{b}.$$

♣ The LinearAlgebra.jl function (G,r)=givens(x,i,j) computes the Givens rotation matrix G and scalar r such that (G*x)[i] equals r and (G*x)[j] equals 0.

▷ **Householder reflections**

While Givens rotations zero out one element at a time, *Householder reflections* speed things up by changing whole columns all at once

$$
\begin{array}{cccc}
\mathbf{A} & \mathbf{Q}_1\mathbf{A} & \mathbf{Q}_2\mathbf{Q}_1\mathbf{A} & \mathbf{Q}_3\mathbf{Q}_2\mathbf{Q}_1\mathbf{A}
\end{array}
$$

$$
\begin{bmatrix} \times & \times & \times & \times \\ \times & \times & \times & \times \\ \times & \times & \times & \times \\ \times & \times & \times & \times \end{bmatrix} \rightarrow
\begin{bmatrix} \times & \times & \times & \times \\ 0 & \times & \times & \times \\ 0 & \times & \times & \times \\ 0 & \times & \times & \times \end{bmatrix} \rightarrow
\begin{bmatrix} \times & \times & \times & \times \\ 0 & \times & \times & \times \\ 0 & 0 & \times & \times \\ 0 & 0 & \times & \times \end{bmatrix} \rightarrow
\begin{bmatrix} \times & \times & \times & \times \\ 0 & \times & \times & \times \\ 0 & 0 & \times & \times \\ 0 & 0 & 0 & \times \end{bmatrix}.
$$

We start with the first column $\mathbf{x}$ of the $n \times n$ matrix. Let's find an orthogonal matrix $\mathbf{Q}_1$ such that $\mathbf{Q}_1\mathbf{x} = \mathbf{y}$, where $\mathbf{y} = \pm\|\mathbf{x}\|_2\boldsymbol{\xi}$ with $\boldsymbol{\xi} = (1, 0, \ldots, 0)$ and the sign $\pm$ taken from the first component of $\mathbf{x}$. We can determine $\mathbf{Q}_1$ with a little geometry.

Let $\mathbf{u} = (\mathbf{x} + \mathbf{y})/2$ and $\mathbf{v} = (\mathbf{x} - \mathbf{y})/2$. Then $\mathbf{u}$ is orthogonal to $\mathbf{v}$ and span$\{\mathbf{u}, \mathbf{v}\}$ = span$\{\mathbf{x}, \mathbf{y}\}$, and we can get $\mathbf{y}$ by subtracting twice $\mathbf{v}$ from $\mathbf{x}$. That is to say, we can get $\mathbf{y}$ by subtracting twice the projection of $\mathbf{x}$ in the $\mathbf{v}$ direction: $\mathbf{y} = (\mathbf{I} - 2\mathbf{P}_\mathbf{v})\mathbf{x}$. In general, for any vector in the direction of $\mathbf{v}$, we define the *Householder reflection matrix*:

$$\mathbf{H}_n = \mathbf{I} - 2\mathbf{P}_\mathbf{v} = \mathbf{I} - 2\mathbf{v}\mathbf{v}^\mathsf{T}/\|\mathbf{v}\|_2^2.$$

Because we want $\mathbf{y}$ to be $\pm\|\mathbf{x}\|_2\boldsymbol{\xi}$, we'll take $\mathbf{v} = \mathbf{x} \pm \|\mathbf{x}\|_2\boldsymbol{\xi}$. Technically, we ought to take $\mathbf{v} = (\mathbf{x} \pm \|\mathbf{x}\|_2\boldsymbol{\xi})/2$, but the one-half scaling factor is drops out when we compute $\mathbf{P}_\mathbf{v}$. Geometrically, the Householder matrix $\mathbf{H}_n$ reflects a vector across the subspace span$\{\mathbf{v}\}^\perp$.

In the second step, we want to zero out the second column's subdiagonal elements, leaving the first column unaltered. To do this, we left multiply by the Householder matrix

$$\mathbf{Q}_2 = \begin{bmatrix} 1 & 0 \\ 0 & \mathbf{H}_{n-1} \end{bmatrix}$$

where $\mathbf{H}_{n-1}$ is the $(n-1) \times (n-1)$ Householder matrix that maps an $(n-1)$-dimensional vector $\mathbf{x}$ to the $(n-1)$-dimensional vector $\pm\|\mathbf{x}\|\boldsymbol{\xi}$.

In the kth step, we use the Householder matrix

$$\mathbf{Q}_k = \begin{bmatrix} \mathbf{I}_k & 0 \\ 0 & \mathbf{H}_{n-k} \end{bmatrix}$$

where $\mathbf{H}_{n-k+1}$ is the Householder matrix that maps an $(n - k + 1)$-dimensional vector $\mathbf{x}$ to an $(n - k + 1)$-dimensional vector $\pm\|\mathbf{x}\|_2\boldsymbol{\xi}$.

♣ The LinearAlgebra.jl function qr computes the QR factorization of a matrix using Householder reflection, returning an object that stores an orthogonal matrix and a sequence of Householder reflectors as an upper triangular matrix.

▷ Least-squares problem (again)

Let's reexamine the least squares problem in the context of QR decomposition without first deriving the normal equation. Suppose that $\mathbf{A} \in \mathbb{R}^{m \times n}$ and $\mathbf{b} \in \mathbb{R}^m$ with $m \geq n$. We want to find the $\mathbf{x} \in \mathbb{R}^n$ that minimizes

$$\|\mathbf{r}\|_2 = \|\mathbf{Ax} - \mathbf{b}\|_2.$$

Using QR decomposition, we can rewrite the 2-norm of the residual as

$$\|\mathbf{r}\|_2 = \|\mathbf{QRx} - \mathbf{b}\|_2,$$

where $\mathbf{R}$ is an upper triangular $m \times n$ matrix. Applying an orthogonal matrix to $\mathbf{r}$ doesn't change its length, so

$$\|\mathbf{r}\|_2 = \|\mathbf{Q}^\mathsf{T}\mathbf{r}\|_2 = \|\mathbf{Rx} - \mathbf{Q}^\mathsf{T}\mathbf{b}\|_2.$$

From this expression, we see that the problem of solving $\mathbf{Ax} = \mathbf{b}$ can be replaced with the equivalent problem of solving the upper triangular system $\mathbf{Rx} = \mathbf{c}$ where $\mathbf{c} = \mathbf{Q}^\mathsf{T}\mathbf{b}$. The residual $\mathbf{r}$ of this system

$$\mathbf{r} = \begin{bmatrix} \mathbf{c}_1 \\ \mathbf{c}_2 \end{bmatrix} - \begin{bmatrix} \mathbf{R}_1 \\ \mathbf{0} \end{bmatrix} \mathbf{x} = \begin{bmatrix} \mathbf{c}_1 - \mathbf{R}_1\mathbf{x} \\ \mathbf{c}_2 \end{bmatrix},$$

where $\mathbf{c}_1 \in \mathbb{R}^n$, $\mathbf{c}_2 \in \mathbb{R}^{m-n}$, and $\mathbf{R}_1 \in \mathbb{R}^{n \times n}$. So

$$\|\mathbf{r}\|_2^2 = \|\mathbf{c}_1 - \mathbf{R}_1\mathbf{x}\|_2^2 + \|\mathbf{c}_2\|_2^2.$$

The term $\|\mathbf{c}_2\|_2^2$ is independent of $\mathbf{x}$—it doesn't change $\|\mathbf{r}\|_2^2$ by any amount regardless of the value of $\mathbf{x}$. So the $\mathbf{x}$ that minimizes $\|\mathbf{c}_1 - \mathbf{R}_1\mathbf{x}\|_2$ also minimizes $\|\mathbf{r}\|_2$. And, if $\mathbf{R}_1$ has full rank, then $\|\mathbf{c}_1 - \mathbf{R}_1\mathbf{x}\|_2$ is minimized when precisely

$$\mathbf{R}_1\mathbf{x} = \mathbf{c}_1.$$

On the other hand, what if $\mathbf{R}_1$ does not have full rank? In this case, $\mathbf{R}_1\mathbf{x} = \mathbf{c}_1$ is

$$\begin{bmatrix} \mathbf{R}_{11} & \mathbf{R}_{12} \\ \mathbf{0} & \mathbf{0} \end{bmatrix} \begin{bmatrix} \mathbf{x}_1 \\ \mathbf{x}_2 \end{bmatrix} = \begin{bmatrix} \mathbf{c}_1 \\ \mathbf{c}_2 \end{bmatrix}$$

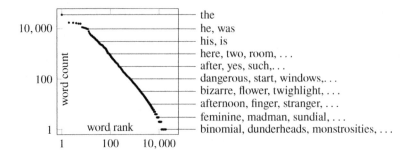

Figure 3.1: Frequency versus rank of words in Sherlock Holmes.

where R_{11} is an upper triangular matrix. Then

$$\|r\|_2^2 = \|c_1 - R_{11}x_1 - R_{12}x_2\|_2^2 + \|c_2\|_2^2,$$

and hence $\|r\|_2^2$ is minimized for any vector x_2 for which

$$R_{11}x_1 = c_1 - R_{12}x_2.$$

In this case, we don't have a unique solution. Instead, we'll need to choose which solution will be the "best" solution. We develop a selection methodology in the next section.

♣ The \ method chooses different algorithms based on the structure of matrices. Solutions to overdetermined systems are computed using pivoted QR factorization.

Example. George Zipf was a linguist who noticed that a few words, like *the*, *is*, *of*, and *and*, are used quite frequently while most words, like *anhydride*, *embryogenesis*, and *jackscrew*, are rarely used at all. By examining word frequency rankings across several corpora, Zipf made a statistical observation, now called Zipf's law. The empirical law states that in any natural language corpus the frequency of any word is inversely proportional to its rank in a frequency table. The most common word is twice as likely to appear as the second most common word, three times as likely to appear as the third most common word, and n times as likely as the nth most common word. For example, 18,951 of the 662,817 words that appear in the canon of Sherlock Holmes by Sir Arthur Conan Doyle are unique. The word *the* appears 36,125 times. *Holmes* appears 3051 times, *Watson* 1038 times, and *Moriarty*[3] appears 54 times. And

---

[3] Professor James Moriarty—criminal mastermind and archenemy of Sherlock Holmes—was a brilliant mathematician who at the age of twenty-one wrote a treatise on the binomial theorem, winning him the mathematical chair at a small university. His book on asteroid dynamics is described as one "which ascends to such rarefied heights of pure mathematics that it is said that there was no man in the scientific press capable of criticizing it."

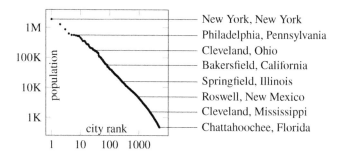

Figure 3.2: Population versus rank of cities in the United States.

there are 6610 words like *binomial, dunderheads, monstrosities, sunburnt,* and *vendetta* that appear only once. See Figure 3.1 on the facing page.

Zipf's power law states that the frequency of the kth most common word is approximately $n_k = n_1 k^{-s}$ where s is some parameter and n_1 is the frequency of the most common word. Let's find the power s for the words in Sherlock Holmes using ordinary least squares and total least squares. First, we'll write the power law in log-linear form: $\log n_k = -s \log k + \log n_1$. The Julia code is

```
using DelimitedFiles
T = readdlm(download(bucket*"sherlock.csv"), '\t')[:,2]
n = length(T)
A = [ones(n,1) log.(1:n)]
B = log.(T)
c = A\B
```

We find that s is -1.165 using least squares. Zipf's law applies to more than just words. We can use it to model the size of cities, the magnitude of earthquakes, and even the distances between galaxies. For example, Figure 3.2 shows the log-log plot of the population of U.S. cities against their associated ranks.[4] We find that s is -0.770.   ◄

3.2   Underdetermined systems

So far, we've assumed that if $\mathbf{A}\mathbf{x} = \mathbf{b}$ has a least squares solution, then it has a unique least squares solution. This assumption is not always valid. If the null space of $\mathbf{A}$ has more than the zero vector, then $\mathbf{A}^{\mathsf{T}}\mathbf{A}$ is not invertible. And the upper triangular submatrix $\mathbf{R}_1$ discussed in the previous section does not have full rank. In this case, the problem has infinitely many solutions. So then,

---

[4]See *UScities.csv* at https://github.com/nmfsc/data

how do we choose which of the infinitely many solutions is the "best" solution? One way is to take the solution $\mathbf{x}$ with the smallest norm $\|\mathbf{x}\|$. This approach is known as *Tikhonov regularization* or *ridge regression*. It works exceptionally well in problems where $\mathbf{x}$ has a zero mean, which frequently appear in statistics by standardizing variables. Let's change our original problem

Find the $\mathbf{x} \in \mathbb{R}^n$ that minimizes $\Phi(\mathbf{x}) = \|\mathbf{A}\mathbf{x} - \mathbf{b}\|_2^2$

to the new problem

Find the $\mathbf{x} \in \mathbb{R}^n$ that minimizes $\Phi(\mathbf{x}) = \|\mathbf{A}\mathbf{x} - \mathbf{b}\|_2^2 + \alpha^2 \|\mathbf{x}\|_2^2$

where α is some regularizing parameter. The result is a solution that fits $\mathbf{x}$ to $\mathbf{b}$ but penalizes solutions with large norms. Minimizing $\|\mathbf{A}\mathbf{x} - \mathbf{b}\|_2^2 + \alpha^2 \|\mathbf{x}\|_2^2$ is equivalent to solving the stacked-matrix equation

$$\begin{bmatrix} \mathbf{A} \\ \alpha\mathbf{I} \end{bmatrix} \mathbf{x} = \begin{bmatrix} \mathbf{b} \\ \mathbf{0} \end{bmatrix}, \tag{3.1}$$

which we can do using least squares methods such as QR factorization.

Let's also examine the normal equation solution to the regularized minimization problem. As before, solve the minimization problem by finding the $\mathbf{x}$ such that $\nabla\Phi(\mathbf{x}) = \mathbf{0}$. We have $2\mathbf{A}^{\mathsf{T}}\mathbf{A}\mathbf{x} - 2\mathbf{A}^{\mathsf{T}}\mathbf{b} + 2\alpha^2\tilde{\mathbf{x}} = \mathbf{0}$, which we can solve to get

$$\mathbf{x} = (\mathbf{A}^{\mathsf{T}}\mathbf{A} + \alpha^2\mathbf{I})^{-1}\mathbf{A}^{\mathsf{T}}\mathbf{b} = \mathbf{R}_\alpha \mathbf{b}. \tag{3.2}$$

When $\mathbf{A}$ has many more columns than rows, computing the QR factorization of the stacked-matrix equation (3.1) or the regularized normal equation (3.2) can be inefficient because we are working with even larger matrices. However, by noting that $\mathbf{A}^{\mathsf{T}}(\mathbf{A}\mathbf{A}^{\mathsf{T}} + \alpha^2\mathbf{I}) = (\mathbf{A}^{\mathsf{T}}\mathbf{A} + \alpha^2\mathbf{I})\mathbf{A}^{\mathsf{T}}$, we have

$$(\mathbf{A}^{\mathsf{T}}\mathbf{A} + \alpha^2\mathbf{I})^{-1}\mathbf{A}^{\mathsf{T}} = \mathbf{A}^{\mathsf{T}}(\mathbf{A}\mathbf{A}^{\mathsf{T}} + \alpha^2\mathbf{I})^{-1}.$$

So we can instead compute $\tilde{\mathbf{x}} = \mathbf{A}^{\mathsf{T}}(\mathbf{A}\mathbf{A}^{\mathsf{T}} + \alpha^2\mathbf{I})^{-1}\mathbf{b}$.

Example.   Photographs sometimes have motion or focal blur and noise, something we might want to remove or minimize. Suppose that $\mathbf{x}$ is some original image and $\mathbf{y} = \mathbf{A}\mathbf{x} + \mathbf{n}$ is the observed image, where $\mathbf{A}$ is a blurring matrix and $\mathbf{n}$ is a noise vector. The blurring matrix $\mathbf{A}$ does not have a unique inverse, so the problem is ill-posed. Compare the following images:

The first image (a) shows the original image $\mathbf{x}$. Blur and noise have been added to this image to get the second image $\mathbf{y} = \mathbf{A}\mathbf{x} + \mathbf{n}$. Image (c) shows the solution using the least squares method $(\mathbf{A}^T\mathbf{A})^{-1}\mathbf{A}^T\mathbf{y}$. Because the blurring matrix $\mathbf{A}$ has a nonzero null space, there are multiple (infinitely many) possible solutions for the least squares algorithm. The method fails. Image (d) shows the regularized least squares solution $(\mathbf{A}^T\mathbf{A} + \alpha^2\mathbf{I})^{-1}\mathbf{A}^T\mathbf{y}$ for a well-chosen α. I think that this one is the winner. Image (e) shows the pseudoinverse $\mathbf{A}^+\mathbf{y}$. This one is also good, although perhaps not as good as the regularized least squares solution. ◄

▷ Multiobjective least squares

A regularized solution to an underdetermined system is a special case of a simultaneous solution to two or more systems of equations—$\mathbf{A}\mathbf{x} = \mathbf{b}$ and $\mathbf{C}\mathbf{x} = \mathbf{d}$. We can solve such a problem by stacking the two systems along with a positive weight α to have the residual

$$\mathbf{r} = \begin{bmatrix} \mathbf{r}_1 \\ \alpha\mathbf{r}_2 \end{bmatrix} = \begin{bmatrix} (\mathbf{A}\mathbf{x} - \mathbf{b}) \\ \alpha(\mathbf{C}\mathbf{x} - \mathbf{d}) \end{bmatrix}.$$

The weight α^2 determines the relative importance of each objective $\|\mathbf{r}_1\|_2^2$ and $\|\mathbf{r}_2\|_2^2$. We then minimize $\|\mathbf{r}\|_2^2 = \|\mathbf{r}_1\|_2^2 + \alpha^2\|\mathbf{r}_2\|_2^2$ by solving

$$\begin{bmatrix} \mathbf{A} \\ \alpha\mathbf{C} \end{bmatrix} \mathbf{x} = \begin{bmatrix} \mathbf{b} \\ \alpha\mathbf{d} \end{bmatrix}$$

using QR decomposition or the normal equations. In the case of $\mathbf{C} = \mathbf{I}$ and $\mathbf{d} = \mathbf{0}$, we simply have the Tikhonov regularized least squares. And, of course, we can extend the problem to any number of objective values.

▷ Constrained least squares

A constrained least squares problem consists of two systems of equations—one $\mathbf{A}\mathbf{x} = \mathbf{b}$ that we are trying to fit as closely as possible and one $\mathbf{C}\mathbf{x} = \mathbf{d}$ that must absolutely fit. For example, $\mathbf{A}\mathbf{x} = \mathbf{b}$ could be a Vandermonde system for points of a piecewise polynomial curve, and $\mathbf{C}\mathbf{x} = \mathbf{d}$ could be the matching conditions at the knots. The number of constraints $\mathbf{C}\mathbf{x} = \mathbf{d}$ must be fewer than the number of variables.

We can solve this problem by using the Lagrangian function

$$\mathcal{L}(\mathbf{x}, \lambda) = \tfrac{1}{2}\|\mathbf{A}\mathbf{x} - \mathbf{b}\|_2^2 + \lambda^T(\mathbf{C}\mathbf{x} - \mathbf{d}),$$

where the λ is a vector of Lagrange multipliers. The pair $(\tilde{\mathbf{x}}, \lambda)$ is a solution to the constrained minimization problem when $\nabla\mathcal{L}(\mathbf{x}, \lambda) = \mathbf{0}$. The zero gradient gives us the systems of equation $\mathbf{A}^T\mathbf{A}\tilde{\mathbf{x}} - \mathbf{A}^T\mathbf{b} + \mathbf{C}^T\lambda = 0$, which we can rewrite along with the system of constraints $\mathbf{C}\tilde{\mathbf{x}} = \mathbf{d}$ in block matrix form

$$\begin{bmatrix} \mathbf{A}^T\mathbf{A} & \mathbf{C}^T \\ \mathbf{C} & \mathbf{0} \end{bmatrix} \begin{bmatrix} \tilde{\mathbf{x}} \\ \lambda \end{bmatrix} = \begin{bmatrix} \mathbf{A}^T\mathbf{b} \\ \mathbf{d} \end{bmatrix}.$$

Using Julia, we have

```
function constrained_lstsq(A,b,C,d)
  x = [A'*A C'; C zeros(size(C,1),size(C,1))]\[A'*b;d]
  x[1:size(A,2)]
end
```

where A is $m \times n$, b is $m \times 1$, C is $p \times n$, and d is $p \times 1$ with $p \le m$.

The method of Lagrange multipliers is generalized by the Karush–Kuhn–Tucker (KKT) conditions. Suppose we want to optimize an objective function $f(\mathbf{x})$ subject to constraints $\mathbf{g}(\mathbf{x}) \ge 0$ and $\mathbf{h}(\mathbf{x}) = 0$, where $\mathbf{x}$ is the optimization variables in a convex subset of $\mathbb{R}^n$. For the corresponding Lagrangian function $\mathcal{L}(\mathbf{x}, \mu, \lambda) = f(\mathbf{x}) + \mu^T\mathbf{g}(\mathbf{x}) + \lambda^T\mathbf{h}(\mathbf{x})$, the value $\mathbf{x}^*$ is a local minimum if the following KKT conditions hold:

- $\nabla\mathcal{L}(\mathbf{x}^*, \mu, \lambda) = \nabla f(\mathbf{x}^*) - \mu^T\nabla\mathbf{g}(\mathbf{x}^*) - \lambda^T\mathbf{h}(\mathbf{x}^*) = \mathbf{0}$ (stationarity)
- $\mathbf{g}(\mathbf{x}^*) \ge 0$ and $\nabla\mathbf{h}(\mathbf{x}^*) = \mathbf{0}$ (primal feasibility)
- $\mu \ge 0$ (dual feasibility)
- $\mu \circ \mathbf{g}(\mathbf{x}^*) = \mathbf{0}$ (complementary slackness)

where $\circ$ is component-wise (Hadamard) multiplication.

▷ Sparse least squares

QR decomposition and Gram matrices both fill in sparse matrices. We can avoid fill-in by rewriting the normal equation $\mathbf{A}^T\mathbf{A}\mathbf{x} = \mathbf{A}^T\mathbf{b}$ as a expanded block system using the residual. Because the residual $\mathbf{r} = \mathbf{b} - \mathbf{A}\mathbf{x}$ is in the left null space of $\mathbf{A}$, it follows that $\mathbf{A}^T\mathbf{r} = \mathbf{0}$. From these two equations, we have

$$\begin{bmatrix} \mathbf{0} & \mathbf{A}^T \\ \mathbf{A} & \mathbf{I} \end{bmatrix} \begin{bmatrix} \mathbf{x} \\ \mathbf{r} \end{bmatrix} = \begin{bmatrix} \mathbf{0} \\ \mathbf{b} \end{bmatrix}.$$

This new matrix maintains the sparsity and can be solved using an iterative method such as the symmetric conjugate-gradient method that will be discussed in Chapter 5. Similarly, a sparse constrained least squares problem can be rewritten as

$$\begin{bmatrix} \mathbf{0} & \mathbf{A}^T & \mathbf{C}^T \\ \mathbf{A} & \mathbf{I} & \mathbf{0} \\ \mathbf{C} & \mathbf{0} & \mathbf{0} \end{bmatrix} \begin{bmatrix} \mathbf{x} \\ \mathbf{r} \\ \lambda \end{bmatrix} = \begin{bmatrix} \mathbf{0} \\ \mathbf{b} \\ \mathbf{d} \end{bmatrix}.$$

3.3   Singular value decomposition

Another way to solve the least squares problem is by singular value decomposition. Recall that for the inconsistent and underdetermined problem

$$\mathbf{A}(\mathbf{x}_{\text{row}} + \mathbf{x}_{\text{null}}) = \mathbf{b}_{\text{column}} + \mathbf{b}_{\text{left null}},$$

we minimize $\|\mathbf{b} - \mathbf{A}\mathbf{x}\|_2$ by forcing $\mathbf{b}_{\text{left null}} = \mathbf{0}$ and ensure a unique solution $\|\mathbf{x}\|_2$ by forcing $\mathbf{x}_{\text{null}} = \mathbf{0}$. We can use singular value decomposition to both zero out the left null space and zero out the null space. A matrix's singular value decomposition is $\mathbf{A} = \mathbf{U}\mathbf{\Sigma}\mathbf{V}^{\mathsf{T}}$, where $\mathbf{U}$ and $\mathbf{V}$ are orthogonal matrices and $\mathbf{\Sigma}$ is a diagonal matrix of singular values. By convention, the singular values σ_i are in descending order $\sigma_1 \geq \sigma_2 \geq \cdots \geq \sigma_n \geq 0$. This ordering is also a natural result of the SVD algorithm, which we study in the next chapter after developing tools for finding eigenvalues. In this section, we look at applications of singular value decomposition.

The SVD of an $m \times n$ matrix $\mathbf{A}$ is an $m \times m$ matrix $\mathbf{U}$, an $m \times n$ diagonal matrix $\mathbf{\Sigma}$, and an $n \times n$ matrix $\mathbf{V}^{\mathsf{T}}$. The columns of $\mathbf{U}$ are called left singular vectors and the columns of $\mathbf{V}$ are called the right singular vectors. When $m > n$, only the first n left singular vectors are needed to reconstruct $\mathbf{A}$. The other columns are superfluous. In this case, it's more efficient to use the *thin* or *economy* SVD—an $m \times n$ matrix $\mathbf{U}$, an $n \times n$ diagonal matrix $\mathbf{\Sigma}$, and an $n \times n$ matrix $\mathbf{V}^{\mathsf{T}}$. See Figure 3.3 on the next page. The same holds for low-rank matrices. For a matrix $\mathbf{A}$ with rank r,

- the first r columns of $\mathbf{U}$ span the column space of $\mathbf{A}$,
- the last $m - r$ columns of $\mathbf{U}$ span the left null space of $\mathbf{A}$,
- the first r columns of $\mathbf{V}$ span the row space of $\mathbf{A}$, and
- the last $n - r$ columns of $\mathbf{V}$ span the null space of $\mathbf{A}$.

We can reconstruct $\mathbf{A}$ using an $m \times r$ matrix $\mathbf{U}$, an $r \times r$ diagonal matrix $\mathbf{\Sigma}$, and an $r \times n$ matrix $\mathbf{V}^{\mathsf{T}}$. This type of a reduced SVD is called a *compact* SVD.

Small singular values do not contribute much information to $\mathbf{A}$. By keeping the k largest singular values and the corresponding singular vectors, we get the closest rank k approximation to $\mathbf{A}$ in the Frobenius norm. The *truncated* SVD of $\mathbf{A}$ is given by an $m \times k$ matrix $\mathbf{U}_k$, an $k \times k$ diagonal matrix $\mathbf{\Sigma}_k$, and an $k \times n$ matrix $\mathbf{V}_k^{\mathsf{T}}$. Truncated SVDs have several different uses—reducing the memory needed to store a matrix, making computations faster, simplifying problems by projecting the data to lower-dimensional subspaces, and regularizing problems by reducing a matrix's condition number.

♣ The LinearAlgebra.jl function svd(A) returns the SVD of matrix A as an object. Singular values are in descending order. When the option full=false (default), the function returns a economy SVD. The function svds(A,k) returns an object containing the first k (default is 6) singular values and associated singular vectors.

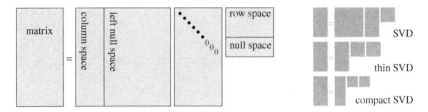

Figure 3.3: The SVD breaks a matrix into the orthonormal bases of its four fundamental subspaces—its column space and left null space along with its row space and null space—coupled through a diagonal matrix of singular values.

▷ **Pseudoinverse**

Let $\mathbf{A}$ be an $m \times n$ matrix with the singular value decomposition $\mathbf{U\Sigma V}^\mathsf{T}$. When $\mathbf{A}$ is nonsingular, its inverse $\mathbf{A}^{-1} = \mathbf{V\Sigma}^{-1}\mathbf{U}^\mathsf{T}$. The matrix $\mathbf{\Sigma}^{-1}$ is a diagonal matrix of the reciprocals of the singular values. The *Moore–Penrose pseudoinverse* of $\mathbf{A}$ is an $n \times m$ matrix defined as $\mathbf{A}^{+} = \mathbf{V\Sigma}^{+}\mathbf{U}^\mathsf{T}$. The matrix $\mathbf{\Sigma}^{+}$ is a diagonal matrix of the reciprocals of the nonzero elements of $\mathbf{\Sigma}$, leaving the zero elements unchanged. The singular vectors corresponding to the zero singular values are in the null space and left null space of $\mathbf{A}$. By fixing the zero elements of $\mathbf{\Sigma}$, we are choosing the zero vectors from the null space and the left null space of $\mathbf{A}$, which ensures that a pseudoinverse exists and that it is unique. For an $m \times n$ matrix $\mathbf{A}$ with rank r:

dimensions	$\mathbf{A}^{+}\mathbf{b}$
$m = n = r$	$\mathbf{A}^{-1}\mathbf{b}$
$m > n = r$	$\arg\min_{\mathbf{x}} \|\mathbf{b} - \mathbf{Ax}\|_2$ and $\mathbf{A}^{+} = (\mathbf{A}^\mathsf{T}\mathbf{A})^{-1}\mathbf{A}^\mathsf{T}$
$n > m = r$	rowspace projection of $\mathbf{b}$ and $\mathbf{A}^{+} = \mathbf{A}(\mathbf{AA}^\mathsf{T})^{-1}$
$n \geq m > r$	$\arg\min_{\mathbf{x}} \|\mathbf{b} - \mathbf{Ax}\|_2$ using the rowspace projection of $\mathbf{b}$

We also can use the pseudoinverse to regularize an ill-conditioned problem. The 2-condition number of a matrix is given by the ratio of the largest to smallest singular values to σ_1/σ_r. By zeroing out the singular values below a threshold α, we lower the condition number to under σ_1/α and solve the problem in a lower-dimensional subspace.

Example. Consider the $n \times n$ Hilbert matrix, whose ij-element equals $(i+j-1)^{-1}$. We examined this matrix and its inverse using Gaussian elimination on page 23. Hilbert matrices are poorly conditioned even for relatively small n. The density plots of the matrices `pinv(hilbert(n))*hilbert(n)` for $n = 0, 15, 20, 25,$ and 50 are below. Zero values are white, values with magnitude one or greater are black, and intermediate values are shades of gray.

$n = 10$ $n = 15$ $n = 20$ $n = 25$ $n = 50$

The pseudoinverse has noticeable error even for small matrices. But unlike Gaussian elimination, which falls flat on its face, the pseudoinverse solution fails with grace. The pseudoinverse truncates all singular values less than 10^{-15} which happens near σ_8, effectively reducing the problem to using a rank-8 matrix. ◄

♣ The LinearAlgebra.jl function `pinv` computes the Moore–Penrose pseudoinverse by computing the SVD with a default tolerance of `minimum(size(A))*eps()`. A tolerance of `sqrt(eps())` is recommended for least squares problems.

▷ Tikhonov regularization

Tikhonov regularization introduced the previous section and the pseudoinverse discussed above each provide ways to solve underdetermined problems. The two procedures are related. Recall Tikhonov regularization $\hat{\mathbf{x}} = \mathbf{R}_\alpha \mathbf{b}$ where $\mathbf{R}_\alpha = (\mathbf{A}^\mathsf{T}\mathbf{A} + \alpha^2\mathbf{I})^{-1}\mathbf{A}^\mathsf{T}$. If $\mathbf{A} = \mathbf{U}\boldsymbol{\Sigma}\mathbf{V}^\mathsf{T}$, then

$$\mathbf{R}_\alpha = (\mathbf{V}\boldsymbol{\Sigma}\mathbf{U}^\mathsf{T}\mathbf{U}\boldsymbol{\Sigma}\mathbf{V}^\mathsf{T} + \alpha^2\mathbf{V}\boldsymbol{\Sigma}\mathbf{I}\mathbf{V}^\mathsf{T})^{-1}\mathbf{V}\boldsymbol{\Sigma}\mathbf{U}^\mathsf{T}$$
$$= (\mathbf{V}\boldsymbol{\Sigma}^2\mathbf{V}^\mathsf{T} + \alpha^2\mathbf{V}\boldsymbol{\Sigma}\mathbf{I}\mathbf{V}^\mathsf{T})^{-1}\mathbf{V}\boldsymbol{\Sigma}\mathbf{U}^\mathsf{T}$$
$$= \mathbf{V}(\boldsymbol{\Sigma}^2 + \alpha^2\mathbf{I})^{-1}\boldsymbol{\Sigma}\mathbf{U}^\mathsf{T}$$
$$= \mathbf{V}\boldsymbol{\Sigma}_\alpha^{-1}\mathbf{U}^\mathsf{T}$$

where $\boldsymbol{\Sigma}_\alpha^{-1}$ is a diagonal matrix with diagonal components

$$\frac{\sigma_i}{\sigma_i^2 + \alpha^2}.$$

It is useful to rewrite these components as

$$\frac{\sigma_i^2}{\sigma_i^2 + \alpha^2}\frac{1}{\sigma_i} = w_\alpha(\sigma_i)\frac{1}{\sigma_i}$$

where $w_\alpha(\sigma_i)$ is the *Wiener weight*. From this, we see that Tikhonov regularization is simply a smooth filter applied to the singular values. The truncated SVD filter

$$w_\alpha^{\text{TSVD}}(\sigma) = \begin{cases} 0, & \sigma \leq \alpha \\ 1, & \sigma > \alpha \end{cases}$$

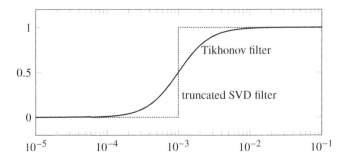

Figure 3.4: Comparison of the Tikhonov filter for $\alpha = 10^{-3}$ and the truncated SVD filter with singular values zeroed out below 10^{-3}.

exhibits a sharp cut-off at α. See Figure 3.4. Because of this, Tikhonov regularization may outperform the pseudoinverse.

▷ Principal component analysis

Principal component analysis, or PCA, is a statistical method that uses singular value decomposition to generate a low-rank approximation of a matrix. We can write an $m \times n$ matrix $\mathbf{A}$ as the sum of rank-one, mutually orthogonal *principal components* $\mathbf{A} = \mathbf{U\Sigma V}^{\mathsf{T}} = \mathbf{E}_1 + \mathbf{E}_2 + \cdots + \mathbf{E}_r$ where $\mathbf{E}_i = \sigma_i \mathbf{u}_i \mathbf{v}_i^{\mathsf{T}}$ and r is the rank of $\mathbf{A}$. We can get a lower rank-k approximation $\mathbf{A}_k$ to $\mathbf{A}$ by truncating the sum $\mathbf{A}_k = \mathbf{E}_1 + \mathbf{E}_2 + \cdots + \mathbf{E}_k$. In fact, the matrix $\mathbf{A}_k$ is the best rank-k approximation to $\mathbf{A}$.

Theorem 9 (Eckart–Young–Mirsky theorem). *Let* $\mathbf{A}_k = \sum_{i=1}^{k} \sigma_i \mathbf{u}_i \mathbf{v}_i^{\mathsf{T}}$ *be a rank-k approximation to* $\mathbf{A} = \sum_{i=1}^{r} \sigma_i \mathbf{u}_i \mathbf{v}_i^{\mathsf{T}}$. *If* $\mathbf{B}$ *is any rank-k matrix, then* $\|\mathbf{A} - \mathbf{A}_k\| \leq \|\mathbf{A} - \mathbf{B}\|$ *in both the spectral and Frobenius norms.*

Proof. Let's start with the spectral norm. A rank-k matrix $\mathbf{B}$ can be expressed as the product $\mathbf{XY}^{\mathsf{T}}$ where $\mathbf{X}$ and $\mathbf{Y}$ have k columns. Then because $\mathbf{Y}$ has only rank k, there is a unit vector $\mathbf{w} = \gamma_1 \mathbf{v}_1 + \cdots + \gamma_{k+1} \mathbf{v}_{k+1}$ such that $\mathbf{Y}^{\mathsf{T}}\mathbf{w} = 0$. Furthermore, $\mathbf{Aw} = \sum_{i=1}^{k+1} \gamma_i \sigma_i \mathbf{u}_i$ from which $\|\mathbf{Aw}\|_2^2 = \sum_{i=1}^{k+1} |\gamma_i \sigma_i|_2^2$. Then

$$\|\mathbf{A} - \mathbf{B}\|_2^2 \geq \|(\mathbf{A} - \mathbf{B})\mathbf{w}\|_2^2 = \|\mathbf{Aw}\|_2^2 \geq \sigma_{k+1}^2 = \|\mathbf{A} - \mathbf{A}_k\|_2^2.$$

Now, consider the Frobenius norm. Let a subscript i denote an approximation using the first i principal components.

$$\sigma_i(\mathbf{A} - \mathbf{B}) = \sigma_1((\mathbf{A} - \mathbf{B}) - (\mathbf{A} - \mathbf{B})_{i-1}) \geq \sigma_1(\mathbf{A} - \mathbf{A}_{k+i-1}) = \sigma_{k+i}(\mathbf{A}),$$

where the inequality follows from the results about the spectral norm above because rank $(\mathbf{B} + (\mathbf{A} - \mathbf{B})_{i-1}) \leq \operatorname{rank} \mathbf{A}_{k+i-1}$. So,

$$\|\mathbf{A} - \mathbf{B}\|_{\mathrm{F}}^2 = \sum_{i=1}^{r} \sigma_i(\mathbf{A} - \mathbf{B})^2 \geq \sum_{i=k+1}^{r} \sigma_i(\mathbf{A})^2 = \|\mathbf{A} - \mathbf{A}_k\|_{\mathrm{F}}^2. \qquad \square$$

Suppose that we measure the heights $\mathbf{h}$ and weights $\mathbf{w}$ of 50 people. Let $\mathbf{A}$ be the 50×2 standardized data matrix, whose first column is the mean-centered heights $\mathbf{h} - \overline{\mathbf{h}}$ and whose second column is the mean-centered weights $\mathbf{w} - \overline{\mathbf{w}}$. The matrix $\mathbf{A}^{\mathsf{T}}\mathbf{A}$ is the covariance matrix. If height is linearly correlated to weight, a variable $\sigma_1 \mathbf{u}_1$ in the direction of the first left singular vector incorporates everyone's heights and weights. The vector $\mathbf{u}_1$ is a point on a 50-dimensional unit sphere, and every person gets their own axis. A second variable $\sigma_2 \mathbf{u}_2$ in the direction of the second left singular vector accounts for the variation in the heights and weights. The vector $\mathbf{u}_2$ is also on the unit sphere, orthogonal to $\mathbf{u}_1$. A rank-one approximation $\mathbf{A}_1 = \sigma_1 \mathbf{u}_1 \mathbf{v}_1^{\mathsf{T}}$ eliminates the contribution from that second variable. Consider the following figures:

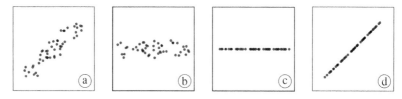

(a) The data in $\mathbf{A}$ lie for the most part along a direction $\mathbf{v}_1$ with a small orthogonal component in direction $\mathbf{v}_2$. (b) The matrix $\mathbf{AV}$ is a rotation of the heights and weights onto the x- and y-axes. (c) We keep only the first principal component— now along the x-axes—and discard the second principal component—the offsets in the y-direction. (d) After rotating back to our original basis, all the data lie along the $\mathbf{v}_1$-direction.

Unlike least squares fit, which would project the data "vertically" onto the height-weight line, principal component analysis projects the data orthogonally onto the height-weight line. Consider the scatter plots below.

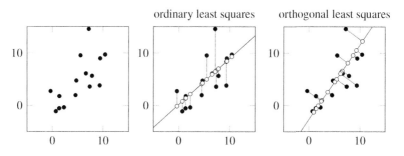

The original data ● are shown in the scatter plot on the left. The least squares approach shown in the center figure is an orthogonal projection of the y-components into the column space of the 15×2 Vandermonde matrix. Principal component analysis is an orthogonal projection into the first right singular vector. Note the difference in the solutions using ordinary least squares fit and orthogonal least squares fit. Neither the points ○ nor the line are the same in either figure.

▷ Total least squares

Let's dig deeper into orthogonal least squares, also known as total least squares. We solved the ordinary least squares problem $\mathbf{A}\mathbf{x} = \mathbf{b}$ by determining the solution to a similar problem: choose the solution to $\mathbf{A}\mathbf{x} = \mathbf{b} + \delta\mathbf{b}$ that has the smallest residual $\|\delta\mathbf{b}\|_2$. We can generalize the problem of finding the solution to $\mathbf{A}\mathbf{X} = \mathbf{B}$ by minimizing the norm of the residual the only with respect to the dependent terms $\mathbf{B}$ but also with respect to the independent terms $\mathbf{A}$. That is, find the smallest $\delta\mathbf{A}$ and $\delta\mathbf{B}$ that satisfies $(\mathbf{A} + \delta\mathbf{A})\mathbf{X} = \mathbf{B} + \delta\mathbf{B}$. Such a problem is called the total least squares problem. In two dimensions, total least squares regression is calledDeming regression or orthogonal regression. Let's examine the general case and take $\mathbf{A}$ to be an $m \times n$ matrix, $\mathbf{X}$ to be an $n \times p$ matrix, and $\mathbf{B}$ to be an $m \times p$ matrix.

We can write the total least squares problem $(\mathbf{A} + \delta\mathbf{A})\mathbf{X} = \mathbf{B} + \delta\mathbf{B}$ using block matrices

$$\begin{bmatrix} \mathbf{A} + \delta\mathbf{A} & \mathbf{B} + \delta\mathbf{B} \end{bmatrix} \begin{bmatrix} \mathbf{X} \\ -\mathbf{I} \end{bmatrix} = \mathbf{0}. \tag{3.3}$$

We want to find

$$\operatorname*{arg\,min}_{\delta\mathbf{A},\delta\mathbf{B}} \left\| \begin{bmatrix} \delta\mathbf{A} & \delta\mathbf{B} \end{bmatrix} \right\|_{\mathrm{F}}.$$

Take the singular value decomposition $\mathbf{U}\boldsymbol{\Sigma}\mathbf{V}^{\mathsf{T}} = \begin{bmatrix} \mathbf{A} & \mathbf{B} \end{bmatrix}$:

$$\begin{bmatrix} \mathbf{A} & \mathbf{B} \end{bmatrix} = \begin{bmatrix} \mathbf{U}_1 & \mathbf{U}_2 \end{bmatrix} \begin{bmatrix} \boldsymbol{\Sigma}_1 & \mathbf{0} \\ \mathbf{0} & \boldsymbol{\Sigma}_2 \end{bmatrix} \begin{bmatrix} \mathbf{V}_{11} & \mathbf{V}_{12} \\ \mathbf{V}_{21} & \mathbf{V}_{22} \end{bmatrix}^{\mathsf{T}},$$

where $\mathbf{U}_1$, $\boldsymbol{\Sigma}_1$, $\mathbf{V}_{11}$, and $\mathbf{V}_{12}$ have n columns like $\mathbf{A}$ and $\mathbf{U}_2$, $\boldsymbol{\Sigma}_2$, $\mathbf{V}_{21}$, and $\mathbf{V}_{22}$ have p columns like $\mathbf{B}$. By the Eckart–Young–Mirsky theorem, the terms $\delta\mathbf{A}$ and $\delta\mathbf{B}$ are those for which

$$\begin{bmatrix} \mathbf{A} + \delta\mathbf{A} & \mathbf{B} + \delta\mathbf{B} \end{bmatrix} = \begin{bmatrix} \mathbf{U}_1 & \mathbf{U}_2 \end{bmatrix} \begin{bmatrix} \boldsymbol{\Sigma}_1 & \mathbf{0} \\ \mathbf{0} & \mathbf{0} \end{bmatrix} \begin{bmatrix} \mathbf{V}_{11} & \mathbf{V}_{12} \\ \mathbf{V}_{21} & \mathbf{V}_{22} \end{bmatrix}^{\mathsf{T}}.$$

By linearity,

$$\begin{bmatrix} \delta\mathbf{A} & \delta\mathbf{B} \end{bmatrix} = -\begin{bmatrix} \mathbf{U}_1 & \mathbf{U}_2 \end{bmatrix} \begin{bmatrix} \mathbf{0} & \mathbf{0} \\ \mathbf{0} & \Sigma_2 \end{bmatrix} \begin{bmatrix} \mathbf{V}_{11} & \mathbf{V}_{12} \\ \mathbf{V}_{21} & \mathbf{V}_{22} \end{bmatrix}^{\mathsf{T}}$$

$$= -\mathbf{U}_2\Sigma_2 \begin{bmatrix} \mathbf{V}_{12} \\ \mathbf{V}_{22} \end{bmatrix}^{\mathsf{T}}$$

$$= -\begin{bmatrix} \mathbf{A} & \mathbf{B} \end{bmatrix} \begin{bmatrix} \mathbf{V}_{12} \\ \mathbf{V}_{22} \end{bmatrix} \begin{bmatrix} \mathbf{V}_{12} \\ \mathbf{V}_{22} \end{bmatrix}^{\mathsf{T}}.$$

Equivalently,

$$\begin{bmatrix} \delta\mathbf{A} & \delta\mathbf{B} \end{bmatrix} \begin{bmatrix} \mathbf{V}_{12} \\ \mathbf{V}_{22} \end{bmatrix} = -\begin{bmatrix} \mathbf{A} & \mathbf{B} \end{bmatrix} \begin{bmatrix} \mathbf{V}_{12} \\ \mathbf{V}_{22} \end{bmatrix}$$

or

$$\begin{bmatrix} \mathbf{A} + \delta\mathbf{A} & \mathbf{B} + \delta\mathbf{B} \end{bmatrix} \begin{bmatrix} \mathbf{V}_{12} \\ \mathbf{V}_{22} \end{bmatrix} = \mathbf{0}.$$

If $\mathbf{V}_{22}$ is nonsingular, then

$$\begin{bmatrix} \mathbf{A} + \delta\mathbf{A} & \mathbf{B} + \delta\mathbf{B} \end{bmatrix} \begin{bmatrix} \mathbf{V}_{12}\mathbf{V}_{22}^{-1} \\ \mathbf{I} \end{bmatrix} = \mathbf{0}.$$

So from (3.3), we have

$$\mathbf{X} = -\mathbf{V}_{12}\mathbf{V}_{22}^{-1}.$$

We can implement the total least squares solution in Julia with

```julia
function tls(A,B)
  n = size(A,2)
  V = svd([A B]).V
  -V[1:n,n+1:end]/V[n+1:end,n+1:end]
end
```

Example.   Let's find the intersections of four lines $2x + 4y = 1$, $x - y = 1$, $3x + y = 4$, and $4x - 8y = 1$. While there is no solution, we can find a best solution. This problem has the matrix form $\mathbf{Ax} = \mathbf{b}$, where the elements of $\mathbf{A}$ are the coefficients of x and y, $\mathbf{x}$ is the coordinates (x, y), and the vector $\mathbf{b}$ is the set of constants.

```julia
A = [2 4; 1 -1; 3 1; 4 -8]; b = [1; 1; 4; 1];
xols = A\b; xtls = tls(A,b)
```

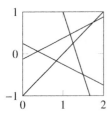 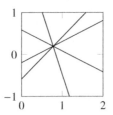 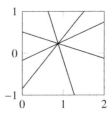

The figure on the left above shows the original lines. The middle one shows the ordinary least squares $\mathbf{A}\mathbf{x} = \mathbf{b} + \delta\mathbf{b}$ solution of around $(0.777, 0.196)$. The solution slides the lines around the plane to find the intersection but does not change their slopes. The one on the right shows the total least squares solution $(\mathbf{A} + \delta\mathbf{A})\mathbf{x} = \mathbf{b} + \delta\mathbf{b}$ solution of around $(0.877, 0.230)$. Now, lines can slide around the plane and change their slopes. ◄

▷ Rank reduction and image compression

Singular value decomposition is sometimes used to demonstrate image compression. In practice, other common approaches are much faster and more effective. For example, JPEG compression uses discrete cosine transforms and JPEG 2000 uses discrete wavelet transforms to significantly reduce file size without a significant reduction in image quality, particularly on images with smooth gradients like photographs. Lossless methods such as PNG and GIF reduce file size without any loss in quality by finding patterns in the data.[5] On the other hand, singular value decomposition is slow, and even moderate compression can result in noticeable artifacts. Furthermore, singular value decomposition produces matrices containing positive and negative floating-point values that must be quantized. Storing these matrices may require more space than the original raw image. Nonetheless, examining SVD image compression is worthwhile because it can help us better understand how an SVD works on other structured data that we might want to reduce in rank using singular value decomposition.

A typical image format such as a JPEG or PNG will use one byte to quantize each pixel for each color. One byte (8 bits) is sufficient for 256 shades of gray, and three bytes (24 bits) are enough for three red-green-blue (RGB) or hue-saturation-value (HSV) channels. Three bytes produce 2^{24} (or roughly 16 million) color variations.[6] We can think of a raw m-by-n grayscale bitmap image as an $m \times n$ matrix and then compute an economy SVD of that matrix, storing the resulting right and left singular matrices along with the corresponding singular

---

[5] Deflate compression used in PNGs combines Huffman coding that generates a dictionary to replace frequently occurring sequences of bits with short ones and Lempel–Ziv–Storer–Szymanski (LZSS) compression that replaces repeated sequences of bits with pointers to earlier occurrences.

[6] A GIF only supports an 8-bit color palette for each image, which results in posterization and makes it less suitable for color photographs. On the other hand, a PNG will support 16 bits per channel.

values. A color image consists of three channels, and the corresponding matrix is $m \times 3n$. Let's consider the SVD of a grayscale image $\mathbf{A} = \mathbf{U\Sigma V}^\mathsf{T}$:

```
using Images
A = load(download(bucket*"laura.png")) .|> Gray
U, σ, V = svd(A);
```

Then a rank-k approximation to $\mathbf{A}$ is $\mathbf{A}_k = \mathbf{U}_k\mathbf{\Sigma}_k\mathbf{V}_k^\mathsf{T}$.

```
Aₖ = U[:,1:k] * Diagonal(σ[1:k]) * V[:,1:k]' .|> Gray
```

See the figure on the following page and the QR code at the bottom of this page. The Frobenius norm, which gives the root mean squared error of two images by comparing them pixel-wise, is the sum of the singular values

$$\|\mathbf{A} - \mathbf{A}_k\|_\mathrm{F}^2 = \sum_{i=1}^{n} \sigma_i^2 - \sum_{i=1}^{k} \sigma_i^2 = \sum_{i=k+1}^{n} \sigma_i^2.$$

We can see this by checking that $\mathrm{norm(A-A_k)} \approx \mathrm{norm(σ[k+1:end])}$ returns the value true. Let's plot the error as a function of rank, shown in the figure on the next page:

```
ε² = 1 .- cumsum(σ)/sum(σ); scatter(ε²,xaxis=:log)
```

A rank k image will require roughly $k(n + m)$ bytes compared to nm bytes for an uncompressed image. So unless k is significantly smaller than n and m, the resulting storage will exceed the storage of the original image. Furthermore, an image compressed as a (lossless) PNG or lossless JPEG will often be much smaller than an SVD-compressed image, without any loss in quality.

▷ Image recognition

Image recognition algorithms have been around since the late 1950s, when psychologist Frank Rosenblatt built the Peceptron, a device with 400 photocells and a rudimentary mathematical model capable of classifying basic shapes. In 1987, mathematicians Lawrence Sirovich and Michael Kirby developed a methodology to characterize human faces. The methodology, initially called *eigenpictures*, was subsequently popularized as *eigenfaces* or *eigenimages*. Two years later, computer scientist Yann LeCun and fellow researchers developed a neural network image classifier called LeNet. We'll return to LeNet in Chapter 10. Here, we examine Sirovich and Kirby's method.

The eigenimage method applies singular value decomposition to training images to produce a smaller set of orthogonal images. Take a set of n $p \times q$-pixel grayscale training images, and reshape each image into a $pq \times 1$ array. We'll denote each as $\mathbf{d}_j$ for $j = 1, 2, \ldots, n$. It is common practice to mean center and

SVD image
compression

relative error versus relative size

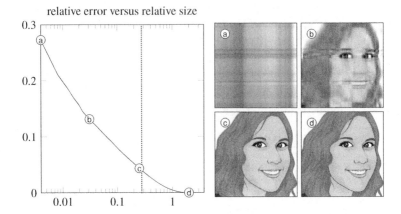

Figure 3.5: The relative error of an SVD-compressed image as a function of relative storage size. The dotted line shows equivalent lossless PNG compression.

standardize these vectors by subtracting the element-wise means of $\{\mathbf{d}_j\}$ and dividing by the element-wise nonzero standard deviations of $\{\mathbf{d}_j\}$ to reduce the condition number. Construct the matrix $\mathbf{D} = \begin{bmatrix} \mathbf{d}_1 & \mathbf{d}_2 & \cdots & \mathbf{d}_n \end{bmatrix}$, which has the singular value decomposition $\mathbf{U}\boldsymbol{\Sigma}\mathbf{V}^\mathsf{T}$.

Although we may include many training images, we can use a substantially lower-dimensional subspace by discarding the singular vectors corresponding to the smallest singular values. By keeping the largest k singular values and discarding the rest, we create a low-rank approximation $\mathbf{U}_k \boldsymbol{\Sigma}_k \mathbf{V}_k^\mathsf{T}$. The projection of $\mathbf{D}$ onto the column space of $\mathbf{U}_k$ is

$$\mathbf{U}_k \mathbf{U}_k^\mathsf{T} \mathbf{D} = \mathbf{U}_k \mathbf{W}_k,$$

where $\mathbf{W}_k = \mathbf{U}_k^\mathsf{T}\mathbf{D} = \boldsymbol{\Sigma}_k \mathbf{V}_k^\mathsf{T}$. We only need to save the $k \times n$ signature matrix $\mathbf{W}_k$ and the $pq \times k$ eigenimage matrix $\mathbf{U}_k$.

Figure 3.6 on page 82 shows a a set of 26 training images—each image $\mathbf{d}_i$ is a 120-by-120 pixel rasterized Times Roman capital letter. These images span a 26-dimensional subspace of a 14400-dimensional space. The matrix $\mathbf{D}$ has the singular value decomposition into a sum of its principal components

$$\mathbf{D} = \mathbf{E}_1 + \mathbf{E}_2 + \cdots + \mathbf{E}_{26} = \sigma_1 \mathbf{u}_1 \mathbf{v}_1^\mathsf{T} + \sigma_2 \mathbf{u}_2 \mathbf{v}_2^\mathsf{T} + \cdots + \sigma_{26} \mathbf{u}_{26} \mathbf{v}_{26}^\mathsf{T}.$$

The eigenimages $\mathbf{u}_i$ and the signatures $\sigma_i \mathbf{v}_i^\mathsf{T}$ contain the information needed to reconstruct the training images.

Take the 8-dimensional projection of $\mathbf{D}$ using the first eight eigenimages and their respective signatures: $\mathbf{D}_8 = \mathbf{E}_1 + \mathbf{E}_2 + \cdots + \mathbf{E}_8$. The projected images are decent representations of the training images, although several—the C and G, the E and F, and the O and Q—are not well differentiated.

Latent (from the Latin for "hidden") refers to variables that are not directly observed yet help explain a model. Latent variables often arise out of dimensionality reduction and tie together underlying concepts. The lower-dimensional space of these variables is called the latent space. Figure 3.7 on page 83 shows the two-dimensional latent space for the set of letter images. Contributions from the first right singular vector are along the horizontal axis, and contributions from the second right singular vector are along the vertical axis. Even in a two-dimensional latent space, we can see quite a bit of clustering. Notice how images (the letters) with similar appearances are close together in the latent space. The O is near the Q—which is simply an O with a tail. The T, I, and J—the only letters with center stems—all live in the same lower-left corner of the latent space. The letters that have left stems—F, P, E, L, R, K, N, D, and U—all reside in the upper half-plane. Letters with left curved strokes C, G, O, and Q are all in the lower-right quadrant. The letters M and W are close together yet away from all the others. Is it perhaps because of their broad stretch?

▷ Latent semantic analysis

Suppose you want to find similar books in a library or a journal article that best matches a given query. One way to do this is by making a list of all possible terms and counting the frequency of each term in the documents as components of a vector (sometimes called a "bag of words"). The jth element of a vector $\mathbf{d}_i$ tells us the number of times that term j appears in document i. The $m \times n$ document-term matrix $\mathbf{D} = \begin{bmatrix} \mathbf{d}_1 & \mathbf{d}_2 & \cdots & \mathbf{d}_n \end{bmatrix}$ maps words to the documents containing those words:

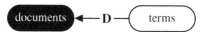

Given a query $\mathbf{q}$, we can find the most relevant documents to the query by finding the closest vector $\mathbf{d}_i$ to $\mathbf{q}$. Ussing *cosine similarity*, we identify the document i that maximizes $\cos \theta_i = \mathbf{q}^\mathsf{T} \mathbf{d}_i / \|\mathbf{q}\| \|\mathbf{d}_i\|$. Values close to one represent a good match, and values close to zero represent a poor match. This approach is called *explicit* semantic analysis.

Searching for a document using only terms is limiting because you need to explicitly match terms. For example, when searching for books or articles about Barcelona, terms like Spain, Gaudi, Picasso, Catalonia, city, and soccer are all conceptually relevant. In this case, rather than clustering documents by explicit variables like terms, it would be better to cluster documents using latent variables like concepts. This is the idea behind *latent* semantic analysis, introduced by computer scientist Susan Dumais in the late-1980s. We can think of concepts as intermediaries between text and documents. Take the singular

Training Images

A B C D E F G H I
J K L M N O P Q R
S T U V W X Y Z

Eigenimages (absolute values)

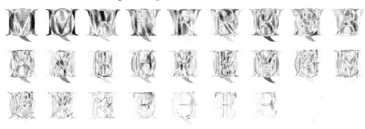

Projected Images (8 singular values)

Singular Values

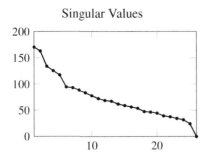

Reconstruction of "G"

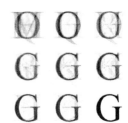

Figure 3.6: These 120×120 pixel images span a 26-dimensional subspace of $\mathbb{R}^{14400}$. Eigenimages (ordered by their associated singular values) form an orthogonal basis for the subspace spanned by the training images. Also, see the QR code below.

alphabet eigenimages
and low rank
projections

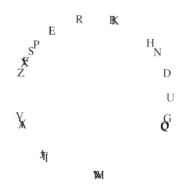

Figure 3.7: Left: The two-dimensional latent space of the letters with the $\mathbf{v}_1$ and $\mathbf{v}_2$-axes of the right-singular vectors shown. Notice how letters with similar appearances are quite close together in the latent space such as the O and Q and the T, I, and J. Right: The directions of the same letters. Also, see the three-dimensional latent space of letters at the QR code at the bottom of this page.

value decomposition of the document-term matrix $\mathbf{D} = \mathbf{U}\Sigma\mathbf{V}^\mathsf{T}$. The transform $\mathbf{V}^\mathsf{T}$ maps from terms to latent concept space, and the mapping $\mathbf{U}\Sigma$ completes the mapping to documents:

$$\boxed{\text{documents}} \leftarrow \mathbf{U}\Sigma - \boxed{\text{concepts}} \leftarrow \mathbf{V}^\mathsf{T} - \boxed{\text{terms}}$$

We don't need or want the full rank of $\mathbf{D}$, so instead, let's take a low rank-k approximation $\mathbf{D}_k$ and its singular value decomposition $\mathbf{U}_k\Sigma_k\mathbf{V}_k^\mathsf{T}$. Then the latent space vectors $\hat{\mathbf{d}}_i$ are the columns of $\mathbf{V}_k^\mathsf{T}$. In other words, $\hat{\mathbf{d}}_i = \Sigma_k^{-1}\mathbf{U}_k^\mathsf{T}\mathbf{d}_i$. We can similarly map a query vector $\mathbf{q}$ to its latent space representation by taking the projection $\hat{\mathbf{q}} = \Sigma_k^{-1}\mathbf{U}_k^\mathsf{T}\mathbf{q}$. In this case, we look for the column i that maximizes $\cos\theta_i = \hat{\mathbf{q}}^\mathsf{T}\hat{\mathbf{d}}_i / \|\hat{\mathbf{q}}\|\|\hat{\mathbf{d}}_i\|$.

3.4   Nonnegative matrix factorization

Singular value decomposition breaks a matrix into orthogonal factors that we can use for rank reduction, such as principal component analysis, or feature extraction, such as latent semantic indexing. One issue with singular value decomposition is that the factors contain negative components. For some applications, negative components may not be meaningful. Another issue is that the factors typically do not preserve sparsity, a possibly undesirable trait. It will be helpful to have a method of factorization that maintains nonnegativity and sparsity. Take an $m \times n$

three-dimensional
latent space of letters

matrix $\mathbf{X}$ whose elements are all nonnegative. Nonnegative matrix factorization (NMF) finds a rank p approximate matrix factorization $\mathbf{WH}$ to $\mathbf{X}$ where $\mathbf{W}$ and $\mathbf{H}$ are nonnegative $m \times p$ and $p \times n$ matrices.

What are the interpretations of the factors $\mathbf{W}$ and $\mathbf{H}$? Suppose that we are using NMF for text analysis. In this case, each column of $\mathbf{X}$ may correspond to one of m words, and each row may correspond to one of n documents. The matrix $\mathbf{W}$ relates p concepts to the n documents, and each element of $\mathbf{H}$ tells us the importance of a specific topic to a specific word.

Nonnegative matrix factorization can also be used for hyperspectral image analysis. A hyperspectral image is an image cube consisting of possibly hundreds of layers of images, each one capturing a wavelength band of a broad spectrum. Hyperspectral remote sensing can detect diseased plants in cropland, mineral ores and oil, or concealed and camouflaged targets. Hyperspectral unmixing tries to identify the constitutive materials such as grass, roads, or metal surfaces (called endmembers) within a hyperspectral image and classify which pixels contain which endmembers and in what proportion. An $m_1 \times m_2 \times n$ image cube can be reshaped into a $m_1 m_2 \times n$ matrix $\mathbf{X}$ with a spectral signature for each pixel. In the nonnegative matrix factorization, $\mathbf{W}$ is the spectral signature of an endmember, and $\mathbf{H}$ is the abundance of the endmember in each pixel.

Nonnegative matrix factorization is a constrained optimization problem. We want to find the matrices $\mathbf{W} \geq 0$ and $\mathbf{H} \geq 0$ that minimize the $\|\mathbf{X} - \mathbf{WH}\|_F^2$. We use the Frobenius norm because we want an element-by-element or pixel-by-pixel comparison. A common approach to constrained optimization problems uses the Karush–Kuhn–Tucker (KKT) conditions introduced on page 70. For an objective function $F(\mathbf{W}, \mathbf{H}) = \frac{1}{2}\|\mathbf{X} - \mathbf{WH}\|_F^2$ and a constraint $g(\mathbf{W}, \mathbf{H}) = (\mathbf{W}, \mathbf{H}) \geq 0$, the KKT conditions can be expressed as

① $\mathbf{W} \geq 0$,　② $\nabla_{\mathbf{W}} F = (\mathbf{WH} - \mathbf{X})\mathbf{H}^{\mathsf{T}} \geq 0$,　③ $\mathbf{W} \circ \nabla_{\mathbf{W}} F = 0$; and

④ $\mathbf{H} \geq 0$,　⑤ $\nabla_{\mathbf{H}} F = \mathbf{W}^{\mathsf{T}}(\mathbf{WH} - \mathbf{X}) \geq 0$,　⑥ $\mathbf{H} \circ \nabla_{\mathbf{H}} F = 0$,

where $\circ$ is component-wise (Hadamard) multiplication. By substituting ② into ③ we have $\mathbf{W} \circ \mathbf{WHH}^{\mathsf{T}} - \mathbf{W} \circ \mathbf{XH}^{\mathsf{T}} = 0$. From this equality, it follows that $\mathbf{W} = \mathbf{W} \circ \mathbf{XH}^{\mathsf{T}} \oslash \mathbf{WHH}^{\mathsf{T}}$ where $\oslash$ is component-wise (Hadamard) division. Similarly, by substituting ⑤ into ⑥, we have $\mathbf{H} = \mathbf{H} \circ \mathbf{W}^{\mathsf{T}} \mathbf{X} \oslash \mathbf{W}^{\mathsf{T}} \mathbf{WH}$. These two equations can be implemented as iterative multiplicative updates:

$$\mathbf{W} \leftarrow \mathbf{W} \circ \mathbf{XH}^{\mathsf{T}} \oslash \mathbf{WHH}^{\mathsf{T}}$$
$$\mathbf{H} \leftarrow \mathbf{H} \circ \mathbf{W}^{\mathsf{T}} \mathbf{X} \oslash \mathbf{W}^{\mathsf{T}} \mathbf{WH}.$$

The method is relatively slow to converge and not guaranteed to converge, but its implementation is simple. Also, we may need to take care to avoid $0/0$ if $\mathbf{W}$ has a zero row or $\mathbf{H}$ has a zero column.

Factors **W**

Reconstruced images **WH**

Figure 3.8: Nonnegative matrix factorization with rank $p = 8$ was applied to the 26 training images in Figure 3.6 on page 82. The reconstructed images are combinations of the eight factors **W** using positive weights **H**.

For a given sparse, nonnegative matrix X, we start with two random, non-negative matrices W and H. A naïve Julia implementation of nonnegative matrix factorization using multiplicative updates is

```
function nmf(X,p=6)
  W = rand(Float64, (size(X,1), p))
  H = rand(Float64, (p,size(X,2)))
  for i in 1:50
    W = W.*(X*H')./(W*(H*H') .+ (W.≈0))
    H = H.*(W'*X)./((W'*W)*H .+ (H.≈0))
  end
  (W,H)
end
```

To set a stopping criterion, we can look for convergence of the residual $\|X - WH\|_F^2$, stopping if the change in the residual from one iteration to the next falls below some threshold. Alternatively, we can stop if $\|W \circ \nabla_W F\|_F + \|H \circ \nabla_H F\|_F$ falls below a threshold or if **W** or **H** becomes stationary. To go deeper into nonnegative matrix factorization, see Nicolas Gillis' article "The Why and How of Nonnegative Matrix Factorization."

♣ The JuliaStats community's NMF.jl package does nonnegative matrix factorization.

3.5   Exercises

3.1. Consider the overdetermined system $x = 1$ and $x = 2$. Find the "best" solution in three ways by minimizing the 1-, 2- and ∞-norms of the residual. Which approaches are well-posed?

3.2. The continuous L^2-norm is

$$(f, g) = \int_0^1 f(x)g(x)\, dx.$$

Use the definition of the angle subtended by vectors

$$\theta = \cos^{-1} \frac{(\mathbf{u}, \mathbf{v})}{\|\mathbf{u}\|\|\mathbf{v}\|}$$

to show that the space of monomials $\{1, x, x^2, \ldots, x^n\}$ is far from orthogonal when n is large. Note that the components $h_{ij} = (x^i, x^j)$ form the Hilbert matrix.

3.3. Prove that the Moore–Penrose pseudoinverse satisfies the properties:

$$\mathbf{A}\mathbf{A}^+\mathbf{A} = \mathbf{A}, \quad \mathbf{A}^+\mathbf{A}\mathbf{A}^+ = \mathbf{A}^+, \quad (\mathbf{A}\mathbf{A}^+)^\mathsf{T} = \mathbf{A}\mathbf{A}^+, \quad \text{and} \quad (\mathbf{A}^+\mathbf{A})^\mathsf{T} = \mathbf{A}^+\mathbf{A}.$$

3.4. Fill in the steps missing from the example on page 68. Hint: let $\mathbf{Y} = \mathbf{A}\mathbf{X}\mathbf{B} + \mathbf{N}$, where $\mathbf{X}$ and $\mathbf{Y}$ are image arrays, $\mathbf{A}$ and $\mathbf{B}$ are appropriately sized Gaussian blur (Toeplitz) matrices, and $\mathbf{N}$ is a random matrix. The matrix $\mathbf{A}$ acts on the columns of $\mathbf{X}$, and the matrix $\mathbf{B}$ acts on the rows of $\mathbf{X}$. ✉

3.5. The Filippelli problem was contrived to benchmark statistical software packages. The National Institute of Standards and Technology (NIST) "Filip" Statistical Reference Dataset[7] consists of 82 (y, x) data points along with a certified degree-10 polynomial

$$y = \beta_0 + \beta_1 x + \beta_2 x^2 + \cdots + \beta_{10} x^{10}.$$

Find the parameters $\{\beta_0, \beta_1, \beta_2, \ldots, \beta_{10}\}$ by first constructing a Vandermonde matrix $\mathbf{V}$ with $\mathbf{V}_{ij} = x_i^{p-j}$ and then using the normal equation, QR decomposition, and the pseudoinverse to solve the system. What happens if you construct the Vandermonde matrix in increasing versus decreasing order or powers? What happens if you choose different cut-off values for the pseudoinverse? What happens if you standardize the data first by subtracting the respective means and dividing

---

[7] http://www.itl.nist.gov/div898/strd/lls/data/Filip.shtml

them by their standard deviations? The Filip dataset and certified parameters are available as *filip.csv* and *filip_coeffs.csv* at https://github.com/nmfsc/data. ✍

♣ The SpecialMatrices.jl function Vandermonde generates a Vandermonde matrix for input $(x_0, x_1, \ldots, x_n)$ with rows given by $\begin{bmatrix} 1 & x_i & \cdots & x_i^{p-1} & x_i^p \end{bmatrix}$.

3.6. The daily temperature of a city over several years can be modeled as a sinusoidal function. Use linear least squares to develop such a model using historical data recorded in Washington, DC, between 1967 to 1971, available as *dailytemps.csv* from https://github.com/nmfsc/data. Or choose your own data from https://www.ncdc.noaa.gov. ✍

3.7. Principal component analysis is often used for dimensionality reduction and as the basis of the eigenface method of image classification. Suppose that we want to identify handwritten digits for automatic mail sorting. Variations in the writing styles would require us to collect a wide range of handwriting samples to serve as a training set. The MNIST (Modified National Institute of Standards and Technology) dataset is a mixture of handwriting samples from American Census Bureau employees and high school students. (LeCun et al. [1998]) Each image is scaled to a 28×28-pixel grayscale image. For reference, the following 9s are sampled from the dataset:

Use the MLDatasets.jl package to load the MNIST dataset.[8] The training set has sixty-thousand images with labels, and the test set has ten-thousand images with labels. Sort and reshape the training data to form ten $28^2 \times n_i$ matrices $\mathbf{D}_i$ using labels $i = \{0, 1, \ldots, 9\}$ where n_i is the number of images for each label. Now, compute a low-rank SVD of $\mathbf{D}_i$ to get $\mathbf{V}_i$. The columns of $\mathbf{V}_i$ form the basis for the low-rank subspace. To classify a new test image $\mathbf{d}$, we find the subspace to which $\mathbf{d}$ is closest by comparing $\mathbf{d}$ with its projection $\mathbf{V}_i \mathbf{V}_i^{\mathsf{T}} \mathbf{d}$

$$\arg\min_{i \in \{0,1,\ldots,9\}} \left\| \mathbf{V}_i \mathbf{V}_i^{\mathsf{T}} \mathbf{d} - \mathbf{d} \right\|_2 .$$

Check how well your method properly identifies the test images. ✍

3.8. Apply Zipf's law to the frequency of surnames in the United States. You can find a 2010 census data set as *surname.csv* from https://github.com/nmfsc/data.

3.9. A model is a simplification of the real world. Take Hollywood actors, for example. We can characterize actors by the roles they often play. Russell Crowe

---

[8]Alternatively, you can download the training and test data as the MAT-file emnist-mnist.mat from https://www.nist.gov/itl/products-and-services/emnist-dataset or https://github.com/nmfsc/data.

is primarily thought of as an action film actor, Ben Stiller as a comedic actor, and Kate Winslet as a dramatic actor. Others have crossed over between comedic roles and serious ones. Build an actor similarity model using film genres to determine which actors are most similar to a given actor. Use the data sets from exercise 2.9 along with the adjacency matrix *movie-genre.csv* that relates movies to genres listed in the file *genres.txt*. Use cosine similarity to determine which actors are most similar to a chosen actor. How well does this approach work in clustering actors? What are the limitations of this model? How does the dimension of the latent space change the model? ✍

3.10. Multilateration determines an object's position by comparing the arrival times of a signal at different monitoring stations. Multilateration can locate a gunshot in an urban neighborhood using a network of microphones or an earthquake's epicenter using seismographs scattered around the world. Consider a two-dimensional problem with n stations each located at (x_i, y_i) and a time of arrival t_i. The source (x, y) and time of transmission t are computed from the intersection of the n circles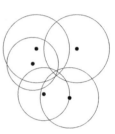

$$(x - x_i)^2 + (y - y_i)^2 = c^2(t_i - t)^2$$

for $i = 1, 2, \ldots, n$ where c is the signal speed. This system can be solved by first reducing it to a system $n - 1$ linear equations. The system will be inconsistent, because of variations in signal speed, the diffraction of waves around objects, measurement errors, etc. We can use least squares to find a best solution. Take $c = 1$ and determine (x, y, t) for the data

$$(x_i, y_i, t_i) = \{(3, 3, 12), (1, 15, 14), (10, 2, 13), (12, 15, 14), (0, 11, 12)\}. ✍$$

3.11. ShotSpotter® is a U.S.-based company that provides gunfire locator services to law enforcement agencies. The company validated the accuracy of their system using a series of live fire tests.[9] A dataset for one round of a 9 mm automatic handgun with a signal-to-noise ratios greater than 12 dB at the reporting sensors is available as *shotspotter.csv* at https://github.com/nmfsc/data. The first eleven rows list the three-dimensional locations of surveyed reporting sensors in meters along with incident times in seconds. The final row lists the surveyed location of the handgun. Modify the method from the previous exercise to locate the handgun using the sensor locations and incident times. Use 328.9 m/s for the sound speed for an air temperature of −4 °C. ✍

---

[9] https://github.com/ShotSpotter/research.accuracy-of-gunshot-location

Chapter 4

Computing Eigenvalues

Using pencil and paper, one often finds the eigenvalues of a matrix by determining the zeros of the characteristic polynomial $\det(\mathbf{A} - \lambda\mathbf{I})$. This approach works for small matrices, but we cannot hope to apply it to a general matrix larger than 4×4. The Abel–Ruffini theorem states states that no general solutions exist to degree-five or higher polynomial equations using a finite number of algebraic operations (adding, subtracting, multiplying, dividing, and taking an integer or fractional power). Consequently, there can be no direct method for determining eigenvalues of a general matrix of rank five or higher. We must find the eigenvalues using iterative methods instead.

Of course, it is possible to compute the characteristic polynomial and then use a numerical method such as the Newton–Horner method to approximate its roots. However, in general, this approach is unstable. In fact, a common technique to find the roots of a polynomial $p(x)$ is to generate the companion matrix of $p(x)$, i.e., the matrix whose characteristic polynomial is $p(x)$, and then determine the eigenvalues of the companion matrix using the QR method introduced in this chapter.

♣ The Polynomials.jl function `roots` finds the roots of a polynomial $p(x)$ by computing the eigenvalues for the companion matrix of $p(x)$.

4.1 Eigenvalue sensitivity and estimation

Before discussing methods for determining eigenvalues, let's look at the estimation and stability of eigenvalues. Suppose that $\mathbf{A}$ is nondefective, with the diagonalization $\mathbf{\Lambda} = \mathbf{S}^{-1}\mathbf{A}\mathbf{S}$. Let $\delta\mathbf{A}$ be some change in $\mathbf{A}$. Then the perturbation in the eigenvalues is

$$\Lambda + \delta\Lambda = S^{-1}(A + \delta A)S$$

and hence

$$\delta\Lambda = S^{-1}\delta A S.$$

Taking the matrix norm, we have

$$\|\delta\Lambda\| \le \|S^{-1}\|\|\delta A\|\|S\| = \kappa(S)\|\delta A\|.$$

So $\delta\Lambda$ is magnified by the condition number of the matrix of eigenvectors.

Let's look at stability again. The *left eigenvector* of a matrix A is a row vector y^H that satisfies

$$y^H A = \lambda y^H.$$

Suppose that A, x and λ vary with some perturbation parameter and let δA, δx and $\delta\lambda$ denote their derivatives with respect to this parameter. Differentiating $Ax = \lambda x$ gives us

$$\delta A x + A \delta x = \delta\lambda x + \lambda \delta x.$$

Multiply by the left eigenvector

$$y^H \delta A x + y^H A \delta x = y^H \delta\lambda x + y^H \lambda \delta x.$$

Since $y^H A \delta x = y^H \lambda \delta x$, we have $y^H \delta A x = y^H \delta\lambda x$, and so

$$\delta\lambda = \frac{y^H \delta A x}{y^H x}.$$

Therefore,

$$\|\delta\lambda\| \le \frac{\|y\|\|x\|}{y^H x}\|\delta A\|.$$

We define the *eigenvalue condition number* as

$$\kappa(\lambda, A) = \frac{\|y\|\|x\|}{y^H x},$$

that is, one over the cosine of the angle between the right and left eigenvectors. We can compute the eigenvalue condition number by using the spectral decomposition $A = S\Lambda S^{-1}$:

```
function condeig(A)
  S_r = eigvecs(A)
  S_l = inv(S_r')
  S_l ./= sqrt.(sum(abs.(S_l.^2), dims=1))
  1 ./ abs.(sum(S_r.*S_l, dims=1))
end
```

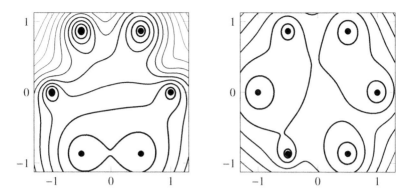

Figure 4.1: Contours of ε-pseudospectra of two similar matrices. Each contour represents a change of $\varepsilon = 0.0005$. For each matrix the 2-condition number is on the order of 10^6 and the condition number of the matrix of eigenvectors is on the order of 10^3.

Finding the spectrum of a matrix $\mathbf{A}$ is the same as asking which values λ make $\mathbf{A} - \lambda\mathbf{I}$ singular, i.e.,

$$\lambda(\mathbf{A}) = \{z \in \mathbb{C} \mid \mathbf{A} - z\mathbf{I} \text{ is singular.}\}.$$

Numerically, such a question may be ill-posed. Instead, we should ask when $\mathbf{A} - \lambda\mathbf{I}$ is close to singular, i.e., when $\|(\mathbf{A} - \lambda\mathbf{I})^{-1}\|$ is large. In this case, it is helpful to talk about the pseudospectrum of the matrix $\mathbf{A}$.

We define the ε-pseudospectrum of $\mathbf{A}$ as the set

$$\lambda_\varepsilon(\mathbf{A}) = \{z \in \mathbb{C} \mid \|(\mathbf{A} - z\mathbf{I})^{-1}\| \geq \frac{1}{\varepsilon}\}.$$

In other words, z is an eigenvalue of $\mathbf{A} + \mathbf{E}$ with $\|\mathbf{E}\| < \varepsilon$. For the Euclidean norm,

$$\lambda_\varepsilon(\mathbf{A}) = \{z \in \mathbb{C} \mid \sigma_{\min}(\mathbf{A} - z\mathbf{I}) \leq \varepsilon\}.$$

See Figure 4.1 above.

Theorem 10 (Gershgorin circle theorem). *Let $\mathbf{A} \in \mathbb{C}^{n \times n}$. Then*

$$\lambda(\mathbf{A}) \subseteq \mathcal{S}_\mathcal{R} = \bigcup_{i=1}^{n} \mathcal{R}_i \quad where \quad \mathcal{R}_i = \{z \in \mathbb{C} : |z - a_{ii}| \leq \sum_{\substack{j=1 \\ j \neq i}}^{n} |a_{ij}|\}.$$

The sets $\mathcal{R}_i$ are called Gershgorin circles.

Proof. Any eigenvalue along the diagonal of $\mathbf{A}$ is clearly in a Gershgorin circle, so we only need to consider eigenvalues that are not diagonal elements of $\mathbf{A}$. For each $\lambda \in \lambda(\mathbf{A})$, we introduce the matrix

$$\mathbf{B}_\lambda = \mathbf{A} - \lambda\mathbf{I} = (\mathbf{D} - \lambda\mathbf{I}) + \mathbf{M},$$

where $\mathbf{D}$ is composed of the diagonal of $\mathbf{A}$ and $\mathbf{M}$ is composed of the off-diagonal elements. There is a nonzero vector $\mathbf{x}$ (an eigenvector of $\mathbf{A}$) in the null space of $\mathbf{B}_\lambda$, so

$$\mathbf{B}_\lambda\mathbf{x} = ((\mathbf{D} - \lambda\mathbf{I}) + \mathbf{M})\mathbf{x} = \mathbf{0}.$$

Equivalently, $\mathbf{x} = (\mathbf{D} - \lambda\mathbf{I})^{-1}\mathbf{M}\mathbf{x}$. In the ∞-norm,

$$\|\mathbf{x}\|_\infty = \|(\mathbf{D} - \lambda\mathbf{I})^{-1}\mathbf{M}\mathbf{x}\|_\infty \leq \|(\mathbf{D} - \lambda\mathbf{I})^{-1}\mathbf{M}\|_\infty\|\mathbf{x}\|_\infty$$

Therefore,

$$1 \leq \|(\mathbf{D} - \lambda\mathbf{I})^{-1}\mathbf{M}\|_\infty = \sup_{1 \leq i \leq n} \sum_{\substack{j=1 \\ j \neq i}}^{n} \frac{|a_{ij}|}{|a_{ii} - \lambda|}.$$

It follows that

$$|a_{ii} - \lambda| \leq \sum_{\substack{j=1 \\ j \neq i}}^{n} |a_{ij}|.$$

Hence, $\lambda \in \mathcal{R}_i$.   □

Corollary 11. *Let* $\mathbf{A} \in \mathbb{C}^{n \times n}$. *Then* $\lambda(\mathbf{A}) \subseteq S_\mathcal{R} \cap S_C$ *where*

$$S_C = \bigcup_{i=1}^{n} C_i \quad \text{where} \quad C_i = \{z \in \mathbb{C} : |z - a_{ii}| \leq \sum_{\substack{j=1 \\ j \neq i}}^{n} |a_{ji}|\}.$$

Proof. Substitute the 1-norm for ∞-norm in the Gershgorin circle theorem to give column circles instead of row circles.   □

Example. The Gershgorin circles are plotted for the following matrix:

$$\mathbf{A} = \begin{bmatrix} 10 & 2 & 3 \\ 1 & 2 & 1 \\ 0 & 1 & 3 \end{bmatrix}$$

Row circles are shaded ▤, column circles are shaded ▥, and the eigenvalues ⊡ lie in their intersections.   ◀

Example. A stochastic or Markov matrix is a square, nonnegative matrix whose rows or columns each sum to one. When the rows each sum to one, it's called a right stochastic matrix; and when the columns each sum to one, it's called a left stochastic matrix. A stochastic or probability vector is a nonnegative vector whose elements sum to one. Stochastic matrices describe the transition in a Markov chain, a sequence of events where the probability of an event occurring depends only on the state of the previous event. It's clear that the ones vector $\mathbf{1} = (1, 1, \ldots, 1)$ is an eigenvector with a corresponding eigenvalue 1 of any right stochastic matrix. Furthermore, from the Gershgorin circle theorem, we know that the spectral radius of a stochastic matrix is at most 1. So 1 is the largest eigenvalue of a stochastic matrix.   ◄

Theorem 12 (Perron–Frobenius theorem). *A positive square matrix (a matrix with all positive elements) has a unique largest real eigenvalue. The corresponding eigenvector has strictly positive components.*

Proof. There are several approaches to proving the Perron–Frobenius theorem. We'll take a geometric approach. Let $\mathbf{A}$ be an $n \times n$ matrix with positive elements. Let X be the set of points $(x_1, x_2, \ldots, x_n)$ on the unit sphere in the nonnegative orthant—the points with $x_1^2 + x_2^2 + \cdots + x_n^2 = 1$ and $x_i \geq 0$. Define the mapping $T : X \rightarrow X$ as $T\mathbf{x} = \mathbf{A}\mathbf{x}/\|\mathbf{A}\mathbf{x}\|_2$. Then T is a contraction mapping over X because the elements of $\mathbf{A}$ are positive. Therefore, by the Banach fixed-point theorem (page 198) the mapping T has a unique fixed point $\mathbf{v} \in X$. That means $\mathbf{A}$ has a *unique* eigenvector $\mathbf{v}$ with strictly positive components. Let the corresponding eigenvalue be λ. We can also consider a similar contraction mapping that generates a unique left eigenvector $\mathbf{u}$ with strictly positive components and eigenvalue λ'. Furthermore, $\lambda' = \lambda$ because $\lambda'\mathbf{u}^T\mathbf{v} = \mathbf{u}^T\mathbf{A}\mathbf{v} = \lambda\mathbf{v}^T\mathbf{u}$ and $\mathbf{u}^T\mathbf{v} > 0$. Now, let μ be any other real eigenvalue of $\mathbf{A}$ and let $\mathbf{w}$ be the corresponding eigenvector. Then at least one component of $\mathbf{w}$ is negative. Let $|\mathbf{w}|$ be the vector whose components are the absolute values of components of $\mathbf{w}$. It follows that

$$|\mu|\mathbf{u}^T|\mathbf{w}| = \mathbf{u}^T|\mathbf{A}\mathbf{w}| < \mathbf{u}^T\mathbf{A}|\mathbf{w}| = \lambda\mathbf{u}^T|\mathbf{w}|.$$

Because $\mathbf{u}$ and $|\mathbf{w}|$ are positive, $\mathbf{u}^T|\mathbf{w}|$ is positive. So $|\mu| < \lambda$.

As an extension, the Perron–Frobenius theorem also holds for primitive matrices. A *primitive matrix* is a square nonnegative matrix, some power of which is a positive matrix.   □

4.2   The power method

Let $\mathbf{A} \in \mathbb{C}^{n \times n}$ be a diagonalizable matrix with eigenvalues ordered by magnitude $|\lambda_1| > |\lambda_2| \geq \cdots \geq |\lambda_n|$. We say that λ_1 is the *dominant eigenvalue* of $\mathbf{A}$. An eigenvector associated with λ_1 is a dominant eigenvector. Consider the iterative method $\mathbf{x}^{(k)} = \mathbf{A}\mathbf{x}^{(k-1)}$ for an initial guess $\mathbf{x}^{(0)}$. As long as $\mathbf{x}^{(0)}$ is not orthogonal to a dominant eigenvector, the sequence $\mathbf{x}^{(0)}, \mathbf{x}^{(1)}, \mathbf{x}^{(2)}, \ldots$ will converge to a dominant eigenvector.

Because $\mathbf{A}$ is diagonalizable, its eigenvectors $\{\mathbf{x}_i\}$ form a basis of $\mathbb{C}^n$, and every vector $\mathbf{x}^{(0)}$ can be represented as a linear combination of the eigenvectors

$$\mathbf{x}^{(0)} = \alpha_1\mathbf{x}_1 + \alpha_2\mathbf{x}_2 + \cdots + \alpha_n\mathbf{x}_n.$$

By applying $\mathbf{A}$ to this initial vector, we have

$$\begin{aligned}
\mathbf{x}^{(1)} = \mathbf{A}\mathbf{x}^{(0)} &= \alpha_1\mathbf{A}\mathbf{x}_1 + \alpha_2\mathbf{A}\mathbf{x}_2 + \cdots + \alpha_n\mathbf{A}\mathbf{x}_n \\
&= \alpha_1\lambda_1\mathbf{x}_1 + \alpha_2\lambda_2\mathbf{x}_2 + \cdots + \alpha_n\lambda_n\mathbf{x}_n.
\end{aligned}$$

After k iterations,

$$\begin{aligned}
\mathbf{x}^{(k)} = \mathbf{A}^k\mathbf{x}^{(0)} &= \alpha_1\lambda_1^k\mathbf{x}_1 + \alpha_2\lambda_2^k\mathbf{x}_2 + \cdots + \alpha_n\lambda_n^k\mathbf{x}_n \\
&= \alpha_1\lambda_1^k\left(\mathbf{x}_1 + \frac{\alpha_2}{\alpha_1}\left(\frac{\lambda_2}{\lambda_1}\right)^k\mathbf{x}_2 + \cdots + \frac{\alpha_n}{\alpha_1}\left(\frac{\lambda_n}{\lambda_1}\right)^k\mathbf{x}_n\right) \\
&= \lambda_1^k\alpha_1\mathbf{x}_1 + O\left(|\lambda_2/\lambda_1|^k\right) \text{ terms.}
\end{aligned}$$

The power method converges linearly as $O(|\lambda_2/\lambda_1|^k)$. Let $\mathbf{x}^{(k)}$ equal the normalized kth iterate and $\mathbf{x}_i$ a unit eigenvalue. Then the error at the kth iterate is

$$\left\|\mathbf{x}^{(k)} - \mathbf{x}_1\right\| = \left\|\sum_{i=2}^n \frac{\alpha_i}{\alpha_1}\left(\frac{\lambda_i}{\lambda_1}\right)^k\mathbf{x}_i\right\| \le \left|\frac{\lambda_2}{\lambda_1}\right|^k\left\|\sum_{i=2}^n\frac{\alpha_i}{\alpha_1}\mathbf{x}_i\right\| \le C\left|\frac{\lambda_2}{\lambda_1}\right|^k.$$

For the Euclidean norm, $C = \alpha_1^{-1}\sqrt{\alpha_2^2 + \alpha_3^2 + \cdots + \alpha_n^2}$.

In practice, the power method is straightforward. We multiply the current eigenvector approximation by our matrix and then normalize to prevent over or underflow at each iteration. Starting with an initial guess $\mathbf{x}^{(0)}$,

$$\begin{cases} \text{multiply} & \mathbf{x}^{(k+1)} = \mathbf{A}\mathbf{x}^{(k)} \\ \text{normalize} & \mathbf{x}^{(k+1)} \leftarrow \mathbf{x}^{(k+1)}/\left\|\mathbf{x}^{(k+1)}\right\|_2 \end{cases}.$$

At each step, the approximate dominant eigenvalue is $\mathbf{x}^{(k)\mathrm{H}}\mathbf{A}\mathbf{x}^{(k)}$. We stop when the difference in iterates $\left\|\left|\mathbf{x}^{(k+1)}\right| - \left|\mathbf{x}^{(k)}\right|\right\|$ or the angle between iterates $1 - \mathbf{x}^{(k+1)\mathrm{H}}\mathbf{x}^{(k)}$ is within a prescribed tolerance.

Example. The results of round-robin chess tournaments are often recorded on square matrices with 1 for a victory, $\frac{1}{2}$ for a draw, and 0 for a defeat. A

Player	Sza	Tai	Gli	Kor	Cas	Ros	Cas	Kle	Pts.	S.B.
Szabó	—	1	1/2	1/2	1/2	1	1	1	5 1/2	16 1/2
Taimanov	0	—	1	1	1	1/2	1	1	5 1/2	16
Gligoric	1/2	0	—	1/2	1	1	1	1	5	12 1/2
Kortchnoi	1/2	0	1/2	—	1/2	1	1	1	4 1/2	11 1/2
Casas	1/2	0	0	1/2	—	1	1/2	0	2 1/2	7 3/4
Rossetto	0	1/2	0	0	0	—	1/2	1	2	5
Casabella	0	0	0	0	1/2	1/2	—	1/2	1 1/2	3
Klein	0	0	0	0	1	0	1/2	—	1 1/2	3 1/4

Figure 4.2: Crosstable of the 1960 Santa Fe chess tournament with the combined scores (*Pts.*) and the tie breaking Sonneborn–Berger score (*S.B.*)

player's tournament score is given by the sum of the scores along the rows. Mathematically, for a matrix $\mathbf{M}$ the combined scores are $\mathbf{r} = \mathbf{M1}$, where $\mathbf{1}$ is a vector of ones. These scores determine ranking and prize money. But what happens when there is a tie?

In 1873, Austrian chess master Oscar Gelbfuhs proposed using a weighted row sum, multiplying each game score by the opponent's cumulative score. In this way, a player earns more points in defeating a strong opponent than a weak one. Take the 1960 Santa Fe tournament (the table above), in which László Szabó and Mark Taimanov both had combined raw scores of $5\frac{1}{2}$. With Gelbfuhs' improved scoring system (now called the Sonneborn–Berger system), Szabó would have

$$1 \cdot 5\tfrac{1}{2} + \tfrac{1}{2} \cdot 5 + \tfrac{1}{2} \cdot 4\tfrac{1}{2} + \tfrac{1}{2} \cdot 2\tfrac{1}{2} + 1 \cdot 2 + 1 \cdot 1\tfrac{1}{2} + 1 \cdot 1\tfrac{1}{2} = 16\tfrac{1}{2},$$

beating Taimanov, who had a score of 16. Mathematically speaking, the Sonneborn–Berger scores are the row sums of $\mathbf{M}^2$, i.e., $\mathbf{r} = \mathbf{M}^2\mathbf{1}$.

If we consider these scores an iterative refinement of the raw scores, we don't need to stop after one go. We might consider $\mathbf{r} = \mathbf{M}^k\mathbf{1}$ for some higher power k. But, what k? In 1895, mathematician Edmund Landau (then seventeen years old) examined the problem and suggested computing $\mathbf{Mr} = \lambda\mathbf{r}$, stating that a player's ranking ought to be a proportional sum of the rankings of those players defeated by that player. Of course, this is simply an eigenvector problem.[1] At the time, it still wasn't known if a meaningful eigenvector would always even exist. Ten years later, Perron and Frobenius independently derived their namesake theorem that guaranteed the unique existence of a solution

---

[1] The March 1902 issue of *British Chess Magazine* praised Landau's formulation as "clear-sighted and precise" but warned "doubtless nevertheless, an accurate estimate of the relative value of games would give extraordinary trouble to a chess player without mathematical training; and such an estimate, even if competently made, would meet with universal distrust."

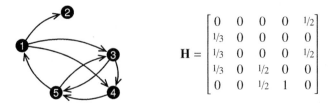

$$\mathbf{H} = \begin{bmatrix} 0 & 0 & 0 & 0 & 1/2 \\ 1/3 & 0 & 0 & 0 & 0 \\ 1/3 & 0 & 0 & 0 & 1/2 \\ 1/3 & 0 & 1/2 & 0 & 0 \\ 0 & 0 & 1/2 & 1 & 0 \end{bmatrix}$$

Figure 4.3: A graph and its normalized hyperlink matrix $\mathbf{H}$.

Centrality is a measure of influence in a network.[2] It could measure the strength of chess masters or the ranking of football teams, it could measure peer status among kindergarteners or trust among colleagues, and it could measure the popularity of websites. Eigenvector centrality measures the influence of a node in a network by computing the principal eigenvector of the network's adjacency matrix. It is the basis of Landau's chess ranking system, and it is the basis for PageRank, the first and best-known algorithm used by Google to sort website pages.[3]

The concept behind the PageRank algorithm arises analogously out of the power method. Imagine that millions of bots (or people) are browsing the internet, each one clicking links at random over and over again. No matter what pages they may have started on, they will eventually limit the probability distribution of all pages they could visit. Pages with more visitors at any given time are arguably more important than those with fewer visitors. This probability is the PageRank.

Suppose that there are n web pages. Let o_j be the number of outgoing links from a page j. Define the hyperlink matrix $\mathbf{H}$ as the weighted incidence matrix where the ij-element equals $1/o_j$ if there is a hyperlink from page j to page i and zero if there isn't. See the figure above. Pages with no outgoing links are problematic because if one of our bots finds its way to such a page, it will get trapped with no way out. Eventually, over time, all of the bots would become trapped. Instead, we'll make the rule that on web pages with no outgoing links—so-called dangling nodes—we'll choose a random page from any of the n possible webpages. We do this by setting all elements in column j to $1/n$. Now, we have the stochastic matrix $\mathbf{S} = \mathbf{H} + \mathbf{ev}^{\mathsf{T}}$ where $\mathbf{e}$ is an $n \times 1$ vector whose components all equal $1/n$ and $\mathbf{v}$ is the $n \times 1$ vector where element $v_j = 1$ if page j is a dangling node and $v_j = 0$ otherwise. Occasionally, someone may decide not to follow any link on the webpage that they are currently viewing and instead opens an arbitrary webpage. To model such a behavior, we define a new matrix $\mathbf{G} = \alpha\mathbf{S} + (1 - \alpha)\mathbf{E}$, where the α is the likelihood of following any link on the

---

[2]The term *prestige* is sometimes used for directed networks, with *measure of influence* for outgoing edges and *measure of support* for incoming edges.

[3]Katz centrality is another variant of eigenvector centrality that adds a damping factor because you might not trust a "friend of a friend" as much as you trust a friend.

page and $\mathbf{E}$ is an $n \times n$ matrix whose elements all equal $1/n$. A typical value for the damping factor α is 0.85. The matrix $\mathbf{G}$ is often called the Google matrix.

A nonnegative vector $\mathbf{x}$ is a *probability vector* if its column sum equals one. The ith element of $\mathbf{x}$ is the probability of being on page i, and the ith element of $\mathbf{Gx}$ is the probability of being on page i a short time later. Since $\mathbf{G}$ is a stochastic matrix, $\lim_{k \to \infty} \mathbf{G}^k$ will converge to a steady-state operator. By the Perron–Frobenius theorem, the eigenvector corresponding to the dominant eigenvalue $\lambda = 1$ gives the steady-state probability of being on a given webpage. This eigenvector is the PageRank.

Because we only need to find the dominant eigenvector, we can use the power method $\mathbf{x}^{(k+1)} \leftarrow \mathbf{Gx}^{(k)}$. The matrix $\mathbf{G}$ is dense and requires $O(n^2)$ operations for every matrix-vector multiplication, but the matrix $\mathbf{H}$ is quite sparse and only requires $O(n)$ operations. Let's reformulate the problem in terms of $\mathbf{H}$. Because $\|\mathbf{x}^{(k)}\|_1 = 1$, it follows that $\mathbf{Ex}^{(k)} = \mathbf{e}$. Now we have

$$\mathbf{x}^{(k+1)} \leftarrow \alpha\mathbf{Hx}^{(k)} + \alpha\mathbf{v}^\mathsf{T}\mathbf{x}^{(k)}\mathbf{e} + (1-\alpha)\mathbf{e}. \tag{4.1}$$

The following Julia code computes the PageRank of the graph in Figure 4.3.

```
H = [0 0 0 0 1; 1 0 0 0 0; 1 0 0 0 1; 1 0 1 0 0; 0 0 1 1 0]
v = all(H.==0,dims=1)
H = H ./ (sum(H,dims=1)+v)
n = size(H,1)
d = 0.85
x = ones(n,1)/n
for i in 1:9
  x = d*(H*x) .+ d/n*(v*x) .+ (1-d)/n
end
```

The full matrix form is fine for smallish matrices like this one, but for larger matrices we should use the sparse form. After a few iterations, the solution x converges to $(0.176, 0.097, 0.227, 0.193, 0.307)$, which we can use to order the nodes as $\{5, 3, 4, 1, 2\}$. If you want to go even deeper, see Vigna [2016] and Langville and Meyer [2004]. ◀

▷ Inverse and shifted power method

The power method itself only gets us the dominant eigenvector. Getting just this one may be enough for some problems, but often we may need more of them or all of them. We can extend the power method to get other eigenvectors.

Suppose that the spectrum of $\mathbf{A}$ is

$$\lambda(\mathbf{A}) = \{\lambda_1, \lambda_2, \cdots, \lambda_{n-1}, \lambda_n\}$$

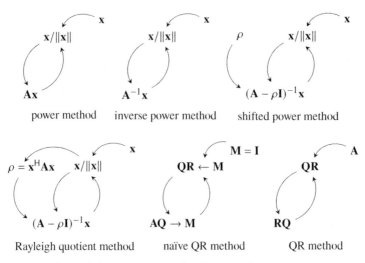

power method   inverse power method   shifted power method

Rayleigh quotient method   naïve QR method   QR method

Figure 4.4: Power method and some of its variations.

where $|\lambda_1| \geq |\lambda_2| \geq \cdots | \geq |\lambda_{n-1}| > |\lambda_n|$. Then, the spectrum of $\mathbf{A}^{-1}$ is

$$\lambda(\mathbf{A}^{-1}) = \left\{ \frac{1}{\lambda_1}, \frac{1}{\lambda_2}, \cdots, \frac{1}{\lambda_{n-1}}, \frac{1}{\lambda_n} \right\}$$

with the same associated eigenspace. We can get the eigenvector associated with the eigenvalue of $\mathbf{A}$ closest to 0 by applying the power method to $\mathbf{A}^{-1}$. The convergence ratio is $O(|\lambda_n / \lambda_{n-1}|)$.

So, now we have the largest and the smallest eigenvalues. What about the rest of them? Recall that for any value ρ, the spectrum of $\mathbf{A} - \rho\mathbf{I}$ is

$$\lambda(\mathbf{A}) = \{\lambda_1 - \rho, \lambda_2 - \rho, \cdots, \lambda_{n-1} - \rho, \lambda_n - \rho\}$$

with the same associated eigenspace as $\mathbf{A}$. We can use this property in a clever approach called *shift-and-invert*. We make a good guess of one of the eigenvalues, say $\rho \approx \lambda_i$ for some i. Then, we apply power iteration to $(\mathbf{A} - \rho\mathbf{I})^{-1}$. We will recover the eigenvector associated with the eigenvalue λ_i. The ratio of convergence is $|\lambda_i - \rho|/|\lambda_k - \rho|$ where λ_k is the next closest eigenvalue to ρ. In practice, for each iteration, we solve

$$(\mathbf{A} - \rho\mathbf{I})\mathbf{x}^{(k+1)} = \mathbf{x}^{(k)}, \quad \text{where} \quad \mathbf{x}^{(k)} \leftarrow \frac{\mathbf{x}^{(k)}}{\|\mathbf{x}^{(k)}\|}.$$

Computation requires $\frac{2}{3}n^3$ flops for LU-decomposition and then only $2n^2$ flops for each iteration

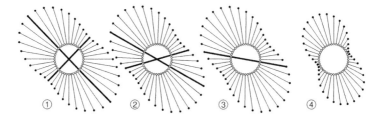

Figure 4.5: Rayleigh quotient $\rho_A(\mathbf{x})\mathbf{x}$ for the matrices in Figure 1.1. Eigenvectors are depicted with thick line segments.

▷ Rayleigh quotient iteration

The convergence rate for the shift-and-invert method depends on having a good initial guess for the shift ρ. It seems reasonable that we could improve the method by updating the shift ρ at each iteration. One way we can do this is by using the eigenvalue equation $\mathbf{Ax} = \rho\mathbf{x}$. Unless $(\rho, \mathbf{x})$ is already an eigenvalue-eigenvector pair of $\mathbf{A}$, this equation is inconsistent. Instead, we will find the "best" ρ. Let's determine which ρ minimizes the 2-norm of the residual

$$\|\mathbf{r}\|_2 = \|\mathbf{Ax} - \rho\mathbf{x}\|_2.$$

At the minimum,

$$0 = \frac{\mathrm{d}}{\mathrm{d}\rho}\|\mathbf{r}\|_2^2 = \frac{\mathrm{d}}{\mathrm{d}\rho}\|\mathbf{Ax} - \rho\mathbf{x}\|_2^2 = -2\mathbf{x}^H\mathbf{Ax} + 2\rho\mathbf{x}^H\mathbf{x}.$$

Therefore, the "best" choice for ρ is

$$\rho_A(\mathbf{x}) = \frac{\mathbf{x}^H\mathbf{Ax}}{\mathbf{x}^H\mathbf{x}}.$$

This number, called the *Rayleigh quotient*, can be thought of as an eigenvalue approximation. The Courant–Fischer theorem, also known as the min-max theorem, establishes bounds on the Rayleigh quotient.

Theorem 13 (Courant–Fischer theorem). *Let* $\mathbf{A}$ *be a Hermitian matrix with eigenvalues* $\lambda_1 \geq \lambda_2 \geq \cdots \geq \lambda_n$ *and corresponding eigenvectors* $\mathbf{v}_1, \mathbf{v}_2, \ldots, \mathbf{v}_n$. *Then* $\lambda_1 = \max_\mathbf{x} \rho_A(\mathbf{x})$, $\lambda_n = \min_\mathbf{x} \rho_A(\mathbf{x})$, *and in general* $\lambda_k = \min_{\mathbf{x} \in S_k} \rho_A(\mathbf{x})$ *where* $S_k = \mathrm{span}\{\mathbf{v}_1, \mathbf{v}_2, \ldots, \mathbf{v}_k\}$.

Proof. Take the spectral decomposition $\mathbf{A} = \mathbf{Q}^H\mathbf{\Lambda Q}$ where $\mathbf{Q}$ is an orthogonal matrix. Because $\mathbf{x}^H\mathbf{Ax} = (\mathbf{Qx})^H\mathbf{\Lambda}(\mathbf{Qx})$ and $\|\mathbf{Qx}\|_2 = \|\mathbf{x}\|_2$, it is sufficient to consider the case of $\mathbf{A} = \mathbf{\Lambda}$, i.e., $\mathbf{A}$ as a diagonal matrix. In this case,

Figure 4.6: Basins of attraction for Rayleigh iteration in the (φ, θ)-plane. Initial guesses in ⬛ regions converge to the eigenvector at ①, guesses in ⬜ regions converge to the eigenvector at ②, and guesses in ☐ regions converge to the eigenvector at ③. See the front cover and the QR code at the bottom of this page.

$\mathbf{x}^H \mathbf{A} \mathbf{x} = \sum_{i=1}^{n} \lambda_i x_i^2$ and $S_k = \mathrm{span}\{\boldsymbol{\xi}_1, \boldsymbol{\xi}_2, \dots, \boldsymbol{\xi}_k\}$, the first k standard basis vectors of $\mathbb{R}^n$. If $\mathbf{x} \in S_k$, then

$$\mathbf{x}^H \mathbf{A} \mathbf{x} = \sum_{i=1}^{n} \lambda_i x_i^2 = \sum_{i=1}^{k} \lambda_i x_i^2 \geq \lambda_k \sum_{i=1}^{k} x_i^2 = \lambda_k \|\mathbf{x}\|_2^2.$$

And, if $\mathbf{x}$ happens to be the eigenvector $\boldsymbol{\xi}_k$, then $\mathbf{x}^H \mathbf{A} \mathbf{x} = \lambda_k$. It follows that $\lambda_k = \min_{\mathbf{x} \in S_k} \rho_A(\mathbf{x})$. Finally consider λ_1.

$$\mathbf{x}^H \mathbf{A} \mathbf{x} = \sum_{i=1}^{n} \lambda_i x_i^2 \leq \lambda_1 \sum_{i=1}^{n} x_i^2 = \lambda_1 \|\mathbf{x}\|_2^2$$

and $\rho_A(\mathbf{x}) = \lambda_1$ for $\mathbf{x} = \boldsymbol{\xi}_1$. So, $\lambda_1 = \max_{\mathbf{x}} \rho_A(\mathbf{x})$. $\square$

By the Courant–Fischer theorem, $\lambda_{\min} \leq \rho \leq \lambda_{\max}$ for a symmetric matrix. Figure 4.5 on the previous page depicts the mapping $\mathbf{x} \mapsto \rho_A(\mathbf{x})\mathbf{x}$ for the matrices from Figure 1.1 on page 13. The Rayleigh quotient is the best approximation to the eigenvalue, and it equals eigenvalues along the eigenvectors. While the Rayleigh quotient is bounded by the largest and smallest eigenvalues in symmetric matrices like ①, in general, it may be larger or smaller than either.

basins of attraction
painted onto the
Rayleigh quotient

The following method combines Rayleigh quotient approximation with the shift-and-invert method, starting with a unit vector $\mathbf{x}^{(0)}$:

$$\begin{cases} \text{calculate} & \rho^{(k)} = \mathbf{x}^{(k)\mathrm{H}}\mathbf{A}\mathbf{x}^{(k)} \\ \text{solve} & \left(\mathbf{A} - \rho^{(k)}\mathbf{I}\right)\mathbf{x}^{(k+1)} = \mathbf{x}^{(k)} \\ \text{normalize} & \mathbf{x}^{(k+1)} \leftarrow \mathbf{x}^{(k+1)} / \left\|\mathbf{x}^{(k+1)}\right\|_2 \end{cases}.$$

Rayleigh quotient iteration is locally cubically convergent if $\mathbf{A}$ is Hermitian and quadratically convergent otherwise. See Demmel [1997]. Like many nonlinear iterative methods (such as Newton's method), Rayleigh quotient iteration exhibits basins of attraction and sensitivity to initial conditions. See Figure 4.6 on the preceding page.

4.3   The QR method

The QR method was invented independently in 1960 by Russian mathematician Vera Kublanovskaya and English computer scientist John Francis. It has since then become "firmly established as *the* most important algorithm for eigenvalue problems" and one of the top ten algorithms of the 20th century.[4] (Watkins [2011]) The QR method extends the power method to get all the eigenvectors all at once rather than one at a time. Recall the idea of the power method. Let $\mathbf{A} \in \mathbb{R}^{n \times n}$ with eigenvalues $|\lambda_1| \geq |\lambda_2| \geq \cdots \geq |\lambda_n|$ and associated eigenvectors $\{\mathbf{v}_1, \mathbf{v}_2, \ldots, \mathbf{v}_n\}$. Choose an initial vector $\mathbf{x}^{(0)}$. At each iteration,

1. Multiply $\mathbf{x}^{(k)}$ by $\mathbf{A}$: $\mathbf{x}^{(k+1)} = \mathbf{A}\mathbf{x}^{(k)}$.

2. Normalize to avoid over- or underflow: $\mathbf{x}^{(k+1)} \leftarrow \mathbf{x}^{(k+1)} / \left\|\mathbf{x}^{(k+1)}\right\|$.

Repeat until convergence. This method finds the dominant eigenvector $\mathbf{v}_1$.

Now, suppose we start with n initial vectors and want to get all n eigenvectors. Let's develop a method so that the first vector sequence converges to $\mathbf{v}_1$, the second vector sequence converges to $\mathbf{v}_2$, and so forth. Of course, we can work with all the vectors at once by treating them as columns of a matrix. It shouldn't matter what set we start with as long it spans $\mathbb{R}^n$. So, let's take the standard unit vectors $\{\mathbf{x}_1^{(0)}, \mathbf{x}_2^{(0)}, \ldots, \mathbf{x}_n^{(0)}\} = \mathbf{I} = \{\boldsymbol{\xi}_1, \boldsymbol{\xi}_2, \ldots, \boldsymbol{\xi}_n\}$ as our initial set of vectors.

If we apply the power method directly to $\mathbf{I}$, all the columns will converge to the dominant eigenvector unless one happens to already be an eigenvector. Let's fix this problem and get all the eigenvectors. We won't do anything to the first column

---

[4]Remarkably, for 45 years, John Francis was entirely unaware of the impact of his contribution. Shortly after publishing his results, he left the field and never looked back. It wasn't until 2007 that Francis was tracked down and learned of his achievements. By then, he was retired and living in a seaside resort on the southeast coast of England, sailing and working on a degree in mathematics. While Francis had briefly attended the University of Cambridge in the 1950s, he never completed a degree. He subsequently received an honorary doctorate from the University of Sussex in 2015.

$x_1^{(k+1)}$ except normalize it to $q_1^{(k+1)}$. It converges to the dominant eigenvector v_1, and within several iterations, it should give us a good approximation to v_1. Let $q_2^{(k+1)}$ be the normalized, orthogonal projection of $Aq_2^{(k)}$ into span$\{q_1^{(k+1)}\}^\perp$. Since $q_1^{(k+1)}$ is close to v_1, this projection will kill off much of the component in the v_1 direction. This means that the change from $q_2^{(k)}$ to $q_2^{(k+1)}$ is now dominated by v_2. Let $q_3^{(k+1)}$ be the orthogonal projection of $q_3^{(k)}$ into span$\{q_1^{(k+1)}, q_2^{(k+1)}\}^\perp$. Since $q_1^{(k+1)}$ is close to v_1 and $q_2^{(k+1)}$ is close to v_2, this projection will ensure that the change from $q_3^{(k)}$ to $q_3^{(k+1)}$ is now dominated by v_3. And so forth.

Our method is now as follows. Take $Q_0 = I$. For each iteration

1. Multiply by A: $M_{k+1} = AQ_k$.

2. Take the QR-decomposition of the resulting matrix: $Q_{k+1}R_{k+1} = M_{k+1}$.

We can write the two-part iteration as

$$Q_{k+1}R_{k+1} = M_{k+1} = AQ_k. \qquad (4.2)$$

It's not yet clear what this equation means. Let's change the basis to Q_k. We simply need to "rotate" by $Q_k^{-1} = Q_k^\mathsf{T}$ to do so. Multiplying (4.2) by Q_k^T yields

$$Q_k^\mathsf{T} Q_{k+1}R_{k+1} = Q_k^\mathsf{T}M_{k+1} = Q_k^\mathsf{T}AQ_k. \qquad (4.3)$$

This equation says that $Q_k^\mathsf{T} Q_{k+1}R_{k+1}$ is unitarily similar to A. So $Q_k^\mathsf{T} Q_{k+1}R_{k+1}$ has the same eigenvalues as A. If the iteration converges, then $Q_k \to Q_{k+1}$ and $Q_k^\mathsf{T} Q_{k+1} \to I$, and we are left with R_{k+1} on the left-hand side. The matrix R_{k+1} is an upper triangular matrix with the eigenvalues along the diagonal, giving us the Schur decomposition of A.

We are not done yet. Define $\hat{Q}_1$ to be the change from Q_k to Q_{k+1}. That is, let $Q_{k+1} = \hat{Q}_{k+1}Q_k$. Then

$$Q_{k+1} = \hat{Q}_{k+1}\hat{Q}_k \cdots \hat{Q}_2\hat{Q}_1$$

and $\hat{Q}_1 = Q_0 = I$. And (4.3) is equivalent to

$$\hat{Q}_{k+1}R_{k+1} = \hat{M}_{k+1} = Q_k^\mathsf{T}AQ_k$$

where $\hat{M}_{k+1} = Q_k^\mathsf{T}M_{k+1}$. From (4.3) we have $R_{k+1}Q_k^\mathsf{T} = Q_{k+1}^\mathsf{T}A$, and hence $R_kQ_{k-1}^\mathsf{T} = Q_k^\mathsf{T}A$. So,

$$\hat{Q}_{k+1}R_{k+1} = \hat{M}_{k+1} = R_kQ_{k-1}^\mathsf{T}Q_k = R_k\hat{Q}_k$$

We are left with the simple implementation. Starting with $T_0 = A$, for each iteration,

$$\begin{cases} \text{factor} & T_k \to Q_kR_k \\ \text{form} & T_{k+1} \leftarrow R_kQ_k \end{cases}.$$

The QR algorithm provides the Schur decomposition of a matrix

$$\mathbf{R} = \mathbf{U}^H \mathbf{A} \mathbf{U}$$

where $\mathbf{U}$ is unitary. At each iteration

$$\mathbf{T}_{k+1} = \mathbf{R}_k \mathbf{Q}_k = \mathbf{Q}_k^H \mathbf{Q}_k \mathbf{R}_k \mathbf{Q}_k = \mathbf{Q}_k^H \mathbf{T}_k \mathbf{Q}_k.$$

If we continue and unravel the terms,

$$\mathbf{T}_{k+1} = (\mathbf{Q}_0 \mathbf{Q}_1 \cdots \mathbf{Q}_k)^H \mathbf{T}_0 (\mathbf{Q}_0 \mathbf{Q}_1 \cdots \mathbf{Q}_k).$$

Because $(\mathbf{Q}_0 \mathbf{Q}_1 \cdots \mathbf{Q}_k)$ is unitary,

$$\lambda(\mathbf{T}_{k+1}) = \lambda(\mathbf{T}_k) = \lambda(\mathbf{T}_{k-1}) = \cdots = \lambda(\mathbf{T}_0) = \lambda(\mathbf{A}).$$

$\mathbf{T}_k$ converges to an upper triangular matrix, and the diagonal of $\mathbf{T}_k$ gives the eigenvalues of $\mathbf{A}$. The eigenvalues don't change, the eigenvectors just rotate. The following figure shows the QR method applied to a matrix at iterations $\mathbf{T}_0$, $\mathbf{T}_5$, $\mathbf{T}_{10}$, $\mathbf{T}_{20}$, and $\mathbf{T}_{100}$:

$\mathbf{T}_0$ $\qquad$ $\mathbf{T}_5$ $\qquad$ $\mathbf{T}_{10}$ $\qquad$ $\mathbf{T}_{20}$ $\qquad$ $\mathbf{T}_{100}$

▷ **Convergence of the QR method**

Because the QR method uses the power method, convergence is generally slow. The diagonal elements of $\mathbf{R}_k$ converge to the eigenvalues linearly. Let $\mathbf{A} \in \mathbb{R}^{n \times n}$ have eigenvalues such that $|\lambda_1| > |\lambda_2| > \cdots > |\lambda_n|$. Then

$$\lim_{k \to \infty} \mathbf{R}_k = \begin{bmatrix} \lambda_1 & r_{12} & \cdots & r_{1n} \\ 0 & \lambda_2 & & \vdots \\ \vdots & & \ddots & \vdots \\ 0 & 0 & \cdots & \lambda_n \end{bmatrix}$$

with convergence

$$|r_{i,i-1}^{(k)}| = O\left(\left|\frac{\lambda_i}{\lambda_{i-1}}\right|^k\right).$$

Each QR decomposition takes $\frac{4}{3}n^3$ operations, and each matrix multiplication takes $\frac{1}{2}n^3$ operations. We need to repeat it $O(n)$ times to get the n eigenvalues. Hence, the net cost of the QR method is $O(n^4)$. We can improve the QR algorithm by making a few simple modifications: reducing the matrix to upper Hessenberg form, shifting the matrix in each iteration to speed up convergence, and deflating.

▷ **The QR algorithm with upper Hessenberg matrices**

Because of Abel's theorem, it is generally impossible to determine the Schur decomposition of a matrix $\mathbf{A}$, i.e., an upper triangular matrix unitarily similar to a matrix $\mathbf{A}$. But we can get an upper Hessenberg matrix—close to being an upper triangular—that is unitarily similar to $\mathbf{A}$. Why would we want to do this?

For nonsingular matrices, upper Hessenberg form is preserved by the QR algorithm. Note that if $\mathbf{Q}_n \mathbf{R}_n = \mathbf{H}_n$ then $\mathbf{Q}_n = \mathbf{H}_n \mathbf{R}_n^{-1}$. The inverse of an upper triangular matrix is an upper triangular matrix, and the product of an upper Hessenberg and a triangular matrix is upper Hessenberg. So, $\mathbf{Q}_n$ is upper Hessenberg. Furthermore, $\mathbf{H}_{n+1} = \mathbf{R}_n \mathbf{Q}_n$ is upper Hessenberg. Reducing a matrix to upper Hessenberg form takes $O(n^3)$ operations. But we only need to do this once.

After putting the matrix in upper Hessenberg form, we will need to do $n-1$ Givens rotations to zero out the subdiagonal elements to get the QR decomposition. So a QR step applied to an upper Hessenberg matrix requires at most $O(n^2)$ operations. Each QR step takes $O(n)$ operations for a Hermitian matrix because we are working on a tridiagonal matrix.

We can use Householder reflectors in a manner similar to QR decomposition to get an upper Hessenberg matrix. We first construct a Householder reflector $\mathbf{Q}_1$ to zero out the elements below the first subdiagonal element. To do this,

$$\text{partition } \mathbf{A} \text{ as } \begin{bmatrix} a_{11} & \mathbf{c}^{\mathsf{T}} \\ \mathbf{b} & \hat{\mathbf{A}} \end{bmatrix} \text{ and let } \mathbf{Q}_i \text{ equal } \begin{bmatrix} \mathbf{I} & \mathbf{0}^{\mathsf{T}} \\ \mathbf{0} & \hat{\mathbf{Q}}_i \end{bmatrix}$$

where $\hat{\mathbf{Q}}_i$ is the reflector that maps a vector $\mathbf{b}$ to $\begin{bmatrix} -\|\mathbf{b}\|_2 & 0 & \cdots & 0 \end{bmatrix}^{\mathsf{T}}$. Because $\hat{\mathbf{Q}}_i$ is a Householder reflector, $\hat{\mathbf{Q}}_i = \hat{\mathbf{Q}}_i^{-1} = \hat{\mathbf{Q}}_i^{\mathsf{T}}$. Note that $\mathbf{Q}_i$ is a block matrix with the identity matrix in the upper-left block. Left-multiplying a matrix by $\mathbf{Q}_1$ does not change the first row, and right-multiplying a matrix by $\mathbf{Q}_1$ does not change the first column. Pictorially, $\mathbf{A}_1 = \mathbf{Q}_1 \mathbf{A} \mathbf{Q}_1^{\mathsf{T}}$ is

We construct a similar Householder reflector $\mathbf{Q}_2$ to zero out the elements below the second subdiagonal. Pictorially, $\mathbf{A}_2 = \mathbf{Q}_2 \mathbf{A}_1 \mathbf{Q}_2^{\mathsf{T}}$ is

Continuing this way, we will form an upper Hessenberg matrix unitarily similar to $\mathbf{A}$. Since it is similar, it has the same eigenvalues. If $\mathbf{A}$ is a Hermitian matrix, the upper Hessenberg matrix is a tridiagonal matrix.

♣ The LinearAlgebra.jl function hessenberg(A) computes the unitarily similar upper Hessenberg form of a matrix **A** and returns a Hessenberg object consisting of a unitary matrix and a Hessenberg matrix. Either can be converted to a regular matrix object using the Matrix method.

▷ Shifted QR iteration

Recall that if the eigenvalues of **A** are $\{\lambda_1, \lambda_2, \ldots, \lambda_n\}$, then the eigenvalues of $\mathbf{A} - \rho\mathbf{I}$ are $\{\lambda_1 - \rho, \lambda_2 - \rho, \ldots, \lambda_n - \rho\}$. The diagonal elements of $\mathbf{A}_k$ converge to the eigenvalues linearly with the values of the subdiagonals given by

$$|a_{i,i-1}^{(k)}| = O\left(\left|\frac{\lambda_i - \rho}{\lambda_{i-1} - \rho}\right|^k\right).$$

We can speed up convergence by applying QR iteration to $\mathbf{A} - \rho\mathbf{I}$ and choosing ρ to be close to an eigenvalue. This is the same idea that we used to pick the Rayleigh iteration shift. Since the diagonal elements of $\mathbf{A}_k$ converge to the eigenvalues of **A**, they are the natural choices for ρ. Once the corresponding diagonal element has converged to an eigenvalue, we move to another one.

Start with the lower right corner $i = n$. Recall that this diagonal element will converge to the smallest eigenvalue. At each iteration,

$$\begin{cases} \text{set} & \rho = a_{ii}^{(k)} \\ \text{factor} & (\mathbf{A}_k - \rho\mathbf{I}) \to \mathbf{Q}_{k+1}\mathbf{R}_{k+1} \\ \text{restor} & \mathbf{A}_{k+1} \leftarrow (\mathbf{R}_{k+1}\mathbf{Q}_{k+1} + \rho\mathbf{I}) \end{cases}.$$

Once $a_{ii}^{(k)}$ has converged to an eigenvalue, move to the previous diagonal element $(i \to i - 1)$ and repeat the process. Note that

$$\mathbf{A}_{k+1} = \mathbf{R}_{k+1}\mathbf{Q}_{k+1} + \rho\mathbf{I} = \mathbf{Q}_{k+1}^\mathsf{T}(\mathbf{A}_k - \rho\mathbf{I})\mathbf{Q}_{k+1} + \rho\mathbf{I} = \mathbf{Q}_{k+1}^\mathsf{T}\mathbf{A}_k\mathbf{Q}_{k+1}.$$

So, the new $\mathbf{A}_{k+1}$ has the same eigenvalues as the old $\mathbf{A}_k$.

The convergence with each shift is $O\left(|\lambda_i - \rho|/|\lambda_{i-1} - \rho|\right)$ where $\rho \approx \lambda_i$. Overall, we get quadratic convergence. We get cubic convergence for Hermitian matrices, where the eigenvectors are orthogonal. This type of shifting is called *Rayleigh quotient shifting*. See the figure on the following page or the QR code below, which shows the convergence of the QR method and convergence of the shifted QR method to eigenvalues of a 6×6 complex matrix. The standard QR method takes 344 iterations to converge to an error of 10^{-3}, while the shifted QR method requires only 16 iterations. Notice that convergence is slower for eigenvalues whose magnitudes are close.

Occasionally, Rayleigh quotient shifting will fail to converge. For example, using $\rho = 2$ on the matrix

$$\mathbf{A} = \begin{bmatrix} 2 & 1 \\ 1 & 2 \end{bmatrix},$$

comparison of QR and shifted QR methods

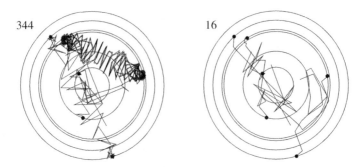

Figure 4.7: Convergence of the QR method (left) and the shifted QR method (right) to eigenvalues of a 6×6 complex matrix. The eigenvectors are depicted by • and line segments show the paths of convergence.

which has eigenvalues $\lambda = 1$ and 3, results in an orthogonal matrix

$$\mathbf{A} - \rho\mathbf{I} = \begin{bmatrix} 1 & 1 \\ 1 & -1 \end{bmatrix},$$

which has eigenvalues ± 1, each of equal magnitude. Each eigenvector pulls equally, and the algorithm cannot decide which eigenvalue to go to. One fix to this problem is to use the *Wilkinson shift*. The Wilkinson shift defines ρ to be the eigenvalue of the submatrix

$$\begin{bmatrix} a_{i-1,i-1}^{(k-1)} & a_{i-1,i}^{(k-1)} \\ a_{i,i-1}^{(k-1)} & a_{i,i}^{(k-1)} \end{bmatrix}$$

that is closest to $a_{i,i}^{(k-1)}$. The eigenvalues of a 2×2 matrix are easily computed by using the quadratic formula to solve the characteristic equation.

▷ **Deflation**

QR decomposition requires $O(n^3)$ operations, and computing the product $\mathbf{RQ}$ takes another $O(n)$ operations. We can speed up the method by using *deflation*. Start with the shift $\rho = a_{i,i}$. When the magnitude subdiagonal element $a_{i,i-1}$ is small, the diagonal element $a_{i,i}$ is a close approximation of the eigenvalue λ_i. At this point set the shift ρ to equal $a_{i-1,i-1}$ and recover λ_i. To reduce the number of computations at the next step, we consider the $(i - 1) \times (i - 1)$ principal submatrix obtained by removing the last row and last column. We continue QR decomposition on this smaller matrix. And continue like this successively with smaller and smaller matrices. Complex eigenvalues of real matrices are extracted in pairs.

4.4 Implicit QR

At each step of the shifted QR method, we compute

$$(\mathbf{A} - \rho\mathbf{I}) = \mathbf{QR}, \qquad \hat{\mathbf{A}} = \mathbf{RQ} + \rho\mathbf{I} \tag{4.4}$$

where $\mathbf{A}$ is in proper upper Hessenberg form. This gives us the similarity transform

$$\hat{\mathbf{A}} = \mathbf{Q}^{\mathsf{T}}\mathbf{AQ}. \tag{4.5}$$

In practice, we don't need (or necessarily want) to compute the QR decomposition (4.4) explicitly. When the shift ρ is close to an eigenvalue (which is what we want it to be), the QR method is sensitive to round-off and may be unstable. The solution is to never explicitly subtract off $\rho\mathbf{I}$ and consequently to never compute $\mathbf{R}$. Instead, we can do this implicitly. But the trick now is determining the sequence of Givens rotations or Householder reflections $\mathbf{Q}_1\mathbf{Q}_2 \cdots \mathbf{Q}_n$ that gives us $\mathbf{Q}$. As it turns out, such an implicit method is no more difficult than the explicit method.

Consider the upper Hessenberg matrix $\mathbf{A} - \rho\mathbf{I}$. We left-multiply by a Givens rotation $\mathbf{Q}_1^{\mathsf{T}}$ to zero out element a_{21}.

$$\begin{bmatrix} a_{11}-\rho & a_{12} & a_{13} & a_{14} & a_{15} \\ a_{21} & a_{22}-\rho & a_{23} & a_{24} & a_{25} \\ & a_{32} & a_{33}-\rho & a_{34} & a_{35} \\ & & a_{43} & a_{44}-\rho & a_{45} \\ & & & a_{54} & a_{55}-\rho \end{bmatrix} \rightarrow \begin{bmatrix} * & * & * & * & * \\ 0 & x & * & * & * \\ & a_{32} & a_{33}-\rho & a_{34} & a_{35} \\ & & a_{43} & a_{44}-\rho & a_{45} \\ & & & a_{54} & a_{55}-\rho \end{bmatrix}$$

The values in the first and second rows are changed. Notably, element $(2, 1)$ is changed from a_{21} to 0 and element $(2, 2)$ is changed from $a_{22} - \rho$ to some value x. Suppose that we were to apply the same Givens rotation $\mathbf{Q}_1^{\mathsf{T}}$ to our original matrix $\mathbf{A}$.

$$\begin{bmatrix} a_{11} & a_{12} & a_{13} & a_{14} & a_{15} \\ a_{21} & a_{22} & a_{23} & a_{24} & a_{25} \\ & a_{32} & a_{33} & a_{34} & a_{35} \\ & & a_{43} & a_{44} & a_{45} \\ & & & a_{54} & a_{55} \end{bmatrix} \rightarrow \begin{bmatrix} * & * & * & * & * \\ \rho s & x + \rho c & * & * & * \\ & a_{32} & a_{33} & a_{34} & a_{35} \\ & & a_{43} & a_{44} & a_{45} \\ & & & a_{54} & a_{55} \end{bmatrix}$$

This time element $(2, 1)$ is changed from a_{21} to ρs and element $(2, 2)$ is changed from a_{22} to $x + \rho c$, where s and c denote $\sin\theta$ and $\cos\theta$ of the Givens rotations. Now, right-multiply by $\mathbf{Q}_1$ to complete the similarity transform.

$$\rightarrow \begin{bmatrix} * & * & * & * & * \\ sx & cx & * & * & * \\ sa_{32} & ca_{32} & a_{33} & a_{34} & a_{35} \\ & & a_{43} & a_{44} & a_{45} \\ & & & a_{54} & a_{55} \end{bmatrix}$$

In the next step, we need a Givens rotation Q_2^T to zero out a_{32}. Exactly the same Q_2^T works for both A and $A - \rho I$. The same is true for Q_3^T and so on.

All we need to do is start the implicit QR step using the same column q as we would have used to start the explicit QR method and then continue by reducing the matrix into upper Hessenberg form. The resulting upper Hessenberg matrix using the implicit method will equal the upper Hessenberg matrix using the explicit method. This idea is closely related to the Implicit Q theorem.

Theorem 14 (Implicit Q theorem). *Let $H = Q^T A Q$ be the reduction of a matrix A to Hessenberg form, and the elements in the lower diagonal of H are nonzero. Then Q and H are uniquely determined by the first column of Q up to a sign.*

Proof. Consider the following pictorial representation of nonzero elements:

$$
A = \begin{bmatrix} \bullet & \bullet & \bullet & \bullet & \bullet & \bullet \\ \bullet & \bullet & \bullet & \bullet & \bullet & \bullet \\ \bullet & \bullet & \bullet & \bullet & \bullet & \bullet \\ \bullet & \bullet & \bullet & \bullet & \bullet & \bullet \\ \bullet & \bullet & \bullet & \bullet & \bullet & \bullet \\ \bullet & \bullet & \bullet & \bullet & \bullet & \bullet \end{bmatrix}, \quad
H = \begin{bmatrix} \bullet & \bullet & \bullet & \bullet & \bullet & \bullet \\ \bullet & \bullet & \bullet & \bullet & \bullet & \bullet \\ & \bullet & \bullet & \bullet & \bullet & \bullet \\ & & \bullet & \bullet & \bullet & \bullet \\ & & & \bullet & \bullet & \bullet \\ & & & & \bullet & \bullet \end{bmatrix}, \quad \text{and} \quad
Q = \begin{bmatrix} \circ & \circ & \circ & \circ & \circ & \circ \\ \bullet & \circ & \circ & \circ & \circ & \circ \\ \bullet & \bullet & \circ & \circ & \circ & \circ \\ \bullet & \bullet & \bullet & \circ & \circ & \circ \\ \bullet & \bullet & \bullet & \bullet & \circ & \circ \\ \bullet & \bullet & \bullet & \bullet & \bullet & \circ \end{bmatrix}.
$$

If A is an $n \times n$ matrix, then A has n^2 degrees of freedom $\bullet$. Additionally, H has $(n-2)(n-1)/2$ explicitly zero elements, so it has $n^2 - (n-2)(n-1)/2$ degrees of freedom. A unitary matrix Q has $n(n-1)/2$ degrees of freedom. To see this, imagine that we build Q, starting with the leftmost column. The first column of Q can be any vector, as long as it has a length of one. So, it has $n-1$ degrees of freedom. The second column can be any vector, as long as it has a length of one and is orthogonal to the first one. So, it has $n-2$ degrees of freedom. The third column gives another $n-3$ degrees of freedom. And so forth, giving $n(n-1)/2$ degrees of freedom. Between H and Q, we have $n^2 + n - 1$ degrees of freedom, which is $n-1$ too many. The missing $n-1$ degrees of freedom are used to determine the first column of Q. □

The algorithm for *one* implicit QR iteration can be summarized as:

1. Let $\tilde{H} = H - \rho I$.

2. Determine a Householder or Givens transformation Q^T that zeros out the $(2, 1)$ element of $\tilde{H}$.

3. Compute $\tilde{H} \leftarrow Q^T \tilde{H} Q$.

4. Now, continue with Householder or Givens transformations to reduce the new $\tilde{H}$ into upper Hessenberg form by "chasing the bulge":

   a) For $i = 1, 2, \cdots, n-2$ determine the Householder or Givens transformation Q_i that zeros out element $(i+2, i)$ using element $(i+1, i)$.

   b) Compute $A \leftarrow Q^T H Q$.

$$\begin{bmatrix} \vdots \end{bmatrix} \rightarrow \begin{bmatrix} \vdots \end{bmatrix} \rightarrow \begin{bmatrix} \vdots \end{bmatrix} \rightarrow \begin{bmatrix} \vdots \end{bmatrix} \rightarrow \begin{bmatrix} \vdots \end{bmatrix}$$

$$\mathbf{H} \qquad \mathbf{Q}_1^\mathsf{T}\mathbf{H}\mathbf{Q}_1 \qquad \mathbf{Q}_2^\mathsf{T}\cdots\mathbf{Q}_2 \qquad \mathbf{Q}_3^\mathsf{T}\cdots\mathbf{Q}_3 \qquad \mathbf{Q}_4^\mathsf{T}\cdots\mathbf{Q}_4$$

By this point, the QR method bears little resemblance to the underlying power method. But just as we could speed up the convergence of the power method by taking multiple steps ($\mathbf{A}^2\mathbf{x}$ versus $\mathbf{A}\mathbf{x}$, for example), we can speed up the QR method using multiple steps. Namely, we can take $(\mathbf{H} - \rho_1\mathbf{I})(\mathbf{H} - \rho_2\mathbf{I})\cdots(\mathbf{H} - \rho_k\mathbf{I})$ in one QR step. In practice, k is typically $1, 2, 4$, or 6. Note that the bulge we need to chase is size k.

Taking multiple steps is especially appealing when working with real matrices with complex eigenvalues because we can avoid complex arithmetic (cutting computation by half). We can formulate a double-step QR method by taking $\rho_1 = \rho$ and $\rho_2 = \bar{\rho}$. In this case, $\tilde{\mathbf{A}} = \mathbf{H}^2 - 2\,\mathrm{Re}(\rho)\mathbf{H} + |\rho|^2\mathbf{I}$.

♣ The LinearAlgebra.jl function `eigen` returns an Eigen object containing eigenvalues and eigenvectors. The functions `eigvecs` returns a matrix of eigenvectors and `eigvals` returns an array of eigenvalues.

4.5   Getting the eigenvectors

We still have not explicitly computed the eigenvectors using the QR method. While we could keep track of the rotator or reflector matrices $\mathbf{Q}_i$ as they accumulate, this approach is inefficient. Instead, computing the eigenvectors after finding the eigenvalues is typically a simple task. This section looks at two methods: using a shifted power method and using the Shur form.

In the shifted power method, we start again from the upper Hessenberg matrix form of the matrix $\mathbf{H} = \mathbf{Q}^\mathsf{T}\mathbf{A}\mathbf{Q}$. Let ρ be our approximation to an eigenvalue. Then using the shifted power method

$$(\mathbf{H} - \rho\mathbf{I})\mathbf{z}^{(k+1)} = \mathbf{q}^{(k)} \quad \text{with} \quad \mathbf{q}^{(k)} = \frac{\mathbf{z}^{(k)}}{\|\mathbf{z}^{(k)}\|}$$

will return an approximation to the associated eigenvector $\mathbf{q}$ of $\mathbf{H}$. Only one iteration is typically needed when ρ is a good approximation. The eigenvector to $\mathbf{A}$ is then $\mathbf{Q}^\mathsf{T}\mathbf{q}$.

We can use an *ultimate shift* strategy to get the eigenvectors using the Schur form $\mathbf{Q}^\mathsf{H}\mathbf{A}\mathbf{Q} = \mathbf{T}$ without accumulating the matrix $\mathbf{Q}$. First, we use the QR method to find only the eigenvalues. Once we have the approximate eigenvalues, we rerun the QR method using these eigenvalues as shifts and accumulate the matrix $\mathbf{Q}$, using two steps per shift to ensure convergence. If the matrix is symmetric, $\mathbf{T}$ is diagonal, and $\mathbf{Q}$ gives us the eigenvectors.

Let's look at the nonsymmetric case. Suppose that λ is the kth eigenvalue of the upper triangular matrix

$$\mathbf{T} = \begin{bmatrix} \mathbf{T}_{11} & \mathbf{v} & \mathbf{T}_{13} \\ \mathbf{0} & \lambda & \mathbf{w}^\mathsf{T} \\ \mathbf{0} & \mathbf{0} & \mathbf{T}_{33} \end{bmatrix},$$

where $\mathbf{T}_{11}$ is a $(k-1) \times (k-1)$ upper triangular matrix and $\mathbf{T}_{33}$ is an $(n-k) \times (n-k)$ upper triangular matrix. Furthermore, suppose that λ is a simple eigenvalue so that $\lambda \notin \lambda(\mathbf{T}_{11}) \cup \lambda(\mathbf{T}_{33})$. Then eigenvector problem $(\mathbf{T} - \lambda\mathbf{I})\mathbf{y} = 0$ can be written as

$$
\begin{array}{rcl}
(\mathbf{T}_{11} - \lambda\mathbf{I}_{k-1})\mathbf{y}_{k-1} \quad + \quad \mathbf{v}y \quad + \qquad\qquad \mathbf{T}_{13}\mathbf{y}_{n-k} & = & \mathbf{0} \\
\mathbf{w}^\mathsf{T}\mathbf{y}_{n-k} & = & 0 \ , \\
(\mathbf{T}_{33} - \lambda\mathbf{I}_{n-k})\mathbf{y}_{n-k} & = & \mathbf{0}
\end{array}
$$

where $\mathbf{y} = \begin{bmatrix} \mathbf{y}_{k-1} & y & \mathbf{y}_{n-k} \end{bmatrix}^\mathsf{T}$. Because λ is simple, $\mathbf{T}_{11} - \lambda\mathbf{I}_{k-1}$ and $\mathbf{T}_{33} - \lambda\mathbf{I}_{n-k}$ are both nonsingular. So, $\mathbf{y}_{n-k} = \mathbf{0}$ and $\mathbf{y}_{k-1} = y(\mathbf{T}_{11} - \lambda\mathbf{I}_{k-1})^{-1}\mathbf{v}$. Since y is arbitrary, we will set it to one. Then

$$\mathbf{y} = \begin{bmatrix} (\mathbf{T}_{11} - \lambda\mathbf{I}_{k-1})^{-1}\mathbf{v} \\ 1 \\ \mathbf{0} \end{bmatrix},$$

which can be evaluated using backward substitution. The eigenvector for $\mathbf{A}$ is then $\mathbf{x} = \mathbf{Q}\mathbf{y}$.

4.6   Arnoldi method

What if we only want a few of the largest eigenvalues of a large, sparse $n \times n$ matrix? The QR method is inefficient when n is large—much larger than say 1000—especially if we only need a few eigenvalues, because it operates on all n dimensions and it fills in the sparse structure. We can do better by restricting ourselves to a low-dimensional subspace. Using a subspace that is one-tenth the size of the original subspace, we'll get an algorithm almost one thousand times faster. Of course, we would need to find a subspace that includes the eigenvectors we want. If we are happy with approximate eigenvalues, we can use the Rayleigh–Ritz method.

The *Rayleigh–Ritz method* computes approximations $(\tilde{\lambda}_i, \tilde{\mathbf{x}}_i)$ of the eigenvalue-eigenvector pair $(\lambda_i, \mathbf{x}_i)$ of $\mathbf{A}$, called Ritz pairs, by solving the eigenvalue problem in a space that approximates an eigenspace of $\mathbf{A}$. Let $\mathbf{A}$ be an $n \times n$ matrix and let $\mathbf{V}$ be an $n \times m$ matrix whose columns are an orthonormal basis that approximates an m-dimensional eigensubspace of $\mathbf{A}$. The Rayleigh–Ritz method goes as follows: take the projection of $\mathbf{A}$ into the column space of $\mathbf{V}$, solve the eigenvalue problem in this space, and finally express the solutions in the canonical basis. That is, take $\mathbf{R} = \mathbf{V}^\mathsf{T}\mathbf{AV}$, solve $\mathbf{Rv}_i = \tilde{\lambda}_i \mathbf{v}_i$, finally calculate $\tilde{\mathbf{x}}_i = \mathbf{Vv}_i$. We still need a way to find a subspace V close to an eigenspace of $\mathbf{A}$. An effective way to do this is by constructing a Krylov subspace. A Rayleigh–Ritz method that uses such a subspace is called an Arnoldi method. The Arnoldi method combines the power method and the Gram–Schmidt process to get the first m eigenvectors approximations.

The power method preserves the sparsity of the matrix. Still, it only gives us one eigenvalue at a time because it throws away information about the other eigenvectors by only keeping the most recent vector. What if we were to keep a history of the vectors at each iteration? An initial guess $\mathbf{q}$ can be expressed in terms of an eigenvector basis $\{\mathbf{v}_1, \mathbf{v}_2, \dots, \mathbf{v}_n\}$. Let's repeatedly multiply this initial guess by $\mathbf{A}$:

$$\mathbf{q} = c_1\mathbf{v}_1 + c_2\mathbf{v}_2 + \cdots + c_n\mathbf{v}_n$$
$$\mathbf{Aq} = c_1\lambda_1\mathbf{v}_1 + c_2\lambda_2\mathbf{v}_2 + \cdots + c_n\lambda_n\mathbf{v}_n$$
$$\mathbf{A}^2\mathbf{q} = c_1\lambda_1^2\mathbf{v}_1 + c_2\lambda_2^2\mathbf{v}_2 + \cdots + c_n\lambda_n^2\mathbf{v}_n$$
$$\vdots$$
$$\mathbf{A}^{k-1}\mathbf{q} = c_1\lambda_1^{k-1}\mathbf{v}_1 + c_2\lambda_2^{k-1}\mathbf{v}_2 + \cdots + c_n\lambda_n^{k-1}\mathbf{v}_n,$$

where k is bigger than m but much smaller than the n. For $|\lambda_1| > |\lambda_2| > \cdots > |\lambda_n|$, we see that (or at least hope that) the subspace

$$\mathrm{span}\{\mathbf{q}, \mathbf{Aq}, \mathbf{A}^2\mathbf{q}, \dots, \mathbf{A}^{k-1}\mathbf{q}\}$$

is close to the subspace spanned by the first m eigenvectors

$$\mathrm{span}\{\mathbf{v}_1, \mathbf{v}_2, \mathbf{v}_3, \dots, \mathbf{v}_k\}.$$

The *Krylov subspace* $\mathcal{K}_k(\mathbf{A}, \mathbf{q})$ is the subspace spanned by

$$\mathbf{q}, \mathbf{Aq}, \mathbf{A}^2\mathbf{q}, \dots, \mathbf{A}^{k-1}\mathbf{q}.$$

These vectors are the columns of the Krylov matrix $\mathbf{K}_k$. This k-dimensional Krylov subspace is much smaller than the original n-dimensional subspace, so it is unlikely to contain our desired eigenvectors. Instead of finding the true eigenvector-eigenvalue pairs in all of $\mathbb{R}^n$, we will instead find approximate eigenvector-eigenvalue pairs in the Krylov subspace $\mathcal{K}_k(\mathbf{A}, \mathbf{q})$.

The k-dimensional Krylov subspace $\mathcal{K}_k \subset \mathbb{R}^n$ does not contain the m-dimensional eigenspace V—only its projection into $\mathcal{K}_k$. If the starting vector $\mathbf{q}$ happens to be already an eigenvector of $\mathbf{A}$, then the Krylov subspace will only consist of the space spanned by $\mathbf{q}$. This is typically not an issue because any vector chosen at random will likely contain components of all eigenvectors of $\mathbf{A}$. By taking a larger Krylov subspace $\mathcal{K}_{k^*}$ with $k^* > k$, we can get a better approximation at the cost of more computing time:

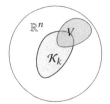 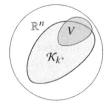

The Krylov subspace approximation introduces another problem. Because $\mathbf{A}^k\mathbf{q}$ converges in direction to the dominant eigenvector, the last several columns of $\mathbf{K}_k$ point in nearly the same direction. So $\mathbf{K}_k$ is ill-conditioned. To fix the ill-conditioning of $\mathbf{K}_k$, we need to replace the vectors $\mathbf{q}, \mathbf{Aq}, \ldots, \mathbf{A}^{m-1}\mathbf{q}$ with the orthonormal set $\mathbf{q}_1, \mathbf{q}_2, \ldots, \mathbf{q}_k$. The process of generating the orthonormal basis for $\mathcal{K}_k(\mathbf{A}, \mathbf{q})$ is called the *Arnoldi method*. The Arnoldi method is similar to the Gram–Schmidt process, except we don't start with a set of m basis vectors already in hand. Instead, we only have $\mathbf{q}$.

First, normalize the first vector $\mathbf{q}_1 \leftarrow \mathbf{q}_1/\|\mathbf{q}_1\|_2$. On the next step, take

$$\mathbf{q}_2 = \mathbf{Aq}_1 - (\mathbf{Aq}_1, \mathbf{q}_1)\,\mathbf{q}_1 = \mathbf{Aq}_1 - h_{11}\mathbf{q}_1$$

and then normalize $\mathbf{q}_2 \leftarrow \mathbf{q}_2/\|\mathbf{q}_2\|$. On the subsequent steps, take

$$\mathbf{q}_{j+1} = \mathbf{Aq}_j - \sum_{i=1}^{j} \mathbf{q}_i h_{ij},$$

where h_{ij} is the Gram–Schmidt coefficient $h_{ij} = (\mathbf{Aq}_j, \mathbf{q}_i)$. In practice, we implement this step using the modified Gram–Schmidt with reorthogonalization. Complete the step by normalizing $\mathbf{q}_{j+1} \leftarrow \mathbf{q}_{j+1}/h_{j+1,j}$ where $h_{j+1,j} = \|\mathbf{q}_{j+1}\|_2$.

The Arnoldi method can be written as the following algorithm,

> Guess an initial $\mathbf{q}^{(1)}$ with $\|\mathbf{q}^{(1)}\|_2 = 1$
> for $j = 1, \ldots, k$
> $\quad\mathbf{q}_{j+1} \leftarrow \mathbf{Aq}_j$
> $\quad\mathbf{q}_{j+1} \leftarrow \mathbf{q}_j/\|\mathbf{q}^{(j+1)}\|$
> $\quad$for $i = 1, \ldots, j$
> $\quad\quad h_{i,j} \leftarrow (\mathbf{q}_i, \mathbf{q}_{j+1})$
> $\quad\quad \mathbf{q}_{j+1} \leftarrow \mathbf{q}_{j+1} - h_{i,j}\mathbf{q}_i$
> $\quad h_{j+1,j} \leftarrow \|\mathbf{q}_j\|$
> $\quad\mathbf{q}_{j+1} \leftarrow \mathbf{q}_{j+1}/h_{j+1,j}$

In matrix form, $\mathbf{AQ}_k = \mathbf{Q}_{k+1}\mathbf{H}_{k+1,k}$ where $\mathbf{Q}_k = \begin{bmatrix} \mathbf{q}_1 & \mathbf{q}_2 & \cdots & \mathbf{q}_k \end{bmatrix}$ and

$$\mathbf{H}_{k+1,k} = \begin{bmatrix} \bullet & \bullet & \bullet & \bullet \\ \bullet & \bullet & \bullet & \bullet \\ & \bullet & \bullet & \bullet \\ & & \bullet & \bullet \\ & & & \bullet \end{bmatrix}$$

is a nonsquare upper Hessenberg matrix. Note we can complete the $\mathbf{H}_{k+1,k}$ by adding a column ξ_1 to get an upper triangular matrix

$$
\mathbf{R} = \begin{bmatrix} 1 & \bullet & \bullet & \bullet & \bullet \\ & \bullet & \bullet & \bullet & \bullet \\ & & \bullet & \bullet & \bullet \\ & & & \bullet & \bullet \\ & & & & \bullet \end{bmatrix}.
$$

In this case, $\mathbf{Q}_k\mathbf{R}$ is the QR decomposition of the Krylov matrix $\mathbf{K}_k$. We can also rewrite the Arnoldi decomposition by separating out the bottom row of $\mathbf{H}_{k+1,k}$ to get

$$
\underbrace{\begin{bmatrix} \end{bmatrix}}_{\mathbf{A}} \underbrace{\begin{bmatrix} \end{bmatrix}}_{\mathbf{Q}_k} = \underbrace{\begin{bmatrix} \end{bmatrix}}_{\mathbf{Q}_k} \underbrace{\begin{bmatrix} \end{bmatrix}}_{\mathbf{H}_k} + \underbrace{\begin{bmatrix} \end{bmatrix} \begin{bmatrix} 0 & \cdots & 0 & h_{k+1,k} \end{bmatrix}}_{\mathbf{q}_{k+1}} \tag{4.6}
$$

Because $\mathbf{Q}_k^{\mathsf{T}}$ is orthogonal to $\mathbf{q}_{k+1}$, multiplying (4.6) by $\mathbf{Q}_k^{\mathsf{T}}$ zeros out the last term and leaves us with $\mathbf{Q}_k^{\mathsf{T}}\mathbf{A}\mathbf{Q}_k = \mathbf{H}_k$. This means that in the projection, the upper Hessenberg matrix $\mathbf{H}_k$ has the same eigenvalues as $\mathbf{A}$, i.e., the Ritz values. More precisely, if $(\mathbf{x}, \mu)$ is an eigenpair of $\mathbf{H}_k$, then $\mathbf{v} = \mathbf{Q}_k\mathbf{x}$ satisfies

$$
\begin{aligned}
\|\mathbf{A}\mathbf{v} - \mu\mathbf{v}\|_2 &= \|\mathbf{A}\mathbf{Q}_k\mathbf{x} - \mu\mathbf{Q}_k\mathbf{x}\|_2 \\
&= \|(\mathbf{A}\mathbf{Q}_k - \mathbf{Q}_k\mathbf{H}_k)\mathbf{x}\|_2 \\
&= h_{k+1,k}\|\xi_{k+1}^{\mathsf{T}}\mathbf{x}\|_2 \\
&= h_{k+1,k}|x_{k+1}|.
\end{aligned}
$$

The residual norm $h_{k+1,k}|x_{k+1}|$ is called the *Ritz estimate*. The Ritz estimate is small if $(\mu, \mathbf{v})$ is a good approximation to an eigenpair of $\mathbf{A}$. See the figure on the next page and the QR code at the bottom of this page.

It is mathematically intuitive that the success of Arnoldi iteration depends on choosing a good starting vector $\mathbf{q}$. A vector chosen at random likely has significant components in all eigenvector directions, not just the first k. So the Krylov subspace is not a great match. In practice, how do we get a good starting vector $\mathbf{q}$ for the Krylov subspace?

One solution is to run the Arnoldi method to get a good starting vector and restart using this better guess. This method is called the *implicitly restarted Arnoldi method*. Suppose that we want to get the m eigenvectors corresponding to the largest eigenvalues. Let's take the Arnoldi subspace to have $k = j + m \approx 2m$ dimensions. First, we run the Arnoldi method to get k Arnoldi vectors $\mathbf{Q}_k$ and $\mathbf{H}_k$. Then, we suppress the components of the eigenvectors of $\lambda_{m+1}, \lambda_{m+2}, \ldots, \lambda_k$ in our k-dimensional Arnoldi subspace. To do this, we run j steps of the shifted QR method, one step for each of the j eigenvectors we are trying to filter out.

Ritz values for
increasing Krylov
dimensions and
eigenvalues

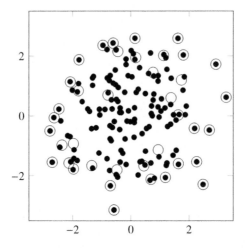

Figure 4.8: The location of the Ritz values ○ of $\mathbf{K}_{40}(\mathbf{A}, \mathbf{q})$ and eigenvalues ● in the complex plane. The matrix $\mathbf{A}$ is a 144×144 complex-valued tridiagonal matrix and $\mathbf{q}$ is a random initial guess. Notice that the Ritz values are closer to eigenvalues with large magnitudes.

For each shift, we use the approximate Ritz value $\{\mu_{k+1}, \ldots, \mu_k\}$. We take the accumulated unitary matrix $\mathbf{V}_k$ from the j QR steps to change the basis to our Arnoldi subspace. Namely,

$$\mathbf{H} \leftarrow \mathbf{V}_k^\mathsf{T} \mathbf{H}_k \mathbf{V}_k$$
$$\mathbf{Q} \leftarrow \mathbf{Q}_k \mathbf{V}_k$$

The first k columns of $\mathbf{Q}$ are our new first k Arnoldi vectors. We zero out the last j Arnoldi vectors (and the last j rows and columns of $\mathbf{H}$) and find new ones by running the Arnoldi method starting with $\mathbf{q}_{k+1}$. We continue like this until convergence.

♣ The Arpack.jl (a wrapper of ARPACK) function `eigs(A,n)` computes n eigenvalues of A using the implicitly restarted Arnoldi method.

The Arnoldi method applied to a symmetric matrix is called the *Lanczos method*. Symmetric matrices have two clear advantages over nonsymmetric matrices. Their eigenvectors are orthogonal, so convergence is fast. And their upper Hessenberg form is tridiagonal, which is $O(n)$ complex.

4.7   Singular value decomposition

Recall that the singular value decomposition of an $m \times n$ matrix $\mathbf{A}$ is $\mathbf{U\Sigma V}^\mathsf{T}$ where $\mathbf{U}$ is an $m \times m$ unitary matrix of eigenvectors of $\mathbf{AA}^\mathsf{T}$, $\mathbf{\Sigma}$ is an $m \times n$ matrix of singular values $\sigma(\mathbf{A}) = \sqrt{\mathbf{A}^\mathsf{T}\mathbf{A}}$, and $\mathbf{V}$ is an $n \times n$ unitary matrix of eigenvectors of $\mathbf{A}^\mathsf{T}\mathbf{A}$. This section examines the Golub–Kahan–Reinisch algorithm for the SVD—there are several others. The algorithm consists of two steps: transforming the matrix to upper bidiagonal form and applying the QR algorithm.

Step 1. Compute

$$\tilde{\mathbf{U}}^\mathsf{T} \mathbf{A} \tilde{\mathbf{V}} = \begin{bmatrix} \mathbf{B} \\ \mathbf{0} \end{bmatrix} = \begin{bmatrix} \bullet\, \bullet \\ \bullet\, \bullet \\ \bullet\, \bullet \\ \bullet \end{bmatrix},$$

where $\mathbf{B}$ is an upper bidiagonal matrix. We use a series of Householder reflections (or Givens rotations).

After $m - 1$ steps, $\tilde{\mathbf{U}} = \tilde{\mathbf{U}}_1 \tilde{\mathbf{U}}_2 \cdots \tilde{\mathbf{U}}_{m-1}$ and $\tilde{\mathbf{V}} = \tilde{\mathbf{V}}_1 \tilde{\mathbf{V}}_2 \cdots \tilde{\mathbf{V}}_{m-1}$.

Step 2. Use the QR method on $\mathbf{B}$ to get the singular values $\mathbf{\Sigma}$. One cycle of implicit QR on $\mathbf{B}^\mathsf{T}\mathbf{B}$ is

1. Take $\rho = b_{n,n}^2 + b_{n-1,n}^2$ (Rayleigh shifting)

2. Compute $\mathbf{AQ}^\mathsf{T}$ for Givens rotation

$$\mathbf{Q} : \begin{bmatrix} b_{11}^2 - \rho & b_{11}b_{12} \end{bmatrix} \to \begin{bmatrix} * & 0 \end{bmatrix}$$

3. "Chase the bulge" using left and right Givens rotations

$$\mathbf{U} : \begin{bmatrix} b_{i,i} \\ b_{i+1,i} \end{bmatrix} \to \begin{bmatrix} * \\ 0 \end{bmatrix} \qquad \mathbf{V} : \begin{bmatrix} b_{i,i+1} & b_{i,i+2} \end{bmatrix} \to \begin{bmatrix} * & 0 \end{bmatrix}.$$

4. Deflate when $|b_{n-1,n}| < \varepsilon$ by using the upper left $n - 1 \times n - 1$ matrix.

We can use the Lanczos method of finding eigenvalues to find the approximate singular values and singular vectors of a large, sparse matrix. If $\mathbf{u}$ is a left singular vector of $\mathbf{A}$ and $\mathbf{v}$ is a right singular vector of $\mathbf{A}$, then combined, they are the eigenvectors of the symmetric block matrix

$$\underbrace{\begin{bmatrix} \mathbf{0} & \mathbf{A} \\ \mathbf{A}^\mathsf{T} & \mathbf{0} \end{bmatrix}}_{\mathbf{M}} \begin{bmatrix} \mathbf{u} \\ \mathbf{v} \end{bmatrix} = \lambda \begin{bmatrix} \mathbf{u} \\ \mathbf{v} \end{bmatrix},$$

where the eigenvalue λ is an eigenvalue of $\mathbf{A}^\mathsf{T}\mathbf{A}$. To see this, note that

$$\left.\begin{matrix} \mathbf{A}\mathbf{v} = \lambda\mathbf{u} \\ \mathbf{A}^\mathsf{T}\mathbf{u} = \lambda\mathbf{v} \end{matrix}\right\} \quad \text{implies} \quad \left\{\begin{matrix} \mathbf{A}^\mathsf{T}\mathbf{A}\mathbf{v} = \lambda\mathbf{A}^\mathsf{T}\mathbf{u} = \lambda^2\mathbf{v} \\ \mathbf{A}\mathbf{A}^\mathsf{T}\mathbf{u} = \lambda\mathbf{A}\mathbf{v} = \lambda^2\mathbf{u} \end{matrix}\right. .$$

The matrix $\mathbf{M}$ is Hermitian, so we can apply the Lanczos method to get the largest eigenvalues.

The *randomized SVD algorithm*, which uses the general Rayleigh–Ritz method, is another technique for computing an approximate, low-rank SVD of a large matrix. We start by choosing a low rank k approximation to the column space of $\mathbf{A}$ with an orthonormal basis: $\mathbf{A} \approx \mathbf{Q}\mathbf{Q}^\mathsf{T}\mathbf{A}$. The k columns of $\mathbf{Q}$ are chosen at random and orthogonalized using Gram–Schmidt projections, Householder reflections, or Givens rotations. Then we compute the SVD of $\mathbf{Q}^\mathsf{T}\mathbf{A}$ as usual. So,

$$\mathbf{A} \approx \mathbf{Q}\left(\mathbf{Q}^\mathsf{T}\mathbf{A}\right) = \mathbf{Q}\left(\mathbf{W}\mathbf{\Sigma}\mathbf{V}^\mathsf{T}\right) = \mathbf{U}\mathbf{\Sigma}\mathbf{V}^\mathsf{T}$$

where $\mathbf{U} = \mathbf{Q}\mathbf{W}$. In practice, instead of computing the randomized SVD of $\mathbf{A}$ we compute the randomized SVD of $(\mathbf{A}\mathbf{A}^\mathsf{T})^r\mathbf{A}$, where r is a small integer power like 1, 2, or 3, to reduce the noise of the principal components that we are removing. Altogether the randomized SVD algorithm for an $n \times n$ matrix $\mathbf{A}$ is

> Generate a random $n \times k$ matrix $\mathbf{\Omega}$
> $\mathbf{Q}\mathbf{R} \leftarrow \mathbf{A}\mathbf{\Omega}$
> for $i = 1, \ldots, r$
> $\quad\left|\begin{matrix} \tilde{\mathbf{Q}}\tilde{\mathbf{R}} \leftarrow \mathbf{A}^\mathsf{T}\mathbf{Q} \\ \mathbf{Q}\mathbf{R} \leftarrow \mathbf{A}\tilde{\mathbf{Q}} \end{matrix}\right.$
> Compute the SVD: $\mathbf{W}\mathbf{\Sigma}\mathbf{V}^\mathsf{T} \leftarrow \mathbf{Q}^\mathsf{T}\mathbf{A}$
> $\mathbf{U} \leftarrow \mathbf{Q}\mathbf{W}$

To dig deeper into probabilistic algorithms for constructing approximate matrix decompositions, see Halko et al. [2011].

4.8 Exercises

4.1. Consider the $n \times n$ matrix $\mathbf{A}$, where the elements are normally distributed random numbers with variance 1. Conjecture about the distribution of eigenvalues $\lambda(A)$ for arbitrary n. ✍

4.2. A square matrix is diagonally dominant if the magnitude of the diagonal element of each row is greater than the sum of the magnitudes of all other elements in that row. Use the Gershgorin circle theorem to prove that a diagonally dominant matrix is always invertible.

4.3. Use the Gershgorin circle theorem to estimate the eigenvalues of

$$\begin{bmatrix} 9 & 0 & 0 & 1 \\ 2 & 5 & 0 & 0 \\ 1 & 2 & 0 & 1 \\ 3 & 0 & -2 & 0 \end{bmatrix}.$$

Then compute the actual values numerically. ✍

4.4. Use Rayleigh iteration to find the eigenvalues of

$$\mathbf{A} = \begin{bmatrix} 2 & 3 & 6 & 4 \\ 3 & 0 & 3 & 1 \\ 6 & 3 & 8 & 8 \\ 4 & 1 & 8 & 2 \end{bmatrix}.$$

Confirm that you get cubic convergence for a symmetric matrix. ✍

4.5. Write a program that implements the implicit QR method using single-step Rayleigh-shifting with deflation for matrices with real eigenvalues. Test your code on the matrix on $\mathbf{R}\Lambda\mathbf{R}^{-1}$, where Λ is a diagonal matrix of integers 1,2, ...,20, and $\mathbf{R}$ is a matrix of normally distributed random numbers. Use a tolerance of $\varepsilon = 10^{-12}$. Compare your approximate eigenvalues with the exact eigenvalues. Are there matrices on which your method fails? ✍

4.6. Exercise 2.9 examined the paths connecting one Hollywood actor with one another. This exercise finds the actors at the center of Hollywood. Compute the eigenvector centrality of the actor-actor adjacency matrix. Explain in plain language what centrality means in the context of the six-degrees game. ✍

4.7. Implement the randomized SVD algorithm. Test your code using a grayscale image of your choosing. How does the randomized SVD compare with the full SVD in accuracy and performance? ✍

4.8. The infinite matrix $\mathbf{A}$ with entries $a_{11} = 1$, $a_{12} = 1/2$, $a_{21} = 1/3$, $a_{13} = 1/4$, $a_{22} = 1/5$, $a_{31} = 1/6$, and so on, is a bounded operator on ℓ^2. What is $\|\mathbf{A}\|_2$? (This problem was proposed by Nick Trefethen as part of his "hundred-dollar, hundred-digit challenge.")   ✍

4.9. Draw a diagram showing the connections between concepts in this chapter. You might wish to include the power method, inverse power method, Rayleigh iteration, QR method, PageRank, Perron–Frobenius theorem, implicit QR method, Arnoldi method, and singular value decomposition.

Chapter 5

Iterative Methods for Linear Systems

For small and medium-sized matrices, Gaussian elimination is fast. Even for a 1000×1000 matrix, Gaussian elimination takes less than a second on my exceptionally ordinary laptop. Now, suppose we want to solve a partial differential equation in three dimensions. We make a discrete approximation to the problem using 100 grid points in each dimension. Such a problem requires that we solve a system of a million equations. Now, Gaussian elimination would take over thirty years on my laptop. Fortunately, such a system is sparse—only 0.001 percent of the elements in the matrix are nonzero. Gaussian elimination is still fast if the matrix has a narrow bandwidth or can be reordered to have narrow bandwidth. But for a matrix with no redeeming features other than its sparsity, a better approach is an iterative method. Iterative methods use repeated matrix multiplications in the place of matrix inversion. Gaussian elimination takes $O(n^3)$ operations. Matrix-vector multiplication takes only $O(n^2)$ operations and as little as $O(n)$ operations if the matrix is sparse. An iterative method will beat a direct method as long as the number of iterations needed for convergence is much smaller than n.

There are other reasons to use an iterative method. While a direct method must always solve each problem from scratch with zero knowledge, we can give an iterative method a good initial guess. Take a time-dependent partial differential equation. At each new time step, the solution may not change much from the solution computed at the previous time step. Using a direct solver with Cholesky decomposition and Cuthill–McKee reordering to avoid fill in, we only need $O(n^2)$ operations to compute the solution. On the other hand, an iterative method can use the solution from the previous step as a good initial guess for the new time step, and it automatically preserves sparsity.

Sometimes we may not need a solution as accurate as the one provided by a direct solver. For example, a finite difference approximation to a partial

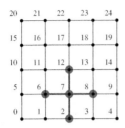 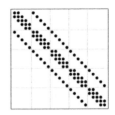

Figure 5.1: The finite difference stencil for the discrete two-dimensional Laplacian on a 5×5 mesh. By labeling the points in lexicon fashion, we can construct a 25×25 block tridiagonal matrix.

differential equation may already have a substantial truncation error. In this case, it may be good enough to use a solver that simply gets us within an error threshold. Or, when solving an optimization problem, finding a close-enough solution might be as good as finding a machine-precision solution, especially if the model contains other errors.

One more reason why iterative methods are helpful is that they reduce the error in the solution with each iteration. Using an iterative method as a corrector to a direct method can help us accurately solve ill-conditioned matrices.

Example. Consider the Poisson equation

$$-\left(\frac{\partial^2 u}{\partial x^2} + \frac{\partial^2 u}{\partial y^2}\right) = f(x, y)$$

with Dirichlet boundary conditions $f(x, y) = 0$ on the unit square. The two-dimensional Poisson equation models several physical systems, such as the steady-state heat distribution $u(x, y)$ given a source $f(x, y)$ or the shape of an elastic membrane $z = u(x, y)$ given a load $f(x, y)$.

The finite difference method is a simple yet effective numerical method for solving the Poisson equation. Consider partitioning a square domain into n intervals each of length h. For the unit square, we would take $h = (n-1)^{-1}$. Using Taylor series approximation, the discrete Laplacian operator can be represented by

$$-\frac{\partial^2 u}{\partial x^2} - \frac{\partial^2 u}{\partial y^2} \approx \frac{4u_{ij} - u_{i-1,j} - u_{i+1,j} - u_{i,j-1} - u_{i,j+1}}{h^2}$$

at each grid point (x_i, y_j). Hence we have a linear system of n^2 equations

$$\frac{4u_{ij} - u_{i-1,j} - u_{i+1,j} - u_{i,j-1} - u_{i,j+1}}{h^2} = f_{ij}$$

for $1 \leq i, j \leq n$ with $u_{ij} \equiv u(x_i, y_j)$ and $f_{ij} \equiv u(x_i, y_j)$. In matrix-vector notation, $\mathbf{Ax} = \mathbf{b}$ where the column vectors

$$\mathbf{x} = \begin{bmatrix} u_{11} & u_{21} & \cdots & u_{n1} & u_{12} & u_{22} & \cdots & u_{nn} \end{bmatrix}^{\mathsf{T}}$$
$$\mathbf{b} = \begin{bmatrix} f_{11} & f_{21} & \cdots & f_{n1} & f_{12} & f_{22} & \cdots & f_{nn} \end{bmatrix}^{\mathsf{T}}.$$

The matrix $\mathbf{A}$ is a sparse, block-tridiagonal matrix with only $5n^2$ nonzero entries out of n^4 elements. See Figure 5.1 on the facing page. ◄

5.1 Jacobi and Gauss–Seidel methods

Suppose that we want to solve $\mathbf{Ax} = \mathbf{b}$. In index format,

$$\sum_{j=1}^{n} a_{ij} x_j = b_i.$$

Let's start by isolating each element x_i:

$$x_i = \frac{1}{a_{ii}} \left(b_i - \sum_{j=1}^{i-1} a_{ij} x_j - \sum_{j=i+1}^{n} a_{ij} x_j \right).$$

The elements of the unknown $\mathbf{x}$ appear on both sides of the equation. One way to solve this problem is by updating x_i iteratively as

$$x_i^{(k+1)} = \frac{1}{a_{ii}} \left(b_i - \sum_{j=1}^{i-1} a_{ij} x_j^{(k)} - \sum_{j=i+1}^{n} a_{ij} x_j^{(k)} \right). \tag{5.1}$$

In this method, called the *Jacobi method*, each element of $\mathbf{x}$ is updated independently, which makes vectorization easy.

Another idea is using the newest and best approximations available, overwriting the elements of $\mathbf{x}$. At each iteration, we compute

$$x_i^{(k+1)} = \frac{1}{a_{ii}} \left(b_i - \sum_{j=1}^{i-1} a_{ij} x_j^{(k+1)} - \sum_{j=i+1}^{n} a_{ij} x_j^{(k)} \right). \tag{5.2}$$

This approach is the *Gauss–Seidel method*. Unlike the Jacobi method, which needs to store two copies of $\mathbf{x}$, the Gauss–Seidel method allows us to use the same array for each iteration, overwriting each element sequentially. Each iteration of the Gauss–Seidel algorithm looks like this

for $i = 1, 2, \ldots, n$
$$\left| \quad x_i \leftarrow \left(b_i - \sum_{j=1}^{i-1} a_{ij} x_j - \sum_{j=i+1}^{n} a_{ij} x_j \right) / a_{ii} \right.$$

At this point, we should ask two questions. When do the Jacobi and Gauss–Seidel methods converge? And how quickly does each converge? To answer these questions, let's look at the Jacobi and Gauss–Seidel methods more generality. The Jacobi and Gauss–Seidel methods are examples of linear iterative methods. Consider using the splitting $\mathbf{A} = \mathbf{P} - \mathbf{N}$ for some $\mathbf{P}$ and $\mathbf{N}$. In this case, the linear system $\mathbf{Ax} = \mathbf{b}$ is the same as

$$\mathbf{Px} = \mathbf{Nx} + \mathbf{b}. \tag{5.3}$$

Given $\mathbf{x}^{(0)}$, we can compute $\mathbf{x}^{(k)}$ by solving the system

$$\mathbf{Px}^{(k+1)} = \mathbf{Nx}^{(k)} + \mathbf{b}. \tag{5.4}$$

We call $\mathbf{P}$ the *preconditioner*. To understand why it's called this, suppose we want to solve the system $\mathbf{Ax} = \mathbf{b}$. Applying $\mathbf{P}^{-1}$ to $\mathbf{Ax} = \mathbf{b}$ gives us $\mathbf{P}^{-1}\mathbf{Ax} = \mathbf{P}^{-1}\mathbf{b}$. The condition number of this new system is $\kappa(\mathbf{P}^{-1}\mathbf{A})$. If we choose $\mathbf{P} \approx \mathbf{A}$, we can get a well-conditioned system. For a general linear iterative method $\mathbf{Px}^{(k+1)} = \mathbf{Nx}^{(k)} + \mathbf{b}$ to be a good method

1. the preconditioner $\mathbf{P}$ should be easy to invert; and

2. the method should converge quickly.

One preconditioner often used for a general matrix is incomplete LU factorization. Incomplete LU factorization takes $\mathbf{P} = \mathbf{LU}$ where $\mathbf{LU} \approx \mathbf{A}$ and the LU decomposition to get $\mathbf{L}$ and $\mathbf{U}$ is fast to compute. For example, we might choose the preconditioner $\mathbf{P}$ that matches $\mathbf{A}$ in certain elements and is otherwise zero.

Let's return to Jacobi and Gauss–Seidel methods. The Jacobi method splits the matrix into diagonal and off-diagonal matrices:

$$\mathbf{A} = \mathbf{P} - \mathbf{N} = \mathbf{D} + \mathbf{M} : \qquad \begin{bmatrix} \bullet\bullet\bullet\bullet\bullet\bullet \\ \bullet\bullet\bullet\bullet\bullet\bullet \\ \bullet\bullet\bullet\bullet\bullet\bullet \\ \bullet\bullet\bullet\bullet\bullet\bullet \\ \bullet\bullet\bullet\bullet\bullet\bullet \end{bmatrix} = \begin{bmatrix} \bullet \\ \ \ \bullet \\ \ \ \ \ \bullet \\ \ \ \ \ \ \ \bullet \end{bmatrix} + \begin{bmatrix} \ \bullet\bullet\bullet\bullet\bullet \\ \bullet\ \bullet\bullet\bullet\bullet \\ \bullet\bullet\ \bullet\bullet\bullet \\ \bullet\bullet\bullet\bullet\ \bullet \end{bmatrix}$$

For an initial guess $\mathbf{x}^{(0)}$, we solve $\mathbf{Dx}^{(k+1)} = -\mathbf{Mx}^{(k)} + \mathbf{b}$. The Gauss–Seidel method splits the matrix into lower triangular and strictly upper triangular matrices:

$$\mathbf{A} = \mathbf{P} - \mathbf{N} = \mathbf{L} + \mathbf{D} + \mathbf{U} : \qquad \begin{bmatrix} \bullet\bullet\bullet\bullet\bullet\bullet \\ \bullet\bullet\bullet\bullet\bullet\bullet \\ \bullet\bullet\bullet\bullet\bullet\bullet \\ \bullet\bullet\bullet\bullet\bullet\bullet \\ \bullet\bullet\bullet\bullet\bullet\bullet \end{bmatrix} = \begin{bmatrix} \bullet \\ \bullet\bullet \\ \bullet\bullet\bullet \\ \bullet\bullet\bullet\bullet \\ \bullet\bullet\bullet\bullet\bullet \end{bmatrix} + \begin{bmatrix} \ \bullet\bullet\bullet\bullet \\ \ \ \bullet\bullet\bullet \\ \ \ \ \bullet\bullet \\ \ \ \ \ \bullet \end{bmatrix}$$

For an initial guess $\mathbf{x}^{(0)}$, we solve $(\mathbf{L} + \mathbf{D})\mathbf{x}^{(k+1)} = -\mathbf{Ux}^{(k)} + \mathbf{b}$.

The error at the kth iteration is $\mathbf{e}^{(k)} = \mathbf{x} - \mathbf{x}^{(k)}$. Subtracting (5.4) from (5.3), gives us $\mathbf{Pe}^{(k+1)} = \mathbf{Ne}^{(k)}$. Equivalently,

$$\mathbf{e}^{(k+1)} = \mathbf{P}^{-1}\mathbf{Ne}^{(k)}.$$

An iterative method creates a *contraction mapping* such that $\mathbf{e}^{(k)} \to \mathbf{0}$ as $k \to \infty$. We can express the initial error $\mathbf{e}^{(0)}$ as a linear combination of the eigenvectors $\mathbf{v}_1, \mathbf{v}_2, \ldots, \mathbf{v}_n$ of $\mathbf{P}^{-1}\mathbf{N}$:

$$\mathbf{e}^{(0)} = c_1\mathbf{v}_1 + c_2\mathbf{v}_2 + \cdots + c_n\mathbf{v}_n.$$

Then

$$\mathbf{e}^{(k)} = \left(\mathbf{P}^{-1}\mathbf{N}\right)^k \mathbf{e}^{(0)} = c_1\lambda_1^k\mathbf{v}_1 + c_2\lambda_2^k\mathbf{v}_2 + \cdots + c_n\lambda_n^k\mathbf{v}_n.$$

It follows that

$$\left\|\mathbf{e}^{(k)}\right\| \leq \left|c_1\lambda_1^k\right|\|\mathbf{v}_1\| + \left|c_2\lambda_2^k\right|\|\mathbf{v}_2\| + \cdots + \left|c_n\lambda_n^k\right|\|\mathbf{v}_n\|.$$

So the method converges if the spectral radius $\rho(\mathbf{P}^{-1}\mathbf{N})$ is less than one. On the other hand, if $\mathbf{P}^{-1}\mathbf{N}$ has an eigenvalue with magnitude greater than or equal to one and the initial error $\mathbf{e}^{(0)}$ has a component in the direction of the corresponding eigenvector, the error will never converge to zero. The error will grow if the eigenvalue is greater than one. We can summarize the discussion above with the following theorem.

Theorem 15. *The iteration* $\mathbf{P}\mathbf{x}^{(k+1)} = \mathbf{N}\mathbf{x}^{(k)} + \mathbf{b}$ *converges if and only if the spectral radius* $\rho(\mathbf{P}^{-1}\mathbf{N}) < 1$.

A matrix is *diagonally dominant* if the magnitudes of the diagonal elements of each row are greater than the sum of the magnitudes of all other elements in that row, i.e., $|a_{ii}| > \sum_{j \neq i} |a_{ij}|$.

Theorem 16. *If a matrix is diagonally dominant, then the Jacobi and Gauss–Seidel methods converge.*

Proof. From theorem 5, all induced matrix norms are bounded below by the spectral radius. Hence, for the Jacobi method,

$$\rho(\mathbf{D}^{-1}\mathbf{M}) \leq \left\|\mathbf{D}^{-1}\mathbf{M}\right\|_\infty = \max_i \sum_{j \neq i} \left|\frac{a_{ij}}{a_{ii}}\right| < 1.$$

So the Jacobi method converges. Put another way, a method $\mathbf{P}\mathbf{e}^{(k+1)} = \mathbf{N}\mathbf{e}^{(k)}$ converges if it is a contraction mapping on the error. For the Jacobi method $a_{ii}e_i^{(k+1)} = \sum_{j \neq i} a_{ij}e_j^{(k)}$, from which

$$\left\|\mathbf{e}^{(k+1)}\right\|_\infty \leq \frac{\sum_{j \neq i} |a_{ij}|}{|a_{ii}|}\left\|\mathbf{e}^{(k)}\right\|_\infty.$$

Intuitively, the Gauss–Seidel should converge even faster because it has even more terms in the denominator. But, because some of the terms might be negative, it's not completely obvious. So, let's be explicit:

$$\left\|\mathbf{e}^{(k+1)}\right\|_{\infty} \leq \frac{\sum_{j>i}|a_{ij}|}{|a_{ii}| - \sum_{j<i}|a_{ij}|}\left\|\mathbf{e}^{(k)}\right\|_{\infty} < \frac{|a_{ii}| - \sum_{j<i}|a_{ij}|}{|a_{ii}| - \sum_{j<i}|a_{ij}|}\left\|\mathbf{e}^{(k)}\right\|_{\infty} = \left\|\mathbf{e}^{(k)}\right\|_{\infty}$$

because the matrix is diagonally dominant.   □

The *convergence factor* r_k of an iterative method is the ratio of errors at each iteration: $r_k = \|\mathbf{e}^{(k)}\|/\|\mathbf{e}^{(k-1)}\|$. The average convergence factor over m iterations is the geometric mean $\left(\prod_{k=1}^{m} r_k\right)^{1/m}$. From this expression, we can compute the average convergence rate: $-\frac{1}{m}\left(\sum_{k=1}^{m} \log r_k\right)$. It is often easier (and just as meaningful) to frame the performance of a method in terms of the long-term convergence rate. We define the *asymptotic convergence rate* as $\lim_{k\to\infty} -\log r_k$.

Example.   Let's examine the convergence rate of the Jacobi and Gauss–Seidel methods on the $n \times n$ discrete Laplacian

$$\mathbf{A} = \begin{bmatrix} -2 & 1 & & & \\ 1 & -2 & 1 & & \\ & \ddots & \ddots & \ddots & \\ & & 1 & -2 & 1 \\ & & & 1 & -2 \end{bmatrix}. \tag{5.5}$$

Let's start with the Jacobi method. The spectral radius of $\mathbf{D}^{-1}(\mathbf{L} + \mathbf{U})$ is $\cos\frac{\pi}{n+1}$, which is approximately $1 - \frac{1}{2}\pi^2(n+1)^{-2}$ when n is large. This value gives us the convergence factor of the Jacobi method. The asymptotic convergence rate (again for large n) is about $\frac{1}{2}\pi^2(n+1)^{-2}$, using the approximation $\log(1 + z) \approx z - \frac{1}{2}z^2 + \cdots$.

The spectral radius of $(\mathbf{L} + \mathbf{D})^{-1}\mathbf{U}$ is $\cos^2\frac{\pi}{n+1}$. So, the convergence factor of the Gauss–Seidel method is approximately $1 - \pi^2(n+1)^{-2}$ when n is large. The asymptotic convergence rate of the Gauss–Seidel method is $\pi^2(n+1)^{-2}$, twice that of the Jacobi method.

If $\mathbf{A}$ is smallish 20×20 matrix, then the convergence factor for the Jacobi method is 0.99. It is 0.98 for the Gauss–Seidel method. The asymptotic convergence rates are 0.01 and 0.02, respectively. Hence, it may conceivably take as many as 450 iterations and 225 iterations, respectively, to get the error to one-hundredth of the initial error.[1] Pretty lousy, especially when naïve Gaussian elimination gives an exact solution in less than one-tenth of the time. For a larger

---

[1] The missing arithmetic is $\log 0.01 / \log 0.99 = 450$ and $\log 0.01 / \log 0.98 = 225$.

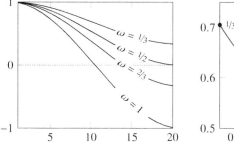
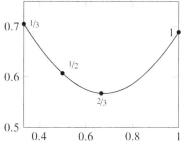

Figure 5.2: Left: eigenvalues of the weighted Jacobi method for the 20×20 discrete Laplacian (5.5) for different weights ω. Right: root mean squared values of the eigenvalues as a function of ω.

matrix, it's much worse. If we double the number of grid points, we'll need to quadruple the number of iterations to achieve the same accuracy. What can we do to speed up convergence?   ◄

5.2   Successive over relaxation

The preconditioners in the Jacobi and Gauss–Seidel methods are easy to invert, but both approaches converge slowly. Our goal in this section will be find a splitting $\mathbf{A} = \mathbf{P} - \mathbf{N}$ that quickly shrinks the error $\mathbf{e}^{(k+1)} = (\mathbf{P}^{-1}\mathbf{N})^k \mathbf{e}^{(0)}$. The initial error $\mathbf{e}^{(0)}$ is a linear combination of the eigenvectors of $\mathbf{P}^{-1}\mathbf{N}$. Each of its components is scaled by their respective eigenvalues at every iteration. A component with a small eigenvalue will swiftly fade away. A component with a magnitude near one will linger like a drunken, boorish guest after a party. If we happen to split the matrix $\mathbf{A}$ in a way that leaves the spectral radius of $\mathbf{P}^{-1}\mathbf{N}$ greater than one, then we'll have an unstable method. While the best splitting will be problem-specific, we can think of a good splitting as one that minimizes all eigenvalues. In the next section, we'll look at a method that systematically targets groups of the eigenvalues at a time.

Let's start by modifying the Jacobi method. Perhaps we can speed things up by weighting the preconditioner $\mathbf{P}^{-1} = \omega \mathbf{D}^{-1}$. This approach is called a *weighted Jacobi method* with the splitting

$$\mathbf{A} = \mathbf{P} - \mathbf{N} = \left(\omega^{-1}\mathbf{D}\right) + \left(\mathbf{A} - \omega^{-1}\mathbf{D}\right).$$

The eigenvalues $\lambda_i(\mathbf{P}^{-1}\mathbf{N})$ of the discrete Laplacian (5.5) are

$$\lambda_i(\mathbf{P}^{-1}\mathbf{N}) = 1 + \omega \left(\cos \tfrac{i\pi}{n+1} - 1\right),$$

or $i = 1, 2, \ldots, n$. See the figure on the previous page. The original, unweighted Jacobi takes $\omega = 1$. The closer an eigenvalue is to zero, the faster its associated component will fade away with each iteration. A good choice for ω might minimize the root mean squared values of the eigenvalues λ_i. For the discrete Laplacian (5.5), that choice for ω happens to be about $\frac{2}{3}$. However, when we reduce the magnitude of some eigenvalues by tuning ω, we are also increase the magnitude of other eigenvalues, including the dominant one.

Before modifying the Gauss–Seidel method, let's think about the meaning of ω. The residual at the kth iteration is

$$\mathbf{r}^{(k)} = \mathbf{A}\mathbf{e}^{(k)} = \mathbf{b} - \mathbf{A}\mathbf{x}^{(k)}.$$

Using this definition and $\mathbf{N} = \mathbf{A} - \mathbf{P}$, we can rewrite $\mathbf{x} = \mathbf{P}^{-1}(\mathbf{N}\mathbf{x} + \mathbf{b})$ as

$$\mathbf{x}^{(k+1)} = \mathbf{P}^{-1}(\mathbf{N}\mathbf{x}^{(k)} + \mathbf{b}) = \mathbf{x}^{(k)} + \mathbf{P}^{-1}\mathbf{r}^{(k)}.$$

We call $\mathbf{x}^{(k+1)} = \mathbf{x}^{(k)} + \delta$ for some vector δ the *relaxation* of $\mathbf{x}$. Think of "relaxation" as $\mathbf{x}^{(k)}$ returning to a steady state from a perturbed state. We can think of an iterative method as an analog to finding the steady-state solution to a time-dependent problem. For example, consider the one-dimensional Poisson equation and its finite difference approximation

$$-\frac{d^2 u}{dx^2} = f(x) \quad \text{and} \quad \frac{-u_{i-1} + 2u_i - u_{i+1}}{h^2} = f_i.$$

The resulting system of equations $\mathbf{A}\mathbf{u} = \mathbf{b}$ can be solved iteratively as

$$\mathbf{P}\mathbf{u}^{(k+1)} + (\mathbf{A} - \mathbf{P})\mathbf{u}^{(k)} = \mathbf{b},$$

which is equivalent to

$$\mathbf{u}^{(k+1)} - \mathbf{u}^{(k)} = \mathbf{P}^{-1}(\mathbf{b} - \mathbf{A}\mathbf{u}^{(k)}).$$

Note the similarity between this system and the forward Euler method

$$\mathbf{u}^{(k+1)} - \mathbf{u}^{(k)} = \Delta t(\mathbf{b} - \mathbf{A}\mathbf{u}^{(k)})$$

used to solve the continuous time-dependent heat equation with a source term

$$\frac{\partial u(t,x)}{\partial t} = f(x) + \frac{\partial^2 u(t,x)}{\partial x^2}.$$

The speed and stability of the forward Euler method are tuned by modifying the step size Δt. Analogously, the speed and stability of an iterative method are tuned by modifying the preconditioner $\mathbf{P}^{-1}$. The Jacobi method simultaneously relaxes $\mathbf{x}^{(k)}$, and the weighted Jacobi method simultaneously under relaxes $\mathbf{x}^{(k)}$ by choosing a weight $0 < \omega \le 1$ to increase stability.

The Gauss–Seidel method successively relaxes $\mathbf{x}^{(k)}$. The *successive over-relaxation* (SOR) method speeds up convergence by choosing $\omega > 1$ to go *beyond* the Gauss–Seidel correction. The naïve algorithm for the SOR method is

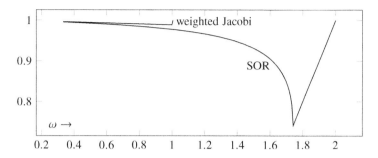

Figure 5.3: The spectral radius $\rho(\mathbf{P}^{-1}\mathbf{N})$ of the weighted Jacobi and SOR methods for the 20×20 discrete Laplacian as functions of the relaxation factor ω.

$$
\begin{aligned}
&\text{for } i = 1, 2, \ldots, n \\
&\quad \left\lfloor \begin{array}{l}
x^* \leftarrow \left(b_i - \sum_{j=1}^{i-1} a_{ij}x_j - \sum_{j=i+1}^{n} a_{ij}x_j \right) / a_{ii} \\
\delta \leftarrow x^* - x_i \\
x_i \leftarrow x_i + \omega\delta
\end{array} \right.
\end{aligned}
$$

The constant ω is called the relaxation factor. The SOR algorithm simply computes the step size δ determined by the Gauss–Seidel algorithm and scales that step size by ω. When $\omega = 1$, the SOR method is simply the Gauss–Seidel method. In general, the SOR method has the splitting

$$
\mathbf{A} = \mathbf{P} - \mathbf{N} = \left(\mathbf{L} + \omega^{-1}\mathbf{D} \right) + \left((1 - \omega^{-1})\mathbf{D} + \mathbf{U} \right).
$$

For an initial guess $\mathbf{x}^{(0)}$, we iterate on

$$
(\mathbf{D} + \omega\mathbf{L})\mathbf{x}^{(k+1)} = \left((1 - \omega)\mathbf{D} - \omega\mathbf{U} \right)\mathbf{x}^{(k)} + \omega\mathbf{b}.
$$

The challenge is to choose an ω so that the SOR method converges quickly, i.e., choose the ω that minimizes $\rho(\mathbf{P}^{-1}\mathbf{N})$. The choice is problem-specific and not trivial. For the discrete Laplacian (5.5), the optimal relaxation factor is $\omega = 2/(1 + \sin \pi/n)$, for which $\rho(\mathbf{P}^{-1}\mathbf{N}) = 1 - 2\pi n^{-1} + O(n^{-2})$. See Watkins [2014].

The convergence factor for a 20×20 discrete Laplacian is computed in the figure above for several values of ω. When $\omega \approx 1.72$, the convergence factor for the SOR method reaches a minimum of about 0.74. By using the SOR method on the example on discrete Laplacian, we can reduce the number of iterations from 225 down to about 15—a significant improvement.[2] Still, a 20×20 matrix is tiny, and we want a method that works well on massive matrices.

---

[2]The missing arithmetic is $\log 0.01 / \log 0.74 \approx 15$.

5.3 Multigrid method

To design a method that works well on big matrices, we need to contend better with the slowly decaying, low-frequency eigenvector components. The solution to the Poisson equation takes so many iterations to converge because the finite difference stencil for the discrete Laplacian only allows mesh points to communicate with neighboring mesh points. Information is shared across adjacent mesh points in the five-point stencil shown in Figure 5.1. A domain with n mesh points in each dimension requires $n/2$ iterations to pass information from one side to the other. As a result, convergence is slow. Of course, we could use a larger stencil. Information would travel more quickly across the domain, but we are adding more nonzero elements to our sparse matrix.

Another idea is to use a coarser mesh. For an $n \times n$ matrix, an optimal SOR method needs $O(n)$ iterations for convergence. The suboptimal Gauss–Seidel and Jacobi methods need $O(n^2)$. So, reducing the size of our system will have a tremendous impact on reducing the number of iterations. But, the solution would not be as accurate with a coarser mesh.

The multigrid method attempts to get both speed and accuracy by iterating on different grid refinements, using a coarse grid to speed up convergence and a fine grid to get higher accuracy. The multigrid method embodies the following idea:

- solve the problem on a coarse mesh to kill off the residual from the low frequencies components;

- solve the problem on a fine mesh for high accuracy; and

- use the solution on the coarse mesh as a starting guess for the solution on the fine mesh (and vice versa).

Consider the one-dimensional Poisson equation. Let A_h have a mesh size h and let A_{2h} be A_h restricted to a mesh size $2h$. One single cycle (with mesh h) has the following steps:

1. Iterate a few times on $A_h u_h = b_h$ using weighted Jacobi, Gauss–Seidel, or SOR. This step shrinks the residual $r_h = b_h - A_h u_h$ from the high-frequency eigenvector components and smooths out the solution.

2. Restrict the residual r_h to a coarse grid by taking $r_{2h} = R_h^{2h} r_h$, where the restriction matrix is

$$
R_h^{2h} = \frac{1}{4}
\begin{bmatrix}
3 & 1 & & & & \\
& 1 & 2 & 1 & & \\
& & 1 & 2 & 1 & \\
& & & & \ddots & \\
& & & & 1 & 3
\end{bmatrix}
$$

mapping a $(2n + 1)$-dimensional vector $\mathbf{r}_h$ to an $(n + 1)$-vector $\mathbf{r}_{2h}$.

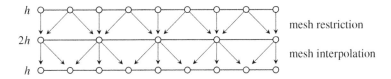

mesh restriction

mesh interpolation

3. Solve (iterate a few times) $\mathbf{A}_{2h}\mathbf{e}_{2h} = \mathbf{r}_{2h}$ where $\mathbf{e}_{2h} = \mathbf{u}_h - \mathbf{u}_{2h}$. Not surprisingly, $\mathbf{A}_{2h} = \mathbf{R}_h^{2h}\mathbf{A}_h$. Because the size of the matrix has changed, we may also need to adjust the relaxation factor ω accordingly.

4. Interpolate the error $\mathbf{e}_{2h}$ back to the fine grid by taking $\mathbf{e}_h = \mathbf{I}_{2h}^h\mathbf{e}_{2h}$ where the interpolation is defined as

$$\mathbf{I}_{2h}^h = \frac{1}{2}\begin{bmatrix} 2 & 1 & & & & \\ & 1 & 2 & 1 & & \\ & & 1 & 2 & 1 & \\ & & & 1 & 2 & 1 \\ & & & & & \ddots \\ & & & & 1 & 2 \end{bmatrix}^{\mathsf{T}}.$$

5. Add $\mathbf{e}_h$ to $\mathbf{u}_h$.

6. Iterate $\mathbf{A}_h\mathbf{u}_h = \mathbf{b}_h$.

Steps 1–6 make up a single cycle multigrid. In practice, one typically uses multiple cycles, restricting to coarser and coarser meshes, before interpolating back. Or, they might start multigrid on a coarse grid. Here are different cycle designs used to restrict and interpolate between an original mesh h and a coarser mesh $16h$:

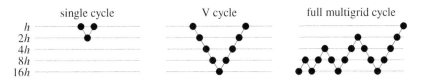

Example.   Let's compare the Jacobi, Gauss–Seidel, SOR, and multigrid methods on a model problem. Take the Poisson equation $u'' = f(x)$ with zero boundary conditions, where the source function is a combination of derivatives of Dirac delta distribution $f(x) = \delta'(x - \frac{1}{2}) - \delta'(x + \frac{1}{2})$. The solution is a rectangle function $u(x) = 1$ for $x \in (-\frac{1}{2}, +\frac{1}{2})$ and $u(x) = 0$ otherwise. We'll take $n = 129$ grid points and choose the relaxation factor ω optimal for the SOR and multigrid

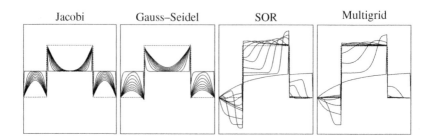

Figure 5.4: Iterative solutions to the Poisson equation converging to the exact solution, the rectangle function. Snapshots are taken every twentieth iteration for a total of 160 iterations. Also, see the QR code at the bottom of this page.

methods. For the multigrid method, use a V-cycle with two restrictions and two interpolations and compute one SOR iteration at each step. Finally, take an initial guess of $u(x) = \frac{1}{2}$. The figure on the current page plots the solution. Notice that the SOR and multigrid methods converge relatively quickly, while the Jacobi and Gauss–Seidel methods still have significant errors after many iterations and convergence slows down. ◀

5.4 Solving the minimization problem

One of the difficulties of the SOR method is that you need to know the optimal relaxation parameter ω. A better approach for symmetric, positive-definite matrices is recasting the problem as a minimization problem. In Chapter 3, we solved an overdetermined system as an equivalent minimization problem. And in the last chapter, we approximated the eigenvalues of sparse matrices by finding the solution that minimized the error in the Krylov subspace. The Poisson equation $-\Delta u = f$ has an equivalent formulation of finding the solution u that minimizes the energy functional $\int_\Omega \frac{1}{2}|\nabla u|^2 - uf \, dV$. This section examines how to solve an iterative method as a minimization problem.

▷ Gradient descent method

Gradient descent is arguably the most commonly used approach to solving minimization problems.[3] Nonlinear functions may have no minimum, multiple minima, saddle-points, and local minima that can cause gradient descent to fail. These difficulties vanish for positive-definite quadratic forms.

---

[3] Augustin–Louis Cauchy proposed gradient descent in 1847—a mere three-page note among his thirteen thousand pages of mathematical writing.

comparison of Jacobi,
Gauss-Seidel, SOR,
and multigrid methods

Theorem 17. *If* $\mathbf{A}$ *is a symmetric, positive-definite matrix, then the solution to the equation* $\mathbf{A}\mathbf{x} = \mathbf{b}$ *is the unique minimizer of the quadratic form*

$$\Phi(\mathbf{x}) = \tfrac{1}{2}\mathbf{x}^\mathsf{T}\mathbf{A}\mathbf{x} - \mathbf{x}^\mathsf{T}\mathbf{b} = \tfrac{1}{2}\|\mathbf{x}\|_\mathbf{A}^2 - (\mathbf{x}, \mathbf{b}).$$

Proof. Take $\mathbf{x} = \mathbf{A}^{-1}\mathbf{b}$ and consider any other vector $\mathbf{y}$. Then

$$
\begin{aligned}
\Phi(\mathbf{y}) - \Phi(\mathbf{x}) &= \tfrac{1}{2}\mathbf{y}^\mathsf{T}\mathbf{A}\mathbf{y} - \mathbf{y}^\mathsf{T}\mathbf{b} - \tfrac{1}{2}\mathbf{x}^\mathsf{T}\mathbf{A}\mathbf{x} + \mathbf{x}^\mathsf{T}\mathbf{b} \\
&= \tfrac{1}{2}\mathbf{y}^\mathsf{T}\mathbf{A}\mathbf{y} - \mathbf{y}^\mathsf{T}\mathbf{A}\mathbf{x} - \tfrac{1}{2}\mathbf{x}^\mathsf{T}\mathbf{A}\mathbf{x} + \mathbf{x}^\mathsf{T}\mathbf{A}\mathbf{x} \\
&= \tfrac{1}{2}\mathbf{y}^\mathsf{T}\mathbf{A}\mathbf{y} - \tfrac{1}{2}\mathbf{y}^\mathsf{T}\mathbf{A}\mathbf{x} - \tfrac{1}{2}\mathbf{y}^\mathsf{T}\mathbf{A}\mathbf{x} + \tfrac{1}{2}\mathbf{x}^\mathsf{T}\mathbf{A}\mathbf{x} \\
&= \tfrac{1}{2}\mathbf{y}^\mathsf{T}\mathbf{A}\mathbf{y} - \tfrac{1}{2}\mathbf{y}^\mathsf{T}\mathbf{A}\mathbf{x} - \tfrac{1}{2}\mathbf{x}^\mathsf{T}\mathbf{A}\mathbf{y} + \tfrac{1}{2}\mathbf{x}^\mathsf{T}\mathbf{A}\mathbf{x} \\
&= \tfrac{1}{2}(\mathbf{y} - \mathbf{x})^\mathsf{T}\mathbf{A}(\mathbf{y} - \mathbf{x}) > 0
\end{aligned}
$$

because $\mathbf{A}$ is symmetric, positive definite. So, $\Phi(\mathbf{y}) > \Phi(\mathbf{x})$. □

We can think of the solution $\mathbf{x}$ as being at the bottom of an n-dimensional "oblong bowl." Let $\mathbf{x}^{(0)}$ be an initial guess for $\mathbf{x}$ and let $\mathbf{x}^{(k)}$ be the kth subsequent estimate

$$\mathbf{x}^{(k+1)} = \mathbf{x}^{(k)} + \alpha_k \mathbf{p}^{(k)} \tag{5.6}$$

for some direction $\mathbf{p}^{(k)}$. The error at the kth step is $\mathbf{e}^{(k)} = \mathbf{x} - \mathbf{x}^{(k)}$. To get to the bottom of the "bowl" knowing only the local topography at $\mathbf{x}^{(k)}$, the best path to take is the steepest descent, i.e., the direction of the negative gradient. The gradient of Φ at $\mathbf{x}^{(k)}$ is

$$\nabla\Phi(\mathbf{x}^{(k)}) = \mathbf{A}\mathbf{x}^{(k)} - \mathbf{b} = -\mathbf{r}^{(k)}.$$

The negative gradient is simply the residual. So we can rewrite the kth subsequent estimate (5.6) as

$$\mathbf{x}^{(k+1)} = \mathbf{x}^{(k)} + \alpha_k \mathbf{r}^{(k)}. \tag{5.7}$$

For now, consider the more general iterative method (5.6) for an arbitrary direction vector $\mathbf{p}^{(k)}$, keeping in mind that $\mathbf{p}^{(k)} = \mathbf{r}^{(k)}$ for the method of gradient descent. Let's find α_k. Since the evaluation of $\mathbf{A}\mathbf{x}^{(k)}$ to get the residual can require a lot of computer processing, we try to reduce the number of times we compute an update to the direction. We will only change direction when we are closest to the solution $\mathbf{x}$ along our current direction. A vector $\mathbf{x}$ is said to be *optimal* with respect to a nonzero direction $\mathbf{p}$ if $\Phi(\mathbf{x}) \leq \Phi(\mathbf{x} + \gamma\mathbf{p})$ for all $\gamma \in \mathbb{R}$. That is, $\mathbf{x}$ is optimal with respect to $\mathbf{p}$ if Φ increases as we move away from $\mathbf{x}$ along the direction $\mathbf{p}$. Put another way, $\mathbf{x}$ is optimal with respect to a direction $\mathbf{p}$ if the directional derivative of Φ at $\mathbf{x}$ in the direction $\mathbf{p}$ is zero, i.e., $\nabla\Phi(\mathbf{x}) \cdot \mathbf{p} = 0$. If $\mathbf{x}$ is optimal with respect to every direction in vector space V, we say the $\mathbf{x}$ is optimal with respect to V. Looking at (5.7), we want to know when $\mathbf{x}^{(k+1)}$ is optimal with respect to a direction $\mathbf{r}^{(k)}$.

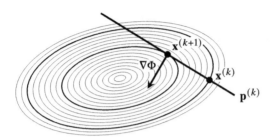

Figure 5.5: The optimal vector $\mathbf{x}^{(k+1)}$ along direction $\mathbf{p}^{(k)}$.

Because $\nabla\Phi(\mathbf{x}^{(k+1)}) = -\mathbf{r}^{(k+1)}$, it follows that $\mathbf{x}^{(k+1)}$ is optimal with respect to $\mathbf{p}^{(k)}$—in the direction of $\mathbf{r}^{(k)}$—if and only if $\mathbf{r}^{(k+1)} \cdot \mathbf{p}^{(k)} = 0$, i.e., if and only if $\mathbf{r}^{(k+1)}$ is orthogonal to $\mathbf{p}^{(k)}$.

$$
\begin{aligned}
\mathbf{r}^{(k+1)} &= \mathbf{b} - \mathbf{A}\mathbf{x}^{(k+1)} \\
&= \mathbf{b} - \mathbf{A}\big(\mathbf{x}^{(k)} + \alpha_k \mathbf{p}^{(k)}\big) \\
&= \mathbf{b} - \mathbf{A}\mathbf{x}^{(k)} - \alpha_k \mathbf{A}\mathbf{p}^{(k)} \\
&= \mathbf{r}^{(k)} - \alpha_k \mathbf{A}\mathbf{p}^{(k)}. \qquad\qquad (5.8)
\end{aligned}
$$

When $\mathbf{r}^{(k+1)} \perp \mathbf{p}^{(k)}$:

$$
0 = \mathbf{p}^{(k)^\mathsf{T}}\mathbf{r}^{(k+1)} = \mathbf{p}^{(k)^\mathsf{T}}\mathbf{r}^{(k)} - \alpha_k \mathbf{p}^{(k)^\mathsf{T}}\mathbf{A}\mathbf{p}^{(k)}.
$$

Therefore, $\mathbf{x}^{(k+1)}$ is optimal with respect to $\mathbf{r}^{(k)}$ when

$$
\alpha_k = \frac{\mathbf{p}^{(k)^\mathsf{T}}\mathbf{r}^{(k)}}{\mathbf{p}^{(k)^\mathsf{T}}\mathbf{A}\mathbf{p}^{(k)}}.
$$

By taking $\mathbf{p}^{(k)} = \mathbf{r}^{(k)}$ (for the gradient descent method), we have

$$
\alpha_k = \frac{\mathbf{r}^{(k)^\mathsf{T}}\mathbf{r}^{(k)}}{\mathbf{r}^{(k)^\mathsf{T}}\mathbf{A}\mathbf{r}^{(k)}}.
$$

At this new vector $\mathbf{x}^{(k+1)} = \mathbf{x}^{(k)} + \alpha_k \mathbf{r}^{(k)}$, we change directions, again taking the steepest descent in the direction of the negative gradient $-\nabla\Phi(\mathbf{x}^{(k+1)})$. We continue like this until either we find the minimum $\mathbf{x}$ or we are close enough. That's the idea. Let's write it out as an algorithm:

make an initial guess $\mathbf{x}$
for $k = 0, 1, 2, \ldots$
$\quad\Big[\;\mathbf{r} \leftarrow \mathbf{b} - \mathbf{A}\mathbf{x}$
$\quad\;$if $\|\mathbf{r}\| <$ tolerance, then we're done
$\quad\;\alpha \leftarrow \mathbf{r}^\mathsf{T}\mathbf{r}/\mathbf{r}^\mathsf{T}\mathbf{A}\mathbf{r}$
$\quad\;\mathbf{x} \leftarrow \mathbf{x} + \alpha\mathbf{r}$

▷ Gauss–Seidel and SOR as descent methods

Let's go back and look at the general descent method (5.6)

$$\mathbf{x}^{(k+1)} = \mathbf{x}^{(k)} + \alpha_k \mathbf{p}^{(k)},$$

where $\mathbf{x}^{(k)}$ is optimal with respect to the direction $\mathbf{p}^{(k)}$ when

$$\alpha_k = \frac{\mathbf{p}^{(k)^T} \mathbf{r}^{(k)}}{\mathbf{p}^{(k)^T} \mathbf{A} \mathbf{p}^{(k)}}.$$

Consider taking the direction $\mathbf{p}^{(k)}$ successively along each coordinate axis $\boldsymbol{\xi}_i$. For example, if $\mathbf{A}$ is 3×3, we take

$$\mathbf{p}^{(1)} = \boldsymbol{\xi}_1 = \begin{bmatrix} 1 \\ 0 \\ 0 \end{bmatrix}, \ \mathbf{p}^{(2)} = \boldsymbol{\xi}_2 = \begin{bmatrix} 0 \\ 1 \\ 0 \end{bmatrix}, \ \mathbf{p}^{(3)} = \boldsymbol{\xi}_3 = \begin{bmatrix} 0 \\ 0 \\ 1 \end{bmatrix}, \ \mathbf{p}^{(4)} = \boldsymbol{\xi}_1, \text{ and so on.}$$

Then for an n-dimensional space

$$\mathbf{x}^{(k+1)} = \mathbf{x}^{(k)} + \frac{\boldsymbol{\xi}_i^T \mathbf{r}^{(k)}}{\boldsymbol{\xi}_i^T \mathbf{A} \boldsymbol{\xi}_i} \boldsymbol{\xi}_i \quad \text{with} \quad i = k \ (\text{mod } n) + 1.$$

We can rewrite this expression in component form by first noting that

$$\boldsymbol{\xi}_i^T \mathbf{r}^{(k)} = b_i - \sum_{j=1}^{n} a_{ij} x_j \quad \text{and} \quad \boldsymbol{\xi}_i^T \mathbf{A} \boldsymbol{\xi}_i = a_{ii}$$

and then noting that $\mathbf{x}^{(k)} + \alpha_k \boldsymbol{\xi}_i$ only updates the ith component of $\mathbf{x}^{(k)}$. In other words,

$$
\begin{aligned}
x_i^{(k+1)} &= x_i^{(k)} + \frac{1}{a_{ii}} \left(-\sum_{j=1}^{i-1} a_{ij} x_j^{(k+1)} - \sum_{j=i}^{n} a_{ij} x_j^{(k)} + b_i \right) \\
&= \frac{1}{a_{ii}} \left(-\sum_{j=1}^{i-1} a_{ij} x_j^{(k+1)} - \sum_{j=i+1}^{n} a_{ij} x_j^{(k)} + b_i \right),
\end{aligned}
$$

which is simply the Gauss–Seidel method (5.2). Depending on the shape of our "bowl," it may be advantageous to take a shorter or longer stepsize than optimal

$$\mathbf{x}^{(k+1)} = \mathbf{x}^{(k)} + \omega \alpha_k \mathbf{p}^{(k)}.$$

By taking our directions successively along the coordinate axes with the scaling factor $0 < \omega < 2$, we have the SOR method. See Figure 5.6 on the following page.

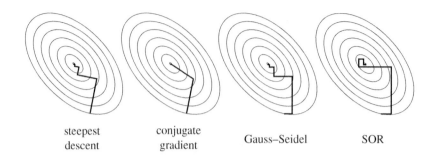

steepest descent   conjugate gradient   Gauss–Seidel   SOR

Figure 5.6: Directions taken by different iterative methods to get to the solution.

Theorem 18. *If a matrix is symmetric, positive definite, then the Gauss–Seidel method converges for any* $\mathbf{x}^{(0)}$. *Furthermore, the SOR method converges if and only if* $0 < \omega < 2$.

Proof. By theorem 17, if $\mathbf{A}$ is a symmetric, positive-definite matrix, then Φ has a unique minimizer. As a descent method, the Gauss–Seidel converges to the bottom of the "bowl." We can consider the bowl as a circular paraboloid sheared and stretched along a coordinate axis. This interpretation follows directly from QR decomposition.

The value $\omega = 2$ takes us in a direction parallel to a coordinate axis to the point at the same elevation on the opposite side of the bowl. Any value $0 < \omega < 2$ positions us lower in the bowl, and $\omega = 1$ positions us optimally along the direction. $\square$

▷ Conjugate gradient method

Locally, gradient descent gives the best choice of directions. Globally, it doesn't— especially when the bowl is very eccentric, i.e., when the matrix's condition number is large. So the gradient descent method doesn't always work well in practice. We can improve it by taking globally optimal directions, not necessarily along the residuals.

What went wrong with the gradient method? Each new search direction $\mathbf{p}^{(k)}$ was determined using *only* information from the most recent search direction $\mathbf{p}^{(k-1)}$. Let $\mathbf{x}^{(k+1)} = \mathbf{x}^{(k)} + \alpha_k \mathbf{p}^{(k)}$ for some direction $\mathbf{p}^{(k)}$, and suppose that $\mathbf{x}^{(k+1)}$ is optimal with respect to $\mathbf{p}^{(k)}$—just as we did in developing the gradient method. So $\mathbf{p}^{(k)} \perp \nabla\Phi(\mathbf{x}^{(k+1)})$ or equivalently $\mathbf{p}^{(k)} \perp \mathbf{r}^{(k+1)}$. Let's impose the further condition that $\mathbf{x}^{(k+1)}$ is also optimal with respect to $\mathbf{p}^{(j)}$ for all $j = 0, 1, \ldots, k$. That is, $\mathbf{r}^{(k+1)} \perp \mathbf{p}^{(j)}$ for all $j = 0, 1, \ldots, k$.

What does this new optimality condition mean? If the position $\mathbf{x}^{(k+1)}$ is optimal with respect to each of the directions $\mathbf{p}^{(k)}, \mathbf{p}^{(k-1)}, \ldots, \mathbf{p}^{(0)}$, then $\mathbf{x}^{(k+1)}$ is optimal with respect to the entire $\mathrm{span}\{\mathbf{p}^{(k)}, \mathbf{p}^{(k-1)}, \ldots, \mathbf{p}^{(0)}\}$ by the linearity of the gradient. As we iterate, the subspace spanned by the directions $\mathbf{p}^{(k)}, \mathbf{p}^{(k-1)}, \ldots, \mathbf{p}^{(0)}$ will continue to grow as long as each new direction is linearly independent. That sounds pretty good. Let's find the directions $\mathbf{p}^{(k)}, \mathbf{p}^{(k-1)}, \ldots, \mathbf{p}^{(0)}$ and show that they are linearly independent.

From the updated residual, we have

$$\mathbf{r}^{(k+1)} = \mathbf{b} - \mathbf{A}\mathbf{x}^{(k+1)} = \mathbf{b} - \mathbf{A}(\mathbf{x}^{(k)} + \alpha_k \mathbf{p}^{(k)}) = \mathbf{r}^{(k)} - \alpha_k \mathbf{A}\mathbf{p}^{(k)},$$

and from our optimality condition, we have

$$0 = \mathbf{p}^{(j)^\mathsf{T}} \mathbf{r}^{(k+1)} = \mathbf{p}^{(j)^\mathsf{T}} \mathbf{r}^{(k)} - \alpha_k \mathbf{p}^{(j)^\mathsf{T}} \mathbf{A}\mathbf{p}^{(k)}$$

for all $j \leq k$. For $j = k$, it follows that

$$\alpha_k = \frac{\mathbf{p}^{(k)^\mathsf{T}} \mathbf{r}^{(k)}}{\mathbf{p}^{(k)^\mathsf{T}} \mathbf{A}\mathbf{p}^{(k)}}.$$

And, because $\mathbf{r}^{(k)} \perp \mathbf{p}^{(j)}$ for all $j < k$, we must have

$$0 = -\alpha_k \mathbf{p}^{(j)^\mathsf{T}} \mathbf{A}\mathbf{p}^{(k)}.$$

In other words, to preserve optimality between iterates, $\mathbf{p}^{(k)}$ and $\mathbf{p}^{(j)}$ must be *A-conjugate* for all $j < k$:

$$\left(\mathbf{p}^{(j)}, \mathbf{p}^{(k)}\right)_\mathbf{A} \equiv \mathbf{p}^{(j)^\mathsf{T}} \mathbf{A}\mathbf{p}^{(k)} = 0 \quad \text{for} \quad j = 0, 1, \ldots, k-1. \qquad (5.9)$$

As before, we'll take the first direction equal to the gradient at $\mathbf{x}^{(0)}$, i.e., we'll take $\mathbf{p}^{(0)} = \mathbf{r}^{(0)}$. Then each subsequent direction will be A-conjugate to this initial gradient. Hence, the name *conjugate gradient method*.

It still makes sense to take the directions as close to the residuals as possible yet still mutually conjugate. Take

$$\mathbf{p}^{(k+1)} = \mathbf{r}^{(k+1)} - \beta_k \mathbf{p}^{(k)} \qquad (5.10)$$

where β_k is chosen so that

$$\left(\mathbf{p}^{(k+1)}, \mathbf{p}^{(j)}\right)_{\mathbf{A}} = 0, \qquad j = 0, 1, \ldots, k. \tag{5.11}$$

It may seem almost magical that by choosing $\mathbf{p}^{(k+1)}$ with explicit dependence only on $\mathbf{p}^{(k)}$, we ensure that $\mathbf{p}^{(k+1)}$ is A-conjugate to all $\mathbf{p}^{(j)}$ for $j = 0, 1, 2, \ldots, k$. Let's see why it works. (We'll better clarify this mathematical sleight-of-hand when discussing Krylov subspaces in the next section.) If we multiply (5.10) by $\mathbf{Ap}^{(k)}$ and enforce (5.11) when $j = k$, then it follows that

$$\beta_k = \frac{\mathbf{r}^{(k+1)^{\mathsf{T}}} \mathbf{Ap}^{(k)}}{\mathbf{p}^{(k)^{\mathsf{T}}} \mathbf{Ap}^{(k)}} = \frac{\left(\mathbf{p}^{(k)}, \mathbf{r}^{(k+1)}\right)_{\mathbf{A}}}{\left(\mathbf{p}^{(k)}, \mathbf{p}^{(k)}\right)_{\mathbf{A}}}.$$

Now, let's show that this choice for β_k ensures that (5.11) holds for all $j < k$. Let

$$V_k = \mathrm{span}\left\{\mathbf{p}^{(0)}, \mathbf{p}^{(1)}, \ldots, \mathbf{p}^{(k-1)}\right\}.$$

Since $\mathbf{p}^{(0)} = \mathbf{r}^{(0)}$, it follows from (5.10) that

$$V_k = \mathrm{span}\left\{\mathbf{r}^{(0)}, \mathbf{r}^{(1)}, \ldots, \mathbf{r}^{(k-1)}\right\}.$$

By our optimality condition we must have $V_k \perp \mathbf{p}^{(k+1)}$. Also,

$$\begin{aligned}
\mathbf{p}^{(k)} &= \mathbf{r}^{(k)} - \beta_{k-1}\mathbf{p}^{(k-1)} \\
&= (\mathbf{b} - \mathbf{Ax}^{(k)}) - \beta_{k-1}\mathbf{p}^{(k-1)} \\
&= \mathbf{b} - \mathbf{A}(\mathbf{x}^{(k-1)} + \alpha_k\mathbf{p}^{(k-1)}) - \beta_{k-1}\mathbf{p}^{(k-1)} \\
&= \mathbf{r}^{(k-1)} - \alpha_k\mathbf{Ap}^{(k-1)} - \beta_{k-1}\mathbf{p}^{(k-1)}
\end{aligned}$$

So, $\mathbf{Ap}^{(k-1)} \in V_{k+1}$ and hence $\mathbf{Ap}^{(j)} \in V_{k+1}$ for all $j = 0, 1, \ldots, k-1$. Therefore, $\mathbf{Ap}^{(j)} \perp \mathbf{p}^{(k+1)}$ or equivalently $\left(\mathbf{p}^{(k+1)}, \mathbf{p}^{(j)}\right)_{\mathbf{A}} = 0$ for $j = 0, 1, \ldots, k-1$. Note that we are performing Arnoldi iteration to generate an A-conjugate set of directions.

Let's summarize the conjugate gradient method by explicitly writing out its algorithm. Compare the following algorithm with the one for the gradient method on page 132.

> make an initial guess $\mathbf{x}$
> $\mathbf{p} \leftarrow \mathbf{r} \leftarrow \mathbf{b} - \mathbf{Ax}$
> for $k = 0, 1, 2, \ldots$
> $\quad\left\lceil \alpha \leftarrow \mathbf{r}^{\mathsf{T}}\mathbf{p}/\mathbf{p}^{\mathsf{T}}\mathbf{Ap}\right.$
> $\quad\;\; \mathbf{x} \leftarrow \mathbf{x} + \alpha\mathbf{p}$
> $\quad\;\; \mathbf{r} \leftarrow \mathbf{r} - \alpha\mathbf{Ap}$
> $\quad\;\;$ if $\|\mathbf{r}\| <$ tolerance, then we're done
> $\quad\;\; \beta \leftarrow \mathbf{r}^{\mathsf{T}}\mathbf{Ap}/\mathbf{p}^{\mathsf{T}}\mathbf{Ap}$
> $\quad\left\lfloor \mathbf{p} \leftarrow \mathbf{r} - \beta\mathbf{p}\right.$

The conjugate gradient method is actually a direct method. If $\mathbf{A}$ is an $n \times n$ symmetric, positive-definite matrix, then the conjugate gradient method yields an exact solution after at most n steps. But when n is large, it is usually unnecessary to run the method for the entire n iterations. Instead, we typically consider the conjugate gradient an iterative method and stop after significantly fewer than n iterations. In particular, the conjugate gradient method converges very quickly if the condition number is close to one. We can also use a symmetric, positive-definite preconditioner $\mathbf{P}$ to reduce the condition number $\kappa(\mathbf{P}^{-1}\mathbf{A}) < \kappa(\mathbf{A})$. For a simple Jacobi preconditioner (diagonal scaling), we take $\mathbf{P} = \mathbf{D}$. The algorithm for the preconditioned conjugate gradient method replaces

$$
\begin{aligned}
\beta &\leftarrow \mathbf{r}^{\mathsf{T}}\mathbf{A}\mathbf{p}/\mathbf{p}^{\mathsf{T}}\mathbf{A}\mathbf{p} \\
\mathbf{p} &\leftarrow \mathbf{r} - \beta\mathbf{p}
\end{aligned}
\qquad \text{with} \qquad
\begin{aligned}
&\text{solve } \mathbf{P}\mathbf{z} = \mathbf{r} \\
\beta &\leftarrow \mathbf{z}^{\mathsf{T}}\mathbf{A}\mathbf{p}/\mathbf{p}^{\mathsf{T}}\mathbf{A}\mathbf{p} \\
\mathbf{p} &\leftarrow \mathbf{z} - \beta\mathbf{p}
\end{aligned}
$$

in the conjugate gradient method above.

♣ The IterativeSolvers.jl function cg implements the conjugate gradient method—preconditioned conjugate gradient method if a preconditioner is also provided.

5.5   Krylov methods

The iterative methods discussed in this chapter can be viewed as Krylov methods. Consider a classical iterative method such as Jacobi or Gauss–Seidel with

$$\mathbf{P}\mathbf{x}^{(k+1)} = \mathbf{N}\mathbf{x}^{(k)} + \mathbf{b}.$$

The error

$$\mathbf{e}^{(k)} = \mathbf{P}^{-1}\mathbf{N}\mathbf{e}^{(k-1)} = (\mathbf{I} - \mathbf{P}^{-1}\mathbf{A})\mathbf{e}^{(k-1)},$$

and so

$$\mathbf{e}^{(k)} = (\mathbf{I} - \mathbf{P}^{-1}\mathbf{A})^{k}\mathbf{e}^{(0)}.$$

Then

$$
\begin{aligned}
\mathbf{x}^{(k)} - \mathbf{x}^{(0)} = \mathbf{e}^{(k)} - \mathbf{e}^{(0)} &= \left[(\mathbf{I} - \mathbf{P}^{-1}\mathbf{A})^{k} - \mathbf{I}\right]\mathbf{e}^{(0)} \\
&= \left[\sum_{j=1}^{k}\binom{k}{j}(-1)^{j}(\mathbf{P}^{-1}\mathbf{A})^{j}\right]\mathbf{e}^{(0)}.
\end{aligned}
$$

This expression says that $\mathbf{x}^{(k)} - \mathbf{x}^{(0)}$ lies in the Krylov space

$$\mathcal{K}_{k}(\mathbf{P}^{-1}\mathbf{A}, \mathbf{z}) = \operatorname{span}\{\mathbf{z}, \mathbf{P}^{-1}\mathbf{A}\mathbf{z}, \ldots, (\mathbf{P}^{-1}\mathbf{A})^{k}\mathbf{z}\}$$

with $\mathbf{z} = \mathbf{P}^{-1}\mathbf{A}\mathbf{e}^{(0)} = \mathbf{P}^{-1}\mathbf{r}^{(0)}$. The gradient descent method is also a Krylov method. Equation (5.8) says that the residuals are elements of the Krylov subspace

$$\mathcal{K}_{k}(\mathbf{A}, \mathbf{r}^{(0)}) = \operatorname{span}\{\mathbf{r}^{(0)}, \mathbf{A}\mathbf{r}^{(0)}, \ldots, \mathbf{A}^{k}\mathbf{r}^{(0)}\}.$$

In the previous sections, we considered a general iterative method

$$\mathbf{x}^{(k+1)} = \mathbf{x}^{(k)} + \alpha_k \mathbf{p}^{(k)} = \mathbf{x}^{(0)} + \sum_{j=1}^{k} \alpha_j \mathbf{p}^{(j)}$$

for some directions $\{\mathbf{p}^{(0)}, \mathbf{p}^{(1)}, \ldots, \mathbf{p}^{(k)}\}$. For the gradient descent method, we took the directions along residuals $\mathbf{p}^{(j)} = \mathbf{r}^{(j)}$. For the conjugate gradient method, we showed that the directions formed a subspace

$$V_{k+1} = \mathrm{span}\big\{\mathbf{p}^{(0)}, \mathbf{p}^{(1)}, \ldots, \mathbf{p}^{(k)}\big\} = \mathrm{span}\big\{\mathbf{r}^{(0)}, \mathbf{r}^{(1)}, \ldots, \mathbf{r}^{(k)}\big\}.$$

Furthermore, we noted that the V_{k+1} is actually a Krylov subspace

$$V_{k+1} = \mathrm{span}\big\{\mathbf{r}^{(0)}, \mathbf{A}\mathbf{r}^{(0)}, \ldots, \mathbf{A}^k \mathbf{r}^{(0)}\big\}.$$

In this section, we'll expand on the idea of using a Krylov subspace to generate an iterative method $\mathbf{x}^{(k+1)} = \mathbf{x}^{(0)} + \delta^{(k)}$, where $\delta^{(k)} \in \mathcal{K}_{k+1}(\mathbf{A}, \mathbf{r}^{(0)})$ with an initial guess $\mathbf{x}^{(0)}$. Let's consider two methods

1. Choose $\mathbf{x}^{(k+1)}$ that minimizes the error $\|\mathbf{e}^{(k+1)}\|_{\mathbf{A}}$.

2. Choose $\mathbf{x}^{(k+1)}$ that minimizes the residual $\|\mathbf{r}^{(k+1)}\|_2$.

The first approach is often called the Arnoldi method or the Full Orthogonalization Method (FOM). When $\mathbf{A}$ is a symmetric, positive-definite matrix, FOM is equivalent to the conjugate gradient method. The second approach is the general minimal residual method (GMRES). It is simply called the minimal residual method (MINRES) when $\mathbf{A}$ is symmetric.

Before looking at either of the two methods, let's recall the Arnoldi process from the previous chapter. The Arnoldi process is a variation of the Gram–Schmidt method that generates an orthogonal basis for a Krylov subspace. By choosing an orthogonal basis, we ensure that the system is well-conditioned. Starting with the residual $\mathbf{r}^{(0)}$, take

$$\mathbf{q}^{(1)} \leftarrow \mathbf{r}^{(0)}/\|\mathbf{r}^{(0)}\|_2$$

and set $h_{11} = \|\mathbf{r}^{(0)}\|_2$. At the kth iteration, take

$$h_{ik} = \big(\mathbf{q}^{(i)}, \mathbf{A}\mathbf{q}^{(k)}\big) \quad \text{for} \quad i = 1, 2, \ldots, k,$$

$$\mathbf{q}^{(k+1)} = \mathbf{A}\mathbf{q}^{(k)} - \sum_{i=1}^{k} h_{ik}\mathbf{q}^{(k)}, \quad \text{and set}$$

$$\mathbf{q}^{(k+1)} \leftarrow \mathbf{q}^{(k+1)}/h_{k+1,k} \quad \text{where} \quad h_{k+1,k} = \|\mathbf{q}^{(k+1)}\|.$$

We can summarize the method pictorially as

$$
\underbrace{\begin{bmatrix} \bullet \cdots \bullet \\ \vdots \ddots \vdots \\ \bullet \cdots \bullet \end{bmatrix}}_{\mathbf{A}} \underbrace{\begin{bmatrix} \bullet \cdots \bullet \\ \vdots \ddots \vdots \\ \bullet \cdots \bullet \end{bmatrix}}_{\mathbf{Q}_k} = \underbrace{\begin{bmatrix} \bullet \cdots \bullet \\ \vdots \ddots \vdots \\ \bullet \cdots \bullet \end{bmatrix}}_{\mathbf{Q}_{k+1}} \underbrace{\begin{bmatrix} \bullet \cdots \bullet \\ \ddots \vdots \\ \bullet \end{bmatrix}}_{\mathbf{H}_{k+1,k}}. \tag{5.12}
$$

By separating the bottom row of $\mathbf{H}_{k+1,k}$ and the last column of $\mathbf{Q}_{k+1}$, we have

$$
\mathbf{A}\mathbf{Q}_k = \mathbf{Q}_k \mathbf{H}_k + h_{k+1,k} \mathbf{q}^{(k+1)} \boldsymbol{\xi}_k^{\mathsf{T}} \tag{5.13}
$$

where $\boldsymbol{\xi}_k = (0, \ldots, 0, 1)$. Note that $\mathbf{H}_k$ is tridiagonal if $\mathbf{A}$ is Hermitian or real symmetric. In this case, the Arnoldi method simplifies and is called the Lanczos method.

▷ **Full orthogonalization method (FOM)**

Let's examine the first Krylov method, in which we choose the $\mathbf{x}^{(k+1)}$ that minimizes the error $\|\mathbf{e}^{(k+1)}\|_{\mathbf{A}}$. At the kth iteration, we choose the approximation $\mathbf{x}^{(k+1)}$ with $\mathbf{x}^{(k+1)} - \mathbf{x}^{(0)} \in \mathcal{K}_k(\mathbf{A}, \mathbf{r}^{(0)})$ to minimize the error in the energy norm

$$
\left\| \mathbf{e}^{(k+1)} \right\|_{\mathbf{A}}^2 = \mathbf{e}^{(k+1)\mathsf{T}} \mathbf{A} \mathbf{e}^{(k+1)}.
$$

Any vector in the Krylov subspace can be expressed as a linear combination of the basis elements $\mathbf{Q}_k \mathbf{z}^{(k)}$ for some $\mathbf{z}^{(k)}$. Take

$$
\mathbf{x}^{(k+1)} = \mathbf{x}^{(0)} + \mathbf{Q}_k \mathbf{z}^{(k)}
$$

with $\mathbf{z}^{(k)}$ to be determined. Then because $\mathbf{e}^{(k)} = \mathbf{x} - \mathbf{x}^{(k)}$, we have

$$
\mathbf{e}^{(k+1)} = \mathbf{e}^{(0)} - \mathbf{Q}_k \mathbf{z}^{(k)}.
$$

So, we need to find the vector $\mathbf{z}^{(k)}$ that minimizes

$$
\left\| \mathbf{e}^{(0)} - \mathbf{Q}_k \mathbf{z}^{(k)} \right\|_{\mathbf{A}}^2 = (\mathbf{e}^{(0)} - \mathbf{Q}_k \mathbf{z}^{(k)})^{\mathsf{T}} \mathbf{A} (\mathbf{e}^{(0)} - \mathbf{Q}_k \mathbf{z}^{(k)}),
$$

which happens when the gradient is zero:

$$
2\left(\mathbf{Q}_k^{\mathsf{T}} \mathbf{A} \mathbf{Q}_k \mathbf{z}^{(k)} - \mathbf{Q}_k^{\mathsf{T}} \mathbf{A} \mathbf{e}^{(0)} \right) = \mathbf{0}.
$$

Hence,

$$
\mathbf{Q}_k^{\mathsf{T}} \mathbf{A} \mathbf{Q}_k \mathbf{z}^{(k)} = \mathbf{Q}_k^{\mathsf{T}} \mathbf{A} \mathbf{e}^{(0)} = \mathbf{Q}_k^{\mathsf{T}} \mathbf{r}^{(0)}.
$$

From (5.13) it follows that $\mathbf{Q}_k^{\mathsf{T}} \mathbf{A} \mathbf{Q}_k = \mathbf{H}_k$ because $\mathbf{Q}_k \perp \mathbf{q}^{(k+1)}$. Also, because $\mathbf{r}^{(0)} = \|\mathbf{r}^{(0)}\|_2 \mathbf{q}^{(1)}$ and $\mathbf{Q}_k^{\mathsf{T}} \mathbf{q}^{(1)} = \boldsymbol{\xi}_1$, it follows that $\mathbf{z}^{(k)}$ must solve the upper Hessenberg system

$$
\mathbf{H}_k \mathbf{z}^{(k)} = \left\| \mathbf{r}^{(0)} \right\|_2 \boldsymbol{\xi}_1
$$

where $\boldsymbol{\xi}_1 = (1, 0, \ldots, 0)$. Note that the norm of the residual

$$\left\|\mathbf{r}^{(k)}\right\|_2 = \left\|\mathbf{b} - \mathbf{A}\mathbf{x}^{(k)}\right\|_2 = \left|h_{k+1,k}\right| \cdot \left|\boldsymbol{\xi}_k^{\mathsf{T}}\mathbf{z}^{(k)}\right| = \left|h_{k+1,k}\right| \cdot \left|z_k^{(k)}\right|,$$

which we can use as a stopping criterion when the value is less than $\varepsilon\|\mathbf{r}^{(0)}\|_2$ for some tolerance ε.

It may not be obvious, but FOM outlined above is just the conjugate gradient method when $\mathbf{A}$ is a symmetric, positive-definite matrix. Start with

$$\mathbf{x}^{(k+1)} = \mathbf{x}^{(0)} + \mathbf{Q}_k \mathbf{z}^{(k)} = \mathbf{x}^{(0)} + \mathbf{Q}_k \mathbf{H}_k^{-1} \left\|\mathbf{r}^{(0)}\right\|_2 \boldsymbol{\xi}_k.$$

Taking the LU decomposition of $\mathbf{H}_k$, we have

$$\mathbf{x}^{(k+1)} = \mathbf{x}^{(0)} + \mathbf{Q}_k \mathbf{U}_k^{-1} \mathbf{L}_k^{-1} \left\|\mathbf{r}^{(0)}\right\|_2 \boldsymbol{\xi}_k = \mathbf{x}^{(0)} + \mathbf{P}_k \mathbf{L}_k^{-1} \left\|\mathbf{r}^{(0)}\right\|_2 \boldsymbol{\xi}_k,$$

where the columns of $\mathbf{P}_k$ are the directions $\mathbf{p}^{(k)}$. For a symmetric matrix $\mathbf{A}$, we have

$$\mathbf{P}_k^{\mathsf{T}} \mathbf{A} \mathbf{P}_k = \underbrace{\mathbf{U}_k^{-\mathsf{T}} \mathbf{Q}_k^{\mathsf{T}} \mathbf{A} \mathbf{Q}_k \mathbf{U}_k^{-1} = \mathbf{U}_k^{\mathsf{T}} \mathbf{H}_k \mathbf{U}_k^{-1}}_{\text{symmetric}} = \underbrace{\mathbf{U}_k^{-\mathsf{T}} \mathbf{L}_k.}_{\text{lower triangular}}.$$

Hence, $\mathbf{P}_k^{\mathsf{T}} \mathbf{A} \mathbf{P}_k$ is a diagonal matrix, and it follows that

$$\left(\mathbf{p}^{(i)}, \mathbf{A}\mathbf{p}^{(j)}\right)_2 = \left(\mathbf{p}^{(i)}, \mathbf{p}^{(j)}\right)_{\mathbf{A}} = 0 \quad \text{for} \quad i \neq j,$$

which says that the directions are A-conjugate.

▷ General minimized residual (GMRES)

This time we will choose $\mathbf{x}^{(k+1)}$ that minimizes the residual $\|\mathbf{r}^{(k+1)}\|_2$. As before, we take

$$\mathbf{x}^{(k+1)} = \mathbf{x}^{(0)} + \mathbf{Q}_k \mathbf{z}^{(k)}$$

for some vector $\mathbf{z}^{(k)}$ to be determined. From $\mathbf{r}^{(k)} = \mathbf{b} - \mathbf{A}\mathbf{x}^{(k)}$, we have

$$\begin{aligned}
\mathbf{r}^{(k+1)} &= \mathbf{r}^{(0)} - \mathbf{A}\mathbf{Q}_k \mathbf{z}^{(k)} \\
&= \mathbf{Q}_{k+1} \mathbf{Q}_{k+1}^{\mathsf{T}} \mathbf{r}^{(0)} - \mathbf{A}\mathbf{Q}_k \mathbf{z}^{(k)} \\
&= \mathbf{Q}_{k+1} \left(\left\|\mathbf{r}^{(0)}\right\|_2 \boldsymbol{\xi}_1 - \mathbf{H}_{k+1,k} \mathbf{z}^{(k)}\right)
\end{aligned}$$

where $\boldsymbol{\xi}_1 = (1, 0, \ldots, 0)$. We now have the problem of finding $\mathbf{z}^{(k)}$ to minimize

$$\left\|\mathbf{r}^{(k+1)}\right\|_2 = \left\| \left\|\mathbf{r}^{(0)}\right\|_2 \boldsymbol{\xi}_1 - \mathbf{H}_{k+1,k} \mathbf{z}^{(k)} \right\|_2.$$

The solution to this problem is the solution to the overdetermined system

$$\mathbf{H}_{k+1,k} \mathbf{z}^{(k)} = \left\|\mathbf{r}^{(0)}\right\|_2 \boldsymbol{\xi}_1,$$

which we can solve using QR decomposition. Because $\mathbf{H}_{k+1,k}$ is upper Hessenberg, we can use a series of Givens rotations to zero out the subdiagonal elements, giving us

$$\hat{\mathbf{R}}\mathbf{z}^{(k)} = \hat{\mathbf{Q}}^{\mathsf{T}} \left\| \mathbf{r}^{(0)} \right\|_2 \boldsymbol{\xi}_1,$$

where $\hat{\mathbf{Q}}$ is an orthogonal matrix and $\hat{\mathbf{H}}$ is an upper triangular matrix. The residual $\|\mathbf{r}^{(k+1)}\|_2$, given by the bottom element of this expression, is

$$\left\| \mathbf{r}^{(0)} \right\|_2 (\boldsymbol{\xi}_1^{\mathsf{T}} \hat{\mathbf{Q}} \boldsymbol{\xi}_{k+1}) = \left\| \mathbf{r}^{(0)} \right\|_2 \hat{q}_{1,k+1}.$$

We stop when $\|\mathbf{r}^{(k)}\|_2 < \varepsilon \|\mathbf{r}^{(0)}\|_2$ for some tolerance ε. Otherwise, we continue by finding the next basis vector $\mathbf{q}^{(k+2)}$ of the Krylov subspace using the Arnoldi process.

♣ The IterativeSolvers.jl function gmres implements the generalized minimum residual method, and minres implements the minimum residual method.

5.6 Exercises

5.1. Confirm that the spectral radius of the Jacobi method is $\cos \frac{\pi}{n+1}$ and the spectral radius of the Gauss–Seidel method is $\cos^2 \frac{\pi}{n+1}$ for the discrete Laplacian (5.5). 🖎

5.2. Consider the 2-by-2 matrix

$$\mathbf{A} = \begin{bmatrix} 1 & \sigma \\ -\sigma & 1 \end{bmatrix}.$$

Under what conditions will Gauss–Seidel converge? For what range ω will the SOR method converge? What is the optimal choice of ω? 🖎

5.3. Show that the conjugate gradient method requires no more than $k+1$ steps to converge for a symmetric, positive-definite matrix with k distinct eigenvalues.

5.4. Consider the three-dimensional Poisson equation $-\Delta u(x, y, z) = f(x, y, z)$ with Dirichlet boundary conditions $u(x, y, z) = 0$ over the unit cube. As in the two-dimensional case, we can use a finite difference approximation for the minus Laplacian $-\partial^2 u/\partial x^2 - \partial^2 u/\partial y^2 - \partial^2 u/\partial z^2$. But instead of a five-point stencil, now we'll use a seven-point stencil

$$\frac{6u_{ijk} - u_{i-1,j,k} - u_{i+1,j,k} - u_{i,j-1,k} - u_{i,j+1,k} - u_{i,j,k-1} - u_{i,j,k+1}}{h^2}.$$

Suppose that we discretize space using 50 points in each dimension. The finite difference matrix $\mathbf{A}$ to the problem $\mathbf{Ax} = \mathbf{b}$ is a 125000×125000 sparse matrix.

Even though **A** has over 15 billion elements, only 0.005 percent of them are nonzero—still, it has almost a million nonzero elements.

Consider the source term

$$f(x, y, z) = (x - x^2)(y - y^2) + (x - x^2)(z - z^2) + (y - y^2)(z - z^2).$$

In this case, the finite difference method will produce an exact solution

$$u(x, y, z) = \tfrac{1}{2}(x - x^2)(y - y^2)(z - z^2).$$

Implement the finite difference scheme using Jacobi, Gauss–Seidel, SOR, and conjugate gradient methods starting with an initial solution $u(x, y, z) \equiv 0$. Take $\omega = 1.9$ for the SOR method. Plot the error of the methods for the first 500 iterations and comment on the convergence. Hint: An easy way to build the finite difference matrix is by using a Kronecker tensor product

$$\mathbf{A} \otimes \mathbf{B} = \begin{bmatrix} a_{11}\mathbf{B} & \cdots & a_{1n}\mathbf{B} \\ \vdots & & \vdots \\ a_{m1}\mathbf{B} & \cdots & a_{mn}\mathbf{B} \end{bmatrix}.$$

The seven-point finite difference operator is $\mathbf{D} \otimes \mathbf{I} \otimes \mathbf{I} + \mathbf{I} \otimes \mathbf{D} \otimes \mathbf{I} + \mathbf{I} \otimes \mathbf{I} \otimes \mathbf{D}$ where **D** is a discrete Laplacian (5.5) and **I** is an identity matrix. ✍

5.5. Let **A** be the 20000×20000 matrix whose entries are zero everywhere except for the primes $2, 3, 5, 7, \ldots, 224737$ along the main diagonal and the number 1 in all the positions a_{ij} with $|i - j| = 1, 2, 4, 8, \ldots, 16384$. What is the $(1, 1)$-entry of $\mathbf{A}^{-1}$? (This problem was proposed by Nick Trefethen as part of his "hundred-dollar, hundred-digit challenge.") ✍

Chapter 6

The Fast Fourier Transform

It's hard to overstate the impact that the fast Fourier transform (FFT) has had in science and technology. It has been called "the most important numerical algorithm of our lifetime" by prominent mathematician Gilbert Strang, and it is invariably included in top-ten lists of algorithms. The FFT is an essential tool for signal processing, data compression, and partial differential equations. It is used in technologies as varied as digital media, medical imaging, and stock market analysis. At its most basic level, the FFT is a recursive implementation of the discrete Fourier transform. This implementation that puts the "fast" in fast Fourier transform takes what would typically be an $O(n^2)$-operation method and makes it an $O(n \log_2 n)$-operation one. In this chapter, we'll examine the algorithm and a few of its applications.

6.1 Discrete Fourier transform

Suppose that we want to find a polynomial $y = c_0 + c_1 z + c_2 z^2 + \cdots + c_{n-1} z^{n-1}$ that passes through the points $(z_j, y_j) \in \mathbb{C}^2$ for $j = 0, 1, \ldots, n - 1$. In this case, we simply solve the system $\mathbf{Vc} = \mathbf{y}$ where $\mathbf{V}$ is the Vandermonde matrix to get the coefficients c_j of the polynomial:

$$
\begin{bmatrix}
1 & z_0 & z_0^2 & \cdots & z_0^{n-1} \\
1 & z_1 & z_1^2 & \cdots & z_1^{n-1} \\
1 & z_2 & z_2^2 & \cdots & z_2^{n-1} \\
\vdots & \vdots & \vdots & \ddots & \vdots \\
1 & z_{n-1} & z_{n-1}^2 & \cdots & z_{n-1}^{n-1}
\end{bmatrix}
\begin{bmatrix}
c_0 \\
c_1 \\
c_2 \\
\vdots \\
c_{n-1}
\end{bmatrix}
=
\begin{bmatrix}
y_0 \\
y_1 \\
y_2 \\
\vdots \\
y_{n-1}
\end{bmatrix}.
$$

Now, suppose that we restrict the $\{z_j\}$ to equally spaced points on the unit circle. That is, take

$$z_j = e^{-i2\pi j/n} = \omega_n^j$$

by choosing nodes clockwise around the unit circle starting with $z_0 = 1$. The value $\omega_n = \exp(-i2\pi/n)$ is called an *nth root of unity* because it solves the equation $z^n = 1$. (In fact, ω_n^k are all nth roots of unity because they all are solutions to $z^n = 1$.) In this case, the Vandermonde matrix is

$$\mathbf{F}_n = \begin{bmatrix} 1 & 1 & 1 & \cdots & 1 \\ 1 & \omega_n & \omega_n^2 & \cdots & \omega_n^{n-1} \\ 1 & \omega_n^2 & \omega_n^4 & \cdots & \omega_n^{n-1} \\ \vdots & \vdots & \vdots & \ddots & \vdots \\ 1 & \omega_n^{n-1} & \omega_n^{2(n-1)} & \cdots & \omega_n^{(n-1)^2} \end{bmatrix}. \tag{6.1}$$

The system $\mathbf{y} = \mathbf{F}_n \mathbf{c}$ expressed in index notation is

$$y_k = \sum_{j=0}^{n-1} c_j e^{-i2\pi jk/n} = \sum_{j=0}^{n-1} c_j \omega_n^{jk}.$$

The matrix $\mathbf{F}_n$, called the *discrete Fourier transform* (DFT), is a scaled unitary matrix—that is, $\mathbf{F}_n^H \mathbf{F}_n = n\mathbf{I}$. This fact follows from a simple application of the geometric series. Recall that if $z \neq 1$, then

$$\sum_{j=0}^{n-1} z^j = \frac{z^n - 1}{z - 1}.$$

Computing $\mathbf{F}_n^H \mathbf{F}_n$,

$$\sum_{j=0}^{n-1} \omega_n^{jk} \overline{\omega_n^{jl}} = \sum_{j=0}^{n-1} \omega_n^{j(k-l)} = \begin{cases} \dfrac{\omega_n^{n(k-l)} - 1}{\omega_n^{k-l} - 1} = \dfrac{1-1}{\omega_n^{k-l} - 1} = 0, & \text{when } k \neq l \\ \displaystyle\sum_{j=0}^{n-1} 1 = n, & \text{when } k = l \end{cases}$$

where $\overline{\omega}$ is the complex conjugate of ω.

It also follows that the *inverse discrete Fourier transform* (IDFT) is simply $\mathbf{F}_n^{-1} = \mathbf{F}_n^H/n = \overline{\mathbf{F}}_n/n$. The DFT is symmetric but not Hermitian. Unlike the usual Vandermonde matrix, which is often ill-conditioned for large n, the DFT is perfectly conditioned because it is a scaled unitary matrix.

The kth column (and row) of $\mathbf{F}_n$ forms a subgroup[1] generated by ω_n^k. That

---

[1] A *group* is a set with an operation that possesses closure, associativity, an identity, and an inverse. A subgroup is any subset of a group, which is itself a group under the same operation.

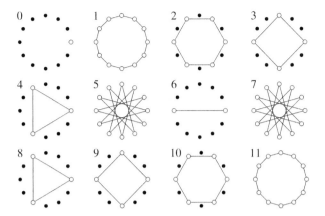

Figure 6.1: Subgroups using the generator ω_{12}^j for $j = 0, 1, \ldots, 11$.

is, $\{kj \mid j = 0, 1, 2, \ldots, n - 1\}$ forms a group under addition modulo n. For example, taking $n = 12$ using 2 as a generator, we have

$$\{2, 4, 6, 8, 10, 12, 14, 16, 18, 20, 22, 24\} \pmod{12} \equiv \{2, 4, 6, 8, 10, 0\}.$$

See Figure 6.1 above. Using 10 as a generator gives us the same group because $10 \equiv -2 \pmod{12}$. In particular, note that this subgroup corresponds to the six 6th roots of unity. That is, the subgroup generated by ω_{12}^2 equals the group generated by ω_6^1.

If the generator k is relatively prime with respect to n, i.e., if k and n are coprime, then the number of elements of the group is n. We say the group has order n. For example, both 5 and 7 are coprime to 12, and they generate subgroups of order 12. Otherwise, k generates a subgroup of order $n/\gcd(k, n)$.

Associated with the subgroup $\{0, 2, 4, 6, 8, 10\}$ is a *coset* formed by taking each element of the group and adding one. So,

$$\{0, 2, 4, 6, 8, 10\} \quad \text{has the coset} \quad \{1, 3, 5, 7, 9, 11\}.$$

Equivalently, for $\omega \equiv \omega_{12}$

$$\{1, \omega^2, \omega^4, \omega^6, \omega^8, \omega^{10}\} \quad \text{times } \omega \text{ equals} \quad \{\omega, \omega^3, \omega^5, \omega^7, \omega^9, \omega^{11}\}.$$

For $k = 3$, the group $\{0, 3, 6, 9\}$ has three cosets: itself, $\{1, 4, 7, 10\}$, and $\{2, 5, 8, 11\}$. For $k = 5$, there is only one coset. The number of cosets of the subgroup generated by k under addition modulo n equals $\gcd(k, n)$. The number of cosets determines the radix, which is the basis for the Cooley–Tukey algorithm.

6.2   Cooley–Tukey algorithm

There are several FFT algorithms. Each works by taking advantage of the group structure of the DFT matrix. The prototypical one, the Cooley–Tukey algorithm, was developed by James Cooley and John Tukey in 1965—a rediscovery of an unpublished discovery by Gauss in 1805. The development of their FFT was prompted by physicist Richard Garwin, designer of the first hydrogen bomb and researcher at IBM Watson laboratory, who at the time was interested in verifying the Soviet Union's compliance with the Nuclear Test Ban Treaty. Because the Soviet Union would not agree to inspections within their borders, Garwin turned to remote seismic monitoring of nuclear explosions. But, time series analysis of the off-shore seismological sensors would require a fast algorithm for computing the DFT, which normally took $O(n^2)$ operations. Garwin prompted Cooley to develop such an algorithm along with Tukey. And with a few months of effort, they had developed a recursive algorithm that took only $O(n \log_2 n)$ operations. When the sensors were finally deployed, they were able to locate nuclear explosions to within 15 kilometers.

In this section, we look at the Cooley–Tukey radix-2 (base-2) algorithm. We'll start with the Danielson–Lanczos lemma,[2] which says that a discrete Fourier transform of even length n can be rewritten as the sum of two discrete Fourier transforms of length $n/2$ (one formed using the even-numbered nodes and the other formed using the odd-numbered ones). By applying this procedure repeatedly, we can recursively break down any power-of-two length discrete Fourier transform. Consider a DFT whose size n is divisible by two:

$$y_j = \sum_{k=0}^{n-1} \omega_n^{kj} c_k = \underbrace{\sum_{k=0}^{n/2-1} \omega_n^{2kj} c_{2k}}_{\text{even index}} + \underbrace{\sum_{k=0}^{n/2-1} \omega_n^{(2k+1)j} c_{2k+1}}_{\text{odd index}}.$$

Let $m = n/2$. Since $\omega_n^2 = \omega_m$, we have

$$y_j = \sum_{k=0}^{m-1} \omega_m^{kj} c_k' + \omega_n^j \sum_{k=0}^{m-1} \omega_m^{kj} c_k''$$

where $c_k' = c_{2k}$ and $c_k'' = c_{2k+1}$. So, the output can be computed by using the sum of two smaller DFTs of size $m = n/2$:

$$y_j = y_j' + \omega_n^j y_j''.$$

---

[2]Cooley and Tukey rediscovered the lemma twenty-three years after Gordon Danielson and Cornelius Lanczos published it the *Journal of the Franklin Institute*, a highly read journal but apparently one that did not enjoy a wide circulation among numerical analysts.

We only need to compute $j = 0, 1, \ldots, m - 1$ because $\omega_m^{k(m+j)} = \omega_m^{km}\omega_m^{kj} = \omega_m^{kj}$ and $\omega_n^{m+j} = \omega_n^m\omega_n^j = -\omega_n^j$. So

$$y_{m+j} = y_j' - \omega_n^j y_j''.$$

Therefore,

$$\begin{cases} y_j = y_j' + \omega_n^j y_j'' \\ y_{m+j} = y_j' - \omega_n^j y_j'' \end{cases} \quad \text{for} \quad j = 0, 1, \ldots, m - 1. \tag{6.2}$$

To get a better picture of the math behind the algorithm, let's look at the matrix formulation of the radix-2 FFT. The $n = 4$ DFT is

$$\mathbf{F}_4 = \begin{bmatrix} 1 & 1 & 1 & 1 \\ 1 & \omega & \omega^2 & \omega^3 \\ 1 & \omega^2 & \omega^4 & \omega^6 \\ 1 & \omega^3 & \omega^6 & \omega^9 \end{bmatrix} = \begin{bmatrix} 1 & 1 & 1 & 1 \\ 1 & i & -1 & -i \\ 1 & -1 & 1 & -1 \\ 1 & -i & -1 & -i \end{bmatrix}.$$

Consider the even-odd permutation matrix (a reverse perfect shuffle[3])

$$\mathbf{P}_4^{-1} = \begin{bmatrix} 1 & 0 & 0 & 0 \\ 0 & 0 & 1 & 0 \\ 0 & 1 & 0 & 0 \\ 0 & 0 & 0 & 1 \end{bmatrix}.$$

Then

$$\mathbf{F}_4\mathbf{P}_4^{-1} = \left[\begin{array}{cc|cc} 1 & 1 & 1 & 1 \\ 1 & -1 & -i & i \\ \hline 1 & 1 & -1 & -1 \\ 1 & -1 & i & -i \end{array} \right] = \begin{bmatrix} \mathbf{F}_2 & \boldsymbol{\Omega}_2\mathbf{F}_2 \\ \mathbf{F}_2 & -\boldsymbol{\Omega}_2\mathbf{F}_2 \end{bmatrix} = \begin{bmatrix} \mathbf{I}_2 & \boldsymbol{\Omega}_2 \\ \mathbf{I}_2 & -\boldsymbol{\Omega}_2 \end{bmatrix}\begin{bmatrix} \mathbf{F}_2 & \\ & \mathbf{F}_2 \end{bmatrix},$$

where

$$\mathbf{F}_2 = \begin{bmatrix} 1 & 1 \\ 1 & -1 \end{bmatrix} \quad \text{and} \quad \boldsymbol{\Omega}_2 = \begin{bmatrix} 1 & 0 \\ 0 & i \end{bmatrix} = \mathrm{diag}(1, \omega_4)$$

The matrix

$$\mathbf{B}_4 = \begin{bmatrix} \mathbf{I}_2 & \boldsymbol{\Omega}_2 \\ \mathbf{I}_2 & -\boldsymbol{\Omega}_2 \end{bmatrix}$$

---

[3]To dig deeper into shuffling, see the article "The mathematics of perfect shuffles" by mathematician Persi Diaconis and others. When he was fourteen, Diaconis dropped out of school and ran off to follow a legendary sleight-of-hand magician. After learning that probability could improve his card skills and that mathematical analysis was necessary to understand probability, Diaconis took up mathematics and later went on to earn a PhD in mathematical statistics from Harvard.

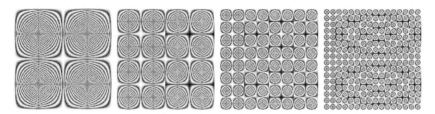

Figure 6.2: $\mathbf{F}_{128}$ (left), after one permutation, after a second permutation, and after a third permutation (right) of the columns.

is called the *butterfly matrix*. The DFT is then

$$
\mathbf{F}_4 = \mathbf{B}_4 \begin{bmatrix} \mathbf{F}_2 & \\ & \mathbf{F}_2 \end{bmatrix} \mathbf{P}_4 = \mathbf{B}_4 \begin{bmatrix} \mathbf{F}_2 \mathbf{P}_2^{-1} & \\ & \mathbf{F}_2 \mathbf{P}_2^{-1} \end{bmatrix} \begin{bmatrix} \mathbf{P}_2 & \\ & \mathbf{P}_2 \end{bmatrix} \mathbf{P}_4 = \mathbf{B}_4 \begin{bmatrix} \mathbf{B}_2 & \\ & \mathbf{B}_2 \end{bmatrix} \mathbf{P}
$$

where $\mathbf{P}$ is the permutation matrix of successive even/odd rearrangements. The pattern reveals itself for larger matrices as well. See the figure above, which shows the first three permutations acting on the DFT matrix $\mathbf{F}_{128}$. Note the emergence of $\mathbf{F}_{64}$, $\mathbf{F}_{32}$ and $\mathbf{F}_{16}$ with each permutation.

The *Kronecker product* of a $p \times q$ matrix $\mathbf{A}$ and an $r \times s$ matrix $\mathbf{B}$ is a $pr \times qs$ matrix equal to

$$
\mathbf{A} \otimes \mathbf{B} = \begin{bmatrix} a_{11}\mathbf{B} & \cdots & a_{1q}\mathbf{B} \\ \vdots & \ddots & \vdots \\ a_p\mathbf{B} & \cdots & a_{pq}\mathbf{B} \end{bmatrix}.
$$

Then for $n = 4$,

$$
\mathbf{F}_4 = (\mathbf{I}_1 \otimes \mathbf{B}_4)(\mathbf{I}_2 \otimes \mathbf{B}_2)\mathbf{P}.
$$

And in general,

$$
\mathbf{F}_n = (\mathbf{I}_1 \otimes \mathbf{B}_n)(\mathbf{I}_2 \otimes \mathbf{B}_{n/2}) \cdots (\mathbf{I}_{n/2} \otimes \mathbf{B}_2)\mathbf{P} \tag{6.3}
$$

where

$$
\mathbf{B}_{2n} = \begin{bmatrix} \mathbf{I}_n & \mathbf{\Omega}_n \\ \mathbf{I}_n & -\mathbf{\Omega}_n \end{bmatrix},
$$

the diagonal matrix $\mathbf{\Omega} = \operatorname{diag}(1, \overline{\omega}_{2n}, \overline{\omega}_{2n}^2, \dots, \overline{\omega}_{2n}^{n-1})$, and the permutation matrix

$$
\mathbf{P} = (\mathbf{I}_{n/4} \otimes \mathbf{P}_4) \cdots (\mathbf{I}_2 \otimes \mathbf{P}_{n/2})(\mathbf{I}_1 \otimes \mathbf{P}_n).
$$

♣ The function kron(A,B) returns the Kronecker tensor product $\mathbf{A} \otimes \mathbf{B}$.

Directly computing the DFT of an n dimensional vector requires $2n^2$ multiplications and additions. We can instead compute it with (6.2) using two DFTs of length $m = n/2$ and an additional $n/2$ multiplications and n additions. That is, a total of $\frac{1}{2}n^2 + \frac{3}{2}n$ operations. But we're not finished yet. If n is a power of two, then we can continue by applying (6.2) this idea recursively, continuing subdividing the nodes in half. For $n = 2^p$, the number of multiplications and additions is

$$M_p = 2M_{p-1} + 2^{p-1}$$
$$A_p = 2A_{p-1} + 2^p.$$

The solution to this difference equation is

$$M_p = p2^{p-1} = \tfrac{1}{2}n \log_2 n$$
$$A_p = p2^p = n \log_2 n.$$

So the number of operations is $O\left(\frac{3}{2}n \log_2 n\right)$. This means that a thousand-point FFT is roughly a hundred times faster than a direct computation $O(2n^2)$. Similar algorithms work for n power of three, five, etc. (radix-3, radix-5, etc.).

Using (6.1) and (6.2), the radix-2 algorithm can be written as a recursive function in Julia for a column vector c:

```
function fftx2(c)
  n = length(c)
  ω = exp(-2im*π/n)
  if mod(n,2) == 0
    k = collect(0:n/2-1)
    u = fftx2(c[1:2:n-1])
    v = (ω.^k).*fftx2(c[2:2:n])
    return([u+v; u-v])
  else
    k = collect(0:n-1)
    F = ω.^(k*k')
    return(F*c)
  end
end
```

We can adapt the FFT using the identity $\mathbf{F}_n^{-1} = \overline{\mathbf{F}}_n/n$ to get the IFFT.

```
ifftx2(y) = conj(fftx2(conj(y)))/length(y);
```

The radix-2 FFT works by recursively breaking the DFT matrix into smaller and smaller pieces. If n is a power of two or a composite of small primes such as $7200 = 2^5 \times 3^2 \times 5^2$, the recursive algorithm is efficient. But if n is a large prime number or a composite with a large prime number, such as $7060 = 2^2 \times 5 \times 353$, the recursion breaks down. In this case, other algorithms must be used. We'll examine two such algorithms in section 6.4.

6.3   Toeplitz and circulant matrices

A *Toeplitz matrix* is constant along each of its descending diagonals, e.g.,

$$
T = \begin{bmatrix}
a_0 & a_{-1} & a_{-2} & \cdots\cdots & a_{-(n-1)} \\
a_1 & a_0 & a_{-1} & a_{-2} & \cdots & a_{-(n-2)} \\
a_2 & a_1 & a_0 & a_{-1} & \ddots & a_{-(n-3)} \\
\vdots & a_2 & a_1 & a_0 & \ddots & \vdots \\
\vdots & \vdots & \ddots & \ddots & \ddots & a_{-1} \\
a_{n-1} & a_{n-2} & a_{n-3} & \cdots & a_1 & a_0
\end{bmatrix}
$$

for some values $\{a_{-(n-1)}, a_{-(n-2)}, \ldots, a_0, \ldots, a_{(n-1)}\}$.

❖ The ToeplitzMatrices.jl function `Toeplitz` constructs a Toeplitz matrix object.

A Toeplitz matrix is *circulant* if it has the form

$$
C = \begin{bmatrix}
c_0 & c_{n-1} & c_{n-2} & \cdots\cdots & c_1 \\
c_1 & c_0 & c_{n-1} & c_{n-2} & \cdots & c_2 \\
c_2 & c_1 & c_0 & c_{n-1} & \ddots & c_3 \\
\vdots & c_2 & c_1 & c_0 & \ddots & \vdots \\
\vdots & \vdots & \ddots & \ddots & \ddots & c_{n-1} \\
c_{n-1} & c_{n-2} & c_{n-3} & \cdots & c_1 & c_0
\end{bmatrix}
$$

for some values $\{c_0, c_1, \ldots, c_{n-1}\}$. Note that C is a Krylov matrix formed by the downshift permutation matrix

$$
R = \begin{bmatrix} \xi_2 & \xi_2 & \cdots & \xi_n & \xi_1 \end{bmatrix} = \begin{bmatrix}
0 & 0 & \cdots & 0 & 1 \\
1 & 0 & \cdots & 0 & 0 \\
0 & 1 & \cdots & 0 & 0 \\
\vdots & \vdots & \ddots & \vdots & \vdots \\
0 & 0 & \cdots & 1 & 0
\end{bmatrix}.
$$

That is,

$$
C = \begin{bmatrix} c & Rc & R^2c & \cdots & R^{n-1}c \end{bmatrix} \text{ with } c = \begin{bmatrix} c_0 & c_1 & \cdots & c_{n-1} \end{bmatrix}^T.
$$

The circulant matrix C can be written as $C = c_0 I + c_1 R + c_2 R^2 + \cdots + c_{n-1} R^{n-1}$, and R is itself a circulant matrix.

❖ The ToeplitzMatrices.jl function `Circulant` constructs a circulant matrix object.

Theorem 19. *A circulant matrix C, whose first column is c, has the diagonalization $C = F^{-1} \operatorname{diag}(Fc) F$, where F is the discrete Fourier transform.*

Proof. Let $\mathbf{F}$ be an $n \times n$ discrete Fourier transform matrix and $\mathbf{R}$ an equally sized downshift permutation matrix. Let's denote $\mathbf{F}$ using its elements as $\left[\omega^{ij}\right]$ where $\omega = e^{-2\pi i/n}$. Define the diagonal matrix $\mathbf{W} = \text{diag}(1, \omega, \omega^2, \ldots, \omega^{n-1})$. Then, $\mathbf{FR} = \left[\omega^{i(j+1)}\right] = \left[\omega^{ij}\omega^i\right]$ and $\mathbf{WF} = \left[\omega^i\omega^{ij}\right]$. So, $\mathbf{R} = \mathbf{F}^{-1}\mathbf{WF}$. For $\mathbf{c} = (c_0, c_1, \ldots, c_{n-1})$,

$$\mathbf{C} = c_0\mathbf{I} + c_1\mathbf{R} + c_2\mathbf{R} + \cdots + c_{n-1}\mathbf{R}^{n-1}$$

and it follows that

$$\mathbf{C} = \mathbf{F}^{-1}\left(c_0\mathbf{I} + c_1\mathbf{W} + c_2\mathbf{W}^2 + \cdots + c_{n-1}\mathbf{W}^{n-1}\right)\mathbf{F}$$

$$= \mathbf{F}^{-1}\,\text{diag}\left(\sum_{j=0}^{n-1}c_j, \sum_{j=0}^{n-1}c_j\omega^j, \ldots, \sum_{j=0}^{n-1}c_j\omega^{j(n-1)}\right)\mathbf{F}$$

Hence, $\mathbf{C} = \mathbf{F}^{-1}\,\text{diag}\,(\mathbf{Fc})\,\mathbf{F}$. $\qquad\square$

▷ Fast convolution

We can think of the convolution of two functions or arrays as their shifted inner products. For continuous functions $f(t)$ and $g(t)$, we have the convolution

$$(f * g)(t) = \int_{-\infty}^{\infty} f(s)g(t - s)\,ds.$$

When $\int_{-\infty}^{\infty} f(s)\,ds = 1$, you can think of $f * g$ as a moving average of g using f as a window function. For arrays $\mathbf{u}$ and $\mathbf{v}$, the kth element of the circular convolution $\mathbf{u} * \mathbf{v}$ is simply

$$(\mathbf{u} * \mathbf{v})_k = \sum_{j=0}^{n-1} u_j v_{k-j \,(\text{mod}\, n)}.$$

Example.   While the definition of a convolution may at first seem foreign to many, we are taught convolutions in grade school. Consider the product of 123 and 241. We compute the product using a convolution

		1	2	3	
×		2	4	1	
		1	2	3	
	4	8	12		.
2	4	6			
2	8	15	14	3	(and carrying...)
2	9	6	4	3	

So $123 \times 241 = 29643$.   ◀

The circular convolution of $\mathbf{u}$ and $\mathbf{v}$ is expressed in matrix notation as $\mathbf{u} * \mathbf{v} = \mathbf{C_u v}$ where $\mathbf{C_u}$ is the circulant matrix constructed from $\mathbf{u}$:

$$\begin{bmatrix} u_0 & u_4 & u_3 & u_2 & u_1 \\ u_1 & u_0 & u_4 & u_3 & u_2 \\ u_2 & u_1 & u_0 & u_4 & u_3 \\ u_3 & u_2 & u_1 & u_0 & u_4 \\ u_4 & u_3 & u_2 & u_3 & u_0 \end{bmatrix} \begin{bmatrix} v_0 \\ v_1 \\ v_2 \\ v_3 \\ v_4 \end{bmatrix}.$$

From theorem 19, the convolution $\mathbf{u} * \mathbf{v} = \mathbf{C_u v} = \mathbf{F}^{-1} \operatorname{diag}(\mathbf{Fu})\mathbf{Fv}$. In practice, we would compute $\mathbf{u} * \mathbf{v}$ as $\mathbf{F}^{-1}(\mathbf{Fu} \circ \mathbf{Fv})$, where $\circ$ denotes the Hadamard (or componentwise) product. Let me repeat—we compute the convolution by taking the IDFT of the component-wise product of the DFTs of $\mathbf{u}$ and $\mathbf{v}$. This evaluation requires three FFTs. Instead of the $2n^2$ operations needed to perform the convolution directly, it only takes $2n \log_2 n$ operations.

⚙ The DSP.jl function conv returns the convolution of two n-dimensional arrays using either direct computation or FFTs, depending on the size of the arrays.

▷ Fast Toeplitz multiplication

The previous section explained how to quickly evaluate circulant matrix multiplication using FFTs. We can do the same for a general Toeplitz matrix by padding it out to become a circulant matrix. For example,

$$\begin{bmatrix} v_1 \\ v_2 \\ v_3 \end{bmatrix} = \begin{bmatrix} a & d & e \\ b & a & d \\ c & b & a \end{bmatrix} \begin{bmatrix} u_1 \\ u_2 \\ u_3 \end{bmatrix} \qquad \longrightarrow \qquad \begin{bmatrix} v_1 \\ v_2 \\ v_3 \\ * \\ * \end{bmatrix} = \begin{bmatrix} a & d & e & c & b \\ b & a & d & e & c \\ c & b & a & d & e \\ e & c & b & a & d \\ d & e & c & b & a \end{bmatrix} \begin{bmatrix} u_1 \\ u_2 \\ u_3 \\ 0 \\ 0 \end{bmatrix}$$

where we discard the $*$ terms in the answer. In general, we need to pad out an $n \times n$ Toeplitz matrix by at least $n-1$ rows and columns to create an $(2n-1) \times (2n-1)$ circulant matrix. It may often be more efficient to overpad the matrix to be a power of two or some other product of small primes. For example,

$$\mathbf{T} = \begin{bmatrix} a & d & e \\ b & a & d \\ c & b & a \end{bmatrix} \qquad \longrightarrow \qquad \mathbf{C} = \begin{bmatrix} a & d & e & 0 & 0 & 0 & c & b \\ b & a & d & e & 0 & 0 & 0 & c \\ c & b & a & d & e & 0 & 0 & 0 \\ 0 & c & b & a & d & e & 0 & 0 \\ 0 & 0 & c & b & a & d & e & 0 \\ 0 & 0 & 0 & c & b & a & d & e \\ e & 0 & 0 & 0 & c & b & a & d \\ d & e & 0 & 0 & 0 & c & b & a \end{bmatrix}.$$

We never need to explicitly construct the full matrix $\mathbf{C}$—instead, we perform a fast convolution using the first column of $\mathbf{C}$.

Example.   Consider the $n \times n$ Toeplitz matrix whose first column is an n-long array $\mathbf{c}$ and whose first row is an n-long array $\mathbf{r}$. Suppose that we also pad the matrix with zeros to get a $2^p \times 2^p$ circulant matrix for some p, so we can efficiently use our radix-2 function fftx2. The naïve Julia code is

```
function fasttoeplitz(c,r,x)
  n = length(x)
  Δ = nextpow(2,n) - n
  x₁ = [c; zeros(Δ); r[end:-1:2]]
  x₂ = [x; zeros(Δ+n-1)]
  ifftx2(fftx2(x₁).*fftx2(x₂))[1:n]
end
```

The ToeplitzMatrices.jl package overloads matrix multiplication with fast Toeplitz multiplication when using a Toeplitz object, so it is quite fast—much faster than the code above.   ◄

6.4 Bluestein and Rader factorization

A k-smooth number (or simply a smooth number) is an integer whose prime factors are less than or equal to k. For example, $720 = 2^4 \times 3^2 \times 5$ is a 5-smooth number, also known as a regular number. A k-rough number is an integer whose prime factors are all greater than or equal to k. The number $721 = 7 \times 103$ is 5-rough. The Cooley–Tukey algorithm is designed to recursively break down composite numbers into their prime factors, so it works best on smooth numbers. And it absolutely does not work on arrays whose lengths are prime numbers. Luckily, there are methods such as Bluestein and Rader factorization when n is a prime number. While not as efficient as the original Cooley–Tukey algorithm, these methods can work in conjunction with the Cooley–Tukey algorithm by smashing through rough numbers. To see this, let's plot several run times of Julia's FFT for smooth numbers and prime numbers:

```
using FFTW, Primes, Plots
N = 10000
smooth(n,N) = (1:N)[all.(x->x<=n,factor.(Set,1:N))]
t₁ = [(x = randn(n); (n,@elapsed(fft(x)))) for n∈primes(N)]
t₂ = [(x = randn(n); (n,@elapsed(fft(x)))) for n∈smooth(5,N)]
plot(t₁,label="prime"); plot!(t₂,label="5-smooth")
```

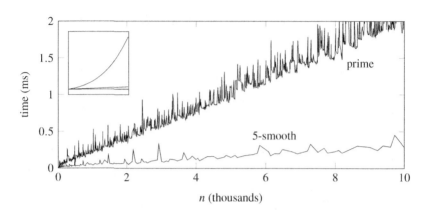

Figure 6.3: FFT run times on vectors of length n. The lower curve shows 5-smooth numbers and the upper curve shows prime numbers. The inset shows both curves relative to the run time of directly computing a DFT.

The figure above shows the plots with several outliers removed. Note that while the FFT is significantly slower on rough numbers than on smooth numbers, it is still orders of magnitude faster than directly computing the DFT.

▷ **Bluestein factorization**

Let's start with the DFT

$$y_j = \sum_{k=0}^{n-1} c_k \omega_n^{jk}.$$

By noting that $(j - k)^2 = j^2 - 2jk + k^2$, we can replace jk in the DFT by $(j^2 - (j - k)^2 + k^2)/2$:

$$y_j = \sum_{k=0}^{n-1} c_k \omega_n^{jk} = \omega_n^{j^2/2} \sum_{k=0}^{n-1} c_k \omega_n^{-(j-k)^2/2} \omega_n^{k^2/2}.$$

Furthermore, since $\sqrt{\omega_n} = \omega_{2n}$, it follows that

$$y_j = \omega_{2n}^{j^2} \sum_{k=0}^{n-1} c_k \omega_{2n}^{-(j-k)^2} \omega_{2n}^{k^2}.$$

This says that the DFT matrix $\mathbf{F}$ equals $\mathbf{WTW}$, where $\mathbf{W}$ is a diagonal matrix whose diagonal elements are given by

$$\mathbf{w} = \begin{bmatrix} 1 & \omega_{2n} & \omega_{2n}^4 & \omega_{2n}^9 & \cdots & \omega_{2n}^{(n-1)^2} \end{bmatrix}$$

and $\mathbf{T}$ is a symmetric Toeplitz matrix whose the first row is given by $\overline{\mathbf{w}}$. For example, for $\mathbf{F}_5$

$$\mathbf{w} = \begin{bmatrix} 1 & \omega & \omega^4 & \omega^9 & \omega^6 \end{bmatrix} \quad \text{and} \quad \overline{\mathbf{w}} = \begin{bmatrix} 1 & \omega^9 & \omega^6 & \omega^1 & \omega^4 \end{bmatrix}$$

where $\omega \equiv \omega_{10}$. Therefore, $\mathbf{F}_5$ equals

$$\begin{bmatrix} 1 & & & & \\ & \omega & & & \\ & & \omega^4 & & \\ & & & \omega^9 & \\ & & & & \omega^6 \end{bmatrix} \begin{bmatrix} 1 & \omega^9 & \omega^6 & \omega^1 & \omega^4 \\ \omega^9 & 1 & \omega^9 & \omega^6 & \omega^1 \\ \omega^6 & \omega^9 & 1 & \omega^9 & \omega^6 \\ \omega^1 & \omega^6 & \omega^9 & 1 & \omega^9 \\ \omega^4 & \omega^1 & \omega^6 & \omega^9 & 1 \end{bmatrix} \begin{bmatrix} 1 & & & & \\ & \omega & & & \\ & & \omega^4 & & \\ & & & \omega^9 & \\ & & & & \omega^6 \end{bmatrix}.$$

So, $\mathbf{y} = \mathbf{Fc}$ equals $\mathbf{w} \circ (\overline{\mathbf{w}} * (\mathbf{w} \circ \mathbf{c}))$ where $\circ$ denotes the Hadamard product.

When computing a Toeplitz product, we can pad the vectors with any number of zeros to get a length for which the Cooley–Tukey algorithm is fast. We need to compute three DFTs over a vector of at least $2n - 1$ elements. The following Julia code implements the Bluestein algorithm using the `fasttoeplitz` function, defined on page 153:

```
function bluestein_fft(x)
  n = length(x)
  ω = exp.((1im*π/n)*(0:n-1).^2)
  ω.*fasttoeplitz(conj(ω),conj(ω),ω.*x)
end
```

▷ **Rader factorization**

The Cooley–Tukey algorithm's superpower is recursively breaking a large matrix into many smaller matrices that can be efficiently multiplied. The algorithm can effortlessly handle an array of 576 elements because 576 is a product of small factors $576 = 2^6 \times 3^2$. But, a prime number like 587 is kryptonite to the Cooley–Tukey algorithm. Luckily, there is an algorithm called Rader factorization whose superpower is prime numbers—and this is only when it works. Rader factorization permutes the rows and the columns of an $n \times n$ DFT matrix to get a matrix

$$\begin{bmatrix} 1 & \mathbf{1}^\mathsf{T} \\ \mathbf{1} & \mathbf{C}_{n-1} \end{bmatrix}$$

where $\mathbf{C}_{n-1}$ is an $(n-1) \times (n-1)$ circulant matrix and $\mathbf{1}$ is a vector of ones. We can replace the circulant matrix with three DFTs of size $n - 1$. If n is prime, then $n - 1$ is at least divisible by two, allowing us to jump-start the Cooley–Tukey algorithm. Say that we start with 587 elements. Rader factorization converts the problem into three 586-element DFTs, each of which can be broken into two

293-element DFTs using the Cooley–Tukey algorithm. Because 293 is a prime, we'll need to use Rader factorization again. We can factor 292 into $2^2 \times 73$, meaning two iterations of Cooley–Tukey followed by Rader again. Finally, 72 factors into 2^3 and 3^2 using the Cooley–Tukey algorithm.

Rader factorization relies on the existence of a permutation. That there is such a permutation is a result of number theory. We take the following theorem as given and demonstrate it with an example.

Theorem 20. *If n is prime, then there is an integer $r \in \{2, 3, \ldots, n-1\}$ such that $\{1, 2, 3, \ldots, n-1\} = \{r, r^2 \pmod{n}, r^3 \pmod{n}, \ldots, r^{n-1} \pmod{n}\}$. The integer r is called a primitive root (or generator) modulo n. There exists an integer s such that $sr \pmod{n} = 1$ for prime n. We call s the inverse of r and denote it by r^{-1}. If r is a primitive root, then so is r^{-1}.*

Example.   The figure on the next page shows the finite cyclic groups of order $n = 13$. We can see that $r = 2$ is a primitive root modulo 13 because

$$2^j \pmod{13} = \{2, 4, 8, 3, 6, 12, 11, 9, 5, 10, 7, 1\}$$

is a permutation of $j = \{1, 2, \ldots, 12\}$. The integer 7 is the inverse of 2 because $2 \cdot 7 = 14 = 1 \pmod{13}$. Notice that the group generated by 7 shares the same cycle graph as the group generated by 2 but in the reverse direction:

$$7^j \pmod{13} = \{7, 10, 5, 9, 11, 12, 6, 3, 8, 4, 2, 1\}.$$

Integers 6 and 11 are also primitive roots modulo 13. The order of the multiplicative group of integers modulo n is given by Euler's totient $\varphi(n)$, which equals $n - 1$ when n is prime. The number of elements in the groups must be a factor of $\varphi(13) = 12$, i.e., $\{2, 3, 4, 6, 12\}$. We see that 12 generates a group of order 2; 3 and 9 generate groups of order 3; 5 and 8 generate groups of order 4; 4 and 10 generate groups of order 6; and the primitive roots 2, 6, 7, and 11 generate groups of order 12.   ◄

Suppose we have the discrete Fourier transform

$$y_k = \sum_{j=0}^{n-1} c_j \omega_n^{jk}$$

where n is prime. If r is a primitive root modulo n, then by theorem 20 we can take the permutation $j \to r^j$ and $k \to r^{-k}$ for $j, k = 1, 2, \ldots, n-1$ giving us

$$y_0 = \sum_{j=0}^{n-1} c_j \quad \text{and} \quad y_{(r^{-k})} = c_0 + \sum_{j=1}^{n-1} c_{(r^j)} \omega_n^{(r^{j-k})}.$$

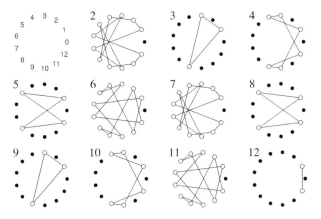

Figure 6.4: Finite cyclic groups of order 13.

We can rewrite the sum as $\mathbf{P}_s^{-1}\mathbf{C}_{n-1}\mathbf{P}_r\mathbf{c}$, where $\mathbf{C}_{n-1}$ is the circulant matrix whose first row is given

$$\begin{bmatrix} \omega_n^r & \omega_n^{r^2} & \cdots & \omega_n^{r^{n-1}} \end{bmatrix},$$

the matrix $\mathbf{P}_r$ is the permutation matrix generated by r

$$\{r, r^2 \,(\mathrm{mod}\,n), r^3 \,(\mathrm{mod}\,n), \ldots, r^{n-1} \,(\mathrm{mod}\,n)\},$$

and the matrix $\mathbf{P}_s$ is the permutation matrix generated by r^{-1}

$$\{r^{-1}, r^{-2} \,(\mathrm{mod}\,n), r^{-3} \,(\mathrm{mod}\,n), \ldots, r^{-n-1} \,(\mathrm{mod}\,n)\}.$$

Finding a primitive root modulo n is not trivial, but it is straightforward. We check each integer r until we find one that works. Let p be the factors of $\varphi(n) = n - 1$. If $r^{p_i} = 1$ for any $p_i \in p$, then we know that r cannot be a primitive root.

```
using Primes
function primitiveroot(n)
  ϕ = n - 1
  p = factor(Set,ϕ)
  for r = 2:n-1
    all( [powermod(r, ϕ÷pᵢ, n) for pᵢ∈p] .!= 1 ) && return(r)
  end
end
```

Now, we can implement the Rader factorization:

```
function rader_fft(x)
```

```
n = length(x)
r = primitiveroot(n)
P₊ = powermod.(r, 0:n-2, n)
P₋ = circshift(reverse(P₊),1)
ω = exp.((2im*π/n)*P₋)
c = x[1] .+ ifft(fft(ω).*fft(x[2:end][P₊]))
[sum(x); c[reverse(invperm(P₋))]]
end
```

While $n - 1$ is even and hence can be factored, it may still be advantageous to pad the matrix $\mathbf{C}_{n-1}$ with zeros to make the evaluation of the three DFTs more efficient. We would need at least another $n - 1$ zeros to use a fast Toeplitz routine plus additional zeros to make the number of elements power smooth.

6.5   Applications

A typical use of the DFT is constructing the frequency components of a time-varying or space-varying function, such as an audio signal. We examine several other applications for the DFT in this section. Before doing so, it's helpful to understand a little more about practical FFT implementation.

▷ **The fast Fourier transform in practice**

The Fastest Fourier Transform in the West (FFTW) is a C library consisting of several FFT algorithms chosen using heuristics and trial. The first time the library is called, it may try several different FFT algorithms for the same problem and use the fastest after that. The FFTW library decomposes the problem using the composite Cooley–Tukey algorithm recursively until the problem can be solved using fixed-size codelets.[4] If n is a prime number, the FFTW library decomposes the problem using Rader decomposition and then uses the Cooley–Tukey algorithm to compute the three $(n - 1)$-point DFTs.

The FFTW library saves the fastest approach for a given array size as the so-called *wisdom*, which it uses when for FFTs on other same-sized arrays. If a problem requires several repeated FFTs, it may be advantageous for FFTW to initially try all of the possible algorithms to see which is fastest. On the other hand, if the FFT is only needed once or twice, it may be better to let FFTW estimate the quickest approach.

⚙ The FFTW.jl package provides several Julia bindings for FFTW. These include `fft` and `ifft` for complex-input transforms and `rfft` and `irfft` for real-input transforms.

Julia's `fft` and `ifft` functions are all multi-dimensional transforms unless an

---

[4]Codelets are small-sized (typically $n \leq 64$), hard-coded transforms that use split-radix, Cooley–Tukey, and a prime factor algorithm.

additional parameter is provided. For example, `fft(x)` performs an FFT overall dimensions of x, whereas `fft(x,2)` only performs an FFT along the second dimension of x. If you expect to use the same transform repeatedly on an array with the shape of A, you can define F = `plan_fft(A)` and then use F*A or F\A—the multiplication and inverse operators are overloaded.

While FFTs of every (or almost every) scientific computing language typically put the zero frequency in the first position output array, it may be more mathematically meaningful or convenient to have the zero frequency in the middle position of the output array. We can do this by swapping the left and right halves of the array.

👀 The FFTW.jl functions `fftshift` and `ifftshift` shift the zero-frequency component to the middle of the array.

Discrete cosine transforms (DCTs) and discrete sine transforms (DSTs) can be constructed using the DFT by extending even functions and odd functions as periodic functions. Because there are different ways to define this even/odd extension, there are different variants for each the DST and the DCT—eight of them (each called type-1 through type-8), although only the first four of them are commonly used in practice. Each of these four types is available through the FFTW.jl real-input/real-output transform `FFTW.r2r(A, kind [, dims])`. The parameter `kind` specifies the type: `FFTW.REDFT`xy where xy, which equals 00, 01, 10, or 11, selects type-1 to type-4 DCT. Similarly, `FFTW.RODFT`xy selects a type-1 to type-4 DST. Because the DCT and DST are scaled orthogonal matrices, we can reuse the same functions for the inverse DCT and inverse DST by dividing by a normalization constant.

👀 The FFTW.jl functions `dct` and `idct` compute the type-2 DCT and inverse DCT

▷ Fast Poisson solver

Recall the three-dimensional Poisson equation $-\Delta u(x, y, z) = f(x, y, z)$ with Dirichlet boundary conditions $u(x, y, z) = 0$ over the unit cube from problem 5.4. This problem $\mathbf{A}\mathbf{u} = \mathbf{f}$ was solved using a nine-point stencil to approximate the Laplacian operator as $\mathbf{A} = \mathbf{D} \otimes \mathbf{I} \otimes \mathbf{I} + \mathbf{I} \otimes \mathbf{D} \otimes \mathbf{I} + \mathbf{I} \otimes \mathbf{I} \otimes \mathbf{D}$, where $\mathbf{D}$ is the tridiagonal matrix $\text{tridiag}(1, -2, 1)/(\Delta x)^2$ and $\mathbf{I}$ is the corresponding identity matrix. Because the matrix was large and sparse, we used an iterative method to find the solution. A faster method is to use a fast Poisson solver. From exercise 1.5, the eigenvalues of $\mathbf{D}$ are

$$\lambda_k = \left(2 - 2\cos\frac{k\pi}{n+1}\right)/(\Delta x)^2$$

where $k = 1, 2, \ldots, n$ and the eigenvectors are given by

$$
\mathbf{x}_k = \left[\sin\left(\frac{k\pi}{n+1}\right) \quad \sin\left(\frac{2k\pi}{n+1}\right) \quad \sin\left(\frac{3k\pi}{n+1}\right) \quad \cdots \quad \sin\left(\frac{nk\pi}{n+1}\right) \right]^{\mathsf{T}}.
$$

Take two arbitrary $n \times n$ matrices $\mathbf{M}$ and $\mathbf{N}$ and an $n \times n$ identity matrix $\mathbf{I}$. If $\mathbf{M}\mathbf{x}_i = \lambda_i \mathbf{x}_i$ and $\mathbf{M}\mathbf{y}_i = \mu_i \mathbf{y}_i$, then

$$
(\mathbf{M} \otimes \mathbf{N})(\mathbf{x}_i \otimes \mathbf{y}_i) = \lambda_i \mu_j (\mathbf{x}_i \otimes \mathbf{y}_i).
$$

Furthermore, the matrix $(\mathbf{I} \otimes \mathbf{M}) + (\mathbf{N} \otimes \mathbf{I})$ has eigenvalues $\{\lambda_i + \lambda_j\}$ with $i, j \in \{1, 2, \ldots, n\}$. From this, it follows that the eigenvalues of $\mathbf{A}$ are

$$
\lambda_{ijk} = \left(6 - 2\cos\frac{i\pi}{n+1} - 2\cos\frac{j\pi}{n+1} - 2\cos\frac{k\pi}{n+1}\right) / (\Delta x)^2
$$

and the i, j, k-component of eigenvalues $\mathbf{x}_{\zeta \xi \eta}$ is

$$
\sin\left(\frac{i\zeta\pi}{n+1}\right) \sin\left(\frac{j\xi\pi}{n+1}\right) \sin\left(\frac{k\eta\pi}{n+1}\right)
$$

with integers $\leq \zeta, \xi, \eta \in \{1, 2, \ldots, n\}$. The diagonalization of equation $\mathbf{A}\mathbf{u} = \mathbf{f}$ is $\mathbf{S}\mathbf{A}\mathbf{S}^{-1}\mathbf{u} = \mathbf{f}$. And the diagonalization of its solution $\mathbf{u} = \mathbf{A}^{-1}\mathbf{f}$ is $\mathbf{u} = \mathbf{S}\Lambda^{-1}\mathbf{S}^{-1}\mathbf{f}$. The operator $\mathbf{S}$ is the discrete sine transform (DST), which in component form is

$$
\hat{f}_{lmn} = \sum_{i=1}^{n} \sum_{j=1}^{n} \sum_{k=1}^{n} f_{ijk} \sin\left(\frac{i\zeta\pi}{n+1}\right) \sin\left(\frac{j\xi\pi}{n+1}\right) \sin\left(\frac{k\eta\pi}{n+1}\right). \qquad (6.4)
$$

We can use an FFT to compute the discrete sine transform by first noting

$$
\sin\frac{k\pi}{n} = \frac{e^{i\pi/n} - e^{-ik\pi/n}}{2i}
$$

and extending the input function (which is zero at the endpoints) to make a periodic function. The indices of the DFT run from 0 to $n-1$, while the indices of the DST run from 1 to n, so we'll need to add a zero to the input vector $\mathbf{f}$ to account for the constant (zero frequency) term. We can compute the discrete sine transform of $(f_1, f_2, \ldots, f_n)$ taking components 2 through $N+1$ of the discrete Fourier transform of $(0, f_1, f_2, \ldots, f_n, 0, -f_n, \ldots, -f_2, -f_1)$. The DST $\mathbf{S}$ is a real symmetric, scaled orthogonal matrix, so its inverse $\mathbf{S}^{-1} = 2/(n+1)\mathbf{S}$. The following Julia code solves exercise 5.4 using a fast Poisson solver. We'll first define a type-1 DST and inverse DST.

```
using FFTW
dst(x) = FFTW.r2r(x,FFTW.RODFT00)
idst(x) = dst(x)/(2^ndims(x)*prod(size(x).+1))
```

Now, we can solve the problem.

```
n = 50; x = (1:n)/(n+1); Δx = 1/(n+1)
v = 2 .- 2cos.(x*π)
λ = [v[i]+v[j]+v[k] for i∈1:n, j∈1:n, k∈1:n]./Δx^2
f = [(x-x^2)*(y-y^2) + (x-x^2)*(z-z^2)+(y-y^2)*(z-z^2)
     for x∈x,y∈x,z∈x]
u = idst(dst(f)./λ);
```

Comparing the numerical solution with the analytic solution,

```
norm(u - [(x-x^2)*(y-y^2)*(z-z^2)/2 for x∈x,y∈x,z∈x])
```

we find an error of 1.5×10^{-14}. It is often much more convenient to operate on the basis functions directly to solve a partial differential equation instead of first discretizing in space. This approach is discussed in Chapter 16.

▷ Data filtering

Suppose that we have noisy data. We can filter out the high frequencies and regularize the data using a convolution with a smooth kernel function, such as a Gaussian distribution. A kernel with a support of m points applied over a domain with n points requires $O(mn)$ operations applied directly. It requires $O(n)$ operations to compute the equivalent product in the Fourier domain, with an additional two $O(n \log n)$ operations to put it in the Fourier domain and bring it back. The extra overhead in computing Fourier transforms may be small when n and m are large. In the example below, noise was added to the data on the left to get the center figure. A Gaussian distribution was used as a convolution kernel to filter the noise and get the figure on the right.

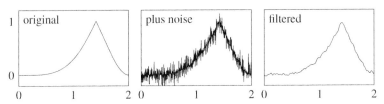

▷ Image and data compression

On page 78, we examined SVD rank reduction as a novel way to compress an image. In practice, photographs are typically saved using JPEG compression, which divides an image into 8×8 pixel blocks and then takes discrete cosine transforms (DCTs) of each of these blocks. Similarly, audio is often compressed as an MP3, using DCT compression of blocks. Using the Fourier series to deconstruct the natural world should be, well, natural. Joseph Fourier introduced

Figure 6.5: Discrete cosine transform (right) of the image (left).

his namesake series as a solution to the heat equation, and a hundred years later, Louis de Broglie suggested that all matter is waves.

The Fourier transform of a smooth function decays rapidly in the frequency domain. So for sufficiently smooth data, high-frequency information can be discarded without introducing substantial error. Since the DFT is a scaled unitary matrix, both the 2-norm and the Frobenius norm are preserved by the DFT: $\|\mathbf{e}\|_2 = \|\mathbf{Fe}\|_2$ and $\|\mathbf{e}\|_F = \|\mathbf{Fe}\|_F$. The pixelwise root mean squared error of an image equals the pixelwise root mean squared error of the DCT of an image.

Figure 6.5 above shows the magnitudes of the discrete cosine transform of a cartoon image. The image isn't an exceptionally smooth one—it has several sharp edges, particularly the eyes, mouth, and chin. The most significant Fourier coefficients are associated with low-frequency components in the upper left-hand corner, and in general, the Fourier coefficients decay as their frequencies increase.

By cropping out the high-frequency components in the Fourier domain, we can keep relevant information with only a marginal increase in the error if the data is smooth. However, if the data is not smooth, important information resides in the higher frequency components and discarding it can result in substantial error. Notice in Figure 6.5 that several slowly decaying rays corresponding to sharp edges and lines in the cartoon emanate from the upper left-hand corner. The so-called Gibbs phenomenon associated with lossy compression of data with discontinuities can result in noticeable JPEG ringing artifacts at sharp edges. As an alternative approach, we can zero out only those Fourier components whose magnitudes are less than some given tolerance regardless of their frequencies. We can store the information efficiently as a sparse array by zeroing out enough components. We'll leave the first approach as an exercise and consider the second approach below.

Consider the following Julia function that compresses a grayscale image A to a factor d from its original array size. We could consider each RGB or HSV channel independently for a color image. The function first computes the DCT B of an image A. It determines the threshold tolerance tol based on the desired density d and then drops the smallest values to get a sparse matrix B_0. Finally, the function returns a reconstruction of the compressed image.

```julia
using Images, FFTW, SparseArrays
function dctcompress(A,d)
  B = dct(Float64.(A))
  idx = d*prod(size(A)) |> floor |> Int
  tol = sort!(abs.(B[:]),rev=true)[idx]
  B₀ = droptol!(sparse(B),tol)
  idct(B₀) |> clamp01! .|> Gray
end
```

Let's compare an original image and a 95-percent compressed image.

```julia
A = Gray.(load(download(bucket*"laura_square.png")))
[A dctcompress(A,0.05)]
```

To be fair, B_0 is a 64-bit floating-point array and would still need to be quantized to 256 discrete values, and the sparse array requires additional overhead for the row-column indices. We can compute the relative compression and error using

```julia
Base.summarysize(B₀)/sizeof(Matrix(B₀)), norm(B - B₀)/norm(B)
```

By computing the errors from several values of d, we can determine the relative efficiency of DCT compression. See the figure on the next page and the QR code below.

6.6   Exercises

6.1. Modify the function fftx2 on page 149 for a radix-3 FFT algorithm. Verify your algorithm using a vector of size $3^4 = 81$.   ✐

6.2. *Fast multiplication of large integers.*   Consider two polynomials

$$p(x) = p_n x^n + \cdots + p_1 x + p_0 \quad \text{and} \quad q(x) = q_n x^n + \cdots + q_1 x + q_0.$$

When $x = 10$, the polynomials $p(x)$ and $q(x)$ return the decimal numbers $p(10)$ and $q(10)$, respectively. We can represent the polynomials as coefficient vectors by using the basis $\{1, x, x^2, \ldots, x^{2n}\}$:

$$\mathbf{p} = (p_0, p_1, \ldots, p_n, 0, \ldots, 0) \quad \text{and} \quad \mathbf{q} = (q_0, q_1, \ldots, q_n, 0, \ldots, 0).$$

an image with
increasing levels of
DCT compressed

relative error versus relative size

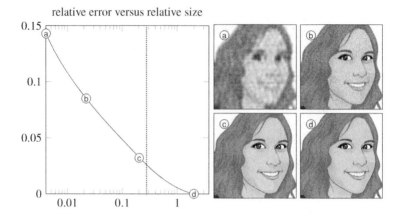

Figure 6.6: The relative error of a DCT-compressed image. The dotted line shows equivalent lossless PNG compression.

The product $p(x)q(x)$ is represented by

$$(p_0 q_0, p_0 q_1 + p_1 q_0, \ldots, p_{n-1} q_n + p_n q_{n-1}, p_n q_n), \tag{6.5}$$

where the jth element is given by $\sum_{i=0}^{j} p_i q_{j-i}$ for $j \leq n$ and $\sum_{i=j-n}^{n} p_i q_{j-i}$ for $j \geq n$. For example, when $n = 2$, the product of $\mathbf{p}$ and $\mathbf{q}$ is computed using

$$\begin{bmatrix} q_0 & & \\ q_1 & q_0 & \\ q_2 & q_1 & q_0 \\ & q_2 & q_1 \\ & & q_2 \end{bmatrix} \begin{bmatrix} p_0 \\ p_1 \\ p_2 \end{bmatrix}.$$

This product is equivalent to the circular convolution

$$\begin{bmatrix} q_0 & 0 & 0 & q_2 & q_1 \\ q_1 & q_0 & 0 & 0 & q_2 \\ q_2 & q_1 & q_0 & 0 & 0 \\ 0 & q_2 & q_1 & q_0 & 0 \\ 0 & 0 & q_2 & q_1 & q_0 \end{bmatrix} \begin{bmatrix} p_0 \\ p_1 \\ p_2 \\ 0 \\ 0 \end{bmatrix}$$

In this case, the jth term of the product vector is $\sum_{i=0}^{2n} p_i q_{j-i \pmod{2n}}$. Recall that the DFT of a circular convolution is a componentwise product. Hence, we can compute the product of two large numbers by

1. Treating each of the n digits as an element of an array.
2. Padding each array with n zeros.

3. Taking the discrete Fourier transform of both arrays, multiplying them componentwise, and then taking the inverse discrete Fourier transform to transform them back.

4. Carrying the digits so that each element only contains a single digit. For example, multiplying 35 and 19 with the array representations $(5, 3, 0, 0, 0)$ and $(9, 1, 0, 0, 0)$ results in $(45, 32, 3, 0, 0)$, which is then adjusted to give $(5, 6, 6, 0, 0)$ or 665.

The benefit of this approach is that we can reduce the number of operations from $O(n^2)$ to $O(n \log n)$. With some modification, this algorithm is called Schönhage–Strassen algorithm.

Write an algorithm that uses FFTs to compute the product of the primes

3276913299326670954996198819083446141317764296799294253979828853 3

and

3490529510847650949147849619903898133417764638493387843990820577.

The product of these two numbers is RSA-129, the value of which can be easily found online to verify that your algorithm works. RSA is one of the first commonly used public-key cryptologic algorithms.   ✍

6.3. We can compute the fast discrete cosine transform using an FFT by doubling the domain and mirroring the signal into the domain extension as we did with the fast sine transform. Alternatively, rather than positioning nodes at the mesh points $\{1, 2, \ldots, n - 1\}$, we can arrange the nodes between the mesh points $\{\frac{1}{2}, \frac{3}{2}, \ldots, n - \frac{1}{2}\}$, counting over every second node and then reflecting the signal back at the boundary. For example, with eight nodes ⓪①②③④⑤⑥⑦⑦⑥⑤④③②①⓪ would have the reordering ⓪②④⑥⑦⑤③①. We need only n points rather than $2n$ points to compute the DCT. In two and three dimensions, the number of points are quartered and eighthed. This DCT

$$\sum_{j=0}^{n-1} f_k \cos\left[\frac{\pi}{n}\left(j + \tfrac{1}{2}\right)k\right] \quad \text{for} \quad k = 0, 1, \ldots, n - 1$$

is called the type-2 DCT or simply DCT-2 and is perhaps the most commonly used form of DCT. Write an algorithm that reproduces an n-point DCT-2 and inverse DCT-2 using n-point FFTs.   ✍

6.4. Compare two approaches to image compression using a DCT—cropping high-frequency components and removing low magnitude components—discussed on page 162.   ✍

Numerical Methods for Analysis

Chapter 7

Preliminaries

This chapter briefly introduces several key ideas that we will use over the next four chapters. Specifically, we examine how functions, problems, methods, and computational error impact getting a good numerical solution.

7.1 Well-behaved functions

Throughout this book, unless otherwise stated, we'll assume that all functions are nice functions to allow us to handwave around formalities. Mathematically, the words *nice* and *well-behaved* are used in an ad-hoc way to allow for a certain laziness of expression. We might reason that an analytic function is better-behaved than a merely continuous function, which itself is better-behaved than a discontinuous one. And that one is surely better-behaved than a function that blows up. But, what is a well-behaved function? Perhaps the easiest way to introduce well-behaved functions is with examples of ones that are not so well-behaved, some rather naughty functions.

Example. Weierstrass functions are examples of mathematical monsters. They are everywhere continuous and almost nowhere differentiable. The following Weierstrass function was proposed by Bernhard Riemann in the 1860s

$$\sum_{n=1}^{\infty} \frac{\sin(\pi n^2 x)}{\pi n^2}.$$

The function is differentiable only at the set of points of the form p/q where p and q are odd integers. At each of these points, its derivative is $-\frac{1}{2}$ (Hardy

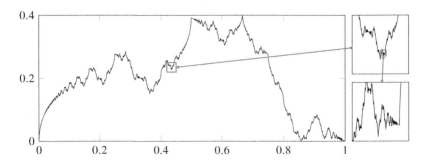

Figure 7.1: The nowhere differentiable Weierstrass function. The callouts depict the fractal nature of this pathological function.

[1916]). The Weierstrass function is also one of the earliest examples of a fractal, a set with repeating self-similarity at every scale and noninteger dimensions. See Figure 7.1 above or the QR link at the bottom of this one.   ◄

Example.   Karl Thomae's function is $f(x) = 1/q$ if x is the rational number p/q (where p and q are coprime) and $f(x) = 0$ if x is irrational.

Thomae's function is discontinuous at rational numbers, continuous at irrational numbers, and everywhere nondifferentiable.   ◄

Example.   We can classify arithmetic operations using a hyperoperation sequence. The simplest arithmetic operation is succession, $x + 1$, which gives us the number that comes after x. Next, the addition of two numbers $x + y$, which is the succession of x applied y times. Then, the multiplication of two numbers xy, which is the addition of x with itself y times. Followed by the exponentiation of two numbers x^y, which is the multiplication of x with itself y times. The next logical operation is raising x to the x power y times. This operation, called *tetration*, is often denoted as $^y x$ or using Knuth's up-arrow notation $x \uparrow\uparrow y$. Tetration can create gargantuan numbers quickly. For example, $^1 3 = 3$, $^2 3 = 27$, $^3 3 = 7625597484987$, and $^4 3 = 1258\ldots9387$ is a number with over three trillion digits. To put this number in perspective, if $^4 3$ were to be written out explicitly in this book, its spine would be over 38 miles thick.   ◄

the Weierstrass
function

To dig deeper into pathological functions, see Gelbaum and Olmstead's *Counterexamples in Analysis*. While mathematically, almost all functions are pathological, the functions important for applications are often quite nice. The typical naughty functions we encounter might have a cusp, a discontinuity, or a blowup. One feature of nice functions is a well-behaved limiting behavior. To help describe the limiting behavior of nice functions, we have Landau notation.

▷ **Landau notation**

Landau notation, often called big O and little o notation, is used to describe the limiting behavior of a function:

$$f(x) \in O(g(x)) \quad \text{if} \quad \lim_{x \to \infty} f(x)/g(x) \text{ is bounded.}$$

$$f(x) \in o(g(x)) \quad \text{if} \quad \lim_{x \to \infty} f(x)/g(x) = 0.$$

One often says that $f(x)$ is on the order of $g(x)$ or $f(x)$ is $O(g(x))$ or simply $f(x) = O(g(x))$ to mean $f(x) \in O(g(x))$. For example, $(n+1)^2 = n^2 + O(n) = O(n^2)$ and $(n+1)^2 = o(n^3)$. Big O notation is often used to describe the complexity of an algorithm. Gaussian elimination, used to solve a system of n linear equations, requires roughly $\frac{2}{3}n^3 + 2n^2$ operations (additions and multiplications). So, Gaussian elimination is $O(n^3)$.

Big O and little o can also be used to notate infinitesimal asymptotics. In this case,

$$f(x) \in O(g(x)) \quad \text{if} \quad \lim_{x \to 0} f(x)/g(x) \text{ is bounded.}$$

$$f(x) \in o(g(x)) \quad \text{if} \quad \lim_{x \to 0} f(x)/g(x) = 0.$$

For example, $e^x = 1 + x + O(x^2)$ and $e^x = 1 + x + o(x)$. We can also use big O notation to summarize the truncation error of finite difference approximation to differentiation. For a small offset h, the Taylor series approximation

$$f(x + h) = f(x) + hf'(x) + \tfrac{1}{2}h^2 f''(x) + \tfrac{1}{6}h^2 f'''(x) + \cdots$$
$$= f(x) + hf'(x) + O(h^2).$$

From this approximation, it follows that

$$f'(x) = \frac{f(x + h) - f(x)}{h} + O(h),$$

where we've taken $O(h^2)/h = O(h)$. So forward differencing provides an $OO[h]1$ approximation (or first-order approximation) to the derivative.

7.2   Well-posed problems

Example.   Just as there are ill-behaved functions, there are also ill-behaved problems. Mathematician Nick Trefethen once offered $100 as a prize for solving ten numerical mathematics problems to ten significant digits. One of them was "A photon moving at speed 1 in the xy-plane starts at t = 0 at (x, y) = (0.5, 0.1) heading due east. Around every integer lattice point (i, j) in the plane, a circular mirror of radius 1/3 has been erected. How far from the origin is the photon at t = 10?" We can solve the problem using the geometry of intersections of lines and circles. At each intersection, we need to evaluate a square root. And each numerical evaluation of a square root adds round-off error to the solution, repeatedly compounding. The solution loses about a digit of precision with every reflection. While the original problem asked for the solution at $t = 10$ to 100-digits of accuracy, we could also think about what happens at $t = 20$. The figure on the left below shows the starting position.

The middle figure shows the solution for a photon at $t = 20$. Instead of just one photon, let's solve the problem using 100 photons each with a minuscule initial velocity angle spread of 10^{-16} for each photon (machine floating-point precision). To put it into perspective, if these photons left from a point on the sun, they would all land on earth in an area covered by the period at the end of this sentence. The figure on the right shows the solution for these hundred photons. Also, see the QR code at the bottom of this page. It's hard to tell which solution is the right one or how accurate our original solution in the middle actually was.   ◄

So, what makes a problem a *nice* problem? To answer this question, let's first think about what makes up a problem. Consider the statement "$F(y, x) = 0$ for some input data x and some output data y." For example, y could equal the value of polynomial F with coefficients $\{c_n, c_{n-1}, \ldots, c_0\}$ of the variable x, e.g., $y = c_n x^n + c_{n-1}x^{n-1} + \cdots + c_1 x + c_0$. Or, $F(y, x) = 0$ could be a differential equation where y is some function and x is the initial condition or the boundary value, e.g., $y' = f(t, y)$ with $y(0) = x$. Or, $F(y, x) = 0$ could be an image classifier where x is a set of training images and y is a set of labels. In a simple diagram, our problem consists of input data, a model, and output data.

photons in a room of circular mirrors

input data   model   output data

We can classify the problem in three ways.

1. *Direct problem*: F and x are given and y is unknown. We know the model and the input—determine the output.

2. *Inverse problem*: F and y are given and x is unknown. We know the model and the output—determine the input.

3. *Identification problem*: y and x are given and F is unknown. We know the input and output—determine what's happening inside the black-box model. For example, what are its parameters?

A direct problem is typically easier to solve than an inverse problem, which itself is easier to solve than an identification problem. What makes a problem difficult to solve (either analytically or numerically)? The function $F(y,x)$ may be an implicit function of y and x. The problem may have multiple solutions. The problem may have no solution. Perhaps the problem is so sensitive that we cannot replicate the output if the input changes by even the slightest amount. How do we know whether a problem has a meaningful solution? To answer this question, French mathematician Jacques Hadamard introduced the notion of mathematical well-posedness in 1923. He said that a problem was *well-posed* if

1. a solution for the problem exists (existence);
2. the solution is unique (uniqueness); and
3. this solution depends continuously on the input data (stability).

If any of these conditions fail to hold, the problem is *ill-posed*.

▷ Condition number

Existence and uniqueness are straightforward. Let's dig into stability. We say that the output y depends continuously on the input x if small perturbations in the input cause small changes in the output. That is to say, there are no sudden jumps in the solution. Let $x + \delta x$ be a perturbation of the input and $y + \delta y$ be the new output, and let $\| \cdot \|$ be some norm. *Lipschitz continuity* says that there is some κ such that $\|\delta y\| \leq \kappa \|\delta x\|$ for any δx. We call κ the Lipschitz constant or the *condition number*. It is simply an upper bound on the ratio of the change in the output data to the change in the input data. We define the *absolute condition number*

$$\kappa_{\mathrm{abs}}(x) = \sup_{\delta x}\left\{ \frac{\|\delta y\|}{\|\delta x\|} \right\}.$$

If $y \neq 0$ and $x \neq 0$, we define the *relative condition number*

$$\kappa(x) = \sup_{\delta x} \left\{ \frac{\|\delta y\|/\|y\|}{\|\delta x\|/\|x\|} \right\}.$$

A problem is *ill-conditioned* if $\kappa(x)$ is large for any x and *well-conditioned* if it is small for all x.

▷ Condition number of a direct problem

For now, consider a problem with a unique solution $y = f(x)$. Perturbing the input data x yields $y + \delta y = f(x + \delta x)$. If f is differentiable, then Taylor series expansion of f about x gives us

$$f(x + \delta x) = f(x) + f'(x)\delta x + o(\|\delta x\|),$$

where f' is the Jacobian matrix. Hence, $\delta y = f'(x)\delta x + o(\|\delta x\|)$. So the absolute condition number is $\kappa_{\text{abs}}(x) = \|f'(x)\|$. Similarly, the relative condition number in the limit as $\delta x \to 0$ is

$$\kappa(x) = \|f'(x)\| \frac{\|x\|}{\|f(x)\|}.$$

Example. Consider the addition of two real numbers $f(a, b) = a + b$. The gradient of f is

$$f'(a, b) = \left(\frac{\partial f}{\partial a}, \frac{\partial f}{\partial b} \right) = (1, 1).$$

In the ℓ^1-norm,

$$\kappa(x) = \|f'(x)\|_1 \frac{\|x\|_1}{\|f(x)\|_1} = \|(1, 1)\|_1 \frac{\|(a, b)^{\mathsf{T}}\|}{\|a + b\|} = \frac{|a| + |b|}{|a + b|}.$$

So, if a and b have the same sign, then the relative condition number is 2. But, if a and b have opposite signs and are close in magnitude, then the condition number can be quite large. For example, for $a = 1000$ and $b = -999$, but $\kappa(x) = 3998$. Subtraction can potentially lead to the cancellation of significant digits.

The quadratic formula

$$x_\pm = \frac{-b \pm \sqrt{b^2 - 4ac}}{2a}$$

is a well-known and frequently memorized solution to the quadratic equation $ax^2 + bx + c = 0$. However, when $b^2 \gg 4ac$, the quadratic formula can be numerically unstable because of subtractive cancellation. A stable alternative makes use of the *citardauq formula* to avoid subtraction:[1]

$$x_\pm = \frac{2c}{-b \mp \sqrt{b^2 - 4ac}}.$$

The combined formula is

$$x_- = \frac{-b - \text{sign}(b)\sqrt{b^2 - 4ac}}{2a} \quad \text{and} \quad x_+ = \frac{c}{ax_-}. \quad \blacktriangleleft$$

▷ Condition of an inverse problem

Consider a differentiable function $y = \varphi(x)$ that is locally invertible. Suppose that we know the output y and want to determine the input $x = \varphi^{-1}(y)$. Then $(\varphi^{-1})'(y) = [\varphi'(x)]^{-1}$. The absolute condition number of the inverse problem $x = \varphi^{-1}(y)$ is

$$\kappa_{\text{abs}}(x) = \left\|(\varphi^{-1})'(y)\right\| = \left\|[\varphi'(x)]^{-1}\right\|,$$

and the relative condition number is

$$\kappa(x) = \left\|[\varphi'(x)]^{-1}\right\| \frac{\|\varphi(x)\|}{\|x\|} \qquad (7.1)$$

for nonzero x. The inverse problem is ill-posed when $\varphi'(x) = 0$, e.g., when $\varphi(x)$ has a double root. Furthermore, it is ill-conditioned when $\varphi'(x)$ is small and well-conditioned if $\varphi'(x)$ is large. One can derive an analogous definition for the condition number of the problem $F(y, x) = 0$ using the implicit function theorem.

Example. The function $(x-1)^3(x-3)$ has zeros at $x = 1$ and $x = 3$, with respective condition numbers $\kappa(1) = \infty$ and $\kappa(3) = 8$. Finding the zeros of this polynomial is ill-conditioned in the neighborhood of $x = 1$ and well-conditioned in the neighborhood of $x = 3$. $\quad \blacktriangleleft$

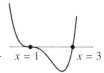

7.3 Well-posed methods

Just as there are pathological functions and pathological problems, there are also pathological solutions, even to well-behaved problems.

------

[1] As you may have deduced, *citardauq* is simply *quadratic* spelled backward.

Example.   The logistic[2] differential equation is a simple model of population dynamics $s(t)$ with a limited carrying capacity, like rabbits competing for food, water, and nesting space:

$$\frac{ds}{dt} = s(1 - s). \tag{7.2}$$

When the population s is small, the derivative $ds/dt \approx s$, and growth is proportional to the population. As the population approaches or exceeds the carrying capacity $s = 1$, starvation occurs, slowing or causing negative population growth. The solution to this differential equation is

$$s(t) = \left[1 - \left(1 - \frac{1}{s(0)} \right) e^{-t} \right]^{-1}$$

The solution is well-behaved and $s(t) \to 1$ as $t \to \infty$, reaching an equilibrium between reproduction and starvation.

The simplest numerical method of solving the differential equation is to use the forward Euler approximation to the derivative and then iteratively solve the resulting difference equation. In this case, we have

$$\frac{s^{(k+1)} - s^{(k)}}{\Delta t} = s^{(k)}(1 - s^{(k)}), \tag{7.3}$$

where Δt is the time step between subsequent evolutions of the solution $s^{(k)}$. By rescaling $s^{(k)} \mapsto (\Delta t)/(1 + \Delta t)x^{(k)}$ and solving for $x^{(k+1)}$, we get an equivalent equation called the logistic map:

$$x^{(k+1)} = rx^{(k)}(1 - x^{(k)}) \quad \text{where} \quad r = (1 + \Delta t). \tag{7.4}$$

This equation has the equilibrium solution $x = 1 - r^{-1}$. Let's examine the solution to (7.3) for $x(0) = 0.25$ with Δt given by 1, 1.9, 2.5, and 2.8:

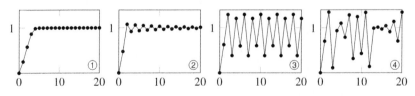

---

[2]The term *logistic* was coined by Belgian mathematician Pierre François Verhulst as *logistique* in his 1845 article on population growth. The name refers to the "log-like" similarities of the logistic function $1/(1 + e^{-t})$, with time t as the dependent variable, to the logarithm function near the origin.

① When $\Delta t = 1$, the solution to (7.3) closely matches the solution to (7.2).
② When $\Delta t = 1.9$, the numerical solution exhibits transient oscillations and converges to the equilibrium solution to (7.2). ③ When $\Delta t = 2.5$, the solution converges to a limit cycle with period 4. As Δt increases, so does the periodicity of the limit cycle. ④ When $\Delta t = 2.8$, the numerical solution is completely chaotic. As Δt continues to increase, the solution eventually becomes unstable and blows up. We'll return to this example when we study dynamical systems in section 8.4.
◀

Again, consider the problem statement:

$$F(y, x) = 0 \text{ for some input data } x \text{ and some output data } y.$$

A numerical method for the problem is

$$F_n(y_n, x_n) = 0 \text{ for some input data } x_n \text{ and some output data } y_n. \qquad (7.5)$$

We can understand x_n as an approximation to the input data x and y_n as an approximation to the output y.

approximate
input

→

numerical
method

→

approximate
output

Analogously to how we defined well-posedness for a problem, we say that the numerical method is well-posed if for any n

1. there is an output y_n corresponding to the input x_n (existence);
2. the computation of y_n is unique for each input x_n (uniqueness);
3. the output y_n depends continuously on the input x_n (stability).

▷ Consistency, stability, and convergence

We say that the numerical method $F_n(y, x) = 0$ is *consistent* if it approaches the original problem $F(y, x) = 0$ as n increases. In this case, it can be made as close to the original problem as we want, such as refining mesh size or iterating longer. Specifically, for every $\varepsilon > 0$ there is an N such that $\|F_n(y, x) - F(y, x)\| < \varepsilon$ for all $n > N$.

Now, suppose we perturb the input data by δx_n, and we let δy_n be the corresponding perturbation in the solution determined by the numerical method $F_n(y + \delta y_n, x + \delta x_n) = 0$. A method is *numerically stable* if a small error or perturbation in the approximate input data produces a small perturbation in the output. That is, if $\|\delta y_n\| \le \kappa \|\delta x_n\|$ for some κ, whenever $\|\delta x_n\| \le \eta$ for some η. We analogously define the absolute condition number as

$$\kappa_{abs,n}(x) = \sup_{\delta x_n} \left\{ \frac{\|\delta y_n\|}{\|\delta x_n\|} \right\}.$$

And if y_n and x_n are nonzero, we define the relative condition number as

$$\kappa_n(x) = \sup_{\delta x_n} \left\{ \frac{\|\delta y_n\|/\|y_n\|}{\|\delta x_n\|/\|x_n\|} \right\}.$$

One would hope that for any good numerical method, the approximate solution y_n would become a better approximation to y as n gets larger. A numerical method is *convergent* if the numerical solution can be made as close to the exact solution as we want—for example, by refining the mesh size and limiting round-off error. That is, for every $\varepsilon > 0$, there is a $\delta > 0$ such that for all sufficiently large n, $\|y(x) - y_n(x + \delta x_n)\| \le \varepsilon$ whenever $\|\delta x_n\| < \delta$. It should come as no surprise that consistency and stability imply convergence. The following theorem, known as the Lax equivalence theorem or the Lax–Richtmyer theorem, is so important that it is often called the fundamental theorem of numerical analysis.

Theorem 21. *A consistent method is stable if and only if it is convergent.*

Proof. Consider a well-posed problem $F(y(x), x) = 0$ and a numerical method $F_n(y_n(x_n), x_n) = 0$. Assume that the numerical method is differentiable and that its Jacobian is invertible and bounded for all n. By the mean value theorem,

$$F_n(y(x), x) = F_n(y_n(x), x) + \left(\frac{\partial F_n}{\partial y} \right) (y(x) - y_n(x)),$$

where the Jacobian $(\partial F_n / \partial y)$ is evaluated at some point in the neighborhood of $y(x)$. Therefore,

$$y(x) - y_n(x) = \left(\frac{\partial F_n}{\partial y} \right)^{-1} \left(F_n(y(x), x) - F_n(y_n(x), x) \right).$$

We can replace $F_n(y_n(x), x)$ with $F(y(x), x)$ in the expression above because both of them are zero. So,

$$y(x) - y_n(x) = \left(\frac{\partial F_n}{\partial y} \right)^{-1} \left(F_n(y(x), x) - F(y(x), x) \right),$$

from which

$$\|y(x) - y_n(x)\| \le M \|F_n(y(x), x) - F(y(x), x)\|$$

where $M = \|(\partial F_n/\partial y)^{-1}\|$. Because the method is consistent, for every $\varepsilon > 0$ there is an N such that $\|F_n(y(x), x) - F(y(x), x)\| < \varepsilon$ for all $n > N$. So, $\|y(x) - y_n(x)\| \leq M\varepsilon$ for all sufficiently large n.

We will use this result to show that convergence implies stability. If a numerical method is consistent and convergent, then

$$
\begin{aligned}
\|\delta y_n\| &= \|y_n(x) - y_n(x + \delta x_n)\| \\
&= \|y_n(x) - y(x) + y(x) - y_n(x + \delta x_n)\| \\
&\leq \|y_n(x) - y(x)\| + \|y(x) - y_n(x + \delta x_n)\| \\
&\leq M\varepsilon + \varepsilon'
\end{aligned}
$$

where the bound $M\varepsilon$ comes from consistency and the bound ε' comes from convergence. Choosing ε and ε' to be less than $\|\delta x_n\|$. Then

$$
\|\delta y_n\| \leq (M + 1)\|\delta x_n\|,
$$

which says that the method is stable. Now, we'll show stability implies convergence.

$$
\begin{aligned}
\|y(x) - y_n(x + \delta x_n)\| &= \|y(x) - y_n(x) + y_n(x) - y_n(x + \delta x_n)\| \\
&\leq \|y(x) - y_n(x)\| + \|y_n(x) - y_n(x + \delta x_n)\| \\
&\leq M\varepsilon + \kappa\|\delta x_n\|,
\end{aligned}
$$

where the bound $M\varepsilon$ comes from consistency and the bound κ comes from stability. By choosing $\|\delta x_n\| \leq \varepsilon/\kappa$, we have

$$
\|y(x) - y_n(x + \delta x_n)\| \leq (M + 1)\varepsilon.
$$

So the method is convergent. $\square$

We can summarize the concepts for well-posed methods as follows:

problem	$F(y, x) = 0$
method	$F_n(y_n, x_n) = 0$
consistency	$F_n(y, x) \to F(y, x)$ as $n \to \infty$
stability	if $\|\delta x_n\| \leq \eta$, then $\|\delta y_n\| \leq \kappa\|\delta x_n\|$ for some κ
convergence	for any ε there are η and N such that if $n > N$ and $\|\delta x_n\| \leq \eta$, then $\|y(x) - y_n(x + \delta x_n)\| \leq \varepsilon$
equivalence	consistency & stability $\leftrightarrow$ convergence

7.4   Floating-point arithmetic

Programming languages support several numerical data types: often 64-bit and 32-bit floating-point numbers for real and complex data; 64-bit, 32-bit, and 16-bit integers and unsigned integers; 8-bit ASCII and up to 32-bit Unicode characters, and 1-bit Booleans for "true" and "false" information. A complex number is typically stored as an array of two floating-point numbers. Other data types exist, including arbitrary-precision arithmetic (also called multiple-precision and bignum), often used in cryptography and in computing algebra systems like Mathematica. For example, Python implements arbitrary-precision integers for all integer arithmetic—the only limitation is computer memory. And it does not support 32-bit floating-point numbers, only 64-bit numbers. The Julia data types BigInt and BigFloat implement arbitrary-precision integer and floating-point arithmetic using the GNU MPFR and GNU Multiple Precision Arithmetic Libraries. The function BigFloat(x,precision=256) converts the value x to a BigFloat type with precision set by an optional argument. The command BigFloat(π,p) returns the first ($p/\log_2 10$) digits of π. The command precision(x) returns the precision of a variable x.

It is important to emphasize that computers cannot mix data types. They instead either implicitly or explicitly convert one data type into another. For example, Julia interprets a=3 as an integer and b=1.5 as a floating-point number. To compute c=a*b, a language like Julia automatically converts (or promotes) 3 to the floating-point number 3.0 so that precision is not lost and returns 4.5. Such automatic, implicit promotion lends itself to convenient syntax. Still, you should be caution to avoid gotchas. In Julia, the calculation 4/5 returns 0.8. In C, the calculation 4.0/5.0 returns 0.8, but 4/5 returns 0. By explicitly defining x=uint64(4) as an integer in Matlab, it is cast as a floating-point number to perform the calculation x/5, returning an integer value 1. In this manner, x/5*4 returns 4 but 4*x/5 returns 3.

⚫⚫ The function typeof returns the data type of a variable.

Floating-point numbers are ubiquitous in scientific computing. So, it is useful to have a basic working understanding of them. The IEEE 754 floating-point representation of real numbers used by most modern programming languages uses 32 bits (4 bytes) with 1 sign bit, 8 exponent bits, and 23 fraction mantissa bits to represent a single-precision number

s	e	m

and 64 bits (8 bytes) with 1 sign bit, 11 exponent bits, and 52 fraction mantissa bits to represent a double-precision number.

s	e	m

The exponents are biased to range between -126 and 127 in single precision and -1022 and 1023 in double precision. This means that single and double precision numbers have about 7 and 16 decimal digits of precision, respectively. The floating-point representation is $(-1)^s \times (1 + \text{mantissa}) \times 2^{(\text{exponent}-b)}$ where the bias $b = 127$ for single precision and $b = 1023$ for double precision. For example, the single-precision numbers

| 0 | 10000011 | 00010100000000000000000 | equals
$$1.000101_2 \times 2^4 = 10001.01_2 = 2^4 + 2^0 + 2^{-2} = 17.25$$

| 1 | 01111110 | 11000000000000000000000 | equals
$$-1.11_2 \times 2^{-1} = -0.111_2 = -(2^{-1} + 2^{-2} + 2^{-3}) = -0.875$$

The mantissa is normalized between 0 and 1 and the leading "hidden bit" in the mantissa is implicitly a one. Normalizing the numbers in this way gives the floating-point representation an extra bit of precision.

♣ The bitstring function converts a floating-point number to a string of bits.

Note that only combinations of powers of 2 can be expressed exactly. For example, the decimal 0.825 can be expressed exactly as $2^{-1} + 2^{-2} + 2^{-4}$, but decimal 0.1 has no finite binary expression. Indeed, typing bitstring(0.1) into Julia returns

```
0011111110111001100110011001100110011001100110011001100110011010
```

Only a finite set of numbers can be represented exactly. All other numbers must be approximated. The *machine epsilon* or *unit round-off* is the distance between 1 and the next exactly representable number greater than 1.

♣ The function eps() returns the double-precision machine epsilon of 2^{-52}. The function eps(x) returns the round-off error at x. For example, eps(0.0) returns 5.0e-324 and eps(Float32(0)) returns 1.0f-45.

Julia and Matlab use double-precision floating-point numbers by default. And Python and R only use double-precision floating-point numbers—they do not use single-precision numbers at all. Python's NumPy adds a type for single-precision. C refers to single-precision numbers as float. Python uses the same term float to refer to double-precision. Julia refers to doubles as Float64 and singles as Float32, and similarly NumPy calls them float64 and float32. Matlab uses double and single. And the current IEEE 754 standard itself uses the terms binary64 and binary32.

IEEE 754 also has a specification for half-precision floating-point numbers that require only 16 bits of computer memory. Such numbers are typically used in GPUs and deep learning applications where there may be a greater need for speed or memory than precision. Julia refers to half-precision numbers as Float16. IEEE 754 also specifies quadruple-precision numbers using 128 bits—one sign bit, 15 exponent bits, and 112 mantissa bits to give about 33 significant digits. IEEE 754 even has a specification for 256-bit octuple-precision floating-point numbers, but it is rarely implemented, in part, because of arbitrary-precision software libraries.

Example.   One algorithm buried in the source code of the 1999 *Quake III Arena* video game has attracted particular notoriety. The cryptic and seemingly obfuscated C code is translated to Julia code below.[3]

```
   function Q_rsqrt(x::Float32)
①      i = reinterpret(Int32,Float32(x))
②      i = Int32(0x5f3759df) - (i>>1)
③      y = reinterpret(Float32,i)
④      y = y * (1.5f0 - (0.5f0 * x * y * y))
   end
```

This function, often called the fast inverse square root function, approximates the reciprocal square root of a single-precision floating-point number, i.e., 1/sqrt(x). Video game developers use the the reciprocal square root to normalize vectors for shading and reflection in 3D generated scenes. In the late 1990s, Q_rsqrt(x) was considerably faster than directly computing 1.0/sqrt(x) and its approximation was good enough for a video game. Subsequent advances in computer hardware in the early 2000s have transcended the need for such a hack, even for video games.

How does the fast inverse square root algorithm work? Lines ①, ②, and ③ make an initial approximation of $y^{-1/2}$ and line ④ performs one iteration of Newton's method to refine that approximation. We'll discuss Newton's method in the next chapter. For now, let's examine the mathematics behind the initial approximation.

Take a single-precision floating-point number $x = (-1)^s 2^{e-127}(1 + 2^{-23}m)$, where s is a sign bit, e is the exponent, and an m is the fractional mantissa. If $y = x^{-1/2}$, then

$$\log_2 y = \log_2 x^{-1/2} = -\tfrac{1}{2}\log_2 x. \tag{7.6}$$

For a positive floating-point number

$$\log_2 x = \log_2\left(2^{e-127}\left(1 + 2^{-23}m\right)\right) = (e - 127) + \log_2\left(1 + 2^{-23}m\right). \tag{7.7}$$

---

[3]The developer's comments that accompanied the source code offered little clarity: "evil floating point bit level hacking" for line ①, "what the fuck?" for the line ②, and "1st iteration" for line ④. The inspiration for the algorithm can be traced through Cleve Moler to mathematicians William Kahan (the principal architect behind the IEEE 754 standard) and K. C. Ng in the mid-1980s.

The logarithm is a concave function—$\log_2(1 + s) \geq s$ with equality exactly when $s = 0$ or $s = 1$. We can approximate $\log_2(1+s)$ as $s+\varepsilon$ where $s = 2^{-23}m$ and ε is some offset. Let's choose an ε that minimizes the uniform norm of the error in the approximation. The maximum of $\log_2(1 + s) - (s + \varepsilon)$ occurs at $s = -1 + (\log 2)^{-1}$, at which point the error in the approximation is

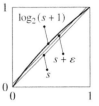

$$\delta = 1 - \frac{1 + \log(\log 2)}{\log 2}.$$

Choosing the shift $\varepsilon = \frac{1}{2}\delta \approx 0.0430$ will minimize the uniform error across $s \in [0, 1]$. Now we just need to compute (7.6) using (7.7) by approximating $\log_2(1 + s)$ with $s + \varepsilon$. By letting $\begin{bmatrix} 0 & e_y & m_y \end{bmatrix}$ and $\begin{bmatrix} 0 & e_x & m_x \end{bmatrix}$ be the single-precision floating-point representations of y and x, respectively, we only need to express e_y in terms of e_x and m_y in terms of m_x

$$(e_y - 127) + \left(2^{-23}m_y + \varepsilon\right)$$
$$= -\frac{1}{2}\left(\left(e_x - 127\right) + \left(2^{-23}m_x + \varepsilon\right)\right)$$
$$= \left(\left(-\tfrac{1}{2}e_x\right) - 127\right) + \left(2^{-23}\left(-\tfrac{1}{2}m_x\right) + \varepsilon\right) + \tfrac{3}{2}(127 - \varepsilon)$$
$$= \left(\left(-\tfrac{1}{2}e_x\right) - 127\right) + \left(2^{-23}\left(-\tfrac{1}{2}m_x\right) + \varepsilon\right) + 2^{-23}\left(2^{23} \cdot \tfrac{3}{2}(127 - \varepsilon)\right).$$

Then, the magic number is

$$2^{23} \cdot \tfrac{3}{2}(127 - \varepsilon) = 2^{23} \cdot \tfrac{3}{2}\left(127 - \tfrac{1}{2}\delta\right) \approx 1597488310 = \text{5f37bcb6}_{16}.$$

This number is close to but doesn't match the magic number used in the Q_rsqrt function. How the original value was chosen is not known.[4]

The expression $e + 2^{-23}m$ is a binary representation $e.m$, where the binary point separates the integer and fractional parts of the number. For example, if $i = 101.101 = 5\frac{5}{8}$, then $\frac{1}{2}i = 10.1101 = 2\frac{13}{16}$ is obtained by simply shifting all of the bits one place to the right i>>1.

To summarize the Q_rqsrt algorithm, line ① reinterprets the floating-point number x as the integer $i = e_x + 2^{-23}m_x$; line ② computes $\log y = -\frac{1}{2}\log x$ using as a linear, integer approximation and overwrites i; line ③ reinterprets floating-point number y from the integer $i = e_y + 2^{-23}m_y$; and line ④ computes one Newton iteration.

How well does the fast inverse square root algorithm work? Let's use the BenchmarkTools.jl library. We'll benchmark it using random input data to prevent Julia from optimizing the function output to a constant during compilation.

---

[4]Jean–Michel Muller argues that the optimal choice of magic numbers is one that minimizes the relative error after one Newton iteration, not the error going to the Newton iteration as is done here. Moroz et. al find the optimal magic number 5f37642f$_{16}$ using an exhaustive search.

```
using BenchmarkTools
@btime Q_rsqrt(Float32(x)) setup=(x=rand()) seconds=3
@btime 1/sqrt(x) setup=(x=rand()) seconds=3
```

We find that both methods take around two nanoseconds, and Q_rsqrt is significantly less accurate. The average relative error is 2×10^{-2} after the first approximation. It is 1×10^{-3} after the Newton iteration—good enough for a late 1990s shooter game. Were we to add another Newton iteration, the relative error would drop to 2×10^{-6}. ◄

▷ **Round-off error**

Example.   Siegfried Rump of the Institute for Reliable Computing posited the following example of catastrophic cancellation. Consider the calculation

$$y = 333.75b^6 + a^2(11a^2b^2 - b^6 - 121b^4 - 2) + 5.5b^8 + \frac{a}{2b}$$

where $a = 77617$ and $b = 33096$. Typing

```
a = 77617; b = 33096
333.75*b^6+a^2*(11*a^2*b^2-b^6-121*b^4-2)+5.5*b^8+a/(2*b)
```

into Julia returns approximately 1.641×10^{21}. Matlab and R both return about -1.181×10^{21}, Python returns about $+1.181 \times 10^{21}$, and Fortran computes it to be about 1.173. What's going on? If we rewrite the calculation as

$$y = z + x + \frac{a}{2b} \text{ where } z = 333.75b^6 + a^2(11a^2b^2 - b^6 - 121b^4 - 2) \text{ and } x = 5.5b^8,$$

then

$$z = -7917111340668961361101134701524942850 \text{ and}$$
$$x = +7917111340668961361101134701524942848.$$

From $z + x = 2$, we have that $y = -\frac{54767}{66192} \approx -0.827396$. The relative condition number for the problem is

$$\kappa = \frac{|z| + |x|}{|z + x|} \approx 10^{36},$$

which is considerably larger than the capacity of the mantissa for double-precision floating-point numbers. ◄

Example. The U.S. Army used Patriot surface-to-air missiles to intercept Iraqi Scud missiles during the Gulf War. In February 1991, a missile battery in Dhahran, Saudi Arabia, failed to track an incoming Scud missile that subsequently hit a barracks. The Patriot missile system's internal clock was based on a 1970s design that used 24-bit fixed-point numbers. The system measured time in tenths of seconds. Because 0.1 cannot be represented exactly in binary, the round-off error introduced by a 24-bit register (by keeping only 24 bits) was approximately 9.5×10^{-8}. So, every second the clock lost 9.5×10^{-7} seconds. After the Patriot computer had run for 100 hours, the clock was off by about 0.34 seconds. A Scud missile travels more than half of a kilometer in this time. Although the system detected an incoming missile, the Scud missile was outside the predicted range-gate because of the round-off error, so the system deemed the initial detection spurious.   ◄

▷ **Underflow, overflow, and NaN**

Because the number of bits reserved for the exponent of a floating-point number is limited, floating-point arithmetic has an upper bound (closest to infinity) and a lower bound (closest to zero). Any computation outside this bound results in either an overflow, producing inf, or an underflow, producing 0.

♣ The command floatmax(Float64) returns the largest floating-point number—one bit less than 2^{1024} or about 1.8×10^{308}. The command floatmin(Float64) returns the smallest normalized floating-point number—2^{-1022} or about 2.2×10^{-308}.

IEEE 754 uses gradual underflow versus abrupt underflow by using denormalized numbers. The smallest normalized floating-point number 2^{-1022} gradually under-flows by $(-1)^s \times (0 + \text{mantissa}) \times 2^{-b}$ and loses bits in the mantissa. Numbers can be as small as eps(0.0) = floatmin(Float64)*eps(1.0) before complete underflow.

Example. A spectacular example of overflow happened in 1996 when the European Space Agency (after spending ten years and $7 billion) launched the first Arianne 5 rocket. The rocket crashed within 40 seconds. An error occurred converting a 64-bit floating-point number to a 16-bit signed integer. The number was larger than 2^{15}, resulting in an overflow. The guidance system shut down, ultimately leading to an explosion and destroying the rocket and cargo valued at $500 million. Three years later, another conversion error—this time between metric and English systems—led to the crash of the $125 million NASA Mars orbiter.   ◄

Some expressions are not defined mathematically—for example, 0/0. IEEE 754 returns NaN (not a number) when it computes these numbers. Other operations that produce NaN include NaN*inf, inf-inf, inf*0, and inf/inf. Note that while mathematically 0^0 is not defined, IEEE 754 defines it as 1.

❖ The commands isinf and isnan check for overflows and NaN. The value NaN can be used to break up a plot, e.g., plot([1,2,2,2,3],[1,2,NaN,1,2]).

7.5 Computational error

Computational error is the sum of rounding error caused by limited-precision data-type representation and truncation error resulting from a finite-dimensional approximation to the original problem. Let's take a look at each in turn.

▷ Rounding error

Let $\mathrm{fl}(x)$ denote the floating-point approximation of x. The relative error of casting a nonzero number as a floating-point number is $\varepsilon = (x - \mathrm{fl}(x))/x$ where $|\varepsilon| \leq$ eps (machine epsilon). We equivalently have that $\mathrm{fl}(x) = (1 + \varepsilon)x$. Let's consider the rounding error caused by floating-point arithmetic: $a + b$. The relative error ε in the floating-point computation is given by $(a + b)(1 + \varepsilon)$:

$$(a + b)(1 + \varepsilon) = \mathrm{fl}[\mathrm{fl}(a) + \mathrm{fl}(b)] = [a(1 + \varepsilon_1) + b(1 + \varepsilon_2)](1 + \varepsilon_3),$$

where ε_i denotes the round-off error. By expanding the expression on the right-hand side and only keeping the linear terms, we have

$$(a + b)(1 + \varepsilon) = a + b + a\varepsilon_1 + b\varepsilon_2 + (a + b)\varepsilon_3.$$

Solving for ε will give us the relative error in the computation

$$\varepsilon = \frac{a\varepsilon_1 + b\varepsilon_2 + (a + b)\varepsilon_3}{a + b}.$$

By taking $|\varepsilon_i| \leq$ eps (machine epsilon), we have the bound

$$|\varepsilon| \leq \frac{|a| + |b| + |a + b|}{|a + b|} \text{eps}.$$

Note that if a approximately equals but is not equal to $-b$ and both numbers are large, then ε can be substantially larger than machine epsilon leading to catastrophic cancellation.

We can extend our analysis to a sum of arbitrarily many numbers. To add n numbers sequentially $x_1 + x_2 + \cdots + x_n$ requires $2n - 1$ rounding operations. We have a rough upper bound on the error

$$\varepsilon \leq \frac{(n + 1)|x_1| + (n + 1)|x_2| + n|x_3| + (n - 1)|x_4| + \cdots + 2|x_n|}{|x_1 + x_2 + \cdots + x_n|} \text{eps},$$

although the actual error is typically much smaller. We see from this expression that we should add smaller terms first to minimize the propagation of rounding error.

Example.   In 1982 the Vancouver Stock Exchange[5] introduced an index starting with a value of 1000.000. After each trade, the index was recomputed using four decimals and truncated to three decimal places. After 22 months, with roughly 2800 transactions per day, the index was 524.881. The index should have been 1098.892. What went wrong? Dropping the least significant decimal value instead of rounding to the nearest value resulted in a bias with each calculation. We can model the least-significant decimal values as discrete independent, uniformly distributed random variables: $10^{-4} \cdot \{0, 1, \ldots, 9\}$. The mean bias is 0.00045 for each trade. Over 1.2 million transactions, the total bias should be down around 554 from the actual index at just under 1099.

Suppose the algorithm had instead used proper rounding to avoid bias. In that case, we should expect the sum of the errors to be normally distributed with zero mean and standard deviation $\sigma \sqrt{n}$, where the σ is the standard deviation of the distribution from which we are sampling. (The variance of the sum of independent random variables is the sum of the variances of those random variables.) The standard deviation for the discrete uniform distribution is $\sigma = 0.0003$. After 1.2 million trades, we should expect a standard deviation of about 0.3 and three standard deviations—with over 99 percent of the distribution—of about 1.0. See Huckle and Neckel [2019].   ◀

Example.   When x is almost zero, the quantity e^x is very close to one, and calculating $e^x - 1$ can be affected by rounding error. We can avoid rounding error when $x = o(\text{eps})$ by instead computing its Taylor series approximation

$$e^x - 1 = (1 + x + \tfrac{1}{2}x^2 + \tfrac{1}{3}x^3 + \cdots) - 1 = x + \tfrac{1}{2}x^2 + o(\text{eps}^2).$$ ◀

☙ The functions expm1 and log1p compute $e^x - 1$ and $\log(x + 1)$ more precisely than exp(x)-1 and log(x+1) in a neighborhood of zero.

▷ **Truncation error**

The truncation error of a numerical method is the error that results from using a finite or discrete approximation to an infinite series or continuous function. For example, we can compute the approximation to the derivative of a function using a first-order finite difference approximation. Consider the Taylor series expansion

$$f(x + h) = f(x) + hf'(x) + \tfrac{1}{2}h^2 f''(\xi)$$

[5]The building of the defunct Vancouver Stock Exchange now has a swanky cocktail bar.

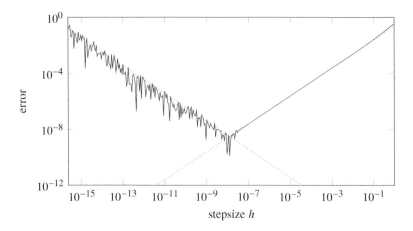

Figure 7.2: The total error for a first-order finite difference approximation. The truncation error decreases as h gets smaller and the round-error increases as h gets smaller. The minimum is near $h = 10^{-8}$.

for $\xi \in (x, x + h)$. Then

$$f'(x) = \frac{f(x+h) - f(x)}{h} + \tfrac{1}{2} h f''(\xi)$$

and we have the finite difference approximation

$$f'(x) \approx \frac{f(x+h) - f(x)}{h}$$

with truncation error bounded by $\varepsilon_{\text{trunc}}(h) = \tfrac{1}{2} h m$ where $m = \sup_{\xi} |f''(\xi)|$. The round-off error is bounded by $\varepsilon_{\text{round}}(h) = 2\,\text{eps}/h$. The total error given by $\varepsilon(h) = \varepsilon_{\text{trunc}}(h) + \varepsilon_{\text{round}}(h)$ is minimized when its derivative is zero:

$$\varepsilon'(h) = \tfrac{1}{2} m - 2\,\text{eps}/h^2 = 0.$$

So, the error has a minimum at $h = 2\sqrt{\text{eps}/m}$.

Example. Consider first-order finite difference approximation of $f'(x)$ for the function $f(x) = \sin x$ at the value $x = 0.5$. We should expect a minimum total error of about 10^{-8} near $h = 10^{-8}$. See Figure 7.2 above. ◄

7.6 Exercises

7.1. By combining the Taylor series expansions

$$f(x - h) = f(x) - hf'(x) + \tfrac{1}{2}h^2 f''(x) - \tfrac{1}{6}h^3 f'''(\xi_1)$$
$$f(x + h) = f(x) + hf'(x) + \tfrac{1}{2}h^2 f''(x) + \tfrac{1}{6}h^3 f'''(\xi_2)$$

where $\xi_1 \in (x - h, x)$ and $\xi_2 \in (x, x + h)$, we get the central difference approximation

$$f'(x) \approx \frac{f(x + h) - f(x - h)}{2h}$$

with truncation error bounded by $\varepsilon_{\text{trunc}} = \tfrac{1}{3}h^2 m$ where m is the upper bound of $|f'''(\xi)|$ for $(x - h, x + h)$. Determine the value h that minimizes the total error (the sum of the truncation error and the round-off error). Then, plot the total error of the central difference approximation of the derivative to $f(x) = e^x$ at $x = 0$ as a function of the stepsize h to confirm your answer.

The round-off error of the central difference method is large when h is small. Another way to compute the numerical derivative of a real-valued function and avoid catastrophic cancellation is by taking the imaginary part of the complex-valued $f(x + ih)/h$. Such an approximation is often called the *complex-step derivative*. Estimate the total error as a function of h using this method. Then verify your estimate by plotting the total error as a function of the stepsize h for $f(x) = e^x$ at $x = 0$. ✍

7.2. One way to determine machine epsilon is by computing $7/3 - 4/3 - 1$. Indeed, typing `7/3 - 4/3 - 1 == eps()` in Julia returns `true`. Use binary floating-point representation to demonstrate this identity. ✍

7.3. We can compute $f(x) = (x - 1)^3$ directly as $(x - 1)^3$ or expanded as $x^3 - 3x^2 + 3x - 1$. The second approach is more sensitive to loss of significance when $x \approx 1$. Plot of $(x-1)^3$ and $x^3 - 3x^2 + 3x - 1$ in the interval $(1 - 10^{-5}, 1 + 10^{-5})$. Then compare the derivative of both expressions of $f(x)$ at $1 + 10^{-5}$ using the central difference approximation $f'(x) \approx (f(x+h) - f(x-h))/2h$ with a log-log plot of the error as a function of h. ✍

7.4. In deriving the Q_rsqrt magic number, we chose ε to minimize the L^∞-norm of $\log(x + 1) - (x + \varepsilon)$. Instead, we could have chosen ε to minimize the L^2-norm, i.e., to minimize the mean error for a number selected at random. What is the magic number in this case? What is the magic number if we apply the Q_rsqrt algorithm to double-precision floating-point numbers?

Chapter 8

Solutions to Nonlinear Equations

An equation like $x = \cos x$ is transcendental and cannot be solved algebraically to get a closed-form. Instead, we rely on numerical methods to find a solution. But it isn't just transcendental equations that require numerical solutions. Even simple polynomial equations like $x^5 + 2x^2 - 1 = 0$ do not have closed-form solutions. Abel's impossibility theorem states that there are no algebraic solutions to general polynomial equations of degree five or higher. So, we also need numerical methods to find the roots of most polynomials. In this chapter, we'll examine techniques to solve such problems.

8.1 Bisection method

Consider a real-valued function $f(x)$ that is continuous but not necessarily differentiable. The bisection method is perhaps the simplest way of finding a zero x^* of $f(x)$. Consider two values a and b such that $f(a)$ and $f(b)$ have opposite signs, say $f(a) < 0$ and $f(b) > 0$. We call the interval $[a, b]$ a bracket. The function f has a zero in the interval $[a, b]$ by the intermediate value theorem. Take $c = (a+b)/2$. If $f(c) > 0$, then the zero is in the interval $[a, c]$. Otherwise, the zero is in the interval $[c, b]$. We choose our new bracket—either $[a, c]$ or $[c, b]$—to be the interval with the zero. We continue iteratively, halving each bracket into smaller brackets until the length is within some tolerance. A naïve Julia implementation of the bisection method is

```
function bisection(f,a,b,tolerance)
  while abs(b-a) > tolerance
```

convergence	sequence	convergence rate	$k \to \infty$
sublinear	$1, \frac{1}{2}, \frac{1}{3}, \frac{1}{4} \ldots, k^{-1}, \ldots$	$\dfrac{(k+1)^{-1}}{k^{-1}}$	1
linear	$1, \frac{1}{2}, \frac{1}{4}, \frac{1}{8} \ldots, 2^{-k}, \ldots$	$\dfrac{2^{-(k+1)}}{2^{-k}}$	$\frac{1}{2}$
superlinear	$1, \frac{1}{4}, \frac{1}{27}, \frac{1}{256} \ldots, k^{-k}, \ldots$	$\dfrac{(k+1)^{-k-1}}{k^{-k}}$	0
quadratic	$1, \frac{1}{16}, \frac{1}{256}, \frac{1}{65536} \ldots, 2^{-k^2}, \ldots$	$\dfrac{2^{-(k+1)^2}}{(2^{-k^2})^{p=2}}$	1

Figure 8.1: Some sequences that converge to zero.

```
    c = (a+b)/2
    sign(f(c)) == sign(f(a)) ? a = c : b = c
  end
  (a+b)/2
end
```

The command `bisection(x->x-cos(x),0,2,0.0001)` solves $x = \cos x$. The bisection method is easy enough to implement, but just how good is it? When does the method work? And when it works, how quickly should we expect the method to converge to a solution? We'll need to define the order and rate of convergence to answer these questions.

▷ Convergence

A sequence $\{x^{(0)}, x^{(1)}, x^{(2)}, \ldots\}$ converges to x^* with order p if there is a positive constant r such that the subsequent error $|x^{(k+1)} - x^*| \le r|x^{(k)} - x^*|^p$ for all k sufficiently large. Likewise, a numerical method that generates such a sequence is said to be of order p. The value p is the *order of convergence*, and the value r is the *rate of convergence*.

A method converges linearly if $p = 1$ and the convergence rate r is strictly less than 1. A method is superlinear if the convergence rate r_k varies with each iteration and $r_k \to 0$ as $k \to \infty$. And a method is sublinear if $r_k \to 1$ as $k \to \infty$. Convergence is quadratic if $p = 2$ Convergence is cubic if $p = 3$. And so on. See Figure 8.1.

A method is *locally convergent* if any $x^{(0)}$ close enough to the zero x^* converges to x^*. A method is *globally convergent* if the method converges to x^* for any initial choice of $x^{(0)}$ in our search interval.

Let's return to the bisection method with an initial bracket $I^{(0)} = [a, b]$. The size of the bracket is $|I^{(0)}| = |b - a|$, and the size of each subsequent bracket is half the size of the previous one. The error at the kth step is $e^{(k)} = x^{(k)} - x^*$. So

$$e^{(k)} \leq |\mathrm{I}^{(k)}| = \tfrac{1}{2}|\mathrm{I}^{(k-1)}| = \tfrac{1}{4}|\mathrm{I}^{(k-2)}| = \cdots = 2^{-k}|b - a|.$$

We see that convergence is linear with a convergence rate $r = \tfrac{1}{2}$. We add one bit of precision to the solution with each iteration. We will need to take about $\log_2(10) \approx 3.3$ iterations to gain a digit of precision in the solution. How many iterations do we need to take to get the error $|e^{(k)}| < \varepsilon$? Since $e^{(k)} \leq 2^{-k}|b - a|$, we will need to take $k = \log_2(|b - a|/\varepsilon)$ iterations.

What's bad about the bisection method is that convergence is relatively slow. What's good about it is that it is globally convergent. The bisection method can help us get close enough to a solution to employ a faster but only locally convergent method such as Newton's method.

8.2 Newton's method

We can build a better root finding method by incorporating more information about the function $f(x)$. Let x^* to be a zero of the function f. If x is sufficiently close to x^*, then the Taylor series expansion of f at x^* about x is

$$0 = f(x^*) = f(x) + (x^* - x)f'(x^*) + \tfrac{1}{2}(x^* - x)^2 f''(\xi)$$

where $\xi \in (x^*, x)$. Solving for x^*, we have

$$x^* = x - \frac{f(x)}{f'(x)} + o(x^* - x).$$

Start with $x^{(0)} = x$ and take the linearized equation

$$x^{(k+1)} = x^{(k)} - \frac{f\left(x^{(k)}\right)}{f'\left(x^{(k)}\right)}. \tag{8.1}$$

This method is called *Newton's method* or the *Newton–Raphson method*.

What's the convergence of Newton's method? The solution after k iterations is $x^{(k)} = x^* + e^{(k)}$ where $e^{(k)}$ is the error. Subtracting x^* from both sides of (8.1) and computing the Taylor series expansion of each term yields the following expression for $e^{(k+1)}$:

$$
\begin{aligned}
e^{(k+1)} &= e^{(k)} - \frac{f\left(x^{(k)}\right)}{f'\left(x^{(k)}\right)} \\
&= \frac{f'\left(x^{(k)}\right) e^{(k)} - f\left(x^{(k)}\right)}{f'\left(x^{(k)}\right)} \\
&= \frac{f'\left(x^* + e^{(k)}\right) e^{(k)} - f\left(x^* + e^{(k)}\right)}{f'\left(x^* + e^{(k)}\right)} \\
&= \frac{\frac{1}{2}f''(x^*)\left(e^{(k)}\right)^2 + \frac{1}{3}f^{(3)}(x^*)\left(e^{(k)}\right)^3 + o\left(\left(e^{(k)}\right)^3\right)}{f'(x^*) + f''(x^*)e^{(k)} + o\left(\left(e^{(k)}\right)\right)} \\
&= \frac{f''(x^*)}{2f'(x^*)}\left(e^{(k)}\right)^2 + o\left(\left(e^{(k)}\right)^2\right)
\end{aligned}
\tag{8.2}
$$

when $f'(x^*) \neq 0$. Therefore, Newton's method converges quadratically. The number of correct digits in the solution more or less doubles with every iteration. With a good starting guess, we should get an answer within machine precision in about six iterations.

Example. The Babylonian method

$$
x^{(k+1)} = \frac{1}{2}\left(x^{(k)} + \frac{a}{x^{(k)}}\right)
$$

is the earliest known algorithm to compute the square root of a number a. The method is a special case of Newton's method applied to $x^2 - a$. Because Newton's method has quadratic convergence, we can expect it to be fast. Let's compute $\sqrt{2}$ with a starting guess of 1:

1.000000000000000000000000000000000000000000000000000000. . .
1.500000000000000000000000000000000000000000000000000000. . .
1.416666666666666666666666666666666666666666666666666666. . .
1.41421568627450980392156862745098039215686274509803. . .
1.414213562374689910626295578890134910116559622115 74. . .
1.414213562373095048801689623502530243614981 92577619. . .
1.41421356237309504880168872420969807856967187537723. . .

The correct digits are in boldface. The first iteration gets one correct digit. The second iteration gets three. Then six. Then 12, 25, and finally 48 at the sixth iteration. As we should expect for a quadratic method, the number of correct decimals doubles with each iteration. ◄

Note from (8.2) that if x^* is a double root, then $f'(x^*) = 0$ and the error $e^{(k+1)} \approx \frac{1}{2}e^{(k)}$. In this case, Newton's method only converges linearly—the

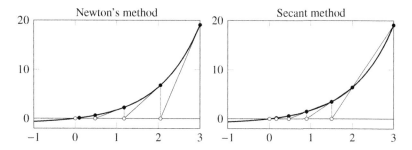

Figure 8.2: Comparison of two methods for finding the zeros of $e^x - 1$.

same as the bisection method. Moreover, if x^* is a root with multiplicity n, then Newton's method converges linearly with convergence rate $r = 1 - \frac{1}{n}$. When n is large, convergence can be slow.

▷ **Secant method**

Newton's method finds the point of intersection of the line of slope $f'(x^{(k)})$ passing through the point $(x^{(k)}, f(x^{(k)}))$. See Figure 8.2 above. Determining the derivative f' can be difficult analytically and numerically. But we can use other slopes $q^{(k)}$ that are suitable approximations to $f'(x^{(k)})$ to get a method:

$$x^{(k+1)} = x^{(k)} - f(x^{(k)})/q^{(k)}. \tag{8.3}$$

By taking the slope defined by two subsequent iterates

$$q^{(k)} = \frac{f(x^{(k)}) - f(x^{(k-1)})}{x^{(k)} - x^{(k-1)}}, \tag{8.4}$$

we have the *secant method*. Note that the method requires two initial values. The secant method's order of convergence is about 1.63—a bit lower than Newton's method.

▷ **Higher-order methods**

We could design methods that converge faster than second order. For example, there are several higher-order extensions of Newton's method called Householder methods. But, it's often unnecessary to go through the trouble of implementing higher-order methods because we can achieve the same net result with multiple iterations of a superlinear method. For instance, two iterations of the second-order Newton's method is a fourth-order method.

The secant method uses linear interpolation to find $x^{(k+1)}$. One way to improve convergence is by interpolating with a quadratic function instead. Consider the parabola $y = ax^2 + bx + c$ which passes through the points $\left(x^{(k-2)}, f\left(x^{(k-2)}\right)\right)$, $\left(x^{(k-1)}, f\left(x^{(k-1)}\right)\right)$ and $\left(x^{(k)}, f\left(x^{(k)}\right)\right)$. Because the parabola likely crosses the x-axis at two points, we'll need to choose the best one. This method, called *Müller's method*, has an order of convergence of about 1.84. A similar method called *inverse quadratic approximation* uses the parabola $x = ay^2 + by + c$, which crosses the x-axis at $x^{(k+1)} = c$. These methods need three points rather than just the two needed for the secant method or the one needed for Newton's method.

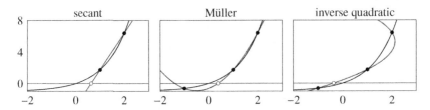

▷ Dekker–Brent method

Newton's method and the secant method are not globally convergent. An iterated initial guess can converge to a different root, go off to infinity, or get trapped in cycles.

Example. The function $\text{sign}(x)\sqrt{|x|}$ is continuous and differential everywhere except at the zero $x = 0$. Applying Newton's method gives the iteration

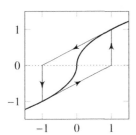

$$x^{(k+1)} = x^{(k)} - 2x^{(k)} = -x^{(k)}.$$

The iteration does not converge. Instead, it oscillates between $x^{(0)}$ and $-x^{(0)}$ for any nonzero starting guess. Newton's method applied to a similar function $\sqrt[3]{x}$ is $x^{(k+1)} = x^{(k)} - 3x^{(k)} = -2x^{(k)}$. Starting at any nonzero guess, such as $x^{(0)} = 1$, sends us off to infinity $\{1, -2, 4, -8, \dots\}$.   ◀

The bisection method is robust, but it is only linearly convergent. The secant method has an order of convergence approaching 1.63, but it is only locally convergent. The Dekker-Brent method, a hybrid of the bisection and secant methods, takes advantage of the strengths of both.

0. Start with a bracket.
1. Perform one secant iteration to get $x^{(k)}$. If the secant step goes outside the bracketing interval, use bisection instead to get $x^{(k)}$.
2. Refine the bracketing interval using $x^{(k)}$.
3. Repeat until convergence.

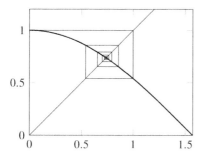 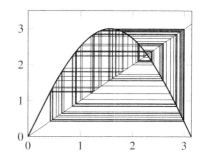

Figure 8.3: The fixed point iterations for $\phi(x) = \cos x$, which converges, and for $\phi(x) = 3\sin x$, which does not converge.

♣ The NLsolve.jl function `nlsolve(f,x0)` uses the trust region method to find the zero of the input function. The Roots.jl library has several procedures, such as `fzero(f,x0)` for finding roots.

8.3 Fixed-point iterations

If you type any number into a calculator and repeatedly hit the cosine button, the display eventually stops changing and gives you 0.7390851s. We call this number a *fixed point*. A fixed point of a function $\phi(x)$ is any point x such that $x = \phi(x)$. The simple geometric interpretation of a fixed point is the intersection of the line $y = x$ and the curve $y = \phi(x)$. We can study Newton's method as a special case of a broader class of numerical methods—fixed-point iterations:

$$\text{Given } x^{(0)}, \quad x^{(k+1)} = \phi(x^{(k)}). \tag{8.5}$$

In fact, for any function f, we can always write the problem $f(x) = 0$ as a fixed-point iteration $x = \phi(x)$ where $\phi(x) = x - f(x)$. But we are not guaranteed that a fixed-point iteration will converge. Suppose we take $\phi(x) = 3\sin x$. The function has fixed points at 0, at roughly $+2.279$, and at roughly -2.279. A fixed-point iteration for any point that does not already start precisely at these three points will never converge. Instead, it will bounce around in the neighborhood of either of the two nonzero fixed points. See the figure above. Let's identify the conditions that do guarantee convergence.

We say that $\phi(x)$ is a *contraction mapping* over the interval $[a, b]$ if ϕ is differentiable function with $\phi : [a, b] \rightarrow [a, b]$ and there is a $K < 1$ such that $|\phi'(x)| \leq K$ for all $x \in [a, b]$. The definition of a contraction mapping can be generalized as a nonexpansive map with Lipschitz constant K of a metric space onto itself. In this generalization, the following contraction mapping theorem is known as the Banach fixed-point theorem.

Theorem 22. *If the function ϕ is a contraction map over $[a, b]$, then ϕ has a unique fixed point $x^* \in [a, b]$ and the fixed-point method $x^{(k+1)} = \phi(x^{(k)})$ converges to x^* for any for any $x^{(0)} \in [a, b]$.*

Proof. We'll start by proving uniqueness. The contraction mapping ϕ is a continuous map from $[a, b]$ to $[a, b]$, so ϕ has at least one fixed point. Now, suppose that there are at least two distinct values $x^*, y^* \in [a, b]$ such that $\phi(x^*) = x^*$ and $\phi(y^*) = y^*$. The first-order Taylor approximation of ϕ expanded about x^* and evaluated at y^* is

$$\phi(y^*) = \phi(x^*) + (y^* - x^*)\phi'(\xi)$$

for some $\xi \in [x^*, y^*]$. Therefore,

$$|y^* - x^*| = |\phi(y^*) - \phi(x^*)| = |(y^* - x^*)\phi'(\xi)| \le K|y^* - x^*|.$$

Since $K < 1$, it must follow that $y^* = x^*$.

Now, we'll prove convergence. The first-order Taylor approximation of ϕ expanded about x^* and evaluated at $x^{(k)}$ is

$$\phi(x^{(k)}) = \phi(x^*) + (x^{(k)} - x^*)\phi'(\xi^{(k)})$$

for some $\xi^{(k)} \in [x^*, x^{(k)}]$. Because $x^{(k+1)} = \phi(x^{(k)})$, it follows that

$$x^{(k+1)} - x^* = \phi(x^{(k)}) - \phi(x^*) = (x^{(k)} - x^*)\phi'(\xi^{(k)}).$$

So, $|x^{(k+1)} - x^*| \le K|x^{(k)} - x^*| \le K^{k+1}|x^{(0)} - x^*| \to 0$ as $k \to \infty$.   □

The set of points $\{x^{(0)}, \phi(x^{(0)}), \phi^2(x^{(0)}), \phi^3(x^{(0)}), \dots\}$ of the iterated function ϕ is called the forward *orbit* of $x^{(0)}$. A fixed point x^* is an *attractive fixed point* if there is an interval (a, b) such that for any $x^{(k)} \in (a, b)$ the forward orbit of $x^{(k)}$ always remains within (a, b) and converges to $x^{(k)}$. A fixed point x^* is a *repulsive fixed point* if for any $x^{(k)} \in (a, b)$ there is a positive k for which $\phi(x^{(k)}) \in (a, b)$. Notably, the fixed point x^* is attractive if $|\phi'(x^*)| < 1$ and repulsive if $|\phi'(x^*)| > 1$.

When a fixed-point iteration converges, the error at each step diminishes. We can compute the ratio of the subsequent errors $e^{(k)}$:

$$\lim_{k \to \infty} \frac{e^{(k+1)}}{e^{(k)}} = \lim_{k \to \infty} \frac{x^{(k+1)} - x^*}{x^{(k)} - x^*} = \lim_{k \to \infty} \frac{\phi(x^{(k)}) - \phi(x^*)}{x^{(k)} - x^*} = \lim_{k \to \infty} \phi'(\xi^{(k)}) = \phi'(x^*).$$

The value $|\phi'(x^*)|$ is called the *asymptotic convergence factor*. In general, we have the following theorem:

Theorem 23. *If $\phi(x)$ is sufficiently smooth in a neighborhood of a fixed point x^*, with $\phi^{(j)}(x^*) = 0$ for $1 \le j < p$ and $\phi^{(p)}(x^*) \ne 0$, then the fixed-point method converges with order p and has an asymptotic convergence factor $\frac{1}{p!}\phi^{(p)}(x^*)$.*

Proof. The Taylor series expansion of ϕ around x^* is

$$\phi(x^{(k)}) = \phi(x^*) + \frac{1}{p!}\phi^{(p)}(\xi^{(k)})(x^{(k)} - x^*)^p$$

for some $\xi^{(k)} \in [x^{(k)}, x^*]$. By definition $x^{(k+1)} = \phi(x^{(k)})$ and $x^* = \phi(x^*)$, so

$$x^{(k+1)} - x^* = \frac{1}{p!}\phi^{(p)}(\xi^{(k)})(x^{(k)} - x^*)^p.$$

Therefore,

$$\lim_{k \to \infty} \frac{e^{(k+1)}}{(e^{(k)})^p} = \lim_{k \to \infty} \frac{x^{(k+1)} - x^*}{(x^{(k)} - x^*)^p} = \lim_{k \to \infty} \frac{1}{p!}\phi^{(p)}(\xi^{(k)}) = \frac{1}{p!}\phi^{(p)}(x^*). \quad \square$$

▷ **Speeding up a linearly convergent method**

Linearly convergent methods can be excruciatingly slow. Fortunately, there are some techniques to accelerate convergence. This section introduces Aitken's Δ^2 process or *Aitken's extrapolation*.[1,2]

For any sequence $x^{(0)}, x^{(1)}, x^{(2)}, \ldots$ that converges linearly to a value x^*, the ratio in errors is more or less constant

$$\frac{x^* - x^{(k+1)}}{x^* - x^{(k)}} \approx \frac{x^* - x^{(k)}}{x^* - x^{(k-1)}}.$$

Solving this expression for x^* yields

$$x^* \approx \frac{x^{(k+1)}x^{(k-1)} - (x^{(k)})^2}{x^{(k+1)} - 2x^{(k)} + x^{(k-1)}}, \tag{8.6}$$

which we can rewrite as a correction to $x^{(k+1)}$ as

$$x^* \approx x^{(k+1)} - \frac{(x^{(k+1)} - x^{(k)})^2}{x^{(k+1)} - 2x^{(k)} + x^{(k-1)}}. \tag{8.7}$$

The difference operator $\Delta x^{(k)} = x^{(k)} - x^{(k-1)}$ simplifies the notation

$$x^* \approx x^{(k+1)} - \frac{(\Delta x^{(k+1)})^2}{\Delta^2 x^{(k+1)}}.$$

---

[1] New Zealand mathematician Alexander Aitken published his namesake process in 1926. The method had earlier been described by the Japanese mathematician Seki Kōwa in his 1642 book *Hatubi Sanpō*. Kōwa used *enri* (円理, circle theory) to approximate π, taking $c_{16} + \frac{(c_{16}-c_{15})(c_{17}-c_{16})}{(c_{16}-c_{15})-(c_{17}-c_{16})}$, where c_n is the perimeter of a 2^n-gon inscribed in a circle of unit diameter.

[2] Alexander Aitken had a prodigious memory. He would recall numbers and long text several decades later. Aitken would also relive the war trauma from his experiences as an infantry soldier. He coped with recurrent psychological breakdowns by writing a memoir *Gallipoli to The Somme*. The acclaimed book was the inspiration behind Anthony Ritchie's 2016 oratorio.

While (8.6) is mathematically identical to (8.7), it is numerically less stable. (Why?) So it's advisable to use (8.7).

By feeding the Aitken's extrapolation to $x^{(k+1)}$ back into the fixed point method, we have an accelerated method

$$u_0 = x^{(k)}, \quad u_1 = \phi(u_0), \quad u_2 = \phi(u_1), \quad x^{(k+1)} = u_2 - \frac{(\Delta u_2)^2}{\Delta^2 u_2}. \tag{8.8}$$

This method is called *Steffenson's method*, and it is quadratically convergent under suitable conditions. Aitken's extrapolation also improves stability. Aitken's method may still converge even if the fixed-point method does not converge.

▷ Stopping criteria

We can stop an iterative method once the error is within our desired tolerance. But without explicitly knowing the solution, we can't explicitly compute the error. Instead, we might use the residual or the increment as a proxy for the error and stop when one of them falls below a prescribed tolerance. The residual $\phi(x^{(k)}) - x^{(k)}$ is the same as the increment $\Delta x^{(k+1)} = x^{(k+1)} - x^{(k)}$ for a fixed-point method. The error of the fixed-point method is

$$e^{(k+1)} = x^* - x^{(k+1)} = \phi(x^*) - \phi(x^{(k)}) \approx \phi'(x^*)e^{(k)}.$$

So

$$\Delta x^{(k+1)} = e^{(k+1)} - e^{(k)} \approx (1 - \phi'(x^*))\, e^{(k)},$$

and hence

$$e^{(k)} \approx \frac{\Delta x^{(k+1)}}{1 - \phi'(x^*)}.$$

For Newton's method, $\phi'(x^*) = 1 - f'(x^*)$ at a simple zero, and the error is approximately $\Delta x^{(k+1)}/f'(x^*)$. If $\phi'(x^*)$ is close to 1 and equivalently $f'(x^*)$ is close to 0, the error could be quite large relative to ε. In this case, using the increment will not be a reliable stopping criterion.

Designing robust stopping criteria is not trivial. For example, consider Newton's method applied to the function $f(x) = e^{-\lambda x}$ for a positive value λ. While there are no solutions, the method will evaluate $x^{(k+1)} = x^{(k)} + \lambda^{-1}$ at each step. In this case, the increment is always λ^{-1}, and using the increment as a stopping criterion will result in an endless loop. Using the residual $e^{-\lambda x}$ as a stopping criterion will eventually terminate the method. Still, the solution will hardly be correct, and if λ is really small, the method may require an unreasonably large number of iterations before it terminates. So, it is advisable to use brackets or some other exception handling when using an iterative method.

8.4   Dynamical systems

Suppose that we want to solve the simple equation $x^2 - x + c = 0$ for a given value c using the fixed-point method. While we could easily compute the solution using the quadratic formula, a toy problem like this will help us better understand the dynamics of the fixed-point method.[3] Start by rewriting the equation as $x = \phi_c(x)$ where $\phi_c(x) = x^2 + c$, and then iterate $x^{(k+1)} = \phi_c(x^{(k)})$. This iterated equation is known as the quadratic map. The quadratic map is equivalent to the logistic map $x^{(k+1)} = rx^{(k)}(1 - x^{(k)})$ introduced on page 176 as a simple model of rabbit population dynamics. If we start with the logistic map and first scale the variables by $-r^{-1}$ and next translate them by $\frac{1}{2}$, we have the quadratic map $x^{(k+1)} = (x^{(k)})^2 + c$ where $c = \frac{1}{4}r(2 - r)$.

By the fixed-point theorem, as long as $|\phi_c'(x)| < 1$ in a neighborhood of a fixed-point x^*, any initial guess in that neighborhood will converge to that fixed point. Because $|\phi_c'(x)| = |2x|$, any fixed point x^* in the interval $\left(-\frac{1}{2}, \frac{1}{2}\right)$ is attractive. This happens when $-\frac{3}{4} < c < \frac{1}{4}$. When $c > \frac{1}{4}$, the equation $x^2 - x + c = 0$ no longer has a real solution. What about when $c < -\frac{3}{4}$? Let's look at a few cases.

① $c = -0.50$: the orbit of $x^{(0)} = 0$ converges to a fixed point.
② $c = -1.00$: the orbit of $x^{(0)} = 0$ converges to an orbit with period 2.
③ $c = -1.33$: the orbit of $x^{(0)} = 0$ converges to an orbit with period 4.
④ $c = -1.38$: the orbit of $x^{(0)} = 0$ converges to an orbit with period 8.

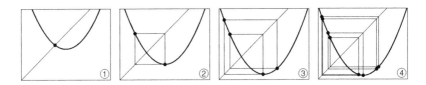

Why does the solution have this periodic limiting behavior? Take the iterated function compositions $\phi_c^2 = \phi_c \circ \phi_c$, $\phi_c^3 = \phi_c \circ \phi_c \circ \phi_c$, and so on. The forward orbit $\{x^{(0)}, \phi_c(x^{(0)}), \phi_c^2(x^{(0)}), \phi_c^3(x^{(0)}), \dots\}$ can be decomposed as

$$\{x^{(0)}, \phi_c^2(x^{(0)}), \phi_c^4(x^{(0)}), \dots\} \cup \{x^{(1)}, \phi_c^2(x^{(1)}), \phi_c^4(x^{(1)}), \dots\}$$

where $x^{(1)} = \phi_c(x^{(0)})$. Plot ② below shows $y = \phi_c^2(x)$ and $y = x$.

---

[3] Robert May's influential 1976 review article "Simple mathematical models with very complicated dynamics," which popularized the logistic map, examined how biological feedback loops can lead to chaos.

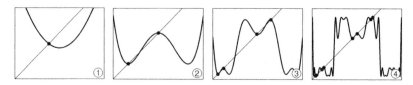

Notice that the function $\phi_c^2(x)$ has three fixed points, two of which are attractive with $|(\phi_c^2)'(x)| < 1$. Starting with $x^{(0)}$ leads us to one fixed point under the mapping ϕ_c^2, and starting with $x^{(1)}$ leads us to the other fixed point. Similarly, we can further decompose

$$\left\{x^{(0)}, \phi_c^2\!\left(x^{(0)}\right), \phi_c^4\!\left(x^{(0)}\right), \ldots\right\} \cup \left\{x^{(1)}, \phi_c^2\!\left(x^{(1)}\right), \phi_c^4\!\left(x^{(1)}\right), \ldots\right\} =$$
$$\left\{x^{(0)}, \phi_c^4\!\left(x^{(0)}\right), \phi_c^8\!\left(x^{(0)}\right), \ldots\right\} \cup \left\{x^{(2)}, \phi_c^4\!\left(x^{(2)}\right), \phi_c^8\!\left(x^{(2)}\right), \ldots\right\} \cup$$
$$\left\{x^{(1)}, \phi_c^4\!\left(x^{(1)}\right), \phi_c^8\!\left(x^{(1)}\right), \ldots\right\} \cup \left\{x^{(3)}, \phi_c^4\!\left(x^{(3)}\right), \phi_c^8\!\left(x^{(3)}\right), \ldots\right\}.$$

Plot ③ above shows $y = \phi_c^4(x)$ and $y = x$. Notice that the function $\phi_c^4(x)$ has four fixed points where $|(\phi_c^4)'(x)| < 1$.

As c is made more and more negative, the period of the limit cycle of the forward orbit of $x^{(0)} = 0$ continues to double at a faster and faster rate. The first doubling happens at $c = -0.75$ and the second doubling at $c = -1.25$. Then at about -1.368, the period doubles again. The rate of period-doubling limits a value called the *Feigenbaum constant*, and when $c \approx -1.401155$, the period of the limit cycle approaches infinity. At this point, the map is *chaotic*. But as c is made still more negative, a finite period cycle re-emerges only to again double and re-double. See the QR code at the bottom of this page and the bifurcation diagram on the next page showing the positions of the attractive fixed points as a function of the parameter c. Finally, when $c < -2$, the sequence escapes to infinity.

Often examining a more general problem provides greater insight into a specific problem. Generalization is one of the techniques that mathematician George Póyla discusses in his classic book *How to Solve It*. We have examined the quadratic map when the parameter c is real-valued. What happens when the c is complex-valued?

Let's take $z^{(k+1)} = \phi_c\!\left(z^{(k)}\right) = \left(z^{(k)}\right)^2 + c$. For what values c does the fixed-point method work? That is to say, when does $z^{(k)}$ converge to a fixed-point z^*? By the fixed-point theorem, z is attractive when $|\phi_c'(z)| < 1$. That is, when $|z| < \frac{1}{2}$. So, let's take the boundary $z = \frac{1}{2}e^{i\theta}$ and determine which values c correspond to this boundary. From the original equation $z^2 - z + c = 0$, we have that $c = z - z^2 = \frac{1}{2}e^{i\theta} - \frac{1}{4}e^{2i\theta}$. The plot of this function $c(z)$ is a cardioid $\bigcirc$, the shape traced by a point on a circle rolling around another circle of the same diameter.[4] For values c inside the cardioid, the orbit $\{0, \phi_c(0), \phi_c^2(0), \ldots\}$ limits a fixed point.

---

[4]There is an interesting related puzzle: "A coin is rolled around a similar coin without slipping.

forward orbit of
quadratic map

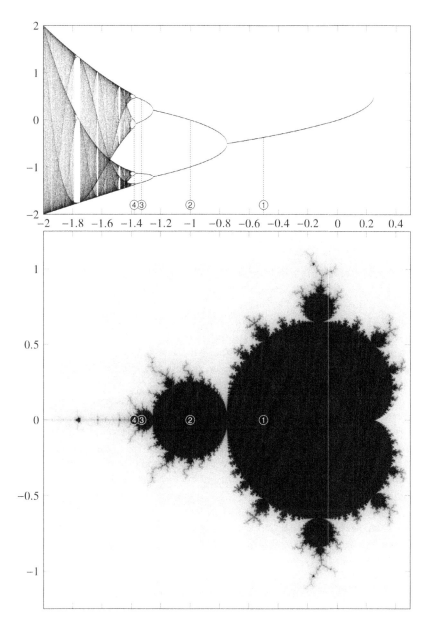

Figure 8.4: Top: The bifurcation diagram showing the limit cycle $\{\phi_c^\infty(0)\}$ of the quadratic map as a function of c. Bottom: The Mandelbrot set is the set of complex values c for which $\phi_c(0)$ has a limit cycle. The cases ①–④ from page 201 are indicated. Pay attention to changes in the period-doubling, bifurcation points, and matching cusps along the real axis of the Mandelbrot set.

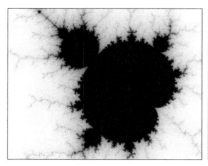 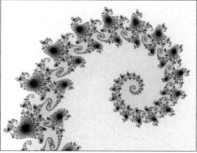

Figure 8.5: Snapshots of the Mandelbrot set showing a self-similar "minibrot" near $c = -0.1602 + 1.0335i$ (left) and a spiral around a Misiurewicz point near $c = -0.7452 + 0.1126i$ (right).

If we extend c to include orbits $\{0, \phi_c(0), \phi_c^2(0), \dots\}$ whose limit sets are bounded, the set of c is called the *Mandelbrot set*. See the figure on the preceding page. At the heart of the Mandelbrot set is the cardioid generated by the fixed points of the quadratic map. There is an infinite set of bulbs for limit sets of period q tangent to the main cardioid at $c = \frac{1}{2}e^{i\theta} - \frac{1}{4}e^{2i\theta}$ with $\theta = 2\pi p/q$ where p and q are relatively prime integers. The Mandelbrot set is one of the best-known examples of fractal geometry, exhibiting recursive detail and intricate mathematical beauty. See the figure above.

If the Mandelbrot set is the set of parameters c that results in bounded orbits given $z^{(0)} = 0$, what can we say about the limit sets themselves? We call the forward orbit for a given parameter c a *Julia set*. Whereas the Mandelbrot set lives in the complex c parameter space, the Julia set lives in the complex z-plane. If the orbit of z is bounded, then the Julia set is connected. If the orbit of z is unbounded, then the Julia set is disconnected and called a *Cantor set*. See Figure 8.6 on the facing page.

Imaging the Mandelbrot set is straightforward. The following functions takes the parameters bb for the lower-left and upper-right corners of a bounding box, xn for the number of horizontal pixels, and n for the maximum number of iterations. The function escape counts the iterations k until $\left|z^{(k)}\right| > 2$ for a given c.

```
function escape(n, c=0, z=0)
  for k in 1:n
    z = z^2 + c
    abs2(z) > 4 && return k
  end
  return n
```

What is the coin's orientation when it is halfway around the stationary coin?" The answer is counter-intuitive, but it is evident in the equation of the cardioid.

Figure 8.6: Julia sets for $-0.123 + 0.745i$ (left) and $-0.513 + 0.521i$ (right).

```
end
```

The function `mandelbrot` returns an array of escape iterations for an array c.

```
function mandelbrot(bb, xn=800, n=200, z=0)
  yn = (xn*(bb[4]-bb[2]))÷(bb[3]-bb[1]) |> Int
  c = LinRange(bb[1],bb[3],xn)' .+ im*LinRange(bb[4],bb[2],yn)
  [escape(n,c,z) for c∈c]
end
```

The following produces the second image of Figure 8.5.

```
using Images
M = mandelbrot([-0.172, 1.0228, -0.1494, 1.0443])
save("mandelbrot.png",1 .- M./maximum(M))
```

Imaging the Julia set uses almost identical code. The Mandelbrot set lives in the c-domain with a given value $z^{(0)} = 0$, and the Julia set lives in the z-domain with a given value c. So the code for the Julia set requires only swapping the variables z and c.

Example.   Orbits that are chaotic, erratic, and unpredictable sometimes have applications. Such behavior makes elliptic curves especially useful in Diffie–Hellman public-key encryption[5] and pseudorandom number generators. An

---

[5] Suppose that Alice and Bob want to communicate securely. If they both have the same secret key, they can both encrypt and decrypt messages using this key. But first, they'll need to agree on a key, and they'll need to do so securely. They can use the Diffie–Hellman key exchange protocol. Both Alice and Bob use a published elliptic curve with a published P. Alice secretly chooses a private key m and sends Bob her public key mP. Bob secretly chooses his private key n and sends Alice his public key nP. When Alice applies her private key to Bob's public key and Bob applies his private key to Alice's public key, they both get the same secret key nmP. With a shared secret key, Alice and Bob can each generate the same cryptographic key to encrypt or decrypt a message. The multiplication is typically modulo some prime.

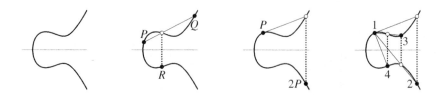

Figure 8.7: An elliptic curve, such as $y^2 = x^3 - 2x + 4$, is symmetric about the x-axis. A secant line through points P and Q passes through another point on the curve, the refection of which about the x-axis is a point $R = P \oplus Q$. A tangent line through a point P passes through another point on the curve, the reflection of which is $2P = P \oplus P$. Continuing these operations we get $3P$, $4P$, and so on.

elliptic curve is any curve of the form

$$y^2 = x^3 + ax + b \tag{8.9}$$

where $x^3 + ax + b$ has distinct roots. Such a curve has two useful geometric properties. First, it is symmetric about the x-axis. And second, a nonvertical straight line through two points on the curve (a secant line) will pass through a third point on the curve. Similarly, a tangent line—the limit of a secant line as two points approach one another—also passes through one other point. Let's label the first two points $P = (x_0, y_0)$ and $Q = (x_1, y_1)$ on the curve, and label the reflection of the third point across the x-axis $R = (x_2, -y_2)$. We can denote $R = P \oplus Q$. Points generated in this way using $\oplus$ (the reflection of the third colinear point on the curve) form a group. The point O at infinity is the identity element in this group. We define $2P = P \oplus P$, $3P = P \oplus 2P$, and so on. See Figure 8.7 above.

The arithmetic is straightforward. To compute $2P$, start by implicitly differentiating (8.9). We have $2y \, dy = (3x^2 + a) \, dx$ from which the slope of the tangent at P is $\lambda = (3x_0^2 + a)/2y_0$. Now, substituting the equation for points along the line $y = \lambda(x - x_0) + y_0$ into (8.9) gives

$$x^3 - (\lambda(x - x_0) + y_0)^2 + ax + b = 0.$$

The coefficient of the x^2 term of the resulting monic cubic equation is $-\lambda^2$. The coefficient of a monic polynomial's second term is the negative sum of the polynomial's roots. Because the polynomial has a double root at x_0, the third root $x = \lambda^2 - 2x_0$. And after reflecting about the x-axis we have that $y = -\lambda(x - x_0) - y_0$.

We can similarly compute $P \oplus Q$. The slope of a line through two points is $\lambda = (y_1 - y_0)/(x_1 - x_0)$. And from the argument above, the third root is given by $x = \lambda^2 - x_0 - x_1$. After reflecting about the x-axis, we have that $y = -\lambda(x - x_0) - y_0$. In this way, we can define $2P = P \oplus P$. Then with $P \oplus 2P$, we can define $3P$ and so on. Computing mP using a double-and-add method takes about $\log_2(m)$ doublings and half as many additions.

Finally, if the coefficients a and b and the point P are rational numbers, then all the points mP in the orbit are rational numbers. And, we can define the group as a quotient group $y^2 = x^3 + ax + b \pmod{r}$ for some r. Undoing the modulo operator equates to solving a discrete logarithm problem, which is a computationally hard problem. Pulling all of this together allows one to build a cryptologic system. ◄

8.5   Roots of polynomials

The quadratic formula has been known in various forms for the past two millennia. During the Renaissance, mathematicians Scipione del Ferro and Niccolò Fontana Tartaglia independently discovered techniques for finding the solutions to the cubic equation.[6] At the time, a mathematician's fame (and fortune?) was tied to winning competitions with other mathematicians, duels of a sort to prove who was the better mathematician. So, while Tartaglia knew a formula for solving a cubic equation, he kept his knowledge of it secret and even obfuscated his formula in a poem, "*Quando chel cubo con le cose appresso. . . .*"

A contemporary, Girolamo Cardano, persuaded Tartaglia to tell him his secret formula with the promise that he would never publish it. Of course, Cardano did exactly that, and it is now known as Cardano's formula (although some give a nod to its original inventor and call it the Cardano–Tartaglia formula). Later, Cardano's student Lodovico de Ferrari developed a general technique for solving quartic equations by reducing them first to cubic equations and then applying Cardano's formula.

And that's where it stops. There is no general algebraic formula for quintic polynomials, nor can there be one. In 1824, the 21-year-old mathematician Niels Henrik Abel proved what would later be known as the Abel–Ruffini theorem or Abel's impossibility theorem by providing a counterexample that demonstrated that there are polynomials for which no root-finding formula can exist. Six years later, 18-year-old Évariste Galois generalized Abel's theorem to characterize which polynomials were solvable by radicals, thereby creating Galois theory.[7] To dig deeper, see Mario Livio's book *The Equation That Couldn't Be Solved*.

---

[6]As a young boy Niccolò Fontana was maimed when an invading French Army massacred the citizens of Brescia, leaving him with a speech impediment, after which people started calling him Tartaglia, meaning "the stutterer."

[7]Évariste Galois died tragically at age 20 in a duel stemming from a failed love affair. During his short life, Galois' theory was largely rejected as incomprehensible. His work would not be published until twelve years after his death. Abel also died tragically young at age of 26 from tuberculosis.

Because we cannot find polynomial roots analytically, we must find them numerically. While any method discussed in the previous section would work, a better design uses the polynomial structure. Namely, because an nth degree polynomial has exactly n complex roots counting multiplicity, once we have found one root, we can factor this root out of the polynomial to simplify the next step. This process is called *deflation*.

▷ **Horner's deflation**

Note that we can write the polynomial $p(x) = x^3 - 6x^2 + 11x - 6$ in the Horner form $x(x(x-6)+11)-6$. This new form allows us to evaluate a polynomial more quickly, requiring fewer multiplications while reducing the propagated round-off error. Synthetic multiplication provides a convenient means of record-keeping when evaluating a polynomial in Horner form. For a general polynomial

$$p(x) = a_n x^n + a_{n-1} x^{n-1} + \cdots + a_1 x + a_0,$$

synthetic multiplication is performed by determining b_0 given the coefficients $\{a_n, a_{n-1}, \ldots, a_0\}$ using the accounting device

$$
\begin{array}{c|cccc}
z & a_n & a_{n-1} & \cdots & a_0 \\
& & b_n z & \cdots & b_1 z \\
\hline
& b_n & b_{n-1} & \cdots & b_0
\end{array}
$$

The coefficients $b_n = a_n$ and $b_k = a_k + z b_{k+1}$ for $k = 0, 1, \ldots, n-1$, and $p(z) = b_0$. Note that if z is a root of $p(x)$, then $b_0 = 0$. To evaluate $p(4)$

$$
\begin{array}{c|cccc}
4 & 1 & -6 & 11 & -6 \\
& & 4 & -8 & 12 \\
\hline
& 1 & -2 & 3 & 6
\end{array}
$$

So, $p(4) = 6$.

∷ The function evalpoly(x,p) uses Horner's method (or Goertzel's algorithm for complex values) to evaluate a polynomial with coefficients p = $[a_0, a_1, \ldots, a_n]$ at x.

By definition $b_k - z b_{k+1} = a_k$ and $b_n = a_n$, so we can rewrite

$$p(x) = a_n x^n + a_{n-1} x^{n-1} + \cdots + a_1 x + a_0$$

as

$$p(x) = b_n x^n + (b_{n-1} - b_n z)x^{n-1} + \cdots + (b_1 - b_2 z)x + (b_0 - b_1 z).$$

By grouping the coefficients b_k, we have

$$p(x) = (x - z)b_n x^{n-1} + (x - z)b_{n-1}x^{n-2} + \cdots + (x - z)b_1 + b_0.$$

So,

$$p(x) = (x - z)q(x) + b_0 \tag{8.10}$$

where $q(x) = b_n x^{n-1} + b_{n-1}x^{n-2} + \cdots + b_2 x + b_1$. This says that if z is the root of $p(x)$, then $b_0 = p(z) = 0$. Therefore, $p(x)$ can be factored as $p(x) = (x - z)q(x)$ for root z. So, $q(x)$ is a polynomial factor. This method of factorization is called synthetic division or Ruffini's rule.

Let's see Ruffini's rule in action by factoring $p(x)$, starting with the root 2:

$$
\begin{array}{r|rrrr}
2 & 1 & -6 & 11 & -6 \\
  &   & 2 & -8 & 6 \\
\hline
  & 1 & -4 & 3 & 0
\end{array}
$$

The factored polynomial is $x^2 - 4x + 3$. We can continue with another root 3:

$$
\begin{array}{r|rrr}
3 & 1 & -4 & 3 \\
  &   & 3 & -3 \\
\hline
  & 1 & -1 & 0
\end{array}
$$

We are left with $x - 1$. So we find that the roots are 3, 2, and 1.

▷ Newton–Horner method

We can use Newton's method to find a root z and then use Horner's method to deflate the polynomial. Newton's method for polynomials is simple. Using (8.10), we have $p(x) = (x - z)q(x) + b_0$ for some z. So, $p'(x) = q(x) + (x - z)q'(x)$, and therefore the derivative of p evaluated at $x = z$ is simply $p'(z) = q(z)$. Newton's method is then simply

$$x^{(n+1)} = x^{(n)} - \frac{p(x^{(n)})}{p'(x^{(n)})} = x^{(n)} - \frac{p(x^{(n)})}{q(x^{(n)})}$$

Example.   Using Newton's method to compute $x^{(1)}$ starting with $x^{(0)} = 4$ for the polynomial $x^3 - 6x^2 + 11x - 6$. Let's determine $p(x^{(0)})$ and $p'(x^{(0)})$:

$$
\begin{array}{r|rrrr}
4 & 1 & -6 & 11 & -6 \\
  &   & 4 & -8 & 12 \\
\hline
  & 1 & -2 & 3 & 6 \\
\end{array}
$$

$$
\begin{array}{r|rrr}
4 & 1 & -2 & 3 \\
  &   & 4 & 8 \\
\hline
  & 1 & 2 & 11 \\
\end{array}
$$

So, $p(4) = 6$ and $p'(4) = 11$. It follows that $x^{(1)} = 4 - \frac{6}{11}$.   ◄

Let's summarize the Newton–Horner method for $a_n x^n + \cdots + a_1 x + a_0$. Start with the coefficients $(a_n, a_{n-1}, \ldots, a_0)$ and an initial guess x for a root. Now, we iterate. First, use Horner's method on $(a_n, a_{n-1}, \ldots, a_0)$ with x to compute $(b_n, b_{n-1}, \ldots, b_0)$. Then, use Horner's method on $(b_n, b_{n-1}, \ldots, b_1)$ with x to compute $(c_n, c_{n-1}, \ldots, c_1)$. Finally, compute one Newton step to update the guess $x \leftarrow x - b_0/c_1$. Once b_0 is sufficiently close to zero, we've found a root. We deflate the polynomial by setting $(a_{n-1}, a_{n-2}, \ldots, a_0) \leftarrow (b_n, b_{n-1}, \ldots, b_1)$ and repeat the method to get the remaining roots. This method only works for real roots—we'd need to add error exceptions for missed complex roots, so we don't get stuck in a neverending loop.

▷ Companion matrix method

Another way to find the roots of a polynomial $p(x)$ is by finding the eigenvalues of a matrix whose characteristic polynomial is $p(x)$. The *companion matrix* of the polynomial

$$p(x) = a_0 + a_1 x + a_2 x^2 + \cdots + a_{n-1} x^{n-1} + x^n$$

is the matrix

$$
\mathbf{C}_n =
\begin{bmatrix}
0 & 0 & \cdots & 0 & -a_0 \\
1 & 0 & \cdots & 0 & -a_1 \\
0 & 1 & \cdots & 0 & -a_2 \\
\vdots & \vdots & \ddots & \vdots & \vdots \\
0 & 0 & \cdots & 1 & -a_{n-1}
\end{bmatrix}.
$$

To show that the polynomial $p(x)$ is indeed the characteristic polynomial of $\mathbf{C}_n$, we can use Laplace expansion (also known as cofactor expansion) to evaluate $\det(\lambda \mathbf{I} - \mathbf{C}_n)$. For instance, consider the Laplace expansion using cofactors from the bottom row

$$\begin{vmatrix} \lambda & 0 & 0 & 0 & a_0 \\ -1 & \lambda & 0 & 0 & a_1 \\ 0 & -1 & \lambda & 0 & a_2 \\ 0 & 0 & -1 & \lambda & a_3 \\ 0 & 0 & 0 & -1 & \lambda + a_4 \end{vmatrix} = (\lambda + a_4)\lambda^4 - (-1)\begin{vmatrix} \lambda & 0 & 0 & a_0 \\ -1 & \lambda & 0 & a_1 \\ 0 & -1 & \lambda & a_2 \\ 0 & 0 & -1 & a_3 \end{vmatrix}.$$

Continuing Laplace expansion in this way yields the characteristic polynomial $p(\lambda) = \lambda^5 + a_4\lambda^4 + a_3\lambda^3 + a_2\lambda^2 + a_1\lambda + a_0$.

♣ The Polynomials.jl, PolynomialRoots.jl, and FastPolynomialRoots.jl libraries all have functions roots that find roots from the eigenvalues of the companion matrix.[8]

▷ Other methods

Other popular methods of finding roots of polynomials include the Jenkins–Traub method, used in Mathematica's NSolve function, and Laguerre's method. These methods typically find a root and then deflate using Horner deflation.

8.6   Systems of nonlinear equations

Systems of equations often arise when finding a nonlinear least squares fit or implementing an implicit solver for a partial differential equation. Adding dimensions adds complexity, and the well-posedness of the problem becomes more complicated.

▷ Newton's method

Consider a system of n nonlinear equations with n unknowns $f : \mathbb{R}^n \to \mathbb{R}^n$, where $f(\mathbf{x})$ is continuously differentiable. Furthermore, consider $\mathbf{x}$ to be sufficiently close to some zero $\mathbf{x}^*$. Then, we only need to determine the offset vector $\Delta\mathbf{x} = \mathbf{x}^* - \mathbf{x}$ to solve the problem. Taylor series expansion of $f(0)$ about the point $\mathbf{x}$ is

$$0 = f(\mathbf{x}^*) = f(\mathbf{x}) + \mathbf{J}_f(\mathbf{x})\Delta\mathbf{x} + O(\|\Delta\mathbf{x}\|^2)$$

where $\mathbf{J}_f(\mathbf{x})$ is the Jacobian matrix with elements given by $\mathbf{J}_{ij} = \partial f_i / \partial x_j$. If the Jacobian matrix is nonsingular, we can invert this system of equations to get

$$\Delta\mathbf{x} = -\left(\mathbf{J}_f(\mathbf{x})\right)^{-1} f(\mathbf{x}) + O(\|\Delta\mathbf{x}\|^2)$$

---

[8]The FastPolynomialRoots.jl package uses a Fortran wrapper of the algorithm by Aurentz, Mach, Vandebril, and Watkins and can be significantly faster for large polynomials by using an eigenvalue solver that is $O(n^2)$ instead of $O(n^3)$.

and since $\mathbf{x}^* = \mathbf{x} + \Delta\mathbf{x}$

$$\mathbf{x}^* = \mathbf{x} - \left(\mathbf{J}_f(\mathbf{x})\right)^{-1} f(\mathbf{x}) + O(\|\Delta\mathbf{x}\|^2).$$

We can use this second-order approximation to develop an iterative method:

$$\mathbf{x}^{(k+1)} = \mathbf{x}^{(k)} - \left(\mathbf{J}_f(\mathbf{x}^{(k)})\right)^{-1} f(\mathbf{x}^{(k)}). \qquad (8.11)$$

In practice, we do not need to or necessarily want to compute the inverse of the Jacobian matrix explicitly. Rather, at each step of the iteration, we

$$\text{evaluate} \quad \mathbf{J}_f(\mathbf{x}^{(k)}), \qquad (8.12a)$$

$$\text{solve} \quad \mathbf{J}_f(\mathbf{x}^{(k)})\Delta\mathbf{x}^{(k)} = -f(\mathbf{x}^{(k)}), \qquad (8.12b)$$

$$\text{update} \quad \mathbf{x}^{(k+1)} = \mathbf{x}^{(k)} + \Delta\mathbf{x}^{(k)}. \qquad (8.12c)$$

If the Jacobian matrix is dense, it will take $O(n^2)$ operations to evaluate $\mathbf{J}_f(\mathbf{x}^{(k)})$ and an additional $O(n^3)$ operations to solve the system. If the system is sparse, the number of operations is $O(n)$ and $O(n^2)$, respectively. There are a few techniques we can do to speed things up.

First, we could reuse the Jacobian. It's not necessary to compute the Jacobian matrix at every iteration. Instead, we can evaluate it every few steps. We can also reuse the upper and lower triangular factors of the LU decomposition of (8.12b), so that each subsequent iteration takes $O(n^2)$ operations.

Alternatively, we could use an iterative method like the SOR or conjugate gradient method to solve the linear system (8.12b). Iterative methods multiply instead of factor, requiring $O(n^2)$ operations per iteration for dense matrices and only $O(n)$ operations per iteration for sparse matrices. They may take many iterations to converge, but because we only want an approximate solution $\mathbf{x}^{(k+1)}$ with each step, we don't need full convergence for the iterative method to be effective. Chapter 5 discusses these methods.

Another way to speed up Newton's method is using a finite difference approximation of the Jacobian matrix. The ij-element of the Jacobi matrix is $J_{ij} = \partial f_i / \partial x_j$. So the jth column of the Jacobian matrix is the derivative of $f(\mathbf{x})$ with respect to x_j. A second-order approximation of the jth column of $\mathbf{J}_f(\mathbf{x})$ is

$$\left[\mathbf{J}_f(\mathbf{x})\right]_j = \frac{f(\mathbf{x} + h\boldsymbol{\xi}_j) - f(\mathbf{x} - h\boldsymbol{\xi}_j)}{2h}, + O(h^2) \qquad (8.13)$$

where h is the step size and $\boldsymbol{\xi}_j$ is the jth vector in the standard basis of $\mathbb{R}^n$. We can typically take the step size h roughly equal to the cube root of machine epsilon For a well-conditioned problem.[9] If $f(\mathbf{x})$ is a real-valued function, we can also approximate the Jacobian using a complex-step derivative

$$\left[\mathbf{J}_f(\mathbf{x})\right]_j = \frac{\operatorname{Im} f(\mathbf{x} + ih\boldsymbol{\xi}_j)}{h} + O(h^2),$$

[9]See exercise 7.1.

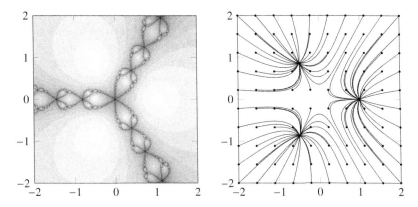

Figure 8.8: Newton fractal (left) for $z^3 - 1$. Darker shades of gray require more iterations to converge. Homotopy continuation (right) for the same problem.

where h is roughly equal to the square root of machine epsilon.

Example.   Consider roots of the polynomial system

$$x^3 - 3xy^2 - 1 = 0$$
$$y^3 - 3x^2y = 0.$$

This problem is equivalent to finding the roots of $z^3 - 1$ in the complex plane, and the roots are $(1, 1)$, $(-\sqrt{3}/2, 1/2)$, and $(-\sqrt{3}/2, -1/2)$. If we use Newton's method to find the roots, then the forward orbit of an initial guess either converges to a root or fails to converge. Even if the orbit does converge, it may not converge to the root closest to the initial guess. A root's *basin of attraction* is the set of starting points for which Newton's method eventually converges to that specific root. A Julia set is the union of the boundaries of each basin of attraction. See Figure 8.8 above.   ◄

▷ Secant-like methods

The secant method used two subsequent iterates $x^{(k)}$ and $x^{(k-1)}$ to approximate the tangent slope used in Newton's method. Just as we extended Newton's method to a system of equations, we can also formally extend the secant method to a system of equations. We have

$$\mathbf{J}^{(k)} \Delta \mathbf{x}^{(k)} = \Delta \mathbf{f}^{(k)} \tag{8.14}$$

where $\mathbf{J}^{(k)}$ is an $n \times n$ approximation to the Jacobian matrix, $\Delta \mathbf{x}^{(k)} = \mathbf{x}^{(k)} - \mathbf{x}^{(k-1)}$, and $\Delta \mathbf{f}^{(k)} = f(\mathbf{x}^{(k)}) - f(\mathbf{x}^{(k-1)})$. We just need to choose a suitable $\mathbf{J}^{(k)}$.

One way to interpret (8.14) is, "Given an output vector $\Delta\mathbf{f}^{(k)}$ and input vector $\Delta\mathbf{x}^{(k)}$, find the matrix $\mathbf{J}^{(k)}$." The matrix $\mathbf{J}^{(k)}$ has n^2 unknowns, and we have only n equations—a bit of a conundrum. How can we determine $\mathbf{J}^{(k)}$? It seems reasonable that $\mathbf{J}^{(k)}$ should be close to the previous $\mathbf{J}^{(k-1)}$, so perhaps we can approximate $\mathbf{J}^{(k)}$ using $\mathbf{J}^{(k-1)}$ with (8.14) as a constraint. In other words, let's minimize $\|\mathbf{J}^{(k)} - \mathbf{J}^{(k-1)}\|$ subject to the constraint $\mathbf{J}^{(k)}\Delta\mathbf{x}^{(k)} = \Delta\mathbf{f}^{(k)}$. What norm $\|\cdot\|$ do we choose? The Frobenius norm is a smart choice because it is an extension of the ℓ^2-norm for vectors, and minimizing the ℓ^2-norm results in a linear problem.

We can use the method of Lagrange multipliers. Take $\lambda \in \mathbb{R}^n$ and define

$$\mathcal{L}(\mathbf{J}^{(k)}, \lambda) = \tfrac{1}{2}\|\mathbf{J}^{(k)} - \mathbf{J}^{(k-1)}\|_{\mathrm{F}}^2 + \lambda^{\mathsf{T}}(\mathbf{J}^{(k)}\Delta\mathbf{x}^{(k)} - \Delta\mathbf{f}^{(k)}).$$

Setting $\nabla\mathcal{L}(\mathbf{J}^{(k)}, \lambda) = 0$ gives us

$$\mathbf{J}^{(k)} - \mathbf{J}^{(k-1)} + \lambda\Delta\mathbf{x}^{(k)\mathsf{T}} = 0 \quad \text{and} \quad \mathbf{J}^{(k)}\Delta\mathbf{x}^{(k)} = \Delta\mathbf{f}^{(k)}.$$

We just need to solve for λ. Right multiply the first equation by $\Delta\mathbf{x}^{(k)}$:

$$\mathbf{J}^{(k)}\Delta\mathbf{x}^{(k)} - \mathbf{J}^{(k-1)}\Delta\mathbf{x}^{(k)} + \lambda\|\Delta\mathbf{x}^{(k)}\|^2 = 0.$$

Now, substitute in the second equation:

$$\lambda = -\frac{\Delta\mathbf{f}^{(k)} - \mathbf{J}^{(k-1)}\Delta\mathbf{x}^{(k)}}{\|\Delta\mathbf{x}^{(k)}\|^2}.$$

Therefore, we have

$$\mathbf{J}^{(k)} = \mathbf{J}^{(k-1)} + \frac{\Delta\mathbf{f}^{(k)} - \mathbf{J}^{(k-1)}\Delta\mathbf{x}^{(k)}}{\|\Delta\mathbf{x}^{(k)}\|^2}\Delta\mathbf{x}^{(k)\mathsf{T}}. \tag{8.15}$$

The finished algorithm is called *Broyden's method*:

> choose an initial guess $\mathbf{x}$
> set $\mathbf{J} \leftarrow \mathbf{J}_f(\mathbf{x})$
> solve $\mathbf{J}\Delta\mathbf{x} = -f(\mathbf{x})$
> update $\mathbf{x} \leftarrow \mathbf{x} + \Delta\mathbf{x}$
> while $\|\Delta\mathbf{x}\| <$ tolerance
> > compute $\mathbf{J}$ using (8.15)
> > solve $\mathbf{J}\Delta\mathbf{x} = -f(\mathbf{x})$
> > update $\mathbf{x} \leftarrow \mathbf{x} + \Delta\mathbf{x}$

Broyden's method requires only $O(n)$ evaluations of $f(\mathbf{x}^{(k)})$ at each step to update the slope rather than $O(n^2)$ evaluations that are necessary to recompute the Jacobian matrix. In practice, errors in approximating an updated Jacobian grow with each iteration, and one should periodically restart the method with a fresh Jacobian.

Rather than solving $\mathbf{J}^{(k)}\Delta\mathbf{x}^{(k+1)} = -f\left(\mathbf{x}^{(k)}\right)$ at each iteration, we can compute $\Delta\mathbf{x}^{(k+1)} = -\mathbf{J}^{(k)}f\left(\mathbf{x}^{(k)}\right)$ directly with the help of the *Sherman–Morrison formula*

$$(\mathbf{A} + \mathbf{u}\mathbf{v}^{\mathsf{T}})^{-1} = \mathbf{A}^{-1} - \frac{\mathbf{A}^{-1}\mathbf{u}\mathbf{v}^{\mathsf{T}}\mathbf{A}^{-1}}{1 + \mathbf{v}^{\mathsf{T}}\mathbf{A}^{-1}\mathbf{u}}$$

to update $\left(\mathbf{J}^{(k)}\right)^{-1}$ given $\left(\mathbf{J}^{(k-1)}\right)^{-1}$:

$$\left(\mathbf{J}^{(k)}\right)^{-1} = \left(\mathbf{J}^{(k-1)}\right)^{-1} + \frac{\Delta\mathbf{x}^{(k)} - \left(\mathbf{J}^{(k-1)}\right)^{-1}\Delta\mathbf{f}^{(k)}}{\|\Delta\mathbf{f}^{(k)}\|^2}\Delta\mathbf{f}^{(k)\mathsf{T}}.$$

⁂ The NonlinearSolve.jl function NewtonRaphson and the NLsolve.jl function nlsolve can be used to find zeros of nonlinear systems.

8.7   Homotopy continuation

One might wonder if we could solve a simpler problem $g(\mathbf{x}) = 0$ as a means to solve $f(\mathbf{x}) = 0$. Well, we can. One way is to use a homotopy continuation. Two functions are *homotopic* if one can be continuously deformed into the other. The deformation is called a homotopy.

Suppose that we have a system of equations $f(\mathbf{x}) = 0$ and a system $g(\mathbf{x}) = 0$, whose roots we know or can easily determine. One way to define a homotopy is $h(t, \mathbf{x}) = tf(\mathbf{x}) + (1 - t)g(\mathbf{x})$ for $t \in [0, 1]$. Then

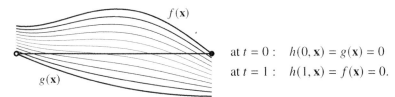

at $t = 0:$ $h(0, \mathbf{x}) = g(\mathbf{x}) = 0$
at $t = 1:$ $h(1, \mathbf{x}) = f(\mathbf{x}) = 0.$

Simply put, when the parameter $t = 0$, the solution $\mathbf{x}$ is a zero of g; and when $t = 1$, the solution $\mathbf{x}$ is a zero of f. We've exchanged the difficult problem of solving $f(\mathbf{x}) = 0$ for the easy problem of solving $g(\mathbf{x}) = 0$. It sounds a little too simple—what's the catch? We still need to track the solutions along the paths $h(t, \mathbf{x})$ for the parameter $t \in [0, 1]$. To do this, we may need to solve a nonlinear differential equation.

Take the homotopy $h(t, \mathbf{x}(t)) = 0$ where $\mathbf{x}(t)$ is a zero of the system h for the parameter t. Let's assume that $\mathbf{x}(t)$ exists and is unique for all $t \in [0, 1]$. Otherwise, the method is ill-posed. This assumption is not trivial—there may be no path connecting a zero of g with a zero of f, or the path may become multivalued as the parameter t is changed:

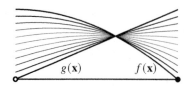 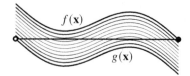

We have $\mathbf{x}(0)$ is a zero of g. We want to find $\mathbf{x}(1)$, which is a zero of f. Differentiating $h(t, \mathbf{x}(t)) = 0$ with respect to t gives us

$$\frac{\partial h}{\partial t} + \mathbf{J}_h(\mathbf{x}) \frac{d\mathbf{x}}{dt} = 0$$

where the Jacobian matrix $\mathbf{J}_h(\mathbf{x}) = \partial h / \partial \mathbf{x}$ and $\partial h / \partial t$ and $d\mathbf{x}/dt$ are both vectors. Therefore,

$$\frac{d\mathbf{x}}{dt} = -\mathbf{J}_h^{-1}(\mathbf{x}) \frac{\partial h}{\partial t}.$$

Solving this differential equation gives us $\mathbf{x}(1)$.

We can make a simple homotopy by choosing $g(\mathbf{x}) = f(\mathbf{x}) - f(\mathbf{x}_0)$ for some $\mathbf{x}_0$. Then $\mathbf{x}_0$ is a known zero of g. In this case

$$h(t, \mathbf{x}) = t f(\mathbf{x}) + (1 - t)[f(\mathbf{x}) - f(\mathbf{x}_0)]$$
$$= f(\mathbf{x}) - (1 - t) f(\mathbf{x}_0). \qquad (8.16)$$

The Jacobian matrix $\mathbf{J}_h(\mathbf{x}) = \mathbf{J}_f(\mathbf{x})$ and $\partial h / \partial t = f(\mathbf{x}_0)$. We'll need to solve the differential equation

$$\frac{d\mathbf{x}}{dt} = -\mathbf{J}_f^{-1}(\mathbf{x}) f(\mathbf{x}_0)$$

with the initial conditions $\mathbf{x}_0$. Solving such a differential equation often requires a numerical solver.

Example.   Suppose that we want to solve the following system:

$$x^3 - 3xy^2 - 1 = 0$$
$$y^3 - 3x^2 y = 0.$$

Define the homotopy as in (8.16), where we can take $\mathbf{x}_0$ to be whatever we want. The Jacobian matrix is

$$\mathbf{J}_f(\mathbf{x}) = \begin{bmatrix} 3x^2 - 3y^2 & -6xy \\ -6xy & 3y^2 - 3x^2 \end{bmatrix}.$$

If we take $\mathbf{x}_0 = (1, 1)$, then $f(\mathbf{x}_0) = (-3, -2)$, and we need to solve

$$\frac{d}{dt} \begin{bmatrix} x(t) \\ y(t) \end{bmatrix} = - \begin{bmatrix} 3x^2 - 3y^2 & -6xy \\ -6xy & 3y^2 - 3x^2 \end{bmatrix}^{-1} \begin{bmatrix} -3 \\ -2 \end{bmatrix}$$

with initial conditions $(x(0), y(0)) = (1, 1)$. We can solve this problem using the following code

```
using DifferentialEquations
f = z -> ((x,y)=tuple(z...); [x^3-3x*y^2-1; y^3-3x^2*y] )
df = (z,p,_) -> ((x,y)=tuple(z...);
  -[3x^2-3y^2 -6x*y; -6x*y 3y^2-3x^2]\p)
z₀ = [1,1]
sol = solve(ODEProblem(df,z₀,(0,1),f(z₀)))
sol.u[end]
```

The numerical solution given by sol.u[end] is $0.999, 0.001$. To reduce the error, we can finish off the homotopy method by applying a step of Newton's method to $f(\mathbf{x})$ using sol.u[end] as the initial guess to get the root $(1, 0)$. See Figure 8.8 on page 213.   ◄

The homotopy continuation method looks similar to Newton's method (8.13). In fact, we can derive Newton's method as a special case of homotopy continuation. Let's define the homotopy

$$h(t, \mathbf{x}) = f(\mathbf{x}) - e^{-t} f(\mathbf{x}_0). \tag{8.17}$$

At $t = 0$, we have $h(0, \mathbf{x}) = f(\mathbf{x}(0)) - f(\mathbf{x}_0) = 0$. And at $t = \infty$, we have $h(\infty, \mathbf{x}) = f(\mathbf{x}(\infty))$. We don't need to find the solution at $t = \infty$. We just need to find a solution for a large enough t so that the residual $e^{-t} f(\mathbf{x}_0)$ is small enough. We want to find the path $\mathbf{x}(t)$ along which $h(t, \mathbf{x}(t)) = 0$. By differentiating (8.17) with respect to t, we have

$$\frac{d}{dt} h(t, \mathbf{x}) = \mathbf{J}_f(\mathbf{x}) \frac{d\mathbf{x}}{dt} + e^{-t} f(\mathbf{x}_0) = \mathbf{J}_f(\mathbf{x}) \frac{d\mathbf{x}}{dt} + f(\mathbf{x}(t)) = 0.$$

We can rewrite this equation as

$$\frac{d\mathbf{x}}{dt} = -\mathbf{J}_f^{-1}(\mathbf{x}) f(\mathbf{x}).$$

Perhaps the simplest way to numerically solve this differential equation is Euler's method, which uses a forward difference approximation for $d\mathbf{x}/dt$ with a step size Δt:

$$\frac{\mathbf{x}^{(k+1)} - \mathbf{x}^{(k)}}{\Delta t} = -\mathbf{J}_f^{-1}(\mathbf{x}^{(k)}) f(\mathbf{x}^{(k)}).$$

By taking $\Delta t = 1$, we simply have Newton's method

$$\mathbf{x}^{(k+1)} = \mathbf{x}^{(k)} - \mathbf{J}_f^{-1}(\mathbf{x}^{(k)}) f(\mathbf{x}^{(k)}).$$

Like Newton's method and other fixed-point methods, Euler's method has stability restrictions. One way to handle the stability restrictions is by taking a smaller step size Δt. Smaller steps, of course, mean more iterations. Homotopy continuation, too, effectively reduces the step size to maintain stability. In Chapter 12, we examine the forward Euler method and other differential equation solvers, many of which rely on Newton's method for their stability properties.

♣ Julia's HomotopyContinuation.jl package can solve systems of polynomial equations.

8.8 Finding a minimum (or maximum)

We find the relative minima and maxima of a function by determining where its derivatives are zero. It shouldn't be surprising that numerical methods for finding a function's extrema are similar to those for finding a function's zeros.

▷ Derivative-free methods

The bisection method, introduced at the beginning of this chapter to find the zero of a univariate function, looked for sign changes to successively choose between two brackets. To find a local minimum (or maximum), we'll see where the function is increasing and where it's decreasing. To do this, we'll need to consider three brackets.

Suppose that $f(x)$ is unimodal (with a unique minimum) on the interval $[a, b]$. Divide this interval into three brackets $[a, x_1]$, $[x_1, x_2]$, and $[x_2, b]$ for some x_1 and x_2. If $f(x_1) < f(x_2)$, then the minimum is in the superbracket $[a, x_2]$. We'll move b to x_2 and select a new x_2 in the new interval $[a, b]$. On the other hand, if $f(x_1) > f(x_2)$, then the minimum is in the superbracket $[x_1, b]$. This time, we'll move a to x_1 and select a new x_1 in the new interval $[a, b]$. So how should we select x_1 and x_2?

Without any additional knowledge about $f(x)$, we can argue by symmetry that the size of bracket $[a, x_1]$ should equal the size of bracket $[x_2, b]$ and that the relative sizes of these brackets should be the same regardless of the scale of the interval $[a, b]$. To simplify calculations, consider the initial interval $[0, 1]$ with points x_1 and x_2 at x and $1 - x$ for an unknown x. The relation $1 : (1 - x) = (1 - x) : x$ maintains equal scaling at every iteration. Equivalently, $x^2 - 3x + 1 = 0$ or $x = (3 - \sqrt{5})/2$. The ratio $\varphi = 1 : (1 - x) = (1 + \sqrt{5})/2$ is the golden ratio, also called the golden section. At each iteration, the intervals are scaled in length by $1/\varphi \approx 0.618$, so the golden section search method has linear convergence with a convergence rate of around 0.6.

A common derivative-free search technique for multivariable functions is the Nelder–Mead simplex method. The Nelder–Mead method uses an $n + 1$ polytope in n-dimensional space—a triangle in two-dimensional space, a tetrahedron in three-dimensional space, and so on. The function is evaluated at each of the vertices of the polytope. Through a sequence of reflections, expansions, and contractions, the polytope crawls like an amoeba across the domain, seeking a downhill direction that takes it to the bottom.

▷ Newton's method

A faster way to get the minimum of a function $f(x)$ is by using Newton's method to find where $f'(x) = 0$:

$$x^{(k+1)} = x^{(k)} - \frac{f'\left(x^{(k)}\right)}{f''\left(x^{(k)}\right)}.$$

Geometrically, each iteration of Newton's method for finding the zero of a function determines a straight line tangent to the function and returns the zero crossing. Each iteration of Newton's method for finding a minimum now determines a parabola tangent to the function and returns its vertex. If the function is convex, then Newton's method has quadratic convergence.

In higher dimensions, we formally replace the Jacobian matrix with the Hessian matrix and vector function with its gradient in (8.11) to get

$$\mathbf{x}^{(k+1)} = \mathbf{x}^{(k)} - \left(\mathbf{H}_f\left(\mathbf{x}^{(k)}\right)\right)^{-1} \nabla f\left(\mathbf{x}^{(k)}\right).$$

The Hessian matrix $\mathbf{H}_f(\mathbf{x})$ has elements $h_{ij} = \partial^2 f / \partial x_i \partial x_j$. When the Hessian matrix is not positive-definite, we can use Levenberg–Marquardt regularization by substituting $(\mathbf{H}_f + \alpha \mathbf{I})$ for $\mathbf{H}_f$ for some positive α.

Computing the Hessian can be costly, particularly when working with many variables. The Broyden–Fletcher–Goldfarb–Shanno (BFGS) algorithm is a quasi-Newton (secant-like) method that approximates the Hessian and updates this approximation with each iteration. Alternatively, we can disregard the Hessian entirely by using a general class of gradient descent methods. Gradient descent methods are standard in machine learning and neural nets, where the number of variables can be pretty large and the data is noisy.

▷ Gradient descent methods

The gradient descent method computes

$$\mathbf{x}^{(k+1)} = \mathbf{x}^{(k)} - \alpha \nabla f\left(\mathbf{x}^{(k)}\right),$$

where the positive parameter α, called the learning rate, controls the relative step size. Imagine descending into a deep valley shrouded in fog. Without any additional knowledge of the terrain, you opt to take the steepest path forward (the negative gradient) some distance. You then reorient yourself and move forward in the direction of the new steepest path. You continue in this manner until, hopefully, you find your way to the bottom. If you choose α to be too small, you'll frequently check your gradient and your progress will be slow. If α is too

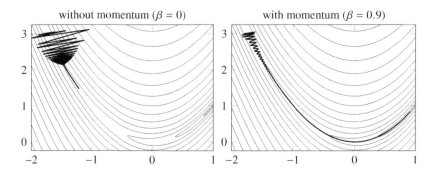

Figure 8.9: The gradient descent method with a learning rate $\alpha = 10^{-3}$ on the Rosenbrock function for 500 iterations without and with momentum.

large and the valley is relatively narrow, you'll likely zigzag back and forth, up and down the valley walls.

In general, we don't need to walk in the direction of the gradient. Instead, we take $\mathbf{x}^{(k+1)} = \mathbf{x}^{(k)} + \alpha \mathbf{p}^{(k)}$ where the vector $\mathbf{p}^{(k)}$ points us in some direction. One approach introduced by Russian mathematician Boris Polyak in the 1960s, often referred to as momentum or the heavy ball method, adds persistence or inertia into the walk

$$\mathbf{x}^{(k+1)} = \mathbf{x}^{(k)} + \alpha \mathbf{p}^{(k)} \quad \text{with} \quad \mathbf{p}^{(k)} = -\nabla f\left(\mathbf{x}^{(k)}\right) + \beta \mathbf{p}^{(k-1)},$$

where β is a parameter usually between zero and one. We are less likely to change directions, a bit like a heavy ball rolling down into the valley. The new factor reduces the oscillations and causes acceleration in the same direction resulting in larger step sizes.

Example. The Rosenbrock function, sometimes called Rosenbrock's banana,

$$f(x, y) = (1 - x)^2 + 100(y - x^2)^2$$

is a narrow valley with rather steep sides and a relatively flat floor along the parabola $y = x^2$. It has a global minimum at $(x, y) = (1, 1)$. When we descend into the valley using gradient descent, the steep valley sides force us to take tiny steps to maintain stability. Once traveling along the valley floor, these tiny steps make for excruciatingly slow progress.

The following code uses the gradient descent method to find the minimum of the Rosenbrock function:

```
∇f = x -> [-2(1-x[1])-400x[1]*(x[2]-x[1]^2); 200(x[2]-x[1]^2)]
x = [-1.8,3.0]; α = 0.001; p = [0,0]; β = 0.9
```

```
for i = 1:100
  p = -∇f(x) + β*p
  x += α*p
end
```

The figure on the facing page shows the trace without momentum ($\beta = 0$) and with momentum ($\beta = 0.9$). Notice that the gradient descent without momentum initially bounces back and forth across the valley and never makes significant progress toward the minimum.

In practice, we can use the Optim.jl library to solve the problem:

```
using Optim
f = x -> (1-x[1])^2 + 100(x[2] - x[1]^2)^2
x₀ = [-1.8,3.0]
result = optimize(f, x₀, GradientDescent())
x = Optim.minimizer(result)
```

Methods include `NelderMead` (the default when no derivatives are provided), `Newton`, `BFGS`, `GradientDescent`, and `GoldenSection` among others.   ◀

⁂ The Optim.jl library includes several methods for finding a local minimum.

8.9 Exercises

8.1. The bisection method takes c at the midpoint of the bracket $[a, b]$. If $f(a)$ is closer to zero than $f(b)$ is to zero, then it seems that we might improve the method were we to take c closer to a than to b, and vice versa. A straightforward way to do this is by linearly interpolating between a and b rather than by averaging a and b:

$$c = \frac{f(a)b - f(b)a}{f(a) - f(b)}.$$

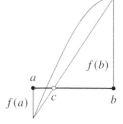

The *regula falsi* method subdivides brackets the same way. Discuss the convergence of the *regula falsi* method. When does it outperform the bisection method? When does it underperform?

8.2. Use theorem 23 to determine the convergence rate of Newton's method.

8.3. Newton's method converges linearly at a root of multiplicity n. Modify it so that it converges quadratically.   ◣

8.4. Newton's method is a special case of a more general class of root-finding algorithms called *Householder methods*:

$$x^{(k+1)} = x^{(k)} + p\frac{(1/f)^{(p-1)}(x^{(k)})}{(1/f)^{(p)}(x^{(k)})}$$

where p is a positive integer and $(1/f)^{(p)}(x)$ denotes the pth derivative of $1/f(x)$. Under suitable conditions, a Householder method has order $p + 1$ convergence. Show that when $p = 1$, we simply have Newton's method. Use a Householder method to extend the Babylonian method for calculating a square root to get a method with cubic order convergence.   ✍

8.5. Edmond Halley, a contemporary of Isaac Newton, invented his own root-finding method:

$$x^{(k+1)} = x^{(k)} - \frac{2f(x^{(k)})f'(x^{(k)})}{2[f'(x^{(k)})]^2 - f(x^{(k)})f''(x^{(k)})}.$$

Derive Halley's method and show that it has cubic-order convergence.

8.6. Prove that, for sufficiently smooth functions, the order of convergence for the secant method is the golden ratio $p = (1 + \sqrt{5})/2$.   ✍

8.7. The Leibniz series, sometimes called the Gregory–Leibniz series or the Madhava–Leibniz series, $4 \cdot (1 - \frac{1}{3} + \frac{1}{5} - \frac{1}{7} + \dots)$ converges sublinearly to π. It's slow. You would need a trillion terms to accurately compute the first 13 digits of π. Compare the Leibniz series and Aitken's extrapolation (8.7) of it.[10] What happens if you use the formulation (8.6) of Aitken's extrapolation?   ✍

8.8. Show that Steffensen's method (8.8) is a quasi-Newton method. Show that this method is quadratically convergent under suitable conditions.   ✍

8.9. Use the Newton–Horner method to compute $x^{(1)}$ given $x^{(0)} = 4$ for the polynomial: $p(x) = 3x^5 - 7x^4 - 5x^3 + x^2 - 8x + 2$.

8.10. Suppose that we want to solve $f(x) = 0$. Taking $x = x - \alpha f(x)$ for some α, we get the fixed-point method $x^{(k+1)} = \phi(x^{(k)})$ where $\phi(x) = x - \alpha f(x)$. How does α affect the stability and convergence of the method?   ✍

8.11. Derive the Newton iteration step of the Q_rsqrt algorithm on page 182.

8.12. Use Newton's method, Broyden's method, and homotopy continuation to find the intersection of

---

[10] Aitken's extrapolation applied to a sequence of partial sums is known as Shanks' transformation.

$$(x^2 + y^2)^2 - 2(x^2 - y^2) = 0$$
$$(x^2 + y^2 - 1)^3 - x^2 y^3 = 0$$

8.13. The elliptic curve secp256k1 $y^2 = x^3 + 7$ (mod r) was popularized when Satoshi Nakamoto used it in Bitcoin's public-key digital signature algorithm. Implement the elliptic curve Diffie–Hellman (ECDH) algorithm using secp256k1. The order of the field is the prime number $r = 2^{256} - 2^{32} - 977$, and the published generator point P can be found in the "Standards for Efficient Cryptography 2 (SEC 2)" at https://www.secg.org/sec2-v2.pdf.

8.14. What are the convergence conditions for the gradient method and Polyak's momentum method applied to the quadratic function $f(x) = \frac{1}{2}mx^2$?

Chapter 9

Interpolation

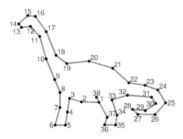

Simple functions such as polynomials or rational functions are often used as surrogates for more complicated ones. These surrogate functions may be easier to integrate, or they might be solved exactly in a differential equation, or they can be plotted as a smooth curve, or they might make computation faster, or perhaps they allow us to fill in missing data points in a consistent manner. Suppose that we have some function $f(x)$, even if it is not explicitly known. We would like to find another function that happens to be a good enough representation of the original one. For now, let's restrict our surrogate function $p_n(x)$ to the space of degree-n polynomials $\mathbb{P}_n$. We can largely break our selection of p_n into two categories:

Interpolation Find the polynomial $p_n \in \mathbb{P}_n$ that coincides with the function f at some given points or nodes $x_0, x_1, \ldots, x_n$.

Best approximation Find the polynomial p_n that is the closest element in $\mathbb{P}_n$ to f with respect to some norm: $p_n = \arginf_{q \in \mathbb{P}_n} \|f - q\|$.

In this chapter, we'll look at interpolation. In the next one, we examine best approximation.

9.1   Polynomial interpolation

Consider the space of degree-n polynomials $\mathbb{P}_n$. By choosing $n+1$ basis elements $\phi_0(x), \phi_1(x), \ldots, \phi_n(x)$ in $\mathbb{P}_n$, we can uniquely express a polynomial $p_n \in \mathbb{P}_n$ as

$$p_n(x) = \sum_{k=0}^{n} c_k \phi_k(x).$$

Our immediate goal is determining constants $c_0, c_1, \ldots, c_n$ such that $p_n(x_i) = y_i$ given $x_0, x_1, \ldots, x_n$ and values $y_0, y_1, \ldots, y_n$. In other words, find the coefficients c_k such that

$$\sum_{k=0}^{n} c_k \phi_k(x_i) = y_i.$$

In matrix form, this says

$$\begin{bmatrix} \phi_0(x_0) & \phi_1(x_0) & \phi_2(x_0) & \cdots & \phi_n(x_0) \\ \phi_0(x_1) & \phi_1(x_1) & \phi_2(x_1) & \cdots & \phi_n(x_1) \\ \phi_0(x_2) & \phi_1(x_2) & \phi_2(x_2) & \cdots & \phi_n(x_2) \\ \vdots & \vdots & \vdots & \ddots & \vdots \\ \phi_0(x_n) & \phi_1(x_n) & \phi_2(x_n) & \cdots & \phi_n(x_n) \end{bmatrix} \begin{bmatrix} c_0 \\ c_1 \\ c_2 \\ \vdots \\ c_n \end{bmatrix} = \begin{bmatrix} y_0 \\ y_1 \\ y_2 \\ \vdots \\ y_n \end{bmatrix}. \tag{9.1}$$

There are several important polynomial bases we might consider. Common ones include the canonical basis, the Lagrange basis, and the Netwon basis, shown in Figure 9.1 on the next page. We can build any degree-n polynomial by using a linear combination of elements from any of these bases. Note that the Newton basis can be defined recursively $v_k(x) = (x - x_k)v_{k-1}(x)$. We'll see that this is a significant advantage of the Newton polynomial basis. Before discussing the bases in-depth, let's prove the uniqueness of a polynomial interpolating function. One way to prove the following theorem is to show that the matrix in (9.1) using the canonical basis (called a Vandermonde matrix) is nonsingular. This approach is left as an exercise. Here we will prove it using Newton bases.

Theorem 24. *Given $n + 1$ distinct points $x_0, x_1, \ldots, x_n$ and arbitrary values $y_0, y_1, \ldots, y_n$, there exists a unique polynomial $p_n \in \mathbb{P}_n$ such that $p_n(x_i) = y_i$ for all $i = 0, 1, \ldots, n$.*

Proof. We'll prove existence using induction. For $n = 0$, choose $p_0(x) = y_0$. Suppose that there is some p_{k-1} such that $p_{k-1}(x_i) = y_i$ for all $i = 0, 1, \ldots, k - 1$. Let

$$p_k(x) = p_{k-1}(x) + c(x - x_0)(x - x_1) \cdots (x - x_{k-1})$$

for some c. Then $p_k \in \mathbb{P}_k$ and $p_k(x_i) = p_{k-1}(x_i) = y_i$ for $i = 0, 1, \ldots, k - 1$. To determine the value c for which $p_k(x_k) = y_k$, take c that solves

$$y_k = p_{k-1}(x_k) + c(x_k - x_0)(x_k - x_1) \cdots (x_k - x_{k-1}).$$

Canonical: $\varphi_k(x) = x^k$

Langrange: $\ell_k(x) = \displaystyle\prod_{\substack{j=0 \\ j \neq k}}^{n} \dfrac{x - x_j}{x_k - x_j}$

Newton: $\nu_k(x) = \displaystyle\prod_{j=0}^{k-1} (x - x_j)$

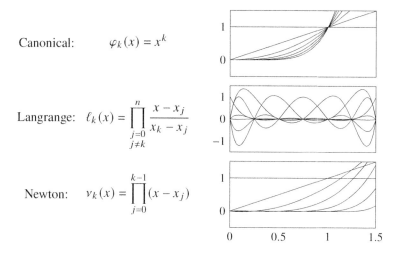

Figure 9.1: Polynomial basis functions for $k = 0, \ldots, 6$ with nodes at $x_j = j/4$.

That is,

$$c = \frac{y_k - p_{k-1}(x_k)}{(x_k - x_0)(x_k - x_1) \cdots (x_k - x_{k-1})}.$$

We now prove uniqueness. Suppose that there were two polynomials p_n and q_n. Then the polynomial $p_n - q_n$ has the property $(p_n - q_n)(x_i) = 0$ for all $i = 0, \ldots, n$. So, $p_n - q_n$ has $n + 1$ roots. But because $p_n - q_n \in \mathbb{P}_n$, it can have at most n roots unless it is identically zero. So, p_n must equal q_n.   □

▷ **Canonical basis**

Consider the problem of fitting a degree-n polynomial $y = c_0 + c_1 x + c_2 x^2 + \cdots + c_n x^n$ to a set of data points $(x_0, y_0), (x_2, y_2), \ldots, (x_n, y_n)$ using the canonical or standard basis $\{1, x, \ldots, x^n\}$. Given $n + 1$ distinct points, we can determine a nth-degree polynomial by solving the *Vandermonde* system $\mathbf{Vc} = \mathbf{y}$. From (9.1),

$$\begin{bmatrix} 1 & x_0 & x_0^2 & \cdots & x_0^n \\ 1 & x_1 & x_1^2 & \cdots & x_1^n \\ 1 & x_2 & x_2^2 & \cdots & x_2^n \\ \vdots & \vdots & \vdots & \ddots & \vdots \\ 1 & x_n & x_n^2 & \cdots & x_n^n \end{bmatrix} \begin{bmatrix} c_0 \\ c_1 \\ c_2 \\ \vdots \\ c_n \end{bmatrix} = \begin{bmatrix} y_0 \\ y_1 \\ y_2 \\ \vdots \\ y_n \end{bmatrix}.$$

Solving the system takes $O(n^3)$ operations. Moreover, the Vandermonde matrix is increasingly ill-conditioned as it gets larger.

✦ It's easy to construct a Vandermonde matrix using broadcasting: `x.^(0:n)'`. For something with more features, try the SpecialMatrices.jl function `Vandermonde` that overloads the `\` operator with the $O(n^2)$-time Björck and Pereyra algorithm.

▷ **Lagrange polynomial basis**

For a Lagrange polynomial,

$$y_j = \sum_{i=0}^{n} y_i \ell_i(x_j) \quad \text{with} \quad \ell_i(x) = \prod_{\substack{j=0 \\ j \neq i}}^{n} \frac{x - x_j}{x_i - x_j}.$$

That is, $\ell_i(x_j) = \delta_{ij}$. For a quick confirmation of this, note where $\ell_i(x)$ is 0 and 1 in the Lagrange basis for $\{x_0, x_1, x_2, x_3\} = \{0, 1, 2, 4\}$:

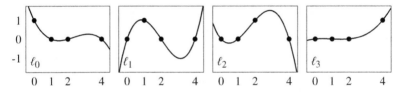

Because $\ell_i(x_j) = \delta_{ij}$, (9.1) becomes simply

$$\begin{bmatrix} 1 & 0 & 0 & \cdots & 0 \\ 0 & 1 & 0 & \cdots & 0 \\ 0 & 0 & 1 & \cdots & 0 \\ \vdots & \vdots & \vdots & \ddots & \vdots \\ 0 & 0 & 0 & \cdots & 1 \end{bmatrix} \begin{bmatrix} c_0 \\ c_1 \\ c_2 \\ \vdots \\ c_n \end{bmatrix} = \begin{bmatrix} y_0 \\ y_1 \\ y_2 \\ \vdots \\ y_n \end{bmatrix}.$$

Hence, it is trivial to find the approximating polynomial using the Lagrange form. But the Lagrange form does have some drawbacks. Each evaluation of a Lagrange polynomial requires $O(n^2)$ additions and multiplications. They are difficult to differentiate and integrate. If you add new data pair (x_n, y_n), you must start from scratch. And the computations can be numerically unstable.

▷ **Newton polynomial basis**

The Newton polynomial basis fixes these limitations of the Lagrange form by recursively defining the basis elements $v_i(x)$:

$$1, \ (x - x_0), \ (x - x_0)(x - x_1), \ \cdots, \ \prod_{i=0}^{n-1} (x - x_i).$$

Defining $f(x_i) = y_i$ and using the Newton basis, (9.1) becomes

$$
\begin{bmatrix}
1 & 0 & 0 & \cdots & 0 \\
1 & (x_1 - x_0) & 0 & \cdots & 0 \\
1 & (x_2 - x_0) & \prod_{i=0}^{1}(x_2 - x_i) & \cdots & 0 \\
\vdots & \vdots & \vdots & \ddots & \vdots \\
1 & (x_n - x_0) & \prod_{i=0}^{1}(x_n - x_i) & \cdots & \prod_{i=0}^{n-1}(x_n - x_i)
\end{bmatrix}
\begin{bmatrix}
c_0 \\ c_1 \\ c_2 \\ \vdots \\ c_n
\end{bmatrix}
=
\begin{bmatrix}
f(x_0) \\ f(x_1) \\ f(x_2) \\ \vdots \\ f(x_n)
\end{bmatrix}.
$$

The lower triangular system can be solved using forward substitution. Note that the coefficient c_i is only a function of $x_0, x_1, \ldots, x_i$. We will use the notation $c_i = f[x_0, x_1, \ldots, x_i]$ to denote this dependency. For example, using forward substitution to find $\{c_0, c_1, c_2\}$ for three nodes

$$f[x_0] = c_0 = f(x_0)$$

$$f[x_0, x_1] = c_1 = \frac{f(x_1) - c_0}{x_1 - x_0} = \frac{f(x_1) - f(x_0)}{x_1 - x_0}$$

$$f[x_0, x_1, x_2] = c_2 = \frac{f(x_2) - c_0 - c_1(x_2 - x_0)}{(x_2 - x_1)(x_2 - x_0)}$$

$$= \frac{\dfrac{f(x_2) - f(x_0)}{x_2 - x_0} - \dfrac{f(x_1) - f(x_0)}{x_1 - x_0}}{x_2 - x_1}.$$

Note that c_2 is the coefficient for x^2 term of $p_2(x)$. Because $p_2(x)$ is unique by theorem 24, it doesn't matter in which order we take the nodes $\{x_0, x_1, x_2\}$ for $f[x_0, x_1, x_2]$. So, by interchanging x_0 and x_1, we have

$$f[x_0, x_1, x_2] = \frac{\dfrac{f(x_2) - f(x_1)}{x_2 - x_1} - \dfrac{f(x_1) - f(x_0)}{x_1 - x_0}}{x_2 - x_0} = \frac{f[x_1, x_2] - f[x_0, x_1]}{x_2 - x_0}.$$

We can compute the rest of the coefficients recursively using *divided differences*, starting with $f[x_i] = f(x_i)$ for $i = 0, 1, \ldots, k$ and then constructing

$$f[x_j, \ldots, x_k] = \frac{f[x_{j+1}, \ldots, x_k] - f[x_j, \ldots, x_{k-1}]}{x_k - x_j}.$$

It's convenient to arrange the divided differences as a table to aid in calculation[1]

x_0	$f[x_0]$	$f[x_0, x_1]$	$f[x_0, x_1, x_2]$	$f[x_0, x_1, x_2, x_3]$
x_1	$f[x_1]$	$f[x_1, x_2]$	$f[x_1, x_2, x_3]$	
x_2	$f[x_2]$	$f[x_2, x_3]$		
x_3	$f[x_3]$			

[1] Nineteenth-century mathematician and inventor Charles Babbage, sometimes called the grandfather of the modern computer, invented a mechanical device he called the "difference engine." The steel and brass contraption was intended to automate and make error-free the mathematical drudgery of computing divided difference tables. Ada Lovelace, enamored by Babbage's even grander designs, went on to propose the world's first computer program.

Then, the coefficients c_i come from each column of the first row

$$\{c_0, c_1, c_2, c_3\} = \{f[x_0], f[x_0, x_1], f[x_0, x_1, x_2], f[x_0, x_1, x_2, x_3]\},$$

and we can use Horner's method to evaluate the interpolating polynomial

$$p_n(x) = c_0 + (x - x_0)\Big(c_1 + (x - x_1)\big(c_2 + (x - x_2)c_3\big)\Big).$$

Example. Let's find the interpolating polynomial for the function $f(x)$ where

$$\begin{array}{rccccc} x & = & 1 & 3 & 5 & 6 \\ f(x) & = & 0 & 4 & 5 & 7 \end{array}.$$

We first build the divided-difference table. We'll use $\square$ to denote unknown values.

From
$$\begin{array}{cc|ccc} 1 & 0 & \square & \square & \square \\ 3 & 4 & \square & \square & \\ 5 & 5 & \square & & \\ 6 & 7 & & & \end{array}$$
we have
$$\begin{array}{cc|ccc} 1 & 0 & 2 & -3/8 & 7/40 \\ 3 & 4 & 1/2 & 1/2 & \\ 5 & 5 & 2 & & \\ 6 & 7 & & & \end{array}.$$

To fill in the upper left value, we take $(4 - 0)/(3 - 1)$ to get 2. The value below it is $(5 - 4)/(5 - 3)$ or $1/2$. Now, we can use these new values to compute to unknown value to their right: $(1/2 - 2)/(5 - 1) = -3/8$. The rest of the table is filled out similarly. From the first row, we have the coefficients of the interpolating polynomial

$$p_n(x) = 0 + 2(x - 1) - 3/8(x - 1)(x - 3) + 7/40(x - 1)(x - 3)(x - 5),$$

which can be evaluated using Horner's method

$$p_n(x) = 0 + (x - 1)\Big(2 + (x - 3)\big(-3/8 + (x - 5) \cdot 7/40\big)\Big). \quad \blacktriangleleft$$

▷ Hermite interpolation

Let's continue our work from the previous section by constructing interpolating polynomials that match a function's values *and* derivatives at a set of nodes. That is, let's find a unique polynomial $p_n \in \mathbb{P}_n$ such that $p_n^{(j)}(x_i) = f^{(j)}(x_i)$ for all $i = 0, 1, \ldots, k$ and $j = 0, 1, \ldots, \alpha_i$. The polynomial p_n is called the *Hermite interpolation* of f at the points x_i.

We are already familiar with Hermite interpolation when we have only one node—it's simply the Taylor polynomial approximation. When we have multiple nodes, we can compute the Newton form of the Hermite interpolation by using a table of divided differences. We'll use the mean value theorem for divided differences.

Theorem 25. *Given $n + 1$ distinct nodes $\{x_0, x_1, \ldots, x_n\}$, there is a point ξ on the interval bounded by the smallest and largest nodes such that the nth divided difference of a function $f(x)$ is $f[x_0, x_1, \ldots, x_n] = f^{(n)}(\xi)/n!$.*

Proof. Let $p_n(x)$ be the interpolating polynomial of $f(x)$ using the Newton basis. The leading term of $p_n(x)$ is $f[x_0, \ldots, x_n](x - x_0) \ldots (x - x_{n-1})$. Take $g(x) = f(x) - p_n(x)$, which has $n + 1$ zeros at each of the nodes $\{x_0, x_1, \ldots, x_n\}$. By Rolle's theorem, $g'(x)$ has at least n zeros on the interval, $g''(x)$ has at least $n - 1$ zeros, and so on until $g^{(n)}$ has at least one zero on the interval. We'll take ξ to be one of these zeros. So,

$$0 = g^{(n)}(\xi) = f^{(n)}(\xi) - p_n^{(n)}(\xi) = f^{(n)}(\xi) - n! f[x_0, x_1, \ldots, x_n]$$

and it follows that $f[x_0, x_1, \ldots, x_n] = f^{(n)}(\xi)/n!$.   □

As a consequence of the mean value theorem, for any node x_i of $n + 1$ nodes, the divided difference is

$$f[x_i, x_i, \ldots, x_i] = \lim_{x_1, \ldots, x_n \to x_i} f[x_0, x_1, \ldots, x_n] = f^{(n)}(x_i)/n!.$$

For example, $f[1] = f(1)$, $f[1, 1] = f'(1)$, $f[1, 1, 1] = f''(1)/2$, and so on.

Example. Compute the polynomial p of minimal degree satisfying

$$p(1) = 2, \quad p'(1) = 3, \quad p(2) = 6, \quad p'(2) = 7, \quad p''(2) = 8.$$

To do this, we compute the divided differences. First note that $p[1, 1] = p'(1) = 3$, $p[2, 2] = p'(2) = 7$, and $p[2, 2, 2] = p''(2)/2! = 8/2 = 4$. Then we fill in the divided difference table starting with □ to denote unknown values.

$$\text{From } \begin{array}{cc|cccc} 1 & 2 & 3 & \square & \square & \square \\ 1 & 2 & \square & \square & \square \\ 2 & 6 & 7 & 4 \\ 2 & 6 & \square \\ 2 & 6 \end{array} \qquad \text{we have} \qquad \begin{array}{cc|cccc} 1 & 2 & 3 & 1 & 2 & -1 \\ 1 & 2 & 4 & 3 & 1 \\ 2 & 6 & 7 & 4 \\ 2 & 6 & \square \\ 2 & 6 \end{array}.$$

By taking the coefficients from the first row, we conclude that $p(x)$ is

$$2 + 3(x - 1) + 1(x - 1)^2 + 2(x - 1)^2(x - 2) - 1(x - 1)^2(x - 2). \qquad \blacktriangleleft$$

9.2 How good is polynomial interpolation?

Theorem 26. *Let $p_n(x)$ be a degree-n interpolating polynomial of a sufficiently smooth function $f(x)$ at $n + 1$ nodes $x_0, x_1, \ldots, x_n$ on the interval $[a, b]$. Then for each $x \in [a, b]$ there is a $\xi \in [a, b]$ such that the pointwise error*

$$f(x) - p_n(x) = \frac{f^{(n+1)}(\xi)}{(n + 1)!} \prod_{i=0}^{n} (x - x_i).$$

Proof. If x is a node, then $f(x) - p_n(x) = 0$, and the claim is clearly true. So, let x be any point other than a node $\{x_0, x_1, \ldots, x_n\}$. Define

$$g(z) = (f(z) - p_n(z)) - (f(x) - p_n(x)) \frac{\prod_{i=0}^{n} (z - x_i)}{\prod_{i=0}^{n} (x - x_i)}.$$

Note that x is now a parameter of $(n + 1)$-differentiable function g and that

$$g(x) = g(x_0) = g(x_1) = \cdots = g(x_n) = 0.$$

That is to say, g has at least $n + 2$ zeros on the interval $[a, b]$. By Rolle's theorem $g'(x)$ has at least $n + 1$ zeros on the interval, $g^{(2)}(x)$ has at least n zeros on the interval, and so on until $g^{(n+1)}$ has at least one zero on the interval. Let's call this zero ξ. We can explicitly compute the $(n + 1)$st derivative of $g(z)$ as

$$g^{(n+1)}(z) = \left(f^{(n+1)}(z) - 0 \right) - \frac{f(x) - p_n(x)}{\prod_{i=0}^{n}(x - x_i)}(n + 1)!,$$

where $p_n^{(n+1)}(z) = 0$ because p_n has degree at most n. At $z = \xi$,

$$0 = g^{(n+1)}(\xi) = f^{(n+1)}(\xi) - \frac{f(x) - p_n(x)}{\prod_{i=0}^{n}(x - x_i)}(n + 1)!.$$

So, it follows that

$$f(x) - p_n(x) = \frac{f^{(n+1)}(\xi)}{(n + 1)!} \prod_{i=0}^{n} (x - x_i). \qquad \square$$

The error estimate above can be extended to Hermite interpolation as well. The proof of the following theorem is similar to that of theorem 26 and is left as an exercise.

Theorem 27. *Let $x_0, x_1, \ldots, x_n$ be nodes on the interval $[a, b]$ and let f be a sufficiently smooth function on that interval. If $p(x)$ is an interpolating polynomial of degree at most $2n + 1$ with $p(x_i) = f(x_i)$ and $p'(x_i) = f'(x_i)$, then for each $x \in [a, b]$ there is a $\xi \in [a, b]$ such that the pointwise error*

$$f(x) - p_n(x) = \frac{f^{(2n+2)}(\xi)}{(2n + 2)!} \prod_{i=0}^{n} (x - x_i)^2.$$

From the expression for pointwise error, we can see that it is affected by the smoothness of the function $f(x)$ and the number and placement of the nodes. We can't control the smoothness of $f(x)$, but we can control the number and position of the nodes. Take a look at the plot of $\prod_{i=0}^{8}(x - x_i)$ for nine equally spaced nodes:

The value $\left|\prod_{i=0}^{8}(x - x_i)\right|$ is quite large near both ends of the interval. And if we add more uniformly spaced nodes, the overshoot becomes larger. This behavior, called *Runge's phenomenon*, explains why simply adding nodes does not necessarily improve accuracy. We can instead choose the position of the nodes to minimize the uniform norm[2] $\left\| \prod_{i=0}^{8}(x - s_i) \right\|_{\infty}$. We do exactly this by choosing nodes s_i that are zeros of the Chebyshev polynomial:

Now, the black curve of $\prod_{i=0}^{8}(x - s_i)$ with Chebyshev nodes s_i overlays the lighter gray curve of $\prod_{i=0}^{8}(x - x_i)$ with uniformly spaced nodes x_i. In exchange for moderately increasing the error near the center of the interval, using Chebyshev nodes significantly decreases the error near its ends.

Let's peek at Chebyshev polynomials and their zeros—we'll come back to them in the next chapter. Chebyshev polynomials can be defined using

$$T_n(x) = \cos(n \arccos x) \tag{9.2}$$

over the interval $[-1, 1]$. While this definition might seem a bit tightly packed, Forman Acton interprets it in a parenthetical comment in his classic 1970 book *Numerical Methods that Work*: "they are actually cosine curves with a somewhat disturbed horizontal scale, but the vertical scale has not been touched." See the figure on the following page. Several important properties can be derived directly from this definition. Chebyshev polynomials can be defined using the recursion formula:

$$T_{n+1}(x) = 2xT_n(x) - T_{n-1}(x),$$

---

[2] Also called the Chebyshev norm, the infinity norm, and the supremum norm.

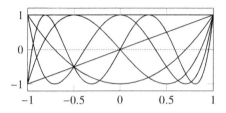
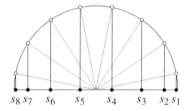

Figure 9.2: Chebyshev polynomials $T_0(x), T_1(x), \ldots, T_5(x)$ (left). Chebyshev nodes of $T_8(x)$ are abscissas of eight equispaced nodes on the unit circle (right).

where $T_0(x) = 1$ and $T_1(x) = x$. The roots of the Chebyshev polynomial, called Chebyshev nodes, occur at

$$ s_i = \cos \frac{\left(i - \frac{1}{2}\right)\pi}{n} \qquad \text{for } i = 1, 2, \ldots, n. $$

These Chebyshev nodes are also the abscissas of equispaced points along the unit semicircle. See the figure above. The Chebyshev polynomial's extrema occur at

$$ \hat{s}_i = \cos \frac{i\pi}{n} \qquad \text{for } i = 0, 1, \ldots, n. $$

and take the values $T_n(\hat{s}_i) = (-1)^{i+1}$. It follows that Chebyshev polynomials are bounded below by -1 and above by $+1$ for $x \in [-1, 1]$. Finally, the leading coefficient of $T_n(x)$ is 2^{n-1}.

Theorem 28. *The maximum magnitude of any degree-n polynomial with a leading coefficient 2^{n-1} must be at least one over the interval $[-1, 1]$.*

Proof. Let p_n be a degree-n polynomial with a leading coefficient 2^{n-1}. Then $T_n - p_n$ is a degree-$(n-1)$ or smaller polynomial. Suppose that $|p_n(x)| < 1$ for all $x \in [-1, 1]$. At the Chebyshev extrema, $T_n(\hat{s}_i) = -1$ for even i and $p_n(\hat{s}_i) > -1$, so it follows that $p_n(\hat{s}_i) - T_n(\hat{s}_i) > 0$. Similarly, $T_n(\hat{s}_i) = +1$ for odd i and $p_n(\hat{s}_i) < 1$, so it follows that $p_n(\hat{s}_i) - T_n(\hat{s}_i) < 0$. This means that the polynomial $p_n - T_n$ is alternating between positive and negative over the $n + 1$ Chebyshev extrema. So it has at least n roots in $[-1, 1]$. But $p_n - T_n$ is a polynomial of degree at most $n - 1$, so it can have at most $n - 1$ roots—a contradiction. Therefore, there must be some $x \in [-1, 1]$ where $|p_n(x)| \geq 1$. □

Example. In 1885, at the age of seventy, Karl Weierstrass proved his famous theorem that any continuous function could be uniformly approximated by a sequence of polynomials. Specifically, the Weierstrass approximation theorem states that if f is a continuous function on the interval $[a, b]$, then for every positive ε, there exists a polynomial p_n such that $|f(x) - p_n(x)| < \varepsilon$ for all $x \in [a, b]$. In 1901, Weierstrass' former student Carl Runge demonstrated that the theorem need not hold for polynomials interpolated through equidistant nodes. Namely, a polynomial interpolant of the function $(x^2 + 1)^{-1}$ using equidistant nodes produces large oscillations near the endpoints that grow unbounded as the polynomial degree increases.

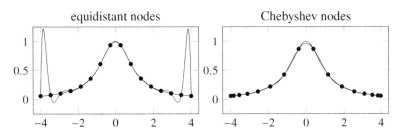

Weierstrass' theorem does hold for a polynomial through Chebyshev nodes. Chebyshev nodes eliminate Runge's phenomenon near the edges but increase the pointwise error around the origin. The function $(x^2 + 1)^{-1}$ is called the Runge function or the witch of Agnesi.[3]   ◀

9.3 Splines

One problem with polynomial interpolation is that polynomials basis elements are smooth and unbounded, so they are ill-suited to approximate functions with predominant local features like discontinuities. We've seen how polynomials lead to Runge's phenomenon. Radial basis functions, examined in exercise 9.3, provide an alternative to polynomial basis functions. Piecewise polynomial functions, called *splines*, provide another. This section will focus on cubic splines, but the ideas will apply to any degree spline.

▷ Cubic splines

A cubic spline $s(x)$ is a C^2-continuous, piecewise-cubic polynomial through points (x_j, y_j) known as *knots*. Let $x_0, x_1, \ldots, x_n$ be $n + 1$ distinct nodes with $a = x_0 < x_1 < \cdots < x_n = b$. And let $\{s_0(x), s_0(x), \ldots, s_{j-1}(x)\}$ be a set of cubic polynomials. We want a function $s(x)$ such that $s(x) = s_j(x)$ over the interval $x \in (x_j, x_{j+1})$ for each j. To determine $s(x)$, we must match the cubic polynomials $s_j(x)$ at the boundaries of the subintervals. A cubic polynomial

---

[3]The witch of Agnesi was named after the Italian mathematician Maria Agnesi, who described it in her 1748 book *Foundations of Analysis for Italian Youth*. The name comes from John Colson's mistranslation of *aversiera* ("versine curve") as *avversiera* ("witch"). The versine (or versed sine) function is versin $\theta = 1 - \cos \theta$. It's one of several oddball trigonometric functions rarely used in modern mathematics: versine, coversine, haversine, archacovercosine, ...

has four degrees of freedom. Hence, we have four unknowns for each of the n subintervals—a total of $4n$ unknowns. Let's look at these constraints. The spline interpolates each of the $n+1$ knots, giving us $n+1$ constraints. Because $s(x) \in C^2$, it follows that $s_{j-1}(x_j) = s_j(x_j)$, $s'_{j-1}(x_j) = s'_j(x_j)$, and $s''_{j-1}(x_j) = s''_j(x_j)$ for $j = 1, 2, \ldots, n-1$. This gives us another $3(n-1)$ constraint for a total of $4n-2$ constraints. We have two degrees of freedom remaining.

We'll need to enforce two additional constraints to remove these remaining degrees of freedom and get a unique solution. Common constraints include the complete or clamped boundary condition where $s'(a)$ and $s'(b)$ are specified; natural boundary condition where $s''(a) = s''(b) = 0$; periodic boundary condition where $s'(a) = s'(b)$ and $s''(a) = s''(b)$; and not-a-knot condition. The not-a-knot condition uses the same cubic polynomial across the first two subintervals by setting $s'''_1(x_1) = s'''_1(x_1)$, effectively making x_1 "not a knot." It does the same across the last two subintervals by setting $s'''_n(x_{n-1}) = s'''_n(x_{n-1})$.

Before computer-aided graphic design programs, yacht designers and aerospace engineers used thin strips of wood called splines to help draw curves. The thin beams were fixed to the knots by hooks attached to heavy lead weights and either clamped at the boundary to prescribe the slope (complete splines) or unclamped so that the beam would be straight outside the interval (natural splines). If $y(x)$ describes the position of the thin wood beam, then the curvature is given by

$$\kappa(x) = \frac{y''(x)}{(1 + y'(x)^2)^{3/2}},$$

and the deformation energy of the beam is

$$E = \int_a^b \kappa^2(x)\, dx = \int_a^b \left(\frac{y''(x)}{(1 + y'(x)^2)^{3/2}} \right)^2 dx.$$

For small deformations, $E \approx \int_a^b [y''(x)]^2\, dx = \|y''\|_2^2$. Physically, the beam takes a shape that minimizes the energy, which implies that the cubic spline is the smoothest interpolating polynomial.

Theorem 29. *Let s be an interpolating cubic spline of the function f at the nodes $a = x_0 < \cdots < x_n = b$ and let $y \in C^2[a, b]$ be an arbitrary interpolating function on f. Then $\|s''\|_2 \le \|y''\|_2$ if the spline has complete, natural, or periodic boundary conditions.*

Proof. Note that $y'' = s'' + (y'' - s'')$ and hence

$$\int_a^b (y'')^2\, dx = \int_a^b (s'')^2\, dx + 2\int_a^b s''(y'' - s'')\, dx + \int_a^b (y'' - s'')^2\, dx.$$

The last term is nonnegative, so we just need to show that the middle term vanishes. Integrating by parts

$$\int_a^b s''(y'' - s'')\, dx = s''(y' - s')\Big|_a^b - \int_a^b s'''(y' - s')\, dx.$$

The boundary terms are zero by the imposed boundary conditions. Over the subinterval $x \in (x_i, x_{i+1})$ the cubic spline $s(x)$ is a cubic polynomial $s_i(x)$ with $s'''(x) = s_i'''(x) = d_i$ for some constant d_i. Then

$$\int_a^b s'''(y' - s')\, dx = \sum_{i=0}^{n-1} \int_{x_i}^{x_{i+1}} d_i(y' - s_i')\, dx$$

$$= \sum_{i=0}^{n-1} d_i\big[(y(x_{i+1}) - s_i(x_{i+1})) - (y(x_i) - s_i(x_i))\big] = 0. \;\square$$

▷ Computation of cubic splines

Let's find an efficient method to construct a cubic spline interpolating the values $y_i = f(x_i)$ for $a = x_0 < x_1 < \cdots < x_n = b$. If $s(x)$ is a C^2-piecewise cubic polynomial, then $s''(x)$ is a piecewise linear function. The second-order derivative of $s_i(x)$ over the subinterval $[x_i, x_{i+1}]$ is the line

$$s_i''(x) = m_{i+1}\frac{x - x_i}{h_i} + m_i\frac{x_{i+1} - x}{h_i},$$

where $h_i = x_{i+1} - x_i$ is the segment length and $m_i = s_i''(x_i)$:

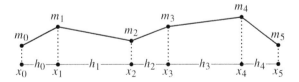

We integrate twice to find

$$s_i(x) = \frac{1}{6}\frac{m_{i+1}}{h_i}(x - x_i)^3 + \frac{1}{6}\frac{m_i}{h_i}(x_{i+1} - x)^3 + A_i(x - x_i) + B_i, \qquad (9.3)$$

where the constants A_i and B_i are determined by imposing the values at the ends of the subintervals $s_i(x_i) = y_i$ and $s_i(x_{i+1}) = y_{i+1}$:

$$y_i = \frac{1}{6}\frac{m_i}{h_i}h_i^3 + B_i \quad \text{and} \quad y_{i+1} = \frac{1}{6}\frac{m_{i+1}}{h_i}h_i^3 + Ah_i + B_i.$$

From this, we have

$$B_i = y_i - \frac{1}{6}m_i h_i^2 \quad \text{and} \quad A_i = \frac{y_{i+1} - y_i}{h_i} - \frac{1}{6}(m_{i+1} - m_i)h_i. \qquad (9.4)$$

We still need to determine m_i. To find these, we match the first derivatives $s(x)$ at x_i: $s'_{i-1}(x_i) = s'_i(x_i)$.

$$s'_i(x) = \frac{1}{2}\frac{m_{i+1}}{h_i}(x - x_i)^2 - \frac{1}{2}\frac{m_i}{h_i}(x_{i+1} - x)^2 + A_i.$$

for $i = 1, 2, \ldots, n - 1$. Substituting in for A_{i-1} and A_i, we have

$$s'_{i-1}(x_i) = \frac{1}{2}\frac{m_i}{h_{i-1}}(h_{i-1})^2 + \frac{y_i - y_{i-1}}{h_{i-1}} - \frac{1}{6}(m_i - m_{i-1})h_{i-1},$$

$$s'_i(x_i) = -\frac{1}{2}\frac{m_i}{h_i}(h_i)^2 + \frac{y_{i+1} - y_i}{h_i} - \frac{1}{6}(m_{i+1} - m_i)h_i.$$

Equating the two, we are left with

$$h_{i-1}m_{i-1} + 2(h_i + h_{i-1})m_i + h_i m_{i+1} = 6\left(\frac{y_{i+1} - y_i}{h_i} - \frac{y_i - y_{i-1}}{h_{i-1}}\right)$$

for $i = 1, 2, \ldots, n - 1$. We have $n - 1$ equations and $n + 1$ unknowns. To close the system, we need to add the boundary conditions. Let's impose natural boundary conditions: $s''_3(a) = s''_3(b) = 0$. Then $m_0 = 0$ and $m_n = 0$, and we have the following system:

$$\begin{bmatrix} 1 & & & & \\ \alpha_0 & \beta_1 & \alpha_1 & & \\ & \ddots & \ddots & \ddots & \\ & & \alpha_{n-2} & \beta_{n-1} & \alpha_{n-1} \\ & & & & 1 \end{bmatrix} \begin{bmatrix} m_0 \\ m_1 \\ \vdots \\ m_{n-1} \\ m_n \end{bmatrix} = \begin{bmatrix} 0 \\ \gamma_1 \\ \vdots \\ \gamma_{n-1} \\ 0 \end{bmatrix}$$

where

$$\alpha_i = h_i, \ \beta_i = 2(h_i + h_{i-1}), \text{ and } \gamma_i = 6\left(\frac{y_{i+1} - y_i}{h_i} - \frac{y_i - y_{i-1}}{h_{i-1}}\right). \qquad (9.5)$$

Note that we can rewrite the $n + 1$ system as an $n - 1$ system by eliminating the first and last equations

$$\begin{bmatrix} \beta_1 & \alpha_1 & & & \\ \alpha_1 & \beta_2 & \alpha_2 & & \\ & \ddots & \ddots & \ddots & \\ & & \alpha_{n-3} & \beta_{n-2} & \alpha_{n-2} \\ & & & \alpha_{n-2} & \beta_{n-1} \end{bmatrix} \begin{bmatrix} m_1 \\ m_2 \\ \vdots \\ m_{n-2} \\ m_{n-1} \end{bmatrix} = \begin{bmatrix} \gamma_1 \\ \gamma_2 \\ \vdots \\ \gamma_{n-2} \\ \gamma_{n-1} \end{bmatrix}. \qquad (9.6)$$

We can use (9.5) and (9.6) to determine the coefficients m of a spline with natural boundary conditions:

```
function spline_natural(xᵢ,yᵢ)
  h = diff(xᵢ)
  γ = 6*diff(diff(yᵢ)./h)
  α = h[2:end-1]
  β = 2(h[1:end-1]+h[2:end])
  [0;SymTridiagonal(β,α)\γ;0]
end
```

The following function computes the interpolating cubic spline using n points through the nodes given by the arrays x and y.

```
function evaluate_spline(xᵢ,yᵢ,m,n)
  h = diff(xᵢ)
  B = yᵢ[1:end-1] .- m[1:end-1].*h.^2/6
  A = diff(yᵢ)./h - h./6 .*diff(m)
  x = range(minimum(xᵢ),maximum(xᵢ),length=n+1)
  i = sum(xᵢ'.≤x,dims=2)
  i[end] = length(xᵢ)-1
  y = @. (m[i]*(xᵢ[i+1]-x)^3 + m[i+1]*(x-xᵢ[i])^3)/(6h[i]) +
      A[i]*(x-xᵢ[i]) + B[i]
  return(x,y)
end
```

▷ Splines in parametric form

We can adapt the work from the previous section to compute a spline through points in a plane. Consider a plane curve in parametric form $f(t) = (x(t), y(t))$ with $t \in [0, T]$ for some T. Take a set of points (x_i, y_i) for $i = 0, 1, \ldots, n$ and introduce the partition $0 = t_0 < t_1 < \cdots < t_n = T$. A simple way to parameterize the spline is by using the lengths of each straight-line segment

$$\ell_i = \sqrt{(x_i - x_{i-1})^2 + (y_i - y_{i-1})^2}$$

for $i = 1, 2, \ldots, n$ and setting $t_0 = 0$ and $t_i = \sum_{j=1}^{i} \ell_j$. We simply need to compute splines for $x(t)$ and $y(t)$. This function is called the *cumulative length spline* and is a good approximation as long as the curvature of $f(t)$ is small.

⚫⚫ The Dierckx.jl function Spline1D returns a cubic spline.

The Julia Dierckx.jl package is a wrapper of the dierckx Fortran library developed by Paul Dierckx, providing an easy interface to building splines. Let's create a function and select some knots.

```
g = x-> @. max(1-abs(3-x),0)
```

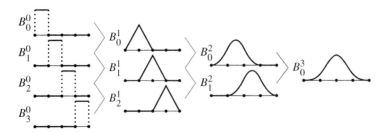

Figure 9.3: B-spline bases generated recursively using de Boor's algorithm.

```
xᵢ = 0:5; yᵢ = g(xᵢ)
x = LinRange(0,5,101);
```

Then we can plot the cubic spline.

```
using Dierckx, Plots
spline = Spline1D(xᵢ,yᵢ)
plot(x,spline(x)); plot!(x,g(x)); scatter!(xᵢ,yᵢ)
```

▷ B-splines

An alternative approach to constructing interpolating splines is by building them using a linear combination of basis elements called basis splines or B-splines. Let $\{B_{0,p}(x), B_{1,p}(x), \ldots, B_{n,p}(x)\}$ be a set of pth-order B-splines, where we use the second subscript to denote the order:

$$B_{0,3} \quad B_{1,3} \quad B_{2,3} \quad B_{3,3} \quad B_{4,3} \quad B_{5,3} \quad B_{6,3} \quad B_{7,3} \quad B_{8,3} \quad B_{9,3}$$

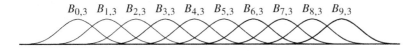

We can interpolate a spline curve $s(x) = \sum_{i=0}^{n} c_i B_{i,p}(x)$ through a set of knots $(x_0, f(x_0)), (x_1, f(x_1)), \ldots, (x_n, f(x_n))$ by determining the coefficients $c_0, c_1, \ldots, c_n$ that satisfies the system of equations $f(x_j) = \sum_{i=0}^{n} c_i B_{i,p}(x_j)$ for $j = 1, 2, \ldots, n$. B-splines have the following properties: each is nonnegative with local support; each is a piecewise polynomial of degree less than or equal to p over $p+1$ subintervals; and together, they form a partition of unity. Degree-0 B-splines are piecewise constant, degree-1 B-splines are piecewise linear, degree-2 B-splines are piecewise quadratic, and so forth.

We can recursively generate splines of any degree, starting with degree-0 splines using *de Boor's algorithm*. Let $a \le x_0 < \cdots < x_n \le b$. The degree-0

B-splines are *characteristic functions*

$$B_{i,0}(x) = \begin{cases} 1, & \text{if } x_i \le x < x_{i+1} \\ 0, & \text{otherwise} \end{cases}.$$

It's easy to see that the set $\{B_{0,0}(x), B_{1,0}(x), \ldots, B_{n-1,0}(x)\}$ forms a partition of unity over $[a, b]$, that is, $\sum_{i=0}^{n-1} B_{i,0}(x) = 1$. We can construct higher degree B-splines that also form a partition of unity by recursively defining

$$B_{i,p}(x) = \left(\frac{x - x_i}{x_{i+p} - x_i}\right) B_{i,p-1}(x) + \left(\frac{x_{i+p+1} - x}{x_{i+p+1} - x_{i+1}}\right) B_{i+1,p-1}(x),$$

which we can rewrite as

$$B_{i,p} = V_{i,p} B_{i,p-1} + (1 - V_{i+1,p}) B_{i+1,p-1} \quad \text{with} \quad V_{i,p}(x) = \frac{x - x_i}{x_{i+p} - x_i}.$$

See Figure 9.3 on the facing page. The constant spline $B_{i,0}(x)$ has one subinterval for its nonzero support. The linear spline $B_{i,1}(x)$ has two subintervals for its nonzero support. The quadratic spline $B_{i,2}(x)$ has three subintervals for its nonzero support. And so forth.

Finally, suppose that the knots are equally spaced with separation h and a node at x_0. A B-spline with equal separation between knots is called a cardinal B-spline. We can generate such a cubic B-spline

$$B_{i,3}(x) = B\left(\frac{x - x_0}{h} - i\right)$$

by translating and stretching the B-spline

$$B(x) = \begin{cases} \frac{2}{3} - \frac{1}{2}(2 - |x|)x^2, & |x| \in [0, 1) \\ \frac{1}{6}(2 - |x|)^3, & |x| \in [1, 2) \\ 0, & \text{otherwise} \end{cases}.$$

At the nodes $x = \{-1, 0, 1\}$, the B-spline takes the values $B(x) = \{\frac{1}{3}, \frac{2}{3}, \frac{1}{3}\}$. The values are zero at every other node. The coefficients c_j of the resulting tridiagonal system $f(x_j) = \sum_{i=0}^{n} c_i B_{i,3}(x_j)$ can be determined quite efficiently by inverting the corresponding matrix equation.

♣ The Interpolations.jl package, which is still under development, can be used to evaluate up through third-order B-splines, but the nodes must be equally spaced.

Let's fit a spline through the knots that we generated earlier:

```
using Interpolations
method = BSpline(Cubic(Natural(OnGrid())))
spline = scale(interpolate(yᵢ, method), xᵢ)
plot(x,spline(x)); plot!(x,g(x)); scatter!(xᵢ,yᵢ)
```

▷ Cubic Hermite spline

Another type of cubic spline is a piecewise cubic Hermite interpolating polynomial or PCHIP. Cubic Hermite polynomials come from a linear combination of four basis functions, each one having either unit value or unit derivative on either end of an interval. Hence, we can uniquely determine a cubic Hermite spline on $[x_i, x_{i+1}]$ by prescribing the values $f(x_i)$, $f(x_{i+1})$, $f'(x_i)$ and $f'(x_{i+1})$. Consider the unit interval, and let $p_0 = f(0)$, $p_1 = f(1)$, $m_0 = f'(0)$ and $m_1 = f'(1)$ at the nodes. In this case,

$$p(x) = p_0 H_{00}(x) + m_0 H_{10}(x) + p_1 H_{01}(x) + m_1 H_{11}(x),$$

where the basis elements are given by

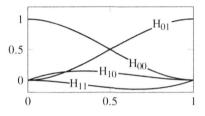

$$H_{00}(x) = 2x^3 - 3x^2 + 1,$$
$$H_{10}(x) = x^3 - 2x^2 + x,$$
$$H_{01}(x) = -2x^3 + 3x^2 = H_{00}(1 - x),$$
$$H_{11}(x) = x^3 - x^2 = -H_{10}(1 - x).$$

We can modify these bases to fit an arbitrary interval $[x_i, x_{i+1}]$ by taking

$$p(x) = p_i H_{00}(t) + m_i h_i H_{10}(t) + p_{i+1} H_{01}(t) + m_{i+1} h_i H_{11}(t)$$

where $h_i = x_{i+1} - x_i$, $t = (x - x_i)/h_i$, and the coefficients $p_i = f(x_i)$ and $m_i = f'(x_i)$. The coefficients m_i can be approximated by finite difference approximation

$$\frac{p_{i+1} - p_{i-1}}{x_{i+1} - x_{i-1}} \quad \text{or} \quad \frac{1}{2} \left(\frac{p_{i+1} - p_i}{x_{i+1} - x_i} + \frac{p_i - p_{i-1}}{x_i - x_{i-1}} \right),$$

using a one-sided derivative at the boundaries.

One practical difference between a PCHIP and a cubic spline interpolant is that the PCHIP has fewer wiggles and doesn't overshoot the knots like the spline is apt to do. On the other hand, the spline is smoother than the PCHIP. A cubic spline is C^2-continuous, whereas a PCHIP is only C^1-continuous. A cubic spline is designed by matching the first and second derivatives of the polynomial segments at knots without explicit regard to the values of those derivatives. A PCHIP is designed by prescribing the first derivatives at knots, which are the same for each polynomial segment sharing a knot, while their second derivatives may be different. Take a look at both methods applied to the knots below:

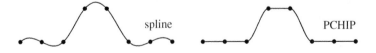

9.4 Bézier curves

Another way to create splines is by using composite Bézier curves. While splines are typically constructed by fitting polynomials through nodes, Bézier curves are constructed by using a set of control points to form a convex hull. A Bézier curve doesn't go through control points except at the endpoints. A Bézier spline is built by matching the position and slopes of several Bézier curves at their terminal control points (○):

Bézier curves are all around us—just pick up a newspaper, and you are bound to see Bézier curves. That's because composite Bézier curves are the mathematical encodings for glyphs used in virtually every modern font, from quadratic ones in TrueType fonts to the cubic ones in the Times font used in each letter of text you are reading right now. Bézier curves are used to draw curves in design software like Inkscape and Adobe Illustrator, and they are used to describe paths in an SVG, the standard web vector image format.

A linear Bézier curve is a straight line segment through two control points $\mathbf{p}_0 = (x_0, y_0)$ and $\mathbf{p}_1 = (x_1, y_1)$:

$$\mathbf{q}_{10}(t) = (1 - t)\mathbf{p}_0 + t\mathbf{p}_1$$

where $t \in [0, 1]$. Note that $\mathbf{q}_{10}(0) = \mathbf{p}_0$ and $\mathbf{q}_{10}(1) = \mathbf{p}_1$. With an additional control point $\mathbf{p}_2$, we can build a quadratic Bézier curve. First, define the linear Bézier curve

$$\mathbf{q}_{11}(t) = (1 - t)\mathbf{p}_1 + t\mathbf{p}_2.$$

Now, combine $\mathbf{q}_{10}(t)$ and $\mathbf{q}_{11}(t)$:

$$\mathbf{q}_{20}(t) = (1 - t)\mathbf{q}_{10}(t) + t\mathbf{q}_{11}(t).$$

String art uses threads strung between nails hammered into a board to create geometric representations, such as a ship's sail. You can think of the Bézier curve as the convex hull formed connecting threads from nails at $\mathbf{q}_{10}(t)$ to corresponding nails at $\mathbf{q}_{11}(t)$. The threads or line segments are tangent to the Bézier curve $\mathbf{q}_{20}(t)$. If we expand the expression for $\mathbf{q}_{20}(t)$, we have

$$\mathbf{q}_{20}(t) = (1 - t)^2 \mathbf{p}_0 + 2t(1 - t)\mathbf{p}_1 + t^2 \mathbf{p}_2$$

with a derivative

$$
\begin{aligned}
\mathbf{q}'_{20}(t) &= -2(1 - t)\mathbf{p}_0 + 2(1 - 2t)\mathbf{p}_1 + 2t\mathbf{p}_2 \\
&= -2\big((1 - t)\mathbf{p}_0 + t\mathbf{p}_1\big) + 2\big((1 - t)\mathbf{p}_1 + t\mathbf{p}_2\big) \\
&= 2\big(\mathbf{q}_{11}(t) - \mathbf{q}_{10}(t)\big).
\end{aligned}
$$

Note that $\mathbf{q}_{20}(0) = \mathbf{p}_0$ and $\mathbf{q}_{20}(1) = \mathbf{p}_2$, which says that the quadratic Bézier curve goes through $\mathbf{p}_0$ and $\mathbf{p}_2$. And, $\mathbf{q}'_{20}(0) = 2(\mathbf{p}_1 - \mathbf{p}_0)$ and $\mathbf{q}'_{20}(1) = 2(\mathbf{p}_2 - \mathbf{p}_1)$, which says that the Bézier curve is tangent to the line segment $\overline{\mathbf{p}_0 \mathbf{p}_1}$ and $\overline{\mathbf{p}_1 \mathbf{p}_2}$ at $\mathbf{p}_0$ and $\mathbf{p}_2$, respectively.

We can continue in the fashion by adding another control point $\mathbf{p}_3$ to build a cubic Bézier curve. Take

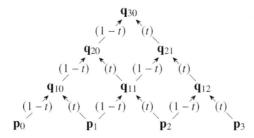

$$
\begin{aligned}
\mathbf{q}_{12}(t) &= (1 - t)\mathbf{p}_2 + t\mathbf{p}_3 \\
\mathbf{q}_{21}(t) &= (1 - t)\mathbf{q}_{11}(t) + t\mathbf{q}_{12}(t) \\
\mathbf{q}_{30}(t) &= (1 - t)\mathbf{q}_{20}(t) + t\mathbf{q}_{21}(t).
\end{aligned}
$$

This time, the cubic Bézier curve $\mathbf{q}_{30}(t)$ is created from the convex hull formed by line segments connecting corresponding points on $\mathbf{q}_{20}(t)$ and $\mathbf{q}_{21}(t)$. These, in turn, are created from the segments connecting $\mathbf{q}_{10}(t)$ and $\mathbf{q}_{11}(t)$, and $\mathbf{q}_{11}(t)$ and $\mathbf{q}_{12}(t)$, respectively. See the QR code at the bottom of this page.

This recursive method of constructing the Bézier curve starting with linear Bézier curves, then quadratic Bézier curves, then cubic (and higher-order) Bézier curves is called *de Casteljau's algorithm*:

$$
\begin{array}{c}
\mathbf{q}_{30} \\
(1-t) \nearrow \quad \nwarrow (t) \\
\mathbf{q}_{20} \qquad\qquad \mathbf{q}_{21} \\
(1-t) \nearrow \quad \nwarrow (t) \quad (1-t) \nearrow \quad \nwarrow (t) \\
\mathbf{q}_{10} \qquad\qquad \mathbf{q}_{11} \qquad\qquad \mathbf{q}_{12} \\
(1-t) \nearrow \ \nwarrow (t) \ (1-t) \nearrow \ \nwarrow (t) \ (1-t) \nearrow \ \nwarrow (t) \\
\mathbf{p}_0 \qquad\qquad \mathbf{p}_1 \qquad\qquad \mathbf{p}_2 \qquad\qquad \mathbf{p}_3
\end{array}
$$

By expanding $\mathbf{q}_{30}$, we have the cubic *Bernstein polynomial*

$$\mathbf{q}_{30}(t) = (1 - t)^3 \mathbf{p}_0 + 3t(1 - t)^2 \mathbf{p}_1 + 3t^2(1 - t)\mathbf{p}_2 + t^3 \mathbf{p}_3.$$

In general, the degree-n Bernstein polynomial is given by

$$\mathbf{q}_{n0}(t) = \sum_{k=0}^{n} \binom{n}{k} (1 - t)^{n-k} t^k \mathbf{p}_k = \sum_{k=0}^{n} B_{nk}(t)\mathbf{p}_k,$$

animation of the cubic
Bézier curve

or simply $\mathbf{q}_{n0}(t) = \mathbf{B}_n(t)\mathbf{p}$, where $\mathbf{B}_n(t)$ is an $m \times (n+1)$ Bernstein matrix constructed by taking m points along $[0, 1]$ and $\mathbf{p}$ is an $(n+1) \times 2$ vector of control points. We can build a Bernstein matrix using the following function, which takes a column vector such as t = LinRange(0,1,20):

```
bernstein(n,t) = @. binomial(n,0:n)'*t^(0:n)'*(1-t)^(n:-1:0)'
```

The bases $\{B_{n0}(t), B_{n1}(t), \ldots, B_{nn}(t)\}$ form a partition of unit, meaning that the points along a Bézier curve are the weighted averages of the control points. From this, we know that the curve is contained in the convex hull formed by control points. The Bernstein polynomials are plotted below as a function of the parameter $t \in [0, 1]$. Notice how the weight changes on each control point as t moves from zero on the left of each plot to one on the right.

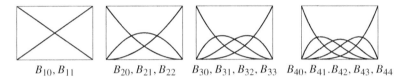

B_{10}, B_{11} B_{20}, B_{21}, B_{22} $B_{30}, B_{31}, B_{32}, B_{33}$ $B_{40}, B_{41}.B_{42}, B_{43}, B_{44}$

▷ **Weierstrass approximation theorem**

Rénault engineer Pierre Bézier popularized Bézier curves in the 1960s for computer-aided geometric design. Paul de Casteljau's contributions occurred around the same time at the competing automobile manufacturer Citroën. Bernstein polynomials, however, appeared much earlier. In 1912, Serge Bernstein introduced his eponymous polynomials in a probabilistic proof of the Weierstrass theorem. We'll conclude the chapter with Bernstein's proof. The proof is elegant, and it provides a nice segue to the material in the next chapter.

It's no coincidence that the terms of the Bernstein polynomial bear a striking similarity to the probability mass function of a binomial distribution. Bernstein's proof invokes Bernoulli's theorem, also known as the weak law of large numbers, which states that the frequency of success of a sequence of Bernoulli trials approaches the probability of success as the number of trials approaches infinity. A Bernoulli trial is a random experiment with two possible outcomes—a success or a failure. A coin flip is either heads or tails. A soccer shot is either a goal or a miss. A student's random guess on a multiple-choice question is either right or wrong.

Theorem 30 (Weierstrass approximation theorem). *If $f(x)$ is a continuous function in the interval $[0, 1]$, then for any $\varepsilon > 0$, there is a polynomial $p_n(x)$ with a sufficiently large degree n such that $|f(x) - p_n(x)| < \varepsilon$ for every $x \in [0, 1]$.*

Proof. Consider an event whose probability equals x. Suppose that we perform n trials and agree to pay out $f(k/n)$ if that event occurs k times. Under these conditions, the expected payout is

$$E_n = \sum_{k=0}^{n} f\left(\frac{k}{n}\right)\binom{n}{k}x^k(1-x)^{n-k}$$

using a binomial distribution. Because $f(x)$ is continuous, we can choose a δ such that $|f(x) - f(\xi)| < \frac{1}{2}\varepsilon$ for any $\xi \in (x - \delta, x + \delta)$. Let $\widehat{f(x)}$ denote the maximum and $\underline{f(x)}$ denote the minimum of $f(x)$ over the interval $(x - \delta, x + \delta)$. Then $\widehat{f(x)} - f(x) < \frac{1}{2}\varepsilon$ and $f(x) - \underline{f(x)} < \frac{1}{2}\varepsilon$.

Let q be the probability that $|x - k/n| > \delta$, and let L be the maximum of $|f(x)|$ in $[0, 1]$. Then

$$\underline{f(x)}(1-q) - Lq < E_n < \widehat{f(x)}(1-q) + Lq,$$

which we can rewrite as

$$f(x) + (\underline{f(x)} - f(x)) - q(L + \underline{f(x)}) < E_n < f(x) + (\widehat{f(x)} - f(x)) - q(L + \widehat{f(x)}).$$

By Bernoulli's theorem, we can choose n sufficiently large such that $q < \varepsilon/4L$. It follows that

$$f(x) - \frac{\varepsilon}{2} - \frac{2L}{4L}\varepsilon < E_n < f(x) + \frac{\varepsilon}{2} + \frac{2L}{4L}\varepsilon,$$

and hence $|f(x) - E_n| < \varepsilon$. Of course, the expected payout E_n is simply a degree-n polynomial $p_n(x)$. □

The Bernstein approximation of a function $f(x)$ is $\sum_{k=0}^{n} f(k/n)B_{nk}(x)$. To be clear, a Bernstein approximant does not interpolate given values, even if $f(x)$ is itself a polynomial. Let's plot the approximation of $f(x) = \sqrt{x}$:

```
n = 20; f = t -> sqrt(t)
y = bernstein(n,t)*f.(LinRange(0,1,n+1))
plot(t,y); plot!(t,f.(t))
```

This code does produce a polynomial approximation to $f(x)$, but it's not a very good one. While Bernstein polynomials are useful in de Casteljau's algorithm to generate Bézier curves, they are not practical in approximating arbitrary functions. Namely, they converge extremely slowly: $|f(x) - p_n(x)| = O(n^{-1})$. In the next chapter, we will examine methods that converge quickly. To dig deeper into the Bernstein polynomials, check out Rida Farouki's centennial retrospective article.

9.5   Exercises

9.1. Prove theorem 24 by using the canonical basis $\{1, x, \ldots, x^n\}$ to construct a Vandermonde matrix. Show that if $\{x_0, x_1, \ldots, x_n\}$ are distinct, then the Vandermonde matrix $\mathbf{V}$ is nonsingular. Hence, the Vandermonde system has a unique solution.   ⊿

9.2. Write a program that constructs a closed parametric cubic spline $(x(t), y(t))$ using periodic boundary conditions. Use it to plot a smooth curve through several randomly selected knots.   ⊿

9.3. A radial basis function is any function ϕ whose value depends only on its distance from the origin. We can use them as interpolating functions:

$$y(x) = \sum_{i=0}^{n} c_i \phi(x - x_i).$$

Compare interpolation using a polynomial basis with the Gaussian and cubic radial basis functions $\phi(x) = \exp(-x^2/2\sigma^2)$ and $\phi(x) = |x|^3$ for the Heaviside function using 20 equally spaced nodes in $[-1, 1]$. The Heaviside function $H(x) = 0$ when $x < 0$ and $H(x) = 1$ when $x \geq 0$.   ⊿

9.4. Collocation is a method of solving a problem by considering candidate solutions from a finite-dimensional space, determined by a set of points called collocation points. The finite-dimensional problem is solved exactly at the collocation points to get an approximate solution to the original problem.

Suppose that we have the differential equation $L u(x) = f(x)$ with boundary conditions $u(a) = u_a$ and $u(b) = u_b$ for some linear differential operator L. We approximate the solution $u(x)$ by $\sum_{j=0}^{n} c_j v_j(x)$ for some basis v_j. Take the collocation points $x_i \in [a, b]$ with $i = 0, 1, \ldots, n$. Then solve the linear system of equations

$$\sum_{j=0}^{n} c_j v_j(x_0) = u_a, \qquad \sum_{j=0}^{n} c_j L v_j(x_i) = f(x_i), \qquad \sum_{j=0}^{n} c_j v_j(x_n) = u_b.$$

Use collocation to solve Bessel's equation $xu'' + u' + xu = 0$ with $u(0) = 1$ and $u(b) = 0$ where b is the fourth zero of the Bessel function (approximately 11.7915344390142) using cubic B-splines with 10 or 20 equally spaced knots over the unit interval $[0, b]$. Comment on the order of convergence of the method as more collocation points are added.   ⊿

9.5. A composite Bézier curve is sometimes used to approximate a circle. One way to do this is by piecing together four cubic Bézier curves that approximate quarter circles, ensuring their tangents match at the endpoints. For a unit quarter circle with endpoints at $(0, 1)$ and $(1, 0)$, this means that we need to choose control points at $(c, 1)$ and $(1, c)$. What value c should we take to ensure that the radial deviation from the unit circle is minimized? How close of an approximation does this value give us?

Chapter 10

Approximating Functions

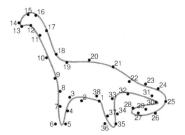

The last chapter used interpolation to find polynomials that coincide with a function at a set of nodes or knots. These methods allowed us to model data and functions using smooth curves. This chapter considers *best approximation*, which is frequently used in data compression, optimization, and machine learning. For a function f in some vector space F, we will find the function u in a subspace U that is closest to f with respect to some norm:

$$u = \arg\inf_{g \in U} \| f - g \|.$$

When the norm is the L^1-norm, i.e., $\int_a^b |f(x) - g(x)|\, dx$, the problem is one of minimizing the average absolute deviation, the one that minimizes the area between curves. When the norm is the L^2-norm, i.e., $\int_a^b (f(x) - g(x))^2\, dx$, the problem is called least squares approximation or *Hilbert approximation*. When the norm is the L^∞-norm, i.e., $\sup_{x \in [a,b]} |f(x) - g(x)|$, the problem is called uniform approximation, minimax, or *Chebyshev approximation*. The least squares approximation is popular largely because it is robust and typically the easiest to implement. So, we will concentrate on the least squares approximation.

10.1 Least squares approximation

An *inner product* is a mapping $(\cdot, \cdot)$ of any two vectors of a vector space to the field over which that vector space is defined (typically real or complex numbers), satisfying three properties: linearity, positive-definiteness, and symmetry.

1. *Linearity* says that for any f, g, and h in the vector space and any scalar α of the field, $(f, \alpha g) = \alpha \cdot (f, g)$ and $(f, g + h) = (f, g) + (f, h)$.

2. *Positive-definiteness* says that $(f, f) > 0$ if f is non-zero (i.e., positive) and that $(f, f) = 0$ if f is identically zero (i.e., definite).

3. Finally, *symmetry* or Hermiticity says that $(f, g) = (g, f)$ for a real vector space and for $(f, g) = \overline{(g, f)}$ for a complex one.

A vector space with an assigned inner product is an *inner product space*. An inner product induces a natural norm $\|f\| = \sqrt{(f, f)}$, so every inner product space is also a normed vector space.

By associating the dot product with the n-dimensional space $\mathbb{R}^n$, we get the Euclidean vector space. The Euclidean inner product $(\mathbf{x}, \mathbf{y}) = \sum_{i=1}^{n} x_i y_i$ has the geometric interpretation as a measure of the magnitude and closeness of two vectors: $(\mathbf{x}, \mathbf{y}) = \|\mathbf{x}\| \|\mathbf{y}\| \cos \theta$. In particular, the inner product of any two unit vectors is simply the angle between those two vectors. In this chapter, we will be interested in the space of continuous functions over an interval $[a, b]$ and its associated inner product

$$(f, g) = \int_a^b f(x) g(x) w(x) \, dx,$$

where $w(x)$ is a specified positive weight function. We can easily verify that the three properties of an inner product space hold. Like the Euclidean vector space, the weighted inner product for the space of functions can also be interpreted as a measure of the magnitude and closeness of the functions.

We say that f is *orthogonal* to g if $(f, g) = 0$. Sometimes, we use the term *w-orthogonal* to explicitly indicate that a weighting function is included in the definition of the inner product. We'll write this as $f \perp g$. If $f \perp g$ for all $g \in G$, we say that f is orthogonal to G and write it as $f \perp G$. For example, consider the space of square-integrable functions on the interval $[-1, 1]$ with the inner product $(f, g) = \int_{-1}^{1} f(x) g(x) \, dx$. In this inner product space, even functions like e^{-x^2} are orthogonal to odd functions like $\sin x$. Even functions form a subspace of square-integrable functions; odd functions form another subspace. In fact, the subspace of even functions is the *orthogonal complement* to the subspace of odd functions. That is to say, every function is the sum of an even function and an odd function.

Theorem 31. *Let U be a subspace of the inner product space F. Take $f \in F$ and $u \in U$. Then u is the best approximation to f in U if and only if $f - u \perp U$.*

Proof. Let's start by proving that if $f - u \perp U$ then u is the best approximation to f. If $f - u \perp U$, then for any $g \in U$

$$\|f - g\|^2 = \|(f - u) + (u - g)\|^2$$
$$= \|f - u\|^2 + 2(f - u, f - g) + \|u - g\|^2 \geq \|f - u\|^2.$$

To prove converse suppose that u is a best approximation to f. Let $g \in U$ and take $\lambda > 0$. Then $\|f - u + \lambda g\|^2 \geq \|f - u\|^2$. So,

$$0 \leq \|f - u + \lambda g\|^2 - \|f - u\|^2$$
$$= \|f - u\|^2 + 2\lambda (f - u, g) + \lambda^2\|g\|^2 - \|f - u\|^2$$
$$= \lambda\left(2 (f - u, g) + \lambda\|g\|^2\right).$$

Because $\lambda > 0$, we have $2 (f - u, g) + \lambda\|g\|^2 \geq 0$. Letting λ shrink to zero, we get $(f - u, g) \geq 0$. Similarly, by replacing g with $-g$, we get $(f - u, -g) \geq 0$ from which it follows that $(f - u, g) \leq 0$. Therefore, $(f - u, g) = 0$. Because g is an arbitrary function of U, it follows that $f - u \perp U$. $\qquad\square$

Let $\{u_1, u_2, \ldots, u_n\}$ be a basis for a subspace $U \subset F$. If we want to find the best approximation to $f \in F$ in U, then we must find the $u \in U$ such that $u - f \perp U$. That is, we must find the u such that $(u - f, u_i) = 0$ for every $i = 1, 2, \ldots, n$. Take $u = \sum_{j=1}^{n} c_j u_j$. Then

$$\left(\sum_{j=1}^{n} c_j u_j - f, u_i\right) = 0,$$

from which it follows that

$$\sum_{j=1}^{n} c_j \left(u_j, u_i\right) = (f, u_i).$$

This system of equations is known as the *normal equation*. In matrix form, the normal equation is

$$\begin{bmatrix} (u_1, u_1) & (u_2, u_1) & \cdots & (u_n, u_1) \\ (u_1, u_2) & (u_2, u_2) & \cdots & (u_n, u_2) \\ \vdots & \vdots & \ddots & \vdots \\ (u_1, u_n) & (u_2, u_n) & \cdots & (u_n, u_n) \end{bmatrix} \begin{bmatrix} c_1 \\ c_2 \\ \vdots \\ c_n \end{bmatrix} = \begin{bmatrix} (f, u_1) \\ (f, u_2) \\ \vdots \\ (f, u_n) \end{bmatrix}.$$

The matrix on the left is called the *Gram matrix*.

Example. Suppose that we want to find the least squares approximation to $f(x)$ over the interval $[0, 1]$ using degree-n polynomials. If we take the canonical basis $\{\varphi_i\} = \{1, x, x^2, \ldots, x^n\}$, then

$$p_n(x) = c_0 + c_1 x + c_2 x^2 + \cdots + c_n x^n = \sum_{i=0}^{n} c_i \varphi_i(x).$$

To determine $\{c_i\}$, we solve $(p_n, \varphi_i) = (f, \varphi_i)$ for $i = 1, 2, \ldots, n$:

$$\left(\varphi_j, \varphi_i\right) = \left(x^j, x^i\right) = \int_0^1 x^{i+j} \, dx = \frac{1}{i + j + 1}.$$

We now must solve the normal equation

$$\begin{bmatrix} 1 & 1/2 & 1/3 & \cdots \\ 1/2 & 1/3 & 1/4 & \cdots \\ 1/3 & 1/4 & 1/5 & \cdots \\ \vdots & \vdots & \vdots & \ddots \end{bmatrix} \begin{bmatrix} c_0 \\ c_1 \\ \vdots \\ c_n \end{bmatrix} = \begin{bmatrix} (f, 1) \\ (f, x) \\ \vdots \\ (f, x^n) \end{bmatrix}$$

This Gram matrix, called the *Hilbert matrix*, is quite ill-conditioned. Even for relatively small systems, the computations can be unstable. For example, the condition number for 7×7 Hilbert matrix is roughly 10^8, meaning that we can expect any error in our calculations to possibly be magnified by as much as 10^8. And the condition number of a 12×12 Hilbert matrix exceeds floating-point precision. Typing

```
using LinearAlgebra; cond([1//(i+j-1) for i∈1:12,j∈1:12])*eps()
```

into Julia returns around 3.89. We can get an intuitive idea of why the canonical basis results in an ill-conditioned problem by just looking at it. The first eight elements of the canonical basis and of the Legendre basis are shown below:

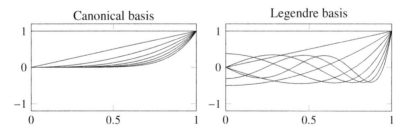

Differences between the elements of the canonical basis get smaller and smaller as the degree of the monomial increases. It is easy to distinguish the plots of 1 from x and x from x^2, but the plots of x^7 and x^8 become almost indistinguishable. On the other hand, the plots of the Legendre polynomial basis elements are all largely different. So, heuristically, it seems that orthogonal polynomials like Legendre polynomials are simply better. ◀

10.2   Orthonormal systems

We say that a set of vectors $\{u_1, u_2, \ldots, u_n\}$ is *orthonormal* in an inner product space if $(u_i, u_j) = \delta_{ij}$ for all i and j. Let's reexamine the normal equation when we use an orthonormal basis. Because $(u_i, u_j) = \delta_{ij}$, we now have

$$\begin{bmatrix} 1 & 0 & \cdots & 0 \\ 0 & 1 & \cdots & 0 \\ \vdots & \vdots & \ddots & \vdots \\ 0 & 0 & \cdots & 1 \end{bmatrix} \begin{bmatrix} c_1 \\ c_2 \\ \vdots \\ c_n \end{bmatrix} = \begin{bmatrix} (f, u_1) \\ (f, u_2) \\ \vdots \\ (f, u_n) \end{bmatrix}.$$

Wow! This means that if $\{u_1, u_2, \ldots, u_n\}$ is an orthonormal system in an inner product space F, then the best approximation p_n to f is simply

$$p_n = \sum_{i=1}^{n} (f, u_i) \, u_i. \tag{10.1}$$

We call this best approximation the orthogonal projection of f. The inner product (f, u_i) is simply the component of f in the u_i direction. We'll denote the orthogonal projection operator by P_n:

$$P_n f = \sum_{i=1}^{n} (f, u_i) \, u_i.$$

We can summarize everything into the following theorem, which will be a major tool for the rest of the chapter.

Theorem 32. *Let $\{u_1, u_2, \ldots, u_n\}$ be an orthonormal system in an inner product space F. Then the best approximation to f is the element $P_n f$, where the orthogonal projection operator $P_n = \sum_{i=1}^{n} (\cdot, u_i) \, u_i$.*

So far, we've only used a finite basis. Let's turn to infinite-dimensional vector spaces. To do this, we'll need a few extra terms. A *Cauchy sequence* is any sequence whose elements become arbitrarily close as the sequence progresses. That is to say, if we have a sequence of projections $P_0 f, P_1 f, P_2 f \ldots$, then the sequence is a Cauchy sequence if given some $\varepsilon > 0$, there is some integer N such that $\| P_n f - P_m f \| < \varepsilon$ for all $n, m > N$. A normed vector space is said to be *complete* if every Cauchy sequence of elements in that vector space converges to an element in that vector space. Such a vector space is called a *Banach space*. Similarly, a complete, inner product space is called a *Hilbert space*. An orthonormal basis $\{u_1, u_2, \ldots\}$ of a Hilbert space F is called a complete, orthonormal system of F or a *Hilbert basis*.

Theorem 33 (Parseval's theorem). *If $\{u_1, u_2, \ldots\}$ is a complete, orthonormal system in F, then $\|f\|^2 = \sum_{i=1}^{\infty} |(f, u_i)|^2$ for every $f \in F$.*

Proof. Because $\{u_1, u_2, \ldots\}$ are orthonormal, we can define the projection operator $P_n = \sum_{i=1}^{n} (\cdot, u_i) u_i$. In the induced norm, we simply have

$$\| P_n f \|^2 = \left\| \sum_{i=1}^{n} (f, u_i) u_i \right\|^2 = \left(\sum_{i=1}^{n} (f, u_i) u_i, \sum_{j=1}^{n} (f, u_j) u_j \right).$$

We expand the inner product to get

$$\| P_n f \|^2 = \sum_{i=1}^{n} \sum_{j=1}^{n} (f, u_i)(f, u_j)(u_i, u_j) = \sum_{i=1}^{n} |(f, u_i)|^2,$$

because $(u_i, u_j) = \delta_{ij}$. Now, because the system is complete,

$$\|f\|^2 = \lim_{n \to \infty} \| P_n f \|^2 = \sum_{i=1}^{\infty} |(f, u_i)|^2. \qquad \square$$

We can generate a Hilbert basis (an orthonormal basis for an inner product space) by using the Gram–Schmidt method. The Gram–Schmidt method starts with an arbitrary basis and sequentially subtracts out the non-orthogonal components. Let $\{v_1, v_2, v_3, \ldots\}$ be a basis for F with a prescribed inner product space.

1. Start by taking $u_1 = v_1$ and normalize $\hat{u}_1 = u_1/\|u_1\|$.

2. Next, define $u_2 = v_2 - P_1 v_2$ where the projection operator $P_1 = (\cdot, \hat{u}_1) \hat{u}_1$, and normalize $\hat{u}_2 = u_2/\|u_2\|$.

3. Now, define $u_3 = v_3 - P_2 v_3$ where the projection operator $P_2 = P_1 + (\cdot, \hat{u}_2) \hat{u}_2$, and normalize $\hat{u}_3 = u_3/\|u_3\|$.

n. We continue in this manner by defining $u_n = v_n - P_{n-1} v_n$ where the projection operator $P_{n-1} = \sum_{i=1}^{n-1} (\cdot, \hat{u}_i) \hat{u}_i$ and normalizing $\hat{u}_n = u_n/\|u_n\|$.

Then $\{\hat{u}_1, \hat{u}_2, \hat{u}_3, \ldots\}$ is an orthonormal basis for F. Directly, applying the Gram–Schmidt process can be a lot of work. Luckily, there's a shortcut to generate orthogonal polynomials. We can use a three-term recurrence relation known as Favard's theorem.[1]

Theorem 34 (Favard's theorem). *For each weighted inner product, there are uniquely determined orthogonal polynomials with leading coefficient one satisfying the three-term recurrence relation*

$$\begin{cases} p_{n+1}(x) = (x + a_n)p_n(x) + b_n p_{n-1}(x) \\ p_0(x) = 1, \quad p_1(x) = x + a_1 \end{cases}$$

[1] Jean Favard proved the theorem in 1935, although it was previously demonstrated by Aurel Wintner in 1926 and Marshall Stone in 1932.

where

$$a_n = -\frac{(xp_n, p_n)}{(p_n, p_n)} \quad and \quad b_n = -\frac{(p_n, p_n)}{(p_{n-1}, p_{n-1})}.$$

Proof. We'll use induction. First, the only polynomial of degree zero with leading coefficient one is $p_0(x) \equiv 1$. Suppose that the claim holds for the orthogonal polynomials $p_0, p_1, \ldots, p_{n-1}$. Let p_{n+1} be an arbitrary polynomial of degree n and leading coefficient one. Then $p_{n+1} - xp_n$ is a polynomial whose degree is less than or equal to n. Because $p_0, p_1, \ldots, p_n$ form an orthogonal basis of $\mathbb{P}_n$

$$p_{n+1} - xp_n = \sum_{j=0}^{n} c_j p_j \quad \text{with} \quad c_j = \frac{(p_{n+1} - xp_n, p_j)}{(p_j, p_j)}.$$

Furthermore, if p_{n+1} is orthogonal to $p_0, p_1, \ldots, p_n$:

$$c_j = \frac{(p_{n+1} - xp_n, p_j)}{(p_j, p_j)} = \frac{(p_{n+1}, p_j)}{(p_j, p_j)} - \frac{(xp_n, p_j)}{(p_j, p_j)} = 0 - \frac{(xp_n, p_j)}{(p_j, p_j)}$$

Let's expand numerator in the right-most term:

$$(xp_n, p_j) = (p_n, xp_j) = \left(p_n, p_{j+1} - \sum_{i=0}^{j-1} c_i p_i\right) = (p_n, p_{j+1}) - \sum_{i=0}^{j-1} c_i (p_n, p_i)^{0}$$

which equals zero for $j = 0, 1, \ldots, n-2$ and equals (p_n, p_n) for $j = n-1$. So, $c_0 = \cdots = c_{n-2} = 0$ and

$$a_n = c_n = -\frac{(xp_n, p_n)}{(p_n, p_n)}, \quad b_n = c_{n-1} = -\frac{(p_n, p_n)}{(p_{n-1}, p_{n-1})}. \qquad \square$$

Example. Legendre polynomials $P_n(x)$ are orthogonal polynomials defined by inner product $\int_{-1}^{1} P_n(x)P_m(x)dx$. It's left as an exercise to show that the coefficients of the three-term recurrence relation are $a_n = 0$ and $b_n = -n^2/(4n^2 - 1)$ and the normalization $\|P_n\|^2 = 2$. We can write a recursive function to compute the Legendre polynomial

```
function legendre(x,n)
  n==0 && return(one.(x))
  n==1 && return(x)
  x.*legendre(x,n-1) .- (n-1)^2/(4(n-1)^2-1)*legendre(x,n-2)
end
```

◄

10.3 Fourier polynomials

So far, we've concentrated on subspaces constructed using polynomial basis elements. When approximating periodic functions, trigonometric polynomials are better suited as a basis. We can define the Fourier polynomials on $(0, 2\pi)$ using the exponential basis elements $\phi_k(x) = e^{ikx}$ for all integers k, positive and negative. We can define cosine polynomials and sine polynomials analogously by taking the real/even and imaginary/odd contributions.

Theorem 35. *The exponential basis elements $\phi_k(x) = e^{ikx}$ form an orthonormal system with the inner product $(f, g) = \frac{1}{2\pi} \int_0^{2\pi} f(x)\overline{g(x)}\, dx$.*

Proof. We'll show that $(\phi_k, \phi_m) = \delta_{km}$.

$$\left(e^{ikx}, e^{imx}\right) = \frac{1}{2\pi} \int_0^{2\pi} e^{ikx} e^{-imx}\, dx = \frac{1}{2\pi} \int_0^{2\pi} e^{i(k-m)x}\, dx$$

$$= \begin{cases} \dfrac{1}{2\pi} \displaystyle\int_0^{2\pi} 1\, dx = 1, & \text{if } k = m \\[2ex] \dfrac{1}{2\pi} \dfrac{e^{i(k-m)x}}{i(k-m)} \Big|_0^{2\pi} = \dfrac{1}{2\pi}\dfrac{1}{i(k-m)}[1-1] = 0, & \text{if } k \neq m \end{cases}$$

So, $\left(e^{ikm}, e^{imx}\right) = \delta_{km}$.   □

Because the Fourier polynomials are orthogonal, there is a projection operator

$$P_n f = \sum_{k=-n}^{n} c_k e^{ikx} \quad \text{with} \quad c_k = \left(f, e^{ikx}\right) = \frac{1}{2\pi} \int_0^{2\pi} f(x) e^{-ikx}\, dx. \quad (10.2)$$

The projection $P_n f$ is called the truncated Fourier series, the set of coefficients $\{c_k\}$ is called the Fourier coefficients, and the inner product (f, ϕ_k) is called the continuous Fourier transform. In practice, the continuous Fourier transform is approximated numerically by taking a finite set of points on the mesh $x_j = 2\pi j/n$ for $j = 0, 1, \ldots, n-1$ and using the trapezoidal method to approximate the integral. By using the piecewise-constant approximation of f and g at $\{x_j\}$ in theorem 35 we arrive at a simple corollary:

Theorem 36. *The exponential basis elements $\phi_k(x) = e^{ikx}$ are orthonormal in the discrete inner product space[2] $(f, g) = \frac{1}{n} \sum_{j=0}^{n-1} f(x_j)\overline{g(x_j)}$.*

---

[2]The bilinear form $(f, g) = \frac{1}{n} \sum_{j=0}^{n-1} f(x_j)\overline{g(x_j)}$ is technically a *pseudo-inner product*. A pseudo-inner product satisfies all requirements to be an inner product except definiteness (nondegeneracy). The bilinear form $(f, g) = \frac{1}{n} \sum_{j=0}^{n-1} f(x_j)\overline{g(x_j)}$ is degenerate because $(f, g) = 0$ for any $f(x)$ that is zero at all nodes $2\pi j/n$, like $\sin nx$. The corresponding "norm" is a *semi-norm*.

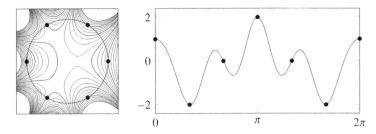

Figure 10.1: A polynomial over the complex plane $\sum_{k=0}^{n-1} c_k z^k$ restricted to the unit circle is a Fourier polynomial $\sum_{k=0}^{n-1} c_k e^{2\pi i k/n}$.

A projection operator in the discrete inner product space, called the *discrete Fourier transform*, can be defined analogously to the continuous Fourier transform (10.2) by taking a discrete inner product at the meshpoints x_j and

$$P_n f(x_j) = \sum_{k=0}^{n-1} c_k e^{ijk} \quad \text{with} \quad c_k = \left(f, e^{ikx}\right) = \frac{1}{n} \sum_{j=0}^{n} f(x_j) e^{-ijk}. \quad (10.3)$$

We call this the *inverse discrete Fourier transform*.

▷ Interpolation with Fourier polynomials

Let's briefly revisit the topic of interpolation discussed in the previous chapter. Suppose that we have equally spaced nodes at $x_j = 2\pi j/n$ with values $f(x_j)$ for $j = 0, 1, \ldots, n-1$. Take the exponential basis functions $\phi_k(x) = e^{ikx}$. Then the interpolating Fourier polynomial satisfies the system of equations

$$f(x_j) = \sum_{j=0}^{n-1} c_k \phi_k(x_j) = \sum_{j=0}^{n-1} c_k e^{i2\pi jk/n} = \sum_{j=0}^{n-1} c_k \omega^{jk} \quad (10.4)$$

for some coefficients c_k. The value $\omega = e^{i2\pi/n}$ is an *nth root of unity*, and we recognize from (10.3) that this transformation is the inverse discrete Fourier transform. So, the coefficients of the Fourier polynomial that interpolates a function f at equally spaced nodes $x_j = 2\pi j/n$ are given by $c_k = (f, \phi_k)$. That is, the solution to the interpolation problem using uniform mesh is the same as the solution to the best approximation problem using the discrete inner product.

We can also establish a connection between Fourier polynomials and algebraic polynomials. Suppose that we want to find the algebraic polynomial interpolant

$$p(z) = c_0 + c_1 z + c_2 z^2 + \cdots + c_{n-1} z^{n-1}$$

passing through the nodes $\{(z_0, y_0), (z_1, y_1), \ldots, (z_{n-1}, y_{n-1})\}$ in $\mathbb{C} \times \mathbb{C}$. In the canonical basis $\{1, z, \ldots, z^{n-1}\}$, we must solve the Vandermonde system

$y_j = \sum_{k=0}^{n-1} c_k z^k$ to get the coefficients of the polynomial c_k. Now, restrict the nodes to equally spaced points around the unit circle—i.e., take $z_k = \omega^k = e^{i2\pi k/n}$, running counterclockwise starting with $z_0 = 1$. In this case, we have (10.4), which means that an algebraic polynomial in the complex plane is a Fourier polynomial on the unit circle. See the figure on the preceding page.

▷ **Approximation error**

Let's finally examine the behavior of the Fourier coefficients for the continuous inner product

$$c_k = \left(f, e^{ikx} \right) = \frac{1}{2\pi} \int_0^{2\pi} f(x) e^{-ikx} \, dx,$$

where $f(x)$ is periodic. The discrete inner product follows analogously. Note that c_0 is simply the mean value of $f(x)$ over $(0, 2\pi)$. Also, note that if $f(x)$ is differentiable, then by integration by parts

$$\left(f', e^{ikx} \right) = \frac{1}{2\pi} \int_0^{2\pi} f'(x) e^{-ikx} \, dx = \frac{ik}{2\pi} \int_0^{2\pi} f(x) e^{-ikx} \, dx = ik c_k$$

because $f(x)$ is periodic. In general, we have $\left(f^{(p)}, e^{ikx} \right) = (ik)^p c_k$ if the function $f(x)$ is sufficiently smooth. A *Sobolev space* is the space of square-integrable functions whose derivatives are also square-integrable functions. Let $H^p(0, 2\pi)$ denote the Sobolev space of periodic functions whose zeroth through pth derivatives are also square-integrable. We can think of Sobolev space as a refinement of the space of C^p-differentiable functions.

Theorem 37. *If $f \in H^p(0, 2\pi)$, then its Fourier coefficients $|c_k| = o(k^{-p-1/2})$ and the L^2-error of its truncated Fourier series is $o(n^{-p})$.*

Proof. By Parseval's theorem,

$$\frac{1}{2\pi} \int_0^{2\pi} |f^{(p)}(x)|^2 \, dx = \sum_{k=1}^{\infty} |k^p c_k|^2.$$

The series to converges only if $|k^p c_k|^2 = o(k^{-1})$ as $k \to \infty$. In other words, $|c_k| = o(k^{-p-1/2})$. We'll use this bound to compute the error in the truncated Fourier series $P_n f$. We have

$$\| f - P_n f \|^2 = \| P_\infty f - P_n f \|^2 = \sum_{k > |n|} |c_k|^2 = \sum_{k > |n|} o(k^{-2p-1}) = o(n^{-2p}).$$

So the error is $o(n^{-p})$.   □

Note that if f is smooth (with infinitely many continuous derivatives), then the error is $o(n^{-p})$ for all integers p. The convergence of the Fourier series will be faster than any polynomial order. In other words, the Fourier series is exponentially convergent.

10.4 Chebyshev polynomials

Chebyshev polynomials are close cousins to Fourier polynomials. While Fourier polynomials are used to approximate periodic functions, Chebyshev polynomials are used to approximate functions with prescribed endpoints. Fourier polynomials are simply polynomials $\sum_{k=0}^{n} c_k z^k$ constrained to the unit circle $z = e^{i\theta}$ in the complex plane. If we take the real part of such a polynomial, we have a function that resides between $[-1, 1]$ along the real axis. Take

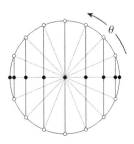

$$x = \operatorname{Re} z = \tfrac{1}{2}(z + z^{-1}) = \cos\theta.$$

For a general kth order monomial z^k, we can define the Chebyshev polynomial

$$T_k(x) = \operatorname{Re} z^k = \tfrac{1}{2}(z^k + z^{-k}) = \cos k\theta.$$

Then a polynomial approximant has the representation

$$p_n(x) = \sum_{k=0}^{n} a_k T_k(x) = \sum_{k=0}^{n} a_k \cos k\theta.$$

The derivative of a Chebyshev polynomial is

$$T'_k(x) = -k \sin k\theta \frac{d\theta}{dx} = \frac{k \sin k\theta}{\sin\theta} = \frac{k \sin k\theta}{\sqrt{1 - x^2}}. \tag{10.5}$$

We use L'Hopital's rule to define the derivative $T'_k(\pm 1) = (\pm 1)^{k+1} k^2$ at the endpoints. Higher-order derivatives can be defined similarly. For example,

$$T''_k(x) = -\frac{k^2 \cos k\theta}{1 - x^2} + \frac{kx \sin k\theta}{(1 - x^2)^{3/2}} \tag{10.6}$$

with $T''_k(\pm 1) = (\pm 1)^{k+1} \tfrac{1}{3}(k^4 - k^2)$. In practice, to compute the Chebyshev derivatives (10.5) or (10.6), we can use discrete cosine and discrete sine transforms. Or, we can extend a function to a periodic domain using its reflection and then take the real components of a discrete Fourier transform. We can efficiently do all of this using a fast Fourier transform.

Another way to differentiate a Chebyshev polynomial is by building a full Chebyshev differentiation matrix with the Lagrange formulation of the polynomials using the Chebyshev extremum points. The Chebyshev extremum points $x_j \in [-1, 1]$ of $T_k(x)$ correspond to equally spaced points on the unit semicircle $\theta_j \in [0, \pi]$ where $\cos k\theta_j = \pm 1$. Computation using a full differentiation matrix is much less efficient than computation using a fast Fourier transform. But, such an approach has the benefit of being easy to manipulate and explore. We'll develop the Chebyshev differentiation matrix over the remainder of this section. See Trefethen's book *Approximation Theory and Approximation Practice* for an in-depth discussion.[3]

In the previous chapter, we used Lagrange basis functions to fit a polynomial through a set of points. A polynomial $p_n(x)$ passing through the points (x_0, y_0), $(x_1, y_1), \ldots, (x_n, y_n)$ can be expressed using a Lagrange polynomial basis

$$p_n(x) = \sum_{i=0}^{n} y_i \ell_i(x_j) \quad \text{with} \quad \ell_i(x) = \prod_{\substack{k=0 \\ k \neq i}}^{n} \frac{x - x_k}{x_i - x_k}.$$

In other words, the vectors $\mathbf{x} = (x_0, x_1, \ldots, x_n)$ and $\mathbf{y} = (y_0, y_1, \ldots, y_n)$ uniquely define the polynomial. At these points $\ell_i(x_j) = \delta_{ij}$, i.e., $\ell_i(x_j)$ is the identity operator. Let's derive the differentiation operator $\mathbf{D}$ such that $\mathbf{y}' = \mathbf{D}\mathbf{y}$, where $\mathbf{y}' = (y_0', y_1', \ldots, y_n')$ are the values of the derivative p_n' at points $\mathbf{x}$.

Start with

$$p_n'(x) = \sum_{k=0}^{n} y_k \ell_k'(x) = \sum_{k=0}^{n} y_k' \ell_k(x).$$

By taking the logarithmic derivative of $\ell_i(x)$, we have

$$\ell_i'(x) = \ell_i(x) \cdot [\log \ell_i(x)]' = \ell_i(x) \sum_{\substack{k=0 \\ k \neq i}}^{n} \frac{1}{x - x_k},$$

where $x_k = \cos k\pi/n$ are Chebyshev extremum points. When $i \neq j$,

$$d_{ij} = \ell_i'(x_j) = \left(\prod_{\substack{k=0 \\ k \neq i}}^{n} \frac{x_j - x_k}{x_i - x_k} \right) \left(\sum_{\substack{k=0 \\ k \neq i}}^{n} \frac{1}{x_i - x_k} \right) = \frac{1}{x_i - x_j} \prod_{\substack{k=0 \\ k \neq i, j}}^{n} \frac{x_j - x_k}{x_i - x_k}.$$

We'll calculate the numerator—the denominator is almost the same:

$$\prod_{\substack{k=0 \\ k \neq i, j}}^{n} (x - x_k) = \frac{\prod_{k=0}^{n}(x - x_k)}{(x - x_i)(x - x_j)}$$

$$= \frac{(x^2 - 1)\prod_{k=1}^{n-1}(x - x_k)}{(x - x_i)(x - x_j)}$$

$$= \frac{(x^2 - 1)T_n'(x)}{(x - x_i)(x - x_j)2^{n-1}}.$$

---

[3]The book is available at http://www.chebfun.org/ATAP as a set of m-files consisting of LaTeX markup and Matlab code. A pdf can be generated from them using the `publish` command in Matlab.

When x_j is an interior Chebyshev point, we take the limit $x \to x_j$ and use (10.6) to get the expression

$$\prod_{\substack{k=0 \\ k \neq i,j}}^{n} (x_j - x_k) = \frac{(x_j^2 - 1)T_n''(x_j)}{2^{n-1}(x_j - x_i)} = \frac{n^2(-1)^{j-1}}{2^{n-1}(x_j - x_i)}.$$

At endpoints $x_0 = 1$ and $x_n = -1$, we have

$$\prod_{\substack{k=0 \\ k \neq i,j}}^{n} (x_j - x_k) = \frac{(x_j^2 - 1)T_n'(x_j)}{(x_j - x_i)(x_j \pm 1)2^{n-1}} = \frac{(\pm 2)T_n'(\pm 1)}{(x_j - x_i)2^{n-1}} = \frac{(\pm 1)^j n^2}{2^{n-2}(x_j - x_i)}.$$

Hence, we can define

$$d_{ij} = \ell_i'(x_j) = \frac{2^{\delta_{i0}+\delta_{in}}(-1)^{i-j}}{2^{\delta_{j0}+\delta_{jn}}\alpha_{ij}}$$

where $\alpha_{ij} = (x_i - x_j + \delta_{ij})$. We haven't yet properly defined the diagonal elements d_{ii}, so let's make that fix. Because the derivative of a constant function is zero, i.e., $\sum_{k=0}^{n} 1 \cdot d_{ik} = 0$, it follows that

$$d_{ii} = -\sum_{\substack{k=0 \\ k \neq i}}^{n} d_{ik}.$$

So we have the following function to compute the Chebyshev differentiation matrix and corresponding Chebyshev points

```
function chebdiff(n)
  x = -cos.(LinRange(0,π,n))
  c = [2;ones(n-2);2].*(-1).^(0:n-1)
  D = c./c'./(x .- x' + I)
  D - Diagonal([sum(D,dims=2)...]), x
end
```

The Chebyshev differentiation matrix is an $n \times n$ matrix with rank $n - 1$. It is also a nilpotent matrix of index n, meaning that $\mathbf{D}^n = \mathbf{0}$. Nilpotency of the differentiation matrix is the same as saying that if we take the nth derivative of a polynomial of degree less than n, we are left with zero.

Example. Let's use the Chebyshev differentiation matrix to compute the derivative of $u(x) = e^{-4x^2}$. If $\mathbf{u}$ is a vector of values at Chebyshev points, then $\mathbf{Du}$ is the derivative of $\mathbf{u}$.

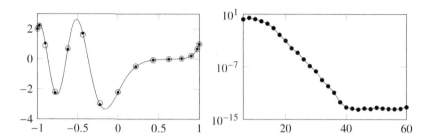

Figure 10.2: Left: Numerical solution ($\circ$) and exact solution ($\rightarrow$) to the Airy equation (10.7). Right: ℓ^∞-error as a function of the number of Chebyshev points.

```
n = 15
D,x = chebdiff(n)
u = exp.(-4x.^2)
plot(x,D*u,marker=:o)
```

We can get higher-order derivatives by composing operators. For example, $\mathbf{D}^2\mathbf{u}$ is the second derivative of $u(x)$. We can compute the antiderivative of $u(x)$ by taking $\mathbf{D}^{-1}\mathbf{u}$ with a constraint. For example, if $u(-1) = 2$, then the antiderivative of $u(x)$ is

```
B = zeros(1,n); B[1] = 1
plot(x,[B;D]\[2;u],marker=:o)
```

We can also use the Chebyshev differentiation matrix to solve a boundary value problem. Take the Airy equation

$$y'' - 256xy = 0 \quad \text{with} \quad y(-1) = 2 \quad \text{and} \quad y(1) = 1. \tag{10.7}$$

We'll prescribe two boundary conditions and then solve the system:

```
n = 15; k² = 256
D,x = chebdiff(n)
L = (D^2 - k²*Diagonal(x))
L[[1,n],:] .= 0; L[1,1] = L[n,n] = 1
y = L\[2;zeros(n-2);1]
plot(x,y,marker=:o)
```

How accurate is the solution? Figure 10.2 above shows a semi-log plot of the ℓ^∞-error as a function of the number of nodes. The solution is already quite good with just 15 points. After that, the solution gains one digit of accuracy for every two points added. The error is $O(10^{-n/2})$. Such a convergence rate is often said to be exponential, geometric, or spectral. With about 40 points, we get a solution close to machine precision.   ◄

These simple examples might spark a brilliant idea. We can represent functions using high-degree polynomials approximations, such as Chebyshev polynomials, to machine precision. Then function manipulation is equivalent to performing operations on the polynomials. In the early 2000s, mathematicians Zachary Battles and Nick Trefethen applied this idea with the vision of creating computational systems that would "feel symbolic but run at the speed of numerics," creating the open-source Matlab suite Chebfun. Numerical operators, such as sum and diff, are overloaded in Chebfun with operators using Chebyshev polynomial approximations, such as integration (using Clenshaw–Curtis quadrature) and differentiation. The backslash operator is overloaded to solve differential equations. Zeros are computed using a "colleague" matrix, the analog to the companion matrix for Chebyshev polynomial roots.[4]

♣ The ApproxFun.jl package includes methods for manipulating functions in Chebyshev and Fourier spaces, similar to the Matlab Chebfun package.

10.5   Wavelets

Wavelets provide yet another orthogonal system for approximating functions. As the "wave" in the word wavelet might suggest, wavelets are oscillatory, and these oscillations balance each other out. Mathematically, their zeroth moments vanish. And as the "let" in the word wavelet might suggest, wavelets are small (like a piglet or a droplet) and localized in space or time. Mathematically, they have finite support or at least quickly decay.

Wavelets are similar to Fourier polynomials, sharing many of the same features and applications, and Fourier polynomials themselves might be viewed as a special case of wavelets. A principal difference is that while Fourier polynomials are only localized in frequency, wavelets are localized in both space and frequency. While Fourier polynomials achieve orthogonality by scaling basis functions, wavelets are orthogonal through both scaling and translation. And while there is just one family of Fourier polynomial, there are perhaps hundreds of families of wavelets.[5] This section provides a condensed introduction to wavelets. Ingrid Daubechies' "Ten Lectures on Wavelets," Adhemar Bultheel's "Learning to Swim in a Sea of Wavelets," and Gilbert Strang's "Wavelets and

---

[4]The matrix analog to the companion matrix for finding the roots of a general orthogonal polynomial is called a "comrade" matrix.

[5]Mathematician Laurent Duval has a compendium of over one hundred "starlets," or wavelets ending in "let."

Dilation Equations: A Brief Introduction" are all approachable primers of this important area of numerical mathematics.

The origins of wavelet theory date back to 1909, when mathematician Alfréd Haar proposed a simple system of orthogonal functions, now called Haar wavelets, in his doctoral dissertation. It took another 75 years for wavelets to emerge in their modern form and be named.[6] In the late 1980s, mathematicians Jean Morlet, Ingrid Daubechies, Stéphane Mallat, and Yves Meyer, motivated by problems in signals processing, developed a systematic theory of multiresolution or multiscale approximation.[7]

What is multiscale or multiresolution approximation intuitively? Right now, I'm looking across the room at a photograph of my beautiful wife. At a distance, I can tell that it is of a woman in a bright city at night. If I walk up to it, I can make out features of her face and smile, enough to confirm that this woman is indeed my wife. And if I examine it even more closely, I see minute details like the glint of a diamond earring I gave her on our wedding day. Each of these successive resolutions adds another layer of detail to the story in the photo. We can similarly find multiscales in music—a score, a motif, a measure, a note—and literature—a novel, a chapter, a paragraph, a sentence, a word.

Mathematically, multiresolution analysis provides a means of breaking up a function into the sum of approximations and details. Consider the following process of multiresolution approximation using a Haar wavelet. Start with the values:

$$1 \quad 3 \quad -3 \quad -1 \quad 5 \quad 9 \quad 8 \quad 10 \quad 23 \quad 25 \quad 21 \quad 19 \quad 16 \quad 16 \quad 19 \quad 21$$

First combine them pairwise, recording the averages and the differences:

$$
\begin{array}{cccccccc}
1,3 & -3,-1 & 5,9 & 8,10 & 23,25 & 21,19 & 16,16 & 19,21 \\
2 \mp 1 & -2 \mp 1 & 7 \mp 2 & 9 \mp 1 & 24 \mp 1 & 20 \mp -1 & 16 \mp 0 & 20 \mp 1
\end{array}
$$

Compute the pairwise averages and differences again:

$$
\begin{array}{cccc}
2,-2 & 7,9 & 24,20 & 16,20 \\
0 \mp -2 & 8 \mp 1 & 22 \mp -2 & 18 \mp 2
\end{array}
$$

And again:

$$
\begin{array}{cc}
0,8 & 22,18 \\
4 \mp 4 & 20 \mp -2
\end{array}
$$

And one more time:

$$
\begin{array}{c}
4,20 \\
12 \mp 8
\end{array}
$$

---

[6] Wavelets were originally called *ondelettes* by the French pioneers Morlet and Grossman after a term frequently used in geophysics for an oscillating localized function.

[7] Electrical engineers had already developed more elaborate algorithms such as the subband decomposition algorithm before the rigorous function-analytic framework caught up.

The value 12 is the average of all the initial numbers. By adding the differences to it, we can reconstruct the original numbers.

$$\{12\} \mp \{8\} \mp \{4, -2\} \mp \{-2, 1, -2, 2\} \mp \{1, 1, 2, 1, 1, -1, 0, 1\}$$

For example, $12 - 8 - 4 - (-2) - 1 = 1$ and $12 - 8 - 4 - (-2) + 1 = 3$ give the first two numbers in the original sequence.

Multiresolution implies that basis functions act on multiple scales and are even self-similar in scale. Fourier polynomial bases $w_n(x) = e^{inx}$ are self-similar in scale. We can construct every one of them by scaling the function $w(x) = e^{ix}$ so that $w_n(x) = w(nx)$. But wavelets ought to also be compactly or almost compactly supported, and Fourier polynomials definitely do not have compact support. We can't construct all functions using merely a combination of scaled copies of a compactly supported function—we also need translations of this function. So, we want basis functions that are also self-similar in space. And, we'll want all of those basis functions to be orthogonal to their translates. Finding a class of functions that possesses all of these properties isn't easy. Before 1985, the Haar wavelet was the only orthogonal wavelet that people knew, and until Yves Meyer and Jan Olov Strömberg independently constructed a second orthogonal wavelet, many researchers believed that the Haar wavelet was the only one.

▷ Scaling function

Let's start with a formal definition and then make it actionable. Take the space of square-integrable functions L^2. A *multiresolution approximation* is a sequence of subspaces $\emptyset \subset \cdots \subset V_{-1} \subset V_0 \subset V_1 \subset \cdots \subset L^2$ such that

1. $f(x) \in V_n$ if and only if $f(2x) \in V_{n+1}$ (dilation)
2. $f(x) \in V_n$ if and only if $f(x - 2^{-n}k) \in V_n$ for integer k (translation)
3. $\bigcup V_n$ is dense in L^2

From this definition, there should exist a basis function $\phi(x) \in V_0$, called the *scaling function* or *father wavelet*. Let's denote the translated copy of the father wavelet as $\phi_{0,k}(x) = \phi(x - k)$ for integer k. Then we can express any function $f \in V_0$ as $f(x) = \sum_{k=-\infty}^{\infty} a_k \phi_{0,k}(x)$ for some coefficients a_k. In particular, we can write the scaled function $\phi(x/2) \in V_{-1} \subset V_0$ as $\phi(x/2) = \sum_{k=-\infty}^{\infty} c_k \phi(x - k)$ for some c_k, and hence the father wavelet satisfies a dilation equation:

$$\phi(x) = \sum_{k=-\infty}^{\infty} c_k \phi(2x - k). \tag{10.8}$$

In general, we'll only consider scaling functions with compact support, and therefore the sum is effectively only over finite k. If we integrate both sides of the dilation equation, then

$$\int_{-\infty}^{\infty} \phi(x)\, dx = \int_{-\infty}^{\infty} \sum_{k=-\infty}^{\infty} c_k \phi(2x - k)\, dx = \sum_{k=-\infty}^{\infty} c_k \int_{-\infty}^{\infty} \tfrac{1}{2}\phi(s)\, ds,$$

where we've made the change of variable $s = 2x - k$. If $\int_{-\infty}^{\infty} \phi(x)\, dx \neq 0$, then we have the condition

$$\sum_{k=-\infty}^{\infty} c_k = 2. \tag{10.9}$$

Example. Let's find solutions to the dilation equation (10.8) that satisfy the constraint (10.9). One approach is to use splines. When $c_0 = 2$ and all other c_k are zero, the solution is a delta function $\phi(x) = \delta(x)$. When $c_0 = c_1 = 1$ and $c_k = 0$ otherwise, the solution is the rectangle function—$\phi(x) = 1$ if $x \in [0, 1]$ and $\phi(x) = 0$ otherwise. This function is the father wavelet of the Haar wavelets. If we set $\{c_0, c_1, c_2\} = \{\tfrac{1}{2}, 1, \tfrac{1}{2}\}$, we get a triangular function as the father wavelet. With coefficients $\{\tfrac{1}{4}, \tfrac{3}{4}, \tfrac{3}{4}, \tfrac{1}{4}\}$, we get the quadratic B-spline. And with $\{\tfrac{1}{8}, \tfrac{1}{2}, \tfrac{3}{4}, \tfrac{1}{2}, \tfrac{1}{8}\}$, we have the cubic B-spline. All of these can be demonstrated by construction. For example, the scaled cubic B-spline (depicted with a dotted line) is the sum of the five translated cubic B-splines:

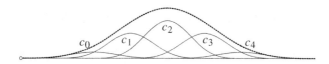

Other than the B_0 Haar wavelet, B-spline wavelets are not orthogonal, limiting their usefulness. ◀

Let's consider scaling functions that are shift-orthonormal:

$$\int_{-\infty}^{\infty} \phi(x)\phi(x - m)\, dx = \delta_{0m}$$

for all integers m. What additional constraints do we need to put on the coefficients c_k? To answer this question, we'll need to take a short detour to examine a few properties of the scaling function. The quickest route is through Fourier space. If we take the Fourier transform of the scaling function

$$\hat{\phi}(\xi) = \frac{1}{2\pi} \int_{-\infty}^{\infty} \phi(x) e^{-ix\xi}\, dx,$$

then the dilation equation is

$$\hat{\phi}(\xi) = \sum_{k=-\infty}^{\infty} \frac{c_k}{2\pi} \int_{-\infty}^{\infty} \phi(2x - k) e^{-ix\xi} \, dx$$

$$= \hat{H}(\tfrac{1}{2}\xi) \cdot \frac{1}{2\pi} \int_{-\infty}^{\infty} \phi(y) e^{-iy\xi/2} \, dy = \hat{H}(\tfrac{1}{2}\xi)\hat{\phi}(\tfrac{1}{2}\xi),$$

where the scaled discrete Fourier transform

$$\hat{H}(\xi) = \frac{1}{2} \sum_{k=-\infty}^{\infty} c_k e^{-ik\xi}. \tag{10.10}$$

If we take $\int_{-\infty}^{\infty} \phi(x) \, d(x) = 1$, then $\hat{\phi}(0) \neq 0$ and it follows that $\hat{H}(0) = 1$. Hence, we must have $\sum_{k=-\infty}^{\infty} c_k = 2$.

Theorem 38. $\sum_{k=-\infty}^{\infty} |\hat{\phi}(\xi + 2\pi k)|^2 = (2\pi)^{-1}$.

Proof. Note that for any function, the autocorrelation

$$\int_{-\infty}^{\infty} \phi(x)\phi(x - m) \, dx = \int_{-\infty}^{\infty} \phi(x) \int_{-\infty}^{\infty} \hat{\phi}(\xi) e^{+i(x-m)\xi} \, d\xi \, dx$$

$$= \int_{-\infty}^{\infty} \hat{\phi}(\xi) e^{-im\xi} \int_{-\infty}^{\infty} \phi(x) e^{+ix\xi} \, dx \, d\xi$$

$$= \int_{-\infty}^{\infty} |\hat{\phi}(\xi)|^2 e^{-im\xi} \, d\xi.$$

Using the orthogonality of the scaling function

$$\int_0^{2\pi} \frac{1}{2\pi} e^{-im\xi} \, d\xi = \delta_{0m} = \int_{-\infty}^{\infty} \phi(x)\phi(x - m) \, dx$$

$$= \int_{-\infty}^{\infty} |\hat{\phi}(\xi)|^2 e^{-im\xi} \, d\xi$$

$$= \int_0^{2\pi} \sum_{k=-\infty}^{\infty} |\hat{\phi}(\xi + 2\pi k)|^2 e^{-im\xi} \, d\xi. \qquad \square$$

Corollary 39. $|\hat{H}(\xi)|^2 + |\hat{H}(\xi + \pi)|^2 = 1$.

Proof. Use the dilation equation $\hat{\phi}(2\xi) = \hat{H}(\xi)\hat{\phi}(\xi)$ with the result from the previous theorem:

$$\frac{1}{2\pi} = \sum_{k=-\infty}^{\infty} |\hat{\phi}(2\xi + 2k\pi)|^2 = \sum_{k=-\infty}^{\infty} |\hat{H}(\xi + k\pi)|^2 |\hat{\phi}(\xi + k\pi)|^2$$

$$= |\hat{H}(\xi)|^2 \sum_{k=-\infty}^{\infty} |\hat{\phi}(\xi + 2k\pi)|^2 + |\hat{H}(\xi + \pi)|^2 \sum_{k=-\infty}^{\infty} |\hat{\phi}(\xi + 2k\pi + \pi)|^2.$$

The last line results from splitting the sum over even and odd values of k and applying the 2π-periodicity of $\hat{H}(\xi)$.   □

Corollary 40. *The following conditions on the dilation equation are necessary for an orthogonal scaling function:*

$$\sum_{k=-\infty}^{\infty} (-1)^n c_k = 0, \quad \sum_{k=-\infty}^{\infty} c_k^2 = 2, \quad and \quad \sum_{k=-\infty}^{\infty} c_k c_{k-2m} = 0. \quad (10.11)$$

Proof. Because $\hat{H}(0) = 1$, it follows that $|\hat{H}(\pi)|^2 = 1 - |\hat{H}(0)|^2 = 0$, and the first condition follows directly. To show the second two conditions, expand $|\hat{H}(\xi)|^2 + |\hat{H}(\xi + \pi)|^2 = 1$ using the definitions of $\hat{H}(\xi)$:

$$\frac{1}{4} \sum_{j=-\infty}^{\infty} \sum_{k=-\infty}^{\infty} c_k c_j e^{-i(k-j)\xi} + \frac{1}{4} \sum_{j=-\infty}^{\infty} \sum_{k=-\infty}^{\infty} c_k c_j (-1)^{k-j} e^{-i(k-j)\xi} = 1.$$

The terms for which $k - j$ is odd cancel, leaving us with

$$\frac{1}{2} \sum_{m=-\infty}^{\infty} \sum_{k=-\infty}^{\infty} c_k c_{k-2m} e^{-im\xi} = 1.$$

This expression is true for all ξ, so it follows that $\sum_{k=-\infty}^{\infty} c_k c_{k-2m} = 2\delta_{0m}$.   □

Example. The Haar scaling functions are orthonormal with $c_0 = 1$ and $c_1 = 1$. But they are piecewise constant. Let's construct a higher-order orthogonal wavelet by determining values c_0, c_1, c_2, and c_3 that satisfy the constraints (10.11):

$$c_0^2 + c_1^2 + c_2^2 + c_3^2 = 2$$
$$c_2 c_0 + c_3 c_1 = 0$$
$$c_0 - c_1 + c_2 - c_3 = 0$$

We'll need to add another constraint for a unique solution. Note that (10.9) can be derived from algebraic manipulation of (10.11), so it will not provide any additional constraint on the coefficients. For fast decaying wavelets, we want as many moments $\int_{-\infty}^{\infty} x^p \psi(x)\, dx$ of the wavelet function $\psi(x)$ discussed in the next section to vanish as possible. To approximate smooth functions with error $O(h^{-p})$, then $\hat{H}(\xi)$ must have zeros of order p at $\xi = \pi$. (See Strang [1989].) So, we'll enforce the additional constraint:

$$0c_0 - 1c_1 + 2c_2 - 3c_3 = 0.$$

The solution to this system of equations is

$$\{c_0, c_1, c_2, c_3\} = \left\{ \tfrac{1}{4}\left(1 + \sqrt{3}\right), \tfrac{1}{4}\left(3 + \sqrt{3}\right), \tfrac{1}{4}\left(3 - \sqrt{3}\right), \tfrac{1}{4}\left(1 - \sqrt{3}\right) \right\}.$$

The corresponding wavelet is called D_4 from the work of Ingrid Daubechies. The D_2 Daubechies wavelet is the Haar wavelet.   ◄

In practice, we don't ever need to construct the scaling functions explicitly, but doing so can help us understand them better. One way to construct the scaling functions $\phi(x)$ is by using the dilation equation $\phi(x) = \sum_{k=-\infty}^{\infty} c_k \phi(2x - k)$ as a fixed-point method starting with $\phi(x)$ initially equal to some guess function, e.g., the rectangle function, and iterating until the method converges. A faster approach is by using recursion. If we know the values of $\phi(x)$ at integer values of x, then we can use the dilation equation to compute $\phi(x)$ at half-integer values of x. Knowing these values, we use the dilation equation to compute the values at quarter-integer values, eighth-integer values, and so on to get $\phi(x)$ at dyadic rational values $x = i/2^j$. Here's a naïve implementation:

```
using OffsetArrays
function scaling(c,ϕₖ,n)
  m = length(c)-1; ℓ = 2^n
  ϕ = OffsetVector(zeros(3*m*ℓ),-m*ℓ)
  k = (0:m)*ℓ
  ϕ[k] = ϕₖ
  for j = 1:n
    for i = 1:m*2^(j-1)
      x = (2i-1)*2^(n-j)
      ϕ[x] = c · ϕ[2x .- k]
    end
  end
  ((0:m*ℓ-1)/ℓ, ϕ[0:m*ℓ-1])
end
```

The OffsetArrays.jl package allows us to simplify notation by starting the scaling function array at $x = 0$. The domain has been padded on the left and right with zeros to simplify implementation.

Let's compute the scaling function for D_4. We'll need to first determine the values $\phi(0), \phi(1), \phi(2), \phi(3)$. The D_4 scaling function is identically zero except over the interval $[0, 3]$, so $\phi(0) = \phi(3) = 0$. From the dilation equation, we then have

$$\phi(1) = c_0\phi(2) + c_1\phi(1)$$
$$\phi(2) = c_2\phi(2) + c_3\phi(1),$$

which says that $(\phi(1), \phi(2))$ is an eigenvector of the matrix with elements (c_1, c_0, c_3, c_2). The eigenvectors of this matrix are $(-1, 1)$ and $(1 + \sqrt{3}, 1 - \sqrt{3})$. Which one do we choose? Here, we'll state a property without proof—the scaling functions form a partition of unity, i.e., the sum of any scaling function taken at integer values equals one: $\sum_{k=-\infty}^{\infty} \phi(k) = 1$. So $(-1, 1)$ cannot be the

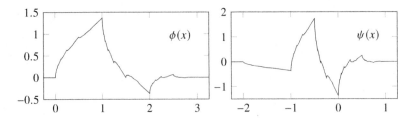

Figure 10.3: Daubechies D_4 scaling function ϕ and wavelet function ψ.

right choice. Instead, we take $\phi(1) = \frac{1}{2}(1 + \sqrt{3})$ and $\phi(2) = \frac{1}{2}(1 - \sqrt{3})$. The Daubechies D_4 scaling function is plotted in the figure above using

```
c = [1+√3, 3+√3, 3-√3, 1-√3]/4
z = [0, 1+√3, 1-√3, 0]/2
(x,ϕ) = scaling(c, z, 8)
plot(x,ϕ)
```

We can define normalized bases functions in V_n as

$$\phi_{nk}(x) = 2^{n/2}\phi(2^n x - k).$$

Furthermore, we can define an orthogonal projection of a function $f \in L^2$:

$$P_n f = \sum_{k=-\infty}^{\infty} (f, \phi_{nk})\phi_{nk} = \sum_{k=-\infty}^{\infty} a_{nk}\phi_{nk} \qquad (10.12)$$

for some coefficients $a_{nk} = (f, \phi_{nk})$. The projection into V_n acts to smooth the data by filtering out finer details. In the following figure, the function $f(x) = \sin \pi x$ is projected into the subspaces generated using Haar wavelets:

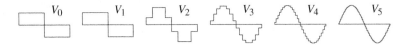

▷ **Wavelet function**

Notice that the scaling functions generate a sequence of nested subspaces $V_0 \subset V_1 \subset V_2 \subset \cdots \subset L^2$. Let W_n be the orthogonal complement of V_n in V_{n+1}. That is, let $V_{n+1} = V_n \oplus W_n$. Then, $V_{n+1} = V_0 \oplus W_0 \oplus W_1 \oplus \cdots \oplus W_n$. For any function $f_{n+1} \in V_n$, we can make the decomposition $f_{n+1} = f_n + g_n$ where $f_n \in V_n$ and $g_n \in W_n$. And continuing, $f_{n+1} = g_n + g_{n-1} + \cdots + g_0 + f_0$ for $f_j \in V_j$ and $g_j \in W_j$. Were we to continue, we would have $V_{n+1} = \bigoplus_{k=-\infty}^{n} W_k$.

$$V_0 \qquad W_0 \qquad W_1 \qquad W_2 \qquad W_3 \qquad W_4$$

We can recursively decompose the V_{n+1}-projection of any function $f \in L^2$ into orthogonal components in V_n and W_n by using orthogonal projection operators

$$P_{n+1} f = P_n f + Q_n f,$$

where $P_n f$ is given by (10.12) and

$$Q_n f = \sum_{k=-\infty}^{\infty} (f, \psi_{nk}) \psi_{nk} = \sum_{k=-\infty}^{\infty} d_{nk} \psi_{nk}$$

for $d_{nk} = (f, \psi_{nk})$ and basis elements $\psi_{nk} \in W_n$:

$$\psi_{nk}(x) = 2^{n/2} \psi(2^n x - k).$$

Specifically, we have $Q_0 f = (P_1 - P_0) f$. From the dilation equation (10.8), we can derive a function $\psi(x) \in W_0$, called the *wavelet function* or *mother wavelet*:

$$\psi(x) = \sum_{k=-\infty}^{\infty} (-1)^k c_{1-k} \phi(2x - k). \tag{10.13}$$

Notice how the mother wavelet differs structurally from the father wavelet—alternating the signs the coefficients, reversing the order of the terms, and shifting them left along the x-axis. Also, unlike the father wavelet, which integrates to one, the mother wavelet integrates to zero. Using this definition, we can generate the wavelet function (in the dotted line below) of the cubic B-spline scaling function on page 266:

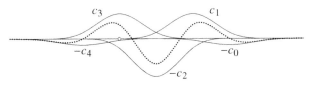

Using the scaling function ϕ from the code on page 269, we can compute the wavelet function ψ with

```
ψ = zero(φ); n = length(c)-1; ℓ = length(ψ)÷2n
for k∈0:n
  ψ[(k*ℓ+1):(k+n)*ℓ] += (-1)^k*c[n-k+1]*φ[1:2:end]
end
```

which we can use to compute the Daubechies D_4 wavelet function in the figure on the preceding page.

▷ **Discrete wavelet transform**

Using the self-similar structure of wavelets, we can develop a recursive formulation for the discrete wavelet transform (DWT). Using the dilation equation (10.8), we have

$$\phi_{nk}(x) = 2^{n/2} \sum_{i=-\infty}^{\infty} c_i \phi(2^n x - 2^n k - i) = \frac{1}{\sqrt{2}} \sum_{j=-\infty}^{\infty} c_{j-2k} \phi_{n+1,j}(x),$$

and similarly, from (10.13) we have

$$\psi_{nk}(x) = \frac{1}{\sqrt{2}} \sum_{j=-\infty}^{\infty} (-1)^{1-j} c_{1-j+2k} \phi_{n+1,j}(x).$$

From these,

$$\left(\phi_{ni}, \phi_{n+1,j}\right) = \frac{1}{\sqrt{2}} c_{i-2j} \quad \text{and} \quad \left(\psi_{ni}, \phi_{n+1,j}\right) = \frac{(-1)^{1-i}}{\sqrt{2}} c_{1-i+2j}.$$

So

$$\begin{aligned}
a_{n+1,k} = \left(f, \phi_{n+1,k}\right) &= \left(P_{n+1}\, f, \phi_{n+1,k}\right) = \left(P_n\, f + Q_n\, f, \phi_{n+1,k}\right) \\
&= \left(P_n\, f, \phi_{n+1,k}\right) + \left(Q_n\, f, \phi_{n+1,k}\right) \\
&= \left(\sum_{i=-\infty}^{\infty} a_{ni} \phi_{ni}, \phi_{n+1,k}\right) + \left(\sum_{i=-\infty}^{\infty} a_{ni} \psi_{ni}, \phi_{n+1,k}\right) \\
&= \frac{1}{\sqrt{2}} \sum_{i=-\infty}^{\infty} c_{k-2i} a_{ni} + \frac{1}{\sqrt{2}} \sum_{i=-\infty}^{\infty} (-1)^{1-k+2i} c_{1-k+2i} d_{ni}.
\end{aligned} \tag{10.14}$$

Similarly, we can write

$$d_{n+1,k} = \frac{1}{\sqrt{2}} \sum_{i=-\infty}^{\infty} c_{k-2i} a_{ni} - \frac{1}{\sqrt{2}} \sum_{i=-\infty}^{\infty} (-1)^{1-k+2i} c_{1-k+2i} d_{ni}.$$

These two expressions allow us to recursively reconstruct a function from its wavelet components. In practice, the algorithm can be computed recursively much like a fast Fourier transform. Reversing these steps allows us to deconstruct a function into its wavelet components.

We can represent (10.14) in matrix notation as

$$\mathbf{a}_{n+1} = \begin{bmatrix} \mathbf{H}^{\mathsf{T}} & \mathbf{G}^{\mathsf{T}} \end{bmatrix} \begin{bmatrix} \mathbf{a}_n \\ \mathbf{d}_n \end{bmatrix} \quad \text{or alternatively} \quad \begin{bmatrix} \mathbf{H} \\ \mathbf{G} \end{bmatrix} \mathbf{a}_{n+1} = \begin{bmatrix} \mathbf{a}_n \\ \mathbf{d}_n \end{bmatrix}.$$

where $\mathbf{H}$ and $\mathbf{G}$ are orthogonal matrices: $\mathbf{H}^{\mathsf{T}}\mathbf{H} = \mathbf{I}$, $\mathbf{G}^{\mathsf{T}}\mathbf{G} = \mathbf{I}$, and $\mathbf{G}^{\mathsf{T}}\mathbf{H} = \mathbf{0}$. Both $\mathbf{G}$ and $\mathbf{H}$ are infinite-dimensional matrices because they extend across the entire real line. We can restrict ourselves to a finite domain while maintaining orthogonality by imposing periodic boundaries. Because the scaling function has compact support, the coefficients c_k are nonzero for finite values of k. Consider the case when $c_k \neq 0$ for $k = 0, 1, 2, 3$. The matrix structure is the same for other orders.

$$\mathbf{H} = \frac{1}{\sqrt{2}} \begin{bmatrix} c_0 & c_1 & c_2 & c_3 & & & \\ & & c_0 & c_1 & c_2 & c_3 & \\ & & & & c_0 & c_1 & c_2 & c_3 \\ c_2 & c_3 & & & & & c_0 & c_1 \end{bmatrix}$$

and

$$\mathbf{G} = \frac{1}{\sqrt{2}} \begin{bmatrix} c_3 & -c_2 & c_1 & -c_0 & & & \\ & & c_3 & -c_2 & c_1 & -c_0 & \\ & & & & c_3 & -c_2 & c_1 & -c_0 \\ c_1 & -c_0 & & & & & c_3 & -c_2 \end{bmatrix}.$$

It's common to write the discrete wavelet transform as a square matrix

$$\mathbf{T} = \mathbf{P} \begin{bmatrix} \mathbf{H} \\ \mathbf{G} \end{bmatrix} = \frac{1}{\sqrt{2}} \begin{bmatrix} c_0 & c_1 & c_2 & c_3 & & & & \\ c_3 & -c_2 & c_1 & -c_0 & & & & \\ & & c_0 & c_1 & c_2 & c_3 & & \\ & & c_3 & -c_2 & c_1 & -c_0 & & \\ & & & & c_0 & c_1 & c_2 & c_3 \\ & & & & c_3 & -c_2 & c_1 & -c_0 \\ c_2 & c_3 & & & & & c_0 & c_1 \\ c_1 & -c_0 & & & & & c_3 & -c_2 \end{bmatrix},$$

where $\mathbf{P}$ is the "perfect shuffle" permutation matrix that interweaves the rows of $\mathbf{H}$ and $\mathbf{G}$. Notice that for $\mathbf{T}$ to be orthogonal, we must have $\frac{1}{2}(c_0^2 + c_1^2 + c_2^2 + c_3^2) = 1$ and $c_2 c_0 + c_3 c_1 = 0$. Furthermore, $c_0 + c_1 + c_2 + c_3 = 2$. And, for vanishing zeroth moment $c_0 + c_2 = 0$ and $c_1 + c_4 = 0$.

♣ The Wavelets.jl package includes several utilities for discrete wavelet transforms.

▷ Image and data compression

One application of discrete wavelet transforms is image compression. The JPEG 2000 format was developed in the late 1990s as a replacement for the discrete-cosine-transform-based JPEG format developed in the early 1990s. JPEG 2000 uses Cohen–Daubechies–Feauveau (CDF) 9/7 wavelets for lossy compression and LeGall–Tabatabai (LGT) 5/3 wavelets for lossless compression. Because of the multiresolution nature of wavelets, lower resolution subsections of JPEG 2000 images can be extracted and downloaded rather than the entire image. This feature is particularly useful when working with massive gigapixel medical, remote sensing, and scientific images, especially where high resolution and

Figure 10.4: Discrete wavelet transform (right) of the image (left).

low edge-compression artifacts are essential. ICER, a similar wavelet-based image compression format, is used by NASA to transmit two-dimensional images and three-dimensional, hyperspectral images back from the Mars Exploration Rovers. (See Kiely et al. [2006].) While JPEG 2000 is arguably a better format than the original JPEG format, it never succeeded in replacing the JPEG format for common applications. One of the reasons it failed to catch on was that it required more memory than a typical late 1990s computer could efficiently process. And because it uses a different algorithm from the JPEG format, there was no backward compatibility. So industry was hesitant to adopt it, especially because the JPEG format already worked quite well.

Let's examine the two-dimensional DWT of a 512×512-pixel image using the Wavelets.jl library. We'll clamp the output values between 0 and 1 and adjust the levels so that small values are more easily seen, especially on a printed page.

```
using Wavelets, Images
img = float.(Gray.(load(download(bucket*"laura_square.png"))))
B = dwt(Float32.(img), wavelet(WT.haar))
[img Gray.(1 .- clamp01.(sqrt.(abs.(B))))]
```

See Figure 10.4 above. Beyond being a little trippy, what's going on in it? Recall the structure of the one-dimensional multiresolution decomposition discussed on page 265

$$\{12\} \mp \{8\} \mp \{4, -2\} \mp \{-2, 1, -2, 2\} \mp \{1, 1, 2, 1, 1, -1, 0, 1\}.$$

This decomposition starts with the sum of the values of the original sequence (the contribution of the father wavelet). The next term tells us the gross fluctuation (the contribution of the mother wavelet). After this, each resolution provides

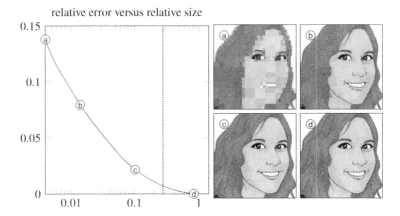

relative error versus relative size

Figure 10.5: The relative error of a DWT (Haar) compressed image as a function of the file size. The dotted line shows equivalent lossless PNG compression.

finer detail with each subsequent generation of daughter wavelets. Figure 10.4 shows a similar decomposition in two dimensions. The tiny pixel in the top-left corner has a value of 325, the sum of the pixel values across the original image. It's surrounded by three one-pixel-sized components that provide the horizontal, vertical, and diagonal details to the next higher resolution. Around these are 2×2 pixels details. Then 4×4, and so on until we get to 256×256-pixel blocks. These three largest blocks show the fluctuations that occur at the pixel level of the original image.

We can compress an image by filtering or zeroing out the coefficients of the DWT of that image whose magnitudes fall below a given threshold. Let's set up such a function.

```
function dwtfilter(channels,wt,k)
  map(1:3) do i
    A = dwt(channels[i,:,:], wavelet(wt))
    threshold!(A, HardTH(), k)
    clamp01!(idwt(A, wavelet(wt)))
  end
end
```

We'll examine the effect of varying the filter threshold on lossy compression error. The following code creates an interactive widget to compare different wavelets and thresholds:

```
using Interact, Wavelets, Images
img = float.(load(download(bucket*"laura_square.png")))
channels = channelview(img)
```

```
func = Dict("Haar"=>WT.haar, "D₄"=>WT.db4, "Coiflet"=>WT.coif4)
@manipulate for wt in togglebuttons(func; label="Transform"),
  k in slider(0:0.05:1.0; value = 0, label = "Threshold")
  colorview(RGB,dwtfilter(channels,wt,k)...)
end
```

The relative Frobenius error, as a function of the percentage of nonzero elements, is plotted in Figure 10.4 on the previous page. Also, see the QR code at the bottom of this page. Compare the DWT image compression with the DCT image compression in Figure 6.6 on page 164. DWT image compression maintains sharp edges without the ringing or nonlocal artifacts characteristic of DCT image compression. Even at high levels of compression, sharp details are well preserved. This feature, in particular, makes DWTs especially relevant in applications such as fingerprint analysis.

10.6   Neural networks

Artificial neural networks provide yet another way of approximating functions. In 1943, neurophysiologist Warren McCulloch and mathematician Walter Pitts, inspired by Bertrand Russell's formal logic and Alan Turing's recent research on computability, teamed up to develop a basic computational model of the brain.[8] They surmised that a brain was simply a biological Turing machine with logic encodings in neurons, and they demonstrated that arbitrary Boolean functions could be represented as a mathematical "nervous net." While McCulloch and Pitt's model sought to mimic the brain, today's artificial neural networks bear as much resemblance to the biological neural networks that inspired them as airplanes do to birds.[9]

An artificial neuron is a function consisting of the composition of an affine transformation and a nonlinear function $\phi(x)$, called an activation function. Often, a second affine transformation is added to the composition. The activation function $\phi(x)$ acts as a basis function. The first affine transformation affects the

---

[8]Bullied as a boy, Walter Pitts spent hours hiding in the library, reading books like Whitehead and Russell's *Principia Mathematica*. When he was 15, he ran away from home and showed up at the University of Chicago, where Bertrand Russell was teaching. He remained at the university for several years, never registering as a student, often homeless and working menial jobs. It's here he met Warren McCulloch and they developed the foundational theory of neural nets. Walter Pitts, enticed to continue his research on modeling the brain, left Chicago to complete his PhD at MIT. Over time he grew increasingly lonely and distraught, eventually setting fire to his dissertation and all of his notes. He tragically died of alcoholism at age 46. To dig deeper, read Amanda Gefter's article in *Nautilus Quarterly*.

[9]Biomimicry looks to nature for insights and inspiration in solving engineering problems. Early unsuccessful pioneers of artificial flight made wings from wood and feathers attached to their arms. Leonardo da Vinci's study of birds led him to devise his ornithopter. Otto Lilienthal did the same in developing his glider. By the time Orville and Wilbur Wright engineered the first successful powered aircraft, it looked very little like a bird other than having wings.

an image compressed using Haar wavelets

input values by stretching and sliding the activation function along the x-axis. The second affine transformation affects the output values by stretching and sliding the activation function in the y-direction. An activation function could be any number of functions—a radial basis function such as a B-spline or Gaussian, a monotonically increasing sigmoid function, a threshold function, a rectifier function, and so on.

sigmoid   ReLu   ramp   swish   Gaussian

McCulloch and Pitts used a step function _⌐ for an activation function to model neurons as logical operators. Sigmoid activation functions ___, which naturally arise from logistic regression, were the most popular until fairly recently. Now, rectified linear units or ReLUs _／ are in vogue, largely do to their simplicity and effectiveness in deep learning.

By taking a linear combination of scaled, translated activation functions

$$f_n(x) = \sum_{i=1}^{n} c_i \phi(w_i x + b_i)$$

we can approximate any continuous function $f(x)$. Furthermore, it doesn't matter which activation function we choose beyond practical considerations because we can linearly combine activation functions to create new ones. For example, consider a rectified linear unit $x^+ = \text{ReLU}(x) = \max(0, x)$ _／. Combining two ReLUs $(x + 1)^+ - x^+$ will make a ramp function _／, an approximation to a sigmoid function. Combining two ramps—or three ReLUs $(x + 1)^+ - 2x^+ + (x - 1)^+$—will make a linear B-spline basis function $\wedge$. Likewise, two step functions will make a rectangle function $\sqcap$, and two sigmoid functions will make a sigmoid bump $\wedge$.

Theorem 41 (Universal approximation theorem). *Let $f(x)$ be a sufficiently smooth function and let $f_n(x)$ be a neural net approximation of $f(x)$ over an interval of length ℓ using a ReLU activation function. For any $\varepsilon > 0$, the error $\|f_n(x) - f(x)\|_\infty \le \varepsilon$ if we use at least $\ell \sqrt{\max |f''(x)|/8\varepsilon}$ neurons.*

Proof. Let $x_1, x_2, \ldots, x_n$ be n equally space nodes over the interval. Then the mesh size h is ℓ/n. A linear B-spline basis function can be built using three ReLU functions, so $f_n(x) = \sum_{i=1}^{n} f(x_i) B_1(h^{-1}(x - x_i))$ is piecewise interpolating polynomial with $f_n(x_i) = f(x_i)$. From theorem 26 on page 232, regarding polynomial interpolation error, on each subinterval

$$|f_n(x) - f(x)| = \tfrac{1}{2} f''(\xi_i)(x - x_i)(x_{i+1} - x) \le \tfrac{1}{8} |f''(\xi)| h^2$$

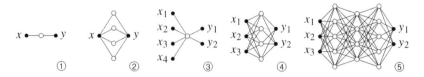

Figure 10.6: Neural networks: ① a simple artificial neuron; ② a simple neural net; ③ a multiple-input/multiple-output neuron; ④ a single layer neural net; and ⑤ a deep neural net.

for some ξ_i in the subinterval. Choose n such that $\frac{1}{8} \max |f''(x)| h^2 \le \varepsilon$. In practice, we need one ReLU function for every line segment. So, we need n ReLU neurons, where $n \ge \ell \sqrt{|f''(\xi)|/8\varepsilon}$.   □

The function $f(x)$ need not be smooth—the proof of a similar result for Lipschitz functions is left as an exercise. George Cybenko's influential 1989 paper "Approximation by superpositions of a sigmoidal function" generalizes the universal approximation theorem for an arbitrary sigmoid function. From the universal approximation theorem, it may appear that neural networks are little different than directly using B-splines, radial basis functions, or any other method we have already discussed. Namely, we can better approximate a function by adding additional neurons into a single layer. The real magic of neural nets emerges by using multiple layers. We can feed the output of one neuron into another neuron. And, we can feed that neuron into yet another one, and that one into another, and so on.

Consider the graphs in Figure 10.6. Input and output nodes are denoted with •. The neurons are denote with ○. The weighted edges, often called synapses, connect the nodes together. The simplest artificial neuron is $y = w_2 \phi(w_1 x + b)$. A neuron can have multiple inputs and multiple outputs $\mathbf{y} = \mathbf{w}_2 \phi(\mathbf{w}_1^\mathsf{T} \mathbf{x} + b)$. For simplicity of notation and implementation, the bias can be incorporated by prepending b into a new zeroth element of $\mathbf{w}_1$ and a corresponding 1 into a zeroth element of $\mathbf{x}$, giving us $y = w_2 \phi(\mathbf{w}_1^\mathsf{T} \mathbf{x})$. We can join neurons in a layer to form a single-layer neural net $\mathbf{y} = \mathbf{W}_2 \phi(\mathbf{W}_1 \mathbf{x})$ where $\mathbf{W}_1$ and $\mathbf{W}_2$ are matrices of synaptic weights. The input and output nodes form input and output layers, and the neurons form a single hidden layer. By feeding one neuron into another, we create a multi-layer neural net called a deep neural net

$$\mathbf{y} = \mathbf{W}_k \phi(\mathbf{W}_{k-1} \phi(\cdots \phi(\mathbf{W}_2 \phi(\mathbf{W}_1 \mathbf{x})) \cdots)).$$

While McCulloch and Pitts forged their neural nets out of the mathematical certainty of formal logic, modern neural nets reign as tools of statistical uncertainty and inference. Deep neural networks are able to classify immense and complicated data sets, thanks in large part to specialized computing hardware and stochastic optimization techniques that allow them to work efficiently in high dimensions. To better understand how a deep neural net partitions data, consider a collection of two thousand (x_1, x_2) points, each one labeled either -1 if it lies outside of the unit circle or $+1$ if it lies inside of it.

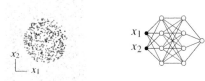

Let's partition the points using the neural net $y = \phi(\mathbf{W}_3\phi(\mathbf{W}_2\phi(\mathbf{W}_1\mathbf{x})))$, with two inputs, two hidden layers (each with four neurons), and one output for the label. We'll use $\phi(x) = \tanh x$ as the activation function.

A single neuron partitions the plane with a line, like a crisp fold in a sheet of paper, called a decision boundary.[10] Each of the four neurons in the first hidden layer produces different partitions in the plane—four separate folds in the paper.

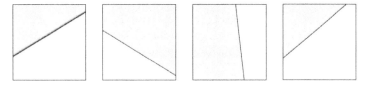

When combined linearly together, these decision boundaries partition a space into a simple, possibly unbound polytope. In a deep neural net, these initial partitions are the building blocks for more complicated geometries with each subsequent layer. The second hidden layer forms curved boundaries by combining the output of the first neural layer using smooth sigmoid and tanh activation functions. The ReLU activation function produces polytopes with flat sides.

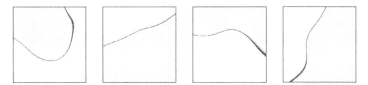

The neural network uses these new shapes to construct the final partition, an almost circular blob that approximates the original data. Had we included more data, used more neurons or more layers, or trained the neural network longer, the blob would have been more circular.

---

[10]Not to be misled by metaphor, the real decision boundary is the result of a smooth sigmoid function, so there is a layer of fuzziness surrounding the line.

Adding more neurons to a layer increases the dimensionality. Just as a four-dimensional space allows us to untie a three-dimensional knot, a wide neural net provides more freedom to move around. Adding more layers increases the depth of recursion. We've seen the power of recursion in dynamical systems and multiresolution analysis. The self-similarity in Mandelbrot sets and Daubechies wavelets comes from recursively feeding the output into the input. As a loose analogy, folding and unfolding a sheet of paper will produce one crease at a time, but folding that sheet again and again before unfolding it will produce a complex pattern of creases.

The manifold hypothesis provides another heuristic for understanding deep neural nets. The manifold hypothesis posits that natural data lie (or almost lie) on lower-dimensional manifolds embedded in high-dimensional space. Intuitively, correlations that exist in data lead to the implicit organization of that data.[11] Each hidden layer successively stretches and squishes space, warping and untangling the manifolds to make them linearly separable. Think about the original light and dark dots from the figure on the preceding page, reproduced on the left below.

 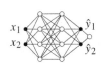

There's no straight line that can partition this data. But, by embedding the data in higher dimensions, we can homeomorphically stretch and fold the space until it can be partitioned with a hyperplane. Imagine that you print the original light and dark dot pattern onto a spandex handkerchief. How might you remove the dark dots with one straight cut using a pair of scissors? Push the middle of the handkerchief up to make a poof, and then cut across that poof. This is what our neural net does. We can visualize the actions of the neural net by examining intermediate outputs $(\hat{y}_1, \hat{y}_2)$ obtained from splitting $\mathbf{W}_3$ into a product of 1×2 and 2×4 matrices. The rightmost figure above shows how the neural net has

---

[11] For example, handwritten digits might be digitized as 28-by-28-pixel images, which are embedded in a 784-dimensional space (one dimension for each pixel). The intrinsic dimension—the minimum degrees of freedom required to describe an object in space—is much smaller than the extrinsic dimensionality. A "3" looks like another "3," and a "7" looks like another "7." Neural networks manipulate low-intrinsic-dimensional data in higher-dimensional space.

stretched, folded, and squashed the data points into the plane, like a used tissue thoughtlessly tossed onto the roadway. The decision boundary can be determined using the 1×2 matrix along with the bias term. Just as the circular blob didn't perfectly partition the original space, the decision boundary doesn't provide a perfect cut between light and dark dots.

We'll return to neural networks when we discuss fitting data in the next section. To dig deeper, see Goodfellow, Bengio, and Courville's text *Deep Learning*, Friedman, Hastie, and Tibshirani's text *Elements of Statistical Learning*, the open-source book project *Dive into Deep Learning* (https://d2l.ai) developed by several Amazon computer scientists, or Christopher Olah's blog post "Neural Networks, Manifolds, and Topology." Also, check out Daniel Smilkov and Shan Carter's interactive visualization of neural networks at http://playground.tensorflow.org.

10.7   Data fitting

We often want to find the "best" function that fits a data set of, say, m input-output values $(x_1, y_1), (x_2, y_2), \ldots, (x_m, y_m)$. Suppose that we choose a model function $y = f(x; c_1, c_2, \ldots, c_n)$ that has n parameters $c_1, c_2, \ldots, c_n$ and that the number of observations m is at least as large as the number of parameters n. With a set of inputs and corresponding outputs, we can try to determine the parameters c_i that fit the model. Still, the input and output data likely come from observations with noise or hidden variables that overcomplicate our simplified model. So, the problem is inconsistent unless we perhaps (gasp!) overfit the data by changing the model function. Fortunately, we can handle the problem nicely using the least squares best approximation.

▷ **Linear least squares approximation**

Suppose that our model is linear with respect to the parameters $c_1, c_2, \ldots, c_n$. That is,

$$f(x; c_1, c_2, \ldots, c_n) = c_1 \varphi_1(x) + c_2 \varphi_2(x) + \cdots + c_n \varphi_n(x),$$

where $\{\varphi_1, \varphi_2, \ldots, \varphi_n\}$ are basis elements that generate a subspace F. To find the best approximation to y in F, we must find the $f \in F$ such that $y - f \perp F$. In this case, we have the normal equation

$$(f, \varphi_i) = \sum_{j=1}^{n} c_j (\varphi_j, \varphi_i) = (y, \varphi_i) \text{ for } i = 1, 2, \ldots, n,$$

where the inner product $(f, \varphi_i) = \sum_{k=1}^m f(x_k)\varphi_i(x_k)$. The matrix form of the normal equation is

$$
\begin{bmatrix}
(\varphi_1, \varphi_1) & (\varphi_2, \varphi_1) & \cdots & (\varphi_n, \varphi_1) \\
(\varphi_1, \varphi_2) & (\varphi_2, \varphi_2) & \cdots & (\varphi_n, \varphi_2) \\
\vdots & \vdots & \ddots & \vdots \\
(\varphi_1, \varphi_n) & (\varphi_2, \varphi_n) & \cdots & (\varphi_n, \varphi_n)
\end{bmatrix}
\begin{bmatrix}
c_1 \\
c_2 \\
\vdots \\
c_n
\end{bmatrix}
=
\begin{bmatrix}
(y, \varphi_1) \\
(y, \varphi_2) \\
\vdots \\
(y, \varphi_n)
\end{bmatrix},
$$

which in vector notation is simply $\mathbf{A}^T\mathbf{A}\mathbf{c} = \mathbf{A}^T\mathbf{y}$, where $\mathbf{A}$ is an $m \times n$ matrix with elements given by $A_{ij} = \varphi_j(x_i)$. In the solution $\mathbf{c} = (\mathbf{A}^T\mathbf{A})^{-1}\mathbf{A}^T\mathbf{y}$, the term $(\mathbf{A}^T\mathbf{A})^{-1}\mathbf{A}^T$ is called the *pseudoinverse* of $\mathbf{A}$ and denoted $\mathbf{A}^+$. Formally, we have replaced the solution $\mathbf{c} = \mathbf{A}^{-1}\mathbf{y}$ with $\mathbf{c} = \mathbf{A}^+\mathbf{y}$. In practice, we don't need to compute the pseudoinverse explicitly. Instead, we can solve $\mathbf{A}\mathbf{y} = \mathbf{c}$ using the QR method. For more discussion of linear least squares and the pseudoinverse, refer back to Chapter 3.

▷ Nonlinear least squares approximation

What do we do if our model cannot be expressed as a linear combination of the basis elements of an inner product space? For example, we may want to determine the Gaussian distribution $y = c_1 e^{-(x-c_2)^2/2c_3^2}$ that best matches some given data by specifying the amplitude c_1, the mean c_2, and the standard deviation c_3. In general, for the given function f, we want to find the parameters $\mathbf{c} = (c_1, c_2, \ldots, c_n)$ such that $y_i = f(x_i; c_1, c_2, \ldots, c_n)$ at given the points $(x_1, y_1), (x_2, y_2), \ldots, (x_m, y_m)$.

Let's switch the roles of $\mathbf{c}$ and $\mathbf{x}$ as variables and parameters and define $f_i(c) = f(c_1, c_2, \ldots, c_n; x_i)$. We can write the system of residuals as

$$r_1 = y_1 - f_1(c_1, c_2, \ldots, c_n)$$
$$r_2 = y_2 - f_2(c_1, c_2, \ldots, c_n)$$
$$\vdots$$
$$r_m = y_m - f_m(c_1, c_2, \ldots, c_n).$$

In vector notation, this system is $\mathbf{r} = \mathbf{y} - f(\mathbf{c})$. If this system were consistent and $m = n$, we could use Newton's method that we developed in section 8.6 to find a $\mathbf{c}$ such that $\mathbf{r} = \mathbf{0}$. In such a case, we would iterate

$$\mathbf{J}_r(\mathbf{c}^{(k)})\Delta\mathbf{c}^{(k+1)} = -\mathbf{r}^{(k)},$$

where $\Delta\mathbf{c}^{(k+1)} = \mathbf{c}^{(k+1)} - \mathbf{c}^{(k)}$ and $\mathbf{J}_r(\mathbf{c})$ is the $m \times n$ Jacobian matrix whose (i, j)-component is $\partial r_i/\partial c_j$. The Jacobian matrix $\mathbf{J}_r(\mathbf{c}) = -\mathbf{J}_f(\mathbf{c})$, so we equivalently have

$$\mathbf{J}_f(\mathbf{c}^{(k)})\Delta\mathbf{c}^{(k+1)} = \mathbf{r}^{(k)} \tag{10.15}$$

where the (i, j)-component of the Jacobian $\mathbf{J}_f(\mathbf{c})$ is $\partial f_i / \partial c_j$. We can solve this overdetermined system using QR factorization to update $\mathbf{c}^{(k+1)} = \mathbf{c}^{(k)} + \Delta \mathbf{c}^{(k+1)}$ at each iteration. The method is called the *Gauss–Newton method*.

By multiplying both sides of (10.15) by $\mathbf{J}_f^\mathsf{T}(\mathbf{c}^{(k)})$ and then formally solving for $\mathbf{c}^{(k+1)}$, we get an explicit formulation for the Gauss–Newton method:

$$\mathbf{c}^{(k+1)} = \mathbf{c}^{(k)} + \mathbf{J}_f^+(\mathbf{c}^{(k)})\mathbf{r}^{(k)}, \tag{10.16}$$

where the pseudoinverse $\mathbf{J}_f^+$ is $(\mathbf{J}_f^\mathsf{T}\mathbf{J}_f)^{-1}\mathbf{J}_f^\mathsf{T}$. The Gauss–Newton method may be unstable. We can regularize it by modifying the $\mathbf{J}_f^\mathsf{T}\mathbf{J}_f$ term of the pseudoinverse to be diagonally dominant. This regularization has the effect of weakly decoupling the system of equations. The *Levenberg–Marquardt method* is given by

$$\mathbf{c}^{(k+1)} = \mathbf{c}^{(k)} + (\mathbf{J}^\mathsf{T}\mathbf{J} + \lambda\mathbf{D})^{-1}\mathbf{J}^\mathsf{T}\mathbf{r}^{(k)}, \tag{10.17}$$

where $\mathbf{J}$ is $\mathbf{J}_f(\mathbf{c}^{(k)})$, the matrix $\mathbf{D}$ is a nonnegative diagonal matrix, and the damping parameter λ is positive. Typical choices for $\mathbf{D}$ include the identity matrix $\mathbf{I}$ or the diagonal matrix $\mathrm{diag}(\mathbf{J}^\mathsf{T}\mathbf{J})$. The damping parameter is typically changed at each iteration, increasing it if the residual increases and decreasing it if the residual decreases. The Levenberg–Marquardt method is analogous to *Tikhonov regularization* used to solve underdetermined, inconsistent linear systems. As mentioned in section 3.2, we don't need to construct the pseudoinverse to implement the method explicitly—we can use a stacked matrix instead. But the explicit formulation (10.17) is more efficient, especially when the number of data points is significantly larger than the number of parameters.

Example. Suppose that we've been handed some noisy data collected from an experiment, which from theory, we expect to be modeled by two Gaussian functions

$$f(x; \mathbf{c}) = c_1 e^{-c_2(x-c_3)^2} + c_4 e^{-c_5(x-c_6)^2} \tag{10.18}$$

for some unknown parameters $\mathbf{c} = \{c_1, c_2, \ldots, c_6\}$. Let's use Newton's method to recover the parameters.

Newton's method is $\mathbf{c}^{(k+1)} = \mathbf{c}^{(k)} - \left(\mathbf{J}^{(k)}\right)^+ (\mathbf{f}(\mathbf{x}; \mathbf{c}^{(k)}) - \mathbf{y})$, where $\left(\mathbf{J}^{(k)}\right)^+$ is the pseudoinverse of the Jacobian. The numerical approximation to the Jacobian using the complex-step derivative is

```
function jacobian(f,x,c)
  J = zeros(length(x),length(c))
  for k in (n = 1:length(c))
    J[:,k] .= imag(f(x,c+1e-8im*(k .== n)))/1e-8
  end
  return J
end
```

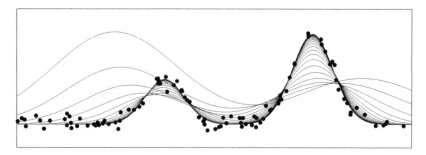

Figure 10.7: The least squares solution for (10.18). Solutions are depicted at intermediate iterations. The input data is represented by •.

Let's implement the Levenberg–Marquardt method:

```
function gauss_newton(f,x,y,c)
  r = y - f(x,c)
  for j = 1:100
    G = jacobian(f,x,c)
    M = G'*G
    c += (M+Diagonal(M))\(G'*r)
    norm(r-(r=y-f(x,c))) < 1e-12 && return(c)
  end
  print("Gauss-Newton did not converge.")
end
```

For this example, we'll take the measured data to be

```
f = (x,c) -> @. c[1]*exp(-c[2]*(x-c[3])^2) +
        c[4]*exp(-c[5]*(x-c[6])^2)
x = 8*rand(100)
y = f(x,[1, 3, 3, 2, 3, 6]) + 0.1*randn(100);
```

Let's take $\{2, 0.3, 2, 1, 0.3, 7\}$ as the initial guess. The problem is solved using

```
c₀ = [2, 0.3, 2, 1, 0.3, 7]
c = gauss_newton(f,x,y,c₀)
```

The plot above shows the intermediate solutions at each iteration, ending with the parameters $\mathbf{c} = \{0.98, 3.25.98, 3.00, 1.96, 2.88, 5.99\}$.

We can also control the stability of Newton's method by shortening the step size by a factor α, called the *learning rate*. For example, we could substitute a Newton step `c += α*G\r` with `α=0.5` in the loop in place of the Levenberg–Marquardt step. Alternatively, we could combine a faster learning rate with the Levenberg–Marquardt method. Because the Levenberg–Marquardt method is more stable than the Gauss–Newton method, we can take a learning rate as large as 2.

In practice, we might use the LsqFit.jl package, which solves nonlinear least squares problems:

```
using LsqFit
cf = curve_fit(f,x,y,c₀)
```

The parameters are given by cf.param. The residuals are given by cf.resid. ◄

    ⁂ LsqFit.jl uses the Levenberg–Marquardt algorithm to fit a function to data.

▷ **Logistic regression**

A *likelihood function* is a probability distribution interpreted as a function of its parameters. We determine parameters that make a distribution most likely to fit observed data by maximizing the likelihood function. We call such values the maximum likelihood estimate.

Consider an experiment with a Boolean-valued outcome—pass or fail, yes or no, true or false—in other words, a Bernoulli trial. We can model such an experiment using a Bernoulli distribution $p^y(1-p)^{1-y}$ where $p(\mathbf{x}, \mathbf{w})$ is the probability for some data $\mathbf{x}$ and some parameters $\mathbf{w}$ and $y \in \{0, 1\}$ is the possible outcome. With several trials, we can define a (scaled) likelihood function as

$$L(\mathbf{w}) = \prod_{i=1}^{n} p^{y_i}(1-p)^{1-y_i}$$

for a probability $p(\mathbf{x}_i, \mathbf{w})$. The log-likelihood function is given by the logarithm of the likelihood:

$$\ell(\mathbf{w}) = \sum_{i=1}^{n} y_i \log p + (1 - y_i)\log(1-p). \tag{10.19}$$

Because the logarithm is a monotonically increasing function, the maximum likelihood estimate is the same as the maximum of the log-likelihood. So we just need to find the parameters $\mathbf{w}$ that maximize $\ell(\mathbf{w})$. We'll first need a model for the probabilities $p(\mathbf{x}_i, \mathbf{w})$ to do this.

A generalized linear model (GLM) relates the expectation of the response $\mu_i = E(y_i)$ to a linear predictor

$$f(\mu_i) = \eta_i = w_0 + w_1 x_{i1} + w_2 x_{i2} + \cdots + w_n x_{in} = \mathbf{w}^\mathsf{T}\mathbf{x}_i.$$

The function f is called a *link function*. We want a link function that is smooth, that is monotonically increasing, and that maps the unit interval $(0, 1)$ to the real line $(-\infty, \infty)$. The link function most commonly associated with the Bernoulli distribution is the logit function

$$\text{logit}\,\mu = \log \frac{\mu}{1-\mu}.$$

While there are other link functions,[12] the logit function is easy to manipulate, it has the nice interpretation of being the log odds ratio, and it is the inverse of the logistic function $\sigma(\eta) = 1/(1+e^{-\eta})$. Using the inverse logit (the logistic function) in the log-likelihood function (10.19) yields

$$\ell(\mathbf{w}) = \sum_{i=1}^{n} y_i \log \sigma(\mathbf{w}^\mathsf{T}\mathbf{x}_i) + (1-y_i)\log\big(1-\sigma(\mathbf{w}^\mathsf{T}\mathbf{x}_i)\big).$$

Now, we can calculate the maximum likelihood estimate. The derivative of the logistic function $\sigma(\eta)$ is $\sigma(\eta)(1-\sigma(\eta))$, from which it follows that the derivative of $y \log \sigma(\eta) + (1-y)\log(1-\sigma(\eta))$ is the remarkably simple expression $y - \sigma(\eta)$. Define $\mathbf{X}$ as the matrix whose ith row is $\mathbf{x}_i^\mathsf{T}$. The contribution from $\mathbf{x}_i$ to the gradient of $\ell(\mathbf{w})$ is

$$\mathbf{g}_i = \big(y_i - \sigma(\mathbf{w}^\mathsf{T}\mathbf{x}_i)\big)\mathbf{x}_i.$$

The corresponding gradient using all data points is

$$\mathbf{g} = \mathbf{X}^\mathsf{T}\big(\mathbf{y} - \sigma(\mathbf{X}\mathbf{w})\big).$$

The contribution from $\mathbf{x}_i$ to the Hessian is

$$\mathbf{H}_i = \mathbf{x}^\mathsf{T}\sigma(\mathbf{w}^\mathsf{T}\mathbf{x})\big(1-\sigma(\mathbf{w}^\mathsf{T}\mathbf{x})\big)\mathbf{x}.$$

After summing over all data points, the Hessian is $\mathbf{H} = \mathbf{X}^\mathsf{T}\mathbf{S}\mathbf{X}$, with the diagonal matrix

$$\mathbf{S} = \sigma(\mathbf{X}\mathbf{w}^{(k)})\big(1-\sigma(\mathbf{X}\mathbf{w}^{(k)})\big).$$

Therefore, following the discussion in section 8.8, Newton's method is

$$\begin{aligned}
\mathbf{w}^{(k+1)} &= \mathbf{w}^{(k)} - \big(\mathbf{H}^{(k)}\big)^{-1}\mathbf{g}^{(k)} \\
&= \mathbf{w}^{(k)} + \big(\mathbf{X}^\mathsf{T}\mathbf{S}^{(k)}\mathbf{X}\big)^{-1}\mathbf{X}^\mathsf{T}\big(\mathbf{y} - \sigma(\mathbf{w}^\mathsf{T}\mathbf{X}^{(k)})\big).
\end{aligned}$$

The terms on the right-hand side are often regrouped as a formula called *iteratively reweighted least squares* (IRLS):

$$\mathbf{w}^{(k+1)} = \big(\mathbf{X}^\mathsf{T}\mathbf{S}^{(k)}\mathbf{X}\big)^{-1}\mathbf{X}^\mathsf{T}\big(\mathbf{S}^{(k)}\mathbf{X}\mathbf{w}^{(k)} + \mathbf{y} - \sigma(\mathbf{w}^\mathsf{T}\mathbf{X}^{(k)})\big).$$

Let's see what the method looks like in Julia. We'll first define the logistic function and generate some synthetic data.

---

[12]Statistician and physician Joseph Berkson introduced the logit function in 1944 as a close approximation to the inverse cumulative normal distribution used ten years earlier by biologist Chester Bliss. Bliss called his curve the probit, a portmanteau of probability and unit, and Berkson followed analogously with logit, a portmanteau of logistical and unit.

 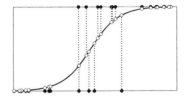

Figure 10.8: Classification data (left). The function fitting the data (right).

```
σ = x -> @. 1/(1+exp(-x))
x = rand(30); y = ( rand(30) .< σ(10x.-5) );
```

Now, we apply Newton's method.

```
X, w = [one.(x) x], zeros(2,1)
for i=1:10
  S = σ(X*w).*(1 .- σ(X*w))
  w += (X'*(S.*X))\(X'*(y - σ(X*w)))
end
```

A more than minimal working example would set a condition to break out the loop once the magnitude of the change in w is less than some threshold. The solution is plotted in Figure 10.8 above. In practice, we might use Julia's GLM library to solve the logistic regression problem.

```
using GLM, DataFrames
data = DataFrame(X=x, Y=y)
logit = glm(@formula(Y ~ X), data, Bernoulli(), LogitLink())
```

⚙ The GLM.jl library fits a generalized linear model to data.

▷ **Neural networks**

Let's pick up from the previous section and examine how to solve a data fitting problem using neural networks. Consider a two-layer neural net $\mathbf{y} = \mathbf{W}_2\phi(\mathbf{W}_1\mathbf{x}_*)$ for some data $\mathbf{x}_*$ and $\mathbf{y}_*$ and some unknown matrices of parameters $\mathbf{W}_1$ and $\mathbf{W}_2$. The vector $\mathbf{x}$ has m elements—$m - 1$ of these elements contain the input variables (called features) and one element, set to 1, is for the bias. The vector $\mathbf{y}$ has n dimensions for the labels. The parameters $\mathbf{W}_1$ and $\mathbf{W}_2$ are $k \times m$ and $n \times k$ matrices, where k is a hyperparameter of the algorithm, independent of the problem. All-in-all, we need to determine kmn parameters, although many of these parameters may be zero.

We'll determine the parameters by finding a $\mathbf{y}$ that minimizes a loss function, also known as a cost function. A typical loss function is the mean squared error—the normalized ℓ^2-error—of the residual

$$L(\mathbf{y}) = N^{-1}\|\mathbf{y} - \mathbf{y}_*\|_2^2,$$

which is minimized when its gradient $[\partial L/\partial \mathbf{y}] = 2N^{-1}(\mathbf{y} - \mathbf{y}_*)$ is zero. We'll use the notation $[\cdot]$ to emphasize that $\partial L/\partial \mathbf{y}$ is a matrix or a vector.

We can solve the minimization problem using the gradient descent method. The gradient descent method iteratively marches along the local gradient some distance and then reevaluates the direction. Start with some random initial guess for the parameters $\mathbf{W}_1$ and $\mathbf{W}_2$. Use these values to compute $\mathbf{y}(\mathbf{x}_*) = \mathbf{W}_2\phi(\mathbf{W}_1\mathbf{x}_*)$. Then use $\mathbf{y}$ to determine the loss and the gradient of the loss. Update the values of the parameters

$$\mathbf{W}_1 \leftarrow \mathbf{W}_1 - \alpha_1 \left[\partial L/\partial \mathbf{W}_1\right]$$
$$\mathbf{W}_2 \leftarrow \mathbf{W}_2 - \alpha_2 \left[\partial L/\partial \mathbf{W}_2\right].$$

The constants α_1 and α_2, called learning rates, are chosen to ensure the stability of the iterative method. Iterate until the method converges to a local minimum. Hopefully, that local minimum is also a global minimum.

We'll use two identities for matrix derivatives in computing the gradients. If $f(\mathbf{C}) = f(\mathbf{AB})$, then

$$\left[\partial f/\partial \mathbf{A}\right] = \left[\partial f/\partial \mathbf{C}\right] \left[\mathbf{B}\right]^{\mathsf{T}} \text{ and } \left[\partial f/\partial \mathbf{B}\right] = \left[\mathbf{A}\right]^{\mathsf{T}} \left[\partial f/\partial \mathbf{C}\right],$$

If $\mathbf{C} = g(\mathbf{A})$, then the chain rule for $f(g(\mathbf{A}))$ is

$$\left[\partial f/\partial \mathbf{A}\right] = \left[g'(\mathbf{A})\right]^{\mathsf{T}} \left[\partial f/\partial \mathbf{C}\right],$$

where $\left[g'(\mathbf{A})\right]$ is a Jacobian matrix. So,

$$\left[\partial L/\partial \mathbf{W}_2\right] = \left[\partial L/\partial \mathbf{y}\right] \left[\phi(\mathbf{W}_1\mathbf{x}_*)\right]^{\mathsf{T}}$$

and

$$\left[\partial L/\partial \mathbf{W}_1\right] = \left[\mathbf{W}_2\phi'(\mathbf{W}_1\mathbf{x}_*)\right]^{\mathsf{T}} \left[\partial L/\partial \mathbf{y}\right] \left[\mathbf{x}_*\right]^{\mathsf{T}}.$$

The Jacobian matrix $[\phi']$ is diagonal. In practice, we'll use a training set consisting of N data points $\mathbf{x}_*$ and $\mathbf{y}_*$. We can treat $\mathbf{x}_*$ as an $m \times N$ matrix and $\mathbf{y}(\mathbf{x}_*)$ and $\mathbf{y}_*$ both as $n \times N$ matrices.

Example.   Let's use neural networks to model the data given by the noisy semicircle $y = \sqrt{1 - x^2} + \sigma(x)$, where $\sigma(x)$ is some random perturbation.[13] We'll pick 100 points.

```
N = 100; θ = LinRange(0,π,N)'
x = cos.(θ); x̃ = [one.(x);x]
y = sin.(θ) + 0.05*randn(1,N)
```

We'll select a neural network with one hidden layer with n neurons, an input layer with two nodes (one for the bias), and one output node. We'll also use a ReLU activation function.

```
n = 20; W₁ = rand(n,2); W₂ = randn(1,n)
φ = x -> max.(x,0)
dφ = x -> (x.>0)
```

We solve the problem using gradient descent with a sufficiently large number of iterations, called epochs. To ensure stability, we take a learning rate $\alpha = 0.1$.

```
α = 0.1
for epoch = 1:1000
    ŷ = W₂ * φ(W₁*x̃)
    ∂L∂y = 2(ŷ-y)/N
    ∂L∂W₁ = dφ(W₁*x̃) .* (W₂' * ∂L∂y) * x̃'
    ∂L∂W₂ = ∂L∂y * φ(W₁*x̃)'
    W₁ -= 0.1α * ∂L∂W₁
    W₂ -= α * ∂L∂W₂
end
```

Now that we have our trained parameters $\mathbf{W}_1$ and $\mathbf{W}_2$, we construct the solution using our neural network model.

```
scatter(x̃[2,:],y',opacity=0.3)
x̂ = LinRange(-1.2,1.2,200)'; x̂ = [one.(x̂);x̂]; ŷ = W₂ * φ(W₁*x̂)
plot!(x̂[2,:],ŷ',width=3)
```

The figure on the next page and the QR code at the bottom of this page show the solution. We can also solve the problem using a sigmoid activation function

```
φ = x -> @. 1 / (1 + exp(-x))
dφ = x -> @. φ(x)*(1-φ(x))
```

---

[13] A neural network on a one-dimensional problem with a small number of parameters is wholly inefficient. Any number of universal approximators like Chebyshev polynomials or B-splines would provide a better solution in a fraction of the compute time. However, these methods quickly get bogged down as the size of the problem increases. We'll return to the curse of dimensionality when we discuss Monte Carlo methods in the next chapter.

best fit using
a neural network

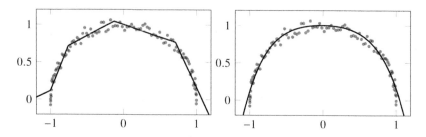

Figure 10.9: The neural network approximation for the data • using ReLU activation functions (left) and sigmoid activation functions (right).

along with alternative loss function $L(\mathbf{y}) = \|\mathbf{y} - \mathbf{y}_*\|_2$. The gradient of this loss function is $\left[\partial L/\partial \mathbf{y}\right] = 2(\mathbf{y} - \mathbf{y}_*)/L(\mathbf{y})$.

```
L = norm(ŷ - y)
∂L∂y = (ŷ-y)/L
```

In practice, one uses a machine learning package. Let's use Flux.jl to solve the same problem. The recipe is as before: build a model with initially unknown parameters, prescribe a loss function, add some data, choose an optimizer such as gradient descent, and then iterate.

```
using Flux
model = Chain(Dense(1, n, relu), Dense(n, 1))
loss(x,y) = Flux.Losses.mse(model(x), y)
parameters = Flux.params(model)
data = [(x,y)]
optimizer = Descent(0.1)
for epochs = 1:10000
  Flux.train!(loss, parameters, data, optimizer)
end
```

The variable parameters is an array of four things: the weights and bias terms of $\mathbf{W}_1$ and the weights and a bias terms of $\mathbf{W}_2$. The object model is the trained model, which we can now use as a function model(x) for an arbitrary input x. ◄

♣ Flux.jl is a deep learning ecosystem built entirely in Julia.

Mathematician Hannah Fry aptly describes a neural network as "an enormous mathematical structure that features a great many knobs and dials" that must be tweaked and tuned so as not to be a "complete pile of junk." Tweaking and tuning all these knobs and dials is no easy task. Even relatively simple neural nets used for handwritten digit classification can have tens of thousands of parameters. One of the largest deep neural nets, GPT-3 (Generative Pre-trained Transformer 3) used for natural language generation, has 96 layers with over 175 billion parameters. On top of that, gradient descent is slow. It can stall on any number of local minimums and saddle points. And the problem is increasingly ill-conditioned as the number of parameters rises. Fortunately, there are several approaches to these challenges.

We can drastically reduce the number of parameters using convolutional layers and pooling layers rather than fully connected layers. Convolutional neural nets (CNNs), frequently used in image recognition, use convolution matrices with relatively small kernels. Such kernels—typical in image processing as edge detection, sharpen, blur, and emboss filters—consist of tunable parameters for novel pattern filtering. Pooling layers reduce the dimensionality by taking a local mean or maximum of the input parameters.

Significant research has led to the development of specialized model architectures. Residual networks (ResNets), used in image processing, allow certain connections to skip over intermediate layers. Recurrent neural networks (RNNs), used in text processing or speech recognition, use sequential data to update intermediate layers. Recent research has explored implicitly defined layers and neural differential equations.

Another way to speed up model training is by starting with a better initial guess of the parameters than simply choosing a random initial state. Transfer learning uses similar, previously trained models to start the parameters closer to a solution. Alternatively, we can embrace randomness. Machine learning often requires massive amounts of data. Stochastic gradient descent uses several batches of smaller, randomly selected subsets of the training data.

We can modify gradient descent to overcome its shortcomings, such as adding momentum to overcome shallow local minimum and saddle points or using adaptive learning rates such as AdaGrad and Adam to speed up convergence. Finally, to speed up the computation of gradients and avoid numerical stability, we can use automatic differentiation, which we discuss in the next chapter.

▷ **Statistical best estimates**

While the focus of this chapter has been on finding the "best" estimate in the ℓ^2-norm, for completeness, let's conclude with a comment on the "best" estimate of sample data in a general ℓ^p-norm. Suppose that we have a set of data $\mathbf{x} = (x_1, x_2, \ldots, x_n)$ consisting of real values. And, suppose that we'd like to find a value $\bar{x}$ that is the "best" estimate of that data set. In this case, we find $\bar{x}$ that is closest to each element of $\mathbf{x}$ in the ℓ^p-norm

$$\bar{x} = \arg\min_{s} \|\mathbf{x} - s\|_p = \arg\min_{s} \left(\sum_{i=1}^{n} |x_i - s|^p \right)^{1/p},$$

where p ranges from zero to infinity. If we further define 0^0 to be 0, then we can strictly include $p = 0$. The ℓ^0-"norm" is simply the count of nonzero elements in the set.[14] Quotation marks are used to emphasize that the ℓ^0-"norm" is not truly a norm because it lacks homogeneity: $\|\alpha \cdot \mathbf{x}\|_0 \neq \alpha \cdot \|\mathbf{x}\|_0$. The value $\bar{x}$ closest to $\mathbf{x}$ in ℓ^0-, ℓ^1-, ℓ^2-, and ℓ^∞-norms is one of the four statistical averages—the mode, median, mean, and midrange, respectively. The mode is the most frequently occurring value in the data set, regardless of its relative magnitude. The midrange is the midpoint of the two extrema of the set, regardless of any other elements of the set. For example, consider the following beeswarm plot of data set sampled from a Rayleigh distribution:

Notice the locations of the mode, median, mean, and midrange relative to the data. How well does each do in summarizing the distribution of the data? Where might they be located on other data? What are the potential biases that arise from using a specific average?

10.8 Exercises

10.1. We can think about orthogonality in geometric terms by using cosine to define the angle between two functions

$$\cos \theta = \frac{(f, g)}{\|f\|\|g\|}$$

and even between two subspaces

$$\cos \theta = \sup_{f \in F, g \in G} \frac{(f, g)}{\|f\|\|g\|}.$$

(a) Find the closest quadratic polynomial to x^3 over $(0, 1)$ with the L^2-inner product

$$(f, g) = \int_0^1 f(x)g(x)\, dx.$$

(b) Use the definition of the angle between two subspaces to show that when n is large, x^{n+1} is close to the subspace spanned by $\{1, x, x^2, \ldots, x^n\}$.

---

[14]Not to be confused with the generalized mean $n^{-1/p} \|\mathbf{x}\|_p$, which in the limit as $p \to 0$ is the geometric mean of $\mathbf{x}$.

10.2. Show that the coefficients in the three-term recurrence relation of the Legendre polynomials are given by a_n and $b_n = -n^2/(4n^2 - 1)$.

10.3. When we learn arithmetic, we are first taught integer values. Only later are we introduced to fractions and then irrational numbers, which fill out the number line. Learning calculus is similar. We start by computing with whole derivatives and rules of working with them, such as

$$\frac{d}{dx}\frac{d}{dx}f(x) = \frac{d^2}{dx^2}f(x).$$

In advanced calculus, we may be introduced to fractional derivatives. For example,

$$\frac{d^{1/2}}{dx^{1/2}}\frac{d^{1/2}}{dx^{1/2}}f(x) = \frac{d}{dx}f(x)$$

One way to compute a fractional derivative is with the help of a Fourier transform. If $\hat{f}(k)$ is the Fourier transform of $f(x)$, then $(ik)^p\hat{f}(k)$ is Fourier transform of the pth derivative of $f(x)$. Compute the fractional derivatives of the sine, piecewise-quadratic, piecewise-linear, and Gaussian functions:

- $\sin x$ for $x \in [-\pi, \pi]$
- $-\frac{1}{4}\text{sign}(x) \cdot ((2|x| - 1)^2 - 1)$ for $x \in [-1, 1]$
- $\frac{1}{2} - |x|$ for $x \in [-1, 1]$
- e^{-6x^2} for $x \in [-2, 2]$

The function e^{-6x^2} is not periodic, but as long as the domain is sufficiently larg Similarly, the piecewise-linear and piecewise-quadratic functions are not smooth. Still, as long as the domain has sufficient resolution to account for the slow decay of the Fourier transform, we minimize the effects of aliasing. Repeat the exercise using a Chebyshev differentiation matrix.

10.4. In 1998, Yann LeCun and fellow researchers published one of the earliest examples of a convolutional neural network, called LeNet-5, in their article "Gradient-based learning applied to document recognition." LeNet-5, which consists of five trainable parameter layers with over 60 thousand parameters combined, was designed to classify handwritten digits. Modern CNN architecture has evolved since LeNet-5 debuted almost 25 years ago—ReLU activation functions have displaced sigmoid activation functions, max pooling or even no pooling is typically used instead of average pooling, depth can reach into the hundreds of layers rather than a handful of them, and GPUs have largely replaced CPUs. This exercise examines the classic LeNet-5, sometimes described as the "Hello, World" program of deep neural nets. Read the LeCun article and

implement LeNet-5 to classify the digits in the MNIST dataset. The dataset is
available through the MLDatasets.jl package.   ✍

10.5. Multilateration finds the source (x, y, t) of a signal by solving a system of
equations
$$(x - x_i)^2 + (y - y_i)^2 = c^2(t_i - t + \varepsilon_i)^2,$$
where (x_i, y_i) are the locations of listening stations, t_i is the signal arrival time
at station i, c is the signal speed, and ε_i is an unknown offset that accounts for
reflection or diffraction by obstacles in the signal pathway. Suppose that the
offset in the transmission times ε_i is normally distributed. Solve $\boldsymbol{\varepsilon}(x, y, t) = \mathbf{0}$
using nonlinear least squares to determine (x, y, t) for locations (x_i, y_i) given
in exercise 3.10. Take $c = 1$. Modify your method to locate the source of the
gunfire described in exercise 3.4.   ✍

Chapter 11

Differentiation and Integration

Numerical approximations to derivatives and integrals appear throughout scientific computing. For example, root-finding methods typically require a derivative. Backpropagation, a necessary step in training neural networks, uses gradients. And collocation computes high-order polynomial approximations of derivative and integral operators. This chapter rounds out many of the topics from the others by examining numerical and automatic differentiation as well as Newton–Cotes, Gaussian, and Monte Carlo integration.

11.1 Numerical differentiation

The previous chapter discussed numerical differentiation using Fourier and Chebyshev polynomials. Now, let's turn to numerical differentiation using Taylor polynomials.

▷ Taylor polynomial approach

Suppose that we want to find the derivative of some sufficiently smooth function f at x. Let h be a small displacement. From Taylor series expansion, we have

$$f(x + h) = f(x) + hf'(x) + \tfrac{1}{2}h^2 f''(x) + O(h^3)$$
$$f(x) = f(x).$$

Taking the difference of these equations gives us

$$f(x + h) - f(x) = hf'(x) + \tfrac{1}{2}h^2 f''(x) + O(h^3),$$

from which we have the approximation

$$f'(x) \approx \frac{f(x+h) - f(x)}{h}$$

with an error of $hf''(x) + O(h^2)$. The error term says that the approximation is first order. To get higher-order methods, we add more nodes. With three equally spaced nodes,

$$f(x+h) = f(x) + hf'(x) + \tfrac{1}{2}h^2 f''(x) + O(h^3)$$
$$f(x) = f(x)$$
$$f(x-h) = f(x) - hf'(x) + \tfrac{1}{2}h^2 f''(x) + O(h^3).$$

We want to eliminate as many terms that could contribute to error. Consider the unknowns a, b, c

$$af(x+h) = af(x) + ahf'(x) + a\tfrac{1}{2}h^2 f''(x) + a\tfrac{1}{6}h^3 f''(x) + O(h^4)$$
$$bf(x) = bf(x)$$
$$cf(x-h) = cf(x) - chf'(x) + c\tfrac{1}{2}h^2 f''(x) - c\tfrac{1}{6}h^3 f''(x) + O(h^4).$$

To ensure consistency, we must eliminate the $f(x)$ terms and keep the $f'(x)$ terms on the right-hand side. To get a second-order method, we must further eliminate the $f''(x)$ terms. So, we have the system of equations

$$a + b + c = 0$$
$$a - c = 1$$
$$\tfrac{1}{2}a + \tfrac{1}{2}c = 0$$

The solution to the system $a = \tfrac{1}{2}$, $b = 0$, and $c = -\tfrac{1}{2}$ gives us

$$\tfrac{1}{2}f(x+h) - \tfrac{1}{2}f(x-h) = hf'(x) + \tfrac{1}{6}h^3 f'''(x) + O(h^4),$$

from which we have

$$f'(x) \approx \frac{f(x+h) - f(x-h)}{2h}$$

with an error of $\tfrac{1}{6}h^2 f'''(x) + O(h^3)$.

Of course, we can extend this process using four nodes to get a third-order method, using five nodes to get a fourth-order method, an so on. We could also use irregularly spaced nodes. And we could generalize the approach to compute derivatives beyond the first derivative. Let's do this. We'll start with Taylor polynomial approximations

$$f(x + \delta_i h) = \sum_{j=0}^{n-1} \frac{1}{j!} (\delta_i h)^j f^{(j)}(x) + O(h^n),$$

where δ_i scales the step size h. We want to find a set of coefficients c_{ki} that satisfy the system of equations for each $k = 0, 1, \ldots, n - 1$:

$$\sum_{i=0}^{n-1} c_{ki} f(x + \delta_i h) = h^k f^{(k)}(x) + O(h^n).$$

That is,

$$\sum_{i=0}^{n-1} \sum_{j=0}^{n-1} c_{ki} \frac{\delta_i^j}{j!} h^j f^{(j)}(x) = h^k f^{(k)}(x) + O(h^n).$$

Hence, we have the system $\mathbf{CV} = \mathbf{I}$, where $\mathbf{C}$ is the matrix of coefficients c_{ki} and $\mathbf{V}$ is the scaled Vandermonde matrix

$$\mathbf{V} = \begin{bmatrix} 1 & \delta_0 & \cdots & \delta_0^{n-1} \\ 1 & \delta_1 & \cdots & \delta_1^{n-1} \\ \vdots & \vdots & \ddots & \vdots \\ 1 & \delta_{n-1} & \cdots & \delta_{n-1}^{n-1} \end{bmatrix} \begin{bmatrix} 1/0! & & & \\ & 1/1! & & \\ & & \ddots & \\ & & & 1/(n-1)! \end{bmatrix}.$$

To determine the coefficient matrix $\mathbf{C}$, we simply need to calculate $\mathbf{V}^{-1}$. The first row of $\mathbf{C}$ is the set of coefficients $\{c_{0i}\}$ for an $O(h^n)$ approximation of $f(x)$, the second row is the set of coefficients $\{c_{1i}\}$ for an $O(h^{n-1})$ approximation of $f'(x)$, and so on. The coefficients of the truncation error are $\mathbf{C}\left[\delta_i^n\right]/n!$.

Example.   Let's compute the third-order approximation to $f'(x)$ using nodes at $x - h, x, x + h$ and $x + 2h$:

```
δ = [-1,0,1,2]
n = length(δ)
V = δ.^(0:n-1)' ./ factorial.(0:n-1)'
C = inv(V)
```

The coefficients of the truncation error are C*δ.^n./factorial(n):

0	1	0	0	0
$-1/3$	$-1/2$	1	$-1/6$	$-1/12$
1	-2	1	0	$1/12$
-1	3	-3	1	$1/2$

From the second row, we have

$$f'(x) = \frac{-\frac{1}{3}f(x - h) - \frac{1}{2}f(x) + f(x + h) - \frac{1}{6}f(x + 2h)}{h} + O\left(\tfrac{1}{12}h^3\right).$$

We can also approximate $f''(x)$ using the third row

$$f''(x) = \frac{f(x - h) - 2f(x) + f(x + h)}{h} + O\left(\tfrac{1}{12}h^2\right)$$

and $f'''(x)$ using the bottom row

$$f'''(x) = \frac{-f(x-h) + 3f(x) - 3f(x+h) + f(x+2h)}{h} + O\left(\tfrac{1}{2}h\right). \quad \blacktriangleleft$$

•• Julia has a rational number type `Rational` that expresses the ratio of integers. For example, `3//4` is the Julia representation for $\frac{3}{4}$. You can also convert the floating-point number 0.75 to a rational using `rationalize(0.75)`.

▷ **Richardson extrapolation**

We can improve the accuracy of a polynomial interpolant by adding more nodes—subdividing the interval into smaller and smaller subintervals. Rather than restarting with a whole new set of nodes and recomputing the approximation to derivative, let's develop a way to add nodes that update the approximation from the previous nodes. We'll use a method called *Richardson extrapolation*. Suppose that we have any expansion

$$\phi(h) = a_0 + a_1 h^p + a_2 h^{2p} + a_3 h^{3p} + \cdots \qquad (11.1)$$

for which we want to determine the value a_0 in terms of function on the left-hand side of the equation. For example, we could have the central difference approximation

$$\phi(h) = \frac{f(x+h) - f(x-h)}{2h} = f'(x) + \tfrac{1}{3!}f''(x)h^2 + \tfrac{1}{3!}f^{(5)}h^4 + \cdots .$$

Richardson extrapolation allows us to successively eliminate the h^p, h^{2p}, and higher-order terms. Take

$$\phi(\delta h) = a_0 + a_1 \delta^p h^p + a_2 \delta^{2p} h^{2p} + a_3 \delta^{3p} h^{3p} + \cdots .$$

where $0 < \delta < 1$. Typically, $\delta = \tfrac{1}{2}$. Then

$$\phi(\delta h) - \delta^p \phi(h) = a_0(1 - \delta^p) + 0 + a_2(\delta^{2p} - \delta^p)h^2 + \cdots ,$$

from which

$$\frac{\phi(\delta h) - \delta^p \phi(h)}{1 - \delta^p} = a_0 + \tilde{a}_1 h^{2p} + \tilde{a}_2 h^{3p} + \tilde{a}_3 h^{4p} + \cdots$$

for some new coefficients $\tilde{a}_1, \tilde{a}_2, \ldots$. This new equation has the same form as the original equation (11.1), so we can repeat the process to eliminate the h^{2p} term. We now have a recursion formula for $a_0 = D_{m,n} + o\left((\delta^m h)^{pn}\right)$ where

$$D_{0,0}$$

$$D_{1,0} \rightarrow D_{1,1}$$

$$D_{2,0} \rightarrow D_{2,1} \rightarrow D_{2,2}$$

$$D_{3,0} \rightarrow D_{3,1} \rightarrow D_{3,2} \rightarrow D_{3,3}$$

$$D_{m,0} = \phi(\delta^m h)$$

$$D_{m,n} = \frac{D_{m,n-1} - \delta^{pn} D_{m-1,n-1}}{1 - \delta^{pn}} \text{ for } m \geq n.$$

Julia code for Richardson extrapolation taking $\delta = \frac{1}{2}$ is

```
function richardson(f,x,m,n=m)
  n > 0 ?
  (4^n*richardson(f,x,m,n-1) - richardson(f,x,m-1,n-1))/(4^n-1) :
  ϕ(f,x,2^m)
end
```

where the finite difference operator is

```
ϕ = (f,x,n) -> (f(x+1/n) - f(x-1/n))/(2/n)
```

We can compute the derivative of $\sin x$ at zero as `richardson(x->sin(x),0,4)`, resulting in an error of 2.4×10^{-14}.

British mathematician Lewis Fry Richardson made several contributions relating to the scales of things, from weather prediction to violent conflict. The success of Richardson's extrapolation is due to smooth functions having a rectifiable length. But not all curves are rectifiable. Richardson observed that measurements of things like seacoasts don't converge by taking progressively smaller scales. Capes and fjords, absent on the large scale, emerge on the small scale. Spits and coves appear at still smaller scales. Richardson found that by dividing a coastline into segments of length h, its total length could be approximated using mh^{1-d}, for some parameters m and d. The Australian coast has a dimensionality $d = 1.13$, and the west coast of Great Britain has $d = 1.25$. Richardson's empirical finding went largely unnoticed until Benoit Mandelbrot wrote about it in 1967. Several years later, Mandelbrot coined the word fractal (from the Latin *fractus* for shattered) and the "Richardson effect" to describe the fractal nature of infinite coastlines.

11.2   Automatic differentiation

There are three common methods of calculating the derivative using a computer: numerical differentiation, symbolic differentiation, and automatic differentiation. Numerical differentiation, which is discussed extensively throughout this book, evaluates the derivative of a function by calculating finite difference approximations of that function or by computing the actual derivative of a simpler approximation of the original function. Because numerical differentiation takes the differences of approximate values or approximate functions, it is affected by truncation error and round-off error. Symbolic differentiation applies rules of differential calculus—the product rule, the power rule, the chain rule, the sine rule, and so on—to manipulate mathematical expressions of symbolic variables. It expands and then simplifies the derivative of that expression in terms of the symbolic variable. By explicitly manipulating the terms, symbolic differentiation produces the closed-form expression of the derivative without numerical approximation error. While such an approach works well for simple expressions, computation time and memory often grow exponentially as the expression size increases. Automatic differentiation, or autodiff, shares features of both numerical and symbolic differentiation. Like symbolic differentiation, automatic differentiation uses explicit rules of calculus to evaluate a derivative of a mathematical expression. Like numerical differentiation, it operates on numerical variables instead of symbolic ones.

Every function evaluated by a computer is a composition of a few basic operations: addition and subtraction, multiplication, exponentiation, some elementary functions, and looping and branching. In Julia, even common functions like sin and exp are computed using high-order Taylor polynomials. Because operations can be represented using a few basic functions, we can develop an arithmetic that differentiates those operators and links them together using the chain rule.

Let's start with a short excursion into nonstandard analysis. A dual number is a number of the form $a + b\varepsilon$ where $\varepsilon^2 = 0$. Dual numbers are the adjunction of a real or complex number a with an infinitesimal number $b\varepsilon$. Just as we could represent a complex number $a + bi$ as an ordered pair of real numbers (a, b) with multiplication and other operations defined in a special way, we can represent a dual number $a + b\varepsilon$ as the ordered pair (a, b) with special rules of arithmetic. First, consider Taylor series expansion:

$$f(x + \varepsilon) = f(x) + \varepsilon f'(x) + \tfrac{1}{2}\varepsilon^2 f''(x) + \cdots = f(x) + \varepsilon f'(x) \equiv (f, f'),$$

where all ε^2 and higher terms are zero. This expression is the formal infinitesimal definition of the derivative using nonstandard analysis

$$f'(x) = \frac{f(x + \varepsilon) - f(x)}{\varepsilon}.$$

Note that the derivative is not defined as the limit as a real number ε goes to zero. Instead, it is defined entirely with respect to an infinitesimal ε. Dual numbers follow the same addition and multiplication rules with the additional rule that $\varepsilon^2 = 0$. For example, for addition,

$$(f, f') + (g, g') \equiv (f + f'\varepsilon) + (g + g'\varepsilon) = (f + g) + (f' + g')\varepsilon$$
$$\equiv (f + g, f' + g');$$

for multiplication,

$$(f, f') \cdot (g, g') \equiv (f + f'\varepsilon) \cdot (g + g'\varepsilon) = fg + (f'g + fg')\varepsilon$$
$$\equiv (fg, f'g + fg');$$

and for division,

$$\frac{(f, f')}{(g, g')} \equiv \frac{f + f'\varepsilon}{g + g'\varepsilon} = \frac{(f + f'\varepsilon)}{(g + g'\varepsilon)} \frac{(g - g'\varepsilon)}{(g - g'\varepsilon)} = \frac{fg + (f'g - g'f)\varepsilon}{g^2}$$
$$\equiv \left(\frac{f}{g}, \frac{f'g - g'f}{g^2} \right).$$

The results are the familiar addition, product, and quotient rules of calculus. We can compute the values of the derivatives at the same time that the values of the functions are evaluated with only a few more operations. When implemented in a programming language such as Julia or Matlab, each function can be overloaded to return its value and derivative. For the chain rule,

$$(f \circ g, (f \circ g)') \equiv f(g(x) + \varepsilon g'(x)) = f(g(x)) + \varepsilon g'(x) f'(g(x))$$
$$\equiv (f \circ g, f'g').$$

When applying the chain rule to several functions $f \circ g \circ h$, we can compute either from the inside out by taking $f \circ (g \circ h)$—a process called forward accumulation—or from the outside in by taking $(f \circ g) \circ h$—a process called reverse accumulation.

Example.   Consider the function $y = x + \sin x$ with the computational graph:

$$v_2 \leftarrow \sin v_1 \qquad v_2' \leftarrow (\cos v_1)v_1'$$
$$v_3 \leftarrow v_1 + v_2 \qquad v_3' \leftarrow v_1' + v_2'$$

We can build a minimal working example of forward accumulation automatic differentiation by defining a structure and overloading the base operators:

```
struct Dual
    value
    deriv
end
```

Let's define a few helper functions:

```
Dual(x) = Dual(x,1)
value(x) = x isa Dual ? x.value : x
deriv(x) = x isa Dual ? x.deriv : 0
```

Now, we'll overload some base functions:

```
Base.:+(u, v) = Dual(value(u)+value(v), deriv(u)+deriv(v))
Base.:-(u, v) = Dual(value(u)-value(v), deriv(u)-deriv(v))
Base.:*(u, v) = Dual(value(u)*value(v),
   value(u)*deriv(v)+value(v)*deriv(u))
Base.:sin(u) = Dual(sin(value(u)), cos(value(u))*deriv(u))
```

We'll define $x = 0$ as a dual number and y as the function of that dual number:

```
x = Dual(0)
y = x + sin(x)
```

which returns `Dual(0.0, 2.0)` as expected. ◄

For a system $f : \mathbb{R}^m \to \mathbb{R}^n$ we have the dual form

$$(f(\mathbf{x}), f'(\mathbf{x})) = f(\mathbf{x} + \varepsilon) = f(\mathbf{x}) + \mathbf{J}_f(\mathbf{x})\varepsilon = (f(\mathbf{x}), \mathbf{J}_f(\mathbf{x})),$$

where $\mathbf{J}_f(\mathbf{x})$ is the $m \times n$ Jacobian matrix evaluated at $\mathbf{x}$. We can choose between forward accumulation and reverse accumulation in constructing the Jacobian matrix. We'll examine each in the following example.

Example.   Consider the system of equations and its accompanying computational graph

$$y_1 = x_1 x_2 + \sin x_2$$
$$y_2 = x_1 x_2 - \sin x_2 \tag{11.2}$$

We can express the derivatives as

$$\begin{bmatrix} y_1' \\ y_2' \end{bmatrix} = \begin{bmatrix} v_5' \\ v_6' \end{bmatrix} = \begin{bmatrix} 1 & 1 \\ 1 & -1 \end{bmatrix} \begin{bmatrix} v_3' \\ v_4' \end{bmatrix} = \begin{bmatrix} 1 & 1 \\ 1 & -1 \end{bmatrix} \begin{bmatrix} v_2 & v_1 \\ 0 & \cos v_2 \end{bmatrix} \begin{bmatrix} v_1' \\ v_2' \end{bmatrix}$$

or equivalently

$$\mathbf{y}' = \begin{bmatrix} 1 & 1 \\ 1 & -1 \end{bmatrix} \begin{bmatrix} v_2 & v_1 \\ 0 & \cos v_2 \end{bmatrix} \mathbf{x}' = \mathbf{J}\mathbf{x}'.$$

Using a standard unit vector $\boldsymbol{\xi}_i$ as our input for $\mathbf{x}'$ will return a column of the Jacobian matrix evaluated at $\mathbf{x}$. In general, for m input variables, we'll need to compute m forward accumulation passes to compute the m columns. Because there are two input variables x_1 and x_2 in the system (11.2), we'll need to do two sweeps. We first start with $(x_1', x_2') = (1, 0)$ to get the first column of the Jacobian matrix. We next start with $(x_1', x_2') = (0, 1)$ to get the second column of the Jacobian matrix. Figure 11.1 shows each node (v_i, v_i') of the computational graph

variables	v		v'		
(v_1, v_1')	x_1	2	x_1'	1	0
(v_2, v_2')	x_2	π	x_2'	0	1
(v_3, v_3')	$v_1 v_2$	2π	$D_{31}v_1' + D_{32}v_2' \rightarrow v_2 v_1' + v_1 v_2'$	π	2
(v_4, v_4')	$\sin v_2$	0	$D_{42}v_2' \rightarrow v_2' \cos v_2$	0	-1
(v_5, v_5')	$v_4 + v_3$	2π	$D_{53}v_3' + D_{54}v_4' \rightarrow v_3' + v_4'$	π	1
(v_6, v_6')	$v_4 - v_3$	2π	$D_{63}v_3' + D_{64}v_4' \rightarrow v_3' - v_4'$	π	3

Figure 11.1: Forward accumulation automatic differentiation of the system (11.2) evaluated at $(x_1, x_2) = (2, \pi)$.

starting with $(x_1, x_2) = (2, \pi)$. The term D_{ij} represents the partial derivative $\partial v_i / \partial v_j$.

Let's use the code developed in the previous example on system (11.2). We can define the dual numbers as:

```
x₁ = Dual(2,[1 0])
x₂ = Dual(π,[0 1])
y₁ = x₁*x₂ + sin(x₂)
y₂ = x₁*x₂ - sin(x₂)
```

The variables y_1.value, y_2.value, y_1.deriv, y_2.deriv returns 6.2832, 6.2832, [3.1416 1.0000], and [3.1416 3.0000] as expected.

Now let's examine reverse accumulation. Reverse accumulation computes the transpose (or adjoint) of the Jacobian matrix

$$\begin{bmatrix} v_2 & 0 \\ v_1 & \cos v_2 \end{bmatrix} \begin{bmatrix} 1 & 1 \\ 1 & -1 \end{bmatrix} = \mathbf{J}^{\mathsf{T}} \bar{\mathbf{x}},$$

where $\bar{\mathbf{x}}$ is called the adjoint value. Using a standard unit vector $\boldsymbol{\xi}_i$ as our input for $\bar{\mathbf{x}}$ will return a row of the Jacobian matrix evaluated at $\mathbf{x}$. In general, for n output variables, we'll need to compute n reverse accumulation passes to compute the n rows. When the number of input variables m is much larger than the number of output variables n, which is often the case in neural networks, reverse accumulation is much more efficient than forward accumulation. We define the adjoint $\bar{v}_i = \partial y / \partial v_i$ as the derivative of the dependent variable with respect to y_i. To compute the Jacobian for a point (x_1, x_2), we first run through a forward pass to get the dependencies and graph structure. The forward pass is the same as forward accumulation and results in the same expression for y_1 and y_2. We then run backward once for each dependent variable, first taking $(y_1', y_2') = (1, 0)$ to get the first row of the Jacobian matrix and then taking $(y_1', y_2') = (0, 1)$ to get the second row of the Jacobian matrix. See Figure 11.2 on the following page. ◄

variables	v		$\bar{v}$		
$(v_1, \bar{v}_1)$	x_1	2	$D_{31}\bar{v}_3 \to v_2\bar{v}_3$	π	π
$(v_2, \bar{v}_2)$	x_2	π	$D_{32}\bar{v}_3 + D_{42}\bar{v}_4 \to v_1\bar{v}_3 + \bar{v}_4 \cos v_2$	1	3
$(v_3, \bar{v}_3)$	$v_1 v_2$	2π	$D_{53}\bar{v}_5 + D_{63}\bar{v}_6 \to \bar{v}_5 + \bar{v}_6$	1	1
$(v_4, \bar{v}_4)$	$\sin v_2$	0	$D_{54}\bar{v}_5 + D_{64}\bar{v}_6 \to \bar{v}_5 - \bar{v}_6$	1	-1
$(v_5, \bar{v}_5)$	$v_4 + v_3$	2π	y_1'	1	0
$(v_6, \bar{v}_6)$	$v_4 - v_3$	2π	y_2'	0	1

Figure 11.2: Reverse accumulation automatic differentiation of the system (11.2) evaluated at $(x_1, x_2) = (2, \pi)$.

Julia has several packages that implement forward and reverse automatic differentiation, including Zygote.jl, ForwardDiff.jl, and ReverseDiff.jl.

11.3 Newton–Cotes quadrature

Numerical integration is often called *quadrature*, a term that seems archaic like many others in mathematics. Historically, the quadrature of a figure described the process of constructing a square with the same areas as some given figure. The English word *quadrature* comes from the Latin *quadratura* (to square). It wasn't until the late nineteenth century that the classical problem of ancient geometers of "squaring the circle"—finding a square with the same area as a circle using only a compass and straightedge—was finally proved to be impossible when the Lindemann–Weierstrass theorem demonstrated that π is a transcendental number. The name quadrature stuck with us, and most scientific programming languages now use some variant of the term `quad` for numerical integration.[1] It wasn't until recently that Matlab started to use the function name `integral`, because many users were having trouble finding `quad`.

The typical method for numerically integrating a smooth function is to approximate the function by a polynomial interpolant and then integrate the polynomial exactly. Recall from Chapter 9 that given a set of $n+1$ nodes we can determine the Lagrange basis for a polynomial

$$f(x) \approx p_n(x) = \sum_{i=0}^{n} f(x_i)\ell_i(x) \quad \text{where} \quad \ell_i(x) = \prod_{\substack{j=0 \\ j\neq i}}^{n} \frac{x - x_j}{x_i - x_j}.$$

[1]The even more archaic-sounding term *cubature* (finding the volume of solids) is sometimes used in reference to multiple integrals.

Therefore, we can approximate the integral of $f(x)$ by

$$\int_a^b p_n(x)\,dx = \int_a^b \left(\sum_{i=0}^n f(x_i)\ell_i(x) \right) dx$$

$$= \sum_{i=0}^n f(x_i) \int_a^b \ell_i(x)\,dx$$

$$= \sum_{i=0}^n w_i f(x_i) \quad \text{where} \quad w_i = \int_a^b \ell_i(x)\,dx. \tag{11.3}$$

For uniformly spaced nodes, the method is called a *Newton–Cotes formula*.
Suppose that we take two nodes at $x = \{0, 1\}$. Then

$$w_0 = \int_0^1 \ell_0(x)\,dx = \int_0^1 (1-x)\,dx = \tfrac{1}{2}$$

$$w_1 = \int_0^1 \ell_1(x)\,dx = \int_0^1 x\,dx = \tfrac{1}{2}.$$

We have that $\int_0^1 f(x)\,dx \approx \tfrac{1}{2}(f(0) + f(1))$. We call this the *trapezoidal rule*.
Over an arbitrary interval $[a, b]$,

$$\int_a^b f(x)\,dx \approx \frac{b-a}{2}(f(a) + f(b)).$$

Now, suppose that we divide the interval $[0, 1]$ in half, giving us three nodes at
$x = \{0, \tfrac{1}{2}, 1\}$. This time the polynomial interpolant will be quadratic. Then

$$w_0 = \int_0^1 \ell_0(x)\,dx = \int_0^1 2(1-x)\left(\tfrac{1}{2} - x\right) dx = \tfrac{1}{6},$$

$$w_1 = \int_0^1 \ell_1(x)\,dx = \int_0^1 4x(1-x)\,dx = \tfrac{2}{3},$$

$$w_2 = \int_0^1 \ell_2(x)\,dx = \int_0^1 2x\left(x - \tfrac{1}{2}\right) dx = \tfrac{1}{6}.$$

We have that $\int_0^1 f(x)\,dx \approx \tfrac{1}{6}\left[f(0) + 4f(\tfrac{1}{2}) + f(1)\right]$. We call this *Simpson's
rule*. Over an arbitrary interval $[a, b]$,

$$\int_a^b f(x)\,dx \approx \frac{b-a}{6}\left[f(a) + 4f\left(\frac{a+b}{2}\right) + f(b)\right].$$

We could continue by dividing each subsegment $[0, \tfrac{1}{2}]$ and $[\tfrac{1}{2}, 0]$ in half, giving
us five equally spaced nodes. The polynomial interpolant is quartic this time,

and the approximation is called *Boole's rule*:

$$\int_0^1 f(x)\,dx \approx \tfrac{2}{45}\left[7f(0) + 32f(\tfrac{1}{4}) + 12f(\tfrac{1}{2}) + 32f(\tfrac{3}{4}) + 7f(1)\right].$$

From theorem 26 on page 232, if an nth degree polynomial $p_n(x)$ interpolates a sufficiently smooth function $f(x)$ at the points $x_0, x_1, \ldots, x_n$ in an interval, then for each x in that interval, there is a ξ in the interval such that the pointwise error

$$f(x) - p_n(x) = \frac{1}{(n+1)!} f^{(n+1)}(\xi) \prod_{i=0}^{n} (x - x_i).$$

The error for the trapezoidal rule over an interval of length h is

$$\int_0^h f(x) - p_1(x) = \tfrac{1}{2} f^{(2)}(\xi) \int_0^h (x)(x - h)\,dx = -\tfrac{1}{12} h^3 f^{(2)}(\xi)$$

for some $\xi \in [0, h]$. Now, consider Simpson's rule over $[-h, h]$—two subintervals each of length h. Simpson's rule is derived using a quadratic interpolating polynomial, so it is exact if $f(x)$ is a quadratic polynomial. Simpson's rule is, in fact, also exact if $f(x)$ is cubic because x^3 is an odd function, and its contribution integrates out to zero. So let's consider a cubic polynomial over the interval $[-h, h]$ with nodes at $-h$, 0, and h and a fourth node at an arbitrary point c. The error of Simpson's rule is

$$\int_{-h}^h f(x) - p_3(x)\,dx = \tfrac{1}{24} f^{(4)}(\xi) \int_{-h}^h x(x - c)(x^2 - h^2)\,dx = -\tfrac{1}{90} h^5 f^{(4)}(\xi)$$

for some $\xi \in [-h, h]$. While we can get more accurate methods by adding nodes and using higher-order polynomials such as Boole's rule, such an approach is not generally good because of the Runge phenomenon. Instead, we can either use a piecewise polynomial approximation (a spline) or pick nodes to minimize the uniform error (such as using Chebyshev nodes). We'll look at both of these options in turn.

▷ **Composite methods**

Composite methods use splines to approximate the integrand. The simplest type of spline is a constant spline. Using these, we get Riemann sums. Linear splines give us the *composite trapezoidal rule*, a more accurate method that applies the trapezoidal rule to each subinterval. For $n + 1$ equally-space nodes

$$\int_a^b f(x)\,dx \approx h\left[\tfrac{1}{2}f(a) + \sum_{i=1}^{n-1} f(a + ih) + \tfrac{1}{2}f(b)\right] \tag{11.4}$$

where $h = (b - a)/n$.

```
function trapezoidal(f,x,n)
  F = f.(LinRange(x[1],x[2],n+1))
  (F[1]/2 + sum(F[2:end-1]) + F[end]/2)*(x[2]-x[1])/n
end
```

The error for the trapezoidal rule is bounded by $\frac{1}{12}h^3|f^{(2)}(\xi)|$ for some ξ in a subinterval. The error for the composite trapezoidal rule is bounded by $\frac{1}{12}(b-a)^3\left|f^{(2)}(\xi)\right|/n^2$ for some $\xi \in (a,b)$. We can derive a much better error estimate with a bit of extra work, which we'll do in a couple of pages. Because the composite trapezoidal rule is a second-order method, if we use twice as many intervals, we can expect the error to be reduced by about a factor of four. And with four times as many intervals, we can reduce the error by about a factor of sixteen.

With a quadratic spline, Simpson's rule becomes the *composite Simpson's rule*. For $n + 1$ equally spaced nodes, Simpson's rule says

$$\int_{x_{i-1}}^{x_{i+1}} f(x)\,dx \approx \frac{2h}{6}\left(f(x_{i-1}) + 4f(x_i) + f(x_{i+1})\right).$$

Therefore, over the entire interval $[a, b]$

$$\int_a^b f(x)\,dx \approx \frac{h}{3}\left(f(x_0) + 4\sum_{i=1}^{n/2} f(x_{2i-1}) + 2\sum_{i=2}^{n/2} f(x_{2i-2}) + f(x_n)\right).$$

The error of Simpson's rule is $\frac{1}{90}h^5 f^{(4)}(\xi)$, so the error of the composite Simpson's rule is bounded by $\frac{1}{180}(b-a)^5 f^{(4)}(\xi)/n^4$ for some ξ over an interval (a, b). By using twice as many intervals, we should expect the error to decrease by a factor of 16. In practice, one often uses an *adaptive* composite trapezoidal or Simpson's rule. But, if we can choose the positions of the nodes at which we integrate, then it's much better to choose Gaussian quadrature.

We can also apply Richardson extrapolation to the composite trapezoidal rule. Such an approach is called *Romberg's method*. Take $\phi(h)$ to be the composite trapezoidal rule using nodes separated by a distance h. Then $D_{m,0}$ extrapolation is equivalent to the composite trapezoidal rule, $D_{m,1}$ extrapolation is equivalent to the composite Simpson's rule, and $D_{m,2}$ extrapolation is equivalent to the composite Boole's rule—all with 2^m subsegments. We can implement a naïve Romberg's method by replacing the definition of ϕ in the Julia code on page 299 with a composite transpose method:

```
φ = (f,x,n) -> trapezoidal(f,x,n)
```

Now, `richardson(x->sin(x),[0,π/2],4)` returns the integral of $\sin x$ from zero to $\pi/2$, with an error of 1.98×10^{-12}.

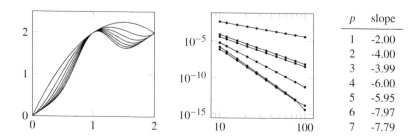

Figure 11.3: Left: Plot of $f_p(x) = x + x^p(2-x)^p$ for $p = 1, 2, \ldots, 7$. Middle: Error using composite trapezoidal rule for $f_p(x)$ as a function of the number of nodes. Right: Slopes of the curves.

Example. Let's examine the error of the composite trapezoidal rule applied to the function $f(x) = x + x^p(2-x)^p$ over the interval $[0, 2]$ with $p = 1, 2, \ldots, 7$.

```
n = [floor(Int,10^y) for y in LinRange(1, 2, 10)]
error = zeros(10,7)
f = (x,p) -> x + x.^p.*(2-x).^p
for p ∈ 1:7,
  S = trapezoidal(x->f(x,p),[0,2],10^6)
  for i ∈ 1:length(n)
    Sₙ = trapezoidal(x->f(x,p),[0,2],n[i])
    error[i,p] = abs(Sₙ - S)/S
  end
end
slope = ([log.(n) one.(n)]\log.(error))[1,:]
info = .*(string.((1:7)'),": slope=",string.(round.(slope')))
plot(n,error, xaxis=:log, yaxis=:log, labels = info)
```

See Figure 11.3 above. We can determine the convergence rate by computing $\begin{bmatrix} \mathbf{x} & \mathbf{1} \end{bmatrix}^{-1} \mathbf{y}$ where $\mathbf{x}$ is a vector of logarithms of the number of nodes, $\mathbf{y}$ is a vector of logarithms of the errors, and $\mathbf{1}$ is an appropriately-sized vector of ones. We had earlier determined that the error of a composite trapezoidal rule should be $O(n^2)$ or better for a smooth function. We find that the error of the trapezoidal rule is $O(n^2)$ when $p = 1$. We find that the error is $O(n^4)$ when p is 2 or 3, $O(n^6)$ when p is 4 or 5, and $O(n^8)$ when p is 6 or 7. What's going on?   ◄

▷ Error of the composite trapezoidal rule

Let's reexamine the quadrature error of the composite trapezoidal rule a little more rigorously. Apply the composite trapezoidal rule to a function $f(x)$ on the interval $[0, \pi]$ with $n + 1$ nodes:

$$S_n = \frac{\pi}{n} \left[\frac{f(0)}{2} + \sum_{i=1}^{n-1} f\left(\frac{i\pi}{n}\right) + \frac{f(\pi)}{2} \right].$$

The interval $[0, \pi]$ might seem a little arbitrary, and in fact, any finite interval would do, but using $[0, \pi]$ will help the mathematical feng shui further on. If we expand $f(x)$ as a cosine series

$$f(x) = \frac{a_0}{2} + \sum_{k=1}^{\infty} a_k \cos kx \quad \text{with} \quad a_k = \frac{2}{\pi} \int_0^{\pi} f(x) \cos kx \, dx,$$

then

$$S = \int_0^{\pi} f(x) \, dx = \frac{a_0 \pi}{2}$$

and

$$S_n = \frac{a_0 \pi}{2} + \frac{\pi}{n} \sum_{k=1}^{\infty} a_k \left(\frac{1 + (-1)^k}{2} + \sum_{i=1}^{n-1} \cos \frac{ik\pi}{n} \right) = S + \pi \sum_{k=1}^{\infty} a_{2nk}.$$

The last equality follows directly from the identity

$$\sum_{j=0}^{n-1} \cos \frac{jk\pi}{n} = \begin{cases} n & \text{if } k \text{ is an even multiple of } n \\ 0 & \text{if } k \text{ is otherwise even} \\ 1 & \text{if } k \text{ is odd} \end{cases}.$$

This identity itself follows from computing the real part of the geometric series

$$\sum_{j=0}^{n-1} e^{ijk\pi/n} = \frac{1 - (-1)^k}{1 - e^{ik\pi/n}}$$

and noting that the real part of $(1 - e^{ix})^{-1}$ equals $\frac{1}{2}$ for any x.

The quadrature error $S_n - S$ is $\pi \sum_{k=1}^{\infty} a_{2nk}$. So the convergence rate of the composite trapezoidal method is determined by the convergence rate of coefficients of the cosine series. If $f(x)$ is a smooth function, then by repeatedly integrating by parts, we get

$$a_{2nk} = \frac{2}{\pi} \int_0^{\pi} f(x) \cos 2nkx \, dx = \frac{2}{\pi} \sum_{j=1}^{\infty} (-1)^j \left. \frac{f^{(2j-1)}(x)}{(2nk)^{2j}} \right|_0^{\pi}.$$

Therefore, the error of the trapezoidal rule can be characterized by the odd derivatives at the endpoints $x = 0$ and $x = \pi$. If $f'(0) \neq f'(\pi)$, then we can expect a convergence rate of $O(n^2)$. If $f'(0) = f'(\pi)$ and $f'''(0) \neq f'''(\pi)$, then we can expect a convergence rate of $O(n^4)$. If the function $f(x)$ is periodic or if each of the odd derivatives of $f(x)$ vanishes at the endpoints, then the composite trapezoidal rule gives us exponential or spectral convergence.[2] If the function $f(x)$ is not periodic or does not have matching odd derivatives at the endpoints, we can still make a change of variable to put it in a form that does. This approach, called Clenshaw–Curtis or Frejér quadrature, will allow us to integrate any smooth function with spectral convergence.

▷ **Clenshaw–Curtis quadrature**

Take any smooth function over an interval $[-1, 1]$ and make a change of variables $x = \cos\theta$,

$$\int_{-1}^{1} f(x)\,dx = \int_{0}^{\pi} f(\cos\theta) \sin\theta\,d\theta.$$

We can express $f(\cos\theta)$ as a cosine series

$$f(\cos\theta) = \frac{a_0}{2} + \sum_{k=1}^{\infty} a_k \cos(k\theta) \quad \text{where} \quad a_k = \frac{2}{\pi}\int_{0}^{\pi} f(\cos\theta) \cos k\theta\,d\theta$$

and integrate analytically

$$S = \int_{0}^{\pi} \left(\frac{a_0}{2} + \sum_{k=1}^{\infty} a_k \cos(k\theta) \right) \sin\theta\,d\theta = a_0 + \sum_{k=1}^{\infty} \frac{2a_{2k}}{1 - (2k)^2}$$

where we now need to evaluate the coefficients a_{2k}. The integrand $f(\cos\theta)\cos k\theta$ is an even function at $\theta = 0$ and $\theta = \pi$, so we can expect spectral convergence. The trapezoidal rule is just the (type-1) discrete cosine transform

$$a_{2k} = \frac{2}{n} \left[\frac{f_0}{2} + \sum_{j=1}^{n-1} f_j \cos\left(\frac{2\pi j k}{n}\right) + \frac{f_n}{2} \right] \quad \text{where} \quad f_j = \cos\left(\frac{\pi j}{n}\right)$$

Extend the function $f(\cos\theta)$ as an even function at π: $f_{n+j} = f_{n-j}$. Then the discrete cosine transform over n nodes is exactly one-half the discrete Fourier

---

[2]The Euler–Maclaurin formula, which relates a sum to an integral, provides an alternative method for estimating the error of the composite trapezoidal rule. The Euler–Maclaurin formula states that if $f \in C^p(a, b)$ where a and b are integers, then

$$\sum_{i=a+1}^{b} f(i) = \int_{a}^{b} f(x)\,dx + \sum_{k=0}^{p-1} \frac{B_{k+1}}{(k+1)!} \left(f^{(k)}(b) - f^{(k)}(a) \right) + R_p$$

where B_k are the Bernoulli numbers and R_p is a remainder term. Odd Bernoulli numbers are zero except for B_1. Ada Lovelace is credited for writing the first computer program in 1843 to calculate the Bernoulli numbers using Charles Babbage's never-built Analytic Engine.

transform of $2n$ nodes because

$$\sum_{j=0}^{2n-1} f_j \exp\left(-\frac{i2\pi jk}{n}\right) = \sum_{j=0}^{n-1} f_j \cos\left(\frac{2\pi jk}{n}\right) + \sum_{j=n}^{2n-1} f_{2n-j} \cos\left(-\frac{2\pi jk}{n}\right)$$

after the sine terms cancel each other out. We can now easily compute the sum using a fast Fourier transform that can be evaluated in $O(n \log n)$ operations.

We can implement the Clenshaw–Curtis quadrature in Julia by computing the discrete cosine transform in

```
using FFTW, LinearAlgebra
function clenshaw_curtis(f,n)
    x = cos.(π*(0:n)'/n)
    w = zeros(n+1,1); w[1:2:n+1] = 2 ./ (1 .- (0:2:n).^2)
    1/n * dctI(f.(x)) · w
end
```

Julia's FFTW package does not have a named type-1 discrete cosine transform—the dct function is a type-2 DCT. We can formulate a type-1 DCT using

```
function dctI(f)
    g = FFTW.r2r!([f...],FFTW.REDFT00)
    [g[1]/2; g[2:end-1]; g[end]/2]
end
```

or we can explicitly construct one as above

```
function dctI(f)
    n = length(f)
    g = real(fft(f[[1:n; n-1:-1:2]]))
    [g[1]/2; g[2:n-1]; g[n]/2]
end
```

Aspects of Clenshaw–Curtis quadrature might seem familiar from the discussion of Chebyshev polynomials over the last two chapters. Note that

$$f(\cos\theta) = \tfrac{1}{2}a_0 + \sum_{k=1}^{\infty} a_k \cos(k \cos^{-1} x) = \tfrac{1}{2}a_0 + \sum_{k=1}^{\infty} a_k T_k(x),$$

where $T_k(x)$ is the kth Chebyshev polynomial. So expanding $f(\cos\theta)$ in a cosine series is the same as expanding $f(x)$ using Chebyshev polynomials. The next section will discuss the expansion of functions in orthogonal polynomial bases.

11.4   Gaussian quadrature

Let's return to the Newton–Cotes formula

$$\int_a^b p(x)\,dx = \sum_{i=0}^n w_i f(x_i) \quad \text{where} \quad w_i = \int_a^b \ell_i(x)\,dx. \qquad (11.5)$$

We can construct higher-order polynomials to approximate the integrand more closely by adding more nodes. The equally spaced nodes of Newton–Cotes quadrature are problematic, specifically because of Runge's phenomenon. Chapter 9 used Chebyshev nodes (the zeros of the Chebyshev polynomial) to minimize Runge's oscillations. This section considers broader families of orthogonal polynomials. The figures below show the difference between the function $(1 + 16x^2)^{-1}$ and polynomials that fit the function at either equally spaced nodes or Legendre–Lobatto nodes:

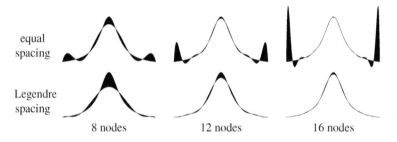

equal spacing			
Legendre spacing			
	8 nodes	12 nodes	16 nodes

Choosing quadrature nodes from the zeros of orthogonal polynomials does more than mitigate Runge's phenomenon. Remarkably, using these carefully selected nodes allows us to determine a polynomial interpolant whose degree is almost *double* the number of nodes.

Suppose that we let the nodes x_i vary freely, still computing the weights w_i based on their positions using the Newton–Cotes formula (11.5). One might ask, "what is the maximum degree of a polynomial $p(x)$ that can be constructed?" This is precisely the question Carl Friedrich Gauss raised in 1814. With $n + 1$ nodes and $n + 1$ weights along with $2n + 2$ constraints, one might rightfully conjecture that $p(x)$ would be uniquely determined using $2n + 2$ coefficients. Hence, the maximum degree is $2n + 1$. A quadrature that carefully chooses nodes to construct a maximal polynomial is called *Gaussian quadrature* (and sometimes Gauss–Christoffel quadrature).

From Chapter 10, we can generate orthogonal polynomials by using different inner product spaces. These orthogonal polynomials are the most important classes of polynomials for Gaussian quadrature and lend their names to Gauss–Legendre, Gauss–Chebyshev, Gauss–Hermite, Gauss–Laguerre, and Gauss–Jacobi quadrature. See the table on the facing page. Gauss–Jacobi quadrature,

polynomial	interval	weight	$\|1\|^2$	a_k	b_k
Legendre	$[-1, 1]$	1	2	0	$k^2/(4k^2 - 1)$
Chebyshev	$[-1, 1]$	$1/\sqrt{1 - x^2}$	$\pi/2$	0	$(1 + \delta_{k0})/4$
Hermite	$(-\infty, \infty)$	$\exp(-x^2)$	$\sqrt{\pi}$	0	$k/2$
Laguerre	$(0, \infty)$	$\exp(-x)$	1	$2k$	k^2

Figure 11.4: Parameters of common Gaussian quadrature methods.

with a weight $(1 - x)^{\alpha}(1 + x)^{\beta}$ with $\alpha, \beta > -1$, is a generalization of Gauss–Legendre quadrature ($\alpha = \beta = 0$) and Gauss–Chebyshev quadrature ($\alpha = \beta = -\frac{1}{2}$) and is suited for functions with endpoint singularities.

Theorem 42 (Fundamental Theorem of Gaussian Quadrature). *Let w be a positive weight function and let $q \in \mathbb{P}_{n+1}$ be a polynomial of degree $n + 1$ that is orthogonal to the space of nth-degree polynomials $\mathbb{P}_n$. Let $x_0, x_1, \ldots, x_n$ be the zeros of q. Then for any $f \in \mathbb{P}_{2n+1}$*

$$\int_a^b f(x)\omega(x)\,\mathrm{d}x = \sum_{i=0}^n w_i f(x_i) \quad where \quad w_i = \int_a^b \ell_i(x)\omega(x)\,\mathrm{d}x$$

with Lagrange basis $\ell_i(x)$ with nodes at $x_0, x_1, \ldots, x_n$.

Proof. Suppose that $f \in \mathbb{P}_{2n+1}$ and $q \in \mathbb{P}_{n+1}$. Then by dividing f by q

$$f(x) = q(x)p(x) + r(x)$$

for some $p, r \in \mathbb{P}_n$. Therefore,

$$\int_a^b f(x)\omega(x)\,\mathrm{d}x = \overbrace{\int_a^b q(x)p(x)\omega(x)\,\mathrm{d}x}^{0} + \int_a^b r(x)\omega(x)\,\mathrm{d}x = \sum_{i=0}^n w_i r(x_i)$$

because $(p, q) = \int_a^b q(x)p(x)\omega(x)\,\mathrm{d}x = 0$ for all $p \in \mathbb{P}_n$ and because $r \in \mathbb{P}_n$. At the zeros of q, $f(x_i) = q(x_i)p(x_i) + r(x_i) = r(x_i)$, and the result follows directly. $\qquad\square$

This theorem says that an n-node Gaussian quadrature yields the exact result for a polynomial of degree $2n - 1$ or less. Therefore, we can get a high-order accuracy with relatively few points—especially nice when $f(x)$ is expensive to compute.

Theorem 43. *For any function $f \in C^{2n+2}[a, b]$, the Gaussian quadrature error*

$$\int_a^b f(x)\omega(x)\,\mathrm{d}x - \sum_{i=0}^n w_i f(x_i) = \frac{f^{(2n+2)}(\xi)}{(2n + 2)!} \int_a^b q^2(x)\omega(x)\,\mathrm{d}x$$

where $q(x) = \prod_{i=0}^{n}(x - x_i)$ and ξ is some point in the interval of integration.

Proof. There exists a polynomial of degree $p(x)$ of degree at most $2n + 1$ with $p(x_i) = f(x_i)$ and $p'(x_i) = f'(x_i)$. From theorem 27

$$f(x) - p(x) = \frac{f^{(2n+2)}(\xi(x))}{(2n + 2)!}q^2(x)$$

from which it follows (after integrating both sides and applying the mean value theorem for integrals to the right-hand side):

$$\int_a^b f(x)\omega(x)\,dx - \int_a^b p(x)\omega(x)\,dx = \frac{f^{(2n+2)}(\xi)}{(2n + 2)!}\int_a^b q^2(x)\omega(x)\,dx.$$

By the fundamental theorem of Gaussian quadrature,

$$\int_a^b p(x)\omega(x)\,dx = \sum_{i=0}^{n} w_i p(x_i) = \sum_{i=0}^{n} w_i f(x_i).$$

And the error formula holds after substitution. $\qquad\qquad\square$

▷ Determining the nodes and the weights

We still need to determine the nodes x_i and the weights w_i. Let's first find the nodes for an arbitrary family of orthogonal polynomials. Recall Favard's theorem on page 254. It says that for each weighted inner product, there exist uniquely determined orthogonal polynomials $p_k \in \mathbb{P}_k$ with leading coefficient one satisfying the three-term recurrence relation

$$\begin{cases} p_{k+1}(x) = (x - a_k)p_k(x) - b_k p_{k-1}(x) \\ p_0(x) = 1, \quad p_1(x) = x - a_1 \end{cases}$$

where

$$a_k = \frac{(xp_k, p_k)}{(p_k, p_k)} \quad \text{and} \quad b_k = \frac{(p_k, p_k)}{(p_{k-1}, p_{k-1})}.$$

It will be useful to use an orthonormal basis. Take $\hat{p}_k = p_k/\|p_k\|$. Then we can rewrite the three-term recurrence relation as

$$\|p_{k+1}\|\hat{p}_{k+1}(x) = (x - a_k)\|p_k\|\hat{p}_k(x) - b_k\|p_{k-1}\|\hat{p}_{k-1}(x).$$

Dividing through by $\|p_k\|$ gives us

$$\frac{\|p_{k+1}\|}{\|p_k\|}\hat{p}_{k+1}(x) = (x - a_k)\hat{p}_k(x) - b_k\frac{\|p_{k-1}\|}{\|p_k\|}\hat{p}_{k-1}(x),$$

and by noting that $\|p_{k+1}\|/\|p_k\| = \sqrt{b_k}$, we have

$$\sqrt{b_{k+1}}\hat{p}_{k+1}(x) = (x - a_k)\hat{p}_k(x) - \sqrt{b_k}\hat{p}_{k-1}(x).$$

We can rearrange the terms

$$\sqrt{b_{k+1}}\hat{p}_{k+1}(x) + a_k\hat{p}_k(x) + \sqrt{b_k}\hat{p}_{k-1}(x) = x\hat{p}_k(x),$$

which is simply the linear system $\mathbf{J}_n\mathbf{p} = x\mathbf{p} + \mathbf{r}$:

$$\begin{bmatrix} a_0 & \sqrt{b_1} & & & \\ \sqrt{b_1} & a_1 & \sqrt{b_2} & & \\ & \ddots & \ddots & \ddots & \\ & & \sqrt{b_{n-1}} & a_{n-1} & \sqrt{b_n} \\ & & & \sqrt{b_n} & a_n \end{bmatrix} \begin{bmatrix} \hat{p}_0(x) \\ \hat{p}_1(x) \\ \vdots \\ \hat{p}_{n-1}(x) \\ \hat{p}_n(x) \end{bmatrix} = x \begin{bmatrix} \hat{p}_0(x) \\ \hat{p}_1(x) \\ \vdots \\ \hat{p}_{n-1}(x) \\ \hat{p}_n(x) \end{bmatrix} - \begin{bmatrix} 0 \\ 0 \\ \vdots \\ 0 \\ \sqrt{b_{n+1}}\hat{p}_{n+1}(x) \end{bmatrix}.$$

The tridiagonal matrix $\mathbf{J}_n$ is called the *Jacobi operator*. This equation says that $p_{n+1}(x) = 0$ if and only if $\mathbf{r} = \mathbf{0}$ if and only if $\mathbf{J}_n\mathbf{p} = x\mathbf{p}$. In other words, the roots of p_{n+1} are simply the eigenvalues of $\mathbf{J}_n$.

Now, let's get the weights. Note that by the fundamental theorem of Gaussian quadrature

$$\sum_{k=0}^{n} w_k\hat{p}_i(x_k)\hat{p}_j(x_k) = \int \hat{p}_i(x)\hat{p}_j(x)\omega(x)\,dx = (\hat{p}_i, \hat{p}_j) = \delta_{ij},$$

because the degree of $\hat{p}_i(x)\hat{p}_j(x)$ is strictly less than $2n$. But this simply says that $\mathbf{Q}^{\mathsf{T}}\mathbf{Q} = \mathbf{I}$ where the elements $Q_{ik} = \sqrt{w_k}\hat{p}_i(x_k)$. Hence, $\mathbf{Q}$ is an orthogonal matrix. So, $\mathbf{QQ}$ also equals the identity operator. Therefore,

$$\sum_{k=0}^{n} \sqrt{w_i w_j}\hat{p}_k(x_i)\hat{p}_k(x_j) = \delta_{ij}$$

which says (for $i = j$) that

$$w_j \sum_{k=0}^{n} \hat{p}_k^2(x_j) = 1.$$

So $\sqrt{w_j}[\hat{p}_0(x_j), \hat{p}_1(x_j), \ldots, \hat{p}_n(x_j)]^{\mathsf{T}}$ is a unit eigenvector of $\mathbf{J}_n$. Let's examine the first component of this unit eigenvector $\sqrt{w_j}\hat{p}_0(x_j)$. Because $p_0(x) \equiv 1$, we have $\hat{p}_0(x) \equiv 1/\|1\|$. Therefore, $\sqrt{w_j}$ simply equals $\|1\|$ times the first component of the unit eigenvector of $\mathbf{J}_n$. We can summarize all of this in the following algorithm.

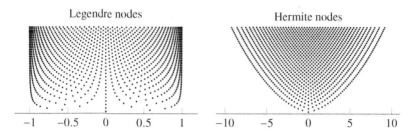

Figure 11.5: Location of Legendre and Hermite nodes for $n = 1, 2, \ldots, 50$.

Theorem 44 (Golub–Welsch algorithm). *The nodes x_i for Gaussian quadrature are the eigenvalues of the Jacobi operator*

$$
\begin{bmatrix}
a_0 & \sqrt{b_1} & & & & \\
\sqrt{b_1} & a_1 & \sqrt{b_2} & & & \\
& \ddots & \ddots & \ddots & & \\
& & \sqrt{b_{n-1}} & a_{n-1} & \sqrt{b_n} & \\
& & & \sqrt{b_n} & a_n &
\end{bmatrix}.
$$

The weights are $\|1\|^2$ times the square of the first element of the unit eigenvectors.

Parameters for common Gaussian quadrature rules are summarized in Figure 11.4 on page 313. The position of the nodes of Gauss–Legendre and Gauss–Hermite quadrature are shown in the figure above. We can directly compute the nodes and weights of Gauss–Chebyshev quadrature using $x_k = \cos((2k-1)\pi/2n)$ and $w_k = \pi/n$, so we don't need the Golub–Welsch algorithm in this case. The Golub–Welsch algorithm takes $O(n^2)$ operations to compute the eigenvalue-eigenvector pairs of a symmetric matrix. More recently, faster $O(n)$ algorithms have been developed that use Newton's method to solve $p_n(x) = 0$ and evaluate $p_n(x)$ and $p_n'(x)$ by three-term recurrence or use asymptotic expansion.[3] We can implement a naïve Gauss–Legendre quadrature with n nodes using

```
f = x -> cos(x)*exp(-x^2)
nodes, weights = gauss_legendre(n)
f.(nodes) · weights
```

where the nodes and weights are computed using the Golub–Welsch algorithm

```
function gauss_legendre(n)
  a = zeros(n)
```

---

[3] Algorithms using Ignace Bogaert's explicit asymptotic formulas can easily generate over a billion Gauss–Legendre nodes and weights to 16 digits of accuracy. See Townsend [2015].

```
b = (1:n-1).^2 ./ (4*(1:n-1).^2 .- 1)
1² = 2
λ, v = eigen(SymTridiagonal(a, sqrt.(b)))
(λ, 1²*v[1,:].^2)
end
```

Alternatively, the Julia library FastGaussQuadrature.jl provides a fast, accurate method of computing the nodes and weights

```
using FastGaussQuadrature
nodes, weights = gausslegendre(n)
```

Gaussian quadrature can be extended to any bounded domain or unbounded domain. To integrate over an interval $[a, b]$, use the affine transformation $x = \varphi(\xi) = \frac{1}{2}(b - a)\xi + \frac{1}{2}(a + b)$ which maps $[-1, 1] \to [a, b]$. Then we have

$$\int_a^b f(x)\, dx = \frac{b - a}{2} \int_{-1}^1 f(\varphi(\xi))\, d\xi,$$

and we perform Gauss–Legendre quadrature as usual. To integrate $\int_{-\infty}^{\infty} f(x)\, dx$, we might try a change of variable using a transformation $x = \tanh^{-1} \xi$ which maps $(-1, 1) \to (-\infty, \infty)$. Then

$$\int_{-\infty}^{\infty} f(x)\, dx = \int_{-1}^1 \frac{f(\tanh^{-1} \xi)}{1 - \xi^2}\, d\xi,$$

and we perform Gauss–Legendre quadrature as usual. Or, instead we might try $x = \tan(\pi \xi / 2)$ or $x = \xi / (1 - \xi^2)$. Gauss–Hermite quadrature can itself be thought of as a change of variable from $(-1, 1) \to (-\infty, \infty)$ with the scaled error function $w = (\sqrt{\pi}/2)\operatorname{erf} x$ and $d\xi = e^{-x^2} dx$. Similarly, Gauss–Laguerre quadrature is a change of variable from $(0, 1) \to (0, \infty)$ with $\xi = -e^{-x}$ and $d\xi = e^{-x} dx$.

▷ **Gauss–Kronrod quadrature**

Gauss–Kronrod quadrature extends Gaussian quadrature by augmenting the original quadrature nodes with an additional set of nodes. Usual Gaussian quadrature is first computed using the original set of nodes for a quadrature rule that is order $2n - 1$. Then quadrature is repeated over both sets of nodes, reusing the function evaluations from the first set of nodes. The resulting quadrature is order $3n + 1$ and can be used in estimating quadrature error. Let's take a closer look.

Consider a polynomial $p(x) \in \mathbb{P}_n$ with n roots in the interval (a, b) and a second polynomial $q(x) \in \mathbb{P}_{n+1}$ with $n + 1$ roots in the same interval. Then $p(x)q(x) \in \mathbb{P}_{2n+1}$. Any polynomial $f(x) \in \mathbb{P}_{3n+1}$ can be written as

$$f(x) = r(x) + p(x)q(x)s(x)$$

for some $s(x) \in \mathbb{P}_n$ and $r(x) \in \mathbb{P}_{2n}$ because the number of coefficients of $f(x)$ must equal the number of coefficients of $r(x)$ plus the number of coefficients of $s(x)$. Furthermore, if

$$\int_a^b p(x)q(x)x^k \omega(x) \, dx = 0 \quad \text{for each } k = 0, 1, \ldots, n \tag{11.6}$$

for some weight function $\omega(x)$, then

$$\int_a^b f(x)\omega(x) \, dx = \int_a^b r(x)\omega(x) \, dx.$$

We just need to find a suitable $q(x)$ so that (11.6) holds. In the 1960s, Aleksandr Kronrod examined this problem for the interval $[-1, 1]$ and unit weight function by taking $p(x) = P_n(x)$ to be a degree-n Legendre polynomial and $q(x) = K_{n+1}(x)$ to be the degree-$(n + 1)$ Stieltjes polynomial associated with $P_n(x)$. In general, if $P_n(x)$ is any degree-n orthogonal polynomial over the interval (a, b) with the associated weight $\omega(x)$, then the *Stieltjes polynomial* $K_{n+1}(x)$ associated with $P_n(x)$ is a degree-$(n + 1)$ polynomial defined by the orthogonality condition

$$\int_a^b K_{n+1}(x)P_n(x)x^k \omega(x) \, dx = 0 \quad \text{for} \quad k = 0, 1, \ldots, n.$$

The family of Stieltjes polynomials $K_0(x), K_1(x), \ldots$ is associated with a family of orthogonal polynomials $P_0(x), P_1(x), \ldots$. While Stieltjes polynomials are not guaranteed to have real zeros, there are important families of Stieltjes polynomials that have both real zeros and interlacing zeros, meaning that between any two zeros of P_n, there is a zero of K_{n+1}. The Stieltjes polynomial associated with Legendre polynomials is one such family.[4] The following figure shows the Legendre polynomial $P_7(x)$ along with the associated Stieltjes polynomial $K_8(x)$, whose roots interlace one another:

We can generate a Kronrod quadrature rule once we determine the $2n+1$ nodes x_i of $K_{n+1}(x)P_n(x)$ along with the associated quadrature weights w_i. One method

---

[4] Another is the Stieltjes polynomials associated with the Chebyshev polynomials of the first kind $T_n(x)$, which happens to be $(1 - x^2)U_{n-2}(x)$, where $U_n(x)$ is a Chebyshev polynomial of the second kind—with weight $\omega(x) = (1 - x^2)$ over $[-1, 1]$. A third—the associated Stieltjes polynomials for the Chebyshev polynomials of the second kind $U_n(x)$—are the Chebyshev polynomials of the first kind $T_n(x)$.

uses Jacobi matrices similar to the Golub–Welsch algorithm described in Laurie [1997]. Because $r(x)$ is a degree-$2n$ polynomial, $r(x)$ can be integrated exactly using $2n + 1$ quadrature nodes. At the roots x_i of $p(x)q(x)$, the function $f(x_i) = r(x_i)$, and we can integrate $f(x)$ as $\sum_{i=0}^{2n} w_i f(x_i)$. A popular implementation of the adaptive Gauss–Kronrod rule is a (15,7)-point pair that couples a 7-point Gauss–Legendre rule with a 15-point Gauss–Kronrod rule, requiring 15 function evaluations. The integral is computed using the Kronrod rule, and the error is estimated by subtracting the two rules. The weights and nodes are simply hard-coded into the algorithm.

▷ Gauss–Radau and Gauss–Lobatto quadratures

Gaussian quadrature nodes are strictly in the interior of the interval of integration. We can modify Gaussian quadrature to add a node to one endpoint, called *Gauss–Radau quadrature*, or to both end endpoints, called *Gauss–Lobatto quadrature*. The nodes and weights for Gauss–Radau and Gauss–Lobatto quadratures can be determined by using the Golub–Welsh algorithm with a modified Jacobi matrix or by using Newton's method. (See Gautschi [2006].)

The Golub–Welsh algorithm can generate the nodes and weights of an $(n+1)$-point Gauss–Legendre–Radau quadrature by replacing $a_n = \pm n/(2n - 1)$ for a node at ± 1. And, the algorithm can generate the nodes and weights of an $(n + 1)$-point Gauss–Legendre–Lobatto quadrature by replacing $b_n = n/(2n - 1)$ for nodes at ± 1.

Because Gauss–Radau quadrature fixes a node to be an endpoint, it removes one degree of freedom from the set of nodes and weights. By using it, we can fit at most a degree-$2n$ polynomial with a set of $n + 1$ nodes. Gauss–Lobatto quadrature fixes nodes at both endpoints, removing two degrees of freedom. So we can fit at most a degree-$(2n - 1)$ polynomial with a set of $n + 1$ nodes.

▷ Quadrature in practice

Every scientific programming language has some sort of quadrature method, typically including a variant of Gaussian quadrature such as Gauss–Lobatto or Gauss–Kronrod quadrature. Julia has several quadrature packages. QuadGK.jl uses adaptive Gauss–Kronrod quadrature. FastGaussQuadrature.jl computes the nodes and weights for n-point Gaussian quadrature in $O(n)$ operations. The routine can compute a billion Gauss–Legendre nodes in under a minute. Matlab includes several methods. The functions `quad`, `quadv`, and `quadl`, which perform the adaptive Simpson's rule, vectorized adaptive Simpson's rule, and Gauss–Lobatto quadrature, are no longer recommended in the documentation. It advises using `integral` instead, which is "just an easier to find and easier to use version of quadgk." The function `quadgk` is an implementation of adaptive Gauss–Kronrod quadrature. Matlab also has `trapz`, which implements the composite trapezoidal rule. The Octave commands are similar to MATLAB commands with a few exceptions. The function quad numerically integrates a function using the Fortran routines from QUADPACK, and the Octave command quadcc uses adaptive Clenshaw–Curtis quadrature. Python's scipy.integrate function quad and quad_vec (for vector-valued functions) use the QUADPACK library, providing a Gauss–Kronrod 21-point rule, Gauss–Kronrod 15-point rule, and a trapezoidal rule. The library also includes simple routines such as simpson, which implements Simpson's rule (for sampled data), and romberg and romb, which implement Romberg's method.

11.5 Monte Carlo integration

Gaussian quadrature uses precisely determined nodes to compute a highly accurate solution. But, sometimes, when there is a great deal of complexity or high numbers of dimensions, you may just want any solution. Monte Carlo integration takes an entirely different approach from the polished grace of orthogonal polynomial quadrature. Instead, it relies on almost brute force application of statistical law, allowing it to tackle problems that other techniques can't touch.

Example. Buffon's needle is one of the earliest problems to pair probability together with geometry. In 1733, French naturalist Georges–Louis Leclerc, Comte de Buffon posed the problem: "Suppose we have a floor made of parallel strips of wood, each the same width, and we drop a needle onto the floor. What is the probability that the needle will lie across a line between two strips?" Let's let ℓ be the length of a needle, d be the width of the strip of wood, θ be the angle of the needle relative to the length of the strip, and x be the distance from the center of the needle to the closest line. Let's also take the length of the needle to be smaller than the width of the strip. Then the needle crosses the line if $x \le (\ell/2) \sin \theta$. By dropping the needle at random, the position x and the angle θ will each come from uniform distributions $U(0, d/2)$ and $U(0, \pi/2)$, where $U(a, b) = 1/(b - a)$ if $x \in [a, b]$ and zero otherwise. To find the probability that the needle lies across a line, we simply integrate over the joint probability density function $U(0, d/2) \cdot U(0, \pi/2)$ to get $4/\pi d$:

$$\int_0^{\pi/2} \int_0^{(\ell/2) \sin \theta} \frac{4}{\pi d} \, dx \, d\theta = \frac{2\ell}{\pi d}.$$

When the length of a needle is exactly half the width of a strip of wood, the probability equals $1/\pi$, giving us an experimental way of computing π, albeit not a very efficient one. Take a large number of needles, perhaps a thousand or more. Drop them on the floor and count those that cross a line. Then, the number of needles divided by that count should give us a rough approximation of π. The more needles we use, the better the approximation. ◄

We could apply Fubini's rule to repeated one-dimensional integrals to compute multidimensional integrals. This approach is perfect for low-dimensional domains, but the complexity grows exponentially as the number of dimensions increases. With N total nodes in d dimensions, we have an equivalent of $N^{1/d}$ nodes per dimension, and a pth-order quadrature method has a convergence rate of $O(N^{-p/d})$. For example, in statistical mechanics, we can compute the energy of a system of particles by integrating over the probability distribution in phase space $f(\mathbf{x})$, where $\mathbf{x}$ is the generalized coordinates of position and velocity. For six particles (each with three position and three velocity coordinates), we would need to integrate over a 36-dimensional space. Using a uniform mesh with only two grid points in each direction, we would still need to compute 2^{36} nodes. With a petaflop supercomputer (one that does 10^{15} floating-point operations per second), we could expect a solution in under a second. But with only two nodes in each dimension, we are likely to get a poor approximation. To reduce the error in the approximation by half, we could use twice as many points in each dimension. Now, we would need 2^{72} nodes—more than two months using the same computer. The problem is afflicted with the so-called *curse of dimensionality*.

Nuclear physicist Stanislaw Ulam developed the Monte Carlo method in 1946. While convalescing and playing solitaire, Ulam asked himself the likelihood that a game of Canfield was winnable. After giving up on solving the problem using pure combinatorial calculations, Ulam wondered whether it might be more practical to simply lay out, say, a hundred hands and then just count the number of wins. With newly developed electronic computers such as ENIAC, the mundane task of statistical sampling could be automated. Furthermore, the approach seemed well suited for exploring neutron diffusion and other problems of mathematical physics.[5]

The *law of the unconscious statistician* provides the expected value of a function $f(X)$ of a random variable X

$$\mathrm{E}[f(X)] = \int_{\Omega} f(\mathbf{x}) p_X(\mathbf{x})\, d\mathbf{x} \tag{11.7}$$

where p_X is the probability density function of the random variable X. A probability density function is a nonnegative function that tells us the probability of the random variable lying within a region $P(X \in \Omega) = \int_{\Omega} p_X(\mathbf{x})\, d\mathbf{x}$. Equation (11.7) is intuitive, and we'll take it as given—for a rigorous proof, see a standard text in probability. Consider the one-dimensional case for a uniform distribution $U(a, b)$. Its probability density function $p_X(x)$ equals $(b - a)^{-1}$ for $x \in (a, b)$

---

[5]The name Monte Carlo, proposed by Ulam's colleague Nicholas Metropolis, was inspired by Ulam's uncle, who would borrow money from relatives because he "just had to go to Monte Carlo," the world-famous gambling destination. The probabilistic programming language Stan (with interfaces in Julia, Python, and Matlab) was named in honor of Stanislaw Ulam.

and zero otherwise. Using (11.7), the integral

$$F = \int_a^b f(x)\,dx = (b-a)\,E\,[f(X)]\,.$$

Now, we need to just estimate the expected value $E\,[f(X)]$, which we can do in practice by sampling. In general, we want to compute $F = \int_\Omega f(\mathbf{x})\,dx$. We'll define the N-sample Monte Carlo estimate for F as

$$\left\langle F^N \right\rangle = \frac{1}{N}\sum_{i=0}^{N-1}\frac{f(X_i)}{p_X(X_i)}.$$

A Monte Carlo estimate has the expected value

$$E\left[\left\langle F^N \right\rangle\right] = E\left[\frac{1}{N}\sum_{i=1}^{N}\frac{f(X_i)}{p_X(X_i)}\right] = \frac{1}{N}\sum_{i=1}^{N}E\left[\frac{f(X_i)}{p_X(X_i)}\right]$$

$$= \frac{1}{N}\sum_{i=1}^{N}\int_\Omega \frac{f(\mathbf{x})}{p_X(\mathbf{x})}p_X(\mathbf{x})\,dx = \frac{1}{N}\sum_{i=1}^{N}\int_\Omega f(\mathbf{x})\,dx = \int_\Omega f(\mathbf{x})\,dx = F.$$

The law of large numbers says that the sample average converges to the expected value as the sample size approaches infinity. For arbitrarily small ε, the probability

$$\lim_{N\to\infty} P\left(|\langle F^N \rangle - E\left[\langle F^N \rangle\right]| > \varepsilon\right) = 0.$$

Hence, the Monte Carlo estimate $\left\langle F^N \right\rangle$ converges to the integral F. To integrate a function $f(\mathbf{x})$ over the bounded domain Ω using a uniform distribution, we take $F = \int_\Omega f(\mathbf{x})\,dx = V(\Omega)\,E\,[f]$ where $V(\Omega)$ is the volume of the domain.

The variance of a Monte Carlo estimate is

$$\sigma^2\left[\left\langle F^N \right\rangle\right] = \sigma^2\left[\frac{1}{N}\sum_{i=1}^{N}\frac{f(X_i)}{p_X(X_i)}\right]$$

$$= \frac{1}{N^2}\sum_{i=1}^{N}\sigma^2\left[\frac{f(X_i)}{p_X(X_i)}\right] = \frac{1}{N^2}\sum_{i=1}^{N}\sigma^2\,[Y_i] = \frac{1}{N}\sigma^2\,[Y]\,,$$

where $\sigma^2\,[Y_i]$ is the sample variance of $Y_i = f(X_i)/p_X(X_i)$. The second equality comes from two properties of variance—that $\sigma^2\,[aX] = a^2\sigma^2\,[X]$ and that $\sigma^2\,[X_1 + X_2] = \sigma^2\,[X_1] + \sigma^2\,[X_2]$ when X_1 and X_2 are independent random variables. The last equality holds because X_i are independent and identically distributed variables. The standard error of the mean is then

$$\sigma\left[\left\langle F^N \right\rangle\right] = \frac{1}{\sqrt{N}}\sigma\,[Y]\,,$$

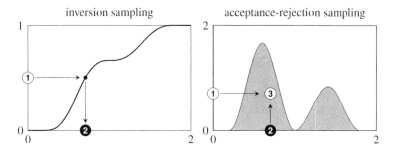

Figure 11.6: Techniques for sampling a variable ❷ from a distribution. Using inversion sampling, a value ① is sampled from $U(0, 1)$ and mapped to ❷ using the inverse cumulative probability function. Using acceptance-rejection sampling, ❷ is uniformly sampled from the domain and ① is sampled from another easy to compute distribution, possibly a uniform distribution. If the corresponding ③ lies within the accept region ▫, then choose ❷. Otherwise, draw ❷ and ① again, repeating until you have one that does.

and the convergence rate is $O(N^{-1/2})$. Such a convergence rate is relatively poor compared to even a simple Riemann sum with a convergence rate of $O(N^{-1})$ for one-dimensional problems. But, the error of the Monte Carlo method does not depend on the number of dimensions!

Using N nodes to integrate a function over a one-dimensional domain using a simple Riemann sum approximation results in an error of $O(1/N)$. For the d-dimensional problem, we would need N^d quadrature points to get an error $O(1/N)$. That is, for N points, we get an error of $O(N^{-1/d})$. When the dimension is more than two, the Monte Carlo method wins out over simple first-order Riemann sums. Furthermore, we can use techniques to reduce the sampling variance $\sigma^2[Y]$. Specifically, by choosing samples from a probability density function $p_X(\mathbf{x})$ that has a similar shape to $f(\mathbf{x})$.

▷ **Sampling**

Often, say in statistical mechanics and molecular dynamics, we want to sample from a probability distribution that is not simply the uniform distribution. In general, for a probability density function, $E[f] = \int_\Omega f(\mathbf{x})p(\mathbf{x})\,d\mathbf{x}$. Let's examine two sampling methods—inversion sampling and acceptance-rejection sampling.

Inversion sampling   A function $p(x)$ is a probability density function if $p(x)$ is nonnegative and $\int_{-\infty}^{\infty} p(x)\,dx = 1$. The cumulative distribution function $P(x) = \int_{-\infty}^{x} p(s)\,ds$, a monotonically increasing function, is the probability that a sampled value will be less than x. The inverse distribution function $P^{-1}(y)$ allows us to sample from $p(x)$ by sampling y from a uniform distribution. For example, the standard normal distribution $p(x) = e^{-x^2/2}/\sqrt{2/\pi}$ has the error function $P(x) = \operatorname{erf} x$ as its cumulative distribution. To sample from a normal distribution, we would compute $P^{-1}(y) = \operatorname{erf}^{-1} y$, where y is sampled from a uniform distribution. To sample from an exponential distribution $p(x) = \alpha e^{-\alpha x}$, we first calculate $P(x) = \int_0^x \alpha e^{-\alpha x} \, ds = 1 - e^{-\alpha x}$. Then taking its inverse, we get $P^{-1}(y) = -\alpha^{-1} \log(1 - y)$.

Acceptance-rejection sampling   Computing the inverse of a cumulative density function is not always easy, especially if the distribution is empirical. Instead, another way to sample from a distribution p is by sampling from a different but close distribution g and using the acceptance-rejection algorithm (developed by von Neumann in 1951). Take M such that $p(x) \leq Mg(x)$ for all x in our domain.

1. Sample x using $g(x)$ and sample y from $U(0, 1)$.

2. If $y < p(x)/Mg(x)$, then accept the value x as a sample drawn from p. Otherwise, reject it and start again with the first step, repeating until you have an x that is accepted.

Metropolis algorithm   The Metropolis algorithm uses acceptance-rejection sampling to generate a sequence of random samples from a distribution $p(x)$. The Metropolis algorithm works by sampling from some arbitrary symmetric test distribution $g(x|y)$. That is, $g(x|y) = g(y|x)$ such as a normal distribution $g(x|y) = e^{-(x-y)^2/2}/\sqrt{2/\pi}$. The extension of the Metropolis algorithm to nonsymmetric test distributions is called the Metropolis–Hastings algorithm. Also, we can use a function $f(x)$ that is proportional to $p(x)$ rather than $p(x)$ itself. In this way, we don't explicitly need to know the normalization constants of $p(x)$. Choose an arbitrary x_0, and for each iteration i:

1. Sample x' from the distribution $g(x'|x_i)$ and compute an acceptance ratio $\alpha = f(x')/f(x_i)$.

2. Now, sample u from $U(0, 1)$. If $u \leq \alpha$, then accept the candidate x' and set $x_{i+1} = x'$. Otherwise, reject the candidate and set $x_{i+1} = x_i$.

Through this process, we get a sequence of values that either remains in place or moves according to the acceptance ratio α. If $\alpha \geq 1$, i.e., if the density $p(x)$ at the candidate point x' is greater than the density at the current point x_i, then we always move to the candidate point. But, if the density at the candidate point is less than the density at the current point, we only move with probability α.

Example.   We don't need to directly compute the inverse error function to sample from the standard normal distribution. We could instead use the Box–Muller transform.[6] Consider

$$p(x)p(y) = \frac{1}{2\pi}e^{-(x^2+y^2)/2}.$$

By making the change of variable $x = r\cos\theta$ and $y = r\sin\theta$, we have the differential element

$$p(x)p(y)\,dx\,dy = \frac{1}{2\pi}e^{-r^2/2}r\,dr\,d\theta = \left(re^{-r^2/2}\,dr\right)\left(\frac{1}{2\pi}\,d\theta\right).$$

We want to sample r from the density $re^{-r^2/2}$ and θ from $1/2\pi$. To do this, we will use inversion sampling:

$$u = \int_0^r re^{-r^2/2}\,dr = 1 - e^{-r^2/2} \quad\text{and}\quad v = \int_0^\theta \frac{1}{2\pi}\,d\theta = \frac{\theta}{2\pi}.$$

Solving for r and θ gives us $r = \sqrt{-2\log(1-u)}$ and $\theta = 2\pi v$ where u and v are independently sampled from the uniform distribution $U(0,1)$. Because u is taken uniformly from $(0,1)$, we could also sample $1-u$ and instead take $r = \sqrt{-2\log u}$. Therefore,

$$x = \sqrt{-2\log u}\cos(2\pi v) \quad\text{and}\quad y = \sqrt{-2\log u}\sin(2\pi v)$$

gives two independent normally distributed samples.   ◄

♣ The Distrtibutions.jl package has an extensive collection of distributions. To draw 20 samples from a Poisson distribution with $\lambda = 6$, use rand(Poisson(6),20).

Example.   Monte Carlo integration chooses quadrature nodes according to some probability distribution using a random number generator. John von Neumann once quipped, "anyone who considers arithmetical methods of producing random digits is, of course, in a state of sin." Still, he conceded that it was far faster than feeding a computer ran dom numbers from punched cards. A sequence of pseudo-random numbers is a sequence of statistically independent numbers sampled from the uniform distribution over the interval $[0,1]$. There are several ways of generating such a sequence. During the latter half of the twentieth century, linear congruence generators were commonly used as pseudo-random number generators until they were, for the most part, replaced by better methods

---

[6]The transform was introduced in 1958 by statistician George E. P. Box, famously known for his aphorism "all models are wrong, but some are useful," and mathematician Mervin Muller.

like the Mersenne twister developed in 1998 by Makoto Matsumoto and Takuji Nishimura and Xoshiro[7] developed in 2018 by David Blackman and Sebastiano Vigna.

A linear congruence generator is given by

$$x_{i+1} = (ax_i + c) \mod m$$

for some integers a, c, m, and seed x_0. The Lehmer formulation, developed by Derrick Lehmer in 1949, takes $c = 0$ and m to be a prime number. By theorem 20 on page 156, by choosing a to be primitive root of m, the sequence has maximal period $m - 1$. For example, by taking $m = 13$ and $a = 2$ with the seed $x_0 = 5$, we get the sequence

$$5 \to 10 \to 7 \to 1 \to 2 \to 4 \to 8 \to 3 \to 6 \to 12 \to 11 \to 9 \to$$

which then repeats. The minimal standard generator developed by Stephen Park and Keith Miller in 1988 takes m as the Mersenne prime $M_{31} = 2^{31} - 1$ and $a = 7^5$ as a primitive root of M_{31}. Responding to criticism of the method, Park later updated a to the prime 48271.   ◄

11.6   Exercises

11.1. Occasionally, one may need to compute a one-side derivative to, say, enforce a boundary condition or model a discontinuity.

1. Find a third-order approximation to the derivative $f'(x)$ with nodes at x, $x + h$, $x + 2h$ and $x + 3h$ for some stepsize h.
2. What choice of stepsize h minimizes the total (round-off and truncation) error of the derivative of $\sin x$ using this approximation with double-precision floating-point numbers?
3. Find a second-order approximation for the second derivative $f''(x)$ for the same set of nodes.   ◿

11.2. The recursive implementation of Richardson extrapolation on page 299 is inefficient when the number of steps n is high. The number of function calls doubles with each step using recursion. We'd need 2^n function calls to evaluate just $n^2 - n$ terms, resulting in excessive duplication. Rewrite the code for Richardson extrapolation as a more efficient nonrecursive function.   ◿

11.3. Find a zero of the function $f(x) = 4 \sin x + \sqrt{x}$ near $x = 4$ using Newton's method with automatic differentiation. Then modify Newton's method to

---

[7] Xoshiro is a portmanteau of XOR, shift, and rotate.

find the local minimum of $f(x)$ near $x = 4$. To compute $f''(x)$ we can use
`f(Dual(Dual(x)).deriv.deriv`.   ✍

11.4. The Cauchy differentiation formula relates the derivative of an analytic
function with a contour integral

$$f^{(p)}(a) = \frac{p!}{2\pi i} \oint_\gamma \frac{f(z)}{(z-a)^{p+1}} \, dz,$$

where γ is any simple, counter-clockwise contour around $z = a$ in the complex
plane. Compute sixth derivative of $e^x (\cos^3 x + \sin^3 x)^{-1}$ evaluated at $x = 0$. The
exact value is 64.   ✍

11.5. Use Newton's method as an alternative to the Golub–Welsh algorithm to
generate nodes and weights for Gauss–Legendre quadrature. Bonnet's recursion
formula

$$nP_n(x) = (2n-1)xP_{n-1}(x) - (n-1)P_{n-2}(x),$$

where $P_0(x) = 1$ and $P_1(x) = x$, is useful in generating the Legendre polynomials.
The derivatives of the Legendre polynomials can be computed using the following
recursion formula

$$(x^2 - 1)P'_n(x) = nxP_n(x) - nP_{n-1}(x).$$

Quadrature weights can be computed using either $w_k = 2/(nP'_n(x_k)P_{n-1}(x_k))$
or $w_k = 2/((1 - x_k^2)(P'_n(x_k))^2)$. To ensure that Newton's method converges to
the right nodes, you'll need to start sufficiently close to each of them. Take
$x_j^{(0)} = -\cos((4j-1)\pi/(4n+2))$.   ✍

11.6. Use Gauss–Legendre quadrature to numerically compute

$$\int_{-1}^{1} e^{-16x^2} \, dx = \frac{\sqrt{\pi}}{4} \operatorname{erf}(4)$$

with an error of less than 10^{-14}. Repeat the exercise using composite Simpson's
quadrature. Determine the convergence rate of the numerical solution to the
exact solution by looping over several different numbers of nodes and plotting
the error as a function of the number of nodes.

11.7. The fundamental solution to the heat equation $u_t = u_{xx}$ with an initial
distribution $u(0,x) = u_0(x)$ is given by

$$u(t,x) = \frac{1}{\sqrt{4\pi t}} \int_{-\infty}^{\infty} u_0(s)e^{-(x-s)^2/4t} \, ds.$$

Use Gauss–Hermite quadrature to compute the solution to the heat equation at
time $t = 1$ for an initial distribution $u_0(x) = \sin x$.   ✍

11.8. One simple application of Monte Carlo integration is computing π by noting that the area of a circle of unit radius is π. Take n samples $(x, y) \in [-1, 1] \times [-1, 1]$ and count the number m of samples where (x, y) is in the unit circle $x^2 + y^2 < 1$. Then $\pi \approx m/n$.

1. Use Monte Carlo integration to compute an approximation for π.
2. Use a log-log plot of the error to confirm the order of convergence.
3. How many samples would be needed to accurately compute 13 digits of π?
4. Modify your solution in part 1 to use Monte Carlo integration to compute the volume of a 9-dimensional unit hypersphere.

11.9. Two cubes, each with equal size and equal uniform density, are in contact along one face. The gravitational force between two point masses separated by a distance r is

$$F = G\frac{m_1 m_2}{r^2},$$

where G is the gravitational constant and m_1 and m_2 are the magnitudes of the two masses. What is the total gravitational force between the two cubes? (This question was proposed by mathematician Nick Trefethen as one of his "ten-digit problems.")

11.10. Spectral methods, also called orthogonal collocation methods, work by projecting problems onto a finite set of orthogonal basis functions (such as Chebeshev, Legendre, or Fourier polynomials) and then solving the new problems exactly in these spaces.[8] Consider the differential equation $u'(t) = f(u, t)$ where $t \in [0, 1]$. We'll solve the approximate problem $p'(t) = f(p, t)$, where $p(t)$ is an n-degree polynomial $c_0 + c_1 t + c_2 t + \cdots + c_n t^n$. Define differentiation as a linear operator

$$\begin{bmatrix} p'(t_1) \\ p'(t_2) \\ \vdots \\ p'(t_n) \end{bmatrix} = \mathbf{M} \left(\begin{bmatrix} p(t_1) \\ p(t_2) \\ \vdots \\ p(t_n) \end{bmatrix} - \begin{bmatrix} p(t_0) \\ p(t_0) \\ \vdots \\ p(t_0) \end{bmatrix} \right), \tag{11.8}$$

where $t_0, t_1, t_2, \ldots, t_n$ are Legende–Gauss–Lobatto nodes or Chebyshev nodes with $t_0 = 0$ and $t_n = 1$. Once we've determined the differentiation matrix $\mathbf{M}$, we solve the system $\mathbf{M}(\mathbf{p} - p(t_0)\mathbf{1}) = f(\mathbf{p}, t)$.

---

[8]Finite element methods work similarly. Whereas spectral methods use global basis functions that span the entire computational domain, finite element methods use basis functions that are only locally non-zero, such as B-splines.

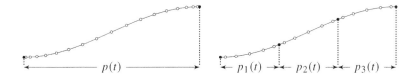

With $n + 1$ nodes, we'll need to solve a system of n nonlinear equations, which involves computing and inverting an $n \times n$ Jacobian at each iteration. Alternatively, we can break the domain up into several smaller intervals and use a low-degree, piecewise-polynomial function $p_1(t)$, $p_2(t)$, ..., $p_m(t)$ matched at knots and solved sequentially for each interval. We call this approach a *pseudospectral* method.

Solve the differential equation $u'(t) = \alpha u^2$ with $\alpha = 0.9$ and $u(0) = 1$ over the interval $t \in [0, 1]$ using the Legendre–Gauss–Lobatto spectral method and pseudospectral methods. Compare the numerical solutions with the analytical solution. What happens with $\alpha = 0.99$? ◿

Numerical Methods for Differential Equations

Chapter 12

Ordinary Differential Equations

Any study of numerical methods for partial differential equations (PDEs) likely starts by examining numerical methods for ordinary differential equations (ODEs). One reason is that numerical techniques used to solve time-dependent partial differential equations often employ the *method of lines*. The method of lines discretizes the spatial component and solves the resulting semi-discrete problem using standard ODE solvers. Consider the heat equation $\frac{\partial}{\partial t} u(\mathbf{x}, t) = \Delta u(\mathbf{x}, t)$, where $\Delta = \sum_i \partial^2/\partial x_i^2$ is the Laplacian operator. The heat equation can be formally solved as a first-order linear ordinary differential equation to get the solution $u(\mathbf{x}, t) = e^{t\Delta} u(\mathbf{x}, 0)$, where $e^{t\Delta}$ is a linear operator acting on the initial conditions $u(\mathbf{x}, 0)$. A typical numerical solution involves discretizing the Laplacian operator Δ in space to create a system of ODEs and then using an ODE solver in time. A second reason to dig deep into ODEs is that the theory of PDEs builds on the theory of ODEs. Understanding stability, consistency, and convergence of numerical schemes for ordinary differential equations will help understand stability, consistency, and convergence of numerical schemes for partial differential equations. To dig even deeper, see Hairer, Nørsett, and Wanner's two-volume compendium *Solving Ordinary Differential Equations*.

12.1 Well-posed problems

Consider the initial value problem $u' = f(t, u)$ with $u(0) = u_0$. An initial value problem is said to be *well-posed* if (1) the solution exists, (2) the solution is unique, and (3) the solution depends continuously on the initial conditions. Let's examine these conditions for well-posedness.

A function $f(t, u)$ is *Lipschitz continuous* if there exists some constant $L < \infty$ such that $|f(t, u) - f(t, u^*)| \le L|u - u^*|$ for all $u, u^* \in \mathbb{R}$. Lipschitz continuity is stronger than continuity but weaker than continuous differentiability. For example, the function $|u|$ is Lipschitz continuous on $\mathbb{R}$, although it isn't differentiable at $u = 0$. The function u^2 is not globally Lipschitz continuous (although it is locally Lipschitz continuous) because its slope becomes unbounded as u approaches infinity. Similarly, the function $\sqrt{|u|}$ is not globally Lipschitz continuous because its slope is unbounded at $u = 0$.

To see why Lipschitz continuity is desirable, let's look at what happens to the solution of $u' = f(t, u)$ when $f(t, u)$ is not Lipschitz continuous. First, take the problem $u' = u^2$ with $u(0) = 1$ over the interval $t \in [0, 2]$. This problem can be solved by the method of separation of variables to get

$$u(t) = \frac{1}{1 - t}.$$

The solution blows up at $t = 1$, so it does not even exist on the interval $[1, 2]$. Now, consider the problem $u' = \sqrt{u}$ with $u(0) = 0$ over the interval $t \in [0, 2]$. This problem has the solution $u(t) = \frac{1}{4}t^2$. It also has the solution $u(t) = 0$. In fact, it has infinitely many solutions of the form

$$u(t) = \begin{cases} 0 & t < t_c \\ \frac{1}{4}(t - t_c)^2 & t \ge t_c \end{cases}$$

where the critical parameter is arbitrary. So, when $f(t, u)$ is not Lipschitz continuous in u, the solution may fail to exist; or if it exists, it may fail to be unique. We state the following theorem without proof.

Theorem 45. *If $f(t, u)$ is continuous in t and Lipschitz continuous in u, then the initial value problem $u'(t) = f(t, u(t))$ with $u(0) = u_0$ has a unique solution.*

We say that an initial value problem is *stable* if a small perturbation in the initial value u_0 or the function $f(t, u)$ produces a bounded change in the solution. That is, $u'(t) = f(t, u)$ with $u(0) = u_0$ is stable if there exists a positive value K such that for any sufficiently small ε the solution $v(t)$ to the perturbed problem $v'(t) = f(t, v) + \delta(t)$ with $v(0) = u_0 + \varepsilon_0$ satisfies $|v(t) - u(t)| \le K\varepsilon$ whenever $|\varepsilon_0|, |\delta(t)| < \varepsilon$ for all $t \in [0, T]$. We can clarify this definition with a theorem.

Theorem 46. *If $f(t, u)$ is Lipschitz continuous in u, then the initial value problem $u'(t) = f(t, u(t))$ with $u(0) = u_0$ is stable.*

Proof. For an error $e(t) = v(t) - u(t)$, we have

$$e'(t) = v'(t) - u'(t) = f(t, v) - f(t, u) - \delta(t)$$

and $e(0) = v(0) - u(0) = \varepsilon_0$. If $f(t, u)$ is Lipschitz continuous in u, then

$$\begin{aligned}
|e'(t)| &= |f(t, v) - f(t, u) - \delta(t)| \\
&\le |f(t, v) - f(t, u)| + |\delta(t)| \\
&\le L|v(t) - u(t)| + |\delta(t)| \\
&\le L|e(t)| + |\delta(t)|.
\end{aligned}$$

Let ε be the maximum of ε_0 and the supremum of $|\delta(t)|$ over $[0, T]$. Then $|e'(t)| \le L|e(t)| + \varepsilon$ and $|e(0)| \le \varepsilon$. It follows that

$$|e(t)| \le \frac{\varepsilon}{L}\left[(L + 1)e^{Lt} - 1\right] \le \frac{\varepsilon}{L}\left[(L + 1)e^{LT} - 1\right] = \varepsilon K.$$

The error is bounded for $0 \le t \le T$, so the initial value problem is stable.   □

Remember the following takeaways over the rest of this chapter and the remainder of this book. First, well-posedness requires existence, uniqueness, and stability. Second, if $f(t, u)$ is continuous in t and Lipschitz continuous in u, then the problem $u' = f(t, u)$ is well-posed.

12.2   Single-step methods

Let $u \equiv u(t)$. Suppose we have the initial value problem

$$u' = f(u) \quad \text{where} \quad u(0) = u_0. \tag{12.1}$$

Let's discretize t by taking n uniform steps of size k, i.e., $t_n = nk$. Except for Chapter 16, the remainder of this book will adopt a fairly standard notation with k representing a step size in time and h representing a step size in space. Using k in place of Δt and h in place of Δx will help tidy some otherwise messier expressions. The derivative u' can be approximated by difference operators:

forward difference $\delta_+ U^n = \dfrac{U^{n+1} - U^n}{k}$

backward difference $\delta_- U^n = \dfrac{U^n - U^{n-1}}{k}$

central difference $\delta_0 U^n = \dfrac{U^{n+1} - U^{n-1}}{2k}$

where U^n is the numerical approximation to $u(t_n)$. Using these operators, we can formulate several finite difference schemes to solve the initial value problem (12.1):

Forward Euler (explicit) $O(k)$

$$\frac{U^{n+1} - U^n}{k} = f(U^n)$$ (12.2)

Backward Euler (implicit) $O(k)$

$$\frac{U^{n+1} - U^n}{k} = f(U^{n+1})$$ (12.3)

Leapfrog (explicit) $O(k^2)$

$$\frac{U^{n+1} - U^{n-1}}{2k} = f(U^n)$$ (12.4)

Trapezoidal (implicit) $O(k^2)$

$$\frac{U^{n+1} - U^n}{k} = \frac{f(U^{n+1}) + f(U^n)}{2}$$ (12.5)

A finite difference scheme has a graphical representation, called a *stencil*, that indicates which terms are employed. We'll use $\bigcirc$ to depict the terms used on the left hand side to discretize the time derivative and $\bullet$ to indicate the terms used on the right hand side to approximate the function $f(u)$. For ODEs, the stencils run vertically with the t_{n+1} terms at the top, the t_n terms below those, then the t_{n-1} terms, and so on. When we move to PDEs, we'll add a horizontal component to the stencil to represent discrete spatial derivatives. In each of the schemes, we can express U^{n+1} in terms of U^n or U^{n-1} either explicitly or implicitly. A numerical method of U^{n+1} is *implicit* if the right-hand side contains a term $f(U^{n+1})$. Otherwise, the numerical method is *explicit*.

Before digging into the consistency and stability of finite difference methods, let's develop more intuition about their behavior. An *integral curve* is a parametric curve representing the solution to an ordinary differential equation for a specified initial condition. We can imagine the set of integral curves as streamlines of a flow. The slope of the tangent at any point is the right-hand-side term $f(t, u)$. A perturbation such as truncation error will bump us from one integral curve to a neighboring one. Existence and uniqueness require that each integral curve be nonintersecting, although they might get close to one another. Let's plot the solutions over one step of the forward Euler, backward Euler, leapfrog, and trapezoidal methods. See the figure on the facing page.

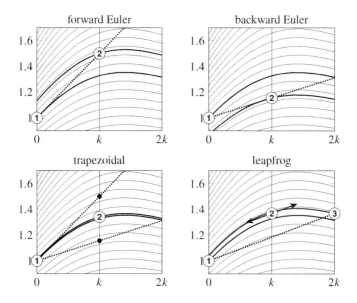

Figure 12.1: Integral curves and numerical solutions using the forward Euler, backward Euler, leapfrog, and trapezoidal methods.

The forward Euler method uses the slope of the integral curve at ① to take a step forward. We are bumped off the original curve and find ourselves at ② on a neighboring one. The backward Euler uses the slope of the integral curve at ② to take a step forward. Finding the slope of the integral curve at ② without explicitly knowing the value of the integral curve at ② is not trivial. Like the forward Euler method, we also find ourselves bumped off the integral curve when using the backward Euler method. The trapezoidal method averages the slopes of the forward Euler and backward Euler to take a step forward. We still get bumped off the original integral curve, but it's not as far this time. The leapfrog method is not a single-step method. It uses the slope of the integral curve at ② to take a double step from ① to ③. Like the trapezoidal method, the leapfrog method performs better than either of the Euler methods.

▷ **Consistency**

To determine $u(t + k)$ for some time step k given a known value $u(t)$, we can use the Taylor series approximation of $u(t + k)$:

$$u(t + k) = u(t) + ku'(t) + \tfrac{1}{2}k^2 u''(t) + O(k^3).$$

Using the relation $u'(t) = f(u(t))$ gives

$$u(t + k) = u(t) + kf(u(t)) + k\tau_k$$

where the truncation $\tau_k = \frac{1}{2}ku'(t) + O(k^2)$. When $k\tau_k \approx 0$, we simply have $u(t + k) \approx u(t) + kf(u(t))$, from which we have the forward Euler method $U^{n+1} = U^n + kf(U^n)$ or equivalently

$$\frac{U^{n+1} - U^n}{k} = f(U^n).$$

The error for each step—given by the local truncation error $k\tau_k$—is $O(k^2)$. The error for the method—given by τ_k—is $O(k)$. We say that a numerical scheme is *consistent* if $\lim_{k \to 0} \tau_k = 0$, that is, we can make the numerical scheme approximate the original problem to arbitrary accuracy.

We can improve the method by using a better approximation of the derivative. Take the Taylor series

$$u(t_{n+1}) = u(t_n) + ku'(t_n) + \frac{1}{2}k^2u''(t_n) + \frac{1}{6}k^3u'''(t_n) + O(k^4)$$
$$u(t_{n-1}) = u(t_n) - ku'(t_n) + \frac{1}{2}k^2u''(t_n) - \frac{1}{6}k^3u'''(t_n) + O(k^4).$$

Subtracting the two expressions yields

$$u(t_{n+1}) - u(t_{n-1}) = 2ku'(t_n) + \frac{1}{3}k^3u'''(t_n) + O(k^4).$$

And for $u'(t_n) = f(u(t_n))$

$$u(t_{n+1}) - u(t_{n-1}) = 2kf(t_n) + k\tau_k$$

where the truncation $\tau_k = \frac{1}{3}k^2u'''(t_n) + O(k^3)$. From this, we have the leapfrog scheme

$$\frac{U^{n+1} - U^{n-1}}{2k} = f(U^n)$$

with truncation error $O(k^2)$.

Figure 12.2 on the next page gives another graphical depiction of consistency in numerical methods. If L is a linear operator, then the differential equation $u' = Lu$ has the solution $u(t) = e^{tL}u(0)$. In particular, $u' = \lambda u$ has the solution $u(t) = e^{\lambda t}u(0)$, and starting with U^n, the exact solution after time k is $U^{n+1} = e^{\lambda k}U^n$. Substituting the ratio $r = U^{n+1}/U^n$ into the numerical schemes (12.2)–(12.5) for the model equation $u' = \lambda u$ and solving for r gives us several approximations for the multiplier $e^{\lambda k}$:

exact solution	forward Euler	backward Euler	trapezoidal	leapfrog
$e^{\lambda k}$	$1 + \lambda k$	$\dfrac{1}{1 - \lambda k}$	$\dfrac{1 + \frac{1}{2}\lambda k}{1 - \frac{1}{2}\lambda k}$	$\lambda k \pm \sqrt{(\lambda k)^2 + 1}$

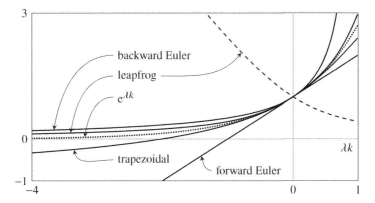

Figure 12.2: Plot of the multiplier $r(\lambda k)$ for several numerical schemes along the real λk-axis compared to the exact solution multiplier $e^{\lambda k}$.

The exact solution $e^{\lambda k}$ is depicted as a dotted curve. Approximations are good when λk is close to zero. The backward Euler and forward Euler methods are both first-order methods. The leapfrog and trapezoidal methods as second-order methods are better approximations. The leapfrog method has two solutions—one that matches the exact solution fairly well and another one that doesn't—the absolute value of this other solution is depicted using a dashed line. This second branch leads to stability issues for the leapfrog method when the real part of λk is negative and not close to zero. The backward Euler method blows up at $\lambda k = \frac{1}{2}$, and the trapezoidal method blows up at $\lambda k = 2$. Note that the backward Euler method limits 0 and the trapezoidal method limits -1 as $\lambda k \to -\infty$. We'll return to this limiting behavior when discussing L-stable and A-stable methods. We'll examine consistency in more depth when we look at multistep methods.

▷ **Stability**

A numerical method is *stable* if, for any sufficiently small step size k, a small perturbation in the numerical solution (perhaps the initial value) produces a bounded change in the numerical solution at a given subsequent time. Furthermore, a numerical method is *absolutely stable* if, for any sufficiently small step size k, the change due to a perturbation of size δ is not larger than δ at any of the subsequent time steps. In other words, a method is stable if perturbations are bounded over a finite time, and it is absolutely stable if perturbations shrink or at least do not grow over time. See the figure on the following page.

Do not equate stability with consistency—a method can be both quite stable and quite wrong. Still, absolute stability is desirable because numerical errors will not only not grow, they will diminish over time. Let's determine a condition under

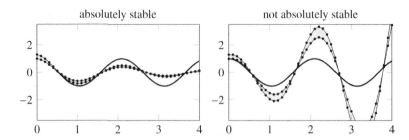

Figure 12.3: A perturbation decreases over time using an absolutely stable method and increases using an absolutely stable one. Neither one is particularly accurate.

which a numerical method is absolutely stable. We'll limit the discussion to linear methods $U^{n+1} = L(U^n, U^{n-1}, \dots)$. The discussion applies to nonlinear methods insofar as those methods can be linearized in a meaningful and representative way. Let U^0 be an initial condition and V^0 be a perturbation of that initial condition. The error in the initial condition is $e^0 = V^0 - U^0$, and the error at time $t_n = nk$ is $e^n = V^n - U^n$. Since

$$|e^{n+1}| = \left|\frac{e^{n+1}}{e^n}\right| \cdot \left|\frac{e^n}{e^{n-1}}\right| \cdots \left|\frac{e^1}{e^0}\right| \cdot |e^0|,$$

a sufficient condition for the error to be nonincreasing is for $|e^{n+1}/e^n| \le 1$ for all n. Because the method is a linear,

$$e^{n+1} = V^{n+1} - U^{n+1} = L(U^n, \dots) - L(V^n, \dots) = L(e^n, \dots).$$

Therefore, to determine the region of absolute stability, we need to determine under what conditions $|r| = |U^{n+1}/U^n| \le 1$.

▷ **Regions of absolute stability**

Consider the simple test problem $u'(t) = \lambda u(t)$ for an arbitrary complex value λ. For what time step k is a numerical scheme absolutely stable? We can answer this question by determining the values $z = \lambda k$ for which the growth factor $|r| = |U^{n+1}/U^n| \le 1$. The region in the λk-plane where $|r| \le 1$ is called the *region of absolute stability*. We'll use it to identify an appropriate numerical method. Let's find the regions of absolute stability for the forward Euler scheme, the backward Euler scheme, the leapfrog scheme, and the trapezoidal scheme.

Forward Euler. The forward Euler method for $u' = \lambda u$ is

$$\frac{U^{n+1} - U^n}{k} = \lambda U^n,$$

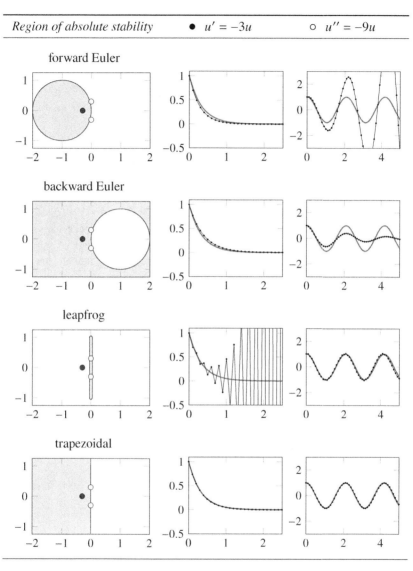

Figure 12.4: Regions of absolute stability and solutions to $u' = -3u$ and $u'' = -9u$ for step size $k = 0.1$. The eigenvalues for these ODEs are -3 and $\pm 3i$, respectively. The value ● $\lambda k = -0.3$ falls outside of the region of absolute stability for the leapfrog method and the value ○ $\lambda k = \pm 0.3i$ falls outside of the region of absolute stability for the forward Euler method resulting in an instability.

from which we have $U^{n+1} = (1 + \lambda k)U^n$, and therefore $|U^{n+1}| \leq |1 + \lambda k||U^n|$. Absolute stability requires $|1 + \lambda k| \leq 1$. That is to say, the region of absolute stability is bounded by the unit circle centered at $\lambda k = -1$. See Figure 12.4 on the previous page. For a given value λ, we may need to limit the size of our step k to ensure that λk is inside the region of absolute stability. Except for the origin, the region of absolute stability for the forward Euler scheme does not contain any part of the imaginary axis, so the method is not absolutely stable for purely imaginary λ.

Backward Euler. The backward Euler method for $u' = \lambda u$ is

$$\frac{U^{n+1} - U^n}{k} = \lambda U^{n+1}.$$

It follows that $(1 - \lambda k)U^{n+1} = U^n$, and therefore $|U^{n+1}| \leq |1 - \lambda k|^{-1}|U^n|$. Absolute stability requires $|1 - \lambda k| \geq 1$. This means that we can take any size step size as long as we are outside of the unit circle centered at $\lambda k = 1$. A numerical method is said to be *A-stable* if the region of absolute stability includes the entire left half λk-plane. The backward Euler method is A-stable.

Note that absolute stability says that the error in a perturbed numerical solution decreases over time (numerical solution minus numerical solution). It does not say anything about the accuracy of a numerical method (numerical solution minus analytic solution). For example, the numerical method $U^{n+1} = 0$ is stable, but the scheme is always inconsistent. Nontrivially, consider the harmonic oscillator $u'' = -9u$ with $u(0) = 1$ and $u'(0) = 0$. The solution is $u(t) = \cos 3t$. This problem can be written as a system by defining $v = u'$ and

$$\frac{d}{dt} \begin{bmatrix} u \\ v \end{bmatrix} = \begin{bmatrix} 0 & 1 \\ -9 & 0 \end{bmatrix} \begin{bmatrix} u \\ v \end{bmatrix} \quad \text{with} \quad \begin{bmatrix} u(0) \\ v(0) \end{bmatrix} = \begin{bmatrix} 1 \\ 0 \end{bmatrix}.$$

The solution using a backward Euler method

$$\begin{bmatrix} U^{n+1} \\ V^{n+1} \end{bmatrix} = \begin{bmatrix} 1 & -k \\ 9k & 1 \end{bmatrix}^{-1} \begin{bmatrix} U^n \\ V^n \end{bmatrix}$$

is a damped sine wave that dissipates within a few oscillations when k is large.

Leapfrog. We can rewrite

$$\frac{U^{n+1} - U^{n-1}}{k} = 2\lambda U^n$$

as $U^{n+1} - 2\lambda k U^n - U^{n-1} = 0$. By letting $r = U^{n+1}/U^n = U^n/U^{n-1}$, then $r^2 = U^{n+1}/U^{n-1}$ and it follows that

$$r^2 - 2\lambda k r - 1 = 0.$$

We want to find when $|r| \leq 1$ in the complex plane, so let's take $r = e^{i\theta}$ as the boundary. We have

$$e^{2i\theta} - 2\lambda k e^{i\theta} - 1 = 0.$$

So $e^{i\theta} - e^{-i\theta} = 2\lambda k$, from which $i \sin \theta = \lambda k$. Therefore, the leapfrog scheme is absolutely stable only on the imaginary axis $\lambda k \in [-i, +i]$.

Trapezoidal. Letting $r = U^{n+1}/U^n$ in the trapezoidal method

$$\frac{U^{n+1} - U^n}{k} = \lambda \frac{U^{n+1} + U^n}{2}$$

gives us $r - 1 = \frac{1}{2}\lambda k(r + 1)$ or equivalently

$$\lambda k = 2\frac{r - 1}{r + 1}.$$

As before, take $r = e^{i\theta}$ to identify the boundary of the region of absolute stability. Then

$$\lambda k = 2\frac{e^{i\theta} - 1}{e^{i\theta} + 1} = 2i \tan \tfrac{1}{2}\theta.$$

That is $\lambda k \in (-i\infty, +i\infty)$. So $|r| = 1$ along the entire imaginary axis, and the region of absolute stability includes the entire left half λk-plane. Therefore, the trapezoidal scheme is A-stable. A method is consistent if and only if the region of stability contains the origin $\lambda k = 0$. We call such a condition *zero-stability*.

12.3   Lax equivalence theorem

Before discussing specific numerical methods in-depth, let's consider the Lax equivalence theorem, which says that a consistent and stable method converges. "Consistency" means that we can get two equations to agree enough, "stability" means that we can control the size of the error enough, and "convergence" means that we can get two solutions to agree enough. The theorem itself is important enough that it's sometimes called the fundamental theorem of numerical analysis. It tells us when we can trust a numerical method for solving linear ordinary or partial differential equations to give us the right results.

Consider the initial value problem $u_t = Lu$, where L is a linear operator. In the next chapter, we'll consider L to be the Laplacian operator, and we'll get the heat equation $u_t = \Delta u$. In Chapter 14, we'll consider $L = \mathbf{c} \cdot \nabla$, and we'll get the advection equation $u_t = \mathbf{c} \cdot \nabla u$. Suppose that $u(t, \cdot)$ is the analytic solution to $u_t = Lu$. We'll use the dot $\cdot$ as a nonspecific placeholder. It could stand-in for some spatial dimensions if we have a partial differential equation. Or, it could be nothing at all if we have an ordinary differential equation. In this case, u is simply a function of t. Let $t_n = nk$ be the uniform discretization of time, and let U^n denote the finite difference approximation of $u(t_n, \cdot)$. Define a finite difference operator H_k such that $U^{n+1} = H_k U^n$. The subscript k in H_k denotes the dependence on the step size k. Of course, $U^{n+1} = H_k^{n+1} U^0$. For a first-order differential equation, U^n and H_k are scalars. For a system of differential equations, U^n is a vector and H_k is a matrix.

Let's restate the definitions of convergence, consistency, and stability with more rigor. Let the error $e_k(t_n, \cdot) = U^n - u(t_n, \cdot)$. A method is *convergent* in a norm $\| \cdot \|$ if the error $\|e_k(t, \cdot)\| \to 0$ as $k \to 0$ for any $t \in [0, T]$ and any initial data $u(0, \cdot)$. Define the *truncation error* as

$$\tau_k(t, \cdot) = \frac{u(t + k, \cdot) - H_k u(t, \cdot)}{k}.$$

A method is *consistent* if $\|\tau_k(t, \cdot)\| \to 0$ as $k \to 0$. Furthermore, a method is consistent of order p if, for all sufficiently smooth initial data, there exists a constant c_τ such that $\|\tau_k(t, \cdot)\| \le c_\tau k^p$ for all sufficiently small step sizes k. Define the operator norm $\| H_k \|$ as the relative maximum $\| H_k u\|/\|u\|$ over all vectors u. A method is *stable* if, for each time T, there exists a c_s and $k_s > 0$ such that $\| H_k^n \| \le c_s$ for all $nk \le T$ and $k \le k_s$. In particular, if $\| H_k \| \le 1$, then $\| H_k^n \| \le \| H_k \|^n \le 1$, which implies stability. But, we can also relax conditions on H_k to $\| H_k \| \le 1 + \alpha k$ for any constant α, since in this case

$$\| H_k^n \| \le \| H_k \|^n \le (1 + \alpha k)^n \le e^{\alpha k n} \le e^{\alpha T}.$$

Theorem 47 (Lax equivalence). *A consistent, stable method is convergent.*

Proof. For a finite difference operator H_k, the truncation error at t_{n-1} is

$$\tau_k(t_{n-1}, \cdot) = \frac{u(t_n, \cdot) - H_k u(t_{n-1}, \cdot)}{k}.$$

We can write the exact solution as $u(t_n, \cdot) = H_k u(t_{n-1}, \cdot) + k\tau_k(t_{n-1}, \cdot)$. Using this expression, the error at t_n is

$$
\begin{aligned}
e_k(t_n, \cdot) &= U^n - u(t_n, \cdot) \\
&= H_k U^{n-1} - H_k u(t_{n-1}, \cdot) - k\tau_k(t_{n-1}, \cdot) \\
&= H_k e_k(t_{n-1}, \cdot) - k\tau_k(t_{n-1}, \cdot) \\
&= H_k [H_k e_k(t_{n-2}, \cdot) - k\tau_k(t_{n-2}, \cdot)] - k\tau_k(t_{n-1}, \cdot),
\end{aligned}
$$

and continuing the iteration

$$e_k(t_n, \cdot) = H_k^n e_k(0, \cdot) - k \sum_{j=1}^{n} H_k^{j-1} \tau_k(t_{j-1}, \cdot).$$

By the triangle inequality

$$\left\| e_k(t_n, \cdot) \right\| \leq \left\| H_k^n \right\| \cdot \left\| e_k(0, \cdot) \right\| + k \sum_{j=1}^{n} \left\| H_k^{j-1} \right\| \cdot \left\| \tau_k(t_{j-1}, \cdot) \right\|.$$

From the stability condition, we have $\left\| H_k^j \right\| \leq c_s$ for all $j = 1, 2, \ldots, n$ and all $nk \leq T$. Therefore,

$$\left\| e_k(t_n, \cdot) \right\| \leq c_s \left(\left\| e_k(0, \cdot) \right\| + k \sum_{j=1}^{n} \left\| \tau_k(t_{j-1}, \cdot) \right\| \right).$$

We have $\left\| \tau_k(t_{j-1}, \cdot) \right\| \to 0$ as $k \to 0$ from the consistency condition. And if the method is pth order consistent, then $\left\| \tau_k(t_{j-1}, \cdot) \right\| \leq c_\tau k^p$. So,

$$\left\| e_k(t_n, \cdot) \right\| \leq c_s \left(\left\| e_k(0, \cdot) \right\| + c_\tau T k^p \right).$$

If the initial error $\left\| e_k(0, \cdot) \right\| \leq c_0 k^p$, then $\left\| e_k(t_n, \cdot) \right\| \leq c_s(c_0 + c_\tau T)k^p$. Hence, the method is convergent.   □

12.4   Multistep methods

The forward and backward Euler methods generate first-order approximations of the solution using piecewise linear functions. We can get more accurate approximations of the derivative by using higher-order piecewise polynomials—piecewise quadratic, piecewise cubic, etc. For an nth-order polynomial approximation, we require n terms of the Taylor series and hence n steps in time. In this section, we examine general multistep methods. Stencils for the backward differentiation formulas (BDF), sometimes called Gear's method, and Adams methods are given below. Note that the first-order BDF method is the same as the backward Euler method, the second-order Adams–Moulton method is the same as the trapezoidal method, and the first-order Adams–Bashforth method is the same as the forward Euler method.

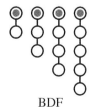

BDF

Adams–Moulton

Adams–Bashforth

▷ **Backward differentiation formulas**

We can get a better approximation to the derivative of $u(t)$ by canceling out more terms of the Taylor series. We've already derived a first-order *backward differentiation formula*, the backward Euler method. Let's derive a second-order implicit method using a piecewise quadratic approximation for u. Consider the nodes $u(t_{n+1})$, $u(t_n)$, and $u(t_{n-1})$:

$$u(t) = u(t)$$
$$u(t - k) = u(t) - ku'(t) + \tfrac{1}{2}k^2 u''(t) + O(k^3)$$
$$u(t - 2k) = u(t) - 2ku'(t) + \tfrac{4}{2}k^2 u''(t) + O(k^3)$$

We want to cancel as many terms as possible by combining the three equations in some fashion. Let a_{-1}, a_0, and a_1 be unknowns, then

$$a_{-1}u(t) = a_{-1}u(t)$$
$$a_0 u(t - k) = a_0 u(t) - a_0 ku'(t) + \tfrac{1}{2}a_0 k^2 u''(t) + O(k^3)$$
$$a_1 u(t - 2k) = a_1 u(t) - 2a_1 ku'(t) + \tfrac{4}{2}a_1 k^2 u''(t) + O(k^3).$$

We have three variables, so we are allowed three constraints. For *consistency*, we require the coefficient of $u(t)$ to be zero and the coefficient of $u'(t)$ to be one; for *accuracy*, we require the coefficient $u''(t)$ to be zero. Therefore

$$a_{-1} + a_0 + a_1 = 0$$
$$0 - a_0 - 2a_1 = k^{-1}$$
$$0 + \tfrac{1}{2}a_0 + \tfrac{4}{2}a_1 = 0.$$

We solve this linear system for (a_{-1}, a_0, a_1), and we get

$$a_{-1} = \tfrac{3}{2}k^{-1}, \qquad a_0 = -2k^{-1}, \qquad a_1 = \tfrac{1}{2}k^{-1}.$$

So

$$\frac{\tfrac{3}{2}u(t_{n+1}) - 2u(t_n) + \tfrac{1}{2}u(t_{n-1})}{k} = u'(t_{n+1}) + O(k^2).$$

Using this approximation for $u'(t)$, we obtain the second-order backward differentiation formula (BDF2)

$$\tfrac{3}{2}U^{n+1} - 2U^n + \tfrac{1}{2}U^{n-1} = kf(U^{n+1}).$$

An r-step (and rth order) backward differentiation formula takes the form

$$a_{-1}U^{n+1} + a_0 U^n + \cdots + a_{n-r+1}U^{n-r+1} = kf(U^{n+1}),$$

where the coefficients $a_{-1}, a_0, \ldots, a_{n-r+1}$ are chosen appropriately.

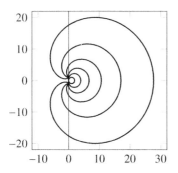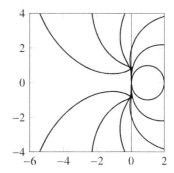

Figure 12.5: Left: internal contours of the regions of absolute stability for BDF1–BDF6. The regions of absolute stability are the areas outside these contours. Right: a close-up of the same contours.

Now, let's determine the region of absolute stability for BDF2. We take $f(u) = \lambda u$. Then letting $r = U^{n+1}/U^n$ in

$$\tfrac{3}{2}U^{n+1} - 2U^n + \tfrac{1}{2}U^{n-1} = kf(U^{n+1}),$$

we have

$$\tfrac{3}{2}r^2 - 2r + \tfrac{1}{2} = k\lambda r^2.$$

For which λk is $|r| \leq 1$? While we can easily compute this answer analytically using the quadratic formula, it becomes difficult or impossible for higher-order methods. So, instead, we will simply plot the boundary of the region of absolute stability. Since we want to know when $|r| \leq 1$, i.e., when r is inside the unit disk in the complex plane, we will consider $r = e^{i\theta}$. Then the variable λk can be expressed as the rational function

$$\lambda k = \frac{\tfrac{3}{2}r^2 - 2r + \tfrac{1}{2}}{r^2}.$$

We can plot this function in Julia using

```
r = exp.(2im*π*(0:.01:1))
plot(@. (1.5r^2 - 2r + 0.5)/r^2); plot!(aspect_ratio=:equal)
```

The regions of absolute stability for backward differentiation formulas are *unbounded* and always contain the negative real axis (well, at least up through BDF6). See Figure 12.5 above. This stability feature makes them particularly nice methods for the stiff problems we'll encounter later. Note that BDF3 and higher are not A-stable, because their regions of absolute stability do not contain the entire left half-plane. Such methods are often referred to as almost A-stable or *A(α)-stable*. A method is A(α)-stable if the region of stability contains the sector in the negative λk-plane between $\pi \pm \alpha$. The regions of absolute stability for the BDF methods get progressively smaller with increased accuracy, and BDF7 and higher are no longer zero-stable. This trade-off between stability and accuracy is typical but not necessary—higher-order Runge–Kutta methods are often more stable than their lower-order counterparts.

▷ **General multistep methods**

The focus of BDF methods is entirely on the left-hand-side term u'. In designing a broader class of methods, we ought to think about the whole equation $u' = f(u)$ and not simply the left-hand side. A general s-step method may be written as

$$\sum_{j=-1}^{s-1} a_j U^{n-j} = k \sum_{j=-1}^{s-1} b_j f(U^{n-j})$$

where the coefficients a_j and b_j may be zero. When $b_{-1} = 0$, the method is explicit; when $b_{-1} \neq 0$, the method is implicit.

The *local truncation error* of the finite difference approximation is defined as

$$\tau_{\text{local}} = \sum_{j=-1}^{s-1} a_j u(t_{n-j}) - k \sum_{j=-1}^{s-1} b_j f(u(t_{n-j})),$$

and it is used to quantify the error for one time step. Error accumulates at each iteration. Because $t_n = nk$, it follows that $n = O(1/k)$. The *global truncation error* of a finite difference approximation is defined as $\tau_{\text{global}} = \tau_{\text{local}}/k$ and quantifies the error over several times steps. For example, the local truncation error of the leapfrog scheme is $O(k^3)$, and the global truncation error is $O(k^2)$.

From Taylor series expansion with $t_{n-j} = t_n - jk$, we have

$$u(t_{n-j}) = u(t_n) - jku'(t_n) + \tfrac{1}{2}(jk)^2 u(t_n) + \cdots$$
$$f(u(t_{n-j})) = u'(t_{n-j}) = u'(t_n) - jku''(t_n) + \tfrac{1}{2}(jk)^2 u'''(t_n) + \cdots.$$

Then the local truncation error at t_n is

$$\sum_{j=-1}^{s-1} a_j u(t_n) - k \sum_{j=-1}^{s-1} (ja_j + b_j)u'(t_n) + k^2 \sum_{j=-1}^{s-1} (\tfrac{1}{2}j^2 a_j + jb_j)u''(t_n) - \cdots$$

$$\cdots - \frac{(-1)^p}{p!} k^p \sum_{j=-1}^{s-1} \left(j^p a_j + pj^{p-1} b_j \right) u^{(p)}(t_n) + \cdots$$

For a consistent method, the global truncation error must limit zero as the step size limits zero. Therefore,

$$\sum_{j=-1}^{s-1} a_j = 0 \quad \text{and} \quad \sum_{j=-1}^{s-1} ja_j + b_j = 0. \tag{12.6a}$$

To further get a method that is $O(k^p)$ accurate, we need to set the first $p + 1$ coefficients of the truncation error to 0:

$$\sum_{j=-1}^{s-1} \left(j^i a_j + i j^{i-1} b_j \right) = 0 \quad \text{for } i = 1, 2, \ldots, p. \tag{12.6b}$$

We can write this system in matrix form $\mathbf{Aa} + \mathbf{Bb} = 0$, where $\mathbf{A}$ is the transpose of a Vandermonde matrix and $\mathbf{B}$ is the transpose of a confluent Vandermonde matrix:

$$\begin{bmatrix} 1 & 1 & 1 & \cdots & 1 \\ 1 & 2 & 3 & \cdots & s \\ 1 & 2^2 & 3^2 & \cdots & s^2 \\ \vdots & \vdots & \vdots & \ddots & \vdots \\ 1 & 2^s & 3^s & \cdots & s^s \end{bmatrix} \begin{bmatrix} 1 \\ a_0 \\ a_1 \\ \vdots \\ a_{s-1} \end{bmatrix} + \begin{bmatrix} 0 & 0 & 0 & \cdots & 0 \\ 1 & 1 & 1 & \cdots & 1 \\ 2 & 4 & 6 & \cdots & 2s \\ \vdots & \vdots & \vdots & \ddots & \vdots \\ s & s2^{s-1} & s3^{s-1} & \cdots & s^{s-1} \end{bmatrix} \begin{bmatrix} b_{-1} \\ b_0 \\ b_1 \\ \vdots \\ b_{s-1} \end{bmatrix} = 0.$$

We can solve this system with a few lines of code in Julia. The following function returns the multistep coefficients for stencils given by m and n:

```
function multistepcoefficients(m,n)
  s = length(m) + length(n) - 1
  A = (m.+1).^(0:s-1) .|> Rational
  B = (0:s-1).*((n.+1).^[0;0:s-2])
  c = -[A[:,2:end] B]\ones(Int64,s)
  [1;c[1:length(m)-1]], c[length(m):end]
end
```

The input m is a row vector indicating nonzero (free) indices of $\{a_j\}$ and n is a row vector of nonzero indices of $\{b_j\}$. The value a_{-1} is always implicitly one, and 0 should not be included in m. By formatting B as an array of rational numbers using // and formatting the ones array as integers, the coefficients c will be formatted as rational numbers. For example, the input m = [1 2] and n = [1 2 3], which corresponds to the third-order Adams–Moulton method, results in the two arrays [1 -1] and [5/12 2/3 -1/12]. We can use these coefficients to plot the boundary of the region of absolute stability:

```
function plotstability(a,b)
  λk(r) = (a · r.^-(0:length(a)-1)) ./ (b · r.^-(0:length(b)-1))
  r = exp.(im*LinRange(0,2π,200))
  plot(λk.(r),label="",aspect_ratio=:equal)
end
```

```
m = [0 1]; n = [0 1 2]
a, b = zeros(maximum(m)+1), zeros(maximum(n)+1)
a[m.+1], b[n.+1] = multistepcoefficients(m,n)
plotstability(a,b)
```

Suppose that we want to maximize the order of a multistep method. The system (12.6) has $s + 1$ equations with $s + 1$ unknown and $s + 1$ prescribed variables. We might be tempted to try something like this

$$
\begin{bmatrix} \mathbf{a}^\mathsf{T} \\ \mathbf{b}^\mathsf{T} \end{bmatrix} = \begin{bmatrix} 1 & a_1 & a_2 & \cdots & a_{s/2} & 0 & \cdots & 0 \\ b_0 & b_1 & b_2 & \cdots & a_{s/2} & 0 & \cdots & 0 \end{bmatrix}.
$$

After all, it works for the trapezoidal method with $\mathbf{a} = (1, -1, 0)$ and $\mathbf{b} = \left(\frac{1}{2}, \frac{1}{2}, 0\right)$, giving a second-order, single-step method. But, in general, such an approach does not ensure the stability of the scheme. In 1956, Germund Dahlquist proved that the order of accuracy of a stable s-step linear multistep formula can be no greater than $s + 2$ if s is even, $s + 1$ if s is odd, and s if the formula is explicit. This theorem is now called the *first Dahlquist barrier*.[1]

Multistep methods may require several starting values, i.e., to compute U^s for an s-step method, we first need $U^0, U^1, \ldots, U^{s-1}$. For example, to implement the leapfrog method, first, use the forward Euler method to compute U^1. Then use the leapfrog after that. The local truncation error from the Euler method is $O\left(k^2\right)$, and the contribution to the global truncation error from that one step is $O\left(k^2\right)$. Therefore, the overall global error from the leapfrog method is $O\left(k^2\right)$.

▷ Adams methods

Whereas BDF methods have complicated approximations for the derivative on the left-hand side, Adams methods have simple left-hand sides and complicated right-hand sides. A BDF method evaluates the derivative at t_{n+1} to match the right-hand side. Adams methods rely on the mean value theorem to find an intermediate time somewhere between t_n and t_{n+1}. To do this, they work by adjusting the right-hand side. The Adams methods have the form $a_{-1} = 1$ and $a_0 = -1$ and $a_j = 0$ for $1 \le j \le s - 1$. That is,

$$
U^{n+1} = U^n + k \sum_{j=-1}^{s-1} b_j f\left(U^{n-j}\right).
$$

The explicit *Adams–Bashforth method* takes $b_{-1} = 0$, and the implicit *Adams–Moulton method* takes $b_{-1} \neq 0$.

Another difference between Adams methods and BDF methods is their regions of absolute stability. Unlike the BDF methods, which have unbounded regions, both the Adams–Bashforth and the Adams–Moulton methods have bounded regions. See Figure 12.6 on the facing page. That the region of absolute stability for an explicit method like the Adams–Bashforth is bounded is expected, but that the region of absolute stability of an implicit method like the Adams–Moulton method is bounded is a little disappointing, especially because

---

[1] In 1963, Dahlquist established his second barrier stating that no explicit scheme can be A-stable.

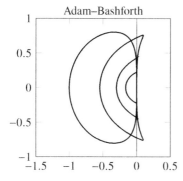
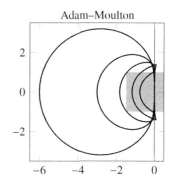

Figure 12.6: External contours of the regions of absolute stability for the explicit Adams–Bashforth methods AB2–AB5 (left) and implicit Adams–Moulton methods AM3–AM7 (right). The plot region of the Adams–Bashforth is shown with the gray rectangle overlaying the plot region of the Adams–Moulton.

the implementation of implicit methods requires significantly more effort. Still, the region of absolute stability of an Adams–Moulton method is about three times larger than that of the corresponding Adams–Bashforth method.

▷ **Predictor-corrector methods**

Nonlinear implicit methods can be difficult to implement because they require an iterative nonlinear solver. One approach is to use an explicit method for one time step to "predict" the implicit term and then use an implicit method to "correct" the solution of the explicit method. Adams methods are particularly well-suited as predictor-corrector methods, using the Adams–Bashforth method as a predictor and one or more functional iterations of the Adams–Moulton method as a corrector—an approach called an Adams–Bashforth–Moulton (ABM) method:

$$\text{predictor:} \qquad \tilde{U}^{n+1} = U^n + k \sum_{j=0}^{s-1} b_j f(U^{n-j}) \qquad (12.7a)$$

$$\text{corrector:} \qquad U^{n+1} = U^n + k b_0^* f(\tilde{U}^{n+1}) + k \sum_{j=0}^{s-1} b_j^* f(U^{n-j}). \qquad (12.7b)$$

The two steps are often expressed as predict–evaluate–correct–evaluate (PECE). The corrector step can always be run a second or third or more times using its output as input to achieve better convergence. In this case, the method is often expressed as PE(CE)^m. If the corrector is run until convergence, PE(CE)^∞ is simply an implementation of the implicit method.

▷ Padé approximation

A *Padé approximation* is a rational-function extension to the Taylor polynomial approximation of an analytic function:

$$R_{m,n}(x) = \frac{P_m(x)}{Q_n(x)} = \frac{\sum_{i=0}^{m} p_i x^i}{1 + \sum_{i=1}^{n} q_i x^i}.$$

For example, the order-(3,4) Padé approximation to $\sin x$ is

$$R_{3,4}(x) = \frac{x - \frac{31}{294}x^3}{1 + \frac{3}{49}x^2 + \frac{11}{5880}x^4}$$

When $n = 0$, the denominator $Q_n(r) = 1$ and the Padé approximation is identical to a Taylor polynomial. Linear multistep methods can be interpreted as Padé approximations to the logarithm function. In particular, $u' = \lambda u$ has the solution $u(t) = e^{\lambda t}u(0)$, and starting with U^n, the exact solution after time k is $U^{n+1} = e^{\lambda k}U^n$. Define the ratio $r = U^{n+1}/U^n = e^{\lambda k}$. If $r(\lambda k)$ is an approximant of the exponential function $e^{\lambda k}$, then the inverse $\lambda k(r)$ is an approximant of the logarithm.

We can compute the Padé approximant of $\log r$ using a symbolic mathematics language like Wolfram.[2] For example, $R_{1,3}(x)$ is constructed using

```
m = 1; n = 3;
Simplify[PadeApproximant[Log[r],{r,1,{m,n}}]]
```

Another way to compute the Padé approximant to $\log r$ is by starting with the Taylor polynomial $T(x)$ of $\log(x+1)$; then determining the coefficients of $P_m(x)$ and $Q_n(x)$ from $P_m(x) = Q_n(x)T(x) + O(x^{m+n+1})$; and finally, substituting $r - 1$ back in for x and grouping coefficients by powers of r. But, perhaps the easiest way to compute the Padé approximant is simply by solving the linear system outlined for general multistep methods using `multistepcoeffs` on page 349.

Implicit methods correspond to the Padé approximations of $\log r$. An order-p BDF method corresponds to $R_{p,0}(r)$ and an order-p Adams–Moulton method corresponds to $R_{1,p-1}(r)$. Explicit methods are associated with $r^{-1}C_{m,n}(r)$, where $C_{m,n}(r)$ is the Padé approximations of $r \log r$. The leapfrog method is $r^{-1}C_{2,0}(r)$, and an order-p Adams–Bashforth method corresponds to $r^{-1}C_{1,p-1}(r)$. The figure on the next page shows the Padé approximants corresponding to the backward Euler, the third-order Adams–Moulton, and the forward Euler methods. Each of these rational functions approximates $\log r$ at $r = 1$ when $\lambda k = 0$.

---

[2]WolframCloud (https://www.wolframcloud.com) provides free, online access to Mathematica.

$$R_{1,0}(r) = \frac{r-1}{1}$$

$$R_{1,2}(r) = \frac{r-1}{-\frac{1}{12}r^2 + \frac{2}{3}r + \frac{5}{12}}$$

$$r^{-1}C_{1,0}(r) = \frac{r-1}{r}$$

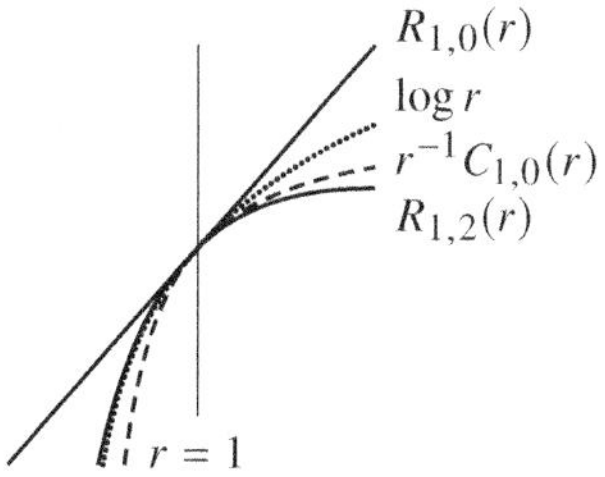

$R_{1,0}(r)$
$\log r$
$r^{-1}C_{1,0}(r)$
$R_{1,2}(r)$
$r = 1$

Figure 12.7: Padé approximant representations of the backward Euler, third-order Adams–Moulton, and forward Euler methods.

12.5 Runge–Kutta methods

By directly integrating $u'(t) = f(u,t)$, we can change the differential equation into an integral equation

$$u(t_{n+1}) - u(t_n) = \int_{t_n}^{t_{n+1}} f(t, u(t))\, dt.$$

The challenge now is to evaluate the integral numerically. One way of doing this is to use the Runge–Kutta method. Unlike multistep methods, Runge–Kutta methods can get high-order results without saving the solutions of previous time steps, making them good choices for adaptive step size. Because of this, Runge–Kutta methods are often methods of choice.

We can approximate the integral using quadrature

$$\int_{t_n}^{t_{n+1}} f(t, u(t))\, dt \approx k \sum_{i=1}^{s} b_i f(t_i^*, u(t_i^*))$$

with appropriate weights b_i and nodes $t_i^* \in [t_n, t_{n+1}]$. In fact, by choosing the s nodes and weights to have a Gaussian quadrature, we can get a method that has order $2s$. We must already know the values $u(t_i^*)$ to apply this method. Such an approach seems circular, but of course, we can always use quadrature at intermediate stages to approximate each of the $u(t_i^*)$.

Example. The simplest quadrature rule uses a Riemann sum:

$$\int_a^b f(x)\, dx \approx (b-a)f(a).$$

Let's use this to compute U^{n+1} given U^n. From

$$u(t_{n+1}) = u(t_n) + \int_{t_n}^{t_{n+1}} f(t, u(t))\, dt,$$

we have $U^{n+1} = U^n + k f(t_n, U^n)$, which is the forward Euler method.   ◄

Example.   The midpoint rule is a more accurate one-point quadrature rule

$$\int_a^b f(x)\, dx \approx (b-a)f\left(\frac{b+a}{2}\right).$$

We'll need to approximate $f(t_{n+1/2}, U^{n+1/2})$ this time. We can use the forward Euler method. Take $K_1 = f(t_n, U^n)$ and

$$K_2 = f(t_n + \tfrac{1}{2}k, U^n + \tfrac{1}{2}k f(t_n, U^n)) = f(t_n + \tfrac{1}{2}k, U^n + \tfrac{1}{2}kK_1).$$

The midpoint rule says

$$u(t_{n+1}) = u(t_n) + \int_{t_n}^{t_{n+1}} f(t, u(t))\, dt = u(t_n) + k f(t_{n+1/2}, u(t_{n+1/2}))$$

from which we have $U^{n+1} = U^n + kK_2$. This second-order method is known as Heun's method.   ◄

Example.   The trapezoidal rule is another one-point quadrature rule

$$\int_a^b f(x)\, dx \approx (b-a)\left[\tfrac{1}{2}f(a) + \tfrac{1}{2}f(b)\right].$$

To compute U^{n+1} given U^n, we'll need to approximate $f(t_{n+1}, U^{n+1})$ using the forward Euler method. Take $K_1 = f(t_n, U^n)$ and

$$K_2 = f(t_n + k, U^n + k f(t_n, U^n)) = f(t_n + k, U^n + kK_1).$$

Combining these yields a second-order rule $U^{n+1} = U^n + k\left[\tfrac{1}{2}K_1 + \tfrac{1}{2}K_2\right]$.   ◄

Example.   To get high-order methods, we add quadrature points. The next step up is Simpson's rule, which says

$$\int_a^b f(x)\, dx \approx (b-a)\left[\frac{1}{6}f(a) + \frac{2}{3}f\left(\frac{b+a}{2}\right) + \frac{1}{6}f(b)\right].$$

We'll need to approximate $f(t_{n+1/2}, U^{n+1/2})$ and $f(t_{n+1}, U^{n+1})$.   ◄

An s-stage Runge–Kutta method is given by

$$U^{n+1} = U^n + k\sum_{i=1}^{s} b_i K_i \quad \text{with} \quad K_i = f\left(t_n + c_i k, U^n + k\sum_{j=1}^{s} a_{ij} K_j\right). \quad (12.8)$$

Computing the coefficients a_{ij} is not a trivial exercise. We need to take $c_i = \sum_{j=1}^{s} a_{ij}$ and $\sum_{i=1}^{s} b_i = 1$ for consistency. These coefficients are often conveniently given as a *Butcher tableau*

$$\begin{array}{c|c} \mathbf{c} & \mathbf{A} \\ \hline & \mathbf{b}^{\mathsf{T}} \end{array}$$

where $[\mathbf{A}]_{ij} = a_{ij}$. If $\mathbf{A}$ is a strictly lower triangular matrix, then the Runge–Kutta method is explicit. Otherwise, the method is implicit. If $\mathbf{A}$ is a lower triangular matrix, the method is a diagonally implicit Runge–Kutta Method (DIRK).

The second-order Heun method (RK2) is given by

$$K_1 = f(t_n, U^n)$$
$$K_2 = f\left(t_n + \tfrac{1}{2}k, U^n + \tfrac{1}{2}kK_1\right)$$
$$U^{n+1} = U^n + kK_2$$

$$\begin{array}{c|cc} 0 & & \\ \tfrac{1}{2} & \tfrac{1}{2} & \\ \hline & 0 & 1 \end{array}$$

The Butcher tableau of the trapezoidal rule is

$$K_1 = f(t_n, U^n)$$
$$K_2 = f\left(t_n + k, U^n + kK_1\right)$$
$$U^{n+1} = U^n + k\left(\tfrac{1}{2}K_2 + \tfrac{1}{2}K_1\right)$$

$$\begin{array}{c|cc} 0 & & \\ 1 & 0 & 1 \\ \hline & \tfrac{1}{2} & \tfrac{1}{2} \end{array}$$

The trapezoidal rule is a DIRK method with an explicit first stage. The fourth-order Runge–Kutta (RK4), sometimes called the classical Runge–Kutta method or simply "the" Runge–Kutta method, is derived from Simpson's rule.

$$K_1 = f(t_n, U^n)$$
$$K_2 = f\left(t_n + \tfrac{1}{2}k, U^n + \tfrac{1}{2}kK_1\right)$$
$$K_3 = f\left(t_n + \tfrac{1}{2}k, U^n + \tfrac{1}{2}kK_2\right)$$
$$K_4 = f\left(t_n + k, U^n + kK_3\right)$$
$$U^{n+1} = U^n + \tfrac{1}{6}k(K_1 + 2K_2 + 2K_3 + K_4).$$

$$\begin{array}{c|cccc} 0 & & & & \\ \tfrac{1}{2} & \tfrac{1}{2} & & & \\ \tfrac{1}{2} & 0 & \tfrac{1}{2} & & \\ 1 & 0 & 0 & 1 & \\ \hline & \tfrac{1}{6} & \tfrac{1}{3} & \tfrac{1}{3} & \tfrac{1}{6} \end{array}$$

Example. Plot the regions of stability for the Runge–Kutta methods given by the following tableaus:

$$\begin{array}{c|c} 0 & 0 \\ \hline & 1 \end{array}$$

$$\begin{array}{c|cc} 0 & & \\ \tfrac{1}{2} & \tfrac{1}{2} & \\ \hline & 0 & 1 \end{array}$$

$$\begin{array}{c|cc} 0 & & \\ \tfrac{1}{2} & \tfrac{1}{2} & \\ 1 & -1 & 2 \\ \hline & \tfrac{1}{6} & \tfrac{2}{3} & \tfrac{1}{6} \end{array}$$

$$\begin{array}{c|cccc} 0 & & & & \\ \tfrac{1}{2} & \tfrac{1}{2} & & & \\ \tfrac{1}{2} & 0 & \tfrac{1}{2} & & \\ 1 & 0 & 0 & 1 & \\ \hline & \tfrac{1}{6} & \tfrac{1}{3} & \tfrac{1}{3} & \tfrac{1}{6} \end{array}$$

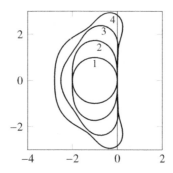

Figure 12.8: External contours of the regions of absolute stability for the explicit Runge–Kutta methods RK1–RK4. The regions of stability get progressively *larger* with increasing order.

The region of absolute stability is bounded by the $|r| = 1$ contour, where $r = U^{n+1}/U^n$ and U^n is the solution to $u' = \lambda u$. For a Runge–Kutta method we can get an explicit expression for λk in terms of r. For $f(t, u) = \lambda u$, a general Runge–Kutta method is by (12.8)

$$U^{n+1} = U^n + k\mathbf{b}^\mathsf{T}\mathbf{K},$$

with $\mathbf{K}$ given implicitly by

$$\mathbf{K} = \lambda(U^n\mathbf{E} + k\mathbf{A}\mathbf{K}) \tag{12.9}$$

where $\mathbf{K}$ is an $s \times 1$ vector, $\mathbf{b}^\mathsf{T}$ is a $1 \times s$ vector, $\mathbf{A}$ is an $s \times s$ matrix, and $\mathbf{E}$ is an $s \times 1$ vector of ones. We solve (12.9) for $\mathbf{K}$ to get

$$\mathbf{K} = \lambda U^n(\mathbf{I} - \lambda k\mathbf{A})^{-1}\mathbf{E}$$

where $\mathbf{I}$ is an $s \times s$ identity matrix. Then

$$r = 1 + \lambda k\mathbf{b}^\mathsf{T}(\mathbf{I} - \lambda k\mathbf{A})^{-1}\mathbf{E}. \tag{12.10}$$

We can use Julia to compute the $|r| = 1$ contours of (12.10) for each tableau. The regions of absolute stability are plotted in Figure 12.8.   ◄

Example.   We can build a second-order Runge–Kutta method by combining the trapezoidal method with BDF2 in two stages, first taking the trapezoidal method for half a time step followed by the BDF method for the remaining half time step:

$$U^{n+1/2} = U^n + \tfrac{1}{4}k\big(f(U^{n+1/2}) + f(U^n)\big)$$
$$U^{n+1} = \tfrac{4}{3}U^{n+1/2} - \tfrac{1}{3}U^n + \tfrac{1}{3}kf(U^{n+1}).$$

Substituting the first equation into the second gives us

$$U^{n+1} = U^n + \tfrac{1}{3}k\left(f\left(U^{n+1}\right) + f\left(U^{n+1/2}\right) + f\left(U^n\right)\right)$$

from which we have the DIRK method.

$$
\begin{aligned}
K_1 &= f(U^n)\\
K_2 &= \tfrac{1}{4}f(U^n) + \tfrac{1}{4}f(U^{n+1/2})\\
K_3 &= \tfrac{1}{3}f(U^n) + \tfrac{1}{3}f(U^{n+1/2}) + \tfrac{1}{3}f(U^{n+1})\\
U^{n+1} &= U^n + k\left(\tfrac{1}{3}K_1 + \tfrac{1}{3}K_2 + \tfrac{1}{3}K_3\right)
\end{aligned}
$$

$$
\begin{array}{c|ccc}
0 & & & \\
\tfrac{1}{2} & \tfrac{1}{4} & \tfrac{1}{4} & \\
1 & \tfrac{1}{3} & \tfrac{1}{3} & \tfrac{1}{3} \\
\hline
 & \tfrac{1}{3} & \tfrac{1}{3} & \tfrac{1}{3}
\end{array}
$$

Instead of breaking the time step into two equal subintervals, we could also take the intermediate point at some fraction α of the time step. In this case, we take the trapezoidal method over a subinterval αk and the BDF2 method over the two subintervals αk and $(1-\alpha)k$ with $0 < \alpha < 1$. Finding an optimal $\alpha = 2 - \sqrt{2}$ is left as an exercise. ◀

   Runge–Kutta methods can seem complicated at first glance. Because of this, it is good to develop an intuition about how they work. For a unit step size, we can interpret c_i as nodes on the interval $[0, 1]$. The terms K_i are the slope of $u(t)$ at the node. Runge–Kutta methods can be viewed as successive approximations combined together at each stage to get a more accurate solution. See Figure 12.9 on the next page.

▷ Adaptive step size

One advantage that Runge–Kutta methods have over multistep methods is the relative ease that the step size can be varied, taking smaller steps when needed to minimize error and maintain stability and larger steps otherwise. Often, a Runge–Kutta method embeds a lower-order method inside a higher-order method, sharing the same Butcher tableau. For example, the Bogacki–Shampine method (implemented in Julia using the function BS3) combines a second-order and third-order Runge–Kutta method using the same quadrature points:

$$
\begin{array}{c|cccc}
0 & & & & \\
\tfrac{1}{2} & \tfrac{1}{2} & & & \\
\tfrac{3}{4} & 0 & \tfrac{3}{4} & & \\
1 & \tfrac{2}{9} & \tfrac{1}{3} & \tfrac{4}{9} & \\
\hline
 & \tfrac{2}{9} & \tfrac{1}{3} & \tfrac{4}{9} & 0 \\
 & \tfrac{7}{24} & \tfrac{1}{4} & \tfrac{1}{3} & \tfrac{1}{8}
\end{array}
$$

The K_i are the same for the second-order and the third-order methods. By subtracting the solutions, we can approximate the truncation error. If the

$$
\begin{array}{c|cccc}
0 \\
\frac{1}{2} & \frac{1}{2} \\
\frac{3}{4} & 0 & \frac{3}{4} \\
1 & \frac{2}{9} & \frac{1}{3} & \frac{4}{9} \\
\hline
& \frac{7}{24} & \frac{1}{4} & \frac{1}{3} & \frac{1}{8}
\end{array}
$$

The Bogacki–Shampine scheme given by the Butcher tableau on the left is implemented in Julia using BS3. It can be implemented as an adaptive step size routine.

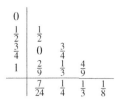

We start with the second row of the Butcher tableau. Using the slope $f(0, u(0))$ at ❶ we find the approximate solution at $t = \frac{1}{2}$ by using a simple forward Euler approximation to arrive at ❷.

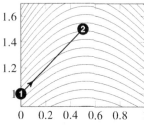

The third row of the Butcher tableau says we now try to find the solution at $t = \frac{3}{4}$ using the slope we just found at ❷ and nothing from ❶. Again, we use a simple linear extrapolation.

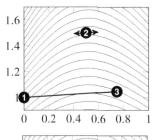

The fourth row says we now try to find the solution at $t = 1$ by first traveling $\frac{2}{9}$ with a slope given by ❶, then a distance $\frac{1}{3}$ with a slope given by ❷, and then a distance $\frac{4}{9}$ with slope from ❸.

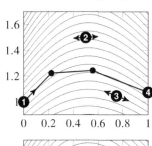

The final row tells us to first travel $\frac{7}{24}$ with a slope from ❶, then $\frac{1}{4}$ with a slope from ❷, then $\frac{1}{3}$ with a slope from ❸, and finally $\frac{1}{8}$ with a slope from ❹. The solution provides a third-order correction over the solution from ❹

Figure 12.9: Runge–Kutta methods can be viewed as successive approximations combined together at each stage to get a more accurate solution. In this example, we take step size $k = 1$ with $u(0) = 1$.

truncation error is above a given tolerance, we set the step size k to $k/2$. If the truncation error is below another given tolerance, we set the step size k to $2k$.

The notation $RKm(n)$ is occasionally used to describe a Runge–Kutta method where m is the order of the method to obtain the solution and n is the order of the method to obtain the error estimate. This notation isn't consistent, and some authors use (m, n) or $n(m)$ instead. At other times a method may have multiple error estimators. For example, the 8(5,3) uses a fifth-order error estimator and bootstraps a third-order estimator.

▷ **Implicit Runge–Kutta methods**

Another approach to Runge–Kutta methods is through collocation. Collocation is a method of problem-solving that uses a lower-dimensional subspace for candidate solutions (often polynomials of a specified degree) along with a set of collocation points. The desired solution is the one that satisfies the problem exactly at the collocation points. With s carefully chosen points, Gaussian quadrature exactly integrates a polynomial of degree $2s - 1$. For an ODE, we define the s-degree collocation polynomial $u(t)$ that satisfies

$$u'(t_0 + c_i k) = f(t_0 + c_i k, u(t_0 + c_i k)) \tag{12.11}$$

for $i = 1, 2, \ldots, s$ where $u(t_0) = u_0$ and the collocation points $c_i \in [0, 1]$. The solution is given by $u(t_0 + k)$. For example, when $s = 1$, the polynomial is

$$u(t) = u_0 + (t - t_0)K_1 \quad \text{where} \quad K_1 = f(t_0 + c_1 k, u_0 + c_1 K_1 k).$$

When $c_1 = 0$ we have the explicit Euler method, when $c_1 = 1$ we have the implicit Euler method, and $c_1 = \frac{1}{2}$ we have the implicit midpoint method:

$$
\begin{array}{c|c}
0 & 0 \\
\hline
 & 1
\end{array}
\qquad\qquad
\begin{array}{c|c}
1 & 1 \\
\hline
 & 1
\end{array}
\qquad\qquad
\begin{array}{c|c}
\frac{1}{2} & \frac{1}{2} \\
\hline
 & 1
\end{array} \ .
$$

Theorem 48. *An s-point collocation method is equivalent to an s-stage Runge–Kutta method* (12.8) *with coefficients*

$$a_{ij} = \int_0^{c_i} \ell_j(z)\,dz \quad \text{and} \quad b_i = \int_0^1 \ell_i(z)\,dz,$$

where $\ell_i(z)$ is the Lagrange polynomial basis function for a node at c_i.

Proof. Let $u(t)$ be the collocation polynomial and let $K_i = u'(t_0 + c_i k)$. The Lagrange polynomial

$$u'(t_0 + zk) = \sum_{j=1}^{s} K_j \ell_j(z) \quad \text{where} \quad \ell_i(z) = \prod_{\substack{l=0 \\ l \neq i}}^{s} \frac{z - c_l}{c_i - c_l}.$$

Integrating with respect to z over $[0, c_i]$ gives us

$$u(t_0 + c_i k) = u_0 + k \sum_{j=1}^{s} K_j \int_0^{c_i} \ell_j(z) \, dz = u_0 + k \sum_{j=1}^{s} a_{ij} K_j.$$

Similarly, integrating over $[0, 1]$ gives us $u(t_0 + k) = u_0 + k \sum_{j=1}^{s} b_j K_j$. Substituting both of these expressions into the collocation method (12.11) gives us the Runge–Kutta method (12.8).   □

A Gauss–Legendre method is an implicit Runge–Kutta method that uses collocation based on Gauss–Legendre quadrature points from the roots of shifted Legendre polynomials. From theorem 43, the error in an n-point Gauss–Legendre quadrature is

$$\frac{f^{(2n)}(\xi)}{(2n)!} \int_a^b \prod_{i=0}^{s-1} (x - x_i) \, dx$$

for nodes $x_0, x_1, \ldots, x_{s-1}$ and for some $\xi \in [a, b]$. Over an interval of length k, the integral is bounded by k^{2s+1}. So the local truncation error is $O(k^{2s+1})$, and the global truncation error is $O(k^{2s})$. Therefore, an s-stage Gauss–Legendre method is order $2s$.

Radau methods are Gauss–Legendre methods that include one of the endpoints as quadrature points—either $c_1 = 0$ (Radau IA methods) or $c_s = 1$ (Radau IIA methods). Such methods have maximum order $2s - 1$. Gauss–Lobatto quadrature chooses the quadrature points that include both ends of the interval. Lobatto methods (Lobatto IIA) have both $c_1 = 0$ and $c_s = 1$ and have maximum order $2s - 2$.

Implicit Runge–Kutta methods offer higher accuracy and greater stability profiles, but they are more difficult to implement because they require solving a system of nonlinear equations. Diagonally implicit Runge–Kutta methods limit the Runge–Kutta method (12.8) to one implicit term

$$K_i = f\left(U^n + k \sum_{j=1}^{i} a_{ij} K_j\right).$$

We can solve these equations successively by applying Newton's method at each stage to handle the one implicit term. We can also go one step further. By linearizing the equation with respect to the implicit term at each stage, we would only need to invert a linear operator. Such an approach, called a Rosenbrock method, is effectively the same as performing one Newton step for each stage. We lose some stability and accuracy but gain speed. In practice, the Rosenbrock method is

$$K_i = f\left(U^n + k \sum_{j=1}^{i-1} a_{ij} K_j\right) + k\mathbf{J} \sum_{j=1}^{i} d_{ij} K_j,$$

where the Jacobian $\mathbf{J} = f'(U^n)$ and the coefficients d_{ij} that arise out of linearization need to be determined.

One can assemble an impressive bestiary of acronyms that have been used to classify implicit Runge–Kutta methods. The figure below summarizes the Butcher tableau structures for common Runge–Kutta methods: fully implicit (FIRK); diagonally implicit (DIRK); single-diagonal-coefficient, diagonally implicit (SDIRK); explicit-first-stage, single-diagonal-coefficient, diagonally implicit (ESDIRK); and explicit (ERK). The glyph • indicates values and the glyph ○ indicates identical nonzero values.

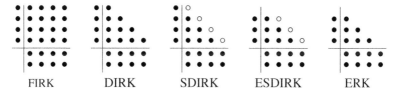

Stability, accuracy, and computational complexity tend to decrease left to right. Implicit methods are often constructed to be stiffly accurate, requiring a Newton solver. Because the diagonal elements of an SDIRK method are identical, the Jacobian matrix may be reused in the Newton iterations. To dig deeper, see the review article by Kennedy and Carpenter.

12.6   Nonlinear equations

Up to now, we've focused on linear differential equations, which can often be solved analytically. This section briefly discusses nonlinear differential equations, starting with the stability condition. For linear differential equations, we used the eigenvalue λ along with the region of absolute stability of the numerical method to determine a stability condition for the step size. If we linearize the right-hand side of a nonlinear differential equation $u' = f(u)$ near a value u^*, we have $f(u) \approx f(u^*) + (u - u^*)f'(u^*)$. Our linearized equation near u^* is

$$u' = f'(u^*)u + \left(f(u^*) - f'(u^*)u^*\right).$$

We should examine $\lambda = |f'(u^*)|$ as our eigenvalue to determine stability and step size. For a system $\mathbf{u}' = \mathbf{f}(\mathbf{u})$ we have the linearization near a value $\mathbf{u}^*$

$$\mathbf{u}' = \nabla\mathbf{f}(\mathbf{u}^*)\mathbf{u} + \left(\mathbf{f}(\mathbf{u}^*) - \nabla\mathbf{f}(\mathbf{u}^*)\mathbf{u}^*\right),$$

where $\nabla\mathbf{f}(\mathbf{u}^*)$ is the Jacobian matrix $\partial f_i/\partial u_j$ evaluated at $\mathbf{u}^*$. The spectral radius of the Jacobian matrix (the magnitude of its largest eigenvalue) now determines the stability condition.

Implicit methods are more difficult to implement, but they are more stable. When the system of differential equations is linear, this often means inverting that system using Gaussian elimination, discrete Fourier transforms, or some other relatively direct method. We may opt for an iterative technique like SOR for large, sparse systems. Implementing implicit methods on a nonlinear system almost always means that we will need to use an iterative solver. Perhaps the simplest iterative solver is functional iteration. Here, one time step of an implicit method like the Adams–Moulton method

$$U^n = U^{n-1} + k \sum_{i=0}^{s} b_i f(U^{n-i})$$

is replaced with a fixed-point iteration

$$U^{n(j+1)} = k b_0 f(U^{n(j)}) + U^{n-1} + k \sum_{i=1}^{s} b_i f(U^{n-i}),$$

initially taking $U^{n(0)} = U^{n-1}$ and iterating until convergence. From theorem 22, a fixed-point iteration $u^{(j+1)} = \phi(u^{(j)})$ only converges if $\phi(u^{(j)})$ is a contraction mapping, i.e., if $|\phi'(u^{(j)})| < 1$. This requirement itself sets a stability condition on any functional iteration method. Namely, for the Adams–Moulton method with functional iteration, we will need to take the time step $k < |b_0 f'(U^{n(j)})|^{-1}$. This approach would be ill-suited for stiff problems, which we'll discuss in the next section. For such problems, Newton's method is preferred.

Newton's method solves $\phi(u) = 0$ by taking

$$u^{(j+1)} = u^{(j)} - \left[\phi'(u^{(j)})\right]^{-1} \phi(u^{(j)}),$$

where $\phi'(u^{(j)})$ is the derivative or Jacobian matrix of $\phi(u)$. We can compute the Jacobian matrix analytically or numerically using a finite difference approximation. We don't necessarily need to compute it at every iteration within a time step. The modified Newton's method

$$u^{(j+1)} = u^{(j)} - \left[\phi'(u^{(0)})\right]^{-1} \phi(u^{(j)})$$

only calculates the Jacobian matrix at the start of each time step and then reuses it for each iteration.

Newton's method and fixed-point iteration may not converge to the correct solution if the initial guess is not sufficiently close to the target. To handle such a situation, one might use an explicit method to get a sufficiently close guess and then an implicit method to get even closer for each time step. These approaches are called predictor-corrector methods and often combine Adams–Bashforth and Adams–Moulton methods.

12.7   Stiff equations

A differential equation is said to be *stiff* if the dynamics of the solution react on at least two vastly different time scales. As we shall see in the next chapter, diffusion equations are stiff. The solution evolves quickly in the presence of a large spatial gradient and then slows to a crawl once it smooths out. Because numerical errors often result in large gradients, the problem remains stiff even after the fast scale is no longer apparent in the solution dynamics.

Example.   In his book *Numerical Computing with MATLAB*, Cleve Moler introduces a simple combustion model, which he credits to Larry Shampine.[3] Imagine striking a match. The ball of flame expands quickly until the amount of oxygen available through the surface balances the amount consumed in combustion. Let $u(t)$ be the radius of the ball of flame. The surface area is proportional to u^2, and the volume is proportional to u^3. Therefore, we can write the toy model as $u' = u^2 - u^3$, where $u(0) = u_0$. By taking an initial condition of $u_0 = \frac{1}{100}$, we have the following dynamics:

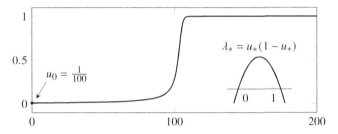

The equation has an unstable equilibrium at $u = 0$ and a stable equilibrium at $u = 1$. The solution evolves slowly when $u(t)$ is near zero until $t \approx 1/u_0$. At this point, the solution rapidly rises to just below 1. Then, the change in the solution slows and asymptotically approaches 1. To get a better idea of what's going on in the nonlinear problem, consider the quasilinear form $u' = \lambda_* u$ with $\lambda_* = u_*(1 - u_*)$ for a value u_*. When u_* is near zero, λ_* is close to zero. As u_* increases, λ_* increases to a maximum of $\frac{1}{4}$ at $u_* = \frac{1}{2}$ and then decreases back to zero as u_* approaches one.

Let's compare solutions using the adaptive Dormand–Prince Runge–Kutta method (RK45) and the adaptive fifth-order BDF methods over the interval $t \in [0, 200]$ starting with $u_0 = 0.999$:

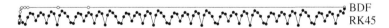

While the dynamics of the equation near $u = 1$ are relatively benign, we need to take many tiny steps using the Runge–Kutta method—124 in total. But, the BDF method takes just 11. And almost all of these steps are early on—the last step is an

---

[3] Shampine himself credits Robert O'Malley, who himself credits Edward Reiss. An explicit solution, given in terms of a Lambert W function, can be found in an article by Corless et al.

enormous leap of $k = 157$. Both methods adjust the step size to ensure stability. To determine the stability conditions for a numerical method, we examine the derivative of the right-hand side $f(u) = u^2(1 - u)$, which is $f'(u) = 2u - 3u^2$. Specifically, when $u(t) \approx 1$, the derivative $f'(u) \approx -1$. The lower limit of the region of absolute stability of the Dormand–Prince Runge–Kutta method is -3. If we use this method, we can take steps as large as $k = 3$ near $u = 1$ and still maintain absolute stability—the solver took an average step size of 1.6. On the other hand, if we use the BDF scheme, which has no lower limit on its region of absolute stability, we can take as large a step as we'd like.   ◄

Chemists Charles Curtiss and Joseph Hirschfelder first referenced "stiff" equations in a 1952 article. They motivated their discussion by describing free radicals that are rapidly created and destroyed compared to an overall chemical reaction. The dynamics of the equations occur faster than the desired resolution of the solution. While these dynamics are not a point of interest, they nonetheless drive the behavior of the numerical solution. Seventy years after Curtiss and Hirschfelder introduced the notion of stiffness, mathematicians still have not settled on its definition.[4]

Like the Reiss combustion model, stiff equations often have a quickly decaying transient solution and an equilibrium solution. A linear system of equations $\mathbf{u}' = \mathbf{Au}$ is stiff if the eigenvalues all lie in the left half-plane and the ratio of the magnitudes of the real parts of the largest and smallest eigenvalues is large. A system of equations $\mathbf{u}' = \mathbf{f}(\mathbf{u})$ is stiff if the same holds for the eigenvalues of its Jacobian matrix $\mathbf{A} = \nabla \mathbf{f}(\mathbf{u})$. This *stiffness ratio*,

$$\kappa = \frac{\max |\operatorname{Re} \lambda(\mathbf{A})|}{\min |\operatorname{Re} \lambda(\mathbf{A})|},$$

is analogous to the condition number of a matrix.

Stiffness is also a property of stability. Ernst Hairer and Gerhard Wanner, in their treatise on stiff differential equations, state simply, "Stiff equations are problems for which explicit methods don't work." Using an explicit method on a stiff problem is like running on cobblestones. You might want to run quite quickly and carefree, and maybe you think you can, but a slight misstep will trip you up and send you flying onto the pavement.

Example.   Consider the behavior of $u' = \lambda(\sin t - u) + \cos t$ where $u(0) = u_0$ and λ is a large, positive value. The solution $u(t) = u_0 e^{-\lambda t} + \sin t$ evolves over two time scales—a slow time scale of $\sin t$ and a fast time scale of $u_0 e^{-\lambda t}$.

---

[4]Söderlind, Jay, and Calvo's review article "Stiffness 1952–2012: Sixty years in search of a definition" addresses the lack of consensus on an adequate definition.

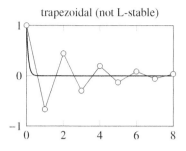

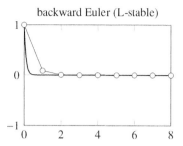

Figure 12.10: The numerical solutions to $u' = -10u$ using the second-order trapezoidal method and first-order backward Euler method with step size $k = 1$.

Take $\lambda = 500$ and $u_0 = 0$. The differential equation has a simple solution $u(t) = \sin t$. Over the interval $t \in [0, 20]$, an adaptive fifth-order BDF method takes 102 time steps. Over the same interval, an adaptive fifth-order Runge–Kutta method takes 3022 steps—roughly 30 times as many as the BDF! ◄

Because stiff equations have relatively large negative eigenvalues, implicit solvers are natural choices for them. In particular, an A-stable method such as the backward Euler or trapezoidal method will ensure stability no matter where the eigenvalues lie in the left-half plane. But, for stiff problems, A-stability is usually not enough. While the trapezoidal method is unconditionally stable in the left-half plane, it typically produces transient oscillations that overshoot and overcorrect along the path of exponential decay for large, negative eigenvalues.

Consider the initial value problem $u' = -\lambda u$ for a positive factor λ. We can write the trapezoidal method $U^{n+1} - U^n = -\frac{1}{2}\lambda k \left(U^{n+1} + U^n\right)$ as

$$U^{n+1} = \left(\frac{1 - \frac{1}{2}\lambda k}{1 + \frac{1}{2}\lambda k}\right)^n U^0 = (r(\lambda k))^n U^0.$$

Because the trapezoidal method is A-stable, we can take a large time step size k and still ensure stability. But when λk is large, the multiplying factor $r(\lambda k) \approx -1$. Consequently, the numerical solution $U^n \approx (-1)^n U^0$ will oscillate for a long time as it slowly decays. See the figure on the current page.

We can write the backward Euler method $U^n - U^{n-1} = -\lambda k U^n$ as

$$U^n = \left(\frac{1}{1 + \lambda k}\right)^n U^0 = (r(\lambda k))^n U^0.$$

Now, when λk is large, the multiplying factor $r(\lambda k) \approx 0$, and the numerical solution decays quickly.

A method is *L-stable* if it is A-stable and $r(\lambda k) \to 0$ as $\lambda k \to -\infty$. We can weaken the definition to say that a method is *almost L-stable* if it is almost A-stable and $|r(\lambda k)| < 1$ as $\lambda k \to -\infty$. In other words, a method is almost L-stable if it is zero-stable and the interior of its region of absolute stability contains the point $-\infty$. Backward differentiation formulas BDF1 and BDF2 are L-stable, and BDF3–BDF6 are almost L-stable. Several third- and fourth-order DIRK and Rosenbrock methods are also L-stable.

12.8   Splitting methods

Partial differential equations often have stiff, linear terms coupled with nonstiff, nonlinear terms. Examples include

Navier–Stokes equation $\qquad \dfrac{\partial \mathbf{v}}{\partial t} + (\mathbf{v} \cdot \nabla)\mathbf{v} = -\dfrac{1}{\rho}\nabla p + \nu \Delta \mathbf{v} + \mathbf{g}$

reaction-diffusion equation $\qquad \dfrac{\partial u}{\partial t} = \Delta u + u(1 - u^2)$

nonlinear Schrödinger equation $\qquad \mathrm{i}\dfrac{\partial \psi}{\partial t} = -\tfrac{1}{2}\Delta \psi + |\psi|^2 \psi$

We can treat the linear terms implicitly to handle stiffness and the nonlinear terms explicitly to simplify implementation—an approach called *splitting*.

▷ Operator splitting

Let's examine the stiff, nonlinear differential equation

$$u' = \cos^2 u - 10u \quad \text{with} \quad u(0) = u_0. \tag{12.12}$$

We can write the problem as $u' = \mathrm{N}\,u + \mathrm{L}\,u$, where $\mathrm{N}\,u = \cos^2 u$ and $\mathrm{L}\,u = -10u$. The solution u is being forced by $\mathrm{N}\,u$ and $\mathrm{L}\,u$ *concurrently*. We can't solve this problem analytically, but we can approximate the solution over a short time interval by considering $\mathrm{N}\,u$ and $\mathrm{L}\,u$ as acting *successively*. We can do this in two ways:

1. First solve $u' = \mathrm{N}\,u$. Then use the solution as initial conditions of $u' = \mathrm{L}\,u$.

2. First solve $u' = \mathrm{L}\,u$. Then use the solution as initial conditions of $u' = \mathrm{N}\,u$.

Let's evaluate each of these approximate solutions after a time k.

1. The solution to $u' = \cos^2 u$ with initial condition u_0 is $u(t) = \tan^{-1}(t + u_0)$. The solution to $u' = -10u$ with initial condition $\tan^{-1}(k + u_0)$ is

$$u(k) = \mathrm{e}^{-10k} \tan^{-1}(k + \tan u_0).$$

2. The solution to $u' = -10u$ with initial condition u_0 is $u(t) = e^{-10t}u_0$. The solution to $u' = \cos^2 u$ with initial condition $e^{-10k}u_0$ is

$$u(k) = \tan^{-1}\left(k + \tan\left(e^{-10k}u_0\right)\right).$$

The natural question is, "how close are these approximations to the exact solution?" Both of these solutions are plotted along curves ❶ and ❺ in Figure 12.11 on the following page.

Take the problem $u' = A\,u + B\,u$, where A and B are arbitrary operators. Consider a simple splitting where we alternate by solving $u' = A\,u$ and then solving $u' = B\,u$ each for one time step k. We can write and implement this procedure as $U^* = S_1(k)U^n$ followed by $U^{n+1} = S_2(k)U^*$, or equivalently as $U^{n+1} = S_2(k)\,S_1(k)U^n$, where $S_1(k)$ and $S_2(k)$ are solution operators.

What is the splitting error of applying the operators A and B successively rather than concurrently? If $S_1(k)$ and $S_2(k)$ are exact solution operators $S_1(k)U^n = e^{k\,A}U^n$ and $S_2(k)U^n = e^{k\,B}U^n$, then

concurrently: $\qquad\qquad U^{n+1} = e^{k(A+B)}U^n$

successively: $\qquad\qquad \tilde{U}^{n+1} = e^{k\,B}e^{k\,A}U^n$

The splitting error is $|U^{n+1} - \tilde{U}^{n+1}|$. By Taylor series expansion, we have

$$e^{k\,A} = I + k\,A + \tfrac{1}{2}k^2\,A^2 + O\left(k^3\right)$$
$$e^{k\,B} = I + k\,B + \tfrac{1}{2}k^2\,B^2 + O\left(k^3\right)$$

and hence

$$e^{k\,B}e^{k\,A} = I + k(A+B) + \tfrac{1}{2}k^2\left(A^2 + B^2 + 2B\,A\right) + O\left(k^3\right)$$
$$e^{k(A+B)} = I + k(A+B) + \tfrac{1}{2}k^2\left(A^2 + B^2 + A\,B + B\,A\right) + O\left(k^3\right).$$

Subtracting these two operators gives us

$$e^{k(A+B)} - e^{k\,B}e^{k\,A} = \tfrac{1}{2}k^2(A\,B + B\,A - 2B\,A) + O\left(k^3\right)$$

There is no splitting error if $A\,B = B\,A$. But, in general, A and B do not commute. So, the splitting error is $O\left(k^2\right)$ for each time step. After n time steps, the error is $O(k)$.

▷ **Strang splitting**

We can reduce the error in operator splitting by using *Strang splitting*. For each time step, we solve $u' = A\,u$ for a half time step, then solve $u' = B\,u$ for a full time step, and finally solve $u' = A\,u$ for a half time step. Because

$$e^{\frac{1}{2}k\,A}e^{k\,B}e^{\frac{1}{2}k\,A} - e^{k(A+B)} = O\left(k^3\right),$$

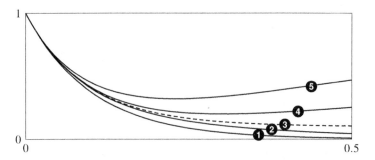

Figure 12.11: Solution to (12.12) using general splitting in ❶ and ❺, Strang splitting in ❷ and ❹, and exactly in ❸. Each operator is inverted without numerical error over a time step $k = 0.5$.

Strang splitting is second order. (The proof of this is left as an exercise.) Note that

$$U^{n+1} = S_1\left(\tfrac{1}{2}k\right) S_2(k) S_1\left(\tfrac{1}{2}k\right) U^n$$
$$= S_1\left(\tfrac{1}{2}k\right) S_2(k) S_1\left(\tfrac{1}{2}k\right) S_1\left(\tfrac{1}{2}k\right) S_2(k) S_1\left(\tfrac{1}{2}k\right) U^{n-1}.$$

But since $S_1\left(\tfrac{1}{2}k\right) S_1\left(\tfrac{1}{2}k\right) = S_1(k)$, this expression becomes

$$= S_1\left(\tfrac{1}{2}k\right) S_2(k) S_1(k) S_2(k) S_1\left(\tfrac{1}{2}k\right) U^{n-1}.$$

Continuing like this, we get

$$= S_1\left(\tfrac{1}{2}k\right) \left[S_2(k) S_1(k)\right]^n S_2(k) S_1\left(\tfrac{1}{2}k\right) U^0$$

So, to implement Strang splitting, we only need to solve $u' = A u$ for a half time step on the initial and final time steps. In between, we can use simple operator splitting. In this manner, the global splitting error is $O(k^2)$ without much more computation. It is impossible to have an operator splitting method with $O(k^3)$ or smaller error.

▷ IMEX methods

Another approach to a stiff problem is an implicit-explicit (IMEX) method. An IMEX method uses the approximation of $u'(t)$ for the implicit, linear term and the explicit, nonlinear term.

A typical second-order IMEX method combines the second-order Adams–Bashforth and the second-order Adams–Moulton methods (the trapezoidal method). Both of these methods approximate the time derivative to second order at $t_{n+1/2}$. For $u' = L u + N u$, we have

$$\frac{U^{n+1} - U^n}{k} = L U^{n+1/2} + N U^{n+1/2} \approx \tfrac{1}{2} L U^{n+1} + \tfrac{1}{2} L U^n + \tfrac{3}{2} N U^n - \tfrac{1}{2} N U^{n-1}. \quad \blacktriangleleft$$

Alternatively, we can build a second-order IMEX scheme using the BDF2 method for the linear part $u' = L u$:

$$\frac{\tfrac{3}{2} U^{n+1} - 2U^n + \tfrac{1}{2} U^{n-1}}{k} = L U^{n+1}.$$

A BDF method approximates the derivative at t_{n+1}. To avoid a splitting error, we should also evaluate the nonlinear term $N U$ at t_{n+1} by extrapolating the terms U^n and U^{n-1} to approximate U^{n+1}. We can use Taylor series to find the approximation:

$$u(t_n) = u(t_{n+1}) - ku'(t_{n+1}) + \tfrac{1}{2}k^2 u''(t_{n+1}) + O(k^3)$$
$$u(t_{n-1}) = u(t_{n+1}) - 2ku'(t_{n+1}) + 2k^2 u''(t_{n+1}) + O(k^3).$$

By combining these equations, we have

$$2u(t_n) - u(t_{n-1}) = u(t_{n+1}) - k^2 u''(t_{n+1}) + O(k^3).$$

So, the IMEX method is

$$\frac{\tfrac{3}{2} U^{n+1} - 2U^n + \tfrac{1}{2} U^{n-1}}{k} = L U^{n+1} + N \left[2U^n - U^{n-1} \right].$$

We can get higher orders by using higher-order extrapolation. To dig deeper into other ways of implementing IMEX methods, see the article by Ascher, Ruuth, and Spiteri.

▷ Integrating factors

Integrating factors provide another way to deal with stiff problems. Consider the problem $u' = L u + N u$ with $u(0) = u_0$, where L is a linear operator and N is a nonlinear operator. If we set $v = e^{-tL} u$, then

$$v' = e^{-tL} N (e^{tL} v) \quad \text{with} \quad v(0) = e^{-tL} u_0.$$

There is no splitting error, but such an approach may only lessen the stiffness.

12.9 Symplectic integrators

The equation of motion of a simple pendulum is $\theta'' + \kappa \sin \theta = 0$, where $\theta(t)$ is the angle and the coefficient $\kappa = g/\ell$ is the acceleration due to gravity divided by the length of the pendulum. To simplify the discussion, we'll take unit mass, length, and gravitational acceleration In this nondimensionalized system with $\kappa = 1$ and with the position $q(t)$ and the angular velocity $p(t)$, we have the system of equations[5]

$$\frac{dq}{dt} = p \quad \text{and} \quad \frac{dp}{dt} = -\sin q.$$

To simply find the trajectory in phase space (q, p), we use conservation of energy. The sum of the kinetic energy T and potential energy V, given by the Hamiltonian $H = T + V = \frac{1}{2}p^2 - \cos q$, is constant along a trajectory. For initial conditions (q_0, p_0), the total energy is given by $H_0 = \frac{1}{2}p_0^2 - \cos q_0$. Because total energy is constant, $p^2 = 2H_0 + 2\cos q$, from which we can plot the trajectories in the phase plane. Suppose that we solve the problem using the forward Euler and backward Euler methods taking $q_0 = \pi/3$ and $p_0 = 0$ with timestep $k = 0.1$. See the figures below or the QR code at the bottom of this page. In both cases, the pendulum starts in the same position. When the pendulum has sufficient momentum $|p_0| > 2$, it has enough energy to swing over the top. Otherwise, the pendulum swings back and forth with $|q(t)| < \pi$.

forward Euler

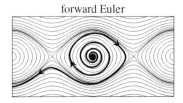

backward Euler

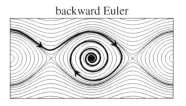

The forward Euler method is unstable, and the total energy grows exponentially in time. Even if the pendulum starts with a tiny swing, it will speed up over time, getting higher and higher with each swing until, eventually, it swings over the top. The backward Euler method is stable, but the total energy decays over time. Even if the pendulum starts with enough energy to swing over the top, over time, energy dissipates until the pendulum all but stops at the bottom of its swing. Energy is not conserved in either method, resulting in unphysical solutions. In problems such as planetary motion and molecular dynamics, a scheme that conserves energy over a long period is essential to getting a physically correct solution. Smaller timesteps and higher-order methods can help, but energy may still not be conserved over time. Let's look at a class of solvers designed to conserve the Hamiltonian.

The pendulum belongs to the general class of Hamiltonian systems

$$\frac{dp}{dt} = -\nabla_q H \quad \text{and} \quad \frac{dq}{dt} = +\nabla_p H.$$

---

[5]This problem can be solved analytically in terms of elliptic functions. See Karlheinz Ochs' article "A comprehensive analytical solution of the nonlinear pendulum."

pendulum using Euler
methods

By defining $\mathbf{r} \equiv (p, q)$:

$$\frac{d\mathbf{r}}{dt} = D_H \mathbf{r} \equiv \mathbf{J}\nabla H(\mathbf{r}) \quad \text{where} \quad \mathbf{J} = \begin{bmatrix} 0 & -\mathbf{I} \\ +\mathbf{I} & 0 \end{bmatrix}.$$

For a time-independent Hamiltonian $H(p, q)$,

$$\frac{dH}{dt} = \nabla_p H \frac{dp}{dt} + \nabla_q H \frac{dq}{dt} = 0,$$

and we see that the Hamiltonian is a conserved quantity.

Symplectic methods are numerical methods that seek to preserve the volume of a differential 2-form $|dp \wedge dq|$ in phase space and conserve the Hamiltonian. Let's start with the semi-implicit or symplectic Euler method, a first-order scheme that combines the implicit forward Euler method and the explicit backward Euler method:

$$P^{n+1} = P^n - k\nabla_q H(P^{n+1}, Q^n) \tag{12.13a}$$
$$Q^{n+1} = Q^n + k\nabla_p H(P^{n+1}, Q^n) \tag{12.13b}$$

or alternatively

$$P^{n+1} = P^n - k\nabla_q H(P^n, Q^{n+1}) \tag{12.14a}$$
$$Q^{n+1} = Q^n + k\nabla_p H(P^n, Q^{n+1}). \tag{12.14b}$$

We'll restrict ourselves to a separable Hamiltonian $H(p, q) = T(p) + V(q)$. In this case, $\nabla_p H(p, q) = \nabla_p T(p)$ and $\nabla_q H(p, q) = \nabla_q V(q)$. It seems reasonable that we could improve the symplectic Euler method by implementing (12.13) for a half-timestep followed by (12.14) for a half-timestep:

$$P^{n+1/2} = P^n - \tfrac{1}{2}k\nabla_q V(Q^n)$$
$$Q^{n+1} = Q^n + k\nabla_p T(P^{n+1/2})$$
$$P^{n+1} = P^{n+1/2} - \tfrac{1}{2}k\nabla_q V(Q^{n+1}).$$

This second-order approach, called the *Verlet method*, was reintroduced by Loup Verlet in 1967 and can be viewed as an application of Strang splitting.

We can continue to build a higher-order method by composing Verlet methods together. For a fourth-order method, take a Verlet with a timestep of αk followed by a Verlet with timestep $(1 - 2\alpha)k$ followed by a Verlet with timestep αk where $\alpha = (2 - 2^{-1/3})^{-1}$. To dig deeper, see Hairer, Lubich, and Wanner's treatise on geometric numerical integration.

12.10   Practical implementation

It should be entirely unsurprising that any scientific computing language would have any number of versatile ODE solvers. While Matlab and Python focus on a few robust ODE solvers, Julia's DifferentialEquations.jl module contains over two hundred—far too many to cover in any depth here.[6] Several of these methods correspond to the standard solvers in Matlab and Python—see the table in Figure 12.12. This section summarizes these standard solvers and their suitability for different problem types. Given Matlab's influence on Python's SciPy and Julia, it makes some sense to start the discussion with it.

▷ **Matlab**

For a complete account of the development of Matlab's ODE suite, see any of the articles authored by Lawrence Shampine in the References. When Lawrence Shampine developed Matlab's ODE suite, he had a principal design goal: the suite should have a uniform interface so the different specialized and robust solvers could be called *exactly* the same way. It's this trade-off between efficiency and convenience that he felt differentiated a "problem solving environment" such as Matlab from "general scientific computation." Instead of simply returning the solution at each timestep, for example, Shampine designed Matlab's ODE suite to provide a smooth interpolation between timesteps (especially) when the high-order solvers took large timesteps. Such a design consideration indeed simplifies plotting nice-looking solutions.

Matlab has four explicit Runge–Kutta methods designed for nonstiff problems. The low-order ode23 routine is the third-order Bogacki–Shampine Runge–Kutta method presented on page 357. The medium-order ode45 routine is the popular Dormand–Prince Runge–Kutta method (sometimes called the DOPRI method), using six function evaluations to compute a fourth-order solution with a fifth-order error correction. This routine is sometimes recommended as the go-to solver for nonstiff problems. The high-order ode78 and ode89 routines—Verner's "most efficient" 7(6) and 8(9) Runge–Kutta methods–often outperform other methods, particularly on problems with smooth solutions. Another routine designed for nonstiff problems, ode113, is a variable-step, variable-order Adams–Bashforth–Moulton PECE. It computes a solution up to order 12 and an error estimate up to order 13 to control the variable step size. The ode15s routine uses a variation on Klopfenstein–Shampine numerical differentiation formulas. These formulas are modifications of BDF methods with variable-step, variable-order to order 5 and have good stability properties, especially at higher orders. The ode15i routine is

---

[6]For a complete list of Julia's ODE solvers, see https://diffeq.sciml.ai/latest/solvers/ode_solve/. Christopher Rackauckas, the lead developer of DifferentialEquations.jl, also provides a comparison of differential equation solvers for the principal scientific programming language in a post in the online journal *The Winnower*.

Method	Julia	Matlab	Python	stiff.	effic.
Rosenbrock (order 4)	Rodas4	—	—	●	●
Radau IIA 5(3)	RadauIIA5	—	Radau	●	●
BDF (DAE/implicit)	DFBDF	ode15i	IDA	●	◑
Rosenbrock (order 2)	Rosenbrock23	ode23s	—	●	○
TR–BDF2 SDIRK	TRBDF2	ode23tb[†]	—	●	○
BDF	FBDF	ode15s	BDF, LSODA, CVODE	◑	◑
Additive IMEX RK	KenCarp4	—	—	◑	◑
Trapezoidal ESDIRK	Trapezoid	ode23t[†]	—	◑	○
Verner 9(8)	Vern9	ode89[†]	—	○	●
Verner 8(7)	Vern8	ode78[†]	—	○	●
Dormand–Prince 8(5,3)	DP8	—	DOP853	○	◑
Tsitouras 5(4)	Tsit5	—	—	○	◑
Dormand–Prince 4(5)	DP5	ode45	RK45	○	◑
ABM	VCABM	ode113[‡]	LSODA, CVODE	○	○
Bogacki–Shampine 2(3)	BS3	ode23	RK23	○	○

○ low   ◑ medium   ● high

Figure 12.12: Equivalent routines in Julia, Matlab, and Python. The table includes only a fraction of all methods available in Julia. Matlab and Python routines are available in Julia using wrappers. [†]Only MATLAB. [‡]Octave uses lsode instead.

a similar variable-step, variable-order BDF method designed for fully implicit problems $f(t, u, u') = 0$. All stiff solvers must solve an implicit difference equation using a Newton method or variation of it, so it is helpful to provide the Jacobian matrix for the right-hand-side function $f(u)$ whenever possible. Otherwise, the routine will compute it using a finite difference approximation. The ode23s routine uses a second-order modified Rosenbrock formula designed especially for stiff problems with sharp changes (quasi-discontinuities) in the solutions. The ode23t routine implements the trapezoidal Runge–Kutta method. Because the method is not L-stable, it's not a good choice for really stiff problems, but it also doesn't have excessive numerical damping. The method doesn't have an embedded error estimate—instead, the routine differentiates a cubic polynomial through prior nodes to estimate the error and adjust the step size. The ode23tb routine is an L-stable trapezoidal-BDF2 SDIRK method discussed on page 356 taking $\alpha = 2 - \sqrt{2}$.

Octave's ODE solvers have some notable differences from the Matlab solvers. In addition to five Matlab-compatible solvers ode23, ode23s, ode45, ode15s, and ode15i, Octave's primary routine is lsode. The routine is an acronym of Livermore Solver for Ordinary Differential Equations and comes from Alan Hindmarsh's family of Fortran ODE solvers developed at Lawrence Livermore

National Laboratory (LLNL). It uses BDF methods for stiff problems and Adams–Moulton methods for nonstiff problems, using functional iteration to evaluate the implicit terms.

▷ Python

Python's scipy.integrate library has several ODE solvers. The RK45 (default), RK23, and BDF routines are equivalent to Matlab's ode45, ode23, and ode15s routines. The DOP853 routine implements the Dormand–Prince 8(5,3) Runge–Kutta. LSODA is similar to the lsode solver available in Octave, except that it automatically and dynamically switches between the nonstiff Adams–Moulton and stiff BDF solvers. The Radau routine is an order-5 Radau IIA (fully-implicit Runge–Kutta) method. The Radau, BDF, and LSODA routines all require a Jacobian matrix of the right-hand side of the system. If none is provided, the Jacobian will be approximated using a finite difference approximation. These routines can also be called from solve_ivp, a generic interface that uses adaptive step size over a prescribed interval of integration, through the method option. These methods can also be called for one time step, allowing them to be integrated into time-splitting routines.

The scikits.odes package provides a few more routines. Two of these routines, CVODE and IDA, come from LLNL's Sundials[7] library. The Sundials routine CVODE[8] includes Adams–Moulton formulas (with orders up to 12) for nonstiff problems and BDFs (with orders up to 5)—similar to LSODA. The Sundials IDA routine solves differential-algebraic equation systems in the form $f(t, u, u') = 0$.

▷ Julia

Julia's flagship ODE package is DifferentialEquations.jl, developed by Chris Rackauckas and Qing Nie. DifferentialEquations.jl includes routines equivalent to those in Matlab and Python and many other methods that may be more efficient than the standard ones. In particular, Tsit5—the Tsitouras 5(4) Runge–Kutta method—is often more efficient than Dormand–Prince DP5; Rodas4—a fourth-order A-stable stiffly stable Rosenbrock method—is often more efficient than Rosenbrock23 and IDA; and Vern7—Verner's "most efficient" 7(6) Runge–Kutta method—is often more efficient than the higher-order VCABM and DP8. For more details and routines, check out the documentation at https://diffeq.sciml.ai.

Julia also has a wrapper for Python's scipy.integrate solve_ivp module (SciPyDiffEq.jl), a wrapper for the Sundials library (Sundials.jl), and a wrapper for licensed MATLAB installations (MATLABDiffEq.jl), among others. The Sundials.jl package has all six Sundials methods, including ARKode. Additive

---

[7]A portmanteau of SUite of Nonlinear and DIfferential/ALgebraic Equation Solvers

[8]The acronym CVODE refers to a C-language implementation of the Fortran VODE, which uses variable-coefficient methods instead of the fixed-step-interpolate methods in LSODE.

Runge–Kutta (ARK) methods are IMEX methods that combine an ERK for nonstiff terms and a DIRK for stiff terms. The routines found in ARKode, a class of ARK methods developed by Christopher Kennedy and Mark Carpenter, are also available through a class of DifferentialEquations.jl routines, such as KenCarp4.

Let's look at a recipe using DifferentialEquations.jl. Suppose that we wish to solve the equation for a pendulum $u'' = \sin u$ with initial conditions $u(0) = \pi/9$ and $u'(0) = 0$ over $t \in [0, 8\pi]$. For this problem, we'll want to use a symplectic or almost symplectic method, so let's use the trapezoidal method. We can solve the problem in Julia using the following steps (see the Back Matter for implementation in Python and Matlab):

1. Load the module
   ```
   using DifferentialEquations, Plots
   ```
2. Set up the parameters
   ```
   pendulum(u,p,t) = [u[2]; -sin(u[1])]
   u₀= [8π/9,0]; tspan = [0,8π]
   ```
3. Define the problem
   ```
   problem = ODEProblem(pendulum, u₀, tspan)
   ```
4. Choose the method
   ```
   method = Trapezoid()
   ```
5. Solve the problem
   ```
   solution = solve(problem,method)
   ```
6. Present the solution
   ```
   plot(solution, xaxis="t", label=["θ""ω"])
   ```

If a method is not explicitly stated, Julia will automatically choose one when it solves the problem. You can help Julia choose a method by telling it whether the problem is stiff (alg_hints = [:stiff]) or nonstiff (alg_hints = [:nonstiff]). The solution can be addressed either as an array where solution[i] indicates the ith element or as a function where solution(t) is the interpolated value at time t. Implicit-explicit (IMEX) problems such as $u_t = f(u, t) + g(u, t)$ can be specified using the SplitODEProblem function and choosing an appropriate solver. When solving a semilinear system of equations, you can define a function $f(u, t) \equiv Lu$ as a linear operator using the DiffEqArrayOperator function from the DiffEqOperators.jl library.

♣ DifferentialEquations.jl is a suite of utilities and hundreds of ODE solvers.

▷ **Efficiency**

No one solver works best for all problems in all scenarios. One routine may be relatively efficient for one class of problems; another one may be better suited for a different class. As we've seen throughout this chapter, a routine's accuracy and computing time are a combination of several competing and compounding factors. Benchmarking different solvers on various standard problems is one approach to measuring performance. Figure 12.12 summarizes the relative efficiencies of routines determined in the following benchmarking example.

Example.   Let's examine the efficiencies of different numerical routines for nonstiff and stiff problems. The Lotka–Volterra equation is a predator-prey population model

$$x' = \alpha x - \beta xy, \qquad y' = -\gamma y + \delta xy.$$

The variable x is the population of the prey (e.g., rabbits) and the variable y is the population of the predators (e.g., lynxes). We'll take the parameters $\{\alpha, \beta, \gamma, \delta\} = \{1.5, 1, 3, 1\}$. Notice how the populations of prey —— and predators ······ fluctuate symbiotically over time:

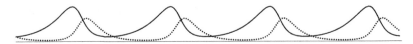

The Van der Pol equation models a nonlinear relaxation oscillator

$$x'' - \mu(1 - x^2)x' + x = 0,$$

where the nonnegative parameter μ controls damping. When μ is zero, the Van der Pol equation is a simple linear oscillator. When μ is large, the Van der Pol equation exhibits slow decay punctuated by rapid phase shifts.[9] The following plot shows the Van der Pol oscillations when $\mu = 100$ with $x(0) = 2$:

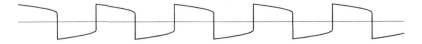

Let's examine the relative efficiencies of some standard routines by comparing the compute times and solution accuracies across a range of tolerances. We'll use Julia's DiffEqDevTools.jl package, which has utilities for benchmarking solvers.[10] The efficiency of several nonstiff solvers and several stiff solvers are depicted using a log-log plot in Figure 12.13. Outliers in the data have been removed using the LinRegOutliers.jl package, and regression lines are fit through the points. More efficient methods are in the lower-right quadrant, and less efficient methods are in the upper-left quadrant. For example, on the Lotka–Volterra problem, Verner's "most efficient" method is, in fact, the most efficient—about 14 times faster than the Adams–Moulton method (CVODE_Adams). The high-order Adams–Moulton method is also relatively inefficient compared to the third-order Bogacki–Shampine method at low tolerances, but it outperforms the Bogacki–Shampine method at high tolerances.   ◄

---

[9]In his original paper, Balthazar van der Pol examined the oscillating current driven by a triode, which required that μ be smaller than one. Van der Pol later studied behavior for large values of μ and coined the term "relaxation oscillation."

[10]The code for this example is available in the Jupyter notebook that accompanies this book. Chris Rackaukas' SciMLBenchmarks.jl project also presents summaries and plots of several benchmarks using the DiffEqDevTools.jl package.

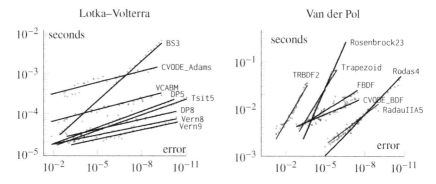

Figure 12.13: Computing time versus precision for the Lotka–Volterra equation (nonstiff) and the Van der Pol equation with $\mu = 1000$ (stiff).

12.11   Differential-algebraic equations

We can reformulate the pendulum problem using Cartesian coordinates and Newton's second law. Let $x(t)$ be the horizontal position and $y(t)$ be the vertical position of the pendulum's bob of mass m, tethered by a rod of length ℓ to a pivot at the origin.

The force on the bob is a combination of gravitational force pulling down and tension of the rod pulling in the direction of the pivot: $m\mathbf{x}'' = m\mathbf{g} - \tau\mathbf{x}$. The position of the bob $\mathbf{x}$ is (x, y), the gravitational acceleration $\mathbf{g}$ is $(0, -g)$ with a constant g, and the tension on the rod is $\tau(t)$. We also have the constraint $x^2 + y^2 = \ell^2$. Let $\mathbf{u} = \mathbf{x}' = (u, v)$ denote the velocity. Then we must solve a differential-algebraic system of equations (DAE) with five unknowns x, y, u, v, and τ:

$$
\begin{aligned}
x' &= u \\
y' &= v \\
mu' &= -\tau x \\
mv' &= -\tau y + mg \\
0 &= x^2 + y^2 - \ell^2
\end{aligned}
$$

This system presents a few challenges. We don't explicitly know the tension $\tau(t)$ on the rod. Also, five variables and one constraint leave us with four degrees of freedom—that's too many. For a pendulum, we only need to prescribe an initial angle and an initial angular velocity. To get down to two degrees of freedom, we'll need two additional constraints.

Let's start by differentiating the equation $0 = x^2 + y^2 - \ell^2$ with respect to time. We get $0 = 2xx' + 2yy'$, from which we have $xu + yv = 0$, or $\mathbf{x}^\mathsf{T}\mathbf{u} = 0$. This

expression says that the motion is perpendicular to the rod. Okay, that's obvious.
Let's take another derivative. After making a few substitutions, we have

$$0 = m(u^2 + v^2) - \tau \ell^2 + mgy. \tag{12.15}$$

This expression says that the centripetal force $m\|\mathbf{v}\|^2/\ell$ equals the sum of the
tension $\tau \ell$ and the radial component of the bob's weight $mgy/\ell = mg \cos \theta$.
    Let's take one more derivative. After a few substitutions, we have

$$0 = -\ell^2 \tau' + 3mgv, \tag{12.16}$$

or $\tau' = -3mgv/\ell^2$, a differential equation for the tension. Note that this equation
is the conservation of energy. The total energy is the sum of kinetic and potential
energies

$$E = \tfrac{1}{2}\|\mathbf{v}\|^2 + \tfrac{1}{2}mgy = \tfrac{1}{2}\tau m^{-1}\ell^2 - \tfrac{1}{2}gy + \tfrac{1}{2}mgy = \tau \ell^2 + \tfrac{3}{2}mgy'.$$

The conservation of energy says that the total energy is constant in time:

$$0 = E' = \ell^2 \tau' + 3mgv.$$

    We now have many equivalent systems. The original problem combines four
differential equations with a constraint for the rod length. We can alternatively
combine the differential equations with the constraint on motion direction. We
can combine them with the constraint balancing the forces on the rod. Or we can
combine them with a fifth differential equation for the conservation of energy.

$$\left.\begin{array}{l} x' = u \\ y' = v \\ mu' = -\tau x \\ mv' = -\tau y + mg \end{array}\right\} \text{ and one of } \left\{\begin{array}{ll} x^2 + y^2 = \ell^2 & \text{index-3} \\ ux + vy = 0 & \text{index-2} \\ m(u^2 + v^2) = \tau \ell^2 - mgy & \text{index-1} \\ \ell^2 \tau' = 3mg & \text{index-0} \end{array}\right.$$

    We can reduce a DAE to a system of purely differential equations using
repeated differentiation as long as the problem is not singular. The *index*
of a DAE is the minimum number of differentiations needed to do so. The
original pendulum DAE required three differentiations to reduce it to a system of
differential equations, so it is index-3. A system of purely differential equations
has index-0. We can immediately solve the index-0 pendulum problem

$$x' = u, \quad y' = v, \quad u' = -\tau x/m, \quad v' = -\tau y/m + g, \quad \tau' = 3mgv/\ell^2, \tag{12.17}$$

as long as the five initial conditions for (x, y, u, v, τ) are consistent. Alternatively,
we can solve the index-1 pendulum problem, first using the algebraic equation to
find the tension τ as a function of (x, y, u, v) to get a system of four differential
equations

$$x' = u, \quad y' = v, \quad u' = -\tau x/m, \quad \text{and} \quad v' = -\tau y/m + g, \tag{12.18}$$

where $\tau = m(u^2 + v^2 + gy)/\ell^2$. Let's solve this pendulum problem in Julia

Figure 12.14: Trace $(x(t), y(t))$ of the pendulum. The drift (left) is removed using manifold projection or mass matrix(right).

```julia
using DifferentialEquations
θ₀ = π/3; ℓ = 1; tspan = (0,30.0)
U₀ = [ℓ*sin(θ₀), -ℓ*cos(θ₀), 0, 0]
function pendulum(dU,U,p,t)
    x,y,u,v = U; ℓ,g,m = p
    τ = m*(u^2 + v^2 + g*y)/ℓ^2
    dU .= (u, v, -τ*x/m, -τ*y/m + g)
end
problem = ODEProblem(pendulum, U₀, tspan, (ℓ,1,1))
solution = solve(problem, Tsit5())
plot(solution, idxs=(1,2), yflip=true, aspect_ratio=:equal)
```

The leftmost plot of Figure 12.14 shows the solution $(x(t), y(t))$. Also, see the QR code at the bottom of this page. While the solution initially traces the arc of the pendulum correctly, it slowly drifts from that arc (a mild instability), and it finally is utter disagreement. Drift isn't specific to the problem (12.18). We also get drift solving (12.17).

We can stabilize the method by controlling the step size, e.g., setting reltol=1e-8 and abstol=1e-8 instead of the default reltol=1e-6 and abstol=1e-3. Alternatively, we can stabilize the problem by orthogonally projecting the solution onto the constraint manifold $x^2 + y^2 - \ell^2 = 0$ and $xu + yv = 0$ to prevent the solution from drifting off. We solve the problem using an explicit solver and use Newton's method at every step (or at every few steps after the residual drifts beyond a tolerance) to find a zero residual.[11] Manifold projection is built into Julia's DifferentialEquations library using a callback function.

```julia
function residual(r,w,p,t)
    x,y,u,v = w; ℓ,g,m = p
    r .= (x^2+y^2-ℓ^2, x*u+y*v, 0, 0)
end
```

---

[11] Note that a Newton solver isn't technically necessary for the pendulum problem because we can explicitly solve the residual equations to add the conditions x = x/ℓ; y = y/ℓ; u = -v*y/x directly into the function pendulum.

pendulum without and
with projection

```
cb = ManifoldProjection(residual)
solution = solve(problem, Tsit5(), callback=cb)
```

The rightmost plot in Figure 12.14 shows the solution using manifold projection. Manifold projection becomes computationally expensive as the system grows larger. Let's instead examine a general strategy for solving DAEs by reducing them to index-1 (or index-0) problems so that they can be solved.

▷ General approach to DAEs

A differential-algebraic equation may appear in semi-explicit form

$$\mathbf{u}' = \mathbf{f}(t, \mathbf{u}, \mathbf{v})$$
$$\mathbf{0} = \mathbf{g}(t, \mathbf{u}, \mathbf{v}),$$

or it may appear in fully-implicit form $\mathbf{F}(t, \mathbf{u}, \mathbf{u}') = \mathbf{0}$. We can always write an implicit DAE in semi-explicit form by assigning $\mathbf{u}' = \mathbf{v}$ and $\mathbf{0} = \mathbf{F}(t, \mathbf{u}, \mathbf{v})$. Similarly, we can rewrite a semi-explicit DAE as a fully implicit one.

Note that the semi-explicit DAE is equivalent to the differential equation

$$\mathbf{u}' = \mathbf{f}(t, \mathbf{u}, \mathbf{v})$$
$$\varepsilon \mathbf{v}' = \mathbf{g}(t, \mathbf{u}, \mathbf{v})$$

in the limit as ε goes to zero. In this way, we can think of a DAE as singularly perturbed a ODE, in which some variables evolve with infinitely fast dynamics (the constraints are instantaneously enforced). When ε is small, the system behaves like a stiff ODE. So we will want to use stiff solvers when solving DAEs.

The semi-implicit form can be written as

$$\mathbf{M} \begin{bmatrix} \mathbf{u}' \\ \mathbf{v}' \end{bmatrix} = \begin{bmatrix} \mathbf{f}(t, \mathbf{u}, \mathbf{v}) \\ \mathbf{g}(t, \mathbf{u}, \mathbf{v}) \end{bmatrix}, \quad \text{where} \quad \mathbf{M} = \begin{bmatrix} \mathbf{I} & \mathbf{0} \\ \mathbf{0} & \mathbf{0} \end{bmatrix}$$

is called a *mass matrix* or a *damping matrix*. The diagonal elements of $\mathbf{M}$ are 1 for rows corresponding to differential equations and 0 for rows corresponding to algebraic ones. Because the system is stiff, we'll use the backward Euler method

$$\mathbf{M} U^{n+1} = \mathbf{M} U^n + k \tilde{\mathbf{f}}(t, U^{n+1}),$$

where $\tilde{\mathbf{f}}$ is vector function $\begin{bmatrix} \mathbf{f} \\ \mathbf{g} \end{bmatrix}$ and U^n is the solution $\begin{bmatrix} \mathbf{u} \\ \mathbf{v} \end{bmatrix}$ at the nth time step. We solve the equation

$$\mathbf{M} U^{n+1} - \mathbf{M} U^n - k \tilde{\mathbf{f}}(t, U^{n+1}) = 0$$

using Newton's method to get U^{n+1} at each time step:

$$U^{n+1} \leftarrow U^{n+1} - \left(\mathbf{M} - k \mathbf{J}_{\tilde{\mathbf{f}}}(U^{n+1}) \right)^{-1} \left(\mathbf{M} U^{n+1} - \mathbf{M} U^n - k \tilde{\mathbf{f}}(t, U^{n+1}) \right).$$

The Jacobian $\mathbf{J}_{\tilde{\mathbf{f}}}$ must be invertible.

Similarly, we can solve the fully implicit DAE $\mathbf{F}(t, \mathbf{u}, \mathbf{u}') = \mathbf{0}$ by replacing $\mathbf{u}'$ with a backward Euler discretization

$$\mathbf{F}\left(t^{n+1}, U^{n+1}, \frac{U^{n+1} - U^n}{k}\right) = 0.$$

Now, we use Newton's method at each time step

$$U^{n+1} \leftarrow U^{n+1} - \left(\frac{\partial \mathbf{F}}{\partial \mathbf{u}} + \frac{1}{k}\frac{\partial \mathbf{F}}{\partial \mathbf{u}'}\right)^{-1}\Bigg|_{U^{n+1}} \mathbf{F}\left(t^{n+1}, U^{n+1}, \frac{U^{n+1} - U^n}{k}\right)$$

to solve the problem.

In practice, we can use any stiff solver. Here's the numerical solution to the pendulum problem using a mass matrix and the fifth-order Rosenbrock method. We'll still need to deal with drift in the solution. So we take a sufficiently small tolerance on the adaptive step size.

```
using DifferentialEquations
θ₀ = π/3; ℓ = 1; tspan = (0,30.0)
u₀ = [ℓ*sin(θ₀), -ℓ*cos(θ₀), 0, 0, -ℓ*cos(θ₀)]
function pendulum(dU,U,p,t)
  x,y,u,v,τ = U; ℓ,g,m = p
  dU .= (u, v, -τ*x/m, -τ*y/m + g, -ℓ^2*τ + m*g*y + m*(u^2 + v^2))
end
M = Diagonal([1,1,1,1,0])
f = ODEFunction(pendulum, mass_matrix=M)
problem = ODEProblem(f,u₀,tspan,(ℓ,1,1))
solution = solve(problem, Rodas5(), reltol=1e-8, abstol=1e-8)
plot(solution, idxs=(1,2), yflip=true, aspect_ratio=:equal)
```

▷ Index reduction

Not all DAEs can be solved using ODE solvers. However, there is a class of DAEs called Hessenberg forms that can be solved systematically.[12] Differential-algebraic equations in Hessenberg form can be reduced to purely differential equations.

Let's start with a DAE in semi-explicit form

$$\mathbf{u}' = \mathbf{f}(t, \mathbf{u}, \mathbf{v})$$
$$\mathbf{0} = \mathbf{g}(t, \mathbf{u}, \mathbf{v}).$$

---

[12]Hessenberg is a reference to upper Hessenberg matrices, which are zero below the diagonal.

If the equation $0 = \mathbf{g}(t, \mathbf{u}, \mathbf{v})$ is solvable for $\mathbf{v}$, we can use it to eliminate $\mathbf{v}$ from $\mathbf{u}' = \mathbf{f}(t, \mathbf{u}, \mathbf{v})$. Differentiating $0 = \mathbf{g}(t, \mathbf{u}, \mathbf{v})$ gives us

$$0 = \frac{\partial \mathbf{g}}{\partial t} + \frac{\partial \mathbf{g}}{\partial \mathbf{u}} \mathbf{u}' + \frac{\partial \mathbf{g}}{\partial \mathbf{v}} \mathbf{v}',$$

which we can solve for $\mathbf{v}'$ as long as the Jacobian $\partial \mathbf{g}/\partial \mathbf{v}$ is not singular, leaving us with the system of differential equations

$$\mathbf{u}' = \mathbf{f}(t, \mathbf{u}, \mathbf{v})$$
$$\mathbf{v}' = -\left(\frac{\partial \mathbf{g}}{\partial \mathbf{v}}\right)^{-1} \left(\frac{\partial \mathbf{g}}{\partial t} + \frac{\partial \mathbf{g}}{\partial \mathbf{u}} \mathbf{u}'\right).$$

An index-2 Hessenberg DAE has the form

$$\mathbf{u}' = \mathbf{f}(t, \mathbf{u}, \mathbf{v})$$
$$0 = \mathbf{g}(t, \mathbf{u}),$$

where the function $\mathbf{g}$ is independent of $\mathbf{v}$ and the Jacobians $\partial \mathbf{g}/\partial \mathbf{u}$ and $\partial \mathbf{f}/\partial \mathbf{v}$ are nonsingular. The incompressible Navier–Stokes equation

$$\frac{\partial}{\partial t} \mathbf{u} + \mathbf{u} \cdot \nabla \mathbf{u} = \nu \Delta \mathbf{u} - \nabla p$$
$$\nabla \cdot \mathbf{u} = 0.$$

is an example of an index-2 DAE. We can solve the Navier–Stokes equation by discretizing it in space to get a system of ODEs and a system of constraints for the incomprehensibility condition. We'll return to the Navier–Stokes equation in Chapter 16, where we use orthogonal projection into the constraint manifold to solve the problem.

An index-3 Hessenberg DAE has the form

$$\mathbf{u}' = \mathbf{f}(t, \mathbf{u}, \mathbf{v}, \mathbf{w})$$
$$\mathbf{v}' = \mathbf{g}(t, \mathbf{u}, \mathbf{v})$$
$$0 = \mathbf{h}(t, \mathbf{v}),$$

where the Jacobians $\partial \mathbf{h}/\partial \mathbf{v}$, $\partial \mathbf{g}/\partial \mathbf{u}$, and $\partial \mathbf{f}/\partial \mathbf{w}$ are nonsingular. These are second-order ODEs, like the pendulum. We need to reduce the differential order to one. Otherwise, the Jacobian is singular, and implicit solvers fail.

While we can reduce the index of a small system like the pendulum equation by hand, manual manipulation is impractical on large systems. Instead, we can use automated methods like the Pantelides algorithm, which uses a graph theoretical approach, to reduce the index. The following Julia code uses ModelingToolkit.jl to reduce the order with the Pantelides algorithm:

```
using ModelingToolkit, DifferentialEquations
θ₀ = π/3; ℓ = 1; tspan = (0,30.0)
u₀ = [ℓ*sin(θ₀), -ℓ*cos(θ₀), 0, 0, 0]
M = Diagonal([1,1,1,1,0])
function pendulum(dU,U,p,t)
  x,y,u,v,τ = U; ℓ,g,m = p
  dU .= (u, v, -τ*x/m, -τ*y/m + g, x^2 + y^2 - ℓ^2)
end
f = ODEFunction(pendulum, mass_matrix=M)
problem = ODEProblem(f, u₀, tspan, [ℓ,1,1])
sys = modelingtoolkitize(problem)
pendulum_sys = structural_simplify(dae_index_lowering(sys))
problem = ODAEProblem(pendulum_sys, [], tspan)
solution = solve(problem, Tsit5(), abstol=1e-8, reltol=1e-8)
plot(solution, idxs=(1,3), yflip=true, aspect_ratio=:equal)
```

⚬⚬ ModelingToolkit.jl provides a high-level modeling language for symbolic-numerical computation, including transformations such as index reduction of DAEs.

▷ Gauss pseudospectral methods

Let's look at one more approach to solving DAEs. Rather than considering a DAE as a system of differential equations with algebraic constraints, we can view it as an algebraic system that incorporates derivative terms.[13] By approaching the problem from this angle, we can use orthogonal collocation, also known as a spectral method, which involves approximating the space of solutions as orthogonal polynomials. Exercise 11.10 used Gauss–Lobatto nodes to define a differentiation operator for Legendre polynomials. Given n nodes (including one endpoint) and m variables, we would need to solve a system of mn equations. To manage the complexity and stability, we can divide the time domain into smaller steps and reduce the number of nodes over each step to get a pseudospectral method.

Let's solve the pendulum problem in Julia using the Gauss pseudospectral method. First, we will define the differentiation matrix for Legendre–Lobatto polynomials. See exercise 11.10 on page 328 and its solution on page 525 for details.

```
using FastGaussQuadrature
function differentiation_matrix(n,Δt=1)
  nodes, _ = gausslobatto(n+1)
  t = (nodes[2:end].+1)/2
```

---

[13]To ponder: Is a zebra white with black stripes or black with white stripes?

```
  A = t.^(0:n-1)'.*(1:n)'
  B = t.^(1:n)'
  (A/B)/Δt, t
end
```

Next, we'll write out our system of equations.

```
function pendulumGLL(U,(U₀,D,n))
  x,y,u,v,τ = U[1:n],U[n+1:2n],U[2n+1:3n],U[3n+1:4n],U[4n+1:5n]
  x₀,y₀,u₀,v₀,_ = U₀
  ℓ,g,m = (1,1,1)
  [D(x,x₀) .- u;
  D(y,y₀) .- v;
  D(u,u₀) .+ τ.*x/m;
  D(v,v₀) .+ τ.*y/m .- g;
  x.^2 + y.^2 .- ℓ^2]
end
```

Now, let's solve the DAE using the NonlinearSolve library by solving a nonlinear system at each time step. We'll use the intermediate nodes as part of our solution.

```
using NonlinearSolve
θ₀ = π/3; ℓ = 1; tspan = (0,30.0)
u₀ = [ℓ*sin(θ₀), -ℓ*cos(θ₀), 0, 0, 0]
n = 5; N = 100; Δt = 30/N
M,_ = differentiation_matrix(n,Δt)
D = (u,u₀) -> M*(u .- u₀)
u = u₀
for i = 2:N
  problem = NonlinearProblem(pendulumGLL,[ones(n)*u₀'...],(u₀,D,n))
  solution = solve(problem,NewtonRaphson(),abstol=1e-12)
  u = [u reshape(solution.u,5,n)']
  u₀ = u[:,end]
end
plot(u[1,:], u[2,:], yflip=true, aspect_ratio=:equal)
```

12.12 Exercises

12.1. A θ-scheme is of the form

$$\frac{U^{n+1} - U^n}{k} = (1 - \theta)f(U^{n+1}) + \theta f(U^n).$$

Find the regions of absolute stability for the θ-scheme.   ⚘

12.2. Plot stability contours for the forward Euler, backward Euler, trapezoidal, and leapfrog methods in the λk-plane using several values of $|r|$ besides $|r| = 1$.

12.3. Show that applying one step of the trapezoidal method to a linear differential equation is the same as applying a forward Euler method for one half time step followed by the backward Euler method for one half time step.

12.4. Plot the region of stability for the Merson method with Butcher tableau

$$
\begin{array}{c|ccccc}
0 \\
\frac{1}{3} & \frac{1}{3} \\
\frac{1}{3} & \frac{1}{6} & \frac{1}{6} \\
\frac{1}{2} & \frac{1}{8} & 0 & \frac{3}{8} \\
1 & \frac{1}{2} & 0 & -\frac{3}{2} & 2 \\
\hline
 & \frac{1}{6} & 0 & 0 & \frac{2}{3} & \frac{1}{6}
\end{array}
$$

12.5. Show that $e^{\frac{1}{2}k\,A}e^{k\,B}e^{\frac{1}{2}k\,A} - e^{k(A+B)} = O(k^3)$, for two arbitrary, linear operators A and B. From this, it follows that the error using Strang splitting is $O(k^2)$.

12.6. The multistage trapezoidal and BDF2 introduced in the example on page 356 are both implicit methods. Implementing each stage typically requires computing a Jacobian matrix for Newton's method when the right-hand-side function $f(u)$ is nonlinear. Thankfully, by choosing α appropriately, we can reuse the same Jacobian matrix across both stages.

1. Write the formulas for the trapezoidal method over a subinterval αk and the BDF2 method over the two subintervals αk and $(1 - \alpha)k$ with $0 < \alpha < 1$.
2. Determine the Jacobian matrices for these methods.
3. Find an α such that the Jacobian matrices are proportional.
4. Plot the region of absolute stability.
5. Show that the multistage trapezoidal–BDF2 method is L-stable for this choice of α.

12.7. Develop a third-order L-stable IMEX scheme. Study the method's stability by writing the characteristic polynomial and plotting the regions of absolute stability in the complex plane for the implicit part and the explicit part of the IMEX scheme.

12.8. Plot the regions of absolute stability for the Adams–Bashforth–Moulton predictor-corrector methods: AB1-AM2, AB2-AM3, AB3-AM4, and AB4-AM5 with $PE(CE)^m$ for $s = 0, 1, \ldots, 4$.

12.9. Compute the Padé approximant $R_{3,2}(x)$ of $\log r$ starting with a Taylor polynomial as outlined on page 352.

12.10. Show that the Verlet method for the system $u' = p$ and $p' = f(u)$ is the same as the central difference scheme $U^n - 2U^{n-1} + U^{n-2} = k f(U^n)$ for $u'' = f(u)$.

12.11. A coupled pendulum is created by connecting two pendulums together with a spring. The Hamiltonian is

$$H = \tfrac{1}{2}(p_1^2 + p_2)^2 - \cos q_1 - \cos q_2 - \varepsilon \cos(q_1 - q - 2),$$

where ε is a coupling parameter. Use a symplectic integrator to solve the system with suitable initial conditions and coupling parameter.

12.12. In 1963, mathematician and meteorologist Edward Lorenz developed a simple model of atmospheric dynamics. The now extensively studied Lorenz equation is

$$\frac{dx}{dt} = \sigma(y - x), \qquad \frac{dy}{dt} = \rho x - y - xz, \qquad \frac{dz}{dt} = -\beta z + xy. \qquad (12.19)$$

Plot the solution $(x(t), z(t))$ when $\sigma = 10, \beta = 8/3, \rho = 28$.

12.13. The SIR model is a simple epidemiological model for infections diseases that tracks the change over time in the percentage of susceptible, infected, and recovered individuals of a population

$$\frac{dS}{dt} = -\beta I S, \qquad \frac{dI}{dt} = \beta I S - \gamma I, \qquad \frac{dR}{dt} = \gamma I$$

where $S(t) + I(t) + R(t) = 1, \beta > 0$ is the infection rate, and $\gamma > 0$ is the recovery rate. The basic reproduction number $R_0 = \beta/\gamma$ tells us how many other people, on average, an infectious person might infect at the onset of the epidemic time $t = 0$. Plot the curves $\{S(t), I(t), R(t)\}$ of the SIR model over $t \in [0, 15]$ starting within an initial state $\{0.99, 0.01, 0\}$ with $\beta = 2$ and $\gamma = 0.4$. ✍

12.14. The Duffing equation

$$x''(t) + \gamma x'(t) + \alpha x + \beta x^3 = \delta \cos \omega t$$

models the motion of a nonlinear damped driven oscillator. Think of a weight attached to a spring attached to a piston. The spring becomes stiffer or softer as it is stretched by adding a cubic term to the linear Hooke's law. The parameter γ is a damping coefficient, α is the stiffness constant of the spring, β is the additional nonlinearity of the spring constant, and δ and ω are the amplitude and angular frequency of the oscillator. Solve the Duffing equation for parameters $\{\alpha, \beta, \gamma, \delta, \omega\}$ equal to $\{-1, 1, 0.37, 0.3, 1\}$. Plot the solution in phase space $(x(t), x'(t))$ for $t \in [0, 200]$. What happens when the damping coefficient is changed from 0.37 to another value? ✍

12.15. One way to solve a boundary value problem $y''(x) = f(y, y', x)$ with boundary values $y(x_0) = y_0$ and $y(x_1) = y_1$ is by using a shooting method. A shooting method solves the initial value problem $y''(x) = f(y, y', x)$ using one of the boundary conditions $y(x_0) = y_0$ and $y'(x_0) = s$ for some guess s. We then compare the difference in the solution at x_1 with the prescribed boundary value y_1 to make updates to our guess s as an initial condition. With this new guess, we again solve the initial value problem and compare its solution with the correct boundary value to get another updated guess. We continue in this manner until our solution $y(x_1)$ converges to y_1. This problem is equivalent to finding the zeros s to the error function $e(s) = y(x_1; s) - y_1$. Use the Roots.jl function find_zero along with an ODE solver to find the solution to the Airy equation $y'' + xy = 0$ with $y(-12) = 1$ and $y(0) = 1$.

12.16. Two balls of equal mass are attached in series to a wall using two springs—one soft and one stiff.

$$x_1'' = -\kappa_1 x_1 + \kappa_2(x_2 - x_1)$$
$$x_2'' = -\kappa_2(x_2 - x_1)$$

Suppose that the soft spring is initially stretched to $x_1(0) = 1$ and the stiff spring is in equilibrium at $x_2(0) = x_1(0)$. Discuss the limiting behavior when $\kappa_2 \to \infty$. Solve the problem numerically when $\kappa_2 \gg \kappa_1$.

Chapter 13

Parabolic Equations

A group of molecules, bacteria, insects, or even people will often move in a random way. As a result, these "particles" tend to spread out. This behavior can be modeled on a large scale by the diffusion process. Let $u(t, \mathbf{x})$ be the concentration of particles in $\mathbb{R}^n$ and consider an arbitrarily shaped but fixed domain $\Omega \subset \mathbb{R}^n$. Then the mass of particles at some time t in Ω is $\int_\Omega u(t, \mathbf{x}) \, dV$. Because the particles are moving, the mass of particles in Ω changes as some particles enter the domain and others leave it. Flux is the number of particles passing a point or through an area per unit time. The change in the number of particles in Ω equals the integral of the flux of particles $\mathbf{J}(t, \mathbf{x})$ through the boundary

$$\frac{d}{dt} \int_\Omega u(t, \mathbf{x}) \, dV = - \int_{\partial\Omega} \mathbf{J}(t, \mathbf{x}) \cdot \mathbf{n} \, dA.$$

By invoking the divergence theorem, we have

$$\int_\Omega \frac{\partial}{\partial t} u(t, \mathbf{x}) \, dV = - \int_\Omega \nabla \cdot \mathbf{J}(t, \mathbf{x}) \, dV.$$

Because the domain Ω was arbitrarily chosen, it follows that

$$\frac{\partial}{\partial t} u(t, \mathbf{x}) = -\nabla \cdot \mathbf{J}(t, \mathbf{x}).$$

Fickian diffusion says that the flux $\mathbf{J}(t, \mathbf{x})$ is proportional to the gradient of the concentration $u(t, \mathbf{x})$. Imagine a one-dimensional random walk in which particles move equally to the right or the left. Suppose that we have two adjacent cells, one at $x - \frac{1}{2}h$ with a particle concentration $u(x - \frac{1}{2}h)$ and one at $x + \frac{1}{2}h$ with a concentration and $u(x + \frac{1}{2}h)$, separated by an interface at x. More particles from the cell with higher concentration will pass through the interface than particles from the cell with lower concentration. If a particle moves through the interface with a positive diffusivity $\alpha(x)$, then the flux across the interface can be approximated by

$$J(t, x) = \frac{-\alpha(x)\left(u\left(t, x + \frac{1}{2}h\right) - u\left(t, x - \frac{1}{2}h\right)\right)}{h}.$$

In the limit as $h \to 0$, we have

$$J = -\alpha(x)\frac{\partial u}{\partial x}.$$

And, in general,

$$\frac{\partial u}{\partial t} = \nabla \cdot (\alpha(\mathbf{x})\nabla u).$$

Consider an insulated heat-conducting bar. The temperature along the bar can be modeled as $u_t = (\alpha(x)u_x)_x$, where $\alpha(x) > 0$ is the heat conductivity and $u(0, x) = u_0(x)$ is the initial temperature distribution. Because the bar is insulated, the heat flux at the ends of the bar is zero. For a uniform heat conductivity $\alpha(x) = \alpha$, the heat equation is simply

$$u_t = \alpha u_{xx}, \quad u(0, x) = u_0(x), \quad u_x(t, x_L) = 0 \quad u_x(t, x_R) = 0. \tag{13.1}$$

This problem is well-posed and can be solved analytically by the method of separation of variables or Fourier series. In the next section, we'll use it as a starting place to examine numerical methods for parabolic partial differential equations, equations that have one derivative in time and two derivatives in space. For now, let's examine the behavior of the solution over time. Take the heat conductivity $\alpha = 1$, and take an initial distribution with $u(x, 0) = 1$ for $x \in [-1, 1]$ and $u(x, 0) = 0$ otherwise along $[-2, 2]$. The following figure and the QR link at the bottom of this page show snapshots of the solution taken at equal time intervals from $t \in [0, 0.1]$:

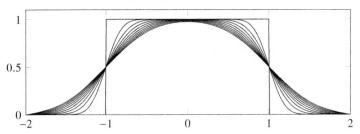

solution to the heat
equation

Notice how initially the solution rapidly evolves and then gradually slows down over time. The height of the distribution decreases and its width increases, steep gradients become shallow ones, sharp edges become smooth curves, and the distribution seems to seek a constant average temperature along the entire domain.

There are several prototypical properties of the heat equation to keep in mind. It obeys a *maximum principle*—the maximum value of a solution always decreases in time unless it lies on a boundary. Equivalently, the minimum value of a solution always increases unless it lies on a boundary. Simply stated, warm regions get cooler while cool regions get warmer. If the boundaries are insulating, then the total heat or energy is conserved, i.e., the L^1-norm of the solution is constant in time. The heat equation is also dissipative. i.e., the L^2-norm of the solution—often confusingly called the "energy"—decreases in time. A third property is that the solution at any positive time is smooth and grows smoother in time. For a complete review, see Lawrence Evans' textbook *Partial Differential Equations*.

Parabolic equations are more than just the heat equation. One important class of parabolic equations is the reaction-diffusion equation that couples a reactive growth term with a diffusive decay term. These equations often model the transitions between disorder and order in physical systems. Reaction-diffusion equations are also used to model the pattern formation in biological systems. Take chemotaxis. Animals and bacteria often communicate by releasing chemicals. Not only do the bacteria spread out due to normal diffusion mechanisms, but the bacteria may also move along a direction of a concentration gradient, following the strongest attractant, which itself is subject to diffusion. The dispersive mechanisms behind parabolic equations also drive stabilizing behavior in viscous fluid dynamics like the Navier–Stokes equation, ensuring that it doesn't blow up like its inviscid cousin, the Euler equation.[1]

13.1   Method of lines

A typical way to numerically solve a time-dependent PDE is by using the *method of lines*. We discretize space while keeping time continuous to derive a semidiscrete formulation. The advantage of this approach is that we can decouple time and space discretizations, thereby combining the best methods for each. Take the grid points $0 = x_0 < x_1 < \cdots < x_m = 1$. For simplicity, define a uniform mesh $x_j = jh$, where h is the grid spacing. Let $U_j(t)$ be a finite difference approximation to $u(t, x_j)$ in space. We can use a central difference

---

[1]That the Navier–Stokes equation does or doesn't blow up is a matter of contention. Olga Ladyzhenskaya, Jacques–Louis Lions, and Giovanni Prodi independently proved the existence of smooth solutions to the two-dimensional Navier–Stokes equation in the 1960s. In 2000, the Clay Mathematics Institute added the three-dimensional Navier–Stokes equation as a one-million-dollar Millennium Prize. It remains unsolved.

approximation

$$D^2 U_j = D \left(\frac{U_{j+1/2} - U_{j-1/2}}{h} \right) = \frac{U_{j+1} - 2U_j + U_{j-1}}{h^2}$$

to get a second-order approximation of the second derivative. Hence, $u_t = \alpha u_{xx}$ becomes

$$\frac{\partial}{\partial t} U_j = \alpha \frac{U_{j+1} - 2U_j + U_{j-1}}{h^2} \tag{13.2}$$

with $j = 0, 1, \ldots, m$. We now have a system of $m + 1$ ordinary differential equations, and we can use any numerical methods for ODEs to solve the problem. Note that the system is not closed. In addition to the interior mesh points at $j = 1, 2, \ldots, m - 1$ and the explicit boundary mesh points at $j = 0$ and $j = m$, we also have mesh points outside of the domain at $j = -1$ and $j = m + 1$. We will use the boundary conditions to remove these *ghost points* and close the system.

This approach of employing the numerical method of lines to solve a partial differential equation is often called *time-marching*. We can combine any consistent ODE solver with any consistent discretization of the Laplacian. The previous chapter discussed the forward Euler, the backward Euler, the leapfrog, and the trapezoidal methods to solve ODEs. Let's apply these methods to the linear diffusion equation. The leapfrog method applied to the diffusion equation is called the Richardson method, and the trapezoidal method applied to the diffusion equation is called the Crank–Nicolson method. British mathematicians John Crank and Phyllis Nicolson developed their method in 1948 as a replacement for the unstable method proposed by Lewis Fry Richardson in 1910.[2] The following stencils correspond to the stencils on page 335.

	Forward Euler	$O(k + h^2)$

$$\frac{U_j^{n+1} - U_j^n}{k} = \alpha \frac{U_{j+1}^n - 2U_j^n + U_{j-1}^n}{h^2} \tag{13.3}$$

[2]Lewis Fry Richardson, hailed as the father of numerical weather prediction, published his visionary book *Weather Forecasting by Numerical Process* in 1923, decades before the invention of digital computers. In this work, Richardson outlines how the planet's weather could be modeled using finite difference approximations of nonlinear partial differential equations. He imagines a fantastic "central-forecast factory" with 64,000 human computers arranged around the inner walls of an enormous painted globe. Each computer works on an equation of the part of the map where they sit, supplied with meteorological data from weather balloons spaced all over the world and informed by numerous little signs displaying the instantaneous values from neighboring computers. A man sits at a pulpit suspended on a tall pillar rising from the pit of the hall "like the conductor of an orchestra in which the instruments are slide-rules and calculating machines. . . instead of waving a baton he turns a beam of rosy light upon any region that is running ahead of the rest, and a beam of blue light upon those who are behind hand." Surely, the hand calculations of the human computers would be tedious, and Richardson commiserates with them, saying, "Let us hope for their sakes that they are moved on from time to time to new operations."

Backward Euler $\qquad O(k + h^2)$

$$\frac{U_j^{n+1} - U_j^n}{k} = \alpha \frac{U_{j+1}^{n+1} - 2U_j^{n+1} + U_{j-1}^{n+1}}{h^2} \tag{13.4}$$

Richardson (*unstable!*) $\qquad O(k^2 + h^2)$

$$\frac{U_j^{n+1} - U_j^{n-1}}{2k} = \alpha \frac{U_{j+1}^n - 2U_j^n + U_{j-1}^n}{h^2} \tag{13.5}$$

Crank–Nicolson $\qquad O(k^2 + h^2)$

$$\frac{U_j^{n+1} - U_j^n}{k} = \tfrac{1}{2}\alpha \frac{U_{j+1}^{n+1} - 2U_j^{n+1} + U_{j-1}^{n+1}}{h^2} + \tfrac{1}{2}\alpha \frac{U_{j+1}^n - 2U_j^n + U_{j-1}^n}{h^2} \tag{13.6}$$

▷ **Boundary conditions**

The method of lines converted the heat equation into a system of $m + 1$ differential equations with $m + 3$ unknowns. In addition to the mesh points at $x_0, x_1, \ldots, x_m$, we also have ghost points outside the domain. We use the boundary constraints to explicitly remove the ghost points and close the system by eliminating the two unknowns U_{-1} and U_{m+1}. There are several common boundary conditions.[3]

A *Dirichlet boundary condition* specifies the value of the solution on the boundary. For example, for a heat-conducting bar in contact with heat sinks of temperatures u_L and u_R at the ends of the bar, we have the boundary conditions $u(t, 0) = u_L$ and $u(t, 1) = u_R$. We can eliminate the left ghost point U_{-1} by using a second-order approximation $\tfrac{1}{2}(U_{-1} + U_1) \approx U_0 = u_L$. In this case, substituting $U_{-1} = 2u_L - U_1$ into (13.2) gives us

$$\frac{\partial}{\partial t} U_0 = \alpha \frac{2U_1}{h^2} + 2\alpha \frac{u_L}{h^2}. \tag{13.7}$$

We can similarly eliminate the right ghost point.

Example. Let's implement a backward Euler scheme for (13.1) that uses Dirichlet boundary conditions. Let $v = \alpha k / h^2$. From (13.4) and (13.7) we have

$$U_0^{n+1} - U_0^n = -2vU_0^{n+1} + 2vu_L$$

$$U_j^{n+1} - U_j^n = v\left(U_{j+1}^{n+1} - 2U_j^{n+1} + U_{j-1}^{n+1}\right)$$

$$U_m^{n+1} - U_m^n = -2vU_m^{n+1} + 2vu_R.$$

---

[3]"Science is a differential equation. Religion is a boundary condition." —Alan Turing

Move U^{n+1} terms to the left-hand side and U^n terms to the right-hand side:

$$\begin{bmatrix} 1+2\nu & & & & \\ -\nu & 1+2\nu & -\nu & & \\ & \ddots & \ddots & \ddots & \\ & & -\nu & 1+2\nu & -\nu \\ & & & & 1+2\nu \end{bmatrix} \begin{bmatrix} U_0^{n+1} \\ U_1^{n+1} \\ \vdots \\ U_{m-1}^{n+1} \\ U_m^{n+1} \end{bmatrix} = \begin{bmatrix} U_0^n \\ U_1^n \\ \vdots \\ U_{m-1}^n \\ U_m^n \end{bmatrix} + \begin{bmatrix} 2\nu u_L \\ 0 \\ \vdots \\ 0 \\ 2\nu u_R \end{bmatrix}.$$

This system is simply $(\mathbf{I} - \nu\mathbf{D})\mathbf{U}^{n+1} = \mathbf{U}^n + \mathbf{b}$ where $\mathbf{D}$ is the modified tridiagonal matrix $(1, -2, 1)$. We need to invert a tridiagonal matrix at each step by using a tridiagonal solver. A tridiagonal solver efficiently uses Gaussian elimination by only operating on the diagonal and two off-diagonals, taking only $O(3m)$ operations to solve a linear system instead of $O\left(\frac{2}{3}m^3\right)$ operations for general Gaussian elimination.

The following Julia code implements the backward Euler method over the domain $[-2, 2]$ with zero Dirichlet boundary conditions and initial conditions $u(0,x) = 1$ for $|x| < 1$ and $u(0,x) = 0$ otherwise.

```julia
Δx = .01; Δt = .01; L = 2; ν = Δt/Δx^2; u₁ = 0; uᵣ = 0;
x = -L:Δx:L; m = length(x)
u = (abs.(x).<1)
u[1] += 2ν*u₁; u[m] += 2ν*uᵣ
D = Tridiagonal(ones(m-1), -2ones(m), ones(m-1))
D[1,2] = 0; D[m,m-1] = 0
A = I - ν*D
for i in 1:20
  u = A\u
end
```

We can compute the runtime by adding `@time begin` before and `end` after the code (or the similar `@btime` macro from the BenchmarkTools.jl package). This code takes roughly 0.0003 seconds on a typical laptop. If a nonsparse matrix is used instead of the Tridiagonal one by setting `D = Matrix(D)`, the runtime is 0.09 seconds—significantly slower but not unreasonably slow. However, for a larger system with $\Delta x = .001$, the runtime using a Tridiagonal matrix is still about 0.004 seconds, whereas for a nonsparse matrix, it is almost 15 seconds. ◄

♣ The LinearAlgebra.jl library contains types such as `Tridiagonal` that have efficient specialized linear solvers. Such matrices can be converted to regular matrices using the command `Matrix`. The identity operator is simply `I` regardless of size.

A *Neumann boundary condition* specifies the value of the derivative or gradient of the solution at the boundary. For example, to model a bar insulated at both ends, we set the heat flux $J(t,x)$ to be zero on the boundary giving $u_x(t,0) = u_x(t,1) = 0$. Zero Neumann boundary conditions are also called reflecting boundary conditions.

Example.   Let's implement a Crank–Nicolson scheme with reflecting boundary conditions. The Crank–Nicolson scheme is second-order in space, so we should also approximate the boundary conditions using the same order. The second-order approximations for the derivatives $u_x(t,x_0)$ and $u_x(t,x_m)$ are $(U_1 - U_{-1})/h$ and $(U_{m+1} - U_{m-1})/h$. For reflecting boundary conditions $u_x(t,x_1) = 0$ and $u_x(t,x_m) = 0$, so we can eliminate the left ghost points by setting $U_{-1} = U_1$ and $U_{m+1} = U_{m-1}$. Let $v = \alpha k / h^2$. Then the Crank–Nicolson method (13.6) is

$$(2+2v)U_0^{n+1} - 2vU_1^{n+1} = (2-2v)U_0^n + 2vU_1^n$$

$$-vU_{j-1}^{n+1} + (2+2v)U_j^{n+1} - vU_{j+1}^{n+1} = vU_{j-1}^n + (2-2v)U_j^n + vU_{j+1}^n$$

$$2vU_{m-1}^{n+1} - (2+2v)U_m^{n+1} = 2vU_{m-1}^n + (2-2v)U_m^n$$

Now, we need to solve the system $(\mathbf{I} - v\mathbf{D})\mathbf{U}^{n+1} = (\mathbf{I} - v\mathbf{D})\mathbf{U}^n$ where $\mathbf{D}$ is a modified tridiagonal matrix $(1, -2, 1)$. The following Julia code implements the Crank–Nicolson method with reflecting boundary conditions over the domain $[-2, 2]$ with initial conditions $u(0,x) = 1$ for $|x| < 1$ and $u(0,x) = 0$ otherwise.

```julia
Δx = .01; Δt = .01; L = 2; ν = Δt/Δx^2
x = -L:Δx:L; m = length(x)
u = float.(abs.(x).<1)
D = Tridiagonal(ones(m-1), -2ones(m), ones(m-1))
D[1,2] = 2; D[m,m-1] = 2
A = 2I + ν*D
B = 2I - ν*D
anim = @animate for i in 1:40
  plot(x,u, legend=:none, ylims=(0,1))
  u .= B\(A*u)
end
gif(anim, "heat_cn.gif", fps = 5)
```

Compare this code with that of the backward Euler method on the preceding page, noting similarities and differences. Running this code, we observe transient spikes at $x = -1$ and $x = 1$, where the initial distribution had discontinuities. Also, see the QR code at the bottom of this page.

Crank-Nicolson
solution to the
heat equation

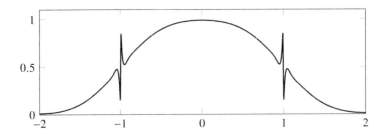

These are clearly numerical artifacts. What causes them, and how can we get a better solution? The Crank–Nicolson method is A-stable but not L-stable. Large eigenvalue components, associated with steep gradients, only slowly decay. See Figure 12.10 on page 365 for comparison. We'll examine numerical stability further in the next section and in the next chapter when we discuss dispersive and dissipative schemes. As a practical matter, we can regularize a problem by replacing a discontinuity in an initial condition with a smooth, rapidly-changing surrogate function. For example, instead of the discontinuous step function, we can take $\frac{1}{2} + \frac{1}{2}\tanh(\varepsilon^{-1}x)$, where the thickness of the interface is $O(\varepsilon)$. ◀

A third type of boundary condition, the *Robin boundary condition*, is a combination of Dirichlet and Neumann boundary conditions $u(t, 0) + au_x(t, 0) = b$ and $u(t, 1) - au_x(t, 1) = b$ for some constants a and b. A Robin boundary condition occurs when the boundary absorbs some of the mass or heat and reflects the rest of it. By contrast, *mixed boundary conditions* apply a Dirichlet boundary condition to one boundary and a Neumann boundary condition to the other.

If the problem has *periodic boundary conditions* $u(t, 0) = u(t, 1)$, we can no longer make the system tridiagonal. We instead have a circulant matrix, which can be inverted quickly using a discrete Fourier transform as we will see in Chapter 16.

A problem can also have *open boundary conditions*, in which the diffusion occurs over an infinite or semi-infinite domain. While we may only be interested in the dynamics in a finite region, we still need to solve the problem over the entire domain. One approach to solving the problem over $(-\infty, \infty)$ is with a nonuniform mesh generated using an inverse sigmoid function such as $\tanh^{-1} x$ or $x/(1 - |x|^p)$ for some $p \geq 1$. A similar approach is mapping the original problem to a finite domain by using a sigmoid function.

13.2 Von Neumann analysis

The previous chapter found the region of absolute stability of a numerical method for the problem $u' = \lambda u$ by determining the values λk for which perturbations of the solution decrease over time. We now want to determine under what conditions a numerical method for a partial differential equation is stable. We can apply a discrete Fourier transform to decouple a linear PDE into a system of ODEs. Because eigenvalues are unaffected by a change in basis, we can use the linear stability analysis we developed in the previous chapter. Furthermore, periodic boundary conditions will not significantly change the analysis because numerical stability is a local behavior.

Take the domain $[0, 2\pi]$ and uniform discretization in space $x_j = jh$ with $h = 2\pi/(2m + 1)$. The discrete Fourier transform is defined as

$$\hat{u}(t, \xi) = \frac{1}{2m + 1} \sum_{j=0}^{2m} u(t, x_j) e^{-i\xi jh},$$

and the discrete inverse Fourier transform is defined as

$$u(t, x_j) = \sum_{\xi=-m}^{m} \hat{u}(t, \xi) e^{i\xi jh},$$

where the wavenumber ξ is an integer (because the domain is bounded).

Use the method of lines to spatially discretize the heat equation $u_t = \alpha u_{xx}$ for $x \in [0, 2\pi]$ to get

$$\frac{\partial}{\partial t} u(t, x_j) = \alpha \frac{u(t, x_{j+1}) - 2u(t, x_j) + u(t, x_{j-1})}{h^2}. \tag{13.8}$$

Substituting the definition of the discrete inverse Fourier transform into this expression gives

$$\sum_{\xi=-m}^{m} \frac{\partial}{\partial t} \hat{u}(t, \xi) e^{i\xi jh} = \sum_{\xi=-m}^{m} \alpha \frac{e^{i\xi(j+1)h} - 2e^{i\xi jh} + e^{i\xi(j-1)h}}{h^2} \hat{u}(t, \xi).$$

Equivalently,

$$\sum_{\xi=-m}^{m} \frac{\partial}{\partial t} \hat{u}(t, \xi) e^{i\xi jh} = \sum_{\xi=-m}^{m} \alpha \frac{e^{i\xi h} - 2 + e^{-i\xi h}}{h^2} \hat{u}(t, \xi) e^{i\xi jh}.$$

This equality is true for each integer j, so

$$\frac{\partial \hat{u}}{\partial t} = \alpha \frac{e^{i\xi h} - 2 + e^{i\xi h}}{h^2} \hat{u}$$

for each $\xi = -m, -m + 1, \ldots, m$. By simplifying the expression

$$\alpha \frac{e^{i\xi h} - 2 + e^{-i\xi h}}{h^2} = \frac{2\alpha}{h^2}(\cos \xi h - 1) = -4\frac{\alpha}{h^2} \sin^2 \frac{\xi h}{2},$$

we have

$$\frac{\partial \hat{u}}{\partial t} = \left(-4\frac{\alpha}{h^2} \sin^2 \frac{\xi h}{2} \right) \hat{u}. \tag{13.9}$$

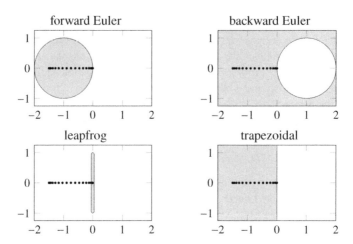

Figure 13.1: Regions of absolute stability (shaded) in the λk-plane for the forward Euler, backward Euler, leapfrog, and trapezoidal methods along with eigenvalues λ_ξ of the central difference approximation with $\alpha k / h^2 = \frac{3}{2}$.

Note that (13.9) is now a linear ordinary differential equation $\hat{u}' = \lambda_\xi \hat{u}$, where the eigenvalues $\lambda_\xi = -4\alpha / h^2 \sin^2(\xi h/2)$ are all nonpositive real numbers.

The regions of absolute stability for the forward Euler, backward Euler, leapfrog, and trapezoidal methods are shown in Figure 13.1 above. A method is stable as long as all $\lambda_\xi k$ lie in the region of absolute stability. The eigenvalues λ_ξ can be as large as $|\lambda_\xi| = 4\alpha / h^2$. We can determine the stability conditions for the different numerical schemes using this bound and the associated regions of absolute stability.

Let's start by determining the stability conditions for the forward Euler method. In the previous chapter, we found that the region of absolute stability for the forward Euler method is the unit circle centered at -1, containing the interval $[-2, 0]$ along the real axis. A numerical method is stable if $\lambda_\xi k$ is in the region of absolute stability for all ξ. Because the magnitude of λ_ξ can be as large as $4\alpha / h^2$, it follows that $\lambda_\xi k$ stays within the region of absolute stability as long as $k \leq h^2/2\alpha$. Such a stability condition is called the *Courant–Friedrichs–Lewy condition* or *CFL condition*. This CFL condition says that if we take a small grid spacing h, we need to take a much smaller time step k to maintain stability. If we double the gridpoints to reduce the error, we need to quadruple the number of time steps to maintain stability. If we increase the number of gridpoints tenfold, we need to increase the number of time steps a hundredfold. Such a restriction is impractical.

There is no constraint on the time step k for the backward Euler method when the eigenvalues are on the negative real axis. The backward Euler method is *unconditionally stable* for (13.8). We need to use a tridiagonal solver at each time step, but this extra effort to get unconditional stability is usually worth it. While the backward Euler method is $O(h^2)$ in space, it is only $O(k)$ in time. We'll still need to keep $k = O(h^2)$ to achieve second-order accuracy overall. We'd be better off pairing (13.8) with a scheme that is $O(k^2)$ in time.

In the above analysis, we used the property that the set $\{e^{i\xi jh}\}$ forms a linearly independent basis, and therefore, we only need to compare the Fourier coefficients. We can abbreviate the stability analysis by formally substituting U_j^n with $Ae^{i\xi jh}$. A method is stable if and only if $|A| \leq 1$. We call this *von Neumann stability analysis*.

Let's use von Neumann analysis to determine the stability condition of the Richardson (leapfrog) method

$$\frac{U_j^{n+1} - U_j^{n-1}}{2k} = \alpha \frac{U_{j+1}^n - 2U_j^n + U_{j-1}^n}{h^2}.$$

Replace U_j^n with $A^n e^{i\xi jh}$:

$$\frac{A^{n+1} e^{i\xi jh} - A^{n-1} e^{i\xi jh}}{2k} = \alpha A^n \frac{e^{i\xi h} - 2 + e^{-i\xi h}}{k^2} e^{i\xi jh}.$$

Then

$$\frac{A^2 - 1}{2k} = -\alpha \frac{4}{h^2} \sin^2 \frac{\xi h}{2} A,$$

from which we have

$$A^2 + 8\alpha \frac{k}{h^2} \sin^2 \frac{\xi h}{2} A - 1 = 0.$$

From the constant term of the quadratic, we know that the product of the roots of this equation is -1. Hence, both roots are real because complex roots would appear in conjugate pairs, the product of which is positive. Since $\{+1, -1\}$ are not the roots, the absolute value of one root must be greater than one. Therefore, the Richardson method is unconditionally unstable! That the Richardson method is unconditionally unstable should be quite clear from Figure 13.1 on the facing page. The eigenvalues λ_ξ of the second-order central difference approximation are negative real numbers, but the region of absolute stability of the leapfrog method is a line segment along the imaginary axis. So, no eigenvalue other than the zero eigenvalue is ever in that region regardless of how small we take k. We can slightly modify to the Richardson method to get the Dufort–Frankel method. As we'll see below, the Dufort–Frankel method is an *explicit* method that is unconditionally *stable*!

Dufort–Frankel (*inconsistent!*) $O(k^2 + h^2 + \frac{k^2}{h^2})$

$$\frac{U_j^{n+1} - U_j^{n-1}}{2k} = \alpha \frac{U_{j+1}^n - (U_j^{n+1} + U_j^{n-1}) + U_{j-1}^n}{h^2} \tag{13.10}$$

Let's determine the stability condition of the Dufort–Frankel method using von Neumann analysis. Replacing U_j^n with $A^n e^{ij\xi h}$ in (13.10) and dividing by $A^{n-1} e^{ij\xi h}$ gives us

$$\frac{A^2 - 1}{2k} = \alpha \frac{A e^{i\xi h} - (A^2 + 1) + A e^{-i\xi h}}{h^2} = \alpha \frac{2A \cos \xi h - (A^2 + 1)}{h^2}.$$

Let $v = \alpha k / h^2$, then

$$(1 + 2v)A^2 - (4v \cos \xi h)A - (1 - 2v) = 0.$$

The roots of this quadratic are

$$A_\pm = \frac{2v \cos \xi h \pm \sqrt{1 - 4v^2 \sin^2 \xi h}}{1 + 2v}.$$

Consider the two cases. If $1 - 4v^2 \sin^2 \xi h \geq 0$, then

$$|A_\pm| \leq \frac{2v + 1}{1 + 2v} = 1.$$

On the other hand, if $1 - 4v^2 \sin^2 \xi h \leq 0$, then

$$|A_\pm|^2 = \frac{(2v \cos \xi h)^2 + 4v^2 \sin^2 \xi h - 1}{(1 + 2v)^2} = \frac{4v^2 - 1}{4v^2 + 4v + 1} \leq 1.$$

So, the Dufort–Frankel scheme is unconditionally stable.

A method that is both explicit and unconditionally stable? That makes the Dufort–Frankel method a unicorn among numerical schemes.[4] But, as the saying goes, "there ain't no such thing as a free lunch." Let's compute the truncation error of the Dufort–Frankel method by substituting the Taylor expansion about (x_j, t_n) for each term. First, note that we can rewrite

$$\frac{U_j^{n+1} - U_j^{n-1}}{2k} = \alpha \frac{U_{j+1}^n - (U_j^{n+1} + U_j^{n-1}) + U_{j-1}^n}{h^2}$$

as

$$\frac{U_j^{n+1} - U_j^{n-1}}{2k} = \alpha \frac{U_{j+1}^n - 2U_j^n + U_{j-1}^n}{h^2} - \alpha \frac{U_j^{n+1} - 2U_j^n + U_j^{n-1}}{h^2}. \tag{13.11}$$

[4]It also violates the second Dahlquist barrier.

Then Taylor expansion simply gives us

$$u_t + \frac{k^2}{6}u_{ttt} + \cdots = \alpha\left(u_{xx} + \frac{h^2}{12}u_{xxxx} + \cdots\right) - \alpha\left(\frac{k^2}{h^2}u_{tt} + \cdots\right).$$

The truncation error is $O(k^2 + h^2 + \frac{k^2}{h^2})$. If $k = O(h)$, then the k^2/h^2 term is $O(1)$, and the method is inconsistent. In this case, we are actually finding the solution to the equation $u_t = \alpha u_{xx} - \alpha u_{tt}$. So, while the Dufort–Frankel scheme is absolutely stable, it is only consistent when $k \ll h$. Furthermore, we don't get second-order accuracy unless $k = O(h^2)$.

13.3   Higher-dimensional methods

The two-dimensional heat equation is $u_t = u_{xx} + u_{yy}$. By making the approximation $U_{ij}^n = u(x_i, y_j, t_n)$ and defining the discrete operators in x and y as

$$\delta_x^2 U_{ij} = (U_{i+1,j} - 2U_{i,j} + U_{i-1,j})/h^2 \tag{13.12a}$$

$$\delta_y^2 U_{ij} = (U_{i,j+1} - 2U_{i,j} + U_{i,j-1})/h^2 \tag{13.12b}$$

where $\Delta x = \Delta y = h$, the Crank–Nicolson method is

$$\frac{U_{ij}^{n+1} - U_{ij}^n}{k} = \tfrac{1}{2}\left(\delta_x^2 U_{ij}^{n+1} + \delta_x^2 U_{ij}^n + \delta_y^2 U^{n+1} + \delta_y^2 U^n\right). \tag{13.13}$$

For von Neumann analysis in two dimensions, we substitute $\hat{U}_{ij}^n = A^n e^{i(i\xi h + j\eta h)}$ and determine the CFL condition such that $|A| \le 1$. The Crank–Nicolson method is second-order in time and space and unconditionally stable.

We no longer have a simple tridiagonal system when moving to two or three dimensions. If we have 100 grid points in the x- and y-directions, then we will need to invert a $10^4 \times 10^4$ block tridiagonal matrix. And we will need to invert a $10^6 \times 10^6$ matrix in three dimensions. A more efficient approach is to use operator splitting. Let's examine two ways of splitting the right-hand operator of (13.13)

$$\tfrac{1}{2}\big(\underset{①}{\delta_x^2 U_{ij}^{n+1}} + \underset{②}{\delta_x^2 U_{ij}^n} + \underset{③}{\delta_y^2 U^{n+1}} + \underset{④}{\delta_y^2 U_{ij}^n}\big)$$

that will ensure that the method remains implicit. The fractional step method splits ① + ② from ③ + ④

$$\frac{U_{ij}^* - U_{ij}^n}{k} = \tfrac{1}{2}\big(\delta_x^2 U_{ij}^* + \delta_x^2 U_{ij}^n\big) \quad \text{and} \quad \frac{U_{ij}^{n+1} - U_{ij}^*}{k} = \tfrac{1}{2}\big(\delta_y^2 U_{ij}^* + \delta_y^2 U_{ij}^{n+1}\big),$$

and the alternate direction implicit (ADI) method splits ① + ③ from ② + ④

$$\frac{U_{ij}^* - U_{ij}^n}{k} = \tfrac{1}{2}\big(\delta_x^2 U_{ij}^* + \delta_y^2 U_{ij}^n\big) \quad \text{and} \quad \frac{U_{ij}^{n+1} - U_{ij}^*}{k} = \tfrac{1}{2}\big(\delta_x^2 U_{ij}^* + \delta_y^2 U_{ij}^{n+1}\big).$$

Let's examine the stability and accuracy of both splitting methods.

▷ Fractional step method

Consider the splitting method $u_t = D u$ where $D = D_1 + D_2 + \cdots + D_p$ and $D_i = \partial^2/\partial^2 x_i$. We solve $u_t = D_i u$ successively for each dimension i, making a multidimensional problem a succession of one-dimensional problems. We can discretize D_i with $\delta^2_{x_i}$ and use the Crank–Nicolson method at each stage

$$\frac{U^{n+i/p} - U^{n+(i-1)/p}}{k} = D_i \frac{U^{n+i/p} + U^{n+(i-1)/p}}{2} \quad \text{for} \quad i = 1, 2, \ldots, p.$$

The Crank–Nicolson method is unconditionally stable at each stage, so the overall method is unconditionally stable. What about the accuracy? At each fractional step,

$$\left(I - \tfrac{1}{2}k\, D_i\right) U^{n+i/p} = \left(I + \tfrac{1}{2}k\, D_i\right) U^{n+(i-1)/p},$$

where I is the identity operator. If $\left\|\tfrac{1}{2}k\, D_i\right\| < 1$, we can expand

$$\left(I - \tfrac{1}{2}k\, D_i\right)^{-1} = I + \tfrac{1}{2}k\, D_i + \tfrac{1}{4}k^2\, D_i^2 + O\!\left(k^3\right)$$

and so

$$\begin{aligned}
U^{n+i/p} &= \left(I + \tfrac{1}{2}k\, D_i + \tfrac{1}{4}k^2\, D_i^2 + O\!\left(k^3\right)\right)\left(I + \tfrac{1}{2}k\, D_i\right) U^{n+(i-1)/p} \\
&= \left(I + k\, D_i + \tfrac{1}{2}k^2\, D_i^2 + O\!\left(k^3\right)\right) U^{n+(i-1)/p}.
\end{aligned}$$

Continuing this expansion for each stage

$$U^{n+1} = \prod_{i=1}^{p} \left(I + k\, D_i + \tfrac{1}{2}k^2\, D_i^2 + O\!\left(k^3\right)\right) U^n,$$

from which it follows that

$$U^{n+1} - U^n = \underbrace{\tfrac{1}{2}k \sum_{i=1}^{p} D_i(U^{n+1} + U^n)}_{\text{Crank–Nicolson}} + \underbrace{\tfrac{1}{4}k^2 \sum_{i,j=1}^{p} D_i\, D_j(U^{n+1} + U^n)}_{O(k^2)} + O\!\left(k^3\right).$$

So, the fractional step method is second order.

▷ Alternating direction implicit method

The ADI method was proposed by Donald Peaceman and Henry Rachford in 1955, while working at Humble Oil and Refining Company, in a short-lived effort to simulate petroleum reserves. The ADI method applied to the heat equation is

$$U^{n+1/2} - U^n = \tfrac{1}{2}\nu\!\left(\delta_x^2 U^{n+1/2} + \delta_y^2 U^n\right), \tag{13.14a}$$

$$U^{n+1} - U^{n+1/2} = \tfrac{1}{2}\nu\!\left(\delta_x^2 U^{n+1/2} + \delta_y^2 U^{n+1}\right), \tag{13.14b}$$

where $v = k/h^2$. We need two tridiagonal solvers for this two-stage method. To examine stability take the Fourier transforms ($x \mapsto \xi$ and $y \mapsto \eta$)

$$\hat{U}^{n+1/2} = \hat{U}^n + \tfrac{1}{2}v\left(-4\sin^2 \tfrac{1}{2}\xi h\right)\hat{U}^{n+1/2} + \tfrac{1}{2}v\left(-4\sin^2 \tfrac{1}{2}\eta h\right)\hat{U}^n$$

$$\hat{U}^{n+1} = \hat{U}^{n+1/2} + \tfrac{1}{2}v\left(-4\sin^2 \tfrac{1}{2}\xi h\right)\hat{U}^{n+1/2} + \tfrac{1}{2}v\left(-4\sin^2 \tfrac{1}{2}\eta h\right)\hat{U}^{n+1}$$

from which

$$\hat{U}^{n+1} = \frac{1 - 2v\sin^2 \tfrac{1}{2}\eta h}{1 + 2v\sin^2 \tfrac{1}{2}\xi h}\hat{U}^{n+1/2} \quad \text{and} \quad \hat{U}^{n+1/2} = \frac{1 - 2v\sin^2 \tfrac{1}{2}\eta h}{1 + 2v\sin^2 \tfrac{1}{2}\xi h}\hat{U}^n.$$

So,

$$\hat{U}^{n+1} = \underbrace{\frac{\left(1 - 2v\sin^2 \tfrac{1}{2}\eta h\right)\left(1 - 2v\sin^2 \tfrac{1}{2}\eta h\right)}{\left(1 + 2v\sin^2 \tfrac{1}{2}\eta h\right)\left(1 + 2v\sin^2 \tfrac{1}{2}\eta h\right)}}_{\lambda}\hat{U}^n.$$

The denominator of λ is always larger than the numerator, so $|\lambda| \leq 1$ from which it follows that the method is unconditionally stable.

To determine the order of the ADI method, we take the difference and sum of (13.14)

$$(a) - (b): \qquad 2U^{n+1/2} = U^{n+1} + \tfrac{1}{2}v\delta_y^2(U^n - U^{n+1}) \tag{13.15a}$$

$$(a) + (b): \qquad U^{n+1} - U^n = v\delta_x^2 U^{n+1/2} + \tfrac{1}{2}v\delta_y^2(U^n + U^{n+1}). \tag{13.15b}$$

Substituting (13.15a) into (13.15b),

$$U^{n+1} - U^n = \tfrac{1}{2}v\delta_x^2\left(U^n + U^{n+1} + \tfrac{1}{2}v\delta_y^2(U^n - U^{n+1})\right) + \tfrac{1}{2}v\delta_y^2(U^n + U^{n+1})$$

$$= \underbrace{v\left(\delta_x^2\frac{U^n + U^{n+1}}{2} + \delta_y^2\frac{U^n + U^{n+1}}{2}\right)}_{\text{Crank–Nicolson}} + \underbrace{\tfrac{1}{4}v^2\delta_x^2\delta_y^2(U^n - U^{n+1})}_{O(v^2 h^4)}.$$

The second term $O(v^2 h^4) = O(k^2)$ because $v = k/h^2$. So the method has the same order as the Crank–Nicolson scheme $O(h^2 + k^2)$. The fractional step method is easier to implement than the ADI method, but the ADI method is generally more accurate.

A three-dimensional problem $u_t = u_{xx} + u_{yy} + u_{zz}$ is treated similarly. Take $\Delta x = \Delta y = \Delta z = h$ and $v = k/h^2$. Then the ADI method is

$$U^{n+1/3} - U^n = \tfrac{1}{6}v(3)\delta_x^2(U^{n+1/3} + U^n) + \delta_y^2(2U^n) + \delta_z^2(2U^n)$$

$$U^{n+2/3} - U^{n+1/3} = \tfrac{1}{6}v(3)\delta_x^2(U^{n+1/3} + U^n) + \delta_y^2(U^{n+2/3} + U^n) + \delta_z^2(2U^n)$$

$$U^{n+1} - U^{n+2/3} = \tfrac{1}{6}v(3)\delta_x^2(U^{n+1/3} + U^n) + \delta_y^2(U^{n+2/3} + U^n) + \delta_z^2(U^{n+1} + U^n)$$

13.4   Nonlinear diffusion equations

Consider the heat equation along a rod for which the heat conductivity $\alpha(u)$ changes as a positive function of the temperature. In this case,

$$\frac{\partial}{\partial t} u = \frac{\partial}{\partial x}\left(\alpha(u)\frac{\partial}{\partial x}u\right) \tag{13.16a}$$

$$u(0, x) = u_0(x) \tag{13.16b}$$

$$u(t, 0) = u(t, 1) = 0. \tag{13.16c}$$

Let's solve the problem by using the method of lines

$$
\begin{aligned}
\frac{\partial}{\partial t} u &= \frac{\partial}{\partial x}\left(\alpha(u)\frac{\partial}{\partial x}u\right)\\
&\approx \frac{1}{h}\left(\alpha(U_{j+1/2})\frac{\partial}{\partial x}U_{j+1/2} - \alpha(U_{j-1/2})\frac{\partial}{\partial x}U_{j-1/2}\right)\\
&\approx \alpha(U_{j+1/2})\frac{U_{j+1} - U_j}{h^2} - \alpha(U_{j-1/2})\frac{U_j - U_{j-1}}{h^2}\\
&\approx \alpha\left(\frac{U_{j+1} + U_j}{2}\right)\frac{U_{j+1} - U_j}{h^2} - \alpha\left(\frac{U_j + U_{j-1}}{2}\right)\frac{U_j - U_{j-1}}{h^2} \tag{13.17}
\end{aligned}
$$

Because the diffusion equation is stiff, the ODE solver should be a stiff solver. Otherwise, we will be forced to take many tiny steps to ensure stability. Because the problem is nonlinear, we will need to solve a system of nonlinear equations, typically using Newton's method. In practice, this means that Julia (or whatever language we might use) must numerically compute and invert a Jacobian matrix. Fortunately, our system of nonlinear equations is sparse, so the Jacobian matrix is also sparse. To help our solver, we can explicitly tell it that the Jacobian is sparse by passing it the sparsity pattern for the Jacobian; otherwise, our solver may foolishly build a nonsparse Jacobian matrix. In this case, the sparsity pattern is a tridiagonal matrix of ones.

Example.   The nonlinear diffusion equation $u_t = (u^p u_x)_x$ for some p is known as the porous medium equation and has been used to model the dispersion of grasshoppers and the flow of groundwater. The following Julia code implements (13.17) with $\alpha(u) = u^2$. We use the Sundials.jl package, which has a BDF routine for stiff nonlinear problems. The routine defaults to using a Netwon's solver, and we can help it by specifying that the Jacobian matrix is tridiagonal.

```
using Sundials
m = 400; L = 2; x = LinRange(-L,L,m); Δx = x[2]-x[1]
α = (u -> u.^2)
Du(u,Δx,t) = [0;diff(α((u[1:end-1]+u[2:end])/2).*diff(u))/Δx^2;0]
```

Method	name	stiff	time steps	runtime (s)
BDF	CVODE_BDF	◑	997	0.1
Bogacki–Shampine 2(3)	BS3	○	19410	1.3
Verner 7(6)	Vern7	○	10513	2.7
Rosenbrock 3(4)	Rodas4	●	430	12.0
Trapezoidal ESDIRK	Trapezoid	◑	948	39.9
Rosenbrock 2(3)	Rosenbrock23	●	554	41.0

○ low   ◑ medium   ● high

Figure 13.2: Solving the porous medium equation with 400 mesh points.

```
u₀ = (abs.(x).<1)
problem = ODEProblem(Du,u₀,(0,2),Δx)
method = CVODE_BDF(linear_solver=:Band, jac_lower=1, jac_upper=1)
solution = solve(problem, method);
```

Because $u^2 u_x = \left(\frac{1}{3}u^3\right)_x$, we could solve $u_t = \left(\frac{1}{3}u^3\right)_{xx}$ instead. In this case, we would simply replace the appropriate lines of code with the following:

```
α = (u -> u.^3/3)
Du(u,Δx,t) = [0;diff(diff(α(u)))/Δx^2;0]
```

There are different ways to visualize time-dependent data in Julia. One is with the @animate macro in Plots.jl, which combines snapshots as a gif

```
anim = @animate for t in LinRange(0,2,200)
  plot(x,solution(t),legend=:none,fill=(0,0.4,:red),ylims=(0,1))
end
gif(anim, "porous.gif", fps = 15)
```

or as an mp4 video with mp4(anim, "porous.mp4", fps = 15). Alternatively, we might save the figures as a set of images in the loop and then make an external call to ffmpeg afterward:

```
savefig("tmp"*lpad(i,3,"0")*".png")
run(`ffmpeg -y -i "tmp%03d.png" -pix_fmt yuv420p porous.mp4`)
```

Another way is with the @manipulate macro in Interact.jl, which creates a slider widget allowing a user to move the solution forward and backward in time.

```
using Interact
@manipulate for t∈slider(0:0.01:2; value=0, label="time")
  plot(x,solution(t), fill = (0, 0.4, :red))
  plot!(ylims=(0,1),legend=:none)
end
```

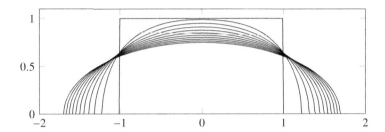

The figure above and the QR link below show the solution to the porous medium equation with an initial distribution given by a rectangular function. The snapshots are taken at equal intervals from $t \in [0, 2]$. Compare this solution with that of the one-dimensional heat equation on page 390.

It's worthwhile to benchmark the performance of the BDF method against other methods. While using an implicit method may reduce the number of steps in time, each step may require significant computation to invert a Jacobian. The runtimes using different stiff and nonstiff methods are shown in Figure 13.2 on the previous page.   ◀

▷ Stability

We cannot use linear von Neumann stability analysis on variable-coefficient and nonlinear problems. Instead, we will use the *energy method* to check stability. We define the "energy" of a system as the L^2-norm of the variable u. A system is stable if the energy is nonincreasing. Multiplying equation (13.16a) by u and integrating over the domain, we have

$$\int_0^1 u \frac{\partial}{\partial t} u \, dx = \int_0^1 u \frac{\partial}{\partial x} \left(\alpha(u) \frac{\partial}{\partial x} u \right) dx.$$

After integrating the right-hand side by parts and applying boundary terms,

$$\frac{1}{2} \frac{\partial}{\partial t} \int_0^1 u^2 \, dx = - \int_0^1 \alpha(u) \left(\frac{\partial}{\partial x} u \right)^2 dx.$$

If u is not a constant function of x, then the right-hand side is strictly negative, and the L^2-norm of u is decreasing in time.

We can use the same approach on the numerical scheme (13.17) with the discrete ℓ^2-norm. Now,

$$\sum_{j=1}^{m-1} U_j \frac{\partial}{\partial t} U_j = \sum_{j=1}^{m-1} \frac{1}{h^2} \left[\alpha_{j+1/2}(U_{j+1} - U_j)U_j - \alpha_{j-1/2}(U_j - U_{j-1})U_j \right],$$

solution to the porous medium equation

from which it follows that

$$\frac{1}{2}\frac{\partial}{\partial t}\sum_{j=1}^{m-1}(U_j)^2 = \frac{1}{h^2}\sum_{j=1}^{m-1}\alpha_{j+1/2}(U_{j+1}-U_j)U_j - \alpha_{j-1/2}(U_j - U_{j-1})U_j$$

$$= -\frac{1}{h^2}\sum_{j=1}^{m-1}\alpha_{j-1/2}(U_j - U_{j-1})^2 \le 0.$$

This inequality tells us that the ℓ^2-norm of the solution is nonincreasing in time.

Because discrete norms are equivalent, we can use other norms besides the ℓ^2-norm to confirm stability. As an example, let's use the ℓ^∞-norm to confirm the CFL condition of the forward Euler method (13.3). Take U_j^0 to be nonnegative for all j. Then letting $\nu = k/h^2$,

$$U_j^{n+1} - U_j^n = \nu\alpha_{j+1/2}(U_{j+1} - U_j) - \nu\alpha_{j-1/2}(U_j - U_{j-1}),$$

from which

$$U_j^{n+1} = \nu\alpha_{j+1/2}U_{j+1}^n + \left(1 - \nu\alpha_{j+1/2} - \nu\alpha_{j-1/2}\right)U_j^n + \nu\alpha_{j-1/2}U_{j-1}^n.$$

If $\nu\alpha_{j+1/2} \le \frac{1}{2}$ for all j, then

$$|U_j^{n+1}| = \nu\alpha_{j+1/2}|U_{j+1}^n| + \left(1 - \nu(\alpha_{j+1/2} + \alpha_{j-1/2})\right)|U_j^n| + \nu\alpha_{j-1/2}|U_{j-1}^n|$$

$$\le \left(\nu\alpha_{j+1/2} + 1 - \nu\alpha_{j+1/2} - \nu\alpha_{j-1/2} - \nu\alpha_{j-1/2}\right)\|U^n\|_\infty = \|U^n\|_\infty$$

for all j. It follows that $\|U^{n+1}\|_\infty \le \|U^n\|_\infty \le \cdots \le \|U^0\|_\infty$ for all n whenever the CFL condition $k \le \frac{1}{2}h^2/\max_j \alpha(U_j^0)$ is met.

13.5 Exercises

13.1. Show that the heat equation $u_t = \alpha u_{xx}$ with a bounded initial distribution $u(0,x) = u_0(x)$ has the solution

$$u(t,x) = \int_{-\infty}^\infty G(t,x-s)u_0(s)\,ds \quad \text{with} \quad G(t,s) = \frac{1}{\sqrt{4\pi\alpha t}}e^{-s^2/4\alpha t}.$$

This expression is known as the fundamental solution to the heat equation.

13.2. Use Taylor series expansion to determine the truncation error of the Crank–Nicolson scheme for $u_t = u_{xx}$.

13.3. Suppose we want to solve the heat equation, but instead of using the values $\{U_{j-1}, U_j, U_{j+1}\}$ to approximate u_{xx} at x_j, we decide to use the values $\{U_j, U_{j+1}, U_{j+2}\}$. For example, the stencil using the backward Euler method would be

Our approach is terrible for several reasons. First, it provides only a first-order approximation, whereas the central difference approximation is second-order. More importantly, it affects stability. Discuss the stability conditions of using such a scheme with various time-stepping methods.

13.4. The Applied Mathematics Panel, an organization established by Vannevar Bush to conduct mathematical research for the U.S. military during World War II, proposed the stencil on the right to solve the heat equation. John Crank and Phyllis Nicolson later dismissed the method as being "very cumbersome." Discuss the stability restrictions of the method.

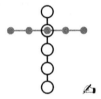

13.5. Prove that the Dufort–Frankel scheme is unconditionally stable by showing that the eigenvalues of the space discretization all lie within the region of absolute stability for the time-marching scheme. Demonstrate that although the scheme is unconditionally stable, it gets the wrong solution when $k = O(h)$.

13.6. Solve the heat equation $u_t = u_{xx}$ over the domain $[0, 1]$ with initial conditions $u(0, x) = \sin \pi x$ and boundary conditions $u(t, 0) = u(t, 1) = 0$ using the forward Euler scheme. Use 20 grid points in space and use the CFL condition to determine the stability requirement on the time step size k.

1. Examine the behavior of the numerical solution if k is slightly above or below the stability threshold.

2. Use the slope of the log-log plot of the error at $t = 1$ to verify the order of convergence. Use several values for the grid spacing h while keeping the time step $k \ll h$ constant. Then, use several values for the time step k, keeping the mesh $h \ll k$.

13.7. The Schrödinger equation

$$i\varepsilon \frac{\partial \psi}{\partial t} = -\frac{\varepsilon^2}{2} \frac{\partial^2 \psi}{\partial x^2} + V(x)\psi$$

models the quantum behavior of a particle in a potential field $V(x)$. The parameter ε is the scaled Plank constant, which gives the relative length and time scales. The probability of finding a particle at a position x is $\rho(t, x) = |\psi(t, x)|^2$ for a normalized wave function $\psi(t, x)$. While the Schrödinger equation is a parabolic PDE, it exhibits behaviors closely related to the wave equation—namely, the

L^2-norm of the solution is constant in time, and the equation has no maximum principle.

1. For constant potential $V(x) \equiv V$, describe the stability conditions using a second-order space discretization with different time-marching schemes, such as forward Euler, Richardson, Crank–Nicolson, and Runge–Kutta.

2. The Crank–Nicolson method does a good job conserving the L^2-norm of the solution. Use it to solve the initial value problem for the harmonic oscillator with $V(x) = \frac{1}{2}x^2$ with initial conditions $\psi(0, x) = (\pi\varepsilon)^{-1/4}e^{-(x-x_0)^2/2\varepsilon}$. The solution for this problem

$$\psi(t, x) = (\pi\varepsilon)^{-1/4}e^{-(x-x_0\exp(-it))^2/2\varepsilon}e^{-(1-\exp(-2it))x_0^2/4\varepsilon}e^{-it/2}$$

is called the coherent state,[5] and it is one of the rare examples of an exact closed-form solution to the time-dependent Schrödinger equation. In particular, at time $t = 2\pi n$, the solution $\psi(2\pi n, x) = (-1)^n\psi(0, x)$. Take $\varepsilon = 0.3$. Choose a wide domain to ensure that interactions with the boundaries are negligible. Compute the slope of the log-log plot of the error with the analytic solution at $t = 2\pi$ to confirm that the method is $O(k^2 + h^2)$. Use several values for the grid spacing h while keeping the time step $k \ll h$ constant. Then use several values for the time step k, keeping the mesh $h \ll k$.

3. What happens when the mesh spacing h or the time step k is about equal to or larger than ε? ◿

13.8. In polar coordinates, the heat equation is

$$\frac{\partial u}{\partial t} = \frac{1}{r}\frac{\partial}{\partial r}\left(r\frac{\partial u}{\partial r}\right) + \frac{1}{r^2}\frac{\partial^2 u}{\partial\theta^2}.$$

For a radially symmetric geometry, this equation simplifies to

$$\frac{\partial u}{\partial t} = \frac{1}{r}\frac{\partial}{\partial r}\left(r\frac{\partial u}{\partial r}\right).$$

Develop a numerical method for this problem and implement it using the regularized step function $\tanh 30(1 - r)$ as initial conditions. Use reflecting boundary conditions at $r = 2$ and symmetry at $r = 0$ to determine an appropriate boundary condition. Implement the method and plot the solution. ◿

[5] Coherent states refer to Gaussian wave packet solutions of the harmonic oscillator. Schrödinger derived them in 1926 in response to criticism that the wave function $\psi(t, x)$ did not display classical motion and satisfy the correspondence principle.

13.9. Suppose we want to model the heat equation $u_t = u_{xx}$ with open boundary conditions. Over time a function will gradually decrease in height and broaden in width while conserving area. The interesting dynamics may all occur near the origin, but we'll still need to solve the equation far from the origin to get an accurate solution. Rather than using equally-spaced gridpoints, we can closely space points near the origin and spread them out away from the origin.

1. Derive a central difference approximation to the Laplacian operator for arbitrarily-spaced gridpoints. Discuss the error of the approximation.

2. Solve the heat equation by approximating open boundary conditions using a nonuniform grid. Use an inverse sigmoid function, such as $x = \tanh^{-1} \xi$, to generate the grid. Use the Gaussian function $u(x, 0) = e^{-sx^2}$ as the initial distribution with $s = 10$. The exact solution over an infinite domain is $u(x, t) = (1 + 4st)^{-1/2} e^{-sx^2/(1+4st)}$. ⚐

13.10. The Allen–Cahn equation

$$u_t = \Delta u + \varepsilon^{-1} u(1 - u^2)$$

is a reaction-diffusion equation that models a nonconservative phase transition. The solution $u(t, x, y)$ has stable equilibria at $u = \pm 1$ with a thin phase interface given by $-1 < u < 1$. As a loose analogy, think of ice melting and freezing in a pool of water with $u = 1$ representing the ice and $u = -1$ representing the water.

Determine the numerical solution to the two-dimensional Allen–Cahn equation using a numerical method that is second order in time and space with the stability condition independent of ε. Consider the domain $[-8, 8] \times [-8, 8]$ with reflecting boundary conditions. Take $\varepsilon = 1/50$ and take the initial conditions

$$u(0, x, y) = \begin{cases} 1, & \text{if } x^4 < 32x^2 - 16y^2 \\ -1, & \text{otherwise} \end{cases}.$$

Also, try initial conditions consisting of an array of normally-distributed random numbers. Observe the behavior of the solution over time. ⚐

Chapter 14

Hyperbolic Equations

Nonlinear hyperbolic equations are synonymous with shock wave formation, from the hydraulic lift of a tsunami approaching the shore to the sonic boom of a jet aircraft to the pressure wave of an atomic blast. Hyperbolic equations also model plasmas, crowds, combustion, earthquakes, and traffic flow.

A principal difference between hyperbolic and parabolic equations is that while solutions to linear parabolic equations are always smooth and become increasingly smoother over time, solutions to hyperbolic equations often are not. In fact, the solutions of nonlinear hyperbolic equations with smooth initial conditions may become discontinuous in time, resulting in shock waves. These discontinuities introduce challenges when we try to approximate them using high-order polynomial interpolants.

Another difference is that the stability condition for explicit schemes for hyperbolic equations are typically $k = O(h)$ rather than the $k = O(h^2)$ that we had for parabolic equations. While there was a significant advantage to using an implicit solver for parabolic equations, there is no significant advantage for hyperbolic equations. Therefore, we only consider explicit schemes.

The subject of numerical methods for hyperbolic equations has developed considerably in the last fifty years. This chapter is an introduction—see Randall LeVeque's textbook *Finite Volume Methods for Hyperbolic Problems* for complete coverage.

14.1 Linear hyperbolic equations

Let $u(t, x)$ be a physical quantity such as density, pressure, or velocity. If the flux of u is given by $f(u)$, then the time evolution of the quantity u is given by

$$\frac{\partial u}{\partial t} + \frac{\partial}{\partial x} f(u) = 0.$$

In the previous chapter, the flux was given by Fick's Law $f(u) = -\alpha(x)\frac{\partial}{\partial x}u$, which led to diffusion that characterized parabolic equations. Hyperbolic equations are characterized by advection. Let's start with the simplest flux $f(u) = cu$ and look at the more general nonlinear case later. Information propagating with velocity c is described by the linear advection equation

$$\frac{\partial u}{\partial t} + c\frac{\partial u}{\partial x} = 0 \quad \text{with} \quad u(x,0) = u_0(x). \tag{14.1}$$

This problem can be solved by the *method of characteristics*. Compare the total derivative of $u(t,x)$ and the advection equation:

$$\frac{d}{dt}u(t,x(t)) = \frac{\partial u}{\partial t} + \frac{dx}{dt}\frac{\partial u}{\partial x} \quad \text{and} \quad \frac{\partial u}{\partial t} + c\frac{\partial u}{\partial x} = 0.$$

By taking $dx/dt = c$, the total derivative

$$\frac{d}{dt}u(t,x(t)) = 0,$$

which says that the solution $u(t,x(t))$ is constant along the *characteristic curves* $x(t)$ for which $dx/dt = c$. The characteristics curves are exactly those for which $x(t) = ct + x_0$ for some x_0. The solution to (14.1) is then given by

$$u(t,x(t)) = u(0,x(0)) = u(0,x_0) = u_0(x_0) = u_0(x - ct).$$

We can find the solution at time t by tracing the characteristic curve back to the initial conditions. The value c is called the *characteristic speed*, and u—which is constant along the characteristic curve—is called the *Riemann invariant*. It's not necessary that c be a constant—the method of characteristics also works for general $f(u)$. We'll come back to the nonlinear case later in the chapter.

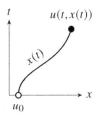

14.2   Methods for linear hyperbolic equations

Let's develop numerical schemes to solve the simple linear problem $u_t + cu_x = 0$. The schemes designed for this linear problem will be prototypic methods that we later extend to solve nonlinear hyperbolic problems.

▷ Upwind method

The most straightforward numerical scheme for solving $u_t + cu_x = 0$ is one that uses a forward Euler approximation in time and a first-order difference in space. Such a scheme is called an *upwind method*.

A natural first question about such a scheme might be, "what is its stability condition?" We can answer this question using the von Neumann analysis developed in the previous chapter. Consider the semidiscrete system of equations

$$\frac{\partial}{\partial t} u(t, x_j) = c \frac{u(t, x_{j-1}) - u(t, x_j)}{h}.$$

We find the corresponding system in the Fourier domain by formally substituting $u(t, x_j)$ with $\hat{u}(t, \xi) e^{i\xi jh}$. In this case, we have the decoupled system

$$\frac{\partial}{\partial t} \hat{u}(t, \xi) = c \frac{e^{-i\xi h} - 1}{h} \hat{u}(t, \xi),$$

whose eigenvalues are $(c/h) \cdot (e^{-i\xi h} - 1)$. The locus of $e^{-i\xi h} - 1$ is a circle of radius one centered at -1. The region of absolute stability for the forward Euler method is also a circle of radius one centered at -1. If the characteristic speed $c > 0$, then $(c/h) \cdot (e^{-i\xi h} - 1)$ is simply a circle of radius c/h centered at $-c/h$. Therefore, the upwind method (14.3) is stable if the *CFL condition* $k < h/c$ holds. We call $|c|k/h$ the *CFL number* for the upwind scheme. A useful method of visualizing the CFL condition of a numerical method is by overlaying the eigenvalues of the right-hand-side operator over the region of absolute stability of the ODE solver:

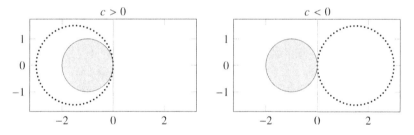

When the characteristic speed c is positive, the upwind method

$$U_j^{n+1} - U_j^n = -\frac{ck}{h}(U_j^n - U_{j-1}^n) \tag{14.2}$$

is made more stable by taking smaller time steps k so that $k < h/c$. But when c is negative, all of the eigenvalues are in the right half-plane. There's nothing we can do to make the method absolutely stable by scaling k, so the method is unconditionally unstable. We can, however, modify (14.2) specifically for the case when the characteristic speed c is negative. The two varieties of upwind methods are listed in the following boxes:

Upwind Method ($c > 0$) $O(k + h)$

$$\frac{U_j^{n+1} - U_j^n}{k} + c \frac{U_j^n - U_{j-1}^n}{h} = 0 \tag{14.3}$$

Upwind Method ($c < 0$) $O(k + h)$

$$\frac{U_j^{n+1} - U_j^n}{k} + c\frac{U_{j+1}^n - U_j^n}{h} = 0 \tag{14.4}$$

To implement the schemes, we must first determine the sign of c. We can combine the two varieties to get a scheme that does this automatically

$$\frac{U_j^{n+1} - U_j^n}{k} + \frac{c + |c|}{2}\frac{U_j^n - U_{j-1}^n}{h} + \frac{c - |c|}{2}\frac{U_{j+1}^n - U_j^n}{h} = 0.$$

To get a sense of why we need two upwind schemes (or one combined automatic-switching scheme), just think about the weather. To predict the weather, we need to look in the upwind direction from which it is coming, not the downwind direction in which it is going. Information propagates at a finite speed c along a characteristic of the advection equation (14.1). In a finite time, the solution at any specific point in space can only be affected by the initial conditions in some bounded region of space. This region is called the *domain of dependence*. Similarly, that same point in space can only influence a bounded region of space over a finite time. This region is called the *domain of influence*. The domain of dependence looks into the past, and the domain of influence looks into the future.

Consider the solution to the advection equation: $u(t_n, x_j) = u_0(x_j - ct_n)$. Take a uniform step size k in time and a uniform grid spacing h. The domain of dependence of the true solution is $[x_j, x_j + cnk]$. The domain of dependence of the numerical solution is $[x_j, x_j + nh]$. By keeping $ck/h < 1$, we ensure that the domain of dependence of the numerical solution contains the domain of dependence of the true solution.

For parabolic equations, like the heat equation, information propagates instantaneously throughout the domain, although its effect may be infinitesimal. If we put a flame to one end of a heat-conducting bar, the temperature at the other end immediately beings to rise, albeit almost undetectably.[1] When we solved the heat equation using an explicit scheme like the forward Euler method, we found a rather restrictive CFL condition. With such a scheme, information at one grid point can only propagate to its nearest neighbor in one time step. The more grid points we have, the greater the number of time steps needed to send the information from one side of the domain to the other. The matrix $\mathbf{I} + k/h^2\mathbf{D}$ associated with the forward Euler method for the heat equation is tridiagonal. On the other hand, the matrix $(\mathbf{I} - k/h^2\mathbf{D})^{-1}$ associated with the backward Euler method is completely filled in. With such as scheme, information at one

---

[1] Such a model is clearly not physical because heat is conducted at a finite velocity and definitely less than the speed of light. But, what mathematical models are perfect?

gridpoint is propagated to every other grid point in one time step. The normalized plots below show the values of a column taken from the matrices $I + k/h^2 D$ with $h = \frac{1}{2}k^2$ and $(I - k/h^2 D)^{-1}$ with $h = k$:

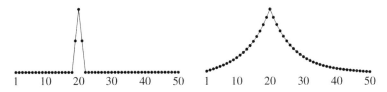

▷ Lax–Friedrichs method

The upwind method is $O(h + k)$. It seems reasonable that we could build a more accurate, $O(k + h^2)$ method by using a central difference approximation for the space derivative while keeping the forward Euler approximation in time. But, what about stability? By formally replacing $u(t, x_j)$ with $\hat{u}(t, \xi)e^{i\xi jh}$, the decoupled central difference system is

$$\frac{\partial}{\partial t}\hat{u}(t, \xi) = c\frac{e^{i\xi h} - e^{-i\xi h}}{2h}\hat{u}(t, \xi) = -\frac{c}{h}(i \sin \xi h)\hat{u}(t, \xi)$$

in the Fourier domain. The eigenvalues of this system are purely imaginary, but the region of stability for the forward Euler scheme is a unit circle in the left half-plane. So the method is unconditionally unstable.

	Centered-difference (*unstable!*)	$O(k + h^2)$
	$\dfrac{U_j^{n+1} - U_j^n}{k} + c\dfrac{U_{j+1}^n + U_{j-1}^n}{2h} = 0$	(14.5)

We can modify the central difference scheme to make it stable. One way to do this is by choosing an ODE solver whose region of absolute stability includes part of the imaginary axis, like the leapfrog scheme. Another way is to somehow push the eigenspectrum into the left half-plane, where we can then shrink them to fit in the region of absolute stability of the forward Euler scheme. The Lax–Friedrichs method approximates the U_j^n term in the time derivative of (14.5) as $\frac{1}{2}(U_{j+1}^n + U_{j-1}^n)$.

	Lax–Friedrichs	$O(k + h^2/k)$
	$\dfrac{U_j^{n+1} - \frac{1}{2}(U_{j+1}^n + U_{j-1}^n)}{k} + c\dfrac{U_{j+1}^n - U_{j-1}^n}{2h} = 0$	(14.6)

The method is accurate to order $O(k + h^2/k)$. What about stability? We can do von Neumann analysis by formally substituting $A^n e^{ij\xi h}$ for U_j^n in (14.6) and simplifying to get

$$A - \frac{e^{i\xi h} + e^{-i\xi h}}{2} = -c\frac{k}{h}i\sin\xi h.$$

We separate out A to get $A = \cos\xi h - i(ck/h)\sin\xi h$, from which we see that $|A|^2 = \cos^2\xi h + (ck/h)^2\sin^2\xi h$. So the Lax–Friedrichs scheme is stable if $|c|k/h \le 1$. Therefore, the CFL number for the Lax–Friedrichs scheme is $|c|k/h$.

▷ Lax–Wendroff method

Let's look at another way to stablize the unstable central difference scheme (14.5). Using the Taylor series expansion about $U_j^n = u(t_n, x_j)$, we have

$$U_j^{n+1} = u + ku_t + \tfrac{1}{2}k^2 u_{tt} + O(k^3)$$
$$U_{j+1}^n = u + hu_x + \tfrac{1}{2}h^2 u_{xx} + \tfrac{1}{6}h^3 u_{xxx} + O(k^4)$$
$$U_{j-1}^n = u - hu_x + \tfrac{1}{2}h^2 u_{xx} - \tfrac{1}{6}h^3 u_{xxx} + O(k^4).$$

The central difference method

$$\frac{U_j^{n+1} - U_j^n}{k} + c\frac{U_{j+1}^n - U_{j-1}^n}{2h} = 0$$

is consistent with

$$u_t + cu_x = -\tfrac{1}{2}ku_{tt} + O(k^2 + h^2). \tag{14.7}$$

Because $u_t + cu_x = 0$, we have $u_t = -cu_x$ from which $u_{tt} = -cu_{tx} = c^2 u_{xx}$. Therefore, (14.7) is the same as

$$u_t + cu_x = -\tfrac{1}{2}c^2 ku_{xx} + O(k^2 + h^2).$$

Note that $u_t = -\tfrac{1}{2}c^2 ku_{xx}$ is a backward heat equation, which is unstable. This term appears to be the source of the instability in the central difference method. We can fix the scheme by counteracting $-\tfrac{1}{2}c^2 ku_{xx}$ with $+\tfrac{1}{2}c^2 ku_{xx}$. Not only will this improve stability, but it also increases the accuracy from $O(k + h^2)$ to $O(k^2 + h^2)$. The new stabilized scheme is

$$\frac{U_j^{n+1} - U_j^n}{k} + c\frac{U_{j+1}^n - U_{j-1}^n}{2h} = \frac{c^2}{2}k\frac{U_{j+1}^n - 2U_j^n + U_{j-1}^n}{h^2}.$$

The original central difference in space, forward Euler scheme (14.5) failed because the eigenvalues were along the imaginary axis and fell entirely outside the region of stability of the forward Euler scheme no matter the size of k. By adding a viscosity term u_{xx} to the problem, we push the eigenvalues into the left-half plane, and by taking k sufficiently small, we can ensure stability.

$$\text{Lax–Wendroff Method} \qquad O(k^2 + h^2)$$

$$\frac{U_j^{n+1} - U_j^n}{k} + c\frac{U_{j+1}^n - U_{j-1}^n}{2h} = \frac{c^2}{2}k\frac{U_{j+1}^n - 2U_j^n + U_{j-1}^n}{h^2} \qquad (14.8)$$

Note that by rearranging the terms of the Lax–Friedrichs scheme, we get a form that looks very similar to the Lax–Wendroff scheme:

$$\frac{U_j^{n+1} - U_j^n}{k} + c\frac{U_{j+1}^n - U_{j-1}^n}{2h} = \frac{h^2}{2k}\frac{U_{j+1}^n - 2U_j^n + U_{j-1}^n}{h^2}.$$

Like the Lax–Wendroff scheme, the Lax–Friedrichs scheme achieves stability by adding a viscosity term onto the unstable central difference scheme. Whereas the Lax–Wendroff scheme adds just enough viscosity ($c^2k/2$) to counteract the unstable second-order term, the Lax–Friedrichs scheme aggressively adds more viscosity ($h^2/2k$). We can generalize the Lax–Wendroff and Lax–Friedrichs methods by using a diffusion coefficient α:

$$\frac{\partial}{\partial t}U_j - c\frac{U_{j+1} - U_{j-1}}{2h} = \alpha\frac{U_{j+1} - 2U_j + U_{j-1}}{h^2}. \qquad (14.9)$$

From earlier in this chapter and the previous chapter, we know that the Fourier transform of this equation is

$$\frac{\partial}{\partial t}\hat{u}(t,\xi) = -4\frac{\alpha}{h^2}\sin^2\frac{\xi h}{2}\,\hat{u}(t,\xi) - i\frac{c}{h}\sin\xi h\,\hat{u}(t,\xi)$$

with eigenvalues

$$-4\frac{\alpha}{h^2}\sin^2\frac{\xi h}{2} - i\frac{c}{h}\sin\xi h.$$

The eigenvalues lie on an ellipse in the negative half-plane bounded by $-4\alpha/h^2$ along the real axis and $\pm c/h$ along the imaginary axis. For a forward Euler method, this ellipse must be scaled by k to lie entirely within the unit circle centered at -1. For the Lax–Friedrichs method, $\alpha = h^2/2k$ and the k-scaled ellipse is

$$-2\sin^2\frac{\xi h}{2} - i\frac{ck}{h}\sin\xi h.$$

The ellipse always goes out to -2 along the real axis no matter the value of k. So, the CFL condition for the Lax–Friedrichs method $k < h/|c|$ is due entirely to the imaginary components of the eigenvalues. For the Lax–Wendroff method, $\alpha = c^2/2k$ and the k-scaled ellipse is

$$-2\left(\frac{ck}{h}\right)^2\sin^2\frac{\xi h}{2} - i\frac{ck}{h}\sin\xi h.$$

When $k < h/|c|$, the k-scaled ellipse is entirely inside the unit circle, and when $k > h/|c|$, the k-scaled ellipse is entirely outside the unit circle. The CFL numbers for the Lax–Wendroff method and the Lax–Friedrichs method are both $|c|k/h$. The following figure shows the eigenvalues for the different methods overlaid on the region of absolute stability of the forward Euler method:

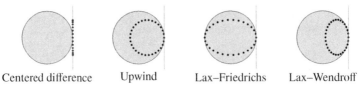

| Centered difference | Upwind | Lax–Friedrichs | Lax–Wendroff |

The eigenvalues of the central difference scheme are outside the region of absolute stability, so the scheme is unconditionally unstable. The eigenvalues for the Lax–Friedrichs scheme extend farther left than those of the upwind scheme, which themselves extend farther left than those of the Lax–Wendroff method. Consequently, the Lax–Friedrichs method is more dissipative than the upwind method, which itself is more dissipative than the Lax–Wendroff method.

14.3   Numerical diffusion and dispersion

We can better understand the behavior of a numerical solution by examining the truncation error of the numerical scheme. Let's start by looking at the upwind scheme. Using Taylor series expansion, we find that the upwind method is a numerical approximation of

$$u_t + cu_x = \tfrac{1}{2}ch\left(1 - \frac{ck}{h}\right)u_{xx} + O(h^2). \tag{14.10}$$

From this expression, the upwind scheme is a first-order approximation to

$$u_t + cu_x = 0, \tag{14.11}$$

but it is a second-order approximation to

$$u_t + cu_x = \tfrac{1}{2}ch\left(1 - \frac{ck}{h}\right)u_{xx}. \tag{14.12}$$

The right-hand side of (14.12) contributes *numerical viscosity* (also called numerical diffusion or numerical dissipation) to the computed solution. You can think of it this way: while the upwind scheme does a decent job matching the original problem (14.11), it does a better job matching the parabolic equation (14.12). Notice what happens if we take tiny step sizes in time (keeping the mesh size in space fixed). As $ck/h \to 0$, we get $u_t + cu_x = \tfrac{1}{2}chu_{xx}$, and the solution is overly dissipative. On the other hand, if we take k equal to the CFL number

($k = h/c$), then not only does the u_{xx} term of (14.10) disappear, but the whole right side disappears. That is, the upwind scheme exactly solves $u_t + cu_x = 0$ when $k = h/c$.

The Lax–Wendroff scheme is a second-order approximation to (14.11), but it is a third-order approximation to

$$u_t + cu_x = -\frac{1}{6}ch^2\left(1 - \left(\frac{ck}{h}\right)^2\right)u_{xxx}. \tag{14.13}$$

The right-hand side of (14.13) contributes *numerical dispersion* to the computed solution.

So, what's the distinction between dissipation and dispersion? Take a Fourier component

$$u(t, x) = e^{i(\omega t - \xi x)}, \tag{14.14}$$

where the value ω is some angular frequency and the value ξ is the wave number of the Fourier component. Let's use the Fourier component as an *ansatz* to the advection equation $u_t + cu_x = 0$. Then

$$i\omega e^{i(\omega t - \xi x)} - ic\xi e^{i(\omega t - \xi x)} = 0,$$

from which we have $\omega = c\xi$. We can plug this relation back into the ansatz to get a solution

$$u(t, x) = e^{i(\omega t - \xi x)} = e^{i\xi(ct - x)}.$$

Each Fourier component moves at a velocity $c = \omega/\xi$, the ratio of the angular frequency and the wavenumber. We call this ratio the *phase velocity*.

Now, let's use the same ansatz (14.14) in the modified upwind equation (14.12) $u_t + cu_x = \alpha u_{xx}$. We get

$$i\omega e^{i(\omega t - \xi x)} - ic\xi e^{i(\omega t - \xi x)} = -\alpha\xi^2 e^{i(\omega t - \xi x)},$$

from which we have $i\omega - ic\xi = -\alpha\xi^2$. From this equation, we can determine a *dispersion relation*

$$\omega = c\xi + i\alpha\xi^2.$$

Plugging this ω back into our ansatz gives us

$$u(t, x) = e^{i(\omega t - \xi x)} = e^{ic\xi t}e^{-\alpha\xi^2 t}e^{-i\xi x} = \underbrace{e^{i\xi(ct - x)}}_{\text{advection}} \cdot \underbrace{e^{-\alpha\xi^2 t}}_{\text{dissipation}}.$$

Dissipation damps out components with high wavenumbers ξ.

The ansatz in the modified Lax–Wendroff equation (14.13) $u_t + cu_x = \beta u_{xxx}$ yields

$$i\omega e^{i(\omega t - \xi x)} - ic\xi e^{i(\omega t - \xi x)} = -i\beta\xi^3 e^{i(\omega t - \xi x)},$$

which we can simplify to derive the dispersion relation

$$\omega = c\xi + \beta\xi^3.$$

For the Lax–Wendroff scheme, we have

$$u(t, x) = e^{i(c\xi + \beta\xi^3)t}e^{-i\xi x} = \underbrace{e^{i\xi(ct-x)}}_{\text{advection}} \cdot \underbrace{e^{i\beta\xi^3 t}}_{\text{dispersion}}.$$

Numerical dispersion causes oscillations in the solution.

Fourier components don't act alone—every function is a linear combination of many (infinitely many) Fourier components of varying wavenumbers. For a function to move as a group of Fourier components, the phase $\omega t - \xi x$ must be independent of wavenumber, i.e.,

$$\frac{d(\omega t - \xi x)}{d\xi} = 0 \quad \text{from which} \quad x = \frac{d\omega}{d\xi} \cdot t.$$

The *group velocity* is the derivative of the angular frequency with respect to the wave number, $v_{\text{group}} = d\omega/d\xi$. See the QR code at the bottom of the page.

A solution is dispersionless when the phase and group velocity are the same $\omega/\xi = d\omega/d\xi = c$. Otherwise, the solution is *dispersive*. For example, the phase velocity of the solution to the modified Lax–Wendroff equation is

$$v_{\text{phase}} = \frac{\omega}{\xi} = c + \beta\xi^2,$$

and group velocity is

$$v_{\text{group}} = \frac{d\omega}{d\xi} = c + 3\beta\xi^2.$$

Let's summarize. Every function is a combination of Fourier components of varying wavenumbers. These components travel at a different speed when the solution is dispersive. High wavenumbers are associated with large derivatives, e.g., functions with discontinuities. A dispersive scheme creates oscillations around a discontinuity, and a dissipative scheme smooths out the discontinuity.

Figure 14.1 on the facing page shows the solution to the advection equation $u_t + u_x = 0$ using the upwind, Lax–Friedrichs, and Lax–Wendroff methods for a rectangle function when k is slightly smaller than h and when $k($ is two-thirds h. (Solutions are unstable when k is greater than h.) When k is much smaller than h, the solutions exhibit significant diffusion in the upwind and Lax–Friedrichs methods and dispersion in the Lax–Wendroff method.

14.4 Linear hyperbolic systems

Let's turn our attention to the one-dimensional linear wave equation

$$u_{tt} - c^2 u_{xx} = 0. \tag{14.15}$$

group and
phase velocities

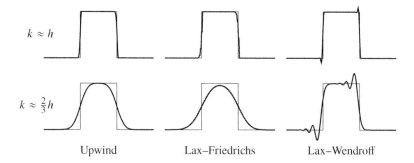

$k \approx h$

$k \approx \frac{2}{3}h$

Upwind   Lax–Friedrichs   Lax–Wendroff

Figure 14.1: Solution to the advection equation for an initial rectangle function. Solutions move from left to right. See the QR code at the bottom of the page.

We can rewrite this equation as the system of partial differential equations by setting $u_t = v$ and $u_x = w$. Then

$$v_t - c^2 w_x = 0$$
$$w_t - v_x = 0,$$

which is equivalent to

$$\begin{bmatrix} v \\ w \end{bmatrix}_t + \begin{bmatrix} 0 & -c^2 \\ -1 & 0 \end{bmatrix} \begin{bmatrix} v \\ w \end{bmatrix}_x = \begin{bmatrix} 0 \\ 0 \end{bmatrix}.$$

In general, one has $\mathbf{u}_t + \mathbf{A}\mathbf{u}_x = \mathbf{0}$ with $\mathbf{u}(t) \in \mathbb{R}^n$ and $\mathbf{A} \in \mathbb{R}^{n \times n}$. This system is called *strictly hyperbolic* if $\mathbf{A}$ has n real eigenvalues. In this case, the matrix $\mathbf{A}$ has a complete set of linearly independent eigenvectors and can be diagonalized in real space as $\mathbf{T}^{-1}\mathbf{A}\mathbf{T} = \mathbf{\Lambda} = \mathrm{diag}(\lambda_1, \lambda_2, \ldots, \lambda_n)$, where $\mathbf{T}$ is a matrix of eigenvectors $\mathbf{v}_1, \mathbf{v}_2, \ldots, \mathbf{v}_n$. That is, $\mathbf{A}\mathbf{v}_i = \lambda_i \mathbf{v}_i$. The eigenvalues λ_i are the *characteristic speeds*. The characteristic speeds for the wave equation (14.15) are $\lambda_{\pm} = \pm c$.

By diagonalizing the matrix $\mathbf{A}$, we completely decouple the system into independent advection equations. Consider

$$\mathbf{u}_t + \mathbf{A}\mathbf{u}_x = \mathbf{0}.$$

Multiply this equation by $\mathbf{T}^{-1}$ to get $\mathbf{T}^{-1}\mathbf{u}_t + \mathbf{T}^{-1}\mathbf{A}\mathbf{u}_x = \mathbf{0}$, which is simply $\mathbf{T}^{-1}\mathbf{u}_t + \mathbf{\Lambda}\mathbf{T}^{-1}\mathbf{u}_x = \mathbf{0}$. By letting $\mathbf{v} = \mathbf{T}^{-1}\mathbf{u}$, we have the equivalent system

$$\mathbf{v}_t + \mathbf{\Lambda}\mathbf{v}_x = \mathbf{0},$$

in which each variable is now uncoupled as

$$\frac{\partial v_i}{\partial t} + \lambda_i \frac{\partial v_i}{\partial t} = 0 \qquad (14.16)$$

solutions to the
advection equation

for $i = 1, 2, \ldots, n$. We get the solution $v_i(t, x) = v_i(0, x - \lambda_i t)$ by using the method of characteristics. The initial conditions are given by $\mathbf{v}(0) = \mathbf{T}\mathbf{u}(0)$. Finally, setting $\mathbf{u}(t) = \mathbf{T}\mathbf{v}(t)$, we've solved the problem.

Now, let's solve the problem numerically. We can discretize the uncoupled system (14.16) using the upwind scheme

$$\frac{(V_i)_j^{n+1} - (V_i)_j^n}{k} + \frac{\lambda_i + |\lambda_i|}{2} \frac{(V_i)_j^n - (V_i)_{j-1}^n}{h} + \frac{\lambda_i - |\lambda_i|}{2} \frac{(V_i)_{j+1}^n - (V_i)_j^n}{h} = 0.$$

If we let $\mathbf{\Lambda}^+$ denote the diagonal matrix whose elements are $\frac{1}{2}(\lambda_i + |\lambda_i|)$ and $\mathbf{\Lambda}^-$ denote the diagonal matrix whose elements are $\frac{1}{2}(\lambda_i - |\lambda_i|)$, then uncoupled upwind scheme is the same as

$$\frac{\mathbf{V}_j^{n+1} - \mathbf{V}_j^n}{k} + \mathbf{\Lambda}^+ \frac{\mathbf{V}_j^n - \mathbf{V}_{j-1}^n}{h} + \mathbf{\Lambda}^- \frac{\mathbf{V}_{j+1}^n - \mathbf{V}_j^n}{h} = 0.$$

By making the substitution $\mathbf{U}_j^n = \mathbf{T}\mathbf{V}_j^n$ and defining $\mathbf{A}^\pm = \mathbf{T}\mathbf{\Lambda}^\pm\mathbf{T}^{-1}$, we can rewrite the above equation as

$$\frac{\mathbf{U}_j^{n+1} - \mathbf{U}_j^n}{k} + \mathbf{A}^+ \frac{\mathbf{U}_j^n - \mathbf{U}_{j-1}^n}{h} + \mathbf{A}^- \frac{\mathbf{U}_{j+1}^n - \mathbf{U}_j^n}{h} = 0$$

We call $\mathbf{A}^\pm = \mathbf{T}\mathbf{\Lambda}^\pm\mathbf{T}^{-1}$ the *characteristic decomposition*.

Let's extend the ideas developed for linear hyperbolic equations to nonlinear hyperbolic equations. Consider the equation

$$\frac{\partial}{\partial t}u + \frac{\partial}{\partial x}f(u) = 0 \tag{14.17}$$

for a function $u(t, x)$ with $u(0, x) = u_0(x)$ and a function $f(u)$ called the *flux*. Such an equation is called a *conservation law*. If we integrate it with respect to x, we have

$$\frac{\mathrm{d}}{\mathrm{d}t}\int_a^b u\,\mathrm{d}x + \int_a^b \frac{\partial}{\partial x}f(u)\,\mathrm{d}x = \frac{\mathrm{d}}{\mathrm{d}t}\int_a^b u\,\mathrm{d}x + \big(f(b) - f(a)\big) = 0.$$

If there is no net flux through the boundary, then $\frac{\mathrm{d}}{\mathrm{d}t}\int_a^b u\,\mathrm{d}x = 0$, from which it follows that $\int_a^b u\,\mathrm{d}x$ is constant. So, u is a conserved quantity.

If the flux $f(u)$ is differentiable, then we can apply the chain rule, and (14.17) becomes

$$\frac{\partial u}{\partial t} + f'(u)\frac{\partial u}{\partial x} = 0,$$

which can be solved using the method of characteristics

$$\frac{\mathrm{d}}{\mathrm{d}t}u(t, x(t)) = \frac{\partial u}{\partial t} + \frac{\mathrm{d}x}{\mathrm{d}t}\frac{\partial u}{\partial x} = \frac{\partial u}{\partial t} + f'(u)\frac{\partial u}{\partial x} = 0.$$

This expression says that the solution $u(t, x)$ is constant (a Riemann invariant) along the characteristics given by

$$\frac{dx}{dt} = f'(u).$$

Because u is invariant along $x(t)$, it follows that

$$\frac{dx}{dt} = f'(u(t, x(t))) = f'(u(0, x(0))) = f'(u_0(x_0)).$$

Integrating this equation, we see that the characteristics are straight lines

$$x(t) = f'(u_0(x_0))t + x_0,$$

and the solution is given by

$$u(t, x) = u_0(x - f'(u_0)t).$$

However, if $u(t, x)$ is not differentiable (or at least not Lipschitz continuous) at some point, the chain rule is no longer valid. Even if $u_0(x)$ is initially smooth, $u(t, x)$ may not necessarily be differentiable for all time if the flux is nonlinear. To see what happens when differentiability falls apart, we'll examine the inviscid Burgers equation, a toy model for fluid and gas dynamics.

▷ **Burgers' equation**

Burgers' equation $u_t + u u_x = \varepsilon u_{xx}$ is a simplification of the Navier–Stokes equation.[2] By neglecting the viscosity, we have the inviscid Burgers equation $u_t + u u_x = 0$. Furthermore, if the solution $u(t, x)$ remains differentiable, we can write Burgers' equation as a conservation law $u_t + f(u)_x = 0$ for a flux $\frac{1}{2}u^2$. We'll take the initial conditions $u(0, x) = u_0(x)$.

Formally, the variable wave speed u in the inviscid Burgers' equation plays the same role as the constant wave speed c in the linear hyperbolic equation $u_t + c u_x = 0$. The wave speed u is a Riemann invariant—the characteristics $x_0(t)$ are straight-line paths with slopes $dx/dt = u(0, x) = u_0(x)$ along which $u(t, x(t)) = u(0, x(0))$ is constant. The larger the value of $u_0(x)$, the faster the solution $u(t, x(t))$ moves; the smaller the value of $u_0(x)$, the slower the solution $u(t, x(t))$ moves.

Given the right initial conditions, it seems plausible that a fast-moving characteristic might eventually catch up with and overtake a slow-moving one. If a characteristic curve with a higher slope is to the left of one with a lower slope, then the two curves will intersect at some point. See Figure 14.2 on page 425 and

---

[2] Jan Burgers: "I have no objection to the use of the term 'Burgers equation' for the nonlinear heat flow equation (provided it is not written 'Burger's equation')."

the QR code at the bottom of this page. The solution at this point would then be multivalued because it comes from two (or possibly more) characteristic curves. Furthermore, at the moment when a multivalued solution in $u(t,x)$ appears, its derivative blows up, and the solution overturns.

We can find the point when the solution overturns by computing when the derivative first becomes infinite.

$$\frac{du}{dx} = \frac{du}{dx_0}\frac{dx_0}{dx} = u_0'(x_0)\left(\frac{dx}{dx_0}\right)^{-1} = \frac{u_0'(x)}{u_0'(x)t + 1} \tag{14.18}$$

If we set the right-hand side to infinity and solve for t, we have $t = -\left(u_0'(x_0)\right)^{-1}$. So, the time at which the solution first becomes multivalued is the infimum of $-\left(u_0'(x_0)\right)^{-1}$. The solution to Burgers' equation becomes singular if and only if the gradient of the initial distribution $u_0(x)$ is ever negative.

Can a faster-moving part really overtake a slower-moving part? No. A multivalued solution is both unphysical and mathematically ill-posed. So, something is wrong with either our formulation or our reasoning. We relied on the fact that $u(t,x)$ is smooth to apply the method of characteristics. But as soon as the derivative of $u(t,x)$ blows up, the method is invalidated. In the next section, we will look at how to solve the ill-posed problem.[3]

▷ Weak solutions

Burgers' equation using the method of characteristics is ill-posed when the solution is multivalued. We need to choose one solution with the most *physical* relevance. We do this mathematically by extending the solution as a "generalized weak solution." A weak solution allows us to solve a differential equation even when that solution is not differentiable. For something like Burgers' equation, this weak solution incorporates a type of discontinuity called a *shock*. To construct a weak solution of $u_t + f(u)_x = 0$, multiply the equation by a sufficiently smooth *test function* φ that vanishes at the boundaries; integrate over space and time; and finally, use integration by parts to pass the derivatives over to φ. There will be no boundary terms because φ vanishes at the boundaries. Essentially, we are using a well-behaved function φ to take the derivatives of $f(u)$ so that we can avoid differentiating $f(u)$, particularly when $f(u)$ becomes non-differentiable. This chapter uses weak solutions to determine an appropriate analytical solution. The next chapter will apply them numerically as the finite element method.

Suppose that we have a test function φ, which is differentiable and has compact support, meaning that the closure of the set over which φ is nonzero

---

[3] An alternative solution starts with the viscous Burgers equation $u_t + uu_x = \varepsilon u_{xx}$ and applies the Hopf–Cole transformation $u = -2\varepsilon\frac{d}{dx}(\log\phi)$, which changes the equation into a heat equation $\phi_t = \varepsilon\phi_{xx}$. The heat equation is solved as a fundamental solution to the Cauchy problem. Finally, the inviscid solution is expressed as the limit as $\varepsilon \to 0$.

multivalued and
weak solutions to
Burgers' equation

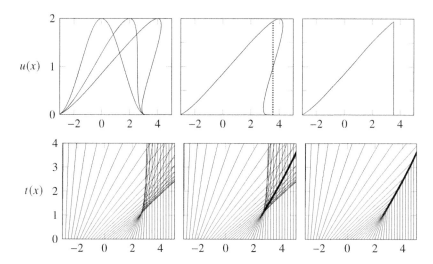

Figure 14.2: Top left: solutions u to Burgers' equation at $t = 0$ (initial shock formation), $t_c = 1$ (initial shock formation), and $t = 2$ (unphysical multivalued solution). Top right: weak solution at $t = 2$. Bottom: characteristic curves $x(t)$.

is bounded. Notably, φ is zero at the boundaries, where we need it to be zero. We denote this by $\varphi = C_0^1(\Omega)$. The C^1 denotes that the function and its first derivative are continuous, and the subscript 0 denotes that the function has compact support over the region $\Omega = \{(x, t)\} \subset \mathbb{R}^2$. In this case, $u_t + f(u)_x = 0$ implies

$$\iint_\Omega \left(\varphi u_t + \varphi f(u)_x\right) \mathrm{d}x\, \mathrm{d}t = 0.$$

We integrate by parts to get

$$\iint_\Omega \left(\varphi_t u + \varphi_x f(u)\right) \mathrm{d}x\, \mathrm{d}t = 0.$$

If this equation holds for all $\varphi \in C_0^1(\Omega)$, then we say that $u(t, x)$ is a *weak solution* of $u_t + f(u)_x = 0$. If $u(t, x)$ is smooth, the weak solution is the classical or *strong solution*.

Consider an arbitrary curve PQ dividing Ω into subdomains Ω_1 and Ω_2.

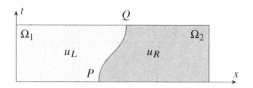

If $u(t, x)$ is a weak solution to $u_t + f(u)_x = 0$, then

$$0 = -\iint_\Omega \varphi u_t + \varphi f(u)_x \, dx \, dt + \iint_\Omega \varphi u_t + \varphi f(u)_x \, dx \, dt$$

$$= \iint_\Omega \varphi_t u + \varphi_x f(u) \, dx \, dt + \iint_\Omega \varphi u_t + \varphi f(u)_x \, dx \, dt$$

Because φ vanishes on the boundary:

$$= \iint_\Omega (\varphi u)_t + (\varphi f(u))_x \, dx \, dt$$

$$= \iint_{\Omega_1} (\varphi u)_t + (\varphi f(u))_x \, dx \, dt + \iint_{\Omega_2} (\varphi u)_t + (\varphi f(u))_x \, dx \, dt.$$

By Green's theorem:

$$= \int_{\partial \Omega_1} -\varphi u \, dx + \varphi f(u) \, dt + \int_{\partial \Omega_2} -\varphi u \, dx + \varphi f(u) \, dt.$$

Because $\varphi(\partial \Omega) = 0$:

$$= \int_P^Q -\varphi u_L \, dx + \varphi f(u_L) \, dt + \int_Q^P -\varphi u_R \, dx + \varphi f(u_R) \, dt$$

$$= \int_P^Q \varphi (u_R - u_L) \, dx - \varphi \left(f(u_R) - f(u_L) \right) \, dt,$$

where u_L is the value of u along PQ from the left and u_R is the value of u along PQ from the right. So, for all test functions $\varphi \in C_0^1(\Omega)$,

$$(u_R - u_L) \, dx - (f(u_R) - f(u_L)) \, dt = 0$$

along PQ. Therefore,

$$s = \frac{dx}{dt} = \frac{f(u_R) - f(u_L)}{u_R - u_L}.$$

This expression is called the *Rankine–Hugoniot jump condition* for shocks, and s is called the *shock speed*. Note that in the limit as $u_L \to u_R$, the shock speed $s \to f'(u)$. To simplify notation, one often uses brackets to indicate difference:

$$s = \frac{f(u_R) - f(u_L)}{u_R - u_L} \equiv \frac{[f]}{[u]}.$$

We can now continue to use the PDE with the weak solution.

▷ The Riemann problem

A *Riemann problem* is an initial value problem with initial data given by two constant states separated by a discontinuity. For the advection equation, it is

$$\frac{\partial u}{\partial t} + \frac{\partial}{\partial x} f(u) = 0 \quad \text{with} \quad u(0, x) = \begin{cases} u_L & x < 0 \\ u_R & x > 0 \end{cases}. \tag{14.19}$$

Notice that if we scale t and x both by a positive constant c, i.e., if we take $\hat{t} = ct$ and $\hat{x} = cx$, then the scaled problem is identical to the original problem

$$\frac{\partial u}{\partial \hat{t}} + \frac{\partial}{\partial \hat{x}} f(u) = 0 \quad \text{with} \quad u(0, \hat{x}) = \begin{cases} u_L & \hat{x} < 0 \\ u_R & \hat{x} > 0 \end{cases}.$$

This symmetry suggests an ansatz for the problem. We'll look for a *self-similar solution* to Burgers' equation to simplify the two-variable PDE into a one-variable ODE. Let $\zeta = x/t = \hat{x}/\hat{t}$. Taking $u(t, x) = u(\zeta)$ in Burgers' equation,

$$0 = u_t + \left(\tfrac{1}{2} u^2 \right)_x = \zeta_t u' + \zeta_x u u' = \left(-\frac{x}{t^2} \right) u' + \left(\frac{1}{t} \right) u u'.$$

Multiplying by t and replacing x/t by ζ, we have

$$-\zeta u' + u u' = u'(u - \zeta) = 0.$$

Either $u' = 0$, in which case $u(x)$ is constant; or $u = \zeta$, in which case $u(t, x) = x/t$. The solution may also be a piecewise combination of these solutions. Let's consider the two cases: when $u_L > u_R$ and when $u_L < u_R$.

1. If $u_L > u_R$, then the Rankine–Hugoniot condition says

$$s = \frac{\tfrac{1}{2} u_R^2 - \tfrac{1}{2} u_L^2}{u_R - u_L} = \tfrac{1}{2}(u_R + u_L),$$

and the exact solution to the Riemann problem is

$$u(t, x) = \begin{cases} u_L, & \text{if } x/t < s \\ u_R, & \text{if } x/t > s \end{cases}$$

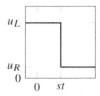

2. If $u_L < u_R$, then one exact solution is

$$u(t,x) = \begin{cases} u_L, & \text{if } x/t < s \\ u_R, & \text{if } x/t > s \end{cases}$$

where $s = (u_R + u_L)/2$ is given by the Rankine–Hugoniot condition.
Another solution is

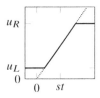

$$u(t,x) = \begin{cases} u_L, & \text{if } x/t < u_L \\ x/t, & \text{if } u_L < x/t < u_R \\ u_R, & \text{if } x/t > u_R \end{cases}$$

A third solution is

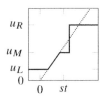

$$u(t,x) = \begin{cases} u_L, & \text{if } x/t < u_L \\ x/t, & \text{if } u_L < x/t < u_M \\ u_M, & \text{if } u_M < x/t < s \\ u_R & \text{if } x/t > s \end{cases}$$

where $s = (u_R + u_M)/2$ is given by the Rankine–Hugoniot condition.

In fact, there are *infinitely* many weak solutions. What is the *physically* permissible weak solution? To find it, we need to impose another condition. Physically, there is a quantity called *entropy*, which is a constant along smooth particle trajectories but jumps to a higher value across a discontinuity. The mathematical definition of entropy $\varphi(u)$ is the negative of physical entropy. For the problem $u_t + f(u)_x = 0$ where $f(u)$ is the convex flux, a solution satisfies the *Lax entropy condition*

$$f'(u_L) > s \equiv \frac{f(u_R) - f(u_L)}{u_R - u_L} > f'(u_R).$$

The Lax entropy condition says that the characteristics with speeds $f'(u_R)$ and $f'(u_L)$ must intersect the shock with speed s from both sides. For Burgers' equation $f(u) = \frac{1}{2}u^2$, so $f'(u) = u$.

1. If $u_L > u_R$, then $f'(u_L) = u_L > \frac{1}{2}(u_R + u_L) > u_R = f'(u_R)$. Therefore, the solution is an entropy shock.

2. If $u_L < u_R$, then the shock does not satisfy the entropy condition. So the only possible weak solution is a continuous, rarefaction wave.

Example.   We can model traffic using a nonlinear hyperbolic equation. Suppose that we have a single-lane road without any on- or off-ramps (no sources or sinks).

Let $\rho(t,x)$ be the density of cars measured in cars per car length. A density $\rho = 0$ says that the road is completely empty, and a density $\rho = 1$ says there is bumper-to-bumper traffic. Then

$$\frac{\partial \rho}{\partial t} + \frac{\partial}{\partial x} f(\rho) = 0$$

models the traffic flow, where the flux $f(\rho)$ tells us the density of cars passing a given point in a given time interval (number of cars per second). We can define flux $f(\rho) = u(\rho)\rho$, where $u(\rho)$ simply tells us the speed of each car as a function of traffic density. Let's make a couple of reasonable assumptions to model $u(\rho)$:

1. Everyone travels as fast as possible while still obeying the speed limit u_{max}.

2. Everyone keeps a safe distance behind the car ahead of them and adjusts their speed accordingly. Drive as fast as possible if there are no other cars on the road. Stop moving if traffic is bumper-to-bumper.

In this case, the simplest model for $u(\rho)$ is $u(\rho) = u_{max}(1 - \rho)$. Notice that the flux $f(\rho) = u(\rho)\rho = u_{max}(\rho - \rho^2)$ is zero when the roads are empty (there are no cars to move) and when the roads are full (no one is moving). The flux $f(\rho)$ is maximum at $f'(\rho) = u_{max}(1 - 2\rho) = 0$ when $\rho = \frac{1}{2}$ (the roads are half-full with the cars traveling at $\frac{1}{2}u_{max}$, half the posted speed limit). Our traffic equation is now

$$\frac{\partial \rho}{\partial t} + \frac{\partial}{\partial x}(u_{max}(1 - \rho)\rho) = 0.$$

This equation is very similar in form to Burgers' equation. Consider two simple examples: cars approaching a red stoplight and cars leaving after the stoplight turns green. Both of these examples are Riemann problems.

Red light. We imagine several cars traveling with density ρ_L approaching a queue of stopped cars with density $\rho_R = 1$. In this case

$$\rho(x,0) = \begin{cases} \rho_L, & x < 0 \\ \rho_R = 1, & x \geq 0. \end{cases}$$

The Rankine–Hugoniot relationship says

$$s = \frac{f(\rho_L) - f(\rho_R)}{\rho_L - \rho_R} = \frac{u_{max}\rho_L(1 - \rho_L) - 0}{\rho_L - 1} = -u_{max}\rho_L.$$

There is a shock wave moving backward as the cars queue up.

Green light. We imagine several cars in a queue with $\rho = 1$ and speed $u_L = 0$. This time the Lax entropy condition tells us that there is a rarefaction wave. The leading car moves forwards with speed u_{max}, and a rarefaction wave moves backward with speed $f'(\rho) = u_{max}(1 - 2\rho)$ with $\rho = 1$, i.e., speed $f'(1) = -u_{max}$. See Figure 14.3 on the following page. ◀

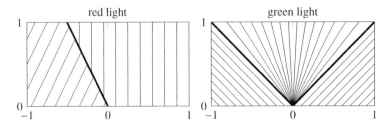

Figure 14.3: Characteristics for traffic flow with $\rho_L = \frac{1}{2}$.

14.5   Hyperbolic systems of conservation laws

Let's extend the discussion of one-dimensional nonlinear equations to a system of n one-dimensional nonlinear conservation laws

$$\frac{\partial \mathbf{u}}{\partial t} + \frac{\partial}{\partial x} \mathbf{f}(\mathbf{u}) = 0, \tag{14.20}$$

with $\mathbf{u}(0, x) = \mathbf{u}_0(x)$, where $\mathbf{u} = (u_1, u_2, \ldots, u_n)$ and $\mathbf{f}(\mathbf{u}) = (f_1, f_2, \ldots, f_n)$. We can write this system in quasilinear form

$$\frac{\partial \mathbf{u}}{\partial t} + \mathbf{f}'(\mathbf{u}) \frac{\partial \mathbf{u}}{\partial x} = 0,$$

where the Jacobian $\mathbf{f}'(\mathbf{u})$ has elements $\partial f_i / \partial u_j$. If the Jacobian $\mathbf{f}'(\mathbf{u})$ has n real eigenvalues and hence a complete set of linearly independent eigenvectors, then the system (14.20) is called *hyperbolic*. In this case, there is an invertible map $\mathbf{T}(\mathbf{u})$ such that $\mathbf{T}^{-1}\mathbf{f}'\mathbf{T} = \mathbf{\Lambda} = \mathrm{diag}(\lambda_1, \lambda_2, \ldots, \lambda_n)$. The eigenvalues λ_i are the characteristic speeds, and $\mathbf{T}$ is the matrix of eigenvectors.

Example.   Let's examine the one-dimensional shallow water equations and show that they form a hyperbolic system. The shallow water equations are

$$h_t + (hu)_x = 0 \tag{14.21a}$$

$$(hu)_t + \left(hu^2 + \tfrac{1}{2}gh^2\right)_x = 0, \tag{14.21b}$$

where g is the gravitational acceleration, h is the height of the water, and u is the velocity of the water. The mass of a column of water is proportional to its height, and we can let $m = hu$ denote the momentum. Then (14.21) becomes

$$h_t + m_x = 0$$

$$m_t + \frac{2m}{h} m_x - \frac{m^2}{h^2} h_x + ghh_x = 0,$$

which can be written as

$$\begin{bmatrix} h \\ m \end{bmatrix}_t + \begin{bmatrix} 0 & 1 \\ gh - u^2 & 2u \end{bmatrix} \begin{bmatrix} h \\ m \end{bmatrix}_x = \begin{bmatrix} 0 \\ 0 \end{bmatrix}.$$

The eigenvalues of the Jacobian matrix $\mathbf{f}'(\mathbf{u})$ are given by the zeros of

$$\begin{vmatrix} -\lambda & 1 \\ gh - u^2 & 2u - \lambda \end{vmatrix} = \lambda^2 - 2u\lambda + u^2 - gh.$$

So $\lambda_\pm = u \pm \sqrt{gh}$. If the height of the water h is positive, then there are two real eigenvalues, and the system is strictly hyperbolic.

The two eigenvalues give us the characteristic speeds for the shallow water equation. Notably, the speed of water waves is a function of the depth of the water h along with the velocity of the current u. For example, a tsunami occurs when a disturbance creates an ocean wave with a wavelength of a hundred or more kilometers and a displacement of a meter or less. The wave travels quickly in the ocean, where the depth may be several kilometers—the speed is $\sqrt{gh}$. Once it reaches the continental shelf, where the depth decreases dramatically, the wave slows considerably, and the height of the wave grows. A shock forms as the faster characteristics intersect the slower characteristics.

Refraction of water waves is also caused by the $\sqrt{gh}$ speed dependence. Ocean waves turn to hit the beach perpendicularly even when the wind is not blowing straight into shore. Waves are produced by a Kelvin–Helmholtz instability resulting from the wind blowing over the water's surface. In the deeper water, waves are driven in the direction of the wind. When they reach shallow water, the wave moves at different speeds. The part of the wave in shallower water moves slower than the part in deeper, turning the wave into shore.   ◀

▷ Riemann invariants

Let's recap what we've discussed so far about Riemann invariants. Information is advected along characteristics, and the quantity that is constant along a characteristic curve is called the *Riemann invariant*. For the advection equation $u_t + cu_x = 0$, the characteristics are given by $dx/dt = c$, and the Riemann invariant is u. For a general scalar conservation law $u_t + f(u)_x = 0$, we have $u_t + f'(u)u_x = 0$ when u is differentiable. The characteristics are given by $dx/dt = f'(u)$, and it follows that

$$\frac{d}{dt}u(t, x(t)) = \frac{\partial u}{\partial t} + \frac{dx}{dt}\frac{\partial u}{\partial x} = \frac{\partial u}{\partial t} + f'(u)\frac{\partial u}{\partial x} = 0.$$

So $u(t, x)$ is the Riemann invariant.

For systems of conservation laws, it's a little more complicated. Once again consider the system

$$\frac{\partial \mathbf{u}}{\partial t} + \frac{\partial}{\partial x}\mathbf{f}(\mathbf{u}) = 0$$

with $\mathbf{u} \in \mathbb{R}^n$. If $\mathbf{u}$ is differentiable,

$$\frac{\partial \mathbf{u}}{\partial t} + \mathbf{f}'(\mathbf{u}) \frac{\partial \mathbf{u}}{\partial x} = \mathbf{0} \qquad (14.23)$$

where $\mathbf{f}'$ is the Jacobian matrix of $\mathbf{f}$ with real eigenvalues $\{\lambda_1, \lambda_2, \dots, \lambda_n\}$. Let $\nabla_{\mathbf{u}} w_i$—for some $w(\mathbf{u})$—be the *left eigenvector* of $\mathbf{f}'(\mathbf{u})$ corresponding to the eigenvalues λ_i. Then left multiplying (14.23) by $\nabla_{\mathbf{u}} w_i$ yields

$$\nabla_{\mathbf{u}} w_i \frac{\partial \mathbf{u}}{\partial t} + \nabla_{\mathbf{u}} w_i \mathbf{f}'(\mathbf{u}) \frac{\partial \mathbf{u}}{\partial x} = \mathbf{0}.$$

Because $\nabla_{\mathbf{u}} w_i$ is the left eigenvector of $\mathbf{f}'(\mathbf{u})$, it follows that

$$\nabla_{\mathbf{u}} w_i \frac{\partial \mathbf{u}}{\partial t} + \lambda_i \nabla_{\mathbf{u}} w_i \frac{\partial \mathbf{u}}{\partial x} = \mathbf{0}.$$

And by the chain rule, we have

$$\frac{\partial w_i}{\partial t} + \lambda_i \frac{\partial w_i}{\partial x} = \mathbf{0}, \qquad (14.24)$$

which is simply the scalar advection equation. So w_i is a Riemann invariant because it is constant along the characteristic curve given by $dx/dt = \lambda_i$. Notice that (14.24) is the diagonalization of the original system.

Example.   Let's find the Riemann invariants for the shallow water equations. The Jacobian matrix

$$\mathbf{f}' = \begin{bmatrix} 0 & 1 \\ gh - u^2 & 2u \end{bmatrix}$$

has eigenvalues $\lambda_\pm = u \pm \sqrt{gh}$. We compute the left eigenvectors to be $(u \mp \sqrt{gh}, 1)$. Recall that we defined $\mathbf{u} = (h, m)$ with $m = hu$. In terms of h and m, the eigenvectors are $(mh^{-1} \mp \sqrt{gh}, 1)$. We need these vectors to be exact differentials, so let's rescale them by $1/h$. We now have

$$\nabla_{\mathbf{u}} w_\pm = \left(\frac{m}{h^2} \mp \sqrt{\frac{g}{h}}, \frac{1}{h} \right).$$

So the Riemann invariants are

$$w_\pm(h, m) = \frac{m}{h} \mp 2\sqrt{gh} = u \mp 2\sqrt{gh},$$

which are constant along the characteristics $dx/dt = u \pm \sqrt{gh}$.   ◀

▷ Open boundary conditions

The advection equation $u_t + cu_x = 0$ has one space derivative, so it needs one influx boundary condition for uniqueness. A hyperbolic system of conservation laws (14.20) with n equations needs n boundary conditions.

Often we want to solve the shallow water equations or the Euler equations using open boundary conditions. For example, we may want to prescribe inflow boundary conditions to model incoming water waves in the ocean. Or we may want to model airflow over an airfoil by injecting a flow upwind of the airfoil. We want the gas to escape the domain downwind of the airfoil without reflecting back into our calculations. Or maybe we may want to model a bomb blast in the semi-infinite domain above the ground. Without an open boundary, information will likely be reflected back into our domain of interest, polluting our solution. It is typically a bad idea to force the boundary to be equal to the external data because the external data does not perfectly match the information leaving the domain.

A straightforward fix is to use a larger domain and stop computation before the reflected information pollutes the solution—effectively putting the boundaries outside the domain of dependence. We could also use a thin sponge layer with added viscosity to absorb energy at the boundary. Another approach, developed by Björn Enquist and Andrew Majda in 1977, creates an artificial boundary that tries to match the reflected waves with waves of opposite amplitude.

We'll examine a characteristics-based approach to implementing open boundary conditions over the next several paragraphs. Recall that the Riemann invariant is constant along a characteristic. For the shallow water equation, we have the Riemann invariant $w_+ = u - 2\sqrt{gh}$ along the characteristic of slope $u + \sqrt{gh}$ and the Riemann invariant $w_- = u + 2\sqrt{gh}$ along the characteristic of slope $u - \sqrt{gh}$. We'll match the Riemann invariants of the two characteristics intersecting at each boundary. We can then determine u and h using the values of the Riemann invariants:

$$u = (w_- + w_+)/2 \qquad \text{and} \qquad h = (w_-^2 - w_+^2)/16g.$$

Take the boundaries at $x = x_L$ and $x = x_R$, and suppose that the external values are given by $h(t, x_L) = h_L$ and $u(t, x_L) = u_L$ on the left and $h(t, x_R) = h_R$ and $u(t, x_R) = u_R$ on the right. Let's partition the domain into m gridpoints at $\{x_1, x_2, \ldots, x_m\}$. If $|u| < \sqrt{gh}$, then the characteristics travel in opposite directions. We'll use extrapolated values to compute the Riemann invariant for the characteristic leaving the domain, and we'll use the boundary values to compute the Riemann invariant for the characteristic entering the domain. So, on the left boundary of the domain

$$w_- = \text{extrapolation of } u + 2\sqrt{gh} \qquad \text{and} \qquad w_+ = u_L - 2\sqrt{gh_L}.$$

To determine w_- at x_0 with second-order accuracy, we extrapolate

$$w_- = (2U_1 - U_2) + 2\sqrt{g(2H_1 - H_2)},$$

where H_i and U_i are the numerical solutions for h and u at x_i. The value $w_+ = u_L - 2\sqrt{gh_L}$ is set according to the external values u_L and h_L. Similarly, on the right boundary of the domain

$$w_- = u_R + 2\sqrt{gh_R} \qquad \text{and} \qquad w_+ = \text{extrapolation of } u - 2\sqrt{gh}.$$

To determine w_+ at x_{m+1} with second-order accuracy, we extrapolate

$$w_+ = (2U_m - U_{m-1}) - 2\sqrt{g(2H_m - H_{m-1})}.$$

The value $w_- = u_R + 2\sqrt{gh_R}$ is set according to the external values u_R and h_R.

If $|u| > \sqrt{gh}$, then both characteristics travel in the same direction, and we match both Riemann invariants on the influx boundary and extrapolate both Riemann invariants on the outflux boundary.

▷ **The Riemann problem**

First-order Godonov schemes approximate a problem using a series of Riemann problems—one for every mesh point in space. These Riemann problems are solved analytically, and the resulting solutions are numerically remeshed. The solution to the Riemann problem is good as long as characteristics don't cross—which happens to determine the CFL condition.

The Riemann problem for a system of hyperbolic equations

$$\mathbf{u}_t + \mathbf{f}(\mathbf{u})_x = 0 \qquad \text{with} \qquad \mathbf{u}(x,0) = \begin{cases} \mathbf{u}_L, & x < 0 \\ \mathbf{u}_R, & x > 0 \end{cases}$$

can be solved analytically using a self-similar solution by taking the ansatz $\mathbf{u}(t,x) = \mathbf{u}(x/t) = \mathbf{u}(\zeta)$. Then

$$\left(-\frac{x}{t^2}\right)\mathbf{u}' + \frac{1}{t}\mathbf{f}'(\mathbf{u})\mathbf{u}' = 0,$$

from which we have

$$(\mathbf{f}'(\mathbf{u}) - \zeta\mathbf{I})\,\mathbf{u}' = 0.$$

So either $\mathbf{u}' = 0$ in which case $\mathbf{u}$ is constant in ζ or $\det(\mathbf{f}'(\mathbf{u}) - \zeta\mathbf{I}) = 0$ in which case ζ is an eigenvalue of $\mathbf{f}'(\mathbf{u})$. The solution is piecewise constant connected by shocks or rarefactions when $\mathbf{u}' = 0$. The solution associated with $\det(\mathbf{f}'(\mathbf{u}) - \zeta\mathbf{I}) = 0$ is a *contact discontinuity* that travels with characteristic speed ζ. Unlike shock discontinuities, across which there is mass flow, contact discontinuities are merely discontinuities that flow with the fluid. Think of the surface separating two different types of fluids that move together.

14.6   Methods for nonlinear hyperbolic systems

A discretization U_j is *conservative* if $\sum_{j=1}^{m} U_j$ is constant in time. Equivalently, a scheme is conservative if it can be written as

$$\frac{\partial}{\partial t} U_j + \frac{F_{j+1/2} - F_{j-1/2}}{h} = 0, \tag{14.25}$$

where $F_{j+1/2}$ is the numerical flux. In this case, by summing (14.25) over all gridpoints, it follows that $\frac{\partial}{\partial t} \sum_{j=1}^{m} U_j = 0$ if there is no net numerical flux through the boundaries. In a foundational 1959 paper, Peter Lax and Burton Wendroff proved their Lax–Wendroff theorem: if a consistent, conservative scheme converges, then it converges to the weak solution of a conservation law.

In particular, we can rewrite the nonlinear Lax–Friedrichs method

$$\frac{U_j^{n+1} - \frac{1}{2}(U_{j+1}^n + U_{j-1}^n)}{k} + \frac{f(U_{j+1}^n) - f(U_{j-1}^n)}{2h} = 0$$

in conservative form

$$\frac{U_j^{n+1} - U_j^n}{k} + \frac{F_{j+1/2}^n - F_{j-1/2}^n}{h} = 0$$

where the numerical flux

$$F_{j+1/2}^n = \frac{f(U_{j+1}^n) + f(U_j^n)}{2} - \frac{h^2}{2k} \frac{U_{j+1}^n - U_j^n}{h}.$$

Recall from the discussion on page 417 that the second term adds artificial viscosity to an otherwise unstable central difference scheme. However, the diffusion coefficient $\alpha = h^2/2k$ tends to make the Lax–Friedrichs scheme overly diffusive. The coefficient of the diffusion term is bounded below by the CFL condition for the Lax–Friedrichs method, which states that h/k must be greater than the characteristic speed. In other words, the diffusion coefficient is bounded below by the norm of the Jacobian matrix $\frac{1}{2}h\|\mathbf{f}'(\mathbf{u})\|$. We can take the magnitude of the largest eigenvalue as a suitable matrix norm. Because we need just enough viscosity to counter the effect of $f'(U_{j+1/2})$, we can lessen the artificial viscosity in the Lax–Friedrichs method by choosing a local diffusion coefficient $\alpha_{j+1/2}$ to be the maximum of $\|\mathbf{f}'(\mathbf{u})\|$ for $\mathbf{u}$ in the interval (U_j, U_{j+1}). Such an approach to defining the numerical flux

$$F_{j+1/2}^n = \frac{f(U_{j+1}^n) + f(U_j^n)}{2} - \alpha_{j+1/2} \frac{U_{j+1}^n - U_j^n}{h}$$

where

$$\alpha_{j+1/2} = \tfrac{1}{2}h \max_{\mathbf{u} \in (U_j, U_{j+1})} \|\mathbf{f}'(\mathbf{u})\|$$

is called the *local Lax–Friedrichs method*. The Lax–Wendroff method defines the diffusion coefficient of the artificial viscosity term as

$$\alpha_{j+1/2} = \tfrac{1}{2}k \left\| \mathbf{f}'(U_{j+1/2}) \right\|^2$$

where the Jacobian matrix is evaluated at $U_{j+1/2} = \frac{1}{2}(U_{j+1} + U_j)$.

▷ Finite volume methods

Rather than solving the problem using Taylor series expansion in the form of a finite difference scheme, we can instead use an integral formulation called a *finite volume method*. In such a method, we consider breaking the domain into cells centered at $x_{j+1/2} = \frac{1}{2}(x_{j+1} + x_j)$ with boundaries at x_j and x_{j+1}. We then compute the flux through the cell boundaries to determine the change inside the cell. Finite volume methods are especially useful in two and three dimensions when the mesh can be irregularly shaped.

The problem $u_t + f(u)_x = 0$ where $u \equiv u(t, x)$ is equivalent to

$$\frac{1}{kh} \int_{t_n}^{t_{n+1}} \int_{x_{j-1/2}}^{x_{j+1/2}} (u_t + f(u)_x) \, dx \, dt = 0,$$

which in turn can be integrated to be

$$\frac{1}{kh} \int_{x_{j-1/2}}^{x_{j+1/2}} u(t, x) \Big|_{t_n}^{t_{n+1}} dx + \frac{1}{kh} \int_{t_n}^{t_{n+1}} f(u(t, x)) \Big|_{x_{j-1/2}}^{x_{j+1/2}} dt = 0$$

or simply

$$\int_{x_{j-1/2}}^{x_{j+1/2}} u(t_{n+1}, x) \, dx - \int_{x_{j-1/2}}^{x_{j+1/2}} u(t_n, x) \, dx$$

$$+ \int_{t^n}^{t^{n+1}} f(u(t, x_{j+1/2})) \, dt - \int_{t^n}^{t^{n+1}} f(u(t, x_{j-1/2})) \, dt = 0. \qquad (14.26)$$

Physically, this says that the change in mass of a cell from time t_n to time t_{n+1} equals the flux through the boundaries at $x_{j+1/2}$ and $x_{j-1/2}$. Let's define

$$U_j^n = \frac{1}{h} \int_{x_{j-1/2}}^{x_{j+1/2}} u(t_n, x) \, dx$$

and the flux at $x_{j+1/2}$ over the time interval $[t_n, t_{n+1}]$ to be

$$F_{j+1/2}^{n+1/2} = \frac{1}{k} \int_{t_n}^{t_{n+1}} f(u(t, x_{j+1/2})) \, dt.$$

Think of u as density and U as mass, and think of f as flux density and F as flux. Then we have

$$\frac{U_j^{n+1} - U_j^n}{k} + \frac{F_{j+1/2}^{n+1/2} - F_{j-1/2}^{n+1/2}}{h} = 0. \tag{14.27}$$

Now, we just need appropriate numerical approximations for these integrals.

For a first-order approximation, we simply take piecewise-constant approximations $u(t, x)$ in the cells. Then

$$U_j^n = \frac{1}{2}\left(U_{j-1/2}^n + U_{j+1/2}^n\right)$$

by the midpoint rule and

$$F_{j+1/2}^{n+1/2} = f\left(U_{j+1/2}^n\right).$$

This gives us a staggered version of the Lax–Friedrichs scheme

$$\frac{U_{j+1/2}^{n+1} - \frac{1}{2}\left(U_j^n + U_{j+1}^n\right)}{k} + \frac{f\left(U_{j+1}^n\right) - f\left(U_j^n\right)}{h} = 0.$$

The CFL condition is given by $k \le h|\lambda_{\max}|$, where $\lambda_{\max}$ is the largest eigenvalue of the Jacobian $f'(u)$. Recall that approximating $U_{j+1/2}^n$ using $\frac{1}{2}\left(U_j^n + U_{j+1}^n\right)$ introduces numerical viscosity into the solution.

We need to use piecewise linear approximations to extend the method to second order (Nessyahu and Tadmor [1990]). Define

$$P_j(x) = U_j^n + \tfrac{\partial}{\partial x}U_j^n \cdot (x - x_j)$$

where $\frac{\partial}{\partial x}U_j^n$ is a slope and $x \in [x_j, x_{j+1}]$. We can approximate

$$U_{j+1/2}^n = \frac{1}{h}\int_{x_j}^{x_{j+1/2}} P_j(x)\,dx + \frac{1}{h}\int_{x_j}^{x_{j+1/2}} P_{j+1}(x)\,dx$$

$$= \frac{1}{2}\left(U_j^n + U_{j+1}^n\right) + \frac{1}{8}h\left(\tfrac{\partial}{\partial x}U_j^n - \tfrac{\partial}{\partial x}U_{j+1}^n\right).$$

From (14.27), we have

$$U_{j+1/2}^{n+1} = \frac{1}{2}\left(U_j^n + U_{j+1}^n\right) + \frac{1}{8}h\left(\tfrac{\partial}{\partial x}U_j^n - \tfrac{\partial}{\partial x}U_{j+1}^n\right) - \frac{k}{h}\left(F_{j+1}^{n+1/2} - F_j^{n+1/2}\right).$$

We still need a second-order approximation for the flux $F_j^{n+1/2}$. Using the midpoint rule,

$$F_j^{n+1/2} = \frac{1}{k}\int_{t_n}^{t_{n+1}} f(u(t, x_j))\,dt \approx f(u(t_{n+1/2}, x_j)),$$

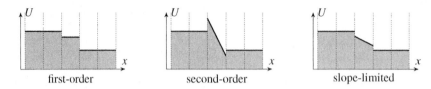

Figure 14.4: A second-order method may introduce oscillations near a discontinuity. A slope limiter is used to minimize oscillations.

with

$$u(t_{n+1/2}, x_j) \approx u(t_n, x_j) + \frac{k}{2}\frac{\partial}{\partial t}u(t_n, x_j) = u(t_n, x_j) - \frac{k}{2}\frac{\partial}{\partial x}f(u(t_n, x_j)),$$

where we use $u_t + f(u)_x = 0$ for the equality above. This approximation gives us the staggered, two-step predictor-corrector method

$$U_j^{n+1/2} = U_j^n - \frac{k}{2}\frac{\partial}{\partial x}f(U_j^n)$$

$$U_{j+1/2}^{n+1} = \frac{1}{2}\left(U_j^n + U_{j+1}^n\right) + \frac{h}{8}\left(\frac{\partial}{\partial x}U_j^n - \frac{\partial}{\partial x}U_{j+1}^n\right) - \frac{k}{h}\left(f(U_{j+1}^{n+1/2}) - f(U_j^{n+1/2})\right).$$

Fitting a higher-order polynomial to a discontinuity introduces oscillations into the solution. Because of this, we need to use slope limiters to approximate the slopes $\frac{\partial}{\partial x}U_j$ and $\frac{\partial}{\partial x}f(U_j)$. For $\frac{\partial}{\partial x}U_j$, we define the slope σ_j to be

$$\sigma_j = \frac{U_{j+1} - U_j}{h}\phi(\theta_j) \quad \text{with} \quad \theta_j = \frac{U_j - U_{j-1}}{U_{j+1} - U_j},$$

where two common limiting functions are the minmod and the van Leer:

minmod $\qquad\qquad \phi(\theta) = \max(0, \min(1, \theta))$

van Leer $\qquad\qquad \phi(\theta) = \dfrac{|\theta| + \theta}{1 + |\theta|}$

The van Leer slope limiter gives a sharper shock than the minmod slope limiter. A slope limiter works by reducing a second-order method (which is typically dispersive) to a first-order method (which is typically dissipative) wherever there appears to be an oscillation, e.g., whenever $U_j - U_{j-1}$ and $U_{j+1} - U_j$ have opposite signs. While the slope limiter removes oscillations and stabilizes the solution, it reduces the method to a first-order approximation near an oscillation. Hence, near discontinuities, we can get at best first-order and, more typically, half-order convergence. To get higher orders, one may use essentially non-oscillatory (ENO) interpolation schemes introduced by Chi-Wang Shu and Stanley Osher in 1988.

Notice that σ_j is a symmetric function of U_{j-1}, U_j and U_{j+1}. That is,

$$\frac{U_{j+1} - U_j}{h} \phi\left(\frac{U_j - U_{j-1}}{U_{j+1} - U_j}\right) = \frac{U_j - U_{j-1}}{h} \phi\left(\frac{U_{j+1} - U_j}{U_j - U_{j-1}}\right).$$

The slope limiter as written above is undefined whenever $U_{j+1} = U_j$. Because this happens precisely when we want the slope to be zero, we can fix it by adding a conditional expression (a promoted BitArray) as in the following code

```
ΔU = [0;diff(U)]
s = @. ΔU*ϕ( [ΔU[2:end];0]/(ΔU + (ΔU==0)) )
```

Notice that ΔU is padded with a zero on the left and then on the right so that s has the same number of elements as U.

    Julia has several packages for modeling and solving hyperbolic problems. Trixi.jl is a numerical simulation framework for hyperbolic conservation laws. Kinetic.jl is a toolbox for the study of computational fluid dynamics and scientific machine learning. Oceananigans.jl is a fluid flow solver for modeling ocean dynamics. ViscousFlow.jl models viscous incompressible flows around bodies of various shapes.

14.7 Exercises

14.1. Show that the error of the Lax–Friedrichs scheme is $O(k + h^2/k)$. Compute the dispersion relation. Taking the CFL condition and numerical viscosity into consideration, how should we best choose h and k to minimize error?   ◿

14.2. Solve the advection equation $u_t + u_x = 0$, with initial conditions $u(0,x) = 1$ if $|x - \frac{1}{2}| < \frac{1}{4}$ and $u(0,x) = 0$ otherwise, using the upwind scheme and the Lax–Wendroff scheme. Use the domain $x \in [0,1]$ with periodic boundary conditions. Compare the solutions at $t = 1$.

14.3. Consider a finite difference scheme for the linear hyperbolic equation $u_t + cu_x = 0$ that uses the following stencil (leapfrog in time and central difference in space):

Determine the order and stability conditions for a consistent scheme. Discuss whether the scheme is dispersive or dissipative. How does dispersion or dissipation affect the scheme's stability? Show that you can derive this scheme starting with (14.5) and counteracting the unstable term.   ◿

14.4. Consider a finite difference scheme for $u_t + u_x = 0$ that uses a fourth-order central difference approximation for u_x and the fourth-order Runge–Kutta method in time. Determine the order and stability conditions of the scheme. Is the scheme is dispersive or dissipative?

14.5. Derive the conservative form of the Lax–Wendroff scheme (page 436).

14.6. The compressible Euler equations of gas dynamics are

$$\rho_t + (\rho u)_x = 0 \qquad \text{conservation of mass}$$
$$(\rho u)_t + (\rho u^2 + p)_x = 0 \qquad \text{conservation of momentum}$$
$$E_t + ((E + p)u)_x = 0 \qquad \text{conservation of energy}$$

where ρ is the density, u is the velocity, E is the total energy, and p is the pressure. This system is not a closed system—there are more unknowns than equations. To close the system, we add the equation of state for an ideal gas

$$E = \tfrac{1}{2}\rho u^2 + \frac{p}{\gamma - 1}.$$

The heat capacity ratio (adiabatic index) γ is constant— for air, γ is around 1.4. Sound speed is given by $c = \sqrt{\gamma p/\rho}$. Show that this system forms a hyperbolic system, and find the eigenvalues of the Jacobian. ✍

14.7. Solve Burgers' equation $u_t + \tfrac{1}{2}(u^2)_x = 0$ over the domain $[-1, 3]$, with initial conditions $u(0, x) = 1$ if $0 < x < 1$ and $u(0, x) = 0$ otherwise, both analytically and numerically using the local Lax–Friedrichs method. Confirm the solutions match by plotting them together at several time steps. ✍

14.8. The dam-break problem. Consider the shallow water equations

$$h_t + (hu)_x = 0 \qquad\qquad (14.29a)$$
$$(hu)_t + (hu^2 + \tfrac{1}{2}gh^2)_x = 0, \qquad\qquad (14.29b)$$

where g is the gravitational acceleration, h is the height of the water, and u is the velocity of the water. Set $g = 1$. Solve the problem with initial conditions $h = 1$ if $x < 0$, $h = 0.2$ if $x > 0$, and $u = 0$ over the domain $[-1, 1]$ using the first- and second-order central schemes with constant boundary conditions. (For the second-order scheme, you will need a slope limiter.) Use 100 and 200 points for space discretization and choose time steps according to the CFL condition. Plot the numerical result at $t = 0.25$ against the "exact" solution obtained using a fine mesh in space and step size in time. ✍

Chapter 15

Elliptic Equations

This chapter introduces the finite element method (FEM) and its applications in
solving elliptic equations. Typical elliptic equations are the Laplace equation
and the Poisson equation, which model the steady-state distribution of electrical
charge or temperature either with a source term (the Poisson equation) or without
(the Laplace equation), and the steady-state Schrödinger equation. Finite element
analysis is also frequently applied to modeling strain on structures such as beams.
Finite element methods, pioneered in the 1960s, are widely used for engineering
problems because the flexible geometry allows one to use irregular elements and
the variational formulation makes it easy to deal with boundary conditions and
compute error estimates.

15.1 A one-dimensional example

Consider a heat-conducting bar with uniform heat conductivity, an unknown
temperature distribution $u(x)$, a known heat source $f(x)$, and constant temperature
$u(0) = u(1) = 0$ at the ends of the bar. Fourier's law tells us that the heat flux
$q(x)$ equals $-u'(x)$, and the law of conservation of energy says $q'(x) = f(x)$.
From these equations, we have the steady-state problem $-u''(x) = f(x)$. We can
solve the problem by formulating it in three different ways—as a *boundary value
problem* Ⓓ, as a *minimization problem* Ⓜ, or as a *variational problem* Ⓥ (also
called the weak formulation).

Ⓓ *Boundary value:* Find u such that $-u'' = f$ with $u(0) = u(1) = 0$.

Let V be the vector space of piecewise-differentiable functions over the interval $[0, 1]$ that vanish on the endpoints. That is, $v(0) = v(1) = 0$ for all $v \in V$. Define the *total potential energy*

$$F(v) = \tfrac{1}{2} \langle v', v' \rangle - \langle f, v \rangle$$

where the inner product $\langle u, v \rangle = \int_0^1 u(x)v(x)\,dx$. In the next section, we'll introduce the notation $a(\cdot, \cdot)$ and $\mathcal{L}(\cdot)$ in the place of these inner products. For now, let's keep things relatively simple.

Ⓜ *Minimization:* Find $u \in V$ such that $F(u) \leq F(v)$ for all $v \in V$.

Ⓥ *Variational:* Find $u \in V$ such that $\langle u', v' \rangle = \langle f, v \rangle$ for all $v \in V$.

Theorem 49. *Under suitable conditions the boundary value problem* Ⓓ, *minimization problem* Ⓜ *and variational problem* Ⓥ *are all equivalent.*

Proof. First, we show Ⓓ is equivalent to Ⓥ. We start by showing Ⓓ implies Ⓥ. If $-u'' = f$, then for all $v \in V$, we have $-\langle u'', v \rangle = \langle f, v \rangle$. After integrating by parts, $-u'v|_0^1 + \langle u', v' \rangle = \langle f, v \rangle$. Because all elements of V vanish on the boundary, it follows that $\langle u', v' \rangle = \langle f, v \rangle$. We reverse the steps to show that Ⓥ implies Ⓓ given that u' is differentiable. For all $v \in V$, we have $\langle u', v' \rangle = \langle f, v \rangle$. Integrating by parts, $u'v|_0^1 - \langle u'', v \rangle = \langle f, v \rangle$. So $\int_0^1 (u'' + f)v\,dx = 0$. Because this expression is true for all $v \in V$, it follows that $-u'' = f$.

Now, we show Ⓜ is equivalent to Ⓥ. First, we'll show that Ⓥ follows from Ⓜ. Define the perturbation $g(\varepsilon) = F(u + \varepsilon w)$ for an arbitrary function w with $\varepsilon > 0$. We define the *variational derivative* of F as $\delta F = dg/d\varepsilon|_{\varepsilon=0}$. The energy $F(u)$ is at a minimum u when its variation derivative equals zero. Let's find out when this occurs. The perturbation

$$g(\varepsilon) = \tfrac{1}{2} \langle u' + \varepsilon w', u' + \varepsilon w' \rangle - \langle f, u + \varepsilon w \rangle$$
$$= \tfrac{1}{2} \langle u', u' \rangle + \varepsilon \langle u', w' \rangle + \tfrac{1}{2}\varepsilon^2 \langle w', w' \rangle - \langle f, u \rangle - \varepsilon \langle f, w \rangle.$$

From this, the variational derivative δF is

$$\left.\frac{dg}{d\varepsilon}\right|_{\varepsilon=0} = \langle u', w' \rangle + \varepsilon \langle w', w' \rangle - \langle f, w \rangle \bigg|_{\varepsilon=0} = \langle u', w' \rangle - \langle f, w \rangle,$$

which is zero when $\langle u', w' \rangle = \langle f, w \rangle$ for all $w \in V$. Finally, we show that Ⓜ follows from Ⓥ. Let $w = v - u$. Then $w \in V$ and

$$F(v) = F(u + w) = \tfrac{1}{2} \langle u' + w', u' + w' \rangle - \langle f, u + w \rangle.$$

Expanding the right-hand side:

$$F(v) = \tfrac{1}{2} \langle u', u' \rangle + \langle u', w' \rangle + \tfrac{1}{2} \langle w', w' \rangle - \langle f, u \rangle - \langle f, w \rangle.$$

Because $\langle u', w' \rangle = \langle f, w \rangle$, it follows that

$$F(v) = F(u) + \tfrac{1}{2} \langle w', w' \rangle \geq F(u). \qquad \square$$

The finite element method finds a solution to the variational problem $\widehat{v}$ or the minimization problem $\widehat{M}$ in a finite-dimensional subspace V_h of V. The finite element solution u_h is a projection of u onto V_h. The minimization problem is called the *Rayleigh–Ritz* formulation, and the variational problem is called the *Galerkin* formulation:

$\widehat{M}$ *Rayleigh–Ritz*: Find $u_h \in V_h$ such that $F(u_h) \leq F(v_h)$ for all $v_h \in V_h$.

$\widehat{v}$ *Galerkin*: Find $u_h \in V_h$ such that $\langle u'_h, v'_h \rangle = \langle f, v_h \rangle$ for all $v_h \in V_h$.

The function v_h is called the *test function*, and u_h is called the *trial function*.

Let's apply the Galerkin formulation to the original boundary value problem. Consider V_h to be the subspace of continuous piecewise-linear polynomials with nodes at $\{x_i\}$. (We might alternatively consider other higher-order splines as basis elements.) We'll restrict ourselves to a uniform partition with nodes at $x_j = jh$ and with $x_1 = 0$ and $x_m = 1$ to simplify the derivations. The finite element solution for a nonuniform partition can similarly be derived. A basis element $\varphi_j(x) \in V_h$ is

$$\varphi_j(x) = \begin{cases} 1 + t_j(x), & t_j(x) \in (-1, 0] \\ 1 - t_j(x), & t_j(x) \in (0, 1] \\ 0, & \text{otherwise} \end{cases} \qquad (15.1)$$

with $t_j(x) = (x - x_j)/h$. Note that $\{\varphi_j(x)\}$ forms a *partition of unity*, i.e., $\sum_{j=1}^{m} \varphi_j(x) = 1$ for all x. Then $v_h \in V_h$ is defined by

$$v_h(x) = \sum_{j=1}^{m} v_j \varphi_j(x)$$

with $v_j = v(x_j)$ and $v \in V$. The finite element solution is given by

$$u_h(x) = \sum_{i=1}^{m} \xi_i \varphi_i(x),$$

where $\xi_i = u(x_i)$ are unknowns. The Galerkin problem to find u_h such that $\langle u'_h, v'_h \rangle = \langle f, v_h \rangle$ now becomes the problem to find ξ_i such that

$$\left\langle \sum_{i=1}^{m} \xi_i \varphi'_i(x), \sum_{j=1}^{m} v_j \varphi'_j(x) \right\rangle = \left\langle f, \sum_{j=1}^{m} v_j \varphi_j(x) \right\rangle.$$

By bilinearity of the inner product, this expression is the same as

$$\sum_{j=1}^{m} v_j \left\langle \sum_{i=1}^{m} \xi_i \varphi_i'(x), \varphi_j'(x) \right\rangle = \sum_{j=1}^{m} v_j \left\langle f, \varphi_j(x) \right\rangle.$$

For this equality to hold for all v_j, we must have

$$\left\langle \sum_{i=1}^{m} \xi_i \varphi_i'(x), \varphi_j'(x) \right\rangle = \left\langle f, \varphi_j(x) \right\rangle$$

for $j = 1, 2, \ldots, m$. Again, by bilinearity

$$\sum_{i=1}^{m} \left\langle \varphi_i'(x), \varphi_j'(x) \right\rangle \xi_i = \left\langle f, \varphi_j(x) \right\rangle.$$

So we have the linear system of equations $\mathbf{A}\boldsymbol{\xi} = \mathbf{b}$ where $\mathbf{A}$ is called the *stiffness matrix* with

$$a_{ij} = \left\langle \varphi_i', \varphi_j' \right\rangle = \begin{cases} \int_0^1 (\varphi_i')^2 \, dx = \dfrac{2}{h}, & i = j \\ \int_0^1 \varphi_i' \varphi_j' \, dx = -\dfrac{1}{h}, & i = j \pm 1 \\ 0, & \text{otherwise.} \end{cases}$$

The vector $\mathbf{b} = (f_1, f_2, \ldots, f_m)$ where $f_j = \langle f, \varphi_j \rangle$ is called the *load vector*. By using regular, piecewise-linear basis functions, the system $\mathbf{A}\boldsymbol{\xi} = \mathbf{b}$ is

$$\frac{1}{h^2} \begin{bmatrix} 2 & -1 & & \\ -1 & 2 & \ddots & \\ & \ddots & \ddots & -1 \\ & & -1 & 2 \end{bmatrix} \begin{bmatrix} \xi_1 \\ \xi_2 \\ \vdots \\ \xi_m \end{bmatrix} = \begin{bmatrix} f_1 \\ f_2 \\ \vdots \\ f_m \end{bmatrix}.$$

15.2   A two-dimensional example

Let's extend the framework we developed in the previous section to the two-dimensional Poisson equation

$$-\Delta u = f \quad \text{where} \quad u\big|_{\partial\Omega} = 0 \tag{15.2}$$

for a region $\Omega \in \mathbb{R}^2$. We'll need a few more concepts before writing the Poisson equation in variational form. A mapping $\mathcal{L} : V \to \mathbb{R}$ is a *linear functional* or linear form if

$$\mathcal{L}(\alpha u + \beta v) = \alpha \mathcal{L}(u) + \beta \mathcal{L}(v)$$

for all real numbers α and β and $u, v \in V$. The mapping $a : V \times V \rightarrow \mathbb{R}$ is a *bilinear form* or bilinear functional if

$$a(\alpha u + \beta w, v) = \alpha a(u, v) + \beta a(w, v), \quad \text{and}$$
$$a(u, \alpha v + \beta w) = \alpha a(u, v) + \beta a(u, w)$$

for all real numbers α and β and $u, v, w \in V$. A bilinear form $a(\cdot, \cdot)$ is *symmetric* if $a(u, v) = a(v, u)$, and it is positive definite if $a(u, u) > 0$ for all nonzero u. An inner product is a bilinear form that is symmetric and positive definite.

The space of L^2-functions, also called square-integrable functions, is

$$L^2(\Omega) = \left\{ v \mid \iint_\Omega |v|^2 \, d\mathbf{x} < \infty \right\}.$$

In this case, we define the L^2-inner product as $\langle v, w \rangle_{L^2} = \iint_\Omega vw \, d\mathbf{x}$ and the L^2-norm as $\|v\|_{L^2} = \sqrt{\langle v, v \rangle}$. A *Sobolev space* is the space of L^2-functions whose derivatives are also L^2-functions:

$$H^1(\Omega) = \left\{ v \in L^2(\Omega) \mid \nabla v \in L^2(\Omega) \right\}.$$

We can further define Sobolev spaces $H^k(\Omega)$ as the space of functions whose kth derivatives are also L^2-functions. We define the Sobolev inner product as

$$\langle v, w \rangle_{H^1} = \iint_\Omega vw + \nabla v \cdot \nabla w \, d\mathbf{x},$$

and the Sobolev norm as

$$\|v\|_{H^1} = \sqrt{\iint_\Omega v^2 + |\nabla v|^2 \, d\mathbf{x}}.$$

Think of the Sobolev norm as an extension of the L^2-norm that includes a measure of the smoothness or regularity of a function. Finally, we define $H^1_0(\Omega)$ to be the set of all Sobolev functions that vanish on the boundary of Ω. Similarly, $H^k_0(\Omega)$ is the set of all Sobolev functions that vanish on the boundary of Ω and whose first $k - 1$ derivatives also vanish on the boundary.

Theorem 50 (Green's first identity).

$$\iint_\Omega v \Delta u \, d\mathbf{x} = \int_{\partial \Omega} v \frac{\partial u}{\partial n} \, ds - \iint_\Omega \nabla v \cdot \nabla u \, d\mathbf{x}$$

where $\dfrac{\partial u}{\partial n} = \nabla u \cdot \hat{\mathbf{n}}$ *is a directional derivative with unit outer normal* $\hat{\mathbf{n}}$.

Proof. Start by noting that

$$\nabla \cdot (v\nabla u) = \nabla v \cdot \nabla u + v\Delta u.$$

Integrating both sides over Ω gives us

$$\iint_\Omega \nabla \cdot (v\nabla u)\, \mathrm{d}\mathbf{x} = \iint_\Omega \nabla v \cdot \nabla u + v\Delta u\, \mathrm{d}\mathbf{x}.$$

From this, it follows that

$$\begin{aligned}
\iint_\Omega v\Delta u\, \mathrm{d}\mathbf{x} &= \iint_\Omega \nabla \cdot (v\nabla u)\, \mathrm{d}\mathbf{x} - \iint_\Omega \nabla v \cdot \nabla u\, \mathrm{d}\mathbf{x} \\
&= \int_{\partial\Omega} (v\nabla u) \cdot \hat{\mathbf{n}}\, \mathrm{d}s - \iint_\Omega \nabla v \cdot \nabla u\, \mathrm{d}\mathbf{x} \\
&= \int_{\partial\Omega} v\frac{\partial u}{\partial n}\, \mathrm{d}s - \iint_\Omega \nabla v \cdot \nabla u\, \mathrm{d}\mathbf{x}. \qquad \square
\end{aligned}$$

Now, let's get back to the two-dimensional Poisson equation. Let $V = H_0^1(\Omega)$, the space of Sobolev functions over Ω that vanish on the boundary $\partial\Omega$. Then from (15.2), for all $v \in V$

$$-\iint_\Omega v\Delta u\, \mathrm{d}x\, \mathrm{d}y = \iint_\Omega fv\, \mathrm{d}x\, \mathrm{d}y. \tag{15.3}$$

Using Green's identity and noting that v vanishes on $\partial\Omega$, we have

$$\iint_\Omega \nabla u \cdot \nabla v\, \mathrm{d}x\, \mathrm{d}y = \iint_\Omega fv\, \mathrm{d}x\, \mathrm{d}y.$$

Define the bilinear form $a(\cdot, \cdot)$ as

$$a(u, v) = \iint_\Omega \nabla u \cdot \nabla v\, \mathrm{d}x\, \mathrm{d}y$$

and the linear functional $\mathcal{L}(\cdot)$ as

$$\mathcal{L}(v) = \iint_\Omega vf\, \mathrm{d}x\, \mathrm{d}y.$$

Then the variational formulation is

ⓥ Find $u \in V$ such that $a(u, v) = \mathcal{L}(v)$ for all $v \in V$.

Let's now look at the implementation using FEM. The finite element method starts with triangulation of the domain—subdividing a two-dimensional domain into triangles and higher-dimensional domains into simplices such as tetrahedrons. Consider some triangulation T_h of Ω. That is, let $T_h = \cup_j K_j$ where K_j are

 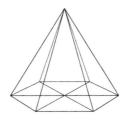 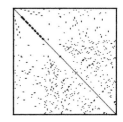

Figure 15.1: Triangulation of a domain Ω (left) using a simple pyramidal basis functions (middle) and the resultant sparse stiffness matrix (right).

triangular elements and $n_j = (x_j, y_j)$ are nodes associated with the vertices of the triangular elements. We'll take the finite element space $V_h \subset H_0^1(T_h)$ as the space of functions that are globally continuous and linear over each element K_j. For all $v_h \in V_h$, we can express

$$v_h(x, y) = \sum_{i=1}^{m} v(n_i)\varphi_i(x, y)$$

where $\{\varphi_i\}$ is a set of pyramidal basis functions with $\varphi_i(n_j) = \delta_{ij}$. Such basis functions are often called *Lagrange elements*. The finite element formulation is

> **Ⓥ** Find $u_h \in V_h$ such that $a(u_h, v_h) = \mathcal{L}(v_h)$ for all $v_h \in V_h$.

Let $u_h(x, y) = \sum_{i=1}^{m} \xi_i \varphi_i(x, y)$ where $\xi_i = u_h(n_i)$, then for all $j = 1, 2, \ldots, m$

$$a\left(\sum_{i=1}^{m} \xi_i \varphi_i, \varphi_j\right) = \mathcal{L}(\varphi_j)$$

from which it follows by linearity that

$$\sum_{i=1}^{m} \xi_i a(\varphi_i, \varphi_j) = \mathcal{L}(\varphi_j),$$

which we can write as $\mathbf{A}\boldsymbol{\xi} = \mathbf{b}$, where elements of the stiffness matrix are

$$a_{ij} = a(\varphi_i, \varphi_j) = \iint_{T_h} \nabla\varphi_i \cdot \nabla\varphi_j \, dx \, dy$$

and elements of the load vector are

$$b_j = \mathcal{L}(\varphi_j) = \iint_{T_h} \varphi_j(x) f(x) \, dx \, dy.$$

The stiffness matrix $\mathbf{A}$ is sparse because n_i can only be a vertex for a small number of triangles.

Example.　Let's write the following problem with Neumann boundary conditions as an FEM problem:

$$-\Delta u + u = f \quad \text{with} \quad \left.\frac{\partial u}{\partial n}\right|_{\partial\Omega} = g.$$

Let $V = H^1(\Omega)$ and take $v \in V$. This time v is allowed to be nonzero on the boundary $\partial\Omega$. Then

$$\iint_\Omega -v\Delta u + vu \, dx \, dy = \iint_\Omega fv \, dx \, dy.$$

Using Green's identity, we have

$$\iint_\Omega \nabla v \cdot \nabla u \, dx \, dy - \int_{\partial\Omega} v \frac{\partial u}{\partial n} \, ds + \iint_\Omega vu \, dx \, dy = \iint_\Omega fv \, dx \, dy.$$

On the boundary $\frac{\partial u}{\partial n} = g$, so

$$\iint_\Omega \nabla v \cdot \nabla u \, dx \, dy + \iint_\Omega vu \, dx \, dy = \iint_\Omega fv \, dx \, dy + \int_{\partial\Omega} gv \, ds.$$

Let

$$a(u, v) = \iint_\Omega \nabla u \cdot \nabla v + uv \, dx \, dy$$

and let

$$\mathcal{L}(v) = \langle f, v \rangle + \langle\langle g, v \rangle\rangle \equiv \iint_\Omega fv \, dx \, dy + \int_{\partial\Omega} gv \, ds.$$

The variational form of the Neumann problem is

> (Ⓥ) Find $u \in V$ such that $a(u, v) = \mathcal{L}(v)$ for all $v \in V$.

Let V_h be the space of continuous, piecewise-linear functions on Ω with a triangulation T_h, and let $\{\varphi_j\}$ be the set of basis functions. Recasting the problem as a finite element approximation

> (●) Find $u_h \in V_h$ such that $a(u_h, v_h) = \mathcal{L}(v_h)$ for all $v_h \in V_h$.

By taking the finite elements $u_h(x, y) = \sum_{i=1}^m \xi_i \varphi_i(x, y)$, then

$$\sum_{i=1}^m \xi_i a(\varphi_i, \varphi_j) = \mathcal{L}(\varphi_j)$$

for $j = 1, 2, \ldots, m$. In other words, we solve the system $\mathbf{A}\xi = \mathbf{b}$ where

$$a_{ij} = a(\varphi_i, \varphi_j) = \iint_{T_h} \nabla\varphi_i \cdot \nabla\varphi_j + \varphi_i\varphi_j \, dx \, dy$$

and

$$b_j = \iint_{T_h} f \varphi_j \, dx \, dy + \int_{\partial T_h} g \varphi_j \, ds.$$

Note that this time our stiffness matrix $\mathbf{A}$ and load vector $\mathbf{b}$ include the boundary elements. ◄

15.3   Stability and convergence

Now that we know how a finite element method works, let's examine when it works and how well it works. To do this, we'll use the Lax–Milgram theorem and Céa's lemma. The Lax–Milgram theorem provides sufficient conditions for the existence and uniqueness of a weak solution of a PDE. Céa's lemma gives a bound on the error between the weak solution of a PDE and the solution of a finite element approximation of the PDE.

Let's begin with a few definitions. A *Hilbert space* is a complete inner product space—a vector space with an inner product, that is complete with respect to the corresponding norm. A space is *complete* if every Cauchy sequence of functions in that space converges to a function in that space. A sequence is *Cauchy* if its elements eventually become arbitrarily close to one another. In other words, the sequence $u_1(x), u_2(x), u_3(x), \ldots$ is Cauchy if, given any positive ε, the norm $\|u_m - u_n\| < \varepsilon$ for all sufficiently large m and n.

Example.   The space of continuous functions over the interval $[-1, 1]$ is not complete in the L^2-norm. Take the scaled sigmoid functions $u_n(x) = \tanh nx$: ⌐, ⌐, ⌐, ⌐, ⌐, etc. These functions form a Cauchy sequence that converge to a discontinuous step function. The broader space of square-integrable functions over the same interval is a Hilbert space. The space of Sobolev functions is also a Hilbert space, though $\{u_1, u_2, u_3, \ldots\}$ is no longer Cauchy in the Sobolev norm because it doesn't converge in the Sobolev norm. ◄

Hilbert spaces provide the framework for the finite element method. The solution to the original PDE is approximated by representing it as a linear combination of basis functions using linear functionals and bilinear forms. And completeness of Hilbert spaces allows for convergence of approximations towards the true solution as the mesh is refined.

A few more definitions. A bilinear form a is *bounded* or *continuous* if there exists a positive γ such that $|a(u, v)| \le \gamma \|u\| \|v\|$ for all $u, v \in V$. On the other hand, a bilinear form a is *coercive* or *elliptic* if there exists a positive α such that $|a(u, u)| \ge \alpha \|u\|^2$ for all $u \in V$. In other words, a bilinear form is coercive if the magnitude of the functional increases at least as fast as the norm of the function. Likewise, a linear functional $\mathcal{L}$ is bounded if there exists a positive Λ such that $|\mathcal{L}(u)| \le \Lambda \|u\|$ for all $u \in V$.

Theorem 51 (Lax–Milgram theorem). *The problem $a(u, v) = \mathcal{L}(v)$ for all v in a Hilbert space V has a unique solution u whenever the bilinear form $a(\cdot, \cdot)$ is a bounded and coercive and the linear functional $\mathcal{L}$ is bounded.*

The Lax–Milgram theorem is a classic result of functional analysis that follows from the Riesz representation theorem, which says every bounded linear functional on a Hilbert space can be represented as an inner product with a fixed element of that space, i.e., $\mathcal{L}(v) = \langle u, v \rangle$ for all v for a unique u in the Hilbert space. In particular, the Lax–Milgram theorem extends the Riesz representation theorem for systems for which the bilinear form $a(\cdot, \cdot)$ may not necessarily be symmetric. For example, the variational form of the stationary convection–diffusion equation $-\Delta u + \mathbf{c} \cdot \nabla u = f$ has a nonsymmetric bilinear form $a(u, v) = \langle \nabla u, \nabla v \rangle + \langle \mathbf{c} \cdot \nabla u, v \rangle$. The proof of the Lax–Milgram theorem is beyond the scope of this introduction to the finite element method. Interested readers are encouraged to check out Lawrence Evan's discussion of the Lax–Milgram theorem in his text *Partial Differential Equations*.

Theorem 52 (Cauchy–Schwarz inequality). $|\langle v, w \rangle| \leq \|v\|\|w\|$

Proof. Note that for any α, $0 \leq \|v - \alpha w\|^2 = \|v\|^2 - 2\alpha \langle v, w \rangle + |\alpha|^2 \|w\|$. By taking $\alpha = |\langle v, w \rangle|/\|w\|^2$, we have $0 \leq \|v\|^2\|w\|^2 - |\langle v, w \rangle|^2$.   □

Theorem 53 (Poincaré inequality). *Let $u \in H_0^1(\Omega)$ for a bounded domain Ω, then*

$$\int_\Omega u^2(\mathbf{x}) \, d\mathbf{x} \leq \beta \int_\Omega |\nabla u(\mathbf{x})|^2 \, d\mathbf{x} \quad \text{for some } \beta.$$

Proof. We'll prove a more straightforward one-dimensional case. Without loss of generality, take $u(0) = 0$ and $x \in [0, 1]$. By the Cauchy–Schwarz inequality,

$$u(x) = \int_0^x u'(x) \, dx \leq \sqrt{\int_0^x 1 \, dx} \sqrt{\int_0^x (u')^2 \, dx} \leq \sqrt{\int_0^1 (u')^2 \, dx}.$$

Squaring and integrating both sides give us

$$\int_0^1 u^2(x) \, dx \leq \int_0^1 \left(\int_0^1 (u')^2 \, dx \right) dx = \int_0^1 (u')^2 \, dx.$$ □

Example. Let's show that the variational formulation of the Poisson equation $-u'' = f$ with $u(0) = 0$ and $u(1) = 0$ is well-posed (a unique solution exists). By setting

$$a(u, v) = \int_0^1 u'v' \, dx \text{ and } \mathcal{L}(v) = \int_0^1 fv \, dx,$$

the variational formulation for the Poisson equation is

ⓥ Find $u \in H_0^1([0, 1])$ such that $a(u, v) = \mathcal{L}(v)$ for all $v \in H_0^1([0, 1])$

To show well-posedness, we'll need to check that the conditions of boundedness and coercivity of the Lax–Milgram lemma hold. By the Cauchy–Schwarz inequality,

$$|a(u, v)| = \left| \int_0^1 u'v' \, \mathrm{d}x \right| \le \sqrt{\int_0^1 |u'|^2 \, \mathrm{d}x} \sqrt{\int_0^1 |v'|^2 \, \mathrm{d}x} \le \|u\|_{H_0^1} \|v\|_{H_0^1},$$

where the Sobolev norm $\|u\|_{H_0^1} = \sqrt{\int_0^1 u^2 + |u'|^2 \, \mathrm{d}x}$. So a is bounded. Similarly,

$$|\mathcal{L}(v)| = \left| \int_0^1 fv \, \mathrm{d}x \right| \le \|f\|_{L^2} \|v\|_{L^2} \le \|f\|_{L^2} \|v\|_{H_0^1}.$$

It follows that $\mathcal{L}$ is bounded. Finally, from the Poincaré inequality, it follows that $a(u, u) = \int_0^1 (u')^2 \, \mathrm{d}x \ge \alpha \int_0^1 u^2 + (u')^2 \, \mathrm{d}x$. So a is coercive. ◀

Theorem 54 (Céa's lemma). *If $a(\cdot, \cdot)$ is bounded and coercive with respective bounding constants γ and α, then $\|u - u_h\| \le (\gamma/\alpha)\|u - v_h\|$ for all $v_h \in V_h$.*

Proof. Let V be a Hilbert space, and consider the problem of finding the element $u \in V$ such that $a(u, v) = \mathcal{L}(v)$ for all $v \in V$. Consider similar problem of finding the element $u_h \in V_h$ such that $a(u_h, v_h) = \mathcal{L}(v_h)$ for all $v_h \in V_h$ for the finite-dimensional subspace V_h of V. The Lax–Milgram theorem says that unique solutions u and u_h exist. Then, $a(u - u_h, v_h) = 0$ for all $v_h \in V_h$. It follows that

$$\alpha \|u - u_h\|^2 \le a(u - u_h, u - u_h) = a(u - u_h, u - v_h) + a(u - u_h, v_h - u_h)$$
$$= a(u - u_h, u - v_h) \le \gamma \|u - u_h\| \|u - v_h\|$$

So, $\|u - u_h\| \le (\gamma/\alpha)\|u - v_h\|$ for all $v_h \in V_h$. □

Céa's lemma says that the finite element solution u_h is the best solution up to the constant γ/α. We can use the lemma to estimate the approximation error. Suppose that $u \in H^2$ is a solution to the Galerkin problem. Let p_h be a piecewise-linear polynomial interpolant of the solution u. Then by Céa's lemma

$$\|u - u_h\|_{H^1} \le \frac{\gamma}{\alpha} \|u - p_h\|_{H^1}.$$

By Taylor's theorem, there is a constant C such that $\|u' - p_h'\|_{L^2} \le Ch\|u''\|_{L^2}$. So

$$\|u - u_h\|_{H^1} \le \frac{\gamma Ch}{\alpha} \|u''\|_{L^2} \le \frac{\gamma Ch}{\alpha} \|u\|_{H^2}.$$

For degree-k piecewise-polynomial basis functions, the H^1-error is $O(h^k)$ if $u \in H^{k+1}$.

15.4 Time-dependent problems

We can also use the finite element method to solve time-dependent problems. Consider the one-dimensional heat equation with a source term $u_t - u_{xx} = f(x)$. Let the initial condition $u(x, 0) = u_0(x)$ and boundary values $u(0, t) = u(1, t) = 0$. Then for all $v \in H_0^1([0, 1])$,

$$\langle u_t, v \rangle - \langle u_{xx}, v \rangle = \langle f, v \rangle$$

where $\langle u, v \rangle = \int_0^1 uv \, dx$. From this we have the Galerkin formulation:

> ❤ Find $u_h \in V_h$ such that $\langle u_t, v \rangle + \langle u_x, v_x \rangle = \langle f, v \rangle$ for all $v \in V_h$.

Let $\{\varphi_1, \varphi_2, \ldots, \varphi_m\}$ be a basis of the finite element space $V_h \subset H_0^1([0, 1])$. Let $u_h(x, t) = \sum_{i=1}^m \xi_i(t) \varphi_i(x)$ and take $v = \varphi_j$. Then we have the system

$$\sum_{i=1}^m \xi_i'(t) \langle \varphi_i, \varphi_j \rangle + \sum_{i=1}^m \xi_i(t) \langle \varphi_i', \varphi_j' \rangle = \langle f, \varphi_j \rangle$$

for $j = 1, 2, \ldots, m$. More concisely, we have the system of differential equations

$$\mathbf{C} \xi'(t) + \mathbf{A} \xi(t) = \mathbf{b},$$

where the elements of $\mathbf{C}$, $\mathbf{A}$, and $\mathbf{b}$ are $c_{ij} = \langle \varphi_i, \varphi_j \rangle$, $a_{ij} = \langle \varphi_i', \varphi_j' \rangle$, and $b_j = \langle f, \varphi_j \rangle$. The matrix $\mathbf{C}$ is a mass matrix. We can rewrite the system as $\xi' = -\mathbf{C}^{-1} \mathbf{A} \xi + \mathbf{C}^{-1} \mathbf{b}$ and solve it using a stiff method, such as the backward Euler method or the Crank–Nicolson method.

We can confirm numerical stability by showing that the energy decreases over time. Consider the heat equation $u_t = u_{xx}$ with boundary conditions $u(0, t) = u(1, t) = 0$. By multiplying by u and integrating over $[0, 1]$, we have $\frac{1}{2} \frac{d}{dt} \|u\|^2 = -\|u_x\|^2 \le 0$. So, $\|u(\cdot, t)\|_{L^2} \le \|u(\cdot, 0)\|_{L^2}$.

The backward Euler scheme for the heat equation is

$$\frac{1}{\Delta t} \langle u_h^{n+1} - u_h^n, v \rangle + a \left(u_h^{n+1}, v \right) = 0$$

for all $v \in V_h$ where $a(u, v) = \int_0^1 u'v' \, dx$. Take $v = u_h^{n+1}$. Then

$$\langle u_h^{n+1}, u_h^{n+1} \rangle - \langle u_h^n, u_h^{n+1} \rangle = -\Delta t a \left(u_h^{n+1}, u_h^{n+1} \right) \le 0.$$

So, $\|u_h^{n+1}\|_{L^2}^2 \le \langle u_h^n, u_h^{n+1} \rangle \le \|u_h^n\|_{L^2} \|u_h^{n+1}\|_{L^2}$ by the Cauchy–Schwarz inequality. Therefore, $\|u_h^{n+1}\|_{L^2} \le \|u_h^n\|_{L^2}$ for all n and all stepsizes Δt. Hence, the scheme is unconditionally stable.

15.5 Practical implementation

In practice, one will typically use a computational software package to manage the tedious, low-level steps of the finite element method. Once we have formulated the weak form of the problem, we can implement a solution by breaking implementation into the following steps:

1. Preprocessing. Define the geometry and generate the mesh.
2. Assembling. Construct the stiffness matrices, boundary conditions, and shape functions.
3. Solving. Use either a direct or iterative sparse linear solver.
4. Postprocessing. Visualize the solution, analyze the results, and estimate the error.

In this section, we'll use FEniCS.jl, a wrapper to the popular, open-source FEniCS[1] platform. FEniCS is written in C++ and designed to run on hardware ranging from laptops to high-performance clusters, with wrappers in Python, Julia, and Matlab. Because FEniCS is an external program, you'll need to download and install it in addition to the wrapper.[2] For a finite-element library in Julia without external dependencies, try the relatively new Gridap.jl library.

⚜ Julia's FEM packages include Ferrite.jl, Gridap.jl, and FEniCS.jl.

Example.   Let's solve the Poisson equation $-\Delta u = f$ over the domain constructed by subtracting the unit square centered at $(0, 0.5)$ from the unit circle centered at $(0, 0)$. Take the source term $f(x, y) = e^{-(2x+1)^2 - (2y+1)^2}$, which models a heat source near $(-0.5, -0.5)$ with Dirichlet boundary conditions $u(x, y) = 0$. The variational form is $a(u_h, v) = \mathcal{L}(v)$ where

$$a(u, v) = \iint_\Omega \nabla u \cdot \nabla v \, dx \, dy \quad \text{and} \quad \mathcal{L}(v) = \iint_\Omega v f \, dx \, dy.$$

We'll first define the geometry, the finite element space consisting of Lagrange polynomials, and the trial and test functions. Given a function space V, FEniCS uses TestFunction(V) for a test function, TrialFunction(V) to define the trial function, and FeFunction(V) to define the solution function where the result will be stored.

---

[1] The letters "FE" stand for "finite element," the letters "CS" stand for "computational software," and the letters "ni" are simply used to string the others together into a homophone of *phoenix*, the mascot of University of Chicago, where the project originated.

[2] https://fenicsproject.org/

Figure 15.2: FEM mesh (left), solution of the Poisson equation with a heat source centered at $(-0.5, -0.5)$ (middle), and solution of the heat equation with initial conditions centered at $(-0.5, -0.5)$ (right). Each contour depicts a 10 percent change in value.

```
using FEniCS
square = Rectangle(Point([-0.5, 0]), Point([0.5, 1]))
circle = Circle(Point([0.0, 0.0]), 1)
mesh = generate_mesh(circle - square,16)
V = FunctionSpace(mesh,"Lagrange",1)
u, v, w = TrialFunction(V), TestFunction(V), FeFunction(V)
```

The mesh is shown in the figure above. Now, define the boundary conditions and the source term. Note that FEniCS requires functions to be entered as C++ expressions.

```
bc = DirichletBC(V,Constant(0),"on_boundary")
f = Expression("exp(-pow(2*x[0]+1,2)-pow(2*x[1]+1,2))", degree=2)
```

Finally, define $a(u_h, v)$ and $\mathcal{L}(v)$ and solve the problem.

```
a = dot(grad(u),grad(v))*dx
L = f*v*dx
lvsolve(a,L,w,bc)
```

The solution w can be exported as a visualization toolkit file (VTK) and later visualized using ParaView:[3]

```
File("poisson_solution.pvd",w)
```

The figure above shows the solution. Notice that the peak temperature is to the right of the heat source peak.   ◀

Example.   Let's modify the example above to solve the heat equation $u_t = \Delta u$ over the same domain with Neumann boundary conditions. We'll take the initial

---

[3] ParaView is an open-source application for visualizing scientific data sets such as VTK.

condition $u(0, x, y) = f(x, y) = e^{-(4x+2)^2-(4y+2)^2}$. The variational form of the heat equation is $\langle u_t, v \rangle + \langle \nabla u, \nabla v \rangle = 0$. We define the geometry, the finite element space, and the test functions as before, adding an expression for the initial condition.

```
using FEniCS, OrdinaryDiffEq
square = Rectangle(Point([-0.5, 0]), Point([0.5, 1]))
circle = Circle(Point([0.0, 0.0]), 1)
mesh = generate_mesh(circle - square,16)
V = FunctionSpace(mesh,"Lagrange",1)
f = Expression("exp(-pow(2*x[0]+1,2)-pow(2*x[1]+1,2))", degree=2)
```

We define variables for the initial condition, trial function, test function, and solution function.

```
u, v = interpolate(f,V), TestFunction(V)
uₜ, wₜ = TrialFunction(V), FeFunction(V)
```

We define the variation form of the heat equation and pass it along with the variables to an in-place function using a named tuple p. The function get_array maps a variable in function space to a one-dimensional array, and the function assign maps the one-dimensional array to a variable in function space. Neumann boundary conditions are the default boundary conditions in FEniCS, and we prescribe them by setting bc = [].

```
F = dot(uₜ,v)*dx + dot(grad(u), grad(v))*dx
p = (u=u, wₜ=wₜ, F=F)
function heat_equation!(uₜ_vec, u_vec, p, t)
  assign(p.u, u_vec)
  lvsolve(lhs(p.F), rhs(p.F), p.wₜ, [])
  copy!(uₜ_vec, get_array(p.wₜ))
end
```

Finally, let's solve the problem for $t \in [0, 0.5]$ using a fourth-order semi-implicit ODE solver and export the solution.

```
problem = ODEProblem(heat_equation!, get_array(u), (0,0.0), p)
method = KenCarp4(autodiff=false)
solution = OrdinaryDiffEq.solve(problem, method)
assign(p.u, solution(0.5))
File("heat_solution.pvd", p.u)
```

The figure on the preceding page shows the solution.   ◀

15.6   Exercises

15.1. Solve the differential equation $u'' + u - 8x^2 = 0$ with Neumann boundary conditions $u'(0) = 0$ and $u'(1) = 1$ using the finite element method with piecewise-linear elements.   ✍

15.2. Consider the boundary value problem

$$u'''' = f \quad \text{with} \quad u(0) = u'(0) = u(1) = u'(1) = 0$$

for the deflection $u(x)$ of a uniform beam under the load $f(x)$. Formulate a finite element method and find the corresponding linear system of equations in the case of a uniform partition. Determine the solution for $f(x) = 384$. You may wish to use the basis elements $\phi_j(t) = H_{00}(|t|)$ and $\psi_j(t) = H_{10}(|t|)$ for $t \in [-1, 1]$ and equal zero otherwise. The Hermite polynomials are $H_{00}(t) = 2t^3 - 3t^2 + 1$ and $H_{10}(t) = t^3 - 2t^2 + t$.   ✍

15.3. Show that bounding constant in Céa's lemma can be improved such that $\|u - u_h\| \leq \sqrt{\gamma/\alpha}\|u - v_h\|$ for all $v_h \in V_h$ when the bilinear form $a(\cdot, \cdot)$ is symmetric and positive-definite.   ✍

Chapter 16

Fourier Spectral Methods

We can improve the accuracy of finite difference methods by using wider stencils that provide better approximations to the derivatives. With each additional grid point added to the stencil, we increase the order of accuracy by one. One might reason that by using all available grid points to approximate the derivatives, we could build a highly accurate method. This is precisely what spectral methods do. If the solution is smooth, the error shrinks faster than any power of grid spacing—something sometimes called exponential or spectral accuracy. If the solution is at most p-times differentiable, convergence is at most $O(h^{p+1})$. This chapter examines an essential class of spectral methods—the Fourier spectral method—which uses trigonometric interpolation over a periodic domain to approximate a solution.

Similar spectral methods, such as the Chebyshev spectral method discussed in Chapter 10, can be used on problems with nonperiodic solutions. Some tricks may also allow us to use Fourier spectral methods if the problem isn't periodic. For example, we can extend the domain so that the solution does not have appreciable boundary interaction. Or we might add absorbing "sponge" layers or reflecting barriers to the problem to prevent the solution from wrapping around the boundaries.

16.1 Discrete Fourier transform

The Fourier transform has already been discussed in sections 6.1 regarding the fast Fourier transform and 10.3 regarding function approximation. This section re-examines the Fourier transform by focusing on trigonometric interpolation and spectral differentiation. Specifically, we'll compare the continuous Fourier transform, discrete Fourier transform, and Fourier series.

▷ Trigonometric interpolation

Let the function $u(x)$ be periodic with period 2π, i.e, $u(x + 2\pi) = u(x)$. We can modify the period of $u(x)$ by rescaling x. We can approximate $u(x)$ by a Fourier polynomial $p(x) = \sum_{\xi=-m}^{m-1} c_\xi e^{-i\xi x}$ by choosing coefficients c_ξ so that $u(x_j) = p(x_j)$ at equally spaced nodes $x_j = j\pi/m$ for $j = 0, 1, \ldots, 2m - 1$. To find the coefficients c_ξ, we'll need the help of an identity.

Theorem 55. $\sum_{j=0}^{2m-1} e^{i\xi x_j}$ equals zero for nonzero integers ξ and $2m$ for $\xi = 0$.

Proof.

$$\sum_{j=0}^{2m-1} e^{i\xi x_j} = \sum_{j=0}^{2m-1} e^{i\xi j\pi/m} = \sum_{j=0}^{2m-1} \omega^{\xi j} = \begin{cases} \dfrac{\omega^{2m} - 1}{\omega - 1}, & \text{if } \xi \neq 0 \\ 2m, & \text{if } \xi = 0 \end{cases}$$

where $\omega = e^{i\pi/m}$. Note that $\omega^{2m} = \left(e^{i\xi\pi/n}\right)^{2m} = e^{i\xi 2\pi} = 1$. □

It follows that

$$\sum_{j=0}^{2m-1} u(x_j)e^{-i\xi x_j} = \sum_{j=0}^{2m-1}\sum_{l=-m}^{m-1} c_\xi e^{i(l-\xi)x_j} = \sum_{l=-m}^{m-1} c_\xi \sum_{j=0}^{2m} e^{i(l-\xi)x_j} = 2mc_\xi.$$

From this expression, we have the discrete Fourier transform and the inverse discrete Fourier transform

$$c_\xi = \frac{1}{2m}\sum_{j=0}^{2m-1} u(x_j)e^{-i\xi x_j} \quad \text{and} \quad u(x_j) = \sum_{\xi=-m}^{m-1} c_\xi e^{i\xi x_j}, \qquad (16.1)$$

where $\xi = -m, -m + 1, \ldots, m - 1$ and $j = 0, 1, \ldots, 2m - 1$. Compare these definitions with the (continuous) Fourier transform and the inverse (continuous) Fourier transform

$$\hat{u}(\xi) = F[u] = \frac{1}{2\pi}\int_{-\infty}^{\infty} u(x)e^{-i\xi x}\,dx \quad \text{and} \quad u(x) = \int_{-\infty}^{\infty} \hat{u}(\xi)e^{i\xi x}\,d\xi.$$

We can think of the discrete Fourier transform as a Riemann sum and the continuous Fourier transform as a Riemann integral.

The 2π-periodization of a function $u(x)$ is the function

$$u_p(x) = \sum_{\xi=-\infty}^{\infty} u(x + 2\pi\xi)$$

if the series converges. If $u_p(x)$ exists, then it is periodic: $u_p(x) = u_p(x + 2\pi\xi)$. Also, if $u(x)$ vanishes outside of $[0, 2\pi)$, then $u_p(x) = u(x)$ for $x \in [0, 2\pi)$. Because $u_p(x)$ is periodic, we can write its Fourier series

$$u_p(x) = \sum_{\xi=-\infty}^{\infty} c_\xi e^{i\xi x} \tag{16.2}$$

with

$$c_\xi = \frac{1}{2\pi} \int_0^{2\pi} u_p(x)e^{-i\xi x}\, dx = \frac{1}{2\pi} \int_{-\infty}^{\infty} u(x)e^{-i\xi x}\, dx,$$

which is simply the Fourier transform $\hat{u}(\xi)$. We are left with

$$\sum_{\xi=-\infty}^{\infty} u(x + 2\pi\xi) = \sum_{\xi=-\infty}^{\infty} \hat{u}(\xi)e^{i\xi x},$$

known as the *Poisson summation formula*. If $u(x)$ vanishes outside of $[0, 2\pi)$,

$$u(x) = \sum_{\xi=-\infty}^{\infty} \hat{u}(\xi)e^{i\xi x}.$$

By truncating the Fourier series (16.2) from $-m$ to $m - 1$ (i.e., restricting the frequency domain), we have the discrete Fourier transform (16.1).

Let's summarize the Fourier transform, the Fourier series, and the discrete Fourier transform over the spatial domain x and the frequency domain ξ.

 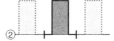 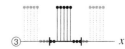

① *Fourier transform:* the spatial domain is the real line $(-\infty, \infty)$
② *Fourier series:* the spatial domain is periodic
③ *discrete Fourier transform:* the spatial domain is periodic and discrete

 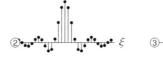 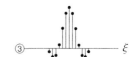

① *Fourier transform:* the frequency domain is the real line $(-\infty, \infty)$
② *Fourier series:* the frequency domain is discrete over the real line $(-\infty, \infty)$
③ *discrete Fourier transform:* the frequency domain is discrete and bounded

▷ Spectral differentiation

Let's find the derivative of the Fourier polynomial approximation of $u(x)$. As before, we take $u(x)$ with period 2π. In this case,

$$\frac{d}{dx}u(x) = \sum_{\xi=-m}^{m-1} c_\xi \frac{d}{dx} e^{i\xi x} = \sum_{\xi=-m}^{m-1} (i\xi c_\xi) e^{i\xi x}.$$

The discrete Fourier transform of the derivative has the memorable form

$$F\left[\frac{d}{dx}u\right] = i\xi\, F[u].$$

From this equation, we can see the origin of the term "spectral method." When we expand a solution $u(t, x)$ as a series of orthogonal eigenfunctions of a linear operator, that solution is related to the spectrum (the set of eigenvalues) of that operator. A *pseudospectral* method solves the problem on a discrete mesh.

When the function $u(x)$ has period ℓ, we make the transform $x \mapsto (2\pi/\ell)x$ and $dx \mapsto (2\pi/\ell)\,dx$, and the discrete Fourier transform of $\frac{d}{dx}u$ is $i(2\pi/\ell)\xi\hat{u}$. Of course, as long as $u(x)$ is smooth, we can differentiate any number of times. So, the Fourier transform of the pth derivative of $u(x)$ is

$$F\left[\frac{d^p}{dx^p}u\right] = \left(i\xi\frac{2\pi}{\ell}\right)^p F[u]. \tag{16.3}$$

Consider the heat equation $u_t = u_{xx}$ with initial conditions $u(0, x)$ and periodic boundary conditions over a domain of length 2π. The Fourier transform $\hat{u}(t, \xi) = F u(t, x)$ of the heat equation is $\hat{u}_t = -\xi^2\hat{u}$, which has the solution

$$\hat{u}(t, \xi) = e^{-\xi^2 t}\hat{u}(0, \xi).$$

We can write the formal solution to the heat equation from this expression as

$$u(t, x) = F^{-1}\left[e^{-\xi^2 t} F u(0, x)\right]. \tag{16.4}$$

We'll use a fast Fourier transform (FFT) to compute the discrete transforms in practice. Let's examine the numerical implementation of the discrete solution in Julia. We need to exercise some care in ordering the indices of ξ. Most scientific computing languages, including Julia, Matlab, and Python, define the coefficients of the discrete Fourier transform c_ξ by starting with the zero-frequency term c_0. For m nodes, we'll take

$$\xi = 0, 1, 2, \ldots, \tfrac{1}{2}(m-1), -\tfrac{1}{2}m, -\tfrac{1}{2}m + 1, \ldots, -2, -1.$$

where we round half toward zero. For a domain of length ℓ, the derivative operator $i\xi \cdot (2\pi/\ell)$ is

```
iξ = im*[0:(m-1)÷2;-m÷2:-1]*(2π/ℓ)
```

Alternatively, we can use the FFTW.jl function `ifftshift`

```
iξ = im*ifftshift(-m÷2:(m-1)÷2)*(2π/ℓ)
```

or the AbstractFFTs.jl function `fftfreq`

```
iξ = im*fftfreq(m,m)*(2π/ℓ)
```

to compute the zero-frequency shift.

We'll use the FFTW.jl package to implement the discrete Fourier transform. The Fastest Fourier Transform in the West (FFTW) library uses heuristics and trials to select from among several FFT algorithms. When first called, the library may try several different algorithms for the same problem and, after that, use the fastest. The Julia implementation of (16.4) using 256 points over a domain of length 4 is

```
using FFTW
m = 256; ℓ = 4
ξ² = (fftshift(-(m-1)÷2:m÷2)*(2π/ℓ)).^2
u = (t,u₀) -> real(ifft(exp.(-ξ²*t).*fft(u₀)))
```

If a problem repeatedly uses Fourier transforms on arrays with the same size as an array u, as is the case in time-marching schemes, then it can be advantageous to have FFTW try out all possible algorithms initially to see which is fastest. In this case, we can define `F = plan_fft(u)` and then use `F*u` or `F\u` where the multiplication and inverse operators are overloaded. For example, we replace the last line in the code above with

```
F = plan_fft(u₀)
u = (t,u₀) -> real(F\(exp.(-ξ²*t).*(F*u₀)))
```

The `fft` and `ifft` functions in Julia are all multi-dimensional transforms unless an additional parameter is provided. For example, `fft(x)` performs an FFT over all dimensions of x, whereas `fft(x,2)` only performs an FFT along the second dimension of x.

▷ Smoothness and spectral accuracy

Smooth functions have rapidly decaying Fourier transforms. The Fourier transform of the smoothest functions, like the constant function or sine function, are Dirac delta distributions. And Gaussian distributions are transformed back into Gaussian distributions. On the other hand, functions with discontinuities have relatively slowly decaying Fourier transforms.

Let's use splines to examine smoothness, starting with a piecewise constant function. The rectangular function

$$B_0(x) = \begin{cases} 1, & x \in [-\tfrac{1}{2}h, \tfrac{1}{2}h] \\ 0, & \text{otherwise} \end{cases}$$

is a zeroth-order B-spline with the Fourier transform $\hat{B}_0(\xi) = F[B_0(x)]$:

$$\int_{-\infty}^{\infty} B_0(x)e^{-i\xi x}\,dx = \int_{-\frac{1}{2}h}^{\frac{1}{2}h} e^{-i\xi x}\,dx = \frac{e^{i\xi/2h} - e^{-i\xi/2h}}{i\xi} = \frac{\sin \xi/2h}{\xi/2} = \frac{1}{h}\operatorname{sinc}\frac{\xi}{2h}.$$

The rectangular function and the sinc function[1] are plotted below.

The rectangular function is not differentiable at $x = \pm\tfrac{1}{2}h$; it is not even continuous at those points. Its Fourier transform decays as $O(|\xi|^{-1})$ as $|\xi| \to \infty$. We can use a linear combination of scaled and translated basis functions $B_0(x)$ to build piecewise constant functions. The Fourier transform of the rectangular function $B_0(x + a)$ is

$$\int_{-\frac{1}{2}h}^{\frac{1}{2}h} e^{-i\xi(x+a)}\,dx = e^{ia\xi}\frac{\sin \xi/2h}{\xi/2} = \frac{1}{h}e^{ia\xi}\operatorname{sinc}\frac{\xi}{2h}.$$

So the Fourier transform a piecewise constant function is a linear combination of sinc functions.

We can use the B_0-spline basis to generate higher-order B-spline bases, starting with a piecewise linear basis $B_1(x)$. One way to do this is to take the self-convolution of $B_0(x)$. Another way is to use de Boor's algorithm, discussed on page 240. A third way is to take the antiderivative

$$B_1(x) = \int_{-\infty}^{x} f(x - h/2) - f(x + h/2)\,dx = \begin{cases} 1 + x/h, & x \in [-h, 0] \\ 1 - x/h, & x \in [0, h] \\ 0, & \text{otherwise} \end{cases}.$$

The Fourier transform of the triangular function $B_1(x)$ is

$$\hat{B}_1(\xi) = (i\xi)^{-1}\left(e^{i\xi/2h} - e^{-i\xi/2h}\right)\frac{1}{h}\operatorname{sinc}\frac{\xi}{2h} = \frac{1}{h^2}\operatorname{sinc}^2\frac{\xi}{2}.$$

[1] British mathematician Phillip Woodward introduced the sinc function (pronounced "sink") in his 1952 paper "Information theory and inverse probability in telecommunication," saying that the function $(\sin \pi x)/\pi x$ "occurs so often in Fourier analysis and its applications that it does seem to merit some notation of its own." It's sometimes called "cardinal sine," not to be confused with "cardinal sin."

The triangular function and the sinc-squared function are plotted below.

The triangular function is not differentiable at $x \in \{-1, 0, 1\}$, but it is weakly differentiable everywhere. The sinc-squared function decays as $O(|\xi|^{-2})$ as $|\xi| \to \infty$. We can use a linear combination of scaled and translated basis functions $B_1(x)$ to build piecewise linear functions. If follows that the Fourier transform of piecewise linear function is a linear combination of sinc-squared functions.

Continuing, we can construct a degree-p piecewise polynomial using B-splines of order p. The Fourier transform of a B-spline with h-separated knots is given by

$$\hat{B}_p(x) = \frac{1}{h^{p+1}} \operatorname{sinc}^{p+1} \frac{\xi}{2h}.$$

In practice, we can't take infinitely many frequencies and must be satisfied with a Fourier polynomial $P_n f$ as our approximation to the Fourier series f:

$$f(x) = \sum_{\xi=-\infty}^{\infty} c_\xi e^{-i\xi x} = \sum_{\xi=-m}^{m-1} c_\xi e^{-i\xi x} + \tau_m(x) = P_m f(x) + \tau_m(x).$$

Because the Fourier series is a complete, orthonormal system, we can use Parseval's theorem on page 253 to compute the ℓ^2-norm of the truncation error

$$\|\tau_m\|^2 = \|f - P_m f\|^2 = \|P_\infty f - P_m f\|^2 = \sum_{\xi > |m|} |c_\xi|^2.$$

Let f be approximated using a spline with knots separated by distance h. Then the Fourier transform of this approximation is a linear combination of terms $h^{-(p+1)} \operatorname{sinc}^{p+1}(\xi/2h)$. It follows that if f has $p-1$ continuous derivatives in L^2 and a pth derivative of bounded variation, then

$$|c_\xi| = O\left(h^{-(p+1)} \operatorname{sinc}^{p+1}(\xi/2h)\right) = O\left(|\xi|^{-(p+1)}\right)$$

and

$$\|\tau_n\|^2 = \sum_{\xi > |m|} |c_\xi|^2 = \sum_{\xi > |m|} O\left(|\xi|^{-2p-2}\right) = O\left(m^{-2p-1}\right).$$

Therefore, the truncation error $\|\tau_m\| = O\left(m^{-p-1/2}\right)$.

For a rectangular function or any function with a discontinuity, $p = 0$ and $|\tau_n| = O\left(n^{-1/2}\right)$. We should expect slow convergence, as we see in the next figure. The original rectangular function f is on the left, the frequency-limited projection $P_n\,f$ is in the middle, and a close-up of $P_n\,f$ near a discontinuity is on the right. The Fourier polynomial approximation results in a *Gibbs phenomenon*, oscillations in the neighborhood of a discontinuity.

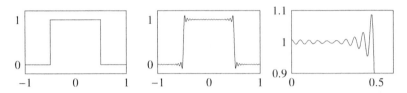

16.2   Nonlinear stiff equations

As seen in previous chapters, some partial differential equations, such as the Navier–Stokes equation, combine a stiff linear term with a nonstiff nonlinear term. Techniques for solving such equations include time splitting, integrating factors, and implicit-explicit (IMEX) methods. Time splitting allows us to avoid the stability issues caused by the stiff linear term. Still, we are typically unable to get beyond second-order-in-time accuracy using them. Integrating factors can bring us high accuracy, but we may not entirely avoid the stability issues caused by the stiffness. IMEX methods can generate moderately accurate solutions with some reduced stability.

▷ **Time splitting**

Time splitting methods are familiar from chapters 12 and 13. Consider the equation $u_t = L\,u + N\,u$, where L is a linear operator and N is a nonlinear operator. Take the splitting

1. $v_t = L\,v$ where $v(0,x) = u(0,x)$,
2. $w_t = N\,w$ where $w(0,x) = v(\Delta t, x)$.

Recall from the discussion on page 366 that after one time step, the solution $u(\Delta t, x) = w(\Delta t, x) + O(\Delta t^2)$. The method has a second-order splitting error with each time step, resulting in a first-order global splitting error. We can increase the order of accuracy by using Strang splitting.

Let's apply time splitting to a spectral method. Let $\hat{u} \equiv F\,u$ and $\hat{v} \equiv F\,v$ be the Fourier transforms of u and v. Then Fourier transform of the equation $v_t = L\,v$ is $\hat{v}_t = \hat{L}\hat{v}$, where $\hat{L}$ is the Fourier transform of the operator L, assuming it exists. This differential equation has the formal solution $\hat{v}(\Delta t, \xi) = e^{\Delta t \hat{L}}\hat{u}(0, \xi)$. Applying the inverse Fourier transform gives us

$$v(\Delta t, x) = F^{-1}\left[e^{\Delta t \hat{L}}\, F\,u(0,x) \right].$$

We now solve $w_t = N\,w$ with initial conditions $w(0, x) = v(\Delta t, x)$ to get the solution $u(\Delta t, x) = w(\Delta t, x) + O(\Delta t^2)$. This solution subsequently becomes the initial condition $v(0, x)$ for the next time step.

Example.   Consider the Allen–Cahn equation

$$u_t = u_{xx} + \varepsilon^{-1} u(1 - u^2)$$

with periodic boundary conditions. We can write the problem as $u_t = L\,u + N\,u$, where $L\,u = u_{xx}$ and $N\,u = \varepsilon^{-1} u(1 - u^2)$. The Fourier transform of u_{xx} is $-\xi^2\,F\,u$, and the differential equation $u_t = \varepsilon^{-1} u(1 - u^2)$ has the analytical solution

$$u(\Delta t, x) = u_0 \left(u_0^2 - (u_0^2 - 1) e^{-2\varepsilon \Delta t} \right)^{-1/2}$$

where the initial conditions $u_0(x) = u(0, x)$. While having an analytic solution is convenient, we could have also solved the differential equation numerically if one didn't exist.

For each time step t_n, we have

1. $v(x) = F^{-1} \left[e^{-\xi^2 \Delta t}\,F\,[u(t_n, x)] \right]$

2. $u(t_{n+1}, x) = u_0 \left(u_0^2 - (u_0^2 - 1) e^{-2\varepsilon \Delta t} \right)^{-1/2}$ where $u_0 = v(x)$.

Each time step has an $O(\Delta t^2)$ splitting error, so we have $O(\Delta t)$ error after n iterations. By using Strang splitting, we can achieve $O(\Delta t^2)$ error.   ◄

Example.   An electron in an external potential $V(x)$ is modeled in quantum mechanics using the Schrödinger equation

$$u_t = \tfrac{1}{2} i\varepsilon u_{xx} - i\varepsilon^{-1} V(x) u,$$

with the scaled Planck constant ε. We can separate the spatial operator into a kinetic term $\tfrac{1}{2} i\varepsilon u_{xx}$ and a potential energy term $-i\varepsilon^{-1} V(x) u$. These terms are linear in u, and we can solve the problem using Strang splitting

$$u(x, t_{n+1}) = e^{-iV(x)\Delta t/2\varepsilon}\,F^{-1}\,e^{-i\varepsilon \xi^2 \Delta t/2}\,F\,e^{-iV(x)\Delta t/2\varepsilon} u(x, t_n)$$

for a spectral-order-in-space and second-order-in-time solution.   ◄

▷ **Integrating factors**

We are unable to get better than second-order accuracy by using time-splitting. We can achieve arbitrary-order accuracy if we don't split the operators. Of course, if the problem is stiff, we must use an implicit L-stable method to avoid stability issues altogether. High-order implicit schemes can be challenging to implement if we have nonlinear terms. So another approach is to use integrating factors to lessen the effect of the stiffness in a high-order explicit scheme.

Suppose that we want to solve $u_t = L\,u + N\,u$, where L is a linear operator, N is a nonlinear operator, and the initial conditions are given by $u(0,x)$. We can rewrite the equation as $u_t - L\,u = N\,u$. Then, taking the Fourier transform, we get

$$\hat{u}_t - \hat{L}\hat{u} = F[N\,u].$$

Multiply both sides of the equation by $e^{-t\hat{L}}$ and simplify to get

$$\left(e^{-t\hat{L}}\hat{u}\right)_t = e^{-t\hat{L}}F[N\,u]. \tag{16.5}$$

Let $\hat{w} = e^{-t\hat{L}}\hat{u}$. Then the solution is

$$u(t,x) = F^{-1}\left[e^{t\hat{L}}\hat{w}(t,\xi)\right]$$

where

$$\frac{\partial}{\partial t}\hat{w}(t,\xi) = e^{-t\hat{L}}F\left[N\left(F^{-1}\left[e^{t\hat{L}}\hat{w}(t,\xi)\right]\right)\right] \tag{16.6}$$

with initial conditions $\hat{w}(0,\xi) = e^{0\cdot\hat{L}}F[u(0,x)] = F[u(0,x)]$.

We can break the time interval into several increments $\Delta t = t_{n+1} - t_n$ and implement integrating factors over each interval. In this case, we have for each interval starting at t_n and ending at t_{n+1} the following set-solve-set procedure

set $\qquad \hat{w}(t_n,\xi) = F u(t_n,x)$

solve $\qquad \dfrac{\partial}{\partial t}\hat{w}(t,\xi) = e^{-\Delta t\hat{L}}F\left[N\left(F^{-1}\left[e^{\Delta t\hat{L}}\hat{w}(t,\xi)\right]\right)\right]$

set $\qquad u(t_{n+1},x) = F^{-1}\left(e^{\Delta t\hat{L}}\hat{w}(t_{n+1},\xi)\right).$

It isn't necessary to switch back to the variable $u(t,x)$ with each iteration. Instead, we can solve the problem in the variable $\hat{u}(t,\xi)$ and only switch back when we want to observe the solution.

The benefit of such integrating factors is that there is no splitting error. But, integrating factors only lessen the effect of stiffness. Cox and Matthews developed a class of exponential time differencing Runge–Kutta (ETDRK) methods that solve (16.5) using matrix exponentials

$$u(t_{n+1}) = e^{\Delta t\hat{L}}u(t_n) + \int_0^{\Delta t} e^{(\Delta t - s)\hat{L}}\hat{N}u(t_n + s)\,ds$$

and evaluate the integral numerically using Runge–Kutta methods. Later, Hochbruck and Ostermann extended these methods to Rosenbrock methods.

▷ IMEX methods

Implicit-explicit (IMEX) methods solve $u_t = L\,u + N\,u$ by using implicit integration on $L\,u$ and explicit integration on $N\,u$ while using the same approximation for the left-hand side. A common second-order IMEX method combines a Crank–Nicolson method with an Adams–Bashforth method. Ascher, Ruuth, and Wetton extended this method to create a class of semi-implicit BDF (SBDF) methods. Later, Kennedy and Carpenter developed a class of high-order additive Runge–Kutta (ARK) methods combining an explicit singly diagonal implicit Runge–Kutta (ESDIRK) scheme for the stiff term and a traditional explicit Runge–Kutta scheme (ERK) for the nonstiff term.

⚬⚬ The DifferentialEquations.jl function `SplitODEProblem` defines a problem to be solved using an IMEX or exponential method, such as `KenCarp4()` or `ETDRK4()`.

⚬⚬ The DiffEqOperators.jl function `DiffEqArrayOperator` can be used to define a spectral operator as a diagonal matrix.

Example.   The Kuramoto–Sivashinsky equation (KSE) combines a nonlinear convection term, a fourth-order diffusion term, and a second-order backward-diffusion term

$$u_t + uu_x + u_{xxxx} + u_{xx} = 0 \tag{16.7}$$

to model small thermal instabilities in a laminar flame front. Imagine a flame fluttering above a gas burner of a kitchen stove. The backward-diffusion term injects instability into the system at large scales. The fourth-order term brings stability back into the system at small scales. The nonlinear convection term transfers stability between scales resulting in the formation of fronts. Eventually, the KSE exhibits chaotic behavior.

The KSE is quite stiff and quite sensitive to perturbations, so we should use a high-order IMEX method. Take $\hat{u} = F\,u$, then the KSE

$$u_t = -u_{xxxx} - u_{xx} - \tfrac{1}{2}\left(u^2\right)_x$$

can be written as

$$\hat{u}_t = (-\xi^4 + \xi^2)\hat{u} - \tfrac{1}{2}\mathrm{i}\xi\, F\!\left(F^{-1}\,\hat{u}\right)^2.$$

Let's solve the KSE using an initial condition $u(0, x) = e^{-x^2}$ over a periodic domain $[-50, 50]$ and a timespan of 200.[2]

```
using FFTW, DifferentialEquations, SciMLOperators
ℓ = 100; T = 200.0; n = 512
x = LinRange(-ℓ/2,ℓ/2,n+1)[2:end]
```

---

[2]In moving from Julia 1.7 to 1.9 and upgrading several packages, this code no longer works. :(

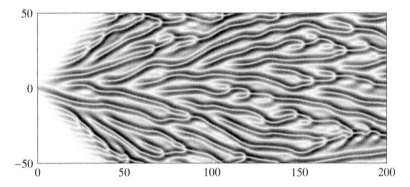

Figure 16.1: Solution to the Kuramoto–Sivashinsky equation for a Gaussian bump. Space is along the vertical axis and time is along the horizontal axis.

```
u₀ = exp.(-x.^2)
iξ = im*[0:(n÷2);(-n÷2+1):-1]*2π/ℓ
F = plan_fft(u₀)
L = DiagonalOperator(-iξ.^2-iξ.^4)
N = (u,_,_) -> -0.5iξ.*(F*((F\u).^2))
problem = SplitODEProblem(L,N,F*u₀,(0,T))
method = KenCarp3(linsolve=KrylovJL(),autodiff=false)
solution = solve(problem,method,reltol=1e-12)
u = t -> real(F\solution(t))
```

We can visualize the time evolution of the solution as a grayscale image with time along the horizontal axis and space along the vertical axis.

```
using ImageShow,ColorSchemes
s = hcat(u.(LinRange(0,T,500))...)
get(colorschemes[:binary],abs.(s),:extrema)
```

Black pixels depict magnitudes close to the maximum, and white pixels depict values close to zero. See the figure above and the animation at the QR code at the bottom of this page.   ◄

16.3   Incompressible Navier–Stokes equation

We can modify a one-dimensional Fourier spectral method to handle two- and three-dimensional problems by replacing the vector ξ with the tuple (ξ_1, ξ_2) and (ξ_1, ξ_2, ξ_3). To see this in practice, we'll solve the two-dimensional Navier–Stokes equation following an approach from Deuflhard and Hohmann [2003].

KSE animation

Consider the incompressible Navier–Stokes equation

$$\frac{\partial \mathbf{u}}{\partial t} + \mathbf{u} \cdot \nabla \mathbf{u} = -\nabla p + \varepsilon \Delta \mathbf{u} \qquad (16.8)$$

$$\nabla \cdot \mathbf{u} = 0, \qquad (16.9)$$

which models viscous fluid flow. The vector $\mathbf{u} = (u(t, x, y), v(t, x, y))$ is the velocity, $p(t, x, y)$ is the pressure, and ε is the inverse of the Reynolds number. Explicitly, the two-dimensional Navier–Stokes equation says

$$u_t + u u_x + v u_y = -p_x + \varepsilon(u_{xx} + u_{yy})$$
$$v_t + u v_x + v v_y = -p_y + \varepsilon(v_{xx} + v_{yy})$$
$$u_x + u_y = 0.$$

To solve the problem, we will find $\mathbf{u}$ using the conservation of momentum equation (16.8) and use the conservation of mass (16.9) as a constraint by forcing $\mathbf{u}$ to be divergence-free. Because (16.8) has stiff linear terms and nonlinear terms, we will use a second-order IMEX Adams–Bashforth/Crank–Nicolson method

$$\frac{\mathbf{u}^{n+1} - \mathbf{u}^n}{\Delta t} = \underbrace{-\tfrac{1}{2}\left(\nabla p^{n+1} + \nabla p^n\right)}_{\text{Crank–Nicolson}} - \underbrace{\left(\tfrac{3}{2}\mathbf{H}^n - \tfrac{1}{2}\mathbf{H}^{n-1}\right)}_{\text{Adams–Bashforth}} + \underbrace{\tfrac{1}{2}\varepsilon\left(\Delta \mathbf{u}^{n+1} + \Delta \mathbf{u}^n\right)}_{\text{Crank–Nicolson}},$$

where convective acceleration $\mathbf{H}^n$ is $\mathbf{u}^n \cdot \nabla \mathbf{u}^n$.

There are a couple of problems with this setup. First, we don't explicitly know p^{n+1}. Second, we haven't enforced the constraint (16.8). So, let's modify the approach by introducing an intermediate solution $\mathbf{u}^*$:

$$\frac{\mathbf{u}^* - \mathbf{u}^n}{\Delta t} = -\tfrac{1}{2}\nabla p^n - \tfrac{3}{2}\mathbf{H}^n + \tfrac{1}{2}\mathbf{H}^{n-1} + \tfrac{1}{2}\varepsilon(\Delta \mathbf{u}^* + \Delta \mathbf{u}^n) \qquad (16.10a)$$

$$\frac{\mathbf{u}^{n+1} - \mathbf{u}^*}{\Delta t} = -\tfrac{1}{2}\nabla p^{n+1} + \tfrac{1}{2}\varepsilon(\Delta \mathbf{u}^{n+1} - \Delta \mathbf{u}^*). \qquad (16.10b)$$

We'll be able to use the intermediate solution so that we don't explicitly need to compute the pressure p. First, solve (16.10a). Formally, we have

$$M_- \mathbf{u}^* = -\tfrac{1}{2}\nabla p^n - \tfrac{3}{2}\mathbf{H}^n + \tfrac{1}{2}\mathbf{H}^{n-1} + M_+ \mathbf{u}^n,$$

where the operators

$$M_- = \left(\tfrac{1}{\Delta t} - \tfrac{1}{2}\varepsilon\Delta\right) \quad \text{and} \quad M_+ = \left(\tfrac{1}{\Delta t} + \tfrac{1}{2}\varepsilon\Delta\right).$$

From this, we have

$$\mathbf{u}^* = M_-^{-1}\left(-\tfrac{1}{2}\nabla p^n - \tfrac{3}{2}\mathbf{H}^n + \tfrac{1}{2}\mathbf{H}^{n-1} + M_+ \mathbf{u}^n\right). \qquad (16.11)$$

We need to determine ∇p^{n+1} in such a way as to enforce the IMEX scheme by using (16.10b):

$$-\tfrac{1}{2}\nabla p^{n+1} = \mathrm{M}_-\left(\mathbf{u}^{n+1} - \mathbf{u}^*\right).$$

Equivalently,

$$-\tfrac{1}{2}\nabla p^n = \mathrm{M}_-\left(\mathbf{u}^n - \mathbf{u}^{*-1}\right), \tag{16.12}$$

where $\mathbf{u}^{*-1}$ is the intermediate solution at the previous time step. Substituting $-\tfrac{1}{2}\nabla p^n$ back into (16.11) yields

$$\begin{aligned}
\mathbf{u}^* &= \mathrm{M}_-^{-1}\left(\mathrm{M}_-\left(\mathbf{u}^n - \mathbf{u}^{*-1}\right) - \tfrac{3}{2}\mathbf{H}^n + \tfrac{1}{2}\mathbf{H}^{n-1} + \mathrm{M}_+\,\mathbf{u}^n\right)\\
&= \mathbf{u}^n - \mathbf{u}^{*-1} + \mathrm{M}_-^{-1}\left(-\tfrac{3}{2}\mathbf{H}^n + \tfrac{1}{2}\mathbf{H}^{n-1} + \mathrm{M}_+\,\mathbf{u}^n\right).
\end{aligned}$$

Finally, we enforce (16.9) by projecting the solution $\mathbf{u}^*$ onto a divergence-free vector field. Note that if we define

$$\mathbf{u}^{n+1} = \mathbf{u}^* - \nabla\Delta^{-1}\nabla\cdot\mathbf{u}^*,$$

then[3]

$$\nabla\cdot\mathbf{u}^{n+1} = \nabla\cdot\mathbf{u}^* - \nabla\cdot\nabla\Delta^{-1}\nabla\cdot\mathbf{u}^* = \nabla\cdot\mathbf{u}^* - \Delta\Delta^{-1}\nabla\cdot\mathbf{u}^* = 0.$$

We now have

$$\begin{aligned}
\mathbf{u}^* &= \mathbf{u}^n - \mathbf{u}^{*-1} + \mathrm{M}_-^{-1}\left(-\tfrac{3}{2}\mathbf{H}^n + \tfrac{1}{2}\mathbf{H}^{n-1} + \mathrm{M}_+\,\mathbf{u}^n\right)\\
\mathbf{u}^{n+1} &= \mathbf{u}^* - \nabla\Delta^{-1}\nabla\cdot\mathbf{u}^*.
\end{aligned}$$

To initialize the multistep method, we'll take

$$\mathbf{u}^{-1} = \mathbf{u}^{*-1} = \mathbf{u}^0.$$

In the Fourier domain, we replace

$$\nabla \to (i\xi_1, i\xi_2) \quad\text{and}\quad \Delta = \nabla\cdot\nabla \to -(\xi_1^2 \oplus \xi_2^2) = -|\xi|^2,$$

where the sum $\xi_1^2 \oplus \xi_2^2$ is broadcasted as $\xi_1^2\mathbf{1}^\mathsf{T} + \mathbf{1}(\xi_2^2)^\mathsf{T}$. From (16.13) we get (using the standard hat notation $\hat{\square}$ for the Fourier transform $F\square$),

$$\hat{\mathbf{u}}^* = \hat{\mathbf{u}}^n - \hat{\mathbf{u}}^{*-1} + \hat{\mathrm{M}}_+^{-1}\left(-\tfrac{3}{2}\hat{\mathbf{H}}^n + \tfrac{1}{2}\hat{\mathbf{H}}^{n-1} + \hat{\mathrm{M}}_-\hat{\mathbf{u}}^n\right) \tag{16.14a}$$

$$\hat{\mathbf{u}}^{n+1} = \hat{\mathbf{u}}^* - \frac{(\xi\cdot\hat{\mathbf{u}}^*)}{|\xi|^2}\xi \tag{16.14b}$$

---

[3] Do you recognize the projection operators $\mathbf{P}_\mathbf{A} = \mathbf{A}(\mathbf{A}^\mathsf{T}\mathbf{A})^{-1}\mathbf{A}^\mathsf{T}$ and $\mathbf{I} - \mathbf{P}_\mathbf{A}$?

where

$$\hat{M}_- = \tfrac{1}{\Delta t} - \tfrac{1}{2}\varepsilon|\xi|^2 \quad \text{and} \quad \hat{M}_+ = \tfrac{1}{\Delta t} + \tfrac{1}{2}\varepsilon|\xi|^2.$$

We must be cautious when dividing by $|\xi|^2$ in (16.14b) because one of the components is zero. In this case, we modify the term by replacing the zeros with ones. This fix is itself fixed when we subsequently multiply by ξ.

We haven't discussed the implementation of the nonlinear term $\hat{H}$ yet. If $\mathbf{u}$ is given by (u, v), the x-component of $\mathbf{H}$ is

$$H(u, v) = uu_x + vu_y,$$

with a similar form for a y-component. The Fourier transform of a product of two functions uv is the convolution $\hat{u} * \hat{v}$—an inefficient operator to implement directly. Therefore, we'll evaluate $\hat{H}$ in the spatial domain rather than the Fourier domain. Hence, we take

$$\hat{H}(\hat{u}, \hat{v}) = F\big(F^{-1}\,\hat{u}\,F^{-1}\,(i\xi_1\hat{u}) + F^{-1}\,\hat{v}\,F^{-1}\,(i\xi_2\hat{u})\big).$$

To visualize the solution, we use a tracer. Imagine dropping ink (or smoke) into a moving fluid and following the ink's motion. Numerically, we can simulate a tracer by solving the advection equation

$$\frac{\partial Q}{\partial t} + \mathbf{u} \cdot \nabla Q = 0 \tag{16.15}$$

using the Lax–Wendroff method, where $\mathbf{u}$ is the solution to the Navier–Stokes equation at each time step.

Consider a stratified fluid moving in the x-direction separated from a stationary fluid by a narrow interface. Suppose we further modulate the speed of the fluid in the flow direction. Think of wind blowing over water. The pressure decreases in regions where the moving fluid moves faster, pulling on the stationary fluid and causing it to bulge. This situation leads to Kelvin–Helmholtz instability, producing surface waves in water and turbulence in otherwise laminar fluids. Kelvin–Helmholtz instability can be seen in the cloud bands of Jupiter, the sun's corona, and billow clouds here on Earth. Some think that the Kelvin–Helmholtz instability in billow clouds may have inspired the swirls in van Gogh's painting "The Starry Night." See the figure on the following page. To model an initial stratified flow in a 2×2 square, we will take zero vertical velocity v and

$$u = \tfrac{1}{4}\,(2 + \sin 2\pi x)\,Q(x, y) \text{ where } Q(x, y) = \tfrac{1}{2} + \tfrac{1}{2}\tanh\big(10 - 20\,|y - 1|\big).$$

The Julia code to solve the Navier–Stokes equation has three parts: defining the functions, initializing the variables, and iterating over time. We start by defining functions for $\hat{H}$ and for the flux used in the Lax–Wendroff method.

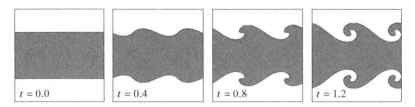

Figure 16.2: The emergence of Kelvin–Helmholtz instability in the Navier–Stokes equation. Also, see the QR code at the bottom of this page.

```
Δ°(Q,step=1) = Q - circshift(Q,(step,0))
flux(Q,c) = c.*Δ°(Q) - 0.5c.*(1 .- c).*(Δ°(Q,1)+Δ°(Q,-1))
H = (u,v,iξ₁,iξ₂) -> F*((F\u).*(F\(iξ₁.*u)) + (F\v).*(F\(iξ₂.*u)))
```

Next, we initialize the variables.

```
using FFTW
ℓ = 2; n = 128; ε = 0.001; Δt = 0.001; Δx = ℓ/n
x = LinRange(Δx,ℓ,n)'; y = x'
Q = (@. 0.5(1 + tanh(10 - 20abs(1 - 2y/ℓ)))).*ones(1,n)
uⁿ = Q .* (1 .+ 0.5sin.(ℓ*π*x))
vⁿ = zeros(n,n)
F = plan_fft(uⁿ)
uⁿ, vⁿ = F*uⁿ, F*vⁿ
u°, v° = uⁿ, vⁿ
iξ₁ = im*fftfreq(n,n)'*(2π/ℓ)
iξ₂ = transpose(iξ₁)
ξ² = iξ₁.^2 .+ iξ₂.^2
H₁ⁿ, H₂ⁿ = H(uⁿ,vⁿ,iξ₁,iξ₂), H(vⁿ,uⁿ,iξ₂,iξ₁)
M₊ = (1/Δt .+ (ε/2)*ξ²)
M₋ = (1/Δt .- (ε/2)*ξ²);
```

Finally, we loop in time.

```
for i = 1:1200
    Q -= flux(Q,(Δt/Δx).*real(F\vⁿ)) + flux(Q',(Δt/Δx).*real(F\uⁿ)')'
    H₁ⁿ⁻¹, H₂ⁿ⁻¹ = H₁ⁿ, H₂ⁿ
    H₁ⁿ, H₂ⁿ = H(uⁿ,vⁿ,iξ₁,iξ₂), H(vⁿ,uⁿ,iξ₂,iξ₁)
    u° = uⁿ - u° + (-1.5H₁ⁿ + 0.5H₁ⁿ⁻¹ + M₊.*uⁿ)./M₋
    v° = vⁿ - v° + (-1.5H₂ⁿ + 0.5H₂ⁿ⁻¹ + M₊.*vⁿ)./M₋
    φ = (iξ₁.*u° + iξ₂.*v°)./(ξ² .+ (ξ².≈ 0))
    uⁿ, vⁿ = u° - iξ₁.*φ, v° - iξ₂.*φ
end
contour(x',y,Q,fill=true,levels=1,legend=:none)
```

Kelvin–Helmholtz
instability

16.4   Exercises

16.1. Solve the Schrödinger equation discussed on page 465 using Strang splitting and using integrating factors. Take a harmonic potential $V(x) = x^2$ with initial conditions $u(0, x) = e^{-(x-3)^2/\varepsilon}$ with $\varepsilon = 0.1$ over a domain $[-8, 8]$.

16.2. Suppose you use a fourth-order Runge–Kutta scheme to solve the Burgers equation $u_t + \frac{1}{2}\left(u^2\right)_x = 0$ discretized with a Fourier spectral method. What order can you expect? What else can you say about the numerical solution?   ✍

16.3. The Kortweg–deVries (KdV) equation

$$u_t + 3(u^2)_x + u_{xxx} = 0 \qquad (16.16)$$

is a nonlinear equation used to model wave motion in a dispersive medium, such as shallow water or optic fiber. This exercise aims to explore the behavior of the KdV equation by first developing a high-order numerical scheme to solve the equation and then using the scheme to simulate soliton interaction.

Dispersion means that different frequencies travel at different speeds, causing a solution to break up and spread out over time. For certain classes of initial conditions, the nonlinearity of the KdV equation counteracts the dispersion, and the solution maintains its shape. We call such a solution a solitary wave or a soliton. It can be easily shown by substitution that

$$\phi(x, t; x_0, c) = \tfrac{1}{2}c \operatorname{sech}^2\left(\frac{\sqrt{c}}{2}(x - x_0 - ct)\right)$$

is a soliton solution to the KdV equation. This solution is a traveling wave solution, which simply moves with speed c and does not change shape.

Solve the KdV equation (16.16) on the interval $[-15, 15]$ for $t \in [0, 2]$ using a fourth-order Runge–Kutta method with integrating factors. Observe the solutions to (16.16) with initial conditions given by $\phi(x, 0; -4, 4)$, $\phi(x, 0; -9, 9)$, and $\phi(x, 0; -4, 4) + \phi(x, 0; -9, 9)$. These initial conditions produce solitons with speeds 4 and 9 centered at $x = -4$ and $x = -9$, respectively. In the two soliton case, the two solitons should combine nonlinearly as the faster one overtakes the slower one. You may also want to observe a three-soliton collision by adding another soliton (say $\phi(x, 0; -12, 12)$).   ✍

16.4. The two-dimensional Swift–Hohenberg equation

$$\frac{\partial u}{\partial t} = \varepsilon u - u^3 - (\Delta + 1)^2 u$$

with $u \equiv u(t, x, y)$ models Rayleigh–Bénard convection, which results when a shallow pan of water is heated from below. Compute the numerical solution for $\varepsilon = 1$ over a square with sides of length 100. Assume periodic boundary conditions with 256 grid points in x and y. Choose $u(0, x, y)$ randomly from the uniform distribution $[-1, 1]$. Output the solution at time $t = 100$ and several intermediate times.   ✍

16.5. Sudden phase separation can set in if a homogeneous molten alloy of two metals is rapidly cooled.[4] The Cahn–Hilliard equation

$$\frac{\partial \phi}{\partial t} = \Delta \left(f'(\phi) - \varepsilon^2 \Delta \phi \right) \quad \text{with} \quad f'(\phi) = \phi^3 - \phi$$

models such phase separation. The dynamics of the Cahn–Hilliard equation are driven by surface tension flow, in which interfaces move with velocities proportional to mean curvature, and the total volumes of the binary regions are constant over time. A convexity-splitting method

$$\frac{\partial \phi}{\partial t} = L\phi + N\phi = \left(-\varepsilon^2 \Delta^2 + \alpha \Delta \right) \phi^{(n+1)} + \Delta \left(f'(\phi^{(n)}) - \alpha \phi^{(n)} \right)$$

balances the terms to ensure energy stability—see Wu et al. [2014] or Lee et al. [2014]. Solve the two-dimensional Cahn–Hilliard equation with $\varepsilon = 0.1$, starting with random initial conditions over a square periodic domain of length 8 over a time $[0, 8]$. Take $\alpha = 1$.   ✍

16.6. The two-dimensional Kuramoto–Sivashinsky equation can be written as

$$\frac{\partial v}{\partial t} + \Delta v + \Delta^2 v + \tfrac{1}{2} |\nabla v|^2 = 0,$$

where $\mathbf{u} = \nabla v$ is the two-dimensional vector-field extension of the variable u in the one-dimensional KSE (16.7). To solve this equation, we'll further impose a mean-zero restriction $\int_\Omega |\nabla v|^2 \, d\Omega = 0$. Solve the two-dimensional KSE using a Gaussian bump or normal random initial conditions over a periodic domain of length 50 and a timespan $t = 150$.

We can enforce the mean-zero restriction by zeroing out the zero-frequency component in the Fourier domain. Kalogirou [2014] develops a second-order IMEX BDF method using the splitting

$$\frac{\partial v}{\partial t} = Lv + Nv = -(\Delta^2 + \Delta + \alpha)v - (\tfrac{1}{2}|\nabla v|^2 - \alpha v),$$

where α is a positive splitting-stabilization constant added to ensure that operator on the implicit term is positive-definite and thus invertible.   ✍

---

[4]Alternatively, imagine vigorously shaking a bottle of vinaigrette and then watching the oil and vinegar separate, first into tiny globules and then coarsening into larger and larger ones.

Back Matter

Appendix A

Solutions

A.1 Numerical methods for linear algebra

1.3. For the Krylov subspace:

(a) If $\mathbf{x}$ is an eigenvector of $\mathbf{A}$, then $\mathbf{Ax} = \lambda\mathbf{x}$, $\mathbf{A}^2\mathbf{x} = \lambda^2\mathbf{x}$, and so on. The subspace is spanned entirely by $\mathbf{x}$, so its dimension is 1.

(b) If $\mathbf{x} = a\mathbf{v}_1 + b\mathbf{v}_2$ for two linearly independent eigenvectors of $\mathbf{A}$, then

$$\mathbf{Ax} = a\mathbf{Av}_1 + b\mathbf{Av}_2 = a\lambda_1\mathbf{v}_1 + b\lambda_2\mathbf{v}_2,$$
$$\mathbf{A}^2\mathbf{x} = a\mathbf{A}^2\mathbf{v}_1 + b\mathbf{A}^2\mathbf{v}_2 = a\lambda_1^2\mathbf{v}_1 + b\lambda_2^2\mathbf{v}_2,$$

and so on. . .

So the Krylov subspace is spanned by linear combinations of the eigenvectors $\mathbf{v}_1$ and $\mathbf{v}_2$, and the dimension is two.

(c) If $\mathbf{A}$ is a projection operator, then $\mathbf{A}^2 = \mathbf{A}$. It follows that the Krylov subspace $\mathcal{K}_r(\mathbf{A}, \mathbf{x}) = \text{span}\{\mathbf{x}, \mathbf{Ax}\}$. If $\mathbf{x}$ is in the null space of $\mathbf{A}$ then $\mathbf{Ax} = \mathbf{0}$. So, the maximum dimension is 2.

(d) For any vector $\mathbf{x}$, the vector $\mathbf{Ax}$ is in the column space of $\mathbf{A}$, which has dimension $n - m$. So, the Krylov subspace is spanned by $\mathbf{x}$ and the column space of $\mathbf{A}$. So, the maximum dimension of the Krylov subspace is $n - m + 1$ (and $n - m$ if $\mathbf{x}$ is in the column space of $\mathbf{A}$).

1.4. The number of invertible $(0,1)$-matrices has been the subject of some research and is a yet unsolved problem. There is an entry in the Online Encyclopedia of Integer Sequences (often called Sloane in reference to its curator Neil Sloane) at http://oeis.org/A055165. We can estimate the number by generating random

(0,1)-matrices and testing them for singularity. The following Julia code generates the accompanying plot:

```julia
using LinearAlgebra, Plots
N = 10000
n = [sum([!(det(rand(Bool,d,d))≈0)
    for i in 1:N]) for d in 1:20]
plot(n/N,marker=:o)
```

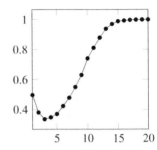

1.5. We'll use a subscript to indicate a matrix's size.

(a) Instead of attacking $\mathbf{D}_n$ head on, let's use $\mathbf{M}_n = \mathbf{D}_n + 2\mathbf{I}$, a matrix with ones along the upper and lower diagonals. If $(\lambda, \mathbf{x})$ is an eigenpair of $\mathbf{M}_n$, then

$$\mathbf{D}_n\mathbf{x} = (\mathbf{M}_n - 2\mathbf{I})\mathbf{x} = (\lambda - 2)\mathbf{x}.$$

So $(\lambda - 2, \mathbf{x})$ is an eigenpair of $\mathbf{D}_n$. The eigenvalues λ of $\mathbf{M}_n$ are zeros of the characteristic polynomial $p_n(\lambda) = \det(\mathbf{M}_n - \lambda\mathbf{I})$, which we can evaluate using Laplace (or cofactor) expansion. We have

$$\begin{aligned}
p_n(\lambda) &= \det(\mathbf{M}_n - \lambda\mathbf{I}) \\
&= -\lambda \det(\mathbf{M}_{n-1} - \lambda\mathbf{I}) - \det(\mathbf{M}_{n-2} - \lambda\mathbf{I}) \\
&= -\lambda p_{n-1}(\lambda) - p_{n-2}(\lambda).
\end{aligned}$$

We can confirm the vaules of $p_2(\lambda)$ and $p_1(\lambda)$ by expanding $p_3(\lambda)$.

$$p_3(\lambda) = \begin{vmatrix} -\lambda & 1 & 0 \\ 1 & -\lambda & 1 \\ 0 & 1 & -\lambda \end{vmatrix} = -\lambda \begin{vmatrix} -\lambda & 1 \\ 1 & -\lambda \end{vmatrix} - 1 \begin{vmatrix} 1 & 1 \\ 0 & -\lambda \end{vmatrix},$$

from which we have $p_2(\lambda) = \lambda^2 - 1$ and $p_1(\lambda) = -\lambda$. With mathematical foresight (or *deus ex machina*?), we may recognize the expression $p_n(\lambda)$ as the three-term recurrence relation for the Chebyshev polynomial of the second kind $U_n(-2\lambda)$. The roots of $U_n(x)$ are

$$x_i = \cos \frac{i\pi}{n+1} \quad \text{for } i = 1, 2, \ldots, n.$$

Therefore, the eigenvalues of $\mathbf{D}_n$ are given by

$$\lambda_i - 2 = -2 - 2\cos \frac{i\pi}{n+1} \quad \text{for } i = 1, 2, \ldots, n.$$

(b) The spectral radius of $\mathbf{D}_n + 2\mathbf{I}$ is

$$\rho(\mathbf{D}_n + 2\mathbf{I}) = \max_{j=1,\ldots,n} \left| -2\cos\frac{i\pi}{n+1} \right| = 2\cos\frac{\pi}{n+1}.$$

(c) The 2-norm condition number for a symmetric matrix is the ratio of the largest eigenvalue to the smallest eigenvalue.

$$\kappa_2(\mathbf{D}_n) = \frac{1 + \cos\frac{\pi}{n+1}}{1 - \cos\frac{\pi}{n+1}} \approx \frac{2 - \frac{1}{2}\left(\frac{\pi}{n+1}\right)^2}{\frac{1}{2}\left(\frac{\pi}{n+1}\right)^2} \approx \frac{4}{\pi^2}(n+1)^2$$

when n is large. So the condition number of D_n is $O(n^2)$.

(d) An easy way to input $\mathbf{D}_n$ in Julia is with

```
D = SymTridiagonal(-2ones(n), ones(n-1))
```

We can compute the eigenvalues and eigenvectors using `eigen(D)`. Alternatively, we can use the pipe operator `D |> eigen`. We confirm the solution of parts (b) and (c) using

```
( 2cos(π/(n+1)) , maximum(eigen(D+2I).values) ) |> display
( 4(n+1)^2/π^2, cond(D) ) |> display
```

1.9. We'll start with (e)

(e) The trace of a matrix equals the sum of its diagonal elements. The ith diagonal element of $\mathbf{A}^\mathsf{T}\mathbf{A}$ equals $\sum_{j=1}^{n} a_{ij}^2$. So $\mathrm{tr}(\mathbf{A}^\mathsf{T}\mathbf{A}) = \sum_{i,j=1}^{n} a_{ij}^2$, which equals $\|\mathbf{A}\|_\mathrm{F}^2$.

(b) The matrix $\mathbf{Q}^\mathsf{T}\mathbf{Q}$ is $n \times n$ identity matrix $\mathbf{I}$. The trace of $\mathbf{I}$ is n. Therefore, using the result from (e), $\|\mathbf{Q}\|_\mathrm{F} = \sqrt{n}$.

(c) Using the result from (e),

$$\|\mathbf{QA}\|_\mathrm{F}^2 = \mathrm{tr}\big((\mathbf{QA})^\mathsf{T}\mathbf{QA}\big) = \mathrm{tr}\big(\mathbf{A}^\mathsf{T}\mathbf{Q}^\mathsf{T}\mathbf{QA}\big) = \mathrm{tr}\big(\mathbf{A}^\mathsf{T}\mathbf{A}\big) = \|\mathbf{A}\|_\mathrm{F}^2.$$

(d) Suppose that $\mathbf{A}$ has the singular value decomposition $\mathbf{A} = \mathbf{U}\mathbf{\Sigma}\mathbf{V}^\mathsf{T}$. Then using the result of (c),

$$\|\mathbf{A}\|_\mathrm{F}^2 = \|\mathbf{U}\mathbf{\Sigma}\mathbf{V}^\mathsf{T}\|_\mathrm{F}^2 = \|\mathbf{\Sigma}\mathbf{V}^\mathsf{T}\|_\mathrm{F}^2 = \|\mathbf{V}\mathbf{\Sigma}^\mathsf{T}\|_\mathrm{F}^2 = \|\mathbf{\Sigma}^\mathsf{T}\|^2 = \sum_{i=1}^{n} \sigma_i^2.$$

(a) By reshaping the $m \times n$ vector $\mathbf{A}$ as an $mn \times 1$ array $\mathbf{a}$, we can interpret the Frobenius norm as simply the 2-norm of $\mathbf{a}$. The 2-norm of a vector satisfies positivity, homogeneity, and the triangle inequality. So the Frobenius norm does, too.

(g) To show submultiplicitivity $\|\mathbf{AB}\|_F \leq \|\mathbf{A}\|_F \|\mathbf{B}\|_F$, we compute

$$\|\mathbf{AB}\|_F^2 = \sum_{i,j} \sum_k (a_{ik} b_{kj})^2 = \sum_{i,j} \sum_k a_{ik}^2 b_{kj}^2 = \sum_k \left(\sum_i a_{ik}^2 \right) \left(\sum_j b_{kj}^2 \right)$$
$$\leq \sum_{i,k} a_{ik}^2 \sum_{k,j} b_{kj}^2 = \|\mathbf{A}\|_F^2 \|\mathbf{B}\|_F^2.$$

(f) $\|\mathbf{Ax}\|_F \leq \|\mathbf{Ax}\|_F \|\mathbf{x}\|$ follows from submultiplicitivity proved in (g).

2.4. The number of n-step walks of a graph G is $\mathbf{A}^n$. So

$$\mathbf{A} = \begin{bmatrix} 0 & 1 & 0 & 1 \\ 1 & 0 & 2 & 1 \\ 0 & 2 & 0 & 0 \\ 1 & 1 & 0 & 0 \end{bmatrix} \quad \text{and} \quad \mathbf{A}^3 = \begin{bmatrix} 2 & 7 & 2 & 3 \\ 7 & 2 & 12 & 7 \\ 2 & 12 & 0 & 2 \\ 3 & 7 & 2 & 2 \end{bmatrix}.$$

Note that

$$\sum_{n=0}^{\infty} \mathbf{A}^n z^n = \sum_{n=0}^{\infty} (z\mathbf{A})^n = (\mathbf{I} - z\mathbf{A})^{-1} \quad \text{for} \quad |z| < \frac{1}{\rho(\mathbf{A})}.$$

Let $\mathbf{B} = (\mathbf{I} - z\mathbf{A})$. We can use Cramer's rule to compute $\mathbf{B}^{-1}$ one entry at a time:

$$w_{ij}(z) = \frac{(-1)^{i+j} \det \mathbf{M}_{ij}}{\det \mathbf{B}},$$

where $\mathbf{M}_{ij}$ is the ij-minor of $\mathbf{B}$, obtained by removing the ith row and jth column. The function $w_{ij}(z)$ is the generating function for walks from $i \to j$. Let's determine $w_{13}(z)$.

$$\det \mathbf{B} = \begin{vmatrix} 1 & -z & 0 & -z \\ -z & 1 & -2z & -z \\ 0 & -2z & 1 & 0 \\ -z & -z & 0 & 1 \end{vmatrix} = -(-2z) \begin{vmatrix} 1 & -z & -z \\ 0 & -2z & 0 \\ -z & -z & 1 \end{vmatrix} + \begin{vmatrix} 1 & -z & -z \\ -z & 1 & -z \\ -z & -z & 1 \end{vmatrix}$$
$$= 2z(-2z + 2z^3) + (1 + 2z^3 - 3z^2) = 4z^4 - 2z^3 - 7z^2 + 1, \quad \text{and}$$

$$\det \mathbf{M}_{13} = \begin{vmatrix} -z & 0 & -z \\ 1 & -2z & -z \\ -z & 0 & 1 \end{vmatrix} = 2z^3 + 2z^2.$$

Hence,

$$w_{13}(z) = \frac{2z^3 + 2z^2}{4z^4 - 2z^3 - 7z^2 + 1} = \frac{2z^2}{4z^3 - 6z^2 - z + 1}.$$

Finally, we can use the identity $(1 - r)^{-1} = 1 + r + r^2 + r^3 + \cdots$ to compute the power series of $w_{13}(z)$.

Alternatively, we could use Wolfram Cloud to do the tedious calculations.[1]

```
A = {{0,1,0,1},{1,0,2,1},{0,2,0,0},{1,1,0,0}};
W = Inverse[IdentityMatrix[4] - z*A];
Simplify[W[[1,3]]]
Series[%,{z,0,10}]
```

$$w_{13}(z) = 2z^2 + 2z^3 + 14z^4 + 18z^5 + 94z^6 + 146z^7 + 638z^8 + 1138z^9 + O(z^{10}).$$

We verify the coefficients by computing the number of walks using Julia

```
A = [0 1 0 1;1 0 2 1;0 2 0 0;1 1 0 0]
walks(A,i,j,N) = [(A^n)[i,j] for n in 1:N]
walks(A,1,3,9)
```

2.3. The determinant of a product equals the product of the determinants. We can use this identity and LU factorization to efficiently determine the compute of a matrix. The LU factorization of a matrix **A** using partial pivoting is given by **PA** = **LU**, where **P** is a permutation matrix, **L** is a lower triangular matrix with ones along its diagonal, and **U** is an upper triangular matrix. The determinant of a triangular matrix is the product of the diagonal elements. So $\det \mathbf{L} = 1$. The determinant of a permutation matrix equals +1, if the permutation matrix was built from identify matrix using an even number of row exchanges (even parity). It equals -1, if it was built using an odd number (odd parity). So

$$\det \mathbf{A} = \det \mathbf{P} \det \mathbf{L} \det \mathbf{U} = \text{sign}(\mathbf{P}) \prod_{i=1}^{N} \text{diag } \mathbf{U}.$$

The LinearAlgebra.jl function `lu` will give us **U** and **P**. We still need to compute the sign of the permutation.

```
function detx(A)
  L,U,P = lu(A)
  s = 1
  for i in 1:length(P)
    m = findfirst(P.==i)
```

---

[1] Wolfram Cloud (https://www.wolframcloud.com) has a free basic plan that provides complete access to Mathematica with a few limitations.

```
    i!=m && ( s *= -1; P[[m,i]]=P[[i,m]] )
  end
  s * prod(diag(U))
end
```

2.5. Let's fill in the steps of the Cuthill–McKee algorithm outlined on page 51. Start with a (0,1)-adjacency matrix **A**, and create a list *r* of vertices ordered from lowest to highest degree. Create another initially empty list *q* that will serve as a temporary first-in-first-out queue for the vertices before finally adding them to the permutation list *p*, also initially empty. Start by moving the first element from *r* to *q*. As long as the queue *q* is not empty, move the first element of *q* to the end of *p*, and move any vertex in *r* adjacent to this element to the end of *q*. If *q* is ever empty, go back and move the first element of *r* to *q*. Continue until all the elements from *r* have been moved through *q* to *p*. Finally, we reverse the order of *p*. The following Julia function produces a permutation vector p for a sparse matrix A using the reverse Cuthill–McKee algorithm.

```
function rcuthillmckee(A)
  r = sortperm(vec(sum(A.!=0,dims=2)))
  p = Int64[]
  while ~isempty(r)
    q = [popfirst!(r)]
    while ~isempty(q)
      q₁ = popfirst!(q)
      append!(p,q₁)
      k = findall(!iszero, A[q₁,r])
      append!(q,splice!(r,k))
    end
  end
  reverse(p)
end
```

We can test the solution using the following code:

```
using SparseArrays
A = sparse(Symmetric(sprand(1000,1000,0.003)))
p = rcuthillmckee(A)
plot(spy(A), spy(A[p,p]), colorbar = false)
```

2.6. Let's plot the graph of the Doubtful Sound dolphins reusing the code on page 49. The figure on the next page shows the sparsity plots and graphs before and after Cuthill–McKee resorting.

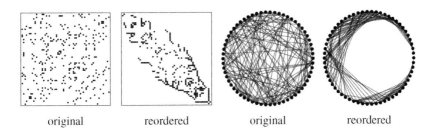

| original | reordered | original | reordered |

Figure A.1: Sparsity plots and graph drawings of the dolphins of Doubtful Sound.

```
p = rcuthillmckee(A)
gplot(Graph(A[p,p]),layout=circular_layout)
```

2.8. Loading the CSV file as a dataframe will allow us to inspect and interpret the data.

```
using CSV, DataFrames
diet = DataFrame(CSV.File(download(bucket*"diet.csv")))
```

We can solve the diet problem as a dual LP problem: "Find the minimum of the objective function $z = \mathbf{b}^\mathsf{T}\mathbf{y}$ subject to constraint $\mathbf{A}^\mathsf{T}\mathbf{y} \geq \mathbf{c}$ and non-negativity restriction $\mathbf{y}, \mathbf{c} \geq 0$." The nutritional value for each of the commodities is given by $\mathbf{A}$, the nutrient minimums are given by $\mathbf{b}$, and because the nutritional values of foods are normalized per dollar of expenditure, $\mathbf{c}$ is a vector of ones.

```
A = Array(diet[2:end,4:end])'
c = ones.(size(A,2))
b = Array(diet[1,4:end])
food = diet[2:end,1]
solution = simplex(b,A',c)
print("foods: ", food[solution.y .!= 0], "\n")
print("daily cost: ", solution.z)
```

We can alternatively use JuMP.jl along with GLPK.jl. The JuMP function `value`, which returns the solution's values, has a name common to other libraries. We'll explicitly call it using `JuMP.value` to avoid confusion or conflicts.

```
using JuMP, GLPK
model = Model(GLPK.Optimizer)
@variable(model, x[1:size(A,2)] ≥ 0)
@objective(model, Min, c' * x)
@constraint(model, A * x .≥ b)
```

```
optimize!(model)
print("foods: ", food[JuMP.value.(x) .!= 0], "\n")
print("daily cost: ", objective_value(model))
```

A combination of the following foods meet the nutritional requirements at the lowest cost: enriched wheat flour, beef liver, cabbage, spinach, and navy beans. The cost is roughly 11 cents per day in 1939 dollars—about $2.12 today.

2.9. Let's write a breath-first search algorithm—we can modify the code for the Cuthill–McKee algorithm in exercise 2.5. We'll keep track of three arrays: an array q that records the unique indices of the visited nodes and their neighboring nodes, an array p of pointers to the parent nodes recorded in this first array, and an array r of nodes that haven't yet been added to array q. Start with a source node a and find all nearest neighbors using the adjacency matrix A restricted to rows r. Then with each iteration, march along q looking for new neighbors until we've either found the destination node b or run out of new nodes to visit, indicating no path. Once we've found b, we backtrack along p to determine the path.

```
function findpath(A,a,b)
  r = collect(1:size(A,2))
  q = [a]; p = [-1]; i = 0
  splice!(r,a)
  while i<length(q)
    k = findall(!iszero, A[q[i+=1],r])
    any(r[k].==b) && return(append!(q[backtrack(p,i)],b))
    append!(q,splice!(r,k))
    append!(p,fill(i,length(k)))
  end
  display("No path.")
end
```

```
function backtrack(p,i)
  s = []; while (i!=-1); append!(s,i); i = p[i]; end
  return(reverse(s))
end
```

Let's import the data and build an adjacency matrix. We'll use the function get_adjacency_matrix defined on page 49 to construct the adjacency matrix, and we'll use get_names to build a list of the names.

```
get_names(filename) = readdlm(download(bucket*filename*".txt"),'\n')
```

```
actors = get_names("actors")
movies = get_names("movies")
B = get_adjacency_matrix("actor-movie");
```

The biadjacency matrix $\mathbf{B}$ indicates which actors (columns) appeared in which movies (rows). The matrix $\mathbf{BB}^\mathsf{T}$ gives us the movie-movie adjacency matrix, and the matrix $\mathbf{B}^\mathsf{T}\mathbf{B}$ gives us the actor-actor adjacency matrix. We can write the adjacency matrix of a bipartite graph as a block matrix

$$\mathbf{A} = \begin{bmatrix} \mathbf{0} & \mathbf{B}^\mathsf{T} \\ \mathbf{B} & \mathbf{0} \end{bmatrix}.$$

Using $\mathbf{A}$ will tell us both the actors and their connecting movies.

```
(m,n) = size(B)
A = [spzeros(n,n) B' ; B spzeros(m,m)];
actormovie = [ actors ; movies ];
```

Let's find the link between actors Emma Watson and Kevin Bacon.

```
index = x -> findfirst(actors.==x)[1]
actormovie[findpath(A, index("Emma Watson"), index("Kevin Bacon"))]
```

Emma Watson appeared in *Harry Potter and the Chamber of Secrets* with John Cleese, who appeared in *The Big Picture* with Kevin Bacon. Let's try another:

```
actormovie[findpath(A, index("Bruce Lee"), index("Tommy Wiseau"))]
```

Bruce Lee appeared in *Enter the Dragon* with Jackie Chan, who appeared in *Rush Hour* with Barry Shabaka Henley, who was in *Patch Adams* with Greg Sestero, who appeared in *The Room* with the great Tommy Wiseau. One might wonder which actor is the center of Hollywood. We'll come back to answer this question in exercise 4.6.

2.10. An $m \times n$ matrix with density d has dmn nonzero elements. Storing a matrix using CSC format requires at most $m + 1$ memory addresses for the column indexes, dmn addresses to identify the rows of each nonzero element, and dmn addresses for each of the values. A 64-bit processor storing double-precision floating-point numbers will need $2dmn + m + 1$ eight-byte blocks to store a CSC matrix and mn blocks for full matrix in memory. The CSC format saves space as long as the density is less than around 0.5. We can check this result by explicitly computing the bytes of memory used in a sparse matrix:

```
d = 0.5; A = sprand(800,600,d)
Base.summarysize(A)/Base.summarysize(Matrix(A))
```

A complex floating-point number is 16-bytes long. We'd need $3dmn + m + 1$ blocks for a CSC matrix versus $2mn$ blocks for a full matrix. The break-even point for the density is around 0.66. We can check this result by with `A .+= 0im`.

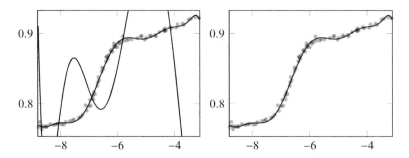

Figure A.2: Solutions to Exercise 3.5. The left plot shows solutions using the Vandermonde matrix built using the original x-data and the right plot shows solutions using the Vandermonde matrix built using the mean-centered x-data.

3.4. Take **X** to grayscale image (with pixel intensity between 0 and 1), **A** and **B** to be Gaussian blurring matrices with standard deviations of 20 pixels, and **N** to be a matrix of random values from the uniform distribution over the interval $(0, 0.01)$.

```
X = load(download(bucket*"laura.png")) .|> Gray
m,n = size(X)
blur = x -> exp(-(x/20).^2/2)
A = [blur(i-j) for i=1:m, j=1:m]; A ./= sum(A,dims=2)
B = [blur(i-j) for i=1:n, j=1:n]; B ./= sum(B,dims=1)
N = 0.01*rand(m,n)
Y = A*X*B + N;
```

We'll compare three deblurring methods: inverse, Tikhonov regulation, and the pseuodinverse. We can find a good value for regulariation parameter $\alpha = 0.05$ with some trial-and-error.

```
α = 0.05
X₁ = A\Y/B
X₂ = (A'*A+α^2*I)\A'*Y*B'/(B*B'+α^2*I)
X₃ = pinv(A,α)*Y*pinv(B,α)
Gray.([X Y X₁ X₂ X₃])
```

3.5. We'll start by defining a function to construct a Vandermonde matrix and evaluate a polynomial using that matrix:

```
vandermonde(t,n) = vec(t).^(0:n-1)'
build_poly(c,X) = vandermonde(X,length(c))*c
```

Now, we'll make a function that determines the coefficients and residuals using three different methods. The command Matrix(Q) returns the thin version of the QRCompactWYQ object returned by the qr function.

```
function solve_filip(x,y,n)
  V = vandermonde(x, n)
  c = Array{Float64}(undef, 3, n)
  c[1,:] = (V'*V)\(V'*y)
  Q,R = qr(V)
  c[2,:] = R\(Matrix(Q)'*y)
  c[3,:] = pinv(V,1e-9)*y
  r = [norm(V*c[i,:]-y) for i in 1:3]
  return(c,r)
end
```

Let's download the NIST Filip dataset, solve the problem, and plot the solutions:

```
using DelimitedFiles
data = readdlm(download(bucket*"filip.csv"),',',Float64)
coef = readdlm(download(bucket*"filip-coeffs.csv"),',')
(x,y) = (data[:,2],data[:,1])
β,r = solve_filip(x, y, 11)
X = LinRange(minimum(x),maximum(x),200)
Y = [build_poly(β[i,:],X) for i in 1:3]
plot(X,Y); scatter!(x,y,opacity=0.5)
[coef β']
```

Let's also solve the problem and plot the solutions for the standardized data:

```
using Statistics
zscore(X,x=X) = (X .- mean(x))/std(x)
c,r = solve_filip(zscore(x), zscore(y), 11)
Y = [build_poly(c[i,:],zscore(X,x))*std(y).+mean(y) for i in 1:3]
plot(X,Y); scatter!(x,y,opacity=0.5)
```

The 2-condition number of the Vandermonde matrix is 1.7×10^{15}, which makes it very ill-conditioned. The residuals are $\|\mathbf{r}\|_2 = 0.97998$ using the normal equation and $\|\mathbf{r}\|_2 = 0.028211$ using QR decomposition, which matches the residual for the coefficients provided by NIST. The relative errors are roughly 11 and 4×10^{-7}, respectively. The normal equation solution clearly fails, which is evident in Figure A.2 on the facing page.

Mean-centering the x-data reduces the 2-condition number of the new Vandermonde matrix to 1.3×10^5. Further scaling the x-data between -1 and 1 reduces the 2-condition number to $\kappa_2 = 4610$. So the matrix is well-conditioned even when using the normal equation method. The residuals of both methods are $\|\mathbf{r}\|_2 = 0.028211$, and both methods perform well.

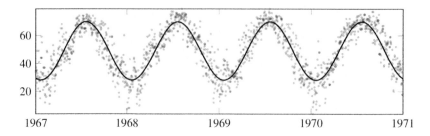

Figure A.3: Daily temperatures of Washington, DC between 1967 and 1971

3.6. Let's start with the model $u(t) = a_1 \sin(a_2 t + a_3) + a_4$. This formulation is nonlinear, but we can work with it to make it linear. First, we know that the period is one year. Second, we can write $\sin(x + y)$ as $\sin x \cos y + \sin y \cos x$. In doing so, we have a linear model

$$u(t) = c_1 \sin(2\pi t) + c_2 \cos(2\pi t) + c_3,$$

where t is the time in units of one year, $a_1 = \sqrt{c_1^2 + c_2^2}$, and $a_3 = \tan^{-1} c_2/c_1$. We can solve this problem using:

```
using CSV, DataFrames, Dates
data = download(bucket*"dailytemps.csv")
df = DataFrame(CSV.File(data))
day = Dates.value.(df[:,:date] .- df[1,:date])/365
u = df[:,:temperature]
tempsmodel(t) = [sin.(2π*t) cos.(2π*t) one.(t)]
c = tempsmodel(day)\u
scatter(df[:,:date],u,alpha=0.3)
plot!(df[:,:date],tempsmodel(day)*c,width=3)
```

The solution is plotted in the figure above.

3.7. The following Julia code reads the MNIST training data and computes the economy SVD of the training set to get singular vectors:

```
using MLDatasets, Arpack, Images
image_train, label_train = MNIST(split=:train)[:]
image_train = reshape(permutedims(image_train,[3,2,1]),60000,:)
V = [( D = image_train[label_train.==i,:];
   svds(D,nsv=12)[1].V ) for i ∈ 0:9];
```

Let's display the principal components of the "digit 3" subspace.

actual class

	0	1	2	3	4	5	6	7	8	9
0	984	8	0	1	6	0	1	0	0	0
1	0	983	2	1	5	0	0	3	6	0
2	12	3	945	10	3	0	7	7	12	1
3	2	1	9	952	0	8	0	5	19	4
4	3	8	5	0	944	1	3	7	4	25
5	2	3	0	46	3	922	7	1	14	2
6	5	3	0	0	1	5	986	0	0	0
7	4	7	6	0	4	1	0	933	5	40
8	6	22	6	16	5	13	5	6	910	11
9	11	4	5	8	12	3	0	20	12	925

(predicted class)

Figure A.4: Confusion matrix for PCA identification of digits in MNIST dataset.

```
pix = -abs.(reshape(V[3+1],28,:))
rescale = scaleminmax(minimum(pix), maximum(pix))
pix .|> rescale .|> Gray
```

The image of any 3 in the training data is largely a linear combination of these basis vectors. We can now predict the best digit associated with each test image using these ten subspaces V. We'll finally build a confusion matrix to check the method's accuracy. Each row of the confusion matrix represents the predicted class, and each column represents the actual class. See Figure A.4. For example, element $(7, 9)$ is 40, meaning that 40 of test images identified as a "7" were actually a "9." Overall, the method is about 95 percent accurate.

```
image_test, label_test = MNIST(split=:test)[:]
image_test = reshape(permutedims(image_test,[3,2,1]),10000,:)
r = [( q = image_test*V[i]*V[i]' .- image_test;
  sum(q.^2,dims=2) ) for i∈1:10]
r = hcat(r...)
prediction = [argmin(r[i,:]) for i∈1:10000] .- 1
[sum(prediction[label_test.== i].== j) for j∈0:9, i∈0:9]
```

3.9. Let **A** be the actor-movie adjacency matrix and **B** be the movie-genre adjacency matrix. We'll compute a truncated singular value decomposition

$\mathbf{U}_k \Sigma_k \mathbf{V}_k^\mathsf{T}$ of $\mathbf{BA}$ to get the projection to a lower-dimensional latent space. Let $\{\mathbf{q}_i\}$ be the columns of $\mathbf{V}_k^\mathsf{T}$. Each column represents the projection corresponding to an actor's genre signature in the latent space. We'll find the closest vectors $\{\mathbf{q}_i\}$ to $\mathbf{q}_j$, i.e., we look for the column i that maximizes $\cos \theta_i = \hat{\mathbf{q}}_j^\mathsf{T} \hat{\mathbf{q}}_i / \|\hat{\mathbf{q}}_j\| \|\hat{\mathbf{q}}_i\|$. Let's start by importing the data and building the adjacency matrices using the functions get_adjacency_matrix and get_names defined on pages 49 and 484

```
actors = get_names("actors")
genres = get_names("genres")
A = get_adjacency_matrix("movie-genre")
A = (A*Diagonal(1 ./ sum(A,dims=1)[:]))
B = get_adjacency_matrix("actor-movie");
```

We'll use the Arpack.jl package to compute the SVD of a sparse matrix, with a suitable small dimensional latent space:

```
using Arpack
X,_ = svds(A*B,nsv=10)
U = X.U; Σ = Diagonal(X.S); Vᵀ = X.Vt
Q = Vᵀ./sqrt.(sum(Vᵀ.^2,dims=1));
```

Now, let's find the actors most similar to Steve Martin:

```
index = x -> findfirst(actors.==x)[1]
q = Q[:,index("Steve Martin")][:]
z = Q'*q
r = sortperm(-z)
actors[r[1:10]]
```

The ten actors most similar to Steve Martin are Steve Martin (of course), Lisa Kudrow, Rob Reiner, Christine Baranski, Patrick Cranshaw, George Gaynes, Jay Chandrasekhar, Alexandra Holden, Luke Wilson, and David Spade. Using the following code, we determine that the Steve Martin's signature is comedy (40%), drama (10%), romance (9%), crime (5%), romantic comedy (4%),...:

```
p = U*Σ*q
r = sortperm(-p)
[genres[r] p[r]/sum(p)]
```

Statistician George Box once quipped: "All models are wrong, but some are useful." How is this actor similarity model wrong? It doesn't differentiate the type or size of roles an actor has in a movie, e.g., such as a character actor appearing in a serious film for comic relief. Actors change over their careers and the data set is limited to the years 1972–2012. Classification of movies into genres is simplistic and sometimes arbitrary. Perhaps using more keywords would add more fidelity. The information was crowdsourced through

Wikipedia editors and contains errors. How does the dimension of the latent space change the model? By choosing a large-dimensional latent space, we keep much of the information about the movies and actors. But we are unable to make generalizations and comparisons. Such a model is overfit. On the other hand, choosing a small-dimensional space effectively removes the underrepresented genres, and we are left with the main genres. Such a model is underfit.

3.10. To simplify the calculations, we'll pick station one (although any station would do) as a reference station and measure all other stations relative to it $(x_i, y_i, t_i) \leftarrow (x_i, y_i, t_i) - (x_1, y_1, t_1)$. For this station, the reference circle is now $x^2 + y^2 = (ct)^2$. We can remove the quadratic terms from the other equations $(x - x_i)^2 + (y - y_i)^2 = (ct - ct_i)^2$ by subtracting the reference equation from each of them to get a system of $n - 1$ linear equations

$$2x_i x + 2y_i y - 2c^2 t_i t = x_i^2 + y_i^2 - c^2 t_i^2.$$

Geometrically, this new equation represents the *radical axis* of the two circles—the common chord if the circles intersect. The system i n matrix form is $\mathbf{Ax} = \mathbf{b}$, which we can solve using ordinary least squares or total least squares. We'll use the function tls defined on page 77.

```
X = [3 3 12; 1 15 14; 10 2 13; 12 15 14; 0 11 12]
reference = X[1,:]; X .-= reference'
A = [2 2 -2].*X; b = (X.^2)*[1; 1; -1]
xₒₗₛ = A\b + reference
xₜₗₛ = tls(A,b) + reference
```

The solution is about $(6.53, 8.80, 7.20)$. Both methods are within a percent of one another.

3.11. We'll start by forming two arrays: X for the (x, y, z, t) data of the sensors and x_0 for the $(x, y, z, \cdot)$ data of the signal source.

```
using CSV, DataFrames
df = DataFrame(CSV.File(download(bucket*"shotspotter.csv")))
X = Array(df[1:end-1,:]); xₒ = Array(df[end,:]);
```

Now, let's solve the system and compute the error.

```
c² = 328.9^2
reference = X[1,:]; X .-= reference'
A = [2 2 2 -2c²].*X; b = (X.^2)*[1; 1; 1; -c²]
xₒₗₛ = A\b + reference
error = xₒₗₛ - xₒ
```

We find that the error is approximately -3.8 m and 3.2 m horizontally and 54.6 m vertically.

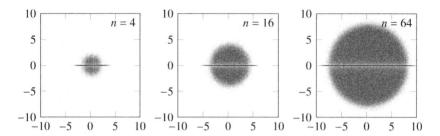

Figure A.5: Distribution of eigenvalues of normal random $n \times n$ real matrices.

4.1. Let's plot the eigenvalues of five thousand random $n \times n$ real matrices:

```
E = collect(Iterators.flatten([eigvals(randn(n,n)) for i∈1:2000]))
scatter(E,mc=:black,ma=0.05,legend=nothing,aspect_ratio=:equal)
```

The figure above shows the distribution for $n = 4$, 16, and 64. The distribution follows Girko's circular law, which says that as $n \to \infty$, eigenvalues are uniformly distributed in a disk of radius $\sqrt{n}$.

4.3. The Gershgorin circles are plotted below.

$$
A = \begin{bmatrix} 9 & 0 & 0 & 1 \\ 2 & 5 & 0 & 0 \\ 1 & 2 & 0 & 1 \\ 3 & 0 & -2 & 0 \end{bmatrix}
$$

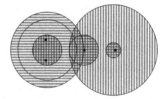

Row circles are shaded ▤, column circles are shaded ▥, and the eigenvalues ⊡ lie in their intersections.

4.4. The following Julia code finds an eigenpair using Rayleigh iteration starting with a random initial vector. We can compute all four eigenpairs by running the code repeatedly for different initial guesses. The method converges rapidly, and $A - \rho I$ becomes poorly conditioned as ρ approaches one of the eigenvalues. So we break out of the iteration before committing the cardinal sin of using an ill-conditioned operator.

```
function rayleigh(A)
  x = randn(size(A,1),1)
  while true
    x = x/norm(x)
    ρ = (x'*A*x)[1]
    M = A - ρ*I
```

```
    abs(cond(M, 1)) < 1e12 ? x = M\x : return(ρ,x)
  end
end
```

4.5. The implicit QR method is summarized as

1. Compute the Hessenberg matrix **H** that is unitarily similar to **A**.

2. One QR-cycle is

   a) Take $\rho = h_{nn}$ (Rayleigh shifting)

   b) Compute $\mathbf{QHQ}^\mathsf{T}$ for Givens rotation $\mathbf{Q} : \begin{bmatrix} h_{11} - \rho \\ h_{21} \end{bmatrix} \rightarrow \begin{bmatrix} * \\ 0 \end{bmatrix}$.

   c) "Chase the bulge" using Givens rotations $\mathbf{Q} : \begin{bmatrix} h_{i+1,i} \\ h_{i+2,i} \end{bmatrix} \rightarrow \begin{bmatrix} * \\ 0 \end{bmatrix}$.

   d) Deflate using the top-left $(n - 1) \times (n - 1)$ matrix if $|h_{n,n-1}| < \varepsilon$.

The LinearAlgebra.jl function hessenberg(A) returns an upper Hessenberg matrix that is unitarily similar to A. The function givens(a,b,1,2) returns the Givens rotation matrix for the vector (a, b). The following code implements the implicit QR method:

```
function implicitqr(A)
  n = size(A,1)
  tolerance = 1E-12
  H = Matrix(hessenberg(A).H)
  while true
    if abs(H[n,n-1])<tolerance
      if (n-=1)<2; return(diag(H)); end
    end
    Q = givens([H[1,1]-H[n,n];H[2,1]],1,2)[1]
    H[1:2,1:n] = Q*H[1:2,1:n]
    H[1:n,1:2] = H[1:n,1:2]*Q'
    for i = 2:n-1
      Q = givens([H[i,i-1];H[i+1,i-1]],1,2)[1]
      H[i:i+1,1:n] = Q*H[i:i+1,1:n]
      H[1:n,i:i+1] = H[1:n,i:i+1]*Q'
    end
  end
end
```

4.6. Let's compute the eigenvector centrality of the actor-actor adjacency matrix. We'll start by importing the data and building the adjacency matrix using the functions get_names and get_adjacency_matrix defined on page 484.

```
actors = get_names("actors")
B = get_adjacency_matrix("actor-movie")
M = (B'*B .!= 0) - I
v = ones(size(M,1))
for k = 1:8
  v = M*v; v /= norm(v);
end
r = sortperm(-v); actors[r][1:10]
```

Eigenvector centrality tells us those actors who appeared in movies with a lot of other actors, who themselves appeared in a lot of movies with other actors. Samuel L. Jackson, M. Emmet Walsh, Gene Hackman, Bruce Willis, Christopher Walken, Robert De Niro, Steve Buscemi, Dan Hedaya, Whoopi Goldberg, and Frank Welker are the ten most central actors. Arguably, Samuel L. Jackson is the center of Hollywood.

```
findfirst(actors[r] .== "Kevin Bacon")
```

Kevin Bacon is the 92nd most connected actor in Hollywood. Let's also look at degree centrality, which ranks each node by its number of edges, i.e., the number of actors with whom an actor has appeared.

```
actors[ -sum(M,dims=1)[:] |> sortperm ][1:10]
```

The ten most central actors are Frank Welker, Samuel L. Jackson, M. Emmet Walsh, Whoopi Goldberg, Bruce Willis, Robert De Niro, Steve Buscemi, Gene Hackman, Christopher Walken, and Dan Aykroyd. The noticeable change is that voice actor Frank Welker moves from tenth to first position.

4.7. The following Julia code implements the randomized SVD algorithm:

```
function randomizedsvd(A,k)
  Z = rand(size(A,2),k);
  Q = Matrix(qr(A*Z).Q)
  for i in 1:3
    Q = Matrix(qr(A'*Q).Q)
    Q = Matrix(qr(A*Q).Q)
  end
  W = svd(Q'*A)
  return((Q*W.U,W.S,W.V))
end
```

Let's import a high-resolution photograph of a fox into Julia as a grayscale image, and convert it to an array:

```
using Images
img = load(download(bucket*"red-fox.jpg"))
A = Float64.(Gray.(img))
U,S,V = randomizedsvd(A,10)
Gray.([A U*Diagonal(S)*V'])
```

Let's also compare the elapsed time for the randomized SVD, the sparse SVD in Arpack.jl, and the full SVD in LinearAlgebra.jl.

```
using Arpack
@time randomizedsvd(A,10)
@time svds(A, nsv=10)
@time svd(A);
```

With rank $k = 10$, the elapsed time for the randomized SVD is about 0.05 seconds compared to 0.1 seconds for a sparse SVD and 3.4 seconds for a full SVD svd(A). We can compute the relative error using

$$\varepsilon_k = \frac{\sqrt{\sum_{i=k+1}^{n} \sigma_i^2}}{\sqrt{\sum_{i=1}^{n} \sigma_i^2}} = 1 - \frac{\sqrt{\sum_{i=1}^{k} \sigma_i^2}}{\|\mathbf{A}\|_F},$$

which can be implemented as

```
ε = 1 .- sqrt.(cumsum(S.^2))/norm(A)
plot(ε,marker=:circle)
```

The relative error in the first ten singular values ranges from 2 percent down to 0.5 percent. The image on the left is the original image A, and the image on the right is the projected image Gray.(U*Diagonal(S)*V').

4.8. We'll approximate **A** with a sufficiently high-dimensional matrix and compute its largest singular value.

```
using Arpack
m = 5000
A = [1/(1 + (i+j-1)*(i+j)/2 - j) for i∈1:m, j∈1:m]
svds(A,nsv=1)[1].S[1]
```

We find $\|\mathbf{A}\|_2 = 1.2742241528\ldots$, which agrees to within 11 digits of the answer given by the Sloane number A117233.

5.1. The Jacobi method's spectral radius was derived in exercise 1.5(b). We will confirm the Gauss–Seidel method's spectral radius using Julia.

```
n = 20; D = SymTridiagonal(-2ones(n),ones(n-1))
P = -diagm(0 => diag(D,0), -1 => diag(D,-1))
N = diagm(1 => diag(D,1))
eigvals(N,P)[end], cos(pi/(n+1))^2
```

5.2. The Gauss–Seidel method converges if and only if the spectral radius of the matrix $(\mathbf{L}+\mathbf{D})^{-1}\mathbf{U}$ is strictly less than one. The eigenvalues of

$$(\mathbf{L}+\mathbf{D})^{-1}\mathbf{U} = \begin{bmatrix} 1 & 0 \\ -\sigma & 1 \end{bmatrix}^{-1} \begin{bmatrix} 0 & \sigma \\ 0 & 0 \end{bmatrix} = \begin{bmatrix} 0 & \sigma \\ 0 & \sigma^2 \end{bmatrix}$$

are 0 and σ^2. So, the Gauss–Seidel method converges when $|\sigma| < 1$.

5.4. Let's start by setting up the problem and defining the exact solution u_e. We can define kron as an infix operator using the Unicode character ⊗ within Julia to improve readability.

```
using SparseArrays, LinearAlgebra
⊗(x,y) = kron(x,y); ϕ = x -> x-x^2
n = 50 ; x = (1:n)/(n+1); Δx = 1/(n+1)
J = sparse(I, n, n)
D = spdiagm(-1 => ones(n-1), 0 => -2ones(n), 1 => ones(n-1) )
A = ( D⊗J⊗J + J⊗D⊗J + J⊗J⊗D ) / Δx^2
f = [ϕ(x)*ϕ(y) + ϕ(x)*ϕ(z) + ϕ(y)*ϕ(z) for x∈x, y∈x, z∈x][:]
uₑ = [ϕ(x)*ϕ(y)*ϕ(z)/2 for x∈x, y∈x, z∈x][:];
```

In practice, we could use routines from IterativeSolvers.jl, but because we want to evaluate the error at intermediate steps, we'll write our own. We define a function that implements the stationary methods—Jacobi ($\omega = 0$), Gauss–Seidel ($\omega = 1$), and SSOR ($\omega = 1.9$)—and returns the error.

```
function stationary(A,b,ω=0,n=400)
    ϵ = []; u = zero.(b)
```

```
    P = (1-ω)*sparse(Diagonal(A)) + ω*sparse(LowerTriangular(A))
    for i=1:n
      u += P\(b-A*u)
      append!(ε,norm(u - uₑ,1))
    end
    return(ε)
end
```

We also define a function for the conjugate gradient method.

```
function conjugategradient(A,b,n=400)
  ε = []; u = zero.(b)
  p = r = b-A*u
  for i=1:n
    Ap = A*p
    α = (r'*p)/(Ap'*p)
    u += α.*p; r -= α.*Ap
    β = (r'*Ap)/(Ap'*p)
    p = r - β.*p
    append!(ε,norm(u - uₑ,1))
  end
  return(ε)
end
```

Finally, we run each method and plot the errors.

```
ε = zeros(400,4)
@time ε[:,1] = stationary(A,-f,0)
@time ε[:,2] = stationary(A,-f,1)
@time ε[:,3] = stationary(A,-f,1.9)
@time ε[:,4] = conjugategradient(A,-f)
method = ["Jacobi" "Gauss-Seidel" "SOR" "Conjugate Gradient"]
plot(ε,yaxis=:log,labels=method,bglegend=RGBA(1,1,1,0.7))
```

Each method takes approximately two seconds to complete 400 iterations. The figure on the following page shows the errors. Notice that the conjugate gradient converges quite quickly relative to the stationary methods—the error is at machine precision after about 150 iterations or about 0.7 seconds. For comparison, using the conjugate gradient method cg from IterativeSolvers.jl takes roughly 0.4 seconds. We can compute the convergence rate by taking the slopes of the lines

```
k = 1:120; ([one.(k) k]\log10.(ε[k,:]))[2,:]
```

The slopes are 0.008, 0.0016, 0.019, and 0.1. The inverse of these slopes tells us the number of iterations required to gain one digit of accuracy—roughly 1200 iterations using a Jacobi method and 10 iterations using the conjugate gradient method. Convergence of the Jacobi method is extremely slow, requiring around

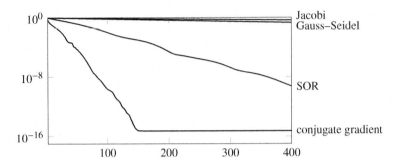

Figure A.6: Relative error as a function of the number of iterations.

18 thousand iterations, or 90 seconds, to reach machine precision. Still, it is faster than the direct solver A\(-f), which takes 130 seconds.

5.5. The $(1, 1)$-entry of $\mathbf{A}^{-1}$ is the first element of the solution $\mathbf{x}$ to $\mathbf{Ax} = \boldsymbol{\xi}$ for $\boldsymbol{\xi} = (1, 0, 0, \ldots, 0)$. We'll use a preconditioned conjugate gradient method to solve the problem.

```
using Primes, LinearAlgebra, SparseArrays, IterativeSolvers
n = 20000
d = 2 .^ (0:14); d = [-d;d]
P = Diagonal(primes(224737))
B = [ones(n - abs(d)) for d∈d]
A = sparse(P) + spdiagm(n ,n, (d .=> B)...)
b = zeros(n); b[1] = 1
cg(A, b; Pl=P)[1]
```

The computed solution $0.7250783\ldots$ agrees with the Sloane number A117237 to machine precision. Using the BenchmarkTools.jl function @btime, we find that the conjugate gradient method takes 11 milliseconds on a typical laptop. If we don't specify the preconditioner, the solver takes 1500 times longer.

6.1. Let $m = n/3$. Then a DFT can be written as a sum of three DFTs

$$y_j = \sum_{k=0}^{n-1} \omega_n^{kj} c_k = \sum_{k=0}^{m-1} \omega_m^{kj} c_k' + \omega_n^j \sum_{k=0}^{m-1} \omega_m^{kj} c_k'' + \omega_n^{2j} \sum_{k=0}^{m-1} \omega_m^{kj} c_k'''$$

with $c_k' = c_{3k}$, $c_k'' = c_{3k+1}$, and $c_k''' = c_{3k+2}$. So, $y_j = y_j' + \omega_n^j y_j'' + \omega_n^{2j} y_j'''$. By computing over $j = 0, \ldots, m - 1$ and noting

$$\omega_m^{k(m+j)} = \omega_m^{km} \omega_m^{kj} = \omega_m^{kj}, \qquad \omega_n^{m+j} = \omega_n^m \omega_n^j = \omega_3 \omega_n^j,$$
$$\omega_m^{k(2m+j)} = \omega_m^{2km} \omega_m^{kj} = \omega_m^{kj}, \qquad \omega_n^{2m+j} = \omega_n^{2m} \omega_n^j = \omega_3^2 \omega_n^j,$$

and

where $\omega_3 = e^{-2i\pi/3}$, $\omega_3^2 = e^{2i\pi/3}$ and $\omega_3^4 = e^{-2i\pi/3}$, we have the system

$$y_j = y_j' + \omega_n^j y_{m+j}'' + \omega_n^{2j} y_{2m+j}'''$$
$$y_{m+j} = y_j' + \omega_3 \omega_n^j y_{m+j}'' + \omega_3^2 \omega_n^{2j} y_{2m+j}'''$$
$$y_{2m+j} = y_j' + \omega_3^2 \omega_n^j y_{m+j}'' + \omega_3^4 \omega_n^{2j} y_{2m+j}'''.$$

Note that when $n = 3$, this system is simply $\mathbf{F}_3$. In matrix notation

$$\mathbf{F}_n \mathbf{c} = \left(\mathbf{F}_3 \otimes \mathbf{I}_{n/3}\right) \mathbf{\Omega}_n \left(\mathbf{I}_3 \otimes \mathbf{F}_{n/3}\right) \mathbf{Pc}$$

were $\mathbf{\Omega} = \mathrm{diag}(1, \omega_n, \omega_n^2, \ldots, \omega_n^{n-1})$.

```
function fftx3(c)
  n = length(c)
  ω = exp(-2im*π/n)
  if mod(n,3) == 0
    k = collect(0:n/3-1)
    u = [transpose(fftx3(c[1:3:n-2]));
         transpose((ω.^k).*fftx3(c[2:3:n-1]));
         transpose((ω.^2k).*fftx3(c[3:3:n]))]
    F = exp(-2im*π/3).^([0;1;2]*[0;1;2]')
    return(reshape(transpose(F*u),:,1))
  else
    F = ω.^(collect(0:n-1)*collect(0:n-1)')
    return(F*c)
  end
end
```

6.2. The following function takes two integers as strings, converts them to padded arrays, computes a convolution, and then carries the digits:

```
using FFTW
function multiply(p_,q_)
  p = [parse.(Int,split(reverse(p_),""));zeros(length(q_),1)]
  q = [parse.(Int,split(reverse(q_),""));zeros(length(p_),1)]
  pq = Int.(round.(real.(ifft(fft(p).*fft(q)))))
  carry = pq .÷ 10
  while any(carry.>0)
    pq -= carry*10 - [0;carry[1:end-1]]
    carry = pq .÷ 10
  end
  n = findlast(x->x>0, pq)
  return(reverse(join(pq[1:n[1]])))
end
```

Arbitrary-precision arithmetic, which also uses the Schönhage–Strassen algorithm, is significantly faster:

```
using Random
p = randstring('0':'9', 100000)
q = randstring('0':'9', 100000)
@time multiply(p,q)
@time parse(BigInt, p)*parse(BigInt, q);
```

6.3. We'll split the DCT into two series, one with even indices running forward $\{0, 2, 4, \ldots\}$ and the other with odd indices running backward $\{\ldots, 5, 3, 1\}$. Doing so makes the DFT naturally pop out after we express the cosine as the real part of the complex exponential. If we were computing a DST instead of a DCT, we would subtract the second series because sine is an odd function at the boundaries.

$$
\begin{aligned}
\hat{f}_\xi &= \sum_{k=0}^{n-1} f_k \cos\left(\frac{(k + \frac{1}{2})\xi\pi}{n}\right) \\
&= \sum_{k=0}^{n/2-1} f_{2k} \cos\left(\frac{(2k + \frac{1}{2})\xi\pi}{n}\right) + \sum_{k=n/2}^{n-1} f_{2(n-k)-1} \cos\left(\frac{(2n - 2k - \frac{1}{2})\xi\pi}{n}\right) \\
&= \mathrm{Re}\left(e^{-i\xi\pi/2n} \sum_{k=0}^{n/2-1} f_{2k} e^{-i2k\xi\pi/n} + e^{-i\xi\pi/2n} \sum_{k=n/2}^{n-1} f_{2(n-k)-1} e^{-i2k\xi\pi/n}\right).
\end{aligned}
$$

Because cosine is an even function, it doesn't matter which sign we choose as long as we are consistent between the two series. We'll choose negative so that the DCT is in terms of a DFT rather than an inverse DFT. We then have DCT $(f_k) = \mathrm{Re}\left(e^{-i\xi\pi/2n} \cdot \mathrm{DFT}\left(f_{P(k)}\right)\right)$, where $P(k)$ is a permutation of the index k. For example, $P(\{0, 1, 2, 3, 4, 5, 6, 7, 8\})$ is $\{0, 7, 2, 5, 4, 3, 6, 1, 8\}$. We can build an inverse DCT by running the steps backward.

Let's define the functions dctII and idctII. Note that the FFTW.jl functions fft and ifft are multi-dimensional unless we specify a dimension.

```
function dctII(f)
  n = size(f,1)
  ω = exp.(-0.5im*π*(0:n-1)/n)
  return real(ω.*fft(f[[1:2:n; n-mod(n,2):-2:2],:],1))
end
```

```
function idctII(f)
  n = size(f,1)
```

```
ω = exp.(-0.5im*π*(0:n-1)/n)
f[1,:] = f[1,:]/2
f[[1:2:n; n-mod(n,2):-2:2],:] = 2*real(ifft(f./ω,1))
return f
end
```

We can verify our code by computing the DCT directly:

```
y₁ = [f[1:n]'*cos.(π/n*k*(0.5.+([0:n-1]...))) for k ∈0:n-1]
```

Alternatively, we can use the FFTW.jl function dct, which includes the additional scaling:

```
y₂ = dct(f)/sqrt(2/n) ; y₂[1] *=sqrt(2)
```

The two-dimensional DCT or IDCT applies the one-dimensional DCT or IDCT in each direction:

```
dct2(f) = dctII(dctII(f')')
idct2(f) = idctII(idctII(f')')
```

6.4. The following function modifies the one on 163, which removes low-magnitude Fourier components, to instead crop high-frequency Fourier components and keep a full subarray. The compressed image A_0 is recovered by padding the cropped components with zeros.

```
function dctcompress2(A,d)
  B = dct(Float64.(A))
  m,n = size(A)
  m₀,n₀ = sqrt(d).*(m,n) .|> floor .|> Int
  B₀ = B[1:m₀,1:n₀]
  A₀ = idct([B₀ zeros(m₀,n-n₀); zeros(m-m₀,n)])
  A₀ = A₀ |> clamp01! .|> Gray
  sizeof(B₀)/sizeof(B), sqrt(1-(norm(B₀)/norm(B))^2), A₀
end
```

The two approaches—∘ cropping high frequency components and • removing low magnitude components—are compared in Figure A.7 on the next page. The lollipops ∘⟋• show the relative compressed size and relative error for the same target density d. Surgically zeroing out low-magnitude components results in lower error than cropping high-frequency components, but it also requires additional overhead for sparse matrix format. As a result, both approaches have similar effective error-compression ratios.

Let's look at the compression artifacts. Figure A.7 shows a close-up of the error at 95 percent compression. See the QR codes at the bottom of this

relative error versus relative size

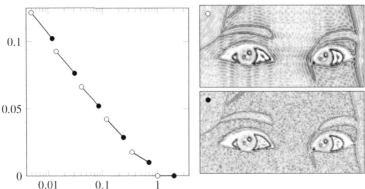

Figure A.7: The relative Frobenius error of a DCT-compressed image as a function of relative storage requirements, by ○ clipping high-frequency Fourier components and by ● zeroing out low-magnitude Fourier components.

page and page 163. Cropping high-frequency components results in the Gibbs phenomenon that appears as local, parallel ripples around the edges in the image that diminish away from the edges. On the other hand, by zeroing out low-magnitude components, instead of the Gibbs phenomenon, we see high-frequency graininess throughout the entire image.

A.2   Numerical methods for analysis

7.1. The truncation error of the central difference approximation is bounded by $\varepsilon_{\text{trunc}} = \frac{1}{3}h^2 m$ where $m = \sup_\xi |f''(\xi)|$. The value of m is approximately one for $f(x) = e^x$. The round-off error is bounded by $\varepsilon_{\text{round}} = 2\,\text{eps}/(2h)$. The total error $\varepsilon(h) = \varepsilon_{\text{trunc}} + \varepsilon_{\text{round}}$ is minimized when $\varepsilon'(h) = 0$, i.e., when

$$\varepsilon'(h) = \tfrac{2}{3}mh - 2\,\text{eps}/h^2 = 0.$$

So, the error is minimum at $h = (3\,\text{eps}/m)^{1/3}$. For $f(x) = e^x$ at $x = 0$, the error reaches a minimum of about $\text{eps}^{2/3} \approx 10^{-11}$ when $h = (3\,\text{eps})^{1/3} \approx 8 \times 10^{-6}$.

By taking the Taylor series expansion of $f(x + ih)$, we have

$$f(x + ih) = f(x) + ihf'(x) - \tfrac{1}{2}h^2 f''(x) - \tfrac{1}{2}ih^3 f'''(\xi)$$

where $|\xi - x| < h$. From the imaginary part, $f'(x) = \text{Im}\, f(x+ih)/h + \varepsilon_{\text{trunc}}$ with truncation error $\varepsilon_{\text{trunc}} \approx \tfrac{1}{2}h^2 |f'''(x)|$. The round-off error $\varepsilon_{\text{round}} \approx \text{eps}|f(x)|$. For $f(x) = e^x$, the total error $\varepsilon(h) = \tfrac{1}{2}h^2 + \text{eps}$, which is smallest when $h < \sqrt{2\,\text{eps}} \approx 10^{-8}$. See Figure A.8 on the facing page.

an image with
increasing levels of
DCT compressed

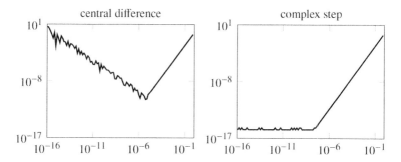

Figure A.8: The total error as a function of the stepsize h in the central difference and complex step approximations of $f'(x)$.

7.2. Let's write the $7/3$, $4/3$, and 1 in binary format. For double-precision floating-point numbers, we keep 52 significant bits, not including the leading 1, and round off the trailing bits. For $7/3$ the trailing bits $0101\ldots$ round up to $1000\ldots$, and for $4/3$ the trailing bits $0010\ldots$ round down to $0000\ldots$. Therefore, we have

$$7/3 = 10.0101010101010101010101010101010101010101010101010101011$$
$$- 4/3 = 1.0101010101010101010101010101010101010101010101010101$$
$$1 = 1.0000000000000000000000000000000000000000000000000000$$

Because binary $10 - 1 = 1$, the double-precision representation of $7/3 - 4/3 - 1$ equals

$$0.0000000000000000000000000000000000000000000000000000001$$

which is machine epsilon.

7.3. See Figure A.9 on the next page. The round-off error dominates the total error when $h < 10^{-5}$ in $x^3 - 3x^2 + 3x - 1$ and when $h < 10^{-9}$ in $(x-1)^3$

8.3. To speed up convergence for multiple roots, we can try taking a larger step

$$x^{(k+1)} = x^{(k)} - m\frac{f\left(x^{(k)}\right)}{f'\left(x^{(k)}\right)}$$

for some $m > 1$. If x^* is a root with multiplicity n, then $f^{(j)}(x^*) = 0$ for $j = 0, 1, \ldots, n-1$ and $f^{(n)}(x^*) \neq 0$. The error computed using (8.2) is

$$e^{(k+1)} = \frac{\frac{n-m}{n!}f^{(n)}(x^*)\left(e^{(k)}\right)^n + \frac{n+1-m}{(n+1)!}f^{(n+1)}(x^*)\left(e^{(k)}\right)^{n+1} + o\left(\left(e^{(k)}\right)^{n+1}\right)}{\frac{1}{(n-1)!}f^{(n)}(x^*)\left(e^{(k)}\right)^{n-1} + o\left(\left(e^{(k)}\right)^{n-1}\right)}.$$

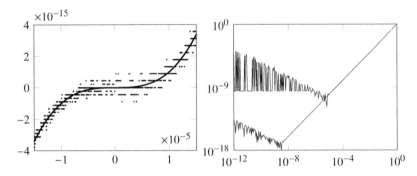

Figure A.9: Left: $(x-1)^3$ (solid line) and $x^3 - 3x^2 + 3x - 1$ (dots). The x-axis is offset from $x = 1$. Right: The total error in the central difference approximation of $f'(x)$ as a function of stepsize h.

By taking $m = n$, we once again get quadratic convergence

$$e^{(k+1)} \approx \frac{f^{(n)}(x^*)}{n(n+1)} \left(e^{(k)}\right)^2.$$

8.4. When $p = 1$,

$$p\frac{(1/f)^{(p-1)}}{(1/f)^{(p)}} = \frac{(1/f)}{(1/f)'} = \frac{1/f}{-f'/f^2} = -\frac{f}{f'}$$

which yields Newton's method $x^{(k+1)} = x^{(k)} - f(x^{(k)})/f'(x^{(k)})$. Take $p = 2$ and let $f(x) = x^2 - a$. Then

$$2\frac{(1/f)'}{(1/f)''} = 2\frac{-\dfrac{2x}{(x^2-a)^2}}{\dfrac{2(3x^2+a)}{(x^2-a)^3}} = 2\frac{-x(x^2-a)}{3x^2+a}$$

from which

$$x^{(k+1)} = \frac{x^{(k)}\left(\left(x^{(k)}\right)^2 + 3a\right)}{3\left(x^{(k)}\right)^2 + a}.$$

Starting with $x^{(0)} = 1$, we get

1.000000000000000000000000000000000000000000000000000...
1.40000000000000000000000000000000000000000000000000...
1.41421319796954314720812182741116751269035532994923...
1.41421356237309504879564008075425994635423824014524...
1.4142135623730950488016887242096980785696718753 7694...

The correct number of decimals—1, 2, 7, 19, and 62, respectively—triples with each iteration.

8.6. When the error is sufficiently small, $\left|e^{(k+1)}\right| \approx r\left|e^{(k)}\right|^{p}$ for some positive r. We can express the secant method

$$x^{(k+1)} = x^{(k)} - f\left(x^{(k)}\right) \frac{x^{(k)} - x^{(k-1)}}{f\left(x^{(k)}\right) - f\left(x^{(k-1)}\right)}$$

in terms of the error $e^{(k)} = x^{(k)} - x^*$ as

$$e^{(k+1)} = e^{(k)} - \frac{f\left(x^* + e^{(k)}\right)\left(e^{(k)} - e^{(k-1)}\right)}{f\left(x^* + e^{(k)}\right) - f\left(x^* + e^{(k-1)}\right)}.$$

The Taylor series expansion of $f\left(x^* + e^{(k)}\right)$ is

$$f'(x^*)e^{(k)} + \tfrac{1}{2}f''(x^*)\left(e^{(k)}\right)^2 + o\left(e^{(k)}\right) = f'(x^*)\left(1 + Me^{(k)}\right)e^{(k)} + o\left(e^{(k)}\right),$$

where $M = f''(x^*)/2f'(x^*)$. It follows that

$$\begin{aligned}
e^{(k+1)} &= e^{(k)} - \frac{e^{(k)} f'(x^*)\left(1 + Me^{(k)}\right)\left(e^{(k)} - e^{(k-1)}\right)}{f'(x^*)\left(e^{(k)} - e^{(k-1)}\right)\left(1 + M\left(e^{(k)} + e^{(k-1)}\right)\right)} + o\left(\left(e^{(k)}\right)^2\right) \\
&= e^{(k)} - \frac{e^{(k)}\left(1 + Me^{(k)}\right)}{1 + M\left(e^{(k)} + e^{(k-1)}\right)} + o\left(\left(e^{(k)}\right)^2\right) \\
&= \frac{Me^{(k)} e^{(k-1)}}{\left(1 + M\left(e^{(k)} + e^{(k-1)}\right)\right)} + o\left(\left(e^{(k)}\right)^2\right) \\
&\approx Me^{(k)} e^{(k-1)}.
\end{aligned}$$

Substituting $\left|e^{(k+1)}\right| \approx r\left|e^{(k)}\right|^{p}$ and $\left|e^{(k)}\right| \approx r\left|e^{(k-1)}\right|^{p}$ into the expression for error yields $r\left|e^{(k)}\right|^{p} \approx |M/r|\left|e^{(k)}\right|\left|e^{(k)}\right|^{1/p}$, from which $r^2 = |M|$ and $p = 1+1/p$. Therefore $p = (\sqrt{5} + 1)/2 \approx 1.618$.

8.7. Formulations (8.7) and (8.6) for Aitken's extrapolation are

```
aitken₁(x₁,x₂,x₃) = x₃ - (x₃-x₂)^2/(x₃ - 2x₂ + x₁)
aitken₂(x₁,x₂,x₃) = (x₁*x₃ - x₂^2)/(x₃ - 2x₂ + x₁)
```

Let's approximate π using the Leibniz formula for values $n = 1, 2, \ldots, 60000$.

```
n = 60000
p = cumsum([(-1)^i*4/(2i+1) for i=0:n])
p₁ = aitken₁.(p[1:n-2],p[2:n-1],p[3:n])
p₂ = aitken₂.(p[1:n-2],p[2:n-1],p[3:n])
plot(abs.(π.-p)); plot!(abs.(π.-p₂)); plot!(abs.(π.-p₁))
plot!(xaxis=:log,yaxis=:log)
```

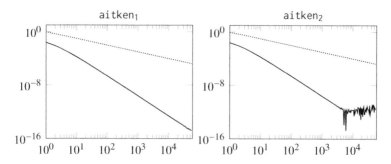

Figure A.10: Error in the nth partial sum of Leibniz's formula (dotted) and Aitken's extrapolation—(8.7) on the left and (8.6) on the right–of that sum (solid).

The left plot of Figure A.10 shows the errors in Leibniz's formula and Aitken's correction. The log-log slopes are 1.0 and 3.0. The errors after the $n$term are approximately $1/n$ and $1/4n^3$, respectively. The methods are both linearly convergent, but using Aitken's acceleration is significantly faster. Instead of a trillion terms to compute the first 13 digits of π, we need nine thousand terms. It's still an exceptionally slow way of approximating π. The right plot of Figure A.10 shows the numerically less-stable Aitken's method.

We can express the Aitken's extrapolation to Leibniz's formula explicitly as

$$\pi_n = \sum_{i=1}^{n} \frac{(-1)^{i+1}4}{2i-1} + r_n \quad \text{where} \quad r_n = (-1)^n \frac{2n-3}{(n-1)(2n-1)}.$$

The 14th-century Indian mathematician Madhava of Sangamagrama formulated a better correction

$$r_n = (-1)^n \frac{4n^2+4}{4n^3+5n}.$$

The error using Madhava's correction goes as $3/4n^7$. With it, we can compute the first 13 digits of π in sixty terms.

Modern methods have quadratic or higher rates of convergence. The Gauss–Legendre algorithm uses iteration with arithmetic and harmonic means to get quadratic convergence—the first 16 digits of π need three terms, and the correct digits double with each additional term. Jonathan and Peter Borwein's algorithm for $1/\pi$ converges quartically, nonically, and even hexadecimally. Each iteration multiplies the correct number of digits by four, nine, and sixteen.

8.8. Consider Newton's method where $f(x) = x - \phi(x) = 0$:

$$x^{(k+1)} = x^{(k)} - \frac{x^{(k)} - \phi\left(x^{(k)}\right)}{1 - \phi'\left(x^{(k)}\right)}.$$

Let's further approximate the slope $\phi'(x^{(k)})$ as

$$\phi'(x^{(k)}) \approx \frac{\phi(x^{(k+1)}) - \phi(x^{(k)})}{x^{(k+1)} - x^{(k)}} = \frac{\phi(\phi(x^{(k)})) - \phi(x^{(k)})}{\phi(x^{(k)}) - x^{(k)}}.$$

Substituting this expression for $\phi'(x^{(k)})$ yields

$$x^{(k+1)} = x^{(k)} - \frac{(\phi(x^{(k)}) - x^{(k)})^2}{\phi(\phi(x^{(k)})) - 2\phi(x^{(k)}) + x^{(k)}}. \tag{A.1}$$

We can further rearrange the terms of this expression to match the form of (8.8)

$$x^{(k+1)} = \phi(\phi(x^{(k)})) - \frac{(\phi(\phi(x^{(k)})) - \phi(x^{(k)}))^2}{\phi(\phi(x^{(k)})) - 2\phi(x^{(k)}) + x^{(k)}}.$$

Note that we can also express Steffenson's method (A.1) in the form

$$x^{(k+1)} = x^{(k)} - \frac{f(x^{(k)})}{q(x^{(k)})} \quad \text{with} \quad q(x) = \frac{f(x + f(x)) - f(x)}{f(x)}$$

where $q(x)$ is an approximation for the slope $f'(x)$.

We'll use Wolfram Cloud to determine the convergence rate.[2]

```
a = Series[ f[x]^2, {x,0,3}] /. f[0]->0;
b = Series[ f[x+f[x]] - f[x], {x,0,3}] /. f[0]->0 /. f[0]->0;
Simplify[x - a/b] /. x->ε
```

We find the error of Steffenson's method is

$$e^{(k+1)} = \frac{(1 + f'(x^*))f''(x^*)}{2f'(x^*)}(e^{(k)})^2 + O((e^{(k)})^3).$$

Recall that Newton's method has a similar error

$$e^{(k+1)} = \frac{f''(x^*)}{2f'(x^*)}(e^{(k)})^2 + O((e^{(k)})^3).$$

8.10. For the fixed-point method to converge, we need $|\phi'(x)| < 1$ in a neighborhood of the fixed point x^*. If $\phi(x) = x - \alpha f(x)$, then $|\phi'(x)| = |1 - \alpha f'(x)| < 1$ when $0 < \alpha f'(x) < 2$. Taking $\alpha < 2/f'(x^*)$ should ensure convergence. The asymptotic convergence factor is given by $|\phi'(x)|$, so it's best to choose α close to $1/f'(x^*)$. The solution x^* is unknown, so we instead could use a known $f'(x^{(k)})$ at each iteration, which is Newton's method $x^{(k+1)} = x^{(k)} - f(x^{(k)})/f'(x^{(k)})$.

---

[2]Wolfram Cloud (https://www.wolframcloud.com) has a free basic plan that provides complete access to Mathematica with a few limitations.

8.12. Define the homotopy as $h(t, \mathbf{x}) = f(\mathbf{x}) + (t - 1)f(\mathbf{x}_0)$ where $\mathbf{x} = (x, y)$.
The Jacobian matrix is

$$\frac{\partial h}{\partial \mathbf{x}} = \frac{\partial f}{\partial \mathbf{x}} = \begin{bmatrix} 4x(x^2 + y^2 - 1) & 4y(x^2 + y^2 + 1) \\ 6x(x^2 + y^2 - 1)^2 - 2xy^3 & 6y(x^2 + y^2 - 1)^2 - 3x^2y^2 \end{bmatrix}.$$

We need to solve the ODE

$$\frac{\mathrm{d}}{\mathrm{d}t}\mathbf{x}(t) = -\left(\frac{\partial f}{\partial \mathbf{x}}\right)^{-1} f(\mathbf{x}_0)$$

with initial conditions $(x(0), y(0)) = \mathbf{x}_0$. Newton's method, which takes

$$\mathbf{x}^{(k+1)} = \mathbf{x}^{(k)} - \left(\frac{\partial f}{\partial \mathbf{x}^{(k)}}\right)^{-1} f(\mathbf{x}^{(k)}),$$

is quite similar to the homotopy continuation. We'll define the two solvers:

```
using DifferentialEquations
function homotopy(f,df,x)
  dxdt(x,p,t) = -df(x)\p
  sol = solve(ODEProblem(dxdt,x,(0.0,1.0),f(x)))
  sol.u[end]
end


function newton(f,df,x)
  for i in 1:100
    Δx = -df(x)\f(x)
    norm(Δx) > 1e-8 ? x += Δx : return(x)
  end
end
```

The routines take a function f, its Jacobian matrix df, and an initial guess x, and
they return one of the zeroes. For our problem, we'll define f and df as

```
f = z -> ((x,y)=tuple(z...);
  [(x^2+y^2)^2-2(x^2-y^2); (x^2+y^2-1)^3-x^2*y^3])
df = z -> ((x,y)=tuple(z...);
  [4x*(x^2+y^2-1) 4y*(x^2+y^2+1);
  6x*(x^2+y^2-1)^2-2x*y^3 6y*(x^2+y^2-1)^2-3x^2*y^2])
```

The solutions are

```
display(homotopy(f,df,[1,1]))
display(newton(f,df,[1,1]))
```

8.13. Let's implement the ECDH algorithm for $y^2 = x^3 + 7 \pmod r$. We'll first define the group operator $\oplus$. Given points $P = (x_0, y_0)$ and $Q = (x_1, y_1)$, the new point is $P \oplus Q$ is (x, y) with

$$x = \lambda^2 - x_0 - x_1$$
$$y = -\lambda(x - x_0) - y_0,$$

where $\lambda = (3x_0^2 + a)/2y_0$ when $P = Q$ and $\lambda = (y_1 - y_0)/(x_1 - x_0)$ otherwise.

```
function ⊕(P,Q)
  a = 0
  r = BigInt(2)^256 - 2^32 - 977
  if P[1]==Q[1]
    d = invmod(2*P[2], r)
    λ = mod((3*powermod(P[1],2,r)+a)*d, r)
  else
    d = invmod(Q[1]-P[1], r)
    λ = mod((Q[2]-P[2])*d, r)
  end
  x = mod(powermod(λ, 2, r) - P[1] - Q[1], r)
  y = mod(-λ*(x-P[1])-P[2], r)
  [x;y]
end
```

We'll use the double-and-add method to compute the product mP. The double-and-add method is the Horner form applied to a polynomial ring. Consider the polynomial

$$x^n + a_{n-1}x^{n-1} + \cdots + a_1 x + a_0.$$

Note that by taking $x = 2$ and $a_i \in \{0, 1\}$, we have a binary representation of a number $m = 1a_{n-1}a_{n-2} \ldots a_2 a_1 a_0$. We can write the polynomial in Horner form

$$x(x(x(\cdots (x + a_{n-1}) + \cdots + a_2) + a_1) + a_0.$$

Similarly, the representation of the number m in Horner form is

$$m = 2(2(2 \cdots 2(2 + a_{n-1}) + \cdots + a_2) + a_1) + a_0.$$

Furthermore, the product of the numbers m and p is

$$mp = 2(2(2 \cdots 2(2p + a_{n-1}p) + \cdots + a_2 p) + a_1 p) + a_0 p.$$

Formally substituting the group operator $\oplus$ and the point P into this expression gives us

$$mP = 2(2(2 \cdots 2(2P \oplus a_{n-1}P) \oplus \cdots \oplus a_2 P) \oplus a_1 P) \oplus a_0 P.$$

We can evaluate this expression from the inside out using an iterative function or from the outside in using a recursive one. Let's do the latter. This approach allows us to right-shift through $m = 1a_{n-1}a_{n-2}\ldots a_2a_1a_0$ and inspect the least significant bit with each function call.

```
Base.isodd(m::BigInt) = ((m&1)==1)
function dbl_add(m,P)
  if m > 1
    Q = dbl_add(m>>1,P)
    return isodd(m) ? (Q⊕Q)⊕P : Q⊕Q
  else
    return P
  end
end
```

Alice chooses a private key m (say 1829442) and sends Bob her public key mP. Similarly, Bob chooses a private key n (say 3727472) and sends Alice his public key nP. Now, both can generate the same cipher using a shared secret key nmP.

```
P₁ = big"0x79BE667EF9DCBBAC55A06295CE87
        0B07029BFCDB2DCE28D959F2815B16F81798"
P₂ = big"0x483ADA7726A3C4655DA4FBFC0E11
        08A8FD17B448A68554199C47D08FFB10D4B8"
P = [P₁; P₂]
m, n = 1829442, 3727472
mP = dbl_add(m,P)
nmP = dbl_add(n,mP)
```

8.14. The derivative of $f(x) = \frac{1}{2}mx^2$ is $f'(x) = mx$. The gradient descent method applied to this function is

$$x^{(k+1)} = x^{(k)} - \alpha f'(x^{(k)}) = (1 - \alpha m)x^{(k)}.$$

The convergence factor for this fixed-point method is $|1 - \alpha m|$. The method converges if and only if the learning rate $0 < \alpha < 2/m$. Convergence is monotonic when the learning rate is less than $1/m$ and zigzagging when it is greater than $1/m$. Convergence is fastest when the learning rate is close to $1/m$, the reciprocal of the second-derivative of $f(x)$—i.e., the inverse of the Hessian.

The momentum method

$$x^{(k+1)} = x^{(k)} + \alpha p^{(k)} \quad \text{with} \quad p^{(k)} = -f'(x^{(k)}) + \beta p^{(k-1)}$$

can be rewritten to explicitly remove $p^{(k)}$ and $p^{(k-1)}$ as

$$x^{(k+1)} = x^{(k)} - \alpha f'(x^{(k)}) + \beta(x^{(k)} - x^{(k-1)}).$$

Hence, we have the system

$$\begin{bmatrix} x^{(k+1)} \\ x^{(k)} \end{bmatrix} = \begin{bmatrix} 1 - \alpha m + \beta & -\beta \\ 1 & 0 \end{bmatrix} \begin{bmatrix} x^{(k)} \\ x^{(k-1)} \end{bmatrix}.$$

The fixed-point system $\mathbf{x}^{(k+1)} = \mathbf{A}\mathbf{x}^{(k)}$ converges if the spectral radius of $\mathbf{A}$ is less than one. The eigenvalues of the system are

$$\lambda_{\pm} = \tfrac{1}{2}(1 - \alpha m + \beta) \pm \tfrac{1}{2}\sqrt{(1 - \alpha m + \beta)^2 - 4\beta}.$$

By taking $\alpha m = 2 + 2\beta$, we have

$$\lambda_{\pm} = \tfrac{1}{2}(-1 - \beta) \pm \tfrac{1}{2}(1 - \beta) = \{-\beta, 1\}.$$

So the method converges if $0 < \alpha < (2 + 2\beta)/m$ and $0 < \beta < 1$. Furthermore, if $(1 - \alpha m + \beta)^2 < 4\beta$, the discriminant is negative and the eigenvalues are complex. From this,

$$|\lambda_{\pm}|^2 = \tfrac{1}{4}(1 - \alpha m + \beta) - \tfrac{1}{4}(1 - \alpha m + \beta)^2 + \beta = \beta.$$

It follows that if $\left(1 - \sqrt{\beta}\right)^2/m < \alpha < \left(1 + \sqrt{\beta}\right)^2/m$, then the spectral radius $\rho(\mathbf{A}) < \sqrt{\beta}$. To dig deeper, see Gabriel Goh's interactive article "Why Momentum Really Works."

9.1. We first show that the Vandermonde matrix is non-singular if the nodes are distinct. Let $\mathbf{V}$ be the Vandermonde matrix using nodes $x_0, x_1, \ldots, x_n$. Consider the relation

$$\det(\mathbf{V}) = \prod_{j=0}^{n} \prod_{i \neq j} (x_i - x_j). \tag{A.2}$$

The relation clearly holds for $n = 1$. Assume that (A.2) is true for n nodes. We will show that it also holds for $n + 1$ nodes by using cofactor expansion with respect to the last column. Let $\mathbf{V}[x_k]$ be the Vandermonde matrix formed using all the nodes $\{x_0, x_1, \ldots, x_n\}$ *except* for x_k. Then

$$\det(\mathbf{V}[x_k]) = \prod_{\substack{j=0 \\ j \neq k}}^{n} \prod_{i \neq j} (x_i - x_j) \tag{A.3}$$

By cofactor expansion $\det(\mathbf{V})$ equals

$$x_0^n \det(\mathbf{V}[x_0]) + \cdots + (-1)^k x_k^n \det(\mathbf{V}[x_k]) + \cdots + (-1)^n x_n^n \det(\mathbf{V}[x_n])$$

By (A.3),

$$\det(\mathbf{V}) = \sum_{k=0}^{n} (-1)^k x_k^n \prod_{\substack{j=0 \\ j \neq k}}^{n} \prod_{i \neq j} (x_i - x_j).$$

9.2. To help visualize periodic boundary conditions, we can imagine repeating the leftmost and rightmost knots onto the right and left sides of our domain:

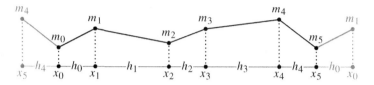

The following code modifies spline_natural on page 238 to determine the coefficients $\{m_0, m_1, \ldots, m_{n-1}\}$ of a spline with periodic boundary conditions. It is assumed that $y_0 = y_n$.

```
function spline_periodic(x,y)
  h = diff(x)
  d = 6*diff(diff([y[end-1];y])./[h[end];h])
  α = h[1:end-1]
  β = 2*(h+circshift(h,1))
  C = Matrix(SymTridiagonal(β,α))
  C[1,end]=h[end]; C[end,1]=h[end]
  m = C\d
  return([m;m[1]])
end
```

Now, we can compute a parametric spline interpolant with nx*n points through a set of n random points using the function evaluate_spline defined on page 239. One solution is shown in Figure A.11 on the facing page.

```
n = 5; nx = 30
x = rand(n); y = rand(n)
x = [x;x[1]]; y = [y;y[1]]
t = [0;cumsum(sqrt.(diff(x).^2 + diff(y).^2))]
X = evaluate_spline(t,x,spline_periodic(t,x),nx*n)
Y = evaluate_spline(t,y,spline_periodic(t,y),nx*n)
scatter(x,y); plot!(X[2],Y[2],legend=false)
```

9.3. First, let's set up the domain x and the function y, which we are interpolating.

```
n = 20; N = 200
x = LinRange(-1,1,n)
y = float(x .> 0);
```

Next, define the radial basis functions and the polynomials bases.

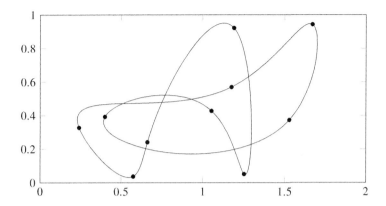

Figure A.11: A closed parametric spline passing through 10 knots.

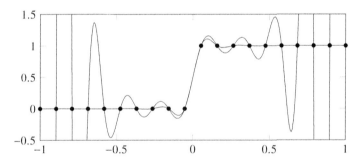

Figure A.12: Interpolation using polynomial and $|x|^3$ radial basis function .

```
φ₁(x,a) = abs.(x.-a).^3
φ₂(x,a) = exp.(-20(x.-a).^2)
φ₃(x,a) = x.^a
```

Finally, we construct and plot the interpolating functions.

```
X = LinRange(-1,1,N)
interp(φ,a) = φ(X,a')*(φ(x,a')\y)
Y₁ = interp(φ₁,x)
Y₂ = interp(φ₂,x)
Y₃ = interp(φ₃,(0:n-1))
scatter(x,y,seriestype = :scatter, marker = :o, legend = :none)
plot!(X,[Y₁,Y₂,Y₃],ylim=[-0.5,1.5])
```

As seen in Figure A.12 on the previous page, the polynomial interpolant suffers from the Runge phenomenon with a maximum error of about 500. On the other hand, the radial basis function gives us a good approximation. The radial basis function $\phi(x) = |x|^3$ generates a cubic spline because the resulting function is cubic on the subintervals and has continuous second derivatives at the nodes.

9.4. Let $v_j(x) = B(h^{-1}x - j)$ be B-splines with nodes equally spaced at $x_i = ih$:

$$
B(x) = \begin{cases} \frac{2}{3} - \frac{1}{2}(2 - |x|)x^2, & |x| \in [0, 1) \\ \frac{1}{6}(2 - |x|)^3, & |x| \in [1, 2) \, . \\ 0, & \text{otherwise} \end{cases}
$$

Every node in the domain needs to be covered by three B-splines, so we'll need to have an additional B-spline centered just outside either boundary to cover each of the boundary nodes. Take the approximation $\sum_{i=-1}^{n+1} c_i v_i(x)$ for $u(x)$. Bessel's equation $xu'' + u' + xu = 0$ at the collocation points $\{x_i\}$ is now

$$
\sum_{j=0}^{n} \left(x_i v_j''(x_i) + v_j'(x_i) + x_i v_j(x_i) \right) c_j = 0
$$

where

	$v_j''(x_i)$	$v_j'(x_i)$	$v_j(x_i)$
when $j = i$	$-2h^{-2}$	0	$\frac{2}{3}$
when $j = i \pm 1$	h^{-2}	$\mp\frac{1}{2}h^{-1}$	$\frac{1}{6}$
othewise	0	0	0

We have the system $\mathbf{Ac} = \mathbf{d}$, where

$$
a_{i,i} = -2x_i h^{-2} + \frac{2}{3}x_i \quad \text{and} \quad a_{i,i\pm 1} = x_i h^{-2} \mp \frac{1}{2}h^{-1} + \frac{1}{6}
$$

and $a_{ij} = 0$ otherwise, and where $d_i = 0$ for $i = 0, 1, \ldots, n$. At the endpoints, we have the boundary conditions

$$
\frac{1}{6}c_{-1} + \frac{2}{3}c_0 + \frac{1}{6}c_0 = u_a = 1 \quad \text{and} \quad \frac{1}{6}c_{n-1} + \frac{2}{3}c_n + \frac{1}{6}c_{n+1} = u_b = 0,
$$

from which

$$
a_{0,-1} = \frac{1}{6}, \ a_{0,0} = \frac{2}{3}, \ a_{0,1} = \frac{1}{6}, \quad \text{and} \quad a_{n,n-1} = \frac{1}{6}, \ a_{n,n} = \frac{2}{3}, \ a_{0,n+1} = \frac{1}{6}
$$

and $d_0 = 1$.

Once we have the coefficients c_j, we construct the solution $\sum_{j=-1}^{n+1} c_j v_j(x)$. We start by defining a general collocation solver for $\mathrm{L}u(x) = f(x)$. This solver takes boundary conditions bc and an array of equally-spaced collocation points x. It returns an array of coefficients c for each node, including two elements for the two B-splines just outside the domain.

```
function collocation_solve(L,f,bc,x)
  h = x[2]-x[1]
  S = L(x)*([1 -1/2 1/6; -2 0 2/3; 1 1/2 1/6]./[h^2 h 1])'
  d = [bc[1]; f(x); bc[2]]
  A = Matrix(Tridiagonal([S[:,1];0], [0;S[:,2];0], [0;S[:,3]]))
  A[1,1:3], A[end,end-2:end] = [1 4 1]/6, [1 4 1]/6
  return(A\d)
end
```

We could have kept matrix A as a Tridiagonal matrix by first using the second row to zero out A[1,3] and the second to last row to zero out A[end,end-2]. Next, we define a function that will interpolate between collocation points:

```
function collocation_build(c,x,N)
  X = LinRange(x[1],x[end],N)
  h = x[2] - x[1]
  i = Int32.(X ./ h .+ 1); i[N] = i[N-1]
  C = [c[i] c[i.+1] c[i.+2] c[i.+3]]'
  B = (x->[(1-x).^3;4-3*(2-x).*x.^2;4-3*(1+x).*(1-x).^2;x.^3]/6)
  Y = sum(C.*hcat(B.((X.-x[i])/h)...),dims=1)
  return(Array(X),reshape(Y,(:,1)))
end
```

Now, we can solve Bessel's equation.

```
using Roots, SpecialFunctions
n = 20; N = 141
L = (x -> [x one.(x) x])
f = (x -> zero.(x) )
b = fzero(besselj0, 11)
x = range(0,b,length=n)
c = collocation_solve(L,f,[1,0],x)
X,Y = collocation_build(c,x,70)
plot(X,[Y besselj0.(X)])
```

The solution is plotted in Figure A.13 on the following page using 15 collocation points. Even with only 15 points, the numerical solution is fairly accurate. Finally, let's measure the convergence rate by increasing the collocation points. A method is order p if the error is $\varepsilon = O(n^{-p})$, where n is the number of points. This means that $\log \varepsilon \approx -p \log n + \log m$ for some m. We'll plot the error as a function of collocation points.

```
N = 10*2 .^(1:7); ϵ = []
for n in N
  x = LinRange(0,b,n)
  c = collocation_solve(L,f,[1,0],x)
```

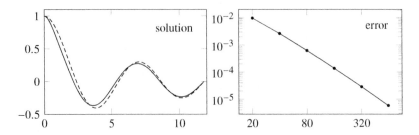

Figure A.13: Numerical solution (solid) and exact solution (dashed) to Bessel's equation for 15 collocation points (left). The log-log plot of the error as a function of number of points (right).

```
    X,Y = collocation_build(c,x,n)
    append!(ε, norm(Y-besselj0.(X)) / n)
  end
plot(N, ε, xaxis=:log, yaxis=:log, marker=:o)
```

The log-log slope will give us the order of convergence. The Julia code

```
([log.(N) one.(N)]\log.(ε))[1]
```

returns approximately -2.18, confirming that the collocation method is second-order accurate.

9.5. The Bernstein polynomial representation of the Bézier curve is

$$\begin{bmatrix} x \\ y \end{bmatrix} = (1-t)^3 \begin{bmatrix} 1 \\ 0 \end{bmatrix} + 3t(1-t)^2 \begin{bmatrix} 1 \\ c \end{bmatrix} + 3t^2(1-t) \begin{bmatrix} c \\ 1 \end{bmatrix} + t^3 \begin{bmatrix} 0 \\ 1 \end{bmatrix}.$$

We want to find the parameter c that minimizes the maximum deviation from the circle $R(t) = x^2 + y^2 - 1$. To do this, we'll find the c for which the magnitude of a local maximum at $t = t_c$ equals the magnitude of the local minimum at $t = \frac{1}{2}$. Before leaping into the problem, there are a few things we can do to make it less messy. Scaling and shifting $t \mapsto \frac{1}{2}(t+1)$ will make R a symmetric function over $(-1, 1)$. Because R is now a symmetric function (with only even powers of t), we can make a second change of variables $t \mapsto \sqrt{t}$ to reduce the function from a sextic polynomial to a cubic polynomial. To find the location t_c, we need to solve $R'(t) = 0$. The function R has another critical point at $t = 1$, so we can factor $(t - 1)$ out of the derivative, leaving us with a linear equation. (The critical point at $t = 0$ naturally falls out because we are differentiating with respect to $\sqrt{t}$.) We now just need to solve $R(t_c) = -R(0)$, which happens to be a sextic equation.

We'll use Wolfram Cloud (https://www.wolframcloud.com) to implement the solution. Wolfram Cloud has a free basic plan that provides complete access to Mathematica with a few limitations, perfect for a problem like this one.

```
x = (1-t)^3 + 3t*(1-t)^2 + 3c*t^2*(1-t);
y = 3c*t(1-t)^2 + 3t^2*(1-t) + t^3;
R = Collect[ (x^2 + y^2 - 1) /. {t->(t+1)/2} /. {t->Sqrt[t]}, t];
R1 = Simplify[ R /. Solve[ D[R,t]/(t-1) == 0, t] ];
R2 = Simplify[ R /. t -> 0 ];
FindRoot[ R1==-R2, {c,0.5}]
Sqrt[ (R1 + 1) /. % ] - 1
```

We find that $c \approx 0.551915$ is the optimal solution, resulting in less than 0.02 percent maximum deviation from the unit circle—not too bad!

10.3. The pth derivative of the sine, piecewise-quadratic, piecewise-linear, and Gaussian functions are plotted below for several values of $p \in [0, 1]$:

Note that the pth derivative for $\sin x$ is $\sin(x + p\pi/2)$, which is simply a translation of the original function. A Julia solution follows.

```
using FFTW
n = 256; ℓ = 2
x = (0:n-1)/n*ℓ .- ℓ/2
ξ = [0:(n/2-1); (-(n/2)):-1]*(2π/ℓ)
f₁ = exp.(-16*x.^2)
f₂ = sin.(π*x)
f₃ = x.*(1 .- abs.(x))
deriv(f,p) = real(ifft((im*ξ).^p.*fft(f)))
```

We can use Interact.jl to create an interactive widget.

```
using Interact
func = Dict("Gaussian"=>f₁,"sine"=>f₂,"spline"=>f₃)
@manipulate for f in togglebuttons(func; label="function"),
  p in slider(0:0.01:2; value=0, label="derivative")
  plot(x,deriv(f,p),legend=:none)
end
```

Alternatively, we could use the Plots.jl `@animate` macro to produce a gif. See the QR code at the bottom of this page.

fractional derivatives
of the Gaussian
function

10.4. The LeNet-5 model consists of several hidden layers—three sets of convolutional layers combined by pooling layers, which are then flattened and followed by two fully-connected layers. The diagram below shows the LeNet-5 architecture:

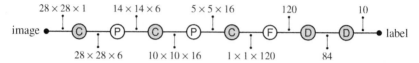

In this diagram, Ⓒ is a trainable convolutional layer, Ⓟ is a pooling layer, Ⓕ is a flattening layer, and Ⓓ is a trainable fully-connected layer. The 28×28 pixel greyscale images are initially padded with two pixels all around the boundary before the first 5×5 convolution layer, creating a set of six 28×28 feature maps. Each of these feature maps is then subsampled to 14×14 maps by an average pooling layer (2×2 subarrays are averaged to 1×1 subarrays). These maps are fed, without padding, through a second convolutional layer with sixteen 5×5 filters. The resultant $10 \times 10 \times 16$ feature map is again halved in size to $5 \times 5 \times 16$. The last (unpadded) convolutional layer consists of 120 filters, producing a $1 \times 1 \times 120$ feature map that is subsequently flattened to 120 values. These values are fed through two fully-connected layers, one with 84 neurons and one with 10 neurons, to an output layer with each of the ten labels.

Let's use the Flux.jl package to develop and train the model. We'll start by defining the model architecture:

```
using MLDatasets, Flux
model = Chain(
  Conv((5,5), 1=>6, tanh, pad=SamePad()),
  MeanPool((2,2)),
  Conv((5,5), 6=>16, tanh),
  MeanPool((2,2)),
  Conv((5,5), 16=>120, tanh),
  Flux.flatten,
  Dense(120, 84, tanh),
  Dense(84, 10))
```

Let's load the MNIST training and test data as single-precision floating-point numbers. Using single-precision numbers can significantly speed performance over double-precision numbers because the memory usage is halved. We'll convert each 28×28-pixel image into a $28 \times 28 \times 1$-element array. We'll also convert each of the labels into one hot arrays—arrays whose elements equal one in positions matching the respective labels and equal zero otherwise.

```
image_train, label_train = MLDatasets.MNIST(split=:train)[:]
image_test, label_test = MLDatasets.MNIST(split=:test)[:]
image_train = Flux.unsqueeze(image_train, 3)
image_test = Flux.unsqueeze(image_test, 3)
```

```
label_train = Flux.onehotbatch(label_train, 0:9)
label_test = Flux.onehotbatch(label_test, 0:9);
```

The categorical cross-entropy, or softmax loss,

$$L(\mathbf{y}) = -\log \frac{e^{y_i}}{\sum_{i=0}^{9} e^{y_i}}$$

is used for multi-label classification. Large datasets can consume significant memory. The Flux.Data.DataLoader function breaks up the dataset and handles iteration over mini-batches of data to reduce memory consumption. Diederik Kingma and Jimmy Ba introduced the Adam optimizer in 2014—well after LeNet's 1998 debut—so its use in LeNet is anachronistic. The Adam optimizer improves the stochastic gradient descent available at the time.

```
loss(x,y) = Flux.Losses.logitcrossentropy(model(x),y)
parameters = Flux.params(model)
data = Flux.Data.DataLoader((image_train,label_train),batchsize=100)
optimizer = ADAM()
```

Now, we can train the model. Let's loop over five epochs. It might take several minutes to train—adding the ProgressMeter.jl macro @showprogress before the for loop will display a progress bar.

```
using ProgressMeter
@showprogress for epochs = 1:5
  Flux.train!(loss, parameters, data, optimizer)
end
```

We use the test data to see how well the model performed. The onecold function is the inverse of the onehot function, returning the position of the largest element.

```
accuracy(x,y) = sum(Flux.onecold(x) .== Flux.onecold(y))/size(y,2)
accuracy(model(image_test),label_test)
```

The LeNet-5 model achieves about a 2 percent error rate—better than the 5 percent error rate obtained using principal component analysis in exercise 3.7. The figure on the following page shows the intermediate layer inputs. The first convolutional layer appears to detect edges in the image. The second convolutional layer then uses this edge detection to identify gross structure in the image.

10.5. We'll minimize the residual $\|\boldsymbol{\varepsilon}\|_2^2 = \sum_i^n \varepsilon_i^2$, where

$$\varepsilon_i = \sqrt{(x - x_i)^2 + (y - y_i)^2} - c(t_i - t). \tag{A.4}$$

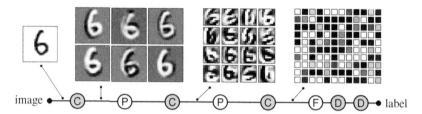

image — label

Figure A.14: An input image and the intermediate transformations of that image following the three convolutional matrices of LeNet-5.

```
using LsqFit
ε = (x,p) -> @. √((x[:,1]-p[1])^2 + (x[:,2]-p[2])^2) - (x[:,3]-p[3])
x = [3 3 12; 1 15 14; 10 2 13; 12 15 14; 0 11 12]
curve_fit(ε,x,zeros(5),zeros(3)).param
```

The solution (x, y, t) is approximately $(6.30, 8.57, 5.46)$. The formulation of the problem is different from that in exercise 3.10, and we should expect a slightly different answer.

Now, let's apply the same method to the ShotSpotter data. We start by forming two arrays: X for the (x, y, z, t) data of the sensors and x_0 for the $(x, y, z, \cdot)$ data of the signal source.

```
using CSV, DataFrames
df = DataFrame(CSV.File(download(bucket*"shotspotter.csv")))
X = Array(df[1:end-1,:]); x₀ = Array(df[end,:]);
```

Then we solve the system and compute the error.

```
using LsqFit
c = 328.6
ε = (x,p)->sqrt.(sum([(x[:,i].-p[i]).^2 for i∈1:3]))-c*(x[:,4].-p[4])
xₙₗₛ = curve_fit(ε,X,zero(X[:,1]),X[1,:]).param
error = xₙₗₛ - x₀
```

The error is approximately -4.7 m and 0.4 m horizontally and 54.0 m vertically.

11.1. The third-order approximation to $f'(x)$ is of the form

$$h^{-1}(c_{10}f(x) + c_{11}f(x+h) + c_{12}f(x+2h) + c_{13}f(x+3h)) + m_1 h^3 f^{(4)}(\xi)$$

where ξ is some point in the interval $[x, x+3h]$. To find the coefficients c_{10}, c_{11}, c_{12}, c_{13}, and m_1, we define d = [0,1,2,3] from nodes at $x, x+h, x+2h$ and $x+3h$ and invert the scaled Vandermonde matrix $C_{ij} = \left[d_i^j / i!\right]^{-1}$. The coefficients of the truncation error are given by C*d.^n/factorial(n):

```
d = [0,1,2,3]; n = length(d)
C = inv( d.^(0:n-1)' .// factorial.(0:n-1)' )
[C C*d.^n/factorial(n)]
```

$$
\begin{array}{cccc c}
1 & 0 & 0 & 0 & 0 \\
-11/6 & 3 & -3/2 & 1/3 & 1/4 \\
2 & -5 & 4 & -1 & -11/12 \\
-1 & 3 & -3 & 1 & 3/2
\end{array}
$$

From the second row, we have

$$
f'(x) \approx \frac{1}{h}\left(-\tfrac{11}{6}f(x) + 3f(x+h) - \tfrac{3}{2}f(x+2h) + \tfrac{1}{3}f(x+3h)\right)
$$

with a truncation error $\frac{1}{4}f^{(4)}(\xi)h^3$ for some $\xi \in [x, x+3h]$. The value $|f^{(4)}(\xi)|$ is bounded by 1 for $f(x) = \sin x$.

The round-off error is bounded by

$$
h^{-1}\left(|-\tfrac{11}{6}| + |3| + |-\tfrac{3}{2}| + |\tfrac{1}{3}|\right)\mathrm{eps} \approx 7h^{-1}\mathrm{eps},
$$

where eps is machine epsilon. The truncation error decreases and round-off error increases error as h gets smaller. Following the discussion on page 187, the total error is minimum when the two are equal, i.e., when $h = (28\mathrm{eps})^{1/4} \approx 3 \times 10^{-4}$.

From the third row, we have

$$
f''(x) \approx \frac{1}{h^2}\left(2f(x) - 5f(x+h) + 4f(x+2h) - f(x+3h)\right)
$$

with a truncation error $\frac{11}{12}h^2 f^{(4)}(\xi)$.

11.2. In practice, we don't need to save every intermediate term. Instead by taking $i = m$, $j = m - n$, and $\bar{D}_j = D_{m,n}$, we have the update

$$
\bar{D}_j \leftarrow \frac{\bar{D}_{j+1} - \delta^{p(i-j)}\bar{D}_j}{1 - \delta^{p(i-j)}} \quad \text{where} \quad j = i-1, \ldots, 1 \quad \text{and} \quad \bar{D}_i \leftarrow \phi(\delta^i h).
$$

The Julia code for Richardson extrapolation taking $\delta = \frac{1}{2}$ is

```
function richardson(f,x,m)
  D = []
  for i in 1:m
    append!(D, ϕ(f,x,2^i))
    for j in i-1:-1:1
      D[j] = (4^(i-j)*D[j+1] - D[j])/(4^(i-j) - 1)
    end
  end
  D[1]
end
```

This reformulated implementation is about 20 times faster when $n = 8$ and about 100 times faster when $n = 12$.

11.3. We'll extend the dual class on page 301 by adding methods for the square root, division, and cosine.

```
Base.:sqrt(u) = Dual(sqrt(value(u)), deriv(u) / 2sqrt(value(u)))
Base.:/(u, v) = Dual(value(u)/value(v),
  (value(u)*deriv(v)-value(v)*deriv(u))/(value(v)*value(v)))
Base.:cos(u) = Dual(cos(value(u)), -sin(value(u))*deriv(u))
```

We can define a function that implements Newton's method.

```
function get_zero(f,x)
  ϵ = 1e-12; δ = 1
  while abs(δ) > ϵ
    fx = f(Dual(x))
    δ = value(fx)/deriv(fx)
    x -= δ
  end
  return(x)
end
```

The call `get_zero(x->4sin(x)+sqrt(x),4)` returns 3.6386... as expected. To find a minimum or maximum, we replace two lines in Newton's method to get

```
function get_extremum(f,x)
  ϵ = 1e-12; δ = 1
  while abs(δ)>ϵ
    fx = f(Dual(Dual(x)))
    δ = deriv(value(fx))/deriv(deriv(fx))
    x -= δ
  end
  return(x)
end
```

The call `get_extremum(x->4sin(x)+sqrt(x),4)` returns 4.6544... as expected.

11.4. Let's take γ to be a circle centered at $z = a$. That is, take $z = a + \varepsilon e^{i\theta}$ with $dz = i\varepsilon e^{i\theta}\, d\theta$. Then

$$f^{(p)}(a) = \frac{p!}{2\pi\varepsilon^p} \int_0^{2\pi} f\!\left(a + \varepsilon e^{i\theta}\right) e^{-ip\theta}\, d\theta.$$

The composite trapezoidal method applied to a smooth, periodic function has spectral convergence:

$$f^{(p)}(a) = \frac{p!}{n\varepsilon^p} \sum_{k=0}^{n-1} f\left(a + \varepsilon e^{2i\pi k/n}\right) e^{-2i\pi pk/n} + O\left((\varepsilon/n)^n\right).$$

We can implement the method as

```
function cauchyderivative(f, a, p, n = 20, ε = 0.1)
    ω = exp.(2π*im*(0:(n-1))/n)
    factorial(p)/(n*ε^p)*sum(@. f(a+ε*ω)/ω^p)
end
```

```
f = x -> exp(x)/(cos(x)^3 + sin(x)^3)
cauchyderivative(f, 0, 6)
```

Note that by taking $n = 2$ and $p = 1$ we have the usual central difference approximation of the derivative:

$$f'(a) = \frac{f(a + \varepsilon) - f(a - \varepsilon)}{2\varepsilon} + O(\varepsilon^2).$$

We don't have to start the contour integral $\theta = 0$. Let's start at $\theta = \pi/2$. Suppose that $f(x)$ is a real function and again take $n = 2$ and $p = 1$. Then

$$f'(a) = \frac{f(a + i\varepsilon) - f(a - i\varepsilon)}{2i\varepsilon} + O(\varepsilon^2) = \frac{\operatorname{Im} f(a + i\varepsilon)}{\varepsilon} + O(\varepsilon^2),$$

which is the complex-step derivative.

11.5. The following function computes the nodes and weights for Gauss–Legendre quadrature by using Newton's method to find the roots of $P_n(x)$:

```
function gauss_legendre(n)
    x = -cos.((4*(1:n).-1)*π/(4n+2))
    Δ = one.(x)
    dPₙ = 0
    while(maximum(abs.(Δ))>1e-16)
        Pₙ, Pₙ₋₁ = x, one.(x)
        for k ∈ 2:n
            Pₙ, Pₙ₋₁ = ((2k - 1)*x.*Pₙ-(k-1)*Pₙ₋₁)/k, Pₙ
        end
        dPₙ = @. n*(x*Pₙ - Pₙ₋₁)/(x^2-1)
        Δ = Pₙ ./ dPₙ
        x -= Δ
    end
    return(x, @. 2/((1-x^2)*dPₙ^2))
end
```

11.7. We'll make a change of variables $\xi = (x - s)/\sqrt{4t}$ and $d\xi = -s/\sqrt{4t}$. Then

$$u(t,x) = \frac{1}{\sqrt{\pi}} \int_{-\infty}^{\infty} u_0(x - 2\xi\sqrt{t})e^{-\xi^2}\,d\xi.$$

We can implement the solution in Julia as

```
using FastGaussQuadrature
ξ,w = gausshermite(40)
u₀ = x -> sin(x)
u = (t,x) -> w · u₀.(x.-2sqrt(t)*ξ)/sqrt(π)
x = LinRange(-12,12,100); plot(x,u.(1,x))
```

11.8. Using the function

```
mc_π(n) = sum(sum(rand(2,n).^2,dims=1).<1)/n*4
```

we compute $\pi \approx 3.138$ using a sample size $n = 10^4$. To confirm the convergence rate for the Monte Carlo method, we further sample over $m = 20$ runs to smooth out the noise inherent in the Monte Carlo method.

```
m = 20; d = []; N = 2 .^ (1:20)
for n ∈ N
   append!(d,sum([abs(π - mc_π(n)) for i∈1:m])/m)
end
s = log.(N.^[0 1])\log.(d)
scatter(N,d,xaxis=:log, yaxis=:log)
plot!(N,exp(s[1]).*N.^s[2])
```

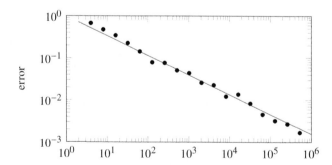

The log-log slope of the error is −0.468, confirming the expected $O(N^{-1/2})$ half-order of convergence. The Monte Carlo method would need roughly 10^{25}

samples for 13 digits of accuracy—taking about 800 years on my laptop. We can compute the area of an eight-dimensional unit hypersphere by a modifying our original code:

```
mc_π(n,d=2) = sum(sum(rand(d,n).^2,dims=1).<1)/n*2^d
```

By taking $n = 10^6$, we get 4.088—close to the actual $\pi^4 r^8/24 \approx 4.059$.

11.10. Substituting the polynomial $p(t_i) = c_0 + c_1 t_i + c_2 t_i^2 + \cdots + c_n t_i^n$ and its derivative $p'(t_i) = c_1 + 2c_2 t_i + \cdots + nc_n t_i^{n-1}$ into (11.8) yields

$$
\begin{bmatrix}
1 & 2t_1 & \cdots & nt_1^{n-1} \\
1 & 2t_2 & \cdots & nt_2^{n-1} \\
\vdots & \vdots & \ddots & \vdots \\
1 & 2t_n & \cdots & nt_n^{n-1}
\end{bmatrix}
\begin{bmatrix} c_1 \\ c_2 \\ \vdots \\ c_n \end{bmatrix}
= \mathbf{M}
\begin{bmatrix}
t_1 & t_1^2 & \cdots & t_1^n \\
t_2 & t_2^2 & \cdots & t_2^n \\
\vdots & \vdots & \ddots & \vdots \\
t_n & t_n^2 & \cdots & t_n^3
\end{bmatrix}
\begin{bmatrix} c_1 \\ c_2 \\ \vdots \\ c_n \end{bmatrix}.
$$

Hence, the differentiation matrix $\mathbf{M}$ is

$$
\mathbf{M} =
\begin{bmatrix}
1 & 2t_1 & \cdots & nt_1^{n-1} \\
1 & 2t_2 & \cdots & nt_2^{n-1} \\
\vdots & \vdots & \ddots & \vdots \\
1 & 2t_n & \cdots & nt_n^{n-1}
\end{bmatrix}^{-1}
\begin{bmatrix}
t_1 & t_1^2 & \cdots & t_1^n \\
t_2 & t_2^2 & \cdots & t_2^n \\
\vdots & \vdots & \ddots & \vdots \\
t_n & t_n^2 & \cdots & t_n^3
\end{bmatrix},
$$

and $c_0 = p(t_0)$ for $t_0 = 0$. Now, we can solve $\mathbf{M}(\mathbf{p} - p(t_0)\mathbf{1}) = f(\mathbf{p}, t)$ using a standard nonlinear solver.

Let's solve the differential equation $u'(t) = \alpha u^2$. First, we'll generate the nodes of Gauss–Legendre–Labotto nodes shifted from $[-1, 1]$ to $[0, 1]$.

```
using FastGaussQuadrature
function differentiation_matrix(n)
  nodes, _ = gausslobatto(n+1)
  t = (nodes[2:end].+1)/2
  A = t.^(0:n-1)'.*(1:n)'
  B = t.^(1:n)'
  A/B,t
end
```

Now, we define the differentiation matrix operator.

```
n = 20
M,t = differentiation_matrix(n)
D = (u,u₀) -> M*(u .- u₀)
```

Finally, we solve the problem.

```
using NLsolve
u₀ = 1.0; α = 0.9
F = (u,u₀,α) -> D(u,u₀) .- α*u.^2
u = nlsolve(u->F(u,u₀,α),u₀*ones(n)).zero
plot([0;t], [u₀;u], marker=:circle, legend=false)
```

The exact solution is $u(t) = (1 - \alpha t)^{-1}$. The value $u(1)$ for $\alpha = 0.9$ and $\alpha = 0.99$ should equal 10 and 100 respectively. Using 20 nodes, we have numerical solutions of approximately 9.984 (not bad) and 21.7 (awful). If we try to increase the number of nodes to get better accuracy, we'll run into trouble because the condition number of differentiation matrix explodes. When $n = 23$, the condition number is 610; when it is $n = 27$, the condition number is 1.35×10^6.

Instead, let's use the pseudospectral method by scaling the differentiation operator and iterating over time. This time, we'll take 20 segments with 5 nodes for each segment (or about 50 nodes overall).

```
N = 30; Δt = 1.0/N; n = 8
M,t = differentiation_matrix(n)
D = (u,u₀) -> M*(u .- u₀)/Δt
u₀ = 1.0; U = [u₀]; T = [0.0]; α = 0.9
for i = 0:N-1
    u = nlsolve(u->F(u,u₀,α),u₀*ones(n)).zero
    u₀ = u[end]
    append!(T,(i.+t)*Δt)
    append!(U,u)
end
plot(T, U, marker=:circle, legend=false)
```

Now, the relative error at $t = 1$ is 1.3×10^{-9} and 0.019 for $\alpha = 0.9$ and $\alpha = 0.99$, respectively.

A.3 Numerical methods for differential equations

12.1. The θ-scheme corresponds to the forward Euler scheme, the trapezoidal scheme, and the backward Euler scheme when $\theta = 1$, $\theta = \frac{1}{2}$, and $\theta = 0$, respectively. So the regions of absolute stability of the θ-scheme will correspond with those three schemes when θ is any of those three values. Let's find the region of absolute stability for a general θ. Take $f(U^n) = \lambda U^n$ and take $r = U^{n+1}/U^n$. Then

$$\frac{r - 1}{k} = (1 - \theta)\lambda r + \theta\lambda.$$

We want to determine the values λk for which $|r| \leq 1$. To do this, we'll find the boundary of the region $\lambda k = x + iy$ where $|r| = 1$.

$$1 = |r|^2 = r\bar{r} = \frac{1 + \theta(x + iy)}{1 - (1 - \theta)(x + iy)} \frac{1 + \theta(x - iy)}{1 - (1 - \theta)(x - iy)}$$

$$= \frac{1 + 2\theta x + \theta^2(x^2 + y^2)}{1 - 2(1 - \theta)x + (1 - \theta)^2(x^2 + y^2)},$$

from which $1 - 2(1 - \theta)x + (1 - \theta)^2(x^2 + y^2) = 1 + 2\theta x + \theta^2(x^2 + y^2)$. After rearranging and combining terms, $(1 - 2\theta)x^2 - 2x + (1 - 2\theta)y^2 = 0$ or equivalently

$$x^2 - \frac{2}{1 - 2\theta}x + y^2 = 0.$$

Completing the square yields

$$\left(x - \frac{1}{1 - 2\theta}\right)^2 + y^2 = \frac{1}{(1 - 2\theta)^2}.$$

So the region of absolute stability is bounded by a circle centered on the real axis at $\lambda k = (1 - 2\theta)^{-1}$ with radius $(1 - 2\theta)^{-1}$, that is, tangential to the imaginary axis. Note that when $\theta \to \frac{1}{2}$, the boundary approaches the imaginary axis.

12.4. The following Julia code produces the accompanying plot:

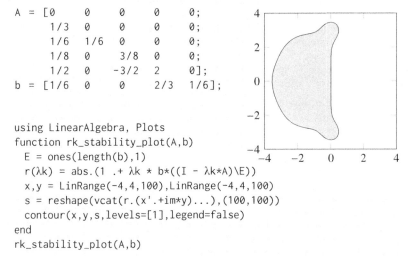

```
A = [0      0      0      0      0;
     1/3    0      0      0      0;
     1/6    1/6    0      0      0;
     1/8    0      3/8    0      0;
     1/2    0     -3/2    2      0];
b = [1/6    0      0      2/3    1/6];

using LinearAlgebra, Plots
function rk_stability_plot(A,b)
    E = ones(length(b),1)
    r(λk) = abs.(1 .+ λk * b*((I - λk*A)\E))
    x,y = LinRange(-4,4,100),LinRange(-4,4,100)
    s = reshape(vcat(r.(x'.+im*y)...),(100,100))
    contour(x,y,s,levels=[1],legend=false)
end
rk_stability_plot(A,b)
```

12.7. To solve $u' = f(u) + g(u)$ with a third-order L-stable IMEX method, we'll pair a BDF3 scheme with an appropriate explicit scheme. The BDF3 method approximates u' at time t_{n+1}, so we'll need to evaluate the explicit scheme at the same time t_{n+1} to avoid a splitting error. To do this, we need a third-order approximation of $g(U^{n+1})$.

The coefficients of the BDF3 scheme can computed using the function multistepcoefficients from page 349 with an input m = [0 1 2 3] and n = [0]. Alternately, we can compute them by solving the Taylor polynomial system

$$u'(t - ik) = u - iku' + \tfrac{1}{2}i^2k^2u'' - \tfrac{1}{6}i^3k^3u''' + O(k^4), \qquad (A.5)$$

keeping the u' term while eliminating the u, u'', and u''' terms.

```
i = 0:3; c = ((-i)'.^i.//factorial.(i))\[0;1;0;0]
```

The coefficients are [11//6 -3//1 3//2 -1//3], and the BDF3 scheme is correspondingly

$$\tfrac{11}{6}U^{n+1} - 3U^n + \tfrac{3}{2}U^{n-1} - \tfrac{1}{3}U^{n-2} = kf(U^{n+1}).$$

To approximate $g(U^{n+1})$, we again solve (A.5). This time, we keeping the u term and eliminate the u', u'' and u''' terms.

```
i = 0:3; c = ((-(i.+1))'.^i.//factorial.(i))\[1;0;0;0]
```

The coefficients are [4 -6 4 -1], and the approximation of $g(U^{n+1})$ is

$$\tilde{g}(U^n, U^{n-1}, U^{n-2}, U^{n-3}) = g\left(4U^n - 6U^{n-1} + 4U^{n-2} - U^{n-3}\right).$$

We combine the implicit and explicit methods to get

$$\frac{\tfrac{11}{6}U^{n+1} - 3U^n + \tfrac{3}{2}U^{n-1} - \tfrac{1}{3}U^{n-2}}{k} = f(U^{n+1}) + \tilde{g}(U^n, U^{n-1}, U^{n-2}, U^{n-3}).$$

The region of absolute stability for the BDF3 is known from Figure 12.5. To determine the region of stability for the explicit scheme, we take $g(u) = \lambda u$ and let $r = U^{n+1}/U^n$:

$$\tfrac{11}{6}r^4 - 3r^3 + \tfrac{3}{2}r^2 - \tfrac{1}{3}r = \lambda k\left(4r^3 - 6r^2 + 4r - 1\right).$$

We express $\lambda k(r)$ as a rational function and find the boundary of the domain $|r| \leq 1$ by taking $r = e^{i\theta}$. Figure A.15 on the next page shows the regions of stability.

12.8. Take $f(u) = \lambda u$ and let

$$\alpha = \frac{1}{b^*_{-1}}\sum_{j=0}^{s-1} b_j U^{n-j} \quad \text{and} \quad \beta = \frac{1}{b^*_{-1}}\sum_{j=0}^{s-1} b^*_j U^{n-j}.$$

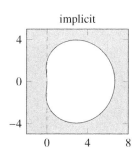
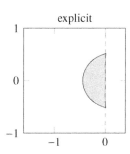

implicit   explicit

Figure A.15: The stencil and regions of absolute stability (in gray) for the implicit and explicit parts of the third-order IMEX method.

Then the Adams–Bashforth–Moulton PECE equation (12.7) can be written as

$$\tilde{U}^{n+1} = U^n + \alpha z \tag{A.6a}$$

$$U^{n+1} = U^n + (\tilde{U}^{n+1} + \beta)z, \tag{A.6b}$$

where $z = \lambda k b^*_{-1}$. Substituting (A.6a) into (A.6b) yields

$$U^{n+1} = U^n + (U^{n+1} + \beta)z + \alpha z^2.$$

For an additional corrector iteration, we substitute this new expression for $\tilde{U}^{n+1}$ in (A.6b), giving us

$$U^{n+1} = U^n + (U^n + \beta)(z + z^2) + \alpha z^3.$$

Continuing for additional corrector iterations produces

$$U^{n+1} = U^n + (z + z^2 + \cdots + z^s)(U^n + \beta) + z^{s+1}\alpha.$$

To find the boundary of the region of absolute stability, we let $r = U^n/U^{n+1}$ and look for the solutions to the following equation when to $|r| = 1$

$$1 = r + (z + z^2 + \cdots + z^s)(r + \beta(r)) + \alpha(r)z^{s+1}, \tag{A.7}$$

where $\alpha(r) = (b^*_{-1})^{-1}\sum_{j=0}^{s-1} b_j r^j$ and $\beta(r) = (b^*_{-1})^{-1}\sum_{j=0}^{s-1} b^*_j r^j$. To do this, we take $r = \exp(i\theta)$ and solve (A.7) by finding the roots of the polynomial. We'll use the function multistepcoefficients from page 349 to compute the coefficients of the Adams–Bashforth and Adams–Moulton. The following function provides the orbit of points in the complex plane for an nth order Adams–Bashforth–Moulton PE(CE)^m.

```
using Polynomials
```

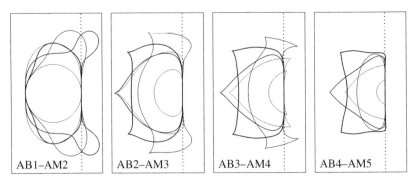

Figure A.16: Regions of stability for Adams–Bashforth–Moulton PE(CE)^m methods for $m = 0$ (thin curve) to $m = 4$ (thick curve). The domain is $[-2.5, .75] \times [-2.75, 2.75]$.

```
function PECE(n,m)
    _,a = multistepcoefficients([0 1],hcat(1:n-1...))
    _,b = multistepcoefficients([0 1],hcat(0:n-1...))
    α(r) = a · r.^(1:n-1)/b[1]
    β(r) = b[2:end] · r.^(1:n-1)/b[1]
    z = [(c = [r-1; repeat([r + β(r)],m); α(r)];
      Polynomials.roots(Polynomial(c)))
      for r in exp.(im*LinRange(0,2π,200))]
    hcat(z/b[1]...)
end
```

We plot the first-order ABM PE(CE)^m using

```
z = vcat([PECE(2,i)[:] for i in 0:4]...)
scatter(z,label="",markersize=.5,aspect_ratio=:equal)
```

After splicing the solution together and snipping off unwanted sections of the curves, we get the regions in Figure A.16 above.

12.9. Let $T(x)$ be the Taylor series for some function. To compute the Padé approximation $P_m(x)/Q_n(x) = T(x) + O(x^{m+n+1})$, we'll find the coefficients of $P_m(x) = Q_n(x)T(x) + O(x^{m+n+1})$:

$$\sum_{i=0}^{m} p_i x^i = \left(1 + \sum_{i=1}^{n} q_i x^i\right)\left(\sum_{i=0}^{\infty} a_i x^i\right) + O(x^{m+n+1}). \qquad (A.8)$$

We need to solve the linear system obtained by collecting the powers of x

$$\sum_{i=0}^{m} p_i x^i - \sum_{i=0}^{m}\sum_{j=1}^{n} a_i q_j x^{i+j} = \sum_{i=0}^{m+n} a_i x^i.$$

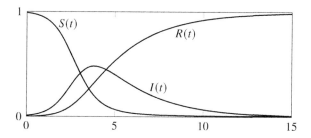

Figure A.17: Solution to the SIR model in problem 12.13.

The Julia Polynomials.jl method `PolyCompat.PadeApproximation.Pade` will do just this for us, but it will be instructive to write our own function to solve (A.8).

```
function pade(a,m,n)
  A = Rational(1)*Matrix(I(m+n+1))
  A[:,m+2:end] = [i>j ? -a[i-j] : 0 for i∈1:m+n+1, j∈1:n]
  pq = A\a[1:m+n+1]
  pq[1:m+1], [1; pq[m+2:end]]
end
```

Let's compute the coefficients of $P_3(x)$ and $Q_2(x)$ of the Padé approximation of $\log(x + 1)$. Its Taylor series is $x - \frac{1}{2}x^2 + \frac{1}{3}x^3 - \frac{1}{4}x^4 + \frac{1}{5}x^5 - \cdots$.

```
m = 3; n = 2
a = [0; ((-1).^(0:m+n).//(1:m+n+1))]
(p,q) = pade(a,m,n)
```

Finally, we substitute $r - 1$ for x in the Padé approximant and regroup by powers of r. This amounts to multiplying the two coefficient vectors by upper inverse Pascal matrices.

```
S = n -> [(-1).^(i+j)*binomial(j,i) for i∈0:n, j∈0:n]
S(m)*p, S(n)*q
```

12.13. The SIR system of equations can be easily solved using a standard explicit ODE solver. While we can write the code that solves this problem succinctly, Julia also lets us write code that clarifies the mathematics. Note that SIR! is an in-place function.

```
function SIR!(du,u,p,t)
  S,I,R = u
  β,γ = p
```

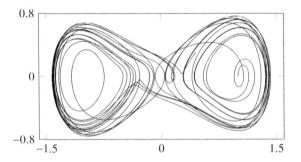

Figure A.18: The phase map of the Duffing equation in problem 12.14.

```
    du[1] = dS = -β*S*I
    du[2] = dI = +β*S*I - γ*I
    du[3] = dR = +γ*I
end
```

Now, we set up the problem, solve it, and present the solution:

```
using DifferentialEquations
u₀ = [0.99; 0.01; 0]
tspan = (0.0,15.0)
p = (2.0,0.4)
problem = ODEProblem(SIR!,u₀,tspan,p)
solution = solve(problem)
plot(solution,labels=["susceptible" "infected" "recovered"])
```

The solution is shown in Figure A.17.

12.14. We can write the Duffing equation as the system of equations $x' = v$ and $v' = -\gamma v - \alpha x - \beta x^3 + \delta \cos \omega t$, which can be solved using a standard, high-order explicit ODE solver:

```
using DifferentialEquations, Plots
function duffing!(dx,x,γ,t)
    dx[1] = x[2]
    dx[2] = -γ*x[2]+x[1]-x[1]^3+0.3*cos(t)
end
problem = ODEProblem(duffing!,[1.0,0.0],(0.0,200.0),0.37)
solution = solve(problem,Vern7())
plot(solution, idxs=(1,2))
```

See Figure A.18 above.

12.15. Implementing the shooting method is straightforward. We define our right-hand side function `airy` along with the domain endpoints x and the boundary conditions bc. Let's take a starting guess of $y'(-12)$ as guess=5. The following code solves the initial value problem and returns the second boundary point:

```
function solveIVP(f,u0,tspan)
  sol = solve(ODEProblem(f,u0,tspan))
  return(sol.u[end][1])
end
```

Now, we can solve the boundary value problem using the shooting method with boundary condition bc and an initial guess guess. Because `find_zero` takes only two arguments, we'll use an anonymous function `shoot_airy` to let us format and pass our additional parameters to `solveIVP`.

```
using DifferentialEquations, Roots
airy(y,p,x) = [y[2];x*y[1]]
domain = (-12.0,0.0); bc = (1.0,1.0); guess = 5
shoot_airy = (guess -> solveIVP(airy,[bc[1];guess],domain)-bc[2])
v = find_zero(shoot_airy, guess)
```

We find the initial condition $v \approx 16.149$. Let's plot the solution:

```
sol = solve(ODEProblem(airy,[bc[1],v],domain))
plot(sol)
```

We can see the shooting method in action by plotting each intermediate solution of `solveIVP`. In the following figure, the lines grow thicker with each iteration until we reach the solution—the widest line.

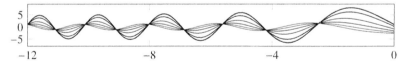

In practice, the BoundaryValueDiffEq.jl package provides a simple interface for solving the boundary problems, using either the shooting method or a collocation method.

13.2. Take the Taylor series approximation

$$U_j^n : \qquad u(t,x) = u$$
$$U_j^{n+1} : \ u(t+k,x) = u + ku_t + \tfrac{1}{2}k^2 u_{tt} + O(k^3)$$
$$U_{j+1}^n : \ u(t,x+k) = u + hu_x + \tfrac{1}{2}h^2 u_{xx} + \tfrac{1}{6}h^3 u_{xxx} + \tfrac{1}{24}h^4 u_{xxxx} + O(h^5)$$
$$U_{j-1}^n : \ u(t,x-k) = u - hu_x + \tfrac{1}{2}h^2 u_{xx} - \tfrac{1}{6}h^3 u_{xxx} + \tfrac{1}{24}h^4 u_{xxxx} - O(k^5).$$

Substituting approximations into the Crank–Nicolson scheme

$$\frac{U_j^{n+1} - U_j^n}{k} = \frac{U_{j+1}^{n+1} - 2U_j^{n+1} + U_{j-1}^{n+1}}{2h^2} + \frac{U_{j+1}^n - 2U_j^n + U_{j-1}^n}{2h^2}$$

gives

$$u_t + \tfrac{1}{2}k + O(k^2) = u_{xx} + \tfrac{1}{12}h^2 u_{xxxx} + O(h^3),$$

which tells us that the Crank–Nicolson is $O(k + h^2)$ to $u_t = u_{xx}$.

13.3. By making the substitution

$$U_{j+2}^n = \hat{u}(t_n, \xi) e^{ijh\xi}$$

in the expression

$$\frac{U_{j+2} - 2U_{j+1} + U_{j-1}}{h^2},$$

we have

$$\frac{1}{h^2}\left(e^{i2h\xi} - 2e^{ih\xi} + 1\right)\hat{u} = \frac{1}{h^2}e^{ih\xi}\left(e^{ih\xi} - e^{-ih\xi}\right)^2 \hat{u} = -\frac{2}{h^2}e^{ih\xi}\sin^2\frac{\xi h}{2}\hat{u}$$

as the right-hand side of $\hat{u}_t = \lambda \hat{u}$. The eigenvalues form a cardioid.

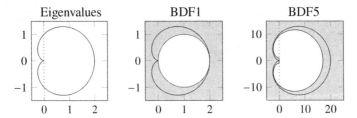

Examining the regions of stability for the methods in Figures 12.5, 12.6, and 12.8, we see that BDF1–BDF5 are the only time-difference schemes that would be absolutely stable and only if we take a sufficiently *large* timestep. For example, for the backward Euler (BDF1) method, we would need to take $k > h^2/2$. And for the BDF5 method, we would need to take $k > 5h^2$. Every other method we've examined is unconditionally unstable.

13.4. We'll use the function `multistepcoefficients`, defined on page 349.

```
m, n = [0 1 2 3 4], [1]
a, b = zeros(maximum(m)+1), zeros(maximum(n)+1)
a[m.+1], b[n.+1] = multistepcoefficients(m,n)
```

The stencil has the following approximation for the time derivative

$$\tfrac{1}{4}U^{n+1} + \tfrac{5}{6}U^{n} - \tfrac{3}{2}U^{n-1} + \tfrac{1}{2}U^{n-2} - \tfrac{1}{12}U^{n-3}. \qquad (A.9)$$

We can examine the stability using the multiplier $r(\lambda k)$ along the negative real axis similar to Figure 12.2 on page 339.

```
λk = r -> (a · r.^-(1:length(a))) ./ (b · r.^-(1:length(b)))
r = LinRange(0.2,6,100)
plot([λk.(r) λk.(-r)],[r r],xlim=[-2,2])
```

The plot on the right shows $|r(\lambda k)|$. One branch of the curve closely matches the exponential function (as we should expect). The other branch increases as λk decreases. The minimum of the maximum of $|r(\lambda k)|$ is around 2.46—it never gets below 1. So the method is unconditionally unstable.

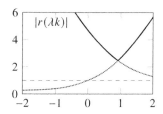

13.5. Start with the Dufort–Frankel scheme as (13.11) and move the second term on the right over to the left-hand side:

$$\frac{U_j^{n+1} - U_j^{n-1}}{2k} + a\frac{U_j^{n+1} - 2U_j^{n} + U_j^{n-1}}{h^2} = a\frac{U_{j+1}^{n} - 2U_j^{n} + U_{j-1}^{n}}{h^2}.$$

Then from (13.9), the eigenvalues from the right-hand side are

$$\lambda = \frac{2a}{h^2}(\cos \xi h - 1).$$

The region of absolute stability determined by the left-hand side is

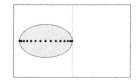

$$\lambda_\xi = i\frac{1}{k}\sin \theta - \frac{2a}{h^2}(\cos \xi h - 1),$$

which is an ellipse in the negative half-plane that extends from 0 to $-4a/h^2$, exactly the size that we need to fit the eigenspectrum.

The Dufort–Frankel requires two starting values U^0 and U^1. In practice, we might use a forward Euler step to generate U^1 from U^0. But, because we are merely demonstrating the consistency of the Dufort–Frankel, we'll simply set U^1 equal to U^0.

```
Δx = 0.01; Δt = 0.01
ℓ = 1; x = -ℓ:Δx:ℓ; m = length(x)
Uⁿ = exp.(-8*x.^2); Uⁿ⁻¹ = Uⁿ
v = Δt/Δx^2; α = 0.5 + v; γ = 0.5 - v
```

```
B = v*Tridiagonal(ones(m-1),zeros(m),ones(m-1))
B[1,2] *=2; B[end,end-1] *=2
@gif for i = 1:300
  global Uⁿ, Uⁿ⁻¹ = (B*Uⁿ+γ*Uⁿ⁻¹)/α, Uⁿ
  plot(x,Uⁿ,ylim=(0,1),label=:none,fill=(0, 0.3, :red))
end
```

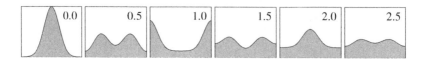

The snapshots above and the QR code at the bottom of the page show the solution to the heat equation using the Dufort–Frankel scheme. While ultimately dissipative, the solution is mainly oscillatory, behaving more like a viscous fluid than a heat-conducting bar.

13.7. Let's determine the CFL condition. We can write the constant-potential Schrödinger equation as

$$\frac{\partial \psi}{\partial t} = \frac{i\varepsilon}{2} \frac{\partial^2 \psi}{\partial x^2} - i\varepsilon^{-1} V\psi.$$

Using (13.9), we have

$$\frac{\partial \hat{u}}{\partial t} = -i \frac{2\varepsilon}{h^2} \sin^2 \left(\frac{\xi h}{2} \right) \hat{u} - \varepsilon^{-1} V\hat{u}. \tag{A.10}$$

So, the eigenvalues λ_ξ of the system $\hat{u}_t = \lambda_\xi \hat{u}$ are

$$\lambda_\xi = -i \left(\frac{2\varepsilon}{h^2} \sin^2 \frac{\xi h}{2} + \varepsilon^{-1} V \right).$$

These eigenvalues lie along the imaginary axis, bounded by $|\lambda_\xi| \le 2\varepsilon/h^2 + \varepsilon^{-1}V$. We'll need to keep h much smaller than ε to model the dynamics of the Schrödinger equation accurately. Consequently, $2\varepsilon/h^2$ will dominate $\varepsilon^{-1}V$. So let's only consider the contribution of $2\varepsilon/h^2$ on stability. Note where the regions of absolute stability intersect the imaginary axis for different methods in the following figures:

forward Euler   backward Euler   leapfrog   trapezoidal

the Dufort–Frankel
solution to the
heat equation

We see that the backward Euler and trapezoidal methods are unconditionally stable and that the forward Euler method is unconditionally unstable. The leapfrog method is stable when $|k\lambda_\xi| < 1$, meaning its CLF condition is $k < h^2/2\varepsilon$. Figure 12.8 shows that the Runge–Kutta method (RK4) is stable when $|k\lambda_\xi| < 2.5$, so its CFL condition is $k < 1.25h^2/\varepsilon$. Figures 12.5 and 12.6 show that the BDF2 method is unconditionally stable and that higher-order BDF and Adams methods are conditionally stable.

The following Julia code solves the Schrödinger equation with $V(x) = \frac{1}{2}x^2$ using the Crank–Nicolson method over the domain $[-3, 3]$ with initial conditions $\psi(0, x) = (\pi\varepsilon)^{-1/4}e^{-(x-1)^2/2\varepsilon}$:

```
function schroedinger(m,n,ε)
    x = LinRange(-4,4,m); Δx = x[2]-x[1]; Δt = 2π/n; V = x.^2/2
    ψ = exp.(-(x.-1).^2/2ε)/(π*ε)^(1/4)
    diags = 0.5im*ε*[1 -2 1]/Δx^2 .- im/ε*[0 1 0].*V
    D = Tridiagonal(diags[2:end,1], diags[:,2], diags[1:end-1,3])
    D[1,2] *= 2; D[end,end-1] *= 2
    A = I + 0.5Δt*D
    B = I - 0.5Δt*D
    for i ∈ 1:n
      ψ = B\(A*ψ)
    end
    return ψ
end
```

To verify the convergence rate of the method, we'll take a sufficiently small time step k so that its contribution to the error is negligible. Then we compute the error for several decreasing values of h. We repeat this process by taking h sufficiently small and computing the error for decreasing values of k.

```
ε = 0.3; m = 20000; eₓ=[]; eₜ=[]
N = floor.(Int,exp10.(LinRange(2,3.7,6)))
x = LinRange(-4,4,m)
ψₘ = -exp.(-(x.-1).^2/2ε)/(π*ε)^(1/4)
for n ∈ N
  x = LinRange(-4,4,n)
  ψₙ = -exp.(-(x.-1).^2/2ε)/(π*ε)^(1/4)
  append!(eₜ,norm(ψₘ - schroedinger(m,n,ε))/m)
  append!(eₓ,norm(ψₙ - schroedinger(n,m,ε))/n)
end
plot(2π./N,eₜ,shape=:circle, xaxis=:log, yaxis=:log)
plot!(8 ./N,eₓ,shape=:circle)
```

The error is plotted in Figure A.19 on the following page. We can compute the slopes of the lines using `polyfit(log(n),log(error_x),1)`. The slope for k is 2.0, and for h, it is 2.5.

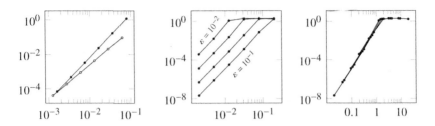

Figure A.19: Left: the error in solution $\rho(t, x)$ as a function of step size h • or time step k ∘. Middle: the error versus step size h for various ε. Right: the error versus step size as a multiple of ε.

Finally, let's examine the effect ε and h have on the solution $\rho(t, x) = |\psi(t, x)|^2$. We find the solution at $t = \pi$ using 10^4 time steps. We compute the error for several values of ε logarithmically spaced between 0.1 and 0.01 and several values of h logarithmically spaced between 0.2 and 0.002. The time step k is sufficiently small, and its contribution to the error is negligible. The middle plot of Figure A.19 shows the error as a function of h for each of the four values of ε, decreasing from right to left. The log-log curves are linear and parallel until they reach a maximum of 2.

How can we explain such behavior? As the mesh spacing h increases relative to ε, the numerical solution doesn't adequately resolve the dynamics of the wave packet. Consequently, the wave packet gradually slows until the numerical solution no longer coincides with the true solution. If we plot the error against h/ε, we see that all of the curves line up with a turning point when h is greater than ε. In general, the Crank–Nicolson method is order $O((k/\varepsilon)^2 + (h/\varepsilon)^2)$.

13.8. We'll start by expanding the derivative

$$\frac{\partial u}{\partial t} = \frac{1}{r} \frac{\partial}{\partial r} \left(r \frac{\partial u}{\partial r} \right) \quad \text{to get} \quad \frac{\partial u}{\partial t} = \frac{\partial^2 u}{\partial r^2} + \frac{1}{r} \frac{\partial u}{\partial r}.$$

This equation is problematic at $r = 0$ because of the division by zero. Because $u(t, r)$ is an even function, odd derivatives are zero at the origin. Therefore, we can apply L'Hopital's rule to get $u_r/r = r_{rr}$ at $r = 0$. At $r = 0$, we have

$$\frac{\partial u}{\partial t} = 2 \frac{\partial^2 u}{\partial r^2}.$$

Let's discretize space to get $\frac{\partial}{\partial t}U_j = D U_j$ where

$$D U_0 = 2\frac{U_1 - 2U_0 + U_{-1}}{h^2}, \text{ and}$$

$$D U_j = \frac{U_{j+1} - 2U_j + U_{j+1}}{h^2} + \frac{1}{r_j}\frac{U_{j+1} - U_{j-1}}{2h} \quad \text{for} \quad j = 1, 2, \ldots, m.$$

Now, let's take care of the boundary conditions. An insulating boundary at $r = 1$ means that $u_r(1) = 0$. We can approximate the derivative to second-order at x_m with $U_{m+1} - U_{m-1} = 0$ by using a ghost point at x_{m+1}. This constraint will allow us to remove U_{m+1} from the system. The derivative at x_0 is also zero—this time because of symmetry. So, we'll replace U_{-1} with U_1 to close the system. We'll use the Crank–Nicolson method $U_j^{n+1} = (I - \frac{1}{2}k\,D)^{-1}(I + \frac{1}{2}k\,D)U_j^n$:

```
t = 0.5; n=100; m = 100
r = LinRange(0,2,m); Δr = r[2]-r[1]; Δt = t/n;
u₀ = @. tanh(32(1 - r)); u = u₀
d = @. [1 -2 1]/Δr^2 + (1/r)*[-1 0 1]/2Δr
D = Tridiagonal(d[2:end,1],d[:,2],d[1:end-1,3])
D[1,1:2] = [-4 4]/Δr^2; D[end,end-1:end] = [2 -2]/Δr^2
A = I - 0.5Δt*D
B = I + 0.5Δt*D
for i = 1:n
 u = A\(B*u)
end
```

A slower but high-order alternative to the Crank–Nicolson method:

```
using Sundials
problem = ODEProblem((u,p,t)->D*u,u₀,(0,t))
method = CVODE_BDF(linear_solver=:Band,jac_upper=1,jac_lower=1)
solution = solve(problem,method)
```

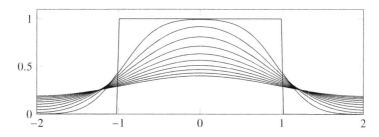

The figure above and the QR code below show the solution with an initial distribution given by a step function. The snapshots are at equal intervals from $t \in [0, \frac{1}{2}]$ of the solution reflected about $x = 0$. Compare this solution to the one-dimensional heat equation on page 390.

the heat equation in
polar coordinates

13.9. Let's take grid points $\{x_1, x_2, x_3\}$ and define $h_1 = x_2 - x_1$ and $h_2 = x_3 - x_1$. The Taylor series expansion about x_1 is

$$f(x_1) = f(x_2 - h_1) = f(x_2) - h_1 f'(x_2) + \tfrac{1}{2}h_1^2 f''(x_2) - \tfrac{1}{6}h_1^3 f'''(x_2) + \cdots$$
$$f(x_3) = f(x_2 + h_2) = f(x_2) + h_2 f'(x_2) + \tfrac{1}{2}h_2^2 f''(x_2) + \tfrac{1}{6}h_2^3 f'''(x_2) + \cdots .$$

We combine $f(x_1)$, $f(x_2)$, and $f(x_3)$ by solving the system of equations to determine $f''(x_2)$ and eliminate $f(x_2)$ and $f'(x_2)$:

$$f''(x_2) = \frac{2f(x_1)}{h_1(h_1 + h_2)} - \frac{2f(x_2)}{h_1 h_2} + \frac{2f(x_3)}{h_2(h_1 + h_2)} + \text{error}$$

where the error is $\tfrac{1}{3}(h_2 - h_1)f'''(x_2) + O\left(h_1^2 + h_2^2\right)$. If $h_2 = h_1$, the method is simply the second-order central difference scheme. As long as $h_2 \approx h_1$, the error will be close to second-order. Otherwise, the error will locally be first-order.

We'll start by defining a logit function equivalent to `LinRange`:

```
logitspace(x,n,p) = x*atanh.(LinRange(-p,p,n))/atanh(p)
```

The parameter $0 < p \le 1$ will control how linear the function behaves. In the limit as $p \to 0$, `logitspace(x,n,p)` will behave like `LinRange(-x,x,n)`. Now, we define a one-dimensional Laplacian operator for gridpoints given by x:

```
function laplacian(x)
    Δx = diff(x); Δx₁ = Δx[1:end-1]; Δx₂ = Δx[2:end]
    d₋ = @. 2/[Δx₁*(Δx₁+Δx₂); Δx₁[1]^2]
    d₀ = @. -2/[Δx₂[end].^2; Δx₁*Δx₂; Δx₁[1].^2]
    d₊ = @. 2/[Δx₂[end].^2; Δx₂*(Δx₁+Δx₂) ]
    Tridiagonal(d₋,d₀,d₊)
end
```

We've used Neumann boundary conditions, but we could also have chosen Dirichlet boundary conditions. We can solve the heat equation using a Crank–Nicolson method.

```
function heat_equation(x,t,n,u)
    Δt = t/n
    D² = laplacian(x)
    A = I - 0.5Δt*D²
    B = I + 0.5Δt*D²
    for i ∈ 1:n
        u = A\(B*u)
    end
    return u
end
```

We define an initial condition and compute the solutions.

```
φ = (x,t,s) -> exp.(-s*x.^2/(1+4*s*t))/sqrt(1+4*s*t)
m = 40; t = 15
x = LinRange(-20,20,m)
plot(x,φ(x,t,10),label="exact",width=3)
u₁ = heat_equation(x,t,m,φ(x,0,10))
plot!(x,u₁,shape=:circle,label="equal")
x = logitspace(20,m,0.999)
u₂ = heat_equation(x,t,m,φ(x,0,10))
plot!(x,u₂,shape=:circle,label="logit")
```

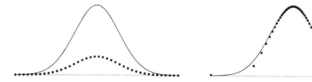

The plots above compare the solution using equally-spaced nodes (left) and the solution using the inverse-sigmoid-spaced nodes (right) with the exact solution.

13.10. We'll solve the Allen–Cahn equation using Strang splitting. The differential equation $u'(t) = \varepsilon^{-1}u(1 - u^2)$ has the analytical solution $u(t) = (u_0^2 - (u_0^2 - 1)e^{-t/\varepsilon})^{-1/2}u_0$. We'll combine this solution with a Crank–Nicolson method for the heat equation applied first in the x-direction and then in the y-direction.

```
L = 16; m = 400; Δx = L/m
T = 4; n = 1600; Δt = T/n
x = LinRange(-L/2,L/2,m)'
u = @. tanh(x^4 - 16*(2*x^2-x'^2))
D = Tridiagonal(ones(m-1),-2ones(m),ones(m-1))/Δx^2
D[1,2] *= 2; D[end,end-1] *= 2
A = I + 0.5Δt*D
B = I - 0.5Δt*D
f = (u,Δt) -> @. u/sqrt(u^2 - (u^2-1)*exp(-50*Δt))
u = f(u,Δt/2)
for i = 1:n
  u = (B\(A*(B\(A*u))')')'
  (i<n) && (u = f(u,Δt))
end
u = f(u,Δt/2); Gray.(u)
```

To watch the solution's evolution, we add the following three commands (the first before the loop, the second inside the loop, and the third after the loop) to the code above.

```
anim = Animation()
(i%10)==1 && (plot(Gray.(u),border=:none); frame(anim))
gif(anim, "allencahn.gif", fps = 30)
```

The figures below show the solutions to the Allen–Cahn equation at times $t = 0.05, 0.5, 2.0$, and 4.0. Also, see the QR code at the bottom of the page.

The solutions with initial conditions u = randn(m,m) are

The limiting behavior of the Allen–Cahn equation evident in these figures is called *motion by mean curvature*, in which an interface's normal velocity equals its mean curvature. Regions of high curvature evolve rapidly to regions of lower curvature, smoothing out any bumps, slowing down, and gradually forming circles, which may finally shrink and disappear.

14.1. The Lax–Friedrichs method is given by

$$\frac{U_j^{n+1} - \frac{1}{2}(U_{j+1}^n + U_{j-1}^n)}{k} + c\frac{U_{j+1}^n - U_{j-1}^n}{2h} = 0.$$

Let's substitute the Taylor series approximation

$$u(t, x) = u$$
$$u(t + k, x) = u + ku_t + \tfrac{1}{2}k^2 u_{tt} + \tfrac{1}{6}k^3 u_{ttt} + O(k^4)$$
$$u(t, x + h) = u + hu_x + \tfrac{1}{2}h^2 u_{xx} + \tfrac{1}{6}h^3 u_{xxx} + O(h^4)$$
$$u(t, x - h) = u - hu_x + \tfrac{1}{2}h^2 u_{xx} - \tfrac{1}{6}h^3 u_{xxx} + O(h^4)$$

in for U_j^n, U_j^{n+1}, U_{j+1}^n, and U_{j-1}^n in terms of the Lax–Friedrichs method

$$\frac{U_j^{n+1} - \frac{1}{2}(U_{j+1}^n + U_{j-1}^n)}{k} = u_t + \tfrac{1}{2}ku_{tt} + O(k^2) - \tfrac{1}{2}\frac{h^2}{k}u_{xx} + O(h^4)$$

the Allen–Cahn
equation

and

$$c\frac{U_{j+1}^n - U_{j-1}^n}{2h} = cu_x + \tfrac{1}{6}ch^2u_{xxx} + O(k^4).$$

By combining these terms, we have

$$u_t + cu_x + \tfrac{1}{2}ku_{tt} - \tfrac{1}{2}\frac{h^2}{k}u_{xx} + \tfrac{1}{6}ch^2u_{xxx} + \{\text{higher order terms}\} = 0,$$

from which we see that the truncation error is $O(k + h^2/k)$.

We examine the leading order truncation

$$u_t + cu_x + \tfrac{1}{2}ku_{tt} - \tfrac{1}{2}\frac{h^2}{k}u_{xx} = 0 \qquad (A.11)$$

to find the dispersion relation. We will eliminate the u_{tt} term by first differentiating (A.11) with respect to t and x and then substituting the expression for u_{tt} back into the original equation, discarding the higher-order terms. We have

$$u_{tt} = -cu_{xt} + O(k + h^2/k)$$
$$u_{tx} = -cu_{xx} + O(k + h^2/k)$$

from which

$$u_{tt} = c^2u_{xx} + O(k + h^2/k).$$

After eliminating higher-order terms, equation (A.11) becomes

$$u_t + cu_x + \tfrac{1}{2}k\left(c^2 - \frac{h^2}{k^2}\right)u_{xx} = 0.$$

Substituting the Fourier component $u(t,x) = e^{i(\omega t - \xi x)}$ into this expression as an ansatz yields

$$\left[i\omega + c(-i\xi) - \tfrac{1}{2}\left(c^2k - \frac{h^2}{k^2}\right)\xi^2\right]e^{i(\omega t - \xi x)} = 0.$$

So

$$i\omega + c(-i\xi) - \tfrac{1}{2}\left(c^2k - \frac{h^2}{k^2}\right)\xi^2 = 0,$$

and the dispersion relation $\omega(\xi)$ is given by

$$\omega = c\xi - i\tfrac{1}{2}k\left(c^2 - \frac{h^2}{k^2}\right)\xi^2.$$

Plugging this ω back into our ansatz gives us

$$u(t,x) = e^{i(\omega t - \xi x)} = e^{ic\xi t}e^{-\alpha\xi^2}e^{-i\xi x} = \underbrace{e^{i\xi(ct-x)}}_{\text{advection}} \cdot \underbrace{e^{-\alpha\xi^2 t}}_{\text{dissipation}}$$

where

$$\alpha = \tfrac{1}{2}k\left(\frac{h^2}{k^2} - c^2\right).$$

So, the Lax–Friedrichs scheme is dissipative, especially when $k \ll h$.

We can minimize the dissipation (and decrease the error) by choosing k and h so that

$$\frac{h^2}{k^2} - c^2 = 0,$$

that is, by taking $k = h/|c|$. Note that if $k > h/|c|$, then α is negative and $e^{-\alpha\xi^2 t}$ grows, causing the solution blows up. This condition is the CFL condition for the Lax–Friedrichs scheme.

14.3. The scheme is

$$\frac{U_j^{n+1} - U_j^{n-1}}{2k} + c\frac{U_{j+1}^n - U_{j-1}^n}{2h} = 0.$$

By Taylor series expansion

$$u(t+k,x) = u + ku_t + \tfrac{1}{2}k^2 u_{tt} + \tfrac{1}{6}k^3 u_{ttt} + O(k^4)$$
$$u(t-k,x) = u - ku_t + \tfrac{1}{2}k^2 u_{tt} - \tfrac{1}{6}k^3 u_{ttt} + O(k^4)$$
$$u(t,x+h) = u + hu_x + \tfrac{1}{2}h^2 u_{xx} + \tfrac{1}{6}h^3 u_{xxx} + O(h^4)$$
$$u(t,x-h) = u - hu_x + \tfrac{1}{2}h^2 u_{xx} - \tfrac{1}{6}h^3 u_{xxx} + O(h^4)$$

from which

$$u_t + \tfrac{1}{2}k^2 u_{ttt} + cu_x + \tfrac{1}{2}h^2 u_{ttt} = O(k^2 + h^2).$$

So, the method is $O(k^2 + h^2)$.

The scheme is leapfrog in time and central difference in space. The Fourier transform of

$$\frac{\partial}{\partial t}U_j = -c\frac{U_{j+1} - U_{j-1}}{2h}$$

is

$$\frac{\partial}{\partial t}\hat{u}(t,\xi) = -c\frac{e^{i\xi h} - e^{-i\xi h}}{h}\hat{u}(t,\xi) = -i\frac{c}{h}\sin(\xi h)\hat{u}(t,\xi).$$

The leapfrog scheme is absolute stability only on the imaginary axis $\lambda k \in [-i, +i]$. The factor $|\sin(\xi h)| \le 1$, so the scheme is stable when $(|c|/h)k \le 1$. That is, when $k \le h/|c|$.

14.6. We can express the compressible Euler equations

$$\rho_t + (\rho u)_x = 0 \tag{A.12a}$$
$$(\rho u)_t + (\rho u^2 + p)_x = 0 \tag{A.12b}$$
$$E_t + ((E + p)u)_x = 0 \tag{A.12c}$$

in semilinear form using ρ, u and p as independent variables. First, rewrite (A.12a) and (A.12b) as

$$\rho_t + u\rho_x + \rho u_x = 0 \tag{A.13}$$

$$u\rho_t + \rho u_t + u^2 \rho_x + 2\rho u u_x + p_x = 0 \tag{A.14}$$

We can eliminate the $u\rho_t$ term in (A.14) by first multiplying (A.13) by u to get

$$u\rho_t + u^2 \rho_x + \rho u u_x = 0$$

and then subtracting this equation from (A.14) to get

$$\rho u_t + \rho u u_x + p_x = 0.$$

$$u_t + u u_x + \frac{1}{\rho} p_x = 0 \tag{A.15}$$

To derive an equation for p, we will use the equation of state

$$E = \tfrac{1}{2}\rho u^2 + \frac{p}{\gamma - 1} \tag{A.16}$$

to eliminate E from (A.12c). Differentiating (A.16) with respect to t yields

$$E_t = \tfrac{1}{2}u^2 \rho_t + \rho u u_t + \frac{1}{\gamma - 1} p_t.$$

Substituting (A.13) and (A.15) in this expression for ρ_t and u_t produces

$$E_t = -\tfrac{1}{2}u^3 \rho_x - \tfrac{3}{2}\rho u^2 u_x - u p_x + \frac{1}{\gamma - 1} p_t. \tag{A.17}$$

By expanding $\big((E + p)u\big)_x$ with the equation of state, we have

$$\big((E + p)u\big)_x = \left(\tfrac{1}{2}u^3 \rho + \frac{\gamma}{\gamma - 1} pu\right)_x$$

$$= \tfrac{1}{2}u^3 \rho_x + \tfrac{3}{2}\rho u^2 u_x + \frac{\gamma}{\gamma - 1} pu_x + \frac{\gamma}{\gamma - 1} up_x \tag{A.18}$$

By combining (A.17) and (A.18), we have

$$E_t + \big((E + p)u\big)_x = \frac{1}{\gamma - 1} p_t + \frac{\gamma}{\gamma - 1} pu_x + \frac{1}{\gamma - 1} up_x.$$

So

$$p_t + \gamma p u_x + u p_x = 0. \tag{A.19}$$

We now can express (A.13), (A.15) and (A.19) in quasilinear matrix form

$$
\begin{bmatrix} \rho \\ u \\ p \end{bmatrix}_t + \begin{bmatrix} u & \rho & 0 \\ 0 & u & 1/\rho \\ 0 & \gamma p & u \end{bmatrix} \begin{bmatrix} \rho \\ u \\ p \end{bmatrix}_x = 0.
$$

The system is hyperbolic if the eigenvalues λ of the Jacobian matrix are real:

$$
\begin{vmatrix} u - \lambda & \rho & 0 \\ 0 & u - \lambda & 1/\rho \\ 0 & \gamma p & u - \lambda \end{vmatrix} = (u - \lambda)^3 - \gamma p \rho^{-1}(u - \lambda)
$$

$$
= (u - \lambda) \left[(u - \lambda)^2 - c^2 \right] = 0
$$

with $c^2 = \gamma p / \rho$. The eigenvalues are $\{u, u + c, u - c\}$ where c is the sound speed.

14.7. The solution starts with a shock beginning at $x = 1$ and moving with speed $\frac{1}{2}$ (half the height, as given by the Rankine–Hugoniot condition). At the same time, a rarefaction propagates from $x = 0$ moving at speed 1 until the rarefaction catches up with the shock at location $x = 2$ and time $t = 2$. We can imagine the trailing edge of a right-angled trapezoid catching up to the leading edge to form a right triangle. Now, the leading edge of the right triangle continues to move forward with speed equal to half the height (again by the Rankine–Hugoniot condition). To compute the leading edge position, we only need to know the height $u(t)$. The area of the triangle is conserved, so $A = \frac{1}{2} x(t) u(t, x) = 1$. That is, $u = 2/x$. The speed is given by

$$
\frac{dx}{dt} = \frac{1}{2} u(t, x) = \frac{1}{x}.
$$

The solution to this differential equation is $x(t) = \sqrt{2t + c}$ for some constant c. At $t = 2$, the leading edge is at $x = 2$. So $c = 0$. Altogether,

$$
\text{when } t < 2 \qquad u(x, t) = \begin{cases} x/t, & 0 < x < t \\ 1, & t < x < 1 + \frac{1}{2}t \\ 0, & \text{otherwise} \end{cases}
$$

$$
\text{when } t \geq 2 \qquad u(x, t) = \begin{cases} x/t, & 0 < x < \sqrt{2t} \\ 0, & \text{otherwise} \end{cases}
$$

because the area is conserved. We can write the exact solution as the function:

```
U = (x,t) -> @. t<2 ?
   (0<x<t)*(x/t) + (t<x<1+t/2) : (x/t)*(0<x<sqrt(2t))
```

We can implement the local Lax–Friedrichs method using the following code:

```
m = 80; x = LinRange(-1,3,m); Δx = x[2]-x[1]; j = 1:m-1
n = 100; Lₜ = 4; Δt = Lₜ/n
f = u -> u.^2/2; df = u -> u
u = (x.>=0).*(x.<=1)
anim = @animate for i = 1:n
  α = 0.5*max.(abs.(df(u[j])),abs.(df(u[j.+1])))
  F = (f(u[j])+f(u[j.+1]))/2 - α.*(u[j.+1]-u[j])
  global u -= Δt/Δx*[0;diff(F);0]
  plot(x,u, fill = (0, 0.3, :blue))
  plot!(x,U(x,i*Δt), fill = (0, 0.3, :red))
  plot!(legend=:none, ylim=[0,1])
end
gif(anim, "burgers.gif", fps = 15)
```

The figure below and the QR code at the bottom of the page show the analytical and numerical solutions.

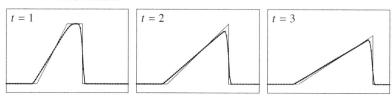

14.8. The Nessyahu–Tadmor scheme

$$U_j^{n+1/2} = U_j^n - \tfrac{1}{2}h\partial_x f(U_j^n)$$

$$U_{j+1/2}^{n+1} = \tfrac{1}{2}\left(U_j^n + U_{j+1}^n\right) - \tfrac{1}{8}h\left(\partial_x U_{j+1}^n - \partial_x U_j^n\right) - \frac{k}{h}\left(f\left(U_{j+1}^{n+1/2}\right) - f\left(U_j^{n+1/2}\right)\right),$$

where we approximate ∂_x using the slope limiter σ_j

$$\sigma_j(U_j) = \frac{U_{j+1} - U_j}{h}\phi(\theta_j) \quad \text{where} \quad \theta_j = \frac{U_j - U_{j-1}}{U_{j+1} - U_j}$$

with the van Leer limiter

$$\phi(\theta) = \frac{|\theta| + \theta}{1 + |\theta|}.$$

We can implement the solution using Julia as

```
δ = u -> diff(u,dims=1)
ϕ = t -> (abs(t)+t)./(1+abs(t))
fixnan(u) = isnan(u)||isinf(u) ? 0 : u
θ = δu -> fixnan.(δu[1:end-1,:]./δu[2:end,:])
∂ₓ(u) = (δu=δ(u);[[0 0];δu[2:end,:].*ϕ.(θ(δu));[0 0]])
F = u -> [u[:,1].*u[:,2] u[:,1].*u[:,2].^2+0.5u[:,1].^2]
```

```
m = 100; x = LinRange(-.5,.5,m); Δx = x[2]-x[1]
T = 0.4; n = ceil(T/(Δx/2)); Δt = (T/n)/2;
U = [0.8*(x.<0).+0.2 zero(x)]
Uⱼ = view(U,1:m-1,:); Uⱼ₊₁ = view(U,2:m,:)
for i = 1:n
  U° = U-0.5*Δt/Δx*∂ₓ(F(U))
  Uⱼ₊₁ .= (Uⱼ+Uⱼ₊₁)/2 - δ(∂ₓ(U))/8 - Δt/Δx*δ(F(U°))
  U° = U-0.5*Δt/Δx*∂ₓ(F(U))
  Uⱼ .= (Uⱼ+Uⱼ₊₁)/2 - δ(∂ₓ(U))/8 - Δt/Δx*δ(F(U°))
end
```

The figure and QR code below show the numerical solution for $h(t, x)$.

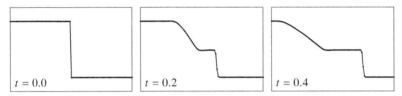

$t = 0.0$ $t = 0.2$ $t = 0.4$

Notice the shock wave moving to the right and the rarefaction wave moving to the left from the initial discontinuity.

15.1. Multiply $-u'' - u = f(x)$ by v and integrate: $\int_0^1 (-u'' - u)v \, dx = \int_0^1 vf \, dx$ where $f = -8x^2$. If we integrate by parts once and move the boundary terms to the right-hand side of the equation, then we have the variational form $a(u_h, v_h) = \mathcal{L}(v_h)$ where

$$a(u, v) = \int_0^1 u'v' - uv \, dx \quad \text{and} \quad \mathcal{L}(v) = \int_0^1 vf \, dx + vu'|_0^1 .$$

The boundary conditions for this problem are $u'(0) = 0$ and $u'(1) = 1$. Take the finite elements $u_h(x) = \sum_{i=0}^{m+1} \xi_i \varphi_i(x)$ and $v_h(x) = \sum_{j=0}^{m+1} v_j \varphi_j(x)$ where $\varphi_j(x)$ are the piecewise basis elements defined in (15.1). Then

$$\sum_{j=0}^{m+1} v_j \sum_{i=0}^{m+1} \xi_i a(\varphi_j, \varphi_i) = \sum_{i=0}^{m+1} v_j \mathcal{L}(\varphi_j) .$$

Because the expression holds for set $\{v_j\}$, it follows that for all j

$$\sum_{i=0}^{m+1} \xi_i a(\varphi_j, \varphi_i) = \mathcal{L}(\varphi_j) .$$

We can compute the integrals using (15.1): $a(\varphi_j, \varphi_i) = -h^{-1} - \frac{1}{6}h$ when $i \neq j$ and $a(\varphi_i, \varphi_i) = 2h^{-1} - \frac{2}{3}h$ except on the two boundaries where it is

the dambreak problem

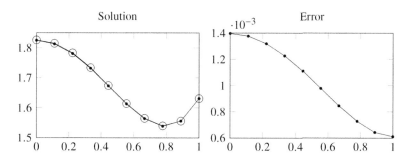

Figure A.20: Solutions to the Neumann problem 15.1. The marker • is used for the finite element solution and ○ for the analytical solution.

half that value. Similarly, $b(\varphi_j) = -\frac{4}{3}h^3 - 8h(jh)^2$, $b(\varphi_0) = -\frac{2}{3}h^3$, and $b(\varphi_{m+1}) = -4h + \frac{8}{3}h^2 - \frac{2}{3}h^3 + 1$, where we've added in the contribution to the boundary term at $x = 1$. In Julia

```
m=10; x=LinRange(0,1,m); h=x[2]-x[1]
α = fill(2/h-2h/3,m); α[[1,m]] /= 2; β = fill(-1/h-h/6,m-1)
A = SymTridiagonal(α,β)
b = [-2h^3/3; -4h^3/3 .- 8h*x[2:m-1].^2; -4h+8h^2/3-2h^3/3+1]
u = A\b
s = -16 .+ 8x.^2 .+ 15csc(1).*cos.(x)
plot(x,s,marker=:o,alpha=0.5); plot!(x,u,marker=:o,alpha=0.5)
```

Figure A.20 shows the finite element solution and the exact solution. The finite element solution has little error even with only ten nodes.

15.2. Let V be the space of twice differentiable functions that take the same boundary conditions as $u(x)$. Multiply the equation $u'''' = f$ by $v \in V$ and integrate by parts twice to get a symmetric bilinear form $\int_0^1 u''v'' \, dx = \int_0^1 fv \, dx$. (The boundary terms vanish when we enforce the boundary conditions.) Define $a(u, v) = \int_0^1 u''v'' \, dx$ and $\mathcal{L}(v) = \int_0^1 fv \, dx$. Then the finite element problem is

> **▼** Find $u_h \in V_h$ such that $a(u_h, v_h) = \mathcal{L}(v_h)$ for all $v_h \in V_h$

The finite elements are

$$u_h(x) = \sum_{i=0}^{m+1} \xi_i \phi_i(x) + \eta_i \psi_i(x) \text{ and } v_h(x) = \sum_{j=0}^{m+1} \alpha_j \phi_j(x) + \beta_j \psi_j(x),$$

where the basis elements $\phi_j(x)$ prescribe the value of $u(x)$ at the nodes, and the basis elements $\psi_j(x)$ prescribe the value of the derivative of $u(x)$ at the nodes. The coefficients ξ_j and η_j are unknown, and the coefficients α_j and β_j are

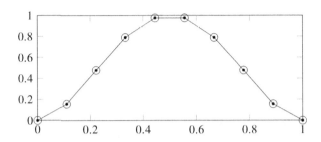

Figure A.21: Solutions to the beam problem. The marker • is used for the finite element solution and ∘ for the analytical solution.

arbitrary. From the boundary conditions, we have $\xi_0 = \xi_{m+1} = \eta_0 = \eta_{m+1} = 0$. Substituting u_h and v_h into $a(u_h, v_h) = \mathcal{L}(v_h)$ yields

$$a\left(\sum_{i=1}^{m} \xi_i \phi_i + \eta_i \psi_i, \sum_{j=1}^{m} \alpha_j \phi_j + \beta_j \psi_j\right) = \mathcal{L}\left(\sum_{j=1}^{m} \alpha_j \phi_j + \beta_j \psi_j\right).$$

Because α_j and β_j are arbitrary, we must have

$$a\left(\sum_{i=1}^{m} \xi_i \phi_i + \eta_i \psi_i, \phi_j\right) = \mathcal{L}(\phi_j) \text{ and } a\left(\sum_{i=1}^{m} \xi_i \phi_i + \eta_i \psi_i, \psi_j\right) = \mathcal{L}(\psi_j)$$

for all $j = 1, 2, \ldots, m$. Finally, by bilinearity and homogeneity, we have

$$\sum_{i=1}^{m} \xi_i a(\phi_i, \phi_j) + \eta_i a(\psi_i, \phi_j) = \mathcal{L}(\phi_j)$$

$$\sum_{i=1}^{m} \xi_i a(\phi_i, \psi_j) + \eta_i a(\psi_i, \psi_j) = \mathcal{L}(\psi_j).$$

We can write the system of $2m$ equations as the block matrix

$$\begin{bmatrix} \mathbf{A} & \mathbf{B} \\ \mathbf{B}^\mathsf{T} & \mathbf{C} \end{bmatrix} \begin{bmatrix} \xi \\ \eta \end{bmatrix} = \begin{bmatrix} \mathbf{f}^{(1)} \\ \mathbf{f}^{(2)} \end{bmatrix},$$

with elements $a_{ij} = \langle \phi_i'', \phi_j'' \rangle$, $b_{ij} = \langle \psi_i'', \phi_j'' \rangle$, and $c_{ij} = \langle \psi_i'', \psi_j'' \rangle$ along with $f_j^{(1)} = \langle f, \phi_j \rangle = h^{-1}$ and $f_j^{(2)} = \langle f, \psi_j \rangle = 0$.

We can compute the solution in Julia using

```
m = 8; x = LinRange(0,1,m+2); h = x[2]-x[1]
σ = (a,b,c) -> Tridiagonal(fill(a,m-1),fill(b,m),fill(c,m-1))/h^3
```

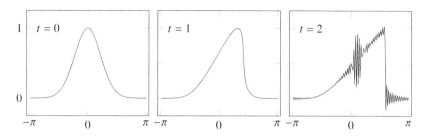

Figure A.22: Solutions to Burgers' equation in exercise 16.2 at $t = 0$, 1, and 2. Gibbs oscillations overwhelm the solution after a discontinuity develops.

```
M = [σ(-12,24,-12) σ(-6,0,6);σ(6,0,-6) σ(2,8,2)];
b = [384h*ones(m);zeros(m)]
u = M\b
s = 16*(x.^4 - 2x.^3 + x.^2)
plot(x,[s [0;u[1:m];0]],marker=:o,alpha=0.5)
```

If we only want the solution at the nodes, we can take $u(x_j) = \xi_j$:

```
s = 16*(x.^4 - 2x.^3 + x.^2)
plot(x,[s [0;u[1:n];0]],marker=:o,alpha=0.5)
```

Figure A.21 shows the solution using 8 interior nodes. Because the problem has a constant load, the finite element solution matches the analytical solution exactly.

15.3. A symmetric, positive-definite bilinear form is an inner product. In this case, u_h is a projection of u onto V_h using $a(\cdot, \cdot)$, and consequently

$$a(u - u_h, u - u_h) = \inf_{v_h \in V_h} a(u - v_h, u - v_h).$$

Because $a(\cdot, \cdot)$ is bounded and coercive with respective bounding constants γ and α,

$$\alpha \|u - u_h\|^2 \le a(u - u_h, u - u_h) \le a(u - v_h, u - v_h) \le \gamma \|u - v_h\|^2.$$

Hence, $\|u - u_h\| \le \sqrt{\gamma/\alpha}\|u - v_h\|$ for all $v_h \in V_h$.

16.2. We can solve Burgers' equation as $u_t = -\frac{1}{2} F^{-1} \left[i\xi \, F(u^2) \right]$ using the Dormand–Prince Runge–Kutta solver:

```
using FFTW, DifferentialEquations
m = 128; x = (1:m)/m*(2π) .- π
ξ = im*[0:(m÷2); (-m÷2+1):-1]
```

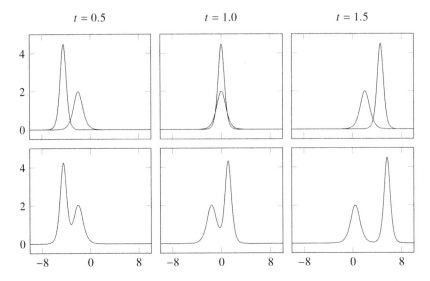

Figure A.23: Solutions of the KdV equation in exercise 16.3. The top row shows independent solitons. The bottom row shows the interacting solitons.

```
f = (u,p,t) -> -real(ifft(ξ.*fft(0.5u.^2)))
u = solve(ODEProblem(f,exp.(-x.^2),(0.0,2.0)),DP5());
```

which can be animated using the Plots.jl macro

```
@gif for t=0:.02:2
  plot(x,u(t),ylim=(-0.2,1.2))
end
```

Figure A.22 and the QR code on the bottom of this page show the solution. Fourier spectral methods have spectral accuracy in space so long as the solution is a smooth function. Space and time derivatives are coupled through Burgers' equation, so we can expect a method that is fourth-order in time and space. However, solutions to Burgers' equation, which may initially be smooth, become discontinuous over time. As a result, truncation error is half-order in space and time once a discontinuity develops. This is bad—and it gets worse. Gibbs oscillations develop around the discontinuity. These oscillations will spread and grow because Burgers' equation is dispersive. Ultimately, the oscillations overwhelm the solution.

16.3. The following Julia code solves the KdV equation using integrating factors. We first set the initial conditions and parameters.

Fourier spectral
soliton interaction in
solution to Burgers'
the KdV equation
equation

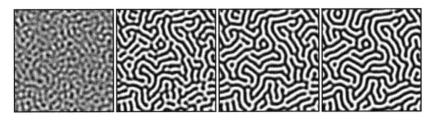

Figure A.24: Solution to the Swift–Hohenberg equation at $t = 3, 10, 25$, and 100.

```
using FFTW, DifferentialEquations
φ = (x,x₀,c) -> 0.5c*sech(sqrt(c)/2*(x-x₀))^2
L = 30; T = 2.0; m = 256
x = (1:m)/m*L .- L/2
u₀ = φ.(x,-4,4) + φ.(x,-9,9)
iξ = im*[0:(m÷2);(-m÷2+1):-1]*2π/L
F = plan_fft(u₀)
```

Next, we define integrating factor G and function f of the differential equation.

```
G = t -> exp.(-iξ.^3*t)
f = (w,_,t) -> -G(t) .\ (3iξ .* (F * (F \ (G(t).*w) ).^2) )
```

Then, we solve the problem.

```
w = solve(ODEProblem(f,F*u₀,(0,T)),DP5())
u = t -> real(F\(w(t).*G(t)))
```

Finally, we animate the solution.

```
@gif for t=0:.01:2
  plot(x,u(t),ylim=(0,5),legend=:none)
end
```

Figure A.23 shows the soliton solution to the KdV equation. The top row shows the two independent solutions with $u(x,0) = \phi(x; -4, 4)$ and $u(x,0) = \phi(x; -9, 9)$ as different initial conditions. The bottom row shows the two-soliton solution for $u(x,0) = \phi(x; -4, 4) + \phi(x; -9, 9)$. After colliding, the tall, fast soliton in the bottom row is about 1 unit in front of the corresponding soliton in the top row. The small, slow soliton in the bottom row is about 1.5 units behind the corresponding soliton in the top row. Each soliton has the same energy after the collision as it had before the collision—its position is merely shifted.

16.4. Let's use Strang splitting on $u' = N u + L u$. There are two reasonable ways to define N and L. The first with $N u = \varepsilon u - u^3$ and $L u = -(\Delta + 1)^2 u$,

the Swift–Hohenberg
equation

and the second with $N u = -u^3$ and $L u = \varepsilon u - (\Delta + 1)^2 u$. In the first case, the analytic solution to $u' = \varepsilon u - u^3$ is

$$u = \frac{u_0}{\sqrt{(1 - \varepsilon^{-1} u_0^2) e^{-2\varepsilon t} + \varepsilon^{-1} u_0^2}};$$

while in the second case, the solution to $u' = -u^3$ is $u = u_0(1 - 2tu_0^2)^{-1/2}$. While the second case seems simpler, it does not accurately model the equilibrium dynamics $u'(x, y, t) = 0$ as $t \to \infty$. The equilibrium solution $\varepsilon u - u^3 - (\Delta + 1)^2 u = 0$ has a reaction component $\varepsilon u - u^3 = 0$ and a diffusion component $(\Delta + 1)^2 u = 0$. The reaction component has two stable equilibria at $u = \pm\sqrt{\varepsilon}$ and the unstable equilibrium at $u = 0$.

Strang splitting uses half-whole-half-step operator splitting at each iteration to get second-order in time error. The solution to $u' = N u$ over $\Delta t/2$ is

$$f(u_0) = \frac{u_0}{\sqrt{(1 - \varepsilon^{-1} u_0^2) e^{-\varepsilon \Delta t} + \varepsilon^{-1} u_0^2}},$$

and the solution to $\hat{u}' = \hat{L}\hat{u}$ over a time interval Δt is

$$E \hat{u}_0 = e^{-(\hat{\Delta}+1)^2 \Delta t} \hat{u}_0.$$

At each time step, we have $u = f\left(F^{-1}\left(E \circ F\left(f(u)\right)\right)\right)$. The following Julia code produces the solution to the Swift–Hohenberg equation shown in Figure A.24 and the QR code on the preceding page.

```
using FFTW, Images
ϵ = 1; m = 256; ℓ = 100; n = 2000; Δt=100/n
U = (rand(m,m).>.5) .- 0.5
ξ = [0:(m÷2);(-m÷2+1):-1]*2π/ℓ
D²= -ξ.^2 .- (ξ.^2)'
E = exp.(-(D².+1).^2*Δt)
F = plan_fft(U)
f = U -> U./sqrt.(U.^2/ϵ + exp(-Δt*ϵ)*(1 .- U.^2/ϵ))
for i=1:600
    U = f(F\(E.*(F*f(U))))
end
```

We can animate the solution by adding the following code inside the loop.

```
save("temp"*lpad(i,3,"0")*".png",Gray.(clamp01.((real(U).+1)/2)))
```

Making a call to ffmpeg produces a movie.

```
run(`ffmpeg -i "temp%03d.png" -pix_fmt yuv420p swifthohenberg.mp4`)
```

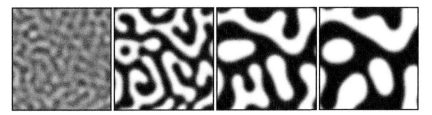

Figure A.25: Solution to the Cahn–Hilliard equation at $t = 0.1, 1, 4,$ and 8.

16.5. We'll use a fourth-order ETDRK scheme.

```
using FFTW, DifferentialEquations, SciMLOperators
ℓ = 8; T = 8.0; m = 256; ε² = 0.01; α = 1
ξ = [0:(m÷2);(-m÷2+1):-1]*2π/ℓ
Δ = -(ξ.^2 .+ ξ'.^2); Δ² = Δ.^2
u₀ = randn(m,m)
F = plan_fft(u₀)
L = DiagonalOperator((-ε²*Δ²+α*Δ)[:])
N = (u,_,_) -> (v = F\reshape(u,m,m); Δ.*(F*(v.^3-(1+α)*v)))[:]
problem = SplitODEProblem(L,N,(F*u₀)[:],(0,T))
solution = solve(problem,ETDRK4(),dt = 0.1)
u = t -> real(F\reshape(solution(t),m,m))
```

We can observe the solution over time using the Interact.jl library.

```
using Interact, ColorSchemes, Images
@manipulate for t in slider(0:0.1:8; value=0, label="time")
  get(colorschemes[:binary], u(t), :extrema)
end
```

Figure A.25 and the QR code on the current page show the solution to the Cahn–Hilliard equation. Observe how the dynamics slow down over time.

16.6. We'll use a fourth-order ETDRK method to solve the KSE.

```
using FFTW, DifferentialEquations, SciMLOperators
ℓ = 50; T = 200.0; n = 128; u₀ = randn(n,n)
x = LinRange(-ℓ/2,ℓ/2,n+1)[2:end]
ξ = [0:(n÷2);(-n÷2+1):-1]*2π/ℓ
Δ = -(ξ.^2 .+ ξ'.^2); Δ² = Δ.^2
F = plan_fft(u₀)
L = DiagonalOperator((-Δ-Δ²)[:])
```

the Cahn–Hilliard
equation

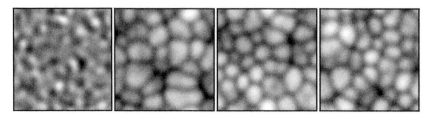

Figure A.26: The Kuramoto–Sivashinsky equation at $t = 1, 50, 100,$ and 150.

```
N = (u,_,_) ->
  ( v = reshape(u,n,n);
    v = -0.5*abs.((F\(im*ξ.*v)).^2 + (F\(im*ξ'.*v)).^2);
    w = (F*v)[:]; w[1] = 0.0; return w )
problem = SplitODEProblem(L,N,(F*u₀)[:],(0,T))
solution = solve(problem, ETDRK4(), dt=0.05, saveat=0.5);
u = t -> real(F\reshape(solution(t),n,n))
```

We can observe the evolution of the solution using the Interact.jl library. See Figure A.26 and the QR code on this page.

```
using Interact, ColorSchemes, Images
@manipulate for t in slider(0:0.5:T; value=0, label="time")
  get(colorschemes[:magma], -u(t), :extrema)
end
```

the two-dimensional
KSE

Appendix B

Computing in Python and Matlab

B.1 Scientific programming languages

▷ The trends

The evolution of modern scientific computing programming languages over the past seventy years is a product of several compounding and reinforcing factors:

- The exponential growth in computing speed and memory, along with the considerable drop in computing cost;
- A paradigm shift towards open-source software and open access research;
- A widespread and fast internet, spurring greater information sharing and cloud computing;
- The shift from digital immigrants to digital natives and increase in diversity;
- The production and monetization of massive quantities of data; and
- The emergence of specialized fields of computational science, like data science, bioinformatics, computational neuroscience, and computational sociology.

In 1965 Gordon Moore, the co-founder of Fairchild Semiconductor and later co-founder and CEO of Intel, observed that the number of transistors on an integrated circuit doubled every year. He revised his estimate ten years later, stating that the doubling occurred every two years. Moore's empirical law has more or less held since then. It is difficult to overstate the impact that technological change and economic growth have had on computing. ENIAC (Electronic Numerical Integrator and Computer), built in the mid-1940s, was the first programmable, digital, electronic computer. It cost $6.6 million in today's dollars, weighed 27 tonnes, and would fill a small house. ENIAC had the equivalent of 40 bytes of internal memory and could execute roughly 500 floating-point operations per second. Cray-1, developed in the late 1970s, was one of the most commercially successful supercomputers with 80 units

557

sold. It cost \$33 million in today's dollars, weighed 5 tonnes, and would fill a closet. Cray-1 had 8 million bytes of memory and could execute 160 million floating-point operations per second. Today, a typical smartphone costs \$500, weighs less than 200 grams, and fits in a pocket. Smartphones often have 6 billion bytes of memory and can execute 10 billion floating-point operations per second. High-performance cloud computing, which can be accessed with those smartphones, has up to 30 trillion bytes of memory and can achieve a quintillion (a billion billion) floating-point operations per second using specialized GPUs. And even now, scientists are developing algorithms that use nascent quantum computers to solve intractable high-dimensional problems in quantum simulation, cryptanalysis, and optimization.

The growth in open data, open standards, open access and reproducible research, and open-source software has further accelerated the evolution of scientific computing languages. Unlike proprietary programming languages and libraries, the open-source movement creates a virtuous innovation feedback loop powered through open collaboration, improved interoperability, and greater affordability. Even traditionally closed-source software companies such as IBM, Microsoft, and Google have embraced the open-source movement through Red Hat, GitHub, and Android. Former World Bank Chief Economist and Nobel laureate Paul Romer has noted, "The more I learn about the open source community, the more I trust its members. The more I learn about proprietary software, the more I worry that objective truth might perish from the earth." Python, Julia, Matlab, and R all have a robust community of user-developers. The Comprehensive R Archive Network (CRAN) features 17 thousand contributed packages, the Python Package Index (PyPI) has over 200 thousand packages, and GitHub has over 100 million repositories. Nonprofit foundations, like NumFOCUS (Numerical Foundation for Open Code and Useable Science), have further supported open-source scientific software projects.

In 1984 Donald Knuth, author of the *Art of Computer Programming* and the creator of TEX, introduced *literate programming* in which natural language exposition and source code are combined by considering programs to be "works of literature." Knuth explained that "instead of imagining that our main task is to instruct a *computer* what to do, let us concentrate rather on explaining to *human beings* what we want a computer to do." Mathematica, first released in the late 1980s, used notebooks that combined formatted text, typeset mathematics, and Wolfram Language code into a series of interactive cells. In 2001, Fernando Pérez developed a notebook for the Python programming language called IPython that allowed code, narrative text, mathematical expressions, and inline plots in a browser-based interface. In 2014, Pérez spun off the open-source Project Jupyter. Jupyter (a portmanteau of Julia, Python, and R and an homage to the notebooks that Galileo recorded his observations on the moons of Jupiter) extends IPython to dozens of programming languages. Projects like Pluto for Julia and Observables for JavaScript have further developed notebooks to make them even more immersive as reactive notebooks. Code everywhere in a reactive notebook re-executes whenever a variable is changed anywhere in the notebook. The impact of notebooks in scientific programming is so significant that James Somers, in an article in *The Atlantic*, declared (too boldly) that the "scientific paper is obsolete."

The widespread availability of high-speed internet has further improved collaboration. Crowdsourcing projects like Wikipedia and StackExchange have transformed how information gets disseminated. Massive open online courses (MOOCs) have made learning available anywhere at any time. Several Jupyter environments now support collaboration by synchronizing changes in real-time, like Google's Colaboratory, Amazon's SageMaker Notebooks, and William Stein's CoCalc. Cloud computing, Software as a Service, and Infrastructure as a Service have all transformed scientific computing and enabled the democratization of data science. The next section provides an overview of the evolution of the major scientific programming languages, from Fortran to Matlab to Python to Julia.

▷ The languages

Fortran (a portmanteau of Formula Translating System) was developed in the 1950s by a team at IBM led by then thirty-year-old John Backus. It came to dominate numerical computation for decades and is still frequently used in high-performance computing and as subroutines called by other scientific programming languages through wrapper functions. Fortran was the first widely-used, high-level "automatic programming" language, invented when computer code was almost entirely written in machine language or assembly language. While "automatic programming" was met with considerable skepticism at the time, the drop in cost of a computer relative to the cost in salaries for computer scientists, who might spend a significant time debugging code, was a significant driver behind the development of Fortran.

Realizing the need for portable, non-proprietary, mathematical software, researchers at Argonne National Laboratory, funded through the National Science Foundation, developed a set of Fortran libraries in the early 1970s. These libraries included EISPACK for computing eigenvalues and eigenvectors and LINPACK for performing linear algebra. The packages were subsequently expanded into a broader set of numerical software libraries called SLATEC (Sandia, Los Alamos, Air Force Weapons Laboratory Technical Exchange Committee). In the 1980s, MINPACK for solving systems of nonlinear equations, QUADPACK for numerical integration of one-dimensional functions, FFTPACK for the fast Fourier transform, and SLAP for sparse linear algebra, among others, were added to the SLATEC Common Mathematics Library. And in the early 1990s, EISPACK and LINPACK were combined into the general linear algebra package

LAPACK. The GNU Scientific Library (GSL) was initiated in the mid-1990s to provide a modern replacement to SLATEC.

Cleve Moler, one of the developers of LAPACK and EISPACK, created MATLAB (a portmanteau of Matrix Laboratory) in the 1970s to give his students access to these libraries without needing to know Fortran.[1] You can appreciate how much easier it is to simply write

```
[1 2; 3 4]\[5;6]
```

and have the solution printed automatically, rather than to write in Fortran

```
program main
    implicit none
    external :: sgesv
    real :: A(2, 2)
    real :: b(2)
    real :: pivot(2)
    integer :: return_code

    A = reshape([ 1., 3., 2., 4. ], [ 2, 2 ])
    b = [ 5., 6. ]
    call sgesv(2, 1, A, 2, pivot, b, 2, return_code)
    if (return_code == 0) then
        print '(a, 2(f0.4, ", "))', 'solution: ', b
    else
        print '(a, i0)', 'error: ', return_code
    end if
end program main
```

which would then still need to be compiled, linked, and run. MATLAB also made data visualization and plotting easy. While at first MATLAB was little more than an interactive matrix calculator, Moler later developed MATLAB into a full computing environment in the early 1980s. MATLAB's commercial growth and evolution coincided with the introduction of affordable personal computers, which were initially barely powerful enough to run software like MATLAB. Over time, other features, like sparse matrix operations and ODE solvers, were added to make MATLAB a complete scientific programming language. Still, matrices are treated as the fundamental data type.

GNU Octave, developed by John Eaton and named after his former professor Octave Levenspiel, was initiated in the 1980s and first released in the 1990s as

---

[1] In this book, "MATLAB" indicates the commercial numerical computing environment developed by MathWorks, and "Matlab" indicates the programming language inclusive of Octave. In modern orthography, uppercase often comes across as SHOUTY CAPS, but before the 1960s, computer memory and printing limitations made uppercase a necessity. In the 1990s, "FORTRAN," on which MATLAB was based and styled, adopted the naming "Fortran," and "MATLAB" stayed "MATLAB."

a free, open-source clone of MATLAB. While the syntax of Octave is nearly identical to MATLAB, there are a few differences. In general, Octave allows a little more freedom in syntax than MATLAB, while MATLAB tends to have more and newer features and functions. For example, Octave permits C-style increment operators such as x++ and addition assignment operators such as + =, but MATLAB does not. MATLAB requires ... for line continuation, while Octave also allows Python-style backslash for line continuation. Octave allows users to merge assignments such as x=y=2. MATLAB uses ~ for a logical negation, while Octave uses either ~ or !. And, MATLAB uses % to start a comment, while Octave can use either % or #. While such syntax provides greater programming flexiblity, it does create greater compatibility issues between MATLAB and Octave.

Dennis Ritchie developed the C programming language at the Bell Telephone Laboratories in the early 1970s. C was named after B, which itself came from "Basic Combined Programming Language." C was followed by D, C++, and C#. While not explicitly developed for scientific computing, C has been widely popular and influential in other derivatives like Python. The GNU Scientific Library (GSL) was written in C and has wrappers in many other languages, including Fortran, Python, R, Octave, and Julia.

The R programming language first appeared in the early 1990s as a GNU GPL modern implementation of the S programming language developed by Bell Laboratories in the mid-1970s. The name "S" is a reference to "statistical" and uses the programming language naming convention at Bell Laboratories at the time. The name "R" comes from both the first names of the language's authors (Ross Ihaka and Robert Gentleman) and from a one-letter nod to S. In the mid-2000s, Hadley Wickham developed tidyverse that helped organize data into more intuitive and more readable syntax and ggplot2 data visualization package that implemented Leland Wilkinson's "grammar of graphics" to help users build visualizations. R has since become a favorite among statisticians and data scientists.

Python is a general-purpose programming, created in the early 1990s by Guido van Rossum with a design philosophy focused on code readability. The name comes from the British comedy troupe Monty Python. While Python was not originally developed for scientific or numerical computing, the language attracted a user base who developed packages for technical computing. A matrix package called Numeric, developed in the mid-1990s, influenced Travis Oliphant to create NumPy in the mid-2000s. SciPy was developed to provide tools for technical computing, such as algorithms for signal processing, sparse matrices, special functions, optimization, and fast Fourier transforms. Matplotlib, first released in 2003, provides a plotting environment with a syntax familiar to Matlab, particularly through the pyplot module. Limited Unicode variable names were introduced in Python 3.0 in 2008. And the matrix multiplication @ operator was introduced in Python 3.5 in 2015, further improving Python's mathematical expressiveness. While Python's improved functionality has made it ubiquitous for scientific computing, it still retains some of its vestigial mathematical clunkiness, such as using ** instead of ^ for exponentiation and @ instead of * for matrix multiplication.² And while Julia has adopted Matlab's syntax of the forward slash and backslash as convenient all-purpose left and right inverse operators, Python's numpy.linalg module requires calls to specific functions such as solve(A,b) and lstsq(A,b). Furthermore, while Fortran, Matlab, Julia, and R all use a column-major order convention for storing and accessing multidimensional arrays in computer memory, Python using NumPy (along with C) uses a row-major convention.

Finally, Python (like C) uses 0-based indexing, whereas many other languages, including Fortran, Matlab, R, and Julia, use 1-based indexing. Arguments can be made supporting either 0-indexing or 1-indexing. When asked why Python uses 0-based indexing, Guido van Rossum stated "I think I was swayed by the elegance of half-open intervals."

Julia debuted in the early 2010s. When asked about the inspiration behind Julia's name, one of the cocreators Stefan Karpinski replied, "There's no good reason, really. It just seemed like a pretty name." What Fortran is to the Silent Generation, what Matlab is to Baby Boomers, and what Python is to Generation X, one might say Julia is to Millennials. While Fortran and Matlab are both certainly showing their age, Julia is a true digital native. It's designed in an era of cloud computing and GPUs. It uses Unicode and emojis that permit more expressive and more readable mathematical notation. The expression 2*pi in Julia is simply 2π, inputted using TEX conventions followed by a tab autocomplete. Useful binary operators, like ≈ for "approximately equal to," are built-in, and you can define custom binary operators using Unicode symbols. Julia is still young, and its packages are still evolving.

While Fortran and C are compiled ahead of time, and Python and Matlab are interpreted scripts, Julia is compiled just in time (JIT) using the LLVM infrastructure. Because Julia code gets compiled the first time it is run, the first run can be slow.³ But after that, Julia runs a much faster, cached compiled version. Julia has arbitrary precision arithmetic (arbitrary-precision integers and

---

²The Python operator ^ is a bit-wise XOR. So 7^3 is 4 (111 XOR 011 = 100).

³Even excruciatingly slow when precompiling some libraries. This compile-time latency is sometimes referred to as "time to first plot" (TTFP) given the amount of time import Plots.jl. But other packages are often slower. For example, DifferentialEquations.jl can take a minute or so the first run and around a second after that. Julia continues to improve and compile-time latency tends to decrease with each version.

floating-point numbers using GNU Multiple Precision Arithmetic Library (GMP) and the GNU MPFR Library) with BigInt and BigFloat.

B.2   Python

This section provides a Python supplement to the Julia commentary and code in the body of this book. The code is written and tested using Python version 3.9.7. Page references to the Julia commentary are listed in the left margins. For brevity, the following packages are assumed to have been imported as needed:

```python
import matplotlib.pyplot as plt
import numpy as np
import scipy.linalg as la
import scipy.sparse as sps
```

We'll also define the following variables:

```python
bucket = "https://raw.githubusercontent.com/nmfsc/data/master/"
π = np.pi
```

Finally, we'll define a few helper functions for downloading and displaying images:

```python
import PIL, requests, io
def rgb2gray(rgb): return np.dot(rgb[...,:3], [0.2989,0.5870,0.1140])
def getimage(url):
  response = requests.get(url)
  return np.asarray(PIL.Image.open(io.BytesIO(response.content)))
def showimage(img):
  display(PIL.Image.fromarray(np.int8(img.clip(0,255)), mode='L'))
```

The Python code in this section is available as a Jupyter notebook at

https://nbviewer.jupyter.org/github/nmfsc/python/blob/main/python.ipynb

The Jupyter viewer has a link in its menu to execute the node on Binder, which you can also access using the inner QR code at the bottom of this page. Note that it may take a few minutes for the Binder to launch the repository. Alternatively, you can download the python.ipynb file and run it on a local computer with Jupyter and Python. Or, you can upload the notebook to Google Colaboratory (Colab), Kaggle, or CoCalc, among others. Perhaps the easiest way to run the code is directly using Colab through the outer QR code at the bottom of this page.

Define the array x = np.arange(n). There are several different ways to create a   5 column vector using NumPy:

Python notebook
on Binder

Python notebook
on Google Colab

```
x[:,None]
x.reshape(n,1)
x.reshape(-1,1)
np.vstack(x)
```

5 Python uses np.array to create an array and np.asarray to cast a list as an array. The operators +, -, *, /, and ** are all element-wise operators and broadcast by implicitly expanding arrays to be of compatible size. For example, by defining A=np.array([[1,2],[3,4]]), then A*np.array([1,2]) is equivalent to A*np.array([[1,2],[1,2]]), and A*np.array([[1],[2]]) is equivalent to A*np.array([[1,1],[2,2]]). NumPy uses the operator @ for matrix multiplication and the operator ^ for matrix power.

6 The transpose of A is produced by A.T, and the conjugate transpose is produced by A.conj().T.

17 The numpy.linalg function norm(A,p) computes the matrix norm of **A**, where the default optional argument p='fro' returns the Frobenius norm. The function returns the induced p-norm when p is a number and the ∞-norm when p=np.inf.

23
```
M = [la.solve(la.hilbert(n),la.hilbert(n)) for n in [10,15,20,25,50]]
fig, ax = plt.subplots(1, 5)
for i in range(len(M)):
    ax[i].imshow(1-np.abs(M[i]),vmin=0,cmap="gray")
plt.tight_layout(); plt.show()
```

23 The numpy.linalg function cond(A,p) returns the p-condition number of A. The command cond(A) is equivalent to cond(A,2), and the ∞-condition number is given by cond(A,np.inf).

29 The getsource function from the inspect module returns the text of the source code for an object.

30 The Jupyter magic command %%timeit can be used to measure execution time.

30 The symbolic math library SymPy command sympy.Matrix(A).rref() returns the reduced row echelon form of A.

33 The following function overwrites the arguments A and b. Pass array copies of these objects gaussian_elimination(A.copy(),b.copy()) if you wish to avoid overwriting them.

```
def gaussian_elimination(A,b):
    n = len(A)
    for j in range(n):
```

```
  A[j+1:,j] /= A[j,j]
  A[j+1:,j+1:] -= np.outer(A[j+1:,j],A[j,j+1:])
for i in range(1,n):
  b[i] = b[i] - A[i,:i]@b[:i]
for i in reversed(range(n)):
  b[i] = ( b[i] - A[i,i+1:]@b[i+1:] )/A[i,i]
return b
```

The following Python code implements the simplex method. We start by defining 42
functions used for pivot selection and row reduction in the simplex algorithm.

```
def get_pivot(tableau):
  j = np.argmax(tableau[-1,:-1]>0)
  a, b = tableau[:-1,j], tableau[:-1,-1]
  k = np.argwhere(a > 0)
  i = k[np.argmin(b[k]/a[k])]
  return i,j


def row_reduce(tableau):
  i,j = get_pivot(tableau)
  G = tableau[i,:]/tableau[i,j]
  tableau -= tableau[:,j].reshape(-1,1)*G
  tableau[i,:] = G


from collections import namedtuple
def simplex(c,A,b):
  m,n = A.shape
  tableau = np.r_[np.c_[A,np.eye(m),b], \
    np.c_[c.T,np.zeros((1,m)),0]]
  while (any(tableau[-1,:n]>0)): row_reduce(tableau)
  p = np.argwhere(tableau[-1,:n] != 0)
  x = np.zeros(n)
  for i in p.flatten():
    x[i] = np.dot(tableau[:,i],tableau[:,-1])
  z = -tableau[-1,-1]
  y = -tableau[-1,range(n,n+m)]
  solution = namedtuple("solution",["z","x","y"])
  return solution(z,x,y)
```

The scipy.optimize function linprog solves the linear programming problem 45
using 'interior-point' (default), 'revised simplex', and 'simplex' (as a legacy
method). Google has also developed a suite of OR-tools. The ortools.linear_solver
function pywraplp is a C++ wrapper for solving linear programming problems.

The scipy.sparse.linalg function spsolve uses the scikit-umfpack wrapper of 46
UMFPACK to solve sparse linear systems.

46 We'll construct a sparse, random matrix, use the nnz method to get the number of nonzeros, and the matplotlib.pyplot function spy to draw the sparsity plot.

```
A = sps.rand(60,80,density=0.2)
print(A.nnz), plt.spy(A,markersize=1)
```

49 The NetworkX package provides tools for constructing, analyzing, and visualizing graphs.

49 The following code draws the dolphin networks of the Doubtful Sound. We'll use dolphin gray (#828e84) to color the nodes.

```
import pandas as pd, networkx as nx
df = pd.read_csv(bucket+'dolphins.csv', header=None)
G = nx.from_pandas_edgelist(df,0,1)
nx.draw(G,nx.spectral_layout(G),alpha=0.5,node_color='#828e84')
plt.axis('equal'); plt.show()
```

We can change layouts using nx.spring_layout(A) and nx.circular_layout(A).

52 The function scipy.sparse.csgraph.reverse_cuthill_mckee returns the permutation vector using the reverse Cuthill–McKee algorithm for sparse matrices.

54 The following code implements the revised simplex method.

```
from collections import namedtuple
def revised_simplex(c,A,b):
    c, A, b = c.astype(float), A.astype(float), b.astype(float)
    m, n = A.shape
    def xi(i): z=sps.lil_matrix((m,1)); z[i] = 1; return z.tocsr()
    N = np.arange(n); B = np.arange(n,n+m)
    A = sps.hstack([sps.csr_matrix(A),sps.identity(m)],format="csr")
    ABinv = sps.identity(m).tocsr()
    b = sps.csr_matrix(b)
    c = sps.vstack([sps.csr_matrix(c),sps.csr_matrix((m,1))])
    while True:
        J = np.argwhere( (c[N].T-(c[B].T @ ABinv) @ A[:,N]) > 0)
        if len(J)==0: break
        j = J[0,1]
        q = ABinv @ A[:,N[j]]
        k = np.argwhere(q>0)[:,0]
        i = k[ np.argmin( ABinv[k,:] @ b/q[k] ) ]
        B[i], N[j] = N[j], B[i]
        ABinv -= ((q - xi(i))/q[i][0,0]) @ ABinv[i,:]
    i = np.argwhere(B<n)
    x = np.zeros(n)
    for k in i.flatten(): x[B[k]] = (ABinv[k,:] @ b)[0,0]
    y=(c[B].T@ABinv).toarray().flatten()
```

```
solution = namedtuple("solution",["z","x","y"])
return solution(z=x@c[:n],x=x,y=y)
```

For a 2000×1999 matrix `la.lstsq(A1,b)` takes 3.4 seconds and `la.pinv(A1)@b`   57
takes 6.3 seconds.

Python does not have a dedicated function for the Givens rotations matrix. Instead,   64
use the scipy.linalg QR decomposition `Q,_ = qr([[x],[y]])`.

The scipy.linalg function `qr` implements LAPACK routines to compute the QR   65
factorization of a matrix using Householder reflection.

The `numpy.linalg` and `scipy.linalg` function `lstsq` solves an overdetermined   66
system using the LAPACK routines `gelsd` (using singular value decomposition)
`gelsy` (using QR factorization), or `gelss` (singular value decomposition).

The Zipf's law coefficients c for the canon of Sherlock Holmes computed using   67
ordinary least squares are

```
import pandas as pd
data = pd.read_csv(bucket+'sherlock.csv', sep='\t', header=None)
T = np.array(data[1])
n = len(T)
A = np.c_[np.ones((n,1)),np.log(np.arange(1,n+1)[:, np.newaxis])]
B = np.log(T)[:, np.newaxis]
c = la.lstsq(A,B)[0]
```

The constrained least squares problem is solved using   70

```
def constrained_lstsq(A,b,C,d):
  x = la.solve(np.r_[np.c_[A.T@A,C.T],
      np.c_[C,np.zeros((C.shape[0],C.shape[0]))]], np.r_[A.T@b,d] )
  return x[:A.shape[1]]
```

The numpy.linalg or scipy.linalg command `U,S,V=svd(A)` returns the SVD de-   71
composition of a matrix A and `la.svd(A,0)` returns the "economy" version of the
SVD. The `scipy.sparse.linalg` command `svds(A,k)` returns the first k singular
values and associated singular vectors.

The NumPy function `la.pinv` computes the Moore–Penrose pseudoinverse by   73
computing the SVD using a default tolerance of `1e-15*norm(A)`.

The following code implements total least squares: 77

```
def tls(A,B):
  n = A.shape[1]
  _,_,Vᵀ = la.svd(np.c_[A,B])
```

```
    return -la.solve(Vᵀ[n:,n:],Vᵀ[n:,:n]).T
```

77
```
A = np.array([[2,4],[1,-1],[3,1],[4,-8]]);
b = np.array([[1,1,4,1]]).T
x_ols = la.lstsq(A,b)[0]
x_tls = tls(A,b)
```

79 We'll use the helper functions getimage and showimage defined on page 563.

```
A = rgb2gray(getimage(bucket+'red-fox.jpg'))
U,σ,Vᵀ = la.svd(A)
```

Take k to be a value such as 20. Let's evaluate $\mathbf{A}_k$ and confirm that the error $\|\mathbf{A} - \mathbf{A}_k\|_F^2$ matches $\sum_{i=k+1}^{n} \sigma^2$.

```
Ak = U[:,:k] @ np.diag(σ[:k]) @ Vᵀ[:k,:]
la.norm(A-Ak,'fro') - la.norm(σ[k:])
```

Finally, we'll show the compressed image and plot the error curve.

```
showimage(np.c_[A,Ak])
r = np.sum(A.shape)/np.prod(A.shape)*range(1,min(A.shape)+1)
error = 1 - np.sqrt(np.cumsum(σ**2))/la.norm(σ)
plt.semilogx(r,error,'.-'); plt.show()
```

85 The following function is a naïve implementation of NMF:

```
def nmf(X,p=6):
    W = np.random.rand(X.shape[0],p)
    H = np.random.rand(p,X.shape[1])
    for i in range(50):
        W = W*(X@H.T)/(W@(H@H.T) + (W==0))
        H = H*(W.T@X)/((W.T@W)@H + (H==0))
    return (W,H)
```

87 The NumPy function vander generates a Vandermonde matrix with rows given by $\begin{bmatrix} x_i^p & x_i^{p-1} & \cdots & x_i & 1 \end{bmatrix}$ for input $(x_0, x_1, \ldots, x_n)$.

89 The NumPy function roots finds the roots of a polynomial $p(x)$ by computing the eigenvalues of the companion matrix of $p(x)$.

90 Python does not have a function to compute the eigenvalue condition number. Instead, we can compute it using:

```
def condeig(A):
    w, vl, vr = la.eig(A, left=True, right=True)
```

```
c = 1/np.sum(vl*vr,axis=0)
return (c, vr, w)
```

The code to compute the PageRank of the graph in Figure 4.3 is   97

```
H = np.array([[0,0,0,0,1],[1,0,0,0,0], \
    [1,0,0,0,1],[1,0,1,0,0],[0,0,1,1,0]])
v = ~np.any(H,0)
H = H/(np.sum(H,0)+v)
n = len(H)
d = 0.85;
x = np.ones((n,1))/n
for i in range(9):
  x = d*(H@x) + d/n*(v@x) + (1-d)/n
```

The scipy.linalg function hessenberg computes the unitarily similar upper Hes- 104
senberg form of a matrix.

Both numpy.linalg and scipy.linalg have the function eig that computes the   109
eigenvalues and eigenvectors of a matrix.

The scipy.sparse.linalg command eigs computes several eigenvalues of a sparse 114
matrix using the implicitly restarted Arnoldi process.

The scipy.sparse.linalg function cg implements the conjugate gradient method— 137
preconditioned conjugate gradient method if a preconditioner is also provided.

The scipy.sparse.linalg function gmres implements the generalized minimum 141
residual method and minres implements the minimum residual method.

The NumPy function kron(A,B) returns the Kronecker product $\mathbf{A} \otimes \mathbf{B}$.   148

The radix-2 FFT algorithm written as a recursive function in Python is   149

```
def fftx2(c):
  n = len(c)
  ω = np.exp(-2j*π/n);
  if np.mod(n,2) == 0:
    k = np.arange(n/2)
    u = fftx2(c[:-1:2])
    v = (ω**k)*fftx2(c[1::2])
    return np.concatenate((u+v, u-v))
  else:
    k = np.arange(n)[:,None]
    F = ω**(k*k.T);
    return F @ c
```

and the IFFT is

```
def ifftx2(y): return np.conj(fftx2(np.conj(y)))/len(y)
```

150 The scipy.linalg function `toeplitz` constructs a Toeplitz matrix.

150 The scipy.linalg function `circulant` constructs a circulant matrix.

152 The scipy.signal function `convolve` returns the convolution of two n-dimensional arrays using either FFTs or directly, depending on which is faster.

153 The following function returns the fast Toeplitz multiplication of the Toeplitz matrix with c as its first column and r as its first row and a vector x. We'll use `fftx2` and `ifftx2` that we developed earlier, although in practice it is much faster to use the built-in NumPy or SciPy functions `fft` and `ifft` the scipy.signals function `convolve`.

```
def fasttoeplitz(c,r,x):
    n = len(x)
    m = (1<<(n-1).bit_length())-n
    x1 = np.concatenate((np.pad(c,(0,m)),r[:1:-1]))
    x2 = np.pad(x,(0,m+n-1))
    return ifftx2(fftx2(x1)*fftx2(x2))[:n]
```

155
```
def bluestein(x):
    n = len(x)
    ω = np.exp((1j*π/n)*(np.arange(n)**2))
    return ω*fasttoeplitz(conj(ω),conj(ω),ω)
```

158 The libraries numpy.fft and scipy.fft both have several functions for computing FFTs using Cooley–Tukey and Bluestein algorithms. These include `fft` and `ifft` for one-dimensional transforms, `fft2` and `ifft2` for two-dimensional transforms, and `fftn` and `ifftn` for multi-dimensional transforms. When `fft` and `ifft` are applied to multidimensional arrays, the transforms are along the last dimension by default. (In Matlab, the transforms are along the first dimension by default.) Similar functions are available to compute FFTs for real inputs and discrete sine and discrete cosine transforms. The PyFFTW package provides a Python wrapper to the FFTW routines. According to the SciPy documentation: "users for whom the speed of FFT routines is critical should consider installing PyFFTW."

159 The scipy.fft functions `fftshift` and `ifftshift` shift the zero frequency component to the center of the array.

160 The following code solves the Poisson equation using a naive fast Poisson solver and then compares the solution with the exact solution.

```
from scipy.fft import dstn, idstn
```

```
n = 50; x = np.arange(1,n+1)/(n+1); Δx = 1/(n+1)
v = 2 - 2*np.cos(x*π)
λ = np.array([[[ (v[i]+v[j]+v[k])/Δx**2 \
  for i in range(n)] for j in range(n)] for k in range(n)])
f = np.array([[[ (x-x**2)*(y-y**2) + \
  (x-x**2)*(z-z**2)+(y-y**2)*(z-z**2) \
  for x in x] for y in x] for z in x])
u = idstn(dstn(f,type=1)/λ,type=1)
U = np.array([[[ (x-x**2)*(y-y**2)*(z-z**2)/2 \
  for x in x] for y in x] for z in x])
la.norm(u - U)
```

The scipy.fft functions dct and dst return the type 1–4 DCT and DST, respectively. 163
The following function returns a sparse matrix of Fourier coefficients along with
the reconstructed compressed image:

```
from scipy.fft import dctn, idctn
def dctcompress(A,d):
  B = dctn(A)
  idx = int(d*np.prod(A.size))
  tol = np.sort(abs(B.flatten()))[-idx]
  B[abs(B)<tol] = 0
  return sps.csr_matrix(B), idctn(B)
```

We'll test the function on an image and compare it before and after using getimage
and showimage defined on page 563.

```
A = rgb2gray(getimage(bucket+"red-fox.jpg"))
_, A0 = dctcompress(A,0.001)
showimage(np.c_[A,A0])
```

The function type returns the data type of a variable.   180

The following function returns a double-precision floating-point representation 181
as a string of bits:

```
def float_to_bin(x):
  if x == 0: return "0" * 64
  w, sign = (float.hex(x),0) if x > 0 else (float.hex(x)[1:],1)
  mantissa, exp = int(w[4:17], 16), int(w[18:])
  return "{}{:011b}{:052b}".format(sign, exp + 1023, mantissa)
```

The NumPy function finfo returns machine limits for floating-point types. For 181
example, np.finfo(float).eps returns the double-precision machine epsilon
2^{-52} and np.finfo(float).precision returns 15, the approximate precision in
decimal digits.

182   The following function implements the Q_rsqrt algorithm to approximate the reciprocal square root of a number. Because NumPy upcasts to double-precision integers, we'll explicitly recast intermediate results to single-precision.

```python
def Q_rsqrt(x):
    i = np.float32(x).view(np.int32)
    i = (0x5f3759df - (i>>1)).astype(np.int32)
    y = i.view(np.float32)
    return y * (1.5 - (0.5 * x * y * y))
```

184
```python
a = 77617; b = 33096
333.75*b**6+a**2*(11*a**2*b**2-b**6-121*b**4-2)+5.5*b**8+a/(2*b)
```

185   The sys command sys.float_info.max returns the largest floating-point number. The command sys.float_info.min returns the smallest normalized floating-point number.

186   To check for overflows and NaN, use the NumPy commands isinf and isnan. You can use NaN to lift the "pen off the paper" in a matplotlib plot as in

```python
plt.plot(np.array([1,2,2,2,3]),np.array([1,2,np.nan,1,2]));plt.show()
```

187   The NumPy functions expm1 and log1p compute $e^x - 1$ and $\log(x + 1)$ more precisely than exp(x)-1 and log(x+1) in a neighborhood of zero.

191   A Python implementation of the bisection method for a function f is

```python
def bisection(f,a,b,tolerance):
    while abs(b-a)>tolerance:
        c = (a+b)/2
        if np.sign(f(c))==np.sign(f(a)): a = c
        else: b = c
    return (a+b)/2
```

197   The scipy.optimize function fsolve(f,x0) uses Powell's hybrid method to find the zero of the input function.

204   The following function takes the parameters bb for the lower-left and upper-right corners of the bounding box, xn for the number of horizontal pixels, and n for the maximum number of iterations. The function returns a two-dimensional array M that counts the number of iterations k to escape $\{z \in \mathbb{C} \mid |z^{(k)}| > 2\}$.

```python
def escape(n,z,c):
    M = np.zeros_like(c,dtype=int)
    for k in range(n):
```

```
    mask = np.abs(z)<2
    M[mask] += 1
    z[mask] = z[mask]**2 + c[mask]
  return M


def mandelbrot(bb, xn=800, n=200, z=0):
  yn = int(np.round(xn*(bb[3]-bb[1])/(bb[2]-bb[0])))
  z = z*np.ones((yn,xn),dtype=complex)
  c = np.linspace(bb[0],bb[2],xn).reshape(1,-1) + \
      1j*np.linspace(bb[3],bb[1],yn).reshape(-1,1)
  return escape(n,z,c)
```

The following commands produce image (c) of Figure 8.5 on page 204:

```
import matplotlib.image as mpimg
M = mandelbrot([-0.1710,1.0228,-0.1494,1.0443])
mpimg.imsave('mandelbrot.png', -M, cmap='magma')
```

The NumPy function polynomial.polynomial.polyval(x,p) evaluates a polyno-   208
mial with coefficients $p = [a_0, a_1, \ldots, a_n]$ at x using Horner's method.

The NumPy function roots returns the roots of a polynomial by finding the   211
eigenvalues of the companion matrix.

The scipy.optimize function fsolve finds zeros of nonlinear systems.   215

The following code finds the roots using homotopy continuation: 217

```
from scipy.integrate import solve_ivp
def f(x): return (np.array([x[0]**3-3*x[0]*x[1]**2-1,
  x[1]**3-3*x[0]**2*x[1]]))
def df(t,x,p):
  A = np.array([[3*x[0]**2-3*x[1]**2,-6*x[0]*x[1]],
      [-6*x[0]*x[1],3*x[1]**2-3*x[0]**2]])
  return la.solve(-A,p)
x0 = np.array([1,1])
sol = solve_ivp(df,[0,1],x0,args=(f(x0),))
sol.y[:,-1]
```

The following code uses the gradient descent method to find the minimum of the   221
Rosenbrock function:

```
def df(x): return np.array([-2*(1-x[0])-400*x[0]*(x[1]-x[0]**2),
  200*(x[1]-x[0]**2)])
x = np.array([-1.8,3.0]); p = np.array([0.0,0.0])
α = 0.001; β = 0.9
for i in range(500):
```

```
p = -df(x) + β*p
x += α*p
```

In practice, we can use the scipy.optimize function `minimize`, which provides several algorithms for finding the minimum of a multivariate function, including the Nelder–Mead method and quasi-Newton methods. The `minimize_scalar` function includes the golden section method for finding the minimum of a univariate function.

```
from scipy.optimize import minimize
def f(x): return (1-x[0])**2 + 100*(x[1] - x[0]**2)**2
x0 = np.array([-1.8,3.0])
x = minimize(f,x0)
```

227   The NumPy function `vander` constructs a Vandermonde matrix. Or you can build one yourself with x**np.arange(n).

238   The following pair of functions determines the coefficients of a cubic spline with natural boundary conditions given arrays of nodes and then evaluates the spline using those coefficients. Because C is a tridiagonal matrix, it is more efficient to use a banded Hermitian solver solveh_banded from from scipy.linalg than the general solver in numpy.linalg.

```
def spline_natural(x,y):
    h = np.diff(x)
    gamma = 6*np.diff(np.diff(y)/h)
    C = [h[:-1],2*(h[:-1]+h[1:])]
    m = np.pad(la.solveh_banded(C,gamma),(1, 1))
    return m


def evaluate_spline(x,y,m,n):
    h = np.diff(x)
    B = y[:-1] - m[:-1]*h**2/6
    A = np.diff(y)/h-h/6*np.diff(m)
    X = np.linspace(np.min(x),np.max(x),n+1)
    i = np.array([np.argmin(i>=x)-1 for i in X])
    i[-1] = len(x)-2
    Y = (m[i]*(x[i+1]-X)**3 + m[i+1]*(X-x[i])**3)/(6*h[i]) \
        + A[i]*(X-x[i]) + B[i]
    return (X,Y)
```

239   The scipy.interpolate function `spline` returns a cubic (or any other order) spline. The `splprep` and `splev` commands break up the steps of finding the coefficients for an interpolating spline and evaluating the values of that spline. Perhaps the easiest approach is the function `CubicSpline` that returns a cubic spline

interpolant class. The Spline classes in scipy.interpolate are wrappers for the Dierckx Fortran library.

The scipy.signal function bspline(x,p) evaluates a pth order B-spline. The 241 scipy.interpolate function Bspline(t,c,p) constructs a spline using pth order B-splines with knots t and coefficients c.

The scipy.interpolate function pchip returns a cubic Hermite spline.   242

We can build a Bernstein matrix using the following function which takes a 245 column vector such as t = np.linspace(0,1,50).[:,None]:

```python
def bernstein(n,t):
  from scipy.special import comb
  k = np.arange(n+1)[None,:]
  return comb(n,k)*t**k*(1-t)**(n-k)
```

```python
def legendre(x,n):                                                          255
  if n==0:
    return np.ones_like(x)
  elif n==1:
    return x
  else:
    return x*legendre(x,n-1)-1/(4-1/(n-1)**2)*legendre(x,n-2)
```

We'll construct a Chebyshev differentiation matrix and use the matrix to solve a 261 few simple problems.

```python
def chebdiff(n):
  x = -np.cos(np.linspace(0,π,n))[:,None]
  c = np.outer(np.r_[2,np.ones(n-2),2],(-1)**np.arange(n))
  D = c/c.T/(x - x.T + np.eye(n))
  return D - np.diag(np.sum(D,axis=1)), x


n = 15
D,x = chebdiff(n)
u = np.exp(-4*x**2);
plt.plot(x,D@u,'.-')


D[0,:] = np.zeros((1,n)); D[0,0] = 1; u[0] = 2
plt.plot(x,la.solve(D,u),'.-'); plt.show()


n = 15; k2 = 256
D,x = chebdiff(n)
L = D@D - k2*np.diag(x.flatten())
```

```
L[[0,-1],:] = 0; L[0,0] = 1; L[-1,-1] = 1
y = la.solve(L,np.r_[2,[0]*(n-2),1].T)
plt.plot(x,y,'o');
```

263 The ChebPy package, a Python implementation of the Matlab Chebfun package, includes methods for manipulating functions in Chebyshev space.

269 The following function returns x and $\phi(x)$ of a scaling function with coefficients given by c and values at integer values of x given z:

```
def scaling(c,z,n):
  m = len(c); L = 2**n
  φ = np.zeros(2*m*L)
  φ[0:m*L:L] = z
  for j in range(n):
    for i in range(m*2**j):
      x = (2*i+1)*2**(n-1-j)
      φ[x] = sum([c[k]*φ[(2*x-k*L)%(2*m*L)] for k in range(m)])
  return np.arange((m-1)*L)/L,φ[:(m-1)*L]
```

Let's use scaling to plot the Daubechies D_4 scaling function.

```
sqrt3 = np.sqrt(3)
c = np.array([1+sqrt3,3+sqrt3,3-sqrt3,1-sqrt3])/4
z = np.array([0,1+sqrt3,1-sqrt3,0])/2
x,φ = scaling(c,z,8)
plt.plot(x,φ); plt.show()
```

271
```
ψ = np.zeros_like(φ); n = len(c)-1; L = len(φ)//(2*n)
for k in range(n):
  ψ[k*L:(k+n)*L] += (-1)**k*c[n-k]*φ[::2]
```

273 The scipy.signals library includes several utilities for wavelet transforms. The PyWavelets (pywt) package provides a comprehensive suite of utilities.

274 We'll use the PyWavelets package. The helper functions getimage and showimage are defined on page 563. The following code gives the two-dimensional Haar DWT of a grayscale image:

```
import pywt
def adjustlevels(x): return 1-np.clip(np.sqrt(np.abs(x)),0,1)
A = rgb2gray(getimage(bucket+"laura_square.png"))/255
A = pywt.wavedec2(A,'haar')
c, slices = pywt.coeffs_to_array(A)
showimage(adjustlevels(c)*255)
```

Let's choose a threshold level of 0.5 and plot the resultant image after taking the inverse DWT.

```
level = 0.5
c = pywt.threshold(c,level)
c = pywt.array_to_coeffs(c,slices,output_format='wavedec2')
B = pywt.waverec2(c,'haar')
showimage(B*255)
```

We first need a numerically approximation for the Jacobian.   283

```
def jacobian(f,x,c):
  J = np.empty([len(x), len(c)])
  n = np.arange(len(c))
  for i in n:
    J[:,i] = np.imag(f(x,c+1e-8j*(i==n)))/1e-8
  return J
```

Now we can implement the Levenberg–Marquardt method.

```
def gauss_newton(f,x,y,c):
  r = y - f(x,c)
  for j in range(100):
    G = jacobian(f,x,c)
    M = G.T @ G
    c += la.solve(M + np.diag(np.diag(M)),G.T@r)
    r, r0 = y - f(x,c), r
    if la.norm(r-r0) < 1e-10: return c
  print('Gauss-Newton did not converge.')
```

The problem can be solved using

```
def f(x,c): return ( c[0]*np.exp(-c[1]*(x-c[2])**2) +
  c[3]*np.exp(-c[4]*(x-c[5])**2) )
x = 8*np.random.rand(100)
y = f(x,np.array([1,3,3,2,3,6])) + np.random.normal(0,0.1,100)
c0 = np.array([2,0.3,2,1,0.3,7])
c = gauss_newton(f,x,y,c0)
```

Assuming that the method converges, we can plot the results using

```
X = np.linspace(0,8,100)
if c is not None: plt.plot(x,y,'.',X,f(X,c))
```

In practice, we can use the scipy.optimize function `curve_fit`, which uses the Levenberg–Marquardt method for unconstrained problems.

```
from scipy.optimize import curve_fit
def g(x,c0,c1,c2,c3,c4,c5): return f(x,[c0,c1,c2,c3,c4,c5])
c,_ = curve_fit(g, x, y, c0)
```

286 We'll first define the logistic function and generate synthetic data. Then, we apply Newton's method.

```
def σ(x): return 1/(1+np.exp(-x))
x = np.random.rand(30)[:,None]
y = (np.random.rand(30)[:,None] < σ(10*x-5))


X, w = np.c_[np.ones_like(x),x], np.zeros((2,1))
for i in range(10):
  S = σ(X@w)*(1-σ(X@w))
  w += la.solve(X.T@(S*X), X.T@(y-σ(X@w)))
```

In practice, we can use the statsmodels module to do logistic regression:

```
import statsmodels.api as sm
results = sm.Logit(y, X).fit()
w = results.params
```

The command results.summary() gives a summary of the results.

289 Let's start by generating some training data and setting up the neural network architecture.

```
N = 100; θ = np.linspace(0,π,N)
x = np.cos(θ); x = np.c_[np.ones(N),x].T
y = np.sin(θ) + 0.05*np.random.randn(1,N)


n = 20; W1 = np.random.rand(n,2); W2 = np.random.randn(1,n)
def φ(x): return np.maximum(x,0)
def dφ(x): return (x>0)
α = 1e-3
```

Now, we train the model to determine the optimized parameters.

```
for epoch in range(10000):
  ŷ = W2 @ φ(W1@x)
  dLdy = 2*(ŷ-y)
  dLdW1 = dφ(W1@x)* (W2.T@ dLdy) @ x.T
  dLdW2 = dLdy @ φ(W1@x).T
  W1 -= 0.1 * α * dLdW1
  W2 -= α * dLdW2
```

After determining the parameters W1 and W2, we can plot the results.

```
plt.scatter(x[1,:],y,color='#ff000050')
x̂ = np.linspace(-1.2,1.2,200); x̂ = np.c_[np.ones_like(x̂),x̂].T
ŷ = W2 @ φ(W1@x̂)
plt.plot(x̂[1,:],ŷ[0],color='#000000')
```

Alternatively, we can swap out the activation and loss functions.

```
def φ(x): return 1/(1+np.exp(-x))
def dφ(x): return φ(x)*(1-φ(x))


L = la.norm(ŷ-y)
dLdy = 2*(ŷ-y)/L
```

Python has several open-source deep learning frameworks. The most popular include TensorFlow (developed by Google), PyTorch (developed by Facebook), and MXNet (developed by Apache). We'll use TensorFlow and the Keras library, which provides a high-level interface to TensorFlow. First, let's load Keras and TensorFlow and generate some training data.

```
import tensorflow as tf
from tensorflow import keras
from tensorflow.keras import layers
n = 20; N = 100;
θ = tf.linspace(0.0,π,N)
x = tf.math.cos(θ); y = tf.math.sin(θ) + 0.05*tf.random.normal([N])
```

Now, we can define the model, train it, and examine the outputs.

```
model = keras.Sequential(
  [
    layers.Dense(n, input_dim=1, activation='relu'),
    layers.Dense(1)
  ]
)
model.compile(loss='mean_squared_error', optimizer='SGD')
model.fit(x,y,epochs=2000,verbose=0)
ŷ = model.predict(x)
plt.plot(x,ŷ,color='#000000'); plt.scatter(x,y,color='#ff000050')
```

This example uses the default gradient descent model. We can also choose a specialized optimizer.

```
optimizer = tf.keras.optimizers.SGD(learning_rate=0.1, momentum=0.9)
```

Coefficients to the third-order approximation to $f'(x)$ using nodes at $x - h$, x,   297
$x + h$ and $x + 2h$ are given by C[1,:] where

```
d = np.array([-1,0,1,2])[:,None]
n = len(d)
V = d**np.arange(n) / [np.math.factorial(i) for i in range(n)]
C = la.inv(V)
```

We can express floating-point numbers as fractions using the following function:

```
from fractions import Fraction
def rats(x): return str(Fraction(x).limit_denominator())
[rats(x) for x in C[1,:]]
```

The coefficients of the truncation are `C@d**n/np.math.factorial(n)`.

298 The `fractions` package allows facilitates arithmetic operations on rational numbers. The command `Fraction(3,4)` returns a representation for $\frac{3}{4}$. You can also convert a float to a rational using `x = Fraction(0.75)`, and express it as a string with `str(x)`.

299 The Python code for Richardson extrapolation taking $\delta = \frac{1}{2}$ is

```
def richardson(f,x,m,n):
  if n==0: return φ(f,x,2**m)
  return (4**n*richardson(f,x,m,n-1)-richardson(f,x,m-1,n-1))/(4**n-1)
```

where we define

```
def φ(f,x,n): return (f(x+1/n) - f(x-1/n))/(2/n)
```

301 The Python package JAX and the older `autograd` implement forward and reverse automatic differentiation. We can build a minimal working example of forward accumulation automatic differentiation by defining a class and overloading the base operators:

```
class Dual:
  def __init__(self, value, deriv=1):
    self.value = value
    self.deriv = deriv
  def __add__(u, v):
    return Dual(value(u) + value(v), deriv(u) + deriv(v))
  __radd__ = __add__
  def __sub__(u, v):
    return Dual(value(u) - value(v), deriv(u) - deriv(v))
  __rsub__ = __sub__
  def __mul__(u, v):
    return Dual(value(u)*value(v),
        value(v)*deriv(u) + value(u)*deriv(v))
  __rmul__ = __mul__
```

```
def sin(u):
    return Dual(sin(value(u)),cos(value(u))*deriv(u))
```

And we'll need some helper functions:

```
def value(x):
    return (x.value if isinstance(x, Dual) else x)
def deriv(x):
    return (x.deriv if isinstance(x, Dual) else 0)
def sin(x): return np.sin(x)
def cos(x): return np.cos(x)
def auto_diff(f,x):
    return f(Dual(x)).deriv
```

We can compute the derivative of $x + \sin x$ at $x = 0$ using

```
auto_diff(lambda x: x + sin(x),0)
```

We can define the dual numbers as   303

```
x1 = Dual(2,np.array([1,0]))
x2 = Dual(π,np.array([0,1]))
y1 = x1*x2 + sin(x2)
y2 = x1*x2 - sin(x2)
```

Python has several packages for automatic differentiation, including dedicated 304
libraries like JAX and machine learning frameworks like TensorFlow and PyTorch

We can use the following trapezoidal quadrature to make a Romberg method 306
using Richardson extrapolation:

```
def trapezoidal(f,x,n):
    F = f(np.linspace(x[0],x[1],n+1))
    return (F[0]/2 + sum(F[1:-1]) + F[-1]/2)*(x[1]-x[0])/n
```

The following code examines the convergence rate of the composite trapezoidal 308
rule using the function $x + (x - x^2)^p$:

```
n = np.logspace(1,2,num=10).astype(int)
error = np.zeros((10,7))
def f(x,p): return ( x + x**p*(2-x)**p )
for p in range(1,8):
    S = trapezoidal(lambda x: f(x,p),(0,2),10**6)
    for i in range(len(n)):
        Sn = trapezoidal(lambda x: f(x,p),(0,2),n[i])
        error[i,p-1] = abs(Sn - S)/S
np.log(error)
```

```
A = np.c_[np.log(n),np.ones_like(n)]
x = np.log(error)
s = np.linalg.lstsq(A,x,rcond=None)[0][0]
info = ['{0}: slope={1:0.1f}'.format(k+1,s[k]) for k in range(7)]
lines = plt.loglog(n,error)
plt.legend(lines, info); plt.show()
```

311
```
def clenshaw_curtis(f,n):
    x = np.cos(π*np.arange(n+1)/n)
    w = np.zeros(n+1); w[0:n+1:2] = 2/(1-np.arange(0,n+1,2)**2)
    return ( 1/n * np.dot(dctI(f(x)), w) )
```

```
from scipy.fft import dct
def dctI(f):
    g = dct(f,type=1)
    return ( np.r_[g[0]/2, g[1:-1], g[-1]/2] )
```

311
```
from scipy.fft import fft
def dctI(f):
    n = len(f)
    g = np.real(fft(np.r_[f, f[n-2:0:-1]]))
    return ( np.r_[g[0]/2, g[1:n-1], g[n-1]/2] )
```

316 We can implement Gauss–Legendre quadrature by first defining the weights

```
def gauss_legendre(n):
    a = np.zeros(n)
    b = np.arange(1,n)**2 / (4*np.arange(1,n)**2 - 1)
    scaling = 2
    nodes, v = la.eigh_tridiagonal(a, np.sqrt(b))
    return ( nodes, scaling*v[0,:]**2 )
```

and then implementing the method as

```
def f(x): return np.cos(x)*np.exp(-x**2)
nodes, weights = gauss_legendre(n)
np.dot(f(nodes), weights)
```

Alternatively, the numpy.polynomial.legendre function `leggauss` computes nodes and weights for Gauss–Legendre quadrature. The function first computes the nodes x_k as eigenvalues of the Jacobi matrix, followed by one Newton step to refine the calculation.

```
nodes, weights = np.polynomial.legendre.leggauss(n)
np.dot(f(nodes), weights)
```

The numpy.random library includes several distributions. Python's Tensor- 325
Flow package also has a large collection in the distributions module of the
tensorflow_probability library.

```
r = np.exp(2j*π*np.linspace(0,1,100))                                       347
z = (3/2*r**2 - 2*r + 0.5)/r**2
plt.plot(z.real,z.imag); plt.axis('equal'); plt.show()
```

The following function determines the coefficients for stencil given by m and n: 349

```
def multistepcoefficients(m,n):
    s = len(m) + len(n) - 1
    A = (np.array(m)+1)**np.c_[range(s)]
    B = [[i*((j+1)**max(0,i-1)) for j in n] for i in range(s)]
    c = la.solve(-np.c_[A[:,1:],B],np.ones((s,1))).flatten()
    return ( np.r_[1,c[:len(m)-1]], c[len(m)-1:] )
```

We'll use the arrays returned by multistepcoefficients to plot the region of
stability.

```
def plotstability(a,b):
    r = np.exp(1j*np.linspace(0,2*π,200))
    z = [np.dot(a,r**np.arange(len(a))) / \
        np.dot(b, r**np.arange(len(b))) for r in r]
    plt.plot(np.real(z),np.imag(z)); plt.axis('equal')
```

The Python recipe for solving a differential equation is quite similar to Julia's 375
recipe, except that the "define the problem" step is merged into the "solve the
problem" step. Python does not have the trapezoidal method, so the Bogacki–
Shampine method is used instead.

1. Load the modules	`import numpy as np;`
	`import matplotlib.pyplot as plt`
	`from scipy.integrate import solve_ivp`
2. Set up the parameters	`def pndlm(t,u): return u[1],-np.sin(u[0])`
	`u0 = [8*π/9,0]; tspan = [0,8*π]`
3. Choose the method	`mthd = 'RK23'`
4. Solve the problem	`sltn = solve_ivp(pndlm,tspan,u0,method=mthd)`
5. Present the solution	`plt.plot(sltn.t,sltn.y[0,:])`
	`plt.plot(sltn.t,sltn.y[1,:])`
	`plt.legend(labels=['θ','ω']); plt.show()`

If a method is not explicitly stated, Python will use the default solver RK45. By
default, the values of sltn.t are those determined and used for adaptive time
stepping. Because such steps can be quite large and far from uniform, especially

for high-order methods, plots using sltn.t and sltn.y may not look smooth. Counterintuitively, higher-order methods such as DOP853 that use smoother interpolating polynomials produce rougher (though still accurate) plots than lower-order methods such as RK23:

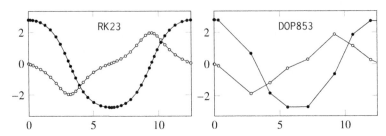

We can request a continuous solution by setting the dense_output flag to True. In this case, solve_ivp returns an additional field sol that retains information from the method so that the solution later be interpolated between the discrete time steps. In practice, we can think of the field sol as a function of the independent variable:

```
sltn = solve_ivp(pndlm,tspan,u0,method=mthd,dense_output=True)
t = np.linspace(tspan[0],tspan[1],200)
y = sltn.sol(t)
plt.plot(t,y[0],t,y[1])
plt.legend(labels=['θ','ω']); plt.show()
```

378 Let's first define the DAE for the pendulum problem. We'll use manifold projection: x = x/ℓ; y = y/ℓ; u = -v*y/x

```
def pendulum(t,U,p):
    x,y,u,v = U; ℓ,g,m = p
    x = x/ℓ; y = y/ℓ; u = -v*y/x # manifold projection
    τ = m*(u**2 + v**2 + g*y)/ℓ**2
    return (u, v, -τ*x/m, -τ*y/m + g)
```

Now, we can solve the problem

```
from scipy.integrate import solve_ivp
θ = π/3; ℓ = 1; tspan = (0,30.0)
U = (ℓ*np.sin(θ), -ℓ*np.cos(θ), 0, 0)
sol = solve_ivp(pendulum, tspan, U, args=((ℓ,1,1),),
    method='RK45',dense_output=True)
t = np.linspace(0,tspan[1],2000);
x,y = sol.sol(t)[:2,:]
plt.plot(x,y); plt.gca().invert_yaxis(); plt.gca().axis('equal');
```

The following code solves the pendulum problem using orthogonal collocation. 383
We'll use the `gauss_legendre` function and `differentiation_matrix` function
defined on page 608 to compute the Gauss–Lobatto nodes and differentiation
matrix.

```python
from scipy.optimize import fsolve
n = 6; N = 100; Δt = 30/N
θ = π/3; ℓ = 1
u0 = [ℓ*np.sin(θ), -ℓ*np.cos(θ), 0, 0, 0]
u = np.concatenate([np.tile(i,n) for i in u0])
M,t = differentiation_matrix(n,Δt)
def D(u,u0): return M@(u - u0)


def pendulum(U,U0,n):
  x,y,u,v,τ = U[:n],U[n:2*n],U[2*n:3*n],U[3*n:4*n],U[4*n:5*n]
  x0,y0,u0,v0,τ0 = U0
  ℓ,g,m = (1,1,1)
  return np.r_[D(x,x0) - u,
    D(y,y0) - v,
    D(u,u0) + τ*x/m,
    D(v,v0) + τ*y/m - g,
    x**2 + y**2 - ℓ**2]


U = u.reshape(5,-1)
for i in range(N):
  u0 = U[:,-1]
  u = fsolve(pendulum,u,args=(u0,n))
  U = np.c_[U,u.reshape(5,-1)]
plt.plot(U[0,:],U[1,:]); plt.gca().axis('equal')
plt.gca().invert_yaxis(); plt.show()
```

Alternatively, we can use GEKKO, a Python front-end to the Advanced
Processing Monitoring (APmonitoring) suite of systems engineering tools,
to solve the pendulum problem using Gauss–Legendre–Lobatto orthogonal
collocation.

```python
from gekko import GEKKO
m = 1; g = 1; ℓ = 1; θ = π/3
model = GEKKO()
x = model.Var(ℓ*np.sin(θ))
y = model.Var(-ℓ*np.cos(θ))
u = model.Var(0)
v = model.Var(0)
τ = model.Var(m*ℓ*g*np.cos(θ)/2)
```

```
model.Equation(x.dt()==u)
model.Equation(y.dt()==v)
model.Equation(m*u.dt()==-τ*x)
model.Equation(m*v.dt()==-τ*y + m*g)
model.Equation(x**2+y**2==ℓ**2)


model.time = np.linspace(0,30,200)
model.options.IMODE=4 # dynamic mode
model.options.NODES=3 # number of collocation nodes
model.solve(disp=False)


plt.plot(x.value,y.value); plt.gca().axis('equal')
plt.gca().invert_yaxis(); plt.show()
```

394 We can use numpy.linalg.solve_banded as a tridiagonal solver.

```
Δx = .01; Δt = .01; L = 2; c = Δt/Δx**2; uL = 0; uR = 0;
x = np.arange(-L,L,Δx); n = len(x)
u = (abs(x)<1)
u[0] += 2*c*uL; u[n-1] += 2*c*uR;
D = np.tile(np.array([[-c,1+2*c,-c]]).T,(1,n))
D[0,1] = 0; D[2,n-2] = 0
for i in range(20):
  u = la.solve_banded((1, 1), D, u)
```

We can compute the runtime by using the timeit package by adding

```
import timeit
start_time = timeit.default_timer()
```

before the block of code and

```
elapsed_time = timeit.default_timer() - start_time
```

after it. This code takes roughly 0.003 seconds on a typical laptop.

394 The scipy.linalg package has several routines for specialized matrices including solve_banded for banded matrices, solveh_banded for symmetric, banded matrices, and solve_circulant for circulant matrices (by dividing in Fourier space). The scipy.sparse.linalg function spsolve can be used to solve general sparse systems.

395 The following code solves the heat equation using the Crank–Nicolson method. While we can use numpy.dot and numpy.linalg.solve_banded for tridiagonal multiplication and inverse, let's use Python's sparse matrix routines instead.

```
from scipy.sparse.linalg import spsolve
Δx = .01; Δt = .01; L = 2; ν = Δt/Δx**2
x = np.arange(-L,L,Δx); n = len(x)
u = (abs(x)<1)
diagonals = [np.ones(n-1), -2*np.ones(n), np.ones(n-1)]
D = sps.diags(diagonals, [-1,0,1], format='csr')
D[0,1] *= 2; D[-1,-2] *= 2
A = 2*sps.identity(n) + ν*D
B = 2*sps.identity(n) - ν*D
for i in range(20):
  u = spsolve(B,A@u)
plt.plot(x,u); plt.show()
```

We'll use the LSODA solver, which automatically switches between Adams– 404
Moulton and BDF routines for stiff nonlinear problems. Using the ipywidgets
package, we can plot the results in a Jupyter notebook as an interactive animation.

```
from scipy.integrate import solve_ivp
n = 400; L = 2; x,Δx = np.linspace(-L,L,n,retstep=True)
def m(u): return u**2
def Du(t,u):
  return np.r_[0,np.diff(m((u[:-1]+u[1:])/2)*np.diff(u))/Δx**2,0]
u0 = (abs(x)<1)
sol = solve_ivp(Du, [0,2], u0, method='LSODA',\
  lband=1,uband=1,dense_output=True)
```

```
from ipywidgets import interactive
def anim(t=0):
  plt.fill_between(x,sol.sol(t),color='#ff9999');
  plt.ylim(0,1);plt.show()
interactive(anim, t = (0,2,0.01))
```

PyClaw is a Python-based interface to Clawpack (Conservation Laws package), 439
a collection of finite volume methods for hyperbolic systems of conservation
laws. The collection was initially developed in Fortran by Randall LeVeque in
the mid-1990s. FiPy is a finite volume PDE solver using Python developed at the
National Institute of Standards and Technology.

The following code solves the heat equation using FEniCS: 453

```
from fenics import *
from mshr import *
square = Rectangle(Point(-0.5, 0), Point(0.5, 1))
circle = Circle(Point(0.0, 0.0), 1)
```

```
mesh = generate_mesh(circle - square, 16)
V = FunctionSpace(mesh, 'P', 1)
u, v, w = TrialFunction(V), TestFunction(V), Function(V)
def boundary(x, on_boundary): return on_boundary
bc = DirichletBC(V, Constant(0), boundary)
f = Expression("exp(-pow(2*x[0]+1,2)-pow(2*x[1]+1,2))", degree=2)
a = dot(grad(u),grad(v))*dx
L = f*v*dx
solve(a == L, w, bc)
File("poisson_solution.pvd") << w
```

460 The numpy.fft function fftfreq returns the DFT sample frequencies.

```
iξ = 1j*np.fft.fftfreq(n,1/n)*(2*π/L)
```

The Python implementation of the solution to the heat equation (16.4) is

```
from numpy.fft import fft,ifft, fftfreq
n = 256; ℓ = 4
ξ2 = (fftfreq(n,1/n)*(2*π/L))**2
def u(t,u0): return np.real(ifft(np.exp(-ξ2*t)*fft(u0)))
```

471 The Python code to solve the Navier–Stokes equation has three parts: define the functions, initialize the variables, and iterate over time. We start by defining functions for $\hat{\mathbf{H}}$ and for the flux used in the Lax–Wendroff scheme.

```
from numpy.fft import fft2,ifft2,fftfreq
def cdiff(Q,step=1): return Q-np.roll(Q,step,0)
def flux(Q,c): return c*cdiff(Q,1) - \
  0.5*c*(1-c)*(cdiff(Q,1)+cdiff(Q,-1))
def H(u,v,iξx,iξy): return fft2(ifft2(u)*ifft2(iξx*u) + \
  ifft2(v)*ifft2(iξy*u))
```

The variable initialization is designed on equal x and y dimensions, but we can easily modify the code for arbitrary domain size.

```
ℓ, n, Δt, ε = 2, 128, 0.001, 0.001; Δx = ℓ/n
x = np.linspace(Δx,ℓ,n)[None,:]; y = x.T
q = 0.5*(1+np.tanh(10*(1-np.abs(ℓ/2 - y)/(ℓ/4))))
Q = np.tile(q, (1,n))
u = Q*(1+0.5*np.sin(ℓ*π*x))
v = np.zeros_like(u)
u,v = fft2(u),fft2(v)
us,vs = u,v
iξx = (1j*fftfreq(n)*n*(2*π/ℓ))[None,:]
iξy = iξx.T
ξ2 = iξx**2+iξy**2
```

```
Hx, Hy = H(u,v,iξx,iξy), H(v,u,iξy,iξx)
M1 = 1/Δt + (ε/2)*ξ2
M2 = 1/Δt - (ε/2)*ξ2
```

Finally, we iterate on (16.14) and the Lax–Wendroff solver for (16.15).

```
for i in range(1200):
  Q -= flux(Q,(Δt/Δx)*np.real(ifft2(v))) + \
    flux(Q.T,(Δt/Δx)*np.real(ifft2(u)).T).T
  Hxo, Hyo = Hx, Hy
  Hx, Hy = H(u,v,iξx,iξy), H(v,u,iξy,iξx)
  us = u - us + (-1.5*Hx + 0.5*Hxo + M1*u)/M2
  vs = v - vs + (-1.5*Hy + 0.5*Hyo + M1*v)/M2
  φ = (iξx*us + iξy*vs)/(ξ2+(ξ2==0))
  u, v = us - iξx*φ, vs - iξy*φ
plt.imshow(Q,'seismic'); plt.show()
```

```
N = 10000; n = np.zeros(20)                                    478
def mat_01(d): return np.random.choice((0,1),size=(d,d))
for d in range(20):
  n[d] = sum([np.linalg.det(mat_01(d))!=0 for i in range(N)])
plt.plot(range(1,21),n/N,'.-'); plt.show()
```

An easy way to input $\mathbf{D}_n$ in Python is with the diag function   479

```
D = np.diag(np.ones(n-1),1) \
  - 2*np.diag(np.ones(n),0) + np.diag(np.ones(n-1),-1)
la.eig(D)
```

Alternatively, to compute the eigenvalues of a real, symmetric tridiagonal matrix we can use the scipy.linalg function eigh_tridiagonal.

```
def det(A):                                                    481
  P,L,U = la.lu(A)
  s = 1
  for i in range(len(P)):
    try:
      m = np.argwhere(P[i+1:,i]).item(0)+1
      P[[i,i+m],:] = P[[i+m,i],:]
      s *= -1
    except:
      pass
  return s*np.prod(np.diagonal(U))
```

481
```
A = np.array([[0,1,0,1],[1,0,2,1],[0,2,0,0],[1,1,0,0]])
def walks(A,i,j,N):
    return [np.linalg.matrix_power(A,n+1)[i-1,j-1] for n in range(N)]
walks(A,1,3,9)
```

482 The following function implements a naïve reverse Cuthill–McKee algorithm for symmetric matrices:

```
def rcuthillmckee(A):
    r = np.argsort(np.bincount(A.nonzero()[0]))
    while r.size:
        q = np.atleast_1d(r[0])
        r = np.delete(r,0)
        while q.size:
            try: p = np.append(p,q[0])
            except: p = np.atleast_1d(q[0])
            k = sps.find(A[q[0],[r]])[1]
            q = np.append(q[1:],r[k])
            r = np.delete(r,k)
    return np.flip(p)
```

The Julia command A[p,p] permutes the rows and columns of A with the permutation array p. But, the similar-looking Python command A[p,p] selects elements along the diagonal. Instead, we should take A[p[:,None],p]. We can test the solution using the following code:

```
A = sps.random(1000,1000,0.001); A += A.T
p = rcuthillmckee(A)
fig, (ax1, ax2) = plt.subplots(1, 2)
ax1.spy(A,ms=1); ax2.spy(A[p[:,None],p],ms=1)
plt.show()
```

482 We'll reuse the code on page 566.

```
A = nx.adjacency_matrix(G)
p = rcuthillmckee(A)
A = A[p[:,None],p]
G = nx.from_scipy_sparse_array(A)
nx.draw(G,nx.circular_layout(G),alpha=0.5,node_color='#828e84')
plt.axis('equal'); plt.show()
```

483 The following code solves the Stigler diet problem using the naïve simplex algorithm developed on page 42.

```
import pandas as pd
```

```
diet = pd.read_csv(bucket+'diet.csv')
A = diet.values[1:,3:].T
b = diet.values[0,3:][:,None]
c = np.ones(((A.shape)[1],1))
food = diet.values[1:,0]
solution = simplex(b,A.T,c)
print("value: ", solution.z)
i = np.argwhere(solution.y!=0).flatten()
print("foods: ", food[i])
```

In practice, we can use the scipy.optimize function `linprog` with a modern method.

```
from scipy import optimize
solution = optimize.linprog(c,-A,-b,method='highs')
solution.fun, food[np.where(solution.x>1e-12)]
```

Let's first define a couple of helper functions to import the data.   484

```
def get_names(filename):
  return np.genfromtxt(bucket+filename+'.txt',delimiter='\n',\
    dtype="str",encoding="utf8").tolist()
def get_adjacency_matrix(filename):
  i = np.genfromtxt(bucket+filename+'.csv',delimiter=',',dtype=int)
  return sps.csr_matrix((np.ones_like(i[:,0]), (i[:,0]-1,i[:,1]-1)))
```

We use the scipy.sparse command `bmat` to form a block matrix. Then we define functions to find the shortest path between nodes a and b.

```
actors = get_names("actors")
movies = get_names("movies")
B = get_adjacency_matrix("actor-movie")
A = sps.bmat([[None,B.T],[B,None]],format='csr')
actormovie = np.r_[actors,movies]


def findpath(A,a,b):
  p = -np.ones(A.shape[1],dtype=np.int64)
  q = [a]; p[a] = -9999; i = 0
  while i<len(q):
    k = sps.find(A[q[i],:])[1]
    k = k[p[k]==-1]
    q.extend(k)
    p[k] = q[i]; i += 1
    if any(k==b): return backtrack(p,b)
  display("No path.")
```

```
def backtrack(p,b):
  s = [b]; i = p[b]
  while i != -9999: s.append(i); i = p[i]
  return s[::-1]
```

```
a = actors.index("Bruce Lee"); b = actors.index("Tommy Wiseau")
actormovie[findpath(A,a,b)].tolist()
```

In practice, we can use the shortest_path function from the scipy.sparse.csgraph library or networkx library.

485   Python formats indices and index pointers in CSR matrices using four-byte integers instead of eight-byte integers as Julia and Matlab do. Storing double-precision floating-point numbers will need $3dmn + m + 1$ four-byte blocks to store a CSR array and $2mn$ blocks for full array in memory—a break-even point of about 0.66. Similarly, double-precision floating-point numbers will need $5dmn + m + 1$ four-byte blocks for the sparse matrix versus $4mn$ blocks for the full matrix—a break-even point of around 0.8.

```
d = 2/3; A = sps.rand(60,80,format='csr',density=d)
nbytes = A.data.nbytes + A.indptr.nbytes + A.indices.nbytes
nbytes, 4*(3*d*np.prod(A.shape) + A.shape[0] + 1)
```

486
```
X = rgb2gray(getimage(bucket+"laura.png"))
m,n = X.shape
def blur(x): return np.exp(-(x/20)**2/2)
A = [[blur(i-j) for i in range(m)] for j in range(m)]
A /= np.sum(A,axis=1)
B = [[blur(i-j) for i in range(n)] for j in range(n)]
B /= np.sum(B,axis=0)
N = 0.01*np.random.rand(m,n)
Y = A@X@B + N
```

```
α = 0.05
X1 = la.lstsq(A,Y)[0]
X2 = la.solve(A.T@A+α**2*np.eye(m),A.T@Y).T
X2 = la.solve(B@B.T+α**2*np.eye(n),B@X2).T
X3 = la.pinv(A,α) @ Y @ la.pinv(B,α)
showimage(np.c_[X,Y,X1,X2,X3])
```

486   The Python code for exercise 3.5 follows:

```
import pandas as pd
df = pd.read_csv(bucket+'filip.csv',header=None)
```

```
y,x = np.array(df[0]),np.array(df[1])
coef = pd.read_csv(bucket+'filip-coeffs.csv',header=None)
β = np.array(coef[0])[None,:]
```

We start by defining a function that determines the coefficients and residuals using three different methods and one that evaluates a polynomial given those coefficients.

```
def solve_filip(x,y):
  V = vandermonde(x,11)
  Q,R = la.qr(V,mode='economic')
  c = np.zeros((3,11),float)
  c[0,:] = la.solve(V.T@V,V.T@y)
  c[1,:] = la.solve(R,Q.T@y)
  c[2,:] = la.pinv(V,1e-14)@y
  r = [la.norm(V@c[i,:].T-y) for i in range(3)]
  return (c,r)
def build_poly(c,x):
  return vandermonde(x,len(c))@c
def vandermonde(x,n):
  return np.vander(x,n,increasing=True)
```

Now, we can solve the problem and plot the solutions.

```
b,r = solve_filip(x,y)
X = np.linspace(min(x),max(x),200)
b = np.r_[b,β]
plt.scatter(x,y,color='#0000ff40')
for i in range(4):
  plt.plot(X,build_poly(b[i],X))
plt.ylim(0.7,0.95);plt.show()
coef.assign(β1=b[0], β2=b[1], β3=b[2])
```

Let's also solve the problem and plot the solutions for the standardized data.

```
def zscore(X,x): return (X - x.mean())/x.std()
k1 = np.linalg.cond(vandermonde(x,11))
k2 = np.linalg.cond(vandermonde(zscore(x,x),11))
print("Condition numbers of the Vandermonde matrix:")
print("{:e}".format(k1))
print("{:e}".format(k2))


c,r = solve_filip(zscore(x,x),zscore(y,y))
plt.scatter(x,y,color='#0000ff40')
for i in range(3):
  Y = build_poly(c[i],zscore(X,x))*y.std() + y.mean()
  plt.plot(X, Y)
```

```
plt.show()
la.norm(c[0]-c[1]),la.norm(c[0]-c[2])
```

488 We'll use pandas to download CSV file. Pandas is built on top of NumPy, so converting from a pandas data frame to a NumPy array is straightforward.

```
import pandas as pd
df = pd.read_csv(bucket+'dailytemps.csv')
t = pd.to_datetime(df["date"]).values
day = (t - t[0])/np.timedelta64(365, 'D')
u = df["temperature"].values[:,None]
def tempsmodel(t): return np.c_[np.sin(2*π*t),\
  np.cos(2*π*t), np.ones_like(t)]
c = la.lstsq(tempsmodel(day),u)[0]
plt.plot(day,u,'o',color='#0000ff15');
plt.plot(day,tempsmodel(day)@c,'k'); plt.show()
```

488 We'll use the Keras library to load the MNIST data. We first compute the sparse SVD of the training set to get singular vectors.

```
from keras.datasets import mnist
from scipy.sparse.linalg import svds
(image_train,label_train),(image_test,label_test) = mnist.load_data()
image_train = np.reshape(image_train, (60000,-1));
V = np.zeros((12,784,10))
for i in range(10):
  D = sps.csr_matrix(image_train[label_train==i], dtype=float)
  U,S,V[:,:,i] = svds(D,12)
```

Let's plot examples of the principal components of "3."

```
pix = [V[i,:,3].reshape(28,28) for i in range(11,-1,-1)]
plt.imshow(np.hstack(pix), cmap="gray")
plt.axis('off'); plt.show()
```

We predict the best digit associated with each test image and build a confusion matrix to check the method's accuracy.

```
image_test = np.reshape(image_test, (10000,-1));
r = np.zeros((10,10000))
for i in range(10):
  q = V[:,:,i].T@(V[:,:,i] @ image_test.T) - image_test.T
  r[i,:] = np.sum(q**2,axis=0)
prediction = np.argmin(r,axis=0)
confusion = np.zeros((10,10)).astype(int)
for i in range(10):
  confusion[i,:] = np.bincount(prediction[label_test==i],minlength=10)
```

Finally, we can view the confusion matrix as a data frame.

```
import pandas as pd
pd.DataFrame(confusion)
```

We use singular value decomposition to find a low-dimensional subspace relating   490
actors and genres. Then we find the closest actors in that subspace using cosine
similarity. We'll use the helper functions get_names and get_adjacency_matrix
from page 591.

```
actors = get_names("actors")
genres = get_names("genres")
A = get_adjacency_matrix("movie-genre"); A /= A.sum(axis=0)
B = get_adjacency_matrix("actor-movie")

from scipy.sparse.linalg import svds
U,S,Vᵀ = svds(A@B, 12)
Q = Vᵀ/np.sqrt((Vᵀ**2).sum(axis=0))

q = Q[:,actors.index("Steve Martin")]
z = Q.T @ q
r = np.argsort(-z)
[actors[i] for i in r[:10]]

p = (U*S) @ q
r = np.argsort(-p)
[(genres[i],p[i]/p.sum()) for i in r[:10]]
```

```
X = np.array([[3,3,12],[1,15,14],[10,2,13],[12,15,14],[0,11,12]])   491
reference = X[0,:]; X = X - reference
A = np.array([2,2,-2])*X
b = (X**2)@np.array([[1],[1],[-1]])
x_ols = la.lstsq(A,b)[0] + reference[:,None]
x_tls = tls(A,b) + reference[:,None]
```

```
import pandas as pd                                                  491
df = pd.read_csv(bucket+'shotspotter.csv')
c = 328.6
X = df.iloc[:-1].to_numpy()
reference = X[0,:]; X = X - reference
A = np.array([2,2,2,-2*c**2])*X
b = (X**2)@np.array([[1],[1],[1],[-1*c**2]])
x_ols = la.lstsq(A,b)[0] + reference[:,None]
error = x_ols.flatten() - df.iloc[-1].to_numpy()
```

```
492    E = [la.eigvals(np.random.randn(n,n)) for i in range(2500)]
       E = np.concatenate(E)
       plt.plot(E.real, E.imag,'.',c='#0000ff10',mec='none')
       plt.axis('equal'); plt.show()
```

```
492    def rayleigh(A,x=[]):
         n = len(A)
         if x==[]: x = np.random.randn(n,1)
         while True:
           x = x/la.norm(x)
           ρ = x.T @ A @ x
           M = A - ρ*np.eye(n)
           if abs(la.det(M))<1e-10:
             return (ρ,x)
           x = la.solve(M,x)
```

493   We'll define a function for implicit QR method and verify it on a matrix with known eigenvalues.

```
def implicitqr(A):
  tolerance = 1e-12
  n = len(A)
  H = la.hessenberg(A)
  while True:
    if abs(H[n-1,n-2]) < tolerance:
      n -= 1
      if n<2: return np.diag(H)
    Q,_ = la.qr([[H[0,0]-H[n-1,n-1]], [H[1,0]]])
    H[:2,:n] = Q @ H[:2,:n]
    H[:n,:2] = H[:n,:2] @ Q.T
    for i in range(1,n-1):
      Q,_ = la.qr([[H[i,i-1]], [H[i+1,i-1]]])
      H[i:i+2,:n] = Q @ H[i:i+2,:n]
      H[:n,i:i+2] = H[:n,i:i+2] @ Q.T
```

```
n = 20; S = np.random.randn(n,n);
D = np.diag(np.arange(1,n+1)); A = S @ D @ la.inv(S)
implicitqr(A)
```

494   We'll use the helper functions get_names and get_adjacency_matrix from page 591.

```
actors = get_names("actors")
B = get_adjacency_matrix("actor-movie")
r,c = (B.T@B).nonzero()
M = sps.csr_matrix((np.ones(len(r)),(r,c)))
v = np.ones(M.shape[0])
for k in range(10):
  v = M@v; v /= np.linalg.norm(v)
r = np.argsort(-v)
[actors[i] for i in r[:10]]
```

The following function approximates the SVD by starting with a set of k random 494 vectors and performing a few steps of the naïve QR method to generate a k-dimensional subspace that is relatively close to the space of dominant singular values:

```
def randomizedsvd(A,k):
  Z = np.random.rand(A.shape[1],k)
  Q,R = la.qr(A@Z, mode='economic')
  for i in range(4):
    Q,R = la.qr(A.T @ Q, mode='economic')
    Q,R = la.qr(A @ Q, mode='economic')
  W,S,Vᵀ = la.svd(Q.T @ A,full_matrices=False)
  U = Q @ W
  return (U,S,Vᵀ)
```

Let's convert an image to an array, compute its randomized SVD, and then display the original image side-by-side with the rank-reduced version.

```
A = rgb2gray(getimage(bucket+'red-fox.jpg'))
U, S, Vᵀ = randomizedsvd(A,10);
img = np.c_[A, np.minimum(np.maximum((U*S)@Vᵀ,0),255)]
showimage(img)
```

```
from scipy.sparse.linalg import svds                              495
m = 5000
A = np.array([[1/((i+j+1)*(i+j+2)/2 - j)
  for i in range(m)] for j in range(m)])
svds(A, 1)[1][0]
```

The following functions solve the Poisson equation: 496

```
n = 50; ξ = np.arange(1,n+1)/(n+1); Δx = 1/(n+1)
I = sps.identity(n)
D = sps.diags([1, -2, 1], [-1, 0, 1], shape=(n, n))
A = ( sps.kron(sps.kron(D,I),I) + sps.kron(I,sps.kron(D,I)) +
```

```
   sps.kron(I,sps.kron(I,D)) )/Δx**2
f = np.array([(x-x**2)*(y-y**2) + (x-x**2)*(z-z**2)+(y-y**2)*(z-z**2)
    for x in ξ for y in ξ for z in ξ])
ue = np.array([(x-x**2)*(y-y**2)*(z-z**2)/2
    for x in ξ for y in ξ for z in ξ])
```

```
from scipy.sparse.linalg import spsolve
def stationary(A,b,ω=0,n=400):
  ε = []; u = np.zeros_like(b)
  P = sps.diags(A.diagonal(),0) + ω*sps.tril(A,-1)
  for i in range(n):
    u += spsolve(P,b-A@u,'NATURAL')
    ε = np.append(ε,la.norm(u - ue,1))
  return ε
```

```
def conjugategradient(A,b,n=400):
  ε = []; u = np.zeros_like(b)
  r = b - A@u; p = np.copy(r)
  for i in range(n):
    Ap = A@p
    α = np.dot(r,p)/np.dot(Ap,p)
    u += α*p; r -= α*Ap
    β = np.dot(r,Ap)/np.dot(Ap,p)
    p = r - β*p
    ε = np.append(ε,la.norm(u - ue,1))
  return ε
```

```
ε = np.zeros((400,4))
ε[:,0] = stationary(A,-f,0)
ε[:,1] = stationary(A,-f,1)
ε[:,2] = stationary(A,-f,1.9)
ε[:,3] = conjugategradient(A,-f)
plt.semilogy(ε);
plt.legend(["Jacobi","Gauss-Seidel","SOR","Conj. Grad."]); plt.show()
```

The three stationary methods take about 13, 34, and 34 seconds to complete 400 iterations. In contrast, the conjugate gradient method takes around 1.2 seconds to complete the same number of iterations—and just 0.5 seconds to reach machine precision. The SciPy routine spsolve uses approximate minimum degree column ordering as the default, which would destroy the lower triangular structure. Instead, stationary sets the option permc_spec = 'NATURAL' to maintain the natural ordering. While SciPy has a dedicated sparse triangular matrix routine spsolve_triangular, it is excruciatingly slow, taking almost a second to complete just one iteration of the stationary method! And directly solving the problem using spsolve(A,-f) takes over 12 minutes.

Python doesn't have a convenient function for generating primes. We could write 498
a function that implements the Sieve of Eratosthenes, but it will be easier to
import a list of the primes (pregenerated using Julia).

```python
from scipy.sparse.linalg import cg
n = 20000
d = 2 ** np.arange(15); d = np.r_[-d,d]
P = sps.diags(np.loadtxt(bucket+"primes.csv"))
B = [np.ones(n - abs(d)) for d in d]
A = P + sps.diags(B, d)
b = np.zeros(n); b[0] = 1
cg(A, b, M=P)[0][0]
```

Python code for the radix-3 FFT in exercise 6.1 is   499

```python
def fftx3(c):
  n = len(c)
  ω = np.exp(-2j*π/n);
  if np.mod(n,3) == 0:
    k = np.arange(n/3)
    u = np.stack((fftx3(c[:-2:3]),\
        ω**k * fftx3(c[1:-1:3]),\
        ω**(2*k) * fftx3(c[2::3])))
    F = np.exp(-2j*π/3)**np.array([[0,0,0],[0,1,2],[0,2,4]])
    return (F @ u).flatten()
  else:
    k = np.arange(n)[:,None]
    F = ω**(k*k.T);
    return F @ c
```

Python code for exercise 6.2 is as follows   499

```python
def multiply(p_,q_):
  from scipy.signal import fftconvolve
  p = np.flip(np.array([int(i) for i in list(p_)]))
  q = np.flip(np.array([int(i) for i in list(q_)]))
  pq = np.rint(fftconvolve(p,q)).astype(int)
  pq = np.r_[pq,0]
  carry = pq//10
  while (np.any(carry)):
    pq -= carry*10
    pq[1:] += carry[:-1]
    carry = pq//10
  return ''.join([str(i) for i in np.flip(pq)]).lstrip('0')
```

We can alternatively use the numpy.fft commands rfft and irfft. We just need to ensure that the zero-padded array has an even length n. In this case, we use

```
from numpy.fft import rfft,irfft
m = (len(p)+len(q)) + (len(p)+len(q))%2
pq = np.round(irfft(rfft(p,m)*rfft(q,m))).astype(int)
```

in the place of pq = convolve(p,q). Note that Python uses arbitrary-precision integers, so we can simply multiply the numbers directly. Python uses the recursive Karatsuba algorithm to multiply integers, which is significantly faster than grade school multiplication but still slower than the Schönhage–Strassen algorithm for larger numbers.

500 Unlike in Julia and Matlab, the SciPy fft and ifft functions operate on the last dimension by default. So we'll need to tell these functions to use the first dimension.

```
from scipy.fft import fft,ifft
def dct(f):
  n = f.shape[0]
  ω = np.exp(-0.5j*π*np.arange(n)/n).reshape(-1,1)
  i = [*range(0,n,2),*range(n-1-n%2,0,-2)]
  return np.real(ω*fft(f[i,:],axis=0))
```

```
def idct(f):
  n = f.shape[0]
  ω = np.exp(-0.5j*π*np.arange(n)/n).reshape(-1,1)
  i = [n-(i+1)//2 if i%2 else i//2 for i in range(n)]
  f[0,:] = f[0,:]/2
  return np.real(ifft(f/ω,axis=0))[i,:]*2
```

The two-dimensional DCT and inverse DCT are

```
def dct2(f): return dct(dct(f.T).T)
def idct2(f): return idct(idct(f.T).T)
```

501 The following function returns a sparse matrix of Fourier coefficients along with the reconstructed compressed image:

```
from scipy.fft import dctn, idctn
def dctcompress2(A,d):
  n = A.shape
  n0 = tuple(int(np.sqrt(d)*i) for i in A.shape)
  B = dctn(A)[:n0[0],:n0[1]]
  return B, idctn(B,s=n)
```

```
def aitken(x1,x2,x3):                                                    505
    return x3-(x3-x2)**2/(x3-2*x2+x1), (x1*x3-x2**2)/(x3-2*x2+x1)
n = 50000
p = np.cumsum([(-1)**i*4/(2*i+1) for i in range(n)])
p1,p2 = aitken(p[:n-2],p[1:n-1],p[2:n])
plt.loglog(abs(π-p)); plt.loglog(abs(π-p2)); plt.loglog(abs(π-p1))
```

We'll find the solution to the system of equations in exercise 8.12. Let's first   508
define the system and the gradient.

```
def f(x,y): return ( np.array([(x**2+y**2)**2-2*(x**2-y**2),
    (x**2+y**2-1)**3-x**2*y**3]) )
def df(x,y): return(np.array([ \
    [4*x*(x**2+y**2-1), 4*y*(x**2+y**2+1)],
    [6*x*(x**2+y**2-1)**2-2*x*y**3, \
     6*y*(x**2+y**2-1)**2-3*x**2*y**2]]))
```

The homotopy continuation method is

```
def homotopy(f,df,x):
    from scipy.integrate import solve_ivp
    def dxdt(t,x,p): return(la.solve(-df(x[0],x[1]),p))
    sol = solve_ivp(dxdt,[0,1],x,args=(f(x[0],x[1]),))
    return sol.y[:,-1]
```

and Newton's method is

```
def newton(f,df,x):
    for i in range(100):
        Δx = -la.solve(df(x[0],x[1]),f(x[0],x[1]))
        x += Δx
        if (la.norm(Δx) < 1e-8): return x
```

We'll write a function that computes point addition and point doubling.   509

```
def addpoint(P,Q):
    a = 0
    r = (1<<256) - (1<<32) - 977
    if P[0] == Q[0]:
        d = pow(2*P[1], -1, r)
        λ = ((3*pow(P[0],2,r)+a)*d) % r
    else:
        d = pow(Q[0] - P[0], -1, r)
        λ = ((Q[1] - P[1])*d) % r
    x = (pow(λ,2,r) - P[0] - Q[0]) % r
    y = (-λ*(x - P[0]) - P[1]) % r
    return [x,y]
```

Now, we can implement the double-and-add algorithm.

```
def isodd(m): return ((m&1)==1)
def dbl_add(m,P):
  if m>1:
    Q = dbl_add(m>>1,P)
    return addpoint(addpoint(Q,Q),P) if isodd(m) else addpoint(Q,Q)
  else:
    return P
```

Finally, we test the algorithm using Alice and Bob.

```
Px = int("79BE667EF9DCBBAC55A06295CE87"\
 + "0B07029BFCDB2DCE28D959F2815B16F81798",16)
Py = int("483ADA7726A3C4655DA4FBFC0E11"\
 + "08A8FD17B448A68554199C47D08FFB10D4B8",16)
P = [Px,Py]
m, n = 1829442, 3727472
mP = dbl_add(m,P)
nmP = dbl_add(n,mP)
```

512 The following function modifies `spline_natural` on page 574 to compute the coefficients $\{m_0, m_1, \ldots, m_{n-1}\}$ for a spline with periodic boundary conditions:

```
def spline_periodic(x,y):
  h = np.diff(x)
  d = 6*np.diff(np.diff(np.r_[y[-2],y])/np.r_[h[-1],h])
  α = h[:-1]
  β = h + np.r_[h[-1],h[:-1]]
  C = np.diag(β)+np.diag(α,1)
  C[0,-1]=h[-1]; C += C.T
  m = la.solve(C,d)
  return np.r_[m,m[0]]
```

Now we can compute a parametric spline interpolant with nx*n points through a set of n random points using the function `evaluate_spline` defined on page 574:

```
n, nx = 10, 20
x, y = np.random.rand(n), np.random.rand(n)
x, y = np.r_[x,x[0]], np.r_[y,y[0]]
t = np.cumsum(np.sqrt(np.diff(x)**2+np.diff(y)**2))
t = np.r_[0,t]
T,X = evaluate_spline(t,x,spline_periodic(t,x),nx*n)
T,Y = evaluate_spline(t,y,spline_periodic(t,y),nx*n)
plt.plot(X,Y,x,y,'o'); plt.show()
```

512 The following code computes and plots the interpolating curves:

```
n = 20; N = 200
x = np.linspace(-1,1,n)[:,None]
X = np.linspace(-1,1,N)[:,None]
y = (x>0)


def φ1(x,a): return abs(x-a)**3
def φ2(x,a): return np.exp(-20*(x-a)**2)
def φ3(x,a): return x**a
def interp(φ,a):
  return φ(X,a.T)@la.solve(φ(x,a.T),y)


Y1 = interp(φ1,x)
Y2 = interp(φ2,x)
Y3 = interp(φ3,np.arange(n))
plt.plot(x,y,X,Y1,X,Y2,X,Y3)
plt.ylim((-.5,1.5)); plt.show()
```

We define a function to solve linear boundary value problems.   514

```
def solve(L,f,bc,x):
  h = x[1]-x[0]
  S = np.array([[1,-1/2,1/6],[-2,0,2/3],[1,1/2,1/6]]) \
          /np.array([h**2,h,1])
  S = np.r_[np.zeros((1,3)),L(x)@S.T,np.zeros((1,3))]
  d = np.r_[bc[0], f(x), bc[1]]
  A = np.diag(S[1:,0],-1) + np.diag(S[:,1]) + np.diag(S[:-1,2],1)
  A[0,:3] , A[-1,-3:] = np.array([1,4,1])/6 , np.array([1,4,1])/6
  return la.solve(A,d)
```

Next, we define a function that will interpolate between collocation points.

```
def build(c,x,N):
  X = np.linspace(x[0],x[-1],N)
  h = x[1] - x[0]
  i = (X // h).astype(int)
  i[-1] = i[-2]
  C = np.c_[c[i],c[i+1],c[i+2],c[i+3]]
  B = lambda x: np.c_[(1-x)**3, 4-3*(2-x)*x**2, \
          4-3*(1+x)*(1-x)**2, x**3]/6
  Y = np.sum(C*B((X-x[i])/h),axis=1)
  return (X,Y)
```

Now, we can solve the Bessel equation.

```
from scipy.special import jn_zeros, j0
```

```
n = 15; N = 141
L = lambda x: np.c_[x,np.ones_like(x),x]
f = lambda x: np.zeros_like(x)
b = jn_zeros(0,4)[-1]
x = np.linspace(0,b,n)
c = solve(L,f,[1,0],x)
X,Y = build(c,x,N)
plt.plot(X,Y,X,j0(X)); plt.show()
```

Finally, we examine the error and convergence rate.

```
N = 10*2**np.arange(6)
ϵ = []
for n in N:
  x = np.linspace(0,b,n)
  c = solve(L,f,[1,0],x)
  [X,Y] = build(c,x,n)
  ϵ = np.r_[ϵ,la.norm(Y-j0(X))/n]
plt.loglog(N,ϵ,'.-'); plt.show()
```

```
from numpy.polynomial.polynomial import polyfit
s = polyfit(np.log(N),np.log(ϵ),1)[1]
print("slope = " + "{:.4f}".format(s))
```

517 Let's compute the fractional derivatives of e^{-16x^2} and $x(1 - |x|)$.

```
from numpy.fft import fft,ifft,fftshift
def f(x): return np.exp(-16*x**2)
def f(x): return x*(1-np.abs(x))
n = 2000; ℓ = 2
x = np.arange(n)/n*ℓ-ℓ/2
ξ = fftshift(np.arange(n)-n/2)*2*π/ℓ
```

We can use Jupyter widgets to create an interactive plot of the derivatives.

```
from ipywidgets import interactive
def anim(derivative=0):
  u = np.real(ifft((1j*ξ)**derivative*fft(f(x))))
  plt.plot(x,u,color='k'); plt.show()
interactive(anim, derivative = (0,2,0.01))
```

518 We can define the model architecture in Keras as

```
import tensorflow as tf
from tensorflow import keras
from keras.layers import Conv2D, AvgPool2D, Dense, Flatten
```

```
model = keras.models.Sequential([
  Conv2D(6,5,activation='tanh',padding='same',input_shape=(28,28,1)),
  AvgPool2D(),
  Conv2D(16, 5, activation='tanh'),
  AvgPool2D(),
  Conv2D(120, 5, activation='tanh'),
  Flatten(),
  Dense(84, activation='tanh'),
  Dense(10, activation='sigmoid')
])
```

Keras provides a summary of the model.

```
model.build(); model.summary()
```

Let's load the MNIST training and test data. We'll convert each 28×28-pixel image into a $28 \times 28 \times 1$-element floating-point array with values between zero and one.

```
from keras.datasets import mnist
(image_train,label_train),(image_test,label_test) = mnist.load_data()
image_train = tf.expand_dims(image_train/255.0, 3)
image_test = tf.expand_dims(image_test/255.0, 3)
```

We compile the model, defining the loss function, the optimizer, and the metrics.

```
loss = keras.losses.SparseCategoricalCrossentropy(from_logits=True)
model.compile(optimizer="adam", loss=loss, metrics=["accuracy"])
```

Now, we can train the model.

```
model.fit(image_train, label_train, epochs=5)
```

Finally, let's see how well the model works on an independent set of similar data.

```
model.evaluate(image_test,label_test)
```

The LeNet-5 model has about a two percent error rate. With more epochs, it has about a one percent error rate.

We'll first solve the toy problem.   519

```
from scipy.optimize import curve_fit
def ε(X, x, y, t):
  return np.sqrt((X[0] - x)**2 + (X[1] - y)**2) - (X[2]-t)
X = np.array([[3,3,12],[1,15,14],[10,2,13],[12,15,14],[0,11,12]])
x_nls = curve_fit(ε, X.T, np.zeros(len(X)), p0 = (0,0,0))
```

Now, let's apply the method to the ShotSpotter data. First, we get the data.

```
import pandas as pd
df = pd.read_csv(bucket+'shotspotter.csv')
X = df.iloc[:-1].to_numpy()
```

Then, we find the solution.

```
def ε(X, x, y, z, t):
    return np.sqrt((X[0]-x)**2+(X[1]-y)**2+(X[2]-z)**2)-328.6*(X[3]-t)
x_nls = curve_fit(ε, X.T, np.zeros(len(X)), p0 = X[0,:])
```

Finally, we compute the error.

```
x_nls[0] - df.iloc[-1].to_numpy()
```

520
```
d = np.array([0,1,2,3])[:,None]; n = len(d)
factorial = [np.math.factorial(i) for i in range(n+1)]
V = d**np.arange(n) / factorial[:-1]
C = la.inv(V)
C = np.c_[C,C@d**n/factorial[-1]]
```

The coefficients of the finite difference approximation of the derivative and coefficient of the truncation error are given by rats(C[1,:]) where the function rats is defined on page 580.

521
```
def richardson(f,x,m):
    D = np.zeros(m)
    for i in range(m):
        D[i] = φ(f,x,2**(i+1))
        for j in range(i-1,-1,-1):
            D[j] = (4**(i-j)*D[j+1] - D[j])/(4**(i-j) - 1)
    return D[1]
```

522 We'll extend the Dual class on page 580 by adding methods for division, cosine, and square root to the class definition.

```
def __truediv__(u, v):
    return Dual(value(u) / value(v),
        (value(v)*deriv(u)-value(u)*deriv(v))/(value(v)*value(v)))
__rtruediv__ = __truediv__
def cos(u):
    return Dual(cos(value(u)),-1*sin(value(u))*deriv(u))
def sqrt(u):
    return Dual(sqrt(value(u)),deriv(u)/(2*sqrt(value(u))))
```

We also define the helper functions.

```
def cos(u): return np.cos(u)
def sqrt(u): return np.sqrt(u)
```

Note that in the definition of cos(u) we multiplied by the -1 instead of using a unitary negative operator because we haven't defined such an operator for the Dual class. Now, we can implement Newton's method.

```
def get_zero(f,x):
    ε = 1e-14; δ = 1
    while abs(δ) > ε:
        fx = f(Dual(x))
        δ = value(fx)/deriv(fx)
        x -= δ
    return x
```

```
get_zero(lambda x: 4*sin(x) + sqrt(x), 4)
```

To find a minimum or maximum of $f(x)$, we substitute the following two lines into the Newton solver:

```
        fx = f(Dual(Dual(x)))
        δ = deriv(value(fx))/deriv(deriv(fx))
```

```
def cauchyderivative(f, a, p, n = 20, ε = 0.1):
    ω = np.exp(2*π*1j*np.arange(n)/n)
    return np.math.factorial(p)/(n*ε**p)*sum(f(a+ε*ω)/ω**p)
```
523

```
f = lambda x: np.exp(x)/(np.cos(x)**3 + np.sin(x)**3)
cauchyderivative(f, 0, 6)
```

The following function computes the nodes and weights for Gauss–Legendre 523 quadrature by using Newton's method to find the roots of $P_n(x)$:

```
def gauss_legendre(n):
    x = -np.cos((4*np.arange(n)+3)*π/(4*n+2))
    Δ = np.ones_like(x)
    dP = 0
    while(max(abs(Δ))>1e-16):
        P0, P1 = x, np.ones_like(x)
        for k in range(2,n+1):
            P0, P1 = ((2*k - 1)*x*P0-(k-1)*P1)/k, P0
        dP = n*(x*P0 - P1)/(x**2-1)
        Δ = P0 / dP
        x -= Δ
```

```
    return ( x, 2/((1-x**2)*dP**2) )
```

524
```
ξ,w = np.polynomial.hermite.hermgauss(40)
def u0(x): return np.sin(x)
def u(t,x):
    return [np.dot(w,u0(x-2*np.sqrt(t)*ξ)/np.sqrt(π)) for x in x]
x = np.linspace(-12,12,100)
plt.plot(x,u(1,x)); plt.show()
```

524 Let's define a general function

```
def mc_π(n,d,m):
    return sum(sum(np.random.rand(d,n,m)**2)<1)/n*2**d
```

that computes the volume of an d-sphere using n samples repeated m times. We can verify the convergence rate by looping over several values of n.

```
m = 20; error = []; N = 2**np.arange(20)
error = [sum(abs(π - mc_π(n,2,m)))/m for n in N]
plt.loglog(N,error,marker=".",linestyle="None")
s = np.polyfit(np.log(N),np.log(error),1)
plt.loglog(N,np.exp(s[1])*N**s[0])
plt.show()
```

525 We can compute Gauss–Lobatto nodes by modifying the function gauss_legendre defined on page 582.

```
def gauss_legendre(n,lobatto=False):
    a = np.zeros(n)
    b = np.arange(1,n)**2 / (4*np.arange(1,n)**2 - 1)
    if lobatto: b[-1] = (n-1)/(2*(n-1) - 1)
    scaling = 2
    nodes, v = la.eigh_tridiagonal(a, np.sqrt(b))
    return ( nodes, scaling*v[0,:]**2 )
```

```
def differentiation_matrix(n,Δt=1):
    nodes, _ = gauss_legendre(n+1,lobatto=True)
    t = (nodes[1:]+1)/2
    A = np.vander(t,increasing=True)*np.arange(1,n+1)
    B = np.diag(t)@np.vander(t,increasing=True)
    return (A@la.inv(B)/Δt, t)
```

We'll use the scipy.optimize function fsolve to solve the nonlinear system

```
from scipy.optimize import fsolve
```

```
n = 20; u0 = 1.0; α = 0.9
M,t = differentiation_matrix(n)
def D(u,u0): return M@(u - u0)
def F(u,u0,α): return D(u,u0) - α*u**2
u = fsolve(F,u0*np.ones(n),args=(u0,α))
plt.plot(t, u, marker="o")
```

Finally, we solve the same problem using the pseudospectral method.

```
N = 20; Δt = 1.0/N; n = 8; α
M,t = differentiation_matrix(n,Δt)
def D(u,u0): return M@(u - u0)
u0 = 1.0; U = np.array(u0); T = np.array(0)
for i in range(N):
  u = fsolve(F,u0*np.ones(n),args=(u0,α))
  u0 = u[-1]
  T = np.append(T,(i + t)*Δt)
  U = np.append(U,u)
plt.plot(T, U, marker="o")
```

The following code plots the region of absolute stability for a Runge–Kutta   527
method with tableau A and b:

```
N = 100; n = b.shape[1]
r = np.zeros((N,N))
E = np.ones((n,1))
x,y = np.linspace(-4,4,N),np.linspace(-4,4,N)
for i in range(N):
  for j in range(N):
    z = x[i] + 1j*y[j]
    r[j,i] = abs(1 + z*b@(la.solve(np.eye(n) - z*A,E)))
plt.contour(x,y,r,[1]); plt.show()
```

```
i = np.arange(4)[:,None]                                                    528
def factorial(k): return np.cumprod(np.r_[1,range(1,k)])
c1 = la.solve(((-i)**i.T/factorial(4)).T,np.array([0,1,0,0]))
c2 = la.solve(((-(i+1))**i.T/factorial(4)).T,np.array([1,0,0,0]))
```

The following function returns the orbit of points in the complex plane for   529
an nth order Adams–Bashforth–Moulton PE(CE)^m.   It calls the function
multistepcoefficients defined on page 583.

```
def PECE(n,m):
  _,a = multistepcoefficients([0,1],range(1,n))
  _,b = multistepcoefficients([0,1],range(0,n))
```

```
def c(r): return np.r_[r-1,\
    np.full(m, r + np.dot(b[1:],r**np.arange(1,n)))/b[0]),\
    (a @ r**np.arange(1,n))/b[0]]
return [np.roots(np.flip(c(r)))/b[0] \
    for r in np.exp(1j*np.linspace(0,2*π,200))]
```

```
for i in range(5):
  z = PECE(4,i)
  plt.scatter(np.real(z),np.imag(z),s=0.5)
plt.axis('equal'); plt.show()
```

529 The scipy.interpolate function pade(a,m,n) computes a Padé approximant from Taylor polynomial coefficients. For instruction, let's write our own.

```
def pade(a,m,n):
  A = np.eye(m+n+1);
  for i in range(n): A[i+1:,m+i+1] = -a[:m+n-i]
  pq = la.solve(A,a[:m+n+1])
  return pq[:m+1], np.r_[1,pq[m+1:]]
```

Now, compute the coefficients of $P_m(x)$ and $Q_n(x)$ for the Taylor polynomial approximation of $\log(x + 1)$.

```
m = 3; n = 2
a = np.r_[0, (-1)**np.arange(m+n)/(1+np.arange(m+n))]
p,q = pade(a,m,n)
```

Finally, shift and combine the coefficients using upper inverse Pascal matrices.

```
def S(n): return la.invpascal(n+1, kind='upper')
S(m)@p, S(n)@q
```

531 The solution to the SIR problem is

```
from scipy.integrate import solve_ivp
def SIR(t,u,β,γ): return (-β*u[0]*u[1],β*u[0]*u[1]-γ*u[1],γ*u[1])
sol = solve_ivp(SIR, [0, 15], [0.99, 0.01, 0],\
   args=(2,0.4), dense_output=True)
t = np.linspace(0,15,200); u = sol.sol(t)
plt.plot(t,u[0,:],t,u[1,:],t,u[2,:]); plt.show()
```

We can add the optional argument t_eval=np.linspace(0,15,100) to solve_ivp to evaluate the solution at additional points for a smoother plot.

532 The solution to the Duffing equation is

```
from scipy.integrate import solve_ivp
def duffing(t,x,g): return(x[1],-g*x[1]+x[0]-x[0]**3+0.3*np.cos(t))
sol = solve_ivp(duffing,[0,200], [1, 0], args=(0.37,),
    method='DOP853',dense_output=True)
t = np.linspace(0,200,2000); y = sol.sol(t)
plt.plot(y[0,:],y[1,:]); plt.show()
```

The following code solves the Airy equation over the domain $x = (-12, 0)$ using   533
the shooting method. The function shoot_airy solves the initial value problem
using two initial conditions—the given boundary condition $y(-12)$ and our guess
for $y'(-12)$. The function returns the difference in the value $y(0)$ computed by
the solve_ivp and our given boundary condition $y(0)$. We then use fsolve to
find the zero-error initial value.

```
from scipy.integrate import solve_ivp
from scipy.optimize import fsolve
def airy(x,y): return (y[1],x*y[0])
domain = [-12,0]; bc = [1,1]; guess = 5
def shoot_airy(guess):
  sol = solve_ivp(airy,domain,[bc[0],guess[0]])
  return sol.y[0,-1] - bc[1]
v = fsolve(shoot_airy,guess)[0]
```

The scipy.integrate function solve_bvp solves the boundary problem using a
different approach, solving a collocation system with Newton's method.

We'll use the function multistepcoefficients, defined on page 583.   534

```
m = [0,1,2,3,4]; n = [1]
a,b = multistepcoefficients(m,n)
b = np.r_[0,b]
```

```
def λk(r): return np.dot(a,r**-np.arange(len(a))) /\
  np.dot(b,r**-np.arange(len(b)))
r = np.linspace(0.2,6,100)
plt.plot([λk(r) for r in r],r)
plt.plot([λk(-r) for r in r],r); plt.xlim([-2,2]);
```

The following code implements the Dufort–Frankel method to solve the heat   535
equation. (As mentioned elsewhere, this approach is not recommended.)

```
dx = 0.01; dt = 0.01; n = 400
L = 1; x = np.arange(-L,L,dx); m = len(x)
U = np.empty((n,m))
U[0,:] = np.exp(-8*x**2); U[1,:] = U[0,:]
```

```
c = dt/dx**2; a = 0.5 + c; b = 0.5 - c
B = c*sps.diags([1, 1], [-1, 1], shape=(m, m)).tocsr()
B[0,1] *=2; B[-1,-2] *=2
for i in range(1,n-1):
  U[i+1,:] = (B@U[i,:]+b*U[i-1,:])/a
```

We can use the ipywidgets library to build an interactive plot of the solution.

```
from ipywidgets import interactive
def anim(i=0):
  plt.fill_between(x,U[i,:],color='#ff9999');
  plt.ylim(0,1);plt.show()
interactive(anim, i=(0,n-1))
```

537 The following code solves the Schrödinger equation:

```
from scipy.sparse.linalg import spsolve
def ψ0(x,ε): return np.exp(-(x-1)**2/(2*ε))/(π*ε)**(1/4)
def schroedinger(n,m,ε):
  x,dx = np.linspace(-4,4,n,retstep=True); Δt = 2*π/m; V = x**2/2
  ψ = ψ0(x,ε)
  D = 0.5j*ε*sps.diags([1, -2, 1], [-1, 0, 1], shape=(n, n))/dx**2 \
    - 1j/ε*sps.diags(V,0)
  D[0,1] *= 2; D[-1,-2] *= 2
  A = sps.eye(n) + (Δt/2)*D
  B = sps.eye(n) - (Δt/2)*D
  for i in range(m):
    ψ = spsolve(B,A*ψ)
  return ψ
```

We'll loop over several values for time steps and mesh sizes and plot the error.

```
ε = 0.3; m = 20000; N = np.logspace(2,3.7,6).astype(int)
x = np.linspace(-4,4,m)
ψ_m = -ψ0(x,ε)
error_t = []; error_x = []
for n in N:
  x = np.linspace(-4,4,n)
  ψ_n = -ψ0(x,ε)
  error_t.append(la.norm(ψ_m - schroedinger(m,n,ε))/m)
  error_x.append(la.norm(ψ_n - schroedinger(n,m,ε))/n)
plt.loglog(2*π/N,error_t,'.-r',8/N,error_x,'.-k'); plt.show()
```

539 We'll solve a radially symmetric heat equation. Although we divide by zero at
$r = 0$ when constructing the Laplacian operator, we subsequently overwrite the
resulting inf term when we apply the boundary condition.

```
from scipy.sparse.linalg import spsolve
T = 0.5; m = 100; n = 100
r = np.linspace(0,2,m); Δr = r[1]-r[0]; Δt = T/n
u = np.tanh(32*(1-r))[:,None]
D = sps.diags([1, -2, 1], [-1, 0, 1], shape=(m,m))/Δr**2 \
    + sps.diags([-1/r[1:], 1/r[:-1]], [-1, 1])/(2*Δr)
D = D.tocsr()
D[0,0:2] = np.array([-4,4])/Δr**2;
D[-1,-2:] = np.array([2,-2])/Δr**2
A = sps.eye(m) - 0.5*Δt*D
B = sps.eye(m) + 0.5*Δt*D
for i in range(n):
  u = spsolve(A,B@u)
plt.fill_between(r,u,-1,color='#ff9999'); plt.show()
```

We'll first define a function as a logit analog to np.linspace.   540

```
def logitspace(x,n,p):
  return x*np.arctanh(np.linspace(-p,p,n))/np.arctanh(p)
```

Next, we define a general discrete Laplacian operator. The following function returns a sparse matrix in diagonal format (DIA). Two inconsequential elements of array d are replaced with nonzero numbers to avoid divide-by-zero warnings.

```
from scipy.sparse.linalg import spsolve
def laplacian(x):
  h = np.diff(x); h1 = h[:-1]; h2 = h[1:]; n = len(x)
  d = np.c_[ \
    np.r_[h1[0]**2, h2*(h1+h2),0], \
    np.r_[-h1[0]**2, -h1*h2,-h2[-1]**2 ], \
    np.r_[h1*(h1+h2), h2[-1]**2,0]].T
  d[0,-1], d[2,-1] = 999, 999
  return sps.diags(2/d,[-1,0,1],shape=(n, n)).T
```

Then, we write a function to solve the heat equation.

```
def heat_equation(x,t,u):
  n = 40; Δt = t/n
  u = φ(x,0,10)
  D = laplacian(x)
  A = sps.eye(len(x)) - 0.5*Δt*D
  B = sps.eye(len(x)) + 0.5*Δt*D
  for i in range(n):
    u = spsolve(A,B@u)
  return u
```

Finally, we compare the uniformly-spaced and logit-spaced solutions.

```
def φ(x,t,s):
  return np.exp(-s*x**2/(1+4*s*t))/np.sqrt(1+4*s*t)
t = 15; m = 40
x = logitspace(20,m,.999)
laplacian(x).toarray()
u = heat_equation(x,t,φ(x,0,10))
plt.plot(x,u,'.-',x,φ(x,t,10),'k'); plt.show()
x = np.linspace(-20,20,m)
u = heat_equation(x,t,φ(x,0,10))
plt.plot(x,u,'.-',x,φ(x,t,10),'k'); plt.show()
```

541 Here's a solution to the Allen–Cahn equation using Strang splitting:

```
from scipy.sparse.linalg import spsolve
L = 16; m = 200; Δx = L/m
T = 8; n = 1600; Δt = T/n
x = np.linspace(-L/2,L/2,m)[None,:]
u = np.tanh(x**4 - 16*(2*x**2-x.T**2))
#u = np.random.standard_normal((m,m))
D = sps.diags([1, -2, 1], [-1, 0, 1], shape=(m,m)).tocsr()/Δx**2
D[0,1] *= 2; D[-1,-2] *= 2;
A = sps.eye(m) + 0.5*Δt*D
B = sps.eye(m) - 0.5*Δt*D
def f(u,Δt):
  return u/np.sqrt(u**2 - (u**2-1)*np.exp(-50*Δt))
u = f(u,Δt/2)
for i in range(n):
  if (i%8==0): U[:,:,i//10] = u
  u = spsolve(B,(A@spsolve(B,A@u).T)).T
  if (i<n): u = f(u,Δt)
u = f(u,Δt/2)
```

We can plot the solution using the code

```
plt.imshow(u, cmap="gray"); plt.axis('off'); plt.show()
```

546 The following code solves Burgers' equation.

```
m = 100; x,Δx = np.linspace(-1,3,m,retstep=True)
n = 100; Lt = 4; Δt = Lt/n; c = Δt/Δx
def f(u): return u**2/2
def fp(u): return u
u = ((x>=0)&(x<=1)).astype(float)
for i in range(n):
  fu = f(np.r_[u[0],u]); fpu = fp(np.r_[u[0],u])
  α = np.maximum(abs(fu[1:-1]),abs(fu[:-2]))
```

```
F = (fu[1:-1]+fu[:-2])/2 - α*(u[1:]-u[:-1])/2
u -= c*(np.diff(np.r_[0,F,0]))
```

Let's first define a few functions.

```
def limiter(t): return (abs(t)+t)/(1+abs(t))
def fixzero(u): return u + (u==0).astype(float)
def diff(u): return np.diff(u,axis=0)
def slope(u):
  du = diff(u)
  return np.r_[np.c_[0,0], \
    np.c_[du[1:,:]*limiter(du[:-1,:]/fixzero(du[1:,:]))],\
    np.c_[0,0]]
def F(u):
  return np.c_[u[:,0]*u[:,1], u[:,0]*u[:,1]**2+0.5*u[:,0]**2]
```

Now, we can solve the dam-break problem.

```
m = 1000; x,Δx = np.linspace(-.5,.5,m,retstep=True)
T = 0.25; n = (T/(Δx/2)).astype(int); Δt = (T/n)/2; c = Δt/Δx
u = np.c_[0.8*(x<0)+0.2,0*x]
for i in range(n):
  v = u-0.5*c*slope(F(u))
  u[1:,:]=(u[:-1,:]+u[1:,:])/2 - diff(slope(u))/8 - c*diff(F(v))
  v = u-0.5*c*slope(F(u))
  u[:-1,:]=(u[:-1,:]+u[1:,:])/2 - diff(slope(u))/8 - c*diff(F(v))
plt.plot(x,u);
```

```
m = 10; x,h = np.linspace(0,1,m,retstep=True)
A = np.tile(np.r_[-1/h-h/6,2/h-2/3*h,-1/h-h/6],(m,1)).T
A[1,0]/=2; A[1,-1] /= 2
b=np.r_[-2/3*h**3,-4/3*h**3-8*h*x[1:-1]**2,-4*h+8/3*h**2-2/3*h**3+1]
u=la.solve_banded((1,1),A,b)
s=(-16)+8*x**2+15*np.cos(x)/np.sin(1)
plt.plot(x,s,'o-',x,u,'.-');
```

```
m = 8; x,h = np.linspace(0,1,m+2,retstep=True)
def tridiag(a,b,c): return np.diag(a,-1)+np.diag(b,0)+np.diag(c,1)
def D(a,b,c):
  return tridiag(a*np.ones(m-1), b*np.ones(m), c*np.ones(m-1))/h**3
M = np.r_[np.c_[D(-12,24,-12),D(-6,0,6)],
  np.c_[D(6,0,-6),D(2,8,2)]]
b = np.r_[np.ones(m)*h*384,np.zeros(m)]
u = la.solve(M,b)
plt.plot(x,16*(x**4 - 2*x**3 + x**2),'o-',x,np.r_[0,u[:m],0],'.-');
```

550

551
```python
from scipy.integrate import solve_ivp
from scipy.fft import fftshift, fft, ifft
m = 128; x = np.linspace(-π,π,m,endpoint=False)
ξ = 1j*fftshift(np.arange(-m/2,m/2))
def f(t,u): return -np.real(ifft(ξ*fft(0.5*u**2)))
sol = solve_ivp(f, [0,1.5], np.exp(-x**2), method = 'RK45')
plt.plot(x,sol.y[:,-1]); plt.show()
```

552 The following code solves the KdV equation using integrating factors. We first
set the parameters.

```python
from scipy.fft import fftshift, fft, ifft
def φ(x,x0,c): return 0.5*c/np.cosh(np.sqrt(c)/2*(x-x0))**2
L = 30; T = 2.0; m = 256
x = np.linspace(-L/2,L/2,m,endpoint=False)
iξ = 1j*fftshift(np.arange(-m/2,m/2))*(2*π/L)
```

Next, we define the integrating factor G and the right-hand side function f.

```python
def G(t): return np.exp(-iξ**3*t)
def f(t,w): return -(3*iξ*fft(ifft(G(t)*w)**2))/G(t)
```

Then we solve the problem using RK45.

```python
from scipy.integrate import solve_ivp
u = φ(x,-4,4) + φ(x,-9,9)
w = fft(u)
sol = solve_ivp(f,[0,T],w,t_eval=np.linspace(0,T,200))
u = [np.real(ifft(G(sol.t[i])*sol.y[:,i])) for i in range(200)]
```

We can animate the solution using matplotlib.animation.

```python
plt.rcParams["animation.html"] = "jshtml"
from matplotlib.animation import FuncAnimation
fig, ax = plt.subplots()
l, = ax.plot([-15,15],[0,5])
def animate(i): l.set_data(x, u[i])
FuncAnimation(fig, animate, frames=len(u), interval=50)
```

The first line of this code block displays the animation as HTML using JavaScript.
Alternatively, we can replace this line with

```python
plt.rcParams["animation.html"] = "html5"
```

to convert the animation to HTML5 (which requires the ffmpeg video codecs).

```
from scipy.fft import fftshift, fft2, ifft2
ε = 1; m = 256; ℓ = 100; n = 2000; Δt=100/n
U = (np.random.rand(m,m)>0.5)-0.5
ξ = fftshift(np.arange(-m/2,m/2))*(2*π/ℓ)
D2 = -ξ[:,None]**2-ξ[None,:]**2
E = np.exp(-(D2+1)**2*Δt)
def f(U):
  return U/np.sqrt(U**2/ε + np.exp(-Δt*ε)*(1-U**2/ε))
for i in range(n):
  U = f(ifft2(E*fft2(f(U))))
plt.imshow(np.real(U), cmap="gray"); plt.axis('off'); plt.show()
```

554

B.3 Matlab

This section provides a Matlab supplement to the Julia commentary and code elsewhere in the book. This book uses *Matlab* to describe the scientific programming language and syntax common to both MATLAB,[4] the proprietary computer software sold by MathWorks, and GNU Octave, the open-source computer software developed by John Eaton and others. The book explicitly uses *MATLAB* or *Octave* when referring to a particular implementation of the language.

The code is written and tested using Octave version 6.4.0. Page references to the Julia commentary are listed in the left margins. For brevity, the variable bucket is assumed throughout. The function rgb2gray is a standard function in MATLAB it is available in Octave in the image toolbox, or we can write it ourselves.

```
bucket = "https://raw.githubusercontent.com/nmfsc/data/master/";
rgb2gray = @(x) 0.2989*x(:,:,1) + 0.5870*x(:,:,2) + 0.1140*x(:,:,3);
```

The Matlab code in this section is available as a Jupyter notebook at

https://nbviewer.jupyter.org/github/nmfsc/octave/blob/main/octave.ipynb

You can download the IPYNB file and run it on a local computer with Octave and Jupyter. You can also run the code directly on Binder using the QR link at the bottom of this page. Note that it may take a few minutes for the Binder to launch the repository.

---

[4]MATLAB® is a registered trademark of The MathWorks, Inc., Python® is a registered trademark of the Python Software Foundation, Julia® is a registered trademark of Julia Computing, Inc., and GNU® is a registered trademark of Free Software Foundation.

Octave notebook
on Binder

5   While Julia's syntax tends to prefer column vectors, Matlab's syntax tends to prefer row vectors. The syntax for a row vector includes `[1 2 3 4]`, `[1,2,3,4]`, and `1:4`. Syntax for a column vector is `[1;2;3:4]`.

5   Matlab broadcasts arithmetic operators and some functions by implicitly expanding arrays to compatible sizes. For example, if we define `A = rand(3,4)`, then `A - mean(A)` will subtract the row vector `mean(A)` from each row of `A`. Similarly, `A - mean(A,2)` subtracts a column vector from each column of `A`. Unlike Julia which explicitly requires a dot (`.-`) to denote broadcasting, Matlab does not. The operator `*` is used for matrix multiplication and `.*` is used for the element-wise Hadamard product. Similarly, `^` is used for matrix power and `.^` is used for element-wise power. Matlab implicitly broadcasts functions such as `sin(A)` across each element of `A`.

23
```
n = [10,15,20,25,50];
set(gcf,'position',[0,0,1000,200])
for i = 1:5,
  subplot(1,5,i)
  imshow(1-abs(hilb(n(i))\hilb(n(i))),[0 1])
end
```

29 The `type` and `edit` commands display the contents of an m-file, if available. Many basic functions are built-in and do not have an m-file.

30 The Matlab command `rref` returns the reduced row echelon form.

33 The corresponding Matlab code is

```
function b = gaussian_elimination(A,b)
  n = length(A);
  for j=1:n
    A(j+1:n,j) = A(j+1:n,j)/A(j,j);
    A(j+1:n,j+1:n) = A(j+1:n,j+1:n) - A(j+1:n,j).*A(j,j+1:n);
  end
  for i=2:n
    b(i) = b(i) - A(i,1:i-1)*b(1:i-1);
  end
  for i=n:-1:1
    b(i) = ( b(i) - A(i,i+1:n)*b(i+1:n) )/A(i,i);
  end
end
```

The following Matlab code implements the simplex method. We start by defining functions used for pivot selection and row reduction in the simplex algorithm.

```
function [tableau] = row_reduce(tableau)
  [i,j] = get_pivot(tableau);
  G = tableau(i,:)./tableau(i,j);
  tableau = tableau - tableau(:,j)*G;
  tableau(i,:) = G;
end


function [i,j] = get_pivot(tableau)
  [_,j] = max(tableau(end,1:end-1));
  a = tableau(1:end-1,j); b = tableau(1:end-1,end);
  k = find(a > 0);
  [_,i] = min(b(k)./a(k));
  i = k(i);
end


function [z,x,y] = simplex(c,A,b)
  [m,n] = size(A);
  tableau = [A eye(m) b; c' zeros(1,m) 0];
  while (any(tableau(end,1:n)>0)),
    tableau = row_reduce(tableau);
  end
  p = find(tableau(end,1:n)==0);
  x = zeros(n,1);
  x(p) = tableau(:,p)'*tableau(:,end);
  z = -tableau(end,end);
  y = -tableau(end,n+(1:m));
end
```

The MATLAB function linprog solves the LP problem. The built-in Octave function glpk (GNU Linear Programming Kit) can solve LP problems using either the revised simplex method or the interior point method.

Matlab's backslash and forward slash operators use UMFPACK to solve sparse linear systems.

We'll construct a sparse, random matrix, get the number of zeros, and draw the sparsity plot.

```
A = sprand(60,80,0.2); nnz(A), spy(A,'.')
```

49   The function gplot plots the vertices and edges of an adjacency matrix. MATLAB, but not Octave, has additional functions for constructing and analyzing graphs.

49   Matlab lacks many of the tools for drawing graphs but we can construct them. First, let's write naïve functions that will draw force-directed, spectral, and circular graphs layouts. Although the force-directed layout can be implemented using a forward Euler scheme, it may be easier to use an adaptive timestep ODE solver to manage stability.

```
function f = spring(A,z)
  n = length(z); k = 2*sqrt(1/n);
  d = z - z.'; D = abs(d)/k;
  F = -(A.*D - 1./(D+eye(n)).^2);
  f = sum(F.*d,2);
end
function xy = spring_layout(A,z)
  n = size(A,1);
  z = rand(n,1) + 1i*rand(n,1);
  [t,z] = ode45(@(t,z) spring(A,z),[0,10],z);
  xy = [real(z(end,:));imag(z(end,:))]';
end


function xy = spectral_layout(A)
  D = diag(sum(A,2));
  [v,d] = eig(D - A);
  [_,i] = sort(diag(d));
  xy = v(:,i(2:3));
end


function xy = circular_layout(A)
  n = size(A,1); t = (2*pi*(1:n)/n)';
  xy = [cos(t) sin(t)];
end
```

Let's also define a function to download and construct an adjacency matrix.

```
function M = get_adjacency_matrix(bucket,filename)
  data = urlread([bucket filename '.csv']);
  ij = cell2mat(textscan(data,'%d,%d'));
  M = sparse(ij(:,1),ij(:,2),1);
end
```

Now, we can draw the dolphin networks of the Doubtful Sound.

```
A = get_adjacency_matrix(bucket,"dolphins");
gplot(A,spring_layout(A),'.-'); axis equal; axis off;
```

The Matlab function `symrcm` returns the permutation vector using the reverse 52 Cuthill–McKee algorithm for symmetric matrices, and `symamd` returns the permutation vector using the symmetric approximate minimum degree permutation algorithm.

The following code implements the revised simplex method. 54

```
function [z,x,y] = revised_simplex(c,A,b)
  [m,n] = size(A);
  N = 1:n; B = n + (1:m);
  A = [A speye(m)];
  ABinv = speye(m);
  c = [c;zeros(m,1)];
  while true
    y = c(B)'*ABinv;
    if isempty(j=find(c(N)'-y*A(:,N)>0,1)), break; end
    k = find((q = ABinv*A(:,N(j))) > 0);
    [_,i] = min(ABinv(k,:)*b./q(k));
    i = k(i);
    p = B(i); B(i) = N(j); N(j) = p;
    ABinv = ABinv - ((q - sparse(i,1,1,m,1))/q(i))*ABinv(i,:);
  end
  i = find(B<=n);
  x = zeros(n,1);
  x(B(i)) = ABinv(i,:)*b;
  z = c(1:n)'*x;
end
```

For a 2000×1999 matrix `A\b` takes 3.8 seconds and `pinv(A)*b` takes almost 56 57 seconds.

The function `givens(x,y)` returns the Givens rotation matrix for (x, y). 64

The function `qr` implements LAPACK routines to compute the QR factorization 65 of a matrix using Householder reflection.

Matlab's `mldivide` (\) solves an overdetermined system using a QR solver. 66

The Zipf's law coefficients c for the canon of Sherlock Holmes computed using 67 ordinary least squares are

```
data = urlread([bucket 'sherlock.csv']);
T = cell2mat(textscan(data,'%s\t%d')(2));
n = length(T);
A = [ones(n,1) log(1:n)'];
```

```
B = log(T);
c1 = A\B
```

70 The constrained least squares problem is solved using

```
function x = constrained_lstsq(A,b,C,d)
    x = [A'*A C'; C zeros(size(C,1))]\([A'*b;d])
    x = x(1:size(A,2))
end
```

64 The command [U,S,V]=svd(A) returns the SVD of a matrix A and svd(A,0)
    returns the "economy" version of the SVD. The command svds(A,k) returns the
    first k singular values and associated singular vectors.

73 The function pinv computes the Moore–Penrose pseudoinverse by computing
    the SVD using a default tolerance of max(size(A))*norm(A)*eps, i.e., machine
    epsilon scaled by the largest singular value times the largest dimension of A.

77 The following code implements total least squares:

```
function X = tls(A,B)
    n = size(A,2);
    [_,_,V] = svd([A B],0);
    X = -V(1:n,n+1:end)/V(n+1:end,n+1:end);
end
```

77
```
A = [2 4; 1 -1; 3 1; 4 -8]; b = [1; 1; 4; 1];
x_ols = A\b
x_tls = tls(A,b)
```

79 Matlab reads a color image as a 3-dimensional RGB array of unsigned integers
    between 0 and 255. It will be easiest to work with floating-point values between 0
    and 1, so we'll first convert to grayscale and normalize. We can use the function
    rgb2gray to make the conversion. Take k to be some nominal value like 20.

```
A = rgb2gray(imread([bucket "laura.png"]));
[U, S, V] = svd(A,0);
sigma = diag(S);
```

We can confirm that the error $\|\mathbf{A} - \mathbf{A}_k\|_F^2$ matches $\sum_{i=k+1}^{n} \sigma^2$ by computing

```
Ak = U(:,1:k) * S(1:k,1:k) * V(:,1:k)';
```

```
norm(double(A)-Ak,'fro') - norm(sigma(k+1:end))
imshow([A,Ak])
```

The values of the compressed image no longer lie between 0 and 1—instead ranging between −0.11 and 1.18. The command imshow(Ak) clamps the values of a floating-point array between 0 and 1. Finally, let's plot the error:

```
r = sum(size(A))/prod(size(A))*(1:min(size(A)));
error = 1 - sqrt(cumsum(sigma.^2))/norm(sigma);
semilogx(r,error,'.-');
```

The following function is a naïve implementation of NMF: 85

```
function [W,H] = nmf(X,p)
  W = rand(size(X,1),p);
  H = rand(p,size(X,2));
  for i=1:50,
    W = W.*(X*H')./(W*(H*H') + (W==0));
    H = H.*(W'*X)./((W'*W)*H + (H==0));
  end
end
```

The function vander generates a Vandermonde matrix for input $(x_0, x_1, \ldots, x_n)$ 87
with rows given by $\begin{bmatrix} x_i^p & x_i^{p-1} & \cdots & x_i & 1 \end{bmatrix}$.

The function roots finds the roots of a polynomial $p(x)$ by computing eig for   89
the companion matrix of $p(x)$.

The Matlab function condeig returns the eigenvalue condition number.   90

The following code computes the PageRank of the graph in Figure 4.3.   97

```
H = [0 0 0 0 1; 1 0 0 0 0; 1 0 0 0 1; 1 0 1 0 0; 0 0 1 1 0];
v = ~any(H);
H = H./(sum(H)+v);
n = length(H);
d = 0.85;
x = ones([n 1])/n;
for i = 1:9
  x = d*(H*x) + d/n*(v*x) + (1-d)/n;
end
```

The function hess returns the unitarily similar upper Hessenberg form of a matrix   104
using LAPACK.

109 The function `eig` computes the eigenvalues and eigenvectors of a matrix with a LAPACK library that implements the shifted QR method.

114 The function `eigs` computes several eigenvalues of a sparse matrix using the implicitly restarted Arnoldi process.

137 The function `pcg` implements the conjugate gradient method—preconditioned conjugate gradient method if a preconditioner is also provided.

141 The function `gmres` implements the generalized minimum residual method and `minres` implements the minimum residual method.

148 The function `kron(A,B)` returns the Kronecker product $\mathbf{A} \otimes \mathbf{B}$.

149 The radix-2 FFT algorithm written as a recursive function in Matlab is

```
function y = fftx2(c)
  n = length(c);
  omega = exp(-2i*pi/n);
  if mod(n,2) == 0
    k = (0:n/2-1)';
    u = fftx2(c(1:2:n-1));
    v = (omega.^k).*fftx2(c(2:2:n));
    y = [u+v; u-v];
  else
    k = (0:n-1)';
    F = omega.^(k*k');
    y = F*c;
  end
end
```

and the IFFT is

```
function c = ifftx2(y)
  c = conj(fftx2(conj(y)))/length(y);
end
```

150 The Matlab function `toeplitz` constructs a Toeplitz matrix.

150 A circulant matrix can be built in Matlab from a vector v using

```
toeplitz(v,circshift(flipud(v),1))
```

152 The convolution of u and v is `ifft(fft(u).*fft(v))`.

```
function y = fasttoeplitz(c,r,x)                                    153
  n = length(x);
  m = 2^(ceil(log2(n)))-n;
  x1 = [c; zeros([m 1]); r(end:-1:2)];
  x2 = [x; zeros([m+n-1 1])];
  y = ifftx2(fftx2(x1).*fftx2(x2));
  y = y(1:n);
end
```

```
function y = bluestein(x)                                           155
  n = length(x);
  w = exp((1i*pi/n)*((0:n-1).^2))';
  y = w.*fasttoeplitz(conj(w),conj(w),w.*x);
end
```

The Matlab function fft implements the Fastest Fourier Transform in the 158
West (FFTW) library. The inverse FFT can be computed using ifft and
multidimensional FFTs can be computed using fftn and ifftn.

The functions fftshift and ifftshift shift the zero frequency component to the 159
center of the array.

Matlab does not have a three-dimensional DST function, so we'll need to build 160
one ourselves. The function dst3 computes the three-dimensional DST (6.4) by
computing the DST over each dimension. The function dstx3 computes a DST in
one dimension for a three-dimensional array. The real command in the function
dstx3 is only needed to remove the round-off error from the FFT. By distributing
the scaling constant $\sqrt{2/(n+1)}$ across both the DST and the inverse DST, we
only need to implement one function for both.

```
function a = dst3(a)
  a = dstx3(shiftdim(a,1));
  a = dstx3(shiftdim(a,1));
  a = dstx3(shiftdim(a,1));
end
```

```
function a = dstx3(a)
  n = size(a); o = zeros(1,n(2),n(3));
  y = [o;a;o;-a(end:-1:1,:,:)];
  y = fft(y);
  a = imag(y(2:n(1)+1,:,:)*(sqrt(2*(n(1)+1))));
end
```

```
n = 50; x = (1:n)'/(n+1); dx = 1/(n+1);
[x,y,z] = meshgrid(x);
v = @(k) 2 - 2*cos(k*pi/(n+1));
[ix,iy,iz] = meshgrid(1:n);
lambda = (v(ix)+v(iy)+v(iz))./dx^2;
f = 2*((x-x.^2).*(y-y.^2) + (x-x.^2).*(z-z.^2) + (y-y.^2).*(z-z.^2));
u = dst3(dst3(f)./lambda);
```

The program takes less than a third of a second to run for $n = 50$.

163 The MATLAB function dct returns the type 1–4 DCT. The equivalent function
     in Octave's signal package returns a DCT-2. The following function returns a
     sparse matrix of Fourier coefficients along with the reconstructed compressed
     image:

```
pkg load signal
function [B,A] = dctcompress(A,d)
  B = dct2(A);
  idx = floor(d*prod(size(A)));
  tol = sort(abs(B(:)),'descend')(idx);
  B(abs(B)<tol) = 0;
  A = idct2(B); B = sparse(B);
end
```

We'll test the function on an image and compare it before and after.

```
A = rgb2gray(imread([bucket "laura.png"]));
[_,A0] = dctcompress(A,0.01);
imshow([A,A0])
```

180 The function class returns the data type of a variable.

181 The Matlab function num2hex converts a floating-point number to a hexadecimal
     string. We can further convert the string to a string of bits using

```
function b = float_to_bin(x)
  b = sprintf("%s",dec2bin(hex2dec(num2cell(num2hex(x))),4)');
  if x<0, b(1) = '1'; end
end
```

181 The constant eps returns the double-precision machine epsilon of $2^{-52} \approx 10^{-16}$.
     The function eps(x) returns the double-precision round-off error at x. For
     example, eps(0) returns $2^{-1074} \approx 10^{-323}$. Of course, eps(1) is the same as eps.

```
function y = Q_rsqrt(x)                                              182
  i = typecast(single(x),'uint32');
  i = 0x5f3759df - bitshift(i,-1);
  y = typecast(i,'single');
  y = y * (1.5 - (0.5 * x * y * y));
end
```

```
a = 77617; b = 33096;                                               184
333.75*b^6+a^2*(11*a^2*b^2-b^6-121*b^4-2)+5.5*b^8+a/(2*b)
```

The command realmax returns the largest floating-point number. The command   185
realmin returns the smallest normalized floating-point number.

To check for overflows and NaN, use the Matlab logical commands isinf and   186
isnan. You can use NaN to lift the "pen off the paper" in a Matlab plot as in

```
plot([1 2 2 2 3],[1 2 NaN 1 2])
```

The functions expm1 and log1p compute $e^x - 1$ and $\log(x + 1)$ more precisely   187
than exp(x)-1 and log(x+1) in a neighborhood of zero.

```
function x = bisection(f,a,b,tolerance)                             191
  while abs(b-a) > tolerance
    c = (a+b)/2;
    if sign(f(c)) == sign(f(a)), a = c; else b = c; end
  end
  x = (a+b)/2;
end
```

The function fzero(f,x0) uses the Dekker–Brent method to find a zero of the   197
input function. The function f can either be a string (which is a function of x),
an anonymous function, or the name of an m-file.

204
```
function M = escape(n,z,c)
    M = zeros(size(c));
    for k = 0:n
        mask = abs(z)<2;
        M(mask) = M(mask) + 1;
        z(mask) = z(mask).^2 + c(mask);
    end
end


function M = mandelbrot(bb,xn,n,z)
    yn = round(xn*(bb(4)-bb(2))/(bb(3)-(bb(1)))));
    z = z*ones(yn,xn);
    c = linspace(bb(1),bb(3),xn) + 1i*linspace(bb(4),bb(2),yn)';
    M = escape(n,z,c);
end


M = mandelbrot([-0.1710,1.0228,-0.1494,1.0443],800,200,0);
imwrite(1-M/max(M(:)),'mandelbrot.png');
```

208   The function polyval(x,p) uses Horner's method to evaluate a polynomial with coefficients $p = [a_0, a_1, \ldots, a_n]$ at x.

211   The function roots returns the roots of a polynomial by finding the eigenvalues of the companion matrix.

215   The function fsolve finds zeros of nonlinear systems.

217
```
f = @(x) [x(1)^3-3*x(1)*x(2)^2-1; x(2)^3-3*x(1)^2*x(2)];
df = @(t,x,p) -[3*x(1)^2-3*x(2)^2, -6*x(1)*x(2);...
    -6*x(1)*x(2), 3*x(2)^2-3*x(1)^2]\p;
x0 = [1;1];
[t,y] = ode45(@(t,x) df(t,x,f(x0)),[0;1],x0);
y(end,:)
```

To reduce the error, we can add the option opt=odeset("RelTol",1e-10) to the solver.

221   The following code uses the gradient descent method to find the minimum of the Rosenbrock function:

```
df = @(x) [-2*(1-x(1))-400*x(1)*(x(2)-x(1)^2), 200*(x(2)-x(1)^2)];
x = [-1.8,3.0]; p = [0,0]; a = 0.001; b = 0.9;
for i = 1:500
```

```
    p = -df(x) + b*p;
    x = x + a*p;
end
```

In practice, we can use the optimization toolbox. The `fminbnd` function uses the golden section search method to find the minimum of a univariate function. The `fminsearch` function uses the Nelder–Mead method to find the minimum of a multivariate function. The `fminunc` function uses the BFGS method to find the minimum of a multivariate function.

```
pkg load optim
f = @(x) (1-x(1)).^2 + 100*(x(2) - x(1)).^2;
x0 = [-1.8,3.0];
fminunc(f, x0)
```

The function `vander` generates a Vandermonde matrix with rows given by $\begin{bmatrix} x_i^n & x_i^{n-1} & \cdots & 1 \end{bmatrix}$. Add `fliplr` to reverse them $\begin{bmatrix} 1 & \cdots & x_{i-1}^{n-1} & x_i^n \end{bmatrix}$. 227

The following function computes the coefficients m of a cubic spline with natural 238 boundary conditions through the nodes given by the arrays x and y.

```
function m = spline_natural(x,y)
    h = diff(x(:));
    gamma = 6*diff(diff(y(:))./h);
    alpha = diag(h(2:end-1),-1);
    beta = 2*diag(h(1:end-1)+h(2:end),0);
    m = [0;(alpha+beta+alpha')\gamma;0];
end
```

We can then use (9.3) and (9.4) to evaluate that spline using n points.

```
function [X,Y] = evaluate_spline(x,y,m,n)
    x = x(:); y = y(:); h = diff(x);
    B = y(1:end-1) - m(1:end-1).*h.^2/6;
    A = diff(y)./h-h./6.*diff(m);
    X = linspace(min(x),max(x),n+1)';
    i = sum(x<=X');
    i(end) = length(x)-1;
    Y = (m(i).*(x(i+1)-X).^3 + m(i+1).*(X-x(i)).^3)./(6*h(i)) ...
        + A(i).*(X-x(i)) + B(i);
end
```

The function takes column-vector inputs for x and y and outputs column vectors X and Y with length N. Note that the line `i = sum(x<=X');` broadcasts the element-wise operator `<=` across a row and a column array.

239 The function `spline` returns a cubic spline with the not-a-knot condition.

241 The function pp = `mkpp(b,C)` returns a structured array pp that can be used to build piecewise polynomials of order n using the function y = `ppval(pp,x)`. The input b is a vector of breaks (including endpoints) with length $p + 1$ and C is an $p \times n$ array of the polynomial coefficients in each segment.

242 The Matlab function `pchip` returns a cubic Hermite spline.

245 We can build a Bernstein matrix in Matlab from a column vector t with the following function.

```
B = @(n,t)[1 cumprod((n:-1:1)./(1:n))].*t.^(0:n).*(1-t).^(n:-1:0);
```

255
```
function P = legendre(x,n)
    if n==0, P = ones(size(x));
        elseif n==1, P = x;
        else P = x.*legendre(x,n-1)-1/(4-1/(n-1)^2).*legendre(x,n-2);
    end
end
```

261 We'll construct a Chebyshev differentiation matrix and use the matrix to solve a few simple problems.

```
function [D,x] = chebdiff(n)
    x = -cos(linspace(0,pi,n))';
    c = [2;ones(n-2,1);2].*(-1).^(0:n-1);
    D = c./c'./(x - x' + eye(n));
    D = D - diag(sum(D,2));
end
```

```
n = 15;
[D,x] = chebdiff(n);
u = exp(-4*x.^2);
plot(x,D*u,'.-')
```

```
B = zeros(1,n); B(1) = 1;
plot(x,[B;D]\[2;u],'.-')
```

```
n = 15; k2 = 256;
[D,x] = chebdiff(n);
L = (D^2 - k2*diag(x));
```

```
L([1,n],:) = 0; L(1,1) = 1; L(n,n) = 1;
y = L\[2;zeros(n-2,1);1];
plot(x,y,'.-')
```

The Chebfun package (https://www.chebfun.org) includes methods for manipu-   263
lating functions in Chebyshev space.

```
function [x,phi] = scaling(c,z,n)                                              269
  m = length(c); L = 2^n;
  phi = zeros(2*m*L,1);
  k = (0:m-1)*L;
  phi(k+1) = z;
  for j = 1:n
    for i = 1:m*2^(j-1)
      x = (2*i-1)*2^(n-j);
      phi(x+1) = c * phi(mod(2*x-k,2*m*L)+1);
    end
  end
  x = (1:(m-1)*L)/L;
  phi = phi(1:(m-1)*L);
end
```

Let's use scaling to plot the Daubechies D_4 scaling function.

```
c = [1+sqrt(3),3+sqrt(3),3-sqrt(3),1-sqrt(3)]/4;
z = [0,1+sqrt(3),1-sqrt(3),0]/2;
[x,phi] = scaling(c,z,8);
plot(x,phi)
```

```
psi = zeros(size(phi)); n = length(c)-1; L = length(phi)/(2*n)        271
for k = 0:n
  psi((k*L+1):(k+n)*L) += (-1)^k*c(n-k+1)*phi(1:2:end);
end
plot(x,psi)
```

The Large Time-Frequency Analysis Toolbox (LTFAT) includes several utilities   273
for wavelet transforms and is available from http://ltfat.github.io under the GNU
General Public License.

We'll use the LTFAT package.   274

```
pkg load ltfat
adjustlevels = @(x) 1 - min(max((sqrt(abs(x))),0),1);
```

```
A = rgb2gray(double(imread([bucket "laura_square.png"])))/255;
c = fwt2(A,"db2",9);
imshow(adjustlevels(c))
```

Let's choose a threshold level of 0.5 and plot the resultant image after taking the inverse DWT.

```
c = thresh(c,0.5);
B = ifwt2(c,"db2",9);
imshow([A,max(min(B,1),0)]);
```

283 The Jacobian can be computed using complex-step approximation.

```
function J = jacobian(f,x,c)
  for k = (n = 1:length(c))
    J(:,k) = imag(f(x,c+1e-8i*(k==n)'))/1e-8;
  end
end
```

We can then implement the Levenberg–Marquardt method.

```
function c = gauss_newton(f,x,y,c)
  r = y - f(x,c);
  for j = 1:100
    G = jacobian(f,x,c);
    M = G'*G;
    c = c + (M+diag(diag(M)))\(G'*r);
    if norm(r-(r=y-f(x,c))) < 1e-10, return; end
  end
  display('Gauss-Newton did not converge.')
end
```

We can solve the problem using the following code:

```
f = @(x,c) c(1)*exp(-c(2).*(x-c(3)).^2) + ...
    c(4)*exp(-c(5).*(x-c(6)).^2);
x = 8*rand([100 1]);
y = f(x,[1 3 3 2 3 6]) + 0.1*randn([100 1]);
c0 = [2 0.3 2 1 0.3 7]';
c = gauss_newton(f,x,y,c0);
```

Assuming that the Gauss–Newton method converged, we can plot the results.

```
X = linspace(0,8,100);
plot(x,y,'.',X,f(X,c));
```

In practice, we can use the lsqcurvefit function in the optim toolkit:

```
pkg load optim
c = lsqcurvefit(@(c,x) f(x,c), c0, x, y)
```

Alternatively, we can use the `leasqr` function in Octave's `optim` toolkit:

```
pkg load optim
[_,c] = leasqr (x, y, c0, f)
```

We'll first define the logistic function and generate synthetic data. Then, we 286 apply Newton's method.

```
sigma = @(x) 1./(1+exp(-x));
x = rand(30,1); y = ( rand(30,1) < sigma(10*x-5) );
```

```
X = [ones(size(x)) x]; w = zeros(2,1);
for i=1:10
  S = sigma(X*w).*(1 - sigma(X*w));
  w = w + (X'*(S.*X))\(X'*(y - sigma(X*w)));
end
```

Let's start by generating some training data and setting up the neural network 289 architecture.

```
N = 100; t = linspace(0,pi,N);
x = cos(t); x = [ones(1,N);x];
y = sin(t) + 0.05*randn(1,N);
n = 20; W1 = rand(n,2); W2 = randn(1,n);
phi = @(x) max(x,0);
dphi = @(x) (x>0);
```

Now, we train the model to determine the optimized parameters.

```
alpha = 1e-3;
for epoch = 1:10000
  s = W2 * phi(W1*x);
  dLdy = 2*(s-y);
  dLdW1 = dphi(W1*x) .* (W2' * dLdy) * x';
  dLdW2 = dLdy * phi(W1*x)';
  W1 -= 0.1 * alpha * dLdW1;
  W2 -= alpha * dLdW2;
end
```

After determining the parameters W1 and W2, we can plot the results.

```
s = W2 * phi(W1*x);
scatter(x(2,:),y,'r','filled'); hold on
plot(x(2,:),s)
```

Alternatively, we can swap out the activation and loss functions.

```
phi = @(x) 1./(1+exp(-x));
dphi = @(x) phi(x).*(1-phi(x));
```

```
L = norm(s- y);
dLdy = 2*(s-y)/L;
```

297 Coefficients to the third-order approximation to $f'(x)$ using nodes at $x - h$, x, $x + h$ and $x + 2h$ are given by C[2,:] where

```
d = [-1;0;1;2];
n = length(d);
V = fliplr(vander(d)) ./ factorial([0:n-1]);
C = inv(V);
```

Coefficients are given by rats(C) and the coefficients of the truncation error is given by rats(C*d.^n/factorial(n)):

298 The command rats returns the rational approximation of number as a string by using continued fraction expansion. For example rats(0.75) returns 3/4.

299 Matlab code for Richardson extrapolation taking $\delta = \frac{1}{2}$ is

```
function D = richardson(f,x,m,n)
  if n > 0
    D = (4^n*richardson(f,x,m,n-1) - richardson(f,x,m-1,n-1))/(4^n-1);
  else
    D = phi(f,x,2^m);
  end
end
```

where the central difference scheme is

```
function p = phi(f,x,n)
  p = (f(x+1/n) - f(x-1/n))/(2/n);
end
```

301 We can build a minimal working example of forward accumulation automatic differentiation in Matlab following an example in Neidinger [2010]. We first

define a class, which we'll call dual, with the properties `value` and `deriv` for the value and derivative of a variable. We can overload the built-in functions + (`plus`), * (`mtimes`), and `sin` to operate on the dual class. We save the following code as the m-file dual.m. When working in Jupyter, we can add `%%file dual.m` to top of a cell to write the cell to a file.

```
%%file dual.m
classdef dual
  properties
    value
    deriv
  end
  methods
    function obj = dual(a,b)
      obj.value = a;
      obj.deriv = b;
    end
    function h = plus(u,v)
      if ~isa(u,'dual'), u = dual(u,0); end
      if ~isa(v,'dual'), v = dual(v,0); end
      h = dual(u.value + v.value, u.deriv + v.deriv);
    end
    function h = mtimes(u,v)
      if ~isa(u,'dual'), u = dual(u,0); end
      if ~isa(v,'dual'), v = dual(v,0); end
      h = dual(u.value*v.value, u.deriv*v.value + u.value*v.deriv);
    end
    function h = sin(u)
      h = dual(sin(u.value), cos(u.value)*u.deriv);
    end
    function h = minus(u,v)
      h = u + (-1)*v;
    end
  end
end
```

Now, let's define a function for the autodiff.

```
x = dual(0,1);
y = x + sin(x);
```

Then `y.value` returns 0 and `y.deriv` returns 2, which agrees with $y(0) = 0$ and $y'(0) = 2$.

We can define the dual numbers as   303

```
x1 = dual(2,[1 0]);
```

```
x2 = dual(pi,[0 1]);
y1 = x1*x2 + sin(x2);
y2 = x1*x2 - sin(x2);
```

306
```
function p = trapezoidal(f,x,n)
  F = f(linspace(x(1),x(2),n+1));
  p = (F(1)/2 + sum(F(2:end-1)) + F(end)/2) * (x(2)-x(1))/n;
end
```

308
```
n = floor(logspace(1,2,10));
for p = 1:7,
  f = @(x) x + x.^p.*(2-x).^p;
  S = trapezoidal(f,[0,2],1e6);
  for i = 1:length(n)
    Sn = trapezoidal(f,[0,2],n(i));
    error(i) = abs(Sn - S)/S;
  end
  slope(p) = [log(error)/[log(n);ones(size(n))]](1);
  loglog(n,error,'.-k'); hold on;
end
```

311
```
function S = clenshaw_curtis(f,n)
  x = cos(pi*(0:n)'/n);
  w = zeros(1,n+1); w(1:2:n+1) = 2 ./ (1 - (0:2:n).^2);
  S = 2/n * w * dctI(f(x));
end
```

```
function a = dctI(f)
  n = length(f);
  g = real( fft( [f;f(n-1:-1:2)] ) ) / 2;
  a = [g(1)/2; g(2:n-1); g(n)/2];
end
```

316 We can implement Gauss–Legendre quadrature by first defining the weights

```
function [nodes,weights] = gauss_legendre(n)
  b = (1:n-1).^2./(4*(1:n-1).^2-1);
  a = zeros(n,1);
  scaling = 2;
  [v,s] = eig(diag(sqrt(b),1) + diag(a) + diag(sqrt(b),-1));
```

```matlab
  weights = scaling*v(1,:).^2;
  nodes = diag(s);
end
```

and then implementing the method as

```matlab
f = @(x) cos(x).*exp(-x.^2);
[nodes,weights] = gauss_legendre(n);
weights * f(nodes)
```

```matlab
r = exp(2i*pi*(0:0.01:1));
plot((1.5*r.^2 - 2*r + 0.5)./r.^2); axis equal;
```
347

The following function returns the coefficients for a stencil given by m and n: 349

```matlab
function [a,b] = multistepcoefficients(m,n)
  s = length(m) + length(n) - 1;
  A = (m+1).^((0:s-1)');
  B = ((0:s-1).*(n+1)'.^[0,0:s-2])';
  c = -[A(:,2:end) B]\ones(s,1);
  a = [1;c(1:length(m)-1)];
  b = [c(length(m):end)];
end
```

We can express floating-point numbers c as fractions using the rats(c).

```matlab
function plotstability(a,b)
  r = exp(1i*linspace(.01,2*pi-0.01,400));
  z = (r'.^(1:length(a))*a) ./ (r'.^(1:length(b))*b);
  plot(z); axis equal
end
```

The Matlab recipe for solving a differential equation is similar to the Julia recipe.   375
But rather than calling a general solver and specifying the method, each method
in Matlab is its own solver. Fortunately, the syntax for each solver is almost
identical.

1. Define the problem   `pendulum = @(t,u)[u(2);-sin(u(1))];`
2. Set up the parameters   `u0 = [8*pi/9,0]; tspan = [0,8*pi];`
3. Solve the problem   `[t,u] = ode23(pendulum,tspan,u0);`
4. Present the solution   `plot(t,u(:,1),'.-',t,u(:,2),'.-')`
                             `legend('\theta','\omega')`

The parameter tspan may be either a two-element vector specifying initial and final times or a longer, strictly increasing or decreasing vector. In the two-vector case, the solver returns the intermediate solutions at each adaptive time step. In the longer-vector case, the solver interpolates the values between the adaptive time steps to provide solutions at the points given in tspan. In MATLAB, we can alternatively request a structure sol as the output of the ODE solver. We can subsequently evaluate sol at an arbitrary array of values t using the function u = deval(sol,t). This approach is similar to the modern approaches in Julia and Python. Octave does not have the function deval.

378   Let's first define the DAE for the pendulum problem. We'll use manifold projection: manifold projection $x = x/\ell$, $y = y/\ell$, and $u = -vy/x$.

```
theta = pi/3; L = 1; tspan = [0,30.0];
U0 = [L*sin(theta), -L*cos(theta), 0, 0];
function dU = pendulum(t,U,p)
  x=U(1); y=U(2); u=U(3); v=U(4); L=p(1); g=p(2); m=p(3);
  x = x/L; y = y/L; u = -v*y/x; % manifold projection
  tau = m*(u^2 + v^2 + g*y)/L^2;
  dU = [u, v, -tau*x/m, -tau*y/m + g];
end
tspan = linspace(0,30,2000);
[t,x] = ode45(@(t,U) pendulum(t,U,[L,1,1]), tspan, U0);
plot(x(:,1),x(:,2)); axis ij; axis equal
```

We can also solve semi-explicit DAEs using ode15s amd fully-implicit DAEs using ode15i. We'll set the parameters ℓ, m, and g to unit values to better see what's happening in the code.

```
theta = pi/3; tspan = [0,30];
u0 = [sin(theta); -cos(theta); 0; 0; -cos(theta)];
function dU = pendulum(t,U)
  x = U(1); y = U(2); u = U(3); v = U(4); tau = U(5);
  dU = [u; v; -tau*x; -tau*y + 1; -tau + y + (u^2+v^2)];
end
M = diag([1,1,1,1,0]);
opt = odeset ("Mass", M, 'AbsTol', 1e-7,'RelTol', 1e-7);
[t,u] = ode15s(@pendulum, tspan, u0, opt);
plot(u(:,1),u(:,2)); axis ij; axis equal
```

The solution gradually drifts off and is eventually entirely wrong. Let's also solve the fully implicit problem using 'ode15i'.

```
function F = pendulum(t,U,dU)
  x = U(1); y = U(2); u = U(3); v = U(4); tau = U(5);
  dx = dU(1); dy = dU(2); du = dU(3); dv = dU(4);
```

```
    F = [dx - u;
       dy - v;
       du + tau*x;
       dv + tau*y - 1;
       -tau + y + (u^2+v^2)];
end
```

We'll use the function decic to *de*termine *c*onsistent *i*nitial *c*onditions for ode15i.

```
theta = pi/3; tspan = [0,30];
u0 = [sin(theta); -cos(theta); 0; 0; 0];
du0 = [0;0;0;0;0];
opt = odeset ('RelTol', 1e-8,'AbsTol', 1e-8);
[u0,du0] = decic(@pendulum,0,u0,[1;1;1;1;0],du0,[0;0;0;0;0]);
[t,y] = ode15i (@pendulum, tspan,u0, du0, opt);
plot(y(:,1),y(:,2)); axis ij; axis equal
```

The following code solves the pendulum problem using orthogonal collocation. 383 we'll use gauss_lobatto and differentition_matrix from page 659 to compute the Gauss–Lobatto nodes and differentiation matrix.

```
function dU = pendulum(U,U0,D,n)
    x = U(1:n); y = U(n+1:2*n); u = U(2*n+1:3*n); v = U(3*n+1:4*n);
    tau = U(4*n+1:5*n); x0 = U0(1); y0 = U0(2); u0 = U0(3); v0 = U0(4);
    dU = [D(x,x0) - u,
       D(y,y0) - v,
       D(u,u0) + tau.*x,
       D(v,v0) + tau.*y - 1,
       x.^2 + y.^2 - 1];
end
```

```
theta = pi/3; tspan = [0,30];
u0 = [sin(theta); -cos(theta); 0; 0; 0];
N = 100; dt = 30.0/N; n = 7;
[M,t] = differentiation_matrix(n,dt);
D = @(u,u0) M*(u - u0);
U = u0;
for i = 1:N
  u = fsolve(@(u) pendulum(u,u0,D,n), repmat(u0',n,1)(:));
  U = [U reshape(u,n,5)'];
  u0 = U(:,end);
end
plot(U(1,:), U(2,:)); axis ij; axis equal
```

The following Matlab code implements the backward Euler method: 394

```
dx = .01; dt = .01; L = 2; lambda = dt/dx^2; uL = 0; uR = 0;
x = (-L:dx:L)'; n = length(x);
u = (abs(x)<1);
u(1) += 2*lambda*uL; u(n) += 2*lambda*uR;
D = spdiags(repmat([1 -2 1],[n 1]),-1:1,n,n);
D(1,2) = 0; D(n,n-1)= 0;
A = speye(n) - lambda*D;
for i = 1:20
  u = A\u;
end
area(x,u,"edgecolor",[1 .5 .5],"facecolor",[1 .8 .8])
```

The runtime using Octave on a typical laptop is about 0.35 seconds. The runtime using a non-sparse matrix is about 0.45 seconds, so there doesn't appear to be a great advantage in using a sparse solver. But, for a larger system with dx = .001, the runtime using sparse matrices is still about 0.35 seconds, whereas for a nonsparse matrix it is almost 30 seconds.

394 The command mldivide (\) will automatically implement a tridiagonal solver on a tridiagonal matrix if the matrix is formatted as a sparse matrix. The command help sparfun returns a list of matrix functions for working with sparse matrices.

395 The following code solves the heat equation using the Crank–Nicolson method:

```
dx = .01; dt = .01; L = 2; lambda = dt/dx^2;
x = (-L:dx:L)'; n = length(x);
u = (abs(x)<1);
D = spdiags(repmat([1 -2 1],[n 1]),-1:1,n,n);
D(1,2) = 2; D(n,n-1) = 2;
A = 2*speye(n) + lambda*D;
B = 2*speye(n) - lambda*D;
for i = 1:20
  u = B\(A*u);
end
plot(x,u);
```

404 The following code implements (13.17) with $m(u) = u^2$ using ode15s, which uses a variation of the adaptive-step BDF methods:

```
n = 400; L = 2; x = linspace(-L,L,n)'; dx = x(2)-x(1);
m = @(u) u.^2;
Du = @(t,u) [0;diff(m((u(1:n-1)+u(2:n))/2).*diff(u))/dx^2;0];
u0 = double(abs(x)<1);
options = odeset('JPattern',spdiags(ones([n 3]),-1:1,n,n));
```

```
[t,U] = ode15s(Du,linspace(0,2,10),u0,options);
for i=1:size(U,1), plot(x,U(i,:),'r'); hold on; ylim([0 1]); end
```

We could also define the right-hand side of the porous medium equation as

```
m = @(u) u.^3/3;
Du = @(t,u) [0;diff(m(u),2)/dx^2;0];
```

We can express the discrete indices of ξ as   460

```
ik = 1i*[0:floor(n/2) floor(-n/2+1):-1]*(2*pi/L);
```

or

```
ik = 1i*ifftshift([floor(-n/2+1):floor(n/2)])*(2*pi/L);
```

The Matlab implementation of the solution to the heat equation (16.4) is

```
n = 256; L = 4;
k2 = ([0:floor(n/2) floor(-n/2+1):-1]*(2*pi/L)).^2;
u = @(t,u0) real(ifft(exp(-k2*t).*fft(u0)))
```

The Matlab code that solves the Navier–Stokes equation has three parts: define   471
the functions, initialize the variables, and iterate over time. We start by defining
functions for $\hat{\mathbf{H}}$ and for the flux used in the Lax–Wendroff scheme.

```
flux = @(Q,c) c.*diff([Q(end,:);Q]) ...
    + 0.5*c.*(1-c).*diff([Q(end,:);Q;Q(1,:)],2);
H = @(u,v,ikx,iky) fft2(ifft2(u).*ifft2(ikx.*u) ...
    + ifft2(v).*ifft2(iky.*u));
```

Now define initial conditions. The variable e is used for the scaling parameter
ε, and k = ξ is a temporary variable used to construct ikx = $i\xi_x$, iky = $i\xi_y$, and
k2 = $-|\xi|^2 = -\xi_x^2 - \xi_y^2$. We'll take the x- and y-dimensions to be the same, but
they can easily be modified.

```
L = 2; n = 128; e = 0.001; dt = .001; dx = L/n;
x = linspace(dx,L,n); y = x';
Q = 0.5*(1+tanh(10*(1-abs(L/2 -y)/(L/4)))).*ones(size(x));
u = Q.*(1+0.5*sin(L*pi*x));
v = zeros(size(u));
u = fft2(u); v = fft2(v);
us = u; vs = v;
ikx = 1i*[0:n/2 (-n/2+1):-1]*(2*pi/L);
iky = ikx.';
```

```
k2 = ikx.^2+iky.^2;
Hx = H(u,v,ikx,iky); Hy = H(v,u,iky,ikx);
M1 = 1/dt + (e/2)*k2;
M2 = 1/dt - (e/2)*k2;
```

Now, we iterate. At each time step, we evaluate (16.14) and use the Lax–Wendroff method to evaluate the advection equation (16.15). The variable Q gives the density Q of the tracer in the advection equation. The variable Hx, computed using the function H, is the x-component of $\mathbf{H}^n$ and Hxo is x-component of $\mathbf{H}^{n-1}$. Similarly, Hy and Hyo are the y-components of $\mathbf{H}^n$ and $\mathbf{H}^{n-1}$. The variables u and v are the x- and y-components of the velocity $\mathbf{u}^n = (u^n, v^n)$. Similarly, us and vs are u^* and v^*, respectively. The variable phi is an intermediate variable for $\Delta^{-1}\nabla \cdot \mathbf{u}^*$. The tracer Q is plotted in Figure 16.2 using a contour plot.

```
for i = 1:1200
  Q = Q - flux(Q,(dt/dx)*real(ifft2(v))) ...
        - flux(Q',(dt/dx)*real(ifft2(u))')';
  Hxo = Hx; Hyo = Hy;
  Hx = H(u,v,ikx,iky); Hy = H(v,u,iky,ikx);
  us = u - us + (-1.5*Hx + 0.5*Hxo + M1.*u)./M2;
  vs = v - vs + (-1.5*Hy + 0.5*Hyo + M1.*v)./M2;
  phi = (ikx.*us + iky.*vs)./(k2+(k2==0));
  u = us - ikx.*phi;
  v = vs - iky.*phi;
end
contourf(x,y,Q,[.5 .5]); axis equal;
```

478   N = 10000; n = zeros([1 20]);
```
      for d = 1:20
        for j = 1:N
          n(d) = n(d) + (det(rand(d)>0.5)~=0);
        end
      end
      plot(1:20,n/N,'.-')
```

479   An easy way to input $\mathbf{D}_n$ in Matlab is with the diag function:

```
D = diag(ones([n-1 1]),1) ...
      - 2*diag(ones([n 1]),0) + diag(ones([n-1 1]),-1);
eig(D)
```

481   The following function implements a naïve determinant:

```
function D = detx(A)
  [L,U,P] = lu(A);
  s = 1;
  for i = 1:length(P)
    m = find(P(i+1:end,i));
    if m, P([i i+m],:) = P([i+m i],:); s = -1*s; end
  end
  D = s * prod(diag(U));
end
```

```
A = [0 1 0 1;1 0 2 1;0 2 0 0;1 1 0 0];                    481
function w = walks(A,i,j,N)
  for n=1:N, w(n) = (A^n)(i,j); end
end
walks(A,1,3,9)
```

The following function implements a naïve reverse Cuthill–McKee algorithm for   482
symmetric matrices:

```
function p = rcuthillmckee(A)
  A = spones(A);
  [_,r] = sort(sum(A));
  p = [];
  while ~isempty(r)
    q = r(1); r(1) = [];
    while ~isempty(q)
      p = [p q(1)];
      [_,k] = find(A(q(1),r));
      q = [q(2:end) r(k)]; r(k) = [];
    end
  end
  p = fliplr(p);
end
```

```
A = sprand(1000,1000,0.001); A = A + A';
p = rcuthillmckee(A);
subplot(1,2,1); spy(A,'.',2); axis equal
subplot(1,2,2); spy(A(p,p),'.',2); axis equal
```

We'll reuse the code on page 620.   482

```
p = rcuthillmckee(A);
```

```
gplot(A(p,p),circular_layout(A),'.-')
axis equal; axis off;
```

483 Reading mixed data into MATLAB or Octave can be frustrating even for
relatively simple structures. In Octave, we can use the csvcell function (from
the io package) to convert a CSV file into a cell. Then, we can use a couple of
loops to divide the cell up into meaningful pieces. The file diet.mat contains
these variables. The solution to the diet problem is

```
urlwrite([bucket "diet.mat"],"diet.mat");
load diet.mat
A = values'; b = minimums; c = ones(size(A,2),1);
[z,x,y] = simplex(b,A',c);
cost = z, food{find(y!=0)}
```

or we can use the built-in Octave glpk function

```
[x,z] = glpk(c,A,b,[],[],repmat("L",size(b')));
cost = z, food{find(x!=0)}
```

484 We'll reuse the function get_adjacency_matrix from page 620. Let's also define
a function to get the names.

```
function r = get_names(bucket,filename)
  data = urlread([bucket filename '.txt']);
  r = cell2mat(textscan(data,'%s','delimiter', '\n')(1));
end
```

We'll create a block sparse matrix and define a function to find the shortest path
between nodes a and b.

```
actors = get_names(bucket,"actors");
movies = get_names(bucket,"movies");
B = get_adjacency_matrix(bucket,"actor-movie");
[m,n] = size(B);
A = [sparse(n,n) B';B sparse(m,m)];
actormovie = [actors;movies];
```

```
function path = findpath(A,a,b)
p = -ones(size(A,2),1);
q = a; p(a) = -9999; i = 1;
while i<=length(q),
    k = find(A(q(i),:));
    k = k(p(k)==-1);
    q = [q k]; p(k) = q(i); i = i + 1;
```

```
    if any(k==b),
      path = backtrack(p,b); return;
    end
  end
  display("No path.");
end


function path = backtrack(p,b)
  s = b; i = p(b);
  while i != -9999, s = [s i]; i = p(i); end
  path = s(end:-1:1);
end


a = find(ismember(actors,"Bruce Lee"));
b = find(ismember(actors,"Tommy Wiseau"));
actormovie(findpath(A,a,b)){:}
```

We can the whos function to determine the bytes of a matrix.   485

```
d = 0.5; A = sprand(60,80,d);
s = whos('A'); nbytes = s.bytes;
nbytes, 8*(2*d*prod(size(A)) + size(A,2) + 1)
```

```
X = rgb2gray(double(imread([bucket "laura.png"])))/255;      486
[m,n] = size(X);
blur = @(x) exp(-(x/20).^2/2);
A = blur([1:m] - [1:m]'); A = A./sum(A,2);
B = blur([1:n] - [1:n]'); B = B./sum(B,1);
N = 0.01*rand(m,n);
Y = A*X*B + N;
```

```
a = 0.05;
X1 = A\Y/B;
X2 = (A'*A+a^2*eye(m))\A'*Y*B'/(B*B'+a^2*eye(n));
X3 = pinv(A,a)*Y*pinv(B,a);
imshow(max(min([X Y X1 X2 X3],1),0))
```

The Matlab code for exercise 3.5 follows. We'll first download the CSV files.   486

```
data = urlread([bucket 'filip.csv']);
T = cell2mat(textscan(data,'%f,%f'));
y = T(:,1); x = T(:,2);
```

```
data = urlread([bucket 'filip-coeffs.csv']);
beta = cell2mat(textscan(data,'%f'));
```

Now, let's define a function that determines the coefficients and residuals using three different methods and one that evaluates a polynomial given those coefficients. The command qr(V,0) returns an economy-size QR decomposition.

```
function [c,r] = solve_filip(x,y,n)
  V = vander(x, n);
  c(:,1) = (V'*V)\(V'*y);
  [Q,R] = qr(V,0);
  c(:,2) = R\(Q'*y);
  c(:,3) = pinv(V,1e-10)*y;
  for i=1:3, r(i) = norm(V*c(:,i)-y); end
end
```

```
build_poly = @(c,X) vander(X,length(c))*c;
```

Now, we can solve the problem and plot the solutions.

```
n = 11;
[c,r] = solve_filip(x,y,n);
X = linspace(min(x),max(x),200);
Y = build_poly(c,X);
plot(X,Y,x,y,'.');ylim([0.7,0.95])
```

Let's also solve the problem and plot the solutions for the standardized data.

```
zscore = @(X,x) (X .- mean(x))/std(x);
[cond(vander(x,11)) cond(vander(zscore(x,x),11))]
[c,r] = solve_filip(zscore(x,x), zscore(y,y), n);
for i=1:3,
  Y(:,i) = build_poly(c(:,i),zscore(X,x))*std(y).+mean(y);
end
plot(X,Y,x,y,'.');ylim([0.7,0.95])
```

```
488  data = urlread([bucket 'dailytemps.csv']);
     T = textscan(data,'%s%f','HeaderLines',1,'Delimiter',',');
     day = datenum(T{1},'yyyy-mm-dd'); temp = T{2};
     day = (day-day(1))/365;
     tempsmodel = @(t) [sin(2*pi*t) cos(2*pi*t) ones(size(t))];
     c = tempsmodel(day)\temp;
     plot(day,temp,'.',day,tempsmodel(day)*c,'k');
```

We'll first load the variables into the workspace and build a matrix $\mathbf{D}_i$ for each   488
$i \in \{0, 1, \ldots, 9\}$. Then we'll use svds to compute the first $k = 12$ singular
matrices. We only need to keep $\{\mathbf{V}_i\}$, which is a low-dimensional column space
of the space of digits.

```
k = 12; V = [];
urlwrite([bucket "emnist-mnist.mat"],"emnist-mnist.mat")
load emnist-mnist.mat
for i = 1:10
  D = dataset.train.images(dataset.train.labels==i-1,:);
  [_,_,V(:,:,i)] = svds(double(D),k);
end
```

Let's display the principal components for the "3" image subspace.

```
pix = reshape(V(:,:,3+1),[28,28*k]);
imshow(pix,[]); axis off
```

Now, let's find the closest column spaces to our test images $\mathbf{d}$ by finding the i
with the smallest residual $\|\mathbf{V}_i \mathbf{V}_i^\mathsf{T} \mathbf{d} - \mathbf{d}\|_2$.

```
r = [];
d = double(dataset.test.images)';
for i = 1:10
  r(i,:) = sum((V(:,:,i)*(V(:,:,i)'*d) - d).^2);
end
[c,predicted] = min(r);
```

We can examine the accuracy of the solution by building a confusion matrix:

```
for i = 1:10
  x = predicted(find(dataset.test.labels == i-1));
  confusion(i,:) = histc(x,1:10);
end
```

Each row of the matrix represents the predicted class and each column represents
the actual class.

We use singular value decomposition to find a low-dimensional subspace relating   490
actors and genres. Then we find the closest actors in that subspace using cosine
similarity. We'll use the helper functions get_names and get_adjacency_matrix
from page 644.

```
actors = get_names(bucket,"actors");
genres = get_names(bucket,"genres");
A = get_adjacency_matrix(bucket,"movie-genre"); A = A/diag(sum(A));
B = get_adjacency_matrix(bucket,"actor-movie");
```

```
[U,S,V] = svds(A*B, 12);
Q = V'./sqrt(sum(V'.^2));
q = Q(:,find(ismember(actors,"Steve Martin")));
[_,r] = sort(Q'*q,'descend');
actors(r(1:10)){:}


[p,r] = sort(U*S*q,'descend');
for i=1:10, printf("%s: %4.3f\n",genres(r(i)){:},p(i)/sum(p)), end
```

491
```
X = [3 3 12; 1 15 14; 10 2 13; 12 15 14; 0 11 12];
reference = X(1,:); X = X - reference;
A = [2 2 -2].*X; b = (X.^2)*[1; 1; -1];
x_ols = A\b + reference'
x_tls = tls(A,b) + reference'
```

491
```
bucket = 'https://raw.githubusercontent.com/nmfsc/data/master/';
data = urlread([bucket 'shotspotter.csv']);
df = cell2mat(textscan(data,'%f,%f,%f,%f','HeaderLines', 1));
X = df(1:end-2,:);
c = 328.6;
reference = X(1,:); X = X .- reference;
A = [2 2 2 -2*c^2].*X; b = (X.^2)*[1; 1; 1; -c^2];
x_ols = A\b + reference';
error = x_ols - df(end,:)'
```

492
```
n = 8; N = 2500; E = zeros(n*N,1);
for i = 0:N-1, E(n*i+(1:n)) = eig(randn(n,n)); end
plot(E,'.'); axis equal
```

492
```
function [rho,x] = rayleigh(A)
  n = length(A); x = randn([n 1]);
  while true
    x = x/norm(x);
    rho = x'*A*x;
    M = A-rho*eye(n);
    if rcond(M)<eps, break; end
    x = M\x;
  end
end
```

The Matlab function hess(A) returns an upper Hessenberg matrix that is unitarily 493 similar to A. The function givens(a,b) returns the Givens rotation matrix for the vector (a, b). The following Matlab code implements the implicit QR method:

```matlab
function eigenvalues = implicitqr(A)
  n = length(A);
  tolerance = 1e-12;
  H = hess(A);
  while true
    if abs(H(n,n-1))<tolerance,
      n = n-1; if n<2, break; end;
    end
    Q = givens(H(1,1)-H(n,n),H(2,1));
    H(1:2,1:n) = Q*H(1:2,1:n);
    H(1:n,1:2) = H(1:n,1:2)*Q';
    for i = 2:n-1
      Q = givens(H(i,i-1),H(i+1,i-1));
      H(i:i+1,1:n) = Q*H(i:i+1,1:n);
      H(1:n,i:i+1) = H(1:n,i:i+1)*Q';
    end
  end
  eigenvalues = diag(H);
end


n = 20; S = randn(n);
D = diag(1:n); A = S*D*inv(S);
implicitqr(A)
```

We'll reuse get_names and get_adjacency_matrix from page 644. 494

```matlab
actors = get_names(bucket,"actors");
B = get_adjacency_matrix(bucket,"actor-movie");
M = sparse(B'*B);
v = ones(size(M,1),1);
for k = 1:10,
  v = M*v; v /= norm(v);
end
[_,r] = sort(v,'descend');
actors(r(1:10)){:}
```

We approximate the SVD by starting with a set of k random vectors and 494 performing a few steps of the naïve QR method to generate a k-dimensional subspace that is relatively close to the space of dominant singular values:

```matlab
function [U,S,V] = randomizedsvd(A,k)
  Z = rand([size(A,2) k]);
  [Q,R] = qr(A*Z,0);
  for i = 1:3
    [Q,R] = qr(A'*Q,0);
    [Q,R] = qr(A*Q,0);
  end
  [W,S,V] = svd(Q'*A,0);
  U = Q*W;
end
```

Let's convert an image to an array, compute its randomized SVD, and then display the original image side-by-side with the rank-reduced version.

```matlab
A = double(rgb2gray(imread([bucket "red-fox.jpg"])));
[U,S,V] = randomizedsvd(A,10);
imshow([A U*S*V'])
```

495
```matlab
m = 5000; j = 1:m;
A = zeros(m,m);
for i = 1:m
  A(i,j) = 1./(1 + (i+j-1).*(i+j)/2 - j);
end
c = svds(A,1)
```

496 The following functions solve the Poisson equation:

```matlab
n = 50; x = (1:n)'/(n+1); dx = 1/(n+1);
[x,y,z] = meshgrid(x);
I = speye(n);
D = spdiags(repmat([1 -2 1],[n 1]),-1:1,n,n);
A = (kron(kron(D,I),I) + kron(I,kron(D,I)) + kron(I,kron(I,D)))/dx^2;
f = ((x-x.^2).*(y-y.^2)+(x-x.^2).*(z-z.^2)+(y-y.^2).*(z-z.^2))(:);
ue = ((x-x.^2).*(y-y.^2).*(z-z.^2)/2)(:);
```

```matlab
function e = stationary(A,b,w,n,ue)
  e = zeros(n,1); u = zeros(size(b));
  P = tril(A,0) - (1-w)*tril(A,-1);
  for i=1:n
    u = u + P\(b-A*u);
    e(i) = norm(u - ue, 1);
  end
end
```

```
function e = conjugategradient(A,b,n,ue)
  e = zeros(n,1); u = zeros(size(b));
  r = b-A*u; p = r;
  for i=1:n
    Ap = A*p;
    a = (r'*p)/(Ap'*p);
    u = u + a.*p; r = r - a.*Ap;
    b = (r'*Ap)/(Ap'*p);
    p = r - b.*p;
    e(i) = norm(u - ue, 1);
  end
end
```

```
tic; err(:,1) = stationary(A,-f,0,400,ue); toc
tic; err(:,2) = stationary(A,-f,1,400,ue); toc
tic; err(:,3) = stationary(A,-f,1.9,400,ue); toc
tic; err(:,4) = conjugategradient(A,-f,400,ue); toc
semilogy(err); legend("Jacobi","Gauss-Seidel","SOR","Conj. Grad.")
```

Each function takes around two seconds to complete 400 iterations. Direct computation tic; A\(-f); toc takes around 20 seconds, considerably shorter than either Julia or Python.

```
n = 20000
d = 2 .^ (0:14); d = [-d;d];
P = spdiags(primes(224737)',0,n,n);
B = spdiags(ones(n,length(d)),d,n,n);
A = P + B;
b = sparse(1,1,1,n,1);
x = pcg(A, b, 1e-15, 100, P); x(1)
```
498

The Matlab code for the radix-3 FFT in exercise 6.1 is   499

```
function y = fftx3(c)
  n = length(c);
  omega = exp(-2i*pi/n);
  if mod(n,3) == 0
    k = 0:n/3-1;
    u = [ fftx3(c(1:3:n-2)).';
        (omega.^k).*fftx3(c(2:3:n-1)).';
        (omega.^(2*k)).*fftx3(c(3:3:n)).'];
    F = exp(-2i*pi/3).^((0:2)'*(0:2));
    y = (F*u).'(:);
  else
```

```
    F = omega.^([0:n-1]'*[0:n-1]);
    y = F*c;
  end
end
```

499 Matlab typically works with floating-point numbers, so we can't easily input
a large integer directly. Instead, we can input it as a string and then convert
the string to an array by subtracting '0'. For example, '5472' - '0' becomes
[5 4 7 2]. Because fft operates on floating-point numbers we use round to
convert the ifft to nearest integer. Putting everything together, we get the
following:

```
function [pq] = multiply(p,q)
  np = [fliplr(p-'0') zeros([1 length(q)])];
  nq = [fliplr(q-'0') zeros([1 length(p)])];
  pq = round(ifft(fft(np).*fft(nq)));
  carry = fix(pq/10);
  while sum(carry)>0,
    pq = (pq - carry*10) + [0 carry(1:end-1)];
    carry = fix(pq/10);
  end
  n = max(find(pq));
  pq = char(fliplr(pq(1:n))+'0');
end
```

500
```
function f = dct(f)
  n = size(f,1);
  w = exp(-0.5i*pi*(0:n-1)'/n);
  f = real(w.*fft(f([1:2:n n-mod(n,2):-2:2],:)));
end
```

```
function f = idct(f)
  n = size(f,1);
  f(1,:) = f(1,:)/2;
  w = exp(-0.5i*pi*(0:n-1)'/n);
  f([1:2:n n-mod(n,2):-2:2],:) = 2*real(ifft(f./w));
end
```

Two-dimensional DCT and IDCT operators apply the DCT or IDCT once in each
dimension.

```
dct2 = @(f) dct(dct(f')');
idct2 = @(f) idct(idct(f')');
```

The following function returns a sparse matrix of Fourier coefficients along with   163
the reconstructed compressed image:

```
pkg load signal
function [B,A] = dctcompress2(A,d)
  n = size(A) ; n0 = floor(n*sqrt(d));
  B = dct2(A)(1:n0(1),1:n0(2));
  A = idct2(B,n);
end
```

We'll test the function on an image and compare it before and after.

```
aitken1 = @(x1,x2,x3) x3 - (x3-x2).^2./(x3 - 2*x2 + x1);          505
aitken2 = @(x1,x2,x3) (x1.*x3 - x2.^2)./(x3 - 2*x2 + x1);
n = 20000;
p = cumsum((-1).^[0:n]*4./(2*[0:n]+1));
p1 = aitken1(p(1:n-2),p(2:n-1),p(3:n));
p2 = aitken2(p(1:n-2),p(2:n-1),p(3:n));
loglog(abs(pi-p)); hold on; loglog(abs(pi-p2)); loglog(abs(pi-p1));
```

We'll find the solution to the system of equations in exercise 8.12. Let's first   508
define the system and the gradient.

```
f = @(x,y) [(x^2+y^2)^2-2*(x^2-y^2); (x^2+y^2-1)^3-x^2*y^3];
df = @(x,y) [4*x*(x^2+y^2-1), 4*y*(x^2+y^2+1);
    6*x*(x^2+y^2 -1)^2-2*x*y^3, 6*y*(x^2+y^2 -1)^2-3*x^2*y^2];
```

The homotopy continuation method is

```
function x = homotopy(f,df,x)
  dxdt = @(t,x) -df(x(1),x(2))\f(x(1),x(2));
  [t,y] = ode45(dxdt,[0;1],x);
  x = y(end,:);
end
```

and Newton's method is

```
function x = newton(f,df,x)
  for i = 1:100
    dx = -df(x(1),x(2))\f(x(1),x(2));
    x = x + dx;
    if norm(dx)<1e-8, return; end
  end
end
```

512 The following function computes the coefficients $\{m_0, m_1, \ldots, m_{n-1}\}$ for a spline
with periodic boundary conditions. It is assumed that $y_0 = y_n$.

```
function m = spline_periodic(x,y)
  h = diff(x);
  C = circshift(diag(h),[1 0]) + 2*diag(h+circshift(h,[1 0])) ...
    + circshift(diag(h),[0 1]);
  d = 6.*diff(diff([y(end-1);y])./[h(end);h]);
  m = C\d; m = [m;m(1)];
end
```

To following script picks n random points and interpolates a parametric spline
with periodic boundary conditions using nx*n points. To evaluate the spline we
use evaluate_spline discussed on page 629.

```
n = 10; nx = 20;
x = rand(n,1); y = rand(n,1);
x = [x;x(1)]; y = [y;y(1)];
t = [0;cumsum(sqrt(diff(x).^2+diff(y).^2))];
[_,X] = evaluate_spline(t,x,spline_periodic(t,x),nx*n);
[_,Y] = evaluate_spline(t,y,spline_periodic(t,y),nx*n);
plot(X,Y,x,y,'.','markersize',6);
```

512 The following code computes and plots the interpolating curves:

```
n = 20; N = 200;
x = linspace(-1,1,n)'; X = linspace(-1,1,N)';
y = (x>0);


phi1 = @(x,a) abs(x-a).^3;
phi2 = @(x,a) exp(-20*(x-a).^2);
phi3 = @(x,a) x.^a;
interp = @(phi,a) phi(X,a')*(phi(x,a')\y);


Y1 = interp(phi1,x);
Y2 = interp(phi2,x);
Y3 = interp(phi3,(0:n-1)');
plot(x,y,X,Y1,X,Y2,X,Y3); ylim([-.5 1.5]);
```

514 We define a function to solve linear boundary value problems.

```
function c = solve(L,f,bc,x)
  h = x(2)-x(1); n = length(x);
  S = ([1 -1/2 1/6; -2 0 2/3; 1 1/2 1/6]./[h^2 h 1])*L(x);
```

```
    A(2:n+1,1:n+2) = spdiags(S',[0 1 2],n,n+2);
    A(1,1:3) = [1/6 2/3 1/6];
    A(n+2,n:n+2) = [1/6 2/3 1/6];
    d = [bc(1) f(x) bc(2)];
    c = A\d';
end
```

Let's also define a function that will interpolate between collocation points.

```
function [X,Y] = build(c,x,N)
    X = linspace(x(1),x(end),N);
    h = x(2) - x(1);
    i = floor(X/h)+1; i(N) = i(N-1);
    C = [c(i) c(i+1) c(i+2) c(i+3)]';
    B = @(x) [(1-x).^3;4-3*(2-x).*x.^2;4-3*(1+x).*(1-x).^2;x.^3]/6;
    Y = sum(C.*B((X-x(i))/h));
end
```

Now, we can solve the Bessel equation.

```
n = 15; N = 141
L = @(x) [x;ones(size(x));x];
f = @(x) zeros(size(x));
b = fzero(@(z) besselj(0, z), 11);
x = linspace(0,b,n);
c = solve(L,f,[1,0],x);
[X,Y] = build(c,x,N);
plot(X,Y,X,besselj(0,X))
```

Finally, we examine the error and convergence rate.

```
n = 10*2.^(1:6);
for i = 1:length(n)
    x = linspace(0,b,n(i));
    c = solve(L,f,[1,0],x);
    [X,Y] = build(c,x,n(i));
    e(i) = sqrt(sum((Y-besselj(0,X)).^2)/n(i));
end
loglog(n,e,'.-');
s = polyfit(log(n),log(e),1);
printf("slope: %f",s(1))
```

517
```
n = 128; L = 2;
x = (0:n-1)/n*L-L/2;
k = [0:(n/2-1) (-n/2):-1]*(2*pi/L);
f = exp(-6*x.^2);
for p = 0:0.1:1
  d = real(ifft((1i*k).^p.*fft(f)));
  plot(x,d,'m'); hold on;
end
```

519 We'll first solve the toy problem.

```
pkg load optim
phi = @(x,p) sqrt((x(:,1)-p(1)).^2+(x(:,2)-p(2)).^2)-(x(:,3)-p(3));
x = [3 3 12; 1 15 14; 10 2 13; 12 15 14; 0 11 12];
[_,x_nls] = leasqr (x, 0*x(:,1), x(1,:), phi)
```

Now, let's apply the method to the ShotSpotter data. First, we get the data.

```
bucket = 'https://raw.githubusercontent.com/nmfsc/data/master/';
data = urlread([bucket 'shotspotter.csv']);
df = cell2mat(textscan(data,'%f,%f,%f,%f','HeaderLines', 1));
X = df(1:end-1,:);
```

Then, we find the solution.

```
pkg load optim
phi = @(x,p) sqrt((x(:,1)-p(1)).^2 + (x(:,2)-p(2)).^2 +
  (x(:,3)-p(3)).^2) - 328.6*(x(:,4)-p(4));
[_,x_nls] = leasqr(X, 0*X(:,1), X(1,:), phi);
```

Finally, we compute the error.

```
x_nls - df(end,:)'
```

520
```
d = [0,1,2,3]; n = length(d);
V = fliplr(vander(d)) ./ factorial([0:n-1]);
coeffs = inv(V);
trunc = coeffs*d'.^n/factorial(n);
```

Coefficients are given by rats(coeffs) and the coefficients of the truncation error is given by rats(trunc).

```
function a = richardson(f,x,m)                                    521
  for i=1:m
    D(i) = phi(f,x,2^i);
    for j = i-1:-1:1
      D(j) = (4^(i-j)*D(j+1) - D(j))/(4^(i-j) - 1);
    end
  end
  a = D(1);
end
```

We'll extend the dual class on page 635 by adding methods for division, square   522
root, and cosine.

```
function h = mrdivide(u,v)
   if ~isa(u,'dual'), u = dual(u,0); end
   if ~isa(v,'dual'), v = dual(v,0); end
   h = dual(u.value/v.value, ...
       (v.value*u.deriv-1*u.value*v.deriv)/(v.value*v.value));
end
function h = cos(u)
  h = dual(cos(u.value), -1*sin(u.value)*u.deriv);
end
function h = sqrt(u)
  h = dual(sqrt(u.value), u.deriv/(2*sqrt(u.value)));
end
```

If an earlier definition of dual is still in our workspace, we may need to refresh
the workspace with the command clear functions. Now, we can implement
Newton's method.

```
function x = get_zero(f,x)
  tolerance = 1e-12; delta = 1;
  while abs(delta)>tolerance,
    fx = f(dual(x,1));
    delta = fx.value/fx.deriv;
    x -= delta;
  end
end
```

```
get_zero(@(x) 4*sin(x) + sqrt(x), 4)
```

To find a minimum or maximum of $f(x)$, we substitute the following two lines
into the Newton solver:

```
fx = f(dual(dual(x,1),1));
delta = fx.deriv.value/fx.deriv.deriv;
```

523 ```
function d = cauchyderivative(f, a, p, n = 20, r = 0.1)
    w = exp(2*pi*1i*(0:(n-1))/n);
    d = factorial(p)/(n*r^p)*sum(f(a+r*w)./w.^p)
end
```

```
f = @(x) exp(x)/(cos(x).^3 + sin(x).^3)
cauchyderivative(f, 0, 6)
```

523 The following function computes the nodes and weights for Gauss–Legendre
quadrature by using Newton's method to find the roots of $P_n(x)$:

```
function [x,w] = gauss_legendre(n)
    x = -cos((4*(1:n)-1)*pi/(4*n+2))';
    dx = ones(n,1);
    dP = 0;
    while(max(abs(dx))>1e-16),
        P = [x ones(n,1)];
        for k = 2:n
            P = [((2*k - 1)*x.*P(:,1)-(k-1)*P(:,2))/k, P(:,1)];
        end
        dP = n*(x.*P(:,1) - P(:,2))./(x.^2-1);
        dx = P(:,1) ./ dP(:,1);
        x = x - dx;
    end
    w = 2./((1-x.^2).*dP(:,1).^2);
end
```

524 We'll modify the implementation of the Golub–Welsch algorithm from page 636
to Gauss–Hermite polynomials.

```
function [nodes,weights] = gauss_hermite(n)
    b = (1:n-1)/2;
    a = zeros(n,1);
    scaling = sqrt(pi);
    [v,s] = eig(diag(sqrt(b),1) + diag(a) + diag(sqrt(b),-1));
    weights = scaling*v(1,:).^2;
    nodes = diag(s);
end
```

Now, we can solve the problem.
```

```
[s,w] = gauss_hermite(20);
u0 = @(x) sin(x);
u = @(t,x) w * u0(x-2*sqrt(t)*s)/sqrt(pi);
x = linspace(-12,12,100);
plot(x,u(1,x))
```

Let's define a general function   524

```
mc_pi = @(n,d,m) sum(sum(rand(d,n,m).^2,1)<1)./n*2^d;
```

that computes the volume of an d-sphere using n samples repeated m times. We
can verify the convergence rate by looping over several values of n.

```
m = 20; error = []; N = 2 .^ (1:20);
for n = N
  error = [error sum(abs(pi - mc_pi(n,2,m)))/m];
end
s = polyfit(log(N),log(error),1);
printf("slope: %f",s(1))
loglog(N,exp(s(2)).*N.^s(1),N,error,'.');
```

We can compute Gauss–Lobatto nodes by modifying the function gauss_legendre   525
defined on page 582.

```
function [nodes,weights] = gauss_lobatto(n)
  b = (1:n-1).^2./(4*(1:n-1).^2-1);
  b(end) = (n-1)/(2*(n-1) - 1);
  a = zeros(n,1);
  scaling = 2;
  [v,s] = eig(diag(sqrt(b),1) + diag(a) + diag(sqrt(b),-1));
  weights = scaling*v(1,:).^2;
  nodes = diag(s);
end
```

```
function [M,t] = differentiation_matrix(n,dt)
  [nodes, _] = gauss_lobatto(n+1);
  t = (nodes(2:end)+1)/2;
  A = (1:n).*fliplr(vander(t));
  B = diag(t)*fliplr(vander(t));
  M = (A/B)/dt;
end
```

Now, let's solve the nonlinear system

```
n = 20; u0 = 1.0; a = 0.9;
[M,t] = differentiation_matrix(n,1);
D = @(u,u0) M*(u - u0);
F = @(u,u0,a) D(u,u0) - a*u.^2;
u = fsolve(@(u) F(u,u0,a),u0*ones(n,1));
plot(t, u, "-o")
```

Finally, we solve the same problem using the pseudospectral method.

```
N = 20; dt = 1.0/N; n = 8; a = 0.9;
[M,t] = differentiation_matrix(n,dt);
D = @(u,u0) M*(u - u0);
F = @(u,u0,a) D(u,u0) - 0.9*u.^2;
u0 = 1.0; U = [u0]; T = [0];
for i = 1:N
  u = fsolve(@(u) F(u,u0,a),u0*ones(n,1));
  u0 = u(end);
  T = [T;(i + t)*dt];
  U = [U;u];
end
plot(T, U, "-o")
```

527 The following code plots the region of absolute stability for a Runge–Kutta
method with tableau A and b:

```
n = length(b);
N = 100;
x = linspace(-4,4); y = x'; r = zeros(N,N);
lk = x + 1i*y;
E = ones(n,1);
for i = 1:N, for j=1:N
  r(i,j) = 1+ lk(i,j) * b*(( eye(n) - lk(i,j)*A)\E);
end, end
contour(x,y,abs(r),[1 1],'k');
axis([-4 4 -4 4]);
```

528
```
i = (0:3)';
a = ((-(i+1)').^i./factorial(i))\[1;0;0;0];
b = ((-i').^i./factorial(i))\[0;1;0;0];
```

529 The following function returns the orbit of points in the complex plane for
an nth order Adams–Bashforth–Moulton PE(CE)^m. It calls the function
multistepcoefficients defined on page 637.

```
function z = PECE(n,m)
  [_,a] = multistepcoefficients([0,1],1:n-1);
  [_,b] = multistepcoefficients([0,1],0:n-1);
  for i = 1:200
    r = exp(2i*pi*(i/200));
    c(1) = r - 1;
    c(2:m+1) = r + r.^(1:n-1)*b(2:end)'/b(1);
    c(m+2) = r.^(1:n-1)*a/b(1);
    z(i,:) = roots(fliplr(c))'/b(1);
  end
end
```

```
for i= 1:4
  plot(PECE(2,i),'.k'); hold on; axis equal
end
```

Let's write a function that computes the Padé coefficients.   531

```
function [p,q] = pade(a,m,n)
  A = eye(m+n+1);
  for i=1:n, A(i+1:end,m+1+i) = -a(1:m+n+1-i); end
  pq = A\a(1:m+n+1);
  p = pq(1:m+1); q = [1; pq(m+2:end)];
end
```

Now, compute the coefficients of $P_m(x)$ and $Q_n(x)$ for the Taylor polynomial approximation of $\log(x + 1)$.

```
m = 3; n = 2;
a = [0 ((-1).^(0:m+n)./(1:m+n+1))]';
[p,q] = pade(a,m,n)
```

Finally, shift and combine the coefficients using upper inverse Pascal matrices.

```
S = @(n) inv(pascal(n,-1)');
S(m+1)*p, S(n+1)*q
```

The solution to the SIR problem is   531

```
SIR = @(t,y,b,g) [-b*y(1)*y(2);b*y(1)*y(2)-g*y(2);g*y(2)];
tspan = linspace(0,15,100); y0 = [0.99, 0.01, 0];
[t,y] = ode45(@(t,y) SIR(t,y,2,0.4),tspan,y0);
plot(t,y(:,1),t,y(:,2),t,y(:,3));
```

We can replace the interval [0 15] in ode45 with linspace(0,15,100) to evaluate the solution at additional points for a smoother plot.

532 The solution to the Duffing equation is

```
duffing = @(t,x,g) [x(2); -g*x(2)+x(1)-x(1).^3+0.3*cos(t)];
tspan = linspace(0,200,2000);
[t,x] = ode45(@(t,x) duffing(t,x,0.37), tspan, [1,0]);
plot(x(:,1),x(:,2));
```

533 The following code solves the initial value problem and computes the error at the second boundary point:

```
function error = shooting(x,f,xspan,bc)
  [t,y] = ode45(f,xspan,[bc(1),x]);
  error = y(end,1)- bc(2);
end
```

The function fsolve calls the function shooting that solves an initial value problem and computes the error in the solutions at the second boundary point.

```
xspan = [-12, 0]; bc = [1, 1]; guess = 5;
airy = @(x,y) [y(2);x*y(1)];
v = fsolve(@(x) shooting(x,airy,xspan,bc),guess)
```

534 We'll use the function multistepcoefficients, defined on page 637.

```
m = [0 1 2 3 4]; n = [1];
a = zeros(max(m)+1,1); b = zeros(max(n)+1,1);
[a(m+1),b(n+1)] = multistepcoefficients(m,n);
```

```
lk = @(r) (r.^-(1:length(a))*a) ./ (r.^-(1:length(b))*b);
r = linspace(0.2,6,100)';
plot([lk(r) lk(-r)],[r r]); hold on; xlim([-2 2])
```

Displaying time-varying dynamics can be challenging. A simple approach in Matlab is adding
a plot command with a drawnow statement inside
a loop. This approach can be slow and doesn't
always work in different Octave environments.
Another approach is saving the plots as PDF or
PNG files, and then using an external program
like ffmpeg to convert the stack of images into
a gif or mp4. A different approach to capturing
time-varying dynamics is layering snapshots
as a still image. Because such a visualization
gets messy when there are many layers, we can
offset each layer horizontally or vertically. The
figure on the right layers the solutions, one on
top of the other like stacked paper cut-outs, each
new one shifted down slightly. From it, we see
the undulating behavior of the Dufort–Frankel
solution.

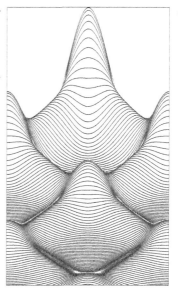

535

```
dx = 0.01; dt = 0.01;
L = 1; x = (-L:dx:L)'; m = length(x);
V = exp(-8*x.^2); U = V;
c = dt/dx^2; a = 0.5 + c; b = 0.5 - c;
B = c*spdiags([ones(m,1),zeros(m,1),ones(m,1)],-1:1,m,m);
B(1,2) = B(1,2)*2; B(end,end-1) = B(end,end-1)*2;
for i = 1:420,
  if mod(i,3)==1, area(x, (V-i/300),-1,'facecolor','w'); hold on; end
  Vo = V; V = (B*V+b*U)/a; U = Vo;
end
ylim([-1,1]); set(gca,'xtick',[],'ytick',[])
```

The following Matlab code solves the Schrödinger equation: 537

```
function psi = schroedinger(n,m,eps)
  x = linspace(-4,4,n)'; dx = x(2)-x(1); dt = 2*pi/m; V = x.^2/2;
  psi = exp(-(x-1).^2/(2*eps))/(pi*eps)^(1/4);
  diags = repmat([1 -2 1],[n 1])/dx^2;
  D = 0.5i*eps*spdiags(diags,-1:1,n,n) - 1i/eps*spdiags(V,0,n,n);
  D(1,2) = 2*D(1,2); D(end,end-1) = 2*D(end,end-1);
  A = speye(n) + (dt/2)*D;
  B = speye(n) - (dt/2)*D;
  for i = 1:m
    psi = B\(A*psi);
  end
```

```
end
```

We'll loop over several values for time steps and mesh sizes and plot the error.

```
eps = 0.3; m = 20000; n = floor(logspace(2,3.7,6));
x = linspace(-4,4,m)';
psi_m = -exp(-(x-1).^2/(2*eps))/(pi*eps)^(1/4);
for i = 1:length(n),
  x = linspace(-4,4,n(i))';
  psi_n = -exp(-(x-1).^2/(2*eps))/(pi*eps)^(1/4);
  error_t(i) = norm(psi_m - schroedinger(m,n(i),eps))/m;
  error_x(i) = norm(psi_n - schroedinger(n(i),m,eps))/n(i);
end
loglog(2*pi./n,error_t,'.-r',8./n,error_x,'.-k');
```

539 Let's solve a radially symmetric heat equation. Although we divide by zero at $r = 0$ when constructing the Laplacian operator, we subsequently overwrite the resulting inf term when we apply the boundary condition.

```
T = 0.5; m = 100; n = 100;
r = linspace(0,2,m)'; dr = r(2)-r(1); dt = T/n;
u = tanh(32*(1-r));
tridiag = [1 -2 1]/dr^2 + (1./r).*[-1 0 1]/(2*dr);
D = spdiags(tridiag,-1:1,m,m)';
D(1,1:2) = [-4 4]/dr^2; D(m,m-1:m) = [2 -2]/dr^2;
A = speye(m) - 0.5*dt*D;
B = speye(m) + 0.5*dt*D;
for i = 1:n
  u = A\(B*u);
end
area(r,u,-1,"edgecolor",[1 .5 .5],"facecolor",[1 .8 .8]);
```

Alternatively, a much slower but high-order BDF routine can be used in place of the Crank–Nicolson routine:

```
options = odeset('JPattern',spdiags(ones([n 3]),-1:1,m,m));
[t,u] = ode15s(@(t,u) D*u,[0 T],u,options);
```

540 We'll first define a function as a logit analogue to linspace.

```
logitspace = @(x,n,p) x*atanh(linspace(-p,p,n)')/atanh(p);
```

Next, we'll define a general discrete Laplacian operator. The following function returns a sparse matrix in diagonal format (DIA). Two inconsequential elements of array d are replaced with nonzero numbers to avoid divide-by-zero warnings.

```
function D = laplacian(x)
  h = diff(x); h1 = h(1:end-1); h2 = h(2:end); n = length(x);
  diags = 2./[h1(1).^2, -h1(1).^2, 0;
  h2.*(h1+h2), -h1.*h2, h1.*(h1+h2);
  0, -h2(end).^2, h2(end).^2];
  D = spdiags(diags,-1:1,n,n)';
end
```

Now, we write a function to solve the heat equation.

```
function u = heat_equation(x,t,u)
  n = 40; dt = t/n;
  D = laplacian(x);
  A = speye(n) - 0.5*dt*D;
  B = speye(n) + 0.5*dt*D;
  for i = 1:n
    u = A\(B*u);
  end
end
```

Finally, we generate a solution using logit spacing.

```
phi = @(x,t,s) exp(-s*x.^2/(1+4*s*t))/sqrt(1+4*s*t);
t = 15; m = 40;
x = logitspace(20,m,.999);
u = heat_equation(x,t,phi(x,0,10));
plot(x,u,'.-',x,phi(x,t,10),'k')
```

Here's a solution to the Allen–Cahn equation using Strang splitting: 541

```
L = 16; m = 400; dx = L/m;
T = 4; n = 1600; dt = T/n;
x = linspace(-L/2,L/2,m);
u = tanh(x.^4 - 16*(2*x.^2-x'.^2));
D = spdiags(repmat([1 -2 1],[m 1]),-1:1,m,m)/dx^2;
D(1,2) = 2*D(1,2); D(end,end-1) = 2*D(end,end-1);
A = speye(m) + 0.5*dt*D;
B = speye(m) - 0.5*dt*D;
f = @(u,dt) u./sqrt(u.^2 - (u.^2-1).*exp(-50*dt));
u = f(u,dt/2);
for i = 1:n
  u = (B\(A*(B\(A*u))')')';
  if i<n, u = f(u,dt); end
end
u = f(u,dt/2);
```

We can plot the solution using the code

```
image((u+1)/2*100);colormap(gray(100));
```

We can animate the time evolution of the solution by adding an `imwrite` command inside the loop to save each iteration to a stack of sequential PNGs and then using a program such as ffmpeg to compile the PNGs into an MP4.

546 The following code solves Burgers' equation.

```
m = 100; x = linspace(-1,3,m); dx = x(2)-x(1);
n = 100; Lt = 4; dt = Lt/n;
lambda = dt/dx;
f = @(u) u.^2/2; fp = @(u) u;
u = (x>=0)&(x<=1);
for i = 1:n
  fu = f([u(1) u]); fpu = fp([u(1) u]);
  a = max(abs(fu(1:n-1)),abs(fu(2:n)));
  F = (fu(1:n-1)+fu(2:n))/2 - a.*diff(u)/2;
  u = u - lambda*(diff([0 F 0]));
end
area(x,u,"edgecolor",[.3 .5 1],"facecolor",[.6 .8 1]);
```

547 Let's first define a few functions.

```
function s = slope(u)
  limiter = @(t) (abs(t)+t)./(1+abs(t));
  du = diff(u);
  s = [[0 0];du(2:end,:).*limiter(du(1:end-1,:)./(du(2:end,:) ...
    + (du(2:end,:)==0)));[0 0]];
end
```

Now, we can solve the dam-break problem.

```
F = @(u) [u(:,1).*u(:,2), u(:,1).*u(:,2).^2+0.5*u(:,1).^2];
m = 1000; x = linspace(-.5,.5,m)'; dx = x(2)-x(1);
T = 0.25; n = ceil(T/(dx/2)); dt = (T/n)/2; c = dt/dx;
u = [0.8*(x<0)+0.2,0*x];
j = 1:m-1;
for i = 1:n
  v = u-0.5*c*slope(F(u));
  u(j+1,:)=(u(j,:)+u(j+1,:))/2 - diff(slope(u))/8-c*diff(F(v));
  v = u-0.5*c*slope(F(u));
  u(j,:)=(u(j,:)+u(j+1,:))/2 - diff(slope(u))/8-c*diff(F(v));
end
plot(x,u(:,1));
```

Other slope limiters we might try include the superbee and the minmod:

```
limiter = @(t) max(0,max(min(2*t,1),min(t,2)));
limiter = @(t) max(0,min(1,t));
```

```
m=10;                                                                    549
x=linspace(0,1,m)'; h=x(2)-x(1);
A=diag(repmat(-1/h-h/6,[m-1 1]),-1)+diag(repmat(1/h-h/3,[m 1]));
A = A + A'; A(1,1)=A(1,1)/2; A(m,m)=A(m,m)/2;
b=[-2/3*h^3;-4/3*h^3-8*h*x(2:m-1).^2;-4*h+8*h^2/3-2*h^3/3+1];
u=A\b;
s=(-16)+8.*x.^2+15.*cos(x).*csc(1);
plot(x,s,'o-',x,u,'.-');
```

```
m = 8;                                                                   550
x = linspace(0,1,m+2); h = x(2)-x(1);
D = @(a,b,c) (diag(a*ones(m-1,1),-1) + ...
   diag(b*ones(m,1),0) + diag(c*ones(m-1,1),1))/h^3;
M = [D(-12,24,-12) D(-6,0,6);D(6,0,-6) D(2,8,2)];
b = [ones([m 1])*h*384;zeros([m 1])];
u = M\b;
plot(x,16*(x.^4 - 2*x.^3 + x.^2),'o-',x,[0;u(1:m);0],'.-');
```

```
m = 128; x = (1:m)'/m*(2*pi)-pi;                                         551
k = 1i*[0:m/2 -m/2+1:-1]';
f = @(t,u) -(ifft(k.*fft(0.5*u.^2)));
[t,u] = ode45(f,[0 1.5],exp(-x.^2));
plot(x,u(end,:))
```

The following Matlab code solves the KdV equation using integrating factors. 552
We first set the parameters:

```
phi = @(x,x0,c) 0.5*c*sech(sqrt(c)/2*(x-x0)).^2;
L = 30; T = 1.0; m = 256;
x = (1:m)'/m*L-L/2;
k = 1i*[0:(m/2) (-m/2+1):-1]'*(2*pi/L);
```

We define the integrating factor and right-hand side of the differential equation.

```
G = @(t) exp(-k.^3*t);
f = @(t,w) -G(t).\(3*k.*fft(ifft(G(t).*w).^2));
```

Then, we solve the problem using ode45.

```
u = phi(x,-4,4) + phi(x,-9,9);
w = fft(u);
[t,w] = ode45(f,linspace(0,T,40),w);
u = real(ifft(G(t').*w.').');
```

Finally, we present the solution as a waterfall plot.

```
for i=40:-1:1,
  area(x, T*(u(i,:)+i)/40,'facecolor','w'); hold on;
end
```

Be careful about the dimensions of the output arrays t and w. My carelessness and use of the conjugate transpose (') instead of a regular transpose (. ') provided me with what seemed like hours of debugging amusement.

554 We'll use Strang splitting to solve the Swift–Hohenberg equation.

```
eps = 1; m = 256; L = 100; n = 2000; dt=100/n;
U = (rand(m)>.5)-0.5;
colormap(gray(256))
k = [0:(m/2) (-m/2+1):-1]*(2*pi/L);
D2 = (1i*k).^2+(1i*k').^2;
E = exp(-(D2+1).^2*dt);
f = @(U) U./sqrt(U.^2/eps + exp(-dt*eps)*(1-U.^2/eps));
for i=1:n
   U = f(ifft2(E.*fft2(f(U))));
end
imshow(real(U))
```

References

Forman S. Acton. *Numerical Methods that Work*. Mathematical Association of America, 1990.

Alexander Craig Aitken. *Gallipoli to the Somme: Recollections of a New Zealand infantryman*. Oxford University Press, 1963.

Uri M. Ascher, Steven J. Ruuth, and Brian T. R. Wetton. Implicit-explicit methods for time-dependent partial differential equations. *SIAM Journal on Numerical Analysis*, 32(3):797–823, 1995.

Uri M. Ascher, Steven J. Ruuth, and Raymond J. Spiteri. Implicit-explicit Runge–Kutta methods for time-dependent partial differential equations. *Applied Numerical Mathematics*, 25(2):151–167, 1997.

Kendall Atkinson and Weimin Han. *Theoretical Numerical Analysis*, volume 39 of *Texts in Applied Mathematics*. Springer, New York, second edition, 2005.

Jared L. Aurentz, Thomas Mach, Raf Vandebril, and David S. Watkins. Fast and backward stable computation of roots of polynomials. *SIAM Journal on Matrix Analysis and Applications*, 36(3):942–973, 2015.

Santiago Badia and Francesc Verdugo. Gridap: An extensible finite element toolbox in Julia. *Journal of Open Source Software*, 5(52):2520, 2020.

Serge Bernstein. Démo istration du théorème de Weierstrass fondée sur le calcul des probabilités. *Communications of the Kharkov Mathematical Society*, 13(1):1–2, 1912.

Michael Blair, Sally Obenski, and Paula Bridickas. Patriot missile defense: Software problem led to system failure at Dhahran. Technical report, GAO/IMTEC-92-26, United States General Accounting Office, 1992.

Ignace Bogaert. Iteration-free computation of Gauss–Legendre quadrature nodes and weights. *SIAM Journal on Scientific Computing*, 36(3):A1008–A1026, 2014.

Max Born. *The Restless Universe.* Courier Corporation, 1951.

Jonathan M. Borwein and Peter B. Borwein. *Pi and the AGM: A study in the analytic number theory and computational complexity.* Wiley–Interscience, 1987.

George E. P. Box and Mervin E. Muller. A note on the generation of random normal deviates. *The Annals of Mathematical Statistics*, 29:610–611, 1958.

Claude Brezinski. *History of continued fractions and Padé approximants*, volume 12. Springer Science & Business Media, 2012.

Daniel R. L. Brown. SEC 2: Recommended elliptic curve domain parameters. *Standards for Efficient Cryptography*, 2010. https://www.secg.org/sec2-v2.pdf.

Adhemar Bultheel. Learning to swim in a sea of wavelets. *Bulletin of the Belgian Mathematical Society*, 2(1):1–46, 1995.

John C. Butcher. *Numerical Methods for Ordinary Differential Rquations.* John Wiley & Sons, 2008.

Robert B. Calhoun, Clark Dunson, Murphey L. Johnson, Scott R. Lamkin, William R. Lewis, Robert L. Showen, Mark A. Sompel, and Lester P. Wollman. Precision and accuracy of acoustic gunshot location in an urban environment. *arXiv preprint arXiv:2108.07377*, 2021.

Emmanuel J. Candè and Michael B. Wakin. An introduction to compressive sampling. *IEEE Signal Processing Magazine*, 25(2):21–30, 2008.

Augustin-Louis Cauchy. Méthode générale pour la résolution des systèmes d'équations simultanées. *Comptes Rendu de à l'Académie des Sciences*, 25:536–538, 1847.

Jean Céa. Approximation variationnelle des problèmes aux limites. In *Annales de l'institut Fourier*, volume 14, pages 345–444, 1964.

Yoonsuck Choe, B. H. McCormick, and W. Koh. Network connectivity analysis on the temporally augmented C. elegans web: A pilot study. In *Society for Neuroscience Abstracts*, volume 30. 2004. Program No. 921.9.

Fan R. K. Chung and Fan Chung Graham. *Spectral Graph Theory.* American Mathematical Society, 1997.

Philippe G. Ciarlet. *The finite element method for elliptic problems.* SIAM, 2002.

Gregory Cohen, Saeed Afshar, Jonathan Tapson, and André van Schaik. EMNIST: an extension of MNIST to handwritten letters. *CoRR*, abs/1702.05373, 2017. http://arxiv.org/abs/1702.05373.

James W. Cooley. How the FFT gained acceptance. In *Proceedings of the ACM conference on History of scientific and numeric computation*, pages 97–100, 1987a.

James W. Cooley. The re-discovery of the fast Fourier transform algorithm. *Microchimica Acta*, 93(1):33–45, 1987b.

James W. Cooley and John W. Tukey. An algorithm for the machine calculation of complex Fourier series. *Mathematics of Computation*, 19(90):297–301, 1965.

Robert M. Corless, Gaston H. Gonnet, David E. G. Hare, David J. Jeffrey, and Donald E. Knuth. On the lambertw function. *Advances in Computational Mathematics*, 5(1): 329–359, 1996.

Steven M. Cox and Paul C. Matthews. Exponential time differencing for stiff systems. *Journal of Computational Physics*, 176(2):430–455, 2002.

John Crank and Phyllis Nicolson. A practical method for numerical evaluation of solutions of partial differential equations of the heat-conduction type. In *Mathematical Proceedings of the Cambridge Philosophical Society*, volume 43, pages 50–67. Cambridge University Press, 1947.

Charles Francis Curtiss and Joseph O. Hirschfelder. Integration of stiff equations. *Proceedings of the National Academy of Sciences of the United States of America*, 38 (3):235, 1952.

Germund Dahlquist. Convergence and stability in the numerical integration of ordinary differential equations. *Mathematica Scandinavica*, pages 33–53, 1956.

Germund Dahlquist. A special stability problem for linear multistep methods. *BIT Numerical Mathematics*, 3(1):27–43, 1963.

Gordon Charles Danielson and Cornelius Lanczos. Some improvements in practical Fourier analysis and their application to x-ray scattering from liquids. *Journal of the Franklin Institute*, 233(5):435–452, 1942.

George B. Dantzig. *Linear Programming and Extensions*. Princeton University Press, 1963.

George B. Dantzig. Reminiscences about the origins of linear programming. Technical report, Stanford University Systems Optimization Laboratory, April 1981. Technical report SOL 81-5.

George B. Dantzig. The diet problem. *Interfaces*, 20(4):43–47, 1990.

George Bernard Dantzig. *Linear Programming and Extensions*, volume 48. Princeton University Press, 1998.

Ingrid Daubechies. *Ten Lectures on Wavelets*. SIAM, 1992.

James W. Demmel. *Applied Numerical Linear Algebra*. Society for Industrial and Applied Mathematics, Philadelphia, PA, 1997.

Peter Deuflhard and Andreas Hohmann. *Numerical Analysis in Modern Scientific Computing*, volume 43 of *Texts in Applied Mathematics*. Springer–Verlag, New York, second edition, 2003.

Persi Diaconis, R. L. Graham, and William M. Kantor. The mathematics of perfect shuffles. *Advances in Applied Mathematics*, 4(2):175–196, 1983.

Paul Adrien Maurice Dirac. A new notation for quantum mechanics. *Mathematical Proceedings of the Cambridge Philosophical Society*, 35(3):416–418, 1939.

Arthur Conan Doyle. *The Complete Sherlock Holmes*. Doubleday Books, 1930.

Susan T. Dumais, George W. Furnas, Thomas K. Landauer, Scott Deerwester, and Richard Harshman. Using latent semantic analysis to improve access to textual information. In *Proceedings of the SIGCHI conference on Human factors in computing systems*, pages 281–285, 1988.

Laurent Duval. WITS = where is the starlet?, 2019. http://www.laurent-duval.eu/siva-wits-where-is-the-starlet.html.

Roger Eckhardt. Stan Ulam, John von Neumann, and the Monte Carlo method. *Los Alamos Science*, 15:131, 1987.

Björn Engquist and Andrew Majda. Absorbing boundary conditions for the numerical simulation of waves. *Mathematics of Computation*, 31(139):629–651, July 1977.

Leonhard Euler. Solutio problematis ad geometriam situs pertinentis. *Commentarii Academiae Scientiarum Imperialis Petropolitanae*, pages 128–140, 1741.

Lawrence C. Evans. *Partial differential equations*. American Mathematical Society, 2010.

Rida T. Farouki. The Bernstein polynomial basis: A centennial retrospective. *Computer Aided Geometric Design*, 29(6):379–419, 2012.

Etienne Forest and Ronald D. Ruth. Fourth-order symplectic integration. *Physica D: Nonlinear Phenomena*, 43(1):105–117, 1990.

John G. F. Francis. The QR transformation a unitary analogue to the lr transformation—part 1. *The Computer Journal*, 4(3):265–271, 1961.

John G. F. Francis. The QR transformation—part 2. *The Computer Journal*, 4(4):332–345, 1962.

Jerome Friedman, Trevor Hastie, and Robert Tibshirani. *The Elements of Statistical Learning: Data Mining, Inference, and Prediction*. Springer Series in Statistics, New York, second edition, 2016.

Matteo Frigo and Steven G. Johnson. The design and implementation of FFTW3. *Proceedings of the IEEE*, 93(2):216–231, 2005.

Uriel Frisch and Jérémie Bec. Burgulence. In *New trends in turbulence*, pages 341–383. Springer, 2001.

Thomas M. J. Fruchterman and Edward M. Reingold. Graph drawing by force-directed placement. *Software: Practice and Experience*, 21(11):1129–1164, 1991.

Hannah Fry. *Hello World: Being Human in the Age of Algorithms*. WW Norton & Company, 2018.

Walter Gautschi. *Orthogonal Polynomials: Computation and Approximation*. Oxford University Press on Demand, 2004.

Walter Gautschi. Orthogonal polynomials, quadrature, and approximation: Computational methods and software (in MATLAB). In *Orthogonal polynomials and special functions*, pages 1–77. Springer, 2006.

Walter Gautschi. *A Software Repository for Orthogonal Polynomials*. SIAM, 2018.

Walter Gautschi. *A Software Repository for Gaussian Quadratures and Christoffel Functions*. SIAM, 2020.

Amanda Gefter. The man who tried to redeem the world with logic. *Nautilus Quarterly*, 21, 2015.

Bernard R. Gelbaum and John M. H. Olmsted. *Counterexamples in Analysis*. Courier Corporation, 2003.

John R. Gilbert, Cleve Moler, and Robert Schreiber. Sparse matrices in MATLAB: Design and implementation. *SIAM Journal on Matrix Analysis and Applications*, 13 (1):333–356, 1992.

Nicolas Gillis. The why and how of nonnegative matrix factorization. *Regularization, Optimization, Kernels, and Support Vector Machines*, 12(257):257–291, 2014.

Gabriel Goh. Why momentum really works. *Distill*, 2017. doi: 10.23915/distill.00006. http://distill.pub/2017/momentum.

Gene Golub and Frank Uhlig. The QR algorithm: 50 years later its genesis by John Francis and Vera Kublanovskaya and subsequent developments. *IMA Journal of Numerical Analysis*, 29(3):467–485, 2009.

Gene H. Golub and Charles F. Van Loan. *Matrix Computations*. Johns Hopkins Studies in the Mathematical Sciences. Johns Hopkins University Press, Baltimore, MD, third edition, 1996.

Ian Goodfellow, Yoshua Bengio, and Aaron Courville. *Deep Learning*. MIT press, 2016.

Joseph F. Grcar. John von Neumann's analysis of Gaussian elimination and the origins of modern numerical analysis. *SIAM Review*, 53(4):607–682, 2011.

John A. Gubner. Gaussian quadrature and the eigenvalue problem. Technical report, University of Wisconsin, 2009.

Alfred Haar. *Zur Theorie der Orthogonalen Funktionensysteme*. Georg-August-Universitat, Gottingen., 1909.

Ernst Hairer and Gerhard Wanner. *Solving Ordinary Differential Equations II: Stiff and Differential-Algebraic Problems*, volume 14. Springer–Verlag, Berlin, 2010.

Ernst Hairer, Syvert Paul Nørsett, and Gerhard Wanner. *Solving Ordinary Differential Equations I: Nonstiff Problems.* Springer–Verlag, Berlin, 1993.

Ernst Hairer, Christian Lubich, and Gerhard Wanner. *Geometric Numerical Integration: Structure-preserving Algorithms for Ordinary Differential Equations,* volume 31. Springer, 2006.

Nathan Halko, Per-Gunnar Martinsson, and Joel A. Tropp. Finding structure with randomness: Probabilistic algorithms for constructing approximate matrix decompositions. *SIAM Review,* 53(2):217–288, 2011.

Paul R. Halmos. How to write mathematics. *L'Enseignement Mathématique,* 16(2): 123–152, 1970.

Godfrey Harold Hardy. Weierstrass's non-differentiable function. *Transactions of the American Mathematical Society,* 17(3):301–325, 1916.

Trevor Hastie, Robert Tibshirani, and Jerome Friedman. *The Elements of Statistical Learning: Data Mining, Inference, and Prediction.* Springer Science & Business Media, 2009.

Deanna Haunsperger and Robert Thompson. *101 Careers in Mathematics,* volume 64. American Mathematical Society, 2019.

Oliver Heaviside. XI. On the forces, stresses, and fluxes of energy in the electromagnetic field. *Philosophical Transactions of the Royal Society of London.(A.),* 183:423–480, 1892.

Michael Heideman, Don Johnson, and Charles Burrus. Gauss and the history of the fast Fourier transform. *IEEE Assp Magazine,* 1(4):14–21, 1984.

Nicholas J. Higham and Françoise Tisseur. A block algorithm for matrix 1-norm estimation, with an application to 1-norm pseudospectra. *SIAM Journal on Matrix Analysis and Applications,* 21(4):1185–1201, 2000.

Marlis Hochbruck and Alexander Ostermann. Exponential integrators. *Acta Numerica,* 19(May):209–286, 2010.

Yifan Hu. Efficient, high-quality force-directed graph drawing. *Mathematica Journal,* 10 (1):37–71, 2005.

T. Huckle and T. Neckel. *Bits and Bugs: A Scientific and Historical Review of Software Failures in Computational Science.* Software, Environments, and Tools. Society for Industrial and Applied Mathematics, 2019.

William Kahan and K. C. Ng. Freely distributable LIBM e_sqrt.c, 1995. Available at the Netlib repository http://www.netlib.org/fdlibm/e_sqrt.c.

Anna Kalogirou. *Nonlinear dynamics of surfactant-laden multilayer shear flows and related systems.* PhD thesis, Queensland University of Technology, 2014.

Aly-Khan Kassam and Lloyd N. Trefethen. Fourth-order time-stepping for stiff PDEs. *SIAM Journal on Scientific Computing*, 26(4):1214–1233, 2005.

Christopher A. Kennedy and Mark H. Carpenter. Additive Runge–Kutta schemes for convection–diffusion–reaction equations. *Applied Numerical Mathematics*, 44(1-2): 139–181, 2003.

Christopher A. Kennedy and Mark H. Carpenter. Diagonally implicit runge-kutta methods for ordinary differential equations, a review. Technical report, National Aeronautics and Space Administration, Langley Research Center, 2016.

A. Kiely and M. Klimesh. The ICER progressive wavelet image compressor. *The Interplanetary Network Progress Report*, 42(155), 2003.

A. Kiely, M. Klimesh, H. Xie, and N. Aranki. Icer-3d: A progressive wavelet-based compressor for hyperspectral images. *The Interplanetary Network Progress Report*, 42 (164), 2006.

David Kincaid and Ward Cheney. *Numerical Analysis: Mathematics of Scientific Computing*. Brooks/Cole Publishing Co., Pacific Grove, CA, third edition, 2001.

Diederik P. Kingma and Jimmy Ba. Adam: a method for stochastic optimization, 2017.

Donald E. Knuth. Literate programming. *The Computer Journal*, 27(2):97–111, 1984.

William H. Kruskal and Stephen M. Stigler. Normative terminology: "Normal" in statistics and elsewhere. *Statistics and Public Policy*, pages 85–111, 1997.

John Denholm Lambert. *Numerical Methods for Ordinary Differential Systems: The Initial Value Problem*. John Wiley & Sons, 1991.

Hans Petter Langtangen and Anders Logg. *Solving PDEs in Python*. Springer, 2017a. ISBN 978-3-319-52461-0. doi: 10.1007/978-3-319-52462-7.

Hans Petter Langtangen and Anders Logg. *Solving PDEs in Python: The FEniCS Tutorial I*. Springer Nature, 2017b.

Amy N. Langville and Carl D. Meyer. Deeper inside PageRank. *Internet Mathematics*, 1 (3):335–380, 2004.

Dirk Laurie. Calculation of Gauss–Kronrod quadrature rules. *Mathematics of Computation*, 66(219):1133–1145, 1997.

D. Lax, P. and N. Milgram, A. IX. Parabolic equations. *Contributions to the Theory of Partial Differential Equations.*, (33):167, 1955.

Peter Lax. *Linear Algebra and Its Applications*. Pure and Applied Mathematics. Wiley-Interscience [John Wiley & Sons], Hoboken, NJ, second edition, 2007.

Peter Lax and Burton Wendroff. Systems of conservation laws. Technical report, Los Alamos National Laboratory, 1959.

Yann LeCun, Léon Bottou, Yoshua Bengio, and Patrick Haffner. Gradient-based learning applied to document recognition. *Proceedings of the IEEE*, 86(11):2278–2324, 1998.

Dongsun Lee, Joo-Youl Huh, Darae Jeong, Jaemin Shin, Ana Yun, and Junseok Kim. Physical, mathematical, and numerical derivations of the Cahn–Hilliard equation. *Computational Materials Science*, 81:216–225, 2014.

Randall J. LeVeque. *Finite Volume Methods for Hyperbolic Problems*. Cambridge Texts in Applied Mathematics. Cambridge University Press, Cambridge, 2002.

Mario Livio. *The Equation that Couldn't Be Solved: How Mathematical Genius Discovered the Language of Symmetry*. Simon and Schuster, 2005.

Anders Logg, Kent-Andre Mardal, Garth N. Wells, et al. *Automated Solution of Differential Equations by the Finite Element Method*. Springer, 2012. ISBN 978-3-642-23098-1. doi: 10.1007/978-3-642-23099-8.

Edward N. Lorenz. Deterministic nonperiodic flow. *Journal of Atmospheric Sciences*, 20 (2):130–141, 1963.

David Lusseau, Karsten Schneider, Oliver J. Boisseau, Patti Haase, Elisabeth Slooten, and Steve M. Dawson. The bottlenose dolphin community of Doubtful Sound features a large proportion of long-lasting associations. *Behavioral Ecology and Sociobiology*, 54(4):396–405, 2003.

James N. Lyness and Cleve B. Moler. Numerical differentiation of analytic functions. *SIAM Journal on Numerical Analysis*, 4(2):202–210, 1967.

Benoit Mandelbrot. How long is the coast of Britain? Statistical self-similarity and fractional dimension. *Science*, 156(3775):636–638, 1967.

Benoit B. Mandelbrot. *The Fractal Geometry of Nature*. W. H. Freeman, New York, 1982.

Kyle T. Mandli, Aron J. Ahmadia, Marsha Berger, Donna Calhoun, David L. George, Yiannis Hadjimichael, David I. Ketcheson, Grady I. Lemoine, and Randall J. LeVeque. Clawpack: Building an open source ecosystem for solving hyperbolic PDEs. *PeerJ Computer Science*, 2:e68, 2016.

Makoto Matsumoto and Takuji Nishimura. Mersenne twister: A 623-dimensionally equidistributed uniform pseudo-random number generator. *ACM Transactions on Modeling and Computer Simulation*, 8(1):3–30, 1998.

Robert M. May. Simple mathematical models with very complicated dynamics. *Nature*, 261:459, 1976.

Warren S. McCulloch and Walter Pitts. A logical calculus of the ideas immanent in nervous activity. *The Bulletin of Mathematical Biophysics*, 5(4):115–133, 1943.

Cleve B. Moler. *Numerical Computing with MATLAB*. Society for Industrial and Applied Mathematics, Philadelphia, PA, 2004.

Cleve B. Moler and Charles Van Loan. Nineteen dubious ways to compute the exponential of a matrix. *SIAM Review*, 20(4):801–836, 1978.

Cleve B. Moler and Charles Van Loan. Nineteen dubious ways to compute the exponential of a matrix, twenty-five years later. *SIAM Review*, 45(1):3–49, 2003.

Leonid V. Moroz, Cezary J. Walczyk, Andriy Hrynchyshyn, Vijay Holimath, and Jan L. Cieśliński. Fast calculation of inverse square root with the use of magic constant—analytical approach. *Applied Mathematics and Computation*, 316:245–255, 2018.

Philip M. Morse. Trends in operations research. *Journal of the Operations Research Society of America*, 1(4):159–165, 1953.

K. W. Morton and D. F. Mayers. *Numerical Solution of Partial Differential Equations*. Cambridge University Press, Cambridge, second edition, 2005.

Jean-Michel Muller. Elementary functions and approximate computing. *Proceedings of the IEEE*, 108(12):2136–2149, 2020.

Richard D. Neidinger. Introduction to automatic differentiation and MATLAB object-oriented programming. *SIAM Review*, 52(3):545–563, 2010.

John A. Nelder and Roger Mead. A simplex method for function minimization. *The Computer Journal*, 7(4):308–313, 1965.

Haim Nessyahu and Eitan Tadmor. Non-oscillatory central differencing for hyperbolic conservation laws. *Journal of Computational Physics*, 87(2):408–463, 1990.

F. T. Nieuwstadt and J. A. Steketee. *Selected Papers of J. M. Burgers*. Springer Science & Business Media, 2012.

Kyle A. Novak and Laura J. Fox. *Special Functions of Mathematical Physics: A Tourist's Guidebook*. Equal Share Press, 2019.

Karlheinz Ochs. A comprehensive analytical solution of the nonlinear pendulum. *European Journal of Physics*, 32(2):479, 2011.

Robert E. O'Malley Jr. *Singular Perturbation Methods for Ordinary Differential Equations*. Springer-Verlag, 1991.

Lawrence Page, Sergey Brin, Rajeev Motwani, and Terry Winograd. The PageRank citation ranking: Bringing order to the web. Technical report, Stanford InfoLab, 1999.

Stephen K. Park and Keith W. Miller. Random number generators: Good ones are hard to find. *Communications of the ACM*, 31(10):1192–1201, 1988.

Thomas N. L. Patterson. The optimum addition of points to quadrature formulae. *Mathematics of Computation*, 22(104):847–856, 1968.

Donald W. Peaceman and Henry H. Rachford, Jr. The numerical solution of parabolic and elliptic differential equations. *Journal of the Society for Industrial and Applied Mathematics*, 3(1):28–41, 1955.

Linda Petzold. Differential/algebraic equations are not ODE's. *SIAM Journal on Scientific and Statistical Computing*, 3(3):367–384, 1982.

Boris T. Polyak. Some methods of speeding up the convergence of iteration methods. *USSR Computational Mathematics and Mathematical Physics*, 4(5):1–17, 1964.

Alfio Quarteroni and Fausto Saleri. *Scientific Computing with MATLAB and Octave*, volume 2 of *Texts in Computational Science and Engineering*. Springer-Verlag, Berlin, second edition, 2006.

Alfio Quarteroni, Riccardo Sacco, and Fausto Saleri. *Numerical Mathematics*, volume 37 of *Texts in Applied Mathematics*. Springer-Verlag, Berlin, second edition, 2007.

Christopher Rackauckas. A comparison between differential equation solver suites in MATLAB, R, Julia, Python, C, Mathematica, Maple, and Fortran, 2018. https://thewinnower.com.

Christopher Rackauckas and Qing Nie. Differentialequations.jl–a performant and feature-rich ecosystem for solving differential equations in julia. *Journal of Open Research Software*, 5(1):15, 2017.

John K. Reid and Jennifer A. Scott. Reducing the total bandwidth of a sparse unsymmetric matrix. *SIAM Journal on Matrix Analysis and Applications*, 28(3):805–821, 2006. https://www.numerical.rl.ac.uk/reports/rsRAL2005001.pdf.

Edward L Reiss. A new asymptotic method for jump phenomena. *SIAM Journal on Applied Mathematics*, 39(3):440–455, 1980.

Lewis Fry Richardson. Ix. the approximate arithmetical solution by finite differences of physical problems involving differential equations, with an application to the stresses in a masonry dam. *Philosophical Transactions of the Royal Society of London. Series A, Containing Papers of a Mathematical or Physical Character*, 210(459-470):307–357, 1911.

Lewis Fry Richardson. *Weather prediction by numerical process*. University Press, 1922.

Philip L. Roe. Modelling of discontinuous flows. *Lectures in Applied Mathematics*, 22, 1985.

Paul Romer. Jupyter, Mathematica, and the future of the research paper, April 2018. https://paulromer.net/jupyter-mathematica-and-the-future-of-the-research-paper.

Frank Rosenblatt. The perceptron: A probabilistic model for information storage and organization in the brain. *Psychological Review*, 65(6):386, 1958.

H. H. Rosenbrock. Some general implicit processes for the numerical solution of differential equations. *The Computer Journal*, 5(4):329–330, 1963.

David E. Rumelhart, Geoffrey E. Hinton, and Ronald J. Williams. Learning representations by back-propagating errors. *Nature*, 323(6088):533–536, 1986.

Siegfried M. Rump. Algorithms for verified inclusions: Theory and practice. In *Reliability in Computing*, pages 109–126. Elsevier, 1988.

Youcef Saad. *Numerical Methods for Large Eigenvalue Problems*. Algorithms and Architectures for Advanced Scientific Computing. Manchester University Press, Manchester, 1992.

Yousef Saad. *Iterative Methods for Sparse Linear Systems*. Society for Industrial and Applied Mathematics, Philadelphia, PA, second edition, 2003.

Lawrence F. Shampine. Design of software for ODEs. *Journal of Computational and Applied Mathematics*, 205(2):901–911, 2007.

Lawrence F. Shampine and Robert M. Corless. Initial value problems for ODEs in problem solving environments. *Journal of Computational and Applied Mathematics*, 125(1-2): 31–40, 2000.

Lawrence F. Shampine and Mark W. Reichelt. The MATLAB ODE suite. *SIAM Journal on Scientific Computing*, 18(1):1–22, 1997.

Chi-Wang Shu and Stanley Osher. Efficient implementation of essentially non-oscillatory shock-capturing schemes. *Journal of Computational Physics*, 77(2):439–471, 1988.

Bonnie Shulman. Math-alive! Using original sources to teach mathematics in social context. *Problems, Resources, and Issues in Mathematics Undergraduate Studies*, 8(1): 1–14, 1998.

Lawrence Sirovich and Michael Kirby. Low-dimensional procedure for the characterization of human faces. *Josa A*, 4(3):519–524, 1987.

Gustaf Söderlind, Laurent Jay, and Manuel Calvo. Stiffness 1952–2012: Sixty years in search of a definition. *BIT Numerical Mathematics*, 55(2):531–558, 2015.

Pavel Šolín. *Partial Differential Equations and the Finite Element Method*. Pure and Applied Mathematics. Wiley-Interscience [John Wiley & Sons], Hoboken, NJ, 2006.

James Somers. The scientific paper is obsolete. *The Atlantic*, 4, 2018.

Peter L. Søndergaard, Bruno Torrésani, and Peter Balazs. The linear time frequency analysis toolbox. *International Journal of Wavelets, Multiresolution Analysis and Information Processing*, 10(4), 2012.

William Squire and George Trapp. Using complex variables to estimate derivatives of real functions. *SIAM review*, 40(1):110–112, 1998.

George J. Stigler. The cost of subsistence. *Journal of Farm Economics*, 27(2):303–314, 1945.

Gilbert Strang. Wavelets and dilation equations: A brief introduction. *SIAM Review*, 31 (4):614–627, 1989.

Gilbert Strang. *Linear Algebra and Its Applications*. Wellesley–Cambridge Press, fifth edition, 2016.

Fabio Toscano. *The Secret Formula: How a Mathematical Duel Inflamed Renaissance Italy and Uncovered the Cubic Equation*. Princeton University Press, 2020.

Alex Townsend. The race for high order Gauss–Legendre quadrature. *SIAM News*, 48: 1–3, 2015.

Lloyd N. Trefethen. The definition of numerical analysis. Technical report, Cornell University, 1992.

Lloyd N. Trefethen. Finite difference and spectral methods for ordinary and partial differential equations. Unpublished text, 1996.

Lloyd N. Trefethen. *Spectral Methods in MATLAB*, volume 10 of *Software, Environments, and Tools*. Society for Industrial and Applied Mathematics (SIAM), Philadelphia, PA, 2000.

Lloyd N. Trefethen. A hundred-dollar, hundred-digit challenge. *SIAM News*, 35(1):1, 2002.

Lloyd N. Trefethen. Ten digit algorithms. In *21st Biennial Conference on Numerical Analysis*. University of Dundee, June 2005. A. R. Mitchell Lecture.

Lloyd N. Trefethen. Computing numerically with functions instead of numbers. *Mathematics in Computer Science*, 1(1):9–19, 2007.

Lloyd N. Trefethen. Is Gauss quadrature better than Clenshaw–Curtis? *SIAM Review*, 50 (1):67–87, 2008.

Lloyd N. Trefethen. Ten digit problems. In *An Invitation to Mathematics*, pages 119–136. Springer, 2011.

Lloyd N. Trefethen. *Approximation Theory and Approximation Practice, Extended Edition*. SIAM, 2019.

Lloyd N. Trefethen and David Bau, III. *Numerical Linear Algebra*. Society for Industrial and Applied Mathematics (SIAM), Philadelphia, PA, 1997.

Lloyd N. Trefethen and Kristine Embree. The (unfinished) PDE coffee table book. https://people.maths.ox.ac.uk/trefethen/pdectb.html, 2001.

Lloyd N. Trefethen and J. A. C. Weideman. The exponentially convergent trapezoidal rule. *SIAM Review*, 56(3):385–458, 2014.

Alan M. Turing. Rounding-off errors in matrix processes. *The Quarterly Journal of Mechanics and Applied Mathematics*, 1(1):287–308, 1948.

Adam Usadi and Clint Dawson. Years of ADI methods: Celebrating the contributions of Jim Douglas, Don Peaceman and Henry Rachford. *SIAM News*, 39(2):2006, 2006.

Charles Van Loan. *Computational Frameworks for the fast Fourier Transform*, volume 10. SIAM, 1992.

Loup Verlet. Computer "experiments" on classical fluids. I. Thermodynamical properties of Lennard–Jones molecules. *Physical Review*, 159(1):98, 1967.

James Hamilton Verner. Explicit Runge–Kutta methods with estimates of the local truncation error. *SIAM Journal on Numerical Analysis*, 15(4):772–790, 1978.

Sebastiano Vigna. Spectral ranking. *Network Science*, 4(4):433–445, 2016.

Pauli Virtanen, Ralf Gommers, Travis E. Oliphant, Matt Haberland, Tyler Reddy, David Cournapeau, Evgeni Burovski, Pearu Peterson, Warren Weckesser, Jonathan Bright, et al. SciPy 1.0: Fundamental algorithms for scientific computing in Python. *Nature Methods*, 17(3):261–272, 2020.

John Von Neumann and Herman H. Goldstine. Numerical inverting of matrices of high order. *Bulletin of the American Mathematical Society*, 53(11):1021–1099, 1947.

David S. Watkins. Francis's algorithm. *The American Mathematical Monthly*, 118(5): 387–403, 2011.

David S. Watkins. *Fundamentals of Matrix Computations*. John Wiley & Sons, third edition, 2014.

X. Wu, G. J. Zwieten, and K. G. Zee. Stabilized second-order convex splitting schemes for Cahn–Hilliard models with application to diffuse-interface tumor-growth models. *International Journal for Numerical Methods in Biomedical Engineering*, 30(2): 180–203, 2014.

Haruo Yoshida. Construction of higher order symplectic integrators. *Physics Letters A*, 150(5):262–268, 1990.

Aston Zhang, Zachary C. Lipton, Mu Li, and Alexander J. Smola. Dive into deep learning, 2021. https://d2l.ai.

Index

Julia Index

Macros

Packages

Python Index

Functions

Packages

Matlab Index

Printed in Great Britain
by Amazon